1978 Writer's Market

1978
Writer's
Market

Edited by
Jane Koester and Bruce Joel Hillman

A Writer's Digest Book
Cincinnati, Ohio

Acknowledgments

The Editors would like to gratefully acknowledge the assistance received on this 1978 edition from the following friends and *Writer's Digest* staff members:

Rose Adkins

Joe Bobbey

John Brady

William Brohaugh

Cathy Bruce

Cecilia Curee

Michael Hoover

Ron Klett

Jeff Lapin

Lynne Lapin

Melissa Milar

Ed Nies

Kirk Polking

Carol Rogers

Bob Rogers

Richard Rosenthal

Doug Sandhage

Paula Arnett Sandhage

Jean Smith

Leon Taylor

Ruby Taylor

Betsy Wones

Budge Wallis

Published by
Writer's Digest Books, 9933 Alliance Rd., Cincinnati, Ohio 45242

Library of Congress Catalog Number 31-20772
International Standard Book Number 0-911654-48-8

Copyright © 1977, Writer's Digest

Printed and bound in the United States of America

Preface

You're on the threshold of the largest, most comprehensive supermarket of opportunities for writers ever assembled—*Writer's Market '78*—and the welcome mat is out ... make that the red carpet.

Folio, a publication which covers magazine management, reports a 30% increase over 1975 in new magazine starts for 1976. This means more markets than ever for anyone who has something to say in writing—*and who can say it well.*

And there we were following up every *Folio* report, advertisement, clipping or writer's tip (and we thank *you* for those), plus a host of other sources to bring you the most up-to-date reference book we could. And, humbly, we think we can say we did OK. There are over 400 brand new entries in this edition, enough alone to keep an active writer in bread and butter (and typewriter ribbons).

But we didn't forget our old acquaintances, either. Earlier this year we sent each entry in *Writer's Market '77* (a total of 4,095 publications and organizations) a copy of its entry for verification, with a special plea to fill out a new questionnaire if there was substantial new data. The response overwhelmed us. Over 20% of the markets completed the questionnaire, and of the remainder, 95% added vital new information to their listing.

In addition to the up-dated market news, we brought in some real heavyweights to share their views on this freelancing world. Leon Taylor, formerly managing editor of *WD* who left us at the bite of the freelance bug, gives insights learned from experience on both sides of the pencil and through hours of interviewing other professionals. Ted Schwarz, author of three books on photography and a hard-working freelance writer/photographer himself, offers help through "Selling Pictures with Your Words." And former *Writer's Market* and *Writer's Digest* editor Kirk Polking steps in with a brief rundown of the new copyright law, plus articles on authors' rights and charging for your freelance services.

This edition has the largest number of total listings in the book's 56-year history. And it continues to grow—even now we have a file a foot thick on leads for the '79 edition. So while we get hopping on *Writer's Market '79,* here's wishing you profitable sales and fine writing.

— *Jane Koester* and *Bruce Joel Hillman*

Contents

The Markets 31

Book Publishers 31

Trade, Technical, and Professional Journals 143

Company Publications   296

Farm Publications   306

Consumer Publications 322

Opportunities & Services   700

Glossary   841

Index   847

Getting Started

How to Use This Book

Using your *Writer's Market* can be as easy as letting your fingers do the walking through the Yellow Pages. The book is constructed in seven major sections: introductory material; book publishers; trade, technical and professional journals; farm publications; company publications; consumer publications; and miscellaneous freelance markets and services. Look at the table of contents.

Under each major section (excepting the introductory material and company publications) are a number of categories. For instance, under consumer publications, you'll find categories ranging from alternative to poetry to women's publications.

After studying the table of contents, then go to the index. This will direct you to any particular publications you already have in mind for your material.

All of the listings in this book are packed with vital information and tips to help you along. If you use this book only as a name-and-address directory, you're missing the point (and probably the buck).

Be sure to study the tips and hints when given under the *How to Break In* subhead under many of the listings; also the subheads *Rejects* and *For '78*. This information is in the editors' own words on what (and how) to write for their magazine or book publishing company.

For example, consider this fictitious listing for *J.D.'s Travelog Magazine*. Little is left to the writer's imagination:

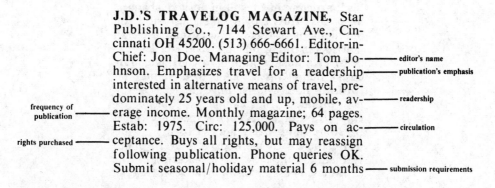

J.D.'S TRAVELOG MAGAZINE, Star Publishing Co., 7144 Stewart Ave., Cincinnati OH 45200. (513) 666-6661. Editor-in-Chief: Jon Doe. Managing Editor: Tom Johnson. Emphasizes travel for a readership interested in alternative means of travel, predominately 25 years old and up, mobile, average income. Monthly magazine; 64 pages. Estab: 1975. Circ: 125,000. Pays on acceptance. Buys all rights, but may reassign following publication. Phone queries OK. Submit seasonal/holiday material 6 months

editor's name
publication's emphasis
readership
circulation
submission requirements

frequency of publication
rights purchased

We use the U.S. Postal Service's two-letter codes for state names in each of the listings, and a few abbreviations that you should know. Tape this to your wall or typewriter for a handy reference guide.

B&W	Black-and-White	MI	Michigan
Estab:	Established	MN	Minnesota
Circ:	Circulation	MO	Missouri
Ms(s)	Manuscript(s)	MS	Mississippi
SASE	Self-addressed	MT	Montana
	stamped envelope	NC	North Carolina
		ND	North Dakota
		NE	Nebraska
STATE CODES		NH	New Hampshire
		NJ	New Jersey
AK	Alaska	NM	New Mexico
AL	Alabama	NV	Nevada
AR	Arkansas	NY	New York
AZ	Arizona	OH	Ohio
CA	California	OK	Oklahoma
CO	Colorado	OR	Oregon
CT	Connecticut	PA	Pennsylvania
DC	District of Columbia	PR	Puerto Rico
DE	Delaware	RI	Rhode Island
FL	Florida	SC	South Carolina
GA	Georgia	SD	South Dakota
HI	Hawaii	TN	Tennessee
IA	Iowa	TX	Texas
ID	Idaho	UT	Utah
IL	Illinois	VA	Virginia
IN	Indiana	VI	Virgin Islands
KS	Kansas	VT	Vermont
KY	Kentucky	WA	Washington
LA	Louisiana	WI	Wisconsin
MA	Massachusetts	WV	West Virginia
MD	Maryland	WY	Wymoning
ME	Maine		

in advance. Simultaneous, photocopied and previously published submissions OK. SASE. Reports in 2 weeks. Free sample ——— *reporting time*

sample copy availability ——— copy and writer's guidelines.

Nonfiction: Jean Adkins, Articles Editor. ——— *department editor's name*

types of articles needed ——— Expose (on public and private transportation companies, rip-offs in the travel field; articles must result in positive changes; no expose for its own sake); historical (on old methods of travel, interesting travelers); how-to (anything on how to travel less expensively; must contain hard facts, including costs); humor (as it relates to traveling); informational (almost anything goes here); new products (that can help people better enjoy traveling); personal experience (must be something that readers can use to improve their own methods of travel); photo feature ("on-the-road" style features); profile (about successful or innovative travelers);

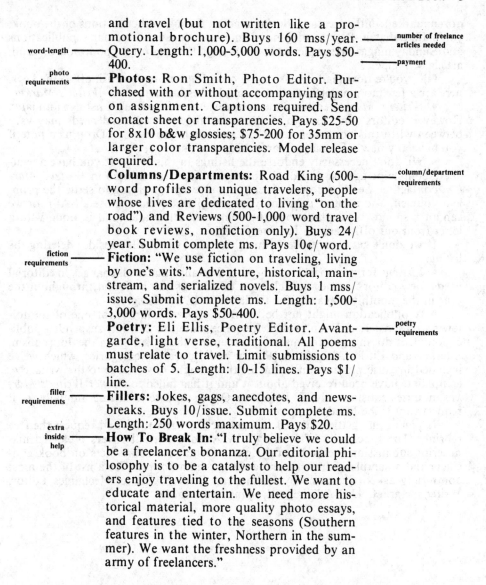

and travel (but not written like a promotional brochure). Buys 160 mss/year.
word-length ——— Query. Length: 1,000-5,000 words. Pays $50-400.

———— number of freelance articles needed

————— payment

photo requirements ——— **Photos:** Ron Smith, Photo Editor. Purchased with or without accompanying ms or on assignment. Captions required. Send contact sheet or transparencies. Pays $25-50 for 8x10 b&w glossies; $75-200 for 35mm or larger color transparencies. Model release required.

Columns/Departments: Road King (500-word profiles on unique travelers, people whose lives are dedicated to living "on the road") and Reviews (500-1,000 word travel book reviews, nonfiction only). Buys 24/year. Submit complete ms. Pays 10¢/word.

——— column/department requirements

fiction requirements ——— **Fiction:** "We use fiction on traveling, living by one's wits." Adventure, historical, mainstream, and serialized novels. Buys 1 mss/issue. Submit complete ms. Length: 1,500-3,000 words. Pays $50-400.

Poetry: Eli Ellis, Poetry Editor. Avant-garde, light verse, traditional. All poems must relate to travel. Limit submissions to batches of 5. Length: 10-15 lines. Pays $1/line.

——— poetry requirements

filler requirements ——— **Fillers:** Jokes, gags, anecdotes, and newsbreaks. Buys 10/issue. Submit complete ms. Length: 250 words maximum. Pays $20.

extra inside help ——— **How To Break In:** "I truly believe we could be a freelancer's bonanza. Our editorial philosophy is to be a catalyst to help our readers enjoy traveling to the fullest. We want to educate and entertain. We need more historical material, more quality photo essays, and features tied to the seasons (Southern features in the winter, Northern in the summer). We want the freshness provided by an army of freelancers."

Take nothing for granted when studying a listing. Consider every requirement, hint, tip and detail before typing the first word or taking the first photo. If a market says it doesn't want unsolicited manuscripts, then query; if it will send a sample copy, then ask for one; and if it won't consider articles over 2,000 words, then don't send them your book-length manuscript. Violation of the rules rarely brings more than a rejection slip—and not even that, if the editor says "Enclose SASE," and you haven't.

When you're looking for the editorial requirements of a particular magazine by name, check the alphabetical index at the back of the book. It also includes cross references for markets that have changed their name in the last year and publishers of one or more magazines.

Don't limit your sales by staying within one category. For example: if your area of main interest is food and drink publications, you're limited to less than a dozen markets in that section. But by reading through other sections of the book, you'll find that in-flight and general interest magazines, woman's publications and Sunday magazine supplements are always looking for a good food or drink article or recipe.

OK, you're now ready to use this book. But before you rush off to the keys, here are a few more pointers to help you take best advantage of *Writer's Market*.

• *Writer's Market* editors research, review and update all listings annually. However, editors come and go, addresses change and editorial needs may vary between when this book was published and when you buy it. (Drop us a note if you have any new information concerning a listing.)

• We don't necessarily endorse the listings in this book. If you have a legitimate complaint against any of the publications or firms listed in *Writer's Market,* contact us. Send us copies of letters you've sent in trying to settle the problem yourself, and a letter detailing your complaint. And enclose a SASE or we cannot respond. We'll photocopy the complaint letter and send it along with a letter from our office asking for a response.

If we don't get a response within three weeks, we will consider deleting the listing.

• Listings for new markets in need of freelance material, changes in editorial needs, new editors' names and changes of address can be found throughout the year in the monthly magazine for freelancers, *Writer's Digest.*

• A publication might not be listed in *Writer's Market* for one of the following reasons: 1. it doesn't solicit freelance material; 2. it has suspended publication; 3. it doesn't pay for material (excepting those listings in the Journalism, Literary and Little, Alternative, Poetry and Education categories, which we've included because publication in any of them might be of value to the writer); 4. complaints have been received about it and it has failed to answer *Writer's Market* inquiries satisfactorily; 5. it fails to OK or update its listing annually; 6. it requests not to be listed.

If you're just getting started in freelancing, write to us and request the free reprint, "The Mechanics of Writing," by Allan Eckert. It covers preferred manuscript submission methods, copyright information, some facts on book contracts and a sample of how to prepare your manuscript. Plus a list of the most commonly asked questions by freelancers. Send SASE to Mechanics Editor, Writer's Market, 9933 Alliance Rd., Cincinnati 45242.

What Every Freelancer Should Know

By Leon Taylor

For Joyce Verrette, freelancing is as compelling as a dream. In fact, her career *began* in a dream one morning some years ago in Chicago.

In the dream she was no longer a TV production assistant, but Nefrytatanen, queen of Tamehu, sailing to the south to marry a prince. "The dream carried me to the point where we were sitting and drinking the wine and getting acquainted. And then I very unhappily woke up."

As it turned out, she merely woke to a larger dream—of finding her characters in a library book about ancient Egypt; turning her dream into a novel, writing on the subway, on her breaks, on her lunch hour; circulating the manuscript for about five years, gathering rejections from 30 to 35 publishers; selling it finally to a paperback house, Avon.

At last count, 1,430,000 copies of *Dawn of Desire* were in print.

Of course, the Verrette Story is extraordinary; few novelists are so lucky on their first shot out of the box. But some are—because they make their own luck. Next time someone tells you the first novel is on its last legs, send him to see Joyce Verrette.

And next time someone tells you (or you tell yourself) that there is simply no room in publishing for one more novelist, one more magazine writer, one more raw voice—haul out *Writer's Market.* Here are a thousand pages of reproof. And if they aren't enough, listen to Charles Brewster, managing editor of *New World Outlook:* "I think there is more roon now [in the Christian field] for good writers than ever before. If a person has good writing ability and can also link up to the basic concerns of a church, then it matters not so much that he is actually a member of that church as that he can communicate what he sees." Charles Henry, editor of *The Dakota Farmer:* "There's a tremendous need for that farm freelancer who can write the production agricultural story." Dave Kaiser, managing editor of *Swimming Pool Weekly/Age:* "There must be hundreds of stories in any given area that would be appropriate for this publication." And Dan Zadra, editor of *Young Athlete:* "I'm still looking for freelance writers that can fulfill what we need. I have one or two that we developed and work well with. Beyond that, I'm still looking."

The competition is enormous—the last edition of *Writer's Market* sold out at 80,000 copies on the first printing—but so are the opportunities. The general interest magazines alone will buy 6,800 manuscripts this year; the sports magazines, 3,800. (And these estimates are extremely conservative; nearly half of the magazines listed in these two subsections don't report how many mss they plan to buy, and they are not included in the figures above.)

So editors are looking for you. But first, you must look for editors. How?

Well, you can narrow your search by keeping these axioms in mind:

The bulk of the market is in nonfiction. You can test the truth of that for magazines by flipping through this directory's listings. For books, *Publishers*

Leon Taylor, former managing editor of Writer's Digest, *is now a fulltime freelancer—and loves it.*

Weekly notes that of 30,004 new volumes published in 1975, only 2,407 were fiction.

The bulk of the magazine nonfiction market is in reportage. Of course, personal experience pieces do move and delight editors; in fact, they're often salt and pepper for the religious magazines. But generally magazines clamor for reporting: how to start your car when all else fails, how to keep your cool when Johnny fails.

This only means that the writer who acquires the reporter's skills of interviewing and digging—and they are largely self-taught skills—should find himself in demand, and find his story possibilities almost limitless. "As [sportswriter] Red Smith said, a good reporter can cover anything," says Claudia Dowling, managing editor of *womenSports*. "You can cover a funeral, you can cover a baseball game."

Ideas

Yet that gift of sight—though broad in its embrace—seems to elude some would-be writers. According to legend, they're the people who linger on the outskirts of a cocktail party and ask the pro, "Where do you get your ideas?"

The question is simple—and nearly impossible to answer. For the writer gets ideas through a process as natural as scratching his head: questioning. Kipling's six honest serving men—*who, what, when, where, how,* and especially *why*—

"I always liked writing, period," says Joyce Verrett. "If you had locked me in a closet, I would have written on the wall."

make the writer proud when they go to work on any intriguing fact or thing. *Why* do we consider a 70-degree thermostat setting more comfortable than one of 65? *Who* invented the paper clip?

One abundant source of ideas is that everyman's almanac, the daily newspaper. Begin with the back page; those cryptic fillers may yield more features than the picked-clean blockbusters on page one. Florida freelancer Lee Butcher found the seed for a book on dolphins in a two-paragraph news story.

But the fastest route to ideas—and to salable articles—may be to take apart *magazines.* Editors say it so often they could mumble it in their sleep: study thy market. "If you realize that the people who read this magazine are young mothers, or elderly people, or well-to-do, or well-educated, then you look for articles that will appeal to those kinds of people," says Tennessee freelancer Marti Hefley. "And you're a lot more apt to sell them."

Ask the editor for a sample issue if the magazine is not available at your newsstand. *Don't* submit a query or manuscript to him first. When the issue arrives, study it closely, page by page, looking for these things:

- *Advertisements.* These make up a quick index to the readers' interests and income. What are the ads selling? Do they appeal to the affluent or the just-getting-by?
- *The masthead*—the list of staff members, published on one of the first pages. Check it against the table of contents. Are the writers usually staff members? If so, this market may be limited for freelancers. But if the writers are often listed as *contributing editors,* be of good cheer—these are simply freelancers who contribute regularly. In fact, you might dissect their articles with particular attention; obviously they have found ways of pleasing their editor.
- *The small print.* It's next to the table of contents, and it's often a mouthful. *Carte Blanche's* is two inches deep, and includes this: "Expressed interest by the editors in unsolicited manuscripts, art, photographs or proposed ideas does not constitute a commitment or an assignment. ... Commitments, assignments and any deviations of the above ... policies must be verified in writing by the publisher or editors." Which is certainly worth knowing.
- *Pictures.* Color? Black and white? How many per article? Who takes them —the writer or a staff photographer?

  If you can't take pictures, learn. Sometimes good pictures will sell a mediocre manuscript. Trade editor Kaiser stresses the importance of getting shots. "They brighten up an article and make it a lot easier for the editor to lay it out in a presentable fashion."
- *Articles.* How long are they? Are they usually essays? features? investigative stories? Are the leads anecdotal or straightforward? Is the style slick or conversational? What is the mix of topics? What is the purpose of each article? And —a fishnet question—what is the magazine's *approach?*

It's all mathematics: there are only so many magazines, and *so* many ideas. You're better off tailoring an article to a market than trying to vice versa.

Queries

Once an idea—a winsome, manageable, salable idea—has taken hold, the writer is tempted to strike *now,* to pillage the libraries, collar the interviewees, before the idea loses its heat. But he really ought to pause before plundering (and maybe blundering) and write a *query* to sell an editor on his notion.

The query is a one-page sales letter summarizing your proposed piece and asking the editor if you may write it for consideration by his publication. Most editors prefer queries to *unsolicited manuscripts.* If the editor gives you a *go-ahead* on your query, he will probably ask you to work *on speculation.* Thus, if he rejects your piece, he will pay nothing. But he might ask an experienced writer to work *on assignment.* Should he reject the assigned piece, he should pay a kill fee (say, a fourth of the full price of the piece. Kill fees are agreed on in advance).

The query is not for the convenience of the editor alone. It also saves you the trouble of writing a piece on the boll weevil rebellion when, unbeknownst to you, your editor has just sent a Special Boll Weevil Issue to the printers. And a go-ahead helps you secure interviews (who would *you* rather talk to—Harry Hagendorf, Freelancer At Large, or Harry Hagendorf, Freelancer for *Herring* magazine?) as well as tailor your piece to the editor's needs. "When a person queries, I can then give him definite ideas on how to get the exact information that I want," says Ben Russell, editor of *American Laundry Digest.* "I often provide freelancers— particularly the younger ones, the more inexperienced— with a list of questions and suggestions for photographs."

Some editors want the writer to query right after he lands his story lead (from, say, a clipping) instead of waiting until after his first interview to gather more goods. "When you're querying, you're facing a pretty good risk that the

editor will say, 'We've got something in the works' or 'It's not quite right for us,'"
says Brian Vachon, editor of *Vermont Life.* "I don't think a writer should spend
an awful lot of time and effort putting together the information in a query, but
rather make it sparkle in itself. And certainly lifting information out of a newspaper article is a perfectly legitimate way to research a query."

But sports editor Zadra thinks the writer should at least sound out his interviewee before sounding out his editor. "It's pretty impressive to me when somebody says, 'I have contacted so-and-so, we've talked about doing an article for
Young Athlete, here's the angle, here's the theme,' That's what I look for."

The writer should at least make sure his interviewee's door is open. "I don't
want to say 'Go ahead' on some story and have the writer get back to me and say
'Gee, I just can't get an interview with this person,'" says *womenSports* managing
editor Dowling. "That's a waste of my time."

The freelancer may also be wasting time if he doesn't ask himself one question before querying: Why would this publication want my article? "To write
successfully for a magazine," says Rev. Jeremy Harrington, editor of *St. Anthony Messenger,* "you must grasp what they're trying to do."

Which recalls our refrain: Study the Market. In studying *Vermont Life,* for
instance, you can't miss the necessity of the Vermont angle for manuscripts. "If
the guy [to be profiled] is a skateboarding champion," says Vachon, "I want to
know if he's going up and down the Green Mountains."

Vachon also wants a quote or two in the query from the subject "to find out
if he is an attractive personality that we would want to present on the pages."

And he wants Style—charms to soothe a savage editor. "When the query is
flat, no matter how exciting the subject is, I tend to get into a negative frame of
mind."

That's understandable. *Vermont Life* is a stylish magazine. But trade publications, more interested in brass tacks than golden words, will often take a mat-
ter-of-fact query. "I've assigned stories to writers whose queries were not impressive, and come up with good stories," says Russell. "And I've assigned stories
to guys who wrote beautiful queries, and got terrible stories."

Neatness counts, cautions *The Lutheran Standard.* Is the query cleanly
typed? Does if offer evidence that the writer takes pride in his product? "Those
subtle things in some ways may have even more importance than what is said on
the paper," says managing editor Lowell Almen. "In that first contact, one of the
questions we have to ask is, 'Can we trust this writer to do a good job for us?'
The impression that is made is part of the query, too."

Some editors are impressed by business letterheads. "If a query comes in
here on a professional-looking letterhead," says trade editor Kaiser, "it gives the
writer quite a bit more of a chance."

But Vachon is unmoved. "In fact, some of them are so pretentious. 'Brian
Vachon, Writer.'"

Even so, a business letterhead saves the writer from typing his name and
address 20 times a week. It may give him a measure of pride in his work; and the
editor, assurance that the writer means business.

For editors, certain gimmicks and gaffes spell *amateur.* Here are some:

• *Misspelling the editor's name.* "And it's a dumb thing—I hate to be prejudiced by it," says Vachon. "But when I see it misspelled, I realize that the person hasn't taken the time to find out how to spell it correctly."

• *Ignorance* is no excuse. "I never cease to be amazed by the number of
writers who begin queries by saying, 'I never read your magazine, but...,'" says
Rebecca E. Greer, articles editor of *Woman's Day.* "It is both presumptuous and
insulting to assume you can write for a magazine you can't be bothered to read."

It's poison to request issues of the magazine and its guidelines for writers in
the query itself. Get them in advance.

• *Don't tip your whole hand* in the query. Be a tease. "Although," warns Vachon, "the one that runs for three paragraphs and then says, 'Want to hear the rest of the story?'—that's just awful."

Vachon recalls with more pleasure a query about an oil rig that once aroused hopes and now sits rusting away. "OK. I know the basic material. I'm intrigued by the fact that there was an oil rig in northern Vermont. And I don't know what happened. The thing was written with such intelligence and music that I wrote back and said, 'You're on.'"

• *Don't bury the editor in trivia.* 'It's easy for a writer to become a pen pal, and that gets to be a drag," says David R. Getchell, editor of *National Fisherman.* "He should get right down to facts. A couple of comments on the time of day or his health is perfectly OK, but he shouldn't go into a long discussion of his personal affairs. ... The editor has enough problems without borrowing those of his writer."

• *Don't be 'umble.* "An amazing number of queries come in that begin with an apology," says Vachon. "'I may not be an expert on wine—in fact, I don't know a Sauvignon 39 from

The freelancer with many credits shouldn't list them *all* in his query, says Brian Vachon, editor of *Vermont Life.* "It's blowing your horn almost too much."

Gallo burgundy—but I'd like to do a story on a Vermont winery.' And my immediate reaction is, 'Why on earth should you of all people get that assignment?'"

Yes, acknowledges Vachon, it's kosher for a writer who knows little about Vermont wine to query on the story, then research it after a go-ahead. "He just shouldn't advertise to me that he doesn't know."

On the other hand, if the freelancer has good wine credentials, "he certainly should get those into the query. It sweetens the offer."

Tearsheets often help. "If you are querying us for the first time, please include three photocopied samples of your published writing," says *womenSports.* "With no indication of your writing ability, we will be quite reluctant to give the go-ahead even on speculation."

Both Vachon and Jack Haring, articles editor of *Guideposts,* advise the beginning writer *not* to mention that he has never been published before. "It sort of sets up a strike against the writer," says Haring. "We're looking primarily at the quality of the person's writing."

But Russell at *American Laundry Digest* wants to know when the writer is new to the turf. Russell can then give him a list of questions to ask, and might call the laundry plant owner before the interview to ask him to help the writer along. "Usually they are very good at that," adds Russell. (That's a comfort; no writer likes to be taken to the cleaners.)

• *Beware of the multiple query.* Sometimes a writer sends copies of a query to several competing magazines, duly informing each editor. That, says Kaiser, "sorta turns you off in a hurry."

Dan Zadra at *Young Athlete* sums up: "If the person really has what he wants to say clearly in mind—there are no spelling errors in the query, it's neatly done, short, to the point, but covers all the information I'll need—that's impressive to me.

"But if something comes in—even if it's a good idea—and it's messy, dashed off, I get the feeling the individual isn't that interested in what he wants to write about, or he's trying to write for 20 or 30 magazines and not just *Young Athlete,* and that I'm liable to get mistakes in the finished piece. The query is so important."

Like an aperitif, the stylish query awakens the editor's appetite for the coming article. Here's a query that led to a $175 sale to *Writer's Digest:*

Take Henny Youngman. Please. Add a machine gun that shoots metaphors. Throw in a pinch of alliteration and sprinkle some sports trivia in between a pair of horn-rimmed glasses. Toss it all together and you have Jim Murray.

For the past decade, Murray has been recognized by his peers as *the* best sportswriter. Despite the fame (Murray is read in over 200 newspapers), he likes the simple life.

Murray on work habits: "I like to get my work out of the way so I can watch TV."

Murray on recreation: "... crossword puzzles, golf, and I like to drink."

Murray on his aspirations: "I'd like to be Jim Brown for about 48 hours. There are a lot of people I'd like to beat up."

Jim Murray is a white shirt and skinny tie in a world of hair dryers and platform shoes. His views on writing, sports and the media would interest the readers of *Writer's Digest.* I'd like to write that story.

I have received several awards in journalism, including best sports page in California, and have been published in *Los Angeles* magazine.

I can supply photos. And pretzels. And dip.

Walt Cieplik
Newhall, California

Short Fiction

Stranger Than Fiction Dept.: Fiction writing, despite the license it affords the writer, may require *more* market study than nonfiction does. The writer may have a passable grasp on the slant of, say, *Prehistoric Woodworking* after studying two issues; then he needs only check back copies to see whether his story idea has been recently covered. But the would-be science fiction writer must read not only the magazines (and more than two issues apiece; as many, in fact, as he can get his hands on) but also the *books:* Bradbury, Clarke, Silverberg, Pohl and Kornbluth—*all* of them. It's the only way he can discover what is new ground and what is as old as the stars; what will bring a check and an editorial shout, and what will bring a crisp note: "Heinlein was here 30 years ago."

Despite the workload—and the limited markets—short stories are well worth tackling. "I think the best way to break into mysteries is with the short story," says Edward D. Hoch, who has published five novels and almost 450 short stories. "Book editors are more likely to read your stuff and give you some consideration if you can say you've published a few short stories."

Hoch notes, "Admittedly, there are only about three mystery magazines. But they still publish probably 30 new stories a month. That's a pretty good market. and *Ellery Queen's* is especially open to new writers."

Ellery Queen's is also especially open to private-eye stories. "Fred Dannay [one half of Ellery Queen; his partner was the late Manfred B. Lee] wants very much to keep up the tradition of the detective story," says managing editor Eleanor Sullivan. "But too many we receive are imitative."

Jean Sharbel, editor of *Secrets,* says: "It's great to get a suspense story or something with humor. It doesn't all have to be gloom and doom, though a beginning writer may think that every story has to be a tragedy.

"A good romance is hard to come by," Sharbel adds wistfully. "I haven't seen a good suspense story in ages. We like some change of pace."

So even fiction magazines have shortages, holes in the inventory. A beginning writer can gain a foothold by locating the holes and plugging them with style. By studying and planning.

In fact, planning the story *before* you write is crucial. "The more you can get together in your head before you start writing," says Sullivan, "the more successful your first draft will be."

Adds Hoch: "I've talked to mystery writers who say that sometimes they don't know where they're going with the story when they start. I think that can be done if you're writing a crime-suspense story—and sometimes it works best if it's done like that. If you're writing a more formal type of whodunit, though, you

have to have at least some idea in mind, even if that idea is going to change along the way."

Not that planning a story means rolled sleeves, compass and blueprint. For science fiction writer George R.R. Martin, it means daydreaming. "I'll start daydreaming about scenes—not at all deliberately, just staring off into space while I'm on a subway train or something," says Martin, one of the brightest new stars in SF. "The scenes will start to come alive. I'll start to hear the characters and such. ... Pretty soon I have a good number of scenes, and I have a rough idea of where the story is going. Then I'll sit down and go with it.

"Sometimes it changes considerably, of course, in the act of being set on paper. The characters lurch off in a different direction than I had anticipated." When that happens, he lets the characters have their own heads.

So Martin plans a story, but not completely. "I've had some stories surprise me in the way they ended."

The freelancer should understand not only what the editor wants to read, but what *readers* want to read. "People have interests that you have to tap," says editor Jeremy Harrington about the range of subjects his magazine, *St. Anthony Messenger,* will undertake. "You don't make their interests. You just try to write about them."

When Hoch is stumped for an ending, he follows one rule: "I try to think of the kind of ending that would satisfy me as a reader. ... That has often caused me to even reject my original ending and do something entirely different."

Satisfying the reader: that's the one unchanging rule. Often that means dispensing with Acts of God and Author. "A story can be quite good, and then the author louses it up by having the narrator's problems solved by fortuitous circumstance rather than by her own efforts," says confessions editor Sharbel. "I read a pretty good story today on wife-beating, and I was very enthusiastic about it. But instead of the narrator doing something about the problem, low and behold, the husband conveniently shot himself. So I killed the whole story."

Another way to cheat the confessions reader is to feed her false medical information. "It's very important for us to convey correct information," says Sharbel. "If you're talking about somebody with leukemia, make sure that your facts are right."

More do's and don'ts:

• If you can't support yourself solely on your writing, get a job *un*related to writing. "Strange as it may seem, the best jobs for a writer are drudgery, dead-end jobs—unloading trucks or something like that," says Martin. "You can daydream while you're doing that, and you're not tired out on writing when you come back."

• If an editor shows interest in your work, keep submitting to him—even if he moves to another magazine or publishing house. Advises Hoch: "Look him up in *Literary Market Place.*" (*LMP* is a directory listing the names and numbers of leading editorial personnel—and much else.)

Finally, don't balk at the slush pile: most fiction editors prefer that you send a complete manuscript rather than query. "I love to get story submissions, because the more I get, the better for me," says Sharbel. "I'm always on the lookout for a good story. And I *do* read that slush pile. Writers think they get lost in slush. But through the years, I've found some damn good writers there. I have a healthy respect for it."

Poetry

Poetry pays poorly—or exceedingly well. It depends on whether one's poetry writing is a search for checks or a search for self. Judson Jerome, poetry columnist for *Writer's Digest,* explains why poets (unlike nonfiction and fiction writers) cannot play the market:

Market is a misnomer for the avenues of publication of poetry; most of the magazines that matter in the career of a poet pay little or nothing beyond contributor's copies, and quality book publication usually pays nothing beyond a small advance, if that. Poets cannot depend upon their writing for economic support, though once their names are known, many derive some income from readings and related benefits.

The poet should distinguish between *subsidy, commercial* and *literary* publication. Subsidy publication usually has absolutely no commercial or literary value, and by succumbing to it a poet is likely to lose both money and reputation. Such publication includes books from many "vanity" publishers, most of the "contests" which a poet pays to enter or which are lures to purchase volumes of "prize-winning" poetry, anthologies in which a poet has to pay (at least by buying a copy of the book) to be included, and "agent" services in which the agent is paid a fee by the writer instead of a fixed percentage (usually ten percent) of monies earned. The public does not buy vanity publications, literary people ignore them, and the only satisfaction poets may derive (and for many this is enough) is that of seeing their work in print. It is cheaper to go to your local printer and pay directly for this service.

Commercial publication is that from which the poet can expect financial return. There is little other reason for getting involved, for, as in the case of most commercial products, the poet must be primarily concerned with what will sell (as opposed to literature, art, self-expression, profundity, or other such considerations). The few commercial successes in poetry (e.g., Rod McKuen, Ogden Nash) tend not to be taken seriously by the literary establishment. Many regard this as snobbism. Whether the situation is just or not, a poet should be aware of it. The most dependable markets for commercial poetry are greeting-card manufacturers and poster publishers. Some successful commercial poets have syndicated newspaper columns or contracts with popular magazines. Some combine their writing with singing or other forms of performance. Note that rates even from high-paying magazine markets are too small to support a poet by freelance sales. If you want to make money with your poetry you will have to explore other forms of publication than magazine sales and book publication.

Literary publication is that which leads to recognition by critics and quality book publishers and the small but intense audience of modern literature. A beginning poet usually starts in the little literary magazines—of which there are dozens open to (some begging for) contributions from unknown writers. When he has a string of credits in such magazines, he may begin submitting book manuscripts to quality publishers or to the few contests of literary significance. (These are announced regularly in the editorial columns of *Writer's Digest, Coda,* and other magazines.) Sometimes the life span of literary magazines is brief. Most pay nothing. They tend to be edited and published by dedicated individuals or groups who are passionately involved—as artists have always been—in the exciting current (and often ephemeral) trends in experimental writing.

For a current listing of these markets, see the latest edition of the *International Directory of Little Magazines and Small Presses* in your library (or from Dustbooks, Box 1056, Paradise, California 95969). For regular announcements of reputable contests and good magazines and book publishers (as well as other information pertinent to poetry), subscribe to *Coda: Poets & Writers Newsletter,* 201 W. 54th St., New York City 10019 —$6 per year. As one reader put it, *Coda* is for poets (and other writers) what the *Wall Street Journal* is for bankers. Request *The Cultural Post* free from the National Endowment for the Arts, Washington, D.C. 20506, and *Poetry Clearinghouse* free from the Poetry Office, 201 E. Capitol St. S.E., Washington, D.C. 20003. Read the review media dealing with the little magazines, such as *Small Press Review, Margins* (write Dustbooks, address above), or *Northeast Rising Sun* (1416 W. Mt. Royal Ave., Baltimore 21217). These will put you in touch with other publications looking for manuscripts and containing good examples of contemporary poetry (as well as information relevant to a literary career). When writing these small journals for sample copies, always enclose a dollar or two: most operate on budgets recorded in red ink. For further guidance, inquire about the creative writing programs at your state and municipal universities, or write *Cedar Rock,* 1121 Madeline, New Braunfels, Texas 78130, for information about their poetry instruction service.

When you are considering book publication, it is important to know that not *all* publishers requiring a subsidy are so-called "vanity" presses. You have to gauge the thickness of the flattery in the correspondence—and the prices and details of the contract. Many reputable subsidy publishers are listed in the *International Directory* (listed above). Self-publication is an honorable alternative. (See *Publishing Poetry,* Trunk Press, Hancock, Maryland 21750 for a general discussion of the problem.)

Basically poets have to recognize that few read poetry, few care about it in any serious way, and even fewer ever buy it. The poet Kenneth

Ross R. Olney, who quit an excellent job to move to California on the strength of one magazine sale because "we thought this was where writers live," has sold over 80 books. "Providing they sell well at all, you draw royalties over a long period of time, which is like having money in the bank."

Patchen once said, "People who say they love poetry but never buy any are cheap SOB's." That includes would-be poets!

Books

Once a freelancer has survived his baptism by fire in magazine writing, he may itch to move on to books: more thoughtful, more lasting work than articles—and more steadily paying. "Providing they sell well at all," says Ross R. Olney, who has sold over 80 books, "you draw royalties over a long period of time, which is like money in the bank."

Sometimes a writer *must* move on to books. "You starve to death in the Christian field on magazine articles," says Marti Hefley, half of a husband-wife team that, singly or in combination, has produced over 30 books. "The first thing you teach people [who want to freelance fulltime by writing articles] is to pray a lot, because they're not going to eat very much."

In the search for book ideas, timing is crucial. Today's fad may fade tomorrow. The trick, of course, is to anticipate tomorrow's lively interests. Olney likes to write about a sport after privately published paperbacks have dealt with it, but before general hardcover books appear. "That's a very very economically sound time," he says.

And you might look out for the offbeat. "California is a pretty zany place, and a lot of things start here," says Olney in Ventura, California. "If you see a sport where some guy is throwing a stick in the air and seeing if it can land on somebody's chimney, you say, 'Well, is this going to spread?'

"No publisher will touch something unless it has spread at least to where it is fairly well-known on the East Coast and accepted in the Midwest."

Once you have a book idea in mind, try to measure its salability by:

• *Checking for similar books listed in the Subject Guide to* Books in Print. *BIP* is a standard reference tool in libraries. Don't wait for your editor to run the check. When Olney queried one publisher on an astronomy book, back came a photocopy out of *BIP*, with a huge area of astronomy books circled—including one by Olney.

- *Reading* Publishers Weekly *assiduously*—particularly its book evaluations, PW Forecasts. "They are marvelous," says Kenneth D. McCormick, senior consultant editor of Doubleday. "If you read them regularly, you begin to see what the flow of ideas are, what's coming. And maybe your idea *is* unique."
- *Studying the publisher's catalog.* It's a handy guide to that house's personality and strengths.

Now write a query to the publisher, sketching your idea and asking whether he would be interested in an outline and a sample chapter. "And then, psychologically, you have the editor asking to see something—and the whole thing becomes reciprocal," says McCormick. "It may be the editor, in writing back, tips his hand and gives the writer a notion of what he wants to see in that outline."

The query should run about 1½ pages unless the subject is so complex it demands more. "We read *so* much mail," says McCormick. "It's a rare letter that can't be stated in 1 to 1½ pages. Most letters are too long, including mine."

Olney recommends this form: at the top of the page, type the book title, and 'a book proposal' in parentheses. Now for "pure sell": 'Did you know that eating grapes is the best possible thing for your health?' Then: 'A book has not been done on this subject.' "This is *very* important to the publisher," says Olney.

Now succinctly outline the book. Chapter one: a basic history of grape-eating. Chapter two: what does this do for your body?...

Three-quarters of the page down, add your credits: 'I've published 14 magazine articles and am an expert on grape-eating.'

Says Olney, "A query like that has never failed me."

George Laycock, who has written over 30 books, warns that even a brief query can require more research than you'd think. "I'm not sure that, in many subjects, you would understand the subject well enough to be sure there's a book in it if you just did enough research to knock out a one-page letter."

Of the three ways to approach a publisher (by sending a query, a sample chapter and an outline, or a complete manuscript), querying is most often preferred by houses—in both fiction and nonfiction. (For a particular house's preference, of course, you should check its listing.)

McCormick suggests that the novelist offer to send the editor thumbnail profiles of his major characters (as well as a sample chapter and an outline). "I find these are very helpful, because you begin to see the cast, the possibilities. I've gotten such a presentation from a fairly well-known writer now—and then the man took a little more trouble and went on for about 40 pages with a complete blueprint of the book. I find it quite engrossing. I plan to recommend it for publication because it's so clear the author knows what he is going to do." The author should also send his credits—"the *Atlantic* monthly, the *National Hardware Manual* or whatever. I wouldn't be afraid to list the specialties, because that might ring a bell in the editor's mind that the writer wouldn't have anticipated."

Even a writer without an idea can get a toehold in a house. "Lively publishing houses often have ideas for which they don't have writers," says McCormick. A seasoned magazine writer can make himself available for assignments by writing a 1½-page letter to the editor-in-chief listed in *Literary Market Place* and asking him to pass the information along do the appropriate editor. Write a letter that seems to invite a reply, "in which the editor might say, 'Have you ever done anything in natural history?'" says McCormick. "As soon as you can get a reply back from the editor, then you're in cahoots, and it becomes give and take instead of you outside pleading."

We'll let McCormick take it from here:

"Let's say your man has written articles in the entertainment field and the financial field and he's also big on ecology. The best thing would be for him to ... write to an editor and say, 'I'm a professional, and I want to break into the field. Here are some tearsheets of what I have done. I believe that these are the fields in which I know something, but I'm a quick study and can work in any field, given a little time to research. I've kept my magazine dates, so I'm pretty dependable on assignments.'

"Then the publisher is intrigued by this man. The publisher might ask him to outline how he would develop an idea an editor is proposing. The writer would be expected to do a thorough outline, and if it's in a field where the author has worked, the publisher would probably ask for a sample chapter. Then there should be a contract, obviously, because the writer shouldn't do any more on spec—other than to prove his ability to do what he is asked to do.

"If he has done a good job and the publisher for some reason has changed his mind, then the author should say, 'OK, I've done my part, but it didn't work out for you. May I take this idea and show it elsewhere?' If the publisher is fair, he will, of course, say yes."

Bookwriting is an attractive trade—for workaholics. An ambitious author may suddenly find himself in the middle of a 20-mile sprint. Paul Little wrote 39 books in 1972. Even Lee Butcher, writing a mere three books at once (and an article a week), worked 12 hours a day, 7 days a week. "I work very hard," he said. "But I'm working for me."

Rejections

Now for a few words about the misery—about getting back a good manuscript, like a kick from an ungrateful horse; about those pitiless inscrutable verdicts—rejection slips.

"I get them as well as give them," says *Vermont Life* editor and freelancer Vachon. "When I get one, I generally shrug my shoulders and wonder where else I can peddle the manuscript. If you start taking them personally, it can be awful, because they're very demeaning little things. I sometimes think the freelance writing profession is pretty demeaning."

It is. And sometimes senseless, too. There's no sense, for instance, in reading a rejection slip backward and right to left and running a chemical analysis on it to figure out what the editor *really* meant by "fails to coincide with our present needs"; he might have meant one of a hundred things. That's why he has rejection slips mass-produced—to cover a hundred situations. You can only send the editor a McGuffey primer (to learn how to read), study your next market, and send the waif out again.

In a sense, *Writer's Market* is a book of dreams, like a Sears, Roebuck

Dan Zadra, editor of *Young Athlete,* is scouting for freelancers. ''We're doing too much revising, rewriting, and I'm still looking for the right people. We're a magazine for young people, and that may be one of the challenges freelancers are having with us. ...They want hard information, yes, but we can't talk down to them. We don't want things too complicated for them, and yet we don't want things that are too far under their expertise level, either.''

Christmas catalog for a child. But don't just fantasize. Get up, Write, fume, write again. No one ever began with a second novel; no law will prevent you, after a hundred and one rejections, from submitting again. After all, what does it cost a writer to keep a manuscript in the mails? A few dimes. But what does it cost him to keep the manuscript locked in his third desk drawer from the top, and future manuscripts locked inside his gut? Against *that* price, a few rejection slips look pitiful indeed.

"Sometimes I'd get very angry," Joyce Verrette reflects about the rejections she received for *Dawn of Desire.* "They'd catch me on the wrong kind of day, and I'd slam doors and things. Sometimes I thought, 'What am I knocking myself out for? They're not going to take it.'

"Then I thought, 'Well, they're certainly not going to take it if you put it in your drawer and forget about it.' And I couldn't forget about it.

"I kept thinking. 'No! It's too good. I'm not going to let it die like this. If I had to do this for the rest of my life, I'm going to keep doing it because on my deathbed I'm not going to lie there and say: 'I wish.''"

Recommended Reading

Here are some valuable books to prop up next to your dictionary:

The Elements of Style, by William Strunk Jr. and E.B. White. A classic primer of grammar and style.

The Careful Writer, by Theodore M. Bernstein. What's the difference between *may* and *might?* Bernstein knows.

Webster's New Dictionary of Synonyms. Defines the shades of meaning separating cousin synonyms.

The Craft of Interviewing, by John Brady. A lively and comprehensive treatment. Helpful both to the pro and to the tenderfoot who was too shy to ask questions even back in health class.

"Confessions of a Children's Book Editor," by James Cross Giblin. In the 1977 *Writer's Yearbook.* How to query the Gentle Editor for fiction or nonfiction.

The World Almanac & Book of Facts. An annual gold mine.

The U.S. Fact Book. The federal census bureau's statistical abstract of the country. Annual.

The People's Almanac, by David Wallechinsky and Irving Wallace. Inspiration for ideas.

Webster's Biographical Dictionary. More than 40,000 succinct biographies.

For fiction writers. ...

Writing Fiction, by R.V. Cassill.

• "How to Please an Editor," by Eleanor Sullivan. In *Mystery Writer's Handbook.* Excellent advice for all fiction writers about to stuff a manuscript into the mailbox.

"Carl Kohler's Checklist for Fiction Writers," by Carl Kohler. In the 1977 *Writer's Yearbook.* For short fiction.

See *Books in Print* for price and ordering information for these books. For free copies of the *Yearbook* articles, send one SASE for each to Freebie Editor, *Writer's Market,* 9933 Alliance Road, Cincinnati 45242.

Selling Pictures With Your Words

By Ted Schwarz

Supposedly one picture is worth a thousand words. I disagree. For a writer, the truth is that a photograph can *sell* a thousand words—or any other article length, for that matter. When you illustrate your work, you are increasing its marketability and *your* income.

We live in a visual age. Newspapers use photographs to show everything from the horrors of war to people enjoying the first day of spring. Advertisements use the faces of beautiful women, handsome men and adorable children to sell everything from laxatives to candy. And both television and the movies are total photographic experiences. We want to see what we are reading about, and that fact is understood by magazine and book publishers. Writing, no matter how strong it may be by itself, is more likely to be read when accompanied by photographs. And if you can supply those pictures, your chance of making a sale will be much greater than if you turn in only an article.

If you have never taken photographs for your articles, your immediate reaction to my statements may be mild panic. "Even if I mortgage my house, sell my car and auction my first-born child, I could never afford the zillion-dollar Moneyflex camera *everyone* knows you *have* to have to take decent pictures," you are probably thinking. Fortunately you would be wrong. The best camera for illustrating your articles is probably the one you now own.

Almost all cameras available today are capable of taking photographs that can be enlarged to 8x10", the standard size for black-and-white when submitting material to an editor. This includes the original 126 Instamatics as well as the "Moneyflex" line. Only cameras using unusually small film, such as the 110 Pocket Instamatic, will present a problem.

The important point about illustrating your work is to know the limitations of your equipment. If your camera is fixed focus and anything closer than five or six feet is a blur, then don't try to take close-up details of a piece of jewelry for a hobby article. If your camera works only with a tiny cube flash, you should not tell an editor you will provide illustrations of a cathedral interior that must be specially illuminated to show details throughout its massive depth.

By limiting your illustrations to what you can handle, you will not need to buy special equipment. Thus, if you are doing an article on jewelry and can't get closer than three or four feet with your camera, you won't offer to show detailed portions of a diamond. Instead you can have a model dress in the jewelry—wearing earrings, bracelets and necklaces—and photograph her.

If you do not own a camera or are planning to buy a better one, the ideal choice is the 35mm single-lens reflex. These are available for as little as $200-300 and take any number of lenses and accessories. Because you look through the lens when focusing, what you see is what you'll get in the final print. The negatives enlarge easily to 8x10, and the 35mm slides are considered standard in the

---

Freelance writer/photographer Ted Schwarz is the author of How to Make Money With Your Camera *and* How to Start a Photography Business, *plus a host of other books. He has sold pictures with his articles to* Modern Bride, Saturday Review, Free Enterprise *and numerous other publications.*

Photographs sent to magazines should be of higher quality than you may be able to obtain in some communities. You can use almost any lab for processing color slide film, but black-and-white processing and printing should be done by a custom lab. Such a lab can make contact prints and will enlarge by hand rather than machine. The custom lab can give you proper contrast for reproduction purposes and correct some of your errors in exposure. The technicians can also do minor retouching to eliminate scratches and other marks.

If your community lacks a custom lab, check the advertisements in magazines like *Modern Photography* and *Popular Photography*. You might also check one of the trade journals for professionals, like *The Rangefinder* magazine, 3511 Centinela Avenue, Los Angeles 90066. Black-and-white processing labs advertising in *The Rangefinder* provide custom services.

business. The day when magazines required 2¼x2¼ or larger transparencies is past. A good 35mm slide is salable most everywhere.

Generally you should use the slowest film you can in order to take pictures that will enlarge well. The amount of existing light will determine your final choice, but try to use Kodachrome for color, and a fine grain film like Kodak's Plus-X for black-and-white. Most professionals tend to use Tri-X, a film made for low light, for all assignments requiring black-and-white, and there is nothing wrong with this. It can be enlarged well beyond the 8x10 limit you will need.

Horizontal or Vertical?

Photographs should be both horizontal and vertical so the editor has some choice when faced with space limitations. If you send only horizontal photographs and he has a tall, narrow hole to fill, your photographs will be valueless. But if you include vertical photos as well, you will make the sale.

When you plan a photo series, keep in mind several facts. First, the photographs will probably be reduced in size when printed. That panoramic print of the marching band which shows vast expanses of sky and ground may be useless when the print is reduced. The band members may be diminished to a point where they look like ants. Thus it is essential that you concentrate on the important elements of the picture, and let them dominate the print or slide. If your story is about a man who carves wooden figures, close in to show the man's hands carving the wood or, at least, the full figure of the man at work. Don't stand back so far that the man is dwarfed by the cabin where he lives, the woods near his home and the creek from which he gets his water. If the story is about a person, *he* is the focal point of your picture.

There are two types of photographs you should include. One type provides an overview of what the story is about. It can stand alone with no other illustrations and still be effective. It ensures the sale of at least one photograph when the space for the article becomes cramped. For instance, this may mean a picture of the wood-carver sitting on a stool working at his craft.

The rest of the photographs should show segments of the story. One should be a close-up of the carver's hands. Another might show raw wood as well as carvings in different stages of completion. Yet another photograph would show the knife blade gouging out the wood; and a fifth, the sanding and smoothing operation. The greater the variety of images you can give the editor, the more prints you are likely to sell.

Be certain your photographs are interesting. Too many times a writer misses the additional sale by sending dull photographs he thinks are important. If he

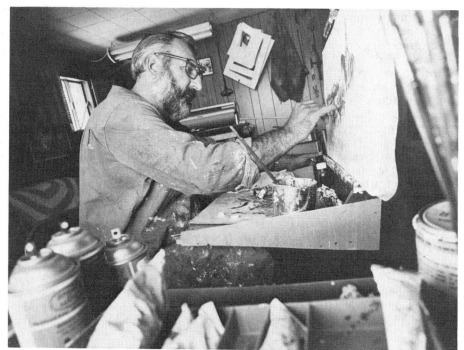

does a story on a prize-winning athlete, he hurts his sales by including a standard, flash-on-camera photo of a grinning athlete holding a trophy and shaking an official's hand. On the other hand, a salable photograph might show the athlete running or jumping in whatever sport it was in which he triumphed.

How you submit your photographs is an important part of selling. Most publications prefer black-and-white prints to costly color reproduction. The 8x10s are considered standard because they can be marked easily for the printer as well as airbrushed when necessary. However, in some cases you may be asked to submit contact sheets from which the editor will select the images to be enlarged.

A contact sheet is just a piece of enlarging paper (8x10 usually) on which all the negatives have been placed. All the exposures are printed the same size as the negative. These are checked with a magnifying glass and the selections for enlarging are made. Unfortunately, unless all the pictures on a roll were exposed exactly the same

When illustrating stories about people in various professions, try for both environmental and more traditional portraits. Artist W.A. Zivic of Tucson was framed by paints, brushes, and canvas in the room where he creates. The second portrait was taken while he was working, this time focusing only on his face.

way, some of the images on the contact sheet will be a little light, and others a little dark. If the editor is experienced in looking at such sheets, he will understand that the final prints will be fine. If the editor isn't experienced, he may assume you did a poor job. To protect yourself when you haven't worked with an editor before, send at least two or three enlargements from the roll in addition to the contact sheet. This will show an inexperienced editor that the work will print well, thus ensuring the sale.

Sending Your Work

Print mailers are the easiest way to send your photographs. These are special envelopes sold by almost all camera stores. They contain two pieces of corrugated cardboard which prevent the mailman from squishing the prints as invariably happens with standard envelopes. I also send the envelope from a second mailer, minus the cardboard, with the prints for their return. The envelope is properly stamped and addressed, and the cardboard from the first mailer is marked "Save For Print Return" so most editors know to reuse the cardboard.

When you send color, the editors want to see slides. You can use the cardboard or plastic boxes in which they are returned, but this is risky. The boxes are easily crushed and you are forcing the editor to handle the slides. This increases the chance of damage.

My solution is to place the slides in heavy-duty plastic pages that hold 20 slides each and fit into standard notebooks. Camera stores sell these as do many coin shops. Compare prices in your area; I have usually found that coin dealers sell the pages for less than the photography stores. Prices range from 15¢ per

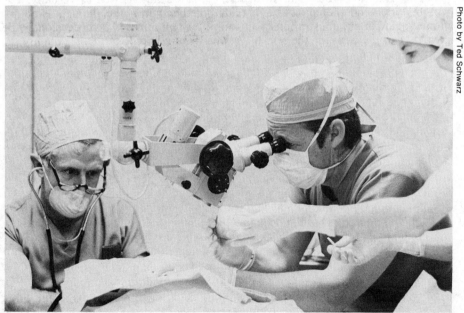

Photo by Ted Schwarz

This photograph was taken to illustrate a story on Surgicenter, a private surgical facility I wrote about for *Physician's Management*. Always frame your subjects tightly, either in the viewfinder or when ordering the print to be cropped. You never know how small the print will have to be reduced. If I had recorded the entire operating room, the important images—the medical personnel—might have been dwarfed by all the nonessentials.

sheet to around a quarter, depending upon the quantity purchased. The sheets even provide protection from spilled coffee.

Some writers like to have duplicate slides made to protect the originals. This is a bad idea. Most duplicate slides lack the original's quality and can be an editorial turn-off. A true duplicate that exactly matches the rich colors of the original can cost as much as $45 at custom labs.

I have an internegative made of any slide I consider highly salable and irreplaceable (cost is $5 to $7.50 for a 4x5 internegative made from a 35mm original). This is a color negative of your slide that can be printed just like regular color negative film. It provides almost perfect color reproduction, and you can have prints and new slides made from the internegative should the original slide be lost.

All prints, contact sheets and slides should have your name and address on them. I have a rubber stamp with full identification. The print shop that made it set the stamp type small enough to fit on the wider cardboard border of 2x2 slides. *Lightly* stamp the prints while they are face down on a hard flat surface to avoid having the ink print through to the front.

Often you can sell photographs used for one story to other, noncompeting publications. The most concise information about multiple sales, as well as extensive market listings for photographs, can be found in the annual *Photographer's Market*. There are also numerous books on the business aspects of such freelancing. Time-Life Books' Library of Photography covers this area as does *How to Make Money With Your Camera*, by Ted Schwarz. *What and How to Sell Your Photograph*, by the late Arvel Ahlers has several chapters on methods for freelancing, though the book is not updated often enough for the market guide to remain accurate.

The next time you write an article, think visually as well as verbally. The pictures you send the editor may decide whether you make the sale. And the money paid for the illustrations you took in a few minutes can occasionally be greater than the cash for the text over which you labored for many hours.

If You Have Any Problems

On Not Getting Paid

When you're getting promises instead of checks from an editor, send him a letter reminding him of his obligation. If he doesn't reply, send him another one —by registered mail—and send his publisher a copy. If there is still no reply, send us a summary of your complaint, copies of your correspondence, and a SASE. We'll probe the matter; if the periodical still refuses to respond, we'll consider deleting its listing from the next *Writer's Market*.

In the meantime, you might also consult with an attorney; or consider a suit in a small claims court.

Sometimes a periodical will close up shop without settling its accounts with writers. When that happens, write the postmaster or the Better Business Bureau office in that periodical's city, asking for a forwarding address.

Mail Fraud

Suppose that *Your Cheatin' Magazine* (fictitious name!) says in its *Writer's Market* listing that it will buy 20 freelance manuscripts annually. You fire an article off, and six days later receive a letter of acceptance, promising $50. Six months later, the piece is published. But you never get paid. Is this mail fraud? Maybe.

Fraud means that someone has intentionally made false claims that resulted in an exchange of money or of something valuable (say, a manuscript). But here's the rub: you (or the prosecutor) must prove that there was an *intent* to defraud. If your errant publisher can prove that he intended to pay, but was later unable to, then intent to defraud would be harder to prove.

According to the Postal Service, however, mail fraud may be involved if: a magazine promises to pay on publication, but never publishes; a magazine solicits manuscripts, but then fails to respond to submissions, and eventually leaves town without a forwarding address; an author's agent claims he has contacts for your manuscript, but fails to substantiate that claim.

If you think you're a victim of mail fraud, ask your local post office for the address of the nearest postal inspection division, or write the Chief Postal Inspection Office, Fraud Branch, 47 L'enfant Plaza, West, S.W., Washington, D.C. 20260.

Describe the nature of your problem, and provide names, addresses, dates, and photocopies of correspondence (excluding the manuscript). If postal inspectors believe you have a case for mail fraud, they'll turn the matter over to the U.S. Attorney. Conviction results in a fine of up to $1,000, or imprisonment of up to five years, or both.

If the inspectors believe that you have a problem—but not a case for mail fraud —they'll turn the matter over to the Postal Service's Consumer Protection Program. The program will then try to mediate the problem—without force of law.

If, in the end, you are dissatisfied with the Postal Service's action, you always have a last resort: take the publisher to court.

Withdrawing a Manuscript

When awaiting a report on your manuscript, be patient; editors are generally overworked, and slow readers to boot. Allow at least two more weeks than the reporting time specified in the *Writer's Market* listing for that editor's periodical. If time passes and your mailbox remains empty, write a letter asking for a report; include the name of your manuscript, the date on which you mailed it, and an S.A.S.E.

If you hear nothing within three weeks, send another query or write the editor that you're withdrawing your ms from consideration. Either way, send the letter registered—return receipt requested—and drop *Writer's Market* a note about your woes. We may be able to help.

File With Care

Doing battle with a recalcitrant periodical can be like challenging Goliath with an empty slingshot. But you'll boost your chances immensely if you'll keep careful records of all editorial correspondence. Photocopy all letters and manuscripts; file them carefully. Sooner or later, you may need them.

Copyright and Rights

By Kirk Polking

Beginning January 1, 1978, the new Copyright Revision Bill will replace the existing law. What does this mean for writers? Primarily these things:

- Works can be copyrighted whether they're published or unpublished.

- Works created after January 1, 1978, can be copyrighted for the author's life plus 50 years. Those works already copyrighted before 1978 under the present term of 28 years can be renewed now for another 47 years, instead of another 28 as previously allowed. (Unpublished works created before January 1, 1978, which were allowed to fall into public domain cannot now be copyrighted, however.)

- The new law specifically recognizes the principle of "fair use" of copyrighted works and indicates factors to be considered in determining "fair use" as opposed to copyright infringement.

- The new law specifies circumstances under which making single copies of works by libraries, for noncommercial purposes, does not constitute copyright infringement.

- The new law raises the statutory royalty on music recordings from 2¢ to 2¾¢ or ½¢ per minute of playing time whichever amount is larger, and makes jukebox operators subject to royalty payments from which they were previously exempt.

Writers who want to obtain information on Highlights of the new copyright law should write for Circulars R99 and R15a to the Copyright Office, Library of Congress, Washington, D.C. 20559. If you want to receive a copy of the complete new statute, you can obtain that also (Public Law 94-553) from the Copyright Office.

Submitting Your Work

Protecting your work is the responsibility of the individual writer and there are still pitfalls to avoid:

Public Domain. If you allow your work to appear in an uncopyrighted publication, it is then in the public domain and the public is free to use it without infringing on your rights. If you're submitting to a publication, look for the copyright notice (such as © 1978 Jones Publishing Co.) which usually appears at the bottom of the contents page. If you're submitting to a publication for which you don't have a sample copy and you're not sure whether it's copyrighted, don't hesitate to ask the editor. If it's not copyrighted and the editor wants to publish your work, you still have the option of copyrighting your work yourself by doing this: Ask the editor to publish your copyright notice (© John Doe, 1978) on the first page of the article, story or poem in the magazine. Meanwhile, write to the Copyright Office for an application form for "Contribution to a Periodical." Fill it out and send it, with two copies of the published magazine, carrying your copyright notice to the Copyright Office with a check for $10. Note: Most newspapers are not copyrighted, so your work appearing in such a newspaper is placed in the public domain.

Kirk Polking was editor of Writer's Digest, *1961-73. She is now director of* Writer's Digest School.

What Rights are You Selling?

The "rights" mentioned by magazine editors refer to the contractual rights they're buying to your work. And what they're buying determines whether you can resell your work, so it's important to know what the terms mean that these editors use:

• *First Serial Rights.* The word serial here does not mean publication in installments, but refers to the fact that libraries call periodicals "serials" because they are published in serial or continuing fashion. *First Serial Rights* means the writer offers the newspaper or magazine (both of which are periodicals) the right to publish his article, story or poem the first time in their periodical. All other rights to the material belong to the writer. Variations on this right are, for example, First North American Serial Rights. Some magazines use this purchasing technique to obtain the right to publish first in both America and Canada since many American magazines are circulated in Canada. If they had purchased only First U.S. Serial Rights, a Canadian magazine could come out with prior or simultaneous publication of the same material. When material is excerpted from a book which is to be published and it appears in a magazine or newspaper prior to book publication, this is also called First Serial Rights.

• *Second Serial (Reprint) Rights.* This gives a newspaper or magazine the opportunity to print an article, poem or story after it has already appeared in some other newspaper or magazine. The term is also used to refer to the sale of part of a book to a newspaper or magazine after a book has been published, whether or not there has been any first serial publication.

• *All Rights.* Some magazines, either because of the top prices they pay for material, or the fact that they have book publishing interests or foreign magazine connections, sometimes buy only *All Rights.* A writer who sells an article, story or poem to a magazine under these terms, forfeits the right to use his material in its present form elsewhere himself. If the magazine has not already made known in its listings in writer's magazines, or in *Writer's Market* that it purchases *All Rights* on material, its check, its voucher or purchase agreement which accompanies the check usually spells out that this is what it is buying. If the writer thinks he may want to use his material later (perhaps in book form) then he must avoid submitting to these types of markets or refuse payment and withdraw his material if he discovers it later. Or ask the editor whether he's willing to buy only first rights instead of all rights.

• *Simultaneous Rights.* This term covers articles and stories which are sold to publications (primarily religious magazines) which do not have overlapping circulations. A Baptist publication, for example, might be willing to buy *Simultaneous Rights* to a Christmas story which they like very much, even through they know a Presbyterian magazine may be publishing the same story in one of its Christmas issues. All publications which will buy simultaneous rights indicate this fact in their listings in *Writer's Market.*

• *Foreign Serial Rights.* Can you resell a story you have had published in America to a foreign magazine? If you sold only First U.S. Serial Rights to the American magazine and you have obtained the assignment of rights to yourself from that original editor, yes, you are free to market your story abroad. This presumes, of course, that the foreign magazine does buy material which has previously appeared in an American periodical.

• *Syndication Rights.* This is a division of serial rights. For example, a book publisher may sell the rights to a newspaper syndicate to print a book in twelve installments in, say, each of twenty of the United States leading newspapers. If they did this prior to book publication it would be syndicating *First Serial Rights* to the book. If they did this after book publication, they would be syndicating *Second Serial Rights* to the book.

A reminder: When a writer sells *First Serial Rights* to a magazine editor on an article, story or poem, the editor is essentially holding all other rights in trust for the author until he asks for them. So writers who do plan to try to resell their work should write the editor who first publishes their work asking for the return of all other rights to their material. The editor's letter is the instrument of transfer of such rights.

How Much Should I Charge?

By Kirk Polking

Freelancers who are asked to take on a specialized writing job, for which no set fee is announced in advance, are in a pickle. How do you know what kind of figure to quote on a job you've never done before?

If the job is locally based, you can try contacting other writers or friends in a related business who have used freelancers, to get some idea of what's been paid for similar jobs in the past.

Otherwise you have to set your fee based on two considerations: (1) how much you think your time is worth and how long you think it will take to do the job; and (2) how much you think the client is willing, or can afford to pay for the job.

Since the rates paid by advertising agencies, businesses, retail stores and other firms who are consistent users of freelance writers vary from city to city, the list which follows can only serve as a rough guideline.

Here are some jobs and the rates writers tell us they have been paid for them.

Advertising copywriting: $10-25/hour or a "package" price which might be just $25 for a press release or small ad on up to several hundred dollars for a more complex assignment.

Associations, writing for, on miscellaneous projects: $10-25/hour or on a project basis.

As-told-to books: author gets full advance and 50% royalties; subject gets 50% royalties.

Audio cassette scripts: $120 for 20 minutes.

Audiovisual scripts: $1,000-$1,500 advance against 5-10% royalties for 5-10 script/visual units.

Biography, writing for a sponsor: $500 up to $3,000 plus expenses over a 4-year period.

Book manuscript copy editing: $3-5/hour.

Book manuscript readers' report: $10 for a half-page summary of the book; half-page recommendation.

Book manuscript rewriting: $1,000 and up; $350/day and up.

Booklets, writing and editing: $500-$1,000.

Business films: 10% of production cost on films up to $30,000. $150/day; $20/hour where % of cost not applicable.

Business writing: $25-50/hour.

Catalogs or brochures for business: $60-75/printed page; more if there are many tables or charts which must be reworked for readability and consistency.

Comedy writing, for night club circuit entertainers: Gags only, $5-7. Routines, $100-300/minute. Some new comics try to get 5-minute routines for $100-150; but top comics may pay $1,500 for a 5-minute bit from a top writer with credits.

Commercial reports, for business, insurance companies, credit agencies, market research firms: $1.85-5/report.

Company newsletters, "house organs": $100-400, 2-4 pages.

Consultation fees: $75-100/hour.

Conventions, public relations for: $500-5,000.

Correspondent, magazine, regional: $5-15/hour, plus expenses.

Criticism, art, music, drama, local: free tickets plus $2-5.

Editing, freelance book: $5/hour and up.

Editing a group of religious publications: $200-500/month.

Editing text copy for business brochures, publications: $20-35/hour.

Educational film strips: $1,200.

Educational films, writing: $200 for one reeler (11 minutes of film); $1,000-1,500 for 30 minutes.

Educational grant proposals, writing: $50-125/day plus expenses.

Family histories, writing: $200-500.

Fiction rewriting: $150 for 10-page short story to $10,000 for complete novel rewrite, under special circumstances.

Folders, announcement, writing: $25-350.

Gallup Poll interviewing: $2.50/hour.

Genealogical research, local: $3-5/hour.

Ghostwriting business speeches, major markets: $2,750.

Ghostwriting a novel rewrite: $500 ($5/hour for 100 hrs. work).

Ghostwriting political speeches: $10-20/hour.

Government, local, public information officer: $10/hour, to $50-100/day.

History, local, lectures: $25-100.

House organs, writing and editing: $200-600, 2-4 pages.

Industrial and business brochures, consultation, research and writing: $3,500.

Industrial films: $500-1,200, 10-minute reel; 5-12% of the production cost of films that run $750-1,000/release minute.

Industrial promotions: $7.50-40/hour.

Industrial slide films: 14% of gross production cost.

Industrial writing: $25-30/hour including conference interview and writing time. Long distance travel time and expenses billed separately.

Library public relations: $5-25/hour.

Magazine stringing, rates recommended by American Society of Journalists and Authors, Inc.: 20¢-$1/word, based on circulation. Daily rate: $200 plus expenses. Weekly rate: $750 plus expenses.

New product releases, writing $300-500 plus expenses.

Newspaper ads, writing, for small businesses: $25 for small 1-column ad; $3.50/hour and up.

Newspaper column: 80¢/column inch to $20/column.

Newspaper stringing: 50¢-2.50/column inch.

Paperback cover copy: $40-75.

Pharmacy newsletters: $125-300.

Photo-brochures: $700-15,000.

Photocomposition on electric typewriter: $6/hour, 5¢/line on short jobs.

Political campaign writing: $200-250/week; $35/page piecework jobs; $10/hour and up.

Programmed instruction materials, writing: $1,000-3,000/hour of programmed training provided. Consulting/editorial fees: $25/hour; $200/day, plus expenses, minimum.

Proofreading paperback book page proofs: 30-40¢/page.

Public relations: $200-400/day plus expenses.

Publicity writing: $30/hour; $100/day.

Radio copywriting: $60-165/week.

Record album cover copy: $100-200.

Retail business newsletters: $200 for 4 pages, writing, picture taking, layout and printing supervision.

Retainer for fund-raising writing for a foundation: $500/month.

Retainer for publicity and PR work for an adoption agency: $200/month.

Retainer for writing for businesses, campaign funds: usually a flat fee but the equivalent of $5-20/hour.

Reviews, art, drama, music, for national magazines: $25-50; $10-20/column for newspapers.

Sales letter, business or industrial: $150 for one or two pages.

School public relations: $3.50-10/hour.

Shopping mall promotion: 15% of promotion budget for the mall.

Slide film, single image photo: $75.

Slide presentation for an educational institution: $1,000.

Speeches by writers who become specialists in certain fields; $50-500 plus expenses.

Sports information director, college: $700-2,000/month.

Syndicated newspaper column, self-promoted: $2 each for weeklies; $5-25/week for dailies, based on circulation.

Teaching creative writing, part-time: $15-25/hour of instruction.

Teaching high school journalism, part-time: % of regular teacher's salary.

Teaching home-bound students: $5/hour.

Technical typing: 50¢-$1/page.

Technical typing masters for reproduction: $3/hour for rough setup then $2-4/page or $5-6/hour.

Technical writing: $10-15/hour.

Textbook and Tradebook copy editing: $3.50-5/hour. Occasionally 75¢/page.

Trade journal articles, ghostwritten for someone else's byline: $250-400.

Translation, literary: $25-50/thousand words minimum.

Travel folder: $100.

TV filmed news and features: $15/film clip.

TV news film still photo: $3-6.

TV news story: $16-25.

If there are substantial differences in the rates paid in your area for any of these jobs—or you'd like to tell us about other job categories with which you have personal experience, please drop a line with the facts to Kirk Polking, Jobs for Writers, care of *Writer's Market,* 9933 Alliance Road, Cincinnati 45242. Your comments will help other freelancers through future editions of this directory.

A book containing more detailed discussions of each of these jobs for writers is planned for publication in 1978 by *Writer's Digest.*

The Markets

Book Publishers

Book publishing is a vast and multi-faceted industry. It is Big Business, employing more than 50,000 persons and operating at almost 4 billion dollars per year. Truly, some of these dollars could be yours.

Publishers Weekly reports that sales for the year's ten bestselling nonfiction and fiction books are among the highest ever recorded. But before giving your manuscript a bag lunch and carfare for making the rounds of the publishing houses, carefully consider the business end of being a craftsman with a typewriter.

The Field

One important question to ask while your book is only a germ of an idea is this: "*What* is being published?" Nonfiction is the industry leader, but *what* nonfiction is making its way from the second assistant copyreader's slush pile to the composing room? Religious titles did well in 1976, as did books on popular health. Psychological self-help books, a recent vogue, lost some of their foothold in the industry. There is also an indication of a swing toward publishing more original paperbacks (these being less costly to produce, but offering less in royalties).

Generally, in today's market, a nonfiction book by an unestablished writer has a better chance of selling well than a like fiction title. Only one first novelist made the 1976 bestsellers' list (*Ordinary People,* by Judith Guest, sold over 98,000 copies). Nonfiction first-timers fared better; in fact, the majority of bestselling nonfiction titles were by names new to the bestseller lists.

The following market listings are chock-full of information to help you find the right publisher for your book. Each listing is subdivided by **boldface** letters as to the kinds of books it is soliciting (fiction, nonfiction, etc.). If you have one type of book in hand or in mind, see how often it pops up in the section. This will give you an idea of the size of the market for your work. Does it surface in the large companies that publish hundreds of titles a year, or solely in the smaller, more specialized houses?

Each listing gives you the essentials for choosing the right publisher. Each contains a contact name and address (and often the department editor for your kind of work), royalty and advance information, submission requirements, how many titles were published in 1976 and 1977, how many are slated for 1978, and detailed information on just *what* that publisher wants to see. Careful examination of these listings can get your manuscript off to a good start.

Baiting the Line

Most publishers prefer to be queried or to be sent an outline/synopsis and sample chapters (see What Every Freelancer Should Know). If you try the latter, type a one- or two-page synopsis of your book, attach it to the first two or three chapters and one other chapter that is particularly well-written, add an outline of the whole work, and send the package off. *Only* in cases where the publisher states in his listing that he's *willing* to consider complete manuscripts should you send one. Many publishing houses now return unsolicited manuscripts unopened.

What you have to say belongs in your book. A cover letter should say only that you're working on a book, part of it is enclosed, and would the editor care to see more? If the editor is impressed, he'll ask for more; if he isn't, your manuscript will be returned via the self-addressed stamped envelope you should always enclose.

Study the listings carefully for what each firm wants, and how it wants it. Don't send a query on the effects of sunburn on Alaskan polar bears to a publisher who wants only material on South Pacific porpoises. That's like personally asking the editor to reject your story.

Getting Paid

Publishers will sometimes offer a writer an *advance* against royalties. An advance is a sum of money paid before the work's completion that is later charged against the author's profit. Advances can vary greatly, depending on who you are, who your publisher is, what you've written, and how well the book is projected to sell. They can range from $100 allowances for typing fees to hundreds of thousands of dollars for major multiple book contracts. Other publishers may pay a flat fee for the manuscript, avoiding royalties.

Usually, hardbound trade books (those which are sold in bookstores) have a minimum royalty arrangement of 10% on the first 5,000-10,000 copies sold, 12½% on the next several thousand, and 15% thereafter. The percentage is based on the retail price of the book. For paperback originals (a fast-growing market), the usual royalty is 4% on the first 150,000 copies and 6% thereafter.

Other rights to be aware of are movie, TV, and book club selection rights. Generally, the first novelist receives 50% of what the publisher contracts for paperback and book club sales, and 90% on movie and television commissions.

Takin' It to Market

OK, you've written a book and now want to join the ranks of the Hemingways and Steinbecks and other writers who have that common denominator — *published books*. One way to market your book is to acquire an agent. Another way is to try marketing it yourself. It's difficult to interest an agent in an unknown writer, and possibly the wisest choice is to try marketing it on your own.

Again (and again and again) be sure to carefully study the requirements and tips found in the following section and to start your book off to the right publisher. Also, study the book catalogs of the publishing houses most likely to be interested in your work. The catalog is an invaluable source of information about what types of books the publisher is interested in, what he's done lately (and so isn't anxious to do again soon) and what he needs. Checking book catalogs before you go to market may seem basic, but the anguished cries of editors wading through inappropriate manuscripts ring loudly on Publishers' Row. You can easily avoid these mistakes by studying catalogs in any major bookstore or library, or by writing directly to the publisher. Each listing states the conditions under which a publisher will send you his current catalog (either free, for SASE, or for some small charge).

Agents don't knock over first-time authors in a rush to represent them. A first book (particularly a novel) is generally not a commercial success, and an established agent will take on a new writer only when he believes in the future sales potential of his client. Some agents are willing to represent you for a fee, which ensures the agent some compensation should the book prove unmarketable.

Don't get discouraged, though frustration is probably the most common trait among unsuccessful writers. It's a tough business — and remember, as beautiful as your art is, selling that art is pure business.

Paying for It

If your book has made all the rounds it (and you) can take, but you still consider it worth publishing, you may want to turn to a subsidy publisher. A subsidy publisher will publish your book only if you pay him. He expects to profit from the venture regardless of how well the book sells. Usually the subsidy publisher lacks the resources for promoting and selling your book that a standard publisher has, and your chances for turning a profit are slim indeed.

Be cautious of the subsidy book contract. Make sure it provides all the essentials, like the number of copies to be printed (and bound), the type of paper to be used, binding, marketing, and hidden costs. Generally, subsidy publishing is a costly venture.

Once you've followed the advice contained in these pages, you're ready to send your prized child into the cement-and-glass world knowing you've done all you can to smooth the way.

Asterisk preceding a listing indicates that individual subsidy publishing (in addition to the firm's regular lines) is also available. Those firms that specialize in subsidy publishing are listed at the end of the book publishers' section.

ABBEY PRESS, St. Meinrad IN 47577. (812)357-6677. Editor: John T. Bettin. Publishes original and reprint paperbacks. Royalty schedule and advances variable. Send query with outline and sample chapter. Reports in 3 weeks. SASE.
Nonfiction: "Primarily books aimed at married and family life enrichment.

ABC-CLIO, INC. (American Bibliographical Center—Clio Press), Riviera Campus, 2040 Almeda Padre Serra, Santa Barbara CA 93103. Clio Book Division. President: Dr. Eric H. Boehm; Publisher and Editor: Lloyd W. Garrison. Publishes hardcover and paperpack originals. Published 16 titles last year. Pays 10% on sales price for first 5,000 copies sold, 12½% for next 5,000 copies, 15% for following 5,000 copies, per contract. "We do not publish on author subsidy. We do publish under subsidy to scholarly institutions with 'joint interests' (e.g., we have published for the Smithsonian Institution, University of Washington, the Carnegie Foundation for International Peace, American Council of Learned Societies, and the Center for the Study of Democratic Institutions, etc.)." Will send a catalog to a writer on request. Query first with prospectus. Enclose return postage. Reports within 2 months.
Bibliography, History, and Politics: Interested in historical bibliography, history, business, economics, library, bibliography, political science, current affairs. No length limitations. Is seeking material for a series in comparative politics and one in war/peace bibliographies.

ABINGDON PRESS, 201 Eighth Ave. S., Nashville TN 37203. (615)749-6403. Editorial Director: Ronald P. Patterson. College Editor: Pierce S. Ellis, Jr.; Editor of Religious Books: Paul M. Pettit; Editor of General Books: Robert J. Hill, Jr.; Juvenile Editor: Ernestine Calhoun; Editor of Fine Arts: Richard Loller; Editor of Research Projects: Jean Hager. Payment in royalties. No advance. Published 90 titles last year. Write for guide to preparation of mss. Query first. Reports in 1 month. Enclose return postage.
Nonfiction, Juveniles, and Textbooks: Publishes religious, children's and general interest books, college texts. Wants books on marriage, the family, Americana, recreation, and social concerns. Length: 32-300 pages.

ACADEMIC PRESS, INC., 111 Fifth Ave., New York NY 10003. (212)741-6836. Editorial Vice-President: James Barsky. Royalty varies. Published 385 titles last year. Will send copy of

current catalog to a writer on request. Submit outline, preface and sample chapter. Reports in 1 month. Enclose return postage.
Science: Specializes in scientific, technical and medical works. Textbooks and reference works in natural, behavioral-social sciences at college and research levels.

ACE BOOKS, Editorial Department, 1120 Avenue of the Americas, New York NY 10036. Publishes paperback originals and reprints. "Terms vary; usually on royalty basis." Published more than 200 titles last year. Must query first, with detailed outline. "Do not send completed ms." Reports in 4 to 8 weeks. Enclose return postage.
Nonfiction and Fiction: Self-help, how-to, nostalgia, puzzle books. Does not want to see poetry or short stories. For fiction, will consider romantic suspense, westerns, science fiction, women's fiction, nurse romances, occult, historical romances. Length: 55,000 to 100,000 words.

ACTIVA PRODUCTS, INC., 582 Market St., Suite 1908, San Francisco CA 94104. Editor-in-Chief: Jane K. Stuppin. Publishes paperback originals and reprints. Royalty is negotiable, but generally runs 6% of net selling price, with $500 advance against earned royalties. Titles published last year: 2. Since books are designed for the craft market, they are generally not sold in the book trade, but are sold to craft, hobby and toy wholesalers, who in turn sell to retail outlets. Will send catalog to writer on request. Query first. If acceptable, will request outline and sample chapters. Queries should be addressed to Jane K. Stuppin, and accompanied by S.A.S.E. Reports on mss accepted for publication in 3 to 4 weeks. Returns rejected material in 1 week.
Hobbies and Crafts: "We are interested in receiving queries about manuscripts dealing with all aspects of adult crafts and hobbies. We serve a definite market, and are only interested in craft and hobby type how-to books. Some examples are mold-making and casting crafts; needle crafts; jewelry crafts; papier-mache, decoupage; flower crafts; ceramics; stained glass; shell craft, tole painting, enameling, quilting. The writer should be acquainted with all aspects of the particular craft, and be able to explain it lucidly to others, particularly the novice. An ability to photograph the various stages of the craft is extremely helpful, but not mandatory. The writer should be able to produce made-up pieces of the craft. In short, should be professional. We stress quality both in format and content." Word length varies with subject matter.

ADDISON-WESLEY PUBLISHING CO., Jacob Way, Reading MA 01867. Editor-in-Chief, Children's Book Depart.: Kathleen Leverich. Publishes hardcover and paperback originals. Offers minimum royalty payment schedule of 10% of list (total for author and illustrator). Submit complete ms. Reports in 4 to 6 weeks. Enclose return postage.
Juveniles: "Fiction should be timely — not trendy — and should focus on precisely and carefully drawn characters, characters so specifically depicted through action, dialogue, and description that a reader would recognize them on a crowded street. Historical fiction, fantasy, mystery and adventure, and wild antics are all fine as long as they focus clearly on ideas and feelings and as long as they can be read by people under 14 years of age and enjoyed by people over that age. The same general guidelines apply to nonfiction. Subjects from continental drift to tree house construction to spelunking are all possibilities as long as they are presented with drama and relevance — with as many specifics and as much human involvement as possible." Length: open.

ADDISONIAN PRESS AND YOUNG SCOTT BOOKS, Juvenile Division of Addison-Wesley Publishing Co., Inc., Reading MA 01867. Editor-in-Chief: Kathleen Leverich. Publishes hardcover originals. Contracts "vary." Advance is negotiable. Published 2 titles last year. Free book catalog. Send complete ms for fiction and nonfiction. Reports in 3-5 weeks. SASE.
Juveniles: Publishes books for 4-16 year olds.

AERO PUBLISHERS, INC., 329 W. Aviation Road, Fallbrook CA 92028. President: Ernest J. Gentle. Offers 10% royalty contract. No advance. Published 12 titles last year. Submit chapter outline and sample chapters. Reports in 3 months. Enclose return postage.
Nonfiction: Books dealing with aviation and space. Length: 50,000 to 100,000 words. Current titles include *Aviation and Space Dictionary* (Gentle and Reithmaier), *U.S. Bombers* (Jones).

AGASCHA PRODUCTIONS, Box 38063, Detroit MI 48238. (313)867-6490. Editor-in-Chief: Schavi M. Diara. Paperback originals. 12% royalty on first 900 copies; 15% thereafter; no advance. Published 1 title in 1976, 2 in 1977; will do 4 in 1978. Query. Simultaneous and photocopied submissions OK. Repors in 3 months. SASE. Book catalog $1.
Nonfiction: Publishes biography; business; cookbooks, cooking and foods (African); eco-

nomics; history (African, African-American); how-to; juveniles; law; music (history of African and African-American); nature; philosophy; photography; politics; psychology; religious (primarily Islamic); scientific; self-help; sociology; technical; textbooks; and travel books. "In all areas we are primarily interested in these subjects as they relate to the African and African-American experience."
Fiction: Publishes religious (primarily Islamic); and historical. Must relate to the African-American experience.
Recent Titles: *Islam and Pan-Africanism,* by A.L. Diara (religion/history); *Song for My Father,* by S.M. Diara (biographical and historical fiction); *An African Tragedy: The Black Woman Under Aparthied,* by P. Ntantala (history and sociology).

ALASKA NORTHWEST PUBLISHING CO., Box 4-EEE, Anchorage AK 99509. Editor: Robert A. Henning. Publishes hardcover and paperback originals. "Contracts vary, depending upon how much editing is necessary. Everybody gets 10% of gross, which averages around 8% because direct mail retail sales are high. Pros may get a flat fee in addition, to increase the percentage. Advances may be paid when ms is completed." Published 16 titles in 1976, 20 in 1977. Free book catalog. "Rejections are made promptly, unless we have 3 or 4 possibilities in the same general field and it's a matter of which one gets the decision. That could take 3 months." Send queries and unsolicited mss to the Book Editor. Enclose return postage.
General Nonfiction: "Alaska, Northern B.C., Yukon, and Northwest territories are subject areas. Emphasis on life in the last frontier, history, outdoor subjects such as hunting and fishing. Writer must be familiar with the North first-hand, from more knowledge than can be gained as a tourist. We listen to any ideas. For example, we recently did a book of woodprints." Art, nature, history, sports, hobbies, recreation, pets, and travel. Length: open.
Recent Titles: *Alaska Sourdough,* by R. Allman (cookbook); *How to Build an Oil Barrel Stove,* by O. Wik (how-to); and *Wild Rivers of Alaska,* by S. Weber (wilderness travel guide).

*ALBA HOUSE, 2187 Victory Blvd., Staten Island, New York NY 10314. (212)761-0047. Editor-in-Chief: Anthony L. Chenevey. Hardcover and paperback originals (90%) and reprints (10%). Specializes in religious books. 10% royalty. No advance. Subsidy publishes 5% of books. Subsidy publishing is offered "if the author is able to promote the sale of a thousand copies of a book which we would not venture on our own." Published 17 titles in 1976, 20 in 1977; will do 25 in 1978. Query. State availability of photos/illustrations. Simultaneous and photocopied submissions OK. Reports in 2-4 weeks. SASE. Free book catalog.
Nonfiction: Publishes philosophy; psychology; religious; sociology; textbooks and Biblical books.
Recent Titles: *Medicine and Christian Morality,* by O'Donnell (theology); *Healing the Unaffirmed,* by Baars and Terruwe (psychology); and *Everlasting Life After Death,* by Fortman (theology).

ALLIANCE PRESS (LONDON) LTD., P.O. Box 593, Times Square Station, New York NY 10036. Affiliate of Diplomatic Press, Inc. Pays 10% of net price. Send query letter with outline and sample chapters to the Editor. Reports in 2 months. Enclose return postage.
Fiction and Nonfiction: Publishes books in every field of human interest—adult fiction, juvenile, history, biography, science, philosophy, the arts, religion and general nonfiction. Length requirements: 65,000 to 80,000 words.

ALLYN AND BACON, INC., 470 Atlantic Ave., Boston MA 02210. Editors: William Roberts (college texts), John DeRemigis (junior college texts), P. Parsons (Elhi texts), John Gilman (professional books). Publishes hardcover and paperback originals. "Our contracts are competitive within the standard industry framework of royalties." Rarely offers an advance. Published 200 titles last year. Letter should accompany ms with author information, ms prospectus, etc. Query first or submit complete ms. Reports in 1 to 3 months. Enclose return postage.
Nonfiction and Textbooks: "We are primarily a textbook, technical and professional book publisher. Authoritative works of quality. No fiction or poetry." Will consider business, medicine and psychiatry, music, reference, scientific, self-help and how-to, sociology, sports and hobbies, technical mss.

AMERICAN ASTRONAUTICAL SOCIETY, Box 28130, San Diego CA 92128 (714)746-4005. Editor: H. Jacobs. Publishes hardcover originals. Offers 10% royalty contract, or "by arrangement. Advance by arrangement." Published 10 titles in 1976, 10 in 1977. Reports in 30 days. SASE.
Reference, Monograph, History and Technical: Monographs in the field of astronautics but

also covering the application of aerospace technology to earth problems. Will consider books only in excess of 100 pages. Historical books or reference books also considered. Books are directed to the specialist or technically oriented layman for use in research establishments, libraries; public, college, or special college-level style. "All our books must relate to astronautics, space sciences and disciplines, and their applications. We have 3 series: Advances in the Astronautical Sciences, American Astronautical Society History and Science and TEchnology." Length: 100-600 pages.
Recent Titles: *End of an Era in Space Exploration,* by B. Blaine; and *200 Years of Flight,* by E. Emme.

AMERICAN CLASSICAL COLLEGE PRESS, P.O. Box 4526, Albuquerque NM 87106. Editor-in-Chief: Leslie Dean. Pays a flat sum plus royalties of 10-15%. Published 27 titles last year. Prefers queries. Enclose return postage.
Nonfiction: Publishes history, biography, scientific phenomena, politics, psychology and philosophy books. Also economics, Wall Street and the stock market. Mss should be short, to the point, informative, and practical. Length: 20,000 to 40,000 words. Publishes The Science of Man Research Books series.

AMERICAN MEDIA, 790 Hampshire Road, Suite H, Westlake Village CA 91361. (213)889-1231. Editor-in-Chief: G. Edward Griffin. Publishes hardcover and paperback originals and reprints. Offers 5% royalties on paperback and 10% on hardback. Advance is negotiable. Published 2 titles in 1976, 5 in 1977. Free book catalog. Will consider photocopied submissions. Query first for nonfiction. Reports in 1 month. Enclose return postage.
General: Specializes in scholarly, documentary books in the following fields: nutrition (favoring organic); creation (favoring the catastrophic, creationist viewpoint as opposed to uniformitarian evolutionist point of view); and ideology (favoring the individualistic conservative point of view as opposed to the collectivistic big government point of view). Point of view is generally controversial and not the orthodox point of view. "Style and structure are open but all points of view must be carefully researched and documented." Publishes biography, book trade, cookbooks, economics, history, medicine and psychiatry, multimedia material, plays, politics, reference, scientific, self-help and how-to, and sociology.
Recent Titles: *Laetrile Case Histories: The Richardson Cancer Clinic Experience,* by J. Richardson M.D./P. Griffin, R.N. (health and medicine) and *Explosion from the Left; Political Terrorism in America,* by L. McDonald.

AMERICAN PHOTOGRAPHIC BOOK PUBLISHING CO., INC., (AMPHOTO), 750 Zeckendorf Blvd., Garden City NY 11530. Editor-in-Chief: Herbert Taylor. Publishes paperback and hardcover originals. Offers standard minimum book contract of 10-12½-15%. Advance varies. Published 40 titles in 1976. Will send free catalog to a writer on request. Will consider photocopied submissions. Query first and submit outline and sample chapters or submit complete ms if possible. Must be neat, double-spaced, typed. Reports on mss accepted for publication in 2 months to 10 weeks. Returns rejected material in 4 to 6 weeks. Enclose return postage.
Nonfiction and Photography: Publishes technical books on photography, camera manuals, simplified photographic guides and pictorials. Would like to see mss on money-making professional photography and darkroom subjects. No non-thematic pictorial material, "photo-philosophy" mss, poetry and picture combinations. Length: 25,000 word minimum. Also publishes art, reference and textbooks,

AMERICAN UNIVERSAL ARTFORMS CORP., Box 2242, Austin TX 78768. Editor-in-Chief: R.H. Dromgoole. Hardcover and paperback originals. 10% (of net invoice) royalty. Possibility of advance "depends on many factors." Published 2 titles in 1976, 4 in 1977; will do 5 in 1978. Send sample print if photos and/or artwork are to accompany ms. Simultaneous submissions OK (if so advised); photocopied submissions OK. Reports in 2-4 weeks. SASE. Book catalog for SASE.
Nonfiction: Publishes textbooks (bilingual educational material, K-12; Spanish/English); books on hobbies, how-to, humor, politics and poetry; juveniles. Submit complete ms.

AMERICANA PUBLICATIONS CO., 212 W. State Highway 38, Moorestown NJ 08057. (609)234-1200. Editor-in-Chief: Patricia F. Yula. Publishes softcover originals and reprints. Will negotiate contract and advance. Published 8 titles in 1976, 8 in 1977. Submit complete ms for nonfiction. Prefers no photocopied submissions. Reports in 2 months for ms; 2 weeks for query. Enclose return postage.
Juveniles and Teaching Aids: Wants juvenile literature for children, ages 5 to 11. Nonfiction. Science and technology preferred. Should be oriented toward learning experience. Illustrations

desirable. Interested in "short, exciting copy; unusual subjects or unusual approach to everyday topics." Mss should be geared to children to enhance learning, but not childish. Outlook must be open to the world, unprejudiced and curious in "how's and why's." Structure must allow for ample illustration. Planning a science-oriented series and vocational arts series. Length: 800 to 1,200 words.

AND/OR PRESS, Box 2246, Berkeley CA 94702. Managing Editor: Peter Beren. Paperback originals (90%); hardcover and paperback reprints (10%). Specializes in "works on counter-culture with youth market interest. We function as an alternative information resource." 5-10% royalty; advance of 10% of first print run. Published 8 titles in 1976, 16 in 1977; will do 15 in 1978. Reports in 2 weeks to 3 months. SASE. Book catalog 25¢.
Nonfiction: Publishes how-to, philosophy, psychology, religious, self-help, sociology, technical, travel, human potential, psycho-pharmacology books. Also alternative lifestyles. Query or submit outline/synopsis and sample chapters.
Special Needs: Planning a series on health, sex and old age.

*ANGLICAN BOOK CENTER, 600 Jarvis St., Toronto, Ontario, Canada M4Y ZJ6. (416)924-9192. Editor-in-Chief: Robert Maclennan. Publisher: Rev. Michael J. Lloyd. Hardcover and paperback originals (90%); hardcover and paperback reprints (10%). Specializes in religious and social issues. 10% royalty; no advance. Subsidy publishes 10% of books for various church and government organizations and private persons. Published 4 titles in 1976, 6 in 1977; will do 8 in 1978. Markets books through all Anglican clergy and diocesan bookstores and trade bookstores and libraries in Canada. State availability of photos to accompany ms. Simultaneous submissions OK. No photocopied submissions unless very clean. SASE. Reports in 2-4 weeks.
Nonfiction: Publishes books on philosophy, psychology and sociology as related to religion. Query or submit clearly typed, double-spaced mss.
Recent Titles: *Moratorium,* by H. and K. McCullum, and J. Olthuis (sociology and religion); *Waswanipi,* by Hugo Muller (poetry).

ANTONSON PUBLISHING CO. (formerly Nunaga Publishing Co., Ltd.) 12165 97th Ave., Surrey, B.C., Canada V3V 2C8. (604)584-9922. EDitor-in-Chief: Richard Antonson. Hardcover and paperback originals. 8-10% royalty; no advance. Published 4 titles in 1976 and 1977; will do 5 in 1978. State availability of photos and/or illustrations to accompany ms. Simultaneous and photocopied submissions OK. Reports in 2-4 weeks. SASE. Free book catalog.
Nonfiction: Publishes Canadiana; biography (Canadian emphasis); how-to (guide books); politics (Canadian perspective); history; nature and wildlife; recreation and conservation, history, reference, how-to, sociology, sports, hobbies, recreation, and travel. "We are developing a strong line of outdoor-oriented books both in the story form and in the guidebook area. Titles vary in length from 40,000 words to 60,000 words. In addition, we are planning more titles on regional and national history."
Recent Titles: *Spatsizi,* by T.A. Walker (biography/wilderness/conservation); *B.C. Cross-Country Ski Routes,* by R. and R. Wright (outdoor guidebook); *Canadian Frontier Annual* by B. Antonson (Canadian history).

THE AQUARIAN PUBLISHING CO. (LONDON) LTD., Denington Estate, Wellingborough, Northamptonshire NN8 2RQ England. Editor-in-Chief: J.R. Hardaker. Hardcover and paperback originals. 8-10% royalty. No advance. Photocopied submissions OK. SAE and International Reply Coupons. Reports in 2-4 weeks. Free book catalog.
Nonfiction: Publishes books on astrology, magic, witchcraft, palmistry and other occult subjects. Length: 15,000-60,000 words.

THE AQUILA PUBLISHING CO., LTD., 9 Skullamus, Breakish, Isle of Skye. Scotland 1V42 8QB. Editor-in-Chief: J.C.R. Green. Hardcover and paperback originals (99%); paperback reprints and pamphlets (1%). 10% royalty. Published 47 titles in 1976, 30 in 1977. If ms is to be illustrated, state availability of prints and send photocopies. Simultaneous submissions OK (if informed); photocopied submissions OK. Reporting time varies with workload. Query. SAE and International Reply Coupons. Free book catalog.
Nonfiction: Publishes books on art, biographies, business; cookbooks, cooking and foods; erotica, hobbies, how-to, humor, music, nature, philosophy, photography, poetry, recreation and self-help. Also publishes translations from any language and work with a Scottish/Celtic bias. Query.
Fiction: Erotica, experimental, fantasy, humorous, mystery, suspense and science fiction. Work with a Scottish/Celtic bias.

Special Needs: "New series of pamphlet/paperbacks of critical essays on American writers and writing; the ecology, humor, etc."
Recent Titles: *Eliot/Language,* by M. Edwards (literary criticism); *God Shave the Queen,* by N. Toczek (humor); *The Counting Stick,* by J. Purser (poetry).

ARCHITECTURAL BOOK PUBLISHING CO., INC., 10 E. 40th St., New York NY 10016. (212)689-5400. Editor: Walter Frese. Royalty is percentage of retail price. Prefers queries, outlines and sample chapters. Reports in 2 weeks. Enclose return postage.
Architecture and Industrial Arts: Publishes architecture, decoration, and reference books on city planning and industrial arts. Also interested in history, biography, and science of architecture and decoration.

ARCO PUBLISHING CO., INC., 219 Park Ave., S., New York NY 10003. Editor-in-Chief: David Goodnough. Education Editor: Edward Turner. Medical Editor: Don Simmons. Hardcover and paperback originals (30%) and reprints (70%). 10-12½-15% royalty. $1,000 advance. Published 130 titles in 1976, 140 in 1977; will do 150 in 1978. Simultaneous and legible photocopied submissions OK. Reports in 4-6 weeks. SASE (must be large enough to contain material in case of return). Book catalog for 8½x11 SASE.
Nonfiction (in order of preference): Publishes hobbies (crafts and collecting); pets (practical and specific); self-help (medical, mental, career guidance, economic); career guidance; medicine and psychiatry (technical and authoritative); study guides and school aids; travel (informative — not "My Trip to   "); sports (but not the usual stories about baseball, football, etc.); psychology and research into parapsychology (scientific); cookbooks, cooking and foods (specialized cookbooks and nutrition); how-to; medical textbooks, military history; reference. Query first or submit outline/synopsis and sample chapters.
Recent Titles: *American First Editions: A Guidebook,* by J. Tannen (history/reference); *Collecting Old Photographs,* by M. Haller (collecting); *The Comprehensive Catalog and Encyclopedia of U.S. Morgan and Peace Silver Dollars,* by VanAllen and Mallis (reference).

ARKHAM HOUSE PUBLISHERS, INC., Sauk City WI 53583. Managing Editor: James Turner. Publishes hardcover originals and reprints. Offers "standard 10% royalties." Average advance is $1,000. Published 8 titles in 1976, 8 in 1977. Will send free catalog to writer on request. Query first. Reports in 4 to 6 weeks. Enclose return postage.
Fiction: "Arkham House is a fantasy imprint, specializing in supernatural horror and weird literature. Mss should be well-written, preferably on original fantastic themes, with particular attention to atmosphere and style."
Recent Titles: *Kecksies and Other Twilight Tales,* by M. Bowen (weird tales); and *And Afterward, the Dark,* by B. Copper (weird tales).

ARLINGTON HOUSE PUBLISHERS, 165 Huguenot St., New Rochelle NY 10801. Hardcover originals (90%) and repints 10%. Specializes in conservative, nostalgia, financial and stock market, film, jazz, religion and history books. 10% royalty on first 7,500 copies, 12½% on next 5,000, and 15% thereafter. Advance averages $1,500. Published 29 titles in 1976, 27 in 1977; will do 28 in 1978. Query or submit outline/synopsis and sample chapters. State availability of photos/illustrations. Simultaneous and photocopied submissions OK. Reports in 1-2 months. SASE. Free book catalog.
Nonfiction: Publishes Americana (Karl Pflock, Richard Band, editors); biography (political or historical; K. Pflock, R. Band, editors); business (P. Pflock, R. Band, editors); economics (K. Pflock, R. Band, editors); history (K. Pflock, R. Band, editors); hobbies (Kathleen Williams, editor); how-to (K. Pflock, R. Band, editors); music (Neil McCaffrey, editor); philosophy (R. Band, editor); politics (R. Band, K. Pflock, editors); reference (K. Williams, editor); religious (Protestant, R. Band, editor; Catholic, Neil McCaffrey, editor); self-help (K. Williams, R. Band, K. Pflock, editors); sociology (R. Band, K. Pflock, editors).
Recent Titles: *The Jack Benny Show,* by J.K. Fitzpatrick (show business biography); *The Reconstruction of the Republic,* by H. Brown (political); *American Dance Band Discography,* by B. Rust (jazz research).

ARTISTS & WRITERS PUBLICATIONS, Box 3692, San Rafael CA 94901. (415)456-1213. Editor-in-Chief: Owen S. Haddock. Paperback originals. Specializes in how-to cookbooks. 5% minimum royalty; no advance. Published 3 titles in 1976, 6 in 1977; will do 12 in 1978. "We prefer all submissions to be in outline/synopsis form, not requiring return, plus a brief resume of the author." State availability of photos/illustrations. Prefers photocopied submissions. Reports in 2-4 months. SASE.

Nonfiction: Publishes business; cookbooks, cooking and foods; hobbies; how-to; law; scientific; and self-help books.
Fiction: Publishes historical books.
Recent Titles: *What About Tea?* by Forsman (tea guide); *Coffee Cuisine,* by MacMillan (coffee cookbook); *The Ghirardelli Chocolate Cookbook,* by Larsen.

ASI PUBLISHERS, INC., 127 Madison Ave., New York NY 10016. Editor-in-Chief: Henry Weingarten. Publishes hardcover and paperback originals and reprints. Offers 9% royalty contract to 10,000 copies, with 10% thereafter for hardcovers; 7½% for paperbacks, with some variations depending on author. Advance varies. Published 6 titles in 1976. Book catalog for SASE. Will consider photocopied submissions. Query first. Submit outline and sample chapters. Mss should be typed, double-spaced. Enclose return postage. Reports in 1 to 3 months.
Nonfiction: "We specialize in guides to balancing inner space, e.g., acupuncture, astrology, yoga, etc. Our editors are themselves specialists in the areas published. We will accept technical material with limited sales potential." Medicine and psychiatry editor: Barbara Somerfield. Astrology editor: H. Weingarten. Recently published titles include *Wisdom of the Tarot* (E. Haich) and *The Study of Astrology* (H. Weingarten).

*ASSOCIATED BOOKSELLERS, 147 McKinley Ave., Bridgeport CT 06606. (212)366-5494. Editor-in-Chief: Alex M. Yudkin. Hardcover and paperback originals. 10% royalty; advance averages $500. Subsidy publishes 25% of books. Subsidy publishing is offered "if the marketing potential is limited." Published 6 titles in 1976, 8 in 1977; will do 9 in 1978. Query. Simultaneous and photocopied submissions OK. Reports in 2-4 weeks. SASE. Book catalog for SASE.
Nonfiction: Publishes how-to; hobbies; recreation; self-help; and sports books.
Recent Titles: *Key To Judo*; *Ketsugo*; and *Kashi-No-Bo.*

ASSOCIATED PUBLISHERS' GUIDANCE PUBLICATIONS CENTER, 1015 Howard Ave., San Mateo CA 94401. Editor: Ivan Kapetanovic. Publishes paperback originals. "Offer standard minimum book contract, but there could be special cases, different from this arrangement. We might give more to an author who can provide competent artwork, less if he uses our resources for basic material. We have not made a practice of giving advances." Published 3 titles last year. Will consider photocopied submissions. Submit outline and sample chapters, or submit complete ms. Reports in 30 days. Enclose return postage.
Education: "In addition to bibliographies, which we develop and publish ourselves, we are interested in most kinds of guidance materials. We distribute these from many sources; but would consider publication of books and pamphlets suitable for high school students, but only in the field of guidance, including occupational information, college entrance and orientation, and personal and social problems. We are less concerned with a single title than a group of related titles or a series of publications which may be developed over a period of time. We would like a series of career materials which can be produced and sold inexpensively for junior and senior high school students, with or without tape and/or filmstrip materials correlated with them. We would like materials relating to the *Dictionary of Occupational Titles* for student use; a first class student study guide or a series for different levels to and including college freshmen; a series of social dramas for junior and senior high school use; a series of pamphlets on occupations, individually and/or in groups. Although we sell to counselors, most of our own materials are aimed at seventh- to twelfth-grade students and those constitute our main market. The vocabulary level usually should be that of average students in the seventh to tenth grades. We prefer not to publish large volumes; stay away from textbooks for school subjects where there are already many books; do not reach markets below or above high school except for additional sales beyond our primary market; do not sell to bookstores, though some buy from us; do not sell to school and public libraries. We are planning a series of occupational pamphlets, a filing system on American colleges. Someone knowledgeable in labor statistics, employment problems, etc., could do the first one; someone familiar with materials on college entrance could do the latter. Interested in publishing about the energy problem and economic conditions in terms of occupations and their impact on the growth or decline of industries over a long range of time. Definitely not interested in poetry, fiction, and pseudo-scientific material. Books published in following categories only: Economics, Self-help and How-to, Sociology, and Guidance. No strict length requirements."

ASSOCIATION PRESS, 291 Broadway, New York NY 10007. (212)374-2127. Editor-in-Chief: Robert W. Hill. Managing Editor: Robert Roy Wright. Hardcover and paperback originals. 10% royalty; advance "varies with nature of project." Published 20 titles in 1976, 25 in 1977; will do 30 in 1978. Query, submit outline/synopsis and sample chapters, or complete ms. State availability of photos/illustrations. Photocopied submissions OK. Reports in 1-2 months. SASE. Free book catalog.

Nonfiction: Publishes general nonfiction, religion, youth leadership, youth problems, recreation, sports, national and international affairs, physical fitness, marriage and sex, crafts and hobbies, social work and human relations. "Word length is a function of the subject matter and market of each book;" ranges from 40,000 words up.

ATHENEUM PUBLISHERS, 122 E. 42nd St., New York NY 10017. Editor-in-Chief: Herman Gollob. Published 28 titles last year. For unsolicited mss prefer query, outline, or sample chapter. Submit complete ms for juveniles. All freelance submissions with the exception of juveniles, should be addressed to "The Editors." Reports in 4 weeks. Enclose return postage.

General Fiction and Nonfiction: Publishes adult fiction, history, biography, science (for the layman), philosophy, the arts and general nonfiction. Length: over 40,000 words.

Juveniles: Juvenile nonfiction books for ages 3 to 18. Length: open. Picture books for ages 3 to 8. "No special needs; we publish whatever comes in that interests us. No bad animal fantasy." Department Editor: Jean Karl. Margaret K. McElderry Books: Fiction and nonfiction preschool through 18. Interested in anything of quality. Editor: Margaret K. McElderry.

ATHLETIC PRESS, Box 2314-D, Pasadena CA 91108. (213)283-3446. Editor-in-Chief: Donald Duke. Paperback originals. Specializes in sports conditioning books. 10% royalty; no advance. Published 2 titles in 1976, 4 in 1977. Query or submit complete ms. "Illustrations will be requested when we believe ms is publishable." Simultaneous and photocopied submissions OK. Reports in 2-4 weeks. SASE. Free book catalog.

Nonfiction: Publishes sports books.

Recent Titles: *Nutrition and Athletic Performance,* by E. Darden; *Wrestling Physical Conditioning Encyclopedia,* by J. Jesse; and *Greco-Roman Wrestling,* by M. Hunt.

ATLANTIC MONTHLY PRESS, 8 Arlington St., Boston MA 02116. (617)536-9500. Director: Peter Davison; Associate Director: Upton Birnie Brady; Associate Director for Children's Books: Emilie McLeod. "Advance and royalties depend on the nature of the book, the stature of the author, and the subject matter." Published 41 titles in 1976, 36 in 1977. Query letters welcomed. Mss preferred, but outlines and chapters are acceptable. Send outline and sample chapters for juvenile nonfiction; send complete ms for juvenile picture books. Enclose return postage.

General Fiction, Nonfiction and Juveniles: Publishes, in association with Little, Brown and Company, fiction, general nonfiction, juveniles, biography, autobiography, science, philosophy, the arts, belles lettres, history, world affairs and poetry. Length: 70,000 to 200,000 words. For juvenile picture books for children 4 to 8, looks for "literary quality and originality."

Recent Titles: *Beautiful Swimmers,* by W. Warner; *FBI,* by S. Ungar; and *Union Dues,* by J. Sayles (fiction).

AUGSBURG PUBLISHING HOUSE, 426 S. Fifth St., Minneapolis MN 55415. (612)332-4561. Director, Book Department: Roland Seboldt. Payment in royalties. Published 40 titles in 1976, 40 in 1977. Prefers queries, outlines and sample chapters. Reports in 1 month. Enclose return postage.

Fiction, Nonfiction, Juveniles, Poetry, and Religion: Publishes primarily religious books. Also nonfiction and fiction, juveniles, and some poetry. Specializes in Christmas literature; publishes "Christmas," an American Annual of Christmas Literature and Art. Length: "varied." Juveniles are usually short.

AURORA PUBLISHERS, INC., 118 16th Ave. S., Nashville TN 37203. (615)254-5842. Publisher: Dominic de Lorenzo. Publishes hardcover and paperback originals and reprints. Offers standard royalty contract. Usual advance is $500 to $1,000 but this varies, depending on author's reputation and nature of book. Published 6 titles last year. Query first or submit outline and sample chapters. Reports on material within 4 to 6 weeks. Enclose return postage.

General Fiction and Nonfiction: Science fiction, sociology, law, art, how-to, religious philosophy, history, cookbooks. Current titles include *Adlai: The Springfield Years.*

Academic: Casebooks on literary works and authors.

Juveniles: Preschool through young adult. Books which foster positive self-image. Editors: William Cannon, Carolyn Aylor.

*AVI PUBLISHING CO., 250 Post Rd., E., Box 831, Westport CT 06880. (203)266-0738. Editor-in-Chief: Norman W. Desrosier, Ph.D. Hardcover and paperback originals. Specializes in publication of books in the fields of food science and technology, food service, nutrition, health, agriculture and engineering. 10% royalty on the first 1,000 copies sold; $200 average advance (paid only on typing bills). Subsidy publishes 2% of titles (by professional organizations) based on "quality of work; subject matter within the areas of food, nutrition and health, endorsed by appropriate professional organizations in the area of our specialty." Published 22 titles in 1976, 45 in 1977; will do 52 in 1978. Reports in 2-4 weeks. SASE. Free book catalog.

Nonfiction: Publishes books on foods, agricultural economics, medicine, scientific, technical, textbooks; nutrition, agriculture and health books. Query or submit outline/synopsis and sample chapters.

Recent Titles: *Food for Thought,* by T.P. Labuza (nutrition); *Commercial Chicken Production Manual,* by M.O. North (agriculture); *The Meat Handbook,* by A. Levie (food technology).

AVIATION BOOK COMPANY, 555 West Glenoaks Blvd., P.O. Box 4187, Glendale CA 91202. (213)240-1771. Editor: Walter P. Winner. Specialty publisher. Publishes hardcover and paperback originals and reprints. No advance. Published 3 titles in 1976, 3 in 1977. Free book catalog. Query with outline. Reports in 2 months. Enclose return postage.

Nonfiction: Aviation books, primarily of a technical nature and pertaining to pilot training. Young adult level and up. Also aeronautical history.

AVON BOOKS, 959 8th Ave., New York NY 10019. (212)262-6252. Editor-in-Chief: Walter Meade. Managing Editor: Judith Riven. Paperback originals (20%) and reprints (80%). 6-8% royalty; advance averages $2,500 "but can go much higher." Publishes about 260 titles a year. State availability of photos and/or illustrations. Simultaneous and photocopied submissions OK. Reports in 2-4 weeks. SASE. Free book catalog.

Nonfiction: Publishes biography; cookbooks, cooking and foods; how-to; juveniles; medicine and psychiatry; music; nature; pets; poetry; religious; scientific; self-help; and sociology books. Query or submit outline/synopsis and sample chapters.

Fiction: Publishes adventure (90-125,000 words); fantasy; historical (100-200,000 words); humorous (85,000 words); mainstream; religious; romance; science fiction; and suspense books. Submit complete ms.

Recent Titles: *Sylvia Porter's Money Book,* by Sylvia Porter; *Irving's Delight,* by Art Buchwald; *The Relaxation Response,* by H. Benson, M.D.

*BADGER CREEK PRESS, Box 728, Galt CA 95632. Editor-in-Chief: James Singer. Managing Editor: Peggy Flynn. Paperback originals. Specializes in how-to (including cookbooks) pamphlets, up to 32 pages and technical health/medicine texts. Flat rate of up to $100 for pamphlets; 15% for technicals. Very small percentage of subsidy publishing. "Each subsidy is usually not paid by the author, but by his/her sponsor (university, foundation, etc.)" Published 2 titles in 1976, 10 in 1977; will do 20 in 1978. Photocopied submissions OK. Reports in 1-2 weeks. SASE.

Nonfiction: Publishes (in order of preference) how-to,; cookbooks, cooking and foods;, self-help; books on small farms; reference, medicine and psychiatry; and technical books. Query. "We do not read unsolicited mss. We send style sheet with go-ahead."

Recent Title: *Rug Tufting — How to Make Your Own Rugs,* by S. Lambert (how-to).

*BAKER BOOK HOUSE CO., Box 6287, Grand Rapids MI 49506. Editor-in-Chief: Dan Van't Kerkhoff. Hardcover and paperback originals (40%); paperback reprints (60%). Specializes in conservative Protestant (religious) nonfiction. 5% royalty on mass market paperbacks; 7½% on trade paperbacks; 10% on hardcover; no advance. Subsidy publishes 5% of titles; prefers religious field. Publishes 150 books a year. All mss follow the MLA Style Sheet and the Chicago *Manual of Style.* State availability of photos and/or illustrations. Simultaneous and photocopied submissions OK. Reports in 1-2 months. SASE. Free book catalog for SASE.

Nonfiction: Publishes books on humor, religion, self-help. Submit outline/synopsis and sample chapters.

Recent Titles: *Salted Peanuts,* by E.C. McKenzie (humor); *Good Morning, Lord: More Five-Minute Devotions,* by R. Hambree; *Survey of the New Testament,* by R. Gromacki (religious textbook).

Special Needs: Booklets of puzzles and activities for children.

BALE BOOKS, Box 2727, New Orleans LA 70176. Editor-in-Chief: Don Bale, Jr. Publishes hardcover and paperback originals and reprints. Offers standard 10-12-15% royalty contract; "no advances." Sometimes purchases mss outright for $500. Published 12 titles last year. "Most books are sold through publicity and ads in the coin newspapers." Will send a book list to writers who send S.A.S.E. Will consider photocopied submissions. "Send ms by registered or certified mail. Be sure copy of ms is retained." Reports usually within several months. Enclose return postage.

Nonfiction and Fiction: "Our specialty is coin and stock market investment books; especially coin investment books and coin price guides. We are open to any new ideas in the area of numismatics. The writer should write for a teenage through adult level. Lead the reader by the hand like a teacher, building chapter by chapter. Our books sometimes have a light, humorous treatment, but not necessarily."

Recent Titles: *Jottings of a Stock Market Jackass,* by J. Penn (stock market); and *How to find Valuable Old and Scarce Coins,* by D. Bale (coins).

BALLANTINE BOOKS, division of Random House, 201 E. 50th St., New York NY 10022. Publishes trade and mass market paperback originals and reprints. Royalty contract varies. Published 350 titles last year; about 1/4 were originals. Query first. Enclose return postage.
General: General fiction and nonfiction, science fiction and fantasy.

*BANNER BOOKS INTERNATIONAL, INC., 13415 Ventura Blvd., Sherman Oaks CA 91423. (213)784-9788. Executive Vice President: Ms. Terry Sherf. Hardcover and paperback originals (90%) and reprints (10%). Specializes in "academic and scholarly books for the world college and university markets." 40% royalty; no advance. "We are co-op publishers, we co-invest with authors in books we accept for publication on a subsidy basis. We are not a vanity press nor are we a 'typical' subsidy publisher. Our co-investment in a book requires that we first substantiate its sales potential and then market it aggressively, to justify our investment." Published 57 books in 1976, 100 in 1977; will do 125 in 1978. State availability of photos or line art. Simultaneous and photocopied submissions OK. Reports in 1-2 months. SASE. Free author's prospectus.
Nonfiction: Publishes Americana; art; biography; business; economics; education; history; law; medicine and psychiatry; military science; music; philosophy; political science; psychology; reference; religious; scientific; sociology; technical; textbooks; language textbooks; and literature translation books. Submit complete ms.
Special Needs: Decision Books (books on business and finance for the business market, including EDP, computer sciences, business law.)
Recent Titles: *Hemingway: A Psychological Portrait,* by Drs. R. Hardy and J. Cull; *Values and the Future,* by Dr. J. Hunter (education) and *Technical Report Writing,* by Drs. L. Harvill and T. Kraft (technical sciences).

BANTAM BOOKS, INC., 666 Fifth Ave., New York NY 10019. Senior Vice President and Editorial Director: Marc H. Jaffe; Associate Editorial Director: Allan Barnard; Executive Editor: Grace Bechtold. Principally reprint. "Will accept unsolicited fiction and nonfiction, only first chapter and one other representative chapter, total no more than 7,500 words." Published 377 titles in 1976. Free book catalog. Reports in 1 month. SASE.
General Fiction and Nonfiction: Publishes adult fiction and general nonfiction education titles. Length: 75,000 to 100,000 words.

*BANYAN BOOKS, INC., Box 431160, Miami FL 33143. (305)665-6011. Director: Ellen Edelen. Hardcover and paperback originals (90%) and reprints (10%). Specializes in publishing regional and natural history books. 10% royalty; no advance. Subsidy publishes 10% of books; "worthwhile books that fill a gap in the market, but whose sales potential is limited." Published 10 books in 1976, 15 in 1977; will publish 15 in 1978. Send prints if illustrations are to be used with ms. Photocopied submissions OK. Reports in 1 month. SASE. Free book catalog.
Nonfiction: Publishes regional history and books on nature and horticulture. Submission of outline/synopsis, sample chapters preferred, but will accept queries.
Recent Titles: *Wild Flowers of Florida,* by Fleming/Genelle/Long (nature); *Lemon City,* by T. Peters (history); *Florida Gardener's Answer Book,* by F. Dickson (nature).

BARLENMIR HOUSE PUBLISHERS, 413 City Island Ave., New York NY 10064. Editor-in-Chief: Barry L. Mirenburg. Managing Editor: Leonard Steffan. Hardcover and paperback originals. 10-12½-15% royalty; varying advance. Published 12 titles in 1976, 14 in 1977; will do 20 in 1978. Submit outline/synopsis and sample chapters. State availability of photos and/or illustrations to accompany ms. Simultaneous (if informed) and photocopied submissions OK. Reports in 2-4 weeks; "sometimes sooner." SASE. Book catalog for SASE.
Nonfiction: Publishes Americana, art, biography, business; cookbooks, cooking and foods;

economics, erotica, history, hobbies, how-to, humor, law; medicine and psychiatry; multimedia material, music, nature, philosophy, photography, poetry, politics, psychology, recreation, reference, scientific, self-help, sociology, sports, technical textbooks, and travel books. "No adherence to specific schools of writing, age, or ethnic group. Acceptance based solely on original and quality work."
Fiction: Publishes adventure, confession, erotica, experimental, historical, humorous, mainstream, mystery, science fiction, suspense. "Always looking for good fiction."
Recent Titles: *UFO, The Eye and The Camera,* by A. Vance (nonfiction); *The Painterly Poets,* by F. Moramarco (nonfiction); *The Beneficence,* by R. Reinhold (fiction).

A.S. BARNES AND CO., INC., Cranbury NJ 08512. (609)655-0190. Editor: Dena Rogin. Publishes hardcover and paperback originals and reprints; occasionally publishes translations and anthologies. Contract negotiable: "each contract considered on its own merits." Advance varies, depending on author's reputation and nature of book. Published 90 titles last year. Will send a catalog to a writer on request. Query first. Reports as soon as possible. Enclose return postage.
General Nonfiction: "General nonfiction with special emphasis on cinema, antiques, sports, and crafts."

BARRE PUBLISHERS, Valley Rd., Barre MA 01005. Editor-in-Chief: Jane West. Publishes hardcover and paperback originals. Offers standard minimum book contract. "We offer small advances." Published 15 titles last year. Will send free catalog to writer on request. Will consider photocopied submissions. Submit outline and sample chapters or complete ms. Reports in 4 weeks. Enclose return postage.
General Nonfiction: "We specialize in fine craftsmanship and design. History, Americana, art, travel, cooking and foods, nature, recreation and pets. No length requirements; no restrictions for style, outlook, or structure. Our emphasis on quality of manufacture sets our books apart from the average publications. Particularly interested in folk art and crafts." Current titles include *Ships' Figureheads* and *Tools That Built America.*

R.O. BEATTY & ASSOCIATES/BEATTY BOOKS, Box 763, Boise ID 83701. (208)343-4949. Publisher: David C. Beatty. Editor: Melissa L. Dodworth. Hardcover and paperback originals. Specializes in photographic documentary books. Royalty and advance negotiable. Published 2 titles in 1976, 2 in 1977; will do 4 in 1978. Query. State availability of photos/illustrations. Simultaneous submissions OK. Reports in 1-2 months. SASE. Free book catalog.
Nonfiction: Publishes Americana; biography; cookbooks, cooking and foods; history; juveniles; nature; photography; and travel books.
Fiction: Publishes fantasy and historical books. No romantic fiction.
Recent Titles: *Nevada: Land of Discovery,* by D. Beatty (Western Americana photographic documentary); *Sun Valley: A Biography,* by D. Oppenheimer and J. Poore (photographic documentary).

BEAU LAC PUBLISHERS, Box 248, Chuluota FL 32766. Publishes hardcover and paperback originals. Query first. Enclose S.A.S.E.
Nonfiction: "Military subjects. Specialist in the social side of service life." Current titles include *Mrs. Lieutenant, Mrs. Field Grade, Mrs. CNO* (Gross).

BELIER PRESS, Box C, Gracie Station, New York NY 10028. Editor-in-Chief: J.B. Rund. Hardcover and paperback originals and reprints. 5-7½-10% royalty; advance depends on work. Send contact sheet or prints to illustrate ms. Photocopied submissions OK. Reports "as soon as possible". SASE. Free book catalog.
Nonfiction: Publishes comics, satire, erotica, and art books. "Strictly adult". Query first.
Recent Titles: *Carload O' Comics,* by R. Crumb; *The Adventure of Sweet Gwendoline,* by J. Willie.

CHARLES A. BENNETT CO., INC., 809 W. Detweiller Dr., Peoria IL 61614. (309)691-4454. Editor-in-Chief: Michael Kenny. Hardcover and paperback originals. Specializes in textbooks and related materials. 10% royalty for textbooks, "less for supplements;" no advance. Published 24 titles in 1976, 20 in 1977; will do 20 in 1978. Query "with a sample chapter that represents much of the book; not a general introduction if the ms is mostly specific 'how-to' instructions." Send prints if photos/illustrations are to accompany the book. Photocopied submissions OK. Reports in 2-4 weeks. SASE. Free book catalog.
Nonfiction: Publishes art (history or appreciation; possibly some how-to intended for students

in junior high or above); foods (textbooks); how-to (textbooks on woodworking, metalworking, etc.); photography (textbook, high school or college level); and textbooks (home economics, industrial education, art).
Recent Titles: *Food for Today,* by H. Kowtaluk and A. Kopan (home economics textbook); *Carpentry and Building Construction,* by Feirer and Hutchings (industrial education textbook).

BERKLEY PUBLISHING CORP., 200 Madison Ave., New York NY 10016. Editor-in-Chief: Page Cuddy. Managing Editor: Robin Rosenthal. Hardcover and paperback originals (50%) and paperback reprints (50%). 6% royalty to 150M copies; 8% thereafter; usually offers advance. Publishes about 165 titles a year. Submit through agent only. State availability of photos/illustrations. Simultaneous and photocopied submissions OK. Reports in 1-2 months. SASE.
Nonfiction: Publishes biography; hobbies; how-to; pets; psychology (popular); and self-help books. "We publish very little nonfiction; the categories above are the ones we are most likely to publish."
Fiction: Publishes fantasy; historical; mainstream; mystery; romance; science fiction; suspense; and western books.
Recent Titles: *Children of Dune,* by F. Herbert (science fiction); *Once an Eagle,* A. Myrer (fiction); and *The Tomorrow File,* by L. Sanders (fiction).

BETHANY FELLOWSHIP, INC., 6820 Auto Club Rd., Minneapolis MN 55438. (612)944-2121. Editor-in-Chief: Alec Brooks. Managing Editor: David Thompson. Hardcover and paperback originals (75%); paperback reprints (25%). 10% royalty on hardcover and original trade paperback; 6% on original mass market book. No advance. Published 41 titles in 1976, 40 in 1977; will do 45 in 1978. Simultaneous and photocopied submissions OK. Reports in 1-2 months. Free book catalog.
Nonfiction: Publishes biography (evangelical Christian), nature, religious (evangelical charismatic) and self-help books. Query.
Fiction: "We are interested in anything that is Christian and evangelical." Query.
Recent Titles: *Your Money Matters* by McGregor (family finances); *Shaping of America* by Montgomery (history).

BETHANY PRESS, Book Division of Christian Board of Education, P.O. Box 179, St. Louis MO 63166. (314)371-6900. Editor-in-Chief: Sherman R. Hanson. Publishes hardcover and paperback originals. Standard 17% royalty contract. Published 13 titles in 1976, 12-14 in 1977. Will consider photocopied submissions. Query first. Reports in 30 days. Enclose return postage.
Nonfiction: Books dealing with Christian experience, church life, devotions, and programming, Christian education, Bible reading and interpretation. Writer should offer clear prose, readable by lay persons, speaking to their concerns as Christians and churchmen or churchwomen. Recent titles include *God Is Never Absent; Feast of Joy;* and *We Saw Stars.*

BETTER HOMES AND GARDENS BOOKS, 1716 Locust St., Des Moines IA 50336. Editorial Director: Don Dooley. Publishes hardcover originals and reprints. "Ordinarily we pay an outright fee for work (amount depending on the scope of the assignment). If the book is the work of one author, we sometimes offer royalties in addition to the fee." Published 17 titles in 1976. Free book catalog. Prefers outlines and sample chapters. Will accept complete ms. Will consider photocopied submissions. Reports in 6 weeks. Enclose return postage.
Home Service: "We publish nonfiction in many family and home service categories, including gardening, decorating and remodeling, sewing and crafts, money management, entertaining, handyman's topics, cooking and nutrition, and other subjects of home service value. Emphasis is on how-to and on stimulating people to action. We require concise, factual writing. Audience is primarily husbands and wives with home and family as their main center of interest. Style should be informative and lively with a straightforward approach. Stress the positive. Emphasis is entirely on reader service. We approach the general audience with a confident air, instilling in them a desire and the motivation to accomplish things. Food book areas that we have already dealt with in detail are currently overworked by writers submitting to us. We rely heavily on a staff of 9 home economist editors for food books. We are interested in non-food books that can serve mail order and book club requirements (to sell at least for $8.95 and up) as well as trade. Rarely is our first printing of a book less than 100,000 copies. Then, new titles must compete with our other titles. 96-, 208- and 400-page books are lengths of 3 most popular lines. Each is heavily interspersed with illustrations ranging from 2-page spreads to 1-column, 5-inch pix." Publisher recommends careful study of specific BH&G book titles before submitting material.

*BINFORD & MORT, PUBLISHERS, 2536 S.E. 11th Ave., Portland OR 97202. (503)238-9666. Editor-in-Chief: L.K. Phillips. Managing Editor: Thomas Binford. Hardcover and paperback originals (50%) and reprints (50%). 10% royalty; advance (to established authors) varies. Occasionally does some subsidy publishing, "when ms merits it, but it does not fit into our type of publishing." Publishes about 24 titles annually. Reports in 2-4 months. SASE. Free book catalog.
Nonfiction: Publishes books about the Pacific Northwest, mainly in the historical field. Also Americana, art, biography; cookbooks, cooking and foods; history, nature, photography, recreation, reference, sports, and travel. Query.
Fiction: Publishes historical and western books. Must be strongly laced with historical background.
Recent Titles: *Seashells of the Pacific Northwest*, by J.S. White; *Grand Era of Cast-Iron Architecture in Portland*, by W. J. Hawkins III.

CLIVE BINGLEY LIMITED, 16 Pembridge Rd., London W11 UK. (01)229-1825. Editor-in-Chief: Clive Bingley. Hardcover and paperback originals (90%); hardcover and paperback reprints (10%). 10% royalty. No advance. Published 19 titles in 1976 and 1977; will do 20 in 1978. State availability of photos if ms is to be accompanied by illustrations. Simultaneous and photocopied submissions OK. SAE and International Reply Coupons. Reports in 1-2 weeks. Free book catalog.
Nonfiction: Publishes bibliographies, reference books and books on library science. Submit outline/synopsis and sample chapters.
Recent Titles: *History: A Reference Handbook* by A. Day (reference); *Third Dictionary of Acronyms and Abbreviations* by E. Pugh (reference); *Classification in the 1970s: A Second Look* by A. Maltby (library science).

JOHN F. BLAIR, PUBLISHER, 1406 Plaza Dr., Winston-Salem NC 27103. (919)768-1374. Editor-in-Chief: John F. Blair. Publishes hardcover originals; occasionally paperbacks and reprints. Royalty to be negotiated. Published 5 titles last year. Free book catalog. Submit complete ms. Reports in 6 weeks; "authors urged to inquire if they have not received an answer within that time." Enclose return postage.
General Fiction, Nonfiction, and Juveniles: In juveniles, preference given to books for ages 10 through 14 and up; in history and biography, preference given to books having some bearing on the southeastern United States. "No poetry this year; give us a chance to catch up." No length limits for juveniles. Other mss may be 140 pages or more.
Recent Titles: *Seven Founders of American Literature* (biography); *Cruise of the Snap Dragon* (fiction); and *Winter Birds of the Carolinas and Nearby states* (nonfiction).

BLAKISTON MEDICAL/NURSING BOOKS, McGraw-Hill Book Co., 1221 Avenue of the Americas, New York NY 10020. Editor-in-Chief; Joseph J. Brehm. Pays on royalty basis. SASE.
Textbooks: Publishes textbooks, major reference books and audiovisual materials in the fields of medicine, dentistry, nursing, and allied health.

THE BOBBS-MERRILL CO., INC., Continuing Education & College Department, 4300 W. 62nd St., Indianapolis IN 46268. (317)291-3100. Editorial Director: Thomas D. Wittenberg. Published 60 titles last year. "Queries are acceptable, but do not send complete manuscripts." Enclose S.A.S.E.
Nonfiction: "We are interested in the following disciplines: business education, humanities, vocational and technical books."

THE BOBBS-MERRILL CO., INC., 4 W. 58th St., New York NY 10019. Editor-in-Chief: Daniel Moses. Publishes hardcover originals. Offers standard 10-12½-15% royalty contract. Advances vary, depending on author's reputation and nature of book. Published about 90 titles last year. Query first. No unsolicited mss. Reports in 4 to 6 weeks. Enclose return postage.
General Fiction and Nonfiction: Publishes American and foreign novels, suspense, science fiction, film, politics, history, and current events, biography/autobiography. No poetry.

THE BOND WHEELWRIGHT COMPANY, Freeport ME 04032. (207)865-4951. Editor: Thea Wheelwright. Offers 10% royalty contract. No advance. Published 6 titles in 1976. Query first. Enclose return postage.
Nonfiction: "We are interested in nonfiction only—books that have a regional interest or specialized subject matter (if the writer is an authority), or how-to-do-it books. Length can vary from 50,000 words up, or start at less if there are a lot of illustrations (b&w only)."

BOOKCRAFT, INC., 1848 W. 2300 South, Salt Lake City UT 84119. Editor: H. George Bickerstaff. Publishes hardcover originals and reprints. Offers standard 10-12½-15% royalty contract. "We rarely make an advance on a new author." Published 20 titles last year. Will send a catalog to a writer on request. Query first. Will consider photocopied submissions. "Include contents page with ms." Reports in about 2 months. Enclose return postage.

Nonfiction: "We publish for members of The Church of Jesus Christ of Latter-Day Saints (Mormons). Our books are directly related to the faith and practices of that church. We will be glad to review such mss, but mss having merely a general religious appeal are not acceptable. Ideal book lengths range from about 64 pages to 200 or so, depending on subject, presentation, and age level. We look for a fresh approach — rehashes of well-known concepts or doctrines not acceptable. Mss should be anecdotal unless truly scholarly or on a specialized subject. Outlook must be positive. We do not publish anti-Mormon works. We almost never publish fiction or poetry. Recently published titles include *How to Live with Your Children and Like Them* (Boyle); *Someone Special, Starring Youth* (Durrant); and *Goals* (Dunn/Eyre).

Teen and Young Adult: "We are particularly desirous of publishing short books for Mormon youth, about ages 14 to 19. Must reflect LDS principles without being 'preachy;' must be motivational. 18,000 to 20,000 words is about the length, though we would accept good longer mss. This is a tough area to write in, and the mortality rate for such mss is high."

BOOKS FOR BUSINESSMEN INC., 744 Broad St., Newark NJ 07102. (201)621-1868. Editor-in-Chief: John Kosarowich. Hardcover and paperback originals (80%) and reprints. Specializes in books on business and international trade. "Usually royalties start at 10%; sometimes 5% for anthologies, but this is not a fixed rule." No advance. Published 4 titles in 1976, 10 in 1977; will do 12 in 1978. Send contact sheets for selection of illustrations. Simultaneous and photocopied submissions OK. Reports in 1-2 months. Book catalog for SASE.

Nonfiction: Publishes books on business, self-help, law, reference, economics, multimedia material and technical subjects. "We can use business material from a 5,000-word pamphlet to a 100,000-word book." Submit complete ms.

Recent Titles: *Tax Havens: What They Are and How They Work,* by Starchild (business); *How the IRS Selects Individual Tax Returns for Audit,* by Starchild (business); *Islamic Law in the Modern World,* by Yemani (law).

BOOKWORM PUBLISHING CO., P.O. Box 655, Ontario CA 91761. Editor-in-Chief: John Burke. Publishes paperback originals and reprints. "We publish limited library hardback editions." Offers royalty of 5% of net publisher revenues. "Author receives 1/3 of all auxillary revenues, e.g., translations, serial, TV rights, etc. We hold all copyrights ourselves in most cases." Advances paid only to previously established authors. Average advance is $500. "We rely on aggressive nontrade promotion to special outlets in addition to regular trade distribution channels, e.g., nurseries for garden books, worm farms for books on vermiculture. Books lending themselves to this additional thrust have an extra edge in our consideration." Query first. First time authors should submit complete ms. Established authors should submit outline and sample chapters. Will consider simultaneous and photocopied submissions. Typed, double-spaced ms essential. "If photos or drawings, send some samples of artists's or photographer's work." Enclose return postage if submitting complete ms on initial contact. Include phone number. Reports usually within 10 days.

Nonfiction: Any subject area related to natural or social ecology. Primary interests are agriculture, horticulture (gardening), waste management, self-sufficiency and organic living. Prefers practical "how-to-do-it" treatment. Mss may range from 7,500 to 30,000 words. "We seek mss from authors having authentic qualifications as 'authorities' in their subject areas, but qualification may be by experience as well as academic training." Interested in "needed" books either covering subjects relatively rare in existing literature or taking an unusual approach to conventional subject matter. Marketability of book is prime consideration. "We dislike issuing books which must compete in too crowded a field." See *The Elements of Style.* "We demand clear, concise, and effective use of English, appropriate to subject and intended audience. Technical terms, if used, should be defined in text on initial appearance and/or in accompanying glossary. We publish for the average person, and wish even our books for specialists to be understandable to the neophyte." Recently published *Earthworms for Ecology and Profit* (Gaddie and Douglas), detailing a step-by-step approach to establishing and operating a successful worm farm. "We're more interested in creating books of lasting value to readers than in following current trends or fads." Abstract philosophy, poetry, fiction are "just not in our fields."

Textbooks: Publishes social science texts for the elementary-high school market, emphasizing traditional values.

Business and Professional: Publishes business and "organization management."

BOREALIS PRESS LTD., 9 Ashburn Dr., Ottawa, Ont., Canada K2E 6N4. Editor-in-Chief: Frank Tierney. Managing Editor: Glenn Clever. Hardcover and paperback originals (90%) and reprints (10%). 10% royalty, no advance. Published 13 titles in 1976, 16 in 1977; will do 20 in 1978. Submit complete ms. Send prints if photos/illustrations are to accompany ms. Photocopied submissions OK. Reports in 6 months. SASE. Book catalog 50¢.
Nonfiction: Publishes juvenile books.
Fiction: Publishes mainstream and romance books.
Recent Titles: *A Visiting Distance,* by P. Anderson (poetry); *Exiles and Pioneers: A Study in Identities,* by T. Farley (criticism); and *Maple Island Mystery,* by J. Cowan (children's fiction).

THE BORGO PRESS, Box 2845, San Bernardino CA 92406. (714)884-5813. Editor-in-Chief: R. Reginald. Publishes paperback originals. "About 80% of our line consists of The Milford Series: Popular Writers of Today, critical studies on modern popular writers, particulary science fiction writers." Royalty: "4% of gross, with a 6% escalator; 6-8% for second books, if the first has sold well." No advance. Published 5 titles in 1976, 11 in 1977; will do 14 in 1978. "At least a third of our sales are to the library market." Reports in 1-2 months. SASE. Free book catalog.
Nonfiction: Publishes literary critiques. Submit outline/synopsis and sample chapters. "We appreciate people who've looked at our books before submitting proposals; all of the books in our author series, for example, are based around a certain format that we prefer using."
Fiction: Fantasy and science fiction. "We only publish fiction by established authors (those with previous book credits)." Query first.
Recent Titles: *Robert A. Heinlein: Stranger in His Own Land,* by G.E. Slusser (critique); *Hasan,* by P. Anthony (fantasy novel); *The Self Condemned,* by G. Wagner (general novel).

THOMAS BOUREGY AND CO., INC., 22 E. 60th St., New York NY 10022. Editor: Ms. Debra Manette. Offers $300 advance on publication date; 10% of retail price on all copies after the original printing of 3,000, to which the $300 applies. Published 60 titles in 1976. Query first with description. Reports in 1 month. SASE.
Fiction: For teenagers and young adults. Publishes romances, nurse and career stories, westerns and gothic novels. Sensationalist elements should be avoided. Length: 50,000 to 55,000 words. Also publishes Airmont Classics Series.
Recent Titles: Inn of the Clowns, by P. Paul (romance/mystery); *Ordeal of Love,* by R.M. Sears (romance); and *Shadow Over Wyndham Hall,* by S.T. Osborn (gothic).

R.R. BOWKER CO., 1180 Avenue of the Americas, New York NY 10036. (212)764-5100. Manager, Book Editorial Department: Desmond F. Reaney; Acquisitions Editor: Judith S. Garodnick. Directories Editor: Olga S. Weber. Royalty basis by contract arrangement. Query first. Reports in 2 to 4 weeks. Enclose return postage.
Book Trade and Reference: Publishes books for the book trade and library field, reference books, and bibliographies.

BOWLING GREEN UNIVERSITY POPULAR PRESS, 101 University Hall, Bowling Green State University, Bowling Green OH 43403. Editor: Ray B. Browne. Publishes hardcover and paperback originals. Offers 10% royalties; no advance. Published 10 titles last year. Will send a catalog to a writer on request. Send complete ms. "Follow MLA style manual." Enclose return postage.
Nonfiction: "Popular culture books generally. We print for the academic community interested in popular culture and popular media." Interested in nonfiction mss on "science fiction, folklore, black culture." Will consider any book-length mss.

BOWMAR PUBLISHING CORP., 4563 Colorado Blvd., Los Angeles CA 90039, (213)247-8995. Editor-in-Chief: Mel Cebulash. Managing Editor: Dolly Hassinbiller. Hardcover and paperback originals (80%) and reprints (20%). Specializes in El-hi educational books. 2-8% royalties or flat fees; "there is no average advance amount, and we don't always give advances." Published 42 titles in 1976, 29 in 1927. "We sell directly to schools; we have very few titles in bookstores." Query or submit outline/synopsis and sample chapters. State availability of photos/illustrations. Photocopied submissions OK. Reports in 1-4 months. SASE. Book catalog for SASE.
Nonfiction: Publishes biography; business; history; juveniles; nature; scientific; sports; and travel books.
Fiction: Publishes adventure; historical; mystery; and science fiction books.

*THE BOXWOOD PRESS, 183 Ocean View Blvd., Pacific Grove CA 93950. Editor-in-Chief: Ralph Buchsbaum. Hardcover and paperback originals (95%) and reprints (5%). 10% royalty; no advance. Subsidy publishes 20% of books. "If the scholarship is sound and the market small, we will consider it." Published 6 titles in 1976, 10 in 1977; will do 10 in 1978. Follow Chicago *Manual of Style.* State availability of photos and/or illustrations to accompany ms. Simultaneous submissions OK, if so advised. Reports in 2-4 weeks. SASE. Free book catalog.
Nonfiction: Publishes Americana, biology, business, economics, education, history, hobbies, how-to, languages, law, mathematics, medicine and psychiatry, music, nature, pets, philosophy, politics, psychology, recreation, reference, scientific, self-help, sociology, sports, technical, textbooks and travel books.
Recent Titles: *First Course in Population Genetics,* by C.C. Li (biology); *Mainstreaming Exceptional Children,* by J. Glover and A. Gary (education); *Woody Plants in Winter,* by E. Core and N. Ammons (biology).

*BRANDEN PRESS, INC., 221 Columbus Ave., Boston MA 02661 (617)267-7471. Editor-in-Chief: Edmund R. Brown. Managing Editor: Janet L. Carpenter. Hardcover and paperback originals (70%) and reprints (30%). 10% royalty up to 5,000 copies; 15% thereafter. "We offer an advance only on important books and cannot give an average amount. We publish some books for which the authors furnish a subsidy, or have grants." Publishes about 50 titles annually. Photos and/or illustrations are generally discussed with the author after ms is received. Photocopied submissions OK. Reports in 2-4 weeks. SASE. Free book catalog.
Nonfiction: "We publish books of all sorts and kinds and are willing to consider any ms, but are not interested in fiction." Query first.
Recent Titles: *Fundamentals of Applied Industrial Management,* by J. Glasser (educational); *Alaska — Not for a Woman,* by M. Carey (autobiographical); *House Plants That Really Grow,* by E.S. Parcher (handbook).

CHARLES T. BRANFORD CO., Box 41, 28 Union St., Newton Centre MA 02159. (617)244-6009. Editor-in-Chief: Ms. Lee F. Jacobs. Hardcover and paperback originals (80%) and reprints (20%). 10% royalty; no advance. Publishes about 10 titles annually. Photocopied submissions OK. Reports in 2 weeks. SASE. Free book catalog.
Nonfiction: Hobbies, how-to, recreation, self-help. Query first.

GEORGE BRAZILLER, INC., 1 Park Ave., New York NY 10016. Offers standard 10-12½-15% royalty contract. Advance varies, depending on author's reputation and nature of book. Published 30 titles in 1976. Prefers completed mss. Reports in 6 weeks. Enclose return postage.
General Fiction and Nonfiction: Publishes fiction and nonfiction; literature, art, philosophy, history, science. Length: 70,000 to 90,000 words.

BREVET PRESS, INC., 519 W. 10th St., Box 1404, Sioux Falls, SD 57101. Editor-in-Chief: Donald R. Mackintosh. Managing Editor: Peter E. Reid. Hardcover and paperback originals (67%) and reprints (33%). Specializes in business management, history, recipes, place names, historical marker series, fiction. 5% royalty; advance averages $1,000. Published 6 titles in 1976, 12 in 1977; will do 15 in 1978. Query; "after query detailed instructions will follow if we are interested." Send copies if photos/illustrations are to accompany ms. Simultaneous and photocopied submissions OK. Reports in 1-2 months. SASE. Free book catalog.
Nonfiction: Publishes Americana (L.S. Plucker, editor); business (D.P. Mackintosh, editor); cookbooks, cooking and foods (Peter Reid, editor); history (B. Mackintosh, editor); and technical books (Peter Reid, editor).
Fiction: Publishes historical books (T.E. Kakonis, editor).
Recent Titles: *Wind Without Rain,* by H. Krause (historical fiction); *Dakota Panorama,* edited by J.L. Jennewein and J. Boorman (history); and *Illinois Historical Markers and Sites* (nonfiction historical series).

BRIGHAM YOUNG UNIVERSITY PRESS, 209 University Press Bldg., Provo UT 84602. (801)374-1211, ext. 2591. Director: Ernest L. Olson. Hardcover and paperback originals (95%) and reprints (5%). Royalty of 15% after basic costs are met. Published 27 titles in 1976, 26 in 1977; will do 26 in 1978. Send samples of photos to illustrate ms. Photocopied submissions OK. Reports in 1-2 months. SASE. Book catalog for SASE.
Nonfiction: "Serious nonfiction in all fields; emphasis on works adding to the scholarly community. No length preferences." Publishes books on Americana, biography, book trade, business, early childhood education, history, nature, outdoor and recreational education, politics, reference, religion, science, sociology, textbooks and travel.

Recent Titles: *Without Fear or Favor,* by L. Harlow (city management); *Custer in '76,* by K. Hammer (western history); *The Great, Great Salt Lake,* by P. Czerny (western environment).

BROADMAN PRESS, 127 Ninth Ave., N., Nashville TN 37234. Editor-in-Chief: Johnnie C. Godwin. Hardcover and paperback originals (85%) and reprints (15%). Specializes in religious publishing (conservative, evangelical, Protestant viewpoint). 10% royalty for original adult hardcover; 5% for original paperbacks; no advance. Published 92 titles in 1976, 96 in 1977; will do 96 in 1978. State availability of photos and/or illustrations to accompany ms. Reports in 1-2 months. SASE.
Nonfiction: Publishes adult religious books (Johnnie C. Godwin, editor) and children's religious books (Grace Allred, editor). Query first.
Fiction: Very limited interest in religious fiction (J.S. Johnson, editor).
Recent Titles: *Why Not the Best?,* by J. Carter (religious autobiography); *The Reluctant Witness,* by K.L. Chafin (evangelism); *God's Miraculous Plan of Economy,* by J.R. Taylor (Christian living).

BROMBACHER BOOKS, 691 S. 31st St., Richmond CA 94804. (415)232-5380. Editor-in-Chief: John C. Tullis. Paperback originals (95%); paperback reprints (5%). Specializes in gardening (how-to) books. Royalty of 4% of retail price. "We also contract by the assignment for a flat, one-time, payment." State availability of photos and/or illustrations to accompany ms, or send contact sheet. Reports in 2-4 weeks. SASE. Free book catalog.
Nonfiction: Publishes books on business, (jobs/employment); cookbooks, cooking and foods; how-to (gardening, building, cooking); pets, reference; scientific (energy conservation, new forms, etc.); travel (budget travel guides). Submit outline/synopsis and sample chapters.
Recent Titles: *A Book About House Plants,* by Basila (gardening); My Face Lift & I, by Wald (cosmetic surgery); *I Love You Clark Gable, etc.,* by Tashman (film history).

WILLIAM C. BROWN CO., PUBLISHERS, 2460 Kerper Blvd., Dubuque IA 52001. Publisher: Richard C. Crews. Royalties vary. Query first. Enclose return postage.
Textbooks: College textbooks.

*C.S.S. PUBLISHING CO., 628 S. Main St., Lima OH 45804. (419)229-1787. Editor-in-Chief: Wesley T. Runk. Managing Editor: Jon L. Joyce. Paperback originals. Specializes in religious books. 4-8% royalty; no advance. Subsidy publishes ½ of 1% of books. Subsidy publishing is offered "to all whose mss we reject, but we do not offer marketing for any ms outside our categories." Published 51 titles in 1976, 60 in 1977; will do 60 in 1978. Markets by direct mail and bookstores. Submit complete ms. Simultaneous submissions OK. Reports in 2-4 months. SASE. Free book catalog.
Nonfiction: "We publish titles geared to helping members of the clergy and lay leaders of all denominations in the work of their parishes. Our titles are practical helps to these leaders: worship resources, sermon books, dramas for church use, stewardship and evangelism materials, youth programming materials, Bible study guides, children's sermon stories, and pastoral care resources. Generally, the more creative and contemporary the ms is, the more likely we are to offer a contract. Length may vary from a 12-page drama to a 200-page book of sermons. Clarity and creativity should be the first consideration."
Recent Titles: *What's Happening Out There in the Dark Tonight?,* by Clausen (drama); *Scales of Rejoicing,* by Taxer (worship); and *Cross Purposes,* by Brokhoff (sermons).

CAMARO PUBLISHING COMPANY, P.O. Box 90430, Los Angeles CA 90009. (213)837-7500. Editor-in-Chief: Garth W. Bishop. Publishes hardcover and paperback originals. "Every contract is different. Many books are bought outright." Published 5 titles last year. Query first. Enclose return postage.
Nonfiction: Books on travel, food, wine and health. Recently published *Total Mind Power: How to use the Other 90% of Your Mind,* by D.L. Wilson, M.D.

CAMBRIDGE UNIVERSITY PRESS, 32 E. 57th St., New York NY 10022. Editor-in-Chief: Walter Lippincott. Publishes hardcover and paperback originals. Offers 10% list worldwide royalty contract; 6% on paperbacks. No advance. Published 350 titles in 1976 in the U.S. and England. Query first. Reports in 2 weeks to 6 months. Enclose return postage.
Nonfiction and Textbooks: Sociology, economics, psychology, upper-level textbooks, academic trade, scholarly monographs, biography, history, music. Looking for academic excellence in all work submitted. Department Editors: Ken Werner (science), Steven Fraser (economics, economic history, American history, social and political theory).

CAPRA PRESS, 631 State St., Santa Barbara CA 93101. Editor-in-Chief: Noel Young. Managing Editor: Robert Sheldon. Hardcover and paperback originals. Specializes in documentary life style and short fiction books. 7½% royalty; advance averages $500. Published 12 titles in 1976 and 1977; will do 15 in 1978. State availability of photos and/or illustrations to accompany ms. Simultaneous submissions OK "if we are told where else it has been sent." Reports in 2-4 weeks. SASE. Book catalog for SASE.

Nonfiction: Publishes Americana (western contemporary, 30,000 words); biography (30,000 words); how-to; nature; self-help; and sociology books. Submit outline/synopsis and sample chapters.

Fiction: Publishes fantasy (like Peter Beagle); and mainstream books. Query.

Special Needs: Condor Series (documentation of ways of life) and novellas. Length not to exceed 25,000 words.

Rejects: "We're getting too much material from the 60's, too much poetry, and too many self-searching mss of no interest to readers who don't know the author."

Recent Titles: *Book of Friends,* by Henry Miller; *Adirondack Stories,* by J. Sanford; and *Sicily Enough,* by C. Rabe.

JAMES F. CARR BOOKS, 227 E. 81st St., New York NY 10028. (212)535-8110. Editor-in-Chief: James F. Carr. Publishes hardcover originals and reprints. Royalty schedule varies. Published 1 title last year. Query first. Enclose return postage.

Art: Books in the area of American art history. Currently compiling a multi-volume biographical dictionary of artists in North America. Always interested in biographical work on American artists. Length is flexible.

CATHOLIC TRUTH SOCIETY, 38/40 Eccleston Square, London SWIV IPD England. (01)834-4392. Hardcover and paperback originals (70%); hardcover and paperback reprints (30%). Specializes in Roman Catholic/ecumenical material. Pays 35 pounds minimum. No advance. Published 40 titles in 1976, 60 in 1977; will do 80 in 1978. If illustrations are to be used, send color slides or b&w glossies. Simultaneous and photocopied submissions OK. SAE and International Reply Coupons. Reports in 2-4 weeks. Free book catalog.

Nonfiction: Publishes books on art (with Roman Catholic/Christian application); biographies (if relevant to Catholics); history, humor, juveniles, medicine and psychiatry; music, philosophy, psychology, reference, religious, sociology, textbooks. Submit complete ms.

Fiction: Religious fiction for children.

Recent Titles: *A Simple Penance Book* (a guide for people to the new rites); *Let's Receive Our Lord* (full-color photographic children's prayer book); *The Lord Is Risen* (a simple coloring book).

CATHOLIC UNIVERSITY OF AMERICA PRESS, 620 Michigan Ave. N.E., Washington DC 20064. (202)635-5052. Manager: Miss Marian E. Goode. 10% royalty. Query first with sample chapter plus outline of entire work, along with curriculum vita, including a list of previous publications. Reports in 60 days. Enclose return postage.

Nonfiction: Publishes history, biography, languages and literature, philosophy, religion, church-state relations, social studies. Length: 100,000 to 500,000 words. Current titles: *Studies in Philosophy and the History of Philosophy - Vol. 6* (Ryan, ed.), *Ancient Patterns in Modern Prayer* (Krosnicki), *Martin John Spalding: American Churchman* (Spalding), *Christian Intitiation* (Riley).

*CAVEMAN PUBLICATIONS LTD., Box 1458, Dunedin, New Zealand. Editor-in-Chief: Trevor Reeves. Hardcover and paperback originals (80%) and reprints (20%). 10% royalty; advance depends on circumstances. Subsidy publishes 50% of books "from government grants only, *not* from authors". Publishes 5 titles a year. Photocopied submissions OK. Reports in 1-2 months. Enclose International Reply Coupons. Free book catalog.

Nonfiction: Publishes books on the environment, conservation, energy systems; technical, nature, poetry, self-help, erotica, how-to; cookbooks, cooking and foods; economics, hobbies, medicine and psychiatry; politics, music, science, music, humor, photography, art. Query first.

Fiction: Publishes experimental, fantasy, erotica, humorous, confession and science fiction. Query first.

Recent Titles: *Body Needs,* by S. Monson (cookbook), *Hospital Shock,* by A. Clark (medicine).

For '78: "Generally, I want books on current matters, such as the environment, alternatives, how-to, experimental fiction, speculative fiction; health and welfare, etc."

THE CAXTON PRINTERS, LTD., P.O. Box 700, Caldwell ID 83605. Publisher: Gordon Gipson. Pays royalties of 10%; advance is negotiable. Published 7 titles last year. Catalog available on request. Query before submitting ms. Publisher does not pass on excerpts or synopses, only complete mss. Reports in 6 to 8 weeks. Enclose return postage.
Americana and Politics: Publishes adult books of nonfiction western Americana or occasionally of conservative political nature. No fiction, scientific mss. Length: 40,000 words and up. Recent titles include *Forked Tongues and Broken Treaties;* and *Uphill Both Ways.*

CELESTIAL ARTS, 231 Adrian Rd., Millbrae CA 94030. (415)692-4500. Editor-in-Chief: David Morris. Paperback originals and reprints. Minimum standard royalty payment schedule; no advance. Published 41 titles in 1976, 40 in 1977; will do 40 in 1978. Send sample prints and/ or state availability of photos and/or artwork to illustrate ms. Simultaneous and photocopied submissions OK. Reports in 1-2 months. SASE. Free book catalog.
Nonfiction: Publishes Americana, art, biography; cookbooks, cooking and foods; erotica, history, hobbies, how-to, humor, medicine and psychiatry; psychology, self-help and sociology books. Query first or submit outline/synopsis, addressed to Gail Hynes.
Fiction: Publishes erotica, fantasy and science fiction. Query first or submit outline/synopsis, addressed to Gail Hynes.
Recent Titles: *The Immortalist,* by A. Harrington; *Selective Awareness,* by P. Mutke.

*CENTURY HOUSE, INC., Watkins Glen NY 14891. Editor: John C. Freeman. Standard royalty contract. Preservation Press, related to Century House, does some subsidy publishing. "Preservation Press will report on such publication costs and related distribution problems if such requests accompany mss." Published 50 titles in 1976. SASE.
Americana and Hobbies: Publishes Americana and books on American decorative arts: history, historical biography, American arts, books on antiques and other collector subjects; hobby handbooks. Pictorial preferred. No fiction.
Recent Titles: *Creative Doll Making,* by D. Gottilly; *Matchcovers: A Guide to Collecting,* by E. Rancier (hobbies) and *Wish You Were Here: Centennial Guide to Postcard Collecting,* by Dr. L. Freeman (hobbies).

CHATEAU PUBLISHING INC., Box 20432, Herndon Station, Orlando FL 32814. (305)898-1641. Editor-in-Chief: Marcia Roen. Managing Editor: Julie Currie. Hardcover originals. 10-12½-15% royalty; no advance. Published 3 titles in 1976 and 1977; will do 5 in 1978. State availability of photos and/or illustrations to accompany ms. Photocopied submissions OK. Reports in 2-4 weeks. SASE. Book catalog for SASE.
Nonfiction: Publishes hobbies, how-to, multimedia material, pets, poetry, politics, recreation, self-help, and sports books. *No* cookbooks. Query, or submit outline/synopsis and sample chapters.
Recent Titles: *Hizzoner the Mayor,* by C.T. Langford (politics); *Look at Me, World,* by G. Roen (poetry).

THE CHATHAM PRESS, a subsidiary of Devin-Adair, 143 Sound Beach Ave., Old Greenwich CT 06310. Editor: Emily Kinder. Publishes hardcover and paperback originals, reprints, and anthologies. "Standard book contract does not always apply if book is heavily illustrated. Average advance is low." Published 15 titles last year. Will send a catalog to a writer on request. Send query with outline and sample chapter. Reports in 2 weeks. Enclose return postage.
General Nonfiction, The Arts, and History and Biography: Publishes mostly "regional history and natural history, involving almost all regions of the U.S., all illustrated, with emphasis on conservation and outdoor recreation, photographic works, the arts." Current titles include *Skiing Colorado, The Soft-Hackled Fly, Green Fun, Seasons of the Salt Marsh, An Age of Flowers.*

CHILDRENS PRESS, 1224 W. Van Buren St., Chicago IL 60607. (312)666-4200. Managing Editor: Joan Downing. Offers outright purchase or small advance against royalty. Published 98 titles in 1976, 65 in 1977. Reports in 3-6 weeks. SASE.
Juveniles: Publishes fiction and nonfiction for supplementary use in elementary and secondary schools; easy picture books for early childhood and beginning readers; high interest, easy reading material. Specific categories include careers, social studies, fine art, plays, and special education. Length: 50-10,000 words. For picture books, needs are very broad. They should be geared from pre-school to grade 3. Length: 50-1,000 words. Send outline with sample chapters or complete ms for picture books. Do not send finished artwork with ms.

Recent Titles: *Jay and the Marigold,* by Robinet; *Artists in our World, Frederic Remington,* by Baker; and *The Halloween Witch,* by Thayer.

CHILTON BOOK CO., 201 King of Prussia Rd., Radnor PA 19089. (215)687-8200. Associate Editorial Director: Glen B. Ruh. Assistant Managing Editor, Automotive: Stephen Davis. Hardcover and paperback originals. Standard royalty; negotiable advance. Published 97 titles in 1976, 60 in 1977; will do 70 in 1978. Simultaneous and photocopied submissions OK. Reports in 2-8 weeks. SASE. Free book catalog.
Nonfiction: Publishes books on arts and crafts (35,000 words minimum; Lydia Driscoll, senior editor). Business; cookbooks, cooking and foods; hobbies, how-to, recreation, reference, self-help, sports, technical, textbooks, current events (50,000 words minimum length; Glen B. Ruh, associate editorial director). Query first or submit outline/synopsis and sample chapters.
Recent Titles: *All God's Children: The New Religious,* by C. Stoner and J. A. Parke (current events); *Indoor Plants: Comprehensive Care and Culture,* by D.F. Hirsch; *Pottery Form,* by D. Rhodes (arts and crafts).

CHOSEN BOOKS, Lincoln VA 22078. (703)338-4131. Executive Director: Leonard E. LeSourd. Managing Editor: Richard Schneider. Hardcover and paperback originals. 10-12½-15% royalty; advance averages $1,000. Published 3-5 titles in 1976; 4 in 1977. Simultaneous submissions OK. SASE. Free book catalog for SASE.
Religion: Seeks out significant developments in the Christian world to present in dramatic book form. Wants quality books that are highly interesting as well as spiritually entertaining. Length: 40,000-60,000 words. Submit outline and sample chapters.
Recent Titles: *Born Again,* by C. Colson; *Adventures in Prayer,* by Marshall; and *The Eye of the Storm,* by Bishop.

CHRISTIAN HERALD BOOKS (formerly Christian Herald House), 40 Overlook Dr., Chappaqua NY 10514. (914)769-9000. Editor-in-Chief: Gary L. Sledge. Hardcover originals. Emphasizes Christian themes. 10% royalty; advance negotiable. Published 11 titles in 1976, 12-15 in 1977; will do 12-15 in 1978. State availability of photos and/or illustrations to accompany ms. Simultaneous and photocopied submissions OK. Reports in 1-2 months. SASE. Book catalog for SASE.
Nonfiction: Publishes Americana, biography, and religious books. Must have Christian slant or theme. Query or submit outline/synopsis and sample chapters.
Fiction: Religious only.
Recent Titles: *Put on a Happy Faith,* by C. Murphey; *The Innermost Room,* by E. Nitsen; *Granny Brand,* by D.C. Wilson.

CHRONICLE BOOKS, 870 Market St., San Francisco CA 94102. A division of the Chronicle Publishing Co., publisher of *The San Francisco Chronicle.* Editor: Phelps Dewey. Publishes hardcover and paperback originals, reprints, and anthologies. Nonfiction only. Offers standard royalty contract. No advance. Published 13 titles in 1976, 15 in 1977. Send query with outline and sample chapter. "We prefer outline and sample chapter to complete ms." Reports in 1 month. Enclose return postage.
General Nonfiction: Current titles are in the fields of animals, architecture, conservation, food, history, the outdoors, sports, travel. Length: 60,000 to 100,000 words.
Recent Titles: *Exploring the Northwest,* by M. Hayden (recreation); *First Horse-Basic Horse Care Illustrated,* by R. Hapgood (self-help) and *Hand Hewn, the Act of Building Your Own Cabin,* by W. Leitch (self-help).

CISTERCIAN PUBLICATIONS, INC., 1749 W. Michigan-WMU, Kalamazoo MI 49008. Managing Editor: E. Rozanne Elder. Hardcover and paperback originals. No royalties. "Most authors are unpaid scholars." No advance. Published 6 titles in 1976, 8 in 1977; will do 8 in 1978. "Our style sheet should be used." Author is responsible for securing glossy prints and permission to use. Photocopied submissions OK. Reports in 1-2 months. SASE. Free book catalog.
Nonfiction: Publishes books on history (monastic); religious (contemplative tradition).
Recent Titles: *Russian Mystics,* by S. Bolshakoff (religion); *Bernard of Clairvaux and the Cistercian Spirit,* by J. Leclerug (history); *The Way of Love,* by P. Hart and E. Elder (religion).

CITADEL PRESS, 120 Enterprise Ave., Secaucus NJ 07094. (212)736-0007. Editor-in-Chief: Allan J. Wilson. Publishes hardcover and paperback originals; paperback reprints. Offers standard minimum book contract of 10-12-15%. Published 65 titles last year. Will consider photo-

copied submissions. Query first or submit outline and sample chapters. Reports in 6 weeks to 3 months. Enclose return postage.
Nonfiction and Fiction: Americana, biography, history, filmography, occult, black studies. Highly selective, offbeat, sensational fiction. Not interested in mss dealing with religion, poetry, theater, or current politics. Length: 70,000 words minimum.

CLARKE, IRWIN & CO., LTD., 791 St. Clair Ave., W., Toronto, Ontario, Canada M6C 1B8. Hardcover and paperback originals (95%) and reprints (5%). Specializes in Canadian subjects. Royalty schedule varies; minimum of 10%. Publishes about 20 titles a year. Submit outline/synopsis and sample chapters or complete ms. Must be typed double-spaced. "Don't send only copy." Send samples of prints for illustration. Photocopied submissions OK. Reports in 1-2 months. SASE.
Nonfiction: Publishes juveniles and books on Canadiana, art, biography, history, how-to, music, nature, poetry, politics, recreation, self-help, sports, textbooks, travel.
Fiction: Publishes adventure, historical, humorous, and mainstream books.
Recent Titles: *Hallowed Walls,* by Adamson/McRae (art/architecture); *Stepping Stones/So Free We Seem,* by J. Brown (fiction); and *Frankenstein,* by A. Nowlan/W. Learning (drama fiction).

CLIFF'S NOTES, INC., Box 80728, Lincoln NE 68501. (402)477-6971. Editor: Harry Kaste. Publishes paperback originals. Outright purchase, with full payment upon acceptance of ms. Published 2 titles in 1976. Free book catalog. Query. Contributors must be experienced teachers with appropriate special interests; usually have Ph.D. degree. Reports in 4 weeks. Enclose return postage.
Nonfiction: Currently expanding a line of paperback texts in the field of speech and hearing handicaps. Also occasional trade or textbooks of special merit.

COBBLESMITH, Route 1, Ashville ME 04607. Editor-in-Chief: Gene H. Boyington. Hardcover and paperback originals (90%); hardcover and paperback reprints (10%). Royalty of 8½% of list price. No advance. Published 2 titles in 1976, 5 in 1977; will do 8 in 1978. Simultaneous and photocopied submissions OK. SASE. Reports in 2-4 months. Free book catalog.
Nonfiction: Americana and art topics (especially New England and antiques); law (popular, self-help); cookbooks, cooking and foods;, gardening, psychology (applied — not theory); how-to (home and homestead crafts); juveniles (illustrated tales for all ages); philosophy (educational and new developments); sociology (applied — not theory); material on alternative life styles; nature, travel (offbeat guide books); self-help. Query. "Unsolicited mss are often treated as though only a little better than unsolicited third class mail."
Fiction: Fantasy, animal stories and humorous fiction.
Recent Titles: *Wood Cook's Cookbook,* by S.D. Haskell (cooking); *Practical Hooked Rugs* by S.H. Rex (how-to, crafts); *Do Your Own Divorce in North Carolina* by M.H. McGee (self-help/law).

COLGATE UNIVERSITY PRESS, Hamilton NY 13346. Editor-in-Chief: R. L. Blackmore. Publishes hardcover originals, reprints, and an annual journal about the Powys family of writers and their circle. No other subjects at this time. Offers standard royalty contract; "rarely an advance." Published 3 titles last year. Will send a catalog to a writer on request. Will consider photocopied submissions. Query first. Reports in 1 month. Enclose return postage.
Biography: "Books by or about the Powyses: John Cowper Powys, T. F. Powys, Llewelyn Powys. Our audience is general and scholarly." Length: open.

COLLECTOR BOOKS, Box 3009, Paducah KY 42001. Editor-in-Chief: Steve Quertermous. Hardcover and paperback originals. 5% royalty of retail; no advance. Published 25 titles in 1976, 25-30 in 1977. Send prints or transparencies if illustrations are to accompany ms. SASE. Reports in 2-4 weeks. Free book catalog.
Nonfiction: "We only publish books on antiques and collectibles. We require our authors to be very knowledgeable in their respective fields and have access to a large representative sampling of the particular subject concerned." Query.

COLLIER MACMILLAN CANADA, LTD., 1125 B Leslie St., Don Mills, Ont., Canada. Publishes both originals and reprints in hardcover and paperback. Advance varies, depending on author's reputation and nature of book. Published 35 titles last year. Always query. Reports in 6 weeks. Enclose S.A.E. and International Reply Coupons.
General Nonfiction: "Topical subjects of special interest to Canadians; how-to books."

Textbooks: History, geography, science, economics, and social studies: mainly texts conforming to Canadian curricular requirements. Also resource books, either paperback or pamphlet for senior elementary and high schools. Length: open.

COLORADO ASSOCIATED UNIVERSITY PRESS, University of Colorado, 1424 Fifteenth St., Boulder CO 80302. (303)492-7191. Editor: Margaret C. Shipley. Publishes hardcover and paperback originals. Offers standard 10-12-15% royalty contract; "no advances." Published 10 titles in 1976 and 1977. Free book catalog. Will consider photocopied submissions "if not sent simultaneously to another publisher." Query first. Reports in 3 months. Enclose return postage.
Nonfiction: "Scholarly and regional." Length: 250 to 500 ms pages.
Recent Titles: *Design and Analysis of Time-Series Experiments,* by Glass et al (scholarly); and *Colorado: A History of the Centennial State,* by Abbott (regional).

COLUMBIA UNIVERSITY PRESS, 562 W. 113th St., New York NY 10025. (212)678-6777. Editor-in-Chief: John D. Moore. Publishes hardcover and paperback originals. Royalty contract to be negotiated. Published 9 titles in 1976, 110 in 1977. Query first. SASE.
Nonfiction: "General interest nonfiction of scholarly value."
Scholarly: Books in the fields of literature, philosophy, fine arts, Oriental studies, history, social sciences, science, law.
Recent Titles: *Khruschev: The Years in Power,* by R. and Z. Medvedev (history) *Skeptical Sociology,* by D. Wrong (sociology).

COMPUTER SCIENCE PRESS, INC., 4566 Poe Ave., Woodland Hills CA 91364. (213)346-2353. Hardcover and paperback originals. 15% minimum royalty; no advance. Published 5 titles in 1976, 7 in 1977; will do 9 in 1978. State availability of photos and/or illustrations to accompany ms. Simultaneous and photocopied submissions OK. SASE. Reports in 1-2 months. Free book catalog.
Nonfiction: "Publish text and reference books in computer science and computer engineering." Submit outline/synopsis and sample chapters or complete ms.
Recent Titles: *Fundamentals of Data Structures,* by Horowitz/Sahni (textbook); *Computer Aided Design of Digital Systems: A Bibliography,* by vanCleemput (reference).

CONCORDIA PUBLISHING HOUSE, 3558 S. Jefferson Ave., St. Louis MO 63118. Pays royalty on retail price; outright purchase in some cases. Current catalog available on request. Published 40 titles last year. Send outline and sample chapter for nonfiction; complete ms for fiction. Reports in 3 months. Enclose return postage.
Religion, Juveniles, and Fiction: Publishes Protestant, general religious, theological books and periodicals; music works, juvenile picture and beginner books and adult fiction. "As a religious publisher, we look for mss that deal with Bible stories, Bible history, Christian missions; and mss that deal with ways that readers can apply Christian beliefs and principles to daily living. Any ms that deals specifically with theology and/or doctrine should conform to the tenets of the Lutheran Church-Missouri Synod. We suggest that, if authors have any doubt about their submissions in light of what kind of mss we want, they first correspond with us."

CONDOR PUBLISHING CO., INC., 521 5th Ave., New York NY 10017. President and Publisher: Gerald Rubinsky. Paperback originals and reprints. 4-8% royalty (based on paperback cover price); advance averages $1,500. Reports in 2 months. SASE.
Fiction and Nonfiction: Publishes adult fiction and general nonfiction titles. Length: 70,000-100,000 words. Query with outline and sample chapters.

DAVID C. COOK PUBLISHING CO., 850 N. Grove, Elgin IL 60120. (312)741-2400. Editor-in-Chief: Lawrence P. Davis. Managing Editor: Dean Merrill. Hardcover and paperback originals (90%) and paperback reprints (10%). Specializes in religious books. 6% royalty on paperbacks, 10% on hardcovers; advance "varies considerably." Published 30 titles in 1976, 35 in 1977; will do 45-50 in 1978. Query. State availability of photos and/or illustrations. Reports in 4-6 weeks. SASE. Free book catalog.
Nonfiction: Publishes juvenile, reference, religious and self-help books. All mss must pertain to religious themes.
Fiction: "We want fiction, especially for ages 8-14, but it should have a religious theme."
Recent Titles: *Open Heart-Open Home,* by K.B. Mains (religious-family); and *There Is Hope,* by L. Gardner (religious).

CORDOVAN CORPORATION, 5314 Bingle Rd., Houston TX 77018. (713)688-8811. Editor-in-Chief: Bob Gray. Publishes hardcover and paperback originals and reprints under the Cordovan Press, Horseman Books, and Fisherman Books imprints. Offers standard minimum book contract of 10-12-15%. Published 8 titles in 1976, 10 in 1977. Marketed heavily by direct mail and through various consumer and trade periodicals. Will consider photocopied submissions. Query first or submit outline and sample chapters. Reports in 1 month. Enclose return postage.

Nonfiction: Cordovan Press, a trade book division, seeks books on Texas history for the history buff interested in Texana. Horseman Books are practical, how-to books on horse training, grooming, feeding, showing, riding, etc., either by experts in the field or as told to a writer by an expert. Fisherman Books are how-to, where-to, when-to books on fishing in Texas and/or the Southwest. Author must be noted expert on fishing, or be retelling what a noted expert told him. "The emphasis is on plain language in all of these lines. Short sentences. Make the verbs sing the song. Pungent quotes. Don't try to snow the readers; they are too sharp and already know most of the score in all areas. Use humor when it isn't forced." Length: 150 ms pages.

CORNELL MARITIME PRESS, INC., Box 109, Cambridge MD 21613. Publisher: Robert F. Cornell. Hardcover and quality paperbacks, both originals and reprints. Payment is on regular trade publishers' royalty basis: 10% for first 5,000 copies, 12% for second 5,000 copies, 15% on all additional. Revised editions revert to original royalty schedule. Subsidy publishing is done only in conjunction with universities. Published 10 titles last year. Free book catalog. Send queries first, accompanied by writing samples and outlines of book ideas. Reports in 2 to 4 weeks. Enclose return postage.

Marine: Nonfiction relating to marine subjects, highly technical; manuals; how-to books on any maritime subject.

Recent Titles: *Marine Transportation of LNG,* by W. Wooler (professional); and *Fiberglass Repairs,* by P. Petrick (how-to).

R.D. CORTINA CO., INC., 136 W. 52nd St., New York NY 10019. General Editor: Mac-Donald Brown. Pays on a fee or a royalty basis. Published 27 titles last year. Do not send unsolicited mss; send outline and sample chapter. Reports in 2 months or less.

Textbooks: Publishes language teaching textbooks for self-study and school; also publishes language teaching phonograph records and tapes. Materials of special ESL interest. Word length varies.

*THE COUNTRYMAN PRESS, INC., Taftsville VT 05073. (802)457-1049. Editor-in-Chief: Peter Jennison. Managing Editor: Chris Lloyd. Hardcover and paperback originals (75%) and paperback reprints (25%). 10% royalty on first 5,000 copies, 12½% on next 2,500 and 15% thereafter; advance averages $500. Subsidy publishes "1 book out of 6. We publish some town histories at the expense of the sponsors; and accept an author's subsidy, in whole or in part, only if we would wish to have published the book anyway and believe we can do an adequate marketing job." Published 6 titles in 1976, 5 in 1977; will do 5 in 1978. Query for fiction or nonfiction, or submit outline/synopsis and sample chapters for nonfiction. Simultaneous and photocopied submissions OK. Reports in 1-2 months. SASE. Free book catalog.

Nonfiction: Publishes (in order of preference) how-to; Americana; hobbies; nature; cookbooks, cooking and foods; history; and recreation books.

Special Needs: "A 'Backyard' series on suburban and rural self-sufficiency."

Recent Titles: *Backyard Livestock: How to Grow Meat for Your Family,* by S. Thomas (how-to); *Lake Champlain: Key to Liberty,* by R.N. Hill (history); and *The Primary State: An Historical Guide to New Hampshire,* by E. Hill (history/travel).

COURIER OF MAINE BOOKS, 1 Park Dr., Rockland ME 04841. (207)549-4401. Director: William E. Dennen. Hardcover and paperback originals (80%) paperback reprints (20%). Specializes in books about Maine only. 10% royalty; "low" advance. Published 5 titles in 1976, 8 in 1977; will do 8 in 1978. Marketing is limited to people and institutions interested in Maine. Submit outline/synopsis and sample chapters. State availability of illustrations and photos. Simultaneous ("if we know about it") and photocopied submissions OK. Reports in 2-4 weeks. SASE. Free book catalog.

Nonfiction: Publishes art; biography; cookbooks, cooking and foods; economics; history; hobbies; how-to; humor; juveniles; nature; poetry; politics; recreation; reference; sociology; and travel books. All mss must pertain to Maine.

Fiction: Adventure; historical; humorous; mainstream; and mystery books.

Recent Titles: *All-Maine All-Seafood,* edited by L. Shibbles and A. Rogers (cookbook); *We Walk on Jewels,* by Blakemore (how-to, nature reference); *Saltwater Farm,* by Coffin (poetry reprint).

COWARD, McCANN & GEOGHEGAN, 200 Madison Ave., New York NY 10016. (212)576-8900. President and Editor-in-Chief: John J. Geoghegan. Pays on a royalty basis. For juveniles, offers 5% to 10% royalties; for juvenile nonfiction, advance is $500 to $3,000. Unsolicited mss will be returned unread. Query the editor, who will advise whether to submit ms. Enclose return postage.

General Fiction and Nonfiction: Publishes novels, including mysteries (no westerns or light or salacious love stories); outstanding nonfiction of all kinds; religious, history, biography (particularly on American figures). Also interested in humor. All should have general appeal. Length: 60,000 words and up.

Juveniles: "We will look at anything. Our needs vary considerably. Want picture books for ages 4 to 12. Want nonfiction for ages 4 and up."

CRAFTSMAN BOOK COMPANY OF AMERICA, 542 Stevens Ave., Solana Beach CA 92075. (714)755-0161. Editor-in-Chief: Gary Moselle. Publishes paperback originals. Royalty of 12½ to 15% of gross revenues, regardless of quantity sold. Published 8 titles last year. "About 75% of our sales are directly to the consumer and since royalties are based on gross revenues, the actual revenue realized is maximized." Will send free catalog to writer on request. Will consider photocopied submissions. Submit outline and sample chapters. Reports in 2 weeks. Enclose return postage.

Technical: "We publish technical books and are aggressively looking for queries and outlines on manuscripts related to construction, carpentry, masonry, plumbing, civil engineering, building estimating, chemical engineering and petroleum technology. Our books are written as practical references for professionals in their respective fields and each book should be written to answer practical questions and solve typical problems. Emphasis is on charts, graphs, illustrations, displays and tables of information. We are producing a series on how to become a successful construction contractor, construction estimator, etc. We can use practical, descriptive information. We don't want to see reprints of magazine articles and isolated essays which do not have the breadth or scope to warrant consideration for publication."

Recent Titles: *Remodelers' Handbook,* by G.B. Smith (professional building); and *Managing Capital Expenditures for Construction Projects,* by K.M. Guthrie (construction management).

CRAIN BOOKS, 740 Rush St., Chicago IL 60611. Editor-in-Chief: Melvin J. Brisk. Hardcover and paperback originals. 10% royalty, "although this varies, depending on the book, its potential and the market". Makes an advance only under exceptional circumstances. Published 10 titles in 1976, 14 in 1977; will do 15-20 in 1978. Send contact sheet if photos/illustrations are to accompany ms. Simultaneous and photocopied submissions OK, "but will rarely receive priority status as compared to the exclusive submission". Reports in 2-4 months. SASE. Free book catalog.

Nonfiction: Publishes business books for the advertising and marketing professional and student, including the academic market. "We're interested in mss that have a definite communications theme, and we usually work on assignment unless the author is a professional or academician. No rehashes. We want innovative ideas that will appeal to business types looking for improvement."

Recent Titles: *100 Best Sales Promotions of 1975/76,* by W. Robinson (promotion); *Advertising Media Planning,* by J. Sissors and R.R. Petray (mdeia); *The advertising Agency Business,* by H.S. Gardner, Jr. (business).

CRANE, RUSSAK & COMPANY, INC., 347 Madison Ave., New York NY 10017. Editor-in-Chief: Ben Russak. Publishes scientific journals and scientific and scholarly books. On monographs, offers no royalty for first 1,500 copies sold, 7% on the second 2,000 copies, and 10% on all copies sold after the first 2,000. No advances. Published 45 titles in 1976, 60 in 1977. "We promote our books by direct mail to the exact market for which each book is intended." Submit outline and sample chapters. Reports in 1 month. Enclose return postage.

Technical and Reference: "We publish scientific and scholarly works at the graduate and reference level: postgraduate textbooks and reference books for scholars and research workers. Our publications also appeal to members of professional societies. We'd like to see manuscripts on large-scale systems analysis in relation to solution of large-scale social problems. But do not send any popular material or matter which is intended for sale to the general public." Length: 60,000 to 120,000 words.

CREATION HOUSE, INC., 499 Gundersen Dr., Carol Stream IL 60187. Editor: Lila Bishop. Publishes hardcover and paperback originals. Offers standard royalty contract. Published 9 titles in 1976. Free book catalog. Follow Chicago *Manual of Style*. Reports in 1 to 2 months. Enclose return postage.

Religion and Philosophy: "We publish exclusively evangelical Christian literature. While we accept a few manuscripts dealing with contemporary issues or subjects of interest to a wide spectrum of Christian readers, our special interest is church growth and renewal. We attempt to be in the forefront in reporting on God at work in the world today. Religious fiction and poetry have only a slim chance with us. Most of our books are written in a popular, rather than a scholarly, style." Current titles include *Disciple* (Ortiz), and *A New Song* (Boone). A small publisher, Creation House will publish "only a few significant titles each year."

CREATIVE BOOK CO., Box 214998, Sacramento CA 95821. (916)489-4390. Editor-in-Chief: Sol H. Marshall. Paperback originals. Payment by flat fee ($50-$200) in the self-improvement category; negotiable for other categories. Pays half of advance on approval of outline; balance on delivery of ms. Published 12 titles in 1976, 12-20 in 1977; will do 12-20 in 1978. "Our catalogs and advertising go only to community organizations and educational fields. We do not use subjects in the field of commerce and industry." Send photocopies of glossy prints to accompany ms. Simultaneous and photocopied submissions OK. Reports in 2-4 weeks. SASE. Free book catalog.

Nonfiction: Publishes recreation, self-help, and textbooks. "We emphasize self-improvement for professionals in education and community organizations; public relations, administration and fund-raising for educational agencies and community organizations; adult education and gerontology. Our audience includes sophisticated lay leaders and professionals. We do not need books on 'how to run a club meeting'." Query or submit complete ms.

Recent Titles: *Public Speaking for Coaches and Other Animals,* by W. Turnbull; *How to Win a Local Issue Election,* by R. Karraker; *How to Produce a Slide/Tape Talk,* by M. Riback.

*****CRESCENDO PUBLISHING CO.**, 132 W. 22nd St., New York NY 10011. Publishes both originals and reprints in hardcover and paperback. Offers standard 10-12½-15% royalty contract. "Advances are rare; sometimes made when we seek out an author." Does less than 1% subsidy publishing a year. Published 20 titles last year. Will send catalog on request. Will look at queries or completed mss, with return postage paid envelope. Address submissions to Gerald Krimm. Reports in 4 weeks.

Music: Trade and textbooks in music. Length: open.

*****CRESCENT PUBLICATIONS, INC.**, 5410 Wilshire Blvd., #400, Los Angeles CA 90036. Editor-in-Chief: Joseph Lawrence. Publishes hardcover and paperback originals. Offers royalty contract "on the basis of the ms published." Does 75% subsidy publishing. Published 15 titles in 1976. Free book catalog. Will consider simultaneous submissions. Submit complete ms for fiction and nonfiction. Mss must be typed, double-spaced, on one side of paper only. Reports in 2 weeks. Enclose return postage.

Fiction, Nonfiction, Juveniles and Poetry: Publishes general trade books which are sold to book publishers and book distributors. Length: open. Also interested in Americana; politics; self-help and how-to; sports, hobbies, recreation and pets. "All subjects."

Recent Titles: *An American Alternative: Steps Toward A More Workable and Equitable Economy,* by Young (economics); and *Waterspout,* by McCain (adventure).

CRESTLINE PUBLISHING CO., Box 48, Glen Ellyn IL 61037. (312)495-9294. Editor-in-Chief: George H. Dammann. Publishes hardcover originals. Offers royalty of negotiable flat rate. "Somewhere between $5,000 and $10,000." No advance, usually. Published 2 titles last year. Will send free catalog to writer on request. Will consider photocopied and simultaneous submissions. Query first. Will not consider submissions from agents. Reports in 1 month. Enclose return postage.

History: Wants "pictorial histories on specific issues — as opposed to general conglomerations of old pictures. So far we have been strictly in automotive history: titles are *Illustrated History of Ford, 70 Years of Buick, 60 Years of Chevrolet, American Fire Engines Since 1900,* etc. For the first time, we are moving out of the automotive scene with a book on agricultural history, *Encyclopedia of American Steam Traction Engines.* This may be the first of a more diverse list of future titles, though automotive history will still be our strong suit." All projects must involve 1,500 photos minimum. "Our average book uses between 1,800 and 2,200 photos." Writer must have thorough knowledge of subject.

CROSSROADS PUBLICATIONS, P.O. Box 504, Palmdale CA 93550. Editor: R.G. Chambers. Publishes paperback originals. Offers 5% minimum royalty, but higher on special arrangements with author. Published 2 titles last year. Will send fliers to writer on request. Will not consider simultaneous or photocopied submissions. Submit complete ms for nonfiction. Must be double-spaced, typed, on 8½x11 paper. Reports in 30 days. Enclose S.A.S.E.

Nonfiction: "Inspirational — Religious (Protestant) Comedy — drawings or Art — Astrology. Also sex books from religious point of view. Paperback books of approximately 20 to 30 thousand words although longer lengths of merit will be considered. Also unusual how-to books, various lengths but generally falling within the length requirements above." No off-color. Recent titles include *Understanding the Sexual Need of Your Mate* (Morse).

THOMAS Y. CROWELL CO., 666 Fifth Ave., New York NY 10019. Send trade submissions to Acquisitions Editor; reference submissions to Pat Barrett. Offers standard royalty contract. Published 230 titles last year. Query first. Reports in 1 to 2 months. Enclose unglued return postage.

Nonfiction, Juveniles, and Textbooks: "Trade and reference books, children's books, college and secondary school reference books. Interested in general books of an informational nature."

CROWN PUBLISHERS, 1 Park Ave., New York NY 10016. (212)532-9200. Editor-in-Chief: Herbert Michelman. Contracts offered on basis of stature of writer, outline, subject and sample material. For juveniles, offers "10% against catalog retail price on books for older children; for picture books, 5% of the catalog retail price to the author and 5% to the artist. However, royalty scales may vary. Advance varies, depending on author's reputation and nature of book." Published 250 titles last year. Will send catalog on request. Prefers queries. Send complete ms for juvenile picture books. Address mss to department editor. Reports in 2 to 6 weeks. Enclose return postage.

General Fiction and Nonfiction: General fiction and nonfiction; pictorial histories, popular biography, science, books on decorative arts and antiques, crafts; some on music, drama and painting. Administrative Editor: Phillip Winsor; Fiction Editor: Larry Freundlich; Arts and Crafts: Brandt Aymar; Collector's Books: Kay Pinney; Science: Paul Nadan.

Juveniles: For juvenile nonfiction for all ages, wants "contemporary issues of a social and political nature. Length depends on the book." Picture books for preschoolers to children 7 years old "should be approached in terms of telling a good story. Length depends on the book." Children's Books Editor: Norma Jean Sawicki.

*CSA PRESS, Lakemont GA 30552. (404)782-3931. Editor-in-Chief: Ed O'Neal. Managing Editor: Bob Ross. Hardcover and paperback originals (25%);and paperback reprints (75%). Royalty of 15% of 43% of the retail price of the book; 5% of mail order sales; no advance. Subsidy publishes 18% of books, depending on quality, originality and current market demand. Published 16 titles in 1976, 8-10 in 1977; will do 8-10 in 1978. Follows Chicago *Manual of Style* guidelines. Send prints to accompany ms. Simultaneous and photocopied submissions OK. Reports in 2-4 weeks. SASE. Free book catalog.

Nonfiction: Publishes cookbooks, cooking and foods (health foods); how-to (special techniques and positive thinking); philosophy (Eastern occult and New Thought); religious (occult, meta-physical, New Thought); and self-help books. Submit complete ms.

Recent Titles: *Health, Healing and Total Living,* by E. Davis (health); *Master Meditations,* by Dr. D. Curtis (meditation); *Religion and the Life of Man,* by Dr. O. Park (religion).

CUSTOMBOOK, INCORPORATED, The Custom Bldg., South Hackensack NJ 07606. A new opportunity for writer-reporters has been developed by Custombook, Inc., nationwide producers of color editions for churches. "These limited editions are produced in conjunction with special occasions such as anniversaries, construction, renovations or for general education. As a result of major technical breakthroughs, such limited color editions are now practical for the first time. The books feature full-color photographs and the story of each church, its history, stained glass, symbolism, services, and organizations. Writers are being sought in most regions of the country to work. Recommendations are being sought from talented writers as to which churches would be the best subject for their initial Custombook. Older churches with major anniversaries (10th, 25th, 50th, 100th), new construction, or renovations (church, religious school, or convent), would be good subjects. The company will then contact the churches recommended by writers. $50 will be paid to any individual whose recommendation of a church eventually results in a Custombook. The organization will at the same time evaluate previous written efforts of this individual. If their editorial staff engages the writer to prepare the ms for the book, and the writer completes the ms himself, he will be paid $200 for his initial effort. Additional assignments may then follow from our own sources or from additional recommendations by the writer." Further details on the program are available from Mrs. Joan Curtis, Editor, at the above address.

DARTNELL CORPORATION, 4660 North Ravenswood Ave., Chicago IL 60640. (312)561-4000. Editorial Director: John Steinbrink. Publishes manuals, reports, hardcovers. Royalties: sliding scale. Published 6 titles last year. Send outline and sample chapter. Reports in 4 weeks. Enclose return postage.

Business: Interested in new material on business skills and techniques in management, supervision, administration, advertising sales, etc.

Recent Titles: *Executive Compensation,* by J. Steinbrink (general business); *How to Participate Profitably in Trade Shows,* by R. Konikow (sales); and *How to Conduct Better Meetings,* by Kirkpatrick (business).

DAUGHTERS PUBLISHING CO., INC., 22 Charles St., New York NY 10014. Paperback originals (80%) and reprints (20%). 10% royalty; negotiable advance. Published 4 titles in 1976, 6 in 1977; will do 6 in 1978. Submit queries to Park Bowman. Simultaneous and photocopied submissions OK. Reports in 2-4 months. SASE. Free book catalog.

Fiction: Publishes radical feminist novels. "We only do novels which reflect the current state of the women's movement."

Recent Titles: *Loner,* by B. Harris (feminist novel); *Sister Gin,* by J. Arnold; and *Ruby Fruit Jungle,* by R.M. Brown.

DAVID & CHARLES (HOLDINGS) LTD., Brunel House, Newton Abbot, Devon, UK. (0626)61121. Editor-in-Chief: Pamela M. Thomas. Hardcover and paperback originals. 10% royalty; advance varies. Publishes about 180 titles annually. "If ms is complete, we like to see all illustrations." Reports in 2-4 weeks. SAE and International Reply Coupons. Book catalog 75¢; author's guide 75¢.

Nonfiction: Publishes art, biography, business; cookbooks, cooking and foods; economics, history, hobbies, how-to, humor, music, nature, pets, photography, recreation, reference, self-help, sociology, sports and travel books. "We like books that deal with their subject in the round without segments idiosyncratically missing, and we like to see only slight use made of the personal pronoun. Our philosophy is sketched out in our Author's Guide, and much frustration would be avoided if the guide and our current catalog were consulted before submissions since most mss received are outside our categories and philosophy."

DAVIS PUBLICATIONS, INC., 50 Portland St., Worcester MA 01608. Published 10 titles last year. Write for copy of guidelines for authors. Submit complete ms. Enclose return postage.

Art and Reference: Publishes art and craft books. "Keep in mind the reader for whom the book is written. For example, if a book is written for the teacher, avoid shifting from addressing the teacher to addressing the student. Include illustrations with text. All illustrations should be collated separately from the text, but keyed to the text. Photos should be good quality original prints. Well-selected illustrations can explain, amplify, and enhance the text. It is desirable for the author's selection of illustrations to include some extras. These may be marked 'optional.' The author should not attempt to lay out specific pages. Poorly selected illustrations or too many competing illustrations in a short space can mar a book. For instance, if you are planning a 125- to 150-page book and you have over 300 photos (more than 2 photos per page, average), you probably have too many."

DAW BOOKS, INC., 1301 Avenue of the Americas, New York NY 10019. Editor: Donald A. Wollheim. Publishes paperback originals and reprints. Standard paperback book contract with advances starting at $2,000. Published 62 titles in 1976. Books are distributed nationally and internationally by The New American Library. Submit complete ms. Will not consider photocopied submissions. Reports in 4 to 8 weeks. Enclose return postage with ms.

Fiction: "Science fiction only, 5 titles a month. About 70% are original works. Mainly novels with occasional collections of the short stories of one author (name authors only). Space flight, future adventure, scientific discovery, unusual concepts, and all the vast range of s-f conceptions will be found in our works. We prefer good narrative presentation without stress on innovations, avant-garde stunts, etc." Length: 55,000 to 75,000 words.

THE JOHN DAY COMPANY, INC., 666 Fifth Ave., New York NY 10019. (212)489-2200. Juvenile Editor: Wendy Barish. Adult Editor: Linda O'Brien. Publishes hardcover originals. Royalty schedule varies. Will send a catalog to writer on request. Query first. Reports in 4 to 7 weeks. Enclose return postage.

General: Publishes adult fiction, juveniles, history, biography, science, special education and other nonfiction. "Adult fiction is not a large field for us; we have never published anything approaching 'pulp' fiction, we we have a rather high general standard of excellence in this field's requirements. Our juvenile books range from intermediate fiction and curriculum-oriented nonfiction, to science, social studies, and special fiction for older readers."

GERRY & HELEN DE LA REE, Scientifantasy Specialists, 7 Cedarwood Lane, Saddle River NJ 07458. (201)327-6621. Editor-in-Chief: Gerry de la Ree. Publishes paperback and hardcover originals. Offers to buy mss outright, since editions are limited. Advance varies. Published 4 titles in 1976. "We do our own retailing through our own mailing list and also sell to wholesalers or other dealers in the fantasy field." Query first for nonfiction and fantasy artwork. Reports in 1 week under normal circumstances. Enclose return postage.
Nonfiction: "We publish books mainly in the nonfiction vein dealing with fantasy, weird, and science fiction. Over the past three years we have done such volumes on writers like the late H.P. Lovecraft, Clark Ashton Smith and Robert E. Howard; art volumes on such fantasy artists as Virgil Finlay, Hannes Bok and Stephen E. Fabian. Our most recent trend has been more toward art books and folios than articles, but we are flexible. Most of our publications have been limited editions — 1,500 or less, with a certain number hardbound and the balance in paper covers. We buy first print rights and would copyright book under author's name if he so desires, and he has all future reprint rights." Not interested in new fiction or poetry. Prefer material of interest to collector in the fantasy field — articles dealing with leading authors of the recent past. Also interested in any unpublished material by these leading authors. Writers should know the fantasy field and its authors and artists. "This is a rather specialized field and we are always willing to discuss in advance any articles a writer is planning. We do not deal with agents."
Recent Titles: *Fantastic Nudes: Second Series,* by S.E. Fabian (folio); *A Hannes Bok Sketch Book,* by H. Bok; and *Finlay's Lost Drawings,* by V. Finlay.

DELL PUBLISHING CO., INC. (including Delacorte Press), 245 E. 47th St., New York NY 10017. Book Division. Publishes hardcover and paperback originals and reprints. Standard royalty schedule. Published 416 titles last year. Query first always. "Mss that arrive without a preceding query answered in the affirmative by a member of our staff will have to be returned unread. On fiction queries, we would like to know what sort of book the author has written or proposes to write—whether straight novel, romance-suspense, mystery, historical, or Gothic. A paragraph further describing the story would also be helpful." Send complete ms for juveniles. Reports in 8 to 10 weeks. Enclose return postage.
General Fiction and Nonfiction: Publishes adult fiction; general nonfiction including philosophy, biography, history, religion, science, the arts.
Juveniles: Delacorte Press children's books: poetry, history, sports and science for ages 12 and over; history, social science and fiction for intermediate level; picture books for the very young. Length: 30,000 to 50,000 words for ages 12 to 16. Juvenile Editor: Ronald Buehl.

*DELTA DESIGN GROUP, 518 Central Ave., Box 112, Greenville MS 38701. (601)335-6148. Editor-in-Chief: Noel Workman. Hardcover and paperback originals. 10-12½-15% royalty; no advance. 25% of books are subsidy published. Published 4 titles in 1976, 6 in 1977; will do 8 in 1978. Send contact sheet to accompany ms. Simultaneous submissions OK, "but tell us what is really going on". Photocopied submissions OK. Reports in 2-4 weeks. SASE.
Nonfiction: Publishes Americana, cookbooks, cooking and foods; history, multimedia material, travel, and regional architectural subject (lower Mississippi Valley) books. "Our market is the lower MIssissippi Valley (Louisiana, Mississippi, Arkansas, Tennessee, Missouri) and we edit for this audience." No autobiographies.
Recent Titles: *Son of a Seacook Cookbook,* by K. Tolliver; *75 Years in Leland,* by N. Workman (history); *A Mississippi Architectural Handbook,* by W. Lack (architecture).

T.S. DENISON & CO., INC., 5100 W. 82nd St., Minneapolis MN 55437. Editor-in-Chief: W.E. Rosenfelt. Hardcover and paperback originals. Specializes in educational publishing, textbooks, supplemental textbooks, and teacher aid materials. Royalty varies, "usually $80-100 per 1,000 copies sold; 10% on occasion; no advance. Published 27 titles in 1976, 30 in 1977; will do 30 in 1978. Send prints if photos are to accompany ms. Photocopied submissions OK. Reports in 2-4 weeks. SASE. Book catalog for SASE.
Nonfiction: Publishes textbooks and teaching aid books. Query.
Recent Titles: *Spanish Bulletin Boards,* by H. Barnell (teaching aids); *Word Enrichment,* by Sullivan (textbook); and *Special Education Teaching Games,* by Schultz (teaching aid).

DENLINGER'S PUBLISHERS, P.O. Box 76, Fairfax VA 22030. (703)631-1501. Editor-in-Chief: Mrs. R. Annabel Rathman. Royalty varies, depending upon type of ms; averages 10%.

Specific information given upon receipt of query indicating type of projected ms. No advance. Published 12 titles last year. Reports in 3 months. Enclose return postage.

Fiction and Nonfiction: Publishes fiction, nonfiction, general publications, books on dog breeds (not dog stories). Length varies, depending upon type of publication.

Recent Title: *Skitch (The Message of the Roses),* by V. Perry (fiction).

THE DEVIN-ADAIR CO., INC., 143 Sound Beach Av., Old Greenwich CT 06870. (203)637-4531. Editor-in-Chief: Devin A. Garrity. Managing Editor: Florence Norton. Hardcover and paperback originals (90%) and reprints (10%). Royalty on sliding scale, 7-12½%. $100-3,500 average advance. Publishes 12 titles annually. Send prints to illustrate ms. Simultaneous submissions OK. SASE. Free book catalog.

Nonfiction: Publishes Americana, art, biography, business, how-to, politics, cookbooks, cooking and foods; history; medicine and psychiatry, nature, economics, hobbies, juveniles, pets, scientific, sports and travel books. Query or submit outline/synopsis and sample chapters.

DIAL PRESS, 1 Dag Hammarskjold Plaza, New York NY 10017. (212)832-7300. Editor-in-Chief: Juris Jurjevics. Hardcover and paperback originals. 10-12½-15% royalty schedule; advance varies. Published 52 titles in 1976, 59 in 1977; will do 60 in 1978. State availability of photos to illustrate ms. Simultaneous and photocopied submissions OK. Submit outline/synopsis and sample chapters. Reports in 2-4 weeks. Free book catalog.

Nonfiction: Publishes biographies, business; cookbooks, cooking and foods; erotica, history, hobbies, how-to, juveniles (Phyllis Fogelman, editor-in-chief); medicine and psychiatry, politics, psychology, self-help, sociology, and sports books.

Fiction: Publishes adventure, historical, mainstream, mystery, romance, science fiction and suspense.

Recent Titles: *Now Playing at Canterbury,* by V. Bourjaily (mainstream fiction); *The Chancellor Manuscript,* by R. Ludlum (suspense/advenure); *Playing for Keeps,* by L. Leamer (politics).

DIANA PRESS, INC., 12 W. 25th St., Baltimore MD 21218. (301)366-9262. Editors: Casey Czanik, Coletta Reid. Publishes paperback originals and reprints. Offers standard minimum book contract of 10-12½-15%. Average advance is $1,000. Published 9 titles in 1976, 7 in 1977. "We sell most of our books to women's bookstores, alternative bookstores, university bookstores and women's studies classes. We do a very lively direct mail-order business for women in remote areas." Will send free catalog and editorial guidelines to writer on request, if S.A.S.E. is enclosed. Will consider photocopied submissions. Query first. Enclose return postage.

Fiction, Nonfiction, Juveniles, Poetry: "We are a feminist publishing house. We publish books by women only. We publish poetry, children's books, nonfiction, fiction and many article anthologies. We are interested in works that aid in building an independent women's culture and consciousness. We don't want to see poetry that is self-indulgent and undisciplined. We welcome mss from black and third world women, working class women and lesbians. Books should be aimed toward women and build women's sense of self, understanding of nppression, or offer possibilities for change. We are interested in practical works for women in areas that they are discriminated against; e.g., how to become an electrician, etc. We specialize in nonfiction, essay type material." Length: 80,000 words maximum.

Recent Titles: *All Our Lives: A Women's Songbook,* edited by Deihl, Cheney and Silverstein (nonfiction); *Selene: the Greatest Bull-leaper on Earth,* by Z. Budapest and C. Clement (nonfiction); and *A Plain Brown Rapper,* by R.M. Brown (nonfiction).

THE DIETZ PRESS, INC., 109 E. Cary St., Richmond VA 23219. Editor: August Dietz, III. Requires preliminary letter stating the subject and briefly outlining the material. Enclose return postage.

Nonfiction: Publishes biography, books of an historical nature, Americana, and Virginiana cookbooks. Length: 40,000 to 50,000 words. No poetry.

*DILLON PRESS, 500 S. 3rd St., Minneapolis MN 55415. Editor-in-Chief: Uva Dillon. Hardcover originals. 5-10% royalty. Published 10 titles in 1977. Photocopied submissions OK. Reports in 6 weeks. SASE. Book catalog $1; free series brochure.

Nonfiction: Publishes mss relating to ethnic heritage, cooking, upper Midwest region. Submit outline/synopsis and sample chapters or complete ms.

Juveniles: Publishes nonfiction mss relating to history, current events, minority groups, women, social problems, environment, gardening, cooking, folk arts and crafts, and folklore. Priority given to mss relating to the culture of native Americans in historical or contemporary context.

Series on the contributions of women includes the biographies of outstanding American women in a specific field. Series on a "story of environmental action" for grades 7 and up focuses on a specific environmental problem in the U.S. Submit outline/synopsis and sample chapters or complete ms.

DIMENSION BOOKS, INC., Box 811, Denville NJ 07834. (201)627-4334. Regular royalty schedule. Advance is negotiable. Published 40 titles in 1976. Book catalog for SASE. Query. Address mss to Thomas P. Coffey. Reports in 1 week on requested mss. SASE.
General Nonfiction: Publishes general nonfiction including religion, principally Roman Catholic. Also psychology and music. Length: 40,000 words and over.

DIPLOMATIC PRESS, INC., Address all communications to: The Editor, P.O. Box 593, Times Square Station, New York NY 10036. (212)222-5464. Royalty schedule: 10% of published price. Reports in 3 months. All subsidiary companies of Diplomatic Press consider mss at the headquarters only. Wants mss only from professional or skilled, if not established, writers. No simultaneous submissions. "Unsolicited mss must be accompanied by self-addressed and stamped envelopes or label. Otherwise they are not returned."
General Nonfiction, Fiction, and Textbooks: General adult nonfiction and fiction. Textbook publisher to different universities and colleges. Considers publications in French, German, Italian and Spanish languages if they are of scholastic or universal appeal. Length: 50,000 to 75,000 words.

DODD, MEAD & CO., 79 Madison Ave., New York NY 10016. (212)685-6464. Executive Editor: Allen T. Klots. Royalty basis: 10% to 15%. Advances vary, depending on the sales potential of the book. A contract for nonfiction books is offered on the basis of a query, a suggested outline and a sample chapter. Write for permission before sending mss. Published 150 titles last year. Adult fiction, history, philosophy, the arts, and religion should be addressed to Editorial Department. Reports in 1 month. Enclose return postage.
General Fiction and Nonfiction: Publishes book-length mss, 70,000 to 100,000 words. Fiction and nonfiction of high quality, mysteries and romantic novels of suspense, biography, popular science, travel, yachting, music, and other arts. Very rarely buys photographs or poetry.
Juveniles: Length: 1,500 to 75,000 words. Children's Books Editor: Mrs. Joe Ann Daly.

THE DONNING CO./PUBLISHERS, INC., 253 W. Bute St., Norfolk VA 23510. Managing Editor: Donna Reiss Friedman. Hardcover and paperback originals. 10-12½-15% royalty. Occasionally makes advance of $500-1,000, but no advance in most cases. Send prints or photocopies of representative samples of photos and/or illustrations. Simultaneous and photocopied submissions (if of good quality) OK. Reports in 2-4 months. SASE. Book catalog for SASE.
Nonfiction: Publishes Americana (Donna R. Friedman, editor); regional cookbooks, cooking and foods (Donna R. Friedman, editor). State histories and travel books (with photos).
Recent Titles: *Savannah: A Historical Portrait,* by M.W. DeBolt (Americana/pictorial history); *New Life Cookbook,* by M. Newton (specialized cookbook); *Historic Fredericksburg: A Pictorial History,* by R.E. Shibley (Americana/pictorial history).

DOUBLEDAY & CO., INC., 245 Park Ave., New York NY 10017. (212)553-4561. Managing Editor: Pyke Johnson, Jr. Publishes hardcover and paperback originals; publishes paperback reprints under Anchor, Dolphin and Image imprints. Offers standard 10-12½-15% royalty contract. Advance varies. Reports in 1 month. Published 650 titles in 1976. Special submission requirements outlined below. Query first with outline and sample chapters for both fiction and nonfiction. "Your letter of inquiry should be addressed to the Editorial Department, Doubleday & Co. Inc., 245 Park Avenue, New York City 10017. The letter may be as short as one page, but no longer than six pages (double-spaced). The first sentence should tell us whether your book is a novel, a biography, a mystery, or whatever. The first paragraph should give us an idea of what your book is about. This description should be clear and straightforward. If your book is a novel, please give us an engaging summary of the plot and background, and a quick sketch of the major characters. If you have already been published, give us details at the end of your letter. You should also tell us of any credentials or experience that particularly qualify you to write your book. For a nonfiction book, it will be helpful to you to consult the *Subject Guide to Books in Print* (available in most libraries) so that you are aware of other books on the same or similar subjects as your own, and can tell us how your book differs from them. Finally, letters of inquiry should be inviting and typed with a good ribbon. If we ask to see your ms, it should be submitted double-spaced on white paper. You should retain a carbon copy, since we cannot assume responsibility for loss or damage to mss. Sufficient postage, in the form of loose stamps, should accompany your submission to insure the return of your ms in the event it is not accepted for publication."

Nonfiction and Fiction: "Doubleday has a policy concerning the handling of manuscripts. We return unopened and unread all complete manuscripts, accompanied by a form telling how we would like submissions made. However, in 2 areas, we will accept complete manuscripts: Mysteries and science fiction. These mss should be addressed to the appropriate editor (for example, Science Fiction Editor) and not just to Doubleday. We have a moratorium on poetry publishing and are not accepting mss."

DOUBLEDAY CANADA LTD., 105 Bond St., Toronto 2, Ont., Canada (416)366-7891. Managing Editor: Betty J. Corson. Publishes hardcover originals. Offers standard royalty contract, with U.S. distribution and full domestic royalty on U.S. export sales; world representation for subsidiary right sales. Advance varies. Published 12 titles in 1976, 10 in 1977. Free book catalog. Send query, outline and sample chapters. Reports in 1 to 2 months. SASE.

General Nonfiction and Fiction, and Juveniles: "We publish trade books of all sorts that are either about Canada or written by Canadian residents." Recent titles include: *The Prairie Years* (Broadfoot), *Snowman* and *Shaking It Rough* (Schroeder). Lengths: 60,000 to 100,000 words for nonfiction; 55,000 to 90,000 words for fiction; open for juveniles.

DOUGLAS, DAVID & CHARLES LTD., 1875 Welch St., North Vancouver, B.C., Canada V7P 1B7. (604)980-7922. Editor: Jim Douglas. Publishes hardcover originals and reprints. Offers "normal" royalty contract. Average advance is $300 to $750. Publishes in association with David & Charles in U.K., whose yearly output is about 350 books. Published 10 titles in 1976, 15 in 1977. Style manual also available on request. Will consider photocopied submissions. No simultaneous submissions. Submit outline and sample chapters. Reports in 6 to 8 weeks. Enclose S.A.E. and International Reply coupons.

Nonfiction: Publishes practical books on all subjects. Nautical, military, gardening, cooking, photography, wildlife, education, Americana, art, business, economics, history, humor, law, library, medicine, music, politics, reference, travel. "Must be authoritative and at the same time readable." Mss should "address themselves to readers in the United Kingdom and Canada as well as the U.S., whenever possible." Planning a new series on Victorian life style. Also planning a series of definitive books on contemporary issues such as unionism and privacy. "A book club is operated from the headquarters of our affiliate company in Britain, and our titles stand a good chance of adoption by the club." Length: 50,000 to 100,000 words.

Recent Titles: *Canals of Canada,* by Legget (communications); *Family Dog Training,* by Wrighteral (how-to); and *Classic Snooker,* by Reardon (recreation).

J.J. DOUGLAS LTD., 1875 Welch St., N. Vancouver B.C., Canada. (604)980-6312. Editor-in-Chief: J.J. Douglas. Managing Editor: Catherine Kerr. Hardcover and paperback originals (90%) and reprints (10%). 10% royalty; $500 average advance. Published 20 titles in 1976, 30 in 1977; will do 30 in 1978. State availability of photos and/or illustrations. Photocopied submissions OK. Reports in 1-2 months. SASE. Free book catalog.

Nonfiction: Publishes reference books and books on Canadian history, nature, hobbies, recreation and sports, how-to, hobbies; cookbooks, cooking and foods; pets, self-help, music and art boks.

Recent Titles: *First Approaches to the Northwest Coast,* by D. Pethick; *Indian Artists at Work,* by L. Stelzer.

DOW JONES-IRWIN, INC., 1818 Ridge Rd., Homewood IL 60430. (312)798-6000. Publishes originals only. Royalty schedule 10% of net. Advance negotiable. Published 25 titles last year. Send completed mss to the attention of Editorial Director. Enclose return postage with mss.

Nonfiction: Business and industrial subjects.

DRAKE PUBLISHERS, 801 Second Ave., New York NY 10017. (212)679-4500. Editor-in-Chief: Robin Kyriakis. Managing Editor: Minon Kerendian. Hardcover and paperback originals (75%) and reprints (25%). 10% royalty; advance averages $1,000. Published 100 titles in 1976 and 1977, and will do 100 in 1978. State availability of photos to accompany ms. Simultaneous submissions OK. SASE. Free book catalog.

Nonfiction: Publishes americana, biography, business; cookbooks, cooking and foods; economics, history, hobbies, how-to, humor, law; medicine and psychiatry; nature, pets, photography, psychology, recreation, reference, scientific, self-help, sports, technical, and travel books. Query or submit outline/synopsis and sample chapters.

Recent Titles: *Lampmaking,* by Murphy and Lope; *Single: How to Live Alone and Like it,* by C. Keel; and *Platform Tennis,* by N. Mochean.

DRAMA BOOK SPECIALISTS (PUBLISHERS), 150 West 52nd St., New York NY 10019. (212)582-1475. Publishes hardcover and paperback originals. Royalties usually 10%. Advance varies. Published 18 titles in 1976. Send query only to Ralph Pine. Do not send complete mss. Reports in 4 to 8 weeks. Enclose S.A.S.E.
Drama: "Theatrical history, texts, film, and books dealing with the performing arts."

DUQUESNE UNIVERSITY PRESS, Pittsburgh PA 15219. (412)434-6610. Royalty schedule is 10%. No advance. Query first. Reports in 8 weeks. Enclose return postage.
Nonfiction: Scholarly books on philosophy and philology and psychology. Length: open.

E.P. DUTTON, 201 Park Ave. S., New York NY 10003. Juvenile Department: Ann Durell. Dutton Paperback: Cyril Nelson. Sunrise: Marian Skedgell. Windmill Books: Robert Kraus. Pays by advances and royalties. Published about 170 titles in 1976. Query. Send letter with outline before submitting mss or sample material. "Policy is not to return materials unless postage is included."
General Fiction and Nonfiction: Publishes novels of permanent literary value, mystery, nonfiction, religious, travel, fine arts, biography, memoirs, belles-lettres, history, science, psychology, translations, quality paperbacks, juvenile books.
Recent Titles: *Bright Stars: American Painting and Sculpture Since 1776,* by J. Lipman/H. Franc (art); *A Death in Canaan,* by J. Barthel (public affairs) and *Psychetypes: A New Way of Exploring Personality,* by M. Malone (psychology).

DUXBURY PRESS (Division of Wadsworth Publishing Co.), 6 Bound Brook Court, North Scituate MA 02060. Publishes hardcover and paperback originals. Contract varies "depending on number of authors involved and degree of involvement. Usually offers 10 to 15% with advance arrangements on a limited basis." Published 29 titles last year. Submit outline, publishing rationale, and sample chapter. Uses Chicago *Manual of Style* . Enclose return postage.
General Nonfiction: "Social science and quantitative methods college texts. Also geography, environmental studies, and interdisciplinary studies; economics, history, politics, sociology, criminal justice, vocational education, and sex education. Some books in these areas of a semi-trade nature as well. Emphasis on pedagogy and quality of thought. Authors mostly Ph.Ds but some work in collaboration with professional writers, researchers, etc., whom we hire. Emphasis on new and exciting approaches to knowledge in these areas; novel formats and varying lengths. We accept a wide latitude of styles, outlooks and structures, as long as each is accompanied by a detailed and thorough rationale and is the embodiment of a responsible trend in the academic field." Length: 50,000 to 200,000 words. Recent titles include: *Sex: Does It Make a Difference?* (Grambs/Waetjen), *Individuals and World Politics* (Isaak), *The American System of Criminal Justice* (Cole).

LES EDITIONS DE L'ETOILE, 325-327 Mont-Royal Est., Montreal H2T 1P8, PQ, Canada. Offers 10% royalty contract. No advance. Enclose S.A.E. and International Reply Coupons for return of submissions.
General Fiction and Nonfiction: General publisher of all types of books in French language only.

ELK GROVE BOOKS, Division of Childrens Press, Box 1637, Whittier CA 90609. (213)697-5637. Editor-in-Chief: Ruth Radlauer. Hardcover originals. Specializes in juvenile nonfiction. Royalty of 10% split between author and illustrator, or outright purchase (negotiable, around $1,000); no advance. Published 5 books in 1976, 6 in 1977; will do 6 in 1978. Marketing emphasis is on schools and libraries. State availability of photos and/or illustrations to accompany ms, or enclose 1 example. Reports in 1-2 months. SASE. Free book catalog from Childrens Press, 1224 W. Van Buren, Chicago IL 60607.
Juveniles: Publishes high-interest, easy to read nonfiction on hobbies, how-to, nature, pets, and sports books. Query first. "I like to know the age level, reading level and word length. See Lee Wyndham's book *Writing for Children and Teenagers* for proper professional ms preparation."
Recent Titles: *You Can Make Good Things to Eat* (Bavels); *You Can Make an Insect Zoo* (Roberts); and *Springboard to Summer* (Bunting).

EMERSON BOOKS, INC., Reynolds Ln., Buchanan NY 10511. (914)739-3506. Managing Editor: Barry Feiden. Hardcover originals (50%) and reprints (50%). Publishes about 5 titles annually. Photocopied submissions OK. Reports in 3 months. SASE.
Nonfiction: Hobbies, how-to, recreation, self-help. Query first.
Recent Titles: *Handbook of Lawn Mower Repair,* by F. Peterson (do-it-yourself); *Designing*

Pictures With String, by R. Sharpton (craft); *Buying Your House (A Complete Guide to Inspection and Evaluation),* by J.C. Davis and C. Walker (self-help).

ENGENDRA PRESS LTD., 4277 Esplanade, Montreal, Quebec, Canada H2W 1T1. (514)845-7502. Editor-in-Chief: Ronald Rosenthal. Hardcover originals. Specializes in literature in translation. "At the present time, a royalty (and if necessary, an advance) is paid to the copyright holder or the translator, *not both.* In addition, each future book will have to be assisted by a grant, preferably from the translator/writer's university." Publishes about 4 titles annually. State availability of photos and/or illustrations to accompany ms. Reports in 1-2 weeks. SASE. Free book catalog.
Translations: "Engendra Press specializes in the publication of translations of quality writing from the languages — though not necessarily the lands — of Continental Europe. Most of the ideas for books originate within the house, but whatever the case, we are most interested either in important authors who will be getting their first 'hearing' in English, or in those already known to English readers but in whose work in translation serious omissions exist." These books are not especially different in subject or theme from the serious side of commercial publishing or from certain of the products of some university presses. "We do, however, stress an imaginative approach to a subject's oeuvre." Query first. No unsolicited mss. "Owing to the nature of the material, only ideas will be entertained."
Recent Titles: *3 Catalan Dramatists,* edited by G. Wellwarth; *The Legacy of Jura Soyfer,* by J. Soyfer.

ENTELEK, Ward-Whidden House/The Hill, Portsmouth NH 03801. Editor-in-Chief: Albert E. Hickey. Publishes paperback originals. Offers royalty contract of 5% trade; 10% textbook. No advance. Published 8 titles last year. Will send free catalog to writer on request. Will consider photocopied and simultaneous submissions. Submit outline and sample chapters or submit complete ms. Reports in 1 week. Enclose return postage.
Nonfiction and Business: Publishes computer, calculator, math, business and how-to books. "We seek books that have not been undertaken by other publishers." Would like to see material for career guides. Length: 3,000 words minimum. Published *Problem Solving with the Computer* (Sage).

ENTERPRISE PUBLISHING CO., 1300 Market St., Wilmington DE 19801. (302)575-0440. President: T.N. Peterson. Publishes hardcover and paperback originals and reprints. Offers 5% royalty contract, usually. Average advance is $1,000. Published 4 titles last year. Mail order comprises 90% of sales. Will send free catalog to writer on request. Will consider photocopied submissions. Query first and submit outline and sample chapters. Submit complete ms on request. Reporting time for rejected material is 30 days; accepted material, 30 to 60 days. Enclose return postage.
Business and Professional: "How-to" books mostly related to business subjects; free market orientation, 30,000 to 60,000 words; practical, usable ideas. Entrepreneurial audience, simplified, clear phraseology, short sentences, short paragraphs. Would especially like to see material on do-it-yourself approach to various matters in business, marriage, divorce, professional incorporation and psychological health. Published titles include *Where the Money Is and How to Get It* (Nicholas) and *How To Do Business Tax Free* (Malone).
Nonfiction: Also publishes books on sports, hobbies and recreation.
Special Needs: Road to success series.

*PAUL S. ERIKSSON, Battell Bldg., Middlebury VT 05753. (302)388-7303. Editor: Paul Eriksson. Publishes hardcover and paperback originals. Pays standard royalty. Does 5% to 10% subsidy annually. Published 8 titles last year. Query first with outline and sample chapters. Reports within 1 month. Enclose return postage.
Fiction and Nonfiction: Trade nonfiction and fiction. Also nature and bird lore. Current leading titles include *The Bird Finder's 3-Year Notebook,* by P. Eriksson; *The Shah,* by Hoyt and *The Phoenix Child* (Viscardi).

*ETC PUBLICATIONS, P.O. Drawer 1627-A, Palm Springs CA 92262. Editor-in-Chief: Dr. Richard W. Hostrop. Managing Editor: LeeOna S. Hostrop. Hardcover and paperback originals. 10-12½-15% royalty of sales for cloth; 5-7½-10% for paperbacks. Only occasional advances; up to $1,200, depending on reputation of author or amount of research. Subsidy publishes 10% of books. "Scholarly works of considerable merit, but of limited economic potential occasionally are published under our imprint on a subsidy basis." Published 10 titles in 1976, 15 in 1977; will do 20 in 1978. Simultaneous submissions OK. Reports in 1-2 months. SASE. Book catalog for SASE.

Nonfiction: Publishes business; cookbooks, cooking and foods; erotica; history; hobbies; how-to; law; medicine and psychiatry; politics; psychology; reference; religious; scientific; self-help; sociology; sports; technical; and textbooks. Query first, addressing it to the editor of the appropriate department.
Recent Titles: *How to Be Self-Employed,* by B. Fregly (how-to); *The Writer's Manual,* by R. Porter (how-to); and *Careers and You,* by R. Ressler (textbook).

M. EVANS AND COMPANY, INC., 216 E. 49 St., New York NY 10017. Editor-in-Chief: Herbert M. Katz. Publishes hardcover originals. Royalty schedule to be negotiated. Publishes 30 titles a year. Will consider photocopied submissions. No mss should be sent unsolicited. A letter of inquiry is essential. Reports on rejected material in 6 to 8 weeks. Reporting time on accepted material varies. Query. SASE.
General Fiction and Nonfiction: "We publish a general trade list of adult fiction and nonfiction, cookbooks and semi-reference works. The emphasis is on selectivity since we publish only 30 titles a year. Our fiction list represents an attempt to combine quality with commercial potential. Our most successful nonfiction titles have been related to the behavioral sciences. No limitation on subject. A writer should clearly indicate what his book is all about, frequently the task the writer performs least well. His credentials, although important, mean less than his ability to convince this company that he understands his subject and that he has the ability to communicate a message worth hearing." Recent titles include: *Dancing Aztecs,* and *Gifford on Courage.*

FAIRCHILD BOOKS & VISUALS, Book Division, 7 East 12th St., New York NY 10003. Manager: Ed Gold. Publishes hardcover and paperback originals. Offers standard minimum book contract. No advance. Pays 10% of net sales distributed twice annually. Published 12 titles last year. Will consider photocopied submissions. Will send free catalog to writer on request. Query first, giving subject matter and brief outline. Enclose return postage.
Business and Textbooks: Publishes business books and textbooks relating to fashion, electronics, marketing, retailing, career education, advertising, home economics, and management. Length: open.

FAR EASTERN RESEARCH AND PUBLICATIONS CENTER, P.O. Box 31151, Washington DC 20031. Publishes hardcover and paperback originals and reprints. "Royalty is based on the standard rate or outright purchase. Pays up to $2,000 advance against standard royalties." Submit a synopsis or table of contents with sample chapter, along with biographical sketches, to editor-in-chief. Reports in 2 months. Enclose return postage with ms—"enough postage to cover registered mail for return of submissions."
Nonfiction: Subject emphasis: reference materials on the Far East, especially on the Chinese, Japanese, and Korean people. All lengths.

FARNSWORTH PUBLISHING CO., INC., 78 Randall Ave., Rockville Centre NY 11570. (516)536-8400. President: Lee Rosler. Publishes hardcover originals. "Standard royalty applies, but 5% is payable on mail order sales." Published 15 titles last year. Will send a catalog to a writer on request. Query first. Reports in 1 to 5 weeks. Enclose return postage.
General Nonfiction, Business and Professional: "Our books generally fall into 2 categories: 1. Books which appeal to executives, lawyers, accountants, and life underwriters. Subject matter may vary from selling techniques, estate planning, taxation, money management, etc. 2. Books which appeal to the general populace which are marketable by direct mail and mail order, in addition to bookstore sales."
Recent Titles: *The Magic of ESOT,* by R. Frisch (finance); *Don't Bank On It,* by M. Meyer/J. McDaniel (consumer); and *Creative Selling for the Seventies,* by B. Feldman (sales methods).

FARRAR, STRAUS AND GIROUX, INC. (including Hill and Wang), 19 Union Square West, New York NY 10003. Published 150 titles last year. Prefers queries. Enclose S.A.S.E.
General Fiction, Nonfiction and Juveniles: Publishes general fiction, nonfiction and juveniles. Publishes Noonday paperbacks, scholarly reprints under Octagon Books imprint and Hill and Wang books.

FAST & McMILLAN PUBLISHERS, 1526 Lilac Rd., Charlotte NC 28209. Editor: Sally Hill McMillan. Hardcover and paperback originals and reprints. 10-12½-15% royalty. If photos are to accompany ms, send prints or contact sheets. Reports in 2-4 weeks. SASE. Free book catalog.
Nonfiction and Fiction: "Our aim is to publish worthy books of general adult fiction and

nonfiction. We offer a unique emphasis on marketing based on experience, in addition to the usual intimate services of a small publisher." Mainstream, adventure, historical and suspense fiction; self-help, how-to, reference books and photographic essays.

FAWCETT PUBLICATIONS, INC.-1/3GOLD MEDAL BOOKS, 1515 Broadway, New York NY 10036. Publishes paperback originals only. Advances and royalties are flexible and competitive. Address query first to the editors before submitting ms. Reports in 3 to 8 weeks. Enclose return postage.
Nonfiction and Fiction: Seeks books of broad, mass-market appeal.

F. W. FAXON COMPANY, INC., 15 Southwest Park, Westwood MA 02090. (617)329-3350. Publisher: Albert H. Davis, Jr. Editor-in-Chief: Beverly Heinle. Publishes hardcover originals. Offers 10% of sales net price for each book sold, payable at the end of each fiscal year. No advance. Books are marketed through advertising, mail campaigns, book reviews, and library conventions. Will send catalog to writer on request. Mss must be original copy, double-spaced, and must be accompanied by a copy. They should contain reference material useful to library users throughout the world. Query first. Enclose S.A.S.E.
Reference: "We publish library reference books. These are primarily indexes but we would also consider bibliographies and other material useful to library users. We would be interested in publishing indexes on topics of current interest which have not been indexed previously." Current titles are *Index to Outdoor Sports, Games and Activities; French Periodical Index.*

FREDERICK FELL PUBLISHING, INC., 386 Park Ave., S., New York NY 10016. (212)685-9017. Editor-in-Chief: Charles Nurnberg. Hardcover and paperback originals (85%) and reprints (15%). 10% royalty. Published 30 titles in 1976, 29 in 1977; 30 in 1978. Query. Send sample prints or contact sheet if photos/illustrations are to accompany ms. Simultaneous and photocopied submissions OK. Reports in 2-4 weeks. SASE. Free book catalog.
Nonfiction: Publishes Americana; business; hobbies; how-to; law; medicine and psychiatry; pets; photography; psychology; recreation; reference; self-help; and sports books.
Special Needs: Pet Lovers Library; Home Medical Library.
Recent Titles: *How To Train Your Dog in Six Weeks,* by Berman and Landesman (pets); *Blocking and Unblocking Plays in Bridge,* by R. Reese and T. Trezel (hobbies); and *Parliamentary Procedures Simplified,* by L. Place (business).

FFORBEZ ENTERPRISES, LTD., Box 35340, Station E, Vancouver B.C., Canada V6M 4G6. (604)872-7325. Editor-in-Chief: P.W. Zebroff. Managing Editor: Tim Udd. Paperback originals. Specializes in how-to books, cookbooks, textbooks, and health-oriented books. 10% royalty; no advance. Published 2 books in 1976, 12 in 1977; will do 12 in 1978. Markets books through health stores. Send at least 1 copy of illustration and 1 print. Simultaneous submissions OK if exclusive to Canada. Photocopied submissions OK. Reports in 2-4 weeks. SASE. Free book catalog.
Nonfiction: Publishes cookbooks, cooking and foods; how-to, multimedia material, nature, recreation, self-help, sports and health books. Submit outline/synopsis, sample chapters and table of contents.
Recent Titles: *Kids, Kids, Kids and Vancouver* by Davis/Wood (recreation); *Beauty Through Yoga,* by K. Zebroff; *Recipes From Karen's Kitchen* by Zebroff/Gabbott (cookbook).

FIDDLEHEAD POETRY BOOKS, Department of English, University of British Columbia, Box 4400, Fredericton, New Brunswick, Canada E3B 5A3. Editor-in-Chief: Fred Cogswell. Paperback originals. Specializes in publishing books of poetry. Royalty of 10% of first run; no advance. Published 16 titles in 1976; 24 in 1977. "We have a fairly large list of standing orders from libraries." State availability of photos and/or illustrations to accompany ms. Simultaneous submissions OK. Reports in 1-2 months. SASE. Free book catalog, if available.
Poetry: "Canadian authors have a better chance of acceptance as our whole publicity and distribution mechanism is geared that way." Submit complete ms. **Recent Titles:** *The Self of Love,* by D. Roberts (poetry); *Living Together,* by J. Finnegan; (poetry); *I Walk by the Harbour,* by N. Levine (poetry).

*FIDES/CLARETIAN, Box F, Notre Dame IN 46556. Editor: James F. Burns. Originals and reprints. Pays 10%, 11%, 12% royalties; reprint in Dome or Spire. 5%, 6%, 7%. No advance. Publishes about 1 subsidy book a year. Published 5 titles in 1976. Free book catalog. Send outline and sample chapter. Reports in 6 weeks. Enclose return postage.
Religion: Publishes religious books (Christian and ecumenical) and general nonfiction with theological, spiritual, pastoral implications. The new look in religion and religious education,

and the attitude of freedom and personal responsibility. Length: religious, 20,000 words and up; general nonfiction, 20,000 words and up.

*THE FILTER PRESS, Box 5, Palmer Lake CO 80133. (303)481-2523. Editor-in-Chief: G.L. Campbell. Managing Editor: Leslie Campbell. Hardcover and paperback originals (50%) and reprints (50%). 10% (of net sales) royalty; no advance. Subsidy publishes 10% of books; "usually family type histories in short runs." Published 6 titles in 1976, 8 in 1977. Will do 8 in 1978. Simultaneous and photocopied submissions OK. Reports in 1-2 weeks. SASE. Book catalog for SASE.
Nonfiction: "At present, most is Western Americana. Books about Indians, early explorations, ghost towns, national parks; good guys and bad guys." Cookbooks, cooking and foods (novelty only); nature, recreation, and travel. Length: 5,000-20,000 words. Query first, with outline. We use the *Chicago Style Manual,* but prefer to omit footnotes where possible and explain in the narrative. If we consider the ms, we would want an entire set of proposed illustrations with it. However, for many, we draw on our own extensive morgue of antique wood engravings."

*FIRST EDITION BOOKS AND FEB COMPANY/PUBLISHERS, W.O. Jacky Bldg., Pittsburgh PA 15236. (412)655-9733. Editor-in-Chief: Jack Dae Check. Paperback originals (90%) and reprints (10%). 10-12½-15% royalty; advance averages $100. Published 12 titles in 1976, 20 in 1977; will do 40 in 1978. "We sell our books not only through retail outlets, but through fund-raising organizations as well." Subsidy publishes 50% of titles. "If we feel that there is a risk factor, we will request that the author consider underwriting initial production, while we provide complete marketing." State availability of photos and/or illustrations to accompany ms. Simultaneous and photocopied submissions OK. SASE. Reports in 2-4 weeks. Free book catalog.
Nonfiction: Dawn Pearson, General Editor. Will consider all types of nonfiction. Complete ms only; must be typed double-spaced.
Fiction: "We will consider all categories."
Recent Titles: *The Climb,* by T. Kern (science fiction); *Our World,* by J.G. Lloyd (political intrigue).

FITZHENRY & WHITESIDE, LIMITED, 150 Lesmill Rd., Don Mills, Ontario, Canada. Editor-in-Chief: Robert Read. Publishes hardcover and paperback originals and reprints. Chiefly educational materials. Royalty contract varies; advance negotiable. Published 40 titles last year. Submit outline and sample chapters. Will consider photocopied submissions. Reports on material accepted for publication in 1 to 2 months. Returns rejected material in 2 to 3 months. Enclose return postage.
General Nonfiction, Drama and Poetry: "Especially interested in topics of interest to Canadians." Biography; business; history; medicine and psychiatry; nature; politics. Canadian plays and poetry are also of interest. Length: open.
Textbooks: Elementary and secondary school textbooks, audiovisual materials in social studies and reading and science.
Recent Titles: *Mackenzie King,* by J.L. Granatstein (biography); *Last Best West,* by J. Bruce (history); and *Bobby Clarke,* by F. McFadden (juvenile).

FLEET PRESS CORPORATION, 160 Fifth Ave., New York NY 10010. (212)243-6100. Editor: Susan Nueckel. Publishes hardcover and paperback originals and reprints. Royalty schedule "varies." Advance "varies." Published 24 titles last year. Will send a catalog to a writer on request. Send query and outline. Reports in 6 weeks. Enclose return postage with ms. Will not evaluate unsolicited mss.
General Nonfiction: "History, biography, arts, religion, general nonfiction, sports." Length: 45,000 words.
Juveniles: Nonfiction only. Stress on social studies and minority subjects; for ages 8 to 15. Length: 25,000 words.
Recent Title: *American Jewish Landmarks,* by Postal/Koppman (Judaica travel/history); and *Defending the Undefendable,* by W. Block (economics/libertarian).

FOLLETT PUBLISHING CO., 1010 W. Washington Blvd., Chicago IL 60607. (312)666-5858. Editorial Director, Children's Book Department: Ms. Marci Ridlon Carafoli. Royalties negotiable. Send outline with sample chapters or send complete ms. Enclose return postage.
Juveniles: "We seriously consider all mss of top professional quality. No heavily moralistic stories. No juvenile fluff or teen romances. No religious material. No biographies that have

been done over and over." Wants juvenile nonfiction books for ages 3 to 16. "Length varies according to subject matter and age group."

Nonfiction: "We are especially interested in mss that deal with contemporary problems at the personal and group level and that offer suggestions for solutions. Health, mental health, survival and coping dynamics, how-to, and psychological self-help mss that are original in content are desirable."

FORTRESS PRESS, 2900 Queen Lane, Philadelphia PA 19129. (215)848-6800. Director and Senior Editor: Norman A. Hjelm. Hardcover and paperback originals. Specializes in general religion for laity and clergy; academic texts and monographs in theology (all areas). 7½% royalty on paperbacks; 10% on hardcover; modest advance. Published 60 titles in 1976, 65 in 1977; will do about 70 in 1978. Mss must follow *Chicago Manual of Style* (17th edition). Photocopied submissions OK. Reports in 60 days. SASE. Free book catalog.

Nonfiction: Publishes philosophy, religious and self-help books. Query. Does not want religious poetry or fiction.

Recent Titles: *Encountering Mary,* by J.M. Lochmann (religious — general academic); *Reading Through Romans,* by C.K. Barrett (religious — laity); a series on Creative Pastoral Counseling and Care, edited by R. Clinebell.

FOUR CORNERS PRESS, 232 Washington St., Hanover MA 02339. Editor-in-Chief: Carl W. Lindsay. Publishes paperback originals. "We buy all material outright. No byline. Payment will vary from a minimum of $25 for simple reports to well over $500 for acceptable book-length material." Published 25 titles, reports and booklets last year. Published material is sold by mail order to the public, or sold to a business and sent to their customers or prospects as if it were published by them. "Do NOT ask for samples, etc. They have no bearing on what we expect from a new submission." Query first. Reports in 2 weeks. Enclose return postage.

Nonfiction: Americana, business, humor, politics, reference, self-help and how-to, technical. "We are always on the lookout for material which can be sold by mail or syndicated." Publishes reports, short books. Most material published in report form, 8½x11 pages, offset printed, stapled rather than bound. Longer material published as saddle-stitched or softcover booklet. "Material must be useful, well researched and, hopefully, unique. This is not a market for off-the-cuff writing. Usually the writer must have some specialized knowledge or be able to do good research." Audience is specialized, but material should also be of interest to a cross-section of professional, business and personal people. Mss must be practical and useful. No preconceived notions. "Household hints are a drug on the market for us. We use no poetry but keep getting it."

FRANCISCAN HERALD PRESS, 1434 West 51st St., Chicago IL 60609. Editor: Paul J. Bernard. "Royalty schedule — 10% and up with volume. Advance depends on nature and length of ms." Published 24 titles last year. Use University of Chicago *Manual of Style.* Send query and outline. Reports in 30 days. Enclose return postage.

Religion: "A Catholic publishing house with a wide range of interests in theology, sociology, culture, art and literature, reflecting, interpreting, directing the socio-religious and cultural aspects of our times." Synthesis Series of booklets (10,000 words maximum) in the field of religion and psychology. Church history, biography and specialized publications on history, purpose and personages of the Franciscan Order. Lengths run from 5,000 to 60,000 words.

THE FREE PRESS, a Division of the Macmillan Publishing Co., Inc., 866 Third Ave., New York NY 10022. President: Edward W. Barry. Editor-in-Chief: Charles E. Smith. Royalty schedule varies. Published 75 titles last year. Send sample chapter, outline, and query letter before submitting mss. Reports in 3 weeks. Enclose return postage.

Nonfiction and Textbooks: Publishes college texts and adult educational nonfiction in the social sciences and humanities.

GARDEN WAY PUBLISHING, Charlotte VT 05445. (802)425-2171. Editor: Roger Griffith. Publishes hardcover and paperback originals. Offers a flat fee arrangement varying with book's scope, or royalty, which usually pays author 6% of book's retail price. Advances are negotiable, but usually range from $1,500 to $2,000. "We stress continued promotion of titles and sales over many years. None of our titles has yet gone out of print." Published 14 titles in 1976. Emphasizes direct mail sales, plus sales to bookstores through salesmen. Will send free catalog and editorial guidelines sheet to writer; enclose S.A.S.E. Will consider photocopied submissions. Query first for nonfiction. Enclose return postage.

Nonfiction: Books on gardening, cooking, animal husbandry, homesteading and energy conservation. Emphasis should be on how-to. Length requirements are flexible. "The writer should remember the reader will buy his book to learn to do something, so that all information to accomplish this must be given. We are publishing specifically for the person who is concerned about natural resources and a deteriorating life style and wants to do something about it." Would like to see energy books with emphasis on what the individual can do.

Recent Titles *Designing and Building a Solar House*, by D. Watson; and *Growing Your Own Mushrooms*, by J. Mueller.

*GENEALOGICAL PUBLISHING CO., INC., 521-523 St. Paul Pl., Baltimore MD 21202. (301)837-8271. Editor-in-Chief: Michael H. Tepper, Ph.D. Publishes hardcover originals and reprints. Offers straight 10% royalty. Does about 10% subsidy publishing. Published 79 titles last year. Will consider photocopied submissions. Prefers query first, but will look at outline and sample chapter or complete ms. Reports "immediately." Enclose S.A.E. and return postage.

Reference, Textbooks and History: "Our requirements are unusual, so we usually treat each author and his subject in a way particularly appropriate to his special skills and subject matter. Guidelines are flexible and generous, though it is expected that an author will consult with us in depth. Most, though not all, of our original publications are offset from camera-ready typescript. Since most genealogical reference works are compilations of vital records and similar data, tabular formats are common. We hope to receive more ms material in the area of census indexes, specifically indexes to statewide decennial censuses. We also anticipate mss documenting the Revolutionary War service of large numbers of early Americans. We would like to have an on-going Revolutionary War genealogy project." Family history compendia, basic methodology in genealogy, and advanced local history (for example, county histories, particularly those containing genealogy); heraldry: dictionaries and glossaries of the art and science, armorials of families entitled to bear coat armor, manuals and craftbooks describing heraldic painting, etc.

Recent Titles: *Index to the 1820 Census of Virginia*, by J. Felldin; *Heraldic Design*, by H. Child; and *Researcher's Guide to American Genealogy*, by V. Greenwood (textbook).

GENERAL AVIATION PRESS, P.O. Box 916, Snyder TX 79549. Editor-in-Chief: M. Gene Dow. Publishes hardcover and paperback originals. Offers standard book contract of 10-12½-15%. Advance is negotiated. Published 1 title last year. Books are marketed through aviation publications. Will consider photocopied submissions. Reports in 1 month. Submit outline and sample chapters or complete ms. Enclose return postage.

Aviation: Subjects pertain strictly to general aviation; non-airline, non-military. How-to, biographies of well-known aviators, safety, organizations, etc. Almost any subject related to private and business aircraft and flying. Must be written with knowledge of aircraft and pilots.

C. R. GIBSON CO., 39 Knight St., Norwalk CT 06856. Publishes gift books in both hardcover originals and anthologies. Offers fixed royalty rate per copy sold. Advance varies according to formats. Query first, with outline and sample chapters. Reports in 4 to 8 weeks. Enclose return postage.

Gift Books: Faith, inspirational and special occasion. Recent titles include *Fields of Gold*.

GINN AND COMPANY, 191 Spring St., Lexington MA 02173. Editor-in-Chief: Richard Morgan. Royalty schedule: from 10% of net on a secondary book to 4% on elementary materials. Published 450 titles last year. Sample chapters, complete or partially complete mss will be considered. Reports in 2 to 6 weeks. Enclose return postage.

Textbooks: Publishers of textbooks and instructional materials for elementary and secondary schools.

GOLDEN WEST BOOKS, Box 8136, San Marino CA 91108. (213)283-3446. Editor-in-Chief: Donald Duke. Managing Editor: Jeff Dunning. Hardcover and paperback originals. 10% royalty contract; no advance. Publishes about 7 titles annually. Simultaneous and photocopied submissions OK. Reports in 2-4 weeks. SASE. Free book catalog.

Nonfiction: Publishes western Americana and transportation Americana. Query first or submit complete ms. "Illustrations and photographs will be examined if we like ms."

Recent Titles: *The Railroad Scene*, by W. Middleton; *Vancouver Island Railroad*, by R.D. Turner; *Southern Pacific Steam Locomotives*. by D. Duke.

GRAY'S PUBLISHING LTD., Box 2160, Sidney, BC, Canada. (604)656-4454. Editor: Maralyn Horsdal. Publishes hardcover and paperback originals. Offers standard royalty contract. Published 6 titles in 1976, 10 in 1977. Free book catalog. Query first with outline. Reports in 6 to 10 weeks. Enclose S.A.E. and International Reply Coupons.

Nonfiction: Wants "nonfiction, Canadiana," especially Pacific Northwest. Biography, natural history, history. Indian culture. Nautical. Length: 60,000 to 120,000 words.
Recent Titles: *The Sea Was Our Village,* by M. Smeeton (adventure); *Prelude to Bonanza,* by A.A. Wright (history); and *The Curve of Time,* by M.W. Blanchet.

GREAT OUTDOORS PUBLISHING CO., 4747 28th St. N., St. Petersburg FL 33714. (813)522-3453. Editor-in-Chief: Charles Allyn. Publishes paperback originals. Offers royalty of 5% of retail price. No advance. Published 8 titles last year. Will send free catalog to writer on request. Will consider photocopied submissions and simultaneous submissions. Query first for nonfiction. Reports in 1 month. Enclose return postage.
Nonfiction: Books of regional interest. Fishing, gardening, shelling in Florida. Also publishes some cookbooks of southern emphasis. Should be straightforward, how-to style with consideration for the hobbyist or sportsman who needs the basic facts without flowery phrasing. "No other publisher is geared to the tourist market in Florida. Our books are low-cost and especially suited to their market." Would like to see more shell books with illustrations. Doesn't want to see personal narratives. Department editors: Patricia Pope, cooking, nature, recreation; Charles Allyn, self-help and how-to. Length: cooking, 9,000 to 17,000 words; nature, 52,000 to 90,000 words; self-help, how-to, sports, hobbies, recreation and pets, 9,000 to 17,000 words.
Recent Titles: *Pelican,* by R. Ovingle (birds); and *Pine Cone Crafts,* by J. McKay (crafts).

THE GREEN TIGER PRESS, 7458 La Jolla Blvd., La Jolla CA 92037. Editor-in-Chief: H.R. Darling. Paperback originals (35%) and reprints (65%). No royalty; flat payment of $500 maximum. No advance. "Our company reproduces pictures from old children's books. We especially want nonfiction of a critical nature in this area." Published 2 titles in 1976 and 1977; will do 6 in 1978. State availability of photos and/or illustrations to accompany ms. Simultaneous and photocopied submissions OK. SASE. Book catalog for 78¢ (in stamps).
Nonfiction: "Only critical or historical studies of some aspect of children's literature or its illustrators." Query first.
Recent Titles: *Kay Nielsen: An Appreciation,* by Poctarness (a critical study of a children's illustrator).

GREEN TREE PUBLISHING CO., LTD., 69 Bathurst St., Toronto, Ont., Canada M5V 2P6. (416)869-3321. Editor-in-Chief: W.H.P. Parr. Hardcover and paperback originals. 10% royalty; advance "depends on how badly we want the book. We've paid up to $3,500 and in many cases just a lunch." Published 8 titles in 1976, 12 in 1977; will publish 12-15 in 1978. Simultaneous submissions OK "if we're given a date by which we must respond and given the book if we offer the best deal." Reports in 1-2 months. SASE. Free book catalog.
Nonfiction: Publishes business; economics; history; hobbies; how-to; humor; juveniles (adventure); politics; psychology (self-help type); reference; self-help; sociology; and textbooks (math). "We are a Canadian firm and publish for our market. In the craft and self-help line, there is no border. We are big on trains and welcome just about anything. No more poetry please." Query.
Special needs: "We are developing an inexpensive line of hobby/craft books. Technically simple and cheap to carry out."

*WARREN H. GREEN, INC., 10 S. Brentwood Blvd., St. Louis MO 63105. Editor: Warren H. Green. Hardcover originals. Offers "10% to 20% sliding scale of royalties based on quantity distributed. All books are short run, highly specialized, with no advance." About 5% of books are subsidy published. Published 43 titles last year. "37% of total marketing is overseas." Will send a catalog to a writer on request. Will consider photocopied submissions. Submit outline and sample chapters. "Publisher requires 300- to 500-word statement of scope, plan, and purpose of book, together with curriculum vitae of author." Reports in 60 to 90 days.
Medical and Scientific: "Specialty monographs for practicing physicans and medical researchers. Books of 160 pages upward. Illustrated as required by subject. Medical books are non-textbook type, usually specialties within specialties, and no general books for a given specialty. For example, separate books on each facet of radiology, and not one complete book on radiology. Authors must be authorities in their chosen fields and accepted as such by their peers. Books should be designed for all doctors in English-speaking world engaged in full- or part-time activity discussed in book. We would like to increase publications in the fields of radiology, anesthesiology, pathology, psychiatry, surgery and orthopedic surgery, obstetrics and gynecology, psychology, and speech and hearing.
Education: "Reference books for elementary and secondary school teachers. Authors must be authorities in their fields. No textbooks."

THE STEPHEN GREENE PRESS, Box 1000, Brattleboro VT 05301. (802)257-7757. Editor-in-Chief: Janet C. Greene. Hardcover and paperback originals (99%); hardcover and paperback reprints (1%). Royalty varies from 8-10-12½% of net to 10-12½-15% of list; no advance. Published 19 titles in 1976, 20 in 1977; will do 20 in 1978. "Ask for our list of submission requirements with your query. Refer to Chicago *Manual of Style; Elements of Style; Words into Type.*" Send contact sheet or prints to illustrate ms. Photocopied submissions OK. Reports in 1-2 months. Book catalog for SASE.
Nonfiction: Publishes Americana, biography; cookbooks, cooking and foods; history, how-to (self-reliance); nature and environment; recreation, self-help, sports (individual outdoor and horse); popular technology; regional (New England); and Belles-lettres.
Recent Titles: *Personal Geography,* by Coatsworth (belles-lettres); *Wind-Catchers,* by Torrey (popular technology); *Wheat Country,* by Heilman (Americana).

GREENLEAF CLASSICS, INC., Box 20194, San Diego CA 92120. Editorial Director: Douglas Saito. Managing Editor: James Koelmel. Paperback originals. Specializes in adult erotic fiction. Pays outright purchase price on acceptance. Published 360 titles in 1976, 360 in 1977; will do 360 in 1978. Submit complete ms. Reports in 1-2 months. SASE. Book catalog for SASE.
Fiction: Publishes erotic books. "Our books are titled (in house) by theme, i.e., unfaithful wife, mother/son incest, women in bondage, etc. Therefore, if a ms doesn't have a commercial erotic theme, we can't give the book a commercial title and we can't buy the ms."
Recent Titles: *Jane's Great Danes; Girl on a Leash;* and *The Family Nurse.*

GREENWICH PRESS, 335 Bleecker St., New York NY 10014. Editor: Anton Hardt. Publishes hardcover originals and reprints. Query first. Enclose return postage.
Nonfiction: "Books only on the subject of antiques and possibly allied fields."

GREGG DIVISION, McGraw-Hill Book Co., 1221 Ave. of the Americas, New York NY 10020. General Manager: Charles B. Harrington. Publishes hardcover originals. "Contracts negotiable; no advances." Query first. "We accept very few unsolicited mss." Reports in 1 to 2 months. Enclose return postage with query.
Textbooks: "Textbooks and related instructional materials for the career education market." Publishes books on typewriting, office education, shorthand, accounting and data processing, distributing and marketing, trade and industrial education, health and consumer education.

GRIFFIN HOUSE PUBLISHERS, 461 King Street West, Toronto, Ontario, Canada M5V 1K7. (416)366-5461. Publishes hardcover and paperback originals. Offers standard royalty contract. Small advance. Published 4 titles in 1976. Free book catalog. Send complete ms. Enclose S.A.E. and International Reply Coupons.
General Fiction, General Nonfiction, History and Biography: Interested in general interest and Canadiana books.

GROSSET AND DUNLAP, INC., (including Tempo Teenage Paperbacks and Universal Library), 51 Madison Ave., New York NY 10010. (212)689-9200. Editor-in-Chief: Robert Markel. Publishes hardcover and paperback originals and reprints, as well as a "very few" translations, and anthologies "on occasion." Royalty and advance terms generally vary. Published "close to 400" titles last year. Will send a catalog to a writer on request. Send query letter, outline, or sample chapter only; do not send complete ms. "We do not accept unsolicited manuscripts." Reports in 3 to 5 weeks. Enclose return postage with query.
General Fiction: "Very seldom —usually only via literary agent."
General Nonfiction and Reference: "No limits—anything and everything that would interest the 'average' American reader: sports, health, ecology, etc." Interested in history, science, religion, biography, the arts, and literature. Favors writers with strong experience and good credits.
Juveniles and Teen: Editor-in-Chief, Children's Picture Books: Doris Duenewald.

*GROSSMONT PRESS, INC., 7071 Convoy Ct., San Diego CA 92111. (714)560-4801. Editor-in-Chief: Joyce Schelling. Publishes hardcover and paperback originals and reprints. Offers royalty contract of 10-12½-15%; no advance. Published 38 titles in 1976, 56 in 1977. 50% of titles are subsidy published. "Books are extensively advertised in national magazines and trade publications, by direct mail, and salesmen. Textbooks are also sold on traveling booktrucks which visit campuses throughout the U.S." Will send free catalog to writer on request. Will consider photocopied submissions. Will consider simultaneous submissions only if solicited. Query first for all material. Reports in 2 weeks. SASE.

Fiction, Business, Nonfiction, Juveniles, Photography, Poetry and Textbooks: "All subjects considered." Fiction and nonfiction length requirements: 15,000 to 20,000 words. Children's books: 1,000 word minimum, "if amply illustrated." Poetry: 30 or 40 poems. "Our poetry list is expanding rapidly because of excellent sales this past year through gift shops. We are anxious to learn about trade and college textbooks, particularly in the business field. Also, we're looking for anthologies on all topics for use as supplementary readers for college level courses." Also interested in Americana; biography; book trade; economics; history; humor; law; library; medicine and psychiatry; nature; philosophy; politics; reference; religion; scientific; self-help and how-to; sociology; sports, hobbies, recreation and pets; travel.

GROUPWORK TODAY, INC., Box 258, South Plainfield NJ 07080. Editor-in-Chief: Harry E. Moore, Jr. Publishes hardcover and paperback originals. Offers $100 advance against royalties on receipt of contract; 10% of gross receipts from sale of book. "If a book is of special value, we will pay 10% of gross earnings on first 1,000 copies and 15% thereafter." Average advance is $100. Books are marketed by direct mail to Groupwork Agency executives and professionals (YMCA, YWCA, Scouts, Salvation Army, colleges, directors of organized camps, and libraries.) Will send catalog to a writer for $1. "Also will answer specific questions from an author considering us as a publisher." Will not consider simultaneous submissions. Submit outline and sample chapters for nonfiction. Reports in 6 to 8 weeks. Enclose return postage.

Nonfiction: "We are publishers of books and materials for professionals and volunteers who work with people in groups. Some of our materials are also suited to the needs of professionals who work with individuals. Groupwork agency management, finance, program development and personnel development are among the subjects of interest to us. Writers must be thoroughly familiar with 'people work' and have fresh insights to offer. New writers are most welcome here. Lengths are open but usually run 30,000 to 50,000 words." Readers are mainly social agency administrators and professional staff members. Groupwork materials are also read by volunteers serving in the social agencies. Mss are judged by experienced professionals in social agencies. The company is advised on policy direction by a council of advisors from national agencies and colleges across the nation. "We are planning what we are tentatively calling our 'Seminar' series to deal with the most important problems with which social work agencies must deal today. We would like to see a good work on 'Management by Objective' as applied to groupwork agency operations."

Recent Titles: *Guide to Successful Fund Raising,* by B. Taylor; and *Communication by Objective,* by L.R. Oaks.

GUIDANCE CENTRE, Faculty of Education, University of Toronto, Suite 304, 1000 Yonge St., Toronto, Ontario, Canada M4W 2K8. Editor-in-Chief: S.J. Totton. Publishes hardcover and paperback originals and paperback reprints. Offers "standard" royalty contract.

Nonfiction: Publishes standardized achievement and personality tests. Also books and journals of interest to guidance counselors and books dealing with topics of concern to professional educators. "We expect an author to write about serious subjects in a readable manner."

GUITAR PLAYER BOOKS, Box 615, Saratoga CA 95030. (408)446-1105. Editor-in-Chief: Jerry S. Martin. Paperback originals (95%) and reprints (5%). 10% royalty; advance averages $500. Published 4 titles in 1976, 10 in 1977; will do 20 in 1978. Simultaneous submissions OK, "but we must be fully informed of identities of all other recipients." Reports in 2-4 weeks. SASE. Free book catalog.

Nonfiction: General interest and instructional books for guitarists of all ages. "We do not want books on chords or fingerpicking or books for fans; no general method books." Query and submit first chapter and outline. "Very clear, straightforward style; minimum personal opinion of author. Music and tablature in pencil only. Permissions for music print rights are responsibility of author. We will consider mss of 15,000-30,000 words; double-spaced on bond paper; author should have intimate knowledge of music, including direct contact with artists, instruments, and technology. Materials should be clearly introduced and fully developed in the text. Ms should convey a sense of authority and support this sense with fresh authenticated information; write for the 18-35-year-old male market of guitar lovers of all styles. We prefer co-authorship with famed and accomplished guitar artists."

Special Needs: A new imprint tentatively titled Keyboard Books will be slanted toward keyboard players.

Recent Titles: *Pedal Steel Handbook,* by R. Young; *British Rock Guitar,* by D. Hedges; *Folk Guitar as a Profession,* by H. Traum.

*GULF PUBLISHING CO., Box 2608, Houston TX 77001. (713)529-4301. Editor-in-Chief: C.A. Umbach, Jr. Hardcover originals. 10% royalty; advance sometimes averages $300-2,500.

Published 20 titles in 1976, 35 in 1977; will do 40 in 1978. Subsidy publishes 1-2 titles a year. Simultaneous and photocopied submissions OK. Reports in 1-2 months. SASE. Free book catalog.
Nonfiction: Publishes business; reference; regional trade; regional gardening; scientific and self-help books.

H.P. BOOKS, Box 5367, Tucson AZ 85703. EDitor-in-Chief: Carl Shipman. Hardcover and paperback originals. Specializes in how-to books in several fields, all photo-illustrated. Pays 12½% of net; advance negotiable. Published 6 titles in 1976, 10 in 1977; will do 14 in 1978. Query. State number and type of illustrations available. Simultaneous and photocopied submissions OK. Reports in 2-4 weeks. SASE. Free book catalog.
Nonfiction: Publishes cookbooks, cooking and foods; hobbies; how-to; leisure activities; photography; recreation; self-help; and technical books. All books 160 pages minimum, "word count varies with format."
Recent Titles: *Crepe Cookery,* by M. Hoffman (cookbook); *Canon SLR Cameras,* by C. Shipman; *How to Make Your Car Handle,* by F. Puhn (automotive).

HAMMOND, INC., 515 Valley St., Mapplewood NJ 07040. (201)763-6000. Editorial Director: Frank Brady. Hardcover and paperback originals. "Books are negotiated from flat fee for outright purchase to advances against standard royalties, depending on subject." Published 20 titles in 1976, 25 in 1977; will do 40 in 1978. Submit outline/synopsis and sample chapters. State availability of photos/illustrations. Simultaneous submissions OK. Reports in 2-4 weeks. SASE. Book catalog for SASE.
Nonfiction: Publishes Americana, art, biography, business; cookbooks, cooking and foods; history, hobbies, how-to, humor, music, nature, photography, psychology, recreation, reference, religious, sports and travel books.
Fiction: "Perhaps mystery fiction with a strong travel or geographical plot. Author must really know the area about which he writes and work that into an intriguing plot."
Recent Titles: *Eyewitness to Disaster,* by D. Perkes (general nonfiction); *Discover Brunch,* by R. MacPherson (cookbook); *The Book of Secrets,* by W. Borosow (general nonfiction).

HANCOCK HOUSE PUBLISHERS LTD., (formerly Hancock Publishers, Ltd.) 3215 Island View Rd., Saanichton, B.C., Canada V05 1MO. Editor-in-Chief: David Hancock. Managing Editor: Robert Sward. Hardcover and paperback originals (97%) and reprints (3%). 10% royalty; $100 minimum advance. Published 17 titles in 1976, 30 in 1977; will do 35 in 1978. State availability of photos and/or illustrations to accompany ms. Reports in 1-2 months. SASE. Free book catalog.
Nonfiction: Publishes (in order of preference): nature, history, biography, reference, Americana (Canadian); cookbooks, cooking and foods; hobbies, how-to, juveniles, photography, recreation, self-help, sports, and travel books. Query first.
Recent Titles: *Wings of the North,* by D. Turner (biography/adventure); *Hawks, Falcons and Falconry,* by F.L. Beebe (nature).

HARBINGER PUBLICATIONS, Box 891, San Francisco CA 94101. Editor-in-Chief: Patrick Fanning. Publishes paperback originals. Offers standard minimum book contract of 10-12½-15%. Published 1 title last year. "At present, our marketing and distribution is mainly by mail, so new book projects for the next year will have to be tailored to a specific market that can be reached by direct mail." Will consider photocopied submissions. Query first for nonfiction. Submit complete ms for fiction. Conform to *Chicago Manual of Style.* Reports in 4 weeks for rejected material; 8 weeks for a manuscript accepted for publication. Enclose return postage.
Fiction: "Would like to see quality experimental fiction or traditional novels with strong personal style.LL
Business and Professional: "No taboos, but dislike seeing commonplace approaches to tired subjects; avoid padding a thin ms out to 'book-length.' We'd rather see the shorter version. Looking for originality and excellence." Would like to see mss in the areas of practical business handbooks, sociology, popular psychology, and alternative life styles.

HARCOURT BRACE JOVANOVICH, 757 Third Ave., New York NY 10017. Director of General Books Department: Kathy Robbins. Publishes hardcover and paperback originals and reprints. "We regret that all unsolicited mss for hardcover trade publication must be returned unread. Only mss submitted by agents or recommended to us by advisors or actively solicited by us will be considered."
Fiction and Nonfiction: Editor-in-Chief: Norman Goldfind. Publishes both adult and juvenile

works. "We have recently merged our subsidiary, Pyramid Publications, with our trade department to form a consolidated General Books Department. Mass market originals and reprints are published under the Pyramid and Pillar Books imprints. Pyramid Books include category fiction plus general fiction and nonfiction. Unsolicited submissions of category fiction should be limited to the areas of romance, gothic, sagas and suspense. Submissions in other areas may be considered for paperback original only, or a combination of hardcover/paperback publication. Refer queries and mss for adult paperbacks to Jeanne Glass or Kay Kidde; young adult or juvenile to Richard Huttner. Pillar Books is interested in titles of a Christian evangelical or inspirational nature, particularly true stories of redeemed lives. No unsolicited mss. Send letter and outline, or sample chapter to Barbara Rogasky, Senior Editor.

Juveniles: Editor: Barbara Lucas. Fiction and nonfiction mss for beginning readers through the young teenager. Length: 5,000 to 60,000 words. "We will be doing more nonfiction than fiction. Fiction must be of exceptional quality. Our list will probably contain fewer picture books, translations and imports."

HARIAN PUBLICATIONS, 1000 Prince St., Greenlawn NY 11740. Editor: Frederic Tyarks. Advances paid on royalties. Published 8 titles last year. Will send copy of current catalog on request. Query first. Reports in 1 week. Enclose S.A.S.E.

Nonfiction: Books on travel, retirement, investments, and health. Length: 50,000 words minimum for completed mss.

HARLEQUIN ENTERPRISES LTD., 240 Duncan Mill Rd., Don Mills, Ontario, Canada M3B 1Z4. Publishing Director: Fred Kerner. Publishes paperback originals. Offers negotiable royalty contract. Published 316 titles in 1976, 208 in 1977. "Marketing by series has provided Harlequin with the lowest return factor in the paperback business." Free sample book. Will consider photocopied submissions. No simultaneous submissions. Submit outline and sample chapters. Acknowledgement is made immediately, followed by full report as soon as possible. Enclose return postage.

Fiction: Publishes romantic fiction. Emphasis on travel. No overt sex or violence. Length: 55,000 to 58,000 words. Suggest authors read several books in Harlequin Romance or Harlequin Presents series before submitting. "In all instances, Harlequin suggests that potential authors for any of its series read books in the series to determine what an acceptable ms is for our audience. All titles appear in paperback and all are carried in our own book club operation, as well as on newsstands, to a wide audience in Canada and the U.S. and the United Kingdom."

HARPER & ROW, PUBLISHERS, INC., (including Torchbooks, Colophon, and Perennial Library, and Barnes & Noble), 10 E. 53rd St., New York NY 10022. Publishes hardcover and paperback originals and reprints. Royalty schedule subject to negotiation, but generally 10% to 5,000; 12½% to 10,000; 15% thereafter. Published 1,700 titles last year. Query letters, sample chapters and outlines preferred. For fiction, prefers completed ms. Address General Trade Department for fiction and nonfiction. Address Junior Books Department for juveniles. Reports in 4 to 6 weeks. Enclose return postage.

General Fiction and Nonfiction: Publishes books between 40,000 and 200,000 words in the following departments: college, elementary and high school, mail order, medical, nature and outdoor, religious, social and economic, and trade. Trade books can cover any subject of general interest, fiction or nonfiction, rather than specialized or scholarly works. Adult Trade Editor: Erwin Gilkes.

Juveniles: Charlotte Zolotow, Patricia Allen.

Textbooks: Publishes elementary and high school textbooks. Address Harrison Bell, School Department, 10 E. 53rd St., New York NY 10022. College textbooks. Address Alvin Abbott, Publisher, College Dept. Harper & Row, 10 E. 53rd St., New York NY 10022. Junior college textbooks. Address Jack Jennings, Publisher, Canfield Press, 1700 Montgomery St., San Francisco CA 94111.

HART PUBLISHING CO., INC., 15 W. 4th St., New York NY 10012. (212)260-2430. Hardcover and paperback originals. Royalty of 5% of list price for paperbacks; 10% for hardcovers. Advance averages $1,000. Published 45 titles in 1976, 50 in 1977; will do 60 in 1978. Reports in 1-2 weeks. SASE. Free book catalog.

Nonfiction: Publishes books on cooking and foods and cookbooks; hobbies, how-to, psychology, recreation, reference, self-help and sociology. Query first, or submit outline/synopsis and sample chapters, or complete me.

Special Needs: "We are beginning a series of activity books for young children. We are looking for crossword puzzles, poems, short bedtime stories, games, things to make and do, puzzles and concept activities. All of these must be extremely easy to do and understand. Art may or may not be included. We pay anywhere from $5-10 per piece, depending on length and merit, more if art is included. Payment is made immediately upon acceptance. All material must be accompanied by SASE. Replies will be made within 2 weeks."

HARVARD UNIVERSITY PRESS, 79 Garden St., Cambridge MA 02138. (617)495-2600. Director: Arthur J. Rosenthal. Published 121 titles in 1976. Prefers queries with outlines. Enclose return postage.
Nonfiction: Publishes scholarly books and monographs and serious nonfiction of general interest, which are based on important scholarship in the following areas: the humanities, social and behavioral sciences, physical science and medicine.

HARVEST HOUSE, LTD., PUBLISHERS, 4795 St. Catherine St. W., Montreal, P. Q., Canada, H3Z 2B9. Editor: Maynard Gertler. Publishes hardcover and paperback originals, reprints, and translations. Royalty schedule varies between 8% and 12%. Published 20 titles last year. Prefers completed ms. Reports in 6 weeks. Enclose S.A.E. and International Reply Coupons.
Nonfiction: History, biography, philosophy, science, social sciences, education, public affairs, and general nonfiction. "We prefer nonfiction to fiction and deal with mss concerning Canadian and general world interest." Minimum length is 35,000 words.

HARVEY HOUSE PUBLISHERS, 20 Waterside Plaza, New York NY 10010. Editor-in-Chief: L. F. Reeves. Hardcover originals. 5% minimum royalty; advance depends on ms. Published 14 titles in 1976, 15 in 1977; will do 14 in 1978. Send prints to accompany ms. Photocopied submissions OK. SASE. Free book catalog.
Juveniles: Nonfiction and fiction with strong values. Query or submit outline/synopsis and sample chapters.
Recent Titles: *If He's My Brother,* by Williams/Paola (picture book); *Navajo Slave,* by Gessner (fiction); and *Mighty Minicycles,* by Butterworth (nonfiction).

HASTINGS HOUSE PUBLISHERS, INC., 10 E. 40th St., New York NY 10016. (212)689-5400. Editor-in-Chief: Walter Frese. Hardcover and paperback originals (80%) and reprints (20%). 10% minimum royalty. Published 76 titles in 1976, 85 in 1977. Reports in 1-2 weeks. SASE. Free book catalog.
Nonfiction: Publishes Americana, biography; cookbooks, cooking and foods; history, humor, juveniles, photography, recreation, sports and travel books. Query or submit outline/synopsis and sample chapters.

HAYDEN BOOK COMPANY, INC., 50 Essex St., Rochelle Park NJ 07662. Editorial Director: S.W. Cook. Advance and royalty arrangements vary; generally 10% to 15% of net. Published 71 titles in 1976. Free book catalog. All book proposals should include complete outline, preface and two representative chapters. Reports in 6 weeks. Enclose return postage.
Technical: Publishes technician-level and engineering texts and references in many subject areas (emphasis on electronics and computer science); text and references for hotel, restaurant and institution management and other personnel (emphasis on management, food preparation, handling).
Textbooks: Texts, references, and visual aids for junior and senior high schools, technical institutes and community colleges in English, computer sciences, mathematics, social studies and other subject areas.

D.C. HEATH & CO., 125 Spring St., Lexington MA 02173. (617)862-6650. Editors: Editor-in-Chief: Joseph Hodges; Economics and Math: Robert Macek; History & Political Science: Ann Knight; Education & Sociology: Lane Akers; Science: Stanley Galek; Biology & Psychology: Robert Clark; Modern Languages: Mario Hurtads; Technical: Michael McCarroll; English: Holt Johnson. General Manager, College Division: John T. Harney. Publishes hardcover and paperback originals. Offers standard royalty rates for textbooks. Free book catalog. Query. Returns rejected material in 2 weeks. "Finished mss accepted are published within 1 year." Enclose return postage.
Textbooks: "Texts at the college level in sociology, psychology, history, political science, chemistry, math, physical science, economics, education, modern language, and English." Length varies.

HEIDELBERG PUBLISHERS, INC., 1003 Brown Bldg., Austin TX 78701. (512)451-3872. Editor-in-Chief: Vijay Parekh. Publishes hardcover originals. Offers standard minimum book contract. Advance varies. Published 4 titles last year. Will consider photocopied submissions. Query first or submit complete ms. Enclose return postage and S.A.E.
General Fiction and Nonfiction: "We are a general interest publisher and willing to see works of fiction (no short stories), nonfiction, biography, journalism, food and health, sociology, book trade, history, philosophy, photography, and travel."

HENDRICKS HOUSE, INC., 488 Greenwich St., New York NY 10013. (212)966-1765. Editorial Office: Putney VT 05346. Editor: Walter Hendricks. Publishes hardcover originals and hardcover and paperback reprints. Published 5 titles last year. Will send a catalog to a writer on request. Gill consider photocopied submissions. Submit complete ms. Reports in 1 month. Enclose return postage with ms.
Nonfiction: "Mainly educational." Publishes Americana, biography, history, philosophy, reference, and textbooks.

HERALD HOUSE, Drawer HH, 3225 S. Noland Rd., Independence MO 64055. (816)252-5010. Editor-in-Chief: Paul A. Wellington. Publishes hardcover originals. Standard royalty contract. Usual advance is $500, but this varies, depending on author's reputation and nature of book. Published 20 titles last year. Will send free catalog to writer on request. Query first. Reports in 2 months. Enclose return postage.
Religion: Publishes religious books for adults and children. Fiction, poetry, doctrinal texts, history, etc. All books must be relevant to the Reorganized Church of Jesus Christ of Latter-Day Saints. Length: 30,000 to 60,000 words.

*HERALD PRESS, 616 Walnut Ave., Scottdale PA 15683. (412)887-8500. (A division of Mennonite Publishing House.) Book Editor: Paul M. Schrock. Publishes hardcover and mass market paperback originals and reprints. Royalty schedule of 10% of retail price of the book. Half royalty on bulk sales sold at more than 50% discount, such as to jobbers and book clubs. Escalator clause to 12% and 15%. Occasional advance of $500; usually, not more. Subsidy publishes 10% of books. "Only books sponsored by our official board or committee of the Mennonite Church to meet discriminating needs when a book is not otherwise economically feasible." Published 31 titles last year. Two or 3 titles a year are subsidized by church organizations. No personal subsidies. Will send catalog to writer for 50¢. No simultaneous submissions. Will consider photocopied submissions. Query first with brief outline and sample chapter. Reports within 1 month. Enclose return postage.
General Nonfiction and Fiction: "We publish books of specific interest to Mennonites, as well as books of general Christian interest in such areas as inspiration, Bible study, self-help, church history, adult fiction, devotionals, peace studies, current issues, personal experience stories showing how the Christian faith provides genuine help in facing life, missions and evangelism, family life, and Christian ethics. Our goal is to publish books which are sound in theology, honest in presentation, clear in thought, stimulating in content, and conducive to the spiritual and intellectual growth of the reader. Length varies from several thousand words (pamphlets, children's storybooks) to hundreds of thousands of words *(Mennonite Encyclopedia)*. We can handle whatever length seems appropriate for the subject matter."
Juveniles: For ages 9 and up. Length: 25,000 to 30,000 words.
Recent Titles: *Divorce, A Liberation Dilemma*, by N. Martin/Z. Levitt; *My Personal Pentecost*, by R. and M. Koch; *Ethics in Business and Labor*, by J. D. Hess.

*HERITAGE HOUSE PUBLISHERS, INC., Box 52298, Jacksonville FL 32203. (904)358-7008. Editor-in-Chief: Leslie E. Ellis. Hardcover and paperback originals. 10% royalty contract; no advance. Subsidy publishes 10% of books. "Generally, if we cannot offer the author a royalty contract because his work does not fit our direct needs, we will give him the option of using our Venture subsidy program. His work must be concise and well done." Published 3 titles in 1976, 20 in 1977; will do 40 in 1978. State availability of photos to illustrate ms. Simultaneous and photocopied submissions OK. SASE. Reports in 6-8 weeks. Free book catalog for SASE.
Nonfiction: Margo Fugeman, Editor. Americana, art, biography, business; cookbooks, cooking and foods; economics, history, hobbies, how-to, humor, juveniles, law; medicine and psychiatry; music, nature, pets, philosophy, poetry, politics, psychology, recreation, reference, religious, scientific, self-help, sociology, sports, technical, textbooks and travel topics. Submit outline/synopsis and sample chapters or complete ms. Mss must be typed double-spaced. If query or outline is sent, prefers complete story line or full description of project.

Fiction: Adventure, historical, humorous, mystery, romance, science fiction, suspense and western fiction.

For '78: "Our primary interest at the present time is in the development of a series of medically oriented books for the lay person. We are always interested in offering royalty contracts for good patient-oriented mss."

HERMAN PUBLISHING, 45 Newbury St., Boston MA 02116. Editor: M.J. Philips. Publishes hardcover and paperback originals and reprints. "Standard 10% royalty up to break-even point; higher beyond." Published 16 titles in 1977. Advance varies, depending on author's reputation and nature of book. Will send copy of current catalog on request. Send query, outline and sample chapter to C.A. Herman. Reports in 2 months. Enclose return postage.

General Nonfiction, Business, and Technical: Business, technical and general nonfiction; reference, science, hi-fi, music, antiques, gardening, cooking, the arts, health, self-improvement, psychology, travel, regional, religion, history, biography, ships, audio, acoustics, electronics, radio, TV. "It might be worth noting that we also perform a unique service. We will market to the book trade (and elsewhere possibly), books which may have been privately published by the author or by a small publisher. Naturally, we must first see a sample copy and be satisfied that we can market it." Writing must be factual and authoritative. No length limits.

LAWRENCE HILL & CO., 24 Burr Farms Rd., Westport CT 06880. (203)226-9392. Editor-in-Chief: Lawrence Hill. Managing Editor: Mercer Field. Hardcover and paperback originals. Specializes in publishing Black Studies and Third-World affairs books. Standard royalty; advance averages $500 and up. Published 8 titles in 1976, 12 in 1977, and will do 15 in 1978. Query or submit outline/synopsis and sample chapters. State availability of photos and/or illustrations unless for children's book. For children's book send samples. Photocopied submissions OK. Reports in 2-4 weeks. SASE. Book catalog for SASE.

Nonfiction: Publishes Americana; art; biography; cookbooks; economics; history; humor; juveniles; law; psychiatry; music; nature; pets; philosophy; poetry; politics; psychology; reference (no dictionaries or encyclopedia—trade book slant); religious (trade book slant); scientific; self-help; sociology; sports; and travel books.

Fiction: Publishes adventure; experimental; historical; humorous; mainstream; mystery; religious; romance; science fiction; suspense; and western books.

Recent Titles: *The Jazz Book,* by J. Berendt (music); *The Kidnapped Saint,* by B. Traven (short stories); *The Land's Lord,* by T.O. Echewa (African fiction).

HOLIDAY HOUSE, INC., 18 E. 53rd St., New York NY 10022. (212)688-0085. Editor: Margery Cuyler. Published 20 titles in 1976, 24 in 1977. Reports in 4 to 6 weeks. Enclose return postage.

Juveniles: Publishes children's books only —fiction and nonfiction, for preschool through teenage boys and girls.

Recent Titles: *The Dog Days of Arthur Cane,* by T.E. Bethancourt (fiction); *The Tyrannosaurus Game,* by S. Kroll (picture book); and *Immunity: How Our Bodies Resist Disease,* by J. Arehart-Treichel (science).

HOLLOWAY HOUSE PUBLISHING CO., 8060 Melrose Ave., Los Angeles CA 90046. (213)653-8060. Editor: Charles D. Anderson. Publishes originals, reprints and translations. "Our payment is comparable to that of all paperback book publishers. We promote heavily, giving each book individual attention. Prefer queries on all submissions. But mss and partials may be submitted provided they are accompanied by an outline covering all salient points. We try to report in 2 weeks if rejected and in 2 months if interested, but this is subject to the volume of mss received. We do not publish poetry, short stories or plays." Published 24 titles last year. Enclose S.A.S.E. with queries or submissions.

Nonfiction: "We're looking for extraordinary works on all subjects of enduring interest which have something to say and which say it well. Prefer 50,000 to 100,000 words. You must query first and all queries or mss must be accompanied by a brief synopsis of the work."

Fiction: "We're looking for general novels." Also particularly interested in realistic, contemporary novels of the Black Experience. "We are not in the market for sex books."

A.J. HOLMAN CO., Division of J.B. Lippincott Co., East Washington Square, Philadelphia PA 19105. Editor-in-Chief: Russell T. Hitt. Publishes hardcover and paperback originals. Offers royalty of 10% of list. Advance negotiable. Published 5 titles in 1976. Free book catalog. Query first. Enclose return postage.

Religious: "Conservative Christian books addressed to popular readership. Devotional. How-

to-do-it approach. Aids to Bible study. Interested in reaching the large, theologically conservative Protestant (primarily) market."
Recent Titles: *A Gift of Love,* by G. Magruder (inspirational); and *I'm in Love with a Married Man,* by H. Vigeveno (self-help).

HOLT, RINEHART AND WINSTON OF CANADA, LTD., 55 Horner Ave., Toronto 18, Ontario, Canada. (416)255-4491. Director, New Product Development: J.C. Mainprize. Publishes hardcover and paperback originals and anthologies. Offers standard royalty contract. "Advance depends on material. Flat fee only in anthologies." Published 73 titles in 1976, 26 in 1977. Free book catalog. Send query with outline and sample chapter for nonfiction and textbooks. Reports in 1 to 3 months. Enclose Canadian postage or International Reply Coupons.
General Nonfiction: "Canadian authors preferred." Buys business and professional, arts, history and biography.
Textbooks: "All fields—elementary, secondary, and college levels. Must be by Canadians or dealing specifically with Canadian materials."
Recent Titles: *Holt Mathematics 1,* by H.A. Elliott (text); *Plants,* by I.S. Carter (science text); and *Golden Trails,* by Dr. J.R. Linn (English-language arts).

HOPKINSON & BLAKE, 185 Madison Ave., New York NY 10016. Editor-in-Chief: Len Karlin. Publishes clothbound and paperback originals. Offers standard 10-12½% royalty contract; average advance $1,000. Published 5 titles last year. Will consider photocopied submissions. Query first. Reports in 2 weeks. Enclose return postage.
Nonfiction: Mainly for college market. "We plan to continue to publish books on motion pictures. Also going into social sciences. Cookbooks, and self-help books will also be considered."

HORIZON PRESS, 156 Fifth Ave., New York NY 10010. Royalty schedule standard scale from 10% to 15%. Published 19 titles in 1976, 22 in 1977. Free book catalog. Prefers complete ms. Reports in 4 weeks. Enclose return postage with ms.
Nonfiction: History, literature, science, biography, the arts, feneral. Length: 40,000 words and up.

HOUGHTON MIFFLIN CO., 2 Park St., Boston MA 02107. (617)725-5000. Editor-in-Chief: Austin G. Olney. Managing Editor: David B. Harris. Hardcover and paperback originals (90%) and paperback reprints (10%). Royalty of 7% for paperbacks; 10-15% on sliding scale for standard fiction and nonfiction; advance varies widely. Published 124 titles in 1976, 160 in 1977; will do 150 in 1978. State availability of photos to accompany ms and show half a dozen sample prints. Simultaneous submissions (if informed) and photocopied submissions OK. Reports in 2-4 weeks. SASE. Book catalog for SASE.
Nonfiction: Publishes (in order of preference): nature, history, biography, juveniles, politics, poetry, hobbies, Americana, how-to; and cookbooks, cooking and foods. Query.
Fiction: Publishes (in order of preference): mainstream, suspense, mystery, and historical books. Submit outline/synopsis and sample chapters.
Recent Titles: *The Age of Uncertainty,* by John Kenneth Galbraith (economic history); *The Genuine Article,* by A. B. Guthrie, Jr. (mystery); *Tolkien,* by Humphrey Carpenter (biography).

HOUSE OF ANANSI PRESS LIMITED, 35 Britain St., Toronto, Ont., Canada M5A 1R7. (416)363-5444. Editor-in-Chief: James Polk. Managing Editor: Ann Wall. Hardcover and paperback originals (99%) and paperback (of out-of-print important Canadiana) reprints (1%). Royalty "varies, depending on whether we publish the book first in hardcover or paperback or both; not less than 8%;" advance averages $500, "but we also participate in the author subsidy plan of the Ontario Arts Council, and through them can offer up to $3,000." Published 5 titles in 1976, 8 in 1977; will do 8-10 in 1978. Query, submit outline/synopsis and sample chapters or complete ms. "We're flexible, but prefer for nonfiction to have a pretty good idea of what we're going to get. Don't send photos or illustrations with first submission. Tell us about them and if we're interested in the writing, we'll talk about those later." Photocopied submissions OK. Reports in 1-2 months. Publishes Canadian authors, only. SASE. Free book catalog.
Nonfiction: Publishes biography; history; law; medicine and psychiatry; music; philosophy; poetry; politics; psychology; and sociology books. "We have no length requirement. A book should be as long as it has to be to cover its topic adequately, and no longer. The slant should be toward the general reader with some university education. We like well-researched but not heavy or over-footnoted books."

Fiction: Publishes experimental books.
Recent Titles: *Coming Through Slaughter,* by M. Ondaatje (fiction); *The Cape Breton Book of the Dead,* D. Domanski (poetry); and *Self-Help Guide to Divorce, Children and Welfare,* by P. Jahn and C. Campbell (nonfiction).

HOUSE OF COLLECTIBLES, INC., P.O. Box D, Florence AL 35630. Publisher: Joel R. Anderson. Publishes hardcover and paperback originals. Royalty is based on the stature of the author, the subject and the ms. Average advance is $1,000. Published 15 titles last year. Complete distribution and marketing range in all fields with heavy coverage on the collectible markets. Will send catalog to writer on request. Submit outline and sample chapters. Will consider photocopied submissions. Mss must be typed, double spaced with sample illustrations, when necessary. Reports within 2 months. Enclose return postage.
Nonfiction: "On the subject of collectibles (antiques, numismatics, philatelics) and how-to-do books. We prefer an author who knows his or her subject thoroughly. Style and general format are left entirely to the author. Any special treatment or emphasis is a matter of decision for the author."

HOWELL-NORTH BOOKS, 1050 Parker St., Berkeley CA 94710. (415)845-4096. President: Mrs. Morgan North. Publishes hardcover and paperback originals. Pays 10% of retail price; no advance. Published 2 titles last year. Current catalog available. Send query, outline and sample chapter. Reports in 10 weeks. Enclose return postage.
Nonfiction: Publishes railroadiana, works on transportation, steamboating, mining, California, marine nonfiction pictorials, histories, Americana, and especially influence of the west. Length: 30,000 words minimum. Recent titles include *Railroads of Arizona, Vol. 1* (Myrick); *Eminent Women of the West* (Richey).

HURTIG PUBLISHERS, 10560-105 St., Edmonton, Alta, Canada T5H 2W7. (403)426-2359. Editor-in-Chief: Sylvia Vance. Hardcover and paperback originals (80%) and reprints (20%). 10% royalty on first 7,000 copies; 12½% on next 1,000; 15% thereafter. Advance averages $500-1,000. Published 12 titles in 1976, 20 in 1977; will do more than 20 in 1978. State availability of photos and/or illustrations to accompany ms. Photocopied submissions OK. Reports in 1-2 months. SASE. Free book catalog.
Nonfiction: Publishes biographies of well-known Canadians; cookbooks, cooking and foods; Canadian history; humor; nature; topical Canadian politics; reference (Canadian); and material about native Canadians. No reminiscences. Query or submit outline/synopsis and sample chapters; or submit complete ms.
Recent Titles: *The Birds of Alberta,* by Salt/Salt (nature); *Colombo's Concise Canadian Quotations,* by J. E. Colombo (reference); *Jewish Life in Canada,* by Kurelek/Arnold (ethnic history).

***HWONG PUBLISHING CO.,** 10353 Los Alamitos Blvd., Los Alamitos CA 90720. Editor-in-Chief: Hilmi Ibrahim. Managing Editor: Ms. Gail Merry. Hardcover and paperback originals. Specializes in social science and the humanities. 10% royalty; no advance. Subsidy publishes 33% of books. Published 22 titles in 1976, 25 in 1977; will do 35 in 1978. Send prints of photos and/or illustrations to accompany ms. Simultaneous and photocopied submissions OK. Reports in 2-4 weeks. SASE. Free book catalog.
Nonfiction: Publishes biography, business, history, humor, politics, psychology, recreation, religious, sociology, sports, and textbooks. Submit outline and sample chapters.

Fiction: Publishes adventure, historical, humorous, mainstream, and suspense. Submit outline and sample chapters.

***IDEAL WORLD PUBLISHING COMPANY,** P.O. Box 1237-EG, Melbourne FL 32935. New Idea Publishing Co. is a division of the Ideal World Publishing Company. Editor: Harold Pallatz. Publishes hardcover and paperback originals and reprints. Offers "10% on hardcover, 5% on softcover; specific contracts can go higher or lower, depending upon material. No advance is ever given." About 25% of books are subsidy published. "If the book looks like it might sell, but we are not certain of exact demand, then, instead of outright rejection, we will try subsidy. Costs vary between $1,000 and $2,000 depending upon number of pages, copies, text, etc." Published 4 titles last year. Will consider photocopied submissions. Query first. Reports in 2 to 4 weeks. "No material will be returned unless S.A.S.E. is attached."
Health: "Natural approaches to good health through nutrition, herbs, vegetarianism, vitamins, unusual medical approaches for specific ailments, particularly from authorities in the field. Any style is acceptable, but it must hold the reader's attention and make for fairly smooth nonintensive (no brain taxation) requirements. Ideas should be in a simple, easygoing pace."

INDEPENDENCE PRESS, 3225 S. Noland Rd., Drawer HH, Independence MO 64055. (816)252-5010. Editor-in-Chief: Paul Wellington. Managing Editor: Margaret Baldwin. Hardcover and paperback originals. 10-12½-15% royalty; advance averages $500. Published 7 titles in 1976, 5 in 1977; will do 7 in 1978. Submit chapter-by-chapter outline and first 6 chapters to Margaret Baldwin. Simultaneous and photocopied submissions OK. Reports in 1-2 months. SASE. Free book catalog.
Nonfiction: Publishes Americana (Midwest); biography (famous Midwesterners); juveniles; medicine and psychiatry; and self-help books. (Author should be well known in the last three fields.)
Juveniles and Young Adult: Publishes adventure, historical, humorous, mystery, religious, science fiction, suspense, western. "No more American Revolution for awhile. No poetry."
Recent Titles: *A Boy Called Hopeless,* by D. Melton (juvenile fiction); *Walk Through the Valley,* by W. Leipold, Ph.D. (adult nonfiction).

*INDIANA UNIVERSITY PRESS, 10th and Morton Sts., Bloomington IN 47401. (812)337-4773. Editorial Director: John Gallman. Publishes hardcover originals and paperback reprints. Normally pays 10% royalty. Does 5% to 10% subsidy publishing. Published 72 titles in 1976 and 1977. Queries should include as much descriptive material as is necessary to convey scope and market appeal of ms. Reports on rejections in 3 weeks or less; on acceptances, in 2 months. Enclose return postage.
Nonfiction: Scholarly books on humanities, public policy, film, music, linguistics, social science; regional materials, serious nonfiction for the general reader.
Recent Titles: *Haydn: Chronicle of Works,* by H. C. Loudon (music); *Don't Make No Waves ... Don't Back No Losers,* by M. Rakove (politics); and *America and the World Political Economy* (politics).

*INTERMEDIA PRESS, Box 3294, Vancouver, B.C., Canada V6B 3X9. (604)681-3592. Editors-in-Chief: Henry Rappaport, Edwin Varney. Hardcover and paperback originals. 7½-10% royalty; occasionally offers advance. Subsidy publishes 50% of books. Subsidy publishing offered "usually on our literary books; those not guaranteed to be commercial successes." Published 8 titles in 1976, 10 in 1977; will do 12 in 1978. Query, or submit outline/synopsis and sample chapters or complete ms. State availability of photos and/or illustrations. Simultaneous and photocopied ("if we can print from the original") submissions OK. Reports in 2-4 months. SASE. Book catalog $1.
Nonfiction: Dona Sturmanis, Managing Editor. Publishes art (avant-garde, personal); business (contemporary, snappy, 50-200 pages); cookbooks, cooking and foods; erotica (in a literary context); humor (absurdist); juveniles; multimedia material; poetry; recreation; sports; textbooks; and travel books.
Fiction: Dona Sturmanis, Managing Editor. Publishes erotica; experimental; fantasy; historical (with a Canadian content); humorous; mainstream; and science fiction books.
Special Needs: "We are especially interested in juvenile and trade books. Anthologies of poetry and fiction also."
Recent Titles: *Tennis Anyone?,* by H. and J. Rappaport (sports); *Canadian Short Fiction Anthology,* edited by C. Ford (fiction anthology); *Sitting on a Lawn with a Lady Twice My Size,* by O. Nations (poetry).

INTERNATIONAL MARINE PUBLISHING COMPANY, 21 Elm St., Camden ME 04843. Editor: Peter Spectre. Publishes hardcover and paperback originals and reprints. "Standard royalties, with advances." Published 15 titles in 1976 and 1977. Free book catalog. "Material in all stages welcome. Query invited, but not necessary." Reports in 4 weeks. Enclose return postage.
Marine Nonfiction: "Marine nonfiction only —but a wide range of subjects within that category: fishing, boatbuilding, yachting, sea ecology and conservation, maritime history, cruising, true sea adventure, etc. —anything to do with boats, lakes, rivers, seas, and the people who do things on them, commercially or for pleasure. No word length requirements. Pictorial books with short texts are as welcome as 60,000-word mss."
Recent Titles: *Singlehanded Sailing,* by R. Henderson (seamanship); *National Watercraft Collection,* by H. I. Chapelle (history); and *Good Boats,* by R. C. Taylor (boat design).

INTERNATIONAL WEALTH SUCCESS, Box 186, Merrick NY 11566. (516)766-5850. Editor: Tyler G. Hicks. Offers royalty schedule of 10% of list price. Usual advance is $1,000, but this varies, depending on author's reputation and nature of book. Published 9 titles in 1976, 12 in 1977. Will consider photocopied submissions. Query first. Reports in 4 weeks. Enclose return postage.

Self-Help and How-to: "Techniques, methods, sources for building wealth. Highly personal, how-to-do-it with plenty of case histories. Books are aimed at the wealth builder and are highly sympathetic to his problems." Financing, business success, venture capital, etc. Length 60,000 to 70,000 words.

*THE INTERSTATE PRINTERS AND PUBLISHERS, INC., 19-27 N. Jackson St., Danville IL 61832. (217)446-0500. Editor-in-Chief: R. L. Guin. Managing Editor: Ronald McDaniel. Hardcover and paperback originals. Usual royalty is 10% of wholesale price; no advance. Occasionally subsidy publishes books depending on the market and financial evaluation. Publishes about 60 titles annually. Markets books by mail to all elementary, junior/middle and high schools in the U.S. Reports in 1-2 months. SASE. Free book catalog.
Nonfiction: Publishes textbooks; agriculture; special education; trade and industrial; home economics; athletics; career education; outdoor education; and learning disabilities books. Query or submit outline/synopsis and sample chapters.
Recent Titles: *Beef Cattle Science,* by M. E. Ensminger (agriculture); and *My Speech Workbook,* by Parker (speech therapy).

INTER-VARSITY PRESS, Box F, Downers Grove IL 60515. (312)964-5700. Editor: Dr. James W. Sire. Publishes hardcover and paperback originals, reprints, translations, and anthologies. Royalty schedule "varies with the ms and the author." Published 30 titles last year. Will send a catalog to a writer on request. Send outline and sample chapter. Reports in 16 weeks. Enclose return postage.
Religion, Philosophy and Textbooks: "Publishes books geared to the presentation of Biblical Christianity in its various relations to personal life, art, literature, sociology, philosophy, history, etc.; college, university, and seminary-level textbooks on any subject within the general religious field. The audience for which the books are published is composed primarily of university students and graduates. The stylistic treatment varies from topic to topic and from fairly simplified popularization for college freshmen to extremely scholarly works primarily designed to be read by scholars." Current leading titles include *Knowing God* (Packer); *The Singer* (Miller).

*IOWA STATE UNIVERSITY PRESS, S. State Ave., Ames IA 50010. (515)294-5280. Director: Merritt Bailey. Managing Editor: Rowena Malone. Hardcover and paperback originals. 10-12½-15% royalty; no advance. Subsidy publishes 10-50% of their titles, based on sales potential of book and contribution to scholarship. Published 20 titles in 1976, 30 in 1977; will do 30 in 1978. Send contrasty b&w glossy prints to illustrate ms. Simultaneous submissions OK, if advised; photocopied submissions OK if accompanied by an explanation. Reports in 2-4 months. SASE. Free book catalog.
Nonfiction: Publishes biography, history, recreation, reference, scientific technical, textbooks and Iowana books. Submit outline/synopsis and sample chapters; must be double-spaced throughout.
Recent Titles: *Graphics for Designers* (Hartman); *Metropolitan Economics* (Tweeten); *Newsletter Editing* (Wales).

THE JOHNS HOPKINS UNIVERSITY PRESS, Baltimore MD 21218. Editor-in-Chief: Michael A. Aronson. Publishes mostly clothbound originals and paperback reprints; some paperback originals. Payment varies; contract negotiated with author. Prompt report, usually 8 weeks. Published 84 titles last year. Prefers query letter first. Enclose S.A.S.E.
Nonfiction: Publishes scholarly books and nonfiction for the intelligent reader; biomedical sciences, history, literary criticism, psychology, political science, and economics. Length: 50,000 words minimum.

JONATHAN DAVID PUBLISHERS, 68-22 Eliot Ave., Middle Village NY 11379. (212)456-8611. General Editor: Alfred J. Kolatch. Publishes hardcover and paperback originals. Offers standard 10-12½-15% royalty contract; "advances according to credentials." Published 23 titles in 1976, 24 in 1977. Free book catalog. Send query with detailed outline and sample chapter. Reports in 2 to 4 weeks. Enclose return postage.
General Nonfiction: "General nonfiction for adults. We feel that we can give the author a more personal relationship than he ordinarily would receive. Our titles must have a mass audience potential. We're always open to solid ideas. We generally recruit our top authors, but we are interested in hearing from able writers with nonfiction book ideas."
Recent Titles: *The Gardener's Hintbook,* by C. Wilson (gardening); and *The Surrealist's Bible,* by D. Luzwick (art/religion).

JOVE/HBJ BOOKS (formerly Pyramid Publications), 757 3rd Ave., New York NY 10017. Editor-in-Chief: Marie R. Reno. Executive Editor: Lucia Staniels. Paperback originals (50%) and reprints (50%). 6-8% royalty; advance averages $2,500. Publishes 200+ titles annually. State availability of photos/illustrations. Simultaneous ("if stated that it is being simultaneously submitted") and photocopied submissions OK. Reports in 1-2 months. SASE. Book catalog for SASE.
Nonfiction: Publishes biography; cookbooks; cooking and foods; history; hobbies; how-to; humor; juveniles; nature; pets; politics; psychology; reference; religious; self-help; and sociology books. Query, or submit outline/synopsis and sample chapters.
Fiction: Publishes adventure; historical; humorous; mainstream; mystery; romance; science fiction and suspense books. Submit complete ms.
Recent Titles: *American Bicentennial Series,* by J. Jakes (historical fiction); *Body Language of,* by J. Fast (pop-psych).

JUDSON PRESS, Valley Forge PA 19481. (215)768-2116. Managing Editor: Harold L. Twiss. Publishes hardcover and paperback originals. Generally 10% royalty on first 7,500 copies; 12½% on next 7,500; 15% above 15,000. "Payment of an advance depends on author's reputation and nature of book." Published 36 titles in 1976 and 1977. Free book catalog. Prefers a query letter accompanied by outline and sample chapter. Reports in 3 months. Enclose return postage.
Religion: Adult religious nonfiction of 30,000 to 200,000 words.
Recent Titles: *Getting Ready for Christmas,* by M. A. Bohrs (religious juvenile); *Free Fall,* J. K. Smith (religious experience); and *Church Administration in the Black Perspective,* by F. Massey/S.B. McKinney (church management).

WILLIAM KAUFMANN, INC., 1 First St., Los Altos CA 94022. Editor-in-Chief: William Kaufmann. Hardcover and paperback originals (90%) and reprints (10%). "Generally offers standard minimum book contract of 10-12½-15% but special requirements of book may call for lower royalties;" no advance. Published 8 titles in 1976, 12 in 1977; will do 10 in 1978. State availability of photos and/or illustrations to accompany ms. Simultaneous and photocopied submissions OK. Reports in 1-2 months. SASE. Free book catalog.
Nonfiction: "We specialize in not being specialized; look primarily for originality and quality." Publishes Americana; art; biography; business; economics; history; how-to; humor; medicine and psychiatry; nature; psychology; recreation; scientific; sports; and textbooks. Does not want to see cookbooks, novels, poetry, inspirational/religious and erotica. Query.
Recent Titles: *What's So Funny About Science?,* by S. Harris (humor); *Ideas Illustrated — (Visualization),* by Belliston/Hanks (drawing, design, art); *The Mystery of B. Traven,* by J. Stone (journalistic biography).

KEATS PUBLISHING, INC., 36 Grove St., P.O. Box 876, New Canaan CT 06840. Editor: Ms. An Keats. Publishes hardcover and paperback originals and reprints. Offers standard 10-12½-15% royalty contract. Advance varies. Published 25 titles in 1976. Free book catalog. Query first with outline and sample chapter. Reports in 2 months. Enclose return postage.
Nonfiction: "Natural health, special interest; industry-subsidy. Also, mss with promotion and premium potential. In natural health, anything having to do with the current interest in ecology, natural health cookbooks, diet books, organic gardening, etc." Length: open.
Religion: "Largely in the conservative Protestant field."

J.J. KELLER & ASSOCIATES, INC., 145 W. Wisconsin Ave., Neenah WI 54956. (414)722-2848. President: John J. Keller. Publishes paperback originals. Payment by arrangement. Published 7 titles in 1976, 5 in 1977. Query. Enclose return postage.
Technical and Reference: "Working guides, handbooks and pamphlets covering the regulatory requirements for the motor carrier industry at both the federal and individual state levels. Technical and consumer publications pertaining to the International System of Units (Metric system of measurement)." Contact must be made in advance to determine applicability of subject matter and method of presentation.
Recent Titles: *National Backhaul Guide* (source directory); *Driver's Guide to Low Underpasses* (reference); and *Metric Yearbook* (reference).

KENT STATE UNIVERSITY PRESS, Kent State University, Kent OH 44242. (216)672-7913. Director: Paul H. Rohmann. Publishes hardcover originals. Standard minimum book contract; rarely gives an advance. Published 10 titles in 1976, 12 in 1977. Free book catalog. "Please always write a letter of inquiry before submitting mss. We can publish only a limited number of titles each year and can frequently tell in advance whether or not we would be interested in a particular ms. This practice saves both our time and that of the author, not to mention postage costs." Reports in 10 weeks. Enclose return postage.

Nonfiction: Especially interested in "scholarly works in history of high quality, particularly any titles of regional interest for Ohio. Also will consider scholarly biographies, social sciences, scientific research, the arts, and general nonfiction."

Recent Titles: *The Obsolete Necessity: America in Utopian Writings, 1888-1900,* by K. Roemer (scholarly); *Laughter in the Wilderness: Early American Humor to 1783,* by W. H. Kenney (scholarly); and *Many Futures, Many Worlds: Theme and Form in Science Fiction,* by T. Clareson (scholarly).

DALE STUART KING, PUBLISHER, 2002 N. Tucson Blvd., Tucson AZ 85716. Publishes hardcover and paperback originals. Royalty schedule: usually 12% of gross sales. Published 1 title last year. Catalog available on request. Send query first, then outline and sample chapter. Reports in less than 30 days. Enclose return postage.

Nonfiction: Publishes specialized history, biography, science, and general nonfiction on the Southwest only. Length: around 60,000 words.

Recent Titles: *Handbook of Rocky Mountain Plants,* by R. A. Nelson (nonfiction); *Early 17th Century Spanish Missions in the Southwest,* by F. A. Parsons (nonfiction).

KIRKLEY PRESS, INC., P.O. Box 200, Timonium MD 21093. Editor: Walter Kirkley. Publishes paperback 16-page booklets. "We buy mss outright and pay upon acceptance. Payment (total) varies between $200 and $300, depending on subject and strength with which written. Sample of our material sent on request." Send complete ms. "Try to answer in 2 weeks." Enclose return postage.

Business: "We publish small booklets which are sold to businesses for distribution to the employee. They attempt to stimulate or motivate the employee to improve work habits. Basically they are pep talks for the employee. We need writers who are so close to the problems of present-day employee attitudes that they can take one of those problems and write about it in a warm, human, understanding, personal style and language that will appeal to the employee and which the employer will find to his advantage to distribute to the employees." Length: 2,400 to 2,600 words.

B. KLEIN PUBLICATIONS, Box 8503, Coral Springs FL 33065. (305)752-1708. Editor-in-Chief: Bernard Klein. Hardcover and paperback originals. Specializes in directories, annuals, who's who type of books; bibliography, business opportunity, reference books. 10% royalty, "but we're negotiable". Advance "depends on many factors". Published 6 titles in 1976 and 1977; will do 6-8 in 1978. Markets books by direct mail and mail order. Simultaneous and photocopied submissions OK. Reports in 1-2 weeks. SASE. Free book catalog for SASE.

Nonfiction: Publishes books on business, hobbies, how-to, reference, self-help, directories, bibliographies. Query or submit outline/synopsis and sample chapters or complete ms.

Current Titles: *Reference Encyclopedia of the American Indian; Your Business, Your Son and You,* by J. McQuaig (nonfiction).

ALFRED A. KNOPF, INC., 201 East 50th St., New York NY 10022. Senior Editor: Ashbel Green. Payment is on royalty basis. Published 115 titles last year. Will consider photocopied submissions. Send query letter for nonfiction; query letter or complete mss for fiction. No unsolicited poetry manuscripts. Reports in 2 to 4 weeks. Enclose self-addressed, stamped envelope.

Fiction: Publishes book-length fiction of literary merit by known or unknown writers. Length: 30,000 to 150,000 words.

Nonfiction: Book-length nonfiction, including books of scholarly merit on special subjects. Preferred length: 40,000 to 150,000 words. A good nonfiction writer should be able to follow the latest scholarship in any field of human knowledge, and fill in the abstractions of scholarship for the benefit of the general reader by means of good, concrete, sensory reporting.

Juveniles: No minimum length requirement. Juvenile Editor: Pat Ross.

JOHN KNOX PRESS, 341 Ponce de Leon Ave., N.E., Atlanta GA 30308. (404)873-1531. Director: Richard A. Ray. Hardcover and paperback originals (90%) and paperback reprints (10%). 7½% royalty on paperbacks; 10% on hardcover; no advance. Published 24 titles in 1976, 25 in 1977; will do 28 in 1978. Photocopied submissions OK. Reporting time varies according to proposal. CASE. Free book catalog.

Nonfiction: Publishes religious, inspirational, inter-personal; and recreation topic books.

KODANSHA INTERNATIONAL, LTD., 2-12-21 Otowa, Bunkyo-Ku, Tokyo 112, Japan. Hardcover originals and a limited number of paperback originals. 3-8% royalty, either against sales or printing; determined case by case. Advance varies. Published 18 titles in 1976, 27 in 1977; will do 25 in 1978. Markets trade books through Harper & Row; by direct mail to Asian studies specialists. State availability of prints or transparencies to illustrate ms. Photocopied submissions OK. SAE and International Reply Coupons. Reports in 2-4 months. Free book catalog but request must be sent to the firm at 10 E. 53 St., New York NY 10022.
Nonfiction: "Books about Japan and the Far East of interest to American general readers or specialists. Books on arts and crafts of highest quality." Oriental arts, crafts of the world; especially ceramics. Books on Oriental cooking; on economics related to Japan and Asia; how-to on arts and crafts and Oriental martial arts. Philosophy, photography, politics, psychology, reference and sociology. Query. "Since we are highly specialized, ge are probably a poor market for American writers, but we would welcome innovative approaches to arts and crafts subjects."
Recent Titles: *Michael Cardew,* by K. Clark (crafts; ceramics); *Dialogue in Art: Japan and the West,* by C. F. Yamada (fine art).

LANTERN PRESS, INC., 354 Hussey Rd., Mount Vernon NY 10552. (914)668-9736. Payment is on royalty basis, or outright purchase, if preferred. Usual advance is $250 on signing, $250 on publication. Published 2 titles last year. No mss should be sent unless authorized. Query first. Reports in 3 to 4 weeks. Enclose return postage.
Nonfiction: Publishes adult nonfiction, mail-order books. Length: 2,000 to 30,000 words.
Juveniles: Especially interested in juveniles for all ages. Juvenile Editor: J.R. Furman.

SEYMOUR LAWRENCE, INC., 90 Beacon St., Boston MA 02108. Publisher: Seymour Lawrence. Editor: Merloyd Lawrence. Publishes hardcover and paperback originals. Seymour Lawrence books are published in association with the Delacorte Press. Royalty schedule: 10% to 5,000 copies; 12½% to 10,000; 15% thereafter on adult hardcover books; 10% on children's books. Published 21 titles in 1976, 14 in 1977. Send outline and sample chapters. Enclose return postage.
Nonfiction, Fiction, Juveniles: Child care and development books for the general reader; no textbooks. Adult fiction. Juvenile fiction and picture books. Recent titles include *Slapstick* (Vonnegut), *Child Health Encyclopedia* (Boston Children's Hospital) and *Doctor and Child* (Brazelton.)
Special Needs: Radcliffe Series of biographies of women.

LAWYERS AND JUDGES PUBLISHING CO., 817 E. Broadway, P.O. Box 6081, Tucson AZ 85733. Editor-in-Chief: David R. DeLano. Publishes paperback originals. "We negotiate each title separately." No advance. Published 5 titles last year. Will consider photocopied submissions. Query first. Reports in 10 days. Enclose S.A.S.E.
Business and Law: Question and answer booklets about the law for laymen. Case organizers for lawyers and their secretaries. How-to books for lawyers and accountants. Question and answer format desired. "Lawyers purchase question and answer booklets to give to their clients at no charge, in order to reduce office time needed to educate the client. How-to books stress practical aspects of complying with the hundreds of different federal government forms. We're planning more Practical Guides, and taxes and government regulations are good themes also."

LEARNING TRENDS, 175 Fifth Ave., New York NY 10010. Director: David A. Katz. Publishes educational hardcover and paperback originals. Contract and advance "subject to negotiation." Published 24 titles in 1976. Free book catalog. Submit outline and sample chapters. Vill consider photocopied submissions. Reports in 6 weeks. Enclose return postage.
Textbooks: "Textbooks, grades K to 12; emphasis on slow learner material. Especially interested in areas lending themselves to a high interest, low reading level approach. Short chapters and study aids recommended. Interested in relevant, original materials in social studies, language arts, science, and other fields represented in school curricula. The high conceptual level and slow learner approach is recommended."

LEBHAR-FRIEDMAN (formerly Chain Store Publishing Corp.), 425 Park Ave., New York NY 10022. (212)371-9400. Editor-in-Chief: Richard J. Staron. Managing Editor: Julie Laitin. Hardcover and paperback originals. 10% (of net) royalty. Advance depends on type of book. Published 5 titles in 1976, 12 in 1977; will do 12 in 1978. Mss must follow Chicago *Manual of Style.* Simultaneous and photocopied submissions OK. Reports in 2-4 weeks. SASE. Free book catalog.

Nonfiction: Business and professional books with emphasis on all aspects of retaining, plus management and marketing. Query or submit outline/synopsis and sample chapters.
Recent Titles: *Retail Advertising: A Management Approach,* by R. J. Gentile; *Managing People: Techniques for Food Service Operators,* by N. R. Sweeney; *Food Purchasing,* by H. Kelly.

LES FEMMES PUBLISHING, 231 Adrian Rd., Millbrae CA 94030. Publisher: Ruth Kramer. Editor: Joycelyn Moulton. Publishes paperback originals. Offers standard royalty payment schedule of "5% to 7% of retail price." Published 10 titles last year. Nationwide distribution, plus distribution to most English-speaking countries. Free book catalog. Will consider photocopied submissions. Query first and submit outline and sample chapters. Must be typed, double spaced. Reports in 6 weeks. Enclose return postage.
Nonfiction and Fiction: Publishes "all subjects of interest to contemporary women, especially those conveying educational or self-help benefits." Will be needing material for the Everywoman's Guide Series. Must be concise, packed with information, presenting guides on subjects of interest to women. Would also like to see material about women in sports, menopause, biographies of famous women. Does not want to see anti-male material. Submit mss about the arts, sociology, sports, hobbies, and special interest material, such as health and history. "Some highly original fiction is possible, such as science fiction, satire, etc."

LESTER AND ORPEN LIMITED, PUBLISHERS, 42 Charles St. E., 8th floor, Toronto, Ontario M4Y 1T4, Canada. (416)961-1812. Editor-in-Chief: Malcolm Lester. Publishes hardcover and paperback originals and reprints. Offers standard minimum book contract of 10-12½-15%. Published 12 titles in 1976. Free book catalog. Will consider photocopied submissions. Query first with outline and one sample chapter showing style and treatment. Submit complete ms only if writer has been published before. Reports in 6 weeks. Enclose S.A.E. and International Reply Coupons.
General Fiction and Nonfiction: "Our basic philosophy of publishing only carefully selected books is stronger than ever; each and every title reflects a uniqueness in concept, careful and imaginative editing and design, and powerful and creative promotion. Our philosophy is that the book should be as long or as short as the subject warrants." Publishes adult trade fiction, biography, sociology, economics and philosophy.

*LIBRA PUBLISHERS, INC., 391 Willets Rd., Box 165, Roslyn Hts NY 11577. (516)484-4950. Hardcover and paperback originals. Specializes in the behavioral sciences. 10-15% royalty; no advance. Published 15 titles in 1976, 20 in 1977. Subsidy publishes a very small percentage of books (those which have obvious marketing problems or are too specialized). Simultaneous and photocopied submissions OK. Reports in 1-2 weeks. SASE. Free book catalog.
Nonfiction and Fiction: Mss in all subject areas will be given consideration, but main interest is in the behavioral sciences. Submit outline/synopsis and sample chapters.·
Recent Titles: *Emotional Aspects of Heart Disease,* by H. Gust, Ph.D.; *The Counseling Process: A Cognitive Behavioral Approach,* by J. Tembo, Ph.D.

LIBRARIES UNLIMITED, INC., Box 263, Littleton CO 80160. (303)770-1220. Editor-in-Chief: Bohdan S. Wynar. Hardcover and paperback originals (95%) and hardcover reprints (5%). Specializes in library science and reference books. 10% royalty; advance averages $500. Published 25 titles in 1976, 30 in 1977; will do 35 in 1978. Marketed by direct mail to 20,000 libraries in this country and abroad. Query or submit outline/synopsis and sample chapters. All prospective authors are required to fill out an author questionnaire. Make inquiry if photos/illustrations are to accompany ms. Reports in 2-4 months. SASE. Free book catalog.
Nonfiction: Publishes reference; textbooks, and library science books.
Recent Titles: *Library Management,* by R.D. Stueart and J. T. Eastlick (textbook); *Government Reference Books 74/75: A Biennial Guide to Government Publications,* by A. E. Schorr (reference); and *The Islamic Near East and North Africa: An Annotated Guide to Books in English for Non-Specialists,* by D. W. Littlefield (reference).

LIGUORI PUBLICATIONS, 1 Liguori Dr., Liguori MO 63057. (314)464-2500. Editor-in-Chief: Christopher Farrell. Managing Editor: David Polek. Paperback originals. Specializes in religion-oriented materials. 8% royalty; no advance. Published 24 titles in 1976, 24 in 1977; will do 24-30 in 1978. Query or submit outline/snyopsis and sample chapters. State availability of photos and/or illustrations. Photocopied submissions OK. Reports in 2-4 months. SASE. Free book catalog.
Nonfiction: Publishes (in order of preference) religious; self-help; juvenile (with religious tone or approach); and how-to (self-help, not mechanical) books.

Recent Titles: *The Spirit and Your Everyday Life,* by R. Chervin (religious); *Living & Loving: A Guide to a Happy Marriage,* by G. Lester (religious family); *How to Face Death Without Fear,* by N. Muckerman (self-help).

LINKS BOOKS, 33 W. 60th St., New York NY 10023. Editors: Jeanette Mall and Jeffrey Weiss. Publishes paperback originals. Published 20 titles in 1976. Query first with sample chapters. Enclose return postage.
Nonfiction: "We publish books we care about, books that will be sold in college bookstores and stores catering to other youth groups, including the counter-culture." Trade books on contemporary culture and society; practical and instructional books; photography and art books.

LION BOOKS, 111 E. 39th St., New York NY 10016. Editor-in-Chief: Harriet K. Ross. Offers royalty contract of 5 to 12½%, depending on subject matter. Advance ranges from $750 to $3,500. Published 17 titles last year. Marketed to trade, libraries and schools. Will send free catalog to writer on request. Will consider photocopied submissions. Submit complete ms. Reports in 4 weeks.
Nonfiction: Activity books, sports, government, biography, self-help, politics for the young reader, recreation, cookbooks; from writers who recognize the world of the young adult reader. "We look at varieties of subjects and choose." Recent titles include *The Care and Treatment of Young Athletes* and *Lost Gold,* the biography of Phyllis Wheatley.

J.B. LIPPINCOTT CO., (General Division), E. Washington Square, Philadelphia PA 19105. General Adult Book Editor: Edward L. Burlingame. Publishes hardcover and paperback originals and reprints. Standard royalty schedule. Published 228 titles last year. Will send catalog on request. Reports in 3 to 4 weeks. No unsolicited mss. Query first. Enclose return postage.
General: Publishes general nonfiction; also history, biography, nature, sports, the arts, adult fiction.

J.B. LIPPINCOTT CO., (Juvenile Division), 521 5th Ave., New York NY 10017. Editor-in-Chief, Books for Young Readers: Dorothy Briley. Publishes trade books for kindergarten through high school. Selected titles published simultaneously in paper and hardcover. Standard royalty schedule. Published 40 titles in 1976. Free book catalog. Reports in 8-10 weeks. Enclose return postage with ms.
Juveniles: Fiction and nonfiction. Current titles include *Trial Valley* (Cleavers); *The Golem* (McDermott).

LITTLE, BROWN AND COMPANY, 34 Beacon St., Boston MA 02106. Editor-in-Chief: Roger Donald. Publishes hardcover and paperback originals and reprints. Offers royalty contract. Published 103 titles in 1976, 92 in 1977. "Contracts for nonfiction offered on basis of an outline and 3 or 4 sample chapters." Reports in 6 weeks. Enclose return postage.
General: "Fiction and general nonfiction book-length mss."
Juveniles: "All ages." Editor of Children's Books: John G. Keller.

LIVING BOOKS, LTD., P.O. Box 593, Times Square Station, New York NY 10036. An affiliate of Diplomatic Press, Inc. Pays "the usual 10% of the published price in accordance with Author's Guild requirements." Advance varies, depending on author's reputation and nature of book. Send query first with outline and sample chapter to the Editor. Reports in 2 to 3 months. "Unsolicited mss are not returned, unless they are accompanied by S.A.S.E."
General: Publishes books in every field of human interest—adult fiction, history, biography, science, philosophy, the arts, religion, and general nonfiction. "List for fiction closed for the time being." Length: 65,000 to 125,000 words.

*LOGOS INTERNATIONAL, 201 Church St., Plainfield NJ 07060. (201)754-0745. Editor: Viola Malachuk. Publishes hardcover and paperback originals and reprints. Offers standard minimum book contract beginning at 10% in trade size. Does 1% to 2% subsidy publishing. Published 35 titles in 1976, 40 in 1977. Book catalog $1; free writer's guidelines. Will not consider photocopied submissions. Submit outline and sample chapters. Chicago *Manual of Style* preferred. "Specify class of mail desired for return of material." Reports in 2 months. Enclose S.A.E. and return postage.
Nonfiction and Fiction: Assistant Editors: Dennis Baker and Craig Lawson. Logos books are primarily written to propagate and inform the charismatic movement within the Christian church. They are typically evangelical in flavor; many are by Roman Catholic authors as well; some are Messianic Jews. Frequently the books are the stories, the testimonies, of leaders in the

charismatic movement; how they came to receive the Baptism of the Holy Spirit and experience the gifts of the Holy Spirit, like speaking in tongues, miracles, prophecy, etc. The first Logos book was a warning against spiritualism, seances, and the occult. The first bestseller was *Run, Baby, Run,* the story of a converted teenage gang leader, Nicky Cruz. The author must be a serious Christian who regards the Bible as authoritative; any attempt to approach this material apart from personal involvement will likely be judged unsuccessful. Especially interested in popular treatments of biblical prophecy, serious trends in discipleship, teaching for children, and biography testimony." Length: 25,000 to 500,000 words.
Recent Titles: *A New Command,* by G. Harris (biography); *Daughter of Destiny,* by J. Buckingham (biography); and *More of Jesus, Less of Me,* by S. Cavanaugh (weight control).

LOLLIPOP POWER, INC., Box 1171, Chapel Hill NC 27514. ()19)929-4857. Collective editorship. Paperback originals; experimenting on some hardcover titles. "We currently pay $100 per book, split between author and illustrator. Hope to increase payment or begin royalties eventually. Payment is made when work is completed, regardless of when book is actually published." No advance. Published 1 title in 1976, 1-2 in 1977. Photocopied submissions OK. Reports in 1-2 months. SASE. Free book catalog and information sheet for authors and illustrators.
Juveniles: Non-sexist, non-racist books for children; fiction and nonfiction. "Because commercial publishers are beginning to incorporate some of our goals into their books, we are now attempting to meet specific needs that continue to exist. We are seeking mss which include: 1) Strong female protagonists, especially Black, Spanish-American or native American girls or women. 2) Females who are struggling to change values and behavior. 3) Friendship and solidarity among girls and women. 4) Non-heterosexist values; e.g., children and lesbian mothers; early childhood sex education materials not limited to heterosexual relationships. 5) Non-traditional family situations; e.g., single mothers, extended families; several women living with children. And we are now especially interested in biographies for children." Submit complete ms for both fiction and nonfiction.
Recent Titles: *The Clever Princess,* by A. Tompert (juvenile picture book).

LONGMAN CANADA LTD., 55 Barber Greene Rd., Don Mills, Ont., M3C 2A1 Canada. (416)444-7331. Query on general nonfiction and science; completed mss preferred in all other categories. Do not need to include return postage. Does return mss and respond to queries.
Fiction: Publishes adult fiction. Fiction mss should run 80,000 words or more.
Nonfiction: History (Canadian preferred), biography (lives of Canadians preferred), popular science, general nonfiction.
Textbooks: Textbooks on all levels.

LOTHROP, LEE & SHEPARD CO., 105 Madison Ave., New York NY 10016. (212)889-3050. Editor-in-Chief: Edna Barth. Hardcover originals. Royalty and advance vary according to type of book. Published 38 titles in 1976, 40 in 1977; will do 40 in 1978. State availability of photos and/or illustrations to accompany ms. Photocopied submissions OK, but originals preferred. Reports in 4-6 weeks. SASE. Free book catalog.
Juveniles: Publishes biography; cooking, cookbooks and foods; history; hobbies; music; poetry; self-help; and sports books. Submit outline/synopsis and sample chapters for nonfiction. Juvenile fiction includes adventure, fantasy, historical, humorous, mystery, science fiction, suspense and contemporary novels. Submit complete ms. for fiction.
Special Needs: "A series we are trying to build is the Fun-To-Read series."
Recent Titles: *Wharton and Morton,* by R. E. Erikson (fantasy); *Detective Mole,* by R. Quackenbush (easy reading); *Bitter Herbs and Honey,* by B. Cohen (novel).

ROBERT B. LUCE, INC., 2000 N St., N.W., Washington D.C. 20036. (202)296-2690. Offers standard 10-12½-15% royalty contract. Published 8 titles in 1976. Free book catalog. Address mss to assistant editor. Submit outline and sample chapter. Reports in 4 weeks. Enclose return postage.
Nonfiction and Fiction: "Books must be authoritative, informative, and written in plain language for the popular audience. Mss should be 60,000 words minimum. General nonfiction: current affairs, how-to-do-it, self-help, controversial subjects. History and biography. Public affairs and social problems. Popular science. Publishes limited fictional works."
Recent Titles: *The Zeal of the Convert,* by B. Wilkinson (biography); *A Plague on Both Your Houses,* by R. Whitaker (history); and *Developing Your Latent Powers,* by F. Gould (psychology).

McCLELLAND AND STEWART LTD., 25 Hollinger Rd., Toronto, Ontario, Canada M4B 3G2. Editor-in-Chief: Anna Porter. Publishes hardcover and paperback originals. Offers sliding scale of royalty on copies sold. Advance varies. Published 105 titles in 1976, 110 in 1977. Free book catalog. Submit outline and sample chapters for nonfiction. Submit complete ms for fiction. Reports in 6 weeks, average. Enclose S.A.E. and International Reply Coupons.
Nonfiction, Poetry and Fiction: Publishes "Canadian fiction and poetry. Nonfiction in the humanities and social sciences, with emphasis on Canadian concerns. Coffee-table books on art, architecture, sculpture and Canadian history." Will also consider adult trade fiction, biography, cookbooks, cooking and foods, history, nature, photography, politics, sociology, textbooks.

McCORMICK-MATHERS PUBLISHING CO., 450 W. 33rd St., New York NY 10001. Executive Vice-President: Anthony J. Quaglia. Publishes paperback originals. Contract negotiated by flat fee. Published 50 titles last year. Will send catalog to writer on request. Will consider photocopied submissions. Submit outline and sample chapters. Reports as soon as possible. Enclose return postage.
Textbooks and Fiction: El-hi textbooks and action fiction within the el-hi age level from short stories to novellas; rural, suburban, city and inner city subject matter; school situations, inter-peer relationships, inter-family situations. Prefers third-person narrative without flashbacks. Value based in outlook, with strong emphasis on ethical good over ethical evil. "Our books are geared primarily to students with reading difficulties who have not profited from traditional reading instructions. We rewrite submitted material."

MCDONALD PUBLISHING HOUSE, INC., 125 Davenport Rd., Toronto, Ontario Canada M5R 7H8. Editor: Daniel McDonald. Publishes originals. "Our contract is the usual publisher's royalty deal. We do offer special royalty where it is warranted." Published 8 titles last year. Will send free catalog to writer on request. Query first and submit outline and sample chapters. Reports immediately. Enclose return postage.
Fiction and Nonfiction: Adult trade fiction, juveniles, law and multimedia material. General publishing, must be Canadian material by Canadians. Interested in material of an educational nature. "More interested in a creative manuscript than formula writing. Please send outline of material and letter." Recent titles include *If I Tell You, Will I Feel Less Scared?* (Sass), dealing with the problems of children in school who are branded "special."

McGRAW-HILL BOOK CO., 1221 Ave. of the Americas, New York NY 10020. Editor-in-Chief: Fred Hills. Hardcover and paperback originals, reprints, translations and anthologies. 10-12½-15% royalty. Submit outline and sample chapter; unsolicited mss rarely accepted. Reports in 3 weeks. SASE.
Professional and Reference: Publishes books for engineers, scientists, and business people who need information on the professional level. Some of these books also find use in college and technical institute courses. This Division also publishes multi-volume encyclopedias (which are usually staff-prepared using work from outside contributors who are specialists in their fields) and one-volume encyclopedias prepared by experts in a given field. The professional books are usually written by graduate engineers or scientists or business people (such as accountants, lawyers, stockbrokers, etc.) Authors of the professional books are expected to be highly qualified in their field. Such qualifications are the result of education and experience in the field; these qualifications are prerequisite for authorship. The multi-volume encyclopedias rarely accept contributions from freelancers because the above education and experience qualifications are also necessary. Single-volume encyclopedias are usually prepared by subject specialists; again freelancers are seldom used unless they have the necessary experience and educational background. Technical and Scientific Book Editor: Tyler G. Hicks; Multi-volume Encyclopedia Editor: Daniel N. Lapedes; Single-volume Encyclopedia Editor: Robert A. Rosenbaum; Business Editor: William H. Mogan; Engineering Editor: Jeremy Robinson; Handbook Editor: Harold B. Crawford.
College Textbooks: The College Division publishes textbooks. The writer must know the college curriculum and course structure. Also publishes scientific texts and reference books in business, economics, engineering, social sciences, physical sciences, mathematics, medicine and nursing. Material should be scientifically and factually accurate. Most, but not all, books should be designed for existing courses offered in various disciplines of study. Books should have superior presentations and be more up-to-date than existing textbooks. Department Publishers: Howard S. Aksen, Business, Economics and Engineering; Joseph J. Brehm, Medicine and Nursing; Bradford Bayne, Science and Mathematics.

High School and Vocational Textbooks: The Gregg Division publishes instructional materials in two main areas, business and office education (accounting, data processing, business communication, business law, business mathematics and machines, management and supervision, secretarial and clerical, records management, shorthand, typing) and career and vocational education (career development, marketing and distribution, public and personal services, applied arts and sciences, technical and industrial education, consumer education, health occupations, and agribusiness). Materials must be accurate, with clearly stated objectives, and should reflect a structuring of technical and interpersonal skills which mesh with both career clustering and course content. A. J. Lemaster, Dditor-in-Chief, Shorthand. E. E. Byers, Editor-in-Chief, Business Management, and Office Education; A. M. Hall, Editor-in-Chief, Accounting, Computing, and Data Processing; P. Voiles, Editor-in-Chief, Typing, Communications, and Record Management; W. A. Sabin, Publisher, Business and Office Education; D. E. Hepler, Editor-in-Chief, Trade and Technical Education; C. O'Keefe, Editor-in-Chief, Career Education.

DAVID McKAY COMPANY, INC., 750 Third Ave., New York NY 10017. Manager, General Book Division: Alan Tucker. Offers standard royalty contract. Query first or submit outline and sample chapter. Reports in about 3 weeks. Enclose return postage.
Nonfiction, Fiction and Juveniles: Nonfiction on themes of human behavior, popular history, social commentary, etc. How-to books on gardening, hobbies, horses, the outdoors, games and cookbooks; books by experts. Mysteries. Mature nonfiction and fiction for young adults. Manager, Juvenile Division: Alexander Whitney.

MACMILLAN COMPANY OF CANADA, LTD., 70 Bond St., Toronto, Ont., Canada M5B 1X3. Trade Editor: D. M. Gibson. Published 25 titles last year. Payment by arrangement. Essential to query first. Unsolicited trade mss not accepted. Reports in 6 weeks. Enclose S.A.E. and International Reply Coupons.
General: Publishes Canadian books of all kinds. Biography, history, art, current affairs, juveniles, poetry and fiction.
Textbooks: Educational Editor: Gladys Neale.
Scientific and Technical: College, Medical, Nursing Editor: Virgil Duff.
Recent Titles: *On Canada, (Volume 2),* by J. G. Defenbaker (political memoirs); and *The Luck of the Irish: A Canadian Fable,* by H. Boyle (fiction).

MACMILLAN PUBLISHING COMPANY, INC., 866 Third Ave., New York NY 10022. Publishes hardcover and paperback originals and reprints. Will consider photocopied submissions. Send query letter before sending ms. Address all mss except juveniles to Trade Editorial Department; children's books to Children's Book Department. Enclose return postage.
Fiction and Nonfiction: Publishes adult fiction and nonfiction. Length: at least 75,000 words.
Juveniles: Children's books.

MACRAE SMITH COMPANY, 225 S. 15th St., Philadelphia PA 19102. Pays 10% of list price. Published 12 titles last year. Will send a catalog on request. Send outline and sample chapters or complete ms and letter reviewing relevant background and experience of author. Address mss to Ruth Allan Miner. Reports in 4 to 6 weeks. Enclose return postage.
General: "Adult trade books, fiction nd nonfiction. Current issues and topical concerns, adventure, mysteries and gothics, history and science, biography."
Juveniles: For nonfiction books, interested in "biographies, history of world cultures, impact of the sciences on human affairs, cultural anthropology, scientific and medical discoveries, ecology, current social concerns and theory, peace research, international cooperation and world order, controversial issues, sports. Future-oriented subjects. For all ages, but prefer 8 to 12 and junior and senior high school." Also buys adventure stories, mysteries, history and science, biography, and girls' fiction. "We have found several of our best authors by reading manuscripts they submitted for themselves. What we want most now is good fiction for girls, middle-elementary age through high school. One word of caution: we look first at writing quality!" Length: 40,000 to 60,000 words.

MADRONA PRESS, INC., Box 3750, Austin TX 78764. (512)327-2683. Editor-in-Chief: Vance Muse. Hardcover and paperback originals. 10% royalty. No advance. Published 5 titles in 1976, 6 in 1977; will do 6 in 1978. Markets heavily by direct mail, as well as book store distribution. Query. State availability of photos/illustrations. Simultaneous and photocopied submissions OK. Reports in 1-2 months. SASE. Book catalog for SASE.
Nonfiction: Americana; art; biography; history; humor; and photography books. "All titles deal with American West, Southwest, and Mexico."

Fiction: Publishes adventure, and historical books. "Must deal in market area."

Special Needs: "We do plan new paperback titles, which simply means we'll be looking for, and hopefully publishing, more books."

Recent Titles: *Chronicles of the Big Bend,* by W. D. Smithers (historical/photography); *Song of the Pedernales,* by J. L. Mortimer (historical novel); and *Bedrock,* by Cauthron and Smith (photography).

MAINE ELVES PRESS, INC., Box 249, Rockport ME 04856. Editor-in-Chief: Julie A. Bragdon. Hardcover and paperback originals. 10-12½-15% royalty. Advance varies, depending on projected sales, generally between $500-1,000. Published 4 titles in 1977; will do 6 in 1978. "We do our own marketing. We go directly to the markets ourselves, sometimes through advertising in magazines; more likely to bookstores and specialty stores." State availability of photos to illustrate ms. Reports in 1-2 months. SASE.

Nonfiction: Publishes how-to, biography, sociology and books on politics. Query. Address it to proper department (How-to Department, Biography Department, etc.).

Special Needs: "We're looking for books that appeal to young people especially. Humor is important in the books we publish."

Recent Titles: *30 Easy Pieces of Furniture* (Made by Elves That You Can Make, Too), by M. P. Boshnack and E. M. Schoon (how-to); *Another 30 Pieces* (a sequel), by M. P. Boshnack.

MAJOR BOOKS, 21335 Roscoe Blvd., Canoga Park CA 91304. (213)999-4100. Editor-in-Chief: Harold Straubing. Managing Editor: John Mitchell. aperback originals (75%) and reprints (15%). 4-6% royalty, breaking at 150M sales mark; average advance of $750-1,000, depending on subject matter of book and literary quality. Published 96 titles in 1976, 100 in 1977; will do 100 in 1978. Submit outline/synopsis and sample chapters or complete ms. Send contact sheets or photos with submissions. Reports in 1-2 months. SASE. Book catalog for SASE.

Nonfiction: John Mitchell, senior editor. Publishes biography; cookbooks, cooking and foods; erotica; how-to; humor; law; pets; politics; self-help; and sports books. No avant-garde material.

Fiction: Yvonne MacManus, senior editor. Publishes adventure, erotica, historical, mystery, romance, science fiction, suspense, and western books.

Recent Titles: *I-Boat Captain,* by Z. Orita and J. Harrington (war); *Rudy Vallee Kisses and Tells,* by R. Vallee (biography); and *Bloody Sundown,* by C. G. Muller (western).

MANOR BOOKS, INC., 432 Park Ave., S., New York NY 10016. (212)686-9100. Editor-in-Chief: William S. Ruben. Publishes hardcover and paperback originals and reprints. Offers standard minimum book contract on hardcover books; other contracts negotiated. Advance varies. Published 200 titles in 1976, 225 in 1977. Free book catalog. Query first to M. Silverman, Managing Editor, for nonfiction and fiction. No unsolicited mss. Reports in 4 to 6 weeks. Enclose return postage.

Nonfiction and Fiction: For adults. Adult trade fiction (gothics, westerns, science fiction). Biography, cookbooks, cooking and foods, history, humor, music, nature, politics, self-help and how-to, sociology, sports, hobbies, recreation and pets, and travel. Length: 55,000 to 70,000 words.

*MANYLAND BOOKS, INC., 84-39 90th St., Woodhaven NY 11421. Editor-in-Chief: Stepas Zobarskas. Publishes hardcover and paperback originals. Offers 5-10-12½-15% royalty contract; average advance, $250 to $500. About 25% of books are subsidy published. Published 6 titles last year. Will consider photocopied submissions. Submit complete ms. Reports in 6 or 8 weeks. Enclose return postage with ms.

Fiction, Nonfiction, Poetry, and Juveniles: "Manyland is concerned primarily with the literature of the lesser known countries. It has already published a score of novels, collections of short stories, folk tales, juvenile books, works of poetry, essays, and historical studies. Most of the publications have more than local interest. Their content and value transcend natural boundaries. They have universal appeal. We are interested in both new and established writers. We will consider any subject as long as it is well-written. No length requirements. We are especially interested in memoirs, biographies, anthologies." Current titles include *The World of Miss Universe* (Cumba); *Fighters for Freedom, Lithuanian Partisans Versus the U.S.S.R.* (Daumantas).

MASON/CHARTER PUBLISHERS, INC., 641 Lexington Ave., New York NY 10022. Editor-in-Chief: Margaret B. Parkinson. Publishes hardcover and paperback originals and hardcover imports. Offers standard minimum book contract of 10-12½-15%. Published 51 titles in

1976, 41 in 1977. No photocopies or simultaneous submissions. Query first. Reports in 2 months. Enclose return postage.
General Trade: Fiction; mainstream, gothic, romance, suspense. Biography, business, history, self-help and how-to, sociology, sports, technical (data processing only), textbooks.
Recent Titles: *Hamilton I & II,* by R. Hendrickson (nonfiction); *Tempestous Peticoat,* by M. A. Gibbs (fiction); and *Search for the Gold of King Tut,* by A. Brackman (nonfiction).

*MASTERCO PRESS, INC., Box 382, Ann Arbor MI 48107. (313)428-8300. Editor-in-Chief: T. S. Roberts. Hardcover and paperback originals. Specializes in books on management. "Payment primarily by royalty;" no advance. Will consider subsidy publishing based on cost and risk. Publishes about 1 title annually. Simultaneous and photocopied submissions OK. SASE. Free book catalog.
Nonfiction: Publishes books on business and economics. Query or submit outline/synopsis and sample chapters.
Recent Titles: *MBO in Mental Health Organizations,* by O. R. Wiethe; *Cost Effective Decision Making,* by R. Pearson.

MASTER'S PRESS, INC., 20 Mills St., Kalamazoo MI 49001. Editor-in-Chief: Earl O. Roe. Paperback originals and reprints. Standard royalty contract. Negotiable advance. Query first for nonfiction; submit outline/synopsis and sample chapters for fiction. Simultaneous submissions OK. Reports in 30-90 days. SASE. Free book catalog.
Nonfiction: "We publish 2 book lines: 1) a small book line using mss of about 15,000 words and 2) a trade-size line requiring mss of 30,000-40,000 words. Within these size ranges, we consider a variety of mss: biography, devotional, inspirational material, Bible studies, both book studies and topical studies; prayer, basic Christian truths (amplified and applied); practical Christian living; contemporary problems and issues viewed from an evangelical perspective; books for juveniles. Writers should avoid a textbook approach to their material and steer clear of technical language or jargon. All materials should express a definite, distinct Christian message and should reflect the evangelical orientation of the company and its constituency. But any emphasis of denominational distinction should be avoided. We use the University of Chicago Press *Manual of Style* and our own style manual."
Recent Titles: *Any Christian Can,* by R. Dunn (religious); *Just Dying to Live,* by J. Hylton (religious).

*MEDCO BOOKS, 1640 S. La Cienega Blvd., Los Angeles CA 90035. Editor-in-Chief: Gil Porter. Hardcover and paperback originals. Specializes "primarily in sex, health, wealth topics, popular medicine such as dealing with diabetes, weight, arthritis, etc." Pays $500-1,500 for outright purchase; advance averages 1/3-½ on contract, balance on acceptance. Subsidy publishes 1% of books. Subsidy publishing offered "if writer has a viable means of selling his book himself, such as personality with media access, etc. We charge our cost plus about 20% for each step of production as a working average." Published 7 titles in 1976. Query. Send prints if photos are to accompany ms. Simultaneous submissions OK. Reports in 1-2 weeks. SASE.
Nonfiction: Publishes erotica; how-to; medicine and psychiatry; pets; and self-help books.
Recent Titles: *Questions and Answers About Diabetes,* by J. Biermann (health); *The Book of Love and Sex,* by Corey (marriage); and *How to Make the Stock Market Make Money,* by Warren (finance).

MEDICAL EXAMINATION PUBLISHING COMPANY, INC., 65-36 Fresh Meadow Lane, Flushing NY 11365. Royalty schedule is negotiable. Will send catalog on request. Send outlines to editor. Reports in 1 month. Enclose return postage.
Medical: Medical texts and medical review books; monographs and training material for the medical and paramedical professions.

*MEMPHIS STATE UNIVERSITY PRESS, Memphis State University, Memphis TN 38152. (901)454-2752. Editor-in-Chief: James D. Simmons. Publishes hardcover and paperback originals and reprints. Offers 10% "unless an exceptional book. Each contract is subject to negotiation. We prefer not to offer an advance." Does about 10% subsidy publishing. "We don't ask a subsidy from the author and do not make subsidy contracts with authors. We do make an effort to obtain outside (other than University) money to assist books which have an identifiable source of public support; associations, commissions, museums and galleries, and the like." Published 7 titles in 1976, 8 in 1977. Free book catalog and writer's guidelines. Will consider photocopied submissions. Query first. Reports in 3 to 6 months. Enclose S.A.S.E.
General Nonfiction: Americana Editor: James D. Simmons; History Editor: Nancy Hurley.

"We publish scholarly nonfiction, books in the humanities, social sciences, and regional material. Interested in nonfiction material within the Mississippi River valley. Tennessee history, contemporary philosophy, modern literature criticism, and regional folklore."
Recent Titles: *Life in the Leatherwoods,* by J. Q. Wolf (regional folklore); *A Radical View,* by J. G. Smart, and *Vision of the Voyage,* R. L. Combs (literary criticism).

ARTHUR MERIWETHER, INC., Box 457, 921 Curtiss St., Downers Grove IL 60515. Editor-in-Chief: Arthur L. Zapel, Jr. Publishes paperback originals. Royalty contract of 10%. Advance by individual negotiation. Marketed by direct mail. Book catalog 25¢. Editorial guidelines also available. Query first. "Do not send ms until after query response from us." Reports in 1 month. Enclose return postage.
Education: Mss for educational use in schools and churches. Mss for business and staff training on subjects related to business communications and advertising. Religious, self-help and how-to, sociology, humor and books on economics are also published.
Drama: Plays on the same subjects as above.

CHARLES E. MERRILL PUBLISHING CO., a Bell & Howell Co., 1300 Alum Creek Dr., Columbus OH 43216. Publishes hardcover and paperback originals. Payment is on acceptance or on a royalty basis. "Our textbooks generally offer 6% at elementary school level; 8% at secondary school level; 10% to 15% at college level. Published 286 titles in 1976. Send brief outline and sample chapter. Reports in 4 to 12 weeks. Enclose return postage.
Textbooks: Education Division publishes texts, workbooks, instructional tapes, overhead projection transparencies and programmed materials for elementary and high schools in all subject areas, primarily language arts and literature, mathematics, science and social studies (no juvenile stories or novels). The College Division publishes texts and instructional tapes in all college areas, specializing in education, business and economics, math, technology, science, and speech. Editor-in-Chief, Educational Division: Buzz Ellis; Editor, College Division: John Buterbaugh.

JULIAN MESSNER (Simon & Schuster Division of Gulf & Western Corp.), 1230 Avenue of the Americas, New York NY 10020. Senior editor for elementary grades: Ms. Lee M. Hoffman. Senior editor for junior and senior high school: Iris Rosoff. Hardcover originals. Royalty varies. Advance averages $1,500. Published 34 titles in 1976, 38 in 1977. State availability of photos and/or illustrations to accompany ms. Simultaneous submissions OK from established authors who may propose two or more book ideas they would like to work on. Reports in 1-2 months. SASE. Free book catalog.
Juveniles: Nonfiction books for young people. Submit outline/synopsis and sample chapters.
Recent Titles: *Katydids: The Singing Insects,* by B. Ford (science); *All the Better to Bite With,* by H. Doss (science); *Eskimos of the World,* by P. M. Elliott (social studies).

MILITARY MARKETING SERVICES, INC., P.O. Box 4010, Arlington VA 22204. President: Mrs. Ann Crawford. Publishes originals. "Usually purchase books outright. Royalties are negotiable if outright purchase is not made. Advance is also negotiable." Published 1 title last year. Query first or submit complete ms. Enclose return postage.
Nonfiction: "Information-type books for military families. Books which show the military family, active or retired, how to save money are needed. Also, books explaining reservist and retiree benefits as well as books on military family travel, will be given special consideration. We're looking for more titles which will help make the military family's life easier and more enjoyable." Length: open.

*MIMIR PUBLISHERS, INC., Box 5011, Madison WI 53705. Editor-in-Chief: Henry H. Bakken. Hardcover and paperback originals. Specializes in books in the social sciences at college level. 15% royalty, "but nearly all titles are determined on a special contract." No advance. Subsidy publishes 50% of books. Subsidy publishing is offered "if the author wishes to proceed on our 50/50 type contract and share in the proceeds. Under this contract the author gets all the proceeds until he recovers his venture capital." Published 4 titles in 1976, 5 in 1977. Query or submit complete ms. Simultaneous ("if indicated") and photocopied submissions OK. Reports in 2-4 months. SASE. Free book catalog.
Nonfiction: Publishes Americana; biography (limited); business; economics; history; law; philosophy; politics; sociology; and textbooks.
Recent Titles: *Mavericks in American Politics,* by E. N. Kearny (political history); *The Wisconsin Income Tax Guide,* by Bower; and *The Hills of Home: A Family History,* by H. H. Bakken.

MITCHELL PRESS LIMITED, Box 6000, Vancouver, B.C. Canada V6B 4B9. Editor-in-Chief: Howard T. Mitchell. Paperback originals. Specializes in travel and Canadian history books. 10% royalty; no advance. Published 4 titles in 1976, 6 in 1977; will do 6 in 1978. Photocopied submissions OK. Reports in 3 months. SASE. Free book catalog.
Nonfiction: Publishes business; history; self-help; sports; and travel books. Query.
Recent Titles: *The Woodwards: a family story of ventures and traditions,* by D. E. Harker; *Fly Fish the Trout Lakes,* by J. Shaw; and *The Strongest Man in History: Louis Cyr,* by B. Weider.

*MODERN BOOKS AND CRAFTS, INC., Box 38, Greens Farms CT 06436. Editor-in-Chief: Robert Paul. Publishes paperback originals and hardcover reprints. 10% royalty; no advance. Subsidy publishes a minimal percentage of books. "We do this only if author is unknown in the field." Published 2 titles in 1976, 3 in 1977; will do 3 in 1978. Photocopied submissions OK. Reports in 1-2 weeks. SASE.
Nonfiction: Publishes erotica, hobbies, and psychology books.
Recent Titles: *Collector's Handbook to Marks on Porcelain and Pottery,* edited by E. Paul and A. Petersen; *Dictionary of American Painters, Sculptors and Engravers,* by M. Fielding.

MODERN CURRICULUM PRESS, INC., 13900 Prospect Rd., Cleveland OH 44136. (216)238-6901. Managing Editor: Barbara K. York. Hardcover and paperback originals. 4% royalty; no advance. Published 24 titles in 1976, 28 in 1977; will do 35 in 1978. Query or submit outline/synopsis and sample chapters. Simultaneous and photocopied submissions OK. Reports in 2-4 weeks. SASE. Free book catalog.
Nonfiction: Educational textbooks and workbooks.

MONARCH PUBLISHING CO., INC., 222 Mamaroneck Ave., White Plains NY 10605. Editor-in-Chief: Kathy Nelson. Publishes hardcover originals. Offers $200 royalty contract, with 2-part payment. Published 35 titles last year. Guidelines furnished on assignment. Enclose return postage.
History and Religion: Limited color editions for church, town, city and county histories. "Generally in conjunction with a major anniversary or dedication." Current titles include *Our Heritage: A History of East Providence, R.I.* and *The History of St. Joseph's Church, Le Mars, Iowa.*

MONITOR BOOK COMPANY, INC., 195 S. Beverly Dr., Beverly Hills CA 90212. (213)271-5558. Editor-in-Chief: Alan F. Pater. Hardcover originals. 10% minimum royalty; also outright purchase, depending on circumstances. No advance. Published 11 titles in 1976, 10 in 1977. Send prints if photos and/or illustrations are to accompany ms. Reports in 2-4 months. SASE. Book catalog for SASE.
Nonfiction: Publishes Americana, biographies (only of vell-known personalities); law and reference books.
Recent Titles: *What They Said in 1976: The Yearbook of Spoken Opinion* (current quotations).

MONTHLY REVIEW PRESS, 62 West 14th St., New York NY 10011. Director: Harry Braverman. Royalty schedule. Published 40 titles last year. Current catalog available on request. Send query letter, table of contents and two sample chapters; enclose return postage. Reports in 1 to 3 months.
Economics, History, and Politics: Publishes books on history, economics, political science, world events. Books should reflect or be compatible with the socialist point of view on world problems.

MOODY PRESS, 820 North LaSalle St., Chicago IL 60610. (312)329-4337. Editor: Leslie H. Stobbe. Publishes hardcover and paperback originals. Royalty schedule is usually 10% of the retail. No advance. Published 80 titles in 1976. Send query with outline and sample chapters. Reports within 3 months. Enclose return postage.
Religion: Publishes books that are definitely Christian in content. Christian education, Christian living, inspirational, theology, missions and missionaries, pastors' helps. Conservative theological position. Clothbound between 45,000 and 60,000 words.
Fiction: Adult; mostly paperback. Length: 25,000 to 40,000 words.
Juveniles: Fiction; mostly paperback. Length: 25,000 to 40,000 words.
Recent Titles: *Failure: The Back Door to Success,* by E. Lutzer (inspirational); *Live Like a King,* by W. Wiersbe (Bible Study); and *In His Steps Today,* by M. Hefley (fiction).

*MOREHOUSE-BARLOW CO., INC., 78 Danbury Rd., Wilton CT 06897. Editor-in-Chief: Margaret L. Sheriff. Hardcover and paperback originals (75%); hardback and paperback reprints (25%). 10% royalty; advance varies. "Subsidy publishing done only in very special cases. We do not encourage subsidy publishing." Published 30 titles in 1976 and 1977. Query first. State availability of photos and/or illustrations to accompany ms. Simultaneous and photocopied submissions OK. Reports in 1-2 months. SASE. Free book catalog.
Nonfiction: Publishes art, how-to, juveniles, and religious books.
Fiction: Only religious material will be considered.
Recent Titles: *The Spirit of God,* by T. Hopko (religious); *The Banner Book,* by B. Wolf (arts and crafts); *Winding Quest,* by A. T. Dale (Old Testament).

MORGAN & MORGAN, INC., 145 Palisade St., Dobbs Ferry NY 10522. Editor-in-Chief: Douglas O. Morgan. Publishes hardcover and paperback originals and reprints. Offers 10% of net sales. No advance. Published 15 titles last year. Will send free catalog to writer on request. Submit outline and sample chapters. Reports "immediately." Enclose S.A.E. and return postage.
Photography: Books on all phases of photography. "We want to see an outline on what the book is about; various chapter headings; and how this material will be covered in various chapters. Would like one chapter in its entirety so that we could better grasp the method of approach in writing and also would like to have writer's reasons why he feels this book would have a good sale potential. We feel that our books go into greater detail on the particular subject and reasons why the book is relevant to the person looking for help in that field. We're looking for mss dealing with the how-to side of photography aimed at the amateur market and the more serious amateur photographer." Length depends on book.

WILLIAM MORROW AND CO., 105 Madison Ave., New York NY 10016. Editor: John C. Willey. Payment is on standard royalty basis. Published 175 titles last year. Query on all books. No unsolicited mss. Address to specific department. Reports in 4 weeks. Enclose return postage.
General: Publishes fiction, nonfiction, history, biography, arts, religion, poetry, how-to books, and cookbooks, all high-quality. Length: 50,000 to 100,000 words.
Juveniles: Juvenile Editor: Connie C. Epstein.

MOTORBOOKS INTERNATIONAL, INC., Box 2, Osceola WI 54020. (715)294-3345. Editor-in-Chief: William F. Kosfeld. Hardcover and paperback originals. Specializes in automotive literature. Escalating royalty begins at "10% retail on each copy; 10% gross where books sold at unusually large discount such as foreign rights sales. Advance depends on reputation of author and the work being considered." Published 4 titles in 1976, 5-6 in 1977; will do 5-6 in 1978. Also markets books through mail order subsidiary. State availability of photos and/or illustrations and include a few photocopied samples. Photocopied submissions OK. Reports in 1-2 months. SASE. Free book catalog.
Nonfiction: Publishes automotive literature written for serious car enthusiasts (histories, biographies, photographic works). Prefers not to see anything on extremely "narrow" topics that would be more suitable for magazine articles.
Recent Titles: *Chrysler & Imperial: The Postwar Years,* by R. Langworth; *Make Money Owning Your Car,* by J. Olson and *Gurney's Eagles,* by K. Ludvigsen.

MOTT MEDIA, Box 236, 305 Caroline, Milford MI 48042. Editor: Diane Zimmerman. Hardcover and paperback originals (90%) and paperback reprints (10%). Specializes in religious books, including trade and textbooks. 7% base royalty with sliding scale for mass sales; usually offers advance, "varies with experience." Published 20 titles in 1976, 25-30 in 1977; will do 30-35 in 1978. Query for fiction and nonfiction or submit outline/synopsis and sample chapters for nonfiction, complete ms for fiction. "Request advance information form with query, return completed form with ms or synopsis." Photocopied submissions OK. Reports in 2-4 months. SASE. Free book catalog.
Nonfiction: Publishes Americana (religious slant); biography (for juveniles on famous Christians, adventure-filled; for adults on Christian people, scholarly, new slant for marketing); how-to (for pastors, Christian laymen); juvenile (biographies, 30,000-40,000 words); politics (conservative, Christian approach); religious (conservative Christian); self-help (religious); and textbooks (all levels from a Christian perspective, all subject fields). No preschool materials or early elementary stories.
Fiction: Publishes adventure; fantasy; historical; and religious. Main emphasis of all mss must be religious.

Recent Titles: *Economics: Principles and Policy; A Christian Perspective,* by T. Rose (college text); *Johannes Kepler: Giant of Faith and Science,* by J. Tiner (juvenile biography); *Pathways for the Poet: Poetry Forms Explained and Illustrated,* by Berg (text-sourcebook).

*MOUNTAIN PRESS PUBLISHING CO., 279 W. Front, Missoula MT 59801. Publisher: David P. Flaccus. Hardcover and paperback originals (90%) and reprints (10%). Royalty of 10% of net amount received; no advance. Subsidy publishes less than 5% of books. "Top quality work in very limited market only." Published 6 titles in 1976, 9 in 1977; will do 10 in 1978. State availability of photos and/or illustrations to accompany ms. Simultaneous submissions OK. Reports in 2-4 weeks. SASE. Free book catalog.
Nonfiction: Publishes history (regional Northwest); hobbies, how-to (angling, hunting); medicine and psychiatry (coronary care and critical care); nature (geology, habitat and conservation); outdoor recreation (backpacking, fishing, etc.); technical (wood design and technology); and textbooks.
Recent Titles: *Roadside Geology of Northern California,* by Alt and Hyndman; *Challenge of the Trout,* by G. J. LaFontaine.

MULTIMEDIA PUBLISHING CORP. (affiliates: Steinerbooks, Rudolf Steiner Publications, Biograf Books), 100 South Western Highway, Blauvelt NY 10913. (914)359-5537. Editor: Paul M. Allen. Publishes paperback originals and reprints. 5% to 7% royalty; average advance, $300. Published 12 titles in 1976, 16 in 1977. Free book catalog. Query first with outline and sample chapters for nonfiction. Will consider photocopied submissions. Reports on ms accepted for publication in 60 days. Returns rejected material in 3 weeks. Enclose return postage.
Nonfiction: "Spiritual sciences, occult, philosophical, metaphysical, E.S.P. These are for our Steiner books division only. Scholarly and serious nonfiction. How-to-do or make books using our patented format of Biograf Books. Examples: origami, breadbaking, calendar. We prefer not to see any more Tarot or religious books." Department Editor, Multimedia Materials and Self-Help: Beatrice Garber; Department Editor, Philosophy and Spiritual Sciences: Paul M. Allen.

MUSEUM OF NEW MEXICO PRESS, Box 2087, Santa Fe NM 87503. (505)827-2352. Editor-in-Chief: Richard L. Polese. Hardcover and paperback originals (90%) and reprints (10%). Royalty of 10% of list after first 1,000 copies; no advance. Published 4 titles in 1976; 6-7 in 1977; will do 9-10 in 1978. Prints preferred for illustrations; transparencies best for color. Sources of photos or illustrations should be indicated for each. Simultaneous and photocopied submissions OK. Submit complete mss, addressed to Richard L. Polese, Editor. Mss should be typed double-spaced, follow Chicago *Manual of Style* and *Words Into Type,* and be accompanied by information about the author's credentials and professional position. Reports in 1-2 months. SASE. Free book catalog.
Nonfiction: "We publish both popular and scholarly books in anthropology, history, fine and folk arts; geography, natural history, the Americas and the Southwest; regional cookbooks; some children's and foreign language books." Art, biography (regional and Southwest); hobbies, how-to, music, nature, photography, reference, scientific, technical and travel.
Fiction: Historical, humorous (regional) and other regional (New Mexico/Southwest) fiction.
Recent Titles: *The Malaspina Expedition: In the Pursuit of Knowledge,* by M. Weber (history, art, anthropology) and *Pueblo Pottery of New Mexico,* by B. Toulouse (art, art history).

THE NAIAD PRESS, INC., Box 5025, Washington Sta., Reno NV 89513. (816)633-4136. Editor-in-Chief: Barbara Grier. Paperback originals. Specializes in Lesbian feminist material. "No royalty. We split profits on a percentage basis;" no advance. Published 4 titles in 1976, 2 in 1977; will do 3-4 in 1978. Reports in 2-4 weeks. SASE. Book catalog for SASE.
Fiction: "We are looking for quality romantic fiction on Lesbian/feminist themes." Query. If response is favorable, sample chapters are requested.
Current Titles: *Speak Out, My Heart,* by S. Jordan; *The Latecomer,* by S. Aldridge.

NATIONAL TEXTBOOK COMPANY, 8259 Niles Center Rd., Skokie IL 60076. Editorial Director: Leonard I. Fiddle. Mss purchased on either royalty or buy out basis. Published 80 titles last year. Free book catalog and writer's guidelines. Send sample chapter. Reports in 6 to 8 weeks. Enclose return postage.
Textbooks: Major emphasis being given to language arts area, especially high interest/low level reading materials. Another important area is career education. Emphasis is on true orientation materials which give an accurate description of a field, its requirements and opportunities, all of which should be written for a 9th-10th grade reading level.

NATUREGRAPH PUBLISHERS, INC., Box 1075, Happy Camp CA 96039. (916)493-5353. Editor-in-Chief: Sevrin Housen. Original paperbacks "We offer 10% of wholesale; 12½% after 10,000 copies are sold." Published 6 titles in 1976 and 1977; will do 10 in 1978. "State what photographs are available in query; send with ms upon request." Simultaneous and photocopied submissions OK. Reports in 1-2 months. SASE. Free book catalog.
Nonfiction: Publishes (in order of preference): nature (plants, mammals, birds, reptiles, amphibians, natural history for American Wildlife Series); history (Indian lore, ethnographic studies on native Americans); how-to (on science-related matters); land and gardening books; seashore life; cookbooks, cooking and foods (modern nutritional knowledge for the layman); hobbies (nature or science-related); religious (Baha'i); geologic studies and recreation books. Query. Follow *Chicago Manual of Style.* "All material must be scientifically well-grounded. Author must not only be professional, but in good command of his/her English. Many of our authors are college professors. Some of our books are used by teachers, particularly for natural science courses and anthropology (special studies)."
Current Titles: *Owls in Field and Legend,* H. A. Tyler (natural history); *The Wintun Indians of California and Their Neighbors,* by P. M. Knudtson (Indian book); *Redwood and National State Parks,* by D. F. Anthrop.

NAZARENE PUBLISHING HOUSE, Box 527, Kansas City MO 64141. Trade name: Beacon Hill Press of Kansas City. Editor: J. Fred Parker. Publishes hardcover and paperback originals and reprints. Offers "standard contract (sometimes flat rate purchase). Advance on royalty is paid on first 1,000 copies at publication date when book is held over for a year. Pays 10% on first 5,000 copies and 12% on subsequent copies at the end of each calendar year." Published 59 titles last year. Send complete ms or query "on larger books." Follow Chicago *Manual of Style.* Address all mss to Book Editor. Reports in 2 to 5 months. "Book Committee meets quarterly to select, from the mss which they have been reading in the interim, those which will be published." Query first. Enclose S.A.S.E.
General Fiction and Juvenile Fiction: "Must have religious content germane to plot not artificially tacked on. At the same time not preachy or moralistic." Publishes 1 adult fiction and 1 juvenile a year. "Currently a moratorium on adult fiction.
Nonfiction: "Basically religious, (Inspirational, devotional, Bible study, beliefs) but of wide scope from college textbook level to juvenile. Doctrinally must conform to the evangelical, Wesleyan tradition. Conservative view of Bible. Personal religious experience. We want the accent on victorious life, definitely upbeat. Social action themes must have spiritual base and motivation. Use both textbook and popular style books, the latter 128 pages and under except in unusual circumstances." Interested in business and professional books on church administration, Sunday school, etc., and church related history and biography. Textbooks are "almost exclusively done on assignment. Send query first." Length: 10,000 to 30,000 words.
Recent Titles: *The Ministry of Sheperding,* by E. L. Stowe (pastoral practice); and *The Occult and the Supernatural,* by M. B. Wynkoop (doctrine).

NELLEN PUBLISHING CO., (formerly DuNellen Publishing Co.), 386 Park Ave., S., New York NY 10016. (212)679-5730. Editor-in-Chief: Robert A. Nicholas. Managing Editor: J. Govak. Hardcover and paperback originals. Specializes in social sciences. 7½-10% royalty; no advance. Published 10 titles in 1976 and 1977; will do 20 in 1978. State availability of photos and/or illustrations to accompany ms. Simultaneous and photocopied submissions OK. Reports in 1-2 months. SASE. Free book catalog.
Nonfiction: Publishes Americana, biography, business, economics, law, multimedia material, philosophy, poetry, politics, psychology, recreation, sociology, sports, and travel books; "and we want books by scholars for the general educational market." Submit outline/synopsis and sample chapters.
Recent Titles: *Mosaics of Organization Character,* by R. Wright (sociology); *Urban Administration,* by Bent and Rossen (public administration).

NC PRESS LTD., Box 4010 Station 10, Toronto, Ont., Canada M5W 1H8. (416)368-1165. Editor-in-Chief: Caroline Perly. Hardcover and paperback originals (90%) and reprints (10%). Specializes in art, poetry, Canadian history, current events, cookbooks and children's books from the Third World and Canada. 00% royalty; advance averages $100. Published 6 titles in 1976, 10 in 1977. Submit outline/synopsis and sample chapters. Simultaneous submissions OK. Reports in 2 months. SASE. Free book catalog.
Nonfiction: Publishes cookbooks, cooking and foods; economics; history; humor; juveniles; multimedia material; philosophy; poetry; politics; self-help; and textbooks.

THOMAS NELSON, INC., 30 E. 42nd St., New York NY 10017. (212)697-5573. Editor-in-Chief: Gloria Mosesson. Hardcover and paperback originals. 7½% royalty; advance offered. Published 70 titles in 1976, 80 in 1977. State availability of photos and/or illustrations. Photocopied submissions OK. Reports in 2-4 months. SASE. Book catalog for SASE.
Nonfiction: Publishes Americana; art; biography; business; cookbooks, cooking and foods; history; hobbies; how-to; humor; juveniles; nature; politics; psychology; recreation; reference; religious; scientific; self-help; and sports books. Query or submit outline/synopsis and sample chapters.
Fiction: Publishes adventure; experimental; fantasy; historical; humorous; mainstream; mystery; religious; science fiction; suspense; and western books. Submit complete ms.

NELSON-HALL INC., 325 West Jackson Blvd., Chicago IL 60606. (312)922-0856. Publisher: V. Peter Ferrara. Editor: Elbert P. Epler. Standard royalty schedule. Rarely offers an advance. Published 84 titles in 1976, 100 in 1977. Free book catalog. Will consider photocopied and simultaneous submissions. Send query accompanied by outline and return postage. "Soundness of subject matter and its treatment more important than just 'good writing.'" Reports in about 3 weeks. Enclose return postage.
Social Sciences, Psychology, History, Biography, Health, and Applied Psychology: Publishes serious works in the behavioral sciences. Also more popular books on practical, applied psychology written by qualified writers; business subjects, employment and personnel, general self-improvement, techniques relating to memory efficiency, retirement, investment, hobbies, etc. Length: 60,000 to 100,000 words.
Special Needs: "Series of individual books on establishing and operating various kinds of independent businesses. Must be authoritative and specific. Full size 256-page texts.
Recent Titles: *Management of Stress* by D. Frew; *Reading Improvement,* by B. Klaeser; and *Cancer & Chemicals,* by T. H. Corbett, M.D.

NEW AMERICAN LIBRARY (including Mentor Books and Signet Books), 1301 Avenue of the Americas, New York NY 10019. Publisher and Editor-in-Chief: Elaine Geiger. Associate Editor-in-Chief: Jerry Gross. Publishes paperback originals and reprints. Published 418 titles in 1976. Pays substantial advances with standard paperback royalties. Send complete ms to Pat Taylor, Managing Editor. Reports in 6 weeks. SASE.
General Nonfiction and Fiction: Under the Signet imprint, publishes adult and young adult fiction. Interested in contemporary romantic novels, gothics, family sagas. Also interested in nonfiction: self-help, psychology, inspirational and topical subjects. Educational books under the Meridian and Mentor imprint. Length: 75,000 words minimum. John F. Thornton, Education Editor.

NEWCASTLE PUBLISHING CO., INC., 13419 Saticoy, No. Hollywood CA 91605. (213)873-3191. Editor-in-Chief: Alfred Saunders. Paperback originals (20%); and reprints (80%). 5% royalty; no advance. Publishes 8 titles a year. Send prints or copies of items to illustrate ms. Simultaneous and photocopied submissions OK. Reports in 2-4 months. SASE. Free book catalog.
Nonfiction: Publishes cookbooks, cooking and foods; how-to; juveniles; multimedia material; pets; psychology; reference; self-help; sports (horse racing); travel; books on the occult, mythology and gambling. Submit outline/synopsis and sample chapters or complete ms. Alfred Saunders and Daryl Jacoby, editors.
Fiction: Fantasy, mystery and science fiction and mythology. Submit outline/synopsis and sample chapters. Doug Menville, editor.
Recent Title: *Celtic Myth,* by C. Squire (mythology).

NEW LEAF PRESS, INC., Box 1045, Harrison AR 72061. Editor-in-Chief: Cliff Dudley. Hardcover and paperback originals (99%); paperback reprints (1%). Specializes in charismatic books. 10% royalty on first 10,000 copies, paid once a year; no advance. Published 14 titles in 1976, 12 in 1977; will do 16 in 1978. Send photos and illustrations to accompany ms. Simultaneous and photocopied submissions OK. SASE. Reports in 30-60 days. Free book catalog.
Nonfiction: Biography; self-help. Charismatic books; life stories; how-to live the Christian life. 100-400 pages. Submit complete ms. B. Springer, editor.
Recent Titles: *The C. M. Ward Story,* by D. Wead (biography); *Christian Catechism,* by E. B. Gentile (curriculum for non-Christians).

NEW VIEWPOINTS, division of Franklin Watts, 730 5th Ave., New York NY 10019. Senior Editor: Will Davison. Hardcover and paperback originals. Specializes in college textbooks.

Standard royalty, "depending on the author's reputation, subject matter and work involved." Advance averages $1,500. Published 15 titles in 0976. Query. Follow MLA *Style Sheet, Words into Type,* or Chicago *Manual of Style.* Simultaneous ("if so advised") and photocopied submissions OK. Reports "immediately on queries; about 2 months on mss." Free book catalog.
Nonfiction: Publishes textbooks on history, political science and sociology. Length: 300 book pages (100,000 words). Publishes textbooks for colleges, junior and community colleges and upper levels of high school.
Recent Title: *The Grass Roots Mind in America: The American Sense of Absolutes,* by Furay.

NEWBURY HOUSE PUBLISHERS, INC., 68 Middle Rd., Rawley MA 01969. Editor-in-Chief: R. H. Ingram. Managing Editor: Jo Alexander. Hardcover and paperback originals (98%) and reprints (2%). 5-10% royalty. Advance against royalties up to $500 in special cases. Published 15 titles in 1976, 17 in 1977; will do 20 in 1978. State availability of photos and/or illustrations to accompany ms. Photocopied and simultaneous submissions OK. Reports in 1-2 months. SASE. Free book catalog.
Nonfiction: "Any topic of motivating interest to the following readers: children, adolescents, university students and adults." Query first.
Fiction: "These materials are intended for students of English as a second language; wanted are materials created especially for the purpose, or simplified and abridged versions of already published materials. Avoid topics which may give offense to persons overseas and topics which are dated or provincial."

NOBLE AND NOBLE, PUBLISHERS, INC., 1 Dag Hammarskjold Plaza, New York NY 10017. Editor-in-Chief: Eleanor Angeles. Royalty and advance vary. Published 125 titles in 1976. Prompt initial reply; subsequent replies may take longer. Enclose return postage with ms.
Textbooks: Elementary and secondary textbooks. Language arts and social studies are among the major areas of interest.

NODIN PRESS, 519 N. Third St., Minneapolis MN 55401. (612)836-1763. Publisher: Norton Stillman. Hardcover and paperback originals (90%); reprints (10%). Specializes in regional (Minnesota) material. 7½-10% royalty. Advance averages $250-500. Published 3 titles in 1976; 5 in 1977. State availability of photos and/or illustrations, or send them with initial query. Photocopied submissions OK. Reports in 2-4 weeks. SASE. Photocopied list of titles available upon request.
Nonfiction: "We specialize in material having to do with the Minnesota area, as long as it is adult work. We prefer not to publish children's books. Aside from this, we have no real requirements as to length or content. New Minnesota writers are welcome."

NORTH RIVER PRESS, INC., Box 241, Croton-on-Hudson NY 10520. Publishes hardcover and paperback originals and hardcover reprints. Offers 10% of cash received on all copies sold and paid for. No advance. Published 3 titles last year. Will consider photocopied submissions. Submit outline and sample page or two. Reports in 3 weeks. Enclose S.A.E. and return postage.
Reference and History: Regional history, literature and lore. Special interest in Hudson Valley material. Reference material, especially psychiatric and psychoanalytic. No special approach. Also interested in politics.

NORTHLAND PRESS, Box N, Flagstaff AZ 86002. (602)774-5251. Hardcover and paperback originals (95%) and reprints (5%). Advance varies. Published 14 titles in 1976, 12 in 1977; will do 12-15 in 1978. Transparencies and contact sheet required for photos and/or illustrations to accompany ms. Simultaneous and photocopied submissions OK. Reports in 2-4 weeks. SASE. Free book catalog.
Nonfiction: Publishes western Americana, western art; and photography books. Query first.

W. W. NORTON CO., INC., 500 Fifth Ave., New York NY 10036. (212)354-5500. Managing Editor: Sterling Lawrence. Hardcover and paperback originals (90%); paperback reprints (10%). 10-12½-15% royalty; advance varies. Publishes about 200 new titles annually. Photocopied and simultaneous submissions OK. Submit outline/synopsis and sample chapters for nonfiction. Submit complete ms for fiction. Reports in 3 weeks. SASE.
Nonfiction, Fiction and Poetry: "General, adult fiction and nonfiction of all kinds on nearly all subjects and of the highest quality possible within the limits of each particular book." Last year there were 52 book club rights sales; 35 mass paperback reprint sales; "Innumerable serializations, second serial, syndication, translations, etc." Would like to have a writer for the fol-

lowing topic: "a demonstration of the fact that our military leaders are consistently wrong in their assessments, bad in execution and an investigation of why our system turns out military leaders of that caliber." Also publishes Americana, biography, history, humor, medicine and psychiatry, music, nature, philosophy, poetry, politics, scientific, self-help and how-to, sports, textbooks. Length: open.

NOYES DATA CORPORATION (including Noyes Press and Noyes Art Books), Noyes Bldg., Park Ridge NJ 07656. Publishes hardcover originals. Pays 10% royalty. Advance varies, depending on author's reputation and nature of book. Published 57 titles in 1976, 62 in 1977. Free book catalog. Query Editorial Department first. Reports in 1 to 2 weeks. Enclose return postage.
Nonfiction: "Art, classical studies, archaeology, history, other nonfiction. Material directed to the intelligent adult and the academic market."
Technical: Publishes practical industrial processing science; technical, economic books pertaining to chemistry, chemical engineering, food and biology, primarily those of interest to the business executive; books relating to international finance. Length: 50,000 to 250,000 words.

OCCUPATIONAL AWARENESS, P.O. Box 948, Los Alamitos CA 90720. Editor-in-Chief: Edith Ericksen. Publishes educational paperback originals. Offers standard minimum book contract of 10-12½-15%. Advance varies. Will consider photocopied submissions. Submit outline and sample chapters for books and textbooks. Reports in 1 month. Enclose return postage.
Nonfiction: Materials should relate to students, careers, personnel, teachers, counselors and administrators. "We are an educational publishing company, relating occupations to curriculum."

OCEANA PUBLICATIONS, INC., Dobbs Ferry NY 10522. (914)693-1394. President: Philip F. Cohen; Managing Editor: William W. Cowan; Legal Editor: Edwin S. Newman; Docket Series Editor: Julius Marke; Editor, Reprint Bulletin: Sam P. Williams. Pays a flat fee of $500 for a legal almanac ms; $250 on receipt of acceptable ms; $250 at date of publication. No advance. Published approximately 50 titles last year. Send outline and sample chapter. Reports in 60 days. Enclose return postage.
Nonfiction: "We publish 5 to 10 legal almanacs a year. Most of them deal with legal aspects of everyday living. The author should have legal training. The prospective author will find sample almanacs in most local libraries."

ODDO PUBLISHING, INC., P.O. Box 68, Beauregard Blvd., Fayetteville GA 30214. (404)461-7627. Managing Editor: Genevieve Oddo. Publishes hardcover and paperback originals. Scripts are usually purchased outright. "We judge all scripts independently." Royalty considered for special scripts only. Will send free catalog to writer on request. Send complete ms, typed clearly. Reports in 3 to 4 months. Return postage and envelope must be enclosed with mss.
Juveniles and Textbooks: Publishes language arts, workbooks in math, writing (English), photophonics, science (space and oceanography), and social studies for schools, libraries, and trade. Interested in children's supplementary readers in the areas of language arts, math, science, social studies, etc. Texts run from 1,500 to 5,000 words. Presently searching for mss carrying the positive mental attitude theme—how to improve oneself, without preaching; material on the American Indian (folklore and background). Ecology, space, oceanography, and pollution are subjects of interest. Books on patriotism. Ms must be easy to read, general, and not set to outdated themes. It must lend itself to full color illustration. No stories of grandmother long ago. No love angle, permissive language, or immoral words or statements.

ODYSSEY PRESS, A Division of Bobbs-Merrill Educational Publishing, 4300 West 62nd St., Indianapolis IN 46268. (317)291-3100. Editorial Director: Thomas D. Wittenberg. Publishes college texts. Published 10 titles last year. "No unsolicited mss at this time, but queries are acceptable."

OHARA PUBLICATIONS, INCORPORATED, 1845-51 W. Empire Ave., Burbank CA 91504. Publishes hardcover and paperback originals, reprints, and translations. Offers standard 10% royalty contract. 5% for first printing if advance is granted. Published 16 titles in 1976. Free editorial guidelines sheet. Query first with outline and sample chapters. Will consider photocopied submissions. Reports in 2 to 4 weeks. Enclose return postage.
Nonfiction: How-to and instructional manuals dealing specifically with the martial arts. Other material includes Oriental religion, philosophy and historical Samurai accounts. "Research our

manuals and follow our basic format. Ohara is the world's largest publisher of martial arts books. Our books use better quality photos and the art layout is professionally handled. We do not want Oriental cookbooks or poetry. Interested in different styles of karate and kung-fu other than those already printed. Psychological, physiological and healthful aspects of the martial arts written by qualified authorities."
Juveniles: Nonfiction only. Deal specifically with the Orient. Illustrations necessary.

OHIO STATE UNIVERSITY PRESS, 2070 Neil Ave., Columbus OH 43210. (614)422-6930. Director: Weldon A. Kefauver. Payment on royalty basis. Published 20 titles last year. Query letter preferred with outline and sample chapters. Reports within 2 months. Ms held longer with author's permission. Enclose return postage.
Nonfiction: Publishes history, biography, science, philosophy, the arts, political science, law, literature, economics, education, sociology, anthropology, geography, and general scholarly nonfiction. No length limitations.

THE OLD ARMY PRESS, 1513 Welch, Ft. Collins CO 80521. (303)484-5535. Editor-in-Chief: Michael J. Koury. Hardcover and paperback originals (90%) and reprints (10%). Specializes in Western Americana. 10% royalty; no advance. Published 7 titles in 1976, 10 in 1977; will do 14 in 1978. State availability of photos and/or illustrations to accompany ms. Simultaneous and photocopied submissions OK. SASE. Free book catalog.
Nonfiction: Publishes Americana (60,000 words or less); history (60,000 words or less). Query first.
Recent Titles: *Centennial Campaign,* by J. S. Gray; *$10 Horse, $40 Saddle,* by D. Rickey; *Carl Akers' Colorado,* by C. Akers (all Western Americana).

OLD TIME BOTTLE PUBLISHING COMPANY, 611 Lancaster Dr., Salem OR 97301. Editors: B.J. Blumenstein and Lynn Blumenstein. Publishes hardcover and paperback originals. Offers standard royalty contract with average $500 advance. Published 1 title last year. Send outline. Reports in 30 days. Enclose return postage.
Hobbies: "Generally new hobbies and any new approach to old hobbies such as treasure hunting, bottle collecting, and artifact collecting. Audience: general public, all ages. Approach is how to get started. Writing should be condensed, very informative, with simple, flowing manner. Step-by-step instructions with inspirational matter and purpose contained in foreword. Profusely illustrated with photos of high quality and identification of items. Average page count (book) 100 to 200 pages."

*OMNI PRESS, INC., Box 2428, Sarasota FL 33578. Editor-in-Chief: Carol A. Vaseff. Paperback originals (80%) and reprints (20%). 10% royalty; no advance. Subsidy publishes 10% of books depending on quality of ms and financial involvement. Published 5 titles in 1976 and 1977; will do 10 in 1978. Query or submit outline/synopsis and sample chapters. Reports in 6-8 weeks.
Nonfiction: Publishes business, economics, history, how-to, law, politics, psychology, recreation, reference, scientific, self-help, technical and textbooks.
Fiction: Adventure, confession, historical and humorous.

101 PRODUCTIONS, 834 Mission St., San Francisco CA 94103. (415)495-6040. Editor-in-Chief: Jacqueline Killeen. Publishes hardcover and paperback originals. Offers standard minimum book contract. Published 8 titles in 1976, 12 in 1977. Free book catalog. Will consider photocopied submissions. Query first. No unsolicited mss will be read. Enclose return postage.
General Nonfiction: All nonfiction, mostly how-to; cookbooks, the home, gardening, outdoors, travel, sports, hobbies, recreation and crafts. Heavy emphasis on graphics and illustrations. Most books are 192 pages.
Recent Titles: *Greenhousing for Purple Thumbs,* by D. Fenten; and *One-Pot Meals,* by M. Gin.

OPEN COURT-LIBRARY PRESS INCORPORATED, Box 599, LaSalle IL 61301. Publisher: M. Blouke Carus. General Manager: Howard R. Webber. Editor: Thomas G. Anderson. Published 44 titles in 1976, 25 in 1977. Royalty contracts negotiable for each book. Query first. Reports in 6 to 8 weeks. Enclose return postage.
Nonfiction: Philosophy, mathematics, comparative religion, history, political science, economics, and related scholarly topics. "This is a publishing house run as an intellectual and cultural enterprise and not as an assembly line industry. Nonetheless, all the books we publish are intended to be at least adequately viable in the market."

Recent Titles: *Hazards of Learning,* by G. R. Urban (education); *The Occult Establishment,* by S. Webb (religion/history); and *Three Questions About Morality,* by W. Frankena (philosophy).

OPTIMUM PUBLISHING CO. LIMITED, 245 rue St-Jacques, Montreal, PQ, Canada H2Y 1M6. (514)282-2491. Editor-in-Chief: Michael S. Baxendale. Hardcover and paperback originals and reprints. 10% royalty. Publishes approximately 25 titles a year. Marketed internationally, mail order and direct mail. Publishes in both official Canadian languages (English and French). Query or submit outline/synopsis and sample chapters. Photocopied submissions OK. Reports in 2-4 weeks. SASE.
Nonfiction: Cookbooks, cooking and foods; history; how-to; medicine and psychiatry; nature; photography; self-help; sports; and travel books.
Recent Titles: *How To Live With Your Heart,* by A. Vineberg, M.D. (health); *The Artic,* by F. Bruemmer (nature);and *Stew and Casserole Cookbook,* by Margo Oliver (cookbook).

ORBIS BOOKS, Maryknoll NY 10545. (914)941-7590. Editor: Philip Scharper. Publishes hardcover and paperback originals. Offers standard 10-12½-15% royalty contract; "standard advance, $500." Published 22 titles in 1976. Query first with outline, sample chapters, and prospectus. Reports in 4 to 6 weeks. Enclose return postage.
Nonfiction: "Christian orientation in the problems of the developing nations. Transcultural understandings, mission theology and documentation."
Recent Titles: *The Liberation of Theology,* B. L. Segundo (theology); *In Search of the Beyond,* by C. Carrette (inspiration); and *The Gospel of Peace and Justice,* by J. Gremillion.

OREGON STATE UNIVERSITY PRESS, Box 689, Corvallis OR 97330. (503)754-3166. Hardcover and paperback originals. "Very seldom pay royalties. Generally, give 40% discount on purchase of books plus a few complimentary copies on publication." No advance. Published 11 titles in 1976, 10 in 1977; will do 10-12 in 1978. Submit contact sheet of photos and/or illustrations to accompany ms. Reports in 2-4 months. SASE. Free book catalog for SASE.
Nonfiction: Publishes Americana; biography; cookbooks, cooking and foods; economics; history; nature; philosophy; energy and recreation; reference; scientific (biological sciences only); technical (energy); and American literary criticism books. Pacific or Northwestern topics only. Submit outline/synopsis and sample chapters.
Recent Titles: *The Fiction of Bernard Malamud,* by Astro/Benson (American literary criticism); *Biology of Tumor Viruses* by Beaudreau (biological science); *Retaliation: Japanese Attacks on the West Coast in WWII,* by Webber (history).

OUR SUNDAY VISITOR, INC., Noll Plaza, Huntington IL 46750. (219)356-8400. Editor-in-Chief: Albert J. Nevins. Original hardcovers and paperbacks (80%); hardcover and paperback reprints (20%). 10% royalty of price received; $500 average advance. Published 57 titles in 1976, 60 in 1977; will do 50 in 1978. Send prints of photos with ms. Reports in 2 weeks on queries; 1-2 months on mss. SASE. Free book catalog.
Nonfiction: Publishes books of some religious connection and value. Biography, history, how-to, philosophy, psychology, reference, religious, textbooks, travel. Submit outline/synopsis and sample chapters.
Recent Titles: *Rome: The Enchanted City,* F. J. Korn (travel); *Depression,* by J. Dominian (psychology);*Alcoholism,* by G. Schomp (self-help).

OXMOOR HOUSE (a division of The Progressive Farmer Co.), P.O. Box 2262, Birmingham AL 35202. Director: Les Adams. Managing Editor: Ann Harvey. Publishes hardcover and paperback originals. Payment on royalty basis or fee. Published 32 titles last year. Send outline and sample chapter. Reports in 3 weeks. Enclose return postage.
General Nonfiction: "Publishes books of general interest to Southern readers—cookbooks, garden books; books on crafts, sewing, photography, art, outdoors, antiques and how-to topics. Their current leading titles include *Jericho: A Southern Album; Tracing Your Ancestry,* and *Southern Antiques and Folk Art.*

P. A. R. INCORPORATED, Abbott Park Place, Providence RI 02903. (401)331-0130. Publisher: Richard P. Thiel. President: Barry M. Smith. Hardcover and paperback originals; reprints of their own texts. Specializes in textbooks for business schools, junior or community colleges, and adult continuing education programs. 10% royalty. Advance of $500-1,000. Published 2 titles in 1976; will do 5 in 1978. Markets through fall and winter workshops throughout the country with special seminars that are periodically held by authors and sales staff. State

availability of photos or illustrations to furnish at a later date. Simultaneous submissions OK. Reports in 2-4 months. SASE. Free book catalog.
Nonfiction: R. P. Thiel, Department Editor. Business, economics, law, politics, psychology, sociology, technical, textbooks.
Recent Titles: *Developing Leadership,* by B. L. Fischman (management); *Study Guide for Personal Selling: Choice Against Chance,* by E. M. Mazze (salesmanship).

PACIFIC BOOKS, PUBLISHERS, P.O. Box 558, Palo Alto CA 94302. (415)323-5529. Editor: Henry Ponleithner. Royalty schedule varies with book. No advance. Published 6 titles last year. Will send catalog on request. Send complete ms. Reports promptly. Enclose return postage with ms.
Nonfiction: General interest, professional, technical and scholarly nonfiction trade books. Specialties include western Americana and Hawaiiana.
Textbooks and Reference: Text and reference books; high school and college.

PADRE PRODUCTIONS, Box 1275, San Luis Obispo CA 93406. Editor-in-Chief: Lachlan P. MacDonald. Hardcover and paperback originals (90%) and reprints (10%). 6% minimum royalty; advance ranges from $200-1,000. Published 4 titles in 1976, 6-8 in 1977; will do 5-10 in 1978. State availability of photos and/or illustrations or include contact sheet or stat. Simultaneous submissions OK. Reports in 2-4 weeks. SASE. Book catalog for SASE.
Nonfiction: Publishes Americana (antiques), art, collectibles; cookbooks, cooking and foods; history (local California); hobbies, how-to, juveniles, nature (with illustrations); photography, poetry (about collectibles); psychology, recreation, reference, self-help, and travel books. Query first or submit outline and sample chapters. "Ample packaging; type all material; don't send slides unless asked."
Fiction: Publishes (in order of preference): adventure, fantasy, experimental, mainstream, and suspense books. Submit complete ms.
Recent Titles: *The New Collector's Directory,* by R. D. Connolly (antiques); *Morro Bay Meanderings,* by H. Weisman (California travel).

PAGURIAN PRESS LTD., Suite 1106, 335 Bay St., Toronto, Ontario, Canada M5H 2R3. Editor-in-Chief: Christopher Ondaatje. Publishes paperback and hardcover originals and reprints. Offers negotiable royalty contract. Advance negotiable. Published 20 titles in 1976, 30 in 1977. Free book catalog. Will consider photocopied submissions. Submit 2-page outline; synopsis or chapter headings and contents. Reports "immediately." Enclose S.A.E. and International Reply Coupons.
Nonfiction: Publishes general interest trade books. Would like to see outdoor topics, sports, instruction. Will consider Americana, biography, cookbooks and cooking, economics, erotic, history, reference, self-help and how-to, sports, travel. Length: 40,000 to 70,000 words.
Recent Titles: *The Agatha Christie Mystery,* by D. Murdoch (biography); and *Wilderness Living,* by B. Berglund (outdoor).

PALADIN PRESS, Box 1307, Boulder CO 80306. (303)443-7250. Editor-in-Chief: Peder C. Lund. Publishes hardcover originals and hardcover and paperback reprints. Offers standard minimum book contract of 10-12½-15%. Published 11 titles last year. Will send free catalog to writer on request. Will consider photocopied submissions. Submit outline and sample chapters. Reports in 1 month. Enclose return postage.
Military: Books on weapons, survival, military science, guerrilla warfare. History, politics, sports, hobbies, recreation, technical.

PALMETTO PUBLISHING CO., INC., 4747 28th St., N., St. Petersburg FL 33714. (813)522-0481. Editor-in-Chief: R. van de Gohm. Hardcover and paperback originals. 10% royalty; advance averages $100. Published 2 titles in 1976, 8 in 1977; will do 15 in 1978. Simultaneous and photocopied submissions OK. Reports in 2-4 weeks. SASE. Free book catalog.
Nonfiction: Publishes natural history, how-to and pet books of high quality. "Authors must have personal experience of their subject. We do not accept mss that have been developed entirely by research." Query first and submit outline/synopsis and sample chapters and example of artwork.
Recent Titles: *Breeding Angelfish,* by S. Dow; *Breeding Snakes,* by R. Roches; *Success With Killfish,* by R. Warner.

PANETH PRESS LTD., P.O. Box 593, Times Square Station, New York NY 10036. Pays the usual 10% of the published price in accordance with Author's Guild requirements. Advance varies. Insists that first query letters with outlines and sample chapters be sent to the Editor. Reports in 2 to 3 months. Enclose return postage and label, "otherwise mss are not returned." **General:** Publishes books in every field of human interest—adult fiction, history, biography, science, philosophy, the arts, religion and general nonfiction. Length: 65,000 to 125,000 words.

PANTHEON BOOKS, Division of Random House, Inc., 201 E. 50th St., New York NY 10022. Managing Editor: Kathleen Macomber. Published over 60 titles last year. Unable to read mss submitted without previous inquiry. Address queries to Wendy Wolf, Adult Editorial Department. Enclose return postage.
Fiction: Publishes fewer than 5 novels each year, including mysteries.
Nonfiction: Books mostly by academic authors. Emphasis on Asia, international politics, radical social theory, history, medicine, and law.
Juveniles: Publishes some juveniles. Address queries specifically to Juvenile Editorial Department.

PAPERJACKS LTD., (formerly Simon & Schuster of Canada), 330 Steelcase Rd., Markham, Ont., Canada L3R 2M1. (416)495-1261. Editor-in-Chief: T. Mulligan. Paperback originals (50%) and reprints (50%). Specializes in mass market paperbacks. 6% royalty; advance averages $1,000. Published 40 titles in 1976, 60 in 1977; will do 60 in 1978. Submit complete ms. "We like to have a covering letter which describes the nature and purpose of the work and states the number of words in the ms." Send contact sheet or prints if photos are to accompany the ms. Simultaneous ("if we are informed and give our prior permission") and photocopied submissions OK. Reports in 1-2 months. SASE. Free book catalog.
Nonfiction: Publishes Canadiana; biography; business; cookbooks, cooking and foods; economics; erotica; history; hobbies; how-to; humor; law; medicine and psychiatry; nature; pets; poetry (if it has broad range popular appeal) politics; psychology (broad appeal); recreation; religious (broad appeal); self-help; sociology (broad appeal); sports; and travel books. "The only requirement is that the work have strong mass-market appeal."
Fiction: Publishes adventure; erotica; fantasy; historical; humorous; mainstream; mystery; religious; romance; suspense; and western books.
Recent Titles: *1977-78 Travel Guide to Canada,* by P. Rowe (travel); *Woman of Ireland,* by J. Barrett (historical fiction); *Wild Goose Jack,* by Jack Miner (autobiography).

PARENTS' MAGAZINE PRESS, 52 Vanderbilt Ave., New York NY 10017. Editor-in-Chief: Selma G. Lanes. Usual advance is $750 minimum (5% to author; 5% to illustrator), but this varies, depending on author's reputation and nature of book. Published 26 titles in 1976, 30 in 1977. Reports in 6 weeks. Enclose return postage with ms.
Juveniles: "Picture books, 500 to 1,500 words, for ages 4 to 8. Although there are no vocabulary restrictions, these stories must combine a high interest level with originality and simplicity of style. It is, of course, essential that the material offer excellent possibilities for illustrations. And we are always interested in new ideas (fiction or nonfiction) for ages 4 to 10, even nursery school age."
Recent Titles: *The Generous Cow,* by B. Letord (picture book); *Penny Tales,* by V. Schone (picture book); and *The Sultan's Perfect Tree,* by J. Yolen (folktale adaptation).

PARKER PUBLISHING CO., West Nyack NY 10994. Publishes hardcover originals and paperback reprints. Offers 10% royalty; 5% mail order and book clubs. Published 90 titles last year. Will send catalog on request. Reports in 3 to 5 weeks.
Nonfiction: Publishes practical, self-help, how-to books. Subject areas include popular health, mystic and occult, inspiration, secretarial, selling, personal and business self-improvement, money opportunities. Length: 65,000 words
Recent Titles: *Extraordinary Healing Secrets from a Doctor's Private Files,* by Van Fleet (health); and *Amazing Power of Solar-Kinetics,* by Morris (mystic/occult).

PAULIST PRESS, 1865 Broadway, New York NY 10023. (212)265-4028. Publishes hardcover and paperback originals and reprints. Standard trade contract with basic royalty open to negotiation. Advance depends on length of ms. Published 70 titles last year. Send outline and sample chapter first to Editorial Department. Reports in 4 weeks. Enclose return postage.
Religion: Catholic and Protestant religious works, both popular and scholarly. Length: 30,000 words and up. "Photo books and multimedia materials, large amounts of contemporary religious education materials." Material tends to avant-garde; no homespun philosophy or pious rehashes.

PAY DAY PRESS, 8208 Vista Dr., Scottsdale AZ 85253. Editor-in-Chief: David L. Markstein. Hardcover and paperback originals. Emphasizes self-help "ranging through all the gamut of human wants, needs, sufferings and hopes." 10% mail order royalty; no advance. Published 1 title in 1976, three in 1977; will do at least 4 in 1978. "We market largely by direct response." State availability of photos, etc., to illustrate ms. Reports in 2-4 weeks. SASE.
Nonfiction: Publishes financial how-to; medicine and psychiatry (if popular); popular psychology; self-help books. Query first.

PEACE & PIECES FOUNDATION, P.O. Box 99394, San Francisco CA 94109. President: M. Custodio. Publishes limited edition paperback originals and chapbooks. Does not offer a royalty contract. Makes outright purchase for a small sum (minimum of $100 honorarium, plus 100 to 200 copies of the book. Publishes 6 to 10 titles a year. No unsolicited mss. Query first. Reports in 3 weeks. Enclose return postage.
Nonfiction and Poetry: "This tax-deductible, nonprofit foundation is concentrating largely on anthologies, California writers, and chapbooks by Bay Area writers and poets, although we will look at mss outside these confines. Serious writers only; no amateurs."
Recent Titles: *The Sixty-nine Days of Easter,* by T. S. Lawson (fiction/humor); *Having Come This Far, ; and Light and Other Poems,* by R. Weiss (poetry).

PEACE PRESS, INC., 3828 Willat Ave., Culver City CA 90230. Editor-in-Chief: Harold Moskovitz. Managing Editor: Bob Zangh. Hardcover and paperback originals (75%) and paperback reprints (25%). Specializes in how-to, ecology, solar change, political and psychological books. 5% royalty; no advance. Published 4 titles in 1976, 6 in 1977; will do 7 in 1978. Submit outline/synopsis and sample chapters or complete ms. State availability of photos and/or illustrations or send contact sheet. Simultaneous and photocopied submissions OK. Reports in 1-2 months. SASE. Free book catalog.
Nonfiction: Publishes biography; cookbooks, cooking and foods; history; how-to; politics; psychology; religious; self-help; sociology; and sports books.
Recent Titles: *The Art of Zen Meditation,* by H. Fast (oriental religion); and *Power of People,* by Woney (political social change).

PEGASUS, (A Division of The Bobbs-Merrill Co., Inc.), 4300 West 62nd Street, Indianapolis IN 46268. (317)291-3100. Editorial Director: Thomas D. Wittenberg. Publishes college texts. Published 10 titles last year. Biological sciences curriculum study series; traditions in philosophy series. "We are not interested in unsolicited mss at this time but queries are acceptable."

*PELICAN PUBLISHING CO., INC., 630 Burmaster St., Gretna LA 70053. (504)368-1175. Editor-in-Chief: James Calhoun. Managing Editor: Garrett Stearns. Hardcover and paperback originals (90%) and reprints (10%). 10% royalty; advance averages $500-1,000. Subsidy publishes 5% of books. Subsidy publishing offered "only if we determine a book is not economically feasible, but subject is of great importance." Published 31 titles in 1976, 25 in 1977; will do 25 in 1978. Submit outline/synopsis and sample chapters. Use Chicago *Manual of Style.* Send prints if photos/illustrations are to accompany ms. Reports in 2-4 months. SASE. Free book catalog.
Nonfiction: Publishes Americana; art; biography; business; cookbooks, cooking and foods; history; hobbies; how-to; humor; juveniles; politics; religious (inspirational); self-help; textbooks; and travel books.
Special Needs: *"Maverick Guide to Hawaii* (Bone) is the first in a series of foreign travel guides. The Pelican Guide Series on domestic themes has long been a staple."
Recent Titles: *See You at the Top,* by Z. Zigler (inspirational and salesmanship); *Patches of Joy,* by V. Daniels (religious inspirational); and *Personal Finance Guide and Workbook,* by R. Stillman (college textbook).

THE PENNSYLVANIA STATE UNIVERSITY PRESS, 215 Wagner Bldg., University Park PA 16802. (814)865-1327. Editor-in-Chief: Jack Pickering. Hardcover and paperback originals. Specializes in books of scholarly value, and/or regional interest. 10% royalty; no advance. Published 52 titles in 1976, 50-60 in 1977; will do 60-70 in 1978. Maintains own distribution company in England which serves the British Empire, Europe, etc. Submit outline/synopsis and sample chapters or complete ms. Send prints if photos/illustrations are to accompany ms. Simultaneous and photocopied submissions OK. Reports in 2-4 months. SASE. Free book catalog.
Nonfiction: Publishes art; biography; business; economics; history; hobbies; medicine and psychiatry; multimedia material; music; nature; philosophy; politics; psychology; recreation; refer-

ence; religious; scientific; sociology; technical; textbooks; women's studies; black studies; and agriculture books.

Special Needs: Keystone Books (a paperback series concentrating on topics of special interest to those living in the mid-Atlantic states.)

Recent Titles: *T. S. Eliot's Personal Wasteland,* by S. Weintraub (literary criticism); *American Liberal Disillusionment,* by S. Rochester (history); and *Seaweeds: Guide to Marine Plants of the East Coast,* by C. J. Hillson (botany).

THE PENNYWORTH PRESS, 114 7th Ave. N.W., Calgary, Alberta, Canada T2M OA2. Editor-in-Chief: David Foy. Publishes paperback and hardcover originals and reprints. Usually offers royalty contract of "20% after costs are covered. Minimal advance." Published 2 titles in 1976, 3 in 1977. Marketed mainly to libraries and university-community bookstores. "Writers seeking mass distribution should consider other publishers first." Send samples of poems from longer ms. Reports in 1 to 2 weeks. Enclose S.A.E. and either Canadian stamps or International Reply Coupons.

Poetry: "We publish books of poetry. Our only restriction is that the work be of high literary quality. All poetry mss, regardless of style, content, or form will be considered, although works in the tradition of this century's major poets, including today's experimentalists, have the best chance of being accepted." Receives too much "poetry which ought to be more carefully directed to publishers who specifically ask to see 'homespun,' 'folksy' material."

Recent Titles: *Poems,* by R. Hoeft and *Writing with Our Blood,* by T. Zimmerman.

THE PEQUOT PRESS, INC., Old Chester Road, Chester CT 06412. (203)526-9571. Publications Director: Sara Ingram. Publishes both hardbound books and several series of paperback monographs; originals and reprints. 7½-10-12½% royalty contract for casebound books; 5-7½% for paperback. Advances individually arranged. Published 20 titles last year. Current catalog available. Send query with sample chapter. Reports in two weeks. Enclose return postage.

Nonfiction: Publishes history, biography, special interest, and "how-to" books. Special field is New England guide books, genealogies, short walks series, New England town histories, New England historical sidelights, railways, maritime, New England arts and crafts, including antiques and architecture. Interested in Connecticut history, biography, the arts. "For book trade and elementary and high school markets." Length: open.

Recent Titles: *Southern New England for Free,* by S. Berman (guidebook); and *Short Walks on Cape Cod,* by P. and R. Sadlier.

PEREGRINE SMITH, INC., 1877 E. Gentile St., Layton UT 84041. Editor-in-Chief: G. M. Smith. Publishes hardcover and paperback originals and reprints. Usually offers standard minimum book contract of 10-12½-15%, but variations differ according to the book and author. Will often tailor a contract to the needs of the project. Published 10 titles last year. Marketed through bookstores. Will send catalog to writer for 25¢. Will consider photocopied submissions. Query first, or submit outline and sample chapters. Follow *Chicago Style Manual.* Reports in 2 weeks to 2 months. Enclose return postage.

Architecture and History: Western American history, western American architecture, western American culture with particular emphasis on the state of California. Culture and history of Latter-Day Saints (Mormon) religion. "Our books are written for the generally intellectual audience, those interested in the arts and history. Many of the books are used for college texts. However, the style should not be stiff or overdone. It should be smooth, interesting reading." No poetry or fiction.

*PERIVALE PRESS, 13830 Erwin St., Van Nuys CA 91401. (213)785-4671. Editor-in-Chief: Lawrence P. Spingarn. Paperback originals (90%) and reprints (10%). Specializes in translations from foreign poetry; regional poetry anthologies. 10% royalty; advance averages $150, "but some books are published without advance." Has subsidy published "one book to date, but we return the investment before taking profits or we return a percentage on regular basis until total is paid. Subsidy publishing is offered if the book is both expensive to produce and not popular. We ask a subsidy of 1/3 the manufacturing cost." Published 3 titles in 1976, 4 in 1977. Query. State availability of photos and/or illustrations. Photocopied submissions OK. Reports in 1-2 months. SASE. Book catalog 13¢.

Nonfiction: Publishes humor; poetry; and translations.

Fiction: Publishes experimental and short story books.

Special Needs: "We are looking for more humorous books, possibly for a new series."

Recent Titles: *Poets West; Contemporary Poems from the Western States,* by L. P. Spingarn (poetry); *Yiddish Sayings Mama Never Taught You,* by G. Weltman and M. S. Zuckerman (folklore and humor); *Epigrams From Martial,* by R. O'Connell.

PETROCELLI/CHARTER, A division of Mason/Charter Publishing Co., 641 Lexington Ave., New York NY 10022. (212)486-8650. Editor-in-Chief: L. S. Marchand. Managing Editor: M. A. Vezzosi. Hardcover and paperback originals. 10-15% royalty; no advance. Publishes 20 titles annually. Query, submit outline/synopsis and sample chapters, or complete ms. State availability of photos/illustrations. Simultaneous and photocopied submissions OK. Reports in 2-4 weeks. SASE. Book catalog for SASE.
Nonfiction: "We specialize in books in computer science, data processing, accounting, marketing, and management. Some of these books are texts, while others are for professionals in the field."
Recent Titles: *Introduction to Computer Science,* by H. Katzen, Jr. (computer science); *Introduction to Decision Science,* by S. M. Lee and L. J. Moore (management science); and *Product/Service Strategy,* by R. T. Hise (marketing).

S.G. PHILLIPS, INC., 305 West 86th St., New York NY 10024. (212)787-4405. Editor: Sidney Phillips. Publishes hardcover originals. "Graduated royalty schedule varies where artists or collaborators share in preparation." Published 2 titles last year. Will send a catalog to a writer on request. "Query first; no unsolicited mss." Reports in 30 to 60 days. Enclose S.A.S.E.
General and Juveniles: "Fiction and nonfiction for children and young adults. Particular interests—contemporary fiction, mysteries, adventure, science fiction; nonfiction: biography, politics, urban problems, international affairs, anthropology, archaeology, geography. Length depends on age group."

PICTORIAL PRESS, 1535 Francisco St., San Francisco CA 94123. (415)362-6979 Editor-in-Chief: T.S. Connelly. Publishes paperback originals. Royalty contract and advance are negotiable. Published 4 titles last year. Will consider photocopied and simultaneous submissions. Query first and include research outline. Reports in 45 days. Enclose return postage.
Nonfiction and Art: Publishes children's art; books about cable television; broadcast radiation; radiation and electromagnetic subjects.

PIGIRON PRESS, Box 237, Youngstown OH 44501. (216)744-2258. Editor-in-Chief: Jim Villani. Paperback originals. Royalty of 15% beyond 5,000 copies; 10% of first printing (1,000 copies); 12½% on second print to 5,000 copies; no advance. Published 1 title in 1977; will do 2 in 1978. Submit outline/synopsis and sample chapters for fiction and nonfiction. Submit contact sheet or prints to accompany ms. Photocopied submissions OK. Reports in 2-4 months. SASE.
Nonfiction: Rose Sayre, editor; Publishes art; cooking, cookbooks and foods; how-to, multimedia material, nature, pets, philosophy, photography, poetry, politics, psychology, and sports books.
Fiction: Rose Sayre, editor: Publishes adventure, experimental, fantasy, mainstream, science fiction, suspense and spacy material.
Recent Title: *Angry Candy,* by J. Parker (poetry).

PILOT BOOKS, 347 Fifth Ave., New York NY 10016. (212)685-0736. Publishes paperback originals. Offers standard royalty contract. Usual advance is $250, but this varies, depending on author's reputation and nature of book. Published 16 titles in 1976, 20 in 1977. Send outline. Reports in 4 weeks. Enclose return postage.
General Nonfiction, Reference, and Business: "Publishes financial, business, travel, career, and personal guides, training manuals. Directories and books on moneymaking opportunities." Wants "clear, concise treatment of subject matter." Length: 8,000 to 20,000 words.
Recent Titles: *National Directory of Budget Hotels,* by Carlson (travel); *Budget Travel Guide,* by Casewit (travel) and *Executive's Guide to Handling a Press Interview,* by Martin.

PINNACLE BOOKS, 1 Century Plaza, Century City CA 90067. Editor: Andrew Ettinger. Publishes paperback originals and reprints. "Contracts and terms are standard and competitive." Published 160 titles in 1976. Will send brochure and requirements memo to a writer if S.A.S.E. is enclosed. "Will no longer accept unsolicited mss. Most books are assigned to known writers or developed through established agents. However, an intelligent, literate, and descriptive letter of query will often be given serious consideration." Enclose return postage with query.
General: "Books range from general nonfiction to commercial trade fiction in most popular

categories. Pinnacle's list is aimed for wide popular appeal, with fast-moving, highly compelling escape reading, adventure, espionage, historical intrigue and romance, science fiction, western, popular sociological issues, topical nonfiction."

PLATT & MUNK PUBLISHERS, division of Questor, 1055 Bronx River Ave., Bronx NY 10475. (212)991-9000. Editor-in-Chief: Kate Klimo. Hardcover originals. Pays flat fee; "if royalty, nothing above 2%; advance averages $500." Published 12 titles in 1976, 36 in 1977; will do 21 in 1978. Submit complete ms. Send prints, photocopies or slides if photos/illustrations are to accompany ms. Photocopied submissions OK. Reports in 2-4 weeks. SASE. Book catalog for SASE.
Nonfiction and Fiction: Publishes juvenile picture books only.

PLAYBOY PRESS Division of Playboy Enterprises, Inc., 919 Michigan Ave., Chicago IL 60611. New York office: 747 Third Ave., New York NY 10017. (212)688-3030. Editorial Director (hardcover): William Adler; Editorial Director (softcover): Mary Ann Stuart. Publishes hardcover and paperback originals and reprints. Royalty contract to be negotiated. Published 60 titles last year. Query first. Enclose return postage.
General: Fiction and nonfiction slanted to the adult male who reads *Playboy* magazine.

PLENUM PUBLISHING CORP., 227 W. 17th St., New York NY 10011. Imprints: Da Capo Press, Consultants Bureau, IFI/Plenum Data Corporation, Plenum Press, Plenum Medical Book Company, Plenum Rosetta. Publishes hardcover and paperback originals and reprints. Offers standard minimum contract of 10-12½-15%. No advance. Published 450 titles last year. Query H. Feldman. Enclose return postage.
Nonfiction: Books on science, medicine, social and behavioral sciences, history, biography, art, music, photography; film, and general trade.

POCKET BOOKS, 1230 Ave. of the Americas, New York NY 10020. Paperback originals and reprints. Published 300 titles last year. Reports in one month. Submit through agent only. All unsolicited mss are returned unread. Enclose return postage.
General: History, biography, philosophy, inspirational, general nonfiction and adult fiction (mysteries, science fiction, gothics, westerns). Reference books, joke books, puzzles.

POET GALLERY PRESS, 224 W. 29th St., New York NY 10001. Editor: E.J. Pavlos. Publishes paperback originals. Offers standard 10-12½-15% royalty contract. Published 4 titles last year. Submit complete ms only. Enclose return postage with ms.
General: "We are a small specialty house, and we place our emphasis on publishing the works of young Americans currently living in Europe. We are interested in creative writing rather than commercial writing. We publish for writers who live overseas, who write and live, who produce writings from the self. Our books might turn out to be commercial, but that is a secondary consideration. We expect to emphasize poetry; however, our list will be concerned with all aspects of literature: the novel, plays, and cinema, as well as criticism." Recent titles include *The Musician; Substituting Memories.*

*POLARIS PRESS, 16540 Camellia Terrace, Los Gatos CA 95030. (408)356-7795. EDitor-in-Chief: Edward W. Ludwig. Paperback originals. Specializes in el-hi books with appeal to general juvenile public. 10% royalty; advance averages $100-300. Will consider subsidy publishing "if the work is of high quality, but of doubtful financial potential, and our funds are limited." Published 1 title in 1976, 2 in 1977; will do 3 in 1978. Send contact sheets or prints if photos and/or illustrations are to accompany ms. Simultaneous and photocopied submissions OK. Reports in 1-2 weeks. SASE. Free book catalog.
Fiction: Publishes some fantasy and science fiction "Please, *no* mss which require extensive (and expensive) use of color in inner pages." Query first.
Recent Titles: *A Mexican-American Coloring Book,* by V. Ranscon; *The California Story: A Coloring Book,* by A. Bernal (both coloring books with history text).

POPULAR LIBRARY/CBS, 600 Third Ave., New York NY 10016. Editor-in-Chief: Patrick O'Connor. Publishes originals and reprints. Royalty contract to be negotiated. Published 252 titles last year. Query first. Enclose return postage.
General: Publishes adult general fiction and nonfiction.

G. HOWARD POTEET, INC., Box 217, Cedar Grove NJ 07009. Editor-in-Chief: Dr. G.H. Poteet. Paperback originals. Specializes in how-to books. 10% royalty; no advance. Published 2 titles in 1976, 5 in 1977; will do 10 in 1978. Markets books by direct mail (and some ads in periodicals) but usually through a network of direct mail order dealers. SASE. Reports in 2-4 weeks. Book catalog for SASE.

Nonfiction: How-to books in the areas of business, hobbies, multimedia material, photography; technical material and textbooks. Query or submit outline/synopsis and sample chapters.

Special Needs: How-to-do-it books in the fields of electronics, woodworking, tools, photos. Books and kits on unusual and offbeat methods of teaching.

Recent Titles: *The Complete Guide to Making Money,* (how-to on making money); and *3-D Spelling Kit.*

CLARKSON N. POTTER, INC., 1 Park Ave., New York NY 10016. (212)532-9200. Editor-in-Chief: Jane West. Managing Editor: Carol Southern. Hardcover and paperback originals. 10% royalty on hardcover; 5% on paperback, varying escalations; advance depends on type of book and reputation or experience of author. Published 26 titles in 1976, 27 in 1977; will do 30 in 1978. Samples of prints may be included with outline. Photocopied submissions OK. Reports in 2-4 weeks. SASE. Free book catalog.

Nonfiction: Publishes Americana; art; biography; cookbooks, cooking and foods; history; how-to; humor; nature; photography; politics; scientific; self-help; and annotated literature books. "Mss must be cleanly typed on 8½x11 bond; double-spaced. Chicago *Manual of Style* is preferred." Query first or submit outline/synopsis and sample chapters.

Recent Titles: *Almanac of Words at Play,* by W. Espy (wordplay); *Six-Minute Souffle,* by C. Cutter (cookbook); *The President's Medal,* by N. McNeil (history).

*A.R. PRAGARE CO., INC., 3695G N. 126th St., Brookfield WI 53005. (414)781-1430. Publisher: Robert W. Pradt. Hardcover and paperback originals (70%) and reprints (30%). Specializes in firearms, hunting, and other topics of interest in this area. 7-10% royalty; no advance. Subsidy publishes a varying percentage of books through Pine Mountain Press, a division of the corporation. "Author must be previously published with good sales record and have some knowledge of publishing (marketing) and the financing to start a publishing venture." Published 4 titles in 1977; will do 6-8 in 1978. Markets books by mail order through gun and hunting magazines. Submit outline/synopsis and sample chapters. "No onion skin paper." Send prints to illustrate ms. Reports in 1-2 months. SASE.

Nonfiction: Publishes Americana, business; cookbooks, cooking and foods; economics, history, humor, recreation, sports (limited to our area); technical (in field of guns); biographies and children's books.

Fiction: Publishes adventure, humorous and western fiction books.

Speical Needs: Guns, hunting, related adventure and historical books for Leather Stocking division; general need for all materials in Business and Economics division.

PRAISE THE LORD PRESS, 2821 E. Ashman, Midland MI 48640. (517)832-3410. Editor-in-Chief: Phil Silva. Managing Editor: Matthew Brown. Paperback originals. Specializes in Christian poetry. Contracts individually negotiated; usually 10% of net profits; no advance. Published 1 title in 1976, 3 in 1977. Send prints to illustrate ms. Reports in 2-4 weeks. SASE. Free book catalog for SASE.

Poetry: Publishes religious poetry. "We publish high-quality, specifically Christian poetry by committted Christian poets. We don't want to see banality or sentimentality passed off as poetry. Our standard of excellence is higher than most contemporary poetry can reach." Submit complete ms.

Recent Titles: *Things New and Old: 33 Sonnets for Jesus,* by P. Silva.

PRENTICE-HALL, INC., Englewood Cliffs NJ 07632. Editor-in-Chief, Trade Division: John Grayson Kirk. Publishes hardcover and paperback originals and reprints. Offers standard 10-12½-15% royalty contract; advance usually $2,500 to $7,000. "A flat royalty is occasionally offered in the case of highly specialized hardcover series. A flat royalty is always offered on house paperbacks. Children's book contracts tend to average around 8% to 10% royalty rate. The advance depends on cost of artwork, but does not usually exceed anticipated first year royalties." Published 80 trade titles and 20 children's book titles last year. Will send a catalog to a writer on request. Submit outlines and sample chapters for nonfiction; submit complete ms for fiction. Will consider photocopied submissions. "Always keep 1 or more copies on hand in case original submission is lost in the mail." Reports in 4 to 6 weeks on trade books; reports in 2 to 4 weeks on juveniles. Enclose return postage.

General: "All types of fiction and trade nonfiction, save poetry, drama, and westerns. Average acceptable length: 80,000 words. The writer should submit his work professionally and be prepared to participate to the extent required in the book's promotion." Publishes adult trade mainstream fiction, Americana, art, biography, business, cookbooks, history, humor, medicine and psychiatry, music, nature, philosophy, politics, reference, religion, science, self-help and how-to, sports, hobbies and recreation. Length: 80,000 to 90,000 words.

Juveniles: "Contemporary fiction for ages 8 and up; high interest, low reading level fiction and nonfiction, project books up to age 15. Style, outlook, and structure requirements vary with each ms. They are as much an integral part of the book as the subject matter itself. In general, writers should make their material as interesting, alive, and simple as possible. We are interested in very simple concept books for preschoolers (*not* alphabet books) about 500 to 1,000 words; books for ages 9 to 14 on one aspect of American history covering a wide time and geographical span. If a book is really good, it can usually survive the fact that the subject has been worked over. Because children's books are so expensive to produce and therefore expensive to buy, the trade market is limited. Libraries are the primary market. At this point, they seem to be showing a decided preference for books in which the child can participate— instructive books, involving books." Length: 15,000 words for teenage books; 5,000 to 15,000 for fiction and nonfiction, ages 7 to 12; Editor-in-Chief, Juvenile Books: Ellen E.M. Roberts.

PRENTICE-HALL OF CANADA, LTD., 1870 Birchmount Rd., Scarborough, Ontario M1P 2J7 Canada. (416)293-3621. Editor-in-Chief: G.B. Halpin. Hardcover and paperback originals (90%); and reprints (10%). Royalty of 10% on first 5,000; 12% on second 5,000; 15% on all copies sold over 10,000 copies. Advance is determined by the publication. Published 23 titles in 1976, 30 in 1977; will do 40 in 1978. Simultaneous and photocopied submissions OK. SASE. Reports in 2-4 weeks. Free book catalog.

Nonfiction: Publishes art, biography, history, hobbies, how-to, humor, nature, photography, politics, recreation, references, self-help, sports, technical. Submit outline and 3-4 representative sample chapters to trade editor with brief author biography including previous publishing experience, if any.

Fiction: Suspense and science fiction.

Recent Titles: *Collecting Canada's Past,* by Smith/Smith/Bell (Canadiana); *Alpine Skiing* by Greene/Raine (sport).

*THE PRESERVATION PRESS, National Trust for Historic Preservation, 740-748 Jackson Pl., N.W., Washington DC 20006. Vice-President and Editor: Mrs. Terry B. Morton. Publishes paperback reprints and originals, and hardcover originals. Offers Author's Guild and other standard publishing contracts. "Past work has generally been on honorarium or fee basis." "Contracts based on flat fees often provide for partial payment upon submission of outline." About 95% of ideas coming from outside the company are published only on a subsidy basis. Also has a cooperative publication program for member organizations, which "can be several options: Shared costs and profits between Press and organizations; subsidized by organization (writing, design and manufacturing costs), with small percentage (10% or so) levied as contribution to editorial and other overhead, with deferred payments (12 to 18 months), with and without Press share in profits." Published 15 titles in 1976. Titles sold and distributed primarily by direct mail. Will send free catalog to writer on request. Will consider simultaneous and photocopied submissions. Query first. Follow Chicago *Manual of Style.* Reports as soon as possible. Enclose return postage.

Nonfiction: Publishes books about historic preservation (saving and reusing the "built" environment such as buildings, structures, sites and objects of architectural and historical importance and character). No general local history. Length: 2,000 to 20,000 words. Also publishes case studies, cookbooks; preservation law; reference and textbooks. Recently published *A Courthouse Conservation Handbook* and *Economic Benefits of Preserving Old Buildings.*

PRINCE PUBLISHERS, 349 E. Northfield Rd., Livingston NJ 07039. Editor-in-Chief: Dick Atkins. Publishes hardcover and paperback originals. Offers standard royalty contract of 10-12½-15%. Advance varies. Published 3 titles last year. "Prince books are headed for the mass market with particular concentration on both coasts." Will consider photocopied and simultaneous submissions. Submit outline and sample chapters for nonfiction and fiction. Address "Fiction Editor" or "Nonfiction Editor." Reports in 1 month. Enclose return postage.

Fiction and Nonfiction: "Prince is very selective and publishes a limited number of books each year. We're looking for mss of quality that have potential mass appeal. Also published mainstream adult trade fiction, sports, hobbies, and recreation.

PROFESSIONAL EDUCATORS PUBLICATIONS, INC., P.O. Box 80728, Lincoln NE 68501. Editor-in-Chief: Harry Kaste. Publishes paperback originals. Offers outright purchase of ms for negotiated fee. Published 2 titles in 1976. Free book catalog. Will consider photocopied submissions; ribbon copy for publication. Mss for publication must be typed on good quality bond stock with generous margins. Everything must be double-spaced, including any extracts, notes, references or bibliographies. Query first. Reports in 1 month. Enclose return postage.

Textbooks: "Short texts treating special topics related to the field of professional education for use by students and faculty in schools of education and by practicing teachers." Presentation should be lucid, with a minimum of professional jargon and scholarly apparatus. Length: 35,000 to 75,000 words. Recent titles include *Lifelong Learning* (Hiemstra) and *Moral Development and Education* (Forisha/Forisha).

PRUETT PUBLISHING COMPANY, 3235 Prairie Ave., Boulder CO 80301. Managing Editor: Gerald Keenan. Royalty contract is "dependent on the price we receive from sales." No advance. Published 18 titles in 1976. "Most books that we publish are aimed at special interest groups. As a small publisher, we feel most comfortable in dealing with a segment of the market that is very clearly identifiable, and one we know we can reach with our resources." Will send free catalog to writer on request. Mss must conform to the Chicago *Manual of Style*. No simultaneous submissions. Legible photocopies acceptable. Query first. Reports in 2-4 weeks. SASE.

General Adult Nonfiction and Textbooks: Pictorial railroad histories; outdoor activities related to the Intermountain West; some Western Americana. Textbooks with a regional (Intermountain) aspect for pre-school through college level. Also, Special Education, with emphasis on student-oriented workbooks. Does not want to see anything with the personal reminiscence angle or biographical studies of little-known personalities. "Like most small publishers, we try to emphasize quality from start to finish, because for the most part, our titles are going to a specialized market that is very quality conscious. We also feel that one of our strong points is the personal involvement ('touch') so often absent in a much larger organization."

Recent Titles: *American Indians in Colorado,* by J.D. Hughes (history); *Northwest Mosaic,* by Halseth/Glasrud (ethnic history); and *Railroad in the Clouds,* by W.H. Wilson (railroadiana).

PSG PUBLISHING COMPANY, INC., 545 Great Rd., Littleton MA 01460. (617)486-8971. Editor-in-Chief: Frank Paparello. Managing Editor: Margery Berube. Hardcover and paperback originals. Specializes in publishing technical medical and scientific books for the professional and graduate student market. 10% royalty; no advance. Published 20 titles in 1976; will do 21-25 in 1977 and 20-25 in 1978. Send prints of photos to accompany ms. Simultaneous submissions OK. Reports in 2-4 weeks. SASE. Free book catalog.

Nonfiction: Margery S. Berube, Department Editor. Publishes scientific books and ones on medicine and psychiatry. "We do not want books directed to the lay person. We are not set up to market consumer oriented books." Query first or submit complete ms.

Recent Titles: *Hemophilia,* by M. Hilgartner (medicine); *Birth Defects and Drugs in Pregnancy,* by D. Stone, O.P. Heinonen, S. Shapiro (epidemialogy).

PULSE-FINGER PRESS, Box 16697, Philadelphia PA 19139. Editor-in-Chief: Orion Roche. Publishes hardcover and paperback originals. Offers standard minimum book contract; less for poetry. Advance varies, depending on quality. "Not less than $100 for poetry; or $500 for fiction." Published 5 titles last year. Query first. No unsolicited mss. Reports in 1 month. Enclose S.A.E. and return postage.

Fiction and Poetry: "We're interested in subjects of general concern with a focus on fiction and poetry. All types considered; tend to the contemporary-cum-avant-garde. No length requirements. Our only stipulation is quality, as we see it." Current titles include *The Icarus to Be* (Sax) and *The Circular Seesaw* (Finkel).

THE PURDUE UNIVERSITY PRESS, South Campus Courts—D. West Lafayette IN 47907. (317)749-6083. Director: William J. Whalen. Managing Editor: Diane R. Dubiel. Publishes hardcover and paperback originals. Specializes in scholarly books from all areas of academic endeavor. 10% royalty on gross; no advance. Published 5 titles in 1976, 5-6 in 1977; will do 6-7 in 1978. Photocopied submissions OK "if author will verify that it does not mean simultaneous submission elsewhere." Reports in 2-4 months. SASE. Free book catalog.

Nonfiction: Publishes Americana, art (but no color plates), biography, cooking and foods, history, law, music, nature, philosophy, photography, poetry, political science, psychology, reference, religious, scientific, technical, and literary criticism. "Works of scholarship only."

Fiction: Experimental. "As a university press, we are interested only in works of academic merit which display creative research and scholarship."

Recent Titles: *The Political Pulpit,* by R. Hart (political rhetoric); *The Social Physics of Adam*

Smith, by V. Foley (economic history); *Advances in Fruit Breeding*, by Janick/Moore (horticulture).

G.P. PUTNAM'S SONS, 200 Madison Ave., New York NY 10016. (212)576-8900. Editor-in-Chief: Phyllis Grann. Juvenile Editor-in-Chief: Charles Mercer. Publishes hardcover and paperback originals. "Payment is on standard royalty basis." Published 281 titles in 1976, 276 in 1977. Free book catalog. "Well-known authors may submit outline and sample chapter." Unsolicited mss not accepted. Reports on queries in 1 week. Enclose S.A.S.E.
Nonfiction, Fiction and Juveniles: Nonfiction in history, biography, exploration, etc. Publishes juvenile fiction and nonfiction. "Adult mss must be a bare minimum of 60,000 words; juveniles vary in length, of course, depending upon whether they are young adult or picture book texts."

QUADRANGLE/THE NEW YORK TIMES BOOK CO., a subsidiary of The New York Times, 3 Park Ave., New York NY 10016. Editor-in-Chief: Roger Jellinek. Hardcover and paperback originals (75%) and reprints (25%). Standard royalty; advance offered "if circumstances require it." Published 60 titles in 1976, 80 in 1977. Submit synopsis and sample chapters. Send prints if photos/illustrations are to accompany ms. Reports in 1-2 weeks. SASE.
Nonfiction: Americana; art; biography; business; cookbooks, cooking and foods; economics; history; how-to; humor; law; medicine and psychiatry; nature; photography; politics; psychology; recreation; reference; scientific; self-help; sociology; sports; and travel.
Fiction: Adventure; fantasy; historical; mainstream; mystery; romance; science fiction; and suspense.
Recent Titles: *Wanted!*, by H. Blum (current affairs); *Life on the Run*, by B. Bradley (biography); and *Food of the Western World*, by Fitzgibbon (cookbook).

QUAIL STREET PUBLISHING CO., 500 Newport Center Dr., Newport Beach CA 92660. Publisher: Jo Newman. Acquisitions Editor: Jeannette Montgomery. Hardcover originals (95%) and reprints (5%). 10-12½-15% royalty; "advance varies widely with author's track record (so far $500-25,000)." Published 6 titles in 1976, 13 in 1977; will do 30 in 1978. Submit outline/synopsis and sample chapters for nonfiction. Submit complete ms for fiction. Agented submissions are read first. Send prints of a representative sample of illustrations. Simultaneous and photocopied submissions OK. Reports in 2-4 months. SASE. Book catalog $1.
Nonfiction: Publishes books on art (only very specialized ones such as current title *I Can Do It, I Can Do It*—arts and crafts for the mentally retarded); biography (should be done with dialogue and "on the scene" feeling; no lengthy accounts of names and dates); business (humorous looks at business today or exposes of our business system); erotica (with a touch of humor—no pulp novels); humor (no cartoon collections, but humorous, full-length mss are welcome); medicine and psychiatry (with a definite point of view); nature (how to conserve water, energy, etc.); psychology (no transactional analysis books—looking for new, but sound, theories); religious (possibly exposes of vast wealth held by churches here and abroad); sociology (on a superficial basis; e.g., TV and violence, but no statistical type studies). 300-1,000 ms pages.
Fiction: Adventure, historical, humorous, mainstream, mystery, romance, science fiction. Will consider a western only if it's really big and more of a historical novel than the usual western.
Special Needs: Planning a special series of books for mentally retarded and/or physically handicapped children.
Current Titles: *Jamaican American*, by B. Cox (fiction); *Our Own Harms*, by J.H. Newman (nonfiction).

QUILL PUBLICATIONS, 1260 Coast Village Circle, Santa Barbara CA 93108. (805)969-2542. Editor: Ben E. Johnson. Publishes hardcover and paperback originals. Offers standard 10-12½-15% royalty contract. No advance, usually. Published 5 titles in 1976, 10 in 1977. Query first with outline and sample chapter. Reports in 1 month. Enclose return postage.
Fiction: Department editor: John Murray. "Must have a foundation in the Christian tradition. Want adult fiction that is realistic, showing characters facing issues that are evaluated through a perspective that is Christian."
Nonfiction: Seeking mss related to social problems, personal ethics, devotional, self-help and Bible study. Must be of interest to a conservative Christian readership. Interested in books which help one Christian communicate feelings and knowledge to large groups of people. Also, books centering on communication skills as they relate to the professional educator and the Christian worker. "75% of our books should be of value to both the secular and religious communities."
Recent Titles: *The Century List*, by M. Baker (novel); *Sunwoman*, by M. Baker (novel); and *What Was That Verse Again?*, by Johnson (nonfiction).

RAINTREE PUBLISHERS LTD., 205 W. Highland, Milwaukee WI 53202. Editorial Director: Jan Celba. Hardcover and paperback originals. Specializes in juvenile supplementary reading and language arts programs. May offer royalty or outright purchase; advance varies; "usually 50% of the contract fee." Published 75 titles in 1976, 100 in 1977; will do 100+ in 1978. Query or submit outline/synopsis and sample chapters. State availability of photos/illustrations. Photocopied submissions OK. Reports in 2-4 weeks. SASE. Free book catalog.
Nonfiction: Publishes biography (juvenile, 1,500 words max); and juvenile (in all categories) books.
Fiction: Publishes juvenile books in all categories.
Recent Titles: *Will I Ever Be Good Enough?,* by J. Conaway (juvenile); *We're Off to See the Lizard,* by B. Brenner (juvenile); and *Photography: Take A Look,* by D.J. Herda (juvenile).

RAND McNALLY, P.O. Box 7600, Chicago IL 60680. Trade Division and Education Division at this address. Variable royalty and advance schedule. Trade books payment on royalty basis or outright; mass market juveniles outright. Reports in 6 to 8 weeks. Enclose return postage.
General Nonfiction: Adult manuscripts should be sent to Stephen P. Sutton, Editor, Adult Books, Trade Division, but query first on the subjects of Americana, travel, natural history, personal adventure, self-help. Contracts are sometimes offered on the basis of outline and sample chapter.
Trade Juveniles: Dorothy Haas, Editor, picture books ages 3-8; fiction and nonfiction ages 8-12; special interest books (no fiction) for young adults; Send picture book manuscripts for review. Query on longer manuscripts.
Mass Market Juveniles: Roselyn Bergman, Editor. Picture book scripts, six years and under; Jr. Elf Books, Elf Books, activity formats. Realistic stories, fantasy, early learning material; not to exceed 600 words and must present varied illustration possibilities.
Textbooks: Education Division publishes books, equipment, other printed materials, and maps for elementary, high schools and colleges in restricted fields. Query Executive Editor, Education Division.

RANDOM HOUSE, INC., 201 East 50th St., New York NY 10022. Also publishes Vintage Books. Publishes hardcover and paperback originals and reprints. Payment as per standard minimum book contracts. Query first. Enclose return postage.
Fiction and Nonfiction: Publishes fiction and nonfiction of the highest standards.
Poetry: Some poetry volumes.
Juveniles: Publishes a broad range of fiction and nonfiction for young readers, including Beginner Books, Step-up Books, Gateway Books, Landmark Books. Particularly interested in high-quality fiction for children.

RD COMMUNICATIONS, Box 683, Ridgefield CT 06877. Editor-in-Chief: Richard Dunn. Publishes paperback originals. Straight book contract of 15%. Advance averages $500 payable in installments from time of contract to publication. Published 3 titles in 1976. Marketed by direct mail and mail order advertising. Will send catalog to writer if professional in one of their fields of specialty. Reports in 2-4 weeks. SASE.
Business, Economics and Technical: Technology, business, professional skills, education. Author should have working background in field in which he writes. Content must have immediate practical value to professionals in the field. Emphasis is on practical application rather than general discussion or theory.

RED DUST, INC., 218 East 81st St., New York NY 10028. Editor: Joanna Gunderson. Publishes hardcover and paperback originals and translations. Specializes in quality work by new writers. Books printed either simultaneously in hard and paper covers or in hardcover alone, in editions of 1,000 copies. 10-12½-15% royalty; the author generally receives $300 on the signing of the contract, as an advance. Published 1 title in 1976, 4 in 1977. Current catalog available on request. Enclose 13¢ stamp with request. Will consider photocopied submissions. "Authors should not submit photos or artwork with mss." Query with sample chaper. Reports in 2 months. SASE.
Fiction: Novels and short stories.
Nonfiction and Poetry: Scholarly, art, art history, film and poetry.

REGAL BOOKS, Division of G/L Publications, Box 1591, Glendale CA 91209. (213)247-2330. Managing Editor: Fritz Ridenour. Publishes paperback originals. 10% royalty contract. Published 49 titles last year. Vill consider photocopied submissions. Query with outline and 1 sample chapter. Reports in 90 days. SASE.
Religion: All material is Christian in content. Christian education, Christian living; theology,

missionary and missions; church growth, family life, Bible study.
Recent Titles: *Your Churning Place* (Wise); and *Creative Christian Marriage* (lee).

THE REGENTS PRESS OF KANSAS, (formerly The University Press of Kansas), 366 Watson Library, Lawrence KS 66045. (913)864-4154. Managing Editor: John Langley. Hardcover and paperback originals. "No royalty until manufacturing costs are recovered." No advance. Published 11 titles in 1976, 10 in 1977; will do 10 in 1978. Markets books by direct mail, chiefly to libraries and scholars. "State availability of illustrations if they add significantly to the ms." Photocopied submissions OK. Reports in 4-6 months. SASE. Free book catalog.
Nonfiction: Publishes biography, history, literary criticism, politics, regional subjects, and scholarly nonfiction books. "No dissertations." Query first.
Recent Titles: *The Presidency of Warren G. Harding,* by E. Trani and D. Wilson (history); *I Am: A Study of E.E. Cummings' Poems,* by G. Lane (literary criticism); *The Prairie People: Potawatomi Indian Culture,* by J. Clifton (ethnohistory).

REGENTS PUBLISHING COMPANY, INC., Two Park Ave., New York NY 10016. Pays 10% to 15% royalty based on net sales. Usual advance is $500, but this varies, depending on author's reputation and nature of book. Published 50 titles last year. Prefers queries, outlines, sample chapters. Reports in 3 to 4 weeks. Enclose return postage.
Textbooks: Publishes foreign language texts, multimedia packages, English books for the foreign-born.

*RESEARCH SERVICES CORP., 5280 Trail Lake Dr., Fort Worth TX 76133. (817)292-4270. Editor-in-Chief: Dr. O.A. Battista, Sc.D. Hardcover and paperback originals. 10% (of list) royalty. Advance averages $1,000. Will consider subsidy publishing after "review of all circumstances; main consideration is quality of work." Published # titles in 1976, 3 in 1977; will do 4 in 1978. Reports in 2-4 weeks. "Return self-addressed package with adequate postage is a must. No mss returned if received otherwise." Book catalog for SASE.
Nonfiction: Publishes self-help books, scientific, humorous, how-to, Americana and humor. Query first.
Fiction: Humorous and science fiction. Query first.

RESTON PUBLISHING COMPANY (Prentice-Hall subsidiary), 11480 Sunset Hills Rd.,, Reston VA 22090. President: Matthew I. Fox. Publishes hardcover originals. Offers standard minimum book contract of 10-12½-15%. Advance varies. "We are a wholly-owned subsidiary of Prentice-Hall, which has the most extensive marketing system in publishing." Published 65 titles last year. Will send free catalog to writer on request. Will consider photocopied submissions. Submit outline and sample chapters. Reports immediately. Enclose return postage.
Textbooks: "Primarily for the junior college and vocational/technical school market. Professionally oriented books for in-service practitioners and professionals. All material should be written to appeal to these markets in style and subject. We are able to attract the best experts in all phases of academic and professional life to write our books. But we are always seeking new material in all areas of publishing; any area that is represented by courses at any post-secondary level."

FLEMING H. REVELL COMPANY, Central Ave., Old Tappan NJ 07675. Editor-in-Chief: Dr. Frank S. Mead. Payment usually on royalty basis. Published 73 titles last year. Reports in a month to six weeks. Enclose return postage with ms.
Religion: Publishers of inspirational and religious books. Also books related to Sunday School and church work. Occasional biography and more general books that might appeal to the religious market. Length: usually 40,000 to 60,000 words.

REYMONT ASSOCIATES, 29 Reymont Ave., Rye NY 10580. Editor-in-Chief: D.J. Scherer. Managing Editor: Felicia Scherer. Paperback originals. 10-12½-15½% royalty; no advance. Published 2 books in 1976, 6 in 1977. Submit outline/synopsis and sample chapters. State availability of photos/illustrations. Simultaneous and photocopied submissions OK. Reports in 2-4 weeks. SASE. Book catalog for SASE.
Nonfiction: Publishes business; how-to; self-help; unique directories and travel books. "Aim for 12-15,000 words."
Recent Titles: *For the Shape of Your Life,* by Felicia Scherer (self-help); and *How the Small Taxpayer Can Take the IRS to Court,* staff-written (how-to).

THE WARD RITCHIE PRESS, 474 S. Arroyo Parkway, Pasadena CA 91105. (213)793-1163. Managing Editor: William Chleboun. •Offers standard 10-12½-15% royalty contract. Advance varies. Published 28 titles in 1976. Free book catalog. Query first and submit outline and 2 chapters. Enclose S.A.S.E.

Nonfiction and Fiction: Broad general interest. "Americana (quality literature pertaining to any period and place in American history). Cookbooks (distincitive cookbooks only). Biography, how-to (on any subject). Photo essay."

Recent Titles: *Running Your Own Business,* by H. Stern (reference); *Big Orange,* by J. Smith (travel); and *Zen and Cross Country Skier,* by D. Blackburn (inspirational).

RONALD PRESS, 79 Madison Ave., New York NY 10016. Publishes hardcover originals. Royalty contract to be negotiated. Query first. Enclose return postage.

Reference and Textbooks: Publishes college textbooks. Also publishes reference books.

RICHARDS ROSEN PRESS, 29 E. 21st St., New York NY 10010. Editor: Ruth C. Rosen. Publishes hardcover originals. "Each project has a different royalty setup." Published 41 titles last year. Wants queries with outline and sample chapter. Reports within 3 weeks. Enclose return postage.

Nonfiction: "Our books are geared to the young adult audience whom we reach via school and public libraries. Most of the books we publish are related to guidance-career and personal adjustment." Also publishes material on the theatre, science, women, as well as journalism for schools. Interested in supplementary material for enrichment of school curriculum. Preferred length: 40,000 words.

ROUTLEDGE & KEGAN PAUL, LTD., 9 Park St., Boston MA 02108. Editorial Director: Brian Southam. Publishes hardcover and paperback originals and reprints. Offers standard 10-12½-15% royalty contract "on clothbound editions, if the books are not part of a series"; usual advance is $250 to $2,500. Published over 200 titles last year. Query first with outline and sample chapters. Submit complete ms "only after going through outline and sample chapters step." Returns rejected material in 1 to 2 months. Reports on ms accepted for publication in 1 to 6 months. Enclose check for return postage.

Nonfiction: "Academic, reference, and scholarly levels: English and European literary criticism, drama and theater, social sciences, philosophy and logic, psychology, parapsychology, oriental religions, mysticism, history, political science, education. Our books generally form a reputable series under the general editorship of distinguished academics in their fields. The approach should be similar to the styles adopted by Cambridge University Press, Harvard University Press, and others." Interested in material for the International Library of Sociology. Length: 30,000 to 250,000 words.

THOMAS J. ROWEN BOOKLET SERVICE, 986 Camino Dr., Santa Clara CA 95050. Editor-in-Chief: Tom Rowen. Publishes paperback originals. "We pay 40% for each booklet sold; no advance. Our books sell for $1.65-3.50, but 25¢ comes off for mailing and handling." Published 2 booklets in 1976, 4 in 1977. Query. Photocopied submissions OK. Reports in 1 month. SASE. Free book catalog.

Nonfiction: "We publish booklets on how to do different skills involved with sports, history and other nonfiction topics. The sports books are done in interviews with coaches and athletes involved with the sport. We have initiated a marketing service for writers who have their booklets published and have difficulties marketing these books themselves."

Recent Titles: *How to Write and Sell to the Juveniel Market,* and *Baseball Drills for Small Groups.*

RUTGERS UNIVERSITY PRESS, 30 College Ave., New Brunswick NJ 08901. Published 20 titles last year in the following categories: history, literary criticism, ornithology, photography, government, geography, science. Free book catalog. Prefers queries. Final decision depends on time required to secure competent professional reading reports. Enclose return postage.

Nonfiction: Books with a New Jersy or regional aspect. Also scholarly books on history, biological science, biographies, philosophy, and criminal justice. Regional nonfiction must deal with mid-Atlantic region with emphasis on New Jersey. Length: 80,000 words and up.

Recent Titles: *Leopold I of Austria,* by Spielman; *A History of Middle Europe,* by Tihany; and *Land and People,* by Wacker.

WILLIAM H. SADLIER, INC., 11 Park Pl., New York NY 10007. Vice President, Editor-in-Chief: William J. Richardson, Ph.D. Offers 6% royalty contract for elementary textbooks; 8% for high school textbooks. Submit outline and sample chapters to Editorial Department. Reports "as soon as possible." Enclose S.A.E. and return postage.

Textbooks: Elementary and secondary textbooks. Whole or significant part of school market should be identified, competition studied, proposal developed and submitted with representative sample. Interested in language arts and social studies. Economics, history, politics, religion, sociology.

ST. ANTHONY MESSENGER PRESS, 1615 Republic St., Cincinnati OH 45210. Editor-in-Chief: Rev. Jeremy Harrington, O.F.M. Publishes paperback originals. Offers 6% to 8% royalty contract. Usual advance is $500. Published 8 titles in 1976, 10 in 1977. Books are sold in bulk to groups (study clubs, high school or college classes). Will send free catalog to writer on request. Will consider photocopied submissions if they are not simultaneous submissions to other publishers. Query first or submit outline and sample chapters. Enclose return postage.
Religion: "We try to reach the Catholic market with topics near the heart of the ordinary Catholic's belief. We want to offer insight and inspiration and thus give people support in living a Christian life in a pluralistic society. We are not interested in an academic or abstract approach. Our emphasis is on the popular approach with examples, specifics, color, anecdotes." Length: 25,000 to 40,000 words.
Recent Titles: *Overcoming Anxiety,* by G. Schomp (psychology/religion); *How To Be Friends With Yourself and Your Family,* by Dr. J. Rosenbaum (psychology); and *Unmarried and Pregnant: What Now?,* by I. Critelli/T. Schick (self-help).

ST. MARTIN'S PRESS, 175 Fifth Ave., New York NY 10010. Editor-in-Chief: Leslie Pockell. Published 350 titles last year. Query first. Reports promptly. Enclose return postage.
General: Publishes general fiction and nonfiction; major interest in adult nonfiction, history, self-help, political science, popular science, biography, scholarly, technical reference, etc. "No children's books." Recently published titles include *All Things Bright and Beautiful* (Herriot).
Textbooks: College textbooks.

HOWARD W. SAMS & CO., INC., 4300 W. 62nd St., Indianapolis IN 46268. Manager, Book Division: C.P. Oliphant. Payment depends on quantity, quality, salability. Offers both royalty arrangements or outright purchase. Prefers queries, outlines, and sample chapters. Usually reports within 30 days. Enclose return postage.
Technical, Scientific, and How-To: "Publishes technical and scientific books for the electronics industry; Audel books for the homeowner, craftsman, and handyman; and books for the amateur radio field."

PORTER SARGENT PUBLISHERS, INC., 11 Beacon St., Boston MA 02108. (617)523-1670. Publishes hardcover and paperback originals, reprints, translations, and anthologies. "Each contract is dealt with on an individual basis with the author." Published 1 title in 1976, 5 in 1977. Free book catalog. Send query with brief description of table of contents, sample chapter and information regarding author's background. Enclose return postage.
General Nonfiction, Reference, Philosophy, and Textbooks: "Handbook Series and Special Education Series offer standard, definitive reference works in private education and writings and texts in special education. The Extending Horizons Series is an outspoken, unconventional series which presents topics of importance in contemporary affairs, viewpoints rarely offered to the reading public, methods and modes of social change, and the framework of alternative structures for the expansion of human awareness and well-being." This series is particularly, although not exclusively, directed to the college adoption market." Contact Martin Blatt or Patricia McGauley.
Recent Titles: *The Politics of Nonviolent Action,* by G. Sharp (political sociology); and *What Is To Be Undone,* by M. Albert (political theory).

SCHENKMAN PUBLISHING CO., INC., 3 Mt. Auburn Pl., Cambridge MA 02138. (617)492-4952. Editor-in-Chief: Alfred S. Schenkman. Managing Editor: Katherine Schlivek. Hardcover and paperback originals. Specializes in textbooks. Royalty varies, but averages 10%. "In some cases, no royalties are paid on first 2,000 copies sold." No advance. Published 50 titles in 1976, over 50 in 1977. State availability of photos and/or illustrations. Simultaneous and photocopied submissions OK. Reports in 1-2 months. SASE. Free book catalog.
Nonfiction: Publishes economics, history, psychology, sociology, and textbooks. Query.
Recent Titles: *Socialization in Drug Abuse,* by R. Coombs (sociology); and *All Their Own: People and the Places They Build,* by J. Wampler (Americana).

SCHIRMER BOOKS, Macmillan Publishing Co., Inc., 866 Third Ave., New York NY 10022. Editor-in-Chief: Ken Stuart. Hardcover and paperback originals (90%); paperback reprints (10%). Specializes in music books for college textbooks, trade, professional and reference and music store markets. 5-15% royalty; small advance. Published 20 titles in 1976 and 1977; will do

20 in 1978. Submit photos and/or illustrations if central to the book, not if decorative or tangential. Photocopied and simultaneous submissions OK. Reports in 1-2 months. SASE. Book catalog for SASE.

Nonfiction: Publishes how-to, music, self-help, and textbooks. Submit outline/synopsis and sample chapters.

Recent Titles: *Boulez; Composer, Conductor, Enigma,* by J. Peyser (trade); *Sound Pleasure: A Prelude to Active Listening,* by D. Ivey (college); *Solo Guitar Playing,* by F. Noad (method book).

SCHOLIUM INTERNATIONAL, INC., 130-30 31st Ave., Flushing NY 11354. Editor-in-Chief: Arthur L. Candido. Publishes hardcover and paperback originals. Standard minimum book contract of 12½%. Published 3 titles last year. Will send free catalog to writer on request. Will consider photocopied submissions. Query first. Reports in 2 weeks. Enclose return postage.

Science and Technology: Subjects covered are cryogenics, electronics, aviation, medicine, physics, etc. "We also publish books in other areas whenever it is felt the manuscript has good sales and reception potential. Contact us prior to sending ms, outlining subject, number of pages, and other pertinent information which would enable us to make a decision as to whether we would want to review the ms."

CHARLES SCRIBNER'S SONS, 597 Fifth Ave., New York NY 10017. Director of Publishing: Jacek K. Galazka. Publishes hardcover originals and hardcover and paperback reprints. "Our contract terms, royalties and advances vary, depending on the nature of the project." Published 300 titles last year. Query first for nonfiction (juvenile and adult), and adult fiction; complete ms preferred for juvenile fiction, "but will consider partial ms and outline." Prefers photocopied submissions. Reports in 1 to 2 months on ms accepted for publication. Returns rejected adult material in 4 to 6 weeks; returns rejected juveniles in 3 to 4 weeks. Enclose return postage.

General: Publishes adult fiction and nonfiction, practical books, garden books, reference sets, cookbooks, history, science. Adult Trade Editors: Elinor Parker, Doe Coover, Patricia Cristol, Susanne Kirk and Laurie Graham.

Juveniles: "We publish books for children of all ages—pre-kindergarten up through high school age. We publish picture books, fiction, and nonfiction in all subjects. We have no special requirements in regard to special treatment or emphasis and length requirements. We're interested in books on any topical subject or theme, assuming we feel the material is exciting enough." Children's Book Editor: Lee Anna Deadrick.

THE SEABURY PRESS, 815 2nd Ave., New York NY 10017. Editors-in Chief: Theodore McConnell, Crossroad Books (religious); Justus G. Lawler, Continuum Books (adult general); and James C. Giblin, Clarion Books (juvenile). 10% royalty; advance "depends on the author's reputation and the nature of the project." Published 100 titles in 1976, 85 in 1977; will do 85-100 in 1978. Query for fiction and nonfiction; submit complete ms for children's picture books and short novels. State availability of photos/illustrations. Photocopied submissions OK. Reports in 1-2 months. SASE. Free book catalog.

Nonfiction: Publishes Americana (adult general, juvenile); biography (adult and juvenile); cookbooks, cooking and foods; history (juvenile); humor (adult, juvenile); juveniles; medicine and psychiatry (adult general); nature (juvenile); philosophy (religious); politics; psychology; reference (adult general); religious; self-help; and sociology (adult general) books.

Fiction: Publishes adventure (juvenile); fantasy (juvenile); historical (juvenile); humorous (juvenile); science fiction (juvenile, adult general); and suspense (juvenile) books.

Recent Titles: *The Irrational Season,* by M. L'Engle (religion, personal philosophy); *Shelter From the Wind,* by M.D. Bauer (realistic juvenile fiction).

E.A. SEEMANN PUBLISHING, INC., P.O. Box K, Miami FL 33156. (305)233-5852. Editor-in-Chief: Ernest A. Seemann. Publishes hardcover originals; rarely paperbacks. Offers standard royalty contract. Advance varies. Published 20 titles in 1976, 20 in 1977. Reports on rejected material within 2 days; accepted material, within 1 to 3 months. Will send free catalog to writer on request.

Nonfiction: Popular history, (particularly pictorial histories); popular natural history, (especially tropical and subtropical); Americana, handcrafts, cookbooks. "Mss must be typed in the normal style that a professional writer would know. Should be written for general, popular audiences. Our popular histories are to be man-centered, rather than date-and-event centered." Does not want to see novels, underground writings, poetry, short stories. Recently published *Yesterday's Cincinnati* (Feck), a pictorial history of Cincinnati dating from the first settlement to the 1950's, featuring a 5,000-word introductory historical essay and 230 authentic, historical photographs with long narrative captions.

'76 PRESS, Box 2686, Seal Beach CA 90740. (213)596-3491. Editor-in-Chief: Wallis W. Wood. Hardcover and paperback originals. 5% royalty; advance averages $2,500. Published 6 titles in 1976, 6-8 in 1977; will do 8-10 in 1978. State availability of photos and/or illustrations. Simultaneous and photocopied submissions OK. SASE. Free book catalog.
Nonfiction: "Economics, politics, and international relations, written from conservative, antibig government perspective. Information on author's credentials on subject matter is very important." Submit outline/synopsis and sample chapters.
Recent Titles: *Jimmy Carter/Jimmy Carter,* by G. Allen (politics); *Wall Street and the Rise of Hitler,* by A.C. Sutton (history); *Freedom from Cancer,* by M.L. Culbert (report on cancer preventative).

SHEED ANDREWS AND McMEEL, INC., 6700 Squibb Rd., MIssion KS 66202. (913)362-1523. Editor-in-Chief: James F. Andrews. Managing Editor: Donna Martin. Standard royalty; negotiable advance. Publishes 30 titles annually. Photocopied submissions OK. Reports in 1-2 months SASE. Book catalog for SASE.
General Nonfiction: Political history and commentary, general interest, popular philosophical, theological, cartoon collections, how-to books in home interests, photography, textbooks. Cookbooks, cooking and foods; economics, humor, politics, psychology, religious, and self-help books.
Recent Titles: *The Formula Book* by N. Stark (how-to); *The Yankee and Cowboy War,* by C. Oglesby (political); *The Church and the Homosexual,* by Fr. J.J. McNeill.

SHOAL CREEK PUBLISHERS, INC., P.O. Box 9737, Austin TX 78766. (512)451-7545. President: W. L. Thompson. Publishes hardcover and paperback originals and reprints. Offers standard minimum book contract of 10-12½-15%. Published 5 titles in 1976, 7 in 1977. Will consider photocopied submissions if they are clear. Query first. Reports as soon as possible. Enclose return postage.
Nonfiction: Regional and western nonfiction, historical interest books; folklore, politics, biographies, collections, cookbooks, Americana, art, biography.
Recent Titles: *Susanna Dickinson; Messenger of the Alamo,* by C.R. King (folklore); *The Yellow Rose of Texas: Her Saga and Her Song,* by M.A. Turner (folklore); and *The Lost Crucifix: Our Lady of Quadalupe,* by F. Alsop (fiction).

THE SHOE STRING PRESS, INC., (Archon Books, Linnet Books), 995 Sherman Ave., Hamden CT 06514. (203)248-6307. President: Mrs. Frances T. Rutter. 10% royalty of net; no advance. Published 68 titles in 1976, 70 in 1977. Query first and include table of contents and sample chapters. Reports in 4 to 6 weeks. Enclose return postage.
Nonfiction: Publishes scholarly books in limited editions, clothbound, etc.; history, biography, literary criticism, reference, philosophy, bibliographies, information science, library science, education, general scholarly nonfiction. Preferred length is 40,000-130,000 words, though there is no set limit.

*GEORGE SHUMWAY PUBLISHER, R.D. 7, Box 388B, York PA 17402. (717)755-1196. Editor-in-Chief: George Shumway. Hardcover and paperback originals (90%) and reprints (10%). Specializes in "nonfiction books concerning antique art and firearms, and Americana." 5-10% royalty; no advance. "We would consider subsidy publishing if a ms is of a particular interest to us for our list, but probably a marginal economic venture." Published 2 titles in 1976, 4 in 1977. Query. Simultaneous and photocopied submissions OK. Reports in 2-4 weeks. SASE. Free book catalog.
Nonfiction: Publishes Americana; art; and history books. "We are particularly interested in well-researched and illustrated mss on early American clothing and costume."
Recent Titles: *Arms Makers of Maryland,* by D.D. Hortzler (Americana, art); and *Rural Pennsylvania Clothing,* by E. Gehret (Americana).

SIGNPOST PUBLICATIONS, 16812 36th Ave. West, Lynnwood WA 98036. Editor-in-Chief: Cliff Cameron. Publishes hardcover and paperback originals. Offers standard minimum book contract of 10%. Advance varies. Published 5 titles in 1976. Free book catalog. Query. Reports in 3 weeks. Enclose S.A.S.E.
Nonfiction: "Books on outdoor subjects. Limited to self-propelled wilderness activity. Also books of general interest to Northwesterners. History, natural science, related to the Pacific Northwest. Books should have strong environmental material for a general audience, where applicable.

Recent Titles: *Pacific Crest Trail Hike Planning Guide,* by Long; and *Packrat Papers,* by Mueller.

SILVER BURDETT, Subsidiary of Scott, Foresman Co., 250 James St., Morristown NJ 07960. Publishes hardcover and paperback originals. "Textbook rates only, El-Hi range." Published approximately 180 titles last year. Query first to Barbara Howell, Editor-in-Chief, Silver Burdett Division. Enclose S.A.S.E.
Education: Produces educational materials for preschoolers, elementary and high school students, and professional publications for teachers. Among materials produced: textbooks, teachers' materials, other print and non-print classroom materials including educational games, manipulatives, and audiovisual aids (silent and sound 16mm films and filmstrips, records, multimedia kits, overhead transparencies, tapes, etc.). Assigns projects to qualified writers on occasion. Writer must have understanding of school market and school learning materials.

SILVERMINE PUBLISHERS INCORPORATED, Comstock Hill, Silvermine, Norwalk CT 06850. President: Marilyn Z. Atkin. Free book catalog. Query. Enclose S.A.S.E.
Nonfiction: Publishes general nonfiction, biography, and books dealing with fine arts and architecture. "We are not interested in name authors, but insist on good writing. Our books are designed to last (that is, they are not 1-season phenomena). Thus, a typical book over a period of 3 to 5 years may earn $3,000 to $6,000 royalties. It is our opinion that books that are solid text, unillustrated, are not salable any longer unless they are news or topical (which we are not interested in), fiction by established writers (which we are not interested in), or books on special subjects."

SIMON AND SCHUSTER, Trade Books Division of Simon & Schuster, Inc., 1230 6th Ave., New York NY 10020. "If we accept a book for publication, business arrangements are worked out with the author or his agent and a contract is drawn up. The specific terms vary according to the type of book and other considerations. Royalty rates are more or less standard among publishers. Special arrangements are made for anthologies, translations and projects involving editorial research services." Published over 200 titles in 1976. Free book catalog. "All unsolicited mss will be returned unread. Only mss submitted by agents or recommended to us by friends or actively solicited by us will be considered. Our requirements are as follows: All mss submitted for consideration should be marked to the attention of the editorial department. Mystery novels should be so labeled in order that they may be sent to the proper editors without delay. It usually takes at least three weeks for the author to be notified of a decision— often longer. Sufficient postage for return by first-class registered mail, or instructions for return by express collect, in case of rejection, should be included. Mss must be typewritten, double-spaced, on one side of the sheet only. We suggest margins of about one inch all around and the standard 8½-by-11-inch typewriter paper." Prefers complete mss.
General: "Simon and Schuster publishes books of adult fiction, history, biography, science, philosophy, the arts and religion, running 50,000 words or more. Our program does not, however, include school textbooks, extremely technical or highly specialized works, or, as a general rule, plays. Exceptions have been made, of course, for extraordinary mss of great distinction or significance."

CHARLES B. SLACK, INC., 6900 Grove Rd., Thorofare NJ 08086. (212)285-9777. Editor-in-Chief: Kenton T. Finch. Managing Editors: Dorothy Love, Kaye Coraluzzo, Peg Carnine. Hardcover and paperback originals (90%) and reprints (10%). Specializes in medical and health education texts. 10% (of net proceeds) royalty; advances are discouraged. Published 9 titles in 1976, 8 in 1977; will do 8 in 1978. State availability of photos and/or illustrations to accompany ms. Simultaneous submissions OK. Reports in 1-2 months. SASE. Free book pamphlet for SASE.
Nonfiction: Publishes medicine and psychiatry; psychology, scientific, and textbooks. Query, or submit outline/synopsis and sample chapters, or submit complete ms. All queries, outlines and mss should be sent to the attention of Kenton T. Finch.

SLEEPY HOLLOW RESTORATIONS, INC., Box 245, Tarrytown NY 10591. (914)631-8200. Editor-in-Chief: Saverio Procario. Managing Editor: Bruce D. MacPhail. Hardcover and paperback originals (85%); hardcover reprints (15%). 5-10% (on net) royalty; no advance. Published 4 titles in 1976, 3 in 1977; will do 5 in 1978. State availability of photos and/or illustrations to accompany ms. Simultaneous and photocopied submissions OK. Reports in 1-2 months. SASE. Free book catalog.
Nonfiction: Publishes Americana, art (American decorative arts); biography; cookbooks, cook-

ing and foods (regional, historic); history (especially American; New York state and colonial through modern times); technical 17th-19th century technology); travel (regional and New York state); American literature and literary criticism, especially 19th century. Query first, addressing it to the Managing Editor.

Recent Titles: *Life Along the Hudson,* by A. Keller (regional history); *Van Cortlandt Family Papers,* edited by J. Judd (American history); *A Century of Commentary on the Works of Washington Irving,* edited by A. Myers (American literary criticism).

THE SMITH, 5 Beekman St., New York NY 10038. Publishes hardcover and paperback originals. The Smith is now owned by The Generalist Association, Inc., a non-profit organization, which gives grants to writers and awards publication. Grants are variable, averaging $500 for book projects. Published 10 titles in 1976. Free book catalog. Send query first for nonfiction; sample chapter preferred for fiction. Reports within six weeks. Enclose return postage.

Nonfiction and Fiction: "original fiction — no specific schools or categories; for nonfiction, the more controversial, the better." Editor of Adult Fiction: Harry Smith. Nonfiction Editor: Sidney Bernard.

*SOCCER ASSOCIATES, P.O. Box 634, New Rochelle NY 10802. Editor: Jeff Miller. Published 95 titles last year. Send finished book to Milton Miller. Enclose return postage.

Sports, Hobbies, and Recreation: Publishes sports, recreation, leisure time, and hobby books under Sport Shelf and Leisure Time Books imprints. Most titles are British and Australian although they do have a special service for authors who publish their own books and desire national and international distribution, promotion, and publicity.

SOUTHERN METHODIST UNIVERSITY PRESS, Dallas TX 75275. (214)692-2263. Director: Allen Maxwell; Associate Director and Editor: Margaret L. Hartley. Payment is on royalty basis: 10% of list up to 2,500 copies; 12½% for 2,500 to 5,000 copies; 15% thereafter. No advance. Published 8 titles in 1976. Free book catalog. Appreciates query letters, outlines and sample chapters. Reports tend to be slow for promising mss requiring outside reading by authorities. Enclose return postage.

Nonfiction: Regional and scholarly nonfiction. History, Americana, economics, banking, literature, and anthologies. Length: open.

SOUTHERN PUBLISHING ASSOCIATION, Box 59, Nashville TN 37202. (615)889-8000. Editor-in-Chief: Richard W. Coffen. Hardcover and paperback originals. Specializes in religiously oriented books. 5-10% royalty; advance averages $100. Published 26 titles in 1976, 30 in 1977; will do 36 in 1978. State availability of photos and/or illustrations to accompany ms. Simultaneous and photocopied submissions OK. SASE. Reports in 2-4 months. Free book catalog.

Nonfiction: Juveniles (religiously oriented only; 20,000-60,000 words; average of 138 pages). Nature (average of 128 pages). Religious (20,000-60,000 words; average of 128 pages). Query or submit outline/synopsis and sample chapters.

Recent Titles: *Yankee on the Yangtze,* by P. Quimby (religious biography); *Life's Greatest Value,* by P. Heubach (inspirational).

*SPORTS CAR PRESS, LTD., Sylvester Court, E. Norwalk CT 06855. (203)866-5450. President: Dorothy H. Greenberg. Editors-in-Chief: Joe Christy (aircraft); Dick Van der Feen (sports cars). Original paperbacks. Specializes in sports cars and small aircraft for private pilots. 12% of net royalty; $400 advance. Occasionally does some subsidy publishing, "if we think a book has merit, but not a wide-range audience to be profitable without subsidy." Published 10 titles in 1976, 8 in 1977. "Author is responsible for all illustrations and must submit them along with ms." Photocopied submissions OK. Reports in 2-4 weeks. SASE. Free book catalog.

Nonfiction: Publishes sports car and private aircraft books. Submit outline/synopsis and sample chapters. "All mss should be 30-33,000 words with about 40 illustrations including b&w photos and line cuts."

Recent Titles: *How to Win at Slalom and Autocross,* by J. Pagel (sports car); *Engines for Home-Built Planes,* by J. Christy (modern aircraft).

STACKPOLE BOOKS, Box 1831, Harrisburg PA 17105. (717)234-5091. Editorial Director: Neil McAleer. Hardcover and paperback originals (90%) and reprints (10%). Specializes in outdoor activity, craft, early Americana, the future, space and space colonization. 10% royalty on hardcover; 5% on paperback. Advance averages $1,000. Published 25 titles in 1976, 30 in 1977; 30-35 in 1978. Query and include author's credentials. Send prints if photos/illustrations

are to accompany ms. Simultaneous ("no more than to 2 other publishers") and photocopied submissions OK. Reports in 2-4 weeks. SASE. Free book catalog.
Nonfiction: Publishes Americana; hobbies; how-to; nature; psychology; recreation; self-help; travel; future; space activities; and energy books.

STANDARD PUBLISHING, 8121 Hamilton Ave., Cincinnati OH 45231. (513)931-4050. Managing Editor: Carol Ferntheil. Hardcover and paperback originals (75%) and reprints (25%). Specializes in religious books. 10% royalty. Advance ("reluctantly") averages $500-1,500. Published 30 titles in 1976, 35 in 1977; will do 40 in 1978. Query or submit outline/synopsis and sample chapters. State availability of photos/illustrations. Reports in 1-2 months. SASE.
Nonfiction: Publishes how-to; history; juveniles; reference; and religious books. All ms must pertain to religion.
Fiction: Publishes religious books.
Recent Titles: *Kicking Against the Goads,* by S. Goad (meditation); *Do You Know Who You Are?,* by R. Huron (devotional); and *Being "Good Enough" Isn't Good Enough,* by J. Cottrell (Christian living).

STATE HISTORICAL SOCIETY OF WISCONSIN PRESS, 816 State St., Madison WI 53706. (608)262-9604. Editor: William C. Marten. Publishes hardcover originals. Pays 10% of gross income. No advance. Published 5 titles in 1976, 3 in 1977. Send complete ms. (No corrasable bond, please.) Reports in eight weeks. Enclose return postage with ms.
History: Research and interpretation in history of the American Middle West—broadly construed as the Mississippi Valley. Must be thoroughly documented. 150,000 to 200,000 words of text, exclusive of footnotes and other back matter.

STEIN AND DAY, Scarborough House, Briarcliff Manor NY 10510. Offers standard royalty contract. Published about 100 titles last year. No unsolicited mss. Nonfiction, send outline or summary and sample chapter; fiction, send first chapter only. Enclose S.A.S.E.
General: Publishes general trade books; no juveniles or college. All types of nonfiction except technical. Quality fiction. Length: 75,000 to 100,000 words.
Recent Titles: *Arabesque,* by T. deKerpely (fiction); *The Children of Ham,* by C. Brown (nonfiction); and *Nightfall,* by S. Crosby (fiction).

STONE WALL PRESS, INC., 5 Byron St., Boston MA 02108. (617)277-6550. Editor-in-Chief: Henry Wheelwright. Publishes paperback and hardcover originals. Offers royalty contract of 5% paperpack; 10% cloth. Rarely offers an advance. Published 2 titles in 1976, 4 in 1977. Free book catalog. Do not send ms. Query first and send prospectus, table of contents, sample chapters and biography. Reports in 1 month. Enclose return postage.
Nonfiction: Nature, sports, recreation, travel. Well-rounded regional outdoor books on specific pursuits. Length: 60,000 to 100,000 words. For an audience of Northeastern U.S. "outdoorspeople."
Recent Titles: *Atlantic Surf Fishing: Maine to Maryland,* by L. Boyd (sports); and *The Northeastern Outdoors: A Field and Travel Guide,* by S. Berman (nature).

STRAVON PUBLISHERS INC., 595 Madison Ave., New York NY 10022. Editor-in-Chief: Robert M. Segal. Hardcover and paperback originals. Specializes in how-to, popular reference books and children's science books. 10% royalty; advance of $1,500-3,000. "Our main publishing interest consists of packaging popular reference books for other publishers. Subjects include medical, general how-to, encyclopedias. Thus, we are always on the lookout for writers on special subjects on a fee or word basis (6-10¢/word)." Published 5 titles in 1976, 7 in 1977; will do 7-10 in 1978. Simultaneous and photocopied submissions OK. Reports in 1-2 weeks. SASE. Free book catalog.
Nonfiction: Publishes art, business,; cookbooks, cooking and foods; history, hobbies, how-to, humor, juveniles, medicine and psychiatry; nature, politics, psychology, reference, religion, scientific, self-help and sociology books. Query.
Recent Titles: *Dinosaur World,* by E. Colbert (science and history); *Cartooning Fundamentals,* by A. Ross (how-to); *Quick Reference Encyclopedia.*

STRUCTURES PUBLISHING CO., P.O. Box 423, Farmington MI 48024. Editor-in-Chief: Shirley M. Horowitz. Publishes hardcover and paperback originals. Offers standard 10-12½-15% royalty contract. Advance varies, depending on author's reputation and nature of book. Published 10 titles last year. Will send a catalog to a writer on request. Submit outline and sample chapters. Will consider photocopied submissions. Reports in 4 to 6 weeks. Enclose return postage.

Technical and How-To: Books related to building. Wants to expand Successful Series which includes books published both for professionals and homeowners in paperback and hardcover. Will consider structure, construction, building and decorating-related topics. "Mss commissioned, usually. Book layout and design expertise of interest."
Recent Titles: *How to Build Your Own Home,* by Reschke; *How to Cut Your Energy Bills,* by Derven; and *Successful Family and Recreation Rooms,* by Cornell.

*SUN PUBLISHING CO., Box 4383, Albuquerque NM 87106. (505)255-6550. Editor-in-Chief: Skip Whitson. Hardcover and paperback originals (40%) and reprints (60%). 10% royalty. No advance. Will subsidy publish "if we think the book is good enough and if we have the money to do it, we'll publish it on our own; otherwise, the author will have to loan the money to us." Published 21 titles in 1976, 50-60 in 1977; will do 100+ in 1978. Query or submit outline/synopsis, table of contents and first and last chapters. Send photocopies if photos/illustrations are to accompany ms. Simultaneous and photocopied submissions OK. Reports in 2-4 months. SASE. Book list for SASE.
Nonfiction: Publishes Americana; art; biography; cookbooks, cooking and foods; history; how-to; politics; scientific; self-help; metaphysical; oriental; and new age books. "40-200 page length ms are preferred."
Fiction: Publishes science fiction books.
Special Needs: "The 'Sun Historical Series' is looking for short, illustrated mss on various U.S. cities and regions."
Recent Titles: *Praying Flute — Song of the Earth Mother,* by T. Shearer (Indian); and *Great Car Rip-Off,* by W. Montage (nonfiction).

SUNSTONE PRESS, P.O. Box 2321, Santa Fe NM 87501. (505)988-4418. Editor-in-Chief: James C. Smith, Jr. Publishes paperback originals; "sometimes hardcover originals." Published 10 titles in 1976. Free book catalog. Query. Reports in 1 month. Enclose return postage.
Nonfiction: How-to series craft books. Books on the history of the Southwest; poetry. Length: open.

SWEDENBORG FOUNDATION, 139 East 23rd St., New York NY 10010. Chairman, Editorial and Publications Committee: C. S. Priestnal. Publishes hardcover and paperback originals and reprints (limited to Swedenborgiana). Royalties negotiable. Published 5 titles last year. Catalog available on request. Will consider photocopied submissions. Query first. Reports in 1 month. Enclose return postage with query.
Nonfiction: The life and works of Emanuel Swedenborg. Studies of Swedenborg's scientific activities as precursors of modern developments. Studies of Swedenborg's contributions to the mainstream of religious thought.

*SYMMES SYSTEMS, Box 8101, Atlanta GA 30306. Editor-in-Chief: E.C. Symmes. Publishes hardcover and paperback originals. Offers royalty contract of 10% of money received. "Contracts are usually written for the individual title and may have different terms." No advance. Published 2 titles in 1976, 3 in 1977. Does 40% subsidy publishing. Will consider photocopied and simultaneous submissions. Acknowledges receipt in 10 days; evaluation within 2 months. Query first. Enclose return postage.
Nonfiction and Nature: "Our books have mostly been in the art of bonsai (miniature trees). We are publishing quality information for laypersons (hobbyists). Most of the titles introduce information that is totally new for the hobbyist." Clear and concise writing style. Text must be topical, showing state-of-the-art and suggestions on how to stay on top. All books so far have been illustrated with photos and/or drawings. Would like to see more material on bonsai, photography, collecting photographica, ferns for neophytes (along with quality photos). Length: open.

SYMPHONY PRESS, INC., Box 515, Tenafly NJ 07670. Editor-in-Chief: Eric Weber. Publishes hardcover originals. Royalty of 5%. Advance varies from $2,000 to $3,000. Published 5 titles last year. Will consider photocopied submissions. Submit complete ms. Reports in 2 weeks. Enclose return postage.
How-To: "Our how-to books are written with extreme simplicity and clarity. Any subject, but must have wide appeal to the general public and be written in a short, punchy, easy-to-read style." Length: 10,000 to 50,000 words.

SYRACUSE UNIVERSITY PRESS, 1011 E. Water St., Syracuse NY 13210. (315)423-2596. Director and Editor: Arpena Mesrobian. The royalty schedule varies, but generally a royalty is

paid on every title. Published 18 titles in 1976, 22 in 1977. Free book catalog. Query first with outline or sample chapters. If the ms is not rejected outright, a decision may be expected in 2-4 months. SASE.
Nonfiction: Publishes nonfiction, scholarly books, including biography, regional (especially on New York State and Iroquois), technical, literary criticism, history, philosophy, politics, religion, and educational books. Approximate minimum length: 50,000 words.
Special Needs: "Contemporary issues in the Middle East, scholarly. Especially looking for material on Iroquois, anything from scholarly to general trade."
Recent Titles: *The Reservation,* by T. Williams (Iroquois); *The Arab Left,* by T.Y. Ismael; and *Woodland Ecology,* by L. Minckler (forest management).

TAB BOOKS, Monterey and Pinola Aves., Blue Ridge Summit PA 17214. (717)794-2191. Pays on fee or royalty basis. Advance varies. Distribution through bookstores, libraries, schools, advertising, direct mail, etc. Wants queries sent to Pete Deksnis; include title, chapter outline, and one-page synopsis describing who book is written for and why. List other books on the subject and how book differs from the others. Reports in 1 to 4 weeks. Enclose return postage.
Technical: Publishes technical and do-it-yourself books. Distribution reaches electronic engineers and technicians; radio and TV broadcasters (chief engineers and managers, program directors, etc.); hobbyists and experimenters; cable TV owners, operators, managers, engineers and technicians; do-it-yourselfers, automotive technicians and repairmen, marine enthusiasts; also electric motor service shops, both independent and in-plant. "We are looking for up-to-date book mss for technical people in these fields, or for nontechnical managers and executives in these fields." Length: "Depends on illustrative content."
Self-Help and How-To: "We are seeking books for the do-it-yourselfer, including crafts, on virtually all subject areas."

TAFNEWS PRESS, Book Division of Track & Field News, Inc., Box 296, Los Altos CA 94022. (415)948-8188. Paperback originals. Specializes in books on track and field athletics. 10% royalty; advance only upon arrangement. Published 6 books in 1976, 6 in 1977; will do 6 in 1978. Simultaneous and photocopied submissions OK. Reports in 2-4 weeks. SASE. Free book catalog.
Nonfiction: Sports; track and field only. Query or submit outline/synopsis and sample chapters.
Recent Titles: *Track & Field: Technique Through Dynamics,* by T. Ecker; *Getting Started in Track and Field,* by R.S. Parker; *How High School Runners Train,* by G. Brock.

TAFT CORPORATION, 1000 Vermont Ave., N.W., Washington DC 20005. (800)424-9477. Editor-in-Chief: Jean Brodsky. Paperback originals. Specializes in books directed toward nonprofit industry. 9% royalty on first 3,000 copies, 11% on next 2,000, 14% over 5,000; advance of $250-500. Published 5 titles in 1976, 5 in 1977; will do 10 in 1978. State availability of photos and/or illustrations to accompany ms "and whether right to use has already been obtained". Simultaneous and photocopied submissions OK. Reports in 1-2 months. SASE. Free book catalog.
Nonfiction: Publishes how-to and technical books. "All dealing with fund-raising and other elements of the nonprofit industry. Query or submit outline/synopsis and sample chapters.
Recent Titles: *Proposal Writers' Swipe File II,* by J. Brodsky (nonprofit industry); *Mediability,* by L. Biegel and A. Lubin (nonprofit media relations); *Up Your Accountability,* by P. Bennett (nonprofit accounting).
Special Needs: Planning textbooks dealing with nonprofit management training.

TAMARACK PRESS, Box 5650, Madison WI 53705. Editor-in-Chief: Jill Weber Dean. Publishes paperback and hardcover originals and reprints. Offers royalty contract of 10% of list price (including text and illustrations). Average advance is $250 to $500. Published 4 titles in 1976. Free book catalog and writer's guidelines. Will consider photocopied submissions. No simultaneous submissions. Query first and submit outline and sample chapters for all material. Reports on query in 1 week; ms in 2 months. Enclose return postage.
Nonfiction and Photography: Books range from local Midwest guidebooks to gift books with four-color photos and national interest subjects. Emphasis is on books that relate in some way to the natural world. "Writer ought to consider the primary audience of Tamarack Press as consisting of those who join such organizations as the Sierra Club, Audubon Society, Defenders of Wildlife, Nature Conservancy, etc. Our books are more specifically regional than national." No heavily technical books or poetry. Interested in Americana; biography; history; self-help and how-to; sports, hobbies, recreation and pets; travel.

Recent Titles: *Easy Going: Door County,* by C. Church (travel guide); *A Season of Birds,* by D. Henderson (nature essay); *A Sand County Almanac Illustrated,* by A. Leopold (nature).

TANDEM PRESS PUBLISHERS, Box 237, Tannersville PA 18372. (717)629-2250. Editor-in-Chief: Judith Keith. Hardcover originals. 10-12½-15% royalty. Sometimes offers an advance. "This is handled with each author individually." Published 2 titles in 1976, 4 in 1977; will do 4 in 1978. Photocopied submissions OK. SASE. Reports in 2-4 weeks. Book catalog for SASE.
Nonfiction: Cookbooks, cooking and foods; how-to, multimedia material, nature, pets, psychology, recreation, self-help and sports books. Query.
Fiction: Adventure, confession, fantasy, historical, mainstream, mystery, religious, romance and suspense. Submit outline/synopsis and sample chapters to Judith Keith.
Recent Titles: *Desires of My Heart,* by J.C. Cruz (romantic fiction); *Candy, Chocolate, Ice Cream 'N How to Lick 'Em,* by S. Spring (humorous diet book); *To You With Love,* by T. Rowe (poetry).

TANGENT BOOKS, 114 7th Ave., N.W., Calgary, Alta., Canada T2M OA2. Editor-in-Chief: David Foy. Hardcover and paperback originals and reprints. Offers "minimum advance against larger than normal royalties after costs have been met. We are the nonfiction imprint of the *Pennyworth Press* and until the 1977 *Writer's Market* came out, we were not active. Expect to contract for at least 4, perhaps 12 titles this year." Query. State availability of photos/illustrations. PHotocopied submissions OK. Ms returned "only if sufficient Canadian postage or International Reply Coupons enclosed."
Nonfiction: Publishes art (especially how-to and crafts); business (oriented twoard small business, especially how-to); how-to (wide open); juveniles; medicine and psychiatry (popularizations, must be authoritative); nature (current issues); photography (technical how-to aspects; no photo books); psychology (popular); reference (wide open); scientific (popular); self-help; sociology (popular); technical (popular, e.g., electronics); textbooks (biology and social sciences); travel (student oriented); Third World and women's movement books.
Special Needs: "We're looking for imaginative nonfiction projects, and particularly encourage mss from Canadians on Canadian subjects."

TAPE 'N TEXT, Williamsville Publishing Co., Inc., P.O. Box 237, Williamsville NY 14221. Editor-in-Chief: William R. Parks. Publishes printed text closely coordinated with narration on cassette tape. Offers royalty contract of 10% minimum. Published 15 titles last year. Marketing currently limited to direct mail to schools and libraries. Will send free catalog to writer on request. Will consider photocopied submissions. Query first. Reports in 6 weeks. Enclose return postage.
Education and Training: "The kind of material we want from prospective authors is either a narration on tape with printed text which is very closely coordinated, *or* taped lectures or talks. Although we are now in English and mathematics, we have plans of going into religious education and, perhaps, other fields such as science, and art. We must have inquiries first before writers send in their material. We also request that writers consider that their educational background and experience are important factors. Authors should examine our existing Tape 'n Text titles so that they can follow this format for their development of material. It is important that the writer establish what his target audience is, i.e., level: elementary school, junior high school, high school, junior college, university, or the general trade market." Current titles include *Basic Language Usage,* by Dr. G.H. Poteet.

J.P. TARCHER, INC., 9110 Sunset Blvd., Los Angeles CA 90069. (213)273-3274. Editor-in-Chief: J.P. Tarcher. Hardcover and paperback originals. 10-12-15% royalty; advance averages $5-7,500. Published 10 titles in 1976, 12 in 1977; will do 15 in 1978. State availability of photos and/or illustrations to accompany ms. Simultaneous and photocopied submissions OK. Reports in 2-4 weeks. SASE. Free book catalog.
Nonfiction: Publishes popular psychology, self-help, sociology, medicine; cookbooks, cooking and foods; and hobbies books. Submit outline/synopsis and sample chapters.
Recent Titles: *Made in Heaven, Settled in Court,* M. Mitchelman; *Sports Psyching,* by T. Tuiko; *With Love From Your Kitchen,* by P. and D. von Welanetz (cookbook).

TEACHERS COLLEGE PRESS, 1234 Amsterdam Ave., New York NY 10027. Publishes originals and reprints. Royalty schedule varies. Published 12 titles in 1976, 35-40 in 1977. Free book catalog. Send outline and sample chapter addressed to the Director.
Nonfiction: Publishes scholarly and professional books in education and allied subjects (psychology, sociology, social studies, etc.) as well as testing materials. Length: open.

Recnt Titles: *Reading Aids Through the Grades,* by Russell/Karp/Meuser (classroom materials); *The Family as Educator,* by Leichter (scholarly); and *Hospitals, Paternalism, and the Role of the Nurse.*

TEN SPEED PRESS, P.O. Box 4310, Berkeley CA 94704. Editor: P. Wood. Publishes hardcover and paperback originals and reprints. Offers royalty of 10% of list price; 12½% after 100,000 copies are sold. Published 8 titles last year. Will send catalog to writer on request. Submit outline and sample chapters for nonfiction. Reports in 1 month. Enclose return postage.
Nonfiction and Poetry: Americana, book trade, cookbooks, cooking and foods, history, humor, juveniles, law, nature, poetry, self-help, how-to, sports, hobbies, recreation and pets, and travel. Publishes mostly trade paperbacks. Subjects range from bicycle books to Wm. Blake's illustrations. No set requirements. Some recipe books, career development books. Recent titles include *What Color Is Your Parachute?* (Bolles) and *Cohabitation Handbook* (King).

TEXAS WESTERN PRESS, The University of Texas at El Paso, El Paso TX 79968. (915)747-5688. Director: E.H. Antone. Publishes hardcover and paperback originals. "We are a university press, not a commercial house; therefore, payment is in books and prestige more than money. Most of our books are sold to libraries, not to the general reading public." Published 10 titles last year. Will send a catalog to a writer on request. Query first. Will consider photocopied submissions. "Follow MLA Style Sheet." Reports in 1 to 3 months. Enclose return postage.
Nonfiction: "Scholarly books. Historic accounts of the Southwest (west Texas, southern New Mexico, and northern Mexico). Some literary works, occasional scientific titles. Our Southwestern Studies use mss of 20,000 words. Our hardback books range from 30,000 words up. The writer should use good exposition in his work. Most of our work requires documentation. We favor a scholarly, but not overly pedantic, style. We specialize in superior book design."
Recent Titles: *Higher Education in Mexico,* by Osborn (education); *Faces of the Borderlands,* by Cisneros (art); and *Geographic Survey of Sinaloa,* by Schmidt (geography).

A. THOMAS & CO., LTD., Denington Estate, Wellingborough, Northamptonshire NN8 2RQ England. Editor-in-Chief: J.R. Hardaker. Hardcover and paperback originals and reprints. Specializes in inspirational, practical psychology and self-improvement material. 8-10% royalty. Photocopied submissions OK. SAE and International Reply Coupons. Reports in 2-4 weeks. Free book catalog.
Nonfiction: Publishes books on how-to methods, psychology and self-help. Submit outline/synopsis and sample chapters.

THORSONS PUBLISHERS, LTD, Denington Estate, Wellington, Northamptonshire NN8 2RQ England. Editor-in-Chief: J.R. Hardaker. Hardcover and paperback originals and reprints. Specializes in health books, psychology, self-improvement, hypnotism, alternative medicine and business success books. 5-10% royalty. Photocopied submissions OK. SAE and International Reply Coupons. Reports in 2-4 weeks. Free book catalog.
Nonfiction: Business; cookbooks, cooking and foods; philosophy, psychology, self-help themes. Submit outline/synopsis and sample chapters.

THREE CONTINENTS PRESS, 1346 Connecticut Ave., N.W., Washington DC 20036. Editor-in-Chief: Donald E. Herdeck. Hardcover and paperback originals (90%) and reprints (10%). 10% royalty; advance "only on delivery of complete ms which is found acceptable; usually $150." Published 10 titles in 1976, 10 in 1977; will do 10 in 1978. Query. Prefers photocopied submissions. State availability of photos/illustrations. Simultaneous submissions OK. Reports in 1-2 months. SASE. Free book catalog.
Nonfiction and Fiction: Specializes in African and Caribbean literature and criticism, third world literature and history. Scholarly, well-prepared mss; creative writing. Fiction, poetry, criticism, history and translations of creative writing. "We search for books which will make clear the complexity and value of African literature and culture, including bilingual texts (African language/English translations) of previously unpublished authors from less well-known areas of Africa. We are always interested in genuine contributions to understanding African and Caribbean culture." Length: 50,000 words.
Recent Titles: *Modern Arab Poets,* edited and translated by I. Bowlata (poetry); *Ghana Talks,* edited by M. Dodds (history, art, geology); and *Shaka-King of the Zulus-in African Literature,* by D. Burmers (criticism).

TIDEWATER PUBLISHERS, Box 109, Cambridge MD 21613. Editor: Mary Jane Cornell. An imprint of Cornell Maritime Press, Inc. Publishes hardcover and paperback originals and reprints. Offers standard 10-12½-15% royalty contract. Published 8 titles in 1976, 6 in 1977. Free book catalog. Query first with outline and sample chapters. Will not consider photocopied submissions. Reports in 2 to 3 weeks. Enclose return postage.
Nonfiction: "General nonfiction nn Maryland and the Delmarva Peninsula." Recent titles include *A Portrait of the Free State, A History of Maryland* and *Chesapeake Kaliedoscope* (Hays/Hazeton).

TIME-LIFE BOOKS INC., 777 Duke St., Alexandria VA 22314. (703)960-5019. Managing Editor: Jerry Korn. Publishes hardcover originals. "We have no minimum or maximum fee because our needs vary tremendously. Advance, as such, is not offered. Author is paid as he completes part of contracted work." Books are almost entirely staff-generated and staff produced, and distribution is primarily through mail order sale. Query first to the Director of Editorial Planning. Enclose return postage.
Nonfiction: "General interest books. Most books tend to be heavily illustrated (by staff), with text written by assigned authors. We very rarely accept mss or book ideas submitted from outside our staff." Length: open. Recent titles include *Violence and Agression* (Human Behavior Series); *The MIners* (Old West Series); and *New York* (Great Cities Series).

TIMES MIRROR MAGAZINES, INC., BOOK DIVISION, (Subsidiary of Times Mirror Company), 380 Madison Ave., New York NY 10017. Publishing books in the Popular Science and Outdoor Life fields. Editor: John W. Sill. Published 12 titles in 1976, 14 in 1977. Royalties and advance according to size and type of book. Wants outlines, sample chapters, author information. Enclose return postage.
How-To and Self-Help: Publishes books in Popular Science field: home renovation, repair and improvement, workshop, hand and power tools, automobile how-to. In the Outdoor Life field: hunting, especially big game and deer; fishing, camping, firearms. Small books to 30,000 words; large books to 150,000 words.
Special Needs: "How-to fishing and hunting books, step-by-step with photos, captions, and text."

THE TOUCHSTONE PRESS, Box 81, Beaverton OR 97005. (503)648-8081. Editor-in-Chief: Thomas K. Worcester. Paperback originals. Specializes in field guide books. Royalty of 10% of retail price; seldom offers an advance. Published 8 titles in 1976, 2-3 in 1977; will do 6-7 in 1978. Photocopied submissions OK. Reports in 1-2 months. SASE. Free book catalog.
Nonfiction: Publishes cookbooks, cooking and foods; history, hobbies, how-to, recreation, sports, and travel books. "Must be within the range of our outdoor styles." Query first.
Recent Titles: *Back Roads and Trails — Willamette Valley,* by Hawkins and Bleything (outdoors); *Cooking of the Prairie Homesteader,* by L. Nickey (cookbook); *Back Country Roads & Trails — San Diego County,* by J. Schad (outdoors).

TRANSACTION BOOKS, Rutgers University, New Brunswick NJ 08903. (201)932-2280. Book Division Director: George E. Magee. Hardcover and paperback originals (65%) and reprints (35%). Specializes in scholarly social science books. Royalty "depends almost entirely on individual contract, we've gone anywhere from 2-15%." No advance. Published 45 titles in 1976, 55 in 1977; will do 60 in 1978. Query or submit outline/synopsis and sample chapters. "Send introduction or first chapter and conclusion or last chapter. Use Chicago *Manual of Style.*" State availability of photos/illustrations and send 1 photocopied example. Photocopied submissions OK "if they are perfectly clear." Reports in 2-4 months. SASE. Free book catalog.
Nonfiction: Publishes Americana; art; biography; economics; history; law; medicine and psychiatry; music; philosophy; photography; politics; psychology; reference; scientific; sociology; technical; and textbooks. "All must be scholarly social science or related."
Recent Titles: *Music in American Society,* by G. McCue (music, sociology); *Fascism,* by R. DeFelice (political science); and *Human Marketplace,* by T. Martinez (sociology, business labor studies).

TRANS-ANGLO BOOKS, P.O. Box 38, Corona del Mar CA 92625. Editorial Director: Spencer Crump. Royalty of 5% to 10%. Published 4 titles last year. Catalog on request. Query required; do not send mss until requested. Reports in three weeks to one month. Enclose return postage.
Nonfiction: Publishes Americana, Western Americana, biography, and railroad books. "We are not interested in family histories or local history that lacks national appeal." Most books are

8½x11 hardcover with many photos supplementing a good text of 5,000 to 100,000 words. Recent titles include *The Real Joaquin Murieta* (biography); *Narrow Gauge Nostalgia* (railroadiana); *California's Spanish Missions* (Western Americana).

TREND HOUSE, Box 2350, Tampa FL 33601. (813)247-5411. Editor-in-Chief: Harris Mullen. Managing Editor: Al Petow. Hardcover and paperback originals (90%) and reprints (10%). Specializes in books on Florida and the South — all categories. 10% royalty; no advance. Published 4 titles in 1976, 4 in 1977. Books are marketed through *Florida Trends* and *The South* magazines. Query or submit complete ms. State availability of photos and/or illustrations. PHotocopied submissions OK. Reports in 2-4 weeks. SASE. Free book catalog.
Nonfiction: Publishes business; economics; history; law; politics; reference; textbooks; and travel books. "Virtually all books pertain to Florida and Southern U.S."
Recent Titles: *300 Most Abused Drugs,* by E. Bludworth (police handbook); *The Power Structure,* by L. Butcher (Florida business); *All About Wills for Florida Residents,* by R. Richards (legal information).

*TRIUMPH PUBLISHING CO., Box 292, Altadena CA 91001. (213)797-0075. Editor-in-Chief: William Dankenbring. Hardcover and paperback originals. 5% royalty; no advance. Subsidy publishes 10% of books; "depends on the ms". Published 2 titles in 1976, 3 in 1977; will do 3 in 1978. State availability of photos and/or artwork to accompany ms. Simultaneous and photocopied submissions OK. Reports in 1-2 months. SASE. Free book catalog.
Nonfiction: Americana (inspirational); business (how-to); history (Biblical); nature (creation); psychology and scientific books (for laymen); religious and self-help.
Recent Titles: *Golden Prince,* by Ramsay (juvenile); *Ascent to Greatness,* by McNair (Americana); *Last Days,* by Dankenbring (religious).

TROUBADOR PRESS, INC., 385 Fremont St., San Francisco CA 94105. (415)397-3717. Editor-in-Chief: Malcolm Whyte. Publishes mostly paperback originals; some hardcover originals and nonfiction, adult trade titles. "Royalties vary from 5% to 10%; also purchase whole mss outright. Advances from $400 to $1,000." Reports within 2 weeks. Published 11 titles in 1976, 12 in 1977. Distributed through book, gift, toy departments and stores, as well as museum stores and education markets. Will consider photocopied submissions. Query first with outline and/or sample illustrations. Address queries to Brenda Shahan. Enclose return postage.
General Nonfiction: "Entertainment, art, activity, nature, self-help, game and cookbooks for adults and children. Titles feature original art and handsome graphics. Primarily nonfiction. Always interested in adding to Puzzlebook line, as well as select (but not esoteric) craft and how-to ideas. Also interested in adding to cookbook line of alternative cooking, such as our vegetarian *Sprouting* and *Yogurt* books. Interested in expanding on themes of 60 current titles. Like books which can develop into a series."
Recent Titles: *Around the World Vegetarian Cookbook,* by M. Boyramian (cookbook); *3-D Mazes,* by L. Evans (puzzle book); and *Ballet Color and Story,* by K. Tichenor (coloring book).

TROY STATE UNIVERSITY PRESS, Troy State University, Troy AL 36081. (205)566-3000. Editor: Martin Kruskopf. Hardcover and paperback originals (80%) and reprints (20%). Royalty of 10% of published price on first 2,000 copies sold; advance averages $250. Published 4 titles in 1976, 5 in 1977; will do 5 or 6 in 1978. State availability of photos and/or artwork to accompany ms. Photocopied submissions OK. Reports in 2-4 months. SASE. Free sample copy.
Nonfiction: Publishes books on Alabama and regional subjects, Americana, economics, history, law, philosophy, politics, psychology, religion, sociology, science; and biographies.
Recent Titles: *The Way of Love,* by J.B. Glubb (religious); *Every Day Is Easter in Alabama,* by R.H. Couch (history); *Devils' Wine,* by S. Scalf (poetry).

TRUCHA PUBLICATIONS, INC., P.O. Box 5223, Lubbock TX 79417. (806)763-3729. Editor-in-Chief: Josie Mora. Publishes paperback originals. Offers standard minimum book contract of 10-12½-15%, but will generally work with author according to individual needs and situation. Published 4 titles in 1976, 6 in 1977. Book catalog 25¢. Query first, or submit outline and sample chapters, or complete ms. Reports in 2 months. Enclose return postage.
Chicano: "The thoughts, expressions, aspirations, and generally esthetic literary creations of oppressed peoples throughout Aztlan, regardless of race, color, creed, nationality or sex. All genre of literature and varying in length. Special emphasis given to bilingual, bicultural literature. Must leave a feeling of hope and self-assertion in subject matter treated. Literature of

despair not our forte, although due to the nature of our literature much suffering is necessarily expressed, but it is certainly not essential for publication. Do not wish to see mss by non-Third World persons jumping on the bandwagon of minorities." Length: Open.

Recent Titles: *Ayer, Hoy, y Manana,* by A. Nada (poetry); *Carlitos,* F. Mireles (bilingual children's); and *Five Plays,* by N. DeLeon (drama).

TURNSTONE BOOKS, 37 Upper Addison Gardens, London W14 8AJ England. (01)602-6885. Editor-in-Chief: Alick Bartholomew. Managing Editor: Robin Campbell. Hardcover and paperback originals (90%) and reprints (10%). 7½% royalty on paperbacks; 10-15% on hardcovers. Advance of 400 pounds. Has subsidy published only one title. "We would really have chosen to publish it anyway, but the investment was too great." Published 7 titles in 1976, 12 in 1977; will do 12 in 1978. Photocopied submissions OK. SASE. Reports in 1-2 months. Free book catalog.

Nonfiction: Pre-history; alternative medicine and psychiatry; practical philosophy, Jungian psychology, alternative technology, mysticism and self-sufficiency topics. Query first or submit outline/synopsis and sample chapters.

Recent Titles: *Dowsing: Techniques & Applications,* by T. Graves (technology); *Food Growing Without Poisons,* by M. Strandberg (organic gardening); *The Way of Non-Attachment,* by D. Abrahamson.

CHARLES E. TUTTLE CO., INC., Publishers & Booksellers, 26-30 S. Main St., Rutland VT 05701. Publishes originals and reprints. Pays $250 against 10% royalty. Advance varies. Published 34 titles in 1976. Book catalog 25¢. Send complete mss or queries accompanied by outlines or sample chapters to Charles E. Tuttle, Inc., Suido 1--Chome, 2-6, Bunkyo-Ku, Tokyo, Japan, where the editorial and printing offices are located. Reports in 4 to 6 weeks. Enclose return postage.

Nonfiction: Specializes in publishing books about Oriental art and culture as well as history, literature, cookery, sport and children's books which relate to Asia, Hawaiian Islands, Australia and the Pacific areas. Also interested in Americana, especially antique collecting, architecture, genealogy and Canadian. Not interested in travel, sociological or topical works even when in subject field. No interest in poetry and fiction except that of Oriental theme. Normal book length only.

Juveniles: Juvenile books are to be accompanied by illustrations.

TWAYNE PUBLISHERS, A division of G. K. Hall & Co., 70 Lincoln St., Boston MA 02111. (617)423-3990. Editor: Alice D. Phalen. Payment is on royalty basis. Published 95 titles in 1976, 115 in 1977. Query first. Reports in three weeks. Enclose return postage.

Nonfiction: Publishes scholarly books in series. Literary criticism and biography.

Special Needs: "We will publish the first 3 titles in Twayne's Theatrical Arts Series. These are consise critical studies of 176-200 pages on film directors, actors, producers, and entertainers, written with scholarly authority, but directed at a literate general audience."

Recent Titles: *Kurt Vonnegut, Jr.,* by S. Schatt (literary criticism and biography); and *The German-Americans,* by L.J. Rippley (history of immigration).

TYNDALE HOUSE PUBLISHERS, 366 Gundersen Dr., Wheaton IL 60187. (312)668-8300. Editor: Dr. Victor L. Oliver. Publishes hardcover and paperback originals and reprints. Offers 10% royalty contract. "We offer a sliding scale on big sellers." Published about 50 titles last year. Will send free catalog to writer on request. Will consider clear photocopied submissions. No simultaneous submissions. Query first, with outline and sample chapters. Follow Chicago *Manual of Style.* Reports in 1 month. Enclose return postage.

Nonfiction: Religion. "We publish conservative evangelical Christian books. One of our foci is to communicate Christianity to secular man. We don't merely publish for other Christians, which is a prime consideration for anyone submitting a ms. We like mss typed, double spaced and complete. Few devotional books or poetry."

Recent Titles: *Norma,* by N. Zimmer; *How to Eat Right and Feel Great, by Rohrer; and The Effective Father,* by McDonald.

FREDERICK UNGAR PUBLISHING CO., INC., 250 Park Ave. S., New York NY 10003. Published 20 titles in 1976, 25 in 1977. Query first. Enclose S.A.S.E.

Nonfiction: "Scholarly books mainly in fields of literature and literary criticism. We do not encourage submission of mss by nonscholars." Mainly literary nonfiction, plus translations from European literature as well as books on films and film literature.

UNITED SYNAGOGUE BOOK SERVICE, 155 Fifth Ave., New York NY 10010. (212)533-7800. Hardcover and paperback originals. Royalty schedule: 10% of list price. No advance. Published 5 titles in 1976. Free book catalog. Send query, outline, sample chapter first. Address juveniles and history to Dr. Morton Siegel; biography, philosophy and adult religion to Rabbi Marvin Wiener. "Address general inquiries to George L. Levine, Director." Reports in one to eight weeks. Enclose return postage.
Religion: Publishes religious books only: textbooks, readers, Hebrew Language books, history, picture books. No length requirements.
Recent Title: *The Jewish Experience, Book I,* by F. Hyman (history).

UNITY PRESS, P.O. Box 1037, Santa Cruz CA 95061. (408)427-2020. Editor-in-Chief: Stephen Levine. Publishes hardcover and paperback originals. Offers standard minimum book contract of 10-12½-15%. Advance "depends; small though." Published 5 titles in 1976, 6 in 1977. Will consider photocopied submissions. Reports in 2 months. Query first. S.A.S.E.
Fiction and Nonfiction: Books of spiritual insight and the coming together of the planet family. Wildlife handling and care. Planet lore. The search for the miraculous. "Planning additions to our Mindfulness Series (meditation books) and original science fiction collections. Only book length mss."
Recent Titles: *Grist for the Mill,* by R. Dass (spiritual growth); *Experience of Insight,* by J. Goldstein (spiritual growth); and *Shoes for Free People,* by D. Runk (crafts).

UNIVELT, INC., American Astrnnautical Society Publications Office, Box 28130, San Diego CA 92128. (714)746-4005. Editor-in-Chief: Dr. Horace Jacobs. Hardcover and paperback originals. Specializes in astronautics and related books; technical communications. 10% royalty; no advance. Published 10 titles in 1976, 10 in 1977; will do 12 in 1978. Simultaneous and photocopied submissions OK. Reports in 1-2 months. SASE. Free book catalog.
Nonfiction: Publishes medicine, reference, scientific, sociology, and technical books. "All must be related to aerospace or communications." Submit outline/synopsis and sample chapters.
Recent Titles: *End of an Era in Space Exploration,* by J.C.D. Blaine (science and technology); *200 Years of Flight (1977),* edited by E.M. Emme (AAS history series).

*UNIVERSAL MAGAZINE PRESS, Box 1537, Palm Desert CA 92260. Editor: Rev. Paul von Johl. Paperback originals. Specializes in short length, softcover books. 10-15% standard royalty; 40-50% on cubsidy publishing. No advance. PUblishes about 5 titles annually. Subsidy publishes 10-25% of titles, based on sales potential of the book and the contribution it makes. "We reject up to 90% of the books that we have received asking for subsidy publishing." Query with outline/synopsis. State availability of photos to illustrate ms when querying. Photocopied submissions OK. Reports in 1-2 months. SASE.
Nonfiction: Art, how-to, self-help, poetry, parapsychology, religious, philosophy. Length: 1,000-10,000 words. Prefers triple-spaced mss.
Fiction: Religious, juveniles, science fiction. Length: 1,000-10,000 words.
Recent Titles: *Gems,* by Detlef Johl (poetry); and *Revelation Book I,* by Rev. M. Lunsford D.D. (religion).

*UNIVERSE BOOKS, 381 Park Ave. S., New York NY 10016. (212)689-0276. Editor-in-Chief: Louis Barron. Hardcover and paperback originals (90%) and reprints (10%). 10% royalty on cloth, 6% on paper. Advance ranges from $500-5,000. Subsidy publishes 5% of books. Subsidy publishing is determined by "size of potential market, cost of production, and significance of material. We won't do a subsidy book unless it contributes significantly to knowledge." Published 35 titles in 1976, 30-40 in 1977; will do 30-40 in 1978. Query or submit outline/synopsis and sample chapters. "Please don't use corrasable bond paper." State availability of photos and/or illustrations. Simultaneous and photocopied submissions OK. Reports in 1-2 weeks. SASE. Free book catalog.
Nonfiction: Publishes art, biography; cookbooks, cooking and foods; erotica, history, how-to, music, nature, philosophy, politics, reference, sociology, alternative lifestyles and survival books.

UNIVERSITY ASSOCIATES, INC., 7596 Eads Ave., La Jolla CA 92037. (714)454-8821. President: J. Gm. Pfeiffer. Vice-President and Editor-in-Chief: John E. Jones. Paperback originals (65%); reprints (35%). Specializes in practical materials for human relations trainers, consultants, etc. 10-15% royalty; no advance. Published 27 titles in 1976, 15 in 1977; will do 15-20 in 1978. Markets books by direct mail. Send prints or completed art or rough sketches to accompany ms. Simultaneous submissions OK. Reports in 2-4 months. SASE. Free book catalog.

Nonfiction: Marion Fusco, Department Editor. Publishes (in order of preference) human relations training and group-oriented material; management education and community relations and personal growth; business, psychology, sociology, and textbooks. Nothing on male/female relations or materials for grammar school or high school classroom teachers. Address query to Marion Fusco, Managing Editor. Use *American Psychological Association Style Manual.*

Recent Titles: *Making Meetings Work,* by L.P. Bradford (community relations); *A Practical Guide to Value Clarification,* by M. Smith (human relations training); *Leaders of Schools,* by W. Schutz (educational).

UNIVERSITY OF ALABAMA PRESS, Drawer 2877, University AL 35486. Managing Editor: James Travis. Publishes hardcover originals. "Maximum royalty is 12½%; no advances made." Published 35 titles last year. Will send a catalog to a writer on request. Will consider photocopied submissions. Submit outlines and sample chapters. Enclose return postage.

Nonfiction: Categories include biography, business, economics, history, philosophy, politics, religion, and sociology. Considers upon merit almost any subject of scholarly investigation, but specializes in linguistics and philology, political science and public administration, literary criticism and biography, philosophy, and history. Also interested in biology, medicine, and agriculture.

UNIVERSITY OF ARIZONA PRESS, Box 3398, Tucson AZ 85722. (602)884-1446. Director: Marshall Townsend. Publishes hardcover and paperback originals and reprints. "Contracts are individually negotiated, but as a 'scholarly publishing house' operating primarily on informational works, does not pay any advances. Also, royalty starting point may be after sale of first 1,000 copies, by virtue of the nature of the publishing program." Published 24 titles in 1976. Marketing methods "are based on 'what is considered best for the book,' giving individual treatment to the marketing of each book, rather than a generalized formula." Will send catalog to writer on request. Write for copy of editorial guidelines sheets. Will consider photocopied submissions if ms is not undergoing consideration at another publishing house. "Must have this assurance." Query first and cubmit outline and sample chapters. Reports on material within 90 days. Enclose return postage

Nonfiction: "Significant works of a regional nature about Arizona, the Southwest and Mexico; and books of merit in subject matter fields strongly identified with the universities in Arizona; i.e., anthropology, arid lands studies, Asian studies, Southwest Indians, Mexico, etc. Each ms should expect to provide its own answer to the question, "Why should this come out of Arizona?" The answer would be that either the work was something that ought to be made a matter of record as a service to Arizona and the Southwest, or that it was presenting valuable information in a subject matter field with which the Arizona institutions hold strong identification. The Press strongly endorses 'the target reader' concept under which it encourages each author to write for only *one* reader, then leave it up to the publisher to reach the thousands—as contrasted with the author's trying to write for the thousands and not 'hitting home' with anyone. The Press believes this approach helps the author come to a consistent level of subject matter presentation. The press also insists upon complete departure of 'time-dating' words such as 'now,' 'recently,' and insists that the author consider how the presentation will read three years hence." Americana, art, biography, business, history, nature, scientific, technical. Length: "what the topic warrants and demands." Not interested in "personal diary types of Western Americana, mainly directed only toward family interest, rather than broad general interest."

Recent Titles: *Prehistoric Indian Craft Arts,* by Tanner; *Lowell and Mars,* by Hoyt; and *The Seris,* by Burkhalter.

UNIVERSITY OF CALIFORNIA PRESS, Berkeley CA 94720; Los Angeles CA 90024. Director: James H. Clark. Los Angeles address is 60 Powell Library, Los Angeles CA 90024. Editor: Robert Y. Zachary. New York Office, Room 513, 50 E. 42 St., New York NY 10017. London Office IBEG, Ltd., 2-4 Brook St., London W1Y 1AA, England. Publishes hardcover and paperback originals and reprints. On books likely to more than return their costs, a standard royalty contract beginning at 10% is paid; on paperbacks it is less. Published 175 titles last year. Queries are always advisable, accompanied by outlines or sample material. Address to either Berkeley or Los Angeles address. Reports vary, depending on the subject. Enclose return postage.

Nonfiction: "It should be clear that most of our publications are hardcover nonfiction written by scholars." Publishes scholarly books including art, literary studies, social sciences, natural sciences and some high-level popularizations. No length preferences.
Fiction and Poetry: Publishes fiction and poetry only in translation. Usually in bilingual editions.

UNIVERSITY OF ILLINOIS PRESS, Urbana IL 61801. Hardcover and paperback originals (95%); paperback reprints (5%). "Royalty varies greatly; from zero on small edition scholarly books to sliding scale beginning at 15% of net income." Very rarely offers advance. Published 48 titles in 1976, 45 in 1977; will do 45 in 1978. State availability of photos and/or illustrations to accompany ms. Simultaneous (in some cases) and photocopied submissions OK. SASE. Reports in 1-2 months. Free book catalog.
Nonfiction: "Particular emphasis on American studies in history, literature, music, and other areas of specialization including anthropology, communications, urban and regional planning, and Western Americana." Query or submit complete ms.
Fiction: "We publish 4 collections of short stories each year in the Illinois Short Fiction series. Should be the kind of stories published in literary journals and quality magazines. Queries to Richard Wentworth."
Recent Titles: *To Byzantium,* by A. Fetler (short stories); *Black Ohio and the Color Line,* by D. Gerber (black history series); *Four Men: An Oral History of Contemporary Cuba,* by O. Lewis et al (anthropology).

UNIVERSITY OF IOWA PRESS, Graphic Services Bldg., Iowa City IA 52242. (319)353-3181. Editor-in-Chief: Art Pflughaupt. Managing Editor: Norman Sage. Hardcover and paperback originals. 10% royalty. Subsidy publishes 5% of books. Subsidy publishing is offered "if a scholarly institution will advance a subsidy to support publication of a worthwhile book." Published 7 titles in 1976, 5 in 1977; will do 5-8 in 1978. "We market mostly by direct mailing of fliers to groups with special interests in our titles." Query or submit outline/synopsis and sample chapters. Chicage *Manual of Style.* State availability of photos/illustrations. Photocopied submissions OK. Reports in 2-4 months. SASE. Free book catalog.
Nonfiction: Publishes art; economics; history; music; philosophy; reference; and scientific books. "We do not publish children's books. We do not publish any poetry or short fiction except the Iowa Translation Series and the Iowa SChool of Letters Award for short fiction."
Recent Titles: *The Black Velvet Girl,* by C.E. Poverman (short stories); *Mark Twain Speaking,* edited by P. Fatout (literature); and *The Nazi Drawings,* by M. Lasanzky (art catalog).

*UNIVERSITY OF MASSACHUSETTS PRESS, Box 429, Amherst MA 01002. (413)545-2217. Hardcover and paperback originals (90%) and reprints (10%). No royalties on first print run except in trade titles; thereafter, 10% of list; advance, if made, averages $500. Subsidy published 15% of titles, based on costs; if deficit large, Press Committee requires outside subsidy. No individual author subsidies accepted. Published 22 titles in 1976, 20 in 1977; will do 20 in 1978. State availability of photos or illustrations. Simultaneous submissions OK, if advised; photocopied submissions OK, but if ms is approved, production copy should be ribbon. Reports in 1-2 months. SASE. Free book catalog.
Nonfiction: Publishes Americana, art, biography, history, philosophy, nature, poetry, politics, psychology, reference, scientific, sociology. Submit outline/synopsis and sample chapters.
Recent Titles: *Young Man Thoreau,* by R. Lebeaux (biography); *Gods and Heroes of the Greeks: The Library of Apollodorus,* translated and edited by M. Simpson; *Party Leadership in the States,* by R.J. Hockshorn (political economics).

UNIVERSITY OF MINNESOTA PRESS, 2037 University Ave., S.E., Minneapolis MN 55455. (612)373-3266. Publishes hardcover and paperback. Royalties vary. Published 28 titles last year. Query letters to Editor highly important. Mss should not be sent unless requested. Reports in three weeks to four months. Enclose return postage.
Nonfiction: Publishes scholarly nonfiction which has wide impact; textbooks; and regional books. No word length requirement, except that only book-length mss are acceptable. Representative titles: *Letters From the Promised Land: Swedes in America, 1840-1914* (Barton) and *Voices From an Empire: A History of Afro-Portuguese Literature* (Hamilton).

UNIVERSITY OF NEBRASKA PRESS, 901 N. 17th St., Lincoln NE 68588. Editor-in-Chief: Virginia Faulkner. Hardcover and paperback originals (60%); hardcover and paperback reprints (40%). Specializes in scholarly nonfiction (particularly literary); some regional books; reprints of western Americana; natural history. Royalty is usually graduated from 10% for original books. No advance. Published 51 titles in 1976, 55 in 1977; will do 55 in 1978. SASE. Reports in 1-2 weeks on rejections; 2-4 months on acceptances. Free book catalog.

Nonfiction: Publishes Americna, biography, history, medicine and psychiatry; nature, photography, psychology, sports, literature, agriculture and American Indian themes. Query.

Recent Titles: *Anatomies of Egotism: A Reading of the Last Novels of H.G. Wells* by R. Bloom (literature); *Oglala Religion* by W.K. Powers (American Indian); *North American Game Birds of Upland and Shoreline* by P.S. Johnsgard (nature).

*THE UNIVERSITY OF NORTH CAROLINA PRESS, Box 2288, Chapel Hill NC 27514. (919)933-2105. Editor-in-Chief: Malcolm Call. Hardcover and paperback originals. Specializes in scholarly books and regional trade books. Royalty schedule "varies greatly. Depends on nature of ms and its marketability; zero to 15% of retail price." No advance. Subsidy publishes 50% of titles; "must first be accepted on qualitative grounds". Published 26 titles in 1976, 35 in 1977; will do 35 in 1978. "As a university press, we do not have the resources for mass marketing books." Send prints to illustrate ms only if they are a major part of the book. Photocopied submissions OK. Reports in 2-5 months on accepted mss, sooner if rejected. SASE. Free book catalog.

Nonfiction: "Our major field is American history." Also scholarly books on Americana, biography, economics; medicine and psychiatry; philosophy, psychology and sociology. History books on art, law, music and religious themes. Books on nature, particularly on the Southeast; literary studies. Submit outline/synopsis and sample chapters. Must follow Chicago *Manual of Style.*

Recent Titles: *Character of John Adams,* by P. Shaw (biography); *The Fledgling Province (Colonial Georgia),* by H. Davis (history); *Fact and Fiction: New Journalism and Nonfiction Novel,* by J. Hollowell (literary studies).

UNIVERSITY OF NOTRE DAME PRESS, Notre Dame IN 46556. Editor: Ann Rice. Publishes hardcover and paperback originals and paperback reprints. Offers standard 10-12½-15% royalty contract; no advance. Published 21 titles in 1976. Free book catalog. Will consider photocopied submissions. Query first. Reports in 2 to 3 months. Enclose return postage.

Nonfiction: "Scholarly books, serious nonfiction of general interest; book-length only. Especially in the areas of philosophy, theology, history, sociology, English literature (Middle English period, and modern literature criticism in the area of relation of literature and theology), government, and international relations. Lately, especially Mexican-American studies. Also interested in books on the heritage of American beliefs and ideas suitable for junior college or high school students." Recent titles include *History of the Mexican American People* (Samora and Vandel); *The Radical Center: Middle Americans and the Politics of Alienation* (Warren); *Compromising of the Constitution* (Tugwell).

*UNIVERSITY OF OKLAHOMA PRESS, 1005 Asp Ave., Norman OK 73019. (405)325-5111. Editor-in-Chief: Luther Wilson. Hardcover and paperback originals (85%); and reprints (15%). Royalty ranges from zero to 15% "depending on market viability of project". No advance. Subsidy publishes 5% of books. "If a book has scholarly merit, but is destined to lose money, we seek a subsidy." Published 83 books in 1976; 85 in 1977; will do 90 in 1978. Submit sample photos or 8x10 glossy prints. Simultaneous and photocopied submissions OK. Reports in 2-4 months. SASE. Book catalog for SASE.

Nonfiction: Publishes Americana and art (western and Indian); biographies of major western and Indian figures; history, hobbies, how-to, music, nature, Politics, reference, sociology, technical, textbooks, archaeology (Mesoamerican); classics, and anthropology books. Query.

*UNIVERSITY OF PENNSYLVANIA PRESS, 3933 Walnut St., Philadelphia PA 19104. (215)243-6261. Director: Robert Erwin. Hardcover and paperback originals (90%) and reprints (10%). Royalty of 10% of list price on first 5,000 copies sold; 12½% on next 5,000 copies sold; 15% thereafter; no advance. Subsidy publishes 10% of books. Subsidy publishing is determined by: a) evaluation obtained by the press from outside specialists b) work approved by Press Editorial Committee c) additional scholarly evaluation obtained by separate funding organization d) subsidy approved by funding organization. Published 18 books in 1976, 20-21 in 1977; will do 25 in 1978. State availability of photos and/or illustrations to accompany ms, with copies of illustrations. Photocopied submissions OK. Reports in 1-3 months. SASE. Free book catalog.

Nonfiction: Publishes Americana, art, biography, business (especially management); economics, history, law, medicine and psychiatry; philosophy, politics, psychology, reference, religious (scholarly only), scientific, sociological, technical, folklore and folk life books. "Serious

books that serve the scholar and the professional." Follow the Chicago *Manual of Style.* Query with outline and sample chapter addressed to the director.
Recent Titles: *Victorian American,* by D. Howe (history); *Red Children in White America,* by A. Beuf (sociology); *The Woman Manager,* by H. Frank (management).

UNIVERSITY OF UTAH PRESS, University of Utah, University Services Building, Salt Lake City UT 84112. (801)581-6771. Director: Norman B. Mikkelsen. Publishes hardcover and paperback originals, reprints, and translations. 10% royalty on first 2,000 copies sold; 12½% on 2,001 to 4,000 copies sold; 15% thereafter. No advance. Published 10 titles last year. Free book catalog. Query first with outline and sample chapter. Reports in 6-8 months. SASE.
Nonfiction: Scholarly books on history, philosophy, religion, anthropology, the arts, poetry, and general nonfiction. Length: author should specify page length in query.
Recent Titles: *Prehistory of the West,* by L.S. Cressman (anthropology); *An Afternoon of Pocket Billiards,* by H. Taylor (poetry); and *On the Meaning of the University,* edited by McMurrin (philosophy of education).

*UNIVERSITY OF WISCONSIN PRESS, P.O. Box 1379, Madison WI 53701. (608)282-4928. Director: Thompson Webb. Editor: Irving E. Rockwood. Publishes hardcover and paperback originals, reprints, and translations. Subsidy publishes 33% of books. "If a ms satisfies our editorial review, we estimate potential income and total publishing costs. If the latter are greater than the former, the difference is the subsidy required." Offers standard royalty contract. No advance. Published 25 titles in 1976 and 1977. Send complete ms. Follow Modern Language Association Style Sheet. Reports in 3 months. Enclose return postage with ms.
Nonfiction: Publishes general nonfiction based on scholarly research.
Recent Titles: *The Great American Blow-Up: Puffery in Advertising and Selling,* by I.L. Preston (academic nonfiction); and *Blue-Collar Aristocrats: Life Styles at a Working Class Tavern,* by E.E. LeMasters (academic nonfiction).

UNIVERSITY PRESS OF KENTUCKY, 102 Lafferty Hall, Lexington KY 40506. (606)258-2951. Editor-in-Chief: William Jerome Crouch. Managing Editor: Evalin F. Douglas. Hardcover originals (95%); paperback reprints (5%). 10% royalty after first 1,000 copies; no advance. Published 30 titles in 1976, 25 in 1977; will do 25 in 1978. State availability of photos and/or artwork to accompany ms. "Author is ultimately responsible for submitting all artwork in camera-ready form." Reports in 2-4 months. SASE. Free book catalog.
Nonfiction: Publishes (in order of preference): history, sociology, literary criticism and history; politics, business, law, philosophy; medicine and psychiatry; nature, psychology, and scientific books. "All mss must receive an endorsement (secured by the press) from a scholar in the appropriate area of learning and must be approved by an editorial board before final acceptance." Query or submit outline/synopsis with sample chapters.
Recent Titles: *The City in Russian History,* by M. Hamm (history); *We Be Here When the Morning Comes,* by B. Woolley (sociology); *The Changing Face of Tibet,* by P.P. Karan (politics).

*UNIVERSITY PRESS OF VIRGINIA, Box 3608, University Station, Charlottesville VA 22903. (804)924-3468. Editor-in-Chief: Walker Cowen. Hardcover and paperback originals (95%) and reprints (5%). Royalty depends on the market for the book; sometimes none is made. We subsidy publish 40% of our books, based on cost vs. probable market." Published 50 titles in 1976, 45 in 1977; will do 45-50 in 1978. Photocopied submissions OK. Returns rejected material within a week. Reports on acceptances in 1-2 months. SASE. Free book catalog.
Nonfiction: Publishes Americana, business, history, law; medicine and psychiatry; politics, reference, scientific, bibliography, and decorative arts books. "Write a letter to the director, describing content of ms, plus length. Also specify if maps, tables, illustrations, etc., are included. Please, no educational or sociological or psychological mss."
Recent Titles: *Papers of George Washington* (history); *Field Guide to Study of American Literature* (bibliography).

URIZEN BOOKS, INC., 66 W. Broadway, New York NY 10007. Editor-in-Chief: Michael Roloff. Publishes paperback and hardcover originals. Offers standard minimum book contract of 10-12½-15%. Average advance is $3,000. Published 30 titles in 1976, 40 in 1977. Book catalog $1. Will consider photocopied submissions. Query first for nonfiction. Reports in 6 weeks. Enclose return postage.
Fiction, Nonfiction, Drama, Poetry: Sociology, philosophy, history of industrialization, history of economics, communication theory, "first class fiction." High caliber writing necessary.

Recent Titles: *Beautiful Days,* by F. Innerhofer (fiction); *Jesus, Son of Man,* by R. Augstein (nonfiction); and *The Soviet Union Against Dr. Mikhail Stern,* by A. Stern (nonfiction).

VALUE COMMUNICATIONS, INC., 11175 Flintcote Ave., San Diego CA 92121. (714)452-8676. Editor-in-Chief: Cynthia B. Tillinghast. Specializes in juvenile books focusing on development of personal values. Pays flat fee; variable. Advance varies. Published 1 title in 1976, 7 in 1977; will do 12 in 1978. Send available prints to illustrate ms. Simultaneous and photocopied submissions OK. Reports in 2-4 weeks. SASE. Free book catalog.
Nonfiction: Publishes juveniles and biographies.
Fiction: Publishes fantasy and themes that emphasize the development of personal values.
Recent Titles: *The Value of Believing in Yourself, The Value of Kindness; The Value of Humor;* all juveniles by S. Johnson.

VANGUARD PRESS, INC., 424 Madison Ave., New York NY 10017. Editor-in-Chief: Mrs. Bernice S. Woll. Publishes hardcover originals and reprints. Offers standard minimum book contract of 10-12½-15%. Published 20 titles last year. Query first with outline and sample chapters. Will not consider photocopied submissions. Reports in 4 months. Enclose correct size envelope and return postage.
General Fiction, General Nonfiction: "We publish both fiction and nonfiction of all types. We stipulate that writers query before sending complete ms. We publish books for all audiences. Overly scholastic, or religious works are rarely published; although some exceptions are made. We seek polished, organized, typed (double-spaced) materials. We are a small, independently run house with a reputation for publishing literate, well-written books. Our size allows us to give more attention to a limited number of authors than is possible in the larger houses. We do not, however, provide free advice or rewrite poorly written material. We rely on the author to come up with a new slant or approach on the subject he is dealing with."

VENTURE PUBLICATIONS, INC., 11157½ W. Washington Blvd., Culver City CA 90230. Editor-in-Chief: Raymond C. Bonaventura. Publishes hardcover and paperback originals. Offers standard minimum royalty. Advance negotiable. Published 2 titles last year. Will consider photocopied submissions. Query first for nonfiction nd juvenile fiction. Address department editor. Reports in 30 to 60 days. Enclose return postage.
Nonfiction, Juvenile Fiction, Biography and General: Americana and art. Department Editor: Ralph Vecchi. Juveniles, crime, Western History. Department Editor: Ray Bonaventura. Length: 1,500 to 3,000 words. "General nonfiction, Americana, originals and reprints should contain reference material useful to library users; accompanied with any photos. Our material is directed toward the general reader. Clean, comprehensive and professional." Would like to see mss on the old West and its heroes; of famous crimes; biographies; general nonfiction accompanied by photos or illustrations. For juveniles: fiction or mystery, adventure, humor, fantasy, science fiction.

*VESTA PUBLICATIONS, Box 1641, Cornwall, Ontario, Canada K6H 5V6. (613)932-2135. Editor-in-Chief: Stephen Gill. Paperback originals. 5% minimum royalty. Subsidy publishes 10% of books. "We ask a writer to subsidize a part of the cost of printing; normally, it is 50%. We do so when we find that the book does not have a wide market, as in the case of university themes and the author's first collection of poems. The writer gets 50 free copies and 10% royalty on paperback editions." No advance. Published 9 titles in 1976, 15 in 1977; will do 25 in 1978. State availabiliy of photos and/or illustrations to accompany ms. Simultaneous submissions OK if so informed. Photocopied submissions OK. Reports in 1-4 weeks. SASE. Free book catalog.
Nonfiction: Publishes Americana, art, biography,; cookbooks, cooking and foods; erotica, history, philosophy, poetry, politics, reference, religious. Query or submit complete ms. "Query letters and mss should be accompanied by synopsis of the book and biographical notes."
Recent Titles: *Why?,* by S. Gill (novel); *Ring Around the Sun,* by N.W. Linder (poetry); *Seaway Valley Cartoons,* by B. Badie (historical art).

VICTOR BOOKS, Box 1825, Wheaton IL 60187. (312)668-6000. Editorial Director: James R. Adair. Editor: Wightman Weese. Paperback originals. 7½-10% royalty; occasionally offers an advance. Published 35 titles in 1976, 40 in 1977; will do 40 in 1978. Prefers outline/synopsis and sample chapters, but queries are acceptable. Reports in 1-2 months. SASE. Free book catalog.
Nonfiction: Only religious themes. "To click with us, writers must have real substance and

know the evangelical market well. Actually, most of our books are by ministers, Bible teachers, seminar speakers. We are looking for freelancers who can help non-writers put together good books."
Recent Titles: *What Happens When Women Pray,* by E. Christenson; *The Happy Housewife,* by E. Baker; *God Can Make It Happen,* by R. Johnston.

THE VIKING PRESS, INC., PUBLISHERS, 625 Madison Ave., New York NY 10022. Royalties paid on all books. Published over 200 titles last year. Juvenile mss should be addressed to Viking Junior Books. Adult mss should be addressed to The Viking Press. Studio mss should be addressed to Viking Studio Books. Reports in 4 to 6 weeks. Enclose return postage with ms.
General: Publishes adult and Studio books (art, photography, etc.). Also publishes Viking Portable Library and Viking Critical Library.
Juveniles: Publishes juvenile books.

VISAGE PRESS, INC., 3409 Wisconsin Ave., N.W., Washington DC 20016. (202)686-5302. Editor-in-Chief: Emilio C. Viano. Managing Editor: Sherry Icenhower. Hardcover and paperback originals. "At this time, interested in particular in how-to books and books about skiing, travel guides to skiing locations in U.S. and abroad. Also looking for a good ms on spouse abuse." 10% royalty on first 5,000 hardcover; 12% next 5,000; 14% thereafter. Paperback royalty depends on the run. "Average advance is $1,000, generally given upon receipt of acceptable ms; rarely given on basis of outline alone." Published 5 titles in 1976, 6 in 1977; will do 10 in 1978. "For scholarly works, please follow the style of the American Sociological Review (see their Notice to Contributors), or send for style sheet." Send contact sheets (if available) or prints to illustrate ms. Pictures must always be captioned and accompanied by proper releases. Photocopied submissions OK. Reports in 1-2 months. SASE. Book catalog for SASE.
Nonfiction: Publishes biography, business; cookbooks, cooking and foods (regional cuisine and Mid-Atlantic and southern states); hobbies, medicine and psychiatry (particularly about emergencies, crisis, rape, child abuse, other victimizations, prevention of victimization); pets (a consumer guide to pet books; "gourmet" foods for pets); politics (books about behind the scenes at United Nations sought); psychology (particularly in the area of the rapist, sex offender and victims repeatedly victimized); recreation (soccer, in particular); religious (books about the coming millenium sought); sports (skiing and soccer, in particular); travel books. Query first or submit outline/synopsis and sample chapters.
Special Needs: "A series on skiing of the travel book variety, telling people where to go, what to expect in terms of facilities, schools, lifts, accommodations, etc. Also books on soccer."

VISTA AND CO., Publication Division, 9056 Santa Monica Blvd., Los Angeles CA 90069. Editor-in-Chief: Cornelius C. Welch, M.D. Hardcover and paperback originals. Specializes in general interest, religious, psychological, occult, social sciences and fiction. 10% royalty. Published 3 titles in 1977; will do 7 in 1978. If ms is to be illustrated, send prints. Simultaneous and photocopied submissions OK. Submit outline and sample chapters. SASE. Reports in 1-2 months. Book catalog for SASE.
Nonfiction: Publishes psychology, religious, occult, philosophy, medicine and psychiatry, self-help, nature and books on sociology.
Fiction: Occult, religious, romance, experimental, suspense and mainstream.

VULCAN BOOKS, Division of Trinity-One, Inc., P.O. Box 25616, Seattle WA 98125. Publisher: Michael H. Gaven. Publishes hardcover and paperback originals and reprints. Offers standard minimum book contract, with quarterly royalty statements. "Advances offered only in special cases." Published 14 titles in 1976. "Our books are marketed by all major occult distributors and we sell them to practically every store in America dealing with our subject matter." Submit outline and sample chapters for nonfiction; complete ms for fiction. Reports in 3 to 6 weeks. Enclose S.A.E. and return postage.
Astrology, Religion, and Metaphysics: Textbooks and books for the student of astrology; no specific religious denomination whatsoever, but religious books that will appeal to all people of all the world; metaphysics. No mediumship, or messages from the other world will be considered. Top priority is material dealing with the interrelationship of man and nature written by qualified experts. "Author must be experienced in above fields, especially in astrology. Will immediately reject material that is called 'entertainment astrology'. We are searching for topics that need to be covered in the field of astrology: weather forecasting, minor aspects, mundane astrology, etc." Current titles include *America: An Astrological Portrait of Its Cities and States* (Penfield) and *Traitmatch: Discovering the Occupational Personality through Handwriting Analysis* (Blazi/Whiting).

WALKER AND CO., 720 5th Ave., New York NY 10019. Editor-in-Chief: Richard Winslow. Managing Editor: Andrea Curley. Hardcover and paperback originals (90%) and reprints (10%). 10-12½-15% royalty or outright purchase; advance averages $1,000-2,500 "but could be higher or lower." Publishes 80 titles annually. Query or submit outline/synopsis and sample chapters. Submit samples of photos/illustrations to accompany ms. Photocopied submissions OK. SASE. Free book catalog.
Nonfiction: Publishes Americana; art; biography; business; cookbooks, cooking and foods; histories; hobbies; how-to; juveniles; medicine and psychiatry; multimedia material; music; nature; pets; psychology; recreation; reference; religious; self-help; sports; travel; and gardening books.
Fiction: Mystery; science fiction; suspense; gothics; and regency books.
Recent Titles: *The New York Philharmonic Guide to the Symphony,* by E. Downs (music nonfiction); *The Santa Claus Book,* by Jones (nonfiction); and *Collapsing Universe,* by Isaac Asimov (nonfiction).

FREDERICK WARNE & CO., INC., 101 Fifth Ave., New York NY 10003. Editor, Books for Young People: Margaret Klee Lichtenberg. Publishes juvenile hardcover originals. Published 10 titles in 1976, 12 in 1977. Offers 10% royalty contract. Minimum advance is $500. Will consider photocopied submissions. No simultaneous submissions. Submit outline and sample chapters for nonfiction. Submit complete ms for fiction. Reports in 6 weeks. "Ms will not be considered unless accompanied by a correct-size S.A.S.E."
Juveniles: Hardcover trade books for children and young adults. Picture books (age 4 to 7), fiction and nonfiction for the middle reader (age 7 to 12) and young adults (ages 11 and up). Mss must combine a high-interest level with fine writing. Prefers to see fewer picture books and more submissions for 8 to 12-year-olds.
Recent Titles: *It's Not Fair!,* by R. Supraner (picture book); *One More Flight,* by E. Bunting (juvenile novel); and *Somebody Else's Child,* by R. Silman (short chapter book).

WATSON-GUPTILL PUBLICATIONS, 1515 Broadway, New York NY 10036. Publishes originals. Reprints foreign or out-of-print art instruction books. Pays, for originals, 10% of first 10,000; 12½% on next 10,000 and over. Usual advance is $1,000, but average varies, depending on author's reputation and nature of book. Published 47 titles last year. Address queries (followed by outlines and sample chapters) to Donald Holden, Editorial Director. Reports on queries within 10 days. Enclose return postage.
Art: Publishes art instruction books. Interested only in books of a how-to-do-it nature in any field of painting, crafts, design, etc. Not interested in biographies of painters, art history books, aesthetic appreciation. Length: open.

FRANKLIN WATTS, INC., 730 Fifth Avenue, New York, NY 10019. Vice-President, Editorial Director: Kathryn F. Ernst. Editor-in-CHief, juvenile books: Jeanne Vestal. Royalty schedule varies according to the type of book. Usual advance for a series title is $1,000. Single title varies according to reputation of author and type of book. Published 130 titles last year. Current catalog available on request. Query before submitting a nonfiction title. Prefers complete manuscript on fiction. Reports in approximately six weeks. Enclose return postage.
Juveniles: Publishes quality juveniles from pre-school through senior high. Especially interested in humorous novels and science fiction for children ages 9-12. Also looking for high interest/low reading level fiction and contemporary teenage fiction. No historical fiction, please. Would suggest that writers check catalog before submitting nonfiction ideas. Recent titles include: *How the Witch Got Alf, Python's Party, The Boy Who Was Followed Home, Knock Knocks: The Most Ever.*

WAYNE STATE UNIVERSITY PRESS, 5980 Cass Ave., Detroit MI 48202. (313)577-4601. Editor-in-Chief: B.M. Goldman. Managing Editor: B. Woodward. Publishes hardcover and paperback originals. "Standard royalty schedule;" no advance. Published 22 titles in 1976, 25 in 1977; will do 30 in 1978. Reports in 1-6 months. SASE. Free book catalog.
Nonfiction: Publishes Americana, biography, economics, history, law; medicine and psychiatry; music, philosophy, politics, psychology, religious, and sociology books. Query first or submit outline/synopsis and sample chapters. "Do not send photos unless requested, or send photocopies."
Recent Titles: *Psychological Criticism,* by Tennenhouse (literature); *Ships of the Great Lakes,* by Kuttruff (Americana); *Artists of Early Michigan,* by Gibson (art).

WEBSTER DIVISION, McGraw-Hill Book Co., 1221 Ave. of the Americas, New York NY 10020. General Manager: Lawrence A. Walsh. Royalties vary. "Our royalty schedules are those of the industry, and advances are not commonly given." Published 349 titles in 1977. Photocopied submissions OK. Reports in 2-4 weeks. SASE.

Textbooks: Publishes school books, films, equipment and systems for elementary and secondary schoolr. Juveniles, social studies, science, language arts, foreign languages, the arts, mathematics. "Material is generally part of a series, system, or program done in connection with other writers, teachers, testing experts, etc. Material must be matched to the psychological age level, with reading achievement and other educational prerequisites in mind. Interested in a Basal Reading program, a Career Education program, a Guidance program, a Health program, and a Special Education program for the elementary schools."

WESTERN ISLANDS, 4 Hill Rd., Belmont MA 02178. Royalty is usually straight 10% on cloth editions; 5% on paper editions. Published 2 titles in 1976, 6 in 1977. Query. Reports in 1 month. SASE.
Nonfiction and Fiction: Specializes in books that have a conservative-political orientation: current events, essays, history, criticism, biography, memoirs, etc. No word length requirement.
Recent Titles: *Betrayal By Rulers,* by M. Sturdza (history); and *How To Read The Federalist,* by H. Alexander (political).

WESTERN PRODUCER PRAIRIE BOOKS, Box 2500, Saskatoon, Saskatchewan, Canada S7K 2C4. Editor-in-Chief: Bob Sanders. Hardcover and paperback originals (95%); and reprints (5%). Specializes in nonfiction historical works set in Western Canada by Western Canadian authors. 10% (of list price) royalty; no advance. Published 5 titles in 1976, 10 in 1977; will do 10 in 1978. Submit contact sheets, prints if illustrations are to accompany ms. Simultaneous submissions OK. Reports in 2-4 months. SASE. Free book catalog.
Nonfiction: Publishes history, nature, photography, biography, reference, economics, politics, cookbooks, cooking and foods books. Submit outline, synopsis and sample chapters.
Recent Titles: *The Battle River Valley,* by J.C. MacGregor (history); *Wildflowers Across the Prairie,* by F. Vance; *Over 2,000 Place Names of Alberta,* by E.J. and P.M. Holmgren (reference).

WESTERN PUBLISHING CO., INC., 1220 Mound Ave., Racine WI 53404. Publishes hardcover and paperback juvenile books only; originals and reprints. Mss purchased outright. Published approximately 95 titles last year. Complete ms may be sent for picture books; query with outline and sample chapter on all mss over 1,000 words. Address mss and query letters for picture books to Miss Betty Ren Wright; query letters for novels, family, Family Funtime activity books to William Larson. Mss should be typed, double-spaced, with S.A.S.E. enclosed. Reports in two to five weeks.
Juveniles: Picture book lines include Whitman Tell-a-Tale books, Big Golden books, Family Funtime books, Little Golden books, Golden Play and Learn books, Golden Shape books, and Golden Touch and Feel books. Material should be concerned with familiar childhood experiences, early learning concepts, favorite subjects (animals, cars and trucks, play activities). Urban, suburban and rural settings welcome. Unless specifically indicated, books are planned to be read to children, but vocabulary should be simple enough for easy understanding and for young readers to handle themselves if they wish. "We are especially interested in stories about animals, humorous stories, and stories that emphasize concepts important to preschool-primary learning. We have board books and cloth books for children two and under; most of our picture books are intended for ages 3 to 6. While we are definitely interested in stories that combine fun and learning, we see too many mss that are forced or uninteresting because the writer has tried too hard to make them 'educational.' Also, we see many stories that are about children without being for children. We would encourage writers to consider always whether the story is genuinely meaningful to children. We are also interested in seeing stories about little girls that enlarge upon the position of women in nur society. It is easy to turn out a 'message' story, and we do not want to do that, but we would like to publish stories in which girls play a wide variety of roles." Length for picture books: 200 to 800 words. Also publishes a limited number of novel-length hardcover books and story anthologies for ages 8-14. Length: 35,000 to 60,000 words. Should deal with subjects of genuine interest to pre-teens and early teens—mystery, adventure, and stories about high school activities.

WESTERNLORE BOOKS, P.O. Box 41073, 5117 Eagle Rock Blvd., Los Angeles CA 90041. Editor: Paul D. Bailey. Pays standard royalties except in special cases. Published 6 titles in 1976, 8 in 1977. Query. Unsolicited mss returned. Reports in 60 days. Enclose return postage with query.
Americana: Publishes Western Americana of the scholarly and basically researched type. "Volumes fitting our Great West & Indian Series, American Survey Series, Ghost Town Series, or Desert Series." Republication of rare and out-of-print books. Scholarly studies of the great West. Length: 25,000 to 65,000 words.

Recent Titles: *Retracing the Butterfield Trail,* by G.A. Ahmerst (history); and *Mining Camps and Ghost Towns Along the Colorado,* by F. Lowe (history).

THE WESTMINSTER PRESS, 902 Witherspoon Bldg., Philadelphia PA 19107. Editor-in-Chief: Barbara S. Bates. Hardcover originals (99%); reprints (1%). Royalty of 10% for hardcover, split with artist for illustrated book. Advance "varies widely depending on amount of advance research and expenses and on author preference." Published 24 titles in 1976, 17 in 1977; will do 16 in 1978. Submit contact sheets or sample prints of photos and/or illustrations to accompany ms. Do not send original artwork; send sketches and sample drawing only. Reports in 2-4 months. SASE. Book catalog for SASE.

Nonfiction: Publishes Americana, biography, economics, history, hobbies, how-to, humor, nature, pets, recreation, scientific, and rports books for ages 10-15. Length: 25,000-45,000 words. Query first or submit outline/synopsis and sample chapters.

Fiction: Publishes adventure, fantasy, historical, humorous, mainstream, mystery, romance, science fiction, suspense. No picture books or didactic or educational fiction. Length: 25,000-45,000 words. Submit outline/synopsis and sample chapters.

Recent Titles: *I Think This Is Where We Came In,* by P.A. Wood (contemporary novel); *How Do They Package It?,* by G. Sullivan (general interest nonfiction); *Who Do You Think You Are?,* by P. Whitney (mystery).

*WESTVIEW PRESS, 1898 Flatiron Ct., Boulder CO 80301. (303)444-3541. Publisher: F.A. Pratger. Managing Editor: Lynne Rienner. Hardcover and paperback originals (90%) and reprints (10%). Specializes in scholarly monographs or conference reports. Zero to 10% royalty, depending on marketing. Subsidy publishes a limited number of books. "Only in the case of top flight, scholarly materials for a limited market and which need to be priced low, or where the mss have unusual difficulties such as Chinese or Sanskrit characters. The usual quality standards of a top-flight university press apply and subsidies must be furnished by institutions and not individuals." Published 100 titles in 1976, 250 in 1977; will do 350 in 1978. Markets books by direct mail. State availability of photos and/or illustrations to accompany ms. Reports in 2-4 months. SASE. Free book catalog.

Nonfiction: Publishes art, business, economics, history, law, politics, psychology, reference, scientific, sociology, and textbooks. Query and submit sample chapters (Chicago *Manual of Style).* "We do not read unsolicited mss."

WEYBRIGHT AND TALLEY, 750 Third Ave., New York NY 10017. President: Truman M. Talley. Publishes hardcover originals and text paperbacks. Usually offers standard 10-12½-15% royalty contract; "there is no average advance—usually $2,000 on up, depending on many factors." Published 25 titles last year. Will consider photocopied submissions "if clear." Query first with outline and sample chapters. Reports in 1 to 2 weeks. Enclose return postage.

General Nonfiction: Publishes books on Wall Street, business, finance, economics, history, Washington, politics, and is expanding its nature and environmental publishing. Length: 120,000 to 160,000 words.

Recent Titles: *The Bankers,* by M. Mayer (nonfiction); and *The Immortal Profession,* by G. Highet (nonfiction).

WHITAKER HOUSE, Pittsburgh and Colfax Sts., Springdale IL 15144. (412)274-4444. Editor: Victoria L. Milnar. Paperback originals (80%) and reprints (20%). "We publish only Christian books, especially dealing with charismatic Christianity. Royalty of a straight percentage (6%) of the cover price of the book. Advance is made only under certain circumstances. Publishes about 12 titles annually. "We market books in Christian book stores and in rack-jobbing locations such as supermarkets and drug stores." Looking for teaching/testimonies; typed, double-spaced, about 200 pages in length. Send prints to illustrate ms. Simultaneous and photocopied submissions OK. Reports in about 2-4 weeks. SASE. Free book catalog.

Nonfiction: Publishes biography or autobiography (testimony of spirit-filled Christians; 60,000 words); how-to (how to move on in your Christian walk; 60,000 words); religious ("don't want heavy theology"; 60,000 words). "Testimonies of drug addicts or ex-convicts are somewhat overworked. Please note that we call our books 'teaching testimonies' because they give the author's life experiences as well as solid Christian teaching."

Recent Titles: *What You Say Is What You Get,* by D. Gossett (how-to); *Yesterday at the Seventh Hour,* by J. Hale (autobiography); *Freedom to Choose,* by E.J. Gruen (how-to).

WHITMORE PUBLISHING COMPANY, 35 Cricket Terrace, Ardmore PA 19003. Contact: Linda S. Peacock. Offers "standard royalty contract, profit-sharing contract, or outright purchase." Published 12 titles last year. Reports in 2 to 3 weeks. Send queries and sample chapters or poems. Enclose return postage.

General Nonfiction and Poetry: Publishing interest focused on books that will provide the reader with insight and techniques to manage his or her life more effectively. Interests include education, nutrition, community life, philosophy, self-improvement, family study and planning, career planning; explanations of significant science and technology not broadly understood.

Recent Titles: *Learning Joy,* by Dickson/Robitscher; *Church Meru: The Tallest Angle,* by Robertson.

THE WHITSTON PUBLISHING CO., INC., Box 322, Tory NY 12181. (518)283-4363. Editor-in-Chief: Stephen Goode. Hardcover originals. 10% royalty after 200 copies; no advance. Published 16 books in 1976, 20 in 1977; will do 25 in 1978. State availability of photos and/or illustrations to accompany ms. Simultaneous and photocopied submissions OK. Reports in 1-2 weeks. SASE. Free book catalog.

Nonfiction: Publishes scholarly books in the arts and humanities. Reference, bibliographies, indexes, history, psychology, reference, and sociology. Query first or submit outline/synopsis and sample chapters.

Recent Titles: *French Novelists Speak Out,* by B. Knapp (interviews with contemporary French novelists); *Between Two Worlds,* by S. Pinsker (essays); *The Italian Theatre Today,* by A. Amoia (interviews with Italian dramatists).

WILDERNESS PRESS, 2440 Bancroft Way, Berkeley CA 94704. Editor: Thomas Winnett. Publishes paperback originals. "We offer 8% to authors who have not published before. Our average advance is $200." Published 5 titles in 1976, 8 in 1977. Will consider photocopied submissions. Query first. Reports in 2 weeks. Enclose return postage.

Nature: "We publish books about the outdoors. So far, almost all our books are drail guides for hikers and backpackers, but we will be publishing how-to books about the outdoors and personal adventures. The ms must be accurate. The author must research an area thoroughly in person. If he is writing a trail guide, he must walk all the trails in the area his book is about. The outlook must be strongly conservationist. The style must be appropriate for a highly literate audience."

JOHN WILEY & SONS, INC., 605 3rd Ave., New York NY 10016. (212)467-9800. Hardcover and paperback originals. 15% (of net receipts) royalty. Advance averages $1,500. Follow MLA Style Sheet. Simultaneous and photocopied submissions OK. Reports in 6 months. SASE. Free book catalog.

Nonfiction: Publishes college textbooks and professional reference titles in engineering, social science, business life sciences, nature, photography, politics, and psychology. Query first or submit outline/synopsis and sample chapters.

Recent Titles: *How to Profitably Buy and Sell Land; Organic Chemistry.*

WILLAMETTE MANAGEMENT ASSOCIATES, INC., 220 S.W. Alder St., Suite 203, Portland OR 97204. (503)224-6004. Query Editor: J. Michael Reid. Publishes paperback and hardcover originals. Offers royalty contract of 10 to 15% of net. Advance varies. "We will consider photocopy, but would like to know the track record of a copied ms. (Turned down texts no problem — if they fit our needs)." Query with outline and sample chapters or completed ms. Reports in 1 month. Enclose return postage.

Business: Interested in business investment books. "They should be technical and of current interest (timing) as well as of good long-range material. We might consider business-related titles. One of our titles is a regional one; another is national in scope. We have several titles in preparation centering about beginning investment and also what women should look for in investments." Will also consider texts in the business field and business histories. Texts slanted to a particular profession acceptable. "For good research and basically well-written texts, we can provide better services to the newer writers than some of the larger houses. We do have a good distribution net. There are presently 3 editors on our staff with several researchers."

WILSHIRE BOOK CO., 12015 Sherman Rd., N. Hollywood CA 91605. (213)875-1711. Editor-in-Chief: Melvin Powers. Paperback originals (50%) and reprints (50%). 5% royalty; no advance. Publishes 50 titles annually. Indicate availability of photos and/or illustrations to accompany ms. Simultaneous and photocopied submissions OK. Reports in 1-2 weeks. SASE. Free book catalog.

Nonfiction: Publishes erotica, hobbies, how-to; medicine and psychiatry; pets, psychology, recreation, reference, self-help, sex and sports books. "Main interest is in self-help, psychological, inspirational books, and those on horses or gambling or of interest to women." Query first.

Recent Titles: *Guide to Rational Living,* by A. Ellis, Ph.D. (self-help); *Play Tennis with Rosewell,* by K. Rosewell (sports); *Just for Women,* by R.E. Sand, M.D.

WINCHESTER PRESS, 205 E. 42 St., New York NY 10017. (212)679-6301. Managing Editor: Jock Bartlett. Hardcover originals. 10-12½-15% royalty; $1,500 average advance. Published 25 titles in 1976, 26 in 1977; will do 26 in 1978. "Submit sample photos and some idea of total number projected for final book." Simultaneous and photocopied submissions OK. Reports in 3 months. SASE. Free book catalog.
Nonfiction: Main interest is in outdoor sports and related subjects. Publishes cookbooks, cooking and foods (if related to their field); how-to (sports and sporting equipment); pets (hunting dogs and horses); recreation (outdoor), sports (hunting, fishing, etc.); and technical (firearms). Submit outline/synopsis and sample chapters.
Recent Titles: *Shotgunning,* by B. Brister (sports); *Trout Hunting,* by F. Woolner (fishing); *Dogsled,* by S. Randles (Americana).

WINTERGREEN PUBLISHING CO., 40 Shallmar Blvd., Toronto, Ontario, Canada M6C 2J9. Editor-in-Chief: Ted Kosoy. Hardcover and paperback originals. Specializes in travel guides. 7½% royalty on paperbacks; 10% on hardcover; $1,500-2,000 average advance. Published 4 titles in 1976, 3 in 1977; will do 2-3 in 1978. Markets books through bookstores. State availability of photos and/or illustrations. Simultaneous and photocopied submissions OK. Reports in 1-2 months. SASE. Free book catalog for SASE.
Nonfiction: Publishes books on recreation and travel. Submit outline/synopsis and sample chapters.
Recent Titles: *Kosoy's Travel Guide to Canada,* by Kosoy; *A Budget Guide to Florida;* and *A Guide to the Orient and the Pacific.*

WISCONSIN HOUSE BOOK PUBLISHERS, P.O. Box 2118, Madison WI 53701. (608)251-3222. Editor-in-Chief: Mark E. Lefebvre. Publishes hardcover and paperback originals and paperback and hardcover reprints. Offers standard minimum book contract of 10-12½-15%. Published 5 titles in 1976 and 1977. Free book catalog. Query. Reports in 6 weeks. Enclose return postage.
Nonfiction and Fiction: Seeking quality book-length nonfiction and fiction. "Close consideration will be given to works with a regional atmosphere which address universal concerns. There is a belief here that one foot can be in the Midwest and another in the world at large. The writer should realize that Wisconsin House does not direct iteslf to a juvenile audience any more. Beyond that, any approach is acceptable from the traditional to the experimental. Our interest is in quality rather than quantity. It is well to note, too, that there are too many books growing out of family histories which obviously appeal to the writer, but do not achieve the necessary distance to create interest for others."
Recent Titles: *The Only Place We Live,* by A. Derleth, J. Stuart, and R.E. Gard (nature); *Wild Goose Country,* by R.E. Gard (nature/wildlife); and *The Biggest, The Smallest, The Longest, The Shortest,* by Jensen (circus).

*ALAN WOFSY FINE ARTS, 150 Green St., San Francisco CA 94111. Hardcover and paperback originals (75%); hardcover reprints (25%). Specializes in art reference books, specifically catalogs of graphic artists; bibliographies related to fine presses and the art of the book; original, illustrated books. Payment usually made on a flat fee basis, which begins at $200. Subsidy publishes 15% of books "where a very high quality of reproduction is necessary for a very limited market, and we feel the book should be published". No advance. Publishes 6 titles annually. SASE. Reports in 2-4 weeks. Free book catalog.
Nonfiction: Publishes reference books on art and photography. Query.

WOODBRIDGE PRESS PUBLISHING CO., P.O. Box 6189, Santa Barbara CA 93111. Editor-in-Chief: Howard B. Weeks. Publishes hardcover and paperback originals. Standard royalty contract. Rarely gives an advance. Published 11 titles in 1976. Will consider photocopied submissions. Query first. Returns rejected material as soon as possible. Reports on material accepted for publication in 3 months. Enclose return postage with query.
General Nonfiction: "How-to books on personal health and well-being. Should offer the reader valuable new information or insights on anything from recreation to diet to mental health that will enable him to achieve greater personal fulfillment, with emphasis on that goal. Should minimize broad philosophy and maximize specific, useful information." Length: Books range from 96 to 300 pages. Also publishes cookbooks and gardening books. Recent titles include *The Oats, Peas, Beans and Barley Cookbook* (Cottrell), *More Food From Your Garden* (Mittleider) and *Butterflies in My Stomach* (Taylor).

THE WRITER, INC., 8 Arlington St., Boston MA 02116. Editor: A.S. Burack. Publishes hardcover originals. Standard royalty schedule. Advance varies. Published 6 titles last year. Catalog on request. Query first. Reports within three weeks. Enclose return postage.
Nonfiction: Books on writing for writers. Length: open.

WRITER'S DIGEST, 9933 Alliance Rd., Cincinnati OH 45242. (513)984-0717. Book Editor: Paula Arnett Sandhage. Hardcover originals. Trade publisher for books about writing, art and photography. Usual royalty contract: 10% of net; advance averages $1,500. Published 4 titles in 1976 (not counting market books); will publish 5 or 6 titles in 1977 and 1978. Books sold in bookstores and by direct mail. Query with outline and sample chapters. Simultaneous (if so advised) and photocopied submissions OK. Reports in 1 month. SASE or enclose return postage. Book catalog for SASE.
Nonfiction: Wants lively, up-to-date treatments of age-old writing problems, for pros and beginners as well. Also books about photography with emphasis on marketing, not technique. Authors should be established, and be able to write from experience — while not merely holding forth. Style should be well researched, instructive, yet conversational and anecdotal.
Recent Titles: *The Craft of Interviewing,* by J. Brady; *A Guide to Writing History,* by D.R. Marston; *Mystery Writer's Handbook,* by Mystery Writers of America; *Writing & Selling Science Fiction,* by Science Fiction Writers of America; *The Poet and the Poem,* by Judson Jerome; and three hardcover annuals — *Writer's Market,* by Koester and Hillman; *Art & Crafts Market,* by Lapin and Wones; and *Photographer's Market,* by Milar and Brohaugh.

WWWWW/INFORMATION SERVICES, INC., 1595 Elmwood Ave., Rochester NY 14620. Editor-in-Chief: Robert A. Fowler. Publishes paperback originals. Offers standard minimum book contract of 10-12½-15%. Advance depends on book's potential. Published 1 title last year. Marketed through paperback distributors. Will send free catalog to writer on request. Will consider photocopied submissions. Query first. Reports quarterly. Enclose return postage.
Special Needs: "Looking for a number of authors to submit chapters for 3 new books and newsletters."
How-To: Consumer/buyer how-to books such as how to buy a business, how to select a career, etc. Length: 60,000 to 70,000 words.

ZONDERVAN PUBLISHING HOUSE, 1415 Lake Drive S.E., Grand Rapids MI 49506. (616)698-6900. Managing Editor: J.E. Ruark. Textbook Editor: Paul Hillman. Publishes hardcover and paperback originals and reprints. Offers standard minimum book contract of 10-12½-15%. Advances paid only on assigned projects. Published 70 titles last year. Will send free catalog to writer on request. Will consider photocopied submissions, if not simultaneous. Query first with outline and sample chapters. Rejects in 3 to 4 weeks; reports in 6 to 8 weeks usually. Enclose return postage.
Religious Nonfiction: For all ages. Material should be aimed at the evangelical Christian reader. Christian adult trade books, bible study, biography, history, humor, marriage and family, nature, philosophy, plays, psychology, reference, scientific, self-help and how-to, sociology, sports, recreation, and textbooks. Conservative and biblical. Length: 12,000 to 100,000 words.
Recent Titles: *Transcendental Hesitation,* by C. Miller (philosophy); *East Wind,* by M.Z. Linke (autobiography); and *The Act of Marriage,* by Tim and Beverly LaHaye (self-help).

Subsidy Book Publishers

The following listings are for book publishing companies who are totally subsidy publishers, meaning they do no standard trade publishing, and will publish a work only if the author is willing to underwrite the entire amount of the venture. This can be costly, and may run into thousands of dollars, usually returning less than 25% of the initial investment.

Read any literature or contracts carefully and thoroughly, being sure that all conditions of the venture (binding, editing, promotion, number of copies to be printed, etc.) are spelled out specifically.

The subsidy publishing firm hasn't the resources of a standard publisher for promotion and marketing. And it is the rare subsidy-published book that gets the exposure of book reviews.

For more information on subsidy publishing, write to us asking for the reprint "Does It Pay to Pay to Have It Published?" Address to *Payin' For It Editor,* 9933 Alliance Rd., Cincinnati OH 45242. Enclose SASE.

The Benjamin Company, Inc., 485 Madison Ave., New York NY 10022.

Dorrance and Company, 1617 J.F. Kennedy Blvd., Philadelphia PA 19003.

Exposition Press, 900 S. Oyster Bay Rd., Hicksville NY 11801.

Helios Publishing Co., Inc., 150 W. 28th St., New York NY 10001.

Mojave Books, 7040 Darby Ave., Reseda CA 91335.

Vantage Press, 516 W. 34th St., New York NY 10001.

William-Frederick Press, 55 East 86 Street, New York NY 10028.

Trade, Technical, and Professional Journals

Trade magazines make up one of the most diverse and challenging segments of the freelance market, ranging from *Convenience Store News* to *Search and Rescue Magazine*. They are numerous, and they pay moderately well. And often they don't require as much technical expertise as you might think.

For instance, Dave Kaiser is an editor at one trade magazine and a stringer for about a dozen other periodicals. But he's not afraid of diving into new trade specialties. "Heck, no," says Kaiser, the managing editor of *Swimming Pool Age/Weekly.* "As long as you have the basic reporting skills, it shouldn't be any problem at all."

That's apparently the key to successful trade freelancing: solid reporting. Although some trade magazines are probably too specialized for the general writer (and their listings usually indicate this), others are open to the freelancer who can grasp a subject quickly and write clearly and tightly.

Most trade journals appeal to one of three audiences: *retailers,* who are interested in unusual store displays, successful sales campaigns, etc.; *manufacturers,* who want stories on how one plant solved an industry problem, how certain equipment performed in production; and *professionals and industry experts,* interested in technical developments.

Whatever its audience, the trade magazine has one purpose: to help its reader do his job better. *Your* job is to find successful businesses in your area — and explain to the reader in detail what accounts for their success.

Where can you find story ideas? "If it's wet, that's where the ideas are," says David R. Getchell, editor of *National Fisherman.* "One of every two people you stop on the waterfront has probably got a first-rate story in him — and he doesn't even know it, in most cases. Almost all of the businesses and certainly all of the boats have stories. It's just the ability to sound out the story."

Kitchen Business advises: "Just go ahead and do it. Select the best-looking kitchen firm in your area, go in and tell the boss you're a writer and want to do a story for *Kitchen Business.* Ask him to let you sit down and read an issue or two. Interview him on a single how-to-do-it topic, shoot some pictures to illustrate the points in the interview, and take a chance. ... It will work for anyone who has any reporting talent at all."

Take a walk through the Yellow Pages, suggests Kaiser of *Swimming Pool Weekly/Age.* "Hop on the wire and call the builder and say, 'Do you have any special sales methods?'"

But "the most valuable thing around is the daily newspaper," says Kaiser. Ben Russell, editor of *American Laundry Digest,* thinks the freelancer can find more than hamburger bargains by flipping through the ads. A creative advertisement indicates a creative plant owner, he says. "Usually it pays off to go in and talk to him."

Ginny Ade, a freelancer with a specialty in camping articles, suggests that the writer begin with the library. Read back copies and make notes on the kinds of articles the camping magazines use; then look for like articles at trade conventions and campgrounds. But Ade adds, "I get the greatest share of my ideas when I go camping."

Generally, of course, the freelancer must approach the editor — but sometimes the editor may approach *you* if you make your presence known. When Kaiser needs a writer in a certain area, he may call a local newspaper for names. So let your newspaper know you're available as a freelancer — both to that paper and to magazines.

"Don't worry about style," says *American Laundry Digest.* "What we want is good writing. We like a lead that grabs the reader's attention, logical development, copy free of cliches, and completeness (all significant details included)."

Although trade magazines want simple writing, they won't tolerate sloppy writing. *Specialty & Custom Dealer* rejects "hyperbolic accounts of business. Those that read like public relations releases. Broad generalizations concerning 'a great product' without technical data behind the information. Lack of detail concerning business operations."

But any trade magazine welcomes concise and informative writing, based on detailed interviewing. Minding the other guy's business can be good business for you.

Accounting

CGA MAGAZINE, Canadian Certified General Accountants Association, #700 535 Thurlow St., Vancouver, B.C., Canada V6E 3L2. Editor-in-Chief: Merrilee Davey. Emphasizes accounting and management. Monthly magazine; 44 pages. Estab: 1967. Circ: 22,000. Pays on acceptance. Buys all rights, but may reassign following publication. Photocopied submissions OK. SASE. Reports in 4 weeks. Free sample copy and writer's guidelines.
Nonfiction: "Accounting and financial subjects of interest to highly qualified professional accountants and other financial officers. Majority of them are industrial (i.e. corporation) accountants as opposed to accountants in public practice. All submissions must be relevant to Canadian accounting. All material must be of top professional quality, but at the same time written simply and interestingly." Publishes how-to; humor; informational; personal experience; personal opinion; and technical. Buys 36 mss/year. Query. Length: 1,500-2,000 words. Pays $100-500.
Fillers: Jokes, gags, anecdotes. Buys 6/issue. Length: "usually one-liners." Pays $5-35.

Advertising and Marketing

Trade journals for professional advertising executives, copywriters and marketing men are listed in this category. Those whose main interests are the advertising and marketing of specific products (such as Groceries or Office Equipment and Supplies) are classified under individual product categories.

AD TECHNIQUES, ADA Publishing Co., 19 W. 44 St., New York NY 10036. (212)986-4930. Managing Editor: Elaine Louie. For advertising executives. Monthly magazine; 50 pages. Estab: 1965. Circ: 4,500. Pays on acceptance. Not copyrighted. Reports in 1 month. Sample copy 85¢.
Nonfiction: Articles on advertising techniques. Buys 10 mss/year. Query. Pays $25-50.

ADVERTISING AGE, 740 N. Rush, Chicago IL 60611. Managing Editor: L.E. Doherty. Currently staff-produced.

ART DIRECTION, Advertising Trade Publications, Inc., 19 W. 44 St., New York NY 10036. (212)986-4930. Managing Editor: Elaine Louie. Emphasis on advertising design for art directors of ad agencies (corporate, in-plant, editorial, freelance, etc.). Monthly magazine; 100 pages. Estab: 1949. Circ: 12,000. Pays on publication. Buys one-time rights. SASE. Reports in 3 months. Sample copy $1.50.
Nonfiction: How-to articles on advertising campaigns. Pays $25 minimum.

THE COUNSELOR, NBS Building, Second and Clearview Aves., Trevose PA 19047. (215)355-5800. Managing Editor: Paul A. Camp. For "the specialty advertising industry." Monthly. Rights purchased vary with author and material. Buys first North American serial rights and reprint rights; may buy simultaneous rights. Pays on publication. Reports in 14 days. SASE.
Nonfiction: Articles on sales, management, market trends, government regulation, interviews with industry suppliers and distributors; articles of interest to small businessmen or women. Length: 1,000-5,000 words. Pays $75 to $100.

INCENTIVE MARKETING/INCORPORATING INCENTIVE TRAVEL, Bill Communications, Inc., 633 Third Ave., New York NY 10017. (212)986-4800. Editor-in-Chief: Murray

Elman. For buyers of merchandise used in motivational promotions. Monthly magazine; 200 pages. Estab: 1905. Circ: 37,000. Pays on acceptance. Buys all rights, but may reassign following publication. SASE. Reports in 2 weeks. Free sample copy and writer's guidelines. **Nonfiction:** Informational, case histories. Buys 60-75 mss a year. Query. Length: 1,500 words minimum. Pays $85-125.

MAC/WESTERN ADVERTISING, 6565 Sunset Blvd., Los Angeles CA 90028. Editor: Lee Kerry. For "people involved in advertising: media, agencies, and client organizations as well as affiliated businesses." Weekly. Buys all rights. Pays on acceptance. Reports in 1 month. Query first; "articles on assignment." Enclose S.A.S.E.
Nonfiction and Photos: "Advertising in the West. Not particularly interested in success stories. We want articles by experts in advertising, marketing, communications." Length: 1,000 to 1,750 words. Pays $100. Photos purchased with mss.

MARK II, THE SALES AND MARKETING MANAGEMENT MAGAZINE, 2175 Sheppard Ave., E., Suite 110, Willowdale, Ont., Canada MJ2 1W8. Editor/Publisher: Harold L. Taylor. For "Canadian marketing, sales management, advertising, and agency executives." Buys first rights. Pays on publication. Will send a sample copy to a writer on request. Reports "in a few days." Enclose S.A.E. and International Reply Coupons.
Nonfiction: "Case histories, conceptual articles. Innovative; lively style. Should have a Canadian slant. Not a market for beginners." Pays $50 for 600-800 words; $125 for 1,500-2,000 words; $150 for 1,500-2,500 words.

THE PRESS, 302 Grote St., Buffalo NY 14207. Managing Editor: Janet Tober. Emphasizes articles of general interest to advertising men from agencies, newspapers and prospective advertisers in the comics. Bimonthly tabloid; 4-8 pages. Estab: 1977. Circ: 3,000. Pays on acceptance. Buys all rights, but may reassign following publication. Submit seasonal or holiday material 2 months in advance. Photocopied and previously published submissions OK. SASE. Reports in 4-8 weeks. Sample copy 50¢; free writer's guidelines.
Nonfiction: Historical; humor; informational; interview; personal experience; profile and travel. Buys 2-3 mss/issue. Query. Length: 1,500-3,000 words. Pays $100-250.

SALES & MARKETING MANAGEMENT, 633 Third Ave., New York NY 10017. (212)986-4800. Editor: Robert H. Albert. For sales and marketing and other business executives responsible for the sale and marketing of their products and services. Magazine published 19 times a year. Established in 1918. Circulation: 43,168. Buys all rights. Buys the occasional outstanding article on selling and marketing; domestic and international. Payment on publication. Will send free sample copy to writer on request. Reports in 2 weeks. Query first. Enclose S.A.S.E.
Nonfiction: "Articles on the sales and marketing operations of companies, concerning the evaluation of markets for products and services; the planning, packaging, advertising, promotion, distribution and servicing of them, and the management and training of the sales force." Informational, how-to, personal experience, interview, profile, humor, think pieces, expose, spot news, successful business operations, new product, merchandising techniques, technical. Length: 500 to 1,800 words. Payment negotiable.

SOUTHWEST ADVERTISING & MARKETING, 5314 Bingle Rd., Houston TX 77092. Editor: Bob Gray. For executives of advertising agencies and corporate ad managers in Texas, Oklahoma, Louisiana, Arkansas and New Mexico; media executives and executives of supplies (printing, litho, and paper plants). Magazine; 40 (7x10) pages. Established in 1946. Monthly. Circulation: 6,000. Buys all rights. Buys about 36 mss per year. Pays on publication. Will send free sample copy to writer on request. No photocopied or simultaneous submissions. Reports in 2 weeks. Query first. Enclose S.A.S.E.
Nonfiction and Photos: How-to articles in advertising and marketing fields, as well as success stories of ad campaigns; new ideas in merchandising; fresh approaches to old selling ideas; how bright people solve their toughest problems in this business. "We emphasize clear, uncomplicated English. This is a sophisticated audience that respects plain language and cannot be snowed. Stick to facts, quotes, and what the writer is absolutely sure of. We always like to see fresh ideas on direct mail shortcuts and merchandising success stories." Informational, interview, profile, think pieces, personal opinion, successful business operations and articles on merchandising techniques are considered. Length: 2,000 words. Pays 7¢ a word. No additional payment for photos used with mss. Captions required.

VISUAL MERCHANDISING, S.T. Publications, 407 Gilbert Ave., Cincinnati OH 45202. Managing Editor: Pamela Gramke. Emphasizes store design and display. Monthly magazine; 72 pages. Circ: 9,500. Pays on publication. Submit seasonal or holiday material 8 months in advance. Simultaneous, photocopied and previously published submissions OK. SASE. Reports in 1 month. Sample copy $1; free writer's guidelines.

Nonfiction: Expose, how-to (display), informational (store design, construction, merchandise display), interview (display directors and shop owners), nostalgia (store architecture, display, etc.), profile (new and remodeled stores), new product, photo feature (window display), technical (store lighting, carpet, wallcoverings, fixtures). Buys 24 mss a year. Query or submit complete ms. Length: 500-2,000 words. Pays $50-100.

Photos: Purchased with or without accompanying ms or on assignment. Pays $5 for 5x7 b&w glossies. Submit contact sheet. Seeks "tongue-in-cheek photos or general subjects on lighting, planning, design and merchandising."

How To Break In: "Be fashion and design conscious and reflect that in the article. Submit finished mss with photos always. Look for stories on department store display directors (profiles, methods, views on the industry, sales promotions and new store design or remodels)."

Agricultural Equipment and Supplies

CANADIAN FARMING, International Harvester, Canada National Marketing Offices, 3228 Service Rd., Burlington, Ont. L7N 3H8. (416)681-1311. Editor: Dennis S. Hladysh. Published by International Harvester Company of Canada, Limited. Audience ranges from agricultural engineers, students, government agencies, agricultural equipment interest groups, 4-H'ers to farmers and dealers. Quarterly magazine; 20 to 24 (8¼x10¾) pages. Established in 1915. Circulation: 150,000 English, 25,000 French. Buys all rights, but will reassign rights to author after publication. Buys about 12 mss a year. Pays on publication. Will send free sample copy to writer on request. Submit seasonal material at least 3 months in advance. Reports within 1 month. Query first with outline of proposed article. Enclose S.A.E. and International Reply Coupons.

Nonfiction and Photos: "Generally, stories are on better farming procedures, machinery management and an occasional safety article or general farm interest story. Prefer stories to deal with people who use International Harvester equipment. We prefer to publish articles on new procedures which have been used by farmers and are of a general successful nature. Minimum tillage, leasing, overbuying, etc. Articles should deal with machinery, planting, harvesting, foraging, etc. Stay away from husbandry or livestock type themes unless machinery has main association." Also uses articles on haying, fall harvest/tillage, winter maintenance, and seasonal articles dealing with better farming and machinery management. Length: 1,000 to 2,000 words. Pays 10¢ per published word. Uses b&w and 35mm or 2¼x2¼ color. Captions optional. Pays a minimum of $15 each for b&w; $35 minimum for color.

CUSTOM APPLICATOR, Little Publications, 6263 Poplar Ave., Suite 540, Memphis TN 38138. Editor: Tom Griffin. For "firms that sell and custom apply agricultural chemicals." Circulation: 17,000. Buys all rights. Pays on publication. "Query is best. The editor can help you develop the story line regarding our specific needs." Enclose S.A.S.E.

Nonfiction and Photos: "We are looking for articles on custom application firms telling others how to better perform jobs of chemical application, develop new customers, handle credit, etc. Lack of a good idea or usable information will bring a rejection. If the idea is good and the information is good (developed), we can always run it through a typewriter." Length: 1,000 to 1,200 words "with 3 or 4 b&w glossies." Pays up to $125.

FARM SUPPLIER, Watt Publishing Co., Sandstone Bldg., Mount Morris IL 61054. (815)734-4171. Editor-in-Chief: Ray Bates. For retail farm supply dealers and managers over the U.S. Monthly magazine; 64 pages. Estab: 1927. Circ: 20,000. Pays on acceptance. Buys all rights in competitive farm supply fields. Phone queries OK. Submit seasonal or holiday material 3 months in advance. Photocopied submissions OK. SASE. Reports in 2 weeks. Free sample copy.

Nonfiction: How-to; informational; interview; new product; and photo feature. "Articles emphasizing product news, how new product developments have been profitably re-sold, or successfully used." Buys 2 mss a year. Query. Length: 300-1,500 words. Pays $20,-100. "Longer articles must include photos, charts, etc."

Photos: Purchased with accompanying ms. Submit 5x7 or 8x10 b&w prints; 35mm or larger color transparencies. Total purchase price for a ms includes payment for photos.

How To Break In: "Query first, preferably by letter, outlining in detail what is proposed. The writer probably should have experience or writing background in the farm supply trade, which is a semi-specialized area. We also require product-news related material, rather than retail management."

Architecture

Architects and city planners whose primary concern is the design of buildings and urban environments are the target audience for the journals in this category. Those that emphasize choice of materials, structural details, and methods of constructing buildings are classified in the Construction and Contracting category.

INLAND ARCHITECT, 1800 S. Prairie, Chicago IL 60616. Editor: M. W. Newman. For architects, planners, engineers, people interested in architecture (buffs) or urban affairs. Monthly magazine; 36 (8½11) pages. Established in 1957. Not copyrighted. Buys 24 mss a year. Payment on publication. Will send sample copy to writer for $1. Will not consider photocopied submissions. Will consider simultaneous submissions. Two triple-spaced copies of each submission are required. Reports in 1 month. Query first. Enclose S.A.S.E.
Nonfiction and Photos: "Articles cover appraisal of distinguished buildings, profiles of individual architects and firms, historic buildings and preservation, related education, architectural philosophy, interior design and furnishing, building technology, architectural education, economics of the architectural field, and the business operation of an architect's office. In addition, periodic articles concern such urban matters as city planning, housing, transportation, population shifts, and ecology. The emphasis is regional (Chicago and Illinois) with occasional forays into the greater Midwest. Approach should be one of serious criticism and investigative journalism in journalistic style." Length: flexible, but is usually 1,000 to 2,500 words. Pays $50 to $100. B&w glossy photos are purchased with mss; no additional payment. Captions (and identifications) required.

PROGRESSIVE ARCHITECTURE, 600 Summer St., Stamford CT 06904. Editor: John M. Dixon. Monthly. Buys first-time rights for use in architectural press. Pays on publication. Enclose S.A.S.E.
Nonfiction and Photos: "Articles of technical professional interest devoted to architecture and community design and illustrated by photographs and architectural drawings. Also use technical articles, which are prepared by technical authorities and would be beyond the scope of the lay writer. Practically all the material is professional, and most of it is prepared by writers in the field who are approached by the magazine for material." Pays $50 to $250. Buys one-time reproduction rights to b&w and color photos.

Auto and Truck

The journals below aim at automobile and truck dealers, repairmen, or fleet operators. Publications for highway planners and traffic control experts are classified in the Government and Public Service category. Journals for traffic managers and transportation experts (who route goods across the continent) will be found in Transportation.

AUTO LAUNDRY NEWS, Columbia Communications, 370 Lexington Ave., New York NY 10017. (212)532-9290. Editor-in-Chief: J.R. Peterson. For sophisticated carwash operators. Monthly magazine; 52 pages. Estab: 1925. Circ: 18,000. Pays on publication. Buys all rights. Phone queries OK. Submit seasonal/holiday material 60 days in advance. Photocopied and previously published submission OK. SASE. Reports in 4 weeks. Free sample copy.
Nonfiction: How-to; historical; humor; informational; new product; nostalgia; personal experience; technical; interviews; photo features; and profiles. Buys 40 mss/year. Query. Length: 1,500-3,000 words. Pays $75-175.

AUTOMOTIVE NEWS, 965 E. Jefferson Ave., Detroit MI 48207. Editor: Robert M. Lienert. For management people in auto making and auto dealing. Veekly. Established in 1925. Circulation: 58,000. Buys all rights. Payment on acceptance. Free sample copy to writer on request. Query first. Enclose S.A.S.E.

Nonfiction and Photos: News material valuable to the auto trade. "Current and complete familiarity with the field is essential, so we don't use much freelance material." Articles must be accurate with the emphasis on the how rather than the what. Ideas must be helpful to dealers, and written in a news style. Pays $1 per inch of type (about 50 words). Photos are purchased with mss. No additional payment.

THE BATTERY MAN, Independent Battery Manufacturers Association, Inc., 100 Larchwood Dr., Largo FL 33540. (813)586-1409. Editor-in-Chief: Dan A. Noe. Emphasizes SLI battery manufacture, applications, new developments. For battery manufacturers and retailers (garage owners, servicemen, fleet owners, etc.). Monthly magazine; 24 pages. Estab: 1919. Circ: 7,000. Pays on acceptance. Buys all rights. Submit seasonal/holiday material 2 months in advance. Simultaneous, photocopied and previously published submissions OK. SASE. Reports in 2 weeks. Free sample copy.
Nonfiction: Technical articles. Submit complete ms. Length: 1,200-1,500 words. Pays $70-90.

BRAKE & FRONT END SERVICE, 11 S. Forge St., Akron OH 44304. (216)535-6117. Editor: Jeffrey S. Davis. For owners of automotive repair shops engaged in brake, wheel, suspension, chassis and frame repair, including: specialty shops; general repair shops; new car and truck dealers; gas stations; mass merchandisers and tire stores. Monthly magazine; 68 pages. Estab: 1931. Circ: 28,000. Pays on publication. Buys all rights. SASE. Reports immediately. Sample copy and editorial schedule $1.
Nonfiction and Photos: Specialty shops taking on new ideas using new merchandising techniques; growth of business, volume; reasons for growth and success. Expansions, and unusual brake shops." Query. Length: about 1,000 words. Pays 4-9¢/word. Pays $5 for b&w glossies purchased with mss.

CANADIAN AUTOMOTIVE TRADE MAGAZINE, MacLean-Hunter, Ltd., 481 University Ave., Toronto, Ontario, Canada M5W 1A7. (416)595-1811. Editor-in-Chief: Edward Belitsky. Emphasizes the automotive aftermarket and for mechanics, service station and garage operators, new car dealers and parts jobbers. Monthly magazine; 60 pages. Estab: 1919. Circ: 39,000. Pays on publication. Buys all rights, but may reassign following publication. Phone queries OK. Submit seasonal/holiday material 2 months in advance. Photocopied submissions OK. SASE. Reports in 2 months. Free sample copy and writer's guidelines.
Nonfiction: Informational; new product; technical; interviews; and profiles. "We can use business articles every month from the 4 corners of Canada. Service articles can come from anywhere." Buys 3 mss/issue. Length: 600-1,400 words. Pays $40-160.
Photos: Purchased with accompanying ms. Captions required. Send contact sheet and/or transparencies. Pays $5-20 for 4x5 b&w prints or 35mm color transparencies. Model release required.

CANADIAN DRIVER/OWNER, 481 University Ave., Toronto, Ont., Canada M5W 1A7. (416)595-1811. Editor: Simon Hally. For owner/operators of heavy-duty trucks in Canada. Magazine; 42 pages. Established in 1972. Quarterly. Circulation: 17,000. Rights purchased vary with author and material. Usually buys first rights. Buys 12 to 15 mss a year. Pays on acceptance. Will send sample copy to writer on request. Will consider photocopied and simultaneous submissions. Reports in 1 to 2 weeks. Query first or submit complete ms. Enclose S.A.E. and International Reply Coupons.
Nonfiction and Photos: Articles on trucks, truck components, maintenance and repair, small business management, CB radio, legal aspects of trucking, country music, etc. Informal, light style. Special emphasis on the Canadian independent trucking scene since the publication is aimed exclusively at Canadian owner-operators, as opposed to company drivers, truck fleets or U.S. truckers. Material on deregulation of trucking and new federal (Canadian) safety legislation would be of interest. Length: 500 to 1,200 words except for how-to material which usually runs from 200 to 1,200 words. Pays 6½¢ to 10¢ a word. B&w photos purchased with or without mss, or on assignment. Pays according to quality. Captions required.

COMMERCIAL CAR JOURNAL, Chilton Way, Radnor PA 19089. Editor: James D. Winsor. Monthly. Buys all rights. Pays on acceptance. "Query first with article outline." Enclose S.A.S.E.
Nonfiction: "Articles and photo features dealing with management, maintenance, and operating phases of truck and bus fleet operations. Material must be somewhat specialized and deal with a specific phase of the operation." Length: open. Pays $50 to $150.
Photos: "Occasionally use separate photos with captions." Pays $10-25.

CONOCO TODAY, Box 2197, Houston TX 77001. Editor: John H. Walker. Continental Oil Company. Bimonthly. Buys all rights. Pays on acceptance. Will send free sample copy on request. Query first. Reports at once. Enclose S.A.S.E.
Nonfiction: Conoco service station operation and wholesale distributor operations, news and ideas. Length: 1,000 words. Pays 7¢ a word.
Photos: Purchased with mss. B&w 8x10, pays $10.

FLEET MAINTENANCE & SPECIFYING, 7300 N. Cicero, Lincolnwood IL 60646. (312)674-7300. Editor: Tom Gelinas. For those directly responsible for specification purchase, repair and maintenance of on-road vehicles of 10,000 GUW or more. Magazine. Established in 1974. Monthly. Circulation: 45,000. Buys all rights. Pays on publication. Will send free sample copy to writer on request. Will consider photocopied submissions. Reports as soon as possible. Query first. Enclose S.A.S.E.
Nonfiction and Photos: Articles on troubleshooting repair and maintenance of vehicles. Articles on fleets and their maintenance programs; management technique stories. "Our publication is technically oriented. Our only interest is in generally superior work." Does not want to see product-oriented job stories, but will consider industry reports or articles on safety. Length: 2,000 to 5,000 words. Pays $25 per printed page minimum, without photos. Pays $50 per page if photos included. No additional payment is made for large format transparencies used with articles.

JOBBER NEWS, Wedham Publications, Ltd., 109 Vanderhoof Ave., Toronto, Ontario, Canada M4G 2J2. (416)425-9021. Editor-in-Chief: Sam Dixon. Emphasizes auto parts merchandising and management for owners and managers of automotive wholesaling establishments, warehouse distributors, and engine rebuilding shops in Canada. Monthly magazine; 58 pages. Estab: 1932. Circ: 8,000. Pays on acceptance. Buys all rights. Phone queries OK. Submit seasonal/holiday material 2 months in advance. Simultaneous, photocopied, and previously published submissions OK. SASE. Reports in 2 weeks. Free sample copy and writer's guidelines.
Nonfiction: How-to articles. Must have authentic Canadian application. Query. Length: 2,000-3,000 words. Pays $50-125.

JOBBER TOPICS, 7300 N. Cicero Ave., Lincolnwood IL 60646. (312)588-7300. Articles Editor: Jack Creighton. For automotive parts and supplies wholesalers. Monthly. Buys all rights. Pays on publication. Query with outline. SASE.
Nonfiction and Photos: Most editorial is staff written. "Articles with unusual or outstanding automotive jobber procedures, with special emphasis on sales and merchandising; any phase of distribution. Especially interested in merchandising practices and machine shop operation." Length: 2,000 words maximum. Pays 4¢ a word minimum. 5x7 or 8x10 b&w glossies purchased with mss. Pays $5 minimum.

MAGIC CIRCLE, c/o Aitkin-Kynett, 4 Penn Center, Philadelphia PA 19102. For the automobile mechanic in his own shop, in the service station, fleet garage, repair shop or new car dealership. Company publication of the Dana Corporation. Magazine; 20 pages. Established in 1955. Quarterly. Circulation: 80,000. Buys all rights, but will reassign rights to author after publication. Buys 2 or 3 mss a year. Pays on acceptance. A free sample copy will be sent only if a viable query is sent at the same time. Will consider photocopied submissions and may consider simultaneous submissions. Reports in 2 weeks. Query first. Enclose S.A.S.E.
Nonfiction and Photos: "Articles on anything that will make the mechanic a better, more efficient, more profitable mechanic and businessman. We need a light style, but with plenty of detail on techniques and methods." Informational, how-to, travel, successful business operations, merchandising techniques, technical articles. Length: 500 to 2,000 words. Pays $150 maximum. B&w and color photos are purchased with or without ms. Captions required. Pays $25 for b&w 8x10 glossies; $50 for 2¼x2¼ or 35mm color.

MERCHANDISER, Amoco Oil Company, P.O. Box 6110-A, Chicago IL 60680. Editor: Robert P. Satkoski. For Amoco service station dealers, jobbers. Quarterly. Circulation: 30,000. Buys all rights, but will reassign after publication. Buys 3 or 4 mss a year. Pays on publication. Query recommended. Enclose S.A.S.E.
Nonfiction and Photos: Short, to-the-point, success stories and how-to stories, that will trigger creative thinking by the reader. Storylines are most often in the merchandising, motivational, and educational areas. Length: 750 words maximum. Payment varies, with minimum of $100. Uses b&w and color photos

MILK HAULER AND FOOD TRANSPORTER, 1604 Chicago Ave., Evanston IL 60201. Editor: Douglas D. Sorenson. For "tank truck haulers who pick up milk from dairy farms and transporters who deliver milk to outlying markets." Buys first rights. Pays on acceptance. Query first. Reports in 2 to 3 weeks. Enclose S.A.S.E.

Nonfiction and Photos: "Particularly interested in success stories on transporters whose operation includes the hauling of cheese and other dairy products, liquid sugar, molasses, citrus juice, and other edible foods. Good photos essential. Pay up to $50 an article, $5 each for sharp b&w photos."

MODERN BULK TRANSPORTER, 4801 Montgomery Lane, Washington DC 20014. (301)654-8802. Editor: Don Sutherland. For "management of companies operating tank motor vehicles which transport liquid or dry bulk commodities." Monthly. Buys first rights only. Pays on acceptance. Will consider photocopied submissions, but "we're prejudiced against them." Enclose S.A.S.E.

Nonfiction and Photos: "Articles covering the tank truck industry; stories concerning a successful for-hire tank truck company, or stories about use of tank trucks for unusual commodities. We especially seek articles on successful operation of tank trucks by oil jobbers or other so-called 'private carriers' who transport their own products. Approach should be about specific tank truck problems solved, unusual methods of operations, spectacular growth of a company, tank truck management techniques, or other subjects of special interest. Articles should speak to management of companies operating tank trucks, *in their terms,* not to truck drivers. Simple description of routine operations not acceptable." Length: 1,000-3,000 words, "preferably accompanied by pictures." Pays minimum 5¢/word. Pays minimum $30/published page "for general articles exclusive in trucking field only (such as maintenance and mechanical subjects)." Pays minimum $25 for reporter assignments — producing fact sheet for rewrite. Pays $7 for 8x10 or 5x7 glossies purchased with exclusive features.

MODERN TIRE DEALER, Box 5417, 77 N. Miller Rd., Akron OH 44313. (216)867-4401. Editor: Stephen LaFerre. For independent tire dealers. Monthly magazine. Pays on publication. Buys all rights. Photocopied submissions OK. Query. Reports in 1 month. SASE.

Nonfiction, Photos, and Fillers: "How TBA dealers sell tires, batteries, and allied services, such as brakes, wheel alignment, shocks, mufflers. The emphasis is on merchandising. We prefer the writer to zero in on some specific area of interest; avoid shotgun approach." Length: 1,500 words. Pays $50 to $100. 8x10, 4x5, 5x7 b&w glossies purchased with mss. Pays $5. Buys 300-word fillers. Pays $5 to $10.

MOTOR, 1790 Broadway, New York NY 10019. Editor: J. Robert Connor. For automobile service and repairshop operators, dealer service managers. Monthly. Buys all rights. Pays on acceptance. Query first. Reports in 1 week. Enclose S.A.S.E.

Nonfiction: Specializes in service and repair of both domestic and foreign cars for professional mechanics. Merchandising, sales promotion and management articles containing ideas that can be adapted by independent garages and service stations. Emphasis on how-to material. Wants stories on wholesalers, jobbers, and interviews with executives for 8-page section in Aftermarket Journal edition. Length: 1,200-1,500 words. Pays $100-300; sometimes higher for exceptional pieces.

Photos: Purchased with mss or with captions, of interest to readership. 8x10 glossies. Pays $25 for single b&w photo; $400 for cover color photo.

MOTOR NORTH MAGAZINE, 6215 Brooklyn Dr., Minneapolis MN 55430. (612)566-6437. Publisher: Gary Jacobson. For service stations, automotive repair garages, parts jobbers, car dealers, fleets. Magazine; 48 pages. Established in 1972. Monthly. Circulation: 12,900. Rights purchased vary with author and material. Usually buys all rights, but may reassign rights to author after publication. Buys 5 to 10 mss a year. Pays on publication. Will send sample copy to writer on request. Will consider photocopied and simultaneous submissions. Submit seasonal material 3 months in advance. Reports on material accepted for publication in 1 month. Returns rejected material at time of decision. Query first or submit complete ms. Enclose S.A.S.E.

Nonfiction and Photos: Technical, sales-oriented, and human interest material relating to the automotive parts and service industry. Articles on transportation-related subjects; fuel shortage, etc. Seasonal material pertaining do automobiles, such as winter-starting, is used. Pays $10 to $40, depending on subject matter. Tips for mechanics used in columns and departments. Length: 1 to 2 double-spaced, typewritten pages. Pays 2¢ a word. Will also accept suggestions for new columns and departments. B&w (8x10) or color (3x5 or 8x10) purchased with mss. Pays $10 for b&w; $20 for color. Captions required.

MUFFLER DIGEST, 1036 S. Glenstone, Springfield MO 65804. (417)866-3917. Editor: William E. Davis. For professional installers and manufacturers of exhaust systems and exhaust system components. Monthly magazine; 26 pages. Estab: 1976. Circ: 5,300. Pays on acceptance. Buys all rights, but may reassign following publication. Simultaneous and photocopied submissions OK. SASE. Reports in 1 week. Free sample copy.
Nonfiction: How-to; humor (in the muffler field); informational; interview (good interviews with shop owners); and profile (industry people). "We're not interested in 'How I Got Ripped Off at....' types of features." Buys 15-20/year. Submit complete ms. Length: 1,000-1,500 words. Pays 3-5¢/word.
Photos: Purchased with accompanying ms. Captions required. Query. Pays $5 for b&w photos.
Columns/Departments: How-To column (could be a shop-talk type of article). Query. Length: 500 words. Pays 3-5¢/word.
How To Break In: "We are covering the professional exhaust system installer in the U.S., Mexico, and Canada. When we talk about professional we are talking about muffler specialty shops—Midas, Tuffy and other franchise chain operators as well as independents. We are not interested in service stations, Sears, Wards, etc. We would prefer to see more stories on successful independent installers; how they got started, what special tricks have they picked up, what is their most successful merchandising tool, etc."

NTDRA DEALER NEWS, 1343 L St., N.W., Washington DC 20005. Editor: Donald L. Thompson. For tire dealers and retreaders. Publication of the National Tire Dealers & Retreaders Association. Weekly magazine; 24 pages. Established in 1935. Circulation: 7,500. Occasionally copyrighted, depending on content. Buys 10 to 15 mss a year. Will send free sample copy on request. Wil consider photocopied and simultaneous submissions. Reports immediately. Query first. Enclose S.A.S.E.
Nonfiction: Articles relating to retailing and marketing, with special emphasis on the tire dealer, retreader and small businessman in general. Industry news, business aids, new products. Dealer and consumer comments regarding this industry. Most articles received are of too general interest. Uses informational, technical, how-to, interview, think pieces and material on successful business operations and merchandising techniques. Pays $150 to $200.

O AND A MARKETING NEWS, P. O. Box 765, LaCanada CA 91011. (213)790-6554. Editor: Don McAnally. For "service station dealers, garagemen, TBA (tires, batteries, accessories) people, oil company marketing management." Bimonthly. Circulation: 15,000. Not copyrighted. Pays on publication. Query first. Reports in 1 week. Enclose S.A.S.E.
Nonfiction and Photos: "Straight news material; management, service, and merchandising applications; emphasis on news about or affecting markets and marketers within the publication's geographic area of the 7 western states. No restrictions on style or slant." Length: maximum 1,000 words. Pays $1 per column inch (about 2¢ a word). Photos purchased with or without mss; captions required. Pays $5.

OHIO TRUCKING TIMES, Mezzanine Floor, Neil House Hotel, Columbus OH 43215. Editor: David F. Bartosic. Publication of the Ohio Trucking Association. Quarterly. Buys material for exclusive publication only. Pays on publication. Free sample copy on request. Query not required. Reports in 30 days. Enclose S.A.S.E.
Nonfiction: Modern developments in truck transportation, particularly as they apply to Ohio industry and truck operators. Length: 1,500 words. Pay negotiable.
Photos: With mss or with captions only. Transportation subjects. Pay negotiable.

OPEN ROAD, 1015 Florence St., Fort Worth TX 76102. Editor: Chris Lackey. For "professional over-the-road truck drivers of America." Monthly. Buys North American serial rights. Pays on publication. Will send a sample copy to a writer on request. Query first. Reports in 2 to 4 weeks. Enclose S.A.S.E.
Nonfiction and Photos: "Pieces on truck drivers—articles about new model heavy trucks and equipment, acts of heroism, humor, unusual events, special driving articles, advice to other drivers, drivers who do good jobs in community life or civic work, etc." Recently sponsored two special events: selection of an outstanding woman trucker, "Queen of the Road," for 1977; and Truck Drivers Country Music Awards Competition, a national poll among professional truck drivers, picked outstanding artists in 10 country music categories. Length: "prefer 1,000 to 1,500 words, usually." Pays "about 6¢ a word." 5x7 or 8x10 b&w glossies purchased with mss. Pays $5 to $10, depending on quality and newsworthiness, "more for covers."
How To Break In: "Best way would be factual articles about unusual experiences of truckers along the highways, either in line of duty or in aiding others. Interviews should be careful, and thorough, and should include full information identifying the trucker, family background, who

employs him, etc. If article deals with operating conditions, it should be based on observations of a veteran trucker with some historical perspective on trucking."

THE PENNSYLVANIA AUTOMOTIVE DEALER, PAA Services, Inc., P.O. Box 2955, Harrisburg PA 17105. Editor: Richard D. Clemmer. For motor vehicle inspection station network that handles periodic motor vehicle inspection; service stations, garages, new and used car dealers. Magazine; 16 pages. Established in 1974. Every 2 months. Circulation: 16,686. Rights purchased vary with author and material. Usually buys all rights, but will reassign rights to author after publication. Pays on publication. Will send free sample copy to writer on request. Write for copy of guidelines for writers. Will consider photocopied and simultaneous submissions. Reports on material accepted for publication on tenth of month prior to publication. Returns rejected material immediately. Query first. Enclose S.A.S.E.
Nonfiction and Photos: Articles on auto inspection regulations, new products, industry regulations, mechanical tips. General interest articles that improve the mind, as well as those on education, tax tips, etc. Programmed P/R material to mold relationships to develop a positive awareness of the auto business, in particular, and auto aftermarket, in general. Nothing on tips to the consumer. Prefers tips to the independent businessman type of ideas. Material on auto-oriented successful business operations and technical material on the servicing of autos and updating of safety. Length: 1,500 words. Pays minimum of $25 per published page. No additional payment for b&w photos used with mss.

REFRIGERATED TRANSPORTER, 1602 Harold St., Houston TX 77006. (713)523-8124. Monthly. Not copyrighted. Pays on publication. Reports in 1 month. Enclose S.A.S.E.
Nonfiction and Photos: "Articles on fleet management and maintenance of vehicles, especially the refrigerated van and the refrigerating unit; shop tips; loading or handling systems, especially for frozen or refrigerated cargo; new equipment specifications; conversions of equipment for better handling or more efficient operations. Prefer articles with illustrations obtained from fleets operating refrigerated trucks or trailers." Pays minimum $45 per page or $2 per inch.
Fillers: Buys newspaper clippings. "Do not rewrite."

SERVICE STATION AND GARAGE MANAGEMENT, 109 Vanderhoof Ave., Suite 101, Toronto, Ont. M4G 2J2, Canada. Editor: Frank Fragan. For "service station operators and garagemen in Canada only." Established in 1956. Monthly. Circulation: 24,000. Buys first Canadian serial rights. Buys 1 or 2 articles a year. Pays on acceptance. Will send a sample copy to a writer for 50¢. Query first. Reports in 2 days. Enclose S.A.E. and International Reply Coupons.
Nonfiction and Photos: "Articles on service station operators in Canada only; those who are doing top merchandising job. Also on specific phases of service station doings: brakes, tune-up, lubrication, etc. Solid business facts and figures; information must have human interest angles. Interested in controversial legislation, trade problems, sales and service promotions, technical data, personnel activities and changes. No general, long-winded material. The approach must be Canadian. The writer must know the trade and must provide facts and figures useful and helpful to readers. The style should be easy, simple, and friendly—not stilted." Length: 1,000 words. Pays 4¢ to 5¢ a word average, "depending on the topic and the author's status." Photos purchased with mss and without mss "if different or novel"; captions required. Pays $5 for 5x7 or 8x10 b&w glossies.

SOUTHERN AUTOMOTIVE JOURNAL, 1760 Peachtree Rd., N.W., Atlanta GA 30309. (404)874-4462. Editor: William F. Vann. For service stations, auto dealers, garages, body shops, fleets, warehouse distributors, and parts jobbers. Monthly. Buys all rights. Will send a sample copy to a writer for $1. Query first. Enclose S.A.S.E.
Nonfiction and Photos: "Articles of interest to the automotive aftermarket." Length: open. Payment varies. Photos purchased with ms.

SOUTHERN MOTOR CARGO, P. O. Box 4169, Memphis TN 38104. Editor: William H. Raiford. For "trucking management and maintenance personnel of private, contract, and for-hire carriers in 16 southern states (Ala., Ark., Del., Fla., Ga., Ky., La., Md., Miss., N.C., Okla., S.C., Tenn., Tex., Va., and W. Va.) and the District of Columbia." Special issues include "ATA Convention," October; "Transportation Graduate Directory," December; "Mid-America Truck Show," February. Monthly. Circulation: 40,000. Buys first rights within circulation area. Pays on publication. Will send a sample copy to a writer on request. "No query necessary." Reports "usually in 3 weeks." Enclose S.A.S.E.
Nonfiction: "How a southern trucker builds a better mousetrap. Factual newspaper style with punch in lead. Don't get flowery. No success stories. Pick one item, i.e. tire maintenance, billing

procedure, etc., and show how such-and-such carrier has developed or modified it to better fit his organization. Bring in problems solved by the way he adapted this or that and what way he plans to better his present layout. Find a segment of the business that has been altered or modified due to economics or new information, such as 'due to information gathered by a new IBM process, it has been discovered that an XYZ transmission needs overhauling every 60,000 miles instead of every 35,000 miles, thereby resulting in savings of $$$ over the normal life of this transmission.' Or, 'by incorporating a new method of record keeping, claims on damaged freight have been expedited with a resultant savings in time and money.' Compare the old method with the new, itemize savings, and get quotes from personnel involved. Articles must be built around an outstanding phase of the operation and must be documented and approved by the firm's management prior to publication." Length: 1,500 to 3,500 words. Pays minimum 4¢ a word for "feature material."
Photos: Purchased with cutlines; glossy prints. Pays $5.

SPECIALTY & CUSTOM DEALER, Babcox Publishing, 11 S. Forge St., Akron OH 44304. (216)535-6117. Editor: Walt Frazier. "Audience is primarily jobbers and retailers of specialty automotive parts and accessories. Average reader has been in business for 10 years, and is store owner or manager. Educational background varies, with most readers in the high school graduate with some college category." Monthly magazine; 56 pages. Estab: 1965. Circ: 18,000. Pays on publication. Buys all rights. Submit seasonal or holiday material 90 days in advance. SASE. Reports in 6 weeks. Sample copy $1.50.
Nonfiction: Publishes informational (business techniques), interview, new product, profile, and technical articles. Buys 24 mss a year. Query. Length: 1,000-2,000 words. Pays $50-100.
How To Break In: "For the most part, an understanding of automotive products and business practices is essential. Features on a specific retailer, his merchandising techniques and unique business methods are most often used. Such a feature might include inventory control, display methods, lines carried, handling obsolete products, etc."
Rejects: "Hyperbolic accounts of business. Those that read like public relations releases. Broad generalizations concerning a 'great product' without technical data behind the information. Lack of detail concerning business operations."

TIRE REVIEW, 11 S. Forge St., Akron OH 44304. (216)535-6117. Editor: William Whitney. For "independent tire dealers and retreaders, company stores, tire company executives, some oil company executives." Monthly. Circulation: 34,000. Buys first rights. Buys 6 or 7 mss a year. Pays on publication. Will send a free sample copy to a writer on request. Query first. Reports in 1 week. Enclose S.A.S.E.
Nonfiction and Photos: "Tire industry news, including new product news, research and marketing trends, legislative news, features on independent tire dealers and retreaders, news of trade shows and conventions, tire and related accessory merchandising tips. All articles should be straightforward, concise, information-packed, and not slanted toward any particular manufacturer or brand name. Must have something to do with tires or the tire industry, particularly independent dealers doing brake and front-end services." Length: "no limitations." Pays 3 ¢ a word. B&w glossies purchased with and without mss. Pays "$5 a photo with story, $8.50 for photos used alone."

TODAY'S TRANSPORT INTERNATIONAL/TRANSPORTE MODERNO, International Publications, Inc., 15 Franklin St., Westport CT 06880. (203)226-7463. Editor: Martin Greenburgh. Emphasizes "fleet operations and materials handling for vehicle fleet operators and materials handling executives in 150 developing countries in Africa, Asia, Middle East, and Latin America." Bimonthly magazine; 48-72 pages. Estab: 1953. Circ: 39,000. Pays on acceptance. Buys all rights, but may reassign following publication. Phone queries OK. Previously published submissions OK. SASE. Free sample copy and writer's guidelines.
Nonfiction: How-to (run a fleet, specify equipment, etc.); informational (fleet operations, new technologies); interview (with fleet executives discussing problem solving); photo feature (fleets and materials handling); and technical (vehicle/bus/truck systems, fork lifts, material handling) articles. Buys 24-30 a year. Query. Length: 1,500-3,000 words. Pays $150-200. No articles about U.S. or developed countries without direct relevance to the 3rd world.
Photos: Purchased with accompanying ms. Captions required. Query. Total purchase price for a ms includes payment for photos.
Columns/Departments: G. Ernsting, column/department editor. Materials Handling (tips and methods for materials handling personnel.) Buys 1 ms an issue. Query. Length: 750-1,500 words. Pays $75-100. Open to suggestions for new columns or departments.
How To Break In: "Articles must be written for readers in the 3rd world. Avoid U.S.-oriented approach. Our readers are administrators and executives — address them."

TOW-LINE, P.O. Box 2586, Framingham MA 01701. (617)879-0383. Editor: J. Kruza. For readers who run their own service business. Established in 1975. Quarterly. Circulation: 15,000. Rights bought vary with author and material. Usually buys all rights, but may reassign rights to author after publication. Buys about 12 mss a year. Pays on acceptance. Will send sample copy to writer for $1. Write for copy of guidelines for writers. Will consider photocopied and simultaneous submissions. Reports in 1 to 4 weeks. Query first or submit complete ms. Enclose S.A.S.E.

Nonfiction and Photos: Articles on business, legal and technical information for the towing industry. "Light reading material; short, with punch." Informational, how-to, personal experience, interview, profile. Length: 200 to 800 words. Pays $20 to $40. Spot news and successful business operations. Length: 100 to 500 words. Pays $20. Technical articles. Length: 100 to 1,000 words. Pays $20. Regular columns sometimes use material of 200 to 400 words. Pays $20. Up to 8x10 b&w photos purchased with or without mss, or on assignment. Pays $15 for first purchase; $5 for each additional purchase.

WARD'S AUTO WORLD, 28 W. Adams, Detroit MI 48226. (313)962-4433. Editor: David C. Smith. For automotive industry executives and engineers; top and middle management. Monthly magazine; 80 pages. Established in 1964. Circulation: 50,000. Buys all rights. Buys 5 to 10 mss a year. Payment on publication. Will send free sample copy to writer on request. Will not consider photocopied or simultaneous submissions. Will accept cassette submissions. Seasonal material is done only on assignment. Reports on material accepted for publication in 4 weeks. Returns rejected material quickly. Query first. Enclose S.A.S.E.

Nonfiction and Photos: News stories or topical features. "Our entire slant is news." Informational, interview, profile, historical, expose, personal opinion, spot news, successful business operations, new product, merchandising techniques, technical, book reviews. No consumer-type, narrowly-focused, or tenuously related stories. Length: open. Pays $100 to $500. Payment varies for 8x10 b&w photos or 4x5 color. Sometimes no additional payment is made for those purchased with mss. Captions required.

WAREHOUSE DISTRIBUTION, 7300 N. Cicero Ave., Lincolnwood, Chicago IL 60646. Editor: Syd Cowan. For "businessmen in the auto parts distribution field who are doing above one million dollars business per year." 10 times a year. Circulation: 27,000. Buys all rights. Pays on publication. Query first. Most material is staff written. Reports "within a reasonable amount of time." Enclose S.A.S.E.

Nonfiction and Photos: "Business management subjects, limited to the automotive parts distribution field." Length: 1,500 to 2,000 words. Pays 4¢ to 10¢ a word, "based on value to industry and the quality of the article." Photos purchased with and without mss; captions required. Wants "sharp 5x7 prints." Pays maximum $6.

WAREHOUSE DISTRIBUTOR NEWS, 11 S. Forge St., Akron OH 44304. Editor: John B. Stoner. For warehouse distributors and redistributing jobbers of automotive parts and accessories, tools and equipment and supplies (all upper management personnel). Magazine; 60 (7x10) pages. Established in 1967. Monthly. Circulation: 13,000. Rights purchased vary with author and material. May buy all rights or simultaneous rights. Buys about 12 mss a year. Pays on publication. Will send sample copy to writer for $1. Will consider photocopied and simultaneous submissions. Reports at once. Query first. Enclose S.A.S.E.

Nonfiction and Photos: Automotive aftermarket distribution management articles and those on general management, success stories, etc., of interest to the industry. Articles on manufacturers and their distributors. Must be aftermarket-oriented. Each issue centers around a theme, such as rebuilt parts issue, import issue, materials handling issue, etc. Schedule changes yearly based on developments in the industry. Does not want to see freelance material on materials handling, or product information. Would be interested in merchandising articles; those on EDP startup, and interviews with prominent industry figures. Recently published articles on the pension reform act. Length: open. Pays 5-9¢/word. B&w (5x7) photos purchased with or without ms. Pays $5 to $8.50. Captions required.

Aviation and Space

In this category are journals for aviation businessmen and airport operators and technical aviation and space journals. Publications for professional and private pilots are classified with the Aviation magazines in the Consumer Publications section.

AIRPORT SERVICES MANAGEMENT, Lakewood Publications, 731 Hennepin Ave. S., Minneapolis MN 55403. (612)333-0471. Managing Editor: Richard A. Coffey. Emphasizes business management of airports and airport services. Monthly magazine; 50 pages. Estab: 1961. Circ: 20,000. Pays on publication. Buys first North American serial rights. Phone queries OK. Submit seasonal or holiday material 3 months in advance. Photocopied submissions OK. Reports in 2 weeks. Sample copy $1; free writer's guidelines.
Nonfiction: How-to (manage airport operations). Buys 24 mss/year. Query. Length: 1,000-2,500 words. Pays $50/page minimum.
Photos: Purchased with accompanying ms. Send 8x10 b&w glossy or semi-matte prints. Total purchase price includes payment for photos. Model release required.

BUSINESS AND COMMERCIAL AVIATION, Hangar C-1, Westchester County Airport, White Plains NY 10604. Editor: Archie Trammell. For "corporate pilots and business aircraft operators." Monthly. Circulation: 52,000. Buys all rights. Buys "very little" freelance material. Pays on acceptance. Will send a sample copy to a writer for $1. Query first. Reports "as soon as an evaluation is made." Enclose S.A.S.E.
Nonfiction and Photos: "Our readers are pilots and we have found general articles to be inadequate. Writers with a technical knowledge of aviation would be most suitable." Wants "reports on business aviation operations, pilot reports, etc." Length: "no limits." Pays $100 to $300. B&w photos of aircraft purchased with mss. Pays $15 to $20. Pays $300 for cover color photos. Uses very little freelance photography.

GENERAL AVIATION BUSINESS, P.O. Box 1094, Snyder TX 79549. (915)573-6318. Editor: M. Gene Dow. For people in business phases of general aviation. Tabloid newspaper; 40 pages. Established in 1973. Monthly. Circulation: 16,000. Buys all rights. Pays on acceptance. Will send sample copy to writer for 50c. Write for copy of guidelines for writers. Will consider photocopied submissions. Reports on material in 1 month. Submit only complete ms. Enclose S.A.S.E.
Nonfiction and Photos: Informative, entertaining, technical, how-to, new products, etc., of general aviation (non-airline, non-military). Knowledgeable aviation articles. All types of articles on aviation subjects. Reviews of aviation books. Pays $25 per 1,000 words. Pays $15 for 30 column inches for regular columns or departments. Photos purchased with accompanying ms or on assignment. Captions required. Pays $5 for b&w and color.
Fiction: Experimental, suspense, adventure, humorous fiction on aviation subjects. Pays $25 per 1,000 words.
Poetry and Fillers: Aviation subjects. Pays $5 for poetry. Newsbreaks, clippings, jokes, short humor and informative items for fillers. Pays $3.

INTERLINE REPORTER, 2 W. 46th St., New York NY 10036. (212)575-9000. Editor: Eric Friedheim. An inspirational and interesting magazine for airline employees. Buys first serial rights. Query first. Enclose S.A.S.E.
Nonfiction and Photos: Wants nontechnical articles on airline activities; stories should be slanted to the sales, reservations and counter personnel. Articles on offbeat airlines and, most of all, on airline employees —those who lead an adventurous life, have a unique hobby, or have acted above and beyond the call of duty. Personality stories showing how a job has been well done are particularly welcome. Length: up to 1,200 words. Payment is $50 to $75 for articles with photographic illustrations.

INTERNATIONAL AVIATION MECHANICS JOURNAL, 211 S. Fourth St., Basin WY 82410. (307)568-2413. Editor: Dale Crane. For governmentally licensed airframe and power-plant mechanics involved in maintaining general aviation airplanes. Magazine; 72 pages. Established in 1970. Monthly. Circulation: 26,489. Buys all rights, but may reassign rights to author after publication. Buys 30-40 mss a year. Pays within 30 days of publication. Free sample copy. Will consider photocopied submissions. No simultaneous submissions. Reports in 30 days. Query first or submit complete ms. Enclose S.A.S.E.
Nonfiction and Photos: Technical articles on aircraft maintenance procedures and articles helping the mechanics to be more efficient and productive. All material should be written from the point of view of an aircraft mechanic, helping him solve common field problems. Informational. Length: 500 to 2,000 words. Pays $25 to $100. How-to. Length: 100 to 500 words. Pays $25. Photo articles. Length: 50 to 100 words. Pays $20. Technical. Length: 500 to 4,000 words. Pays $25 to $150.

JET CARGO NEWS, 5314 Bingle Rd., Houston TX 77092. (713)688-8811. Editor: Britt Martin. For "traffic and distribution managers, marketing executives, sales executives, and corporate management who use or may sometime use air transportation to ship their company's products." Established in 1968. Monthly. Circulation: 20,333. Buys all rights. Buys 6 to 10 mss a year. Pays on publication. Will send a sample copy to a writer on request. Write for copy of guidelines for writers. Will not consider photocopied submissions. Submit seasonal material 2 weeks in advance of issue date. Reports within a month, if postage is included. Submit complete ms. Enclose S.A.S.E.

Nonfiction and Photos: "Air marketing success stories, cargo rate changes, new ideas on packaging and/or sales. The writer's message should be to the shipper, not to or about airlines. We feel the shipper wants to know how an airline can help him, and that he's not particularly interested in the airline's economics. Use a tight, magazine style. The writer must know marketing. We want depth, how-to material. We don't like the 'gee whiz' approach to product marketing by air. We are not particularly interested in rare items moving by air frieght. Rather, we are interested in why a shipper switches from surface to air transportation." Buys informational articles, how-to's, interviews, and coverage of successful business operations. Length: maximum 2,500 words. Pays 5¢/word; 7¢/word for air marketing success stories. 7x10 b&w glossies purchased with and without mss; captions required. Pays $7.50.

Baking

BAKING INDUSTRIES JOURNAL, Maclaren Publishers, Ltd., Box 109, Davis House, 69-77 High St., Croydon, CR9 1QH, England. (01)688-7788. Editor: Chris Whitehorn. For the large scale bakery industry. Monthly magazine; 36 pages. Circ: 2,500. Copyrighted. SAE and International Reply Coupons. Sample copy $1.
Nonfiction: Features on baking and allied subjects. Length: 1,000-3,000 words. Submit complete ms. Pays $25/1,000 words.
Photos: B&w glossies used with mss. Captions required. Query.

PACIFIC BAKERS NEWS, Route 2, Belfair WA 98528. (206)275-6421. Publisher: Leo Livingston. Business newsletter for commercial bakeries in the western states. Monthly. Pays on publication. "We don't require S.A.S.E."
Fillers: Uses bakery business reports and news about bakers. Buys only brief "boiled-down news items about bakers and bakeries operating only in Alaska, Hawaii, Pacific Coast and Rocky Mountain states. Welcome clippings. Need monthly news reports and clippings about the baking industry and the donut business. "We don't use how-to and think pieces or feature articles." Length: 10 to 200 words. Pays 4¢ a word for clips and news used.
How To Break In: "Send brief news reports or clippings on spot business news about bakers and bakeries in the following western states: California, Arizona, Nevada, New Mexico, Colorado, Utah, Wyoming, Montana, Idaho, Oregon, Washington, Alaska, and Hawaii."

SPECIALTY BAKERS VOICE, 299 Broadway, New York NY 10007. Editor: Jack Posner. For "bakery management." Monthly.
Nonfiction: "Articles geared to the single unit and multi-unit retail bake shop on topics such as merchandising, management techniques, store layout, production, employee-employer relations, bakery sanitation, customer service.

Beverages and Bottling

The following journals are for manufacturers, distributors, retailers of soft drinks and alcoholic beverages. Publications for bar and tavern operators and managers of restaurants are classified in the Hotels, Motels, Clubs, Resorts, and Restaurants category.

BEVERAGE WORLD, 10 Cutter Mill Rd., Great Neck NY 11021. Editor: Richard V. Howard. (516)829-9210. Magazine: 60 pages. Established in 1882. Monthly. Buys all rights. Pays on publication. Buys about 6 mss per year. Will send free sample copy to writer on request. Will not consider photocopied or simultaneous submissions. Reports in 1 month. Enclose S.A.E.S.
Nonfiction and Photos: "Articles on any subject pertaining to manufacturers of carbonated and non-carbonated soft drinks, wine or beer. Emphasis should be on sales, distribution, merchandising, advertising, and promotion. Historical articles and 'how-to dissertations' are not desired; no shorts, fillers or rewritten newspaper clippings." Most mss rejected because the writers usually don't have a "thorough understanding of what they're writing about. Pieces

often shallow and too generalized." Should be written in crisp, clear style. Pays $35 per printed page (about 1,200 words). "Illustrations should be supplied where possible." Pays $5 for each photo used.

MARYLAND-WASHINGTON BEVERAGE JOURNAL, 2 W. 25th St., Baltimore MD 21218. (301)235-1716. Editor: Anna A. Pumphrey. For retailers in the alcohol beverage industry in Maryland-Washington-Delaware. Magazine; 210 pages. Established in 1938. Monthly. Circulation: 12,300. Not copyrighted. Buys about 5 mss a year. Pays on publication. Will send sample copy to writer for $1. No photocopied submissions. Will consider simultaneous submissions. Submit seasonal material (for December holiday sales) 3 months in advance. Reports promptly. Query first or submit complete ms. Enclose S.A.S.E.
Nonfiction and Photos: Articles of local interest regarding the beer, wine, liquor industry. Biographical stories on local retailers, stories on bars, package goods, restaurants, etc. Emphasis on innovative trends in the industry; articles to interest and educate Maryland-Washington-Delaware retailers. Merchandising trends; advertising; informational, how-to, interview, profile, successful business operations, merchandising techniques. Length: 1,000 to 2,000 words. Pays $15 to $25. No additional payment for b&w photos used with mss.

MICHIGAN BEVERAGE NEWS, 24681 Northwestern Highway, Suite 408, Southfield MI 48075. Editor: Steve McGregor. For "owners of bars, taverns, package liquor stores, hotels, and clubs in Michigan." Semimonthly. Buys exclusive rights to publication in Michigan. Pays on publication. Will send a sample copy to a writer on request. Query first. Reports "immediately." Enclose S.A.S.E.
Nonfiction and Photos: "Feature stories with pictures. Unusual attractions and business-building ideas in use by Michigan liquor licensees. Profit tips, success stories, etc., slanted to the trade, not to the general public. Especially interested in working with freelancers in Grand Rapids, Flint, Kalamazoo, Marquette, Saulte Ste. Marie, and Bay City areas." Length: 500 to 750 words. Pays $1/column inch. Buys photos of Michigan licensees engaged in business activities. Pays $1/column inch.

MID-CONTINENT BOTTLER, Box 2298, Shawnee Mission, Kansas City MO 66201. (913)384-0770. Publisher: Floyd E. Sageser. For "soft drink bottlers in the 18-state midwestern area." Bimonthly. Not copyrighted. Pays on acceptance. Will send a sample copy to a writer on request. Reports "immediately." Enclose S.A.S.E.
Nonfiction and Photos: "Items of specific soft drink bottler interest with special emphasis on sales and merchandising techniques. Feature style desired." Length: 2,000 words. Pays $15 to $50. Photos purchased with mss.

MODERN BREWERY AGE, 80 Lincoln Ave., Stamford CT 06902. Editor: Stanley N. Vlantes. For "brewery executives on the technical, administrative, and marketing levels." Bimonthly. Buys North American serial rights. Pays on publication. Query first. Reports "at once." Enclose S.A.S.E.
Nonfiction and Photos: "Technical and business articles of interest to brewers." Length: "no more than 6 or 7 double-spaced typewritten pages." Pays "$35 per printed page (about 3 to 3½ pages double-spaced typewritten ms)." Photos purchased with mss; captions required. Pays $7.50.

REDWOOD RANCHER, 756 Kansas St., San Francisco CA 94107. (415)824-1563. Editor: Sally Taylor. For winemakers, grape growers, and other north coast ranchers. Magazine; 48 pages. Special issues: Vintage (September). Viticulture (February). Established in 1945. Bimonthly. Circulation: 7,000. Buys 20 to 35 mss a year. Pays on publication. Free sample copy (to writers "in our area"). Photocopied and simultaneous submissions OK. Submit special issue material at least 2 months in advance. Reports on material accepted for publication in 2 to 4 weeks. Returns rejected material as soon as possible. Query first. Enclose S.A.S.E.
Nonfiction and Photos: Technical articles on the wine industry viticulturists, and country people. "Down-to-earth, humorous, with technical savvy." Articles on pest control, carbonic maceration, pruning, chemical control, new equipment. Informational, personal opinion, how-to, interview, profile, exposes run from 100 to 3,000 words. Pays $15 to $300. Pays $10 to $150 for historical articles of 100 to 2,000 words. Pays $10 to $50 for spot news, articles on successful business operations, new products, merchandising techniques; technical. Length: 25 to 200 words. 8x10 b&w glossies and color (separations preferred) purchased with mss or on assignment. Pays $7.50 for b&w; $25 for color.

SOUTHERN BEVERAGE JOURNAL, P. O. Box 561107, 13225 S. W. 88th Ave., Miami (Kendall) FL 33156. Managing Editor: Raymond G. Feldman. For "operators of package stores, bars, restaurants, hotel lounges, and dining rooms in Florida, Georgia, South Carolina, Texas, Tennessee, Arkansas, Louisiana, Mississippi." Established in 1944. Monthly. Circulation: about 23,000. Buys "exclusive rights for the 8 southern states." Buys about 12 mss a year. Pays on acceptance or on publication. Will send a sample copy to a writer on request. Write for copy of guidelines for writers. No photocopied or simultaneous submissions. Query first. SASE.

Nonfiction and Photos: "How operators of package stores, bars, restaurants, hotels, and dining rooms merchandise—what they do to attract customers, keep them coming back, and how they promote their operations and the products they sell. We are different from other beverage journals because of our regional circulation and because of our emphasis on merchandising and promotion." Length: open. Pays 4¢ to 6¢ a word, "but it really depends on the article itself; sometimes we don't count words, but we pay for value." Photos purchased with mss only. Prefers 8x10 b&w glossies, but will consider 5x7. Pays $5.

WINES & VINES, 703 Market St., San Francisco CA 94103. Editor: Philip Hiaring. For everyone concerned with the wine industry including winemakers, wine merchants, suppliers, consumers, etc. Monthly magazine. Established in 1919. Circulation: 5,500. Rights purchased vary with author and material. May buy first North American serial rights or simultaneous rights. Buys 4 or 5 mss a year. Payment on acceptance. Will send free sample copy to writer on request. Will not consider photocopied or simultaneous submissions. Submit special material (brandy, January; vineyard, February; champagne, June; marketing, September; aperitif/dessert wines, November) 3 months in advance. Reports in 2 weeks. Query first. Enclose S.A.S.E.

Nonfiction and Photos: Articles of interest to the trade. "These could be on grapegrowing in unusual areas; new winemaking techniques; wine marketing, retailing, etc." Interview, historical, spot news, merchandising techniques, technical. Does not want to see stories with a strong consumer orientation as against trade orientation. Author should know the subject matter, i.e., know proper winegrowing/winemaking terminology. Length: 1,000 to 2,500 words. Pays $25 to $50. Pays $5 to $10 for 4x5 or 8x10 b&w photos purchased with mss. Captions required.

Book and Book Store Trade

AB BOOKMAN'S WEEKLY, Box AB, Clifton NJ 07015. (201)772-0020. Editor-in-Chief: Jacob L. Chernofsky. For professional and specialist booksellers, acquisitions and academic librarians, book publishers, book collectors, bibliographers, historians, etc. Weekly magazine; 140 pages. Estab: 1948. Circ: 8,000. Pays on publication. Buys all rights. Phone queries OK. Submit seasonal or holiday material 1-2 months in advance. Simultaneous and photocopied submissions and previously published work OK. SASE. Reports in 4 weeks. Sample copy $2.

Nonfiction and Photos: Jacob L. Chernofsky, Articles Editor. How-to (for professional booksellers); historical (related to books or book trade or printing or publishing). Personal experiences, nostalgia, interviews, profiles. Query. Length: 4,000 words minimum. Pays $60 minimum. Photos used with mss.

BOOK COLLECTOR'S MARKET, P.O. Box 50, Cooper Station, New York NY 10003. Editor: Denis Carbonneau. For booksellers and book collectors. Magazine; 40 pages. Established in 1975. Bimonthly. Circulation: 4,800. Buys all rights. Pays on acceptance. Free sample copy and writer's guidelines. Will consider photocopied submissions. No simultaneous submissions. Reports almost immediately. Query first. Enclose S.A.S.E.

Nonfiction: "We publish articles about the rare, out-of-print and antiquarian book market from a business/finance point of view. Material must appeal to book collectors and rare book dealers. Emphasis is placed on determining market forces in the trade." Length varies. Pays $25 minimum.

How To Break In: "Write to us; tell us of your interest, and indicate any special areas you would like to work in."

CHRISTIAN BOOKSELLER, Gundersen Dr. and Schmale Rd., Wheaton IL 60187. "The business magazine of religious retailing." Monthly. Buys all rights. Pays on publication. Will send sample copy to writer on request. Query first. "Writers urged to study magazine before submitting." Reports in 2 weeks. Enclose S.A.S.E.

Nonfiction: "Success stories, illustrated with glossy photos, about established Christian booksellers. Stories should highlight specific techniques and managerial policy contributing to the success of the store. We use how-they-did-it articles on phases of bookstore administration and management with an anecdotal approach, and articles presenting proven techniques for seasonal or year-round items. These must be based on actual bookstore experience or sound sales techniques. Features focusing on trends in the Christian book and supply trade; short news articles, with photos if possible, reporting significant developments in the bookstore or publishing field; comprehensive reports on successful store layouts, traffic flow, with glossy illustrations or diagrams. Approach articles from a 'how-they-did-it' rather than 'how-to-do-it' point of view." Length: 1,500 to 2,000 words "with 2 or 3 photos." Pays $50-70/article.

COLLEGE STORE EXECUTIVE, 211 Broadway, Lynbrook NY 11563. Editor: Melanie Ann Kubat. For "managers, buyers, and business operators of campus stores." 10 times a year. Circulation: 9,500. Buys North American serial rights. Pays on publication. Will send a sample copy to a writer on request. Query first. Reports "immediately." Enclose S.A.S.E.
Nonfiction and Photos: "Descriptions of unusual displays, merchandising techniques, student trends, industry news, etc., used in a specific 'bookstore' on campus. (We refer to these stores as college stores.) Best source of information is the manager of the store." Length: 1,000 words. Pays 5¢ a word. Photos purchased with mss. Should be "of college stores, expansion, unusual displays, unusual lines being carried in the store, etc. Should be sharp and clear." Pay negotiable, generally $5.
Poetry and Fillers: "Can pertain to any phase of bookselling or retailing to college students." Length: open. Pays 5¢ a word.

PUBLISHERS WEEKLY, 1180 Ave. of the Americas, New York NY 10036. Editor-in-Chief: Arnold W. Ehrlich. Weekly. Buys first North American rights only. Pays on publication. Reports "in several weeks." Enclose S.A.S.E. for return of submissions.
Nonfiction and Photos: "We rarely use unsolicited mss because of the highly specialized audience and their professional interests, but we can sometimes use news items of bookstores or store promotions for books, or stories of book promotion and design." Payment negotiable; generally $50 to $75 per printed page. Photos purchased with and without mss "occasionally."

QUILL & QUIRE, 59 Front St., E., Toronto, Ont. M5E 1B3, Canada. Editor: Susan Walker. For professional librarians, writers, booksellers, publishers, educators, media people; anyone interested in Canadian books. Newspaper; 32 (11½x17) pages. Established in 1935. Monthly. Circulation: 12,000. Rights purchased vary with author and material. May buy all rights or second serial (reprint) rights. Buys 120 mss a year. Pays on acceptance. Will send free sample copy to writer on request. Reports in 1 week. Query first. Enclose S.A.E. and International Reply Coupons.
Nonfiction and Photos: Interviews, profiles, commentary. Strong emphasis on information. Subject must be of Canadian interest. Length: 1,000 to 2,000 words. Pays $75-150. B&w photos purchased with mss. Pays $15.

Brick, Glass, and Ceramics

AMERICAN GLASS REVIEW, 1115 Clifton Ave., Clifton NJ 07013. (201)779-1600. Editor: Donald Doctorow. For manufacturers, fabricators, and distributors of glass and glass products. Monthly. Pays on publication. Reports in 3 to 4 weeks. Enclose S.A.S.E.
Nonfiction and Photos: "Illustrated articles on uses of glass, application in new buildings, new container uses, products using fiber glass, glass factory operations, etc." Pays $35/printed page.

AUTO AND FLAT GLASS JOURNAL, 1929 Royce Ave., Beloit WI 53511. Editor: Lester E. Battist. For owners and employees of glass shops. Magazine; 36 (6x9) pages. Established in 1953. Monthly. Circulation: over 3,500. Rights purchased vary with author and material; usually buys all rights. Buys 12 mss a year. Pays on acceptance. Will send sample copy to writer for 50c (plus S.A.S.E. and 7x10 envelope). Will consider photocopied submissions only with guarantee of priority within the trade. Submit seasonal material 3 months in advance. Reports on material accepted for publication in 2 weeks. Returns rejected material in 10 days. Query first or submit complete ms. Enclose S.A.S.E.
Nonfiction and Photos: Self-help pieces and successful shop features. Emphasis is on what another shop owner/manager would gain from what a particularly successful owner/manager has to say. Would like to see something on a catchy, successful way of promoting a shop;

offbeat angles within the trade. Holiday-oriented features of substance. No locally oriented stories about kind-hearted persons who made good. Length: 1,000 to 2,000 words. Pays minimum of 3¢ per word. Buys 8x10 b&w photos, with or without ms. Pays $5.
Fillers: Jokes and short humor related to the trade. Length: 100 words minimum. Pays $5.

BRICK AND CLAY RECORD, 5 S. Wabash Ave., Chicago IL 60603. (312)372-6880. Managing Editor: Phil Jeffers. For "the heavy clay products industry." Monthly. Buys all rights. Pays on publication. Query first. Reports in 15 days. Enclose S.A.S.E.
Nonfiction and Photos: "News concerning personnel changes within companies; news concerning new plants for manufacture of brick, clay pipe, refractories, drain tile, face brick, glazed tile, lightweight clay aggregate products and abrasives; news of new products, expansion, new building." Pays minimum 8¢ "a published line. Photos paid for only when initially requested by editor."
Fillers: "Items should concern only news of brick, clay pipe, refractory, or clay lightweight aggregate plant operations. If news of personnel, should be only of top-level plant personnel. Not interested in items such as patio, motel, or home construction using brick; of weddings or engagements of clay products people, unless major executives; obituaries, unless of major personnel; items concerning floor or wall tile (only structural tile); of plastics, metal, concrete, bakelite, or similar products; items concerning people not directly involved in clay plant operation." Pays $3 "per published 2- or 3-line brief item." Pays minimum $3 for "full-length published news item, depending on value of item and editor's discretion. Payment is only for items published in the magazine. No items sent in can be returned."

CERAMIC INDUSTRY, 5 S. Wabash, Chicago IL 60603. Editor: J. J. Svec. For the ceramics industry; manufacturers of glass, porcelain, enamel, whitewares and electronic/industrial newer ceramics. Magazine; 50 to 60 pages. Established in 1923. Monthly. Circulation: 7,500. Buys all rights. Buys 10 to 12 mss a year (on assignment only). Pays on acceptance. Will send free sample copy to writer on request. Reports immediately. Query first. Enclose S.A.S.E.
Nonfiction and Photos: Semitechnical, informational and how-to material purchased on assignment only. Length: 500 to 1,500 words. Pays $35 per published page. No additional payment for photos used with mss. Captions required.

CERAMIC SCOPE, Box 48643, Los Angeles CA 90048. (213)939-4821. Mel Fiske. For "ceramic hobby teachers, dealers, and distributors." 11 times a year, including annual *Buyers Industry Guide.* Buys all rights. Pays on acceptance. Query first. Reports "immediately." Enclose S.A.S.E.
Nonfiction and Photos: "Articles on all phases of studio management (such as merchandising, promotion, pricing, credit and collection, recordkeeping, taxes, display, equipment and layout); case histories of actual studio operation; discussion of ceramic business practices and policies; news about traveling teachers, studios, shows, books, ceramic associations; reports on manufacturers' aids, products, services, displays, and literature. We reject poorly written stories that allegedly apply to all fields and actually apply to none." Length: open. Pays 5¢/word. Photos purchased with mss. "Show interior of ceramic studios, workshops, and classes." Pays $7.50.
How To Break In: "Submit samples of well-written stories and articles from other fields, plus detailed summary of proposed story."

GLASS DIGEST, 15 E. 40th St., New York NY 10016. (212)685-0785. Editor: Oscar S. Glasberg. Monthly. Buys all rights. Pays on publication "or before, if ms held too long." Will send a sample copy to a writer on request. Reports "as soon as possible." Enclose S.A.S.E. for return of submissions.
Nonfiction and Photos: "Items about firms in glass distribution, personnel, plants, etc. Stories about outstanding jobs accomplished—volume of flat glass, storefronts, curtain walls, auto glass, mirrors, windows (metal), glass doors; special uses and values; who installed it. Stories about successful glass jobbers, dealers, and glazing contractors—their methods, promotion work done, advertising, results." Length: 1,000 to 1,500 words. Pays 6¢/word, "occasionally more. No interest in bottles, glassware, containers, etc., but leaded and stained glass OK." B&w photos purchased with mss; "8x10 preferred." Pays $6, "occasionally more."
How To Break In: "Find a typical dealer case history about a firm operating in such a successful way that its methods can be duplicated by readers everywhere."

Building Interiors

DECOR, The Magazine of Fine Interior Accessories, 408 Olive, St. Louis MO 63102. (314)421-5445. Editor: Bill Humberg. For retailers, including individual gallery owners, managers of picture and interior accessory departments of department stores, mirror store owners, home furnishings stores and picture framers. Monthly magazine; 200 pages. Estab: 1875. Circ: 14,000. Buys "rights exclusive to our field". Buys 36 mss a year. Payment on acceptance. Will send free sample copy to writer on request. Write for copy of guidelines for writers. Will not consider photocopied submissions. Will consider simultaneous submissions. Submit special issue material (framing, April; clocks and lamps, June; original art, October; mirrors, November; holiday displays, stories, Christmas) three months in advance. Reports in 1 week. Query first. Enclose S.A.S.E.

Nonfiction and Photos: "How-to articles (how to advertise, how to use display space, how to choose product lines, how to use credit) giving, in essence, new and better ways to show a profit. Most often in the form of single store interviews with a successful store manager. No editorializing by the freelancer, unless he has proper credentials. Our emphasis is on useful material, not merely general interest. How does this businessman keep his customers, get new ones, please the old ones, etc." Length: open. Pays $65 to $125. No additional payment for 5x7 or 8x10 b&w photos used with mss.

KITCHEN BUSINESS, 1515 Broadway, New York NY 10036. Editor and Publisher: Patrick Galvin. For "kitchen cabinet and countertop plants, kitchen and bath planning specialists, and kitchen—bath departments of lumber, plumbing, and appliance businesses." Monthly. Buys all rights. Pays on acceptance. Will consider photocopied submissions. Often overstocked. Reports in 1 month. Enclose S.A.S.E.

Nonfiction and Photos: "Factual case histories with illustrative photos on effective selling or management methods; picture tours of outstanding kitchen showrooms of about 1,000 words; articles on management methods for kitchen distributorships which handle a full range of kitchen products; 'how-to' shop stories on kitchen cabinet shops or countertop fabricators, or stories on how they adapt to growth problems." Length: "600 words and 2 photos to 2,000 words and 10 photos." Pays $50 "first published page, minimum $30 each succeeding page, as estimated at the time of acceptance." Photos purchased with mss.

How To Break In: "Just go ahead and do it. Select the best looking kitchen firm in your area, go in and tell the boss you're a writer and want to do a story for *Kitchen Business*, ask him to let you sit down and read an issue or two, interview him on a single how-to-do-it topic, shoot some pictures to illustrate the points in the interview, and take a chance. Include his phone number so I can check with him. If it's good, you'll get paid promptly. If it shows promise, I'll work with you. If it's lousy, you'll get it back. If it's in between, you might not hear for a while because I hate to send them back if they have any value at all. This worked for me through a dozen years of highly successful freelancing. It will work for anyone who has any reporting talent at all."

PROFESSIONAL DECORATING & COATING ACTION, Painting and Decorating Contractors of America, 7223 Lee Hwy., Falls Church VA 22046. (703)534-1201. Editor-in-Chief: Heskett K. Darby. Emphasizes professional decorating, painting, wallcovering and sandblasting for painting contractors and their top assistants. Monthly magazine; 48-56 pages. Estab: 1938. Circ: 12,000. Pays on acceptance. Buys all rights, but may reassign following publication. Submit seasonal or holiday material 2 months in advance. SASE. Reports in 3 weeks. Free sample copy.

Nonfiction: Publishes how-to and informational articles. Buys 17-20 mss a year. Query. Length: preferably under 1,000 words. Pays 10¢/word maximum.

Photos: Purchased with accompanying ms. Captions required. Pays $7.50-9.50 for professional quality 8½x11 or 4x5 glossy b&w prints. Model release required.

WALLS AND CEILINGS, 14006 Ventura Blvd., Sherman Oaks CA 91423. (213)789-8733. Editor: Robert F. Welch. For "contractors involved in lathing and plastering, drywall, acoustics, fireproofing, curtain walls, movable partitions and their mechanics, together with manufacturers, dealers, and architects." Monthly. Circulation: 9,500. Not copyrighted. Buys 25 mss a year. Pays on publication. Free sample copy to a qualified writer. Query first. Reports in 30 days. Enclose S.A.S.E.

Nonfiction and Photos: "As technical as possible. Should be helpful to professional operator—diagrams, sketches, and detail pictures should illustrate material." Interested in interviews, spot news, successful business operations and new products. Length: maximum 1,000 words. Pay "depends upon value to our readers—maximum usually $50 to $75." B&w glossies purchased with and without mss; captions required. Pays $3 to $5.

How To Break In: "Interview a contractor about an unusual job or his principles of business management."

Business Management

The publications listed here are aimed at owners of businesses and top level business executives. They cover business trends and general theory and practice of management. Publications that use similar material but have a less technical or professional slant are listed in Business and Finance in the Consumer Publications section. Journals dealing with banking, investment, and financial management are classified in the Finance category in this section.

Publications dealing with lower level management (including supervisors and office managers) will be found in Management and Supervision. Journals for industrial plant managers are listed under Industrial Management, and under the names of specific industries such as Machinery and Metal Trade or Plastics. Publications for office supply store operators will be found with the Office Equipment and Supplies Journals.

ADMINISTRATIVE MANAGEMENT, Geyer-McAllister Publications, Inc., 51 Madison Ave., New York NY 10010. Editor: Walter A. Kleinschrod. For middle to upper level executives responsible for office administration, including record-keeping systems, data processing, word processing, reprographics, telecommunications, personnel and clerical functions. Monthly magazine; 100 pages. Estab: 1960. Circ: 53,000. Pays on publication. Buys all rights or first North American serial rights. Photocopied submissions OK. Reports in 1 month. Free editorial guidelines.
Nonfiction and Photos: "Material tailored to top, upper and middle managers responsible for office-based functions collectively known as 'administration'. Topics include business systems, personnel management, office environment, trends." Informational articles and think pieces on successful administrative developments and operations. Length: 500 to 2,500 words. Pays up to $1.75 per column inch in 13-pica measure and $2.50 per column inch in 20-pica measure. Photos purchased with accompanying ms with no additional payment.

BUSINESS DIGEST OF FLORIDA, P.O. Drawer 23729, Oakland Park FL 33307. Editor: Mary Lathrop. For executives and general managers of business and industry. Established in 1973. Circulation: 15,000. Not copyrighted. Buys 20 mss a year. Pays on publication. Will send free sample copy to writer on request. Will consider photocopied and simultaneous submissions. Reports on material accepted for publication in 3 months. Returns rejected material immediately. Query first or submit complete ms. Enclose S.A.S.E.
Nonfiction: Articles on profits, business management, business psychology, morale, motivation, better methods of operation. Emphasis is on writing about successes and failures from past experiences; analyzing present needs in business; future trends, general problems management and employees are faced with. "Must be adaptable to Florida thinking and ways of functioning, and at the same time generate new ideas and thinking." Length: 1,200 to 1,500 words. Pays $25 per published page. Also buys tongue-in-cheek business articles.
How To Break In: "The writer must have enough insight into the future and be able to produce an article that covers present day problems constructively."

EXECUTIVE REVIEW, 224 S. Michigan, Chicago IL 60604. (312)922-4083. Editor-in-Chief: Franklin E. Sobes. For management of small and middle-class companies, middle management in larger companies and enterprises. Monthly magazine; 32 pages. Estab: 1955. Circ: 25,000. Pays on publication. Buys second (reprint) rights. Submit seasonal or holiday material 4 months in advance. Simultaneous, photocopied, and previously published submissions OK. SASE. Reports in 2 weeks. Free sample copy.
Nonfiction: "As they apply to business", publishes historical, how-to, informational, inspirational, nostalgia, personal experience and travel articles; interviews. Buys about 7 mss an issue. Length: 1,000-1,500 words. Submit complete ms or copies of printed material. Pays $15-50.

HARVARD BUSINESS REVIEW, Soldiers Field, Boston MA 02163. (617)495-6800. Editor: Ralph F. Lewis. For top management in U.S. industry, and in Japan and Western Europe; younger managers who aspire to top management responsibilities; policymaking executives in government, policymakers in noncommercial organizations, and professional people interested in the viewpoint of business management. Published 6 times a year. Buys all rights. Payment on publication. Query first. Reports in 2 to 6 weeks. Enclose S.A.S.E.
Nonfiction: Articles on business trends, techniques and problems. *"Harvard Business Review*

seeks to inform executives about what is taking place in management, but it also wants to challenge them and stretch their thinking about the policies they make, how they make them, and how they administer them. It does this by presenting articles that provide in-depth analyses of issues and problems in management and, wherever possible, guidelines for thinking out and working toward resolutions of these issues and problems." Length: 3,000 to 6,000 words. Pays $100.

MARKETING COMMUNICATIONS, United Business Publications, Inc., 750 Third Ave., New York NY 10017. Editor-in-Chief: Ronnie Telzer. Emphasizes marketing and promotion. Monthly magazine; 90 pages. Estab: 1976. Circ: 25,000. Pays on publication. Buys all rights, but may reassign (with credit to *MC*) following publication. Submit seasonal or holiday material 2-3 months in advance. Photocopied submissions OK (if exclusive). Reports in 2 months. Sample copy $1.25. Free writer's guidelines.
Nonfiction: "The preferred format for feature articles is the case history approach to solving marketing problems. Critical evaluations of market planning, premium and incentive programs, point-of-purchase displays, direct mail campaigns, dealer/distributor meetings, media advertising, and sales promotion tools and techniques are particularly relevant." How-to articles (develop successful product campaigns); informational (marketing case histories); personal opinion (guest editorials by marketing executives); profiles (on a given industry, i.e., tobacco, razors, food); technical articles (technology updates on a field of interest to marketing people). Buys 1 ms/issue. Length: 750-1,250 words. Pays $75-250.
Photos: Prefers 8x10 b&w glossies with mss, or 2¼x2¼ color transparencies; other formats acceptable. Submit prints and transparencies. Captions required. No additional payment.
How To Break In: "Competitive or comprehensive industry profiles by people qualified to do the reporting (experienced in marketing communications) are desired. Simple, one-sided case histories are *not* needed since we can get an adequate supply free."

MAY TRENDS, 111 S. Washington St., Park Ridge IL 60068. (312)825-8806. Editor: J.J. Coffey, Jr. For chief executives of businesses, trade associations, government bureaus, Better Business Bureaus, educational institutions, newspapers. Publication of George S. May International Company. Magazine published 3 times a year; 28 to 30 pages. Established in 1967. Circulation: 10,000. Buys all rights. Buys 15 to 20 mss a year. Payment on acceptance. Will send free sample copy to writer on request. Reports on material accepted for publication in 1 week. Returns rejected material immediately. Query first or submit complete ms. Enclose S.A.S.E.
Nonfiction: "We prefer articles dealing with problems of specific industries (manufacturers, wholesalers, retailers, service businesses) where contact has been made with key executives whose comments regarding their problems may be quoted." Avoid material on overworked, labor-management relations. Interested in small supermarket success stories vs. the "giants"; automobile dealers coping with existing dull markets; contractors solving cost—inventory problems. Will consider material on successful business operations and merchandising techniques. Length: 1,500 to 3,000 words. Pays $100 to $250.
How To Break In: "Submit an article idea or the article in its entirety. A prompt reply will be forthcoming."

SMALL BUSINESS MAGAZINE, Small Business Service Bureau, Inc., 544 Main St., Box 1441, Worcester MA 01601. (617)756-3513. Managing Editor: Stewart Alsop II. Emphasizes small businesses with 1-100 employees. "Audience is primarily self-employed or small business people with fewer than 50 employees; generally their only interest is surviving and making money." Monthly magazine; 28 pages. Estab: 1976. Circ: 18,000. Pays on acceptance. Buys all rights, but may reassign following publication. SASE. Reports in 4 to 6 weeks. Free sample copy.
Nonfiction: How-to (business related, bookkeeping, retail display, direct mail, advertising, etc.); informational (about using government resources, new programs, loan sources, etc.); interview (legislators and regulators are prime interviewees); personal experience (short pieces on how you improved your business — i.e. "how I outwitted bad checks"); and profile (of highly unusual and/or successful businesses and how they got that way). Buys 15-20 mss/year. Query. Length: 1,200-1,500 words. Pays $75-200.
Photos: Photos purchased with accompanying ms. Captions required. Total purchase price for a ms includes payment for 8x10 b&w glossies.
Columns/Departments: Consultus (how-to, especially on technical and legal subjects). Buys 1 ms/issue. Query. Length: 1,000 words maximum. Pays $50 minimum. Open to suggestions for new columns/departments (except ones on taxes and retail management).
How To Break In: "We are looking for people to contribute regularly and grow with us. Please

try to be original and easy to read. You would have to be patient with our payment schedule and lack of space, but we do intend to grow fairly rapidly over the next few years."

TRAINING MANAGEMENT & MOTIVATION, 401 N. Broad St., Philadelphia PA 19108. Editor: John Denlinger. For training department administrators and managers in industrial and non-industrial organizations. Magazine; 55 (8½x11) pages. Established in 1974. 3 issues a year. Circulation: 30,000. Not copyrighted. Pays on publication. Free sample copy. Will consider photocopied and simultaneous submissions. Reports on material accepted for publication in 2 weeks. Returns rejected material in 6 weeks. Enclose S.A.S.E.
Nonfiction and Photos: Features informational articles on training programs and purchasing techniques, new training materials, and management techniques as applicable to training managers. "We rely more heavily on editorial features than other publications in this field." Informational, how-to, personal experience, interview, profile, spot news, successful business operations, and new product articles. Length: 250 to 3,000 words. Pays $50. Photos desired.

Church Administration and Ministry

THE CHAPLAIN, General Commission on Chaplains and Armed Forces Personnel, 5100 Wisconsin Ave., N.W., Suite 310, Washington DC 20016. (202)686-1957. Editor-in-Chief: Norman G. Folkers. For active duty military and full-time Veterans Administrations Chaplains. Quarterly magazine; 80 pages. Estab: 1944. Circ: 5,000. Pays on acceptance. Buys all rights, but may reassign following publication. Phone queries OK. Submit seasonal/holiday material 6 months in advance. Photocopied and previously published submissions OK. SASE. Reports in 4 weeks. Free sample copy and writer's guidelines.
Nonfiction: Publishes informational articles (trends in ministries and related fields); historical (relating to chaplains and chaplaincy; inspirational (only if pertinent to the specialized attention of chaplains); interviews with noted professionals in theology relating to chaplaincy); personal opinion (of an academic nature, in defense of a theory or new idea); profile (of noted chaplains or church figure of outstanding repute); articles on general theology relating to the specialized chaplain ministry. Length: 1,000 words minimum. Query first. Pays $20 minimum.
Photos: B&w (8x10) glossies purchased with mss. Pays $3 minimum. Query.
How To Break In: "Prospective contributors should have a solid background in military life and the unique ministry performed by chaplains. Good scholarship and careful, precise writing are essential."

THE CHRISTIAN MINISTRY, 407 S. Dearborn St., Chicago IL 60605. (312)427-5380. Editorial Director: James M. Wall. For the professional clergy (primarily liberal Protestant). Bimonthly magazine; 40 pages. Estab. 1925. Circ: 12,000. Buys all rights. Buys about 50 mss a year. Pays on publication. Free sample copy. Reports in 2 weeks. Query. SASE.
Nonfiction: "We want articles by clergy-theologians who know the clergy audience. We are interested in articles on local church problems and in helpful how-to as well as "think" pieces. Length: 1,200-1,800 words. Pay varies, $10/page minimum.

CHURCH ADMINISTRATION, 127 Ninth Ave., N., Nashville TN 37234. (615)254-5461, Ext. 363. Editor: George Clark. For Southern Baptist pastors, staff, and volunteer church leaders. Monthly. Buys all rights. Will also consider second rights. Uses limited amount of freelance material. Pays on acceptance. Will send a free sample copy to a writer on request. Write for copy of guidelines for writers. Reports in ! month. Enclose S.A.S.E.
Nonfiction and Photos: "How-to-do-it articles dealing with church administration, including church programming, organizing, and staffing, administrative skills, church financing, church food services, church facilities, communication, pastoral ministries, and community needs." Length: 750 to 1,200 words. Pays 2½¢ a word. Pays $7.50 to $10 for 8x10 b&w glossies purchased with mss.
How To Break In: "A beginning writer should first be acquainted with organization and policy of Baptist churches and with the administrative needs of Southern Baptist churches. He should perhaps interview one or several SBC pastors or staff members, find out how they are handling a certain administrative problem such as 'enlisting volunteer workers' or 'sharing the administrative load with church staff or volunteer workers.' I suggest writers compile an article showing how *several* different administrators (or churches) handled the problem, perhaps giving meaningful quotes. Submit the completed manuscript, typed 54 characters to the line, for consideration."

CHURCH MANAGEMENT-THE CLERGY JOURNAL, 4119 Terrace Lane, Hopkins MN 55340. (612)933-6712. Editor: Manfred Holck, Jr. For ministers, rabbis and priests. Magazine. Published 10 times a year. Estab. 1924. Circ. 10,000. Rights purchased vary with author and material. Usually buys all rights, but will reassign rights to author after publication. Will consider photocopied submissions. Will not consider simultaneous submissions. Submit seasonal material 4 months in advance. Reports on material accepted for publication in 4 weeks. Returns rejected material in 2-6 weeks. Query first. Enclose S.A.S.E.
Nonfiction and Photos: Professional how-to articles slanted to ministers. Avoid theological emphasis. Interested in coverage of seasonal church services (Christmas, Lent, Easter, vacation schools). Also informational, profile, inspirational, humorous and historical articles; personal opinion, reviews of religious books. Length: 1,200 words maximum. Pays $2.50 to $25. Pays $1 to $5 for 7x10 b&w glossies purchased with mss. Captions required.

CHURCH TRAINING, 127 Ninth Ave., N., Nashville TN 37234. (254)546-1393. Publisher: The Sunday School Board of the Southern Baptist Convention. Editor: Richard B. Sims. For all workers and leaders in the Church Training program of the Southern Baptist Convention. Established in 1926. Monthly. Circulation: 40,000. Buys all rights. Buys about 25 freelance mss a year. Pays on acceptance. Will send sample copy to writer on request. Write for copy of guidelines for writers. No photocopied or simultaneous submissions. Reports on material accepted for publication in 2 weeks. Returns rejected material immediately. Query first, with rough outline. Enclose S.A.S.E.
Nonfiction: "Articles that pertain to leadership training in the church. Success stories that pertain to Church Training. Associational articles. Informational, how-to's that pertain to Church Training." Length: 500 to 1,500 words. Pays 2½¢ a word.

THE EDGE on Christian Education, Nazarene Publishing House, 6401 The Paseo, Kansas CIty MO 64131. Editor: Melton Wienecke. Emphasizes Christian/religious education for Sunday School teachers, pastors Sunday School superintendents, supervisors and workers. Quarterly magazine; 48 pages. Estab: 1973. Circ: 40,000. Pays on acceptance. Buys all rights, second serial (reprint) rights, or one-time rights. Submit seasonal/holiday material 10 months in advance. Simultaneous, photocopied, and previously published submissions OK. SASE. Reports 10-12 weeks. Free sample copy and writer's guidelines.
Nonfiction: Publishes how-to, humor, informational, inspirational new product, personal experience, and technical articles; interviews, profiles of trends, photo features, and articles on philosophy of Christian education. Length: 1,000 words maximum. Buys 150 mss a year. Query first with tearsheets of published work. Pays 2¢/word.
Photos: B&w and color purchased with or without mss, or on assignment. Send prints and transparencies. Pays $6 minimum.
Fiction: Considered if it is short and deals with a problem in the field. Length: 1,000 words maximum. Pays 2¢/word.
Poetry: Publishes light verse or poetry in traditional forms. Buys 10 a year. Submit complete ms. Pays $10 minimum.

EMMANUEL, 194 E. 76th St., New York NY 10021. (212)861-1076. Editor: Rev. Paul J. Bernier, S.S.S. Monthly. For the Catholic clergy. Established in 1895. Circulation: 17,000. Rights to be arranged with author. Buys 5 or 6 mss a year. Pays on publication. Will consider photocopied submissions. No simultaneous submissions. Submit seasonal material 3 to 4 months in advance. Reports in 5 weeks. Enclose S.A.S.E.
Nonfiction: Articles of Catholic (especially priestly) spirituality; can be biographical, historical or critical. Articles on Eucharistic theology, and those which provide a solid scriptural and/or theological foundation for priestly spirituality (prayer, applied spirituality, etc.). Aims at providing today's priest with an adequate theology and philosophy of ministry in today's church. Length: 1,500 to 3,000 words. Usually pays $50.

ENDURING WORD ADULT TEACHER, 6401 The Paseo, Kansas City MO 64131. (816)333-7000. Editor: John B. Nielson. For teachers of adults. Quarterly. Buys first and second rights; will accept simultaneous submissions. Pays on acceptance. Will consider photocopied submissions. Reports in 6 weeks. Enclose S.A.S.E.
Nonfiction: Department Editor: John B. Nielson. "Articles of interest to teachers of adults and articles relevant to the Enduring Word Series Sunday school lesson outline." Length: 1,300 words maximum. Pays minimum $20 per 1,000 words.
Photos: Purchased with captions only. Pays minimum $5; 4 color up to $100.
Poetry: Inspirational, seasonal, or lesson-related poetry. Length: 24 lines maximum. Pays minimum 25¢ per line.

KEY TO CHRISTIAN EDUCATION, Standard Publishing, 8121 Hamilton Ave., Cincinnati OH 45231. (513)931-4050. Editor-in-Chief: Marjorie Miller. For "church leaders of all ages; Sunday school teachers and superintendents; ministers; Christian education professors; youth workers." Quarterly magazine; 48 pages. Estab: 1962. Circ: 65,000. Pays on acceptance. Buys first North American serial rights. Phone queries OK. Submit seasonal/holiday material 15 months in advance. Photocopied and previously published submissions OK. SASE. Reports in 4 weeks. Free sample copy and writer's guidelines.

Nonfiction: How-to (programs and projects for Christian education), informational; interview; personal opinion; and personal experience. Buys 10 mss an issue. Query or submit complete ms. Length: 700-2,000 words. Pays $20-50.

Photos: Purchased with or without accompanying ms. Submit prints. Pays $5-25 for any size glossy finish b&w prints. Total price for ms includes payment for photos. Model release required.

Fillers: Purchases short ideas on "this is how we did it" articles. Buys 10 mss an issue. Submit complete ms. Length: 50-250 words. Pays $5-10.

For '78: "Themes: Summer: Recreation for Christians; Fall: Recruitment and training of church workers; Winter: Relationships. We work over a year in advance."

PASTORAL LIFE, Society of St. Paul, Route 224, Canfield OH 44406. Editor: Victor L. Viberti, S.S.P. For priests and those interested in pastoral ministry. Magazine; 64 pages. Monthly. Circulation: 8,600. Buys first rights. Payment on acceptance. Will send sample copy to writer on request. "Queries appreciated before submitting mss. New contributors are expected to accompany their material with a few lines of personal data." Reports in 7 to 10 days. Enclose S.A.S.E.

Nonfiction: Professional review, principally designed to focus attention on current problems, needs, issues and all important activities related to all phases of pastoral work and life. Avoids merely academic treatments on abstract and too controversial subjects." Length: 2,000 to 3,400 words. Pays 3¢ a word minimum.

SUCCESS, P.O. Box 15337, Denver CO 80215. (303)988-5300. Editor: Mrs. Edith Quinlan. For persons engaged in or interested in Christian education. Established in 1951. Quarterly. Circulation: 15,000. Rights purchased vary with author and material. Usually buys all rights, but may reassign rights to author after publication. Pays on acceptance. Will send free sample copy and editorial guidelines sheet to writer on request. Will occasionally consider simultaneous submissions, "depending on where the other submissions are." Submit seasonal material 9 months in advance. Reports in 2 to 3 weeks. Enclose S.A.S.E.

Nonfiction: "Should write on Christian education subjects, within the framework of Baptist doctrines and distinctives." Mss should provide ideas and information for Sunday School superintendents, teachers and youth workers, with a view to helping them achieve excellence in their work. "Articles may be of general nature slanted to all Christian education workers, or may be slanted to specific age groups such as preschool, elementary, youth and adult. We are more interested in receiving articles from people who know Christian education, or workers who have accomplished something worthwhile in Sunday School and/or 'Training Time,' than from experienced writers who do not have such experience. A combination of both, however, is ideal." Length: 500 to 2,000 words. Pays 2¢ to 3¢ per word. "When submitting ms enclose short biographical sketch, especially if engaged in Christian education work."

Photos: Purchased with accompanying ms with extra payment. Captions optional. Pays $1 to $10. "Sharp jumbo snapshots or Polaroid are acceptable." Prefers b&w. "Photos accompanying articles are helpful."

SUNDAY SCHOOL COUNSELOR, General Council of the Assemblies of God, 1445 Boonville Ave., Springfield MO 65802. (417)862-2781, ext. 433. Editor-in-Chief: Sylvia Lee. "Our audience consists of local church school teachers and administrators. These are people who, by and large, have not been professionally trained for their positions but are rather volunteer workers. Most would have not more than a high school education." Monthly magazine; 32 pages. Estab: 1939. Circ: 45,000. Pays on acceptance. Buys all rights, but may reassign following publication; or simultaneous rights. Submit seasonal/holiday material 9 months in advance. Simultaneous and previously published submissions OK. SASE. Reports in 4-6 weeks. Free sample copy and writer's guidelines.

Nonfiction: How-to (Sunday school teaching, crafts, discipline in the Sunday school, building student-teacher relationships); inspirational (on the teaching ministry); and personal experience (as related to teaching ministry or how a Sunday school teacher handled a particular situation). Buys 70 mss/year. Submit complete ms. Length: 400-1,000 words. Pays 1-3¢/word.

Photos: Purchased with accompanying ms or on assignment. Send prints or transparencies.

Pays $5-8 for 5x7 b&w photos; $10-70 for 2¼x2¼ color transparencies. Model release required. **How To Break In:** "A freelancer can break into our publication by submitting a first person account of a Sunday school experience. This must be actual, and contain a new slant or insight on an old topic. We are a good freelance market providing the person has taken time to study our publication first and to see our needs and slant."

YOUR CHURCH, 198 Allendale Rd., King of Prussia PA 19406. (215)265-9400. Editor: Richard L. Critz. For the ministers of America's churches. "We reach 2 out of 3 of them; all faiths; Protestant, Catholic, Jew." Magazine published every 2 months; 48 (8¼x11) pages. Established in 1955. Circulation: 192,000. Buys all rights, but may reassign after publication. Buys 20 to 30 mss a year. Pays on publication. Free sample copy. Photocopied submissions OK. No simultaneous submissions. Reports "as soon as we can." Query or submit complete ms. Enclose S.A.S.E.
Nonfiction and Photos: "News material for pastors; informative and cogently related to some aspect of being a pastor (counseling, personal finance, administration, building, etc.). No special approach required, but we seldom use liturgical material. We stress the personal, the informal, and avoid the pretentious. Would like to see good material on music, the arts and crafts in the church." Informational, how-to, inspirational, think pieces. Length: 2 to 15 typewritten pages. Pays $25 to $75. No additional payment made for b&w photos.
How To Break In: "The best way is to treat a relevant subject with humor and the personal touch."

THE YOUTH LEADER, 1445 Boonville Ave., Springfield MO 65802. Editor: Glen Ellard. For "ministers of youth (Christian)." Evangelical Christianity and Christian activism. Special issues at Christmas and Easter. Established in 1944. Monthly. Circulation: 5,000. Buys all rights, but will reassign rights to author after publication. Buys first North American serial rights, second serial (reprint) rights and simultaneous rights. Buys 20 to 30 mss a year. Payment on acceptance. Will send free sample copy to a writer on request. Will consider photocopied submissions. Submit seasonal material 4 months in advance. Submit only complete ms. Reports in 6 weeks. Enclose S.A.S.E.
Nonfiction: "How-to" articles (e.g., "How to Evangelize Youth Through Music," "How to Study the Bible for Personal Application," "How to Use the Media for the Christian Message"); skits and role-plays; Bible raps, original choruses, Bible verses set to music, ideas for youth services, socials, and fund raising; interviews with successful youth leaders. Avoid cliches (especially religious ones); educational philosophy; youth (or student) centered instead of adult (or teacher) centered; relational approach instead of preaching. Length: 500 to 2,500 words. Pays 2½¢ to 3½¢ a word.

Clothing and Knit Goods

APPAREL INDUSTRY MAGAZINE, 112 W. 9th St., Los Angeles CA 90015. (215)626-0486. Managing Editor: Julie Barker. For executive management in apparel companies with interests in equipment, government intervention in the garment industry; finance, management and training in industry. Magazine; 70 to 100 pages. Established in 1946. Monthly. Circulation: 16,000. Not copyrighted. Buys 40 to 50 mss a year. Pays on publication. Will send sample copy to a writer for $1. Will consider legible photocopied submissions. No simultaneous submissions. Reports in 3 to 4 weeks. Query first. Enclose S.A.S.E.
Nonfiction and Photos: Articles dealing with equipment, training, finance; state, federal government, consumer interests, etc., related to the industry. "Use concise, precise language that is easy to read and understand. In other words, because the subjects are technical, keep the language comprehensible. No general articles on finance and management. Material must be precisely related to the apparel industry." Informational, interview, profile, successful business operations, technical articles. Length: 500 to 1,000 words. Pays 2½¢ to 3¢ a word. No additional payment for b&w photos.

BODY FASHIONS/INTIMATE APPAREL, Harcourt Brace Jovanovich Publications, 757 Third Ave., New York NY 10017. Editor-in-Chief: Ms. Deane L. Moskowitz. Emphasizes information about men's and women's hosiery and underwear; women's undergarments, lingerie, sleepwear, robes, hosiery, leisurewear. For merchandise managers and buyers of store products, manufacturers and suppliers to the trade. Monthly tabloid insert, plus 7 regional market issues called Market Maker; 24 pages minimum. Estab: 1913. Circ: 13,500. Pays on publication. Buys all rights. Phone queries OK. Submit seasonal/holiday material 2 months in advance. Previously published submissions OK. SASE. Reports in 4 weeks. Free sample copy.

Columns/Departments: New Image (discussions of renovations of Body Fashions/Intimate Apparel department); Creative Retailing (deals with successful retail promotions); Ad Ideas (descriptions of successful advertising campaigns). Buys 1 feature/issue. Query first. Length: 500-2,500 words. Pays 15¢/word. Open to suggestions for new columns and departments.

Photos: B&w (5x7) photos purchased without mss. Captions required. Send contact sheet, prints or negatives. Pays $5-25. Model release required.

KNITTING TIMES, National Knitted Outerwear Association, 51 Madison Ave., New York NY 10010. (212)683-7520. Editor-in-Chief: Charles Reichman. For the knitting industry, from the knitter to the cutter and sewer to the machinery manufacturer, to the fiber and yarn producer, chemical manufacturer, and various other suppliers to the industry. Weekly magazine; 58 pages. Estab: 1933. Circ: 6,100. Pays on publication. Buys all rights. Submit seasonal or holiday material 1 month in advance. SASE. Reports in 4 weeks. Free sample copy and writer's guidelines.

Nonfiction: Historical (various parts of the knitting industry; development of machines, here and abroad); how-to (cut and sew various outer garments; knit, dye and finish; needle set-outs for various knit constructions); informational (market or show reports, trends, new fabrics, machine, fiber, yarn, chemical developments); interviews (with leading figures in the industry; may be knitter, head of fiber company etc. Must say something significant such as new market development, import situation, projections and the like). New product (on anything in the industry such as machines, fibers, yarns, dyeing and finishing equipment, etc.). Photo features (on plants or plant layouts, how to cut and sew sweaters, skirts, etc.). Profiles (can be on industry leaders, or on operation of a company; specifically plant stories and photos). Technical (on machines, chemical processes, finishing, dyeing, spinning, texturing, etc.) Length: 750 words minimum. Query first. Pays 70¢ an inch.

Photos: B&w glossies (8x10) purchased with mss. Query first. Pays $3 for glossies; $5/diagram.

MEN'S WEAR, Fairchild Publications, 7 E. 12th St., New York, NY 10003. Editor-in-Chief: Becki Levine. Emphasizes men's and boy's apparel retailers. Semimonthly magazine; 46 pages. Estab: 1896. Circ: 26,700. Pays on acceptance. Buys all rights. SASE. Reports in 3 weeks. Free sample copy.

Nonfiction: Expose (pertaining to men's wear industry companies or issues), how-to (on making men's wear retailing more profitable, sales promotions, advertising, displays). Buys 2-3 mss a year. Query. Length: Flexible, from 1,000 words. Pays $100-200.

TACK 'N TOGS MERCHANDISING, P.O. Box 67, Minneapolis MN 55440. Address mss to The Editor. For "retailers of products for horse and rider and Western and English fashion apparel." Estab. 1970. Monthly. Circ: 16,000. Rights purchased vary with author and material; may buy all rights. Buys 10-15 mss/year. Pays on acceptance. Will send a sample copy to a writer on request. Write for copy of guidelines for writers. Query first. Enclose S.A.S.E.

Nonfiction and Photos: "Case histories, trends of industry." Buys informational articles, how-to's, interviews, profiles, coverage of successful business operations, new product pieces, and articles on merchandising techniques. Length: open. Pays "up to $100." B&w glossies and color transparencies purchased with mss.

TEENS & BOYS, The Boys's Outfitter, 71 W. 35th St., New York NY 10001. (212)594-0880. Editor-in-Chief: Ellye Bloom. Emphasizes boys' and young men's apparel merchandising/retailing. Monthly magazine; 70 pages. Estab: 1919. Circ: 8,200. Pays on publication. Submit seasonal or holiday material 3 months in advance. Photocopied submissions OK. SASE. Free sample copy and writer's guidelines.

Nonfiction: *"Teens & Boys* is edited for merchants of apparel for boys and male teenage students, aged 4-18. It forecasts style trends, reports on retail merchandising, stock control, promotion, display, new products and industry news. All factual, carefully researched, pertinent articles presented in a lively style will be considered." Query or submit complete ms. Length: 1,000-2,000 words. Pays $50-150. No straight fashion stories.

Photos: Purchased with accompanying ms. Captions required. Pays $7.50-10 for 4x5 or larger b&w glossies. Query.

How To Break In: "Send query and/or samples of work. We prefer articles accompanied by clear, clean glossy photos or proof sheets and negatives. Freelancers should have some experience in our market or with business writing. Look for stores with exceptional decor or with an unusual approach to retailing for the male youth market. We need additional coorespondents and require coverage in all regions of the country."

WESTERN OUTFITTER, 5314 Bingle Rd., Houston TX 77092. (713)688-8811. Publication Manager: Tad Mizwa. For "owners and managers of retail stores in all 50 states and Canada. These stores sell clothing for riders and equipment for horses, both Western and English style. Mostly Western." Monthly. Buys all rights. Pays on publication. Query first. Enclose S.A.S.E.

Nonfiction: Method stories; "in-depth treatment of subjects each merchant wrestles with daily. We want stories that first describe the problem, then give details on methods used in eliminating the problem. Be factual and specific." Subjects include merchandising, promotion, customer contact, accounting and finance, store operation, merchandise handling, and personnel. "To merit feature coverage, this merchant has to be a winner. It is the uniqueness of the winner's operation that will benefit other store owners who read this magazine." Length: 1,000 to 1,500 words for full-length feature; 500 to 600 words for featurette. Pays 3¢ per published word for shortcut featurettes; 5¢ per published word for full-length feature, and featurettes. "Send us copies of stories you have done for other trade magazines. Send us queries based on visits to Western dealers in your territory."

Photos: "Excellent photos make excellent copy much better. Plan photos that bring to life the key points in your text. Avoid shots of store fixtures without people. Submit photos in glossy finish, in 8x10 size or smaller. Sharp focus is a must." Captions required. "Cover photos: We will pay $40 for a 2¼x2¼ color transparency if used for a cover. Your 35mm shots are fine for interior b&w art." Pays $6 per photo used with ms. Also uses "single photos, or pairs of photos that show display ideas, tricks, promotional devices that are different and that bring more business." Pays $10.

Coin-Operated Machines

AMERICAN COIN-OP, 500 N. Dearborn St., Chicago IL 60610. (312)337-7700. Editor: Earl Fischer. For businessmen and businesswomen who own coin-operated laundry and drycleaning stores; operators, distributors and industry leaders. Monthly magazine; 51 (8¼x11¼) pages. Established in 1960. Circulation: 24,000. Rights purchased vary with author and material but are exclusive to the field. Buys 50 mss per year. Pays on publication. Free sample copy. Reports decision on material as soon as possible; usually in 2 weeks. SASE.

Nonfiction and Photos: "We emphasize store operation and management and use features on industry topics: utility use and conservation, maintenance, store management, customer service, and advertising. A case study should emphasize how the store operator accomplished whatever he did — in a way that the reader can apply in his own operation. Mss should have no-nonsense, businesslike approach and be brief. Uses informational, how-to, interview, profile, think pieces, spot news, successful business operations articles. Length: 500 to 3,000 words. Pays minimum of 3¢ per word. Pays minimum $5 for 8x10 b&w glossy photos purchased with mss. Must be clear and have good contrast.

Fillers: Newsbreaks, clippings. Length: open. Pays 3¢ per word; $3 minimum.

How To Break In: "Query first about subjects of current interest. Be observant of coin-operated laundries — how they are designed and equipped; how they serve customers; how (if) they advertise and promote their services. Report anything unusual. Even one-sentence query reports themselves are sometimes bought and published. Most general articles turned down because they are not aimed well enough at audience. Most case histories turned down because of lack of practical purpose (nothing new or worth reporting)."

COIN LAUNDERER & CLEANER, 525 Somerset Dr., Indianapolis IN 46260. For owners, operators, and managers of coin-operated and self-service laundry and drycleaning establishments. Monthly. Buys all rights. Enclose S.A.S.E.

Nonfiction: "Our requirements are for self-service coin laundry and drycleaning store management articles which specify the promotion, service, or technique used by the store owners; the cost of this technique; and the profit produced by it. Freelance writers must be familiar with coin laundry and drycleaning industry to prepare an article of sufficient management significance." Pays 5¢ per printed word.

COINAMATIC AGE, 60 E. 42nd St., New York NY 10017. (212)682-6330. Editor: C. F. Lee. For operators/owners of coin-operated laundries; dry cleaners. Bimonthly. Buys all rights. Pays on publication. "Queries get same-day attention." Enclose S.A.S.E.

Nonfiction and Photos: "We are currently considering articles on coin-operated laundries, and/or in combination with drycleaners. Slant should focus on the unusual, but at the same time should stress possible adaptation by other coinamat operators. Particular interest at this time centers on energy conservation methods. We are interested in promotional and advertising techniques; reasons for expansion or additional locations; attached sidelines such as carwashes and other businesses; Main Street vs. shopping center operations; successes in dealing with permanent press garment laundering and cleaning; ironing services; and, primarily, financial success, personal satisfaction, or any other motivation that the owner derives from his business. Give the story punch, details, and applicability to the reader. Include a list of specifications, detailing the number of units (washers, dryers, etc.), the different pound-loads of each machine and the make and model numbers of all of these, as well as any vending machines, change-makers, etc. Three action photos (preferably a minimum of 6) must accompany each article. At this time, we are especially interested in combined laundry/drycleaning articles. Submitted photos must include an exterior shot of the installation and interior shots showing customers. Where possible, a photo of the owner at work is also desired. If you have a far-out slant, query first." Pays 3¢ to 4¢ a word, depending on need to rewrite. Length: 1,200 to 2,000 words. No "plugola" for manufacturers' products, please. Photos purchased with mss. Pays $12 for 3 photos and $6 for each additional photo.

PLAY METER, P.O. Box 24170, New Orleans LA 70184. Editor and Publisher: Ralph C. Lally. For the coin-op amusement industry. Established in 1974. Monthly. Circulation: 5,000. Copyrighted. Buys about 12 mss a year. Pays on publication. Will send free sample copy to writer on request. Write for copy of guidelines for writers. No photocopied or simultaneous submissions. Reports in 1 month. Query first or submit complete ms. Enclose S.A.S.E.
Nonfiction and Photos: "We publish news and features about the coin-op amusement industry: how to's, what's happening, new concepts. Possible new subjects worthy of spot news coverage: 'New state tax hurts operators'; 'Ops gather for seminar'; 'Distributor hosts tournament'. Features can be about the industry's manufacturers, distributors or operators but all our material is aimed at the operator. We don't want to see articles glibly portraying this industry as a mob-run or controlled industry. We don't mind news or features on persons of criminal background or intent who enter the business. We recognize they exist, but want to know the facts. We might consider something on players' preferences of types of games. the vicissitudes of the video game market: new avenues of profit for the operator." Length: 3,500 word maximum. Pays $25 to $150, depending on length. "For photos used in conjunction with articles, we pay $10 per printed photo (5x7 or 8x10 glossies, preferred, or negatives with contact sheet)."

VENDING TIMES, 211 E. 43rd St., New York NY 10017. Editor: Arthur E. Yohalem. For operators of vending machines. Monthly. Circulation: 13,500. Buys all rights. Pays on publication. Query first; "we will discuss the story requirements with the writer in detail." Enclose S.A.S.E.
Nonfiction and Photos: Feature articles and news stories about vending operations; practical and important aspects of the business. "We are always willing to pay for good material. Primary interest is photo fillers." Pays $5 per photo.

Confectionery and Snack Foods

CANDY AND SNACK INDUSTRY, 777 Third Ave., New York, NY 10017. (212)838-7778. Editor: Myron Lench. For confectionery and snack manufacturers. Monthly. Buys all rights. Query first. Reports in 2 weeks. Enclose S.A.S.E.
Nonfiction: "Feature articles of interest to large scale candy, cookie, cracker, and other snack manufacturers that deal with activities in the fields of production, packaging (including package design), merchandising; financial news (sales figures, profits, earnings), advertising campaigns in all media, and promotional methods used to increase the sale or distribution of candy and snacks." Length: 1,000 to 1,250 words. Pays 5¢ a word; "special rates on assignments."
Photos: "Good quality glossies with complete and accurate captions, in sizes not smaller than 5x7." Pays $5. Color covers.
Fillers: "Short news stories about the trade and anything related to candy and snacks." Pays 5¢ per word; $1 for clippings.

CANDY MARKETER, 777 Third Ave., New York NY 10017. (212)838-7778. Editor: Mike Lench. For owners and executives of wholesale and retail businesses. Monthly magazine. Established in 1967. Circulation: 14,000. Buys all rights. Buys 20 mss a year. Payment on acceptance. Will send free sample copy to writer on request. Will consider photocopied submissions. Will not consider simultaneous submissions. Submit seasonal material at least 6 weeks in advance. Reports within 2 weeks. Query first. Enclose S.A.S.E.

Nonfiction, Photos, and Fillers: News and features on the candy trade. "Describe operation, interview candy buyer or merchandise manager; quote liberally. More interested in mass operations, than in unusual little shops." Informational, how-to, interview, profile, spot news, successful business operations, merchandising techniques. Annual issues on Halloween merchandising, Christmas merchandising and Easter merchandising are published in May, June and November (respectively). Length: 1,000 to 2,500 words. Pays 5¢ a word. 5x7 or 8½x11 b&w photos and color transparencies or prints purchased with or without mss. Captions required. Pays $5 for b&w; $15 for color. Pays $1 for each clipping used.

Construction and Contracting

Journals aimed at architects and city planners will be found in the Architecture category. Those for specialists in the interior aspects of construction are listed under Building Interiors.

ABC AMERICAN ROOFER AND BUILDING IMPROVEMENT CONTRACTOR, Shelter Publications, Inc., 915 Burlington St., Downers Grove IL 60515. (312)964-6200. Editor-in-CHief: J.C. Gudas. For roofing industry contractors. Monthly magazine; 20-32 pages. Estab: 1911. Circ: 28,800. Pays on publication. Buys all rights. Submit seasonal/holiday material 4 months in advance. SASE. Reports in 1 week. Free sample copy.
Nonfiction: Publishes how-to (apply various kinds of material on roofs, preferably unusual kinds of data), historical, humor (if original), interview, photo feature (unusual types of roofing), profile (on industry men), and technical. Buys 5 mss a year. Query. Length: 1,500 words maximum. Pays $10-50. Editorial schedule available.
Photos: Purchased with accompanying ms. Captions required. Pays $5-25 for any size b&w glossy prints. Query or submit prints.
How To Break In: "Mss must pertain to our industry. Be consise and brief. Spaced-out wordings are not tolerated — articles must be well condensed, yet carry all the pertinent facts."
Rejects: "No generalized industry articles; no women in industry stories unless the job is the important part of the article."

AUTOMATION IN HOUSING & SYSTEMS BUILDING NEWS, CMN Associates, Inc., 3740 Dempster St., Skokie IL 60076. (312)674-8392. Editor-in-Chief: Don Carlson. Specializes in management for industrialized (manufactured) housing and volume home builders. Bi-monthly magazine; 44 pages. Estab: 1964. Circ: 23,000. Pays on acceptance. Buys first North American serial rights or one-time rights. Phone queries OK. SASE. Reports in 2 weeks. Free sample copy and writer's guidelines.
Nonfiction: Case history articles on successful home building companies which may be 1) production (big volume) home builders; 2) mobile home manufacturers; 3) modular home manufacturers; 4) prefabricated home manufacturers or 5) house component manufacturers. Also uses interviews, photo features and technical articles. Buys 6-8 mss/year. Query. Length: 2,500 words maximum. Pays $250 minimum.
Photos: Purchased with accompanying ms. Captions required. Query. No additional payment for 4x5, 5x7 or 8x10 b&w glossies or 35mm or larger color transparencies.

BATIMENT, 625 President Kennedy Ave., Montreal 111, Que., Canada. (514)845-5141. Editor: Marc Castro. Published in French for "contractors, architects." Established in 1927. Monthly. Circulation: 6,000. Rights purchased vary with author and material. Buys about 25 mss a year. Pays on acceptance. Will send a sample copy to a writer on request. Write for copy of guidelines for writers. Enclose S.A.E. and International Reply Coupons.
Nonfiction: "Articles on new techniques in construction and subjects of interest to builders. Interested in residential, apartment, office, commercial, and industrial buildings—not in public works. Generally, articles written in English are rejected." Length: 500 to 1,000 words. Pays $75-100.

CALIFORNIA BUILDER & ENGINEER, 363 El Camino Real, South San Francisco CA 94080. Senior Editor: Mahlon R. Fisher. For "contractors, engineers, machinery distributors for construction industry." Seeks material for water development and heavy construction. Established in 1894. Biweekly. Circulation: 12,500. Not copyrighted. Buys 30 to 40 mss a year. Pays on publication. Will send a sample copy to a writer on request. Will consider photocopied submissions. Submit seasonal material 2 months in advance. Reports in 2 weeks. Query first. Enclose S.A.S.E.

Nonfiction: "How-to articles: how can a contractor save time or money. Compared to similar publications, we give greater California coverage well within the regional framework." Interested in material on "the highway trust fund." Buys "normally only feature-type articles": how-to articles, interviews, profiles, humor, personal experience articles, photo features, coverage of successful business operations. Length: 1,000 to 5,000 words. Pays "$50 a printed page."
Photos: "We prefer 8x10 b&w glossies. By arrangement only."

CONSTRUCTION EQUIPMENT OPERATION AND MAINTENANCE, P.O. Box 1689, Cedar Rapids IA 52406. (319)366-1597. Editor: C.K. Parks. For users of heavy construction equipment. Bimonthly. Buys all rights. Pays on acceptance. Query first. Reports in 1 month. SASE. Free writer's guidelines.
Nonfiction and Photos: "Articles on selection, use, operation, or maintenance of construction equipment; articles and features on the construction industry in general; job safety articles." Length: "3 to 4 printed pages." Pays $200. Also buys a limited number of job stories with photos, and feature articles on individual contractors in certain areas of U.S. and Canada. Length varies. Pays $50 to $200.

CONSTRUCTION SPECIFIER, 1150 17th St., N.W., Washington DC 20036. Editor: Thomas A. Cameron. Professional society journal for architects, engineers, specification writers, contractors. Monthly. Circulation: 12,000. Buys all rights. Pays on publication. Will send a sample copy to a writer on request. Deadlines are 45 days preceding publication on the 10th of each month. Reports in 4 to 7 days. Query required. Enclose S.A.S.E.
Nonfiction and Photos: "Articles on building techniques, building products and material." Length: minimum 3,500 words. Pays $200-400. Photos "purchased rarely; if purchased, payment included in ms rate." 8x10 glossies.

CONSTRUCTIONEER, 1 Bond St., Chatham NJ 07928. Editor: Ken Hanan. For contractors, distributors, material producers, public works officials, consulting engineers, etc. Established in 1945. Biweekly. Circulation: 18,000. Rights purchased vary with author and material. Usually buys all rights but will reassign rights to author after publication. Buys 10 to 15 mss a year. Payment on acceptance. Will send a sample copy to writer for $1. Write for copy of guidelines for writers. Will consider photocopied submissions. Submit seasonal material 2 months in advance. Reports on material accepted for publication in 30 to 60 days. Returns rejected material in 30 days. Query first. Enclose S.A.S.E.
Nonfiction and Photos: Construction job stories; new methods studies. Detailed job studies of methods and equipment used; oriented around geographical area of New York, New Jersey, Pennsylvania and Delaware. Winter snow and ice removal and control; winter construction methods. Current themes: public works, profiles, conservation. Length: 1,500 to 1,800 words. Pays $100 to $200. B&w photos purchased with or without accompanying ms or on assignment. Pays $5 to $8.

CONSTRUCTOR MAGAZINE, 1957 E St., N.W., Washington DC 20006. Editor: Elena Cunningham. Publication of the Association of General Contractors of America for "men in the age range of approximately 25 to 70 (predominantly 40's and 50's), 50% with a college education. Most own or are officers in their own corporations." Established in 1902. Monthly. Circ. 27,500. Buys all rights, but will reassign after publication. Buys about 30 mss a year. Pays on publication. Will send a sample copy to a writer for 50¢. Query first or submit complete ms. Reports in 30 days. Enclose S.A.S.E.
Nonfiction: "Feature material dealing with labor, legal, technical, and professional material pertinent to the construction industry and corporate business. We deal only with the management aspect of the construction industry. No articles on computers and computer technology." Buys informational articles, interviews, think pieces, exposes, photo features, coverage of successful business operations, and technical articles. Length: "no minimum or maximum; subject much more important than length." Pays $50 to $300.

DIXIE CONTRACTOR, P.O. Box 280, Decatur GA 30031. (404)377-2683. Editor: Russell K. Paul. For readers in heavy construction: building, road construction, water/sewer contractors, construction materials producers, equipment dealers, public works officials. Magazine: 100 pages. Established in 1926. Every 2 weeks. Circulation: 8,700. Buys all rights, but may reassign rights to author after publication. Buys about 10 mss a year. Pays on publication. Will send free sample copy to writer on request. Will consider photocopied submissions. Rarely considers simultaneous submissions. Reports on material accepted for publication immediately. Query first or submit complete ms. Enclose S.A.S.E.

Nonfiction and Photos: New methods articles; current events. "Note that we are a regional trade journal. All material would have to come from Alabama, Florida, Georgia, South Carolina or middle or eastern Tennessee." How-to, interview, successful business operations, new product, technical articles. Length: 1,000 to 1,500 words. Pays $50 minimum. Also uses material for columns and departments. Length: 1 page. Pays $25 per page. 8x10 b&w photos and color transparencies are purchased with mss. Pays $5 for b&w; $10 for color. Captions required.

ENGINEERING AND CONTRACT RECORD, 1450 Don Mills Road, Don Mills, Ont., Canada M3B 2X7. (416)445-6641. Editor: Brandon Jones. For contractors in engineered construction and aggregate producers. Established in 1889. Monthly. Circulation: over 18,000. Buys first and second Canadian rights. Buys 12 to 15 mss a year. Pays on publication. Will send free sample copy to writer on request. Query first. Reports in 2 weeks. Enclose S.A.E. and International Reply Coupons.
Nonfiction and Photos: "Job stories. How to build a project quicker, cheaper, better through innovations and unusual methods. Articles on construction methods, technology, equipment, maintenance and management innovations. Management articles. Stories are limited to Canadian projects only." Length: 1,000 to 1,500 words. Pays 13¢/printed word and $5/8x10 printed photo. B&w glossies purchased with mss. 8x10 preferred.

FARM BUILDING NEWS, 733 N. Van Buren, Milwaukee, WI 53202. Managing Editor: Don Peach. For farm structure builders and suppliers. 6 times a year. Buys all rights. Pays on acceptance. Will send a free sample copy on request. Query suggested. Deadlines are at least 4 weeks in advance of publication date; prefers 6 to 8 weeks. Reports immediately. Enclose S.A.S.E.
Nonfiction and Photos: Features on farm builders and spot news. Length: 600 to 1,000 words. Pays $150 to $200. Buys color and b&w photos with ms.

FENCE INDUSTRY, 461 Eighth Ave., New York NY 10001. (212)239-6285. Editor: Lawrence Moores. For retailers of fencing materials. Magazine; 48 to 80 pages. Established in 1958. Monthly. Circulation: 12,000. Buys all rights. Buys 25 to 35 mss a year. Pays on publication. Will send free sample copy to writer on request. No photocopied or simultaneous submissions. Reports on material accepted for publication in 3 months. Returns rejected material in 2 weeks. Query first or submit complete ms. Enclose S.A.S.E.
Nonfiction and Photos: Case histories, as well as articles on fencing for highways, pools, farms, playgrounds, homes, industries. Surveys, and management and sales reports. Interview, profile, historical, successful business operations, and articles on merchandising techniques. Length: open. Pays 5¢ a word. Pays $10 for 8x10 b&w photos purchased with mss. Captions required.

JOURNAL OF COMMERCE, 2000 West 12th Ave., Vancouver, B.C., Canada. V6J 2G2. Editor: L.F. Webster. For engineers, architects, contractors, developers and construction industry specialists. Weekly. General business newspaper, tabloid 20 pages, with emphasis on construction. Established in 1911. Circulation: 9,000. Buys all rights. Payment on publication. Query first. Enclose S.A.E. and International Reply Coupons.
Nonfiction and Photos: Specialized technical articles on construction methodology and equipment. Take the approach of writing a newspaper feature, interview, or report. "Many publications deal with construction projects, etc., but not for an audience that knows the field thoroughly; we go beyond 'daily' style of how much, how big, etc." Particularly interested in articles about Canadian products being employed in the U.S. construction field. Length: 2,000 words maximum. Pays 8¢ a word. Captioned photos are purchased with accompanying ms. Pays $5 each.

MID-WEST CONTRACTOR, Box 766, Kansas City MO 64141. (816)842-2902. Editor: Gilbert Mulley. Buys all rights. Pays on acceptance. Query first. Enclose S.A.S.E.
Nonfiction and Photos: "Limited market for articles relating to large construction contracts in the Midwest only — Iowa, Nebraska, Kansas, and Missouri. Such articles would relate to better methods of building various phases of large contracts, ranging anywhere from material distribution to labor relations. Also interested in articles on outstanding construction personalities in territory." Length: open. Pays $50 minimum per article. Photos purchased with and without mss. Captions required. Pays $5 minimum per photo.

MODERN STEEL CONSTRUCTION, American Institute of Steel Construction, 1221 Avenue of the Americas, New York NY 10020. Editor: Mary Anne Stockwell. For architects and engineers. Quarterly. Not copyrighted. Pays on acceptance. Query first. Enclose S.A.S.E.

Nonfiction and Photos: "Articles with pictures and diagrams, of new steel-framed buildings and bridges. Must show new and imaginative uses of structural steel for buildings and bridges; new designs, new developments." Length: "1 and 2 pages." Pays $100. Photos purchased with mss.

WESTERN CONSTRUCTION, Box 2328, Eugene OR 97402. (503)689-2711. Editor: Gene Sheley. For "heavy constructors and their job supervisors." Monthly. Buys all rights and simultaneous rights. Pays on acceptance. Query first. Enclose S.A.S.E.
Nonfiction and Photos: "Methods articles on street, highway, bridge, tunnel, dam construction in 13 western states. Slant is toward how it was built rather than why." Writers in this field should have a background in civil engineering, heavy machine operation, or writing experience in associated fields such as commercial building construction. Academic training not as important as field experience and firsthand knowledge of the writer's subject. Length: 1,500 to 2,500 words and 6 photos. Pays minimum $40 "per printed magazine page."

WORLD CONSTRUCTION, 666 Fifth Ave., New York NY 10019. (212)489-4652. Editor: Donald R. Cannon. For "English-speaking engineers, contractors, and government officials in the Eastern hemisphere and Latin America." Monthly. Buys all rights. Pays on publication. Will send a sample copy to a writer on request. Query first. Reports in 1 month. Enclose S.A.S.E.
Nonfiction and Photos: "How-to articles which stress how contractors can do their jobs faster, better, or more economically. Articles are rejected when they tell only what was constructed, but not how it was constructed and why it was constructed in that way." Length: about 1,000 to 6,000 words. Pays $75/magazine page, or 4 typed ms pages. Photos purchased with mss; b&w glossies no smaller than 4x5.
How To Break In: "Send something from overseas. We're not distributed in North America, so we're very interested in writers who are living or traveling abroad and who know how to spot an engineering story."

Dairy Products

DAIRY RECORD, 3460 John Hancock Center, Chicago IL 60611. (312)943-5300. Editor: Herb Saal. Monthly. For the dairy processing industry. Not copyrighted. Pays on publication. Enclose S.A.S.E.
Nonfiction: Contributions must be confined to spot news articles and current events dealing with the dairy processing industry, especially news and news commentary of fluid milk distribution and the manufacturing and processing of dairy products. "Newsclips are okay. Not interested in items dealing with cows, dairy farms, herd management, etc." Pays $1 for every item published.

DAIRY SCOPE, 756 Kansas St., San Francisco CA 94107. (415)824-1563. Editor: Linda Clark. For dairy executives in the western part of the U.S. Bimonthly magazine; 16 pages. Estab: 1901. Circ: 5,000. Pays on publication. Buys one-time rights. SASE. Reports in 1 month.
Nonfiction: News stories pertaining to distribution and sales of milk and cream and manufacture and distribution of manufactured dairy products in 11 western states, plus Alaska and Hawaii. Also news stories pertaining to meetings, legal actions and other activities connected with the dairy industry in this area, including news of people in industry (promotion, retirement, etc.) Query. Length: open. Pays 4¢/word ($2/column inch).
Photos: Purchased with mss or with captions only. Pays $5 for b&w.

Data Processing

CANADIAN DATASYSTEMS, 481 University Ave., Toronto, Ont., Canada M5W 1A7. (416)595-1811. Editor: Tom Kelly. For data processing managers, computer systems managers, systems analysts, computer programmers, corporate management and similar people concerned with the use of computers in business, industry, government and education. Magazine; 70 pages. Established in 1969. Monthly. Circulation: 15,000. Buys first Canadian rights. Buys about 20 mss a year. Pays on acceptance. Will send sample copy to writer on request. No photocopied or simultaneous submissions. Reports in 1 month. Query first or submit complete ms. Enclose S.A.E. and International Reply Coupons.

Nonfiction: Articles of technical, semi-technical and general interest within thd general area of data processing. How-to features, application reports, descriptions of new techniques, surveys of equipment and services. Emphasis should be placed on the use of data processing equipment and services in Canada. Articles must be technical enough to satisfy an informed readership. Length: 2,000 words maximum. Pays $50 per feature article minimum.

COMPUTER DECISIONS, 50 Essex St., Rochelle Park NJ 07662. Editor: Hesh Wiener. For computer professionals, computer-involved managers in industry, finance, academia, etc. Well-educated, sophisticated, highly paid. Computer trade journals; 64 pages plus supplements. Established in 1969. Monthly. Circulation: 110,000. Buys first serial rights. Buys 12-24 mss/year. Pays on publication. Free sample copy to writer "who has a good background." Will consider photocopied submissions. Reports in 4 weeks. Enclose S.A.S.E.
Nonfiction and Fiction: Department Editor: Larry Lettieri. "Mainly serious articles about technology, business practice. Interviews. Informational, technical, think pieces, exposes, spot news. Fiction with a moral about technology and society. News pieces about computers and their use. Articles should be clear and not stylized. Assertions should be well-supported by facts. We are business-oriented, witty, more interested in the unusual story, somewhat less technical than most. We'll run a good article with a computer peg even if it's not entirely about computers. We want social issues involving computers —welfare, equal employment, privacy. Business analysis done by people with good backgrounds. Investigative stories on computers and crime." Length: 300 to 1,000 words for news; 1,000 to 5,000 words for features. Pays 3¢ to 10¢ per word. Mainstream, mystery, science fiction, fantasy, humorous, and historical fiction must have computer theme. Length: 1,000 to 3,000 words. Pays 3¢ to 6¢ per word for one-time rights.

COMPUTER DESIGN, 11 Goldsmith St., Littleton MA 01460. Editor: John A. Camuso. For digital electronic design engineers. Monthly. Buys all rights and simultaneous rights. Pays on publication. Will send sample copy on request. Query first. Reports in 4 to 8 weeks. Enclose S.A.S.E.
Nonfiction: Publishes engineering articles on the design and application of digital circuits, equipment, and systems used in computing, data processing, control and communications. Pays $30 to $40 per page.

COMPUTERWORLD, 797 Washington St., Newton MA 02160. Editor: E. Drake Lundell, Jr. For management-level computer users, chiefly in the business community, but also in government and education. Established in 1967. Weekly. Circulation: 76,000. Buys all rights, but may reassign rights to author after publication. Buys about 100 mss a year. Pays on publication. Will send free sample copy to writer on request, if request is accompanied by story idea or specific query. Write for copy of guidelines for writers. Will consider photocopied submissions only if exclusive for stated period. No simultaneous submissions. Submit special issue material 2 months in advance. Reports on material accepted for publication in 2 to 4 weeks. Returns rejected material immediately. Query first. Enclose S.A.S.E.
Nonfiction and Photos: Articles on problems in using computers; educating computer people; trends in the industry; new, innovative, interesting uses of computers. "We stress impact on users and need a practical approach. What does a development mean for other computer users? Most important facts first, then in decreasing order of significance. We would be interested in material on factory automation and other areas of computer usage that will impact society in general, and not just businesses. We prefer *not* to see executive appointments or financial results. We occasionally accept innovative material that is oriented to unique seasonal or geographical issues." Length: 250 to 1,200 words. Pays 10¢/word. B&w (5x7) glossies purchased with ms or on assignment. Captions required. Pays $5 to $10.
Fillers: Newsbreaks, clippings. Length: 50 to 250. Pays 10¢/word.

CREATIVE COMPUTING, Box 789-M, Morristown NJ 07960. Publisher: David Ali. Managing Editor: Burchenal Green. Emphasizes the use of computers in homes and schools for students, faculty, hobbyists, everyone interested in the effects of computers on society and the use of computers in school, at home, or at work. Bimonthly magazine; 128 pages. Estab: 1974. Circ: 30,000. Pays on acceptance. Buys all rights, but may reassign following publication. Submit seasonal/holiday material at least 4 months in advance. SASE. Reports in 4-5 weeks. Sample copy $1.50.
Nonfiction: How-to articles (building a computer at home; getting a computer system to work); informational (computer careers, simulations on computers, problem solving techniques, use in a particluar institution or discipline such as medicine, education, music, animation, space exploration or home use); historical articles (history of computers, or of a certain discipline, like

computers and animation); interviews with personalities in the hobbyist field, old-timers in the computer industry or someone doing innovative work. Personal experience (first person account of using hardware or software actively sought). Technical articles on programs, games, simulations (with printout) also actively sought. Buys 300 mss/year. Length: 500-3,000 words. Pays $10-300.

Photos: Usually purchased with mss, with no additional payment, but sometimes pays $3-50 for b&w glossies or $3-110 for any size color.

Columns/Departments: Compendium uses interesting, short articles about crazy, silly, unfortunate, interesting uses of computers (some human interest) about use in menu planning, pole vaulting, exploring, mistakes in computer programming, etc. Length: 50-500 words. Pays $5-30. Pays in copy of book for book reviews (all books on computer use). Complete Computer Catalog accepts only press releases on new products.

Fiction: Humorous fiction, mysteries, science fiction. "Must be specifically related to computer use. Stories that are of an interesting style that show how computers can benefit society are sought. Stories must keep in mind that people program computers and should program them for people's benefit. Stories dealing with new field of computers in the home are also sought." Buys 30 mss/year. Submit complete ms. Length: 500-3,000 words. Pays $15-400.

Poetry: Avant-garde, free verse, haiku, light verse, traditional forms and computer-generated poetry. Buys about 30/year. Submit complete poem. Pays $10-100.

Fillers: Jokes, gags, anecdotes, puzzles, short humor. Buys 20/year. Send fillers in. Pays $3-25.

JOURNAL OF SYSTEMS MANAGEMENT, 24587 Bagley Road, Cleveland OH 44138. (216)243-6900. Publisher: James Andrews. For systems and procedures and management people. Monthly. Buys all serial rights. Pays on publication. Will send a free sample copy on request. Query first. Reports as soon as possible. Enclose S.A.S.E.

Nonfiction: Uses articles on case histories, projects on systems, forms control, administrative practices, computer operations. Length: 3,000 to 5,000 words. Maximum payment is $25.

MINI-MICRO SYSTEMS, 5 Kane Industrial Dr., Hudson MA 01749. (617)562-9305. Editor: Stanley Klein. For systems engineers, computer users, and computer systems designers and manufacturers. Established in 1968. Monthly. Circulation: 86,000. Buys all rights but usually shares republication rights with author. Payment 30-60 days after publication. Free sample copy. Will consider photocopied submissions. Query first. Reports in 30 days. Enclose S.A.S.E.

Nonfiction and Photos: "Equipment surveys, application stories; expository articles on general methods and techniques. Will consider short (750 words) articles on varied aspects of computer technologies; areas of specialization are mini- and microcomputers and data communications. When we reject freelance material it's because the material is either 'old hat', irrelevant or unsophisticated, or generally contains insufficient substantive, supportive data." Informational, historical, think pieces, reviews of computer equipment, successful business operations, new products and applications. Length: 1,500 words maximum. Pays $35-50/magazine page.

Dental

CAL MAGAZINE, 3737 West 127th St., Chicago IL 60658. Editor: T.G. Baldaccini. Coe Laboratories, manufacturers of dental supplies. For dentists, dental assistants and dental technicians. Established in 1935. Monthly. Circulation: 50,000. Buys all rights, but will reassign to author after publication. Pays on acceptance. Will send free sample copy on request. Submit complete ms only. Reports in 6 weeks. Enclose S.A.S.E.

Nonfiction and Photos: Articles pertaining to or about dentists and dentistry; accomplishments of dentists in other fields. History, art, humor, adventure, unusual achievements, successful business operations, new products, merchandising techniques and technical. Length: 1,500 to 2,000 words. Pays $25 to $100. B&w photos only, 8x10 or 5x7 glossy, purchased with mss or captions only. Pays $25 to $50.

Fiction: "Related in some way to dentistry." Length: 1,500 to 2,000 words. Pays $25 to $100.

Poetry and Fillers: Light verse. "Related to dentistry." Puzzles, short humor. Pays $3 minimum.

CONTACTS, Box 407, North Chatham NY 12132. Editor: Joseph Strack. For laboratory owners, managers, and dental technician staffs. Established in 1938. Published every 2 months. Circulation: 1,200. Not copyrighted. Pays on acceptance. Will send sample copy to writer on request. No photocopied or simultaneous submissions. Reports on material accepted for publi-

cation in 1 or 2 weeks. Returns rejected material immediately. Query first. Enclose S.A.S.E.
Nonfiction and Photos: Writer should know the dental laboratory field or have good contacts there to provide technical articles, how-to, and successful business operation articles. Length: 1,500 words maximum. Pays 3¢ to 5¢ a word; higher for top material. Willing to receive suggestions for columns and departments for material of 400 to 800 words. Payment for these negotiable.

DENTAL ECONOMICS, P.O. Box 1260, Tulsa OK 74101. (918)835-3161. Editor: Richard L. Henn, Jr. For practicing dentists in the U.S. Established in 1911. Monthly. Circulation: 104,000. Buys first North American serial rights. Buys 75 mss a year. Payment on acceptance when material has been assigned. Payment on publication for unsolicited material. Will send free sample copy to writer on request. Query first or submit complete ms. Reports on material in 4 to 6 weeks. Enclose S.A.S.E.
Nonfiction and Photos: "Business side of a dental practice; patient and staff relations, taxes, investments, professional image; original 'case history' articles on means of conducting a dental practice more efficiently or more successfully (preferably with a D.D.S. byline). Lively writing style; in-depth coverage. Mss must be oriented to the dental profession and non-clinical in nature." Length: 1,000 to 2,500 words. Pays $50-300, "depending on material." B&w glossy photos; contact prints. Captions required.

DENTAL MANAGEMENT, 757 Third Ave., New York NY 10017. Editor: M.J. Goldberg. For practicing dentists. Monthly. Buys all rights. Buys two or three articles per issue. Pays on acceptance. Query first. Enclose S.A.S.E.
Nonfiction and Photos: "No clinical or scientific material. Magazine is directed toward the business side of dentistry—management, collections, patient relations, fees, personal investments and life insurance. Writing should be clear, simple, direct. Like lots of anecdotes, facts and direct conclusions." Pays 10-20¢/word, depending on quality and research. Photos purchased with ms. Pays $10.

THE JOURNAL OF ORAL IMPLANTOLOGY, 469 Washington St., Abington MA 02351. Editor: Dr. Isaih Lew. Executive Director: John P. Winiewicz. For the dental profession and related areas of medicine and technology. Magazine; 150 pages. Established in 1970. Quarterly. Circulation: 2,000. Not copyrighted. Time of payment depends on arrangements made to the convenience of the author. Will send sample copy to writer on request. Write for copy of guidelines for writers. Will consider photocopied submissions. May consider simultaneous submissions. Submit complete ms. Enclose S.A.S.E.
Nonfiction and Photos: Technical articles on all related areas of dental implantology to include materials and devices, medical research that relates to this field. Basic research, basic technology and any new research being done on new materials. Length: open. Pays $25 minimum, based on acceptability of material supplied and approval by the editorial board. No additional payment for photos used with mss.

PROOFS, The Magazine of Dental Sales, Box 1260, Tulsa OK 74101. (918)835-3161. Editor: Richard Henn. Monthly. Pays on acceptance. Will send free sample copy on request. Query first. Reports in a week. Enclose S.A.S.E.
Nonfiction: Uses short articles, chiefly on selling to dentists. Must have understanding of dental trade industry, and problems of marketing and selling to dentists and dental laboratories. Pays about $75.

TIC MAGAZINE, Box 407, North Chatham NY 12132. (518)766-3047. Editor: Joseph Strack. For dentists, dental assistants, and oral hygienists. Monthly. Buys first publication rights in the dental field. Pays on acceptance. Reports in 2 weeks. Query first. Enclose S.A.S.E.
Nonfiction: Prefers a simple, almost popular style. Uses articles (with illustrations, if possible) as follows: 1. Lead feature: Dealing with major developments in dentistry of direct, vital interest to all dentists. 2. How-to-do-it pieces: Ways and means of building dental practices, improving professional techniques, managing patients, increasing office efficiency, etc.; 3. Special articles: Ways and means of improving dentist-laboratory relations for mutual advantage, of developing auxiliary dental personnel into an efficient office team, of helping the individual dentist to play a more effective role in alleviating the burden of dental needs in the nation and in his community, etc. 4. General articles: Concerning any phase of dentistry or dentistry-related subjects of high interest to the average dentist. Length: 800 to 3,200 words. Pays 4¢ minimum per word.
Photos: Photo stories: four to ten pictures of interesting developments and novel ideas in dentistry. B&w only. Pays $10 minimum per photo.

How To Break In: "We can use fillers of about 300 words or so. They should be pieces of substance on just anything of interest to dentists. A psychoanalyst broke in with us recently with pieces relating to interpretations of patients' problems and attitudes in dentistry. Another writer just broke in with a profile of a dentist working with an Indian tribe. If the material's good, we'll be happy to rewrite."

Department Store, Variety, and Dry Goods

JUVENILE MERCHANDISING, 370 Lexington Ave., New York NY 10017. (212)532-9290. Editor: Lee Clarke Neumeyer. For buyers and merchandise managers in nursery furniture, wheel goods, preschool toys and related lines, including juvenile specialty shops, department stores, chain stores, discount stores, rated PX's, leading furniture stores with juvenile departments, and resident buying offices. Monthly. Circulation: 11,000. Buys all rights, but will reassign rights to author after publication; buys second serial (reprint) rights. Buys 18 mss a year. Payment on publication. Will send free sample copy to writer on request. Reports in 1 week. Query first. Enclose S.A.S.E.
Nonfiction and Photos: "Stories should emphasize how sales and profits can be increased. How-to articles, merchandising stories, juvenile store coverage, etc. Solid features about a phase of juvenile operation in any of the above-mentioned retail establishments. Not interested in store histories. Mss on successful displays, methods for more efficient management; also technical articles on stock control or credit or mail promotion—how a specific juvenile store uses these, why they were undertaken, what results they brought. Factual material with pertinent quotes. Emphasis on benefits to other retail operations. Illustrated interviews with successful dealers." Length: 1,000 to 1,500 words. Pays $50 to $75.

MILITARY MARKET, Army Times Publishing Co., 475 School St., S.W., Washington DC 20024. (202)554-7180. Editor-in-Chief: Gerald F. McConnell. For store managers, headquarters personnel, Pentagon decision-makers, Congressional types, wholesalers to the military, manufacturers. Monthly magazine; 56 pages. Estab: 1954. Circ: 13,500. Pays on acceptance. Buys all rights, but may reassign following publication. Phone queries OK. Submit seasonal or holiday material 4 months in advance. Simultaneous and photocopied submissions and previously published work OK. SASE. Reports in 2 months. Free sample copy.
Nonfiction: Publishes how-to articles (directed toward improving management techniques or store operations); humor (funny aspects of the business); informational (implementation of policies and directions); interviews (notables in the field); technical (store operations). Buys 1 ms a year. Length: 1,000-4,000 words. Query first. Pays $75-300.

SEW BUSINESS, 1271 Avenue of the Americas, New York NY 10020. Editor: Linda Nicastro. For retailers of home-sewing merchandise. Monthly. Circulation: 14,000. Not copyrighted. Buys about 100 mss a year. Pays on publication. Will send a sample copy to a writer on request. Query first. Reports in 1 month. Enclose S.A.S.E.
Nonfiction and Photos: Articles on department store or fabric shop operations, including coverage of art needlework, piece goods, patterns, sewing accessories and all other notions. Interviews with buyers—retailers on their department or shop. "Unless they are doing something different or offbeat, something that another retailer could put to good use in his own operation, there is no sense wasting their or your time in doing an interview and story. Best to query editor first to find out if a particular article might be of interest to us." Length: 500 to 1,500 words. Pays $85 minimum. Photos purchased with mss. "Should illustrate important details of the story." Sharp 8x10 b&w glossies. Pays $5.
Fillers: $2.50 for news items less than 100 words. For news item plus photo and caption, pays $7.50.

Drugs, Health Care, and Medical Products

CANADIAN PHARMACEUTICAL JOURNAL, 175 College St., Toronto, Ontario, Canada M5T 1P8. (416)979-2431. Editor-in-Chief: N.R. McIver. For pharmacists. Monthly magazine;

32 pages. Estab: 1918. Circ: 9,200. Pays on publication. Buys all rights, but may reassign following publication. Phone queries OK. Previously published work OK. SASE. Reports in 1 month. Free sample copy and writer's guidelines.

Nonfiction: Publishes exposes (pharmacy practice, education and legislation); how-to (pharmacy business operations); historical (pharmacy practice, legislation, education); interviews with and profiles on pharmacy figures. Buys 2-4 mss a year. Length: 1,000-3,000 words. Query first. Payment is contingent on value; usually 5¢/word.

Photos: B&w (5x7) glossies and color transparencies purchased with mss. Captions required. Payment by arrangement. Model release required.

DRUG SURVIVAL NEWS, c/o Do It Now Foundation, P.O. Box 5115, Phoenix AZ 85010. (602)257-0797. Editor: Vic Pawlak. For directors and workers in drug abuse and alcoholism field; schools, counselors, nurses, state and local mental health agencies, military drug and alcohol programs, and interested people concerned with the problems of drug and alcohol abuse. Tabloid newspaper; 12 pages. Established in 1970. Every 2 months. Circulation: 20,000. Buys all rights, but may reassign rights to author after publication. Retains the option of publishing later as a pamphlet or part of a collection. Pays on publication. Will send free sample copy to writer on request. Will consider photocopied submissions. Simultaneous submissions are considered only when they know name of publication to which other submission was sent. Reports on material accepted for publication in 1 month. Returns rejected material in 2 to 3 weeks. Query first. Enclose S.A.S.E.

Nonfiction and Photos: Research, news and articles about effects of various chemicals. In-depth articles about prominent programs and the people who run them. Writers should have experience with these subjects, either professionally or subjectively (as a former user, etc., but not prejudiced against the topics beforehand). Would like to see over-the-counter drug stories, but nothing on marijuana, or articles by ex-addicts or ex-alcoholics telling about their lives. Informational, interview, profile, historical, personal opinion, photo, book reviews, spot news, successful program operations, new product and technical articles. Length: 100 to 2,000 words. Pays $5 to $50. B&w photos purchased with mss or on assignment. Captions required. Pays $5 to $10.

Fillers: Newsbreaks, jokes, gags, anecdotes. Length: 100 to 300 words. Pays $5 to $10. Pays less for clippings.

DRUG TOPICS, 550 Kinderkamack Rd., Oradell NJ 07649. (201)262-3030. Editor-in-Chief: David W. Sifton. Executive Editor: Ralph M. Thurlow. For retail drug stores and wholesalers, manufacturers, and hospital pharmacists. Monthly. Circulation: over 50,000. Buys all rights. Query first. Pays on acceptance. Enclose S.A.S.E.

Nonfiction: News of local, regional, state pharmaceutical assocations, legislation affecting operation of drug stores, news of pharmacists in civic and professional activities, etc. Query first on drug store success stories which deal with displays, advertising, promotions, selling techniques. Length: 1,500 words maximum. Pays $5 and up for leads, $25 and up for short articles, $50 to $200 for feature articles, "depending on length and depth."

Photos: May buy photos submitted with mss. May buy news photos with captions only. Pay $20.

N.A.R.D. JOURNAL, 1 E. Wacker Dr., Chicago IL 60601. Editor: Richard W. Lay. Monthly. Buys all rights. Query first. Enclose S.A.S.E.

Nonfiction and Photos: Uses success stories about independent retail drug stores; novel methods used in promotion and display of front and departments; how to compete effectively with large chains. Length: 2,100 words. Pays $50 per page; $25 for photos from "pro" photographers.

PATIENT AID DIGEST, 2009 Morris Ave., Union NJ 07083. (201)687-8282. Editor: Laurie N. Cassak. For pharmacists, home health care managers and manufacturers of patient aid products. Established in 1970. Published every 2 months. Circulation: 11,000. Buys all rights. Buys about 10 mss per year. Pays on publication. Will send free sample copy and editorial guidelines sheet to writer on request. Will consider photocopied and simultaneous submissions. Reports on material accepted for publication in 8 weeks. Returns rejected material in 2 weeks. Query first. Enclose S.A.S.E.

Nonfiction and Photos: "Articles about existing home health care centers or opportunities for proprietors; human interest stories that deal with health care; helpful hints for the pharmacist. It is essential to understand your reading audience. Articles must be informative, but not extremely technical." Buys informational, how-to, interview, photo articles. Length: 1,000 to

1,500 words. Pays 5¢ per word. Photos purchased with accompanying ms with no additional payment. Captions optional.

WHOLESALE DRUGS, 1111 E. 54th St., Indianapolis IN 46220. Editor: William F. Funkhouser. Bimonthly. Buys first rights only. Query first. Enclose S.A.S.E.
Nonfiction and Photos: Wants features on presidents and salesmen of Full Line Wholesale Drug Houses throughout the country. No set style, but subject matter should tell about both the man and his company—history, type of operation, etc. Pays $50 for text and pictures.

Education

Professional educators, teachers, coaches, and school personnel read the journals classified here. Publications for parents, or the general public interested in education-related topics are listed under Education in the Consumer Publications section.

THE AMERICAN SCHOOL BOARD JOURNAL, National School Boards Association, 1055 Thomas Jefferson St., N.W., Washington DC 20007. (202)337-7666. Editor-in-Chief: James Betchkal. Emphasizes public school administration and policymaking. For elected members of public boards of education throughout the U.S. and Canada, and high level administrators of same. Monthly magazine; 64 pages. Estab: 1891. Circ: 50,000. Pays on acceptance. Buys all rights. Phone queries OK. Submit seasonal or holiday material 4-6 months in advance. Photocopied submissions OK. SASE. Reports in 3 months. Free sample copy.
Nonfiction: Publishes how-to articles (solutions to problems of public school operation including political problems); interviews with notable figures in public education. Buys 20 mss a year. Query first. Length: 400-2,000 words. Payment varies, "but never less than $100."
Photos: "B&w glossies (any size) and color purchased on assignment. Captions required. Pays $10-50. Model release required.

AMERICAN SCHOOL & UNIVERSITY, North American Publishing Co., 401 N. Broad St., Philadelphia PA 19108. Editor-in-Chief: Rita Robison. Emphasizes "facilities and business office matters of schools, colleges, and universities (no curriculum, etc)." For "administrators such as superintendents of buildings and grounds, business officials, school superintendents, college vice-presidents of operations, etc." Monthly magazine; 70-120 pages. Estab: 1928. Circ: 41,000. Pays on publication. Buys all rights, but may reassign following publication. Reports in 3-6 weeks.
Nonfiction: Photo feature (new or renovated buildings, with architectural/engineering description), technical (energy conservation measures, solar energy applications, business practices that save money). "We prefer the 'this was the problem and this is how it was solved' approach." Buys 3-4 mss a year. Query. Length: 500-1,800 words. Pays $25/page minimum.
Photos: Used with accompanying ms for no additional payment. Submit 8x10 b&w glossies or 4x5 color transparencies.

ARTS AND ACTIVITIES, 8150 N. Central Park Ave., Skokie IL 60076. (312)675-5602. Editor: Marjorie S. Sarnat. For "art teachers in elementary, junior high, and senior high schools." Monthly, except July and August. Buys all rights. Pays on publication. Free sample copy. Reports in 3 weeks. SASE.
Nonfiction and Photos: "Articles for teachers on creative art activities for students in elementary, junior high, and senior high schools, with illustrations such as artwork or photos of activity in progress. Payment is determined by length, nature of photos and educational value." Pays minimum $30.

CATECHIST, Peter LI, Inc., 2451 E. River Rd., Dayton OH 45439. Editor: Patricia Fischer. Emphasizes religious education for professional and volunteer religious educators working in Catholic schools. Monthly (September-May) magazine; 40 pages. Estab: 1966. Circ: 82,000. Pays on publication. Buys all rights. Submit seasonal or holiday material 3 months in advance. SASE. Reports in 1 month. Sample copy, 50¢; free writer's guidelines.
Nonfiction: Publishes how-to articles (methods for teaching a particular topic or concept; informational (theology and church-related subjects, insights into current trends and developments); personal experience (in the religious classroom). Length: 1,500 words maximum. Buys 45 mss a year. Query first. Pays $30-75.
Photos: B&w (8x10) glossies purchased without mss. Send contact sheet. Pays $15-25.

How To Break In: "By writing articles that would be of practical use for the teacher of religion or an article that results from personal experience and expertise in the field."

CHILDREN'S HOUSE, P.O. Box 111, Caldwell NJ 07006. Editor: Kenneth Edelson. For teachers and parents of young children. Magazine; 32 (8½x11) pages. Established in 1966. Every 2 months. Circulation: 50,000. Buys all rights. Buys 20 to 30 mss a year. Pays on publication. Sample copy for $1.25; free writer's guidelines. Will consider photocopied submissions. Reports on material accepted for publication in 3 to 6 months. Returns rejected material immediately. Query first or submit complete ms. Enclose S.A.S.E.
Nonfiction and Photos: Department Editor: Margery Mossman. Articles on education, open (and closed) education, Montessori, learning disabilities, atypical children, innovative schools and methods; new medical, psychological experiments. "We're not afraid to tackle controversial topics such as sex education, integration, etc., but we don't want to see personal or family histories. No 'why-Johnny-can't-read' articles." Informational, how-to, profile, think articles. Length: 1,200 to 2,000 words. Pays 2¢ to 5¢ a word "conditionally". 5x7 or 7x9 b&w glossies purchased on assignment. Pays minimum of $5.
Fillers: Newsbreaks, clippings. Length: 1 or 2 paragraphs. Pays minimum of $1 per column inch "conditionally".

CHRISTIAN TEACHER, Box 550, Wheaton IL 60187. (312)665-0786. Editor: Phil Landrum. For "members of the National Association of Christian Schools. They are mostly grade school teachers; also, high school teachers, principals, board members, parents." Established in 1964. Bimonthly, except during summer. Circulation: 3,500. Not copyrighted. Will send a sample copy to a writer on request. Query first. Reports "quickly." Enclose S.A.S.E.
Nonfiction and Photos: "Educational trends, reports, how-to—mostly informative or inspirational. Our publication deals with education from a Christian point of view." Length for articles: 500 to 2,000 words. Payment: "no set rate; work on assignment only. We are unable to pay standard prices for articles, and we like to specify to writers what we want them to write so our time and theirs is not wasted." Photos purchased with and without mss.

COLLEGE STUDENT JOURNAL, Project Innovation, 1362 Santa Cruz Ct., Chula Vista CA 92010. (714)421-9377. Editor: Dr. Russell N. Cassel. For college students, faculty, teachers, educators, psychologists. Magazine; 96 pages. Established in 1962. Quarterly. Circulation: 1,000. Acquires all rights, but may reassign rights to author after publication. Pays in contributor's copies. Will send sample copy to writer on request. Write for copy of guidelines for writers. Reports on material accepted for publication in about 30 days. Returns rejected material in about 6 weeks. Query first. Enclose S.A.S.E.
Nonfiction: Theory, practice, and research bearing on the college student, which includes professional preparation and schools. Research assignments available on yearbook summaries, research, theory, practice, and proposals related to college and professional school students and schools. All material must follow the *APA Publications Manual.*

COMMUNITY COLLEGE FRONTIERS, Sangamon State University, Shepherd Rd., Springfield IL 62708. Editor-in-Chief: J. Richard Johnston. For all persons interested in two-year post-secondary educational institutions, especially faculty, administrators, trustees and students in public community colleges. Quarterly magazine; 56 pages. Estab: 1972. Circ: 5,000. Pays in contributor's copies. Acquires all rights, but will reassign following publication. Phone queries OK. All material should be given minimum of 3 months' lead time. SASE. Reports in 6-8 weeks. Free sample copy and writer's guidelines.
Nonfiction: Publishes historical articles (of community colleges); how-to (college teaching strategies to organize subject material and motivate students); humor (satire on stuffy, pompous educators); informational (analytical reports on college instructional programs; inspirational (individual students/adults; sincerity, handicapped, etc.). Query first.
Photos: Uses B7w glossies (8x10) with captions and credit line. Send contact sheet.
Columns, Departments: Say It With Words (stuffy, pretentious, academic language and style; funny errors; play on words, etc.); Frontiers Exchange (brief information on special programs, techniques, or ideas. "We are especially interested in informal learning networks for adults, cooperatives, collective, non-profit enterprises, etc." Length: 50-100 words. Query with sample lead paragraph.
How To Break In: "Writing fresh viewpoints (critical views are welcome) upon college education in clear, simple language. Personal experience related to important general principles make good material for us."

CURRICULUM REVIEW, Curriculum Advisory Service, 500 S. Clinton St., Chicago IL 60607. (312)939-1333. Editor-in-Chief: Irene M. Goldman. For teachers K-12, curriculum planners, librarians, graduate schools of education. 5 times yearly magazine; 68 pages. Estab: 1961. Circ: 2,000. Pays on publication. Buys all rights, but will reassign following publication. Phone queries OK. Photocopied submissions OK. Reports in 4 weeks. Free sample copy and writer's guidelines.
Nonfiction: Charlotte H. Cox, Articles Editor. Informational (on education or curriculum for K-12, current trends, methods, theory). Buys 20 essay mss a year. Query. Length: 1,000-2,000 words. Pays $30-50. Alos publishes 300-400 book reviews per year on an assigned basis; classroom text materials in language arts, mathematics, science, social studies. Pays $10-50 a review depending on scope and difficulty of materials. Send educational vita. "We are especially interested in innovative articles by curriculum planners, school superintendents, deans of graduate education, or interdisciplinary specialists on new educational approaches.
For '78: "We will feature environmental studies, women's studies, career education, values education, and media studies, among other topics. Schedule available on request."

EDUCATION, Projection Innovation, 1362 Santa Cruz Ct., Chula Vista CA 92010. (714)421-9377. Editor: Dr. Russell N. Cassel. For educators, psychologists, college students, teachers, etc. Magazine; 96 pages. Established in 1880. Quarterly. Circulation: 3,500. Acquires all rights, but may reassign rights to author after publication. Pays in contributor's copies. Will send sample copy to writer on request. Write for copy of guidelines for writers. Reports on material accepted for publication in about 30 days. Returns rejected material in about 6 weeks. Query first. Enclose S.A.S.E.
Nonfiction: Theory and practices in relation to innovations in education and learning; all levels of education, and in every area. Assignments are sometimes made for book summaries, research reports, theoretical articles, and practices. All material follows the *APA Publication Manual.*

EDUCATIONAL STUDIES: A Journal in the Foundations of Education, 107 Quadrangle, Ames IA 55011. (515)294-7327. Editor-in-Chief: DR. L. Glenn Smith. Emphasizes research, reviews and opinions in the foundations of education. Quarterly magazine; 120 pages. Estab: 1970. Circ: 1,500. Pays on publication. Buys all rights, but may reassign following publication. Phone queries OK. Photocopied submissions OK. SASE. Reports in 2 months. Free sample copy and writer's guidelines.
Nonfiction: Historical and informational articles; must relate to the Foundations of Education. Also uses pieces on experimental research. Buys 8-12 mss/year. Submit complete ms. Length: 1,000-3,500 words. Pays $25 maximum, but sometimes no payment is made.
Photos: No additional payment for 8x10 b&w glossies used with mss. Captions required. Send contact sheet or prints. Model release required.
Poetry: Traditional forms, free verse, haiku and light verse. Length: 4-24

FORECAST FOR HOME ECONOMICS, 50 W. 44th St., New York NY 10036. (212)867-7700. Address mss to Gloria Spitz, Editor. For home economics professionals and educators in junior and senior high schools. Established in 1956. Monthly. September through May-June. Circ. 75,000. Buys all rights. Pays on publication. Free writer's guidelines. "Query or outline strongly recommended." Reports in 2 months. Enclose S.A.S.E.
Nonfiction and Photos: "Articles of interest to home economists in education, family relations, child development, clothing, textiles, grooming, foods, nutrition, career awareness, consumerism, economy, finance, ecology, and home management." Length: 1,500 to 3,000 words. Pays average $75, "depending on the author and length." B&w photos accepted with mss.

HOSPITAL/HEALTH CARE TRAINING MEDIA PROFILES, Olympic Media Information, 71 W. 23 St., New York NY 10010. (212)675-4500. Publisher: Walt Carroll. For hospital education departments, nursing schools, schools of allied health, paramedical training units, colleges, community colleges, local health organizations. Serial, in loose leaf format, published every 2 months. Established in 1974. Circulation: 1,000 plus. Buys all rights. Buys about 240 mss a year. Payment on publication. Will send free sample copy to writer on request. "Send resume of your experience to introduce yourself." Will not consider photocopied or simultaneous submissions. Reports in 1 month. Query first. Enclose S.A.S.E.
Nonfiction: "Reviews of all kinds of audiovisual media. We are the only existing review publication devoted to evaluation of audiovisual aids for hospital and health training. We have a highly specialized, definite format that must be followed in all cases. Samples should be seen by all means. Our writers should first have a background in health sciences, secondly, some experience with audiovisuals; and third, follow our format precisely. Besides basic biological sciences, we are interested in materials for nursing education, in-service education, continuing

education, personnel training, patient education, patient care, medical problems." Pays $5 to $15 per review.

How To Break In: "Contact us and send a resume of your experience in writing for hospital, science, health fields. We will assign audiovisual aids to qualified writers and send them these to review for us. Unsolicited mss not welcome."

ILLINOIS SCHOOLS JOURNAL, Chicago State University, 95th St. at King Drive, Chicago IL 60628. Editor: Virginia McDavid, Department of English, room E-356. Primarily for teachers and professional educators. Magazine; 64 to 80 (6x9) pages. Established in 1906. Quarterly. Circulation: 7,000. Acquires all rights, but will reassign rights to author after publication. Pays in contributor's copies. Will send free sample copy and editorial guidelines to a writer on request. Will consider photocopied submissions. No simultaneous submissions. Reports on material accepted for publication within 3 months. Returns rejected material in 1 month. Submit only complete ms. Enclose S.A.S.E.

Nonfiction: Educational subject matter. Concentrate on practical aspects of education. Length: 2,000 to 3,000 words.

INDUSTRIAL EDUCATION, 1 Fawcett Place, Greenwich CT 06830. (203)869-8585. For administrators and instructors in elementary, secondary, and post-secondary education in industrial arts, vocational, industrial and technical education. Monthly, except July and August and combined May-June issue. Buys all rights. Pays on publication. Write for copy of guidelines for writers. Deadline for Shop Planning Annual is Dec. 29; for Back to School and Projects, July 1. Reports in 5 weeks. Enclose S.A.S.E. for return of submissions.

Nonfiction and Photos: "Articles dealing with the broad aspects of industrial arts, vocational, and technical education as it is taught in our junior and senior high schools, vocational and technical high schools, and junior college. We're interested in analytical articles in relation to such areas as curriculum planning, teacher training, teaching methods, supervision, professional standards, industrial arts or vocational education, industrial practice, relationship of industrial education to industry at the various educational levels, current problems, trends, etc. How-to-do, how-to-teach, how-to-make articles of a very practical nature which will assist the instructor in the laboratory at every level of industrial education. Typical are the 'activities' articles in every instructional area. Also typical is the article which demonstrates to the teacher a new or improved way of doing something or of teaching something or how to utilize special teaching aids or equipment to full advantage—activities which help the teacher do a better job of introducing the industrial world of work to the student." Length: maximum 2,500 words. Pays $30 "per printed page." 8x10 b&w photos purchased with ms.

Fillers: Short hints on some aspect of shop management or teaching techniques. Length: 25 to 250 words.

INSTRUCTOR MAGAZINE, 7 Bank St., Dansville NY 14437. (716)335-2221. Editor: Leanna Landsman. For elementary classroom teachers and supervisors. Established in 1891. Monthly except July and August. Circulation: 275,000. Rights purchased vary with author and material. Buys all rights or first serial rights. Payment on acceptance. Will send free sample copy to writer on request. Write for copy of guidelines for writers. Submit seasonal material 6 months in advance. Reports on material accepted for publication in 4 months. Returns rejected material in 1 month. Submit complete ms. Enclose S.A.S.E.

Nonfiction and Photos: "Professional articles on various aspects of education; ideas and suggestions about effective teaching activities. Descriptive work about a program, emphasizing the specific techniques necessary for teachers to follow. Need seasonal articles on teaching suggestions and art activities. Informational and technical. Interviews." Length: 600 to 1,500 words. "Payment rates vary so much depending upon length, quality, and how the material is to be used. For a one-paragraph idea we may pay as little as $5 and as much as $500 for a long, full-length feature." 8x10 glossies and color transparencies purchased with ms.

Fiction, Poetry and Drama: Department Editor: Kathryn Eldridge. Stories, poems, plays for elementary classroom use. Historical, real life, holidays, Length: 600 to 1,000 words. Payment varies.

JGE: The Journal of General Education, Penn State University Press, 215 Wagner Bldg., University Park PA 16802. Editors-in-Chief: Caroline and Robert Eckhardt. Emphasizes general education for teachers of undergraduates in colleges and universities. Quarterly magazine; 104 pages. Estab: 1946. Circ: 1,600. Acquires all rights, but may reassign following publication. Simultaneous and photocopied submissions OK. SASE. Reports in 4 weeks. Free sample copy and writer's guidelines.

Nonfiction: How-to (teaching specific topics), informational (new ideas, fresh approaches, findings). Uses 30 mss a year. Query. Length: No limits. Pays in 25 offprints of the article.

JOURNAL OF ENGLISH TEACHING TECHNIQUES, University of Michigan, Flint MI 48503. (313)767-4000. Editor: Dr. F.K. Bartz. For public school English teachers, English professors in colleges and universities. Established in 1968. Quarterly. Circulation: 500. Acquires all rights. Pays in contributor's copies. Will send sample copy to writer for $1. Reports in 6 weeks. Query first or submit complete ms. Enclose S.A.S.E.
Nonfiction: Articles on the teaching of English. Book reviews. Short features. Bibliographies. Exercises. Anything of interest to English teachers. All material must follow the *M.L.A. Style Sheet.*

JOURNAL OF READING, THE READING TEACHER, International Reading Association, 600 Barksdale Rd., Newark DE 19711. (302)731-1600. Editor-in-Chief: Dr. Janet R. Binkley. For teachers, reading specialists, or other school personnel; college and university faculty, independent researchers. Monthly (October-May) magazines; 132 pages *(The Reading Teacher);* 96 pages *(Journal of Reading).* Estab: 1948 *(The Reading Teacher);* 1957 *(Journal of Reading).* No payment. Phone queries OK. Submit seasonal or holidy material 1 year in advance. Photocopied submissions OK. SASE. Reports in 3 months. Sample copy $2.
Nonfiction: Publishes articles that deal with reading, teaching reading, learning to read; about children or adults. Theory, techniques, research, mental processes, history, humor; current events in reading education, etc. Articles about learners through grade 6 go to *The Reading Teacher;* articles about secondary and adult learners, go to *Journal of Reading.* Length: 100-3,000 words. Submit complete ms.
Photos: "We have no budget for photos, but are delighted to use reading-related photos (b&w) with articles and on *Journal of Reading* covers, when donated."
Columns/Departments: Tips on effective teaching techniques for Interchange *(The Reading Teacher)* and Open to Suggestion *(Journal of Reading).*
Poetry: "We don't buy poetry, but would gladly publish more than is contributed at present." Avant-garde, free verse, haiku, light verse and traditional forms acceptable.

LEARNING, 530 University Ave., Palo Alto CA 94301. (415)321-1770. Editor: Morton Malkofsky. For elementary school teachers. Established in 1972. Monthly. Circulation: 225,000. Buys all rights, but will reassign rights to author after publication. Buys 100 to 150 mss a year. Payment on acceptance. Will consider photocopied submissions. Reporting time "depends on story." Rejected material is returned in 1 to 4 weeks. Query first. Enclose S.A.S.E.
Nonfiction and Photos: "We publish manuscripts that describe innovative teaching strategies or probe controversial and significant social/political issues related to the professional and classroom interests of preschool to 8th grade teachers. Reports of classroom action and/or documentation of claims should be an integral part of all submitted manuscripts." Length: 300 to 3,000 words. Pays $50 to $500. Photos purchased with accompanying mss or on assignment. Captions required. "Contact sheets and negs."

THE LIVING LIGHT, 1312 Massachusetts Ave., N.W., Washington DC 20005. An interdisciplinary review for "professionals in the field of religious education, primarily Roman Catholics." Established in 1964. Quarterly. Buys all rights but will reassign rights to author after publication. Buys 4 mss a year. Payment on publication. Sample copy $3.50. Submit complete ms. Reports in 30-60 days. SASE
Nonfiction: Articles that "present development and trends, report on research and encourage critical thinking in the field of religious education and pastoral action. Academic approach." Length: 2,000 to 5,000 words. Pays $40 to $100.

THE MANITOBA TEACHER, 191 Harcourt St., Winnipeg, Manitoba, Canada R3J 3H2. (204)888-7961. Editor: Mrs. Miep van Raalte. For public school teachers and others in the public school system of Manitoba. 10 times a year; tabloid; 8-12 pages. Estab: 1919. Circ: 17,000. No payment. Phone queries OK. Submit seasonal or holiday material 3 months in advance. Photocopied submissions OK. SASE. Reports in 4 weeks. Free sample copy and writer's guidelines.
Nonfiction: Publishes historical and how-to articles; humor, informational, nostalgia, personal experience, personal opinion, technical and travel articles; interviews and profiles. All ms must relate to the interests of teachers in the Manitoba public schools. Length: 50-1,500 words. Query first or submit complete ms.
Photos: "We do not purchase photos, but are glad to consider b&w glossies; any size." Captions required.

THE MASSACHUSETTS TEACHER, 20 Ashburton Place, Boston MA 02108. Editor: Russell P. Burbank. For Massachusetts educators. Established in 1921. Monthly. Circulation: 67,000. Buys all rights. Buys "very few — one or two" mss per year. Pays on publication. Will send free sample copy and editorial guidelines sheet to writer on request. Will consider photocopied submissions. No simultaneous submissions. Reports in 1 month. Query first. Enclose S.A.S.E.

Nonfiction and Photos: "We want provocative education articles, features on classroom innovations that are two steps above the ordinary; well-researched authoritative articles (we check your facts) on items of interest to Massachusetts classroom public school teachers." Pays $25 minimum. Photos purchased with accompanying mss with extra payment and also purchased without accompanying mss. Captions required. Pays $5. B&w only. Size 7x9.

MEDIA & METHODS, 401 N. Broad St., Philadelphia PA 19108. Editor: Anthony Prete. For English and social studies teachers who have an abiding interest in humanistic and media-oriented education, plus a core of librarians, media specialists, filmmakers; the cutting edge of educational innovators. Magazine; 56 to 64 (8½x11) pages. Established in 1964. Monthly (September through May). Circulation: 50,000. Rights purchased vary with author and material. Normally buys all rights. About half of each issue is freelance material. Pays on publication. Free writer's guidelines to qualified writers. Will consider photocopied submissions. No simultaneous submissions. Reports on material in 2-4 months. Submit complete ms or query first. Enclose S.A.S.E.

Nonfiction: "We are looking for the middle school, high school or college educator who has something vital and interesting to say. Subjects include practical how-to articles with broad applicability to our readers, and innovative, challenging, conceptual-type stories that deal with educational change. Our style is breezy and conversational, occasionally offbeat. We make a concentrated effort to be non-sexist; mss filled with 'he', 'him', and 'mankind' (when the gender is unspecified) will pose unnecessary barriers to acceptance. We are a trade journal with a particular subject emphasis (media-oriented English and social studies), philosophical bent (humanistic, personal), and interest area (the practical and innovative)." Length: 2,500 words maximum. Pays $15 to $100.

MOMENTUM, National Catholic Educational Association, 1 Dupont Circle, Suite 350, Washington DC 20036. (202)293-5954. Editor: Carl Balcerak. For Catholic administrators and teachers, some parents and students, in all levels of education (preschool, elementary, secondary, higher). Quarterly magazine; 56 to 64 (8½x11) pages. Established in 1970. Circulation: 14,500. Buys all rights. Buys 28 to 36 mss per year. Payment on publication. Will send free sample copy to writer on request. Will consider photocopied and simultaneous submissions. Submit special issue material 2 months in advance. Query first. Reports in 2 weeks. Enclose S.A.S.E.

Nonfiction and Photos: "Articles concerned with educational philosophy, psychology, methodology, innovative programs, teacher training, etc. Catholic-oriented material. Book reviews on educational-religious topics. Innovative educational programs; financial and public relations programs, management systems applicable to nonpublic schools. No pious ruminations on pseudoreligious ideas. Also, avoid general topics, such as what's right (wrong) with Catholic education. In most cases, a straightforward, journalistic style with emphasis on practical examples, is preferred. Some scholarly writing, but little in the way of statistical. All material has Catholic orientation, with emphasis on professionalism; not sentimental or hackneyed treatment of religious topics." Length: 2,500 to 3,000 words. Pays 2¢ per word. Pays $5 for b&w glossy photos purchased with mss. Captions required.

NATIONAL ON-CAMPUS REPORT, 621 N. Sherman Ave., Suite 4, Madison WI 53704. (608)249-2455. Editor: William H. Haight. For education administrators, corporate marketing executives, journalists, directors of youth organizations. Established in 1972. Monthly. Not copyrighted. Buys 100 mss a year. Payment on publication. Will send free sample copy to writer on request. Write for copy of guidelines for writers. Will consider photocopied submissions. Reports on material in 1 month. Submit complete ms. Enclose S.A.S.E.

Nonfiction and Fillers: Short, timely articles relating to events and activities of college students. "No clippings of routine college news, only unusual items of possible national interest." Also buys newsbreaks and clippings related to college students and their activities. "We particularly want items about trends in student media: newspapers, magazines, campus radio, etc." Length: 25 to 800 words. Pays 10¢ to 12¢ per word.

NJEA REVIEW, New Jersey Education Association, 180 W. State St., Trenton NJ 08608. Editor-in-Chief: George Adams. For members of the association employed in New Jersey schools; teachers, administrators, etc. Monthly (September-May) magazine; 56 pages. Estab: 1922. Circ: 105,000. Pays on acceptance. Buys all rights, but may reassign following publication. Previously published submissions OK. SASE. Reports in 1-2 months. Free sample copy and writer's guidelines.

Nonfiction: How-to (classroom ideas), informational (curriculum area), personal opinion articles (on educational issues) and interviews with "names" in education. Length: 2,500-3,000 words maximum. Buys 15-20 mss a year. Query first or submit complete ms. Pays $35 minimum.

Photos: B&w (5x7 or 8x10) glossies purchased with ms. Query first. Pays $5 minimum. Model release required.

How To Break In: "Needed are well-researched articles (but no footnotes, please) on new trends in education (such as teaching and curriculum experimentation) and subject area articles. These are especially suitable if they grow directly out of experience in a New Jersey school or college. Human interest stories about people, teaching situations, or education in general also often acceptable."

PHI DELTA KAPPAN, 8th & Union Sts., Bloomington IN 47401. Editor: Stanley Elam. For educators, especially those in leadership positions, such as administrators; mid-forties; all hold BA degrees; one-third hold doctorates. Magazine; 72 (8½x11) pages. Established in 1915. Monthly, 10 issues, September through June. Circulation: 118,000. Generally buys all rights, but will sometimes reassign rights to author after publication (this varies with the author and material). Buys 10 to 15 mss a year. Payment on publication. Will send free sample copy to a writer on request. No photocopied or simultaneous submissions. Reports on material accepted for publication in 1 to 2 months. Returns rejected material within 2 months. Submit complete ms. Enclose S.A.S.E.

Nonfiction and Photos: Feature articles on education, emphasizing policy, trends, both sides of issues, controversial developments. Also, informational, how-to, personal experience, interview, profile, inspirational, humor, think articles, expose. "Our audience is scholarly but hardheaded." Length: 500 to 3,000 words. Pays $25 to $250 per ms. Pays average photographer's rates for b&w photos purchased with mss, but captions are required. Will purchase photos on assignment. Sizes: 8x10 or 5x7 preferred.

How To Break In: "We want research-based, informative material. Analysis, not opinion, is our emphasis. Submit the complete ms."

THE PROGRESSIVE TEACHER, 2678 Henry St., Augusta GA 30908. Editor: M.S. Adcock. For teachers, school superintendents, school board members, and others engaged in the instruction of children and youth. Magazine. Established in 1899. Every 2 months. Circulation: 4,350. Copyrighted. Pays on publication. Will send free sample copy to writer on request. Submit complete ms. Enclose S.A.S.E.

Nonfiction: Material of interest and help to teachers and other professional educators on methods, units of work. Professional articles for school administrators and others engaged in guidance and instruction. Especially interested in material other educators have found helpful. Length: 1,500 to 2,000 words. Pays $1 per column inch.

READING IMPROVEMENT, Project Innovation, 1362 Santa Cruz Ct., Chula Vista CA 92010. (714)421-9277. Editor: Dr. Russell N. Cassel. For teachers, educators, reading teachers, and persons interested in the improvement of the teaching of reading. Magazine; 64 pages. Established in 1962. Circulation: 2,500. Acquires all rights, but may reassign rights to author after publication. Pays in contributor's copies. Will send sample copy to writer on request. Write for copy of guidelines for writers. Reports on material accepted for publication in 30 days. Returns rejected material in 6 weeks. Query first. Enclose S.A.S.E.

Nonfiction: Materials dealing with the teaching of reading-theory, research, and innovations in actual practice; foreign language and bilingual teaching, and matters pertaining to early childhood education. Assignments are sometimes made for book summaries, research, theory, practices, and matters pertaining to the teaching of reading. All material follows the *APA Publications Manual.*

SCHOOL ARTS MAGAZINE, 72 Printers Bldg., Worcester MA 01608. Editor: George F. Horn. For art and craft teachers and supervisors from grade school through high school. Monthly, except July and August. Will send a sample copy to a writer on request. Pays on publication. Reports in 90 days. Enclose S.A.S.E.

Nonfiction and Photos: Articles, with photos, on art and craft activities in schools. Length: 1,000 words. Payment is negotiable but begins at $20 per article.

SCHOOL SHOP, 416 Longshore Dr., Ann Arbor MI 48107. Editor: Lawrence W. Prakken. For "industrial and technical education personnel." Special issue in April deals with varying topics for which mss are solicited. Monthly. Circulation: 45,000. Buys all rights. Pays on publication. Query first: "direct or indirect connection with the field of industrial and/or technical education preferred." Submit mss to Howard Kahn, Managing Editor. Submit seasonal material 3 months in advance. Reports in 6 weeks. SASE.

Nonfiction and Photos: Uses articles pertinent to the various teaching areas in industrial education (woodwork, electronics, drafting, machine shop, graphic arts, computer training, etc.). "Outlook should be on innovation in educational programs, processes, or projects which directly apply to the industrial-technical education area." Buys how-to's, personal experience and think pieces, interviews, humor, coverage of new products. Length: 500 to 2,000 words. Pays $15 to $40. 8x10 photos purchased with ms.

SCIENCE ACTIVITIES, Room 510, 4000 Albermarle St., N.W., Washington DC 20016. (202)362-6445. Publisher: Cornelius W. Vahle, Jr. Editor: Jane Powers Weldon. For science teachers (high school, junior high school, elementary and college). Bimonthly magazine; 40-48 pages. Estab. 1969. Circ. 6,500. Buys 50 mss/year. Pays on publication. Sample copy for $2. Reports in 90 days. SASE.

Nonfiction and Photos: "Articles on creative science projects for the classroom, including experiments, explorations, and projects in every phase of the biological, physical and behavioral sciences." Length: 1,500-3,000 words. Pays $10/printed page. Photos purchased with ms; no additional payment. Captions required.

SCIENCE AND CHILDREN, National Science Teachers Association, 1742 Connecticut Ave., N.W., Washington DC 20009. (202)265-4150. Editor-in-Chief: Phyllis Marcuccio. Emphasizes elementary school science for teachers and educational personnel of all levels, kindergarten through college. Monthly (8 issues during academic year) magazine; 48 pages. Estab: 1963. Circ: 23,000. No payment except for subscription. Phone queries OK. Submit seasonal/holiday material 6-8 months in advance. Photocopied submissions OK. SASE. Reports in 2-3 months. Free sample copy and writer's guidelines.

Nonfiction: How-to (science projects and activities for elementary students); informational (relating to science or elementary science programs); inspirational (relating to children and science); personal experience (with an aspect of elementary school science); photo feature (relating to science); research on science education. Submit complete ms. Length: 1,500 words maximum.

Photos: Used with mss. Send prints. Prefers 8x10 b&w glossies. Model release required.

Columns, Departments: Research in Education. Current research, in particular, relating to science at the elementary level. Send complete ms. Length: 1,200-1,500 words.

Rejects: "Material that would not be appropriate for elementary school level. The magazine is read by teachers. It is not a children's audience. However, the teachers look for material they can use in the classroom or material that would be relevant to them."

SIGHTLINES, Educational Film Library Association, Inc., 43 W. 61st St., New York NY 10023. (212)246-4533. Editor: Nadine Covert. Emphasizes the non-theatrical film world for librarians in university and public libraries, independent filmmakers, film teachers on the high school and college level, film programmers in the community, university, religious organizations, film curators in museums. Quarterly magazine; 32 pages. Estab: 1967. Circ: 3,000. Pays on publication. Buys all rights, but may reassign following publication. Phone queries OK. SASE. Reports in 2 months. Free sample copy.

Nonfiction: Informational (on the production, distribution and programming of non-theatrical films), interview (with filmmakers who work in 16mm, video; who make documentary, avantgarde, children's, and personal films), new product, personal opinion (for regular Freedom To View column), and profile (of filmmakers in the 16mm, video non-commercial field). Buys 4 mss/issue. Query. Length: 4,000-6,000 words. Pay 2½¢/word.

Photos: Purchased with accompanying ms. Captions required. Offers no additional payment for photos accepted with accompanying ms. Model release required.

Columns/Departments: Who's Who in Filmmaking (interview or profile of filmmaker or video artist who works in the non-commerical field). Buys 1 ms/issue. Query. Pays 2½¢/word. Open to suggestions for new columns or departments.

SPECIAL EDUCATION: FORWARD TRENDS, 12 Hollycroft Ave., London NW3 7QL., England. Editor: Margaret Peter. Quarterly. Estab: 1974. Circ: 6,500. Pays on publication. Free sample copy. SAE and International Reply Coupons.

Nonfiction: Articles on the education of all types of handicapped children. "The aim of this journal of the National Council for Special Education is to provide articles on special education and handicapped children which will keep readers informed of practical and theoretical developments not only in education but in the many other aspects of the education and welfare of the handicapped. While we hope that articles will lead students and others to further related reading, their main function is to give readers an adequate introduction to a topic which they may not have an opportunity to pursue further. References should therefore be selective and mainly easily accessible ones. It is important, therefore, that articles of a more technical nature (e.g., psychology, medical, research reviews) should, whenever possible, avoid unnecessary technicalities or ensure that necessary technical terms or expressions are made clear to nonspecialists by the context or by the provision of brief additional explanations or examples." Length: 750 to 3,750 words. Payment by arrangement.

TEACHER, Macmillan Professional Magazines, 1 Fawcett Place, Greenwich CT 06830. (203)869-8585. Editor-in-Chief: Joan S. Baranski. Emphasizes education at the elementary school level. Monthly magazine; 150 pages. Estab: 1883. Circ: 250,000. Pays on publication. Buys all rights, but may reassign following publication. Submit seasonal/holiday material 6 months in advance. Photocopied submissions OK. SASE. Reports in 3 months. Free sample copy and writer's guidelines.
Nonfiction: Jeanette Moss, articles editor. "In evaluating potential articles for *Teacher,* we try to keep one thought uppermost in mind: Can an elementary school teacher gain some practical help from this material? We're most interested in the article that says, 'Here's how I did it and it works.' We want teachers talking to teachers as peers who understand and face similar problems. We are not interested in material that is basically theoretical or in the form of a research paper or a textbook-style unit. If you want to describe a successful project or unit, put it into article form." Publishes interviews, personal experience and personal opinion articles; photo features and profiles. Length: 1,000-1,500 words. Buys 15 mss per issue. Query first. Pays $50 minimum.
Photos: Vincent Ceci, department editor. B&w and color used with mss. Query first. No additional payment. Model release required.

TODAY'S CATHOLIC TEACHER, 2451 E. River Rd., Suite 200, Dayton OH 45439. (513)294-5785. Editor: Ruth A. Matheny. For educators (teachers, administrators, school board members) and parents interested in the nonpublic school, particularly the Catholic school. Magazine published 8 times during the school year; 48 to 96 (8¼x11) pages. Established in 1967. Circulation: 70,000. Not copyrighted. Buys 25 mss a year. Payment on publication. Will send sample copy to writer for 50¢. Write for copy of guidelines for writers. Will not consider photocopied or simultaneous submissions. Submit seasonal material (Christmas, Thanksgiving, Easter—successful programs or celebrations) 2 to 3 months in advance. Reports on material accepted for publication in 2 months. Returns rejected material promptly if not to be considered at all. Query first or submit complete ms. Enclose S.A.S.E.
Nonfiction and Photos: "Informative features describing philosophy, innovative practices, practical solutions to common problems of Catholic schools. Successful public relations programs that lead to increased parental and community involvement in the Catholic school are of special interest. Too many of the mss coming to us are of a too general nature, offering nothing new to inspire readers to thought or action. At the same time, anything too localized has no place in a national magazine. Anything that is sound pedagogically is of interest to us, but we prefer that it have a Catholic or other nonpublic school application. Prefer straightforward, readable, lively style, as opposed to profound, scholarly approach. First-person reactions and direct quotations are a 'plus'." Length: 500 to 1,500 words. Pays $15 to $75. No additional payment is made for b&w photos used with mss.

TODAY'S EDUCATION: NEA JOURNAL, National Education Association, 1201 16th St., N.W., Washington DC 20036. (202)833-5442. Editor: Walter A. Graves. Copyrighted. "We buy one-time editorial use of freelance photos." Does not pay for submissions, except photos. No query necessary. Enclose S.A.S.E.
Nonfiction: Articles on teaching methods and practices; human interest, popular style. "We generally accept manuscripts from teachers who are members of the local, state, and national education associations since the magazine belongs to those teachers. However, we occasionally buy mss from freelance writers who are not eligible to be regular members of the National Education Association since they are not teachers. Such writers are, of course, not eligible to be active NEA members and therefore we do not require membership in those cases." Length: 800 to 2,000 words. No payment.

Photos: Photo Editor: Walter Graves. Buys singles and photo series of school situations and scenes. Requires model releases. 8x10 b&w. Pays $25 for b&w.

TRAINING FILM PROFILES, Olympic Media Information, 71 W. 23 St., New York NY 10010. (212)675-4500. Editor: Walt Carroll. For colleges, community colleges, libraries, training directors, manpower specialists, education and training services, career development centers, audiovisual specialists, administrators. Serial in looseleaf format, published every 2 months. Established in 1967. Circulation: 1,000. Buys all rights. Buys 200 to 240 mss a year. Payment on publication. Will send free samples to writer on request. "Send resume of your experience to introduce yourself." Will not consider photocopied or simultaneous submissions. Reports on material accepted for publication in 2 months. Returns rejected material in 1 month. Query first. Enclose S.A.S.E.
Nonfiction: "Reviews of instructional films, filmstrips, videotapes and cassettes, sound-slide programs and the like. We have a highly specialized, rigid format that must be followed without exception. Ask us for sample 'Profiles' to see what we mean. Besides job training areas, we are also interested in the areas of values and personal self-development, upward mobility in the world of work, social change, futuristics, management training, problem solving, and adult education." Pays $5 to $15 per review.
How To Break In: "Contact us first. Unsolicited manuscripts are not wanted. If part of your full-time work is to preview audiovisual materials, you probably can do something for us."

Electricity

Publications classified here aim at electrical engineers, electrical contractors, and others who build, design, and maintain systems connecting and supplying homes, businesses, and industries with power. Journals dealing with generating and supplying power to users will be found in the Power and Power Plants category. Publications for appliance servicemen and dealers will be found in the Home Furnishings classification.

ELECTRICAL APPARATUS, Barks Publications, Inc., 400 N. Michigan Ave., Chicago IL 60611. (312)321-9440. Editorial Director: Elsie Dickson. Editor-in-Chief: H.B. Barks. Emphasizes industrial electrical maintenance and repair. Monthly magazine; 60 pages. Estab: 1948. Circ: 15,000. Pays on acceptance. Buys all rights, but may reassign following publication. Phone queries OK. Submit seasonal/holiday material 3 months in advance. SASE. Reports in 2 weeks. Sample copy $1.50.
Nonfiction: Publishes how-to, informational, and technical articles. Buys 1-2/issue. Length: 1,000-2,000 words. Query first. Pays $50-200.
Photos: B&w glossies (5x7 or 8x10) purchased with mss or on assignment. Query first. Pays $10-25.

ELECTRICAL CONTRACTOR, 7315 Wisconsin Ave., Washington DC 20014. (301)657-3110. Editor: Larry C. Osius. For electrical contractors. Monthly. Buys first rights, reprint rights, and simultaneous rights. Will send free sample copy on request. Freelance material bought on assignment following query. Usually reports in 1 month. Enclose S.A.S.E.
Nonfiction and Photos: Installation articles showing informative application of new techniques and products. Slant is product and method contributing to better, faster, more economical construction process. Length: "1 column to 4 pages." Pays $60 per printed page, including photos and illustrative material. Photos should be sharp, reproducible glossies, 5x7 and up.

ELECTRICAL CONTRACTOR & MAINTENANCE SUPERVISOR, 481 University Ave., Toronto, Ont., M5W 1A7, Canada. Editor: George McNevin. For "middle-aged men who either run their own businesses or are in fairly responsible management positions. They range from university graduates to those with public school education only." Established in 1952. Monthly. Circ. 13,400. Rights purchased vary with author and material. "Depending on author's wish, payment is either on acceptance or on publication." Will send a sample copy to a writer on request. Query first. Enclose S.A.E. and International Reply Coupons.
Nonfiction and Photos: "Articles that have some relation to electrical construction or maintenance and business management. The writer should include as much information as possible pertaining to the electrical field. We're not interested in articles that are too general and philosophical. Don't belabor the obvious, particularly on better business management. We're interested in coverage of labor difficulties." Buys informational articles, how-to's, profiles, coverage

of successful business operations, new product pieces, and technical articles. Length: "no minimum or maximum." Pays "8¢ a published word or 6¢ a word on submitted mss, unless other arrangements are made." Photos purchased with mss or on assignment; captions optional. Pays "$7 for the first print and $2 for each subsequent print, plus photographer's expenses."

Electronics and Communications

Listed here are publications for electronics engineers, radio and TV broadcasting managers, electronic equipment operators, and builders of electronic communication systems and equipment, including stereos, television sets, and radio-TV broadcasting systems. Journals for professional announcers or communicators will be found under Journalism; those for electronic appliance retailers will be found in Home Furnishings; publications on computer design and data processing systems will be found in Data Processing. Publications for electronics enthusiasts or stereo hobbyists will be found in Hobby and Craft or in Music in the Consumer Publications section.

BROADCAST, Communications Software Limited, 111A Wardour St., London W1V 3TD, U.K. (01)439-9756. Editor-in-Chief: Rod Allen. Emphasizes broadcasting for a totally professional audience in the TV and radio industries in the U.K. and Europe. Weekly magazine; 28 pages. Estab: 1973. Circ: 3,500. Buys first British serial rights. Enclose International Reply Coupons.
Nonfiction: Information articles (professional only); interviews with important industry figures; new product articles (if genuinely new and not promotional); technical articles (by broadcast professionals). Length: 3,000 words maximum. Query first. Pays £20-27/1,000 words.
Fillers: Newsbreaks are published only if they're important to the trade. Length: 25-250 words. Query first. Pays £2-10.
How To Break In: "The problem is finding people who understand the needs of our European readership, who aren't particularly interested in the internal wranglings of the U.S. broadcasting industry. There aren't too many of them around, but we'd sure like to be in touch with anyone who fills the bill."

BROADCAST ENGINEERING, 1014 Wyandotte, Kansas City MO 64105. Editor: Ron Merrell. For "owners, managers, and top technical people at AM, FM, TV stations, cable TV operators, educational and industrial TV and business communications, as well as recording studios." Established in 1959. Monthly. Circulation: 30,000. Buys all rights, but will reassign rights to author after publication. Buys about 50 mss a year. Pays on acceptance; "for a series, we pay for each part on publication." Will send a sample copy to a writer on request. Write for copy of guidelines for writers. Will not consider photocopied submissions. Submit seasonal material at least 3 months in advance. Reports in 2 weeks. Query first. Enclose S.A.S.E.
Nonfiction and Photos: Wants technical features dealing with design, installation, modification, and maintenance of radio and television broadcast station equipment; interested in features on educational and cable TV systems, other material of interest to communications engineers and technicians, and on self-designed and constructed equipment for use in broadcast and communications fields. "Currently looking for business, industrial, and medical application of video systems. This includes the use of video equipment in varied security systems; and instructional TV how-to's with pictures; articles on overcoming problems. Articles start with the evolution of the problem and resolve with the solution. We use a technical, but not textbook, style. Our publication is mostly how-to and it operates as a forum, talking with readers, not down to them. We reject material when it's far too general, not on target, or not backed by evidence or proof. Some articles and photos need releases and they are seldom included. We're overstocked with build-it-yourself articles, except for our 'Station to Station' column, where we take short-shorts and pay up to $25. We're especially interested now in articles on recording studios and improving facilities and techniques." Length: 1,500 to 2,000 words for features, with drawings and photos, if possible. Pays $75 to $200 for features and $15 to $25 for "Station to Station." Photos purchased with and without mss; captions required. Pays $5 to $10 for b&w, pays $10 to $35 for color (2¼x2¼ color transparencies or larger).
How To Break In: "Offer new solutions to old problems and include pictures of people in action on these problems."

BROADCAST EQUIPMENT TODAY, Diversified Publications Limited, Box 423, Station J, Toronto, Ont., Canada M4J 4Y8. (416)463-5304. Editor-in-Chief: Doug Loney. Emphasizes broadcast engineering. Bimonthly magazine; 50 pages. Estab: 1975. Circ: 3,600. Pays on publi-

cation. Buys all rights. Phone queries OK. Photocopied and previously published submissions OK. SASE. Free writer's guidelines.
Nonfiction: Technical articles on developments in broadcast engineering, especially pertaining to Canada. Query. Length: 1,000-2,000 words. Pays $50-150.
Photos: Purchased with accompanying ms. Captions required. Query for b&w or color. Total purchase price for a ms includes payment for photos.

BROADCAST MANAGEMENT/ENGINEERING, 295 Madison Ave., New York NY 10017. (212)685-5320. Editor: J. Lippke. For general managers, chief engineers, program directors of radio and TV stations. Established in 1964. Monthly. Circulation: 28,000. Buys all rights, but will reassign rights to author after publication. Buys 1 to 3 mss a year. Pays on publication. Reports in 4 weeks. Query first. Enclose S.A.S.E.
Nonfiction: Articles on cost-saving ideas; use of equipment, new programming ideas for serving the public. Tone of all material is professional to professional. "We're interested in the profile or program sound of competitive stations in a market." Length: 1,200 to 3,000 words. Pays $25 to $100.

BROADCASTER, 77 River St., Toronto, Ont. M5A 3P2 Canada. (416)363-6111. Editor: Michael L. Pollock. For the Canadian "communications industry — radio, television, cable, ETV, advertisers, and their agencies." Established in 1942. Monthly. Circulation: 10,000. Buys all rights, but may reassign rights to writer after publication. Buys 50 to 60 mss per year. Pays on publication. Will send sample copy to writer for $2. Will not consider photocopied or simultaneous submissions. Reporting time for mss accepted for publication: variable. Returns rejected material "as soon as possible." Enclose S.A.E. and International Reply Coupons.
Nonfiction: "Publish profiles, some technical and general interest articles about the broadcasting industry almost exclusively Canadian. Style is relatively free but articles should follow, for the most part, format of magazine. Although the magazine is basically a trade publication, it has far more general appeal than magazines of this type." Length: 1,000 to 2,000 words. Pays $25 to $200.
Photos: "Depending on circumstances, ways of purchase vary." Captions required. Pays $25 for b&w; $100 to $150 for color. Print or negative should be submitted for b&w; submit transparency for color.

CANADIAN ELECTRONICS ENGINEERING, 481 University Ave., Toronto M5W 1A7, Ont., Canada. (416)595-1811, Ext. 636. Editor: Cliff Hand. For technically trained users of professional electronics products. Monthly. Buys Canadian serial rights. Pays on acceptance. Will send free sample copy to a writer on request. Will consider cassette submissions. Query first with brief outline of article. Reports in 2 to 4 weeks. Enclose S.A.E. and International Reply Coupons.
Nonfiction: Science and technology involving professional electronic products and techniques. Must have direct relevance to work being done in Canada. Length: maximum about 1,500 words. Pays 5¢ to 8¢ per word depending on importance of subject, amount of research, and ability of writer.
Photos: Purchased with mss. 4x5 to 8x10 b&w glossy prints; must provide useful information on story subject. Pays average professional rates for time required on any particular assignment.

COMMUNICATIONS NEWS, 402 W. Liberty Drive, Wheaton IL 60187. (312)653-4040. Editor: Bruce Howat. For managers of communications systems including telephone companies, CATV systems, broadcasting stations and private systems. Established in 1964. Monthly. Circulation: 36,000. Buys all rights. Buys 3 to 10 mss a year. Payment on publication. Will send free sample copy to writer on request. Will consider photocopied submissions. Will not consider simultaneous submissions. Reports on material accepted for publication in 4 weeks. Returns rejected material in 3 weeks. Query first or submit complete ms. Enclose S.A.S.E.
Nonfiction: Case histories of problem-solving for communications systems. Factual reporting about new communications products, systems and techniques. Must be terse, factual, helpful. Informational news and how-to articles; think pieces. Length: 1,600 words maximum. Pays 3¢ per word.
Photos: Department Editor: Ken Bourne. Purchased with accompanying ms with no additional payment or without accompanying ms. Captions optional. Pays $10 for b&w glossy prints.

COMMUNICATIONS RETAILING, 375 E. 75th St., New York NY 10021. Publisher: Richard Ekstract. Editor: Walter Salm. For retailers who sell citizens' band radios, monitor scanners, and phone answerers Newspaper; 56 (10x14) pages. Special show issues include CES

(January and June) and PC Show (February). Estab. 1975. Monthly. Circ. 25,000. Buys all rights. Pays on publication. Free sample copy. Photocopied submissions OK. Submit material for special issues 6 weeks in advance. Reports in 2 weeks. Query first. Enclose S.A.S.E.

Nonfiction: "Anything applicable to the trade we serve, but not generalized pieces. Articles should be specifically oriented to the personal communications trade." Informational, how-to, personal experience, interview, profile, humor, travel, reviews of equipment, spot news, successful business operations, new products, merchandising techniques, technical articles. Length: 100 to 2,000 words. Pays 7¢ to 10¢ a word.

How To Break In: "The person who writes successfully for us must have an intimate knowledge of 2-way radio merchandising, and he must be able to write fluently on the subject. We are in greatest need of freelance material in December, January, early February, and May."

ELECTRONIC BUYERS' NEWS, 280 Community Dr., Great Neck NY 11021. (516)829-5880. Editor: James Moran. The purchasing publication for the electronics industry. Newspaper; 48 pages. Estab: 1972. Circ: 35,000. Pays on publication. Usually buys first rights. SASE. Reports on accepted material in 2-3 months. Rejected material not returned unless requested. Free sample copy.

Nonfiction: "Each issue features a specific theme or electronic component. Articles are usually accepted from companies involved with that component. Other stories are accepted occasionally from authors knowledgeable in that field." All material is aimed directly at the purchasing profession. Length: open. Pays $100 minimum.

ELECTRONICS INDUSTRY, Lester Star, Ltd., 375 Upper Richmond Rd., W., London SW14 FNX England. (01)878-4852. Editor-in-Chief: Mike Dance. Managing Editor: Simon Henley. For professional electronic engineers. Monthly magazine; 70 pages. Circ: 20,000. Pays on publication. Buys all United Kingdom rights. Phone queries OK. SAE and International Reply Coupons. Reports in 1 month. Sample copy $5 plus postage. Free writer's guidelines.

Nonfiction: How-to articles (make best use of electronics devices); informational (comprehensive or specialist studies on some aspect of electronics technology); technical articles. Buys 2/issue. Query. Length: 1,000-4,000 words. Pays $40/published page (about 1,300 words).

Photos: No additional payment for b&w glossies used with ms. Send prints with ms.

How To Break In: "The freelancer will generally be an electronics graduate in order to be able to write in sufficient depth about the subject chosen."

ELECTRONIC PACKAGING AND PRODUCTION, 222 W. Adams St., Chicago Il 60606. (312)263-4866. Editor: Donald J. Levinthal. For engineers and designers involved in electronic equipment prototype design and volume production. Magazine; 175 (8x11) pages. Established in 1960. Circulation: 26,500. Buys all rights. Buys 40 mss a year. Pays on publication. Will send free sample copy to writer on request. Write for copy of guidelines for writers. Will consider photocopied submissions. No simultaneous submissions. Reports in 2 to 3 weeks. Query first. Enclose S.A.S.E.

Nonfiction and Photos: Subject matter to be related to the physical design, production and testing of electronic equipment — PC boards, cooling, artwork generation, microelectronics fabrication, etc. New and interesting techniques in packaging, production and testing. Semiconductor and hybrid design and fabrication; systems packaging techniques; QC/QA and production testing. Should be detailed and technical and of benefit to the reader. "We specialize in the physical design and implementation of electronic equipment and are not concerned with electronic circuit design. An initial outline and abstract should be submitted for approval." Prefers not to see lab report style or articles that are sales pitch oriented. Length: about 2,000 words. Pays $25 per published page. Columns and departments use news items involving up-to-date happenings in packaging and production, trends, etc. Length: 500 words. Payment to be negotiated. No additional payment for photos used with mss. Captions optional.

How To Break In: "Must be involved in science or engineering and be qualified to write on a given subject. Send outline, abstract and affiliations."

ELECTRONIC TECHNICIAN/DEALER, 1 E. First St., Duluth MN 55802. (218)727-8511. Editor: J.W. Phipps. For owners, managers, technician employees of consumer electronic sales and/or service firms. Magazine; 72 pages. Established in 1953. Monthly. Circulation: 70,000. Buys all rights. Buys about 12 mss a year. Pays on acceptance. Will send sample copy to writer on request. Write for copy of guidelines for writers. Will consider simultaneous submissions. No photocopied submissions. Reports immediately. Query first or submit complete ms. Enclose S.A.S.E.

Nonfiction and Photos: Feature articles of a practical nature about consumer electronic technology and servicing techniques; business profiles and/or business management. No generalization; must have concise, practical orientation; a specific approach. No business management articles which are too general and superficial. Informational, how-to, interview, profile, technical articles and those on successful business operations. Length: 1,200 to 2,500 words. Pays $100 to $175. No additional payment for b&w photos purchased with mss. Captions required. Will also consider suggestions for new columns or departments.

ELECTRONICS, 1221 Avenue of the Americas, New York NY 10019. Editor: Kemp Anderson. Biweekly. Buys all rights. Query first. Reports in 2 weeks. Enclose S.A.S.E.
Nonfiction: Uses copy about research, development, design and production of electronic devices and management of electronic manufacturing firms; articles on "descriptions of new circuit systems, components, design techniques, how specific electronic engineering problems were solved; interesting applications of electronics; step-by-step, how-to design articles; nomographs, charts, tables for solution of repetitive design problems." Length: 1,000 to 3,500 words. $30 per printed page.

ELECTRONICS RETAILING, 645 Stewart Ave., Garden City NY 11530. Editor: Tom Ewing. For independent, department, chain and discount stores; buyers of consumer electronics (hi-fi, TV, autosound, calculators, electronic watches, and related products). Tabloid; 24 pages. Established in 1975. Monthly. Circulation: 35,000. Buys all rights, but will reassign rights to author after publication. Buys about 500 mss a year. Pays on publication. Will send free sample copy to writer on request. Write for copy of guidelines for writers. No photocopied or simultaneous submissions. S.A.S.E.
Nonfiction and Photos: "We are looking primarily for hard news stories about the retailers in our audience. We prefer a straight news style and more extensive coverage of broader product areas. Length: 100-500 words. Pays 10¢ a word. B&w photos (5x7 or larger; no Polaroids) should support accompanying ms. Pays $10.
How To Break In: "Query first. We have occasional openings for stringers in some parts of the country."

MICROWAVES, 50 Essex St., Rochelle Park NJ 07662. (201)843-0550. Editor-in-Chief: Stacy Bearse. For microwave engineers and engineering managers. Monthly magazine; 80 to 100 (8x10) pages. Established in 1962. Circulation: 40,000. Buys all rights. Buys 24 to 36 mss a year. Payment on publication. Will send sample copy to writer on request. Write for copy of guidelines for writers. Will consider photocopied submissions. Reports in 2 months. Query first. "Submit outline and send resume of technical writing experience."
Nonfiction: Interested in material on research and development in microwave technology and economic news that affects the industry. Pays $30 per published page (approximately 840 words per published page) plus "25% bonus if you are a second-time author and a 50% bonus if you publish with us 3 times or more."
How To Break In: "Ask yourself these questions: Does my subject have broad appeal to microwave designers? Is my subject timely? Does my information have practical value in design, application or management? If you can explain your design ideas to fellow engineers at your lab, you can be sure you can do the same to readers of *MicroWaves*."

P. D. CUE, Box 5348, Lancaster PA 17601. For television station program executives who are in charge of local programming. Magazine published every 2 months; 36 to 48 (7½x10) pages. Established in 1974. Circulation: 1,500. Buys all rights for 6 months. Buys 2 or 3 mss per issue. Payment on acceptance. Will send sample copy to writer for $1. Reports on accepted material in 10 days. Returns rejected material in 1 week. Query first. Enclose S.A.S.E.
Nonfiction and Photos: Unique ideas on local television programs (not network) with cost figures, amount of film used, manpower, audience acceptance, camera techniques, equipment used, amount of time spent planning and producing. Interested in any unique approach to local television programs that are comparatively new on the scene. "Many submissions are just too general. Sound like they have been rewritten from a news clipping." Uses interviews and material on successful business operations and technical aspects of the industry. Length: 1,000 to 1,500 words. Pays $25 to $50. No additional payment is made for b&w (3x5, 5x7 or 8x10) photos used with mss. Captions required.

PAY TELEVISION MAGAZINE, P.O. Box 2430, Hollywood CA 90028. (213)876-2219. Editor: Al Preiss. For management executives of the communications industry. Magazine; 52 pages. Established in 1975. Every 2 months. Circulation: 5,000. Rights purchased vary with author and material. Usually buys "magazine" rights. Pays on publication. Will send sample copy to writer for $5. Write for copy of guidelines for writers. No photocopied or simultaneous submissions. Reports in 30 days. Query first. Enclose S.A.S.E.

Nonfiction and Photos: Articles on the need for pay television. Profiles. Length: 5 double-spaced, typed pages. Pays minimum of $150. B&w photos purchased with or without mss. Captions required. Pays minimum of $25.

RADIO & TELEVISION WEEKLY, BMT Publications, Inc., 254 W. 31st St., New York NY 10001. (212)594-4120. Editor-in-Chief: Edward J. Walter. For "management and sales personnel of electronics distributors, who buy component parts from manufacturers and resell them to end users. Wo do not cover radio, TV, or appliance firms." Weekly tabloid; 32 pages. Estab: 1918. Circ: 10,000. Pays on publication. Buys simultaneous rights. Phone queries OK. Submit seasonal or holiday material 2 months in advance. Simultaneous and photocopied submissions OK. SASE. Reports in 2 weeks. Free sample copy and writer's guidelines.
Nonfiction: Publishes informational and historical articles, news items and success stories.
Photos: Purchased with or without accompanying ms or on assignment. Captions required. Pays $5-10 for 8½x11 b&w glossy prints. Query. Total purchase price for a ms includes payment for photos.

RADIO-TV EDITORIAL JOURNAL, Foundation for American Communications, 20121 Ventura Blvd., Woodland Hills CA 91364. (213)999-6772. Editor-in-Chief: George Mair. For editorial writers, news directors, and general managers of radio and television stations. Monthly magazine; 32 pages. Estab: 1976. Circ: 10,600. Pays on publication. Buys all rights. Phone queries OK. Submit seasonal/holiday material 2 months in advance. Simultaneous, photocopied and previously published submissions OK. SASE. Reports in 1 month. Free sample copy and writer's guidelines.
Nonfiction: Informational (political and social issues), personal opinion. Buys 12 mss a year. Query. Length: 1,000-2,000 words. Pays $25.

TELEPHONY MAGAZINE, 53 W. Jackson Blvd., Chicago IL 60604. Editor: Leo Anderson. For people employed by telephone operating companies. Weekly. Buys all rights. Pays on publication. Query first. Enclose S.A.S.E.
Nonfiction: Technical or management articles describing a new or better way of doing something at a telephone company. "Feature articles range from highly technical state-of-the-art presentations to down-to-earth case studies. Case-history articles should cover a new or particularly efficient way of handling a specific job at a specific telephone company." Length: 1,500 words. Generally pays $30 per published magazine page.

TELEVISION INTERNATIONAL MAGAZINE, P.O. Box 2430, Hollywood CA 90028. (213)876-2219. Editor: Al Preiss. For management/creative members of the TV industry. Established in 1956. Every 2 months. Circulation: 8,000 (USA); 4,000 (foreign). Rights purchased vary with author and material. Pays on publication. Will send sample copy to writer for $2. Will consider photocopied submissions. No simultaneous submissions. Reports in 30 days. Query first. Enclose S.A.S.E.
Nonfiction and Photos: Articles on all aspects of TV programming. "This is not a house organ for the industry. We invite articles critical of TV." Pays $150 to $350. Column material of 600 to 800 words. Pays $75. Will consider suggestions for new columns and departments. Pays $25 for b&w photos purchased with mss; $35 for color transparencies.

VIDEO SYSTEMS, Intertec Publishing Corp., Box 12901, Overland Park KS 66212. (913)888-4664. Editor/Publisher: George Laughead. For qualified persons engaged in various applications of closed-circuit communications who have operating responsibilities and purchasing authority for equipment and software in the video systems field. Monthly magazine; 56 pages. Estab: 1976. Circ: 15,000. Pays on acceptance. Buys all rights, but may reassign following publication. Phone queries OK. Photocopied submissions and previously published work OK. SASE. Reports in 2 months. Free sample copy and guidelines for writers.
Nonfiction: "All material must present an authoritative view of the professional video/audio/visual media field. Must be useful information for persons working in the field. We do not want equipment roundups or listings. We are not a personality magazine. We do not care much about which people are using video, but want to know what people are doing with it — on jobs, in schools, etc." Publishes how-to articles (any area of video/audio production); informational (new video systems; use of equipment); historical (any area of television or visual media); interviews (with leaders of media field); new product (video/audio); personal experience (use of video equipment); technical articles (video/audio equipment). Length: 1,500-4,000 words. Buys 4 mss an issue. Query first. Pays $100-200.
Photos: B&w glossies (8x10) purchased with or without mss, or on assignment. Payment for

b&w varies, but pays maximum of $100 for 35mm or 2¼x2¼ color transparencies used on cover. Model release required.
Fillers: Buys 2 jokes, gags, or anecdotes on CCTV television per issue. Pays $10-25.

Engineering and Technology

Publications for electrical engineers are classified under Electricity; journals for electronics engineers are classified with the Electronics and Communications publications.

CANADIAN CONSULTING ENGINEER, 1450 Don Mills Rd., Don Mills, Ont. M3B 2X7, Canada. Managing Editor: Russell B. Noble. For private engineering consultants. Buys exclusive rights preferably; occasionally exclusive to field or country. Payment on publication. Reports in 15 days. Enclose S.A.E. and International Reply Coupons.
Nonfiction: "We serve our readers with articles on how to start, maintain, develop and expand private engineering consultancies. Emphasis is on this management aspect. We are not a how-to magazine. We don't tell our readers how to design a bridge, a high rise, a power station or a sewage plant. Paradoxically, we are interested if the bridge falls down, for engineers are vitally interested in Errors and Omissions claims (much like journalists are about libel suits). We have articles on income tax, legal problems associated with consulting engineering, public relations and interviews with political figures. When we write about subjects like pollution, we write from a conceptual point of view; i.e., how the environmental situation will affect their practices. But because our readers are also concerned citizens, we include material which might interest them from a social, or educational point of view. The word to remember is *conceptual* (new concepts or interesting variations of old ones)." Usually pays $50 to $175, but this is dependent on length and extent of research required.

DESIGN ENGINEERING, Maclean-Hunter, Ltd., 481 University Ave., Toronto, Ontario, Canada M5W 1A7. (416)595-1811. Editor-in-Chief: Bryan S. Rogers. Emphasizes O.E.M. and in-plant design engineering for professional engineers, consultants, engineering schools, draftsmen, plant engineers, product development engineers, R&D departments. Monthly magazine; 60 pages. Estab: 1955. Circ: 14,000. Pays on acceptance. Buys first North American serial rights. Phone queries OK. Previously published submissions OK. SASE. Reports in 2 weeks. Free sample copy and writer's guidelines.
Nonfiction: How-to (on use of materials, new techniques in successful design engineering, value engineering); informational (new products, trends, state-of-the-art articles on fluid power, mechanical power, electric/electronics, drawing office, automation (in-plant). ecology-oriented products, energy-conservative products, etc.). Length: 750-1,500 words. Buys up to 12 mss/year. Query. Pays $75-200.
Photos: B&w photos (5x7 or 8x10) purchased with mss or on assignment. Pays $5 minimum. Query or send contact sheet, or send prints. Color used only on cover, by assignment. Model release required.
Columns, Departments: World Design, Ottawa Report, Careers. Query first. Length: 500 words maximum. Pays $40 minimum. Open to suggestions for new columns and departments.

DETROIT ENGINEER, 18226 Mack, Grosse Pointe MI 48236. Editor: Jack Weller-Grenard. For "members of the Engineering Society of Detroit. They are engineers, architects, and persons in other related fields. The median age is about 45; mostly affluent, with wide-ranging interests." Established in 1945. Monthly. Circulation: 7,000. Rights purchased vary with author and material; may buy all rights, but will reassign rights to author after publication. Buys about 20 mss/year. Pays on publication. Will send a sample copy to a writer for $1. Submit complete ms. Will not consider photocopied submissions. Submit seasonal material 3 to 4 months in advance. Returns rejected material "usually in 2 weeks." Acknowledges acceptance of material in 4 to 6 weeks. Enclose S.A.S.E.
Nonfiction: "*Detroit Engineer* publishes articles on subjects of regional, southeastern Michigan interest not covered in other publications. We are only interested in the unusual and highly specific technical or man-oriented pieces, such as an expose on the Wankel engine or a new way to harness solar energy—subjects of wide interest within the scientific community." Buys exposes and technical articles. Length: 500 to 1,000 words. Pays $50.
Photos: Buys 4x5 to 8x10 b&w glossies; "any surface." Pays $5 to $15. Buys 8x10 color prints or larger transparencies for cover use. Pays minimum $25.

ELECTRO-OPTICAL SYSTEMS DESIGN MAGAZINE, Room 900, 222 W. Adams St., Chicago IL 60606. (312)263-4866. Editor: Richard Cunningham. Monthly. Circulation: 26,000. Buys all rights. Pays on publication. Will send a sample copy to a writer on request. Write for copy of guidelines for writers. Will consider cassette submissions. Query required. Editorial deadlines are on the 5th of the month preceding publication. Enclose S.A.S.E.

Nonfiction and Photos: Articles and photos on lasers, laser systems, and optical systems aimed at electro-optical scientists and engineers. "Each article should serve a reader's need by either stimulating ideas, increasing technical competence, improving design capabilities in the following areas: natural light and radiation sources, artificial light and radiation sources, light modulators, optical components, image detectors, energy detectors, information displays, image processing, information storage and processing, system and subsystem testing, materials, support equipment, and other related areas." Rejects flighty prose, material not written for type of readership, and irrelevant material. Pays $30 per page. Submit 8x10 b&w glossies with ms.

LIGHTING DESIGN & APPLICATION, 345 E. 47th St., New York NY 10017. (212)644-7922. Editor: Chuck Beardsley. For "lighting designers, architects, consulting engineers, and lighting engineers." Established in 1971. Monthly. Circulation: 13,500. Rights purchased vary with author and material. Buys about 20 mss/year. Pays on acceptance. Will not consider photocopied submissions. Query first. Enclose S.A.S.E.

Nonfiction: "Lighting application, techniques, and trends in all areas, indoors and out. Our publication is the chief source of practical illumination information." Buys informational and think articles. Length: 500 to 2,000 words. Pays $150.

How To Break In: "Interview authorities in the field of illuminating engineering."

NEW ENGINEER, 730 Third Ave., New York NY 10017. (212)557-9855. For "engineering school students at the graduate and undergraduate levels and young professional engineers, recent graduates, engineers in management." 11 times a year with combined July/August issue. Circulation: 100,000. Buys first rights. Buys 20 to 30 mss a year. Pays on publication. Will send a sample copy to a writer on request. Submit seasonal material 4 months in advance. Query first with outline or abstract. Enclose S.A.S.E.

Nonfiction and Photos: Articles on "engineering trends, employment patterns, outlook, profiles of successful engineers, social responsibility, engineering education. Articles should interest young engineers in general. Our publication approaches the engineer as a professional person—as a member of an elite group." Publishes issues on "minority groups and engineering and environment and the engineer." Buys how-to's, personal experience articles, interviews, profiles, humor, coverage of successful business operations, and new product articles. Does not want to see articles that are too technical or with too limited an appeal. Style should be more for consumer readership. Length: 1,500 to 4,000 words. Pays 6-20¢/word. B&w glossies, 35mm color, and color transparencies purchased with mss. Payment "usually $20 to $25."

Fiction: Humorous; "engineering related." Length: 1,000 to 2,000 words. Pays 6-15¢/word. Buys 6-8 fiction mss/year.

PARKING MAGAZINE, National Parking Association, 1101 17th St., N.W., Washington DC 20036. (202)296-4336. Editor-in-Chief: Norene Dann Martin. "The bulk of our readers are owners/operators of commercial, off-street parking facilities in major metropolitan areas. The remainder is made up of architects, engineers, city officials, planners, retailers, contractors, service/equipment suppliers, etc." Quarterly magazine; 50-56 pages. Dstab: 1952. Circ: 5,500. Pays on acceptance. Buys one-time rights. Phone queries OK. Submit seasonal/holiday material 3 months in advance. SASE. Reports in 1 week. Free sample copy.

Nonfiction: David L. Ivey, associate editor. Historical articles (a study of a particularly interesting parking facility, history of the industry or a particular company, etc.); how-to (new parking construction methods, design innovations, etc.); informational (virtually any aspect of parking operation, design, impact, construction, etc.); interviews (with a new/old/typical parking operator or other person associated with the industry); personal experience (must deal with parking); personal opinion (accepted only if especially original or from recognized authority); travel articles (parking facilities around the world). Length: 1,000-15,000 words. Query first. Pays $25 minimum.

Photos: B&w (8x10) glossies and color transparencies (35mm) purchased with or without mss, or on assignment. Captions required. Query first or send contact sheet or transparencies. Pays $5 minimum for b&w; $10 minimum for color.

Fillers: Clippings, jokes, gags, anecdotes, newsbreaks. Pays $1-10.

How To Break In: "Being small and flexible, we wouldn't be hard to please if the piece is relatively well-written and pertinent, to some extent, to the parking industry. Perhaps the most readily acceptable material would be informative pieces dealing with a new parking structure or facility that is somehow unique."

Finance

The magazines listed below deal with banking, investment, and financial management. Magazines that use similar material but have a less technical or professional slant are listed in the Consumer Publications under Business and Finance.

BANK SYSTEMS & EQUIPMENT, 1515 Broadway, New York NY 10036. Editor: Alan Richman. For bank and savings and loan association operations executives. Monthly. Circulation: 22,000. Buys all rights. Pays on publication. Query first for style sheet and specific article assignment. Mss should be triple spaced on one side of paper only with wide margin at left-hand side of the page. Enclose S.A.S.E.
Nonfiction: Third-person case history articles and interviews as well as material relating to systems, operations and automation. Charts, systems diagrams, artist's renderings of new buildings, etc., may accompany ms and must be suitable for reproduction. Prefers one color only. Length: open. Pays $75 for first published page, $45 for second page, and $40 for succeeding pages.
Photos: 5x7 or 8x10 single-weight glossies. Candids of persons interviewed, views of bank, bank's data center, etc. Captions required. "We do not pay extra for photos."

BURROUGHS CLEARING HOUSE, Box 418, Detroit MI 48232. (313)972-7936. Managing Editor: Norman E. Douglas. For bank and financial officers. Monthly. Buys all publication rights. Pays on acceptance. Will send a sample copy on request. Query first on articles longer than 1,800 words. Enclose S.A.S.E.
Nonfiction: Uses reports on what banks and other financial institutions are doing; emphasize usable ideas. "We reject an article if we question its authenticity." Length: 1,000 to 2,000 words; also uses shorter news items. Pays 10¢ a word. Additional payment of $5 for usable illustrations.
Photos: Should be 8x10 glossy b&w. Also buys pix with captions only. Pays $5.

THE CANADIAN BANKER & ICB REVIEW, The Canadian Bankers' Association, Box 282, Toronto, Dominion Centre, Ontario, Canada M5K 1K2. Editor: Brian O'Brien. Emphasizes banking in Canada. Bimonthly magazine; 72 pages. Estab: 1893. Circ: 45,000. Buys first North American serial rights. SASE. Reports in 1 month. Free sample copy.
Nonfiction: Informational articles on international banking and economics; interviews, nostalgic and personal opinion articles; book reviews. Query. Length: 750-2,000 words. Pays $100-250. "Freelancer should be an authority on the subject. Most contributors are bankers, economists and university professors."

COMMODITIES MAGAZINE, 219 Parkade, Cedar Falls IA 50613. (319)677-6341. Publisher: Merrill Oster. Editor: Darrell Jobman. For private, individual futures traders, brokers, exchange members, agri-businessmen; agricultural banks; anyone with an interest in commodities. Monthly magazine; 48-64 pages. Estab. 1971. Circ. 17,000. Buys all rights, but will reassign rights to author after publication. Buys 30 to 40 mss a year. Payment on publication. Free sample copy. Photocopied submissions OK. Will not consider simultaneous submissions. Reports on material accepted for publication within 1 month. Returns rejected material within 2 months if accompanied by S.A.S.E. Query first or submit complete ms. Enclose S.A.S.E.
Nonfiction and Photos: Articles analyzing specific commodity futures trading strategies; fundamental and technical analysis of individual commodities and markets; interviews, book reviews, "success" stories; news items. Material on new legislation affecting commodities, trading, any new trading strategy (results must be able to be substantiated); personalities. Does not want to see "homespun" rules for trading and simplistic approaches to the commodities market. Treatment is always in-depth and broad. Informational, how-to, interview, profile, technical. "Articles should be written for a reader who has traded commodities for one year or more; should not talk down or hypothesize. Relatively complex material is acceptable." Length: No maximum or minimum; 2,500 words optimum. Pays 6¢ per word. Pays $15 for glossy print b&w photos. Captions required.

COMMODITY JOURNAL, The American Association of Commodity Traders, 10 Park St., Concord MA 03301. Editor-in-Chief: Arthur R. Economou. Mainly for members of the Ameri-

can Association of Commodity Traders, the journal serves an educational function for them, because of its design as a clearinghouse for exchanges of ideas and opinions. Bimonthly magazine. Estab: 1965. Circ: 4,000. Pays on acceptance. Buys all rights. Simultaneous submissions OK. SASE. Reports in 1 month.
Nonfiction: "Only feature articles dealing with commodities; preferably of a technical nature. We are interested in fresh material concerning alternatives to the commodity futures industry operant in the U.S. today. Special emphasis should be given the spot and forward selling methods and markets. Rather than assigning specific articles, we prefer to consider the ideas of interested writers." Length: 2,500 words maximum. Pays 5-10¢/word. Query.

FINANCIAL QUARTERLY, P. O. Box 14451, North Palm Beach FL 33408. Editor: Thomas A. Swirles. For "bank and savings and loan presidents, vice-presidents, etc. We now go to major credit unions as well." Established in 1969. Quarterly. Circulation: 64,000. Rights purchased vary with author and material. Pays on publication. Will send a sample copy to a writer on request. Submit complete ms. Will consider photocopied submissions. Reports on material accepted for publication "at closing." Returns rejected material in 1 month. Enclose S.A.S.E.
Nonfiction and Photos: "Bank product information, trends in banking, etc." Buys informational articles, how-to's, interviews, and coverage of merchandising techniques. Length: 500 to 750 words. Pays $200 to $500. Photos purchased with mss.

THE INDEPENDENT BANKER, Box 267, Sauk Centre MN 56378. Editor-in-Chief: Al Blair. Emphasizes banking. Monthly magazine; 32 pages. Circ: 10,000. Pays on acceptance. Buys all rights. Reports in 1-2 weeks. Free sample copy.
Nonfiction: How-to and informational articles "that will appeal to officers of independent banks in small communities." Query or send complete ms. Pays 5¢ per published word.
Photos: Pays $5 each for 8x10 or 5x7 b&w glossies.

MERGERS & ACQUISITIONS, 1621 Brookside Rd., McLean VA 22101. Editor: Stanley Foster Reed. For presidents and other high corporate personnel, financiers, buyers, stockbrokers, accountants, and related professionals. Quarterly. Buys all rights. Pays 21 days after publication. Will send a free sample copy to a writer on request. Highly recommends query with outline of intended article first. Include 50-word autobiography with mss. Enclose S.A.S.E.
Nonfiction: "Articles on merger and acquisition techniques (taxes, SEC regulations, anti-trust, etc.) or surveys and roundups emphasizing analysis and description of trends and implications thereof. Articles should contain 20 to 60 facts per 1,000 words (names, dates, places, companies, etc.). We reject articles that are badly researched. We can fix bad writing but not bad research. Accurate research is a must and footnote references should be incorporated into text. Avoid 'Company A, Company B' terminology." Length: maximum 10,000 to 15,000 words. Pays $50 to $100 per 1,000 printed words for freelance articles; $200 honorarium or 200 reprints for articles by professional business persons, such as lawyers, investment analysts.

Fishing

CANADIAN FISHERMAN AND OCEAN SCIENCE, Gardenvale, Que., HOA 1BO, Canada. (514)457-3250. Editor: Allan Muir. Not copyrighted. Pays on publication. Will send a sample copy to a writer on request. Reports in 1 month. Enclose S.A.E. and International Reply Coupons.
Nonfiction: Articles describing new developments in commercial fisheries and oceanography. Will also consider sketches and controversial articles about Canadian fisheries and oceanological developments. Style should be strictly factual and easy to read. Length: up to 1,000 words. Pays 3¢ to 5¢ per word.
Photos: Buys photos with mss and with captions only. Pays $3 and up.

MAINE COMMERCIAL FISHERIES, Box 37, Stonington ME 04681. (207)367-5590. Managing Editor: Nat Barrows. Emphasizes commercial fisheries. Monthly newspaper; 24 pages. Estab: 1974. Circ: 3,200. Pays on publication. Copyrighted. SASE. Reports in 2 weeks. Sample copy $1.
Nonfiction: "Material strictly limited to coverage of commerical fishing, technical and general; occasional environment, business, etc., articles as they relate to commercial fishing." Query first. Pays $50-75.

NATIONAL FISHERMAN, 21 Elm St., Camden ME 04843. (207)236-4344. Editor: David R. Getchell. For "amateur and professional boat builders, commercial fishermen, armchair sailors, bureaucrats and politicians. Age 18 to 98." Newspaper: 88 pages. Estab: 1946. Monthly. Circ: 65,000. Buys first serial rights. Buys about 350 mss per year. Pays within a month of acceptance. Will send free sample copy and editorial guidelines sheet to writer on request. Will not consider photocopied or simultaneous submissions. Reports on mss accepted for publication in 2 weeks to 1 month. Returns rejected material in 5 or 6 weeks. Article propnsals should be accompanied by sample of work. Enclose S.A.S.E.

Nonfiction: Department Editor: Stephen Saft. Publishes "News stories and features on such topics as unusually large or small catches by local commercial fishermen, political action by individual or commercial fishermen groups, small boat disasters, the construction and launching of boats, etc. We do not insist on a set style, but we do insist on good writing. We want the human element. We carry book reviews, and we are always looking for good short features. We refuse to glamorize the sea. We are not afraid to criticize new boats, boat-building methods, politicians, etc., when it is deserved. We do not print as gospel advertising or PR copy on new products." Not interested in material on sportfishing, routine cruising or conventional sail and powerboat racing. Buys informational, how-to, personal experience, profile, interview, historical, "think" pieces, expose, nostalgia, personal opinion, photo, reviews on marine books, spot news, successful business operations, new product and technical articles. Length: 3,000 words maximum. Pays $1 per column inch of copy published, "which figures to over 2.5¢ per word."

Photos and Fillers: B&w photos purchased with accompanying mss with extra payment, purchased without mss or purchased on assignment. Captions required. Pays $5 "or more, depending on quality." Buys newsbreaks and clippings for fillers, pertaining to commercial fishing, boat building and general marine subjects. Pays 2¢ per word.

How To Break In: "We are always open to good writing. Good writing to us is not just a case of grammar, punctuation and style, but of feel for the subject being written about. The writer trying to break in with us shouldn't attempt, for example, doing a story about a new boat unless he's spent some time with a boat builder and has observed what's involved in building a boat. If he's going to write a commercial fishing story for us, then he should spend some time watching commercial fishermen doing some aspect of their job." Principal reasons for rejecting submissions are: the writer does not show sufficient respect for the sea, the feel of what it's like to travel it or an understanding of what is really involved in trying to make a living from it.

Florists, Nurserymen, and Landscaping

FLORAFACTS, Florafax International, Inc., Box 45745, Tulsa OK 74145. (918)622-8415. Editor-in-Chief: Angela H. Caruso. For retail florists, wholesalers, suppliers, students of floriculture, horticulture, floral designers. Monthly magazine; 70 pages. Estab: 1961. Circ: 22,500. Pays on acceptance. Buys all rights, but may reassign following publication. Phone queries OK. Submit seasonal/holiday material 6 months in advance. Previously published submissions OK. SASE. Free sample copy and writer's guidelines.

Nonfiction: Expose (floral industry), how-to (floral designs, business, staff, and customer relations), informational, historical, humor (floral trade), interview, nostalgia, personal opinion, profile, travel, new product, personal experience, photo feature, technical. Buys 48 mss/year. Query or submit complete ms. Length: 1,000-3,000 words. Pays 3-8¢/word.

Photos: Elaine Simpson, Photo Editor. Purchased with or without accompanying ms or on assignment. Captions required. Query or submit prints, negatives, or transparencies. Pays $10-25 for 8x10 b&w glossy prints; $15-35 for 2¼x2¼ color transparencies. Model release required.

Columns, Departments: Length: 500-1,000 words. Pays $15. Open to suggestions for new columns and departments.

FLORIST, Florists' Transworld Delivery Association, Box 2227, 29200 Northwestern Hwy., Southfield MI 48037. (313)355-9300. Editor-in-Chief: William P. Golden. Emphasizes matters of interest to retail and wholesale florists and commercial flower and plant growers. Monthly magazine; 100 pages. Estab: 1967. Circ: 23,000. Pays on acceptance. Buys all rights. Submit seasonal or holiday material 3-4 months in advance. Photocopied submissions and previously published work OK. SASE. Reports in 3 weeks. Free sample copy.

Nonfiction: Historical and how-to articles; humor, informational, interviews, photo features and profiles. Buys 1-2 an issue. Submit complete ms. Length: 500-1,500 words. Pays $20 minimum.

Photos: B&w (5x7 or 8x10) glossies and color (2¼x2¼ or 4x5) purchased on assignment. Query. Pays $10 minimum for b&w; $25 minimum for color. Model release required.

FLOWER NEWS, 549 W. Randolph St., Chicago IL 60606. (312)236-8648. Managing Editor: Jean Onerheim. For retail, wholesale florists, floral suppliers, supply jobbers, growers. Weekly newspaper; 40 pages. Estab: 1947. Circ: 13,060. Pays on acceptance. Not copyrighted. Submit seasonal/holiday material at least 2 months in advance. Photocopied submissions and previously published work OK. SASE. Reports immediately. Free sample copy.
Nonfiction: How-to articles (increase business, set up a new shop, etc.; anything floral-related without being an individual shop story); informational (general articles of interest to industry); and technical (grower stories related to industry, but not individual grower stories). Submit complete ms. Length: 3-5 typed pages. Pays $10.
Photos: "We do not buy individual pictures. They may be enclosed with ms at regular ms rate (b&w only).

TELEFLORA SPIRIT, 2400 Compton Blvd., Redondo Beach CA 90278. Editor: Jorian Clair. Official publication of Teleflora, Incorporated, for retail florist subscribers to Teleflora's flowers-by-wire service. Positioned as "The Magazine of Professional Flower Shop Management." Monthly. Circulation: 16,000. Buys one-time rights in floral trade magazine field. Most articles are staff-written. Pays on publication. Reports in 2 to 3 weeks. Enclose S.A.S.E.
Nonfiction and Photos: Articles dealing with buying and selling profitably, merchandising of product, management, designing, shop remodeling, display techniques, etc. Also, allied interests such as floral wholesalers, growers, tradespeople, gift markets, etc. All articles must be thoroughly researched and professionally relevant. Any florist mentioned must be a Teleflorist. Length: 1,000 to 3,000 words. Pays 8¢ per published word. Photos purchased with mss or with captions only. 8x10 b&w glossies preferred. Captions required. Pays $7.50.

WEEDS TREES & TURF, Harvest Publishing Co., 9800 Detroit Ave., Cleveland OH 44102. Editor-in-Chief: Gail D. Hogan. For "turf managers, parks, superintendents of golf courses, airports, schools, landscape architects, landscape contractors, and sod farmers." Monthly magazine; 64 pages. Estab: 1968. Circ: 45,000. Pays on publication. Buys all rights. Submit seasonal/holiday material 4 months in advance. Photocopied submissions OK. SASE. Reports in 6 weeks. Free sample copy.
Nonfiction: Publishes how-to, informational, and technical articles. Buys 24 mss a year. Query or submit complete ms. Length: 750-2,000 words. Pays $50-150.

Food Products, Processing, and Service

In this list are journals for food wholesalers, processors, warehousers, caterers, institutional managers, and suppliers of grocery store equipment. Publications for grocery store operators are classified under Groceries. Journals for food vending machine operators will be found under Coin-Operated Machines.

FAST SERVICE, Harcourt Brace Jovanovich, Inc., 757 Third Ave., New York NY 10017. (212)754-4324. Editor: Tom Farr. Established in 1940. Monthly. Circulation: 50,800. Buys all rights. Buys 20 mss a year. Pays on acceptance. Reports on material accepted for publication in 2 weeks. Returns rejected material immediately. Query first. Enclose S.A.S.E.
Nonfiction and Photos: Articles on operations and case histories of all phases of fast service restaurant operations. Length: 1,500 to 2,000 words. Pays 10¢ a word. B&w photos (5x7 or 8x10) purchased with mss or with captions only. Pays $7 to $10. Color transparencies used for cover and for feature article illustration. Fee is negotiated for all color photography. Prefers 2¼x2¼ transparencies or larger, but will accept 35mm work if of high quality.

KITCHEN PLANNING, 757 Third Ave., New York NY 10017. Editor: Thomas Farr. Buys all rights. Pays on acceptance. Query first. Enclose S.A.S.E.
Nonfiction and Photos: How-to, in-depth articles on designing commercial and institutional kitchens—installations based on actual experience of specific operation—with quotes, facts, figures. Length: 1,000 to 1,500 words. Kitchen floor plans must accompany ms. B&w glossies purchased with ms. Pays 7¢ to 10¢ a word. Pays $5 for each photo.

MEAT MAGAZINE, 66 Carter Lane, London EC4V 5EA, England. (01)248-4256. Editor-in-Chief: John Spence. For meat product manufacturers, wholesale and multiple butchers, self-help stores, supermarkets, freezer centers and poultry packers. Magazine; 10 times a year; 68 pages. Pays on publication. Buys all rights, but will reassign following publication. Phone queries OK. Submit seasonal/holiday material 2 months in advance. Photocopied submissions OK. SAE and International Reply Coupons. Reports in 2 weeks. Free sample copy and writer's guidelines.

Nonfiction: Exposes (any problem areas revealed in the meat industry in the U.S. or Canada); interviews (in-depth insights into "meat" men in America, especially heads of meat processing companies); profiles (of successful meat companies or people); technical articles (meat packing, processing, storing, transporting, cutting, etc.). Length: 1,500-3,500 words. Buys 4 mss/issue. Query or submit complete ms. Pays $36-100.

Photos: B&w glossies purchased with mss. Captions required. Send contact sheet. Pays $5-15.

MEAT PLANT MAGAZINE, 8678 Olive Blvd., St. Louis MO 63132. (314)993-5638. Editor: Albert Todoroff. For meat processors, locker plant operators, freezer provisioners, portion control packers, meat dealers, and food service (food plan) operators. Bimonthly. Pays on acceptance. Reports in 2 weeks. Enclose S.A.S.E. for return of submissions.

Nonfiction, Photos, and Fillers: Buys feature-length articles and shorter subjects pertinent to the field. Length: 1,000 words for features. Pays 1½¢ a word. Pays $3.50 for photos.

PRODUCE NEWS, 6 Harrison St., New York NY 10013. Editor: Harold B. Mers. For "commercial growers and shippers, receivers, and distributors of fresh fruits and vegetables, including chain store produce buyers and merchandisers." Established in 1897. Weekly. Circulation: 5,300. Not copyrighted. Pays on publication. Will send a sample copy to a writer on request. "Our deadline is Wednesday afternoon before Friday press day each week." Query first. Enclose S.A.S.E.

Nonfiction, Fillers and Photos: "News is our principal stock in trade, particularly trends in crop growing, distributing, and marketing. Tell the story clearly, simply, and briefly." Buys informational articles, how-to's, profiles, spot news, coverage of successful business operations, new product pieces, articles on merchandising techniques. Length: "no special length." Pays 50¢ a column inch for original material, 40¢ a column inch for clippings. 8½x11 b&w glossies purchased with ms.

QUICK FROZEN FOODS, 757 Third Ave., New York NY 10017. (212)754-4335. Co-Publisher and Editor: Sam Martin. Monthly. Buys all rights but will release any rights on request. Pays within 30 days after acceptance. Query first. Guaranteed assignments by special arrangement. Will accept names for file of correspondents who would be given assignments when and if story breaks in their locality. Reports in 30 days. Enclose S.A.S.E.

Nonfiction and Photos: Uses feature articles and short articles on frozen food operations in processing plants, wholesalers' warehouses, chain stores and supermarkets. Good articles on retailing of frozen foods. Most rejected mss are "too general in nature for a magazine catering to a specialized industry." Pays 3¢/word. Pays $5 a photo.

Fillers: Pays $1 minimum for clippings.

SNACK FOOD, HBJ Publications, Inc., 1 E. 1st St., Duluth MN 55802. (218)727-8511. Editor-in-Chief: Jerry L. Hess. For manufacturers and distributors of snack foods. Monthly magazine; 60 pages. Estab: 1912. Circ: 10,000 Pays on acceptance. Buys all rights, buy may reassign following publication. Phone queries OK. Submit seasonal/holiday material 2-3 months in advance. Photocopied submissions OK. SASE. Reports in 2-3 weeks. Free sample copy and writer's guidelines.

Nonfiction: Informational, interview, new product, nostalgia, photo feature, profile and technical articles. "We are beginning a new format which will allow us to use a greater variety of mini news-features and personality sketches." Length: 300-600 words for mini features; 1,000-1,500 words for longer features. Pays $50-300.

Photos: Purchased with accompanying ms. Captions required. Pays $10-15 for 5x7 b&w photos; $15-50 for 4x5 color transparencies. Total purchase price for a ms includes payment for photos.

How To Break In: "We are looking for regional correspondents who will be able to move quickly on leads furnished as well as develop articles on their own. A directory of processors in their areas will be furnished upon making working agreement."

Fur

FUR TRADE JOURNAL, Bewdley, Ont., Canada. K0L 1EO. (416)797-2281. Editor: Charles

Clay. For fur ranchers in mink, chinchilla, rabbit, nutria; and for all aspects of fur pelt sales, garment manufacture, garment retailing. Monthly. Buys first Canadian rights. Pays on publication. Very little freelance material used. Mostly staff-written. Query first. Reports "immediately." Enclose S.A.E. and International Reply Coupons.

Nonfiction: Articles on anything of practical value and interest to fur ranchers. Length: up to 1,500 words. Pays 2¢ per word.

Photos: Purchased with mss; dealing with fur ranching. Pays $3 to $5.

U.S. FUR RANCHER, 3055 N. Brookfield Rd., Brookfield WI 53005. (414)786-7540. Publisher: Bruce W. Smith. For mink farmers. Monthly. Buys first world rights. Pays on publication. Will send free sample copy on request "by letter, not postcard. Queries imperative, including names and addresses of proposed interview subjects." Reports "immediately." Enclose S.A.S.E.

Nonfiction and Photos: "Articles and photos on mink-ranch operations, based on interviews with manager or owner. Not interested in any fur-bearing animals except mink. Opportunities for freelancers traveling to foreign nations in which mink are raised. We reject an article if we find factual errors resulting from carelessness in interviewing and research." Length: 1,000 to 2,000 words. Pays $30 to $75 per article, including four contact prints at least 2¼ square.

Gas

BUTANE-PROPANE NEWS, P.O. Box 1408, Arcadia CA 91006. (213)446-4607. Editor-Publisher: William W. Clark. For LP-gas distributor dealers with bulk storage plants, LP bottled gas dealers and manufacturers of appliances and equipment. Monthly. Buys all rights. Pays on publication. Will send free sample copy on request. Will consider cassette submissions. Query preferred. Reports in 1 week. Enclose S.A.S.E.

Nonfiction: Articles on advertising and promotional programs; plant design, marketing operating techniques and policies; management problems; new, unusual or large usages of LP-gas; how LP-gas marketers are coping with the energy crisis. Completeness of coverage, reporting in depth, emphasis on the why and the how are musts. "Brevity essential but particular angles should be covered pretty thoroughly." Pays $50 per magazine page. "We also publish *The Weekly Propane Newsletter,* which is a market for newsclippings on propane, butane, and other energy related matters." Will send clipping tips on request.

Photos: Purchased with mss. 8x10 desired but not rdquired; can work from negatives. Pays $6.

Fillers: Clippings and newsbreaks pertinent to LPG industry. Clippings regarding competitive fuels (electricity, oil) with relationship that would have impact on LPG industry. Pays $5 minimum for clippings.

GAS DIGEST, Box 35819, Houston TX 77035. (713)723-7456. Editor: Ken Kridner. For operating personnel of the gas industry. Magazine; 50 pages. Established in 1975. Monthly. Circulation: 6,500. Rights may be retained by the author. Pays on publication. Sample copy for $2; free writer's guidelines. Will consider photocopied submissions. No simultaneous submissions. Reports in 10 days. Query first. Enclose S.A.S.E.

Nonfiction and Photos: Applications stories; new developments. All material must be operations oriented and meaningful to one working in the gas industry. How-to, interviews, technical articles. Length: 1,000 words. Pays 2.5¢ per word minimum. B&w and color photos purchased with mss or on assignment. Pays $5 minimum for b&w; $7.50 minimum for color.

LP-GAS, 1 East First St., Duluth MN 55802. Editor: Zane Chastain. For liquefied petroleum gas (propane, 'bottled gas') marketers. Monthly. Buys all rights. Pays on acceptance. Query first. Enclose S.A.S.E.

Nonfiction: Uses dealer and LP-gas utilization articles, how-to features on selling, delivery, service, etc. Tersely written, illustrated by photo or line for documentation. Length: maximum 1,500 words. Pays 5 ¢ a word.

Photos: Pix with mss or captions only; not less than 2¼x2¼. Pays $5 to $7.

SOONER LPG TIMES, 2910 N. Walnut, Suite 114-A, Oklahoma City OK 73105. (405)525-9386 Editor: John E. Orr. For "dealers and suppliers of LP-gas and their employees." Monthly. Not copyrighted. Pays on publication. Reports in 3 weeks. Enclose S.A.S.E.

Nonfiction: "Articles relating to the LP-gas industry, safety, small business practices, and economics; anything of interest to small businessmen." Length: 1,000 to 2,000 words. Pays $10 to $15.

Government and Public Service

Below are journals for individuals who provide governmental services, either in the employ of local, state, or national governments or of franchised utilities. Included are journals for city managers, politicians, civil servants, firemen, policemen, public administrators, urban transit managers, utilities managers, etc.

Publications that emphasize the architectural and building side of city planning and development are classified in Architecture. Publications for lawyers are found in the Law category. Journals for teachers and administrators in the schools are found in Education. Publications for private citizens interested in politics, government, and public affairs are classified with the Politics and World Affairs magazines in the Consumer Publications section.

CAMPAIGN INSIGHT, Campaign Associates, Inc., 516 Petroleum Bldg., Wichita KS 67202. (316)265-7421. Editor-in-Chief: Hank Parkinson. Emphasizes political techniques. For readers who are interested in new politics methodology. Monthly newsletters; 16 pages. Estab: 1969. Circ: 4,300. Pays on acceptance. Buys all rights. Phone queries OK. Previously published submissions OK. SASE. Reports in 6 weeks. Free sample copy and writer's guidelines.
Nonfiction: How-to (projects other candidates used that have application in most other campaigns); informational (campaign overviews, if replete with how-to examples); interviews ("Playboy-style" interviews are used to lead off every issue and are in great demand). Length: 100-1,000 words. Buys about 75 mss a year. Query first. Pays 5¢/word.
How To Break In: "We work only from queries and assigned items. A new writer should request a free copy of the newsletter, study the style and format; then query. He must have a grasp of new political technologies and be interested in modern campaigning."

THE CRIMINOLOGIST, Box No. 18, Bognor, Regis, Sussex, UK P022 7AA. For professionals and students interested in public affairs, criminology, forensic science, the law, penology, etc. Quarterly. Query. SAE and International Reply Coupons. Sample copy $3.
Nonfiction: Considers articles of very high standards, authoritatively written and factually sound, informative and sober, and not in a popular or sensational style. All material must have attached list of references or sources (title of source, author or editor, town of publication, date, and, if a periodical, page number, issue number, and volume). Articles from police officials, experts, etc., are welcomed. Length: 2,000 to 4,000 words.
Photos: Purchased with mss. Payment negotiable.

FIRE CHIEF MAGAZINE, 625 N. Michigan Ave., Chicago IL 60611. (312)642-9862. Editor: William Randleman. For chiefs of volunteer and paid fire departments. Buys all rights. Will not consider simultaneous submissions or material offered for second rights. Pays on publication. Reports in 10 days. Enclose S.A.S.E.
Nonfiction: Wants articles on fire department administration, training, or fire-fighting operations. Will accept case histories of major fires, extinguished by either volunteer or paid departments, detailing exactly how the fire department fought the fire and the lessons learned from the experience. "Prefer feature articles to be bylined by a fire chief or other fire service authority." Writing must be simple, clear, and detailed, preferably conversational in style. Pays $1 to $1.50 per column inch.
Photos: Used with mss or with captions only. 4x5 or larger; Polaroid or other small prints of individuals or small subjects accepted. Pays up to $35 for acceptable color photos. Pays nothing for public domain photos, up to $5 for exclusives, $1 for mug shots.

FIRE ENGINEERING, 666 Fifth Ave., New York NY 10019. Editor: James F. Casey. For commissioners, chiefs, senior officers of the paid, volunteer, industrial, and military fire departments and brigades. Buys first serial rights. Pays on publication. Reports in 3 weeks. Enclose S.A.S.E. for return of submissions.
Nonfiction and Photos: Wants articles on fire suppression, fire prevention, and any other subject that relates to fire service. Length: 750 to 1,500 words. Pays minimum 3¢ a word and up. Good photos with captions always in demand. Particular need for color photos for cover; small print or slide satisfactory for submission, but must always be a vertical or capable of being cropped to vertical. Transparency required if accepted. Pays $75 for color shots used on cover, $15 and up for b&w shots.

FIRE TIMES, American Fire Fighters Association, 1100 N.E. 125th St., North Miami FL 33161. (305)891-9800. Editor-in-Chief: Tom Moore. Emphasizes fire fighting services. Bimonthly magazine; 24 pages. Estab: 1975. Circ: 22,000. Pays on publication. Buys all rights, but may reassign following publication. Phone queries OK. Submit seasonal/holiday material 3 months in advance. SASE. Reports in 4 weeks. Sample copy 50¢; free writer's guidelines.

Nonfiction: How-to, informational, historical, interview, profile, new product, personal experience, photo feature, technical articles. Buys 15-20 ms/issue. Send complete ms. Length: 400-1,200 words. Pays $5-25.

Photos: Purchased with ms. Captions required. Send prints. Pays $5-25 for 8x10 b&w glossies. Except for photos of public officials, captions are required.

How To Break In: "By remembering that this publication is aimed at the volunteer fire fighters in the small towns and that we need pictures of new buildings, equipment and activity."

FOREIGN SERVICE JOURNAL, 2101 E St., N.W., Washington DC 20037. (202)338-4045. Editor: Shirley R. Newhall. For Foreign Service officers and others interested in foreign affairs and related subjects. Monthly. Buys first North American rights. Pays on publication. Query first. Enclose S.A.S.E.

Nonfiction: Uses articles on "international relations, internal problems of the State Department and Foreign Service, informative material on other nations. Much of our material is contributed by those working in the fields we reach. Informed outside contributions are welcomed, however." Length: 2,500 to 4,000 words. Pays 2¢ to 3¢ a word.

MODERN GOVERNMENT (SERVICIOS PUBLICOS), P.O. Box 1256, Stamford CT 06904. (203)327-9340. Editor: Philip R. Moran. For government officials, private contractors and executives of public utilities and corporations in Latin America and Spain (Spanish) and Asia, Australasia, Africa, the Middle East and the Caribbean (English). 9 times a year. Circulation: 42,000. Buys international rights. Pays on acceptance. Will send free sample copy on request. Query advised. Reports in 1 week. Enclose S.A.S.E.

Nonfiction and Photos: All material should be of interest to government officials in developing nations. Strong "how to do it" (but not highly technical) angle on infrastructure development, public works, public transportation, public health and environmental sanitation, administrative skills, etc. Avoid strictly U.S. orientation. Publications go only overseas. Articles are bought in English and translated into Spanish. Length: 1,500 to 2,000 words. Pays $100 to $150 for article with up to 6 photos.

PASSENGER TRANSPORT, 1100 17th St. N.W., Washington DC 20036. Editor: Albert Engelken. Published by the American Public Transit Association for those in urban mass transportation. Pays on publication. Very little material bought. Enclose S.A.S.E.

Nonfiction: Uses short, concise articles which can be documented on urban mass transportation. Latest news only. No airline, steamship, intercity bus or railroad news. Pays 40¢ per column inch.

Photos: Sometimes buys photographs with mss and with captions only, but standards are high. 8x10's preferred. No color.

POLICE TIMES MAGAZINE, 1100 N. E. 125th St., N. Miami FL 33161. (305)891-1700. Editor: Donald Anderson. For "law enforcement officers; federal, state, county, local, and private security." Monthly. Circulation: 50,000. Buys all rights. Buys 10 to 20 mss a year. Pays on publication. Sample copy for 50¢ postage. No query required. Reports "at once." Enclose S.A.S.E.

Nonfiction and Photos: Interested in articles about local police departments all over the nation. In particular, short articles about what the police department is doing, any unusual arrests made, acts of valor of officers in the performance of duties, etc. Also articles on any police subject from prisons to reserve police. "We prefer newspaper style. Short and to the point. Photos and drawings are a big help." Length: 300 to 1,200 words. Payment is $5 to $15—up to $25 in some cases based on 1¢ a word." Uses b&w Polaroid and 8x10 b&w glossies, "if of particular value." Pays $5-15 for each photo used.

PUBLIC UTILITIES FORTNIGHTLY, Suite 500, 1828 L St. N.W., Washington, DC 20036. Editor-in-Chief: Neil H. Duffy. For utility executives, regulatory commissions, lawyers, etc. Semimonthly. Pays on publication. "Study our publication." Reports in 3 weeks. Enclose S.A.S.E.

Nonfiction: Length: 2,000 to 3,000 words. Pays $25 to $200.

RESERVE LAW, P.O. Box 17807, San Antonio TX 78217. Editor: Otto Vehle. Publication of Reserve Law Officers Association of America. For sheriffs, chiefs of police, other law enforcement officials and their reserve components. Established in 1969. Bimonthly. Circulation: "over 10,000." Not copyrighted. Payment on publication. Will send free sample copy to writer on request. Submit complete ms. Will consider photocopied submissions. Enclose S.A.S.E.

Nonfiction and Photos: "Articles describing police reserve and sheriff reserve organizations and their activities should be informative and interesting. Style should be simple, straightforward, and with a touch of humor when appropriate. We need current features on outstanding contemporary lawmen, both regular officers and reserves." Length: 500 to 2,000 words. "In most cases, ms should be accompanied by high contrast 8x10 b&w action photos, properly identified and captioned." Pays minimum of $10; plus $5 for first photo and $2.50 for additional photos used in same article. Also seeks material for the following columns: "Ichthus," a chaplain's column dealing with Christian law officers (100 to 500 words); "Law-Haw," humorous anecdotes about police work (40 to 60 words); "Fundamentals," basic "how-to's" of law enforcement (100 to 500 words). Payment in contributor's copies or a maximum of $50.

Fiction: "Fictionalized accounts of true police cases involving reserve officers will be accepted if they meet our needs." Length: 200 to 800 words. Pays maximum of $50.

Fillers: Jokes and short humor "of the law enforcement type." Length: 20 to 80 words. Pays maximum of $10.

ROLL CALL, 428 8th St., S.E., Washington DC 20003. (202)546-3080. Editor: Sidney Yudain. For U.S. Congressmen, political buffs, editors and TV commentators. Newspaper. Established in 1955. Weekly. Circulation: 9,000. Buys first North American serial rights. Buys about 10 mss a year. Pays on acceptance. Will consider photocopied and simultaneous submissions. Reports in 1 week. Query first or submit complete ms. Enclose S.A.S.E.

Nonfiction and Photos: Profiles, humor, historical, and nostalgic articles. "Political satire material must measure up to the work of the noted satirists we usually publish." Length: 500 to 2,000 words. Pays $5 to $25. No additional payment for b&w photos used with articles.

Poetry and Fillers: Light verse related to subject matter. Puzzles on a Congressional or political theme and short humor on political topics are used as fillers. Pays $2 minimum.

SEARCH AND RESCUE MAGAZINE, P.O. Box 153, Montrose CA 91020. (213)248-3057. Publisher: Dennis Kelley. Editor: M.P. Sweeney. For volunteer and paid professionals involved in search and rescue. Estab: 1973. Quarterly. Circ: 10,000. Buys all rights, but will reassign rights to author after publication. Buys about 40 mss/year. Pays on acceptance. Will send sample copy to writer for $1.25. Reports in 2 weeks. Query first or submit complete ms. Enclose S.A.S.E.

Fiction, Nonfiction and Photos: All material must be related to search and rescue work. Particularly likes photo essays. Pays $25 to $100. No additional payment for b&w photos used with mss. Captions required.

STATE & COUNTY ADMINISTRATOR, P.O. Box 272, Culver City CA 90230. For "top officials, managers, administrators and legislators at the state level in the government of all 50 states and 3,106 counties." Published 12 times a year. Circ: 31,000. Buys all rights. Pays on publication. Will send a sample copy to a writer on request. Submit seasonal material at least 2 months in advance of issue date. Reports in 4 to 6 weeks. Query first or submit complete ms. Enclose S.A.S.E.

Nonfiction and Photos: "A great amount of free material comes in from states, counties, and PR departments. Innovative methods that states are employing to increase the efficiency of administration, personnel management and training, revenue programs, issues facing states, new methods, procedures, and systems to reduce costs. We are management and administration oriented, as opposed to public works oriented. We are interested in environmental/pollution coverage." Length: 1,000 to 1,500 words. Pays 2¢ a word. 8x10 b&w glossies purchased with mss; captions required. Pays $2.50.

TODAY'S FIREMAN, P.O. Box 594, Kansas City MO 64141. (816)474-3495. Editor: Donald Mack. For persons involved in and interested in fire service. Magazine. Established in 1960. Quarterly. Circulation: 10,000. Copyrighted. Buys about 6 mss per year. Pays on acceptance or publication. Will send sample copy to writer for $2. Will consider photocopied and simultaneous submissions. Query first. Reports in 1 month. Enclose S.A.S.E.

Nonfiction, Photos and Fillers: Approach should be expository with research. Interested in psychological and philosophical aspects of current problems. Buys informational, interview, humor, nostalgia, new product, merchandising techniques, technical articles. Length: 50 to 1,500 words. Pays $15 to $40. Historical. Length: 500 to 2,500 words. Pays $20 to $40. Expose. Length: 500 words. Pays $15 to $40. Would like to see humorous articles with photos. Occasionally buys material for 2 regional editions, covering the Eastern U.S. and Western U.S. Writers may also submit suggestions for new columns or departments. Photos purchased with accompanying mss with no additional payment. Also purchased without ms. Pays $10 for b&w glossies. Captions required. Puzzles, jokes, gags, short humor. Pays $5 to $25.

VIRGINIA MUNICIPAL REVIEW, Review Publishing Co., Inc., Box 100, Richmond VA 23201. (804)643-1113. Editor-in-Chief: Ralph L. Dombrower, Sr. Emphasizes governmental subjects: federal, state, city, town and county. Monthly magazine; 32 pages. Estab: 1921. Circ: 2,500. Pays on publication. Buys all rights. Submit seasonal/holiday material 3 months in advance. Photocopied submissions OK. SASE. Free sample copy and writer's guidelines.
Nonfiction and Photos: Articles on governmental subjects. Well-researched, informative; current problems. Length: 500 words maximum. Pays 10¢ a word. No additional payment made for b&w photos used with mss.

WESTERN FIRE JOURNAL, 9072 E. Artesia Blvd., Suite 7, Bellflower CA 90706. (213)866-1664. Editor: Dick Friend. For fire chiefs, fire-fighters, paramedics, members of paid and volunteer departments in Montana, Utah, Colorado, Wyoming, Idaho, Nevada, New Mexico, Washington, Oregon, California, Alaska, Arizona, Texas, Hawaii, as well as rescue squad members (EMTs) affiliated with a fire department. Magazine; 34 (8½x11) pages. Established in 1959. Monthly. Circulation: 4,500. Rights purchased vary with author and material. Usually buys all rights, but will reassign rights to author after publication. Pays on publication. Will send sample copy to writer for $1. Will consider photocopied submissions. No simultaneous submissions. Reports on material in 1 week. Query first or submit complete ms. Enclose S.A.S.E.
Nonfiction and Photos: Innovations in equipment and techniques; reviews of major incidents; informative articles on individual departments or agencies which have something to tell to other similar agencies or departments; training aids. "Be technical enough to adequately explain what is being done and how it can be done by others." Length: open. Pays 2¢ per word. B&w photos (any size) purchased with or without mss. Pays $3 to $25.

WORKLIFE, Dept. of Labor PH 10141, Washington DC 20213. Editor: Walter Wood. For employment training, poverty and education specialists. Monthly. Circulation: 30,000. Not copyrighted. Pays on publication. Will send a free sample copy on request. Query preferred. Enclose S.A.S.E.
Nonfiction: Articles on government and private efforts to solve human resources, training, and education problems, particularly among the disadvantaged. Length: 600 to 4,000 words. "Payment for unsolicited articles used in the magazine is $100 to $200. For articles done by outside writers on assignment, payment is negotiable."

Groceries

The journals that follow are for owners and operators of retail food stores. Journals for food wholesalers, packers, warehousers, and caterers are classified with the Food Products, Processing, and Service journals. Publications for food vending machine operators are found in the Coin-Operated Machines category.

CHAIN STORE AGE SUPERMARKETS, 425 Park Ave., New York NY 10022. (212)371-9400. Editor: David Pinto. For chain, cooperative and voluntary executives; buyers, store supervisors, managers, food brokers, rack jobbers, associations, colleges and government agencies. Magazine; 80 pages. Established in 1925. Monthly. Circulation: 105,000. Buys all rights. Pays on publication. Will consider photocopied submissions. No simultaneous submissions. Reports in 2 weeks. Query first. Enclose S.A.S.E.
Nonfiction and Photos: News magazine technique of reporting and interpreting trends, developments and events of interest to chain supermarket segment of industry. This technique is combined with feature articles especially suited for chain supermarket headquarters and multiunit stores. Articles of interest to buyers, merchandisers, trainers, supervisors, as well as management and operations. At the store level, article emphasis is on store management, meat management and produce management; display, training, and supervision. Assigns articles to freelance writers as need for coverage arises. Pays $75 per printed page minimum. No additional payment for b&w photos used with mss. Captions optional.

CONVENIENCE STORE NEWS, 254 W. 31 St., New York NY 10001. (212)594-4120. Editor:

Jesse Stechel. For executives and buyers of convenience store retailing organizations and owners of individual stores. Established in 1969. Biweekly. Circulation: 8,000. Not copyrighted. Payment on publication. Will send free sample copy to writer on request. Enclose S.A.S.E.

Nonfiction and Photos: "News stories on developments in convenience store industry or developments that affect it, such as new laws and regulations; feature articles on successful operations." Pays $2 per column inch. B&w photos. Pays $5.

How To Break In: "The best way for a newcomer to break in would be with a news story from his area. They run an average of several hundred words. News material could be a new advertising campaign, an effective new promotion, the opening of a new store, or the promotion of an executive. Someone who can send us this sort of thing from outside New York can easily develop into a regular correspondent to whom we would assign feature work. We are, however, basically a news publication and seek coverage of news stories and items pertaining, directly or indirectly, to convenience stores. We like to see photos, and again, it helps if you're outside the New York area."

FOODSMAN, 1001 E. Main St., Richmond VA 23219. (804)644-0731. Editor: Brian F. Daly. For food retailers, wholesalers, distributors. Monthly magazine; 40 to 50 pages. Established in 1939. Circulation: 7,000. Not copyrighted. Payment on publication. Will send free sample copy to writer on request. Query first. Queries handled immediately. Enclose S.A.S.E.

Nonfiction and Photos: "Consumer articles; anything of interest to food people. From attitude surveys, operational studies, general interest articles or photo layouts on store design. Emphasis is on mid-Atlantic region and helpful ideas to be implemented by either food retailers, wholesalers or distributors." Informational, interviews with government officials, profiles, think pieces, training reviews, spot news, successful business operations, new product, merchandising techniques. Length: open. Payment varies.

PENNSYLVANIA GROCER, 3701 N. Broad St., Philadelphia PA 19140. (215)228-0808. Editor: John McNelis. For grocers, their families and employees, store managers; food people in general. Magazine; 16 pages. Established in 1913. Monthly. Circulation: 3,500. Copyrighted. Buys 10 to 15 mss a year. Pays on publication. Will send sample copy to writer for 75¢. Reports on material accepted for publication in 30 days. Returns rejected material in 30 days. Query first or submit complete ms. Enclose S.A.S.E.

Nonfiction and Photos: Articles on food subjects in retail food outlets; mainly local, in Pennsylvania and surrounding areas. Informational, interviews, profiles, historical, successful business operations, new product, merchandising technique and technical articles. Length: 500 to 900 words. Pays $25. Pays $25 maximum for minimum of 2 b&w photos purchased with mss.

PROGRESSIVE GROCER, 708 Third Ave., New York NY 10017. (212)490-1000. Editor: Edgar B. Walzer. For supermarket operators, managers, buyers; executives in the grocery business. Monthly magazine; 150 pages. Established in 1922. Circulation: 90,000. Rights purchased vary with author and material. May buy all rights, but will reassign rights to author after publication; first North American serial rights; first serial rights; second serial (reprint) rights or simultaneous rights. Buys about 20 mss a year. Pays on acceptance. Will consider photocopied and simultaneous submissions. Submit seasonal merchandising material (spring, summer, fall, holiday) 3 months in advance. Reports in 2 to 3 weeks. Query first. Enclose S.A.S.E.

Nonfiction and Photos: Department Editor: Mary Ann Linsen. Articles on supermarket merchandising; success stories; consumer relations pieces; promotional campaigns; personal pieces about people in the business. How grocers manage to relate and communicate with consumers via smart programs that really work. Tight, direct, informal, colorful writing needed. Does not want to see anything about quaint little "mom and pop" stores or "run of mill" stores with nothing more than half-hearted gourmet sections. Length: open. Pays minimum of 5¢ a word. Pays minimum of $15 for b&w glossies; $25 for color. Captions required.

SUPERMARKETING MAGAZINE, 1515 Broadway, New York NY 10036. (212)869-1300. Editor: Howard S. Rauch. For supermarket retailers; chains, independents, convenience stores, supermarket wholesalers; voluntaries, cooperatives. Magazine; 60 to 68 pages. Established in 1945. Monthly. Circulation: over 80,000. Rights purchased vary with author and material. Buys 10 to 20 mss a year. Pays on publication. Will consider photocopied submissions. No simultaneous submissions. Immediate reports on queries. Unsolicited material is not returned. Query first. Enclose S.A.S.E.

Nonfiction and Photos: Material with a heavy retail orientation, usually based on interviews with buyers at retail and/or wholesale operations. "I don't like to see the canned management or how-to-do-it material that a writer is trying to sell to umpteen different magazines. Material must exhibit a special knowledge of our field's problems. Do not submit on speculation. Material will not be returned. Await detailed instructions in reply to your query." Length: 5 to 6 double-spaced, typewritten pages. Pays $120 to $170. No additional payment for b&w photos used with mss.

TELEFOOD MAGAZINE, Davies Publishing Co., 136 Shore Dr., Hinsdale IL 60521. (312)325-2930. Managing Editor: Barbara Pattarozzi. Emphasizes only specialty and gourmet foods for retailers, supermarkets, gourmet shops and delicatessens, manufacturers/distributors, food brokers, media and advertisers. Monthly magazine; 50-60 pages. Estab: 1935. Circ: 15,000. Pays on acceptance. Buys all rights, but may reassign following publication. Phone queries OK. Submit seasonal or holiday material 2-3 months in advance. Photocopied submissions and previously published work OK. SASE. Reports in 1-3 weeks. Free sample copy and writer's guidelines.
Nonfiction: "Our needs are for articles on issue themes as determined by demands of readership; for interviews and coverage of gourmet and specialty food shops, business, manufacturers, distributors, large delicatessen operations including those within major supermarket chains or department stores. Prefer contributions from various geographical areas particularly the West and Southwest." Can be in the form of informational articles or interviews. Buys 1-2/issue. Length: 500-2,000 words. Query. "We must approve subject covered." Pays $50 minimum.
Photos: B&w glossies must accompany articles; 5x7 or 8x10. Captions required. Query and send contact sheet. Additional payment.

Grooming Products and Services

AMERICAN HAIRDRESSER/SALON OWNER, 100 Park Ave., New York NY 10017. (212)532-5588. Editor: Louise Cotter. For beauty shop owners and operators. Monthly. Buys all rights. Pays on publication. Reports "6 weeks prior to publication." Enclose S.A.S.E.
Nonfiction: "Technical material; is mainly staff-written." Pays $25 per magazine page.

HAIRSTYLIST, Allied Publications Inc., P.O. Box 23505, Fort Lauderdale FL 33307. Associate Editor: Marie Stilkind. Buys North American serial rights only. Pays on acceptance. Query not necessary. Reports in 2 to 4 weeks. Enclose S.A.S.E.
Nonfiction and Photos: Wants "articles of general interest to the professional beautician." Interested in how-to's, interviews, and profiles. Length: 500 to 1,000 words. Payment is 5¢ a word. Pays $5 for b&w glossy photos of hairstyles.

PROFESSIONAL MEN'S HAIRSTYLIST, 100 Park Ave., New York NY 10017. Editor: Sandra Kosherick. For "men and women serving the men's hairstyling and barbering profession." Monthly. Circulation: 65,000. Rights purchased vary with author and material. Buys 10 to 12 mss a year. Pays on publication. Will send a sample copy to a writer on request. Write for copy of guidelines for writers. Query first. Submit seasonal material 2 months in advance of issue date. Enclose S.A.S.E.
Nonfiction and Photos: "Matter only relating to the hairstyling profession. Material should be technical—written from the viewpoint of professionals. Currently overworked are articles on female barbers or hairstylists and unisex salons. We're interested in articles on new trends in men's hairstyling." Buys informational articles, how-to's, interviews, coverage of successful business operations, articles on merchandising techniques, and technical articles. Length: 750 to 2,500 words. Pays $25 to $50. 8x10 b&w glossies purchased with mss and on assignment. Pays $25.

WOMAN BEAUTIFUL, Allied Publications, Inc., P.O. Box 23505, Fort Lauderdale FL 33307. Associate Editor: Marie Stilkind. For "students at beauty schools and people who go to beauty salons." Buys North American serial rights only. Pays on acceptance. Reports in 2 to 4 weeks. Enclose S.A.S.E. with all submissions.
Nonfiction and Photos: "Articles on hairstyling, beauty, and fashion." Length: 500 to 1,000 words. Pays 5¢ per accepted word. Pays $5 for photos of hairstyles.

Hardware

In this classification are journals for general hardware wholesalers and retailers, lock-

smiths, and retailers of miscellaneous special hardware items. Journals specializing in the retailing of hardware for a certain trade, such as plumbing or automotive supplies, are classified with the other publications for that trade.

CHAIN SAW AGE, 3435 N.E. Broadway, Portland OR 97232. Editor: Norman W. Raies. For "mostly chain saw dealers (retailers); small businesses—typically small town, typical ages, interests, education." Monthly. Circulation: 15,000. Not copyrighted. Buys "very few" mss a year. Payment on acceptance or publication—"varies." Will send a sample copy to a writer on request. Will consider photocopied submissions. Query first. Enclose S.A.S.E.
Nonfiction and Photos: "Must relate to chain saw use, merchandising, adaptation, manufacture, or display." Buys informational articles, how-to's, personal experience articles, interviews, profiles, inspirational articles, personal opinion articles, photo features, coverage of successful business operations, and articles on merchandising techniques. Length: 500 to 1,000 words. Pays $20 to $50 ("2½¢ a word plus photo fees"). Photos purchased with mss, without mss, or on assignment; captions required. For b&w glossies, pay "varies."

CHAIN SAW INDUSTRY AND POWER EQUIPMENT DEALER, Louisiana Bank Bldg., P.O. Box 1703, Shreveport LA 71166. (318)222-3062. Editor: O.M. Word. For chain saw and outdoor power equipment dealers. Monthly. Buys first rights. Buys 1 or 2 articles per issue. Pays on publication. Will send free sample copy on request. Reports as quickly as possible. Enclose S.A.S.E. for return of submissions.
Nonfiction: Articles on successful or unusual chain saw and other small outdoor power equipment dealers, explaining factors which make them so. Human interest material necessary. Articles on unusual uses or unusual users of these tools. Articles on dealers whose profits have increased through diversification of stock. Information on new markets and accessory items. Slant to help dealers do a better job of merchandising. Reader audience varies from large hardware dealers in major cities to crossroad filling station shops in rural areas. Length: 1,000 to 1,500 words. Pays 3½¢ a word.
Photos: Purchased with mss or with captions. B&w, sharp, action if possible; caption must include identification. Pays $5.

HARDWARE AGE, Chilton Way, Radnor PA 19089. (215)687-8200. Editor: Jon P. Kinslow. For "manufacturers, wholesalers, and retailers in the hardware/housewares/lawn and garden industry. About half of our circulation is independent hardware retailers, and another significant portion is mass merchandisers." Established in 1857. Monthly. Circulation: 55,000. Buys all rights. Buys about 10 mss a year. Pays on acceptance. Will send a sample copy to a writer for $1. Write for copy of guidelines for writers. Will not consider photocopied submissions. Submit seasonal material 3 months in advance. Reports in 3 weeks. Query first or submit complete ms. Enclose S.A.S.E.
Nonfiction: Department Editor: Jay Holtzman, Managing Editor. "Articles relating how hardlines retailers increase sales and profits through better management, merchandising, etc. Generally these articles are built around a specific product category. Field research by our own editorial staff is quite thorough." Does not want to see "the round-up story on a single store which tells how that one store does a good job—usually, a good job on everything! Tell us how one store does one thing well. Better yet, tell us how several stores in different parts of the country do one thing well. We have a strong emphasis on the large volume hardlines outlet. Also, we aim for features that are more in-depth—both in the information and the geographic coverage. We have on occasion covered such non-merchandising subjects as product liability, consumerism, and black employment in the hardware industry." Length: open. Pays $100 to $125 "for a good piece with text and photos filling three pages." Captioned photos purchased with mss, without mss, or on assignment. "Photo subjects should be the same as nonfiction, and no people in the photos, please." For b&w, submit enlargements or proof sheets and negatives. Pays $10 to $15 per b&w photo, "more for series of related photos." Pays $15 minimum for color. "Prefer proof sheets. We will select for enlargements."
Fillers: "Short fillers on management/merchandising." Pays $10 to $15.

HARDWARE MERCHANDISING, 481 University Ave., Toronto 1, Ont., Canada. Editor: John O'Keefe. For "hardware retailers and hardware and houseware buyers across Canada." Monthly. Circulation: 8,900. Rights purchased vary with author and material. Buys about 12 mss a year. Pays on acceptance. Will consider cassette submissions. Query first. Enclose S.A.E. and International Reply Coupons.
Nonfiction and Photos: "Any articles demonstrating ways to increase profit for the above audience. The approach must be geared to management improving profit/image picture in retailing.

This is a Canadian book for Canadians." Buys informational articles, how-to's, coverage of successful business operations and merchandising techniques, new product articles, and technical articles. Length: open. Pays 8¢ minimum per word. 8x10 b&w glossies purchased with mss; captions optional.

NORTHERN HARDWARE TRADE, 5901 Brooklyn Blvd., Suite 203, Minneapolis MN 55429. (612)533-0066. Editor: Edward Gonzales. For "owners, managers of hardware and discount stores and lumber yards and home centers; hardware, sporting good, wholesalers." Estab: 1890. Monthly. Circ: 16,500. Not copyrighted. Pays on publication. Submit seasonal material 3 months in advance of issue date. Query first or submit complete mss. Enclose S.A.S.E.
Nonfiction and Photos: "Case histories on successful retail stores." Buys how-to's and articles on successful business operations. Pays 4¢ a word. B&w photos purchased with mss. Pays $5.

OUTDOOR POWER EQUIPMENT, 3339 W. Freeway, P. O. Box 1570, Fort Worth TX 76101. Publisher: Bill Quinn. Established in 1959. Monthly. Circulation: 10,000. Not copyrighted. Pays on publication. Query first. Enclose S.A.S.E.
Nonfiction and Photos: Photo-story of a single outstanding feature on power equipment stores (lawnmower, snowblower, garden tractors, chain saws, tiller, snowmobiles, etc.). Feature can be a good display, interior or exterior; sales tip; service tip; unusual sign; advertising or promotion tip; store layout; demonstrations, etc. Photos must be vertical. One 8x10 photo sufficient. Length: 200 to 300 words. Pays $32.50 to $37.50.

OUTDOOR POWER PRODUCTS/EQUIPEMENT MOTORISE PLEIN AIR, 481 University Ave., Toronto 1, Ont., Canada. (416)595-1811. Editor: John O'Keefe. 8 times a year. Usually buys first North American rights, but it varies. Pays on acceptance or on publication "as per agreement." Will consider cassette submissions. Query first. Enclose S.A.E. and International Reply Coupons.
Nonfiction: "We're interested in any new approach to increase the profitability of an outdoor power products dealer." Material is rejected if not Canadian in content or if it's poor quality. Length: open. Pays 8¢ minimum per word.

SOUTHERN HARDWARE, W.R.C. Smith Publishing Co., 1760 Peachtree Rd., N.W., Atlanta GA 30357. (404)874-4462. Editor-in-Chief: Ralph E. Kirby. Circulated to retailers of hardware in the 16 southern and southwestern states: independent retail hardware stores, home centers, hardware departments of building material stores. Monthly magazine; 65 pages. Estab: 1920. Circ: 16,000. Pays on the first of the month following acceptance. Buys all rights. Submit seasonal/holiday material 2-3 months in advance. SASE. Reports in 2-3 weeks. Free sample copy and writer's guidelines.
Nonfiction: Informational (how and why a store is successful with a given line), and photo feature (of a new and modern store with outstanding displays). Buys 5 mss/issue. Query or submit complete ms. Length: 500-1,000 words. Pays $60-200.
Photos: Purchased with accompanying ms. Captions required. Pays $10-20 for 5x7 or 8x10 b&w glossy prints. Model release "helpful but not required."
How To Break In: "Study a sample copy and supplementary material. Select a subject store that offers enough hard facts upon which to base an in-depth report. Good photographs should illustrate points in text. We reject shallow reporting with insufficient facts to justify article, sloppy organization of material and poor photographs."

Home Furnishings and Appliances

APPLIANCE SERVICE NEWS, 5841 Montrose Ave., Chicago IL 60634. Editor: J.J. Charous. For professional service people whose main interest is the repairing of major and portable household appliances. Their jobs consists of either service shop owner, service manager, or service technician. Monthly "newspaper style" publication; 24 pages. Established in 1950. Circulation: 41,350. Buys all rights. Buys about 2 mss per issue. Payment on publication. Will send free sample copy to writer on request. Write for copy of guidelines for writers. Will not consider photocopied submissions. Will consider simultaneous submissions. Reports in about 1 month. Query first. Enclose S.A.S.E.
Nonfiction and Photos: Department Editor: James J. Hodl. "The types of articles we publish directly relate to the business of repairing appliances. We want articles that affect service and the business it involves. We don't want articles explaining how one can get the most out of salesmen or how to increase sales. We do, however, want articles on how a servicer can better

operate his service business and how to increase his service business in his community. Each month, we run a technical article explaining how a specific appliance is repaired. Others inform the service person about how he can improve his business operation. We prefer that the freelancer write in a straightforward, easy-to-understand style about the appliance repair industry. Writing should be crisp and interesting, as well as highly informational. We prefer that articles concern appliance service people, i.e., people who repair refrigerators, ranges, washing machines, toasters, microwave ovens, etc. Electronics, like TV's, radios, etc., are not our territory." Length: open. Pays 5-7¢/word. Pays $10 for b&w photos used with mss. Captions required.

BEDDER NEWS, 322 Main St., Lewiston ID 83501. (208)746-3130. Editor: Kenny Wayne. Emphasizes the waterbed industry for waterbed retailers, distributors, manufacturers, including furniture stores and decorators. Monthly tabloid; 20 pages. Pays on publication. Buys all rights, but may reassign following publication. Phone queries OK. Submit seasonal or holiday material 3 months in advance. Simultaneous submissions and previously published work OK. SASE. Reports in 2 weeks. Sample copy $1.
Nonfiction: Medical stories relating to waterbeds, interviews with people in the waterbed industry, material on old types or use of waterbeds, new product, photo feature and technical. Buys about 25 mss a year. Length: 500-1,500 words. Submit complete ms. Pays $25-100.
Photos: B&w glossies (5x7) purchased with ms or on assignment. Captions required. Send prints. Pays $2-15.
Fillers: Clippings, jokes, anecdotes related to waterbeds. Pays $1-5.

CASUAL LIVING MAGAZINE, Time & Life Bldg., 1271 Avenue of the Americas, New York NY 10020. (212)586-2806. Editor: Marvin L. Wilder. For retailers and manufacturers of summer and casual furniture and accessories. Monthly. Circulation: 10,500. Buys all rights. Pays on acceptance. Query first. Reports in 2 weeks. Enclose S.A.S.E.
Nonfiction: "Articles on how various department stores, discount houses and specialty stores used advertising, promotion and display to improve business. Should be well-written, well-slanted, non-blurb material with good b&w photos." Length: 500 to 1,000 words. Pays $85 minimum.
Photos: Anything pertaining to outdoor and casual furniture industry; purchased with mss. Pays $5 each for 8x10's.

CHINA GLASS & TABLEWARE, 1115 Clifton Ave., Clifton NJ 07013. Editor: Susan Grisham. For tableware retailers and merchandise managers of the home furnishings department of department stores. Magazine; 40 pages. Seeks special material on January and June bridal promotions in tableware. Monthly. Circulation: 6,000. Buys all rights. Buys about 24 mss per year. Pays on publication. Will send free sample copy and editorial guidelines sheet to writer on request. Will not consider photocopied submissions. Will consider simultaneous submissions. Submit seasonal material 3 months in advance. Reports on mss accepted for publication in 4 weeks. Returns rejected material "immediately." Query first. Enclose S.A.S.E.
Nonfiction: Interested in articles on department store and specialty shop china, glass, silverware and tableware merchandising ideas; special promotion, display techniques, advertising programs, and retail activities in this field. "Writer should emphasize specific reasons why one dealer is more successful than another in tableware — or why he thinks he's better. We spotlight individuals and their efforts as opposed to a general operation's successes." Overworked subjects include specialty shops in the tableware field (especially in the Dallas area). Does not want to see articles by persons who have not been in the field of tableware retailing. Would like to see mss about department store competition in major cities and department store bridal fairs. Length 1,000 to 2,000 words. Pays $35 per printed page.
Photos: Purchased with accompanying ms with no additional payment, without accompanying ms or on assignment. Captions required. B&w only. Size 5x7 or 8x10. "Must be clear." Pays $10.

FLOORING MAGAZINE, 757 Third Ave., New York NY 10017. Editor: Michael Korsonsky. For floor covering retailers, wholesalers, floor covering specifiers, architects, etc. Monthly. Circulation: 20,000. Buys all rights. Buys 10 to 12 mss a year. Payment on acceptance. Will send free sample copy to writer on request. Query first. Reports on material in 2 to 4 weeks. Enclose S.A.S.E.
Nonfiction and Photos: "Merchandising articles, new industry developments, unusual installations of floor coverings, etc. Conversational approach; snappy, interesting leads; plenty of quotes." Informational, how-to, interview, successful business operations, merchandising techniques, technical. Length: 1,500 to 1,800 words. Pays 5¢ to 7¢ a word. 5x7 or 8x10 b&w photos. Pays $5. Color transparencies (when specified). Pays $7.50. Captions required.

FURNITURE & FURNISHINGS, 1450 Don Mills Rd., Don Mills, Ontario, M3B 2X7, Canada. (416)445-6641. Editor: Ronald H. Shuker. For an audience that includes all associated with making and selling furniture, floorcoverings and fabrics, as well as suppliers in the trade; lamps and accessories manufacturers and dealers; decorators and designers; domestic and contract readers (not consumers). Monthly magazine; 40-150 pages. Established in 1910. Circulation: 11,500. Buys first Canadian serial rights. Buys 20 mss a year. Payment on publication. Will send free sample copy to writer on request. Will not consider photocopied submissions if they have been made to other Canadian media. Submit special material for Market Previews and Product Reports 1 month in advance. Reports on material accepted for publication in 1 month. Returns rejected material immediately. Query. SASE.

Nonfiction and Photos: "The magazine is not news-oriented. Rather, it is more feature-oriented, covering various subjects in depth. Very much a merchandising magazine for home furnishings retailers in Canada. We publish merchandising and retailer success stories; product trends; management articles; promotion/advertising programs. Styles, designs, color trends. Emphasis is on how-to—what retailers can learn from what others are doing. Writing is tight, semi-aggressive, and interesting. We'd like to see feature reports analyzing the retail situation in various cities and towns in Canada; who are the top retailers in each center and why; or personality profiles of people in this industry. We do not want U.S. or foreign-oriented articles unless they report on trends in styles, designs, colors and materials used in furniture, floorcoverings, fabrics appearing in major trade shows in the U.S. and Europe with photos showing examples of these trends. Must be aimed at Canadian readers." Length: 500 to 2,000 words. Pays $100 or more, "depending on length and use of real examples." Pays $10 for b&w photos purchased with mss. Captions required.

GIFT & TABLEWARE REPORTER, 1515 Broadway, New York NY 10036. (212)764-7317. Editor: Jack McDermott. For "merchants (department store buyers, specialty shop owners) engaged in the resale of giftwares, china and glass, decorative accessories." Monthly. Circ: 36,000. Buys all rights. Pays on acceptance. Will send a sample copy to a writer on request. Query first or submit complete ms. Will consider photocopied submissions. Reports "immediately." Enclose S.A.S.E.

Nonfiction: "Retail store success stories. Be brief, be factual, describe a single merchandising gimmick. Our distinguishing factor is conciseness, fast-moving factuality. We are a tabloid format—glossy stock. Descriptions of store interiors are less important than a sales performance. We're interested in articles on aggressive selling tactics. We cannot use material written for the consumer." Buys coverage of successful business operations and merchandising techniques. Length: 300 words.

Photos: Purchased with and without mss and on assignment; captions optional. "Individuals are to be identified."

GIFTS & DECORATIVE ACCESSORIES, 51 Madison Ave., New York NY 10010. (212)689-4411. Editor: Phyllis Sweed. For the "quality gift and decorative accessories retailer, independent store and department store." Estab: 1917. Monthly. Circ: about 30,000. Buys all rights. Buys 10 to 12 mss a year. Payment on publication. Write for copy of guidelines for writers. Submit seasonal material 2 to 3 months in advance of the following deadlines: Bridal, February 15 or July 15; Christmas, July 1; resort merchandising, January 15. Reports on material in 3 months. Query first. Enclose S.A.S.E.

Nonfiction and Photos: "Our features deal with all retail phases of the gift industry; dealer case histories (a store problem and how someone solved it); and dealer activities (displays, promotions, new stores, enlargements, remodelings). Stories also deal with subjects of direct interest to gift retailers: shifts in consumer buying habits, statistical surveys and other 'think piece' subjects that have documentation of gift retailors. In case histories, be clear with detailed step-by-step descriptions of the 'how' angle. In dealer activity pieces, probe beneath obvious surface things to the 'reasons why'. In opinion articles, offer positive solutions to problems, or at least present both sides. In all stories, remember that nothing works better than short, declarative sentences with an entertaining lilt where possible." Most acceptable are case history stories with good photos. Length: 1,000 to 5,000 words. Pays $25 to $100. 5x7 or 8x10 clear and sharp b&w photos purchased with ms. Pays $7.50. Prefers 4x5 transparencies (or sharp color prints) or 35mm. Pays $7.50 for 35mm; $15 for 4x5 color transparencies.

HOME LIGHTING & ACCESSORIES, 1115 Clifton Ave., Clifton NJ 07013. (201)779-1600. Editor: Herbert M. Ballinger. A 60-page magazine for lighting retailers in all categories; specialty lighting stores, department stores, and furniture stores. Established in 1923. Circulation: 8,000. Buys First North American serial rights. Buys 60 articles a year. Pays on publication.

Will send free sample copy to writer on request. Will not accept photocopied or simultaneous submissions. Reports on submissions in 3 to 4 weeks, however, seasonal material must be sent in 3 months early or the magazine "will hold until the following year." Enclose S.A.S.E.

Nonfiction and Photos: "Ours is the only trade publication specially dedicated to lighting retailers. The way to break in with us is to report and photograph the successful, contemporary experience of lighting retailers, emphasizing display and merchandising." Seeks articles on howto, interviews, profiles, personal opinion, successful business operations, and merchandising techniques. Mr. Ballinger "would welcome any retailing feature of substance that deals with lighting." Photos are purchased alone, and with accompanying ms with extra payment. Articles including photos bring $35 to $50 per published page, while b&w shots bring $5 to $10 each. Captions are required.

LINENS, DOMESTICS AND BATH PRODUCTS, 370 Lexington Ave., New York NY 10017. (212)532-9290. Editor: Ruth Lyons. For department store, mass merchandiser, specialty store and bath boutique. 6 times a year. Buys all rights. Pays on publication. Reports in 4 to 6 weeks. Query first. Enclose S.A.S.E.

Nonfiction and Photos: Merchandising articles or personal interviews which educate the buyer on sales trends, success stories, industry news, styles; in-depth articles with photos on retail sales outlets for bath accessories, linens and sheets, towels, bedspreads. Length: 700 to 900 words. Pays $35 a published page ("the average article is 1 to 3 pages long"). Photos purchased with mss. For b&w glossies, pays $5. For Ektachrome color, pays $30.

MART MAGAZINE, Berkshire Common, Pittsfield MA 01201. Editor: Wallis E. Wood. For retailers of consumer electronics (TV, stereo, CB, etc.), major appliances (refrigerators, washers, etc.), electric housewares (toasters, blenders, coffee makers, etc.), floor care and personal care appliances (hair dryers, shavers, etc.). Semimonthly magazine. Circ: 45,000. Pays on acceptance. Buys exclusive rights in appliance/TV retailing field. SASE. Reports in 2 weeks. Free sample copy and writer's guidelines.

Nonfiction: Articles and case histories showing how retailers (appliance/TV stores, department stores, mass merchandisers, hi-fi/radio specialists, catalog showrooms and others) successfully merchandise appliances, consumer electronics, or electric housewares. Looking for stories about retail promotions, store openings and closings, and how an individual retailer solved some business problem. Length: 500-750 words for a news story; 1,200-2,500 words for a feature. Query first. Pays on a sliding scale with a $50 minimum. $250 maximum.

Photos: Submit b&w proofsheet with the negatives and brief identifications. Pays $15.

NHFA REPORTS, 405 Merchandise Mart, Chicago IL 60654. (312)527-3070. Editor: Peggy Heaton. For top management of stores specializing in all home furnishings products. Monthly magazine; 80 to 100 pages. Established in 1923. Circulation: 15,000. Buys all rights. Buys 2 to 3 mss a year. Payment on publication. Will send free sample copy to writer on request. Reports immediately. Query first. Enclose S.A.S.E.

Nonfiction and Photos: Articles on managing, merchandising, operating the home furnishings store in all facets from advertising to warehousing. Concise and very factual reporting of new developments or activities within the retail store with explanation of why and how something was accomplished, and results or benefits. "We largely present 'success' stories that give ideas the reader might want to adapt to his own individual operation." Interested in material on special services to consumers, internal cost-cutting measures, traffic-building efforts; how the small store competes with the giants; unusual display techniques or interesting store architecture. Does not want to see straight publicity or "puff" articles about store owners or their operations, with no news value or interest to others on a national basis, or articles that are too general with no specific point. Length: 800 to 2,000 words. Pays 4½ ¢ per word. 5x7 b&w glossy photos are purchased with or without mss, or on assignment. Pays $5. Captions optional.

RETAILER AND MARKETING NEWS, P.O. Box 57194, Dallas TX 75207. (214)528-5910. Editor: Michael J. Anderson. For "retail dealers and wholesalers in appliances, television, and furniture." Monthly. Circulation: 10,000. Free sample copy. No query required. Will consider photocopied submissions. Mss will not be returned unless S.A.S.E. is enclosed.

Nonfiction: "How a retail dealer can make more profit" is the approach. Wants "sales promotion ideas, advertising, sales tips, business builders, and the like, localized to the southwest and particularly to north Texas." Length: 100 to 500 words. Payment is $5-10.

SOUTHWEST HOMEFURNISHINGS NEWS, 4313 N. Central Expressway, Dallas TX 65206. Editor: Shelby L. Smith, Jr. For retail home furnishing business people; home furnishings manufacturers, and others in related fields. Magazine; 50 to 100 pages. Established in 1923. Circulation: 12,000. Not copyrighted. Buys 2 mss a year. Pays on publication. Sometimes pays in copies only. Will send a free sample to writer on request. No photocopied or simultaneous submissions. Reports in 2 weeks. Query first. Enclose S.A.S.E.

Nonfiction: Informational articles about selling, construction of furniture, credit, business, freight, and transportation. "Must have honest, well-researched approach." Interview, nostalgia, new product, merchandising techniques, technical. Length: 750-2,000 words. Pays $50 maximum. Prior agreement must be reached before submitting.

Hospitals, Nursing, and Nursing Homes

In this section are journals for nurses; medical and nonmedical nursing home, clinical, and hospital staffs; and laboratory technicians and managers. Journals for physicians in private practice or that publish technical material on new discoveries in medicine will be found in the Medical category.

DOCTORS' NURSE BULLETIN, 9600 Colesville Rd., Silver Spring MD 20901. (301)585-1056. Editor: Bob Bickford. Quarterly. Occasionally copyrighted. Pays on publication. Reports in a few days. Enclose S.A.S.E.

Nonfiction: Uses articles of interest to the doctor's nurse. Pays from $5 to $50, depending on length and value.

Photos: Buys photographs with mss and with captions only. B&w only. Pays $3 minimum.

HOSPITAL FORUM, Association of Western Hospitals, 830 Market St., San Francisco CA 94102. (415)421-8720. Editor-in-Chief: Richard Tuggle. Emphasizes hospital administration. Monthly magazine; 24 pages. Estab: 1959. Circ: 10,000. Buys one-time rights. Phone queries OK. SASE. Reports in 2 months. Free guidelines for writers.

Nonfiction: Publishes informational and how-to articles on hospitals. Length: 500-5,000 words. Pays $50 maximum. Query first.

HOSPITAL PROGRESS, The Catholic Hospital Association, 1438 S. Grand Blvd., St. Louis MO 63104. (314)773-0646. Editor: Robert S. Stephens. For hospital and nursing home administrators, trustees and department heads. Monthly magazine; 100 pages. Estab: 1920. Circ: 15,000. Buys all rights. Phone queries OK. SASE. Photocopied submissions OK. SASE. Reports in 3 months. Free guidelines for writers.

Nonfiction: Publishes how-to, and informational articles and interviews with government and hospital leaders. Must be in-depth (not superficial) reports of hospital administration. Buys 5 mss a year. Length: 1,000-2,000 words. Query first. Pays $1 per column inch.

HOSPITAL SUPERVISOR'S BULLETIN, Bureau of Business Practice, 24 Rope Ferry Rd., Waterford CT 06386. Editor: Barbara Kelsey. For hospital supervisors. Semimonthly newsletter; 8 pages. Estab: 1968. Circ: 8,000. Pays on acceptance. Buys all rights. Submit seasonal/holiday material 6 months in advance. Photocopied submissions OK. SASE. Reports in 4 weeks. Free sample copy and writer's guidelines.

Nonfiction: Publishes interviews with hospital department heads. "You should ask supervisors to pinpoint current problems in supervision, tell how they are trying to solve these problems and what results they're getting — backed up by real examples form daily life." Also publishes articles on people problems and good methods of management. People problems include the areas of training, planning, evaluating, counseling, discipline, motivation, supervising the undereducated, getting along with the medical staff, etc., with emphasis on good methods of management. "We prefer 4- to 6-page typewritten articles, based on interviews." Pays 10¢/word after editing.

JOURNAL OF PRACTICAL NURSING, 122 E. 42 St., New York NY 10017. Editor: Candace S. Gulko, R.N. For practical nurses, practical nurse educators, registered nurses, hospital and nursing home administrators, and other allied health professionals. Monthly magazine; 32 to 44 pages. Established in 1951. Circulation: 50,000. Buys, or acquires, all rights. Buys, or accepts, 10 to 20 mss a year. Payment, when made, is on publication. Seventy percent of the material is contributed without any payment, except for contributor's copies. Will send free sample copy to writer on request. Write for copy of guidelines for writers. Will not consider photocopied or simultaneous submissions. Reports in 1 month. Query first. Enclose S.A.S.E.

Nonfiction and Photos: "Clinical articles on new developments in treatment, new approaches to patient care, research in medicine, learning approaches, books, nursing experience, human interest. Special emphasis should be on the attitude or approach of the practical nurse." Uses informational, how-to, personal experience, interviews, historical, think pieces, personal opinion and technical articles. Length: 800 to 2,000 words. Rate of payment is $10 to $50. No additional payment for b&w photos used with mss. Captions required.

NURSING CARE, 75 E. 55th St., New York NY 10022. (212)688-7110. Editor: Serena Stockwell. For licensed practical nurses. 12 times a year. Circulation: 70,000. Buys North American serial rights. Pays on acceptance. Will send free sample copy on request. Query first. Enclose S.A.S.E.
Nonfiction: Nursing articles geared specifically to licensed practical nurses and their profession. "We prefer clinical teaching material from which our readers can learn, keep up to date on new medical developments, or refresh their skills. I would also like more articles on the nurse as a person; articles that improve her self-esteem and relationships with people (not just with patients); assertiveness, training, supervisory skills, coping with a career and a family at the same time, etc. I'd like more first-person stories from nurse-writers and more on nutrition." Length: maximum 2,500 words. Pays $20 per published page; 2 to 3 typewritten pages usually equal 1 published page.

PROFESSIONAL MEDICAL ASSISTANT, One East Wacker Dr., Chicago IL 60601. Editor: Susan S. Croy. "About 95% of our subscribers belong to the American Association of Medical Assistants. They are professional people employed by a doctor of medicine." Established in 1957. Bimonthly. Circulation: 18,000. Rights purchased vary with author and material. Buys about 2 mss/year. Pays on publication. Free sample copy. Will consider photocopied submissions. Reports in 2 weeks. Submit complete ms. Enclose S.A.S.E.
Nonfiction and Photos: "Articles dealing with clinical and administrative procedures in a physician's office. Request our publication to study for the style we require." Buys informational articles, how-to's, and humor. Length: 500 to 2,500 words. Pays $15 to $50.
Fillers: "Crosswords for allied health personnel, find the word," or "word-search" puzzles. Pays $7.50.

RN, 680 Kinderkamack Rd., Oradell NJ 07649. (201)262-3030. Editor: Don L. Berg. For registered nurses, mostly hospital-based but also in physicians' offices, public health, schools, industry. Monthly magazine of 100 pages. Established in 1937. Circulation: 240,000. Buys all rights. Buys 20 to 30 mss a year. Payment on acceptance. Will send free sample copy on request. Write for copy of guidelines for writers. Will not consider photocopied or simultaneous submissions. Reports in 2 to 3 weeks. Query first or submit complete ms. Enclose S.A.S.E.
Nonfiction: "If you are a nurse who writes, we would like to see your work. Editorial content: diseases, clinical techniques, surgery, therapy, research, equipment, drugs, etc. These should be thoroughly researched and sources cited. Personal anecdotes, experiences, observations based on your relations with doctors, hospitals, patients and nursing colleagues. Our style is simple, direct, not preachy. Do include examples, case histories that relate the reader to her own nursing experience. Talk mostly about people, rather than things. Dashes of humor or insight are always welcome. Include photos where feasible." Length: 8 to 10 double-spaced, typewritten pages. Pays up to 10¢ per word.
How To Break In: "Most material we buy is written by R.N.'s. A freelancer has to have some technical expertise in our field and understand our audience. Best bet: study the magazine before trying to write for it."

Hotels, Motels, Clubs, Resorts, Restaurants

Journals which emphasize retailing for bar and beverage operators are classified in the Beverages and Bottling category. For publications slanted to food wholesalers, processors, and caterers, see Food Products, Processing, and Service.

CLUB & FOOD SERVICE, P.O. Box 788, 211 Broadway, Lynbrook NY 11563. Editor: Glenn E. Flood. For men and women who are managers and supervisors of U.S. military clubs and food service operations and Washington policy writers regarding military welfare and recreation; Congressmen, etc. Monthly magazine; 48 pages. Established in 1967. Circulation: 11,000.

Buys all rights. Buys 2 mss a year. Payment on publication. Free sample copy. Will not consider simultaneous or photocopied submissions. Reports in 1 month. Query first or submit complete ms. Enclose S.A.S.E.

Nonfiction and Photos: Interested in new ideas in management; interviews with club and food service leaders; how certain businesses operate; facilities; budget managing; how to increase profits. Informational, how-to, think pieces, spot news, merchandising techniques. Length: 500 to 2,500 words. Pays 5¢ to 8¢ a word. Pays $5 to $7 for b&w and color photos purchased with or without accompanying mss. Captions required.

CLUB EXECUTIVE, 1028 Connecticut Ave. N.W., Washington DC 20036. (202)296-4514. Editor: Paul E. Reece. For military club managers. Monthly. Not copyrighted. Pays on publication. Reports in 2 weeks. Enclose S.A.S.E.

Nonfiction: Articles about food and beverages, design, equipment, promotional ideas, etc. Length: 1,500 to 2,000 words. Pays 4¢ a word.

EXECUTIVE HOUSEKEEPER, North American Publishing Co., 401 N. Broad St., Philadelphia, PA 19108. (215)574-9600. Editor-in-Chief: Marsha Gaspar. For "professionals in the field of institutional housekeeping." Monthly magazine; 64 pages. Estab: 1964. Circ: 15,000. Payment on publication. Buys all rights, but may reassign following publication. Submit seasonal or holiday material 3 months in advance. Photocopied submissions OK. SASE. Reports in 3 weeks. Free sample copy and writer's guidelines.

Nonfiction: Expose (government legislation/regulations relevant to housekeeping), informational (management, housekeeping topics), interview (with innovative executive housekeepers), new product (must be relevant), and technical. Buys 6 mss per issue. Query. Length: 1,000-3,500. Pays $40-100.

Photos: Purchased with mss; no additional payment. Captions required. B&w or color;5x7 preferred. Model release required.

Columns, Departments: Feedback and Reader Rap-Up. Buys 3 columns per issue. Submit complete ms. Length: 200-1,000 words. Pays $10-50. Open to suggestions for new columns and departments.

How To Break In: "Our audience takes themselves, their jobs and our publication seriously. Every major hotel/motel, hospital and nursing home has a housekeeping department whose responsibilities include more than washing windows. Recognize their self-respect and you'll stand a good chance of understanding what we'll publish."

FOOD EXECUTIVE, 508 IBM Building, Fort Wayne IN 46805. (219)484-1901. Associate Editor: Carleton B. Evans. For restaurant, hotel, cafeteria owners and managers. Bimonthly. Not copyrighted. Pays on acceptance. Query first. Enclose S.A.S.E.

Nonfiction: Material dealing with restaurant, institutional, industrial, and catering food service (includes government and military) operation and techniques such as cost control, personnel, portion control, layout and design, decor, merchandising. Also new trends in the food service industry, general economic problems, labor situations, training programs for personnel. Must be written for professionals in the field. Length: 500 to 2,000 words. Pays 1½¢ per word.

Photos: "Pertinent photos." Pays $3 to $5.

KANSAS RESTAURANT MAGAZINE, 359 South Hydraulic St., Wichita KS 67211. (316)267-8383. Editor: Neal D. Whitaker. For food service operators. Special issues: Christmas, October Convention, Who's Who in Kansas Food Service, Beef Month, Dairy Month, Wheat Month. Monthly. Circulation: 1,400. Not copyrighted. Pays on publication. Will send sample copy for 50¢. Reports "immediately." Enclose S.A.S.E.

Nonfiction and Photos: Articles on food and food service. Length: 1,000 words maximum. Pays $10. Photos purchased with ms.

LODGING AND FOOD SERVICE NEWS, 131 Clarendon St., Boston MA 02116. Managing Editor: Mrs. Susan G. Holaday. For managers and executives of hotels, motels, restaurants, fast food operations, contract feeders, country clubs, etc. Established in 1925. Every 2 weeks. Circulation: 8,000. Not copyrighted. Pays on publication. Will send sample copy to writer on request. Submit seasonal material 6 months in advance. Reports in 1 month. Query first. Enclose S.A.S.E.

Nonfiction and Photos: News relating to hotels, restaurants, etc. Travel and tourism trends. Features on unusual operations. Stories on new chains and expansions. Must have hard-breaking news orientation. Stories on food service promotions for the holidays and summer merchandising news. Length: 16 to 80 double-spaced lines. Pays $25 minimum. Pays $5 for 8x10 b&w glossies used with mss.

MOTEL/MOTOR INN JOURNAL, Box 769, Temple TX 76501. (817)778-1311. Editor: Walter T. Proctor. For owners and managers of motels, motor inns and resorts in the U.S. Magazine; 42 to 100 pages. Established in 1937. Monthly. Circulation: 28,000. Buys all rights. Buys about 15 mss a year. Pays on acceptance. Will send free sample copy to writer on request. Write for copy of guidelines for writers. No photocopied submissions. Will consider simultaneous submissions. Submit seasonal (holiday) material 2 months in advance. Reports in 10 days. Query first. Enclose S.A.S.E.
Nonfiction and Photos: Factual articles designed to help owners/managers to be more effective, and to become more profitable operators of such properties. How-to articles on profitable holiday promotions. "We stress less emphasis on big hotels; more on medium-sized to large motels and motor inns and resorts. We don't want general articles on community relations, or how to be a better manager, etc." Length: "4 to 6 pages, double-spaced." Pays $10 per double-spaced, typed page. B&w photos (5x7 or 8x10) and top-quality color transparencies purchased with mss. Pays $5 for b&w; $10 for color.

NATION'S RESTAURANT NEWS, 425 Park Ave., New York NY 10022. Editor: Charles Bernstein. "National business newspaper for food service chains and independents." Published every 2 weeks. Circulation: 52,000. Pays on acceptance.
Nonfiction: "News and newsfeatures, in-depth analyses of specific new types of restaurants, mergers and acquisitions, new appointments, commodity reports, personalities. Problem: Most business press stories are mere rehashes of consumer pieces. We must have business insight. Sometimes a freelancer can provide us with enough peripheral material that we'll buy the idea, then assign it to staff writers for further digging." Length: 500 words maximum. Pays $5 to $75.
Photos: B&w glossies purchased with mss and captions only. Pays $10 minimum.
How To Break In: "Send most wanted material, such as personality profiles, business-oriented restaurant news articles, but no how-to stories."

PIZZA AND PASTA, 23 N. Washington, Suite 201, Ypsilanti MI 48197. Editor: Lynda L. Boone. For pizzeria owners and managers, Italian restaurateurs, and manufacturers and wholesalers in related fields. Publication of the Pizza and Pasta Association. Magazine; 58 (8½x11) pages. Established in 1969. Quarterly. Circulation: 24,500. Buys first rights. Buys 4 mss a year. Payment on acceptance. Will send free sample copy to writer on request. Will consider photocopied submissions. Reports in 3 weeks. Query first. "We will give consideration to a completed article, but a query first would be helpful, both to the writer and to us." Enclose S.A.S.E.
Nonfiction and Photos: "Articles dealing with the operation of pizzerias and Italian restaurants; decor, customer relations, advertising, community service, management, employee training ... all aspects of running a successful food service establishment. Humor, unless both the slant and content are exceptional, is not used. Interviews with successful owners and operators are used in each issue, but these are not accepted from freelancers. The point of view should be from that of the store owner and operator; generally, an article from the customer's point of view would not be used. A direct and businesslike approach is a necessity with our readers. Style should be easy to read and concise. Must have cohesiveness and flow. Don't pad the article to the nth degree in an attempt to camouflage a lack of knowledge of the market. We'd be quite interested in seeing a survey-type article done on what the general public thinks of pizza; specifically, pizza is a very nutritious food, but the public probably doesn't think of it as such. If a freelancer has an inexpensive way of contacting people in various parts of the country, this could be great." Uses informational articles, how-to and those on merchandising techniques. Length: 500 words minimum; 7 double-spaced typed pages, maximum. Pays $15 to $20 for short articles; $35 for feature articles. Photos are not usually needed, but can use 5x7 b&w glossies. Pays $3. "Photos are only purchased if they illustrate a point made in the article; they are not usually needed with the type of article we purchase from freelance writers."

RESORT & MOTEL MAGAZINE, Page Publications, Ltd., 380 Wellington St., W., Toronto, Ontario, Canada M5V 1E3. (416)366-4608. Editor: John Burry. For resort owners and managers; hotels, motels, etc. Magazine; 50 to 60 pages. Established in 1962. Every 2 months. Circulation: 7,000. Buys one-time rights. Buys 10 to 20 mss a year. Pays on publication. Will send sample copy to writer on request. Write for copy of guidelines for writers. Reports on material accepted for publication in 6 weeks. Returns rejected material in 2 weeks. Query first. Enclose S.A.E. and International Reply Coupons.
Nonfiction: Informational, technical and how-to articles. Interviews. Articles on travel, successful business operations, new products, merchandising techniques. Length: open. Pays 6¢ a word or $40 per published page.

RESORT MANAGEMENT, P.O. Box 4169, Memphis TN 38104. (901)276-5424. Editor: Allen J. Fagans. For "the owners and/or managing executives of America's largest luxury vacation resorts." Monthly. Buys first rights only. Pays on publication. Will send free sample copy on request. Query first. "Editorial deadline is the 1st of the month; i.e., January material must be received by December 1." Reports in 10 days. Enclose S.A.S.E.

Nonfiction and Photos: "This is not a travel or tourist publication. It is a 'how-to-do-it' or 'how-it-was-done' business journal. Descriptive background of any sort used to illustrate the subject matter must be held to a minimum. Our material helps managers attract, house, feed and provide entertainment for guests and their friends, and bring them back again and again. Any facet of the resort operation could be of interest: guest activities, remodeling, advertising and promotion, maintenance, food, landscaping, kitchen, personnel, furnishings, etc. We do not want to see material relating to any facet of commercial hotels, motels, motor courts, fishing and hunting camps, housekeeping or other facilities serving transients. Material submitted must be accurate, to the point, and supported by facts and costs, plus pertinent examples illustrating the subject discussed." Length: 800 to 1,000 words. Pays 60¢ per inch for a 20-em column; 40¢ per inch for a 13-em column. "Photos of the resort and of its manager, and the subject(s) being discussed are a must." Pays $5/photo.

Fillers: Uses clippings related to resorts and resort area organizations only. Promotions: president, general manager, resident manager (including changes from one resort to another). Resort Obituaries: president, owner, general manager. Resort construction: changes, additions, new facilities, etc. New resorts: planned or under construction. Changes in resort ownership. Resort news: factual news concerning specific resorts, resort areas, state tourism development. Not interested in clippings about city hotels, roadside motels, motor inns or chain (franchise) operations. Clippings must be pasted on individual sheets of paper, and addressed to Clipping Editor. Your complete mailing address (typed or printed) must be included, as well as the name of the newspaper or magazine and date of issue. Do not send advertisements or pictures. Clippings will not be returned unless a self-addressed envelope and sufficient postage is enclosed. Pays $1 per clipping used.

Industrial Management

The journals that follow are for industrial plant managers, executives, distributors, and buyers; some industrial management journals are also listed under the names of specific industries, such as Machinery and Metal Trade. Publications for industrial supervisors are listed in Management and Supervision.

COMPRESSED AIR, 253 E. Washington Ave., Washington NJ 07882. Editor: C.W. Beardsley. Emphasizes the technologies and applications of pneumatics, hydraulics and associated energy forms, processes, and equipment that do the world's work; allied subjects. Monthly magazine. Estab: 1896. Circ: 100,000. Pays on publication. Buys all rights, but may reassign following publication. Photocopied submissions OK. SASE. Reports in 2 weeks. Free sample copy.

Nonfiction and Photos: "Case histories of pneumatic and hydraulic applications; in-depth articles about companies using pneumatics and hydraulics in construction and mining projects. Unusual and unique applications of air power. Must be factually and technically accurate, but in a quasi-technical style. This is not a 'how-to' magazine." Informational, historical, think articles, successful business operations, technical. Length: open. Pays $60 per published page. Photos purchased with ms. Captions required.

ENERGY NEWS, P.O. Box 1589, Dallas TX 75221. (214)748-4403. Editor: Claribel Simpson. For natural gas industry and oil industry executives and management personnel and related industries' management (suppliers, consultants). Newsletter; 4 (8½x11) pages. Established in 1970. Every 2 weeks. Circulation: 500. Buys all rights. Pays on publication. Will send free sample copy to writer on request. Will consider simultaneous and photocopied submissions. Reports in 2 weeks. Submit complete ms. Enclose S.A.S.E.

Nonfiction: Latest news about the industry; discoveries, government regulations, construction projects, new trends, supplies, prices of natural gas. Concise, personal style (as to a certain small group, as opposed to mass media style). Length: 250 to 500 words maximum. Pays 10¢ a word.

ENERGY WEEK, P.O. Box 1589, Dallas TX 75221. Publisher: Ernestine Adams. For general industry executives who need to know about the energy situation to make decisions, obtain supplies; energy industry executives, suppliers, consultants, etc., to energy industry. Newsletter; 4 (8½x11) pages. Estab: 1969. Buys all rights. Pays on publication. Will consider photocopied and simultaneous submissions. Reports in 2 weeks. S.A.S.E.

Nonfiction: News about new trends, energy supply, prices for all energy items (crude, LPG, natural gas, gasoline, etc.), research of all branches of the energy industry; oil, coal, gas, solar, etc. Must be concise and aimed at general industry. Length: 250 words maximum. Pays 10¢ a word.

HANDLING AND SHIPPING, 614 Superior Ave. W., Cleveland OH 44113. (216)696-0300. Executive Editor: John F. Spencer. For operating executives with physical distribution responsibilities in transportation, material handling, warehousing, packaging, and shipping. Monthly. Buys all rights. Pays on publication. "Query first with 50-word description of proposed article." Enclose S.A.S.E.

Nonfiction and Photos: Material on aspects of physical distribution management, with economic emphasis. Informational and successful business operations material. Writer must know the field and the publications in it. Not for amateurs and generalists. Length: 1,500 to 3,000 words. Pays minimum of $30 per published page. Additional payment is made for b&w photos used with mss, but they must be sharp, for good reproduction. No prints from copy negatives. Any size. Color used may be prints or transparencies.

INDUSTRIAL DISTRIBUTION, 205 E. 42 St., New York NY 10017. (212)573-8100. Editor: George J. Berkwitt. Monthly. Buys all rights. Will consider cassette submissions. Enclose S.A.S.E.

Nonfiction: "Articles aimed at making industrial distributor management, sales and other personnel aware of trends, developments and problems and solutions in their segment of industry. Articles accepted range widely; may cover legislation, sales training, administration, Washington, marketing techniques, case histories, profiles on industry leaders, abstracted speeches — any area that is timely and pertinent and provides readers with interesting informative data. Use either roundups or bylined pieces." Length: 900 words minimum. Pays "flat fee based on value; usually $100 per published page."

INDUSTRIAL DISTRIBUTOR NEWS, 1 West Olney Ave., Philadelphia PA 19120. Managing Editor: Stephen A. Albertini. For industrial distributors, wholesalers of industrial equipment and supplies; business managers and industrial salesmen. Established in 1959. Monthly. Circulation: 29,500. Will send free sample copy to writer on request. Reports on material within 6 weeks. "Company policy dictates no bylined articles except when noted by publisher. Therefore, no freelance material used unless assigned through initial query first." Enclose S.A.S.E.

Nonfiction and Photos: "Factual feature material with a slant toward industrial marketing. Case studies of distributors with unusual or unusually successful marketing techniques. Avoid triteness in subject matter. Be sure to relate specifically to industrial distributors." Informational, how-to, interview. Length: 500 to 3,000 words. B&w 8x10 or 2¼x2¼ color transparencies.

INDUSTRIAL NEWS *(Southern California Industrial News, North California Electronic News, Northern California Industrial News, Southwest Industrial News, Pacific Northwest Industrial News, Pacific Coast Plastics, Southern California Electronics News),* P.O. Box 3631, Los Angeles CA 90051. Editor: Larry Liebman. For manufacturing executives and industrial suppliers, as well as technical people (engineers and chemists). Tabloid newspapers. Established in 1948. *Southern California Industrial News* is published weekly. The balance are monthlies. Circulation: over 50,000. Buys simultaneous rights. Payment on publication. Will send free sample copy to writer on request. Will consider photocopied and simultaneous submissions. Reports in 2 weeks. Query first. Enclose S.A.S.E.

Nonfiction and Photos: Hard news, industry oriented. Should pertain to the area of each publication. Should be to the point, not long-winded or overly technical. Not interested in energy crisis stories by instant experts. Does like to see the how-to approach in all industrial situations, without it being a "puff" for a particular producer. Informational, interview, profile, expose, spot news, successful business operations, new products, merchandising techniques. Length: 50 to 100 typewritten lines. Pays $10 to $50. No additional payment for b&w photos used with mss. Captions required.

INDUSTRIAL WORLD, 386 Park Ave., S., New York NY 10016. (212)689-0120. Editor and Publisher: S. W. Kann. For plant managers abroad. Monthly. Buys first world rights. Pays on publication. Will send a sample copy to a writer on request. Query first. Formal outlines not required; paragraph of copy sufficient. Reports in 30 days. Enclose S.A.S.E.

Nonfiction and Photos: "Interested primarily in articles dealing with application of U.S. industrial machinery and know-how abroad. Clear, factual data necessary. Articles of more than passing interest to plant managers on production tools, techniques, unusual installation, new or novel solutions to production problems, etc. Should be slanted for the overseas plant manager." Length: 1,000 to 3,000 words. Pays "$75 for first printed page of article, $50 for each subsequent page." Photos purchased with mss. 5x7 or 8x10 glossies only; must be clean, professional, quality. ("If necessary, we will make prints from author's negatives which will be returned. Photos supplied, however, are usually not returned.")

How To Break In: "Concentrate on the adaptations of industrial know-how in the developing nations. Your best chance of getting an assignment will be if you are planning to travel in one of the less frequently traveled areas and have an idea for a story of this kind. We tend to rely on regular contributors in certain areas and if you plan to stay abroad, you could become a stringer."

INDUSTRY WEEK, Penton/IPC, Inc., 1111 Chester Ave., Cleveland OH 44114. (216)696-7000. Editor-in-Chief: Stanley Modic. Emphasizes manufacturing and related industries for top or middle management (administrating, production, engineering, finance, purchasing or marketing) throughout industry. Biweekly magazine; 100 pages. Estab: 1882. Circ: 230,000. Pays on publication. Buys all rights. Phone queries OK. Submit seasonal or holiday material 3 months in advance. Simultaneous and photocopied submissions OK. Previously published work OK. SASE. Reports in 4 weeks. Sample copy $2.

Nonfiction: How-to and informational articles (should deal with areas of interest to manager audience, e.g., developing managerial skills or managing effectively). Length: 1,000-4,000 words. Buys 15-20 a year. Query first. Pays $60/published page.

Photos: Chris Nehlen, department editor. B&w and color purchased with ms or on assignment. Query first. Pays $35 minimum. Model release required.

Rejects: Product news and clippings.

MODERN PLANT OPERATION AND MAINTENANCE, 209 Dunn Ave., Stamford CT 06905. (203)322-7676. Editor: Kenneth V. Jones. For plant engineers and managers. Quarterly. Circulation: 55,000. Buys all rights. Pays on acceptance. "We reject all unsolicited material unseen, as we are not set up to handle it. All assignments come from us and we can use only the people who truly know the field. Send letter stating qualifications and availability." Enclose S.A.S.E. Do not send query letters.

Nonfiction and Photos: Length: 600 to 1,000 words. Pays $100 to $150.

NORTHEASTERN INDUSTRIAL WORLD, 2 Penn Plaza, Suite 2360, New York NY 10001. (212)564-0340. Editor-in-Chief: David T. Paul. For senior executives in northeastern manufacturing, service and industrial development. Monthly magazine; 40 pages. Estab: 1955. Circ: 150,000. Pays on publication. Buys all rights, but may reassign following publication. Phone queries OK. Submit seasonal or holiday material 2 months in advance. Previously published work OK. SASE. Reports in 2 weeks. Free sample copy and writer's guidelines.

Nonfiction: "Feature articles deal vith energy, finance, legislation, economic and community development and innovations in industrial techniques and theories." Expose, historical, how-to, informational, new product and technical articles; interviews and profiles. "Best potential area for freelancers are expose and historical." Length: 1,800-2,700 words. Query. Purchases very few mss; must be material unavailable from industry sources. Pays $50-200.

Photos: B&w glossies (8x10) used with mss. Captions required. Query. No additional payment.

THE PHILADELPHIA PURCHASOR, 1518 Walnut St., Suite 610, Philadelphia PA 19102. Editor-in-Chief: Howard B. Armstrong, Jr. For buyers of industrial supplies and equipment, including the materials of manufacture, as well as the maintenance, repair and operating items; and for buyers of office equipment and supplies for banks and other industries. Magazine; 65 (8¼x11¼) pages. Established in 1926. Monthly. Circulation: 4,000. Not copyrighted. Buys 25 to 35 mss a year. Pays on acceptance. Will send free sample copy to writer on request. Write for copy of guidelines for writers. Will consider photocopied and simultaneous submissions. Reports in a month. Query first or submit complete ms. Enclose S.A.S.E.

Nonfiction and Photos: "We use articles on industrial, service and institutional purchasing — *not* consumer. We also use business articles of the kind that would interest purchasing personnel. Ours is a regional magazine covering the middle Atlantic area, and if material takes this into account, it is more effective." Length: 900 to 1,200 words. Pays minimum of $15. No additional payment for b&w photos used with mss.

PRODUCTION ENGINEERING, Penton Plaza, 1111 Chester Ave., Cleveland OH 44114. (216)696-7000. Editor: Larry L. Boulden. "The production engineering magazine; interested in concepts, procedures and hardware involving production processes and machines, handling equipment, controls, and manufacturing information handling plus personal and professional development." Established in 1954. Circulation: 90,000. Buys all rights. Buys less than 20 mss a year. Payment on publication. Will send sample copy to writer for $1. Write for copy of guidelines for writers. Will consider photocopied submissions. Submit seasonal material 4 months in advance. Reports on material in "about a month." Query first or submit complete ms. Enclose S.A.S.E.

Nonfiction and Photos: "Feature articles and short items describing new equipment, new components and free new literature related to our readers' interests. Keep the interests and characteristics of our readers in mind. Try to supply illustrations or ideas for good graphics." Length: 3,000 to 5,000 words. Pays average of $25 per printed page. 8x10 b&w glossies; 3x5 or larger transparencies (8x10 prints) purchased with mss. Captions required.

PURCHASING, 221 Columbus Ave., Boston MA 02116. Editorial Director: Robert Haavind. For purchasing specialists, primarily in manufacturing industries. Semimonthly. Circulation: 72,000. Buys all rights. Buys about 20 mss a year. Payment on publication. Will send free sample copy to writer on request. Submit seasonal material 3 months in advance. Reports in 10 days. Query first. Enclose S.A.S.E.

Nonfiction: Some news items (on price shifts, purchasing problems, etc.) from stringers. Features on better purchasing methods (with real examples), on evaluating or specifying. Items must be generalized and objective. Back up topics with good data, examples, charts, etc. No product pitches. Particularly interested in contract writing, negotiating techniques. Informational, how-to, and spot news. Length: 500 to 1,500 words. Pays $50 to $150.

THE WASHINGTON PURCHASER, P.O. Box 9038, Seattle WA 98109. Production Editor: Norman P. Bolotin. Associate Editor: Cristine Laing. For readers doing purchasing for commercial, government and industrial firms. Magazine; 32 to 80 pages. Established in 1925. Monthly. Circulation: 2,500. Buys first North American serial rights. Pays on publication. Will send sample copy to writer on request. Write for copy of guidelines for writers. No photocopied or simultaneous submissions. Reports in 1 week to 1 month. Query first. Enclose S.A.S.E.

Nonfiction: Articles on techniques for buying, from office supplies to heavy industrial materials and general business and economic trends. "Use of freelance material is limited and writers must follow typical rules of style, remembering that readers want concise material that must benefit them in their jobs as buyers of various commodities." Informational, how-to, interview, new product, merchandising techniques, technical articles. Pays $10 to $25.

Insurance

BUSINESS INSURANCE, 740 N. Rush Street, Chicago IL 60611. Editor: Susan Alt. For "corporate risk managers, insurance brokers and agents, insurance company executives. Interested in insurance, safety, security, consumerism, employee benefits." Special issues on safety, pensions, health and life benefits, international insurance. Biweekly. Circulation: 35,000. Buys all rights. Buys 75 to 100 mss a year. Pays on publication. Submit seasonal or special material 2 months in advance. Reports in 2 weeks. Query required. Enclose S.A.S.E.

Nonfiction: "We publish material on corporate insurance and employee benefit programs and related subjects. We take everything from the buyers' point of view, rather than that of the insurance company, broker, or consultant who is selling something. Items on insurance company workings do not interest us. Our special emphasis on corporate risk management and employee benefits administration requires that freelancers discuss with us their proposed articles before going ahead. Length is subject to discussion with contributor." Payment is $2.50 a column inch.

EQUIFAX, Box 4081, Atlanta GA 30302. (404)875-8321. Editor: H.A. McQuade. For "management employees of most American corporations, especially insurance companies. This includes Canada and Mexico. Pass-along readership involves sub-management and non-management people in these firms. Distributed by Equifax, Inc." Quarterly. Circulation: 89,000. Copyrighted; "we allow customer publications free reprint privileges. Author free to negotiate fee independently, however." Buys 3 to 5 mss a year. Pays on acceptance. Will send a sample copy to a writer on request. Query first: "present idea in paragraph outline form. Accepted queries should result in authors' submitting double-spaced copy, typed 35 characters to the line, 25 lines to the page." Reports in 2 to 3 weeks. Enclose S.A.S.E.

Nonfiction and Photos: "Insurance-related articles —new trends, challenges, and problems facing underwriters, actuaries, claim men, executives, and agents; articles of general interest in a wide range of subjects —the quality of life, ecology, drug and alcohol-related subjects, safe driving, law enforcement, and insurance-related Americana; inspirational articles to help managers and executives do their jobs better. Write with our audience in mind. Only articles of the highest quality will be considered. Especially interested in material written by insurance underwriters, executives, college instructors, and college professors on previously unpublished or updated facets of our area of interest. More than 90% of our readers are customers f Equifax, Inc., or its various affiliates, and they expect to see articles that help them know and understand the business information business." Buys inspirational articles, think pieces about insurance industry needs for business information services, etc. Length: 1,000 to 2,000 words. Pays 1¢ to 2¢ a word, "depending on quality and importance of material, but not less than $25." B&w glossies relating to theme of article purchased with mss; 5x7 or 8x10. Pays $5 to $15.

Jewelry

AMERICAN HOROLOGIST & JEWELER, Roberts Publishing Co., 2403 Champa St., Denver CO 80205. (303)572-1777. Managing Editor: Kathleen P. Eagan. Specializes in watch/clock making and repair/jewelry. For professional watch and clock repairmen; jewelers, retail store owners, manufacturing wholesalers, students and hobbyists. Monthly magazine; 84 pages. Estab: 1936. Circ: 13,000. Pays on publication. Buys first North American serial rights. Phone queries OK. Submit seasonal/holiday material 2 months in advance. Previously published mss OK. Reports in 3 weeks. SASE. Free sample copy and editorial guidelines.

Nonfiction: How-to articles on various watch, clock or jewelry repairs; informational (industry news or features and management articles on retailing); interviews (with industry personalities); photo features (if timely); and technical articles (must pertain to horological or jewelry field). Buys 8-10 mss/year. Length: 1,000-3,500 words. Pays $10-100.

Photos: Patricia Barnes, Art Director. B&w and color purchased with or without mss or on assignment. Query first. Total purchase price usually includes payment for photos. Pays $10-50 for b&w purchased on assignment; $25-150 for color.

Special Needs: "Would love to begin a new technical column on watch or clock repair, but must have knowledgeable writer." Query first. Length: 1,500-3,000 words. Pays $35-150.

AMERICAN JEWELRY MANUFACTURER, 340 Howard Bldg., 155 Westminster St., Providence RI 02903. (401)274-3840. Editor: Steffan Aletti. For manufacturers of supplies and tools for the jewelry industry; their representatives, wholesalers and agencies. Established in 1956. Monthly. Circulation: 5,000. Buys all rights (with exceptions). Buys 2 to 5 mss a year. Will send free sample copy to writer on request. Write for copy of guidelines for writers. Will consider photocopied submissions. Submit seasonal material 3 months in advance. Reports on material within a month. Query first. Enclose S.A.S.E.

Nonfiction and Photos: "Topical articles on manufacturing; company stories; economics (i.e., rising gold prices). Story must inform or educate the manufacturer. Occasional special issues on timely topics, i.e., gold; occasional issues on specific processes in casting and plating. We reject material that is not specifically pointed at our industry; i.e., articles geared to jewelry retailing, not the manufacturers." Informational, how-to, interview, profile, historical, expose, successful business operations, new product, merchandising techniques, technical. Length: open. Payment "usually around $25." B&w photos purchased with ms. 5x7 minimum.

CANADIAN JEWELLER, The Giftware and Jewellry Magazine, 481 University Ave., Toronto, Ontario, Canada MW5 1A7. (416)595-1811. Editor: Dennis Mellersh. For retail jewellers. Magazine; 75 pages. Established in 1876. Monthly. Circulation: 4,000. Rights purchased vary with author and material. May buy all rights, but will reassign rights to author after publication; or first North American serial rights. Pays on acceptance. Write for copy of guidelines for writers. No photocopied or simultaneous submissions. Reports in 2 weeks. Query first. "Speculative material is generally not on target for our specific requirements." Enclose S.A.E. and International Reply Coupons.

Nonfiction and Photos: Informative articles which help jewellers buy more effectively. Length: open. Pays 10¢ a word. B&w photos purchased with mss. Pays minimum of $7.50. "If photography is assigned, the custom is to pay the photographers a daily, half-day, or hourly fee and a nominal charge for prints."

JEWELER'S CIRCULAR-KEYSTONE, Chilton Company, Radnor PA 19089. Editor: George Holmes. For "retail jewelers doing over $30,000 annual volume." Monthly. Circulation: 28,000. Buys all rights. Buys 10 or 12 mss a year. Pays on publication. SASE.
Nonfiction: Wants "how-to-articles, case history approach, which specify how a given jeweler solved a specific problem. No general stories, no stories without a jeweler's name in it, no stories not about a specific jeweler and his business." Length: 1,000 to 2,000 words.

MODERN JEWELER, 15 W. 10th St., Kansas City MO 64105. Managing Editor: Dorothy Boicourt. For retail jewelers and watchmakers. Monthly. Pays on acceptance. Will send sample copy only if query interests the editor. Reports in 30 days. Enclose S.A.S.E.
Nonfiction and Photos: "Articles with 3 or 4 photos about retail jewelers—specific jewelers, with names and addresses, and how they have overcome certain business problems, moved merchandise, increased store traffic, etc. Must contain idea adaptable to other jewelry operations; 'how-to' slant. Informal, story-telling slant with human interest. We are not interested in articles about how manufacturing jewelers design and make one-of-a-kind jewelry pieces. Our readers are interested in retail selling techniques, not manufacturing processes. Photos must include people (not just store shots) and should help tell the story. We reject poor photography and articles written as local newspaper features, rather than for a business publication." Pays average $70 to $90 for article and photos.

THE NORTHWESTERN JEWELER, Washington and Main Sts., Albert Lea MN 56007. Publisher: John R. Hayek. Monthly. Not copyrighted. Pays on publication. Enclose S.A.S.E.
Nonfiction and Photos: Uses news stories about jewelers in the Northwest and Upper Midwest and feature news stories about the same group. Also buys retail jeweler "success" stories with the "how-to-do" angle played up, and occasionally a technical story on jewelry or watchmaking. Pictures increase publication chances. Pays 1¢ a published word. Pays $2.50 per photo.

PACIFIC GOLDSMITH, 41 Sutter St., San Francisco CA 94104. (415)986-4323. Editor: Robert B. Frier. For jewelers and watchmakers. Magazine; 80 to 90 pages. Established in 1903. Monthly. Circulation: 6,000. Not copyrighted. Buys about 12 mss a year. Pays on acceptance. Will send sample copy to writer for $1. No photocopied or simultaneous submissions. Submit seasonal (merchandising) material 3 to 4 months in advance. Reports on material accepted for publication in 1 week. Returns rejected material immediately. Query first or submit complete ms. Enclose S.A.S.E.
Nonfiction and Photos: "Our main interest is in how western jewelers can do a better selling job. We use how-to-do-it merchandising articles, showing dealers how to sell more jewelry store items to more people, at a greater profit. Seasonal merchandising articles are always welcome, if acceptable." Length: 1,500 to 2,000 words. Pays 2¢ a word. Pays $5 for b&w photos used with mss; 3x5 minimum. Captions required.

SOUTHERN JEWELER, 75 Third St., N.W., Atlanta GA 30308. (404)881-6442. Editor: Charles Fram. For southern retail jewelers and watchmakers. Monthly. Circulation: 4,400. Not copyrighted. Pays on publication. Submit seasonal material 2 months in advance. Enclose S.A.S.E. for return of submissions.
Nonfiction: Articles relating to southern retail jewelers regarding advertising, management, and merchandising. Buys spot news about southern jewelers and coverage of successful business operations. Prefers *not* to see material concerning jewelers outside the 14 southern states. Length: open. Pays 1¢ per word.
Photos: Buys b&w glossies. Pays $4.

Journalism

Because many writers are familiar with the journals of the writing profession and might want to submit to them, those that do not pay for contributions are identified in this list. Writers wishing to contribute material to these publications should write the editors for their requirements or query before submitting work.

THE CALIFORNIA PUBLISHER, 1127 11th St., Suite 1040, Sacramento CA 95814. (916)443-5991. Editor: Harvi Callahan. Does not pay.

CANADIAN AUTHOR & BOOKMAN, Canadian Authors Association, Box 120, Niagara-on-the-Lake, Ontario, Canada L0S 1J0. (416)468-7391. Editor-in-Chief: Duncan S. Pollock. For writers, young and old; beginning and established — primarily Canadian and interested in the Canadian writing scene. Quarterly magazine; 40 pages. Estab: 1921. Circ: 3,000. Pays on publication. Buys first North American serial rights. Phone queries OK. Submit holiday/seasonal material 9 months in advance. Simultaneous submissions OK, if so identified. Photocopied submissions and previously published work OK. Reports in 2 months. Free sample copy and writer's guidelines.

Nonfiction: Publishes how-to articles (how to write; how to sell; the specifics of the different genre — what they are and the how of them); informational articles (the writing scene — mainly Canadian — who's who and what's what); interviews (with writers, mainly leading ones, but also those with a story that can help others write/sell more/more often); personal opinion and personal experience (only if helpful to other writers). Buys 10 mss per issue. Query preferred. Length: 100-5,000 words (average: 1,000-5,000 words). Pays $5-75.

Photos: B&w glossies are only purchased with mss. Prefers 8x10. No additional payment (as such), but value of article will increase 10-20%.

Columns, Departments: Publishes serious or lighthearted pieces about language and its uses in A Matter of Language; book reviews in All About Books. Length: 100-500 words. Query first since these are assigned. Pays $5.

Poetry: Peggy Fletcher, department editor. Publishes all forms of poetry, free verse and light verse; must be of very high quality. Buys 12 per issue. Submit complete ms. Length: open. Pays $2-5.

How To Break In: "With something that will teach other writers. You don't have to be an established pro in order to teach (most of them are too busy to write for a writer's magazine, anyway), but you must have learned something about how to do it more often. Pass the lesson on and you're in with CA&B."

THE CATHOLIC JOURNALIST, 119 N. Park Ave., Rockville Center NY 11570. "We are no longer buying freelance material."

COLLEGE PRESS REVIEW, Department of Journalism, Bradley University, Peoria IL 61625. (309)676-7611. Editor: John W. Windhauser. For members of the National Council of College Publications staffs, editors, and faculty advisers; staff members of student publications, journalism professors and others interested in the student communication media. Established in 1956. Quarterly. Circulation: 1,000. Acquires all rights, but may reassign rights to author after publication. No payment. Will send sample copy to writer for $1.50. Write for copy of guidelines for writers. Will consider photocopied submissions. No simultaneous submissions. Reports in 1 to 4 months. Query first or submit complete ms. Enclose S.A.S.E.

Nonfiction and Photos: Articles by, about, and of interest to college publication staffs, editors, and faculty advisers. Articles should focus on the editing, advising, and production of college newspapers, magazines, and yearbooks. "We like to use articles on research and opinion in the student communications media and related areas. We also like to use features on journalism techniques. The writer should write in a readable style. We will accept no manuscripts that read like term papers." Topical subjects of interest include use of new technology on campus publications; case studies of censorship problems at private schools, tips on purchasing new equipment; the adviser's role in revitalizing a dying publication. Length: 3,000 words maximum. B&w glossy photos used with ms. Captions required.

COLUMBIA JOURNALISM REVIEW, 700 Journalism Building, Columbia University, New York NY 10027. (212)280-3872. Editor: Kenneth M. Pierce. "We welcome queries concerning the media, as well as subjects covered by the media. All articles are assigned. We reject sloppy, incomplete reporting and lack of clear, carefully thought-out point of view (judgment and analysis)."

EDITOR & PUBLISHER, 850 Third Ave., New York NY 10022. (212)752-7050. Editor: Robert U. Brown. For newspaper publishers, editors, executives, employees and others in communications, marketing, advertising, etc. Magazine: 60 pages. Established in 1884. Weekly. Circulation: 26,000. Pays on publication. Will send sample copy to writer for 50¢. Query first. Enclose S.A.S.E.

Nonfiction: Department Editor: Jerome H. Walker, Jr. Uses newspaper business articles and news items; also newspaper personality features.

Fillers: "Amusing tyographical errors found in newspapers." Pays $2.

FEED/BACK, THE JOURNALISM REPORT AND REVIEW, Journalism Department, San Francisco State University, 1600 Holloway, San Francisco CA 94132. (415)469-1689. Editors: B.H. Liebes, Lynn Ludlow. Managing Editor: David M. Cole. For the working journalist, the journalism student, the journalism professor, and the journalistic layman. Magazine; 60 pages. Established in 1974. Quarterly. Circulation: 1,750. Not copyrighted. Pays in subscriptions and copies. Will send free sample copy to writer. Will consider photocopied and simultaneous submissions. Reports on material accepted for publication in 1 month. Returns rejected material in 2 weeks. Query first. Enclose S.A.S.E.
Nonfiction and Photos: In-depth views of journalism in Northern California. Criticism of journalistic trends throughout the country, but with a local angle. Reviews of books concerning journalism. Informational, interview, profile, humor, historical, think pieces, expose, nostalgia, spot news, successful (or unsuccessful) business operations, new product, technical; all must be related to journalism. Rejects articles that are not documented, or those in which the subject matter is not pertinent or those which show personal prejudice not supported by evidence. Length: 1,000 to 10,000 words. B&w glossies (8x10 or 11x14) used with or without mss. Pays in subscriptions and/or copies, tearsheets for all material.

FOLIO, 125 Elm St., P.O. Box 697, New Canaan CT 06840. (203)972-0761. Editor: Howard S. Ravis. For publishing company executives. Monthly magazine; 80 pages. Estab: 1972. Circ: 5,900. Pays on publication. Acquires all rights. Query. SASE.
Nonfiction: "Covers 6 specific areas of interest to executives of magazine publishing companies: management (including finances), sales, circulation and fulfillment, production, editing, and graphics. All material should be written with our audience in mind. Above all, we are a how-to magazine, and stories should have information that can be applied by publishers and/or other magazine management people." Length: 3,500 words maximum for most; "articles for each of the departments (1 department for each of the areas mentioned above) run to about 1,800 words." Pays $50 minimum.

THE JOURNALISM EDUCATOR, Department of Journalism, University of Wyoming, Laramie WY 82071. (307)766-3122. Editor: William Roepke. For journalism professors and a growing number of news executives in the U.S. and Canada. Published by the Association for Education in Journalism. Founded by the American Society of Journalism Administrators. Quarterly. Enclose S.A.S.E.
Nonfiction: "We do accept some unsolicited manuscripts dealing with our publication's specialized area — problems of administration and teaching in journalism education. Because we receive more articles than we can use from persons working in this field, we do not need to encourage freelance materials, however. A writer, generally, would have to be in journalism/communications teaching or in some media work to have the background to write convincingly about the subjects this publication is interested in. The writer also should become familiar with the content of recent issues of this publication." Maximum length: 2,500 words. Does not pay.

JOURNALISM QUARTERLY, School of Journalism, Ohio University, Athens OH 45701. (614)594-6710. Editor: Guido H. Stempel, III. For members of Association for Education in Journalism; also, other academicians and journalism practitioners. Established in 1923. Quarterly. Usually acquires all rights. Circulation: 4,000. Write for copy of guidelines for writers. Will consider photocopied submissions. Submit only complete ms "in triplicate." Reports in 4 to 6 months. Enclose S.A.S.E. for return of submissions.
Nonfiction: Research in mass communication. Length: 4,000 words maximum. No payment.
How To Break In: "There's no best way other than to write the best article you can based on the best research you can do. We do not solicit mss, and we judge all submissions on the same basis."

MEDICAL COMMUNICATIONS, School of Journalism, College of Communication, Ohio University, Athens OH 45701. (614)594-2671. Editor: Byron T. Scott. For medical libraries, members of the American Medical Writers Association, physicians, journal and magazine editors, medical illustrators and pharmaceutical advertising people. Quarterly, 24- to 32-page digest size magazine. Established in 1971. Circulation: over 2,000. Acquires first North American serial rights. Uses 6 to 8 freelance mss per issue. Payment in contributor's copies. Will send sample copy for $1.25. Will not consider photocopied or simultaneous submissions. Submit seasonal or special material 2 to 3 months in advance. Reports on material accepted for publication in 6 weeks. Returns rejected material in 4 weeks. Query first. Enclose S.A.S.E.
Nonfiction and Photos: Articles relating to any aspect of medical communications including inter- and intra-personal writing. May be either philosophic or how-to with the proviso that it

must tell the medical communicator something that will enrich his professional goals and achievements. "We are more of a journal than a magazine, but like to take a less formal approach in the hopes of improving an article's readability across the broad range of AMWA membership." Uses fairly serious, straightforward style. Humor accepted, but rarely. Footnotes may be required. Does not want to see anything on "how doctors can't communicate with their patients. We know this, and improving the situation is a major purpose of our organization." Length: 1,500 to 3,000 words. Charts and photos are used with mss, if needed. Payment in copies.

MILITARY MEDIA REVIEW, Defense Information School, Bldg. 400, Ft. Benjamin Harrison, Indianapolis IN 46216. (317)542-2173. Editor-in-Chief: Connie McKean. For military and Civil Service employees of the Department of Defense and all military branch services in the field of information/public affairs; print, broadcast and photojournalism. Quarterly magazine; 32 pages. Estab: 1972. Circ: 6,000. Pays in contributor's copies. Not copyrighted. Phone queries OK. Submit seasonal/holiday material 3 months in advance. Simultaneous and photocopied submissions and previously published work OK. Reports in 1 month. Free sample copy and writer's guidelines.
Nonfiction: "Basically, our magazine prints how-to articles in the fields of military public affairs, print, broadcast and photojournalism. An example topic might be 'How to run a military press center', or 'How to illustrate a military newspaper', or 'How to design a post newspaper', etc. Occasionally, we run an interview or profile of an outstanding figure in our field. Personal opinion and experience features must be informative. They must relate information which our readers will find useful in the field. Photo features and technical articles also must relate to the field." Length: 1,000-4,000 words. Query first or submit complete ms.
Photos: Uses b&w photos with or without mss. Prefers 8x10 glossies. Query first or send prints. Model release required.
How To Break In: "Practical and theoretical experience in the field is almost a must."

MORE, A Critical Review of the Nation's Media, 750 Third Ave., New York NY 10017. Editor: Richard Pollak. For "both men and women active in media, and readers and viewers interested in how media operates." Monthly. Circulation: 20,000. Rights purchased vary with author and material. Usually buys all rights, but will reassign them to author after publication. Buys 70 mss a year. Pays on publication. Will send a copy to writer for $1. Query first. Reports promptly. Enclose S.A.S.E.
Nonfiction: Publishes "critical evaluations of the media—print and electronic, overground and underground. Heavy emphasis on solid reporting and good writing. Essayists need not apply. With the exception of the generally scholarly *Columbia Journalism Review*, there is no publication doing what we do." Length: "ordinarily 4,000 words." Pays 10¢ a word.

THE PEN WOMAN MAGAZINE, 1300 17th St., N.W., Washington DC 20036. Editor: Wilma W. Burton. For women who are professional writers, artists, composers. Publication of National League of American Pen Women. Magazine: 32 to 36 (6x9) pages. Established in 1920. Published 9 times a year, October through June. Circulation: 6,000. Rights purchased vary with author and material. Buys 2 or 3 mss per year. Pays on publication. Will send free sample copy to writer if S.A.S.E. is enclosed with request. Will "sometimes" consider photocopied submissions. No simultaneous submissions. Submit seasonal material 3 to 4 months in advance. Reports on mss accepted for publication in 6 weeks. Returns rejected material immediately. Enclose S.A.S.E.
Nonfiction: "We are overstocked from our own members. Only on occasion do we accept freelance material which must be of unusual appeal in both information and inspiration to our readers." Mss (slanted toward the professional writer, composer and artist) should be 300 to 1,500 words.
Fiction: Department Editor: Rosemary Stephens. "Usually purchase or use reprints from recognized magazines; use some original materials."
Poetry: Department Editor: Anne Marx. Uses traditional forms, blank verse, experimental forms, free verse, light verse and haiku. "We encourage shorter poems under 36 lines. Usually reprints from members."

PHILATELIC JOURNALIST, P.O. Box 150, Clinton Corners NY 12514. (914)266-3150. Editor: Gustav Detjen, Jr. For "journalists, writers, columnists in the field of stamp collecting." Established in 1971. Bimonthly. Circulation: 1,000. Not copyrighted. Pays on publication. Will send a sample copy to a writer on request. Will consider photocopied submissions. Submit seasonal material 2 months in advance. Reports in 2 weeks. Query first. Enclose S.A.S.E.
Nonfiction and Photos: "Articles concerned with the problems of the philatelic journalist, how

to publicize and promote stamp collecting, how to improve relations between philatelic writers and publishers and postal administrations. Philatelic journalists, many of them amateurs, are very much interested in receiving greater recognition as journalists. Any criticism should be coupled with suggestions for improvement." Buys profiles and personal opinion articles. Length: 250 to 500 words. Pays $15 to $30. Photos purchased with ms; captions required.

PNPA PRESS, 2717 N. Front St., Harrisburg PA 17110. (717)234-4067. Editor: Ruth E. Kuhn. No payment.

PUBLISHERS' AUXILIARY, 491 National Press Bldg., Washington DC 20004. Editor: Jeffrey Colin Van. For newspaper publishers, general managers, other newspaper executives. Publication of the National Newspaper Association. 24-page newspaper published twice a month. Established in 1865. Circulation: 13,000. Copyrighted. Payment on publication. Will consider photocopied submissions. Submit special issue material 1 month in advance. Reporting time varies. Returns rejected material immediately. Query first. Enclose S.A.S.E.
Nonfiction and Photos: "We are a newspaper for newspaper people. We use only items that relate to some aspect of newspaper publishing, written in newspaper style. Since our audience is almost exclusively management people, all material is geared toward management. All work is assigned and is primarily coverage of newspaper organization meetings." Does not want to see features on "old-time" journalists. Is interested in material on newspaper plant design. How-to, interview, profile, successful business operations, new product, merchandising techniques; book reviews. Length: open. Pays $25 to $50. B&w photos purchased on assignment. Pays minimum of $5.

THE QUILL, National Magazine for Journalists, 35 E. Wacker Dr., Chicago IL 60601. (312)236-6577. Editor: Charles Long. For newspaper reporters and editors, broadcast newspeople, photographers, magazine writers and editors, freelance writers, journalism educators and students, public relations and advertising executives and others interested in journalism. Established in 1912. Monthly. Circulation: 30,000. Payment for assigned feature articles only. Rights acquired vary. Will send free sample copy to writer on request. Query first. Enclose S.A.S.E.
Nonfiction: "Articles relating to all aspects of journalism; particularly those dealing with freedom of information matters and issues dealing with professionalism and ethics, freedom of the press articles, profiles of people and places in the media; news items. Regardless of the subject matter, write in a readable style and a structure understandable to a lay audience; nothing that appears like a term paper or thesis."

ST. LOUIS JOURNALISM REVIEW, 928 N. McKnight, St. Louis MO 63132. (314)991-1698. A critique of St. Louis media, print and broadcasting, by working journalists. Bimonthly. Buys all rights. Enclose S.A.S.E.
Nonfiction: "We buy material which analyzes, critically, local (St. Louis area) institutions, personalities, or trends. Payment starts at $20."

SCHOLASTIC EDITOR, 720 Washington Ave., S.E., Suite 205, University of Minnesota, Minneapolis MN 55414. Editor: Judy Schell. For high school and college journalism students, publications editors, staffs and advisers as well as mass media people. Monthly (Sept.-May with Dec.-Jan. issues combined) magazine; 32 pages, 8½x11. Special issue in April, Summer Workshop issue; articles on summer journalism workshops would be appropriate. Established in 1921. Circulation: 3,000. Buys all rights, but will reassign rights to author after publication. Buys about 30 mss each year. Pays in contributor's copies. Will send free sample copy to writer on request. Will consider photocopied submissions. Query or submit complete ms for nonfiction. Reports in 2 to 4 weeks. Enclose S.A.S.E.
Nonfiction and Photos: "How-to articles on all phases of publication work, photography, classroom TV and the general field of communications. How to save money setting up a darkroom, make your yearbook layouts exciting with press-on lettering, etc. Style should avoid using first person. Looking for articles that have a lively, exciting approach. Especially interested in articles that suggest interesting illustration possibilities." Informational, how-to, personal experience, profile, photo feature, spot news, successful business operations, new product articles, merchandising techniques, technical; journalism and mass media topics book reviews. Length: 10 to 20 typed, double-spaced pages for articles. Regular columns are Reading Between the Lines (book reviews), and People, Products, Etc., Publicity (news releases) and Down the Road in Time (futuristics). Length: 2 pages, double-spaced, typed. 8x10 b&w glossies wanted, but will accept smaller if not accompanied by ms. Captions optional. Have occasional use for mood photos.

THE WRITER, 8 Arlington St., Boston MA 02116. Editor: A.S. Burack. Monthly. Pays on acceptance. Uses very little freelance material. Enclose S.A.S.E.
Nonfiction: Articles of instruction for writers. Length: about 2,000 words. Pays minimum $35.

WRITER'S DIGEST, 9933 Alliance Rd., Cincinnati OH 45242. (513)984-0717. Editor: John Brady. For writers. Estab: 1919. Monthly. Circulation: 120,000. Buys first magazine rights. Buys about 65 mss/year. Pays on acceptance. Free sample copy. Photocopied submissions OK. Submit seasonal material at least 5 months in advance of issue date. Reports in 3 weeks. "Query first for in-depth features." SASE.
Nonfiction: "Practical, instructional features on specific types of writing for the freelance market. In-depth market features on major magazine and book publishing houses; interviews with outstanding writers. Discussions of specialized fields of writing, such as greeting cards, wire service reporting, comedy writing, script writing, new potential freelance markets, etc. Regular columns cover poetry, cartooning, nonfiction, fiction, and photojournalism. We also publish articles on subjects related to the business aspects of writing for publication. Our style is lively and anecdotal. We see—and reject—too many articles that *tell,* but do not *show.* Our motto here at camp: No generalizations without examples. We also prefer articles with *solid reportorial underpinning.* Our writers should treat how-to articles as they would feature assignments for a city or business magazine. They should interview other writers for their hints and stories, and dig in the library for material that will give the article perspective. The freelancer who *reports* as well as writes for us will stand a much better chance than the freelancer who merely draws from personal experience and holds forth on a topic. At the moment we're short on articles on writing techniques—writing transistions, plotting in fiction, characterization, organizing an article. We also need more material on writing books and juvenile fiction and nonfiction. Profiles and Q&A's *must* be accompanied by candid and tight mug shots, taken against the background of the interview." Length: 500 to 3,000 words. Pays 10¢/word; "more for outstanding pieces."
Photos: "Well-known writers, the writing life, for inside and cover use." B&w only. Send contact sheet first. Pays $20-50.
Fillers: Clippings, etc., about well-known writers. Will not be returned. Pays $2 to $5.
How To Break In: "We have several editorial departments that are fertile ground for a hardworking freelancer. The Writing Life uses brief, robust items that are offbeat and on-the-scene. Items are generally 100 to 500 words—the shorter the better. The reporting must be fresh, the writing polished. Light verse welcome, too. We pay $20 to $50 for articles; $10 to $20 for verse. How I Do It is open to writers who have a valuable hint to share in 500 words or less. We're more interested in pieces on researching and writing techniques than in pieces on how to convert old envelopes into files. We pay $25-50. Biolines uses short and pointed profiles of writers —the famous, the infamous and the obscure. Must be likely and balanced; no valentines, please —and no brickbats. Piece won't sell here without fresh and lively quotes from the subject—as well as tight and crisp shots that have a sense of place as well as of person. Package is usually a 500-word ms and one or two contrasting b&w photos. We pay $75. We're always looking for freelancers who can deliver responsible reporting and lively writing. A writer who can produce polished and balanced spots for our editorial departments stands a good chance of getting an assignment when she/he queries us later on a useful full-length feature. You might go to market for us. Is your specialty wine magazines, or Tasmanian religious journals? Let's see an article— 1,5000 words or less — on how to write for that market. We're interested in your material on researching and *writing* techniques for a particular field. And — last and never least — *read the magazine.*Our slant is simple: how the freelancer can turn out good work and make money. Any manuscript that does not satisfy that slant will be rejected—no matter how well-written it is. Your best bet is to sit down with a year's backlog of *WD* and study it. What areas have we missed? What questions have we left unanswered? What new opportunities for the freelancer are we leaving untouched? Tell us that, and you'll have our full attention. And maybe our money."

WRITER'S YEARBOOK, 9933 Alliance Rd., Cincinnati OH 45242. Editor: John Brady. For writers, writer/photographers and cartoonists. Established in 1930. Annual. Buys first rights only. Buys about 20 mss a year. Pays on acceptance. Will send sample copy to writer for $2.50. "Writers should query in summer with ideas for the following year." Will consider *good-quality* photocopied submissions. Enclose S.A.S.E.
Nonfiction: "I want articles that reflect the current state of writing in America," says editor Brady. "Trends, inside information, money-saving and money-making ideas for the freelance writer. Material on writer's hardware—typewriters, cameras, recorders, etc.—and how they can be used to make writing easier or more lucrative. I'm also interested in the writer's spare time—

what she/he does to retreat occasionally from the writing wars; where to refuel and replenish the writing spirit. I also want a big interview (or profile) or two, always with *good* pictures. Articles on writing techniques that are effective today are always welcome." Length: 750 to 3000 words. Pays 10¢/word.

Photos: Usually purchased with manuscripts as part of package; b&w only; depending on use, pay is $20 to $50 per published photo.

WRITING, Sean Dorman Manuscript Society, 4 Union Pl., Fowey, Cornwall, U.K. PL23 1BY. Editor-in-Chief: Sean Dorman. For writers of all ages and education. Quarterly tabloid; 52 pages. Estab: 1959. Circ: 500. Pays on publication. All rights reserved to the author. Simultaneous and photocopied submissions and previously published work OK. Reports in 1 month. Sample copy $1.

Nonfiction: How-to and informational articles about writing in any form. Buys 4 mss/issue. Length: 300-350 words. Submit complete ms. Pays 2 pounds for double use in linked issues. ("The same articles appear in the spring and summer issues, and in the linked autumn and winter issues.")

Poetry: Traditional forms, free verse and light verse. Buys 4/issue. Submit poems. Pays 2 pounds for double use in a pair of linked issues.

Laundry and Dry Cleaning

Some journals in the Coin-Operated Machines category are also in the market for material on laundries and dry cleaning establishments.

AMERICAN DRYCLEANER, 500 N. Dearborn St., Chicago IL 60610. (312)337-7700. Editor: Paul T. Glaman. For professional drycleaners. Monthly. Circulation: 30,000. Buys all rights. Pays on publication. Will send free sample copy on request. Reports "promptly." Enclose S.A.S.E.

Nonfiction and Photos: Articles on merchandising, diversification, sales programs, personnel management, consumer relations, cost cutting, workflow effectiveness, drycleaning methods. "Articles should help the drycleaner build his business with the most efficient utilization of time, money and effort, inform the drycleaner about current developments within and outside the industry which may affect him and his business, introduce the drycleaner to new concepts and applications which may be of use to him, teach the drycleaner the proper methods of his trade. Tight, crisp writing on significant topics imperative. Eliminate everything that has no direct relationship to the article's theme. Select details which add depth and color to the story. Direct quotes are indispensable." Pays 3¢ to 5¢ per word. Photos purchased with mss; quality 8x10 b&w glossies. Photos should help tell story. No model releases required. Pays $5.

AMERICAN LAUNDRY DIGEST, American Trade Magazines, Inc., 500 N. Dearborn St., Chicago IL 60610. (312)337-7700. Editor-in-Chief: Ben Russell. For a professional laundering, linen rupply, uniform rental audience. Monthly magazine; 52 pages. Estab: 1936. Circ: 16,000. Pays 2 weeks prior to publication. Buys all rights. Phone queries OK. Photocopied submissions OK. SASE. Reports in 2 weeks. Free sample copy and writer's guidelines.

Nonfiction: How-to articles about how laundrymen have cut costs, increased production, improved safety, gained sales, etc. "Interviews with laundrymen about how they run a successful plant would be welcome." Query. Length: 300-3,000 words. Pays 4¢/word.

Photos: B&w glossies (8x10 preferred; 5x7 acceptable) purchased with mss. Send contact sheet. Pays $5.

INDUSTRIAL LAUNDERER, 1730 M St., N.W., Suite 613, Washington DC 20036. (302)296-6744. Editor: James W. Roberts. For decisionmakers in the industrial laundry industry. Publication of the Institute of Industrial Launderers, Inc. Magazine; 124 pages. Established in 1949. Monthly. Circulation: over 3,000. Buys all rights, but will reassign rights (with some exceptions) to author after publication. Buys 15 to 20 mss a year. Pays on publication. Will send free sample copy to writer on request. Write for copy of guidelines for writers. No photocopied or simultaneous submissions. Reports in 1 week. Query first. Enclose S.A.S.E.

Nonfiction and Photos: General interest pieces for the industrial laundry industry; labor news, news from Washington; book reviews on publications of interest to people in this industry. Technical advancements and "people" stories. Informational, personal experience, interview, profile, historical, successful business operations, merchandising techniques. Length: no less than 750 words. Payment negotiable. No additional payment for 8x10 b&w glossies used with ms. Pays minimum of $5 for those purchased on assignment. Captions required.

How To Break In: "Send covering letter, outlining article and describing photos available, along with copies of published material."

Law

BARRISTER, American Bar Association Press, 1155 E. 60th St., Chicago IL 60637. (312)947-4072. Managing Editor: Elizabeth H. Cameron. For young lawyers who are members of the American Bar Association, concerned about practice of law, improvement of the profession and service to the public. Quarterly magazine; 80 pages. Estab: 1974. Circ: 105,000. Pays on acceptance. Buys all rights, but may reassign following publication; or first serial rights or second serial (reprint) rights, or simultaneous rights. Photocopied submissions OK. SASE. Reports in 4-6 weeks. Free sample copy.
Nonfiction: "As a magazine of ideas and opinion, we seek material that will help readers in their inter-related roles of attorney and citizen. Major themes in legal and social affairs. Reference to legal questions in a topic may be helpful; we examine the inter-relationship between law and society. Expository or advocacy articles welcome; position should be defended clearly in good, crisp, journalistic prose." Length: 1,000-3,000 words. Query first, Pays $150-400.
Photos: Donna Tashjian, department editor. B&w (8x10) glossies and 35mm color transparencies purchased without accompanying ms. Pays $35 minimum for b&w; $50 minimum for color.

JURIS DOCTOR MAGAZINE FOR THE NEW LAWYER, 730 Third Ave., New York NY 10017. Editor: Zachary Sklar. For "young lawyers, ages 25 to 37." 11 times per year. Circulation: 160,000. Buys first rights. Buys 30 mss a year. Pays on publication. Will send a free sample copy to a writer on request. Query first "with 2 short writing samples and an outline." Reports in 5 weeks. Enclose S.A.S.E.
Nonfiction: Wants articles on the legal profession, as well as travel and leisure items. Writer should show a knowledge of law, but should not be overly technical. Willing to research. "Most articles are muckraking pieces about the profession—the organized bar, law schools, new areas of legal practice. We also run book reviews." Interested in how-to, interviews, and profiles. Length: 1,000 to 3,500 words. Book reviews, 900 words. Payment is 10¢ a word. $50 for reviews.
Photos: B&w glossies purchased with mss and with captions only. Payment is $25.

LAWYER'S NEWSLETTER, 1180 S. Beverly Dr., Los Angeles CA 90035. Editor: Stephan Z. Katzan. For attorneys. Bimonthly. Buys all rights. Pays on publication. Will send a sample copy to a writer on request. Reports in 2 weeks. Enclose S.A.S.E.
Nonfiction: "Our publication's main purpose is to increase the efficiency of attorneys and of law office operations. We are interested in suggestions and ideas for improvement of office operations as well as articles on legal economics." Length: 2,000 words maximum. Pays $100 per article.

LEGAL ECONOMICS, 1155 E. 60th St., Chicago IL 60637. Editor: Robert P. Wilkins. For the practicing lawyer. Magazine; 52-64 pages. Established in 1975. Quarterly. Circulation: 18,000. Rights purchased vary with author and material. Usually buys all rights, but may reassign rights to author after publication for special purposes. Pays on publication. Free sample copy and writer's guidelines. Returns rejected material in 90 days, if requested. Query first. Enclose S.A.S.E.
Nonfiction and Photos: "We assist the practicing lawyer in operating and managing his office in an efficient and economical manner by providing relevant articles and editorial matter written in a readable and informative style. Editorial content is intended to aid the lawyer by informing him of management methods which will allow him to provide legal services to his clients in a prompt and efficient manner at reasonable cost." Pays $50-100. Pays $10-20 for b&w photos purchased with mss; $15-25 for color.

STUDENT LAWYER, American Bar Association, 1155 E. 60th St., Chicago IL 60637. (312)947-4077. Editor-in-Chief: David Martin. For law students. Monthly (except summer) magazine; 56 pages. Estab: 1952. Circ: 30,000. Pays on publication. Buys all rights, but may reassign following publication. Submit seasonal/holiday material 2 months in advance. Photocopied submissions OK. SASE. Reports in 2 weeks. Sample copy $1; free writer's guidelines.
Nonfiction: Expose (government, law, education, corporate), how-to (get through law school, take the bar exam, establish a practice), humor (pertaining to law students' lives, lawyers),

interview (government and legal individuals of prominence), personal experience (surviving law school, practice, bar exam), personal opinion (government, law, legal education), photo feature (a day in the life of a lawyer), and profile (lawyers, government officials) articles. Buys 8 mss/ issue. Query. Length: 3,000-5,000 words. Pays $150-300.

Photos: Purchased with or without accompanying ms or on assignment. Query. Pays $35-75 for 5x7 b&w photos; $50-150 for color. Model release required. "Photos should center around ideas of the law, justice, education, etc., and may be used to illustrate any number of articles."

Columns/Departments: Book Reviews (reviews of legal biographies, consumer interest books on government, corporate interests, etc.), Status (news stories on legal education), Briefly (short subjects on new legal developments), Legal Aids (highlighting office products, books, mags, new services that will help lawyers). Buys 4 mss/issue. Query. Length: 100-1,500 words. Pays $25-50.

Fiction: "We run fiction that deals with lawyers." Buys 10 mss/year. Query or submit complete ms. Length: 1,000-3,000 words. Pays $50-150. No mystery stories.

How To Break In: "The writer should not think we are a law review; we are somewhere between *Newsweek* and *Rolling Stone* with articles on social and legal concerns, from gay rights to the death penalty, from affirmative action in legal education to highlighting office products."

TODAY'S POLICEMAN, P.O. Box 594, Kansas City MO 64141. (816)474-3495. Editor: Donald Mack. For persons employed in and interested in police services. Magazine. Established in 1960. Quarterly. Circulation: 10,000. Copyrighted. Buys about 6 mss per year. Pays on acceptance or publication. Will send sample copy to writer for $2. Will consider photocopied and simultaneous submissions. Query first. Reports in 1 month. Query first or submit complete ms. Enclose S.A.S.E.

Nonfiction, Photos and Fillers: Buys informational, interview, humor, nostalgia, new product, merchandising techniques, technical articles. Length: 500 to 1,500 words. Pays $15 to $40. Historical. Length: 500 to 2,500 words. Pays $20 to $40. Expose. Length: 500 words. Pays $15 to $40. Approach should be expository with research. Interested in psychological and philosophical aspects of current problems. Would like to see humorous articles with photos. Occasionally buys material for 2 regional editions, covering the eastern U.S. and western U.S. Writers may also submit suggestions for new columns or departments. Photos purchased with accompanying ms with no additional payment. Also purchased without ms. Pay: $10 for b&w glossy. Captions required. Fillers: puzzles, jokes, gags, short humor. Pays $5 to $25.

Leather Goods

CANADIAN LUGGAGE AND LEATHERGOODS NEWS, Page Publications, Ltd., 380 Wellington St., W., Toronto, Ontario, Canada M5V 1E3. (416)366-4608. Editor: Henry Wittenberg. For retailers, wholesalers, importers, manufacturers and suppliers in the luggage, leathergoods and handbag trade. Tabloid newspaper; 12 pages. Established in 1966. 10 issues a year. Circulation: 4,500. Pays on publication. Will send sample copy to writer on request. Will consider photocopied and simultaneous submissions. Reports in 2 months. Query first. Enclose S.A.E. and International Reply Coupons.

Nonfiction: Informational and technical articles and those on successful business operations, new products, merchandising techniques. Length: open. Pays 4¢ a word, or $25 per published page.

Library Science

AMERICAN LIBRARIES, 50 E. Huron St., Chicago IL 60611. (312)944-6780. Editor: Arthur Plotnik. For librarians. "A highly literate audience. They are for the most part practicing professionals with high public contact and involvement interest." 11 times a year. Circulation: 36,000. Buys first North American serial rights. Will consider photocopied submissions if not being considered elsewhere at time of submission. Submit seasonal material 9 months in advance. Reports within 12 weeks. Enclose S.A.S.E.

Nonfiction, Photos, and Fillers: "Material reflecting the special and current interests of the library profession. Non-librarians should browse recent journals in the field, available on request in medium-sized and large libraries everywhere. Topic and/or approach must be fresh, vital, or highly entertaining. Stereotyped stories about old maids, overdue books, fines, etc., are unacceptable. Our first concern is with the American Library Association's activities, and how they relate to the 36,000 reader/members. Tough for an outsider to write on this topic, but not to supplement it with short, offbeat library stories and features. Will look at all good b&w, natural light photos of library situations, and at color transparencies for possible cover use." Pays $5 to $150 for fillers and articles. Pays $5 to $50 for photos.

How To Break In: "With a sparkling, 300-word report on a true, offbeat library event, or with an exciting photo and caption."

CATHOLIC LIBRARY WORLD, 461 W. Lancaster Ave., Haverford PA 19041. (215)649-5251. Editor-in-Chief: John T. Corrigan, CFX. Emphasizes libriarianship for librarians and educators in academic, school, public, special, seminaries, medical and health, archives/libraries. Monthly magazine; 48 pages. Estab: 1929. Circ: 3,500. Not copyrighted. No payment. Phone queries OK. Submit seasonal or holiday material 3 months in advance. SASE. Reports in 2 weeks. Free sample copy and writer's guidelines.

Nonfiction: "We cover a broad range of library services on a thematic approach (e.g., library services to the poor) and use materials of interest to librarians and educators; research bibliographies and comments on the library profession."

THE HORN BOOK MAGAZINE, 585 Boylston St., Boston MA 02116. (617)536-3145. Editor: Ethel Heins. For librarians, teachers, parents, authors, illustrators, publishers. Bimonthly. Circulation: 27,500. Buys all rights, "subject to author's wishes." Buys 24 mss a year. Pays on publication. Will send a sample copy to a writer for $3. No query required. Reports in 3 months. Enclose S.A.S.E.

Nonfiction: Uses four or five articles per issue about children's books or children's pleasure reading, both in this country and others. Material must have originality and the ability to give inspiration to those working with children and books. Does not want articles on techniques of reading or articles aimed at the education market. Read the magazine before submitting. "it is a literary magazine. Good writing required as well as suitable subject." Length: 3,000 words maximum. Pays $20 a page.

LIBRARY JOURNAL, 1180 Avenue of the Americas, New York NY 10036. Editor: John N. Berry III. For librarians (academic, public, special, school). 115-page (8½x11) magazine published every 2 weeks. Established in 1876. Circulation: 40,000. Buys all rights. Buys 50 to 100 mss a year (mostly from professionals in the field). Payment on publication. Submit complete ms. Enclose S.A.S.E.

Nonfiction and Photos: Professional articles on criticism, censorship, professional concerns, library activities, historical articles and spot news. Outlook should be from librarian's point of view. Length: 1,500 to 2,000 words. Pays $50 to $250. Payment for b&w glossy photos purchased without accompanying mss is $25. Must be at least 5x7. Captions required.

How To Break In: *"Library Journal* is a professional magazine for librarians. Freelancers are most often rejected because they submit one of the following types of article: 1) 'A wonderful, warm, concerned, loving librarian who started me on the road to good reading and success'; 'How I became rich, famous, and successful by using my public library'; 'Libraries are the most wonderful and important institutions in our society, because they have all of the knowledge of mankind — praise them.' We need material of greater sophistication, dealing with issues related to the transfer of information, access to it, or related phenomena. (Current hot ones are copyright, censorship, the decline in funding for public institutions, the local politics of libraries, trusteeship, etc.)"

MEDIA: LIBRARY SERVICES JOURNAL, 127 Ninth Ave., N., Nashville TN 37234. (615)251-2752. Editor: Floyd B. Simpson. For adult leaders in church organizations and people interested in library work (especially church library work). Quarterly magazine; 50 pages. Estab: 1970. Circ: 17,500. Pays on publication. Buys all rights. Phone queries OK. Submit seasonal/holiday material 14 months in advance. Previously published submissions OK. SASE. Reports in 1 month. Free sample copy and writer's guidelines.

Nonfiction: "Primarily interested in articles that relate to the development of church libraries in providing media and services to support the total program of a church and in meeting individual needs. We publish personal experience accounts of services provided, promotional ideas, exciting things that have happened as a result of implementing an idea or service; human interest stories that are library related; media education (teaching and learning with a media mix). Articles should be practical for church library staffs and for teachers and other leaders of the church." Buys 15-20 mss per issue. Query first. Pays 2½¢/word.

MICROFORM REVIEW, 520 Riverside Ave., Box 405 Saugatuck Station, Westport CT 06880. (203)226-6967. Editor-in-Chief: Allen B. Veaner. For librarians and educators at the college and university level. Bimonthly magazine; 64 pages. Estab: 1972. Circ: 1,800. Pays on publication. May buy all rights. Phone queries OK. Submit seasonal material 3 months in advance. Simultaneous, photocopied, and previously published submissions OK. SASE. Reports in 3 weeks. Free sample copy and writer's guidelines.

Nonfiction: How-to articles (technical, dealing with micrographic equipment; innovative use of microform in libraries; new product articles (in photographic field); photo features and technical articles; profiles and interviews. "We are interested in articles dealing with micropublication libraries and research using micropublications. Also problems libraries have using microforms, and solutions to those problems." Buys 1 ms per issue. Length: 1,000-3,000 words. Query first. Pays $10-50.

Photos: B&w glossies purchased with mss. Captions required. Query first. Pays $5-10.

THE PAMPHLETEER MONTHLY, 55 E. 86 St., New York NY 10028. (212)722-7272. Editor: William Frederick. A review source for paper-covered materials; from single-page leaflets to booklets and pamphlets/books up to and beyond 160 pages. For the library trade; buying guide for public school, college, university and special libraries; book review source. Magazine; 48 (6x9) pages. Established in 1940. Monthly except July/August. Circulation: 6,000. Buys all rights. Pays on assignment. Query. Send in a resume and clips of previous reviews or published writing.

Nonfiction: Book reviews on assignment only. Length: 50 words, average. Pays $1. (Usually, 50 to 100 assigned reviews at a time.)

SCHOOL LIBRARY JOURNAL, 1180 Avenue of the Americas, New York NY 10036. Editor: Lillian N. Gerhardt. For librarians in schools and public libraries. 88-page (8x11) magazine published monthly from September to May. Established in 1954. Circulation: 45,000. Buys all rights. Buys about 6 mss a year. Payment on publication. Will not consider photocopied or simultaneous submissions. Reports on material in 3 months. Enclose S.A.S.E.

Nonfiction: Articles on library services, local censorship problems, how-to articles on programs that use books or films. Informational, personal experience, interview, expose, successful business operations. "Interested in history articles on the establishment/development of children's and young adult services in schools and public libraries." Length: 2,500 to 3,000 words. Pays $100.

WILSON LIBRARY BULLETIN, 950 University Ave., Bronx NY 10452. (212)588-8400. Editor: William R. Eshelman; Associate Editor: E. Harriet Rosenfeld. For professional librarians and those interested in the book and library worlds. Monthly, September through June. Circulation: 33,000. Buys North American serial rights only. Pays on publication. Sample copies may be seen on request in most libraries. "Ms must be original copy, double spaced; additional Xerox copy or carbon is appreciated. Deadlines are a minimum 2 months before publication." Reports in 2 to 8 weeks. Enclose S.A.S.E. for return of submissions.

Nonfiction: Uses articles "of interest to librarians throughout the nation and around the world. Style must be lively, readable and sophisticated, with appeal to modern professionals; facts must be thoroughly researched. Subjects range from the political to the comic in the world of media and libraries, with an emphasis on the human as well as the technical aspects of any story. No condescension: no library stereotypes." Length: 3,000 to 6,000 words. Pays about $50 to $150, "depending on the substance of article and its importance to readers."

How To Break In: "With a first rate b&w photo and caption information on a library, library service, or librarian that departs completely from all stereotypes and the commonplace. Note: Libraries have changed! You'd better first discover what is now commonplace."

Lumber and Woodworking

THE BRITISH COLUMBIA LUMBERMAN, 2000 West 12th Ave., Vancouver 9, B.C., Canada. (604)731-1171. Editor: Brian Martin. For forest industries (logging, sawmilling, plywood, marine and forest management). Monthly. Buys first rights. Pays on publication. Send resume, query, and topic outline first. Each issue has a specific theme. For example, sawmill trends, marine review, etc. Reports in 2 weeks. Enclose S.A.E. and International Reply Coupons.

Nonfiction: In-depth research articles on new developments, theories, practical applications, new methods, equipment usage and performance, etc., in the industry. Must be specific and accurate; especially applicable to forestry in British Columbia. Length: maximum 1,500 words. Pays 8¢/word.

Photos: Purchased with mss or with captions only. B&w glossy; minimum 4x5 (8x10 preferred). Pays $5.

CANADIAN FOREST INDUSTRIES, 1450 Don Mills Rd., Don Mills, Ont., M3B 2X7, Canada. Editor: Rich Letkeman. For forest companies, loggers, lumber-plywood-board manufacturers. Established in 1882. Monthly. Circulation: 12,000. Buys first North American serial rights. Buys about 20 mss a year. Pays on publication. Will send free sample copy to writer on request. Will consider cassette submissions. Reports within 1 month. Query first. Enclose S.A.E. and International Reply Coupons.
Nonfiction: Uses "articles concerning industry topics, especially how-to articles that help businessmen in the forest industries. All articles should take the form of detailed reports of new methods, techniques and cost-cutting practices that are being successfully used anywhere in Canada, together with descriptions of new equipment that is improving efficiency and utilization of wood. It is very important that accurate descriptions of machinery (make, model, etc.) be always included and any details of costs, etc., in actual dollars and cents can make the difference between a below-average article and an exceptional one." Length: 1,200 to 2,500 words. Pays 12¢/word minimum, more with photos.
Photos: Buys photos with mss, sometimes with captions only. Should be 8x10, b&w glossies or negatives.

NATIONAL HARDWOOD MAGAZINE, P.O. Box 18436, Memphis TN 38118. (901)362-1700. Editor: Floyd Keith. For "hardwood lumber mills and furniture manufacturers; their education varies, as do their interests." Estab: 1927. Monthly. Circ: 5,000. Buys all rights. Buys 12-24 mss/year. Pays on acceptance. Free sample copy and writer's guidelines. Will not consider photocopied submissions or clippings. Returns rejected material "usually right away." Reports on ms accepted for publication "usually within 3-4 months." Query. SASE.
Nonfiction and Photos: "Furniture plant stories on those using large amounts of hardwood lumber; also, other plants that use hardwoods: casket firms, etc. We're the only publication dealing exclusively with hardwood lumber producers and users." Each plant story should include the following: Name of company and location, names of officers and plant manager, products manufactured, size of plant, number of employees, average number of hours per week the plant runs, sales force (do they have their own? Where's the sales office located? Where are the showrooms?). Complete descriptions of outstanding features or production ideas (how they work; what has been accomplished since their installation, etc.) Quantities, grades, thicknesses of lumber purchased annually; kinds of dimension used and for what purpose. Species of veneer purchased and for what purpose. Make of dry kilns, number, their capacity and moisture content of the lumber dried. Size of lumberyard and average inventory carried. History of the company and its growth; future plans. Dollar value of plant. Description of the flow of material through the plant from the back door to the front (lumberyard to the shipment of the finished product). In human interest articles, look for the following: An unusual request from a customer which the company fulfilled. The struggles the infant company went through to get established. The life of the man behind the company; how he got started in the business, etc. Has the company a unique record or reputation throughout the industry? What is it and how did it come about? 5x7 (or smaller) b&w glossies purchased with mss; captions required. Usually pays $150 for complete story and photographs.

PLYWOOD AND PANEL MAGAZINE, P.O. Box 567B, Indianapolis IN 46206. (317)634-1100. Editor: James F. Burrell. For manufacturers and industrial fabricators of plywood and veneer and particleboard. Monthly. Buys all rights. Pays on publication. Enclose S.A.S.E.
Nonfiction: "Factual and accurate articles concerning unusual techniques or aspects in the manufacturing or processing of veneer, plywood, particleboard, hardboard; detailing successful and/or unusual marketing techniques for wood panel products; or concerning important or unusual industrial end-uses of these materials in the production of consumer goods." Length: maximum 1,000 words. Pays maximum 5¢ a word.
Photos: Of good quality and directly pertinent to editorial needs. Action photos; no catalog shots. No in-plant photos of machinery not operating or not manned in natural fashion. Must be completely captioned; 5x7 b&w or larger preferred. Pays up to $5 per photo.

WOOD & WOOD PRODUCTS, 300 W. Adams St., Chicago IL 60606. Editor: Monte Mace. "For management and operating executives of all types of wood product manufacturers normally employing minimum of 20 persons." Monthly. Circulation: 30,000. Buys first rights. Pays on acceptance. Will send fact sheet on request. "Detailed query imperative." Reports in 2 to 4 weeks. Enclose S.A.S.E.

Nonfiction: "Semitechnical to technical articles, manufacturing process descriptions, safety, management. Prefer an in-depth treatment of how one company solved one or more problems. No handicraft articles. Must be entirely factual and accurate. Photos essential." Length: 1,500 words maximum. Pays $100 and up for feature articles, based on merit, not length.
Photos: Purchased with mss. "Must have complete descriptive captions. Photos of employees and machinery in natural operating positions. No mug shots, no catalog shots wanted. Any size negative from 35mm up; prints 5x7 or 8x10." Color only on assignment.

WOODWORKING & FURNITURE DIGEST, Hitchcock Bldg., Wheaton IL 60187. (312)665-1000. Editor: Richard D. Rea. For industrial manufacturers whose products employ wood as a basic raw material. Monthly. Buys all rights. Pays on publication. Will send free sample copy to serious freelancer on request. Query first. Reports in 10 days. Will sometimes hold ms for further evaluation up to 2 months, if it, at first, appears to have possibilities. Enclose S.A.S.E.
Nonfiction and Photos: "Articles on woodworking and furniture manufacturing with emphasis on management concepts, applications for primary raw materials (including plastics, if involved with wood), technology of remanufacturing methods and machines, and news of broad industry interest. Articles should focus on cost reduction, labor efficiency, product improvement, and profit. No handcraft, do-it-yourself or small custom shopwork. Present theme, or why reader can benefit, in first paragraph. Cover 'feeds and speeds' thoroughly to include operating data and engineering reasons why. Leave reader with something to do or think. Avoid mechanically handled case histories and plant tours which do not include management/engineering reasons." Photos, charts and diagrams which tell what cannot be told in words should be included. "We like a balance between technical information and action photos." Length: "no length limit, but stop before you run out of gas!" Pays $35 to $50 per published page. Photos purchased with mss. Good technical quality and perception of subject shown. No posed views. Prefers candid action or tight closeups. Full-color cover photo must be story-related.

Machinery and Metal Trade

ASSEMBLY ENGINEERING, Hitchcock Publishing Co., Wheaton IL 60187. Editor: Robert T. Kelly. For design and manufacturing engineers and production personnel concerned with assembly problems in manufacturing plants. Monthly. Buys first publication rights. Pays on publication. Sample copy will be sent on request. "Query first on leads or ideas. We report on ms decision as soon as review is completed and provide edited proofs for checking by author, prior to publication." Enclose S.A.S.E.
Nonfiction and Photos: Wants features on design, engineering and production practices for the assembly of manufactured products. Material should be submitted on "exclusive rights" basis and, preferably, should be written in the third person. Subject areas include selection, specification, and application of fasteners, mounting hardware, electrical connectors, wiring, hydraulic and pneumatic fittings, seals and gaskets, adhesives, joining methods (soldering, welding, brazing, etc.), and assembly equipment; specification of fits and tolerances; joint design; design and shop assembly standards; time and motion study (assembly line); quality control in assembly; layout and balancing of assembly lines; assembly tool and jig design; programming assembly line operations; working conditions, incentives, labor costs, and union relations as they relate to assembly line operators; hiring and training of assembly line personnel; supervisory practices for the assembly line. Also looking for news items on assembly-related subjects, and for unique or unusual "ideas" on assembly components, equipment, processes, practices and methods. Requires good quality photos or sketches, usually close-ups of specific details. Pays $30 minimum/published page.

AUTOMATIC MACHINING, 65 Broad St., Rochester NY 14614. (716)454-3763. Editor: Donald E. Wood. For metalworking technical management. Buys all rights. Query first. Enclose S.A.S.E.
Nonfiction: "This is not a market for the average freelancer. A personal knowledge of the trade is essential. Articles deal in depth with specific job operations on automatic screw machines, chucking machines, high production metal turning lathes and cold heading machines. Part prints, tooling layouts always required, plus written agreement of source to publish the material. Without personal background in operation of this type of equipment, freelancers are wasting time." Length: "no limit." Pays $20 per printed page.

CANADIAN MACHINERY AND METALWORKING, 481 University Ave., Toronto Ont., Canada M5W 1A7. (416)595-1811. Editor: A. Whitney. Monthly. Buys first Canadian rights.

Pays on publication. Will consider cassette submissions. Query first. Enclose S.A.E. and International Reply Coupons.

Nonfiction: Technical and semitechnical articles dealing with metalworking operations in Canada and in the U.S., if of particular interest. Accuracy and service appeal to readers is a must. Pays minimum 7¢ a word.

Photos: Purchased with mss and with captions only. "Color for covers only." Pays $5 minimum for b&w features, $50 to $100 for color covers.

CUTTING TOOL ENGINEERING, P.O. Box 937, Wheaton IL 60187. (312)653-3210. Editor: N.D. O'Daniell. For metalworking industry executives and engineers concerned with the metal-cutting/metal-removal/abrasive engineering function in metal working. Bimonthly. Circulation: 33,000. Buys all rights. Pays on publication. Will send free sample copy on request. Query required. Enclose S.A.S.E.

Nonfiction: "Intelligently written articles on specific applications of all types of metal cutting tools—mills, drills, reamers, etc. Articles must contain all information related to the operation, such as feeds and speeds, materials machined, etc. Should be tersely written, in-depth treatment. In the Annual Diamond Directory, published in September, we cover the use of diamond cutting tools and diamond grinding wheels." Length: 1,000 to 2,500 words. Pays "$35 per published page, or about 5¢ a published word."

Photos: Purchased with mss. 8x10 b&w glossies preferred.

DETROIT INDUSTRIAL MARKET NEWS, Brochures Unlimited, Inc., 2951 Greenfield Rd., Southfield MI 48076. (313)559-8357. Editor: Lowell Cauffiel. Emphasizes industrial manufacturing (largely metalworking). For industrial entrepreneurs and men in executive, managerial and engineering levels in the Midwest's manufacturing industry. Wide age range; educated mostly in technical and marketing areas. "These men work in, or own, small, mid-level firms, ranging from tool and die 'job shops' to steel processors and suppliers. Monthly tabloid; 40 pages. Estab: 1976. Circ: 32,000. Pays on acceptance. Buys all rights, but may reassign following publication. Phone queries OK. Submit seasonal/holiday material 2 months in advance. Photocopied and previously published submissions OK. SASE. Reports in 3 weeks. Free sample copy.

Nonfiction: Expose, how-to, informational, inspirational (success stories), interviews, personal experience, profiles, new product and technical articles. Buys 30-40 mss/year. Query. Length: 500-1,500 words. Pays $25-100.

Photos: Purchased with or without ms. Captions required. Send prints. Pays $20 for 8x10 b&w glossies. 1 color cover/issue. Query. Pays $75.

Columns, Departments: Viewpoint (authoritative, opinion columns on various aspects, trends, problems, etc., of manufacturers or the auto industry). Buys 1/issue. Query or send complete ms. Length: 700-1,000 words. Pays $50 minimum. Open to suggestions for new columns or departments.

Fillers: Clippings, newsbreaks. Length: 150 words maximum. Pays $5 maximum.

How To Break In: "Request and study a copy of the publication. Query with a proposal that's specific and not a fishing expedition for a story approach. And remember that our readers have little time to read and are bombarded daily with highly technical trade publications. Our aim is to provide a breezy, enlightening and entertaining look at the highly competitive realm of the smaller industrial manufacturer, often ignored in daily newspaper business news."

FOUNDRY MAGAZINE, Penton Plaza, Cleveland OH 44114. (216)696-7000. Editor: J. C. Miske. Monthly. Reports in 2 weeks. Enclose S.A.S.E.

Nonfiction and Photos: Uses articles describing operating practice in foundries written to interest companies producing metal castings. Length: maximum 3,000 words. Pays $35 a printed page. Uses illustrative 8x10 photographs with article.

INDUSTRIAL FINISHING, Hitchcock Building, Wheaton IL 60187. (312)665-1000. Editor: Matt Heuertz. Monthly. Circulation: 35,000. Buys first rights. Buys 3 or 4 mss a year. Pays on acceptance. Will send a free sample copy to a writer on request. Query first. Enclose S.A.S.E.

Nonfiction and Photos: Wants "technical articles on finishing operations for oem products." Style should be "direct and to the point." Photos purchased with mss, "as part of the complete package which we purchase at $100 to $150."

How To Break In: "Remember that we cover the oem (original equipment manufacturers, such as Ford or General Motors). We do not cover the after-market which is concerned with supplying equipment, materials, and services for repair or replacement."

INDUSTRIAL MACHINERY NEWS, 29516 Southfield Rd., C.S. #5002, Southfield MI 48037. (313)557-0100. Editor-in-Chief: Lucky D. Slate. Emphasizes metalworking for buyers, specifiers, manufacturing executives, engineers, management, plant managers, production managers, master mechanics, designers and machinery dealers. Monthly tabloid; 200 pages. Estab: 1953. Circ: 65,000. Pays on publication. Buys first North American serial rights. Phone queries OK. Submit seasonal/holiday material 3 months in advance. Simultaneous, photocopied, and previously published submissions OK. SASE. Reports in 3-5 weeks. Sample copy $1.50. Free guidelines for writers.

Nonfiction and Photos: Articles on "metal removal, metal forming, assembly, finishing, inspection, application of machine tools, technology, measuring, gauging equipment, small cutting tools, tooling accessories, materials handling in metalworking plants, safety programs. We give our publication a newspaper feel — fast reading with lots of action or human interest photos." Buys how-to's. Pays $25 minimum. Length: open. Photos purchased with mss; captions required. Pays $5 minimum.

Fillers: Newsbreaks, puzzles, jokes, short humor. Pays $5 minimum.

How To Break In: "Stories on old machine tools — how they're holding up and how they're being used."

MODERN MACHINE SHOP, 600 Main St., Cincinnati OH 45202. Editor: Fred W. Vogel. Monthly. Pays 30 days following acceptance. Query first. Reports in 5 days. Enclose S.A.S.E.
Nonfiction: Uses articles dealing with all phases of metal manufacturing and machine shop work, with photos. Length: 1,500 to 2,000 words. Pays current market rate.

ORNAMENTAL METAL FABRICATOR, Suite 106, 443 E. Paces Ferry Rd., N.E., Atlanta GA 30305. Editor: Blanche Blackwell. For fabricators of ornamental metal who are interested in their businesses and families, their community and nation. Most are owners of small businesses employing an estimated average of 10 persons, usually including family members. Official publication of the National Ornamental and Miscellaneous Metals Association. Magazine published every 2 months; 24 pages. Established in 1958. Circulation: 5,500. Not copyrighted. Buys 6 mss a year. Payment on acceptance. Will send free sample copy to writer on request. Will not consider photocopied or simultaneous submissions. Submit seasonal material 2 months in advance. Reports immediately. Query first. Enclose S.A.S.E.
Nonfiction and Photos: "Our publication deals solely with fabrication of ornamental metal, a more creative and aesthetic aspect of the metals construction industry. Special emphasis on ornamental metal trade. How-to articles that will help our readers improve their businesses. Articles on use and history of ornamental metal; on better operation of the business; on technical aspects. News about the association and its individual members and about 6 regional chapters affiliated with the national association. Articles on the effects of steel shortage on ornamental metal fabricator and how a typical firm is handling the problem; the search for qualified employees; successful prepaint treatments and finishes." Prefers not to see "character study" articles. Length: 1,000 to 5,000 words. Pays 3¢ per vord. B&w glossy photos purchased with accompanying mss. Pays $4. Color is not accepted.

POWER TRANSMISSION DESIGN, 614 Superior Ave. West, Cleveland OH 44113. (216)696-0300. Editor: Tom Hughes. For design engineers and persons who buy, operate, and maintain motors, drives, bearings, and related controls. Monthly. Circulation: 48,500. Buys all rights, but may reassign rights to author after publication. Pays on publication. Reports in 3 weeks. Enclose S.A.S.E.
Nonfiction and Photos: "The article should answer these questions: What does the machine do? What loads and load changes, speed and speed changes, does the operation impose upon the drive system? What drive system do you use and why? What were the alternatives, and why did you reject them? How did the operating environment affect the selection of motors, drives, bearings, and controls? How is the machine designed for easy maintenance? What are the sizes and capacities of the motors, drives, bearings, and controls? How does the drive system design make the machine superior to competitive machines? To previous models of your manufacture? What specific advances in motors, drives, bearings, and controls have led to improvements in machines like this one? What further advances would you like to see? Accompany your write-up with a photo of the machine and close-ups of the drive system and schematic drawings and blueprints, if necessary." Length: 600 to 6,000 words; "anything longer we'll break up and serialize." Pays $35 "per published magazine page (about 600 words to a page)."

PRODUCTION, Box 101, Bloomfield Hills MI 48013. (313)647-8400. Editor: Robert F. Huber. For "managers of manufacturing." Monthly. Circulation: 80,000. Buys all rights. Buys "a few" mss a year. Pays on acceptance. Query first. Enclose S.A.S.E.
Nonfiction and Photos: "Trends, developments, and applications in manufacturing." Length: open. Pays $50 to $350. Photos purchased with mss; captions required.

PRODUCTS FINISHING, 600 Main St., Cincinnati OH 45202. Editor: Gerard H. Poll, Jr. Monthly. Buys all rights. Pays within 30 days after acceptance. Reports in 1 week. Enclose S.A.S.E. for return of submissions.

Nonfiction: Uses "material devoted to the finishing of metal and plastic products. This includes the cleaning, plating, polishing and painting of metal and plastic products of all kinds. Articles can be technical and must be practical. Technical articles should be on processes and methods. Particular attention given to articles describing novel approaches used by product finishers to control air and water pollution, and finishing techniques that reduce costs." Pays 8¢ minimum per word.

Photos: Wants photographs dealing with finishing methods or processes. Pays $10 minimum for each photo used.

STEEL '77, 1000 16th St., N.W., Washington DC 20036. Editor: Thomas D. Patrick. For "opinion leaders; all ages and professions." Established in 1933. Quarterly. Circulation: 110,000. Buys all rights. Buys 4 to 6 mss a year. Payment on acceptance. Will send free sample copy to writer on request. Query first. Enclose S.A.S.E.

Nonfiction and Photos: Articles on the environmental, energy, economics, international trade, new technology aspects of the steel industry. "No product articles." Interviews, think pieces, technical. Length: 50 to 2,000 words. Pays $25 to $400. Photos purchased with or without accompanying ms or on assignment. Proofsheets and negatives. Color transparencies. Pays $15 to $100. Captions required. Freelance articles on assignment only.

33 MAGAZINE, McGraw-Hill Bldg., 1221 Avenue of the Americas, New York NY 10020. (212)997-3330. Editor: Joseph L. Mazel. For "operating managers (from turn foreman on up), engineers, metallurgical and chemical specialists, and corporate officials in the steelmaking industry. Work areas for these readers range from blast furnace and coke ovens into and through the steel works and rolling mills. *33's* readers also work in nonferrous industries." Monthly. Buys all rights. Pays on publication. Will send free sample copy on request. Query required. Reports in 3 weeks. Enclose S.A.S.E.

Nonfiction and Photos: Case histories of primary metals producing equipment in use, ruch as smelting, blast furnace, steelmaking, rolling. "Broadly speaking, *33 Magazine* concentrates its editorial efforts in the areas of technique (what's being done and how it's being done), technology (new developments), and equipment (what's being used). Your article should include a detailed explanation (who, what, why, where, and how) and the significance (what it means to operating manager, engineer, or industry) of the techniques, technology or equipment being written about. In addition, your readers will want to know of the problems you experienced during the planning, developing, implementing, and operating phases. And, it would be especially beneficial to tell of the steps you took to solve the problems or roadblocks encountered. You should also include all cost data relating to implementation, operation, maintenance, etc., wherever possible. Benefits (cost savings; improved manpower utilization; reduced cycle time; increased quality; etc.) should be cited to gauge the effectiveness of the subject being discussed. The highlight of any article is its illustrative material. This can take the form of photographs, drawings, tables, charts, graphs, etc. Your type of illustration should support and reinforce the text material. It should not just be an added, unrelated item. Each element of illustrative material should be identified and contain a short description of exactly what is being presented. We reject material that lacks in-depth knowledge of the technology on operations involved in metal producing." Pays $35 per published page. Minimum 5x7 b&w glossies purchased with mss.

TOOLING & PRODUCTION, 5821 Harper Rd., Solon OH 44139. (216)248-1125. Editor: Jim Keebler. For production, engineering and management people within the metalworking industries, who are responsible for the tooling and manufacturing techniques to make their products. Magazine; 144 pages. Established in 1934. Monthly. Circulation: 70,000. Buys all rights. Buys 6 to 12 mss a year. Pays on publication "or when edited to our style and in layout." Will send free sample copy to writer on request. Will consider photocopied and simultaneous submissions. "Author will be notified after review board meeting, first week of each month." Query first or submit complete ms. Enclose S.A.S.E.

Nonfiction and Photos: "Ferret out and report on machine tools, machine systems and tooling developments that will provide the readers with the know-how needed to make better products at less cost. How-to material with drawings/photos to help illustrate. Articles are always edited to our style." Would be interested in material on automotive manufacturing, cutting tools, holemaking, toolmaking, grinding and finishing, quality assurance, machine controls, automation, parts feeding and assembly, pressworking, turning; materials in metalworking. Informational, how-to, think pieces, case histories of new products; technical articles. Recently published material includes "Sharp-pointed Stamping by Subterfuge." Length: open. "Payment is established after material is edited to our style and in layout. It has been averaging $30 per page."

THE WELDING DISTRIBUTOR, 614 Superior Ave., W., Cleveland OH 44113. Executive Editor: Charles Berka. For wholesale and retail distributors of welding equipment and safety supplies and their sales staffs. Bimonthly. Buys all rights. Pays on publication. Enclose S.A.S.E. for return of submissions.
Nonfiction: Categories of editorial coverage are: management, process/product knowledge, profiles, selling and safety. Pays 2½¢ a word.

Maintenance and Safety

BUILDING SERVICES CONTRACTOR, 101 W. 31st St., New York NY 10001. (212)279-4455. Editorial Director: John Vollmuth. For management personnel in the contract cleaning field. Magazine; 80 pages. Established in 1964. Every 2 months. Circulation: 6,000. Not copyrighted. Buys about 12 mss a year. Pays 1 month after publication. Will send free sample copy to writer on request. Will consider photocopied and simultaneous submissions. "Author is informed whether material will or will not be used within 10 working days after receipt of release." Query first or submit complete ms. Enclose S.A.S.E.
Nonfiction and Photos: Articles on new methods, new equipment, new cleaning materials, information for training field personnel, information on labor relations and collective bargaining, as well as explaining how contracting firms maintain specific buildings, submit estimates and allocate work. A direct approach in a simple style encompassing anything a building services contractor would find of interest. No general sales articles. Would like to see material on time/motion studies with the use of automatic cleaning equipment; new cleaning devices and new approaches to cleaning familiar objects. Length: 800 to 2,000 words. Pays $100 to $110. Photos increase the possibility of material being used. No additional payment.

HEAVY DUTY EQUIPMENT MAINTENANCE, 7300 N. Cicero Ave., Lincolnwood IL 60646. (312)588-7300. Editor: Greg Sitek. Magazine; 76 to 110 pages. Established in 1972. Monthly. Circulation: 47,000. Rights purchased vary with author and material. Usually buys all rights, but may reassign rights to author after publication. Buys about 12 mss a year. Pays on publication. Free sample copy. No photocopied or simultaneous submissions. Reports in 4 weeks. Query first, with outline. Enclose S.A.S.E.
Nonfiction and Photos: "Our focus is on the effective management of equipment through proper selection, careful specification, correct application and efficient maintenance. We use job stories, technical articles, safety features, basics and shop notes. No product stories." Length: 2,000 to 5,000 words. Pays $25 per printed page minimum, without photos. Uses 35mm and 2¼ or larger color transparencies with mss. Pays $50 per printed page when photos are furnished by author.

MAINTENANCE SUPPLIES, 101 W. 31 St., New York NY 10001. (212)279-4455. Editorial Director: John Vollmuth. For distributors of sanitary supplies. Monthly. Circulation: 10,000. Not copyrighted. Payment on publication. Will send free sample copy to writer on request. Submit complete ms. Reports "as soon as possible." Enclose S.A.S.E.
Nonfiction and Photos: All news stories are staff-written. "Articles pointing out trends in the sanitary supply fields; stories about distributors, possible markets and merchandising. We expect a writer to turn out an article about some aspect of the sanitary supply field for readers who sell the products of this industry. General sales articles are sometimes accepted, but stories geared to the specific industry are much preferred." Length: 1,500 words. Pays $90-120. 8x10 b&w photos purchased with accompanying ms. Captions required.
How To Break In: "Probably the best way to break in would be with a story on the cleaning of an unusual establishment. For instance, we've had stories on cleaning the World Trade Center, cleaning Rockefeller Center, and cleaning Trinity Church. Should be done from the point of view of what supplies were used. Another good type of piece is the profile of someone in the field, such as a distributor of janitorial supplies. It would ideally be a good, sound company with an office-showroom-warehouse that lends itself to photos, and it would help if they also have some unusual procedures or selling techniques."

OCCUPATIONAL HAZARDS, 614 Superior Ave. W., Cleveland OH 44113. (216)696-0300. Editor: Peter J. Sheridan. "Distributed by function to middle management officials in industry who have the responsibility for accident prevention, occupational health, plant fire protection, and plant security programs. Job titles on our list include: safety directors, industrial hygienists, fire protection engineers, plant security managers, and medical directors." Monthly. Buys first rights in field. Pays on publication. Reports in 30 days. Enclose S.A.S.E.

Nonfiction: "Articles on industrial health, safety, security and fire protection. Specific facts and figures must be cited. No material on farm, home, or traffic safety. All material accepted subject to sharp editing to conform to publisher's distilled writing style. Illustrations preferred but not essential. Work is rejected when story is not targeted to professional concerns of our readers, but rather is addressed to the world at large." Length: 300 to 2,000 words. Pays 5¢/word minimum.

Photos: Accepts 4x5, 5x7 and 8x10 photos with mss. Pays $5.

PEST CONTROL MAGAZINE, 9800 Detroit Ave., Cleveland OH 44102. (216)651-5500. Editor: Bruce F. Shank. For professional pest control operators and sanitation workers. Magazine; 44 pages. Established in 1933. Monthly. Circulation: 14,000. Buys all rights. Buys about 6 mss a year. Pays on publication. Will send sample copy to writer for $1. Submit seasonal material 2 months in advance. Reports in 30 days. Query first or submit complete ms. Enclose S.A.S.E.

Nonfiction and Photos: Business tips, unique control situations, personal experience articles. Must have trade or business orientation. No general information type of articles desired. "Remember that we are oriented toward the owner-manager more than the serviceman. We might consider something on the view of an outsider to the pest control operator's job, or a report by an outsider after spending a day with a PCO on a route." Length: 4 double-spaced pages. Pays $25 minimum. Regular columns use material oriented to this profession. Length: 8 double-spaced pages. Pays 4¢ a word. No additional payment for photos used with mss. Pays $5 to $25 for 5x7 b&w glossies purchased without mss; $15 to $50 for 8x10 color or slide.

SDM: SECURITY DISTRIBUTING & MARKETING, 2639 S. La Cienega Blvd., Los Angeles CA 90034. Editor: Robert J. Bargert. For security products dealers, distributors, manufacturers; electrical and electronics engineering background; technically oriented. Magazine; 96-150 pages; 8½x11. Buys all rights. Buys 10 to 12 mss a year. Pays on publication. Will send free sample copy to writer on request. Submit complete ms. Submit special or seasonal material 3 months in advance. Reports in 1 week. Enclose S.A.S.E.

Nonfiction and Photos: News stories, case history success stories, how-to stories (how to advertise and promote, etc.). Length: 1,500 to 5,000 words. Pays $45 per printed page. Photos purchased with accompanying ms. Captions required. Pays $7.50 for b&w; $15 for color.

How To Break In: "New writers should obtain some working knowledge of the security products field. Interested in obtaining stories about dealers who installed burglar alarms that worked when needed. Can be obtained from news stories in papers and followed up with personal interview with dealer."

Management and Supervision

This category includes trade journals for lower level business and industrial managers, including supervisors and office managers. Journals for business executives and owners are classified under Business Management. Those for industrial plant managers are listed in Industrial Management.

THE BUSINESS QUARTERLY, School of Business Administration, University of Western Ontario, London, Ontario N6A 3K7, Canada. (519)679-3222. Editor: Doreen Sanders. For persons in upper and middle management, university education, interested in continuing and updating their management education. Estab: 1933. Quarterly. Circ: 10,000. Buys all rights. Buys 35 mss a year. Payment on publication. Reports in 3 months. Query first with brief outline of article. Enclose S.A.E. and International Reply Coupons.

Nonfiction: Articles pertaining to all aspects of management development. Must have depth. "Think" articles and those on successful business operations. Length: 2,000 to 5,000 words. Pays $100.

How To Break In: "Submit an idea for an article that has academic validity supported by either research or experience. Our principal reasons for rejecting freelance mss are that material submitted is not suitable for sophisticated readership; often tends to be a re-hash of what has already been published; does not offer fresh, original approach to management problems."

CONSTRUCTION FOREMAN'S & SUPERVISOR'S LETTER, Bureau of Business Practice, 24 Rope Ferry Rd., Waterford CT 06386. (203)442-4365. Emphasizes all aspects of construction supervision. Semimonthly newsletter; 4 pages. Estab: 1967. Circ: 9,000. Buys all rights. Phone queries OK. Submit seasonal or holiday material at least 4 months in advance. SASE. Reports in 4-6 weeks. Free sample copy and writer's guidelines.

Nonfiction: Publishes solid interviews with construction managers or supervisors on how to improve a single aspect of the supervisor's job. Buys 100 a year. Length: 360-720 words. Pays 7-10¢/word.

Photos: B&w head and shoulders "mug shots" of person interviewed purchased with mss. Send prints. Pays $7.50.

CONSTRUCTION LETTER, Bureau of Business Practice, 24 Rope Ferry Rd., Waterford CT 06386. (203)442-4365. For front-line supervisors and foremen of construction workers. Newsletter; 4 pages. Established in 1967. Published every 2 weeks. Circulation: 8,000. Buys all rights. Buys about 100 mss per year. Pays on acceptance. Will send free sample copy and editorial guidelines sheet to writer on request. Will not consider photocopied or simultaneous submissions. Reports on mss accepted for publication in 4 to 8 weeks. Returns rejected material in 3 to 6 weeks. Query first. Enclose S.A.S.E.

Nonfiction and Photos: "Material must deal with a single aspect of a supervisor's (foreman's) job — preferably: How to improve that aspect of his or her job." Length: 360 to 720 words. Pays 7¢ to 10¢ per word. Open to suggestions for new columns and departments. Query editor. Photos purchased with accompanying ms with extra payment. Pays $5. No color. Photos should be of head and shoulders of interviewee.

THE FOREMAN'S LETTER, National Foremen's Institute, 24 Rope Ferry Rd., Waterford CT 06386. (203)442-4365. Editor: Frank Berkowitz. For industrial supervisors. Semimonthly. Buys all rights. Pays on acceptance. "Query preferred only if out-of-pocket expenses may be involved." Interested in regular stringers (freelance) on area exclusive basis. Enclose S.A.S.E.

Nonfiction: Interested primarily in direct in-depth interviews with industrial foremen in the U.S. and Canada, written in newspaper feature or magazine article style, with concise, uncluttered, non-repetitive prose as an essential. Subject matter would be the interviewee's techniques for managing people, bolstered by illustrations out of the interviewee's own job experiences. Slant would be toward informing readers how their most effective contemporaries function, free of editorial comment. "Our aim is to offer information which, hopefully, readers may apply to their own professional self-improvement." Pays 8¢ to 10½¢ a word "after editing."

Photos: Buys photos submitted with mss. "Captions needed for identification only." Head and shoulders, any size b&w glossy from 2x3 up. Pays $7.50.

LE BUREAU, 625 President Kennedy, Montreal H3A 1K5, Que., Canada. (514)845-5141. Editor: Paul Saint-Pierre. For "office executives." Established in 1965. 6 times per year. Circulation: 7,500. Buys all rights, but will reassign rights to author after publication. Buys about 10 mss a year. Pays on acceptance. Will send a sample copy to a writer on request. Query first or submit complete ms. Submit seasonal material "between 1 and 2 months" of issue date. Enclose S.A.E. and International Reply Coupons for return of submissions.

Nonfiction and Photos: "Our publication is published in the French language. We use case histories on new office systems, applications of new equipment, articles on personnel problems. Material should be exclusive and above-average quality." Buys personal experience articles, interviews, think pieces, coverage of successful business operations, and new product articles. Length: 500 to 1,000 words. Pays $50 to $75. B&w glossies purchased with mss. Pays $10 each.

MANAGE, The National Management Assn., 2210 Arbor Blvd., Dayton OH 45439. (513)294-0421. Editor-in-Chief: Don Vendely. For first line and middel management and scientific/technical lanagers. Bimonthly magazine; 32 pages. Estab: 1925. Circ: 51,736. Pays on acceptance. Buys all rights, but may reassign following publication. Phone queries OK. Submit seasonal/holiday material at least 6 months in advance. Photocopied submissions and previously published work OK. SASE. Reports in 6 weeks. Free sample copy and writer's guidelines.

Nonfiction: How-to (make a management principle or practice work for you); informational (new techniques in middle management); interview (with a well-known management authority with specific material for our readers). Buys 42 mss a year. Query or submit complete ms. Length: 600-2,500 words. Pays 5¢/word.

How To Break In: "Develop or find some new material and present it well. We're primarily looking for informative, how-to material on motivation, productivity, human relations, communications, leadership and how it relates to first line and middle management."

MODERN BUSINESS REPORTS, Alexander Hamilton Institute, 605 Third Ave., New York NY 10016. (212)557-5203. Editor: J. M. Jenks. For management and business methods personnel. Newsletter; 8 pages. Established in 1972. Monthly. Buys all rights. Buys 40 mss a year. Pays on acceptance. Will send free sample copy to writer on request. No photocopied or simultaneous submissions. Reports in 2 weeks. Query first. Enclose S.A.S.E.

Nonfiction: Articles on management methods and practices, management by objectives, cost reduction methods, administration. All material must give readers a piece of information on a management or business practice that can be used or put to use in a company. "Our principal reasons for rejecting freelance submissions are: Failure of the writer to query us first on our needs, failure of the writer to study our publication; material written below the level of our readers." Length: 1,000 to 1,500 words. Pays 15¢ a word.

OFFICE SUPERVISOR'S BULLETIN, Bureau of Business Practice, 681 Fifth Ave., New York NY 10022. (212)758-8210. For first and second line office supervisors. Semimonthly. Buys all rights. Pays on acceptance. Will send a free sample copy to a writer on request. Query first. Address mss to the Editor. Reports in 1 week. Enclose S.A.S.E.

Nonfiction: Buys only interview-based articles. "Emphasis is on good methods of getting things done through others. Articles give practical how-to tips to help office supervisors increase productivity, cut absenteeism and tardiness, raise morale, cut costs, and generally do their jobs better. From freelancers, we need interview-based articles quoting, by name, top-notch (but lower level) office supervisors in industry, business and government. You should ask interviewees to pinpoint current problems in supervision, discuss how they're solving these problems in their company, what results they're getting. Illustrate with real examples from daily office life. We're interested only in 'people problems' common to all offices, not systems or machinery problems. Sample subjects: Planning, training, disciplining, listening, motivating, evaluating performance, counseling, getting along with the boss, reducing errors, enriching jobs, controlling costs, affirmative action, upward and downward communication. For current subjects, keep yourself informed by checking lists of seminars offered by universities, American Management Association, chambers of commerce, and by regularly checking management publications. If you're serious about writing in this field, spend some time in the library reading about management. We do not give assignments. You must find interviewees yourself. For leads, look for stories about successful new methods or training programs in: financial pages of your local paper, house organs (ask friends for their company publications), announcements of business seminars. Please don't interview management consultants or professors. But you can ask them what companies are doing great things in supervision. If you have a subject in mind, contact the public relations department of a likely company. Utilities, banks, insurance companies, any firms with lots of paperwork are good prospects. To stay on target as you write and interview, keep saying to yourself: 'How is this important to the lower level office supervisor?' Avoid topics he has no control over (changing company salary policies, moving to another location, buying computers). Keep in mind the problem/solution/result format. Don't talk down to readers; they know more than you do about supervising." Recently published articles include "To Get the Job Done — Ask — Don't Tell — Employees" and "Effective Training Teaches Self-Control." Length: 900 to 1,350 words. Pays $35 per published page (about 450 words). Prefers 2- to 3-page articles.

SUPERVISION, 424 N. 3rd Street, Burlington IA 52601. (319)752-5415. Editor: G.B. McKee. For foremen, personnel managers, supervisors, and department heads. Monthly. Buys all rights. Pays on publication. Sample copy sent on request. Query first. Reports in 10 days. Enclose S.A.S.E.

Nonfiction and Photos: Wants "how-to articles dealing with manufacturing plant situations relating to improving production, cutting costs, handling grievances, eliminating waste, building morale. Case study situations preferred, showing how a specific problem was overcome and what benefits resulted. Clear style wanted; article must contain practical information." Length: 1,000 to 1,200 words. Payment is 2¢ a word. Occasionally buys b&w photos with mss. Payment is $5.

TRAINING, The Magazine of Human Resources Development, 731 Hennepin Ave., Minneapolis MN 55403. (612)333-0471. Editor: Philip Jones. For persons who train people in business, industry, government and health care. Age 25 to 65. Magazine; 75 pages. Established in 1964. Monthly. Circulation: 40,000. Rights purchased vary with author and material. Usually buys all rights, but may reassign rights to author after publication; first North American serial rights; first serial rights; or all rights. Buys 30 to 50 mss per year. Payment on acceptance. Will send sample copy to writer for $1. Write for editorial guidelines sheet. Will consider photocopied submissions. No simultaneous submissions. Reports in 4 weeks. Query. SASE.

Nonfiction and Photos: Articles on management and techniques of employee training. "Material should discuss a specific training problem; why the problem existed; how it was solved, the alternative solutions, etc. Should furnish enough data for readers to make an independent judgment about the appropriateness of the solution to the problem. We want names and specific details on all techniques and processes used." Would like to see "interesting examples of successful training and management development programs; articles about why certain types of the above seem to fail; articles about trainers and training directors who have become company presidents or top execs." Most mss should be 200 to 3,000 words. Informational. Length: 200 to 2,000 words. Book reviews. Length: 50 to 1,000 words. Successful business operations. Length: 50 to 3,000 words. Pays maximum of $75 per printed page. "In general, we pay more for tightly written articles." No extra payment for photos. B&w only. Captions optional.

UNIROYAL MANAGEMENT, Uniroyal, Inc., Oxford Management & Research Center, Middlebury CT 06749. Editor: Renee Follett. Published by Uniroyal, Inc. for "management employees, including sales, engineers, scientists and general management." Established in 1967. Published 8 times a year. Circulation: 9,500. Buys all rights. Pays on acceptance. Will send sample copy to writer on request. Write for copy of guidelines for writers. Will consider photocopied submissions. Reports in 3 weeks. Enclose S.A.S.E.
Nonfiction and Photos: "How-to-manage articles, industry and management trend articles. This publication primarily deals with Uniroyal — its people, places and products." Buys informational articles, how-to's, personal experience articles, interviews, profiles, inspirational articles, humor, think pieces, coverage of successful business operations and merchandising techniques. Length: 600 to 1,200 words. Pays $50 to $200. 8x10 b&w glossies purchased with mss; captions required. Pays $20 per photo.

UTILITY SUPERVISION, Bureau of Business Practice, 24 Rope Ferry Rd., Waterford CT 06386. (203)442-4365. Editor-in-Chief: Peter W. Hawkins. Emphasizes all aspects of construction supervision. Semimonthly newsletter; 4 pages. Estab: 1966. Pays on acceptance. Buys all rights. Phone queries OK. Submit seasonal or holiday material 4 months in advance. SASE. Reports in 4-6 weeks. Free sample copy and writer's guidelines.
Nonfiction: Publishes how-to (nterview on a single aspect of supervision: how can reader/supervisor improve in that area?) and interview (how-to interview with utility manager/supervisor concentrating on how reader/supervisor can improve in that area) articles. Buys 100 mss/year. Query. Length: 360-720 words. Pays 6-10¢/word.
Photos: Purchased with accompanying ms. Captions required. Pays $7.50 for b&w prints of "head and shoulders 'mug shot' of person interviewed." Total purchase price for ms includes payment for photos.
How To Break In: "Write solid interview articles on a single aspect of supervision in the utility field. Concentrate on how the reader/supervisor can improve his/her own performance in that area. Articles should concentrate on 'outside' operations; stay away from office operations."

Marine Industries and Water Navigation

In this list are journals for seamen, boatbuilders, navigators, boat dealers, and others interested in water as a means of travel or shipping. Journals for commercial fishermen are classified with Fishing journals. Publications for scientists studying the ocean will be found under Oceanography.

AMERICAN SHIPPER, Box 4728, Jacksonville FL 32201. Editor: David A. Howard. For businessmen in shipping, transportation and foreign trade. Monthly magazine; 48 pages. Established in 1958. Circulation: 12,000. Not copyrighted. Buys 12 mss/year. Pays on acceptance. Reports in 1 month. Enclose S.A.S.E.
Nonfiction and Photos: "In-depth features. Analytical pieces (based on original data or research). Port finances. Other transportation (in-depth) with solid figures. News approach, basically. No 'old salt' human interest." Length: "depends on need of subject." Pays $100 to $150. Photos purchased with accompanying ms.

THE BOATING INDUSTRY, 205 E. 42nd St., New York NY 10017. Editor: Charles A. Jones. For "boating retailers and distributors." Established in 1929. Monthly. Circulation: 26,000. Buys all rights, but will reassign rights to author after publication. Buys 10 to 15 mss a year. Pays on publication. "Best practice is to check with editor first on story ideas for go-ahead."

Submit seasonal material 3 to 4 months in advance of issue date. Returns rejected material in 2 months. Acknowledges acceptance of material in 1 month. Enclose S.A.S.E.

Nonfiction and Photos: Uses "boat dealer success stories." No clippings. Pays 7¢ to 10¢ a word. B&w glossy photos purchased with mss.

MARINA MANAGEMENT/MARKETING, Box 373, Wilmette IL 60091. (312)256-4560. Editor: E.E. DuVernet. For marina owners, operators and other personnel. Monthly magazine; 64 pages. Estab: 1975. Circ: 15,000. Pays on publication. Buys all rights, but may reassign following publication, or second serial (reprint) rights). Simultaneous and photocopied submissions OK. SASE. Reports in 3 weeks. Free sample copy.

Nonfiction: Publishes material relating to the operation of marinas, boatyards and yacht clubs; including articles on dockage, maintenance, repair services, rentals, marina stores, boat dealerships; adjoining motels and recreational facilities. Informational, how-to, successful business operations, new product, merchandising techniques and technical articles; interviews and profiles. Length: 1,000-5,000 words. "Study previous issues." Pays $30-200.

Photos: B&w glossies (8x10) purchased with mss. Captions required. Pays $5-10. Color by assignment only

For '78: "We would like to see more articles on business practices of specific marinas—accounting procedures, financing problems, sales efforts in marina stores and boat dealerships."

SEAWAY REVIEW, Harbor Island, Maple City Postal Station MI 49664. Senior Editor: Jacques LesStrang. Professional journal dealing with the St. Lawrence Seaway, Great Lakes, Lake ports and shipping. Quarterly. Buys North American serial rights. Pays on acceptance. Sample copy available for $1. "Query first on features as these are usually assigned to experts in their respective fields. From time to time will have assignments for writers in the states covered by the journal and will keep on file the names of qualified writers in these areas. Writers should support their listings with either credits or samples of their work. Deadlines fall on the 10th of the months preceding April, July, Oct. and Jan." Reports in two weeks. Enclose S.A.S.E.

Nonfiction: Articles of a professional nature relating to Great Lakes shipping, the economics of the eight states which comprise the Seaway region (Minnesota, Ohio, Wisconsin, Michigan, New York, Pennsylvania, Indiana and Illinois), port operation, the Seaway's role in state economic development, etc. Length: 1,000-3,000 words. "Payment varies with the knowledgeability of the author and the value of the subject matter; up to $250."

Photos: Purchased both with lss and with captions only. 8x10 glossy b&w or 4x5 or 2½x2¼ Ektachrome on Lake shipping or port activity, if newsworthy. Pays $25 maximum per accepted b&w photo, and "$100 maximum for color—scenic as well as news photos."

Fillers: Uses spot news items relating to Lake ports only. Length: 50 to 500 words. Pays $5 to $50.

SHIP & BOAT INTERNATIONAL, S-15030 Mariefred, Sweden. For naval architects, shipbuilders, owners, consultants, engineers, equipment manufacturers. Monthly. Estab: 1947. Pays on publication. Buys all rights. Submit seasonal material 2 months in advance. Enclose SAE and International Reply Coupons for reply to queries.

Nonfiction: Technical material regarding design and construction of commercial craft. Does not wnat to see "anything with a personal angle." Buys coverage of successful business operations and new products. Length: 500 to 1,500 words. Pays 0.25 Swedish krona per word as published.

THE WORK BOAT, Box 217, Mandeville LA 70448. (504)626-3151. Publisher/Editor: Harry L. Peace. Monthly. Buys first rights. Pays on publication. Query first. Reports in 2 week. Enclose S.A.S.E.

Nonfiction and Photos: "Articles on waterways, river terminals, barge line operations, work boat construction and design, barges, dredges, tugs. Best bet for freelancers: One-angle article showing in detail how a barge line, tug operator or dredging firm solves a problem of either mechanical or operational nature. This market is semitechnical and rather exacting. Such articles must be specific, containing firm name, location, officials of company, major equipment involved, by name, model, power, capacity and manufacturer; with b&w photos." Length: 1,000 to 5,000 words. Pays $90 minimum. 5x5 or 5x7 b&w; 4x5 color prints only. No additional payment for photos.

Medical

Publications that are aimed at private physicians or which publish technical material on new discoveries in medicine are classified here. Journals for nurses, laboratory

technicians, hospital resident physicians, and other medical workers will be found with the Hospitals, Nursing, and Nursing Homes journals. Publications for druggists and drug wholesalers and retailers are grouped with the Drugs, Health Care, and Medical Products journals.

AMERICAN FAMILY PHYSICIAN, 1740 W. 82nd St., Kansas City MO 64114. (816)333-9700. Publisher: Walter H. Kemp. Monthly. Circulation: 126,000. Buys all rights. Pays on publication. "Most articles are assigned." Query first. Reports in 2 weeks. Enclose S.A.S.E.
Nonfiction: Interested only in clinical articles. Length: 2,500 words. Pays $50 to $200.

AUDECIBEL, Journal of the National Hearing Aid Society, 20361 Middlebelt, Livonia MI 48152. (313)478-2610. Editor: Anthony DiRocco. Assistant Editor: Lila R. Johnson. For "otologists, otolaryngologists, hearing aid specialists, educators of the deaf and hard of hearing, clinical audiologists, and others interested in hearing and audiology." Established in 1951. Quarterly. Circulation: 12,600. Buys all rights. "Most articles published are from authorities in the field who publish for professional recognition, without fee." Pays on publication. Will send a sample copy to a writer on request. Write for copy of guidelines for writers. Query first or submit complete ms. Enclose S.A.S.E.
Nonfiction and Photos: "Purpose of the magazine is to bring to the otologist, the clinical audiologist, the hearing aid audiologist and others interested in the field authoritative articles and data concerned with current issues, research, techniques, education and new developments in the field of hearing and hearing aids. In general, *Audecibel's* editorial policy emphasizes a professional and technical approach rather than a sales and merchandising approach. Eight types of articles are used: technical articles dealing with hearing aids themselves; technical articles dealing with fitting hearing aids; case histories of unusual fittings; technical articles dealing with sound, acoustics, etc.; psychology of hearing loss; medical and physiological aspects; professional standards and ethics, and current issues in the hearing health care fields. We are not interested in human interest stories, but only in carefully researched and documented material." Length: 200 to 2,000 words; "will consider longer articles if content is good." Pays 1¢ to 2½¢ per word. Photos purchased with mss; captions optional. Pays $3 to $5.
How To Break In: "Before you submit an article, it's a good idea to send a query. Let us know what your idea is. It may be that we're overstocked with the type of article you want to write. Or, it may be that it's just what we need, and we may be able to give you some information from our files, or suggestions of names of people to contact."

CANADIAN DOCTOR, 310 Victoria Ave., Montreal, P.Q., Canada H32 2M9. (514)487-2302. Editor: Peter Williamson. For all Canadian physicians. Monthly magazine; 125 (8x10) pages. Established in 1935. Circulation: 31,712. Buys all rights, but will reassign rights to author after publication. Buys 50 mss a year. Payment on publication. Will send sample copy to writer for $2. Guidelines for writers are sent only after a story idea has been accepted. Will consider photocopied submissions. Will not consider simultaneous submissions. Reports in 2 weeks. Query first. Enclose S.A.E. and International Reply Coupons.
Nonfiction and Photos: Articles concerning financial planning for Canadian physicians; practice management, professional relations. Some travel and retirement material. Tax and estate planning would be of interest, as well as informational articles. All material must be "informal and anecdotal, but with authority. Freelancers should really know the subject. Unassigned articles usually miss the specialized tone we use with our audience. We reject material when the subject is too general." Length: 2,000 words maximum. Pays 5¢ to 10¢ a word. Also looking for shorter material on Canadian real estate. Length: 1,000 to 1,500 words. Pays $100. Pays $15 for 8x10 b&w photos purchased with mss. $25 for color transparencies used with mss. Captions required.
Fillers: Jokes. Length: 100 words. Pays $5.

DRUG THERAPY MEDICAL JOURNAL, Biomedical Information Corp., 919 Third Ave., New York NY 10022. (212)758-6104. Editor-in-Chief: Dr. Rhoda Michaels. Published in 2 editions: Office edition for practicing physicians; Hospital edition for hospital personnel. Emphasizes drug therapy for physicians in all the clinical specialties as well as internists, residents and attendants in the hospital setting throughout the U.S. Monthly magazine; 175 pages. Estab: 1970. Circ: 100,000. Pays on publication. Phone queries OK. Submit seasonal or holiday material 4 months in advance. Simultaneous and photocopied submissions OK. Previously published work acceptable as long as reprint rights are clear. SASE. Reports in 1-3 weeks. Free sample copy and editorial guidelines.
Nonfiction: How-to (diagnosis and treatment as clinical entity); informational (use of drugs,

new drugs, how a drug works, etc.). Technical and new product articles. Buys 10-15 mss per issue. Query. Length: 1,000 words minimum. Pays $300.
Photos: No additional payment for b&w or color used with mss.

HOSPITAL PHYSICIAN MAGAZINE, 405 Lexington Ave., New York NY 10017. Editor: Peter Frishauf. For doctors. Monthly magazine; 60 pages. Circulation: 80,000. Rights purchased vary with author and material. Usually buys all rights or First North American serial rights. Buys 35 mss a year. Payment on acceptance. Will send free sample copy to writer on request. Will consider photocopied submissions and simultaneous submissions. Reports in 1 month. Query first or submit complete ms. Enclose S.A.S.E.
Nonfiction: Uses medical information stories, "the patient's view" and clinical tips. Must be of interest to interns and residents in hospitals throughout the country. "We deal with the patient's view, with ethical questions in medicine, and especially with the particular problems of house-staff." Not interested in "one-shot" interviews. Length: 700-3,000 words. Pays $50.

JOURNAL OF INTERNATIONAL PHYSICIANS, 1030 N. Kings Highway, Cherry Hill NJ 08034. (609)667-7526. Editor: Mark Pratter. For physicians who have received their degrees in foreign countries. Published every 6 weeks. Estab: 1976. Circ: 4,000. Pays on acceptance. Buys all rights, but may reassign following publication; or first North American serial rights. SASE. Sample copy $2.
Nonfiction: Publishes news of interest to foreign educated physicians including U.S. citizens who went to medical school abroad. "We seek profiles of outstanding, interesting foreign educated physicians. Stories on American culture of interest too. Interviews with developers of U.S. medical policy are featured." Length: 1,000-1,500 words. Query. Pays $75-200.
Photos: B&w and color purchased with mss, or on assignment. Captions required. Pays $100 per day on assignment.
Columns/Departments: Immigration news, legislation affecting foreign graduates, news of medicine in foreign countries (particularly India, Phillippines, Italy, S. Korea, and Iran), items from foreign physician organizations. Length 200-500 words. Pays $30 a column.

MEDICAL DIMENSIONS, 730 Third Ave., New York NY 10017. (212)557-9854. Editor: Decia Fates. For physicians under 40 years of ge; medical students and faculty. Magazine; 56 pages. Established in 1972. Monthly. Circulation: 80,000. Rights purchased vary with author and material. Usually buys all rights, but may reassign rights to author after publication; or all rights. Buys 50 to 75 mss per year. Payment on publication. Will send free sample copy to writer on request. Will consider photocopied submissions. No simultaneous submissions. Reports in 2-5 weeks. Query first or submit complete ms. Enclose S.A.S.E.
Nonfiction and Photos: Wants mss of professional but non-technical nature; career opportunities and help; medical politics; travel and leisure; consumer information on luxury and leisure goods; investigative reports on "doings and trends within the profession, not medical breakthroughs." Also humor with heavy medical content. "Keep in mind the highly educated, sophisticated reader." Does not want to see material on patients' complaints or experiences. Would like to see mss about changes in medical practice in any individual community. Also profiles of interesting young doctors. Length: 1,000-4,000 words. Pays 10¢/word.

MEDICAL OPINION, 575 Madison Ave., New York NY 10022. Editor: Genell Subak-Sharpe. For physicians primarily in private practice. Monthly. Circulation: 130,000. Buys all rights. Buys 30-55 mss/year. Pays on acceptance. Query first. Reports in 4 to 6 weeks. Enclose S.A.S.E.
Nonfiction: "Interested in articles written by physicians which are reflective and informative on specific aspects of modern medical practice. "Clinical topics are preferred, with an emphasis on topics of practical interest to medical practitioners. We are not a news magazine. Wo do not feature products or immediate breakthroughs, but rather subjects and therapeutic areas that have been at least partially exposed to our audience. No fiction, poetry, or 'cute pieces'. All articles should offer a clearly defined opinion. Style is not technical, but follows the more lively consumer magazine style. Be careful not to oversimplify or to confuse medical terms with clear writing." Length: 1,500 to 2,500 words. Pays $150 to $350.

THE MEDICAL POST, 481 University Ave., Toronto, Ont., M5W 1A7, Canada. Editor: Earl Damude. For the medical profession. Published every 2nd Tuesday. Will send sample copy to medical writers only. Send query first to Derek Cassels, Clinical Editor. Buys first North American serial rights. Pays on publication. Enclose S.A.E. and International Reply Coupons.
Nonfiction: Uses "newsy, factual reports of medical developments Must be aimed at pro-

fessional audience, and not written in 'popular medical' style." Length: 300 to 800 words. Pays 9¢ a word.
Photos: Uses photos with mss or captions only, of medical interest; pays $5 up.

THE NEW PHYSICIAN, 1171 Tower Rd., Schaumburg IL 60195 (312)882-1680. Editor: Dianne Rafalik. For medical students, interns and residents. Magazine; 72 (8½x11) pages. Established in 1952. Monthly. Circulation: 78,000. Buys all rights. Buys 6 to 12 mss a year. Pays on publication. Will send free sample copy to writer on request. No photocopied submissions. Will consider simultaneous submissions. Reports on material accepted for publication in 4 to 6 weeks. Returns rejected material immediately. Query first. Enclose S.A.S.E.
Nonfiction and Photos: "Articles on social, political, economic issues in medicine/medical education. Our readers need more than a superficial, simplistic look into issues that affect them. We want skeptical, accurate, professional contributors to do well-researched, comprehensive reports, and offer new perspectives on health care problems." Not interested in material on "my operation," or encounters with physicians, or personal experiences as physician's patient. Occasionally publishes special topic issues, such as those on emergency care and foreign medical graduates. Informational articles, interviews, and exposes are sought. Length: 500 to 2,500 words. Pays $25 to $250. Pays $10 to $25 for b&w photos used with mss. Captions required.

OSTEOPATHIC PHYSICIAN, Box 340, North Madison OH 44057. Publication and official office: 733 Third Ave., New York NY 10017. (212)867-7520. Editor: Dr. J. Dudley Chapman. For osteopathic physicians and students with 4 years of college and 4 years of medical school and internship, as a minimum; specialists have an additional 4 years. The major portion of the audience are general or family physicians. Some 2,000 doctors of medicine also receive this publication. Established in 1933. Circulation: 18,000. Rights purchased vary with author and material. Usually buys all rights, but will reassign rights to author after publication. Buys 25 mss a year. Payment on publication. Will send sample copy to writer for $1. Will consider photocopied submissions. Submit special issue (December) material 4 months in advance. Reports on material accepted for publication in 21 days. Returns rejected material in 30 days. Query first or submit complete ms. Enclose S.A.S.E.
Nonfiction and Photos: "This is a journal dedicated to the psychological, philosophical and social aspects of medicine as they relate to the physician in private practice. There is a special emphasis on the role of human sexuality in the series, as well as other family life topics." Prefers material on social changes that affect practice of medicine, philosophical issues directed toward doctors; marital and social issues affecting health and medicine; occasional political matters affecting health care, and the third party matter. A special issue is published in December on the personal life of physicians: hobbies, travel, aesthetics, recreation. Prefers that the opening paragraph of all manuscripts define the topic and problem to be discussed. Likes individual style and variation that deliver the message. Dislikes stylized, formal writing. Does not want to see material on medical economics and business management. Current interest is in articles on the future of marriage, the government's influence on the rising cost of medicine, the organization's defense and hiding of bad medicine. Maximum length is 10 double-spaced pages with wide margins. Pays $50 to $125.
Poetry: Free verse and avant-garde forms. "We do publish poetry, but in theme with all of our material; not poetry for poetry's sake but poetry with a message and meaning. We limit poetry very restrictively." Maximum length of 54 lines. Pays up to $100.
How To Break In: "Know thy subject and material — we are not interested in words be they poetry or essay — we want a message that is of value to justify a physician spending his most expensive commodity — time. We have found too often that the author knows little or nothing about the subject material, leaving a myriad of words and no authentic message or reason for putting such valueless words into print."

PHYSICIAN'S MANAGEMENT, Harcourt Brace Jovanovich Health Care Publications, 757 Third Ave., New York NY 10017. (212)754-2938. Editor-in-Chief: Patrick Flanagan. Emphasizes finances, investments, small office administration, practice management and taxes for physicians in private practice. Quarterly magazine; 120 pages. Estab: 1960. Circ: 180,000. Pays on acceptance. Buys all rights, but may reassign following publication. Submit seasonal or holiday material 5 months in advance. SASE. Reports in 2-4 weeks. Sample copy $2. Free writer's guidelines.
Nonfiction: "*Physician's Management* is a socio-economic publication, not a clinical one." Publishes how-to articles (limited to medical practice management); informational (when relevant to audience); personal experience articles (if written by a physician). Length: 500-3,000 words. Buys 3-5 an issue. Query first. Pays $50-400.

How To Break In: "Talk to doctors first about their practice, financial interests, and day-to-day non-clinical problems and then query us. Use of an MD byline helps tremendously! Also, the ability to write a concise, well-structured and well-researched magazine article is essential. Most freelancers think like patients and fail with us. Those who can think like MD's are successful."

PRACTICAL PSYCHOLOGY FOR PHYSICIANS, Magazines for Medicine, Inc., 475 5th Ave., New York NY 10017. (212)889-1050. Editor-in-Chief: Robert McCrie. Emphasizes behavioral sciences for physicians. Monthly magazine; 66 pages. Estab: 1972. Circ: 109,000. Pays on publication. Buys all rights, but may reassign following publication. Phone queries OK. Submit seasonal/holiday material 3 months in advance. Simultaneous and photocopied submissions OK. SASE. Report in 2 weeks. Free writer's guidelines.

Nonfiction: "Useful information from the behaviorial sciences for primary care physicians. We need one type of article more than any other: practical, clinical-related, slightly offbeat mss that are of value to busy primary care physicians." Buys 1-3 mss/issue. Query. Length: 1,500-2,000 words. Pays $200-300.

Photos: Purchased with or without accompanying ms. Captions required. Query. Offers additional payment for photos accepted with accompanying ms up to $350 per complete article. "We like to use photo articles of physicians in practice. Would also like picture articles that tell a story of interest to physicians."

Rejects: "Articles in which author 'tells off' physicians for bad techniques or communications. Also, we never use highly personal articles from physicians about patients. Mss on depression or general psychosomatic complaints have been done to death."

PRIVATE PRACTICE, 5100 N. Brookline, Suite 700, Oklahoma City OK 73112. Editor: Llewellyn H. Rockwell, Jr. For "medical doctors in private practice." Monthly. Buys first North American serial rights. Pays on acceptance. Puery first. Enclose S.A.S.E.

Nonfiction and Photos: "Articles which indicate importance of maintaining freedom of medical practice or which detail outside interferences in the practice of medicine, including research, hospital operation, drug manufacture, etc. Straight reporting style. No cliches, no scare words such as 'socialists,' etc. No flowery phrases to cover up poor reporting. Stories must be actual, factual, precise, correct. Copy should be lively and easy-to-read. Also publish historical, offbeat, and humorous articles of medical interest." Length: up to 2,500 words. Pays "usual minimum $150." Photos purchased with mss only. B&w glossies, 8x10. Payment "depends on quality, relevancy of material, etc."

SURGICAL BUSINESS, 2009 Morris Ave., Union NJ 07083. Editor: Adrian Comper. For medical/surgical dealers and dealer/salesmen. Magazine; 92 pages. Established in 1938. Monthly. Circulation: 7,000. Buys exclusive industry rights. Buys 5 to 10 mss a year. Pays on publication. Will send free sample copy to writer on request. Write for copy of guidelines for writers. Will consider photocopied and simultaneous submissions. Reports in 3 months. Query first or submit complete ms. Enclose S.A.S.E.

Nonfiction and Photos: "We publish feature-length articles dealing with manufacturers within the industry, as well as meeting coverage and general information within the industry. We do not desire promotional material about a company or product. Mss should be objective and to the point." No additional payment for b&w photos used with mss. Recently published "Medical Supplier Gets Tax Benefits for Exports" and "Scoring High Through Promotions." Length: approximately 2,500 words. Pays 5¢ a word.

UROLOGY TIMES, OPHTHALMOLOGY TIMES, RADIOLOGY TIMES, Murray Publications, 79 Madison Ave., New York NY 10016. (212)889-6210. Editor: Zee King. Magazine; 40 pages. Established in 1973. Monthly. Circulations: 8,200, 10,727 and 15,000 respectively. Buys about 12 mss a year. Pays on publication. Will send sample copy to writer on request. Write for copy of guidelines for writers. Will consider photocopied submissions. No simultaneous submissions. Reports on material accepted for publication in 8 weeks. Returns rejected material in 2 weeks. Query first. Enclose S.A.S.E.

Nonfiction: "Our object is to act as the bridge between the academician and the clinician. We use reports on work in urology-hypertension-radiology; all with a reportorial approach." Recently published articles include "Immunologic Effects of Surgery." Length: 1,000 to 5,000 words. Pays $80 to $320.

Milling, Feed, and Grain

FEED INDUSTRY REVIEW, 3055 N. Brookfield Rd., Brookfield WI 53005. (914)786-7540. Publisher: Bruce W. Smith. For manufacturers of livestock and poultry feed. Quarterly. Circulation: 8,000. Buys all rights. Pays on publication. Will send a free sample copy on receipt of letter only, no postcards. Query first. Reports in one week. Enclose S.A.S.E.

Nonfiction: "Profile articles on progressive feed manufacturing operations, including data on plant layout and equipment, research, and distribution. This is a market for factual reporters, not creative writers. Market extremely limited; queries imperative prior to submitting completed articles." Length: 1,500 to 2,200 words. Pays $20 to $75.

Photos: Usually buys only with mss, occasional exceptions. Subject matter should be agribusiness, plants, or other physical facilities. B&w glossies, horizontal prints. Pays $7 to $10.

THE WHEAT SCOOP, 606 25th St. North, Box 6699, Great Falls MT 59406. Editor: Ray Fenton. 8 times a year. Not copyrighted. Query first. "Very little freelance material purchased." Enclose S.A.S.E.

Nonfiction: Uses "articles on grain research, freight rates, fertilizers, domestic markets and foreign markets as they pertain to Montana. Clarity and precision necessary. Authenticity, definite Montana tie-in are musts." Length: 100 to 1,000 words. Payment negotiated.

Photos: Buys photos with mss and with captions only. Particularly needs art wheat photos, from seeding to harvesting, b&w or color; unusual or art type.

Mining and Minerals

AMERICAN GOLD NEWS, P.O. Box 457, Ione CA 95640. (209)274-2196. Editor: Cecil L. Helms. For anyone interested in gold, gold mining, gold companies, gold stocks, gold history, gold coins, the future of gold in our economy. Tabloid newspaper; 20 pages. Established in 1933. Monthly. Circulation: 3,500. Not copyrighted. Pays on acceptance. Will send free sample copy to writer on request. Write for copy of guidelines for writers. No photocopied or simultaneous submissions. Submit seasonal material (relating to seasonal times in mining country) 2 months in advance. Reports in 2 to 4 weeks. Query first or submit complete ms. Enclose S.A.S.E.

Nonfiction and Photos: "This is not a literary publication. We want information on any subject pertaining to gold told in the most simple, direct, and interesting way. How to build gold mining equipment. History of mines (with pix). History of gold throughout U.S. Financial articles on gold philosophy in money matters. Picture stories of mines, mining towns, mining country. Would like to see more histories of mines, from any state. Length: 500 to 2,000 words. Pays $10 to $25. B&w photos purchased with or without ms. Must be sharp, if not old, historical photos. Pays $2.50 to $25. Captions required.

Fiction and Fillers: Western, adventure, humorous fiction related to gold mining. Length: 500-2,000 words. Pays $10-$25. Also buys newsbreaks, puzzles related to gold; jokes, gags and anecdotes. Length: open. Pays $2.50 to $5.

COAL AGE, 1221 Avenue of the Americas, New York NY 10020. Editor: Joseph F. Wilkinson. For supervisors, engineers and executives in coal mining. Monthly. Circulation: 20,000. Buys all rights. Pays on publication. Query. Reports in two-three weeks. SASE.

Nonfiction: Uses some technical (operating type) articles; some how-to pieces on equipment maintenance; management articles. Pays $150 per page.

COAL WEEK, 441 National Press Bldg., Washington DC 20045. (202)624-7375. Editor: Michael Morrison. For executives in coal producing, consuming and related industries, observers in the financial and academic communities, and government officials. Newsletter; 10 pages. Established in 1975. Weekly. Buys all rights. Pays on acceptance. Will send sample copy to writer on request. Write for copy of guidelines for writers. No photocopied or simultaneous submissions. Query first. Enclose S.A.S.E.

Nonfiction: Spot news; brief news reports on developments which will affect the coal market. Length: 500 words maximum. Pays $5 to $7.50 per inch.

Miscellaneous

AMERICAN CANDLEMAKER, P.O. Box 22227, San Diego CA 92122. (714)755-1410. Editor: A. Paul Theil. For "high school age through retirees who engage in candlemaking, either as a hobby or a semiprofessional endeavor. Usually have accompanying interest in allied crafts." Monthly magazine; 12 (8½x11) pages. Established in 1972. Circulation: 1,000. Buys all rights. Payment is usually made 2 weeks after acceptance. Will send sample copy to writer for 75¢.

Will not consider photocopied or simultaneous submissions. Submit seasonal material (Easter, Thanksgiving, Christmas) at least 3 months in advance. Reports in 2 weeks. Submit complete ms. Enclose S.A.S.E.

Nonfiction, Photos and Poetry: "All phases of material directly related to candlecrafting, either in the creation of the candle, decoration, techniques; the how-to. The latter is tested, however, before we publish it to assure accuracy. Writer may use his own approach, but nothing 'far out.' Special emphasis is helpful, of course, since we receive large numbers of manuscripts from reputable, professional candlemakers." Uses informational, how-to, historical, successful business operations, new product, merchandising techniques and technical material. Especially interested in material on the use of candles for all occasions in foreign lands. Length: no minimum; 1,500 words maximum. Pays 2½¢ per word. B&w photos are used with mss. No additional payment. Captions required. Also uses traditional forms of poetry related to the subject.

THE ANTIQUES DEALER, 1115 Clifton Ave., Clifton NJ 07013. Editor: Stella Hall. For antiques dealers. Monthly magazine. Established in 1949. Circulation: 10,000. Rights purchased vary with author and material. May buy all rights or first North American rights or exclusive rights in this field. Buys 40 mss a year. Payment on publication. Will send free sample copy to writer on request. Will consider photocopied submissions "if clear". Enclose S.A.S.E.

Nonfiction: "Remember that we are a trade publication and all material must be slanted to the needs and interests of antique dealers. We publish nothing of a too general or too limited nature." Only articles of interest to dealers; may be tutorial if by authority in one specific field; otherwise of broad general interest to all dealers. Glass, china, porcelain, furniture, oriental, Americana, and news of the international antique trade. Emphasis is currently on heirlooms (50-100 years old), art nouveau, art deco, jewelery and miniatures. Length: no minimum; maximum 2-part article, about 7,000 words; 3,500 words if one-part. Pays $30 a page for features; $1.50 for few sentence obit. Columns cover Trade News; anything from a couple of sentences to about 200 words, with photo or two. Usually pays just $1.50 if very short.

Photos: Purchased with or without accompanying mss, or on assignment. Pays $5 per b&w, no smaller than 5x7 (glossy). Professional quality only; no Polaroids.

Fillers: Suitable for professional dealers; any type of fillers. Length: 300 to 400 words. Pays approximately $15 for half-page.

How To Break In: "Submit 'hard news'—brief one-paragraph items are used in Trade News column. Also, for feature articles, knowledge of antiques and/or antiques business more important than writing ability. Photos always help sell a ms."

APA MONITOR, 1200 17th St., N.W., Washington DC 20036. Editor: Pamela Moore. For psychologists, interested in behaviorial science and mental health. Newspaper; 32 (11x16) pages. Established in 1970. Monthly. Circ: 55,000. Buys all rights. Buys about 25 mss/year. Pays on publication. Will send free sample copy to writer on request. Will not consider photocopied or simultaneous submissions. Query.

Nonfiction and Photos: News and features about psychology and political, social, economic developments that affect psychology; APA (American Psychological Association) affairs. "We put more emphasis on organizational and political aspects of psychology as a profession; less on interpretation of scientific findings to the public. Keep in mind that the reader is probably better informed about the substantive science and practice of psychology than the writer." Informational, interview, profile, humor, historical, think articles, expose, new product, photo. Length: 300 to 1,000 words.

CANADIAN FUNERAL DIRECTOR, Peter Perry Publishing, Ltd., 1658 Victoria Park Ave., Suite 5, Scarboro, Ontario, Canada M1R 1P7. (416)755-7050. Managing Editor: Peter Perry. Emphasizes funeral home operation. Monthly magazine; 60 pages. Estab: 1924. Circ: 1,700. Pays on publication. Buys one-time rights. Phone queries OK. Reports in 30-60 days. Simultaneous and photocopied submissions and previously published work OK. SASE. Reports in 3 weeks. Free sample copy.

Nonfiction: Informational, historical, humor, interview, personal opinion, profile, photo feature, technical. Buys 12 mss a year. Query. Length: 200-1,500 words. Pays $40 per 1,000 words.

Photos: Purchased with or without ms. Captions required. Query or send contact sheet. Pays $5-10 for 5x7 or 8x10 b&w glossies.

CANADIAN RENTAL SERVICE, J. Peter Watkins, Ltd., 49 Queens Dr., Weston, Ontario, Canada M9N 2H3. (416)241-4724. Editor-in-Chief: L.C. Brown. Emphasizes general rental business. Bimonthly magazine; 44 pages. Estab: 1976. Circ: 2,500. Pays on publication. Buys one-time rights. Phone queries OK. Submit seasonal/holiday material 2 months in advance.

Photocopied submissions and previously published work OK. SASE. Reports in 12 weeks. Free sample copy.

Nonfiction: J. Stiff, Department Editor. Profiles and technical articles. Buys 1-2 per issue. Query. Length: 1,000 words maximum. Pays $50/page minimum.

Photos: Purchased with ms or on assignment. Captions required. Query. Pays $20 minimum for 5x7 b&w glossies. Model release required.

Columns, Departments: Trade News, Association News, Appointments. Query. Length: 1 typewritten page. Open to suggestions for new columns and departments.

Fillers: Clippings, newsbreaks. Buys 1-2 per issue. Send complete ms. Pays $10-20.

Rejects: Material relating to rental of items not rented by the field involved. Material relating to renting in the U.S.A.

COACHING: MEN'S ATHLETICS, Intercommunications, Inc., 50 S. Main Rd., Box 867, Wallingford CT 06492. (203)265-0937. Editor/Publisher: William J. Burgess. Emphasizes school athletics for high school and college administrators of athletic programs. Every 2 months except July/August. Magazine; 48 pages. Estab: 1977. Circ: 3,500. Buys all rights. SASE. Reports in 2 weeks. Sample copy $2. Free writer's guidelines.

Nonfiction: "Knowledge of school athletics essential." Expose, how-to, humor (only if combined with more technical material); informational, inspirational, interview, personal experience, personal opinion, photo feature, profile, technical articles. Buys 10/issue. Send complete ms. Length: 1,500-3,500 words. Pays 2½-5¢/word.

Photos: Purchased with mss or on assignment. Query. Pays $2/b&w (4x5 glossy or larger); $25-100/color (35mm or larger).

COACHING: WOMEN'S ATHLETICS, Intercommunications, Inc., Box 867, Wallingford CT 06492. (203)265-0937. Editor-in-Chief: William J. Burgess. For athletic and/or physical education departments of public, private and parochial elementary, junior and senior high schools, preparatory schools, junior colleges and universities. Bimonthly (except July/August) magazine; 60 pages. Estab: 1975. Circ: 10,000. Pays on publication. Buys all rights. Phone queries OK. Previously published submissions OK. SASE. Reports in 0 month. Free sample copy and writer's guidelines.

Nonfiction: How-to; interview; personal experience; and profile. Buys 60 mss/year. Length: 2,500 words maximum. Pays 5¢/word.

Photos: Purchased with or without accompanying ms. Captions required. Query. Uses 4x5, 5x7, or 8x10 clear finish glossy prints; 35mm, 2¼x2¼ or 4x5 color transparencies. Model release required.

EMERGENCY PRODUCT NEWS, P.O. Box 159, Carlsbad CA 92008. (714)438-3456. Editor: Linda Olander. For paramedics, emergency medical technicians, emergency physicians and nurses, fire departments, hospitals, law enforcement agencies, industries, governmental agencies, schools, sports trainers, etc. Magazine; 96 pages. Established in 1968. Published every 2 months. Circulation: 60,000. Buys first North American serial rights. Buys 10 to 20 mss per year. Payment on publication. Will send free sample copy to writer on request. Write for editorial guidelines sheet. Will consider photocopied submissions. No simultaneous submissions. Reports on mss accepted for publication "immediately." Returns rejected material in 2 weeks. Query first. Enclose S.A.S.E.

Nonfiction and Photos: "Articles dealing with emergency care and transportation of the sick and injured; techniques in treatment, first aid techniques, organizational structure on care institutions, human interest. Writer must be knowledgeable in the field. Material must be technically sound and related to the emergency medical field. Emphasis is on first aid treatment or emergency medical transportation." Open to suggestions for new columns and departments. Recently published "Child Abuse and the EMT," "The Hollowpoint Bullet," "Lightning Injuries" and "Wilderness Rescue." "Payment is determined by review board. Payment depends on material content and importance to Journal." Average pay is $75 to $200. Length: at least 8 typed pages, not exceeding 30. Photos purchased with or without accompanying ms, or purchased on assignment. Captions required. Pays $10 for b&w glossy prints. Pays $75 for color cover shot. Color photos should be 35mm or 2¼ transparencies only.

HOUSEHOLD AND PERSONAL PRODUCTS INDUSTRY, 26 Lake St., Ramsey NJ 07446. Editor: Hamilton C. Carson. For "manufacturers of soaps, detergents, cosmetics and toiletries, waxes and polishes, insecticides, and aerosols." Established in 1964. Monthly. Circulation: 14,000. Not copyrighted. Buys 3 to 4 mss a year, "but would buy more if slanted to our needs." Pays on publication. Will send a sample copy to a writer on request. Will consider photocopied submissions. Submit seasonal material 2 months in advance. Query first. Enclose S.A.S.E.

Nonfiction and Photos: "Technical and semitechnical articles on manufacturing, distribution, marketing, new products, plant stories, etc., of the industries served. Some knowledge of the field is essential in writing for us." Buys informational articles, interviews, photo features, spot news, coverage of successful business operations, new product articles, coverage of merchandising techniques, and technical articles. Length: 500 to 2,000 words. Pays $5 to $125. 5x7 or 8x10 b&w glossies purchased with mss. Pays $3 to $5.

THE INDIAN TRADER, Box 867, Gallup NM 87301. (505)863-4300. Editor-in-Chief: Ms. Jo Smith. For traders in the Indian arts, crafts and culture. Monthly tabloid; 88 pages. Estab: 1970. Circ: 10,000. Pays on publication. Buys all rights, but may reassign following publication. Phone queries OK. Submit seasonal/holiday material 2 months in advance. Reports in 3-6 weeks. Free sample copy and writer's guidelines.
Nonfiction: Historical (must be accurately researched and of special interest to collectors of Indian artifacts, traders, or those interested in current American activities); informational (characters of historical interest, their descendants, etc.); interviews (with exceptional Indian craftsmen, collectors, shows, pow-wows, etc.); photo features (coverage of Indian affairs, reservation happenings, etc.); and travel (visits to Indian ruins, trading posts, similar material in areas of the Northwest or Northeast, or Canada). Buys 8-10 mss/issue. Pays 50¢-$1.50/column inch. "This usually works out to about 2-4¢/word, but we do pay by the column inch."
Photos: B&w (8x10) glossies preferred. Purchased with or without mss or on assignment. Captions optional, but information must be included if captionless. Query or send prints. Pays $2-15 when additional payment is made. Total purchase price sometimes includes payment for photos.
Columns/Departments: Buys 1-3 book reviews/issue. Query. Pays 50¢-$1.50/column inch.

MEETINGS & CONVENTIONS, Ziff-Davis Publishing Co., 1 Park Ave., New York NY 10016. Editor-in-Chief: Mel Hosansky. For association and corporate executives who plan sales meetings, training meetings, annual conventions, incentive travel trips, and any other kind of off-premises meeting. Monthly magazine; 130 pages. Estab: 1966. Circ: 73,500. Pays on acceptance. Buys all rights. Submit seasonal or holiday material 6 months in advance. Photocopied submissions and previously published work (if not published in a competing publication) OK. SASE. Reports in 6 months.
Nonfiction: "Publication is basically how-to. We tell them how to run better meetings; where to hold them, etc. Must be case history, talking about specific meeting." Query. Length: 250-2,000 words. Pays $35-300.
Photos: Purchases 8x10 b&w glossies with mss. Captions required. No additional payment. Query.

MEETINGS & EXPOSITIONS, 22 Pine St., Morristown NJ 07960. (201)538-9470. Editorial Director: William F. Kaiser. For corporate and trade association meeting planners, exhibit managers and incentive travel program managers. Bimonthly. Magazine; 64 (8½x11) pages. Established in 1972. Circulation: 40,000. Rights purchased vary with author and material. May buy all rights, first serial rights or second serial (reprint) rights. Buys 5 to 8 mss a year. Payment is usually made on acceptance, but payment for filler material is sometimes made on publication. Will consider photocopied and simultaneous submissions. Reports quickly. Query first. Enclose S.A.S.E.
Nonfiction: "We need well-written, informative articles on all aspects of meeting planning. Short, snappy articles, rather than tomes. We assume a certain competence in our area of specialization on the part of our readers. Articles dealing with meeting planning, expositions and incentive travel. We are especially seeking humorous material about meetings and/or trade shows." How-to, interview, profile, humor, think pieces, successful business operations. Length: 1,200 words maximum. Pays $100.
How To Break In: "Attend meetings, conventions, trade shows; work with planners, managers and designers to understand basics of business. Learn what makes a good program; what causes a bad program — then write about it simply and straightforwardly."

MILLIMETER MAGAZINE, 12 E. 46th St., New York NY 10017. Publishers: William Blake, George Cooper and Monte Stettin. Editors: Robert Avrech and Larry Gross. For advertising people, as well as filmmakers, technicians, writers, animators, directors, sound men, students. "We're paying equal attention to business, craft, and art with a special emphasis on the personalities involved." Monthly, 52 (8½x11) pages. Established in 1973. Circulation: 10,000. Buys all rights but will reassign rights to author after publication. Buys 30 mss a year. Pays on publication. Will send sample copy to writer for $1. Will consider photocopied and simultaneous submissions. Submit special material (some issues are built around a particular theme: TV, animation, advertising, etc.) 3 months in advance. Reports within 5 weeks. Qiery first. Enclose S.A.S.E.

Nonfiction: Emphasis on off-camera personalities or new developments and trends in the film industry, advertising, cable TV, video tape or animation. Interested in articles pertaining to the history of motion pictures, videotapes, and the related technology. "We like to think of ourselves as having a style similar to *New York* magazine but our range includes all the major filmmaking centers around the country and in Europe. We encourage queries and make quick decisions on all articles." Informational, personal experience, interview, profile. Length: 800 to 2,000 words. Pays $50 to $100 per ms.

NATIONAL MALL MONITOR, Suite 104, Arbor Office Center, 1321 U.S. 19 S., Clearwater FL 33516. (813)531-5893. Editor: Barbara D. Engel. For shopping center developers, mall managers, insurance agencies, architects, engineers, retailers. Bimonthly magazine; 46 pages. Estab. 1970. Circ. 5,000. Buys all rights. Buys about 40 mss per year. Pays on publication. Will send free brochure to writer on request. Write for editorial guidelines. No photocopied or simultaneous submissions. Reports on mss accepted for publication in 2 weeks. Returns rejected material in 1 month. Query first. Enclose S.A.S.E.

Nonfiction, Photos and Fillers: Wants concise, factual, well-written mss that will keep readers informed of the latest happenings within the industry and allied fields. "The pieces should be cleared through the proper channels for accuracy and authenticity and must be written in a free and easy style, similar to consumer magazines." Buys how-to articles, (such as the best way to enlarge or build a shopping center for less money, or how to maintain a center to keep it up to date); human interest (such as a recent ms about the first auctioneer ever to set up shop in a mall). Stories about unusual specialty centers always in demand. Personality profiles are also purchased. "Always looking for articles about noted architects, engineers, designers, as long as they have something to say to the industry that it doesn't already know. In one issue, a freelance wrote a piece on John Portman, nationally known architect who believes shopping malls must be part of the total environment and must inter-relate with the lifestyle of individuals." Does not want to see material on pageants, auto shows, band concerts or local promotional activities "dreamed up by a center's resident public relations man." Length: 700 words for how-to's; 1,000 to 1,500 for interviews; 1,000 to 1,200 for profiles; 1,200 to 1,800 for "think" pieces; 500 to 800 words for photo mss. Pays 7½¢ per word for first sale; 10¢ per word for each subsequent sale. "Bonuses, usually 25% additional, are sometimes paid for exceptional pieces or articles commissioned at the last moment and gotten to us before deadline." Photos purchased with mss with extra payment; without mss, or on assignment. Captions required. "Unusual mall interiors are needed and headshots should accompany the personality profiles. We pay $9 for each 8x10 b&w glossy we use. And don't forget the photo feature. It's a must. Keep your eye open for anything that might make a good photo spread for us." Also buys clippings. Pays $10 to $25.

PROBLEMS OF COMMUNISM, IPS/MC, U.S. Information Agency, 1776 Pennsylvania Ave., N.W., Washington DC 20547. (202)632-5119. Editor: Paul A. Smith, Jr. For scholars and decisionmakers in all countries of the world with higher education and a serious interest in foreign area studies and international relations. Established in 1952. Circulation: 25,000. Not copyrighted. Buys 60 to 70 mss a year. Payment on acceptance. Will send free sample copy to writer on request. Will consider photocopied submissions. Reports in 3 months. Query first or submit complete ms. Enclose S.A.S.E.

Nonfiction and Photos: "*Problems of Communism* is one of a very few journals devoted to objective, dispassionate discourse on a highly unobjective, passionately debated phenomenon: communism. It is maintained as a forum in which qualified observers can contribute to a clearer understanding of the sources, nature and direction of change in the areas of its interest. It has no special emphasis or outlook and represents no partisan point of view. Standards of style are those appropriate to the field of international scholarship and journalism. We use intellectually rigorous studies of East-West relations, and/or related political, economic, social and strategic trends in the USSR, China and their associated states and movements. Length is usually 5,000 words. Essay reviews of 1,500 words cover new books offering significant information and analysis. Emphasis throughout *Problems of Communism* is on original research, reliability of sources and perceptive insights. We do not publish political or other forms of advocacy or apologetics for particular forms of belief." Pays $400 for articles; $175 for essay reviews. Pays $35 for b&w glossies.

SANITARY MAINTENANCE, 407 E. Michigan St., Milwaukee WI 53201. (414)271-4105. Editor: Jack Pomrening. For distributors of sanitary supplies. Magazine; 60 pages. Special May issue on floor maintenance; Special January Buyers' Guide. Established in 1943. Monthly.

Circulation: 11,700. Buys all rights. Buys about 4 mss per year. Payment on publication. Will send free sample copy to writer on request. Write for editorial guidelines sheet for writers. Will consider photocopied and simultaneous submissions. Submit seasonal mss 2 months in advance. Query first. Reports on mss accepted for publication in 1 month. Returns rejected material "immediately." Enclose S.A.S.E.

Nonfiction and Photos: Wants mss on salesmen incentives and case studies of distributors of sanitary supplies. No "how-to clean up" themes. Interested in the "personal side" of the business. Buys informational, interview, successful business operations, new product, merchandising techniques and technical articles. Length: 2,500 words. Pays $80 to $100. Photos purchased with accompanying ms with no additional payment. B&w glossy prints only.

SHOPFITTING INTERNATIONAL, (incorporating *Display International),* Link House, Dingwall Ave., Croydon CR9 2TA England. Editor: Martin Staheli. Monthly newspaper for retailers with purchasing and specifying powers, property and premises managers, architects, designers, shopfitters, display managers, woodworking and metalworking equipment manufacturers, management and executive staffs in all retail trades and in most major commercial organizations which meet the public on their premises. Estab: 1955. Circ: 10,000. Pays on publication. Copyrighted. SAE and International Reply Coupons. Query or submit complete ms. Free sample copy.

Nonfiction: News items and features on the fitting-out of shops, departmental stores, restaurants, hotels (public areas only), showrooms, offices, board rooms, bars, night clubs, theaters, banks, building societies; the materials and techniques used; the design brief for interior and exterior; use of sub-contractors, cost of job. Pays 30 pounds minimum.

SOLAR ENERGY DIGEST, P.O. Box 17776, San Diego CA 92117. Editor: William B. Edmondson. For manufacturers, scientists, engineers, architects, builders, developers, technicians, energy experts, teachers, inventors, and others interested in solar energy conversion. Newsletter; 12 pages. Established in 1973. Monthly. Circulation: 15,000. Buys all rights, but may reassign rights to author after publication. Buys 60 to 75 mss per year. Payment on publication. Will send free sample copy to writer on request, if S.A.S.E. is enclosed. Will not consider photocopied or simultaneous submissions. Reports on mss accepted for publication in 2 to 3 weeks. Returns rejected material in 1 to 2 weeks. Enclose S.A.S.E.

Nonfiction and Fillers: Wants mss about new developments in any facet of solar energy conversion, including applications in agriculture, architecture, cooking, distillation, mechanical engines and pumps, photo-electricity, steam generation, flat plate and concentrating collectors, sea thermal plants, furnaces, heat and energy storage, photosynthesis, wind power, wave power, etc. "Assume that the reader knows the fundamentals of the subject and plunge right in without a long introduction. Keep it simple, but not simplistic." No generalized papers on solar energy. "We like to cover a specific new development in each story." Length: 100 to 1,000 words. Length preferred for regular columns: 1,000 words maximum. Pays 2¢ to 5¢ per word. Also buys news clippings on solar energy. Pays $2.50 maximum for accepted clips. Buys fillers; shorts on solar energy. Length: 25 to 200 words. Pays $1 to $5.

Photos: Purchased with accompanying ms with extra payment or without ms. Captions required. Pays $1 to $5 for b&w. Size: 4x5 minimum.

TOBACCO REPORTER, 424 Commercial Square, Cincinnati OH 45202. (513)621-0835. Editor: F. Lee Stegemeyer. For tobacco growers, processors, warehousemen, exporters, importers, manufacturers and distributors of cigars, cigarettes, and tobacco products. Monthly. Buys all rights. Pays on publication. Enclose S.A.S.E.

Nonfiction and Photos: Uses original material on request only. Pays approximately 2½¢ a word. Pays $3 for photos purchased with mss.

Fillers: Wants clippings on new tobacco product brands, local tobacco distributors, smoking and health, and the following relating to tobacco and tobacco products: job promotions, obituaries, honors, equipment, etc. Pays minimum 25¢ a clipping on use only.

WEIGHING & MEASUREMENT, Key Markets Publishing Co., Box 4476, Rockford IL 61110. (815)965-0015. Editor: David M. Mathieu. For users of industrial scales and meters. Monthly tabloid; 24 pages. Estab: 1913. Circ: 25,000. Pays on acceptance. Buys all rights, but may reassign following publication. Reports in 2 weeks. Free sample copy.

Nonfiction: Interview (with presidents of companies), personal opinion (guest editorials on government involvement in business, etc.), profile (about users of weighing and measurement equipment) and technical. Buys 25 mss/year. Query on technical articles; submit complete ms for general interest material. Length: 750-2,500 words. Pays $45-125.

Music

THE CANADIAN COMPOSER, Creative Arts Co., #904, 40 St. Clair Ave., W., Toronto, Ont., Canada M4V 1M2. (416)925-5138. Editor-in-Chief: Richard Flohil. For "composers of music in Canada; 10% 'serious', the rest involved in various kinds of popular music." Published 10 times/year. Magazine; 48 pages. Estab: 1966. Pays on publication. Buys one-time rights. Phone queries OK. Submit seasonal/holiday material 3 months in advance. Photocopied submissions OK. SASE. Reports in 1 week. Free sample copy.
Nonfiction: Informational, interview and profile. Buys 4 mss/issue. Query. Length: 2,500 words. Pays $90-125.
Photos: Purchased with accompanying ms or on assignment. Captions required. Query or submit contact sheet. Pays $10-20 for 8x10 b&w glossies.

THE CHURCH MUSICIAN, 127 Ninth Ave. N., Nashville TN 37234. (615)251-2953. Editor: William Anderson. Southern Baptist publication. For Southern Baptist church music leaders. Monthly. Circulation: 20,000. Buys all rights. Pays on acceptance. Will send a sample copy to a writer on request. Will consider cassette submissions. No query required. Reports in 2 months. Enclose S.A.S.E.
Nonfiction: Leadership and how-to features, success stories, articles on Protestant church music. "We reject material when the subject of an article doesn't meet our needs. And they are often poorly written, or contain too many 'glittering generalities' or lack creativity." Length: maximum 1,300 words. Pays up to 2½¢ a word.
Photos: Purchased with mss; related to mss content only.
Fiction: Inspiration, guidance, motivation, morality with Protestant church music slant. Length: to 1,300 words. Pays up to 2½¢ a word.
Poetry: Church music slant, inspirational. Length: 8 to 24 lines. Pays $5 to $10.
Fillers: Puzzles, short humor. Church music slant. Pays $3 to $5.
How To Break In: "I'd advise a beginning writer to write about his or her experience with some aspect of church music; the social, musical, and spiritual benefits from singing in a choir; a success story about their instrumental group; a testimonial about how they were enlisted in a choir—especially if they were not inclined to be enlisted at first. A writer might speak to hymn singers—what turns them on and what doesn't. Some might include how music has helped them to talk about Jesus as well as sing about Him. We would prefer most of these experiences be related to the church, of course, although we include many articles by freelance writers whose affiliation is other than Baptist. We are delighted to receive their manuscripts, to be sure. A writer might relate his experience with a choir of blind or deaf members. Some people receive benefits from working with unusual children—retarded, or culturally deprived, emotionally unstable, and so forth. Photographs are valuable here."

CLAVIER, 1418 Lake Street, Evanston IL 60204. (312)328-6000. Editor: Mrs. Dorothy Packard. Magazine; 54 pages. Established in 1962. 9 times a year. Buys all rights, but may reassign rights to author after publication. Pays on publication. Will send free sample copy on request. No simultaneous submissions. "Suggest query to avoid duplication." Reports in 2 weeks on very good or very bad mss, "quite slow on the in-betweens." Enclose S.A.S.E.
Nonfiction and Photos: Wants "articles aimed at teachers of piano and organ. Must be written from thoroughly professional point of view. Avoid, however, the thesis-style subject matter and pedantic style generally found in scholarly journals. We like fresh writing, practical approach. We can use interviews with concert pianists and organists. An interview should not be solely a personality story, but should focus on a subject of interest to musicians. Any word length. Photos may accompany ms." Pays 1½¢ per word. Need color photos for cover, such as angle shots of details of instruments, other imaginative photos, with keyboard music themes."

HIGH FIDELITY TRADE NEWS, 6 E. 43rd St., New York NY 10017. Editor: Ronald Marin. For "retailers, salesmen, manufacturers, and representatives involved in the high fidelity/home entertainment market." Established in 1956. Monthly. Circulation: 23,000. Buys all rights. Buys about 36 to 50 mss a year. Pays on acceptance. Will send a sample copy to a writer on request. Query first; "all work by assignment only." Enclose S.A.S.E.
Nonfiction: "Dealer profiles, specific articles on merchandising of high fidelity products, market surveys, sales trends, etc." Length: "open." Pay varies "as to type of article."
How To Break In: "We prefer to rely on our own resources for developing story ideas. Let us know about your willingness to work and submit, if possible, some samples of previous work. Even if you're a new writer, we're still likely to try you out, especially if you know the business

or live in a market area where we need coverage. Articles on merchandising, product reports, and dealer profiles."

THE INSTRUMENTALIST, 1418 Lake St., Evanston IL 60204. Editor: Kenneth L. Neidig. For instrumental music educators. Established in 1946. Monthly except in July. Circulation: 20,547. Buys all rights. Buys 200 mss a year. Payment on publication. Will send sample copy to writer for $1 postpaid. Will consider photocopied submissions. Submit seasonal material 3 months in advance. New Products (February); Summer Camps, Clinics, Workshops (March); Marching Bands (June); Back to School (September); Music Industry. (August). Reports on material accepted for publication within 4 months. Returns rejected material within 3 months. Query first. Enclose S.A.S.E.

Nonfiction and Photos: "Practical information of immediate use to instrumentalists. Not articles 'about music and musicians,' but articles by musicians who are sharing knowledge, techniques, experience. 'In-service education.' Professional help for instrumentalists in the form of instrumental clinics, how-to articles, new trends, practical philosophy. Most contributions are from professionals in the field." Interpretive photojournalism. Length: open. Pays $10 to $100, plus 3 contributor's copies. Quality b&w prints. Pays $5. Color: 35mm and up. Pays $25 if used for cover.

How To Break In: "With a topic of immediate, practical application to the work of the school band/orchestra director—clear, concise, lacking in 'educationese'."

MUSIC EDUCATORS JOURNAL, 1902 Association Dr., Reston VA 22091. (703)860-4000. Editor: Malcolm E. Bessom. For professional music educators in elementary and secondary schools and universities. Monthly (September-May) magazine; 120 pages. Estab: 1914. Circ: 70,000. Pays on acceptance. Buys all rights, but may reassign following publication. SASE. Reports in 1-8 weeks. Free sample copy and 9-page author's guidesheet.

Nonfiction: "We publish articles on music education at all levels — not about individual schools, but about broad issues, trends, instructional techniques. Also articles on music, aside from teaching it. Particularly interested in solid, heavily researched pieces on individual aspects of American music, and interviews with important but lesser known composers, performers and educators. We do not want to see articles about 'the joys of music', or about personal experiences. We are not a homey type of publication." Length: 1,000-3,000 words. Query first. Pays $75-200 for assigned articles.

Photos: Purchased with or without mss. Captions required. Pays about $40 for b&w; maximum of $250 for color used on cover.

MUSIC JOURNAL, 370 Lexington Ave., New York NY 10017. Editor: Guy Freedman. For music faculties and students of universities, colleges, libraries, and professionals, music lovers, in general. 50-page magazine published 10 times a year; monthly, September through May, plus summer and winter annuals. Established in 1943. Circulation: 24,170. Rights purchased vary with author and material. Usually buys first North American serial rights. Buys 30 to 35 mss a year. Payment on publication. Will send sample copy to writer for 50¢. Will not consider photocopied or simultaneous submissions. Submit special issue material (folk, country/western, rock, jazz) 3 months in advance. Reports on material accepted for publication in 3 weeks. Returns rejected material immediately. Query first or submit complete ms. Enclose S.A.S.E.

Nonfiction and Photos: "We embrace all musical subject areas, exploring the many mansions of the composer, conductor, performer, private teacher, student, educator, artist, manager and music lover." Does not solicit material on the opera. Uses informational articles, personal experience, humorous, historical and nostalgic articles, as well as those dealing with personal opinion, spot news, new products, technical. Length: 500 to 1,200 words. Pays $25 to $50. No additional payment is made for photos used with mss.

Poetry: Traditional forms, blank verse, free verse, avant-garde forms, light verse. Must relate to music. Length: open. Pays $5.

How To Break In: "Stories of special interest to instrumentalists are the hardest to come by and would be the best way to break in. Otherwise, the key thing to keep in mind is that we are trying to be timely."

MUSIC TRADES, 80 West St., P.O. Box 432, Englewood NJ 07631. (201)871-1965. Editor: John F. Majeski, Jr. For "music store owners and salesmen; manufacturers of pianos, organs, band instruments, guitars, etc." Magazine; 100 pages. Established in 1890. Monthly. Circulation: 6,500. Copyrighted, "but rights remain with author." Pays on publication. Enclose S.A.S.E.

Nonfiction and Photos: Uses news and features on the musical instrument business. Also uses case history articles with photos, dealing specifically with musical instrument merchandising,

not including record or hi-fi shops. No limit on length. Payment negotiable, minimum $1.
Fillers: Clippings of obituaries of music store people. Music store openings. Pays $1 minimum.

THE MUSICAL NEWSLETTER, 654 Madison Ave., Suite 1703, New York NY 10021. Editor: Patrick J. Smith. For "amateur and professional music lovers who wish to know more about music and be given more specific information." Established in 1971. Quarterly. Circulation: 600. Rights purchased vary with author and material; may buy first serial rights in English or second serial rights. Pays on acceptance. Will send a sample copy to a writer for $1. Will consider photocopied submissions. Query first for nonfiction, "giving a list of subjects of possible interest and outlines, if possible." Enclose S.A.S.E.
Nonfiction: "Articles on music and the musical scene today. The bulk of articles are on 'classical' music, but we also publish articles on jazz and pop. Articles need not pertain to music directly, such as socio-economic articles on performing entities. As the level of our publication is between the musicological quarterly and the record review magazine, what we want is readable material which contains hard-core information. We stress quality. We are always happy to examine freelance material on any aspect of music, from articles on composers' works to philosophical articles on music or reportorial articles on performing organizations. We discourage reviews of performances and interviews, which we feel are adequately covered elsewhere." Length: 3,000 words maximum. Pays 10¢ a word.

OPERA NEWS, 1865 Broadway, New York NY 10023. Editor: Robert Jacobson. For all people interested in opera; opera singers, opera management people, administrative people in opera, opera publicity people, artists' agents; people in the trade and interested laymen. Magazine; 32 to 72 pages. Established in 1933. Weekly. (Monthly in summer.) Circulation: 76,000. Copyrighted. Pays on publication. Will send sample copy to writer for $1. Query first. Enclose S.A.S.E.
Nonfiction and Photos: Most articles are commissioned in advance. In summer, uses articles of various interests on opera; in the fall and winter, articles that relate to the weekly broadcasts. Emphasis is on high quality in writing and an intellectual interest in the opera-oriented public. Informational, how-to, personal experience, interview, profile, humor, historical, think pieces, personal opinion; opera reviews. Length: 300 words maximum. Pays 10¢ per word for features; 8¢ a word for reviews. Pays minimum of $25 for photos purchased on assignment. Captions required.

SOUTHWESTERN MUSICIAN, P.O. Box 9908, Houston TX 77015. Editor: J.F. Lenzo. For music teachers. Monthly (August through May). Buys all rights. Pays on acceptance. Reports in 30 days. Enclose S.A.S.E.
Nonfiction: Wants "professionally slanted articles of interest to public school music teachers." Pays $25 to $50.

Oceanography

The journals below are intended primarily for scientists who are studying the ocean. Publications for ocean fishermen will be found under Fishing. Those for persons interested in water and the ocean as a means of travel or shipping are listed with the Marine Industries and Water Navigation journals.

OCEAN INDUSTRY, P.O. Box 2608, 3301 Allen Parkway, Houston TX 77001. (713)529-4301. Editor: Donald M. Taylor. Publication of Gulf Publishing Company. For persons working for offshore industries — oil, mining, oceanography. Magazine; 150 pages. Established in 1966. Monthly. Circulation: 34,000. Buys first serial rights. Buys about 130 mss per year. Pays on publication. Will send free sample copy to a writer on request. Write for editorial guidelines. No photocopied submissions. Reports on mss accepted for publication in 30 days. Returns rejected material in 45 days. Query first with short summary. Enclose S.A.S.E.
Nonfiction and Photos: Wants technical mss on the industry in the ocean. (No stories or poems). Recently published "How the Scene in International Offshore Oil Is Changing" and "Coldwater Survival Techniques Advance by Canadian Researchers." Buys personal experience, interview, successful business operations in the ocean and new product. Length: 1,000 to 1,500 words. Photos purchased with accompanying ms with no additional payment. Uses b&w and color.

SEA FRONTIERS, 3979 Rickenbacker Causeway, Virginia Key, Miami FL 33149. (305)361-5786. Editor: F. G. W. Smith. For "members of the International Oceanographic Foundation.

People with an interest in the sea; professional people for the most part; people in executive positions and students." Established in 1954. Bimonthly. Circulation: 70,000. Buys all rights. Buys 20 to 25 mss a year. Payment on publication. Will send free sample copy to writer on request. Write for copy of guidelines for writers. Will consider photocopied submissions "if very clear." Reports on material within 6 weeks. Query first. Enclose S.A.S.E.

Nonfiction and Photos: "Articles (with illustrations) covering explorations, discoveries or advances in our knowledge of the marine sciences, or describing the activities of oceanographic laboratories or expeditions to any part of the world. Emphasis should be on research and discoveries rather than personalities involved." Length: 500 to 3,000 words. Pays 5¢ to 8¢ a word. 8x10 b&w glossy prints and 35mm (or larger) color transparencies purchased with ms. Pays $25 for color used on front and back cover. Pays $15 for color used on inside covers.

How To Break In: "The best way for a beginning writer to break into *Sea Frontiers* would be to study our style, query us concerning a subject and then submit a short article, with photographs. Before being submitted, the manuscript should be checked by a scientist doing work in the area with which the manuscript is concerned. The writer should also be sure that his sources are authoritative and up to date."

Office Equipment and Supplies

GEYER'S DEALER TOPICS, 51 Madison Ave., New York NY 10010. (212)689-4411. Editor: Neil Loynachan. For individual office equipment and stationery dealers, and special purchasers for store departments handling stationery and office equipment. Monthly. Buys all rights. Pays on acceptance. Query first. Reports "immediately." Enclose S.A.S.E.

Nonfiction and Photos: Articles on merchandising and sales promotion; programs of stationery and office equipment dealers. Problem-solving articles relating to retailers of office supplies, social stationery items, gifts (if the retailer also handles commercial supplies), office furniture and equipment and office machines. Minimum payment, $35, but quality of article is real determinant. Length: 300 to 1,000 words. B&w glossies are purchased with accompanying ms with no additional payment.

OFFICE PRODUCTS, Hitchcock Building, Wheaton IL 60187. (312)665-1000. Editorial Director: Thomas J. Trafals. For "independent dealers who sell all types of office products—office machines, office furniture, and office supplies." Established in 1904. Monthly. Circulation: 24,000. Buys all rights, but will reassign rights to author after publication. Pays on acceptance. Article deadlines are the 1st of the third month preceding date of issue. News deadlines are the 1st of each month. Will consider photocopied submissions. Reports in 3 to 4 weeks. Query first on any long articles. Enclose S.A.S.E.

Nonfiction: "We're interested in anything that will improve an office product dealer's methods of doing business. Some emphasis on selling and promotion, but interested in all phases of dealer operations." Length: "that which tells the story, and no more or less." Pays $25 to $150 "based on quality of article."

Photos: Purchased with mss. "Some news photos. Also, photos of new stores, promotions, etc., but we're not actively looking for these now." Pays $10.

OFFICE WORLD NEWS, 645 Stewart Ave., Garden City NY 11530. Editor: Robert R. Mueller. For independent office products dealers. Monthly; 24 to 60 tabloid pages. Established in 1972. Circulation: 16,000. Buys all rights. Payment on publication. Will send free sample copy to writer on request. Will not consider photocopied or simultaneous submissions. Reports on material accepted for publication in 2 weeks. Returns rejected material immediately (if requested and S.A.S.E. is enclosed). Query first. Enclose S.A.S.E.

Nonfiction and Photos: "Most freelance material is written on assignment or following queries by our freelance 'stringers'. There are occasional openings in some parts of the country for experienced newswriters. Our published material consists of news and news-related features. Straight news reporting, with emphasis on the effect on office product dealers. No textbook management articles will be accepted." Uses interviews, personal opinion, spot news and new product material. "We try to limit our content to hard news." Length: 100 to 500 words. Pays 10¢ per word. B&w and color photos are purchased with mss or on assignment. $10 for 5x7 (minimum) b&w; $15 for 4x5 color transparencies, but will consider slides and 5x7 or 8x10 prints.

How To Break In: "Will consider any experienced newswriter for stringer assignments, except in New York metropolitan area."

PACIFIC STATIONER, 41 Sutter St., San Francisco CA 94104. Editor: Robert B. Frier. Magazine; 60 to 70 pages. Established in 1908. Monthly. Circulation: 5,000. Not copyrighted. Buys about 12 mss a year. Pays on acceptance. Will send sample copy to writer for $1. No photocopied or simultaneous submissions. Submit seasonal (merchandising) material 3 to 4 months in advance. Reports on material accepted for publication in 1 week. Returns rejected material immediately. Query first or submit complete ms. Enclose S.A.S.E.
Nonfiction and Photos: "Our main interest is in how western retailers of stationery and office products can do a better selling job. We use how-to-do-it merchandising articles showing dealers how to sell more stationery and office products to more people at a greater profit. Seasonal merchandising articles always welcome, if acceptable." Informational, how-to, personal experience, interview, successful business operations. Length: 1,000 to 1,500 words. Pays 2¢ a word. Pays $5 for b&w photos used with mss; 3x5 minimum. Captions required.

SOUTHERN STATIONER AND OFFICE OUTFITTER, 75 Third St. N.W., Atlanta GA 30308. Editor: Earl Lines, Jr. For retailers of office products in the Southeast and Southwest. Monthly. Not copyrighted. Pays on publication. Will send free sample copy on request. Query required. Reports promptly. Enclose S.A.S.E.
Nonfiction: Can use articles about retailers in the Southeast and Southwest regarding problems solved concerning store layout, inventory, personnel, etc. "We want articles giving in-depth treatment of a single aspect of a dealer's operation rather than superficial treatment of a number of aspects." Must be approved by subject. Length: 1,000 to 1,400 words. Pays 2¢ to 4¢ a word.
Photos: Purchased with mss. Pays $5.

Optical

THE DISPENSING OPTICIAN, Opticians Association of America, 1250 Connecticut Ave., N.W., Washington DC 20036. Editor: James M. McCormick. For dispensing opticians. Published 11 times a year. Magazine; 36-48 pages. Estab: 1950. Circ: 5,800. Pays "somewhere between acceptance and publication." Buys all rights, but may reassign following publication. Photocopied submissions OK. SASE. Reports in 10-40 days. Will send sample copy to writer "only when we're interested in an article suggestion."
Nonfiction: Publishes informational, how-to, interview, profile, historical, photo feature, successful business operations, merchandising techniques, and technical articles. "All must specifically pertain to or interest the dispensing optician." Query. Buys 6-15 mss/year. Length: 400-1,500 words. Pays 9-15¢/word.
Photos: Purchased with or without accompanying ms, or on assignment. Caption material required. Pays $5-50 for 5x7 or 8x10 b&w prints. Query.

N.J. JOURNAL OF OPTOMETRY, County Line Professional Bldg., W. County Line Rd., Jackson NJ 08527. (201)364-4111. Editor: Errol Rummel, O.D. For doctors of optometry practices located in New Jersey. Magazine; 35 to 40 pages. Established in 1955. Quarterly. Circulation: 1,200. Not copyrighted. Will consider photocopied submissions. No simultaneous submissions. Reports in 3 weeks. Query first. Enclose S.A.S.E.
Nonfiction and Photos: Technical articles on eye care, exam techniques, etc.; news reports on eye care, either national or local; practice management articles. Writer must remember that this is a professional, knowledgeable audience. Length: 1,000 to 2,000 words. Pays 3¢ per word minimum.

OPTICAL JOURNAL & REVIEW OF OPTOMETRY, Chilton Way, Radnor PA 19089. (215)687-8200. Editor: Chris Kelly. Magazine; 72 pages. For optometrists, opticians, optical wholesalers and manufacturers. Established in 1891. Monthly. Circulation: 21,500. Buys all rights, but may reassign rights to author after publication. Buys about 30 mss per year from doctors in the optometry field. Pays on publication. Will send free sample copy to writer on request. Write for guidelines sheet. Will not consider photocopied or simultaneous submissions. Reports in 2 to 4 weeks. Enclose S.A.S.E.
Nonfiction: Uses technical articles on optometric practice. "We are a very special interest book and most freelancers cannot produce the kind of material we need. We solicit mss only from those within the field." Will consider book reviews by members of the profession. Interested in news and activities of optometrists, opticians, and optical manufacturers, importers, and wholesalers. Pays 50¢ per printed inch minimum.

Packing, Canning, and Packaging

Journals in this category are for packaging engineers and others concerned with new methods of packing, canning, and packaging foods in general. Other publications that buy similar material will be found under the Food Processing, Products, and Services heading.

FOOD AND DRUG PACKAGING, 777 Third Ave., New York NY 10017. Editor: Ben Miyares. For packaging decisionmakers in food, drug, cosmetic firms. Established in 1959. Biweekly. Circulation: 45,000. Rights purchased vary with author and material. Pays on acceptance. "Queries only." Enclose S.A.S.E.
Nonfiction and Photos: "Looking for news stories about local and state (not federal) packaging legislation, and its impact on the marketplace. Newspaper style." Length: 1,000 to 2,500 words; usually 500 to 750 words. Payments vary; usually 5¢ a word. Photos purchased with mss. 5x7 glossies preferred. Pays $5.
How To Break In: "1) Get details on local packaging legislation's impact on marketplace/sales/consumer/retailer reaction, etc. 2) Keep an eye open for *new* packages. Query when you think you've got one. New packages move into test markets every day, so if you don't see anything new this week, try again next week. Buy it; describe it briefly in a query."

MODERN PACKAGING, Morgan Grampian Publishing Corp., 205 E. 42nd St., New York NY 10017. (212)573-8109. Editor-in-Chief: Paul E. Mullins. For product manufacturers who package or have contract-packaged their product lines, suppliers of packaging material and equipment. Monthly magazine; 70 pages. Estab: 1927. Circ: 56,000. Pays on publication. Buys all rights. Photocopied submissions OK. SASE. Reports in 6 weeks. Free sample copy. Guidelines for writers (only on technical articles).
Nonfiction: How-to, informational and new product articles. Trend reports, engineering and technical reports. Length: open. Query first. Pays $30 per printed page.
Photos: B&w photos (5x7 minimum) purchased with mss or on assignment. Query, or send contact sheets or prints. Pays $5 minimum. Model release required.

THE PACKER, 1 Gateway Center, Kansas City KS 66101. (913)281-3073. Editor: Paul Campbell. For shippers, fruit and vegetable growers, wholesalers, brokers, retailers. Newspaper; 36 pages. Established in 1893. Weekly. Circulation: 16,500. Buys all rights, but may reassign rights to author after publication. Buys about 10 mss a year. Pays on publication. Will send free sample copy to writer on request. Write for copy of guidelines for writers. Will consider simultaneous submissions. No photocopied submissions. Reports on material accepted for publication in 2 weeks. Returns rejected material in 1 month. Query first or submit complete ms. Enclose S.A.S.E.
Nonfiction: Articles on growing techniques, merchandising, marketing, transportation, refrigeration. Emphasis is on the "what's new" approach in these areas. Length: 1,000 words. Pays $40 minimum.

PACKING AND SHIPPING, 735 Woodland Ave., Plainfield NJ 07062. Editor: C.M. Bonnell, Jr. For "packaging engineers, traffic managers, shipping managers, and others interested in physical distribution, industrial packaging and shipping." 9 times a year. Buys all rights. Pays on publication. A sample copy will be sent on request. Query first. Reports "promptly." Enclose S.A.S.E.
Nonfiction: Packing, handling and physical distribution procedure by land, water and air as related to large company operations. Pays 1¢ a word.

Paint

Additional journals that buy material on paint, wallpaper, floor covering, and decorating products stores are listed under Building Interiors.

AMERICAN PAINT & COATINGS JOURNAL, American Paint Journal Co., 2911 Washington Ave., St. Louis MO 63103. (314)534-0301. Editor: Fred Schulenberg. For the coatings industry (paint, varnish, lacquer, etc.); manufacturers of coatings, suppliers to coatings in-

dustry, educational institutions, salesmen. Weekly magazine; 78 pages. Estab: 1916. Circ: 7,300. Pays on publication. Buys all rights. Phone queries OK. Simultaneous and photocopied submissions OK. SASE. Reports in 3 weeks. Free sample copy and writer's guidelines.
Nonfiction: Informational, historical, interview, new product and technical articles and coatings industry news. Buys 2 mss/issue. Query before sending long articles; submit complete ms for short pieces. Length: 75-1,200 words. Pays $5-100.
Photos: B&w (5x7) glossies purchased with or without mss, or on assignment. Query first. Pays $3-10.

AMERICAN PAINT & WALLCOVERINGS DEALER, 2911 Washington Ave., St. Louis MO 63103. (314)534-0301. Editor-in-Chief: Clark Rowley. Specializes in information about paint and wallcoverings. Monthly magazine; 70 pages. Estab: 1908. Circ: 33,000. Pays on publication. Buys all rights. Submit seasonal/holiday material 2 months in advance. Previously published submissions OK. SASE. Reports in 2 weeks. Free sample copy and writer's guidelines.
Nonfiction: Informational articles (how a certain store is successful; new and different departments). Buys 1-2 mss/issue. Submit complete ms. Length: open. Pays $75-100.
Photos: Purchased with mss. Captions required. Send transparencies. Pays $10 for b&w glossies; $25 for color transparencies.
How To Break In: "Concentrate on stories that will be of interest to the paint and wallcoverings retailer—what one store owner did to make his sales pick up."

AMERICAN PAINTING CONTRACTOR, American Paint Journal Co., 2911 Washington Ave., St. Louis MO 63103. (314)534-0301. Editor-in-Chief: John L. Cleveland. For painting and decorating contractors, in-plant maintenance painting department heads, architects and paint specifiers. Monthly magazine; 80 pages. Estab: 1923. Circ: 33,000. Buys all rights, but may reassign following publication. Phone queries OK. Submit seasonal/holiday material 2 months in advance. Simultaneous and photocopied submissions OK. SASE. Reports in 3 weeks. Free sample copy and writer's guidelines.
Nonfiction: Historical, how-to, humor, informational, new product, personal experience, personal opinion and technical articles; interviews, photo features and profiles. Buys 4 mss an issue. "Freelancers should be able to write well and have some understanding of the painting and decorating industry. We do not want general theme articles such as 'How to Get More Work Out of Your Employee' unless they relate to a problem within the painting and decorating industry. Query before submitting copy." Length: 1,000-2,500 words. Pays $75-100.
Photos: B&w and color purchased with mss or on assignment. Captions required. Send contact sheets, prints or transparencies. Pays $15-35.

CANADIAN PAINT AND FINISHING MAGAZINE, 481 University Ave., Toronto 2, Ont., Canada M5W 1A7. (416)595-1811. Editor: James O'Neill. Monthly. Buys first North American serial rights. Pays on acceptance for mss, on publication for photos. Query first. Reports in 1 week. Enclose S.A.E. and International Reply Coupons.
Nonfiction and Photos: "Semitechnical and news articles on paint manufacturing, industrial finishing techniques, new developments. Also interested in electroplating. Mostly Canadian material required." Accompanied by photos. Length: 800 to 1,500 words. Pays minimum 5¢ a word. Pays $5 for 8x10 b&w glossies.

WESTERN PAINT REVIEW, 2354 W. 3rd St., Los Angeles CA 90057. (213)389-4151. Editor: Ernest C. Ansley. For painting and decorating contractors, retail paint dealers and paint manufacturers. Established in 1920. Monthly. Circulation: 18,000. Buys first North American serial rights. Buys 25 to 30 mss a year. Payment on publication. Will consider photocopied submissions. Submit seasonal material 2 months in advance. Reports on material within 3 weeks. Query first. Enclose S.A.S.E.
Nonfiction and Photos: Articles on successful business operations, merchandising techniques. Technical articles. Length: 500 to 3,000 words. Pays 4¢ a word minimum. 4x5 minimum glossy b&w photos purchased with ms. Captions required. Pays $4.

Paper

FORET ET PAPIER, 625 President Kennedy Ave., Montreal, Quebec, Canada H3A 1K5. (514)845-5141. Editor: Paul Saint-Pierre, C. Adm. For engineers and technicians engaged in the making of paper. Magazine; 50 pages. Established in 1975. Quarterly. Circulation: 7,000. Rights purchased vary with author and material. Buys first North American serial rights, second serial (reprint) rights, and simultaneous rights. Buys about 12 mss per year. Pays on acceptance. Will consider photocopied submissions. Reports on mss accepted for publication in 1 week. Returns rejected material in 2 days. Enclose S.A.S.E.

Nonfiction and Photos: Uses technical articles on papermaking. Buys informational, how-to, personal experience, interview, photo, and technical articles. Length: 1,000 words maximum. Pays $25 to $150. Photos purchased with accompanying ms with extra payment or purchased on assignment. Captions required. Pays $25 for b&w. Color shots must be vertical. Pays $150 maximum for color cover shots.

PAPERBOARD PACKAGING, 777 Third Ave., New York NY 10017. (212)838-7778. Editor: Joel J. Shulman. For "managers, supervisors, and technical personnel who operate corrugated box manufacturing and folding cartons converting companies and plants." Established in 1916. Monthly. Circulation: 10,000. Buys all rights. Pays on publication. Will send a sample copy to a writer on request. Will consider photocopied submissions. Submit seasonal material 3 months in advance. Query first. Enclose S.A.S.E.

Nonfiction and Photos: "Application articles, installation stories, etc. Contact the editor first to establish the approach desired for the article. Especially interested in packaging systems using composite materials, including paper and other materials." Buys technical articles. Length: open. Pays "$50 pdr printed page (about 1,000 words to a page), including photos. We do not pay for commercially oriented material. We do pay for material if it is not designed to generate business for someone in our field. Will not pay photography costs, but will pay cost of photo reproductions for article."

Petroleum

ENERGY MANAGEMENT REPORT, P.O. Box 1589, Dallas TX 75221. (214)748-4403. Editor: Ernestine Adams. Newsletter/magazine; 16 pages. For operating management in the oil and gas industry. Established in 1929. Monthly. Circulation: 42,000. Buys all rights. Buys "few" mss from freelance writers. Pays on publication. Will send free sample copy to writer on request. Reports "immediately." Enclose S.A.S.E.

Nonfiction: Uses energy briefs and concise analysis of energy situations. "Across-the-board interpretive reporting on current events." Publishes briefs about energy world news, international design and engineering, offshore energy business, environmental action, energy financing, and new products. Pays 10¢ per word.

FUELOIL AND OIL HEAT, 200 Commerce Rd., Cedar Grove NJ 07009. (201)239-5800. Feature Editor: M. F. Hundley. For distributors of fueloil, heating and air conditioning equipment dealers. Monthly. Buys first rights. Pays on publication. Reports in 2 weeks. Enclose S.A.S.E.

Nonfiction: Management articles dealing with fueloil distribution and oilheating equipment selling. Length: up to 2,500 words. Pays $35 a printed page.

HUGHES RIGWAY, Hughes Tool Co., Box 2539, Houston TX 77001. Editor-in-Chief: Tom Haynes. For oilfield drilling personnel. Quarterly magazine; 28 pages. Estab: 1963. Circ: 14,000. Pays on acceptance. Buys first North American serial rights. Simultaneous and photocopied submissions OK. SASE. Reports in 1 month. Free sample copy and writer's guidelines.

Nonfiction and PHotos: "Character-revealing historical narratives about little-known incidents, heroes, or facts, particularly those which contradict conventional concepts. Also, topical reportorial features about people in oil or drilling. Must be thoroughly documented." Length: 2,000 to 2,500 words. Pays 10¢ a word. Photos purchased with mss.

Fiction: "Top-quality fiction in oilfield settings." Length: 2,000 to 2,500 words. Pays 10¢ a word.

HYDROCARBON PROCESSING, P.O. Box 2608, Houston TX 77001. Editor: Frank L. Evans. For personnel in oil refining, gas and petrochemical processing or engineering-contractors, including engineering, operation, maintenance and management phases. Special issues: January, Maintenance; April, Natural Gas Processing; September, Refining Processes; November, Petrochemical Processes. Monthly. Buys all rights. Write for copy of guidelines for writers. Enclose S.A.S.E.

Nonfiction: Wants technical manuscripts on engineering and operations in the industry which will be of help to personnel. Also nontechnical articles on management, safety and industrial relations that will help technical men become managers. Length: open, "but do not waste words." Pays about $25 per printed page.

How To Break In: "Articles must all pass a rigid evaluation of their reader appeal, accuracy and overall merit. Reader interest determines an article's value. We covet articles that will be of real job value to subscribers. Before writing—ask to see our Author's Handbook. You may save time and effort by writing a letter, and outline briefly what you have in mind. If your article will or won't meet our needs, we will tell you promptly."

NATIONAL PETROLEUM NEWS, 1221 Avenue of the Americas, New York NY 10020. (212)997-2361. Editor: Frank Breese. For businessmen who make their living in the oil marketing industry, either as company employees or through their own business operations. Monthly magazine; 90 pages. Established in 1909. Circulation: 20,000. Rights purchased vary with author and material. Usually buys all rights. Buys 2 mss a year. Payment on acceptance if done on assignment. Payment on publication for unsolicited material. "The occasional freelance copy we use is done on assignment." Query first. Enclose S.A.S.E.

Nonfiction and Photos: Department Editor: Carolyn DeWitt. Material related directly to devlopments and issues in the oil marketing industry and "how-to" and "what-with" case studies. Informational; successful business operations. Length: 2,000 words maximum. Pays $60 per printed page. Payment for b&w photos "depends upon advance understanding".

OFFSHORE, The Petroleum Publishing Co., 1200 S. Post Oak Rd., Houston TX 77056. (713)621-9720. Editor-in-Chief: Robert Burke. Emphasizes offshore operations—oil, marine, construction, marine transportation, diving, engineering for management, engineers, operational people, geologists, technicians. Monthly (2 June issues) magazine. Estab: 1959. Circ: 19,000 Pays on publication. Buys all rights. Phone queries OK. Submit seasonal and holiday material 3 months in advance. Photocopied submissions OK. SASE. Reports in 3 weeks. Free sample copy.

Nonfiction: Publishes how-to and informational articles (specific operational articles; how to do a job better); new product articles, photo features, interviews; technical articles (good, strong details). Length: 800-2,500 words.

Photos: B&w glossies and color purchased with or without mss, or on assignment. Captions required. Query first. Pays minimum.

OILWEEK, 918 6th Ave., S.W., #200, Calgary, Alberta, Canada T2P 0V5. Editor: Vic Humphreys. For senior management, engineers, etc., in the energy industries. Magazine; 36 to 100 pages. Established in 1948. Weekly. Circulation: 11,000. Rights purchased vary with author and material. Usually buys all rights. Pays on publication. Will send free sample copy to writer on request. Write for copy of guidelines for writers. Reports on material accepted for publication in 2 weeks. Returns rejected material in 2 weeks. Query first. Enclose S.A.E. and International Reply Coupons.

Nonfiction: News or semitechnical articles which have a Canadian content or Canadian application, directed toward the petroleum, or in some instances, energy field. Length: 1,500 words maximum. Pays 10¢ a word minimum.

PETROLEUM INDEPENDENT, 1101 16th St., N.W., Washington DC 20036. (202)466-8240. Editor-in-Chief: Robert Gouldy. For "college-educated men and women involved in high-risk petroleum ventures. Contrary to popular opinion, they are not all Texans. They live in almost every state. These people are politically motivated. They follow energy legislation closely and involve themselves in lobbying and electoral politics." Bimonthly magazine; 64-88 pages. Estab: 1929. Circ: 13,000. Pays on acceptance. Buys all rights but may reassign following publication. Photocopied submissions OK. SASE. Reports in "5-15 minutes." Free sample copy; individualized writer's guidelines sent with acceptance of query.

Nonfiction: "Articles need not be limited to oil and natural gas—can reflect on other energy." Expose (bureaucratic blunder), informational, historical (energy-related, accurate, with a witty twist), humor (we're still looking for a good humor piece), interview (with energy decisionmakers. Center with questions concerning independent petroleum industry. Send edited transcript plus tape), personal opinion, profile (of Independent Petroleum Association of America members), photo feature. Buys 30 mss/year. Query. Length: 750-3,000 words. Pays $40-300.

Photos: Purchased with or without accompanying ms or on assignment. Pays $15-75 for b&w glossies; $50-200 (for cover only) for 35mm or 2¼x2¼ transparencies. Send contact sheet, prints or transparencies.

Fiction: Experimental, historical, science fiction. Buys 1 ms an issue. Submit complete ms. Length: 750-2,000 words. Pays $40-200.

For '78: Taxation and its impact on domestic energy; intrastate natural gas exploration; political impact on drilling plans and investments; prospects for deregulation of natural gas; effects of crude oil pricing; energy and domestic security; energy agencies.

PETROLEUM MARKETER, 636 First Ave., West Haven CT 06516. (203)934-5288. Editor: Henry F. Harris. For "independent oil jobbers, major oil company operations and management personnel, and petroleum equipment distributors." Bimonthly. Circulation: 20,000. Buys North American serial rights. Pays on publication. Will send a sample copy to a writer on request. Query first. Reports in 1 week. Enclose S.A.S.E.
Nonfiction and Photos: "Success stories on how an oil jobber did something; interpretive marketing stories on local or regional basis. We want straightforward, honest reporting. Treat the subject matter with dignity." Length: 1,200 to 2,500 words. Pays "$35 per printed page." Photos purchased with and without mss; captions required. "Glossies for reproduction by engraving; subject matter decided after consultation." Pays $5.

PETROLEUM TODAY, 2101 L St., N.W., Washington DC 20037. "For what we call opinion leaders; may be clergymen, legislators, newspapermen, club leaders, professors; but few oil industry people." Established in 1959. Quarterly. Circulation: 80,000. Not copyrighted. Buys 8 to 10 mss a year. Payment on publication. Will send free sample copy to writer on request. Query first. Reports on material in 2 to 6 weeks. Enclose S.A.S.E.
Nonfiction and Photos: "Articles on issues that currently face the petroleum industry on the energy crisis, marine drilling, the environment, taxation, the Alaska pipeline, offshore drilling, consumerism, coastal zone management. Also like to use a few short, light articles; oil-related." Informational, personal experience, interview, profile, think pieces. Length: open. Pays $200 to $750. 8x10 b&w glossy photos purchased with or without accompanying mss, or on assignment. Captions required. Pays $25. 35mm (or larger) color transparencies. Pays $50 a quarter page; $250 for cover. Must be petroleum-related.

PIPELINE & GAS JOURNAL, Box 1589, Dallas TX 75221. For "key management, engineering/operating and construction influences engaged in cross-country pipeline (oil, natural gas, LPG, chemical, and slurry) and urban gas distribution utility operations — plus related contractors, consultants, and engineering firms." Magazine. Established in 1859. Monthly. Circulation: 25,000. Rights purchased vary with author and material. Usually buys all rights, with the possiblity of reassigning rights to author after publication. Buys 5 to 10 mss per year. Pays on publication. Will send free sample copy to writer on request. Write for editorial guidelines. Query first. Enclose S.A.S.E.
Nonfiction and Photos: Technical and semitechnical articles about the petroleum industry, but not about the marketing of oil. Must concern methods in pipeline construction and operation and gas distribution. Knowledge of the oil industry is essential. Pictures and illustrations help." Length: 2 to 10 typed pages. Pays $35 to $250.

PIPE LINE INDUSTRY, P.O. Box 2608, Houston TX 77001. Editor: Don Lambert. For gas and oil pipeline and distribution industry. Monthly. Circulation: about 22,000. Buys all rights. Pays on publication. Will send free sample copy to a writer on request. Query preferred; include outline indicating approach, depth, and probable photos or other illustrations to be submitted. Reports in 10 days. Enclose S.A.S.E.
Nonfiction: Gas and Engineering Editor: Carrington Mason; Associate Editor: Lee J. Corkill. Short, technical features; ideas for doing a job easier, cheaper, and safer; operating hints, etc. Length: "varies." Pays $40 per page; higher rates upon advance agreement.
Photos: Purchased with mss; construction and operations of facilities in the gas and pipeline industry. 8x10 glossies preferred. Payment depends on space and manner in which photo is used.

PIPELINE & UNDERGROUND UTILITIES CONSTRUCTION, Box 22267, Houston TX 77027. (713)622-0676. Editor: William R. Quarles. Magazine; 48 pages. For underground utilities construction market; "mostly management and supervision level ... international level." Established in 1945. Monthly. Circulation: 13,500. Buys all rights, but may reassign rights to author after publication. Buys 10 to 15 mss per year. Pays on publication. Will send free sample copy to writer on request. Write for editorial guidelines. Submit seasonal material 3 months in advance. Reports in 1 month. Enclose S.A.S.E.
Nonfiction and Photos: Uses how-to, technical and semi-technical articles on construction of underground facilities. Does not want to see copies of newspaper articles, general success stories, articles not pertaining to the construction market. Length: 750 to 1,500 words. Pays $50 per

printed page. Photos purchased with accompanying ms with no additional payment. Captions required.

THE REVIEW, 111 St. Clair Ave. W., Toronto, Ont. M5W 1K3, Canada. Editor: Kenneth Bagnell. Bimonthly. Buys all rights. Payment on acceptance. Will send a sample copy to a writer on request. Query first. Reports in 1 week. Enclose SAE and International Reply Coupons.
Nonfiction: "Subject matter is general. Articles specifically about the oil industry are generally staff-written. Material must be Canadian." Length: 2,500 words maximum. Pays $300 minimum.

Pets

Listed here are publications for professionals in the pet industry; wholesalers, manufacturers, suppliers, retailers, owners of pet specialty stores, pet groomers. Also aquarium retailers, distributors, manufacturers and those interested in the fish industry.

AQUARIUM INDUSTRY, Toadtown, Magalia CA 95954. Editor: Robert Behme. For aquarium retailers, distributors, manufacturers. Tabloid newspaper published 12 times a year; 16 (9x13½) pages. Established in 1973. Circulation: 12,400. Not copyrighted. Buys 2 to 4 mss per issue. Payment within 30 days of acceptance. Will send free sample copy to writer on request. Will not consider photocopied or simultaneous submissions. Reports in 10 days. Query first. Enclose S.A.S.E.
Nonfiction: News-oriented shorts; how-to features. Interviews with retailers on ways to improve stores, sales, etc. Material must be "most concise piece possible. No fat. No (or very few) superlatives. Facts and description when important to the story." Interested in retailer and distributor stories, personnel changes, new shops opening up, etc. Length: 700 to 1,000 words. Pays $30 to $50. Also open to column ideas from those who know fish and the fish business.

FROM THE KENNELS, Box 1369, Vancouver WA 98660. (206)696-2971. Editor-in-Chief: J.C. Perkins. Emphasizes material of interest to owners of purebred dogs. Semimonthly newspaper; 16-32 pages. Pays on publication. Not copyrighted. Simultaneous, photocopied, and previously published submissions OK. SASE. Reports in 2 weeks. Sample copy 50¢. Guidelines for writers for SASE.
Nonfiction: Exposes (of dog show behaviour of individuals). Must be related to the showing of purebred dogs. Query.
Photos: Purchased with accompanying ms. Captions required. Uses b&w only. Query. No additional payment for photos accepted with ms.

THE PET DEALER, 225 W. 34 St., New York NY 10001. (212)279-0800. For owners and managers of pet specialty stores, departments and dog groomers and their suppliers. Monthly magazine, 100 pages. Established in 1950. Circulation: 7,800. Buys 12 mss a year. Buys all rights. Payment on publication, when length is determined. Write for copy of guidelines for writers. Will not consider photocopied or simultaneous submissions. Reports on material in 10 days. Query first or submit complete ms. Enclose S.A.S.E.
Nonfiction and Photos: Success stories about pet shops, and occasional stories about distributors and jobbers in the pet field. Articles about retail management, marketing and merchandising trends and innovations. Stories about pets themselves are of no possible interest. Pays $25 per printed page. Photos (no smaller than 5x7) or negatives, are purchased with mss, with no additional payment. Captions required.
How To Break In: "We're interested in store profiles outside the New York area. Photos are of key importance. Good photos and lots of them can sell an otherwise inadequate piece. The story we can always fix up, but we can't run out and take the photos. The best thing to do is send a sample of your work and some story proposals. Even if your proposals are not that strong, we still might want to use you on one of our own ideas. Articles focus on new techniques in merchandising or promotion."

PETS/SUPPLIES/MARKETING, Harcourt Brace Jovanovich Publications, 1 E. First St., Duluth MN 55802. (218)727-8511. Editor-in-Chief: Paul Setzer. For pet retailers (both small, "mom-and-pop" stores and chain franchisers); livestock and pet supply wholesalers, manufacturers of pet products. Monthly magazine; 100 pages. Estab: 1946. Circ: 14,500. Pays on acceptance. Buys all rights. Phone queries OK. Submit seasonal/holiday material 2 months in advance. Photocopied submissions OK. SASE. Reports in 4 weeks. Free sample copy and writer's guidelines.

Nonfiction: How-to (merchandise pet products, display, set up window displays, market pet product line); humor (pertaining to pets and/or their retail sale); interviews with pet store retailers); personal opinion (of pet industry members or problems facing the industry); photo features (of successful pet stores or effective merchandising techniques and in-store displays); profiles (of successful retail outlets engaged in the pet trade); technical articles (on more effective pet retailing; i.e., building a central filtration unit, constructing custom aquariums or display areas). Length: 1,000-2,500 words. Buys 5-6 per issue. Query. Pays 5-10¢/word.

Photos: Purchased with or without mss or on assignment. "We prefer 5x7 or 8x10 b&w glossies. But we will accept contact sheets and standard print sizes. For color, we prefer 35mm transparencies or 2¼x2¼." Pays $6-7.50 for b&w; $12.50-15 for color.

Columns/Departments: Barbara Trelevan, Department Editor. Short, human interest items on the pet trade for Up Front; factual news items on members of the pet industry for Industry News. Buys 3/issue. Submit complete ms. Length: 25-100 words. Pays 5-10¢/word. Suggestions for new columns or departments should be addressed to Paul Setzer.

Fillers: Terry Kreeger, Department Editor. Clippings, jokes, gags, anecdotes, newsbreaks, puzzles, short humor; anything concerned with the pet industry. Buys 3-4/issue. Send fillers in. Length: 25-100 words. Pays $10-25.

How To Break In: "Send a letter of introduction and we will send our guidelines for writers and a sample copy of the magazine. After studying each, the freelancer could visit a number of pet stores and if any seem like interesting material for *PSM,* query us. We will check them out through our wholesalers and, if recommended by them, will assign the article to the freelancer. Once we have bought several articles from a writer, we will send the person out on specific assignments."

Photography

AMERICAN CINEMATOGRAPHER, A.S.C. Holding Corp., 1782 N. Orange Dr., Hollywood CA 90028. (213)876-5080. Editor-in-Chief: Herb A. Lightman. Specializes in coverage of 16mm and 35mm motion picture production. For an audience ranging from students to retirees; professional interest or advanced amateurs in cinematorgraphy. Monthly magazine; 116 pages. Estab: 1921. Circ: 18,500. Time of payment depends on nature of article. Buys all rights, but may reassign rights after publication. Phone queries OK. Simultaneous and photocopied submissions OK. SASE. Free sample copy.

Nonfiction: How-to articles must be unusual type of treatment, or technique used in filming a production. Interviews with cinematographers. New product pieces on 16mm and 35mm cinematographic items. "The articles we use are primarily those submitted by the photographers of motion pictures. Other material is submitted by the manufacturers of equipment important in our industry. The magazine is technical in nature and the writer must have a background in motion picture photography to be able to write for us." Buys 1 ms per issue. Query first. Length varies with interest. Pays $75-125.

Photos: B&w and color purchased with mss. No additional payment.

BUSINESS SCREEN, 165 W. 46th St., New York NY 10036. For sponsors, producers and users of business, commercial advertising and industrial motion pictures, slidefilms and related audiovisual media. Bimonthly. Buys all rights. Pays on publication. Query first. Reports in 2 weeks. Enclose S.A.S.E.

Nonfiction: "Short articles on successful application of these 'tools' in industry and commerce, but only when approved by submission of advance query to publisher's office. Technical articles on film production techniques, with or without illustrations, science film data and interesting featurettes about application or utilization of films in community, industry, etc., also welcomed." Pays up to 5¢ a word.

THE CAMERA CRAFTSMAN, 2000 W. Union Ave., Englewood CO 80110. Editor: Ann McLendon. For camera repair technicians, or people with a specialized interest in photographic equipment. Magazine; 32 to 40 pages. Established in 1955. Every 2 months. Circulation: 16,000. Rights purchased vary with author and material. Usually buys first rights. Buys about 6 mss a year. Pays on acceptance. Will send sample copy to writer on request. Will consider photocopied and simultaneous submissions. Reporting time on mss accepted for publication varies, but tries to report in 30 days. Returns rejected material in 1 week. Query first on technical articles. On others, will consider complete mss. Enclose S.A.S.E.

Nonfiction and Photos: "Technical articles on camera disassembly repair and service; articles of interest to small service businesses (on business management or other appropriate subjects). "We do not want superficial or outdated business management articles, many of which are rehashes of publications issued by the Small Business Administration. We are interested in seeing current, problem-solving articles for small businesses. However, our principal interest is in technical articles on photographic equipment; also on related fields, such as optics. We are not interested in reviewing how-to articles on picture taking, or photography as such." Length: 1,000 to 5,000 words. Pays minimum of 5¢ a word. B&w glossies purchased with mss. Captions preferred. Pays minimum of $1.50.

FUNCTIONAL PHOTOGRAPHY, The Magazine of Photographic Applications in Science, Technology and Medicine, 250 Fulton Ave., Hempstead NY 11550. Editor: David A. Silverman. For scientists, engineers, doctors, etc., who must use image-production techniques to document or present their work. Magazine; 36 pages. Established in 1966. Every 2 months. Circulation: 34,000. Not copyrighted. Pays on publication. Will send free sample copy to writer on request. Write for copy of guidelines for writers. No photocopied or simultaneous submissions. Reports on material accepted for publication in 1 month. Query first or submit complete ms. Describe illustrations to be supplied. Enclose S.A.S.E.
Nonfiction and Photos: "We publish reports of major conferences of interest to our readers, 'spectrum' features discussing overall photographic set-ups; specific application articles discussing any field where an image making process is involved; reports of interesting and new techniques developed in the field and portfolios in both b&w and color of work done by our readers. Use of videotape, CCTV and other audiovisual equipment is also of interest, as well as 'exotic' uses of photographic technology which might be applied to other areas." Length: 8 to 10 pages, typed, double-spaced. "Minimum payment is $35 per display page."

INDUSTRIAL PHOTOGRAPHY, 750 Third Ave., New York NY 10017. Editor: Barry Ancona. For professional photography specialists who fulfill the visual communications needs of business, industry, government, science, medical and other organizations. Magazine; 64 (8½x11) pages. Established in 1951. Monthly. Circulation: 40,000. Rights purchased vary with author and material. May buy all rights, but occasionally will reassign rights to author after publication; or first North American serial rights. Buys 25 mss a year. Pays on publication. Will consider photocopied submissions. No simultaneous submissions. Reports in 4 weeks. Query first.
Nonfiction and Photos: Features describing ideas, applications and techniques for all types of still photography, motion pictures, audiovisuals, industrial video. Material is balanced from how-to articles to discussion of visual communication trends. "Freelancer should write only about subjects he is fully qualified to handle from a strictly professional orientation. Will specify needs in personal letter providing contributor describes his general qualifications and suggests a specific story idea — subject, event, person to interview, etc. — with outline of author's qualifications to handle the subject or subjects." Informational, how-to, interview, profile, think articles, technical pieces and coverage of successful photo department operations. Length: 750 to 3,000 words. Pays $50 to $275. Good b&w prints (minimum 5x7) and color transparencies (35mm minimum) or good color prints should amply illustrate articles. No additional payment.

PHOTOMETHODS, Ziff-Davis Publishing Co., 1 Park Ave., New York NY 10016. (212)725-3942. Editor-in-Chief: Fred Schmidt. For professional, in-plant image-makers (still, film, video, graphic arts, micrographics) and functional photographers. Monthly magazine; 64 pages. Estab: 1958. Circ: 50,000. Pays on publication. Buys all rights, but may reassign following publication. Phone queries OK. Submit seasonal/holiday material 4 months in advance. SASE. Reports in 2 months. Free sample copy and writer's guidelines.
Nonfiction: How-to and photo features (solve problems with image-making techniques—photography, etc.); informational (to help the reader in his use of photography, cine and video); interviews (with working pros); personal experience (in solving problems with photography, cine and video); profiles (well-known personalities in imaging); and technical (on photography, cine and video). Buys 5 mss/issue. Length: 1,500-3,000 words. Pays $75 minimum.
Photos: Mary Sealfon, Department Editor. B&w photos (8x10 matte) and color (35mm minimum or 8x10 print, matte) purchased with or without mss, or on assignment. Captions required. Query or submit contact sheet. Pays $25 for b&w; $35 for color. Model release required.

THE RANGEFINDER MAGAZINE, 3511 Centinela Ave., Los Angeles CA 90066. (213)390-3688. Editor-in-Chief: Janet Marshall Victor. Emphasizes professional photography. Monthly magazine; 100 pages. Estab: 1952. Circ: 42,500. Pays on publication. Buys first North American serial rights. Phone queries OK. Submit seasonal/holiday material 3 months in advance. Previously published submissions OK "if in different field." SASE. Reports in 2-3 weeks. Sample copy $1.50; free writer's guidelines.

Nonfiction: How-to (of new photographic techniques); informational; interview; new product; photo feature and technical articles. Buys 3 mss/issue. Query or submit complete ms. Length: 1,500-2,500 words. Pays $24-36/printed page, including white space and illustrations. "If you wish to be paid for the article, be sure to so indicate by stating on the ms the words 'your usual rates'. Otherwise, it will be assumed that the material is contributed at no cost to us by one of our readers who wishes to share his knowledge with his fellow photographers."

Photos: Purchased with accompanying ms. Query, or send contact sheet, prints (5x7 or 8x10 glossy for b&w, 35mm—8x10 color transparency or up to 8x10 color prints), negatives or transparencies. Total purchase price includes payment for photos.

How To Break In: "Feature material is judged on the basis of its real benefit to professional photographers. Does it help them improve their status either quality-wise or business-wise? Any contributor should be well versed in the needs of the professional photographer."

TECHNICAL PHOTOGRAPHY, PTN Publishing Corp., 250 Fulton Ave., Hempstead NY 11550. Editor-in-Chief: David A. Silverman. Publication of the "on-staff (in-house) industrial, military and government still, cine, and AV professional who must produce (or know where to get) visuals of all kinds." Monthly magazine; 64 pages. Estab: 1968. Circ: 36,000. Pays on publication. Buys first North American Serial rights. SASE. Reports in 4 weeks. Free sample copy and writer's guidelines.

Nonfiction: Publishes how-to, humor, interview, photo feature, profile (detailed stories about in-house operations), and technical articles. "All mss must relate to industrial, military or government production of visuals." Buys 12-20 mss a year. Query. Length: "As long as needed to get the information across." Pays $35 minimum/display page.

Photos: Purchased with accompanying ms. Captions required. Query.

How To Break In: "Best approach is through query letter. If familiar with TP, they should submit ideas and treatment prepared in a professional manner."

Plastics

CANADIAN PLASTICS, 1450 Don Mills Rd., Don Mills, Ont., Canada. (416)445-6641. Editor: Geoffery Spark. For management people in the plastics industry. Monthly. Buys first rights. Pays on publication. Query first. Reports in 2 to 4 weeks. Enclose S.A.E. and International Reply Coupons.

Nonfiction: Accurate technical writing. Accuracy is more important than style. "We reject some freelance material because of lack of Canadian relevance; we like to publish articles that are meaningful to the reader; something he can use for his benefit as a businessman." Pays 7¢ a word.

Photos: Buys photos submitted with ms. Pays $5.

Fillers: Buys newsbreaks. Pays $5 for news items; $15 for longer features.

PLASTICS TECHNOLOGY, 633 3rd Ave., New York NY 10017. (212)986-4800. Editor: Malcolm W. Riley. For plastic processors. Circulation: 40,000. Buys all rights. Pays on publication. Will send free sample copy on request. Query preferred. Reports in 2 weeks. Enclose S.A.S.E.

Nonfiction and Photos: Articles on plastics processing. Length: "no limits." Pays $30 to $35 per published page. Photos and all artwork purchased with ms with no additional payment.

Plumbing, Heating, Air Conditioning, and Refrigeration

Publications for fuel oil dealers who also install heating equipment are classified with the Petroleum journals.

CONTRACTOR MAGAZINE, Berkshire Common, Pittsfield MA 01201. Editor: Seth Shepard. For mechanical contractors, wholesalers, engineers. Newspaper; 70 (11x15) pages. Established in 1954. Twice a month. Circulation: 43,000. Not copyrighted. Buys 30 mss a year. Pays on publication. Will send sample copy to writer for $1.50. Write for copy of guidelines for writers. Will consider photocopied submissions. No simultaneous submissions. Reports in 1 month. Query first or submit complete ms. Enclose S.A.S.E.

Nonfiction and Photos: Articles on materials, use, policies, and business methods of the air conditioning, heating, plumbing industry. Topics covered include: interpretive reports, how-to, informational, interview, profile, think articles, expose, spot news, successful business operations, merchandising techniques, technical. Pays $150 maximum. 5x7 b&w glossies purchased with or without ms. Pays $5. Captions required.

DE/JOURNAL, 110 N. York Rd., Elmhurst IL 60126. Editor: Stephen J. Shafer. For independent businessmen who sell and install plumbing, heating, air conditioning, process piping systems. Established in 1889. Monthly. Circulation: 45,000. Rights purchased vary with author and material. Lay buy all rights, but usually will reassign rights to author after publication. Buys 30 mss a year. Payment on publication. Will send sample copy to writer for $2. Will consider photocopied and simultaneous submissions. Reports in 1 month. Query first or submit complete ms. Enclose S.A.S.E.

Nonfiction and Photos: "Only management and technical articles, pertaining to industry. Familiarity with industry described most important. Emphasis is on management." Interview, successful business operations, merchandising techniques, technical. Payment varies with quality, but the usual rate is $25 per published page. B&w photos.

EXPORT, 386 Park Ave., S., New York NY 10016. Editor: M. Downing. For importers and distributors in 165 countries who handle hardware, air conditioning and refrigeration equipment and related consumer hardlines. Magazine; 60 to 80 pages in English and Spanish editions. Established in 1877. Every 2 months. Circulation: 38,500. Buys first serial rights. Buys about 10 mss a year. Pays on acceptance. Reports in 1 month. Query first. Enclose S.A.S.E.

Nonfiction: News stories of products and merchandising of air conditioning and refrigeration equipment, hardware and related consumer hardlines. Informational, how-to, interview, profile, successful business operations. Length: 1,000 to 3,000 words. Pays 10¢ a word, maximum.

How To Break In: "One of the best ways to break in here is with a story originating outside the U.S. or Canada. Our major interest is in new products and new developments —but they must be available and valuable to overseas buyers. We also like company profile stories. A key thing we look for in writers is some kind of expertise in our field. Departments and news stories are staff written."

HEATING/PIPING/AIR CONDITIONING, Two Illinois Center, Chicago IL 60601. (312)861-0880. Editor: Robert T. Korte. Monthly. Buys all rights. Pays on publication. Query first. Reports in 2 weeks. Enclose S.A.S.E.

Nonfiction: Uses engineering and technical articles covering design, installation, operation, maintenance, etc., of heating, piping and air conditioning systems in industrial plants and large buildings. Length: 3,000 to 4,000 words maximum. Pays $30 per printed page.

HEATING, PLUMBING, AIR CONDITIONING, 1450 Don Mills Rd., Don Mills, Ont., Canada. (416)445-6641. Editor: Alan Gooding. For mechanical contractors; plumbers; warm air heating, refrigeration and air conditioning contractors; wholesalers; architects; consulting and mechanical engineers who are in key management or specifying positions in the plumbing, heating, air conditioning and refrigeration industries in Canada. Monthly. Circulation: 13,500. Buys North American serial rights only. Pays on publication. Will send free sample copy to a writer on request. Reports in 1 to 2 months. Enclose S.A.E. and International Reply Coupons.

Nonfiction and Photos: News, technical, business management and "how-to" articles which will inform, educate and motivate readers who design, manufacture, install, service, maintain or supply fuel to all mechanical components and systems in residential, commercial, institutional and industrial installations across Canada. Length: 1,000 to 1,500 words. Pays 10¢/word. Photos purchased with mss. Prefers 5x7 or 8x10 glossies.

IOWA PLUMBING, HEATING, COOLING CONTRACTOR, Box 56, Boone IA 50036. Editor: Dick Hunter. For those in the plumbing-heating-cooling contracting industry plus state procurement authorities. Monthly. Circulation: 1,100. Not copyrighted. Pays on publication. Will send sample copy to a writer on request. "Study publication." Enclose S.A.S.E. for return of submissions.

Nonfiction, Photos, and Fiction: Articles on development, engineering problems and improvements in general covering new equipment, new materials, legal review, state news, national news; other topics. Photos and fiction appropriate to format. Pays 2½¢ a word; $5 each for photos.

SNIPS MAGAZINE, 407 Mannheim Rd., Bellwood IL 60104. (312)544-3870. Editor: Nick Carter. For sheet metal, warm air heating, ventilating, air conditioning, and roofing contractors. Monthly. Buys all rights. "Write for detailed list of requirements before submitting any work." Enclose S.A.S.E.

Nonfiction: Material should deal with information about contractors who do sheet metal, warm air heating, air conditioning, ventilation and roofing work; also about successful advertising campaigns conducted by these contractors and the results. Length: "prefers stories to run less than 1,000 words unless on special assignment." Pays 2¢ each for first 500 words, 1¢ each for additional words.

Photos: Pays $2 each for small snapshot pictures, $4 each for usable 8x10 pictures.

Power and Power Plants

Publications in this listing aim at company managers, engineers, and others involved in generating and supplying power for businesses, homes, and industries. Journals for electrical engineers who design, maintain, and install systems connecting users with sources of power are classified under the heading Electricity.

DIESEL AND GAS TURBINE PROGRESS, P.O. Box 26308, 11225 West Blue Mound Rd., Milwaukee WI 53213. (414)771-4562. Publisher: Robert E. Schulz. For engineers, purchasers, and users of diesel and natural gas engines and gas turbines. Monthly. Pays on acceptance. Will send free sample copy to a writer on request. "Query with brief details about engine system and location. Send queries to Tony Alberte, Managing Editor." Reports in 4 weeks. Enclose S.A.S.E.

Nonfiction and Photos: Illustrated on-the-job articles detailing trend-setting application of diesel, gas (not gasoline) engines, gas turbine engines in industrial and commercial service. Material must thoroughly describe installation of the prime mover and auxiliary equipment, special system requirements, and controls. Articles must be slanted to the viewpoint of the user. Length: 2,500 words. Pays $75 and up per page.

ELECTRIC LIGHT AND POWER, Cahners Building, 221 Columbus Ave., Boston MA 02116. Editorial Director: Robert A. Lincicome. 2 editions (Energy/Generation and Transmission/Distribution) for electric utility engineers, engineering management and electric utility general top management. Monthly. Buys all rights. Pays on publication. Will send free sample copies to a writer on request. "Query not required, but recommended." Reports in 1 week. Enclose S.A.S.E.

Nonfiction and Photos: Engineering application articles, management subjects, electric utility system design, construction and operation, sales, etc. Articles may be case histories, problem-solutions, general roundups, state-of-the-art, etc. Must be technically oriented to industry. Length: 500 to 3,000 words. Pays $75 first published page, $50 second and succeeding pages. Photos purchased with mss as package; no separate photos accepted. Prefers 8x10 glossy prints, b&w; color transparencies, 2 ¼x2¼ or larger.

POWER ENGINEERING, 1301 S. Grove Ave., Barrington IL 60010. (312)381-1840. Editor: John Papamarcos. Monthly. Buys first rights. "Must query first." Enclose S.A.S.E.

Nonfiction and Photos: Articles on electric power field design, construction, and operation. Length: 500 to 1,500 words. Pays $80 to $200, "depending on published length." Uses 8x10 glossies with mss.

How To Break In: "We do not encourage freelance writers in general. We do review anything that is sent to us, but will generally accept articles only from people who are involved in the power field in some way and can write to interest engineers and management in the field."

PUBLIC POWER, 2600 Virginia Ave., N.W., Washington DC 20037. (202)333-9200. Editor: Ron Ross. Established in 1942. Bimonthly. Not copyrighted. Pays on publication. Query first. Enclose S.A.S.E.

Nonfiction: News and features on municipal and other local publicly owned electric systems. Payment negotiable.

RURAL ELECTRIFICATION, 2000 Florida Ave., N.W., Washington DC 20009. Editor: J. C. Brown, Jr. For managers and boards of directors of rural electric systems. Monthly. Buys all rights or reprint rights. Pays on acceptance. Will send sample copy on request. Query first. Reports in one month. Enclose S.A.S.E.

Nonfiction: Uses articles on the activities of rural electric systems which are unusual in themselves or of unusually great importance to other rural electric systems across the country. Length: "open." Pay "negotiable, but usually in $50 to $250 range."
Photos: Uses photos gith or without mss, on the same subject matter as the articles; 8x10 glossies. Pays $5 for b&w; $10 for color.

Printing

AMERICAN INK MAKER, 101 W. 31st St., New York NY 10001. Editor: John Vollmuth. For those in managerial and technical positions in the printing ink and pigment industries. Monthly. Circulation: 3,500. Buys all rights. Pays on acceptance. Will send free sample copy to a writer on request. Query first. Reports "immediately." Enclose S.A.S.E.
Nonfiction and Photos: Articles on new products for printing inks and pigment producers; articles on companies in these fields. Length: 1,200 words. Pays 3¢ per word. Pays $5 per b&w photo (unless on assignment, in which case payment is negotiated).
Fillers: Newsbreaks, clippings, short humor on ink and pigment industries. Pays $1 minimum.

GRAPHIC ARTS MONTHLY, 222 S. Riverside Plaza, Chicago IL 60606. (312)648-5900. Editor: B.D. Chapman. Monthly. Buys all rights. Pays on publication. Query first. Reports in 30 days. Enclose S.A.S.E.
Nonfiction: Uses articles of interest to management, production executives, and craftsmen in printing and allied plants. Length: maximum 2,500 words.

GRAPHIC ARTS SUPPLIER NEWS, 401 N. Broad St., Philadelphia PA 19108. (215)574-9600. Editor: Peggy Bicknell. For dealers, salesmen, and manufacturers of printing equipment and supplies. 6 times a year. Buys first publication rights. Query preferred. Reports in 2 months. Enclose S.A.S.E.
Nonfiction: Feature articles with heavy emphasis on sales, marketing, profiles and promotion techniques, and some news related to graphic arts supply. Pays flat fee of $100 with photos.
Photos: On assignment only; payment varies with assignment.

THE INLAND PRINTER/AMERICAN LITHOGRAPHER, 300 W. Adams St., Chicago IL 60606. Editor: Richard H. Green. For qualified personnel active in any phase of the graphic arts industry. Established in 1883. Monthly. Circulation: 59,000. Buys all rights, unless otherwise specified in writing at time of purchase. Pays on publication. Free sample copy to a writer on request. Submit seasonal material 2 months in advance. "Study publication before writing." Query first. Enclose S.A.S.E.
Nonfiction: Articles on management; technical subjects with illustrations with direct bearing on graphic arts industry. Length: 1,500 to 3,000 words. Pays $50 to $200.
Photos: Purchased with mss; also news shots of graphic arts occurrences. 5x7 or 8x10 glossy. Pays $5 to $10.
Fillers: Newsbreaks, clippings, short humor; must relate to printing industry. Length: 100 to 250 words. Pays $10 minimum.

NEWSPAPER PRODUCTION, North American Publishing Co., 401 N. Broad St., Philadelphia PA 19108. (215)574-9600. Editor-in-Chief: Jeffrey Markow. For the newspaper industry; production personnel through management to editor and publisher. Monthly magazine; 56 pages. Estab: 1972. Circ: 16,000. Pays on publication. Buys all rights. Phone queries OK. Photocopied submissions OK. SASE. Reports in 3 weeks. Free sample copy.
Nonfiction: Publishes historical articles (production case histories) and how-to articles (production techniques). Length: 1,500 words minimum. Query first or submit complete ms. Pays $35 minimum.
Photos: B&w and color purchased with or without mss, or on assignment. Captions required. Query first or submit contact sheet or prints. No additional payment for those used with mss. Model release required.

PLAN & PRINT, International Repro Graphic Blueprhnt Association, Inc., 10116 Franklin Ave., Franklin Park IL 60131. (312)671-5356. Editor: James C. Vebeck. For in-plant reproduction, printing, drafting and design departments of business and industry. Monthly magazine; 42 pages. Estab: 1929. Circ: 20,333. Pays on acceptance. Buys all rights. Phone queries OK. SASE. Reports in 2 weeks. Free sample copy and writer's guidelines.
Nonfiction: How-to articles (problems and how and why they were solved; benefits to customer

and to company in time and costs); interviews, photo features and technical articles. Pays $35-200.

Photos: B&w (8x10) glossies purchased with mss. Captions required. Pays $5 minimum. Model release required.

Poetry: Light verse related to the industry. Buys 4 per year. Limit submissions to 3 at a time. Pays $5-7.50.

Fillers: Jokes, gags, anecdotes, crossword puzzles related to the industry. Pays $5-30.

PRINTING IMPRESSIONS, 401 N. Broad St., Philadelphia PA 19108. Editor: James F. Burns, Jr. For production people who also sell and manage. "Write for journeyman-level production people when discussing processes and procedures; in management discussions, address problems on college-level basis." Monthly tabloid size magazine; 100 (11x16) pages. Established in 1958. Circulation: 70,000. Buys all rights. Buys 2 or 3 mss a year. Payment on publication. Will consider photocopied submissions, if legible enough. Will not consider simultaneous submissions. Reports within a month or so. Query first. Enclose S.A.S.E.

Nonfiction and Photos: Personal experience, interview, profile, successful business operations. "Ask for an assignment after 1) outlining topic and suggesting reason for merit; 2) supply sample of work you've done; 3) mention payment expected. Only expository writing wanted. Chances of hitting with a speculative article are 100 to 1." Length: 1,000 to 2,000 words. Pays 4¢ a word. Pays $10 for b&w photos published with mss. Captions required.

PRINTING SALESMAN'S HERALD, Champion Papers, Champion International, 245 Park Avenue, New York NY 10017. Editor: G. Steven Read. For printing, graphic arts industries. Published 3 times/year. Buys all rights. Pays on acceptance. Reports in 1 to 4 weeks. Enclose S.A.S.E.

Nonfiction: Articles on salesmanship as applicable to the selling of printing; technical pieces relating to printing production; sales incentive material as seen from both sides of the desk. Material must be valid to the publication's audience and well-written. Pays $75 if material is worth developing but needs rewriting; $100 to $150 if copy is meaty and well-written.

SCREEN PRINTING, 407 Gilbert Ave., Cincinnati OH 45202. (513)421-2050. Editor: Jonathan E. Schiff. For the screen printing industry, including screen printers (commercial, industrial and captive shops), suppliers and manufacturers, ad agencies and allied professions. Monthly magazine; 64 to 68 pages. Established in 1953. Circulation: 7,000. Rights purchased vary with author and material. Usually buys all rights, but may reassign rights to author after publication. Copyrighted. Pays on publication. Free writer's guidelines. Will not consider photocopied submissions. Will consider simultaneous submissions. Reporting time varies for material accepted for publication. Returns rejected material immediately. Query first. Enclose S.A.S.E.

Nonfiction and Photos: "Since the screen printing industry covers a broad range of applications and overlaps other fields in the graphic arts, it's necessary that articles be of a significant contribution, preferably to a specific area of screen printing. Subject matter is fairly open, with preference given to articles on administration or technology; trends and developments. We try to give a good sampling of technical articles, business and management articles; articles about unique operations. We also publish special features and issues on important subjects, such as material shortages, new markets and new technology breakthroughs. While most of our material is nitty-gritty, we appreciate a writer who can take an essentially dull subject and encourage the reader to read on through concise, factual, flairful and creative, expressive writing. Interviews are published after consultation with and guidance from the editor." Interested in stories on unique approaches by some shops on how to lick the problems created by the petroleum shortage (the industry relies heavily on petrol products). Length: 1,500 to 2,000 words. Pays minimum of $125 for major features; minimum of $50 for minor features; minimum of $35 for back of book articles. Pays $15 for photos used on cover; b&w only. Published material becomes the property of the magazine.

SOUTHERN PRINTER & LITHOGRAPHER, 75 Third St., N.W., Atlanta GA 30308. Editor: Charles Fram. For commercial printing plant management in the 14 southern states. Established in 1924. Monthly. Circulation: 3,600. Not copyrighted. Payment on publication. Reporting time on submissions varies. Query first. Enclose S.A.S.E.

Nonfiction and Photos: Feature articles on commercial printing plants in the 14 southern states and their personnel. Length: 1,000 to 1,500 words. Pays 1¢ a word. B&w photos. Pays $4.

Public Relations

PUBLICIST, Published by Public Relations Aids, Inc., 221 Park Ave. S. New York NY 10003. Editor-in-Chief: Lee Levitt. Devoted entirely to professional publicity/public relations. For "a controlled circulation of people engaged in publicity on a national or major regional scale." Bimonthly tabloid. Estab: 1976. Circ: 14,000. Pays on acceptance. Buys all rights, but may reassign to author following publication. Submit seasonal/holiday material 6 months in advance. Simultaneous photocopied and previously published material OK. SASE. Reports in 1 month. Free sample copy and writer's guidelines.

Nonfiction: How-to, informational, humor, interview, nostalgia, profile, personal dxperience, photo feature and technical. "The subject of every article must be publicity, or organizations or persons engaged in publicity. We cover only national projects." Buys 5 mss/issue. Query. Length: 400-1,500 words. Pays $30-250.

Photos: Purchased with or without accompanying ms or on assignment. Captions required. Uses b&w only. Query. Prefers 8x10's. Pays $20-50 per photo.

Fiction: Humorous, condensed novels, mainstream, serialized novels. "All fiction must concern publicity people in a realistic, professional situation; must exhibit sophisticated comprehension of big time PR practice." Query. Length: 500 words minimum. Pays $50-400.

Fillers: Clippings, jokes, gags, anecdotes, newsbreaks, short humor or professional public relations. Buys 2 an issue. Query. Length: 50-400 words. Pays $15-40.

How To Break In: "We are most likely to accept case histories of national publicity projects; the article must include details of the project's cost; you must send documentation of the project. All our articles are in newspaper style: flat, abrupt leads, attributions for all important statements, no editorial comment."

Railroad

THE SIGNALMAN'S JOURNAL, 601 West Golf Rd., Mt. Prospect IL 60056. (312)439-3732. Editor: Robert W. McKnight. Monthly. Buys first rights. Query first. Reports in 3 weeks. Enclose S.A.S.E.

Nonfiction: Can use articles on new installations of railroad signal systems, but they must be technically correct and include drawings and photos. "We do not want general newspaper type writing, and will reject material that is not of technical quality." Length: 3,000 to 4,000 words. Pays $10 per printed page, and up.

Photos: Photographs dealing with railroad signaling. Pays $5.

Real Estate

APARTMENT MANAGEMENT NEWSLETTER, Mattco Equities, Inc., 48 W. 21st St., New York NY 10010. Editor: Ann Redlin. Emphasizes apartment management. Monthly newsletter; 8 pages. Estab: 1975. Circ: 5,000. Pays on publication. Buys all rights. Submit seasonal/holiday material 2 months in advance. Photocopied submissions OK. SASE. Reports in 8 weeks. Sample copy $2.25.

Nonfiction: How-to (maintenance, occupancy, cost-cutting); informational (taxes, gas, oil, trends affecting apartments) interviews (with successful managers); profiles (successful apartment complexes), new products (snow throwers, rugs, windows, etc.); and technical (for all the foregoing; can include graphs, charts). Query or submit complete ms. Length: 250-1,000 words. Pays $5-10/page.

AREA DEVELOPMENT, 432 Park Ave. S., New York NY 10016. (212)532-4360. Editor: Albert H. Jaeggin. For chief executives of leading firms in the U.S., Canada, western Europe, Japan and Latin America. Monthly. Buys all rights, reprint rights, and, possibly, simultaneous rights. Query first. Enclose S.A.S.E.

Nonfiction: Wants articles on all subjects related to facility planning, including: finding new sites, building new plants and/or expanding and relocating existing facilities; community and employee relations; political climate; transportation, recreational and educational facilities; financing; insurance; plant design and layout; safety factors; water and air pollution controls; case histories of companies which have moved or built new plants. Must be objective (no puffery) and useful to executives. Must avoid discussions of merits or disadvantages of any

particular community, state or area. Also carries news items on activities, people, areas, books on facility planning, based on releases. Pays $40 per printed page.
Photos: Buys glossy photos. Pays $40 per page.

COMMUNITY DEVELOPMENT DIGEST, 399 National Press Bldg., Washington DC 20045. (202)638-6113. Managing Editor: Byron Fielding. Predominantly for Federal/state/local agencies interested in housing and community development. Semimonthly newsletter; 18 pages. Estab: 1965. Pays end of month following publication. Not copyrighted. Phone queries OK. Simultaneous and photocopied submissions OK. SASE. Reports in 2 weeks. Sample copy and writer's guidelines for SASE.
Fillers: Uses contributions of newspaper clippings on housing and community development; substantive actions and litigations, that would be of interest to housing and community development professionals beyond immediate area. "We reject material when the territory has already been covered; material not of interest to our needs." Particularly wants regular contributors for multistates, region, or at least a full state, especially state capitals. Normally pays $1.50 for each clipping used.

PROPERTIES MAGAZINE, 4900 Euclid Ave., Cleveland OH 44103. (216)431-7666. Editor: Gene Bluhm. Monthly. Buys all rights. Pays on publication. Query first. Enclose S.A.S.E.
Nonfiction and Photos: Wants articles of real estate and construction news value. Interested primarily in articles relating to northeastern Ohio. Length: up to 700 words. Pays $25 minimum. Buys photographs with mss, 8x10 preferred.

PROPERTY MANAGEMENT JOURNAL, P.O. Box 853, Temple City CA 91780. Editor: Gladys Dickholtz. For owners and managers of rental property in the San Gabriel Valley, realtors and property management firms. Tabloid newspaper. Established in 1971. Monthly. Circulation: 7,000. Buys first serial rights. Buys about 5 mss each issue. Pays on acceptance. Will send sample copy to writer for $1. Reports in 4 weeks. Query first or submit complete ms. Enclose S.A.S.E.
Nonfiction and Photos: How-to articles of vital interest to owners and property managers who control the purchasing of services and products in the rental housing industry. Topics could be on carpet care, painting, draperies, appliance sales and service, electrical and plumbing repair, decorating, swimming pool maintenance, roof repair, laundry services, fire and building safety, etc. Writers should remember that subjects should be applicable to southern California readers — no snowplows or storm window stories. Length: 3 pages, typed, double-spaced. Also uses shorter humorous articles about apartment hunting, resident managers, tenant relations, etc. Length: 1, 2 or 3 pages, typed, double-spaced. Pays $5 to $15. Will buy b&w photos, if applicable, at $5 each. "Enclose S.A.S.E. with all correspondence for which you wish a reply."

SHOPPING CENTER WORLD, Communication Channels, Inc., 461 8th Ave., New York NY 10001. (212)239-6221. Editor-in-Chief: Eric C. Peterson. Emphasizes shopping center/retailing world for shopping center developers, builders, owners and managers; chain store executives, store planners, and others in the industry. Monthly magazine; 72 pages. Estab: 1972. Circ: 20,000. Pays on acceptance. Buys all rights. Phone queries OK. Submit seasonal/holiday material 8 weeks in advance. Photocopied and previously published submissions OK. SASE. Reports in 4 weeks. Free sample copy. Editorial schedule available.
Nonfiction: How-to (improve efficiency, cut costs, etc., in construction and operation of shopping centers); informational (discussion of interesting new projects, concepts, etc.); interview (with top industry leaders only); and technical (as relates to operation and construction of shopping centers). Buys 30 mss/year. Query. Length: 500-1,500 words. Pays $50-150.
Photos: Purchased with accompanying ms. Captions required. Submit (with ms) contact sheet, prints, or transparencies. Pays $5-10 for 3x5 or larger b&w glossies; $10-15 for 3x5 or larger color glossy prints or any size transparencies. Total purchase price for ms includes payment for photos.
Columns/Departments: Joya Woolley, column/department editor. New locations (new and expanding shopping centers); Sales, Leases, Mortgages (sales, financing, and leasing of centers); and People & Places (general industry news). No length requirement. Pays $5-25.
Fillers: Joya Woolley, fillers editor. Clippings. Buys 25/issue. Pays $1.50.
How To Break In: "A freelancer should come up with something 'nuts and bolts' with plenty of hard facts and figures including dollar figures. Anything less gets too puffy."

Recreation Park and Campground Management

CAMPGROUND AND RV PARK MANAGEMENT, Rt. 1, Box 780, Quincy CA 95971. (916)283-0666. Editor: Bill Shepard. 8 times a year. Circulation: 14,000. Buys all rights. Pays on publication. Will send a free sample copy on request. "Best to query first." Reports in 1 month. Enclose S.A.S.E.

Nonfiction and Photos: Success stories and management information articles for owners of campgrounds and recreation vehicle parks. News stories about campgrounds, campground associations, campground chains and any other subjects helpful or of interest to a campground operator. Also uses features about such subjects as a specialized bookkeeping system for campground operations, an interesting traffic circulation system, an advertising and promotion program that has worked well for a campground, an efficient trash collection system. Successful operation of coin-operated dispensing machines, successful efforts by a campground owner in bringing in extra income through such means as stores, charge showers, swimming fees, etc. Use newspaper style reporting for news items and newspaper feature style for articles. Length: 500 to 700 words, news stories; 300 to 1,200 words, features. Pays $20 to $50. "B&w photos should accompany articles whenever practicable."

Fillers: Pays $2 to $5 for ideas which eventually appear as stories written by staff or another writer; $5 to $10 for newsbreaks of one paragraph to a page.

CAMPING INDUSTRY, Market Communications, Inc., 225 E. Michigan, Milwaukee WI 53202. (414)276-6600. Editor-in-Chief: Connie B. Howes. Magazine; 7 times a year; 48 pages. Estab: 1960. Circ: 15,000. Pays on acceptance. Buys all rights, but may reassign following publication. Phone queries OK. Submit seasonal material 2-3 months in advance. Simultaneous submissions OK if exclusive in the area. Photocopied submissions OK. SASE. Reports in 3 weeks. Free sample copy and writer's guidelines.

Nonfiction: How-to (run your business better); informational and technical (regarding camping products); interviews and profiles (camping oriented); photo features (successful dealer stories). Buys 2-3/issue. Length: 500-2,000 words. Query. Pays $50-150.

Photos: B&w glossies purchased with mss. Prefers 8x10, but will consider 5x7. Send contact sheets, prints or negatives. Pays $5-15.

PARK MAINTENANCE, P.O. Box 1936, Appleton WI 54911. (414)733-2301. Editor: Erik L. Madisen, Jr. For administrators of areas with large grounds maintenance and outdoor recreation facilities. Special issues include March, Swimming Pool and Beach; July, Turf Research and Irrigation Annual; October, Buyer's Guide issue. Established in 1948. Monthly. Circulation: 17,000. Buys all rights. Buys 4 or 5 mss a year. Pays on acceptance. Will send a sample copy to a writer on request. Write for copy of guidelines for writers. Will consider photocopied submissions "if exclusive to us." Query first. "Outline material and source in letter, and include S.A.S.E." Deadlines are the first of the month preceding publication. Reports in 2 weeks.

Nonfiction: How-to, case history, technical or scientific articles dealing with maintenance of turf and facilities in parks, forestry, golf courses, campuses. These may be new or unique ideas adopted by park systems for greater use or more efficient and economical operation. Also, methods of dealing with administrative, financial, personnel and other problems; new phases of landscape architecture and building design. Buys how-to's and interviews. Length: up to 1,000 words. Pays 2¢ a word.

Photos: Purchased with mss if applicable; 8x10 or 5x7 b&w glossies. "Captions required." Pays minimum of $2 each; $5 for front cover.

TOURIST ATTRACTIONS AND PARKS, 327 Wagaraw Rd., Hawthorne NJ 07506. (201)423-2266. Editor: Martin Dowd. For owners and managers of theme parks, amusement parks, national and state parks, zoos, etc. Published 2 times a year; magazine, 52 pages, 8½x11. Established in 1972. Circulation: 6,130. Buys first North American serial rights. Buys 3 or 4 mss a year. Payment on acceptance. Will send free sample copy to writer on request. Query first or submit complete ms. Reports in 2 weeks. Enclose S.A.S.E.

Nonfiction, Photos, and Fillers: "Articles on the science of managing a tourist attraction. How to increase the number of visitors, how to handle crowds best, how to train people to handle crowds, operate rides, feed large masses of tourists. We prefer articles about how a specific manager has solved a specific problem in the operation of a tourist attraction. Prefer quotes, specific examples." Informational, how-to, personal experience, interview, profile, and successful business operations and technical articles. Length: 500 to 2,000 words. Pays 4¢ minimum a word. Regular columns use items on advertising, promotion, training, maintenance, rides, food. Length: 500 to 2,500 words. Pays 4¢ minimum per word, plus $10 for each photo used. 8x10 or 5x7 b&w photos purchased with mss for $10. "Will pay for photos even if attraction supplies them to writers." Captions optional. Pays 80¢ a printed inch for clippings.

WOODALL'S CAMPGROUND MANAGEMENT, Rt. 1, Box 780, Quincy CA 95971. (916)283-0666. Editor-in-Chief: Bill Shepard. Audience is the owners and managers of private campgrounds in the U.S., Canada and Mexico. Monthly tabloid; 20 pages. Estab: 1970. Circ: 16,000. Pays on publication. Buys all rights, but may reassign following publication. Phone queries OK. Submit seasonal/holiday material 2 months in advance. Photocopied (if statement is enclosed stating that material has not been published or accepted elsewhere) and previously published submissions OK. SASE. Reports in 4 weeks. Sample copy 25¢; free writer's guidelines.
Nonfiction: Expose (governmental practices detrimental to private campground industry); how-to (any type that will provide practical, usable information in operation of campgrounds); informational; interview; new product; personal experience (experiences of campground owners/managers); photo feature; and technical. Buys 40-50 mss/year. Query. Length: 1,000-2,500 words. Pays $35-100.
Photos: Purchased with or without accompanying ms or on assignment. Captions required. Query. Pays $2.50-7.50 for 5x7 minimum b&w glossy; $20 minimum for 120mm and larger color transparencies. Offers no additional payment for photos accepted with ms "except for page 1 color transparencies; pays $20 additional whether part of editorial package or not." Model release required.
Fillers: Clippings and newsbreaks. Buys 10-12/year. Length: 50-250 words. Pays $2.50-15.
How To Break In: "We are seeking freelancers from throughout the country who can provide factual, useful articles pertinent to the private campground industry; new ideas that work, success stories, how to solve a problem. Facts and figures must be included."

Secretarial

MODERN SECRETARY, Allied Publications, P.O. Box 23505, Fort Lauderdale FL 33307. Associate Editor: Marie Stilkind. Monthly. Buys North American serial rights only. Pays on acceptance. Query not necessary. Reports in 2 to 4 weeks. Enclose S.A.S.E.
Nonfiction and Photos: "Office tips, articles and photos about secretaries. Also articles about secretaries to famous personalities, or other material of interest to secretaries." Length: 500 to 1,000 words. Payment is 5¢ a word, and $5 for b&w glossy photos purchased with mss.

TODAY'S SECRETARY, 1221 Avenue of the Americas, New York NY 10020. Editor: Lauren Bahr. For students (mostly female, age 16 to 21) training for careers in the business world. Magazine; 32 pages. Established in 1898. Monthly. Circulation: 80,000. Buys all rights. Buys about 40 mss a year. Pays on acceptance. Will send free sample copy to writer on request. Write for copy of guidelines for writers. Will consider photocopied submissions. No simultaneous submissions. Query first for articles; submit complete ms for fiction. Enclose S.A.S.E.
Nonfiction: Articles on business trends, secretarial procedure; articles of general interest to young women (communications, human relations; beauty and fashion). Should be informational in nature. An imaginative manner of presentation is encouraged with emphasis away from factual, textbooklike approach. Material must have professional slant, reaching for the informed, contemporary, young businesswoman. Length: 800 words minimum. Pays $75 to $150. Columns are staff written, but new ideas for columns are always welcome.
Fiction: Any good story line acceptable. Length: 800 to 900 words. Pays $35.
How To Break In: "The best way to break in would be with a short piece of fiction (800 words). Keep in mind that our audience is mostly women, age 16 to 22, in high school or business school. Also, the stories shouldn't be too heavy —we print them in shorthand as a skills exercise for our readers. Other good freelance possibilities include profiles of secretaries with unusual job responsibilities or in an unusual field, and secretarial procedure stories —tips on filing, making travel arrangements for your boss, etc."

Selling and Merchandising

In this category are journals for salesmen and merchandisers who publish general material on how to sell products successfully. Journals in nearly every other category of this Trade Journal section will also buy this kind of material if it is slanted to the specialized product or industry they deal with, such as clothing or petroleum. Publications for professional advertising and marketing men will be found under Advertising and Marketing Journals.

AGENCY SALES MAGAZINE, Box 16878, Irvine CA 92713. (714)752-5231. Editor: Linda Hamner. For independent sales representatives and the manufacturers they represent. Publication of Manufacturers' Agents National Association. Magazine; 40 pages. Established in 1950. Monthly. Circulation: 11,000. Rights purchased vary with author and material. May buy all rights, with the possibility of reassigning rights to author after publication, or simultaneous rights. Buys about 36 mss/year. Pays on publication. Free sample copy and writer's guidelines. Will consider photocopied and simultaneous submissions. Reports on mss accepted for publication in 1 to 2 months. Returns rejected material in 1 month. Query first. Enclose S.A.S.E.
Nonfiction and Photos: Articles on independent sales representatives, the suppliers and customers, and their operations. Must be about independent selling from the agent's point of view. Uses how-to, profile, interview, successful business techniques. "Articles about selling should not be too general — specifics a must." Length: 500 to 2,500 words. Ideal length is 1,500 words. Pays $50 to $100. Photos purchased with accompanying ms with extra payment. Captions required. B&w glossies only. Pays $10 to $15. Size: 3x5, 8x10.

AMERICAN FIREARMS INDUSTRY, American Press Media Association, Inc., 7001 N. Clark St., Chicago IL 60626. Specializes in the sporting arms trade. Monthly magazine; 58 pages. Estab: 1972. Circ: 19,000. Pays on publication. Buys all rights, but may reassign following publication. Submit seasonal/holiday material 60 days in advance. SASE. Reports in 2 weeks. Sample copy, $1.
Nonfiction: Milo Yelesiyevich, Department Editor. Publishes informational, technical and new product articles. Buys 60 mss/year. Query first. Length: 900-1,500 words. Pays $75.
Photos: B&w (8x10) glossies. Mss price includes payment for photos.

ARMY/NAVY STORE AND OUTDOOR MERCHANDISER, 225 W. 34 St., New York NY 10001. (212)279-0800. Editor: Michael Spielman. For the owners of army/navy surplus and outdoor goods stores. Established in 1947. Circulation: 3,000. Buys all rights. Buys 30 mss a year. Pays on publication. Enclose S.A.S.E.
Nonfiction and Photos: Articles on the methods stores use to promote items; especially on how army/navy items have become fashion items, and the problems attendant to catering to this new customer. Sources of supply, how they promote, including windows, newspapers, etc. "If the guy wants to tell his life story, listen and take notes. Use simple words. Stick to a single subject, if possible. Find out how the man makes money and tell us. The true 'success' story is the most frequently submitted and the most dreadful; yet nothing is of more interest if it is done well. No one truly wishes to tell you how he earns money." Length: open. Pays $50 minimum. No additional payment for 5x7 photos or negatives.
How To Break In: "Am anxious to build our coverage of camping departments. The best material always has a unique—but not forced—slant to most routine store stories."

THE AUDIO RETAILER, Maclean-Hunter, Ltd., 481 University Ave., Toronto, Ontario, Canada M5W 1A7. (416)595-1811. Editor: Greg Gertz. For retailers of high-quality audio equipment and operators of stereo stores. Monthly tabloid; 24 pages. Estab: 1972. Circ: 6,000. Pays on publication. Buys first North American serial rights. Phone queries OK. Submit seasonal/holiday material 3 months in advance. Previously published submissions OK. SASE. Reports in 3 weeks.
Nonfiction: How-to (run a successful audio retail outlet); profiles (successful dealers); interviews (with top executives in the audio equipment manufacturing industry). Buys 2 mss/issue. Length: 500-2,000 words. Query. "Most freelance material comes to us from regular contributors. Anything else must be either very new, very exciting, or very controversial. Strong Canadian angle required." Pays 10¢/word average.
Photos: Purchased with mss B&w only. Captions required. Query. Pays $10/photos.

AUTOMOTIVE AGE, Freed-Crown Publishing, 6931 Van Nuys Blvd., Van Nuys CA 92405. (213)873-1320. Editor: Art Spinella. For a primarily male audience with income in the upper middle and upper brackets; sole owners or partners in multi-million dollar businesses. Monthly magazine; 80-90 pages. Estab: 1967. Circ: 47,000. Pays on publication. Buys all rights, but may reassign after publication. Phone queries OK. Simultaneous submissions OK, if list of other publications receiving same or similar story is furnished. SASE. Reports in 2 weeks. Free sample copy.

Nonfiction: Publishes humorous articles relating to retail sales, auto repair, or of general interest to men meeting readers' demographics; informational articles (sales techniques, dealership/retail promotions); interviews (with men in government or industry; auto dealers); nostalgia (automotive and sales related); travel (to places where men meeting their demographics would find new and different). "Clean, sophisticated copy that talks to the audience on a professional level." Buys 10 mss per issue. Query first. Length: 300-2,000 words. Pays $5 per column inch, or $7 per hour, plus expenses.

Photos: Pays $25 per b&w photo used with articles, columns or departments.

Columns/Departments: Promo Beat (unique auto dealership promotions for new and used car sales, service or parts departments). Buys 12 items per issue. Query. Length: 700-1,000 words. Pays $5 per column inch. Open to suggestions for new columns and departments.

Fillers: Buys 15 clippings per issue. Pays $1 per clipping or tip leading to a published item.

CAMPGROUND MERCHANDISING, 327 Wagaraw Rd., Hawthorne NJ 07506. Editor: Debby Roth. For owners and managers of recreation vehicle campgrounds who sell merchandise or equipment to people who vacation in recreation vehicles. Magazine published 3 times a year; 56 (5½x8½) pages. Established in 1972. Circulation: 6,500. Buys first North American serial rights. Buys 5 mss a year. Payment on acceptance. Free sample copy to writer on request. Will not consider photocopied or simultaneous submissions. Submit seasonal material 3 months in advance. Reports in 2 weeks. Query first or submit complete ms. Enclose S.A.S.E.

Nonfiction and Photos: "We specialize in RV campgrounds that resell equipment or merchandise to RV'ers who are visiting the RV campground. We use articles about how to best operate a recreation vehicle campground. The best approach is to interview managers of recreation vehicle campgrounds about their operations. Not interested in RV campgrounds selling, bread, milk, ice cream. Main interest is in their sales of equipment or merchandise wanted only by RV'ers, and how the resale of merchandise and equipment in an RV campground made it profitable." Informational, how-to, personal experience, interview, successful business operations, merchandising techniques. Length: 800 to 1,500 words. Pays about 4¢ a word. Prefers 8x10 b&w glossies, but can use 5x7. Pays $10 for each one used with ms. No color. Captions optional.

Fillers: Clippings are purchased only if about RV parks and newsworthy. Pays 80¢ per inch used.

CHAIN STORE AGE, GENERAL MERCHANDISE EDITION, 425 Park Ave., New York NY 10022. Publisher: Paul J. Reuter. Editor: John Lightfoot. For major chain store executives, field and store management personnel in the general merchandise chain field. Established in 1925. Monthly. Circulation: 33,500. Buys all rights. Purchases of mss are limited to special needs and commitments: "12 columns in fashions (from London), 12-plus pages of government news from Washington." Pays on publication. Will send free sample copy to writer on request. Reports in 2 weeks. Submit complete ms. Enclose S.A.S.E.

Nonfiction: Retail-related news across a wide band of merchandise categories (housewares, home sewing, toys, stationery, fashionwear, etc.). News about companies, promotions, people-on-the-move. Sharp, to the point, strong on facts. Subjects that are on the tip of chain retailers' minds about their business. How chain retailers are coping with traffic fall-off by tightening productivity screws in day-to-day operations. "We have one definite 'no-no' —sloppy copy that is not proofread." Length: 250 to 300 words. Pays minimum of $10 per page.

CONVENIENCE STORE MERCHANDISER, Associated Business Publications, 101 Park Ave., Suite 1838, New York NY 10017. (212)685-5111. Editor-in-Chief: Michael R. Ball. For owners of convenience stories, suppliers, manufacturers of products sold in convenience stores. Monthly magazine; 68 pages. Estab: 1973. Circ: 28,000. Pays on publication. Buys all rights, but may reassign following publication. Phone queries OK. Submit seasonal/holiday material 2½ months in advance. Simultaneous submissions OK, if not competing. Photocopied submissions and previously published work OK. SASE. Reports in 2 weeks. Free sample copy and writer's guidelines.

Nonfiction: Publishes how-to articles (wholesaler, or manufacturer who does something different or better and makes money with it); interviews; new product items; personal opinion; profiles of stores or manufacturers; technical articles. "We don't care how clean the store is, how

pretty it is, or how the manager used to be a clerk. As similar as many of the stores are in appearance and items stocked, we need the unique or superior." Buys 2 mss/issue. Length: "Whatever it takes to tell the story." Pays $100.
Photos: Purchased with or without mss, or on assignment. B&w, 5x7 or larger; glossy or semi-matte. "We work with b&w veloxes and need properly exposed pix." Pays $10 minimum. Color transparencies; 35mm or 2¼x2¼ slides. Pays $50 minimum for those used on cover.

CRAFT & ART MARKET, 1615 E. Catalina Dr., Phoenix AZ 85016. (602)263-0634. Managing Editor: Mike Skerlak. For retail store owners, wholesalers, mass merchandise buyers. Bimonthly magazine; 44 pages. Estab: 1975. Circ: 15,000. Pays on publication. Buys one-time rights. Submit seasonal/holiday material 2 months in advance. Simultaneous and photocopied submissions OK. SASE. Reports in 4 weeks. Free sample copy.
Nonfiction: Rebecca Ford, Department Editor. How-to articles, interviews and photo features. Buys 3/issue. Submit complete ms. Length: 500-3,000 words. Pays $50-200.
Photos: B&w glossies (5x7) purchased with mss. Captions required. Pays $5.

GIFTWARE NEWS, 1111 E. Touhy Ave., Des Plaines IL 60018. Editor: Cholm Houghton. For retailers, gift stores, florists, stationers, department stores, jewelry and home furnishings stores. Magazine; 80 (11x15) pages. Established in 1975. Every 2 months. Circulation: 41,000. Rights purcahsed vary with author and material. Buys about 12 mss a year. Pays on publication. Will send sample copy to writer for $1. Write for copy of guidelines for writers. Submit seasonal material (related to the gift industry) 2 months in advance. Reports in 1 to 2 months. Query first or submit complete ms. Enclose S.A.S.E.
Nonfiction and Photos: Trade material. Only informative articles written in a manner applicable to daily business and general knowledge; not mere rhetorical exercises. Articles on store management, security, backgrounds (history) of giftwares, i.e., crystals, silver, (methods, procedures of manufacture); porcelain, etc. Informational, interview, profiles, material on new products and merchandising techniques. Length: 500 words minimum. Pays $40 minimum. Pays $10 minimum for b&w photos used with mss. Captions optional.

HEALTH FOODS BUSINESS, Howmark Publishing Corp., 225 W. 34th St., New York NY 10001. (212)279-0800. Editor-in-Chief: Michael Spielman. For owners and managers of health food stores. Monthly magazine; 100 pages. Estab: 1954. Circ: over 5,000. Pays on publication. Buys simultaneous rights, second serial (reprint) rights or first North American serial rights. Phone queries OK. Simultaneous and photocopied submissions OK if exclusive to their field. Previously published work OK. SASE. Reports in 1 month. Sample copy $1.
Nonfiction: Exposes (government hassling with health food industry); how-to (unique or successful retail operators); informational (how or why a product works; technical aspects must be clear to laymen); historical (natural food use); interviews (must be prominent person in industry or closely related to the health food industry); and photo features (any unusual subject related to the retailer's interests). Buys 2-3 mss/issue. Query first for interviews and photo features. Will consider complete ms in other categories. Length: 1,000 words minimum. Pays $25/published page minimum.
Photos: "Most articles must have photos included"; minimum 5x7 b&w glossies. Captions required. Send contact sheet, prints or negatives. No additional payment.
How To Break In: "Best way, in fact, the only way, is to submit a piece that is geared to retailers, and helps them do a better job. The more specifically it speaks to the reader, the better. Will not consider any article, no matter how well written or how germane the subject, if it does not truly inform the reader."

HOUSEWARES, Harcourt Brace Jovanovich Publications, Inc., 757 Third Ave., New York NY 10017. Editor: Jack BenAry. Emphasizes the retail merchandising of housewares. Monthly tabloid; 50 pages. Estab: 1892. Circ: 12,500. Pays on publication. Buys all rights. SASE. Reports in 3 weeks. Free sample copy.
Nonfiction: Photo features. "Articles without photos are rarely acceptable. We are picture-oriented." Buys 35 mss a year. Query. Length: 1,000-2,500 words. Pays 15¢/word maximum.
Photos: Purchased with accompanying ms. Captions required. Query. Submit 5x7 or 8x10 b&w glossy; transparencies for color. Total price for ms includes payment for photos. Model release required.
How To Break In: "Articles that show (with pictures) and explain (with details) successful merchandising strategies and promotions in housewares will be considered. Writers must have a working knowledge of retail merchandising. They *must* speak the language."

PHOTO MARKETING, 603 Lansing Ave., Jackson MI 49202. Managing Editor: James L. Crawford. For camera store dealers, photofinishers, manufacturers and distributors of photographic equipment. Publication of the Photo Marketing Association, International. Magazine; 42 pages. Established in 1924. Monthly. Circulation: 12,250. Buys all rights. Pays on publication. Reports in 5 days. Query first with outline and story line. Enclose S.A.S.E.

Nonfiction and Photos: Business features dealing with photographic retailing or photofinishing operations, highlighting unique aspects, promotional programs, special problems. Length: 300 to 500 typewritten lines. Pays 6¢ per word minimum. Pays $5 to $7 per published 5x7 glossy photo.

SALESMAN'S OPPORTUNITY MAGAZINE, 1460 John Hancock Center, Chicago IL 60611. (312)337-3350. Editor: Jack Weissman. For "people who are eager to increase their incomes by selling or through an independent business of their own." Established in 1923. Monthly. Buys all rights. Buys about 50 mss a year. Payment on publication. Will send free sample copy to writer on request. Write for copy of guidelines for writers. Submit complete ms. Will consider photocopied submissions, but must have exclusive rights to any article. Enclose S.A.S.E.

Nonfiction: "Our editorial content consists of articles dealing with sales techniques, sales psychology and general self-improvement topics that are inspirational in character." Should be tightly written, very specific. "We prefer case history type articles which show our readers how to do the same things that have helped others succeed in the direct selling industry. We are particularly interested in articles about successful women in the direct selling door-to-door field, particularly for our annual women's issue which is published each August." Length: 250 words for column features; maximum of 1,000 words for full-length articles. Pays $20 to $35.

SOLUTION, One Jake Brown Road, Old Bridge NJ 08857. (201)679-4000. Editor: George S. Bahue. For persons involved in television servicing; most own their own stores. Also for trade school graduates. Publication of Blonder-Tongue Labs. Established in 1967. Quarterly. Circulation: 30,000. Buys all rights. Buys about 6 mss per year. Pays on publication. Will send free sample copy to writer on request. Will consider photocopied and simultaneous submissions. Reports in 1 month. Enclose S.A.S.E.

Nonfiction and Photos: General interest articles on TV and signal distribution, MATV systems, and cable television systems. General knowledge of electronics is a must. Author must be able to talk the language. "Will consider short features." Buys informational, new product and technical articles. Length: 750 to 1,500 words. Pays $250 minimum. Photos purchased with accompanying mss with no additional payment.

SPECIALTY SALESMAN AND BUSINESS OPPORTUNITIES, 307 N. Michigan Ave., Chicago IL 60601. (312)726-0743. Editor: Ms. J. Taylor. Magazine; 70 pages. For independent businessmen and women who sell door-to-door, store-to-store, office-to-office and by the party plan method as well as through direct mail and telephone solicitation; selling products and services. Established in 1915. Monthly. Buys all rights. Buys about 120 mss per year. Pays on acceptance. Will send free sample copy to writer on request. Write for editorial guidelines sheet. Will consider photocopied submissions. No simultaneous submissions. Submit seasonal material 3 months in advance. Reports in 1 month. Enclose S.A.S.E.

Nonfiction and Photos: Uses articles offering advice and/or suggestions on how to improve the individual's direct selling business. Mss should discuss a specific subject only. Subject should be applicable to all direct selling specialists. "Examples: 'How to Meet and Beat Competition,' 'The Persuasive Power of Demonstration.' Write in practical, down-to-earth terms emphasizing the positive approach to selling success." Length: 600 to 2,000 words. Pays 3¢ per word; $100 maximum. Photos purchased with accompanying ms with extra payment. Captions optional. B&w glossies only. Pays $5. Size: open.

WALLCOVERINGS MAGAZINE, Publishing Dynamics, Inc., 209 Dunn Ave., Stamford CT 06905. Managing Editor: Joe Conlin. Emphasizes retail merchandising of wallcoverings. Monthly magazine; 60 pages. Estab: 1921. Circ: 9,000. Pays on publication. Buys all rights. SASE. Reports in 2 weeks. Sample copy $1.50; free writer's guidelines.

Nonfiction: Janet Verdeguer, articles editor. Informational (retail merchandising of wall coverings) and interview (with innovative retailers). Buys 2 mss/year. Submit complete ms. Length: 1,000-4,000 words. Pays $20-50/published page.

Photos: Purchased with or without accompanying ms or on assignment. Captions required. Submit 5x7 or 8x10 b&w prints. Total purchase price for ms includes payment for photos. Model release required.

Show People and Amusements

THE BILLBOARD, 9000 Sunset Blvd., Los Angeles CA 90069. Editor-in-Chief and Publisher: Lee Zhito. Managing Editor: Eliot Tiegel. Special Issues Editor: Earl Paige. (All Los Angeles). Record Review Editor: Nat Freedland. Talent Editor: Nat Freedland; Marketing News Editor: John Sippel; Radio/TV Editor: Claude Hall; Country Music Editor: Gerry Wood (Nashville); Classical: I. Horowitz (NY). Weekly. Buys all rights. Payment on publication. Enclose S.A.S.E.
Nonfiction: "Correspondents are appointed to send in spot amusement news covering phonograph record programming by broadcasters and record merchandising by retail dealers. Concert reviews, interviews with artists; stories on discotheques. We are extremely interested in blank tape, and tape playback, and record hardware stores." Length: short. Pays 25¢ to $1 per published inch; $5 per published photo.

G-STRING BEAT, Atlanta Enterprises, Box 2007, Peabody MA 01960. Editor-in-Chief: Rita Atlanta. Emphasizes burlesque and allied fields of entertainment. Quarterly magazine; 48 pages. Estab: 1973. Circ: 12,000. Pays on publication. Buys all rights. SASE. Reports in 2-3 weeks.
Nonfiction: Publishes in-depth, hard-edged profiles of performers. Buys 6-10 mss/year. Submit complete ms. Length: 1,000-2,500 words. Pays $75-150.
Photos: Query first. "We have about 5,000 pix on hand and pix must be exceptional for us to buy."
Fiction: John Bane, Department Editor. Publishes mystery, humorous and suspense fiction. "Very little fiction is accepted because freelance writers have a limited 'feel' (no pun intended) of burlesque. The tensions of the business are rarely understood by outsiders. Would say that this is one of the hardest markets to please." Buys 2-3 a year. Submit complete ms. Length: 2,500-5,000 words. Pays $100-250.

VARIETY, 154 W. 46th St., New York NY 10036. Executive Editor: Syd Silverman. Does not buy freelance material.

Sport Trade

AMERICAN BICYCLIST AND MOTORCYCLIST, 461 Eighth Ave., New York NY 10001. (212)563-3430. Editor: Stan Gottlieb. For bicycle sales and service shops. Established in 1879. Monthly. Circulation: 7,854. Buys all rights. Pays on publication. Query first. Reports within 10 days. Enclose S.A.S.E.
Nonfiction and Photos: Typical story describes (very specifically) unique traffic-builder or merchandising ideas used with success by an actual dealer. Articles may also deal exclusively with moped sales and service operation within conventional bicycle shop. Emphasis is on showing other dealers how they can follow a similar pattern and increase their business. Articles may also be based entirely on repair shop operation, depicting efficient and profitable service systems and methods. Length: 1,800 to 2,800 words. Pays 4¢ a word, plus bonus for excellent manuscript. Relevant b&w photos illustrating principal points in article purchased with ms. 5x7 minimum. No transparencies. Pays $5 per photo.

THE APBA JOURNAL, Box 12502, Research Triangle Park NC 27709. Editor: Tom Heiderschiet. For an extremely varied audience; all with dedicated interest in the APBA/sports games; median age of 28; moderate income. Established in 1967. Monthly. Circulation: 2,000. Rights purchased vary with author and material. May buy all rights, first serial rights, or second serial (reprint) rights. Accepts a limited number of freelance mss. Payment on acceptance. Will send sample copy to writer for 50¢. Will consider photocopied submissions. Will consider cassette submissions; taped interviews. Submit seasonal material 3 months in advance. Reports on material in 2 weeks. Query first. Enclose S.A.S.E.
Nonfiction and Photos: Research/analysis features on APBA sports games, especially baseball. Personality type articles, personal experience, game results, regular columnists, etc. Looking for more articles specifically on research into sports history relevant to the table sports world of APBA games. "Material is accepted all year round, though we stress baseball January through August; golf, football, horse racing, and basketball August through January." Departments seeking material include AJ Focus on personalities, oddities, newsworthy events, etc.; APBA Scene, brief tidbits on personalities, etc. Q/A Forum, questions and answers; Front Page Fea-

ture, in-depth research/analysis. Length for Focus and Front Page Feature: 650 words maximum. Pays 1¢ to 3¢ a word. No payment for APBA Scene or Q/A Forum. Photos are purchased only on assignment and a query is required for photographic assignments.
Fillers: Relevant newsbreaks and clippings. No payment.

ARCHERY RETAILER, Market Communications, Inc., 225 E. Michigan, Milwaukee WI 53202. (414)276-6600. Editor-in-Chief: Glenn Helgeland. Emphasizes archery retailing. Published 5 times a year. Magazine; 54 pages. Estab: 1976. Circ: 9,000. Pays between acceptance and publication. Buys one-time rights. Phone queries OK, "but prefer mail queries." Submit seasonal/holiday material 4 months in advance. SASE. Reports in 3 weeks. Free sample copy and writer's guidelines.
Nonfiction: How-to (better buying, selling, displaying, advertising, etc.); interview, profile. Buys 1-2 mss/issue. Query. Length: 500-2,000 words. Pays $35-125.
Photos: Purchased with or without accompanying ms. Captions required. Pays $10-25 for 8x10 b&w glossies.
Rejects: "Stories about dinky shops selling because they love archery but have no idea of profitability."

BICYCLE DEALER SHOWCASE, 2070 Business Center Dr., Suite 125, Irvine CA 92664. Editor: Steve Ready. For bicycle dealers and distributors. Magazine: 48 pages. Established in 1972. Monthly. Circulation: 9,000. Buys all rights. Buys about 12 mss a year. Pays on publication. Will send free sample copy on request. Write for copy of guidelines for writers. Submit seasonal material 2 months in advance. Reports on material in 3 to 4 weeks. Query first or submit complete ms. Enclose S.A.S.E.
Nonfiction and Photos: Articles dealing with marketing bicycle products; financing, better management techniques, current trends, as related to bicycle equipment or selling. Material must be fairly straightforward, with a slant toward economic factors or marketing techniques. Informational, how-to, interview, profile, humor, successful business operations, merchandising techniques, technical. Length: 1,000 to 1,500 words. Pays $35 to $50. 8x10 b&w glossies purchased with mss. Pays $5 for each published b&w photo.

BICYCLE JOURNAL, 3339 W. Freeway, Fort Worth TX 76101. Publisher: Bill Quinn. Established in 1947. Monthly. Circulation: 7,500. Not copyrighted. Pays on publication. Enclose S.A.S.E. for return of submissions.
Nonfiction and Photos: Wants stories only about dealers who service what they sell. Stories of a single outstanding feature of a bike store, such as a good display, interior or exterior; sales tip; service tip; unusual sign; advertising or promotion tip; store layout, etc. Photo must be vertical. One 8x10 photo is sufficient. Length: 200 to 300 words. Pays $32.50 to $37.50.

THE BOWLING PROPRIETOR, Bowling Proprietors' Association of America. Box 5802, 615 Six Flags Dr., Arlington TX 76011. Editor-in-Chief: Enid G. Barron. Magazine; 11 monthly issues (July/August combined); 72 pages. Estab: 1954. Circ: 4,300. Buys simultaneous rights. Submit seasonal/holiday material 3 months in advance. Simultaneous submissions OK. SASE. Reports in 3 months. Sample copy, $1.
Nonfiction: Publishes how-to articles (how to remodel, conserve energy, manage employees, check cash flow, motivate customers; handle promotions). Profiles (with bowling proprietors who are members of BPAA). Query. Pays $25 minimum.

GOLF BUSINESS (formerly *Golfdom*), Harvest Publishing Co./Div. of Harcourt Brace Jovanovich, 9800 Detroit Ave., Cleveland OH 44102. (216)651-5500. Editor-in-Chief: David J. Slaybaugh. Emphasizes golf and country club industry. For the management personnel at golf courses and country clubs. Monthly magazine; 60 pages. Estab: 1927. Circ: 35,000. Pays on publication. Buys all rights. Phone queries OK. Submit seasonal/holiday material 4 months in advance. SASE. Reports in two months. Free sample copy and writer's guidelines.
Nonfiction: Expose (may focus on industry problem that would uncover information new and beneficial to business); how-to (find something new that a club or course is doing that can be applied to whole industry); informational (new concepts in club management); interview (with industry or governmental individual involved in business); new product (also interested in new services which are in the news; photo feature (if it demonstrates a new technique in course or club operation, new food service or turfgrass operations). Buys 7 mss/year. Query. Length: 1,500-3,000 words. Pays $50-100.
Photos: Used with ms with no additional payment. Query or send contact sheet. B&W glossies, at least 5x7 or color transparencies.

How To Break In: "Calling first is important. If we know what the story idea is, we can guide the writer directly without further hangups due to correspondence. We can find out about the writer quicker. After contact, submission, including photos, is important as soon as possible."
Rejects: "We don't want to see articles that may have originally been speeches, digested into pieces and then, warmed over."
For '78: Budgeting and planning issue (September) — technical articles on how to prepare for a new year. Profile of today's golfer (November) — regional reports on what the golfer/customer thinks of his facility.

GOLF INDUSTRY, Industry Publishers, Inc., 915 N.E. 125th St., Suite 2-C, North Miami FL 33161. (305)893-8771. Editor: Michael J. Keighley. Emphasizes the golf industry for country clubs, pro-owned golf shops, real estate developments, municipal courses, military and schools. Bimonthly magazine; 75 pages. Estab: 1975. Circ: 17,000. Pays on publication. Buys all rights. Submit seasonal/holiday material 2-3 months in advance. SASE. Reports "usually in 6-8 weeks." Free sample copy and writer's guidelines.
Nonfiction: Publishes informational articles "dealing with a specific facet of golf club or pro shop operations, i.e., design, merchandising, finances, etc." Buys 20 mss/year. Submit complete ms. Length: 2,500 words minimum. Pays 5¢/word.
How To Break In: "Since we don't make freelance assignments, a query is not particularly important. We would rather have a complete ms which conforms to our policy of general, but informative, articles about one specific facet of the business of golf merchandising, financing, retailing, etc. Well done mss, if not used immediately, are often held in our files for use in a future issue."
Rejects: "We never publish articles concentrating on one specific manufacturer, or extolling the virtues of one product over another. We seldom feature one club or retail outlet. We don't deal with the game itself, but with the business end of the game."

GOLF SHOP OPERATIONS, 495 Westport Ave., Norwalk CT 06856. (203)847-5811. Editor: James McAfee. For golf professionals at public and private courses, resorts, driving ranges. Magazine; 36 pages. Published 6 times a year. Established in 1963. Circulation: 10,700. Copyrighted. Buys 12 mss a year. Payment on publication. Free sample copy on request. Will consider photocopied submissions. Will not consider simultaneous submissions. Submit seasonal material (for Christmas and other holiday sales) 3 months in advance. Reports in 4 weeks. Query first or submit complete ms. Enclose S.A.S.E.
Nonfiction and Photos: "We emphasize improving the golf professional's knowledge of his profession. Articles should describe how pros are buying, promoting, merchandising and displaying wares in their shops that might be of practical value to fellow professionals. Must be aimed only at the pro audience. We would be interested in seeing material on how certain pros are fighting the discount store competition." How-to, profile, successful business operations, merchandising techniques. Pays $50 to $100. Pays $15 for b&w photos purchased with or without mss. Captions required.

MOTORCYCLE DEALER NEWS, Box 19531, Irvine CA 92713. Editor: John Rossmann. For motorcycle dealers and key personnel of the industry. Monthly. Buys first serial rights. Payment on publication. Will send free sample copy to writer on request. Write for copy of guidelines for writers. Query first. Reports in 4 weeks. Enclose S.A.S.E.
Nonfiction and Photos: "Looking for articles that examine problems of dealers and offer a solution. These dealer articles are not a history of the business, but one unique aspect of the store and its attempt to hurdle an obstacle that may aid other dealers in a similar situation. This is not to be a success story, but rather a fresh look at tackling problems within the industry. Tips for dealers on selling merchandise, creating new displays and improving basic business knowledge are also needed. In-depth articles regarding liability insurance, warranty, land usage, noise pollution and advertising. Usually, in-depth articles about current problems are staff written. However, do not hesitate to query. We do not use articles of a general or unspecific nature. Concrete examples are a must. Photos help sell the article." Length: 750 to 2,500 words. Pays $50 to $100. 8x10 b&w glossy photos purchased with mss or with captions only. Modern stores, dealer awards, etc. Minimum payment for photo not accompanied by ms is $5.

MOTORCYCLE INDUSTRY NEWS, 6226 Vineland Ave., P.O. Box 978, North Hollywood CA 91603. (213)877-1195. Editor: Carol Sims Ashworth. For motorcycle retail dealers, manufacturers and distributors of motorcycles and accessories, and key industry personnel. Monthly. January issue is devoted to motorcycle accessory trade; April issue, chrome accessories; May issue, displays and floor plans; June issue, retail marketing; September issue, motorcycle apparel. Established in 1972. Circulation: 15,000. Buys all rights. Buys 15 to 20 mss a year. Payment on publication. Will send free sample copy to writer on request. Will not consider photocopied or simultaneous submissions. Submit material for special issues 3 months in advance. Reports as soon as possible. Submit complete ms. Enclose S.A.S.E.

Nonfiction and Photos: "Manufacturer, distributor, and dealer profiles; features related to business management, retail marketing and advertising techniques, training, and customer relations. Particularly interested in success stories, seasonal displays, relationship of motorcycles to other industries. Current and complete familiarity with the field is essential, as are good photos. Must be lively, informative and knowledgeable. Should take a positive approach to methods of building a successful retail motorcycle business and be based on in-depth reporting on marketing conditions." Does not want to see dealer profiles that do not have strong themes in retail merchandising. Informational, successful business operations, merchandising techniques, technical. Length: 750 to 1,500 words. Pays 5¢ a word; maximum of $75. No additional payment is made for photos used with mss. Captions required.

NATIONAL BOWLERS JOURNAL AND BILLIARD REVUE, 875 N. Michigan Ave., Chicago IL 60611. (312)266-7171. Editor-in-Chief: Mort Luby. For tournament bowlers and billiard players and a trade audience of proprietors, dealers, distributors. Monthly magazine; 90 pages. Estab: 1913. Circ: 17,000. Pays on publication. Buys all rights, but may reassign following publication. Phone queries OK. Submit seasonal/holiday material 1 month in advance. Simultaneous and photocopied submissions OK. SASE. Reports in 3 weeks.

Nonfiction: Uses illustrated articles about successful bowling and billiard room proprietors who have used unusual promotions to build business, profiles of interesting industry personalities (including bowlers and billiard players), and coverage of major competitive events, both bowling and billiards. "We publish some controversial matter, seek out outspoken personalities. We reject material that is too general; that is, not written for high average bowlers and bowling proprietors who already know basics of playing the game and basics of operating a bowling alley." Length: 1,500 to 2,500 words. Pays $150 to $75.

Photos: B&w (8x10) glossies and color (35mm or 120 or 4x5) transparencies purchased with mss. Captions required. Pays $5-10 for b&w; $15-25 for color.

POOL NEWS, Leisure Publications, 3923 W. 6th St., Los Angeles CA 90020. (213)385-3926. Editor-in-Chief: Fay Coupe. Emphasizes swimming pools for pool builders, pool retail stores, and pool service firms. Monthly magazine; 56 pages. Estab: 1961. Circ: 10,000. Pays on publication. Buys all rights, but may reassign following publication. Phone queries OK. Photocopied submissions OK. SASE. Reports in 2 weeks. Free writer's guidelines.

Nonfiction: Interview, new product, profile, and technical. Length: 500-2,000 words. Pays 5¢/word. Pays $5 per b&w photo used.

RVR, RECREATIONAL VEHICLE RETAILER, 23945 Craftsman Rd., Calabasas CA 91302. (213)888-6000. Editorial Director; Alice Robison. For men and women of the RV industry, primarily those involved in the sale of trailers, motorhomes, pickup campers, to the public. Also, owners and operators of trailer supply stores, plus manufacturers and executives of the RV industry nationwide and in Canada. Magazine; 100 pages, 8¼x11. Established in 1972. Monthly. Circulation: 28,000. Buys all rights. Buys 100 to 150 mss a year. Pays on publication. Will send free sample copy to writer on request. Write for copy of guidelines for writers. Reports on material in 3 weeks. Query first. Enclose S.A.S.E.

Nonfiction and Photos: "Stories that show trends in the industry; success stories of particular dealerships throughout the country; news stories on new products; accessories (news section); how to sell; how to increase profits, be a better businessman. Interested in broadbased, general interest material of use to all RV retailers, rather than mere trade reporting." Informational, how-to, personal experience, interview, profile, humor, think articles, successful business operations, and merchandising techniques. Length: 1,000 to 2,000 words. Pays $50 to $125. Shorter items for regular columns or departments run 800 words. Pays $50 to $75. Photos purchased with accompanying ms with no additional payment. Captions required.

Fillers: Dealer/industry items from over the country; newsbreaks. Length: 100 to 200 words; with photos, if possible. Payment based on length.

SELLING SPORTING GOODS, 717 N. Michigan Ave., Chicago IL 60111. (312)944-0205. Managing Editor: Thomas B. Doyle. For owners and managers of retail sporting goods stores. Established in 1945. Monthly. Circulation: 20,000. Buys all rights. Buys 12 mss/year. Pays on acceptance. Free writer's guidelines. Submit seasonal material 3 months in advance. Enclose S.A.S.E.

Nonfiction and Photos: Articles on "full-line and specialty sporting goods stores. Informational articles, how-to's; articles on retail sporting goods advertising, promotions, in-store clinics/ workshops; employee hiring and training; merchandising techniques. Articles should cover one aspect of store operation in depth." Length: 750 to 1,000 words. Pays 8-10¢/word.. B&w glossy photos purchased with or without accompanying ms. 5x7 minimum. Captions required. Color transparencies acceptable. Pays $100 for cover transparency.

How To Break In: "Practice photography! Most stories, no matter how good, are useless without quality photos. They can be submitted as contact sheets with negatives to hold down writers' cost."

THE SHOOTING INDUSTRY, 8150 N. Central Park Blvd., Skokie IL 60076. (312)675-5602. Editor: J. Rakusan. For manufacturers, dealers, sales representatives of archery and shooting equipment. 12 times a year. Buys all rights. Buys about 135 mss a year. Pays on publication. Will send free sample copy to a writer on request. Query first. Reports in 2 to 3 weeks. Enclose S.A.S.E.

Nonfiction and Photos: Articles that tell "secrets of my success" based on experience of individual gun dealers; articles of advice to help dealers sell more guns and shooting equipment. Also, articles about and of interest to manufacturers and top manufacturers' executives. Length: up to 3,000 words. Pays $50 to $150. Photos essential; b&w glossies. Purchased with ms.

SKI BUSINESS, 380 Madison Ave., New York NY 10017. (212)687-3000. Editor: Seth Masia. Tabloid newspaper; 28 pages. For ski retailers and instructors Established in 1960. Monthly. Circulation: 15,000. Buys about 150 mss per year. Pays on publication. Will send free sample copy to writer on request. Write for guidelines for writers. Will consider photocopied submissions. No simultaneous submissions. Submit seasonal material 3 weeks in advance. Reports on mss accepted for publication in 1 month. Returns rejected material in 1 week. Query first or submit complete ms. Enclose S.A.S.E.

Nonfiction and Photos: Will consider ski shop case studies; mss about unique and succesful merchandising ideas, and ski area equipment rental operations. "All material should be slanted toward usefulness to the ski shop operator. Always interested in interviews with successful retailers." Uses round-ups of pre-season sales and Christmas buying across the country during September to December. Would like to see reports on what retailers in major markets are doing. Length: 800 to 1,500 words. Pays $35 to $75. Photos purchased with accompanying mss. Buys b&w glossy 8x10 photos. Pays $10.

SKI INFO, 20 Hill St., Morristown NJ 07960. (201)267-9088. Editor: Jim Avalanche Smith. For the skiing public. Soft-cover book; 300 (8½x11) pages. Established in 1975. Annually. Circulation: 20,000. Buys all rights, but may reassign rights to author after publication. Buys 5 to 7 mss a year. Pays on publication. Sample copy for $3.50. Will consider photocopied submissions. No simultaneous submissions. Submit seasonal material 6 to 8 months in advance. Reports on material accepted for publication in 4 weeks. Returns rejected material in 3 weeks. Query first or submit complete ms. Enclose S.A.S.E.

Nonfiction and Photos: Technical articles are used in this ski reference book on equipment, and other ski related topics. Helpful hints, etc. Length: 2,000 words minimum. Pays 5¢ a word. B&w photos purchased with mss, or on assignment. Pays $10 minimum.

SKIING TRADE NEWS, One Park Ave., New York NY 10016. Editor: William Grout. For ski shop owners. Annual magazine; 150 pages. Established in 1964. Circulation: about 5,000. Buys first North American serial rights. Buys 14 mss/year. Payment on acceptance. Reports in 30 days. Query first. Enclose S.A.S.E.

Nonfiction: Factual how-to or success articles about buying at the ski trade shows, merchandising ski equipment, keeping control of inventory, etc. Length: 2,000 words. Pays 10¢ a word.

How To Break In: "Find a ski shop that is a success, one that does something (merchandising, etc.) differently and makes money at it. Research the reasons for the shop's success and query."

THE SPORTING GOODS DEALER, 1212 North Lindbergh Blvd., St. Louis MO 63166. (314)997-7111. Editor: C. C. Johnson Spink. For members of the sporting goods trade; retailers, manufacturers, wholesalers, representatives. Monthly magazine. Established in 1899. Circulation: 15,746. Buys second serial (reprint) rights. Buys about 15 mss a year. Payment on publication. Sample copy $1 (refunded with first mss); free writer's guidelines. Will not consider photocopied or simultaneous submissions. Reports in 2 weeks. Query first. Enclose S.A.S.E.

Nonfiction and Photos: Steve Blackhurst, Managing Editor. "Articles about specific sporting goods retail stores, their promotions, display techniques, sales ideas, merchandising, timely news of key personnel; expansions, new stores, deaths—all in the sporting goods trade. Specific details on how specific successful sporting goods stores operate. What specific retail sporting goods stores are doing that is new and different. We would also be interested in features dealing with stores doing an outstanding job in retailing of baseball, fishing, golf, tennis, camping, firearms/hunting and allied lines of equipment. Query first on these." Successful business operations, merchandising techniques. Does not want to see announcements of weddings and engagements. Length: open. Pays $2 per 100 published words. Also looking for material for the following columns: Terse Tales of the Trade (store news); Selling Slants (store promotions); Open for Business (new retail sporting goods stores or sporting goods departments). All material must relate to specific sporting goods stores by name, city, and state; general information is not accepted. Pays minimum of $3.50 for sharp and clear b&w photos; size not important. These are purchased with or without mss. Captions optional, but identification requested.
Fillers: Clippings. These must relate directly to the sporting goods industry. Pays 1¢ to 2¢ per published word.

SPORTING GOODS TRADE, Page Publications, Ltd., 380 Wellington St., W., Toronto, Ontario, Canada M5V 1E3. (416)366-4608. Editor: John Burry. For sporting goods retailers, manufacturers, wholesalers, jobbers, department and chain stores, camping equipment dealers, bicycle sales and service, etc. Magazine; 50 to 100 pages. Established in 1972. Every 2 months. Circulation: 9,000. Pays on publication. Will send sample copy to writer on request. Reports in 2 months. Query first. Enclose S.A.E. and International Reply Coupons.
Nonfiction: Technical and informational articles. Articles on successful business operations, new products, merchandising techniques; interviews. Length: open. Pays 4¢ a word or $25 per published page.

SPORTS MERCHANDISER, W.R.C. Smith Publishing Co., 1760 Peachtree Rd., N.W., Atlanta GA 30357. (404)874-4462. Editor: Ralph E. Kirby. "For retailers of sporting goods in all categories: independent stores, chains, specialty stores, department store departments; wholesalers, manufacturers, sales personnel in all categories." Monthly tabloid; 85 pages. Estab: 1969. Circ: 24,000. Pays on acceptance. Buys all rights. Phone queries OK. Submit seasonal/holiday material 3-4 months in advance. SASE. Reports in 2-3 weeks. Free sample copy and writer's guidelines.
Nonfiction: Informational (how a store is successful in selling a line of merchandise), and photo feature (on a new, modern store, carefully captioned). Buys 5 mss/issue. Query or submit complete ms. Length: 500-1,000 words. Pays $60-200.
Photos: Purchased with accompanying ms. Captions required. Send contact sheet. Pays $10-20 for 8x10 b&w glossies; $10-25 for 2⅛x2⅛ color transparencies. Total purchase price for ms includes payment for photos. Model release is "helpful but not required."

SWIMMING POOL WEEKLY/AGE, Hoffman Publications, Inc., Box 11299, Fort Lauderdale FL 33339. (305)566-8401. Managing Editor: Dave Kaiser. Emphasizes pool industry. Bimonthly tabloid; 36 pages. Estab: 1928. Circ: 16,000. Pays on acceptance. Buys all rights for industry. Phone queries OK. Submit seasonal/holiday material 1 month in advance. SASE. Reports in 2 weeks. Writer's guidelines for SASE.
Nonfiction: Expose (if in industry, company frauds), how-to (stories on installation techniques done with an expert in a given field); interview (with important poeple within the industry); photo feature (pool construction or special pool use); technical (should be prepared with expert within the industry). Buys 50-80 mss/year. Query. Length: 1,000 words maximum. Pays $35-50.
Photos: Purchased with or without accompanying ms or on assignment. Captions required. Query or send contact sheet. Pays $5-20 for any size larger than 5x7 b&w photo; $15-25 for any size above 35mm color transparencies.
Columns/Departments: "Short news on personality items always welcome at about $10-15 for 25-100 words."

TENNIS INDUSTRY, Industry Publishers, Inc., 915 N.E. 125th St., Suite 2-C, North Miami, FL 33161. (305)893-8771. Editor: Michael J. Keighley. Emphasizes the tennis industry for teaching pros, pro shop managers, specialty shop managers, country club managers, coaches, athletic directors, etc. Monthly magazine; 200 pages. Estab: 1972. Circ: 18,000. Pays on publication. Buys all rights. Submit seasonal or holiday material 2-3 months in advance. Previously published submissions OK. SASE. Reports "usually in 6-8 weeks." Free sample copy and writer's guidelines.

Nonfiction: Publishes informational articles dealing "with specific facets of the tennis club or pro shop operation, i.e., design, merchandising, finances, etc." Buys 20 mss a year. Submit complete ms. Length: 2,500 words maximum. Pays 5¢/word.

How To Break In: "Since we do not make freelance assignments, a query is not particularly important. We would rather have a complete ms which conforms to our policy of general, but informative articles about one specific facet of the business of tennis merchandising, financing, retailing, etc. Well done ms, if not used immediately, are often held in our files for use in a future issue."

Rejects: "We never publish articles concentrating on one specific manufacturer, or extolling the virtues of one product over another. We seldom feature one club or retail outlet. We don't deal with the game itself, but with the business end of the game."

TENNIS TRADE, 370 Seventh Ave., New York NY 10001. Managing Editor: Marilyn Nason. For the tennis industry, club owners, park recreation leaders. Magazine; 40 pages minimum. Established in 1971. Monthly. Circulation: 28,000. Rights purchased vary with author and material. Usually buys all rights. Buys about 20 mss a year. Pays on publication. Will send sample copy to writer for $1.25. Reports on material accepted for publication in 6 to 8 weeks. Query first, briefly stating credentials. Enclose S.A.S.E.

Nonfiction: How-to articles related to the tennis industry. Length: open. Pays $2 per published page minimum.

Stone and Quarry Products

ASBESTOS, 131 North York Road (P.O. Box 471), Willow Grove PA 19090. Editor: Mrs. Doris M. Fagan. For the vertical asbestos industry. Monthly. Copyrighted. Pays on publication. Will send free sample copy to a writer on request. Query first. Enclose S.A.S.E.

Nonfiction: "Interested only in items concerning some phase of the international asbestos industry, i.e., new asbestos mines and mills, progress reports on asbestos mines and mills, new or improved techniques in processing asbestos fiber and the manufacture of asbestos-based products, personnel changes and expansions within asbestos firms, asbestos vs. industrial and public health (including techniques to control the emanation of asbestos dust), findings from research into new uses for asbestos (including utilization of the fiber as a reinforcement to improve the effectiveness of plastics, synthetics, and composite materials), improvements in already existing asbestos-based products, etc. We are not interested in news of the asbestos workers union or in advertisements. We make little use of photographs or other graphics." Length: 500 to 3,000 words. Pays 1¢ to 1½¢ per word "as the article appears in the journal."

Fillers: Newsbreaks and clippings related to asbestos industry. Length: maximum 500 words. Pays 1¢ a word, "as published in *Asbestos*".

CONCRETE, Cement and Concrete Association, 52 Grosvenor Gardens, London SW1W OAQ. (01)235-6661. Editor-in-Chief: R.J. Barfoot. Emphasizes civil engineering and building and construction. Monthly magazine; 60 pages. Estab: 1969. Circ: 13,000. Pays on publication. Phone queries OK. Submit seasonal/holiday material 6 weeks in advance. Photocopied submissions OK. Free sample copy and writer's guidelines.

Nonfiction: Historical, new product, and technical articles dealing with concrete and allied industries. Buys 12 mss/year. Query or submit complete ms. Length: 1,000-3,000 words. Pays $10-30.

CONCRETE CONSTRUCTION MAGAZINE, 329 Interstate Rd., Addison IL 60101. Editor: William C. Panarese. For general and concrete contractors, architects, engineers, concrete producers, cement manufacturers, distributors and dealers in construction equipment, testing labs. Monthly magazine; 52 pages. Established in 1956. Circulation: 60,000. Buys all rights. Buys 50 mss/year. Payment on acceptance. Will send free sample copy to writer on request. Write for copy of guidelines for writers. Will consider photocopied and simultaneous submissions. Reports on material accepted for publication in an indefinite time. Returns rejected material in 1 to 2 months. Submit complete ms. Enclose S.A.S.E.

Nonfiction and Photos: "Our magazine has one topic to discuss: cast-in-place (site cast) concrete. Our articles deal with tools, techniques and materials which result in better handling, better placing, and ultimately an improved final product. We are particularly firm about not using proprietary names in any of our articles. Manufacturers and products are never mentioned; only the processes or techniques that might be of help to the concrete contractor, the architect or the engineer dealing with the material. We do use 'bingo cards' which accomplish the purpose of relaying reader interest to manufacturers, but without cluttering up the articles themselves with a lot of name dropping." Does not want to see job stories or promotional material. Length: 300 to 3,500 words. Pays 7¢ per published word. Pays $10 for b&w glossy photos and color used with mss. Photos are used only as part of a completed ms.

MINE AND QUARRY, Ashire Publishing Ltd., 42 Gray's Inn Rd., London WC1X 8LR, England. Editor-in-Chief: Cyril G. Middup. For senior management at mines and quarries. Monthly magazine; 80 pages. Estab: 1924. Circ: 4,600. Buys all rights, but may reassign following publication. Phone queries OK. Submit seasonal/holiday material 2 months in advance. Simultaneous, photocopied, and previously published submissions OK. SAE and International Reply Coupons. Reports in 2 months. Free sample copy and writer's guidelines.
Nonfiction: Technical and new product articles related to the industry. Buys 144 mss/year. Submit complete ms. Length: 200-1,000 words. Pays $10-20.
Photos: B&w glossies and color transparencies purchased with or without mss. Captions required. Send contact sheet, prints, or transparencies. Pays $3-6.

MONUMENTAL NEWS REVIEW, American Monument Association, 6902 N. High St., Worthington OH 43085. (614)885-2713. Editor-in-Chief: William A. Kistner. Emphasizes the granite and marble memorial industry for quarriers and manufacturers of memorial stone products in the U.S. and Canada; retail memorial dealers, cemetarians and funeral directors. Monthly magazine; 40 pages. Estab: 1889. Circ: 2,375. Pays on publication. Buys all rights, but may reassign following publication. Phone queries OK. Submit seasonal or holiday material 2 months in advance. Simultaneous and photocopied submissions and previously published work OK. SASE. Reports in 2 weeks. Free sample copy and writer's guidelines, but adequate postage must accompany request.
Nonfiction: How-to (setting memorials, carving memorials, selling, managing); historical, informational, inspirational, new product, nostalgia, photo features, profiles; anything of interest to the industry. Technical articles on abrasive technology, diamond technology; tool/machine and product technology. Buys 15 mss/year. Length: 300-5,000 words. Query first or submit complete ms. Pays 2¢/word.
Photos: Uses b&w glossies (5x7) with or without mss. Send contact sheet or prints. Captions required. No additional payment for those used with mss. Model release required.
Columns, Departments: Buys 50- to 500-word items for Tool Chest, Films (Business/Technical), Commerative Art, Marketing — Sales Techniques, Small Business Management, Stone (Granite & Marble). Buys 15/year. Query first or submit complete ms. Pays 2¢/word. Open to suggestions for new columns/departments.
Fiction: Adventure, experimental, historical, humorous, mystery, religious, suspense; appropriate to the industry. Length: 1,000-5,000 words. Pays 2¢/word.
Poetry: Published avant-garde forms, haiku, free verse and light verse; epitaphs. Buys 10/year. Limit submissions to batches of 20. Length: 5-65 lines. Pays $5-50.

ROCK PRODUCTS, 300 W. Adams St., Chicago IL 60606. (312)726-2802. Editor: Roy A. Grancher. For nonmetallic minerals mining producers. Monthly. Buys all rights. Pays on publication. Query first. Reports within 4 weeks. Enclose S.A.S.E.
Nonfiction and Photos: "Covers the construction minerals segment of the non-metallic (industrial) minerals industry. Uses articles on quarrying, mining, and processing of portland cement, lime, gypsum, sand and gravel, crushed stone, slag, and expanded clay and shale. Other non-metallic metals covered include dimension stone, asbestos, diatomite, expanded fly ash, vermiculite, perlite. Equipment and its applications are emphasized in the operating and technical coverage. Feature articles describe complete plant operations, design and planning, company profiles, marketing, and management techniques." Length: open. $35 per published page.
How To Break In: "Articles for *Rock Products* are prepared by specialists or authorities in their particular field. For the beginning writer, an engineering or technical background is a major prerequisite. For 'professional' freelancers, I suggest what the pro already knows: 'Study the book.'"

Textile

AMERICA'S TEXTILE REPORTER/BULLETIN, P.O. Box 88, Greenville SC 29602. Editor: Prentice Thomas. For "officials and operating executives of manufacturing corporations and plants in the basic textile yarn and fabric industry." Established in 1878. Monthly. Circulation: 22,000. Not copyrighted. Buys "very few" mss a year. Pays on publication. Will send a sample copy to a writer for $1. Write for copy of guidelines for writers "only if background is suitable." Query first. "It is extremely difficult for non-textile industry freelancers to write for us." Enclose S.A.S.E.

Nonfiction: "Technical and business articles about the textile industry." Length: open. Pays $25 to $50 per printed page.

TEXTILE WORLD, 1175 Peachtree St., N.E., Atlanta GA 30361. Editor-in-Chief: Laurence A. Christiansen. Monthly. Buys all rights. Pays on acceptance. Enclose S.A.S.E.

Nonfiction and Photos: Uses articles covering textile management methods, manufacturing and marketing techniques, new equipment, details about new and modernized mills, etc., but avoids elementary, historical, or generally well-known material. Pays $25 minimum per page. Photos purchased with accompanying ms with no additional payment, or purchased on assignment.

Toy, Novelty, and Hobby

MODEL RETAILER, Clifton House, Clifton VA 22024. (703)830-1000. Editor-in-Chief: David Ritchey. For owners and managers of retail hobby stores stocking models and model supplies. Magazine: 100 (8¼x10⅞) pages. Established in 1975. Monthly. Circulation: 5,400. Rights purchased vary with author and material. Buys 70 mss a year. Pays on publication. Sample copy $1. Photocopied submissions OK. Reports on material accepted for publication and returns rejected material as soon as possible. Query first or submit complete ms. Enclose S.A.S.E.

Nonfiction and Photos: "Business articles of a general nature, of interest to small retailers. Hobby shop interviews, merchandising techniques. Information specifically relating to the hobby industry." Doesn't want to see articles concerning business insurance. Length: 1,000 to 3,000 words. Pays 4¢ a word. Photos purchased with ms. Captions optional. Pays $5 for b&w. No color.

How To Break In: "Write an article which will help a small retailer make more money."

PROFITABLE CRAFT MERCHANDISING, News Plaza, Peoria IL 61601. (309)682-6626. Editor: Ellen M. Dahlquist. For craft retailers. Monthly magazine; 112 pages. Circulation: 17,500. Buys all rights. Buys 40 to 50 mss a year. Payment on acceptance. Will send free sample copy to writer on request. Write for copy of guidelines for writers. Will not accept photocopied submissions. Will consider simultaneous submissions only if not submitted to a competitive publication. Submit seasonal material for Christmas merchandising issue, which is published in August, 6-8 months in advance. Reports in 6 to 8 weeks. Query first. Enclose S.A.S.E.

Nonfiction and Photos: Articles on store management techniques. Craft retailer success stories. Coverage of news events such as trade shows and conventions and better consumer shows that have heavy retailer participation. Store management oriented articles. Does not want to see interviews of craft retailers. "Keep in mind that the primary purpose of *Profitable Craft Merchandising* is to tell the retailer how to make money." Informational, how-to, personal experience, spot news, new product, successful business operations, and merchandising techniques. Length: 1,000 to 2,500 words. Pays $45 to $250. 4 to 10 good quality 8x10 or 5x7 b&w glossy photos are usually used with mss. No additional payment. Captions required. Color photos are not used unless especially requested.

SOUVENIRS AND NOVELTIES, 327 Wagaraw Rd., Hawthorne NJ 07506. (201)423-2266. Editor: Martin Dowd. For "owners and managers of tourist attractions and souvenir shops who buy and sell souvenirs and novelties at resorts, parks, museums, airports, etc." Special issues include parks, museums, attractions (April), tourist travel terminals shops (June), free attractions (December). Established in 1962. Bimonthly. Circulation: 6,143. Buys first North American serial rights. Buys about 15 mss/year. Pays on acceptance when copy and photos are to be published. Free sample copy and writer's guidelines. Query first or submit complete ms. Will consider photocopied submissions. Submit seasonal material 3 months in advance of issue date, "if possible." Reports in 2 weeks. Enclose S.A.S.E.

Nonfiction and Photos: "Articles about how to buy and sell souvenirs and novelties. How to manage a souvenir or novelty shop. How to handle inventory, pilferage, prices, etc. The writer should interview managers and owners and report on what they say about how to sell and buy souvenirs and novelties. How to display merchandise, how to train employees, etc. We specialize in a narrow field of merchandising for tourists, generally. I am not really interested in travel articles." Buys informational articles, how-to's, interviews, and coverage of successful business operations. Length: 500 to 1,500 words. Pays minimum $1 per column inch. Photos purchased with ms; captions required. For 8x10 or 5x7 b&w glossies, pays $5 "for amateur photos" and $10 "for professional photos. Will pay for photos even if supplied by the park or attraction or museum, as long as we use them and the writer obtains them."

Fillers: Clippings. "Must be about souvenir or novelty business, or don't bother to send them, please. We pay 80¢ a published inch if we use the clipping."

THE STAMP WHOLESALER, P.O. Box 529, Burlington VT 05402. Editor: Lucius Jackson. For small-time independent businessmen; many are part-time and/or retired from other work. Published 21 times a year; 68 (8½x11) pages. Established in 1936. Circulation: 9,300. Buys all rights. Buys 40 mss a year. Payment on acceptance. Will send free sample copy to writer on request. Will not consider photocopied or simultaneous submissions. Reports on material accepted for publication in 1 day to 1 year. Returns rejected material when decision is reached. Submit complete ms. Enclose S.A.S.E.

Nonfiction: How-to information on how to deal more profitably in postage stamps for collections. Emphasis on merchandising techniques and how to make money. Does not want to see any so-called "humor" items from nonprofessionals. Length: 1,500 to 2,000 words. Pays 3¢ per word minimum.

TOY & HOBBY WORLD, 124 E. 40th St., New York NY 10016. For everyone in the toy and hobby and craft industry from manufacturer to retailer. Magazine. Monthly. Established in 1961. Circulation: 16,500. Not copyrighted. Buys 5 mss a year. Payment on publication. Will send sample copy to writer for 50¢. Will consider photocopied submissions. Will not consider simultaneous submissions. Returns rejected material when requested. Query first. Enclose S.A.S.E.

Nonfiction and Photos: Merchandising and news. Informational, how-to, new product. Technical articles for manufacturers; features about wholesalers, retailers, chains, department stores, discount houses, etc., concerned with their toy operations. Prefers stories on toy wholesalers or retailers who have unusual success with unusual methods. Also interested in especially successful toy departments in drug stores, supermarkets, hardware stores, gas stations, etc. No interest in mere histories of run-of-the-mill operators. Use a news style. Length: 1,000 to 3,000 words. Payment commensurate with quality of material. Buys 8x10 b&w photos with mss and with captions only. Must be glossy on singleweight paper. No color. Pays $6 plus word rate. Prefers captions.

TOYS & GAMES, Page Publications, Ltd., 380 Wellington St., W., Toronto, Ontario, Canada M5V 1E3. (416)366-4608. Editor: Henry Wittenberg. For toy retailers, wholesalers and jobbers; owners of department stores, variety stores, hobby and handicraft stores, drug stores; arts and crafts suppliers. Magazine; 50 to 100 pages. Established in 1972. Every 2 months. Circulation: 6,500. Pays on publication. Will send sample copy to writer on request. Reports in 2 months. Query first. Enclose S.A.E. and International Reply Coupons.

Nonfiction: Interviews and profiles. Informational and technical articles. Articles on successful business operations, new products, merchandising techniques. Length: open. Pays 4¢ a word or $25 per published page.

Trailers, Mobile Homes

MOBILE HOME MERCHANDISER, RLD Group, Inc., 2602 Grosse Point Rd., Evanston IL 60201. Editor-in-Chief: Jim Mack. Emphasizes the mobile/modular housing industry for retailers of manufactured housing, and suppliers to manufactured homes, as well as park operators. Monthly magazine; 60-70 pages. Estab: 1952. Circ: 20,000. Pays on publication. Buys one-time rights. Submit seasonal/holiday material 6 months in advance. Photocopied submissions OK. SASE. Sample copy $2. Free writer's guidelines.

Nonfiction: How-to and informational articles (examination of a mobile home retailer's operation—how he does something better than others); interviews. Buys 6 mss/year. Length: 750-2,500 words. Query first. Pays $35/printed page.

Photos: B&w glossies (5x7) accepted only with mss. Captions required. Send prints. No additional payment.

MOBILE-MODULAR HOUSING DEALER MAGAZINE, 6229 Northwest Highway, Chicago IL 60631. (312)774-2525. Editor: James Kennedy. For dealers, manufacturers and suppliers concerned with the industry. Monthly magazine; 130 (8¼x11¼) pages. Established in 1949. Circulation: 15,200. Buys all rights, but will reassign rights to author after publication. Payment on publication. Will send free sample copy to writer on request. Write for copy of guidelines for writers. Reports as soon as possible. Query first. Enclose S.A.S.E.

Nonfiction and Photos: "Dealer success stories; in-depth techniques in dealership operations; service articles; financing, features; dealer/manufacturer relationships. Every article should be dealer oriented, pointed to the dealer for the benefit of the dealer. Focus on some one or two aspects of the dealer operation largely responsible for the company's success. A general overall description of the dealership is necessary for a well-rounded story, but an important aspect of the firm's operation should be developed, such as merchandising the product, unique inventory control; before and after sales service; financing procedures; salesmen programs, accessories and parts success." Also uses warrantee features, material on manufacturers and dealer franchise agreements; consumerism and service articles. Length: 500 to 2,000 words. Pays $2 per column inch (13 picas wide). 7x10 b&w glossy photos purchased with mss or on assignment. Pays $7. Captions required.

TRAILER/BODY BUILDERS, 1602 Harold St., Houston TX 77006. (713)523-8124. Editor: Paul Schenck. For the manufacturers and builders of truck trailers, truck bodies, truck tanks, vans, cargo containers, plus the truck equipment distributors. Monthly. Not copyrighted. Pays on publication. Will send free sample copy to a writer on request. Reports in 30 days. Enclose S.A.S.E.

Nonfiction: "Material on manufacturers of truck trailers, and truck bodies, school bus bodies, also their sales distributors. These also go under the names of semitrailer manufacturing, custom body builders, trailer sales branch, or truck equipment distributor. No travel trailers, house trailers, mobile homes, or tire companies, transmission people or other suppliers, unless it directly affects truck body or truck trailer. Need shop hints and how-to features. Many stories describe how a certain special truck body or truck trailer is built." Length: 900 to 1,000 words. Pays $2 per inch or $50 per page.

Photos: Buys photos appropriate to format. Study publication. Pays $10.

Fillers: "New products and newspaper clippings appropriate to format. Do not rewrite clippings." Pays $2 per inch or better on news items.

Transportation

These journals aim at traffic managers and transportation experts (who route goods across the continent). Publications for automobile and truck dealers, repairmen, or fleet operators are classified in the Auto and Truck category. Journals for highway planners and traffic control experts are in the Government and Public Service listings.

DEFENSE TRANSPORTATION JOURNAL, 1612 K St., N.W., Washington DC 20006. Publisher and Editor: Gerald W. Collins. For "transportation executives and managers of all ages and military transportation officers. Generally educated with college degree." Established in 1945. Bimonthly. Circulation: 13,000. Rights purchased vary with author and material; may buy all rights, but may reassign rights to author after publication. Buys 5 to 10 mss a year. Pays on acceptance. Will send a sample copy to a writer on request. Write for copy of guidelines for writers. Submit seasonal material 2 to 3 months in advance. Reports in 2 to 3 weeks. Enclose S.A.S.E.

Nonfiction: "Articles on transportation, distribution, and traffic management in the U.S. and abroad. This publication emphasizes transportation as it relates to defense and emergency requirements." Buys informational and personal experience articles. Length: 2,500 words. Pays $100.

How To Break In: "Study the magazine very carefully, perhaps even discuss the editorial goals with the editor, and then come up with creative ideas or a new approach to an old idea, that would be valuable to the magazine. Whether it be a new column, a research article or new ideas along other lines, I believe a fresh, imaginative view is the most helpful to an editor."

TRAFFIC MANAGER MAGAZINE, 206 Graphic Arts Bldg., 108 N.W. 9th, Portland OR 97209. (503)222-9794. Editor: C.R. Hillyer. For professionals in the freight transportation industry in the Pacific Northwest; shipper and carrier firms. Magazine; 32 pages. Special issue: National Transportation Week issue annually in May. Established in 1925. Every 2 months. Circulation: 3,500. Not copyrighted. Buys no more than 6 mss a year. Pays on publication. Will send sample copy to writer on request. Will consider photocopied and simultaneous submissions. Submit special issue material 2 months in advance. Reports in 2 weeks. Query first or submit complete ms. Enclose S.A.S.E.

Nonfiction and Photos: Industry news, semi-technical features about traffic management, materials handling, carrier services. Regionally oriented, personal coverage of management individuals and specific firms. Profiles of firms or executives; personal opinion articles on transportation regulation topics, or related. Length: 300 to 700 words. Pays $10 to $25. Technical articles. Length: 200 to 500 words. Pays $10 to $20. Pays $5 for each b&w glossy (5x7 or larger) used with mss. Captions required.

Travel

ASTA TRAVEL NEWS, 488 Madison Ave., New York NY 10022. (212)826-9461. Editor: Coleman Lollar. For international audience of travel agents (all members of American Society of Travel Agents), tour operators, airline executives, national tourist office directors. Magazine: 100 (8½x11) pages. Established in 1931. Monthly. Circulation: 17,500. Buys all rights. Buys about 24 mss a year. Pays on acceptance. Free sample copy. Reports in 1 month. Query first, with writing samples and detailed description of proposed article. Enclose S.A.S.E.

Nonfiction and Photos: "Feature articles on trends in tourism. These range from investigative reporting on government or industry decision to 'color' features on foreign destinations. Most destination stories are on assignment. We have a particular need for profiles of agencies or individuals who have developed unusual, successful approaches for marketing travel. A new writer's best bet with us is with short features on travel marketing. Knowledge of IATA fares and industry practices would be helpful. Small business how-to pieces, geared to travel agents; articles on air fares, regional promotional organizations, travel industry personalities. All submissions *must* be organized and written expressly for the information needs of the travel agent and his associates in the industry — not the traveling public." Informational and how-to articles. Length: 500 to 3,000 words. Pays $75 to $150. Profiles of 500 to 2,000 words. Pays $75 to $150. Articles on successful business operations. Length: 600 to 1,500 words. Pays $75 to $150. No additional payment is usually made for b&w (5x7 or 8x10) photos or 35mm (or larger) color transparencies used with mss. Additional payment would depend on quality and capability.

PACIFIC TRAVEL NEWS, 274 Brannan St., San Francisco CA 94107. (415)397-0070. Editor: Frederic M. Rea. For travel trade—travel agencies, transportation companies. Monthly. Buys one-time rights for travel trade publications. Pays on publication unless material is for future use; then on acceptance. Will send sample copy on request. All material purchased on assignment following specific outline. Query about assignment. "Do not send unsolicited mss or transparencies." Reports in 1 to 3 weeks. Enclose S.A.S.E.

Nonfiction: Writer must be based in a country in coverage area of the Pacific from Hawaii west to India, south to Australia and New Zealand. "We are not interested in how-to articles, such as how to sell, decorate your windows, keep your staff happy, cut costs." Pays $200 maximum.

Photos: Purchased with mss or captions only. Related to travel attractions, activities within Pacific area. Sometimes general travel-type photos, other times specific photos related to hotels, tours, tour equipment, etc. Buys mainly b&w glossy, 5x7 or larger. Also buys about 18 color transparencies a year, 35mm top quality. Pays up to $10 for b&w; up to $50 for inside color; $75 for color used on cover.

THE STAR SERVICE, Sloane Agency Travel Reports, Box 15610, Ft. Lauderdale FL 33318. (305)472-8794. Editor: Robert D. Sloane. Editorial manual sold to travel agencies on subscription basis. Buys all rights. Buys about 2,000 reports a year. Pays on publication. Write for instruction sheet and sample report form. Initial reports sent by a new correspondent will be examined for competence and criticized as necessary upon receipt, but once established, a correspondent's submissions will not usually be acknowledged until payment is forwarded, which can often be several months, depending on immediate editorial needs. Query first. Enclose S.A.S.E.

Nonfiction: "Objective, critical evaluations of worldwide hotels and cruise ships suitable for North Americans, based on inspections. Forms can be provided to correspondents so no special writing style is required, only perceptiveness, experience, and judgment in travel. No commercial gimmick—no advertising or payment for listings in publication is accepted." With query, writer should "outline experience in travel and specific forthcoming travel plans, time available for inspections. Leading travel agents throughout the world subscribe to Star Service. No credit or byline is given correspondents due to delicate subject matter often involving negative criticism of hotels. We would like to emphasize the importance of reports being based on current experience and the importance of reporting on a substantial volume of hotels, not just isolated stops (since staying in hotel is not a requisite) in order that work be profitable for both publisher and writer. Experience in travel writing is desirable." Length: "up to 350 words, if submitted in paragraph form; varies if submitted on printed inspection form." Pays $5 per report used. "Guarantees of acceptance of set numbers of reports may be made on establishment of correspondent's ability and reliability (up to about $400, usually), but always on prior arrangement. Higher rates of payment sometimes arranged, after correspondent's reliability is established."

TRAVELAGE WEST, The Reuben H. Donneley Corp., 582 Market St., San Francisco CA 94104. Managing Editor: Donald C. Langley. For travel agency sales counselors in the western U.S. and Canada. Weekly magazine; 60 pages. Estab: 1969. Circ: 13,500. Pays on publication. Buys all rights. Submit seasonal/holiday material 2 months in advance. SASE. Reports in 4 weeks. Free writer's guidelines.
Nonfiction: Travel. Buys 15 mss/year. Query. Length: 1,000 words maximum. Pays $1.50/ column inch. "No promotional tones of voice or any hint of do-it-yourself travel."

THE TRAVEL AGENT, 2 W. 46th St., New York NY 10036. Editor: Eric Friedheim. For "travel agencies and travel industry executives." Established in 1929. Semiweekly. Circulation: 22,000. Not copyrighted. Pays on acceptance. Query first. Reports "immediately." Enclose S.A.S.E.
Nonfiction and Photos: Uses trade features slanted to travel agents, sales and marketing people, and executives of transportation companies such as airlines, ship lines, etc. No travelogues such as those appearing in newspapers and consumer publications. Articles should show how agent and carriers can sell more travel to the public. Length: up to 2,000 words. Pays $50 to $100. Photos purchased with ms.

TRAVELSCENE MAGAZINE, 888 Seventh Ave., New York NY 10019. Managing Editor: Hank Herman. For three diverse audiences: airline reservationists, travel agents, and corporate travel planners. Magazine; 60 (8½x11) pages. Established in 1965. Monthly. Circulation: 97,000. Buys all rights. Buys 30 to 40 mss a year. Payment on acceptance. Will send free sample copy to writer on request. No photocopied or simultaneous submissions. Submit special issue material 5 months in advance. Reports in 2 to 6 weeks. Query first. Enclose S.A.S.E.
Nonfiction and Photos: "*TravelScene* is the largest circulation magazine in the travel industry and runs articles on important trade issues, destinations, personalities, how-to's and other topics designed to help professional travel planners do a better job and gain a better perspective on their profession." Recently published articles have dealt with the politician/travel agent, women's roles in the airlines, and how tipping can run up the cost of a business meeting. B&w and color photos purchased with or without ms, or on assignment. Pays $10 to $15.
How To Break In: "Writer should submit past samples of work, an outline of proposal(s), and include S.A.S.E. and phone number. Getting a first assignment may not be too difficult, if the writer can write. We are looking for and need good writers. If stories are submitted, they must be an average of 8 to 12 pages, double spaced; 13 to 15 maximum. Please do not send queries for destination pieces unless you have a specific angle. We have never given an assignment to someone who merely writes, 'I'm going to London. Can I give you something on it?' Also, we rarely buy destination pieces since we can get those articles in exchange for the trips we offer."

Veterinary

CANINE PRACTICE JOURNAL, FELINE PRACTICE JOURNAL, Veterinary Practice Publishing Co., P.O. Box 4506, Santa Barbara CA 93103. (805)965-1028. Editor: Dr. Anna P. Clarke. For graduate veterinarians working primarily in small animal practice, or in mixed practices (large and small) which do a substantial volume of dog and cat practice. Published every two months; magazines, 60 pages, 7x10. *Feline Practice Journal* established in 1971. Circulation: 6,800. *Canine Practice Journal* established in 1974. Circulation: 5,230. Rights purchased vary with author and material. Buys all rights, but will reassign rights to author after publication. Buys second serial (reprint) rights. "Strictly technical medical and surgical content written so far exclusively by graduate veterinarians." Payment on publication. Will send free sample copy to writer on request, if an apparently legitimate author in this field. Write for copy of editorial guidelines for writers. Will consider photocopied submissons. Query first. Reports within 4 weeks. Enclose S.A.S.E.

Nonfiction and Photos: "Strictly technical medical and surgical articles for veterinarians, by veterinarians. One of our magazines deals exclusively with feline (cat) medicine and surgery; the other, with canine (dog) medicine and surgery. Writer would first have to be a veterinarian, or a scientist in one of the life sciences fields (for example, biology, nutrition, zoology). We send an author's guide on request. Our journals are specifically vertical magazines in a field heretofore served by horizontal magazines. That is, we publish single-species journals, the others publish multi-species journals." Length: 300 to 5,000 words. Pays $10 per published page. 4x5 to 8x10 b&w matte or glossy. 35mm or 4x5 color transparencies or negatives.

How To Break In: "We welcome long or short articles from veterinarians in clinical work so long as these are practice-oriented and not research-oriented. The content (diagnosis and treatment) is much more important than style, syntax or grammar."

MODERN VETERINARY PRACTICE, American Veterinary Publications, Inc., Drawer KK, 300 E. Canon Perdido, Santa Barbara CA 93102. For graduate veterinarians. Monthly magazine; 90 pages. Estab: 1920. Circ: 15,400. Pays on publication. Buys all rights, but may reassign following publication. Phone queries OK. Submit seasonal/holiday material 3 months in advance. SASE. Reports in 4 weeks. Sample copy $1.50.

Nonfiction: How-to articles (clinical medicine, new surgical procedures, business management); informational (business management, education, government projects affecting practicing veterinarians, special veterinary projects); interviews (only on subjects of interest to veterinarians; query first); technical articles (clinical reports, technical advancements in veterinary medicine and surgery). Buys 25-30 mss/year. Submit complete ms, but query first on ideas for pieces other than technical or business articles. Pays $15/page.

Photos: B&w glossies (5x7 or larger) and color transparencies (5x7) used with mss. No additional payment.

How To Break In: "Contact practicing veterinarians or veterinary colleges. Find out what interests the clinician, and what new procedures and ideas might be useful in a veterinary practice. Better yet, collaborate with a veterinarian. Most of our authors are veterinarians or those working with veterinarians in a professional capacity. Knowledge of the interests and problems of practicing veterinarians is essential."

NORDEN NEWS, Norden Laboratories, 601 W. Cornhusker Hwy., Lincoln NE 68521. (402)475-4541. Editor-in-Chief: Patricia Pike. Emphasizes veterinary medicine for licensed veterinarians, practicing veterinary clinicians and veterinary students. Quarterly magazine; 36 pages. Estab: 1925. Circ: 28-30,000. Buys one-time rights or second serial (reprint) rights. Photocopied submissions and previously published work OK. SASE. Reports in 3 weeks. Free sample copy and writer's guidelines.

Nonfiction: How-to articles (relating to veterinary medicine; for example, case histories, clinical tips on procedures and treatment); interviews (with veterinarians); profiles (of veterinarians); technical articles (anything relevant or of interest to the veterinary practice). Buys 4-8 mss/year. Length: 1,000-1,500 words. Will review unsolicited mss, but prefers to be queried. Pays $100-150.

Photos: B&w (8x10) glossies and color (35mm or larger) transparencies purchased with mss. Send contact sheet and/or transparencies. Pays $7.50 minimum for b&w; $50 minimum for color. Model release required.

Columns, Departments: Buys 4-6 items/year for Business Practices/Tips and Tap Tips. Length: 250-500 words. Query first. Pays $50 minimum.

VETERINARY ECONOMICS MAGAZINE, 2728 Euclid Ave., Cleveland OH 44115. Editorial Director: John D. Velardo. For all practicing veterinarians in the U.S. Monthly. Buys exclusive rights in the field. Pays on publication. Enclose S.A.S.E.

Nonfiction and Photos: Uses case histories telling about good business practices on the part of veterinarians. Also, articles about financial problems, investments, insurance and similar subjects of particular interest to professional men. "We reject articles with superficial information about a subject instead of carefully researched and specifically directed articles for our field." Pays $15 to $25 per printed page depending on worth. Pays maximum $100. Photos purchased with ms. Pays $7.50.

VETERINARY MEDICINE/SMALL ANIMAL CLINICIAN, 144 North Nettleton Ave., Bonner Springs KS 66012. (913)422-5010. Editor: Dr. C.M. Cooper. For graduate veterinarians, research, libraries, schools, government agencies and other organizations employing veterinarians. Monthly. Circulation: 15,992. Buys North American serial rights. Occasionally overstocked with business/investment type mss. Pays on publication. Reports in 2 weeks. Enclose S.A.S.E.

Nonfiction: Managing Editor: Ray E. Ottinger, Jr. Accepts only articles dealing with medical case histories, practice management, business, taxes, insurance, investments, etc. Length: 1,500 to 2,500 words. Pays $15 per printed page.

How To Break In: "Write up clinical reports for local veterinarians. We prefer to carry veterinarian as author."

Water Supply and Sewage Disposal

GROUND WATER AGE, 110 N. York Rd., Elmhurst IL 60126. (312)833-6540. Editor: Gene Adams. For water well drilling contractors and systems specialists. Established in 1965. Monthly. Circulation: 15,000. Rights purchased vary with author and material. Buys all rights but will reassign rights to author after publication. Buys first North American serial rights, first serial rights (reprint) or simultaneous rights. Buys 12 to 18 mss a year. Payment on acceptance. Will send free sample copy to writer on request. Will consider photocopied submissions. Submit seasonal material 3 to 6 months in advance. Reports on material within 2 weeks. Query first. Enclose S.A.S.E.

Nonfiction and Photos: Technical articles on business operation. Informational, how-to, interview, historical, merchandising techniques. Length: open. Pays 4¢ to 8¢ a word. B&w photos. Minimum 4x5. Prefers 8x10. Pays $5 to $15. Purchased with accompanying ms. Captions required. Pays $25 to $75 for color.

SOLID WASTES MANAGEMENT, Communication Channels, Inc., 461 8th Ave., New York NY 10001. (212)239-6200. Editor-in-Chief: Kevin Lynch. Emphasizes refuse hauling, landfill transfer stations, and resource recovery for private haulers, municipal sanitation and consulting engineers. Monthly magazine; 100 pages. Estab: 1958. Circ: 21,000. Pays on acceptance. Buys all rights, but may reassign following publication. Phone queries OK. Submit seasonal or holiday material 3 months in advance. Photocopied submissions OK. SASE. Reports in 4 weeks. Sample copy 50¢. Free writer's guidelines.

Nonfiction and Photos: Case studies of individual solid wastes companies. Material must include details on all quantities handled, statistics, equipment used, etc. Informational, how-to, interview, historical, think pieces and technical articles. Length: 1,500 words minimum. Pays $75 to $100.

Company Publications

The company publications field began in the United States in 1840 with the *Lowell Offering,* a modest house organ which printed news of the women employed by the Lowell Cotton Mills of Massachusetts. From this beginning was spawned one of the largest publishing ventures in the country today, totaling nearly 20,000 publications with an annual estimated circulation of 180 million readers. Conservative estimations place the figure for the monies invested in this field at a *billion* dollars per year. In a field of this size and magnitude, freelance opportunities abound.

Company publications are those magazines, newspapers, newsletters and tabloids that are sponsored by a particular company to keep employees, customers and interested parties informed of the activities of that company. Basically, there are six kinds of company publications: *employee magazines* published to keep employees abreast of company policy and the goings-on of their co-workers; *customer magazines* edited to remind customers of the desirability of owning or using that company's products or services; *stockholder or corporate magazines* put out for the shareholder keeping him informed of financial or policy matters; *sales magazines* telling the company's field representatives how to better push their wares; *dealer magazines* published to maintain open channels of communication between manufacturer and independent dealers; and *technical service magazines* sponsored by companies to whom technical data is important in the use and application of products. A single company may publish any or all of these types, enlarging their need for well-written information regarding their products, employees and services.

What interests the editors of these publications? The trick to successful (meaning selling) writing in the field is the word *company.* These magazines are published for the sole purpose of performing a useful service to the sponsor, be that service in an *internal* publication (which is a controlled circulation magazine distributed only among the employees of a company) or an *external* publication (published for the public relations benefits to the company and circulated among the customers and users of that company's products or services). These publications vary in emphasis, some giving more space to company product-related information, and others highlighting the interesting activities or unique doings of company personnel. Manuscripts lacking a strong company tie-in, or derogatory material about the company or its goods are worthless to company publication editors.

Ideas for writing for company publications are as numerous as the number of companies that publish magazines. Stay alert for new businesses or unique applications of company's products in your own home town. Quite often, an out-of-the-ordinary use of a company's product is the way to a sure sale. Due to the limited nature of the publication, and the fact that editors have run stories on the use of their company's goods in all the conventional ways, an article about some merchant in your town who uses products in an offbeat manner will catch the editor's eye.

Photos are a must for most company publications. When doing your photo planning, be sure to ensure that your photos contain concrete references to the company's product. Show off the product in a manner which compliments its qualities. Remember, the story is about the *product* and its use, not the store owner or manager who uses it.

Company publications aren't the "puffy" magazines they were years ago. Editors are looking for articles that do more than praise the merits of their companies. They want well-developed, lively pieces that will make the reader more aware of aspects of the firm other than his own job. Writing for these publications can be profitable (paying fairly competitive rates in comparison with other publishing fields) and rewarding. The freelancer who can turn in polished copy to these busy editors may find himself more often than not on the company's payroll.

ACF HORIZONS, ACF Industries, Corporate Communications, 620 N 2nd St., St. Charles MO 63301. (314)723-9600. Editor: William W. Wallace. For "employees and the public." Quarterly. Circulation: 18,000. Buys "non-exclusive" rights. Pays on publication. Will send a sample copy to a writer on request. Query first. Reports in 1 month. Enclose S.A.S.E.

Nonfiction, Photos, and Fillers: "Articles related to the products and operations of the divisions of ACF Industries: railroad equipment, automotive fuel systems, valves and fittings. Material must have ACF tie-in." Length: "the shorter the better." Pays $5 minimum. Buys 8x10 single-weight b&w glossies.

BAROID NEWS BULLETIN, P.O. Box 1675, Houston TX 77001. (713)527-1182. Editor: Marvin L. Brown. Publication of the Baroid Petroleum Services Division of N L Industries, Inc. "Our readership consists of employees of the petroleum industry worldwide." Established in 1941. Quarterly. Circulation: 18,000. Buys North American rights, but will reassign rights to author after publication. Buys 12 mss/year. Pays on acceptance. Will send free sample copy to writer on request. Reports on material in 3 weeks. Submit complete ms. Enclose S.A.S.E.

Nonfiction and Photos: "We prefer feature articles. Topic needs fluctuate, but quality of writing is most important factor. Each quarterly publication includes feature articles and art plus technical articles written by our employees." Length: 1,000 to 3,000 words. Pays 6¢ to 10¢ per word. B&w glossies or color transparencies purchased with ms.

BARTER COMMUNIQUE, Full Circle Marketing Corp., Box 2527, Sarasota FL 33578 (813)349-2242. Editor-in-Chief: Robert J. Murely. Emphasizes bartering for radio and TV station owners, cable TV, newspaper and magazine publishers and select travel and advertising agency presidents. Semiannual tabloid; 32-40 pages. Estab: 1975. Circ: 30,000. Pays on publication. Rights purchased vary with author and material. Phone queries OK. Simultaneous photocopied and previously published submissions OK. SASE. Reports in 4 weeks. Free sample copy and writer's guidelines.

Nonfiction: Articles on "barter" (trading products, good, and services), primarily travel and advertising. Length: 1,000 words. "Would like to see travel mss on southeast U.S. and the Bahamas, and unique articles on media of all kinds. Include photos where applicable." Pays $30-50.

THE BEAVER, 77 Main St., Winnipeg, MB, Canada. Editor: Helen Burgess. Publication of Hudson's Bay Company for "mature students and adults". Established in 1920. Quarterly. Circulation: 40,000. Buys all rights. Buys about 30 mss a year. Pays on acceptance. Will send a sample copy to a writer on request. Submit seasonal material at least 6 months in advance. Reports in 2 weeks. "Content is quite specialized; suggest query first." Enclose S.A.E. and International Reply Coupons.

Nonfiction and Photos: "Well-illustrated, authentic articles on life in the Arctic and areas of early Hudson's Bay Company activities; historical and present-day fur trade, nature subjects, Indians, and Eskimos. Accurate information must be presented in a readable way. No more articles on Arctic canoe trips." Buys informational articles, personal experience pieces, profiles, and historical articles. Length: 1,000 to 4,000 words. Pays minimum 5¢ a word. Photos purchased with mss; captions required. Pays minimum $5 for 8x10 b&w glossies. Pays minimum $10 for 35mm or 4¼x4¼ color slides.

BUSINESS ON WHEELS, P.O. Box 13208, Phoenix AZ 85002. (602)264-1579. Editor: Frederick H. Kling. "External house organ of Goodyear Tire and Rubber Company for distribution to owners and operators of truck fleets, both common carrier trucking systems and trucks used in connection with businesses of various types." Quarterly. Not copyrighted. Pays on acceptance. "Stories on assignment only. We like to choose our own subjects for case history stories." Query first. Enclose S.A.S.E.

Nonfiction and Photos: "Freelance writers and photographers (especially writer-photographer teams or individuals) are invited to send in their qualifications for assignment of articles on truck-fleet operators in their territory. Payment from $250 to $300, plus expenses, for complete editorial-photographic coverage, additional for color, if used."

THE CARAVANNER, 600 S. Commonwealth Ave., Los Angeles CA 90005. Editor: Frank Quattrocchi. For persons in the 50 to 60 year age class; retired or semi-retired who have expressed a definite interest in the Airstream make of travel trailer. Publication of Airstream, a Division of Beatrice Foods Co., Chicago IL. Newspaper; 8 pages, 11¼x16¼. Established in 1954. Circulation: 450,000. Not copyrighted. Pays on acceptance. Will send free sample copy to writer on request. Write for copy of guidelines for writers. Will consider photocopied submissions. No simultaneous submissions. Returns rejected material in 2 to 3 weeks. Reports on material in 3 to 4 weeks "unless I'm on vacation." Query first. Enclose S.A.S.E.

Nonfiction: "Interesting uses of the Airstream make of travel trailers. Material must be entirely factual and not exaggerated, but upbeat. Writer must know what we usually print in our pages. We're really looking for truth; sharp analysis. The recreational vehicle, of which a travel trailer is one kind, has really encouraged or engendered a new life style in modern America —I'd like to see that examined." Personal experience, interview, profile, nostalgia, travel, and spot news. Length: 250 to 2,500 words. Usually pays $50 to $150.

Photos: Purchased with accompanying ms with no additional payment. Photos generally required with ms. Pays $5 minimum if photos are exceptional, and without accompanying ms. 8x10 b&w. Captions required.

CHANNELS MAGAZINE, Northwestern Bell Telephone Co., 100 S. 19th St., Omaha NE 68102. Editor: G.T. Metcalf. For top level executives in Iowa, Minnesota, Nebraska, North and South Dakota. Quarterly magazine. Estab: 1966. Circ: 47,000. Pays on acceptance. Buys all rights, but may reassign following publication. SASE. Reports in 1 month.

Nonfiction: Wants mss designed to keep executives up to date on new developments and techniques in business communications such as WATS, data transmission, time-shared computers, industrial television. Also uses occasional general interest features on sports, hobbies, personalities, events and points of interest in the five states covered. "Writing must be good and it must be tight." Length: 500-1,500 words. Query. Pays $150 minimum.

CIBA-GEIGY JOURNAL, 4002 Basel, Switzerland. Editor: Stanley Hubbard. For "employees of Ciba-Geigy, together with 'opinion leaders,' customers, educational institutions, etc., in most English-speaking countries." Established in 1971. Circulation: 27,000. Rights purchased vary with author and material; may buy all rights, but will reassign rights to author after publication. Buys 4 to 6 mss a year. Pays on publication. Will send a sample copy to a writer on request. Will consider photocopied submissions. Submit seasonal material 5 months in advance. Reports in 4 weeks. Query first.

Nonfiction and Photos: "Popularized scientific and technical presentations, international cooperation subjects, regional and historical contributions related to group activities, human interest with product or operational tie-in. The approach should be literate; no writing down. The internationalism of our company is the basic determining factor — we are interpreting from continent to continent rather than talking to a homogeneous, neatly defined readership." Buys informational articles, think pieces, photo features, and technical articles. Length: 500 to 3,000 words. Pays minimum of $50. Photos purchased with mss; captions required. Pays $10.

THE COMPASS, Mobil Sales and Supply Corp., 150 E. 42nd St., New York NY 10017. (212)883-3639. Editor: R.G. MacKenzie. For ship owners, ship operators and agents for shipping companies. Established in 1920. Quarterly. Circulation: 25,000. Buys first serial rights. Pays on acceptance. Will consider photocopied and simultaneous submissions. Reports in 2 weeks. Query first. Enclose S.A.S.E.

Nonfiction and Photos: "Various marine or maritime subjects, with particular emphasis on history, origin, and scientific developments." Length: 2,000 to 4,000 words. Pays $125 to $250. Photos purchased with accompanying ms, with no additional payment. Must be on marine subjects. B&w glossies, any size; color, 35mm or larger.

Fiction: Experimental, mainstream, mystery, suspense, adventure, fantasy, historical. Must be marine oriented. Length: 2,000 to 4,000 words. Pays $125 to $250.

CORVETTE NEWS, 2-129 General Motors Bldg., Detroit MI 48202. For Corvette owners worldwide. Bimonthly. Circulation: 170,000. Buys all rights. Pays on acceptance. Write for sample copy and editorial guidelines. Query first. Enclose S.A.S.E.

Nonfiction and Photos: "Articles must be of interest to this audience. Subjects considered include: (1) Technical articles dealing with engines, paint, body work, suspension, parts searches, etc. (2) Competition, 'Vettes vs. 'Vettes, or 'Vettes vs. others. (3) Profiles of Corvette owners/drivers. (4) General interest articles, such as the unusual history of a particular early model Corvette, and perhaps its restoration; one owner's do-it-yourself engine repair procedures, maintenance procedures; Corvettes in unusual service; hobbies involving Corvettes; sports involving Corvettes. (5) Road hunts. (6) Special Corvette events such as races, drags, rallies, concourse, gymkhanas, slaloms. (7) Corvette club activities." Length: 800 to 2,400 words. Pays $50 to $500, including photos illustrating article. Color transparencies or b&w negatives preferred. Pays additional fee of $35 for cover shot which is selected from photos furnished with article used in that issue.

EARTH/SPACE NEWS, 4151 Middlefield, Palo Alto CA 94303. Editor-in-Chief: Paul L. Siegler. Managing Editor: Mark Frazier. Emphasizes free enterprising in space. Audience ranges from educated space enthusiasts to managers in major corporations. Primary interest is in learning how to get to space quickly and cheaply, and once there how to make profit (as business) or explore (as individual). Newsletter; every 2 months; 8-16 pages. Estab: 1975. Circ: 1,000. Pays on acceptance. Buys all rights, but may reassign following publication. Simultaneous, photocopied, and previously published submissions OK. SASE. Free sample copy.

Nonfiction: How-to (use space profitably as a business or individual); informational (innovative but realistic means of living, working and transporting in space which are not government-oriented); interviews (with any space entrepreneur); travel (to earth orbit); new product (especially low-cost launch and satellite techniques); technical (private launch systems and satellite systems). Buys 12 mss/year. Submit complete ms. Length: 1,000-5,000 words. Pays $15-30.

Fillers: Newsbreaks relating to commercial space activities. Buys 20/year. Send fillers in. Pays $1-5.

How To Break In: "The freelancer should best understand the difference between free enterprise and government projects; how they work and what motivates them. He should have an innate feel of space as potentially the most expansive frontier mankind has ever faced."

Rejects: "I do not want to see a listing of NASA plans and activities or anything written about tax-funded projects."

EUA SPECTRUM, EUA Service Corp., Box 212, Lincoln RI 02865. (401)333-1400. Editor: Jerry Campbell. Monthly. Circ: 2,500. Pays on publication. Not copyrighted. Submit seasonal or holiday material 2 months in advance. SASE. Reports in 4-6 weeks.

Nonfiction: How-to articles, humor, think pieces, new product coverage; photo and travel and safety articles. Length: open. Pays $10-50.

Photos: No additional payment for b&w glossies purchased with mss.

THE EDUCATIONAL FOCUS, Optics Center SOPD Division, Bausch & Lomb, 1400 N. Goodman St., Rochester NY 14602. (716)338-6470. Editor: R.I. Fiester. For "high school and college science teachers and professors, and advanced students." Established in 1929. Annual. Circulation: 25,000. Buys all rights. Pays "within 2 weeks following acceptance." Will send a sample copy to a writer on request. Write for copy of guidelines for writers. Reports in 2 weeks. Enclose S.A.S.E. for return of submissions.

Nonfiction and Photos: "We are primarily interested in articles dealing with new or unusual uses of scientific optical equipment, new approaches to teaching, or interesting adaptations and accessories devised for use with such equipment. Obviously, we prefer that the story be concerned with Bausch and Lomb equipment, but we will not reject an article simply because it makes a reference to the use of competitive optical equipment. Serious consideration will be given to any article that advances the cause of science in any area —in schools, industry, hospitals, research labs, etc. —whether or not scientific optical equipment is used (although, obviously, that is preferred). How-to stories describing the construction of scientific optical equipment by students are very much to our liking. Such articles should be accompanied by drawings and photographs so that another student can easily duplicate the equipment from information contained in the article. We do not buy highly technical articles delineating unsupported scientific theories. No articles that 'run down' competitive optical equipment, even if unnamed." Length: 1,500 to 3,000 words. Pays "3¢ per word as published. We do pay more for articles, depending on the type of material, ease of bringing it to finished form, etc." Photos purchased with mss. "A picture story is particularly appealing to us." Uses b&w for inside use, color for cover "if it illustrates a point about an inside article." Pays $5 minimum per photo. "When we give the author permission to have photos taken, we pay the photographer's fee, including the cost of prints, without further reimbursement to the author."

THE ENTHUSIAST, 3700 W. Juneau, Milwaukee WI 53208. (414)342-4680. Editor: Bob Klein. Published by Harley-Davidson Motor Co., Inc. for "motorcycle riders of all ages, education, and professions." Established in 1920. Quarterly. Circulation: 150,000. Not copyrighted. Pays on publication. Will send a sample copy to a writer on request. Write for copy of guidelines for writers. Will consider photocopied submissions. Submit seasonal material 2 months in advance. Reports in 2 to 4 weeks. Query first or submit complete ms. Enclose S.A.S.E.

Nonfiction and Photos: "Stories on motorcycling or snowmobiling—humor, technical, racing, touring, adventures, competitive events. All articles should feature Harley-Davidson products and not mention competitive products. We do not want stories concerning sex, violence, or anything harmful to the image of motorcycling. We use travel stories featuring Harley-Davidson motorcycles, which must be illustrated with good quality photos of the motorcycle and travelers with scenic background taken on the trip. Also needed are stories of off-road usage, e.g., scrambles, racing, motocross, trail riding, or any other unusual usage. We use snowmobile stories in fall and winter." Informational articles, how-to's, personal experience articles, interviews, profiles, inspirational pieces, humor, historical articles, photo features, travel articles, and technical articles. Length: 3,000 words. Pays 5¢ "per published word, or as previously agreed upon." Photos purchased with mss and without mss; captions optional. Uses "quality b&w or color 4x5 prints or larger." Pays $7.50 to $15.

Fiction: "Good short stories with the image of clean motorcycling fun. No black leather jacket emphasis." Buys adventure and humorous stories. Length: 3,000 words maximum. Pays 5¢ "per published word, or as previously agreed upon."

Fillers: Jokes, short humor. Length: open. Pays $15.

GOULDS PUMPS INDUSTRIAL NEWS, 240 Fall St., Seneca Falls NY 13148. Editor: William Romano. Published by Goulds Pumps, Inc. for "industrial engineers, maintenance people, designers, purchasing agents for chemical process, paper, marine, mining, utility, municipal industries." Established in 1937. Bimonthly. Circulation: 22,000. Not copyrighted. Write for copy of guidelines for writers. Query first. Enclose S.A.S.E.

Nonfiction and Photos: "Case histories, industrial pump related human interest: old replaces new, solves the problem, out-of-the-ordinary application, assisting in scientific breakthrough, used in state-of-the art service, etc." Buys historical articles, coverage of successful business operations, and technical articles. Length: maximum 700 words. Pays $25 to $50 per article. Photos purchased with or without mss.

HOBART WELDWORLD, Hobart Brothers Co., Troy OH 45273. (513)339-6509. Editor: Daniel Lea. For "men and women with engineering degrees or technical education who are practicing a technical profession related to welding fabrication or who have moved into manufacturing management posts." Established in 1941. Quarterly. Circulation: 50,000. Usually buys first rights only. Buys "a few" mss a year. Pays on publication. Will send a sample copy to a writer on request. Will consider photocopied submissions. Reports in 1 month. Query first or submit complete ms. Enclose S.A.S.E.

Nonfiction and Photos: "Technical articles on arc welding applications. The writer should submit items only about exotic or unusual applications, give full technical information, and describe the benefits of equipment or process for the application as compared with other welding methods. Give figures, if possible. Unless a specific product benefit is involved, we worry about the application and let the product references come as they may. We're interested in coverage of big construction projects, in which welding plays a major part." Length: 300 to 1,000 words. Pays $50 minimum. Mss must be accompanied by photos illustrating the application. Buys color negatives or transparencies, only. Pays $20 minimum each.

How To Break In: "We are trying to upgrade our photos as to artistic quality, impact, and information value, and will be impressed by submissions which help do this."

INDUSTRIAL PROGRESS, P.O. Box 13208, Phoenix AZ 85002. (602)264-1579. Editor: Frederick H. Kling. External house organ of Goodyear Tire and Rubber Company, for "executives, management, and professional men (designers, engineers, etc.) in all types of industry." Bimonthly. Not copyrighted. Pays on acceptance. Enclose S.A.S.E. for return of submissions.

Nonfiction and Photos: Male-interest features: hobbies, sports, novelty, mechanical, do-it-yourself, personalities, adventure, etc. Must be strongly photographic. Some color features used. Pays from $25-50 for a single photo caption item to $125 for full-length features (up to 1,000 words) with 4 or 5 b&w photos; more for full-length color features.

INLAND, The Magazine of the Middle West, Inland Steel Co., 30 W. Monroe St., Chicago IL 60603. (312)346-0300. Managing Editor: Sheldon A. Mix. Emphasizes steel products, services and company personnel. Quarterly magazine; 24 pages. Estab: 1953. Circ: 12,000. Pays on acceptance. Buys one-time rights. Submit seasonal/holiday material at least a year in advance. Simultaneous submissions OK. SASE. Reports in 6-8 weeks. Free sample copy.

Nonfiction: Articles, essays, humorous commentaries, pictorial essays. "We like well-done individuality. Half of each issue deals with staff-written steel subjects; half with widely ranging nonsteel matter. Articles and essays related somehow to Midwest (basically Illinois, Wisconsin, Minnesota, Michigan, Missouri, Iowa, Indiana, Ohio) in such subject areas as history, folklore, sports, humor, the seasons, current scene generally; nostalgia and reminiscence if appeal is broad enough. But subject less important than treatment. Encourage individuality, thoughtful writing, fresh ideas, and approaches. Please don't send slight, rehashed historical pieces or any articles of purely local interest." Personal experience, profile, inspirational, humor, historical,

think articles, nostalgia, personal opinion, photo articles. Length: 1,200 to 5,000 words, but this may vary. Pays $200 minimum.
Photos: Purchased with or without mss. Captions required. "Payment for pictorial essay same as for text feature."

ITEMS, Federal Reserve Bank of Dallas, Station K, Dallas TX 75275. (214)651-6300. Editor: Mildred Hopkins. For employees and retirees of the bank and its branches in El Paso, Houston and San Antonio. Publication of Federal Reserve Bank of Dallas. Magazine; 16 pages. Established in 1921. Every 2 months. Circulation: 1,850. Not copyrighted. Buys 3 or 4 mss per year. Pays on acceptance. Will send free sample copy to writer on request. Write for editorial guidelines sheets. Submit seasonal material 3 months in advance. Reports on mss accepted for publication in 8 to 10 weeks. Returns rejected material in 4 weeks. Enclose S.A.S.E.
Nonfiction and Photos: Buys mss on banking and finance, Federal Reserve System, historical, patriotic themes (tied in with seasonal holidays) and civic responsibility. Length: 800 to 1,000 words. Pays 3¢ per word. Photos purchased with ms with extra payment. No color. Pays $15 to $20. Size: 8x10 glossy; or 5x7 glossy.

LLOYD'S LISTENING POST, P.O. Box 4476, Rockford IL 61110. (815)965-0015. Editor: David M. Mathieu. For persons age 50 and over. Publication of Lloyd Hearing Aid Corp. Tabloid; 8-12 pages. Established in 1972. Quarterly. Circulation: 180,000. Not copyrighted. Buys about 25 mss per year. Pays on acceptance. Will send free sample copy to writer on request. Will consider photocopied and simultaneous submissions. Reports in 2 weeks. Submit only complete ms. Enclose S.A.S.E.
Nonfiction, Photos and Crossword Puzzles: Uses "self-help; inspirational; stories on active and happy people; solutions to senior citizens' problems; nostalgia; travel; profile; how-to and informational. Keep material positive — and short. We use short features and wide variety of subjects in each issue." Would like to see mss on social security problems; travel (places and costs); "handyman" ideas around the home; relationships between old and young; profiles of active senior citizens. Length: 500 to 1,500 words. Pays 3¢ to 5¢ per word. Photos used with accompanying ms with no additional payment. Captions required. Also buys crossword puzzles. Pays $10.

MARATHON WORLD, Marathon Oil Company, 539 S. Main St., Findlay OH 45840. (419)422-2121. Editor-in-Chief: Robert Ostermann. Emphasizes petroleum/energy; for shareholders, educators, legislators, government officials, libraries, community leaders, students and employees. Quarterly magazine; 28 pages. Estab: 1964. Circ: 72,000. Pays on acceptance. Buys first North American serial rights. Photocopied submissions OK. SASE. Reports in 3 weeks. Free sample copy and writer's guidelines.
Nonfiction: Informational; interview and photo feature. Buys 2-3 mss/issue. Query. Length: 800-2,500 words. Pays $300-1,000.
Photos: Photos purchased with accompanying ms or on assignment. Pay negotiable for b&w and color photos. Total purchase price for a ms includes payment for photos.
How To Break In: "Because of the special nature of the *World* as a corporate external publication and the special limits imposed on contents, suggest best approach is through initial query."

ONAN NEWS BRIEF/ONAN NEWS, 1400 73rd Ave., N.E., Minneapolis MN 55432. (612)574-5000. Editor: Patricia Halsten. For "Onan employees, distributors, dealers, and customers." Monthly *(Onan News Brief)*; bimonthly *(Onan News)*. Circulation: 8,000. Not copyrighted. Buys about 12 mss a year. Pays on acceptance. Will send a sample copy to a writer on request. Will not consider photocopied submissions. Reports on material accepted for publication in 30 days. Returns rejected material in 15 days. Query first. Enclose S.A.S.E.
Nonfiction and Photos: "Application stories on Onan products and feature stories on Onan employees, distributors, and dealers. The story should be readable, informative, and interesting. It should be able to stand alone, and the mention of Onan products should not necessarily be important to the story line. We do not want material on recreational vehicles —our marketing emphasis has shifted." Length: "about 1,000 words, but we will look at anything on the subject, no matter how short. And if it takes 5,000 well-chosen words to put a message across, we'll consider that, too. Remuneration depends on so many things other than the number of words: difficulty in obtaining the material, accompanying photographs (we prefer contact sheets and require negatives —b&w with captions only), quality of article, timeliness, and degree of importance of theme to our audience. Our normal pay for a four-page typed article accompanied by 8 to 12 b&w negatives is $150. This includes expenses, unless an additional allowance is authorized in advance by the editor."

OUR SUN, Sun Co., 1608 Walnut St., Philadelphia PA 19103. For "local, state, and national government officials; community leaders; news and financial communicators; educators, shareholders, customers, and employees of Sun Company." Established in 1923. Published three times a year. Circulation: 140,000. Not copyrighted. Buys 1 or 2 articles a year. "Most are staff written." Pays on acceptance. Will send a sample copy to a writer on request. Reports in 3 to 6 weeks. Query first. Enclose S.A.S.E.
Nonfiction: "Articles only. Subject matter should be related to Sun Company, oil industry, or national energy situation. Articles should be directed toward a general audience. Style: magazine feature. Approach: nontechnical. Travel themes are currently being overworked." Buys informational articles, interviews, profiles, historical articles, think pieces, coverage of successful business operations. Length: 1,000 to 3,000 words. Pays $300 to $800.
Photos: Purchased on assignment; captions optional. "We do not buy photos on spec." Pays $100 to $400 a day for photographic assignments.

PENNEY NEWS, JCPenny, 1301 Ave. of the Americas, New York NY 10019. (212)957-6508. Publication of JC Penney. For employees and retirees. Tabloid newspaper; 16 pages. Established in 1902. Monthly. Circulation: 200,000. Buys all rights. "Very few unsolicited mss accepted. Most freelance work on assignment." Pays on acceptance. Will send free sample copy to writer on request. Will consider simultaneous submissions. No photocopied submissions. Query first. Enclose S.A.S.E.
Nonfiction and Photos: News and features about JC Penney, employees, retirees, retail industry. "Exercise highest journalistic standards." No poems, cartoons, crossword puzzles, fillers or public service material. Would like to see news of stores, employees in freelancers' own communities. "Length and payment depend on value of material to us." Usually pays $5 to $350. Photos purchased with or without ms with extra payment or on assignment. Captions required. No color. Payment for b&w "depends on value of photo to us. Usually $3 to $250."

PGW NEWS, Philadelphia Gas Co., 1800 N. 9th St., Philadelphia PA 19122. (215)796-1260. Editor-in-Chief: William B. Hall, III. Emphasizes gas utility; for employees, retirees, their families, suppliers, other utility editors in U.S. and abroad. Monthly magazine; 24 pages. Estab: 1928. Circ: 5,000. Pays on acceptance. Buys one-time rights. Submit seasonal/holiday material 3-4 months in advance. SASE. Reports in 1-2 months. Free sample copy.
Nonfiction: How-to (being a better employee); informational; inspirational (from a job approach). Send complete ms. Length: 1,000-2,000 words. Pays $5 minimum.

ROSEBURG WOODSMAN, 1220 S. W. Morrison St., Portland OR 97205. (503)227-3693. Publication of Roseburg Lumber Company. Editor: Rodger Dwight. For wholesale and retail lumber dealers and other buyers of forest products, such as furniture manufacturers and paper products companies. Magazine; 8 pages, (8¼x11). Publishes a special Christmas issue. Established in 1955. Monthly. Circulation: 10,000. Buys all rights, but will reassign rights to author after publication. Buys approximately 20 mss per year. Pays on publication. Will send free sample copy to a writer on request, as well as editorial guidelines sheet. Will not consider photocopied or simultaneous submissions. Submit seasonal material 3 months in advance. Reports on material accepted for publication in 1 week. Returns rejected material immediately. Query first, or submit complete mss. Enclose S.A.S.E.
Nonfiction and Photos: Features on the "residential, commercial and industrial applications of Roseburg's wood products, such as lumber, plywood, prefinished wall paneling, and flakeboard —vinyl-laminated and printed." Informational, how-to, interview, profile, new products, technical and merchandising techniques articles. Length: 500 to 1,000 words. Pays 10¢ per word. Pays $10 per b&w glossies purchased with mss, 8x10. Pays $25 to $50 per color transparency or print.
How To Break In: "We seek the short story approach in our mss, showing successful applications of our wood products."

RURALITE, P.O. Box 1731, Portland OR 97207. (503)357-2105. Editor: Aaron C. Jones. For "rural people served by our member utilities in Oregon, Washington, Idaho, Nevada and Alaska." Established in 1953. Monthly. Circulation: 145,000. Rights purchased vary with author and material. Usually buys first rights. Buys 300 mss a year. Payment on acceptance. Will send free sample copy to Northwest writers on request. Will consider photocopied submissions. Submit seasonal material 3 months in advance. Reports on material in 15 days. Query first. Enclose S.A.S.E.
Nonfiction and Photos: "Human interest stories about member-owners of the public utilities that send *Ruralite* to their members. Articles that offer good advice to rural people; how to

repair or how to live more safely, etc. Must have some connection with utility or members of utility." How-to, inspirational. Length: 500 to 3,000 words. Pays $50 to $150. B&w photos purchased with accompanying mss or without ms. Captions required. Pays $7.50.

SAFECO AGENT, (Safeco Insurance Co.), Safeco Plaza, Seattle WA 98185. (206)545-5973. Editor-in-Chief: Jack C. High. Emphasizes insurance for independent agents. Magazine; bimonthly; 32 pages. Estab: 1923. Circ: 13,500. Pays on acceptance. Buys all rights, but may reassign following publication. Phone queries OK. SASE. Reports in 1 month. Free sample copy and writer's guidelines.
Nonfiction: How to (run an insurance agency; prospect, sell, develop accounts, recruit new producers); informational articles, interviews and profiles. Buys 4-8 mss/year. Query. Length: 900-1,500 words. Pays $250 maximum.
Photos: B&w glossies (8x10) purchased on assignment. Query or send contact sheet. Pays $40 maximum. Model release required.

SEVENTY SIX MAGAZINE, P.O. Box 7600, Los Angeles CA 90051. Editor: Karen Saunders. For employees, politicians, retirees and community leaders. Publication of Union Oil Company. Established in 1920. Every 2 months. Circulation: 32,000. Not copyrighted. Buys 2 or 3 mss per year. Pays on acceptance. Will send free sample copy to writer on request. Write for editorial guidelines. Reports "as soon as possible." Enclose S.A.S.E.
Nonfiction and Photos: "Articles about the petroleum industry, Union Oil Co., or Union Oil's employees or retirees. No articles about service stations or dealers. The history of oil or the unusual uses of petroleum are good subjects for freelancers." No straight news. People-oriented. Does not want to see travel features. Buys informational, profile, humor, historical mss. Pays 10¢ a word minimum. Photos purchased with ms with extra payment. 8x10 b&w; 35mm color transparencies. Captions required.

SMALL WORLD, Volkswagen of America, 818 Sylvan Ave., Englewood Cliffs NJ 07632. Editor: Burton Unger. For "Volkswagen owners in the United States," Magazine; 24 pages. Circulation: 400,000. 5 times a year. Buys all rights. Buys about 20 mss a year. Payment on acceptance. Free writer's guidelines. Reports in 6 weeks. "If you have a long feature possibility in mind, please query first. Though queries should be no longer than 2 pages, they ought to include a working title, a short, general summary of the article, and an outline of the specific points to be covered. Where possible, please include a sample of the photography available. We strongly advise writers to read at least 2 past issues before working on a story." Enclose S.A.S.E.
Nonfiction and Photos: "Interesting stories on people using Volkswagens; useful owner modifications of the vehicle; travel pieces with the emphasis on people, not places; Volkswagenmania stories, personality pieces, inspirational and true adventure articles. VW arts and crafts, etc. The style should be light. All stories must have a VW tie-in. Our approach is subtle, however, and we try to avoid obvious product puffery, since *Small World* is not an advertising medium. We prefer a first-person, people-oriented handling. Length: 1,500 words maximum; shorter pieces, some as short as 450 words, often receive closer attention." Pays $100 per printed page for photographs and text; otherwise, a portion of that amount, depending on the space allotted. Most stories go 2 pages; some run 3 or 4. Photos purchased with ms; captions required. "We prefer color transparencies, particularly 35mm slides. All photos should carry the photographer's name and address. If the photographer is not the author, both names should appear on the first page of the text. Where possible, we would like a selection of at least 40 transparencies. It is recommended that at least one show the principal character or author; another, all or a recognizable portion of a VW in the locale of the story. Quality photography can often sell a story that might be otherwise rejected. Every picture should be identified or explained." Model releases required. Pays $250 maximum for cover photo.
Fillers: "Short, humorous anecdotes about Volkswagens." Pays $15.

SPERRY NEW HOLLAND PUBLIC RELATIONS NEWSFEATURES, New Holland PA 17557. (717)354-1274. Contact: Don Collins, Press Relations Supervisor. For farm families. Special Thanksgiving, Christmas and July 4 issues. Established in 1895. Buys all rights. Buys about 40 mss per year. Pays on acceptance. Write for editorial guidelines. Will consider photocopied submissions. No simultaneous submissions. Submit seasonal material 4 months in advance. Reports on mss accepted for publication in 2 weeks. Returns rejected material "immediately." Query first. Enclose S.A.S.E.
Nonfiction and Photos: "We send releases on how-to; getting the most out of; new twists in old practices; good management practices; work and time saving tips; safety tips — as these topics

apply to farming and ranching. Most subjects will be owners of Sperry New Holland agricultural machinery. Give us an outline of a story of interest to a farmer magazine editor. Tell us about the operation and the farmer and equipment involved. Always looking for good freelancers we can contact with our own leads and get coverage." This publication contains newsfeature articles for farm publications and newspapers. Circulation is to various farm publications. "We discuss rates before assignment is made. We usually pay expenses involved in gathering articles. Payment for unsolicited materials, which are accepted, depends on quality and value to us. We're fair, but want only good materials that don't require a lot of rework." Buys informational mss on new farming practices, profiles of good farmers who use Sperry New Holland equipment, spot news, successful business operations of farms and Sperry New Holland dealers, and new product applications. Photos purchased with ms with extra payment, without ms, or on assignment. Captions required. Uses "good cover shots in which our equipment appears" and agricultural photos. Payment: "no set figure for photos. If they are good we'll pay a fair price." Size: 8x10 for b&w; 2¼x2¼ for color.

THINK, 7-11 S. Broadway, White Plains NY 10601. (914)696-4755. Editor: C.B. Hansen. For company employees with interests in science, business, technology and other topics. Publication of IBM. Established in 1935. Every 2 months. Circulation: 170,000. Rights purchased vary with author and material. Usually buys first serial rights. Buys about 20 mss per year. Pays on acceptance. Will send free sample copy to writer on request. Will consider photocopied submissions. No simultaneous submissions. Reports in 6 to 8 weeks. Enclose S.A.S.E.
Nonfiction and Photos: Art Director: Ben Carucci. Wants mss on science, technology, business, data processing and other business-related topics. Would like to see any topical themes in business such as privacy, international corporations and consumerism. Buys informational, how-to, interview, profile, "think" pieces. "Most stories done on assignment. Length: 500 to 2,000 words. Payment "varies with writer's experience. Generally adhere to going market rate." Photos purchased with accompanying ms with extra payment or on assignment. Captions required. B&w only. Payment "depends on quality and experience."

TRACK TALK, Kershaw Manufacturing Co., Inc., 2205 W. Fairview, Montgomery AL 36108. (205)263-5581. Editor-in-Chief: Mike Murrell. Emphasizes "railroad maintenance-of-way for a male audience; primarily engineers, formally educated or self-made; straight shooters who know their work inside and out; usually railroad buffs." Quarterly magazine; 20 pages. Estab: 1947. Circ: 7,500. Pays on publication. Buys one-time rights. Phone queries OK. Submit seasonal/holiday material 6 months in advance. Simultaneous, photocopied and previously published submissions OK. SASE. Reports in 6 weeks. Free sample copy and writer's guidelines.
Nonfiction: Articles on historical cars, events, people in railroading; how-to (on various manners in which engineering departments on different railroads maintain their rights-of-way); informational (innovations in track maintenance); interviews (with chief engineers of railroads making favorable comments on Kershaw machinery); articles on Kershaw machinery in operation worldwide, profiles and technical articles. Buys 1-2 mss/issue. Query. Length: 500-1,250 words. Pays $25-60.
Photos: B&w and color purchased with or without mss or on assignment. Captions required. Query or send transparencies. Pays $5-25 for 5x7 or 8x10 b&w glossies; $25-50 for 2¼x2¼ color transparencies.

UNIROYAL WORLD, Oxford Management and Research Center, Middlebury CT 06749. (203)573-2218. Editor: Renee Follett. Published by Uniroyal, Inc. for "wage and salary employees, all ages and educations; they are plant, office, and management employees." Established in 1964. 8 times a year. Circulation: 65,000. Copyrighted. Pays on acceptance. Will send a sample copy to a writer on request. Will consider photocopied submissions. Reports in 3 weeks. Enclose S.A.S.E.
Nonfiction and Photos: "This publication deals primarily with Uniroyal —its people, places and products. We publish general information dealing with specific aspects of Uniroyal and the rubber industry. Articles must relate to Uniroyal employees." Buys informational articles, how-to's, personal experience articles, interviews, profiles, humor, think articles, coverage of successful business operations and merchandising techniques. Length: 600 to 1,200 words. Pays $10-200. 8x10 b&w glossies purchased with mss; captions required. Pays $10-50/photo.

UNITED HORSEMEN, United Horsemen of America, Inc., Drawer 690, Middleboro, MA 02346. (617)947-8314. Editor-in-Chief: Chris Wirtzburger. Managaing Editor: Ruth LaPergola. For all horsemen and horse lovers. Quarterly magazine; 36 pages. Estab: 1976. Circ: 6,500. Pays on publication. Buys all rights, but may reassign rights following publication. Photocopied and previously published submissions OK. SASE. Reports in 3 months. Free sample copy.

Nonfiction: How-to (training, riding, etc.); humor (horse-related); informational; interview (with nationally known trainers, riders, etc.); personal experience; profile (current, horse-related); and travel. Buys 1-2 mss/issue. Send complete ms. Length: 500-2,500 words. Pays $20-75.

Photos: Photos purchased with accompanying ms. Captions required. Uses b&w and color 8x10 or 5x7. Total purchase price includes payment for photos.

Fillers: Jokes, gags, anecdotes and children's word games. Buys 1-2 mss/issue. Pays $1-5.

VICKERS VOICE, Box 2240, Wichita KS 67201. (316)267-0311. Editor: Derald Linn. For employees of Vickers Petroleum Corp. Quarterly magazine; 24 pages. Established in 1956. Quarterly. Circulation: 2,000. Not copyrighted. Payment on publication. Will send free sample copy to writer on request. Query first or submit complete ms. Enclose S.A.S.E.

Nonfiction and Photos: Articles about activities of the company, its parent company, and its subsidiaries. Articles showing, by example, how a service station owner or manager can make more money from an existing outlet; travel articles. Length: 500 to 1,000 words. Pays $100-150. Photos purchased with or without mss or on assignment. Captions required. Pays $10 for 8x10 b&w glossies.

Farm Publications

Today's farmer is a businessman in bib-overalls with a six-figure investment in producing foodstuffs for the country and the world. Today's farm magazines reflect this, and the successful farm freelance writer is the person who grasps this fact and turns his attentions to the business end of farming. "We need management articles," says Dick Hanson, editor of *Successful Farming.* "We don't need nostalgic treatises or ax-grinding material. Our readers are interested in dollars and cents, profit and loss."

Do you need to be a farmer to write about farming? The general consensus is yes, and no, depending on just what you're writing about. For more technical articles, most editors feel that you should have a farm background (and not just summer visits to Aunt Rhodie's farm, either) or some technical farm education. But there are plenty of writing opportunities for the general freelancer, too. Easier stories to undertake for farm publications include straight reporting of agricultural events; meetings of national agricultural organizations; or coverage of agricultural legislation. "Something that would come straight off a city news desk, almost, but would pertain strictly to agriculture," says *Dakota Farmer* editor Charles Henry. Other ideas might be articles on rural living, rural health care or transportation in small towns.

Always a commandment in any kind of writing, but possibly even more so in the farm field, is the tenet *"Study Thy Market."* The following listings for farm publications are broken down into seven categories, each specializing in a different aspect of farm publishing: crops and soil management; dairy farming; general interest farming and rural life (both national and local); livestock; miscellaneous; and poultry.

The best bet for a freelancer without much farming background is probably the general interest, family-oriented magazines. These are sort of the *Saturday Evening Posts* of the farm set. The other six categories are more specialized, dealing in only one aspect of farm production. If you do choose to try a specialized magazine, heed this advice from Richard Krumme, managing editor of *Successful Farming:* "The writer must know what he's talking about. If he doesn't, it's terribly easy to look foolish in the trade (farming) business when you're dealing with readers who are specialists."

Where should a writer go for information about farming specialities? Go to a land-grant university; there's one in every state. According to Krumme, "there's a wealth of information there, from a variety of sources. He (the writer) could start with the information branch that each land-grant university has. They have literally thousands, probably millions, of publications about current agriculture. An assortment of these would give him the fastest and best background in a short period of time that he could get anywhere." Also try farming seminars or the county extension offices.

Armed with all this information, and the knowledge that there just aren't many bumpkin farmers anymore, the ambitious freelancer can find a niche for himself in the farm publishing world. "There's a tremendous need for that farm freelancer who can write the production agricultural story. I don't need any more history or general agricultural information. I need production agriculture that pertains to my magazine," says *Dakota Farmer* editor Henry. "I want all my questions answered. I want facts, figures, dollars, cents, yields, acres, numbers. What we're trying to do for our readers is say, 'Hey, here's what this fella over here is doing. His whole program may not work for you, but some part may be applicable.' We're trying to pass on management techniques, cultural practices. I think a lot of people have a tendency to take farm magazines for granted and say, 'Hey, I can get by with murder. This is not *Time-Life.'* So, they'll send me anything and I have no choice but to put it back in the envelope and send it back."

So as you can see, there's no room for hayseeds in the farm writing field. But for the freelance writer who is willing to plow in and study, there's a good chance he'll find himself in the middle of a cash crop.

Crops and Soil Management

COTTON FARMING MAGAZINE, Little Publications, 6263 Poplar Ave., Memphis TN 38138. Editor: Tom Griffin. Buys all rights. Pays on publication. Will send a free sample copy and outline of requirements to a writer on request. Reports in approximately 3 to 6 weeks. Enclose S.A.S.E. for return of submissions.
Nonfiction and Photos: Continually looking for material on large-acreage cotton farmers (200 acres or more). Likes stories on one phase of a grower's production such as his weed control program, insect control, landforming work, or how he achieves higher than average yields. Length: 1,000 to 1,200 words with at least 3 in-the-field photos. Payment is 10¢ a word.

THE FLUE CURED TOBACCO FARMER, 559 Jones Franklin Rd., Suite 150, Raleigh NC 27606. Editor: Stephen Denny. For farmers who produce 4 or more acres of flue cured tobacco. Magazine; 40 pages. Established in 1964. Eight times a year. Circulation: 45,500. Buys all rights, but will reassign rights to author after publication. Buys 24 mss a year. Pays on publication. Will send free sample copy to writer on request. Reports immediately. Query first. Enclose S.A.S.E.
Nonfiction and Photos: Production and industry-related articles. Emphasis is on a knowledge of the industry and the ability to write specifically for it. All material must be in-depth and be up to date on all industry activities. Informational, how-to, personal experience, interview, profile, personal opinion, successful business operations. Length: open. Pays $2 per column inch. B&w glossies (5x7) purchased with mss. Pays $10. Captions required.

THE PEANUT FARMER, 559 Jones Franklin Rd., Suite 150, Raleigh NC 27606. Editor: Stephen Denny. For peanut farmers with 15 or more acres of peanuts. Magazine; 32 pages. Established in 1965. Eight times a year. Circulation: 28,500. Buys all rights, but will reassign rights to author after publication. Buys about 24 mss a year. Pays on publication. Will send free sample copy to writer on request. Query first or submit complete ms. Enclose S.A.S.E.
Nonfiction and Photos: Production and industry-related articles. Must be in-depth and up to date on all industry activities. Informational, how-to, personal experience, interview, profile, personal opinion, successful business operations. Length: open. Pays $2 a column inch. Pays $10 for 5x7 b&w glossies purchased with mss. Captions required.

POTATO GROWER OF IDAHO, Harris Publishing, Inc., Box 981, Idaho Falls ID 83401. (208)522-5187. Editor-in-Chief: Loel H. Schoonover. Emphasizes material slanted to the potato grower and the business of farming related to this subject — packing, shipping, processing, research, etc. Monthly magazine; 32-56 pages. Estab: 1972. Circ: 14,500. Pays on publication. Buys all rights, but may reassign following publication. Phone queries OK. Submit seasonal/holiday material 6 weeks in advance. Photocopied submissions and previously published work OK. SASE. Reports in 1 month. Free sample copy and editorial guidelines.
Nonfiction: Expose (facts, not fiction or opinion, pertaining to the subject); how-to (do the job better, cheaper, faster, etc.); informational articles; interviews (can use one of these a month, but must come from state of Idaho since this is a regional publication, though serving the nation, tells the nation "how Idaho grows potatoes"); all types of new product articles pertaining to the subject; photo features (story can be mostly photos, but must have sufficient outlines to carry technical information); technical articles (all aspects of the industry of growing, storage, processing, packing, and research of potatoes in general, but must relate to the Idaho potato industry. Buys 24 mss/year. Query. Length: 750 words minimum. Pays 3¢/word.
Photos: B&w glossies (any size) purchased with mss or on assignment; use of color limited. Captions required. Query if photos are not to be accompanied by ms. Pays $5 minimum; $25 for color used on cover. Model release required.
How To Break In: "Choose one vital, but small, aspect of the industry; research that subject, slant it to fit the readership and/or goals of the magazine. All articles on research must have valid source for foundation. Material must be general in nature about the subject or specific in nature about Idaho potato growers. Write a query letter, noting what you have in mind for an article; be specific."

RICE FARMING MAGAZINE, Little Publications, 6263 Poplar Ave., Suite 540, Memphis TN 38138. Editor: Tom Griffin. Buys all rights. Pays on publication. Will send a free sample copy and outline of requirements to a writer on request. Reports in approximately 3 to 6 weeks. Enclose S.A.S.E. for return of submissions.
Nonfiction and Photos: Continually looking for material on large acreage rice farmers (200

acres or more). Stories on one phase of grower's production such as his weed control program, insect control, landforming work, or how he achieves higher than average yields. Include at least 3 in-the-field photos. Length: 1,000 to 1,200 words. Payment is 10¢ a word.

THE RICE JOURNAL, Box 714, Mclean VA 22101. Editor: Gordon Carlson. For readers interested in rice and rice farming and marketing. Magazine; 40 to 120 (8½x11) pages. Established in 1897. Monthly. Circulation: 10,000. Buys all rights, but will reassign rights to author after publication. Buys about 12 mss a year. Pays on publication. Reports in 10 days. Query first. Enclose S.A.S.E.

Nonfiction and Photos: Informational, profile, humor and travel; related to rice industry. Articles on duck hunting. Length: open. Pays minimum of $40 for articles, less for fillers. B&w photos and color transparencies purchased without mss. Pays $25 for b&w; $50 for color.

SOYBEAN DIGEST, American Soybean Association, Box 158, Hudson IA 50643. (319)988-3295. Editor: James L. Bramblett. Emphasizes soybean production and marketing. Monthly magazine; 60 pages. Estab: 1940. Circ: 22,000. Pays on acceptance. Buys all rights, but may reassign following publication. Phone queries OK. Submit seasonal or holiday material 2 months in advance. Photocopied submissions OK. SASE. Reports in 2-3 weeks. Sample copy 50¢.

Nonfiction: How-to (produce or market soybeans); informational articles (concerning soybean production and marketing); personal opinion (farmer-related stories on soybean production and marketing). Buys 120 mss/year. Query or submit complete ms. Length: 300-1,200 words. Pays $50-250.

Photos: Grant Mangold, Editor. B&w semi-glossies (8x10) and color transparencies (35mm or larger) purchased with or without mss. Need for captions depends on subject matter. Query or send contact sheets or transparencies. Pays $5-35 for b&w; $5-100 for color.

How To Break In: "We like 'people' copy. Use live people in your stories, especially successful farmers. Growing soybeans is a subjective science. We don't like to say 'Plant beans 2 inches deep' but rather, 'John Jones has had greatest success planting 2 inched deep in silt loam soil'."

THE SUGAR BEET, The Almalgamated Sugar Co., Box 1520, Ogden UT 84402. (801)399-3431. Editor-in-Chief: A.L. Hanline. "Primarily for beet growers in Idaho, Oregon, and Utah. Also goes to research personnel, agricultural companies, local bankers, equipment dealers, etc., and other beet sugar companies." Quarterly magazine; 24 pages. Estab: 1937. Circ: 4,500. Pays on publication. Not copyrighted. Phone queries OK. Submit seasonal/holiday material 3-6 months in advance. Previously published submissions OK, "if timely and appropriate." Reports in 2 weeks. Free sample copy and writer's guidelines.

Nonfiction: How-to, informational, interview, personal experience, technical. Buys 3-4 mss/year. Query. Length: 500-2,000 words. Pays $50-100.

Photos: Purchased with accompanying ms. Captions required. No additional payment for photos accepted with ms. Send 5x7 b&w glossies. Query. Model release required.

WESTERN FRUIT GROWER, 300 Valley St., Sausalito CA 94965. (415)332-5006. Editor: Harold T. Rogers. For commercial fruit and nut growers in the Western U.S. Magazine; 50 pages. Established in 1950. Monthly. Circulation: 22,000. Not copyrighted. Buys 10 to 15 mss per year. Pays on publication. Will send free sample copy to writer on request. No photocopied or simultaneous submissions. Reports in 2 weeks. Query first. Enclose S.A.S.E.

Nonfiction and Photos: Wants mss dealing with production and marketing operations, semi-technical production research and farm experience operation. Prefers business magazine approach. Pays $50 to $100 for nonfiction mss. Length: 700 to 1,000 words. B&w photos used with mss with no extra payment. Color purchased only on assignment.

Dairy Farming

Publications for dairymen are classified here. Publications for farmers who raise animals for meat, wool, or hides are included in the Livestock category. Other magazines that buy material on dairy herds will be found in the General Interest Farming and Rural Life classification. Journals for dairy products retailers will be found under Dairy Products in the Trade Journals section.

DAIRY GOAT JOURNAL, P.O. Box 1908, Scottsdale AR 85252. Editor: Kent Leach. Monthly for breeders and raisers of dairy goats. Generally buys exclusive rights. Pays on acceptance. Sample copy will be sent on request. Reports in ten days. Query first. Enclose S.A.S.E.

Nonfiction and Photos: Uses articles, items, and photos that deal with dairy goats, and the people who raise them. Goat dairies and shows. How-to-do-it articles up to 1,000 words. Pays 7¢/word. Also buys 8x10 b&w photos for $1 to $15.

DAIRY HERD MANAGEMENT, Miller Publishing Co., Box 67, Minneapolis MN 55440. (612)374-5200. Editor: George Ashfield. Emphasizes dairy farming. Monthly magazine; 60 pages. Estab: 1963. Circ: 55,000. Pays on acceptance. Buys all rights, but may reassign following publication. Submit seasonal/holiday material 2 months in advance. Photocopied and previously published submissions OK. SASE. Reports in 3-6 weeks. Free sample copy and writer's guidelines.

Nonfiction: How-to, informational, technical. Buys 12-15 mss/year. Query. Length: 1,000-3,000 words. Pays $75-200. "Articles should concentrate on useful management information. Be specific rather than general."

THE DAIRYMAN, P.O. Box 819, Corona CA 91720. Editor: Dolores Davis Mullings. For large herd dairy farmers. Monthly. Buys reprint rights. Pays on publication. Will send a sample copy to a writer on request. Reports in 3 weeks. Enclose S.A.S.E.

Nonfiction and Photos: Uses articles on anything related to dairy farming, preferably anything new and different or substantially unique in operation, for U.S. subjects. Acceptance of foreign dairy farming stories based on potential interest of readers. Pays $1.50 per printed inch. Buys photos with or without mss. Pays $5 each.

DAIRYMEN'S DIGEST (Southern Region Edition), P.O. Box 809, Arlington TX 76010. Editor: Phil Porter. For commercial dairy farmers and their families, throughout the central U.S., with interests in dairy production and marketing. Magazine; 32 (8½x11) pages. Established in 1969. Monthly. Circulation: 9,000. Not copyrighted. Buys about 34 mss a year. Pays on publication. Will send free sample copy to writer on request. Reports in 3 weeks. SASE.

Nonfiction and Photos: Emphasis on dairy production and marketing. Buys articles of general interest to farm families, especially dairy-oriented. Seeks unusual accomplishments and satisfactions resulting from determination and persistence. Must be positive and credible. Needs newsbreaks, fresh ideas, profile, personal experience articles. Buys some historical, inspirational or nostalgia. Also articles of interest to farm wives. Length: 50 to 1,500 words. Pay varies from $10 to $125 per article, plus additional amount for photos, depending on quality.

General Interest Farming and Rural Life

The publications listed here aim at farm families or farmers in general and contain material on sophisticated agricultural and business techniques. Magazines that specialize in the raising of crops will be found in the Crops and Soil Management classification; publications exclusively for dairymen are included under Dairy Farming; publications that deal exclusively with livestock raising are classified in the Livestock category; magazines for poultry farmers are grouped under the Poultry classification. Magazines that aim at farm suppliers are grouped under Agricultural Equipment and Supplies in the Trade Journals section.

National

AGWAY COOPERATOR, Box 1333, Syracuse NY 13201. (315)477-6488. Editor: James E. Hurley. For farmers. Monthly. Pays on acceptance. Usually reports in 1 week. Enclose S.A.S.E. for return of submissions.

Nonfiction: Should deal with topics of farm or rural interest in the northeastern U.S. Length: 1,200 words maximum. Payment is $75, usually including photos.

Photos: Payment is $10 for photos purchased singly.

AG WORLD, 20 E. Kent St., St. Paul MN 55102. (612)225-6211. Editor-in-Chief: Ed Jackson. Emphasizes economic and social aspects of agriculture. Monthly tabloid; 24 pages. Estab: 1975. Circ: 6,000. Pays on publication. Buys all rights, but may reassign following publication. Phone queries OK. Simultaneous, photocopied, and previously published submissions OK. SASE. Reports in 4 weeks. Sample copy $1.

Nonfiction: Expose, informational and personal opinion articles; interviews and profiles. Submit complete ms. Length: 750-3,000 words. Pays 10¢/word.

CAPPER'S WEEKLY, Stouffer Publications, Inc., 616 Jefferson St., Topeka KS 66607. (913)357-4421. Editor-in-Chief: Dorothy Harvey. Emphasizes home and family. Biweekly tabloid; 24 pages. Estab: 1879. Circ: 425,000. Pays for poetry and cartoons on acceptance; articles on publication. Buys first North American serial rights. Submit seasonal/holiday material 2 months in advance. SASE. Reports in 2-3 weeks, 6-8 months for serialized novels. Sample copy 35¢.
Nonfiction: Historical (local museums, etc.), inspirational, nostalgia, travel (local slants) and people stories (accomplishments, collections, etc). Buys 2-3 mss/issue. Submit complete ms. Length: 700 words maximum. Pays $1/inch.
Photos: Purchased with accompanying ms. Submit prints. Pays $5 for 8x10 b&w glossy prints. Total purchase price for ms includes payment for photos.
Columns, Departments: Heart of the Home (homemakers' letters, hints), Hometown Heartbeat (descriptive). Submit complete ms. Length: 500 words maximum. Pays $2-10.
Fiction: Novel length mystery and romance mss. Buys 2-3 mss/year. Query. Pays $200.
Poetry: Free verse, haiku, light verse, traditional. Buys 7-8/issue. Limit submissions to batches of 5-6. Length: 4-16 lines. Pays $3-5.

THE COUNTRY GENTLEMAN, 1100 Waterway Blvd., Indianapolis IN 46202. Editor-in-Chief: Starkey Flythe, Jr. Managing Editor: Michael New. Emphasizes country living. Quarterly magazine; 120 pages. Circ: 250,000. Pays on publication. Usually buys all rights, first rights or second serial (reprint) rights. Photocopied submissions OK. SASE. Reports in about 4 weeks. Sample copy, $1.
Nonfiction: Articles and stories on how to acquire and care for a country place. How-to's, personalities, travel, food and humor. Recent articles have dealt with greenhouses, iris propagation, English country houses, keeping a horse in the suburbs, recycling log cabins, the American rifle, Teddy Roosevelt's Bully Hilltop and fly tying. Length: 2,000 words maximum. Pays $50-200.
Photos: "We buy color photographs and illustrations having to do with rural life in America and abroad." Pays $25-75.
Fiction: Mainstream, mystery, adventure, western and humorous stories. Length: 2,000 words maximum. Pays $75-200.
Poetry: Traditional forms of poetry, blank verse, free verse, light verse and humorous or serious poetry on country or outdoor themes. Length: 5-30 lines. Pays $10-50.

COUNTRYSIDE, 312 Highway 19 E., Waterloo WI 53594. (414)478-2118. Editor: Jerome D. Belanger. Emphasizes practical small farming and organic agriculture; homesteading. Monthly magazine; 88 pages. Estab: 1917. Circ: 29,000. Pays on publication. Buys all rights, but may reassign following publication. Submit seasonal/holiday material 6 months in advance. SASE. Reports in 2 months. Free sample copy and writer's guidelines.
Nonfiction: Expose (agri-business); how-to (organic farming and gardening, practical self-sufficiency); informational (soil science, biological insect control, intermediate technology, alternative sources of energy, nutrition); interviews (farmers, researchers, agricultural consultants, politicians); and personal experience (as it relates to farming on a small scale or using organic methods). Buys 70-100 mss/year. Query or submit complete ms. Length: 750-3,500 words. Pays $25-250.
Photos: Lea Landmann, Photo Editor. Purchased with or without accompanying ms or on assignment. Send contact sheet or transparencies. Pays $2.50-5 for b&w photos; $35 for color transparencies. Total purchase price for ms includes payment for photos.
Columns/Departments: Cow Barn (material on keeping a family cow or small dairy herd) and Pig Pen (small scale commercial swine production or for family meat supply). Also needs material on sheep, bees, poultry, rabbits and small farm machinery. Buys 10-12/year. Query or submit complete ms. Length: 750-1,500 words. Pays $25-50. Open to suggestions for new columns/departments.
Fillers: Clippings, jokes, gags, anecdotes, newsbreaks, and short humor. Buys 24/year. Submit complete ms. Length: 25-100 words. Pays $10-25.

FARM JOURNAL, Washington Square, Philadelphia PA 19105. Editor: Lane Palmer. Many separate editions for different parts of the U.S. Material bought for one or more editions depending upon where it fits. Buys all rights. Payment made on acceptance and is the same regardless of editions in which the piece is used. Query before submitting material. Enclose S.A.S.E.
Nonfiction: Timeliness and seasonableness are very important. Material must be highly prac-

tical and should be helpful to as many farmers as possible. Farmers' experiences should apply to one or more of these 8 basic commodities: corn, wheat, milo, soybeans, cotton, dairy, beef, and hogs. Technical material must be accurate. Pays $25 minimum.

Photos: Much in demand either separately or with short how-to material in picture stories and as illustrations for articles. Warm human interest pix for covers—activities on modern farms. For inside use, shots of homemade and handy ideas to get work done easier and faster, farm news photos, and pictures of farm people with interesting hobbies. In b&w, 8x10 glossies are preferred; color submissions should be 2¼x2¼ for the cover, and 35mm for inside use. Pays $50 and up for b&w shot; $75 and up for color.

THE FURROW, Deere & Co., John Deere Rd., Moline IL 61265. Executive Editor: Ralph E. Reynolds. For commercial farmers and ranchers. Magazine; 8 times/year; 40 pages. Estab: 1895. Circ: 1.2 million. Buys all rights, but may reassign following publication. Phone queries OK. Submit seasonal/holiday material at least 6 months in advance. SASE. Reports in 2 weeks. Free sample copy and writer's guidelines.

Nonfiction: George R. Sollenberger, North American Editor. "We want articles describing new developments in the production and marketing of crops and livestock. These could be classified as how-to, informational and technical, but all must have a news angle. All articles should include some interviews, but we rarely use straight interviews. We publish articles describing farmers' personal experiences with new practices. We occasionally use photo features related to agriculture, as well as occasional guest editorials on the Commentary page." Buys 10-15 mss/year. Submit complete ms. Length: 300-1,000 words. Pays $100-400.

Photos: Wayne Burkart, Art Editor. Original color transparencies (no copies) or color negatives of any size used only with mss. Captions required. Send negatives or transparencies with ms. No additional payment.

How To Break In: "By studying our publication and knowing what type of articles we publish. He/she should also know what the farm press in general has been publishing lately."

THE NATIONAL FUTURE FARMER, Box 15130, Alexandria VA 22309. (703)360-3600. Editor-in-Chief: Wilson W. Carnes. For members of the Future Farmers of America who are students of vocational agriculture in high school, ranging in age from 14-21; major interest in careers in agriculture/agribusiness and other youth interest subjects. Bimonthly magazine; 52 pages. Estab: 1952. Circ: 533,684. Pays on acceptance. Buys all rights, but may reassign following publication. Phone queries OK. Submit seasonal/holiday material 3-4 months in advance. SASE. Usually reports in 2 weeks. Free sample copy and writer's guidelines.

Nonfiction: How-to for youth (outdoor type such as camping, hunting, fishing); informational (getting money for college, farming; other help for youth). Informational, personal experience and interviews are used only if FFA members or former members are involved. Buys 2-3 mss/issue. Query or send complete ms. Length: 1,200 words maximum. Pays 2½-4¢/word.

Photos: Purchased with mss (5x7 or 8x10 b&w glossies; 35mm or larger color transparencies). Pays $5-7.50 for b&w; $25-35 for inside color; $100 for cover.

How To Break In: "Find an FFA member who has done something truly outstanding which will motivate and inspire others, or provide helpful information for a career in farming, ranching or agribusiness."

REPORT ON FARMING, Free Press, 300 Carlton St., Winnipeg, Manitoba, Canada R3C 3C1. (204)269-4237. Managing Editor: Leo Quigley. For "upper income, progressive farmers." Weekly tabloid; 32 pages. Estab: 1880. Circ: 180,000. Pays on acceptance. Buys one-time rights. Phone queries OK. Submit seasonal/holiday material 5 weeks in advance. Simultaneous, photocopied and previously published submissions OK. SASE. Reports in 4 weeks. Free sample copy.

Nonfiction: Expose (with direct impact on Canadian farmers), how-to, informational (analysis, background, think pieces), interview (agriculturally important individuals, power brokers, progressive farmers), profile, technical, agricultural market analysis. "We also use *many* short, hard news stories." Submit complete ms. Length: 1,500 words maximum. Pays $20 for news items, $50-150 minimum for "solid features."

Photos: Purchased with accompanying ms. Captions required. Pays $5-20 for b&w prints.

For 1978: "We have a large number of special supplements dealing with farm management, chemical use, machinery, travel, dairy and beef and hogs."

SUCCESSFUL FARMING, 1716 Locust St., Des Moines IA 50336. (515)284-9204. Editor: Dick Hanson. For top farmers. Established in 1902. 13 times a year. Circulation: 750,000. Buys all rights. Pays on acceptance. No photocopied or simultaneous submissions. Reports in 4 to 6 weeks. Query first. Enclose S.A.S.E.

Nonfiction: Semi-technical articles on the aspects of farming with emphasis on how to apply this information to one's own farm. "Most of our material is too limited and unfamiliar for freelance writers — except for the few who specialize in agriculture, have a farm background and a modern agricultural education." Length: about 1,500 words maximum. Pays competitive rates.

Photos: Ralph Figg, Art Director, prefers 8x10 b&w glossies to contacts; color should be 2¼x2¼, 4x5 or 8x10. Buys exclusive rights and pays $20 for b&w, more for color. Assignments are given, and sometimes a guarantee, provided the editors can be sure the photography will be acceptable. Pays for meals, phone, lodging.

Local

AGROLOGIST, Agricultural Institute of Canada, 151 Slater St., Suite 907, Ottawa, Ontario, Canada K1P 5H4. Managing Editor: W. E. Henderson. For professionals in agriculture: scientists, researchers, economists, teachers, extension workers; most are members of the Agricultural Institute of Canada. Magazine; 40 pages. Established in 1934. Quarterly. Circulation: 6,500. Not copyrighted. Buys 1 or 2 mss a year. Pays on acceptance; occasionally in contributor's copies. Will send free sample copy to writer on request. No photocopied submissions but will consider simultaneous submissions, if so identified. Reports in 1 to 2 weeks. Query first or submit complete ms. Enclose S.A.E. and International Reply Coupons.

Nonfiction and Photos: Articles on subjects of interest to a wide range of disciplines within agriculture, such as results and applications of new research, economic implications, international agricultural trends, overviews, transportation, education, marketing, etc. Highly technical and specialized material presented as much as possible in layman's language. Main interest is not in new facts, but in the interpretation and implication of facts and situations. "We don't publish 'as is' technical papers (such as those prepared for symposia) or scientific journal material. But we will look at it. If the information is of interest, we could suggest how it might be rewritten for our use. We are particularly interested in articles that highlight how some action of agriculture is affecting nonagriculture areas; e.g., ecology topics, food crisis, etc." Length: 500 to 2,500 words. Most articles are not paid for; those that are average $100 for 1,500 words. No additional payment for b&w photos used with mss. Pays $5 to $15 for 8x10 b&w glossies purchased without mss or on assignment.

AMERICAN AGRICULTURALIST AND THE RURAL NEW YORKER, P.O. Box 370, Ithaca NY 14850. Editor: Gordon Conklin. Monthly. Copyrighted. Pays on acceptance. Will send a free sample copy to a writer on request. Reports immediately. Enclose S.A.S.E. for return of submissions.

Nonfiction and Photos: Short articles on farm subjects of general interest to farm and suburban dwellers. Pays 2¢ to 3¢ a word. Photos purchased with mss and with captions only. Pays $5.

BUCKEYE FARM NEWS, Ohio Farm Bureau Federation, 245 N. High St., Columbus OH 43216. (614)225-8906. Editor-in-Chief: S.C. Cashan. Emphasizes agricultural policy. Monthly magazine; 53 pages. Estab: 1922. Circ: 85,000. Pays on acceptance. Buys all rights, but may reassign following publication. Phone queries OK. Submit holiday/seasonal material 3 months in advance. Simultaneous, photocopied, and previously published submissions OK. SASE. Reports in 3 weeks. Free sample copy.

Nonfiction: Exposes (on government, agriculture); humor (light pieces about farm life); informational (but no nuts-and-bolts farming); inspirational (as long as they're not too heavy); personal opinion; and interview. Buys 20 mss/year. Query. Length: 500-2,000 words. Pays $25-$100.

Photos: B&w and color purchased with mss or on assignment. Captions required. Send prints and transparencies. Pays $5-10 for b&w.

Poetry: Traditional forms and light verse. Buys 12/year. Limit submissions to batches of 3. Pays $10-25.

Fillers: Buys about 6 newsbreaks/year. Length: 100-250 words. Pays $10-$25.

CAROLINA COOPERATOR, 125 E. Davie, Raleigh NC 27601. (919)828-4411. Editor: Robert J. Wachs. For Carolina farmers. Monthly. Buys all rights. Not many freelance articles bought. Pays on publication. Will send a free sample copy to a writer on request. Reports as soon as possible. Enclose S.A.S.E.

Nonfiction: Interested only in material related to Carolina agriculture, rural living, and farmer co-ops. Newsy features on successful or unusual farmers and their methods, with the intent to entertain or inform. Length: 1,200 words maximum. Payment is $35 to $50 per published page.

COUNTRY WORLD, (formerly *Oklahoma Ranch and Farm World*), Box 1770, Tulsa OK 74102. (918)583-2161, Ext. 230. Editor: Herb Karner. For a rural, urban, and suburban readership. Monthly. Buys first serial rights. Pays on publication. Query first. Enclose S.A.S.E.
Nonfiction and Photos: Wants farm and ranch success stories; also suburban living, home-making, youth, 4-H, and F.F.A. Effective photo illustrations necessary. Preferred length: 700 to 800 words. Pays $7.50 a column, sometimes more for exceptional copy. Photos purchased with mss and occasionally with captions only. Prefers b&w glossies, at least 5x7.

THE DAKOTA FARMER, P.O. Box 1950, Aberdeen SD 57401. (605)225-5170. Editor: Russ Oviatt. For farmers and families in North and South Dakota. "All have agriculturally related occupations and interests." Special issues include Beef issue (August). Monthly. Circulation: 80,000. Rights bought "depend on story and author. We are flexible." Buys 15 to 25 mss a year. Pays on publication. Will send a sample copy to a writer on request. Submit seasonal material 3 to 4 months in advance. Returns rejected material in approximately 15 days. Query first. Enclose S.A.S.E.
Nonfiction: "Human interest features of Dakota farm people, history, or events. Keep in mind we write for Dakotans. Stories should be geared to that audience. Articles should be objective. We take sides on controversial issues on our editorial page only." Buys how-to's, personal experience stories, interviews, new product articles, photo essays, historical and travel pieces, and successful business operation coverage. Length: 500 to 2,000 words. Payment based on "sliding scale."
Photos: Purchased with mss. With captions only. B&w glossies.
Poetry: Department Editor: Karen Buechler. Buys traditional and contemporary poetry and light verse. Length: 5 to 15 lines. Pays $5 to $8 per poem.

FARM AND COUNTRY, 30 Bloor St., W., Toronto, Ontario M4W 1AE Canada. Editor: John Phillips. News Editor: Michael Sage. For Ontario farmers. Tabloid newspaper; 40 pages. Established in 1894. 19 times a year. Circulation: 86,000. Buys all rights, but will reassign rights to author after publication. Buys 120 mss a year. Payment on publication. Write for copy of guidelines for writers. Will consider photocopied submissions. Submit seasonal material 4 weeks in advance. Reports in 1 week. Query first. Enclose S.A.E. and International Reply Coupons.
Nonfiction and Photos: Informational articles on farm business, how-to-do-it around the farm; practical application of agricultural research. "Keep to the subject. We like crisp, short sentences, an original approach, simple style. Nothing folksy or homespun." Length: 250 to 600 words. Pays $2 to $4 per 37 words. Buys 5x7 glossies with mss. Pays $8. Captions required.

FARMFUTURES, 225 E. Michigan, Milwaukee WI 53202. (414)276-6600. Editor: Royal Fraedrich. For high income farmers. Magazine; 32 (8½x11) pages. Established in 1973. Monthly. Circulation: 42,500. Buys all rights. Buys 60 to 100 mss a year. Pays on publication. Will send free sample copy to writer on request. No photocopied or simultaneous submissions. Reports on material accepted for publication in 30 days. Returns rejected material in 2 weeks. Query first. Enclose S.A.S.E.
Nonfiction and Photos: "Ours is the only national farm magazine devoted exclusively to marketing and the financial management side of farming. We are looking for case histories of successful use of commodity futures markets by farm operators. Major articles deal with marketing and financial strategies of high income farmers. Major commodity interests include corn, cattle, hogs, soybeans, wheat, cotton, and other grains. Market material must be current; thus, must be written within 2 to 3 weeks of publication." Interviews, profiles, personal experience and successful business operation articles pertaining to agricultural commodity markets. Length: 1,000 to 2,000 words. Pays $50 to $250. No additional payment for b&w photos used with mss.

FARMLAND NEWS, P.O. Box 7305, Kansas City MO 64116. Editor: Frank C. Whitsitt. For rural members of farmer co-ops. Tabloid newspaper; 24-32 pages. Estab: 1932. Not co-pyrighted. Buys 25 to 50 mss/year. Will send free sample copy to writer on request. No photocopied or simultaneous submissions. Submit seasonal material (Christmas, Thanksgiving, Easter) 6 months in advance. Reports on material accepted for publication in 1 to 2 weeks. Returns rejected material in a few days. Query first. Enclose S.A.S.E.
Nonfiction: "We try to personalize and humanize stories of broad significance. We use features of interest to our rural audience, as well as holiday-slanted material (Christmas, Thanksgiving, Easter)." Length: open. Pays $25-125.

FLORIDA GROWER & RANCHER, 559 Jones Franklin Rd., Suite 150, Raleigh NC 27606. Editor: Stephen Denny. For citrus grove managers and production managers; vegetable growers and managers. Magazine; 24 pages. Established in 1912. Monthly except for combined June/July issue. Circulation: 12,000. Buys all rights, but will reassign rights to author after publication. Buys about 40 mss a year. Pays on publication. Will send free sample copy to writer on request. Reports on material immediately. Query first or submit complete ms. Enclose S.A.S.E.

Nonfiction and Photos: Articles on production and industry-related topics. In-depth and up to date. Writer must know the market and write specifically for it. Informational, how-to, personal experience, interview, profile, personal opinion, successful business operations. Length: open. Pays $2 a column inch. Pays $10 for 5x7 b&w glossies used with mss. Captions required.

FLORIDAGRICULTURE, P.O. Box 730, Gainesville FL 32602. (904)378-1321, ext. 307. Editor: Andy Williams. For members of the Florida Farm Bureau Federation. Monthly magazine; 32-40 pages. Estab: 1941. Circ: 60,000. Pays on acceptance. Buys first North American serial rights. Phone queries OK. Submit seasonal/holiday material 3 months in advance. Previously published submissions OK. SASE. Reports in 4 weeks.

Nonfiction and Photos: "We cover the broad spectrum of Florida farming and use articles of general interest to Florida farmers. We can't stress the word 'Florida' enough. The outlook is always toward the Florida farmer. The Federation serves all farmers, not specialized interests. Our theme is 'The Voice of Agriculture.' Articles on the economic problems facing the farmer and how he can best meet them would be of interest. And remember, understand your subject matter thoroughly because the farmer will. We like crisp, provocative writing. Don't make it so folksy as to appear to be writing down to your reader. Please, no stories on why the farmer isn't to blame for high food prices. And, no stories on part-time farmers, or on people who have moved from the big city to get back to rural life." Length: 750-2,000 words. Pays $50-250. No additional payment for b&w photos used with mss. But b&w photo essays of Florida farm scenes will be considered. Payment negotiable.

GEORGIA FARMER, 500 Plasamour Dr., P.O. Box 13449, Atlanta GA 30324. (404)876-1800. Editor: Ron Edmundson. For commercial farmers of Georgia. Monthly. Not copyrighted. Pays on publication. Reports immediately. Query helps, but must have meat in it. Enclose S.A.S.E.

Nonfiction and Photos: Concise how-to and success farm stories localized to Georgia. Subject can vary anywhere within the areas of interest to farm readers or agribusiness readers. Length: 1,200 words maximum. Payment is $5 to $50. Photos are occasionally bought with mss; payment included in price of article. Any size; color used.

MICHIGAN FARMER, 3303 W. Saginaw St., Lansing MI 48917. (517)372-4407. Editor: Richard Lehnert. Semimonthly. Buys first North American rights. Pays on acceptance. Reports in 1 month. Query first. Enclose S.A.S.E.

Nonfiction: Uses articles of interest and value to Michigan farmers, which discuss Michigan agriculture and the people involved in it. "These are fairly technical. Also articles for home section about Michigan farm housewives and what they are doing. Although articles are technical, lucid easy-to-understand writing is desired. Length depends on topic." Rates are 2¢ a word minimum; special stories bring higher rates.

Photos: Buys some b&w singles; also a few color transparencies, for cover use. Pays $2 to $5 each for b&w, depending on quality. Pays $60 for selected cover transparencies of identifiable Michigan farm or rural scenes.

MONTANA RURAL ELECTRIC NEWS, Montana Associated Utilities, Inc., Box 1641, Great Falls MT 59403. (404)454-1412. Managing Editor: Russell J. Cox. Emphasizes rural life. For farmers, ranchers and rural dwellers. Monthly magazine; 32 pages. Estab: 1951. Circ: 40,000. Pays on publication. Buys one-time rights. Phone queries OK. Simultaneous photocopied, and previously published submissions OK. SASE. Reports in 3 weeks. Free sample copy.

Nonfiction: How-to, informational, historical, humor, inspirational, nostalgic and travel articles; interviews and photo features. Query. Length: 500-2,000 words. Pays $15 minimum.

Photos: Purchased with mss or on assignment. Captions required. Query. Pays $10 minimum for 8x10 (or 5x7 minimum) b&w glossies. Model release required.

THE OHIO FARMER, 1350 W. 5th Ave., Columbus OH 43212. (614)486-9637. Editor: Andrew Stevens. For Ohio farmers and their families. Magazine; 50 pages. Established in 1848.

Every 2 weeks. Circulation: 103,000. Rights purchased vary with author and material. Usually buys all rights, but may reassign rights to author after publication. Buys 15 to 20 mss per year. Pays on publication. Will send sample copy to writer for $1. Write for editorial guidelines. Will consider photocopied submissions. No simultaneous submissions. Reports in 2 weeks. Submit complete ms. Enclose S.A.S.E.

Nonfiction and Photos: Technical and on-the-farm stories. Buys informational, how-to, personal experience. Length: 600 to 700 words. Pays $15. Photos purchased with ms with no additional payment, or without ms. Pays $5 to $25 for b&w; $35 to $100 for color. Size: 4x5 for b&w glossies; transparencies or 8x10 prints for color.

RURAL ELECTRIC MISSOURIAN, 2722 E. McCarty St., Jefferson City MO 65101. (314)635-6857. Editor: Don Yoest. For rural readers (farm and nonfarm). Monthly. Not copyrighted. Buys exclusive Missouri first rights. Pays on acceptance. Usually reports in 30 to 120 days. Query. SASE. Sample copy 50¢.

Nonfiction: Buys articles on electrical equipment—new applications in home, farm, shop, business, or cooperative business. Also needs human interest material, preferably with a humorous rural flavor. Length: 500-1,500 gords. Payment varies and is negotiated.

Photos: 8x10 b&w glossies occasionally purchased either with mss or with captions only. Payment varies; minimum $5 a photo.

Poetry: "Short, human interest, rural items needed." Pays $7.

SOUTH CAROLINA FARMER-GROWER, 500 Plasamour Dr., Box 13449, Atlanta GA 30324. (404)876-1800. Editor: Ron Edmundson. For commercial farmers of South Carolina. Monthly. Not copyrighted. Pays on publication. Reports immediately. Query helps, but must have meat in it. Enclose S.A.S.E.

Nonfiction and Photos: Wants concise how-to and success farm stories localized to South Carolina. Subject can vary anywhere within the areas of interest to farm readers or agribusiness readers. Length: 1,200 words maximum. B&w or color photos, any size, occasionally bought with mss. Payment (including photos) is $5 to $50.

WALLACES FARMER, 1912 Grand Ave., Des Moines IA 50305. (515)243-6181. Editor: Monte N. Sesker. For Iowa farmers and their families. Semimonthly. Buys Midwest States rights (Nebraska, Minnesota, Wisconsin, Illinois, Missouri, South Dakota, and Iowa). Pays on acceptance. Reports in 2 weeks. Enclose S.A.S.E.

Nonfiction and Photos: Occasional short feature articles about Iowa farming accompanied by photos. Payment varies. Length: 500 to 750 words. Pays about $50. Photos purchased with or without mss. Should be taken on Iowa farms. Pays $7 to $15 for 8x10 b&w; $50 to $100 for 4x5, 2¼x2¼ color transparencies. See recent issue covers for examples.

WISCONSIN AGRICULTURIST, Farm Progress Publications, 2976 Triverton Pike, Box 4420, Madison WI 53711. (608)274-9400. Editor: Ralph Yohe. For Wisconsin farmers. Semimonthly tabloid; 60 pages. Estab: 1848. Circ: 102,000. Pays on acceptance. Rights purchased vary, depending on state and situation. Phone queries OK. Submit holiday or seasonal material 3-4 months in advance. Simultaneous submissions and previously published work OK if advised of circumstances. SASE. Reports in 1 month.

Nonfiction: Frank Hill, Managing Editor. How-to articles useful to Wisconsin farmers and informational articles about what is going on in farming are primary needs. "We also buy quite a bit for our home section (women or family interest)." Buys 15-20 mss/year. Submit complete ms. Length: 900-3,000 words. Pays $30-$250 "depending on value to us".

Photos: B&w glossies (5x7 or 8x10) and color transparencies (2¼x2¼ or 35mm) purchased with or without mss. Captions required. Send prints and transparencies. Pays $10-50 for b&w; $50-200 for color.

WYOMING RURAL ELECTRIC NEWS, 301 Pacific Western Bldg., Casper WY 82601. (307)234-6152. Editor: Anne Fitzstephens. For rural farmers and ranchers. Magazine; 16 pages. Established in 1954. Monthly. Circulation: 21,000. Not copyrighted. Buys about 12 mss per year. Pays on publication. Will send free sample copy to writer on request. Will consider photocopied and simultaneous submissions. Submit seasonal material 2 months in advance. Reports on mss accepted for publication in 1 week. Returns rejected material immediately. Enclose S.A.S.E.

Nonfiction, Photos and Fiction: Wants "feature material, historical pieces about the West, things of interest to Wyoming's rural people." Recently published "One Woman, Many Legends," a history piece on Sacajawea, and "Of Bullets, Barrooms and Bygone Days," fiction based on fact about Lost Springs WY. Buys informational, humor, historical, nostalgia and photo mss. Length for nonfiction and fiction: 1,500 words. Pays $25. Photos purchased with accompanying ms with no additional payment, or purchased without ms. Captions required. Pays $25 for cover photos. B&w preferred. Buys experimental, western, humorous and historical fiction. Pays $25.

Livestock

Publications in this section are for farmers who raise cattle, sheep, or hogs for meat, wool, or hides. Publications for farmers who raise other animals are listed in the Miscellaneous category; also many magazines in the General Interest Farming and Rural Interest classification buy material on raising livestock. Magazines for dairymen are included under Dairy Farming. Publications dealing with raising horses, pets, or other pleasure animals will be found under Animal in the Consumer Publications section.

AMERICAN HEREFORD JOURNAL, 715 Hereford Dr., Kansas City MO 64105. Editor: Bob Day. Monthly. Buys first North American serial rights. Pays on publication. Reports in 30 days. Always query first. Enclose S.A.S.E.
Nonfiction and Photos: Breeding, feeding, and marketing of purebred and commercial Herefords, with accent on well-substantiated facts; success-type story of a Hereford cattleman and how he did it. Length: 1,000 to 1,500 words. Pays average of 2½¢ to 3¢ a word. Buys 5x7 b&w glossy photos for use with articles. Pays $3 each.

ARKANSAS CATTLE BUSINESS, 208 Wallace Bldg., Little Rock AR 72201. (501)372-3197. Editor: Mary Hinkle. For beef cattlemen. Not copyrighted. Buys 2 to 3 mss a year. Pays on acceptance. Will send a free sample copy to a writer on request. Reports in 2 weeks. Query first. Enclose S.A.S.E.
Nonfiction and Photos: Articles related to beef cattle production and allied interests, with an Arkansas slant. Could also use historical articles on Arkansas. Length: 1,000 to 2,000 words. Pays 2¢ a word maximum. Photos purchased with mss. Payment varies.

BEEF, The Webb Co., 1999 Shepard Rd., St. Paul MN 55116. (612)647-7374. Editor-in-Chief: Paul D. Andre. Managing Editor: William D. Fleming. For readers who have the same basic interest—making a living feeding cattle. Monthly magazine; 40 pages. Estab: 1964. Circ: 61,000. Pays on acceptance. Buys one-time rights. Phone queries OK. Submit seasonal material 3 months in advance. SASE. Reports in 6-8 weeks. Free sample copy and writer's guidelines.
Nonfiction: How-to and informational articles on doing a better job of feeding cattle, market building, managing, and animal health practices. Buys 8-10 mss/year. Query. Length: 500-2,000 words. Pays $25-200.
Photos: B&w glossies (8x10) and color transparencies (35mm or 2¼x2¼) purchased with or without mss. Captions required. Query or send contact sheet or transparencies. Pays $10-50 for b&w; $25-100 for color. Model release required.
How To Break In: "Be completely knowledgeable about cattle feeding. Know what makes a story. We want specifics, not a general roundup of an operation. Pick one angle and develop it fully."

BIG FARMER CATTLE, DAIRY AND HOG GUIDES, 131 Lincoln Highway, Frankfort IL 60423. (815)469-2163. Editor: Greg Northcutt. "To qualify for this controlled circulation publication, the reader must gross $20,000-plus annually." Established in 1970. Monthly, except June, July and December. Circulation: 100,000. Rights purchased vary with author and material; may buy all rights, but will reassign rights to author after publication. Pays on acceptance. Will send a sample copy to a writer on request. Will not consider photocopied submissions. Will consider cassette submissions. "We prefer articles typed at 37 characters wide and no longer than 6 typewritten pages." Submit seasonal material 3 months in advance. Reports in 1 month. Query first or submit complete ms. Enclose S.A.S.E.
Nonfiction and Photos: "Management articles must be on specific areas; not general features about an operator's operation. Articles must be to the point and acceptable for livestock producers across the country. We'd like to see articles on marketing strategies." Buys informational and how-to articles, interviews, and coverage of successful business operations. Length: 2,000 words maximum. Pays $100 minimum. Captioned photos purchased with and without mss. Pays $15 for 8x10 or 5x7 glossy prints "if not submitted with ms." Pays $25 minimum for color transparencies "from 35mm and up."

THE CATTLEMAN MAGAZINE, Texas & Southwestern Cattle Raisers Association, 410 E. Weatherford, Ft. Worth TX 76102. (817)332-7155. Editor-in-Chief: Paul W. Horn. Emphasizes beef cattle production and feeding. "Readership consists of commercial cattlemen, purebred seedstock producers, cattle feeders, horsemen in the Southwest." Monthly magazine; 200 pages. Estab: 1914. Circ: 27,000. Pays on acceptance. Buys all rights but may reassign following publication. Submit seasonal/holiday material 3 months in advance. SASE. Reports in 3 weeks. Free sample copy and writer's guidelines.

Nonfiction: Need informative, entertaining feature articles on specific commercial ranch operations, cattle breeding and feeding, range and pasture management, profit tips. Will take a few historical western lore pieces. Must be well-documented. No first person narratives or fiction. Buys 36 articles/year. Query. Length open. Pays $25-200. No articles pertaining to areas outside of southwestern U.S.

Photos: Photos purchased with or without accompanying ms. Captions required. Pays $10-25 for 8x10 b&w glossies; $25-100 for color photos. Total purchase price for ms includes payment for photos. Model release required.

CATTLEMEN, The Beef Magazine, Public Press, 1760 Ellice Ave., Winnipeg, Manitoba R3H 0B6 Canada. (204)774-1861. Editor-in-Chief: Harold Dodds. For beef producers. Monthly magazine; 50 pages. Estab: 1938. Circ: 38,900. Pays on publication. Buys all rights. Phone queries OK. Submit seasonal/holiday material 3 months in advance. Reports in 2 weeks. Free sample copy and writer's guidelines.

Nonfiction: Industry articles, particularly those on raising and feeding beef in Canada. Also how-to-do-it and success stories with good management slant. Writer must be informed. Uses an occasional historical item. Pays up to $150 for industry and historical articles, more for special assignments.

Photos: Canadian shots only, purchased with mss and for cover. B&w and color for cover. Pays up to $10 for b&w; up to $75 for color.

FEEDLOT MANAGEMENT, P.O. Box 67, Minneapolis MN 55440. Editorial Director: George Ashfield. For agri-businessmen who feed cattle and/or sheep for slaughter. Special issues include easte management (May); feeder cattle (September); nutrition (November). Monthly. Circulation: 20,000. Not copyrighted. Pays on acceptance. Will send a free sample copy to a writer on request. Reports in 1 to 5 weeks. Query first. Enclose S.A.S.E.

Nonfiction: Wants detailed, thorough material relating to cattle or lamb feeding and related subject areas—waste management, nutrition, marketing and processing, feeding, animal health. "Write for a copy of the magazine. Writers should know something about the industry in order to get the information that's important. We can accept highly technical articles, but there's no room for simple cursory articles. Feature articles on feedlots should include photos." No length restriction. Pays $30 to $200.

Photos and Fillers: 8x10 and 5x7 b&w glossies purchased with mss and with captions only. Pays 50¢ an inch for newsbreaks and clippings.

HOG FARM MANAGEMENT, Box 67, Minneapolis MN 55440. (612)374-5200. Managing Editor: John Byrnes. For "large-scale hog producers who make raising hogs their primary business. Average age: 43.5. Average education: 12.5 years. Average investment: $174,000. Average acres farmed: 558.2." Special issue in July seeks farrowing-related material for a farrowing issue. Established in 1964. Monthly. Circulation: 46,000. Not copyrighted. Buys 12 to 15 mss a year. Payment on acceptance. Will send a sample copy to a writer for $1. Will send editorial guidelines sheet to a writer on request. Will consider photocopied submissions. Submit seasonal material 3 to 4 months in advance. Reports in 2 to 4 weeks. Query first. Enclose S.A.S.E.

Nonfiction and Photos: General subject matter consists of "management-oriented articles on problems and situations encountered by readers. Subjects include marketing, management, nutrition, disease, waste management, buildings and equipment, accounting and recordkeeping." Articles on a hog producer's operation should focus on one unique aspect or angle, and not give a general description of the producer's entire operation. Controversial articles OK, as are industry articles (trends) and round-ups on new developments. Edited for the largest, most business-like producers. More semitechnical and in-depth management information. Prefers not to see articles describing a producer's entire operation, written very general and shallow. Looks for articles that focus on only one subject. Length: up to 2,000 words. Pays $75 to $200 "for maximum feature article." Buys 5x7 or 8x10 b&w glossies. Also buys color transparencies that are at least 2¼x2¼. Must relate to subject matter. Pays $10 to $20 per b&w photo. Pays $25 to $50 for color photos.

IBIA NEWS, Box 1127, Ames IA 50010. Publisher: Angus Stone. Published for the Iowa Beef Improvement Association. For cow-calf producers (farmers) in the Corn Belt states. Tabloid style magazine; 24 (11½x17) pages. Established in 1968. Monthly. Circulation: 48,000. Not copyrighted. Pays on acceptance. Will send free sample copy to writer on request. Will consider photocopied and simultaneous submissions. Returns rejected material immediately. Query first or submit complete ms. Enclose S.A.S.E.

Nonfiction and Photos: "Our only interest is genetic improvement of beef cattle and updated cattle raising procedures. Success stories on beef cattle producers (not feeders) who participate in a program of performance testing. Articles on new equipment, products or procedures applicable to cow-calf operations. We prefer a conservative, typical Midwest farm approach." Interview, profile, successful business operations and technical articles. Length: 1,000 to 1,500 words. Pays $40 to $100. Photos are purchased with mss or on assignment. No additional payment is made for those purchased with mss.

THE KANSAS STOCKMAN, Kansas Livestock Association, 2044 Fillmore, Topeka KS 66604. Editor-in-Chief: Rich Wilcke. Emphasizes cattle ranching and feeding for farmers, ranchers and feeders (over 3 million cattle). Monthly magazine; 75 pages. Estab: 1916. Circ: 8,500. Buys one-time rights. Submit seasonal/holiday material 2 months in advance. Simultaneous, photocopied, and previously published submissions OK. Reports in 3 months. Sample copy 50¢.

Nonfiction: Exposes (government—added costs or inefficiencies, etc.); historical (livestock business, ranching in 19th century—*not* just cattle drives); how-to (management/scientific); humor (cattle business oriented—must be esoteric); interviews. Buys 6 mss/year. Query. Length: 750-2,000 words. Pays 3¢/word minimum.

Photos: B&w and color purchased with mss. Captions required. Send contact sheet or prints. Pays $5 minimum for b&w; $25 minimum for color.

Special Issues: Cow/calf/stocker issue (March); beef month (May); cattle feeder emphasis (July); marketing emphasis (September); convention and trade show (November).

NATIONAL WOOL GROWER, 600 Crandall Bldg., Salt Lake City UT 84101. (801)363-4484. Editor: Vern Newbold. Not copyrighted. A very limited market. Best to query first here. Reports in 4 to 5 days. Enclose S.A.S.E.

Nonfiction: Material of interest to sheepmen. Length: 2,000 words. Pays 1¢ per word for material used.

NEW MEXICO STOCKMAN, Livestock Publications, Inc., Box 7127, Albuquerque NM 87104. (505)247-8192. Editor: Carol Cohen. For ranchers, farmers, horsemen, feedlot operators of all ages. "Women and youngsters are some of our best supporters." Monthly magazine; 70 pages. Estab: 1935. Circ: 11,000. Pays on publication. Buys one-time rights. Phone queries OK. Simultaneous, photocopied, and previously published submissions OK. Reports on material accepted for publication on first of month prior to publication. Free sample copy and writer's guidelines.

Nonfiction: Historical (articles relating the rich culture and heritage of southwestern agriculture, the people and events that made it so); how-to (articles that teach people who depend on agriculture for a living how to better manage their resources); informational (articles that relate new concepts and research in agricultural management techniques); interviews (with anyone who has made a contribution to southwestern agriculture); material on ag-related new products; profiles (which relate the goals, accomplishments and achievements of the movers of southwestern agriculture); technical articles (horse pedigrees, artificial insemination, research on crops and animals that may lead to more profitable management). Buys 3-8 mss/issue. Query. Unsolicited mss are not returned. Length: 250-1,250 words. Pays 5-10¢/word.

Photos: B&w glossies (5x7 or 8x10) or color (35mm or 2¼x2¼) purchased with mss. Captions required. Query. Pays $5-10 for b&w; $25-40 for color.

How To Break In: "A freelancer should have a broad background in agriculture. That doesn't mean that he made frequent trips to granny's farm. Rather, he should have a solid grasp of the management problems, government policies, and technological challenges that face agribusinessmen."

THE OKLAHOMA COWMAN, 2500 Exchange Ave., Oklahoma City OK 73108. For cattle producers and feedlot owners (mostly within Oklahoma) who are members of the Oklahoma Cattlemen's Association and are deeply involved in the actual business of producing and selling beef cattle. Magazine; 40 (8½x11) pages. Established in 1961. Monthly. Circulation: 6,300. Buys all rights, but will reassign rights to author after publication. Buys 2 or 3 mss a year. Pays on publication. Will send sample copy to writer for $1. Will consider photocopied submissions.

Simultaneous submissions considered if assured of first publication rights. Submit seasonal material (geared to management practices) 1 month in advance. Reports on material accepted for publication in 2 weeks. Returns rejected material immediately. Query first. Enclose S.A.S.E.

Nonfiction and Photos: "We are exclusively interested in beef cattle and centered around field crops, horses, etc., as they relate directly to cattle production. Mostly reports of state activity in education, extension, etc., to inform the cattleman. Also, regular feature stories on historical significance of Oklahoma's cattle background. All material dealing with management practices should be geared to season. New ideas on more intensive production practices and 'success' stories on Oklahoma cattle people, as well as adaptability of cattle people to the current economic drain on their land, labor and capital. No Wild West fictionalized articles." Length: 500 to 750 words. Pays $10 to $25. "Photos may make the difference in acceptance of articles. They should be an integral part of the subject." No additional payment. Captions required.

POLLED HEREFORD WORLD, #1 Place, 4700 E. 63rd St., Kansas City MO 64130. (816)333-7731. Editor: Ed Bible. For "breeders of polled Hereford cattle—about 80% registered breeders, about 5% commercial cattle breeders; remainder are agri-businessmen in related fields." Established in 1947. Monthly. Circulation: 20,000. Not copyrighted. Buys "very few mss at present." Pays on publication. Will send a sample copy to a writer on request. Will consider photocopied submissions. Submit seasonal material "as early as possible; 2 months preferred." Reports in 1 month. Query first for reports of events and activities. Query first or submit complete ms for features. Enclose S.A.S.E. for return of submissions or reply to queries.

Nonfiction: "Features on registered or commercial polled Hereford breeders. Some on related agricultural subjects (pastures, fences, feeds, buildings, etc.). Mostly technical in nature; some human interest. Our readers make their living with cattle, so write for an informed, mature audience." Buys informational articles, how-to's, personal experience articles, interviews, profiles, inspirational articles, humor, historical and think pieces, nostalgia, photo features, coverage of successful business operations, articles on merchandising techniques, and technical articles. Length: "varies with subject and content of feature." Pays about 5¢ a word ("usually about 50¢ a column inch, but can vary with the value of material").

Photos: Purchased with mss, sometimes purchased without mss, or on assignment; captions required. "Only good quality b&w glossy prints accepted; any size. Good color prints or transparencies." Pays $2 for b&w photos, $2 to $25 for color. Pays $25 for color covers.

THE RECORD STOCKMAN, 105 Livestock Exchange Bldg., Denver CO 80216. Editor: Fred Wortham Jr. For purebred and commercial ranchers and feeders, and others in fields related to the cattle industry. Weekly newspaper; annual magazine. Established in 1889. Circulation: 20,000. Copyrighted. Pays on publication. Will send free sample copy to writer on request. Reports in 2 weeks. Query first or submit complete ms. Enclose S.A.S.E.

Nonfiction and Photos: Wants "interesting, informative articles on commercial ranchers, feedlot operators, etc., who are doing something innovative in their field. Writers should be familiar with livestock and the cattle industry. Query for magazine by October 15. Copy deadline is November 15." Buys informational, how-to, interview, successful business operations mss. Length: 500 to 1,000 words for newspaper; 1,500 to 4,000 words for magazine. Pays about $35 for newspaper-length mss; more for magazine articles. Photos purchased with accompanying mss. Captions required.

SIMMENTAL JOURNAL, Box 410, Cody WY 82414. (307)587-5987. Editor: John McGee. For cattle breeders. Tabloid; 16 pages. Established in 1975. Every two weeks. Circulation: 7,000. Buys first serial rights. Buys about 20 mss a year. Pays on publication. Will consider photocopied and simultaneous submissions. Reports in 1 month. Query first or submit complete ms. Enclose S.A.S.E.

Nonfiction and Photos: Articles on individual Simmental ranches or ranchers. Informational, how-to, personal experience, profile, interview, successful business operations. Length: 1,000 words maximum. Pays 80¢/column inch. Pays $15 for 8x10 b&w glossy prints purchased with or without ms; $25 for color transparencies or negatives.

SIMMENTAL SCENE, 310 9th Ave., S.W., Suite 120, Calgary, Alberta, Canada T2P 1K5. Editor-in-Chief: B.A. Sharp. Emphasizes Simmental cattle. Monthly magazine; 72 pages. Estab: 1973. Circ: 6,000. Pays on publication. Buys all rights, but may reassign following publication. Submit seasonal or holiday material 3 months in advance. Simultaneous submissions OK. SASE. Reports in 1-4 weeks. Free sample copy.

Nonfiction: Keith Wilson, Articles Editor. How-to (breeding, feeding, management of cattle, equipment maintenance and repair), informational (scientific and technological advances, ranching methods), humor (pertaining to cattle), interview (with Simmental cattlemen, agriculture industry leaders, government people with influence on agriculture), profile, travel (of interest to rural people), new product, photo feature (on herds throughout the world), technical. Buys 5-12 mss a year. Query or submit complete ms. Length: 2,000 words maximum. Pays 2-5¢/word.

Photos: Keith Wilson, Photo Editor. Purchased with or without accompanying ms. Captions required. Query or send contact sheet, or prints. Pays $25-100 for 5x7 or larger b&w glossy; $25-200 for 11x14 or larger glossy for color. Model release required.

Columns/Departments: Keith Wilson, column/department editor. Canadian Scene, U.S. Scene, Scene Downunder, Research & Retail. Query. Length; 500 words maximum. Pays 2-5¢/word. Open to ideas for new columns or departments.

Fillers: Keith Wilson, Fillers Editor. Clippings, newsbreaks. Query. Length: 500 words maximum. Pays 2-5¢/word for original material.

SIMMENTAL SHIELD, P.O. Box 511, Lindsborg KS 67456. Editor: Chester Peterson, Jr. Official publication of American Simmental Association. Readers are purebred cattle breeders and/or commercial cattlemen. Monthly; 180 pages. Circulation: 6,500. Buys all rights. Pays on publication. Will send free sample copy to writer on request. February is AI issue; August is herd sire issue; November is brood cow issue. Submit material 3 to 4 months in advance. Reports in 1 week. Query first or submit complete ms. Enclose S.A.S.E.

Nonfiction, Photos, and Fillers: Farmer experience; management articles with emphasis on ideas used and successful management ideas based on cattleman who owns Simmental. Research: new twist to old ideas or application of new techniques to the Simmental or cattle business. Wants articles that detail to reader how to make or save money or pare labor needs. Buys informational, how-to, personal experience, interview, profile, humor, think articles. Rates vary, but equal or exceed those of comparable magazines. Photos purchased with accompanying ms with no additional payment. Interested in cover photos; accepts 35mm if sharp, well-exposed. Also buys puzzles and short humor as filler material.

Miscellaneous

GLEANINGS IN BEE CULTURE, 623 West Liberty St., Medina OH 44256. Editor: Lawrence R. Goltz. For beekeepers. Monthly. Buys first North American serial rights. Pays on publication. Reports in 15 to 90 days. Enclose S.A.S.E.

Nonfiction and Photos: Interested in articles giving new ideas on managing bees. Also uses success stories about commercial beekeepers. Length: 3,000 words maximum. Pays $23 a published page. Sharp b&w photos pertaining to honeybees purchased with mss. Can be any size, prints or enlargements, but 4x5 or larger preferred. Pays $3 to $5 a picture.

How To Break In: "Do an interview story on commercial beekeepers who are cooperative enough to furnish accurate, factual information on their operations."

THE SUGAR PRODUCER, Harris Publishing, Inc., 520 Park, Box 981, Idaho Falls ID 83401. (208)522-5187. Editor-in-Chief: Loel H. Schoonover. Emphasizes the growing, storage, use and by-products of the sugar beet. Magazine published 7 times a year; 32 pages. Estab: 1975. Circ: 20,000. Pays on publication. Buys all rights, but may reassign following publication. Phone queries OK. Photocopied submissions and previously published work OK. SASE. Reports in 30 days. Free sample copy and writer's guidelines.

Nonfiction: Expose (pertaining to the sugar industry or the beet grower); how-to (all aspects of growing, storing and marketing the sugar beet); interview, profile, personal experience; technical (material source must accompany story—research and data must be from an accepted research institution). Query or send complete ms. Length: 750-2,000 words. Pays 3¢/word.

Photos: Purchased with mss. Captions required. Pays $5 for any convenient size b&w; $25 for color print or slide used on cover. Model release required.

How To Break In: "This is a trade magazine, not a farm magazine. It deals with the business of growing sugar beets, and the related industry. All articles must tell the grower how he can do his job better, or at least be of interest to him, such as historical, because he is vitally interested in the process of growing sugar beets, and the industries related to this."

Poultry

The publications listed here specialize in material on poultry farming. Other publications that buy material on poultry will be found in the General Interest Farming and Rural Life classification.

CANADA POULTRYMAN, 605 Royal Avenue, New Westminster B.C. Canada V3M 1J4. Editor: Fred W. Beeson. For poultry producers and those servicing this industry. Magazine; 56 pages. Established in 1912. Monthly. Circulation: 12,000. Buys all rights. Pays on publication. Will send free sample copy to writer on request. Submit seasonal material 2 months in advance. Reports on material accepted for publication in 1 month. Returns rejected material in 1 month. Submit complete ms to Ken Larson, Managing Editor. Enclose S.A.E. and International Reply Coupons.
Nonfiction and Photos: Canadian market facts, management material, pieces on persons in the industry. Length: 200 to 2,000 words. Pays 4¢ to 5¢ a word. Photos (up to 5x7) purchased with mss for $3. Captions required.

INDUSTRIA AVICOLA (Poultry Industry), Watt Publishing Co., Mt. Morris IL 61054. (815)734-4171. Editor: Gary Buikema. For "poultry producers (minimum 1,000 hens and/or 20,000 broilers annually and/or 1,000 turkeys annually) who have direct affiliation with the poultry industry in Latin America." Circulation: 12,100. Buys all rights. Pays on acceptance. Will send a free sample copy to a writer on request. Will consider cassette submissions. "Prefer mss written in English." Reports in 10 days. Query first. Enclose S.A.S.E.
Nonfiction and Photos: Specialized publication "for poultry businessmen of Latin America. Printed only in Spanish. Emphasis is to aid in production, processing, and marketing of poultry meat and eggs. Keep readers abreast of developments in research, breeding, disease control, housing, equipment, marketing production and business management. Analytical and trend articles concerning the poultry industry in Latin countries are given preference." Length: up to 1,000 to 1,500 words. Pays $40 to $130 depending on content and quality. Photos are purchased with mss. No size requirements.

TURKEY WORLD, Mount Morris IL 61054. Editor: Bernard Heffernan. Monthly. Reports on submissions in two weeks. Buys all rights. Pays on acceptance. Query first. Enclose S.A.S.E.
Nonfiction and Photos: Clear, concise, simply written, factual articles beamed at producers, processors and marketers of turkeys and turkey products. Length: 1,200 to 2,000 words. Pays $50-150.

Consumer Publications

Consumer publications are the "meat and potatoes" of the freelance diet. These magazines purchase hundreds of thousands of manuscripts annually for a few dollars to over $4,000. Many have small, belabored staffs, and so rely solely on freelancers for material.

For almost every interest, there is a magazine; for every magazine, an editor who is constantly looking for new ideas. This section contains 52 categories packed with magazines and editors who are looking for ideas from *you*.

Folio magazine reports an increase of over 30% for magazine start-ups in 1976. A total of 334 publications were given breath (as opposed to 254 in 1975), including *Quest '77*, a general interest magazine dedicated to the pursuit of human excellence (which pays over $2,000 for a major feature) and *Heavy Metal*, a science-fiction/fantasy magazine from the people at *National Lampoon*, which pays 20¢/word for "far out pieces...with lots of dots...and ohs and ahs." In fact, 191 of these new publications were in the consumer/special interest field.

These new magazines are often good jumping-in points for talented freelancers on the rise because they haven't as yet established good freelance contacts to feed their word mills. By signing on early with the kinds of submissions the editor wants to see, a writer can grow and prosper with these magazines as they increase in size and stature.

Traditionally, religious publications have been good springboards for new writers. Although payment is generally low, these publications offer the exposure that an unestablished writer needs, and more important, they offer a vehicle in which to practice and *perfect* the craft of writing. Opportunities are plentiful. "I think there is more room now [in the Christian field] for good writers than ever before," says Charles Brewster, managing editor of *New World Outlook*. This edition lists over 100 religious publications that need freelance material.

Regional publications are increasing in number by leaps and bounds. Of the 334 new magazines of 1976, 72 were directly tied to a specific geographic region. A quick check through the 100-plus regional markets (excluding Sunday magazine supplements and op-ed pages) shows that more than 4,500 manuscripts will be bought from freelancers this year in nonfiction *alone*.

What do regional magazines do? According to Monty Joynes, editor of *Metro, The Magazine of Southeastern Virginia*, "city magazines must surprise and entertain, as well as inform and challenge their readership." Says *Boston* editor George M. Gendron: "Remember that we consider ourselves in the entertainment business, so the emphasis here is on compelling, entertaining writing. The one thing this or any other magazine can never afford to do is to bore the reader."

What's being bought by editors in the consumer field? Everything—so long as it's good. The consumer field is immense, and encompasses interests from every point of the compass. Would you like to write about sports? *Writer's Market* lists 21 subcategories under the general heading Sport and Outdoor. Want to put puzzles together for fun and profit? There's a section for that, too.

Generally, people watch TV to get their fiction, and turn to magazines for their facts. For this reason, in magazines, nonfiction is more salable than fiction. But if you're a fiction afficionado, don't despair; the Literary and Little section is packed with publications that will consider your story. They may not pay as well as some of the larger markets (which *do* use a limited amount of fiction) but chances of being accepted there are much greater than if you submit your fiction to the few larger markets (such as men's and women's publications, or the general interest section).

Few people earn their bread by writing poetry. But because many people enjoy writing poetry for its own sake, the Poetry and Literary & Little categories include publications that *don't* pay for material. Often these magazines are small (some have circulations under 1,000), but they do offer exposure for the beginning writer.

Magazine editors want their submissions in one of two ways: by query, or by submitting the completed manuscript. Before sending *anything* to a publication, check its listing to see how the editor wants material sent to him. If he says to query, write a knowledgeable, cleanly typed, one-page letter outlining your article idea. (See "What Every Freelancer Should Know.") If the editor is interested, he'll get back to you, often with ideas for slanting your story to his publication. If the listing states that he'll consider complete manuscripts (as is usually the case for fiction and poetry), be sure to package your article *neatly*. Always include the proper return postage in *any* correspondence with an editor.

When waiting to hear from a publication on the outcome of a query or article, it's a good idea to allow a few more weeks than what the listing states as a reporting time. Editors *are* busy—constantly. However, once you've allowed an editor the allotted time (and a bit more), drop a gentle reminder in the mail, asking for a progress report on your submission.

The most important tenet of the freelance business is this: *Know Thy Market*. The best way to do this is to read recent back issues of the publication at which you're aiming. Usually a magazine will send a sample copy (free or at some cost) to a writer; to be sure, check its listing. Before writing for an issue, check your library or local newsstand to see if you can obtain a copy there.

For the latest marketing tips and information—including news of new markets— read *Writer's Digest*. One *WD* column, The Markets, is like a monthly edition of *Writer's Market*. The magazine also includes other marketing columns and features.

Alternative Publications

Publications in this section offer writers a forum for expressing anti-establishment or minority ideas and views that wouldn't necessarily be published in the commercial or "establishment" press. Included are a number of "free press" publications that do not pay except in contributor's copies. Writers are reminded that these publications sometimes remain at one address for a limited time or prove unbusinesslike in their reporting on, or returning of, submissions. However, the writer will also find a number of well-established, well-paying markets in this list.

THE ADVOCATE, Liberation Publications, Inc., 1 Peninsula Place, Bldg. 1730, Suite 225, San Mateo CA 94402. Editor-in-Chief: Robert I. McQueen. For gay men and women, age 21-40; middle-class, college educated, urban. Biweekly tabloid; 64 pages. Estab: 1968. Circ: 60,000. Pays on publication. Rights purchased vary with author and material. Submit seasonal/holiday material 3-6 months in advance. Simultaneous and photocopied submissions OK. SASE. Reports in 1 month. Free sample copy and writer's guidelines.
Nonfiction: "Basically, the emphasis is on the dignity and joy of the gay lifestyle." News articles, interviews, lifestyle features. "Major interest in interviews or sketches of gay people whose names can be used, but who are not in The Movement." Informational, how-to, personal experience, profile, humor, historical, photo feature, reviews of books and records, spot news, new product. Query. Length: open. Pays $10 minimum.
Photos: "Payment for b&w photos purchased without ms or on assignment depends on size of the reproduction."

THE ARTS OBJECTIVELY, Podium II, Box 15716, Philadelphia PA 19103. Editor-in-Chief: Frederic C. Kaplan. Quarterly magazine; 35-50 pages. Estab: 1975. Circ: 1,000. Pays on publication. Buys all rights, but may reassign following publication; simultaneous rights or second serial (reprint) rights. Query about holiday/seasonal material 4 months in advance. Simultaneous and photocopied submissions OK. Previously published work OK. SASE. Reports in 6-8 weeks. Sample copy $1. Writer's guidelines for SASE.
Nonfiction: Exposes (of governmental interference into the arts of communications);

informational (advice to professionals on arts of communications); interviews (with individuals involved in the arts or who have made an impact in this area). Buys 10-15/issue. Pays 1-1½¢/word.

Photos: "We are seeking photo essays of about 12 pictures." On assignment only; query. Pays $2-5.

Fiction: "Good, fast-paced stories reflecting objectivist values." Adventure, fantasy, historical, humorous, mainstream, mystery, science fiction, suspense. Buys 1-2/issue. Submit complete ms. Length: 1,500-5,000 words. Pays 1-1½¢/word.

Fillers: Clippings, newsbreaks. Buys 8-10/issue. Send fillers in. Length: 50-100 words. Pays 1-1½¢/word.

BERKELEY BARB, International News Keyus, Inc., Box 1247, Berkeley, CA 94701. (415)849-1040. Editor-in-Chief: Ray Riegert. Alternative weekly newspaper. Audience ranges from college age to upper 40s, well educated, interested in leftist politics, avant-garde art, sex, drugs and the counter-culture. Estab: 1965. Circ: 20,000. Pays on publication. Buys all right, but may reassign following publication. Phone queries OK. Submit seasonal/holiday material 6 weeks in advance. Simultaneous and photocopied submissions OK. SASE. Reports in 4 weeks. Free sample copy and writer's guideline.

Nonfiction: Expose (mainly political, but must be hard-hitting, well substantiated, investigative journalism); historical (San Francisco Bay area historical sketches only); how-to (make a freelance living, grow your own dope, make it outside the establishment); interview (with leftist, political leaders, avant-garde artists and other counter-culture figures; write in prose narrative, not Q & A form); nostalgia (Bay area only); photo feature (counter-culture related); and profile (of individuals, groups or movements which are leftist, avant-garde or part of the counter-culture). Buys 10 mss/issue. Send complete ms. Length: 500-2,000 words. Pays 3-5¢/word.

Photos: Tom Glass, Photo Editor. Photos purchased with or without accompanying ms. Captions required. Pays $10-70 for b&w and color photos. Send prints and contact sheet.

Columns/Departments: Gar Smith, Columns/Departments Editor. Alternatives (lifestyles, energy, scams); Off-The-Wall (uncommon people, events, enterprises); Reviews (unsung heroes/heroines, innovators, writers). Buys 10 mss/year. Query. Length: 300-800 words. Pays 3¢/word.

Poetry: Tom Plante, Poetry Editor. Avant-garde, free verse, haiku, and satirical. Buys 15 poems/year. Limit submissions to batches of 2. Length: 1-30 lines. Pays $10.

Fillers: Jokes, gags, anecdotes and newsbreaks. Buys 6 fillers/issue. Length: 100-300 words. Pays 3¢/word.

BLACK MARIA, 815 W. Wrightwood, Chicago IL 60614. (312)929-4883. Collective editorship. Mostly for women interested in redefining women's position in society and in the family. Magazine; 64 pages. Established in 1971. Published 3 to 4 times per year. Circulation: 1,000. Rights acquired vary with author and material. May acquire all rights, with the possibility of reassigning rights to author after publication, or second serial (reprint) rights. Uses about 40 mss a year. Pays in contributor's copies and a subscription. Will send sample copy to writer for $1.50. Will consider photocopied submissions, but would prefer the original. Will consider simultaneous submissions. Reports on material accepted for publication in 1 month. Returns rejected material in 2 months. Query first or submit complete ms. Enclose S.A.S.E.

Nonfiction and Photos: "Articles must be written by women. Subjects include those pertinent to women's liberation (e.g., redefining history to include women); life style changes through role reversals in family. Articles which are pro woman and define her as active, intelligent; a complete human being. We prefer a more subtle approach than political rhetoric. We do not want immediate, newsy articles about specific events. We prefer more general, non-transitory themes for articles." B&w photos (2x3 or 8x10) used with mss.

Fiction and Poetry: "Writer should use understatement in stories; gutsy and to the point, with a moral." Experimental, mainstream, science fiction, fantasy, humorous and historical fiction. Traditional forms of poetry, free verse, light verse and avant-garde forms. Submit at least 3 poems. Length: 4 to 75 lines.

THE BOSTON PHOENIX, 100 Massachusetts Ave., Boston MA 02115. (617)536-5390. Editor: William Miller. For 18-35 age group, educated middle class and post-counterculture. Weekly alternative newspaper. Circulation: 115,000. Buys all rights. Pays on publication. Sample copy $1. Photocopied submissions OK. Reports in 4 to 6 weeks. Query. SASE.

Nonfiction: "No set theme. Anything well written; people interest. Unsentimental; not corny or folksy; high-quality writing and observation. No humor." Pays $50 to $100.

BROTHER, A Forum for Men Against Sexism, P.O. Box 4387, Berkeley CA 94704. Collective editorship. For a predominantly young, male audience concerned about sexism and sexual oppression; older males and a substantial number of women. "Most of the staff, much of the material, and many of the readers are gay." Quarterly newspaper and newsletter; 16 to 24 (12x16) pages. Established in 1971. Circulation: 3,000 to 4,000. Not copyrighted. Payment in contributor's copies. Sample copy 50¢. Photocopied and simultaneous submissions OK. Reports in 2 months. Query or submit complete ms. Enclose S.A.S.E.
Nonfiction: "We're relatively unique. There are no other regular men's anti-sexist publications. We print analytical articles and reminiscences around the theme of men struggling with sexism in their own lives. We look for personal treatments, critical of standard male sex role, men and class (economic class relationships and sex roles); men and women (articles on inter-personal relationships). No sexist trash; no anti-woman; no windy, generalized over-views of sex role differences." Length: 1,000 to 1,500 words maximum.
Fiction and Poetry: Experimental and "confession" type stories. All forms of poetry.

COMMUNITY, 343 S. Dearborn St., Room 317, Chicago IL 60604. (312)939-3347. Editor: Albert Schorsch. For teachers, religious, students and movement types (high school age up) interested in social change through nonviolent action. Magazine; 32 pages. Established in 1937. Quarterly. Circulation: 1,000. Acquires all rights, but will reassign rights to author after publication. Uses about 40 mss a year. Pays in contributor's copies. Will send sample copy to writer for 60¢. Will consider clear photocopied submissions. Occasionally considers simultaneous submissions. Reports on material accepted for publication in 6 to 8 weeks. Returns rejected material as soon as possible. Query first. Enclose S.A.S.E.
Nonfiction and Photos: "All types of material concerning movements of liberation and how to achieve such through nonviolence. Our approach is from the viewpoint of the Catholic left. We like to publish material extracted from personal experience whether theoretical or practical. All facets of the women's struggle; men's liberation. No term paper types. We also use book reviews and photo essays." Length: 2,400 words. B&w glossies are used with mss.
Poetry: Nothing trite. Traditional forms. Blank verse, free verse, avant-garde forms and haiku. Length: 3 to 30 lines.

COSMOPOLITAN CONTACT, Pantheon Press, Box 1566, Fontana CA 92335. Editor-in-Chief: Romulus Rexner. Managing Editor: Nina Norvid. "It is the publication's object to have as universal appeal as possible—students, graduates and others interested in international affairs, cooperation, contacts, travel, friendships, trade, exchanges, self-improvement and widening of mental horizons through multicultural interaction. This publication has worldwide distribution and participation, including the Communist countries." Irregularly published 3 or 4 times a year. Magazine; 32 pages. Estab: 1962. Circ: 1,500. Pays on publication in copies. Simultaneous, photocopied and previously published submissions OK. SASE. Reports in 6 weeks. Sample copy $1.
Nonfiction: Expose (should concentrate on government, education, etc.); how-to; informational; inspiration; personal experience; personal opinion and travel. Submit complete ms. Maximum 500 words. "Material designed to promote across all frontiers bonds of spiritual unity, intellectual understanding and sincere friendship among people by means of correspondence, meetings, publishing activities, tapes, records, exchange of hospitality, books, periodicals in various languages, hobbies and other contacts."
Poetry: Haiku and traditional. Length: Maximum 40 lines.
Rejects: "We are not interested in any contribution containing vulgar language, extreme, intolerant, pro-Soviet or anti-American opinions."

DOING IT!, Urban Alternative Group, Box 303, Worthington OH 43085. (614)885-8964. Editor-in-Chief: Ruth Kaswan. Emphasizes alternatives in environment, education, lifestyle, and economics. "We hope to breach the walls of specialization and demonstrate the continuity of the humanistic impulse over its various and disparate manifestations." Bimonthly magazine; 80 pages. Estab: 1976. Circ: 4,000. Pays on publication. Buys publication rights only. Phone queries OK. Simultaneous, photocopied, and previously published submissions OK. SASE. Reports in 4 weeks. Free sample copy and writer's guidelines.
Nonfiction: How-to (anything from medical self-help to building energy-efficient houses), informational (people exploring ways of working, living, relating to others, and functioning in society that emphasizes human aspects over material aspects—i.e., working for pleasure, not money—concern for ecology, justice, and opposition to greed, violence and abuse of power) personal experience. Buys 1-2 mss/issue. Query or submit complete ms. Length: 1,000-2,000 words. Pays $5-35.

Photos: Photos purchased with accompanying ms. Query or send contact sheet. No additional payment for photos accepted with accompanying ms.
Columns/Departments: Jaques Kaswan, Columns/Departments Editor. Resources, Hints, The Exchange, and Newsbits. Send complete ms. Length: 50-700 words. Pays $5 maximum. Open to suggestions for new columns/departments.
Poetry: Avant-garde, free verse, haiku. Buys 4-6 poems/issue. Length: 4-70 lines.

EARTH'S DAUGHTERS, 944 Kensington Ave., Buffalo NY 14215. Editors: Myrna Ford, Judith Kerman, Lillian Robinson, Elaine Rollwagen. For women and men interested in literature and feminism. Establish in 1971. Publication schedule varies from 2 to 4 times a year. Circulation: 1,000. Acquires first North American serial rights. Pays in contributor's copies. Will send sample copy to writer for $1. Will consider clear photocopied submissions and clear carbons. Reports in 10 weeks. Submit complete ms. Enclose S.A.S.E.
Nonfiction and Photos: "Our subject is the experience and creative expression of women. We require a high level of technical skill and artistic intensity; although we work from a left-feminist political position, we are concerned with creative expression rather than propaganda. On rare occasions we publish feminist work by men. We rarely use nonfiction, but might be interested in reviews of work by women for an occasional review issue. Length: 1,000 words maximum. We are generally interested in photos more as free-standing artistic works than as illustrations." Pays in copies only.
Fiction: Feminist fiction of any and all modes. Length: 2,500 words maximum.
Poetry: All modern, contemporary, avant-garde forms. Length: 6 pages maximum.

EAST WEST JOURNAL, 233 Harvard St., Brookline MA 02146. (617)738-1760. Editor-in-Chief: Sherman Goldman. Emphasizes alternative living for "people of all ages seeking to live harmoniously in a world of change." Monthly magazine; 80 pages. Estab: 1971. Circ: 30,000. Pays on publication. Buys one-time rights. Phone queries OK. Submit seasonal/holiday material 4 months in advance. Simultaneous, photocopied and previously published submissions OK. SASE. Reports in 4 weeks. Free sample copy.
Nonfiction: Gala Lachman, Articles Editor. Expose (medicine, agribusiness), how-to (self-healing, martial arts, crafts, alternative energy), informational (American Indians, social and political alternatives, natural foods, macrobiotics), historical (mythology, nutrition and diet, cultural rise and fall, sacred wisdom), interview (spiritual leaders), photo feature (traditional cultures). Buys 60 mss/year. Query. Length: 500-5,000 words. Pays $25-250.
Photos: Purchased on assignment. Query. Pays $5-25 for b&w prints; $125-175 for color transparencies (cover only).
Columns/Departments: Alex Jack, Columns/Departments Editor. Books, Music, Cooking (natural foods), Healing (wholestic therapies, martial arts), Compass (current news items). Buys 48 mss a year. Submit complete ms. Length: 500-1,000 words. Pays $5-50. Open to suggestions for new columns and departments.
Fiction: Gala Lachman, Fiction Editor. Experimental (alternative lifestyles), religious (yoga, natural therapies, meditation). Buys 10 mss/year. Query. Length: 500-2,500 words. Pays $25-100.
Poetry: Gala Lachman. Poetry Editor. All types. Buys 10/year. Query. No length requirement. Pays $5-50.

EDCENTRIC MAGAZINE, Box 10085, Eugene OR 97401. Collective editorship. For administrators and teachers; others interested in education from day care through college. Magazine; 32 to 64 pages. Estab: 1969. Quarterly. Circ: 2,500. Acquires all rights. No payment. Will send sample copy to writer for $1. Reports in 1 month. Query first. Enclose S.A.S.E.
Nonfiction and Photos: Articles dealing with political, social and educational issues. "This is a radical journal, relating educational change to other social change movements." Will also consider articles on rural education, bilingual education and alternative schools. Length: 16 to 24 typewritten, double-spaced pages. B&w photos are used with or without mss.

EGO, Box 31312, San Francisco CA 94131. Editor-in-Chief: Kristen Hillary. "Our audience is made up of people of varied backgrounds and interests, all of whom are committed to reason. Most are students of the Objectivist philosophy and are advocates of laissez-faire capitalism." Quarterly magazine; 85 pages. Estab: 1975. Circ: 1,000. Pays in contributor's copies on publication. Acquires second serial and first North American serial rights. Submit seasonal/holiday material 3 months in advance. Photocopied and previously published submissions OK. SASE. Reports in 1 month. Sample copy $1.50; free writer's guidelines.
Nonfiction: Especially likes articles on psychology, education, the arts, and philosophical

articles that are logically developed rather than asserting conclusions. Uses 10 mss/year. Query or submit complete ms. Length: 1,000-7,000 words. Pays in copies based on number of words.
Fiction: Mystery, suspense, condensed novels, science fiction, serialized novels. "Fiction should project an image of a heroic, efficacious man. It should be well-plotted and written in a dramatic, interesting manner." Uses 10-12 mss/year. Query or submit complete ms. Length: 1,500-8,000 words. Pays in copies based on number of words.
Poetry: Traditional. No length limit. Pays in copies.
Fillers: Joseph Robert Neri, Fillers Editor. Newsbreaks. Submit complete ms. No length requirement. Pays in 1 copy.

THE EMISSARY, Eden Valley Press, Box 328, Loveland CO 80537. Editor-in-Chief: Robert Moore. Managing Editor: Theodore Black. Emphasizes general reading, "dedicated to the practical art of living." Monthly magazine; 48 pages. Estab: 1975. Circ: 2,000. Acquires one-time rights. Pays in contributor's copies. Seasonal/holiday material must be submitted 3 months in advance. Photocopied and previously published submissions OK. SASE. Reports in 1 week. Free sample copy and writer's guidelines.
Nonfiction: Historical (how modern experience is connected to a historical event/person); humor; inspirational (not religious or moralistic); interview (with well-known personalities or leader in such fields as solar energy development, ecology, education, etc.); personal experience and photo feature. Uses 12 mss/year. Length: 2,500 words maximum.
Photos: B&w and color. Send contact sheet.
Columns, Departments: Historical connection, awareness forum, TV, movie and book reviews. Buys 12 mss/year. Length: 1,500 words maximum.
Fiction: Adventure. fantasy; humorous and science fiction. Uses 6 mss/year.
Poetry: Most types. Uses 12 poems/year. Limit submissions to batches of 6.
Fillers: Clippings, puzzles and short humor. "Would use more of this type material if contributors knew magazine and sent fillers that fit our format and general tone."

FOCUS: A JOURNAL FOR GAY WOMEN, Daughters of Bilitis, Room 323, 419 Boylston St., Boston MA 02116. Emphasizes lesbian art and literature for gay women of all ages and interests. Monthly magazine; 16 pages. Estab: 1970. Circ: 350. Pays in contributor's copies. Buys all rights. Seasonal/holiday material must be submitted 3 months in advance. Simultaneous and photocopied submissions OK. SASE. Reports in 3 months. Sample copy 60¢.
Nonfiction: Historical; humor; informational; interview; personal experience; personal opinion; profile and book reviews (includes monthly D.O.B. calendar). Send complete ms. Length: 2,500 maximum words.
Fiction: Relating to magazine theme. Confession; erotica; fantasy; historical; humorous; romance and science fiction. Send complete ms. Length: 2,500 words maximum.
Poetry: Avant-garde; free verse; haiku; light verse and traditional. Length: 2,500 words maximum.
Fillers: Clippings, jokes, gags, anecdotes, newsbreaks, short humor, graphics, cartoons and drawings. Send fillers. Length: 200 words maximum.

GAY SUNSHINE, A Journal of Gay Liberation, P.O. Box 40397, San Francisco CA 94140. (415)824-3184. Editor: Winston Leyland. For gay people of all ages throughout North America and abroad. "We especially appeal to people interested in the radical, political and literary aspects of the gay liberation movement." Newspaper. Quarterly; 28 to 36 pages. Established in 1970. Circulation: 10,000. Rights purchased vary with author and material; negotiable. Payment in contributor's copies, or negotiable. Will send sample copy to writer for $1. Will consider photocopied submissions. Will not consider simultaneous submissions. Will consider cassette submissions; "interviews only." Reports in 2 to 4 weeks. Submit complete nonfiction mss; query first for short fiction and graphics. Enclose S.A.S.E.
Nonfiction and Photos: Interviews, personal articles, political articles, literary essays. Particularly interested in in-depth interviews with gay people from different backgrounds. "Material should relate to gay people and the gay consciousness. Author should write to us first regarding style, structure, etc." Length: maximum of 10 to 15 double-spaced, typed pages. B&w photos are purchased on assignment. Captions required.
Fiction: Experimental and erotica. Must relate to theme. Length: maximum of 10 to 15 double-spaced, typed pages.
Poetry: Blank verse, free verse, avant-garde forms.

GNOSTICA MAGAZINE (formerly *Gnostica: News of the Aquarian Frontier*), Box 3383, St. Paul MN 55165. (612)291-1970. Editor: P.S. Teply. For people interested in astrology, parapsychology, psychic phenomena, magic, witchcraft and alternative religions, tantra and Eastern philosophy, the tarot and the occult. Bimonthly tabloid; 100-150 pages. Estab: 1971. Circ: 10,000. Pays within a month of publication. Usually buys first serial rights. Photocopied and simultaneous submissions OK. SASE. Reports in 2 months. Free sample copy.

Nonfiction: All articles deal with astrology, parapsychology and the occult. Prefers articles with a how-to or instructional theme. Length: 500-10,000 words. Will consider serializing some book-length mss. Pays 2¢/word, except by arrangement. Reviews of occult books. Length: 200-1,000 words. Pays 2¢/word.

Photos: Purchased with mss, or on assignment.

Columns/Departments: Material on astrology, parapsychology and the occult. Length: 500-2,000 words. Pays $10-50/column. Submit several columns at one time.

Fiction and Poetry: Will consider occult fiction that is instructional in nature, but use of fiction is severely limited. Poetry is purchased as filler material only and must be occult oriented. Length: 1-100 lines. Pays 2¢/word or $10, whichever is higher.

GRASS ROOTS FORUM, P.O. Box 472, San Gabriel, CA 91778. Editor: Henry Wilton. For "ages 14 to 70; from thinking, intelligent craftsmen, to Ph.D.'s, M.D.'s, etc." Estab: 1967. Monthly. Circ: 5,000. Rights acquired are open. Payment in contributor's copies. Will send sample copy to writer for 25¢. Submit only complete ms. Will consider photocopied submissions. Reports in 2 weeks. Enclose S.A.S.E. for return submissions.

Nonfiction, Photos, Poetry and Fillers: Publishes material on "political, economic, social subjects; all aspects of our culture; current events. In prose or verse; from liberal perspective. Emphasis on truth, reality, justice as it would serve the underdog. We do not want erotica, trivia, falsehoods, etc. We are seeking cogent, astute observations regarding national issues, political events; activities of dissenting groups and minorities." Buys informational, interview, humor, expose articles; book and music reviews. B&w photos must be of general interest and authentic. Photos used with or without ms and on assignment. Accepts traditional, avant-garde, blank, and free verse. Buys jokes and short humor. Payment in contributor's copies.

HARROWSMITH, Camden House Publishing Ltd., Camden East, Ont, Canada K0K 1J0. (613)378-6618. Editor-in-Chief: James M. Lawrence. Emphasizes country living, gardening and alternative energy. Audience is 90% Canadian, 10% American; mostly college educated; interests are gardening, alternative energy, back-to-land subjects, folk arts, ecology. Bimonthly magazine; 96 pages. Estab: 1976. Circ: 60,000. Pays on acceptance. Buys all rights, but may reassign following publication. Submit seasonal/holiday material 4 months in advance. SAE and International Reply Coupons. Reports in 2 weeks. Free sample copy and writer's guidelines.

Nonfiction: Expose (ecology, land use, agriculture, food additives), how-to (garden, alternative architecture, folk arts, natural cooking, animal husbandry, homesteading), informational, humor (subtle, sophisticated), interview, personal experience, personal opinion (query first), photo feature, profile and technical. Buys 10-15 mss/issue. Query. Length: 500-3,500 words. Pays $50-300.

Photos: Barry Estabrook, Photo Editor. Photos purchased with or without accompanying ms or on assignment. Captions required. Pays $15-35 for 8x10 matte or glossy b&w photos; $25-200 for 35mm or larger color transparencies (color negatives must be accompanied by color contact sheet.) Total purchase price for ms includes payment for photos.

Columns/Departments: Last Word (humor, opinion), Windowsill Gardener (indoor gardening), Pantry (natural cooking, food preservation, canning, old-time recipes). Buys 2 mss/issue. Query. Length: 400-750 words. Pays $50-150. Open to suggestions for new columns/departments.

Fiction: Experimental, historical, humorous, mainstream, science fiction, serialized novels. Buys 1 ms/issue. Query. Length: 1,500-3,500 words. Pays $150-300.

Fillers: Barry Estabrook, Fillers Editor. Clippings and newsbreaks. Pays $10-25.

How To Break In: "We are especially looking for well-written gardening material. Must be thorough, either informational or how-to (or a combination) and geared to northern U.S. and Canadian growing conditions. We expect more depth and research than some other magazines in this field. We are repelled by the 'shucks-folks' pseudo-hillbilly approach."

HIGH TIMES, Trans-High Corporation, Box 386, Cooper Station, New York NY 10003. (212)481-0120. Managing Editor: Susan Wyler. For persons under 35 interested in lifestyle changes, personal freedom, sex and drugs. Monthly magazine; 116 pages. Estab: 1974. Circ: 450,000. Buys second serial (reprint) rights. Submit seasonal/holiday material 6 months in advance. Pays on publication. SASE. Reports in 6-8 weeks. Sample copy $1.75.

Nonfiction: Expose; historical; humor; informational; interview; new product; photo feature; profile and travel. Buys 4 mss/issue. Send complete ms. Length: 3,000-4,000 words. Pays $250-750. Wants material on drugs and consciousness expansion; other subjects of interest to a young, hip audience. "Brevity and clarity appreciated." Also, new drugs, dope-dealing, business news, glamor drugs. Nothing on "my drug bust."

Photos: Annie Toglia, Photo Editor. Photos purchased with or without accompanying ms or on assignment. Pays $25-150 for b&w photos; $50-250 for color photos. Query. No additional payment for photos accepted with accompanying ms. Model release required.

Fiction: Adventure; erotica; experimental; fantasy; humorous; mystery and serialized novels. Buys 1 ms/issue. Send complete ms on spec. Length: 2,500-4,000 words. Pays $100-750.

INTEGRITY: GAY EPISCOPAL FORUM, 701 Orange St., #6, Fort Valley GA 31030. (912)825-7287. Editor: Louie Crew, Ph.D. For "gay Episcopalians and friends. About one-fourth of our readers are clergy, many of them gay themselves, and others of them trying thereby to become more informed of our basically gay point of view. We also have many non-Christian gays seeking to be informed of our Christian witness. We have now developed chapters in over 35 cities, meeting regularly for eucharist and other programs." Newsletter; 10 pages. Established in 1974. 10 times a year. Circulation: 1,000. Rights acquired vary with author and material. Usually acquires all rights, but may reassign rights to author after publication. Uses 15 to 20 mss a year. Pays in contributor's copies. Will send sample copy to writer for $1. Will consider photocopied submissions. Will consider simultaneous submissions only if other distribution is explained. Reports in 2 weeks. Query first or submit complete ms. Enclose S.A.S.E.

Nonfiction: "Personal experience items, particularly with a Christian (but not sentimental) focus, and particularly with the poignancy to be forceful about the truth of the gay experience. We like materials that discuss gay sexuality in the broader context of human sexuality." Length 25 to 2,000 words.

Poetry and Fillers: Traditional forms of poetry, blank verse, free verse, avant-garde forms, haiku. Length 2 to 25 lines. Newsbreaks, clippings, jokes, gags, anecdotes, short humor used as fillers. Length: 1 to 10 lines.

JIM'S JOURNAL, Box 1885, Rockford IL 61110. Editor: James E. Kurtz. For young adult to middle-age readers. All professions. Interested in controversial themes. Established in 1962. Monthly. Circulation: 5,000. Not copyrighted. Payment in contributor's copies. Will send sample copy to writer for 25¢. Will not consider photocopied submissions. Reports on material accepted for publication in 4 weeks. Returns rejected material in 3 to 5 weeks. Query first or submit complete ms. Enclose S.A.S.E.

Nonfiction and Photos: Controversial, underground material, sociology, philosophy, current events, religion, men's liberation, sex. "We honestly invite stimulating material. We want well-written material and we favor the new writer. Be bold, speak out with confidence; no punches pulled. All subjects are carefully read." Informational, personal experience, inspirational, think pieces, personal opinion, expose. Length: 2,500 words maximum. 5x7 or 8x10 b&w photos used with accompanying mss. Captions required.

Fiction: Experimental, mainstream, adventure, erotica, humor, confession, condensed novels. Length: 3,000 words maximum.

THE LADDER, P.O. Box 5025, Washington Station, Reno NV 89503. (816)633-4136. Editor: Gene Damon. For lesbian and women's liberation audience that is "serious, and much more concerned with reform than revolution." Subject matter includes "any and all material that pertains to the gaining of full human status for all women, including lesbians." Bimonthly. Circulation: 3,900. Acquires one-time use rights, insists on acknowledgement when material is reprinted. Pays in contributor's copies. Will send a sample copy to a writer for $1.25. Query preferred for articles and photos. Reports in 20 days. Enclose S.A.S.E. for return of submissions or reply to queries.

Nonfiction: "Any article dealing with women or lesbians, having to do with women's rights, women's liberation, any civil rights violation that particularly affects women, biographical articles on famous women. No particular slant. Prefer clean, concise style." Length: 1,500 to 5,000 words.

Photos: "Use many, as illustrations for stories and articles." Mostly pictures of women. B&w glossies.

Fiction: "Prefer fiction connected to lesbians in some way, but will accept relevant sensitive portraits of women, especially those that show their limitations in a male-ordered, male-run world. No limitations except no pornography. Can be either sympathetic or not, but must be well-written. Need many short-shorts. Using increasing amount of fiction with future issues." Length: 300 to 5,000 words.

Poetry: "By and about women, all and any women. Probable preference given to lesbian themes but quality is the primary criterion. Using increasing amounts of poetry."

Fillers: Especially needs short humor. Also wants newsbreaks, clippings, jokes, and other fillers.

THE LESBIAN TIDE, 8855 Cattaragus Ave., Los Angeles CA 90034. (213)839-7254. Collective editorship. Managing Editor: Jeanne Cordova. For feminist lesbians of any age, educational level, interests, or political viewpoints. Magazine; 40 pages. Estab: 1971. Bimonthly. Circ: 6,700. Not copyrighted. Uses about 50 mss a year. No payment. Sample copy $1. Will consider photocopied and simultaneous submissions. Reports on material accepted for publication upon publication. Returns rejected material in 60 days. Submit complete ms. Enclose S.A.S.E.

Nonfiction and Photos: News regarding lesbian organizations, conferences, social alternatives, "zaps," etc.; civil rights, historical/political analyses; book, film, and music reviews; interviews, profiles, instructional pieces. "Writers must be women writing for a readership of feminist lesbians of any political orientation. We will not consider material written by men." Will consider articles on lesbian child custody cases, job and credit discrimination against women, armed services discharge battles, abuse of women in prison, and general oppression of lesbians and other feminists by the legal power structure. Length: 250 to 1,500 words. B&w photos (any size) used with or without mss or on assignment.

Fiction, Poetry and Fillers: Stories of interest to lesbians and other feminists; all types, except religious fiction. Length: 250 to 1,500 words. Traditional and avant-garde forms of poetry; blank verse, light verse, free verse and haiku. Short humor (100 to 200 words), jokes, gags, anecdotes, clippings, newsbreaks used as fillers.

LIBERATION, New Perspectives, Inc., 186 Hampshire St., Cambridge MA 02139. (617)354-0492. Editor-in-Chief: Michael Nill. Managing Editor: Jan Edwards. Emphasizes politics and culture for college educated audience, and those with interest in politics and culture. 10 times a year; magazine; 36 pages. Estab: 1956. Circ: 10,000. Pays, on publication, 1¢/word, a year's subscription and 10 copies of issue in which article appears. Buys all rights, but may reassign rights to author following publication. Phone queries OK. Seasonal/holiday material must be submitted 3 months in advance. Photocopied submissions OK. SASE. Reports in 1 month. Free sample copy.

Nonfiction: Expose (investigative reporting that challenges the status quo, all areas); historical (if it makes connections to the present); informational; interview; personal experience (if connected with social forces and realities); profile and analysis. Buys 4 mss/issue. Query. Length: 1,400-5,000 words.

Columns, Departments: Reviews—books, film, TV. Length: 700-2,400 words.

Fiction: Should deal with personal relations or social realities. Submit complete ms. Length: 1,400-5,000 words.

Poetry: Avant-garde and free verse. Buys 40 poems/year. Limit submissions to batches of 6.

LOS ANGELES FREE PRESS, New Way Enterprises, 5850 Hollywood Blvd., Los Angeles CA 90028. (213)466-5431. Editor-in-Chief: Roger J. Gentry. Managing Editor: Salley Rayl. Primarily for southern Californians, 20-40 years old; college educated. Weekly newspapers; 52 pages. Estab: 1964. Circ: 75,000. Pays on publication. Buys first rights. Photocopied submissions OK. SASE. Sample copy 25¢.

Nonfiction: News; in-depth investigative articles; consumer news; features (entertainment and news-related); public service articles. Liberal viewpoint; thorough investigation and substantion of statements. Of particular interest are articles on the economy; consumer issues. Length: 4,000 words maximum. Pays $20-50.

Photos: Purchased with or without accompanying ms or on assignment. Pays $5 minimum for b&w glossies.

THE MOTHER EARTH NEWS, Box 70, Hendersonville NC 28739. (704)692-4256. Editor-in-Chief: John Shuttleworth. Emphasizes "back-to-the-land self-sufficiency for the growing number of individuals who seek a more rational self-directed way of life." Bimonthly magazine; 180 pages. Estab: 1970. Circ: 400,000. Pays on publication. Buys all rights, but will reassign following publication. Submit seasonal/holiday material 3-4 months in advance. Simultaneous, photocopied and previously published submissions OK. SASE. Reports in 2-3 months. Free sample copy and writer's guidelines.

Nonfiction: How-to (*Mother* is always looking for good, well documented home business pieces and reports on alternative energy systems as well as low cost ($100 and up) housing stories and seasonal cooking and gardening articles) and profile (250-400-word thumbnail biographies of "doers" are always welcome). Buys 150-200 mss/year. Query. Length: 300-3,000 words. Pays $40-500.

Photos: Purchased with accompanying ms. Captions required. Send prints or transparencies. Uses 8x10 b&w glossies; any size color transparencies. Include type of film, speed and lighting used. Total purchase price for ms includes payment for photos.

Columns/Departments: "Mother's Down-Home Country Lore: Nancy Bubel and Successful Swaps are contributed in return for a one-year subscription; Bootstrap Business pays a two-year suscrittion; Profiles and Newsworthies." Length: 100-500 words. Pays $25-50. Open to suggestions for new columns/departments.

Fillers: Short how-to's on any subject normally covered by the magazine. Query. Length: 150-300 words. Pays $7.50-25.

How To Break In: "Probably the best way is to send a tightly written, short (1,000 words), illustrated (with color slides) piece on a slightly offbeat facet of gardening, cooking or country living. It's important that the writer get all the pertinent facts together, organize them logically, and present them in a fun to read fashion. It's also important that the ms be accompanied by top-notch photos, which is why, as a matter of policy, we reimburse authors for the cost of hiring professional photographers."

MOUTH OF THE DRAGON, Box 107, Cooper Station, New York NY 10003. Editor: Andrew Bifrost. For those in the literary, academic movement. Established in 1974. Quarterly. Circulation: 1,000. Acquires all rights. Reassigns rights to author after publication. Uses about 100 mss a year. Pays in contributor's copies. Will send sample copy to writer for $1.50. Will consider photocopied submissions. No simultaneous submissions. Reports on material accepted for publication in 2 months. Returns rejected material immediately. Submit complete ms. Enclose S.A.S.E.

Poetry: "We publish poetry and criticism of poetry on and by gay males only."

NORTH COUNTRY ANVIL, Anvil Press, Box 37, Millville MN 55957. Editor-in-Chief: Jack Miller. Emphasizes alternatives, lifestyles, back-to-the-soil movements, and social justice. For a "midwestern audience interested in subject matter, distributed among all ages, but 25-40 age group most predominant." Bimonthly magazine; 40-44 pages. Estab: 1972. Circ: 2,200. Pays in copies. Acquires all rights, but may reassign following publication. Submit seasonal or holiday material 6-9 months in advance. Simultaneous and photocopied submissions OK. SASE. Reports in 12 weeks. Sample copy $1.

Nonfiction: Expose (mistreament and triumphs of minorities), historical (populist and land reform movements). how-to (gardening, alternative sources of energy, small scale farming), humor and informational (lifestyles). Uses 20 mss/issue. Length: 3,000 words maximum.

Poetry: Mara and Ray Smith, Poetry Editors. Uses all kinds. Uses 20 poems/issue. Pays in copies.

How To Break In: "Start by being well-informed on the subject matter, then present it in clear, concise fashion. We want our writers to touch all the bases without dying on them. We're always on the lookout for people-oriented articles, particularly when the people involved are accomplishing something worthwhile in spite of the 'establishment,' and not because of it."

SAN FRANCISCO BAY GUARDIAN, 2700 19th St., San Francisco CA 94110. (415)824-7660. Editor: Bruce Brugmann. For "a young liberal to radical, well-educated audience." Established in 1966. Weekly. Circulation: 25,000. Buys all rights, but will reassign them to author after publication. Buys 200 mss a year. Payment on publication. Will consider photocopied submissions. Query first for nonfiction with sample of published pieces. Enclose S.A.S.E.

Nonfiction and Photos: Department Editors: Louis Dunn and Michael E. Miller. Publishes "investigative reporting, features, analysis and interpretation, how-to and consumer reviews, and stories must have a Bay Area angle." Freelance material should have a "public interest advocacy journalism approach (on the side of the little guy who gets pushed around by large institutions). More interested in hard investigative pieces. Fewer stories about isolated suffering welfare mothers and other mistreated individuals; should be put in context (with facts) of groups and classes. We would like to see articles on how to survive in the city—in San Francisco." Reviews of 800 to 1,500 words pay $25 minimum; short articles of 1,500 to 2,500 words pay $35 minimum; long articles of over 2,500 words pay $50 minimum. Photos purchased with or without mss. B&w full negative prints, on 8x10 paper. Pays $15 per published photo, $40 minimum photo essay.

How To Break In: "Working with our summer volunteer projects in investigative reporting, in which we teach the techniques and send new reporters out to do investigations in the Bay Area. Submit applications in mid-Spring each year."

THE SECOND WAVE, Box 344, Cambridge A., Cambridge MA 02139. (617)491-1071. Editors: Women's Editorial Collective. For women concerned with issues of women's liberation. Quarterly magazine; 44 (8x10) pages. Established in 1971. Circulation: 5,000. Acquires first serial rights. Uses about 20 mss a year. Pays in contributor's copies. Sample copy $1.25. Photocopied and simultaneous submissions OK. Reports in 1 to 3 months. Query first or submit complete ms. Enclose S.A.S.E.
Nonfiction and Photos: All material must be related to the theme of women's liberation. "She (the writer) should write only on issues involving women's struggle for liberation, or women's relationships with other women. We do not want work glorifying men, marriage, traditional women's roles, etc. Would like to see articles on the women's liberation movement outside the big cities and in other countries; new issues being dealt with by women, etc." Informational, personal experience, interview, historical and think articles. Length: varies. B&w photos are used with or without accompanying mss. Captions optional.
Fiction and Poetry: Must relate to women's liberation theme. Experimental, mainstream, science fiction, fantasy. Free verse.

SIPAPU, Route 1, Box 216, Winters CA 95694. Editor: Noel Peattie. For "libraries, editors and collectors interested in Third World studies, the counterculture and the underground press." Established in 1970. Semi-annually. Circulation: 500. Buys all rights, but will reassign rights to author after publication (on request). Payment on publication. Will send sample copy to writer for $1. Will consider photocopied submissions. Reports on material in 3 weeks. Query first. Enclose S.A.S.E.
Nonfiction: "Primarily book reviews, interviews, descriptions of special libraries and counterculture magazines and underground papers. We are an underground 'paper' about underground 'papers.' We are interested in personalities publishing dissent, counterculture and Third Vorld material. Informal, clear and cool. We are not interested in blazing manifestos, but rather a concise, honest description of some phase of dissent publishing, or some library collecting in this field, that the writer knows about from the inside." Personal experience, interview, successful library operations. "We usually pay in contributor's copies, but will pay 2¢ per word if payment is required."

THE UNSPEAKABLE VISIONS OF THE INDIVIDUAL, Tuvoti, Inc., Box 439, California PA 15419. Editors-in-Chief: Arthur Winfield Knight, Kit Knight. For "an adult audience, generally college-educated (or substantial self-education) with an interest in Beat (generation) writing." Annual magazine/book; 176 pages. Estab: 1971. Circ: 2,000. Payment (if made) on publication. Acquires first North American serial rights. Reports in 2 months. Sample copy $2.
Nonfiction: Interviews (with Beat writers), personal experience, photo feature. Uses 20 mss/year. Query or submit complete ms. Length: 300-1,000 words. Pays 2 copies, "sometimes a small cash payment, i.e., $10."
Photos: Used with or without ms or on assignment. Captions required. Send prints. Pays 2 copies to $10 for 8x10 b&w glossies.
Fiction: Uses 10 mss/year. Submit complete ms. Length: Pays 2 copies to $10.
Poetry: Avant-garde, Free verse, traditional. Uses 15/year. Limit submissions to batches of 10. Length: 100 lines maximum. Pays 2 copies to $10.

VILLAGE VOICE, New York Magazine, Inc., 80 University Plaza, New York NY 10003. Editor-in-Chief: Marianne Partridge. Emphasizes arts and politics. Weekly tabloid; 125 pages. Estab: 1956. Circ: 156,000. Pays on publication. Buys all rights. SASE. Reports in 2 weeks.
Nonfiction: Expose, how-to, informational, historical, humor, interview, nostalgia, personal opinion, profile, personal experience, photo feature. Query. Length: 2,500 words maximum. Pays $150 minimum.
Photos: Charles P. Whitin, Department Editor. Purchased with ms or on assignment. Send prints. No additional payment for 8x11 b&w glossies purchased with ms. $25 for assigned photos. Model release required.
Poetry: Avant-garde and traditional forms. Pays $25 minimum.
Fillers: Alan Weitz, Managing Editor. Jokes, gags, anecdotes, newsbreaks. Length: 25-1,000 words. Pays $35 minimum.

WOMEN: A JOURNAL OF LIBERATION, 3028 Greenmount Ave., Baltimore MD 21218. (301)235-5245. Collective editorship. For women and men; high school education; specifically

feminists. Quarterly magazine; 56 pages. Estab: 1969. Circ: 20,000. Payment in contributor's copies. Acquires all rights. Phone queries OK. Simultaneous and photocopied submissions OK. SASE. Reports in 4-5 months. Sample copy $1.25.
Nonfiction: "All articles should be related to upcoming themes and reflect nonsexist and, hopefully, a socialist/feminist approach." Uses 60 mss/year. Submit complete ms. Length: 1,000-3,000 words.
Photos: Photos used with or without mss or on assignment; 5x7 (or larger) b&w.
Columns/Departments: Uses reviews of feminist press books about women. Letters from readers are used in Our Sisters Speak column. Uses 6/year. Length: 1,000-2,000 words.
Fiction: Adventure, confession, erotica, experimental, fantasy, historical, humorous, mainstream, mystery, suspense and science fiction. Uses 6/year. Length: 4,000-5,000 words.
Poetry: Avant-garde and traditional forms; free verse, blank verse, haiku and light verse. Submit complete ms. Length: open.

WOMEN AS WOMEN AS WOMEN, 1218 E. 49th St., Kansas City MO 64110. Collective editorship. For women in the Midwest who are interested in feminism. A Journal of the K.C. Women's Liberation Union. 28 (8½x11) pages. Established in 1972. Published every two months. Circulation: 200. Not copyrighted. Payment in contributor's copies. Will send sample copy to writer for 60¢. Will consider photocopied and simultaneous submissions. Reports on material accepted for publication and returns rejected material in 2 months. Query first or submit complete ms. Enclose S.A.S.E.
Fiction, Poetry, Nonfiction and Photos: Uses material on current feminist movements taken from any angle, topic, style. Societal change, non-sexist. Will consider informational, how-to, interview, expose, reviews, successful business operations. Length: open. Uses b&w photos with accompanying ms. Also uses material for columns and departments.
How To Break In: "Be familiar with what movement papers print and submit an article which reflects that life value."

WOMEN'S RIGHTS LAW REPORTER, 180 University Ave., Newark NJ 07102. (201)648-5320. Managing Editors: Dara Klassel, Gerry O'Kane. Legal journal emphasizing law and feminism for lawyers, students and feminists. Quarterly magazine; 48 pages. Estab: 1971. Circ: 1,500. No payment. Acquires all rights. Phone queries OK. Submit seasonal/holiday material 3-4 months in advance. Photocopied submissions OK. SASE. Reports in 1 month. Sample copy $3.50.
Nonfiction: Historical and legal articles. Query or submit complete ms. Length: 20 pages plus footnotes.
How To Break In: "We'd prefer to have people inquire on topics we'd like to have articles on, but will consider any legal article submitted to us."

Animal Publications

These publications deal with pets, racing and show horses, and other pleasure animals. Magazines about animals bred and raised for food are classified in Farm Publications.

AMERICAN HUMANE MAGAZINE (formerly *National Humane Review*), 5351 S. Roslyn St., Englewood CO 80110. (303)779-1400. Editor: Anne A. Brennan. Monthly magazine. Estab: 1913 (as *National Humane Review*). Pays on publication. Copyrighted. SASE. Reports in 3 months. Sample copy 50¢.
Nonfiction: "Freelance material is accepted on speculation and must be typed triple-spaced. Study recent issues before submitting material." Pays $25 for 1,000 words or less; $50 for 2,000 words or less.
Photos: "Whenever possible, articles should be accompanied by suitable photographs or illustrations. Single photographs, color photographs for possible cover use, photo series with introduction and captions and original artwork will also receive consideration." Pays $15 for b&w glossies; $30 for color used on cover.
How To Break In: "Remember that the purposes of the magazine are: To publicize the activities of the association, and to report on trends, news and accomplishments in the humane movement, including activities in child and animal protection."

ANIMAL KINGDOM, New York Zoological Park, Bronx NY 10460. (212)220-5121. Editor: Eugene J. Walter, Jr. For individuals interested in wildlife, zoos, aquariums, and members of zoological societies. Bimonthly. Buys first North American serial rights. Pays on acceptance. Reports in 1 month. Enclose S.A.S.E.

Nonfiction and Photos: Wildlife articles dealing with animal natural history, conservation, behavior. No pets, domestic animals, or botany. Articles should be scientifically well-grounded but written for a general audience, not scientific journal readers. No poetry, cartoons, or fillers. Length: 1,500 to 3,000 words. Pays $100-$450. Payment for photos purchased with mss is negotiable.

How To Break In: "It helps to be a working scientist dealing directly with animals in the wild. Or a scientist working in a zoo such as the staff members here at the New York Zoological Society. Most of the authors who send us unsolicited mss are non-scientists who are doing their research in libraries. They're simply working from scientific literature and writing it up for popular consumption. There are a fair number of others who are backyard naturalists, so to speak, and while their observations may be personal, they are not well grounded scientifically. It has nothing to do with whether or not they are good or bad writers. In fact, some of our authors are not specially good writers but they are able to provide us with fresh, original material and new insights into animal behavior and biology. That sort of thing is impossible from someone who is working from books. Hence, I cannot be too encouraging to anyone who lacks field experience."

ANIMAL LOVERS MAGAZINE, Box 918, New Providence NJ 07974. (201)665-0812. Editor-in-Chief: Anita Coffelt. Emphasizes animals, pets for readership of animal lovers, pet owners, veterinarians, school/public libraries and 2-3 universities. Quarterly magazine; 24 pages. Estab: 1969. Circ: 3,500+. Payment on acceptance. Buys all rights, but may reassign rights to author following publication. Seasonal/holiday material must be submitted 3 months in advance. Photocopied submissions OK. SASE. Reports in 6 weeks. Sample copy 75¢. Free writer's guidelines.

Nonfiction: How-to; humor (between pet and owner; two pets, etc.); informational, personal experience; personal opinion (on euthanasia, veterinarian fees, cruelty, hunting, etc.) and profile (animal lovers who have gone to extraordinary lengths to help animals). Buys 60 mss/year. Submit complete ms. Length: 300-600 words. Pays 1¢ per published word; $3-6 article.

Photos: Purchased with or without accompanying ms. Captions required. Send b&w or color prints. Pays maximum $2 for b&w or color.

Fiction: Humorous. Buys 5 mss/year. Length: 300-600 words. Pays 1¢ per word; $3-6/ms. Send complete ms.

Fillers: Short Humor (brief incidents involving animals). Buys 5-10/year. Length: 75-200 words. Pays 1¢ per word; $1-2, maximum.

Rejects: "Poetry, cartoons, puzzles, articles or stories which depict cats stalking their prey; gory details about dying animals; stories which contain profanity or sexual overtones. We particularly do not want inconsequential accounts of pets. Manuscripts that are 1,000 words+. No poetry or foreign markets."

ANIMALS, MSPCA, 350 S. Huntington Ave., Boston MA 02130. Editor-in-Chief: Deborah Salem. For members of the MSPCA. Bimonthly magazine; 40 pages. Estab: 1868. Circ: 18,000. Pays on publication. Buys all rights, but may reassign to author following publication. Photocopied and previously published submissions OK. Reports in 2 weeks. Sample copy 75¢ with 8½x11 SASE; writers's guidelines for SASE.

Nonfiction, Fiction, Photos and Poetry: Articles Editor: Jean-Alice Uehlinger. Uses practical articles on animal care and breeding, animal profiles, articles on humane/animal protection issues, true stories of pets and their people, articles on cultural subjects relating to animals, such as "Animals in American Folk Art." Uses some original fiction with animal protagonists. Also pictorial essays. Emphasis should be on animals. Non-sentimental approach. "Humorous, as well as serious articles appreciated when in good taste." Recently published "Your Dog's Senses" and "The Irish Setter in Your Life." Length: 300 to 3,000 words. Pays 2¢ per word. Photos purchased with accompanying ms with extra payment, without accompanying ms or on assignment. Captions required. Payment: $5 for b&w; $7.50 for color. Size: 5x7 minimum for b&w; color transparencies or prints. Buys light verse. Pays $5 to $10.

APPALOOSA NEWS, Box 8403, Moscow ID 83843. (208)882-5578. Emphasizes appaloosa horses for appaloosa owners, breeders and people interested in horses. Monthly magazine; 186 pages. Estab: 1950. Circ: 25,000. Buys all rights, but may reassign rights to author following publication. Phone queries OK. Seasonal/holiday material should be submitted 90 days in advance. Simultaneous, photocopied and previously published submissions OK. SASE. Reports in 6 weeks. Free sample copy.

Nonfiction: How-to (horse-related articles); historical (history of appaloosa); humor (cartoons);

informational; interview (horse-related persons—trainer, owner, racer, etc.); personal opinion (we have a form); photo feature; profile (must be authentic) and technical. Submit complete ms. Pays $35 minimum, however most are gratis by owners.

Photos: Purchased with accompanying manuscript for article, without accompanying manuscript for cover. Captions are required. Send prints or transparencies. 8x10 or 5x7 b&w glossies or color transparencies for cover. No additional payment for photos accepted with accompanying ms, total purchase price for ms includes payment for photos.

Columns, Departments: For regional reports for appaloosa horse club, horse shows or sales. Send complete ms. No payment.

THE CANADIAN HORSE, 48 Belfield Rd., Rexdale, Ontario, Canada M9W 1G1. (416)249-7278. Editor: P.G. Jones. For thoroughbred horsemen. Monthly magazine. Estab: 1961. Circ: 4,500. Buys all rights. Pays on publication. Query first. Enclose S.A.S.E.

Nonfiction: Material on thoroughbred racing; racing results. Length: 2 pages. Pays $20 per page.

CAT FANCY, Fancy Publication, Inc., Box 4030, San Clemente CA 92672. (714)498-1600. Editor: Mike Criss. For men and women of all ages interested in all phases of cat ownership. Bimonthly magazine; 40 pages. Estab: 1967. Circ: 55,000. Pays on publication. Buys all rights, but may reassign following publication. Submit seasonal/holiday material 4 months in advance. Previously published submissions OK. SASE. Reports in 3 months. Sample copy $1.25; free writer's guidelines.

Nonfiction: Historical; how-to; humor; informational; personal experience; photo feature and technical. Buys 5 mss/issue. Send complete ms. Length: 500-3,500 words. Pays 3¢/word.

Photos: Photos purchased with or without accompanying ms. Pays $7.50-25 for 8x10 b&w glossies: $50-100 for 35mm or 2¼x2¼ color photos. Send prints and transparencies. No additional payment for photos accepted with accompanying ms. Model release required.

Fiction: Adventure; fantasy; historical and humorous. Buys 1 mss/issue. Send complete ms. Length: 500-5,000 words. Pays 3¢/word.

Poetry: Avant-garde, free verse, haiku, light verse and traditional. Buys 4 poems/issue. Length: 5-50 lines. Pays $10.

Fillers: Short humor. Buys 10 fillers/year. Length: 100-500 words. Pays 3¢/word.

CATS MAGAZINE, P.O. Box 4106, Pittsburgh PA 15202. Editor: Jean Amelia Laux. For men and women of all ages; cat enthusiasts, vets, geneticists. Monthly magazine. Established in 1945. Circulation: 50,000. Buys first North American serial rights. Buys 50 mss per year. Payment on acceptance. Will send free sample copy to writer on request. Write for copy of guidelines for writers. Will "reluctantly" consider photocopied submissions. No simultaneous submissions. Submit seasonal Christmas material 4 to 6 months in advance. Reports within 6 weeks. Enclose S.A.S.E.

Nonfiction and Photos: "Cat health, cat breed articles, articles on the cat in art, literature, history, human culture, cats in the news. Cat pets of popular personalities. In general how cats and cat people are contributing to our society. We're more serious, more scientific, but we do like an occasional light or humorous article portraying cats and humans, however, as they really are. Would like to see something on psychological benefits of cat ownership; how do cat-owning families differ from others? Also movie and book reviews." Length: 800 to 2,500 words. Pays $15 to $75. Photos purchased with or without accompanying ms. Captions optional. Pays $15 minimum for 4x5 or larger b&w photos; $100 minimum for color. Prefers 2¼x2¼ minimum, but can use 35mm (transparencies only). "We use color for cover only. Prefer cats as part of scenes rather than stiff portraits."

Fiction and Poetry: Science fiction, fantasy and humorous fiction; cat themes only. Length: 800 to 2,500 words. Pays $15 to $100. Poetry in traditional forms, blank or free verse, avant-garde forms and some light verse; cat themes only. Length: 4 to 64 lines. Pays 30¢/line.

DOG FANCY, Fancy Publications, Inc., Box 4030, San Clemente CA 92672. (714)498-1600. Editor: Mike Criss. For men and women of all ages interested in all phases of dog ownership. Bimonthly magazine; 40 pages. Estab: 1969. Circ: 40,000. Pays on publication. Buys all rights, but may reassign following publication. Submit seasonal/holiday material 4 months in advance. Previously published submissions OK. Sample copy $1.25; free writer's guidelines.

Nonfiction: Historical; how-to; humor; informational; interview; personal experience; photo feature; profile and technical. Buys 5 mss/issue. Length: 500-3,500 words. Pays 3¢/word.

Photos: Photos purchased with or without accompanying ms. Pays $7.50-25 for 8x10 b&w glossies: $50-100 for 35mm or 2¼x2¼ color photos. Send prints and transparencies. No additional payment for photos accepted with accompanying ms. Model release required.

Fiction: Adventure; fantasy; historical and humorous. Buys 5 mss/year. Send complete ms. Length: 500-5,000 words. Pays 3¢/word.
Fillers: Jokes, gags, anecdotes, newsbreaks and short humor. Buys 10 fillers/year. Length: 100-500 words. Pays 3¢/word.

DRESSAGE, The National Magazine, Box 2460, Cleveland OH 44112. Editor: Ivan I. Bezugloff, Jr. For a readership interested in classical horsemanship and/or combined training. Monthly magazine; 36-52 pages. Estab: 1971. Circ: 5,000. Pays on publication. Buys first North American serial rights. Reports in 4 weeks. Free sample copy.
Nonfiction: Educational material on training horses and riders in using the principles of dressage (classical horsemanship), for both dressage and/or combined training. Pays 14¢/ published line.
Fiction: Humorous, equestrian fiction, particularly amusing and entertaining short stories for the 'Hayseed' column. Must be related to dressage or combined training. Length: 700-1,200 words. Pays $21-26.

THE EQUESTRIAN IMAGE, Image Publications and Promotions, R.R. 5, Fenwick, Ontario, Canada L0S 1CO. (416)892-2222. Editor-in-Chief: Pat Mellen. Emphasizes equine world; from novice to professional, all breeds from pony to draft, all facets from breeding to clipping. Monthly magazine; 56 pages. Estab: 1973. Circ: 4,700. Pays on publication. Buys one-time rights. Submit seasonal/holiday material 1 month in advance. Simultaneous, photocopied and previously published submissions OK. SAE and International Reply Coupons. Reports in 6 weeks. Free sample copy.
Nonfiction: "All topics open to writers." Buys 6-12 mss/year. Send complete ms. Pays 60¢/ column inch.
Photos: Photos purchased with accompanying ms or on assignment. Captions required. Pays $2 minimum for b&w and color photos. Send prints.
Fiction: Historical and humorous. Buys 6-12 mss/year. Send complete ms. Pays 60¢/column inch.
Fillers: Jokes, gags, anecdotes, puzzles and short humor. Buys 6-12 mss/year. Pays $3.

FAMILY PET, Box 22964, Tampa FL 33622. Editor-in-Chief: M. Linda Sabella. Emphasizes pets and pet owners in Florida. "Our readers are all ages; many show pets, most have more than one pet, and most are in Florida." Quarterly magazine; 16-24 pages. Estab: 1971. Circ: 3,000. Pays on acceptance. Buys one-time rights. Previously published submissions OK. SASE. Reports in 3-4 weeks. Free sample copy and writer's guidelines.
Nonfiction: Historical (especially breed histories); how-to (training and grooming hints); humor (or living with pets); informational; personal experience; photo feature and travel (with pets). Buys 1-2 mss/issue. Send complete ms. Length: 500-1,200. Pays $5-20.
Photos: Photos purchased with or without accompanying ms. Captions required. Pays $3-5 for 5x7 b&w glossies. Send prints. Total purchase price for ms includes payment for photos.
Columns/Departments: New Books (reviews of recent issues in pet field). Send complete ms. Length: 200-400 words. Pays $3-5. Open to suggestions for new columns/departments.
Poetry: Light verse, prefers rhyme. Buys 1/issue. Length: 25 lines maximum. Pays $3-5.
Fillers: Jokes, gags, anecdotes, puzzles and short humor. Buys 4-5 fillers/year. Length: 100-400 words. Pays $2-5.

HORSE AND HORSEMAN, P.O. Box HH, Capistrano Beach CA 92624. Editor: Mark Thiffault. For owners of pleasure horses; predominantly female with main interest in show/ pleasure riding. Monthly magazine; 74 pages. Estab: 1973. Circ: 96,000. Buys all rights, but will reassign rights to author after publication. Buys 40 to 50 mss a year. Payment on acceptance. Will send free sample copy to writer on request. Write for copy of guidelines for writers. Will not consider photocopied or simultaneous submissions. Submit special material (horse and tack care; veterinary medicine pieces in winter and spring issues) 3 months in advance. Reports within 1 month. Query first or submit complete ms. Enclose S.A.S.E.
Nonfiction and Photos: Training tips, do-it-yourself pieces, grooming and feeding, stable management, tack maintenance, sports, personalities, rodeo and general features of horse-related nature. Emphasis must be on informing, rather than merely entertaining. Aimed primarily at the beginner, but with information for experienced horsemen. Subject matter must have thorough, in-depth appraisal. Interested in more English (hunter/jumper) riding/training copy, plus pieces on driving horses and special horse areas like Tennessee Walkers and other gaited breeds. More factual breed histories. Uses informational, how-to, personal experience, interview, profile, humor, historical, nostalgia, successful business operations, technical articles. Length: 2,000 words minimum. Pays $75 to $200. B&w photos (4x5 and larger) purchased with

or without mss. Pays $4 to $10 when purchased without ms. Uses original color transparencies (35mm and larger). Will not consider duplicates. Pays $100 for cover use. Payment for inside editorial color is negotiated.

HORSE LOVER'S NATIONAL MAGAZINE, Uniplan Publishing Corp., 899 Broadway, Redwood City CA 94063. (415)367-8282. Editor-in-Chief: Robert J. Lydon. Emphasizes horses and horse owners. Bimonthly magazine; 64 pages. Estab: 1936. Circ: 120,000. Pays on publication. Buys first North American serial rights. Phone queries OK. Submit seasonal/holiday material 6 months in advance. Photocopied and previously published submissions OK. SASE. Reports in 6 weeks. Sample copy $1.25. Free writer's guidelines.
Nonfiction: Jack Foley, Managing Editor. Historical, how-to; informational; interview (well known and respected horse people only); personal experience; photo feature; profile and medical (related to horses). Buys 15 mss/year. Query. Length: 1,000-2,500 words. Pays 5-10¢/word.
Photos: Photos purchased with or without accompanying ms or on assignment. Captions required. Pays $10-25 for 35mm color transparencies; no payment for 5x7 b&w glossies submitted with ms. Model release required.
Fiction: Jack Foley, Managing Editor. Adventure; historical; humorous; mainstream; mystery; suspense and western. Buys 1 ms/issue. Send complete ms. Length: 1,000-2,000 words. Pays $25-75. Buys some column space (800-1,200 words at 5¢/word) and poetry (for the Junior Section; no payment involved).
Fillers: Mike Antonucci, Fillers Editor. Jokes, gags, anecdotes, newsbreaks and short humor. Buys 6 fillers/issue. Length: 25-200 words. Pays $5-10.

HORSE, OF COURSE, Derbyshire Publishing Co., Temple NH 03084. (603)654-6126. Editor-in-Chief: R.A. Greene. For novice, backyard horsemen, mostly female. Monthly magazine; 72 pages. Estab: 1972. Circ: 120,000. Pays on publication. Buys all rights. Submit seasonal/holiday material 6 months in advance. SASE. Reports in 3 weeks. Sample copy $1; free writer's guidelines.
Nonfiction: How-to (about all aspects of horsemanship, horse care, and horse owning), historical (on breeds, famous horse-related people, etc., would be particularly saleable if they include some tips on riding and horse care), interview (with trainers, riders giving their methods), photo feature ('how-to' photo features). Buys 35-50 mss/year. Submit complete ms. Length: 800-3,500 words. Pays $10-200.
Photos: Purchased with accompanying ms. Captions required. Submit prints. Pays minimum $3 for 4x5 or larger b&w glossies; pays $10-50 for 33mm or 8x10 glossy color prints (for cover). Model release required.

HORSE PLAY, 443 N. Frederick Ave., Gaithersburg MD 20760. (301)840-1866. Editor-in-Chief: Carolyn Banks. Managing Editor: Cordelia Doucet. Emphasizes horses and horse sports for a readership interested in horses, especially people who show, event and hunt. Monthly magazine; 48 pages. Estab: 1975. Circ: 10,000. Pays on publication. Buys first North American serial rights. Phone queries OK. Submit seasonal/holiday material 3 months in advance. SASE. Reports in 6 weeks. Sample copy $1.50; free writer's guidelines.
Nonfiction: Expose; how-to (various aspects of horsemanship, course designing, stable management, putting on horse shows, etc.); historical; humor; interview; nostalgia; personal experience; personal opinion; photo feature; profile; technical; and travel. Buys 40 mss/year. Length: 1,000-3,000 words. Pays $35-75.
Photos: Margaret Thomas, Photo Editor. Purchased on assignment. Captions required. Query or send contact sheet, prints, or transparencies. Pays $5 for 8x10 b&w glossies; $50 maximum for color transparencies.
Columns/Departments: Book Reviews, Roundup, and News Releases. Pays $10.

HORSEMAN, The Magazine of Western Riding, 5314 Bingle Rd., Houston TX 77092. (713)688-8811. Editor: Tex Rogers. For people who own and ride horses for pleasure and competition. Majority own western stock horses and compete in western type horse shows as a hobby or business. Monthly. "We have 6 special emphasis issues per year, but they're not standard. Subjects may vary from year to year." Established in 1954. Circulation: 175,000. Rights purchased vary with author and material. Buys all rights, first North American serial rights, or second serial (reprint) rights. Buys approximately 110 mss per year. Payment on publication. Will send free sample copy to writer on request. Write for copy of guidelines for writers. Will not consider photocopied submissions. Submit seasonal material 4 months in advance. Reports in 3 weeks. Query first. Enclose S.A.S.E.
Nonfiction, Photos, and Poetry: "How-to articles on horsemanship, training, grooming,

exhibiting, nutrition, horsekeeping, mare care and reproduction, horse health, humor and history dealing with horses. We really like articles from professional trainers, or 'as told to' articles by pro horsemen to freelancers. The approach should always be to provide information which will educate and inform readers as to how they can ride, train, keep and enjoy their horses more. Compared to other horse publications, we try to be more professional in our writing and really have meaningful articles in the magazine." Length: 1,000 to 3,500 words. Pays 4¢/word (one time); 5¢/word for all rights; 7¢/word for "as told to" with professional horseman. Photos purchased with accompanying ms with no additional payment. Captions required. Also purchased on assignment. Pays $6 minimum for b&w 8x10 and negs; 35mm or 120 negs. Color negative film. "We make prints." Pays $200 for covers; all rights. Buys some traditional forms of poetry. Pays $10 for all rights.

HORSEMEN'S JOURNAL, 6000 Executive Bldg., Suite 317, Rockville MD 20852. Editor: William McDonald. For an audience composed entirely of thoroughbred running-horse owners, trainers and breeders. Monthly magazine; standard (8x11), 72 pages. Special issues: May (Kentucky Derby issue); December, July and August (material relating to racehorse breeding and bloodlines); September (material relating to training). Established in 1949. Circulation: 34,000. Rights purchased vary with author and material. Buys all rights, first North American serial rights, and second serial (reprint) rights. Buys "less than 6 unsolicited mss a year; over 50 mss on assignment basis." Payment on publication. Will send sample copy to writer for $1. Will not consider photocopied or simultaneous submissions. Submit seasonal material first of month preceding cover date. Reports "as soon as possible." Query first. Enclose S.A.S.E.
Nonfiction and Photos: "Any material which our readership can relate to on a professional level. This includes personality pieces, interviews, how-to articles, veterinary stories and generally material relating to happenings and economics within the racehorse industry." Length: 1,000 to 3,000 words. Pays $45 minimum. 8x10 b&w glossies are purchased with accompanying ms. Captions optional. Pays $10 each.
How To Break In: "Because of our monthly deadline and competition from dailies and weeklies, 'current events' pieces are of little use. Material should be incisive, should quote the people involved in their words and should have national import and interest."

HORSEMEN'S YANKEE PEDLAR NEWSPAPER, Wilbraham MA 01095. (413)589-9088. Editor-in-Chief: Beverly Foisy. For "horse enthusiasts of all ages, all incomes from one horse owners to large private show and hunt stables and public commercial stables." Monthly newspaper; 104 pages. Estab: 1962. Circ: 12,500. Pays on publication. Buys one-time rights. Submit seasonal/holiday material 2-3 months in advance. Simultaneous, photocopied and previously published submissions OK. SASE. Reports in 4 weeks. Sample copy $1; free writer's guidelines.
Nonfiction: How-to, humor, informational, inspirational, interview, nostalgia, and profile. Buys 25-30 mss/year. Submit complete ms. Length: 1,500-2,500 words. Pays $50-100.
Photos: Purchased with or without accompanying ms. Captions required. Query. Total purchase price for ms includes payment for photos.
Columns/Departments: Area news column and Equine Activities. Buys 85-95 mss/year. Query. Length: 1,200-1,400 words. Pays $25.
Fillers: Puzzles and short humor. Pays $10-25.

HUNTING DOG MAGAZINE, 9714 Montgomery Rd., Cincinnati OH 45242. (513)891-0060. Editor-in-Chief: George R. Quigley. Emphasizes sporting dogs. Monthly magazine; 52 pages. Estab: 1965. Circ: 24,000. Pays on publication. Buys all rights but may reassign following publication. Phone queries OK. Submit seasonal/holiday material 5-6 months in advance. Photocopied submissions OK. Reports in 3-4 weeks. Free sample copy and writer's guidelines.
Nonfiction: How-to (training dogs, hunting with dogs, building dog-related equipment), informational, interview (with well-known outdoor and dog-related persons), personal opinion (by the experts), profile, new product, photo feature, technical (guns, dog-related items). Buys 175-200 mss/year. Query or submit complete ms. Length: 1,500-2,200 words. Pays 2¢/word minimum.
Photos: Purchased with or without accompanying ms. Captions required. Send contact sheet, prints or transparencies. Pays $5 minimum for 8x10 b&w glossy prints; $50 for 35mm vertical transparencies (for cover).
Fillers: "Short (200-700 words) pieces about hunting dogs or new uses for equipment." Buys 100 mss/year. Submit complete ms. Pays "generally more than 2¢/word."

PRACTICAL HORSEMEN, The Pennsylvania Horse, Inc., 225 S. Church St., West Chester PA 19380. Editor-in Chief: Pamela Goold. For knowledgeable horsemen interested in breeding, raising and training thoroughbred and thoroughbred-type horses for show, eventing, dressage, race or hunt and field. Monthly magazine; 56-64 pages. Estab:1973. Circ:18,000. Pays on publication. Buys all rights. Simultaneous and photocopied submissions OK, but will not use any submission unless withdrawn from other publishers. SASE. Reports in 2 months. Free sample copy and writer's guidelines.
Nonfiction: How-to-do-it interviews with top professional horsemen in the hunter/jumper field; vetinary and stable management articles; and photo features and step-by-step ideas for barn building, grooming, trimming, and feeding and management tips. Buys 3-4/issue. Query with sample of writing or complete ms. Length: open. Pays $100.
Photos: Purchased on assignment. Captions required. Query. Pays $5 minimum for b&w glossies (5x7 minimum size); $40 maximum or 35mm or 2¼x2¼ color transparencies for covers.
How To Break In: "Freelancers with horse experience absolutely required. Submit background (writing and horse) and samples of writing, preferably of a how-to-do-it nature. Suggestions for interviews or story topics are also appreciated."

THE QUARTER HORSE JOURNAL, Box 9105, Amarillo TX 79105. (806)376-4811. Editor-in-Chief: Audie Rackley. Official publication of the American Quarter Horse Association. Monthly magazine; 500 pages. Estab: 1948. Circ: 67,000. Pays on acceptance. Buys all rights, but on occasion will buy first rights. Phone queries OK. Submit seasonal/holiday material 2 months in advance. SASE. Reports in 2 weeks. Free sample copy and writer's guidelines.
Nonfiction: Historical (those that retain our western heritage); how-to (fitting, grooming, showning, clipping, or anything that relates to owing, showing, or breeding); informational (educational clinics, current news); interview (feature-type stories; must be on established people who have made a contribution to the business); new product; personal opinion; and technical (medical updates, new surgery procedures, etc.). Buys 25 mss/year. Length: 800-2,500 words. Pays $40-100.
Photos: Purchased with accompanying ms. Captions required. Send prints or transparencies. Uses 5x7 or 8x10 b&w glossies; 2¼x2¼ or 3x5 color transparencies. Offers no additional payment for photos accepted with accompanying ms.

THE QUARTER HORSE OF THE PACIFIC COAST, Pacific Coast Quarter Horse Assn., Box 254822, Gate 12 Cal Expo, Sacramento, CA 95825. Editor-in-Chief: Jill L. Scopinich. Emphasizes quarter horses for owners, breeders and trainers on the west coast. Monthly magazine; 150 pages. Estab: 1945. Circ: 8,200. Pays on publication. Buys all rights and first North American serial rights. Simultaneous submissions OK. SASE. Reports in 4 weeks. Sample copy $1.
Nonfiction: How-to; informational; interview; personal experience; photo feature and profile. Buys 2 mss/issue. Send complete ms. Length: 500-3,000 words. Pays $50-150.
Photos: Photos purchased with or without accompanying ms. Captions required. Pays $3-5 for 8x10 b&w glossies. Model release required.
Columns/Departments: Of Course, A Horse; Racing Room and The Stable Pharmacy. Buys 3 mss/issue. Send complete ms. Length: 500-2,000 words. Pays $50-100.
Fiction: Humorous and western. Buys 6 mss/year. Send complete ms. Length: 500-3,000 words. Pays $50-150.

TODAY'S ANIMAL HEALTH, (formerly *Animal Cavalcade*), Animal Health Foundation, 8338 Rosemead, Pica Rivera CA 90660. (213)682-3080. Editor-in-Chief: R.S. Glassberg, D.V.M. Emphasizes animal health for laymen. Bimonthly magazine; 32-40 pages. Estab: 1970. Circ: 50,000. Pays on publication. Buys all rights. Submit seasonal/holiday material 6 months in advance. Simultaneous, photocopied and previously published submissions OK. SASE. Reports in 2 months. Sample copy $2, free writer's guidelines.
Nonfiction: How-to, informational, historical, interview, profile, travel, photo feature. Buys 1-3 mss/issue. Submit complete ms. Length: 250-2,000 words. Pays $5-20.
Photos: D.M. Diem, Department Editor. No additional payment for those used with mss. Captions required. Pays $5-20 for 5x7 (minimum) b&w glossies purchased without ms. Model release required.
Fillers: Purchases clippings only with permission to reprint from original source. Buys 6-12/year. Send fillers in. Length: 50-200 words. Pays $2.50-10.

TROPICAL FISH HOBBYIST, 211 W. Sylvania Ave., Neptune City NJ 17753. Editor: Neal Pronek. For tropical fish keepers; mostly male, mostly young. Monthly magazine; 100

(5½x8½) pages. Established in 1952. Circ: 40,000. Rights purchased vary with author and material. Usually buys all rights, but buys only serial rights in some cases. Buys 50 mss a year. Payment on acceptance. Will send sample copy to writer for $1. Will not consider photocopied or simultaneous submissions. Reports within 1 week. Query first or submit complete ms. Enclose S.A.S.E.

Nonfiction and Photos: "Don't submit material unless you're an experienced keeper of tropical fishes and know what you're talking about. Offer specific advice about caring for and breeding tropicals and related topics. Study the publication before submitting." Informal style preferred. Can use personality profiles of successful aquarium hobbyists, but query first on these. Pays from 1½¢ to 3¢ a word. Pays $5 for b&w glossy photos purchased with or without accompanying mss. No size limitation. Captions optional. Pays $10 for color; 35mm transparency, or larger.

THE WESTERN HORSEMAN, Box 7980, Colorado Springs CO 80933. Editor: Chan Bergen. Emphasizes western horsemanship. Monthly magazine. Estab: 1936. Circ: 195,000. Pays on acceptance. Buys one-time rights. Submit seasonal/holiday material 3 months in advance. SASE. Reports in 2-3 weeks. Sample copy $1.

Nonfiction: How-to (horse training, care of horses, tips, etc.); and informational (on rodeos, ranch life, historical articles of the west emphasizing horses). Buys 15-20/issue. Submit complete ms. Pays $35-75; "sometimes higher by special arrangement."

Photos: Purchased with accompanying ms. Captions required. Uses 5x7 or 8x10 b&w glossies. Total purchase for ms includes payment for photos.

Art Publications

THE AMERICAN ART JOURNAL, Kennedy Galleries, Inc., and Israel Sack, Inc., 40 W. 57th St., 5th Floor, New York NY 10019. (212)541-9600. Editor-in-Chief: Jane Van N. Turano. Scholarly magazine of American art history of the 17th, 18th, 19th and 20th centuries, including painting, sculpture, architecture, decorative arts, etc., for people with a serious interest in American art, and who are already knowledgeable about the subject. Readers are scholars, curators, collectors, students of American art, or persons who have a strong interest in Americana. Quarterly magazine; 112 pages. Estab: 1969. Circ: 2,000. Pays on acceptance. Buys all rights, but may reassign following publication. Photocopied submissions OK. SASE. Reports in 2 months. Sample copy $6.

Nonfiction: "All articles are historical in the sense that they are all about some phase or aspect of American art history." Buys 25-30 mss/year. Submit complete ms "with good cover letter." Length: 2,500-8,000 words. Pays $250-300.

Photos: Purchased with accompanying ms. Captions required. Uses b&w only. Offers no additional payment for photos accepted with accompanying ms.

How To Break In: "Actually, our range of interest is quite broad. Any topic within our time frame is acceptable if it is well-researched, well-written, and illustrated. Whenever possible, all mss must be accompanied by b&w photographs which have been integrated into the text by the use of numbers."

Rejects: No how-to articles or reviews of exhibitions. No book reviews or opinion pieces. No human interest approaches to artists' lives.

AMERICAN ART REVIEW, P.O. Box 65007, Los Angeles CA 90065. (213)254-7301. Editor: Martha Hutson. For libraries, museums, professional art historians, artists, collectors; persons interested in American art history heritage. Magazine; 144 (8½x11) pages. Established in 1973. Every 2 months. Special student issue; date varies. Circulation: 10,000. Rights purchased vary with author and material. May buy all rights, but will reassign rights to author after publication; or simultaneous rights. Buys 35 to 40 mss a year. Pays on publication. Will send sample copy to writer for $3.75. Write for copy of guidelines for writers. Will consider photocopied and simultaneous submissions. Submit special issue material 6 months in advance. Reports on material accepted for publication in 2 weeks. Returns rejected material immediately. Query first. Enclose S.A.S.E.

Nonfiction and Photos: Articles must be well-researched and documented, but can be interpretive. Should be highly readable and directed toward art historians/collectors, and concern American art history from the Colonial period to 1950. Would like to see material on American art as an investment; articles about collectors and collections; interpretations of American art history; collecting possibilities. Quality of artists or collectors must be high. Length: 1,500 to 5,000 words. Pays $25 to $150. Student issue uses papers written by undergraduate or graduate art students. Also uses reviews of exhibitions and art books. Length: 1,500 to 3,000 words. Pays $35 to $100. No additional payment for 8x10 b&w glossies or 4x5, 5x7 or 8x10 color transparencies used with mss. Captions required.

THE ART GALLERY, Ivoryton CT 06442. (203)767-0151. Editor: William C. Bendig. For an art-oriented audience; collectors with an auction and antique interest; museum directors and curators. Established in 1957. Circ: 40,000. Buys all rights. Pays on publication. Will send free sample copy to writer on request. Reports in 2 weeks. Query first. Enclose S.A.S.E.
Nonfiction: Highly specialized or unique approach required for material on fine arts, antiques, collecting all decorative arts objects plus coins, medals, books, etc. "Current news approach; crisp, clear, concise writing; intelligent, but not stuffy. Normally, everything is commissioned." Length: 1,000 to 4,000 words. Pays $50 to $250.

ART NEWS, 750 Third Ave., New York NY 10017. Editor: Milton Esterow. For persons interested in art. Monthly. Circ: 50,000. Query first. Enclose S.A.S.E.
Nonfiction: "I'm buying in-depth profiles of people in the art world—artists, curators, dealers. And investigative pieces, including some on antiques. The format is very flexible to cover personalities, trends, a single painting." Wants "humanized" art coverage. Length: 800 words; "some major pieces as long as 8,000 words." Pays $75 to $300.

ARTS MAGAZINE, 23 E. 26th St., New York NY 10010. (212)685-8500. Editor: Richard Martin. A journal of contemporary art, art criticism, and art history, particularly for artists, scholars, museum officials, art teachers and students, and collectors. Established in 1926. Monthly, except July and August. Circulation: 28,500. Buys all rights. Pays on publication. Query first. Study magazine before querying. Enclose S.A.S.E.
Nonfiction and Photos: Art criticism, art analysis, and art history. Topical reference to museum or gallery exhibition preferred. Length: 1,500 to 2,500 words. Pays $100, with opportunity for negotiation. B&w glossies or color transparencies customarily supplied by related museums or galleries.

ARTS MANAGEMENT, 408 West 57th St., New York NY 10019. (212)245-3850. Editor: A.H. Reiss. For cultural institutions. Five times annually. Circulation: 6,000. Buys all rights. Pays on publication. Mostly staff written. Query first. Reports in several weeks. Enclose S.A.S.E.
Nonfiction: Short articles, 400 to 900 words, tightly written, expository, explaining how art administrators solved problems in publicity, fund raising, and general administration; actual case histories emphasizing the how-to. Also short articles on the economics and sociology of the arts and important trends in the nonprofit cultural field. Must be fact-filled, well-organized and without rhetoric. Payment is 2¢ to 4¢ per word. No photographs or pictures.

DESIGN MAGAZINE, 1100 Waterway Blvd., Indianapolis IN 46202. (313)634-1100, Ext. 209. Editor: Terry K. Cristy. For junior high and high school students, art educators to beginning college level, craftsmen, home hobbyists. Art journal; 40 pages. Established in 1898. Every 2 months. Circulation: 7,200. Buys all rights unless otherwise specified with submission. Buys about 75 mss per year. Pays on publication. Will send sample copy to writer for $1.25. Free writer's guidelines. Photocopied submissions OK. Submit seasonal material 4 months in advance. Reports in 2 months. Enclose S.A.S.E. for return of photos.
Nonfiction and Photos: Wants demonstrative art projects, new art materials and concepts, craft ideas, articles about unusual artists. Approach should be how-to aiming toward adaptation in art classes or duplication by home hobbyists. Length: 3 to 5 typed, double-spaced pages. Pays 3-1/3¢/word. Short features used for arts and crafts. Mostly photo articles; some copy. No emphasis on educational syntax. Length for arts and crafts: 200 words. Payment for photos included in total editorial payment. Captions optional. B&w only.

GLASS (formerly *Glass Art Magazine*), 7830 S.W. 40th Ave., Portland OR 97219. For artists working in blown glass, stained glass, conceptual glass; collectors, museum curators, gallery and shop owners, art critics, high school and college students in the arts; general public. Monthly magazine; 52 pages. Estab: 1973. Circ: 3,500. Pays on publication. Buys all rights, but may reassign following publication. Simultaneous, photocopied and previously published submissions OK. SASE. Reports in 4 weeks. Sample copy 50¢.
Nonfiction: "We want articles of a general nature treating the arts and crafts in the U.S. and abroad; psychology of art; urban artist. We'll gladly look at anything dealing with the arts and crafts, especially contemporary glass in the U.S. We confine our main interest to contemporary

glass arts, and to subjects touching thereon, viz., the energy crisis. Art-oriented themes, reviews of shows including glass arts. Successful business operations (glass blowing or stained glass only). New product (glass oriented only). Pays 4¢ minimum per word; $125 maximum.
Photos: No additional payment made for 8x10 b&w glossies used with mss. Captions required.

METROPOLITAN MUSEUM OF ART BULLETIN, Metropolitan Museum of Art, Fifth Ave. and 82nd St., New York NY 10028. Editor: Joan K. Holt. Quarterly. Query first. "Writers contributing must write entirely on speculation. Most of our writers are scholars or have some reputation in the field, and we commission most of our freelance material." Enclose S.A.S.E.
Nonfiction: Each issue usually covers a single theme. Writers must be acknowledged experts in their fields. "Our museum experts scrutinize everything very carefully." Length: 750 words; 1,500 to 2,000 words. Pays $75 for short pieces, $150 for longer articles.

NEW YORK ARTS JOURNAL, Manhattan Arts Review, Inc., 560 Riverside Dr., New York NY 10027. (212)663-2245. Editors-in-Chief: Richard Burgin and Holland Cotter. Emphasizes the arts: visual arts, fiction, poetry, music, etc. Bimonthly tabloid; 44 pages. Estab: 1976. Circ: 15,000. Buys one-time rights. Phone queries OK. Simultaneous, photocopied and previously published submissions OK. SASE. Reports in 4 weeks. Sample copy $1.
Nonfiction: Historical, informational, interview, photo feature and profile. Buys 3-6 mss/issue. Send complete ms. Pays $3/page.
Photos: Purchased with or without accompany ms. Pays $10 for b&w photos. Send prints. "We publish full-page portfolios of photos which stand on their own, not necessarily as illustration."
Columns/Departments: Richard Kuczkowski, Book Review Editor, 15 Forest Glen Rd., Valley Cottage NY 10989. Book Review, Music Review and Art Review. Send complete ms. Pays $3/page.
Fiction: Adventure, confession, erotica, experimental, fantasy, historical, humor, mystery, romance, science fiction. Buys 2 mss/issue. Send complete ms. Pays $3/page.
Poetry: David Lehman, Poetry Editor. Avant-garde, free verse and traditional. Buys 6-8 poems/issue. Pays $15/poem.

THE ORIGINAL ART REPORT, Box 1641, Chicago IL 60690. (312)588-6897. Editor and Publisher: Frank Salantrie. Emphasizes "visual art conditions for visual artists, art museum presidents and trustees, collectors of fine art, art educators, and interested citizens." Monthly newsletter; 6-8 pages. Estab: 1967. Circ: 1,000. Pays on publication. Buys all rights. Phone queries OK. SASE. Reports in 2 weeks. Sample copy $1.
Nonfiction: Expose (art galleries, government agencies ripping off artists, or ignoring them), historical (perspective pieces relating to now), humor (whenever possible), informational (material that is unavailable in other art publications), inspirational (acts and ideas of courage), interview (with artists, other experts; serious material), personal opinion, technical (brief items to recall traditional methods of producing art), travel (places in the world where artists are welcome and honored) philosophical, economic, aesthetic, and artistic. Query or submit complete ms. Length: 1,000 words maximum. Pays 1¢/word.
Columns/Departments: WOW (Worth One Wow), Worth Repeating, and Worth Repeating Again. "Basically, these are reprint items with introduction to give context and source, including complete name and address of publication. Looking for insightful, succinct commentary." Submit complete ms. Length: 500 words. Pays ½¢/word. Open to suggestions for new columns/departments.

SOUTHWEST ART, Art Magazine Publishers, Box 13037, Houston TX 77019. (713)529-3533. Editor-in-Chief: Vicki Baucum. Emphasizes art: painting and sculpture. Monthly magazine; 112 pages. Estab: 1971. Circ: 17,500. Pays on 10th of month following publication. Buys all rights, but may reassign following publication. Photocopied submissions OK. SASE. Reports in 6 weeks. Sample copy $3.
Nonfiction: Informational, interview, personal opinion, and profile. "We publish articles about artists and art trends. We primarily concentrate on artists living west of the Mississippi and on art trends occurring within the same geographical region. The articles should be informative, but not biographical. They should be in-depth pieces about the artist's opinions as to why he does what he does, and how this has developed." Buys 72 mss/year. Query; also submit 10 8x10 b&w glossies, 4 8x10 color prints and a short biography of the artist. Length: 2,000 words minimum. Pays $100-150.

TODAY'S ART, 6 E. 43rd St., New York NY 10017. Editor: George A. Magnan. For "artists (professional and amateur), art teachers, and museums." Monthly. Circulation: 86,000. Buys first rights. Pays on publication. Query first. Enclose S.A.S.E.

Nonfiction and Photos: "Only items referring to art and how-to articles in all fields of art with b&w and some color illustrations. Articles should be easy to follow. Most articles we receive are not sufficiently detailed and a lot have to be rewritten to make them more informative." Length: 400 to 850 words. Pays $25 to $50.

How To Break In: "Every now and then, someone comes up with a good idea, even if no idea can be completely new, of course. But there are many technical and esthetic possibilities in art. Indeed, there's no limit to them. If a writer, young or old, is sure he has something like that, and knows how to present it in an easily comprehensible manner, we are glad to consider the article. But we don't want philosophizing about art, and we do not wish to promote unknown artists."

WESTART, Box 1396, Auburn CA 95603. (916)885-3242 or 0960. Editor-in-Chief: Jean L. Couzens. Emphasizes art for practicing artists and artist/craftsmen; students of art and art patrons. Semimonthly tabloid; 20 pages. Estab: 1962. Circ: 7,500. Pays on publication. Buys all rights, but may reassign following publication. Phone queries OK. Submit seasonal/holiday material 2 months in advance. Photocopied submissions OK. Sample copy 50¢; free writer's guidelines.
Nonfiction: Informational; photo feature; and profile. Buys 6-8 mss/year. Query or submit complete ms. Length:7-800 words. Pays 30¢/column inch.
Photos: Purchased with or without accompanying ms. Send b&w prints. Pays 30¢/column inch.

Association, Club, and Fraternal

The following publications exist to publicize—to members, friends, and institutions— the ideals, objectives, projects, and activities of the sponsoring club or organization. Club-financed magazines that carry material not directly related to the group's activities (for example, Manage *magazine in the Management and Supervision Trade Journals) are classified by their subject matter in the Consumer, Farm, and Trade Journals sections of this book.*

THE AMERICAN LEGION MAGAZINE, 1608 K St., N.W., Washington DC 20006. (202)393-4811. Monthly. Circulation: 2.6 million. Reports on most submissions promptly; borderline decisions take time. Buys first North American serial rights. Pays on acceptance. Include phone number with ms. Enclose S.A.S.E. for ms return.
Nonfiction: Most articles written on order. Some over transom. Writers may query for subject interest. Subjects include national and international affairs, American history, reader self-interest, great military campaigns and battles, major aspects of American life, vignettes of servicemen, veterans and their families, etc. Length: maximum of 20 double-spaced typewritten pages. Pay varies widely with length and worth of work. Research assignments for some skilled reporters. Proven pros only.
Photos: Chiefly on assignment. Some over-transom stories or photos click.
Poetry and Humor: Limited market for short, light verse, and short, humorous anecdotes, epigrams, jokes, etc. No serious verse. Taboos: old material; bad taste; amateurish work. Short humorous verse: $2.50 per line, minimum $10. Epigrams: $10. Anecdotes: $20.

AUTOMOTIVE BOOSTER OF CALIFORNIA, P.O. Box 765, LaCanada CA 91011. (213)790-6554. Editor: Don McAnally. For members of Automotive Booster clubs, automotive warehouse distributors and automotive parts jobbers in California. Established in 1967. Monthly. Circulation: 4,000. Not copyrighted. Pays on publication. Submit complete ms. Enclose S.A.S.E.
Nonfiction and Photos: Will look at short articles and pictures about successes of automotive parts outlets in California. Also can use personnel assignments for automotive parts people in California. Pays $1 per column inch (about 2¢ a word); $5 for b&w photos used with mss.

CALIFORNIA HIGHWAY PATROLMAN, California Association of Highway Patrolmen. 1225 8th St., Suite 150, Sacramento CA 95814. (916)442-0411. Editor-in-Chief: Richard York. Monthly magazine; 100 pages. Estab: 1937. Circ: 16,000. Pays on publication. Buys all rights, but may reassign following publication. SASE. Reports in 1 month. Free sample copy.
Nonfiction: Publishes articles on transportation safety and driver education. "Topics can include autos, boats, bicycles, motorcycles, snowmobiles, recreational vehicles and pedestrian safety. We are also in the market for travel pieces and articles on early California. We are *not* a

technical journal for teachers and traffic safety experts, but rather a general interest publication geared toward the layman. Please note that we are not a law enforcement magazine." Submit complete ms. Pays 2½¢/word.

Photos: "Illustrated articles always receive preference." Pays $2.50/b&w.

CIRCLE, Canadian Red Cross Society/National Youth Programme, 95 Wellesley St. E., Toronto, Ontario, Canada M4Y 1H6. (416)923-6692. For elementary school teachers and children of Canada. Focuses on educational themes of health, safety, community service and relief aids organized by children. Bimonthly newsletter; 11 pages. Estab: 1973. Circ: 17,000. Pays on acceptance. Buys second serial (reprint) and first North American serial rights. Phone queries OK. Accepts material only from March-June. Simultaneous, photocopied and previously published submissions OK. SAE and International Reply Coupons. Reports in 1 month. Free sample copy and writer's guidelines.

Nonfiction: Must be educational and Canadian in content. Aimed at a child's level, but not too simplistic. Buys 2 mss/issue. Query. Length: 60-800 words. Pays $10-80.

Fiction: Educational and ethical fiction. Buys 1-2 mss/issue. Send complete ms. Length: 60-800 words. Pays $5-80.

Fillers: Jokes, gags, anecdotes, participation games/experiments and puzzles. Buys 1-2 fillers/issue. Pays $5-30.

EASY LIVING MAGAZINE, The Webb Company, 1999 Shepard Rd., St. Paul MN 55116. (612)647-7304. Executive Editor: Don Picard. Editor: Jerry Bassett. Emphasizes international travel, profiles, lifestyles, family activities, and consumer and food articles; for an audience between 35 and 65; fairly high income. Distributed by Savers Travel Club, Ltd. Quarterly magazine; 36 pages. Estab: 1974. Circ: 300,000. Pays on acceptance. Buys all rights, but will reassign following publication. Submit seasonal/holiday material 6 months-1 year in advance. Photocopied submissions OK. SASE. Reports on queries in 3 weeks; on mss in 6 weeks. Free sample copy and writer's guidelines.

Nonfiction: Informational (about popular activities, new trends), profile (of known or unknown), and travel (international, Europe, Caribbean, Mexico, Far East, and Hawaii only). Query. Length: 1,000-2,500 words. Pays $150-400.

Photos: Photos purchased with or without accompanying ms (but only to illustrate ms already purchased). Captions required. Pays $35 for 8x10 b&w glossies; $75 minimum for 35mm color photos; $250 for color cover photos. Total purchase price for a ms includes payment for photos. Model release "preferred, but in some circumstances may be dispensed with."

THE ELKS MAGAZINE, 425 W. Diversey, Chicago IL 60614. Editor-in-Chief: Jeffrey Ball. Emphasizes general interest with family appeal. Monthly magazine; 56 pages. Estab: 1922. Circ: 1,600,000. Pays on acceptance. Buys first North American serial rights. Submit seasonal/holiday material 4-6 months in advance. Previously published submissions OK. SASE. Reports in 3 weeks. Free sample copy and writer's guidelines.

Nonfiction: Expose; historical (no textbook stuff); informational; and new product (like ESP breakthroughs). Buys 3-4 mss/issue. Query. Length: 2,000-3,500. Pays $250-350.

Photos: Purchased with or without accompanying manuscript (for cover). Captions required. Query with photos or send transparencies. Uses 8x10 or 5x7 b&w glossies and 35mm or 2x2 color transparencies (for cover). Pays $250 minimum for color (cover). Total purchase price for ms includes payment for photos.

Fiction: Adventure, fantasy, historical, humorous, mainstream, mystery, science fiction, suspense and western. Buys 6 mss/year. Submit complete ms. Length: 1,500-2,500 words. Pays $150 minimum.

How To Break In: "In the past, TEM has used very little fiction. A freelancer desiring to break in would do best to think in terms of nonfiction. Since we continue to offer sample copies and guidelines for the asking there is no excuse for being unfamiliar with TEM. A submission, following a go ahead would do best to include several b&w prints, if the piece lends itself to illustration, and a short cover letter. It's not wise to try to sneak through by implying the submission is in answer to a go ahead (i.e., Here's the piece you asked to see). If we didn't ask to see it, we'll know. Short humor (1,500-2,000) has been a best bet in fiction. While TEM has not been a big fiction market, we hope to include more. Family appeal is the watchword. No query is necessary for fiction."

For '78: "The big item on the editorial schedule is our January business issue. Also, around July of each year we start looking for a suitable Christmas piece for the December issue."

FUTURE MAGAZINE, P.O. Box 7, Tulsa OK 74102. Official publication of the United States Jaycees. Editor: Jim Brasher. For 18- to 36-year-old young men. Well-educated, affluent, with varied interests. Magazine published bimonthly; 32 pages. Estab: 1938. Circ: 353,000. Acquires all rights, but will reassign rights to author after publication. Payment in contributor's copies. Free sample copy. Query first. Enclose S.A.S.E.

Nonfiction: "General editorial features that follow Jaycees programming. Success stories of nationally known (usually former or current) Jaycees, articles concerning Jaycee chapter projects or accomplishments.

KANSAS MOTORIST, 4020 W. 6th, Topeka KS 66606. Editor: Ronald M. Welch. For Kansas members of the American Automobile Association. Magazine; 16 pages. Estab: 1952. Bimonthly. Circ: 50,000. Buys second serial (reprint) rights. Pays on acceptance. Will send free sample copy to writer on request. Will consider photocopied and simultaneous submissions. Reports in 3 weeks. Query first or submit complete ms. Enclose S.A.S.E.

Nonfiction and Photos: Informative and entertaining articles of interest to the Kansas motoring public. Primarily interested in features with regional travel, especially Kansas. Length: 1,500 words maximum. Pays 2¢ a word. High quality 8x10 or 5x7 b&w glossies purchased with mss. Captions required. Pays $2.50 to $10. The higher rate of payment is for cover shots of Kansas subjects.

THE KEY MAGAZINE, 144 W. 12th Ave., Denver CO 80204. (303)222-7734. Publication of the Inter-Community Action Association. Editor: Lou Thomas. For the general public interested in news analysis as well as news reporting. Published 6 times a year. Circulation: 12,000. Buys all rights. Buys about 50 mss a year. Payment on publication. Will send sample copy to writer for 75¢. Mss must be double-spaced, with 55-character line. Reports in 3 to 4 weeks. Enclose S.A.S.E.

Nonfiction and Photos: "News summary materials of events or activities happening (or that have happened) that have national relevance though of local origin. Analysis must be included. Reports on government, culture(s), crime, law, economy, etc. All materials must provide more than one point of view. Seek freelance book, movie, and concert reviews." Buys interviews, profiles, spot news, historical and essay pieces, and photo features. Length: 2,000 to 4,000 words. Pays 1¢ to 3 ¢ a word. B&w glossies and color transparencies purchased with mss. Pays $5 to $20.

Fillers: Newsbreaks, letters to the editor. Analysis preferably included. Length: 500 to 1,500 words. Pays $5 minimum.

How To Break In: "New writers can best 'break into' our publication by providing fresh approaches to subjects not normally covered by the established news periodicals. Prefer the perspectives of cultural and ethnic groups not represented in the larger publications. Material is selected depending on how well the viewpoint (extremist or conformist) is clearly stated and the position taken is defended."

THE KIWANIS MAGAZINE, 101 E. Erie St., Chicago IL 60611. Executive Editor: David B. Williams. For business and professional men. Published 10 times a year. Buys first North American serial rights. Pays on acceptance. Will send free sample copy on request. Query first. Reports on submission in 4 weeks. SASE.

Nonfiction and Photos: Articles about social and civic betterment, business, education, religion, domestic affairs, etc. Emphasis on objectivity, intelligent analysis and thorough research of contemporary problems. Concise writing, absence of cliches, and impartial presentation of controversy required. Length: 1,500 words to 3,000 words. Pays $300 to $600. "No fiction, personal essays, fillers, or verse of any kind. A light or humorous approach welcomed where subject is appropriate and all other requirements are observed. Detailed queries can save work and submission time. We sometimes accept photos submitted with mss, but we do not pay extra for them; they are considered part of the price of the ms. Our rate for a ms with good photos is higher than for one without."

How To Break In: "We have a new staff and we're trying to do new things. I'm dying to hear from pros with fresh ideas and the rare ability to say a lot in a few words."

LEADER, The Order of United Commercial Travelers of America, 632 N. Park St., Columbus OH 43215. (614)228-3276. Editor-in-Chief: James R. Eggert. Emphasizes fraternalism for its officers and active membership. Magazine; 8 times a year; 32 pages. Estab: 1976. Circ: 25,000. Pays on publication. Rights purchased vary with author and material; usually buys first North American serial rights. Submit seasonal/holiday material 4 months in advance. Photocopied submissions and previously published work OK. SASE. Reports in 2 weeks. Free sample copy and writer's guidelines.

Nonfiction: Exposes and informational articles in the areas of special education, safety and cancer research, historical articles, interviews concerning fraternalism, retardation, safety,

cancer, youth, nostalgia, personal experience, personal opinion, photo features and profiles.
Buys 18 mss/year. Query. Length: 500-2,000 words. Pays 1½¢/word minimum.
Photos: Additional payment for 5x7 b&w glossies or color transparencies or 5x7 prints. Model
release required.
Rejects: "Material that does not relate to our fraternal organization and its specific civic
projects."

THE LION, 300 22nd St., Oak Brook IL 60521. (312)986-1700. Editor-in-Chief: W.L. Wilson.
Senior Editor: Robert Kleinfelder. Emphasizes service club organization for Lions club
members and their families. Monthly magazine; 48 pages. Estab: 1918. Circ: 670,000. Pays on
acceptance. Buys all rights. Phone queries OK. Submit seasonal/holiday material 4 months in
advance. Photocopied submissions OK. SASE. Reports in 2 weeks. Free sample copy and
writer's guideline.
Nonfiction: Humor; informational (stories of interest to civic-minded men); and photo feature
(must be of a Lions club service project). Buys 4 mss/ issue. Query. Length: 500-2,200. Pays
$50-400.
Photos: Purchased with or without accompanying ms or on assignment. Captions required.
Query first for photos. B&w glossies at least 5x7. Total purchase price for ms includes payment
for photos.

THE LOOKOUT, Seaman's Church Institute, 15 State St., New York NY 10004. (212)269-
2710. Editor: Carlyle Windley. "Basic purpose is to engender and sustain interest in the work of
the Institute and to encourage monetary gifts in support of its philanthropic work among
seamen." Monthly, except combined February-March and July-August issues. Magazine; 20
pages, (6x9). Established in 1909. Buys first North American serial rights. Payment on
publication. Will send sample copy to writer on request. Query first. Reports in 1 month.
Enclose S.A.S.E.
Nonfiction: Emphasis is on the merchant marine; not Navy, pleasure yachting, power boats,
commercial or pleasure fishing, passenger vessels. Buys freelance marine-oriented articles on
the old and new, oddities, adventure, factual accounts, unexplained phenomena. Length: 200 to
1,000 words. Pays $40 maximum, depending on quality, length, etc.
Photos: Buys vertical format b&w (no color) cover photo on sea-related subjects. Pays $20;
lesser amounts for miscellaneous photos used elsewhere in the magazine.
Poetry: Buys small amount of short verse; seafaring-related but not about the sea per se and the
cliches about spume, spray, sparkle, etc. Pays $5.

MR. LONGEARS MAGAZINE, The Noteworthy Company, 100 Church St., Amsterdam, NY
12010. (518)842-2660. Editor-in-Chief: Thomas B. Constantino. Official publication of the
American Donkey and Mule Society. "For people that own donkeys or are interested in
equines and history and role of animals." Quarterly magazine; 48 pages. Estab: 1971. Circ:
1,500. Pays on acceptance. Buys all rights, but may reassign following publication. Submit
seasonal/holiday material 3 months in advance. Simultaneous, photocopied, and previously
published submissions OK. SASE. Reports in 1 month. Free sample copy.
Nonfiction: Informational, historical, humor, personal experience, photo feature, and travel.
Buys 2 mss/issue. Query. Pays $25.
Photos: Photos purchased with or without accompanying ms or on assignment. Send prints.
Total purchase price for ms includes payment for photos.

NATIONAL 4-H NEWS, 150 N. Wacker Dr., Chicago IL 60606. (312)782-5021, Ext. 44.
Editor: Bonnie B. Sarkett. For "young to middle-aged adults and older teens (mostly women)
who lead 4-H clubs; most with high school, many with college education, whose primary reason
for reading us is their interest in working with kids in informal youth education projects,
ranging from aerospace to swimming, and almost anything in between." Monthly. Circulation:
90,000. Buys first serial or one-time rights. Buys about 48 mss a year. Pays on acceptance. Will
send a sample copy to a writer on request. Write for copy of guidelines for writers. Query first.
"We are very specialized, and unless a writer has been published in our magazine before, he
more than likely doesn't have a clue to what we can use. When query comes about a specific
topic, we often can suggest angles that make it usable." Submit seasonal material 6 months to 1
year in advance. Reports in 3 weeks. Enclose S.A.S.E. with manuscript. Postage for responses
to queries paid by the magazine.
Nonfiction: "Education and child psychology from authorities, written in light, easy-to-read
fashion with specific suggestions how layman can apply them in volunteer work with youth;
how-to-do-it pieces about genuinely new and interesting crafts of any kind. "This is our

primary need now but articles must be fresh in style and ideas, and tell how to make something worthwhile ... almost anything that tells about kids having fun and learning outside the classroom, including how they became interested, most effective programs, etc., always with enough detail and examples, so reader can repeat project or program with his or her group, merely by reading article. Speak directly to our reader (you) without preaching. Tell him in a conversational text how he might work better with kids to help them have fun and learn at the same time. Use lots of genuine examples (although names and dates not important) to illustrate points. Use contractions when applicable. Write in a concise, interesting way—our readers have other jobs and not a lot of time to spend with us. Will not print stories on 'How this 4-H club made good' or about state or county fair winners. Reasons for rejection of freelance submissions include: failure of the writer to query first; failure of the writer to study back issues; and mss submitted on subjects we've just covered in depth." Length: 1,700 to 3,400 words. Payment up to $100, depending on quality and accompanying photos or illustrations."
Photos: "Photos must be genuinely candid, of excellent technical quality and preferably shot 'available light' or in that style; must show young people or adults and young people having fun learning something. How-to photos or drawings must supplement instructional texts. Photos do not necessarily have to include people. Photos are usually purchased with accompanying ms, with no additional payment. Captions required. If we use an excellent single photo, we generally pay $25 and up."

PERSPECTIVE, Pioneer Girls, Inc., Box 788, Wheaton IL 60187. (312)293-1600. Editor-in-Chief: Alyce Van Til. "All subscribers are volunteer leaders of clubs, anywhere from 1-12 grade. Clubs are sponsored by evangelical, conservative churches throughout North America." Quarterly magazine; 32 pages. Estab: 1964. Circ: 20,000. Pays on acceptance. Buys first North American serial rights. Submit seasonal/holiday material 9 months in advance. Simultaneous submissions OK. SASE. Reports in 3 weeks. Sample copy $1; writer's guidelines for SASE.
Nonfiction: Julie Smith, Articles Editor. How-to (projects for girls' clubs, crafts, cooking service), informational (relationships, human development, mission education, outdoor activities), inspirational (Bible studies, women leading girls), interview (Christian education leaders), personal experience (women working with girls). Buys 12-24 mss/year. Query. Length: 200-1,500 words. Pays $5-40.
Columns/Departments: Julie Smith, Column/Department Editor. Storehouse (craft, game, activity, outdoor activity suggestions — all related to girls' club projects for any age between grades 1-12). Buys 8-10 mss/year. Submit complete ms. Length: 150-250 words. Pays $5.
Fiction: Julie Smith, Fiction Editor. Humorous (women leading girls' clubs), religious (Christian education — message inherent, not tacked on). Buys 1-2 mss/year. Query. Length: 1,000-2,000 words. Pays $20-40.
How To Break In: "Submit articles directly related to club work, practical in nature, i.e., ideas for leader training in communication, Bible knowledge, teaching skills. They must have practical application. We want substance—not ephemeral ideas."

PLANNING, 1313 E. 60th St., Chicago IL 60637. (312)947-2103. Editor: Robert Cassidy. Publication of the American Society of Planning Officials. For urban planners, public officials, and citizens active in community groups. Magazine; 40 (8x11) pages. Established in 1972. 11 times a year. Circulation: 15,000. Buys first serial rights. Buys about 50 mss a year. Payment on publication. Free sample copy and writer's guidelines. Photocopied submissions OK. Reports in 1 month. Query first. Enclose S.A.S.E.
Nonfiction and Photos: Articles of high quality on architecture, environment, energy, housing, health care, planning, historic preservation, land use, transportation, urban renewal, neighborhood conservation and zoning. "Articles should be written in magazine feature style. Topics should be current and stress issues, not personalities, though quotes should be used. We are national and international in perspective and are interested in stories from all parts of the country and the world." Length: 100 to 1,200 words for news; 1,200 to 3,000 for features; 300 to 800 words for book reviews. Pays $25 for book reviews; $50 for news articles, and $125 for features. B&w (8x11) glossies purchased on assignment. Pays $5 minimum.

PORTS O' CALL, P.O. Box 530, Santa Rosa CA 95402. (707)542-0898. Editor: William A. Breniman. Newsbook of the Society of Wireless Pioneers. Society members are mostly early-day wireless "brass-pounders" who sent code signals from ships or manned shore stations handling wireless or radio traffic. Twice yearly. Not copyrighted. Payment on acceptance. Query suggested. Editorial deadlines are May 15 and October 15. Reports on submissions at once. Enclose S.A.S.E.
Nonfiction: Articles about early-day wireless as used in ship-shore and high power operation.

Early-day ships, records, etc. "Writers should remember that our members have gone to sea for years and would be critical of material that is not authentic. We are not interested in any aspect of ham radio. We are interested in authentic articles dealing with ships (since about 1910)." Oddities about the sea and weather as it affects shipping. Length: 500 to 2,000 words. Pays 1¢ per word.

Photos: Department Editor: Dexter S. Bartlett. Purchased with mss. Unusual shots of sea or ships. Wireless pioneers. Prefers b&w, "4x5 would be the most preferable size but it really doesn't make too much difference as long as the photos are sharp and the subject interests us." Fine if veloxed, but not necessary. Payment ranges from $2.50 to $10 "according to our appraisal of our interest." Ship photos of various nations, including postcard size, if clear, 25¢ to $1 each.

Poetry: Ships, marine slant (not military), shipping, weather, wireless. No restrictions. Pays $1 or $2.50 each.

THE ROTARIAN, 1600 Ridge Ave., Evanston IL 60201. (312)328-0100. Editor: Willmon L. White. For Rotarian business and professional men and their families; for schools, libraries, hospitals, etc. Monthly. Circulation: 466,000. Usually buys all rights. Payment on acceptance. Will send free sample copy and editorial fact sheet to writer on request. Query preferred. Reports in 2 to 4 weeks. Enclose S.A.S.E. with queries and submissions.

Nonfiction: "The field for freelance articles is in the general interest category. These run the gamut from inspirational guidelines for daily living to such weighty concerns as world hunger, peace, and control of environment. Articles should appeal to an international audience and should in some way help Rotarians help other people. An article may increase a reader's understanding of world affairs, thereby making him a better world citizen. It may educate him in civic matters, thus helping him improve his town. It may help him to become a better employer, or a better human being. We carry debates and symposiums, but we are careful to show more than one point of view. We present arguments for effective politics and business ethics, but avoid expose and muckraking. Controversy is welcome if it gets our readers to think but does not offend ethnic or religious groups. In short, the rationale of the organization is one of hope and encouragement and belief in the power of individuals talking together." Length: 2,000 words maximum. Payment varies.

Photos: Purchased with mss or with captions only. Prefers 2¼ square or larger color transparencies, but will consider 35mm also. B&w singles and small assortments. Vertical shots preferred to horizontal. Scenes of international interest. Color cover.

Poetry and Fillers: "Presently overstocked." Pays $2 a line. Pays $10 for brief poems. "We occasionally buy short humor pieces."

How To Break In: "We prefer established writers, but a beginner who has a crisp style, is accurate, and can write with some authority on a subject of international interest has a chance of publication in *The Rotarian*."

THE SPIRIT, 601 Market St., St. Genevieve MO 63670. Newsletter of Lindbergh Association. Editor: Bob Hammack. For collectors of Charles A. Lindbergh memorabilia, conservationists, and aviators (many "pioneer"); admirers of Lindbergh with high school to post-graduate backgrounds; ages from 15 to 75. Magazine; 24 (8½x11) pages. Established in 1975. Every 2 months. Circulation: 1,000. Buys all rights, but may reassign rights to author after publication. Buys all material from freelancers. "Writers are eligible for Reader Survey Awards for, 'Best Collector Interest Article,' and/or, 'Best Historical Article.'" Pays on acceptance. Will send sample copy to writer on request. Will send editorial guidelines on request. Will consider photocopied and simultaneous submissions. Reports on material accepted for publication in 1 month. Returns rejected material within 2 weeks. Submit complete mss. Enclose S.A.S.E.

Nonfiction and Photos: This publication is the first to concern itself with Lindbergh memorabilia, history, research, etc., and seeks anything connected with the "Lone Eagle." "We are especially interested in material dealing with his contributions to archaeology, and his scientific and medical research. If submitting collector material, give sources of supply; if historical, give addresses of museums, displays, individual authors, etc." Anniversaries of "first flights," genealogical material and new memorials or tributes are desired. Also, personal experience, nostalgia, personal opinion, spot and photo news, and book reviews are needed. Length: 250 to 1,000 words. Pays $3 to $10 per ms. When photos are purchased with ms, they should be the same as the nonfiction article, but photos *are* purchased without accompanying ms with captions required. Pays approximately $5. No color shots. Numismatic, philatelic, and bibliographic items are needed for regular columns; pays $5 per contribution. Length: 500 words.

Poetry: "Would like to see good narrative work regarding the 1927 Trans-Atlantic Flight." Will consider some traditional poetic forms, and blank and free verse. Payment varies.

Fillers: Will use newsbreaks and clippings. Length: 50 to 100 words. Pays $1 per item.
How To Break In: "Do something on Lindbergh's 'advisory role' in either commercial or military aviation. All submitted information must show detailed research."

STEERING WHEEL, P.O. Box 1669, Austin TX 78767. (512)478-2541. Editor: Kellyn R. Murray. Published by the Texas Motor Transportation Association for transportation management, high school libraries, state agencies, doctors, legislators, mayors, county judges, newspapers. Monthly magazine; 28 pages, (7x10). Established in 1936. Circulation: 7,200. Not copyrighted. Buys about 10 mss a year. Payment on publication. Will send free sample copy to writer on request. Write for copy of editorial guidelines for writers. Submit seasonal holiday material 3 months in advance. Will consider photocopied and simultaneous submissions. Query first. Reports immediately. Enclose S.A.S.E.
Nonfiction and Photos: "Material related to motor transportation in Texas, and other subjects as they relate; highway safety, energy, etc." Buys interviews, profiles, historical, travel, spot news, and coverage of successful business operations. Length: 1,000 to 2,500 words. Pays $15 to $50. Photos purchased with ms. Captions required.

THE TOASTMASTER, 2200 N. Grand Ave., Box 10400, Santa Ana CA 92711. (714)542-6793. Editor-in-Chief: Michael J. Snapp. Emphasizes communication and leadership techniques; self-improvement. For members of Toastmasters International, Inc. Monthly magazine; 32 pages. Estab: 1932. Circ: 60,000. Pays on acceptance. Buys all rights, but may reassign following publication. Photocopied submissions and previously published work OK. SASE. Reports in 2 weeks. Free sample copy and writer's guidelines.
Nonfiction: How-to (improve speaking, listening, thinking skills; on leadership or management techniques, meeting planning, etc., with realistic examples), humor (on leadership communications or management techniques), interviews (with communications or management experts that members can directly apply to their self-improvement efforts; should contain "how to" information). Buys 15-20 mss/year. Query. Length: 1,500-3,000 words. Pays $25-150.
Photos: Purchased with or without ms. Query. Pays $10-50 for 5x7 or 8x10 b&w glossies; $35-75 for color transparencies. No additional payment for those used with ms.
How To Break In: "By studying our magazine and sendin us (after a query) material that is related. Since we get a number of articles from our members on 'how to build a speech', freelancers should concentrate on more specific subjects such as body language, time management, etc. We're a non-profit organization, so if they're looking to get rich on one article, they can probably forget it. But we do provide a good place for the inexperienced freelancer to get published."

V.F.W. MAGAZINE, Broadway at 34th St., Kansas City MO 64111. (816)561-3420. Editor: James K. Anderson. For members of the Veterans of Foreign Wars, men who served overseas, and their families. They range in age from the 20's to veterans of World War I and Spanish-American War veterans. Interests range from sports to national politics. Monthly magazine; 48 pages (8½x11). Established in 1913. Circulation: 1,900,000. Buys all rights. Buys 40 mss a year. Payment on acceptance. Will send sample copy to writer for 50¢. Write for copy of editorial guidelines for writers. Seasonal material should be submitted 3 months in advance. Query first to "The Editor." Reports in 1 week. Enclose S.A.S.E.
Nonfiction and Photos: "Nonfiction articles on sports, personalities, and historical pieces. Special emphais within a subject, special outlook related to veterans. The Veterans of Foreign Wars organization is geared to the man who has served overseas, a distinction that other veterans organizations do not make." Buys informational, how-to, personal experience, interview, profile, historical, think articles, and travel articles. Length: 1,000 to 1,500 words. Pays 5¢ to 10¢ per word. B&w and color photos purchased with accompanying ms. Captions required. Pays $5 each.

Astrology and Psychic Publications

The following publications regard astrology, psychic phenomena, ESP experiences, and related subjects as sciences or as objects of serious scientific research. Semireligious, occult, mysticism, and supernatural publications are classified in the Alternative category.

AMERICAN ASTROLOGY, 2505 N. Alvernon Way, Tucson AZ 85712. (602)327-3476. Editor: Joanne S. Clancy. For all ages, all walks of life. Magazine; 116 (9x6) pages. Established in 1933. Monthly. Circulation: 265,000. Buys all rights. Buys 50 to 75 mss a year. Pays on publication. Write for copy of guidelines for writers. No photocopied or simultaneous submissions. Reports in 4 weeks. Submit complete ms. Enclose S.A.S.E.

Nonfiction: Astrological material, often combined with astronomy. More interested in presenting results of research material and data based on time of birth, instead of special Sun sign readings. Source of birth data must be included. Length: 3,500 words. "Payment is made according to the astrological knowledge and expertise of the writer."

ASTROLOGY GUIDE, Sterling's Magazines, Inc., 355 Lexington Ave., New York NY 10017. (212)391-1400, Ext. 21. Editor: Marsha Kaplan. For a special interest audience involved in astrology, parapsychology and the occult on all levels, from the merely curious to the serious student and practitioner. Bimonthly magazine; 96 (6½x9½) pages. Established in 1937. Circulation: 55,000. Buys all rights. Buys 30 mss/year. Pays on acceptance. Will not consider photocopied or simultaneous submissions. Submit seasonal (Christmas, vacation-time, etc.) and special (major astrological events) material 5-6 months in advance. Reports in 8-12 weeks minimum. Query first or submit complete ms. Enclose S.A.S.E.

Nonfiction: "Mostly astrological articles: Sun-sign, mundane, speculative or research. Slightly more technical for advanced readers, but prefer intelligent popular approach. Emphasis is on use of astrology and the related psychic and occult arts for self betterment in the reader's life. Very interested in buying articles on timely themes in these fields. We are more interested in featuring new ideas and new writers than in repeating what has been done in the past. We are attempting to develop a more personal, intimate approach." Would also like to see astrological "portraits" or interviews with current celebrities. Does not want to see articles based only on the writer's knowledge of Sun signs. "They are superficial and boring. Even Sun-sign articles on the traditional themes (health, money, love) should refer (at least in preparation) to other aspects of the birth chart, and should be written by a practicing astrologer, or serious student. Length: 2,000 to 3,000 words, but will accept shorter articles. Also uses book reviews and will consider new ideas for new departments. Pays 3¢ a word minimum.

Fillers: Short humor and material on strological experiences and insights are used as fillers. Length: 750 words maximum. Pays 3¢ per word.

ASTROLOGY '78, ASI Publications, Inc., 127 Madison Ave., New York NY 10016. Editor-in-Chief: Henry Weingarten. Emphasizes astrology. Quarterly magazine; 64 pages. Estab: 1969. Circ: 2,500. Pays on publication. Buys all rights but may reassign to author following publication. Submit holiday and seasonal material 3-4 months in advance. Simultaneous and photocopied submissions OK. SASE. Reports in 1 month. Sample copy for $1.

Articles: How-to, informational, historical, humor, interview, technical. Buys 4 mss an issue. Submit complete ms. Length: Variable; can be serialized. Pays $2/page.

Fillers: Jokes, gags, anecodtes. Must be on astrology. Buys 5 a year. Length: Varies. Pays $2/page.

Rejects: Sun sign articles.

ASTROLOGY—YOUR DAILY HOROSCOPE, 383 Madison Ave., New York NY 10017. Monthly. Buys all rights. Pays on acceptance. Enclose S.A.S.E.

Nonfiction: Articles on astrology, either popularized or moderately technical. Anxious to attract new writers and can promise a steady market plus a great deal of help from the editor. Knowledge of astrology is necessary. Length: 1,500 to 3,500 words. Pays 2¢ a word, or by arrangement.

BEYOND REALITY MAGAZINE, 303 W. 42nd St., New York NY 10036. (212)265-1676. Editor: Harry Belil. Primarily for university students interested in astronomy, archaeology, astrology, the occult (the whole range); UFO's, ESP, spiritualism, parapsychology, exploring the unknown. Magazine published every 2 months; 64 (8½x11) pages. Established in 1971. Circulation: 50,000. Buys all rights. Buys 30 to 35 mss a year. Payment on publication. Will send sample copy to writer for $1. Write for copy of guidelines for writers; enclose S.A.S.E. with request. Will consider photocopied submissions. Will not consider simultaneous submissions. Will consider cassette submissions. Query first or submit complete ms. Enclose S.A.S.E.

Nonfiction and Photos: Interested in articles covering the range of their readers' interests, as well as any new discoveries in parapsychology. How-to, interview, inspirational, historical, think pieces, spot news. Length: 1,000 to 2,000 words. Pays 3¢ per word maximum, or whatever the editor feels such a feature warrants. No additional payment for b&w photos used with mss.

Fillers: "We pay $1 for clippings used."

How To Break In: "Show me some pieces you've written and if I like your style, I'll provide you with the subjects to write on. Also looking for current ideas from the campuses, so student writers should give us a try." Lack of research documentation, or re-hashing old material will bring a rejection here.

BREAKTHROUGH! Institute of Psychic Science, Inc., 2015 S. Broadway, Little Rock AR 72206. (501)372-4278. Editor-in-Chief: Korra L. Deaver. Emphasizes personal psychic development. Bimonthly magazine; 20 pages. Estab: 1971. Circ: 1,000. Pays in copies on publication. Buys all rights, but may reassign following publication. Phone queries OK. Simultaneous, photocopied and previously published submissions OK. SASE. Reports in 2 months. Free sample copy and writer's guidelines.
Nonfiction: How-to (explaining how one acquires an understanding of, and personal use of, such psychic gifts as clairvoyance, precognition, astral projection, etc.); informational, personal experience, inspirational and think articles. Length: 5,000 words maximum.
Poetry: Any form; upbeat and inspirational. Buys 1/issue. Length: 4-41 lines. Pays in copies.

FATE, Clark Publishing Co., 500 Hyacinth Place, Highland Park IL 60035. Editor: Mary Margaret Fuller. Monthly. Buys all rights; occasionally North American serial rights only. Pays on publication. Query first. Reports on submissions in 4 to 8 weeks. Enclose S.A.S.E.
Nonfiction and Fillers: Personal psychic experiences, 300 to 500 words. Pays $10. New frontiers of science, and ancient civilizations, 2,000 to 3,000 words; also parapsychology, occultism, witchcraft, magic, spiritual healing miracles, flying saucers, etc. Must include complete authenticating details. Prefers interesting accounts of single events rather than roundups. Pays minimum of 3¢ per word. Fillers should be fully authenticated. Length: 100 to 300 words.
Photos: Buys good glossy photos with mss or with captions only. Pays $5 to $10.
How To Break In: "We very frequently accept manuscripts from new writers; the majority are individuals' first-person accounts of their own psychic experience. We do need to have all details, where, when, why, who and what, included for complete documentation."

HOROSCOPE, 1 Dag Hammarskjold Plaza, 245 E. 47th St., New York NY 10017. Editor: Julia A. Wagner. Monthly magazine; 130 pages. Established in 1939. Circulation: 300,000. Buys all rights. Buys 100 mss a year. Payment on acceptance. Free sample copy and writer's guidelines. All submissions must be accompanied by a carbon copy. Submit material dealing with major astrological sign changes at least 6 months in advance. Reports in 2 months. Query first or submit complete ms. Enclose S.A.S.E.
Nonfiction: Articles on astrology only. "Love, family, money, employment, and health are our most popular subjects. Must appeal to general readers with some knowledge of astrology. Articles dealing with prevailing conditions are always considered. We will not accept any articles relating to witchcraft." Informational, how-to, profile, inspirational. Length: 3,000 to 3,500 words. Pays 5¢ a word.
Fillers: On astrology only. Length: 25 to 150 words. Submissions must consist of a minimum of 10 fillers. Pays 5¢ a word.

HOROSCOPE GUIDE, 350 Madison Ave., Cresskill NJ 07626. (201)568-0500. Editor: Jim Hendvyx. For persons interested in astrology as it touches their daily lives; all ages. Established in 1967. Monthly. Circulation: 60,000. Buys all rights, but may reassign rights to author after publication "for non-competitive use. That is, for book publication, but never for magazine resale." Buys about 40 mss per year. Pays on acceptance. Will send sample copy to writer for $1. Will consider photocopied submissions. No simultaneous submissions. Submit seasonal material 5 months in advance. Submit complete ms. Enclose S.A.S.E.
Nonfiction, Poetry and Fillers: No textbook-type material. Wants anything of good interest to the average astrology buff, preferably not so technical as to require more than basic knowledge of birth sign by reader. Mss should be light, readable, entertaining and sometimes humorous. Not as detailed and technical as other astrology magazines, "with the astro-writer doing the interpreting without long-winded reference to his methods at every juncture. We are less reverent of astrological red tape." Does not want to see a teacher's type of approach to the subject. Wants mss about man-woman relationships, preferably in entertaining and humorous fashion. Length: 900 to 4,000 words. Pays 1½¢ to 2¢ per word. Buys traditional forms of poetry. Length: 4 to 16 lines. Pays $2 to $8. Also buys newsbreaks on astrology. Wants historical newsbreaks and quotes from notable persons favorable to astrology. Length: 25 to 500 words. Pays $2 to $7.50.
How To Break In: "Best way to break in with us is with some lively Sun-sign type piece involving some area of man-woman relationships — love, sex, marriage, divorce, differing views on money, religion, child-raising, in-laws, vacations, politics, life styles, or whatever."

MOON SIGN BOOK, P.O. Box 3383, St. Paul MN 55165. (612)291-1970. Editor: Carl Weschcke. For "persons from all walks of life with interests in the occult." Established in 1906. Annual. Circulation: 100,000. Rights purchased vary with author and material. Pays on publication. Query first or submit complete ms. Reports in 8 weeks. Enclose S.A.S.E.

Nonfiction and Photos: "Astrology (with emphasis on the moon) is the primary subject, but we can use material in any field of the occult, and living in intelligent cooperation with nature. We are a yearly publication dealing with farming, gardening, yearly forecasts for all types of activities, with informative articles on astrology. We try to be educational as well as practical." Length: 3,000 to 10,000 words. Pays 2¢ to 5¢ a word. Photos on assignment.

How To Break In: "The *Moon Sign Book* is a farming and gardening almanac emphasizing astronomical effects on planting, growing, harvesting and using crops to maximum advantage. Since 80% of the book is taken up with tables, we have room for only a few outside articles. Those articles should have something to do with either astrology or gardening (we are also interested in herbs, herbal remedies). Since most freelancers are not astrologers I would suggest that they concentrate on the many aspects of organic gardening or possibly how-to-do features that relate in some way to farming and gardening. Short articles on the occult phenomena (enhancing growth psychically), are also good possibilities for the beginning writer. We are continually looking for astrologers capable of writing 'Sun Sign' predictions for *Moon Sign Book*. Also astrological predictions for weather, stock and commodity markets, news and political developments, etc. We generally stick with one, but we find that quality depends on a variety, and would like to find a few more writers to back us up."

NEW REALITIES (formerly *Psychic*), 680 Beach St., Suite 408, San Francisco CA 94109. (415)776-2600. Editor-in-Chief and Publisher: James Bolen. Editor: Alan Vaughan. For general public interested in holistic approach to living and being—body, mind, and spirit—and straightforward, entertaining material on parapsychology, consciousness research, and the frontiers of human potential and the mind. Bimonthly. Buys all rights. Pays on acceptance. Will send sample copy to writer for $1.50. Reports in 4 to 6 weeks. Query first. Enclose S.A.S.E.

Nonfiction and Photos: "Documented articles on ESP research and the psychic, holistic dimensions of man. Balanced reporting, no editorializing. No personal experiences as such. Accept profiles of leaders in the field. Must have documented evidence about holistic leaders, healers, researchers. Short bibliography for further reading." Length: 3,000 to 4,000 words. Pays $100 to $150. Photos purchased only with ms.

How To Break In: "Read the magazine for approach and style. Keep in mind that you are writing for the magazine of new realities, 'the field's popular authority'."

THE PSYCHIC EYE, Heflin Printing Company, 236 10th St., Toledo OH 43624. Editor-in-Chief: Charlie R. Brown. Managing Editor: Colleen Sawyers. Emphasizes parapsychology for readership age 18 and up. Quarterly magazine; 26-30 pages. Estab: 1972. Circ: 5,000. Pays on publication. Buys all rights, but may reassign rights to author following publication. Submit seasonal/holiday material 3 months in advance. Simultaneous and previously published submissions OK. SASE. Reports in 6 weeks. Sample copy, $1.

Nonfiction: Personal experience (in psychic/occult fields clairvoyance, etc., healing, psychic development). Buys 12 mss/year. Submit complete ms.

Photos: Purchased with accompanying manuscript. Captions required. Submit b&w prints.

Columns, Departments: Buys 1-2 mss/issue. Submit complete ms. Length: 250-500 words. Pays 1¢-2¢ per word; may also pay in contributor's copies. Open to suggestions for new columns/departments; address to C.R. Brown.

Fillers: Newsbreaks (in psychic field).

For '78: Looking for material on magnetic healing, color and sound therapy and pyramid energy and other related subjects.

PSYCHIC WORLD, CBS Publications, Popular Magazine Group, a Division of Columbia Broadcasting System, Inc., 383 Madison Ave., New York NY 10017. (212)975-7407. Editor: Anne Keffer. General field of psychic phenomena. Bimonthly. Buys all rights. Pays on acceptance. Do not send for sample copy. Query first. Reports in 3 weeks. Enclose S.A.S.E.

Nonfiction: "Altered states of consciousness, psychic healing, telekinesis, hauntings, spiritualism, ESP, astral projection, etc. No fiction. Subject matter is based on documented evidence or substantiated by scientific research." Length: 2,500 to 3,500 words. Payment is $60 to $105.

QUEST, North American UFO Organization, Box 2485, Cedar Rapids IA 52406. Editor-in-Chief: Kevin D. Randle. Emphasizes unusual phenomena. Bimonthly magazine; 45-60 pages.

Estab: 1975. Circ: 100,000. Pays on acceptance. Buys all rights, but may reassign following publication. Phone queries OK. Simultaneous and photocopied submissions OK. SASE. Reports in 2 weeks. Free sample copy.

Nonfiction: "Exposes should show how good UFO cases have been 'edited' so the public gets only one side, either pro or con. We are interested in articles showing how information in the field differs from the public belief. All facts must be verified. Interviews, personal opinion, photo features." Length: 3,000-12,000 words. Pays $150-500.

YOUR PERSONAL ASTROLOGY, Sterling's Magazines, Inc., 355 Lexington Ave., New York NY 10017. (212)391-1400, Ext. 33. Editor: Marsha Kaplan. For a special interest audience involved in astrology, parapsychology and the occult on all levels, from the merely curious to the serious student and practitioner. Quarterly magazine; 96 pages. Estab: 1940. Circ: 60,000. Buys 35 mss/year. Payment on acceptance. Will not consider photocopied or simultaneous submissions. Submit seasonal (Christmas, vacation-time, etc.) and special (major astrological events) material 5-6 months in advance. Reports in 8-12 weeks minimum. Query first or submit complete ms. Enclose S.A.S.E.

Nonfiction: "Mostly astrological articles: Sun-sign, mundane, speculative or research. Slightly more technical for advanced readers, but prefer intelligent popular approach. Emphasis is on use of astrology and the related psychic and occult arts for self betterment in the reader's life. Very interested in buying articles on timely themes in these fields. We are more interested in featuring new ideas and new writers than in repeating what has been done in the past. We are attempting to develop a more personal, intimate approach." Would also like to see astrological "portraits" or interviews with current celebrities. Does not want to see articles based only on the writer's knowledge of Sun signs. "They are superficial and boring. Even Sun-sign articles on the traditional themes (health, money, love) should refer (at least in preparation) to other aspects of the birth chart, and should be written by a practicing astrologer or a serious student." Length: 2,000 to 3,500 words, but will accept shorter articles. Also uses book reviews and will consider new ideas for new departments. Pays 3¢ a word minimum.

Fillers: Short humor and material on astrological experiences and insights are used as fillers. Length: 750 words maximum. Pays 3¢ per word.

Automotive and Motorcycle

Publications listed in this section are concerned with the maintenance, operation, performance, racing, and judging of automobiles and motorcycles. Publications that treat vehicles as a means of transportation or shelter instead of as a hobby or sport are classified in the Travel, Camping, and Trailer category. Journals for teamsters, service station operators, and auto dealers will be found in the Auto and Truck classification of the Trade Journals section.

AMA NEWS, American Motorcyclist Association, Box 141, Westerville OH 43081. (614)891-2425. Managing Editor: Jeffery A. John. For "enthusiastic motorcyclists, investing considerable time and money in the sport." Monthly magazine; 48 pages. Estab: 1947. Circ: 116,000. Pays on publication. Rights purchased vary with author and material. Phone queries OK. Submit seasonal/holiday material 2 months in advance. SASE. Reports in 4 weeks. Free sample copy.

Nonfiction: How-to (different and/or unusual ways to use a motorcycle or have fun on one), historical (the heritage of motorcycling, particularly as it relates to the AMA), interviews (with interesting personalities in the world of motorcycling), photo feature (quality work on any aspect of motorcycling), technical (well-researched articles on safe riding techniques). Buys 10-20 mss/year. Query. Length: 500 words minimum. Pays $2/published column inch.

Photos: Bob Pluckebaum, Photo Editor. Purchased with or without accompanying ms, or on assignment. Captions required. Query. Pays $10 per photo published; $50 for cover.

How To Break In: "Unique feature approaches which lend themselves to attractive graphic presentation will receive more favorable consideration than mundane accounts of 'where we went on summer vacation' or 'who beat who in the first turn'. Give us a complete editorial and photo package; making it easy on us certainly won't hurt."

AUTOMOBILE QUARTERLY, 221 Nassau St., Princeton NJ 08540. (609)924-7555. Editor-in-Chief: Beverly Rae Kimes. Senior Editor: Stan Grayson. Emphasizes automobiles and automobile history. Quarterly hardbound magazine; 112 pages. Estab: 1962. Circ: 40,000. Pays on acceptance. Buys all rights. SASE. Reports in 2 weeks. Sample copy $7.95.

Nonfiction: Articles relating to the automobile and automobile history. Historical, humor,

interview and nostalgia. Buys 5 mss/issue. Query. Length: 2,000-10,000 words. Pays $200-400.
Photos: Purchased on assignment. Captions required. Query. Uses 8x10 b&w glossies and 4x5 color transparencies. "Payment varies with assignment and is negotiated prior to assignment."

AUTOWEEK, Real Resources Group, Inc., Box A, Reno NV 89506. Editor-in-Chief: Cory Farley. Managing Editor: Charles L. Cannon. Emphasizes automobile racing and the auto industry, domestic and international. Weekly tabloid; 32 pages. Estab: 1965. Circ: 95,000. Pays on publication. Buys all rights, or simultaneous rights, or by agreement with author. Simultaneous and previously published submissions OK. SASE. Reports in 2-4 weeks. Free sample copy.
Nonfiction: Informational (group-based vs. assembly line system; does Volvo/Kalmar plant really work?, etc.); historical (the first Indy race, first successful Ferrari, first European assembly line, etc.); nostalgia ("we'd have room for 2-3/month if we had them on tap." Technical articles on radical design changes. News reports on auto racing. Length: 2,000 words maximum. Query. Pays $1.20/column inch.
Photos: Purchased with or without mss, or on assignment. Pays $5 minimum for b&w glossies (5½x9 minimum); $15 minimum for color slides.
Fillers: Clippings ("rewrite clips and enclose"); newsbreaks. Buys 3/issue. Send fillers in. Length: 50-500 words. Pays $1.20/column inch.
How To Break In: "Any literate auto racing enthusiast can offer articles to *Autoweek*. If the beginner is at a local race and he sees no *AW* reporter around, he might try covering the event himself. If he's going to a big race, he should query first since we undoubtedly already have it covered. A number of stringers got started just that way. Industry stories may range from General Motors to consumerists. In either case, remember we're not the auto section in a family paper."

BIKER, Cycle News, Inc., 2201 Cherry Ave., Long Beach CA 90801. (213)595-4753. Editor-in-Chief: Charles Clayton. Emphasizes road motorcycle recreation, transportation and touring. For outdoorsmen (18-50); average education. Semimonthly tabloid; 24 pages. Estab: 1975. Circ: 6,000. Pays 15th of month following publication. Buys one-time rights and rights to reprint in any other CN publication. Submit seasonal/holiday material 3 weeks in advance. Photocopied submissions OK. SASE. Reports in 6 weeks. Sample copy 60¢.
Nonfiction: Expose (government, industry); how-to (nuts and bolts, plus pix and diagrams); informational; interviews (with remarkable bikers of all ilk, except racers and off-road riders); travel (specific travel and touring experiences); photo features (custom bikes, parties — no races); technical (any type, but road only); political action by bikers, oddball news bits, trivia. Buys 5-15 mss/issue. Submit complete ms. Length: 2,500 words maximum. Pays 50¢-$1/ column inch.
Photos: Clear, sharp 5x7 or 8x10 b&w glossies purchased with or without mss. Captions required. Pays $2-5.
Columns/Departments: Runs Around the Nation. Road rides, meets, organized road recreation reports. "This is dated material and should not be more than 1 week old." Submit complete ms. Length: 100-500 words. Pays 50 cents/column inch.
How To Break In: "First, be interested in what modern day bikers are into. Become a correspondent by covering local motorcycle road runs, rallies, etc. Use sense of humor, even on serious subjects."
Rejects: Anything about death or dismemberment.

BMW JOURNAL, A. Christ Zeitschriftenverlag GmbH, Pettenkoferstrasse 22, 8000 Munich 2, W. Germany. (089)53.59.11. Editor-in-Chief: Udo Wust. An automobile customer magazine for owners and enthusiasts of BMW automobiles; upper income audience; generally, people with active life styles and an eye for the unusual. Bimonthly magazine; 52 pages. Estab: 1962. Circ: 50,000. Pays on publication. Buys all rights, but may reassign following publication. Phone queries OK. SASE. Reports in 4 weeks. Free writer's guidelines.
Nonfiction: Historical (having to do with places or with history of automobiles if related to BMW); informational; nostalgia, photo features; profiles (of interesting BMW owners); travel (by automobile, BMW in photos). Buys 3-5/issue. Query. Length: 500-1,500 words. Pays $75-150.
Photos: Used with or without ms, or on assignment. Captions required. Query. No additional payment for 5x7 b&w glossies or 35mm minimum (larger preferred) color transparencies. Model release required. Need not relate to publication's subject matter; can encompass a broad range of life style themes.
Fiction: Adventure, experimental, historical mystery, science fiction, suspense. Buys 1/issue. Query. Length: 500-1,500 words. Pays $75-150.

How To Break In: "Author must know the magazine, available at local BMW dealers. Articles must be submitted with excellent photos, captioned."

CAR AND DRIVER, One Park Ave., New York NY 10016. (212)725-3763. Editor: David E. Davis. For auto enthusiasts; college educated, professional, median 26 to 28 years of age. Monthly magazine; 100 pages. Established in 1957. Circulation: 725,000. Rights purchased vary with author and material. Buys all rights, but may reassign rights to author after publication, or first North American serial rights. Buys 10-12 unsolicited mss/year. Pays on acceptance. No photocopied or simultaneous submissions. Submit seasonal material 4 months in advance. Query and include samples of previous work. Reports in 2 months. Enclose S.A.S.E.
Nonfiction and Photos: Nonanecdotal articles about the more sophisticated treatment of autos and motor racing. Exciting, interesting cars. Automotive road tests, informational articles on cars and equipment; some satire and humor. Personalities, past and present in the automotive industry and automotive sports. Treat readers as intellectual equals. Emphasis on people as well as hardware. Informational, how-to, humor, historical, think articles, and nostalgia. Length: 750 to 2,000 words. Pays $200 to $1,000. B&w photos purchased with accompanying mss with no additional payment. Also buys book reviews for book review department, and mini-features for FYI department. Length: about 500 words. Pays $50.
How To Break In: "It is best to start off with an interesting query and to stay away from nuts-and-bolts stuff since that will be handled in-house or by an acknowledged expert. Probably the very best way for a new writer to break in with us is with a personal, reasonably hip approach which shows a real intimacy with what we are trying to do. A while back, for instance, we ran a freelance piece on automobiles in Russia, which was the product of an interesting query. We are not like other automotive magazines inasmuch as we try to publish material which could just as well appear in the general magazines. We're not interested in unusual cars. To us the Ford Mustang is infinitely more important than a 1932 Ruxton wicker-seat five-passenger touring car. Good writing and unique angles are the key."

CAR CRAFT, 8490 Sunset Blvd., Los Angeles CA 90069. (213)657-5100, ext. 345. Editor: Rick Voegelin. For men and women, 18 to 34, automotive oriented. Monthly magazine; 124 pages, 8x11. Established in 1953. Circulation: 300,000. Buys all rights. Buys 12 mss per year. Payment on acceptance. Will not consider photocopied or simultaneous submissions. Query first. Enclose S.A.S.E.
Nonfiction and Photos: Photo Department Editor: Charlie Hayward. Drag racing articles, technical car features, how-to articles, and general car features. Interview, profile, and photo features. Length: open. Pays $100 to $125 per page. Photos are purchased with or without accompanying ms. Captions optional. 8x10 b&w glossy; 35mm or 2¼ color transparencies. Pays $12.50 for b&w photos; $100 minimum (one page) color.

CARS MAGAZINE, Popular Publications, Inc., 420 Lexington Ave., Suite 2540, New York NY 10017. (212)687-1234. Editor-in-Chief: Rich Ceppos. Emphasizes hot rods, muscle cars, drag racing for auto freaks from early teens through twenties and thirties; some older. High school education, plus a fair amount of technical knowledge about cars. Monthly magazine; 76 pages. Estab: 1957. Circ: 100,000. Pays on publication. Buys all rights. Phone queries OK. SASE. Reports in 2 months. Sample copy $1.
Nonfiction: How-to (budget hop-ups, customizing, repair, maintenance, body work, race car building); informational and new product (on magazine's subject); humor (on hot rods, muscle cars, drag racing); interviews and profiles (of prominent people in drag racing or automotive field); historical and nostalgia (looking back on hot rods; muscle cars of the 50's and 60's); technical (drivetrain and suspension subjects); race coverage (big drag racing events). Buys 12 mss/issue. Send complete ms. Length: 500-3,000 words, Pays $100-300.
Photos: No additional payment for 8x10 b&w glossies or 35mm (or larger) transparencies used with mss. Owner's release required.
How To Break In: "Read the magazine to get an idea of what we're about. A writer doesn't have much chance unless he knows cars well and is complete and clear with his information."
Rejects: "A story with no photos."

THE CLASSIC CAR, Box 3013, Orange CA 92665. Editor: William S. Snyder. For the classic car enthusiast, highly specialized in his interest. Uses writing with a "good nonfiction prose style. More interested in clear, factual writing than a lot of 'flash.'" The publication has a "finer focus than general automotive magazines. The reader is extremely knowledgeable to begin with. Accuracy is of utmost importance." Quarterly. Circulation: 5,000. Buys first rights. Buys 4 to 8 mss a year from freelancers. Pays on publication. Query first. Reports in a week to 10 days. Enclose S.A.S.E.

Nonfiction and Photos: Wants "historical articles on various makes and models of classic cars (high quality cars of 1925-1942 vintage), photo articles on classics, restoration how-to articles, interviews, and profiles." Length: 500 to 5,000 words. Pays $25 to $100. 8x10 b&w glossy photos, 4x5 color transparencies. Preferred with captions only. Pays $1 to $5 for b&w; $5 to $25 for color.

CUSTOM VANS MAGAZINE, Twentieth Century Publications, Box 547, 8943 Fullbright Ave., Chatsworth CA 91311. (213)998-7411. Editor/Publisher: Pat Mackie. Emphasizes custom vans. Monthly magazine; 76 pages. Estab: 1976. Circ: 120,000. Pays on publication. Buys first North American serial rights. Phone queries OK. SASE. Reports in 4 weeks. Free sample copy. **Nonfiction:** How-to and van features. Buys 10 mss/issue. Query. Length: 350-1,500 words. Pays $35-50/published page.
Photos: Purchased with accompanying ms. Captions required. Send b&w prints (8x10 for feature vans; 5x7 for how-to's) or color transparencies (2¼x2¼). Offers no additional payment for photos accepted with mss. Model release required.
How To Break In: "Offer us some original ideas and approaches, especially with how-to stories that can save the customizer money. We're always looking for outstanding custom vans to feature, with good quality color transparencies and b&w prints."

CYCLE NEWS, WEST, 2201 Cherry Ave., Box 498, Long Beach CA 90801. (213)427-7433. Editor-in-Chief: John D. Ulrich. Publisher: Sharon Clayton. Emphasizes motorcycle recreation for motorcycle racers and recreationists west of Mississippi River. Weekly tabloid; 48 pages. Estab: 1963. Circ: 60,000. Payment on 15th of month for work published in issues cover dated previous month. Buys all rights, but may reassign rights to author following publication. SASE. Reports in 4 weeks. Free writer's guidelines. **Nonfiction:** Expose; how-to; historical; humor; informational; interview (racers); personal experience (racing, non-racing with a point); personal opinion (land use, emission control, etc.); photo feature; profile (personality profiles); technical; and travel (off-road trips, "bikepacking"). Buys 1,000 mss/year. Submit complete ms. Pays $1/column inch.
Photos: Purchased with or without accompanying manuscript. Captions required. Submit contact sheet, prints, negatives or transparencies. Pays $5 minimum for 5x7 or 8x10 glossies; $10 minimum for 35mm slides or 2¼ color transparencies. Model release required. No additional payment for photos accepted with accompanying ms.

CYCLE TIMES, Multi-Media Publications, 222 W. Adams St., Suite 895, Chicago IL 60606. (312)236-5550. Managing Editor: Denis Schmidlin. For "midwestern motorcyclists, early teens and up, probably race oriented." Monthly tabloid; 24 pages (winter); 40 (summer). Estab: 1975. Circ: 50,000. Pays on publication. Submit seasonal/holiday material 3 months in advance. SASE. Reports in 2-3 weeks. Free sample copy and writer's guidelines.
Nonfiction: How-to (motorcycle maintenance, performance modifications, repairs); informational (race coverage, event reports); interview (with midwesterners); personal opinion; new product; personal experience (no first m/c rides, no crash/death stories); and technical. Buys 5-10 mss/issue. Submit complete ms. Length: 500-2,000 words. Pays $1/column inch.
Photos: Purchased with accompanying ms. Captions required. B&w only. Submit 5x7 (minimum size) glossy or matte. Pays $2.50/photo.
Columns/Departments: Tech Talk (mechanical engineer takes the jargon out of m/c topics). Buys 1-2/issue. Submit complete ms. Length: 1,500-2,500. Pays $15-30. Open to suggestions for new columns or departments.
How To Break In: "Start covering the races in our 10-state circulation area. Include usable photos and a sufficient re-cap of the day's events. All of us started this way. Once we know who you are, you'll get all the work you can handle."
Rejects: "I'm very open to new submissions, but slander pieces, poetry, or too short treatments get automatic rejects."
For '78: "We're looking for a lot more contributors who like to (or have to) go to motorcycle races. If you're a literary genius, so much the better, but that's secondary to your ability to provide consistent, on-time, race coverage."

CYCLE WORLD, 1499 Monrovia Ave., Newport Beach CA 92663. Editor: Allan Girdler. For active motorcyclists, "young, affluent, educated, very perceptive." Subject matter includes "road tests (staff-written), features on special bikes, customs, racers, racing events; technical and how-to features involving mechanical modifications." Monthly. Circulation: 250,000. Buys all rights, but will reassign rights to author after publication. Buys 200 to 300 mss a year from freelancers. Payment on publication. Will send sample copy to a writer for 75¢. Write for copy of guidelines for writers. Submit seasonal material 2½ months in advance. Reports in 4 to 6 weeks. Query first. Enclose S.A.S.E.

Nonfiction: Buys informative, well-researched travel stories; technical, theory, and how-to articles; interviews, profiles, humor, spot news, historical pieces, think pieces, new product articles and satire. Taboos include articles about "wives learning to ride; 'my first motorcycle.'" Length: 800 to 5,000 words. Pays $75 to $100 per published page. Columns include Competition, which contains short, local racing stories with photos. Column length: 300 to 400 words. Pays $75 to $100 per published page.

Photos: Purchased with or without ms, or on assignment. Captions optional. Pays $50 for 1 page; $25 to $35 for ½ page. 8x10 b&w glossies, 35mm color transparencies.

Fiction: Needs mystery, science fiction, and humorous stories. Does not want to see racing fiction or "rhapsodic poetry." Length: 1,500 to 3,000 words. Pays $75 minimum per published page.

DIRT BIKE MAGAZINE, P.O. Box 317, Encino CA 91436. Editor: Bruce Woods. For dirt bike riders. Magazine; 100 (8x10) pages. Established in 1971. Monthly. Circulation: 175,000. Buys all rights. Buys about 24 mss a year. Will consider photocopied submissions. No simultaneous submissions. Submit special material 3 months in advance. Query first. SASE.

Nonfiction and Photos: Competition reports outside of southern California of national interest. Light, humorous style, but accurate facts. Informational, how-to, expose, spot news, technical. Length: 1,000 to 8,000 words. Pays 3¢ to 5¢ a word. Hole Shot column uses opinions of general interest. Length: 1,200 to 1,500 words. Payment is the same as for articles. Photos are used in special Crash & Burn issues. Also purchased with or without ms, or on assignment. Pays $5 to $7 for 8x10 b&w glossies. Pays $25 to $50 for 35mm (or larger) transparencies.

DUNE BUGGIES & HOT VWS, Wright Publishing Co., Inc., P.O. Box 2260, Costa Mesa CA 92626. Editor: Tom Chambers. Monthly magazine; 100 pages. Estab: 1967. Circ: 50,000. Pays on publication. Buys one-time rights. Submit seasonal or holiday material 3 months in advance. SASE. Free sample copy.

Nonfiction: Technical how-to and informational articles. Buys 6-8 per issue. Submit complete ms. Length: 500-2,000 words. Pays $50 per published page.

Photos: Purchased with ms. Captions required. Send contact sheet. Pays $10 maximum for 8x10 b&w glossies; $10 minimum for color negs or slides.

Rejects: First person articles.

EASYRIDERS MAGAZINE, Entertainment for Adult Bikers, Box 52, Malibu CA 90265. (213)880-4240. Editor: Lou Kimzey. For "adult men—men who own, or desire to own, expensive custom motorcycles. The individualist—a rugged guy who enjoys riding a chopper and all the good times derived from it." Monthly. Circulation: 285,000. Buys all rights. Buys 12 to 20 mss a year. Payment on acceptance. Will send a sample copy to a writer for 25¢. Reports in 2 to 3 weeks. Enclose S.A.S.E. for return of submissions.

Nonfiction, Fiction, and Fillers: Department Editor: Louis Bosque. "Masculine, candid material of interest to men. Must be bike-oriented, but can be anything of interest to a rugged man. It is suggested that everyone read a copy before submitting—it's not *Boy's Life*. Light, easy, conversational writing style wanted, like guys would speak to each other without women being around. Gut level, friendly, man-to-man. Should be bike-oriented or of interest to a guy who rides a bike. *Easyriders* is entirely different from all other motorcycle magazines in that it stresses the good times surrounding the owning of a motorcycle—it's aimed at the rider and is nontechnical, while the others are nuts and bolts. Not interested in technical motorcycle articles. We carry no articles that preach to the reader, or attempt to tell them what they should or shouldn't do." Buys personal experience, interviews, humor, expose (motorcycle-oriented) articles. Length: 1,000 to 3,000 words. Payment is usually 10¢/word, depending on length and use in magazine. "It's the subject matter and how well it's done—not length, that determines amount paid." Risque joke fillers, short humor. Length: open. Payment: open.

Photos: Department Editor: Pete Chiodo. B&w glossies, 35mm color, 2¼x2¼ color transparencies purchased with mss. "We are only interested in *exclusive* photos of exclusive bikes that have never been published in, or photographed by, a national motorcycle or chopper publication. Bikes should be approved by editorial board before going to expense of shooting. Submit sample photos—Polaroids will do. Send enough samples for editorial board to get good idea of the bike's quality, originality, workmanship, interesting features, coloring." Payment is $50 to $150 for cover, $75-$150 for centerspread, $20 for b&w and $35 for color for "In the Wind," $25 up for arty, unusual shots, and $100 to $225 for a complete feature.

Fiction: "Gut level language okay. Any sex scenes, not to be too graphic in detail. Dope may be implied, but not graphically detailed. Must be bike-oriented, but doesn't have to dwell on that fact. Only interested in hard-hitting, rugged fiction." Length: 2,000-5,000 words. Payment is usually 10¢/word, depending on quality, length and use in magazine.

How To Break In: "There is no mystery about breaking into our publication, as long as the material is aimed at our specific audience. We suggest that the writer read the requirements indicated above and seriously study a current copy of the magazine before submitting material."

FOUR WHEELER MAGAZINE, Box 547, 8943 Fullbright, Chatsworth CA 91311. (213)998-7411. Editor-in-Chief: Bill Sanders. Associate Editor: Lynette McDonald. Emphasizes four-wheel-drive vehicles. Monthly magazine; 108 pages. Estab: 1956. Circ: 120,000. Pays on publication. Buys all rights. Phone queries OK. Submit seasonal/holiday material at least 4 months in advance. SASE. Reports in 6-12 months. Free sample copy and writer's guidelines.

Nonfiction: Historical (4 wheeling in ghost towns), how-to, interview (4WD industry), new product, profile (prominent 4WD enthusiast), technical and travel. Query or send complete ms. Length: 5-6 pages. Pays $50-250.

Fillers: Newsbreaks, cartoons and 4WD outings for "campfire". Submit fillers. Pays $15 minimum for cartoons.

HOT ROD, 8490 Sunset Blvd., Los Angeles CA 90069. (213)657-5100. Editor: John Dianna. For readers 10 to 60 years old with automotive high performance and racing interest, truck and van interest, drag racing and street machines. Magazine; 120 pages. Established in 1948. Monthly. Circulation: 800,000. Buys all rights. Buys 30 mss per year. Pays on publication. Will send free sample copy and editorial guidelines on request. Will not consider photocopied or simultaneous submissions. Submit seasonal material 3 to 4 months in advance. Reports on accepted and rejected material "as soon as possible." Enclose S.A.S.E.

Nonfiction and Photos: Wants how-to, interview, profile, photo, new product and technical pieces. Length: 2 to 12 ms pages. Pays $100 to $125 per printed page. Photos purchased with accompanying ms with no additional payment, with extra payment, without accompanying ms and on assignment. Captions required. Pays $15 for b&w prints and $25 minimum for color.

How To Break In: "Freelance approach should be tailored for specific type and subject matter writer is dealing with. If it is of a basic automotive technical nature, then story slant and info should be aimed at the backyard enthusiasts. If the story is dealing with a specific personality, then it must include a major portion of human interest type of material. What we do is attempt to entertain while educating and offer exceptional dollar value."

KEEPIN' TRACK, Box 5445, Reno NV 89513. Editor-in-Chief: Frank Kodl. Managing Editor: Fredi Kodl. Emphasizes Corvettes. Monthly magazine; 40-48 pages. Estab: 1976. Circ: 12,000. Pays on publication. Buys all rights. Submit seasonal/holiday material 2-3 months in advance. Previously published submissions OK. SASE. Reports in 3 weeks. Free sample copy and writer's guidelines.

Nonfiction: Expose (telling of Corvette problems with parts, etc.); historical (any and all aspects of Corvette developments); how-to (restorations, engine work, suspension, race, swapmeets); humor; informational; interview (query); nostalgia; personal experience; personal opinion; photo feature; profile (query); technical; and travel. Buys 2-3 mss/issue. Submit complete ms. Pays $25-100.

Photos: Purchased with accompanying ms. Send contact sheet or transparencies. Offers no additional payment for photos accepted with ms.

MOTOCROSS ACTION MAGAZINE, 16200 Ventura Blvd., Encino CA 91436. (213)981-2317. Editor: Dick Miller. For "primarily young and male, average age 12 to 30, though an increasing number of females is noticed. Education varies considerably. They are interested in off-road racing motorcycles, as either professional or hobby." Magazine; 72 pages. Established in 1973. Monthly. Circulation: 85,000. Buys all rights but may reassign them to author after publication. Buys 20 to 25 mss a year. Pays on publication. Will send sample copy for $1. Write for editorial guidelines. Will consider photocopied but no simultaneous submissions. Reports on material accepted for publication in 1 to 6 months. Returns rejected material immediately. Query first. Enclose S.A.S.E.

Nonfiction and Photos: Wants "articles on important national and international motocross events, interviews with top professionals, technical pieces, and in-depth investigative reporting. Short stories and/or poetry will be greeted with a heartfelt yawn. It's best to obtain a copy of the magazine and read recent stories. Stories should be brief and to the point, though flair is appreciated. Top photography is a must." No blatant hero worship. For the coming year, Miller also wants to see articles on "the evolution of motocross from a backyard to a big time, multi-million dollar sport and business." Takes informational, how-to, profile, humor and photo pieces. Length: 500 to 2,000 words. Pays $25 to $200. Photos purchased with accompanying ms with extra payment and on assignment. Captions optional. Pays $8 to $10 for b&w, 8x10 glossies. $25 to $50 for 35mm or 2¼ color slides.

MOTOR TREND, 8490 Sunset Blvd., Los Angeles CA 90069. (213)657-5100. Managing Editor: Cliff Creager. For automotive enthusiasts, backyard mechanics and general interest consumers. Monthly. Circulation: 650,000. Buys all rights, except by negotiation. "Fact-filled query suggested for all freelancers." Reports in 30 days. Enclose S.A.S.E.
Nonfiction: Automotive and related subjects that have national appeal. Emphasis on money-saving ideas for the motorist, high-performance and economy modifications, news tips on new products, pickups, RVs, long-term automotive projects. Packed with facts. Pays $100 per printed page in magazine, or as negotiated.
Photos: Buys photos, particularly of prototype cars in Detroit area. Other automotive matter. 8x10 b&w glossies or transparencies. Pays $25 minimum.
Fillers: Automotive newsbreaks. Any length. Payment open.

MOTORCYCLIST MAGAZINE, Petersen Publishing, 8490 Sunset Blvd., Los Angeles CA 90069. Editor-in-Chief: Dave Ekins. Emphasizes motorcycles for motorcycle enthusiasts. Monthly magazine; 100 pages. Estab: 1912. Circ: 150,000. Pays on publication. Buys all rights. Submit seasonal/holiday material 90 days in advance. SASE. Reports in 1 month. Free writer's guidelines.
Nonfiction: How-to, humor, informational, interview, new product, photo feature, profile and technical. Buys 12 mss/year. Query. Length: 500-2,000 words. Pays $100/published page.

NORTHEAST VAN, 95 N. Main St., Waterbury CT 06702. (203)757-8731. Editor: John Florian. Established in 1975. Readers are people interested in vanning in the Northeast. Ages vary, though most are in early to late twenties, in the process of customizing a van, or a member of a van club. Tabloid newspaper. 32-plus pages. Seasonal features considered; no specific plans for them. Monthly. Not copyrighted. Expects to buy 3 or 4 mss per issue. Pays on publication. Will send free sample copy and editorial guidelines to writer on request. Will not consider photocopied or simultaneous submissions. Submit seasonal material 3 months in advance. Reports on accepted and rejected material in 2 weeks. Query first. Enclose S.A.S.E.
Nonfiction and Photos: "We publish 'how-to' articles about customizing vans, features about what others in the Northeast have done to their vans, and other features of interest to readers, like truck-ins, club news, maintenance/safety advice. We are open to all ideas. Material should be snappy and easy-reading, yet without a load of cliches." Wants informational, how-to, personal experience, humor, and travel articles. Length: 800-2,000 words. Pays $20 to $60; up to $60 maximum with b&w photos. "Good photos are very important to complement any article, though manuscripts will be considered without them." For photos alone, pay is $7.50 for each b&w 8x10. Photo layouts bring $40. Captions optional. Freelance article recently purchased: "Black Beauty", a feature about a customized van, which had good photos of the van, and what the owner did to customize it. Florian says, "If you have any questions or wish to cover some event live and ask about it first, please feel free to write or call me."

1001 CUSTOM & ROD IDEAS, Argus Publishers Corporation, 12301 Wilshire Blvd., Los Angeles CA 90025. (213)820-3601. Editor: Jay Amestoy. For hobbyists who build modified American cars (hot rods); ages 15 to approximately 45, mechanically inclined. Magazine published every two months; 68 pages. Established in 1967. Circulation: 145,000. Rights purchased vary with author and material. Buys all rights or first North American serial rights. Buys 90 mss per year. Payment on publication. Will send free sample copy to writer on request. Write for copy of guidelines for writers. Will not consider simultaneous submissions except to other Argus magazines. Reports within 2 months. Query first; send sample of copy and photos. Enclose S.A.S.E.
Nonfiction and Photos: "Technical articles on engine building, tuning, installation of performance equipment. Car features on unusual street rods, both early and late models. Read the magazine, pay special attention to quality and type of photos used. We do not accept copy only. Special emphasis on quality photos, how-to articles, no superfluous wordage in copy. We have adequate car features on early street rods from freelancers at present. We don't want rough-looking, dirty cars or technical articles that are written by persons without automotive experience. Our most efficient method of assuring material use is to assign subject matter, or be asked by freelancer about our needs." Length: 300 to 4,000 words. Pays $50 per page, including photos. Photos purchased with accompanying ms with no additional payment. Captions required. Also purchased without ms or on assignment. Prefers 8x10 b&w glossies (occasionally

takes proof sheets with negatives). Pays $10 minimum for b&w photo. Color transparencies; pays $50 minimum.

1001 TRUCK AND VAN IDEAS MAGAZINE, Argus Publishers Corp., 12301 Wilshire Blvd., Los Angeles CA 90025. (213)820-3601. Editor-in-Chief: Phillip E. Carpenter. Emphasizes use of trucks, RVs, vans and mini-trucks for drivers who use, modify, customize and 'go fun truckin' with these vehicles. Monthly magazine; 96 pages. Estab: 1975. Circ: 200,000. Pays either on acceptance or publication. Phone queries OK. Submit seasonal/holiday material 3 months in advance. SASE. Reports in 2 weeks. Free writer's guidelines.
Nonfiction: How-to (on building interiors for custom vans and pickups, engine swaps, suspension work, etc.); informational; interview, new product, photo feature (for *Van Idea Notebook* and *Tricks For Trucks*); technical (step-by-step) and travel (tie in with type of vehicle). Buys 6-7 mss/issue. Query. Length: 1,500 maximum. Pays $50-75/page.
Photos: Steve Reyes, Photo Editor. Photos purchased with or without accompanying ms or on assignment. Captions required. Pays $10-25 for 5x7 minimum b&w glossies; $25-75 for 2¼x2¼ or 35mm color transparencies. Total purchase price for ms includes payment for photos. Model release required.
How To Break In: "If a writer cannot furnish professional photos with his copy, he shouldn't bother with us. He or she must know vans and pickups from a semi-technical viewpoint. No copy without photo, and no 'look, world, here's my very own custom van I built and captured on my polaroid for you' articles."

PICKUP, VAN & 4WD MAGAZINE, CBS Consumer Publishing, 1499 Monrovia Ave., Newport Beach CA 92663. (714)646-4451. Editor: Don E. Brown. Managing Editor: Dave Epperson. For off-road vehicle enthusiasts. Monthly magazine; 96 pages. Estab: 1972. Circ: 180,000. Pays on publication. Buys all rights. Submit seasonal/holiday material 3-4 months in advance. Photocopied submissions OK. SASE. Reports 1-2 months. Free writer's guidelines.
Nonfiction: How-to (modifications to light duty trucks, such as extra seats, tool storage, etc.), historical, nostalgia (old restored trucks and 4-wheel drives), technical and travel (4-wheel drive travel only, must show vehicle being used). Buys 4-5 mss/issue. Submit complete ms. Length: 1,000-3,000 words. Pays $50 minimum.
Photos: Purchased with accompanying manuscript or on assignment. Captions required. Query for photos. Pays $12.50-75 for 8x10 b&w glossies; $25-75 for 35mm or 2¼ color transparencies. Total purchase price for ms includes payment for photos. Model release required.

RACING CARS, Carl Hungness & Associates, Box 1341, Marion IN 46952. Editor-in-Chief: Jerry Miller. For automobile racing fans; 30-50; blue collar. Quarterly magazine; 64 pages. Estab: 1977. Circ: 5,000. Pays on publication. Buys first North American serial rights. Submit seasonal/holiday material two months in advance. SASE. Reports in 3 weeks.
Nonfiction: Historical (on racing in general, race cars, speedways, etc,; humor (anything to do with racing); informational (on racing personalities, profiles or specific enterprises); interviews (major racing personality; hard-hitting; not restricted to questions on racing subjects); nostalgia (old races, drivers, mechanics, cars, etc.); profiles (any racing personalities of national interest). "Remember, we cover only oval racing in America and personalities, cars, tracks associated with it. No road racing, please." Buys 24 mss/year. Query. Length: 2,000-5,000. Pays $50-100.
Photos: Purchased with or without mss or on assignment. Captions required. Send contact sheet, prints or transparencies. Pays $5-15 for 5x7 or 8x10 b&w glossies; $25 minimum for color transparencies, any size.

RIDER, 23945 Craftsman Rd., Calabasas CA 91302. Editor: Bill Estes. For owners and prospective buyers of motorcycles to be used for touring and commuting. Magazine: 100 to 120 pages. Established in 1974. Bimonthly. Buys all rights. Pays on acceptance. Will send sample copy to writer for $1. Write for copy of guidelines for writers. Submit seasonal material 3 months in advance. Will consider photocopied submissions. Query first. Reports in 1 month. Enclose S.A.S.E.
Nonfiction and Photos: Articles directly related to motorcycle touring, commuting and sport riding including travel, human interest, safety, novelty, do-it-yourself and technical. "Articles which portray the unique thrill of motorcycling." Should be written in clean, contemporary style aimed at a sharp, knowledgeable reader. Buys informational, how-to, personal experience, profile, historical, nostalgia, personal opinion, travel and technical. Length is flexible. Pays $100-200. Photos purchased with ms with no additional payment. Captions required.

ROAD & DRIVER, Box 326, Northport NY 11768. Editor: Mel Shapiro. For car owners who are interested in getting more for their driving dollars. Magazine; 84 (8½x11) pages.

Established in 1974. Every 2 months. Circulation: 250,000. Buys all rights. Buys 60 mss per year. Payment on publication. Will send sample copy to writer for 50¢. Will consider photocopied submissions. No simultaneous submissions. Submit seasonal/holiday material 4 to 5 months in advance. Reports on material accepted for publication in 3 weeks. Returns rejected material in 4 weeks. Query first. Enclose S.A.S.E.
Nonfiction and Photos: Articles on anything to do with auto economy. Safety and better driving tips. New products. Maintenance. Informational, how-to, personal experience, interview, profile, humor, travel, spot news. Length: 500 to 3,000 words. Pays $50 to $60. No additional payment is made for photos submitted with mss.
Fillers: Newsbreaks, clippings, short humor on themes pertinent to economical driving. Length: 50 to 200 words. Pays $5 to $25.

ROAD & TRACK, 1499 Monrovia Avenue, Newport Beach CA 92663. Editor: Tony Hogg. For knowledgeable car enthusiasts. Monthly magazine. Buys all rights, but may be reassigned to author after publication. Query first. Reports in 6 weeks. Enclose S.A.S.E.
Nonfiction: "The editor welcomes freelance material, but if the writer is not thoroughly familiar with the kind of material used in the magazine, he is wasting both his time and the magazine's time. *Road & Track* material is highly specialized and that old car story in the files has no chance of being accepted. More serious, comprehensive and in-depth treatment of particular areas of automotive interest." Payment is minimum 12¢ per word but often reaches 20¢ per word.

ROAD KING MAGAZINE, Box 319, Park Forect IL 60466. (312)664-2959. Editor-in-Chief: George Friend. Publication of The Union Oil Co. For independent truckers and their families. Quarterly magazine; 48 pages. Estab: 1963. Circ: 195,000. Pays on acceptance. Buys one-time rights. Phone queries OK. Submit seasonal/holiday material 3-4 months in advance. Simultaneous and photocopied submissions OK. SASE. Reports in 3 weeks. Sample copy for SASE.
Nonfiction: Jeanne Lynch, Articles Editor. How-to and historical "related to the trucking industry." Buys 1-2 mss/year. Submit complete ms. Length: 500-1,500 words. Pays $50-100.
Columns, Departments: Joan Nash, Department Editor. Wives Are Winners (recipe column) Loads of Laughs (cartoons, jokes). Buys 15-20/year. Pays $5 for jokes, $10 for recipes, $25 for cartoons.
Fiction: Joan Nash, Fiction Editor. Adventure, fantasy, historical, humorous, mystery, suspense, science fiction, western. Buys 4-5 mss/year. Submit complete ms. Length: 1,000-2,500. Pays $100.
Fillers: Joan Nash, Fillers Editor. Jokes, gags, anecdotes, short humor. Buys 25/year. Length: 50-75 words. Pays $5.
Rejects: "Erotica, experimental, or unnecessary violence. Our readers like straight reading for entertainment."

ROAD RIDER, Box 678, South Laguna CA 92677. Editor-in-Chief: Roger Hull. Managing Editor: R.L. Carpenter. Emphasizes touring on motorcycles for family style and fellow enthusiasts. Monthly magazine; 88 pages. Estab: 1969. Circ: 35,000. Pays on publication. Buys all rights, but may reassign rights to author following publication. Submit seasonal/holiday material 4 months in advance. "We schedule seasonal material 1 year in advance". SASE. Reports in 4 weeks. Free sample copy and writer's guidelines.
Nonfiction: How-to (researched method for improving facet of motorcycling/touring); informational (verified references when applicable); humor; nostalgia ("yesterday cycling", accompanied by photos); personal experience; photo feature; travel (biggest market) and technical (by assignment, must have prior outline). Buys 50 mss/year. Query. Length: maximum 2,000 words. Pays $75 minimum.
Photos: Purchased with accompanying manuscript. Captions required. B&w 5x7 glossies; 35mm or 2¼x2¼ color transparencies. Pays $50 maximum for covers. Total purchase price for ms includes payment for photos.
How To Break In: "We are an enthusiast publication—as such, it is virtually impossible to sell here unless the writer is also an enthusiast and actively involved in the sport. A good, well-written, brief item dealing with a motorcycle trip, accompanied by top quality b&w photos receives prime time editorial attention. We are always on the lookout for good material from eastern seaboard or Midwest. Best way to hit this market is to request sample and study same prior to submitting. Most of our contributors are Road Rider People. If you are unsure as to what "Road Rider People" refers, you will propably not be able to sell to this magazine."
Rejects: We continue to be overstocked on following: beginner articles (all ages, sexes, etc.), Journal-format travel articles (not welcome), travel articles from southwestern U.S.

ROAD TEST, Quinn Publishing Company, 1440 W. Walnut St., Compton CA 90220. (213)537-0857. Editor-in-Chief: Jon F. Thompson. Managing Editor: Dick Falk. Emphasizes automobiles for college-educated, professional readership. Monthly magazine; 72 pages. Estab: 1964. Circ: 80,000. Pays on publication. Buys first North American serial rights. Submit seasonal/holiday material 3 months in advance. SASE. Reports in 3 weeks. Free sample copy.
Nonfiction: How-to (make cars more reliable, responsive, economical, etc.); humor; informational; interview (racing or industry); nostalgia (old car stuff) and profile. Buys 3-4 mss/issue. Query. Length: 1,500-3,000 words. Pays $250-500.
Photos: Purchased with accompanying manuscript. Captions required. Query for photos. B&w 35mm/2¼ proof sheets and negatives; 35mm kodachrome color. Model release required.

STOCK CAR RACING MAGAZINE, 1420 Prince St., Alexandria VA 22314. Editor: Richard S. Benyo. For blue-collar audience from 16 to 60. Magazine; 80 pages. Established in 1966. Monthly. Circulation: 120,000. Buys all rights, but may reassign rights to author after publication. Buys about 75 mss per year. Pays on publication. Sample copy $1. Will consider photocopied and simultaneous submissions. Reports in 2 to 6 weeks. Query first. Enclose S.A.S.E.
Nonfiction, Photos and Fiction: Photo Editor: Neil Britt. Fiction Editor: Richard S. Benyo. Uses primarily nonfiction on stock car drivers, cars and races. Writers should study the magazine before submitting. Will consider book reviews and short features. "We really don't need any more race articles. What we do need most are features from the southwest. Would like to see more lifelike portrayals of drivers instead of stories that leave the impression they are cardboard gods." Length: 100 to 500 words for book reviews; 600 to 5,000 words for expose; 600 to 2,500 words for historical; 1,000 to 6,000 words for profiles; 1,000 to 5,000 words for interviews. Pays $10 to $175. Regular columns are staff-written. Photos purchased with or without ms with extra payment and on assignment. Captions required. Payment: $15 for b&w; $50 to $150 for color. Size: 8x10 for b&w; 35mm color slides. Fiction must be about racing and should be written with knowledge and understanding of the sport. Length: 1,000 to 5,000 words. Pays $50 to $150.

STREET CHOPPER, 1132 No. Brookhurst, Anaheim CA 92801. (714)635-9040. Editor: Bob Clark. For custom and high-performance motorcycle enthusiasts. Monthly magazine; 84 pages. Established in 1969. Circulation: 100,000. Buys all rights. Buys 25 to 35 mss a year. Payment on acceptance. Will not consider photocopied or simultaneous submissions. Reports within 3 months. Query first. Enclose S.A.S.E.
Nonfiction and Photos: Technical-oriented stories dealing with all aspects of motorcycles. "We deal strictly with custom and high-performance motorcycles. No off-road or dirt bikes." Material must be written in laymen's terminology. Greatest interest is in technical stories and how-to articles on motorcycles. Length: open. Pays maximum of $50/published page. Columns using freelance material include "Checkered Flag" and "Cafe Corner." Length: 2 to 5 double-spaced, typed pages. Pays $40 per published page. Pays $40 to $75 for b&w photos purchased with mss; $50 for color; 2¼ only.
Fillers: Newsbreaks and jokes. Length: 1 to 3 typed, double-spaced pages.

STREET RODDER MAGAZINE, TRM Publications, Inc., 1132 N. Brookhurst, Anaheim CA 92801. Editor: Patrick Ganahl. For the automotive enthusiast with an interest in street-driven, modified old cars. Magazine; 76 (8x11) pages. Established in 1972. Monthly. Circulation: 105,000. Buys all rights, but will reassign rights to author after publication. Buys 25 to 35 mss a year. Payment on acceptance. Sample copy $1.50; free writer's guidelines. No photocopied or simultaneous submissions. Reports in 1 month. Query first or submit complete ms. Enclose S.A.S.E.
Nonfiction and Photos: "We need coverage of events and cars that we can't get to. Street rod events (rod runs); how-to technical articles; features on individual street rods. We don't need features on local (Southern California) street rods, events or shops. We stress a straightforward style; accurate and complete details; easy to understand (though not 'simple') technical material. We are currently overstocked with individual car features. Need good, clear, complete and well-photographed technical and how-to articles on pertinent street rod modifications or conversions. We very seldom accept a story without photos." Length: 250 to 1500 words. Pays $25 to $150. Average payment for 2- to 3-page 5x7, 8x10 b&w feature: $75-150.
How To Break In: "The best way to break in is to carefully and objectively study recent past issues, and to submit the same type of material contained in the magazine. I wouldn't mind receiving something that's well-written and ready to print, for a change, too."

SUPER CHEVY MAGAZINE, Argus Publishers Corporation, 12301 Wilshire Blvd.,, Los Angeles CA 90025. (213)820-3601. Editor: Jay Amestoy. For high-performance automotive enthusiasts who build and race their own cars. Magazine published every 2 months; 84 pages. Established in 1973. Circulation: 100,000. Buys first North American serial rights. Buys 90 mss a year. Pays on publication. Will send free sample copy to writer on request. Will not consider photocopied and simultaneous submissions except to other Argus magazines. Reports in 2 months in most cases. Query first or submit complete ms. Enclose S.A.S.E.

Nonfiction and Photos: All articles should be slanted to high-performance-minded individuals. Car features, technical articles dealing with the automobile. New car introductions, new product features, and a few race reports. All cars or pickups must be 100% Chevrolet. Informational, how-to, interview, profiles. Length: open. Pays $40 per printed page. No additional payment is made for b&w photos (8x10 prints) purchased with mss. Pays $10 to $20 for those purchased separately. Pays $50 to $150 for 2¼x2¼ color transparencies.

How To Break In: "Send for freelancer guidelines and publisher's requirements sheet. Then, submit proposed article idea with snapshots to editor before going ahead."

SUPERSTOCK AND DRAG ILLUSTRATED, Lopez Publications, 1420 Prince St., Alexandria VA 22314. Editor-in-Chief: Richard Benyo. Executive Editor: Neil Britt. For "mostly blue-collar males between 12-35 years old; high performance, drag racing oriented. Monthly magazine; 80 pages. Estab: 1964. Circ: 140,000. Pays on publication. Buys all rights, but may reassign following publication. Simultaneous and photocopied submissions OK. SASE. Reports in 2-6 weeks. Sample copy $1.

Nonfiction: Interview (with prominent drag racers); nostalgia (of famous drag racing events); profile (on local or national drag racers); photo features (on drag racing cars or racing events); and technical. Buys 120 mss/year. Query or submit complete ms. Length: 500-5,000 words. Pays $50-250.

Photos: Neil Britt, Photo Editor. Purchased with accompanying ms. Captions required. Submit prints or transparencies. Pays $15 for 8x10 b&w glossies; $50-150 for 35mm color transparencies.

Fiction: Adventure, humorous. Must be drag racing oriented. Submit complete ms. Length: 500-5,000 words. Pays $50-250.

TRAVELIN' 4x4's, MINIS & PICKUPS, E-Go Enterprises, Inc., 13510 Ventura Blvd., Sherman Oaks CA 91423. (213)990-2510. Editor: Jay Sadler. Emphasizes off-road vehicles and related activities. Monthly magazine; 72 pages. Estab: 1976. Circ: 135,000. Pays on publication. Buys all rights, but may reassign following publication. Phone queries OK. Submit seasonal/holiday material 4 months in advance. SASE. Reports in 2 weeks. Free sample copy and writer's guidelines.

Nonfiction: Expose (on government bills and such related to off roaders); how-to; informational; technical and travel (off-road areas). Buys 5-7 mss/issue. Query of send complete ms. Length: 1,500-3,000 words. Pays $20-35/published page.

Photos: Photos purchased with accompanying ms. Captions required. Uses 8x10 b&w photos and 35mm or 2¼x2¼ color photos. Send prints and transparencies. Total purchase price for ms includes payment for photos.

Columns/Departments: Dirt Freak (off-road motorcycle column); Willie's Work Bench (budget mechanical tips); Blood, Sweat and Gears (tips, news events, etc.). Buys 3-4/issue. Query or send complete ms. Length: 400-1,000 words. Pays $25-50.

Fillers: Clippings, jokes, gags, anecdotes and short humor. All off-road related. Buys 2/issue. Query or send fillers in. Length: 50-200 words. Pays $5-10.

How To Break In: "Follow through after query—don't keep us waiting for months after we give approval. We are always looking for out-of-state and foreign material."

VAN WORLD MAGAZINE, Hi-Torque Publications Inc., 16200 Ventura Blvd., Encino CA 91436. Editor-in-Chief: Chris Hosford. Managing Editor: Tiff Ford. Emphasizes custom vans for enthusiasts. Monthly magazine; 76 pages. Estab: 1973. Circ: 85,000. Pays on publication. Buys all rights. Submit seasonal/holiday material 4 months in advance. Photocopied submissions OK. SASE. Reports in 3 weeks. Sample copy $1.50. Free writer's guidelines.

Nonfiction: CB (non-technical articles enabling vanners to get the most from their CBs); feature vans: (photo features with brief description); how-to (interior/exterior customizing and engine/mechanical with emphasise on economy); and photo feature (b&w, color with short article on custom vans). Buys 30-50 mss/year. Query. Length: 200-1,000 words. Pays $40 maximum/page.

Photos: Purchased with or without accompanying manuscript or on assignment. Captions required. Submit contact sheet or transparencies. Pays $5-10 for 8x10 b&w glossies; $10-25 for 35mm or 2¼ color transparencies. Total purchase price for ms includes payment for photos. Model release required.

Aviation Publications

Publications in this section aim at professional and private pilots, and at aviation enthusiasts in general. Magazines intended for the in-flight passengers of commercial airlines are grouped in a separate In-Flight category. Technical aviation and space journals, and those for airport operators, aircraft dealers, or other aviation businessmen are listed under Aviation and Space in the Trade Journals.

AIR LINE PILOT, 1625 Massachussetts Ave., N.W., Washington DC 20036. (202)797-4176. Editor-in-Chief: C.V. Glines. Managing Editor: Esperison Martinez. Emphasizes commercial aviation. Monthly magazine; 52 pages. Estab: 1933. Circ: 42,000. Pays on acceptance. Buys all rights, but may reassign following publication. Submit seasonal/holiday material 4 months in advance. SASE. Reports in 4 weeks. Free sample copy and writer's guidelines.
Nonfiction: Historical (aviation/personal or equipment, aviation firsts); informational (aviation safety, related equipment or aircraft aids); interview (aviation personality); nostalgia (aviation history); photo feature; profile (airline pilots; must be ALPA members); and technical. Buys 25 mss/year. Query. Length: 1,000-2,500 words. Pays $100-300.
Photos: Purchased with or without accompanying ms. Captions required. Query. Pays $10-25 for 8½x10 b&w glossies; $20-250 for 35mm or 2¼x2¼ color transparencies.
How To Break In: "Unless a writer is experienced in aviation, he is more likely to score with a pilot profile or aviation historical piece."

THE AOPA PILOT, 7315 Wisconsin Ave., Bethesda MD 20014. (301)654-0500. Editor: Robert I. Stanfield. For plane owners, pilots, and the complete spectrum of the general aviation industry. Official magazine of the Aircraft Owners and Pilots Association. Monthly. Circulation: 195,000. Pays on acceptance. Reports promptly. Enclose S.A.S.E. for return of submissions.
Nonfiction: Factual articles up to 2,500 words that will inform, educate and entertain flying enthusiasts ranging from the student to the seasoned professional pilot. These pieces should be generously illustrated with good quality photos, diagrams or sketches. Quality and accuracy essential. Topics covered include maintenance, how-to features, pilot reports on new or unusual aircraft or aeronautical equipment, places to fly (travel), governmental policies (local, state or federal) relating to general aviation. Additional features on weather in relation to flying, legal aspects of aviation, flight education, pilot fitness, aviation history and aero clubs are used periodically. Short features of 100 to 300 words written around a single photograph, and strong photo features are always in demand. Payment is up to $300.
Photos: Pays $10 to $25 for each photo or sketch used. Exceptionally good cover color transparencies also purchased.
How To Break In: "Be aviation oriented and study the magazine (available at most airport pilots' lounges). And remember that our audience consists solely of pilots; thus a writer must speak the 'language' and be knowledgeable in the subject area."

AVIATION QUARTERLY, Box 7070, Arlington VA 22207. Publisher and Editor: Brad Bierman. For the serious aviation enthusiast, interested in the history of aviation. Quarterly. Hard-bound volume with four-color illustrations. Established in 1974. Circulation: 9,500. Buys all rights. Buys about 20-25 mss/year. Pays on publication. Query first to editorial and production office, Box 606, Plano, Texas 75074. Enclose S.A.S.E.
Nonfiction and Photos: "We accept only the highest quality articles and photos. Photos with captions must be included or available. Subject matter should be a specific topic within the history of aviation. Writer must have acknowledged experience in his particular field, and must treat his subject in a unique way. Technical articles must also be readable. Nontechnical mss acceptable. It is our intent to make each volume a definitive source of information on a given event, aircraft, person or period within the history of aviation. Preferred length: 4,000 words. Payment varies, depending on subject matter and quality and acceptability of text and photos." Pays $150 to $400 per article.

AVIATION TRAVEL, P.O. Box 7070, Arlington VA 22207. For owners of business and private aircraft; ages 30 to 50; interested in fishing, hunting, boating, photography, golf, sightseeing, beaches, resorts, outdoor and other sports. Offers a substantial market for writers slanting their material to aviation buffs. Bimonthly magazine. Established in 1972. Circulation: 30,000. Buys all rights. Buys about 20 to 30 mss a year. Payment on publication. Will send sample copy to writer for $1. Write for copy of guidelines for writers. Will consider photocopied submissions. Submit seasonal material 3 to 4 months in advance. Query first or submit complete ms. Reports in 2 months. Enclose S.A.S.E.

Nonfiction and Photos: "Short travel articles—where to go, what to see and do. We may feature a general area or special activity, event, or resort which must be accessible by private or business plane. The U.S.A., Canada, Mexico and the Bahamas are preferred. Airport and flight info are helpful, but not required. The style should be light and nontechnical. Stories must be short, informational, and specific enough to be helpful to the traveler. Destinations must be emphasized, rather than flight. Dates, admission, what to take, etc., increase the value of a story. We're the only travel-oriented aviation magazine, featuring places and events accessible by general aviation. We're interested in fly-in wilderness, fishing, hunting, golfing and camping stories at specific locations. Each issue features items of particular interest during the period immediately following." Buys informational articles, how-to's, personal experience articles, interviews, humor, historical articles, photo features, new product articles, and technical articles. Length: 200 to 1,200 words. Pay "varies: about 5¢ per word, depending on subject and quality." Photos purchased with mss or without mss; captions required. Pay "$5 and up, depending on photo, for b&w glossies 5x7 and larger." Pays $5 and up, "depending on photo and use for transparencies only."

EXXON AIR WORLD, Exxon International Co., Div. of Exxon Corp., 1251 Avenue of the Americas, New York NY 10020. (212)398-5644. Editor: E.A.C. Wren. For worldwide audience of technical and semitechnical aviation readers. Quarterly. Buys reprint rights. Payment on publication. Query first. Reports "quickly." Enclose S.A.S.E.
Nonfiction and Photos: Uses articles on aviation in action, worldwide; especially the offbeat aviation operation; technical articles. Style should be "unsensational, good 'international' English, informative. accurate." Length 300 to 2,000 words. Must be accompanied with good photos. Pays about 10¢ a word. Photos must be of good quality, interesting subject, striking composition, and adequately captioned. Pays $10 minimum for photos.

FLIGHT LINE TIMES, Data Publications, Box 186, Brookfield CT 06804. (203)792-5800. Editor: David A. Shugarts. Emphasizes national issues and broad interest features from within the aviation community of pilots, student pilots, airplane owners, controllers, aviation specialists, etc. Weekly tabloid; 16 pages. Estab: 1974. Pays on publication. Buys all rights. Phone queries OK. Submit seasonal/holiday material 1½ months in advance. Photocopied submissions OK. SASE. Reports in 4 weeks. Free sample copy and writer's guidelines.
Nonfiction: Exposes (on government and industry as their decisions affect the lives of aviation people); how-to (e.g., how to fly in certain tricky conditions, such as wind shear); informational; interviews (with outstanding, important and unusual people in aviation); travel (about the features—resorts, museums, vacation spots, etc.—of places to fly.) "Our outlook is not as formal as most publications. We would rather have the material in hand to look at than to answer queries and talk about writing. We have been stung too many times by people who like to promise, but don't come across with the story. On the other hand, we provide special help and advice for non-writers, when they show they have a commitment to fair, quick and accurate aviation reporting." Buys 10 mss/issue. Length: 800 words maximum. Pays $1/ column inch (maximum $10) for news stories; $20 for features at least 15 column inches long.
Photos: Mark Lacagnina, Photo Editor. Purchased with or without mss. Captions required. Pays $2.50-5 for b&w or color prints.
Columns/Departments: Restaurant reviews. Buys 1/issue. Send complete ms. Length: 400-800 words. Pays $20. Open to suggestions for new columns/departments.
Fillers: Clippings and newsbreaks. Buys 1/issue. Length: 40-60 words. Pays $1.

GENERAL AVIATION NEWS, P.O. Box 1094, Snyder TX 79549. (915)573-6318. Editor: M. Gene Dow. For pilots and aircraft owners. Tabloid newspaper; 40 pages. Established in 1950. Published every 2 weeks. Circulation: 30,000. Buys all rights. Buys 50 mss a year. Pays on acceptance. Will send sample copy to writer for 50¢. Write for copy of guidelines for writers. Will consider photocopied submissions. Reports within 1 month. Submit only complete ms. Enclose S.A.S.E.
Nonfiction and Photos: Informative, entertaining, technical, how-to, new products, etc., of general aviation (non-airline, non-military). Knowledgeable aviation articles. Informational, how-to, personal experience, interview, profile, humor, historical, think articles, expose, nostalgia, photo, travel, reviews (aviation books), spot news, successful business operations, new product, merchandising techniques, technical —all on aviation subjects. Any length. Pays $25 for 1,000 words. Pays $15 for 30 column inches for regular columns or departments. Photos purchased with accompanying ms or on assignment. Captions required. Pays $5 for b&w and color.
Fiction: Experimental, suspense, adventure, and humorous fiction on aviation subjects. Pays $25 for 1,000 words.

Poetry and Fillers: Aviation subjects. Pays $5 for poetry. Newsbreaks, clippings, jokes, short humor, and informative filler material. Pays $3.

GREAT LAKES AIRCRAFT BULLETIN, Data Publications, Box 186, Brookfield CT 06804. (203)789-5800. Editor: David A. Shugarts. Aimed at airplane owners and would-be owners in the Great Lakes states; uses articles on safety, accident reporting, features on people, places and events in the region. For further details, see the listing for *Flight Line Times.*

NORTH ATLANTIC AIRCRAFT BULLETIN, Data Publications, Box 186, Brookfield CT 06804. (203)789-5800. Editor: David A. Shugarts. For further details, see listing for *Flight Line Times,* bearing in mind that this publication puts less emphasis on accident reporting than the others in the group.

PLANE & PILOT MAGAZINE, Werner & Werner Corp., 606 Wilshire, Suite 100, Box 1136, Santa Monica CA 90401. (213)451-1423. Editor-in-Chief: Don Werner. Managing Editor: Bill Cox. Emphasizes all aspects of general aviation. Monthly magazine; 80 pages. Estab: 1965. Circ: 75,000. Pays on publication. Buys all rights. Phone queries OK. Submit seasonal/holiday material 6 months in advance. SASE. Reports in 3 months. Sample copy $1.25.
Nonfiction: How-to articles (emergency procedures); informational (proficiency); humor (strongly encouraged); personal experience (regular features on "Flight I'll Never Forget"). Buys 150 mss/year. Query. Length: 1,000-2,200 words. Pays $50-250.
Photos: Purchased with mss; no additional payment. Only uses 8x10 b&w. Prefers 2¼x2¼ slides or larger, but will consider 35mm. Query.
How To Break In: "Always query first to avoid duplication of effort. A good short query is far preferable to a complete manuscript. And good photos are almost essential to a sale."

PRIVATE PILOT, Macro/Comm Corp., 2377 S. El Camino Real, San Clemente CA 92672. (714)498-1600. Editor: Dennis Shattuck. For owner/pilots of private aircraft, for student pilots and others aspiring to attain additional ratings and experience. Established in 1955. Circulation: 90,000. Buys first North American serial rights. Buys about 60 mss/year. Pays on publication. Sample copy $2; writer's guidelines for SASE. Will consider photocopied submissions if guaranteed original. Will not consider simultaneous submissions. Reports in 30 days. Query first. Enclose S.A.S.E.
Nonfiction and Photos: Material on techniques of flying, developments in aviation, product and specific airplane test reports, travel by aircraft, development and use of airports. All must be related to general aviation field. "Freelancer must know the subject about which he is writing; use good grammar; know the publication for which he's writing; remember that we try to relate to the middle segment of the business/pleasure flying public. We see too many 'first flight' type of articles. Our market is more sophisticated than that. Most writers do not do enough research on their subject. Would like to see more material on business-related flying, more on people involved in flying." Length: 1,000 to 4,000 words. Pays $25 to $200. Material is also used in the following columns: Business Flying, Homebuilt/Experimental Aircraft, Pilot's Logbook. Length: 1,000 words. Pays $25 to $100. 8x10 b&w glossies purchased with mss or on assignment. Pays $10. Color transparencies of any size are used for the cover. Pays $75.

SOUTHERN AVIATION TIMES, Data Publications, Box 186, Brookfield CT 06804. (203)789-5800. Editor: David A. Shugarts. For airplane owners and would-be owners in the Southeastern states; uses articles on safety, accident reporting, features on people, places and events in the region. For further details, see the listing for *Flight Line Times.*

WINGS MAGAZINE, (formerly *Canadian Wings*), Corvus Publishing Group Ltd., 203-2003 McKnight Blvd., Calgary, Alberta, Canada T2E 6L2. (403)277-2337 or 277-0078. Editor-in-Chief: Wayne D. Ralph. Emphasizes aviation-private, commercial & military. The audience would range from age 15-70 and are predominately employed in aviation or with a hobbyist's interest in the field. Monthly magazine; 52 pages. Estab: 1958. Circ: 7,500. Pays on publication. Buys all rights, but may reassign following publication; one-time rights for photo material. Phone queries OK. Submit seasonal/holiday material 2 months in advance. Simultaneous, photocopied and previously published submissions OK. SASE. Reports in 1 month. Sample copy $1.
Nonfiction: Historical (mainly Canadian history); how-to (technical); humor (cartoonists' drawings); informational (technical aviation); interview (Canadian personalities in aviation circles); new product, nostalgia (historical vein); personal experience; photo feature; profile (Canadian individuals); technical; travel (flying related); aircraft handling tests and technical evaluation on new products. Buys 25 mss/year. Query. Length: 500-2,000 words. Pays $50-200.

Photos: Purchased with or without accompanying ms. Captions required. Query for photos. Pays $5-20 for 5x7 b&w glossies; $25-50 for 35mm color transparencies. No additional payment for photos accepted with accompanying ms. Total purchase price for a ms includes payment for photos.
Fillers: Clippings and newsbreaks.
How To Break In: "It helps to be a professional pilot or someone with an expert's grounding. We are a specialist publication, written by professionals for the technical aviation community. Canadian material takes priority, but news items can have a world wide slant."

Black Publications

Black general interest publications are listed in this category. Additional markets for black-oriented material are in the following sections: Business and Finance Publications, Confession Publications, Juvenile Publications, Literary and Little Publications, Poetry Publications, Politics and World Affairs Publications, Sport and Outdoor Publications, Teen and Young Adult Publications; Theater, Movie, TV and Entertainment Publications; Play Publishers, Book Publishers, Greeting Card Publishers, and Syndicates.

BLACK AMERICA MAGAZINE, Fashionable Productions Inc., 24 W. Chelten Ave., Philadelphia PA 19121. Editor-in-Chief: J. Morris Anderson. Managing Editor: Albert Cassorla. General interest for blacks. Quarterly magazine; 48 pages. Estab: 1969. Circ: 125,000. Pays on publication. Buys all rights. Photocopied submissions OK. Free sample copy and writer's guidelines.
Nonfiction: Expose; historical; informational; photo feature and profile. Buys 3-5 mss/issue. Query or submit complete ms. Length: maximum 1,750 words. Pays $25 maximum.
Photos: Purchased without accompanying manuscript. Submit contact sheet or b&w prints. Pays $15 minimum for b&w glossies. Model release required.
Fiction: Fantasy and historical (social problems-related). Length: 1,750 words. Pays $25 minimum.
Poetry: All types. Buys 6 poems/issue. Limit submissions to batches of 3. Pays $10 minimum.

BLACK FORUM MAGAZINE, Box 1090, Bronx NY 10451. Editor-in-Chief: Revish Windham. Managing Editor: Julia Coaxum. For unpublished black writers interested in literary subjects. Semiannual magazine; 48 pages. Estab: 1975. Circ: 2,000. Pays on publication. Buys first North American serial rights. Photocopied submissions OK. SASE. Reports in 1-2 months. Sample copy $1.25; free writer's guidelines.
Nonfiction: Informational; interview (with black writers, artists, etc.); and profile. Buys 2 mss/issue. Submit complete ms. Length: 750-1,000 words. Pays $15 minimum.
Photos: Reginald Ward, Photo Editor. Purchased on assignment. Query for photos.
Columns, Departments: Movie, book, theater and dance reviews. Submit complete ms. Open to suggestions for new columns/departments; address to Revish Windham.
Fiction: Fred Richardson, Fiction Editor. Adventure, experimental, historical, humorous and suspense. Buys 2 mss/issue. Submit complete ms. Length: 500-750 words. Pays $15 maximum.
Poetry: Horace Mungin, Poetry Editor. Avant-garde, free verse, light verse and traditional. Limit submissions to batches of 5. Length: maximum 20 lines. Pays in copies of magazine.
Fillers: Puzzles (subject should deal with black history). Send fillers.
How To Break In: "All material will be personally read by the editor of each department. Comments and notations will accompany all returned material. We ask that freelancers read and note our comments and continue to send in material."

CORE, 200 W. 135 St., New York NY 10030. (212)368-8104. Editor: Denise Mitchell. Publication of the Congress of Racial Equality. Estab: 1970. Bimonthly. Circ: 30,000. Rights acquired vary with author and material. Uses about 60 freelance articles/year. "Most of our articles are donated." Will send free sample copy to writer on request. Will consider photocopied submissions. Submit seasonal/holiday material at least 2 months in advance. Query. Reports in 6 months. SASE.
Nonfiction and Photos: "Articles about or related to the black movement, black people's oppression, projected or attempted solutions. Also profiles of Black Movement people. Interviews. Health, food, books, sports. Also interested in travel, fashion, movies or African affairs. The writer's style and emphasis is up to him. We like variety. Of course, it helps if his outlook is black nationalist, but it's not mandatory. We try to make black nationalism (a little

understood concept) digestible for the common man as well as the intellectual. Most articles are donated." Length: 500-5,000 words. Pays $25 for b&w photos on assignment. Captions optional.

Fiction: Should relate to magazine's theme. Length: 500-5,000 words. "Most are donated."

Poetry and Fillers: Free verse and avant-garde forms. Should relate. Length: open. Short humor and anecdotes. Length: 500-1,500 words. "Most are donated."

THE CRISIS, 1790 Broadway, New York NY 10019. (212)245-2100. Editor: Warren Marr, II. Official publication of the NAACP. "Our audience includes government officials, schools and libraries, representative of the leadership group in the black community across the nation, and persons involved in the broad area of human relations." Established in 1910 by W. E. B. Du Bois. Monthly (June/July, August/September issues are combined). Circulation: 114,000. Acquires all rights. "In most situations, upon request, we will grant permission to reprint provided proper credit is included." Uses 50 freelance mss a year. "Our payment to writers at this time is in contributor's copies only." Submit complete ms. Reports on material within a month. Enclose S.A.S.E.

Nonfiction: "Articles dealing with civil rights and general welfare of Negroes and other minorities." Informational, interview, profile, historical, think pieces, exposes. Length: 3,000 words maximum.

Fiction: Short stories with a constructive racial theme.

Poetry: Traditional forms, blank verse and free verse. Should relate to magazine's theme. Length: 40 lines maximum.

How To Break In: "What we don't get and would appreciate is material dealing with Blacks in the arts and sciences. And that means all the arts —performing, graphic, etc. We haven't had any material on Blacks in the classical music area, for instance. When dealing with other minorities, stick to material that is applicable across the board —to minorities in general. For example, how does the struggle of a Puerto Rican writer relate to the struggle of all third world writers?"

EBONY MAGAZINE, 820 S. Michigan Ave., Chicago IL 60605. Editor: John H. Johnson. Address mss to Charles L. Sanders, Managing Editor. For black readers of the U.S., Africa, and the Caribbean. Monthly. Circulation: 1,300,000. Buys all rights. Buys about 20 mss a year from freelancers. Pays on publication. Submit seasonal material 2 months in advance. Query first. Usually reports in less than 30 days, but this varies. Enclose S.A.S.E.

Nonfiction: Achievement and human interest stories about, or of concern to, black readers. Photo essays, interviews, think pieces, profiles, humor, inspirational and historical pieces are bought. Length: 2,500 words minimum. Pays $150 and up.

Photos: Purchased with mss, and with captions only. Buys 8x10 glossies, color transparencies, 35mm color. Submit negatives and contacts when possible. Photo stories. Pays $150 and up.

JET, 820 S. Michigan Ave., Chicago IL 60605. Executive Editor: Robert E. Johnson. For black readers interested in current news and trends. Weekly. Circulation: 700,000. Study magazine before submitting. Enclose S.A.S.E. for return of submissions.

Nonfiction and Photos: Articles on topics of current, timely interest to black readers. News items and features: religion, education, African affairs, civil rights, politics, entertainment. Buys informational articles, interviews, profiles, spot news, photo pieces, and personal experience articles. Length: varies. Payment to be negotiated.

PENNSYLVANIA BLACK OBSERVER, P.O. Box 72, Reading PA 19603. Editor: J. Murphy. For black audience. Established in 1972. Quarterly. Buys all rights. Payment on publication. Will send sample copy to writer for $1. Reports in 30 days. Enclose S.A.S.E.

Nonfiction, Photos, and Poetry: Articles, poetry, photos relating to black people. "We prefer short articles." Personal experience, interview, profile, humor, personal opinion, photo, and travel articles. Length: 800 to 1,500 words. Pays $10, $15, $25, depending on value of article. B&w photos purchased with accompanying ms with no additional payment. Captions required. Blank verse, free verse, and avant-garde forms of poetry; not too long. Pays $5 minimum for poetry.

SEPIA, Box 600, Wilmette IL 60091. Editor: Ben Burns. For "black readers of all age groups and interests." Monthly. Circulation: 160,000. Buys all rights. Buys about 75 mss a year from freelancers. Pays on acceptance. Will send a sample copy to a writer for $1. Will consider photocopied submissions. Submit seasonal material 3 months in advance. Reports in 1 week. Query first. Enclose S.A.S.E.

Nonfiction and Photos: "We are in the market for well-written, provocative, factual articles on the role of black Americans in all phases of American life. We look for a good writing style, no different from any popularly written publication. We are constantly in need of articles with current news value, but strictly projected for future publication. In this respect, we specifically look for queries on events that will be in the news when our magazine reaches its readers. Articles may be on interesting personalities, entertainers, sports figures, human interest or controversial topics. We will consider any subject if it has good reader appeal for a black audience. It cannot be overemphasized that contributors should study recent issues for general content and style." Buys interviews, profiles, historical articles, exposes, coverage of successful business operations, photo essays. Length: 3,000 words. Pays $200-$250. Photos are required with mss. B&w glossies, color transparencies.

Business and Finance Publications

National and regional publications of general interest to businessmen are listed here. Those in the National grouping cover national business trends, and include some material on the general theory and practice of business and financial management. Those in the Regional grouping report on the business climate of specific regions.

Magazines that use material on national business trends and the general theory and practice of business and financial management, but which have a technical, professional slant, are classified in the Trade Journals section, under the Business Management, Finance, Industrial Management, or Management and Supervision categories.

National

BARRON'S NATIONAL BUSINESS AND FINANCIAL WEEKLY, 22 Cortlandt St., New York NY 10007. (212)285-5245. Editor: Robert M. Bleiberg. For business and investment people. Weekly. Will send free sample copy to a writer on request. Buys all rights. Pays on publication. Enclose S.A.S.E.
Nonfiction: Articles about various industries with investment point of view; shorter articles on particular companies, their past performance and future prospects as related to industry trends for "News and Views" column. "Must be suitable for our specialized readership." Length: 2,000 words or more. Pays $200 to $500 for articles; $100 and up for "News and Views" material. Articles considered on speculation only.
How To Break In: "News and Views might be a good way, but the key thing to remember here is these pieces must be fully researched and thoroughly documented."

BLACK ENTERPRISE, 295 Madison Ave., New York NY 10017. Managing Editor: Phil W. Petrie. For black executives, professionals, and independent businessmen. Monthly. Established in 1970. Circulation: 215,000. Rights purchased vary with author and material. Buys 20 to 30 mss per year. Pays on acceptance. Will send free sample copy to writer on request. Will consider photocopied submissions. Will not consider simultaneous submissions. Reports in 6 to 8 weeks. Query first. Enclose S.A.S.E.
Nonfiction: Informational articles addressed to business and business-related interests of audience. Stress is on black perspective and economic framework. Unique, exclusive focus on black economic interests. Informational, how-to, personal experience, interview, profile, think articles, and successful business operations. Length: 1,500 words minimum. Pays up to $500 maximum.

BUSINESS WEEK, 1221 Avenue of the Americas, New York NY 10020. Does not solicit freelance material.

COMMODITY JOURNAL, American Assoc. of Commodity Traders, 10 Park St., Concord NH 03001. Editor-in-Chief: Arthur N. Economou. Emphasizes commodities, agriculture and energy for a highly educated and informed audience with specific interests in mind. Bimonthly magazine; 45 pages. Estab: 1965. Circ: 5,000. Pays on acceptance. Buys all rights. Phone queries OK. Simultaneous and photocopied submissions OK. SASE. Reports in 2 months.
Nonfiction: Robert J. Reinert, Nonfiction Editor. Informational (of technical nature) and technical (commodities, agriculture and alternative energy). Query. Length: 2,500 words maximum. Pays 5-10¢/word.
How To Break In: "We do not deal with futures markets, but with spot, deferred and forward contracting of commodities."

DOLLARS & SENSE, National Taxpayers Union, 325 Pennsylvania Ave., S.E., Washington DC 20003. Editor-in-Chief: Stephen J. Chapman. Emphasizes taxes and government spending for a diverse readership. Monthly newsletter; 8-12 pages. Estab: 1970. Circ: 30,000. Pays on publication. Buys all rights. Submit seasonal/holiday material 1 month in advance. Previously published submissions OK. SASE. Free sample copy and writer's guidelines.

Nonfiction: Expose (dealing with wasteful government spending, excessive regulation of the economy), and personal opinion. Buys 10 mss/year. Query. Length: 600-2,000 words. Pays $15-100. "We look for original material on subjects overlooked by the national press and other political magazines. Probably the best approach is to take a little-known area of government mismanagement and examine it closely. The articles we like most are those that examine a federal program that is not only poorly managed and wasteful, but also self-defeating, hurting the very people it is designed to help. We are also interested in the long term harm done by different kinds of taxation. Articles on IRS harassment and abuses are always needed and welcome. We have no use for financial or investment advice or broad philosophical pieces."

DUN'S REVIEW, Dun & Bradstreet Publications Corp., 666 5th Ave., New York NY 10019. (212)489-2200. Editor: Clem Morgello. Emphasizes business, management and finances for a readership "concentrated among senior executives of those companies that have a net worth of $1 million or more." Monthly magazine; 90-140 pages. Estab: 1893. Circ: 225,000. Pays on acceptance. Buys all rights. Submit seasonal/holiday material 3 months in advance. Photocopied submissions OK. Reports in 1 month. Sample copy $1.50.

Nonfiction: Expose (business and government), historical (business; i.e., law or case history), how-to (hobby that would appeal to readership), humor (business), informational (business and government), interview (assigned only), personal opinion (submitted to The Forum, opinion from high ranked sources), and profile (companies, turnarounds, etc). Buys 12 mss/year. Query. Length: 1,500-3,000 words. Pays $200 minimum.

Photos: Gene Landino, Art Director. Purchased with accompanying ms. Query. Pays $75 for b&w photos; $150 for color.

Columns/Departments: Footnotes (historical or important issues impacting business world) and The Economy (by invitation only). Buys one mss/issue. Query. Length: 1,000-1,500 words. Pays $200.

ENTERPRISING WOMEN, A Business Monthly, Artemis Enterprises, Inc., 525 West End Ave., New York NY 10024. Editor-in-Chief: Ava Stern. Monthly newsletter; 8-20 pages. Estab: 1975. Circ: 10,000. Buys all rights. Submit seasonal/holiday material 60 days in advance. Photocopied submissions OK. SASE. Reports in 2 weeks. Sample copy $1.

Nonfiction: How-to articles (on any technical aspect of small business management); informational (any topical information regarding women in business); inspirational (profiles and interviews with women business owners). Buys about 5 mss/issue. Submit complete ms. Length: 800-1,200 words. Pays $10-50.

Columns/Departments: Occasionally uses book reviews and question/answer type of material for The Forum, as well as news items (about 400 words) for Businesswomen in the News. Buys 2/issue. Query. Length: 800-1,000 words. Pays $10-30. Open to suggestions for new columns/departments.

How To Break In: "Research subjects in specific geographic locale, i.e., interview several women business owners and professionals and identify common problems for various types of articles. Write concisely and with humor on practical and applicable topics. Summarize legal, business or finance news; explain complex technical issues in simple terms."

FINANCE, Magazine of Money & Business, 8 W. 40th St., New York NY 10018. (212)682-3500. Editor: B.K. Thurlow. For managements of industrial corporations, banks and other financial companies. Magazine; 48 pages. Estab: 1940. Circ: 45,000. Buys all rights. Buys about 50 mss per year. Pays on publication. Will send free sample copy to writer on request. Write for editorial guidelines. No photocopied or simultaneous submissions. Reports on mss accepted for publication in 2 weeks. Returns rejected material in 1 week. Query first. Enclose S.A.S.E.

Nonfiction and Photos: Wants mss on a broad range of business and financial subjects. No first person mss. "Fairly sophisticated articles on business and finance. Occasional picture-text features of general interest to businessman/financier audience. Get in touch with us first: assignments may vary in this regard. *Finance* has traditionally been banking (both commercial and investment) oriented. But increasingly, we have broadened our scope to embrace a wide range of subjects of interest to our readers. Our special areas of interest are investment management, notably by bank trust departments, and international trends." Also features the column, "The Good Things in Life Besides Money" that focuses on personal interests of readers. Length for regular articles: 1,500 to 2,500 words. Pays $100 to $250. Photos purchased with ms with extra payment. Captions optional. Payment: $10 for b&w; $30 for color. Art Director: Bill Nirenberg.

FORBES, 60 Fifth Ave., New York NY 10011. "We do not buy freelance material." But, on occasion, when a writer of some standing (or whose work is at least known to them) is going abroad or into an area where they don't have regular staff or stringer coverage, they have given assignments or sometimes helped on travel expenses.

FORTUNE, 1271 Ave. of the Americas, New York NY 10020. Staff-written, but they do buy a few freelance articles (by Irwin Ross, for example) and pay extremely well for them.

FRANCHISING INVESTMENT & BUSINESS OPPORTUNITY NEWS, P.O. Box 610097, North Miami FL 33161. Editor: Edward J. Foley. For people interested in investment and business opportunities. Newspaper. Established in 1974. Monthly. Circulation: over 50,000. Buys all rights, but will reassign rights to author after publication. Buys about 10 mss a year. Pays on publication. Will send free sample copy to writer on request. Will consider photocopied submissions. No simultaneous submissions. Reports on material accepted for publication in 30 days. Does not return unsolicited material which is rejected. Query first. Enclose S.A.S.E.
Nonfiction and Photos: Business and financial articles. New ideas for money-making opportunities. Articles should tie in with current market conditions and should be preceded with an outline and query. Avoid emphasis on "old" times. Informational, spot news, successful business operations, new product. Length: 1,000 to 3,000 words. Pays 2¢ a word. $5 for b&w glossies purchased with mss. Captions required.

FREE ENTERPRISE, 800 2nd Ave., New York NY 10017. (212)697-3200. Publisher: Patrick H.W. Garrard. Emphasizes business opportunities and money making. Bimonthly magazine. Estab: 1971. Circ: 350,000. Pays on publication. Buys all rights. Free sample copy and writer's guidelines.
Nonfiction: "We are about business opportunities and money making—but we stay away from the ordinary, the dull, and corporate doings. We want stories about new fads and trends, told either in the second person or, as an inspirational profile, in the third person; both though, must contain in the text or in sidebars enough information (names, address, sources of information) for readers to go forth and prosper. We also want articles about individuals fighting big business (Washington, unions, City Hall, or big media) and exposes where the victim is the little guy." Query. Buys 150 mss/year. Length: 2,500 words maximum. Pays 10¢/ words minimum.

MBA MAGAZINE, 730 3rd Ave., New York NY 10017. (212)557-9240. Editor-in-Chief: Thomas J. Goff. Emphasizes business management. Monthly magazine; 80 pages. Estab: 1966. Circ: 160,000. Pays on the tenth of the month of publication. Buys all rights. Submit seasonal/ holiday material 4 months in advance. Simultaneous and photocopied submissions OK. SASE. Reports in 3 months. Sample copy $1.25.
Nonfiction: William West, Articles Editor. Expose (business and government regulations); how-to (business management and career planning); interview (business and government executives); profile; new product (for management market, e.g., calculators, computers); photo feature (business or economic); and technical (management science). Buys 5 mss/issue. Submit outline. Length: 500-2,000 words. Pays 10¢/word.
Photos: John Jay, Photo Editor. Purchased on assignment. Captions required. Query. Pays $25-50 per b&w photo; $75-100 for color. Model release required. Will make appointments to see portfolios.

MONEY, Time-Life Building, Rockefeller Center, New York NY 10020. Managing Editor: William Simon Rukeyser. "For the middle to upper middle income, sophisticated, well-educated reader. We picture our readers as neither insiders or idiots." Established in 1972. No freelance material.

MONEY STRATEGIES, Alexander Hamilton Institute, 605 Third Ave., New York NY 10016. Editor: Joseph R. Tigue. For high income individuals. Newsletter published every 2 weeks. Established in 1909. Buys all rights. Pays on acceptance. Will send free sample copy to writer on request. Query first. Enclose S.A.S.E.
Nonfiction: Ways to save and invest money; investment alternatives, real estate, precious

metals, art, antiques. Pithy, newsletter style of writing. No puffery. Solid copy with concrete examples. Length: 500 words average. Pays 15¢ per word.

Regional

ALASKA CONSTRUCTION & OIL MAGAZINE, 109 W. Mercer St., Seattle WA 98119. Executive Editor: Roscoe E. Laing. Production Editor: Norman P. Bolotin. For management level personnel in construction/oil/timber/mining. Monthly magazine; 100 pages. Estab: 1959. Circ: 9,500. Pays on publication. Buys first North American serial rights. Submit seasonal/holiday material 3-4 months in advance. Previously published work OK. SASE. Reports in 2 weeks. Sample copy $1. Free writer's guidelines.
Nonfiction: "Only informational articles on the fields we cover." Buys 10-15/year. Query. Length: 500-2,000 words. Pays $1.50/column inch.
Photos: Purchased with mss. Pays $10-25/5x7 or 8x10 b&w glossies; $25-50/color positives of any size.

AUSTIN MAGAZINE, Austin Chamber of Commerce, P.O. Box 1967, Austin TX 78767. Editor: Hal Susskind. A business and community magazine dedicated to telling the story of Austin and its people to Chamber of Commerce members and the community. Magazine published monthly by the Chamber; 48-64 pages, 8½x11. Established in 1960. Circulation: 5,000. Not copyrighted. Will send sample copy to writer for $1. Will consider original mss only. Reports in 1 month. Enclose S.A.S.E.
Nonfiction and Photos: Articles should deal with interesting businesses or organizations around town with emphasis on the Austin community and Chamber of Commerce members. Articles are also accepted on Austin's entertainment scene. Length: 1,000 to 2,000 words. Pays 2½¢ per word. B&w photos are purchased with mss.

B.C. BUSINESS MAGAZINE, Pacific Rim Publications Ltd., 200 1520 Alberni St., Vancouver, B.C. Canada V6G 1A3. (604)685-2376. Editor-in-Chief: J.R. Martin. Emphasizes business people in British Columbia for readership of male business executives in upper management. Monthly magazine; 48 pages. Estab: 1973. Circ: 18,000. Pays on publication. Buys all rights, but may reassign following publication. Phone queries OK. Submit seasonal/holiday material 2 months in advance. Photocopied submissions OK. SASE. Reports in 2 weeks. Sample copy $1.
Nonfiction: Expose; how-to; informational; interview; new product; personal opinion and profile. "All mss must be about companies and people in the province of British Columbia and must have a business angle." Buys 6-8 mss/issue. Query. Length: 1,000-4,000 words. Pays $50-300.

CALIFORNIA BUSINESS, 1060 Crenshaw Blvd., Los Angeles CA 90019. (213)937-1714. Editor: Paul Keil. For management executives, investors, bankers, other financial executives. Tabloid newspaper; 32 to 40 pages. Established in 1965. Every 2 weeks. Circulation: 35,000. Buys all rights, but will reassign rights to author after publication. Buys 30 to 40 mss a year. Payment within 1 to 3 weeks after publication. Will send free sample copy to writer on request. No photocopied or simultaneous submissions. Reports on material accepted for publication in 1 to 4 weeks. Returns rejected material in 2 weeks. Query first. Enclose S.A.S.E.
Nonfiction: Department editor: Arthur Garcia. Specializes in regionalized business coverage of the West. Uses business and financial news and feature stories; management, marketing,investment trend stories. Nearly all have a California or west coast angle. Virtually all stories are keyed to western readers. Informational, how-to, interview, profile, expose, personal opinion and coverage of successful business operations. Length: 250 to 2,000 words. Pays $25 to $250. Photos purchased with mss; no additional payment.
How To Break In: "Query by mail, or telephone."

CANADIAN BUSINESS MAGAZINE, 1080 Beaver Hall Hill, Montreal, H2Z 1T2, Quebec, Canada. Editor: Robin Schiele. For senior and middle management men in business and industry in late 40s or early 50s, usually educated to at least bachelor degree level. We also have significant readership among business students and university and government people. Monthly magazine. Established in 1927. Circulation: 50,000. Buys first Canadian serial rights. Buys second serial (reprint) rights, on occasion. Buys 60 to 80 mss per year. Payment on acceptance. Will send free sample copy to writer on request. Will consider photocopied submissions. Simultaneous submissions, "if so indicated." Reports within 8 weeks. Query first. Enclose S.A.S.E.

Nonfiction and Photos: Subjects pertaining directly to Canadian business, including the economic performance of the nation, a region, an industry, or a company; finance; corporate management; investments; trade relations; personnel; government action, particularly planned or newly passed legislation; how-to stories helpful to the reader in his capacity as businessman. Non-academic style, written with a complete familiarity with the Canadian scene (and how it differs from the American). Length: 1,000 to 2,500 words. Pays $100 minimum. Photos purchased with accompanying ms with no additional payment. Captions optional.

COMMERCE MAGAZINE, 130 S. Michigan Ave., Chicago IL 60603. (312)786-0111. Editor: Gordon A. Moon II. For top businessmen and industrial leaders in greater Chicago area. Also sent to chairmen of and presidents of Fortune 1,000 firms throughout United States. Monthly magazine; varies from 100 to 400 pages, (8¼x11¼). Established in 1904. Circulation: 12,000. Buys all rights, but will reassign rights to author after publication. Buys 30 to 40 mss per year. Pays on acceptance. Will send sample copy to writer for $1. Query first. Enclose S.A.S.E.
Nonfiction: Business articles and pieces of general interest to top business executives. "We select our freelancers and assign topics. Many of our writers are from local newspapers. Considerable freelance material is used but almost exclusively on assignment from Chicago area specialists within a particular business sector." Pays 4¢ to 8¢ a word.

THE FINANCIAL POST, Maclean-Hunter Ltd., 481 University Ave., Toronto, Ontario Canada M5W 1A7. Editor and Publisher: Paul S. Deacon. Managing Editor: Neville J. Nankivell. Emphasizes business, investments and public affairs for management and investors and written from a Canadian point of view for a Canadian audience. Weekly newspaper; 42 pages. Estab: 1907. Circ: 155,000. Pays on publication. Buys first Canadian rights. Phone quries OK. SASE. Reports in 6 weeks. Free sample copy.
Nonfiction: How-to; informational; and new product. Query. Length: 200-1,000 words. Pays $50-200.

HOUSTON BUSINESS JOURNAL, Cordovan Corp., 5314 Bingle Rd., Houston TX 77092. (713)688-8811. Editor-in-Chief: Mike Weingart. Emphasizes Houston business. Weekly tabloid; 36 pages. Estab: 1971. Circ: 15,000. Pays on publication. Purchases all rights. Phone queries OK ("but prefer mail"). Submit seasonal/holiday material 2 months in advance. Previously published submissions OK. SASE. Reports in 1 month. Free sample copy.
Nonfiction: Expose (business, if documented), How-to (finance, business, management, lifestyle), informational (money-making), interview (local business topics), nostalgia (possible, if business), profile (local business execs), personal experience and photo feature. Buys 100+ mss/year. Query or submit complete ms. Length: 500-2,000. Pays $2/column inch.
Photos: Purchased with or without accompanying ms or on assignment. Captions required. B&w only. Submit prints; 4x5 minimum, 11x14 maximum glossy. Pays $7.50-25.
Columns, Departments: Profile, Restaurants. Buys 100 mss/year. Query. Pays $2. Open to suggestions for new columns and departments.

NEAR EAST BUSINESS, 386 Park Ave., S., New York NY 10016. Editor: Joseph Fitchett. U.S. Editor: Martha Downing. Magazine; 60 to 80 pages. For business and government leaders (English speaking) in the Arab Middle East, Iran and Turkey. Established in 1976. Every 2 months. Circulation: 14,000. Buys first serial rights. Buys 6 to 8 mss per year. Pays on publication. Will send a sample copy to a writer on request. Will consider photocopied submissions. Reports in 1 month. Enclose S.A.S.E.
Nonfiction: Stories and news items relating to business, industry, markets, management in the Middle East, Iran and Turkey. Length: 1,000 to 2,000 words. Pays average of $250.

THE NEW ENGLANDER, Dublin NH 03444. (603)563-8111. Editor-in-Chief: Brad Ketchum, Jr. Emphasizes business and public affairs in New England. For "executives and public officials in 6 New England states, age 25-65, college educated, upper income." Monthly magazine; 80 pages. Estab: 1953. Circ: 17,400. Pays on acceptance or publication. Purchases all rights, but may reassign following publication. Submit seasonal/holiday material 6 weeks in advance. Previously published submissions OK. SASE. Reports in 2 weeks. Free sample copy (if in New England).
Nonfiction: Expose (government regulation, business); How-to (business, management); informational (regional needs); interview (key business and public leaders); personal opinion; profile; travel (recreation in New England); personal experience; and photo feature (any related to New England business or regional interest). Buys 7 mss/issue. Query. Length: 500-3,000. Pays $75/printed page.

Photos: Bruce Hammond, photo editor. Purchased with accompanying ms or on assignment. Captions required. Submit 5x7 or 8x10 glossy for b&w, 2¼x2¼ or 4x5 for color. Query or send contact sheet. Pays $25-150 per photo for both color or b&w. Photos must relate to publication's subject matter.

Columns, Departments: Booked for Business (reviews), Business Update (regional economy), Talking Stock (investments) Notes & Comments (misc.). Buys 30 columns an issue. Query. Length: 1,000-2,000 words. Pays $25/10" column. Open to suggestions for new columns or departments.

How To Break In: "Submit article idea in brief written outline staying with New England topics."

NORTHWEST INVESTMENT REVIEW, 220 S.W. Alder St., Portland OR 97212. (503)224-6004. Editor-in-Chief: Shannon P. Pratt. For investors and corporate leaders who pay $135 a year to read about the 200 plus northwestern publicly held corporations covered by this publication. Newsletter; 6-20 pages. Established in 1971. Semimonthly. Not copyrighted. Pays on publication. Will send sample packet of newsletters to writer for $2.50. No photocopied or simultaneous submissions. Reports on material accepted for publication in 2 to 4 weeks. Returns rejected material as soon as possible. Query first to J. Michael Reid. Enclose S.A.S.E.

Nonfiction: "We need top articles, appealing to investors." Corporate profiles, personnel changes, industry surveys. "If well researched in our field, we will consider freelance work; ideally, from business page writers, individuals with finance/security backgrounds." Length: 500 to 2,500 words. "With query first, we would quote what the piece would be worth to us. Many are done for a fee. No set minimum."

PACIFIC BUSINESS MAGAZINE, P.O. Box 1736, Sacramento CA 95808. (916)444-6670. Editor: Carla Goodman. For top executives from all California businesses; most are members of the California Chamber of Commerce. Magazine; 36 pages. Established in 1910. Bimonthly. Circulation: 10,000. Buys one-time rights. Buys about 7 mss a year. Pays on publication. Will send sample copy to writer on request. Will consider photocopied submissions. No simultaneous submissions. Reports on material accepted for publication in 1 month. Returns rejected material in 2 weeks. Query first or submit complete ms. Enclose S.A.S.E.

Nonfiction: Articles on California business and economy, individual companies, trends in all California industries, governmental and legislative developments affecting California business, and human interest articles with a business slant. Regular interviews with California legislators and business executives. Emphasis on clear, factual approach, well-documented material, written in feature style. Length: 1400-1600 words. Pays $75. Not interested in product production, how-to, and technical articles.

PERSPECTIVE ON MONEY, Financial Times of Canada, 1885 Leslie St., Toronto, Ontario (Don Mills) Canada M3B 3J4. Editor: Paul Nowack. Emphasizes spending, saving and investing money for high income — in middle or upper management as well as professionals and self-employed readership. Quarterly magazine; 40-48 pages. Estab: 1974. Circ: 200,000. Pays on acceptance. Buys all rights. Submit seasonal/holiday material 3 months in advance. SASE. Reports in 3 weeks. Free sample copy.

Nonfiction: How-to and informational (Canadian angle). Buys 16 mss/year. Query. Length: 1,500-3,000 for features. Pays $250-500.

THE SOUTH MAGAZINE, Trend Publications, Inc., Box 2350, Tampa FL 33601. Editor-in-Chief: Roy B. Bain. Emphasizes "business and urban affairs for 25-60-year-old business and community leaders across the South." Bimonthly magazine; 64 pages. Estab: 1973. Circ: 45,000. Pays on acceptance. Buys first North American serial rights. SASE. REports in 1 month. Sample copy $1; free writer's guidelines.

Nonfiction and Photos: Business and economic trends, industry stories affecting the South, profiles, articles on urban growth patterns and problems, major restorations (example, Atlanta's Inman Park or Underground Atlanta), articles with government/agency interplay with community or business patterns, education articles. Length: 300 to 2,000 words. Pays $75 to $300. Photos purchased with or without accompanying ms. Captions required. 5x7 or 8x10 b&w glossies; high contrast. High quality, sharp color, 35mm or 2¼x2¼ transparencies. "Payment depends on prearrangements at our discretion."

SOUTHERN CALIFORNIA JOURNAL OF COMMERCE, 4000 Westerly Place, Newport Beach CA 92660. Editor: Jim Wolcott. For business executives. Business news magazine; 32 (8½x11) pages. Established in 1975. Monthly. Circulation: 30,000. Buys all rights. Buys 40 to

50 mss a year. Pays on acceptance. Will send sample copy to writer for $1. Will consider photocopied submissions. Reports in 4 weeks. Query first. Enclose S.A.S.E.

Nonfiction and Photos: Business news and features with a local (Southern California) angle or slant. Journalistic style. Industry trend stories and profiles of interesting executives, including success stories and how success was achieved. Informational, how-to, interview, profile, humor, think articles, spot news, successful business operations, and new product articles. Length: 800 words. Pays 3¢ a word. Photos purchased with accompanying ms. Captions required. Pays $5 for each 5x7 or 8x10 b&w photo.

TIDEWATER VIRGINIAN, (formerly *New Norfolk*), P.O. Box 327, Norfolk VA 23501. Editor: Marilyn Goldman. For members of Norfolk, Portsmouth, Chesapeake and Virginia Beach chambers of commerce. Magazine; 48 pages. Established in 1943. Monthly. Circulation: 10,000. Copyrighted. Buys about 24 mss a year. Pays on publication. Will send sample copy to writer for $1. Will consider photocopied and simultaneous submissions. Reports in 2 to 3 weeks. Query first or submit complete ms. Enclose S.A.S.E.

Nonfiction: Articles dealing with business and industry in Norfolk, Virginia, and surrounding area of southeastern Virginia (Tidewater area only). Profiles, successful business operations, new product, merchandising techniques, book reviews. Length: 500 to 1,500 words. Pays $25 to $100.

CB Radio

CB GUIDE, Jess Publishing, 16146 Covello St., Van Nuys CA 91406. Editor-in-Chief: Kenneth Doe. Emphasizes CB radios, scanners, etc. Monthly magazine; 100 pages. Estab: 1976. Circ: 200,000. Pays on publication. Buys all rights, but may reassign following publication. Phone queries OK. Submit seasonal/holiday material 3 months in advance. Previously published submissions OK. SASE. Reports in 1 month.

Nonfiction: Michael McCready, Articles Editor. How-to (building CB radio accessories, unique radio installations, etc.; informational (original, interesting uses of CB radios and personalities who use CB). Buys 2-3 mss per issue. Query. Length: 500-5,000 words. Pays $20-175.

Photos: David Weeks, Department Editor. No additional payment for 3x7 or 8x10 b&w glossies. Send prints. Rarely buys color. Model release required.

How To Break In: "Our most serious need from freelancers is good, detailed how-to mss with several close-up photos of the work."

Rejects: "Mss without accompanying photos. Articles that encourage or explain how to violate FCC regulations concerning CB radio."

CB LIFE, Petersen Publishing Co., 8490 Sunset Blvd., Los Angeles CA 90069. (213)657-5100. Editor-in-Chief: Johann William Rush. For CB radio users of all ages, all interests. Monthly magazine; 76 pages. Estab: 1976. Circ: 200,000. Pays on acceptance. Buys all rights but may reassign following publication. Phone queries OK. Submit seasonal/holiday material 4 months in advance. SASE. Reports in 3 weeks. Free sample copy and writer's guidelines.

Nonfiction: Bob Mann, Articles Editor. Expose ("unusual" application of CB radio); how-to (install, make installations work better, CB rigs, antennas—base and mobile); informational (how different parts of CB operate—semi-technical); humor (true, but funny CB stories); inspirational (how CB has helped save lives and helped shut-ins); interviews (famous people who use CB, people with interesting rigs); nostalgia (crude radio communications in the old days); personal experience (lifesaving cases, truckers' true stories); personal opinion (mainly reports on FCC activities in Washington); photo features (all freelance articles should be illustrated); profile (with REACT, ALERT and other Channel 9 teams); technical (semi-technical reports on how transmitters, receivers, antennas work); travel (on the road with CB, vacations, camping, must be CB-oriented). Buys 10 mss/issue. Query. Length: 1,000-3,000 words. Pays $50-800 (average is $100/magazine page).

Photos: Purchased with or without mss. Captions required. Query or send contact sheet. No additional payment for 8x10 b&w glossies or color purchased with mss.

Columns/Departments: Sideband, Boating With CB, Antenna, Outdoors columns. Buys 4/issue. Query. Length: 1,000-2,000 words. Pays $100-200. Open to suggestions for new columns/departments.

Poetry: Traditional forms of poetry, free verse, light verse. Buys 4/year. Send poems in — "but it better be funny". Limit submissions to 5. Length: 200-1,000 words. Pays $50-150.

How To Break In: "The quickest way to break in is to write a news-type report on a specific CB related event such as a major 'jamboree'. We always need good photos to go with the story. We can run photo-only stories if caption info is complete. Meeting deadlines and exclusivity are more important in some cases than clean copy."

CB MAGAZINE, 531 N. Ann Arbor, Oklahoma City OK 73127. Editor-in-Chief: Leo G. Sands (212)986-6596, New York City). Managing Editor: Edward K. Minderman (405)947-6113 Oklahoma City). For operators of citizens band 2-way radiotelephones for personal and business communications. Established in 1964. Monthly. Circulation: 305,000. Full rights purchased worldwide. May buy all rights but will sometimes reassign rights to author after publication. Buys 4 or more mss/year. Payment on publication. Will send sample copy to writer for $1.50. Will consider photocopied and cassette submissions. Will not consider simultaneous submissions. Reports on material in 30 days. Query first. Enclose S.A.S.E.
Nonfiction and Photos: Case histories of use of citizens band radio in saving lives, etc. Semitechnical articles about equipment installation and repair. Interested in true life stories where CB radio was used to render public service. Not interested in social events concerning CB radio operator clubs. Uses informational, how-to, personal experiences articles; expose and technical. Length: 500 to 1,500 words. Payment varies. B&w photos purchased with accompanying mss; no additional payment.
How To Break In: "Report on a significant incident such as the use of CB radio in a search and rescue operation or at the scene of an accident or disaster. We cannot use material about social and fund raising activities of CB radio users."

CB TIMES, Charlton Publications, Inc., The Charlton Bldg., Derby CT 06418. (203)735-3381. Editor-in-Chief: John E. Bartimole. For anyone involved in CBing. Bimonthly magazine; 64 pages. Estab: 1976. Circ: 150,000. Pays on publication. Buys all rights. Phone queries OK. Submit seasonal/holiday material 4 months in advance. SASE. Reports in 2 weeks. Sample copy 50¢.
Nonfiction: "We want any type of article which would interest CBers. In other words, nothing to do with CBs is out of bounds. In fact, some of our most popular articles have been extremely offbeat. We pride ourselves on being the only CB magazine which devotes itself primarily to the 'human' side of CB. So, we're interested in humor, expose, information—just about anyting—as long as it has a shred of CB in it." Buys 8-10 mss/issue. Query or submit complete ms. Length: 1,000-11,000 words. Pays $25 minimum.
Photos: B&w (8½x11 glossies) and color 2¼x2¼ or 35mm) purchased with or without mss. Captions required. "If someone's thinking about submitting a color transparency for a cover, he might be better off querying, but we'll look at unsolicited cover shots, too." Pays $5 minimum for b&w; $25 minimum for color.
Fiction: "We pioneered the field in CB fiction—and we're always looking for fiction pieces dealing with CB and its people. We'll look at any type of fiction dealing with CB." Buys 1 ms/ issue. Query or submit complete ms. Length: 1,000 words minimum. Pays $50 minimum.
Fillers: Clippings, jokes, gags, anecdotes, newsbreaks, short humor. "This is a new area for us. We're giving it a try, experimentally." Send complete ms. Length: 500 words maximum. Pays $5 minimum.
How To Break In: "Just write the best you can on any subject dealing with CB. We'll look at everything. We feel every manuscript deserves an equal shot. Everyone started out as an 'unknown' writer once—we're always looking for fresh new talent. We are currently in need of freelance material, and we sincerely hope that need never diminishes. Freelancers will be a constant source of new ideas for us. We ask freelancers to remember one thing, and this keys our whole editorial philosophy: We emphasize the 'human' side of CB. CBers are people who are interested in other people, in communicating. That's what keys our contents, good buddies!"
Rejects: Super-technical articles and unprofessional looking mss. "Neatness does count!"

Child Care and Parental Guidance Publications

The following publications are concerned with child care and parental guidance. Other categories that include markets that buy items about child care for special columns and features are: Confession, Religious, and Women's in Consumer Publications; Education Journals in Trade Journals.

AMERICAN BABY MAGAZINE, 575 Lexington Ave., New York NY 10022. (212)752-0775. Editor-in-Chief: Judith Nolte. Emphasizes infant care. Monthly magazine; 58 pages. Estab: 1938. Circ: 1,600,000. Pays on publication. Buys all rights, but may reassign following publication. Phone queries OK. Submit seasonal/holiday material 3-4 months in advance. Photocopied and previously published submissions OK. SASE. Reports in 2-3 weeks. Free sample copy and writer's guidelines.
Nonfiction: How-to (all aspects of infant care); informational (medical, psychological, emotional aspects of pregnancy, birth, child care); humor (related to child raising up to age 3); inspirational (personal experience related to pregnancy, childbirth, child care); interview (medical experts, celebrities, relating to pregnancy, birth); profile; new product; and personal experience. Buys 50 mss/year. Submit complete ms. Length: 300-2,000 words. Pays $50-300. No breast feeding or childbirth experience articles.
Photos: Jeanne Dzienciol, Photo Editor. Purchased with accompanying ms or on assignment. Query. Pays $25-100 for 8x10 b&w prints; $100-300 for 35mm color transparencies. Model release required.
Columns, Departments: Frankly for Father (male slant on any aspect of parenthood); My Own Experience (reader personal experience related to pregnancy, birth or child care. Must illustrate how experience changed writer's attitude or taught lesson). Buys 25 mss/year. Submit complete ms. Length: 500-1,000 words. Pays $50-150.
Fillers: Jokes, gags, anecdotes, short humor, household tips, cute kids' sayings. Length: 50-200 words. Pays $5-50.

BABY CARE, 52 Vanderbilt Ave., New York NY 10017. Editor: Evelyn A. Podsiadlo. Assistant Editor: Doris Youdelman. For "mothers of babies from birth through the first year." Quarterly. Circulation: 500,000. Rights purchased vary with author and material. May buy all rights, first North American serial rights, or second serial rights. Payment on acceptance. Will send a free sample copy to a writer on request. Will send editorial guidelines sheet to a writer on request. Submit seasonal material 5 to 6 months in advance. Reports in 1 to 4 weeks. Enclose S.A.S.E.
Nonfiction: Feature articles "include basic infant care (bathing, feeding, common illness, safety); emotional and physical development; how-to's; effect of new baby on family relations; seasonal topics (travel, summer or winter care). Shorter features with a humorous, narrative or reflective approach. Articles can be first-person accounts by mothers and fathers, but prefer medical subject to be written by M.D.'s and R.N.'s or writer who can work well with doctors." Worthy material is used to aid mothers of the very young child. Buys informational, how-to, personal experience, inspirational, humor, nostalgia and travel. Length: 1,000 to 1,800 words. Pays $50 to $125; and slightly higher to professionals such as M.D.'s. Regular columns that seek freelance material are: "Family Corner" —shorter anecdotes about life with the new baby. Pays $10. "Focus on You" —500-word mss focusing on a mother's feelings, personal interests or family relationships in regard to the baby. Pays $25.
Poetry: Uses poetry occasionally; all forms. Length: 4 to 24 lines. Pays $5 to $10. Should relate to subject matter.

BABY TALK, 66 E. 34th St., New York NY 10016. Editor: Patricia Irons. For new and expectant mothers interested in articles on child development and baby care. Monthly. Established in 1934. Circulation: over 750,000. Buys first North American serial rights. Payment on acceptance. Submit only complete ms. Enclose S.A.S.E.
Nonfiction and Photos: "Articles on all phases of baby care. Also true, unpublished accounts of pregnancy, life with baby or young children. Write simple, true experience articles, not too lengthy. Informational, how-to, personal experience, inspirational, humor, think pieces, personal opinion, photo, travel (with babies), and new product articles. Pays $20-50. B&w and color photos are sometimes purchased with or without ms. Payment varies.

EXCEPTIONAL PARENT, Room 708, Statler Office Bldg., 20 Providence St., Boston MA 02116. (617)482-0480. Editors: Dr. Stanley D. Klein, Dr. Maxwell J. Schleifer. Associate Editor: Dr. Lewis B. Klebanoff. Managing Editor: John Griffin. Magazine provides practical guidance for parents and professionals concerned with the care of children with disabilities (physical disabilities, emotional problems, mental retardation, learning disabilities, perceptual disabilities, deafness, blindness, chronic illness, etc.). Established in 1971. Bimonthly. Circulation: 12,000. Buys all rights. Buys about 20 mss/year. Pays on publication. Sample copy for $2.50; writer's guidelines for SASE. Send query with outline. Reports in 6 months. Enclose S.A.S.E.
Nonfiction and Photos: "The general intent of the magazine is to provide practical guidance for the parents and professionals concerned with the care of children with disabilities. We print

articles covering every conceivable subject within this area, including legal issues, tax information, recreation programs, parent groups, etc. This is a consumer publication within a very specialized market. That we provide practical guidance cannot be stressed too strongly. Articles should be jargon-free. Articles within special areas are checked by an advisory board in the medical and allied professions. There is no other magazine of this type." Buys how-to's, personal experience articles. Length: 200 words maximum. Pays 5¢ a word. Photos accompanied by signed releases are of interest.

EXPECTING, 52 Vanderbilt Ave., New York NY 10017. Editor: Evelyn A. Podsiadlo. Assistant Editor: Doris Youdelman. Issued quarterly for expectant mothers. Buys all rights. Pays on acceptance. Reports in 2 to 4 weeks after receipt of ms. Enclose S.A.S.E.
Nonfiction: Prenatal development, layette and nursery planning, budgeting, health, fashions, husband-wife relationships, naming the baby, minor discomforts, childbirth, expectant fathers, working while pregnant, etc. Length: 800 to 1,600 words. Pays $50 to $125 for feature articles, somewhat more for specialists.
Fillers: Short humor and interesting or unusual happenings during pregnancy or at the hospital; maximum 100 words, $10 on publication; submissions to "Happenings" are not returned. Other fillers pay up to $40.

HOME LIFE, Sunday School Board, 129 Ninth Ave., N., Nashville TN 37234. (615)251-2271. Editor-in-Chief: George W. Knight. Emphasizes Christian family life. For married adults of all ages, but especially newlyweds and middle-aged marrieds. Monthly magazine; 64 pages. Estab: 1947. Circ: 850,000. Pays on acceptance. Buys all rights. Phone queries OK, but written queries preferred. Submit seasonal/holiday material 9-10 months in advance. SASE. Reports in 6 weeks. Free sample copy and writer's guidelines.
Nonfiction: How-to (good articles on child care and marriage); informational (about some current family-related issue of national significance such as "Our Drinking Teenagers" or "Mainstreaming a Common Sense Approach to Unemployment in the Family"); personal experience (informed articles by people who have solved family problems in healthy, constructive ways). Buys 10 mss/month. Submit complete ms. Length: 1,200-3,000 words. Pays $25-50.
Fiction: "Our fiction should be family related and should show a strong moral about how families face and solve problems constructively." Buys 12/year. Submit complete ms. Length: 1,600-2,400 words. Pays $35-60.
How To Break In: "Study the magazine to see our unique slant on Christian family life. We prefer a life-centered case study approach, rather than theoretical essays on family life."
For '78: "Particularly interested in marriage articles directed to newlyweds and middle-aged marrieds."

MOTHERS' MANUAL MAGAZINE, 176 Cleveland Dr., Croton-on-Hudson NY 10520. (914)271-8926. Editor-in-Chief: Beth Waterfall. Emphasizes parenting. Magazine published every 2 months; 52 pages. Estab: 1964. Circ: 900,000. Pays on publication. Buys all rights. Submit seasonal/holiday material 5-6 months in advance. SASE. Reports in 6 weeks. Sample copy 50¢.
Nonfiction: How-to, humor, informational, inspirational, interview, personal experience and personal opinion. Submit complete ms. Length: 500-2,500 words. Pays 2-5¢/published word; $10-500/article.
Poetry: Lorraine Morris, Poetry Editor. Free Verse, light verse and traditional. Buys 72/year. Pays 50¢/line; $3-30.

PARENTS' MAGAZINE, 52 Vanderbilt Ave., New York NY 10017. Editor: Genevieve Millet Landau. Special issues: March (Nutrition); September (Education); November (Health). Monthly. Circulation: 1,500,000. Usually buys all rights; sometimes buys North American serial rights only. Pays on acceptance. Free sample copy. Reports on submissions in 3 weeks. Query first; enclose outline and sample opening. Enclose S.A.S.E.
Nonfiction: "We are interested in well-documented articles on the problems and success of preschool, school-age, and adolescent children —and their parents; good, practical guides to the routines of baby care; articles which offer professional insights into family and marriage relationships; reports of new trends and significant research findings in education and in mental and physical health; articles encouraging informed citizen action on matters of social concern. We prefer a warm, colloquial style of writing, one which avoids the extremes of either slanginess or technical jargon. Anecdotes and examples should be used to illustrate points which can then be summed up by straight exposition." Length: up to 2,500 words. Payment varies, starting from a base of $350.

Fillers: Anecdotes for "Family Clinic," illustrative of parental problem solving with children and teenagers. Pays $10.

YOUNG FAMILY, J.L. Hunt Publications, Ltd., 37 Hanna Ave., Box 8, Station C, Toronto, Canada M6J 3M8. Editor-in-Chief: Mrs. Myroslava Baker. Emphasizes issues of interest to parents with young children. Quarterly magazine; 48 pages. Estab: 1975. Circ: 300,000. Pays on publication. Buys first Canadian serial rights. Submit seasonal/holiday material 4 months in advance. Simultaneous, photocopied and previously published submissions OK. Free sample copy and writer's guidelines.
Nonfiction: Larry Osborn, Nonfiction Editor. How-to (home improvements, redecorating, gardening, landscaping); humor (directly relating to theme); informational (investigative and social nature pertaining to young Canadian family). Buys 15 mss/year. Query. Length: 450-3,150 words. Pays 5-10¢/word.
Fiction: Larry Osborn, Fiction Editor. Humor and mainstream. Buys 3 mss/year. Query. Length: 350-2,000 words. Pays 10¢/word.
Photos: Pays $50 for b&w glossies; $100-150 for 35mm color transparencies.

YOUR BABY (service section of *Modern Romances* magazine), *Modern Romances*, 1 Dag Hammarskjold Plaza, New York NY 10017. Buys all rights. Pays on acceptance. Reports in 1 month. Enclose S.A.S.E.
Nonfiction: Uses warmly written, genuinely helpful articles of interest to mothers of children from birth to three years of age, dealing authoritatively with pregnancy problems, child health, child care and training. Should open with an illustrative incident. Editors recommend you study this market before trying to write for it. Length: about 1,000 words. Pays $100. Submissions should be addressed to Service Director, *Modern Romances*. "We continuously receive letters addressed to Your Baby. There is no magazine called Your Baby. This is simply a department within *Modern Romances* magazine."

College, University, and Alumni

The following publications are intended for students, graduates, and friends of the institution. Publications for college students in general are found in the Teen and Young Adult category.

ALCALDE, P.O. Box 7278, Austin TX 78712. (512)476-6271. Editor: Sarah Jane English. The University of Texas at Austin Alumni Magazine for ex-students from the University of Texas with interests in travel, arts, theatre, sports, education; any aspect of life. Magazine; 64 pages. Established in 1913. Bimonthly. Circulation: 28,000. Not copyrighted. Buys 10-15 mss a year. Pays on acceptance. Will consider photocopied submissions. No simultaneous submissions. Reports on material accepted for publication in time to meet their deadline. Returns rejected material immediately. Query first. Enclose S.A.S.E.
Nonfiction and Photos: Articles must be connected with the University of Texas in some way and feature its interests, purposes, history, etc. Informational, personal experience, interview, profile, humor, historical, nostalgia, photo, travel. Length: 500 to 2,000 words; 1,000 words preferred. Pays 4¢ a word. Additional payment for 8x10 b&w glossies used with ms if requested in advance. Captions optional.

CLIFTON MAGAZINE, University of Cincinnati, 204 Tangeman University Center, University of Cincinnati, Cincinnati OH 45221. (513)475-6379. Editor-in-Chief: David A. Ginter. For the university community, students, faculty, administrators, residents of the area. Published once each academic quarter (autumn, winter, spring). Magazine; 52 pages. Estab: 1972. Circ: 1,200. Pays on publication. Buys all rights, but may reassign following publication. Phone queries OK, but written queries preferred. Submit seasonal/holiday material 3 months in advance, but query first. Photocopied submissions OK. SASE. Reports in 4 weeks. Sample copy $1. Free writer's guidelines.
Nonfiction: Joe Bobbey, Articles Editor. Expose (government, education, environmental, consumer, life style, industry); historical (but only if community of Clifton or old Cincinnati); how-to (survival type, but no recipes); humor (especially satire); informational (especially dealing with the bureaucracy); interviews, profiles and photo features. Buys 5/issue. Query. Length 1,000-1,400 words. Pays $10-20.
Photos: B&w glossies (5x7 or 8x10) used with mss. No additional payment. Captions required. Query.

Fiction: John Ficociello, Department Editor. Erotica (if responsible and in good taste, i.e., esthetically); experimental (thematic, not formal); fantasy (but not sci-fi); humorous (short); mainstream (not cliche). Buys 1-2/issue. Send complete ms. Length: 1,000-1,600 words. Payment: 2 contributor's copies.

Poetry: Avant-garde and traditional forms of poetry, free verse, or formal poems. Buys 10-15/issue. Send poems in. Limit submissions to 6. Length: open. Payment: 2 contributor's copies.

MISSISSIPPI STATE UNIVERSITY ALUMNUS, Mississippi State Univ. Alumni Assoc., Editorial Office, Box 4930, Mississippi State MS 39762. (601)325-6343. Editor-in-Chief: Bob V. Moulder. Emphasizes articles about Mississippi State graduates and former students. For well-educated and affluent audience. Quarterly magazine; 32 pages. Estab: 1921. Circ: 13,875. Pays on publication. Buys one-time rights. Phone queries OK. Submit seasonal/holiday material 3 months in advance. Simultaneous, photocopied and previously published submissions OK. SASE. Reports in 1 month. Free sample copy.

Nonfiction: Historical, humor (with strong MSU flavor; nothing risque), informational, inspirational, interview (with MSE grads), nostalgia (early days at MSU), personal experience, profile and travel (by MSU grads, but must be of wide interest). Buys 2-3 mss/year ("but welcome more submissions.") Send complete ms. Length: 500-2,500 words. Pays $10-25 (including photos, if used).

Photos: Photos purchased with accompanying ms. Captions required. No additional payment for photos accepted with accompanying ms. Uses 8x10 b&w photos.

Columns/Departments: Statesmen "A section of the Alumnus that features briefs about alumni achievements and professional or business advancement. We do not use engagements, marriages or births. There is no payment for Statemen briefs.")

How To Break In: "We welcome articles about MSU grads in interesting occupations and have used stories on off-shore drillers, miners, horse trainers, etc. We also want profiles on prominent MSU alumni and have carried pieces on Senator John C. Stennis, comedian Jerry Clower and baseball manager, Alex Grammas."

Comic Book Publications

GOLD KEY COMICS, 850 Third Ave., New York NY 10022. Editor: Wallace I. Green. For children, ages 6 to 15. "Most titles are issued every 2 months or quarterly." Circulation: 150,000 to 250,000. Buys all rights. Payment on acceptance. Enclose S.A.S.E.

Comics: "Our main product is comic books; 65 titles. We publish our own animated and adventure titles as well as licensed animated and adventure properties; e.g., Bugs Bunny, Heckle and Jeckle. I would prefer that potential authors *do not write us just to inquire* as to whether or not we are interested and what kind of material to submit. I suggest the following procedure: Buy copies of our various comics, particularly those you think you can write. If you don't know which ones suit you, you can determine that after reading them. Become familiar with the characters and the kinds of stories we use in particular titles. Write a number of story synopses (keep them brief, please) aimed for particular publications. At the same time, let us know whether you have had any experience writing comics so we'll know how much instruction to give you about the form to follow when writing a script. This last applies only if we like the synopses. We prefer to deal personally with authors, rather than through the mails. But I'd rather anyone who is interested send in his first synopses. We can meet personally later if it seems worthwhile. Our manuscript rate is $10 per page (mss are written page for page with the printed comic). Since we have several writers who produce stories on a more or less regular basis, I do not want to sound overly encouraging. But ours is not a closed shop. There's always room for someone with original and imaginative ideas who can turn them into sound, workable scripts."

Confession Publications

The confession market has come a long way since the old hide-under-the-mattress days, upgrading itself to "family counselor" status. Although a very lucrative market for writers (especially personal experience stories), editors still invent titles that often make even a veteran confession writer blush. Such titles are usually come-ons.

Another concern among freelancers is the cheaper looking appearance of even the best confession magazines. Those magazines that used to be slick are apparently caught in the paper crunch, using part pulp and part coated stock. What's ahead if the paper shortage continues? Will a cheapened appearance cost the reader and writer the respect the markets have gained in recent years? This is unlikely since readers are becoming used to this stock in other publications, as well.

Marketing Tip: Confession magazines may use psychic phenomena and supernatural stories, even though some use them very rarely. These stories should not be in the realm of fantasy; they must be plausible. Male-narrator or humorous stories might be another type they'll consider. Suspense crime yarns are always well received if the confessional tone is preserved. Courtroom stories and mental health problems are usually sure sales. It might be wise to query the confession editor first about these out-of-the ordinary stories.

BRONZE THRILLS, 1220 Harding St., Ft. Worth TX 76102. Editor: Mrs. Edna K. Turner. Monthly magazine; 96 pages. Established in 1957. Circulation: 80,000. Buys all rights. Buys 60 mss a year. Payment on acceptance. Will send free sample copy to writer on request. Write for copy of guidelines for writers. Reports in 90 days. Submit complete ms. Enclose S.A.S.E.
Fiction: All material must relate to blacks. Romance or confession; black-oriented. Particularly interested in occult themes or those concerned with UFO's or mental illness. Does not want to see anything dealing with pregnancy, venereal disease, virginal girls getting pregnant after "first mistake" or old woman/young man love affairs unless the story has an unusual angle. Length: 4,000 to 6,000 words. Pays $30.
Photos: B&w and color photos are purchased on assignment. 8x10 b&w glossies. 2¼x2¼ or 4x5 color transparencies. Pays $35 for b&w; $50 for color.

DARING ROMANCES, Ideal Publishing Corp., 575 Madison Ave., New York NY 10022. For women 14-70; some men, blue collar. Monthly magazine; 68 pages. Estab: 1976. Pays on publication. Buys all rights. Submit seasonal/holiday material 6 months in advance. SASE. Reports in 2 months.
Fiction: Confession and romance; nothing hopeless or depressing.
How To Break In: "Come up with a good, original confession idea, or try a new twist on an old theme."

EXCITING CONFESSIONS, Ideal Publishing Corp., 575 Madison Ave., New York NY 10022. Editor: Johanna Roman Smith. Emphasizes sex, romance, human relations. Monthly magazine; 68 pages. Estab: 1976. Pays on acceptance. Buys all rights. Submit seasonal/holiday material 5 months in advance. SASE. Reports in 6-8 weeks. Free writer's guidelines.
Fiction: Confessions and romances. Prefers strong sex theme, but not pornography. Buys 10/ issue. Submit complete ms. Length: 2,000-6,000 words. Pays 3¢/word; $175 maximum.

INTIMATE ROMANCES, Magazine Management, 575 Madison Ave., New York NY 10022. Editorial Director: Cara Sherman. Requirements same as *Intimate Secrets.*

INTIMATE SECRETS, Magazine Management, 575 Madison Ave., New York NY 10022. Editorial Director: Cara Sherman. For women between the ages 16-30. Magazine. Circ: 170,000. Pays on acceptance. Buys all rights. Submissions addressed to *Intimate Secrets* are also considered for publication for *Intimate Romances, My Romance,* and *True Secrets.* Reports in 4-6 weeks. Free writer's guidelines.
Nonfiction: "Though wo do not purchase much nonfiction, if the subject is of interest, relevance, and handled appropriately for our readership, we'll consider it." Length: 3,000-5,000 words. Pays $125-150.
Fiction: "We look primarily for tender love stories, touching baby stories, and stories dealing with identifiable marital problems, particularly sexual. We are interested in realistic teen stories, and on occasion, male-narrated stories, and tales with supernatural overtones. Stories should be written in the first-person. They should deal with a romantic or emotional problem that is identifiable and realistically portrays how the narrator copes with her conflict and resolves it. We reject stories based on hackneyed themes and outdated attitudes. In our contemporary society, stories condemming premarital sexual experience, abortion, and those that preach chastity, etc., are unsuitable for our needs." Length: 1,500-6,000 words. Pays $75-150.
How To Break In: Avoid the "sin-suffer-repent" syndrome. Tailor your needs to suit a young, rural audience who, though unsophisticated, no longer live by Puritanical values."

INTIMATE STORY, 575 Madison Ave., New York NY 10022. Editor: Janet Wandel. For women; 14- to 70-years-old; small minority men; blue-collar. Magazine; 74 pages. Established in 1948. Monthly. Circulation: 170,000. Buys all rights. Buys about 100 mss per year. Pays on acceptance. Rarely sends sample copies. No photocopied or simultaneous submissions. Submit seasonal material 6 months in advance. Reports in 2 months. Enclose S.A.S.E.

Fiction: "Sex oriented and human interest stories; all types of fictional confession stories. Always first person; always enough dialogue. Our stories are within the realm of the believable." Does not want to see anything with the theme of hopelessness. No depressing situations. All titles are house-generated. Length: 2,000 to 7,000 words. Pays 3¢ per word; $175 maximum.

LOPEZ ROMANCE GROUP: REAL ROMANCES, REAL STORY, 21 W. 26th St., New York NY 10010. (212)689-3933. Editor: Ardis Sandel. For housewives and working women. Magazines; 72 pages. Monthly. Buys all rights. Buys about 350 mss/year. Pays on publication. Will send sample copy to writer for 60¢. No photocopied or simultaneous submissions. Reports in 6 to 8 weeks. Submit seasonal or holiday material 6 months in advance. Submissions addressed to individual publications in this listing will be considered by all of the publications. Enclose S.A.S.E.

Nonfiction and Fiction: "First person confession stories and service articles on sex, decorating, arts and crafts, fashions, homemaking, beauty, cooking, children, etc. Stories must be well-plotted, have realistic situations, motivation and characterization." Writer should read several issues for style and approach. Strong emphasis on realism. No racial stories. "Sexy passages and dialogue are okay." Mss should feature a different twist or angle to make the story usable. Lengths from short-shorts to 7,500 words maximum. Pays $150 maximum, depending on length.

MODERN ROMANCES, 1 Dag Hammarskjold Plaza, New York NY 10017. Editor: Rita Brenig. For blue collar class women. Monthly. Buys all rights. Buys over 100 mss a year. Payment on acceptance. Write for copy of guidelines for writers, enclosing S.A.S.E. No photocopied or simultaneous submissions. Reports on submissions within 6 weeks. Rejects are accompanied by individual critiques designed to help writers in preparing future submissions. Although only a few lines in length, these point out the basic flaw or flaws of the story. "Please do not send story queries; just complete mss." Enclose S.A.S.E.

Fiction: "First-person confession stories. Feminine narrator greatly preferred, but masculine not completely taboo; in either case, narrator should belong to the working class and be someone a reader will like and root for. Narrator should also be believable, memorable, and someone reader can identify with. We like stories to have strong conflicts, emotion, warmth, good dialogue, and dramatic tension. We want very good characterization. A sense of reality is important. Write about what's happening right now." Length: 7,000 words maximum. Pays approximately 5¢ a published word. "Quality of a manuscript might increase or decrease our payment slightly."

How To Break In: "Read several issues of *Modern Romances*. Perhaps you might start to plan your story by thinking of real people, real situations, and backgrounds you are familiar with. Add (or change or omit) the appropriate character traits, plot twists, details, etc., so the story becomes sharp and clear, dramatic, warm. Use a maximum of dialogue and action, and a minimum of passive narration. Avoid flashbacks."

Rejects: "We don't want to see stories with thin plots and thin characterization."

MY ROMANCE, Magazine Management, 575 Madison Ave., New York NY 10022. Editorial Director: Cara Sherman. Requirements same as *Intimate Secrets*.

PERSONAL ROMANCES, Ideal Publishing Corp., 575 Madison Ave., New York NY 10022. Editor: Johanna Roman Smith. Monthly. Buys all rights. Pays on acceptance. Reports on submissions in 6-8 weeks. Enclose S.A.S.E.

Fiction: First-person stories told in strong up-to-date terms by young marrieds, singles, and teens revealing their emotional, sexual, and family conflicts and their search to resolve personal problems. Blue-collar, white collar group identification. Length: 2,000 to 6,000 words. Top pay is up to $175, based on 3¢ a word.

REAL CONFESSIONS, MODERN LOVE CONFESSIONS, Sterling Library Inc., 261 Fifth Ave., New York NY 10016. Editor: Susan Silverman. For female readers from teenage on up. Monthly. Circulation: 300,000. Buys all rights. Payment on publication. Will not consider photocopied or simultaneous submissions. Submit seasonal material 5 months in advance. Reports within 1 month. Submit only complete ms. Enclose S.A.S.E.

Fistion: "Current sexual themes; quantity of description, although it should not be too explicit." Payment: "In the area of 3¢/word."

REAL ROMANCES, 21 W. 26th St., New York NY 10010. See Lopez Romance Group.

REAL STORY, 21 W. 26th St., New York 10010. See Lopez Romance Group.

SECRETS, Macfadden Women's Group, 205 E. 42nd St., New York NY 10017. (212)983-5644. Editor: Jean Sharbel. For blue-collar family women, ages 18 to 35. Magazine; 72 pages. Established in 1936. Monthly. Buys all rights. Buys about 150 mss per year. Pays on publication. No photocopied or simultaneous submissions. Submit seasonal material 4 to 5 months in advance. Submit only complete ms. Reports in 4 weeks. Enclose S.A.S.E..
Nonfiction, Fiction and Poetry: Wants confession stories; self-help or inspirational fillers. Stories should have realistic plotting with strong emotional tone. Length: 300 to 1,000 words for nonfiction; 1,500 to 7,500 words for confession mss. Pays 3¢ a word for confession mss. Greatest need: 2,000-5,000 words. Also buys light, romantic verse. Length: 24 lines maximum.

TRUE CONFESSIONS, Macfadden Women's Group, 205 E. 42 St., New York NY 10017. Editor: Jean Press Silberg. For blue-collar women, teens through maturity. Magazine. Established in 1922. Monthly. Circulation: 350,000. Buys all rights., Pays on publication. No photocopied or simultaneous submissions. Submit seasonal material at least 5 or 6 months in advance. Reports on material accepted for publication in about 8 weeks. Returns rejected material in 6 to 8 weeks. Submit complete ms. Enclose S.A.S.E.
Fiction, Nonfiction, and Fillers: Realistic life stories within the confession frame. Humor, romance, suspense, adventure fiction. All must be of interest to women in their new and ever-changing role in today's world. Some stories may have a seasonal tone. Careful study of a current issue is suggested. Length: 6,000 to 7,500 words average, but shorter fiction of 1,500 to 2,000 words is also used, as book-lengths of 12,000 words. Pays 5¢ a word. Also, articles, regular features, and short fillers.

TRUE EXPERIENCE, Macfadden Women's Group, 205 E. 42 St., New York NY 10017. Editor: Lydia E. Paglio. For young marrieds, blue-collar, high school education. Interests: children, home, arts, crafts, family and self-fulfillment. Magazine; 72 pages. Established in 1925. Monthly. Circulation: 225,000. Buys all rights. Buys about 150 mss a year. Pays on publication. "Study the magazine for style and editorial content." No photocopied or simultaneous submissions. Submit seasonal material for holiday issues 5 months in advance. Reports in 3 months. Submit complete ms. Enclose S.A.S.E.
Fiction and Nonfiction: Stories on life situations, i.e., death, love, sickness. Romance and confession, first-person narratives with strong identification for readers. Articles on health, self-help, child care. "Remember that we are more contemporary. We deal more with women's self-awareness, and consciousness of their roles in the seventies." Length: 250 to 1,000 words for nonfiction; 1,000 to 7,500 words for fiction. Pays 3¢ a word.
Poetry: Only traditional forms. Length: 4 to 20 lines. Payment varies.

TRUE LOVE, Macfadden Women's Group, 205 E. 42 St., New York NY 10017. Editor: Erma E. Benedict. For young, blue-collar women. Magazine; 72 pages. Established in 1924. Monthly. Circulation: 225,000. Buys all rights. Buys about 150 mss a year. Pays on publication. Will send sample copy to writer for 90¢. No photocopied or simultaneous submissions. Submit seasonal material (Christmas, Easter, Thanksgiving Day, Mother's Day, Father's Day, Valentine's Day) at least 6 months in advance. Reports in 3 months. Submit complete ms. Enclose S.A.S.E.
Fiction: Confessions, true love stories; problems and solutions. Graphic sex is to be avoided. Stories dealing with reality, current problems, everyday events, with emphasis on emotional impact. Length: 1,500 to 8,000 words. Pays 3¢ a word.
Nonfiction: Informational and how-to articles. Length: 250 to 800 words. Pays 5¢ a word minimum.

TRUE ROMANCE, Macfadden Women's Group, 205 E. 42nd St., New York NY 10017. (212)983-8893. Editor: Barbara J. Brett. "Our readership ranges from teenagers to senior citizens. The vast majority of them, however, are young, high school educated, blue-collar wives, the mothers of young children. They have high moral values, are family and love oriented." Monthly magazine; 80 pages. Estab: 1923. Circ: 225,000. Pays on publication. Buys all rights. Submit seasonal/holiday material at least 4 months in advance. SASE. Reports in 1-2 weeks on queries; 8-12 weeks on mss. Free writer's guidelines.
Nonfiction: How-to; informational; and personal experience (inspirational—300-500 words). Submit complete ms. Length: 300-1,000 words. Pays 3¢/word, special rates for short features and articles.

Fiction: Confession. Buys 10 stories/issue. Submit complete ms. Length: 2,000-7,500. Pays 3¢/word; slightly higher flat rate for short-shorts.

Poetry: Free verse and traditional. Buys 20/year. Length: 4-20 lines. Pays minimum $10.

How To Break In: "The freelance writer is needed and welcomed. A timely, well-written story that is centered around sympathetic characters, that reaches a strong climax and that sees the central problem through to a satisfying resolution is all that is needed to 'break into' *True Romance.*"

TRUE SECRETS, Magazine Management, 575 Madison Ave., New York NY 10022. Editorial Director: Cara Sherman. Requirements same as *Intimate Secrets.*

TRUE STORY, Macfadden Women's Group, 205 E. 42 St., New York NY 10017. Editor: Helen Vincent. For young married, blue-collar women, 20 to 35; high school education; increasingly broad interests; home-oriented, but increasingly looking beyond the home for personal fufillment. Magazine; 104 (8¼x11⅛) pages. Monthly. Established in 1919. Circulation: 1,700,000. Buys all rights. Buys about 125 full-length mss a year. Pays on publication. No photocopied or simultaneous submissions. Submit seasonal material 4 months in advance. Make notation on envelope that it is seasonal material. Query first for nonfiction. Submit only complete mss for fiction. Reports in 2 to 3 months. Enclose S.A.S.E..

Nonfiction, Photos, Fiction, and Fillers: "First-person stories covering all aspects of women's interest: love, marriage, family life, careers, social problems, etc. Nonfiction would further explore same areas. The best direction a new writer can be given is to carefully study several issues of the magazine; then submit a fresh, exciting, well-written story. We have no taboos. It's the handling that makes the difference between a reject and an accept." How-to, personal experience, inspirational. Length: 1,000 to 2,500 words. Pays 5¢ to 10¢ or more per word. Also seeks material for Women are Wonderful column. Length: 1,500 words maximum. Pays 5¢ per word. Pays a flat rate for column or departments, announced in the magazine. Query Art Director, Gus Gazzola, about all possible photo submissions. Fiction; romance and confession. Length: 1,500 to 8,000 words. Pays 5¢ a word; $100 minimum. Regular departments, New Faces and Children's Corner, bring $5 each item.

Consumer Service and Business Opportunity Publications

Magazines in this classification are edited for individuals who don't necessarily have a lot of money, but who want maximum return on what they do have—either in goods purchased or in earnings from investment in a small business of their own. Publications for business executives are listed under Business and Finance. Those on how to run specific businesses are classified in Trade, Technical, and Professional Journals.

BUYWAYS, 1000 Sunset Ridge Rd., Northbrook IL 60062. (312)777-7000. Editor: Charles E. McKillip. For members of NACT, Inc.; National Association of Consumers and Travelers, United Farmers Association and United Builders Association. Association members are middle income, high school graduates. They joined their association to save money or a variety of products (for example, new cars, motels, group travel, car rental, appliances, etc.). Quarterly magazine; 16 pages. Estab: 1972. Circ: 126,000. Buys first North American serial rights. Buys 12 to 16 mss a year. Payment on acceptance. Will send free sample copy to writer on request. Will consider photocopied and simultaneous submissions. Query first. Reports in 3 weeks. Enclose S.A.S.E.

Nonfiction and Photos: "Consumer-oriented articles on how to save, how to buy wisely (money and management); travel articles (domestic and foreign). Emphasis on wise buying for home and travel. Looking for well-researched articles. We prefer third-person to first-person articles. We like articles on regionalized weekend travel, recommended restaurants on regional or specialty basis." Informational, how-to, personal experience, interview, profile, humor, historical, photo, travel, successful business operations, and new product articles. Length: 500 to 2,500 words. Pays 10¢ to 20¢ per word. Color transparencies purchased with or without ms, or on assignment. Captions optional. Payment depends on size and use.

How To Break In: "Query first. Send samples of published work. We prefer xerox copies for our files."

CONSUMER REPORTS, 256 Washington St., Mt. Vernon NY 10550. Editor: Irwin Landau. Staff-written.

CONSUMERS DIGEST, 4001 W. Devon, Chicago IL 60646. Editor: Arthur Darack. For high school and college educated do-it-yourselfers. Magazine, published every 2 months; 32 (8½x11) pages. Established in 1958. Circulation: 370,000. Buys all rights. Buys 15 to 20 mss a year. Payment on acceptance. Will send sample copy to writer for 50¢. Query first. Enclose S.A.S.E.
Nonfiction: Material on investments, self-help, products and services, health and food, best buys, analysis of cars, appliances, etc. Also how-to's on car, appliance and house repair. Approach is systematic with mass appeal. Not interested in exposes, but will consider material on successful business operations and merchandising techniques and for legal and medical columns. Article length: 1,000 words minimum. Column length: 3,000 words. Pays 5¢ a word.

CONSUMERS' RESEARCH MAGAZINE, Washington NJ 07882. Editor: F.J. Schlink. Monthly. Copyrighted. Limited amount of freelance material used. Query first. Enclose S.A.S.E.
Nonfiction and Photos: Articles of practical interest to ultimate consumers concerned with tests and expert judgment of goods and services which they buy. Must be accurate and careful statements, well-supported by chemical, engineering, scientific, medical, or other expert or professional knowledge of subject. Pays approximately 2¢ per word. Buys b&w glossies with mss only. Pays $5 minimum. "Photos are accepted only if they are clearly relevant to the article being published."

FDA CONSUMER, 5600 Fishers Lane, Rockville MD 20852. (301)443-3220. Editor: Ellis Rottman. For "all consumers of products regulated by the Food and Drug Administration." A Federal Government publication. Magazine, 40 pages. Established in 1967. Monthly. December/January and July/August issues combined. Circulation: 20,000. Not copyrighted. "All purchases automatically become part of public domain." Buys 4 to 5 freelance mss a year, by contract only. Payment on publication. Query first. "We cannot be responsible for any work by writer not agreed upon by prior contract." Enclose S.A.S.E.
Nonfiction and Photos: "Articles of an educational nature concerning purchase and use of FDA regulated products and specific FDA programs and actions to protect the consumer's health and pocketbook. Authoritative and official agency viewpoints emanating from agency policy and actions in administrating the Food, Drug and Cosmetic Act and a number of other statutes. All articles subject to clearance by the appropriate FDA experts as well as the editor. The magazine speaks for the Federal Government only. Articles based on facts and FDA policy only. We cannot consider any unsolicited material. All articles based on prior arrangement by contract. The nature and subject matter and clearances required are so exacting that it is difficult to get an article produced by a writer working outside the Washington DC metropolitan area." Length: average, 2,000 words. Pays $500. B&w photos are purchased on assignment only.

INCOME OPPORTUNITIES, 229 Park Ave., South, New York NY 10003. Editor: Joseph V. Daffron. Managing Editor: Robert Brown. For all who are seeking business opportunities, full- or part-time. Monthly magazine; (8½x11). Established in 1956. Buys all rights. Buys 100 mss per year. Will not consider photocopied or simultaneous submissions. Two special directory issues contain articles on selling techniques, mail order, import/export, franchising and business ideas. Reports in 1 to 2 weeks. Always query first. Enclose S.A.S.E.
Nonfiction and Photos: Regularly covered are such subjects as mail order, direct selling, franchising, party plans, selling techniques and the marketing of handcrafted or homecrafted products. Wanted are ideas for the aspiring entrepreneur; examples of successful business methods that might be duplicated. No material that is purely inspirational. "Payment rates vary according to length and quality of the submission from a minimum of $50 for a short of a maximum of 800 words, to $200 for a major article of 2,000 to 3,000 words. Illustrations are considered part of the manuscript purchase."
How To Break In: "Study recent issues of the magazine. Best bets for newcomers: Interview-based report on a successful small business venture."

MONEYTREE NEWSLETTER, Task Bldg., Kerrville TX 78028. Editor: Marshall Sideman. Pays on acceptance. Send #10 S.A.S.E. and $1.00 for sample copy.
Fillers: "Items dealing with money. How to invest it, make it grow rapidly, how to get big savings—these have the best chance of acceptance. Our readers want to get rich, or if wealthy already, stay rich." Also uses capsule articles on health, self-help, vocational training, practical

science, money-making opportunities, etc. Also capsulized write-ups about free publications, product samples, items of value, etc. All submissions must be documented by author. Length: 10 to 60 words. Payment is $5.

Detective and Crime Publications

Publications listed in this section provide markets for nonfiction accounts of true crimes. Markets for criminal fiction (mysteries) are listed in Mystery Publications.

DETECTIVE CASES, Detective Files Group, 1440 St. Catherine St., W., Montreal, Quebec, Canada H3G 1S2. Editor-in-Chief: Dominick A. Merle. Managing Editor: Art Ball. Monthly magazine; 72 pages. See *Detective Files.*

DETECTIVE DRAGNET, Detective Files Group, 1440 St. Catherine St., W., Montreal, Quebec, Canada H3G 1S2. Editor-in-Chief: Dominick A. Merle. Managing Editor: Art Ball. Monthly magazine; 72 pages. See *Detective Files.*

DETECTIVE FILES, Detective Files Group, 1440 St. Catherine St., W., Montreal, Quebec, Canada H3G 1S2. Editor-in-Chief: Dominick A. Merle. Managing Editor: Art Ball. Monthly magazine; 72 pages. Pays on acceptance. Buys all rights. Phone queries OK. Submit seasonal/holiday material 4 months in advance. Photocopied submissions OK. SASE. Reports in 4 weeks. Free sample copy and writer's guidelines.
Nonfiction: True crime stories. "Do a thorough job; don't double-sell (sell an article to more than one market), and deliver and you can have a steady market. Neatness, clarity and pace will help you make the sale." Query. Length: 3,500-6,000 words. Pays $175-300.
Photos: Purchased with accompanying ms; no additional payment. B&w only. Model release required.

FRONT PAGE DETECTIVE, INSIDE DETECTIVE, Official Detective Group, R.G.H. Publishing Corp. 235 Park Ave., S., New York NY 10003. Editor-in-Chief: Albert P. Govoni. Editor: Diana Lurvey.
Nonfiction: The focus of these two newly acquired publications will be quite similar to the others in the Official Detective Group, but will concentrate less on pre-trial stories. For further details, see *Official Detective.*

HEADQUARTERS DETECTIVE, Detective Files Group, 1440 St. Catherine St., W., Montreal, Quebec, Canada H3G 1S2. Editor-in-Chief: Dominick A. Merle. Managing Editor: Art Ball. Monthly magazine; 72 pages. See *Detective Files.*

MASTER DETECTIVE, Official Detective Group, R.G.H. Publishing Corp., 235 Park Ave., S., New York NY 10003. Editor-in-Chief: Albert P. Govoni. Managing Editor: Walter Jackson. Monthly. Estab: 1929. Circ: 350,000; Buys 9-10 mss/issue. See *Official Detective.*

OFFICIAL DETECTIVE, Official Detective Group, R.G.H. Publishing Corp., 235 Park Ave., S., New York NY 10003. Editor-in-Chief: Albert P. Govoni. Manager Editor: Walter Jackson. "For detective story or police buffs whose tastes run to *true*, rather than fictional crime/mysteries." Monthly magazine; 80 pages. Estab: 1930. Circ: 500,000. Pays on acceptance. Buys all rights. Phone queries OK. Buys 11-12 mss/issue. SASE. Reports in 2 weeks.
Nonfiction: "Only *fact* detective stories. We are actively trying to develop new writers, and we'll work closely with those who show promise and can take the discipline required by our material. It's not difficult to write, but it demands meticulous attention to facts, truth, clarity, detail. Queries are essential with us, but I'd say the quickest rejection goes to the writer who sends in a story on a case that should never have been written for us because it lacks the most important ingredient, namely solid, superlative detective work. We also dislike pieces with multiple defendants, unless all have been convicted." Buys 150 mss/year. Query. Length: 4,500-6,500 words. Pays $200-400.
Photos: Purchased with accompanying mss. Captions required. Send prints for inside use; transparencies for covers. Pays $12.50 minimum for b&w glossies, 4x5 minimum. Pays $200 minimum for 2¼x2¼ or 35mm. Model release required for color used on cover.

TRUE DETECTIVE, Official Detective Group, R.G.H. Publishing Corp., 235 Park Ave., S., New York NY 10003. Editor-in-Chief: Albert P. Govoni. Managing Editor: Walter Jackson. Monthly. Estab: 1924. Circ: 500,000. Buys 11-12 mss/issue. See *Official Detective.*

STARTLINE DETECTIVE, Detective Files Group, 1440 St. Catherine, W., Montreal, Quebec, Canada H3G 1S2. Editor-in-Chief: Dominick A. Merle. Managing Editor: Art Ball. Bimonthly magazine; 72 pages. See *Detective Files.*

TRUE POLICE CASES, Detective Files Group, 1440 St. Catherine St., W., Montreal, Quebec, Canada H3G 1S2. Editor-in-Chief: Dominick A. Merle. Managing Editor: Art Ball. Bimonthly magazine; 72 pages. See *Detective Files.*

Education Publications

Magazines in these listings approach the subject of education with the interests of parents and the general public in mind. Journals for professional educators and teachers are included under Education in the Trade Journals section.

AMERICAN EDUCATION, U.S. Office of Education, 400 Maryland Ave. SW, Washington DC 20202. (202)245-8907. Editor-in-Chief: William A. Horn. Associate Editor: Gertrude Mitchell. Emphasizes federal government role in education for readership of mature adult professionals engaged in education or with special interest in the field. Monthly magazine; 32 pages. Estab: 1965. Circ: 40,000. Pays on acceptance. Buys one-time rights. Submit seasonal/holiday material 4 months in advance. Photocopied submissions OK. SASE. Reports in 2-3 weeks. Free sample copy and writer's guidelines.
Nonfiction: Informational (successful projects or programs with federal involvement). Buys 30 mss/year. Query. Length: minimum 2,500 words. Pays $350-500.
Photos: Mark Travaglini, Photo Editor. Purchased with accompanying manuscript. Submit b&w photos and contact sheet. Pays $15-50.
How To Break In: Because most of our articles are made on assignment, we are constantly looking for those who can write a clear and detailed description of an education program, using enough thoughtfully selected anecdotal material and quotes to give the article pace and increased readability. Thus, queries should be accompanied by writing samples demonstrating this ability.

AMERICAN TEACHER, 11 Dupont Circle, N.W., Washington DC 20036. Editor: Gail Miller. For "members of the American Federation of Teachers, AFL-CIO, and other classroom teachers." Monthly except July and August. Buys first North American serial rights; will buy simultaneous rights. Pays on publication. Will send a sample copy to a writer on request. Prefers query first. Reports in 4 months. Enclose S.A.S.E.
Nonfiction and Photos: "We want material directly concerned with our primary interests: educational innovation, academic freedom, the teacher union movement, better schools and educational methods, legislation concerning teachers, etc. Pays $25 to $70. Photos purchased with and without mss; captions required. "Stock photos of classroom scenes." Subjects must be in range of subject interest. No specific size. Pays $15.

CANADIAN CHILDREN'S MAGAZINE, 4150 Bracken Ave., Victoria B.C. Canada, V8X 3N8. (604)479-6906. Editor-in-Chief: Evelyn Samuel. "This magazine is geared toward children 6-12 years old in Canada or interested in Canadian materials." Quarterly magazine; 48 pages. Estab: 1976. Circ: 25,000. Pays in copies. Acquires one-time rights. Phone queries OK. Submit seasonal/holiday material 6 months in advance. Photocopied submissions OK. SASE. Reports in 1 month. Sample copy $1.25; free writer's guidelines.
Nonfiction: How-to (always with a Canadian slant—ethnic, Indian, or regional), historical (Canadian material only), and informational (current Canadian contributions, inventions, etc). Uses 25 mss/issue. Query. Length: 500-1,500 words. Pays in copies.
Fiction: Uses 2 mss/year. Query. Length: 500-1,500 words. Pays in copies.

CAREER WORLD, Curriculum Innovations, Inc., 501 Lake Forest Ave., Highwood IL 60040. (312)432-2700. Editor: Whayne Dillehay. Emphasizes career education for junior and senior high school students at approximately 9th grade reading level. Teacher's edition aimed at guidance and career education personnel. Monthly (September-May) magazine; 32 pages. Estab: 1972. Circ: 130,000. Pays on publication. Buys all rights. Submit seasonal/holiday material 4 months in advance. Simultaneous, photocopied or previously published submissions OK. SASE. Reports in 2 weeks. Free sample copy.
Nonfiction: How-to, informational, interview, profile, photo feature. Buys 9 mss/year. Query. Length: 750-3,000 words. Pays 4¢/word minimum.

Photos: Purchased with or without accompanying ms or on assignment. Query. Pays $10 minimum for 8x10 b&w glossies; $25 for 35 or 120mm transparencies. Model release usually required.

Columns, Departments: Lifestyle (worker profile), Opening Door (profile of minority or handicapped worker), New Careers, Teachers' Edition (activities and news for teachers). Buys 9/year. Query. Length: 500-1,500 words. Pays 4¢/word and up. Open to suggestions for new columns or departments.

Poetry: Traditional (subjects must relate to the world of work). Buys 15/year. Length: 4 lines minimum. Pays $10/poem and up.

Fillers: Clippings and short humor applicable to the world of work. Buys 9-18/year. Pays $5-15. Also has poetry contest.

CHANGE MAGAZINE, Educational Change, Inc., NBW Tower, New Rochelle, NY 10801. Editor-in-Chief: George W. Bonham. Emphasizes higher learning/higher education. *"Change* is an opinion magazine broadly concerned with academic matters, social issues, and subject matter of intellectual interest." Monthly magazine; 69 pages. Estab: 1969. Circ: 26,000. Pays on acceptance. Buys all rights. Simultaneous and photocopied submissions OK. SASE. Reports in 6 weeks. Sample copy $1.

Nonfiction: Joyce Hermel, Articles Editor. Informational; interview; personal opinion; and profile. Buys 150 mss/year. Length: 1,200-10,000 words. Pays $100-300.

Columns, Departments: Cullen Murphy, Column, Department Editor. Book Reviews (top-notch reviews of books on education, social issues, intellectual interests), Community Colleges (first-rate reports on community colleges and their programs and problems), Media (broad-based pieces on all forms of media, educational and others). Buys 2/issue. Query. Length: 1,600-2,000 words. Pays $100-150. Open to suggestions for new columns and departments.

CURRENT CONSUMER, Curriculum Innovations, Inc., 501 Lake Forest Ave., Highwood IL 60040. (312)432-2700. Editor: Whayne Dillehay. Emphasizes consumer education. For junior and senior high school students at approximately 9th grade reading level. Teacher's edition aimed at home economics, business, economics and consumer education teachers. Monthly during the school year (Sept-May). Magazine; 32 pages. Estab: 1976. Circ: 50,000. Pays on publication. Buys all rights. Submit seasonal/holiday material 4 months in advance. Simultaneous, photocopied or previously published submissions OK. SASE. Reports in 2 weeks. Free sample copy.

Nonfiction: How-to (on ways to becoming a more effective and confident consumer); informational (on anything a junior or senior high school student should know as a future consumer); interview; profile (of a consumer who has a valuable story to tell or lesson to teach); new product (that offers unique alternatives or advantages to the consumer); personal experience, and photo feature. Buys 9/year. Query. Length: 750-3,000 words. Pays 4¢/word and up.

Photos: Purchased with or without accompanying ms or on assignment. Query. Pays $10 minimum for 8x10 b&w glossies; $25 minimum for 35mm or larger transparencies. Model release required.

Columns, Departments: Marketplace (guide to buying goods and services—no product listing or rating), Money Management, Consumer Law, Teacher's Edition (activities for teachers). Buys 10-15/year. Query. Length: 500-1,500 words. Pays 4¢/word and up. Open to suggestions for new columns or departments.

Fillers: Clippings, puzzles (consumer related), short humor. Buys 20/year. Pays $5-15.

How To Break In: "Our editorial philosophy is to educate young people toward becoming effective and aware consumers. We do not take an advocacy stance or endorse singular viewpoints. Material submitted for our consideration must correspond to this philosophy."

DAY CARE AND EARLY EDUCATION, 72 Fifth Ave., New York NY 10011. Editor: Allen J. Sheinman. For "day care workers, parents, community boards, educators, students, political action groups." Magazine; 48 pages. Established in 1973. Every 2 months. Circulation: 25,000. Rights purchased vary with author and material. May buy all rights, with the possibility of reassigning rights to author after publication, first North American serial rights, first serial rights, or second serial (reprint) rights. Buys 35 to 40 mss per year. Will send free sample copy to writer on request. Write for editorial guidelines sheet. Will consider photocopied submissions. No simultaneous submissions. Submit seasonal material 3 months in advance. Reports on mss accepted for publication in 4 to 8 weeks. Returns rejected material in 2 to 8 weeks. Query first. Enclose S.A.S.E.

Nonfiction, Photos and Fillers: "Instructional methods and materials, child development trends, funding and administrative issues, program planning, the politics of day care, parental participation, personnel development and standards. Always consider how the article can be of practical use to others in the field." Does not need fiction or poetry at this time. Would like to see mss on how big cities are coping with day care cut-backs; new moves toward meaningful child care legislation; how localities are transcending stubborn federal and/or state attitudes toward day care. Length: 500 to 2,000 words. Pays $35 to $150. Photos purchased with accompanying ms with or without extra payment. Captions optional. No color. Submit b&w glossies. Buys newsbreaks. Length: 25 to 500 words. Pays $35 maximum.

READ MAGAZINE, 245 Long Hill Rd., Middletown CT 06457. (209)347-7251. Editor: Jacqueline A. Ball. For high school students. Magazine; 32 pages. Established in 1951. Every 2 weeks. Circulation: 796,305. Rights purchased vary with author and material. May buy second serial (reprint) rights or all rights. Buys about 20 mss a year. Pays on acceptance. Will send sample copy to writer on request. Write for copy of guidelines for writers. Will consider photocopied submissions. No simultaneous submissions. Reports in 3 to 4 weeks. Submit complete ms. Enclose S.A.S.E.
Drama and Fiction: First emphasis is on plays; second on fiction with suspense, adventure, or teenage identification themes. "No preachy material. Plays should have 12 to 15 parts and not require complicated stage directions, for they'll be used mainly for reading aloud in class. Remember that we try to be educational as well as entertaining." No kid detective stories or plays. No obscenity. Pays $50 minimum.

Food and Drink Publications

Magazines classified here aim at individuals who are interested in and appreciate fine wines and fine foods. Journals aimed at food processors, manufacturers, and retailers will be found in the Trade Journals.

GOURMET, 777 Third Ave., New York NY 10017. Managing Editor: Miss Gail Zweigenthal. For moneyed, educated, traveled, food-wise men and women. Monthly. Purchases copyright, but grants book reprint rights with credit. Pays on acceptance. Suggests a study of several issues to understand type of material required. Reports within 2 months. Query first. "We prefer published writers, so if you haven't written for us before, you should enclose some samples of previous work." Enclose S.A.S.E.
Nonfiction: Uses articles on subjects related to food and wine—travel, adventure, reminiscence, fishing and hunting experiences. Prefers personal experiences to researched material. Recipes included as necessary. Not interested in nutrition, dieting, penny-saving, or bizarre foods, or in interviews with chefs or food experts, or in reports of food contests, festivals, or wine tastings. Buys recipes only as part of an article with interesting material to introduce them and make them appealing. "Gourmet Holidays" written by staff contributors only. The same is true for material including specific hotel or restaurant recommendations. Sophisticated, light, nontechnical. Length: 2,500 to 3,000 words. Current needs include American regional pieces (no restaurants). Pays $500 minimum.
Poetry and Verse: Light, sophisticated with food or drink slant. Pays $50 minimum.
How To Break In: "Personal reminiscences are the easiest way to break in, since we always use staff writers when recommending hotels or restaurants. Our biggest problem with freelancers is that they are not familiar with our style or that they fail to treat their material with enough sophistication or depth. We don't want pieces which sound like press releases or which simply describe what's there. We like to really cover a subject and literary value is important. We'd very much like to see more regional American material. It seems to be much easier to get people traipsing around Europe."

WINE WORLD MAGAZINE, 15101 Keswick St., Van Nuys CA 91405. (213)785-6050. Editor-Publisher: Dee Sindt. For the wine loving public (adults of all ages) who wish to learn more about wine. Magazine published every 2 months; 48 (8½x11) pages. Established in 1971. Buys first North American serial rights. Buys about 72 mss a year. Payment on publication. Will send sample copy to writer on request. Write for copy of guidelines for writers. Will not consider photocopied submissions. Will consider simultaneous submissions, "if spelled out." Reports in 30 days. Query first. Enclose S.A.S.E.
Nonfiction: "Wine-oriented material written with an in-depth knowledge of the subject, designed to meet the needs of the novice and connoisseur alike. Wine technology advancements, wine history, profiles of vintners the world over. Educational articles only. No first-person accounts. Must be objective, informative reporting on economic trends, new technological developments in vinification, vine hybridizing, and vineyard care. New wineries and new market-

ing trends. We restrict our editorial content to wine, and wine-oriented material. No restauran or food articles accepted. No more basic wine information. No articles from instant wine experts. Authors must be qualified in this highly technical field." Length: 750 to 2,000 words. Pays $50 to $100.

WOMEN'S CIRCLE HOME COOKING, Box 338, Chester MA 01011. Editor: Barbara Hall Pedersen. For women (and some men) of all ages who really enjoy cooking. "Our readers collect and exchange recipes. They are neither food faddists nor gourmets, but practical women and men trying to serve attractive and nutritious meals. Many work full-time, and most are on limited budgets." Magazine; 72 (5x7¼) pages. Monthly. Circulation: 225,000. Buys all rights, but will reassign rights to author after publication. Buys about 50 mss a year. Pays on publication. Will send sample copy to writer for S.A.S.E. Holiday food articles are always welcome, especially if accompanied by photos, and should be submitted 6 months in advance. Submit complete ms. Reports in 2 to 8 weeks. Enclose S.A.S.E.

Nonfiction and Photos: "We like a little humor with our food, for the sake of the digestion. Keep articles light. Stress economy and efficiency. Remember that at least half our readers must cook after working a full-time job. Draw on personal experience to write an informative article on some aspect of cooking. We're a reader participation magazine. We don't go in for fad diets, or strange combinations of food which claim to cure anything." Informational, how-to, inspirational, historical, expose, nostalgia, photo, and travel also considered. Length: 50 to 1,000 words. Pays 2¢ to 5¢ per word. Columns and regular features by arrangement. Photos purchased with ms or on assignment. Captions optional. 4x5 b&w, sharp, glossy. 2¼ color, but prefers 4x5. Pays $5 for b&w, $20 or more for color, by arrangement.

Fiction, Poetry, and Fillers: Humorous fiction, related to cooking and foods. Length: 1,200 words maximum. Pays 2¢ to 5¢ per word. Light verse related to cooking and foods. Length: 30 lines maximum. No payment. Short humorous fillers, 100 words maximum. Pays 2¢ to 5¢ per word.

General Interest Publications

Publications classified here are edited for national, general audiences and carry articles on any subject of interest to a broad spectrum of people. Other markets for general interest material will be found in the Black, In-Flight, Men's, Newspapers and Weekly Magazine Sections, Regional, and Women's classifications in the Consumer section.

ACCENT, 1720 Washington Blvd., P.O. Box 2315, Ogden UT 84404. (801)394-9446. Editor: Helen S. Crane. For "a wide segment, from the young couple to the retired one." Established in 1968. Monthly. Circulation: 500,000. Rights purchased vary with author and material. Buys about 18 mss a year. Pays on acceptance. Will send a sample copy to a writer on request. Submit seasonal/holiday material 11 months in advance. Query. Enclose S.A.S.E. for reply to queries and return of submissions.

Nonfiction and Photos: "The majority of our articles are written on assignment by professonal writers knowledgeable in their fields. We do, however, consider interest-capturing, short features from freelancers. Since our emphasis is on pictures, and our copy space limited, we require concise, informative, yet lively writing that covers a lot in a few words. We want pieces of lasting general interest suitable for the family. We do not need rambling experience pieces, or ecology features; nor do we want holiday material. We use a few travel vignettes about exciting yet well-known spots and pieces showing glimpses of life and unusual activities. Writing should be in a fresh, sparkling style." Pays about 10¢ per word. Photos purchased with mss; captions required. "For the most part, we prefer views without people, particularly if they tend to date the views. If people are present, they should be actively engaged in interesting ways. Subjects must be eyecatching and colors sharp." For 8x10 b&w glossies, pays $20. For color transparencies ("some 35mm, prefer larger"), pays $25 minimum ("more for larger views or covers").

How To Break In: "The only way to break in to our magazine is with queries that cover something we feel our readers will be interested in, backed up by sharp pictures and entertaining yet informative writing. "Principal reason for rejecting freelance submissions is that "writers disregard what we have stated in our listing and write loosely and subjectively (diary style) or they tend to preach or moralize. We like an upbeat, positive approach."

THE ATLANTIC MONTHLY, 8 Arlington St., Boston MA 02116. (617)536-9500. Editor-in-Chief: Robert Manning. For a professional, academic audience. Monthly. Circulation: 325,000. Buys first North American serial rights. Pays on acceptance. Will send a sample copy to a writer for $1. Reports in 2 weeks to several months. Enclose S.A.S.E. for return of submissions.

Nonfiction: "We prefer not to formulate specifications about the desired content of *The Atlantic* and suggest that would-be contributors examine back issues to form their own judgment of what is suitable." Length: 2,000 to 5,000 words. Rates vary from $100 per magazine page base rate. Author should include summary of his qualifications for treating subject.

Fiction: Short stories by unestablished writers, published as Atlantic "Firsts" are a steady feature. Two prizes of $750 and $250 are awarded to the best of these when a sufficient number of stories are published. Candidates should so label their submissions and list their previous publications, if any, as authors whose stories have appeared in magazines of national circulation are not considered eligible. Will also consider stories by established writers in lengths ranging from 2,700 to 7,500 words. Payment depends on length, but also on quality and author.

Poetry: Uses three to five poems an issue. These must be of high literary distinction in both light and serious poetry. Interested in young poets. Base rate for poetry is $2 per line.

BLACKWOOD'S MAGAZINE, William Blackwood & Sons, Ltd., 32 Thistle St., Edinburgh, Scotland EH2 1HA. (031)225-3411. Editor-in-Chief: David Fletcher. Monthly magazine; 96 pages. Estab: 1817. Circ: 8,500. Pays on publication. Buys first British serial rights. Phone queries OK. Submit seasonal/holiday material 3 months in advance. SAE and International Reply Coupons. Reports in 1 week. Sample copy $1.50.

Nonfiction: Historical; nostalgia; personal experience; personal opinion; and travel. "Would-be contributors should first study the magazine." Buys 50 mss/year. Submit complete ms. Length: 2,500-9,000 words. Pays 5-8 pounds/1,000 words.

Fiction: Adventure, historical; humorous; mainstream; mystery; and religious. Buys 50 mss/year. Submit complete ms. Length: 2,500-9,000 words. Pays 5-8 pounds/1,000 words.

Poetry: Traditional forms, free verse and light verse. Buys 12/year. Length: 14-69 lines. Pays 8 pounds/poem.

How To Break In: "*Blackwood's* is one of the world's oldest monthlies and we are always keen to see work by U.S. and Canadian writers. But writers must, first of all, have studied the magazine and remember that material must not have appeared in print before submission to us."

CARTE BLANCHE, 3460 Wilshire Blvd., Los Angeles CA 90010. (213)480-3210. Editor: Margaret M. Volpe. For affluent professional people and their families; highly educated, well-read, well-traveled; have much leisure time; interested in fine food and drink. Bimonthly magazine; 60-72 pages. Estab: 1964. Circ: 700,000. Pays on acceptance. Buys one-time reproduction rights. Submit seasonal/holiday material 5-6 months in advance. Photocopied submissions OK. SASE. Reports in 4 weeks. Sample copy and writer's guidelines for SASE.

Nonfiction: "We publish articles relating to our travel, dining and entertaining format. Photos are very important. Food stories should have expnsitory text, recipes and photos. No fillers or cartoons. Some articles on crafts, hobbies, sports, art, or personality profiles (no film stars). We rarely give assignments." Buys 12-20 mss/year. Query or submit complete ms. Length: 1,500-2,000 words. Pays $300-400.

Photos: Purchased with or without accompanying ms. Captions required. Send list of stock photos. Uses any size color transparencies from 35mm and larger.

CHANGING TIMES, The Kiplinger Service for Families, 1729 H St., N.W., Washington DC 20006. Editor: Sidney Sulkin. For general, adult audience interested in personal finance, family money management and personal advancement. Established in 1947. Monthly. Circulation: 1,500,000. Buys all rights. Pays on acceptance. Reports in 30 days. Enclose S.A.S.E.

Items: "Original topical quips and epigrams for our monthly humor feature, 'Notes on These Changing Times.' All other material is staff-written." Pays $10.

COMMENTARY, 165 East 56th St., New York NY 10022. Editor: Norman Podhoretz. Monthly magazine, 96 pages. Established in 1945. Circulation: 60,000. Buys aall rights. "All of our material is done freelance, though much of it is commissioned." Payment on publication. Query first, or submit complete ms. Reports in 4 weeks. Enclose S.A.S.E.

Nonfiction and Fiction: Nonfiction Editor: Brenda Brown. Fiction Editor: Marion Magid. Thoughtful essays on political, social, theological, and cultural themes; general, as well as with special Jewish content. Informational, historical, and think articles. Length: 3,000 to 7,000 words. Pays approximately $30 a page. Uses some mainstream fiction. Length: flexible.

How To Break In: "We're hungry for material in every field, especially good fiction (which we don't see enough of anywhere). Book reviews are a good way to start. We've found that it gives us an opportunity to assess the new writer without undertaking a major project. Book reviews should be about 1,500 words; on most subjects with obvious exceptions like gothic novels and cookbooks. Also don't assume it's mostly Jewish-oriented material. That accounts for only about 15 to 20 percent of our writing in the course of a year."

FORD TIMES, Ford Motor Company, Room 332, 3000 Schaefer Rd., Dearborn MI 48121. Managing Editor: Richard L. Routh. "Family magazine designed to attract all ages." Monthly. Circulation: 1,700,000. Buys first serial rights. Buys about 150 mss/year. Pays on acceptance. Will send a sample copy to a writer on request. Write for copy of guidelines for writers. Query first. Submit seasonal material 6 months in advance. Reports in 2 to 4 weeks. Enclose S.A.S.E.
Nonfiction and Photos: "Almost anything relating to American life, both past and present, that is in good taste and leans toward the cheerful and optimistic. Topics include motor travel, sports, fashion, where and what to eat along the road, vacation ideas, reminiscences, big cities and small towns, the arts, Americana, nostalgia, the outdoors. We strive to be colorful, lively and engaging. We are particularly attracted to material that presents humor, anecdote, first-person discourse, intelligent observation and, in all cases, superior writing. We are committed to originality and try as much as possible to avoid subjects that have appeared in other publications and in our own. However, a fresh point of view and/or exceptional literary ability with respect to an old subject will be welcomed." Length: 1,500 words maximum. Pays $250 and up for full-length articles. "We prefer to have a suitable ms in hand before considering photos or illustration. Speculative submission of good quality color transparencies and b&w photos is welcomed. We want bright, lively photos showing people in happy circumstances. Writers may send snapshots, postcards, brochures, etc., if they wish."

GOOD READING, Henry F. Henrichs Publications, Litchfield IL 62056. (217)324-2322. Editor: Mrs. Monta Crane. "A magazine with the human touch." Monthly. Not copyrighted. Estab: 1964. Circ: 75,000. Buys 50-75 mss/year. Pays on acceptance. Sample copy 50¢; free writer's guidelines. Submit seasonal/holiday material 4 months in advance. Reports in 1 to 2 months. Enclose S.A.S.E.
Nonfiction and Photos: Articles on "current or factual subjects, and articles based on incidents related to business, personal experiences that reveal the elements of success in human relationships. All material must be clean and wholesome and acceptable to all ages. Material should be uplifting, and non-controversial." Length: 500-1,000 words. Pays $10-35. B&w glossies purchased with mss occasionally.

GREEN'S MAGAZINE, Box 313, Detroit MI 48231. Editor: David Green. For a general audience; the more sentient, literate levels. Quarterly magazine; 100 pages. Estab: 1972. Circ: 1,000. Buys first North American serial rights. Buys 48 mss a year. Payment on publication. Will send sample copy to writer for $1.50 Will not consider photocopied or simultaneous submissions. Reports in 6 weeks. Submit complete ms. Enclose S.A.S.E.
Fiction: Mainstream, suspense, humorous, must have a realistic range in conflict areas. Slice of life situations enriched with deep characterization and more than superficial conflict. Avoid housewife, student, businessmen problems that remain "so what" in solution. Open on themes as long as writers recognize the family nature of the magazine. Length: 1,000 to 3,000 words. Pays $15 to $25.
Poetry: Haiku, blank verse, free verse. Length: about 36 to 40 lines. Pays $2 to $3.

GRIT, 208 W. Third St., Williamsport PA 17701. (717)326-1771. Editor: Terry L. Ziegler. For "residents of all ages in small-town and rural America who are interested in people and generally take a positive view of life." Tabloid newspaper; 44 pages. Established in 1882. Weekly. Circulation: 1,300,000. Buys first serial rights and second serial (reprint) rights. Buys 800 to 1,000 mss per year. Pays on acceptance for freelance material; on publication for reader participation feature material. Will send free sample copy to writer on request. No photocopied or simultaneous submissions. Reports in 2 to 4 weeks. Query first or submit complete ms. Enclose S.A.S.E.
Nonfiction and Photos: Feature Editor: Kenneth D. Loss. "Stories of small towns recovering from adversity; small towns which can be examples for other communities in specific accomplishments; small-town celebrations. Stress unique and unusual features and their significance. Inspiring stories of personal courage and devotion; individuals and groups who are making an important contribution to their neighbors, community, or American way of life." Also wants mss demonstrating the power of free enterprise as a desirable and vital aspect of life in the U.S., with emphasis on specific examples. Mss should show "value of honesty, thrift, hard work and generosity as keys to better living." Also wants patriotic stories which have an immediate tie-in

with a patriotic holiday. Avoid sermonizing, but mss should be interesting and accurate so that readers may be inspired. Also mss about men, women and teenagers involved in unusual occupations, hobbies or significant personal adventures. "*Grit* seeks to present the positive aspect of things. When others point out the impending darkness, *Grit* emphasizes the beautiful sunset or approaching rest before another day." Does not want to see mss promoting alcoholic beverages, immoral behavior, narcotics, unpatriotic acts. Wants good Easter, Christmas and holiday material. Mss should show some person or group involved in an unusual and/or uplifting way. "We lean heavily toward human interest, whatever the subject. Writing should be simple and down-to-earth." Length: 300 to 800 words. Pays 5¢ a word for first or exclusive rights; 2¢ a word for second or reprint rights. Photos purchased with or without ms. Captions required. Size: prefers 8x10 for b&w, but will consider 5x7; color transparencies or slides only. Pays $10 for b&w photos accompanying ms; for accompanying color transparencies, $35 each.
Fiction and Poetry: Department Editor: Mrs. Fran Noll. Buys only reprint material for fiction. Western, romance. Pays 2¢ per word. Buys traditional forms of poetry and light verse. Length: 32 lines maximum. Pays $4 for 4 lines and under, plus 25¢ per line for each additional line.

HARPER'S MAGAZINE, 2 Park Ave., Room 1809, New York NY 10016. (212)481-5220. Editor: Lewis H. Lapham. For well-educated, socially concerned, widely read men and women and college students who are active in community and political affairs. Monthly. Circulation: 325,000. Rights purchased vary with author and material. Buys all rights, but will reassign rights to author after publication; first North American serial rights; first serial rights; or second serial (reprint) rights. Buys approximately 12 non-agented, non-commissioned, non-book-excerpted mss a year. Pays on acceptance. Will send a sample copy to a writer for $1. Will look only at material submitted through agents or which is the result of a query. Reports in 2 to 3 weeks. Enclose S.A.S.E. with all queries and submissions.
Nonfiction: "For writers working with agents or who will query first only, our requirements are: Public affairs, literary, international and local reporting, humor." Also buys exposes, think pieces, and profiles. Length: 1,500 to 6,000 words. Pays $200 to $1,500.
Photos: Department Editor: Sheila Berger. Occasionally purchased with mss. Others by assignment. Pays $35 to $400.
Fiction: On contemporary life and its problems. Also buys humorous stories. Length: 1,000 to 5,000 words. Pays $300 to $500.
Poetry: 60 lines and under. Pays $2 per line.

HOLIDAY, 1100 Waterway Blvd., Indianapolis IN 46202. (317)634-1100. Managing Editor: Kathryn Klassen. For a mature audience, travel and leisure oriented. Established in 1946. Every 2 months. Circulation: 475,000. Pays on publication. Rights purchased vary with author and material. Write for editorial guidelines. S.A.S.E. must be enclosed with request. Submit seasonal material 5 months in advance. Send query or complete ms (by certified mail if acknowledgement of receipt is desired). "We prefer 1-page queries written in the style the proposed article will take, telling why this special approach merits space." Enclose S.A.S.E.
Nonfiction: "Articles on a wide range of subjects related to travel or free-time activities: regions, communities, resorts (foreign and domestic); cultural and historical places and events; sports and hobbies; entertainment; shopping; food, drink, restaurants; personalities; humor; service articles concerning travel facilities and accessories; vacation houses. We look for sophisticated humor rather than slapstick, for a literary style (as opposed to newspaper objective reportage) and hope to include some emotional content — drama, charm, enchantment, excitement — along with in-depth exploration and interpretation." Recently published articles include George Plimpton's "Oriental Hotels" and "Princess Grace's Monaco" by Joyce Winslow. Length: 1,000 to 2,000 words. Payment varies according to length, quality, need: from $5 for fillers to $1,200 for a feature article.
Photos: Technically perfect, well-composed color transparencies, 35mm or larger (or b&w prints) on subjects related to article needs. Specific subjects only, with caption notes. No general scenics. Prefers photos with interesting people, activity, drama. Payment per photo ranges from $50 to $200 for b&w, depending on size, quality, usage; $100 to $300 for 35mm (or larger) transparencies. Address stock lists and samples (may be duplicates) to Anne McAndrews, Art Director.
Fillers: Department Editor: Lynne McPherson. Short humor. Length: 300 to 1,000 words. Pays $50 to $300.
How To Break In: "Write like Faulkner, Wolfe, Arthur Miller, Thurber. Send us an article on any travel or free-time related subject that is so fascinating, in terms of style and information, that no reader could pass it by. Study back issues. Style must be crisp, compact, ultimately entertaining. Don't send an article on Bangkok when we ran a feature on it two issues ago.

Avoid first-person travelogues. Assume the reader is a college graduate, fast-moving professional who has already been there and read all the guide books. Then give him something he will delight in and make use of on his next vacation. Rather than focus on a single hotel, park, tour, museum, festival, discuss trends, give evaluations, comparisons, individual atmospheres (with specific examples)."

HORIZON, 10 Rockefeller Plaza, New York NY 10020. Managing Editor: Priscilla Flood. Bimonthly. Copyrighted. Circulation: 100,000. Pays on acceptance. Reports within 4 weeks. Enclose S.A.S.E. for ms return.
Nonfiction: History, the arts, archaeology, science, contemporary society and urban life, with emphasis on extremely high-quality writing. Length: 3,000 to 5,000 words. Payment: depends on material; $100 minimum.

MACLEAN'S, 481 University Ave., Toronto, Ont., Canada M5W 1A7. (416)595-1811. Editor: Peter C. Newman. For general interest audience. Biweekly. Newsmagazine; 90 pages. Circulation: 750,000. Buys first North American serial rights. Pays on acceptance. Will send free sample copy to writer on request. Will consider photocopied submissions; no simultaneous submissions. "Query with 200- or 300-word outline before sending any material." Reports in 2 weeks. Enclose S.A.E. and International Reply Coupons.
Nonfiction: "We have the conventional newsmagazine departments (science, medicine, law, art, music, etc.) with slightly more featurish treatment than other newsmagazines. We usually have 3 middle-of-the-book features on politics, entertainment, etc. We buy short features, but book reviews and columns are done by staffers or retainer freelancers. Freelancers should write for a free copy of the magazine and study the approach." Length ranges from 400 to 3,500 words. Pays $300 to $1,000.

MIDNIGHT, 200 Railroad Ave., Greenwich CT 06830. Editor: Selig Adler. For everyone in the family over 18. *Midnight* readers are the same people you meet on the street, and in supermarket lines, the average hard-working American who finds easily digestible tabloid news the best way for his information. Weekly national tabloid newspaper. Established in 1954. Circulation: 1,400,000. Buys more than 1,000 mss a year. Payment on acceptance. "Writers should advise us of specializations on any submission so that we may contact them if special issue or feature is planned." Submit special material 2 months in advance. Submit only complete ms. Reports within 1 week. Enclose S.A.S.E.
Nonfiction, Photos, and Fillers: Photo Department Editor: Alistair Duncan. "Sex and violence are taboo. We want upbeat human interest material, of interest to a national audience. Stories where fate plays a major role are always good. Always interested in features on well-known personalities, offbeat people, places, events and activities. Current issue is best guide. Stories are best that don't grow stale quickly. No padding. Grab the reader in the first line or paragraph. Tell the story, make the point and get out with a nice, snappy ending. Don't dazzle us with your footwork. Just tell the story. We don't require queries if the material is professionally written and presented. And we are always happy to bring a new freelancer or stringer into our fold. No cliques here. If you've got talent, and the right material—you're in. Remember—we are serving a family audience. All material must be in good taste. If it's been written up in a major newspaper or magazine, we already know about it." Buys informational, how-to, personal experience, interview, profile, inspirational, humor, historical, expose, nostalgia, photo, spot news, and new product articles. Length: 1,000 words maximum; average 500 to 800 words. Pays $50 to $300. Photos are purchased with or without ms, and on assignment. Captions are required. Pays $25 minimum for 8x10 b&w glossies. "Competitive payment on exclusives." Buys puzzles, quizzes, and short humor.
How To Break In: "*Midnight* is constantly looking for human interest subject material from throughout the United States and much of the best comes from America's smaller cities and villages, not necessarily from the larger urban areas. Therefore, we are likely to be more responsive to an article from a new writer than many other publications. This, of course, is equally true of photographs. A major mistake of new writers is that they have failed to determine the type and style of our content and in the ever-changing tabloid field, this is a most important consideration. It is also wise to keep in mind that what is of interest to you or to the people in your area may not be of equal interest to a national readership. Determine the limits of interest first. And, importantly, the material you send us must be such that it won't be 'stale' by the time it reaches the readers."

MODERN PEOPLE, Aladdin Dist., 11058 W. Addison St., Franklin Park IL 60131. Editor-in-Chief: Ray Bachar. Emphasizes celebrities, consumer affairs and offbeat stories for white lower and middle class, blue collar, non-college educated people with religious, patriotic, conservative background. Weekly tabloid; 32 pages. Estab: 1969. Circ: 200,000. Pays on acceptance. Buys all rights. Submit seasonal/holiday material 6-8 weeks in advance. Photocopied submissions OK. SASE. Reports in 2 weeks. Free sample copy and writer's guidelines.

Nonfiction: Bernard Whalen, Nonfiction Editor. Expose (consumer ripoffs); how-to (get rich, save money, be healthy, etc.); interviews (celebrities); photo feature (offbeat subjects). Buys 10 mss/issue. Query. Length: 150-500 words. Pays $10-150.

Photos: Bernard Whalen, Photos Editor. Photos purchased with accompanying ms. Pays $5-15 for 8½x11 b&w glossies; $25-200 for 8x5.5 pica color slides or transparencies. Total purchase price for ms includes payment for photos. Model release required.

Columns/Departments: Bernard Whalen, Columns/Departments Editor. Psychic Prediction; TV Soap Operas, Celebrity Gossip and Dieting. Buys 2 mss/issue. Query. Length: 15-300 words. Pays $25-50. Open to suggestions for new columns/departments.

NATIONAL ENQUIRER, Lantana FL 33464. Editor: Iain Calder. Weekly tabloid. Circ: 5,000,000. Pays on publication. Buys first North American serial rights. Query. "Story idea must be accepted first. No longer accepting unsolicited mss and all spec material will be returned unread." SASE.

Nonfiction and Photos: Wants story ideas on any subject appealing to a mass audience. Requires fresh slant on topical news stories, waste of taxpayers' money by government, the entire field of the occult, how-to articles, rags to riches success stories, medical firsts, scientific breakthroughs, human drama, adventure, personality profiles. "The best way to understanding our requirements is to study the paper." Pays $300 for most completed features; more with photos. "Payments in excess of $500 are not unusual; will pay more for really top, circulation-boosting blockbusters." Uses single or series b&w photos that must be attention-grabbing. Wide range; anything from animal photos to great action photos. "We'll bid against any other magazine for once-in-lifetime photos."

NATIONAL GEOGRAPHIC MAGAZINE, 17th and M Streets, N.W., Washington DC 20036. Senior Assistant Editor: James Cerruti. Editor: Gilbert M. Grosvenor. For members of the National Geographic Society. Monthly. Circulation: 9,325,000. Buys first publication rights with warranty to use the material in National Geographic Society copyrighted publications. Buys 40-50 mss/year. Pays on acceptance. Sample copy $1.25. Returns rejected material and acknowledges acceptance of material in 2 to 4 weeks. Query first. Writers should study several recent issues of *National Geographic* and send for leaflets "Writing for National Geographic" and "National Geographic Photo Requirements." Enclose S.A.S.E.

Nonfiction and Photos: "First-person narratives, making it easy for the reader to share the author's experience and observations. Writing should include plenty of human-interest incident, authentic direct quotation, and a bit of humor where appropriate. Accuracy is fundamental. Contemporary problems such as those of pollution and ecology are treated on a factual basis. The magazine is especially seeking short American place pieces with a strong regional 'people' flavor. The use of many clear, sharp color photographs in all articles makes lengthy word descriptions unnecessary. Potential writers need not be concerned about submitting photos. These are handled by professional photographers. Historical background, in most cases, should be kept to the minimum needed for understanding the present." Length: 8,000 words maximum for major articles. Shorts of 2,000 to 4,000 words "are always needed." Pays from $1,500 to $4,000 (and, in some cases, more) for acceptable articles; from $250 per page for color transparencies. A paragraph on an article idea should be submitted to James Cerruti, Senior Assistant Editor. If appealing, he will ask for a one- or two-page outline for further consideration. Photographers are advised to submit a generous selection of photographs with brief, descriptive captions to Mary G. Smith, Assistant Editor.

How To Break In: "Send 4 or 5 one-paragraph ideas. If any are promising, author will be asked for a one- to two-page outline. Read the latest issues to see what we want."

THE NATIONAL INFORMER, 11058 W. Addison St., Franklin Park IL 60131. Editor: Jack Steele. For "the sophisticated, mature adult, who likes to be informed on topics he usually doesn't find in the daily papers." Weekly Circulation: 500,000. Buys all rights. Buys about 600 mss a year. Occasionally overstocked. Pays on acceptance. Will send a sample copy to a writer for $1. Reports in about 3 weeks. Enclose S.A.S.E.

Nonfiction and Photos: "Our readers like human interest, self-help, and do-it-yourself types of features, particularly if these are sex-oriented. Also, our readers like to be shocked by sex expose features. We're looking for shocking features that expose and titillate. The writer should keep his article fast-paced, informative, and exciting without losing track of his main theme. We don't like slow, plodding features that inform but don't entertain. Our stories need to do both. We do not buy consumer articles or stories with settings in foreign countries." Length: 600 to 1,200 words. Pays 2¢ per word. B&w glossies purchased with mss. Pays $5 to $100.

NATIONAL INSIDER, 2713 N. Pulaski Rd., Chicago IL 60639. Editor: Robert J. Sorren. For a general audience. Weekly newspaper; 20 pages. Established in 1962. Rights purchased vary with author and material. Usually buys all rights but will sometimes reassign rights to author after publication. Buys 500 to 600 mss a year. Payment on acceptance. Will send free sample copy to writer on request. Write for copy of guidelines for writers. Will not consider photocopied or simultaneous submissions. Reports in 2 weeks. Query first. Enclose S.A.S.E.
Nonfiction and Photos: "We are looking for a variety of human interest stories. These generally should be upbeat human interest stories about persons who have overcome handicaps, or beat City Hall, or made millions from a small investment, etc. We're also interested in articles on wasteful government practices, unexplained phenomena, murder mysteries. (The emphasis here must be on the mystery surrounding the crime and good detective work. No gore photos or stories with the emphasis on sex crimes. No fictionalized accounts.) In the past we have published articles relating to sex and sex scandals. We are no longer interested in such material." B&w photos (8x10) purchased with or without mss, or on assignment. Captions required. Payment varies.

NEW TIMES, 1 Park Ave., New York NY 10016. Editor: Jonathan Z. Larsen. For general audience, mostly single, college educated, and in their 30's. News magazine published every 2 weeks; 72 pages. Established in 1973. Circulation: 130,000. Buys first North American serial rights. Buys 100 mss a year. "Guarantee; full payment on acceptance." Query first. Reports in 2 to 3 weeks. Enclose S.A.S.E.
Nonfiction: "News features, light in style. Fast-paced, individualistic and highly personal coverage of what's happening and why. The news dictates the contents of *New Times.*" Buys informational, humor, expose, and spot news. Feature length: 3,000 words. Pays $400 minimum for feature articles. Special "Insider" feature uses short items (200 words). Pays $25.

THE NEW YORKER, 25 W. 43rd St., New York NY 10036. Editor: William Shawn. Weekly. Reports in two weeks. Pays on acceptance. Enclose S.A.S.E.
Nonfiction, Fiction, and Fillers: Single factual pieces run from 3,000 to 10,000 words. Long fact pieces are usually staff-written. So is "Talk of the Town," although ideas for this department are bought. Pays good rates. Uses fiction, both serious and light, from 1,000 to 6,000 words. About 90 percent of the fillers come from contributors with or without taglines (extra pay if the tagline is used).

PAGEANT, P.O. Box 704, 21 Elm St., Rouses Point NY 12979. Editor: Nat K. Perlow. For a general audience. Established in 1945. Monthly magazine. Circulation: 250,000. Buys all rights. Buys 250 mss a year. Payment on publication. Query first. Will read only 1-page queries which include brief outline of articles. No unsolicited mss. Enclose S.A.S.E. with queries.
Nonfiction: General interest articles. Articles about people in the news. Medical breakthroughs. Consumer-oriented features, Offbeat briefs. "We find that many articles submitted to us are rewrites from other magazines. We want a fresh approach, new material and an interesting angle." Informational, how-to, personal experience, interview, profile, inspirational, humor, historical, think pieces, exposes, nostalgia, personal opinion. Length: 1,500 words. Pays $100 minimum.

PEOPLE ON PARADE, Meridian Publishing Co., 1720 Washington Blvd., Box 2315, Ogden UT 84404. (801)394-9446. Senior Editor: Dick Harris. For employees, stockholders, customers and clients of 2,000 business and industrial firms. Monthly magazine; 28 pages. Estab: 1976. Circ: 450,000. Pays on acceptance. Buys one-time rights. Submit seasonal/holiday material 9 months in advance. SASE. Reports in 3-4 weeks. Sample copy 35¢; free writer's guidelines.
Nonfiction: Melissa Arlene Hamblin, Articles Editor. "*POP* focuses on people—active, interesting, exciting, busy people; personality profiles on people succeeding, achieving, doing things." Humorous, informational, inspirational. "We want material from all regions of the country and about all types of people. Big name writers are fine, but we know there is a lot of talent among the little knowns, and we encourage them to submit their ideas. We read everything that comes in, but writers will save their time and ours by writing a good, tantalizing query." Buys 10 mss/issue. Length: 400-1,000 words. Pays 10¢/word.
Photos: Purchased with or without mss or on assignment. Captions required. Pays $20/8x10 b&w glossy; $25 for 35mm, 2¼x2¼ or 4x5 color used inside; $50 for cover color. Model release required.

Fillers: "We welcome fillers and shorts with a humorous touch, featuring interesting, successful, busy people." Buys 1-2/issue. Send fillers in. Length: 200-300 words. Pays 10¢/word.

How To Break In: *"POP* has a strong family-community orientation. Without being maudlin or pious, we cherish the work ethic, personal courage and dedication to the American dream. So we look for material that reflects positively on the man/woman who succeeds through diligence, resourcefulness, and imagination, or finds fulfillment through service to community or country. He/she may be a captain of industry, a salvage yard operator, country school teacher, medical technician, or bus driver. Tell us about people whose lives and accomplishments inspire and encourage others. We like humor and nostalgia. We want tight writing, with lively quotes and anecdotes. Pictures should be fresh, sharp, unposed, showing action, involvement."

PEOPLE WEEKLY, Time Inc., Time & Life Bldg., Rockefeller Center, New York NY 10020. Editor: Richard B. Stolley. For a general audience. Established in 1974. Weekly. Circulation: 2,000,000. Rights purchased vary with author and material. Usually buys first North American serial rights with right to syndicate, splitting net proceeds with author 50/50. Payment on acceptance. Query first. Enclose S.A.S.E.

Nonfiction and Photos: "Short pieces on personalities in all fields (sports, politics, religion, the arts, business) centered on individuals of current interest. We deal exclusively with personality pieces, in all career areas. We accept specific story suggestions only, not manuscripts." Uses question and answer interviews of 1,500 to 2,000 words. Pays $500. Biographies of 2,000 words. Pays $1,000. Payment for other assigned articles varies with amount of material used. Pays $200 per page for b&w photos purchased with or without mss. Prefers minimum 8x10 from original negatives. Captions required. Photos are also purchased on assignment.

How To Break In: "The new writer is best off aiming for a story on an unknown but extremely interesting person. The little guy out there in the hinterlands that we might overlook and that our stringers might miss. The freelancer in the boondocks is at an advantage here and a success with a story like this will make it easier to approach us with another idea. We like pieces which portray someone who reacts to the trials and tribulations of everyday life in a unique and unusual way —who does something which the rest of us perhaps should, but don't. Famous personalities are mostly handled in-house, but try us if you have a new twist or special access. Remember —we like story suggestions only, so query first."

QUEST/77, 1133 Avenue of the Americas, New York NY 10036. Editor-in-Chief: Robert Shnayerson. Managing Editor: Molly McKaughan. Emphasizes "the pursuit of human excellence for an educated, intelligent audience, interested in the positive side of things; in human potential, in sciences, the arts, good writing, design and photography. We have no connection with the feminist magazine, *Quest.*" Bimonthly magazine; 112 pages. Estab: 1977. Circ: 250,000. Pays on acceptance. Buys all rights. Submit seasonal/holiday material 4 months in advance. Photocopied submissions OK. Free writer's guidelines.

Nonfiction: Jed Horne, Molly McKaughan, Articles Editors. Humor (short pieces deflating or satirizing world views or "good" things), interviews (with fascinating individuals in government, the arts, business, science), personal experience (adventures, unusual experiences), profiles (of risk taking people, great craftsmen, adventurers), reviews (books, products, thoughts, places, etc.), and technical (new inventions, applications of science). Query. Length: 500-5,000 words. Pays $600-2,500.

Columns/Departments: Book Reviews (William Plummer, Editor); Potentials (Tony Jones, editor). Also reviews of all other cultural, political, art, or commercial events. Buys 100 mss/year. Length: 500-2,000 words. Pays $100-1,000.

Fiction: Molly McKaughan, Fiction Editor. Adventure, fantasy, humorous, mainstream, science fiction. Buys 6 mss/year. Query. Length: 500-6,000 words. Pays$600-2,000.

Poetry: Molly McKaughan, Poetry Editor. Avant-garde and free verse. Buys 6-12 poems/year. Query. Limit submissions to batches of 5. Length: 5-50 lines. Pays $5/line.

READER'S DIGEST, Pleasantville NY 10570. Monthly. Buys all rights to original mss. "Items intended for a particular feature should be directed to the editor in charge of that feature, although the contribution may later be referred to another section of the magazine as seeming more suitable. Manuscripts cannot be acknowledged, and will be returned —usually within eight or ten weeks —only when return postage accompanies them."

Nonfiction: *"Reader's Digest* is interested in receiving First Person and Premonition articles. An article for the First Person series must be a previously unpublished narrative of an unusual personal experience. It may be dramatic, inspirational or humorous, but it must have a quality of narrative and interest comparable to stories published in this series. An article for the Premonition series must be a previously unpublished narrative of an unusual psychic experience, verifiable through witnesses or appropriate documentation. Contributions for either series must be typewritten, double-spaced, no longer than 2,500 words, and accompanied by SASE. Pays $3,000 on acceptance. Address: Premonition or First Person Editor. Base rate for *general* articles is $2,400 for first sale."

Fillers: "Life in These United States contributions must be true, unpublished stories from one's own experience, revelatory of adult human nature, and providing appealing or humorous side-lights on the American scene. Maximum length: 300 words. Address Life in U.S. Editor. Payment rate on publication: $300. True and unpublished stories are also solicited for Humor in Uniform, Campus Comedy and All in a Day's Work. Maximum length: 300 words. Payment rate on publication: $300. Address Humor in Uniform, Campus Comedy or All in a Day's Work Editor. Toward More Picturesque Speech: The first contributor of each item used in this department is paid $30. Contributions should be dated, and the sources must be given. Address: Picturesque Speech Editor. For items used in Laughter, the Best Medicine, Personal Glimpses, Quotable Quotes, and elsewhere in the magazine, payment is made at the following rates: to the *first* contributor of each item from a published source, $30. For original material, $15 per *Digest* two-column line, with a minimum payment of $30. Address: Excerpts Editor."

Special Needs: Reader's Digest Educational Division can use stories and articles (1,000-2,000 words) on a variety of subjects of high interest and low readability for junior high and senior high students. Pays $100-350 on acceptance. For specifications and word list, write to Editor, *Point 31 Program,* Reader's Digest Educational Division, Pleasantville NY 10570.

READER'S NUTSHELL, Allied Publications, Inc., P.O. Box 23505, Fort Lauderdale FL 33307. Associate Editor: Marie Stilkind. Bimonthly. Buys North American serial rights only. Pays on acceptance. Query not necessary. Reports in 2 to 4 weeks. Enclose S.A.S.E. for return of submissions.

Nonfiction and Photos: "Family magazine for all ages." Wants "humorous articles of general interest." Length: 500 to 1,000 words. Pays 5¢ per accepted word. Pays $5 for photos purchased with mss; b&w glossies.

THE SAMPLE CASE, 632 N. Park St., Columbus OH 43215. (614)228-3276. Editor: James R. Eggert. For members of the United Commercial Travelers of America, located throughout the U.S. and Canada; 18 years of age and older, with a wide range of interests, educations, and occupations. Established in 1891. Quarterly. Rights purchased vary with author and material. Buys all rights, but will reassign rights to author after publication; buys first North American serial rights; first serial rights; second serial (reprint) rights; simultaneous rights. Buys 12-25 mss/year. Payment on publication. Free sample copy and writer's guidelines. Will consider photocopied submissions. Submit seasonal material 6 months in advance. Reports in 4 months. Enclose S.A.S.E.

Nonfiction and Photos: "Especially interested in general interest nonfiction. We pay special attention to articles about mental retardation, youth, safety, and cancer." Informational, personal experience, interview, some humor. Length: 500 to 2,000 words. Pays 1½¢ per word. Additional payment for good quality color and b&w glossies purchased with mss. Captions required.

THE SATURDAY EVENING POST, The Curtis Publishing Co., 1100 Waterway Blvd., Indianapolis, IN 46202. (317)634-1100. Editor-in-Chief: Cory Ser Vaas M.D. Managing Editor: Starkey Flythe. For general readership. Magazine, published 9 times a year; 120 pages. Estab: 1728. Circ: 460,000. Pays on publication. Buys all rights. Phone queries OK. Simultaneous, photocopied and previously published submissions OK. SASE. Reports in 1 month. Sample copy $1; free writer's guidelines.

Nonfiction: Ms. Betty White, Nonfiction Editor. Historical (especially nostalgia and Americana); how-to (health, general living); humor; informational (people; celebrities and ordinary but interesting personalities); inspirational (for religious columns); interview; nostalgia; personal experience (especially travel, yachting, etc.); personal opinion; photo feature; profile (especially government figures); travel and small magazine "pick-ups." Buys 10 mss/issue. Query. Length: 1,500-3,000 words. Pays $100-1,000.

Photos: Noreen Flynn, Photo Editor. Photos purchased with or without accompanying ms. Pays $25 minimum for b&w photos; $50 minimum for color photos. Total purchase price for ms includes payment for photos. Model release required.

Columns/Departments: Thomas Satrom, Columns/Departments Editor. Editorials ($100 each); Food ($150-450); Medical Mailbox ($50-250); Religion Column ($100-250) and Travel ($150-450). Open to suggestions for new columns/departments.

Fiction: Ms. Connie Schmidt, Fiction Editor. Adventure; fantasy; humorous; mainstream; mystery; romance; science fiction; suspense; western and condensed novels. Buys 5 mss/issue. Query. Length: 1,500-3,000 words. Pays $150-750.
Poetry: Ms. Astrid Henkels, Poetry Editor. Free verse, light verse and traditional. Buys 1 poem/issue. Pays $15-150.
Fillers: Ms. Louise Folsom, Fillers Editor. Jokes, gags, anecdotes, cartoons, postscripts and short humor. Buys 1 filler/issue. Length: 500-1,000 words. Pays $10-100.
How To Break In: "Keenly interested in topics relating to science, government, the arts, personalities with inspirational careers and humor. We read unsolicited material."

SATURDAY REVIEW, 1290 Ave. of the Americas, New York NY 10022. Editor-in-Chief: Norman Cousins. Managing Editor: Peter Young. "A review of ideas, the arts, and the human condition for above average educated audience. Biweekly magazine; 64 pages. Estab: 1924. Circ: 550,000. Usually pays on publication. Buys first North American serial rights. Photocopied submissions OK. SASE. Reports in 3-4 weeks. Free writer's guidelines.
Nonfiction: Expose (government, education, science); informational (analytical pieces on national or international affairs, sciences, education, and the arts); interview; and profile. Buys 100 mss/year. Query. Length: 2,500 words maximum. Pays $200/page.

SIGNATURE—The Diners' Club Magazine, 260 Madison Ave., New York NY 10016. Managing Editor: Robin Nelson. For Diners' Club members—"businessmen, urban, affluent, traveled, and young." Monthly. Circulation: 800,000. Buys first rights. Buys approximately 75 mss a year. Pays on acceptance. Write for copy of guidelines for writers. Submit seasonal material, including seasonal sports subjects, at least 3 months in advance. Returns rejected material in 2 weeks. Query first to Josh Eppinger, Executive Editor. Enclose S.A.S.E.
Nonfiction: "Articles aimed at the immediate areas of interest of our readers—in travel, social issues, personalities, sports, entertainment, food and drink, business, humor. *Signature* runs 5 to 8 nonfiction articles an issue, all by freelancers." Subjects covered in past issues of *Signature* include profiles of Norman Lear and Pete Rose. Articles on secretarial crisis, Wall Street reform, British TV invasion, natural foods dispute and small town U.S.A. restoration. Travel pieces require a *raison d'etre,* a well-defined approach and angle. Eschew destination or traditional travel piece. Feature articles run 2,500 words maximum and pay $650. Also buy shorter 1,500-word pieces which are a slice of some travel experience and usually written in very personal style. These pay $450. It's important that writer be familiar with our magazine."
Photos: "Picture stories or support art are usually assigned to photographers who have worked with in the past. We rarely ask a writer to handle the photography also. But if he has photos of his subject, we will consider them for use." Pays $50 minimum per photo.

THE STAR, 730 Third Ave., New York NY 10017. For every family; all the family—kids, teenagers, young parents and grandparents. Weekly newspaper, 48-page tabloid. Established in 1974. Circulation: 1,500,000. Rights purchased vary with author and material. Buys all rights, but will reassign rights to author after publication; buys first North American serial rights, first serial rights, second serial (reprint) rights. Buys up to 1,000 mss a year. Payment on acceptance. Submit Christmas material 2 months in advance. Query first with brief, one-paragraph outline. Reports "soon as possible." Enclose S.A.S.E.
Nonfiction and Photos: "News stories, features of topical interest, especially on personalities. No fiction or poetry. Be direct, factual, colorful." Informational, how-to, interview, profile, expose, nostalgia, photo, spot news, successful business operations, and new product articles. Not interested in first-person narratives. Length: 100 to 1,500 words. Pays $20 to $1,000. B&w photos purchased with or without ms. Captions required. Pays from $25 to $250.
Fillers: Newsbreaks and puzzles. Address to Mike Nevard.

SUNSHINE MAGAZINE, Henry F. Henrichs Publications, Litchfield IL 62056. (217)324-2322. Editor: Mrs. Monta Crane. For general audience of all ages. Monthly magazine. Established in 1924. Circulation: 225,000. Not copyrighted. Buys 75 to 100 mss per year. Payment on acceptance. Sample copy 50¢; free writer's guidelines. Submit seasonal material 6 months in advance. Reports in 1-3 months. SASE.
Nonfiction: "We accept some short articles, but they must be especially interesting or inspirational. *Sunshine Magazine* is not a religious publication, and purely religious material is rarely used. We desire carefully written features about persons or events that have real human interest—that give a 'lift'." Length: 250 to 1,200 words. Pays $10 to $40.
Fiction: "Stories must be wholesome, well-written, with clearly defined plots. There should be a purpose for each story, but any moral or lesson should be well-concealed in the plot development. Avoid trite plots that do not hold the reader's interest. A surprising climax is most

desirable. Material should be uplifting, and non-controversial." Length: 400 to 1,300 words. Pays $10-40.

SWINGERS WORLD, 8060 Melrose Ave., Los Angeles CA 90046. Editors: Gerald Vall and Elaine Stanton. For "swingers and would-be swingers." Established in 1972. Subject matter must be "swinger oriented." Bimonthly. Buys first North American serial rights. Buys 50 mss a year. Payment on publication. Will send a sample copy to a writer for $1.50. Will send editorial guidelines sheet to a writer on request (enclose S.A.S.E.). Reports in 2 weeks. Query first required. Enclose S.A.S.E.
Nonfiction: "Articles must be pro-swinger. Slick. We like new information on sex-oriented subjects, with an occasional allied subject acceptable. Even if it is humorous in treatment (which we do like), your research must be thorough." Length: approximately 2,500 words. Pays $150-225.

TOWN AND COUNTRY, 717 Fifth Ave., New York NY 10022. Managing Editor: Jean Barkhorn. For upper-income Americans. Monthly. Not a large market for freelancers. Always query first. Enclose S.A.S.E.
Nonfiction: Department Editors: Richard Kagan and Frank Zachary. "We're always trying to find ideas that can be developed into good articles that will make appealing cover lines." Wants provocative and controversial pieces. Length: 1,500 to 2,000 words. Pays $300. Also buys shorter pieces for which pay varies.

WOODMEN OF THE WORLD MAGAZINE, 1700 Farnam St., Omaha NE 68102. (402)342-1890, Ext. 302. Editor: Leland A. Larson. Published by Woodmen of the World Life Insurance Society for "people of all ages in all walks of life. We have both adult and children readers from all types of American families." Established in 1891. Monthly. Circulation: 460,000. Not copyrighted. Buys 25 mss a year. Pays on acceptance. Will send a sample copy to a writer on request. Will consider photocopied and simultaneous submissions. Submit complete ms. Submit seasonal material 3 months in advance. Reports in 5 weeks. Enclose S.A.S.E. for reply to queries or return of submissions.
Nonfiction: "General interest articles which appeal to the American family —travel, history, art, new products, how-to-do-it, sports, hobbies, food, home decorating, family expenses, etc. Because we are a fraternal benefit society operating under a lodge system, we often carry stories on how a number of people can enjoy social or recreational activities as a group. No special approach required. We want more 'consumer type' articles, humor, historical articles, think pieces, nostalgia, photo articles." Length: 10 to 1,800 words. Pays $10 minimum, 2½¢ a word depending on word count.
Photos: Purchased with or without mss; captions optional "but suggested." Uses 8x10 glossies, 4x5 tranparencies ("and possibly down to 35mm"). Payment "depends on use." For b&w photos, pays $25 for cover, $10 for inside. Color prices vary according to use and quality. Minimum of $25 for inside use; up to $100 for covers.
Fiction: Humorous and historical short stories. Length: 600 to 2,000 words. Pays "$10 or 2½¢ a word, depending on count."

Health Publications

Nearly every publication is a potential market for an appropriate health article, particularly the General Interest publications.

ACCENT ON LIVING, P.O. Box 700, Bloomington IL 61701. (309)378-4213. Editor: Raymond C. Cheever. For physically disabled persons and rehabilitation professionals. Quarterly magazine, 112 pages, (5x7). Established in 1956. Circulation: 17,000. Buys all rights. Buys 40 to 60 mss per year. Payment on publication. Sample copy $1; free writer's guidelines. Will consider photocopied submissions. Will not consider simultaneous submissions. Reports in 2 weeks. Enclose S.A.S.E.
Nonfiction: Articles about seriously disabled people who have overcome great obstacles and are pursuing regular vocational goals. Home business ideas with facts and figures on how someone confined to their home can run a business and make an average income. Especially interested in new technical aids, assistive devices, devised by an individual or available commercially, such as: bathroom and toilet aids and appliances, clothes and aids for dressing and undressing, aids for eating and drinking, as would be helpful to individuals with limited physical mobility. Intelligent discussion articles concerning the public image of and acceptance or non-acceptance

of physically disabled in normal living situations. Articles reporting on lawsuits, demonstrations or protests by handicapped individuals or consumer groups to gain equal rights and opportunities. Length: 200 to 750 words. Pays $5-100.

Photos: B&w photos purchased with accompanying ms. Captions required. Pays $5 to $25.

BESTWAYS MAGAZINE, 466 Foothill Blvd., La Canada CA 91011. (213)790-5370. Editor: Patricia Bassett. For housewives, students and those with an interest in health and nutrition. Monthly magazine; 64 pages. Established in 1973. Circulation: 125,000. Buys all rights, but may reassign rights to author after publication. Buys 100 or more mss a year. Payment on publication. Will send free sample copy to writer on request. Will consider photocopied submissions. No simultaneous submissions. Reports on material in 3 weeks. Query first or submit complete ms. Enclose S.A.S.E.

Nonfiction and Photos: Articles on vitamins, minerals, exercise, nutrition. Easy to comprehend articles, based on products sold through health food stores. New information or new applications for understanding vitamin and mineral supplementation. Family feeding. Informational, how-to, personal experience, interview, profile, crafts. Length: 1,600 to 5,000 words. Pays $75 to $150. No additional payment is usually made for b&w photos used with mss, but exceptions are sometimes made.

BODY FORUM MAGAZINE, Cosvetic Laboratories, Box 80883, Atlanta GA 30305. Editor: Paul Hagan. Emphasizes "health from standpoint of nutrition for an audience mid 20's to 60's with 50% below 38. Education level high school to post grad. Average income $16,000." Monthly magazine; 48 pages. Estab: 1976. Circ: 2.2 million. Pays on acceptance. Buys all rights. Phone queries OK "from authors whose written inquiries we follow up." Submit seasonal/holiday material 3 months in advance. Photocopied and previously published submissions OK. SASE. Reports in 4 weeks. Free sample copy.

Nonfiction: Expose, how-to, informational, interview and technical. "We are trying to interpret what is happening in governmental and university research projects for the general public. We focus on nutrition, exercise physiology, relaxation techniques and congressional legislation affecting nutrition. The aim is for each article to show the reader how this new piece of information can be used to give him a better, more healthy life style." Buys 12 mss/issue. "Prefer ms, but will work with query." Length: 750-1,200 words. Pays $100-225; "specialist articles at negotiated rates."

How To Break In: "We are particularly interested in new developments from reputable scientists. These would discuss how some new piece of research can be applied by the average person to better his life. An example would be a report by a university researcher showing that 200 mg of vitamin E per day could cut heart attacks in half."

THE CRITICAL LIST, 32 Sullivan St., Toronto, Ontario, Canada M5T 1B9, Dept. WM. (416)923-0716. Publisher: Jerry Green, M.D. For anyone interested in health in its broadest sense, and the politics of it. Established in 1975. Quarterly. Circulation: 12,000. Rights purchased vary with author and material. Usually buys first North American serial rights. Buys about 15 mss a year. Pays on publication. Will send free sample copy to writer on request. Write for copy of guidelines for writers. No photocopied or simultaneous submissions. Reports in 2-3 months. Query first. Enclose S.A.E. and International Reply Coupons.

Nonfiction and Photos: "Very interested in original, investigative work in health area; exposes and articles that are critical of establishment medicine; articles on alternate forms of health care." Analysis, criticism, muckraking on topics in the health field; especially Canadian. Informational, how-to, personal experience, interview, profile, humor, historical, think pieces, expose, nostalgia, personal opinion, reviews, spot news, technical articles. Length: 500 to 2,000 words. Pays 3-10¢/word, if requested. B&w photos purchased with or without mss or on assignment. Pays $5 to $10. Captions optional.

Poetry and Fillers: Traditional and avant-garde forms of poetry, blank verse, free verse, light verse, haiku. Length: open. Pays $5-10. Newsbreaks, puzzles related to health, clippings, jokes, gags, anecdotes, short humor used as fillers. Length: brief. Pays $5-10.

CURRENT HEALTH, Curriculum Innovations, Inc., 501 Lake Forest Ave., Highwood IL 60040. (312)432-2700. Managing Editor: Laura Ruekberg. For junior high and high school health education classes; written at about 9th grade reading level. Monthly during school year (September-May); magazine; 32 pages. Estab: 1974. Circ: 150,000. Pays on publication. Buys all rights. Submit seasonal/holiday material 4 months in advance. Simultaneous, photocopied and previously published submissions OK. SASE. Reports in 1 month. Free sample copy.

Nonfiction: Informational, interview, personal opinion, personal experience, photo feature, and technical. Query. Length: 750-3,000 words. Pays 4¢/word and up.

Photos: Purchased with or without accompanying ms or on assignment. Query. Pays $10 minimum for 8x10 b&w glossy; $25 for 35 or 120mm transparencies. Model release usually required.

Columns/Departments: Drugs, Personal Health (insomnia, acne, warts, exercise, etc.), Disease Focus (close examination), First Aid & Safety, Psychology, Nutrition. Query and submit writing samples. Length: 500-1,500 words. Pays 4¢/word and up. Open to suggestions for new columns or departments.

FAMILY HEALTH, 149 Fifth Ave., New York NY 10010. Editor: Caroline Stevens. For health-minded young parents. Magazine; 66 pages. Special issues: April and November (food and nutrition); October (baby and child care). Established in 1969. Monthly. Circulation: 1,000,000. Rights purchased vary with author and material. May buy all rights but may reassign rights to author after publication; first North American serial rights. Buys most of their articles from freelance writers. Pays within 6 weeks of acceptance. Will send sample copy to writer for $1. No photocopied or simultaneous submissions. Submit special issue material 3 months in advance. Reports in 6 weeks. Query first for most nonfiction. Submit complete ms for first-person articles. Enclose S.A.S.E.

Nonfiction: Articles on all aspects of health, both mental and physical; safety, new advances in medicine. Fresh, new approaches essential. No "all about" articles (for example, "All About Mental Health"). Informational, how-to, personal experience, interview, profile, think articles, expose; book reviews. Length: 500 to 3,000 words. Pays $350 to $750.

FITNESS MAGAZINE, T. Fleming Associates, Box 4473, Pittsburgh PA 15205. Editor-in-Chief: Thomas J. Fleming. Emphasizes physical fitness and nutrition. Monthly magazine; 24 pages. Estab: 1975. Circ: 100,000. Pays on publication. Buys all rights. Simultaneous, photocopied and previously published submissions OK. SASE. Reports in 6 months. Sample copy $3.

Nonfiction: Expose (fad diets, exercise equipment, spas, health clubs); historical (old-time exercise programs, ancient diets); how-to (be fit); humor; informational; inspirational (report on people who have benefitted from fitness programs); interview; nostalgia; personal experience and personal opinion. Query. Pays $25-500.

Photos: Photos purchased with accompanying ms. Captions required. Pays $10-20 for 8x10 b&w matte photos; $20-100 for color photos (no 35mm). No additional payment for photos accepted with accompanying ms. Model release required.

Columns/Departments: Books (review). Query. Length: 50-200 words. Pays $10-50. Open to suggestions for new columns/departments.

Fillers: Clippings, jokes, gags, anecdotes and newsbreaks. Query. Length: 50-200 words. Pays $25-150.

How To Break In: "Writers must put themselves in the reader's place. I'd like to see writers become reporters. Report happenings in their area that would be of importance to 'fitness' readers. Dig around grade and high schools, interview gym teachers, find out how good or bad the health programs are. Visit YMCA's, YWCA's, health clubs, spas, look for interesting people, tell the readers about bricklayers, lawyers, doctors, teachers, plumbers, etc., who practice the good healthy life."

HEALTH, American Osteopathic Association, 212 E. Ohio St., Chicago IL 60611. (312)944-2713. Managing Editor: Mary Anne Klein. For patients of osteopathic physicians. Magazine; 28 pages, 8½x5½. Established in 1955. Published every 2 months. Circulation: 24,000. Buys first serial rights. Pays on acceptance. Will send free sample copy to writer on request. Write for copy of guidelines for writers. Query first. Reports within 6 weeks. Enclose S.A.S.E.

Nonfiction and Photos: "Primarily educational material on health and health-related subjects (ecology, community health, mental health). We do not use first-person or fictional material. We use some feature-type articles on unusual events or situations. Material must be carefully researched (and documented by bibliography to the editor) but must be geared to the layman. We try to gear all material (even though the subject may be concerned with general medicine) to the philosophy of osteopathic medicine. We are especially concerned with preventive medicine, personal health care, nutrition, exercise, etc." Length: 1,000-1,200 words. Pays 4¢/word. B&w photos purchased with ms. Pays $2.50 to $5, depending on quality and originality.

HEALTHWAYS, American Chiropractic Association, 2200 Grand Ave., Des Moines IA 50312. Editor-in-Chief: Maryann Smith. Emphasizes chiropractic and general health. For readers interested in maintaining their health, "probably in the most natural way possible—sans drugs, surgery, etc." Magazine published 6 times a year; 50 pages. Estab: 1946. Circ: 115,000. Pays on publication. Buys one-time rights. Submit seasonal/holiday material 6 months in advance. If advised, will consider simultaneous submissions. SASE. Reports in 3 weeks. Free sample copy and editorial guidelines.

Nonfiction: Informational (chiropractic; general health, nutrition, exercise); inspirational (if it's realistic in that it offers practical advice on how one can be inspired—nothing on religious themes); interview (if of informational nature); travel (short pieces; specific on dates of special events and some idea of costs); photo features (but query on these); technical (chiropractic and health, if person is versed in subject area and can write to a lay audience). Buys 30 mss/year. Query or send complete ms. Length: 400-2,000 words. Pays $10-50.

Photos: Purchased with or without mss. Captions required. Query for b&w. Send transparencies. Pays $2.50-25 for b&w glossies; 5x7 minimum. Pays $15-50 for 35mm color transparencies, but prefers larger sizes. Good color prints also acceptable. Model release required. Covers need not relate to subject matter. "Our covers are general interest type, usually outdoor subjects."

How To Break In: "Portray knowledge in those areas of interest to us; know how to write in a succinct, reportorial manner with some humor, if appropriate. Submit articles in accepted manner. Would particularly welcome pieces that deal with some aspect of chiropracty in a knowledgeable way as it relates to the receiver of those services. We are particularly interested in writers who specialize in health articles: nutrition, exercise, recreational activities that involve exercising; how to live a 'normal' everyday life and still keep oneself in good physical and mental condition."

LIFE AND HEALTH, 6856 Eastern Ave., N.W., Washington DC 20012. Editor: Don Hawley. Established in 1884. Monthly. Circulation: 100,000. Buys all rights. Buys 100 to 150 mss a year. Payment on acceptance. Will send editorial guidelines sheet to a writer on request. Will send sample copy to writer for 50¢. Complimentary copies automatically to authors published. No query. Submit seasonal health articles 6 months in advance. Reports on material within two months. Enclose S.A.S.E.

Nonfiction, Photos, Poetry, and Fillers: General subject matter consists of "short, concise articles that simply and clearly present a concept in the field of health. Emphasis on prevention; faddism avoided." Approach should be a "simple, interesting style for laymen. Readability important. Medical jargon avoided. Material should be reliable and include latest findings. We are perhaps more conservative than other magazines in our field. Not seeking sensationalism." Buys informational, interview, some humor. "Greatest single problem is returning articles for proper and thorough documentation. References to other lay journals not acceptable." Regular columns that seek freelance material are Youth Corner and Man and His Spirit. Length: up to 1,500 words. Pays $50 to $150. Purchases photos with mss. 5x7 or larger b&w glossies. Pays $7.50. Color photos usually by staff. Pays $75. Buys some health-related poetry, minimum of $10.

LISTEN MAGAZINE, 6830 Laurel St., N.W., Washington DC 20012. (202)723-0800. Editor: Francis A. Soper. Slanted primarily for teens. *Listen* is used in many high school curriculum classes, in addition to use by professionals; medical personnel, counselors, law enforcement officers, educators, youth workers, etc. Monthly magazine, 28 pages. Established in 1948. Circulation: 200,000. Buys all rights. Buys 100 to 200 mss per year. Payment on acceptance. Will send free sample copy to writer on request. Write for copy of guidelines for writers. Will not consider photocopied submissions or simultaneous submissions. Reports within 4 weeks. Query first. Enclose S.A.S.E.

Nonfiction: Specializes in preventive angle, presenting positive alternatives to various drug dependencies. Especially interested in youth-slanted articles or personality interviews encouraging nonalcoholic and nondrug ways of life. Teenage point of view is good. Popularized medical, legal, and educational articles. "We don't want typical alcoholic story/skid-row bum, AA stories." Length: 500 to 1,500 words. Pays 2-5¢/word.

Photos: Purchased with or without accompanying ms. Captions required if photos accompany ms; captions optional on general photo submissions. Pays $5-15 per b&w (5x7, but 8x10 preferred). Color done mostly on assignment; some general color photos (2x2 transparencies).

Poetry and Fillers: Blank verse and free verse only. Some inspirational poetry; short poems preferred. Word square/general puzzles are also considered. Pays $5 for poetry. Payment for fillers varies according to length and quality. Pays $15 for puzzles.

How To Break In: "Personal stories are good, especially if they have a unique angle. Other authoritative articles need a fresh approach."

MUSCLE MAGAZINE INTERNATIONAL, Unit 1, 270 Rutherford Rd., S., Brampton, Ontario, Canada. L6W 3K7. Editor: Robert Kennedy. For 20- to 30-year-old men interested in physical fitness and overall body improvement. Magazine; 116 pages. Established in 1974.

Quarterly. Circulation: 110,000. Buys all rights. Buys 80 mss a year. Pays on acceptance. Will send sample copy to writer for $1. No photocopied or simultaneous submissions. Reports in 1 week. Submit complete ms. Enclose S.A.E. and International Reply Coupons.

Nonfiction and Photos: Articles on ideal physical proportions and importance of protein in the diet. Should be helpful and instructional and appeal to young men who want to live life in a vigorous and healthy style. "We do not go in for huge, vein-choked muscles and do not want to see any articles on attaining huge muscle size. We would like to see articles for the physical culturist or an article on fitness testing." Informational, how-to, personal experience, interview, profile, inspirational, humor, historical, expose, nostalgia, personal opinion, photo, spot news, new product, merchandising technique articles. Length: 1,200 to 1,600 words. Pays 6¢ per word. Columns purchasing material include Nutrition Talk (eating ideas for top results) and Shaping Up (improving fitness and stamina). Length: 1,300 words. Pays 6¢ per word. B&w and color photos are purchased with or without ms. Pays $8 for 8x10 glossy exercise photos; $16 for 8x10 b&w posing shots. Pays $100 for color; 2¼x2¼ or larger.

Fillers: Newsbreaks, clippings, puzzles, jokes, short humor. Length: open. Pays $5, minimum.

How To Break In: "Best way to break in is to seek out the muscle-building 'stars' and do in-depth interviews with biography in mind. Picture support essential."

NUTRITION HEALTH REVIEW, Box 221, Haverford PA 19041. Editor-in-Chief: Frank Ray Rifkin. Emphasizes nutrition, vegetarianism and health for all ages. Quarterly tabloid; 30 pages. Estab: 1976. Circ: 110,000. Pays on publication. Buys all rights, but may reassign following publication. Submit seasonal/holiday material 90 days in advance. Photocopied and previously published submissions OK. SASE. Reports in 5 weeks. Sample copy 75¢.

Nonfiction: William Renaurd, Nonfiction Editor. Expose, historical, how-to, humor, informational, interview, new product, personal experience, photo feature, technical and travel. All must be related to nutrition and health. Buys 15-20 mss/issue. Send complete ms. Length: 400 words maximum. Pays $10 minimum.

Photos: Purchased without accompanying ms. Pays $15 minimum for b&w photos. Send prints. Total purchase price for ms includes payment for photos. Model release required.

Columns/Departments: Vegetarianism, Health Hints and Medical Research. Buys 15-20 mss/issue. Send complete ms. Length: 400 words maximum. Pays $10 minimum. Open to suggestions for new columns/departments.

WEIGHT WATCHERS MAGAZINE, 149 FIfth Ave., New York NY 10011. (212)838-8964. Editor: Bernadette Carr. For middle class females, mostly married, with children. Monthly magazine, 64 pages. Established in 1968. Circulation: 780,000. Buys all rights. Buys 3-5 mss per month. Payment on acceptance. Sample copy for 75¢. Will not consider photocopied or simultaneous submissions. Submit seasonal material 5 months in advance. Reports within 4 weeks. Enclose S.A.S.E.

Nonfiction: "Subject matter should be related to weight control, although we are not interested in diet pieces. We are interested in developing medical and psychological pieces related to weight, or humor, or weight control articles with a male slant. We are not interested in women's articles per se, or in fiction, or in fashion or beauty pieces. We don't want recipes, either." Informational, how-to, humor, think articles. Particularly open to new material on both children and money, but stay away from narrow, personal experience pieces like "How to Have a Garage Sale." Length: 3,000 words maximum. Pay varies, usually $300-600.

WELL-BEING MAGAZINE, 833 W. Fir, San Diego CA 92101. (714)234-2211. Editors: Barbara Salat and Allan Jaklich. Managing Editor: Dean Plummer. Reports on "do-it-yourself" healing techniques for readers interested in change for the better, for the individual and the planet. Monthly magazine; 56 pages. Estab: 1975. Circ: 19,000. Pays on publication. Phone queries OK. Submit seasonal/holiday material 1 month in advance. Photocopied and previously published submissions OK. Reports in 2-3 weeks. Sample copy $1; free writer's guidelines.

Nonfiction: Reports on various life styles and healing techniques, alternative and traditional. Subjects include diet, massage, herbs, exercise, positive thought, life styles, gardening, recycling, alternative energy, wild foods, wholistic medicine, home birth, etc. How-to (use solar energy, recycling methods, garden naturally, conserve, improve health); informational (effects of common foods, drugs, additives, flavorings, colorings); inspirational (achieving inner peace; outer harmony through relationship; work, prayer, positive thought, service, sharing); interviews (with folks who live natural, positive, healthy, active lives; healers, doctors, midwives, inventors, musicians, "new age" business people); new products (natural — can be made at home); nostalgia (living on the land, homesteading); personal experience (self-healing, home birth, new herbal uses); profiles (natural life style personalities); photo features (related to indi-

vidual and/or planetary healing) and technical (how to build single, inexpensive solar devices, composters, etc., for the home). Buys 2-3/issue. Length: 500-5,000 words. Pays $5-100.
Photos: Purchased with or without mss, or on assignment. Query. Pays $5/page (published). Send 8x10 b&w glossies. Color slides by arrangement.

History Publications

THE ALASKA JOURNAL, Alaska Northwest Publishing Co., Box 4-EEE, Anchorage AK 99509. (907)279-1723. Editor-in-Chief: William S. Hanable. Quarterly magazine; 64 pages. Estab: 1971. Circ: 10,000. Pays on publication. Buys first North American serial rights. SASE. Reports in 3 weeks. Sample copy $1.
Nonfiction: Historical (Alaska and Yukon Territory), and articles on Alaskan art and artists, present and past. Buys 30-36 mss/year. Query. Length: 1,000-6,000 words. Pays 2-4¢/word.
Photos: Purchased with accompanying ms. Captions required. Pays $2-5 for 5x7 or 8x10 b&w photos; $5-10 for 35mm color transparencies.

AMERICAN HERITAGE, 10 Rockefeller Plaza, New York NY 10020. Editor: Alvin M. Josephy, Jr. Established in 1954. Bimonthly. Circulation: 170,000. Buys all rights. Buys about 20 uncommissioned mss a year. Pays on acceptance. Before submitting, "check our five- and ten-year indexes to see whether we have already treated the subject." Submit seasonal material 8 months in advance. Returns rejected material in 1 month. Acknowledges acceptance of material in 1 month, or sooner. Query first. Enclose S.A.S.E.
Nonfiction: Wants "historical articles intended for intelligent lay readers rather than professional historians." Emphasis is on authenticity, accuracy, and verve. Style should stress "readability and accuracy." Length: 4,000 to 5,000 words. Pays $350 minimum.
Fillers: "We occasionally buy shorts and fillers that deal with American history."
How To Break In: "Our needs are such that the criteria for a young, promising writer are unfortunately no different than those for an old hand. Nevertheless, we have over the years published quite a few 'firsts' from young writers whose historical knowledge, research methods, and writing skills meet our standards from the start. Everything depends on the quality of the material. We don't really care whether the author is twenty and unknown, or eighty and famous."

AMERICAN HISTORICAL REVIEW, Ballantine Hall, Indiana University, Bloomington IN 47401. Editor: Otto Pflanze. Associate Editor: Barbara A. Hanewalt. For professional historians, educators, others interested in history. Established in 1895. Five times a year. Circulation: 23,000. Acquires all rights. Uses about 20 mss per year. No payment. Will consider photocopied submissions. No simultaneous submissions. Reports in 2 to 3 months. Submit complete ms. Enclose S.A.S.E.
Nonfiction: Scholarly articles of historical nature to appeal to a general audience (not specialized). Reviews of history books.

AMERICAN HISTORY ILLUSTRATED, CIVIL WAR TIMES ILLUSTRATED, Box 1831, Harrisburg PA 17105. (717)234-5091. Editor: William C. Davis. Aimed at general public with an interest in sound, well-researched history. Monthly except March and September. Buys all rights. Pays on acceptance. Will send a sample copy of either for $1.25. Write for copy of guidelines for writers. Suggestions to freelancers: "Do not bind ms or put it in a folder or such. Simply paperclip it. We prefer a ribbon copy, not a carbon or xerox. No multiple submissions, please. It is best to consult several back issues before submitting any material, in order to see what we have already covered and to get an idea of our editorial preferences. Please include informal annotations and a reading list of materials used in preparing the article." Reports within two weeks. Query first. Enclose S.A.S.E.
Nonfiction: U.S. history, pre-historic to the 1960's, biography, military, social, cultural, political, etc. Also the U.S. in relation to the rest of the world, as in World Wars I and II, diplomacy. The Civil War, military, biography, technological, social, diplomatic, political, etc. Style should be readable and entertaining, but not glib or casual. Slant generally up to the author. Taboos: shallow research, extensive quotation. 2,500 to 5,000 words. Pays $50 to $350.
Photos: Buys only occasionally with mss; 8x10 glossies preferred. Does welcome suggestions for illustrations. Address to Frederic Ray, Art Director.

THE AMERICAN WEST, 20380 Town Center Ln., Suite 160, Cupertino CA 95014. Senior Editor: Pamela Herr. Editor: Ed Holm. Emphasizes Western American history. Sponsored by the Western History Association. Bimonthly magazine; 64 pages. Estab: 1964. Circ: 35,000. Pays within 30 days of acceptance. Buys all rights. Submit seasonal/holiday material 6 months in advance. Photocopied submissions OK. SASE. Reports in 4 weeks. Free sample copy and writer's guidelines.

Nonfiction: Historical (carefully researched, accurate, lively articles having some direct relationship to Western American history) and photo feature (essays relating to some specific historical theme). Buys 5 mss/issue. Length: 2,000-5,000 words. Pays $100-250.

Photos: Purchased with or without accompanying ms. Captions required. Query. Pays $25 for 8x10 b&w photos; $50 for 4x5 color transparencies.

How To Break In: "We publish a relatively small number of articles, emphasizing careful research (preferably based in primary resources) and historical accuracy. The articles should be written with a general audience in mind and should be lively in tone. Most accepted mss fall into the following subject areas: biography (noteworthy men and women figuring in the Western American heritage), historical narrative; personal experience (accounts by senior citizens having some relation to the Western heritage); and 'living history' (articles on museums, historical reenactments, or other events). Geographic subjects area is limited to anything west of the Mississippi River."

ART AND ARCHAEOLOGY NEWSLETTER, 243 East 39 St., New York NY 10016. Editor: Otto F. Reiss. For people interested in archaeology; educated laymen, educators, some professional archaeologists. Quarterly newsletter, 20 pages, (5½x8½). Established in 1965. Circulation: 1,800. Buys all rights, but will reassign rights to author after publication; buys second serial (reprint) rights. Buys 1 or 2 mss per year. Payment on publication. Will send sample copy to writer for $1.50 in 13¢ stamps. Will consider photocopied or simultaneous submissions. Reports in 2 weeks. Query first. Enclose S.A.S.E.

Nonfiction: "Ancient history, archaeology, new discoveries, new conclusions, new theories. Our approach is similar to the way *Time Magazine* would treat archaeology or ancient history in its science section. A lighter tone, less rigidly academic. Don't avoid mystery, glamor, eroticism. Primarily interested in old world antiquity. Would like intriguing articles on Aztecs, Mayas, Incas, but not travel articles a la *Holiday*. Definitely not interested in Indian arrowheads, Indian pots, kivas, etc." Length: 400 to 2,500 words. Pays $20.

Photos: Purchased with accompanying ms with no additional payment. Purchased also without ms for $5 minimum for b&w. Information (data) required for all b&w photos. No color. Will write own captions.

How To Break In: "Spend five years reading books about archaeology and ancient history so that you become something of an expert on the subject. Be prepared to give precise sources, with page and paragraph, for factual statements. Some freelance writers, pretending to submit nonfiction, invent their material. Don't know what is on their mind, perhaps the ambition to be a pocket-size Clifford Irving. Altogether, dealing with freelance people in this field is more trouble than it is worth. But hope blooms eternal. Perhaps there's another enthusiast who sneaked his way into an Alexander's Tomb."

CANADA WEST MAGAZINE, Stagecoach Publishing Co., Ltd., Box 3399, Langley, B.C. Canada V3A 4R7. (604)534-8222. Editor-in-Chief: T.W. Paterson. Emphasizes Canadian pioneer history. Quarterly tabloid; 16 pages. Estab: 1969. Circ: 6,000. Pays on publication. Buys first North American serial rights. SASE. Reports in 6-8 weeks. Free sample copy and writer's guidelines.

Nonfiction: Historical (any subject of Canadian history: shipwrecks, battles, massacres, pioneers, exploration, etc.), and travel (Canadian historical sites). Buys 7 mss/issue. Query or submit complete ms. Length: 400-2,500 words. Pays 1½¢/word.

Photos: Purchased with accompanying ms. Captions required. Pays $5 for 5x7 or larger b&w photos. Offers no additional payment for photos accepted with accompanying ms.

CANADIAN FRONTIER, P.O. Box 157, New Westminster, British Columbia, Canada V3L 4Y4. Editor: Brian Antonson. For people of all ages interested in Canadian history. Annual magazine; 112 pages. Estab: 1972. Circ: 2,000. Copyrighted. Buys 24 mss/year. Pays on publication. Sample copy $3.50; free writer's guidelines. Photocopied and simultaneous submissions OK. Query first or submit complete ms, including a brief author's biography and bibliography. SAE and International Reply Coupons. Annual submissions deadline: April 1.

Nonfiction and Photos: Authoritative, accurate accounts of people, incidents, etc., in Canada's history. Completely factual material, with complete bibliographies, where possible. Length: 3,000 words maximum. Pays $35 minimum, and $2/photo used. Captions required.

CHICAGO HISTORY, Chicago Historical Society, Clark St. at North Ave., Chicago IL 60614. (312)642-4600. Editor-in-Chief: Fannia Weingartner. Emphasizes history for history scholars, buffs and academics. Quarterly magazine; 64 pages. Estab: 1970. Circ: 5,000. Pays on acceptance. Buys all rights (but may reassign following publication), second serial (reprint) rights and one-time rights. Submit seasonal/holiday material 6 months in advance. Simultaneous and photocopied submissions OK. SASE. Reports in 2 weeks. Free sample copy and writer's guidelines.

Nonfiction: Historical (of Chicago and the Old Northwest). Buys 6 mss/issue. Query. Length: 4,000 minimum. Pays $75-250.

How To Break In: "Query first. Articles must be both scholarly and lively."

EL PALACIO, QUARTERLY JOURNAL OF THE MUSEUM OF NEW MEXICO, Museum of New Mexico Press, Box 2087, Santa Fe NM 87503. (505)827-2352. Editor-in-Chief: Richard L. Polese. Emphasizes anthropology, history, folk and fine arts, natural history and geography. Quarterly magazine; 48 pages. Estab: 1913. Circ: 2,500. Pays on publication. Buys all rights, but may reassign following publication. Phone queries OK. Submit seasonal/holiday material 9 months-1 year in advance. Photocopied submissions OK. SASE. Reports in 2-6 weeks. Sample copy $2; free writer's guidelines.

Nonfiction: Historical (on Southwest; technical approach OK); how-to (folk art and craft, emphasis on the authentic); informational (more in the fields of geography and natural history); photo feature; technical; and travel (especially if related to the history of the Southwest). Buys 1 ms/issue. Send complete ms. Length: 1,750-5,000 words. Pays $15 minimum.

Photos: James Mafchir, Photo Editor. Photos purchased with or without accompanying ms or on assignment. Captions required. Pays $10 minimum for 5x7 (or larger) b&w photos; $10 minimum for 5x7, 8½x11 or 35mm color transparencies. Send prints. Total purchase price for ms includes payment for photos.

Columns/Departments: Museum Notes, Books (reviews of interest to *El Palacio* readers). The following pertains to Books: Query or send complete ms. Length: 750-1,500 words. Pays in copies. Open to suggestions for new columns/departments.

How To Break In: "*El Palacio* magazine offers a unique opportunity for writers with technical ability to have their work reach publication and be seen by influential professionals as well as avidly interested lay readers. The magazine is highly regarded in its field, despite the fact that we still infrequently pay for articles, except on contract."

FRONTIER TIMES, Western Publications, Inc., Box 3338, Austin TX 78764. Bimonthly. See *Old West.*

HISTORIC PRESERVATION, National Trust for Historic Preservation, 740-748 Jackson Place, N.W., Washington DC 20006. Vice President and Editor: Mrs. Terry B. Morton. Organizational publication emphasizing historic preservation. For members of the National Trust for Historic Preservation and others interested in or involved with historic preservation efforts. Quarterly magazine; 48 pages. Estab: 1949. Circ: 110,000. Pays on publication. Rights purchased vary; may buy all, second serial (reprint), or one-time rights. Photocopied and previously publishes submissions OK. SASE. Reports in 2-4 weeks. Free sample copy and writer's guidelines.

Nonfiction: "Little freelance work used, but willing to review queries on subjects directly related to historic preservation, including efforts to save buildings, structures, neighborhoods of historical, architectural and cultural significance. No local history; must relate to sites, objects, buildings and neighborhoods specifically. Most material prepared on a commission basis. Writer must be very familiar with our subject matter, which deals with a specialized field, in order to present a unique publication idea." Length: 1,000-2,500 words. Pays $250 maximum.

Photos: Additional payment not usually made for photos purchased with mss. Query or send contact sheet. Pays $10-50 for 8x10 b&w glossies purchased without mss or on assignment; $50 maximum for color.

JOURNAL OF AMERICAN HISTORY, Ballantine Hall, Indiana University, Bloomington IN 47401. (812)337-3034. Editor: Martin Ridge. For professional historians of all ages. Quarterly journal, 350 pages. Established in 1907. Circulation: 12,500. Buys all rights. Buys over 300 mss per year. Payment on acceptance. Reports in 10 to 12 weeks. Submit only complete ms. Enclose S.A.S.E.

Nonfiction: Material dealing with American history; analytical for the audience of professional historians. Length: 900 to 1,500 words. Pays $5 per page.

JOURNAL OF GENEALOGY, Anderson Publishing Co., Inc., Box 31097, Omaha NE 68131. (402)554-1800. Editor-in-Chief: Robert D. Anderson. Emphasizes genealogy and history. Monthly magazine; 48 pages. Estab: 1976. Circ: 10,000. Pays on publication. Buys all rights, but may reassign following publication. Submit seasonal/holiday material 4 months in advance. Previously published submissions OK. SASE. Reports in 4 weeks. Sample copy $1; writer's guidelines for SASE.

Nonfiction: Historical (on places or obscure pioneers, place names, etc), how-to (new or different ways to trace ancestors, new ways to keep notes, or new ways to diagram a pedigree chart), interview (of well-known persons involved in genealogy), new product (about innovations in capturing, storing, indexing, and retrieving data—such as computors and microfiche relating to historical or genealogical data), personal experience (must have profound impact on genealogical research), personal opinion (must be in-depth and scholarly dealing with genealogy and/or history), profile, travel (genealogists like to combine a vacation with genealogical research), and scholarly (we need thought provoking articles on the science of genealogy and how it relates to other sciences). Buys 20 mss/year. Query. Length: 750-4,500 words; "longer considered, but need natural breaks for serialization." Pays 2¢/word.

Photos: Purchased with or without accompanying ms or on assignment. Captions required. Query. Pays $5-25 for 8x10 b&w photos. Model release required.

Columns/Departments: Society Station (this column is devoted to helping genealogical and historical societies in their day-to-day activities, i.e., "How to Write a News Release" or "Should We File for Non-Profit Status?"). Query. Length: 750-2,000 words. Pays 2¢/word. Open to suggestions for new columns/departments.

How To Break In: "We want articles that will help the most people find the most genealogy. Always ask yourself, as we do, 'is it meaningful?' We need good articles on researching in foreign countries."

MANKIND, The Magazine of Popular History, 8060 Melrose Ave., Los Angeles CA 90046. Editor: Robert Edward Brown. Primarily college graduate reader audience. Quarterly. Buys North American serial rights only. Buys about 50 mss a year. Pays on publication. Will send sample copy for $1.25. Query first. Enclose S.A.S.E.

Nonfiction: "Queries are preferred and should be extensive enough so the editors may determine where the article is going. We have found that most of the over-the-transom submissions are poorly researched for this market. Assignments are given only to writers who have sold here before or have a reputation in the field of historical writing. We are looking for articles on any aspect of history that can be rendered meaningful and alive and which lends itself to illustration. We would like to emphasize high quality writing together with accurateness and a fresh approach to history. We do not wish to see superficiality, survey generalizations or material of a shocking nature. We see far too many articles on the Civil War and most other aspects of American history." Prefers 5,000 words or less. Pays $200 maximum.

Photos: Purchased with mss. Pays $35 per page for b&w. Pays $75 per page for color.

How To Break In: "There are no special departments for the beginner who wants to break in, save 'Guest Column', which runs usually to 2,000 words and takes current events and compares them to similar happenings in the past. Check the magazine. A new writer can break in only by submitting an article precisely fitting current format. Best way is to read the magazine and submit queries. Warning: we are really overstocked. That is not just a rejection ploy."

MONTANA, The Magazine of Western History, Montana Historical Society, 225 N. Roberts, Helena MT 59601. (406)449-2694. Editor: Mrs. Vivian Paladin. Quarterly. Circulation: 14,000. Prefers to buy first rights. Pays on acceptance. Will send a sample copy to a writer on request. Write for copy of guidelines for writers. Query first. Reports in 1 month. Enclose S.A.S.E. for reply to queries.

Nonfiction and Photos: "Interested in authentic articles on the history of the American and Canadian West which show original research on significant facets of history rather than the rewriting of standard incidents generally available in print. Evidence of research must accompany articles, either in the form of footnoting or bibliography. Strict historical accuracy is a must for us: we cannot use fictional material, however authentic the background may be. Unless it is very skillfully and authentically employed, contrived dialog is not acceptable." Length: 3,500 to 6,500 words with rare photographs if possible. Photos (b&w) purchased with ms. Pays $40 to $100, "depending on length and quality."

NORTH CAROLINA HISTORICAL REVIEW, Historical Publications Section, Archives and History, 109 E. Jones St., Raleigh NC 27611. (919)733-7442. Editor-in-Chief: Memory F. Mitchell. Emphasizes scholarly historical subjects for students and others interested in history. Quarterly magazine; 100 pages. Estab: 1924. Circ: 2,500. Buys all rights, but may reassign following publication. Phone queries OK. Submit seasonal/holiday material 6-12 months in advance. SASE. Reports in 3 months. Free writer's guidelines.

Nonfiction: Articles relating to North Carolina history in particular, southern history in general. Topics about which relatively little is known or are new in interpretations of familiar subjects. All articles must be based on primary sources and footnoted. Length: 15-25 typed pages. Pays $10/article.

NORTH SOUTH TRADER, 8020 New Hampshire Ave., Langley Park MD 20783. (301)434-2100. Editor: Wm. S. Mussenden. For Civil War buffs, historians, collectors, relic hunters, libraries and museums. Magazine; 52 to 68 (8 ½x11) pages. Established in 1973. Every 2 months. Circulation: 5,000. Rights purchased vary with author and material. Usually buys all rights. Buys 70 mss a year. Pays on publication. Sample copy and writer's guidelines $1. Will consider photocopied and simultaneous submissions. Reports within 2 weeks. Query first or submit complete ms. Enclose S.A.S.E.

Nonfiction and Photos: General subject matter deals with battlefield preservation, relic restoration, military artifacts of the Civil War (weapons, accoutrements, uniforms, etc.); historical information on battles, camp sites and famous people of the War Between the States. Prefers a factual or documentary approach to subject matter. Emphasis is on current findings and research related to the places, people, and artifacts of the conflict. Not interested in treasure magazine type articles. Length: 500 to 3,000 words. Pays 2¢ a word.

Columns/Departments: Columns and departments include Relic Restoration, Lost Heritage and Interview. Length: 1,000 to 1,500 words. Pays 2¢ a word. B&w photos are purchased with or without ms. Captions required. Pays $2.

OLD WEST, Western Publications, Inc., Box 3338, Austin TX 78764. (512)444-3674. Editor: Pat Wagner. Established in 1953. Bimonthly. Circulation: 175,000. Buys first North American serial rights. Payment on acceptance. Will send sample copy to writer for 60¢. Query first. Enclose S.A.S.E.

Nonfiction and Photos: "Factual accounts regarding people, places and events of the frontier West (1850 to 1910). Sources are required. If first-hand account based on family papers, records, memoirs, etc., reminiscences must be accurate as to dates and events. We strive for accounts with an element of action, suspense, heroics and humor. Stories derived solely from printed sources about the better known outlaws, Indians, lawmen, explorers will probably overlap material we have already run." Preferred length: 750 to 4,000 words. Pays 2¢ a word minimum. Buys color cover photos. "We usually buy mss and accompanying photos as a package. All photos are returned after publication."

Rejects: "At present we are receiving too much material from the 1920's, '30's, and '40's. We regret that many first-hand accounts have to be returned because the happenings are too recent for us."

PERSIMMON HILL, 1700 N.E. 63rd St., Oklahoma City OK 73111. Editor: Dean Krakel. Managing Editor: Richard Muno. For a Western art and Western history and rodeo oriented audience; historians, artists, ranchers, art galleries, schools, libraries. Publication of the National Cowboy Hall of Fame. Established in 1970. Quarterly. Circulation: 20,000. Buys all rights. Buys 20 to 30 mss a year. Pays on publication. Will send a sample copy to writer for $3. Will consider photocopied submissions. No simultaneous submissions. Reporting time on mss accepted for publication varies. Returns rejected material immediately. Submit complete ms. Enclose S.A.S.E.

Nonfiction and Photos: Historical and contemporary articles on famous Western figures connected with pioneering the American West, or biographies of such people; stories of Western flora and animal life, famous ranches and early manufacturers. Only thoroughly researched and historically authentic material is considered. May have a humorous approach to subject. Not interested in articles that re-appraise, or in any way put the West and its personalities in an unfavorable light. Length: 2,000 to 3,000 words. Pays a minimum of $150, maximum of $750. B&w glossies or color transparencies purchased with or without ms, or on assignment. Pays according to quality and importance for b&w and color. Suggested captions appreciated.

TRUE WEST, Western Publications, Inc., Box 3338, Austin TX 78764. Bimonthly. See *Old West.*

VIRGINIA CAVALCADE, Virginia State Library, Richmond VA 23219. Primarily for Virginians and others with an interest in Virginia history. Quarterly magazine; 48 pages. Established in 1951. Circulation: 17,000. Buys all rights. Buys 15 to 20 mss a year. Payment on acceptance. Will send sample copy to writer for $1. Write for copy of "Invitation to Authors."

Rarely considers simultaneous submissions. Submit seasonal material 15 to 18 months in advance. Reports in 4 weeks to 1 year. Query first. Enclose S.A.S.E.

Nonfiction and Photos: "We welcome readable and factually accurate articles that are relevant to some phase of Virginia history. Art, architecture, literature, education, business, technology, and transportation are all acceptable subjects, as well as political and military affairs. Articles must be based on thorough, scholarly research. We require footnotes but do not publish them. Authors should avoid contemporary political and social topics on which people hold strong and conflicting opinions. Any period from the age of exploration to the mid-twentieth century, and any geographical section or area of the state may be represented. Must deal with subjects that will appeal to a broad readership, rather than to a very restricted group or locality. Fresh and little known themes are preferred; manuscripts on more familiar subjects must treat them in a new light or rest on new documentary evidence. Articles must be suitable for illustration, although it is not necessary that the author provide the pictures. If the author does have pertinent illustrations or knows their location, the editor appreciates information concerning them." Uses 8x10 b&w glossies; color transparencies should be at least 4x5. Length: approximately 3,500 words. Pays $100.

How To Break In: "First, query. Then send a thoroughly researched, well-organized, well-written, fully annotated, interesting article of no more than 15 to 20 pages. Relatively unfamiliar but reasonably significant aspects of Virginia history, based on original research, are preferred. We especially welcome articles from graduate students and professional historians. Authors must avoid a fictionalized or overly popularistic style."

VIRGINIA MAGAZINE OF HISTORY AND BIOGRAPHY, Virginia Historical Society, P.O. Box 7311, Richmond VA 23221. Editor: William M.E. Rachal. Quarterly for serious students of Virginia history. Usually buys all rights. Pays on publication. Reports in one month. Enclose S.A.S.E. for return of submissions.

Nonfiction: Carefully researched and documented articles on Virginia history, and well-edited source material relating to Virginia. Must be dignified, lucid, scholarly. Length: 1,500 to 15,000 words. Appropriate illustrations are used. Pays $2 per printed page.

THE WESTERN PRODUCER, Box 2500, Saskatoon, Sask., S7K 2C4, Canada. (306)242-7651. For "mainly rural, farm-ranch oriented" audience. Circulated in 4 western Canadian provinces. Weekly. Newspaper. Circulation: 150,000. Buys first rights. Pays on acceptance. Reports in 1 month. Enclose S.A.E. and International Reply Coupons for return of submissions.

Nonfiction: Publishes authentic, pioneering western Canadiana, history, memoirs, real experiences. Preferred length not over 2,500 words for short features, longer for serials. Payment varies from 1¢ to 5¢ per word, depending on need and quality.

Photos: Good pioneering photos, Canadian scenic, or seasonal photos accepted. Uses color pix features in addition to b&w. Color transparencies (2¼x2¼) of good quality, all subjects. Pays $5 to $75, depending on use. Query first for photos.

Fiction: Based on western situations (not shooting stories), humorous and otherwise, light love stories. Payment varies from 1¢ to 5¢ a word.

How To Break In: "Bombard the editor with good, brightly written stories tailored to his journal—which means—read the journal first."

Hobby and Craft Publications

Publications in this section are for collectors, do-it-yourselfers, and craft hobbyists. Publications for electronics and radio hobbyists will be found in the Science classification.

ACQUIRE: THE MAGAZINE OF CONTEMPORARY COLLECTIBLES, 170 5th Ave., New York NY 10010. Editor: R. C. Rowe. For collectors, mostly 30 to 65 in age, many rural and suburban, affluent and reasonably well educated. Published 5 times a year. Established in 1973. Circulation: 50,000. Rights purchased vary with author and material. Buys all rights, but will reassign rights to author after publication; first North American serial rights; first serial rights; second serial (reprint) rights; simultaneous rights. Buys 15 to 30 mss a year. "First assignments are always done on a speculative basis." Payment on acceptance. Will send sample copy to writer for $1. Will consider photocopied submissions and simultaneous submissions. Query first, with an outline. Reports within 1 month. Enclose S.A.S.E.

Nonfiction: "Short features about collecting, written in tight, newsy style. We specialize in contemporary (postwar) collectibles. Particularly interested in items affected by scarcity." Informational, how-to, interview, profile, expose, nostalgia. Length: 500 to 2,500 words. Pays $50 to $150. Columns cover stamps, cars, porcelains, glass, western art, and graphics. Length: 750 words. Pays $75.

Photos: Department Editor: S. Linden. B&w and color photos purchased with accompanying ms with no additional payment. Also purchased without ms and on assignment. Captions are required. Wants clear, distinct, full frame image that says something. Pays $10 to $50.

AIRFIX MAGAZINE, PSL Publications Limited, Bar Hill, Cambridge CB3 8EL England. (0954)80010. Editor-in-Chief: Bruce Quarrie. Emphasizes plastic modeling. Monthly magazine; 68 pages. Estab: 1960. Circ: 42,000. Pays on publication. Buys all rights. Phone queries OK. Photocopied submissions OK. SASE. Reports in 2 months. Free sample copy and writer's guidelines.

Nonfiction: How-to (on plastic model construction and conversion); historical (military, aviation, naval); photo features and technical (military, aeronautical, naval). Buys 120 mss/year. Query. Length: 500-3,000 words. Pays $10-100.

Photos: Purchased with or without mss or on assignment. Pays $1-10 for half plate b&w glossies; $10-25 for 35mm, 2¼x2¼ or 4x5 color.

How To Break In: "By covering air shows, military rallies, etc., outside the United Kingdom and submitting illustrated write-ups."

AMERICAN ANTIQUES, (incorporating *Antiques Gazette* and *National Antiques Review*), Lindencroft Publishing, Inc., R.D. 1, New Hope PA 18938. Editor-in-Chief: Willis M. Rivinus. For antique collectors, history buffs, dealers, and lovers of old things. Monthly magazine; 72 pages. Estab: 1973. Circ: 40,000. Pays on publication. Buys all rights. Phone queries OK. Submit seasonal/holiday material 3 months in advance. Photocopied and previously published submissions OK. SASE. Reports in 2 weeks. Free sample copy and editorial guidelines.

Nonfiction: How-to, informational and historical articles about American antiques, history and our national heritage. Examples of the type of feature used are: "Winslow Homer Prints" a survey of a unique collection at the Cooper-Hewitt Museum in New York; "We the People", a review of the Bicentennial exhibition mounted by the Smithsonian Institution. Buys 20 mss/year. Query. Length: 1,000-2,500 words. Pays $15-50.

Photos: Purchased with mss. Captions required. Query. Total purchase price usually includes photo payment, but sometimes pays $2-5 for 8x10 b&w glossies.

AMERICAN COLLECTOR, Real Resources Group, Box A, Reno NV 89506. Editor-in-Chief: John F. Maloney. Emphasizes collecting for antique buffs, dealers, and investors. Monthly tabloid; 40 pages. Estab: 1970. Circ: 180,000. Pays on publication. Buys one-time rights. Submit seasonal/holiday material 3 months in advance. Photocopied submissions OK. SASE. Reports in 2 weeks. Free sample copy and writer's guidelines.

Nonfiction: Expose; historical; how-to; informational; interview; photo feature; and profile. Buys 120 mss/year. Query. Length: 100-2,000 words. Pays $1.20/column inch.

Photos: Purchased with accompanying ms. Captions required. Query. Pays $5 for any format b&w photos ("we even accept daguerreotypes"); $10-20 for 35mm or 2¼x2¼ color transparencies. Model release required.

AMERICANA, 10 Rockefeller Plaza, New York NY 10020. Editor: Michael Durham. For "a very well-educated, mature audience, interested in American history, especially such things as architecture, design, crafts, travel, etc." Established in 1973. Bimonthly. Circulation: 250,000. Buys all rights. Payment on acceptance. Query first. Enclose S.A.S.E.

Nonfiction: "Materials of the broadest range of American creation from gardens to cut glass; from collecting Revere silver to automobile hood ornaments. We are interested in anything Americans have created. Our special approach is that, although we are interested in the creative American past, we are a contemporary magazine. The ideal reaction to any story is that the reader will want to and be able to do something about it now; to go to that place, prepare that meal, collect that object, now." Length: 1,500 to 2,500 words. Pays $200 to $300.

THE ANTIQUE TRADER WEEKLY, P.O. Box 1050, Dubuque IA 52001. (319)588-2073. Editor: Kyle D. Husfloen. For collectors and dealers in antiques and collectibles. Weekly newspaper; 90-120 pages. Established in 1957. Circulation: 80,000 to 90,000. Buys all rights, but will reassign rights to author after publication. Buys about 200 mss a year. Payment at end of month following publication. Will send free sample copy to writer on request. Write for copy of guidelines for writers. Will consider photocopied and simultaneous submissions. Submit seasonal material (holidays) 3 to 4 months in advance. Prompt reports. Query first or submit complete ms. Enclose S.A.S.E.

Nonfiction and Photos: "We invite authoritative and well-researched articles on all types of antiques and collectors' items. Submissions should include a liberal number of good b&w photos. We also welcome feature cover stories which are accompanied by a good, clear color transparency which illustrates the feature. The feature should also have several b&w photos to illustrate the inside text. A color transparency of 4x5 is desirable for use as cover photo, but a smaller transparency is sometimes acceptable." Pays $5 to $35 for feature articles; $35 to $100 for feature cover stories. "We do not pay for brief information on new shops opening or other material printed as service to the antiques hobby."

ANTIQUES JOURNAL, Babka Publishing Co., Box 88129, Dunwoody GA 30338. Editor-in-Chief: John Mebane. Emphasizes antiques and collecting for "experienced and incipient antiques collectors and dealers from age 20-80 interested in learning the background of both the older antiques and thd more recent collectible objects." Monthly magazine; 68 pages. Estab: 1946. Circ: 36,000. Pays on acceptance. Buys first North American serial rights. Submit seasonal/holiday material 10 months in advance. SASE. Reports in 2 weeks. Sample copy $1. Free writer's guidelines.

Nonfiction: Historical; informational; interview (only occasionally); and nostalgia (if related to collectible objects of the 1920s-50s. Buys 100 mss/year. Query. Length: 300-2,000 words. Pays $35-105.

Photos: Photos purchased with accompanying ms. Captions required. Uses 4x5 or 8x10 b&w glossies; pays $35-40 for 35mm-4x5 color transparencies (for cover). Total purchase price for ms includes payment for photos (excluding color transparencies for cover). Model release required.

CANADA CRAFTS, Page Publications Ltd., 380 Wellington St., W., Toronto, Ontario, Canada M5V 1E3. (416)366-4608. Publisher: Gwen P. Dempsey. For craftspeople; individuals; shops; galleries; libraries, guilds, craft organizations. Magazine; 50 pages. Established in 1975. Published every 2 months. Circulation: 5,000. Buys 6 to 12 mss per year. Pays on publication. Will send sample copy to writer on request. Will send editorial guidelines sheet to writer on request. Reports on material accepted for publication 2 weeks before publication date. Returns rejected material in approximately 1 month. Query first. Enclose S.A.E. and International Reply Coupons.

Nonfiction: Interested in mss about crafts. Publishes informational, how-to, interview, technical articles. Pays $25 per published page or 4¢ per word. Open to suggestions for new columns and departments.

COIN WORLD (incorporating *World Coins* and *Numismatic Scrapbook Magazine),* Box 150, Sidney OH 45365. Editor: Margo Russell. For "coin collectors, mostly specialists in U.S. or world coins, or related numismatic items such as medals, tokens, and paper money. Mostly middle income or high income brackets." Weekly. Circ: 106,000. Buys first rights. Buys 100 mss/year. Pays on publication. Returns rejected material in 2 weeks. Acknowledges acceptance of material in 4 weeks. Query first. Enclose S.A.S.E.

Nonfiction and Photos: "Articles on U.S. and world coins or related subjects, especially those based on original research or personal experience." Buys personal experience and historical pieces. Length: 250 to 4,000 words. Pays 2¢ per published word with additional allowance for art. Photos purchased with mss. B&w glossies.

COLLECTORS NEWS, P.O. Box 156, 606 8th St., Grundy Center IA 50638. (319)824-5456. Editor: Mary E. Croker. For dealers in, and collectors of, antiques. Tabloid newspaper; 60 pages. Established in 1960. Monthly. Circulation: 30,000. Buys 12-20 mss/year. Pays on publication. Free Sample copy. No photocopied or simultaneous submissions. Submit seasonal material (holidays) 2 months in advance. Reports on material accepted for publication in 30 days. Returns rejected material as soon as possible. Query first or submit complete ms. Enclose S.A.S.E.

Nonfiction and Photos: Only factual articles pertaining to some phase of collecting or interesting collections. Informational, profile, nostalgia. Length: 1,200 words minimum; 1,600 words average. Pays 50¢ per column inch. No additional payment for b&w photos used with mss. Captions required.

CRAFT HORIZONS, 44 West 53rd St., New York NY 10019. Editor-in-Chief: Rose Slivka. Bimonthly. Circ: 40,000. Published by American Crafts Council for professional craftspeople, artists, teachers, architects, designers, decorators, collectors, connoisseurs and the consumer public. Copyrighted. Pays on publication. Will send free sample copy to writer on request. Reports as soon as possible. Query first. Enclose S.A.S.E.

Nonfiction and Photos: Articles and accompanying photos on the subject of creative work in ceramics, weaving, stitchery, jewelry, metalwork, woodwork, etc. Discussions of the technology, the materials and the ideas of artists throughout the world working in the above media. Length: 1,000 words. Pays $75 to $100 per article. Accompanying photos should be 8x10 b&w glossies. Pays $7.50 per b&w glossy.

CREATIVE CRAFTS, Carsten's Publications, Inc., Box 700, Newton NJ 07860. Editor-in-Chief: Sybil C. Harp. Emphasizes crafts for the serious adult hobbyist. Bimonthly (with a Christmas annual) magazine; 76 pages. Estab: 1967. Circ: 75,000. Pays on publication. Buys all rights. Submit seasonal/holiday material 7 months in advance. SASE. Reports in 4 weeks. Sample copy $1; free writer's guidelines.

Nonfiction: How-to (step-by-step of specific projects or general techniques; instructions must be clearly written and accompanied by b&w procedural photos and/or drawings). Buys 50-60 mss/year. Query. Length: 1,200 words average. Pays $50/magazine page. No human interest articles.

Photos: Purchased with accompanying ms. "We give $35 maximum allowance for photo expenses."

Columns/Departments: Going Places (articles dealing with annual fairs, craft "villages" or museums of special interest to craft enthusiasts). Buys 1 mss/issue. Query. Length: 1,200 words average. Pays $50/magazine page without advertising; $25/page mixed. Open to suggestions for new columns/departments.

Special Needs: "In the market for articles on dollhouse miniatures for a special 'miniature' section of each issue. Must be written by serious miniaturists who understand the hobby and do miniature crafts themselves."

DECORATING & CRAFT IDEAS MADE EASY, 1303 Foch, Ft. Worth TX 76107. (817)338-4401. Editor: Fredrica Daugherty. For women whose main interests are crafts, decorating and sewing. Magazine; 80 (8½x10¾) pages. Established in 1970. Monthly except January and July. Circulation: 650,000. Buys all rights, but may reassign rights to author after publication. Buys 10 mss a year. Pays on publication. Will send free sample copy to writer on request. Submit seasonal (Christmas) material 6 months in advance. Reports as soon as possible. Query first, with snapshot of project. Enclose S.A.S.E.

Nonfiction and Photos: Material on craft projects, craft-related travel, sewing projects, needlework projects. Simple, straightforward approach; clear, concise, complete instructions. In crafts, the emphasis must be on what makes the project unique. "We explain a craft project, show it close-up, in a decorative manner and completely explain how a reader can reproduce the project. We do a '100 Ideas' type article for Christmas, so we're on the lookout for small Christmas projects." Length: 600 to 1,000 words, not including instructions. Rate of payment is variable and is negotiated with each writer. Payment for photos depends on article.

How To Break In: "Query first with an explanation of the project and clear snapshots of the completed object. Projects offering *original* patterns for unique, well-made items are of highest interest and appeal."

DELTIOLOGY, 3709 Gradyville Rd., Newtown Square PA 19073. (215)353-1689. Editor: James L. Lowe. For collectors of antique picture postcards from around the world. Magazine; 16 (8½x11) pages. Established in 1960. Every 2 months. Circulation: 2,600. Rights purchased vary with author and material. Usually buys first U.S. rights. Buys 6 to 10 mss a year. Pays on publication. Will send a sample copy to writer for 50¢. Will consider photocopied and simultaneous submissions. Reports on material accepted for publication in 2 months. Returns rejected material promptly. Query first or submit complete ms. Enclose S.A.S.E.

Nonfiction and Photos: Informative articles pertaining to antique picture postcards, primarily those issued prior to 1915, dealing with specific publishers and artists. Length: 500-2,000 words. Pays $10/article minimum. No additional payment for b&w photos used with mss.

EARLY AMERICAN LIFE, Early American Society, P.O. Box 1831, Harrisburg PA 17105. Editor: Robert G. Miner. For "people who are interested in capturing the warmth and beauty of the 1600 to 1850 period and using it in their homes and lives today. They are interested in arts, crafts, travel, restoration, collecting." Magazine published every 2 months; over 100 pages. Estab: 1970. Circ: 260,000. Buys all rights. Buys 50 mss a year. Payment on acceptance. Will send free sample copy to writer on request. Write for copy of guidelines for writers. Will consider photocopied submissions. Will not consider simultaneous submissions. Reports in 1 month. Query first or submit complete ms. Enclose S.A.S.E.

Nonfiction and Photos: "Social history (the story of the people, not epic heroes and battles);

crafts such as woodworking and needlepoint; travel to historic sites; country inns; antiques and reproductions; refinishing and restoration; architecture and decorating. We try to entertain as we inform, but always attempt to give the reader something he can do. While we're always on the lookout for good pieces on any of our subjects, the 'travel to historic sites' theme is most frequently submitted. Would like to see more how-to-do-it (well-illustrated) on how real people did something great to their homes." Length: 750 to 4,000 words. Pays $50-300. Pays $10 for 5x7 (and up) b&w photos used with mss; minimum of $25 for color. Prefers 2¼ and up, but can work from 35mm.

How To Break In: "Get a feeling for 'today's early Americans', the folks who are visiting flea markets, auctions, junkyards, the antiques shops. They are our readers and they hunger for ideas on how to bring the warmth and beauty of early America into their lives. Then, conceive a new approach to satisfying their related interests in arts, crafts, travel to historic sites, and the story of the people of the 1600 to 1850 period. Write to entertain and inform at the same time, and be prepared to help us with illustrations, or sources for them."

FLEA MARKET QUARTERLY, Box 243, Bend OR 97701. Editor: Kenneth Asher. For flea market owners, dealers and shoppers. All ages, walks of life and educational backgrounds. Magazine (almanac), (8½x11), 50 pages. "Our publication is seasonal; for example, spring, summer, fall, and winter." Established in 1973. Circulation: 5,000. Buys all rights. Buys 20 to 30 mss a year. Payment on acceptance. Will send sample copy to writer for $1. Will consider photocopied submissions. Submit seasonal material 2 months in advance. Submit only complete ms. Reports in 1 month. Enclose S.A.S.E.

Nonfiction and Photos: "Short items of wit; money-making, money-saving tips; recycling ideas; practical ecological news; collecting trends; alternate lifestyle ideas; consumer affairs and health briefs. Use inspirational, optimistic approach, but be frank. There is no other nationwide flea market publication. We particularly like articles giving money-making ideas that require little capital to get started." Informational, how-to, personal experience, interview, profile, inspirational, humor, nostalgia, photo, travel, book reviews, successful business operations, new product, and merchandising techniques. Pays $20 a published page or $5 to $15 an item. Regular column, "Money Page," pays $5 for money-making ideas. B&w photos are purchased with or without accompanying ms. Captions optional. Pays $5.

Fillers: Newsbreaks and clippings; jokes and short humor. Pays $5 an item.

How To Break In: "Attend a local flea market and find a brief item that would be helpful to our readers."

GEMS AND MINERALS, P.O. Box 687, Mentone CA 92359. (714)794-1173. Editor: Jack R. Cox. Monthly for the amateur gem cutter, jewelry maker, mineral collector, and rockhounds. Buys first North American serial rights. Buys 15 to 20 mss a year. Payment on publication. Will send free sample copy to writer on request. Write for copy of guidelines for writers. Query first. Reports within a month. Enclose S.A.S.E.

Nonfiction and Photos: Material must have how-to slant. No personality stories. Field trips to mineral or gem collecting localities used; must be accurate and give details so they can be found. Instructions on how to cut gems; designs and creations of jewelry. Four to eight typed pages plus illustrations preferred, but do not limit if subject is important. Frequently good articles are serialized if too long for one issue. Pays 50¢ per inch for text and pix as published.

How To Break In: "Because we are a specialty magazine, it is difficult for a writer to prepare a suitable story for us unless he is familiar with the subject matter: jewelry making, gem cutting, mineral collecting and display, and fossil collecting. Our readers want accurate instructions on how to do it and where they can collect gemstones and minerals in the field. The majority of our articles are purchased from freelance writers, but most of them are hobbyists (rockhounds) or have technical knowledge on one of the subjects. Infrequently, a freelancer with no knowledge of the subject interviews an expert (gem cutter, jewelry maker, etc.) and gets what this expert tells him down on paper for a good how-to article. However, the problem here is that if the expert neglects to mention all the steps in his process, the writer does not realize it. Then, there is a delay while we check it out. My best advice to a freelance writer is to send for a sample copy of our magazine and author's specification sheet which will tell him what we need. We are interested in helping new writers and try to answer them personally, giving any pointers that we think will be of value to them. Let us emphasize that our readers want how-to and where-to stories. They are not at all interested in personality sketches about one of their fellow hobbyists."

HOBBY ARTIST NEWS, R. #2, Fort Atkinson IA 52144. Editor: Ray Gillem. For artists, hobbyists and authors. Magazine; 8 to 12 (8½x11) pages. Established in 1970. Every 2 months. Circulation: 500. Not copyrighted. Pays on publication. Will send sample copy to writer for

75¢. Write for copy of guidelines for writers. Reports on material accepted for publication in 2 to 3 weeks. Returns rejected material immediately. Submit complete ms. Enclose S.A.S.E.
Nonfiction: How-to and moneymaking idea type of articles on art, artists, handicrafts, song writing. Should be informative, educational, entertaining, first-person material on actual experiences. How-to articles on greeting cards and "new ways for an artist to make a buck." Length: 300 to 500 words. Pays ½¢ a word.

JOEL SATER'S ANTIQUES & AUCTION NEWS, 225 W. Market St., Marietta PA 17547. (717)426-1956. Managing Editor: Joel Sater. Editor: Denise Murphy. For dealers and buyers of antiques, nostalgics, and collectibles; and those who follow antique shows and shops. Biweekly tabloid; 24 pages. Estab: 1967. Circ: 80,000. Pays on publication. Buys all rights. Phone queries OK. Submit seasonal/holiday material 6 weeks to 3 months in advance. Simultaneous (if so notified), photocopied and previously published submissions OK. SASE. Reports in 6 weeks. Free sample copy (must identify *Writer's Market*).
Nonfiction: Historical (related to American artifacts or material culture); how-to (restoring and preserving antiques and collectibles); informational (research on antiques or collectibles; "news about activities in our field"); interview; nostalgia; personal experience; photo feature; profile; and travel. Buys 100-150 mss/year. Query or submit complete ms. Length: 500-2,500 words. Pays $5-25.
Photos: Purchased with or without accompanying ms. Captions required. Send prints. Pays $2-10 for b&w photos. Total purchase price for ms includes payment for photos.

LAPIDARY JOURNAL, P.O. Box 80937, San Diego CA 92138. Editor: Pansy D. Kraus. For "all ages interested in the lapidary hobby." Established in 1947. Monthly. Circ: 66,250. Rights purchased vary with author and material. Buys all rights, or first serial rights. Payment on publication. Will send free sample copy to writer on request. Will send editorial guidelines to a writer on request. Will consider photocopied submissions. Query first. Enclose S.A.S.E.
Nonfiction and Photos: Publishes "articles pertaining to gem cutting, gem collecting and jewelry making for the hobbyist." Buys informational, how-to, personal experience, historical, travel, and technical articles. Pays 1¢ a word. Buys good contrast b&w photos. Contact editor for color. Payment varies according to size.

LOST TREASURE, Box 328, Conroe TX 77301. Editor: John H. Latham. For treasure hunting hobbyists, bottle and relic collectors, amateur prospectors and miners. Magazine; 72 (8½x11) pages. Monthly. Established in 1969. Circulation: 100,000. Buys all rights, but will reassign rights to author after publication. Buys 180 mss a year. Payment on acceptance. Will send free sample copy to writer on request. Write for copy of guidelines for writers. Will consider photocopied submissions. Will not consider simultaneous submissions. Reports in 3 to 4 weeks. Submit complete ms. Enclose S.A.S.E.
Nonfiction and Photos: Articles about lost mines and buried and sunken treasures. Avoid writing about the more famous treasures and lost mines. Length: 100 to 3,000 words. Pays 2¢ per word. Pays $5 for b&w glossies purchased with mss. Captions required. Pays $100 for color transparencies used on cover; 2¼x2¼ minimum size. "Treasure Nuggets" section uses short articles on publication's theme. Length: 100 to 250 words. Pays $12.50.

McCALL'S NEEDLEWORK AND CRAFTS MAGAZINE, 230 Park Ave., New York NY 10017. Managing Editor: Margaret GIlman. Quarterly. All rights bought for original needlework and handcraft designs. Enclose S.A.S.E.
Nonfiction: Accepts the made-up items accompanied by the directions, diagrams, and charts for making them. Preliminary photos may be submitted. Variety of payment depends on items sent in. The range of payment could be from a few dollars to a few hundred dollars.

MAINE ANTIQUE DIGEST, Box 358, Waldoboro ME 04572. (207)832-7534. Editor: Samuel Pennington. For collectors and dealers in early Americana, antique furniture (country and formal), marine, redware, folk art, "Shaker things." Tabloid newspaper; 84 pages. Estab: 1973. Monthly. Circ: 10,000. Buys first North American serial rights. May buy second serial (reprint) rights for use in their annual. Buys about 60 mss a year. Pays on acceptance. Will send free sample copy to writer on request. No photocopied or simultaneous submissions. Reports in 1 week. Query first or submit complete ms. Enclose S.A.S.E.
Nonfiction and Photos: Auction and show articles (mostly assigned); on antiques from 1700 to 1875. "We want writers who are very knowledgeable about antiques; writers who can write with feeling and 'tell it like it is' about the antiques business and collecting. We would be particularly interested in articles (chapters or selections) by authors of forthcoming antique books." Length:

1,000 words minimum. Pays $35 to $50. No additional payment for b&w photos used with mss. Captions required.

MAKE IT WITH LEATHER, P.O. Box 1386, Fort Worth TX 76101. (817)335-8500. Editor: Earl F. Warren. Buys all rights. Bimonthly. Established in 1956. Circ: 60,000. Buys 60 mss a year. Payment on publication. Will send free sample copy to writer on request. Write for copy of guidelines for writers. Reports on material in 6 to 8 weeks. Enclose S.A.S.E. for return of submissions.

Nonfiction and Photos: "How-to-do-it leathercraft stories illustrated with cutting patterns, carving patterns. First-person approach even though article may be ghosted. Story can be for professional or novice. Strong on details; logical progression in steps; easy to follow how-to-do-it." Length: 2,000 words maximum. Payment starts at $25 to $50 plus $5 to $10 per illustration. "Most articles judged on merit and may range to '$200 plus' per ms. Depends on project and work involved by author." 5x7, or larger, b&w photos of reproduction quality purchased with mss. Captions required. Pays $5 minimum. Color of professional quality is used. Ektachrome slides or sheet film stock. Negs needed with all print film stock. Pays $8.50 minimum. All photos are used to illustrate project on step-by-step basis, and also finished item. "We can do photos in our studio if product sample is sent. No charge, but no payment for photos to writer. Letting us 'do it our way' does help on some marginal story ideas and mss since we can add such things as artist's sketches or drawings to improve the presentation."

Fillers: "Tips and Hints." Short practical hints for doing leathercraft or protecting tools, new ways of doing things, etc. Length: 100 words maximum. Pays $5 minimum.

How To Break In: "There are plenty of leathercraftsmen around who don't feel qualified to write up a project or who don't have the time to do it. Put their ideas and projects down on paper for them and share the payment. We need plenty of small, quick, easy-to-do ideas; things that we can do in one page are in short supply."

MILITARY COLLECTORS NEWS, P.O. Box 7582, Tulsa OK 74105. Editor: Jack Britton. For amateur and advanced collectors of all types of military items. Established in 1967. Monthly. Circulation: 3,200. Buys or acquires all rights. Buys or uses about 12 mss a year. Payment in contributor's copies or cash. "Since we receive many articles from our readers for which no payment other than contributor's copies is made, writers should let us know whether or not payment is expected." Sample copy 25¢. Reports in 1 week. Submit complete ms. Enclose S.A.S.E.

Nonfiction and Photos: Articles on the identification of military items (insignia, medals, uniforms, flags, weapons, aircraft, armor), anything that is of a military nature. Covers all periods (Vietnam, Korea, WW I, WW II, Civil War; all earlier periods). Also, military history. Informational, humor, historical, nostalgia. Length: 100 to 2,000 words. Pays 1¢ per word, or 2 to 20 copies of the magazine. "We need photos of WW II, men in uniform, foreign weapons, tanks, etc. (WW I, or earlier). Captions optional. Pays 50¢ to $1, or 2 to 4 copies of the magazine.

Fillers: Clippings, jokes. Length: half page or less. Pays 50¢ to $1, or 2 to 4 copies of the magazine.

MODEL RAILROADER, 1027 N. 7th St., Milwaukee WI 53233. Editor: Linn H. Westcott. For adult hobbyists interested in scale model railroading. Monthly. Buys rights "exclusive in model railroad and rail fan field." Study publication before submitting material. Reports on submissions within 4 weeks. Query first. Enclose S.A.S.E.

Nonfiction: Wants construction articles on specific model railroad projects (structures, cars, locomotives, scenery, benchwork, etc.). Also photo stories showing model railroads. First-hand knowledge of subject almost always necessary for acceptable slant. Pays base rate of $36 per page. (Page is typically 960 words plus 30 sq. in. of illustration, both getting same rate for area.)

Photos: Buys photos with detailed descriptive captions only. Pays $7.50 and up, depending on size and location. Color: double b&w rate. Full color cover: $112.

THE OLD BOTTLE MAGAZINE, Box 243, Bend OR 97701. (503)382-6978. Editor: Shirley Asher. For collectors of old bottles, insulators, relics. Monthly. Circulation: 11,000. Buys all rights. Buys 35 mss a year. Pays on acceptance. Will send a sample copy to a writer on request. No query required. Reports in 1 month. Enclose S.A.S.E. for return of submissions.

Nonfiction, Photos, and Fillers: "We are soliciting factual accounts on specific old bottles, canning jars, insulators and relics." Stories of a general nature on these subjects not wanted. "Interviews of collectors are usually not suitable when written by non-collectors. A knowledge of the subject is imperative. Would highly recommend potential contributors study an issue before makiig submissions. Articles that tie certain old bottles to a historical background are desired." Length: 250 to 2,500 words. Pays $20 per published page. B&w glossies and clippings purchased separately. Pays $5.

POPULAR HANDICRAFT HOBBIES,,Tower Press, Inc., Box 428, Seabrook NH 03874. Editor-in-Chief: Karen P. Sherrer. "Our readers are primarily women interested in crafts and hobbies. Many are looking for projects suitable for sale at church bazaars and fund-raising events. They also like crafts that are easy and inexpensive to do." Bimonthly magazine; 72 pages. Estab: 1966. Circ: 140,000. Pays on acceptance. Buys all rights, but may reassign following publication. Submit seasonal/holiday maatepial 8-10 months in advance. SASE. Reports in 6-8 weeks. Free sample copy and writer's guidelines.
Nonfiction: How-to (illustrated with color slides and b&w photos; craft projects to make); informational (about new craft projects or techniques); historical (material about collecting as a hobby); humor (craft-related); profile (people who have an interesting hobby or do an unusual craft); new product; and photo feature. Buys 15 mss/issue. Query. Length: 200-1,500 words. Pays 2¢/word.
Photos: Purchased with accompanying ms. Submit prints or transparencies. Pays $5 minimum for x5 or larger b&w glossy prints; $20 minimum for 35mm, 2¼x2¼ or 4x5 color transparencies. Model release required.
Columns/Departments: Designers Workshop (useful, decorative crafts for the home), The Magpie's Nest profiles or how-to's about collecting as a hobby), Junior Handicrafters (projects for children to make). Buys 1-2 mss/issue. Submit complete ms. Length: 100-1,500 words. Pays 2¢/word, extra for photos.
Fillers: Craft-related tips or hints. Buys 10/year. Pays $2.

THE PRINTER, Log Cabin Press, R.R. 4, Findlay OH 45840. (419)422-4958. Editor-in-Chief: Michael J. Phillips. Managing Editor: Diana J. Phillips. Emphasizes printing history for collectors, hobby printers and historians. Monthly magazine; 16-20 pages. Estab: 1975. Circ: 1,200. Pays on acceptance. Buys one-time rights. Submit seasonal/holiday material 2 months in advance. Simultaneous, photocopied and previously published submissions OK. SASE. Reports in 1 month. Free sample copy and writer's guidelines.
Nonfiction: Historical; how-to; personal opinion; interview (with hobby printers, collectors, etc.); new product (books, services, etc.); nostalgia (museum exhibits or store displays, etc.). Buys 3 mss/year. Query. Length: 100-1,200 words. Pays $5-25.
Photos: Purchased with mss. B&w only. Captions required. Query. No additional payment.
Fiction: Historical and humorous (pertaining to printing, writing, etc.). Buys 3/year. Query. Length: 300-1,200 words. Pays $5-25.
Poetry: Avant-garde, traditional and free verse. Buys 3/year. Pays $5-25.
Fillers: Clippings and newsbreaks. Buys 3/issue. Send fillers in. Length: 25-200 words. Pays $5-10.

QUILTER'S NEWSLETTER MAGAZINE, Box 394, Wheatridge CO 80033. Editor: Bonnie Leman. Established in 1968. Monthly. Circulation: 80,000. Buys first or second North American serial rights. Buys about 15 mss a year. Pays on acceptance. Will send free sample copy to writer on request. Will consider photocopied submissions. No simultaneous submissions. Reports in 2 to 3 weeks. Submit complete ms. Enclose S.A.S.E.
Nonfiction, Photos and Fillers: "We re interested in articles, fillers and photos on the subject of quilts and quiltmakers *only*. We are not interested in anything relating to 'Grandma's Scrap Quilts', but could use material about contemporary quilting." Pays 1½¢ a word minimum. Additional payment for photos depends on quality.

RAILROAD MODEL CRAFTSMAN, P.O. Box 700, Newton NJ 07860. (201)383-3355. Managing Editor: Tony Koester. For "adult model railroad hobbyists, above average, including mature youngsters. All gauges, scales, plus collecting, railfanning." Established in 1933. Monthly. Circulation: 88,000. Buys all rights. Buys 50 to 100 mss a year. Payment on publication. Will send a sample copy to a writer for 75¢. Submit seasonal material six months in advance. Enclose S.A.S.E. for return of submissions.
Nonfiction and Photos: "How-to model railroad features written by persons who did the work. They have to be good. Glossy photos a must. Drawings where required must be to scale, accurately and completely rendered. Some railroad prototype features if of interest to modelers and wit modelers' slant. All of our features and articles are written by active model railroaders familiar with the magazine and its requirements. 'Outsiders' don't have the technical know-how to write for us. Non-model railroad writers invariably write up some local hobbyist as 'Joe Doaks has a railroad empire in his basement made all by himself,' treating him as some kind of

nut. We do not want the cartoon of little men tying the little girl to model railroad track. We do want topnotch how-to model railroading articles." Purchases photos with and without mss. Captions required. Buys sharp 8x10 glossies and 35mm transparencies. Minimum payment: $1 per column inch of copy ($30 per page); $5 for photos ($1 per diagonal inch of published b&w photos, $3 for color transparencies); $50 for covers (must tie in with feature material in that issue).

How To Break In: "Frankly, there is virtually no chance of making a sale to us unless the author is a very experienced hobbyist in our field. I doubt that a non-model railroad hobbyist has authored a single line of copy for us in the past 40 years, so it's 'hobbyist first, author second' as far as we're concerned. Our material is for the serious hobbyist, not the general public trying to better understand our hobby, as a rule."

RAPIDFIRE REVIEW, Box 779, Glendora CA 91740. Editor-in-Chief: Ted Mauritzen. Emphasizes automatic weaponry collecting. Bimonthly magazine; 34 pages. Estab: 1977. Circ: 5,000. Pays on publication. Buys all rights, but may reassign following publication. Submit seasonal/ holiday material 6 months in advance. Photocopied submissions OK. SASE. Reports in 4 weeks. Sample copy $2. Free writer's guidelines.

Nonfiction: Historical (information on all types of automatic and semiautomatic firearms. Museum collections with photos; how-to (shooting and servicing automatic firearms and ammunitions); informational; interview (with important collectors and ATF officials); new product; nostalgia, personal experience (military combat experience especially); personal opinion (range reports, etc.); photo feature (on special historical guns); technical (ballistics, etc.); and travel (museums around the world with gun collections). Buys 4-6 mss/issue. Query. Length: 1,000-3,500 words. Pays $50-175.

Photos: Photos purchased with or without accompanying ms. Captions required. Pays $3-5 for 8x10 b&w glossies; $2-25 for 35mm, 2¼x2¼ or 4x5 color photos. Query. Send contact sheet. Total purchase price for ms includes payment for photos.

Fillers: Clippings and newsbreaks. Buys 10-15 fillers/issue. Length: 200-500 words. Pays $2-15.

How To Break In: "Have factual material that is timely. Come up with new ideas for articles that would be of interest to the automatic weapons buff. No dry writing or warmed over stories from other publications. This is a trial balloon. Ve are on a tight budget and are starting slowly. If all goes well, *Rapidfire Review* should be a fertile market for the novice who has an interest in guns and military ordnance. Those who stick with us will reap the rewards as we grow."

RELICS, Western Publications, Inc., P.O. Box 3338, Austin TX 78764. (512)444-3674. Editor: Pat Wagner. Bimonthly to collectors of Americana. Buys N.A. serial rights and occasionally reprint rights based on where the article originally appeared. Will send sample copy for 35¢. Pays on acceptance. Query appreciated. Reports in 4 to 6 weeks. Enclose S.A.S.E. for reply to queries.

Nonfiction and Photos: "General subject matter includes collectibles of any kind except those of museum quality. We are not as much devoted to the coverage of true antiques as to the myriad assortment of nostalgic items. Also pieces pertaining to personal collections if specific information is given, such as current value, how to judge, where to find, how to preserve. Articles must contain useful hints for the collector. 2,500 words is tops." Pays 2¢/word minimum. No mss considered unless accompanied by photos (b&w preferably) or drawings of item. Photos and drawings are returned after publication.

How To Break In: "Many submissions seem to have been taken from encyclopedias or other reference books. We appreciate authors familiarizing themselves with the subject, but prefer articles to have some element beyond what is available at the library — a more personal touch."

ROCK & GEM, 16001 Ventura Blvd., Encino CA 91436. (213)788-7080. Senior Editor: W.R.C. Shedenhelm. For amateur lapidaries and rockhounds. Magazine; 94 pages. Established in 1971. Monthly. Circulation: 70,000. Rights purchased vary with author and material. May buy first North American serial rights or first serial rights. Pays on publication. Will send sample copy to writer for $1. No photocopied or simultaneous submissions. Reports on material accepted for publication in 1 month. Returns rejected material immediately. Query first or submit complete ms. Enclose S.A.S.E.

Nonfiction and Photos: Knowledgeable articles on rockhounding and lapidary work; step-by-step how-to articles on lapidary and jewelry making. Length: open. Pays $40 per published page. No additional payment for 8x10 b&w glossies used with mss. Color for cover is by assignment only.

ROCKHOUND, P.O. Box 328, Conroe TX 77301. Editor: John H. Latham. For gem and mineral hobbyists. Magazine published every 2 months; 52 (8 ½x11) pages. Established in 1971. Circulation: 20,000. Buys all rights, but will reassign rights to author after publication. Buys 75 to 100 mss a year. Payment on acceptance. Will send free sample copy to writer on request. Write for copy of guidelines for writers. Will consider photocopied submissions. Will not consider simultaneous submissions. Reports in 3 to 4 weeks. Submit complete ms. Enclose S.A.S.E.

Nonfiction and Photos: Articles on where and how to find gems and minerals. "We cover only where and how to collect gems and minerals; not the whole lapidary field." Length: 250 to 3,000 words. Pays 2¢ per word. B&w glossies of any size purchased with mss. Captions required. Pays $5. Pays $5 to $35 for color transparencies used on cover.

How To Break In: "Write about collecting sites anywhere in the U.S., except the western states. We receive a glut of mss from the West. We particularly welcome new writers who write about the East, North, South, or Midwest. A bit of research on collecting sites (for gems and minerals) in these parts of the country will really sell us."

SCOTT'S MONTHLY STAMP JOURNAL, 530 Fifth Ave., New York NY 10036. (212)391-1500. Editor: Jane Goldman. For stamp collectors, from the pre-teenage beginner to the sophisticated philatelist. Monthly magazine; 64 pages. Estab: 1922. Circ: 24,000. Rights purchased vary with author and material. Usually buys all rights. Buys 12-24 mss/year. Pays on publication. Free sample copy. Will consider photocopied and simultaneous submissions. Submit seasonal or holiday material 3 months in advance. Reports in 4 weeks. Query first. Enclose S.A.S.E.

Nonfiction and Photos: "Stories about *stamps only*. Human interest and historical perspective very mportant. Must be lively, well-researched articles. Emphasize philatelic detail and human interest at the same time. Stamps capture the time and place of events. An interesting article might be one of a period in a country's stamp history such as 'Sweden, 1800 to 1900' or whatever historical events define as a period. We recently published a story about stamp collecting in the U.S.S.R." Length: 500 to 4,000 words. Pays $50 to $250. No additional payment is made for b&w photos used with mss.

How To Break In: *"Scott's Monthly Stamp Journal* is undergoing a complete change. Although all material deals with stamps, new writers are invited to seek assignments. It is not necessary to be a stamp collector or a published professional. You must (1) be a good writer, and (2) be willing to do careful research on strong material. Because our emphasis is on lively, interesting articles about stamps, including historical perspectives and human interest slants, we are open to writers who can produce the same. Of course, if you are an experienced philatelist, so much the better. We do *not* want to see finished manuscripts. What we *do* want is this: A query letter with paragraph summaries of suggested articles, followed by a phone call. Because our magazine does require philatelic detail, phone contact throughout the assignment is necessary. Long distance — please call collect."

THE SPINNING WHEEL, Everybodys Press, Inc., Hanover PA 17331. (717)632-3535. Editor: A. Christian Revi. For antique collectors and dealers. 10 times a year. Pays on publication. Buys exclusive rights unless author wishes some reservations. Enclose S.A.S.E

Nonfiction: Authentic, well-researched material on antiques in any and all collecting areas; home decorating ideas with antiques. Prefers combined scholar-student-amateur appeal. No first-person or family history. Prefers draft or outline first. Requires bibliography with each ms. Quality illustrations. Length: 500 to 1,500 words. Pays minimum $1 per published inch, including pictures.

Photos: Photos and professional line drawings accepted. Photos should be top quality b&w, no smaller" th n 5x7. If of individual items shown in groups, each should be separated for mechanical expediency. Avoid fancy groupings.

STITCH 'N SEW, Tower Press, Box 338, Chester MA 01011. Editor: Barbara Hall Pedersen. For women of all ages who like to sew. Magazine published every 2 months; 64 pages, (8x11). Established in 1968. Circulation: 200,000. Buys all rights. Buys 50 mss a year. Payment on publication. Will send free sample copy to writer on request, if large S.A.S.E. is enclosed. Write for copy of guidelines for writers. Submit holiday crafts, especially Christmas, 6 months in advance. Query first or submit complete ms. Reports in 2 to 8 weeks. Enclose S.A.S.E.

Nonfiction, Photos, and Fillers: "Articles on various facets of needlework; knitting, crocheting, garment construction, embroidery, tatting, gift and toy making, decorative items for the home. Our emphasis is on old-fashioned practicality. Our projects appeal to the woman on a tight budget. We like 'scratch' projects which utilize readily available materials which do not cost much. How-to articles must include either a sharp photograph, or drawing or actual sample."

Length: 1,500 words maximum. Pays $5 to $50. B&w and color photos purchased with accompanying ms. Captions required. Pays $35 for 4x5 color transparency used on cover.

TODAY'S FILM MAKER, 250 Fulton Ave., Hempstead NY 11550. Editor: Barry Tanenbaum. For amateur movie makers and hobbyists. Magazine; 50 pages. Established in 1971. Every 4 months. Circulation: 40,000. Rights purchased vary with author and material. May buy all rights, but will reassign rights to author after publication; first North American serial rights or first serial rights. Buys 25 to 30 mss a year. Pays on publication. Will send free sample copy to writer on request. Write for copy of guidelines for writers. Will consider photocopied submissions. No simultaneous submissions. Reports in 1 week. Query first. Enclose S.A.S.E.
Nonfiction and Photos: How-to articles; Super 8 film techniques. All material should tell the amateur how to better use his equipment to achieve professional results. Informational, personal experience, interviews, think pieces, personal opinion, reviews. Captions required for photos used with mss. Pays minimum of $35 per published page; $5 for accompanying photos.

TREASURE, Jess Publishing, 16146 Covello St., Van Nuys CA 91406. (213)988-6910. Editor-in-Chief: Kenneth Doe. Managing Editor: Bob Grant. Emphasizes treasure hunting and metal detecting. Monthly magazine; 74 pages. Estab: 1969. Circ: 100,000. Pays on publication. Buys all rights, but may reassign following publication. Phone queries OK. Submit seasonal/holiday material 4 months in advance. Previously published submissions OK. SASE. Reports in 1 month. Free writer's guidelines.
Nonfiction: Michael McCready, Articles Editor. How-to (coinshooting and treasure hunting tips); informational and historical (location of lost treasures with emphasis on lesser known); interviews (with treasure hunters); profiles (successful treasure hunters and metal detector hobbyists); personal experience (treasure hunting); technical (advice on use of metal detectors and metal detector designs). Buys 6-8 mss/issue. Send complete ms. Length: 300-3,000 words. Pays $15-150. "Our rate of payment varies considerably depending upon the proficiency of the author, the quality of the photographs, the importance of the subject matter, and the amount of useful information given."
Photos: David Weeks, Department Editor. No additional payment for 5x7 or 8x10 b&w glossies used with mss. Pays $50 minimum for color transparencies (120 or 2¼x2¼). Color for cover only. Model release required.

TRI-STATE TRADER, 27 N. Jefferson St., Knightstown IN 46148. (317)345-5134. Managing Editor: Kevin Tanzillo. Editor: Elsie Kilmer. For persons interested in antiques, history, restorations, etc. Newspaper; 40 (11x16) pages. Established in 1968. Weekly. Circulation: 27,000. Not copyrighted. Pays on 10th of month following publication. Will send free sample copy to writer on request. Write for copy of guidelines for writers. Submit seasonal (Christmas, Easter, Halloween) material 4 months in advance. Query first. Enclose S.A.S.E.
Nonfiction and Photos: Prefers material that deals with antiques, collectibles, or places of historical interest; restored homes, etc. Chiefly in the North Central and border states. Interested in material on less commonly found antiques, but not museum type pieces; including origin, date of manufacture, unique features; pattern names of glassware; ceramics with dates and origin (including foreign ceramics); trademarks. Much of the material received is too general in content and omits dates, styles, names of firms, etc. Also uses auction reports and nostalgic material related to antiques and collectibles. Length: 1,200 words maximum. Pays $5 to $25. Pays $3 to $5 for b&w photos purchased with or without ms. $2 for Polaroids.
Fillers: In areas of this newspaper's interests; specific information on subjects of antique and historical interests; used as fillers. Length: 500 words maximum. Pays 25¢ per published inch.

WOMEN'S CIRCLE, Box 428, Seabrook NH 03874. Editor: Marjorie Pearl. For women of all ages. Monthly magazine; 72 pages. Buys all rights. Buys 150 mss/year. Pays on acceptance. Sample copy 75¢. Submit seasonal material 7 months in advance. Reports in 1 to 3 months. Query first or submit complete ms. Enclose S.A.S.E.
Nonfiction: How-to articles on hobbies, handicrafts, etc. Also food, recipes, needlework, dolls, home, family and children. Informational approach. Needs Christmas crafts for Christmas annual. Length: open. Pays 3¢ per word.

THE WORKBASKET, 4251 Pennsylvania, Kansas City MO 64111. Editor: Mary Ida Sullivan. Issued monthly. Buys first rights. Pays on acceptance. Query. Reports in six weeks. Enclose S.A.S.E.
Nonfiction and Photos: Uses articles, 400 to 500 words, which explain how a person or a family has benefited, financially or otherwise, by sewing, needlecraft, etc. Interested in step-by-step directions for making project. Also has a how-to short-stuff section which uses material on

hobbies, ideas for pin-money and the like. These are limited to 250 words or under and bring a flat sum of $5. Pays 4¢ a word for articles, plus $5 to $7 for accompanying art. 5x7 or 8x10 pix with mss.

WORKBENCH, 4251 Pennsylvania Ave., Kansas City MO 64111. (816)531-5730. Editor: Jay W. Hedden. For woodworkers. Estab: 1946. Circ: 500,000. Pays on publication. Buys all rights, but returns all but first magazine rights on request, after publication. Reports in 10-14 days. Query. SASE.
Nonfiction and Photos: "In the last couple of years, we have increased our emphasis on home improvement and home maintenance, and now are getting into alternate energy projects. Ours is a nuts-and-bolts approach, rather than telling how someone has done it. Because most of our readers own their own homes, we stress 'retrofitting' of energy-saving devices, rather than saying they should rush out and buy or build a solar home. Energy conservation is another subject we cover thoroughly; insulation, weatherstripping, making your own storm windows. We still are very strong in woodworking, cabinetmaking and furniture construction. Projects range from simple toys to complicated reproductions of furniture now in museums. We pay a minhmum of $150/published page. Shop tips bring $20 maximum with drawing and/or photo. If we pay less than the rate, it's because we have to supply photos, information, drawings or details the contributor has overlooked. Contributors should look over the published story to see what they should include next time. Our editors are skilled woodworkers, do-it-yourselfers and photographers. We have a complete woodworking shop at the office and we use it often to check out construction details of projects submitted to us."

WORKING CRAFTSMAN, Box 42, 1500 Shermer Rd., Northbrook IL 60062. Editor: Marilyn Heise. For craftsmen (both professional and part-time), teachers, shopowners who sell handcrafted items, suppliers; others seriously interested in crafts. Magazine; 36 pages. Established in 1971. Quarterly. Circulation: 5,000. Buys all rights, but may reassign rights to author after publication. Buys about 8 mss a year. Pays on publication. Will send free sample copy to writer on request. Reports on material accepted for publication by return mail. Returns rejected material in 3 months. Query first. Enclose S.A.S.E.
Nonfiction and Photos: Emphasis is on how to market crafts. Also, ideas for teaching for art departments or home studio teachers; new products; trends in the crafts field; new books, careers in crafts, ideas for operating successful shops or galleries. Does not want to see anything on crafts as a hobby, or how-to pieces on individual crafts. Uses articles based on personal experience, and those dealing with successful business operations and merchandising techniques. Interviews, profiles, inspirational, humorous and historical articles. Length: 50 to 1,500 words. Pays $5 to $35, except for humorous and historical material. Payment for these is $5 to $20 or $25. Pays $5 to $50 for photo articles of 25 to 1,500 words. $5 to $25 for reviews of craft shows; 50 to 600 words; 5x7 or 8x10 b&w photos of craftsmen seriously involved in crafts; teachers, schools. These are purchased with mss or on assignment. Pays $5 minimum. Captions required.

Home and Garden Publications

AMERICAN HOME, 641 Lexington Ave., New York NY 10022. (212)644-0300. Editor: Nancy Love. For busy homemakers. Magazine; 100 pages. Monthly. Circulation: 2.5 million. Buys all rights. Address queries to the Features Editor. SASE.
Nonfiction: "The new *American Home* tries to present alternative life styles and support for people going through transitions that affect their homes and families. Editorial focus is on subjects dealing with the home and home management, but freelance material is also used on subjects such as health, beauty, gardening, antiques, travel, family problems and relationships, singlehood, working women. Regular features include Emerging Woman (profiles of interesting women) and Men at Home (either a profile or a personal opinion piece by or about men). Home Front News (100-500 words). Front of book articles (1,000 words). Major features (2,000 words minimum)." Payment depends on quantity and quality.
Photos: Query required for photos to accompany mss since most are done on assignment.

APARTMENT LIFE, 1716 Locust, Des Moines IA 50336. Editor: David Jordan. For apartment residents. Monthly magazine; 108 pages. Estab: 1968. Circ: 850,000. Buys all rights. Buys 60 to 100 mss a year. Payment on acceptance. Will not consider photocopied or simultaneous submissions. Submit seasonal material 5 to 6 months in advance. Reports in 2 months. Query first. Enclose S.A.S.E.

Nonfiction and Photos: "Service material specifically for people who live in cities and apartments. Thorough, factual, informative articles always slanted toward the apartment situation." Informational, how-to, travel. Length: 300 to 1,000 words. Pays $250 to $400. B&w photos and color are purchased only on assignment.

BETTER HOMES AND GARDENS, 1716 Locust St., Des Moines IA 50336. (515)284-9011. Editor: James A. Autry. For "middle-and-up income, homeowning and community-concerned families." Monthly. Circulation: 8,000,000. Buys all rights. Pays on acceptance. Query preferred. Submit seasonal material 1 year in advance. Mss should be directed to the department where the story line is strongest. Enclose S.A.S.E.
Nonfiction: "Freelance material is used in areas of travel, health, cars, money management, and home entertainment. Reading the magazine will give the writer the best idea of our style. We do not deal with political subjects or areas not connected with the home, community and family." Pays top rates based on estimated length of published article; $100 to $2,000. Length: 500 to 2,000 words.
Photos: Shot under the direction of the editors. Purchased with mss.
How To Break In: "Follow and study the magazine, to see what we do and how we do it. There are no secrets, after all; it's all there on the printed page. Having studied several issues, the writer should come up with one or several ideas that interest him, and, hopefully, us. We consider freelance contributions in the areas of health, education, cars, money matters, home entertainment, and travel. The next step is to write a good query letter. It needn't be more than a page in length (for each idea), and should include a good stab at a title, a specific angle, and a couple of paragraphs devoted to the main points of the article. This method is not guaranteed to produce a sale, of course; there is no magic formula. But it's still the best way I know to have an idea considered."

THE CANADIAN LOG HOUSE, Box 1205, Prince George, B.C., Canada V2L 4V3. Editor-in-Chief: B. Allan Mackie. "For a middle and upper income audience; well educated, otherwise all ages and sexes. Everyone needs a home, but these are the people who have the energy, the drive, the intelligence to want to create a superior home with their own hands." Annual magazine; 70 pages. Estab: 1974. Circ: 20,000. Pays on acceptance. Buys one-time rights. Annual deadline is October 1. Reports in 1 week.
Nonfiction: Historical (on excellent log construction methods), how-to (do any part/portion of a good solid timber house), informational, humor, inspirational, interview (with a practicing, professional builder, or a factual one on an individual who built a good house), new product (if relevant), personal experience (house building), photo feature (on good log buildings of a permanent residential nature; absolutely no cabins or rotting hulks), and technical (preservatives, tools). Query. Length: 3,000 words maximum. Pays $50 minimum.
Photos: Mary Mackie, Photo Editor. Purchased with accompanying ms. Captions required. Send contact sheet. Pays $3 minimum for 5x7 b&w glossy photos (negatives appreciated); $10 minimum for 2¼x2¼ transparencies.
How To Break In: "Very simple: either he/she is, or knows what it means to be, an excellent log builder. It is very difficult to write intelligently in this subject without this prerequisite."

FAMILY FOOD GARDEN, P.O. Box 1014, Grass Valley CA 95945. (916)273-3354. Editor: Elaine McPherson. For gardeners. Magapaper (magazine in newspaper format) published 10 times a year; 24 (9½x13½) pages. Established in 1973. Circulation: 250,000. Buys all rights, but will reassign rights to author upon request. Buys about 50 mss a year. Payment on publication. Will send sample copy to writer on request. Write for copy of guidelines for writers. Will not consider photocopied or simultaneous submissions. Submit seasonal material 3 months in advance. Reports in 3 weeks. Query first. Enclose S.A.S.E.
Nonfiction and Photos: "Our approach is 'practical' food growing. We prefer gardening advice based on personal experience, or sometimes third-person accounts. Not interested in inspirational approach, but in practical, usable advice on all aspects of growing fruit, vegetables and meat. We do not cover flower gardening except very incidentally. We are interested in articles in which the economics of home raising of food are spelled out; exact costs, food budget savings, etc. We do not want recipes, except as inclusions in articles about particular foods. Inspirational gardening articles or very long articles do not have much chance." Length: 300 to 1,200 words. Pays $25-50 for illustrated articles. No additional payment for b&w used with mss. Snapshot size acceptable for b&w; any size color transparencies, but b&w is more often used.
How To Break In: "A query is the best avenue, since it is difficult for a writer to know our needs without suggestions from us."

FLOWER AND GARDEN MAGAZINE, 4251 Pennsylvania, Kansas City MO 64111. Editor-in-Chief: Rachel Snyder. For home gardeners. Monthly. Picture magazine. Circulation: 600,000. Buys first rights. Pays on acceptance. Will send a sample copy to a writer on request. Write for copy of guidelines for writers. Query first. Reports in 6 weeks. Enclose S.A.S.E.

Nonfiction: Interested in illustrated articles on how-to-do certain types of gardening, descriptive articles about individual plants. Flower arranging, landscape design, house plants, patio gardening are other aspects covered. "The approach we stress is practical (how-to-do-it, what-to-do-it-with). We try to stress plain talk, clarity, economy of words. We are published in 3 editions: Northern, Southern, Western. Some editorial matter is purchased just for single edition use. Most, however, is used in all editions, so it should be tailored for a national audience. Material for a specific edition should be slanted to that audience only." Length: 1,000 to 1,200 words. Pays 4½¢ a word or more, depending on quality and kind of material.

Photos: Buys photos submitted with mss or with captions only. Pays up to $12.50 for 5x7 or 8x10 b&w's, depending on quality, suitability. Also buys color transparencies, 35mm and larger. Pays $20 to $125 for these, depending on size and use.

How To Break In: "Prospective author needs good grounding in gardening practice and literature. Then offer well-researched and well-written material appropriate to the experience level of our audience. Illustrations help sell the story."

HOMEMAKER'S MAGAZINE, Comac Communications Ltd., Yonge Eglinton Centre, 2300 Yonge St., Toronto, Ontario M4P 1E4. (416)482-8260. Editor-in-Chief: Ms. Jane Hughes. Emphasizes social issues and women's topics. Magazine, published 9 times/year; 146 pages. Estab: 1966. Circ: 2.2 million. Pays on acceptance. Buys first North American serial rights (English and French). Submit seasonal/holiday material 6 months in advance. Photocopied submissions OK. SASE and International Reply Coupons. Reports in 2 weeks. Free sample copy and writer's guidelines.

Nonfiction: Expose (of interest to suburban housewife), informational, interview, personal experience, personal opinion, profile. Buys 3-6 mss/issue. Query. Length: 2,000-6,000 words. Pays $600 minimum.

HOMEOWNERS HOW TO HANDBOOK, The Make-It, Fix-It, Grow-It Magazine, Box 4630, Stamford CT 06907. Editor: Jim Liston. A Popular Science publication of Times Mirror Magazines. Established in 1974. Quarterly. Circulation: 250,000. Buys all rights. Pays on acceptance. Will send sample copy to writer for $1.50. Address request to: Milton J. Norcross, Homeowners How To Handbook Subscription Department, 380 Madison Ave., New York NY 10017. No photocopied or simultaneous submissions. Submit seasonal material 7 months in advance. Reports on material accepted for publication in 2 to 3 weeks. Returns rejected material in 1 week. Enclose S.A.S.E.

Nonfiction and Photos: Wants how-to information based on facts and experience — not theory. "Design ideas should be original and uncomplicated. They should be directed at young homeowners working with simple tools, and, if possible, the kind of project that can be completed on a weekend. All articles should contain a list of necessary materials and tools. Photos are as important as words. B&w preferred. 4x5's are OK, but 8x10's are better." Length: 1,800 words maximum. Pays $150 per published page maximum. No additional payment for b&w photos used with mss.

Fillers: Problem Solvers, a regular filler feature, pays $25 per captioned photo that contains a work-saving hint or solves a problem.

HORTICULTURE, 300 Massachusetts Ave., Boston MA 02115. Editor: Paul Trachtman. Published by the Massachusetts Horticulture Society. Monthly. "We buy only first and exclusive rights to mss; one time use rights for photos." Pays after publication. Query first. Reports in 6 weeks. Enclose S.A.S.E.

Nonfiction and Photos: Uses authentic articles from 500 to 1,000 words on plants and gardens, indoors and out, based on actual experience. Study publication. Pays 2¢ to 3¢ per word, more for special features. Photos: color must be accurate tones, transparencies only, preferably not Ektachromes "and accurately identified."

HOUSE AND GARDEN, The Conde Nast Building, 350 Madison Ave., New York NY 10017. Editor-in-Chief: Mary Jane Pool. For homeowners and renters in middle and upper income brackets. Monthly. Circulation: 1,136,444. Buys all rights. Pays on acceptance. Will not send sample copy. "Study magazine before querying." Reports immediately. Query first and include sample of previous writing. Enclose S.A.S.E.

Nonfiction and Photos: Subjects of interest to "families concerned with their homes. Nothing for young marrieds specifically." Anything to do with the house or garden and affiliated subjects such as music, art, books, cooking, etc. Length: about 1,500 words. Payment varies. Jerome H. Denner, Assistant Managing Editor, is department editor. Photos purchased with mss only.

How To Break In: "This is a very tough market to break into. We very seldom use unsolicited material, but if anything is going to have a chance of making it here, it should be on a news breaking item. It must be something which has not already been covered in the other major magazines. It must have a new slant. Read the magazine closely for style and avoid things we've already done. We get too many freelancers sending us material on subjects for which the crest of wave has already passed. There's no guarantee that providing a short item (say, for Gardener's Notes, which is mostly staff-written) will be an easier way in, but if you understand our needs and provide something that's really good, there's always a chance. It's best to send a query and a sample of previous writing."

HOUSE BEAUTIFUL, 717 Fifth Ave., New York NY 10022. Editor: Wallace Guenther. For women of all ages. "Women with families are in the majority. Women who are interested in all aspects of modern living and creating a purposeful environment for their families." Monthly magazine; 180 pages. Established in 1896. Circulation: 900,000. Rights purchased vary with author and material. Buys all rights or first North American serial rights. Payment on acceptance. Will send sample copy to writer for $1.50. Will not consider photocopied or simultaneous submissions. Submit seasonal material (entertaining issue in November; personal histories related to remodeling for May and September) 6 to 7 months in advance. Reports in 1 month. Submit complete ms "unless writer has worked with us in the past". Submit articles to Linda B. Downs, Editor. S.A.S.E.

Nonfiction and Photos: "Because all food and travel material and much of the gardening material we use is prepared by the staff, we are not in the market for articles on these subjects. Other than that, we are interested in almost anything related to the home and modern living, but we avoid health and religious articles. Approach depends on the nature of the subject. We do buy some straight how-to and idea pieces, but even there we look for some expression of insight or relationship to others who might be interested in the same topic. Style and structure are entirely up to the writer. If it works for the story, it will work for us. Crafts are in today, but a lot of people are turning out straight how-to craft stories without realizing that most of those we do use must offer good design as well. Design orientation is very important to us. Others fail to realize that the slice-of-life or humorous features we buy should make a point and not just be a vignette on an amusing or strange incident that happened to that individual. For example, Leonard S. Bernstein is a frequent contributor of lightheartedly styled stories. We don't use little amusing stories with no point or human interest profiles. What I mostly look for from freelancers are slice-of-life stories, but which make a point." Length: 750 to 2,000 words. Pays $150 to $400. "Shorter material for our Insight section (primarily a straight news/feature type of section) should be sent to John H. Ingersoll, Senior Editor. Anyone who is interested in contributing to this section should look over a couple of copies of *House Beautiful* to see the range of material this encompasses." Length: 700 to 1,500 words. Pays $100 to $300. 8x10 b&w glossies purchased with or without mss, or on assignment. Should be 8x10. High-quality color transparencies are also used. Size: 35mm, 2¼x2¼ or 4x5. Payment varies.

How To Break In: "The Insight section is mostly service oriented and there we recently bought a piece from a woman whom we had never published before on dangerous craft materials. Insight is one place to aim shorter pieces. It's not necessarily an easy way to break in, but it is a way for us to see your work without doing a major manuscript."

HOUSE PLANTS AND PORCH GARDENS, Scrambling Press, Inc., 355 Lancaster Ave., Haverford PA 19041. (215)642-8883. Editor-in-Chief: Peter Tobey. Emphasizes house plants and porch or terrace gardens. Monthly magazine; 96 pages. Estab: 1976. Circ: 250,000. Pays on publication. Buys all rights. Phone queries OK. Submit seasonal/holiday material 5-6 months in advance. Photocopied submissions OK. SASE. Reports in 3 weeks. Sample copy $1.25. Writer's guidelines.

Nonfiction: Kim Mac Leod, Managing Editor. How-to (building plant-oriented projects, i.e., making terrariums, work areas, containers, etc.); informational (care and culture of specific plant families or individual plants); profile (on renowned horticulturists who have done interesting or unusual things in the plant world, generally in interview format). Buys 2-3 mss/issue. Send sample of writing along with resume, outline of proposed article, with a 1-2 page introduction, and a list of areas of expertise. Length: 1,200-6,000 words. Pays $100/1,000 words, pre-editing.

Photos: Purchased with or without mss, or on assignment. Captions required. Send b&w prints or color transparencies. Pays $10-25 for 8x10 b&w glossies; $25-50 for color used inside.

Columns, Departments: Artificial Light Gardening (all aspects); Basics (of indoor gardening); Potpourri (short, interesting bits about all aspects of gardening); Weird but Lovable (house or greenhouse plants that are odd in color, size, shape); Greenhouse (all aspects of greenhouse gardening); All columns are geared to amateur gardeners. Buys 20% of column material per year. Length: 1,200-3,500 words. Send sample of writing, with resume, outline of proposed article, with a 1-2 page introduction. Pays $100/1,000 words, pre-editing. Open to suggestions for new columns and departments.

Fillers: Clippings, jokes, gags, anecdotes. All plant-oriented. Send fillers in. Buys 2-3/issue. Length: 25-200 words. Pays 10¢/word, pre-editing.

How To Break In: "Carefully study the present writing style of our magazine, and follow this style when sending outline of proposed article idea and introductory pages. Work must be accurate and carefully researched. We generally accept work only from professional horticulturists, but if the freelancer is good, we'll be happy to look at his/her work."

Rejects: "Articles pertaining to particular locales(i.e., Arizona problems, etc.) And no 'how I did it myself' kind of articles."

HOUSEHOLD GARDENING AND HOUSE PLANTS, Box 874, Oak Bluffs MA 02557. Editor: Louise Aldrich Bugbee. For growers of home gardens and house plants. Magazine; 72 pages. Established in 1975. Buys all rights. Pays on publication. Will send free sample copy to writer on request. Write for copy of guidelines for writers. Will consider photocopied submissions. Submit seasonal material 6 to 8 months in advance. Reports in 2 months. Submit complete ms. Enclose S.A.S.E.

Nonfiction, Photos and Fillers: How-to articles on gardens and house plants, unusual flowers and vegetables. Either serious or light material. Should be slanted to appeal to ordinary readers, interested in gardens and plants. "Our aim is garden talk among friends and neighbors." Length: About 500 words for articles; 25 to 100 words for fillers. Pays 2¢ a word minimum. Pays $2 to $5 for b&w glossies purchased with mss.

HOUSTON HOME AND GARDEN, Bayland Publishing, Inc., Box 66469, Houston TX 77006. Editor-in-Chief: Karleen Koen. Emphasizes shelter. Monthly magazine; 160 pages. Estab: 1974. Circ: 60,000. Pays on publication. Buys all rights, but may reassign following publication. Submit seasonal/holiday material 4-6 months in advance. Photocopied and previously published submissions OK. SASE. Reports in 2 months. Sample copy $1.50. Free writer's guidelines.

Nonfiction: How-to (home maintenance and repairs); informational (city, tax information) and new product (short description). Buys 40 mss/year. Query. Length: 1,000-2,000 words. Pays $2.50/published inch.

Photos: Photos purchased with accompanying ms. Captions required. Pays $15-20 for 8x10 b&w glossies. Model release required.

Fillers: Informative, how-to pieces. Buys 2 fillers/issue. Length: 500-1,000 words. Pays $25-50.

ORGANIC GARDENING AND FARMING, Rodale Press Publications, 33 E. Minor St., Emmaus PA 18049. (215)967-5171. Managing Editor: M.C. Goldman. For a readership "ranging the full scope of public now aware and interested in growing plants, vegetables and fruits, as well as concerned about environmental problems." Monthly magazine; 160 to 240 (6x9) pages. Established in 1942. Circulation: 1,300,000. Buys all rights and the right to reuse in other Rodale Press Publications with agreed additional payment. Buys 300 to 350 mss a year. Payment on publication (actually, on preparation for publication). Will send free sample copy to writer on request. Write for copy of guidelines for writers. Reports in 4 to 6 weeks. Query first or submit complete ms. Enclose S.A.S.E.

Nonfiction, Photos and Fillers: "Factual or informative articles or fillers on both backyard gardening and family farming, stressing organic methods. Interested in all crops, soil topics, livestock, indoor gardening, greenhouses; natural foods preparation, storage, etc.; biological pest control; variety breeding, nutrition, recycling, energy conservation; community and club gardening. Strong on specific details, step-by-step how-to, adequate research. Good slant and interesting presentation always help. We do not want to see generalized garden success stories. And some build-it-yourself topics are often repeated. We would like to see material on development, techniques, different approaches to organic methods in producing fruit crops, grains, new and old vegetables; effective composting, soil building, waste recycling, food preparation. Emphasis is on interesting, practical information, presented effectively and accurately." Length: 1,200 to 2,500 words for features. Pays $75-250. B&w and color purchased with mss or on assignment. Enlarged b&w glossy print and/or negative preferred. Pays $15-25. 2¼x2¼ (or larger) color transparencies. Fillers on above topics are also used. Length: 150 to 500 words. Pays $35 to $50.

PERFECT HOME MAGAZINE, 427 6th Ave., S.E., Cedar Rapids IA 52401. Editor: Donna Nicholas Hahn. For "homeowners or others interested in building or improving their homes." Established in 1929. Monthly. Buys all rights. Pays on acceptance. Study magazine carefully before submitting. No seasonal material used. Submit editorial material at least 6 months in advance. Reports "at once." Will send free sample copy to a writer on request. Query first. Enclose S.A.S.E.

Nonfiction: "Ours is a nationally syndicated monthly magazine sponsored in local communities by qualified home builders, real estate companies, home financing institutions, and lumber and building supply dealers. We are primarily a photo magazine that creates a desire for an attractive, comfortable home. We need homebuilding, decorating, and remodeling features, decorating idea photographs, complete home coverage, and plans on homes." No do-it-yourself features. Length: 1 to 3 meaty paragraphs. No set price. "Each month we feature one nationally known guest editor on the theme 'What Home Means to Me.' Check with us before contacting a celebrity since we have had so many of them." Length: 500 to 1,000 words. Pays $50, including copy, photos, signature, and signed release from individual.

Photos: Purchases photos with articles on home building, decorating and remodeling; also purchases photos of interest to homeowners with captions only. Buys either b&w or color; color 3¼x4¼ up. "We return color; keep b&w unless return is requested as soon as issue has been printed. May hold photos 1 year." Photos must be well-styled and of highest professional quality. No models in pictures. Interested in series (for example, several pictures of gates, bay windows, window treatment, fireplaces, etc.). Pays $25 minimum.

PLANTS ALIVE, 5509 1st Ave., S., Seattle WA 98108. Publisher and Editor-in-Chief: Theodore R. Marston. Managing Editor: John McClements. Emphasizes houseplants, greenhouses and some outdoor gardening. For an audience extremely interested in gardening (indoors and outdoors). Monthly magazine; 52 pages. Estab: 1972. Circ: 125,000. Pays on publication. Buys all rights, but may reassign following publication. Submit seasonal/holiday material at least 3 months in advance. Photocopied submissions OK. SASE. Reports in 4 weeks-12 months. Free sample copy and writer's guidelines.

Nonfiction: Chris Miller, Assistant Editor. How-to (related to growing plants, building plant equipment, greenhouses); informational (to help readers with all aspects of gardening); histories (of popular flowers, usually combined with useful information); interviews (with leading growers or horticulturists, especially if article includes useful information for readers); travel (pieces on unique and unusual gardens around the world); new product (will it help our readers or is it a dud?) and newsworthy, first person accounts on gardening; capillary watering, plant photography and personality articles (how this person built a greenhouse or an indoor atrium, etc.). Buys 150 mss/year. Query or submit complete ms. Length: 300-2,000 words. Pays 4¢/word.

Photos: Norm Comp, Art Director. Purchased with mss. Pays $10 for 8x10 b&w glossies; $35 for color transparencies (35mm minimum). Model release required.

Columns/Departments: How-to (ideas on building plant stands, light units, greenhouses, planters). Plant Propagation (how to increase plants in general or a specific kind of plant, or by one particular method). Buys 24 mss/year. Query or send complete ms. Pays 4¢/word plus $10 for each drawing or b&w photo used.

How To Break In: "Freelancer should be specific, know subject and be accurate. Article shouldn't be too technical, though. Organize thoughts and present in logical manner. Ideas should be somewhat newsworthy; not something that has appeared in other publications. Leads should be snappy. Copy should be clear with no extra baggage."

POOL 'N PATIO, 3923 W. 6th St., Los Angeles CA 90020. Editor: Fay Coupe. Issued once yearly, in April, to residential owners of swimming pools. Buys all rights. Pays on publication. Reports on submissions at once. Enclose S.A.S.E.

Nonfiction and Photos: Articles on how to make pool maintenance easier; technical articles on equipment, unusual use of pools, or unusual pools; human interest or glamour stories on pool owners. Pays 5¢/word. Length: 500 to 1,500 words. Photos purchased with mss. Pays $5 minimum.

REAL ESTATE, P.O. Box 1689, Cedar Rapids IA 52406. (319)366-1597. Editor: C.K. Parks. For community leaders, homemakers and well-educated individuals. Magazine; 16 pages. Special Christmas issue. Established in 1972. Published every 2 mont. Circulation: 80,000. Buys all rights. Buys about 24 mss per year. Payment on acceptance. Will send free sample copy to

writer on request. Will consider photocopied submissions. No simultaneous submissions. Submit seasonal material 4 months in advance. Reports in 30 days. Enclose S.A.S.E.
Nonfiction and Photos: Wants mss about how-to projects that can be done around the home, decorating in the home, and investing in real estate. Length: 700 to 1,200 words. Pays $100 to $150. Photos purchased with accompanying ms with extra payment. No color. Pays $10 for first photo; $5 per additional photo. Size: 5x7.

WOMAN TALK MAGAZINE, P.O. Box 356, Blackwood NJ 08012. Editor: Jo P. Italiano. For homemakers of all ages with interests in all areas of homemaking. Bimonthly; 24 pages. Estab: 1973. Circ: 1,200. Not copyrighted. Buys 10 mss/year. Pays on publication. Will send sample copy to writer for 50¢. Will consider photocopied submissions. Will not consider simultaneous submissions. Submit seasonal material 3 to 4 months in advance. Reports in 2 to 3 months. Query first or submit complete ms. Enclose S.A.S.E.
Nonfiction and Photos: Articles on goal achievement, interesting women, homemakers, garage sales, gardening, animals, spare-time earning. "We emphasize a person-to-person relationship between our book and the reader and try gently to broaden the horizons of our readers. Our size makes it absolutely necessary that articles be concise. Style is open, but we do prefer a light approach. This does not preclude thoughtful subject matter, but nothing on the sensational side." Informational, how-to, interview, profile, humor, historical. Length: no minimum; 1,000 words maximum. Prefers 400 to 600 words. Pays ½¢ a word. Columns and departments include: Garden Corner, Pet Page, Of Interest to Boys and Girls. Items on needlework of all kinds are always needed. Length: 200 to 400 words. Pays ½¢ a word.

YOUR HOME, P.O. Box 2315, Ogden UT 84403. (801)394-9446. Editor: Helen S. Crane. For young marrieds of middle income and better than average education who own their homes and are interested in improving them. Magazine; 16 pages. Established in 1945. Monthly. Circ: 500,000. Buys all rights, but may reassign rights to author after publication. Buys about 20 mss/year. Pays on acceptance. Free sample copy. Query first, with copies of published material. Enclose S.A.S.E.
Nonfiction and Photos: "Articles on decorating the home, simple gourmet touches for foods, small vignettes on lifestyles past or present. Our emphasis is on articles that can be illustrated effectively. We want short, but pertinent, pieces that give the reader new ideas. Articles must be general in scope and timeless in appeal; short, yet meaty. We don't want to see amateur photos of one's own do-it-yourself project, nor do we want heavy, pedantic tomes on nutrition or any household tips." Length: 400-700 words. Pays $40-70. Pays $15-20 for b&w glossies purchased with mss. Can use 35mm color transparencies, but prefers larger. "Must be sparkling." Pays $25 minimum.

Humor Publications

Publications in this category specialize in humor. Other publications that use humor can be found in nearly every category in this book. Some of these have special needs for major humor pieces; some use humor as fillers; many others are simply interested in material that meets their ordinary fiction or nonfiction requirements but has a humorous slant.

BELCH & FART, Box 6342, Terra Linda CA 94903. Editor: Marcia Blackman. For young readers with a sense of humor. 36 (8x11) pages. Established in 1974. Every 2 months. Circulation: 10,000. Not copyrighted. Buys 60 mss a year. Payment on publication. Will send sample copy to writer for $2. Will consider photocopied submissions. No simultaneous submissions. Reports on material accepted for publication in 1 month. Returns rejected material immediately. Query first. Enclose S.A.S.E.
Nonfiction: "This is a spoof on *Gourmet Magazine,* using food as a humorous topic. Our profile is probably the same as *Mad Magazine* and *Lampoon.* We use only humorous articles with the emphasis on food, eating, restaurants, cooking, etc. We'd also like to see something on depression cooking and eating." Informational, how-to, personal experience, interview, profile, inspirational, humor, personal opinion, photo, travel, successful business operations, new products, merchandising techniques and reviews of restaurants. Length: 1,600 to 2,000 words. Pays $20-40.

MAD MAGAZINE, 485 Madison Ave., New York NY 10022. Editor: Al Feldstein. Buys all rights.
Nonfiction: "You know you're *almost* a *Mad* writer when: You include a self-addressed, stamped envelope with each submission. You realize we are a visual magazine and we don't print prose, text or first/second/third person narratives. You don't send us stuff like the above saying, 'I'm sure one of your great artists can do wonders with this.' You first submit a 'premise' for an article, and show us how you're going to treat it with three or four examples, describing the visuals (sketches not necessary). You don't send in 'timely' material, knowing it takes about 6 months between typewriter and on-the-stands. You don't send poems, song parodies, fold-ins, movie and/or TV show satires, Lighter Sides or other standard features. You understand that individual criticism of art or script is impossible due to the enormous amount of submissions we receive. You don't ask for assignments or staff jobs since *Mad* is strictly a freelance operation. You concentrate on new ideas and concepts other than things we've done (and over-done), like 'You Know You're a . . . . When . . .'."

ORBEN'S CURRENT COMEDY, ORBEN COMEDY FILLERS, 2510 Virginia Ave., N.W., Apt. 701-N, Washington DC 20037. (202)338-8281. Editor: Robert Orben. For "speakers, toastmasters, businessmen, public relations people, communications professionals." Biweekly; monthly. Buys all rights. Pays at the end of the month for material used in issues published that month. "Material should be typed and submitted on standard size paper. Please leave 3 spaces between each item. Unused material will be returned to the writer within a few days if S.A.S.E. is enclosed. We do not send rejection slips. Please do not send us any material that has been sent to other publications. If S.A.S.E. is not enclosed, all material will be destroyed after being considered except for items purchased."
Fillers: "We are looking for funny, performable one-liners, short jokes, and stories that are related to happenings in the news, fads, trends, and topical subjects. The accent is on comedy, not wit. Ask yourself, 'Will this line get a laugh if performed in public?' Material should be written in a conversational style and, if the joke permits it, the inclusion of dialogue is a plus. We are particularly interested in material that can be used by speakers and toastmasters: lines for beginning a speech, ending a speech, acknowledging an introduction, specific occasions, anything that would be of use to a person making a speech. We can use lines to be used at sales meetings, presentations, conventions, seminars, and conferences. Short, sharp comment on business trends, fads, and events is also desirable. Please do not send us material that's primarily written to be read rather than spoken. We have little use for definitions, epigrams, puns, etc. The submissions must be original. If material is sent to us that we find to be copied or rewritten from some other source, we will no longer consider material from the contributor." Pays $3.

In-Flight Publications

This list consists of publications read by commercial air ine passengers. They use freelance material of general interest such as travel articles, etc., as well as general interest material on aviation.

AIR CALIFORNIA MAGAZINE, The Ppblishing Co., Box 707, South Laguna CA 92677. (714)494-9393. Editor-in-Chief: Michael McFadden. Emphasizes all aspects of California for airline passengers on the world's 2nd largest intra-state airline. Monthhly magazine; 84 pages. Estab: 1967. Circ: 200,000. Pays on publication. Buys one-time rights. Phone queries OK. Submit seasonal/holiday material 3 months in advance. Simultaneous, photocopied and previously published submissions OK. SASE. Reports in 2 months. Sample copy $1.
Nonfiction: Sheldon Kilbane, Nonfiction Editor. Historical; humor; informational (travel); inspirational (if not sentimental); interview (California personalities); nostalgia; photo feature; profile and travel (California or international). Buys 65 mss/year. Query. Length: 1,500-5,000 words. Pays $50-150.
Photos: Photos purchased with accompanying ms or on assignment. Captions required. Pays $10-25 for 8x10 b&w photos; $25-50 for 35mm color photos. No additional payment for photos accepted with accompanying ms. Model release required.

ALOFT, Wickstrom Publishers, Inc., 2701 South Bayshore Dr., Suite 501, Miami FL 33133. (305)858-3546. Editor: Karl Wickstrom. For National Airlines passengers. Tr vel-oriented. Offbeat places, things to see and do along NAL route or connecting areas. Designed for light upbeat entertainment. Quarterly. Rights to be negotiated. Pays on publication. Will send sam-

ple copy to a writer for 25¢. Will consider photocopied submissions. Reports in 4 to 6 weeks. Query first. Address query to Ms. Pat Pinkerton, Executive Editor. Enclose S.A.S.E.
Nonfiction and Photos: Articles on unusual or little-known places rather than national monuments, historical sites, and the usual commercial attractions. New emphasis on leisure activity of interest to the affluent male. Each issue contains at least one piece by or about a known personality. NAL city restaurant dining (with recipes), book reviews and fashion, are handled by staff or contributing editors. No controversial or expose articles. Length: 800 to 1,500 words. Pays $150 and up for articles. Color transparencies are purchased with mss or captions on travel, sports, adventure. Must be top quality with imaginative approach. Payment negotiated. Photo Editor: Theodore R. Baker.

THE AMERICAN WAY, 633 Third Ave., New York NY 10017. For businessmen and vacation travelers aboard American Airlines. Monthly. Circulation: 2,000,000. Rights purchased vary with author and material. May buy all rights. Payment on acceptance. Query firrst to the attention of the Articles Editor. Submit seasonal material 7 months in advance. Reports 4 months prior to an issue. Enclose S.A.S.E. with queries.
Nonfiction: "*The American Way,* in addition to articles on travel, sports, food and the arts, tries to provide its readers stimulating and thought-provoking material that deals with current issues. First off, we like queries rather than actual mss. Also we like writing samples which more or less show a writer's abilities and scope. These will not be returned. We seek out the unusual aaspects of both the relatively unknown and the familiar. We are essentially a news magazine, not a travel magazine. We want articles on news events, business, ecology, the environment; art, culture; important historical events." Informational, how-to, interview, profile, humor, historical, think articles, nostalgia, travel, successful business operations and new product articles. Regular columns include: This Month, Beard on Food. Length: 1,500 to 2,000 words. Pays $200 minimum, $400 maximum.
How To Break In: "Come up with new insights into a major news story well in advance of its breaking (solar energy developments, business techniques, etc.)."

ASPEN, Blevins Publishing Co., Box 60033, Houston TX 77205. (713)443-2510. Managing Editor: Claire Hubbard. An in-flight publication for commuter airlines. Monthly. Estab: 1977. Pays on publication. Buys first rights. Phone queries OK. Submit seasonal/holiday material 3 months in advance. Simultaneous and photocopied submissions OK. SASE. Reports in 1 month. Free sample copy.
Nonfiction: Informational; historical; humor; interviews; nostalgia; profile; travel; new product (but no specific products—an article might cover the variety of solar energy products, for example); photo features and technical articles (if directed toward laymen). Articles should be aimed at the traveling salesman whose first interest is to learn about the area to which he is traveling. Also needs general interest material. Buys 8-12 mss/year. Query. Length: 500-1,200 words. Pays 5¢/word.
Photos: Purchased with or without ms, or on assignment. Query. Captions required. Pays $5-25 for 8x10 b&w glossy prints. Fee for color negatives or transparencies is negotiable.

THE CALIFORNIA MAGAZINE, East/West Network, 590 Wilshire Blvd., Suite 300, Los Angeles 90036. See *East/West Network.*

CLIPPER, East/West Network, 488 Madison Avenue, New York NY 10022. Editorial Director: Fred R. Smith. See *East/West Network.*

COMPANION, East/West Network, 488 Madison Ave., New York NY 10022. Editorial Director: Fred R. Smith. See *East/West Network.*

EAST/WEST NETWORK, INC., 5900 Wilshire Blvd., Suite 300, Los Angeles CA 90036. (213)937-5810. Editorial Director: Fred R. Smith. Publishes *The California Magazine, Clipper, Flightime, Mainliner, ReView, Sky, Sundancer, Companion* and *Reflections.* In-flight magazines for Allegheny Airlines, Continental Airlines, Delta Airlines, Eastern Airlines, Hughes Airwest, Ozark Airlines, Pacific Southwest Airlines, Pan Am and United Airlines. In-room magazines for Holiday Inn and Ramada Inn. Monthly magazines. Estab: 1968. Circ: (combined) 18 million. Pays within 60 days of acceptance. Buys all *East/West Network* rights. SASE. Reports in 1 month. All inquiries except for *The California Magazine* and *Sundancer* should be sent to Fred R. Smith, 488 Madison Ave., New York NY 10022.
Nonfiction: "On business, topical subjects, sports, personalities, trends, and destinations." Length: 1,000-2,000 words. Pays $75-1,000.

FIESTA, Travel Network International, 1182 N.W. 159th Dr., Miami FL 33169. (305) 624-5299. Editor-in-Chief: Sue Skeoch. Official in-flight magazine of TACA Airlines (El Salvador, C.A.) Emphasizes travel. Published every 4 months; 48 pages. Bilingual; Spanish and English. Estab: 1976. Circ: 1 million. Buys all rights or one-time rights. Phone queries OK. Submit seasonal/holiday material 3 months in advance. Previously published submissions OK. SASE. Reports in 3 weeks. Free sample copy and writer's guidelines.

Nonfiction: "Articles on broad range of topics relative to countries and cities to which the airline flies. Nearly any topic acceptable if it pertains to geographical area specified, but nothing ponderous or political. Food, fashions, crafts, archaeology, art, sports, game fishing, Indians, etc." Historical, humor (greatly appreciated) interview, nostalgia, personal experience, photo features, profiles. Buys 18/year. Query or submit complete ms. Length: 500-2,000 words. Pays $50-200.

Photos: Robert C. Skeoch, Photo Editor. Purchased with or without mss, or on assignment. Captions required. Query or send transparencies. Pays $10-100 for 2¼x2¼ (or larger) color transparencies. Some 35mm accepted if extremely sharp. Model release required.

How To Break In: "Make sure subject matter deals in some way with the geographical area served by the airline. Accuracy of facts is crucial. All submissions in English. We have translations made. Important for author to know the area, customs, tourist attractions, out-of-the-way and little known attractions, etc., through research. Brief background sketch of new contributors appreciated."

FLAIR MAGAZINE, 6500 Midnight Pass Rd., Penthouse Suite 504, Sarasota FL 33581. (813)921-5513. Editor: Robert J. Murley. For the passengers of Florida Air Lines, Air South and Shawnee Airlines. Tabloid; 24 pages. Established in 1975. Monthly. Circulation: 20,000. Acquires all rights. Buys about 36 mss a year. Pays on publication. Will send sample copy to writer on request. Write for copy of guidelines for writers. Will consider photocopied submissions. No simultaneous submissions. Reports in 30 days. Query first or submit complete ms. Enclose S.A.S.E.

Nonfiction and Photos: Upbeat articles on travel and vacation. Items of regional interest (the Southeast and the Bahamas), business-oriented articles. Short, personal experience articles on travel and leisure activities. Length: 1,000 words. Pays 2¢ to 3¢ a word; $50 maximum. No additional payment for b&w photos used with mss. Captions required.

FLIGHTIME, East/West Network, 488 Madison Ave., New York NY 10022. Editorial Director: Fred R. Smith. See *East/West Network.*

FLYING COLORS, Halsey Publishing Co., 15383 N.W. 7th Ave., Miami FL 33021. Editor-in-Chief: Seymour Gerber. In-flight magazine of Braniff International Airlines. Monthly magazine; 40 pages. Estab: 1972. Circ: 900,000. Pays on publication. Buys all rights, but may reassign following publication. Previously published submissions OK. SASE. Reports in 2 months. Sample copy $2; free writer's guidelines.

Nonfiction: Humor; informational, interview (question and answer); and travel (Braniff International destination cities). Buys 24 mss/year. Query. Length: 1,500-2,000 words. Pays $175-250.

Photos: Purchased with accompanying ms. Captions required. Send transparencies. Uses 35mm, 2¼x2¼ or 4x5 color transparencies. Total price for ms includes payment for photos. Model release required.

Fillers: Jokes, gags, anecdotes and puzzles. Buys 12/year. Submit complete ms. Length: 100-150 words. Pays $35-70.

FUTURO, Travel Network International, 1182 N.W. 159th Dr., Miami FL 33169. (305)624-5299. Editor-in-Chief: Sue Skeoch. Official in-flight magazine of LACSA Airlines (Costa Rica, C.A.) Emphasizes travel. For further details, see the *Fiesta* listing.

INTERLUDE, Westworld Publications, Ltd., Box 6680, Vancouver, B.C., Canada V6B 4L4. (604)732-1371. Editor-in-Chief: Bill Mayrs. Emphasizes local material on Pacific Western Airlines destinations. Bimonthly magazine; 32 pages. Estab: 1976. Circ: 50,000. Pays on publication. Buys first North American serial rights. Phone queries OK. Submit seasonal/holiday material at least 3 months in advance. Photocopied submissions OK. Free sample copy and writer's guidelines.

Nonfiction: Elspeth Woodske, Assistant Editor. How-to (very short; usually on travel or activities); humor; informational; interview (non-political; should be B.C. or Alberta person); and travel (P.W.A. charter destinations or travel tips). Length: 500-1,500 words. Pays $25-100.

Photos: Purchased with accompanying ms. Captions required. Uses 5x7 or larger b&w glossies; 35mm or larger color transparencies. Total purchase price for ms includes payment for photos.
Fillers: Jokes, gags, anecdotes, puzzles and Fancy That (short pieces of interesting trivia, suitable for illustration with cartoons). Buys 2-3/issue. Length: 50-100 words. Pays $10.
How To Break In: "We could use more good interesting material on Alberta, especially Edmonton. More urban-oriented material on Alberta: entertainment, business, etc. Should be relatively light and noncontroversial."
Rejects: "Anything on aircraft dangers. Prefer to keep the passengers minds off flying altogether. No U.S. or eastern Canada material. Nothing too heavy."

KOA'E KEA, Inflight Marketing, Inc., 1649 Kapiolani Blvd., Honolulu HI 96814. Editor-in-Chief: Rita Witherwax. Emphasizes travel/aviation/Hawaiiana. Bimonthly magazine; 36 pages. Estab: 1975. Circ: 15,000. Pays on publication. Buys first Hawaii rights. Submit seasonal/holiday material 6 months in advance. Photocopied submissions OK. SASE. Reports in 6 weeks. Sample copy $1.
Nonfiction: Historical (relating to Hawaii); informational (travel-related and practical articles); interview (Hawaii personalities); photo feature (Hawaii/travel); profile and aviation (particularly Hawaii related). Buys 2-3 mss/issue. Send complete ms. Length: 450-1,500 words. Pays $35-50.
Photos: Photos purchased with or without (for covers only) accompanying ms. No extra payment for b&w photos; pays $80 for color cover photos. Model release required.
How To Break In: "Submit articles that reflect a knowledge of Hawaii and its people. Also a love and knowledge of small plane aviation—Hawaii related."

LA CONEXION, Travel Network International, 1182 N.W. 159th Dr., Miami FL 33169. (305) 624-5299. Editor-in-Chief: Sue Skeoch. Official in-flight magazine of Air Panama (Panama). Emphasizes travel. For further details, see the *Fiesta* listing.

LATITUDE/20, 1649 Kapiolani Blvd., #27, Honolulu HI 96814. Editor: Rita Witherwax. For Hawaiian Air passengers; affluent tourists and local people traveling inter-island. Magazine; 34-48 pages. Established in 1974. Every 2 months. Circulation: 2,500,000. Not copyrighted. Buys about 30 mss a year. Pays on publication. Will send sample copy to writer for $1. Will consider photocopied submissions. No simultaneous submissions. Reports in 1 month. Query first. Enclose S.A.S.E.
Nonfiction and Photos: Primarily interested in Hawaiiana. Practical information and historical facts. Self-improvement articles. Travel-related humor. Ethnic stories are always welcome (Japanese, Chinese, Korean, Filipino, Hawaiian, Samoan, Portuguese). No word pictures of swaying palms and scarlet sunsets. Length: 1,000 to 1,500 words. Pays $50. No additional payment for photos used with mss.

MAINLINER, East/West Network, 488 Madison AVe., New York NY 10022. Editorial Director: Fred R. Smith. See *East/West Network.*

METRO, Blevins Publishing Co., Box 60033, Houston TX 77205. (713)443-2510. Managing Editor: Claire Hubbard. In-flight publication for commuter airlines covering east Texas and the Gulf coast. For further details, see the *Aspen* listing.

NORTHWEST EXPERIENCE, 7020 125th S.E., Renton WA 98055. Editor: Troy Bussey. For professional and general public interested in travel and vacation in the Northwestern states of Washington, Oregon and Idaho. Distributed as in-flight magazine for several regional airlines and paid subscribers. Established in 1972. Bimonthly. Circulation: 10,000. Not copyrighted. Will send sample copy to writer for $1. Uses only a limited number of mss per year. Pays on publication. Will consider photocopied submissions. Reports in 30 days. Query first. Enclose S.A.S.E.
Nonfiction and Photos: Travel, sports, outdoor recreation, points of interest, crafts, informational, how-to and nostalgia. "We want in-depth, investigative writing — including who, what, when, where and how to experience this activity." Length: 250 to 500 words. Pays $10 to $35 per story. Photos purchased with or without mss. B&w; very seldom uses color. Query first on color photos. Pays from $5 per photo to $50 for photo story.

NORTHWEST PASSAGES (formerly *Passages*), The Webb Co., 1999 Shepard Rd., St. Paul MN 55116. Editor-in-Chief: Jean Marie Hamilton. Managing Editor: Jim Carney. For Northwest Orient Airlines passengers. Monthly magazine. Pays on acceptance. Buys all rights, but may reassign following publication. Buys 61 mss/year. Reports in 2-4 weeks. Query with samples of published work. No complete mss accepted. SASE. Sample copy $1; free writer's guidelines.

Nonfiction: Controversial ("rather than pure expose, but we want to explore both sides of any controversy"); how-to (on business, health, etc.,—no crafts); informational (sports, business trends, modern living, current issues); historical (with current peg); humor (on current topics, not personal experiences); interviews and profiles (on interesting people who are saying things of significance); personal opinion (only from writers with the proper credentials); travel (no broadbrush, what-to-see, where-to-stay pieces) and business management. Length: 1,500-1,700 words. Pays $75-500.

Photos: Purchased with mss and on assignment. Query. Pays $25-75/b&w; $50-100/color; $200/cover shots. For photos purchased with mss, "the package price is negotiated ahead of time." Model release required.

REFLECTIONS, East/West Network, 488 Madison Ave., New York NY 10022. Editorial Director: Fred R. Smith. See *East/West Network.*

REVIEW, East/West Network, 488 Madison Ave., New York NY 10022. Editorial Director: Fred R. Smith. See *East/West Network.*

ROYALE, Blevins Publishing Co., Box 60033, Houston TX 77205. (713)443-2510. Managing Editor: Claire Hubbard. An in-flight publication for commercial airlines in Louisiana. For further details, see the *Aspen* listing.

SKY, East/West Network, 488 Madison Ave., New York NY 10022. Editorial Director: Fred R. Smith. See *East/West Network.*

SUNDANCER, East/West Network, 5900 Wilshire Blvd., Suite 300, Los Angeles CA 90036. See *East/West Network.*

TIME ZONES, 15383 N. W. 7th Ave., Miami FL 33169. Semiannual. See *Flying Colors.*

TWA AMBASSADOR (for Trans World Airlines), The Webb Co., 1999 Shepard Rd., St. Paul MN 55116. Editor-in-Chief: James Morgan. "For TWA passengers, top management executives, professional men and women, world travelers; affluent, interested and responsive." Monthly magazine. Estab: 1968. Circ: 321,000. Pays on acceptance. Buys all rights, but may reassign following publication. Submit seasonal/holiday material 6 months in advance. SASE. Reports in 2-4 weeks. Sample copy $1; free writer's guidelines.

Nonfiction: Controversial (rather than the pure expose; we insist on exploring all sides in any topic), historical (with current peg), how-to (in business subjects, health; no crafts or hobbies), humor (on current topics), informational (sports, business, modern living, current issues, etc.), interview (with interesting people who are saying something of significance), personal opinion (from writers with the proper credentials), profile (people who're topical, timely; covered in-depth. Not just what they do, but why they do it), travel (no "where-to-go, what-to-see" pieces) and business management. Buys 72 mss/year. Query. Length: 800-2,000 words. Pays $100-600.

Photos: Purchased with accompanying ms. Query. Pays $25-75 for b&w photos; $50-150 for 35mm and larger color transparencies ($250 for cover). "We often buy photos with mss; the package price is negotiated ahead of time." Model release required.

Columns/Departments: Health, Travel, Sports, Food and Drink, Technology, Management, Education, Art, etc. "We buy short (800-900 words) pieces and run them as columns, under the appropriate heading." Pays $150 maximum. Open to suggestions for new columns/departments.

T Z, Transair's In-Flight Magazine, Canasus Publications, 129 12th St., Brandon, Manitoba, Canada R7A 5Z8. (204)727-2421. Editor-in-Chief: R.A. Murray. For "traveling businessmen between 30-50; highly educated, above average income, broad interests in travel, leisure and articles affecting executive lifestyles." Bimonthly magazine; 32 pages. Estab: 1977. Circ: 50,000. Pays on publication. Buys all rights, but may reassign following publication. Phone queries OK. Submit seasonal/holiday material 2 months in advance. Simultaneous and previously published submissions OK. SASE. Free sample copy and writer's guidelines.

Nonfiction: Informational, humor, interview, new product, photo feature, profile, travel. Buys 4 mss/issue. Submit complete ms. Length: 500-2,000 words. Pays 10-25¢/word.

Photos: T.J. Fowler, Photo Editor. Purchased with accompanying ms. Captions required. Send

contact sheet. Pays $10-30 for 5x7 or 8x10 b&w glossies; $50-75 for 2¼x2¼ color transparencies. Total purchase price for ms includes payment for photos.
Fiction: Adventure, erotica, humorous and mainstream. Submit complete ms. Length: 500-2,000 words. Pays 10-25¢/word.

VOYAGER, Trent Press, Ltd., 63 Shrewsbury Ln., Shooters Hill, London, England SE18 3JJ. Editor: Dennis Winston. 20% of material from American/Canadian writers. Emphasizes travel for "a reasonably sophisticated audience, middle to upper income and intelligence, both sexes, all ages." Quarterly magazine; 32 pages. Estab: 1973. Circ: 15,000. Pays on publication. Buys one-time rights. Submit seasonal/holiday material 6 months in advance. Photocopied and previously published submissions OK ("if not previously published in U.K."). SASE. Reports in 1 month.
Nonfiction: Humor (real-life travel experiences), informational (articles concerning business and/or holidays in areas with which magazine is concerned), and travel (relevant to area served by magazine). "*Voyager* is the free in-flight magazine for passengers of British Midland Airways, which has several domestic routes within the U.K., and international routes to France, West Germany, Belgium, Holland, and the Republic of Ireland. Our need is for well-informed, entertaining articles about business, tourism, and facets of life in those countries and in others for which those countries are gateways." Buys 6 mss/issue. Submit complete ms. Length: 1,000-2,000 words maximum. Pays 25-45 pounds.
Photos: Purchased with accompanying ms. Captions required. Submit prints or transparencies. Pays 3-12 pounds for 8x6 b&w glossies; 7-20 pounds for color transparencies. Total purchase price for ms includes payment for photos.
How To Break In: "Articles must be informative, specific (e.g., name hotels and restaurants, give prices), not outdated, entertaining. First person material is welcomed."

WESTERN'S WORLD, 141 El Camino, Beverly Hills CA 90212. (213)273-1990. Editor: Frank M. Hiteshew. Published by Western Airlines for the airline traveler. Established in 1970. 6 times a year. Circulation: 250,000. Buys all rights. Buys 20 to 25 mss a year. Pays on publication. Will consider photocopied submissions. Submit seasonal material 12 months in advance of issue date. Reports in 1 to 3 months. Query first. Enclose S.A.S.E.
Nonfiction: "Articles should relate to travel, dining, or entertainment in the area served by Western Airlines: Hawaii, Minneapolis/St. Paul, Alaska to Mexico, Miami and between. Compared to other airline magazines, *Western's World* strives for a more editorial approach. It's not as promotional-looking; all articles are bylined articles. Some top names in the field." Buys photo features and travel articles. Length: 1,000 to 2,000 words. Pays 10¢ a word.
Photos: Department Editor: Tom Medsger. Purchased with or without mss or on assignment; captions required. Uses 8x10 b&w glossies, but "rarely." Pays $25. Uses 35mm, 4x5, and larger color transparencies. Pays $25 to $125; "more for cover, subject to negotiation."
Fiction: Western short stories, fantasy, humor. "Rarely printed because we've seen so few good ones. Should relate to *Western's World*." Length: 1,000 to 2,000 words. Pays 10¢ a word.
Fillers: Department Editor: Tom Medsger. "Travel-oriented or brain-teasers. We have a page of children's puzzles every issue, as well as one for adults. We welcome ideas for both. Pay ranges from $10-25."

Jewish Publications

The publications which follow use material on topics of general interest slanted toward a Jewish readership. Publications using Jewish-oriented religious material are categorized in Religious Publications.

AMERICAN JEWISH TIMES-OUTLOOK, P.O. Box 10674, Charlotte NC 28234. (704)372-3296. Editor: Ronald D. Unger. For Jewish middle and upper class; religious; primarily own their own businesses or ccorporations; most of the women are club oriented. Magazine; 24 pages. Special issues for Rosh Hashanah, Hanukkah, Purim and Passover. Monthly. Circulation: 5,000. Not copyrighted. Buys 12 to 15 mss a year. Pays on publication. Will send sample copy to writer on request. Write for copy of guidelines for writers. Will consider photocopied and simultaneous submissions. Submit special holiday material at least 2 months in advance; usually earlier. Length of time in which reports are given on material accepted for publication depends on material. Returns rejected material in 7 to 10 days. Query first. Enclose S.A.S.E.

Nonfiction and Photos: Articles primarily dealing with Jewish topics of interest: economic news, Israel, Soviet Jewry, holy days, Jewish personalities, art, music, sports, etc. Book reviews and short features. Articles usually take an analytical, rather than reportive, style. A more condensed style is preferred. Length: maximum of 3 typed, double-spaced pages. Pays $10 per article. No additional payment for b&w photos used with mss.

Fiction, Poetry and Fillers: Fantasy, humorous, religious, and historical fiction. If timely, may be linked to Holy Days. Pays $25. Traditional and avant-garde forms of poetry, blank verse, free verse, haiku. Must relate to publications's theme. Pays $10 minimum. Groups of jokes, gags, anecdotes; and short humor used as fillers. Pays $10 minimum.

THE AMERICAN ZIONIST, Zionist Organization of America, 4 E. 34th St., New York NY 10016. Editor-in-Chief: Elias Cooper. Political journal pertaining to Israel, Middle East, and Jewish affairs. Monthly magazine; 40 pages. Estab: 1910. Circ: 44,000. Pays "some time after publication." Buys all rights, but may reassign following publication. Submit seasonal/holiday material 2 months in advance. Photocopied submissions OK. SASE.

Nonfiction: Expose, historical, humor, informational, inspirational, interview, nostalgia, profile, and travel. Buys 64 mss/year. Length: 2,000-3,000 words. Pays $50-100.

Poetry: Traditional "mainly used as filler material." Buys 4 poems/year. Pays $15.

CANADIAN ZIONIST, 1310 Greene Ave., Montreal, Quebec, Canada H3Z 2B2. Editor: Dr. Leon Kronitz. Associate Editor: Rabbi S. Shizgal. For a cross-section of Canada's Jewish community. Publication of the Canadian Zionist Federation. Magazine; 40 to 56 pages. Special issues: Passover, Rosh Hashana and Hanukkah. Established in 1939. Monthly. Circulation: 30,000. Copyrighted. Pays on publication. Will send free sample copy to writer on request. Will consider photocopied submissions. No simultaneous submissions. Submit special issue material 2 months in advance. Reports on material accepted for publication in about 6 weeks. Returns rejected material in 1 to 2 weeks. Query first. Enclose S.A.S.E.

Nonfiction and Photos: Articles on Zionism, Israel and the Middle East; Jewish culture and literature. Human interest stories. Articles on Jews in far-flung communities, the campus scene, dialogue with Arabs. Personal experience, interview, profile, historical, expose and travel articles. Length: 2,000 to 3,000 words. Pays $50-250. No additional payment for b&w photos used with mss. Captions required.

DAVKA MAGAZINE, Los Angeles Hillel Council, 900 Hilgard Ave., Los Angeles CA 90024. (213)474-7717. Editor-in-Chief: Neil Reisner. Emphasizes Jewish community life. For "an audience of actively identifying Jews, ages 18-40. Mostly students, Jewish communal workers or lay people and others interested in the Jewish community." Quarterly magazine; 60 pages. Estab: 1970. Circ: 3,500. Pays in contributor's copies. Acquires all rights, but may reassign after publication. Phone queries OK. Submit seasonal/holiday material 3-4 months in advance. Simultaneous, photocopied and previously published submissions OK. SASE. Reports in 3 weeks. Sample copy $1.40; free writer's guidelines.

Nonfiction: How-to (new or alternate rituals, religious or secular Jewish observance); informational (all facets of Jewish community); historical (on little known Jewish communities or people, especially concerning the West Coast), humor, interview, nostalgia, personal opinion (query first), profile, travel (exotic Jewish communities), and photo feature. Buys 15-20 mss/issue. Query or submit complete ms. Length: 250-3,000 words.

Photos: Ellen Lampert, Photo Editor. Purchased with accompanying ms or on assignment. Query. Will consider 5x7 or 8x10 matte or glossy for b&w or color.

Fiction: Howard Kaplan, Fiction Editor. Adventure, historical, religious, science fiction. "All fiction must relate to Jewish themes." Buys 2 mss/issue. Length: 1,000-5,000 words. Pays in copies.

Poetry: Avant-garde, free verse, traditional. Buys 3/issue. Submit maximum of 5 poems at one time. Length: 4 lines minimum.

Rejects: "Jewish humor, stereotypes, or anything which is mainstream."

JEWISH CURRENT EVENTS, 430 Keller Avenue, Elmont NY 11003. Editor: S. Deutsch. For Jewish children and adults; distributed in Jewish schools. Biweekly. Pays on publication. No sample copies available. No query required. Reports in 1 week. Enclose S.A.S.E.

Nonfiction: All current event items of Jewish content or interest; news; featurettes; short travel items (non-Israel) relating to Jewish interests or descriptions of Jewish communities or personalities; life in Jewish communities abroad; "prefer items written in news-style format." Length must be short. Pays anywhere from $10 to $300, depending on content, illustrations, length and relevance.

Photos: Purchased with mss, if available, but not required. All items of Jewish content or interest. B&w snapshots only. Payment varies.

THE JEWISH DIGEST, 1363 Fairfield Ave., Bridgeport CT 06605. Editor: Bernard Postal. For "urban, well-educated families, interested in topics of Jewish interest." Established in 1955. Monthly. Circulation: 15,000. Occasionally buys first North American serial rights. Payment on acceptance. Will send a sample copy to writer for $1. Submit seasonal material (Jewish holidays) six months in advance. Will consider photocopied submissions. Reports in 2 weeks. Enclose S.A.S.E.
Nonfiction: Subject matter should be of "Jewish interest. Jewish communities around the world, and personality profiles. Contemporary topics about and relating to Jews in the U.S. and abroad. We would like to see personal experiences, biographic sketches, impressions of the Jewish community here and abroad." Length: 2,000 words. Pays 1¢ to 2¢ a word with $30 maximum.

JEWISH TELEGRAPH, Levi House, Bury Old Rd., Manchester M8 6HR, England. Editor: Frank Harris. Weekly. Estab: 1950. Circ: 11,500, Copyrighted. Pays on publication. SAE and International Reply Coupons. Free sample copy.
Nonfiction: Exclusive news and humorous and historical articles of Jewish interest. Pays 3 pounds minimum.

MIDSTREAM, 515 Park Ave., New York NY 10022. Editor: Joel Carmichael. Monthly. Circulation: 12,000. Buys first rights. Pays on publication. Reports in 2 weeks. Enclose S.A.S.E.
Nonfiction and Fiction: "Articles offering a critical interpretation of the past, searching examination of the present, and affording a medium for independent opinion and creative cultural expression. "Articles on the political and social scene in Israel, on Jews in Russia and the U.S.; generally it helps to have a Zionist orientation. If you're going abroad, we would like to see what you might have to report on a Jewish community abroad." Buys historical and think pieces and fiction, primarily of Jewish and related content. Pays 7¢ minimum per word.
How To Break In: "A book review would be the best way to start. Send us a sample review or a clip, let us know your area of interest, suggest books you would like to review."

MOMENT MAGAZINE, 55 Chapel St., Newton MA 02160. (617)964-2512. Editor-in-Chief: Leonard Fein. Emphasizes Jewish affairs. Monthly magazine; 80 pages. Estab: 1975. Circ: 25,000. Pays on publication. Buys all rights. Phone queries OK. Submit seasonal/holiday material 6 months in advance. Reports in 4 weeks. Sample copy $2.
Nonfiction: Expose, how-to, informational, historical, humor, nostalgia, profile, personal experience. Top literary quality only. Buys 100 mss/year. Query or submit complete ms. Length: 1,000-5,000 words. Pays $50-400.
Fiction: William Novak, Fiction Editor. "We use only the highest quality fiction. If you wouldn't send it to the *New Yorker,* don't send it to us. Stories must have high Jewish content." Buys 8 mss/year. Submit complete ms. Length: 1,000-5,000 words. Pays $100-400.
How To Break In: "We rarely publish beginners. Best way to break in is to have published in other quality magazines."
Rejects: "We don't want anything sentimental or cliched. We receive far too many mss on the Holocaust. No room for memoirs or family stories."

THE NATIONAL JEWISH MONTHLY, 1640 Rhode Island, N.W., Washington DC 20036. (202)857-6645. Editor: Charles Fenyvesi. Published by B'nai B'rith. Monthly magazine. Buys North American serial rights. Pays on publication. Enclose S.A.S.E.
Nonfiction: Articles of interest to the Jewish community: economic, demographic, political, social, biographical. Length: 4,000 words maximum. Pays 10¢ per word maximum.

RECONSTRUCTIONIST, 432 Park Ave., S., New York NY 10016. (212)889-9080. Editor: Dr. Ira Eisenstein. A general Jewish religious and cultural magazine. Monthly. Established in 1935. Circulation: 6,000. Buys all rights. Buys 10 mss a year. Payment on publication. Will send free sample copy to writer on request. Query first. Enclose S.A.S.E.
Nonfiction: Publishes literary criticism, reports from Israel and other lands where Jews live, and material of educational or communal interest. Also uses interviews and features dealing with leading Jewish personalities. Preferred length is 3,000 words and payment is from $15 to $25.
Fiction and Poetry: Uses a small amount of poetry and fiction as fillers.

SOUTHERN JEWISH WEEKLY, P.O. Box 3297, Jacksonville FL 32206. (904)355-3459. Editor: Isadore Moscovitz. For a Jewish audience. Established in 1924. General subject matter is human interest and short stories. Weekly. Circulation: 28,500. Not copyrighted. Buys 15 mss a year. Payment on acceptance. Will send a free sample copy to a writer on request. Will send editorial guidelines sheet on request. Submit seasonal material one month in advance. Reports in 10 days. Enclose S.A.S.E.

Nonfiction and Photos: Approach should be specifically of "Southern Jewish interest." Length· 250 to 500 words. Pays $10 to $25. Buys b&w photos with mss.

WORLD OVER, 426 W. 58th St., New York NY 10019. Editor: Ezekiel Schloss. Buys first serial rights only. Pays on acceptance. Reports within three to four weeks. Query first. Enclose S.A.S.E.

Nonfiction, Photos, and Fiction: Uses material of Jewish interest, past or present for ages 9 to 13 and up. Articles up to 1,300 words. Fiction should have an ethical or moral slant and be Jewish in content. Length: 600-1,350 words. Pays 6¢/word minimum. B&w glossies purchased with mss.

Juvenile Publications

This section of Writer's Market *includes publications for children ages 2 to 12. Magazines for young people 12 to 25 appear in a separate Teen and Young Adult category.*

Most of the following publications are produced by religious groups, and wherever possible, the specific denomination is given. For the writer with a story or article slanted to a specific age group, the sub-index which follows is a quick reference to markets for his story in that age group.

Those editors who are willing to receive simultaneous submissions are indicated. (This is the technique of mailing the same story at the same time to a number of low-paying religious markets of nonoverlapping circulation. In each case, the writer, when making a simultaneous submission, should so advise the editor.) The few mass circulation, nondenominational publications included in this section which have good pay rates are not interested in simultaneous submissions and should not be approached with this technique. Magazines which pay good rates expect, and deserve, the exclusive use of material.

Writers will also note in some of the listings that editors will buy "second rights" to stories. This refers to a story which has been previously published in a magazine and to which the writer has already sold "first rights." Payment is usually less for the reuse of a story than for first-time publication.

Juvenile Publications Classified by Age

Two- to Five-Year Olds: *Children's Playmate, Children's Service Programs, The Friend, Happy Times, Highlights for Children, Humpty Dumpty's Magazine, Jack and Jill, The Kindergartner, Let's Find Out, Nursery Days, Our Little Friend, Ranger Rick's Nature Magazine, Story Friends.*

Six- to Eight-Year-Olds: *Child Life, Children's Playcraft, Children's Playmate, Children's Service Programs, Cricket, Crusader, Daisy, The Friend, Highlights for Children, Humpty Dumpty's Magazine, It's Our World, Jack and Jill, Jet Cadet, Let's Find Out, Primary Treasure, Ranger Rick's Nature Magazine, Story Friends, Video-Presse, The Vine, Weekly Bible Reader, Wonder Time, Wow, Young Crusader, Young Judaean.*

Nine- to Twelve-Year-Olds: *The Beehive, Child Life, Children's Playcraft, Children's Service Programs, Climb, Cricket, Crusader, Crusader Magazine, Discoveries, Discovery, Ebony, Jr., The Friend, The Good Deeder, Highlights for Children, It's Our World, Jack and Jill, Jet Cadet, Mill Street Journal, On the Line, Primary Treasure, Rainbow, Ranger Rick's Nature Magazine, Sprint Magazine, Story Friends, Trails, Video-Presse, The Vine, Wee Wisdom, Young Crusader, Young Judaean, Young Musicians.*

THE BEEHIVE, 201 8th Ave., S., Nashville TN 37203. Editor: Martha Wagner. Published monthly in weekly format for children in grades five and six in United Methodist Church schools. Will send free sample copy to a writer on request. Buys all rights. Pays on acceptance. Submit double-spaced copy, 36-character line count. Reports on submissions within three months. Enclose S.A.S.E.
Nonfiction and Photos: Most articles requested by editor from writers. Subject matter relates to or correlates with church school curriculum and interests of children in grades 4, 5 and 6. Should not be overly moralistic or didactic. May provide information to enrich cultural understanding in religion and in relationships with other people. Also well-written biography, not composed from encyclopedias. Length: 200 to 800 words. Pays 3¢ a word. Photos purchased with mss. B&w glossies; color transparencies. Pays $1 to $25.
Fiction and Poetry: Modern day life, problems. Unusual historical stories; church history. No slang, references to drinking, or smoking. Might-have-happened Biblical stories. "I am rejecting many manuscripts because of our low budget. Many stories are too long, too unrealistic, or goody-goody." Length: about 800 words. Poetry to 20 lines. Pays 50¢ per line.

CHILD LIFE Mystery and Science Fiction Magazine, Saturday Evening Post Co., Youth Publications, 1100 Waterway Blvd., Box 567B, Indianapolis IN 46206. Editor: Peg Rogers. For children to age 14. Monthly (except bimonthly issues in June/July, August/September) magazine; 48 pages. Estab: 1921. Pays on publication. Buys all rights. Submit seasonal/holiday material 8 months in advance. Photocopied submissions OK. SASE. Reports in 8-10 weeks. Sample copy 50¢; free writer's guidelines.
Nonfiction: How-to (crafts for children up to 14, using easy to find items or articles around the home); informational (science, mysteries of nature, space-related subjects); historical (mysterious happenings); humor (always needed and appreciated); interview (famous TV personalities connected with space and mystery). Buys 1-2 mss/issue. Submit complete ms. Length: 500-1,000 words. Pays 3¢/word.
Photos: Purchased with accompanying ms. Captions required. Submit prints or transparencies. Pays $2.50 for b&w glossy prints; $5 for color transparencies. Model release required.
Fiction: Adventure; fantasy; humorous; mystery; suspense; and science fiction. All fiction must appeal to children to age 14. Buys 3-6 mss/issue. Submit complete ms. Length: 1,200-5,000 words. Pays 3¢/word.
How To Break In: "We encourage new authors. The most important factors are interest levels and length of ms. Good mystery and science fiction stories are accepted. Authors must remember that our readers are up to 14 years old, and endeavor to keep their words and sentence lengths to that level. We're looking for a good mini-mystery writer. Word limit: 500 words and answers should be short enough to be placed on another page. Queries and samples are requested."

CHILDREN'S PLAYCRAFT, 52 Vanderbilt Ave., New York NY 10017. Editor: Michaela Muntean. Published 10 times a year by Parents' Magazine Enterprises, Inc., as an arts and crafts, activities and hobbies magazine for children ages 6-12. *Playcraft* is primarily a reprint magazine.

CHILDREN'S PLAYMATE, 1100 Waterway Blvd., P.O. Box 567B, Indianapolis IN 46206. (317)634-1100, Ext. 296. Editor: Beth Wood Thomas. For children, ages 3 to 8. 10 times a year. Buys all rights. Pays on publication. Will send sample copy for 50¢. Write for copy of guidelines for writers. No query. "We do not consider resumes and outlines. Reading the whole ms is the only way to give fair consideration. The editors cannot criticize, offer suggestions, or review unsolicited material that is not accepted." Submit seasonal material 8 months in advance. Simultaneous submissions not accepted. Reports in 8 to 10 weeks. Sometimes may hold mss for up to 1 year. "Material will not be returned unless accompanied by a self-addressed envelope and sufficient postage."
Fiction: Short stories, not over 600 words for beginning readers. No inanimate, talking objects. Humorous stories, unusual plots. Vocabulary suitable for ages 3 to 8. Pays about 3¢ per word.
Nonfiction: Beginning science, not more than 600 words. Monthly "All About...." feature, 300 to 500 words, may be an interesting presentation on animals, people, events, objects, or places. Pays about 3¢ per word.
Fillers: Puzzles, dot-to-dots, color-ins, mazes, tricks, games, guessing games, and brain teasers. "Attention to special holidays and events is sometimes helpful." Payment varies.

CHILDREN'S SERVICE PROGRAMS, Concordia Publishing House, 3558 S. Jefferson Ave., St. Louis MO 63118. (314)664-7000. Issued annually by The Lutheran Church—Missouri

Synod, for children, aged three through eighth grade. Buys all rights. Receipt of children's worship scripts will be acknowledged immediately, but acceptance or rejection may require up to a year. All mss must be typed, double-spaced on 8½x11 paper. S.A.S.E. must be enclosed for ms return. Write for details.

Nonfiction and Drama: "Three Christmas worship service programs for congregational use published yearly. Every script must include usual elements embodied in a worship service. Children lead the worship with adults participating in singing some of the hymns. Youth and adult choir selections optional. Every script must emphasize the Biblical message of the Gospel through which God shares His love and which calls for a joyful response from His people. Services requiring elaborate staging or costumes not accepted." Pays $125 but buys few mss.

CLIMB, Warner Press, 1200 E. Fifth St., Anderson IN 46011. Editor: William A. White. For "ten-year-old boys and girls from across the U.S.A. and Canada." Publishes material "dealing with Christian living and example." Weekly. Circulation: 19,000. Not copyrighted. Buys 225 mss a year. Pays on publication. Will send a sample copy to a writer on request. Write for copy of guidelines for writers. No query required. Will consider photocopied submissions. Submit seasonal material 6-8 months in advance. Reports in 2 weeks. Enclose S.A.S.E. for return of submissions.

Nonfiction and Photos: "These stories might deal with current situations of 10- and 11-year-olds who have done something about a problem in their community; current Christian laymen and how they see their job as a Christian; current Christian athletes," etc. Writer should use a 10-year-old's vocabulary and "lots of dialog." Buys how-to's, interviews, profiles, think pieces, travel pieces, humor, historical articles, and personal experience nonfiction. Length: 250 to 1,000 words. Pays $10 per 1,000 words. B&w glossy photos purchased with mss. Pays $5 to $25; one-time use.

Fiction: "Should challenge and guide readers in the meaning of living a winsome, Christian life." Stories of adventure; also, religious, contemporary problem stories. Length: 800 to 1,200 words. Pays $10 per 1,000 words.

Poetry: Prefers "readers' poems." Length: 4 to 20 lines. Pays 20¢ per line or $2 per poem.

CRICKET, P.O. Box 100, LaSalle IL 61301. Editor: Marianne Carus. For children ages 6 to 12. Monthly magazine; 96 pages. Established in 1973. Rights purchased vary with author and material. May buy all rights, first serial world rights, or second serial (reprint) rights. Buys about 100 mss per year. Pays on publication. Sample copies of magazine available; $1.50 each. Send S.A.S.E. for copy of guidelines for writers. Will consider photocopied and simultaneous submissions. Special material should be submitted 9 to 12 months in advance. "We work 1 year in advance of publication." Reports on material accepted for publication in 6 to 8 weeks. Returns rejected material in 6 to 8 weeks. Submit complete ms. Enclose S.A.S.E.

Nonfiction: "We are interested in high-quality material written for children, not down to children." Biography, science, history, foreign culture, informational, humor, travel. Pays up to 25¢ per word.

Fiction: Realistic and historic fiction; fantasy, myth, legend, folk tale. Does not want to see animal stories or rewritten or retold folk tales that appear in standard story collections and anthologies. Length: 200 to 2,000 words. Pays up to 25¢ per word.

Poetry: Traditional forms, light verse, limericks, nonsense rhymes. Length: 100 lines maximum. Pays up to $3 per line.

Fillers: Short humor, puzzles, songs, crafts, recipes. Length: 200 words maximum. Pays up to 25¢ per word.

CRUSADER, 1548 Poplar Ave., Memphis TN 38104. (901)272-2461. Editor: Lee Hollaway. For boys ages 6 through 11, who are part of a boys' program in Southern Baptist Churches called Royal Ambassadors. Established in 1970. Monthly. Circulation: 100,000. Rights purchased vary with author and material. May buy first North American serial rights, first serial rights, second serial (reprint) rights, simultaneous rights. Buys 25-50 mss/year. Pays on acceptance. Free sample copy and writer's guidelines. Will consider photocopied submissions. Submit seasonal material 8 to 10 months in advance. Reports within 3 months. Enclose S.A.S.E.

Nonfiction and Photos: "Articles of general interest to the age group. Articles should often aid the child's interest in the world around him and increase his appreciation for cultures other than his own." Informational, how-to (simple), humor, historical (limited), photo, and travel articles. Nature articles almost always require photos. Query. Length: maximum 900 words, but prefers 500. Pays minimum $5, no maximum. Photos are purchased with or without manuscripts, and on assignment. Captions optional. Prefers 5x7 b&w or larger glossy. Pays $5 and up per photo. "Nonfiction photo stories involving boys as well as self-explanatory photos without copy involving boys."

Fiction and Fillers: 12 to 15 short stories are purchased each year. Mainstream, mystery, adventure, humorous, and religious fiction (no sermonizing!). Length: no minimum, maximum 900 words. Pays 2½¢ a word. Prefers simple puzzles involving drawing.

Rejects: "Please avoid the 'new kid in the neighborhood' theme. We see it almost daily. Also avoid use of corrasable bond paper. It definitely prejudices us against the piece."

CRUSADER MAGAZINE, Box 7244, Grand Rapids MI 49510. Editor: Michael R. McGervey. For boys, age 9 to 14. Magazine; 32 (5½x8½) pages, in cartoon format. Established in 1962. Seven times a year. Circulation: 10,300. Rights purchased vary with author and material. Buys 15 to 20 mss a year. Pays on acceptance. Will send free sample copy to writer on request. Write for copy of guidelines for writers. Will consider photocopied and simultaneous submissions. Submit seasonal material (Christmas, Easter) at least 4 months in advance. Reports on material accepted for publication in 30 days. Returns rejected material in 30 to 60 days. Query first or submit complete ms. Enclose S.A.S.E.

Nonfiction and Photos: Articles about young boys' interests: sports, outdoor activities, bike riding, science, crafts, etc., and problems. Emphasis is on a Christian perspective, but no simplistic moralisms. Material appropriate to Christmas and Easter. Informational, how-to, personal experience, interview, profile, inspirational, humor. Length: 500 to 1,500 words. Pays 2¢ to 5¢ a word. Pays $4 to $25 for b&w photos purchased with mss.

Fiction and Fillers: "Fiction is used sparingly, but fast-moving stories that appeal to a boy's sense of adventure or sense of humor are always welcome. Avoid 'preachiness'. Avoid simplistic answers to complicated problems. Avoid long dialog and little action." Length: 500 to 1,200 words. Pays 2¢ to 5¢ a word. Uses short humor and any type of puzzles as fillers.

DASH, Box 150, Wheaton IL 60187. Editor: Paul Heidebrecht. For boys 8 to 11 years of age. Most subscribers are in a Christian Service Brigade program. Monthly magazine; 32 pages. Established in 1972. Circulation: 32,000. Rights purchased vary with author and material. Usually buys all rights, but will sometimes reassign rights to author after publication. Buys 5 mss a year. Payment on publication. Submit seasonal material 4 months in advance. Reports on material accepted for publication as soon as possible. Returns rejected material in 4 weeks. Query first. Enclose S.A.S.E.

Nonfiction and Photos: "Our emphasis is on boys and how their belief in Jesus Christ works in their everyday life." Uses short articles about boys of this age; problems they encounter. Material on crafts and games. Interview, profile. Length: 1,000 to 1,500 words. Pays $30 to $60. Pays $7.50 for 8x10 b&w photos purchased with ms. Captions required.

Fiction: Religious. Length: 1,000 to 1,500 words. Pays $20 to $60.

DISCOVERIES, 6401 The Paseo, Kansas City MO 64131. Editor: Ruth Henck McCreery. For boys and girls 8 to 12. Weekly. Buys first and some second rights. No query required. "No comments can be made on rejected material." Enclose S.A.S.E. for return of submissions.

Nonfiction: Articles on nature, travel, history, crafts, science, Christian faith, biography of Christian leaders, Bible manners and customs, home craft ideas. Should be informal, spicy, and aimed at fourth and fifth grade vocabulary. Sharp photos and artwork help sell features. Length: 400 to 800 words. Pays 2¢ a word.

Photos: Sometimes buys pix submitted with mss. Buys them with captions only if subject has appeal. Send quality photos, 5x7 or larger.

Fiction: Stories with Christian emphasis on high ideals, wholesome social relationships and activities, right choices, Sabbath observance, church loyalty, goodwill, and missions. Informal style. Length: 1,000 to 1,250 words. "Or serials of 2 to 4 parts, average 1,250 words per installment." Pays 2¢ a word.

Poetry: Nature and Christian thoughts or prayers, 4 to 16 lines. Pays 50¢ for each 4 lines.

DISCOVERY, Free Methodist Publishing House, 999 College Ave., Winona Lake IN 46590. (219)267-7161. Editor-in-Chief: Vera Bethel. For "57% girls, 43% boys, age 9-11; 48% city, 23% small towns." Weekly magazine; 8 pages. Estab: 1929. Circ: 15,000. Pays on acceptance. Rights purchased vary; may buy simultaneous, second serial or first North American serial rights. Submit seasonal/holiday material 3 months in advance. Simultaneous and previously published submissions OK. Reports in 4 weeks. Free sample copy and writer's guidelines.

Nonfiction: How-to (craft articles, how to train pets, party ideas, how to make gifts); informational (nature articles with pix); historical (short biographies except Lincoln and Washington); and personal experience (my favorite vacation, my pet, my hobby, etc.). Buys 150 mss/year. Submit complete ms. Length: 300-1,000 words. Pays 2¢/word.

Photos: Purchased with accompanying ms. Captions required. Submit prints. Pays $5-10 for 8x10 b&w glossy prints. $2 for snapshots.

Fiction: Adventure; humorous; mystery; and religious. Buys 100 mss/year. Submit complete ms. Length: 1,200-2,000 words. Pays 2¢/word.

Poetry: Free verse; haiku; light verse; traditional; devotional; and nature. Buys 100/year. Limit submissions to batches of 5-6. Length: 4-16 lines. Pays 25¢/line.

How To Break In: "Send interview articles with children about their pets, their hobbies, a recent or special vacation—all with pix if possible. Kids like to read about other kids."

EBONY JR!, Johnson Publishing Co., 820 S. Michigan Ave., Chicago IL 60605. (312)786-7722. Managing Editor: Karen Odom Gray. For all children, but geared toward black children, ages 6-12. Monthly magazine (except bimonthly issues in June/July and August/September); 48 pages. Estab: 1973. Circ: 75,000. Pays on acceptance. Buys all rights, but may reassign following publication, or second serial (reprint) rights or first North American serial rights. Submit seasonal/holiday material 4 months in advance. Previously published work OK. SASE. Reports in 3 weeks to 3 months. Sample copy 75¢. Free writer's guidelines.

Nonfiction: How-to (make things, gifts and crafts; cooking articles); informational (science experiments or articles explaining how things are made or where things come from); historical (events or people in black history); inspirational (career articles showing children they can become whatever they want); interviews; personal experience (taken from child's point of view); profiles (of black Americans who have done great things—especially need articles on those who have not been recognized). Buys 3/issue. Query or submit complete ms. Length: 500-1,500 words. Pays $75-400.

Photos: Purchased with or without mss. Must be clear photos; no instamatic prints. Pays $10-15/b&w; $25 maximum/color. Send prints and transparencies. Model release required.

Columns/Departments: Ebony Jr! News uses news of outstanding black children, reviews of books, movies, TV shows, of interest to children. Pays $25-100.

Fiction: Must be believable and include experiences black children can relate to. Adventure, fantasy, historical (stories on black musicians, singers, actors, astronomers, scientists, inventors, writers, politicians, leaders; any historical figures who can give black children positive images. Buys 2/issue. Query or submit complete ms. Length: 300-1,500 words. Pays $75-200.

Poetry: Free verse, haiku, light verse, traditional forms of poetry. Buys 2/issue. Send poems in. No specific limit on number of submissions, but usually purchase no more than two at a time. Length: 5-50 lines; longer for stories in poetry form. Pays $15-100.

Fillers: Jokes, gags, anecdotes, newsbreaks and current events written at a child's level. Brain teasers, word games, crossword puzzles, guessing games, dot-to-dot games; games that are fun, yet educational. Pays $15-85.

THE FRIEND, 50 East North Temple, Salt Lake City UT 84150. (801)531-2210. Managing Editor: Lucile C. Reading. Appeals to children from age 4 to 12. Publication of the Church of Jesus Christ of Latter-day Saints. Each issue features a different country of the world, its culture, and children. Special issues: Christmas and Easter. Established in 1970. Monthly. Circulation: 180,000. Pays on acceptance. Sample copy and guidelines for writers will be sent free upon request. Submit only complete ms. Submit seasonal material 6 months in advance. Enclose S.A.S.E. for return nf submissions.

Nonfiction: Subjects of current interest, science, nature, pets, sports, foreign countries, and things to make and do. Length: 1,000 words maximum. Pays 3¢ a word and up.

Fiction: Seasonal and holiday stories; stories about other countries and children in them. Wholesome and optimistic; high motive, plot, and action. Also simple, but suspense-filled mysteries. Character-building stories preferred. Length: 1,200 words maximum. Stories for younger children should not exceed 700 words. Pays 3¢ a word and up.

Poetry: Serious or humorous; holiday poetry. Any form. Good poetry, with child appeal. Pays 25¢ a line and up.

How To Break In: "Do you remember how it feels to be a child? Can you write stories that appeal to children ages four to twelve in today's world? We're interested in stories with an international flavor and those that focus on present day problems."

THE GOOD DEEDER, c/o Your Story Hour, Berrien Springs MI 49103. Editor: Colleen S. Garber. For young pdople, age 9 to 13, who are members of the Good Deeds Club and listeners to Your Story Hour radio program. Established in 1950. Published 10 times a year. Circulation: 13,000. Not copyrighted. Buys 30 mss a year. Pays on publication. Will send sample copy to writer if 13¢ in coin or stamps is enclosed. Will consider photocopied submissions. No simultaneous submissions. Submit special material for temperance, anti-drug, anti-alcohol,

anti-tobacco (March) issues 3 to 5 months in advance. Submit complete ms. Enclose S.A.S.E.
Nonfiction and Photos: Character building stories for kids. "No lost dogs or cats. No windows broken by a baseball followed by the little boy's confession to the cross old lady who forgave him and let him play there every day." Lengths: 500, 750, 1,000 words. Freelance photos are rarely purchased, but pays $8 for 8x10 b&w glossies used on cover; $1 to $3 for inside use.
Fiction: Adventure and Sunday school type religious fiction. Length: 750, 1,000 or 1,500 words. Pays 1¢ to 2¢ per word.

HAPPY TIMES, Concordia Publishing House, 3558 S. Jefferson Ave., St. Louis, MO 63118. Editor: Carol Greene. Emphasizes religion for Christian preschoolers 3-5. Monthly magazine; 16 pages. Estab: 1964. Circ: 60,000. Pays on acceptance. Buys all rights, but may reassign following publication. Submit seasonal/holiday material 8-12 months in advance. Previously published submissions OK. Free sample copy and writer's guidelines.
Photos: Photos purchased without accompanying ms. Pays $30 for 35mm slides or transparencies for cover only. "Should show preschoolers doing something, not posed. Occasional animal shots." Model release required.
Fiction: "Interested in material that strengthens and supports Christian home training by showing characters living with and growing in Christian principles. Strong, easily-illustrated plots are important. Avoid Santa, Easter Bunny, fairies and elves, animals that want to be something other than what they are, little trees that become Christmas trees, new pets, goody-goody children and moralizing." Buys 12 mss/issue. Send complete ms. Length: 400 maximum. Pays $10-25.
Poetry: Light verse, prayers for children, humorous verse, action poems and finger plays. Buys 2 poems/issue. Limit submissions to batches of 10. Length: 2-16 lines. Pays $5-15.

HIGHLIGHTS FOR CHILDREN, 803 Church St., Honesdale PA 18431. Editors: Walter B. Barbe and Caroline C. Myers. For children 2 to 12. 11 times a year. One of the better juvenile markets, but strong competition here. Circulation: approximately 1,000,000. Buys all rights. Pays on acceptance. Write for copy of guidelines for writers. No query. Submit complete ms only. Reports in 2 months. Enclose S.A.S.E.
Nonfiction: Most factual features, including history and science, are written on assignment by persons with rich background and mastery in their respective fields. But contributions always welcomed from new writers, especially science teachers, engineers, scientists, historians, etc., who can interpret to children useful, interesting, and authentic facts, but not of the bizarre or "Ripley" type; also writers who have lived abroad and can interpret well the ways of life, especially of children in other countries, and who don't leave the impression that our ways are always the best. Sports material, biographies, articles about sports of interest to children. Direct, simple style, interesting content, without word embellishment; not rewritten from encyclopedias. State background and qualifications for writing factual articles submitted. Include references or sources of information with first submission. Length: 1,000 words maximum. Pays minimum $50. Also buys original party plans for children 7 to 12, clearly described in 600 to 800 words, including pencil drawings or sample of items to be illustrated. Also, novel but tested ideas in arts and crafts, with clear directions, easily illustrated, preferably with made-up models. Projects must require only salvage material or inexpensive, easy-to-obtain material. Especially desirable if easy enough for early primary grades and appropriate to special seasons and days. Also, fingerplays with lots of action, easy for very young children to grasp and parents to dramatize, step-by-step, with hands and fingers. Avoid wordiness. Pays minimum $30 for party plans; $10 for arts and crafts ideas; $25 for fingerplays.
Fiction: Unusual, wholesome stories appealing to both girls and boys. Vivid, full of action and word-pictures, easy to illustrate. Seeks stories that the child 8 to 12 will eagerly read, and the child 2 to 6 will like to hear when read to him. "We print no stories just to be read aloud; they must serve a two-fold purpose. We encourage authors not to hold themselves to controlled word lists. Especially need humorous stories, but also need winter stories; urban stories; horse stories; and especially some mystery stories void of violence; and stories introducing characters from different ethnic groups; holiday stories void of Santa Claus and the Easter Bunny. Avoid suggestion of material reward for upward striving. Moral teaching should be subtle. The main character should preferably overcome difficulties and frustrations through his own efforts. The story should leave a good moral and emotional residue. War, crime, and violence are taboo. Some fanciful stories wanted." Length: 400 to 1,000 words. Pays minimum 5¢ a word.
How To Break In: "We are pleased that many authors of children's literature report that their first published work was in the pages of *Highlights*. It is not our policy to consider fiction on the strength of the reputation of the author. We judge each submission on its own merits. With factual material, however, we do prefer either authorities in their fields or people with first-hand experience. In this manner we can avoid the encyclopedic-type article which merely re-

states information readily available elsewhere. A beginning writer should first become familiar with the type of material which *Highlights* publishes. We are most eager for the easy-type story for very young readers, but realize that this is probably the most difficult kind of writing. The talking animal kind of story is greatly overworked. A beginning writer should be encouraged to develop first an idea for a story which must involve only a small number of characters and likely a single-incident plot. The story must contain a problem or a dilemma which is clearly understood and presented early. It is then clearly resolved at the end of the story. Description should be held to a minimum. Dialogue is a requirement for it is a means by which children can identify with the characters in the story."

HUMPTY DUMPTY'S MAGAZINE, Parents' Magazine Enterprises, Inc., 52 Vanderbilt Ave., New York NY 10017. Editor: Karen Craig. For children, 3 to 7 years of age. Magazine published monthly except June and August. Established in 1952. Circulation: 1,000,000. Rights purchased vary with author and material. Usually buys all rights. Buys 25 or more freelance story mss a year. Payment on acceptance. Write for copy of guidelines for writers enclosing self-addressed, stamped envelope. No sample copies. Will consider photocopied submissions. Will not consider simultaneous submissions. Submit seasonal material 6 to 8 months in advance. Reports in 2 to 6 weeks. Submit complete ms. Enclose S.A.S.E.
Fiction: "Like stories with real-life children, not all suburban types; more urban material. One thing that's always anathema to me is the animated inanimate object. Yet I just bought an excellent piece in that genre. I also dislike cliche pieces about sugar girls with dolls at tea parties. We use old-fashioned stories and folk tales — but real children must be up-to-date. We're cautious about adaptations because we don't want to give our readers something they have seen before." Length: 900 to 1,000 gords maximum. Pays $50 minimum.
Poetry: Rhyme or free verse. Length: 4 to 16 lines. Pays $10.

IT'S OUR WORLD, 800 Allegheny Ave., Pittsburgh PA 15233. Editor: Thomas F. Haas. For boys and girls in Catholic elementary schools in the United States, ages 6 to 13. Quarterly. Two-color, four-page (8½x11) newsletter. Established in 1974 by the Holy Childhood Association as a replacement for *Annals of the Holy Childhood,* which is no longer being published. Circulation: 3.1 million. Buys simultaneous rights. Buys 4 or 5 mss a year. Payment on acceptance. Will send free sample copy to writer on request. Write for copy of guidelines for writers. Will consider photocopied and simultaneous submissions. Submit seasonal material 4 months in advance. Reports on material within a month. Submit complete ms. Enclose S.A.S.E.
Nonfiction: "Ours is a publication of mission news for children, dealing with children in other countries, especially those in the developing countries (Third World or mission countries). Stories about children in other countries should show an appreciation for that country's culture, and not give the impression that our culture is better." Interested in current events reports, stories about life in other countries, stories about the legends, culture or customs of various countries (with documentation). Not interested in stories that use animal characters like Sally Squirrel, Charlie Chicken or Oscar Owl. Uses informational, how-to, personal experience, interview, profile, inspirational, humor, adventure, biographical, historical, travel and think articles. Length: 600 to 800 words. Pays minimum of $25.
Fiction: Experimental, mainstream, mystery, suspense, adventure, science fiction, fantasy, humorous, religious and historical fiction. Length: 600 to 800 words. Pays minimum of $25.
Poetry: Traditional forms, light verse and poems written by children. Length: open. Pays $15 to $25.

JACK AND JILL, 1100 Waterway Blvd., Box 567B, Indianapolis IN 46206. (317)634-1100. Editor: William Wagner. For children 5 to 12. 10 times a year. Buys all rights. Pays on publication. Will send sample copy to writer for 50¢. Write for copy of guidelines for writers. Submit seasonal material 8 months in advance. Reports in approximately 8 weeks. May hold material seriously being considered for up to 6 months or 1 year. "Material will not be returned unless accompanied by self-addressed envelope with sufficient postage."
Nonfiction and Photos: "*Jack and Jill's* primary purpose is to encourage children to read for pleasure. The editors are actively interested in material that will inform and instruct the young reader and challenge his intelligence, but it must first of all be enjoyable reading. Submissions should appeal to both boys and girls." Current needs are for "short factual articles concerned with nature, science, and other aspects of the child's world. Longer, more detailed features: 'My Father (or My Mother) Is a ...'; first-person stories of life in other countries; some historical and biographical articles." Where appropriate, articles should be accompanied by good 35mm color transparencies, when possible. Pays approximately 3¢ a word. Pays $2.50 for each b&w photo. Pays $5 each for color photo.

Fiction: "May include, but is not limited to, realistic stories, fantasy, adventure—set in the past, present, or future. All stories need plot structure, action, and incident. Humor is highly desirable." Length: 500 to 1,200 words, short stories; 1,200 words per installment, serials of 2 or 3 parts. Pays approximately 3¢ a word.

Fillers and Drama: "Short plays, puzzles (including varied kinds of word and crossword puzzles), riddles, jokes, songs, poems, games, science projects, and creative construction projects. Instructions for activities should be clearly and simply written and accompanied by models or diagram sketches. We are also in need of projects for our feature, For Carpenters Only. Projects should be of the type our young readers can construct with little or no help. Be sure to include all necessary information—materials needed, diagrams, etc. Whenever possible, all materials used in projects should be scrap materials that can be readily found around the workshop and home." Payment varies for fillers. Pays approximately 3¢ per word for drama.

How To Break In: "We have been accused of using the same authors over and over again, not keeping an open mind when it comes to giving new authors a chance. To some extent, perhaps we do lean a little heavier toward veteran authors. But there is a good reason for this. Authors who have been published in *Jack and Jill* over and over again have shown us that they can write the kind of material we are looking for. They obtain *current* issues of the magazine and *study* them to find out our present needs, and they write in a style that is compatible with our current editorial policies. That is the reason we use them over and over; not because they have a special 'in.' We would reject a story by the world's best known author if it didn't fit our needs. After all, our young readers are more interested in reading a good story than they are in reading a good by-line. We are constantly looking for new writers that have told a good story with an interesting slant—a story that is not full of outdated and time-worn expressions. If an author's material meets these requirements, then he stands as good a chance of getting published as anyone."

JET CADET, 8121 Hamilton Ave., Cincinnati OH 45231. (513)931-4050. Editor: Dana Eynon. For children 8 to 11 years old in Christian Sunday schools. Weekly. Rights purchased vary with author and material. Buys first serial rights or second serial (reprint) rights. Occasionally overstocked. Pays on acceptance. Will send a sample copy to a writer on request. Submit seasonal material 12 months in advance. Reports in 4 to 6 weeks. Enclose S.A.S.E. for return of submissions.

Nonfiction: Articles on hobbies and handicrafts, nature (preferably illustrated), famous people, seasonal subjects, etc., written from a Christian viewpoint. Length: 500 to 1,000 words. Pays up to 1½¢ a word.

Fiction: Short stories of heroism, adventure, travel, mystery, animals, biography. True or possible plots stressing clean, wholesome, Christian character-building ideals, but not preachy. Make prayer, church attendance, Christian living a natural part of the story. "We correlate our fiction and other features with a definite Bible lesson." Length: 900 to 1,200 words; 2,000 words complete length for 2-part stories. Pays up to 1½¢ per word.

Fillers: Bible puzzles and quizzes. Pays up to 1½¢ a word.

How To Break In: "We give the same consideration to a new writer as we do to regular contributors. We just checked our files, and this past year purchased mss from 35 new writers. We look for (1) Christian character-building stories, filled with action and conversation, based on true-to-life situations; (2) articles on a wide range of subjects, filled with accurate facts, and written from a Christian viewpoint. Writers may send for list of themes coming up, and submit stories that correlate with the lesson stressed in a particular issue."

Rejects: Talking animal stories, science fiction, Halloween stories, first-person stories from an adult's viewpoint, non-Biblical puzzles, and articles about saints of the opposite, or historical figures with an absence of religious implication.

THE KINDERGARTNER, The United Methodist Publishing House, 201 Eighth Ave. S., Nashville TN 37202. Editor: Arba O. Herr. For children of kindergarten age. Monthly in weekly parts. Magazine; 4 pages per week. Estab: 1964. Circ: 160,000. Pays on acceptance. Buys all rights. Submit seasonal/holiday material 1½ years in advance. SASE. Reports in 4 weeks. Free sample copy and writer's guidelines for SASE.

Nonfiction: How-to (inexpensive craft ideas, simple science discoveries that kindergartners can experiment with, gift ideas, games); informational (about nature, animals, or community services such as doctors, plumbers, etc.); inspirational (prayers and Biblical stories); personal experience (any that would be of interest to a kindergarten age child); and photo feature. Buys 60 mss/year. Query. Length: 250-300 words. Pays 2-3¢/word.

Photos: Purchased with or without accompanying ms. Query. Pays $10-15 for 8x10 glossy b&w photos; $35-40 for 2x2 color transparencies. Model release required.

Fiction: Adventure; experimental ("in the area of Bible stories there often is not sufficient dialogue or background to make a story. Therefore, we add experiences typical of the historical period—but not really authentic as to the Biblical account. Also, since the child learns by experience, we often use stories about children whose experiences are typical but at the same time fictitious"); humorous; and religious. Buys 60 mss/year. Query. Length: 200-300 words. Pays 2-3¢/word.

Poetry: Free verse, traditional. Buys 60/year. Query. Length: 8-12 lines. Pays $.50-1/line.

MILL STREET JOURNAL, Mill Street Publishing Co., Box 10562, Eugene OR 97401. Editor-in-Chief: Gary Bond. Emphasizes entertainment for children 7-12. Monthly tabloid; 16 pages. Estab: 1975. Circ: 10,000. Pays on acceptance. Buys all rights. Submit seasonal/holiday material 6 months in advance. Photocopied submissions OK. Writer's guidelines $1.

Nonfiction: Alan Boye, Nonfiction Editor. How-to (projects children can do at home or school); humor; interview (of popular TV and movie stars); new product; photo feature (animals). Buys 12 mss/issue. Send complete ms. Length: 100-500 words. Pays $25-200.

Photos: Dan Berg, Photo Editor. Photos purchased with or without accompanying ms. Captions required. Pays $10-50 for 5x7 b&w glossies. Total purchase price for ms includes payment for photos. Model release required.

Fiction: Carol Baker, Fiction Editor. Adventure; fantasy; humor; mystery; science fiction and suspense. Buys 25 mss/issue. Submit complete ms. Length: 100-500 words. Pays $25-200.

Poetry: Carol Otis, Poetry Editor. Light verse. Buys 25 poems/issue. Limit submissions to batches of 3. Length: 4-20 lines. Pays $5-100.

Fillers: Marilyn Swanson, Fillers Editor. Jokes, gags, anecdotes and short humor. Buys 25 fillers/issue. Length: 10-50 words. Pays $5-25.

How To Break In: "Children want high interest, familiar material. Something that will make them laugh, cry and will arouse their interest."

MY DEVOTIONS, Concordia Publishing House, 3558 S. Jefferson Ave., St. Louis MO 63118. For young Christians, 8 through 13 years of age. Buys little freelance material. Write for guidelines, enclosing 13¢ postage. Material is rejected here because of poor writing, lack of logic, and lack of Lutheran theology. Pays $7.50 per printed devotion.

NURSERY DAYS, The United Methodist Publishing House, 201 8th Ave., S., Nashville TN 37202. Editor-in-Chief: Dr. Ewart Watts. Children's Editor: Leo Kisrow. A story paper for children 2-4 years of age, distributed through Sunday school classes of the United Methodist Church. Weekly magazine; 4 pages. Circ: 125,000. Pays on acceptance. Buys all rights. Submit seasonal/holiday material 12 months in advance. SASE. Reports in 1-2 months. Free sample copy and writer's guidelines.

Nonfiction: Doris Willis, Nursery Editor. Informational (Biblical, nature, seasonal); inspirational (Biblical, church, family, prayers, etc.); and personal experience (familiar to children 2-4 years old). Buys 1 ms/issue. Length: 250 words maximum. Pays 2¢/word.

Photos: Dave Dawson, Photo Editor. Purchased without accompanying ms. Send prints or transparencies. Pays $10-25 for 8x10 b&w glossies; $25-125 for 35mm color transparencies. Model release required.

Fiction: Religious (Jesus, God, prayer, church, Bible). Buys 1 ms/issue. Submit complete ms. Length: 250 words. Pays 2¢/word.

Poetry: Doris Willis, Nursery Editor. Free verse and light verse. Buys 3-4/issue. Length: 4-12 lines. Pays 50¢/line.

ON THE LINE, Menonite Publishing House, 616 Walnut Ave., Scottdale PA 15683. (412)887-8500. Editor: Helen Alderfer. For 10-14-year-olds. Weekly magazine; 8 pages. Estab: 1970. Circ: 17,650. Pays on acceptance. Buys one-time rights. Submit seasonal/holiday material 6 months in advance. Simultaneous, photocopied and previously published submissions OK. SASE. Reports in 2 weeks.

Nonfiction: How-to (things to make with easy-to-get materials); informational (500-word articles on wonders of nature, people who have made outstanding contributions); photo features and travel (short pieces on places of churchwide interest). Buys 25-40 mss/issue. Length: 500-1,200 words. Pays $10-24.

Photos: Photos purchased with or without accompanying ms. Pays $5-25 for 8x10 b&w photos. Total purchase price for a ms includes payment for photos.

Columns/Departments: Fiction; adventure; humorous and religious. Buys 25 mss/year. Send complete ms. Length: 800-1,200 words. Pays $15-24.

Poetry: Light verse and religious. Length: 3-12 lines. Pays $5-15.

Fillers: Puzzles and all types of religious fillers. Buys 100 fillers/year. Length: 50-190 words. Pays $6-12.

OUR LITTLE FRIEND, PRIMARY TREASURE, Pacific Press Publishing Association, 1350 Villa St., Mountain View CA 94042. (415)961-2323, Ext. 335. Editor: Louis Schutter. Published weekly for youngsters of the Seventh-Day Adventist church. *Our Little Friend* is for children ages 2 to 6; *Primary Treasure*, 7 to 9. Rights purchased vary with author and material. Buys first serial rights (international); second serial (reprint) rights (international). "The payment we make is for one magazine right. In most cases, it is for the first one. But we make payment for second, third rights also." Query on serial-length stories. Will accept simultaneous submissions. "We do not purchase material during June, July, and August." Enclose S.A.S.E. for return of submissions or reply to queries.

Nonfiction and Fiction: All stories must be based on fact, written in story form. True to life, character-building stories; written from viewpoint of child and giving emphasis to lessons of life needed for Christian living. True to life is emphasized here more than plot. Nature or science articles, but no fantasy; science must be very simple. All material should be educational or informative and stress moral attitude and religious principle. Honesty, truthfulness, courtesy, health and temperance, along with stories of heroism, adventure, nature and safety are included in the overall planning of the editorial program. *Our Little Friend* uses stories from 700 to 1,000 words. *Primary Treasure*, 600 to 1,500 words. Fictionalized Bible stories are not used. Pays 1¢ per word.

Photos, Poetry, and Fillers: 8x10 glossies for cover. "Photo payment: sliding scale according to quality." Juvenile poetry; up to 12 lines. Puzzles.

PRIMARY TREASURE, Pacific Press Publishing Association, 1350 Villa St., Mountain View CA 94042. See *Our Little Friend.*

RAINBOW, American Baptist Board of Educational Ministries, Valley Forge PA 19481. Editor-in-Chief: Gracie McCay. Emphasizes religion for children in Baptist churches; ages 8-11. Monthly magazine; 32 pages. Estab: 1974. Circ: 10,000. Pays on acceptance. Buys first North American serial rights. Submit seasonal/holiday material 8 months in advance. Simultaneous and previously published submissions OK. SASE. Reports in 6 months. Free sample copy and writer's guidelines.

Nonfiction: Historical; how-to (projects of interest to children, including recipes); humor; informational; inspirational; and photo feature. Buys 10-12 mss/year. Length: 800-1,000 words. Pays 3¢/word.

Photos: Purchased without accompanying ms. Send contact sheet or prints. Pays $7.50-15 for 8x10 b&w glossies. Model release required.

Fiction: Adventure; historical; humorous; religious; science fiction; and suspense. Buys 200 mss/year. Submit complete ms. Length: 800-1,500 words. Pays 3¢/word.

Poetry: Free verse; haiku; light verse and traditional. Buys 25-30/year. Limit submissions to batches of 5. Pays 25¢/line.

Fillers: Puzzles appropriate for children—wide variety. Buys 30/year. Pays $8/puzzle.

RANGER RICK'S NATURE MAGAZINE, National Wildlife Federation, 1412 Sixteenth St., N.W., Washington DC 20036. (202)797-6800. Editorial Director: Trudy D. Farrand. For "children from ages 4 to 12, with the greatest concentration in the 7-10 age bracket." Monthly. Buys all rights. Pays 3 months prior to publication. "Anything written with a specific month in mind should be in our hands at least 8 months before that issue date." Query first. Enclose S.A.S.E.

Nonfiction and Photos: "Articles may be written on any phase of nature, conservation, environmental problems, or natural science. Do not try to humanize wildlife in features. We limit the attributing of human qualities to animals in our regular feature, 'Ranger Rick and His Friends.' The publisher, National Wildlife Federation, discourages wildlife pets because of the possible hazards involved to small children. Therefore, pets of this kind should not be mentioned in your copy." Length: 900 words maximum. Pays from $10 to $250 depending on length. "If photographs are included with your copy, they are paid for separately, depending on how they are used. However, it is not necessary that illustrations accompany material."

SPRINT MAGAZINE, Scholastic Magazines, Inc., 50 W. 44th St., New York NY 10036. Editor: Vicky Chapman. Magazine (14 times/school year); 16 pages. Pays on acceptance. Usually buys all rights. SASE. Reports as soon as possible.

Nonfiction and Fiction: Phyllis Keaton, Assistant Editor. Accepts some feature articles on sports, career education, other topics of interest to pre-teens. "Main need is for very short fiction, plays (450-900 words), short stories (200-450 words), unique and creative items teaching reading skills (word games, etc.) Fiction subjects include action, adventure, mystery, science fiction, sports, humor, family, friend, and school situations. Stories often work best when they

(1) are heavy on dialogue; (2) concentrate on developing insight into at least one character, and/or (3) have a 'twist' ending. No overt moralizing. No talking animals." Pays $80 minimum.

STORY FRIENDS, Mennonite Publishing House, 616 Walnut Ave., Scottdale PA 15683. (412)887-8500. Editor: Alice Hershberger. For children, 4 to 9 years of age. Published monthly in weekly parts. Not copyrighted. Payment on acceptance. Will send sample copy to writer on request. Submit seasonal material 6 months in advance. Enclose S.A.S.E.
Nonfiction and Photos: "The over-arching purpose of this publication is to magnify Jesus Christ and His way in terms a child can grasp. Children of this age group are full of questions about God and Jesus, the Bible, prayer. Stories of everyday experiences at home, at church, in school, at play help provide answers. Of special importance are relationships: patterns of forgiveness, respect, honesty, trust, caring. Emphasis is on spiritual values, but not from a purely humanistic viewpoint; rather, recognizing Jesus Christ as a source of power to live out 'goodness'." Length: 150 words. Pays $3.50 to $15. Pays $7.50 to $15 for b&w photos purchased with or without ms. Captions optional. Photo Department Editor: Joyce Millslagle.
Fiction: Suspense, adventure, religious. Should be based on the application of Christian principles on a child's level of understanding. Prefer short stories; exciting but plausible; spiritual values intrinsic to the story; wide variety of settings and racial backgrounds. Avoid preachiness, but have well-defined spiritual values as an integral part of each story. Realistic stories with spiritual value needed for Christmas and Easter. Nothing about Santa Claus or Easter bunnies. Length: 300 to 900 words. Pays 2½-3¢/word.
Poetry and Fillers: Traditional forms of poetry and free verse. Length: 3 to 12 lines. Pays $5. Uses crossword puzzles and quizzes.

TOUCH, P.O. Box 7244, Grand Rapids MI 49510. Editor: Joanne Ilbrink. Assistant Editor: Carol Slager. For girls, usually members of Calvinette clubs, ages 8-15. Monthly magazine; 24 pages. Estab: 1970. Circ: 14,000. Pays on acceptance. Buys simultaneous, second serial and first North American serial rights. Submit seasonal/holiday material 3-5 months in advance. Simultaneous, photocopied or previously published submissions OK. SASE. Reports in 3 weeks. Free sample copy and writer's guidelines.
Nonfiction: How-to (crafts girls can make easily and inexpensively), informational (write for issue themes), humor (needs much more), inspirational (seasonal and holiday), interview, travel, personal experience (avoid the testimony approach), and photo feature (query first). Buys 20 mss a year. Submit complete ms. Length: 100-1,000 words. Pays 2¢/word, depending on the amount of editing.
Photos: Purchased with or without ms. Submit 3x5 clear glossy prints. B&w only. Pays $5-25.
Fiction: Adventure (that girls could experience in their home towns or places they might realistically visit), fantasy (fables welcome), humorous, mystery (believable only), romance (stories that deal with awakening awareness of boys are appreciated), suspense (can be serialized), and religious (nothing preachy). Buys 20 mss/year. Submit complete ms. Length: 300-1,500 words. Pays 2¢/word.
Poetry: Free verse, haiku, light verse, traditional. Buys 10/year. Length: 50 lines maximum. Pays $5 minimum.
Fillers: Jokes, gags, anecdotes, puzzles, short humor and cartoons. Buys 6/issue. Pays $2.50-7.
How To Break In: "Because our magazine is published around a monthly theme, requesting the letter we send out twice a year to our established freelancers would be most helpful."
Rejects: "We do not want easy solutions or quick character changes from bad to good. No pietistic characters. Constant mention of God is not necessary, if the moral tone of the story is positive. We do not want stories that always have a good ending."

TRAILS, Pioneer Girls, Inc., Box 788, Wheaton IL 60187. Editor-in-Chief: Sara Robertson. Managing Editor: Frances Price. Emphasizes Christian education for girls, 7-12, most of whom are enrolled in the Pioneer Girls club program. It is kept general in content so it will appeal to a wider audience. Bimonthly magazine; 32 pages. Estab: 1962. Circ: 23,000. Pays on acceptance. Buys first, second, or simultaneous rights. Submit seasonal/holiday material 6 months in advance. Simultaneous and previously published submissions OK. SASE. Reports in 4 weeks. Sample copy $1; free writer's guidelines.
Nonfiction: How-to (crafts and puzzles); humor; informational; inspirational; and interview. Query or submit complete ms. Length: 800-1,500 words. Pays $20-30.
Fiction: Adventure; fantasy; historical; humorous; mainstream; mystery; and religious. Buys 6 mss/issue. Query or submit complete ms. Length: 800-1,500 words. Pays $20-30.
Fillers: Jokes, gags, anecdotes, and short humor. Buys 4/issue. Pays $5-15.

VIDEO-PRESSE, 3965 est, boul. Henri-Bourassa, Montreal H1H 1L1, Que., Canada. Editor: Pierre Guimar. For "French Canadian boys and girls of 8 to 15." Monthly. Circulation: 45,000. Buys all rights. Buys 20 to 30 mss a year. Pays on publication. Will send a sample copy to a writer on request. Reports in 2 weeks. Enclose S.A.S.E.
Nonfiction: "Material with a French Canadian background. The articles have to be written in French, and must appeal to children aged 8 to 15." Buys how-to's, personal experience articles, interviews, profiles, humor, historical articles, photo features, travel pieces. Length: 1,500 to 3,000 words. Pays 3¢ a word.
Photos: B&w glossies, color transparencies; with captions only. Pays $7.50.
Fillers: Puzzles, jokes, short humor.

THE VINE, 201 Eighth Ave., S., Nashville TN 37203. (615)749-6369. Editor: Betty M. Buerki. Publication of The United Methodist Church. For children in grades 3 and 4. Monthly in weekly parts. Buys all rights. Pays on acceptance. Will send a sample copy to a writer on request. Deadlines are 18 months prior to publication date. Reports in 1 month. Enclose S.A.S.E. for return of submissions.
Nonfiction and Photos: Desires articles about science, nature, animals, customs in other countries, and other subjects of interest to readers. Length: approximately 500 words. Pays 3¢ a word. Photos usually purchased with manuscripts only. Uses photo features. Prefers 8x10 glossies. Also uses transparencies.
Fiction: Historical stories should be true to their setting. Stories which make a point about values should not sound moralistic. Also accepts stories written just for fun. Length: 500 to 800 words. Writers must know children. Fictionalized Bible stories must be based upon careful research. Pays 3¢ a word.
Poetry: Accepts light verse or religious verse. Pays 50¢ to $1 per line.
Fillers: Puzzles, quizzes, and matching games. Pays 3¢ minimum per word. Pays more for clever arrangements. Puzzles, such as crossword, mazes, etc.; pays $4.50 to $12.50.

WEE WISDOM, Unity Village MO 64065. Editor: Jim Leftwich. Character-building monthly magazine for boys and girls. Designed to help child develop positive self-image and strength to function successfully in tomorrow's world. Free sample copy, editorial policy on request. Buys first North American serial rights only. Pays on acceptance. Enclose S.A.S.E. for return of submissions.
Nonfiction: Entertaining science articles or projects, activities to foster creativity. Pays 3¢ per word minimum.
Fiction: Short and lively stories, education for living without moralizing. "Although entertaining enough to hold the interest of the older child, they should be readable by the third grader. Character-building ideals should be emphasized without preaching. Language should be universal, avoiding the Sunday school image." Length: 500 to 800 words. Pays 3¢ per word minimum.
Poetry: Very limited. Pays 50¢ per line. Prefers short, seasonal or humorous poems. Also buys rhymed prose for "read alouds" and pays $15 up.
Fillers: Pays $3 up for puzzles and games.

WEEKLY BIBLE READER, Standard Publishing, 8121 Hamilton Ave., Cincinnati OH 45231. Editor: Barbara Curie. For children 6 and 7 years of age. Quarterly in weekly parts; 4 pages. Established in 1965. Circulation: 95,459. Buys first serial rights. Payment on acceptance. Will send free sample copy to writer on request. Write for copy of guidelines for writers. Will not consider photocopied or simultaneous submissions. Submit seasonal material 18 months in advance. Reports on material accepted for publication in about 1 month. Returns rejected material in about 2 weeks. Query first or submit complete ms. Enclose S.A.S.E.
Nonfiction, Photos, and Poetry, and Fillers: Religious-oriented material. Stories with morals, short fiction (150 to 250 words in length) fun poems, puzzles and other interesting items. Emphasis is on material that can be read by children themselves. "No fanciful material, superstitions or luck, things that talk, fairies, Easter rabbits, or Santa Claus. We'd like to see material on things children can do to help others; to be pleasing to God, etc." Do not send Bible stories or Buzzy Bee items, as these are staff-written from preplanned outlines. Length for fiction and nonfiction: 300 words maximum. Pays $1 to $10. B&w photos purchased with or without mss. Pays $10. Light verse. Length: 12 lines maximum. Very simple puzzles for this age group. Pays 50¢ to $10.

WONDER TIME, 6401 The Paseo, Kansas City MO 64131. (816)333-7000. Editor: Elizabeth B. Jones. Published weekly by Church of the Nazarene for children ages 6 to 8. Will send free sample copy to a writer on request. Buys first rights. Pays on acceptance. Enclose S.A.S.E. for return of submissions.

Fiction and Poetry: Buys stories portraying Christian attitude, without being preachy. Uses stories for special days, stories teaching honesty, truthfulness, helpfulness or other important spiritual truths, and avoiding symbolism. God should be spoken of as our Father who loves and cares for us: Jesus, as our Lord and Savior. Length: 500 to 750 words. Pays 2¢ a word on acceptance. Uses verse which has seasonal or Christian emphasis. Length: 8 to 12 lines. Pays 25¢/line minimum.

WOW, American Baptist Board of Educational Ministries, Valley Forge PA 19481. Editor-in-Chief: Gracie McCay. Emphasizes religion for children in Baptist churches, ages 6-7. Weekly magazine; 4 pages. Estab: 1974. Circ: 10,000. Pays on acceptance. Buys simultaneous, first North American and one-time rights. Submit seasonal/holiday material 8 months in advance. Simultaneous and previously published submissions OK. SASE. Reports in 6 months. Free sample copy and writer's guidelines.

Photos: Purchased without accompanying ms. Send contact sheet or prints. Pays $7.50-15 for 8x10 b&w glossies. Model release required.

Fiction: Adventure; fantasy; historical; humorous; religious; science fiction and suspense. Buys 100 mss/year. Length: 200-400 words. Pays 3¢/word.

Poetry: Free verse; haiku; light verse; and traditional. Buys 25-30/year. Limit submissions to batches of 5. Pays 25¢/line.

Fillers: Jokes, gags, anecdotes and puzzles. Buys 25-30/year. Pays $5-8.

THE YOUNG CRUSADER, 1730 Chicago Ave., Evanston IL 60201. (312)864-1396. Managing Editor: Michael Vitucci. For children 6 to 12 who are junior members of National WCTU. Monthly. Not copyrighted. Pays on publication. Will send a sample copy to a writer on request. Submit seasonal material 6 months in advance. Enclose S.A.S.E.

Nonfiction and Fiction: Uses articles on total abstinence, character building, love of animals, Christian principles, world friendship. Also science stories. Length: 650 to 800 words. Pays ½¢ per word.

YOUNG JUDAEAN, 817 Broadway, New York NY 10003. (212)260-4700. Editor: Barbara Gingold. For Jewish children aged 8 to 13, and members of Young Judaea. Publication of Hadassah Zionist Youth Commission. All material must be on some Jewish theme. Special issues for Jewish/Israeli holidays, or particular Jewish themes which vary from year to year; for example, Hassidim, Holocaust, etc. Established in 1916. Monthly (November through June). Circulation: 8,000. Rights purchased vary with author and material. Buys all rights, but will reassign rights to author after publication; buys first North American serial rights; buys first serial rights. Buys 10 to 20 mss a year. Payment in contributor's copies or small token payment. Sample copy and annual list of themes for 25¢. Prefers complete ms only. Will consider photocopied and simultaneous submissions. Submit seasonal material 4 months in advance. Reports in 3 months. SASE.

Nonfiction and Photos: "Articles about Jewish-American life, Jewish historical and international interest. Israel and Zionist-oriented material. Try to awaken kids' Jewish consciousness by creative approach to Jewish history and religion, ethics and culture, politics and current events. Style can be didactic, but not patronizing." Informational (300 to 1,000 words), how-to (300 to 500 words), personal experience, interview, humor, historical, think articles, photo, travel, and reviews (books, theater, and movies). Length: 500 to 1,200 words. Pays $5-25. "Token payments only, due to miniscule budget."

Photos: Photos purchased with accompanying mss. Captions required. 5x7 maximum. B&w prefered. Payment included with fee for article. Illustrations also accepted.

Fiction: Experimental, mainstream, mystery, suspense, adventure, science fiction, fantasy, humorous, religious, and historical fiction. Length: 500 to 1,000 words. Pays $5 to $25. Must be of specific Jewish interest.

Poetry and Fillers: Traditional forms, blank verse, free verse, avant-garde forms, and light verse. Poetry themes must relate to subject matter of magazine. Length: 25-100 lines. Pays $5-15. Newsbreaks, jokes, and short humor purchased for $5.

How To Break In: "Think of an aspect of Jewish history/religion/culture which can be handled in a fresh, imaginative way, fictionally or factually. Don't preach; inform and entertain."

YOUNG MUSICIANS, 127 Ninth Ave., N., Nashville TN 37234. Editor: Jimmy R. Key. For boys and girls age 9 to 11, and their leaders in children's choirs in Southern Baptist churches (and some other churches). Monthly magazine; 52 (7x10½) pages. Established in 1963. Buys all rights. Buys 5 or 6 mss a year. Payment on acceptance. Will send free sample copy to writer on request. Will not consider photocopied or simultaneous submissions. Query first. Enclose S.A.S.E.

Nonfiction: "All material is slanted for use with and by children in church choirs. Music study materials related to study units in *The Music Leader*. Ours is a curriculum magazine written almost entirely on assignment." Informational, how-to, historical. Length: 300 to 900 words. Pays approximately 2½¢ per word.

Fiction: Child-centered stories related to church music and music in the home. Length: 600 to 900 words. Pays approximately 2½¢ per word.

Literary and "Little" Publications

Many of the publications in this category do not pay except in contributor's copies. Nonpaying markets are included because they offer the writer a vehicle for expression that often can't be found in the commercial press. Many talented American writers found first publication in magazines like these. Writers are reminded that many "littles" remain at one address for a limited time; others are notoriously unbusinesslike in their reporting on, or returning of submissions. University-affiliated reviews are conscientious about manuscripts but some of these are also slow in replying to queries or returning submissions.

Magazines that specialize in publishing poetry or poetry criticism are found in the Poetry category. Many "little" publications that offer contributors a forum for expression of minority opinions are classified in the listings for Alternative Publications.

AMERICAN MERCURY, P.O. Box 1306, Torrance CA 90505. Managing Editor: La Vonne Furr. Quarterly. Write for copy of guidelines for writers. "All mss must be typed, double-spaced, clean, ready for printer, left margin at least 1½ inches. Break up articles with periodic italicized paragraphs and/or subheads. Authors should submit biographical material to aid editor in preparing a suitable introduction." Enclose S.A.S.E. for return of submissions.

Nonfiction: *Mercury's* editorial policy is nonpartisan but generally conservative. "It will stress the positive and hopeful aspects of life and Western tradition through reliable and well-written exposes. Articles on fads, dances, narcotics, crime, entertainers are generally unwanted." Wants Americana, nature briefs, humorous comment on everyday life, politics, science, health; particular emphasis on heroic and patriotic themes; satire. "Precede book reviews with a very brief title, then describe book: Title of book in caps, by (name of author), number of pages, publisher, date of publication." Length: 1,000 words maximum for book reviews; 900 to 2,000 words for articles. Payment ranges from one-year complimentary subscription to $50 for unsolicited articles.

AMERICAN NOTES AND QUERIES, Erasmus Press, 225 Culpepper, Lexington KY 40502. (606)266-1058. Book Review Editor: Lee Ash, 61 Hudson Drive, Bethany CT 06525. Ten times a year. No payment. Enclose S.A.S.E.

Nonfiction: Historical, artistic, literary, bibliographical, linguistic and folklore matters, scholarly book reviews and reviews of foreign reference books; items of unusual antiquarian interest.

AMERICAN QUARTERLY, Van Pelt Library, University of Pennsylvania, 3420 Walnut St., Philadelphia PA 19174. (215)243-6252. Editor: Dr. Bruce Kuklick. For college professors, teachers, museum directors, researchers, students, college and high school libraries. Readers professionally interested in American studies. Acquires all rights. Does not pay. Reports in 2-4 months. SASE and 2 copies of article.

Nonfiction and Photos: Scholarly, interdisciplinary articles on American studies, about 20 pages. August issue contains bibliographic essays, dissertation listings, American Studies programs. Occasionally uses photos.

THE AMERICAN SCHOLAR, 1811 Q St., N.W., Washington DC 20009. (202)265-3808. Editor: Joseph Epstein. For college educated, mid-20's and older, rather intellectual in orientation and interests. Quarterly magazine, 144 pages. Estab: 1932. Circ: 40,000. Buys all rights, but will reassign rights to author after publication. Buys 20 to 30 mss a year. Payment on publication. Will send sample copy to writer for $2. Write for copy of guidelines for writers. Will consider photocopied submissions. Will not consider simultaneous submissions. Reports within 3 weeks. Query first, with samples, if possible. Enclose S.A.S.E.

Nonfiction and Poetry: "The aim of the *Scholar* is to fill the gap between the learned journals and the good magazines for a popular audience. We are interested not so much in the definitive analysis as in the lucid and creative exploration of what is going on in the fields of science, art, religion, politics, and national and foreign affairs. Advances in science particularly interest us." Informational, interview, profile, historical, think articles, and book reviews. Length: 3,500 to 4,000 words. Pays $250 per article and $50 for reviews. Pays $35 to $75 for poetry on any theme. Approximately 5 poems published per issue. "We would like to see poetry that develops an image or a thought or event, without the use of a single cliche or contrived archaism. The most hackneyed subject matter is self-conscious love; the most tired verse is iambic pentameter with rhyming endings. The usual length of our poems is 10-12 lines. From 1-4 poems may be submitted at one time; *no more* for a careful reading. We urge prospective contributors to familiarize themselves with the type of poetry we have published by looking at the magazine."

ANTHELION, Box 614, Costa Madera CA 94925. Editor: Wm. Whitney. For "a university level readership." Bimonthly. Purchases all rights with return of reprint rights upon request. Pays on publication. Reports in 4 to 6 weeks. Authors should include a brief resume and cover letter with submissions. Enclose S.A.S.E.
Nonfiction and Fiction: "Devoted in alternate months to the fields of literature, social and cultural comment, and philosophy. January and July issues are devoted to literary articles and stories. Interviews, reviews and like articles are used to augment our basic copy. We stress that all copy must be verifiable and logical. We seek the new writer with new insights into our modern world. Our pay for articles varies from contributor's copies up to 5¢ a word." Length: 2,500 words maximum.

ANTIOCH REVIEW, P.O. Box 148, Yellow Springs OH 45387. Editor: Paul Bixler. For general, literary and academic audience. Quarterly. Buys all rights. Pays on publication. Reports in 4 to 6 weeks. Enclose S.A.S.E.
Nonfiction: Contemporaneous articles in the humanities and social sciences, politics, economics, literature and all areas of broad intellectual concern. Somewhat scholarly, but never pedantic in style, eschewing all professional jargon. Lively, distinctive prose insisted upon. Length: 2,000 to 8,000 words. Pays $8 per published page.
Fiction: No limitations on style or content. Pays $8 per published page.
Poetry: No light or inspirational verse. Contributors should be familiar with the magazine before submitting. Rarely uses traditional, or rhymed verse.

APALACHEE QUARTERLY, P.O. Box 20106, Tallahassee FL 32304. Editor: P.V. LeForge. For an artistic/critical audience; 20 to 60 years of age. Magazine; 44 to 60 (7½x10) pages. Established in 1972. Quarterly. Circulation: 400. Acquires all rights. Uses about 80 mss a year. Payment in contributor's copies. Will send sample copy to writer for $1. No simultaneous submissions. Reports in 1 to 10 weeks. Submit complete ms. Enclose S.A.S.E.
Nonfiction and Photos: Emphasis is on creative writing, rather than criticism. Uses interviews and reviews of fiction and poetry. Length: 300 to 3,000 words. B&w photos purchased without ms. Captions optional.
Fiction and Poetry: Short stories, experimental or mainstream. Length: 300 to 6,000 words. Traditional forms of poetry, blank verse, free verse, avant-garde forms. Length: 3 to 100 lines.

ARION, University Professors, Boston University, Rm. 608-610, 745 Commonwealth Ave., Boston MA 02215. (617)353-4025. Editors-in-Chief: William Arrowsmith and D. S. Carne-Ross. "Journal of humanities and classics for persons interested in literature of the classical periods of Greece and Rome." Established in 1962. Quarterly journal, 128 pages, (8½x5). Circulation: 1,000. No payment. Acquires all rights, but will reassign rights to author after publication. Sample copy for $3. Query first or submit complete ms. Will consider photocopied submissions. Reports in 3 months. SASE.
Nonfiction: Uses articles on literature, Greece and Rome. The articles printed are in the form of literary essays. "We deal with the classics as literature, rather than philology." Length: 10 to 40 pages.

ARIZONA QUARTERLY, University of Arizona, Tucson AZ 85721. Editor: Albert F. Gegenheimer. For a university-type audience. Quarterly. "We acquire all rights, but freely give authors permission to reprint. We require editors of anthologies, etc., to obtain permission of authors as well as of ourselves." Payment is in copies and a one-year subscription to the magazine. There are annual awards for the best poem of the year, the best article of the year, the best story of the year and the best book review of the year. Reports in 3 to 4 weeks except during summer. Enclose S.A.S.E.

Nonfiction: "Always interested in articles dealing with the Southwest, but open to articles on any topic of general interest."

Fiction: "Quality" fiction. Southwestern interest preferred, but not essential. Length: normally not over 3,000 words.

Poetry: Uses 4 or 5 poems per issue on any serious subject. Prefers short poems; up to 30 lines can be used most readily. The author must have something to say and be equipped to say it.

THE ARK RIVER REVIEW, c/o A. Sobin, English Department, Wichita State University, Wichita KS 67208. Editors-in-Chief: Jonathan Katz, A.G. Sobin. For "the well-educated, college age and above; poets, writers, and the readers of contemporary poetry and fiction." Published 3-4 times a year. Magazine; 52 pages. Estab: 1971. Circ: 1,000. Pays on publication. Buys all rights, but will reassign to author following publication. Photocopied submissions OK. Reports in 1-3 weeks. Sample copy $1.

Fiction: "Conventional fiction stands little chance. We are interested only in highly innovative and sophisticated material. Type and subject matter is far less important to us than the way in which the story is written. We are looking for freshness in approach, style and language. We suggest strongly that you read back issues before submitting." Buys 3 mss/issue. Send complete ms. No length limit (no novels). Pays $3/page (minimum $20/story) and contributor's copies.

Poetry: "Poetry should be substantial, intelligent and serious (this doesn't mean it can't be funny). Any form is OK, though we almost never print rhyming poems." Buys 30/issue. Limit submissions to batches of 5. No length limits. Pays 20¢/line, $5/poem minimum and copy.

How To Break In: "Your work should demonstrate to us that you know what has gone on in literature in the last 50 years, and that you're doing something better."

ART AND LITERARY DIGEST, Summer address: Madoc-Tweed Art Centre, Tweed, Ontario, Canada. Winter address: 1109 N. Betty Lane, Clearwater FL 33515. Editor: Roy Cadwell. "Our readers are the public and former students of the Art and Writing Centre. As an educational publication we welcome new writers who have something to say and want to see their name in print and get paid for it." Quarterly. Estab: 1969. Circ: 1,000. Not copyrighted. Payment on publication. Will send sample copy for $1. Photocopied mss are accepted, but not returned. Unless notified, you may submit elsewhere after 30 days. Original mss must be accompanied by return envelope and unattached postage. Enclose S.A.S.E.

Nonfiction and Fiction: How-to articles, inspirational, humorous, travel and personality improvement. "Good writing is essential with integrity and knowledge. Ask yourself, 'What have I to say?' Slant toward students and alumni. Our readers want to be informed and, hopefully, learn how to live better." Personal experience articles and "I was there" type of travel articles are appreciated. Length: 500 words. Pays $5. "We need digests of articles on art, music, poetry and literary subjects." Pays 1¢ per word.

Fillers: Ideas and short humor. Length: 500 words or less. Pays 1¢ per word.

Poetry: All types. Free verse, light verse, blank verse, traditional and avant-garde. Length: usually 12 lines, but no limit. Payment in contributor's copies.

ASPECT, 66 Rogers Ave., Somerville MA 02144. Editors: Edward Hogan, Miriam Sagan, Kathryn Van Spanckeren. Primarily for people interested in new and experimental, as well as traditional and widely accepted writing. Many readers are themselves involved in the field of writing. Quarterly magazine; 80-100 pages. Estab: 1969. Circ: 650. Pays in copies. Acquires first North American serial and one-time anthology rights. Photocopied submissions OK. SASE. Reports in 1-3 months. Sample copy $1.50.

Nonfiction: Informational; historical (social, political or literary subjects); humor; interview (with emerging, exciting poets and writers or people involved in alternative literary publishing); personal experience; personal opinion (social,, political or literary subjects); photo feature (social, political, literary, historical focus). Buys 6-8 mss/year. Query. Length: 5,000 words maximum. Pays in copies.

Columns/Departments: News & Reviews (short news pieces about the field of alternative literary publishing; magazine and small press manuscript needs; Reviews of little magazines and small press books). Uses 15/issue. Submit complete ms. Length: 400 words for news; 300-1,000 for reviews.

Fiction: Adventure; experimental; historical; humorous; mainstream; and science fiction.

Poetry: Avant-garde; free verse; traditional. Uses 25/issue. Limit submissions to batches of 3-6.

How To Break In: "Subject area is broad, but tends to focus most on literature, and secondly, politics, broadly defined. We are a mature (in growth stage) independent literary magazine that still publishes, almost entirely, work by unknowns. Know what you're doing, and try to do it very well."

ASPEN ANTHOLOGY, The Aspen Leaves Literary Foundation, Box 3185, Aspen CO 81611. (303)925-8750. Editor-in-Chief: Kurt N. Brown. For poets, novelists, teachers, and literate readers. Biannual magazine; 130 pages. Estab: 1973. Circ: 1,000. Pays in contributor's copies. Acquires all rights, but may reassign following publication. Phone queries OK. SASE. Reports in 4 weeks. Sample copy $2.75.
Fiction: Rosemary Thompson, Hancel McCord, Fiction Editors. Experimental. Uses 2 mss/issue. Submit complete ms. No length requirement. Pays in 2 copies.
Poetry: Bruce Berger, Donna Disch, Poetry Editors. Any style. Uses 50/issue. No length limit. Pays in two copies.

ATARAXIA, 291 Pine St., Madison GA 30650. Editors: Phil and Linda Williams. Magazine. Established in 1972. Three times a year. Circulation: about 400. Acquires first serial rights. Uses about 100 mss a year. Pays in contributor's copies. Will send sample copy to writer for $2. No photocopied or simultaneous submissions. Reports in 3 to 6 weeks. Submit complete ms. Enclose S.A.S.E.
Fiction and Poetry: Only serious work, of high quality. Experimental and mainstream fiction. Length: 500 to 1,000 words. Blank verse, free verse and avant-garde forms.

BACHY, Papa Bach Bookstore, 11317 Santa Monica Blvd., Los Angeles CA 90025. Established in 1972. Semiannual. Circulation: 800. Average number of pages per issue: 96. Buys first North American serial rights only. Will send sample copy to writer for $2.50. Submit complete ms. Will consider photocopied submissions. Reports within 8 weeks. Enclose S.A.S.E.
Fiction, Poetry: Serious poetry and fiction of highest quality, avant-garde or traditional forms of poetry; any length: *"Bachy* is dedicated to the discovery and continued publication of serious new writers and poets."

BALL STATE UNIVERSITY FORUM, Ball State University, Muncie IN 47306. (317)285-7255. Editors: Merrill Rippy and Frances Mayhew Rippy. For "educated readers interested in nontechnical studies of humanities, fine arts, sciences, social sciences, history, and education." Quarterly. Established in 1959. Acquires all rights, "but author may always reprint at his own request without charge, so long as *Forum* is notified and international copyright held by *Forum* is acknowledged." Pays in 5 contributor's copies. Will send a sample copy to a writer on request. Contributors should accompany their entries with a 2-sentence description of their academic background or position, their other publications, and their special competence to write on their subject. Contributors submitting multiple copies cut 1 month from reading time: poems, 7 copies; short stories, 9 copies; plays, 9 copies; articles, 2 copies. Special issues planned on American literature, British literature, education. Reports in 2 weeks to 4 months. Enclose S.A.S.E. for return of submissions.
Nonfiction, Fiction, Drâma, and Poetry: Articles that are reasonably original, polished, and of general interest. Length: 50 to 3,000 words. Short stories, 1-act plays. Length: 50 to 2,000 words. Uses 5 to 30 poems per issue. Length: 5 to 200 lines.

BARBEQUE PLANET, 2513-B Ashwood Ave., Nashville TN 37212. Editor: Bob Millard. For an educated, literate, general readership (ages 18 to 50), including many people who are not ordinarily attracted to literary magazines. Magazine; 20 to 36 pages. Established in 1975. Quarterly. Circulation: 500. Acquires all rights, but will reassign rights to author after publication. Buys about 8 short stories and 100 poems a year. Pays in contributor's copies, unless otherwise arranged. Will send sample copy to writer for $1. No photocopied or simultaneous submissions. Reports in 2 to 6 weeks. Submit complete ms. Enclose S.A.S.E.
Fiction and Poetry: "We would like to see imaginative, straightforward and to-the-point material. We appreciate irreverence, irony and humor, but we also want serious material. All material should share images, episodes, emotions, and/or laughter with the reader." Experimental, mainstream, suspense, fantasy and humorous fiction. Length: 1,000 to 3,000 words. Traditional forms of poetry, blank and free verse. Length 5 to 55 lines.

BLACK AMERICAN LITERATURE FORUM, (formerly *Negro American Literature Forum*), Indiana State University, Parsons Hall 237, Terre Haute IN 47809. (812)232-6311, ext. 2664. Editor-in-Chief: Joe Weixlmann. Emphasizes black American literature. Quarterly magazine; 36 pages. Estab: 1967. Circ: 750. Pays in copies. Acquires simultaneous rights. Phone queries OK. Submit seasonal/holiday material at least 3 months in advance. Simultaneous and

photocopied submissions OK. SASE. Reports in 3 months. Free sample copy and writer's guidelines.
Nonfiction: "We publish scholarly criticism and bibliographies of black American writers, also pedagogical articles and curricular evaluations. We also use poetry by black writers and original graphic work by black artists."
Photos: Sketches and photos used without accompanying ms. Pays $15/graphic work.

BLACK SCHOLAR, P.O. Box 908, Sausalito CA 94965. Editor: Robert Allen. Mainly for black professionals, educators, and students. Monthly journal of black studies and research, 64 pages, (10x7). Established in 1969. Circulation: 20,000. Acquires all rights. Uses about 60 mss per year. Payment in contributor's copies. Will send free sample copy to writer on request. Write for copy of guidelines for writers. Will consider photocopied submissions. Will consider simultaneous submissions, "but must be so informed." Reports within 2 months. Query first about upcoming topics. Enclose S.A.S.E.
Nonfiction: "We seek essays discussing issues affecting the black community (education, health, economics, psychology, culture, literature, etc.). Essays should be reasoned and well-documented. Each issue is organized around a specific topic: Black education, health, prisons, family, etc., with a variety of viewpoints." Informational, interview, profile, historical, think articles, and book and film reviews. Length: 1,500 to 7,000 words.

THE BLACK WARRIOR REVIEW, The University of Alabama, Box 2936, University AL 35486. (205)348-7839. Editor-in-Chief: Sarah DeMellier. Emphasizes fiction and poetry. Semiannual magazine; 80 pages. Estab: 1974. Circ: 1,000. Pays in copies. Acquires all rights, but may reassign following publication. Phone queries OK. Submit seasonal material for fall/August 1; for spring/January 1. SASE. Reports in 2 months. Sample copy $2.00.
Nonfiction: Interview and criticism of contemporary literature. Buys 2 mss/year. Query.
Fiction: Ric Dice, Fiction Editor. Experimental and mainstream. "Acceptance depends on quality, not subject matter, genre or treatment." Buys 1-3 mss/issue. Submit complete ms.
Poetry: Richard Weaver, Poetry Editor. Avant-garde, free verse and traditional. Buys 20/issue.

BLACKBERRY, P.O. Box 4757, Albuquerque NM 81706. Editor: Jeanne Shannon. For readers interested in literature, especially poetry. Established in 1975. Quarterly. Circulation: 100. Acquires first North American serial rights. Uses about 90 mss a year. No payment, but contributors may buy copies of issues containing their work at reduced rate. Sample copy $1.25. Photocopied and simultaneous submissions OK. Reports in 2 weeks. Enclose S.A.S.E.
Nonfiction and Poetry: "We use a few reviews, primarily of poetry books and magazines. Howto articles; i.e., lessons in poetry and fiction writing. Personal experiences of writers in learning their craft. Interviews with writers and poets." Length: 800 words maximum. Traditional and avant-garde forms of poetry; blank verse, free verse and haiku. Length: 30 lines maximum.

BOOK ARTS, The Center For Book Arts, 15 Bleeker St., New York NY 10012. (212)260-6860. Editor-in-Chief: Patricia Nedds. Managing Editor: Joanne Deveraux-Caputi. Emphasizes bookbinding and exploring the arts of the book. Quarterly magazine; 60 pages. Estab: 1974. Circ: 5,000. Pays in copies. Acquires all rights, but may reassign following publication. Submit seasonal/holiday material 3 months in advance. Simultaneous, photocopied, and previously published submissions OK. Reports in 2 months. Sample copy $3.
Nonfiction: Expose (on banning books in schools, other censorship, etc.); historical (bookburnings, looking at the history of watermarks and any other book experience); interview (with book artists) and technical (e.g. "William Blake's Method of Printing"). Query. Pays in copies.

BOSTON UNIVERSITY JOURNAL, Room 333, West Tower Three, 775 Commonwealth Ave., Boston MA 02215. (617)353-2699. Editor: Paul Kurt Ackermann. For libraries, universities, college educated people. Magazine; 72 pages. Established in 1966. Three times a year. Circulation: 3,000. Buys all rights, but may reassign rights to author after publication. Buys 30 mss a year. "Read the magazine and query first before submitting mss." Reports in 1 month. Enclose S.A.S.E.
Nonfiction, Photos, Fiction, and Poetry: "Literary criticism, poetry (all forms), scholarly, well-written and lively articles on a variety of subjects (must be written clearly, without jargon), a few short stories." No limitations on length. "We also take reviews and b&w photos." Pays $10 per printed page; $25 minimum.

BOX 749, Box 749, Old Chelsea Station, New York NY 10011. (212)989-0519. Editor: David Ferguson. For "people of diverse background, education, income and age—an audience not necessarily above or underground. Such an audience is consistent with our belief that literature (plus art and music) is accessible to and even desired by a larger and more varied portion of society than has generally been acknowledged." Biannual magazine; 68-100 pages. Estab: 1972. Circ: 2,500. Acquires all rights, but will reassign rights to author after publication. Uses about 100 mss a year. Payment in contributor's copies. Will send sample copy to writer for $2. Will consider photocopied submissions. Will not consider simultaneous submissions. Reports in 1 to 4 months. Submit complete ms. Enclose S.A.S.E.

Fiction, Drama, Music and Poetry: "We publish poetry and fiction of every length and any theme; satire, belles-lettres, plays, music and any artwork reproducible by photo-offset. We will consider (and have serialized) long fiction. We will consider full-length plays. We have no particular stylistic or ideological bias."

BULLETIN OF BIBLIOGRAPHY AND MAGAZINE NOTES, F. W. Faxon Company, Inc., Publishing Division, 15 Southwest Park, Westwood MA 02090. Editor: Sandra J. Conrad. For college and university professors, undergraduate and graduate students, reference and serials librarians and the general public. Quarterly scholarly journal. 56 pages. Established in 1897. Circulation: 1,500. Copyrighted. Pays in contributor's copies. Uses about 30 mss a year. Reports within 12 weeks. Enclose S.A.S.E.

Bibliographies: "We publish bibliographies (primary and/or secondary, annotated or unannotated) on a wide range of topics within the humanities and social sciences. Articles are indexed or abstracted in 9 indexes and abstracting journals every year."

How To Break In: "We publish many bibliographies by researchers in specialized fields who find themselves hampered by incomplete or inaccurate bibliographies on particular subjects. Librarians, high school and college teachers, and graduate students often compile checklists for their own use which would be of value to scholars or the general public."

THE CALIFORNIA QUARTERLY, 100 Sproul, University of California, Davis CA 95616. Editor: Elliot Gilbert. "Addressed to an audience of educated, literary and general readers, interested in good writing on a variety of subjects, but emphasis is on poetry and fiction." Quarterly. Usually buys first North American serial rights. Reports in 4 to 6 weeks but the editorial office is closed from July 1 to September 30. Enclose S.A.S.E.

Fiction and Nonfiction: Department Editor: Diane Johnson. "Short fiction of quality with emphasis on stylistic distinction; contemporary themes, any subject." Experimental, mainstream. Length: 8,000 words. Original, critical articles, interviews and book reviews. Length: 8,000 words maximum. Pays $2 per published page.

Poetry: Department Editor: Sandra M. Gilbert. "Original, all types; any subject appropriate for genuine poetic expression; any length suitable to subject." Pays $3 per published page.

CANADIAN FICTION MAGAZINE, Box 46422, Station G, Vancouver B.C., Canada V6R 4G7. Editor-in-Chief: Geoffrey Hancock. Emphasizes Canadian fiction, short stories and novel excerpts. Quarterly magazine; 128 pages. Estab: 1971. Circ: 1,800. Pays on publication. Buys first North American serial rights. SASE (Canadian stamps). Reports in 4-6 weeks. Sample copy $2.50 (in Canadian funds); free writer's guidelines.

Nonfiction: Interview (must have a definite purpose, both as biography and as a critical tool focusing on problems and techniques) and book reviews (Canadian fiction only). Buys 35 mss/year. Query. Length: 1,000-3,000 words. Pays $3/printed page plus one-year subscription.

Photos: Purchased on assignment. Send prints. Pays $5 for 5x7 b&w glossies; $20 for cover. Model release required.

Fiction: "No restrictions on subject matter or theme. We are open to experimental and speculative fiction as well as traditional forms. Style content and form are the author's prerogative. We also publish self-contained sections of novel-in-progress and French-Canadian fiction in translation. Please note that *CFM* is an anthology devoted exclusively to Canadian fiction. We publish only the works of writers and artists residing in Canada and Canadians living abroad."

THE CANADIAN FORUM, 3 Church St., Suite 401, Toronto, Ont., Canada M5E 1M2. Editor-in-Chief: Denis Smith. Managing Editor: Jane Somerville. Emphasizes Canadian arts, letters, affairs for a highly educated readership interested in and committed to Canadian affairs. Monthly magazine; 60 pages. Estab: 1920. Circ: 20,000. Pays on publication. Buys one-time rights. SASE. Reports in 1-2 months. Sample copy $1.

Nonfiction: Canadian political and literary commentary. Must be intellectual. Preferred subjects are research, politics, sociology and art. Length: 2,000-3,000 words.

Poetry: Avant-garde; free verse; haiku; light verse; and traditional.

How To Break In: "We accept very little material from the U.S. and are not a 'commercial' market for writers. However, we have published poetry and occasional articles about politics, economics, social analysis, etc., written by Americans."

CANADIAN LITERATURE, University of British Columbia, Vancouver V6T 1W5, B.C, Canada. Editor: George Woodcock. Quarterly. Circulation: 2,500. No fiction, fillers or photos. Not copyrighted. Pays on publication. Study publication. Query advisable. Enclose S.A.E. and International Reply Coupons.
Nonfiction: Articles of high quality on Canadian books and writers only. Articles should be scholarly and readable. Length: 2,000 to 5,500 words. Pays $40 to $120 depending on length.

CAROLINA QUARTERLY, P. O. Box 1117, Chapel Hill NC 27514. (919)933-0244. Editor: Robert Gingher. 3 issues per year. Reprint rights revert to author on request. Pays on publication. Will send sample copy to a writer for $1.50. Reports in 6 to 8 weeks. Submissions should be marked Fiction or Poetry on envelope. Enclose S.A.S.E.
Fiction: "Quality, primary emphasis on stylistic achievement as well as character development and interesting point of view. A place for both the new writer and the professional. Mainly interested in new writers who demonstrate both control of material and sophistication of language. We publish a significant number of unsolicited mss." Pays $3 a printed page. A contest in fiction and poetry for new writers, with cash prizes and publication, is held annually with a deadline of February 1. Only major restriction is that entrant not have published a book-length ms in the field of entry.
Poetry: "Quality; poems must have original subjects or points of view and demonstrate maturity in technique and in use of language. Popular or conventional verse not wanted." Pays $5 per poem.
How To Break In; "Writer, first of all, needs experience in writing even if unpublished. We publish only those pieces that show evidence of craft. Second, writer would benefit from perusal of recent copy of magazine to appreciate the type of thing we publish. After that, it's a matter of quality and editorial taste."

CHELSEA, P.O. Box 5880, Grand Central Station, New York NY 10017. Editor: Sonia Raiziss. Acquires first North American serial rights, but returns rights to author on request. Payment in copies. Enclose S.A.S.E.
Nonfiction, Fiction, and Poetry: "Poetry of high quality; short fiction; occasional nonfiction articles, interviews, and special issues. Accent on style. Interested in fresh, contemporary translations also."
How To Break In: "Best thing to do: Read several issues of the magazine to get the tone/content, themes, penchants, and range of contributions."

CHICAGO REVIEW, University of Chicago, Faculty Exchange, Box C, University of Chicago, Chicago IL 60637. (312)753-3571. Editors-in-Chief: Mary-Ellis Gibson, David S. Shields. Managing Editor: Margaret Yntema. Readership is primarily college educated with a strong interest in cultural questions and contemporary literature. Quarterly magazine; 200 pages. Estab: 1946. Circ: 3,000. Pays in copies. Acquires all rights, but may reassign following publication. Photocopied submissions OK. SASE. Reports in 2 months. Sample copy $2.45. Free writer's guidelines.
Nonfiction: David L. Smith, Articles Editor. Informational and interview. "We consider essays on and reviews of contemporary writing and the arts." Submit complete ms. Length: 500-5,000 words.
Photos: Lee Lordeaux, Photo Editor. Accepted without accompanying ms. Send b&w prints or transparencies. "We welcome experimental photography and graphics."
Fiction: Brian Stonehill, Fiction Editor. Experimental and mainstream. "We welcome the work of younger, less established writers." Uses 3-12 mss/issue. Submit complete ms.
Poetry: Richard Hagen, Poetry Editor. Avant-garde; free verse; haiku; and traditional. Uses 120/year. Limit submissions to batches of 3-5.
How To Break In: "We are very sympathetic to over-the-counter submissions. Many major American writers received their first publication with *Chicago Review*—Susan Sontag, Philip Roth, William Burroughs and others."

CHICAGO SUN-TIMES SHOW/BOOK WEEK, Chicago Sun-Times, 401 N. Wabash Ave., Chicago IL 60611. (312)321-2659. Editor: Jean Adelsman. Emphasizes entertainment, arts and books. Weekly newspaper; 10 pages. Circ: 750,000. Pays on publication. Buys all rights. Submit seasonal/holiday material at least 2 months in advance. Photocopied and previously published work OK. SASE. Reports in 2 weeks.
Nonfiction: "Articles and essays dealing with all the serious and lively arts—movies, theater

(pro, semipro, amateur, foreign), filmmakers, painting, sculpture, music (all fields, from classical to rock—we have regular columnist in these fields). Our Book Week columns have from 5 to 10 reviews, mostly assigned. Material has to be very good because we have our own regular staffers who write almost every week. Writing must be tight. No warmed-over stuff of fan magazine type. No high schoolish literary themes." Query. Length: 500-800 words. Pays $50-100.

CIMARRON REVIEW, Oklahoma State University, Stillwater OK 74074. Editor-in-Chief: Clinton Keeler. Managing Editor: Jeanne Adams Wray. For educated readers, college and university oriented. Quarterly magazine, small and humanistic, 72 pages, (6x9). Established in 1967. Circulation: 1,500. Acquires all rights. Payment in contributor's copies. Will send free sample copy to writer on request. Reports within 5 months. Submit only complete ms. Enclose S.A.S.E.

Nonfiction and Fiction: "Stories, articles, often grouped in specific issues around a theme; such as women, aging, the dignity of work, etc. We are particularly interested in articles that show man triumphant in a polluted, technological world. Contemporary. Grace, lucidity in style; optimistic or positive in outlook. We prefer to do theme issues. No adolescent, adjustment problems in fiction."

THE COLORADO QUARTERLY, Hellems 134, University of Colorado, Boulder CO 80302. Editor: Walter Simon. Established in 1952. Quarterly. Circulation: 700. Buys all rights. Pays on acceptance. Reports in 3 to 4 weeks. Enclose S.A.S.E.

Nonfiction: Articles on a wide range of subjects that concern themselves with regional, national and educational matters, written by specialists, for the general reader, in a nontechnical, nonacademic style. Length: 4,000 to 6,000 words. Pays $50.

Fiction: With plots and well-defined, believable characters. No esoteric or experimental writing. Length: 4,000 to 6,000 words. Pays $50.

CONFRONTATION, Long Island University, 1 University Plaza, Brooklyn NY 11201. (212)834-6170. Editor-in-Chief: Martin Tucker. Emphasizes creative writing for a literate, educated, college graduate audience. Semiannual magazine; 160 pages. Estab: 1968. Circ: 2,000. Pays on publication. Buys all rights, but may reassign following publication. Phone queries OK. Simultaneous and photocopied submissions OK. SASE. Reports in 2 months. Sample copy $1.

Nonfiction: "Articles are, basically, commissioned essays on a specific subject." Memoirs wanted. Buys 6 mss/year. Query. Length: 1,000-3,000 words. Pays $10-50.

Fiction: Ken Bernard, Fiction Editor. Fantasy, experimental, humorous, mainstream. Buys 20 mss/year. Submit complete ms. Length: "completely open." Pays $20-75.

Poetry: W. Palmer, Poetry Editor. Avant-garde, free verse, haiku, light verse, traditional. Buys 40/year. Limit submissions to batches of 10. No length requirement. Pays $10-40.

CONNECTICUT FIRESIDE AND REVIEW OF BOOKS, Box 5293, Hamden CT 06518. (203)248-1023. Editor-in-Chief: Albert E. Callan. Emphasizes writing and literary subjects for an intelligent, well-educated readership interested in writing. Quarterly magazine; 96 pages. Estab: 1972. Circ: 1,500. Pays in copies on publication. Acquires first North American serial rights. Phone queries OK. Simultaneous, photocopied and previously published submissions OK. Reports in 2 weeks. Sample copy $1.25.

Nonfiction: Historical (have had an article about a Connecticut person, usually literary, in each issue so far); and humor. Uses 4 mss/year. Submit complete ms. Length: 1,000-2,500 words.

Photos: "We would use good art photos if offered, otherwise we take our own. We are interested in anything of artistic nature."

Columns/Departments: L.R. Langley, Reviews Editor. "We have about 20 pages of tradebook reviews/issue. Also 5 pages of small press books and poetry chapbooks." Length: 500 words minimum.

Fiction: Confession; experimental; fantasy; historical; humorous; mystery; and suspense. Uses 16-20/issue. Submit complete ms. Length: 1,500-5,000 words.

Poetry: Avant-garde; free verse; haiku; light verse; and traditional. Uses 160/year. Length: 30 lines or less.

How To Break In: "We need articles about Connecticut literary people, or literary people associated with Connecticut in some way, or with New England. Such articles should have a fresh viewpoint, or new information to offer. We also need good serious fiction, nothing commercial."

CONTEMPORARY LITERATURE, Dept. of English, Helen C. White Hall, University of Wisconsin, Madison WI 53706. Editor: L.S. Dembo. Quarterly. "All details should conform to those recommended by the *MLA Style Sheet.*" Does not encourage contributions from freelance writers without academic credentials. Enclose S.A.S.E.
Nonfiction: A scholarly journal which examines various aspects of contemporary literature, from generalizations on current trends and themes, to studies of a writer, his technique, and/or his work, to other specialized treatments or studies in modern literature.

CONTEMPORARY REVIEW, 62 Carey St., London, W.C. 2, England. Editor: Rosalind Wade. Monthly magazine. Estab: 1866. SAE and International Reply Coupons. Reports within a week or so.
Nonfiction, Fiction, and Poetry: "We are completely 'independent' although 'liberal' in origin. We can provide a platform for a very wide range of ideas. Our circulation is greater in the U.S.A. than in England. Freshness of approach and some new and authoritative information is essential. Only material written with authority can be considered." Buys interviews, profiles, and personal experience articles on "the arts, history, home and international politics, domestic subjects, theology, etc." Occasionally buys "short stories and poems of the highest literary merit." Length: 1,500 to 3,000 words for articles; 4,000 words maximum for fiction. Pays 3 pounds per 1,000 words.

CRITICISM, Wayne State University, Dept. of English, Detroit MI 48202. Editor: Alva Gay. For college and university audience of humanities scholars and teachers. Quarterly. No payment. Reports in 3 months. Enclose S.A.S.E.
Nonfiction: Articles on literature, music, visual arts; no particular critical "school." Style should be clear and to the point. Length: 15 to 20 typewritten pages.

CRITIQUE: STUDIES IN MODERN FICTION, Department of English, Georgia Institute of Technology, Atlanta GA 30332. Editor: James Dean Young. For college and university teachers and students. Established in 1956. Triannual. Circulation: 1,500. Acquires all rights. Pays in contributor's copies. Submit complete original ms. Writers should follow the *MLA Style Sheet.* Reports in 4 to 6 months. Enclose S.A.S.E.
Nonfiction: "Critical essays on writers of contemporary fiction. We prefer essays on writers from any country who are alive and without great reputations. We only rarely publish essays on well-known, established writers such as Conrad, James, Joyce, and Faulkner." Uses informational articles and interviews. Length: 4,000 to 8,000 words.

CTHULHU CALLS, Northwest Community College, Powell WY 82435. (307)754-5151. Editor: Terry L. Shorb. For readers with a broad background in science fiction/fantasy/horror literature. Magazine; 48 pages. Established in 1973. Quarterly. Circulation: 1,000. Acquires first serial rights. Pays in contributor's copies. Will send sample copy to writer for $1. Write for copy of guidelines for writers. No photocopied or simultaneous submissions. Reports on material accepted for publication in 2 to 4 weeks. Returns rejected material in 4 to 5 weeks. Submit complete ms. Enclose S.A.S.E.
Nonfiction: "We use essays and personal experience features on teaching science fiction in the classroom; sources of material connected with the SF genre (including audiovisual, books, textbooks, tapes, etc.). Practical, informative stuff. Writer should be familiar with the field, or be aware of educational trends in the field." Occasionally uses book reviews. Book review length: 500 words maximum. Length for other material: 200 to 2,000 words.
Fiction and Poetry: "Open to any solid fiction of a SF or fantasy nature. But extrapolate with care!" Poetry is limited to science fiction, fantasy and horror poetry, with emphasis on SF poetry. Submissions of poetry should be sent to Peter Dillingham, 2272 S. Bannock, Denver CO 80223.

DARK HORSE, c/o Barnes, 47 Stearns, Cambridge MA 02138. (617)544-2663. Editor: Bob Knox. Estab: 1974. Quarterly. Circ: 3,000. Not copyrighted. Uses about 120 mss a year. Pays in contributor's copies. Will send sample copy to writer for 75¢. No photocopied or simultaneous submissions. Reports on material accepted for publication in 1 to 12 weeks. Returns rejected material in 1 to 3 months. "Read most recent issue. Then query." Enclose S.A.S.E.
Nonfiction and Photos: "We welcome intelligent reviews of poetry and fiction books of New England writers. Priority is given to New England writers. We accept only a minimum of non-New England work, unless of exceptional quality. We use material on minorities, translations, collaborations, sensitive topics. News about literary events in New England; small press publishing. Techniques of printing, running a small press, distribution, literary cooperatives, setting type, etc." Length: 50 to 4,000 or 5,000 words. B&w and color photos used with mss.

Fiction and Poetry: Experimental, mainstream and science fiction; serialized novels. Length: 5,000 words maximum. Payment varies; usually 10¢ a word. Traditional and avant-garde forms of poetry. Blank verse, free verse, haiku. "Open to all non-cliched poetry. Fold poems together. Identify each page with name and address." Length: 200 lines maximum.

DARK TOWER MAGAZINE, University Center, Cleveland State University, Cleveland OH 44115. (215)687-2056. Editor: Linda Unger. For those interested in literature, poetry, etc. Annual magazine. Estab: 1972. Circ: 700. Acquires first serial rights. Uses 6 mss/year. Pays on publication in copies, or up to $5. Sample copy $1.50. Simultaneous and photocopied submissions OK. Submit no more than 6 poems at one time. Reports within 2 months. Enclose S.A.S.E.
Nonfiction, Photos, Fiction, Drama and Poetry: "We have no thematic restrictions and no structural or stylistic restrictions. Poetry, short stories, literary criticism, and plays. But no pornography or political treatises, and nothing occult." Length: 3,000 words maximum. Pays in copies or up to $5. Pays $5 for 5x7 b&w prints. Captions optional. Experimental, erotica, fantasy, humorous, and prose poems, poetic fiction considered. Length: 3,000 words maximum. Traditional forms of poetry, blank verse, free verse, light verse, or avant-garde forms. Concrete poetry. Length: 2 to 250 lines. Pays in copies or up to $5.

DE KALB LITERARY ARTS JOURNAL, 555 N. Indian Creek Dr., Clarkston GA 30021. (404)292-1520. Editor: William S. Newman. For those interested in poetry, fiction and/or art. Quarterly. Magazine; 100 pages. Established in 1966. Circulation: 5,000. Acquires first serial rights. Payment in contributor's copies. Will send sample copy to writer for $1.40 (cost plus postage). "Look for announcements of special issues." Seeking material for National Poets Issue. Submit complete ms. Reports in 2-3 months. SASE.
Nonfiction, Fiction, Photos, and Poetry: Subject matter is unrestricted. "We consider all types of nonfiction and fiction. Our decisions are based on quality of material. Traditional, blank verse, free verse, light verse, and avant-garde forms of poetry." B&w photos are used with mss; 8x10 glossies preferred.

THE DENVER QUARTERLY, University of Denver, Denver CO 80210. (303)753-2869. Editor-in-Chief: Burton Raffel. Managing Editor: Audrey Haerlin. For an intellectual/university readership. Quarterly magazine; 175-200 pages. Estab: 1965. Circ: 800. Pays on publication. Buys first North American serial rights. Phone queries OK. Photocopied (if explained as not simultaneous) submissions OK. SASE. Reports in 2 weeks. Sample copy $2.
Nonfiction: Expose (if actually relevant); historical; humor; personal opinion and profile. Buys 10-12 mss/year. Send complete ms. Pays $5/printed page.
Fiction: Adventure; fantasy; experimental; historical; humorous; mainstream and science fiction. Buys 12-15 mss/year. Send complete ms. Pays $5/printed page.
Poetry: Avant-garde, free verse and traditional. Buys 60 poems/year. Send poems. Pays $5/ printed page.
How To Break In: "We decide on the basis of quality only. Prior publication is irrelevant. Promising material, even though rejected, will receive some personal comment from the editor; some material can be revised to meet our standards, through such criticism. Rejection via a printed form only means the editor sees nothing worth encouraging.
For '78: Winter, 1978 issue will focus on the West. One of the subsequent issues may deal with colonial experience.

DESCANT, Texas Christian University Press, Department of English, TCU, Fort Worth TX 76129. (817)926-2461. Editor-in-Chief: Betsy Feagan Colquitt. Quarterly magazine; 48 pages. Estab: 1956. Circ: 650. Pays in contributor's copies on publication. Acquires all rights, but will reassign following publication. Phone queries OK. Simultaneous and photocopied submissions OK. SASE. Reports in 6 weeks. Sample copy $1; free writer's guidelines.
Nonfiction: Informational (articles used are literary criticism, with examination of modern literature as principal concern of the essay). Use 4 mss/year. Submit complete ms. Length: 3,000-5,000 words.
Fiction: Fantasy, confession, experimental, historical. Uses 10-12 mss/year. Submit complete ms. Length: 2,000-6,000 words.
Poetry: Avant-garde, free verse, traditional. Uses 40/year. Limit submissions to batches of 6. Length: 10-40 lines.

THE DRAMA REVIEW, New York University, 51 W. 4th St., Rm. 300, New York NY 10012. (212)598-2597. Editor-in-Chief: Michael Kirby. Emphasizes avant-garde performance art for professors, students and the general theater and dance-going public as well as professional practitioners in the performing arts. Quarterly magazine; 144 pages. Estab: 1955. Circ: 10,000. Pays on publication. Buys all rights, but may reassign following publication. Phone queries OK. Submit seasonal/holiday material 4 months in advance. Photocopied and previously published (if published in another language) submissions OK. SASE. Reports in 3 months. Sample copy $3.50. Free writer's guidelines.

Nonfiction: Kate Davy, Managing Editor. Historical (the historical avant-garde in any performance art, translations of previously unpublished plays, etc.) and informational (documentation of a particular performance). Buys 10-40 mss/issue. Query. Pays 1¢/word for translations; 2¢/word for other material.

Photos: Kate Davy, Managing Editor. Photos purchased with or without accompanying ms or on assignment. Captions required. Pays $10 for b&w photos. No additional payment for photos accepted with accompanying ms.

Rejects: "No criticism in the sense of value judgments—we are not interested in the author's opinions. We are only interested in documentation theory and analysis."

EL VIENTO, 348 7th Street, Huntington WV 25701. Editor: William Lloyd Griffin. Established in 1967. Semiannual. "All rights revert to the authors." Pays in contributor's copies. Will consider photocopied submissions. Reports in 6 weeks. Enclose S.A.S.E.

Fiction, Nonfiction, Poetry, and Drama: "We use fiction, nonfiction, poetry, and one-act plays. No taboos except low quality material." Length: 500 to 3,000 words for fiction and nonfiction.

EPOCH, A Magazine of Contemporary Literature, 245 Goldwin Smith Hall, Cornell University, Ithaca NY 14853. 3 times yearly. Acquires first serial publication rights. Payment in copies. Reports in 2 months or more. Enclose S.A.S.E. for return of submissions.

Fiction: "Quality. Would like to see more stories which combine a fresh, honest transcription of human experience with power or meaningfulness, but are not adverse to experimental forms." Length: 1,500 to 5,000 words.

Poetry: Approximately 30 to 40 pages each issue devoted to poetry.

EVENT, Douglas College, Box 2503, New Westminster, B.C., Canada V3L 5B2. For "those interested in literature, writing, etc." Biannual magazine; 135-150 pages. Estab: 1970. Circ: 800. Uses 65-75 mss/year. Token payment and contributor's copies. Photocopied and simultaneous submissions OK. Reports in 4 months. Submit complete ms. Enclose S.A.E. and International Reply Coupons.

Nonfiction, Fiction, Poetry and Drama: "Only professional, high-quality work." Reviews, essays, the novella, the short story, poetry, drama.

THE FAULT, 33513 6th St., Union City CA 94587. (415)487-1383. Editors-in-Chief: Terrence Ames, Rustie Cook. Emphasizes innovative literature for the small press collector, libraries, anyone interested in experimental and contemporary works of art. Semiannual magazine; 125 pages. Estab: 1971. Circ: 500. Payment 1 year after publication "if grant is awarded." Buys 1-time and reprint rights. Phone queries OK. Submit seasonal/holiday material 2 months in advance. Photocopied and previously published submissions OK. SASE. Reports in 2 weeks. Sample copy $1.50. Free writer's guidelines.

Photos: Purchased without accompanying manuscript. Send prints. Pays $5-10 for 5x7 b&w; $5-10 for color. No additional payment for photos accepted with accompanying ms.

Fiction: Science fiction, dada, visual, erotica, experimental, fantasy and mainstream. Buys 10 mss/year. Send complete ms. Length: 100-5,000 words. Pays $5-10.

Poetry: Avant-garde and free verse. Buys 40 poems/year. Limit submissions to batches of 20. Length: 2-100. Pays $5-10.

Fillers: Collages. Buys 10/year. Submit fillers. Length: 1-100 words. Pays $5-10.

How To Break In: "No need for formula fiction filled with cliches and unimaginative writing. Poetry with end rhymes filled with abstractions and archaic ideas. Any work that lacks style, invention, originality."

For '78: Issues with an emphasis on science fiction and fantasy.

FICTION, City College, English Department, 138th St. and Convent Ave., New York NY 10031. (212)690-8170. Editor: Mark Mirsky. Published by a cooperative of writers. For individual subscribers of all ages; college libraries, bookstores, and college bookstores. Published 3 times a year. Magazine, 28 to 32 pages. Established in 1972. Circulation: 5,000. Acquires all rights, but will reassign rights to author after publication. Payment in contributor's copies only. Will send free sample copy to writer on request. Submit complete ms. Reports as soon as possible, but time "depends on the backlog of material." Enclose S.A.S.E.

Fiction and Photos: "We publish only fiction, up to 3,000 words. There really is no minimum or maximum length, because we edit many pieces. No payment for writers." Photos purchased without accompanying ms. Photo Editor: Inger Grytting.

FICTION INTERNATIONAL, Department of English, St. Lawrence University, Canton NY 13617. Editor: Joe David Bellamy. For "readers interested in the best writing by talented writers working in new forms or working in old forms in especially fruitful new ways; readers interested in contemporary literary developments and possibilities." Semiannual. Circulation: 5,000. Buys all rights (will reassign rights to author after publication), first North American serial rights, first serial rights. Buys 15 fiction and interview mss/year. Pays on publication. Sample copy $3. Query or submit complete ms for interviews; submit only complete ms for fiction or reviews. Prefers not to see photocopied submissions. Reports in 1 to 2 months; sometimes longer. Enclose S.A.S.E.

Nonfiction and Photos: "Regularly use interviews with well-known fiction writers." Length: 1,000 to 10,000 words. "Also use book reviews of new fiction, though these are usually assigned." Length: 300 to 500 words. Photos accompanying interviews purchased to illustrate interviews. 8x10 b&w glossies. Payment varies.

Fiction: "Almost no taboos or preconceptions, but highly selective. Not an easy market for unsophisticated writers. Especially receptive to innovative forms or rich personal styles. Easily bored by nineteenth-century narratives or predictable, plot-ridden fictions. Originality and the ability to create living characters are highly desirable qualities." Portions of novels acceptable if reasonably self-contained. Length: no length limitations for fiction but "rarely use short-shorts or mss over 30 pages." Payment is $25 to $150, sometimes higher.

FIRELANDS ARTS REVIEW, Firelands Campus, Huron OH 44839. Editor: Joel D. Rudinger. For general educated audience. Annual magazine, 64 pages, (5½x7½). Established in 1972. Circulation: 1,000. Acquires first serial rights or second serial (reprint) rights. Uses 50 mss a year. Pays in copies. Will send sample copy to writer for $2.20. Submit only complete ms. Accepts mss from October to March of each year. Reports within 8 weeks. Enclose S.A.S.E.

Fiction: "Any style and approach and subject matter as long as the quality is professional and mature. Length: 3,000 words maximum. Will also accept short prose sketches and characterizations sensitive to the human condition. We also need stories that display a sense of humor or clever ironic twist."

Photos: 5x7 or 8x10 b&w's. Any non-cliched subject or style. Unusual perspective, high contrast, experimental materials are of interest as well as fresh approaches to traditional photography.

Poetry: Poems must be original and mature in use of language. Any subject, any theme, any style, any length. High quality and awareness of the art of writing poetry essential.

FOLKLORE FORUM, 504 North Fess, Bloomington IN 47401. For folklorists, graduate students in the humanities and social sciences. Quarterly magazine; 80 pages, (8½x11). Established in 1968. Circulation: 350. Not copyrighted. Payment in contributor's copies. Will send sample copy to writer for $2. Will consider photocopied and simultaneous submissions. Query first or submit complete ms. Reports within 2 months. Enclose S.A.S.E.

Nonfiction: Articles, bibliographies; book, record, and ethnographic film reviews on topics in folklore. "We encourage short comments and queries. Our objective is to serve as a medium of communication among folklorists. We have a special interest in popular culture and folklore."

FORUM, University of Houston, Cullen Blvd., Houston TX 77004. (713)749-4710. Editor: William Lee Pryor. Primarily for a sophisticated audience; most of the contributors are university professors. Quarterly. Acquires all rights, but will reassign rights to author after publication. Pays in contributor's copies. "A query letter is a welcome courtesy, although we do not specifically request one." Enclose S.A.S.E.

Nonfiction: "We feature articles in the humanities, fine arts, and the sciences, but we also welcome those bearing on business and technology. Specialized interests involving highly technical or special vocabularies are usually not within our range, however. For articles, we stress the scholarly approach and originality. We recommend use of the *MLA Style Sheet.* An informal style is not objectionable, but research, if any, should be accurate, thorough, and carefully documented. Our format differs from those publications of a similar orientation in that we attempt to combine scholarship with an appealing, aesthetic setting. We are very much interested in good articles on music, dance, architecture, sculpture, etc., not only for our regular issues, but also for special numbers like recent ones featuring French culture and Renaissance." Length: open.

Fiction: "We are open on story themes, and we stress originality. Up to now we have not found it possible to publish condensed or serialized novels."

FOUR QUARTERS, La Salle College, Olney Ave. at 20th St., Philadelphia PA 19141. Editor: John J. Keenan. For college educated audience with literary interest. Quarterly. Circulation: 700. Buys all rights; grants permission to reprint on request. Buys 10 to 12 short stories, 30 to 40 poems, 4 articles a year. Pays on publication. Will send a sample copy to a writer for 50¢. Reports in 4 to 6 weeks. "Do not submit during July and August." Enclose S.A.S.E.
Nonfiction: "Lively critical articles on particular authors or specific works. Think pieces on history, politics, the arts. Prefer footnotes incorporated. Style must be literate, lively, free of jargon and pedantry." Length: 1,500 to 5,000 words. Payment is up to $25.
Fiction: "Technical mastery gets our attention and respect immediately. We admire writers who use the language with precision, economy, and imagination. But fine writing for its own sake is unsatisfying unless it can lead the reader to some insight into the complexity of the human condition without falling into heavy-handed didacticism." Length: 2,000 to 5,000 words. Pays up to $25.
Poetry: "Quality poetry from 8 to 32 lines. Some shorter ones used as fillers without payment." Payment is up to $5.

GALLIMAUFREY PRESS, 3208 N. 19th Rd., Arlington VA 22201. Editor-in-Chief: Mary MacArthur. Emphasizes literature. Semiannual magazine; 56 pages. Estab: 1973. Circ: 5,000. Pays on publication in copies. Acquires all rights, but may reassign to author following publication. Seasonal/holiday material should be submitted 6 months in advance. Simultaneous submissions (if notified) OK. SASE. Reports in 3 months. Sample copy $1.
Fiction: Contemporary—both traditional and experimental. Uses 50 mss/year. Send complete ms.

GRAFFITI, English Department, Box 418, Lenoir Rhyne College, Hickory NC 28601. Editor: Kermit Turner. For writers, college students, faculty and all persons interested in literature. Semiannual magazine; 44 pages. Estab: 1972. Circ: 250. Acquires first serial rights. All rights return to author after publication. Uses 6 to 8 short story mss a year; about 80 poems. Payment in contributor's copies. Will send sample copy to writer for $1. Will not consider photocopied or simultaneous submissions. Reports on material accepted for publication in 4 months. Returns rejected material in 6 weeks. Submit complete ms. Enclose S.A.S.E.
Fiction: Short stories; experimental, mainstream. Length: 2,000 to 5,000 words.
Poetry: Traditional forms; free verse. Will consider any length.

GRAY DAY, Point Blanc Press, 2830 Napier Ave., Macon GA 31204. Editor-in-Chief: Roger Charles. Emphasizes creative writing for a literary readership. Semiannual magazine; 44 pages. Estab: 1975. Circ: 300. Pays on publication in copies. Buys first North American serial rights. Photocopied submissions OK. SASE. Reports in 4 weeks. Sample copy $1. Free writer's guidelines.
Photos: B&w. Send prints.
Fiction: Uses 6 mss/year. Send complete ms. Length: maximum 3,000 words.
Poetry: Uses 20 poems/year. Limit submissions to batches of 6.

THE GREAT LAKES REVIEW, Northeastern Illinois University, Chicago IL 60625. (312)583-4050, Ext. 8145. Editor: Gerald Nemanic. Mostly for scholars and academics who are interested in Midwest studies. Semi-annual magazine, 100 pages. Estab: 1974. Circ: 1,000. "We require no rights outside of copyright." Payment in contributor's copies. Write for editorial guidelines for writers. Query first or submit complete ms. Will consider photocopied and simultaneous submissions. Reports in 6 months. Enclose S.A.S.E.
Nonfiction and Poetry: Scholarly articles, bibliographies, interviews, poetry features, personal narratives.

GRUB STREET, Grub Street Press, Box 91, Bellmore NY 11710. (212)733-3922. Editor: Alan Ball. For anyone interested in modern literature. Semiannual magazine; 48 pages. Estab: 1969. Circ: 1,000. Pays on publication. All rights revert to author. Phone queries OK. Simultaneous, photocopied, and previously published submissions OK. SASE. Reports in 3-6 weeks. Sample copy 50¢; writer's guidelines for SASE.
Fiction: "We are a magazine of modern culture, which publishes mainly, but is not restricted to, verse, fiction, and graphics. We do seek mss of high quality from professional as well as relatively unknown writers. We are a literary magazine, hoping to appeal to a diverse audience. At the same time we seek readable material of significant interest, we encourage experimentation. No taboos, no restrictions on subject matter or length, except that we try to publish a diverse collection, so shorter works have a certain advantage." Buys 1-2 mss/issue. Send first 2 pages only if ms is over 2,000 words. Length: 5,000 maximum. Pays in copies.

Poetry: Avant-garde, free verse and traditional. Buys 20 poems/issue. Pays in copies. 1 featured poet per issue is paid a cash award.
Rejects: No racist or sexist material.

HANGING LOOSE, 231 Wyckoff St., Brooklyn NY 11217. Editors: Dick Lourie, Emmett Jarrett, Ron Schreiber, Robert Hershon. Quarterly. Acquires first serial rights. Payment in copies. Will send sample copy to writer for $1.50. Reports in 2 to 3 months. Enclose S.A.S.E.
Poetry and Fiction: Fresh, energetic poems of any length. Excellent quality. Experimental fiction. "Space for fiction very limited."

HARVEST, P.O. Box 78, Farmington CT 06032. Editor: Robert T. Casey. For "people who are interested in reading poetry and fiction, and, perhaps, discovering some new talent in an otherwise stagnant literary society." Magazine; 75 pages. Established in 1974. Annually (October). Circulation: 1,000. Acquires first North American serial rights. No payment. Will send sample copy to writer for $1.95. Will consider photocopied and simultaneous submissions. Writer's guidelines available. Enclose S.A.S.E.
Nonfiction, Fiction and Poetry: Essays, short fiction, parts of novels, poetry. Satire and other types of humor would also be welcome. Length for fiction: 2,000 words. No limit on length for poetry.

HEIRS MAGAZINE, 657 Mission St., Room 205, San Francisco CA 94105. Editor: Alfred Durand Garcia. For educators, artists, students, professionals, poets, libraries and public institutions; specifically people interested in art and literature viewed from a multi-culture perspective. Magazine; 80 (8½x11) pages. Established in 1968. Published 3 or 4 times a year. Circulation: 2,000. Rights acquired vary with author and material. May acquire first North American serial rights, first serial rights, or all rights. Token monetary payment and/or copies. Will send sample copy to writer for $3. Write for copy of guidelines for writers. Will consider photocopied submissions. No simultaneous submissions. Reports in 6 to 8 weeks. Submit complete ms. Enclose S.A.S.E.
Nonfiction and Photos: Art criticism, feature articles on art and artists. Must be written from a humanistic perspective. Book reviews. Reviews of Third World literature and women's literature. B&w photos used with or without mss. "Because of our unique format, we suggest that writers see a sample copy first since we publish major articles in English, Spanish and Chinese." Length: 1,500 words.
Fiction and Poetry: Experimental fiction. Length: 1,500 words. Blank verse, free verse and avant-garde forms of poetry.

THE HUDSON REVIEW, 65 E. 55th St., New York NY 10022. Managing Editor: Marianne Clay. Quarterly. Buys first North American serial rights. Pays on publication. Reports in 6 to 8 weeks. Enclose S.A.S.E. for return of submissions.
Nonfiction, Fiction, and Poetry: Uses "quality fiction up to 10,000 words, articles up to 8,000 words; translations, reviews and poetry." Pays 2½¢ a word for prose, and 50¢ a line for poetry.

THE HUMANIST, 923 Kensington Ave., Buffalo NY 14215. (716)837-0306. Editor: Paul Kurtz. For college graduates; humanists with a wide range of interests. Published every 2 months; 48 to 64 pages, (8½x11). Established in 1941. Circulation: 28,000. Copyrighted. Pays on publication. Will send free sample copy to writer on request. Will consider photocopied submissions. Query first. Reports "immediately." Enclose S.A.S.E.
Nonfiction: "General informative articles of an intellectual nature. A thorough treatment of the subject material covered. We're considered to be quite innovative in the types of articles published. Particularly interested in articles on frontier issues, especially on changing ethical and value issues." Informational, think articles, and book, movie, and TV reviews. Length: 1,000 to 5,000 words. Pays $50 to $150.

HYACINTHS AND BISCUITS, Box 392, Brea CA 92621. Editor: Jane R. Card. Magazine; 56 (8½x11) pages. Special issues: Young Poets, Prison Poets, Peace/War. Established in 1969. Every 2 months. Circulation: 1,000. Buys first North American serial rights. Buys about 500 mss a year. Pays on acceptance. Will send sample copy to writer for $1. Write for copy of guidelines for writers (enclosing S.A.S.E.). Will consider photocopied submissions. No simultaneous submissions. Reports in 1 to 4 weeks. Submit complete ms. Enclose S.A.S.E., or material will not be returned.
Poetry: "*Hyacinths and Biscuits* emphasizes quality, but does not stand for any particular school. It is, therefore, a mixture of traditional and modern; sonnets and free verse. One page is

usually devoted to haiku, another to light verse and limericks." Length: 1 to 100 lines. Pays $1 for 5 lines or less; $2 for more than 5 lines. Moratorium on poems until January 1978.

Nonfiction: "General subject matter is the human condition. General theme of bettering man's worth and circumstances on earth, whether in business, in prison; or a woman, black, Indian, or whatever. Biographies of poets; short sketches of local happenings that are interesting to the world at large. Prison reform. Arms reduction. Over-population. Lack of food. Inflation, and what it has done to the impoverished nations." Length: 300 words. Pays $2.

IN A NUTSHELL, Hibiscus Press, Box 22248, Sacramento CA 95822. (916)428-2766. Editor-in-Chief: Margaret Wensrich. Emphasizes poetry and fiction. Quarterly magazine; 40 pages. Estab: 1975. Circ: 5,000. Pays on publication. Buys one-time rights. Submit seasonal/holiday material 6 months in advance. Photocopied submissions OK. SASE. Reports in 4 weeks. Sample copy $1; writer's guidelines free, if SASE is enclosed.

Fiction: Adventure, fantasy, confession, experimental, historical, humorous, mystery, romance, suspense, mainstream, science fiction, western. Buys 12 mss/year. Submit complete ms. Length: 1,500-5,000 words. Pays ½¢/word.

Poetry: Joyce Odam, Poetry Editor. Free verse, haiku, light verse, traditional. "We put no restrictions on poetry." Buys 60-80/year. Limit submissions to batches of 4-6. No length limit. Pays $2 minimum. "We have an annual poetry and short story contest. We give cash and other awards. Winners are published *In A Nutshell.* Send SASE for contest rules and entry form."

INLET, Virginia Wesleyan College, Norfolk VA 23502. Editor: Joseph Harkey. Emphasizes poetry and fiction for liberally educated readership of all ages. Annual magazine; 30 pages. Estab: 1971. Circ: 700. Pays in copies. Acquires all rights, but will reassign rights to author following publication. Photocopied submissions OK. Submissions accepted September 1-March 15. SASE. Reports in 2 months. Sample copy for SASE.

FIction: Adventure; experimental; fantasy; historical; humorous; mainstream and suspense. Buys 1-2 mss/issue. Send complete ms. Length 500-3,000 words.

Poetry: Avant-garde; free verse; haiku; light verse and traditional. Buys 20-40 poems/year. Limit submissions to batches of 5. Length: very short.

INTER-AMERICAN REVIEW OF BIBLIOGRAPHY, Organization of American States, Washington DC 20006. Editor: Elena Castedo-Ellerman. Quarterly magazine; 120-150 pages. Estab: 1951. Circ: 3,000. Pays in subscription to magazine. Sample copy $1.50; free writer's guidelines.

Nonfiction: Historical (scholarly only, literature and philosophy). Uses 16 mss/year. Query.

Columns/Departments: Book reviews on serious literature and humanistic studies dealing with the American continent. Also News and Notes about cultural news dealing with the American continent, especially in the humanities. Submit complete ms. Length: 2 pages for book reviews; 1 paragraph for news. Pays in copy of book to be reviewed.

THE INTERCOLLEGIATE REVIEW, Intercollegiate Studies Institute, 14 S. Bryn Mawr Ave., Bryn Mawr PA 19010. (215)525-7501. Editor-in-Chief: Robert A. Schadler. Emphasizes intellectual conservatism on cultural, economic, political, literary and philosophical issues. Quarterly magazine; 64 pages. Estab: 1975. Circ: 30,000. Pays on publication. Buys all rights. Phone queries OK. SASE. Reports in 6 months. Free sample copy.

Nonfiction: Historical; informational and personal. Buys 4 mss/issue. Query. Length: 1,000-5,000 words. Pays $50-150.

How To Break In: "Read back issues and thoroughly understand our purpose and format."

INTERMEDIA, Century Club Educational Arts Project, 10508 W. Pico Blvd., Los Angeles CA 90026. Editor-in-Chief: Harley W. Lond. Emphasizes art and literature for college educated vriters and artists interested in new literature. Triquarterly magazine; 48 pages. Estab: 1974. Circ: 2,000. Pays on publication. Acquires all rights, but may reassign following publication. Simultaneous, photocopied, and previously published submissions OK. SASE. Reports in 1 month. Sample copy $1.

Nonfiction: Informational articles on art groups, media groups, dance, theater, etc. Interviews, personal opinion articles, profiles, photo features on the same themes. "We're wide open on articles on art and media, particularly those covering avant-garde art of all disciplines; video, film, theater, dance, etc." Buys 9-15 mss/year. Query. Length: 5,000 words. Pays in contributor's copies.

Photos: B&w only. Used with or without mss. Query. Pays in contributor's copies.

Fiction and Poetry: "Both should be highly experimental." Buys 1-2 mss/issue. Query. Pays in contributor's copies.

INTERSTATE, Box 7068, University Station, Austin TX 78712. Editors: Loris Essary and Mark Loeffler. For "anyone interested in creative arts." Quarterly magazine; 54 pages. Estab: 1974. Circ: 500. Acquires all rights, but will reassign rights to author after publication. Payment in contributor's copies. Sample copy $2. Photocopied submissions OK. Reports in 1-3 weeks. "Occasionally longer." No query necessary. Enclose S.A.S.E.

Nonfiction and Photos: "We actively seek nonfiction in the form of 'creative essays.' Such work is best defined by reference to John Cage, Norman O. Brown and Merleau-Ponty. We accept mss and then fit them to the issues for the year. Frequently, we have holdover." Photos used with and without mss. Size: open. "Must be b&w glossies."

Fiction and Poetry: All forms and subjects open. Length: open. "Piece should be creative in either terms of style or theme. We are interested in seeing all forms of creative material, particularly experimental. We are not interested in ill-thought-through political diatribes or material that is totally sexually centered. These latter groups are overworked. We must admit a preference of the surrealists and Dadaists."

THE IOWA REVIEW, EPB 321, The University of Iowa, Iowa City IA 53342. (319)353-6048. Editor: Thomas R. Whitaker. For persons "interested in modern literature, aware of the sophisticated relationships in the critical-creative dialogue." Magazine; 126 pages. Established in 1970. Quarterly. Circulation: 1,000. Buys all rights, but may reassign rights to author after publication. Buys about 100 mss per year. Pays on publication. Will send sample copy to writer for $2. Will consider photocopied submissions. No simultaneous submissions. Reports on mss accepted for publication in 3 to 4 months. Returns rejected material in 1 day to 3 months. Enclose S.A.S.E.

Nonfiction, Fiction and Poetry: "We publish poetry, fiction and criticism. Our interest is with modern (not necessarily contemporary) literature. It is best for a writer to study some recent issues, available through our office. We attempt to achieve a conversation between poetry, fiction and critical pieces or interviews." Does not want to see "domestic poetry" or "overly self-conscious cover letters." Length for interviews and reviews: 10,000 words maximum. Pays $5/page. Fiction. Length: 10,000 words maximum. Pays $5/page. Department Editor: Robert Coover. Poetry Editor: William Matthews. Pays $1 per line.

JOHNSONIAN NEWS LETTER, 610 Philosophy Hall, Columbia University, New York NY 10027. Co-editors: James L. Clifford and John H. Middendorf. For scholars, book collectors and all those interested in 18th century English literature. 4 times a year. No payment. Reports immediately. Enclose S.A.S.E.

Nonfiction: Interested in news items, queries, short comments, etc., having to do with 18th century English literature. Must be written in simple style. Length: maximum 500 words.

THE JOURNAL OF MEXICAN AMERICAN HISTORY, Box 13861-UCSB, Santa Barbara CA 93107. (805)968-5915. Editor-in-Chief: Joseph Peter Navarro. Emphasizes history for specialists in Mexican American history, including professors, graduate and undergraduate students. Annual magazine; 150-200 pages. Estab: 1970. Circ: 1,500. No payment. Acquires simultaneous rights. Phone queries OK. Submit seasonal/holiday material 6-12 months in advance. Photocopied submissions OK. SASE. Reports in 2 weeks. Sample copy $17.50.

Nonfiction: Historical (Mexican American history from 1848 to present); interview; personal experience (documented carefully); personal opinion; photo feature (if historical and pertinent). Send complete ms. Length: 1,500-4,500 words. Prize of $100 for best article. Captions required for b&w photos used.

JOURNAL OF MODERN LITERATURE, Temple University, 1241 Humanities Bldg., Philadelphia PA 19122. (215)787-8505. Editor-in-Chief: Maurice Beebe. Managing Editor: Kathleen Morgan. Emphasizes scholarly literature for academics interested in literature of the past 100 years. Quarterly magazine; 160-200 pages. Estab: 1970. Circ: 2,000. Buys all rights, but may reassign rights to author following publication. Phone queries OK. Photocopied submissions OK. SASE. Reports in 8 weeks. Free sample copy.

Nonfiction: Historical (20th century literature); informational (20th century literature); and photo feature on art and literature. Buys 30 mss/year. Query or send complete ms. Pays $50-100.

Photos: Purchased only with accompanying nonfiction manuscript. Total purchase price for ms includes payment for photos.

For '78: "Articles on John Fowles or pornography as literature."

JOURNAL OF THE NORTH AMERICAN WOLF SOCIETY, Box 118, Eatonville WA 98328. Editor: Sandra L. Gray. For audience with interest in "conservation issues and a strong concern for the preservation and promotion of the wolf and its habitat, and other wild canids of North America." Established in 1975. Quarterly. Circ: 200. Rights acquired vary with author and material. Acquires all rights, but may reassign rights to author after publication; first North American serial rights; or simultaneous rights. Payment in contributor's copies. Will send sample copy to writer for $1. Write for editorial guidelines sheet. Will consider simultaneous and photocopied submissions. Reports in 4 to 6 weeks. Query not necessary. Enclose S.A.S.E.

Nonfiction: "Subject matter must be relevant to wolves, or other wild canids such as coyotes, their prey, their habitat, or activities of individuals or groups on their behalf. Our approach is factual and objective. We try to provide space for as many positions as possible in this complex and emotional subject, as long as these positions have their bases in fact and are rationally presented. We generally like to see sources and references though they may not be published with the article." Length: 600 to 1,800 words. For personal opinion, 300 to 600 words. For reviews, 150 to 300 words. Regular columns: "Thinking It Over" and "Views and Reviews."

Photos and Fillers: "No specific requirements yet for photos, will negotiate on individual basis." Uses newsbreaks and clippings.

JOURNAL OF POPULAR CULTURE, University Hall, Bowling Green State University, Bowling Green OH 43402. (419)372-2610. Editor: Ray B. Browne. For students and adults, interested in popular culture, TV, films, popular literature, sports, music, etc. Quarterly magazine, 256 pages, (6x9). Established in 1967. Circulation: 3,000. Acquires all rights, but will reassign rights to author after publication. Payment in copies. Will send sample copy to writer for $4. Will consider photocopied submissions. Reports within 3 to 6 months. Enclose S.A.S.E.

Nonfiction and Photos: "Critical essays on media, books, poetry, advertising, etc." Informational, interview, historical, think pieces, nostalgia, reviews of books, movies, television. Length: 5,000 words maximum. Payment in contributor's copies (25 reprints). Uses b&w glossies.

JOURNALISM MONOGRAPHS, School of Journalism, University of Kentucky, Lexington KY 40506. (606)258-2671. Editor: Bruce H. Westley. For all journalism educators in the U.S., Canada and the world. Magazine; 30 to 85 (6x9) pages. Established in 1966. Published serially, 1 ms per issue; 4 to 6 issues per year. Circulation: 1,600. "Author grants all rights." Uses 4 to 6 mss a year. No payment. Will send sample copy to writer for $2.50. Write for copy of guidelines for writers. Will consider photocopied submissions. No simultaneous submissions. Reports on material accepted for publication in 1 to 6 months. Query first or submit complete ms. Enclose S.A.S.E.

Nonfiction: "Scholarly articles (any methodology) in the field of journalism and mass communications. We do not encourage freelancers without scholarly discipline."

KANSAS QUARTERLY, Dept. of English, Kansas State University, Manhattan KS 66502. (913)532-6716. Editors: Harold W. Schneider and Ben Nyberg. For "adults, mostly academics, and people interested in creative writing, literary criticism, midwestern history, and art." Established in 1968. Quarterly. Circulation: 1,100. Acquires all rights, but will reassign them to author after publication. Pays in contributor's copies. Sample copy $2.50. Query first for nonfiction. "Follow *MLA Style Sheet* and write for a sophisticated audience." Reports in about 2 to 4 months. Enclose S.A.S.E. for return of submissions or reply to queries.

Nonfiction, Photos, Fiction, and Poetry: Accepts poetry, short stories; art, history and literary criticism on special topics. "We emphasize the history, culture, and life style of the Mid-Plains region. We do not want children's literature, 'slick' material, or special interest material not in keeping with our special numbers." Accepts historical articles on "special topics only." Photos should have captions; 4x6 b&w preferred. Accepts experimental and mainstream fiction. Length: 250 to 10,000 words. Accepts traditional and avant-garde forms of poetry, blank verse, and free verse. Poetry themes open.

KARAMU, English Department, Eastern Illinois University, Charleston IL 61920. (217)345-5013. Editor: Allen Neff. For literate, university-educated audience. Established in 1967. Annually. Circulation: 300. Acquires first North American serial rights. Uses 25 mss a year. Payment in 2 contributor's copies. Will send sample copy to writer for $1. Submit complete ms. Reports on material in 5 months. Enclose S.A.S.E.

Nonfiction: Articles on contemporary literature. Length: open.

Fiction: Experimental, mainstream. Length: 2,000 to 8,000 words. Dept. Editor: Gordon Jackson.

Poetry: Traditional forms, free verse, avant-garde. "Quality with visual perception or with fresh language." Length: 3 to 80 lines, "but we do publish longer poems." Dept. Editor: Carol Elder.

KENTUCKY FOLKLORE RECORD, Box U-169, College Heights Station, Western Kentucky University, Bowling Green KY 42101. (502)745-3111. Editor: Charles S. Guthrie. For libraries and individuals having a professional or personal interest in folklore as a learned discipline. Established in 1955. Quarterly. Circulation: 400. Copyrighted. Acquires all rights. Will grant reprint rights, provided full credit is given to *KFR*. Uses 20 mss a year. Payment in contributor's copies. Sample copy 25¢ postage. Will not consider photocopied submissions. Follow *MLA Style Sheet*. Usually reports on material in 4 weeks. Query first or submit complete ms. Enclose S.A.S.E.
Nonfiction and Photos: "Our main emphasis is on Kentucky material. Articles dealing primarily with folklife, folk speech, folktales, folksong (songs collected from oral tradition) of Kentucky. Some material pertaining to other areas is used also. Book reviews dealing with recent publications that treat some aspect of folklore. Study an issue of the journal." Also interested in Child ballads, folk children's games, nursery rhymes, black folklore, folklore in literature. Not interested in seeing anything pertaining to "Nashville" music. Length: 200 to 2,000 words. B&w photos with good contrast, 8x10 preferred, used with mss. Must relate to the journal's theme.

THE LAKE SUPERIOR REVIEW, Box 724, Ironwood MI 49938. (906)667-3781. Editors: Faye Korp, Cynthia Willoughby, and Lee Merrill. Emphasizes contemporary poetry and short stories for readership interested in good contemporary literature. Published 3 times a year; 48 pages. Estab: 1970. Circ: 300. Pays on publication in copies. Buys first North American serial rights. Phone queries OK. Reports in 2 weeks-4 months. Sample copy $1.50.
Photos: Dail Willoughby, Photo Editor. Purchased without accompanying manuscript. Maximum size b&w without reduction 5x8. "Can be an expression or piece of art in itself."
Fiction: Adventure; erotica; experimental; fantasy; historical; humorous; mainstream; mystery and science fiction. Uses 12 mss/year. Length: 4,000 words maximum.
Poetry: Avant-garde; free verse; haiku; light verse and traditional. Uses 90 poems/year. Limit submissions to batches of 6-8.

L'ESPRIT CREATEUR, Box 222, Lawrence KS 66044. (913)864-3164. Editor: John D. Erickson. Bilingual journal for persons interested in French literature (educators, critics). Quarterly, 95 to 100 pages, (8¾x6). Established in 1961. Circulation: 1,250. Acquires all rights, but will reassign rights to author after publication. Uses about 30 mss a year. Payment in 5 contributor's copies. Will send sample copy to writer for $2.25. Prefers the *MLA Style Sheet* style. "All issues are devoted to special subjects, though we print book reviews and review articles of critical works that do not correspond to the issue subject. Please note subjects of coming issues, listed in each issue. Submit July 1 for spring issue, Oct. 1 for summer issue, Feb. 1 for fall issue, and April 1 for winter issue." Reports within 3 to 6 months. Query first or submit complete ms. Enclose S.A.S.E.
Nonfiction: "Criticism of French literature centered on a particular theme each issue; interviews with French writers or critics that appear irregularly; book reviews of critical works on French literature. Critical studies of whatever methodological persuasion that observe the primacy of the text. We notice a bit too much emphasis on extra-literary matters and a failure to note the special issues scheduled. Interested in new critical practices in France. We prefer articles that are direct, honest, avoid pedantry, respect the integrity of the literary work and have something intelligent to say." Length: 12 to 15 double-spaced typed pages, or 3,500 to 4,000 words.

LETTERS, Mainspring Press, Box 82, Stonington ME 04681. (207)367-2484. Editor-in-Chief: Helen Nash. For general literary audience. Quarterly magazine; 4-10 pages. Estab: 1972. Circ: 6,500. Pays on acceptance. Buys all rights. Submit seasonal/holiday material 5 months in advance. Simultaneous and photocopied submissions OK. SASE. Reports in 1 month. Free sample copy.
Nonfiction: "Any subject within moral standards and with quality writing style." Query. Length: 100-500 words. Pays 5¢/word.
Fiction: No porno or confession and no religious or western. Buys 5 mss/year. Query. Pays 5¢/word.
Poetry: G.F. Bush, Poetry Editor. Avant-garde, free verse, haiku, light verse, traditional, blank verse, humorous and narrative. Buys 15/year. Length: 30-42 lines. Pays $1/line maximum.

LITERARY REVIEW, Fairleigh Dickinson University, 285 Madison Ave., Madison NJ 07940. (201)377-4050. Editors: Martin Green, Harry Keyishian. For international literary audience, largely libraries, academic readers and other poets and writers. Quarterly magazine; 100 pages. Estab: 1956. Circ: 1,000. Pays in copies. Acquires first North American serial rights.

Phone queries OK. Photocopied submissions OK. Reports in 2-3 months. Sample copy $2; free writer's guidelines.
Nonfiction: Literary criticism on contemporary American and world literature; themes, authors and movements aimed at non-specialist audience. Uses 2-3 mss/issue.
Fiction: Experimental or traditional. "We seek high literary stories, not slick types." Uses 3-4/issue.
Poetry: Avant-garde, free verse and traditional. Buys 5-10/issue.

LITERARY SKETCHES, P.O. Box 711, Williamsburg VA 23185. (804)229-2901. Editor: Mary Lewis Chapman. For readers with literary interests; all ages. Monthly magazine; 16 pages. Estab: 1961. Circ: 500. Not copyrighted. Buys about 24 mss a year. Pays on publication. Will send free sample copy to writer on request, if a stamped, self-addressed envelope is enclosed. Will consider photocopied and simultaneous submissions. Reports in 1 month. Submit complete ms. Enclose S.A.S.E.
Nonfiction: "We use only interviews of well-known writers and biographical material on past writers. Very informal style; concise. Centennial or bicentennial pieces relating to a writer's birth, death, or famous works are usually interesting. Look up births of literary figures and start from there." Length: 1,000 words maximum. Pays ½¢ per word.

LONG ISLAND REVIEW, 360 W. 21st St., New York NY 10011. Editors: Stephen Sossaman and Edward Faranda. For those interested in contemporary literature and criticism. Biased only toward the well-crafted and intelligent. Semiannual magazine. Estab: 1973. Circ: 500. Acquires first or second (reprint) serial rights; all rights are returned to author. Payment in contributor's copies. Will consider photocopied submissions. "We're open to new writers, but send a cover letter telling us who you are. We advise writer to see a sample issue first." Will send sample copy to writers for $1. Uses 50 mss a year. Reports in 4 to 5 weeks. Enclose S.A.S.E.
Nonfiction: Literary criticism and articles on literature as craft or as art; psychology of the creative process; sociology of literary forms; any length. Book reviews to about 800 words. Seeks articles for occasional special issues which are announced in the magazine.
Fiction: Experimental or traditional. Length: 3,500 words maximum.
Poetry: Any form, style, or length, but content or message cannot make up for deficiencies in language. Poetry as social criticism, and poetry by Vietnam veterans.

LOOK QUICK, Quick Books, Box 4434, Boulder CO 80306. Editor-in-Chief: R. Rubinstein. Poetry magazine published irregularly; 28 pages. Estab: 1975. Circ: 500. Pays in copies. Acquires first North American serial rights. SASE. Reports in 1 month. Sample copy $1.
Poetry: Avant-garde, free verse, haiku, light verse, traditional and blues lyrics. Uses 20 poems/issue.

MARK TWAIN JOURNAL, Kirkwood MO 63122. Editor: Cyril Clemens. For those interested in American and English literature. Semiannual magazine. Estab: 1936. Not copyrighted. SASE. Sample copy $1. Pays in contributor's copies. Reports in 2 weeks. "Queries welcome."
Nonfiction: Critical and biographical articles dealing with Mark Twain and other American, English, and foreign authors.

THE MARKHAM REVIEW, Horrmann Library, Wagner College, Staten Island NY 10301. (212)390-3000. Editor: Joseph W. Slade. For academics; specialists in American culture. Newsletter; 20 pages. Established in 1968. Quarterly. Circulation: 1,000. Rights purchased vary with author and material. Usually buys all rights, but may reassign rights to author after publication. Buys 15 to 20 mss a year. Pays in contributor's copies. Will send free sample copy to writer on request. No photocopied or simultaneous submissions. Reports in 4 weeks. Query first or submit complete ms. Enclose S.A.S.E.
Nonfiction: Inter-disciplinary treatments of any aspect of American culture between 1965 and 1940. Scholarly approach following *MLA* style. Does not want articles on Henry James or Ernest Hemingway or other major writers. Would consider material on the history of science and technology. Length: 6,000 words maximum.

THE MASSACHUSETTS REVIEW, Memorial Hall, University of Massachusetts, Amherst MA 01002. Editors: Lee R. Edwards, Mary T. Heath, John Hicks, and Robert Tucker. Quarterly. Buys first North American serial rights. Pays on publication. Reports promptly. Enclose S.A.S.E.
Nonfiction: Articles on literary criticism, women, public affairs, art, philosophy, music, dance. Average length: 6,500 words. Pays $50.

Fiction: Short stories or chapters from novels when suitable for independent publication. Pays $50.

MICHIGAN QUARTERLY REVIEW, 3032 Rackham Bldg., University of Michigan, Ann Arbor MI 48109. Editor: Radcliffe Squires. Quarterly. Circulation: 2,000. Buys all rights. Payment on acceptance. Reports in 4 weeks. Enclose S.A.S.E.
Nonfiction: "We are open to general articles directed at an intellectual audience. We especially welcome serious criticism in the field of the humanities." Length: 2,000 to 5,000 words. Payment is 2¢ a word (occasionally $100 to $300).
Fiction and Poetry: "No restrictions on subject matter or language. Experimental fiction welcomed." Length: 2,000 to 5,000 words. Payment is 2¢ a word (occasionally $200 to $300). Pays 50¢ to $1 a line for poetry.

THE MIDWEST QUARTERLY, Kansas State College of Pittsburg, Pittsburg KS 66762. (316)231-7000. Editor: V. J. Emmett, Jr. Pubblished "for an educated adult audience interested in contemporary thought in a variety of scholarly disciplines." Magazine; 100 pages. July issue is all literary analysis. Established in 1959. Quarterly. Circulation: 1,000. Acquires all rights, but may reassign rights to author after publication. Uses 24 articles; 48 poems per year. Payment in contributor's copies. Will send free sample copy to writer on request. Will consider photocopied submissions. No simultaneous submissions. Submit seasonal material 6 to 9 months in advance. Reports in 3 months for prose; 6 months for verse. Enclose S.A.S.E.
Nonfiction and Poetry: "Literary analysis, history, social sciences, art, musicology, natural science in nontechnical language. Write standard literary English without jargon or pedantry. No footnotes, minimum parenthetical documentation and a short bibliography. We do not use fiction. Would like to see more history and social science." Length: 3,500 to 5,000 words. Publishes traditional forms of poetry, blank verse, free verse, avant-garde forms and haiku. Subject: open. Length: 4 to 200 lines. Poetry Editor: Michael Heffernan.

MISSISSIPPI REVIEW, Center for Writers, University of Southern Mississippi, Box 37, Southern Station, Hattiesburg MS 39401. (601)261-7180. Editor-in-Chief: Bernard Kaplan. For "college students, educated adults, general audiences, libraries, writers." Published 3 times a year, magazine; 120 pages. Estab: 1972. Circ: 300-500. Pays on publication. Buys all rights but may reassign following publication. SASE. Reports in 8-10 weeks. Sample copy $1.75. No submissions in June, July, or August.
Fiction: Jean Todd Freeman, Fiction Editor. Adventure, erotica, fantasy, confession, experimental, historical, humorous, mystery, romance, suspense, condensed novels, mainstream, religious, science fiction, western. Buys 10 mss a year. Submit complete ms. No length requirement. Pays $3/printed page.
Poetry: D.C. Berry, Poetry Editor. Avant-garde, free verse, traditional. Buys 50 a year. Length: 2-1,000 lines. Pays $5.

MISSISSIPPI VALLEY REVIEW, Department of English, Western Illinois University, Macomb IL 61455. Editor: Forrest Robinson. For persons active in creating, teaching, or reading poetry and fiction. Magazine; 64 pages. Established in 1971. Published twice a year. Circulation: 400. "Permission to reprint must be gained from individual authors." Accepts 80 to 100 mss per year. Payment in 2 contributor's copies, plus a copy of the next 2 issues. Will send sample copy to writer for $1.50 plus postage. Will consider "only excellent" photocopied submissions. Will consider simultaneous submissions only if the author "notifies us immediately upon receipt of an acceptance elsewhere. We try to return mss within 3 months. We do not mind writers asking for progress reports if we are a bit late. Allow for no ms reading during summer." Submit complete ms. Enclose S.A.S.E.
Fiction and Poetry: Publishes stories and poems. Not interested in long poems. Tries to provide a range and variety of style and subject matter. "*Writer's Market* guidelines for ms submission suggested. We take pride in trying to help those who are breaking in. Perversion or sensationalism for its own sake holds no interest for us. We publish no articles. We usually solicit our reviews." Fiction Editor: Loren Logsdon. Long poems are discouraged. Length: 2 printed pages, maximum. Poetry Editor: John Mann.

MODERN FICTION STUDIES, Dept. of English, Purdue University, W. Lafayette IN 47907. (317)493-1684. Editors: William T. Stafford and Margaret Church. For students and academic critics and teachers of modern fiction in all modern languages. Quarterly magazine, 140 to 160 pages, (6x9½). Established in 1955. Circulation: 4,500. Acquires all rights, but with written stipulated agreement with author permitting him or her to republish anywhere, any time as long as *MFS* is cited, and splitting 50/50 with him reprints by others of his agreed-to-be-reprinted material. No payment. Reports in 2 to 4 months. "Every other issue is a special issue. See current copy for future topics. Submit material any time before announced deadline for special issue." Enclose S.A.S.E.

Nonfiction: Interested in critical or scholarly articles on American, British, and Continental fiction since 1880. Length: notes, 500 to 2,500 words; articles, 3,000 to 7,000 words.

MOONS AND LION TAILES, Permanent Press, Box 8434, Lake St. Station, Minneapolis MN 55408. (612)377-4384. Editor-in-Chief: H. Schjotz-Christensen. Emphasizes contemporary literature for professional people, teachers, high school and college students. Quarterly magazine; 100 pages. Estab: 1973. Circ: 1,500. Pays on publication. Buys all rights. Submit seasonal/holiday material 2-3 months in advance. SASE. Reports in 2 months. Sample $1.75. Free writer's guidelines.

Nonfiction: Informational (reviews of current poetry publications) and profile (each issue publishes an article or essay on the work on a contemporary poet). Buys 8-10 mss/issue. Query. Length: 800-1,600 words. Pays $15-50.

Photos: Photos purchased on assignment. Pays $10 maximum for b&w photos. No additional payment for photos accepted with accompanying ms.

Columns/Departments: Poets on Poetry. Buys 1-2 mss/issue. Query. Length: 800-1,000 words. Pays $15-50. Open to suggestions for new columns/departments.

Fiction: Experimental. Buys 1-2 mss/issue. Send complete ms. Length: 2,000-5,000 words. Pays in copies for fiction. Buys some translations (pays $15/page).

Poetry: Avant-garde, free verse, haiku; "poetry in free forms preferred." Buys 35-40 poems/issue. Limit submissions to batches of 10. Pays in copies. Buys some translations (pays $15/page).

MOUNTAIN REVIEW, Box 660, Whitesburg KY 41858. (606)633-4811. Editor: Betty Edwards. For Appalachians of all ages and backgrounds and others interested in life in the mountains. Magazine; 48 pages. Established in 1974. Quarterly. Circulation: 500. Acquires all rights, but may reassign rights to author after publication. Uses about 50 mss a year. No payment. Will send sample copy to writer for $1.50. Will consider photocopied submissions. No simultaneous submissions. Submit seasonal material (spring, summer, fall, winter) 4 months in advance. Reports on material accepted for publication in 1 month. Returns rejected material in 1 to 3 months. Query first or submit complete ms. Enclose S.A.S.E.

Nonfiction and Photos: "We publish articles, preferably by mountain people, about some aspect of life in the mountains; life — not repetitions of old stereotypes. The material we choose deals with Appalachia, but in a fresh (often surprising) way." Personal experience, interview, historical, think pieces, expose, nostalgia, personal opinion articles and reviews of books about the mountains. Length: open. B&w glossies used with or without mss.

Fiction and Poetry: Open to all writing by Appalachian writers, including, but not limited to, themes that deal with some aspect of mountain life. Traditional and avant-garde forms of poetry, blank verse, free verse, haiku.

MOUNTAIN SUMMER, Glen Antrim, Sewanee TN 37375. (615)595-5931 Ext. 665. Editor: Don Keck DuPree. For literary, college and university audience. Established in 1972. Published annually. Circulation: 1,000. Acquires all rights, but may reassign rights to author after publication. Uses 12 to 16 mss per year. Pays in contributor's copies. Will send sample copy to writer for $1.50. Will consider photocopied and simultaneous submissions. Reports in 2 to 4 weeks. Enclose S.A.S.E.

Poetry and Nonfiction: "We publish material which shows an interest in traditional English forms." Likes "good sound material." Poetry and essays. Preferred submission time: March 15 to July 15. Length for poetry: 4 to 48 lines.

MOVING OUT, Wayne State University, 4866 3rd, Detroit MI 48202. (313)577-3355. Editors: Margaret Kaminsk and Gloria Dyc. Feminist literary and arts journal for college and career women and others interested in women's studies and writing. Magazine; 2 times a year; 50 pages. Estab: 1971. Circ: 800. Pays in contributor's copies. Acquires all rights, but may reassign following publication. Phone queries OK. Simultaneous and photocopied submissions OK. SASE. Reports in 3-6 months. Sample copy $1.25. Writer's guidelines for 13¢ stamp.

Nonfiction: Literary criticism (not too academic in style); reviews of women's books; magazines, records or film reviews of interest to women. Historical (papers on famous women writers, artists, etc.). Interviews and personal experience (diary excerpts). Photo features (portfolios of fine art photography or artwork, graphics, paintings, etc.); uses 1/issue. Query or submit complete ms. Length: about 20 pages.

Fiction: Must be related to women's experience. Also uses novel excerpts. Query or submit complete ms. Length: 20 pages.
Poetry: Free verse, haiku, prose poems, feminist poetry.

MUNDUS ARTIUM, A Journal of International Literature and the Arts, University of Texas at Dallas, Box 688, Richardson TX 75080. Editor: Rainer Schulte. For all levels except the scholarly, footnote-starved type. Semiannual magazine; 160 pages. Estab: 1967. Circ: 2,000. Buys all rights, but will reassign rights to author after publication. Buys about 50 mss a year. Pays on publication. Will send sample copy to writer for $3. Will consider photocopied submissions. No simultaneous submissions. Reports in 30 days. Submit complete ms. Enclose S.A.S.E.
Nonfiction and Photos: "In articles, we look for people who are able to talk about our nontraditional, conceptual kind of orientation from a broad, esthetic point of view. We like interdisciplinary emphasis. We don't want scholarly articles, kitsch, or social-political material, or descriptive, representational work." Length: open. Pays $15 to $100. Only avant-garde photography is acceptable.
Fiction: Experimental and fantasy. Must be non-traditional and conceptual. Length: open. Pays minimum of $5 per page.
Poetry: Avant-garde forms. Prefers to publish young, outstanding poets from the international and American scene who, as yet, are unrecognized. Pays minimum of $5 per page.
How To Break In: "Since we have a bilingual format, translations of contemporary international poets is a good way. Otherwise, creative work which goes beyond description and regional, national restrictions."

NATCHEZ TRACE LITERARY REVIEW, The Bluff Press, Box 6945, Jackson MS 39212. Editor-in-Chief: Rosalie Daniels. Emphasizes poetry and fiction. For an educated, literary audience. Semiannual magazine; 16-20 pages. Estab: 1976. Circ: 200. Pays on acceptance. Acquires all rights. Submit seasonal/holiday material 3 months in advance. SASE. Reports in 2 months. Sample copy $2; writer's guidelines $2.
Fiction: Experimental. Buys 3 mss/issue. Send complete ms. Length: 3,000-3,500 words. Pays in copies.
Poetry: Avant-garde, free verse, haiku and traditional. Buys 14 poems/issue. Limit submissions to batches of 2. Pays in copies.

NEBULA, 970 Copeland St., North Bay, Ontario, Canada P1B 3E4. (705)472-5127. Editor-in-Chief: Ken Stange. Managing Editor: Ursula Stange. Emphasizes literature for an intellectually sophisticated readership. Semiannual magazine; 88 pages. Estab: 1974. Circ: 500. Pays on publication in copies and grants. Buys first North American serial rights. Phone queries OK. SAE and International Reply Coupons. Reports in 5 weeks. Sample copy and writer's guidelines $1.00.
Nonfiction: Interview (with literary figures); and personal opinion (critical essays). Submit complete ms.
Fiction: Erotica; experimental; fantasy; mainstream and science fiction. Submit complete ms.
Poetry: Quality poetry of all kinds. Limit submissions to batches of 5. Length: 1-50 lines.
How To Break In: We do thematic issues, the themes announced in preceeding issues, so a would-be contributor is advised to send for a recent sample. Seeing the type of material we publish generally and learning what specific themes we will be exploring in future issues is the best guide to any writer considering our publication.
Rejects: "We are very tired of receiving submissions from the states where the return postage affixed to the return envelope is American. Canada is a separate country and has its own postal system. Canadian postage or International Reply Coupons should accompany submissions."

NEW BOSTON REVIEW, 77 Sacramento St., Somerville MA 02143. (617)547-1878. Editors: Gail Pool and J. M. Alonso. For "people interested in arts." Magazine; 36 pages. Established in 1975. Quarterly. Circulation: 12,000. Acquires all rights, but may reassign rights to author after publication. Accepts about 20 lss per year. No payment. Will send sample copy to writer for $1. Will consider photocopied and simultaneous submissions. Reports in 4 months. Enclose S.A.S.E.
Nonfiction, Fiction and Poetry: Critical essays, interviews, book reviews, reviews of classical records. Length: 3,000 to 6,000 words for interviews; 600 to 1,500 words for reviews; 500 to 5,000 words for experimental and mainstream fiction; 1,000 to 5,000 words for serialized novels. Poetry. Length: 10 to 40 lines.

THE NEW ENGLAND QUARTERLY, Hubbard Hall, Brunswick ME 04011. (207)725-8731, Ext. 289. Managing Editor: Herbert Brown. For historians and scholars. Established in 1928. Quarterly. Acquires all rights. Does not pay. Usually reports in 4 weeks. Enclose S.A.S.E. for return of submissions.
Nonfiction: Wants scholarly articles on New England life and letters. Length: "essays should be limited to 25 pages, including documentation."

THE NEW INFINITY REVIEW, Box 412, South Point OH 45680. (614)377-4182. Editor: James R. Pack. Manuscript Editor: Ron Houchin. For the lovers of new writing with "pizzazz and verve." Quarterly magazine; 48 pages. Estab: 1969. Circ: 500. Acquires North American serial rights. Pays in copies. "We feature one writer in every issue." Free sample copy and writer's guidelines. Photocopied submissions OK "if readable." All submissions should be accompanied by a brief autobiography, stressing the individual and his/her unique personality, and including current activities and publication credits. Reports in 4 weeks. SASE.
Nonfiction and Photos: Essays and articles on literature, drama and art. Articles on psychic phenomena and the occult, myths and legends, and human sociology. Length: 3,000 words maximum. Accompanying photos or illustrations are welcome.
Fiction: "We publish stories that are mentally exciting. Mystery, science fiction and fantasy find an eager eye." Length: 4,000 words maximum.
Poetry: "Submit 4-12 poems to give us a clear perspective of your talent. Free verse, experimental or avant-garde forms welcome with the exception of pointless obscenity. We encourage all poetry approaching the visual. Above all, we seek poetry with honest vision and a clear, natural voice. No length limit."
How To Break In: "We especially need good short fiction, 3-6 pages, that deals with the new and the strange."

NEW ORLEANS REVIEW, Loyola University, New Orleans LA 70118. (504)865-2294. Editor: Marcus Smith. Editorial Associate: Christina Ogden. For anyone interested in literature and culture. Quarterly magazine, 96 pages, (9x13). Established in 1968. Circulation: 1,500. Buys all rights, but will reassign rights to author after publication, on request. Buys 200 mss a year. Payment on publication. Will send sample copy to writer for $1.50. Write for copy of editorial guidelines for writers. Will consider photocopied submissions. Query first or submit complete ms. Study a current issue before submitting material. Reports in 2 weeks to 2 months. Enclose S.A.S.E.
Nonfiction: Articles Editor: Peter Cangelosi. Book Review Editor: C.J. McNaspy. General interest articles. Culture. Avoid too specialized literary analyses. Likes ecology, economics, current political topics. Informational, interview, profile, historical, think articles, personal opinion, and book reviews. Length: 5,000 to 10,000 words. Pays $50. Regular column, Perspective, uses multiple book review with unifying topic. Length: 3,000 words. Pays $25.
Photos: 8x10 glossies purchased with or without ms. Pays $10 for single photos; $75 for portfolios.
Fiction and Poetry: Department Editors: Dawson Gaillard (fiction); Shael Herman (poetry). High quality fiction, any themes. Experimental and mainstream. Length: 5,000 to 10,000 words. Pays $50. Highest quality poetry. Length: 2 to 100 lines. Pays $10.

THE NEW YORK CULTURE REVIEW, 128 E. 4th St., New York NY 10003. Editor: Daniel M. J. Stokes. Monthly newsletter. Established in 1974. Circulation: 2,000. Buys first North American serial rights. Pays on publication. Will send sample copy to writer for $1. Write for copy of guidelines for writers. Reports within 1 month. Submit complete ms. Enclose S.A.S.E.
Nonfiction: Anything that will interest a culturally alive person; publishing, painting, interviews with people in the arts, science, politics, drama, literary criticism, ecology. Informational, profile, exposes, personal opinion, book, theatre and music reviews. Length: 500 to 2,500 words. Pays ½¢ to 5¢ a word. Contributor's copies are the only payment for reviews.
Fiction and Poetry: Experimental, mainstream, fantasy and science fiction. Length: 500 to 3,000 words. Pays ½¢ to 5¢ a word. Blank verse, free verse, avant-garde and concrete forms of poetry. Pays 20¢ a line; $10 maximum.

THE NEW YORK TIMES BOOK REVIEW, 229 West 43rd St., New York NY 10036. Editor: Harvey Shapiro. Weekly.
Nonfiction: "Occasional book reviews and essays. Almost all reviewing is done on an assignment basis."

NEWSART, 5 Beekman St., New York NY 10038. Editor: Harry Smith. Newspaper. Established in 1974. Published 2 times a year, as a supplement to *The Smith.* Circulation: 5,000.

Buys first rights. Buys 50 to 100 mss per year. Pays on acceptance. Will send sample copy to writer for $1. Will consider photocopied and simultaneous submissions. Reports in 4 weeks. Query first for nonfiction. Submit complete ms for fiction and poetry. Enclose S.A.S.E.

Nonfiction, Fiction and Poetry: Essays, book reviews, humor, interviews. Pays $15 minimum for nonfiction. Fiction "should be reasonably short for newspaper format — newsy element helpful." Pays $15 minimum for fiction. Poetry should be short, though occasional longer poems are used. Pays $5 for poetry.

Photos: Purchased with accompanying ms with extra payment and purchased without accompanying ms. B&w only. "8x10 best but not exclusively used." Pay: open.

NIMROD, University of Tulsa, 600 South College, Tulsa OK 74104. (918)939-6351. Editor: Francine Ringold. For readers and writers interested in good literature and art. Semiannual magazine; 96 (6x9) pages. Established in 1955. Circulation: 1,000. Acquires all rights but will return rights to author on request. Payment in contributor's copies and $5/page when funds are available. Will consider photocopied submissions, but they must be very clear. No simultaneous submissions. Reports in 3 to 6 months. Query first or submit complete ms. Enclose S.A.S.E.

Nonfiction: Interviews and essays. Length: open.

Fiction and Poetry: Experimental and mainstream fiction. Traditional forms of poetry; blank verse, free verse and avant-garde forms. "We are interested in quality and vigor. We often do special issues. Writers should watch for announced themes and/or query."

NITTY-GRITTY, Goldermood Rainbow Publisher, 331 W. Bonneville, Pasco WA 99301. (509)547-5525. Editor-in-Chief: W.R. Wilkins. Each issue has a "tool-theme" subject. Triannual magazine; 100 pages. Estab: 1975. Circ: 3,000. Pays on acceptance. Buys all rights, but may reassign following publication. Submit seasonal/holiday material 2 months in advance. Simultaneous and photocopied submissions OK. SASE. Reports in 2 months. Sample copy $4; free writer's guidelines.

Nonfiction: Humor; interview; personal experience; personal opinion and profile. Buys 60-70 mss/issue. Send complete ms. Length: 100-3,000 words. Pays $2-15.

Fiction: Adventure; experimental, fantasy, historical; humorous; mainstream; mystery; romance; science fiction and suspense. Send complete ms. Length: 1,000-10,000 words. Pays $15 minimum.

Poetry: Free verse. Buys 50 poems/issue. Limit submissions to batches of 4. Length: 100 lines maximum. Pays $2.

Fillers: Clippings, jokes, gags, anecdotes and short humor. Buys 20 fillers/issue. Length: 50-1,000 words. Pays $2-15.

NORTH AMERICAN MENTOR MAGAZINE, 1745 Madison St., Fennimore WI 53809. (608)822-6237. Editors: John Westburg, Mildred Westburg. For "largely mature readers, above average in education, most being fairly well-to-do; many being retired persons over 60; college personnel and professional writers or aspirants to being professional." Quarterly. Acquires all rights, but may reassign rights to author after publication. Payment in contributor's copies. Sample copy $1. Photocopied and simultaneous submissions OK. Reports in 1 week to 6 months. Enclose S.A.S.E. for return of submissions.

Nonfiction: "Desire writing to be in reasonably good taste; traditional is preferable to the vulgar, but emphasis should be on creativity or scholarship. I know of no other of the small magazine genre that is like this one. We make no claim to being avant-garde, but have been accused of being a rear guard periodical, for we try to follow the general traditions of western civilization (whatever that might be). Would be interested in readable articles on anthropology, archaeology, American Indians, black or white Africa. Do not want vulgarity or overworked sensationalism. No stuff on riots, protests, drugs, obscenity, or treason. We do not want to discourage a writer's experimental efforts. Let the writer send what he thinks best in his best style. Study a current issue first, though." Length: "maximum about 5,000 words."

Photos: "Please make inquiry about photographs in advance. We like to use them if they can be reproduced on multilith offset masters."

Fiction: "Short stories should have a plot, action, significance, and depth of thought, elevating rather than depressing; would be glad to get something on the order of Dickens, Thackeray or Dostoyevsky rather than Malamud, Vidal or Bellow. Sustained wit without sarcasm would be welcome; propaganda pieces unwelcome." Length: 1,000 to 4,000 words.

Poetry: Accepts traditional, blank and free verse, avant-garde forms and light verse. "Poetry from many cultures." Length: 50 lines maximum.

THE NORTH AMERICAN REVIEW, University of Northern Iowa, Cedar Falls IA 50613. (319)273-2681. Editor: Robley Wilson, Jr. Quarterly. Circulation: 3,000. Buys all rights for nonfiction and North American serial rights for fiction and poetry. Pays on publication. Will send sample copy for $1. Familiarity with magazine helpful. Reports in 8 to 10 weeks. Query first for nonfiction. Enclose S.A.S.E.

Nonfiction: No restrictions, but most nonfiction is commissioned by magazine. Rate of payment arranged.

Fiction: No restrictions; highest quality only. Length: open. Pays minimum $10 per page.

Poetry: Department Editor: Peter Cooley. No restrictions; highest quality only. Length: open. Pays 50¢ per line minimum.

NORTHWEST REVIEW, 369 P.L.C., University of Oregon, Eugene OR 97403. (503)686-3957. Editor-in-Chief: Michael Strelow. For literate readership whether university or non-university. "We have one issue per year with Northwest emphasis, the other two are of general interest to those who follow American/world poetry and fiction." Published 3 times/year; 130 pages. Estab: 1958. Circ: 1,000. Pays on publication in copies. Buys all rights, but may reassign rights to author following publication. Phone queries OK. Submit seasonal/holiday material 6 months in advance. Photocopied submissions OK. SASE. Reports in 6-8 weeks. Sample copy $1.50. Free writer's guidelines.

Photos: Purchased without accompanying manuscript. Send prints. Pays $5 maximum per b&w. Total price for ms includes payment for photos.

Fiction: Christine McQuitty, Fiction Editor. All types. Buys 5 mss/issue. Send complete ms.

Poetry: John Ackerson, Poetry Editor. Buys 30-35 poems/issue. Limit submissions to batches of 10-15. Pays $5 minimum.

NORTHWOODS JOURNAL, A Magazine for Writers, R.D. #1, Meadows of Dan VA 24120. (703)952-2388. Editor-in-Chief: Robert W. Olmstead. Readers are all writers. Monthly (except summer and January) magazine; 35-52 pages. Estab: 1972. Circ: 2,000. Pays on acceptance. Buys all rights. Submit seasonal or holiday material 4-6 months in advance. Reports in 4 weeks. Sample copy 25¢.

Nonfiction: Expose (about writing con games); historical; how-to; humor; informational; interview; nostalgia; personal opinion; profile; technical (as pertains to small press publishing only). Buys 1-2 mss/issue. Submit complete ms. Length: 400-2,400 words. Pays $5-40.

Photos: Purchased with accompanying ms. Captions required. Query. Pays $5-25 for 8x10 b&w photos. Total purchase price for ms includes payment for photos. Model release required.

Columns/Departments: Paul Hodges, Review Editor. Reviews (small press and self-published books only). Submit complete ms. Length: 100-1,000 words. Pays $1-4. Open to suggestions for new columns/departments.

Fiction: "Anything that is superb." Buys 8 mss/year. Submit complete ms. Length: 500-5,000 words. Pays $5-25.

Poetry: Avant-garde; free verse; haiku; and traditional. Buys 80/year. Pays 50¢-$3.

THE NOTEBOOK & OTHER REVIEWS, The Notebook Press, Box 180, Birmingham MI 48012. Editor-in-Chief: Michael O'Neill. Emphasizes the arts, literature and humanities (and "intelligent writing"). Magazine, published 10 times yearly; 32 pages. Estab: 1975. Circ: 300. Pays on acceptance. Buys all rights. Submit seasonal/holiday material 6 months in advance. Photocopied submissions OK. SASE. Reports in 2-4 weeks. Sample copy 75¢.

Nonfiction: Humor; interview and personal opinion. Buys 1-2 mss/issue. Query. Length: 400-4,000 words. Pays $10-50.

Photos: Photos purchased without accompanying ms. Pays $5-10 for 5½x8½ b&w glossies. Send contact sheet. Model release required.

Columns/Departments: Reviews (new books); Reports (a look at various publications) and Hindsight (reviews of previous issue by readers). Buys 3 mss/issue. Query. Length: 250-1500 words. Pays $5-25. Open to suggestions for new columns/departments.

Fiction: Rottinger McTaggert, Fiction Editor. Experimental, humorous; mainstream; mystery and suspense. Buys 1 ms/issue. Send complete ms. Length: 750-4,000 words. Pays $5-100.

Poetry: Avant-garde, free verse, light verse and traditional. Buys 5/issue. Pays $1-25.

Fillers: Clippings, jokes, gags, anecdotes, newsbreaks, and short humor. Buys 5/year. Length: 25-250 words. Pays $1-5.

THE OHIO JOURNAL, A Magazine of Literature and the Visual Arts, Department of English, Ohio State University, 164 W. 17th Ave., Columbus OH 43210. Editor: William Allen. Magazine; 3 times a year. Estab: 1972. Circ: 1,250. Pays in contributor's copies. Acquires all rights, but will reassign rights following publication. Photocopied and simultaneous submissions OK. SASE. Reports in 6 weeks.

Nonfiction and Photos: Material of interest to an audience knowledgeable of literature and the arts, but not of an academic nature. Interviews and photo essays welcome. No color reproductions.

Fiction and Poetry: Gordon Grigsby, Poetry Editor. No restrictions as to category or type. Maximum length for fiction: 10,000 words.

THE OHIO REVIEW, Ellis Hall, Ohio University, Athens OH 45701. (614)594-5889. Editors: Wayne Dodd, S.W. Lindberg. For the general, educated reader. Published 3 times yearly. Established in 1959. Circulation: 1,000. Rights acquired vary with author and material. Acquires all rights or first North American serial rights. Will send sample copy to writer for $2. Submit complete ms. Unsolicited material will be read only September-June. Reports in 6 to 8 weeks. Enclose S.A.S.E.

Nonfiction, Fiction, and Poetry: Buys essays of general intellectual appeal. Not interested in narrowly focused scholarly articles. Seeks writing that is marked by clarity, liveliness, and perspective. Buys only excellent fiction and poetry. Pays minimum $5 a page, plus copies.

OHIOANA QUARTERLY, Martha Kinney Cooper Ohioana Library, 65 S. Front St., 1105 Ohio Departments Bldg., Columbus OH 43215. (614)466-3831. Editor-in-Chief: Bernice Williams Foley. Quarterly magazine; 60 pages. Estab: 1943. Circ: 1,800. No payment. Phone queries OK. Reports in 2 days.

Nonfiction: "Limited to articles about Ohio authors and current book reviews; or articles by published Ohio authors." Query. Length: 500-1,000 words.

OMEGA, 145 E. Main St., Cambridge NY 12816. Editor: J. Geoffrey Jones. For "people interested in literature and art in a permanent way; collectors of literary rarities." Magazine; 30 pages. Established in 1975. Published irregularly. Circulation: 1,000. Acquires first serial rights. Uses 40 mss a year. Payment in contributor's copies. Will send sample copy to writer for $2. Reports in 4 weeks. Query first for nonfiction. Submit complete ms for fiction and poetry. Enclose S.A.S.E.

Nonfiction, Fiction and Poetry: "*Omega* is the voice of the Graycroft Press, founded in memory of Elbert Hubbard's Roycroft Press. We are concerned with printing as a permanent art form and enjoy combining high quality literature with high quality format. All the type is set by hand and the sheets hand-pulled from an 1890 press. *Omega* wishes to explore the work of well-known creators in areas not as often noticed (see Vol. 1, No. 1, 'Ray Bradbury As Poet'). We also wish to bring light to gifted unknowns, and forgotten writers of importance. We publish articles, short stories and serious poetry, which must be clear and without contrived obscurity."

OPINION, P.O. Box 1885, Rockford IL 61110. Editors: Dr. James E. Kurtz and Sue Northrup. For readers from 18 and older; people who have an appetite for invigorating, inspiring, thought-provoking articles. Numerous teachers, clergymen, and professional people. Monthly magazine, 16 (8½x11) pages. Established in 1957. Circulation: 3,700. Not copyrighted. Uses about 38 mss a year. Pays in contributor's copies. Will send sample copy to writer for 30¢. Will consider photocopied submissions and simultaneous submissions. Submit complete ms. Reports in 3 to 5 weeks. Enclose S.A.S.E.

Nonfiction: "We publish articles dealing with social problems, philosophical themes, theological studies. Our articles are on current subjects but inspirational as well. Controversy but not just for the sake of being 'different'. Our writers believe in what they write. Be yourself. Take a deep subject and make it simple—don't write down to people but lift people up to a higher level of understanding. *Opinion* is down to earth. We carry some in-depth essays but for the most part we present to our readers, articles that hit the nail on the head. We are informal but we adhere to the old principles of good writing. Articles on marriage problems are a bit heavy and we prefer to see more material on philosophy and theology. Common sense philosophy. Particularly we want articles on religious adventure; new trends, new happenings." Informational, personal experience, profile, inspirational, historical, think articles, expose, nostalgia, personal opinion, spot news, and new product. Length: 1,500 words maximum.

Photos: Uses 5x7 or 8x10 b&w glossies. Captions optional.

Poetry: Traditional forms, free verse and light verse.

OUT THERE MAGAZINE, 552 25th Ave., San Francisco CA 94121. Editor: Stephen M. H. Braitman. For a literary audience with science fiction interests. Quarterly; 25 (8½x11) pages. Established in 1967. Circulation: 1,000. Acquires first North American serial rights. Uses 4 mss a year. Payment in contributor's copies. Will send sample copy to writer for 75¢. Will consider photocopied and simultaneous submissions. Reports in 1 month. Submit complete ms. Enclose S.A.S.E.

Nonfiction: Informational, interview, humor, historical, nostalgia, personal opinion and book and film reviews. Length: 1,500 words.

Fiction: Science fiction and fantasy; anything above the average of "tameness." Must be quality writing; literature, not pulp. Uses experimental, mainstream, mystery, suspense, adventure, erotica, science fiction, fantasy and humorous fiction. Length: 500 to 2,000 words maximum.

Poetry and Fillers: Sci-fi poetry, blank verse, free verse, avant-garde forms; light verse. Length: open. Jokes and relevant short humor used as fillers.

PAINTBRUSH, Comparative Literature, State University of New York, Binghampton NY 13901. (607)758-2319. Editor: B. M. Bennani. For professional and "up-and-coming" writers, college and university groups; teachers. Magazine; 65 (5½x8½) pages. Established in 1974. Semiannually. Circulation: 500. Buys all rights, but may reassign rights to author after publication. Buys about 50 mss a year. Pays on publication. Will send sample copy to writer for $2. No photocopied or simultaneous submissions. Reports in 2 to 4 weeks. Query first for interviews. Enclose S.A.S.E.

Nonfiction and Photos: Criticism, nonscholarly articles, translations from any language. Interviews with known writers and poets. Length: 2,000 to 3,000 words. Book reviews are usually assigned. Length: 300 words maximum. "No soul-searching, back-scratching junk. No book reviews that begin with 'This is a terrific book'. No politically inspired propaganda. Only the best goes." Would like to see work on "popularizing poetry without barbarizing it." Pays $5 per published page. B&w glossies (minimum 3x5) are used only with interviews.

Poetry: "All schools are welcome but, please, no four-letter rhymes or jingles." Traditional forms of poetry, blank verse, free verse, prose poems. Short lyrics preferred; 30 lines maximum. Pays $5 per poem per page.

PANACHE, Box 77, Sunderland MA 01375. Editor-in-Chief: David Lenson. "A small press publication specializing in experimental and other fiction and poetry. For a small but sophisticated audience, by and large educated." Semiannual magazine; 64 pages. Estab: 1965. Circ: 800. Pays on acceptance. Buys all rights, but may reassign following publication. Photocopied submissions OK. SASE. Reports in 6 weeks. Sample copy $1.

Fiction: Robert Steiner, Fiction Editor. Adventure, erotica (of literary quality), fantasy, experimental, historical (if imaginative), humorous, mainstream. Buys 10 mss/year. Submit complete ms. Length: 1-50 pages. Pays $25-100.

Poetry: Avant-garde, free verse. Buys 40/year. Limit submissions to batches of 7. No length requirements. Pays $5-40.

How To Break In: *"Panache* is an eclectic publication belonging to no school or movement, or, better yet, to all schools and movements. We rely on freelance material as a matter of principle, in order to bring to a discriminating audience that which is new and exciting at the grass roots level of American literature. In addition, we are also interested in poetry translations, line drawings, and word-pictures."

PARABOLA, 150 Fifth Ave., New York NY 10011. Editors: John Loudon and James Odell. "Audience is educated, and shares a fascination with the mythopoeic process." Magazine; 96 (7x10) pages. Established in 1974. Quarterly. Circulation: 10,000. Rights purchased vary with author and material. Usually buys all rights, but will reassign rights to author after publication; first North American serial rights; or second serial (reprint) rights. Buys about 24 mss per year. Pays on publication. Free writer's guidelines. Photocopied submissions OK. Reports in 3-5 weeks. Query first or submit complete ms. Enclose S.A.S.E.

Nonfiction: "Handles work from a wide range of perspectives — from comparative religion and anthropology to psychology and literary criticism — but focus rests on the mythic dimensions of the contemporary quest for meaning. Examples: *The Narcissus Myth, Modern Day Gods and Goddesses.* Don't be scholarly, don't footnote, don't be dry. We want fresh approaches to timeless subjects." Length: 5,000 words maximum. Pays $25 to $150. Length preferred for regular columns: 750 words for short reviews or 3,000 words for major review essay.

Photos and Fiction: Purchased with accompanying ms with extra payment or purchased without accompanying ms. No color. Pays about $25. Prefers traditional stories, legends, myths, etc., or modern teaching stories (a la John Gardner or Isaac Singer). Length for fiction: 1,500 to 5,000 words. Payment: negotiable.

How To Break In: "Send a readable, substantial article in the area of myth, comparative religion, the quest for meaning."

THE PARIS REVIEW, 45-39 171 Place, Flushing NY 11358. Editor: George A. Plimpton. Quarterly. Buys all rights. Pays on publication. Address submissions to proper department. Enclose S.A.S.E. for return of submissions.
Fiction: Study publication. No length limit. Pays up to $150. Fiction should be sent to Flushing office. Makes award of $500 in annual fiction contest.
Poetry: Study publication. Pays $10 to 25 lines; $15 to 50 lines; $25 to 100 lines; $50 thereafter. Poetry mss must be submitted to Michael Benedikt at 541 E. 72nd St., New York NY 10021.

THE PENNY DREADFUL, c/o The Department of English, Bowling Green State University, Bowling Green OH 43403. Editors: Robert W. Johnson, Jr. and Michael McCall. Tabloid format. Estab: 1972. Published irregularly. Circulation: 500. "All rights returned to author after publication." Pays in contributor's copies. Will send a sample copy to a writer for 50¢. Reports in 2 weeks. Enclose S.A.S.E. for return of submissions.
Nonfiction, Fiction, Drama and Poetry: The editors encourage submission of poems, fiction, one-act plays, book reviews, interviews, and critical essays. No particular themes. Length: 500 to 3,500 words for fiction and nonfiction; 2 to 120 lines for poetry.

PERFORMING ARTS REVIEW, The Journal of Management and Law of the Arts, 453 Greenwich St., New York NY 10013. Editor: Joseph Taubman. Established in 1970. For lawyers, theater managers, academic libraries in law and arts. Quarterly. Circulation: 2,200. Acquires primary or secondary U.S. or Canadian rights. Payment in contributor's copies (10 to each author). Will send free sample copy to writer on request. Will consider photocopied submissions. Reports in 2 months. Query first. Enclose S.A.S.E.
Nonfiction: "Articles on theater, law-management, and creativity in the arts. Academic outlook; professional tone. Writer should be experienced in the field of entertainment law or the theater (pro or amateur)." Length: 1,000 to 7,000 words.

THE PERSONALIST, School of Philosophy, University of Southern California, Los Angeles CA 90007. Editor: John Hospers. Quarterly. No honorarium. Follow the *MLA Style Sheet.* Put footnotes at end of article. Reports in approximately 4 months. Enclose S.A.S.E. for return of rubmissions.
Nonfiction: Uses critical articles pertaining only to the field of philosophy.

PERSPECTIVES, English Department, West Virginia University, Morgantown WV 26506. (304)293-5525. Editor: Arthur C. Buck. A page of literature, philosophy, and education. Associated with the Charleston *Gazette-Mail State Magazine.* Circ: 110,000. Appears on a space-available basis. Not copyrighted. Space for freelance material is strictly limited. Pays after publication. No sample copies available. Reports in 1 month. Enclose S.A.S.E.
Nonfiction: Short, informal personal essays on literature, philosophy, higher education, and linguistics. Interesting, informal style desired. Preference is given to informational or interpretive essays or essays of personal opinion. Pays on the average of 2¼¢ per word. Length: 500 to 900 words preferred. Longer articles are rarely used. Satire is sometimes used.
Poetry: Length: 30 lines maximum. Any style. No payment. Limit submissions to batches of 3.
Rejects: Seasonal material, formal research or scholarly articles, previously published work, poorly prepared mss, simultaneous submissions, photocopied submissions.

PIERIAN SPRING, Brandon University Press, Brandon University, Brandon, Manitoba, Canada R7A 6A9. Editor: Dr. Robert W. Brockway. For a readership of all ages, predominantly university level, aimed at readers interested in the products of fledgling writers. Published autumn and spring. Magazine; 70-100 pages. Estab: 1969. Circ: 200. Pays in copies. Buys all rights. Submit seasonal/holiday material 3 months in advance. Photocopied and previously published submissions OK. SASE. Reports in 4 weeks. Free sample copy and writer's guidelines.
Nonfiction: Linda West, Articles Editor. Historical; humor; interview; nostalgia; personal experience; personal opinion; photo feature (if brief); profile; inner self-expression. "In general, imaginative, subjective, experimental, observations, vignettes, and memoirs. We are less interested in political or religious writing, not at all in polemics of any kind or crank articles." Uses 4-6 mss/issue. Submit complete ms. Length: 2,000 words maximum.
Photos: Curt Shoultz, Art Editor. "We can publish pen and ink drawings, possibly photography, whatever can be done on university offset press." Captions required. Send b&w prints. "In general, we would be interested in art photos, photography as an art medium."
Fiction: Darlene Perkin, Barbara Farough, Fiction Editors. "Any type of short fiction (up to 2,000 words) or short prose, vignettes, memoirs, etc." Submit complete ms.

Poetry: Frances Spafford, Barbara Farough, Poetry Editors. Avant-garde; free verse; haiku; light verse; traditional. Uses 70/issue. Limit submissions to batches of 5.
How To Break In: "Our publication was founded to provide another outlet for the beginning writer, although we very much welcome poems and brief articles from established writers as well. We publish in order of priority poetry, short short stories, subjective prose such as personal experiences or observations, and fillers."

PIGIRON, Box 237, Youngstown OH 44501. (216)744-2258. Emphasizes literature/art for university and young adult audience. Magazine, published 1-3 times a year; 100 pages. Estab: 1975. Circ: 1,000. Pays on publication. Buys one-time rights. Phone queries OK. Photocopied and previously published submissions OK. SASE. Reports in 6 months. Sample copy $2. Free writer's guidelines.
Photos: Jim Villani, Photo Editor. Photos purchased with or without accompanying ms. Pays $2 minimum for 8½x10-11x14 b&w semigloss photos. Model release required.
Columns/Departments: Jim Villani, Columns/Departments Editor. Fascia (editorial and fictional feature that pursues the role of art and artist in culture. Accent on the process of art rather than the finished product). Buys 20 pages/issue. Query. Pays $2 minimum.
Fiction: Rose Sayre, Fiction Editor. Adventure; experimental; fantasy; humorous; mainstream; science fiction and suspense. Buys 4 mss/issue. Send complete ms. Pays $2 minimum.
How To Break In: "Take great care with minor details; oftentimes a negative decision stems from the writer's negligence. Don't submit fresh mss; allow them to lie dormant for a while and then revise. Don't write materials that are in any way similar to the materials you read."

PLOUGHSHARES, Box 529, Dept. M., Cambridge MA 02139. (617)926-4174. Editor: DeWitt Henry. For "readers of serious contemporary literature; students, educators, adult public." Quarterly magazine; 300 pages. Estab: 1971. Circulation: 3,000. Rights purchased vary with author and material. Usually buys all rights, but may reassign rights to author after publication; or may buy first North American serial rights. Buys 50 to 100 mss per year. Pays on publication. Sample copy $3.50. Will consider photocopied submissions. No simultaneous submissions. Reports in 3 months. Enclose S.A.S.E.
Nonfiction, Poetry and Fiction: "Highest quality poetry, fiction, criticism." Interview and literary essays. Length: 5,000 words maximum. Pays $50. Reviews (assigned). Length: 500 words maximum. Pays $15. Fiction. Experimental and mainstream. Length: #00 to 6,000 words. Pays $5 to $50. Poetry. Buys traditional forms, blank verse, free verse, avant-garde forms. Length: open. Pays $10 per poem.

POETRY AUSTRALIA, South Head Press, 350 Lyons Rd., Five Dock, Sydney NSW 2046. Editor-in-Chief: Grace Perry. Emphasizes poetry. Quarterly magazine; 72 pages. Estab: 1972. Circ: 2,000 (50% in U.S. and Canada). Pays on publication. Buys all rights, but may reassign following publication. Submit seasonal/holiday material 4 months in advance. Photocopied submissions OK. SASE. "International Reply Coupons are rarely enough for ms return. Best to send enough coupons for air letter reply and U.S. surface mail. Prefer photocopies that do not need to be returned." Reports in 3 months. Sample copy $2.
Poetry: Uses all kinds. Buys 32/issue. Limit submissions to batches of 4-6. Length: 7 pages maximum. Pays $8,56/page. New poets appear each issue.

PRAIRIE SCHOONER, Andrews Hall, University of Nebraska, Lincoln NE 68588. Editor: Bernice Slote. Quarterly. Usually acquires all rights, unless author specifies first serial rights only. Small payment, depending on grants, plus copies of the magazine, offprints, and prizes. Reports usually in a month. Enclose S.A.S.E.
Nonfiction: Uses 2 or 3 articles per issue. Subjects of general interest. Seldom prints extremely academic articles. Length: 5,000 words maximum.
Fiction: Uses several stories per issue.
Poetry: Uses 20 to 30 poems in each issue of the magazine. These may be on any subject, in any style. Occasional long poems are used, but the preference is for the shorter length. High quality necessary.

PRISM INTERNATIONAL, Department of Creative Writing, University of British Columbia, Vancouver, B.C., Canada V6T 1W5. Editor-in-Chief: Michael Bullock. Emphasizes contemporary literature, including translations. For university and public libraries, and private subscribers. Semiannual magazine; 200 pages. Estab: 1959. Circ: 1,000. Pays on publication. Buys first North American serial rights. Photocopied submissions OK. SAE and International Reply Coupons. Reports in 10 weeks. Sample copy $2.75.

Fiction: Experimental and fantasy. Buys 12 mss/issue. Send complete ms. Length: 5,000 words maximum. Pays $5/printed page.
Poetry: Avant-garde, free verse and haiku. Buys 60 poems/issue. Limit submissions to batches of 6. Pays $5/printed page.
How To Break In: "Study back issues. The magazine is subtitled, A Journal of Contemporary Literature. Keep this in mind."

PULP, c/o Sage, 720 Greenwich St., 4H, New York NY 10014. Editors: Howard Sage and Regina Vogel. For writers and any persons interested in quality fiction, poetry, art. Quarterly tabloid; 12 pages. Estab: 1975. Circ: 2,000. Acquires all rights, but will reassign rights to author after publication. Payment in contributor's copies. Will send sample copy to writer for 25¢. Will consider photocopied submissions. No simultaneous submissions. Reports in 1 month. Submit complete ms. Enclose S.A.S.E.
Fiction and Poetry: "Fiction topics of human relations (especially intercultural relations)." Experimental fiction and serialized novels. Length: open. "Poems on all topics as long as subject is well handled and control is deft." Traditional and avant-garde forms; free verse. Length: open.

PULP: FICTION & POETRY, P.O. Box 243, Narragansett RI 02882. Editor: Robert E. Moore. For a general, educated audience. Established in 1975. Quarterly. Circulation: 600. Acquires all rights, but will reassign rights to author after publication. Payment in contributor's copies. Will consider photocopied submissions. No simultaneous submissions. Reports on material accepted for publication in 6-8 weeks. Returns rejected material in 4-8 weeks. Submit complete ms. Enclose S.A.S.E.
Fiction and Poetry: Mainstream, mystery, suspense, adventure, fantasy, humorous, historical and science fiction. Will consider serialized novels and continuing sagas. Length: 10,000 words maximum. All forms of poetry. Length: Open — but no one-liners. "Our only criterion is that material be well written and well thought-out."

QUARTET, 1119 Neal Pickett Dr., College Station TX 77840. (713)846-9079. Editor-in-Chief: Richard Hauer Costa. Emphasizes fiction, poetry and nonfiction for a fairly sophisticated collegiate, literary audience; devoting about 40% of issues to Texas writers, culture and materials. Quarterly magazine; 40 pages. Estab: 1962. Circ: 1,000. Buys all rights. SASE. Reports in 6-8 weeks. Sample copy $1.
Fiction: Any subject matter, provided language is in good taste. Stress the integrity of the individual. "We prefer the well-crafted story but will often accept a sensibly experimental story." Length: 2,000-6,000 words.
Poetry: "We have enough poetry on hand for the foreseeable future; no unsolicited poetry until further notice."

QUEEN'S QUARTERLY, Queen's University, Kingston, Ont., Canada. (613)547-2608. Editor: J.K. McSweeney. For well-informed readers both within and beyond Canada. Established in 1893. Quarterly. Buys or acquires first North American serial rights. Pays on publication. "Follow the *MLA Style Sheet* in preparing articles." Deadlines: Spring (January 2); Summer (April 1); Autumn (July 1); Winter (October 1). Reports in 3 weeks. Enclose S.A.E. and International Reply Coupons for return of submissions.
Nonfiction: Articles on literary, social, political, economic, educational and other subjects. "Articles must be well considered and show some distinction of presentation, and should be addressed to the intelligent and well-informed general reader, not to the specialist." Length: about 4,000 words. "We no longer pay for nonfiction but provide 50 free offprints."
Fiction: Short stories. Priority to Canadian authors. Length: 2,000 to 4,000 words. Pays $3 a printed page for fiction.
Poetry: "Shorter poems preferred. Priority to Canadian poets." Pays $10 per poem, regardless of length.

THE REMINGTON REVIEW, 505 Westfield Ave., Elizabeth NJ 07208. Editors: Joseph A. Barbato and Dean Maskevich. Published 2 times a year. All rights revert to author upon publication. Reports as soon as possible. Pays in contributor's copies. Enclose S.A.S.E.
Fiction, Poetry, and Photos: Department Editors: Joseph A. Barbato (fiction); Dean Maskevich (poetry). "A magazine of new writing and graphics; short stories, poems, parts of novels, and art which, we hope, have a spark of life. We will look at quality fiction and poetry of any school, by new as well as established writers. However, we tend to shy away from work that indicates the contributor has just learned how toes freeze when it gets too cold outside. But if you and your work are alive, by all means let us see something. We want to do what we can to bring promising talent and an appreciative audience together." Fiction length: 1,500 to 10,000

words. Poetry length should not exceed 100 lines. Drawings and photos suitable for b&w, offset reproduction.

RENASCENCE, Essays on Values in Literature, Marquette University, Milwaukee WI 53233. Editor: Dr. John D. McCabe. For college teachers of English, French and theology. Quarterly magazine, 56 (7x10) pages. Established in 1949. Circulation: 675. Acquires all rights. Payment in contributor's copies. Submit only complete ms for literary essays. Reports in 4 to 6 weeks. Enclose S.A.S.E.
Nonfiction: Scholarly and critical articles on literary works of the nineteenth century and, especially, of the twentieth century. Primarily devoted to the study of values in literature. Often invites papers on special topics through announcements in its issues. Length: 2,500 to 5,000 words.

REVISTA/REVIEW INTERAMERICANA, G.P.O. Box 3255, San Juan, Puerto Rico 00936. (809)767-4240. Editor: John Zebrowski. For "mostly college graduates and people with higher degrees." Publication of the Inter American University of Puerto Rico. Established in 1971. Quarterly. Circulation: 2,000. Acquires all rights, "but will pay 50% of money received if reprinted or quoted." Uses about 75 mss a year. Payment in reprints (25) mailed to author. Will send a sample copy to a writer on request. Query first or submit complete ms. Will consider photocopied submissions. No simultaneous submissions. Submit seasonal material at least 3 months in advance. Reports in 3 months. Enclose S.A.S.E. for return of submissions or reply to queries.
Nonfiction: "Articles on the level of educated laymen; bilingual. Also book reviews. Multidisciplinary with preference to Puerto Rican and Caribbean and Latin American themes from multidisciplinary approach." Length: maximum 10,000 words. ·
Photos: B&w glossies, 4x5 minimum. Captions required. No color.
Fiction and Poetry: "Bilingual; Spanish or English." Experimental, fantasy, humorous and historical fiction. Blank verse, free verse; experimental, traditional and avant-garde forms of poetry.

ROMANCE PHILOLOGY, University of California, Berkeley CA 94720. Editor: Yakov Malkiel, Department of Linguistics. For college and university professors, including graduate students. Quarterly magazine, 120 pages. Established in 1947. Circulation: 1,200. Copyrighted. No payment. Write for copy of editorial guidelines for writers. Query first. Reports within 6 weeks. Enclose S.A.S.E.
Nonfiction: "Scholarly articles, notes, review articles, book reviews, brief reviews, editorial comments, and technical essays. Examine very carefully some of the recent issues." General linguistics, theory of literature, historical grammar; dialectology, textual criticism applied to older Romance materials.

RUSSIAN LITERATURE TRIQUARTERLY, 2901 Heatherway, Ann Arbor MI 48104. (313)971-2367. Editors: Carl R. and Ellendea Proffer. For "readers of material related to Russian literature and art." Established in 1971. 3 times a year. Circulation: 1,000. Acquires all rights. Uses about 50 mss a year. Except for photographs, payment is made in contributor's copies. Will send sample copy for $5. Query first or submit complete ms. Will consider photocopied and simultaneous submissions. Reports on material in 1 to 2 months. Enclose S.A.S.E.
Nonfiction and Photos: Translations of Russian criticism, bibliographies, parodies, texts and documents from English literature. Critical articles. All in English. Interviews and reviews of Russia-related books. Payment by arrangement for b&w glossies or negatives. "Only requirement is relation of some kind to Russian art, literature."

THE RUSSIAN REVIEW, Hoover Institution, Stanford CA 94305. (415)497-2067. Editor: Terence Emmons. Quarterly journal; 128 pages. Estab: 1941. Circulation: 1,850. Buys all rights, but will reassign rights to author after publication. Buys 2 or 3 mss a year. Pays on acceptance. Will send free sample copy to writer on request. Will consider photocopied submissions. No simultaneous submissions. Reports on material accepted for publication in 4 to 6 weeks. Returns rejected material immediately after decision is made. Query first. Enclose S.A.S.E.
Nonfiction: A forum for work on Russian-American and Soviet-American relations. Uses material of high quality in the fields of Russian history, politics and society, literature and the arts. Personal experience and historical articles. Scholarly reviews. Length: 2,500 to 7,500 words. Pays $50 minimum.

ST. CROIX REVIEW, Religion Society Inc., Box 244, Stillwater MN 55082. Editor-in-Chief: Angus MacDonald. For an audience from college presidents to students. Bimonthly magazine;

48 pages. Estab: 1968. Circ: 2,000. Pays in copies. Buys all rights. Submit seasonal/holiday material 2 months in advance. Simultaneous, photocopied and previously published submissions OK. SASE. Reports in 2 weeks. Free sample copy.

Nonfiction: "Articles must be germane to today's problems." Scholarly, but not pedantic articles on religion and/or society for intelligent and concerned American and foreign audience. Must analyze and evaluate current problems in terms of West European intellectual heritage. Editorial viewpoint is classical liberalism. Length: 5,000 words maximum.

SAINT LOUIS LITERARY SUPPLEMENT, 3523 Itaska St., St. Louis MO 63111. (314)832-0770. Editor-in-Chief: John Heindenry. Emphasizes literature, politics, and the arts. Bimonthly tabloid; 32 pages. Estab: 1976. Circ: 10,000. Pays on acceptance. Buys all rights, but may reassign following publication. Phone queries OK. Submit seasonal/holiday material 2 months in advance. Photocopied submissions OK. SASE. Reports in 2-3 weeks. Free sample copy.

Nonfiction: Informational (or critical piece relating to the arts or literature); interview (mainly with personalities in the arts and literature; in depth); personal experience (a recent example told of a writer's 9-day pilgrimage in Mexico); personal opinion (if well-written and fact-filled); profile; and technical (some musical or philosophical pieces considered). Buys 15 mss/year. Query or submit complete ms. Pays $25-75.

Columns/Departments: Film, Feminist Movement, Law, Book Reviews, Music, Politics, Architecture, and Visual Arts. Buys 5 mss/issue. Pays $25-75. Open to suggestions for new columns/departments.

Fiction: "Any serious fiction; no restrictions in length or kind." Buys 1-2 mss/issue. Query or submit complete ms. Pays $25-75.

Poetry: "Any kind; no restrictions." Buys 3 poems/issue. Pays $5-30.

How To Break In: "The *Literary Supplement* is especially interested in promoting Midwestern arts and culture and welcomes critical opinion, interviews, book reviews on this theme."

SALT LICK PRESS, Box 1064, Quincy IL 62301. Editor-in-Chief: James Haining. Emphasizes literature. Published irregularly; magazine; 68 pages. Estab: 1969. Circ: 1,500. Pays by arrangement. Buys second serial (reprint) rights. Photocopied and previously published submissions OK. SASE. Reports in 2 weeks. Sample copy $2.

Nonfiction: Informational and personal opinion. Send complete ms. Pays $5 minimum.

Photos: Photos purchased with accompanying ms. Pays $5 minimum for b&w matte or glossy prints. Send contact sheet. Total purchase price for ms includes payment for photos.

Fiction: Experimental. Send complete ms. Pays $5 minimum.

Poetry: Open to all types. Limit submissions to batches of 4. Pays $5 minimum.

Fillers: Query. Pays $5 minimum.

SAMISDAT, Box 231, Richford VT 05476. Editor-in-Chief: Merritt Clifton. Emphasizes literature, art and aesthetics for a primarily college-educated audience "alienated from commercial and academic tastes, yet not aligned with the conventional underground either. Highly demanding, most are themselves well published writers with a lifelong commitment to alternative and rebel literature." Monthly magazine; 60-80 pages. Estab: 1973. Circ: 500. Pays in copies on publication. Previously published submissions OK. SASE. Reports in 1 month. Sample copy $1.

Nonfiction: Robin Clifton, Nonfiction Editor. Expose (of commercial publishing practices; corruption in both big and little publishing circles; name names and be accurate); historical (background on little magazine and small pressmanship; contemporary small press criticism within historical context); interview; personal opinion; and profile. Buys 6 mss/year. Send complete ms, "but be familiar with the publication." Length: 1,000-5,000 words.

Fiction: June Kemp, Fiction Editor. Experimental; fantasy; humorous; mainstream; and science fiction. "We do not use mere 'genre' material; give us stories that make us think and rouse our emotions as well as our intellects. No mock Henry James or James Joyce." Uses 50 mss/year. Send complete ms. Length: 500-3,000 words.

Poetry: Avant-garde and free verse. "Read and understand our critical manifesto, *The Pillory Poetics*. We are open to imagism and surrealism, but only so long as the devices make a point and statement beyond themselves." Uses 200 poems/year.

SAN FRANCISCO REVIEW OF BOOKS, 2140 Vallejo St., #10, San Francisco CA 94123. Editor: Ron Nowicki. For a college-educated audience interested in books and publishing. Magazine; 28 (8½x11) pages. Established in 1975. Monthly. Circulation: 10,500. Acquires all rights, but will reassign rights to author after publication. Uses about 24 to 36 mss a year. Payment in contributor's copies and subscription. Will send sample copy to writer for 75¢. No photocopied or simultaneous submissions. Reports on material accepted for publication in 2 to 4 weeks. Returns rejected material in 1 month. Query first for nonfiction; submit complete ms for book reviews and poetry. Enclose S.A.S.E.

Nonfiction: Book reviews; articles about authors, books, and their themes. "No glib, slick writing. Primarily serious; humor occasionally acceptable. No restrictions on language provided it is germane to the book or article." Interviews, profiles, historical and think articles. Length: 1,000 words maximum for reviews; 2,000 words maximum for articles.

SAN JOSE STUDIES, San Jose State University, San Jose CA 95192. (408)277-3460. Editor: Arlene H. Okerlund. For the educated, literate reader. Academic journal; 112 (6x9) pages. Established in 1975. Three times a year; February, May and November. Circulation: 500. Acquires first serial rights. Uses about 40 mss a year. Pays in contributor's copies. Will send sample copy to writer for $3.50. No photocopied or simultaneous submissions. Reports in 2 to 3 months. Submit complete ms. Enclose S.A.S.E.

Nonfiction and Photos: In-depth, erudite discussions of topics in the arts, humanities, sciences, and social sciences. Review essays of authors. Informational, interview, profile, humor. Photo essays can be free-wheeling. "We need more science articles and more in-depth review essays of significant, but little known, contemporary writers." Recently published articles include previously unpublished letters of William James; "Deriddling Tillie Olsen's Writings," "Of Mice and Marshes" and "The Political Odyssey of George D. Herron". Length: 5,000 words maximum. Payment consists of 2 copies of the journal.

Fiction and Poetry: Experimental, mainstream, fantasy, humorous, mystery and science fiction. Length: 5,000 words maximum. Traditional and avant-garde forms of poetry; blank verse and free verse. Themes and length are open.

SCHOLIA SATYRICA, Department of English, University of South Florida, Tampa FL 33620. (813)974-2421. Editor: R. D. Wyly. For professors of English in American universities and scholars having an interest in satire. Magazine; 40 (5½x8½) pages. Established in 1975. Quarterly. Acquires first North American serial rights or second serial (reprint) rights. Uses about 40 mss a year. Pays in contributor's copies. Will send sample copy to writer for $1. Will consider photocopied submissions. No simultaneous submissions. Reports in 1 month. Submit complete ms. Enclose S.A.S.E.

Nonfiction: Serious, critical articles on the nature of satire itself, and original satire that mocks the scholarly community, its 4 horsemen, and its sacred cows. Length: 5,000 words maximum; shorter length preferred.

Fiction, Poetry and Fillers: Humorous fiction and erotica. Length: 5,000 words maximum, but prefers shorter material. Satiric blank verse and free verse. Satiric fillers.

SCIMITAR AND SONG, Box 151, Edgewater MD 21037. Editor: Dr. Jean Sterling. Features special issues on ecology, poetry in other countries, and youth's voices. Annual. Pays in copies. Acquires first rights. Submit seasonal material "as soon as possible in advance." Reports in 4-5 weeks. SASE. Sample copy (back issue) $2; current issue, $6.

Nonfiction: Inspirational; historical; humor; and travel. Query. Length: determined by type and content of article.

Fiction: Mystery; science fiction; adventure; historical; humorous; contemporary problems; religious; and juvenile. Length: determined by type and content of story.

Poetry: Traditional; contemporary; avant-garde; and light verse. "No restriction on length. Annual cash prizes and trophies for best published poems."

Fillers: Puzzles and short humor on poets, writers or poetry. Length: 50 words.

SECOND COMING, Box 31249, San Francisco CA 94131. Editor-in-Chief: A.D. Winans. Semiannual magazine; 80-120 pages. Estab: 1972. Circ: 1,000. Pays in copies. Acquires one-time rights. Previously published submissions OK, if accompanied by release. SASE. Reports in 1-4 weeks. Sample copy $1.50.

Fiction: Experimental (avant-garde), humorous, science fiction. Uses 2-4 mss/year. Submit complete ms. Length: 1,000-3,000 words. Pays in copies.

Poetry: Avant-garde, free verse, traditional, surrealism. Uses 160-200/year. Limit submissions to batches of 6. No length requirement. Pays in copies.

SEWANEE REVIEW, University of the South, Sewanee TN 37375. (615)598-5931. Editor: George Core. For audience of "variable ages and locations, mostly college-educated and with interest in literature." Quarterly. Circulation: 3,900. Buys all rights. Pays on publication. Will send a sample copy to a writer for $2.75. Returns rejected material in 2 months. Enclose S.A.S.E. for return of submissions.

Nonfiction and Fiction: Short fiction (but not drama), essays of critical nature on literary subjects (especially modern British and American literature), essay-reviews and reviews (books and reviewers selected by the editors). Payment varies: averages $10 per printed page.
Poetry: Selections of 4 to 6 poems preferred. In general, light verse and translations are not acceptable. Maximum payment is 60¢ per line.

THE SHAKESPEARE NEWSLETTER, University of Illinois at Chicago Circle, English Department, Chicago IL 60680. (312)996-3289. Editor: Louis Marder. For professors of English, students, and Shakespeare enthusiasts. Published 6 times per academic year. Estab: 1951. Circ: 2,675. Not copyrighted. Payment in contributor's copies. Will send sample copy to writer for $1. Will consider photocopied submissions. Will not consider simultaneous submissions. Query first or submit complete ms. "Send the conclusions and I will tell you if I want the facts." Enclose S.A.S.E.
Nonfiction: Solid, original articles. Wants new facts on Shakespeare. Scholarly, yet popular. Length: 1,500 words maximum.
Poetry and Fillers: Occasional poems. No abstract poetry. Shakespeare only; anything that works. Length: 20 lines maximum. Newsbreaks, clippings, jokes, and short humor. Length: 75 words or so.

SHAW REVIEW, S-234 Burrowes Bldg., University Park PA 16802. (814)865-4242. Editor: Stanley Weintraub. For scholars and writers and educators interested in Bernard Shaw and his work, his milieu, etc. Published every 4 months. Estab: 1954. Circ: 600. Not copyrighted. Payment in contributor's copies. Will consider photocopied submissions. Submit complete ms. Reports in 1 month. SASE.
Nonfiction: "Articles must pertain to G.B. Shaw, his writing life and environment." Uses informational and historical articles and interviews. Length: open.

SIGNS: Journal of Women in Culture & Society, Barnard College, 307 Barnard Hall, New York NY 10027. Editor: Catharine R. Stimpson. For academic and professional women; women and men interested in the study of women. Journal; 196 (6x9) pages. Established in 1975. Quarterly. Circulation: 7,000. Acquires all rights. Payment in copies and offprints. Write for copy of guidelines for writers. Will consider photocopied submissions. No simultaneous submissions. Reports on material accepted for publication in 4 to 6 months. Returns rejected material in 2-3 months. SASE.
Nonfiction: "Scholarly essays exploring women, their roles and culture, their relations with society, etc. We are especially looking for articles with larger theoretical implications." Length: 20 to 45 typed, double-spaced pages.

THE SMALL POND MAGAZINE OF LITERATURE, 10 Overland Dr., Stratford CT 06497. (203)378-9259. Editor: Napoleon St. Cyr. For "high school students, mostly poets, the rest college and college grad students who read us in college libraries, or in general the literati." Published 3 times a year. 40 pages; (5½x8½). Established in 1964. Circulation: 300. Acquires all rights. Uses about 100 mss a year. Payment in contributor's copies. Sample copy $1.25. Will consider photocopied submissions. Will not consider simultaneous submissions. Query first or submit complete ms. Reports within 1 month. Enclose S.A.S.E.
Nonfiction, Photos, and Poetry: "About 2/3 poetry, the rest is open to any and all subjects, essays, articles, and stories such as you'd find in *Harper's, Atlantic*, etc. We've had an uncanny knack for discovering talent which has gone on and risen rapidly in the literary field. We don't want anything on the high school and college drug scene, or fiction based on 'love story'. Particularly interested in authoritative inside exposes (not rabid yellow journalism) of some aspect of business, government, international affairs, or even the world of literature and performing arts." Nonfiction length: 2,500 words maximum. Experimental, mainstream, fantasy, historical, and humorous fiction. Length: 200 to 2,500 words. Traditional and avant-garde forms of poetry, blank, free and light verse. Length: 100 lines maximum.

SMALL PRESS REVIEW, P.O. Box 1056, Paradise CA 95969. Editor: Len Fulton. Associate Editor: Ellen Ferber. For "people interested in small presses and magazines, current trends and data; many libraries." Monthly. Circ: 3,000. Accepts 50-200 mss/year. Will send a sample copy to a writer on request. "Query if you're unsure." Reports in 1 to 2 months. Enclose S.A.S.E. for return of submissions or reply to queries.
Nonfiction and Photos: "News, short reviews, photos, short articles on small magazines and presses and underground papers. Get the facts and know your mind well enough to build your opinion into the article." Uses how-to's, personal experience articles, interviews, profiles, spot

news, historical articles, think pieces, photo pieces, and coverage of merchandising techniques. Length: 100 to 200 words. Uses b&w glossy photos.

THE SMITH, 5 Beekman St., New York NY 10038. Editor: Harry Smith. For students, writers, professors, librarians, others who are interested in literature as art and revolutionary thought. 3 book-size issues, plus supplements. Book format magazine. Established in 1964. Circulation: 2,500. Buys first North American serial rights and second serial (reprint) rights. Buys 200 mss a year. Payment on acceptance. Will send sample copy to writer for $1. Will consider photocopied and simultaneous submissions. Query first for nonfiction. Submit complete ms for fiction and poetry. Reports within 4 weeks. Enclose S.A.S.E.
Nonfiction: Department Editor: Sidney Bernard. Speculative essays. No taboos. Length: 5,000 words or less. Payment is "modest," by arrangement.
Fiction and Poetry: Department Editor (fiction): Raphael Taliaferro. Long stories and novellas as well as short-shorts and vignettes of under 2,000 words. Modest payment by arrangement. Has published poems as long as 52 pages. Pays $5 per short poem.
How to Break In: "The only thing I can say about the trend in this office in the use of over-the-transom mss is that the best chance lies in poetry and fiction. We don't tend to encourage new people to do reviews for a couple of reasons—they usually tend to be too formalistic and conventional (in the style of *Saturday Review, The Yale Review,* or *The New York Review*), and besides we have a number of people in the office and outside who have been doing them. Newcomers might want to try their hands at topical essays, perhaps with a polemical stroke, on the aesthetics of literature. But query first. I should point out that we prefer the unknown to the known. It's partly the sense of discovery—that's very important here—and also because we're not that crazy about many of the knowns."

SOUTH ATLANTIC QUARTERLY, Box 6697, College Station, Durham NC 27708. Editor: Oliver W. Ferguson. For the academic profession. Quarterly. No payment. Proceeds of sale of rights to reprint divided with author. Reports in 6 weeks. Enclose S.A.S.E. for return of submissions.
Nonfiction: Articles on current affairs, literature, history and historiography, art, education, essays on most anything, economics, etc. — a general magazine. No taboos. Length: 4,500 words maximum.

SOUTH CAROLINA REVIEW, English Dept., Clemson University, Clemson SC 29631. (803)656-3229. Editors-in-Chief: R. Calhoun, R. Hill. Managing Editor: F. Day. Publishes in April and November. Magazine; 72 pages. Estab: 1965. Circ: 500. Pays in copies. Acquires all rights, but may reassign following publication. Phone queries OK. Submit seasonal/holiday material 3 months in advance. Simultaneous and photocopied submissions OK. SASE. Reports in 2 months. Free sample copy.
Nonfiction: Literary criticism, literary history and history of ideas. Submit complete ms. Pays in copies.
Fiction: "We have no set types; if it's fiction, we'll look at it." Submit complete ms.
Poetry: "If it's poetry, we'll look at it."

SOUTH DAKOTA REVIEW, Box 11, University Exchange, Vermillion SD 57069. (605)677-5229. Editor: John R. Milton. For a university audience and the college educated, although reaches others as well. Quarterly. Acquires North American serial rights and reprint rights. Pays in contributor's copies. Will send sample copy to writer for 50¢. Reports within 4 weeks. Enclose S.A.S.E.
Nonfiction: Prefers, but does not insist upon, Western American literature and history; especially critical studies of western writers. Open to anything on literature, history, culture, travel, the arts, but selection depends on patterns and interests of individual numbers within each volume. Contents should be reasonably scholarly, but style should be informal and readable. All well-written mss will be considered. Length: 6,000 words maximum, but at times has used longer.
Fiction: Western setting preferred (Great Plains, Rockies, Southwest), but receptive to almost anything that is disciplined and original. Quality is more important than subject or setting. No excessive emotions. Rarely uses hunting, fishing, or adolescent narrator or subject studies. Open to paramyth, Jungian treatments, serious themes. Length: 6,000 words maximum, but has used longer at times.
Poetry: Prefers poetry which is disciplined and controlled, though open to any form (tends to prefer traditional free verse). Any length considered, but prefers 10 to 30 lines.

THE SOUTHERN REVIEW, Drawer D, University Station, Baton Rouge LA 70893. (504)388-5108. Editors: Donald E. Stanford and Lewis P. Simpson. For academic, professional, literary, intellectual audience. Quarterly. Circulation: 3,000. Buys first rights. Pays on publication. Will send sample copy to writer for $1.50. No queries. Reports in 2 to 3 months. Enclose S.A.S.E. for return of submissions.

Nonfiction: Essays; careful attention to craftsmanship and technique and to seriousness of subject matter. "Willing to publish experimental writing if it has a valid artistic purpose. Avoid extremism and sensationalism. Essays exhibit thoughtful and sometimes severe awareness of the necessity of literary standards in our time." Emphasis on contemporary literature, especially Southern culture and history. Minimum number of footnotes. Length: 4,000 to 10,000 words. Pays 3¢ per word minimum.

Fiction and Poetry: Short stories of lasting literary merit, with emphasis on style and technique. Length: 4,000 to 8,000 words. Pays minimum of 3¢ per word. Pays $20 per page for poetry.

SOUTHWEST REVIEW, Southern Methodist University, Dallas TX 75275. (214)692-2263. Editor: Margaret L. Hartley. For adults, college graduates, literary interests, some interest in the Southwest, but subscribers are from all over America and some foreign countries. Quarterly magazine; 120 pages, (6x9). Established in 1915. Circulation: 1,000. Buys all rights, but will reassign rights to author after publication. Buys 65 mss a year. Payment on publication. Will send free sample copy to writer on request. Query first for nonfiction. Submit only complete ms for fiction and poetry. Reports within 3 months. Enclose S.A.S.E.

Nonfiction and Photos: "Articles, literary criticism, social and political problems, history (especially Southwestern), folklore (especially Southwestern), the arts, etc. Articles should be appropriate for a literary quarterly; no feature stories. Critical articles should consider a writer's whole body of work, not just one book. History should use new primary sources or a new perspective, not syntheses of old material. We're regional but not provincial." Interviews with writers, historical articles, and book reviews of scholarly nonfiction. Length: 1,500 to 5,000 words. Pays ½¢ a word. Regular columns are Regional Sketchbook (southwestern) and Points of View (excellent personal essays). Uses b&w photos only occasionally for cover.

Fiction: No limitations on subject matter for fiction. No experiences of adolescents—that's overworked. Experimental (not too far out), and mainstream fiction. Length: 1,500 to 5,000 words. Pays ½¢ per word. The John H. McGinnis Memorial Award is made in alternate years for fiction and nonfiction pieces published in *SR*.

Poetry: No limitations on subject matter. "We don't care for most religious and nature poetry." Free verse, avant-garde forms (not too far out), and open to all serious forms of poetry. Length: prefers 18 lines or shorter. Pays $5 per poem.

SOU'WESTER, Department of English, Southern Illinois University, Edwardsville IL 62025. Editor: Lloyd Kropp. For "poets, fiction writers, teachers, and anyone else connected with or interested in the small press scene." Magazine; 92 pages. Established in 1960. Three times a year. Circulation: 500. Acquires all rights, but will return rights to author after 12 months, upon request. Uses about 70 mss a year. Payment in contributor's copies. Several prizes are offered yearly for fiction and poetry. Will send sample copy to writer for $1.50. Will consider photocopied submissions. Reluctantly considers simultaneous submissions. Reports in 4 to 6 weeks except in the summer. "We do not read mss during June, July and August." Submit complete ms. Enclose S.A.S.E.

Fiction and Poetry: "We publish mostly fiction and poetry. We do not have any particular editorial bias, but we do insist on meaningful, imaginative development and technical proficiency. No doggerel; no old-fashioned magazine fiction aimed at old-fashioned housewives." Experimental, mainstream, fantasy, historical and science fiction. Length: 10,000 words maximum. Traditional and avant-garde forms of poetry; blank verse, free verse, haiku. Length: 80 lines maximum.

SUNSTONE REVIEW, Box 2321, Sante Fe NM 87501. Publisher: James Clois Smith, Jr. Editor: Marcia Muth Miller. Estab: 1974. Quarterly. Circ: 500. Acquires all rights, but will give permission to reprint. Payment in contributor's copies. Will send sample copy to writer for $1.50. Reports in 6 weeks. Enclose S.A.S.E.

Nonfiction, Fiction, Poetry, and Photos: "Interested in new writers as well as those well known. Material selected on merit only. Accepts poetry (any form, any length), short fiction, b&w photos, drawings, criticism and short articles."

THE TEXAS ARTS JOURNAL, Box 7458, Dallas TX 75209. (214)528-5008. Editor: Cameron Northouse. Emphasizes art, literature, history and biography. Quarterly magazine; 112 pages.

Estab: 1977. Circ: 4,000. Pays on publication. Buys one-time rights. Photocopied submissions OK. SASE. Reports in 3 weeks. Sample copy $2.95.

Nonfiction: Donna M. Northouse, Articles Editor. Historical; informational; interview; personal experience; personal opinion; photo feature; profile and travel. Buys 5 mss/issue. Send complete ms. Pays $8/page.

Photos: Britt C. Brown, Photo Editor. Photos purchased with or without accompanying ms or on assignment. Pays $10 minimum for 5x7 b&w glossies. Model release required.

Fiction: Experimental, mainstream, science fiction and serialized novels. Buys 6 mss/year. Send complete ms. Length: open. Pays $8/page.

Poetry: J.W. Brown, Poetry Editor. Avant-garde, free verse and traditional. Buys 30 poems/year. Pays 40¢/line.

13TH MOON, Box 3, Inwood Station, New York NY 10034. Editor-in-Chief: Ellen Marie Bissert. Emphasizes quality work by women for a well-read, collegiate audience of professors and graduates. Semiannual magazine; 96 pages. Estab: 1973. Pays in copies. Acquires all rights, but may reassign following publication. SASE. Reports in 2 months. Sample copy $1.75.

Nonfiction: Literary criticism and aesthetics. Query.

Photos: Photos used without accompanying ms. Uses b&w photos. Sent prints.

Fiction: Experimental. "Send complete ms, but study magazine first."

Poetry: Avant-garde and free verse.

THOUGHT, The Quarterly of Fordham University, Fordham University Press, Box L, Fordham University, The Bronx NY 10458. Editor: Joseph E. Grennen. Acquires all rights. Payment in copies. Reports within a month. Enclose S.A.S.E.

Nonfiction and Poetry: A review of culture and idea, *Thought* discusses questions of permanent value and contemporary interest in every field of learning and culture in a scholarly but not excessively technical way. Articles vary from 5,000 to 10,000 words. Publishes a page or 2 of poetry in each issue.

TOWN AND COUNTRY JOURNAL, 101½ Mill St., Coudersport PA 16915. Editor: Geraldine R. Miller. For natives and newcomers of this area. Special double winter issue, January/February. Established in 1972. Monthly. Circulation: 2,000. Not copyrighted. Pays in contributor's copies. Will send free sample copy to writer on request. Will consider photocopied submissions. Submit special issue material 3 months in advance. Reports on material accepted for publication in 1 month. Returns rejected material in 2 weeks. Query first or submit complete ms. Enclose S.A.S.E.

Nonfiction and Photos: Articles on the history of the area, local government, nature, real estate, antiques, gardening, subdivision, zoning. May have inspirational or mild ecology theme. Snowmobile and other winter sport material is used for the winter issue; material on fairs is used for the August issue. Other interests include informational, how-to, interviews, profile, nostalgia, merchandising techniques, successful business operations, book reviews. Length: 1,500 to 5,000 words. 8x10 b&w glossy photos purchased with mss. Captions required.

Poetry: Free verse, light verse. Length: 4 to 20 lines.

TRI-QUARTERLY, University Hall, 101 Northwestern University, Evanston IL 60201. (312)492-3490. Editor: Elliott Anderson. 3 times yearly. For an intellectual and literary audience. "Our format is extremely eclectic. The tone and intentions of each issue may vary." Buys first serial rights. Reports on unsolicited mss within 8 weeks; solicited mss immediately. Pays on publication. Study publication before submitting mss; enclose S.A.S.E.

Fiction and Photos: No length limits. "We are not committed to the short story as the only publishable form of fiction. Frequently excerpts from longer works tell us more about an author and his work." Payment at $10 per page, if possible. Occasionally uses photos.

UNICORN, A Miscellaneous Journal, 345 Harvard St., #3B, Cambridge MA 02138. Editor: Karen S. Rockow. Established in 1967. Mainly for college and graduate school students and faculty. "Well-educated and sophisticated. Not jaded." Published irregularly. Circulation: 700. Acquires all rights, but will reassign rights to author after publication. Uses 15 to 25 freelance mss a year. Pays an honorarium only for nonfiction. Submit complete ms. Generally reports in 3 to 4 weeks, longer over summer, and for poetry and short stories. Will send sample copy to writer for $1. Will consider photocopied submissions. Enclose S.A.S.E. for return of submissions.

Nonfiction and Photos: "*Unicorn* is a community of writers and readers brought together to share their favorite books and topics. Primarily, we publish essays. These range from personal

essays to graceful, scholarly papers directed at a general audience. Areas of greatest interest are folklore, popular culture (especially fantasy literature, detective fiction, children's books) and medieval studies, but we will consider mss on any subject. Scholarly and semischolarly papers may include footnotes (use *MLA* form). The supporting scholarship must be rigorous, but avoid 'intellectualese'. Also have a very offbeat foods column, The Galumphing Gourmet, and publish many reviews, long and short. We are looking for crisp, honest prose and stand committed against pretentiousness. We pay $5 honorarium for each article and essay accepted." B&w glossies, any size. Payment in cost of film plus extra roll and offprints. Optimum length: 2,500 to 5,000 words; 7,500 words maximum, but will break longer articles and consider series.
Fiction: Department Editor: Stuart Silverman. Satire, short stories. Fantasy, detective fiction. Experimental, mainstream, science fiction, humorous fiction. "We publish 1 short story per issue, plus perhaps, a parody or humorous piece." Length: 2,500 words maximum. Payment in copies plus offprints.
Poetry: Department Editor: Stuart Silverman. "We are heavily overstocked with poetry at present time. This does not preclude any current acceptances, but does make us more selective. Please limit number of submissions at any one time to 3 poems, unless they are very short. Publication of poetry may be delayed several issues." Traditional forms, blank verse, free verse, avant-garde forms, light verse and "concrete" poetry. Length: 1 line to 1 single-spaced page. Payment in copies plus offprints.

UNIQUEST, The Search for Meaning, First Unitarian Church, 1 Lawson Rd., Berkeley CA 94707. Editor: Joseph Fabry. For those in search of meaning in their own lives, and for a world in which survival as a fulfilled human being is possible. Publication of the Uniquest Foundation. Semiannual magazine; 44 pages. Estab: 1974. Circ: 1,000. Copyrighted. Uses about 8 mss a year. Payment in contributor's copies. Will send sample copy to writer for $2. Simultaneous and photocopied submissions OK. Reports in 4 weeks. Submit complete ms. Enclose S.A.S.E.
Nonfiction: Main interest is in articles that help individuals discover meaning in the inward and outward journey of personal life. Also to serve as a basis for adult discussion in groups concerned with ethical and moral issues. Especially interested in "Life Scripts," "Biography as Theology," and why people make a decision to join a new religious group. How can small groups be more effective in helping their members discover meaning? Techniques to make your organization come alive. Questions of intimate ethics: sex, marriage, religion (non-dogmatic), and death. Also ethics and ecology, the future of human life on earth. Distribution is largely to Unitarian Universalist Churches and to those interested in the ethical questions of ecology.

UNIVERSITY OF TORONTO QUARTERLY, University of Toronto, Ontario M5S 1A6. Editor-in-Chief: W.J. Keith. Emphasizes literature and the humanities for the university community. Quarterly magazine; 96 pages. Estab: 1931. Pays on publication. Buys all rights. Photocopied submissions OK. SASE. Sample copy $3.50.
Nonfiction: Scholarly articles on the humanities; literary criticism and intellectual discussion. Buys 15 mss/year. Pays $50 maximum.

UNIVERSITY OF WINDSOR REVIEW, Windsor, Ontario, Canada. N9B 3P4 (519)253-4232. Editor: Eugene McNamara. For "the literate layman, the old common reader." Established in 1965. Biannual. Circulation: 300 plus. Acquires first North American serial rights. Accepts 50 mss/year. Sample copy $1.25 plus postage. Follow *MLA Style Sheet*. Reports in 4 to 6 weeks. Enclose S.A.E. and International Reply Coupons.
Nonfiction and Photos: "We publish articles on literature, history, social science, etc. I think we reflect competently the Canadian intellectual scene, and are equally receptive to contributions from outside the country; I think we are good and are trying to get better. We are receiving too many poems, too many short stories. Everybody in the world is writing them. Too many articles on literature itself. Not enough in the other areas: history, etc." Seeks informational articles. Length: about 6,000 words. Pays $25. For photos, please inquire to Evelyn McLean.
Fiction: Department Editor: Alistair MacLeod. Publishes mainstream prose with open attitude toward themes. Length: 2,000-6,000 words. Pays $25.
Poetry: Department Editor: John Ditsky. Accepts traditional forms, blank verse, free verse, and avant-garde forms. No epics. Pays $10.

UNMUZZLED OX, Box 840, Canal St. Station, New York NY 10013. (212)431-8829. Editor-in-Chief: Michael Andre. Emphasizes art and poetry. Quarterly magazine; 140 pages. Estab: 1971. Circ: 4,000. Pays on publication. Buys all rights, but may reassign following publication. Photocopied submissions OK. SASE. Reports in 1 month. Sample copy $3.
Nonfiction: Interviews (artists, writers and politicians). Buys 1 ms/issue. Query. Pays $1-50.

Photos: Photos purchased on assignment only. Pays $1-25 for photos. Model release required.
Fiction: Ellen Kahow, Fiction Editor. Experimental. Buys 1 ms/issue. Mostly solicited. Pays $1-50.
Poetry: Avant-garde. Pays $1-25.

VAGABOND, P.O. Box 879, Ellensburg WA 98926. Editor: John Bennett. For "libraries, poets, writers, sensitive and free spirits, minority groups, people of all ages, varied education and with an interest in life ..." Established in 1966. Quarterly. Circulation: 700. Acquires all rights, but will reassign them to author after publication. Uses about 80 mss/year. Pays in contributor's copies. Sample copy $1.25. Cassette submissions OK. Query first for nonfiction. Reports in 3 to 4 weeks. Enclose S.A.S.E.
Nonfiction: "I would prefer not to see work that was written with a market in mind. I would like to see material that deals with life and death and all their accoutrements ... joy, laughter, love and hate." Accepts interviews, reviews and personal opinion articles. Length: not more than 5,000 words.
Fiction and Poetry: Publishes genuine experimental, suspense, adventure, erotica, fantasy, humorous fiction. Length: 5,000 words maximum. Traditional and avant-garde forms of poetry; blank verse, free verse and haiku.

VALLEY VIEWS MAGAZINE, Box 39096, Solon OH 44139. (216)248-4048. Editor: Patricia R. Yunkes. Managing Editor: Nelson P. Bard. Quarterly magazine; 44 pages. Estab: 1964. Circ: 5,000. Pays in copies on publication. "Author retains all rights except for those we need to print the story." Submit seasonal/holiday material 6 months in advance. SASE. Reports in 2 months.
Nonfiction: Historical; humor; new product; nostalgia; personal experience; photo feature; and travel. Uses 8 mss/year. Submit complete ms. Length: 3,000 words maximum.
Photos: Purchased with accompanying ms. Send prints. Uses b&w prints (at least 3 inch square) and 5x7 or 8x10 color glossy prints. Model release required.
Fiction: Adventure; historical; humorous; mystery; science fiction; suspense and western. Uses 110 mss/year. Submit complete ms. Length: 3,000 words maximum.
Poetry: Free verse; light verse; traditional; and humorous. Uses 15/issue. Limit submissions to batches of 10.

THE VILLAGER, 135 Midland Ave., Bronxville NY 10708. (914)337-3252. Editor: Amy Murphy. Publication of the Bronxville Women's Club. For club members and families; professional people and advertisers. Established in 1929. Monthly, October through June. Circulation: 850. Acquires all rights. Uses 40 mss a year. Pays in copies only. Will send sample copy to writer for 35¢. Submit seasonal material (Thanksgiving, Christmas, Easter) 2 months in advance. Submit only complete ms. Reports within 2 weeks. Enclose S.A.S.E.
Nonfiction, Fiction, and Poetry: Short articles about interesting homes, travel, historic, pertinent subjects, sports, etc. Informational, personal experience, inspirational, humor, historical, nostalgia, travel. Mainstream, mystery, suspense, adventure, humorous, romance, and historical fiction. Length: 900 to 2,500 words. Traditional forms of poetry, blank verse, free verse, avant-garde forms, light verse. Length: 20 lines.

VILTIS (Hope), P.O. Box 1226, Denver CO 80201. (303)534-2025. Editor: V.F. Beliajus. For teenagers and adults interested in folk dance, folk customs and folklore; all professions and levels of education. Published every 2 months. Magazine; 40 pages, (12x9). Established in 1942. Circulation: 2,500. Acquires all rights, but will reassign rights to author after publication on request. No payment. Will send free sample copy to writer on request. Query first. Enclose S.A.S.E.
Nonfiction: Uses articles on folklore, legends, customs and nationality backgrounds. Folkish (not too erudite) but informative. Can be any length. Everything must be based on custom, interview, profile, humor, expose reportage. Length: 500 to 3,500 words. Dept. Editor: Robert Friedman.

THE VIRGINIA QUARTERLY REVIEW, 1 West Range, Charlottesville VA 22903. (804)924-3124. Editor: Staige Blackford. Quarterly. Pays on publication. Reports on submissions in 2 weeks. Enclose S.A.S.E. for return of submissions.
Nonfiction: Articles on current problems, economic, historical; literary essays. Length: 3,000-6,000 words. Pays $10/345-word page.
Fiction: Good short stories, conventional or experimental. Length: 2,000-7,000 words. Pays $10/350-word page. Prizes offered for best short stories and poems published in a calendar year, beginning in 1978.

Poetry: Generally publishes 10 pages of poetry in each issue. No length or subject restrictions. Pays $1/line.

WALT WHITMAN REVIEW, Business Office: Wayne State University Press, Detroit MI 48202. (313)626-6404. Editorial Office: Journalism Program, Communication Arts Department, Oakland University, Rochester MI 48063. Editors: William White and Charles E. Feinberg. For specialists in American literature. Quarterly. Payment in contributor's copies. Wayne State University Press and author share all rights. Reports within a few days. Enclose S.A.S.E. for return of submissions.
Nonfiction: All articles and book reviews, notes and queries should deal with Walt Whitman and his writings. Length: 500 to 6,000 words.

WASCANA REVIEW, University of Regina, Saskatchewan, Canada. Editor-in-Chief: W. Howard. Emphasizes literature and the arts for readers interested in serious poetry, fiction and scholarship. Semiannual magazine; 90 pages. Estab: 1966. Circ: 300. Pays on publication. Buys all rights. Photocopied submissions OK. SAE and International Reply Coupons. Reports in 6-8 weeks.
Nonfiction: Literary criticism and scholarship in the field of English, American, Canadian, French or German literature and drama; reviews of current books (2,000-6,000 words). Buys 1-4 mss/issue. Send complete ms. Pays $3-4/page.
Fiction: Quality fiction with an honest, meaningful grasp of human experience. Any form. Buys 5-10 mss/issue. Send complete ms. Length: 2,000-6,000 words. Pays $3/page.
Poetry: Avant-garde, free verse, haiku, light verse and traditional. Buys 10-15 poems/issue. Length: 2-100 lines. Pays $10.

WAVES, Room 128, Founders College, York University, 4700 Keele St., Downsview, Ontario, Canada L4J 1P2. Editor: Bernice Lever. For university and high school English teachers and readers of literary magazines. Magazine published 3 times a year; 80 (5x8) pages. Established in 1972. Circulation: 1,000. Acquires first North American serial rights. Payment in contributor's copies. Will send sample copy to writer for $1. Will consider photocopied submissions. Will not consider simultaneous submissions. Reports in 6 weeks. Submit complete ms. Enclose S.A.E. and International Reply Coupons.
Nonfiction and Photos: "Intelligent, thorough, unique, humanitarian material. Good quality; yet wide variety of genres and styles. Avoid pornography and carelessness. No 'copies' of Jonathan Livingston Seagull." Uses interviews, essays, literary think pieces and book reviews. Length: 250 to 7,000 words. B&w photos and graphics are used.
Fiction: Experimental, mainstream, fantasy, humorous and science fiction. Length: 500 to 5,000 words.
Poetry and Drama: Free verse and avant-garde forms. Playlets. Length: 2,000 words maximum.

WAYSIDE QUARTERLY, P.O. Box 475, Cottonwood AZ 86326. Editors: Joan Atwater and Mary Radcliffe. Quarterly magazine; 72 pages. Estab: 1972. Circulation: 350. Not copyrighted. No payment. Uses 4 or more articles a year; 30-50 poems. Pays in contributor's copies. Free sample copy. Will consider photocopied and simultaneous submissions. Reports on material accepted for publication in 6-8 weeks. Submit complete ms. Enclose S.A.S.E.
Nonfiction: "Articles should reflect some interest in self-understanding, personal growth. Material should reflect some serious thought on the part of the writer, contribute some real experience of the writer that can be shared with others." Informational, personal experience, inspirational, nutritional information, nutritional recipes. Length: flexible, but averages 1,200 to 1,500 words.
Poetry: Same themes as for nonfiction; also nature or descriptive poems. Traditional forms, blank verse, free verse, light verse, haiku.

WEBSTER REVIEW, Webster College, Webster Groves MO 63119. (314)432-2657. Editor: Nancy Schapiro. For "academics, students, all persons interested in contemporary international literature." Magazine; 64 pages. Established in 1974. Quarterly, Circulation: 400. Not copyrighted. Uses about 200 mss per year. Pays in copies. Will send free sample copy to writer on request. Will consider photocopied and simultaneous submissions. Reports on mss accepted for publication in 1 month. Returns rejected material in 3 weeks. Enclose S.A.S.E.
Fiction and Poetry: "Stories, poems, excerpts from novels, essays and English translations of foreign contemporary literature. Subject matter is not important, but quality is. Our emphasis is on international as well as American contemporary quality writing." No restrictions on length.

WEST END MAGAZINE, Box 354, Jerome Ave. Station, Bronx NY 10468. Editor-in-Chief: Gail Darrow Kaliss. Emphasizes poetry, short fiction and politics for readers interested in poetry and in the movement for social change in America. "We hope to appeal to working people." Quarterly magazine; 48 pages. Estab: 1971. Acquires all rights, but may reassign following publication. Pays in copies. Simultaneous and photocopied submissions OK. SASE. Reports in 1-3 months.
Nonfiction: Stories about people's lives: realistic with a social message. Proletarian writings. We don't really want protest literature. We want material telling us how it feels to work in America." Personal experience. Also uses fiction.
Poetry: Free verse and avant-garde. Length: 1-200 lines.

WESTERN HUMANITIES REVIEW, University of Utah, Salt Lake City UT 84112. (801)581-7438. Editor-in-Chief: Jack Garlington. For educated, university-centered, sophisticated readers. Quarterly magazine; 96 pages. Estab: 1947. Circ: 1,000. Pays on acceptance. Buys all rights, but may reassign following publication. Phone queries OK. Simultaneous and photocopied submissions OK. SASE. Reports in 4 weeks.
Nonfiction: Historical; informational; interview; personal experience; personal opinion; profile and travel. "We need articles related to issues in the humanities." Buys 2-5 mss/issue. Send complete ms. Pays $25-100.
Fiction: Adventure; experimental; fantasy; historical; and humorous. Buys 2 mss/issue. Send complete ms. Pays $25-100.
Poetry: Avant-garde; free verse; haiku; light verse and traditional. Buys 5-10 poems/issue. Pays $25-35.

WIND/LITERARY JOURNAL, R.F.D. 1, Box 810, Pikeville KY 41501. (606)437-6936. Editor: Quentin R. Howard. For literary people. Magazine; 96 pages. Established in 1971. Quarterly. Circulation: 500. Copyrighted. Uses about 500 mss a year. Payment in contributor's copies. Will send sample copy to writer for $1.25. No photocopied or simultaneous submissions. Reports on material accepted for publication in 5 to 15 days. Returns rejected material in 5 days. Submit complete ms. Enclose S.A.S.E.
Nonfiction, Fiction, Drama and Poetry: Short essays and book reviews are used, as well as short stories and 1-act plays. Blank verse, traditional and avant-garde forms of poetry, free verse, haiku. Length: 30 lines maximum.

WISCONSIN REVIEW, Box 245, Dempsey Hall, University of Oshkosh, Oshkosh WI 54901. (414)424-2267. Editors: Charles Dahlen, Karen Waugh and Judith Wittig. For persons interested in literature. Quarterly magazine; 60-80 pages. Estab: 1966. Circ: 500. Acquires all rights, but will reassign following publication. Pays in contributor's copies. Sample copy 75¢. Reports in 2-3 months. Submit complete ms. SASE.
Nonfiction, Photos, Fiction and Poetry: Book reviews and occasional essays. Interviews. B&w photos used with mss. "In fiction, I prefer a well-structured short story, although I do, occasionally, accept a piece of automatic writing." No romance, confession or religious fiction or serialized novels. Length: 6,000 to 8,000 words. Avant-garde forms of poetry, blank verse, free verse, haiku.

WOMEN ARTISTS NEWSLETTER, Midmarch Associates, Box 3304 Grand Central Station, New York NY 10025. Editor-in-Chief: Cynthia Navaretta. For "artists, museum and gallery personnel, students, teachers, crafts personnel, art critics, writers." Monthly newsletter; 8 pages. Estab: 1975. Circ: 5,000. Pays on publication. "Payment is modest and is based on a recent grant from the New York State Council of the Arts to pay authors. When grant runs out, we may be forced to revert to 'no payment'." Buys all rights, but may reassign following publication. Submit seasonal/holiday material 1-2 months in advance. SASE. Reports in 1 month. Free sample copy.
Nonfiction: Judy Seigel, Articles Editor. Expose; how-to; informational; historical; interview; personal opinion; profile; personal experience; photo feature; and technical. Buys 4-6 mss/issue. Query or submit complete ms. Length: 500-1,000 words. Pays $5-10.
Photos: Susan Schwalb, Photo Editor. Purchased with or without accompanying ms. Captions required. Query or submit contact sheet or prints. Pays $5 for 5x7 b&w prints.

WORLD LITERATURE TODAY (formerly *Books Abroad*), 630 Parrington Oval, Room 109, University of Oklahoma, Norman OK 73019. Editor: Ivar Ivask. University of Oklahoma holds all rights to materials published unless otherwise noted. Enclose S.A.S.E. for return of submissions.

Nonfiction: Articles (maximum length 3,000 words) concerned with contemporary literature; book reviews of 200 to 300 words on new, important, original works of a literary nature in any language. All contributions in English. Payment only in offprints (25) of a major article, plus 3 complimentary copies.

THE YALE REVIEW, 1902A Yale Station, New Haven CT 06520. Editor: J.E. Palmer. Managing Editor: Mary Price. Buys all rights. Pays on publication. Enclose S.A.S.E.
Nonfiction and Fiction: Authoritative discussions of politics, literature, and the arts. Pays $75 to $100 per article. Buys quality fiction. Length: 3,000 to 5,000 words. Pays $75 to $100 per story.

Men's Publications

ADAM, Publishers Service Inc., 8060 Melrose Ave., Los Angeles CA 90046. For the adult male. General subject: "Human sexuality in contemporary society." Monthly. Circulation: 500,000. Buys first North American serial rights. Occasionally overstocked. Pays on publication. Writer's guidelines for SASE. Reports in 3-6 weeks, but occasionally may take longer. Query. SASE.
Nonfiction: "On articles, please query first. We like hard sex articles, but research must be thorough." Length: 2,500 words. Pays $100 to $200.
Photos: All submissions must contain model release including parent's signature if under 21; fact sheet giving information about the model, place or activity being photographed, including all information of help in writing a photo story, and S.A.S.E. Photo payment varies, depending upon amount of space used by photo set.

AFFAIR, Sunway Periodicals, Inc., 21322 Lassen St., Chatsworth CA 91311. Editor: Herb Hills. For uninhibited young men from about 21 to 35, with above average interest in erotic entertainment and improving their sex lives. Magazine; 84 pages. Established in 1975. Every 2 months. Circulation: 65,000. Buys first North American rights. Buys about 75 mss a year. Pays on acceptance. No photocopied or simultaneous submissions. Reports in 3 to 4 weeks. Query first or submit complete ms. Enclose S.A.S.E.
Nonfiction and Fiction: "We're looking for things that are warm and enjoyable, not so super-slick that they're over the heads of most of our readers. Articles and fiction pieces with sexual and erotic themes. Areas covered are self-help, do-it-yourself or how-to articles; new trends, humor, entertainment (of the reader), all with a strong man-woman orientation. Articles should be helpful to the male reader and give him insights and appraoches to better relations with women. Writers with interesting personal experiences should have an edge in this approach. Fiction must have strong, action plots with erotic orientation and activity." Length (for both fiction and nonfiction): 2,500 to 3,000 words. Pays $75 minimum.
How To Break In: "Submit an article or a piece of fiction for our consideration, and then suggest several other ideas that could be developed (with our approval) into other submissions.

ALL MAN, DEBONAIR, E-GO Enterprises, Inc., 13510 Ventura Blvd., Sherman Oaks CA 91423. (714)990-2510. Editor: Virginia Del Lago. For a male audience, age 21 and older. Monthly. Buys original and second rights. Pays on publication. Material not suitable is rejected the same day it's received. SASE. Reports in 3 weeks.
Nonfiction and Fiction: Anything of strong sexual interest to men, generally with a male-female slant. Strong narrative hook preferred with a conclusive ending. "All material—straight heterosexual or lesbian (no male homosexual angle)—must be of a strong, explicitly sexual nature. Eroticism is the primary importance. Four-letter words and far-out sex rituals welcome. No science fiction of any kind accepted. Humor with strong sexual angle acceptable." Length: 500-2,000 words. Pays 1¢/word.

ARGOSY, 420 Lexington Ave., New York NY 10017. Editor: Lou Sahadi. For the "adult male, with at least high school education, interested in outdoors, nature, adventure, exploration, camping, hunting, fishing, travel, history, automobiles, sports." Monthly. Circulation: 1,400,000. Rights bought "depend on individual arrangements." Buys 100 mss a year. Payment upon publication; sometimes later. Reports in 1 month. Query first. Enclose S.A.S.E.
Nonfiction: Articles of personal adventure—humor, offbeat and exotic travel, treasure hunts, unusual outdoor stories—everything of interest to the active, intelligent male except overly sexy material. Must be documented and authentic. "We like to feel that the author was actually on

the scene. We don't need anything on the movies or for our regular columns." Length: 2,500 to 3,000 words. Pays $250 to $500.

Photos: Major areas for photo stories are outdoor adventure, leisure, and recreation. "Before submitting, photographers should thumb through back issues of *Argosy* to see the type of stories we run." Send color transparencies as well as b&w contact sheets. Pays $150 a page for full-page b&w, $200 for full-page color, and, generally, $500 for a cover. "But we will pay much more for exceptional material." Photographer is responsible for identifying and explaining his photos. Send pictures; queries cannot describe photos fully. Expenses, if any, must be arranged specifically for each assignment. Picture Editor: Bernie White.

How To Break In: "To break into the pages of *Argosy* for the first time, a new writer would first have to submit a story idea that we like. It could be just 2 or 3 paragraphs. And he would also have to include the possibility of good photos. If he's a photographer himself, this would be to his credit. Then, if his story idea is accepted, we would ask him to do the piece on speculation, obviously because we have no idea of how well he can write since, as a beginner, he will have no samples of published stories. In *Argosy* there is no such thing as a small sale; we run only full-length features, no shorts."

BEAVER, Reese Publishing Co., Inc., 235 Park Ave., S., New York NY 10003. Editor: Jayson Rollands. For men, age 18 to 34; high school education; interested in sex, cars, scandal in government, etc. Magazine; 80 pages. Established in 1976. Every 2 months. Circulation: 200,000. Buys first North American serial rights. Buys about 24 mss a year. Pays on acceptance. Will consider photocopied submissions. Reports in 1 month. Query first for nonfiction. Submit complete ms for fiction. Enclose S.A.S.E.

Nonfiction and Photos: "Articles of interest to our male readers." Informational, personal experience, humor, historical, expose. Length: 5,000 words. Pays $300-500. Spot news (humorous items). Pays $25 maximum. Sets of nudes are purchased without mss. Pays $500 for 35mm or 2¼ transparencies.

Fiction: "Short, erotic fiction. The approach should be fresh, explicit and very erotic. It should be a real turn on. We don't want to see anything like the typical fiction run in other men's books." Experimental, adventure, erotica, science fiction. Length: 5,000 words. Pays $300-500.

CAVALIER, Suite 209, 316 Aragon Ave., Coral Gables FL 33134. Editor: Douglas Allen. For "young males, 18 to 29, 80% college graduates, affluent, intelligent, interested in current events, ecology, sports, adventure, travel, clothing, good fiction." Monthly. Circulation: 250,000. Buys first and second rights. Buys 35 to 40 mss a year. Pays on publication or before. See past issues for general approach to take. Submit seasonal material at least 3 months in advance. Reports in 3 weeks. Query first except on fiction. Enclose S.A.S.E. for return of submissions or reply to query.

Nonfiction and Photos: Personal experience, interviews, humor, historical, think pieces, expose, new product. "Frank—open to dealing with controversial issues." Does not want material on Women's Lib, water sports, hunting, homosexuality, or travel, "unless it's something spectacular or special." Length: 2,800 to 3,500 words. Payment to $300. Photos purchased with mss or with captions. No cheesecake.

Fiction: Department Editor: Nye Willden. Mystery, science fiction, humorous, adventure, contemporary problems. Length: 3,000 to 4,000 words. Payment to $300, "higher for special."

How To Break In: "Our greatest interest is in originality—new ideas, new approaches; no tired, overdone stories—both feature and fiction. We do not deal in sensationalism but in high-quality pieces. Keep in mind the intelligent 18- to 29-year-old male reader."

CHIC MAGAZINE, Larry Flynt Publications, 1888 Century Park East, Suite 1606, Los Angeles CA 90067. Editor-in-Chief: Peter Brennan. For affluent men, 20-35 years old, college educated and interested in current affairs, luxuries, entertainment, sports, and fashion. Monthly magazine; 115 pages. Estab: 1976. Circ: 450,000. Pays 30 days after acceptance. Buys all rights, but may reassign following publication. Submit seasonal/holiday material 5-6 months in advance. SASE. Reports in 3-4 weeks. Writer's guidelines for SASE.

Nonfiction: Expose (national interest only); how-to (male-oriented consumer interest) historical (sexual slant only); humor (parody, satire); informational (entertainment, fashion, food, drink, etc.); interview (personalities in news and entertainment); celebrity profiles; travel (rarely used, but will consider). Buys 90 mss/year. Query. Length: 750-3,200 words. Pays $500-1,200.

Photos: Bob Elia, Photo Editor. Purchased with or without mss, or on assignment. Query or send transparencies. Pays $35-100/8x11 b&w glossies; $50-150/transparency. Model release required.

Columns/Departments: Hank Nuwer, Associate Editor: Chic Thrills (front of the book shorts; study the publication first). Pays $50-75/250-450 words. Media (trends in TV, journalism, radio, etc.). Pays $250/1,200 words. Close Up (profiles of celebrities and future celebrities; one Q/A interview/month) pays $100-150/300-700 words. Buys 150/year. Query. Open to suggestions for new columns/departments.

Fiction: "No porn. Only *Chic* characters in *Chic* situations." Buys 14/year. Send complete ms. Length: 2,000-3,000 words. Pays $500-750.

How To Break In: "Break in with short pieces for the front-of-the-book section (Chic Thrills). Study the magazine. Don't send us your worst stuff if you want to receive serious consideration now or in the future."

CLUB, Fiona Press, 919 Third Ave., 27th floor, New York NY 10022. Editor-in-Chief: Anthony Power. Managing Editor: David Jones. Emphasizes sex for the 20-30-year-old male, from truck driver to corporate executive. Monthly magazine; 100 pages. Estab: 1975. Circ: "Over 1 million". Pays on publication. Buys all rights. SASE. Reports in 4 weeks.

Nonfiction: Marvin Bevans, Department Editor. Expose (any kind involving sex ala Liz Ray); informational (anything bizarre); humor (sexual fantasies while fasting at a fat farm, etc.); interviews; personal experience (sodomy in the services, etc.). Buys 50 mss/year. Query. Length: 2,000-3,000 words. Pays $600-1,250.

Photos: Alan Walton, Department Editor. Color purchased on assignment. Query.

Fiction: Marvin Bevans, Department Editor. Erotica; fantasy; confession; experimental humor; mystery; and science fiction. Buys 2 stories/issue. Send complete ms. Length: 2,000-3,000 words Pays $600 minimum.

How To Break In: "The magazine has an open door policy to freelancers and it is very eager to establish contacts. We depend upon freelancers as much as they depend on us. But out of courtesy to the editor and in all fairness to the writer, a quicker and more professional route would be to query first thereby eliminating a lot of wasted time and energy."

DAPPER, Sunway Periodicals, Inc., 21335 Roscoe Blvd., Canoga Park CA 91401. Editor-in-Chief: Kent Roland. Managing Editor: Lewis J. Klett. Emphasizes adult male topics. For the active, sexually motivated male; 21-40. Magazine published every 2 months; 84 pages. Estab: 1972. Pays about 6 weeks after acceptance. Buys all rights, but may reassign following publication. Submit seasonal/holiday material 3 months in advance. Reports in 2-3 weeks. Free writer's guidelines.

Nonfiction: Expose; how-to; informational; humor. Buys about 65 mss/year. Query or submit complete ms. Length: 2,500-3,500 words. Pays $100.

Photos: B&w and color purchased on assignment. Query or send prints and/or transparencies. Pays $10 maximum for b&w; payment for color varies. Model release usually required.

Fiction: Adventure; erotica; fantasy; confession; experimental; humorous; mystery; suspense; and mainstream. Buys 25 mss/year. Query or send complete ms. Length: 2,500-3,500 words. Pays $100.

DUDE, GENT, NUGGET, Suite 209, 316 Aragon Ave., Coral Gables FL 33134. (305)443-2378. Editor: Bruce Arthur. "For men 21 to ?; adventure and sex are their interests." Male-oriented subject matter. Every 2 months. Buys first North American serial rights. Buys about 100 mss a year. Pays on publication. Submit complete ms. Reports on material in 6 to 8 weeks. Enclose S.A.S.E.

Nonfiction and Photos: "Articles which are male oriented; primarily concerning sex or adventure." Informational, how-to, personal experience, interview, humor, historical, personal opinion and travel. Length: 1,500-4,000 words. Pays $100-200. Photos purchased with mss.

Fiction: Adventure, erotica, science fiction, humorous. Length: 1,500 to 3,500 words. Pays $100-200.

ELITE MAGAZINE, J.E.M. Publishing Co., Ltd., 606 Avenue Rd., Suite 404, Toronto, Ontario, Canada. (416)487-7183. Editor-in-Chief: David Wells. Managing Editor: Chris Curl. For 18-35-year-old, sophisticated males. Bimonthly magazine; 100 pages. Estab: 1975. Circ: 180,000. Pays on publication. Buys all rights, but may reassign following publication; or first North American serial rights. Phone queries OK. Simultaneous and photocopied submissions OK. SASE. Reports in 4 weeks. Sample copy $1; free writer's guidelines.

Nonfiction: Expose (topical, today's living); how-to (living life); humor (basic, sexually oriented); interview (known personalities); personal experience (sexually oriented or humorous); and profile. Buys 30 mss/year. Submit complete ms. Length: 1,500-3,000 words. Pays $150-400.

Photos: Gerry L'orange, Photo Editor. Purchased with or without accompanying ms. Send contact sheet or transparencies. Pays $20-100 for standard size b&w photos; $40-400 for 35mm or 2¼x2¼ transparencies. Offers no additional payment for photos accepted with ms. Model release required.

Columns/Departments: Reviews of film, books and pop music. Submit complete ms. Length: 500-1,000 words. Pays $50-100. Open to suggestions for new column/departments.
Fiction: Adventure; erotica; fantasy; humorous; and science fiction. Buys 12 mss/year. Length: 1,500-3,000 words. Pays $150-400.
Fillers: Clippings; jokes, gags, anecdotes; and newsbreaks. Pays $20-50.

ESCAPADE MAGAZINE, Escapade Corp., 210 E. 35th St., New York NY 10016. Editor-in-Chief: Christopher Watson. Emphasizes sophisticated sex. Readers are 18-40, high school educated, interested in sexual entertainment. Monthly magazine; 100 pages. Estab: 1955. Circ: 150,000. Pays 2-3 weeks after scheduling for specific issue. Buys first North American serial rights. Submit seasonal/holiday material 6 months in advance. SASE. Reports in 2-3 weeks.
Nonfiction: "Material in keeping with contemporary 'sophisticate' magazine standards; must be frank in sexual detail without being tasteless (racist, etc.). Expose (of sexual nature); interviews (with sex personalities); photo features (nudes). Buys about 6 mss/issue. Send complete ms. Length: 2,500-3,500 words. Pays $75-125.
Photos: B&w and color purchased with or without mss. Send contact sheet or transparencies. Pays $10 minimum for b&w contacts; $15-20 for 2¼x2¼ or 35mm color. Model release required. All photos must relate to theme of magazine.
Columns, Departments: Offbeat sex news, sex puzzles (crossword), pieces with reader involvement (sexual). Buys 1-2/issue. Length: 1,000-1,500 words. Pays $35-50. Open for suggestions from freelancers for new columns or departments.
Fiction: Adventure, erotica, fantasy, confession, experimental (sexual). Buys 3 mss/issue. Send complete ms. Length: 2,500-4,000 words. Pays $100-150.

ESQUIRE, 488 Madison Ave., New York NY 10022. Editor: Byron Dobell. Monthly. Usually buys all rights. Payment on acceptance. Reports in 3 weeks. "We depend chiefly on solicited contributions and material from literary agencies. Unable to accept responsibility for unsolicited material." Query first. Enclose S.A.S.E.
Nonfiction: Articles vary in length, but usually average 4,000 words and rarely run longer than 5,000 words. Articles should be slanted for sophisticated, intelligent readers; however, not highbrow in the restrictive sense. Wide range of subject matter. Rates run roughly between $350 and $1,250, depending on length, quality, etc. Expenses are sometimes allowed, depending on the assignment.
Photos: Art Director Michael Gross. Accepts both contacts and 11x14 b&w matte prints. Uses 35mm and larger Ektachrome and Kodachrome color transparencies. Buys all rights. Payment depends on how photo is used, but rates are roughly $25 for single b&w; $100 to $150 for b&w full page; $150 to $200 for full color page. Guarantee on acceptance. Prefers to be queried. Gives assignments and pays some expenses.
Fiction: Gordon Lish, Fiction Editor. "Literary excellence is our only criterion, but we accept only solicited contributions and material from literary agents." Length: about 1,000 to 6,000 words. Payment: $350 to $1,500.

FLING, 1485 Bayshore Blvd., San Francisco CA 94124. Editor/Publisher: Arv Miller. For male readership, 25- to 35-years old, college-educated and "hip in the sense that he knows what rings true and what sounds phony." Magazine. Estab: 1957. Bimonthly. Buys first rights (additional payment if reprinted in Fling Festival annual); first or second rights for photos, with additional payment for reprint use. Pays on acceptance. Query for nonfiction. SASE. Sample copy $2; free writer's guidelines.
Nonfiction: "We want contemporary subjects that have a special interest to men. Areas such as crime, film reviews, sport figures, personality profiles, new sexual activities, foreign travel, pornography, health-diets, making money and sexual news items are currently needed. Style of text should reflect a modern-day, sophisticated approach to prose. No long-winded, scholarly sentences or paragraphs. We want the writer's personal feelings to come through." Quotes and anecdotes important to mss. Also buys humor-fillers, personalities and investigative reporting. Length: 2,500 to 4,500 words. Pays $125 to $500 on acceptance.
Fiction: Wants "up-beat, happy-goofy pieces that contain elements of sharp, contemporary dialogue and spaced-out sexual expisodes." Fiction should be slightly fantasized without being too far-fetched.

GALLERY, Montcalm Publishing Corp., 99 Park Ave., New York NY 10016. (212)986-9600. Editorial Director: Eric Protter. For men; 18-34. Monthly magazine; 132 pages. Estab: 1972. Circ: 800,000. Pays in-part before publication. Rights purchased vary. May buy first North American serial rights or all rights. Submit seasonal/holiday material 4-6 months in advance. Photocopied submissions OK. SASE. Reports in 4-8 weeks.

Nonfiction: F. Joseph Spieler, Executive Editor. Investigative articles, informational, humor, interview, profile, new product, photo features and expose. Buys about 80 mss/year. Send complete ms. Length: 2,500-6,500 words. Pays $300-750. Special arrangements for higher fees.
Photos: Payment varies for color sets of nude female photography. Model release required.
Columns/Departments: On movies, music, books. Query. Length: 800-1,500 words. Pays $150-200. Open to suggestions for new columns/departments.
Fiction: Adventure, erotica, fantasy, humorous, suspense. Buys 12 mss a year. Length: 2,500-6,000 words. Pays $300-500.

GENESIS MAGAZINE, 770 Lexington Ave., New York NY 10021. Editor: Sherry Armstrong. Monthly magazine; 110 pages. Estab: 1973. Circ: 600,000. Buys all rights. Submit seasonal material 8 months in advance. Query. Reports in 2-3 weeks. SASE.
Nonfiction, Photos and Fiction: "Newsmaking articles and interviews with world celebrities—political and entertainment; photo essays of beautiful women. Remember that we are, male-pleasure oriented. We want top quality first and foremost. Nothing downbeat, depressing or nostalgic."

GENTLEMEN'S QUARTERLY, Esquire, Inc., 488 Madison Ave., New York NY 10022. Editor-in-Chief: Jack Haber. Managing Editor: Roger C. Sharpe. Emphasizes fashion and service features for men in their late 20's, early 30's, with a large amount of discretionary income. Published 8 times/year. Pays between acceptance and publication. Submit seasonal/holiday material 4-6 months in advance. Photocopied submissions OK. SASE. Reports in 3 weeks.
Nonfiction: "Content is mostly geared toward self-help and service areas. Subject should cover physical fitness, psychological matters (different types of therapy, etc), health, money and investment, business matters—all geared to our audience and filling our format." Buys 6-10 mss/issue. Query with outline of story content. Length: 1,500-2,500 words. Pays $300-450.
Columns/Departments: Aileen Stein, Associate Editor. Shaping Up (physical fitness); Money (investments); Selling Yourself; Business Wise; and Living (catchall for various stories that fit magazine format). Buys 5-8/issue. Query. Length: 1,500-2,500 words. Pays $300-400. Open to suggestions or new columns/departments.

HUSTLER MAGAZINE, 40 W. Gay St., Columbus OH 43215. (614)464-2068. Editor: Bruce David. For "the working man, 30-years-old, high school educated." Monthly magazine; 140 pages. Estab: 1974. Circ: 3 million. Rights purchased vary with author and material. Usually buys all rights, but may reassign rights to author after publication, or first world serial rights. Buys about 72 mss per year. Pays on acceptance. Write for editorial guidelines. Will consider photocopied submissions (although original is preferred) and simultaneous submissions. Reports in 4 to 6 weeks. Query first for nonfiction. Query first or submit complete ms for other material. Enclose S.A.S.E.
Nonfiction, Photos and Fiction: Department Editors: Mark Baker, articles; Francis DeLia, photos. Will consider expose, profiles, interviews. Should be hard-hitting, probing, behind-the-scenes material. "We do not want fluff pieces or P.R. releases. Avoid complex sentence structure. Writing should nonetheless be sophisticated and contemporary, devoid of any pretensions, aggressively masculine and down-to-earth, exhibiting no-nonsense attitude. We deal in a realistic world where people sweat and pick their noses. We mirror the reality of the 70's." The publication is "sexually explicit but no pornography. No interviews or profiles on porno actors or actresses." Wants expose material, particularly sexual exposes/in political/celebrity world. Length: 4,000 to 5,000 words. Pays $500 to $1,500. Material also needed for regular columns, "Kinky Korner" and "Sex Play." Length: 2,000 words for "Korner"; 1,500 to 2,000 words for "Play." Pays $100 for 'Korner'; $250 for "Play." Photos used with mss with no additional payment. Size: 35mm Kodachrome. Buys "total exclusive rights." Pays $300 per page for color. "Check a recent copy to see our style. Slides should be sent in plastic pages. Soft-focus and diffusion are not acceptable." Buys erotica and humorous fiction. Length: 4,000 to 5,000 words. Pays $500 to $1,000.

KNIGHT, Publishers Service Inc., 8060 Melrose Ave., Los Angeles CA 90046. For male adults. Monthly. Buys all rights, but author may ask for and receive all rights other than first North American serial rights after publication. Pays on publication. Query first on articles. Enclose S.A.S.E.
Nonfiction: "Broad variety of subjects of interest to male adults. Sophisticated, sexual slant preferred. Profiles of contemporary personalities; reports on new life styles; latest trends in erotic films, art, theater; photojournalism, coverage of current social movements. Interested in articles in the subjective 'new journalism' style, as well as carefully researched reportage, but all

must be erotically oriented. No interest in true adventure pieces or how-to-do-it material."
Length: 2,500 to 4,000 words. Pays $50-250, based on quality and editorial needs.
Photos: All photo submissions must contain the following: 1) An acceptable release (containing the model's name and signature) for all models used. If the model is under 21 years old (18 if married), the signature of a parent or guardian is required. A sample model release is available on request. 2) A stamped, self-addressed envelope. 3) A fact sheet giving information about the model. 4) Place or activity being photographed. Include all information that may be of help in writing an interesting text for photo story. Sample fact sheet available on request. Uses b&w photo stories for personality profiles; photo stories covering events, places, or unusual activities, plus special material, such as erotic art, nude theater, etc. Photos bring $15 each when used to illustrate a story. Purchased separately at time issue goes to press. If submitting an entire layout, an effort should be made to capture a model in the midst of various activities; clothed and unclothed shots should be intermingled; interesting settings and backgrounds are essential. "Keep in mind that the model will become a personality if used in the magazine and emphasis should be as much on who she is as what her body looks like. Natural, real girls with whom men can easily identify are most desirable."

MACHO, Relim Publishing Co., Inc., 1485 Bayshore Blvd., San Francisco CA 94124. Managing Editor: David Harrison. For "liberated men — young, hip, somewhat sophisticated guys." Magazine. Published every other month. Enclose S.A.S.E..
Nonfiction: "If it's not offbeat, upbeat, or a bit on the kinky side — it's not right for Macho." Expects top-notch writing. Uses "investigative reporting, celebrity profiles, sexposes, New Journalism, photojournalism and controversial articles on contemporary topics. Articles submitted to *Macho* should reflect the male chauvinistic attitude." Length: 2,000 to 5,000 words. Pays $100 to $350.
Fiction: Publishes "one solid fictional story per issue, along with one or two humor pieces. Fiction must be offbeat, kinky, fast-paced and contemporary in theme, subject matter and dialogue. Characters must be sharply drawn figures from the modern American landscape. First person stories which are obviously thinly-veiled vignettes from the writer's life are immediately rejected." Rarely accepts any mss written in the first person. Also wants "hilarious spoofs of modern fads and foibles, biting satire that is funny as well as pungent, offbeat tales of, humorous sexual episodes." Length: 2,000 to 4,000 words. Pays $100 to $200.

MAN TO MAN, MR., SIR, 280 Madison Ave., New York NY 10016. (212)889-0878. Editor: Adam Blake. Monthly. Buys all rights, but usually returns specific rights to author on request. Usually pays on publication. Enclose S.A.S.E.
Nonfiction and Photos: Sharply angled articles that reflect contemporary trends in such subjects as travel, music, sex, new art forms, unusual entertainment, and other activities of interest to men. Length: 2,000 to 5,000 words. Pays $100 and up. Typical payment for article with 1 or 2 good b&w photos, $150.
Fiction: "Strong, imaginative stories in modern mood that include man-woman relationships; no one stereotype is demanded. Taboos are against hackneyed plotting and dull writing rather than particular themes or points of view. No rewriting is done in this market, so the original must be mature and professional in execution, as well as fresh in concept." Length: 1,500-5,000 words. Pays $100 minimum.
Fillers: Jokes for male audience. Pays $5.

MAN'S DELIGHT, MAN'S PLEASURE, E-GO Enterprises, Inc., 13510 Ventura Blvd., Sherman Oaks CA 91423. (714)990-2510. Editor: Sam H. Stritch. For a male audience, age 21 and older. Monthly. Buys original and second rights. Pays on publication. Reports in 3 weeks. Material not suitable is generally rejected the same day it's received. Enclose S.A.S.E.
Nonfiction and Fiction: Anything of strong sexual interest to men, with a male-female slant. Strong narrative hook preferred with a conclusive ending. "All material—straight heterosexual or lesbian (no male homosexual angle)—must be of a strong, explicitly sexual nature. Eroticism is of primary importance. Four-letter words and far-out sex rituals welcome. No science fiction of any kind accepted. Humor with strong sexual angle acceptable." Length: 500-2,000 words. Pays 1¢/word.

NATIONAL SCREW, Rorjor, Inc., 116 W. 14th St., New York NY 10011. (212)741-900600. Editor-in-Chief: Al Goldstein. "For young, college-educated, not necessarily exclusively, but predominantly male audience, 18-35." Monthly magazine; 100 pages. Estab: 1976. Circ: 500,000. Pays on commencement of production of issue in which material is to appear. Buys all rights, but may reassign following publication, and first North American serial rights. Submit seasonal/holiday material 4 months in advance. Simultaneous and photocopied submissions OK. SASE. Reports in 6 weeks. Sample copy $2.

Nonfiction: Expose (especially crime, politics, consumer fraud, drugs, etc.); historical (with sex/drugs/pop culture slant); how-to (especially sex, unusual sports—i.e. boomerangs—gambling, investing); humor (this is the key; parody, satire, lampoon, irreverence); informational (consumer-oriented); interview (media figures, cultural heroes, rock personalities, writers, artists); new product (electronics); nostalgia (primarily 50s and 60s); personal experience (related to sex, drugs, travel, unusual experiences); photo feature (art-photo portfolios, travel); profile (preferred over interviews); travel (youth-oriented, off the beaten track); and occult (fads, 'scenes', and trends). Buys 7-10 mss/issue. Query. Length: 3,000-3,500 words. Pays $200 minimum.

Fiction: Adventure (with erotic flavor), erotica, experimental, fantasy, humor, mystery, science fiction and suspense. "Interested in reprinting sections of books by top-qualityy, op-name writers." Buys 1 ms/issue. Send complete ms. Length: 1,500-3,500 words. Pays $200 minimum.

How To Break In: "Query first, outlining your ideas, plan of attack; include publishing credits. Read a few issues of the magazine carefully. It's something like a cross between *Oui* and *National Lampoon:* sex with tongue in cheek. Articles should be fresh, outrageous, off the wall, and well-written. We're especially interested in parody."

NYMPHET, Sunway Periodicals, Inc., 21335 Roscoe Blvd., Canoga Park CA 91401. Editor-in-Chief: Kent Roland. Managing Editor: Ross Knight. Emphasizes adult male topics, particularly as they relate to young women. For the active, sexually motivated man; 21-40. Bi-monthly magazine; 84 pages. Estab: 1972. Pays 6 weeks after acceptance. Buys all rights, but may reassign following publication. Submit seasonal/holiday material 6 months in advance. Reports in 2-3 weeks. Free editorial guidelines.

Photos: Kevin Rawls, Department Editor. Purchased on assignment. Query preferred. Pays $10 maximum. Model release usually required.

Fiction: Adventure, erotica, fantasy, confession, experimental, humorous, mystery, suspense, mainstream. Buys 25 mss/year. Query or send complete ms. Length: 2,500-3,500 words. Pays $100 maximum.

ONE MAN'S OPINION, Box 1885, Rockford IL 61110. Editor-in-Chief: K. Hamilton. For young to middle-age men; semi-professional. Monthly magazine; 32 pages. Estab: 1972. Circ: 5,000. Pays on publication. Buys all rights, but may reassign following publication. Simultaneous submissions OK. SASE. Reports in 6 weeks. Writer's guidelines 25¢.

Nonfiction: Expose (all types); personal opinion (provocative); personal experience; photo feature (men's type). Buys 48 mss/year. Submit complete ms. Length: 250-1,500 words. Pays $100-500.

Photos: Purchased with or without mss. Query first. Pays $5-25 for 5x7 or 8x10 b&w glossies. Model release required.

Fiction: Erotica, confession, romance, mainstream. Buys 25 stories a year. Query or submit complete ms. Length: 500-1,500 words. Pays 4¢/word.

How To Break In: "We are looking for strong fiction/nonfiction. No punches pulled. Heavy on man/woman relationships, sex, forceful and fast-moving stories—good dialogue."

Rejects: "Clever" or "cute" approaches. Wants the "meat and potatoes", not the overly intellectual stuff.

OUI MAGAZINE, 919 North Michigan Ave., Chicago IL 60611. (312)649-0800. Executive Editor: Mark Zussman. For young, well-educated, urban-oriented men. Monthly. Established in 1972. Circulation: over 1½ million. Buys all rights. Buys over 100 mss a year. Payment on acceptance. Seasonal material for year-end holidays must be submitted 6 months in advance. Reports within 4 weeks. Query first for nonfiction. Submit only complete ms for fiction and humor. Enclose S.A.S.E.

Nonfiction and Photos: "Articles dealing with subjects of national and international interest (including travel) as well as pop culture (including entertainment), sex, sports, service, human behavior. Humor and satire are welcome. All material should be characterized by friskiness, irreverence, wit, humor." Informational, interview, profile, humor, nostalgia, photo, travel, and spot news. Length: 5,000 words maximum. Pays $750 to $1,200 for full-length article. Spot news is used for regular column, Openers. Photos (both b&w and color) are purchased without accompanying ms or on assignment. Pays $200 to $400.

Fiction: Experimental, mainstream, mystery, suspense, erotica, science fiction, fantasy, and humorous fiction. Length: 500 to 5,000 words. Pays $500 to $1,200.

Fillers: Department Editor: John Rezek. Newsbreaks, clippings and short humor. Pays $25.

PENTHOUSE, 909 Third Ave., New York NY 10022. Executive Editor: Art Cooper. For male (18 to 34) audience; upper income bracket, college educated. Established in 1965. Monthly. Circulation: 5,350,000. Buys all rights. Buys 60 to 70 mss a year. Payment on acceptance. Will consider photocopied submissions. Reports in 6 to 8 weeks. Query first. Enclose S.A.S.E.

Nonfiction: Department Editor: Peter Bloch. Articles on general themes, but not sport or family orientated; money, sex, politics, health, crime, etc. No first person. Male viewpoint only. Length: 3,500 to 5,000 words. General rates: $250 per 1,000 words.

Fiction: Department Editor: Gerard Van Der Leun. Fiction with some sex content. Experimental, mainstream; mystery, suspense and adventure with erotic flavor; erotica, and science fiction. Length: 3,500 to 5,000 words. Pays $750 and up.

Photos: Purchased without mss and on assignment. Nude girl sets. Pays $200 minimum for b&w; $250 for color. Spec sheet available from Art Director Joe Brooks.

PIX, Publishers Service, Inc., 8060 Melrose Ave., Los Angeles CA 90046. (213)653-8060. Editor: Sean Stephens. Bimonthly. For the young adult male. Buys first North American serial rights. Pays on publication. Sample copy $1.50; free writer's guidelines. Query. Reports in 3-6 weeks, but may take longer. SASE.

Nonfiction: Wants hard-hitting articles with strong sexual slant, ribald humor, articles on erotica, etc. Articles with a very bizarre sexual slant. Humor, too, should be of an erotic, but kinky or far-out nature. The whole spectrum of Krafft-Ebing's writings on sexuality can be considered in articles and fiction. Length: 3,000 words maximum. Pays 5¢ per word minimum.

PLAYBOY, 919 N. Michigan, Chicago IL 60611. Editor-Publisher: Hugh M. Hefner; Editorial Director: Arthur Kretchmer; Managing Editor: Sheldon Wax. Monthly. Reports in 2 weeks. Buys first rights and others. Enclose S.A.S.E. with mss and queries.

Nonfiction: Department Editors: Laurence Gonzales and Peter Ross Range. "Articles should be carefully researched and written with wit and insight; a lucid style is important. Little true adventure or how-to material. Check magazine for subject matter. Pieces on outstanding contemporary men, sports, politics, sociology, business and finance, games, all areas of interest to the urban male." A query is advisable here. Length is about 4,000 to 6,000 words. On acceptance, pays $2,000 minimum. If a commissioned article does not meet standards, will pay a turn-down price of $400. The Playboy interviews run between 8,000 and 15,000 words. After getting an assignment, the freelancer outlines the questions, conducts and edits the interview, and writes the introduction. Pays $2,500 on acceptance. Also, selected shorts pays $750 for 1,000-word essays on contemporary topics; query first. For interviews and selected shorts, contact G. Barry Golson, Executive Editor.

Photos: Gary Cole, Photography Editor, suggests that all photographers interested in contributing make a thorough study of the photography currently appearing in the magazine. Generally all photography is done on assignment. While much of this is assigned to *Playboy's* staff photographers, approximately 50% of the photography is done by freelancers and *Playboy* is in constant search of creative new talent. Qualified freelancers are encouraged to submit samples of their work and ideas. All assignments made on an all rights basis with payments scaled from $600 per color page; $300 per b&w page; cover, $1,000. Playmate photography for entire project: $6,000. Assignments and submissions handled by Associate Editor: Janice Moses, Chicago; Hollis Wayne, New York; Marilyn Grabowski, Los Angeles. Assignments made on a minimum guarantee basis. Film, processing, and other expenses necessitated by assignment honored.

Fiction: Department Editor: Robie Macauley. Both light and serious fiction. Entertainment pieces are clever, smoothly written stories. Serious fiction must come up to the best contemporary standards in substance, idea, and style. Both, however, should be designed to appeal to the educated, well-informed male reader. General types include comedy, mystery, fantasy, horror, science fiction, adventure, social-realism, "problem," and psychological stories. One special requirement for science fiction is that it deal—in fresh and original ways—with human dilemmas more than technological problems. "We prefer stories that would appeal to the general reader, not to the science fiction specialists alone." Fiction on controversial topics is welcome; the only taboo is against formless sketches and excessively subjective writing. *Playboy* has serialized novels by Ian Fleming, Vladimir Nabokov, Graham Greene, Michael Crichton, and Irwin Shaw. Other fiction contributors include Saul Bellow, John Cheever, Bernard Malamud, and Kurt Vonnegut. Fiction lengths are from 3,000 to 6,000 words; occasionally short-shorts of 1,000 to 1,500 words are used. Pays $3,000 for lead story; $2,000 regular; $1,000 short-short. Rates rise for additional acceptances. Rate for Ribald Classics is $400. Unsolicited mss must be accompanied by stamped, self-addressed envelope.

Fillers: Party Jokes are always welcome. Pays $50 each on acceptance. Also interesting items for Playboy After Hours, front section (best check it carefully before submission). The After

Hours, front section, pays anywhere from $50 for a two-line typographical error (submissions not returned) to $350 for an original essay. Subject matter should be humorous, ironic. Has movie, book, record reviewers but solicits queries for short (1,000 words or less) pieces on art, places, people, trips, adventures, experiences, erotica, television—in short, open-ended. Ideas for Playboy Potpourri pay $75 on publication. Query first.

PLAYERS MAGAZINE, Players International Publications, 8060 Melrose Ave., Los Angeles CA 90046. (213)653-8060. Editor-in-Chief: Michael St. John. Managing Editor: Meronda Jones. For the black male. Monthly magazine; 94 pages. Estab: 1973. Circ: 400,000. Pays on publication. Buys all rights. Phone queries OK. Submit seasonal/holiday material 4-6 months in advance. Photocopied submissions OK. SASE. Reports in 3 months. Free writer's guidelines.
Nonfiction: *"Players* is *Playboy* in basic black." Expose; historical; humor; inspirational; sports; travel; reviews of movies, books and records; profile and interview (on assignment). Length: 1,000-5,000 words. Pays 6¢/word. Photos purchased on assignment (pays $25 minimum for b&w; $500 and expenses for 100 shots). Model release required.
Fiction: Adventure; erotica; fantasy; historical (black); humorous; science fiction and experimental. Length: 1,000-4,000 words. Pays 10¢/word.

RAMPAGE, 11058 West Addison St., Franklin Park IL 60131. Editor: Jack Tyger. For sophisticated, cosmopolitan adults. Weekly. Circulation: 300,000. Buys all rights. Buys 600 mss a year. Pays on acceptance. Will send a sample copy to a writer for $1. Query first or submit complete ms. Enclose S.A.S.E.
Nonfiction and Photos: "Our audience consists of sophisticated, cosmopolitan adult readers who enjoy reading witty, humorous and satirical sex-oriented articles. Our readers also prefer reading shocking expose features. We're always in the market for features on current trends in sex. These features should have a strong humorous or satirical slant. Humorous first-person confession stories are also in order. Writer should know how to put humor, wit and satire to good use in his features. Features must be entertaining. Rather than treating readers as groups of buyers, we try to reach each and every reader on an individual basis." Length: 600 to 1,200 words. Payment is up to 2¢ a word. B&w glossy photos purchased with mss. Payment is $5 to $100.

SAGA, Gambi Publications, Inc., 333 Johnson Ave., Brooklyn NY 11206. (212)456-8600. Editor-in-Chief: David J. Elrich. General interest men's magazine. "We offer an alternative to the many 'skin' magazine across the country in that we give an exciting, contemporary look at America today without the porn. A man's magazine that can be read by the entire family." Monthly magazine; 80 pages. Estab: 1950. Circ: 300,000. Pays on acceptance. Buys all rights, but may reassign following publication. Phone queries OK. Submit seasonal/holiday material 3 months in advance. SASE. Reports in 3-4 weeks. Sample copy $1.
Nonfiction: Expose (government); how-to (save money); humor (topical); interview; new product; profile and travel. Buys 12 mss/issue. Query. Length: 1,500-3,500 words. Pays $250-600.
Photos: Photos purchased with accompanying ms or on assignment. Captions required. Pays $35 minimum for b&w photos; $75 minimum for 35mm color photos. Query for photos. Model release required.

SCREW, P.O. Box 432, Old Chelsea Station, New York NY 10011. Managing Editor: M.V. Clayton. For a predominantly male, college-educated audience; 21 through mid-40's. Tabloid newspaper; 48 pages. Established in 1968. Weekly. Circulation: 125,000. Buys all rights. Buys 150 to 200 mss a year. Pays on publication. Will send free sample copy to writer on request. Write for copy of guidelines for writers. Reports in 2 to 4 weeks. Submit complete ms for first-person, true confessions. Query first on all other material. Enclose S.A.S.E.
Nonfiction and Photos: "Sexually related news, humor, how-to articles, and first-person, true confessions. Frank and explicit treatment of all areas of sex; outrageous and irreverent attitudes combined with hard information, news and consumer reports. Our style is unique. Writers should check several recent issues." Length: 1,000-3,000 words. Pays $100-200. Will also consider material for "Letter From...", a consumer-oriented wrapup of commercial sex scene in cities around the country; and "My Scene," a sexual true confession. Length: 1,000 to 1,200 words. Pays about $40. B&w glossies (8x10 or 11x14) purchased with or without mss or on assignment. Pays $10 to $50.

STAG MAGAZINE, 575 Madison Ave., New York NY 10022. (212)838-7900. Editorial Director: Noah Sarlat. Issued monthly. Reports in 2 weeks. Buys all rights. Pays on acceptance. Query first. Enclose S.A.S.E.

Nonfiction: Uses fast, suspenseful, dramatic, true stories. Also uses articles on personalities and crime which run up to 3,500 words. "Our emphasis is on sophisticated, sex-oriented articles of interest to men." Pays up to $500.

Photos: B&w: singles, illustrations, series. Up to $25 for each article illustration; up to $50 per page for series. Color for covers, cheesecake and inside illustrations.

Fiction: "Sex-oriented fiction only." The editor suggests that the inexperienced writer stick to the well-plotted story. Length: 3,500 words. Pays up to $300.

How To Break In: "Most of our material is based on successful queries and we read everything that comes in. We have plenty of openings. We're a good market for the freelancer, but unfortunately many of the stories and ideas we get show a lack of familiarity with what we're trying to do. The key thing is to make your story current and based on something newsworthy. When there were a lot of drug busts, we were running a lot of drug bust stories. We also base our stories on current movie themes. The plots can be the old stuff, but we want to be able to develop the story into an eye-catching, new, newsworthy title. We only do 1 consumer-oriented piece a month and 1 sex-fiction piece, so they are more difficult to break into. However, 1 of our regular freelancers started with a 'true' adventure piece and we have since developed him into an excellent sex-fiction writer. Try to familiarize yourself with our formula and absorb what we want."

SWANK, 888 7th Ave., New York NY 10019. Editor-in-Chief: Ben Pesta. Managing Editor: Rita Rowzee. For urban men, ages 18-40. Monthly magazine; 98 pages. Circ: 250,000. Pays 60 days following acceptance. Buys first North American serial rights and second serial (reprint) rights (for books). Submit seasonal/holiday material 4 months in advance. SASE. Reports in 4 weeks. Sample copy $2.

Nonfiction: Expose (on government, big business, and organized crime); how-to (get a raise, find a divorce lawyer, seduce women); humor; interview (must be established names); photo feature (usually nude sets); profile; and travel (with a strong men's slant). Buys 5-6 mss/issue. Length: 3,000 words maximum (except for *very* strong investigative pieces). Pays $200 minimum.

Photos: Leo McCarthy, Art Director. Purchased without accompanying ms. Send transparencies. Pays $400/set for 2x2 color transparencies. Model release required. "There should be some notation here that the photos we're looking for are female nudes, not your kids, your puppy, your vacation, etc."

Fiction: Adventure; erotica; humorous; mystery; science fiction; suspense; western. Buys 1 mss/issue. Length: 3,000 words. Pays $100 minimum.

How To Break In: "The best way is to read several issues which will give you an idea of what we do. Local events and celebrities that are singular enough to be of national interest are usually good query material. With your query, enclose tearsheets of pieces you've written that are fairly close in style to what you'd like to do for us. Don't just list your credits. We have to know if you can write."

TOPPER, Top-Flight Magazines, 13510 Ventura Blvd., Sherman Oaks CA 91423. Editor: Eric Thomas. For a male audience, all ages. Bimonthly. Buys original rights. Pays on publication. Material not suitable is generally reported on within 2 weeks. SASE.

Nonfiction and Fiction: "Anything of interest to men. Male-female slant required." Buys only strongly erotic pieces. All material should be contemporary. No historical surveys. No personality pieces, sci-fi or fantasy. Length: 500-2,500 words. Pays 1¢/word.

WEEKDAY, Enterprise Publications, 20 N. Wacker Dr., Suite 3417, Chicago IL 60606. For the average employee in business and industry. Established in 1953. Circulation: 30,000. Buys all rights. Pays on acceptance. Enclose S.A.S.E.

Nonfiction and Photos: Uses articles slanted toward the average man, with the purpose of increasing his understanding of the business world and helping him be more successful in it. Also uses articles on "How to Get Along with Other People." and informative articles on meeting everyday problems — consumer buying, legal problems, community affairs, real estate, education, human relations, etc. Length: approximately 1,000 words or less. Pays $10 to $40 for these. Uses b&w human interest photos.

Military Publications

Technical and semitechnical publications for military commanders, personnel, and planners, as well as those for military families and civilians interested in Armed

Forces activities are listed here. All of these publications require submissions emphasizing military subjects or aspects of military life.

AIR UNIVERSITY REVIEW, United States Air Force, Air University, Bldg. 1211, Maxwell Air Force Base AL 36112. (205)293-2773. Editor: Glenn E. Wasson, Col., USAF. Professional military journal for military supervisory staff and command personnel and top level civilians. Circulation: 20,000. Not copyrighted, Buys no mss, but gives cash awards on publication. Reports in 6 weeks. Query first.
Nonfiction and Photos: "Serves as an open forum for exploratory discussion. Purpose is to present innovative thinking and stimulate dialogue concerning Air Force doctrine, strategy, tactics, and related national defense matters. Footnotes as needed. Prefer the author to be the expert. Reviews of defense related books. Expository style. B&w glossy photos or charts to supplement articles are desired. Length: 2,500 to 4,000 words. Cash awards up to $120 unless written by U.S. Federal personnel on duty time.

ARMED FORCES JOURNAL, 1414 22nd St., N.W., Washington DC 20037. Editor: Benjamin F. Schemmer. For "senior career officers of the U.S. military, defense industry, Congressmen and government officials interested in defense matters, international military and defense industry." Established in 1863. Monthly. Circulation: 12,000. Buys all rights. Buys 25-45 mss/year. Pays on publication. Sample copy $1.25. Photocopied submissions OK. Reports in 2-4 weeks. Submit complete ms. SASE.
Nonfiction: Publishes "national and international defense issues: weapons programs, research, personnel programs, international relations (with emphasis on defense aspect). Also profiles on retired military personnel. We do not want broad overviews of a general subject; more interested in detailed analysis of a specific program or situation. Our readers are decision makers in defense matters—hence, subject should not be treated too simplistically. Be provocative. We are not afraid to take issue with our own constituency when an independent voice needs to be heard." Buys informational, profile, think articles. Length: 1,000 to 3,000 words. Pays $50 per page.

ARMY MAGAZINE, 1529 18th St., N.W., Washington DC 20036. (202)483-1800. Editor: L. James Binder. For active military, reserves, retired military, defense-oriented industry, government personnel and their families. Monthly magazine; 64 pages. Established in 1899. Circ: 92,000. Buys all rights. Buys 125 mss/year. Pays on publication. Will send free sample copy to writer on request. Write for copy of guidelines for writers. Query first. Reports within 6 weeks. Enclose S.A.S.E.
Nonfiction and Photos: "Military subjects; contemporary, historical. While most of our material is of a serious nature, we use as much good humor as we can find, both very short and feature length. We like our articles to get to the point quickly, although we like interesting, attention-getting leads. We are very aware of the 'why' of things and prefer to go deeply into an aspect of a topic rather than carrying a superficial survey type of article which probably already has been done in publications that come out oftener and may have more space. History, specifically well-known history, is overworked. We like new slants within this area, previously unpublished information or material that is little known. Personality profiles in which the writer discovers military types are human and bright are also a drag." Length: 4,000 words maximum. Pays 7¢ to 9¢ per word. Regular columns cover book reviews and editorial opinion. 8x10 b&w glossies and 8x10 color prints or 35mm transparencies purchased with or without ms, or on assignment. Captions required. Pays $10 minimum for b&w; $50 minimum for color. Photo Department Editor: Michael Dunbar.
Fillers: Uses short humorous fillers. Length: 500 words maximum. Pays $5 to $25.
How To Break In: "We would like to publish more material from writers who do not specialize in military topics and I believe they have much to say to our readers. Gee-whiz approaches and historical pieces recounting events that would obviously be well known to a professional military readership never get very far with us. Best advice: avoid these, query first and tell us what you have published or anything that will give us an idea about your credibility."

ARMY RESERVE MAGAZINE, DAAR-PA, The Pentagon, Washington DC 20310. (202)697-2470. Editor: Bernard F. Halloran. For civilians who find the military a hobby. Magazine; 32 pages. Established in 1954. Every 2 months. Circulation: 720,000. Not copyrighted. Payment in contributor's copies. Various prizes are awarded from time to time. Will send free sample copy to writer on request. Write for copy of guidelines for writers. Reports on accepted or rejected material in 6 weeks. Answers queries in 1 week. Query first. Enclose S.A.S.E.
Nonfiction: "We use news and personality features, consumer information, articles on happenings in world military affairs, weapons, foreign armies, off-duty activities, and happenings

in the Army, Army Reserve and ROTC units. And good, amusing military history. Since *Reserve* is designed for a primarily non-military audience, buzz words are not used; humor is. We assume the reader knows nothing about the subject and develop it carefully attempting to find a universal level of interest. Articles are short, to the point, filled with information and often written tongue in cheek." Length: 1,200 to 2,500 words.
Fillers: Newsbreaks, anecdotes; short humor. Length: 150 to 500 words.

AT EASE, Division of Home Missions, Assemblies of God, 1445 Boonville Ave., Springfield MO 65802. Editor: T.E. Gannon. For military personnel. Magazine; 4 (14x17) pages. Every 2 months. Circulation: 10,000. Buys all rights. "We are quite limited in what we would accept from freelance writers. Everything has to be slanted to Assemblies of God readers." Pays on publication. Will send free sample copy to writer on request. Write for copy of guidelines for writers. "If we can't use a submission and we think another department can, we usually let them see it before replying. Otherwise, as soon as we reject it, we return it." Query first. Enclose S.A.S.E.
Nonfiction and Photos: Materials that will interest military men and women. Must have some religious value. Length: 500 to 800 words. Pays minimum of 2¢ a word. Payment for b&w and color photos subject to author's stated fee and size of picture.

INFANTRY, P.O. Box 2005, Fort Benning, GA 31905. (404)545-2350. Editor: LTC Thomas J. Barham. For young Infantry officers and senior noncommissioned Infantry officers. Oriented toward the United States professional military man. Bimonthly magazine, 64 pages. Established in 1921. Circulation: 21,000. Not copyrighted. Accepts about 75 mss a year. Payment for articles on publication at a rate determined by the Editor; no payment for book reviews. Payment cannot be made to U.S. Government employees. Will send free sample copy to writers on request. Write for copy of guidelines for writers. Submit only complete ms. Reports within 30 days.
Nonfiction and Photos: Interested in current information on U.S. military organization, weapons, equipment, tactics, and techniques; foreign armies and their equipment; solutions to problems encountered in the Active Army, National Guard, and Army Reserve. *Infantry* is the only magazine in the U.S. that deals specifically with the foot soldier and his problems, and is used by officers and noncommissioned officers as a reference book, especially when new techniques and equipment are introduced. Interested in any subject related to military affairs that is of current interest and significance. Departments include letters, Features and Forum, Training Notes, Book Reviews. Illustrations and photos help to sell the product. Length of articles: 1,500 to 3,500 words. Length of Book Reviews: 500 to 1,000 words. Send query to Book Review editor for book reviews. To save time, query Editor on article ideas. Explain intended scope, theme, and organization." Prefers concise and direct wording, expressed in the active voice. Also prefers precision and clarity of expression to flowery prose. All ms edited as needed to conform to magazine's style and standards of expression. Likes clean, double-spaced mss typed on one side of sheet. "Acceptance and publication by *Infantry* conveys to the magazine the right for subsequent reproduction and use of published material for training purposes."

LADYCOM, Downey Communications, Inc., 1800 M St. NW, Suite 650 S., Washington DC 20036. Editor-in-Chief: Anne Taubeneck. For wives of military men who live in the U.S. or overseas. Published eight times a year. Magazine; 64 pages. Estab: 1969. Circ: 390,000. Pays on publication. Buys first North American serial rights. Phone queries OK. Submit seasonal/holiday material 4 months in advance. Previously published submissions OK. SASE. Reports in 2-3 weeks. Free sample copy and writer's guidelines.
Nonfiction: All articles must have special interest for military wives. How-to (crafts, food), humor, interview, personal experience, personal opinion, profile and travel. Buys 10-12 mss/issue. Query. Length: 1,200-3,000 words. Pays $75-400/article.
Photos: Purchased with accompanying ms and on assignment. Captions required. Query for photos. 5x7 or 8x10 b&w glossies; 35mm or larger color transparencies. Total purchase price for a ms includes payment for photos. Model release required.
Columns, Departments: It Seems to Me—"personal experience" pieces by military wives. Pros & Cons—opinion pieces on a controversial topic of interest to military wives. Buys 2-3/issue. Query. Length: 1,200-1,800 words. Pays $75-175. Open to suggestions for new columns/departments; address to Anne Taubeneck.
Fiction: Mystery, romance and suspense. Buys 6-8 mss/year. Query. Length: 1,800-2,500 words. Pays $100-250.
How To Break In: "Our ideal contributor is a military wife who can write. However, I'm always impressed by a writer who has analyzed the market and can suggest some possible new angles for us."

LEATHERNECK, Box 1775, Quantico VA 22134. (703)640-6161. Managing Editor: Ronald D. Lyons. Usually buys all rights, but will sometimes reassign rights to author under certain circumstances. Pays on acceptance. Query first. Enclose S.A.S.E.

Nonfiction and Photos: Interested in articles covering present-day Marine activities. Photos are mandatory. *Leatherneck's* slant today is toward the young Marine. Large percentage of subscribers are parents and dependents of enlisted Marines, consequently material used must be impeccable in taste. Pays $150 up. Length: 2,000 to 3,000 words.

Fiction: "Stories must have a strong Marine Corps slant and be in good taste. Humor encouraged. Mss must be accompanied by S.A.S.E." Length: 1,500 to 3,000 words. Pays $150 minimum.

Poetry: Poems with Marine themes. Pays $10 each.

How To Break In: "Like most publications, we're interested in young writers. And, if their writing is good, we smile when we sign the check. More than one beginner has 'broken in' with us, and we've watched them go on to bigger and better things. That's happiness. Unhappiness is vhen we receive manuscripts from young freelancers—and older ones too—who have not done their homework. The manuscripts come in, and our rejection slips go out. On many of them we pen a note: 'We are sorry to be returning your manuscript, but *Leatherneck* is a magazine published for Marines. Perhaps one of the other service publications would like to see your story about the Navy, Army, Air Force, etc.' Yes, there are opportunities for young freelancers at *Leatherneck*. But they must remember that we are specialized. Our main interest is United States Marines, their problems, their interests and their accomplishments. If a young freelancer thinks he can write professionally about the Marine Corps, without having served in it, he is more than welcome to step up to our firing line. If he can't hit the target, his manuscript will be given a 'Maggie's Drawers' and returned. If he comes anywhere near the 'bull's-eye,' he will be encouraged. Our poetry column (Gyrene Gyngles) is a good opportunity for 'recruits' in the writing field to break in with us. Occasionally we buy short human interest items concerning Marines and their acts of heroism. And, of course, we're always interested in humor pieces, in good taste. You may have seen the Marine Corps' recruiting slogan: 'The Marines are looking for a few good men!' We go along with that. *Leatherneck* is looking for a few good freelancers."

MARINE CORPS GAZETTE, Marine Corps Association, Box 1775, MCB, Quantico VA 22134. Editor: Col. Bevan G. Cass, U.S.M.C. (Ret.). May issue is aviation oriented. November issue is historically oriented. Monthly. Circulation: 25,000. Buys all rights. Buys 140 to 160 mss a year. Pays on publication. Will send free sample copy on request. "Will send writer's guide on request." Submit seasonal or special material at least 2 months in advance. Query first. Reports in 30 to 60 days. Enclose S.A.S.E.

Nonfiction: Uses articles up to 5,000 words pertaining to the military profession. Keep copy military, not political. Wants practical articles on military subjects, especially amphibious warfare, close air support and helicopter-borne assault. Also uses any practical article on artillery, communications, leadership, etc. Particularly wanted are articles on relationship of military to civilian government, in-depth coverage of problem areas of the world, Russian and Chinese military strategy and tactics. Also historical articles about Marines are always needed for the November issue, the anniversary of the Marine Corps. Otherwise, historical articles not wanted unless they have a strong application to present day military problems. All offerings are passed on by an editorial board as well as by the editor. Does not want "Sunday supplement" or "gee whiz" material. Pays 3¢ to 6¢ per word.

Photos: Purchased with mss. Pays $5 each. 4x5 glossies preferred.

THE MILITARY ENGINEER, Suite 905, 740 15th St., N.W., Washington DC 20005. (202)638-4010. Editor: Brig. Gen. William C. Hall, USA, Ret. Managing Editor: John J. Kern. Bimonthly magazine. Estab: 1919. Circ: 22,000. Pays on publication. Buys all rights. Phone queries OK. SASE. Reports in 1 month. Sample copy and writer's guidelines $3.

Nonfiction: Well-written and illustrated semi-technical articles by experts and practitioners of civil and military engineering, constructors, and architect/engineers on these subjects and on subjects of military biography and history. "Subject matter should represent a contribution to the fund of knowledge, concern a new project or method, be on R&D in these fields; investigate planning and management techniques or problems in these fields, or be of militarily strategic nature." Buys 80-100 mss/year. Length: 2,000-4,000 words. Query.

Photos: Mss must be accompanied by 6-8 well-captioned photos, maps or illustrations; b&w, generally. Pays $20/page.

MILITARY LIFE, c/o Taylor & Ives, Inc., 30 E. 42nd St., New York NY 10019. (212)687-9040. Editor: Will Lieberson. For the young serviceman. Monthly. Circulation: 300,000. Buys

all rights. Pays on publication. Will send a sample copy to a writer on request. Query first, with synopsis. Reports in 1 month. Enclose S.A.S.E.
Nonfiction and Photos: Articles dealing with topics that would interest men who are either currently in the service or have been in the service and are doing something that would be of interest to other servicemen. The subject areas are limitless. "We prefer to see a synopsis of the article." Length: 750 to 1,200 words. Pays $75. B&w glossies and color transparencies (35mm) are purchased with ms. Pays $15 for b&w; $50 for color.

MILITARY LIVING AND CONSUMER GUIDE, P.O. Box 4010, Arlington VA 22204. (703)521-7703. Editor: Ann Crawford. For military personnel and their families. Monthly. Circulation: 30,000. Buys first serial rights. "Very few freelance features used last year; mostly staff-written." Pays on publication. Sample copy for 50¢ in coin or stamp. "Slow to report due to small staff and workload." Submit complete ms. Enclose S.A.S.E.
Nonfiction and Photos: "Articles on military life in greater Washington DC area. We would especially like recreational features in the Washington DC area. We specialize in passing along morale boosting information about the military installations in the area, with emphasis on the military family—travel pieces about surrounding area, recreation information, etc. We do not want to see depressing pieces, pieces without the military family in mind, personal petty complaints or general information pieces. Prefer 700 words or less, but will consider more for an exceptional feature. We also prefer a finished article rather than a query." Payment is 1¢ to 1½¢ a word. Photos purchased with mss. 8x10 b&w glossies. Payment is $5 for original photos by author.

MILITARY LIVING AND CONSUMER GUIDE'S R&R REPORT, P.O. Box 4010, Arlington VA 22204. Publisher: Ann Crawford. For "military consumers worldwide who are subscribers to the Military Living R&R Report." Newsletter. Bimonthly. "Please state when sending submission that it is for the *R&R Report Newsletter* so as not to confuse it with our monthly magazine which has different requirements." Buys first rights, but will consider other rights. Pays on publication. Sample copy 50¢. SASE.
Nonfiction: "We use information on little-known military facilities and privileges, discounts around the world and travel information. Items must be short and concise. Stringers wanted around the world. Payment is on an honorarium basis—1¢ to 1½¢ a word."

MILITARY REVIEW, US Army Command and General Staff College, Fort Leavenworth KS 66027. (913)684-5642. Editor-in-Chief: Col. Ruby R. Stauber. Managing Editor: Cpt. John W. Ball. Emphasizes the military for senior military officers, students and scholars. Monthly magazine; 112 pages. Estab: 1922. Circ: 21,000. Pays on publication. Buys one-time rights. Phone queries OK. Photocopied and previously published submissions OK. SASE. Reports in 4 weeks. Free sample copy and writer's guidelines.
Nonfiction: Historical, humor, informational, new product, personal opinion and technical. Buys 5-7 mss/issue. Query. Length: 2,000-4,000 words. Pays $10-50.
Photos: Purchased on assignment. Captions required. Send b&w/color prints. Offers no additionaal payment for photos accepted with accompanying ms. Model release required.

NATIONAL DEFENSE, 819 Union Trust Bldg., Washington DC 20005. (202)347-7250. Editor: R.E. Lewis. For members of industry and U.S. Armed Forces. Publication of the American Defense Preparedness Association. Magazine; 80 pages. Established in 1920. Every 2 months. Circulation: 30,000. Buys all rights. Buys 6 to 12 mss a year. Pays on publication. Will send sample copy to writer for $2. Write for copy of guidelines for writers. Will consider photocopied submissions. No simultaneous submissions. Reports on material accepted for publication in 2 to 3 weeks. Returns rejected material in 4 weeks. Query first or submit complete ms. Enclose S.A.S.E.
Nonfiction: Military-related articles: weapons, systems, management, production. "We emphasize industrial preparedness for defense and prefer a news style, with emphasis on the 'why'." Length: 1,500 to 2,500 words. Pays $25 per published page. Book reviews are sometimes used, but query is required first and no payment is made.

NATIONAL GUARDSMAN, 1 Massachusetts Ave., N.W., Washington DC 20001. (202)347-0341. Editor: Luther L. Walker. For officers and enlisted men of the Army and Air National Guard. Monthly except August. Circulation: 62,000. Rights negotiable. Buys 10-12 mss/year. Pays on publication. Query first. Enclose S.A.S.E.
Nonfiction and Photos: Military policy, strategy, training, equipment, logistics, personnel policies: tactics, combat lessons learned as they pertain to the Army and Air Force (including Army National Guard and Air National Guard). No history. Material must be strictly accurate from a

technical standpoint. Writer must have military knowledge. "It helps if he knows enough about Guard or other reserve forces to orient his piece toward the Guardsman's frame of reference. Style should be easy to read, serious but not pedantic." Does not want exposes. Length: 2,000 to 3,000 words. Payment is 3¢ a word and up, depending on originality, amount of research involved, etc. B&w glossy photos occasionally purchased with mss. Payment is $5 to $10.

Fillers: True military anecdotes (but not timeworn jokes). Length: 50 to 200 words. Payment is $10.

OFF DUTY, 250 E. 63rd St. New York NY 10021. Editor: Jim Shaw. For members of he U.S. military and dependents living overseas and the mainland West Coast, with much interest in travel and hobbies. Monthly magazine; 56-60 pages. Estab: 1971. Circ: 275,000. Pays on publication in most cases, but sometimes pays on acceptance. Buys one-time rights. Submit seasonal or holiday material 4 months in advance. Simultaneous and photocopied submissions OK. Previously published work OK. SASE. Reports in 6 weeks. Free sample copy and writer's guidelines.

Nonfiction: How-to articles on getting started in hobbies, getting around in exotic countries, household hints for women, latest travel information, shopping bargains, etc. Travel articles (how to get there, what to see and do, tariffs, hidden costs, anecdotes, etc.) New product (chiefly cars, hobby and recreational equipment). Personal experience (only to enlighten readers on pitfalls or discoveries in travel stories). Buys 8-100/year. Query or submit complete ms. Length: 300-2,500 words. Pays 7-10¢/word.

Photos: Purchased with mss. Captions required. Pays $10-20/5x7 b&w glossies; $15-100/35mm (and up) transparencies. Query or send contact sheet or transparencies.

OFF DUTY EUROPE, Eschersheimer Landstrasse 69, 6-D Frankfurt/Main, West Germany. Editor-in-Chief: Patricia Graves. (Submissions may be sent through New York. Address to Graves, Off Duty, 250 E. 63rd St., New York NY 10021). For "U.S. servicemen and their families, mostly between 18-30 years old. Interested in travel, sports, audio and sports equipment, cars, hobbies." Monthly magazine; 104 pages. Estab: 1969. Circ: 100,000. Pays on acceptance. Buys second serial or one-time rights. Submit seasonal or holiday material 2-3 months in advance. Photocopied and previously published (if not in conflicting distribution) submissions OK. SASE. Free sample copy and writer's guidelines.

Nonfiction: "We like articles on travel, hobbies, recreation, entertaining, motoring, family activities, the home, and budget saving ideas. Emphasis is on things to do. In travel articles we like anecdotes, lots of description, color and dialogue. Our readers are not looking to relax in unspoiled scenery. They want to know what to do." Buys 8-10 mss/issue. Query. Length: 850-2,500 words. Pays 10-12¢/word.

Photos: Clothild Lucey, Photo Editor. Purchased with accompanying ms. Captions required. Send contact sheet. Pays $20 for b&w photos; $40-100 for color transparencies. More for covers. Model release required. Photos often decisive in acceptance of article.

Columns, Departments: For Her Section (articles of interest to modern women, keeping in mind our audience of military wives and servicewomen). Open to suggestions for new columns or departments.

Rejects: "No fiction, poetry, war stories, GI humor, personality feature, cartoons, medicine, diets, occult or mysticism."

OVERSEAS LIFE, Verlagsgesellschaft Ogh., Otto-Hahn Strasse 9, 6382 Friedrichsdorf/Koppern, West Germany. Editor-in-Chief: Bruce Thorstad. Travel magazine serving American and Canadian military personnel and their families stationed throughout Europe and the U.K. Monthly magazine; 60 pages. Estab: 1973. Circ: 80,000. Pays on publication. Buys all rights, but may reassign following publication. Submit seasonal/holiday material 3 months in advance. Simultaneous, photocopied and previously published submissions OK, "but we won't touch anything which might also have gone to our competitors." SASE. Reports in 2 weeks. Enclose International Reply Coupons for sample copy.

Nonfiction: How-to (travel by bike, van, foot; how to photograph travel subjects, hang glide, ski, kayak, sail, etc.), informational (setting up stereo, darkroom; best place to sun and swim, ski, shop, etc.), new product (not specific brand, but new category, i.e., sound super-8), photo feature (recently bought 'Photographing Rock Stars,' a how-to on front of stage photography), and travel (spots in Europe today, for our audience). Buys 36 mss/year. Query. Length: 1,000-2,000 words. Pays $60-100.

Photos: Purchased with accompanying ms. Captions required. Send prints or transparencies with ms. Pays DM 15 minimum/photo for 8x10 b&w glossies; DM 15 minimum/35mm or larger color transparencies (DM 50 for cover). Total purchase price for ms includes payment for photos.

Rejects: "We get far too many mss written by would-be 19th century aristocrats for other would-be 19th century aristocrats. Our military readers are not taking the Grand Tour, they are on a tour of duty and travel when they can. Seeing the best of Europe cheaply takes information and ingenuity."

PARAMETERS: JOURNAL OF THE U.S. ARMY WAR COLLEGE, U.S. Army War College, Carlisle Barracks PA 17013. (717)245-4943. Editor: Colonel Paul R. Hilty, Jr., U.S. Army. For military audience (large percentage of graduate level degrees) interested in national and international security affairs, defense activities and management; also a growing audience among civilian academicians. Quarterly. Circ: 6,500. Not copyrighted. Unless copyrighted, articles may be reprinted. Please credit the author and *Parameters, Journal of the U.S. Army War College*. Payment on publication. Reports in 2 months.
Nonfiction and Photos: The purpose of *Parameters* is to provide a forum for the expression of mature, professional thought on national and international security affairs, military history, military strategy, military leadership and management, the art and science of land warfare, and other topics of significant and current interest to the U.S. Army and the Department of Defense. Further, it is designed to serve as a vehicle for continuing the education, and thus the professional development, of War College graduates and other military officers and civilians concerned with military affairs. Military implications should be stressed whenever possible. Length: 5,000-7,000 words. B&w glossies purchased with mss. Pays $25 minimum; $100 maximum (to include half-tones, artwork, charts, graphs, maps, etc.).

PERIODICAL, Council on Abandoned Military Posts, 4970 N. Camino Antonio, Tucson AZ 85718. Editor-in-Chief: Dan L. Thrapp. Emphasizes old and abandoned forts, posts and military installations; military subjects for a professional, knowledgeable readership interested in one-time defense sites or other military installations. Quarterly magazine; 40-64 pages. Estab: 1967. Circ: 1,500. Pays on publication. Buys one-time rights. Simultaneous, photocopied and previously published (if published a long time ago) submissions OK. SASE. Reports in 3 weeks. Sample copy 50¢.
Nonfiction: Historical; personal experience; photo feature; technical (relating to posts, their construction/operation and military matters) and travel. Buys 4-6 mss/issue. Query or send complete ms. Length: 300-4,000 words. Pays minimum $2/page.
Photos: Purchased with or without accompanying ms. Captions required. Query. Glossy, single weight, b&w up to 8x10. Offers no additional payment for photos accepted with accompanying ms.

THE RETIRED OFFICER MAGAZINE, 1625 Eye St., N.W., Washington DC 20006. (202)331-1111. Editor: Colonel Minter L. Wilson, Jr., USA-Ret. For "officers of the 7 uniformed services and their families." Estab: 1945. Monthly. Circ: 241,000. Rights purchased vary with author and material. May buy all rights or first serial rights. Pays on publication. Will send free sample copy to writer on request. Will consider photocopied submissions "if clean and fresh." Submit seasonal material (holiday stories in which the Armed Services are depicted) at least 3 months in advance. Reports on material accepted for publication within 6 weeks. Returns rejected material in 4 weeks. Submit complete ms. Enclose S.A.S.E.
Nonfiction and Photos: History, humor, cultural, second-career opportunities and current affairs. "Currently topical subjects with particular contextual slant to the military; historical events of military significance; features pertinent to a retired military officer's milieu (second career, caveats in the business world; wives' adjusting, leisure, fascinating hobbies). True military experiences (short) are also useful, and we tend to use articles less technical than a single-service publication might publish." Length: 1,000 to 2,500 words. Pays $25 to $250. 8x10 b&w photos (normal halftone). Pays $5. Color photos must be suitable for color separation. Pays $25 if reproduced in color; otherwise, same as b&w. Department Editor: Sharon F. Golden.

RUSI JOURNAL, Royal United Services Institute for Defense Studies, Whitehall SW1A 2ET, England. Editor: Rear Admiral E.F. Gueritz. Deputy Editor: Jenny Shaw. Emphasizes defense and military history. Quarterly magazine; 100 pages. Estab: 1857. Circ: 7,000. Pays on publication. Buys all rights, but may reassign following publication. Photocopied submissions OK. SAE and International Reply Coupons. Sample copy, $5.
Nonfiction: Informational articles on British and U.S. defense; historical military articles with particular reference to current defense problems; weapon technology; international relations and civil/military relations. Buys 10/issue. Query. Length: 2,500-6,000 words. Pays 8 pounds/printed page.
Photos: No additional payment is made for photos, but they should accompany articles whenever possible.

SEA POWER, 818 Eighteenth St., N.W., Washington DC 20006. Editor: James D. Hessman. Issued monthly by the Navy League of the U.S. for naval personnel and civilians interested in naval maritime and defense matters. Buys all rights. Pays on publication. Will send free sample copy to a writer on request. Reports in 1 to 6 months. Query first. Enclose S.A.S.E.

Nonfiction and Photos: Factual articles on sea power in general, and the U.S. Navy, the U.S. Marine Corps, U.S. Coast Guard, U.S. merchant marine and naval services and other navies of the world in particular. Should illustrate and expound the importance of the seas and sea power to the U.S. and its allies. Wants timely, clear, nontechnical, lively writing. Length: 500 to 2,000 words. Does not want to see historical articles, commentaries, critiques, abstract theories, poetry or editorials. Pays $50 to $200, depending upon length and research involved. Purchases 8x10 glossy photos with mss.

U.S. NAVAL INSTITUTE PROCEEDINGS, Annapolis MD 21402. (301)268-6110. Editor: Clayton R. Barrow, Jr. Managing Editor: Paul Stillwell. Emphasizes sea services (Navy, Marine Corps, Coast Guard) for sea services officers and enlisted personnel, other military services in the US and abroad and civilians interested in naval/maritime affairs. Monthly magazine; 120 pages. Estab: 1873. Circ: 65,000. Pays on acceptance. Buys all rights. Phone queries OK, but all material must be submitted on speculation. Submit seasonal/holiday material 6 months in advance. Photocopied submissions OK. SASE. Reports in 2 weeks (queries); 3 months (manuscripts). Free sample copy.

Nonfiction: Historical (based on primary sources, unpublished and/or first-hand experience); humor; informational; nostalgia; personal experience; personal opinion; photo feature; technical; professional notes; and book reviews. Query. Length: 4,000 words maximum. Pays $200-400.

Photos: Purchased with or without accompanying ms or on assignment. Captions required. Query. Pays $15 maximum for b&w 8x10 glossies. "We pay $2 for each photo submitted with articles by people other than the photographer."

Columns/Departments: Fred Rainbow, Column/Department Editor. Comment and Discussion (comments 500-700 words on new subjects or ones previously covered in magazine); Professional Notes; Nobody Asked Me, But... (700-1,000 gords, strong opinion on naval/maritime topic); and Book Reviews. Buys 35 Book Reviews; 35 Professional Notes; 100 Comment and Discussion and 10 NAMB/year. Pays $25-50.

Fillers: Patricia Perry, Fillers Editor. Jokes, gags, anecdotes. Buys 25 fillers/year. Length: maximum 200 words. Pays $25 flat rate.

How To Break In: "The Comment and Discussion section is our bread and butter. It is a glorified letters to the editor section and exemplifies the concept of the *Proceedings* as a forum. We particularly welcome comments on material published in previous issues of the magazine. This offers the writer of the comment an opportunity to expand the discussion of a particular topic and to bring his own viewpoint into it. This feature does not pay particularly well, but it is an excellent opportunity to get one's work into print."

US MAGAZINE, c/o Taylor & Ives, 30 E. 42nd St., New York NY 10017. Editor: Will Lieberson. For the young military wife and her family. Estab: 1966. Monthly. Circ: 67,000. Buys all rights. Pays on acceptance. Will send free sample copy to writer on request. Reports in 1 month. Query first, with synopsis. Enclose S.A.S.E.

Nonfiction: "Looking for articles that will appeal to the military wife and family. They should be general enough so that they will interest all 3 services. As a rule, these women are young with small children." Length: 750 to 1,200 words. Pays $75.

Photos: Purchased with mss; prefers captions but not necessary. Wants b&w glossies and 4-color transparencies. Pays minimum of $15 for b&w; $50 for color.

Miscellaneous Publications

ALTERNATIVE SOURCES OF ENERGY MAGAZINE, Route 2, Box 90A, Milaca MN 56353. (612)983-6892. Editor-in-Chief: Donald Marier. Emphasizes alternative energy sources and appropriate technology for a predominately male, age 36, college educated audience, conscious of environmental and energy limitations. Bimonthly magazine; 64 pages. Estab: 1972. Circ: 4,000. Pays on acceptance. Buys all rights, but may reassign following publication. Phone queries OK. Simultaneous, photocopied, and previously published submissions OK, "if specified at time of submission." SASE. Reports in 2 weeks. Sample copy $1.

Nonfiction: Expose (government, industry), historicaal, (solar, wind, water, etc.), how-to (plans, kits, etc.), humor, informational (new sources of data, products, etc.), interview (any active person), and technical (plans, kits, designs). Buys 90 mss/year. Submit complete ms. Length: 500-6,000 words. Pays $20 minimum, "generally $15-30/page."

Photos: Susan Pauls, Photo Editor. Photos purchased with or without accoompanying ms or on assignment. Captions required. Send contact sheet or prints. Pays $5-25 for 8x10 b&w glossy photos. Total ppurchase price for ms includes payment for photos. Model release required. "We prefer to purchase pix with mss rather than alone."

Fillers: Susan Pauls, Fillers Editor. Clippings, jokes, gags, anecdotes, newsbreaks. Length: 25-100 words. Pays $5 minimum.

How To Break In: "We need well-researched articles emphasizing alternative or appropriate sourcess f energy; solar, water, wind, biofuels, etc."

For '78: "We have plans for a water power development special issue.'"

THE AMERICAN ATHEIST, Society of Separationists Inc., 4408 Medical Pkqy., Austin TX 78756. (512)458-1244. Editor-in-Chief: Dr. Madalyn Murray O'Hair. Emphasizes American atheism for independent businessmen/women, educators, politicians; most are middle aged, republican and conservative. Monthly magazine; 32 pages. Estab: 1963. Circ: 30,000. Pays on publication. Rights purchased vary with author and material. Phone queries OK. Submit seasonal/holiday material 3 months iin advance. SASE. Simultaneous, photocopied and previously published submissions OK. Reports in 1 month. Sample copy $1; fbree writer's guidelines.

Nonfiction: W.J. Murray, Articles Editor. Expose (activities of organized religion); historical (American atheist, agnostic freethought activities); humor (anti-theistic); informational (current separation of state/church controversies); interview (with atheist personalities or those of importance to separation of state/church movement); personal experience (relating to persecution of persons for their beliefs) and technical (on longevity, birth control, human sexuality and psychiatry). Buys 2 mss/issue. Query. Length: 1,000-4,000 words. Pays $10-150.

Photos: Ralph Shirley, Photo Editor. Purchased with accompanying ms. Captions required. Query for photos or send negatives. Pays $1-20 for b&w smooth finish 8x10 photos. Total purchase price for ms includes payment for photos. Model release required.

Fiction: Jon Murray, Fiction Editor. Experimental (situations based on historical facts with interpretation as to "what may have happened"), historical (religious figures, events); humorous (viewing the troubles of atheists, agnostics and the foolery of religion) and religious (emphasizing the faults of various denominations). Buys 4 mss/year. Submit complete ms. Length: 1,000-5,000 words. Pays $10-100.

Poetry: Jon Murray, Poetry Editor. Avant-garde, light verse and traditional. Buys 4-6 poems/issue. Limit submissions to batches of 6. Length: maximum 200 words. Pays $5-25.

Fillers: Jon Murray, Fillers Editor. Jokes, gags, anecdotes and short humor. Buys 2-8 fillers/issue. Length: 25 words maximum. Pays $1-5.

For '78: "We celebrate 4 natural holidays for which we need special submissions every year. They are the winter and summer solstices and the vernal and autumnal equinoxes."

AMERICAN DANE MAGAZINE, Danish Brotherhood in America, Box 31748, Omaha NE 68131. (402)341-5049. Editor-in-Chief: Gary Eilts. Emphasizes Danish heritage and traditions. Monthly magazine; 24-36 pages. Estab: 1920. Circ: 11,000. Pays on publication. Buys all rights, but will reassign to author following publication. Submit seasonal/holiday material 4 months in advance (particularly Christmas). Photocopied or previously published submissions OK. SASE. Reports in 1 month. Sample copy 50¢. Free writer's guidelines.

Nonfiction: Historical; humor (satirical, dry wit notoriously Scandinavian); informational (Danish items, Denmark or Danish-American involvements); inspirational (honest inter-relationships); interview; nostalgia; personal experience; personal opinion (very limited, query first); photo feature and travel. Buys 35-40 mss/year. Query. Length: maximum 1,500 words. Pays $25-100.

Photos: Purchased on assignment. Query. Pays $10-50 for b&w; $25-100 for color. Total purchase price for a ms includes payment for photos. Model release required.

Columns, Departments: Grandmother's Kitchen (unusual, unique, or traditional Danish or Scandinavian recipes); Book, film, play reviews (relating to Denmark or the Danes, Danish authors, playwrights, etc.). Buys 20/year. Query. Length: maximum 500 words. Pays $10-50. Open to suggestions for new columns/departments; address Gary Eilts.

Fiction: Adventure; historical; humorous; mystery; romance; and suspense. Buys 12 mss/year. Query. Length: 500-2,000 words. Pays $25-100.

Poetry: Avant-garde, free verse, haiku, light verse and traditional. Buys 6-8 poems/year. Query. Limit submissions to batches of 5. Length: maximum 40 lines. Pays $25-75.

Fillers: Clippings, jokes, gags, anecdotes, puzzles (crossword, anagrams etc.) and short humor. Buys 10-12 fillers/year. Query. Length: 50-300 words. Pays $10-50.

ANDY WARHOL'S INTERVIEW MAGAZINE, 860 Broadway West, New York NY 10003. (212)533-4700. Editor: Bob Colacello. For those interested in fashion, movies, art and music. Established in 1970. Monthly. Circulation: 82,000. All rights purchased but will negotiate on individual basis. Buys 25 mss a year. Payment on publication. Will send sample copy for $1. Query first. Enclose S.A.S.E.

Nonfiction and Photos: Features exclusive interviews with interesting people in fashion, art, movies, television, music, books, and whatever is happening now. Length: 10,000 words maximum. Pays $25. Prefer 8x10 or larger b&w photos.

How To Break In: "We are interested in interviews with entertainment figures as well as with *entertaining* figures. Usually with famous people with whom I want an interview, I'll assign it to someone I know. So the best way to break in is either with a well-known person to whom you happen to have some kind of access or, more likely, a lesser known *entertaining* person who you can get to yourself. If we like what you do —and I don't know how to describe it; basically what you need is a good interviewing personality rather than writing skill —then I will certainly want to use you in the future and will arrange access for you when it comes to interviewing the more famous types."

ARARAT, The Armenian General Benevolent Union, 628 2nd Ave., New York NY 10016. Editor-in-Chief: Leo Hamalian. Emphasizes Armenian life and culture for Americans of Armenian descent; Armenian immigrants. "Many are well-educated; some are Old World." Quarterly magazine; 48 pages. Estab: 1960. Circ: 900. Pays on publication. Buys first North American serial rights. Submit seasonal/holiday material at least 3 months in advance. Photocopied, and previously published submissions OK. SASE. Reports in 6 weeks. Sample copy $1.50.

Nonfiction: Historical (history of Armenian people, of leaders, etc.); interviews (with prominent or interesting Armenians in any field, but articles are preferred); profile (on subjects relating to Armenian life and culture; personal experience (revealing aspects of typical Armenian life); travel (in Soviet Armenia). Buys 3 mss/issue. Query. Length: 1,000-6,000 words. Pays $25-100.

Columns/Departments: Reviews of books by Armenians or relating to Armenians. Buys 6 per issue. Query. Pays $20. Open to suggestions for new columns/departments.

Fiction: Any stories dealing with Armenian life in America or in the old country. Religious stories relating to the Armenian Church. Buys 2 mss/year. Query. Length: 2,000-5,000 words. Pays $35-75.

Poetry: Any verse that is Armenian in theme. Buys 6 per issue. Pays $10.

How To Break In: "Read the magazine, and write about the kind of subjects we are obviously interested in, i.e., Kirlian photography, Aram Avakian's films, etc. Remember that we have become almost totally ethnic magazine in subject matter, but we want articles that present the Armenian to the rest of the world in an interesting way."

C.S.P. WORLD NEWS, Editions Stencil, Box 2608, Station D, Ottawa, Ontario, Canada K1P 5W7. Editor-in-Chief: Guy F. Claude Hamel. Emphasizes book reviews. Monthly newsletter; 20 pages. Estab: 1965. Circ: 200,000. Buys all rights. Photocopied submissions OK. SASE. Reports in 2 months. Sample copy $1.

Nonfiction: Publishes exposes about law enforcement and courts. Buys 12/year. Send complete ms. Length: 2,600-5,000 words. Pays $1-2 per typewritten, double-spaced page. Submit complete ms.

Columns, Departments: Writer's Workshop material. Buys 12 items/year. Send complete ms. Length: 20-50 words. Pays $1-2.

Poetry: Publishes avant-garde forms. Buys 12/year. Submit complete ms; no more than 2 at a time. Length: 6-12 lines. Pays $1-2.

Fillers: Jokes, gags, anecdotes. Pays $1-2.

CANADIAN GEOGRAPHICAL JOURNAL, 488 Wilbrod St., Ottawa, Ontario, Canada K1N 6M8. (613)236-7493. Editor: David Maclellan. Publication of The Royal Canadian Geographical Society. Bimonthly magazine; 84 pages. Estab: 1930. Circ: 40,000. Buys first serial rights. Buys 45-50 mss/year (few from outside Canada). Pays on publication. Free writer's guidelines. No photocopied or simultaneous submissions. Reports in 1 to 3 months. Query first with outline of proposed article.

Nonfiction and Photos: "We seek to advance geographical knowledge in the Canadian context by serving as a bridge between the academic-scientific community and the interested lay public. Although we carry many articles of an historical or largely historical character (because geography and history explain so much of one another) our prime orientation must and should be to the present and the future. What is happening now and what may happen hold maximum interest for most readers. We welcome queries and outlines on historical narratives which have broad national interest, e.g., dealing with such subjects as early exploration of different regions, settlement, land use, historic sites, architecture, Indians and Eskimos, development of Canadian education, etc. Of most interest are illustrated articles written in a popular vein. Illustrations are important and wanted (b&w or color photos)." Length: 1,000-3,000 words. Pays 5½-6¢/word; $6-15 for b&w photos; higher rates for color (from $10-35). Minimum $50/color photo. "Usual payment for articles (with illustrations) ranges from $150-500."

CA$H NEWSLETTER, 2232 Arrowhead Ave., Brooksville FL 33512. Editor-in-Chief: G. Douglas Hafely, Jr. Managing Editor: K.R. Baker. Emphasizes "making, saving, and investing money." Monthly newsletter; 8 pages. Estab: 1976. Pays on acceptance. Buys all rights. Submit seasonal/holiday material 2 months in advance. Simultaneous and photocopied submissions OK. SASE. Reports in 2 weeks. Sample copy 50¢.
Nonfiction: Expose (rags to riches, how the little guy got started and made it big; need full details on how); humor (pertaining to making and saving money); how-to (make, save, keep, use, and invest money; how to get services, information and goods free); informational (ways for anyone to succeed); inspirational (hope for the small man); interview (with successful people who started small), new product (hot items for resale, new items of interest to mass audience, how to buy and save), personal experience (if from small to successful); technical (on interesting new ways to invest; market projections and contacts); and travel (any inexpensive and/or unusual vacations). Buys 2-10 mss/isue. Submit complete ms. Length: 100-1,000 words. Pays $2-10.
Photos: Purchased with or without accompanying ms. Captions required. Send prints. Pays $2-5 for 4x5 b&w glossies. No additional payment for photos accepted with accompanying ms.
Fillers: Clippings, newsbreaks. Buys 1-10/issue. Length: 5-50 words. Pays 50¢-$2.

C-ME MAGAZINE, P.O. Box 48487, Los Angeles CA 90048. (213)382-6341 and (213)382-9857. Editor: Freeda C. Jordan. Monthly magazine; 50 pages. For general audience. Estab: 1975. Circ: 10,000. Buys all rights. Pays on acceptance. Sample copy 75¢. Will consider simultaneous submissions. Submit seasonal material 6 months in advance. Reports in 4 weeks. Query first. Enclose S.A.S.E.
Nonfiction, Photos, Fiction, Poetry and Fillers: Wants mss dealing with music, the arts and entertainment fields; inspiration, "you can do it." Writers should "study and become familiar with format." Length: 3,000 words maximum for fiction and nonfiction. Pays $125 maximum for fiction and nonfiction. 8x10 b&w photos used with accompanying ms with no additional payment. Captions required. Poetry. Length: 50 words maximum. Pays $5 to $10. Buys various types of fillers. Length varies. Payment varies.

CREATIVE LIVING, 488 Madison Ave., New York NY 10022. (212)752-4530. Editor: Robert H. Spencer. Published by Northwestern Mutual Life. Established in 1972. Quarterly. Circulation: 200,000. Rights purchased vary with author nd material. Usually buys all rights but may reassign rights to author after publication. Buys 40 to 50 mss a year. Occasionally overstocked. Payment on publication. Will send free sample copy to writer on request. Write for copy of guidelines for writers. Prefers items not written in first person. Will not consider photocopied submissions. Submit seasonal sports material 6 months in advance. Reports on material in 2 to 3 months. Query first4 with writing sample. Enclose S.A.S.E.
Nonfiction: "We publish *Creative Living* because we think it helps turn people on to themselves. We think it totally conceivable that people who read articles about others living their lives to the hilt might be motivated to think of themselves in a brighter, more creative light. Writers should bone up a bit on what makes the creative process tick. Get behind the facts. Many people lead creative lives. Importantly, we want to know their philosophical basis for living. Stress individuality and use specific examples. Give advice to the reader for gaining greater self-fulfillment. We try to avoid sex and partisan politics." Length: 600 to 2,500 words with greater need for short manuscripts. Pays $50 to $300, sometimes more for complex assignments.

CREDIT UNION LIFE, Division of Video Learning Systems, Inc., 3934 Tower Dr., Eau Claire WI 54701. (715)832-3463. Editor-in-Chief: Stephen A. Franzmeier. Quarterly magazine; 64 pages. Estab: 1977. Circ: 40,000. Pays on acceptance. Buys one-time rights. Phone queries OK. Submit seasonal/holiday material 2 months in advance. Photocopied submissions OK. SASE.. Reports in 1 week. Free writer's guidelines.
Nonfiction: Informational (fresh subject matter, offbeat angle, upper Midwest locale); interview (remarkable philosophies of life, spectacular achievement by an unsung and unusual personality); personal experience (escapist in nature); photo feature (people at work, body language,

facial expressions, gestures are important); profile (unique but unknown personalities, men or women great in their own domain); pieces on non-ordinary life styles and leisure-time activities. Buys 2/issue. Send complete ms. Length: 750-1,500 words. Pays $200-250.

Photos: Purchased without mss. Captions required. Send contact sheet. Pays $30-50/5x7 or 8x10 b&w glossy; $45-65/35mm or 4x5 or 2¼x2¼ color transparency.

Columns/Deparrtments: Ms. Lucille Schaff, Department Editor. Strange and Unexplained column buys 750 words/issue. Send complete ms. Length: 500-750. Pays $100-175. Open to suggestions for new columns/departments.

How To Break In: "Send a people-centered article that deals with people who live in Wisconsin, but not Milwaukee residents. Column ideas are in particular demand. We need, especially, columns about leisure-time activities that appeal to a large proportion of the population."

THE DEAF CANADIAN MAGAZINE, Box 1016, Calgary, Alta., Canada T2P 2K4. Editor-in-Chief: Lynette Burnett. For "general consumers who are deaf, parents of deaf children/adults, professionals on deafness, teachers, ministers, and government officials." Bimonthly magazine; 24 pages. Estab: 1972. Circ: 125,000. Pays on publication. "Although the publication is copyrighted, we do not purchase any rights which are reserved to the individual contributor." Submit seasonal/holiday material 2 months in advance. Simultaneous, photocopied and previously published submissions OK. SASE. Reports in 4 months. Free sample copy and writer's guidelines.

Nonfiction: Expose (education), how-to (skills, jobs, etc.), historical, humor, informational (deafness difficulties), inspirational, interview, new product, personal experience, personal opinion, photo feature (with captions), profile, technical and travel. "Mss must relate to deafness or the deaf world." Buys 1-10 mss/issue. Submit complete ms. Length: 3,000 words maximum. Pays $20-75. "Articles should be illustrated with at least 4 good b&w photos."

Photos: David Burnett, Photo Editor. Purchased with accompanying ms or on assignment. Captions required (not less than 25 words). Query. Pays $5 for 5x7 b&w glossy or matte finish photos; $20 for color transparencies used as cover. Total purchase price for ms includes payment for photos.

Columns/Departments: David Burnett, Column/Department Editor. Here and There, Sports and Recreation, Foreign, Cultural, Events and Books. Submit complete ms. Length: 1 page maximum. Pays $25-100. Open to suggestions for new columns/departments.

Fiction: Adventure, experimental, historical, humorous, mystery, mainstream, religious, romance, science fiction, suspense, condensed novels, and serialized novels. Buys 1-10 mss/issue. Length: 3,000 words maximum. Pays $25-100.

Fillers: Clippings, jokes, gags, anecdotes, newsbreaks, puzzles, and short humor. Must be related to deafness or the deaf world. Buys 1-20 mss/issue. Submit complete ms. Length: ½ page maximum. Pays $5-30.

DIRECTORS & BOARDS, The Journal of Corporate Action, Information for Industry Inc., 1621 Brookside Rd., McLean VA 22101. Editor-in-Chief: Stanley Foster Reed. Emphasizes corporate decisionmaking at board level. Quarterly magazine; 64 pages. Estab: 1976. Circ: 3,000. Pays 21 days after publication. Buys all rights. Photocopied submissions OK. SASE. Reports in 2 weeks. Free sample copy and writer's guidelines.

Nonfiction: Expose; how-to; informational; historical; interview (question and answer type); personal experience. Buys 16 mss/year. Query. Length: 3,000-10,000 words. Pays $100-1,000.

How To Break In: "The best way is to talk to someone experienced with directors' problems. Then, do a very thorough research job on the previously published literature on the subject and talk to other directors and executives. Then, sit down and write a query."

EL EXCENTRICO MAGAZINE, Garcia Enterprises, 274 Terrriine St., San Jose CA 95110. (408)294-4040. Editor-in-Chief: Marc Garcia. "Our audience is almost exclusively Mexican-American, family-orientated, non-radical, lower to middle income, conscious of Chicano strife. We distribute in Santa Clara County CA." Biweekly magazine; 40 pages. Estab: 1949. Circ: 12,000. Pays on publication. Buys simultaneous, second serial and one-time rights. Submit seasonal/holiday material 2 months in advance. Simultaneous, photocopied and previously published submissions OK. SASE. Free sample copy and writer's guidelines.

Nonfiction: Historical (of interest to Mexican-Americans), humor, informational (on any Chicano-related issue), inspirational (written by a Hispanic), interview (any prominent Latino, local or national), foods (Mexican recipes), personal experience (personal struggle as a Chicano), photo feature (Mexican politicians or related news events), profile, sports, and travel

(Mexico, Spain, Latin America). Buys 50-75 mss/year. Submit complete ms. Length: 50-1,000 words. Pays $5-60.

Photos: Purchased with accompanying ms. Captions required. Query. Pays $5-15 for 4x5 or 8x10 b&w photos. Model release required.

Columns/Departments: Profiles of prominent Chicanos, Foods (Mexican recipes), Movies, and interviews with successful Chicanos, business or political. Buys 50-100 mss/year. Submit complete ms. Length: 250-750 words. Pays $5-50. Open to suggestions for new columns/departments.

Poetry: "Poems must be relating to issues concerning Mexican-Americans." Buys 5 poems/year. Pays $5-20.

How To Break In: "In the past we have dealt with local people and issues. We are now expanding our coverage to include state and national concerns. Additionally, we are interested in regular departments such as Foods, Music, News Brief; this is an excellent opportunity for interested writers because we are very much in need of their services."

FAR WEST, Wright Publishing Co., Inc., 2949 Century Place, Costa Mesa CA 92626. (714)979-2560. Editor-in-Chief: Scott R. McMillan. Emphasizes fiction about the Old West (1840-1900) for a readership encompassing a wide range of incomes, ages, and educational backgrounds. Monthly magazine; 128 pages. Estab: 1977. Press run: 200,000. Pays on publication. Rights purchased "outlined in publishing agreement sent to author with notice of acceptance." Phone queries OK. Submit seasonal/holiday material 6 months in advance. Previously published submissions OK. SASE. Reports in 6 weeks. Sample copy for cost of postage; free writer's guidelines.

Photos: "We will consider photos for our cover, but prefer original western art." Query. Pays $150 minimum for 4x5 color transparencies. Model release required.

Fiction: Western and serialized novels. "We are looking for fast-moving, well-crafted fiction dealing with the Old West, 1840-1900." Buys 150 mss/year. Submit complete ms. Length: 1,500-60,000 words. Pays $150-700.

Poetry: Traditional verse, dealing with period western themes. Pays $75.

How To Break In: "An error-free manuscript is important. We will work with first-time writers, but not those who appear lazy. We read every ms that comes in, and most are rejected because the story lacks action, or there are too many technical errors. We are interested in developing new talent. Our concern is that every story be historically accurate and technically correct. Beyond that it must be imaginative, and well-written.

Rejects: "No range romances, please. Also, no avant-garde writing styles, or animal stories. Further, no way out westerns that take place in some cowboy's bedroll. No overuse of dialect. The 'iffin y'all bin a-hunkerin' round about them thar gullies' type of dialogue gets returned pronto."

FIREHOUSE MAGAZINE, 4 W. 57th St., New York NY 10014. (212)541-7262. Editor-in-Chief: Dennis Smith. For volunteer firefighters, as well as paid firefighters and their families. Monthly magazine; 72 pages. Estab: 1976. Circ: 80,000. Pays on publication. Buys all rights, but may reassign following publication. Submit seasonal or holiday material 4 months in advance. Photocopied submissions OK. SASE. Reports in 6 weeks. Sample copy $1.50. Free writer's guidelines.

Nonfiction: How-to (firefighting); informational (family activities); historical (great fires); profiles (achieving firefighters); new product; personal experience (firefighting); photo features (recent fires); technical (fire science and medicine). Buys 6 mss/year. Query. Length: 1,000-3,000 words. Pays 10¢/word.

Photos: Purchased with or without ms, or on assignment. Captions required. Query. Pays $10-25 for 8x10 glossies or color transparencies.

GREEN PAGES, 641 W. Fairbanks, Winter Park FL 32789. (305)644-6326. Managing Editor: John Erving. Emphasizes physical rehabilitation for disabled consumers (and families) and professionals in the rehabilitation field. Quarterly magazine; 80-96 pages. Estab: 1975. Circ: 22,000. Pays on publication. Buys first North American serial and one-time rights. Phone queries OK. Submit seasonal/holiday material 3 months in advance. Simultaneous submissions OK. SASE. Reports in 3-4 weeks. Free sample copy and writer's guidelines.

Nonfiction: "We are a news magazine styled after *Time* magazine with up to 50 "departments". We rewrite and condense, so need stringers and correspondents for special assignments, photos, etc." Query. Pays $1.75-2.50/column inch.

Photos: Purchased with or without accompanying ms or on assignment. Captions required. Submit contact sheet. Pays $7.50-25 for 5x7 or 8x10 b&w glossies. "We will not use obviously posed shots, only action."

THE HARD HAT DIGEST, P.O. Box 230, Kemmerer WY 83101. Editor: Gene Vickrey. For persons involved in the construction industry. Magazine; 48 pages. Established in 1975. Published every 2 months. Circulation: 2,500. Rights purchased vary with author and material. Usually buys all rights, but will reassign rights to author after publication or second serial (reprint) rights. Buys about 12 mss per year. Payment on acceptance. Will send free sample copy to writer on request. Will consider photocopied and simultaneous submissions. Submit seasonal mss 3 months in advance. Submit only complete ms. Reports in 2 weeks. Enclose S.A.S.E.

Nonfiction and Fiction: Varied contents. Buys "all forms of short stories, science fiction, western, as well as timely news articles. We invite submissions of most any type with the exception of risque stories with out-and-out sex themes." Keep in mind that audience is a "rugged, outdoors type, with a love for the outdoor life." Would like to see mss on hunting, fishing, snowmobiling, skiing and off-the-road vehicles. Length for nonfiction: 1,500 to 3,000 words. Pays 5¢ a word minimum. Also seeks freelance material for columns, "Construction News" and "Labor Reports." Length: 2,000 words. Pays 5¢ per word. Length for fiction: 3,000 to 5,000 words. Pays $300 minimum.

Photos: Purchased with accompanying ms with extra payment and purchased without accompanying ms. Captions optional. Pays $10 for b&w; $50 for color. Color photos should be 35mm transparencies.

IDENTITY, 420 Madison Ave., New York NY 10017. (212)688-4580. Editor: Raffaele Donato. For "Italian-Americans of all ages, primarily 20-40 years old, earns over $20,000. Also 'Italophiles'." Monthly magazine; 80 pages. Estab: 1976. Circ: 100,000. Pays on publication. Buys all rights but may reassign following publication. Submit seasonal/holiday material 6 months in advance. Previously published submissions OK "in rare circumstances." SASE. Reports in 3 weeks. Sample copy $1; free writer's guidelines.

Nonfiction: Robert Fierro, Articles Editor. Expose (government, media, industry, education), how-to (food, gardening, fashion), informational, historical (little known Italian contributions to American history), humor, interview, profile, travel, personal experience, photo feature. Buys 50 mss/year. Query. Length: 1,000-5,000 words. Pays 10¢/word minimum.

Photos: Angelo Marfisi, Photo Editor. Purchased with or without accompanying ms or on assignment. Captions required. Pays $15 minimum for b&w prints; $25 minimum for color transparencies. Query. Model release required. "We will consider photo essays on any subject *if* the photographer is Italian-American. Other photos must relate to our subjects."

Fiction: Fantasy, experimental, historical, humorous, condensed novels, mainstream. Buys 6 mss/year. Query. Length: 2,000-5,000 words. Pays 10¢/word minimum.

Poetry: Avant-garde, free verse, haiku, light verse, traditional, original or translated in Italian language. Buys 10/year. Limit submissions to batches of 3. Pays 10¢/word.

INTRO, Interplay International Ltd., Box 501, Station S, Toronto, Ontario, Canada M5M 3L8. (416)487-3101. Editor-in-Chief: Russel Aldridge. Emphasizes personal relationships and social life of the unattached. Audience is middle-upper income singles (25-45) interested in "dating, mating, relating, self-improvement, social behavior, entertainment and lifestyle." Monthly magazine; 32 pages. Estab: 1976. Circ: 15,000. Pays on publication (exceptions made for timely material). Buys all rights (but may reassign following publication), simultaneous rights, and second serial (reprint) rights. Submit seasonal/holiday material 4 months in advance. Simultaneous, photocopied, and previously published submissions OK. SASE and International Reply Coupons. Reports in 4-8 weeks. Sample copy $1. Free writer's guidelines.

Nonfiction: Expose (dating agencies, dance studios; those that take advantage of the unattached person's need for company), historical (anything on a personal level that is relevant to today, with a current hook), how-to (practical; such as beauty, health, finance, psychological, etc.); informational (where to go, what to do for fun and entertainment; reviews of movies, books, happenings; law, tax, finance, related business operations and products), inspirational (nothing religious, insights into personal relationships), interview, new product (health, beauty, sex, clothing), nostalgia, personal experience (must have a positive tone and entertaining style; personal opinion, photo feature, profile, travel (where the action is), pieces on divorce, separation and widowhood. Open to new department ideas. Buys 30-50 mss/year. Query. Length: 1,500-3,000 words. Pays $15-60.

Photos: Photos purchased with or without accompanying ms or on assignment. Captions required. Pays $6-30 for 8x10 b&w glossies (2¼ preferred, but 35mm OK); $15-60 for 2¼ or 35mm color transparencies. Total purchase price for a ms includes payment for photos. Model release required.

Columns/Departments: The Night-Spotter (reviews of Ontario clubs, pubs, dance halls, shows, coffeehouses, etc., from the standpoint of mixing and meeting), Screen (movies opening in

Toronto area. These are assigned), and Books (new books related to the singles scene). Buys 1-3 mss/issue. Query or send complete ms. Pays 1-3¢/word. Open to suggestions for new columns/departments.

Fiction: Adventure (strong man-woman romantic or erotic; modern setting, North American locale), erotica (subtle), humorous (man-woman theme), mystery, romance (must reflect today's emancipated attitudes), suspense, and serialized novels. Query or send complete ms. Length: 1,000-2,000. Pays $10-40.

Poetry: Free verse, light verse and traditional. Buys nil-2/issue. Length: 30-150 lines. Pays $3-8.

Fillers: Clippings, jokes, gags, anecdotes, newsbreaks, short humor, and humorous observations. Length: 100-800 words. Pays $1-8.

How To Break In: Professionalism first—"include name, address, phone and rights offered on top of each ms. Also word count. Each item should be on a separate sheet. Articles should be upbeat, positive, helpful, original and have a fresh twist. No tirades or preachiness. Write to stimulate the passions without overdoing it. Nothing that leaves a bad taste in the mouth or treats the readers as lonely hearts. Sex is wanted but it must be educational in a provocative manner. The readers are fun-loving, aware singles and should be approached as such. No 'downers' or how-rotten-life-is types."

JOURNAL OF GRAPHOANALYSIS, 325 W. Jackson Blvd., Chicago IL 60606. Editor: V. Peter Ferrara. For audience interested in self-improvement. Monthly. Buys all rights. Pays on acceptance. Reports on submissions in 1 month. Enclose S.A.S.E.

Nonfiction: Self-improvement material helpful for ambitious, alert, mature people. Applied psychology and personality studies, techniques of effective living, etc.; all written from intellectual approach by qualified writers in psychology, counseling and teaching, preferably with degrees. Length: 2,000 words. Pays about 5¢ a word.

MASTHEAD, Box 1009, Marblehead MA 01945. (617)581-0198. Editor-in-Chief: Walter A. Day, Jr. "A journal for teaching history with old newspapers" for teachers, genealogists, collectors and people interested in printing, journalism and general history. Tabloid; 9 times/year; 20 pages. Estab: 1977. Circ: 6,000. Pays on publication. Not copyrighted. Phone queries OK. Simultaneous, photocopied, and previously published submissions OK. SASE. Reports in 2 weeks. Sample copy $1.

Nonfiction: Informational; historical; humor (in historical vein); interviews (with people in history field); nostalgia, profile; travel; personal experience. Length: 500-5,000 words. Query. Pays 1¢/word.

Photos: Used with mss with no additional payment for 5x7 glossies. Model release required.

Columns/Departments: Open Forum (letters on developments in printing, journalism and collecting history); The Hidden Side to History (articles tracing the original, firsthand account in a newspaper of an historical event tempered with a current perspective). Length: 100-750 words. Pays 1¢/word. Open to suggestions for new columns/departments.

MONEYPLAN, 516 Petroleum Bldg., Wichita KS 67202. Editor: Hauk Parkinson. For political fund raisers. Newsletter; 4 to 6 (8½x11) pages. Established in 1975. Monthly. Circ: 6,300. Buys all rights. Buys about 45 mss/year. Pays on acceptance. Will send free sample copy to writer on request. Write for copy of guidelines for writers. Will consider photocopied and simultaneous submissions. Reports in 1 month. Query first. Enclose S.A.S.E.

Nonfiction and Photos: Political fund-raising stories, stressing the how-to of raising funds for political campaigns. Some case histories acceptable, as well as brief articles on techniques that really raise funds for politics. Length: 50 to 800 words. Pays 5¢ a word. No additional payment for b&w (5x7) photos used with mss.

How To Break In: "Send us concise, well-written material, with step-by-step instructions our readers can use in their fund-raising efforts."

THE NEW HARBINGER: A Journal of the Cooperative Movement, NASCO, Box 1301, Ann Arbor MI 48106. (313)663-0889. Editor-in-Chief: Margaret Lamb. Managing Editor: Jonathan Klein. Emphasizes consumer cooperatives. Readership is mostly consumer co-op members and leaders, and others interested in social change. Quarterly magazine; 64 pages. Estab: 1971. Circ: 2,000. Pays on publication. Buys all rights, but may reassign following publication. Phone queries OK. Simultaneous, photocopied, and previously published submissions OK. SASE. Sample copy $1; free writer's guidelines.

Nonfiction: Interview, personal opinion; personal experience; technical; investigative reporting; and theory analysis. "We want articles on consumer cooperatives and related efforts at democratic social change." Buys 5 mss/year. Query. Length: 1,000-4,000 words. Pays $10-50.

THE NEW YORK ANTIQUE ALMANAC, The New York Eye Publishing Co., Inc., Box 335, Lawrence NY 11559. (516)371-3300. Editor-in-Chief: Carol Nadel. Emphasizes antiques, art, investments, nostalgia for an audience above average in income and intelligence. Monthly tabloid; 24 pages. Estab: 1975. Circ: 18,000. Pays on publication. Buys all rights, but may reassign following publication. Phone queries OK. Submit seasonal/holiday material "whenever available." Previously published submissions OK. SASE. Reports in 2 weeks. Free sample copy.

Nonfiction: Expose (fraudulent practices), historical (museums, exhibitions, folklore, background of events), how-to (clean, restore, travel, shop, invest), humor (jokes, cartoons, satire), informational, inspirational (essays), interviews (authors, shopkeepers, show managers, appraisers), nostalgia ("The Good Old Days" remembered various ways), personal experience (anything dealing with antiques, art, investments, nostalgia), personal opinion, photo feature (antique shows, art shows, fairs, crafts markets, restorations), profile, technical (repairing, purchasing, restoring), travel (shopping guides and tips) and investment, economics, and financial reviews. Buys 9 mss/issue. Query or submit complete ms. Length: 3,000 words maximum. Pays $15-35. "Expenses for accompanying photos will be reimbursed."

Photos: "Occasionally, we have photo essays (auctions, shows, street fairs, human interest) and pay $3/photo with caption."

Fillers: Jokes, gags, anecdotes. "Limited only by author's imagination." Buys 45 mss/year. Pays $5-15.

How To Break In: "While keeping our readers abreast of the current scene, our publication is a unique magazine which reflects the charm of bygone days with bits of yesteryear to help you cope with the present year."

THE NEWS CIRCLE, Box 74637, Los Angeles CA 90004. (213)469-7004. Editor: Joe Haiek. For Arab Americans. Newspaper; 16 pages. Established in 1972. Monthly. Circulation: 5,000. Not copyrighted. Buys 18 to 35 mss per year. Payment on publication. Will send free sample copy to writer on request. Will consider photocopied and simultaneous submissions. Reports in 1 week. Query first with title of proposed article. Enclose S.A.S.E.

Nonfiction, Photos and Fillers: Wants mss about Middle East issues; mainly business, and economic conditions. Would like to see mss on Mideast business conferences and expos. Length: 400 words maximum. Pays 5¢ to 10¢. Photos purchased with accompanying ms with extra payment and purchased on assignment. Captions required. Pays $5 to $10. Also buys newsbreaks, clippings on Mideast business. Pays 10¢ to 15¢ a word.

PRACTICAL KNOWLEDGE, 325 W. Jackson Blvd., Chicago IL 60606. Editor: Lee Arnold. Bimonthly. A self-advancement magazine for active and involved men and women. Buys all rights, "but we are happy to cooperate with our authors." Pays on acceptance. Reports in 2 to 3 weeks. Enclose S.A.S.E.

Nonfiction and Photos: Uses success stories of famous people, past or present; applied psychology; articles on mental hygiene and personality by qualified writers with proper degrees to make subject matter authoritative. Also human interest stories with an optimistic tone. Up to 5,000 words. Photographs and drawings are used when helpful. Pays a base rate of 5¢ a word; $10 each for illustrations.

RAILROAD MAGAZINE, 420 Lexington Ave., New York NY 10017. Editor: Freeman Hubbard. "Our magazine has a double-barreled appeal, for railroad men, active or retired; and railfans." Monthly magazine; 64 (8x11) pages. Established in 1906. Circulation: about 35,000. Buys all rights, but will reassign rights to author after publication. Rarely buys second serial (reprint) rights. Buys between 100 and 150 mss a year. Payment on acceptance; occasionally, shortly afterward. Will send free sample copy and guidelines for writers only if the writer is a more or less established writer in the railroad field. A sample copy may be purchased for $1. Query first. Enclose S.A.S.E.

Nonfiction and Photos: Would be interested in a story of passenger station train sheds in the U.S. and Canada or a story of the commissary railroad car that the U.S. Bureau of Indian Affairs used to deliver supplies to Indian reservations. Length: 1,500 to 3,500 words. Pays minimum of 5¢ a word, depending on the subject and how well it is handled. Pays $5 to $10 for b&w photos purchased with accompanying mss, and will return photos on request. Any size, if sharply detailed. "Not in the market for photos apart from articles, except that we would pay a good price for a photo of the Jefferson Davis funeral train."

REVIEW, Center for Inter-American Relations, 680 Park Ave., New York NY 10021. (212)249-8950. Editor-in-Chief: Ronald Christ. Emphasizes "views, reviews, interviews, news on Latin-American literature and arts." Published spring, fall, and winter. Magazine; 95 pages. Estab: 1968. Circ: 2,000. Pays on publication. Buys all rights, but may reassign following publication. Phone queries OK. Previously published submissions OK (if originally published in Spanish). Reports in 2 months. Free sample copy.

Nonfiction: Interview, personal opinion, personal experience, literary esays on Latin-American authors, art, film. Buys 30 mss/year. Length: 8-14 pages. Pays $35-75.

Fiction: "All types—but has to be by Latin-Americans." Buys 3/issue. Query. No length requirement. Pays $6.50/1,000 words.

Poetry: Uses all types. Buys 3/issue. Limit submissions to batches of 3.

ROSICRUCIAN DIGEST, Rosicrucian Order, AMORC, Rosicrucian Park, San Jose CA 95191. (408)287-9171. Editor-in-Chief: Robin M. Thompson. Emphasizes mysticism, science, the arts. For "men and women of all ages, many well-educated, and into alternative answers to life's questions." Monthly magazine; 40 pages. Estab: 1916. Circ: 70,000. Pays on acceptance. Buys first rights and rights to reprint. Phone queries OK. Submit seasonal or holiday material 5 months in advance. Photocopied and previously published submissions OK. SASE. Reports on submissions in 4 weeks. Free sample copy and writer's guidelines.

Nonfiction: How-to (deal with life's problems and opportunities in a positive and constructive manner); informational (new ideas and developments in science, the arts, philosophy, and thinking), historical (biographies, historical sketches, human interest), inspirational (no religion articles—we are looking for articles with a constructive, uplifting outlook; philosophical approach to problem solving), interview (occasionally, but we would definitely have to work with author on this), philosophy, psychology. Buys 40-50 mss a year. Query. Length: 1,000-1,700 words. Pays 4¢/word for first rights.

Photos: Purchased with accompanying ms. Send prints. Pays $3 per 8x10 b&w glossy.

Fillers: Short inspirational or uplifting (not religious) anecdotes or experiences. Buys 6 a year. Query. Length: 25-250 words. Pays 2¢/word.

How To Break In: "Be specific about what you want to write about—the subject you want to explore—and be willing to work with editor. Articles should appeal to worldwide circulation.

Rejects: Religious, political, or articles promoting a particular group or system of thought.

SCANDINAVIAN REVIEW, American-Scandinavian Foundation, 127 E. 73rd St., New York NY 10021. (212)879-9779. Editor-in-Chief: Howard E. Sandum. "The majority of our readership is over 30, well educated, and in the middle income bracket. Most similar to readers of *Smithsonian* and *Saturday Review*. Have interest in Scandinavia by birth or education." Quarterly magazine; 112 pages. Estab: 1913. Circ: 7,000. Pays on publication. Buys all rights. Phone queries OK. Submit seasonal/holiday material 6 months in advance. Previously published material (if published abroad) OK. SASE. Reports in 2 months. Sample copy $3. Free writer's guidelines.

Nonfiction: Historical, informational, interview, photo feature and travel. "Modern life and culture in Scandinanvia." Buys 25 mss/year. Send complete ms. Length: maximum 2,500 words. Pays $50-150.

Photos: Purchased with accompanying ms. Captions required. Submit prints or transparencies. Prefers sharp, high contrast b&w enlargements. Total purchase price for ms includes payment for photos.

Fiction: Adventure, fantasy, historical. Prefers work translated from the Scandinavian. Buys 8 mss/year. Send complete ms. Length: 2,500 words maximum. Pays $75-150.

Poetry: Free verse, light verse and traditional. Buys 4 poems/year. Pays $35-50.

SMITHSONIAN MAGAZINE, 900 Jefferson Drive, Washington DC 20560. Editor: Edward K. Thompson. For "associate members of the Smithsonian Institution; 87% with college education." Monthly. Circ: 1,500,000. "Our material is automatically copyrighted. In the case of selling off second rights *Smithsonian* keeps half, gives the rest to writer. Payment for each article to be negotiated depending on our needs and the article's length and excellence." Pays "first half on assignment or tentative acceptance, remainder on acceptance." Submit seasonal material 3 months in advance. Reports "as soon as possible." Query first. Enclose S.A.S.E.

Nonfiction: "Our mandate from the Smithsonian Institution says we are to be interested in the same things which now interest or should interest the Institution: folk and fine arts, history, natural sciences, hard sciences, etc." Length and payment "to be negotiated."

Photos: Purchased with or without ms and on assignment. Captions required. Pays "$300 a color page, $250 b&w."

STEREO, ABC Leisure Magazines, Inc., The Publishing House, State Rd., Great Barrington MA 01230. (413)528-1300. Editor-in-Chief: John W.P. Mooney. Managing Editor: Wayne Armentrout. Emphasizes high quality home audio equipment. Quarterly magazine; 96 pages. Estab: 1960. Circ: 50,000. Pays on acceptance. Buys all rights. Phone queries OK. Submit seasonal/holiday material 6 months in advance. Photocopied submissions OK. SASE. Reports in 2 weeks. Free writer's guidelines.

Nonfiction: How-to (technically expert articles dealing with audio equipment), humor, interview (with personalities in audio field) and technical (workings of audio equipment). Buys 1-2 mss/year. Query. Length: 2,000-5,000 words. Pays 8¢-10/word.

How To Break In: "We are interested in the small minority of freelancers who are genuine audio experts with the training and experience that qualifies them to write with real authority. *Stereo* is almost entirely staff-written. At the moment, we buy very few manuscripts. However, we would buy more if material meeting our very high technical standards were available. Because every issue is themed to a specific aspect of audio, and all articles are written on assignment, it is *imperative* that freelancers query us before writing."

Rejects: "We are not interested in record buffs with 'golden ears'."

SUCCESS UNLIMITED, 6355 Broadway, Chicago IL 60660. Executive Editor: Diana Maxwell. "Average reader is 25-40, married with 2 children; working in professional, sales or management capacity; college educated (85%), with a strong motivation to go into business for himself. Financially, he's doing fine—but wants to do even better." Monthly magazine; 122 pages. Estab: 1954. Circ: 180,000. Pays on acceptance. Rights purchased vary with author and material. Submit seasonal (Christmas) material 4 months in advance. Free sample copy and writer's guidelines. SASE.

Nonfiction: "Our publication continues to stress the importance of a positive mental attitude (PMA) in all areas of endeavor." Uses material on self-motivation and the psychology of success; profiles of business leaders and successful (not necessarily wealthy) persons of all types—especially individuals who have overcome adversity to achieve success. How-to articles on entrepreneurship, management techniques, health, moneymaking ideas and investments. Length: 500-2,500 words. Pays 10¢/word; $250 maximum. Query.

Photos: Purchases 8x10 b&w glossies and color transparencies; $10 minimum for b&w; $25 minimum for color. Captions required.

VEGETARIAN TIMES, P.O. Box A3104, Chicago IL 60690. Editor: Paul Obis, Jr. For "non meat eaters and people interested in organic food. Well educated, sincere, ecologically minded. Interests in do-it-yourself food preservation, preparation, cooking, growing, and with a compassion for animals other than homo sapiens." Monthly magazine; 60 pages. Estab: 1973. Circ: 10,000. Rights purchased vary with author and material. Will reassign all rights to author after publication, or will buy first serial or simultaneous rights. Buys 50 mss/year. Pays on acceptance. Sample copy $1. Will consider photocopied and simultaneous submissions. Submit seasonal material 2 to 3 months in advance. Reports in 8 weeks. Query first. Enclose S.A.S.E.

Nonfiction and Photos: Features concise articles related to "vegetarianism (cooking, humanism, pacifism), environment, self-sufficiency, animal welfare and liberation, articles about vegetarian nutrition — all material should be well-documented and researched. It would probably be best to see a sample copy — remember that despite our name, we are beholden to our readers and we do not want the health food stores to sell more vitamins. We are not in the business of selling health foods. We are strongly pro consumer and this means making your own Granola. We are not interested in personal pet stories or wonder cure all foods." Informational, how-to, personal experience, interview, profile, historical, expose, personal opinion, successful health food business operations, and restaurant reviews. Length: 500 to 3,000 words. Pays 1¢ per word minimum. Will also use 500- to 1,000-word items for regular columns. Pays $10 apiece. Pays $5 total for photos purchased with accompanying ms. No color; b&w ferrotype preferred.

WEIRD TRIPS, Krupp Comic Works, Inc., Box 7, Princeton WI 54968. (414)295-5972. Editor-in-Chief: Denis Kitchen. Emphasizes the bizarre and exotic for young and hip audience. Annual magazine; 48 pages. Estab: 1971. Circ: 50,000. Pays on acceptance. Buys all rights, but may reassign following publication. Phone queries OK. Simultaneous, photocopied, and previously published submissions OK. SASE. Reports in 2 weeks. Sample copy $1.

Nonfiction: Expose (government, institutions, Army); historical and humor (relating to hip and drug culture); profile (subculture figures); travel (to exotic places—Nepal, etc.); new product (if unusual); personal experience (UFO's, drugs, bizarre sex); photo feature (of bizarre nature). Buys 6-8/issue. Query or submit complete ms. Pays $25-400.

Photos: Michael Jacobi, Department Editor. Purchased with or without mss. Captions required. Send b&w prints. Query for color. Pays $10-30 for 8x10 b&w glossies. Model release required.

How To Break In: "By offering items usually too bizarre or offbeat to be accepted in most other publications, but writing must be of good quality as well."

WESTERN & EASTERN TREASURES, People's Publishing, Inc., 1440 W. Walnut St., Box 7030, Compton CA 90224. (213)537-0896. Managing Editor: Ray Krupa. Emphasizes treasure hunting for all ages, entire range in education, coast-to-coast readership. Monthly magazine; 68 pages. Estab: 1966. Circ: 70,000. Pays on publication. Buys all rights, but may reassign rights to author following publication. SASE. Reports in 2-3 weeks. Free sample copy and writer's guidelines.
Nonfiction: How-to (use of equipment, how to look for rocks, gems, prospect for gold, where to look for treasures, rocks, etc., "first person" experiences). Buys 150 mss/year. Submit complete ms. Length: maximum 1,500 words. Pays maximum 2¢ per word.
Photos: Purchased with accompanying ms. Captions required. Submit prints or transparencies. Pays $5 maximum for 3x5 and up b&w glossies; $10 maximum for 35mm and up color transparencies. Model release required.
Columns/Departments: Treasures in the Headlines, Look What They Found, Off Road/This & That and Around the Campfire. Buys 50/year. Send complete ms. Length: 800-1,500 words. Pays maximum 2¢ per word. Open to suggestions from freelancers for new columns or departments; address Ray Krupa.

THE WITTENBURG DOOR, 861 Sixth Ave., Suite 411, San Diego CA 92101. (714)234-6454. Editor: Denny Rydberg. For men and women, usually connected with the church. Magazine; 36 pages. Established in 1968. Published every 2 months. Circulation: 9,100. Buys all rights, but may reassign rights to author after publication. Buys about 12 mss per year. Payment on publication. Will send free sample copy to writer on request. Reports in 2 weeks. Query first or submit complete ms. Enclose S.A.S.E.
Nonfiction: Articles on church renewal, the Christian life, book reviews, satire and humor. Length: 2,500 word maximum. Pays $15 to $40.

Music Publications

AUDIO MAGAZINE, 401 N. Broad St., Philadelphia PA 19108. Editor: Gene Pitts. For persons interested in high fidelity components, electronics and music. Monthly magazine; 110 pages. Estab: 1947. Circ: 125,000. Buys all rights. Buys about 15 mss/year. Pays on publication. Will send free sample copy to writer on request. Will consider photocopied submissions. No simultaneous submissions. Reports in 3 to 6 weeks. Query recommended, but not required. Enclose S.A.S.E.
Nonfiction and Photos: Articles on hi-fi equipment, design technique, hi-fi history; explanations for buffs and of widely known commercial uses. Pays $35 per published page minimum. No additional payment made for photos used with mss.

BLUEGRASS UNLIMITED, Box 111, Broad Run VA 22014. (703)361-8992. Editor-in-Chief: Peter V. Kuykendall. Managing Editor: Marion C. Kuykendall. Emphasizes old-time traditional country music for musicians and devotees of bluegrass, ages from teens through the elderly. Monthly magazine; 48 pages. Estab: 1966. Circ: 13,000. Pays on publication. Buys all rights, but may reassign to author following publication. Phone queries OK. Submit seasonal/holiday material 2-3 months in advance. Photocopied and previously published submissions OK. SASE. Reports in 1 month. Free sample copy and writer's guidelines.
Nonfiction: Historical, how-to, humor, informational, interview, nostalgia, personal experience, personal opinion, photo feature, profile and technical. Buys 20-40 mss/year. Query. Length: 500-5,000 words. Pays 3¢-3½/word.
Photos: Purchased with or without accompanying ms. Query for photos. Pays $15-20/page for 5x7 or 8x10 b&w glossies, 35mm or 2¼ color transparencies; $25 for covers.
Columns, Departments: Record and book reviews. Buys 5-10/year. Query. Length: 100-500 words. Pays 3¢-3½/word.
Fiction: Adventure and humorous. Buys 5-7 mss/year. Length: 500-2,500 words. Pays 3¢-3½/word.

CONCERT LIFE, Division of Baldwin Sound Productions, Inc., Box 1152, Mechanicsburg PA 17055. (717)766-2901. Editor-in-Chief: Cheri J. Mummert. Emphasizes gospel music. Bimonthly magazine; 48 pages. Estab: 1974. Buys all rights, but may reassign following publication. Submit seasonal/holiday material 2-4 months in advance. Simultaneous submissions OK. SASE. Reports in 6 months. Sample copy 30¢ (stamps only).

Nonfiction: Informational; inspirational; interview; nostalgia (in gospel field); and personal experience. Buys 5 mss/issue. Query. Length: 600-1,000 words. Pays $5 minimum.

Fiction: Religious. Query. Length: 600-1,000 words. Pays $5 minimum.

CONTEMPORARY KEYBOARD MAGAZINE, The GPI Corp., Box 907, Saratoga CA 95070. (408)446-3220. Editor: Tom Darter. For those who play piano, organ, synthesizer, accordion, harpsichord, or any other keyboard instrument. All styles of music; all levels of ability. Monthly magazine; 60 pages. Estab: 1975. Circ: 51,000. Pays on acceptance. Buys all rights. Phone queries OK. SASE. Reports in 1 week. Free sample copy and writer's guidelines.

Nonfiction: "We publish articles on a wide variety of topics pertaining to keyboard players and their instruments. In addition to interviews with keyboard artists in all styles of music, we are interested in historical and analytical pieces, how-to articles dealing either with music or with equipment, profiles or well-known instrument makers and their products. In general, anything that amateur and professional keyboardists would find interesting and/or useful." Buys 6-7 mss/issue. Query. Length: 8-12 double-spaced pages. Pays $50-100.

Photos: Purchased with or without accompanying ms. Captions required. Pays $25-40 for 5x7 or 8x10 b&w glossies; $75-100 for 35mm transparencies (for cover).

COUNTRYSTYLE, 11058 W. Addison, Franklin Park IL 60131. (312)455-7178. Editor: Vince Sorren. Emphasizes country music and country life style. Bimonthly tabloid; 48 pages. Estab: 1976. Circ: 425,000. Pays on acceptance. Buys all rights, but may reassign following publication. Phone queries OK. Submit seasonal/holiday material 3 months in advance. Photocopied submissions and previously published work OK. SASE. Reports in 2 weeks. Sample copy $1. Free writer's guidelines.

Nonfiction: Harry Morrow, Department Editor. Expose, informational, interview, nostalgia, profile, photo feature. Buys 100 mss/year. Query. Length: 500-2,000 words. Pays minimum of $10 per ms page.

Photos: Purchased with or without ms, or on assignment. Send contact sheet, prints or transparencies. Pays $15-100 for 8x10 b&w glossies; $35-250 for color. Prefers 2¼x2¼, but color negatives OK.

Columns, Departments: Country Music. Record Review. Send complete ms. Length: 100-500 words. Pays 5-10¢/word.

Fiction: Western. Buys 10/year. Query. Pays minimum of $10/ms page.

Fillers: Newsbreaks. Buys 40/year. Length: 100-300 words. Pays $5-15.

How To Break In: "With a timely (in the sense that the artist has a hot song on the charts) feature with good color art. But, no microphones, please."

CREEM, 187 S. Woodward Ave., Suite 211, Birmingham MI 48011. (313)642-8833. Editor: Susan Whitall. Estab: 1969. Buys all rights. Pays on publication. Query first. Reports within 2 weeks. Enclose S.A.S.E.

Nonfiction and Photos: Freelance photos and articles, mostly music oriented. "We bill ourselves as America's Only Rock 'n' Roll Magazine." Pays $125 minimum, more for the right story. Pays $35 minimum for reviews.

FORECAST!, 8615 Ramsey Ave., Silver Spring MD 20910. Editor-in-Chief: Richard W. Mostow. Emphasizes FM radio, Fine Arts, Performing Arts. Monthly magazine; 112 pages. Estab: 1963. Circ: 23,000. Pays on publication. Buys all rights. Submit seasonal/holiday material 45 days in advance. SASE. Reports in 2-4 weeks. Free sample copy and writer's guidelines.

Nonfiction: Faith P. Moeckel, Articles Editor. Expose, historical, how-to, humor, informational, interview, new product, nostalgia, personal experience, personal opinion, photo feature, profile and technical. "Fine Arts, Performing Arts, Music—concentrating on events occurring locally in the Washington/Baltimore area to preview outstanding performances and/or performers of the month and to enhance enjoyment of performing and fine arts in general." Buys 5-6 mss/issue. Query. Length: 1,000-2,000. Pays $25-75.

Photos: Purchased with accompanying ms or on assignment. Query. Pays minimum $10 for 8x10 b&w glossies. Model release required.

Fillers: Anne Hubbard, Fillers Editor. Newsbreaks. Query. Length: maximum 200 words.

GUITAR PLAYER MAGAZINE, Box 615, 12333 Saratoga-Sunnyvale Rd., Saratoga CA 95070. (408)446-1105. Editor: Jim Crockett. For persons "interested in guitars and guitarists." 12 times a year. Circulation: 102,000. Buys all rights. Buys 30 to 35 mss a year. Pays on acceptance. Will send a sample copy to a writer on request. Returns rejected material in 1 week. Acknowledges acceptance in 1 week. Query first. Enclose S.A.S.E.

Nonfiction and Photos: Publishes "wide variety of articles pertaining to guitars and guitarists: interviews, guitar craftsmen profiles, how-to features—anything amateur and professional guitarists would find fascinating and/or helpful. On interviews with 'name' performers, be as technical as possible regarding strings, guitars, techniques, etc. We're not a pop culture magazine, but a music magazine." Also buys features on such subjects as a "guitar museum, the role of the guitar in elementary education, personal reminiscences of past greats, technical gadgets and how to work them, analysis of flamenco, etc." Length: open. Pays $50 to $85. Photos purchased with mss. B&w glossies. Pays $25 to $35. Buys 35mm color slides. Pays $100 (for cover only). Buys all rights.

HI-FI STEREO BUYERS' GUIDE, 229 Park Ave., South, New York NY 10003. Editor-in-Chief: Julian S. Martin. Bimonthly magazine whose function is to assist the prospective buyer of high fidelity components in their purchase. Writers are advised to obtain a copy of the magazine and examine it carefully for content. "If you think you can write for us, we suggest you submit to us a precis of the story you would like to write, and await our comments. We pay on impulse before publication." Enclose S.A.S.E.

Nonfiction: "We run a short jazz column and a comprehensive record-review column on classical music. Also, we have a continuing series on opera which takes about 2 pages in the magazine. We don't plan to increase this coverage, nor do we plan to take on additional freelancers to assist us in this area. We are interested in discovering new authors who are familiar with the buying habits of the audiophile and know the current audio marketplace. Average payment is about $200."

HIGH FIDELITY, The Publishing House, State Road, Great Barrington MA 01230. Editor: Leonard Marcus. For well-educated, young, affluent readers, interested in home recording and playback systems (all disc and tape formats) and the music to play on them. Special issues: August, tape; June, speakers; September, new recordings and new equipment; December, year's best recordings. Monthly magazine. Estab: 1951. Circ: 315,000. Buys all rights. Buys 12 mss/year. Payment on acceptance. Will consider photocopied submissions, "if they are legible." Submit seasonal material 5 months in advance. Reports in 1 month. Query first or submit complete ms. Enclose S.A.S.E.

Nonfiction: "Material for feature articles is divided between audio equipment and music makers. Audio equipment articles should be backed up with as many technical specifications as possible and appropriate and readily understandable to the lay reader. Music articles should be slanted toward the musician's recording career or recordings of his works or to increase the reader's understanding of music. Articles are sophisticated, detailed, and thoroughly backgrounded." Regular columns include: interviews with noted music and recording personalities about their work and favorite recordings; Behind the Scenes, reports of in-progress recording sessions here and abroad. Length: 1,000 to 3,000 words. Pays $150 to $300.

Photos: Purchased with accompanying manuscripts. Captions required. 8x10 b&w glossy payment included in ms payment. Color rarely used; inquire first.

HIGH FIDELITY/MUSICAL AMERICA, The Publishing House, State Road, Great Barrington MA 01230. Editor-in-Chief: Leonard Marcus. Monthly. Established in 1888. Circulation: 20,000. Buys all rights. Pays on publication. Enclose S.A.S.E.

Nonfiction and Photos: Articles, musical and audio, are generally prepared by acknowledged writers and authorities in the field, but does use freelance material. Length: 3,000 words maximum. Pays $25 minimum. New b&w photos of musical personalities, events, etc.

INTERNATIONAL MUSICIAN, 1500 Broadway, New York NY 10036. (212)869-1330. Editor: J. Martin Emerson. For professional musicians. Monthly. Not copyrighted. Pays on acceptance. Will send a sample copy to a writer on request. Reporting time varies. Query first. Enclose S.A.S.E.

Nonfiction: Articles on prominent instrumental musicians (classical, jazz, rock, or country). Pays $75 minimum.

KEYBOARD WORLD (formerly *The Organist Magazine*), Box 4399, Downey CA 90241. (213)923-0331. Editor-in-Chief: Bill Worrall. Emphasizes organ, piano and synthesizer music. Monthly magazine; 48-52 pages. Estab: 1972. Circ: 18,000 U.S. and Canada; 10,000 Australia. Pays on acceptance. Buys all rights, but may reassign following'ppublication. Phone queries OK. Submit seasonal/holiday material at least 4 months in advance. Simultaneous and photocopied submissions OK. Previously published work OK, if author owns rights. SASE. Reports in 4 weeks. Sample copy $1.

Nonfiction: Linda S. Peck, Articles Editor. How-to (playing technique, forming clubs, fixing, building instruments, theory of music, information for teachers); informational (profiles of teachers, news of concerts, conventions); historical (keyboard instrument history, history of composers, songs—but related to the present, restoring old instruments); inspirational (human interest on handicapped, etc., musicians who are nevertheless outstanding); interview (with organ/piano and all keyboard teachers and musicians, and others related to this field); nostalgia (old theatre organs, older songs, musicians of the past); personal opinion (letters to the editor welcomed); profile (of teachers and musicians); new product (reviews of books and records); personal experience (human interest about relationships with teachers, musicians, students overcoming difficulties); photo feature (good, clear pix of concerts, etc., especially candid shots, rather than posed); technical (advice on fixing/turning instruments and on teaching/practice/learning methods). Query. Length: 500-4,000 words. Pays ½-1¢/word.

Photos: David Rivas, Art Director. Purchased with or without mss or on assignment. Captions optional, "but must have names and situation info". Send prints or negatives. Pays $2 minimum fnr b&w and color; $25 for cover use. Model release required.

Fillers: Clippings, jokes, anecdotes, newsbreaks, short humor related to keyboard music. Send fillers in. Pays $1 minimum.

How To Break In: "Read *Keyboard World*. Most of our material is contributed free. Therefore, we want something we can't readily get from the experts who write for us. Well-researched and slanted material, especially on pianos and synthesizers, and for children."

THE LAMB, 2352 Rice Blvd., Houston TX 77005. (713)526-7793. Editor-in-Chief: Michael Point. Emphasizes music for a readership interested in the current shape and future course of contemporary music. Primary readership lies in the 20-30-year-old bracket with some college affiliation (past or present) and a serbous interest in music. Monthly tabloid; 28 pages. Estab: 1976. Circ: 30,000. Pays on publication. Buys all rights, but ay reassign rights to author following publication. Phone queries OK. Photocopied (if clean and clear) submissions OK. SASE. Reports in 4 weeks. Sample copy 50¢.

Nonfiction: Historical, informational, interview, nostalgia, personal opinion, photo feature and profile. "All articles must deal with music, musicians or the music world." Buys 100 mss/year. Query. Length varies. Pays minimum $10.

Photos: Geary Davis, Photo Editor. Purchased with or without accompanying ms or on assignment. Captions required. Pays minimum $5 for 8x10 b&w glossies. Send contact sheet or prints. Total purchase price for ms includes payment for photos.

Columns/Departments: Bill Whiting, Editor. Cinema (music-related movies reviewed). Buys 20 mss/year. Query. Length varies. Pays minimum $5. Open to suggestions from freelancers for new columns/departments.

Fiction: Adventure, confession, erotica, experimental, fantasy, historical, humorous and science fiction. Buys 10 mss/year. Query. Pays minimum $10.

Poetry: Nancy McKinney, Poetry Editor. Avant-garde, free verse, haiku, light verse and traditional. Buys 50 poems/year. Send poems. Pays minimum $5.

How To Break In: *"The Lamb* is not a teen or pop music oriented publication. It deals with "progressive music" of all styles (jazz, rock, classical, etc.) and requires writers able to communicate to an audience of musically informed and interested readers. *The Lamb* is open to all forms of alternative expression dealing with music and invites writers, photographers, etc., to use their creativity when submitting material. Remember that this is a music magazine and, as such, concentrates almost exclusively on the permutations of the music world. Album reviews and performance reviews are customary starting points for new writers."

LIVING BLUES, 2615 N. Wilton Ave., Chicago IL 60614. (312)281-3385. Editors: Jim and Amy O'Neal. For blues fans and people in the blues business (record companies, agents, disc jockeys, etc.) Bimonthly magazine; 44-52 pages. Estab: 1970. Circ: 5,000. Buys first North American serial rights. Buys 20 mss a year. Payment for feature articles and interviews is made on publication. Payment in contributor's copies is made for news and reviews. Will send complimentary sample copy to writer. Will consider photocopied submissions. Will not consider simultaneous submissions. Reports in 2 to 12 weeks. Query first or submit complete ms. Enclose S.A.S.E.

Nonfiction and Photos: "Mainly detailed biographies (including Q&A-format interviews) of black blues musicians and singers but we are open to any articles pertaining to the black blues traditions. We look for in-depth articles, well-researched and usually based on personal interviews with blues personalities. Record, concert, book and film reviews; short, local 'blues news' reports. We would like articles on blues artists in the South, and in cities such as St. Louis, Detroit and Indianapolis. We do not want articles on John Mayall, the Allman Bros., or other blues-rock or pseudo-blues artists." Also interested in how-to's on musical tablature and instruction: Length: 750 words minimum for articles; 100 to 500 words for reviews. Pays $10 to $25 for articles and interviews; contributor's copies for reviews and news. Payment for departmental material is in contributor's copies. Pays $3 to $5 for b&w photos. Send positive prints. Captions required. Photos are purchased with or without accompanying mss or on assignment. Must relate to theme.

How To Break In: "Send new information about local blues artists and the blues scenes in various cities, or send thorough interviews/features on important blues personalities. Especially looking for substantial features on contemporary blues artists who are still popular with black audiences."

MELODY MAKER, IPC Specialist & Professional Press Ltd., 24/34 Meymott St., London SE1 9LU, England. Editor-in-Chief: Ray Coleman. Emphasizes popular music. Weekly magazine; 64 pages. Estab: 1926. Circ: 153,709. Pays on publication. Buys all rights. Submit seasonal/holiday material 2-3 weeks in advance. SAE and International Reply Coupons.
Nonfiction: Concert reviews; folk, rock, pop, jazz, country artists. Interviews with personalities. Length: 400-1,000 words. Pays $17-100.

MODERN DRUMMER, 47 Harrison St., Nutley NJ 07110. (201)667-2211. Editor-in-Chief: Ronald Spagnardi. For "student, semi-pro, and professional drummers at all ages and levels of playing ability, with varied specialized interests within the field." Quarterly magazine; 32 pages. Estab: 1975. Circ: 5,000. Pays on publication. Buys all rights. Phone queries OK. Photocopied and previously published submissions OK. SASE. Reports in 8 weeks. Free sample copy and writer's guidelines.
Nonfiction: How-to; informational; interview; personal opinion; new product; personal experience; and technical. "All submissions must appeal to the specialized interests of drummers." Buys 5-10 mss/issue. Query or submit complete ms. Length: 500-2,000 words. Pays 4-8¢/word.
Photos: Purchased with accompanying ms. Considers 8x10 b&w and color glossies. Submit prints or negatives. Total ms purchase price includes payment for photos. Model release required.
Columns, Departments: Jazz Drummers Workshop, Rock Perspectives, Rudimental Symposium, Complete Percussionist, Teachers Forum, Drum Soloist, Record, Book and Live Action Review, Shop Talk. "Technical knowledge of area required for all columns." Buys 5-8 mss/issue. Query or submit complete ms. Length: 500-1,500 words. Pays 4-8¢/word. Open to suggestions for new columns and departments.
Fillers: Jokes, gags, anecdotes. Buys 3 fillers an issue. No length requirement. Pays $2-5.

MUSIC CITY NEWS, 1302 Division St., Nashville TN 37203. (615)244-5187. Managing Editor: Lee Rector. Emphasizes country music. Monthly tabloid; 40 pages. Estab: 1963. Circ: 40,000. Buys all rights. Phone queries OK. Submit seasonal or holiday material 2 months in advance. Photocopied submissions OK. SASE. Reports in 6 weeks. Free sample copy.
Nonfiction: "We prefer interview type articles with country music personalities, not question/answer but narrative/quote interviews leaning toward the personality telling his own story. Prefer new slants to biographical." Buys 4-5 mss per issue. Query. Length: 500-1,250 words. Pays $1.05/column inch.
Photos: Purchased on assignment. Query. Pays $10 maximum for 8x10 b&w glossies.

OPERA CANADA, 366 Adelaide St., E., Suite 533, Toronto, Ontario Canada M5A 1N4. (416)363-0395. Editor: Ruby Mercer. For readers who are interested in serious music; specifically, opera. Magazine; 52 pages. Established in 1960. Quarterly. Circulation: 5,000. Not copyrighted. Buys about 10 mss a year. Pays on publication. Will send sample copy to writer for $2. Will consider photocopied and simultaneous submissions. Reports on material accepted for publication within 1 year. Returns rejected material in 1 month. Query first or submit complete ms. Enclose S.A.E. and International Reply Coupons.
Nonfiction and Photos: "Because we are Canada's opera magazine, we like to keep 75% of our content Canadian, i.e., by Canadians or about Canadian personalities/events. We prefer informative and/or humorous articles about any aspect of music theatre, with an emphasis on opera. The relationship of the actual subject matter to opera can be direct or barely discernible. We accept record reviews (*only* operatic recordings); book reviews (books covering any aspect of music theatre) and interviews with major operatic personalities. Please, no reviews of performances. We have staff reviewers." Length (for all articles except reviews of books and

records): 350 to 5,000 words. Pays $50. Length for reviews: 50 to 100 words. Pays $10. No additional payment for photos used with mss. Captions required.

Fillers: Opera quiz puzzles, anecdotes, short humor. Length: 50 to 350 words. Pays $5 to $20.

PAID MY DUES: JOURNAL OF WOMEN AND MUSIC, Woman's Soul Publishing, Inc., P.O. Box 11646, Milwaukee WI 53211. Editor: Althea Majajna. For everyone interested in feminist and women's music; all aspects from technical to "herstorical," as well as coverage of the contemporary scene. Magazine; 48 pages. Established in 1974. Circulation: 1,200. Rights purchased vary with author and material. Buys all rights, but may reassign rights to author after publication; first serial rights or simultaneous rights. Buys about 15 mss per year. Pays on publication. Sample copy $1.50; free writer's guidelines. Will consider photocopied submissions. May consider simultaneous submissions. Reports in 6 weeks. Query first. Enclose S.A.S.E.

Nonfiction and Photos: "We focus exclusively on women and use articles about women (alive or dead) who are prominent in music (or should be prominent in music); interviews with musicians who are women; songs, reviews of records, concerts. Emphasis is on the work itself (concert, musician, etc.), as well as the approach of the woman to her music. No articles on 'how bad things are for women in music'." Informational, how-to, personal experience, profile, humor, historical, think pieces, personal opinion and travel articles. All must relate to women in music. Length: 300 words minimum. Pays $5-10/ms. B&w photos purchased with or without mss. 2x2, minimum size. Prefers 5x7 or larger. Pays $2.

ROLLING STONE, 78 E. 56 St., New York NY 10022. Editor: Jann S. Wenner. "Seldom accept freelance material. All our work is assigned or done by our staff."

SONO, 625 President Kennedy Ave., Montreal, Quebec, Canada H3A 1K5. (514)845-5141. Editor: Paul Saint-Pierre. For amateurs and fanatics of music and of musical instruments. Although this publication is in French, English mss are considered. Annual magazine; 100 pages. Estab: 1973. Circulation: 15,000. Buys all rights, but will reassign rights to author after publication. Pays on acceptance. Reports in 1 week. Query first or submit complete ms. Enclose S.A.E. and International Reply Coupons.

Nonfiction: Interviews with singers, technical articles on quadraphony; on new equipment, trends; reviews of new records, audiolab, etc. Informational, how-to, profile, technical. Length: 600 to 1,200 words. Pays $100 minimum.

SOUNDS, 332 E. Camelback, Phoenix AZ 85012. (602)265-4830. Editor-in-Chief: William Niblick. Managing Editor: Bart Bull. Emphasizes music, audio, performing and visual arts entertainment for audiophiles, music listeners and anyone interested in what is "happening" in music, dance, theater, film, audio both nationally and locally (Arizona). Monthly tabloid; 24 pages. Estab: 1973. Circ: 25,000. Pays on acceptance. Buys all rights, but may reassign rights to author following publication. Phone queries OK. Simultaneous, photocopied and previously published submissions OK. SASE. Reports in 3 weeks. Free sample copy and writer's guidelines.

Nonfiction: Expose (music); interview; new product (audio or music); essays; record and performance reviews. Buys 12-25 mss/year. Query or send complete ms. Length: 100-700 words for record reviews; 600-10,000 words for articles. Pays 2¢-10/word.

Photos: Purchased with or without accompanying ms. Query or send contact sheet. Pays maximum $10 for b&w any finish at least 4x5. Total purchase price for ms includes payment for photos.

Mystery Publications

ALFRED HITCHCOCK'S MYSTERY MAGAZINE, Davis Publications Inc., 229 Park Ave., S., New York NY 10003. (212)073-1300. Editor: Eleanor Sullivan. Associate Editor: Mimi H. Pardo. Emphasizes mystery fiction. Monthly magazine; 130 pages. Estab: 1956. Circ: 115,000. Pays on acceptance. Buys all rights. Submit seasonal/holiday material 7 months in advance. Simultaneous and photocopied submissions OK. SASE. Reports in 6 weeks. Free sample copy and writer's guidelines.

Fiction: Original and well-written mystery, suspense and crime fiction. No reprints or true crimes. "A 'now' feeling is preferred for every story, both as to plot urgency and today's world. Plausibility counts heavily even in supernatural stories." Length: 1,000-10,000 words. Rates are basically the same as those paid by *Ellery Queen's Mystery Magazine.*

How To Break In: "Think Hitchcock. It's the master's brand of suspense that we want. Avoid gore, profanity and explicit sex. It's not needed."

ELLERY QUEEN'S MYSTERY MAGAZINE, Davis Publications, Inc., 229 Park Ave., S., New York NY 10003. (212)673-1300. Editor-in-Chief: Ellery Queen. Managing Editor: Eleanor Sullivan. Monthly magazine; 160 pages. Estab: 1941. Circ: 310,000. Pays on acceptance. Buys first North American serial rights. Submit seasonal/holiday material 7 months in advance. Simultaneous, photocopied and previously published submissions OK. SASE. Reports in 6 weeks. Free sample copy and writer's guidelines.

Fiction: "We publish every type of mystery: the suspense story, the psychological study, the deductive puzzle—the gamut of crime and detection from the realistic (including the policeman's lot and stories of police procedure) to the more imaginative (including 'locked rooms' and impossible crimes). We need private-eye stories, but do not want sex, sadism, or sensationalism-for-the-sake-of-sensationalism'" Buys 13 mss/issue. Length: 6,000 words maximum. Pays 3-8¢/word.

How To Break In: "We have a department of First Stories to encourage writers whose fiction has never before been in print. We publish an average of 24 first stories a year."

MIKE SHAYNE MYSTERY MAGAZINE, Renown Publications, Inc., Box 69150, Los Angeles CA 90069. Editor-in-Chief: Cylvia Kleinman. Monthly magazine; 128 pages. Estab: 1956. Pays on acceptance. Buys magazine serial rights only. Submit seasonal/holiday material 4 months in advance. Photocopied submissions OK. SASE. Reports in 2 weeks.

Fiction: Strong, fast-moving mystery stories. Buys 8 mss/issue. Length: 1,000-6,000 words. Pays 1¢/word minimum.

How To Break In: "Study the type of material we use. Know pace of story, type of mystery we buy. Best to send very short material to start, as the new author doesn't handle novelette lengths convincingly."

Nature, Conservation, and Ecology Publications

The magazines classified here are "pure" nature, conservation, and ecology publications—that is, they exist to further the study and preservation of nature and do not publish recreational or travel articles except as they relate to conservation or nature. Other markets for this kind of material will be found in the Regional; Sport and Outdoor; and Travel, Camping, and Trailer categories, although the magazines listed there require that nature or conservation articles be slanted to their specialized subject matter and audience.

AUDUBON, 950 Third Avenue, New York NY 10022. "Not soliciting freelance material; practically all articles done on assignment only. We have a backlog of articles from known writers and contributors. Our issues are planned well in advance of publication and follow a theme."

ENVIRONMENT, 560 Trinity Ave., University City MO 63130. (314)863-6560. Editor: Julian McCaull. For citizens, scientists, teachers, high school and college students interested in environment or effects of technology and science in public affairs. Magazine; 48 pages. Established in 1958. Ten times a year. Circulation: 25,000. Buys all rights, but may reassign rights to author after publication. Pays on acceptance to professional writers. Free sample copy. Will consider photocopied submissions. No simultaneous submissions. Reports in 2 to 4 weeks. Query first or submit complete ms. Enclose S.A.S.E.

Nonfiction and Photos: Scientific and environmental material; effects of technology on society. Pays $100-150, depending on material. Department Editor: Julian McCaull. 8x10 b&w photos purchased with or without mss. Pays $3 on acceptance, $7 on publication. Photographer must submit an invoice. Department Editor: Patricia DeJoie.

Poetry: Environmental and satiric poems. Pays $10.

THE EXPLORER, Cleveland Museum of Natural History, Wade Oval, University Circle, Cleveland OH 44106. (216)231-4600. Editor: Bill Baughman. For readers with a strong interest in natural science. Established in 1938. Quarterly. Circ: 20,000. Audience are members of 14 museums and many independent subscribers. Buys one-time rights. Payment in contributor's

copies. Submit seasonal material 6 months in advance. Reports on material accepted for publication in 3 to 4 weeks. Returns rejected material in 3 to 4 weeks. Query first. Enclose S.A.S.E.
Nonfiction and Photos: "We are especially concerned with interpreting the natural history and science of North America, but mostly U.S. We endeavor to give a voice to the natural scientists and naturalists functioning within these geographical boundaries and feel an obligation to make our readers aware of the crucial issues at stake in the world regarding conservation and environmental problems. Now assigning most articles, but will consider articles by scientists, naturalists and experts in nature, ecology, and environmental areas. Writing should have a lively style and be understandable to scientists of all ages. Exploring nature can be exciting. Your writing should reflect and encourage the exploring mind." Length: 1,000 to 4,000 words. B&w (8x10) photos. Some color transparencies and color prints are used. 35mm Kodachrome color, 2¼x2¼, and 4x5 transparencies are acceptable for inside editorial and cover illustrations. All photos, particularly close-ups of birds and animals, must be needle-sharp. Also interested in b&w photo essays (12 photos maximum) on natural history topics.

FRONTIERS, A Magazine of Natural History, Academy of Natural Sciences, 19th and the Parkway, Philadelphia PA 19103. Editor: Mrs. Vi Dodge. Published 4 times per year. Circulation: 6,000. Rights purchased vary with author and material. May buy first North American serial rights or all rights, but may reassign rights to author after publication. Pays on acceptance. Will send a sample copy to writer for $1. Reports in 4 to 6 weeks. Enclose S.A.S.E.
Nonfiction and Photos: Articles on natural science and ecology, written for high school and adult laymen, but scientifically accurate. Length: 500 to 3,000 words. Pays $50 to $100. Articles with b&w photos usually given preference. Accuracy, originality, and neatness all weigh heavily. 8x10 b&w photos purchased with mss.
Fillers: Natural science puzzles and short humor. Length: 10 to 50 words. Pays $15 to $25.

INTERNATIONAL WILDLIFE, 225 E. Michigan, Milwaukee WI 53202. Editor: John Strohm. For persons interested in natural history, outdoor adventure and the environment. Bimonthly. Buys all rights to text; usually one-time rights to photos and art. Payment on acceptance. Query first. "Now assigning most articles but will consider detailed proposals for quality feature material of interest to broad audience." Reports in 2 weeks. Enclose S.A.S.E.
Nonfiction and Photos: Focus on world wildlife, environmental problems and man's relationship to the natural world as reflected in such issues as population control, pollution, resource utilization, food production, etc. Especially interested in articles on animal behavior and other natural history, little-known places, first-person experiences, timely issues. "Payment varies according to value and use of feature articles, but usually begins at $500. Purchase top-quality color and b&w photos; prefer 'packages' of related photos and text, but single shots of exceptional interest and sequences also considered. Prefer Kodachrome transparencies for color, 8x10 prints for b&w."

THE LIVING WILDERNESS, 1901 Pennsylvania Ave., N.W., Washington DC 20006. (202)293-2732. Editor: James G. Deane. For members of The Wilderness Society, libraries and educational institutions. Established in 1935. Quarterly. Circulation: 80,000. Buys all rights, but may reassign rights to author after publication. Buys one-time rights to photos. Buys about 20 mss a year. Pays on publication. Will send sample copy to a writer for $1.25. Query first or submit complete ms. Enclose S.A.S.E.
Nonfiction, Photos and Poetry: Articles on wilderness preservation and appreciation; wildlife conservation, environmental issues and natural history; photographs relevant to these subjects, usually to illustrate specific articles. special interest in threats to North American wild areas. Occasional nature-oriented essays and poetry. Some book reviews are assigned. Payment depends on character of material. Pays $25 minimum for b&w; $75 minimum for color, except when bought in article/photo package.

LOUISIANA CONSERVATIONIST, 400 Royal St., Room 126-D, New Orleans LA 70130. Editor: Bob Dennie. For the outdoorsman and his family. Publication of Louisiana Wildlife and Fisheries Commission. Established in 1931. Bimonthly. Circulation: 190,000. Not copyrighted. Payment in contributor's copies. Will send free sample copy to writer on request. Write for copy of guidelines for writers. Will not consider photocopied submissions. Submit seasonal material (for Christmas issue only) 6 months in advance. Returns rejected material in 2 weeks. Reports on mss accepted for publication in 6 to 8 weeks. Query first. "We will look at outlines with query letters." Enclose S.A.S.E.
Nonfiction and Photos: "We use feature-length articles, including how-to's if they are informative and concisely written, of the outdoor variety. We also consider 'offbeat' pieces if they are written to interest a general outdoor audience. Studying the style of the staff writers and pub-

lished authors in the magazine is the best advice interested writers could get. To be avoided are wordiness, cute tricks, writing with adjectives, and the outmoded 'me and Joe' articles. It is important that a writer be active in the outdoor writing field in order to submit to our magazine." Length: 800 to 2,000 words. Mss should be illustrated with color slides (originals only); 35mm or 2¼x2¼.

NATIONAL PARKS & CONSERVATION MAGAZINE, 1701 18th St., N.W., Washington DC 20009. (202)265-2217. Editor: Eugenia Horstman Connally. For a mature, high-education audience interested in out-of-doors and environmental matters. Monthly magazine; 32 (8½x11) pages. Established in 1919. Circ: 45,000. Buys all rights. Almost all material used is purchased from freelance writers. Payment on acceptance. Will send sample copy to writer for $1.50. Write for copy of guidelines for writers. Submit seasonal material 4 months in advance. Reports on material accepted for publication in 3 weeks. Returns rejected material promptly. Query first. Enclose S.A.S.E.
Nonfiction and Photos: Articles about national parks and monuments, stressing threats confronting them or their particularly significant floral, faunal, geological, or historical features; endangered species of plants or animals and suggestions to save them; protection of natural resources; environmental problems and programs to solve them. Short articles on nature appreciation. Informational, personal experience, think pieces. Length: 1,500 to 2,000 words. Short article length (nature appreciation): 500 to 1,000 words. Pays $75 to $100 for acceptable illustrated articles. No additional payment for b&w and color used with mss, unless selected for cover. Pays $15-50 for 8x10 b&w glossies purchased without mss; $25 to $75 for 4x5 color transparencies (some slides) purchased without mss. Captions required. "Photos generally not purchased unless a relevant article is on file. Send list of subjects and a few samples for files."
How To Break In: "Excellent market for new writers. 'Adventures in the national parks' articles are welcome, particularly those on backcountry hiking, mountain climbing, river running, spelunking. Emphasize conservation and protection of natural resources."

NATIONAL WILDLIFE, 225 E. Michigan Ave., Milwaukee WI 53202. Editor-in-Chief: John Strohm. Emphasizes wildlife. Bimonthly magazine; 56 pages. Estab: 1962. Circ: 610,000. Pays on acceptance. Buys all rights. Submit seasonal/holiday material 6 months in advance. Previously published submissions OK. SASE. Reports in 3 weeks. Free writer's guidelines.
Nonfiction: Mark Wexler, Nonfiction Editor. How-to; humor; informational; interview; personal experience; photo feature and profile. Buys 5 mss/issue. Query. Length: 2,000-3,000 words. Pays $500-1,000.
Photos: Karen Altpeter, Photo Editor. Photos purchased with or without accompanying ms or on assignment. Pays $35-100 for 8x10 b&w glossies; $75-150 for 35mm color kodachromes. Total purchase price for ms includes payment for photos.

NATURAL HISTORY, 79th and Central Park West, New York NY 10024. Editor: Alan Ternes. For "well-educated, ecologically aware audience. Includes many professional people, scientists, scholars." Monthly. Circulation: 425,000. "Copyright on text of articles is held by The American Museum of Natural History." Buys 20 mss a year. Pays on publication. Will send a sample copy to a writer for $1. Submit seasonal material 6 months in advance. Query first or submit complete ms. Enclose S.A.S.E.
Nonfiction: Uses all types of scientific articles except chemistry and physics—emphasis is on the biological sciences and anthropology. Prefers professional scientists as authors. "We always want to see new research findings in almost all the branches of the natural sciences —anthropology, archaeology, zoology, ornithology. We find that it is particularly difficult to get something new in herpetology (amphibians and reptiles) or entomology (insects) and we would like to see material in those fields. We lean heavily toward writers who are scientists or professional science writers. High standards of writing and research. Favor an ecological slant in most of our pieces, but do not generally lobby for causes, environmental or other. Writer should have a deep knowledge of his subject. Then submit original ideas either in query or by ms. Should be able to supply high-quality illustrations." Length: 2,000 to 4,000 words. Pays $300-750, plus additional payment for photos used.
Photos: Uses some 8x10 b&w glossy photographs; pays up to $50 per page. Much color is used; pays $125 for inside and up to $200 for cover. Photos are purchased for one-time use.
How To Break In: "Learn about something in depth before you bother writing about it."

THE NATURALISTS' DIRECTORY AND ALMANAC (INTERNATIONAL), Box 505, Kinderhook NY 12106. (518)758-9021. Editor-in-Chief: Ross H. Arnett, Jr. Emphasizes outdoor natural history recreation. Annual magazine; 250 pages. Estab: 1877. Circ: 5,000. Pays on publication. Buys all rights. Phone queries OK. Submit seasonal or holiday material any time. Xeroxed submissions and previously published work OK. SASE. Reports in 2 months. Sample copy $4. Free writer's guidelines.

Nonfiction: Informational (sources must be documented) and historical articles. "Some suggested subjects are: nature sayings; records such as tallest trees, smallest living organisms; value of minerals; where and what to collect; poisonous plants and animals; state trees, state birds, state fish, state mammals, state insects, etc." Buys 40 mss a year. Pays $10 minimum.

Photos: Purchased with or without mss, or on assignment. Captions required. Send b&w prints and color transparencies. Pays $5-50 for b&w glossies (at least 5x7); $10-50 for 35mm, 2¼x2¼ or 2¼x3¼ color transparencies. No prints.

How To Break In: "Material must be technically accurate. Most freelance material is too elementary or is written in newspaper style, and is not acceptable."

Rejects: Humorous or sensational material; hunting and fishing themes.

PACIFIC DISCOVERY, California Academy of Sciences, Golden Gate Park, San Francisco CA 94118. (415)221-5100. Editor: Bruce Finson. A journal of nature and culture around the world, read by scientists, naturalists, teachers, students, and others having a keen interest in knowing the natural world more thoroughly. Established in 1928. Published every 2 months by the California Academy of Science. Circulation: 12,000. Buys first North American serial rights of articles, one-time use of photos. Usually reports within 3 months; publishes accepted articles in 2 to 4 months. Pays on publication. Send query first, with 100-word summary of projected article for review before preparing finished ms. Enclose S.A.S.E.

Nonfiction and Photos: "Subjects of articles include behavior and natural history of animals and plants, ecology, anthropology, geology, paleontology, biogeography, taxonomy, and related topics in the natural sciences. Occasional articles are published on the history of natural science, exploration, astronomy, and archaeology. Types of articles include discussions of individual species or groups of plants and animals that are related to or involved with one another, narratives of scientific expeditions together with detailed discussions of field work and results, reports of biological and geological discoveries and of short-lived phenomena, and explanations of specialized topics in natural science. Authors need not be scientists; however, all articles must be based, at least in part, on firsthand fieldwork." Length: 1,000 to 3,000 words. Pays $50 to $150. B&W photos or color slides must accompany all mss or they will not be reviewed. Send 15 to 30 with each ms. Photos should have both scientific and aesthetic interest, be captioned in a few sentences on a separate caption list keyed to the photos and numbered in story sequence. Some photo stories are used. Pays $10 per photo. All slides, negatives, and prints are returned soon after publication.

SAERCH, Social Science and Environmental Research, Box 614, Corte Madera CA 94925. Editor: William Whitney. For professionals in the environmental and sociological fields. Magazine; 52 pages. Established in 1975. Every 2 months. Circulation: 5,000. Rights purchased vary with author and material. Buys all rights, but may reassign rights to author after publication, or first serial rights, or simultaneous rights. Buys about 20 mss a year. Pays on acceptance. Will send sample copy to writer for $1. No photocopied submissions. Will consider simultaneous submissions. Reports in 8 to 10 weeks. Query first or submit complete ms. Enclose S.A.S.E.

Nonfiction, Photos and Fillers: "Our material centers on the subjects of environmental science, impacts on sociological areas, etc. All material should be up-to-date and informative. Our readers are aware of their fields and the need to stay abreast of new developments. The writer's approach and outlook should be problem oriented with stress on solutions to the multi-faceted sciences of today. Nothing trite or generalized. We would like to see more coverage of current debates in the fields of environmental and sociological science. Our recent coverage has included activities of the Sierra Club, as well as specific topics such as shell oil retrieval." Informational, interview, profile, historical, think pieces, expose and technical articles. Length: 2,000 to 3,500 words. Pays 3¢ to 10¢ a word. Spot news. Length: 500 to 750 words. Pays 3¢ to 10¢ a word. Pays $5 to $20 for 8x10 b&w glossies used with mss. Pays $10 to $50 for color transparencies used with mss. 35mm minimum. Newsbreaks of 500 to 750 words used as fillers. Same rate of payment as for other material.

SNOWY EGRET, 205 S. Ninth St., Williamsburg KY 40769. (606)549-0850. Editor: Humphrey A. Olsen. For "persons of at least high school age interested in literary, artistic, philosophical, and historical natural history." Semiannual. Circulation: less than 500. Buys first North American serial rights. Buys 40-50 mss/year. Pays on publication. Sample copy $1. Usually reports in 1 month. Enclose S.A.S.E.

Nonfiction: Subject matter limited to material related to natural history, especially literary, artistic, philosophical, and historical aspects. Criticism, book reviews, essays, biographies. Pays $2 per printed page.

Fiction: "We are interested in considering stories or self-contained portions of novels. All fiction must be natural history or man and nature. The scope is broad enough to include such stories as Hemingway's 'Big Two-Hearted River' and Warren's 'Blackberry Winter.'" Length: maximum 10,000 words. Payment is $2 a printed page. Send mss and books for review to Dr. William T. Hamilton, Dept. of English, Otterbein College, Westerville OH 43081. "It is preferable to query first."

Poetry: No length limits. Pays $4 per printed page, minimum of $2. Send poems and poetry books for review to Dr. Hamilton, Literary Editor, and to West Coast Editor, Gary Elder, 22 Ardith Ln., Alamo CA 94507.

Newspapers and Weekly Magazine Sections

This section includes daily newspapers as well as Saturday and Sunday magazine sections of daily newspapers. They are listed geographically by state headings although some cover wider areas (such as Michiana which serves both Michigan and Indiana).

Most of these markets require submissions to be about persons, places, and things in their specific circulation areas. However, some large city and national newspapers that welcome general interest material from nonlocal writers are also included in this list. Newspapers with specialized subject matter or audiences, like The Wall Street Journal are classified with magazines dealing with the same subject matter or audience.

A few editors report that some correspondents in their area are attracted to small feature items but let big news stories from their communities slip through their fingers. Freelancers, on the other hand, report that some busy newspaper editors return their submissions without even a rejection slip—or in a few cases, fail to return it at all, even when it's accompanied by a stamped, self-addressed envelope. (Since newspaper editors receive many submissions from public relations firms and other individuals who do not expect return of their material, they sometimes automatically toss material they're not interested in publishing. That means a retyping job for the freelancer. It also means you should be wary of sending photographs which are your only copies.)

Arizona

ARIZONA MAGAZINE, 120 E. Van Buren, Phoenix AZ 85016. (602)271-8291. Editor: Bud DeWald. For "everyone who reads a Sunday newspaper." Weekly; 60 pages. Estab: 1953. Circ: 333,000. Not copyrighted. Buys 250 mss/year. Payment on scheduling. Free sample copy. Write for copy of guidelines for writers. Will consider photocopied submissions. Will consider simultaneous submissions if exclusive regionally. Reports on material accepted for publication in 2 weeks. Returns rejected material in 1 week. Query first or submit complete ms. Enclose S.A.S.E.

Nonfiction and Photos: "General subjects that have an Arizona connection. Should have a bemused, I-don't-believe-it approach. Nothing is that serious. Should have an abundance of quotes and anecdotes. Historical and travel subjects are being overworked. We don't need someone's therapy." Length: 1,000 to 3,000 words. Pays $50-$200. B&w and color photos purchased with or without mss or on assignment. Pays $10 to $25 for 8x10 b&w glossies; $15 to $65 for color (35mm or 8x10).

How To Break In: "Find a good personal subject and write about him so the reader will feel he is with the subject. Describe the subject in anecdotes and let him describe himself by his quotes."

California

CALIFORNIA TODAY, 750 Ridder Park Dr., San Jose CA 95131. (408)289-5441. Editor: Fred Dickey. For a general audience. Weekly newspaper. Circulation: 250,000. Not copyrighted. Buys 100 mss a year. Payment on acceptance. Will send free sample copy to writer on request. Will consider photocopied and simultaneous submissions, if the simultaneous submission is out of their area. Submit seasonal material (skiing, wine, outdoor living) 3 months in

advance. Reports on material accepted for publication in 1 week. Returns rejected material imediately. Query first or submit complete ms. Enclose S.A.S.E.
Nonfiction and Photos: A general newspaper requiring that all subjects be related to California and interests in that area. Length: 500 to 3,000 words. Pays $25 to $200. Payment varies for b&w and color photos purchased with or without mss. Captions required.

THE SACRAMENTO BEE, Box 15779, Sacramento CA 95813. For a general readership; higher than average education; higher than average interest in politics, government; outdoor-activity oriented. Newspaper; 48 pages. Established in 1857. Daily. Circulation: 170,000 daily; 200,000 Sunday. Not copyrighted. Buys about 200 mss/year. Pays on publication. Will consider simultaneous submissions if they are not duplicated in Northern California. Reports in 2 weeks. Query or submit complete ms to Features Editor. SASE.
Nonfiction and Photos: Human interest features, news background. Prefers narrative feature style. Does not want to see sophomoric humor. Will consider interviews, profiles, nostalgic and historical articles; expose; personal experience. Length: 100 to 1,500 words. Pays $20 to $100. B&w glossies and color (negatives) purchased with or without mss. Pays $15 to $75 for b&w; $25 to $100 for color. Captions required.

SACRAMENTO WEEKENDER, *Sacramento Union,* 301 Capitol Mall, Sacramento CA 95812. Editor: Jackie Peterson. Weekly. Not copyrighted. Buys about 50 mss a year. "We cannot be responsible for return of unsolicited material." Query first. Enclose S.A.S.E.
Nonfiction and Photos: "We are becoming more and more local in our approach to all subjects, such as leisure activities, outings, travel, the arts, music, entertainment, hobbies, how-to crafts, area personalities." Length: 1,200 words maximum. Pays $25 minimum; $35 to $50 with b&w photos; $45-90, depending on number used, with color photos.

Colorado

CONTEMPORARY MAGAZINE, Sunday supplement to *The Denver Post,* 650 15th St., Denver CO 80201. Editor: Joan White. For "young adults to senior citizens (both sexes), aware of today's world." Newspaper format. Buys first rights. Pays on publication. Will send a free sample copy to a writer on request. No query required. "We are being very selective and use a very limited amount of freelance material." Submit seasonal material 3 months in advance. Reporting time varies. Enclose S.A.S.E. for return of submissions.
Nonfiction: "Mostly a family and women's interest magazine." Articles of 500 to 1,500 words. Payment is $50 to $75.

EMPIRE MAGAZINE, *The Denver Post,* P.O. Box 1709, Denver CO 80201. (303)297-1687. Editor: Carl Skiff. Weekly. Estab: 1950. Buys about 250 mss a year. Buys first rights. Payment on acceptance for nonfiction; on publication for photos. Query first. Enclose S.A.S.E.
Nonfiction and Photos: "A rotogravure magazine covering the general scene in our circulation area. We are looking for material of national magazine quality in interest and writing style, but with a strong, regional peg. Our region focuses on Colorado, Wyoming, Utah, New Mexico, western Kansas and Nebraska. We need solidly researched articles about exciting things, personalities and situations. We also need light humor and reminiscences." Length: 2,500 words maximum. Pays about 5¢ per word. "Photographs can help sell a story." B&w photos are purchased with ms or as singles or series or as picture stories (500 words). Five to 8 photos are used with picture stories. Query first about these. Pays $50 for color transparencies used for cover; $100 for double spread; $25 for singles (color) used inside; $10 for b&w.

District of Columbia

PRESERVATION NEWS, National Trust for Historic Preservation, 740-748 Jackson Place, N.W., Washington DC 20006. Vice President and Editor: Mrs. Terry B. Morton. Organizational publication for members of the National Trust for Historic Preservation. Emphasizes historic preservation. Monthly newspaper; 12-16 pages. Estab: 1961. Circ: 110,000. Pays on publication. Rights purchased vary; may buy all, second serial (reprint) or one-time rights. Photocopied submissions and previously published work OK. SASE. Reports in 4-6 weeks. Free sample copy and editorial guidelines.
Nonfiction: Carleton Knights, Articles Editor. "Most of our material is prepared in-house, but willing to review queries on subjects directly related to historic preservation, including efforts to save and re-use buildings, structures, and to restore neighborhoods of historical, architectural and cultural significance. Writer must be very familiar with our subject matter, which deals with a specialized field, in order to present a unique publication idea." Length: 740 words maximum. Buys about 20 mss a year. Pays $50 maximum.

Photos: Additional payment not usually made for photos used with mss. Pays $10-25 for 8x10 b&w photos purchased without mss or on assignment. Query or send contact sheet. No conversions from slides.

Florida

THE FLORIDIAN, Box 1211, St. Petersburg FL 33731. Editor: Anne L. Goldman. For upper-middle income readers with contemporary outlook. Weekly magazine; 24-40 pages. Estab: 1967. Circ: 200,000. Pays on acceptance. Buys first North American serial, second serial, and simultaneous rights. Simultaneous and photocopied submissions OK. SASE. Free writer's guidelines.
Nonfiction: "Useful articles should be focused on Florida, exploring provocative lifestyles. Subject areas include imaginative leisure and recreational activities, business and financial advice, consumer articles, health and medical articles of use to the sophisticated, energetic household, and food, fashion, interior design, and architecture articles — all with good taste as the prime ingredient. Articles that deal with urban life — not only surviving it, but enjoying it. High interest, upbeat, success oriented personalities. Presentation of all subjects should be crisp, original, innovative. No once-over lightly general features. Articles must be validated by substantial research and a high degree of professionalism is expected in all articles." Buys 200 mss/year. Length: 1,500-3,000 words. Pays $75-300.
Photos: Purchased with or without accompanying ms or on assignment. Captions required. Pays $25 minimum for b&w glossies or color transparencies.

THE TAMPA TRIBUNE, P.O. Box 191, Tampa FL 33601. Features Editor: Leland. Hawes. For a general circulation, newspaper audience. Newspaper; 80 to 160 pages. Established in 1894. Daily. Circulation: 175,000 to 210,000. Not copyrighted, but special stories are co-pyrighted. Buys limited number of mss (primarily from area freelancers). Pays 2-4 weeks after acceptance. Will consider photocopied submissions. Simultaneous submissions considered (but not if made to nearby publications). Reports on material accepted for publication within a month. Returns rejected material within 2 weeks. Query first or submit complete ms. Enclose S.A.S.E.
Nonfiction and Photos: Articles on travel, history, news events, sports, fashion, profiles, trends, etc. Must have central Florida emphasis or tie-in. Open to any literate style. Informational, how-to, personal experience, interview, humor, think pieces, spot news. Length: 150-3,000 words. Pays $25-200. Pays $5 to $25 for b&w glossies purchased with or without ms. Pays $15 to $50 for color transparencies purchased with or without ms.

Illinois

CHICAGO SUN-TIMES' MIDWEST MAGAZINE, 401 N. Wabash, Chicago IL 60611. Editor: Richard Takeuchi. Reports on submissions in 2 weeks. Buys first rights. Pays on publication. Enclose S.A.S.E. with mss and queries.
Nonfiction and Photos: General interest articles, preferably topical, focusing on Chicago or Chicago area. Timeliness is essential for the development of all stories. "No articles on hobbies; no straight narratives." Length: 750 to 2,500 words. Pays $50 to $300. Full color and 8x10 b&w photos purchased as package with mss.

CHICAGO TRIBUNE MAGAZINE, 435 N. Michigan Ave., Chicago IL 60611. Editor: Robert Goldsborough. "The magazine is largely staff-written, but we do use a limited number of freelance articles. Query first, however." Pays $200 minimum. Length: 1,500 to 3,000 words.

Indiana

INDIANAPOLIS STAR MAGAZINE, 307 N. Pennsylvania St., Indianapolis IN 46206. Editor-in-Chief: Fred D. Cavinder. Emphasizes subjects of interest in Indiana. Weekly magazine section of newspaper; 40 pages. Estab: 1947. Circ: 380,000. Pays on publication. Buys one-time rights. Phone queries OK. Submit seasonal/holiday material 2 months in advance. Simultaneous and photocopied submissions OK. SASE. Reports in 2 weeks. Free sample copy.
Nonfiction: Informational; historical and interview (Indiana only); profiles (Hoosiers or ex-Hoosiers only); and technical (health/medical developments). Buys 50/year. Query. Length: 5,000 words maximum. Pays $25-75.
Photos: Purchased with mss. Query or send prints or transparencies. Pays $5-7.50 for 5x7 or larger b&w glossies or mattes; $7.50-10 for 35mm (or larger) color transparencies.
How To Break In: "Find a good, solid subject related to Indiana, such as a native Hoosier who now has an important or offbeat role elsewhere."
Rejects: "Too many freelancers send us too general material. We are not interested in house-

hold hints, consumer tips, oddities, celebrities, etc. We want stories which would be of specific interest to Indiana readers. That is, if the story doesn't include some relationship to Indiana, the subject must be of significant universal interest. An example would be a health breakthrough, major social development, or a new national trend. But our overwhelming topic is Indiana, her people or her former residents."

MICHIANA, *The South Bend Tribune,* Colfax at Lafayette, South Bend IN 46634. (219)233-6161. Editor: Tom Philipson. For "average daily newspaper readers; perhaps a little above average since we have more than a dozen colleges and universities in our area." Weekly; 24 pages. Established in 1873. Circulation: 125,000. Rights purchased vary with author and material. May buy first North American serial rights or simultaneous rights providing material offered will be used outside of Indiana and Michigan. Buys about 200 mss a year. Payment on publication. Will consider photocopied submissions if clearly legible. Submit special material for spring and fall travel sections at least 1 month in advance. Reports within a week. Submit complete ms. Enclose S.A.S.E.

Nonfiction and Photos: "Items of general and unusual interest, written in good, clear, simple sentences with logical approach to subject. We like material oriented to the Midwest, especially Indiana, Michigan, Ohio and Illinois; also some religious material if unusual." Humor, think pieces, travel, photo articles with brief texts. "We avoid all freelance material that supports movements of a political nature. We do not like first-person stories, but use them on occasion. We can use some offbeat stuff if it isn't too far out." Length: 800 to 3,000 words. Payment is $50 to $60 minimum, with increases as deemed suitable. All mss must be accompanied by illustrations or b&w photos or 35mm or larger color transparencies.

Iowa

DES MOINES SUNDAY REGISTER PICTURE MAGAZINE, *Des Moines Register,* 715 Locust St., Des Moines IA 50309. Editor: Charles J. Nettles. For mass newspaper audience, metropolitan and rural. Established in 1950. Weekly. Circulation: 440,000. Buys first serial rights. Buys 15 to 20 mss a year. Payment on publication. Query first preferred. Submit seasonal material 6 to 8 weeks in advance. Enclose S.A.S.E. for reply to queries.

Nonfiction and Photos: "Articles heavily concentrated on Iowa, about what's going on in Iowa; how to survive in the modern world. General interest material. Anything interesting in Iowa, or interesting elsewhere with some kind of tie to Iowans." Length: 1,500 words maximum, but prefers shorter mss. Material must lend itself to strong photographic presentation. If the idea is good, a photographer will be assigned, if writer does not have professional quality photos. Pays $60 to $150. Photos purchased with or without mss. Captions required. Prefers 8x10 b&w glossies. Pays $15 minimum. 35mm or larger transparencies. Pays $50 minimum for cover; $25 for inside use.

How To Break In: "Good local human interest stories should be what a new writer should be looking for. Would suggest you write for free sample copy of magazine. Frequently need short-short articles that will go with one photo. This is a good place for a new writer to get that first hit. Our suggestion always is to write about people, not things."

Kentucky

COURIER-JOURNAL AND TIMES MAGAZINE, 525 W. Broadway, Louisville KY 40202. (502)582-4674. Editor: Geoffrey Vincent. Not soliciting freelance material.

THE VOICE-JEFFERSONIAN, Chenoweth Sq., St. Matthews KY 40207. (502)895-5436. Editor: Bruce B. VanDusen. For middle and upper income suburban audience. Family readership, but no taboos. Weekly. "No copyright unless the story is super-special and exclusive to us." Will consider cassette submissions. Address all inquiries to the editor. Enclose S.A.S.E.

Nonfiction and Photos: News and Features departments. 300 to 1,500 words on local (East Jefferson County) subjects. "Manuscripts must have a local angle. Writers persistently ignore this fundamental standard." 5x7 b&w glossies. Pays 25¢ to $1 per inch; $5 to $15 for photos.

How To Break In: "Find a present resident of our area with an interesting story, and tell it, with one good picture to illustrate."

Louisiana

SUNDAY ADVOCATE MAGAZINE, Box 588, Baton Rouge LA 70821. (504)383-1111, Ext. 262. Editor: Charles H. Lindsay. Buys no rights. Pays on publication. Enclose S.A.S.E. for return of submissions.

Nonfiction and Photos: Well-illustrated, short articles; must have local, area or Louisiana angle, in that order of preference. Photos purchased with mss. Rates vary.

Massachusetts

THE CHRISTIAN SCIENCE MONITOR, 1 Norway St., Boston MA 02115. (617)262-2300, Ext. 2321. Editor: John Hughes. International newspaper issued daily except Saturdays, Sundays and holidays in North America; weekly international edition. Special issues: travel, winter vacation and international travel, summer vacation, autumn vacation, and cruise section. February and September: fashion; May and October: food. Established in 1908. Circulation: 188,000. Buys all rights. Buys about 3,700 mss a year. Payment on acceptance or publication, "depending on department." Submit seasonal material 1 to 2 months in advance. Reports within 4 weeks. Submit only complete ms. Enclose S.A.S.E.

Nonfiction: Features Editor: Alan Bance. In-depth news analysis, features, and essays. Style should be bright but not cute, concise but thoroughly researched. Try to humanize news or feature writing so the reader identifies with it. Avoid sensationalism, crime and disaster. Accent constructive, solution-oriented treatment of subjects. Can use news-in-the-making stories not found elsewhere if subject has sufficient impact on current history (600 to 1,500 words). Feature pages as follows: People, Places, Things page uses colorful human interest material not exceeding 800 words, and humorous anecdotes. Home Forum page buys essays of 400 to 800 words; education, arts, real estate, travel, women, fashion, furnishings, consumer, environment, and science-technology pages will consider articles not usually more than 800 words appropriate to respective subjects." Pays from $20 to $100. Some areas covered in travel pages include: Swiss, N.E., British, Canadian, Hawaiian, and Caribbean.

Photos: Department Editor: Gordon Converse. Purchased with or without mss. Captions required. Pays $10 to $50 depending upon size and where used in paper.

Poetry: Home Forum Editor: Henrietta Buckmaster. Home Forum uses poetry. Wide variety of subjects and treatment; traditional forms, blank and free verse, but the poetry must be of high quality and proficiency. Short poems preferred. Pays $20-40.

NEW ENGLAND MAGAZINE, *Boston Globe,* Boston MA 02107. Editor-in-Chief: Anthony C. Spinazzola. Weekly magazine; 44 pages. Estab: 1936. Circ: 606,353. Pays on publication. Buys one-time rights. Submit seasonal/holiday material 3 months in advance. Reports in 2 weeks.

Nonfiction: Karen Dobkin, Articles Editor. Expose (variety of issues including political, economic, and scientific); informational; humor (limited use, but occasionally published in short columns of 1,000 words); interview; personal opinion (1,000 words); and profile. Buys 100-150 mss/year. Query. Length: 1,000-3,000 words. Pays $150-300.

Photos: Purchased with accompanying ms or on assignment. Captions required. Send contact sheet. Pays $25-75 for b&w photos; $50-225 for color. Total purchase price for ms includes payment for photos.

Columns/Departments: Karen Dobkin, Column/Department Editor. In Personal Terms (humor, personal experiences, opinion). "This column is a magazine op-ed page, which allows the opportunity to air views, joys, angers, and experiences through quality writing." Buys 52 mss/year. Submit complete ms. Length: 1,000-1,200 words. Pays $175.

SUNDAY MORNING MAGAZINE, Worcester Sunday Telegram, 20 Franklin St., Worcester MA 01613. (617)755-4321. Sunday News Editor: Charles F. Mansbach. Sunday supplement serving a broad cross-section of Central Massachusetts residents; 16 pages. Estab: 1933. Circ: 110,000. Pays on acceptance. Buys first North American serial rights. Phone queries OK. Submit seasonal/holiday material 2 months in advance. SASE. Free sample copy.

Nonfiction: Expose (related to circulation area); informational (should have broad application; personal experience (something unusual); photo feature and profile. Buys 2 mss/issue. Query. Length: 600-2,400 words. Pays $50-100. "All pieces must have a local angle."

Photos: Photos purchased with or without accompanying ms or on assignment. Captions required. Pays $5 for 5x7 b&w glossies.

Columns/Departments: City Life ("a brief slice-of-life piece that says something about life in our city; heavy on dialogue and description.") Query. Length: 600-1,200 words. Pays $32-50. Open to suggestions for new columns/departments.

Michigan

DETROIT MAGAZINE, *The Detroit Free Press,* 321 Lafayette Blvd., Detroit MI 48231. (313)222-6490. Editor: Rogers Worthington. For a general newspaper readership; urban and suburban; relatively high educational level. Weekly magazine. Estab: 1965. Circ: 714,000. Pays within 6 weeks of publication. Buys first rights. Reports in 3-4 weeks. SASE. Sample copy for SASE.

Nonfiction: "Seeking quality magazine journalism with a Greater Detroit (extending to Ann

Arbor) and Michigan focus, or elsewhere, provided the subject is a Michiganian or Michigan issue or event. Looking for well-written crime narratives; 'what-happened-here?' stories; and good business and political intrigue stories. Articles that hinge on burgeoning public issues (in Michigan), trends, lifestyles, science behavior, health and medicine, sports, art and entertainment. Also uses well-researched interviews, with Detroit and other Michigan figures. *Detroit Magazine* is bright and cosmopolitan in tone. Most desired writing style is the 'new journalism' genre, and reporting must be unimpeachable. We also use guides or service pieces." Buys 65-75 mss/year. Query or submit complete ms. Length: 3,500 words maximum. Pays $125-250.

Photos: Purchased with or without accompanying ms. Pays $25 for b&w glossies or color transparencies used inside; $100 for color used as cover. (Covers are usually free-standing, non-story related.)

FENTON INDEPENDENT, 112 E. Ellen St., Fenton MI 48430. (313)629-2203. Editor: Robert G. Silbar. Weekly. Newspaper, not a magazine supplement. Buys all rights. Query first. Enclose S.A.S.E.

Nonfiction and Photos: News stories, features, photos of local interest. Wants local material on local people, not generalized articles. Appreciates opinion articles on local topics. All material must have local flavor. Pays 25¢ per column inch.

Montana

THE BILLINGS GAZETTE, Billings MT 59101. Sunday Editor: Kathryn Wright. Weekly. Buys first rights. Pays on publication. Enclose S.A.S.E. with mss and queries.

Nonfiction and Photos: Features stories and photos about circulation area—northern Wyoming and eastern and central Montana—or people from it and now someplace else doing interesting things. Length: 1,000 words plus photos. Pays 25¢ per inch and up depending on quality. $3 to $5 each for action photos.

New Jersey

SOUTH JERSEY LIVING, Abarta, Inc., 1900 Atlantic Ave., Atlantic City NJ 08404. (609)345-1111. Editor-in-Chief: Charles Reynolds. Weekly magazine section; 12 pages. Estab: 1965. Circ: 70,000. Pays after publication. Buys all rights but may reassign following publication. Phone queries OK. Submit seasonal/holiday material 1 month in advance. SASE. Reports in 1 month. Free sample copy and writer's guidelines.

Nonfiction: "All material must have a strong, direct relationship to South Jersey, which in this case comprises the counties of Atlantic, Cape May, Cumberland, Salem, and the southern portion of Burlington and Ocean. All topics range full spectrum: profiles, public issues, controversial and non-controversial sports; hobbies, occupations; fashions, recipes (South Jersey recipes); gardening, ecology, history; geography, anthropology, science and so on." Query preferred, but not essential. Length: 1,000-3,000 words. Pays $20 minimum.

Photos: Department Editor: Paul Learn. B&w glossies (8x10) purchased with mss. Captions required. Send prints. Pays $5-10.

New Mexico

VIVA, The New Mexican (Gannett Group), Box 2048, Santa Fe NM 87501. Editor: Peter H. Eichstaedt. For a general Sunday newspaper audience. "We are the Sunday magazine for *The New Mexican,* Santa Fe's daily paper." Weekly tabloid; 24 pages. Estab: 1971. Circ: 25,000. Pays on publication. Buys one-time rights. Phone queries OK if local. Submit seasonal/holiday material 1 month in advance. Photocopied submissions OK. Reports in 2 weeks. Free sample copy and writer's guidelines.

Nonfiction: Historical (northern New Mexico towns); humor (life in and around Santa Fe and northern New Mexico); informational (what's happening in a line of work, or town, or area of art); interviews and profiles (unique people or people with unique talent). Buys 1-2/issue. Query (in writing). Length: 1,500-2,000 words. Pays $25-35.

Photos: B&w glossies (8x10) purchased with or without mss. Captions required. Query or send prints. Pays $5.

How To Break In: "All material must be about something or someone in Santa Fe or northern New Mexico only."

New York

FAMILY WEEKLY, 641 Lexington Ave., New York NY 10022. Managing Editor: Tim Mulligan. No longer accepting unsolicited mss, but will consider queries. SASE.

Fillers: Will consider short jokes and humor items. Pays $10.

LI MAGAZINE, *Newsday,* 550 Stewart Ave., Garden City NY 11530. (516)222-5126. Managing Editor: Stanley Green. For well-educated, affluent suburban readers. Established in 1972. Weekly. Circulation: 450,000. Buys all rights. Pays on publication. Query. SASE.
Nonfiction and Photos: Art Director: Cliff Gardiner. "Stories must be about Long Island people, places or events." Length: 600 to 2,500 words. Pays $100 to $600. B&w contacts and 35mm transparencies purchased on assignment. Pays up to $100 per page for b&w; $200 per page for color, including cover.

NATIONAL EXAMINER, Box 711, Rouses Point NY 12979. (514)866-7744. Editor-in-Chief: John Elder. For a contemporary, upbeat audience. Weekly color tabloid. Pays on acceptance or publication. Buys first North American serial rights. Phone queries OK. SASE. Reports immediately by letter or phone. Free sample copy.
Nonfiction: Informational; how-to; personal experience; interview; profile; inspirational; humor; historical; expose; nostalgia; photo feature; spot news; and new product. Especially interested in pieces on ghosts, psychics and astrology. Sex and violence OK if handled in a "sophisticated, non-sleazy manner." Query. Buys 1,000 mss/year. Pays $50-300.
Photos: Purchased with or without accompanying ms. "Celebrities, off-beat shots, humorous and spot news photos always in demand." Send prints or transparencies. Pays $25 minimum for 8x10 b&w glossies; pay negotiable for 35mm or 2¼x2¼ color transparencies.

NEW YORK NEWS MAGAZINE, *New York Daily News,* 220 E. 42 St., New York NY 10017. Editor: Richard C. Lemon. For general audience. Weekly. Circulation: over 3 million. Buys first serial rights. Buys about 40 mss a year. Payment on acceptance. Will send free sample copy to a writer on request. Submit seasonal material 2 months in advance. Will consider photocopied submissions. Reports in 4 weeks. Query first. "If you have published before, it is best to include a sample clip." Enclose S.A.S.E.
Nonfiction and Photos: "Interested in all sorts of articles: most interested in human interest stories, articles about people (famous or unknown) and service pieces; least interested in essays and discussion pieces. Continuing need for New York City area subjects. Freelancer should use his own approach to material. Entertainment pieces seem to be over-abundant. We use a number, but they are mostly staff written." Buys informational, personal experience, interview, profile, humor, nostalgia, and photo articles. Length: 600 to 3,000 words. Pays $50 to $750. Photos purchased with or without mss. Captions are required. Specifications for b&w glossies or jumbo contacts: 8x10. Pays $25 for single, $150 for complete picture story. Color specifications: 2½, 4x5 or 35mm transparency. Pays from $35 for single, $200 for set.
How To Break In: "For new writers, the key thing to remember is to start with a suggestion that grabs us and keep your material within screaming distance of New York City."

THE NEW YORK TIMES, 229 W. 43 St., New York NY 10036. Enclose S.A.S.E. for reply to queries or return of mss.
Nonfiction and Photos: *The New York Times Magazine* appears in *The New York Times* on Sunday, and is edited by Edward Klein. "We are looking for fresh, lively and provocative writing on national and international news developments, science, education, family life, social trends and problems, arts and entertainment, personalities, sports, the changing American scene. Freelance contributions are invited. Articles must be timely. They must be based on specific news items, forthcoming events, significant anniversaries, or they must reflect trends. Our full-length articles run from 2,500-5,000 words, and for these we pay $850 on acceptance. ($1,000 after two prior acceptances). Our shorter pieces run from 1,500-2,500 words, and for these, we pay $500 on acceptance. We pay a basic minimum of $50 for photos." *Travel and Resorts* section buys "literate, sophisticated, factual articles, evoking the experience of travel with quotes, anecdotes and even-handed reportage. Authors must be personally familiar with subjects about which they write, free to praise or criticize; under no circumstances will we publish articles growing out of trips in any way subsidized by airlines, hotels or other organizations with direct or indirect interest in the subjects. All submissions are to be considered on speculation; payment upon publication is approximately 10¢ a word; maximum $250 per article; additional $50 for each photo used." *Travel and Resorts* Editor: Robert Stock. *Arts and Leisure* section of *The New York Times* appears on Sunday. Wants "to encourage imaginativeness in terms of form and approach —stressing ideas, issues, trends, investigations, symbolic reporting and stories delving deeply into the creative achievements and processes of artists and entertainers —and seeks to break away from old-fashioned gushy, fan magazine stuff." Length: 750-2,000 words. Pays $100-$250 depending on length. Pays $50 for photos. *Arts and Leisure* Editor: William H. Honan.
How To Break In: "The Op Ed page is always looking for new material and publishes many people who have never been published before. We want material of universal relevance which

people can talk about in a personal way. When writing for the Op Ed page there is no formula but the writing itself should have some polish. Don't make the mistake of pontificating on the news. We're not looking for more political columnists. Op Ed length runs about 700 words, and pays about $150."

NEWSDAY, 550 Stewart Ave., Garden City NY 11566. Travel Editor: Steve Schatt. For general readership of Sunday Travel Section. Newspaper. Estab: 1947. Weekly. Circ: 460,000. Buys all rights for the New York area only. Buys 100 mss a year. Pays on publication. Will consider photocopied submissions. Simultaneous submissions considered if others are being made outside of New York area. Reports in 4 weeks. Submit complete ms. Enclose S.A.S.E.
Nonfiction and Photos: Travel articles with strong focus and theme for the Sunday Travel Section. Emphasis on accuracy, service, quality writing to convey mood and flavor. Must involve visit or experience that typical traveler can easily duplicate. Skip diaries, "My First Trip Abroad" pieces or compendiums of activities; downplay first person. Length: 600 to 1,750 words, but use more 800-1,000—word pieces. Pays $60-175. Also, regional "weekender" pieces of 700-800 words plus service box, but query subject first.

PARADE, The Sunday Newspaper Magazine, 733 Third Ave., New York NY 10017. (212)953-7557. Weekly. Circulation: over 19 million. Buys first North American serial rights. Pays on acceptance. Query first. Enclose S.A.S.E.
Nonfiction: "Interested in features that will inform, educate or entertain a mass circulation domestic audience. Exclusive, news-related articles and photos are required. Subjects may include: well-known personalities, sports, religion, education, community activities, family relations, science and medicine. Articles should be current, factual, authoritative." Length: about 1,500 words. Pays up to $1,000.
Photos: "Photos should have visual impact and be well composed with action-stopping qualities. For the most part, color is used on cover. Transparencies of any size are accepted. Either b&w 8x10 enlargements or contact sheets may be submitted. Accurate caption material must accompany all photos."
How To Break In: "A good way to start out with us is if you have an expertise in some field. For instance, I was speaking to a young writer just the other day who has mainly done work for science publications and textbooks and wants to break into the general field. He's just the kind of person we're looking for. Someone else did a piece for us on the stock market recently. He had expert knowledge in the field and applied it to a general audience. Another thing that would be of advantage to the new writer would be competence with a camera. We are always on the lookout for short features with good illustrations, say 1,000 to 1,500 words. Then there are our short report sections: Intelligence Report and Keeping Up With Youth. These are items of about 250 words and provide a good opportunity for us to get to know a new writer. Intelligence Report deals with things like new inventions, new technologies, new acts of government that the reader should be familiar with. Keeping Up With Youth is an ideal slot for someone who is close to campus life and can fill us in briefly on cultural trends and avant-garde directions. Also youth personalities."

Ohio

THE BLADE SUNDAY MAGAZINE, 541 Superior St., Toledo OH 43660. (419)259-6132. Editor-in-Chief: Mike Tressler. General readership. Weekly magazine; 32 pages. Estab: 1948. Circ: 210,000. Pays on publication. Buys one-time rights. Phone queries OK. Submit seasonal/holiday material 6 months in advance. Simultaneous, photocopied and previously published submissions OK. SASE.
Nonfiction: Historical (about Ohio); humor; informational; interview; personal experience and photo feature. Buys 1 ms/issue. Query. Length: 600-2,000 words. Pays $35-100.
Photos: Photos purchased with accompanying ms. Captions required. Pays $7.50-15 for 8x10 b&w glossies; $10-45 for 35mm, 2¼x2¼ or 8x10 color glossies. Total purchase price for ms includes payment for photos. Model release required.

COLUMBUS DISPATCH SUNDAY MAGAZINE, 34 South Third St., Columbus OH 43216. (614)461-5250. Editor: Robert K. Waldron. Buys one-time rights. Payment after publication. Enclose S.A.S.E.
Nonfiction and Photos: "We accept offerings from beginning writers, but they must be professionally written, and a good picture helps." Strong Ohio angle is essential in all material. Buys singles, photo series, and illustrated articles. Length: 1,000 to 1,500 words. Pays minimum of 3¢ per word. B&w photos only. Pays $5 per photos. "Pay is flexible, depending on how good the piece is, how much effort has apparently been put into it, etc."

DAYTON LEISURE, *Dayton Daily News*, Fourth and Ludlow Sts., Dayton OH 45401. (513)225-2240. Editor: Jack M. Osler. Sunday supplement. Circulation: 225,000. Pays on publication. Usually reports within 1 week. Enclose S.A.S.E.
Nonfiction and Photos: Magazine focuses on leisure time activities particularly in Ohio—that are interesting and unusual. Emphasis is on photos supplemented by stories. Up to 1,000 words. Photos should be glossy. "*The Daily News* will evaluate articles on their own merits. Likewise with photos. Average payment per article: $25." Payments vary depending on quality of writing.
Rejects: "Packages of photos *only* for photo layouts. I only use photos with regular mss, *not* alone."

THE ENQUIRER MAGAZINE, 617 Vine St., Cincinnati OH 45201. (513)721-2700. Editor: Graydon DeCamp. Weekly; 52 pages. Established originally as the Pictorial Section in 1924. Circ: 288,000. Not copyrighted. Buys about 150 to 200 mss a year. Pays after publication. Will send free sample copy to writer on request. Write for editorial guidelines. Will consider photocopied and simultaneous submissions. Submit holiday material 2 months in advance. Query first, or submit complete ms. Reports in 2 to 3 weeks. Enclose S.A.S.E.
Nonfiction, Photos, and Fillers: Photo Department Editor: Allan Kain. "Primarily interested in local stories about people, places or events of Cincinnati area and Tri-State; also interested in stories of universal appeal and stories of national interest. Prefer factual stories rather than fiction. No short stories or poems. Prefer researched, documented stories told from an objective point of view. Do not like first-person or opinion stories. Anything topical, particularly contemporary issues, will be considered." Informational, how-to, interview, profile, humor, historical, think articles, nostalgia, and photo. Length: 1,500-3,000 words. A reader participation column of writer's views on a controversial subject is published regularly. Pays $25 for column. Photos purchased with or without accompanying ms. Captions optional. Prefers 8x11 glossies or contact sheets or color transparencies. Pays $10 for b&w; $20 for color. Also buys puzzles, short humor, and quizzes. Length: 100 to 1,000 words.
Rejects: Travel, nostalgia, poems, single photos.

Oklahoma
ORBIT MAGAZINE, *The Sunday Oklahoman*, Box 25125, Oklahoma City OK 73122. (405)232-3311. Editor: W.U. McCoy. "*Orbit* is a Sunday newspaper magazine serving the western two-thirds of Oklahoma, including Oklahoma City, and an audience of general readers of all ages living in that area." Weekly magazine; 24 pages. Estab: 1961. Circ: 328,000. Pays on publication. Buys first North American serial rights. SASE. Reports in 2 weeks. Sample copy 25¢; free writer's guidelines.
Nonfiction: Informational, historical, humor, inspirational, interview, nostalgia, profile, personal experience, photo feature. Buys 6-8 an issue. Query. Length: 200-3,000 words. Pays $20-200. "All material must relate to Oklahoma."
Photos: Purchased with or without accompanying ms. Captions required. Submit prints or transparencies. Pays $5-35 per b&w photo; $30-100 for 35mm or 2¼x2¼ color transparencies.

Oregon
NORTHWEST MAGAZINE, *The Sunday Oregonian*, 1320 S.W. Broadway, Portland OR 97201. Editor: Joseph R. Bianco. For a family type of audience with somewhat higher education level in Oregon than average. Weekly Sunday supplement magazine; 28 to 40 pages. Established in 1965. Circulation: about 400,000. Buys all rights, but will reassign rights to author after publication. Buys 600 to 650 mss a year. Pays in the closest period to the 15th of the month following publication. Will not consider photocopied submissions. Will consider simultaneous submissions. Reports on material accepted for publication in 10 days. Returns rejected material in 2 weeks. Query first or submit complete ms. Enclose S.A.S.E.
Nonfiction and Photos: "Articles of interest to the Northwest. Topical and (sometimes) controversial. Periodically, issue is devoted to a theme. For example, the theme of 'Outdoors' is how-to. How to do the hockey stop in skiing, how to find a remote hiking ridge, etc. Keep Northwest articles short, topical, and of interest to the Northwest. Ecology, environment, and social mores are always subjects of interest. Also, personality profiles of people of interest." Length: 800 to 1,500 words. Pays $40. 8x10 b&w glossies are purchased with mss or on assignment. Captions required. Pays $15.

Pennsylvania
THE PITTSBURGH PRESS, 34 Blvd. of Allies, Pittsburgh PA 15230. (412)263-1100. Features Editor: William Allan. For general newspaper readers. Established in 1920. Publishes 3

536 Writer's Market '78

weekly magazines. Circulation: 700,000. Not copyrighted. Buys 25 to 50 mss a year. Pays on publication. Reports in 2 weeks. Submit complete ms. Enclose S.A.S.E.

Nonfiction and Photos: Picture-oriented material for the Roto Magazine; family type stories for Family Magazine. Must be local subjects with good general interest. Informational, how-to, personal experience, profile, inspirational, humor, historical, nostalgia. Pays $25 per published page. Some additional payment for b&w photos used with mss.

How To Break In: "Submit good copy."

TODAY MAGAZINE, *Philadelphia Inquirer,* 400 N. Broad St., Philadelphia PA 19101. Editor-in-Chief: David Boldt. Managing Editor: Michael Shoup. Sunday magazine section for big city audience. Weekly magazine; 42 pages. Circ: 183,000. Pays on publication. Buys first North American serial rights. Submit seasonal/holiday material 3 months in advance. Photocopied submissions OK. SASE. Reports in 1 month. Free sample copy.

Nonfiction: Rebecca Sinkler, Nonfiction Editor. Informational; interview; personal experience; personal opinion and profile. Buys 2-3 mss/issue. Query. Length: 500-5,000 words. Pays $250-500.

How To Break In: "A good way to break in is to submit an excellent, flashy short piece for our Finale section. We use local stories only and we're looking for sophisticated material about Philadelphia and its people; its institutions. Excellent writing a must."

Rhode Island

RHODE ISLANDER, *The Providence Journal,* Providence RI 02902. (401)277-7263. Editor: Douglas Riggs. Sunday magazine section. Circulation: 210,000. Buys first rights. Payment on publication. Will send free sample copy to writer on request. Reports in 2 weeks. Query first or submit complete ms. Enclose S.A.S.E.

Nonfiction and Photos: "Always looking for new writers with real talent. Prefer articles with 'new journalism' flavor (anecdotal, subjective, highly descriptive, thought-provoking, etc.). Strongly oriented toward Rhode Island and southern New England." Pays $50 to $200. Photos purchased with mss. Their weekly "Speaking Out" feature uses expressions of opinions on any topic. Length: 1,000 words maximum. Pays $50.

Poetry: "We publish short poems once a month. No restrictions on subject matter or style." Pays $20.

How To Break In: "A phone call or personal visit is better than a query letter. If you have some specific story ideas, you are always welcome. Read the magazine first; sample copies sent on request. Personal contact with writer may mean difference between rejection slip and letter suggesting revisions. But if your stuff is really good, we'll buy it if it comes in by pony express. We're always looking for new talent, especially in southern New England."

Rejects: "Light" essays on homey topics, historical narrations unrelieved by anecdotes, commentary on national events, single photographs.

Texas

THE DALLAS SUN, Buddy, Inc., PO Box 8366, Dallas TX 75205. (214)526-6049. Editor-in-Chief: Ken Badt. Emphasizes Dallas-based features. For "North Dallas readers; 30-45 years old, consumers, media freaks." Monthly tabloid; 16 pages. Estab: 1976. Circ: 25,000. Payment on publication. Buys one-time rights. Phone queries OK. Submit seasonal/holiday material 2 months in advance. Simultaneous and photocopied submissions OK. SASE. Reports in 2 weeks. Free sample copy.

Nonfiction: Expose (possible, but we stay out of politics); how-to, informational; historical; humor (if localized); interview (local); profile; and photo feature. Buys 120 mss/year. Query or send complete ms. Length: 500-1,500 words. Pays 3¢/word.

Photos: Purchased with or without accompanying ms or on assignment. Captions optional. B&w only. Submit contact sheet, or 8x10 glossies. Pays $2/column inch; $10/assignment fee. Model release required.

Columns/Departments: Movie and book reviews. Buys 2/issue. Send complete ms. Length: 450-1,600 words. Pays 3¢/word. Open to suggestions for new columns/departments.

Fillers: Newsbreaks, short humor. Buys 12-20/year. Submit complete ms. Length: 200-700 words. Pays 3¢/word.

How To Break In: "Our paper is entertainment. Copy should be snappy, witty, informative, locally oriented and slightly irreverent."

Rejects: "Politics and great causes."

THE ICONOCLAST, Box 7013, Dallas TX 75209. (214)528-4031. Editor-in-Chief: Douglas D. Baker Jr. News and review. Weekly tabloid; 24 pages. Estab: 1969. Circ: 10,000. Pays 2 weeks after publication. Buys all rights. Submit seasonal/holiday material 2 months in advance. Simultaneous and photocopied submissions OK. SASE. Reports in 4 weeks. Free sample copy and writer's guidelines.

Nonfiction: Expose; historical; how-to; humor; informational; inspirational; interview; new product; nostalgia; personal experience; personal opinion; photo feature; profile and travel. Buys 7 mss/issue. Send complete ms. Length: 150-2,000 words. Pays $10-250.

Photos: Photos purchased with or without accompanying ms. Pays $2.50-50 for 8x11 b&w glossies. No additional payment for photos accepted with accompanying ms. Model release required.

Columns/Departments: Dining; Dallas Notes; Sports and Music. Buys 5 mss/issue. Send complete ms. Length: 150-1,000 words. Pays $5-50. Open to suggestions for new columns/departments.

MIDLAND REPORTER-TELEGRAM, Box 1650, Midland TX 79701. Managing Editor: Tom Rutland. City Editor: Larry Hitchcock. Primarily for oilmen, ranchers, office workers; all ages, varied interests. Daily newspaper. Estab: 1890. Circ: 23,000. Pays on publication. Buys one-time rights. Query. Phone queries OK. Submit seasonal/holiday material 1 month in advance. Reports in 2-3 weeks. Sample copy 50¢.

Nonfiction: Informational, historical, interviews, profiles, travel articles; photo features. Should be related to the oil business or be of interest to West Texas readers. Query. Length: 200 words minimum. Pays $5-10.

Photos: Purchased with or without mss or on assignment. Captions required. Query. Pays $3-10 for 8x10 b&w glossies. Model release required.

Columns/Departments: Material for Oil/Energy, Travel and Outdoors columns. Buys 60-75 items/year. Query. Length: 200 words minimum. Pays $3-10. Address suggestions for new columns and departments to Tom Rutland.

Utah

VALLEY MAGAZINE, The Herald Journal, Box 487, Logan UT 84321. (801)752-2121. Editor-in-Chief: C.P. Cheney. For readers of the *Herald Journal.* Weekly newspaper magazine section; 12 pages. Estab: 1975. Circ: 11,000. Pays on publication. Buys one-time rights. Submit seasonal/holiday material 2 months in advance. Photocopied, simultaneous, and previously published submissions OK. SASE. Reports in 4 weeks. Free writer's guidelines.

Nonfiction: Expose; how-to; informational; historical; humor; inspirational; interview; nostalgia; personal opinion; profile; travel; personal experience; and photo feature. Buys 1 ms/issue. Query or submit complete ms. Length: 700-2,000 words. Pays $10-30.

Photos: Purchased with or without mss. Send contact sheet. Pays $2-7.50 for b&w. "We run a regular photo feature which is simply one b&w photo that can stand alone. Local subject or local interest is essential."

Fiction: Adventure, fantasy, experimental, historical, humorous, mainstream, religious, science fiction, western. Buys 10 stories/year. Query or send complete ms. Length: 700-2,000 words. Pays $10-30.

How To Break In: "Subject matter is open, but articles should be of interest to newspaper-reading audience in northern Utah/southern Idaho area."

Rejects: Fiction without a strong local tie-in to Cache Valley.

Virginia

THE JOURNAL MESSENGER, Prince William Publishing Co., Inc., 9009 Church St., Manassus VA 22110. (203)368-3101. Managing Editor: Bennie Scarton, Jr. For young, suburban families ages 25-30. Daily newspaper; 20 pages. Estab: 1869. Circ: 10,000. Pays on publication. Buys all rights but may reassign following publication. Phone queries OK. Submit seasonal/holiday material 2 weeks in advance. Simultaneous, photocopied, and previously published submissions OK. SASE. Reports in 2 weeks. Free sample copy and editorial guidelines.

Nonfiction: Bruce Elbert, News Editor. Expose and interview. Buys 5/issue. Query. Length: 300-500 words. Pays $15-25.

Photos: Tom Kane, Department Editor. Purchased with or without mss or on assignment. Captions required. Query or send prints. Pays $10-15 for 8x10 b&w glossies.

Columns/Departments: Government. Editorial. Buys 3/issue. Query. Length: 300-500 words. Pays $10-15. Open to suggestions for new columns and departments.

Washington

PANORAMA MAGAZINE, *The Everett Herald,* Box 930, Everett WA 98206. (206)259-5151. Editor: Jeanne Metzger. Weekly magazine section; 20 pages. Estab: 1973. Circ: 51,000. Pays on publication. Buys one-time rights. Phone queries OK. Submit seasonal/holiday material 6 weeks in advance. Simultaneous, photocopied and previously published submissions OK. SASE. Reports in 1 month.

Nonfiction: Historical (Pacific Northwest history); humor; interview and profile; nostalgia; personal experience; photo feature and some travel. Query or send complete ms. Pays $15-60.

Photos: Photos purchased with or without accompanying ms. Pays $30 for good color photos to go with 'people' covers. No payment for b&w photos accompanying ms.

SEATTLE TIMES MAGAZINE, Seattle Times Co., Box 70, Seattle WA 98111. (206)464-2283. Editor: Larry Anderson. For people 20-80, above average in education and income. Weekly newspaper supplement; 16 pages. Estab: 1910. Circ: 300,000. Pays on publication. Buys first rights. Submit seasonal/holiday material 2 months in advance. Photocopied and previously published submissions OK. SASE. Reports in 1 week. Free sample copy and writer's guidelines.

Nonfiction: Humor; informational; inspirational; interview; personal experience and profile. Buys 3 mss/issue. Query or send complete ms. Length: 200-1,500 words. Pays $40-60/page.

Photos: Photos purchased with accompanying ms. Captions required. Pays $10-20 for b&w glossies. Query or send prints.

SEATTLE TIMES PICTORIAL, P.O. Box 70, Seattle WA 98111. Editor: Tom Stockley. For a general audience, above average in education. Sunday newspaper supplement. Circ: 325,000. Buys first rights. Pays on publication. Reports in 1 week. Enclose S.A.S.E.

Nonfiction and Photos: Looking for pictorial essays on regional (Washington, British Columbia) material. Uses b&w photos inside with possible tie-in color (4x5 transparencies) cover. B&w, submit negatives with contact sheets. Text length: 500 to 1,000 words. Pays $30 to $50 for text. Pays $125 for color cover; $30/page for b&w. Unused negatives and transparencies returned after publication.

SUNDAY MAGAZINE, *Tacoma News Tribune,* 1950 S. State St., Tacoma WA 98411. (206)597-8671. Editor: Dick Kunkle. Sunday supplement. Circulation: 100,000. Pays on publication. Query first. Reports immediately. Enclose S.A.S.E.

Nonfiction and Photos: Articles and photos about Pacific Northwest, particularly the Puget Sound area. Historical, biographical, recreational stories. Length: 1,000 words maximum. Pays $50/printed tabloid page, whether pictures, text or both. Also occasionally buys a color cover transparency for $60. Northwest subjects only.

TOTEM TIDINGS MAGAZINE, *The Daily Olympian,* P.O. Box 407, Olympia WA 98507. Editor: Dennis Anstine. For newspaper readers. Sunday tabloid; 16 pages. Estab: 1974. Weekly. Circ: 27,000. Not copyrighted. Buys about 35 mss a year. Pays on publication. Will send free sample copy to writer on request if postage is included. Write for copy of guidelines for writers. No photocopied or simultaneous submissions. Reports in 30 days. Query first or submit complete ms. Enclose S.A.S.E.

Nonfiction and Photos: Washington state-oriented articles, preferably from southwestern part of state. Must be bright and fast-paced material. People, places or things —but no first-person articles. Historical, water-oriented and topical pieces dealing with the immediate area. Informational, how-to, interview, profile, humor, historical, nostalgia, travel (but only in the northwest). Length: 1,440 words maximum. Pays $25. Buys color transparencies or b&w (8x10) prints with mss. Pays $5 for both b&w and color.

West Virginia

PANORAMA, *The Morgantown Dominion-Post,* Greer Bldg., Morgantown WV 26505. Sunday supplement issued weekly. Editor: Sarah Stevenson. Rights purchased are negotiable. Pays on publication. Reports in 2 weeks. Query first. Enclose S.A.S.E.

Nonfiction: "While we have considerable material from our regular sources, we are interested in 1,500- to 2,000-word nonfiction about West Virginia places, people, customs and events and about the Appalachian area immediately surrounding the state. We are always looking for the regional tie-in, no matter how slim." Pays $7.50 to $25.

STATE MAGAZINE, *Sunday Gazette-Mail,* 1001 Virginia St., E, Charleston WV 25330. Editor: Harold C. Gadd. For family newspaper readers. Newspaper magazine; (11x14). Established in 1952. Weekly. Circulation: 110,000. Not copyrighted. Buys 150 to 200 mss a year. Pays on publication. Will send sample copy to writer for 25¢. Will consider photocopied submissions. Simultaneous submissions are considered, if not made to other West Virginia newspapers. Submit special issue material by May 1. Reports in 30 to 90 days. Query first. Enclose S.A.S.E.

Nonfiction and Photos: Emphasis is on West Virginia material; articles and photo essays. "Simple, lucid, tight writing with a logical organization. Writer must want to catch and hold readers' attention in a busy, busy world. We do not want to see material that has obviously been rejected by other publications. We're easy to sell, but not that easy. We would like to see some West Virginia animal profiles slanted to the family hiker, camper or picnicker; or toward youth outdoors." Length: 500 to 1,500 words. Pays $10 to $50. Annually publishes a special issue on West Virginia: Vacationland, in which articles on enjoyable West Virginia vacation locales are used. Length: 500 to 1,000 words. Pays $10 to $50. B&w photos with good contrast, good composition, and sharp focus purchased with or without ms. Pays $5. Ultra-sharp, bright, 35mm (or up to 4x5) color transparencies purchased with or without ms. Pays $20.
How To Break In: "Always query first. Beginning West Virginia writers have best chance. Our freelance policy is designed to encourage them to write about their home state."

Wisconsin

INSIGHT MAGAZINE, *Milwaukee Journal,* 333 W. State, Milwaukee WI 53201. (414)224-2341. Editor: Mike Moore. Emphasizes general interest reading for a cross-section of Milwaukee. Weekly magazine; 40 pages. Estab: 1969. Circ: 550,000. Pays on acceptance. Buys one-time rights. Phone queries OK. Submit seasonal/holiday material at least 2 months in advance. Simultaneous, photocopied and previously published submissions OK. SASE. Reports in 1-2 weeks. Free sample copy.
Nonfiction: Humor; interview; nostalgia; personal experience; personal opinion; and profile. Buys 50 mss/year. Query. Length: 1,000-3,000 words. Pays $50-250.
How To Break In: "We are not a good market for out-of-state writers. We may buy reprints from time to time from established writers."

MIDWEST ROTO, (formerly *Rural Gravure),* Rural Gravure Service, Inc., 2564 Branch St., Middleton WI 53562. (608)836-1525. Editor-in-Chief: Jerry C. Carren. Managing Editor: Deena Schneider. Emphasizes "hometown midwest America. A newspaper supplement which carries human interest articles about the midwest and midwest people. Circulates in 150 newspapers." Monthly magazine; 16 pages. Estab: 1936. Circ: 651,000. Pays on publication. Buys simultaneous rights. Submit seasonal/holiday material 6 months in advance. Simultaneous and previously published submissions OK. SASE. Reports in 1 week.
Nonfiction: Historical; humor; interview; nostalgia; photo feature; and profile. Mss must relate to midwest people and places. Buys 4-6/issue. Submit complete ms. Length: 1,000-3,000 words. Pays $50-300.
Photos: Purchased with accompanying ms. Captions required. Send prints. Pays $15-150 for 8x10 b&w glossies. Total purchase price for ms includes payment for photos. Model release required.

Canada

THE CANADIAN MAGAZINE, The Simpson Tower, 401 Bay St., Toronto M5H 2Y8, Ontario, Canada. (416)363-7151. Editor: Don Obe. Buys North American serial rights. Pays on acceptance. "We only consider mss written with a very strong Canadian slant." Query first. Enclose S.A.E. and International Reply Coupons.
Nonfiction: Department Editor: Alan Walker, Managing Editor. Looking for articles of interest to Canadians from coast to coast, on Canadian subjects, written in a lively and informative manner with plenty of human interest. Effective use of anecdotes quite frequently provides this human interest; therefore, use an anecdotal approach to the subject. Articles submitted may cover a wide range of topics—human affairs, religion, science, politics, personalities, humor and sport, hobbies, cookery and fashion. Looking for good literary quality. Strongly recommend an outline letter, of 200 to 300 words, staking out the extent and burden of the article. Length: 2,000 to 4,000 words. Pays $300 to $800.

THE ISLANDER MAGAZINE, *The Daily Colonist,* Victoria B.C., Canada. (604)383-4111. Editor: Alec Merriman. For "just about everyone who lives on Vancouver Island". Weekly; 16 (9x14) pages. Established in 1858. Circulation: 50,000. Not copyrighted. Buys 400 to 500 mss a year. Payment on publication. Will send free sample copy to writer on request. Will not consider simultaneous submissions. Reporting time varies "from a week or two to a year, if it is an article we hope to use." Submit complete ms. Enclose S.A.E.
Nonfiction and Photos: "*The Islander* is very personally Pacific Northwest, mainly Vancouver Island, and takes a folksy, homespun, almost chatty outlook. We aim at our local market and don't try to compete with the syndicated magazine sections with articles of wide-ranging general interest. We use feature articles about people, places and things, with a Pacific Northwest

slant, plus a heavy interest in Northwest history. All material must have the Pacific Northwest angle." Length: 500 to 2,000 words. Pays about $25/magazine page. Prefers 5x7 or 8x10 b&w glossies, but sometimes uses snapshots. Pays $3 for photos used with ms; $7.50 for cover use (always a local scene). Captions required.

How To Break In: "*The Islander* leans heavily toward the local slant which is an advantage for Pacific Northwest writers. But, a person from this area who is doing something unique or making a success of living elsewhere always makes an acceptable feature. Travel literature is distributed freely by the yard, so a local and different slant must be sought."

WEEKEND MAGAZINE, The Montreal Standard Limited/Limitee, 231 St. James St. West, Montreal, PQ Canada. (514)282-2457. Editor: John Macfarlane. Weekly section of 23 newspapers. Circ: 1,700,000. Buys first North American rights. Buys 100 mss a year. Pays on acceptance. "All mss and photos sent in are done so on a speculative basis only and should be addressed to the Editor or Art Director respectively." Query before submitting material. Enclose S.A.E. and International Reply Coupons with mss and queries.

Nonfiction and Photos: "Articles should be about some person, event or activity of interest to Canadians. We don't use travel articles or fillers." Length: 1,500 to 2,500 words. Pays $400-800. If photos or transparencies are sent in and used in addition to the ms, payment is adjusted accordingly. "Our photographic requirements are for all sizes of color from 35mm up; we prefer color transparencies and b&w prints." Pays from $75-250.

Op-Ed Pages

Within the last few years, a new forum for opinion and observation (and freelance opportunity) has emerged—the Op-Ed Page. The Op-Ed page is that page in a newspaper opposite the editorial page which solicits commentary on any subject concerning its readers.

Here are the requirements for three of the largest and best known newspapers who solicit material for their Op-Ed pages. Be sure to check with your own local newspaper to see if it contains an Op-Ed page, or if it solicits freelance material for use on its editorial page.

CHICAGO SUN TIMES, 401 N. Wabash Ave., Chicago IL 60611. Editorial Page Editor: Donald K. Coe. Published 6 times/week. Copyrighted. Submit complete ms. SASE. "Primarily intelligent comments, but we also read things sent to us by kneejerk liberals and mossback conservatives and dull middle-of-the-roaders. Every so often, we print them as well. Any subject of general interest." Send submissions to John Teets in care of the editorial page. Length: 500-700 words. Pays $35 minimum.

NEW YORK TIMES, 229 W. 43rd St., New York NY 10036. Op-Ed Page Editor: Charlotte Curtis. Daily. Copyrighted, if requested. Submit complete ms. SASE. "No limit to topics, just something of interest to the public. However, it should be an opinion or commentary. No news reports. We are always looking for new and exciting writers to add to the page." Length: 700 words maximum. Pays $150 maximum.

NEWSDAY, 550 Stewart Ave., Garden City NY 11550. Editorial Page Editor: William C. Sexton. Daily. Copyrighted. SASE. Seeks "opinion on current events, trends, issues—whether national or local government or lifestyle. Must be timely, pertinent, articulate and opinionated. Strong preference for authors within the circulation area, and it's best to consult before you start writing." Length: 600-2,000 words. Pays $50-500.

Photography Publications

CAMERA 35, Popular Publications, 420 Lexington Ave., New York NY 10017. (212)687-1234. Editor: Willard Clark. "A very special magazine within a vertical field, directed at thinking photographers." Semiannual magazine. Estab: 1957. Circ: 115,000. Buys first North American serial rights. Pays on publication. Query first. Reports in 1 to 3 months. Enclose S.A.S.E.

Photos: "Photography published in form of portfolios and essays. No taboos for either words or pictures, as long as they fit our needs. To determine needs, study at least 3 recent issues. Good literate writing mandatory." Payment rates negotiable prior to acceptance.

FREELANCE PHOTOGRAPHY, FREELANCE PHOTO NEWS, 4 East State St., Doylestown PA 18901. Acting Editor: William Cameron. For "amateur and professional photographers, all ages and with various educational backgrounds." Established in 1972 and 1968, respectively. Monthly (FP); every two months (FPN). Circulation: over 25,000. Rights purchased vary with author and material, but may buy all rights. Buys "hundreds" of mss a year. Payment on acceptance or publication. Will send free sample copy to a writer on request. Will send editorial guidelines sheet to a writer on request. "If photographs are to accompany the article, they should be clearly marked with the photographer's name and address, necessary captions or pertinent information must be also clearly available, and if identifiable persons appear in any photo, the proper model release must be attached. Used photos, stories, etc., will not be returned after use unless specifically requested." Reports in two weeks. Query first. Enclose S.A.S.E.
Nonfiction: Interested in articles in the following categories: "A how-to approach toward taking photos or a unique device designed to aid in certain picture situations. It could be with regard to cameras, lighting, studio setup, backdrops, model handling, etc. Included in this could be new darkroom techniques or innovations which would make use of a darkroom more efficient. Aside from the equipment and supporting areas of how-to, an article could be designed from experiences such as 'Promotion sells photos,' 'Linking your camera to a business,' 'A hobby becomes a profitable business,' etc. Unusual experiences which one may have had with a camera or other equipment. Personalities. We'd like to hear about any unique or special happenings by well-known personalities and their involvement in photography. These may be of political figures, TV and movie stars, etc., and their use of cameras and related equipment. Human interest stories. We are interested in stories which illustrate people with unusual or unique job situations and their use of cameras and related equipment. Travel stories. We are not interested in general travel items. They must be geared to a person or group of people and their experience with photography. Articles which inform the reader of how-to or what-to photograph when visiting . . . (city or country) are encouraged and acceptable. Humorous articles are welcome and should be short. These could be of any item which relates to photography, on the lighter side." Also interested in "almost any idea which is photography related." Length: 500 to 5,000 words. Pays $5 to $50.
Photos: "'The Photo Gallery' is a section of selected photographs submitted by our members and readers at large for display on a space available basis in each issue. Individual photos or a series of photos with captions are considered. Credit line will be given. No payment is usually made for photos appearing in this section. 'Photo Story' is devoted to a series of photographs which would be self-explanatory and contain captions only. A short explanatory paragraph may accompany the series." Photos purchased with and without mss. Captions required. Buys 5x7, but prefers 8x10 b&w glossies. Pays $5 and up.

PETERSEN'S PHOTOGRAPHIC MAGAZINE, Petersen Publishing Co., 8490 Sunset Blvd., Los Angeles CA 90069. (213)657-5100. Editor-in-Chief: Paul R. Farber. Managing Editor: Karen Geller. Emphasizes photography. Monthly magazine; 112 pages. Estab: 1972. Circ: 230,000. Pays on publication. Buys one-time rights. Submit seasonal/holiday material 4 months in advance. Photocopied submissions OK. SASE. Reports in 2 months. Sample copy $1.
Nonfiction: Joan Yarfitz, Nonfiction Editor. How-to. Buys 3 mss/issue. Send story outline. Pays $60/printed page.
Photos: David B. Brooks, Photo Editor. Photos purchased with or without accompanying ms. Pays $25-35 for b&w and color photos. Model release required.

PHOTO CONTEST NEWS, Box 1269, Glendora CA 91740. Editor: David C. Fitzgerald, Jr. For amateur and professional photographers interested in photography contests. Readership ranges from the novice photographer to professionals." Newsletter; 6 to 8 pages. Established in 1971. Monthly. Circulation: 1,000. Buys all rights. Buys 12 to 24 mss per year. Payment on publication. Will send sample copy to writer for $1. Will consider photocopied submissions. No simultaneous submissions. Reports on mss accepted for publication in 1 month. Returns rejected mss "immediately upon rejection." Enclose S.A.S.E.
Nonfiction and Fillers: Wants detailed rules and information of use to photographers interested in competitions. Subject matter should be slanted toward "how-to-win." Also interested in articles explaining how competitions work; judging, etc. "Remember this is a knowledgeable audience." Will accept articles and book reviews from new writers as long as they know the subject. Length: 300 to 1,000 words for articles; 100 to 300 words for book reviews. Pays 5¢ a word for articles; $10 for book reviews. Open to suggestions for new columns or departments. Also buys clippings and historical photography contest fillers. Length: 25 to 100 words. Pays

$3. "Clippings must be related to contests offering cash or merchandise and be outside the U.S. Payment to $15 depending on complete information."

PHOTO INSIGHT, Suite 2, 91-24 168th St., Jamaica NY 11432. Editor-in-Chief: Conrad Lovelo, Jr. Emphasizes photography. For amateur and professional photographers interested in photography contests. Bimonthly newsletter; 8 pages. Estab: 1975. Circ: 1,000. Pays on publication. Buys one-time rights. Submit seasonal or holiday material 3 months in advance. Simultaneous and previously published submissions OK. SASE. Reports in 1 month. Sample copy $1.

Nonfiction: How-to (tips on winning contests), humor, inspirational and new products (related to photography). Buys 2 mss/issue. Length: 800-1,000 words. Pays $30.

Photos: Photos purchased with accompanying ms. Captions required. Pays $35 for 8x10 or 4x5 b&w glossies. Total purchase price for ms includes payment for photos. Model release required.

Columns/Departments: Gallery Insight (photo show reviews) and In The News (new products or seminars). Buys 1 ms/issue. Query. Length: 100-300 words. Pays $10. Open to suggestions for new columns/departments.

Poetry: Edwardo Braithwaite, Poetry Editor. Traditional. Length: 4-12 lines. Pays $5.

Fillers: Jokes, gags and anecdotes. Pays $5.

POPULAR PHOTOGRAPHY, 1 Park Ave., New York NY 10016. Editor: Kenneth Poli. "Mostly for advanced hobby photographers; about 90% are men." Also publishes 6 annuals or one-shots. Monthly. Circ: 750,000. "Rights purchased vary with author and material, but usually buys one-time if story is author's idea, not ours." Buys 35 to 50 mss a year, "mostly from technical types already known to us." Pays on acceptance. Submit seasonal material 4 months in advance. Reports in 3 to 4 weeks. Query first. Enclose S.A.S.E.

Nonfiction: This magazine is mainly interested in instructional articles on photography that will help photographers improve their work. This includes all aspects of photography, from theory to camera use and darkroom procedures. Utter familiarity with the subject is a prerequisite to acceptance here. It is best to submit article ideas in outline form since features are set up to fit the magazine's visual policies. "Style should be very readable but with plenty of factual data when a technique story is involved. We're not quite as 'hardware' oriented as some magazines. We use many equipment stories, but we give more space to cultural and aesthetic aspects of the hobby than our competition does." Buys how-to's, interviews, profiles, historical articles, new product coverage, photo essays. Length: 500 to 2,000 words. Pays $100 per display page.

Photos: Interested in seeing b&w prints of any type finish that are 8x10 or larger. Also uses any size color transparency. Buys one-time rights except when assigned, then all-time. No additional payment is made. Gives few assignments.

Fillers: Uses featurettes that run from 1 to 2 columns to 1-pagers and "Photo Tips," which are short how-to-do-its, illustrated by a single picture. Featurette length should be from 500 to 1,000 words; for the "Photo Tips," less than 100 words or whatever is necessary to give all pertinent information. Pays $25 to $75 for featurettes, depending on use; $25 for illustrated "Photo Tips."

Poetry Publications

This category includes publications that exist to discuss and publish poetry. A few newspapers and other special media using poetry are also included. Many publications in the Literary and Little category are also interested in poetry submissions. Various other poetry markets are listed in other categories throughout the Consumer section.

Many of the markets that follow pay in contributor's copies, prizes or some form of remuneration other than money. We have included such markets because there are limited commercial outlets for poetry and these at least offer the poet some visibility.

Poetry manuscripts should have the poet's name and address typed in the upper left-hand corner. Total number of lines in the poem should appear in the upper right-hand corner. Center the title of the poem 8 to 10 lines from the top of the page. The poem should be typed, double-spaced. The poet's name should again appear at the end of the poem. In the case where the poet submits more than one poem to the editor, each poem should always be typed on a separate sheet of paper. Always enclose SASE with poetry submissions.

ADVENTURES IN POETRY MAGAZINE, 3915 SW Military Dr., San Antonio TX 78211. (512)923-8407. Editor-in-Chief: Dr. Stella Woodall. Bimonthly magazine; 60 pages. Estab: 1968. Circ: 300. Submit seasonal/holiday material 3 months in advance. Simultaneous, photocopied and previously published submissions OK. SASE. Reports in 8 weeks. Sample copy $2.
Poetry: Free verse; haiku; light verse; traditional and sonnet. Uses 60 poems/issue. "We have prizes for each issue, contest prizes of $25, $15 and $10 and annual prizes for those registering for Patriotic Poetry Seminar, up to $300 in prizes."

ALBIREO QUARTERLY, P.O. Box 4345, Albuquerque NM 87106. Editors: Thomas Lyons and Leroy Stradford. Established in 1975. Circulation: 1,000. Not copyrighted. Pays in contributor's copies. Uses 50 to 60 mss per year. Will send free sample copy to writer on request. Reports in 4 to 6 weeks. Enclose S.A.S.E.
Poetry: "We will consider any type of good poetry. We prefer poems under 30 lines, and we hesitate on poems that follow religious lines." Writers should read a sample copy before submitting. Will consider traditional forms of poetry, blank verse, free verse, light verse, avantgarde forms and haiku. Length: 30 lines maximum.

AMERICAN POETRY LEAGUE MAGAZINE, 3925 SW Military Dr., San Antonio TX 78211. (512)923-8407. Editor-in-Chief: Dr. Stella Woodall. Quarterly magazine. See *Adventures in Poetry Magazine.*

ASFA POETRY QUARTERLY, Alabama School of Fine Arts, 800 8th Ave., W., Box A-16, Birmingham Southern College, Birmingham AL 35204. Editor: Charles Ghigna. For high school and college audience. Poetry quarterly. Established in 1975. Circulation: 1,000. Pays in contributor's copies. Submit complete poem and brief biography. Enclose S.A.S.E.
Poetry: Wants poetry that is "fresh, concise; strong use of imagery." No sentimental lyrics.

BARDIC ECHOES, 1036 Emerald Ave., N.E., Grand Rapids MI 49503. (616)454-9120. Editor: Clarence L. Weaver. Quarterly. Not copyrighted. Payment in contributor's copies. Will send sample copy to writer for 50¢. Reports in 1 to 3 months. Limit submissions to no more than 5 poems. Occasionally overstocked. Enclose S.A.S.E.
Poetry: Poetry may be on any subject, but in good taste. Varied style. Length: 40 lines maximum including title, byline, and stanzaic spaces (one full page).

BELOIT POETRY JOURNAL, Box 2, Beloit WI 53511. Editorial Board: Robert Glauber, David Stocking, Marion Stocking. "Our readers are people of all ages and occupations who are interested in the growing tip of poetry." Quarterly magazine; 40 pages. Estab: 1950. Circ: 1,100. Pays in copies on publication. Acquires all rights, but may reassign following publication. Photocopied submissions OK. SASE. Reports in 4 months; "actually most rejections are within a week; four months would be the maximum for a poem under serious consideration." Sample copy 75¢; free writer's guidelines.
Poetry: Avant-garde; free verse; haiku; and traditional. Uses 60/year. Limit submissions to batches of 12. "We publish the best contemporary poetry submitted, without bias as to length, form, school, or subject. We are particularly interested in discovering fresh new poets, with strong imagination and intense, accurate language."

BIRTHSTONE MAGAZINE, Box 27394, San Francisco CA 94127. (415)334-4681. Editor-in-Chief: Daniel Brady. Emphasizes poetry, graphics, and photography. Quarterly magazine; 16 pages. Estab: 1975. Circ: 500. Pays in copies. Acquires all rights but may reassign following publication. Photocopied and previously published submissions OK.
Photos: B&w glossies, maximum size 7x10. No additional payment for photos accepted with accompanying ms. "We use pen and ink graphics.
Poetry: Avant-garde, free verse, haiku, light verse, traditional, and "anything that we agree is good." Buys 20-25 poems/issue. Limit submissions to batches of 5. Length: 1-48 lines, but "will consider longer if very good." Pays in copies.

BITTERROOT, International Poetry Magazine, Blythebourne Station, P.O. Box 51, Brooklyn NY 11219. Editor: Menke Katz. Quarterly. Copyrighted. Payment in 1 contributor's copy. Enclose S.A.S.E.
Poetry: "We need good poetry of all kinds. If we think a poem is very good, we will publish a two-page poem; mostly however, we prefer shorter poems, not longer than one page. We always discourage stereotyped forms which imitate fixed patterns and leave no individual mark. We inspire all poets who seek their own selves in original forms of many moods, in harmony

with their poems which may be realistic or fantastic, close to earth and cabalistic." We have an annual contest with awards amounting to $325. December 31 of each year is the deadline for the Kaitz award; deadline for the William Kushner and the Albert Tallman awards is June 30."

BONSAI, A QUARTERLY OF HAIKU, Bonsai Press, Box 7211, Phoenix AZ 85011. Editors-in-Chief: Jan and Mary Streif. Emphasizes haiku poetry and related prose. Quarterly magazine; 36 pages. Estab: 1975. Circ: 350. Pays in awards. Buys one-time rights. Photocopied submissions OK. SASE. Reports in 1-2 weeks. Sample copy 75¢. Free writer's guidelines.
Nonfiction: "We are looking for penetrating essays dealing with the haiku of the 1970's, some reviews and other contemporary work in the haiku/senryu field. Length: short or long; no limit."
Poetry: "All schools of haiku are welcome, but the standard is high. We look for haiku that captures a moment, not just talks about it."

THE CAPE ROCK, Southeast Missouri State University Press, English Department, Cape Girardeau MO 63701. (314)334-8211, Ext. 278. Editor: R.A. Burns. For libraries and persons interested in poetry. Established in 1964. Semiannual. Circulation: 500. Acquires all rights, but may reassign rights to author after publication. Uses about 100 mss per year. Pays in contributor's copies. Will send sample copy to writer for $1. Write for editorial guidelines sheet, enclosing S.A.S.E. Will consider photocopied submissions. No simultaneous submissions. Reports in 1 to 4 months. Enclose S.A.S.E.
Poetry, Fiction and Photos: "Publish primarily poetry — any style, subject. Avoid obscene or profane diction, sentimentality, didacticism. Fiction for special issues only — require query. We have summer and winter issues and try to place poetry in the appropriate issue, but do not offer strictly seasonal issues." Photos acquired with accompanying ms with no additional payment; also used without accompanying ms. B&w only. Pays 2 copies. Length: 70 lines maximum. Pays 2 copies.

CEDAR ROCK, 1121 Madeline, New Braunfels TX 78130. (512)625-6002. Editor-in-Chief: David C. Yates. For "persons with an active interest in poetry." Quarterly tabloid; 20 pages. Estab: 1975. Circ: 400. Pays on publication. Buys all rights but may reassign following publication. Phone queries OK. Photocopied submissions OK. SASE. Reports in 3 weeks. Sample copy $1.25; free writer's guidelines.
Poetry: Avant-garde; free verse; haiku; light verse; and traditional. "No deliberately obscure poems." Buys 200 poems/year. Limit submissions to 6 at one time. Length: 3-75 lines. Pays 2 contributor's copies. "Cash prizes sometimes offered for outstanding poems—usually no more than $25."

CHOOMIA Collections of Contemporary Poetry, Yarrow Press, Box 107, Framingham MA 01701. Editor-in-Chief: Jay Barwell. Managing Editor: Ann Guido. Semiannual magazine; 60 pages. Estab: 1975. Circ: 400. Pays in copies on publication. Acquires all rights, but may reassign following publication. Photocopied submissions OK. SASE. Reports in 3 months. Sample copy $1.
Poetry: "We have an extremely high standard and are not interested in seeing poetry that is written "out of fun and enjoyment" rather than commitment." Any form. No length restrictions.

CIRCUS MAXIMUS, Garretson Graphics, Box 3251, York PA 17402. Editor-in-Chief: Peter J. Garretson, Jr. For an intellectual readership of all ages. Quarterly magazine; 40 pages. Estab: 1975. Circ: 400-500. Pays on acceptance. Buys one-time rights. Photocopied and previously published submissions OK. SASE. Reports in 2 weeks. Sample copy $2. Free writer's guidelines.
Poetry: Free verse, haiku and traditional. Buys 40-50 poems/issue. Limit submissions to batches of 5. Pays $2/poem.
How To Break In: "We prefer imaginative language poems which use concrete imagery to create a 'scene' with a beginning, a middle and an end. The message or experience should suddenly come alive for the reader so that he/she can leave the poem with a fresh emotional/intellectual perception that was not present in the mind's eye before reading the poem."

COLD MOUNTAIN PRESS PUBLICATIONS, 4705 Sinclair Ave., Austin TX 78756. Editor: Ryan Petty. For "the community of people who love fine poetry, and fine printing." Poetry published in pamphlets, broadsheets and postcards. Established in 1973. "We have distributed more than 1,000 copies of a single pamphlet of poems." Rights purchased vary with author and material. "Rights and payments are subject to negotiation and are occasionally set out in written contract." Buys 10 to 15 mss per year. Will send catalog to writer on request. No photocopied submissions. Will consider simultaneous submissions. Reports in 60 days. "Either send the ms with a cover letter or, in the case of a bulky ms, send a query with a sample excerpt." Enclose S.A.S.E.

Poetry and Fiction: Publishes poetry, mainly. "We have published a tape cassette of a poetry reading by Michael Hogan and are interested in other tape cassettes. We have contracted to publish a novel by Joseph Brudiac. Interested in seeing essays and public letters of interest to the literary community. In addition to Cold Mountain publications, we distribute fine poetry publications from the nation's other small presses." Interested also in interviews with poets. Payments and word length negotiable. No seasonal material. Buys free verse and avant-garde forms of poetry. "We like Bly, Snyder, Stafford, Kooser, Bruchac, Berry, Piercy, Levertov, Hogan, etc. Payment is negotiable. Minimum is $5 per poem."

CONNECTIONS MAGAZINE, Bell Hollow Rd., Putnam Valley NY 10579. Editor-in-Chief: Toni Ortner-Zimmerman. Annual magazine; 70 pages. Estab: 1971. Circ: 600. Pays in copies. SASE. Reports in 2 weeks. Sample copy $2.
Poetry: Avant-garde, free verse and traditional. Limit submissions to batches of 5. Length: 50 lines maximum.

CREATIVE MOMENT, Poetry Eastwest Publications, P.O. Box 391, Sumter SC 29150. Editor: Dr. Syed Amanuddin. For "creative writers, poets, and those who are interested in the international scene in contemporary poetry." Established in 1972. Biannual. Circulation: 500. Acquires first serial rights. Payment in contributor's copy. Will send a sample copy to a writer for $1. Will not consider photocopied submissions. Reports in 6 to 8 months. Query first for articles and reviews. Enclose S.A.S.E.
Nonfiction: "We specialize in world poetry written in English and we need intelligent and provocative articles on contemporary English-language poetry of all the regions of the world including Canada, India, Nigeria, Rhodesia, South Africa, and West Indies. We also need short articles on poetry by American minority groups. Articles should be under 3,000 words with all notes worked into the text. We refuse to read articles with footnotes."
Poetry: "We are interested only in original unpublished poems under 30 lines, but our primary interest is criticism."

CREATIVE REVIEW, 1718 S. Garrison, Carthage MO 64836. Editor: Glen Coffield. For hobbyists, educated, retired, handicapped, educators. Quarterly mimeographed magazine; 14 to 18 pages. Established in 1961. Not copyrighted. Uses 250 poems a year. Payment in contributor's copies. Will send sample copy to writer for 50¢. Reports within 3 months. Submit complete ms; "one poem to a page (8½x11)." Enclose S.A.S.E.
Poetry: "Poems on creativity, good description, local history, examples of good writing, pictures of life, positive approach, good taste, simple and clear. Good grammar and punctuation, logical structure, understandable to the average reader; interesting beginnings, strong endings, objective imagery, not too abstract. We're perhaps more selective and demanding; more traditional in a knowledgeable sense. We don't want anything risque, no negativism or tearing down, no difficult typographical experiments, no excess verbosity and repetition, no intellectual snobbery or trite sophistication. No personal frustrations. Not especially interested in the topical, except positive suggestions on current problems." Length: 32 lines maximum. "Quality demands are greater the longer the poem."

DRAGONFLY: A QUARTERLY OF HAIKU, 4102 NE 130th Pl., Portland OR 97230. Editor-in-Chief: Lorraine Ellis Harr. For all ages. Quarterly magazine; 68 pages. Estab: 1965. Circ: 500. Pays in copies. Some awards. Reassigns rights on request. SASE. Reports in 1 month. Sample copy $1.25. Free writer's guidelines.
Nonfiction: 300-word articles on haiku or related matter. "Must be concise and have something to say." Uses 2-3 mss/issue.
Poetry: Uses some senryu poetry and oriental forms, but mostly haiku. Uses 150 poems/issue. Limit submissions to batches of 5.

EN PASSANT POETRY QUARTERLY, 1906 Brant Rd., Wilmington DE 19810. Editor: James A. Costello. For an audience interested in poetry. Magazine; 44 pages. Established in 1975. Quarterly. Circulation: 500. Acquires all rights, but will reassign rights to author after publication. Uses about 25 to 30 mss per issue. Payment in contributor's copies. Will send a sample copy to writer for $1.50. Reports in 3 weeks. Submit complete ms. Enclose S.A.S.E.
Poetry: Poetry of insight and clear imagery. Poetry in translation.

ENCORE, A Quarterly of Verse and Poetic Arts, 1121 Major Ave., N.W., Albuquerque NM 87107. (505)344-5615. Editor: Alice Briley. For "anyone interested in poetry from young people in high school to many retired people. Good poetry on any theme." Established in 1966. Quarterly. Circulation: 600. Acquires all rights but will reassign rights to author after publication. Uses 300 mss a year. Payment in contributor's copies. Will send sample copy to a writer for 25¢. Will consider photocopied submissions "provided the author is free to assign rights to *Encore.* Will require assurance if poem is accepted." Submit seasonal material 6 to 9 months in advance. Reports on material within a month. Submit complete poetry ms. Query first, for short reviews. Enclose S.A.S.E.

Nonfiction, Poetry and Photos: "Particularly like poetry which illustrates the magazine's theme that poetry is a performing art. Fresh approach greatly desired. Poetry by students as well as established poets." Traditional forms, blank verse, free verse, avant-garde and light verse. Limit submissions to batches of 4. Some articles on related subjects. Profiles of poets, poetry reviews, technical verse writing. Length: open, but "very long articles rarely used." Prefer no larger than 5x8 b&w glossy photos with good contrast. Pays in contributor's copies. Also has poetry contests. "My poetry contests have grown considerably. Continuous contests have November 1 and May 1 deadlines. In addition, there are often very good special contests."

4 ELEMENTS, Egret Press, 504 Inverness Ct., St. Simons Island GA 31522. Editor: Patrick Garner. For persons interested in modern, quality poetry and book reviews. Established in 1972. Published 3 times a year. Circulation: 500. Acquires all rights, but will reassign rights to author after publication. Acquires 50 to 60 poems per year. Pays in contributor's copies. Will send sample copy to writer for $1.75. Will not consider photocopied or simultaneous submissions. Enclose S.A.S.E. Reports in 2 weeks.

Poetry and Fiction: "We publish anything that reflects a poet's sensitivity and ability to translate his feelings into a unique experience. We don't want theme poetry, seasonal, or greeting card couplets. Most of what we print is national in origin, though we welcome good regional work." Publishes experimental and mainstream fiction. Length: 300 words maximum. Does not want to see epic poetry. Publishes traditional forms of poetry, blank verse and avant-garde forms.

THE FREE LANCE, A Magazine of Poetry & Prose, 6005 Grand Ave., Cleveland OH 44104. Editors: Russell Atkins, Casper L. Jordan. For college students, teachers and persons who practice the creative arts. Established in 1950. Published irregularly. Circulation: 600. Copyrighted. Pays in contributor's copies. No sample copies. Will not consider photocopied or simultaneous submissions. Reports in 6 months. Query first for book reviews. Enclose S.A.S.E.

Nonfiction, Fiction and Poetry: "Largely avant-garde, emphasis on literary techniques and ideas, should be experimental. Book reviews. We are more creative than 'topical,' consequently there are not many themes we would single out." Fiction. Length: 3,000 words maximum. Poetry; mainstream, contemporary and avant-garde forms. "Not in the market for poetry or verse that rhymes, or verse that has a message on social problems, or work that is rigidly traditional in form, etc." Length: open.

GRAVIDA, Box 76, Hartsdale NY 10530. Editor: Lynne Savitt. Quarterly magazine; 44-60 pages. Estab: 1973. Circ: 1,000. Pays in copies on publication. Acquires all rights, but may reassign following publication. Submit seasonal/holiday material 6 months in advance. Photocopied submissions OK. SASE. Reports in 2 weeks. Sample copy $1; free writer's guidelines.

Poetry: Avant-garde; free verse; haiku; light verse; traditional. Uses 120/year. Limit submissions to batches of 5. Pays in 2 copies and a $25 prize for best poem in each issue.

HAPPINESS HOLDING TANK, 1790 Grand River Ave., Okemos MI 48864. Editors: Albert and Barbara Drake. For "poets of various ages, interests; other editors; students." Triannual magazine; 45 pages, (8 ½x11). Established in 1970. Circulation: 300 to 500. All rights revert to author automatically. Payment in contributor's copies. Will send a sample copy to a writer for $1. Reports in 1 to 3 weeks. Not reading during summer months. Submit complete ms. Enclose S.A.S.E.

Nonfiction and Poetry: Publishes "poems of various kinds, somewhat eclectic—looking for 'excellence.' Essays and articles on modern poetry. Emphasis on younger but unestablished poets: their work to date. Emphasis on information of various kinds—to make magazine useful. Interested in printing methods of all kinds." Buys informational, how-to, and poetry book reviews. Uses all forms of poetry except light verse. Now doing chapbooks and poetry posters.

How To Break In: "We are eclectic, and have published all kinds of poetry. What we are looking for is freshness, a lively imagination, the kind of poem that you remember later. It's a good idea for any writer to read what's being written and published."

Rejects: "What we see repeatedly, and do not want, is a kind of poem which can best be described as a 'beginner's poem.' It's usually entitled 'Reflections' or 'Dust' or 'Spring' and has to do with death, love, etc. These are abstractions and the poet treats them in an abstract way. This kind of poem has to be written, but shouldn't be published."

THE HARTFORD COURANT, THIS SINGING WORLD, 285 Broad St., Hartford CT 06115. Poetry Editor: Malcolm L. Johnson. For a general audience. Weekly poetry column in newspaper. Established in 1764. Circulation: 180,000. Not copyrighted. Uses about 200 poems a year. Payment in tearsheets. "We are not set up to send free copies." Will consider photocopied submissions and simultaneous submissions. "Christmas poetry is wanted for the weekend before Christmas. Seasonal poetry is usually not used out of season." Submit seasonal poetry 1 month in advance. Reports usually within 2 weeks, unless it is being considered for publication; may take up to 3 months. Submit complete ms. Enclose S.A.S.E.
Poetry: "Any sort of poetry is eligible, but the general readership means that graphically erotic or violent poetry cannot be used. In general, we strive for the same sort of poetry that might be published in a literary magazine. The only guideline would be that the poetry must necessarily be rather short. 50 lines is about the maximum. Seasonal and poet's soul poetry always seem overworked, but creative approaches to these subjects are still welcome. It would be pleasant to receive more light or satirical verse, but these seem difficult genres for many poets." Length: 2 to 50 lines.

HIRAM POETRY REVIEW, P.O. Box 162, Hiram OH 44234. (216)569-3211. Editor: David Fratus. Published 2 times a year; magazine, 40 to 60 pages, (6x9). "Since our chief subscribers are libraries in major cities or libraries of colleges and universities, our audience is highly literate and comprises persons who are actively interested in poetry of high quality." Established in 1967. Circulation: 500. Copyrighted. Acquires all rights, but will reassign rights to author upon written request. Uses approximately 75 poems a year. Payment in 2 contributor's copies plus one year's subscription. Will send free sample copy to writer on request. Reports in 8 weeks. Submit only complete ms. Enclose S.A.S.E.
Poetry: "All forms of poetry used. No special emphasis required. Length: open, but we have printed few very long poems." Limit submissions to 4-6 to a batch.

HUERFANO, Daran, Inc., Box 49155, University Station, Tucson AZ 85717. Editor-in-Chief: Randell Shutt Semiannual magazine; 40 pages. Estab: 1972. Circ: 250. Pays in copies. Acquires all rights, but may reassign following publication. Photocopied submissions OK. SASE. Reports in 1 month. Sample copy $1. Free writer's guidelines.
Poetry: Vicki Thompson, Poetry Editor. Free verse, light verse and traditional. Uses 50-60 poems/year. Length: 4-50 lines. "Daran Award of $50 to one of our published poets annually."

ICARUS, P.O. Box 8, Riderwood MD 21139. Editor: Margaret Diorio. For readers of poetry. Established in 1973. Quarterly. Circulation: 600. Acquires all rights, but will reassign rights to author after publication. Payment in contributor's copies. Will send sample copy to writer for 75¢. Reports on material in 1 month. Enclose S.A.S.E.
Poetry: Will consider poetry from all schools. Serious poetry, any and all forms. Open on themes. Length: 30 lines or less preferred, but will consider longer poems.

IDEALS, 11315 Watertown Plank Rd., Milwaukee WI 53201. Editor: Maryjane Hooper Tonn. Managing Editor: Ralph Luedtke. Payment for poems or articles made at time of publication ($10 and a copy of the issue). Buys one-time rights. Will send sample copy to writer on request. Reports in 2 weeks. Enclose return postage.
Nonfiction, Poetry and Photos: "*Ideals* are books containing clean, wholesome, old-fashioned American ideals, homey philosophy and general inspirational, patriotic, religious, seasonal, family, childhood or nostalgic material. Poems and articles submitted will be carefully reviewed, and such material that we believe will lend itself to use in *Ideals* will be retained in our permanent review files. Such material is carefully reviewed during the preparation of each new book. We cannot definitely guarantee that we will feature the poems or articles which we retain, but we shall make a sincere effort to do so. We assume the privilege of editing retained material where necessary. If, for any reason, you do not want us to enter your material into our review files, kindly advise us when submitting it so that we can promptly return it to you. Please do not send us your original poems or articles. Send only copies. We cannot return your submitted material after it has been entered into our review files. B&w photos should be sharp, clear 8x10 glossies. We pay $20 minimum when purchased for immediate use. We prefer 4x5 or 8x10 color transparencies, for which pay is $75 minimum. 35mm transparencies are accepted,

provided they are mounted on a sheet of acetate in groups of at least 20 so they may be easily reviewed."

KOSMOS, Milky Way Press, 130 Eureka, San Francisco CA 94114. (415)863-4861. Editor: Kosrof Chantikian. Biannual magazine; 64 pages. Estab: 1975. Circ: 300. Pays in copies on publication. Acquires all rights, but may reassign following publication. Previously published submissions OK. SASE. Reports in 7-9 weeks. Sample copy $1.75.
Poetry: No restrictions.

LIGHT: A POETRY REVIEW, Box 1105, Stuyvesant PO, New York NY 10009. Editor-in-Chief: Roberta C. Gould. Annual magazine; 64 pages. Estab: 1973. Circ: 800. Pays in copies. Acquires first North American serial rights. Submit seasonal/holiday material 3 months in advance. SASE. Reports in 3 months. Sample copy $1.25. Uses graphics and some 7½x5 b&w photos.
Poetry: Avant-garde, free verse, haiku and traditional. Uses 40 poems/issue. Limit submissions to batches of 4. Length: 5-40 words.

THE LITTLE MAGAZINE, Box 207, Cathedral Station, New York NY 10025. Editor-in-Chief: Barbara Damrosch. Managing Editor: Felicity Thoet. Quarterly magazine; 64 pages. Circ: 1,000. Pays in copies. Acquires all rights, but may reassign following publication. Photocopied submissions OK. SASE. Reports in 2-6 weeks. Sample copy $1.50; free writer's guidelines.
Fiction: Uses all types. Uses 12 mss/year.
Poetry: Avant-garde; free verse; haiku; light verse; traditional. Uses 75/year. Limit submissions to batches of 10.

THE LITTLE REVIEW, English Department, Marshall University, Huntington WV 25701. Editor: John McKernan. Biannual. Circulation: 1,000. Acquires first rights. No payment. Will send a sample copy to a writer for $1.25. Reports in 2 months or more. Enclose S.A.S.E. for return of submissions.
Nonfiction and Poetry: "Poetry, translations, critical reviews of contemporary poets, parodies, and satire. We are mainly a poetry magazine."

LOON, P.O. Box 11633, Santa Rosa CA 95406. Editors: D. L. Emblen, Richard Speakes, Richard Welin. For educated readers of any age from 18 up. Magazine published twice a year. Established in 1973. Circulation: 500. Acquires all rights, but will reassign rights to author upon request. Uses 80 poems a year. Payment in contributor's copies. Will send sample copy to writer for $1. Will not consider photocopied or simultaneous submissions. Reports in 1 to 2 months. Submit complete ms. Enclose S.A.S.E.
Poetry: Original poems and translations of poems from other languages. No restrictions on form or subject matter. Traditional forms, blank verse, free verse, avant-garde forms, light verse. Prospective contributors are advised to "read a lot of first-rate modern poetry and read a copy of *Loon*."

THE LYRIC, 307 Dunton Dr., SW, Blacksburg VA 24060. Editor-in-Chief: Leslie Mellichamp. Quarterly magazine; 26 pages. Estab: 1921. Circ: 1,000. Pays in prizes only $25-100. Acquires first North American serial rights. Submit seasonal/holiday material 3-6 months in advance. Photocopied submissions OK. SASE. Reports in 2 weeks.
Poetry: Light verse and traditional. Uses 40 poems/issue. Limit submissions to batches of 5. Length: 36 lines maximum.

MARILYN; A MAGAZINE OF NEW POETRY, 150 W. Ninth St., Claremont CA 91711. Editor-in-Chief: P. Schneidre and Jeffrey Wells-Powers. Magazine, published in spring and autumn; 72 pages. Estab: 1975. Circ: 400. Pays on acceptance. Buys first world rights, reassigned to author on request. SASE. Reports in 1 month. Sample copy $1.95.
Poetry: All contemporary poetry. Buys 100 poems/year. Limit submissions to batches of 7. Pays $5-50.

MODERN HAIKU, 260 Vista Marina, San Clemente CA 92672. Editor: Kay Titus Mormino. Quarterly magazine; 48 pages, (8½x5½). Established in 1969. Circulation: 600. Acquires all rights, but will reassign rights to author after publication. No payment, but several cash prizes are awarded each issue. Sample copy $2.25; writer's guidelines for SASE.
Nonfiction, Poetry, and Fillers: "Mostly haiku. Also senryu and haibun. Articles dealing with any aspect of reading or writing the above. Reviews of books on any of the above. No special

requirements or approach, but poetic quality is a must. *MH* is a showcase for haiku from traditional to experimental. The editors don't play favorites. We would prefer not to see prose written in 3 lines and called haiku. Line unity, essence of haiku, distinction between haiku and senryu are of interest." Length: 500 to 3,000 words. "Students, up to and including Grade 12 should submit haiku, giving name, address, teacher's name, name of school and grade in school to Student Section Editor Willene H. Nusbaum, Bern KS 66408. S.A.S.E. required.

THE MODULARIST REVIEW, Wooden Needle Press, 65-45 Yellowstone Blvd., #3-D, Forest Hills NY 11375. Editor: R.C. Morse. Annual magazine. Estab: 1972. Circ: 1,000. Pays in contributor's copies. Acquires all rights but may reassign following publication. SASE. Reports in 3 months.
Fiction, Photos, Poetry: "All literary—visual and plastic arts. Work submitted must be Modularist: Based on the concept that time is not the fourth dimension, but is composed of our dimensional elements, the simultaneous, contiguous, recursive and disparate (which correspond to length, width and depth, the dimensional elements of space) and thereby conceived from a seven-dimensional space/time perspective." Length: Short fiction mss preferred, but will consider long poems.

NEW COLLAGE MAGAZINE, 5700 N. Trail, Sarasota FL 33580. (813)355-7671, Ext. 203. Editor: A. McA. Miller. For poetry readers. Magazine; 24 pages minimum. Established in 1971. Triquarterly. Circulation: 2,000. Acquires all rights, but usually reassigns rights to author after publication. Uses 80 poems per year. Token payment or 3 contributor's copies. Will send sample copy to writer for $1, together with editorial guidelines sheet. Will consider photocopied submissions. No simultaneous submissions. Reports in 3 weeks. Enclose S.A.S.E..
Poetry: "We want poetry as a fresh act of language. No tick-tock effusions about everyday sentiments, please. First, read a sample copy. Then, and only then, send us poems. We especially want strong poems, more in Yeats' vein than in W. C. Williams, but we are open to any poem that sustains clear imagery and expressive voice." Length: 150 lines maximum.

NEW EARTH REVIEW, Box 83, Murfreesboro NC 27855. (919)398-3341. Editor: Robert G. Mulder. For "wide audience of readers." Most readers are women poets, although many men subscribe. Magazine; 20 to 30 pages. Established in 1975. Quarterly. Circulation: 500. Acquires all rights, but may reassign rights to author after publication. Uses 200 to 300 poems per year. Pays in contributor's copies for most poetry. Will send sample copy to writer for $1. Write for editorial guidelines sheet. Will consider photocopied submissions. No simultaneous submissions. Reports in 2 weeks. Enclose S.A.S.E.
Poetry: "We only publish poems of our selection trying to get a good representation of poets across the U.S." Sometimes publishes essays pertinent to poetry. Uses traditional forms, blank verse, free verse, light verse, avant-garde forms, haiku, experimental forms and prose poetry. Length: 4 to 16 lines. Pays $5 per poem "in some cases for poem-of-the-issue. Other payment in contributor's copies."

NEW POETRY, Poetry Society of Australia, Box N110, Grosvenor Post Office, Sydney, N.S.W. 2000. (02)421-861. Editor-in-Chief: Cheryl Adamson. For serious poetry writers and readers. Quarterly magazine; 100 pages. Estab: 1952. Circ: 2,000. Pays on acceptance. Buys one-time rights. Phone queries OK. Photocopied submissions OK. SAE and International Reply Coupons. Reports in 12 weeks. Sample copy and writer's guidelines $3 each (in Australian dollars).
Nonfiction: Interviews with major poets. Photo features on poetry readings and poetry events. Informational articles about small presses and poetry. Buys 8/year. Query. Length: 500-5,000 words. Pays $10-100.
Photos: Purchased with or without mss. Pays $5-20 for 8x10 b&w glossies. Query or send prints.
Poetry: Avant-garde and traditional forms of poetry; free verse. Buys 50/issue. Send poems in. Limit submissions to 6 at a time. Length: open. Pays $10-100.

NORTHERN LIGHT, University of Manitoba Printers, 605 Fletcher Argue Bldg., University of Manitoba, Winnipeg, Manitoba R3J 2E4. (204)474-8145. Editor-in-Chief: George Amabile. Audience is poets, libraries, professors, teachers, English students and lighthouse keepers. Semiannual magazine; 64 pages. Estab: 1968. Circ: 1,000. Pays on either acceptance or publication. Buys all rights, but may reassign following publication. Phone queries OK. Simultaneous submissions OK. SASE and International Reply Coupons. Reports in 4 weeks. Sample copy $1.50. Free writer's guidelines.

Nonfiction: Reviews of recent poetry publications and interviews with poets. Buys 2 mss/issue. Send complete ms. Length: 1,000-1,800 words. Pays $5/page.
Photos: Pamela McLeod, Photo Editor. Photos purchased without accompanying ms. Pays $5/page for 8x10 b&w photos.
Poetry: Avant-garde, free verse, haiku, light verse and traditional. Buys 30 poems/issue. Pays $5/page.
How To Break In: "We prefer to publish Canadians, so Americans have to be good."

OINK!, 7021 Sheridan, Chicago IL 60626. Editors: Paul Hoover and Maxine Chernoff. Semi-annual magazine; 92 pages. Established in 1971. Circulation: 600. Acquires all rights, but will reassign rights to author after publication. Payment in contributor's copies. Will send sample copy to writer for $2. Reports on material accepted for publication in 1 to 2 weeks. Returns rejected material immediately. Enclose S.A.S.E.
Poetry and Fiction: Avant-garde forms of poetry. Imaginative writing only. Short fiction; preferably experimental.

OUTPOSTS, 72 Burwood Rd., Walton-on-Thames, Surrey KT12 4AL. Editor-in-Chief: Howard Sergeant. Quarterly magazine; 40 pages. Estab: 1946. Circ: 1,500. Pays on publication. Buys first serial rights. Photocopied submissions OK. SAE and International Reply Coupons. Reports in 2 weeks. Sample copy $1.50.
Nonfiction: Articles on poetry or critical studies of poetry. Buys 4/year. Length: 1,000-2,500 words. Pays about 1 pound/page.
Poetry: Any type of poetry, but not of epic length. Buys 25-50/issue. Limit submissions to 6. Length: 80 lines maximum. Pays about 1 pound/page.

POEM, P.O. Box 1247, West Station, Huntsville AL 35807. Editor: Robert L. Welker. For adults; well-educated, interested in good poetry. Published 3 times a year; magazine, 65 pages. Established in 1967. Circulation: 500. Acquires all rights, but will reassign rights to author after publication. Uses 200 poems a year. Payment in contributor's copies. Reports within 2 months. Submit complete ms only. Enclose S.A.S.E.
Poetry: "We use nothing but superior quality poetry. Good taste (no pornography for its own sake) and technical proficiency. We give special attention to young and less well-known poets. Do not like poems about poems, poets, and other works of art." Traditional forms, blank verse, free verse, and avant-garde forms. Length and theme: open.

THE POET, 2314 W. 6th St., Mishawaka IN 46544. (219)255-8606. Editor: Doris Nemeth. For professional people, freelance writers, students, etc. Anthology; 200 pages. Established in 1963. Twice a year. Circulation: 25,000. Acquires first North American serial rights. Uses about 1,000 mss a year. No payment. Will send sample copy to writer for $4.50. Will consider photocopied and simultaneous submissions. Reports on material accepted for publication in 4 to 6 weeks. Returns rejected material immediately. Submit complete ms. Enclose S.A.S.E.
Poetry and Photos: "All forms of poetry. No set rules. We read all manuscripts. We prefer not to see religious material." Length: 16 lines maximum. Uses 8x10 (or smaller) b&w glossies.

POETRY, The Modern Poetry Association, 1228 N. Dearborn Pkwy., Chicago IL 60610. Editor-in-Chief: Daryl Hine. Monthly magazine; 64 pages. Estab: 1912. Circ: 7,000. Pays on publication. Buys all rights, but may reassign following publication. Submit seasonal/holiday material 9 months in advance. SASE. Reports in 4-6 weeks. Sample copy $2; writer's guidelines for SASE.
Poetry: "We consistently publish the best poetry being written in English. All forms may be acceptable." Buys 500/year. Limit submissions to batches of 6-8. Pays $1/line.

POETRY NEWSLETTER, Department of English, Temple University, Philadelphia PA 19122. (215)787-1778. Editor: Richard O'Connell. For readers of serious poetry. Quarterly newsletter; 20-40 pages. Estab: 1971. Circulation: 500 to 1,000. Not copyrighted. Payment in contributor's copies. Will send sample copy to writer for $1. Will consider photocopied submissions. No simultaneous submissions. Reports in 1 to 3 months. Submit complete ms. Enclose S.A.S.E.
Poetry: "Poetry of high literary quality. No biases. Commercial verse will not be considered. The news is the poetry."

POETRY NORTHWEST MAGAZINE (formerly *Oregonian Verse*), *The Oregonian,* Portland OR 97201. Editor: Penny Avila. Poetry column in Sunday magazine of newspaper. Pays on

10th of month following publication. Buys first newspaper rights which revert to poet after publication. SASE. Reports in 2-3 weeks.

Poetry: "We publish 3 poems/week from many schools and disciplines old and new. Rarely use religious poems. Seek fresh metaphor and imagery in issue and ethic oriented poems. Welcome the new and experimental, but in good taste." Length: 10 lines maximum. Pays $5.

POETRY I, II, Poetry Press, Box 42, Meta Sta., Pikeville KY 41501. Editor-in-Chief: Lillie D. Chaffin. Semiannual magazine; 24 pages. Estab: 1976. Circ: 500. Payment in contributor's copies. Acquires all rights. SASE. Reports in 1 month. Sample copy $1.50.

Poetry: Avant-garde forms only. Uses 20-30/issue. Send poems in. Length: 4-20 lines.

POETRY VENTURE, Valkyrie Press, Inc., 8245 26th Ave., N., St. Petersburg FL 33710. Editor and Publisher: Marjorie Schuck. For poets, writers, scholars. Semiannual magazine; 64 to 72 (6x8¾) pages. Established in 1968. Circulation: 1,000 to 2,000. Acquires all rights, but will reassign rights to author after publication. Payment in contributor's copies and subscription. Will send sample copy to writer for $1.25. Will consider photocopied submissions. Will not consider simultaneous submissions. Reports on material within 6 months. Query first on poetry essays. Enclose S.A.S.E.

Nonfiction and Poetry: Poetry essays on poetry and/or related topics (the literary scene, contemporary poetry, etc.). Brief articles on individual poets. Commentaries, anthology reviews, poetical analyses. Often features foreign poetry published in both the original and the English translation. Length: 100 to 1,500 words. Traditional forms of poetry, blank verse, free verse, innovative poetry. Length: 112 lines maximum.

POETRY VIEW, 1125 Valley Rd., Menasha WI 54952. Editor: Dorothy Dalton. Published weekly as half-page in *View*, magazine section of the *Post-Crescent*. Estab: 1970. Circ: 50,000. Not copyrighted. Buys 250 poems per year. Payment on 10th of month following publication. Prefers original submissions; not photocopies. Will not consider simultaneous submissions. Submit seasonal material 2 to 3 months in advance. Reports in 2 to 3 months. Enclose S.A.S.E.

Poetry: Well-written poetry, showing a fresh use of language. No religious poetry or poetry that is overly sentimental. Uses some traditional forms, free verse, and light verse. Length: serious poetry, to 24 lines; light verse, 4 to 8 lines. Pays $3 per poem.

QUOIN, 1226 W. Talmage, Springfield MO 65803. (417)869-3223. Editor: Arlis M. Snyder. Quarterly magazine; 40 pages. Estab: 1964. Circ: 300. Pays in copies. Acquires first North American serial rights. Phone queries OK. Simultaneous and photocopied submissions OK. SASE. Reports in 10 days. Sample copy $1.50.

Poetry: "Any poetry written in accurate English (translations used, with poem in original language) with language in good taste." Uses 200/year. Limit submissions to batches of 5.

SEVEN, 115 South Hudson, Oklahoma City OK 73102. Editor: James Neill Northe. Published 4 times a year on an irregular basis. Established in 1954. Circulation: 1,000. Buys all rights. Payment on acceptance. Will send sample copy to writer for $1.25. Will not consider photocopied submissions. Will consider simultaneous submissions. Reports on material accepted for publication in 10 days. Returns rejected material immediately. Submit complete ms. Enclose S.A.S.E.

Poetry: "We strive to present only the most sheerly lyrical, poignant and original material possible. Seven poems and 1 reprint are used in each issue. We prefer the classical sonnet over the variations, accenting adherence to the form. Free verse is acceptable, but not as chopped prose. Good ballads are always acceptable. We like titles, punctuation and capitalization where needed. We like well-written and finely expressed spiritual poems, but they must be spiritual (not religious). We prefer the universal approach, rather than the personal. We want lines that communicate; not rambling, disjointed, chopped prose in or out of rhyme, lacking the rhythm and power of free verse." No restrictions as to form or subject. Length: open. Pays $4 per poem.

SEVEN STARS POETRY, Realities Library, Box 33512, San Diego CA 92103. Editor-in-Chief: Richard A. Soos, Jr. Emphasizes poetry/modern literature. Monthly magazine; 40 pages. Estab: 1975. Circ: 800-1,000. Pays on acceptance. Buys all rights, but may reassign following publication. Photocopied and previously published submissions OK. SASE. Reports in 3 weeks. Sample copy $1.50; writer's guidelines for SASE.

Poetry: Avant-garde, free verse, haiku, dada/surreal. Buys 50-60 poems/issue. Limit submissions to batches of 5. Pays 50¢-$1.

Nonfiction: Interviews with any modern poet, or fictional interview with a historic poet. Query. No length requirement. Pays $1/printed page.
Columns, Departments: Reviews on poetry books and TV poetry. Buys 10 mss/issue. Query. No length requirements. Pays 1¢/word. Open to suggestions for new columns, departments.
Fiction: Adventure, erotica, fantasy, experimental, humorous, suspense, science fiction, serialized novels. Buys "1 or less" an issue. Query. No length requirements. Pays $1/printed page.

THE SOLE PROPRIETOR, 2770 N.W. 32 Ave., Miami FL 33142. Editor-in-Chief: Al Fogel. For lovers of quality contemporary poetry. Semi-annual magazine; 48 pages. Estab: 1974. Circ: 700. Acquires all rights, but reassigns following publication. Photocopied submissions OK. Sample copy $2.
Poetry: "Beginners have small chance of acceptance unless familiar with recent innovations, i.e., meta-poetic, found, surreal, post-objectivist, prose poems, developmental/sequence." Uses 100/year. Submit complete poems. Limit submissions to 15 at a time. Pays in contributor's copies.

SOUTHERN EROTIQUE, P.O. Box 2303, Baton Rouge LA 70821. Editor: N.F. Franks. For a male, blue collar audience, 30 to 60 years old, living in Louisiana, Texas, Mississippi, Alabama, Arkansas, beginning to notice an increase in female interest. Magazine; 52 (5½x8½) pages. Established in 1974. Monthly. Circulation: 12,000. Buys all rights. Buys about 50 mss a year. Pays on publication. Will consider photocopied and simultaneous submissions. Reports on material accepted for publication in 30 days. Returns rejected material in 5 weeks. Submit complete ms. Enclose S.A.S.E.
Nonfiction, Fiction and Poetry: "We are looking for good erotic writing, both fiction and nonfiction, and some poetry. But, not trash or words used for shock value. Simply send us something we can use — erotic writing with a professional touch." Length for fiction and nonfiction: 1,500 to 4,000 words. Pays $200 to $400. Only avant-garde forms of poetry. Pays $100.

SPARROW POVERTY PAMPHLETS, (formerly *Sparrow*), Sparrow Press, 103 Waldron St., West Lafayette, IN 47906. Editor-in-Chief: Felix Stefanile. Semiannual magazine; 32 pages. Estab: 1954. Circ: 800. Pays on publication. Buys first North American serial rights. "We retain anthology rights." Previously published submissions OK. SASE. Reports in 6 weeks. Sample copy $1.50.
Poetry: "No form bias. Mature, serious work in the modern manner. Poetry must be human and relevant." Buys 20-30 poems/issue. Pays $15 plus royalties.

SPEAK OUT, P.O. Box 737, Stamford CT 06904. Editor: Agnes D'Ottavio. For "people who write vocationally and avocationally; many new poets; all are concerned citizens." Quarterly magazine; 40 pages. Established in 1972. Circulation: 100 and growing. Acquires all rights. Uses 200 mss a year. Payment in contributor's copies. Sample copy $2; writer's guidelines for SASE. Will not consider photocopied submissions. Will not consider simultaneous submissions. Reports in 2 to 6 weeks. Submit complete ms. Enclose S.A.S.E.
Poetry: Topics include "anything that is an unveiling of social and moral injustice, drug abuse, ecology/pollution, poverty, prison reform, justice in the courts." Humane treatment of animals, conditions in mental hospitals, urban renewal, police brutality, etc. No prose; only poetry which has a definite purpose and is not sentimental and self-indulgent. Poets are urged to "come to the point. Don't start a poem and not follow through on the idea. Any form is fine as long as the idea is a complete statement within the poem. Present work clearly and neatly." Length: 24 lines maximum.
Photos: Department Editor: Ms. Leonie Haviland. B&w photos are sometimes used without ms.
How To Break In: "Present work clearly and neatly, maintain patience and type mss if possible. If incarcerated, note on ms and print clearly. Always enclose S.A.S.E. If incarcerated and cannot send S.A.S.E., so note on work submitted."

SPRING RAIN PRESS, P.O. Box 15319, Seattle WA 98115. Editor: Karen Sollid. Yearly anthology. 50 to 60 (8½x5) pages. Established in 1971. Circulation: 500. Acquires all rights, but will reassign rights to author after publication. Payment in contributor's copies. Will send sample copy to writer for $3. Write for copy of guidelines for writers, but S.A.S.E. must be enclosed. Will consider photocopied submissions. Will not consider simultaneous submissions. Reports in June each year. Submit representative sample ms. Enclose S.A.S.E.
Poetry: Traditional forms, blank verse, free verse, avant-garde forms, lyric poetry. "We avoid sentimental poetry." Length: open.

STAR WEST, P.O. Box 731, Sausalito CA 94965. Editor: Leon Spiro. Semiannual newspaper, with mini-supplements. Established in 1963. Circulation: 1,000. Not copyrighted. Payment in contributor's copies. Will send sample copy to writer for $1. Reports in 2 to 4 weeks. Enclose S.A.S.E.
Poetry: Traditional, contemporary, avant-garde, light verse, surrealism. "Poetry that's dynamic, from Black English to haiku." Length: 16 lines maximum.

STONE COUNTRY, 20 Lorraine Rd., Madison NJ 07940. (201)377-3727. Editor: Judith Neeld. For mature and young adults who have a participating interest in all forms of poetry. Magazine, published 3 times a year; 40 (8½x5½) pages. Circ: 400. Acquires first North American serial rights. Accepts 100 to 150 poems a year. Payment in contributor's copies. Sample copy $1.50. Reports in 1 month, "more or less". Query first or submit complete ms. Enclose S.A.S.E.
Poetry and Graphics: Art Editor: Pat McCormick. "We publish poetry, poetry criticism, and graphics. No thematic or stylistic limitations, but we are unable to publish long narrative poems in full. Overworked approaches include adolescent love, explicit sex, or use of Anglo-Saxonisms. (Have no objections to these poems, just not in quantity, usually badly done.) All themes must be handled maturely and with a search for language, not just the first word that comes to mind or the obvious shocker." Traditional forms, blank verse, free verse, avant-garde forms. Length: 40 lines maximum. No minimum. Limit submissions to 5 poems at a time. Graphic work (b&w only) must be clearly drawn; preferably small (4x4). Larger drawings are used occasionally. Pays $10.

UT REVIEW, University of Tampa, Tampa FL 33606. Editor-in-Chief: Duane Locke. Quarterly magazine; 32 pages. Estab: 1972. Circ: 500. Pays in copies on publication. Buys all rights, but may reassign following publication. Photocopied and previously published submissions OK. SASE. Reports in 1 week. Sample copy $1.50.
Poetry: Avant-garde. Buys 32-128 poems/issue. "Each issue is devoted to the work of one poet. Write poetry similar to that of Alan Britt, Silvia Schiebli, Nico Suarez, or Paul Roth."

VOICES INTERNATIONAL, South and West Inc., 6804 Cloverdale Dr., Little Rock AR 72209. Editor-in-Chief: Clovita Rice. Quarterly magazine; 32 pages. Pays in copies on publication. Acquires all rights. Submit seasonal/holiday material 1 year in advance. SASE. Reports in 3 weeks. Sample copy $1.50.
Poetry: Free verse. Uses 50-60 poems/issue. Limit submissions to batches of 5. Length: 3-40 lines. Will consider longer ones if good.
How To Break In: "We accept poetry with a new approach, haunting word pictures and significant ideas. Language should be used like watercolors to achieve depth, to highlight one focal point, to be pleasing to the viewer, and to be transparent, leaving space for the reader to project his own view."

WEST COAST POETRY REVIEW, 1127 Codel Way, Reno NV 89503. Editor-in-Chief: William L. Fox. Emphasizes conventional and experimental literature. *WCPR* if often used in college writing courses. Semiannual magazine; 80 pages. Estab: 1970. Circ: 750. Pays in copies on publication. Acquires first North American serial rights. Photocopied submissions OK. SASE. Reports in 1 week. Sample copy $2.
Nonfiction: Criticism of contemporary poetry only. Query. Uses some fiction. Must query.
Poetry: Avant-garde and free verse. Uses 50 poems/issue. Limit submissions to batches of 10.

WESTERN POETRY, 3253-Q San Amadeo, Laguna Hills CA 92653. Editor: Joseph Rosenzweig. For a well-educated audience with a wide range of interests. Quarterly; 32 to 40 (5½x8½) pages. Established in 1974. Circulation: 200. Acquires first North American serial rights. Uses 120 to 160 mss a year. Payment in 1 contributor's copy. Will send sample copy for $1.25. Reports in 10 days. Submit complete ms. Enclose S.A.S.E.
Poetry: "We accept all types of quality poetry; traditional, contemporary, free form and humorous verse and are not limited as to theme. Contributors are asked to submit at least 3 poems for consideration." Length: 8 to 24 lines, but exceptions are made on very high quality poems. Best of issue cash awards are also made.

THE WINDLESS ORCHARD, English Department, Indiana-Purdue University, Ft. Wayne IN 46805. Editor: Dr. Robert Novak. For poets and photographers. Established in 1970. Quarterly. Circulation: 300. Acquires all rights, but will reassign rights to author after publication. Payment in contributor's copies. No photocopied or simultaneous submissions. Reports in 3 to 14 weeks. Submit complete ms. Enclose S.A.S.E.

Poetry and Photos: Avant-garde forms of poetry, free verse and haiku. Use of photos restricted to b&w.

THE WORMWOOD REVIEW, P.O. Box 8840, Stockton CA 95204. Editor: Marvin Malone. Quarterly. Circulation: 700. Acquires all rights, but will reassign rights to author on request. Pays in copies or cash equivalent. Pays on publication. Will send sample copy to writer for $1.50. Reports in 2 to 8 weeks. Enclose S.A.S.E.
Poetry: Modern poetry and prose poems that communicate the temper and depth of the human scene. All styles and schools from ultra avant-garde to classical; no taboos. Especially interested in prose poems or fables. 3 to 500 lines.
How To Break In: "Be original. Be yourself. Have something to say. Say it as economically and effectively as possible. Don't be afraid of wit and intelligence."

XANADU, L.I Poetry Collective Inc., 1704 Auburn Rd., Wantagh NY 11793. (516)826-4964. Editors: Charles Fishman, George William Fisher, Beverly Lawn, Cord Gordon. For a college-educated audience, interested in reading the best new poetry being written. Magazine; 60 (5½x8½) pages. Established in 1974. Biannually. Circulation: 1,000. Acquires all rights, but will reassign rights to author after publication if proper credit line is given. Uses about 90 poems a year. Payment in 3 contributor's copies. Will send sample copy to writer for $1.50. No photocopied or simultaneous submissions. Reports in 2 months. *Query first for nonfiction.* Submit complete poetry mss. Enclose S.A.S.E.
Poetry, Nonfiction, Graphics, and Photos: "We publish only poems and materials related to poetry; intelligent criticism, interviews with up-and-coming poets we respect; possible reviews of new books. Our main criteria for poetry are excellence of craft and clarity and force of vision. Only the highest quality contemporary poetry. We like to see at least 5 poems by a contributor at one time. Strongly realized poems rooted in human experience have an edge. We would prefer not to see sloppy, poorly crafted work. Any theme is acceptable, if it is approached with integrity, although we are not a good market for pornographic material pretending to be erotic, or for tedious avant-garde experiments, or for trite or sentimental verse. Poems incorporating recent scientific knowledge, poems confronting important political, moral, and ethical issues, and poems reaching into the realm where the ordinary and the dramatic or visionary are one would be most welcome." B&w photos and line drawings appropriate to size of publication are used without mss.

Politics and World Affairs Publications

Other categories in Writer's Market *include publications that will also consider articles about politics and world affairs. Some of these categories are Business and Finance, General Interest, and Newspapers and Weekly Magazine Sections.*

AFRICA REPORT, 833 United Nations Plaza, New York NY 10017. (212)949-5731. Editor: Anthony J. Hughes. For U.S. citizens, residents with a special interest in African affairs for professional, business, academic or personal reasons. Not tourist-related. Established in 1956. Every 2 months. Circulation: 10,500. Rights purchased vary with author and material. Usually buys all rights. Buys about 70 mss per year. Pays on publication. Will send sample copy to writer for $2. Write for editorial guidelines sheet. Enclose S.A.S.E.
Nonfiction and Photos: Interested in mss on "African political, economic and cultural affairs, especially in relation to U.S. foreign policy and business objectives. Style should be journalistic but not academic or light. Articles should not be polemical or long on rhetoric but may be committed to a strong viewpoint. I do not want tourism articles." Would like to see in-depth topical analyses of lesser known African countries, based on residence or several months stay in the country." Pays $150 for nonfiction. Photos purchased with or without accompanying mss with extra payment. B&w only. Pays $25. Submit 12x8 "half-plate."

AMERICAN OPINION MAGAZINE, Belmont MA 02178. Managing Editor: Scott Stanley, Jr. "A conservative, anti-communist journal of political affairs." Monthly except August. Circulation: 50,000. Buys all rights. Pays on publication. Sample copy $1. SASE.
Nonfiction: Articles on matters of political affairs of a conservative, anti-communist nature. "We favor highly researched, definitive studies of social, economic, political and international problems which are written with verve and originality of style." Length should not exceed 4,000 words nor be less than 3,000. Pays $25 per published page.

AMERICAS, Organization of American States, Washington DC 20006. Managing Editor: Flora L. Phelps. Official organ of Organization of American States. Audience is persons interested in inter-American relations. Editions published in English, Spanish, Portuguese. Monthly. Circulation: 100,000. Buys first publication and reprint rights. Pays on publication. Will send free sample copy on request. Articles received only on speculation. Include cover letter with writer's background. Reports within two months. Not necessary to enclose S.A.S.E.
Nonfiction: Articles of general hemisphere interest on history, art, literature, music, development, travel, etc. Taboos are religious and political themes or articles with non-international slant. Photos required. Length, about 3,000 words. Pays about $75.

THE ASIA MAIL, Potomac-Asia Communications, Inc., Box 1044, Alexandria VA 22313. (703)548-2881. Editor and Publisher: Edward Neilan. Associate Editor: Donna Gays. Emphasizes "American perspectives on Asia and the Pacific" for business executives, opinion leaders, diplomats, scholars, and other Americans who travel, do business or have demonstrated an interest in Asia and Asian affairs. Monthly tabloid; 28 pages. Estab: 1976. Circ: 30,000. Pays on publication. Buys first North American serial rights. SASE. Reports in 2 weeks. Free sample copy and writer's guidelines.
Nonfiction: "The *Asia Mail* will purchase about 4-5 mss from freelance writers each month. The Asia-related articles must show a U.S. interest in an Asian country or Asian interests within the U.S. The publication is comprehensive in business and scholarly aspects and includes articles of information, nostalgia, personal interest, historic interest, as well as reviews of books, art and theatre." Query. Length: 1,500 words maximum for features; 800 words maximum for reviews. Pays $50-150, "higher by special assignment."

CALIFORNIA JOURNAL, California Center for Research and Education in Government. 1617 10th St., Sacramento CA 95814. (916)444-2840. Editor-in-Chief: Ed Salzman. Managing Editor: Leah Cartabruno. Emphasizes California politics and government. Monthly magazine; 40 pages. Estab: 1970. Circ: 13,500. Pays on publication. Buys all rights. Phone queries OK. SASE. Reports immediately. Free sample copy.
Nonfiction: Profiles and state and local government and political analysis. No outright advocacy pieces. Buys 75 mss/year. Query. Length: 900-6,000 words. Pays $50/printed page.

CONSERVATIVE DIGEST, Jefferson Communications, Inc., 7777 Leesburg Pike, Falls Church VA 22043. (703)790-8020. Editor-in-Chief: Brien Benson. Emphasizes politics and social issues. Monthly magazine; 56 pages. Estab: 1975. Circ: 100,000. Pays on publication. Buys all rights. Submit seasonal/holiday material 2½ months in advance. Simultaneous, photocopied and previously published submissions OK. SASE. Reports in 3 weeks. Free writer's guidelines.
Nonfiction: Expose (government, waste, over-regulation), historical (vignettes about political and cultural figures), how-to, humor (politics and personal life), informational (political and social issues), inspirational (religious, people overcoming obstacles, people helping people), nostalgia (of American life), new product (if used in the household or office), personal experience (inspirational), photo feature (political or social subjects), and profile (of political figures). Buys 2 mss/issue. Submit complete ms. Length: 600-1,800 words. Pays $75-300.
Fillers: Clippings, jokes, gags, anecdotes, newsbreaks, word and number puzzles, short humor. Buys 2 mss/issue. Query. Length: 50-300 words. Pays $15.

CURRENT HISTORY, 4225 Main St., Philadelphia PA 19127. Editor: Carol L. Thompson. Monthly. Pays on publication. Reports in one to two weeks. Query preferred. "All articles contracted for in advance." Enclose S.A.S.E.
Nonfiction: Uses articles on current events, chiefly world area studies, stressing their historical, economic, and political background, 3,500 to 4,000 words in length. Academician contributions almost exclusively. Pays an average of $100.

EUROPEAN COMMUNITY, 2100 M St., N.W., Washington DC 20037. Editor: Walter Nicklin. For anyone with a professional or personal interest in Western Europe and European U.S. relations. Monthly magazine; 50 pages. Estab: 1954. Circ: 40,000. Copyrighted. Buys about 50 mss/year. Pays on acceptance. Will send free sample copy to writer on request. Will consider photocopied and simultaneous submissions. Submit seasonal material 3 months in advance. Reports in 2 weeks. Query first or submit complete ms. Include resume of author's background and qualifications with query or ms. Enclose S.A.S.E.
Nonfiction and Photos: Interested in current affairs (with emphasis on economics and politics), the Common Market and Europe's relations with the rest of the world. Publishes occasional

travel and cultural pieces, with European angle. High quality writing a must. "Please, no more M.A. theses on European integration. Looking for European angle in topics current in the U.S." Length: 250 to 3,000 words. Average payment is $250. Photos purchased with or without accompanying mss. Also purchased on assignment. Captions optional. Buys b&w and color. Average payment is $25 to $35 per b&w print, any size; $100 for inside use of color transparencies; $200 to $300 for color used on cover.

FOREIGN AFFAIRS, 58 E. 68th St., New York NY 10021. (212)734-0400. Editor: William P. Bundy. For academics, businessmen (national and international), government, educational and cultural readers especially interested in international affairs of a political nature. Established in 1922. Quarterly. Circulation: 75,000. Buys all rights. Buys 45 mss a year. Payment on publication. Will send sample copy to writer for $3. Will consider photocopied submissions. Reports in 2 to 4 weeks. Submit complete ms. Enclose S.A.S.E.
Nonfiction: "Articles dealing with international affairs; political, educational, cultural, philosophical and social sciences. Develop an original idea in depth, with a broad basis on topical subjects. Serious, in-depth, developmental articles with international appeal." Length: 2,500 to 6,000 words. Pays $300.

THE FREEMAN, 30 S. Broadway, Irvington-on-Hudson NY 10533. (914)591-7230. Editor: Paul L. Poirot. For "fairly advanced students of liberty and the layman." Monthly. Buys all rights, including reprint rights. Buys about 44 mss a year. Pays on publication. Enclose S.A.S.E.
Nonfiction: "We want nonfiction clearly analyzing and explaining various aspects of the free market, private enterprise, limited government philosophy, especially as pertains to conditions in the United States. Though a necessary part of the literature of freedom is the exposure of collectivistic cliches and fallacies, our aim is to emphasize and explain the positive case for individual responsibility and choice in a free economy. Especially important, we believe, is the methodology of freedom; self-improvement, offered to others who are interested. We try to avoid name-calling and personality clashes, and find satire of little use as an educational device. Ours is a scholarly analysis of the principle underlying a free market economy." Length: not over 3,500 words. Payment is 5¢ a word.

THE NATION, 333 Sixth Ave., New York NY 10014. Editor: Blair Clark. Weekly. Query first. Enclose S.A.S.E.
Nonfiction and Poetry: "We welcome all articles dealing with the social scene, particularly if they examine it with a new point of view or expose conditions the rest of the media overlooks. Poetry is also accepted." Length and payment to be negotiated.
How To Break In: "I'm absolutely committed to the idea of getting more material from the boondocks. For instance, a fellow in Denver just sent us a piece we're printing on the firings that are going on at the newspaper there. Right now we're getting stuff at the ratio of about 10 to one from the New York area and I would like to reverse that ratio. If you live somewhere where you think nothing is going on, look again! If you do a piece for us from someplace where we don't have anyone, you could develop into a stringer."

NATIONAL DEVELOPMENT, Intercontinental Publications, Inc., 15 Franklin St., Westport CT 06880. (203)226-7463. Editor-in-Chief: Martin Greenburgh. Emphasizes 3rd world infrastructure. For government officials in 3rd world—economists, planners, engineers, ministers. Monthly magazine; 120 pages. Estab: 1960. Circ: 23,000. Pays on acceptance. Buys all rights, but may reassign following publication. Phone queries OK. Previously published submissions OK. SASE. Reports in 4 weeks. Free sample copy and writer's guidelines.
Nonfiction: How-to (tourism, case studies, government management, planning, telecommunications), informational (agriculture, economics, public works, construction management), interview, photo feature, technical. Buys 6-10 mss/issue. Query. Length: 1,800-3,000 words. Pays $150-250.
Photos: B&w and color. Captions required. Query. Total price for ms includes payment for photos.
Columns, Departments: Gail Ernsting, Column/Department Editor. Managing Maintenance (public works maintenance from managerial viewpoint), Financial Technology (finances as they might affect 3rd world governments). Buys 4 mss/issue. Query. Length: 750-1,500 words. Pays $75-150. Open to suggestions for new columns/departments.

NATIONAL JOURNAL, 1730 M St., N.W., Washington DC 20036. (202)857-1400. Editor: Richard Frank. "Very limited need for freelance material because full-time staff produces virtually all of our material."

NATIONAL REVIEW, 150 E. 35th St., New York NY 10016. (212)679-7330. Editor: Wm. F. Buckley, Jr. Issued fortnightly. Buys all rights. Pays on publication. Will send sample copy. Reports in a month. Enclose S.A.S.E.
Nonfiction: Uses articles, 1,000 to 3,500 words, on current events and the arts, which would appeal to a politically conservative audience. Pays about 7½¢/word. Inquiries about book reviews, movie, play, TV reviews, or other cultural happenings, or travel should be addressed to Chilton Williamson, Jr., 150 E. 35th St., New York NY 10016.
Poetry: Uses only short, satirical poems of a political nature. Should not run over 30 lines.

NEW GUARD, Young Americans for Freedom, Woodland Rd., Sterling VA 22170. (703)450-5162. Editor-in-Chief: David Boaz. Managing Editor: Pam Dutton. Emphasizes libertarian or conservative political ideas for readership of mostly young people with a large number of college students. Age range 14-39. Virtually all are politically conservative or libertarian with interests in politics, economics, philosophy, current affairs. Mostly students or college graduates. Monthly magazine; 32 pages. Estab: 1961. Circ: 12,000. Pays on publication. Buys all rights. Phone queries OK. Seasonal/holiday material should be submitted 2-3 months in advance. Simultaneous and photocopied submissions OK. SASE. Reports in 1 month. Free sample copy.
Nonfiction: Expose (government waste, failure, mismanagement, problems with education or media); historical (illustrating political or economic points); humor (satire on current events); interview (politicians, academics, people with conservative viewpoint or something to say to conservatives); personal opinion and profile. Buys 40 mss/year. Submit complete ms. Length: 2,500 words maximum. Pays $10-60/article.
Photos: Purchased with accompanying manuscript.
Fiction: Humorous (satire or current events). Buys 5 mss/year. Submit complete ms. Length: 1,800 words maximum. Pays $10-40.

THE NEW REPUBLIC—A Weekly Journal of Opinion, 1220 Nineteenth St., N.W., Washington DC 20036. Managing Editor: Michael Kinsley. Estab: 1914. Circ: 90,000. Buys all rights. Pays on publication. Enclose S.A.S.E.
Nonfiction: This liberal, intellectual publication uses 1,000- to 1,500-word comments on public affairs and arts. Pays 8¢ per published word.

NEWSWEEK, 444 Madison Ave., New York NY 10022. Staff-written. Unsolicited mss accepted for "My Turn," a column of personal opinion. Length: 1,100 words maximum.

PRESENT TENSE: THE MAGAZINE OF WORLD JEWISH AFFAIRS, 165 E. 56th St., New York NY 10022. (212)751-4000. Editor: Murray Polner. For college-educated, Jewish-oriented audience interested in foreign affairs and Jewish life abroad. Quarterly magazine; 80 (8½x11) pages. Established in 1973. Circulation: 25,000. Buys all rights, but will reassign rights to author after publication. Buys 60 mss a year. Payment on acceptance. Will send sample copy to writer for $2.50. Will not consider photocopied or simultaneous submissions. Reports in 6 to 8 weeks. Query first. Enclose S.A.S.E.
Nonfiction: Quality reportage of contemporary events (a la *Harper's, Atlantic, New Yorker,* etc.) and well-written memoirs. Personal experience, profiles, essay reviews. Length for essay reviews: 1,500 words maximum. Length for other material: 4,000 words maximum. Pays $150 to $300.

THE PROGRESSIVE, 408 W. Gorham St., Madison WI 53703. (608)257-4626. Editor: Erwin Knoll. Issued monthly. Buys all rights. Pays on publication. Reports in two weeks. Query first. Enclose S.A.S.E.
Nonfiction: Primarily interested in articles which interpret, from a progressive point of view, domestic and world affairs. Occasional lighter features. Up to 3,000 words. Pays $50-$200 per ms.

REASON MAGAZINE, Box 40105, Santa Barbara CA 93103. (805)969-6290. Editor: Robert Poole, Jr. For a readership interested in individual liberty, economic freedom, private enterprise alternatives to government services, protection against inflation and depressions. Monthly; 52 pages. Estab: 1968. Circ: 19,000. Rights purchased vary with author and material. May buy all rights; but will sometimes reassign rights to author after publication; first North American serial rights or first serial rights. Buys 40 mss a year. Payment on publication. Will send sample copy to writer for $1. Write for copy of guidelines for writers. "Manuscripts must be typed, double- or triple-spaced on one side of the page only. The first page (or a cover sheet) should contain an aggregate word count, the author's name and mailing address, and a brief (100- to 200-word) abstract. A short biographical sketch of the author should also be included." Will consider photocopied submissions. Reports in 3 months. Query first. Enclose S.A.S.E.

Nonfiction and Photos: "*Reason* is specifically a libertarian publication, dealing with social, economic and political problems, and supporting both individual liberty and economic freedom. Articles dealing with the following subject areas are desired: analyses of current issues and problems from a libertarian viewpoint (e.g., education, pollution, victimless crimes, regulatory agencies, foreign policy, etc.). Discussions of social change, i.e., strategy and tactics for moving toward a free society. Discussions of the institutions of a free society and how they would deal with important problems. Articles on self-preservation in today's environment (economic, political, cultural). Lessons from the past, both revisionist history and biographical sketches of noteworthy individuals. Case studies of unique examples of the current application of libertarian/free-market principles." Length: 1,500-5,000 words. Pays $25 minimum plus 10 copies of the issue and a 1-year subscription. Book reviews are also used and compensation for these consists of $10 plus a 1-year subscription and 10 copies of the issue containing the review. No additional payment is made for b&w photos. Captions required.

TIME, Rockefeller Center, New York NY 10020. Staff-written.

WASHINGTON MONTHLY, 1028 Connecticut Ave., N.W., Washington DC 20036. Editor: Charles Peters. For "well-educated people interested in politics and government; well-read." Monthly. Circulation: 30,000. Rights purchased depend on author and material. Buys all rights or first rights. Buys about 40 mss a year. Pays on publication. Sample copy $1.75. Sometimes does special topical issues. Query or submit complete ms. Tries to report in 2-4 weeks. SASE.
Nonfiction and Photos: Responsible investigative or evaluative reporting about the U.S. government, business, society, the press, and politics. Length: "average 2,000 to 6,000 words." Pays 5¢ to 10¢ a word. Buys b&w glossies.

WORLD POLITICS, Corwin Hall, Princeton NJ 08540. Editors: Klaus Knorr, Cyril E. Black, Gerald Garvey, Walter F. Murphy, Leon Gordenker. Issued quarterly to academic readers in social sciences. Pays on publication. Buys all rights. Reports in one to six months. Enclose S.A.S.E.
Nonfiction: Uses articles based on original scholarly research on international aspects of the social sciences. Mss should be double-spaced throughout (including footnotes), and have wide margins. Footnotes should be placed at the end of article. Length: 3,000 to 5,000 words. Pays $50 per article.

WORLDVIEW, 170 E. 64th St., New York NY 10021. Phone: (212)838-4120. Managing Editor: Susan Woolfson. For "the informed and concerned reader who insists that discussion of public issues must take place within an ethical framework." Monthly. Buys all rights. Pays on publication. Study the magazine and query first. Enclose S.A.S.E.
Nonfiction: Articles on public issues, religion, international affairs, world politics, and moral imperatives. "The editors believe that any analysis of our present cultural and political problems which ignores the moral dimension is at best incomplete—at worst, misleading. *Worldview* focuses on international affairs, puts the discussion in an ethical framework, and relates ethical judgment to specifically religious traditions." Article length: 2,500 to 5,000 words; "Excursus", 300-1,000 words; Book reviews: 1,000 words. Payment depends on length and use of material.
How To Break In: "Short pieces for the 'Excursus' section must be as well written and have the same degree of ethical orientation as the longer ones, but it is one way to break in. Book reviews are also a possibility. If a writer sends some samples of previous work and a list of the types of literature he is interested in, we might try him out with an assignment."

Puzzle Publications

This category includes only those publications devoted entirely to puzzles. The writer will find many additional markets for crosswords, brain teasers, acrostics, etc., by reading the Filler listings throughout the Consumer, Farm, Trade, Technical, and Professional sections of this book. Especially rich in puzzle markets are the Religious, Juvenile, Teen and Young Adult, and General Interest classifications in the Consumer section.

OFFICIAL CROSSWORDS, DELL CROSSWORDS, POCKET CROSSWORDS, DELL WORD SEARCH PUZZLES, DELL PENCIL PUZZLES AND WORD GAMES, DELL CROSSWORD ANNUALS, DELL CROSSWORD PUZZLES, PAPERBACK BOOK SERIES, DELL PUZZLE PUBLICATIONS, 245 East 47 St., New York NY 10017. Editor: Kathleen Rafferty. For "all ages from '8 to 80'—people whose interests are puzzles, both crosswords and variety features." Beys all rights. Enclose S.A.S.E.

Puzzles: "We publish puzzles of all kinds, but the market here is limited to those who are able to construct quality pieces which can compete with the real professionals. See our magazines. They are the best guide for our needs. We publish quality puzzles, which are well-conceived and well edited, with appeal to solvers of all ages and in about every walk of life. We are the world's leading publishers of puzzle publications and are distributed in many countries around the world in addition to the continental U.S. However, no foreign language puzzles, please! Our market for crosswords and anacrostics is very small, since long-time contributors supply most of the needs in those areas. However, we are always willing to see material of unusual quality, or with a new or original approach. Since most of our publications feature variety puzzles in addition to the usual features, we are especially interested in seeing quizzes, picture features, and new and unusual puzzle features of all kinds. Please do not send us remakes of features we are now using. We are interested only in new ideas. Kriss Krosses are an active market here. However, constructors who wish to enter this field must query us first before submitting any material whatever. Prices vary with the feature, but ours are comparable with the highest in the general puzzle field."

ORIGINAL CROSSWORD, EASY-TIME, CROSSWORD'S WORD HUNT, 575 Madison Ave., New York NY 10022. (212)838-7900. Editorial Director: Arthur Goodman. Bimonthly. Buys all rights. Pays on acceptance. Refer to current issue available on newsstand as guide to type of material wanted. Submissions must be accompanied by self-addressed, stamped envelope for return.

Puzzles: Original adult crossword puzzles; sizes 15x15 and 13x13; medium and not hard. Same requirements for diagramless, but 15x15 irregular patterns only. Pays $7 to $20.

Regional Publications

General interest publications slanted toward residents of and visitors to a particular city or region are listed below. Since they publish little material that doesn't relate to the area they cover, they represent a limited market for writers who live outside their area. Many buy manuscripts on conservation and the natural wonders of their area; additional markets for such material will be found under the Nature, Conservation, and Ecology, and Sport and Outdoor headings.

Publications that report on the business climate of a region are grouped in the regional division of the Business and Finance category. Newspapers and weekly magazine sections, which also buy material of general interest to area residents, are classified separately under that category heading. Magazines for farm audiences which buy regional general interest material are found in the local division of the General Interest Farming and Rural Life category in the Farm Publications section.

ADIRONDACK LIFE, Box 137, Keene NY 12942. Editor-in-Chief: Bernard R. Carman. Emphasizes the Adirondack region of New York State for a readership aged 30-60, upper-educated, whose interests include outdoor activities, history, and natural history directly related to the Adirondacks. Bimonthly magazine; 64 pages. Estab: 1970. Circ: 40,000. Pays on publication. Buys all rights, but may reassign following publication. Submit seasonal/holiday material 4 months in advance. Previously published book excerpts OK. SASE. Reports in 4 weeks. Free sample copy and writer's guidelines.

Nonfiction: Historical (Adirondack relevance only); how-to (should relate to activities and lifestyles of the region, e.g., how to make your own maple syrup); informational (natural history of the region); interview (Adirondack personalities); personal experience; photo feature (Adirondack relevance required); profile; and travel (Adirondacks only). Buys 10 mss/issue. Query. Length: 1,500-3,500 words. Pays $75-250.

Photos: Purchased with or without mss or on assignment. Captions required (Adirondacks locale must be identified). Submit contact sheet or transparencies. Pays $10 for 8x10 glossy, semi-glossy or matte photos; $25-50 for 35mm or larger color transparencies.

How To Break In: "Start with a good query that tells us what the article offers—its narrative line and, most importantly, its relevance to the Adirondacks. We tolerate all sorts of aberrations at least once. The exception: failure to determine what the magazine is all about. At the risk of being tiresome, let me repeat again: it's all about the Adirondacks, broadly concieved—and not about anything else."

ARIZONA HIGHWAYS, 2039 W. Lewis Ave., Phoenix AZ 85009. (602)258-6641. Editor: Tom C. Cooper. For persons who have lived in Arizona, tourists and potential tourists; with 90% of circulation out-of-state. Magazine; 48 pages. Established in 1925. Monthly. Circulation: 700,000. Buys first North American serial rights. Buys about 100 mss per year. Pays on publication. Will send free sample copy to writer on request. No simultaneous submissions. Reports in 1 month. Query first. Enclose S.A.S.E.
Nonfiction and Photos: Wants mss about Arizona people, places and things, from historical to contemporary subjects of interest to tourists. Buys informational, historical, nostalgia and travel mss. Pays 10¢ to 20¢ per word. Photos purchased with mss with extra payment or on assignment. Captions required. Pays $25 for 8x10 b&w photos. Pays $40 to $150 for color transparencies.

THE ATLANTIC ADVOCATE, University Press of New Brunswick Ltd., Gleaner Bldg., Fredericton, NB., Canada E3B 5A2. (506)455-6671. Editor-in-Chief: James D. Morrison. Editor: H.P. Wood. Emphasizes The Atlantic Provinces for junior high school to octogenarian. Monthly magazine; 64 pages. Estab: 1950. Circ: 21,000. Pays on publication. Buys first North American serial rights. Phone queries OK. Submit seasonal/holiday material 3 months in advance. SASE. Reports in 2 weeks. Sample copy 50¢.
Nonfiction: Historical, humor, informational, interview, nostalgia, personal experience and profile. Buys 150-200 mss/year. Send complete ms. Length: 500-2,000 words. Pays 5¢/word.
Photos: Purchased with accompanying ms. Submit transparencies. Pays $5-10 for b&w; $25 for color (covers only). Model release required. "Our cover shots are scenes taken in the Atlantic Provinces. We try to be seasonal."
Fiction: Adventure, historical and humorous. Buys 15-30 mss/year. Send complete ms. Length: 1,500-2,000 words. Pays 5¢/word.
Poetry: Free verse and traditional. Buys 12-20 poems/year. Limit submissions to batches of 6. Length: 15-50 lines. Pays $10-50.
How To Break In: "We encourage new writers and read every manuscript that is relevant to the Atlantic area. We write letters, even if brief, and have no rejection cards or slips. We're friendly people with a sincere love for writers, artists and photographers, but don't abuse our good nature."

AVENUE M, 100 E. Walton, Apt. 36-A, Chicago IL 60611. (312)787-9415. Editor-in-Chief: Art Desmond. Emphasizes news and features around dhe Magnificent Mile in Chicago for all ages. Monthly magazine; 24 pages. Estab: 1975. Circ: 15,000. Pays on publication. Buys all rights, but may reassign to author following publication. Phone queries OK. Photocopied and previously published submissions OK. SASE. Reports in 3 weeks. Sample copy $1; free writer's guidelines.
Nonfiction: Historical, humor, informational, inspirational, interview, nostalgia, personal experience, personal opinion, photo feature, profile and travel. Buys 80 mss/year. Query. Length: 500-750 words. Pays $25-50.
Photos: Purchased with accompanying ms. Captions required. Pays $5-10 for 8x10 b&w glossies. Offers no additional payment for photos accepted with accompanying ms. Total purchase price for ms includes payment for photos.

BC OUTDOORS, Box 900, Postal Station A, Surrey, B.C., Canada. (604)574-5211. Editor: Art Downs. Magazine, published every 2 months; 68 (8½x11) pages. Established in 1945. Circulation: 30,000. Buys first North American serial rights. Buys 30 to 40 mss a year. Payment on acceptance. Free sample copy. Submit seasonal material 4 months in advance. Reports in 2 to 4 weeks. Query first or submit complete ms. Enclose S.A.E. and International Reply Coupons.
Nonfiction and Photos: Anything of a factual nature about B.C./Yukon, including conservation, history, travel, fishing, camping and wildlife. Must be of general interest. Length: 1,500 to 3,000 words. Pays $50-125. 8x10 or 6x9 b&w photos purchased with or without accompanying ms. Pays $5. 35mm color used for covers. Pays $25.

BEND OF THE RIVER MAGAZINE, Box 239, Perrysburg OH 43551. (419)874-1691. Editors: Christine Raizk Alexander and Lee Raizk. For readers interested in history, antiques, etc. Monthly magazine; 24 (9x11) pages. Established in 1972. Circ: 2,000. Rights purchased vary with author and material. Usually buys all rights, but will reassign rights to author after publication. Buys 50 to 60 mss a year. Payment on publication. Will send free sample copy to writer for 10¢. Will not consider photocopied or simultaneous submissions. Submit seasonal material 2 months in advance; deadline for holiday issue is October 15. Reports in 2 months. Submit complete ms. Enclose S.A.S.E.

Nonfiction and Photos: "We deal heavily in Ohio history. We are looking for articles about modern day pioneers, doing the unusual. Another prime target is the uplifting feature, spiritual and/or religious sketch or interview. Don't bother sending anything negative; other than that, we can appreciate each writer's style. We'd like to see interviews with historical (Ohio) authorities; travel sketches of little known but interesting places in Ohio; grass roots farmers; charismatic people. Nostalgic pieces will be considered. Our main interest is to give our readers happy thoughts. We strive for material that says 'yes' to life, past and present." Length: open. Pays minimum of $5. Purchases b&w photos with accompanying mss. Pays minimum of $1. Captions required.

How To Break In: "Send us any unusual piece that is either cleverly humorous, divinely inspired or thought provoking. We like articles about historical topics treated in down-to-earth conversational tones. And *any* Toledo area history will be put on top of the heap!"

BIRMINGHAM MAGAZINE, 1914 Sixth Ave. N., Birmingham AL 35203. (205)323-5461. Editor: Donald A. Brown. For civic, political, cultural, and business leaders; affluent audience. Monthly. Circulation: 10,000. Buys all rights. Pays on publication. Will send free sample copy on request. Editorial deadlines are 45 days prior to publication. Reports in 2 to 3 weeks. Prefers to see samples of work in advance and usually works by assignment. Query preferred. Enclose S.A.S.E.

Nonfiction: Timely, interpretive, objective articles of Birmingham and the South; progress and problems. Professional, imaginative style, 1,500 to 5,000 words. Pays $75 to $200.

Photos: Purchased with mss. Subject matter, specifications, and payment rate worked out according to the particular story.

BOSTON MAGAZINE, Municipal Publications, 1050 Park Square Bldg., Boston MA 02116. (617)357-4000. Editor-in-Chief: George M. Gendron. For young, upscale readers; vast majority are professionals, college-educated and affluent. Monthly magazine; 160 pages. Estab: 1910 as a Chamber of Commerce publication, becoming an independent publication in 1971. Pays on acceptance. Buys all rights, but may reassign following publication. Submit seasonal/holiday material 3 months in advance. Simultaneous and photocopied submissions OK. SASE. Reports in 2 weeks.

Nonfiction: Expose (subject matter varies); profiles (of Bostonians; sometimes, New Englanders); travel (usually only in New England or eastern Canada); personal experience. Buys about 40 mss/year. Query. Length: 1,000-10,000 words. Pays $100-500.

Photos: Ronn Campisi, Design Director. B&w and color purchased on assignment only. Query. Specifications vary. Pays $25-150 for b&w; payment for color (which is only used on cover) averages $275.

Fillers: Nancy Pomerene, Department Editor. Newsbreaks. Short items of interest about Boston personalities, institutions or phenomena. Buys about 5 per issue. Send fillers in. Length: 100-500 words. Pays $5-25.

How To Break In: "If we are unfamiliar with a writer's work, we want to see clips that are representative of his/her style and range of interest and expertise. Remember, we consider ourselves in the entertainment business, so the emphasis here is on compelling, entertaining writing. The one thing that this or any other magazine can never afford to do is bore the reader."

BOULDER DAILY CAMERA FOCUS MAGAZINE, Box 591, Boulder CO 80306. (303)442-1202. Editor-in-Chief: Phil Gruis. Emphasizes subjects of particular interest to Boulder County residents. Weekly tabloid.; 40 pages. Estab: 1964. Circ: 28,000. Pays on first of month following publication. Buys one-time rights. Phone queries OK. Submit seasonal/holiday material 6-8 weeks in advance. Photocopied submissions OK. SASE. Reports in 2 weeks.

Nonfiction: Expose (anything relevant to Boulder County that needs exposing); informational (emphasis on good writing, warmth and impact); historical (pertaining to Boulder County or Colorado in general); interview and profile (stress local angle); photo feature (featuring Boulder County or areas in Colorado and Rocky Mountain West where Boulder County residents are apt to go). Buys 35 mss/year. Query. Length: 700-3,300 words. Pays 30-50¢ a column inch.

Photos: Purchased with or without mss, or on assignment. Captions required. Query. Pays $3-6 for 8x10 b&w glossies; $4-8 for 35mm or 2¼x2¼ (or larger) color transparencies.

BROWARD LIFE, Brenda Publishing Co., 3081 E. Commercial Blvd., Fort Lauderdale FL 33308. (305)491-6350. Editor-in-Chief: Joanne Myers. Emphasizes leisure activities in Broward County. Monthly magazine; 72 pages. Estab: 1974. Circ: 20,000. Pays on publication. Rights purchased vary with author and material; buys all rights, but may reassign following publication, or first North American serial rights. Phone queries OK. Submit seasonal/holiday material 1 month in advance. Simultaneous, xeroxed and previously published submissions OK. SASE. Reports in 6 weeks. Sample copy for $1.

Nonfiction: Expose (must pertain to persons or events in Broward County), how-to (must appeal to high-income lifestyles), humor (especially *New Yorker* type), interview (Broward County oriented), profile (Broward County resident), travel, new product, photo feature. Buys 2 mss/issue. Submit complete ms. Length: 1,000-2,000 words. Pays $25-100. "We will consider students' work for credits only. Writers previously published in other magazines will be given preference."

Photos: Michael O'Bryon, Photo Editor. Purchased with or without accompanying ms or on assignment. Captions required. Pays $5-50 for b&w or 35mm color transparencies. Query or send contact sheet. Model release required.

Columns, Departments: Movies, Books, Theatre, Cooking, Business (taxes, new laws), quizzes. Buys 6 mss/issue. Submit complete ms. Length: 500-1,500 words. Pays $25-75.

Poetry: Avant-garde, free verse, haiku, light verse, humorous. Buys 4/issue. Limit submissions to 6 at one time. Length: 50 line maximum. Pays $5-25.

Fillers: Jokes, gags, anecdotes, crossword puzzles, short humor. Buys 3/issue. Length: 100 words maximum. Pays $5-25.

BUCKS COUNTY PANORAMA MAGAZINE, GBW Publications Inc., 57 W. Court St., Doylestown PA 18901. (215)348-9505. Editor/Publisher: Mrs. Gerry Wallerstein. Regional magazine serving Bucks County/Delaware valley for an upscale readership. Monthly magazine; 56 pages. Estab: 1959. Circ: 8,000. Pays on acceptance (written work); on publication (photos). "All rights usually purchased, but may make exceptions depending on author and material." Submit seasonal/holiday material 6 months in advance. Photocopied submissions OK. SASE. Reports in 2-4 weeks. Sample copy $1.25. Free writer's guidelines.

Nonfiction: Expose (dealing with our coverage area and well researched and documented); historical (must be well researched, in-depth and written in lively manner; queries advisable on subject matter); how-to; humor (should be 750-1,200 words; themes must have relevance to our audience/geographical area); informational; interview; nostalgia; personal experience; photo feature; profile and travel. "We are a regional magazine—all these types must be relevant to our audience and coverage area." Buys 60 mss/year. Query or send complete ms. Length: 750-2,500 words. Pays $15-25. (Occasionally pays higher fee for articles requiring considerable research).

Photos: Jeanne E. Stock, Art Director. Purchased with or without accompanying ms or on assignment. Captions required. Pays $15 maximum for 8½x11 b&w glossies. Model release required. Photos accompanying ms should be sent to Gerry Wallerstein.

Fiction: Adventure, historical, humorous, mainstream, mystery, romance, science fiction and suspense. "All fiction must relate to our audience and/or geographic area." Buys 3-5 mss/year. Send complete ms. Length: 1,000-2,500 words. Pays $15-25.

Poetry: Free verse, haiku, light verse, traditional and historical. Buys 15-20 poems/year. Limit submissions to batches of 4. Length: maximum 16 lines. Pays $5 maximum.

For '78: Suitable article and/or story for Halloween, Christmas, Thanksgiving, Easter, July 4th.

BUFFALO SPREE MAGAZINE, P.O. Box 38, Buffalo NY 14226. (716)839-3405. Editor: Richard G. Shotell. For "a highly literate readership." Established in 1967. Quarterly. Circulation: 18,000. Buys first serial rights. Buys 30 to 35 mss a year. Enclose S.A.S.E.

Nonfiction and Fiction: Department Editor: Gary Goss. "Intellectually stimulating prose exploring contemporary social, philosophical, and artistic concerns. We are not a political magazine. Matters of interest to western New York make up a significant part of what we print." Length: 3,000 words maximum. Pays about $75 for a lead article. "We print fiction, but it must be brilliant." Length: 3,000 words maximum. Pays $75.

Poetry: Department Editor: Nik Mistler. "Serious, modern poetry of nature and of man's relationship with nature interests us, provided it is of the highest quality." Pays $15 minimum.

CANADIAN FRONTIER ANNUAL, Antonson Publishing Ltd., Box 157, New Westminster, B.C., Canada V3L 4Y4. (604)584-9922. Editor-in-Chief: Brian Antonson. Emphasizes Canadian history (pre-1900). For "anybody at all who is interested in Canadian history." Annual magazine; 112 pages. Estab: 1972. Circ: 1,200. Pays on publication. Buys all rights. "All material

should be submitted by April of publication year." Simultaneous, photocopied and previously published submissions OK. Reports in 1 month. Sample copy $3.50; free writer's guidelines.
Nonfiction: Historical (Canadian history, pre-dating 1900. Only true, accurate and factual material will be accepted). Buys 24 mss/issue. Length: 2,000-3,000 words. Pays $35 minimum.
Photos: Purchased with accompanying ms. Captions required. Send prints. Pays $2 for any size b&w photos.

CANADIAN GOLDEN WEST MAGAZINE, Suite 115, 818-16 Ave. N.W., Calgary, Alberta, Canada T2M 0K1. (403)289-4022. Editor: Pat Donaldson. For residents and visitors to Western Canada. Magazine; 40 to 48 pages. Established in 1965. Quarterly. Circulation: 9,750. Buys first North American serial rights. Buys about 50 mss per year. Pays on acceptance. Will send free sample copy to writer on request. Submit seasonal material 3 months in advance. Reports in 4 weeks. Enclose S.A.S.E.
Nonfiction and Photos: "Emphasis on the history, fine arts, people, places and opinions of Western Canada; well-illustrated with b&w photos. No Wild West cowboy and Indian stuff!" Prefers informal, relaxed writing in third person, but first-person narratives considered if the writer was personally involved in an event of major importance. "Golden Notes" features true anecdotes and original humor. Pays $5 to $15 for 100 to 600 words. Indian stories accepted only if they are written by Indians. Would like to see personality profiles on public figures. "The magazine, being quarterly, likes to run material that corresponds to the seasons — historical slant appreciated." Length: 1,000-3,000 words. Pays 3-5¢/word. "Regular contributors are paid more, as are writers who have done original historical research." Photos purchased with mss with no additional payment. Captions optional, but some explanation preferred.
Fiction and Fillers: Buys fiction with Western Canadian slant. Will consider mystery, suspense, adventure, Western, science fiction and historical. Buys 1 ms/issue. Pays 1¢ to 5¢ per word. "Average article is paid 3¢/word." Will consider fillers with Canadian slant. Buys crossword and word puzzles, jokes, gags, anecdotes, and short humor. Pays $5 to $15.

CHICAGO MAGAZINE, 500 N. Michigan Ave., Chicago IL 60611. Editor-in-Chief: Allen H. Kelson. Editor: John Fink. For an audience which is "95% from Chicago area; 90% college-trained; upper income; overriding interests in the arts, dining, good life in the city. Most are in 30 to 50 age bracket and well-read and articulate. Generally liberal inclination." Monthly. Circulation: 160,000. Buys first rights. Buys about 50 mss/year. Pays on acceptance. Sample copy $1. Submit seasonal material 3 months in advance. Reports in 2 weeks. Query first. Enclose S.A.S.E.
Nonfiction and Photos: "On themes relating to the quality of life in Chicago ... past, present, future." Writers should have "a general awareness that the readers will be concerned, influential native Chicagoans reading what the writer has to say about their city. We generally publish material too comprehensive for daily newspapers or of too specialized interest for them." Buys personal experience and think pieces, interviews, profiles, humor, spot news, historical articles, exposes. Length: 2,000 to 6,000 words. Pays $100 to $500. Photos purchased with mss. B&w glossies, color transparencies, 35mm color, color prints.
Fiction: Mainstream, fantasy, and humorous fiction. Preferably with Chicago orientation. No word length limits, but "no novels, please". Pays $250 to $500.

CHICAGO READER, Box 11101, Chicago IL 60611. (312)828-0350. Editor: Robert A. Roth. "The *Reader* is distributed free in Chicago's lakefront neighborhoods. Generally speaking, these are Chicago's best educated, most affluent neighborhoods—and they have an unusually high concentration of young adults living there." Weekly tabloid; 60 pages. Estab: 1971. Circ: 76,000. Pays "by 15th of month following publication." Buys all rights. Phone queries OK. Photocopied submissions OK. SASE. Reports in 12 months.
Nonfiction: "We want magazine features on Chicago topics. Will also consider reviews." Buys 500 mss/year. Submit complete ms. Length: "whatever's appropriate to the story." Pays $18-200.
Photos: By assignment only.
Columns/Departments: By assignment only.

CINCINNATI MAGAZINE, Greater Cincinnati Chamber of Commerce, 120 W. 5th St., Cincinnati, OH 45202. (513)721-3300. Editor-in-Chief: J. P. O'Connor. Features Editor: Leslie Major. Emphasizes Cincinnati living. Monthly magazine; 64-80 pages. Estab: 1967. Circ: 15,000. Pays on acceptance. Buys all rights, but may reassign following publication. Phone queries OK. Submit seasonal/holiday material 2 months in advance. Simultaneous, photocopied and previously published submissions OK. SASE. Reports in 3 weeks. Free sample copy and writer's guidelines.

Nonfiction: How-to; informational; interview; photo feature; profile and travel. Buys 3-4 mss/issue. Query. Length: 2,000-4,000 words. Pays $200-500.

Photos: Theo Kouvatsos, Photo Editor. Photos purchased on assignment only. Model release required.

Columns/Departments: Travel; How-To; Sports and Consumer Tips. Buys 6 mss/issue. Query. Length: 750-1,500 words. Pays $75-150. Open to suggestions for new columns/departments.

COAST, Box 2448, Myrtle Beach SC 29577. Editor: Mary Miller. For tourists to the Grand Strand. Magazine; 180 (5½x8½) pages. Established in 1955. Weekly. Circulation: 17,500. Buys all rights. Buys 5 or 6 mss a year. Pays on acceptance. Will send free sample copy to writer on request. Will consider photocopied and simultaneous submissions. Reports on material accepted for publication in 60 to 90 days. Returns rejected material in 2 weeks. Query first. SASE.

Nonfiction and Photos: "Timely features dealing with coastal activities and events, and an occasional historical article related to the area. Submit an idea before a manuscript. It should be directly related to this coastal area. No vague, general articles." Emphasis is on informational and historical articles. Length: 800 to 1,000 words. Pays $25 to $30. B&w photos purchased with mss. Prefers 5x7. Pays $5 to $10 for b&w. Buys come solor for editorial purposes. Must relate to area. Pays $15 to $25.

COAST MAGAZINE, Boardwalk Publications Inc., 509 N. Fairfax Ave., Suite 212, Los Angeles CA 90036. Editor-in-Chief: Stephen M. Silverman. Managing Editor: Judy Pataky. For young, involved, Western Americans in active and intelligent pursuit of the good life along the Pacific Coast. Monthly magazine. Estab: 1959. Pays on publication. Buys first North American serial rights. Submit seasonal/holiday material 4 months in advance. Photocopied submissions OK. SASE. Reports in 2-3 weeks. Sample copy $2; free writer's guidelines.

Nonfiction: Expose (ecology along the coast); historical ("old Hollywood"); how-to (build your own furniture, etc.); humor (set at the beach); informational (where to go, what to do); interview (personalities along the coast); nostalgia (old Hollywood); photo feature (beaches); profile and travel ("coasts" around the world). Buys 3-4 mss/issue. Query. Length: 1,000-3,000 words. Payment open to discussion.

Photos: Randy Robinson, Photo Editor. Purchased on assignment. B&w. Query for photos.

Columns/Departments: Modes (other coasts); media (places); art; metiers; theatre and wine. Buys 2-3/issue. Query. Length: 500-1,000 words. Payment open to discussion. Open to suggestions from freelancers for new columns/departments; address to Stephen M. Silverman.

Fiction: Adventure, experimental, historical, humorous, mystery, science fiction, suspense and condensed novels. Buys 2-3 mss/year. Length: 1,000-3,000 words. Payment open to discussion.

Poetry: Avant-garde, free verse, haiku, light verse and traditional (*all* about the beach). Buys 3-5 poems/issue. Send poems. Payment open to discussion.

COASTLINE MAGAZINE, P.O. Box 914, Culver City CA 90230. (213)839-7847. Editor/Publisher: Robert M. Benn. For zone 9 audience in major urban complexes; age 24-48. Quarterly magazine; 64 pages. Estab: 1973. Rights purchased vary with author and material. May buy all rights, with the possibility of reassigning rights to author after publication, first North American serial rights, first serial rights, or second serial (reprint) rights. Pays on publication. Will send sample copy to writer for $1. Write for editorial guidelines sheet. Will consider photocopied submissions. No simultaneous submissions. Reports on mss accepted for publication in 3 to 7 weeks. Returns rejected mss in 4 to 6 weeks. Query first. Enclose S.A.S.E.

Nonfiction: Department Editor: Stephen Lawrence Berger. Will consider mss about regional lifestyles, investigative articles (municipal to international); socially significant trends in the arts (reviews, columns, events); and expanded print/electronic media-related mss. Establishment, avant-garde approach. Writer should study sample copy and contributor guidelines before submitting. Favors regional artists and writers. "We favor in-depth over gimmick and consider all, not merely a portion of our region." Interested in non-specific promotion of travel, restaurants and specific city cultural events. Length: 400 to 6,000 words. Pays $10 to $600. Length preferred for regular columns: 200 to 300 words. Pays minimum of $45.

Photos: Contact: Art Director. Purchased with ms with extra payment, without ms, or on assignment. Captions required. B&w only. Pays $5 to $25. Size: 8x10 b&w glossies or very clear 35mm transparencies.

Fiction and Poetry: Poetry Editor: Charles Price. Uses "significant fiction (especially novel excerpts); and major poetry tied in with West Coast slant." Buys experimental, mainstream, erotica, science fiction, humorous, historical, condensed novels and serialized novels. Length: 500 to 4,000 words. Pays $25 minimum. Buys blank verse, free verse, traditional forms, and avant-garde forms of poetry. Length: 4 to 50 lines (2 columns wide). Pays $5 to $50.

COLORADO MAGAZINE, Titsch Publication, Inc., 1139 Delaware Plaza, Suite 200, Denver CO 80204. (303)573-1433. Editor-in-Chief: Paul S. Maxwell. Managing Editor: Rich Marschner. Emphasizes the scenic/lifestyle Rocky Mountain West, (Colorado, Wyoming, Utah, Montana, Idaho, New Mexico, Nevada and Arizona only). Bimonthly magazine; 100 pages. Estab: 1965. Circ: 175,000. Pays on acceptance. Buys all rights (one-time rights for photos). Submit seasonal/holiday material 3-6 months in advance. Simultaneous, photocopied and previously published submissions OK. SASE. Reports in 4 weeks. Free sample copy and writer's guidelines.
Nonfiction: Historical (old West); how-to (Rocky Mt. flavor); informational (useful 'where-to' lifestyle); personal experience (adventure, sports, recreation); photo feature; and profile ("Faces"—people who are fascinating and from the Western states). Buys 5-8 mss/issue. Query or send complete ms. Length: 1,500-2,500 words. Pays 12¢/word.
Photos: Ann Tait, Photo Editor. Photos purchased with or without accompanying ms or on assignment. Captions required. Uses b&w and 35mm color photos. Total purchase price for a ms includes payment for photos. Model release required. "Attractive views of Western mountains, lakes, streams, ranches, ghost towns, sunsets, flowers, animals, outdoor sports."

COMMONWEALTH, Virginia State Chamber of Commerce, 611 E. Franklin St., Richmond VA 23219. (804)643-7491. Editor-in-Chief: James S. Wamsley. Emphasizes Virginia. Monthly magazine; 48 pages. Estab: 1934. Circ: 11,000. Pays on publication. Buys all rights, but may reassign following publication. Submit seasonal/holiday material 4 months in advance. Photocopied submissions OK. SASE. Reports in 6 weeks. Sample copy 75¢.
Nonfiction: Informational; historical; humor; interview; nostalgia; profile; travel; and photo feature. Buys 25-30 mss/year. Query or submit complete ms. Length: 1,200-3,000 words. Pays $75-150.
Photos: Purchased with or without accompanying ms or on assignment. Captions required. Query. Pays $5-10 for 8x10 b&w glossy prints; $50 maximum for 35mm color transparencies.
How To Break In: "Very difficult for a non-Virginian, or one not familiar with the magazine. We always need good ideas but find most outside freelancers want to provide subjects which are cliches to our readers."

CUE MAGAZINE, 545 Madison Ave., New York NY 10022. (212)371-6900. Editor-in-Chief: Jeremiah E. Flynn. Emphasizes leisure and entertainment for sophisticated New Yorkers knowledgeable in all areas of the arts. Biweekly magazine; 144 pages. Estab: 1935. Circ: 300,000. Pays on publication. Buys all rights, but may reassign to author following publication or buys first North American serial rights. Phone queries OK. Submit seasonal/holiday material 2 months in advance. SASE. Reports in 2 weeks. Free sample copy.
Nonfiction: Informational, interview and travel. Buys 3 mss/issue. Query. Length: 500-2,500. Pays $100 minimum.
Photos: Judy Greer, Photo Editor. Purchased with accompanying ms. Query for photos. Offers no additional payment for 8x10 b&w/color photos accepted with accompanying ms. Model release required.

D MAGAZINE, Dallas Southwest Media Corp., 2902 Carlisle, Dallas, TX 75204. Editor-in-Chief: Wick Allison. Managing Editor: Gay Yellen. For readers in the Dallas metropolitan area; primarily the middle to upper income group. Monthly magazine; 136 pages. Estab: 1974. Circ: 45,000. Pays on publication. Buys all rights. Submit seasonal/holiday material 2 months in advance. Photocopied submissions OK. SASE. Reports in 1 month. Sample copy $2.
Nonfiction: Informational; new product; profile; travel and business. Buys 2-3 mss/issue. Query. Length: 750-4,000 words. Pays $50-400.
Photos: Photos purchased with accompanying ms or on assignment. Pays $25-150 for 8x10 b&w glossies; $50-150 for color transparencies. Model release required.
Columns/Departments: Keeping Up (arts, entertainment, books, movies, and concert reviews); Everybody's Business (business and gossip); Dining (reviews); Back Page (personal observation); Windfalls (special products and services). "All pieces must relate to Dallas and the Fort Worth area." Open to suggestions for new columns/departments.

DELAWARE TODAY MAGAZINE, 2401 Pennsylvania Ave., Wilmington DE 19806. (302)655-1571. Editor-in-Chief: Leondard A. Quinn. Monthly magazine; 68 pages. Estab: 1962. Circ: 8,000. Pays on publication. Buys all rights, but may reassign following publication. Submit seasonal/holiday material 3 months in advance. Photocopied submissions OK. SASE. Reports in 4-6 weeks. Free sample copy.
Nonfiction: Expose, historical, informational, inspirational, interview, new product, nostalgia, personal experience, profile, arts/crafts, hobbies and fashion. "The material must always relate to Delaware; it must have substance and holding power. Contemporary articles on social or

political issues will be considered as well as consumer, ecological and economic pieces that are bright in style and locally oriented, especially in-depth, well-researched work." Buys 65 mss/year. Query or send complete ms. Length: 500-6,000 words. Pays $15-200.

Photos: Purchased with accompanying manuscript. Captions required. Pays $5-50 for b&w; $5-50 for color. Query for photos. Total purchase price for ms includes payment for photos. Model release required.

DELTA SCENE, Box B-3, Delta State University, Cleveland MS 38733. (601)846-1976. Editor-in-Chief: Dr. Curt Lamar. Managing Editor: Ms. Cary Thomas Cefalu. For an art-oriented or history-minded audience wanting more information (other than current events) on the Delta region. Quarterly magazine; 32 pages. Estab: 1973. Circ: 700. Pays on publication. Buys one-time rights. Submit seasonal/holiday material at least 4 months in advance. Simultaneous, photocopied, and previously published submissions OK. SASE. Reports in 2 weeks. Sample copy 50¢.

Nonfiction: Historical and informational articles; interviews, profiles and travel articles; technical articles (particularly in reference to agriculture). "We have a list of articles available free to anyone requesting a copy." Buys 2-3 mss/issue. Query. Length: 1,000-2,000 words. Pays $5-20.

Photos: Purchased with or without ms, or on assignment. Pays $5-15 for 5x7 b&w glossies or any size color transparency.

Fiction: Humorous and mainstream. Buys 1/issue. Submit complete ms. Length: 1,000-2,000 words. Pays $10-20.

Poetry: Traditional forms, free verse and haiku. Buys 1/issue. Submit unlimited number. Pays $5-10.

DENVER MAGAZINE, Stevens Publishing, 8000 E. Girard, Suite 210, Denver CO 80231. (303)755-1296. Editor-in-Chief: Jan Golab. For an urban, well-educated audience interested in all aspects of contemporary living. Monthly; 74 pages. Estab: 1971. Circ: 25,000. Pays on publication. Buys all rights, but may reassign following publication. Submit seasonal/holiday material 3 months in advance. Photocopied submissions OK. SASE. Reports in 1 month. Sample copy $1.35.

Nonfiction: Expose (anything that is a genuine scoop); informational (anything that will enhance life; happiness and well-being of Denver and Colorado residents; where to go, what to do, etc.) interviews and profiles (famous Coloradoans). Buys 70 mss/year. Query. Length: 1,000-5,000 words. Pays $50-250.

Photos: B&w and color used with or without mss, or on assignment. No additional payment. Query.

Fillers: Clippings, jokes, gags, anecdotes, newsbreaks, short humor for "Town Square", the newsletter section of the magazine. Buys 10/year. Send fillers in. Length: 25-500 words. Pays $10-25.

How To Break In: "Queries are very important. *Denver* is always searching for an exciting story idea. A talented writer with a *great* idea is far more likely to break in than one without. We look for excitement, flair and punch in writing style. Newspaper copy will not do. Knowledge of local trends is obviously necessary, and many stories require extensive local contact."

DOWN EAST MAGAZINE, Bayview St., Camden ME 04843. (207)236-4354. Editor-in-Chief: Dave Thomas. Emphasizes Maine people, places and events. Monthly (except December & February) magazine; 116 pages. Estab: 1954. Circ: 70,000. Pays on acceptance. Buys first North American serial rights. Phone queries OK. Submit seasonal/holiday material at least 6 months in advance. SASE. Reports in 3 weeks. Free sample copy and writer's guidelines.

Nonfiction: Dale Kuhnert, Articles Editor. Historical; humor (clean); informational; interview (in-depth profile); nostalgia and photo feature (limited); Buys 6-8 mss/issue. Query or send complete ms. Length: 1,200-2,400 words. Pays $75 and up depending on subject and quality.

Photos: Norman Gibbons, Photo Editor. Purchased with accompanying ms or on assignment. Captions required. Pays $5 minimum for 4x5 or 8x10 b&w; $5 minimum for 35mm, 2¼ transparencies, 4x5 or larger color prints. Total purchase price for ms includes payment for photos (text/photos figured separately). Model release required.

Columns/Departments: Dale Kuhnert, Column/Department Editor. "Room With A View" (800-word essay—usually first person experience); "I Remember" (short nostalgic piece with 1 photo—200-300 words at most); "It Happened Down East" (humorous, short piece—1 to 2 paragraphs). Buys 3-4 mss/issue. Send complete ms. Pay depends on subject and length.

THE DRUMMER, 4221 Germantown Ave., Philadelphia PA 19140. Editor: Bob Ingram. Tabloid newspaper; 24 pages. Established in 1967. Weekly. Circulation: 60,000. Rights purchased vary with author and material. Usually buys all rights, but will reassign rights to author after publication. Buys about 50 mss a year. Pays on publication. Will send free sample copy to writer on request. Will consider photocopied submissions. No simultaneous submissions. Reports as soon as possible. Query first. Enclose S.A.S.E.

Nonfiction and Photos: "Articles that, we hope, will either edify or entertain, with a decided emphasis on Philadelphia. This emphasis is most important. We like clarity and brevity and would prefer not to see think pieces." Interview, profile, humor, expose. Length: 750 to 1,000 words. Pays $5 to $50. 8x10 b&w glossies purchased with or without ms. Pays $5 to $10.

EMPIRE STATE REPORT, 99 Washington Ave., Albany NY 12210. Editor: Timothy B. Clark. For taxpayers and others with an interest in New York State government and politics. Monthly magazine; 40 pages. Estab: 1974. Circ: 6,500. Rights purchased vary with author and material. Usually buys all rights, but may reassign rights to author after publication. Buys about 70 mss/year. Pays on acceptance. Will send free sample copy to writer on request. Will consider photocopied and simultaneous submissions. Reports in 3 weeks. Query first or submit complete ms. Enclose S.A.S.E.

Nonfiction: Uses well-researched articles on issues, such as welfare, environment, taxes, energy, labor relations. Also uses some articles on politics. All must concern New York State. Would like to see political-economic profiles of major cities and counties of New York State. Length: 1,000 to 7,000 words. Payment is negotiated on an individual basis.

ENCHANTMENT MAGAZINE, 614 Don Gaspar Ave., Santa Fe NM 87501. (505)982-4671. Editor: John Whitcomb. For diversified audience. Established in 1950. Monthly. Circulation: 65,000. Rights purchased vary with author and material. May buy all rights, with the possibility of returning rights to author after publication, or second serial reprint rights, or simultaneous rights. Buys 12 to 15 mss per year. Pays on publication. Will send free sample copy to writer on request. Will consider photocopied and simultaneous submissions. Reports as soon as possible. Enclose S.A.S.E.

Nonfiction, Fiction and Photos: Buys historical features about rural New Mexico. Also occasional short stories on wide range of subjects. Length: 600-1,200 words. Pays $15 maximum. Photos purchased with accompanying ms with extra payment. Captions required. Pays $5. B&w only.

FAIRFIELD COUNTY MAGAZINE, County Communications, Inc., Playhouse Square, Box 269, Westport, CT 06880. (203)227-3706. Editor-in-Chief: Elizabeth Hill O'Neil. Emphasizes regional material of interest to high-salaried, well-educated readers. Monthly magazine; 72-96 pages. Estab: 1959. Circ: 26,500. Pays on publication. Buys all rights, but may reassign rights following publication. Phone queries OK. Submit seasonal/holiday material 3-4 months in advance. Photocopied submissions OK. SASE. Reports in 3 weeks. Sample copy $1.

Nonfiction: How-to, informational, historical, interview, profile, travel. Buys 5 mss/issue. Query. Length: 750-2,000 words. Pays $50-200.

Photos: Photos purchased with accompanying ms or on assignment. Pays $15-30 for 5x7 b&w glossies. Color photos for cover only. Total purchase price for ms includes payment for photos.

Columns/Departments: Travel, Nature, Sports, Music, Books, At Home, Executive Profile, and Lifestyle. Buys 3-4 mss/issue. Query. Length: 750-1,000 words. Pays $75-150. Open to suggestions for new columns/departments.

How To Break In: "Make your presence known, via resume or phone call. Tell of any specialty or experience. Write on-target articles."

FIESTA MAGAZINE, 140 N. Federal Hghwy., P.O. Box 820,. Boca Raton, FL 33432. Editor: Paul T. Hutchens. For a Gold Coast of Florida audience. Monthly magazine; 64 to 80 pages. Estab: 1970. Circ: 20,000. Buys simultaneous rights provided articles are not submitted to other south Florida periodicals or newspapers. Buys about 130 mss a year. Pays on publication. Will send free sample copy to writer on request. Will consider photocopied and simultaneous submissions. Submit seasonal material 3 months in advance. Reports on material accepted for publication in 60 days. Returns rejected material in 30 days. Submit complete ms. Enclose S.A.S.E.

Nonfiction: "Our general subject matter is regionally oriented to the south Florida area. We prefer articles with historical, cultural, or social slants. They should have a local color approach. Above all, we prefer historical vignettes about events that occurred in our region. Topical subjects are covered by local writers who are close to the south Florida pulse." Pays approximately $30 per ms.

FOCUS/MIDWEST, 928a N. McKnight, St. Louis MO 63132. Editor: Charles L. Klotzer. For an educated audience in Illinois, Missouri and the Midwest. Magazine; 28 to 42 (8½x11) pages.

Established in 1962. Every 2 months. Circulation: 7,500. Buys all rights. Pays on publication. Reports in 4-6 weeks. SASE.

Nonfiction: Controversial articles; main emphasis on Illinois and Missouri. Facts, interpretation, analyses presenting political, social, cultural and literary issues on the local, regional and national scene of direct interest to the reader in or observer of the Midwest. Informational, interview, profile, think pieces. Length: open. Pays minimum of $25.

Poetry: Blank verse and free verse. Length: open. Pays minimum of $10.

GLIMPSES OF MICRONESIA AND THE WESTERN PACIFIC (formerly *Glimpses of Guam*), Box 3191, Agana, Guam 96910. Editor-in-Chief: Robert Kiener. "A regional publication for Micronesia lovers, travel buffs and readers interested in the United States' last frontier. Our audience covers all age levels and is best described as well-educated and fascinated by our part of the world." Quarterly magazine; 80 pages. Estab: 1974. Circ: 15,000. Pays on publication. Buys one-time rights. Submit seasonal/holiday material 8 months in advance. Previously published work OK. SASE. Reports in 2 weeks. Sample copy $2; free writer's guidelines.

Nonfiction: Expose (well-documented of Micronesian cover-ups; mismanagement of funds, etc. CIA bugging is recent example); historical (anything related to Micronesia and the Western Pacific that is lively and factual); interviews; personal experience (first person adventure as in our recently published piece about 1,000 open-ocean outrigger canoe trip across Micronesia). Photo features (very photo-oriented magazine—query us on Island or Pacific themes); profiles (of outstanding Micronesian or Western Pacific individuals—e.g., looking for Lee Marvin's relationship with Micronesia); travel (use one/issue about areas reachable from Micronesia). Buys 30 mss/year. Query. Length: 5,000 words maximum. Pays 5¢/word.

Photos: Thomas E. Walsh, Jr., Photo Editor. Purchased with or without accompanying ms. Pays minimum of $10 for 8x10 b&w prints or 4x5 color transparencies or 35mm slides. Captions required. Model release required.

Fiction: Adventure (believable; related to Micronesia); historical (as long as it's related to our part of the world). Buys 2 mss/year. "Most fiction is rejected because of poor quality." Submit complete ms. Length: 4,000 words maximum. Pays 10¢/word.

Poetry: "Use very little, but willing to look at Pacific-related themes to be used with photos." Only traditional forms. Pays $10 minimum.

How To Break In: "Writers living in or having first-hand experience with Micronesia and the Western Pacific are scarce. (That's because we *truly* are the United States' last frontier). Therefore, we'll work with a writer on making his manuscript suitable for publishing in *Glimpses*. If a writer has a good idea and is willing to work, we have the time to spare."

GULFSHORE LIFE, Gulfshore Publishing Co., Inc., 1039 Fifth Ave., N., Naples FL 33940. (813)649-9125. Editor: Jean Clarke Denmead. For an upper income audience; largely retirees of varied business and academic backgrounds. Published monthly, November through April. Magazine; 48 pages. Established in 1970. Circulation: 15,000. Buys all rights, with permission in writing to reproduce. Buys 6 mss a year. Payment on publication. Will not consider photocopied or simultaneous submissions. Submit seasonal material 3 months in advance. Reports on material accepted for publication within 4 months. Returns rejected material as soon as possible. Query first. Enclose S.A.S.E.

Nonfiction: "Basically personal journalism of people, sports, homes, boats; pinpointing all features to seasonal residents, year-round residents and visitors. Travel, fishing, environmental articles are also used, but must be tied into personalities. Platinum Coast community activities. Emphasis on "at home" life styles. Yachting, personality profiles; some historical material. Everything must be localized in line with our personal journalism concept." Length: 500 to 1,000 words. Pays $15 to $50.

How To Break In: "Only to be on location: Naples, Marco Island, Ft. Myers, Ft. Myers Beach, Sanibel-Captiva, Whiskey Creek, Punta Gorda Isles, Port Charlotte."

HOUSTON, Houston Chamber of Commerce, 1100 Milam Bldg., 25th Floor, Houston TX 77002. Editor: Richard Stanley. Emphasizes the Houston business community. Monthly magazine; 64-90 pages. Estab: 1929. Circ: 15,000. Pays on acceptance or publication. Buys all rights. Phone queries OK, "but prefer mail." Submit seasonal/holiday material 2-3 months in advance. Photocopied submissions OK. SASE. Reporting time varies; "writer should contact us sometime after query." Free sample copy.

Nonfiction: How-to (managing a company, starting a business, motivating employees, etc.); informational (on economy, business, people, etc.); interview; profile (on business people); travel (include economy and business attitudes of destination); and new product. Buys 12 mss/year. Query. Length: 30-120 inches. Pays $30-300. "Experienced business writers needed for assignment stories on such topics as oil, aviation, housing, banking, etc. We encourage ideas about individuals or firms in Houston's business community. Profiles and success stories preferable."

How To Break In: "Best chance for a freelancer who has expertise in a specific area of business, or who has many good contacts in the Houston business community."

HOUSTON SCENE MAGAZINE, 3600 Yoakum, Houston TX 77006. (713)529-2131. Editor: Elroy Forbes. For creative people interested in the arts, entertainment and the people involved in them. Estab: 1972. Monthly. Circ: 30,000. Buys all rights, but may reassign rights to author after publication. Buys about 20 mss/year. Pays on publication. Free sample copy and editorial guidelines sheet. Submit seasonal material 1 month in advance. SASE.

Nonfiction, Photos and Poetry: Buys profiles; antiques articles; mss about music, art; and how-to stories. Wants direct, to-the-point writing. "A photo is used if it saves words." Does not want to see record reviews. Would like to see more humorous mss. Length: 2-3 double-spaced, typed pages. Pays minimum of $5. Photos purchased with ms with no additional payment. Captions optional. Pays $5 for b&w glossies. No color. Will consider free verse and avant-garde forms of poetry. Length: "short." Pays $5.

HUDSON VALLEY MAGAZINE, Suburban Publishing Inc., Box 265, Main St., Pleasant Valley NY 12569. (914)635-8822. Editor: Marilyn Bontempo. Managing Editor: Ron Rozman. Emphasizes regional entertainment and leisure. Monthly magazine; 42 pages. Estab: 1972. Circ: 22,000. Pays 2-4 weeks after publication. Buys all or first North American serial rights. Submit seasonal/holiday material 2-3 months in advance. Simultaneous and photocopied submissions OK. SASE. Reports in 4-6 weeks. Sample copy $1; free writer's guidelines.

Nonfiction: All types of articles if regionally oriented to Hudson Valley. Buys 1-4 mss/issue. Query with tentative short outline and sample tentative introduction. Send samples of previous work. Length: 1,200-3,000 words. Pays 3¢/word.

Photos: Purchased on assignment. Uses b&w; payment depends on assignment. Query for photos. Offers no additional payment for photos accepted with accompanying ms. Model release required.

Fillers: Jokes, cartoons. Buys 1-2 fillers/issue. Send fillers. Pays about $5/cartoon.

ILLINOIS ISSUES, Sangamon State University, 226 CC, Springfield IL 62708. Publisher: William L. Day. Managing Editor: Caroline Gherardini. Emphasizes Illinois government and issues for state and local government officials and staff plus citizens and businessmen concerned with Illinois and its government (local government also). Monthly magazine; 32 pages. Estab: 1975. Circ: 4,500. Pays on publication. Buys all rights. Submit seasonal/holiday material 4 months in advance. SASE. Reports in 4 weeks. Sample copy $1.50; free writer's guidelines.

Nonfiction: How-to (use state services and processes as a citizen); informational (explaining state/local government agency in Illinois, detailing new process initiated by state legislation, city or county ordinance); interview (Illinois government or political leaders) and technical (relating to government policy, services with issues stressed, i.e., energy). Buys 7 mss/issue. Query. Length: 800-2,500 words (best chance: 1,200 words). Pays 5¢-10¢/word.

How To Break In: "Local issues tied to state government in Illinois have a good chance, but writer must research to know state laws, pending legislation and past attempts that relate to the issue."

INDIANAPOLIS MAGAZINE, 320 N. Meridian St., Indianapolis IN 46204. (317)635-4747. Editor: Craig J. Beardsley. Publication of the Indianapolis Chamber of Commerce for members and others interested in Indianapolis. Established in 1964. Monthly. Buys first rights. Buys about 50 mss a year. Pays on publication. Will consider photocopied submissions. Seasonal material should be sent 6 months in advance. Reports on material within 10 days. Query first, "but if story is already completed, mail it on in." Enclose S.A.S.E.

Nonfiction and Photos: In-depth features of and about Indianapolis. Also interested in people who once lived in Indianapolis. Controversial articles welcomed, but must have Indianapolis-oriented slant to them. Anything that deals with informational, how-to, personal experience, interview, profile, humor, historical, think pieces, exposes, nostalgia, personal opinion, travel, successful business operations, new product, merchandising techniques. Length: 500 to 5,000 words. Pays $100 and as high as $200 for an exceptional article. Editor will make arrangements for photography after ms has been accepted. Uses both b&w and color photos. Pays between $50 and $100.

Fiction and Fillers: Uses very little fiction, unless it's Indianapolis oriented. Short (500 to 1,500 words) humor pieces welcome. Pays $50 to $100.

THE IRON WORKER, Lynchburg Foundry (A Mead Company), Drawer 411, Lynchburg VA 24501. (804)847-1724. Editor-in-Chief: Patrick M. Early. Emphasizes the iron industry and Virginia history for customers of the Lynchburg Foundry and, to a lesser extent, the general public. Quarterly magazine; 28 pages. Estab: 1919. Circ: 10,000. Pays on acceptance. Buys all rights. Submit seasonal/holiday material 1 year in advance. Simultaneous and photocopied submissions OK. SASE. Reports in 3 months. Free sample copy and writer's guideline.
Nonfiction: Historical—Virginia-related history with national appeal; well-documented; action-oriented stories on previously unresearched subjects. Buys 6 mss/year. Query. Length: 2,500-5,000 words. Pays $200-600.

JACKSONVILLE MAGAZINE, P.O. Drawer 329, Jacksonville FL 32201. (904)353-6161. For civic-minded, concerned community types; business, community oriented interest, Jacksonville subjects. Estab: 1963. Bimonthly. Circ: 7,000. Buys all rights, Buys 20 to 25 mss/year. Pays on publication. Query. Submit seasonal material 3 to 6 months in advance. Reports in 3 weeks. Enclose S.A.S.E.
Nonfiction and Photos: Buys historical, photo, business articles. Length: usually 1,500 to 3,000 words. Pays $50 to $150. "We accept b&w glossies, good contrast; color transparencies." Pays $15 minimum for b&w; color terms to be arranged.

JAPANOPHILE, Box 223, Okemos MI 48864. Editor: Earl R. Snodgrass. For people who have visited Japan or are interested in Japan; all ages. Magazine; 50 (7x10) pages. Established in 1974. Quarterly. Circulation: 800. Rights purchased vary with author and material. Buys all rights, but will reassign rights to author after publication; buys first North American serial rights; second serial (reprint) rights. Buys 50 mss a year. Pays on acceptance. Sample copy $1.75; free writer's guidelines. Will consider photocopied and simultaneous submissions. Submit seasonal material (each issue is built around a season) 4 months in advance. Reports in 2 months. Query preferred, but not required. Enclose S.A.S.E.
Nonfiction and Photos: Department Editors: Robert Cavera (nonfiction); Robert Copland (photos). "Articles that have to do with Japan or Japanese culture. We welcome material about Americans and other non-Japanese who practice a Japanese art in their own country. Hawaii, Los Angeles, and other locations have activity in the Japanese arts as well as Tokyo. Stories must be informed and accurate. We would like more on how Japan retains its culture and tradition while becoming a modern nation." Buys informational, personal experience, interview, profile, inspirational, humor, historical, think articles, nostalgia, personal opinion, photo, travel, book and film reviews, successful business operations. Length: 1,200 words maximum. Pays $5 to $20. Regular columns and features are San Francisco Scene, Tokyo Scene and Profiles of Artists. Length 1,000 words. Pays $20 maximum. Photos purchased with or without accompanying ms. Captions required. Pays $5 for b&w.
Fiction, Poetry, and Fillers: Department Editors: Earl Snodgrass (fiction and fillers); Carol Schumacher (poetry). Experimental, mainstream, mystery, adventure, science fiction, humorous, romance, and historical. Themes should relate to Japan. Length: 1,000 to 3,000 words. Pays $20. "We particularly need profiles of people practicing Japanese art forms, and well-written short stories with a setting in Japan." Traditional forms of poetry; avant-garde forms, and light verse. Should relate to Japan and to a season. Length: 3 to 50 lines. Pays $1 to $10. Newsbreaks, puzzles, clippings, short humor. Length: 200 words maximum. Pays $1 to $5.

KANSAS CITY MAGAZINE, Box 2298, Shawnee Mission KS 66201. (913)384-0770. Editor-in-Chief: Floyd E. Sageser. Managing Editor: Steve Cameron. Emphasizes Kansas City lifestyle and business. Monthly; 64 pages. Estab: 1976. Circ: 16,000. Pays on publication. Buys one-time rights. Phone queries OK. Submit seasonal/holiday material 90 days in advance. Simultaneous and photocopied submissions OK. SASE. Reports in 3 weeks. Sample copy $1.
Nonfiction: Expose, historical, informational, interview, nostalgia, photo feature and profile. Buys 4 mss/issue. Query. Pays 5¢/word.
Photos: Captions required. Pays $10 minimum for 5x7 or 8x10 b&w glossies; $25 minimum for color. Query for photos.

LAS VEGAS REVIEW-JOURNAL, Donrey Media Group, Inc., Box 70, Las Vegas NV 89101. (702)385-4241. Editor-in-Chief: Don Digilio. Emphasizes stories about Nevada, either a timely or interesting feature or a historical piece. "We accept freelance work only for our Sunday Nevada magazine." Daily newspaper; 64 pages. Circ: 72,000. Pays on publication. Buys all rights, but may reassign following publication. Phone queries OK. Submit seasonal/holiday material 1 month in advance. Photocopied submissions OK. SASE. Reports in 1 month. Free sample copy.

Nonfiction: Bill Vincent, Nonfiction Editor. Historical (on Nevada only); how-to; informational; interview; photo feature (on Nevada only). Send complete ms. Length: 800 words. Pays $30 minimum.

Photos: Rene Germanier, Photo Editor. Photos purchased with accompanying ms. Captions required. Pays $10 minimum for 8x10 b&w glossies; $10 minimum for color photos. Send prints and transparencies.

LOS ANGELES MAGAZINE, 1888 Century Park East, Los Angeles CA 90067. Editor: Geoff Miller. Monthly. Buys first North American serial rights. Query first. Enclose S.A.S.E.

Nonfiction: Uses articles on how best to live (i.e., the quality of life) in the changing, growing, diverse Los Angeles urban-suburban area; ideas, people, and occasionally places. Writer must have an understanding of contemporary living and doing in Southern California; material must appeal to an upper-income, better-educated group of people. Fields of interest include urban problems, pleasures, personalities and cultural opportunities, leisure and trends, candid interviews of topical interest; the arts. Solid research and reportage required. No essays. Length: 1,000-3,000 words. Also uses some topical satire and humor. Pays 10¢/word minimum.

Photos: Buys photographs with mss. B&w should be 8x10. Pays $15-50 for single article photos.

How To Break In: "Prefer multiple ideas in a single query *letter,* briefly stated."

MADISON SELECT, 114 N. Carroll St., Madison WI 53703. Editor: Gertrude M. Struck. For business, civic and social leaders of Madison. Magazine; 32-40 pages. Estab: 1958. Monthly. Circ: 13,000. Buys all rights, but may reassign rights to author after publication. Buys 10 to 15 mss a year. Pays on publication. Will send sample copy to writer for $1. Reports on material accepted for publication 10 days after publication. Returns rejected material immediately. Query first. Enclose S.A.S.E.

Nonfiction and Photos: "Subjects of interest to the business, civic and social leaders in the Madison metropolitan area. We regularly review one aspect each of the business, arts, sports, society, fashion and travel scene. We like humor as well as serious material, as long as it relates to Madison or Madisonians." Length: 350 to 1,250. Pays $10 to $500. No additional payment for b&w photos used with mss. Pays $5 to $10 for b&w, $25 for color, when purchased without mss. Captions required.

MAINE LIFE, RFD 1, Liberty ME 04949. (207)589-4351. Editor: Dave Olson. For middle age and over, urban or rural, 70% Maine; balance in other states to persons who have either an interest or love for the state of Maine. Monthly magazine; 64 pages. Estab: 1946. Circ: 26,000. Rights purchased vary with author and material. May buy all rights, but will reassign rights to author after publication or second serial (reprint) rights. Buys 110 mss a year. Payment on publication. Will send sample copy to writer for 30¢ in stamps. Will consider photocopied submissions and simultaneous submissions. Submit seasonal material 2 months in advance. Reports in 1 week. Query first. Enclose S.A.S.E.

Nonfiction and Photos: "Largely historical (Maine), non-controversial 'good-news' type of publication. Slogan is "For Those Who Love Maine.' Down-to earth material; more general interest, historical type." Interview, profile, humor, historical, nostalgia, personal opinion. Length: 500 to 2,000 words. Pays $10 to $35. B&w photos purchased with accompanying ms. Captions required. Pays $2 to $3.

MAINE MAGAZINE, Box 494, Ellsworth ME 04605. (207)667-4616. Editor-in-Chief: John Buchanan. Emphasizes "editorial coverage of the state of Maine aimed at young professionals, 20-40 years old, who live in the state year-around." Monthly magazine; 84 pages. Estab: 1977. Circ: 30,000. Pays on acceptance. Buys first North American serial rights. Submit seasonal/ holiday material 3-4 months in advance. Photocopied submissions OK. Reports in 1 month. Sample copy $1.50; free writer's guidelines.

Nonfiction: Gunnar Hansen, Articles Editor. How-to (service features, particularly housing); informational (in-depth examination of what is happening in the state politically, economically, and socially); interview (mostly political); personal opinion (each month we feature a personal essay); and profile (mainly arts). Buys 7 mss/issue. Query. Length: 2,000-3,000 words. Pays $150-300.

Photos: Buddy Chase, Photo Editor. Purchased on assignment. Query. Uses 8x10 b&w glossy, 35mm and larger color transparencies. "We pay per assignment, not per photo." Offers no additional payment for photos purchased with accompanying ms.

Columns/Departments: Christine Plumer, Columns/Department Editor. Business (in-state business), Media, Arts (a specific artist or performing enterprise), Outdoors (what year-round residents can do; this far north it must be seasonal), Science, and Making It (on enterprises that are making it (or not) in Maine—and why). Buys 4 mss/issue. Query. Length: 1,000-1,500 words. Pays $125-150.

Fiction: Susan Knott, Fiction Editor. "Our main interest is mainstream, serious work, but we are willing to look at just about any quality work." Buys 1 mss/issue. Submit complete ms. Length: 2,500-4,000 words. Pays $150 minimum.

Poetry: Annabelle Robbins, Poetry Editor. Avant-garde and traditional. Buys 1 poem/issue. Limit submissions to batches of 4. Length: 60 lines maximum. Pays $20. "Quality! We get too much that isn't."

MARYLAND MAGAZINE, 2525 Riva Rd., Annapolis MD 21401. Editor: M. E. Dougherty. Published by the State's Department of Economic and Community Development. Quarterly. Established in 1968. Circulation: 19,500. Buys North American serial rights only. Buys about 30 mss a year. Pays on publication. Editorial deadlines 6 to 12 months in advance. Send S.A.S.E. for sample copy and author's or photographer's guidelines. Query first with outline. Reports in 6 to 8 weeks. Enclose S.A.S.E.

Nonfiction and Photos: Features exclusively places, events, and personages in Maryland. Articles on any facet of life in Maryland except conservation/ecology pieces. Well-researched agricultural, cultural, economic, ethnic, human interest, and travel-in-Maryland features. Length: 600-2,000 words. Pays 6¢ a word. Theme photos purchased with or without mss. Captions required. 8x10 b&w glossies; 35mm or 2¼x2¼ color transparencies. Pays $20 for b&w; $25 for color.

METRO, THE MAGAZINE OF SOUTHEAST VIRGINIA (formerly *Metro Hampton Roads Magazine*), Suite 304, Holiday Inn Scope, Norfolk VA 23510. (804)622-4122. Editor-in-Chief: St. Leger "Monty" Joynes. For urban adults with a concern for a lifestyle that provides cultural and social enrichment. Monthly magazine; 100 pages. Estab: 1970. Circ: 20,000. Pays on publication. Buys all rights, but may reassign following publication. Phone queries OK. Submit seasonal/holiday material 3 months in advance. Simultaneous, photocopied and previously published submissions OK. SASE. Reports in 2 weeks. Sample copy $1. Free writer's guidelines.

Nonfiction: Expose (regional controversies), historical (regional events, personalities), how-to (purchasing consumer goods), interview (regional), photo feature (society), and travel (major cities, sun and ski spots). Buys 4 mss/issue. Query. Length: 2,000-5,000 words. Pays $100-150.

Photo: Coco Smith, Photo Editor. Photos purchased with accompanying ms or on assignment. Captions required. Pays $25-100 for 8x10 b&w glossies. $50-150 for 35mm, 2¼x2¼ or 4x5 color transparencies. No additional payment for photos accepted with accompanying ms. Model release required.

Columns/Departments: Coco Smith, Columns/Departments Editor. Fashion (trends, male and female), Gourmet (restaurant reviews), Business (regional commentary), Books (by Southern authors), Arts (reviews, personalities), and Newsmakers. Buys 6 mss/issue. Query. Length: 1,000-1,750 words. Pays $75-100. Open to suggestions for new columns/departments.

How To Break In: "Know the city magazine genre. Have a dramatic approach to the subject. Review back issues of the publication. Nearly all features and photos pertain to the geographic region served by *Metro*. No generalized 'seat-of-the-pants' writing."

MIAMI MAGAZINE, 3361 S.W. Third Ave., Miami FL 33145. (305)856-5011. Executive Editor: James R. Kukar. For affluent, involved citizens of South Florida; generally well educated. Magazine. Established in 1975. Monthly. Circulation: 27,000. Rights purchased vary with author and material. Usually buys first publication rights. Buys about 200 mss a year. Pays on publication. Will send sample copy to writer for $1.50. Reports in 60 to 90 days. Query first or submit complete ms. Enclose S.A.S.E.

Nonfiction: Investigative pieces on the area; thorough, general features; sprightly, spirited writing. Informational, how-to, personal experience, interview, profile, humor, expose, travel. Length: 2,000 words maximum. Pays $100 minimum. Sports, wine and music columns use appropriate material for these departments. Length: 700 words maximum. Payment ranges from $25 to $50.

Fiction, Poetry and Fillers: Erotica and humorous fiction. Length: 700 to 900 words. Pays $15 to $200. Traditional and avant-garde forms of poetry, blank verse, free verse, light verse and haiku. Length: 14 to 80 lines. Pays $10 to $50. Jokes, gags, anecdotes and short humor used as fillers. Length: 100 to 1,000 words. Pays $10 to $20.

MPLS. MAGAZINE, Realization, Inc., 512 Nicollet Mall, Minneapolis MN 55402. (612)339-7571. Editor-in-Chief: Bill Kienzle. For "people of upper middle income; 25-49 years old; residing in Minneapolis areas of known affluence." Monthly magazine; 88 pages. Estab: 1971. Circ: 25,000. Pays on publication. Buys one-time rights. Phone queries OK. Submit seasonal/holiday material 4 months in advance. Simultaneous and photocopied submissions OK. SASE. Reports in 3 weeks. Free sample copy and writer's guidelines.

Nonfiction: Expose; how-to; informational; historical; humor; interview; profile; new product; and photo feature. "We can use any of these as long as they are Minneapolis-related." Buys 3 mss/issue. Query. Length: 800-4,000 words. Pays $20-200.

Photos: Ann Sundet, Photo Editor. Purchased on assignment. Query. Pays $25-100 for b&w; $25-150 for color.

Fiction: Adventure; historical; serialized novels. Buys 2 mss/year. Query. Length: 2,000 words. Pays $100 minimum.

Fillers: Kate Richardson, Fillers Editor. Clippings, newsbreaks. Buys one filler/issue. Length: 250 words. Pays $50.

MISSOURI LIFE, 1209 Elmerine Ave., Jefferson City MO 65101. (314)635-4011. Editor: W. R. Nunn. For readers whose ages range from the upper twenties to retirees; education varies from high school to Ph.D's. Occupations range from farmers to professionals, such as doctors, lawyers, engineers, etc. Bimonthly magazine; 56 (9x12) pages. Estab: 1973. Circ: 33,000. Buys all rights, but will reassign rights to author after publication. Buys 20 mss a year. Payment on publication. Sample copy $2.50. Will consider photocopied and simultaneous submissions. Submit seasonal material 3 months in advance. Reports on material in 3 weeks. Query first or submit complete ms. Enclose S.A.S.E.

Nonfiction and Photos: "Almost any kind of material if it's about Missouri or Missourians. History, travel, recreation, human interest, personality profiles, business, scenic, folklore. The emphasis is on the approach and quality. Because it is a bimonthly, *Missouri Life* must look for the different angle, the human interest, the long-lasting information and appeal, the time-lessness of quality and beauty. Prospective contributors would best be guided by recent issues of *Missouri Life*." Does not want to see "the stereotyped Ozark hillbilly piece, the travelogue with no feel of the country, the 'social message'." Seasonal material should have a different approach, with a seasonal flavor. Back issues are the best reference. Length: 1,200 to 2,500 words. 8x10 b&w glossy prints and color transparencies purchased with mss. Pays $50 for ms with b&w; $75 for mss with color transparencies; more if exceptional.

MONTANA MAGAZINE, Box 5630, Helena MT 59601. (406)443-2842. Editor: Rick Graetz. For residents of Montana and out of state residents with an interest in Montana. Estab: 1970. Quarterly. Pays on publication. Will send sample copy to writer for $1. Write for copy of guidelines for writers. Will consider photocopied and simultaneous submissions. Reports in 8 weeks. Query first. Enclose S.A.S.E.

Nonfiction and Photos: Articles on life in Montana; history, recreation. "How-to, where and when type articles." Limited usage of material on Glacier and Yellowstone National Park. Prefers articles on less publicized areas. Informational, profile, think pieces, nostalgia, travel, history. Length varies. Pays $20-35 for short articles with b&w photos; $35-125 for longer articles and accompanying b&w photos. Photo size: 5x7 or 8x10. "We can make b&w photos from color transparencies at a cost of $5 each. This amount would be deducted from the fee for the article."

MONTREAL CALENDAR MAGAZINE, 300 Place d' Youville, Montreal, Quebec, Canada H2Y 2B6. (514)844-3931. Editor: James Chouinard. For an audience in the top 25% income bracket in Montreal. Magazine; 80 pages. Established in 1971. Monthly. Circulation: 100,000. Buys all rights, but may reassign rights to author after publication. Buys about 30 mss a year. Pays on acceptance. Will send free sample copy to writer on request. Will consider photocopied and simultaneous submissions. Submit seasonal material 1 month in advance. Reports in 2 weeks. Query first or submit complete ms. Enclose S.A.E. and International Reply Coupons.

Nonfiction: Informational, how-to, personal experience, interview, humor, think pieces, expose and travel pieces. Articles on money and events for children. Theater, stage, movies, restaurant dining, shopping bag, clubs. "Be brief, to the point, and include all essential information: addresses, phones, prices, etc. — in essence, *digest*. And remember that we speak only of subjects of interest to people who live in Montreal. Will pay from $75 to $400, depending on length, and from there, it depends on professionalism."

NASHVILLE! Plus Media, Inc., 1 Vantage Way, Suite 238, Nashville TN 37228. (615)259-4600. Editor-in-Chief: C. Turney Stevens, Jr. For "upper middle class families who live in Nashville/Davidson County; business people, professionals in management positions; intelligent, educated, well-read." Monthly magazine; 100 pages. Estab: 1973. Circ: 15,500. Pays on publication. Phone queries OK. Submit seasonal/holiday material 4-5 months in advance. Simultaneous and photocopied submissions OK. SASE. Reports in 6-8 weeks. Sample copy $1.25; free writer's guidelines.

Nonfiction: Wayne Gurley, Articles Editor. Expose (politics, government); how-to (hobbies, gardening, recreational activities); historical (local only); interview; nostalgia; profile; travel; and business. Buys 80 mss/year. Query. Length: 2,000-4,000 words. Pays $75-200.

Photos: Don Milstead, Photo Editor. Purchased with or without accompanying ms or on assignment. Captions required. Query. Pays $5.50-15 for 5x7 or 8x10 b&w prints; $12.50-25 for 35mm or 2¼x2¼ color transparencies. Model release required.

Columns/Departments: Wayne Gurley, Column/Department Editor. Politics, People, Complete Consumer, Science, Medicine, After Hours (entertainment, recreation). Buys 36 mss/year. Query. Length: 1,500-2,500 words. Pays $75-125. Open to suggestions for new columns or departments.

NEVADA MAGAZINE, Carson City NV 89710. For travel or vacation-minded people. Quarterly. Buys North American serial rights only. Pays on publication. Query first. Enclose S.A.S.E.

Nonfiction and Photos: Nevada-related articles only. Pays $100 minimum, depending on quality and length. Photos of Nevada subject matter only; scenery, tours, recreation, activities such as ranching and mining; special events such as rodeos. Photos purchased with either mss or captions only. 4x5 color preferred; 35mm accepted. Pays $15 to $35 on acceptance for b&w prints; $20 minimum for color transparencies.

NEW ALASKAN, Rt. 1, Box 677, Ketchikan AK 99901. Editor: R. W. Pickrell. For residents of southeast Alaska. Tabloid magazine; 28 pages. Established in 1964. Monthly. Circulation: 15,000. Rights purchased vary with author and material. May buy all rights, but will reassign rights to author after publication; or second serial (reprint) rights. Buys about 40 mss a year. Pays on publication. Will send sample copy to writer for 40¢. Will consider photocopied submissions. Reports on material accepted for publication in 60 days. Returns rejected material in 60 to 80 days. Submit complete ms. Enclose S.A.S.E.

Nonfiction and Photos: Feature material about southeast Alaska. Emphasis is on full photo or art coverage of subject. Informational, how-to, personal experience, interview, profile, inspirational, humor, historical, nostalgia, personal opinion, travel, successful business operations, new product. Length: minimum of 1,000 words. Pays 1½¢ a word. B&w photos purchased with or without mss. Minimum size: 5x7. Pays $5 per glossy used. Pays $2.50 per negative (120 size preferred). Negatives are returned. Captions required.

Fiction: Historical fiction related to Alaska. Length: open. Pays 1½¢ per word.

NEW ENGLAND GALAXY, Old Sturbridge Village, Sturbridge MA 01565. Editor: Catherine Fennelly. For all ages, people interested in New England history and museums. Quarterly magazine; 60 pages, (5½x7½). Established in 1959. Circulation: 11,500. Rights purchased vary with author and material. Buys all rights, but will occasionally reassign rights to author after publication; buys first North American serial rights. Buys 26 mss a year. Payment on publication. Will send free sample copy to writer on request. Will consider photocopied submissions. Reports within 6 weeks. Query first for nonfiction. Enclose S.A.S.E.

Nonfiction and Photos: "Articles on any aspect of New England history, but not on a specific historic house open to the public. We're aimed at the general public, but emphasize the historical knowledge, original research and accuracy. We like to see the author's bibliography, which, however, will not be published." Biography, social customs, etc. Profile, historical, occasionally nostalgia articles. Length: 2,000 to 3,500 words. Pays $75 to $150. B&w photos purchased with or without ms. 8x10 photos of New England subjects. Pays $10.

Poetry and Fillers: Traditional forms, blank verse, and free verse. New England themes. Length: 6 to 30 lines. Pays $50. Pays $10 for quotes from New England historical sources.

THE NEW ENGLAND GUIDE, Stephen W. Winship & Co., Box 1108-12 Green St., Concord NH 03301. (603)224-4231. Editor-in-Chief: Stephen W. Winship. Detailed travelers'/vacationers' guide to New England. Annual magazine; 166 pages. Estab: 1958. Circ: 133,000. Pays on publication. Buys one-time rights. Deadline for queries is October 1. Reports in 2-3 weeks. Sample copy $1.50. Free writer's guidelines.

Nonfiction: Historical (New England subjects only, off-beat material preferred. "We didn't run a piece on Paul Revere's ride, but we did on the man who hung the lanterns"); humor (as an essay); informational (personal experience while traveling in New England, or a piece on a New

England institution, such as antiquing, auctions, country fairs); nostalgia (this is tricky going); and profile (of little known but unusual people). Buys 6 mss/issue. Query. Length: 400-700 words. Pays $40-75.

Fillers: Anecdotes "one paragraph long, short and sharp history info is preferred. These tend to have a bit of wry humor to them, and that is preferred." Buys 10 mss/year. Length: 20-110 words. Pays $10.

How To Break In: "There is such a vast reservoir of history, legend and folklore on New England that we want the more off-beat variety. We don't pan individuals, groups, or hotels. Writing is to a large extent expository and sources are needed."

NEW HAMPSHIRE PROFILES, 2 Reservoir Rd., Hanover NH 03755. (603)643-5505. Editor-in-Chief: Sharon L. Smith. For middle and upper income, college-educated homeowners who live in New Hampshire, did live in New Hampshire, or dream of living in New Hampshire. Monthly magazine; 80 pages. Estab: 1951. Circ: 16,000. Pays on publication. Buys first North American serial rights. Submit seasonal/holiday material 4 months in advance. Simultaneous submissions OK. SASE. Reports in 4 weeks. Sample copy 75¢; free writer's guidelines.

Nonfiction: Historical, how-to, humor, informational, nostalgia, photo feature, profile, travel (within the state), contemporary events/activities, antiques, natural history, country living, recreation and crafts. "New Hampshire material only." Buys 10 mss/issue. Query. Length: 1,500-2,000 words. Pays $50-100.

Photos: Purchased with accompanying ms, or with captions for photo essay. Captions required. Pays $5-10 for 8x10 b&w glossies; $25 minimum for 35mm color transparencies. Total purchase price for ms includes payment for photos. Model release required.

How To Break In: "We still cover many of the traditional subjects, but we're looking for new ways of treating the old stories, preferably by narrowing in on a single aspect. Country fairs, for instance, might be done from the angle of the young 4Her winning his first blue ribbon with his pet sheep, or (as we did recently) heating with wood could be approached as a photo essay on contrasting woodpiles. We do use color in each issue, but we deal much more with black and white. If you send color, your story has a much better chance of acceptance or better play in the magazine if you also include black and white."

NEW HAVEN INFO MAGAZINE, 53 Orange St., New Haven CT 06510. (203)562-5413. Editor: Sol D. Chain. For those interested in art, music, theater, recreational activities, etc. Monthly magazine; 40 (6x9) pages. Established in 1952. Circulation: 5,000. Not copyrighted. Buys 20 mss per year. Payment on publication. Will send sample copy to writer for 50¢. Will consider photocopied and simultaneous submissions. Reports on material accepted for publication in 30 days. Returns rejected material in 2 weeks. Query first. Enclose S.A.S.E.

Nonfiction: "Most of our material is on assignment. We publish articles dealing with New Haven area events and people." Personal experience, interview, profile, historical, nostalgia. Length: 350 to 700 words. Pays $10 per page (about 350 words).

NEW MEXICO MAGAZINE, Bataan Memorial Bldg., Santa Fe NM 87503. (505)827-2642. Editor-in-Chief: Sheila Tryk. Associate Editor: Richard Sandoval. Emphasizes the Southwest, especially New Mexico, for a college-educated readership above average income, interested in the Southwest. Monthly magazine; 48 pages. Estab: 1923. Circ: 80,000. Pays on acceptance for mss; on publication for photos. Buys first North American serial or one-time rights for photos/compilation. Submit seasonal/holiday material 8 months in advance. SASE. Reports in 10 days-4 weeks. Sample copy $1.

Nonfiction: How-to (Southwestern food, recipes; "how to build an outdoor oven"); informational (events, celebrations, parks, recreational interests); historical (little known or new light on New Mexico historical events); humor; interview; nostalgia (the way it was in the early days); personal experience (a greenhorn on a pack trip); profile; photo feature (New Mexico subjects; feature work of individual photographers—how they see the state); travel (specific places, events to see in New Mexico). Buys 5-7 mss/issue. Query. Length: 500-2,000 words. Pays $25-300.

Photos: Purchased with or without accompanying ms or on assignment. Captions required. Query, or send contact sheet or transparencies. Pays $15-30 for 8x10 b&w glossies; $20-30 for 35mm; prefers Kodachrome; (photos in plastic pocketed viewing sheets). Model release required.

How To Break In: "Send a superb short (1,000 words) manuscript on a little known event, aspect of history or place to see in New Mexico. Inaccurate research, faulty 'facts' will immediately ruin a writer's chances for the future. Good style, good grammar, please!"

Rejects: No generalized odes to the state or the Southwest. No Anglo, sentimentalized, paternalistic views of the Indians or of the Hispanos. No glib, gimmicky "travel brochure" writing.

NEW YORK AFFAIRS/URBAN AMERICA, Institute for the Study of the City, 342 Madison Ave., Suite 1100, New York NY 10017. (212)953-1713. Editor-in-Chief: Dick Netzer. Emphasizes urban problems. "Readers tend to be academics, public officials, corporation presidents and intellectual types." Quarterly magazine; 128 pages. Estab: 1973. Circ: 5,000. Pays on publication. Buys all rights, but may reassign following publication. Phone queries OK. Photocopied submissions OK. SASE. Reports in 4 weeks. Sample copy $3; free writer's guidelines.
Nonfiction: Marlys J. Harris, Articles Editor. Expose; interview (figures who are key to urban policymaking); and personal opinion. Buys 8 mss/year. Query. Length: 3,000-7,500 words. Pays $50-200. "We also have a section for short articles (250-3,000 words) called 'Side Streets' in which we run just about anything that is good about cities—humor especially. Most of our authors are academics whom we don't pay. For those whom we can't afford to pay, which includes most articles and Side Streets, we pay in copies of the magazine."
Columns/Departments: Harold Kollmeier, Book Review Editor. Book reviews. "We don't pay reviewers. They just get to keep the book." Uses 30 pages/year. Query.
How To Break In: "We are looking for hard-hitting, well-written articles on general urban problems. We especially like articles that take the unconventional approach—that transit fares should be raised, or that the cost of welfare should *not* be picked up by the Federal Government."

NEW YORK MAGAZINE, 755 2nd Ave., New York NY 10017. (212)986-4600. Editor: James Brady. For intelligent readers in the New York area. Circ: 375,000. Buys all rights. Pays on publication. Query first. Reports in 1 month. Enclose S.A.S.E.
Nonfiction: Articles with ample reportage (not essays) about genuinely new or important aspects of the New York scene. Length: 1,000 to 3,500 words. Pays $250 to $1,000.

NORTH/NORD, 110 O'Connor St., Ottawa, Ontario, Canada K1A OH4. (613)995-6206. Editor: Robert F.J. Shannon. For a varied audience, from libraries and educational institutions to businessmen and diplomats, Canadian and international. Special issues on various special subjects in the North. Bimonthly. Established in 1959. Circulation: 19,500. Rights purchased vary with author and material. Buys full rights to publish and permit to be republished. Buys 100 mss a year. Payment on acceptance. Will send free sample copy to writer on request. Write for copy of guidelines for writers. Submit seasonal material 4 months in advance. Reports in 6 to 8 weeks. Submit only complete original mss.
Nonfiction: "Subjects must pertain to Canada's north or other northern areas of the world such as Alaska and Scandinavia. Topics can include resource development (business, mining, pipeline, construction and oil and gas industries); history (exploration, archaeology, fur trade); conservation (wilderness, wildlife, national parks, geology); adventure and human interest stories; the arts (folklore, sculpture, print making, etc.); life in the north (housing, transportation, education, communications, health and welfare, government, entertainments); native peoples (customs, life styles, organizations etc.); features on outstanding personalities of the north as well as northern communities." Length: 500-2,500 words. Pays $50-300.
Photos: Purchased with or without mss. "We use mainly color transparency or print film; some black and white." Pays from $10-50 for single shot; $50 for "Face of the North," a photo feature profile of a northern personality. Pays $100-200 for cover photo and center spread scenic.

NORTHERN VIRGINIAN, Virginia Cardinal Publications, Box 334, 138 Church St., Vienna VA 22180. (703)938-0666. "In the past we have relied on writers' queries and blind freelance submissions for editorial content. In the future, we'll do the proposing and will direct writers step-by-step. We are always looking for more and better, willing writers in our market area. Call us and ask for an assignment."

OREGON TIMES MAGAZINE, New Oregon Publishers, Inc., 1000 S.W. 3rd Ave., Portland OR 97204. (503)223-0304. Editor-in-Chief: Tom Bates. Managing Editor: David Kelly. Emphasizes Oregon for an adult, college-educated readership. Monthly magazine; 72 pages. Estab: 1971. Circ: 18,500. Pays on publication. Buys all rights, but may reassign following publication. Phone queries OK. Submit seasonal/holiday material 3 months in advance. Photocopied submissions OK. SASE. Reports in 3 weeks. Free sample copy and writer's guidelines.
Nonfiction: Expose; historical; how-to; humor; inspirational; interview; new product; nostalgia; personal experience; photo feature; profile; and travel. All articles must have an Oregon focus. Buys 4 mss/issue. Query. Length: 1,500-10,000 words. Pays $45-300.
Photos: Bruce McGillivray, Photo Editor. Purchased with or without accompanying ms. Query. Pays $5-30 for 8x10 b&w glossies, uncropped, preferably full frame print; $10-40 for any size color transparencies. Model release required.

Columns/Departments: Grass Mountain Lookout (short news, interesting facts, bizarre opinion); Guest Editorial; Grapevine (gossip). Query. Pays 3¢/word. Open to suggestions for new columns/departments.
Poetry: Henry Morrison, Poetry Editor. Avant-garde, free verse, traditional. Buys 12/year. Pays $5-25.

OREGON VOTER DIGEST, 108 N.W. 9th, Portland OR 97209. (503)222-9794. Editor: C. R. Hillyer. For top echelon of leaders and decisionmakers in private industry and government in Oregon. Magazine; 40 pages. Frequent topical issues; apply for schedule. Estab: 1915. Monthly. Circ: 3,000. Not copyrighted. Pays on publication. Will send sample copy to writer on request. Will consider photocopied and simultaneous submissions. Submit topical issue material 1 month in advance. Reports on material accepted for publication in 1 month. Returns rejected material in 1 week. Query first or submit complete ms. Enclose S.A.S.E.
Nonfiction and Photos: News of business and industry, public affairs, legislation; statewide or affecting Oregon. Land use planning, forest industry, big government, economic trends, political items. "Looking for short political items (in state or affecting Oregon) of an expose or investigative nature. A writer's approach should be traditional, conservative stance, in support of private enterprise, against sprawling bureaucracy of government. Remember that this is not a mass consumer readership." Length: 500 words maximum. Pays 4¢ per word minimum. B&w glossies purchased with mss. Pays $7 minimum.

ORLANDO-LAND MAGAZINE, Box 2207, Orlando FL 32802. (305)644-3355. Editor-in-Chief: E.L. Prizer. Managing Editor: Carole De Pinto. Emphasizes central Florida information for a readership made up primarily of people new to Florida—those here as visitors, traveling businessmen, new residents. Monthly magazine; 112 pages. Estab: 1946. Circ: 28,000. Pays on acceptance. Buys all rights, but may reassign following publication; or first North American serial rights. Phone queries OK. Submit seasonal/holiday material 2 months in advance. Photocopied and previously published submissions OK. SASE. Reports in 6 weeks. Sample copy $1.
Nonfiction: Historical, how-to, informational. "Things involved in living in Florida."
How To Break In: "Always in need of *useful* advice-type material presented as first person experience. Central Florida subjects only."

OUTDOOR INDIANA, Room 612, State Office Building, Indianapolis IN 46204. (317)633-4294. Editor: Herbert R. Hill. For subscribers who seek information regarding programs, projects, services and facilities of the Indiana Department of Natural Resources. Published 10 times/year. Circ: 33,000. Buys first serial rights. Pays on publication. Reports on submissions in 1 to 4 weeks. Query preferred. Enclose S.A.S.E.
Nonfiction and Photos: Informative, concise, illustrative, bright articles on Indiana-related topics only. No fiction, essays or verse. Length: 1,000 to 2,000 words. Usually pays 2¢ a word. Photos of Indiana interest only; purchased with mss or with captions only. B&w photos, 8x10; color transparencies, 2¼x2¼ or larger. Pays $5 for b&w; $25 for color; $50 for color cover.

OUTDOORS IN GEORGIA, 270 Washington St., S.W., Atlanta GA 30334. (404)656-5660. Editor: Bill Morehead. For a male audience of hunters, fishermen, campers, environmentalists. Magazine; 32 pages. Established in 1966. Monthly. Circulation: 35,000. Not copyrighted. Buys 5 or 6 mss a year. Pays on publication. Will send sample copy to writer on request. Write for copy of guidelines for writers. No photocopied or simultaneous submissions. Reports on material accepted for publication in 4 to 6 weeks. Returns rejected material 2 weeks after decision. Query first. Enclose S.A.S.E.
Nonfiction and Photos: Department Editor: Aaron Pass. "Material designed for reader use and relating to the outdoors (how-to and where-to in Georgia), the environment and natural/cultural history. Currently interested in environment/energy issues and how they affect natural resources." Informational, how-to, personal experience, interview, profile, inspirational, humor, historical articles. No "me and Joe" type articles. Length: 900 to 1,500 words. Pays $20 to $75, but payment depends on length, quality, and editorial needs. No additional payment made for b&w glossies or color transparencies used with mss, but "number and quality of photos may result in higher offer for story."

PALM BEACH LIFE, Post Office Box 1176, Palm Beach FL 33480. (305)655-5755. Editor: Kathryn Robinette. "*Palm Beach Life* caters to society (America's oldest society journal) and reflects its interests. Readers are affluent ... usually over 40, well-educated." Special issues on the arts (February), travel (March), and yachting (November), and elegant living, home, family, etc. (September-October). Established in 1906. Monthly with combined September-October issue. Circulation: 12,000. Buys first North American and occasional second rights from noncompetitive publication. Payment on acceptance. Will consider photocopied submissions. Submit seasonal material 5 months in advance. Reports in 3 weeks. Query first. Enclose S.A.S.E.

Nonfiction and Photos: Subject matter involves "articles on fashion, travel, music, art and related fields; subjects that would be of interest to the sophisticated, well-informed reader; especially personality sketches of those in society or those who cater to it. We feature color photos, 'but are crying for good b&w'; also emphasize life in Palm Beach itself. Parties are overdone. Trying to show 'doers' in society." Buys informational, interview, profile, humor, historical, think, photo, and travel articles. Length: 1,000 to 2,500 words. Pays $50 to $250. Purchases photos with and without mss, or on assignment. Captions are required. Buys 8x10 b&w glossies at $5 each. Also buys 35mm or 2¼x2¼ transparencies and photo stories. Pay is negotiable.

PENINSULA LIVING, Box 300, Palo Alto CA 94302. (415)326-1200. Editor: Carolyn Snyder. For higher educated newspaper readers; median income over $20,000. Tabloid newspaper; 24 pages. Established in 1952. Weekly. Circulation: 65,000. Not copyrighted. Buys 20 to 30 mss a year. Pays 10th of month after publication. No photocopied or simultaneous submissions. Reports in 1 to 3 weeks. Query first. Enclose S.A.S.E.

Nonfiction and Photos: "Regional 'soft news'. Unusual hobbies, community trends, personalities, regional travel, regional history with popular 'hook', homes and gardens, TV interviews and features. No rigid structure. We seek good writing, unusual approach, impeccable accuracy. We don't want to see weak Erma Bombeck-type humor pieces, or out-of-area travel and history pieces, or themes not applicable to our audience." Length arranged with author after query is approved. Pays 3¢ to 5¢ a word. B&w glossies (8x10) purchased with mss. Pays $10 minimum.

PENINSULA MAGAZINE, Box 11701, Palo Alto CA 94306. (415)327-6666. Executive Editor: Ted Bache. Managing Editor: Dave Fuller. "For alert, active and aware individuals who have a strong desire to know what's going on right in their own backyard." Monthly magazine; 56 pages. Estab: 1975. Circ: 12,000. Pays on publication. Buys first North American serial rights. Phone queries OK. Photocopied submissions OK. SASE. Reports in 4 weeks. Free sample copy and writer's guidelines.

Nonfiction: Expose, how-to, informational, humor, interview, new product (El Camino or Bird Dog!), personal experience, photo feature, profile and travel. Buys 3 mss/issue. Query or send complete ms. Length: 1,500-3,500 words. Pays 3¢/word.

Photos: Michael Parks, Photo Editor. Purchased with or without accompanying ms or on assignment. Captions required. Pays $5-10 for b&w 5x7 or 8x10. Query for photos.

Columns/Departments: Knute O. Berger, Assistant Managing Editor. Profiles buys 3 mss/issue, 350-500 words. Notable, interesting Peninsula residents, business, professional, civic, artistic. Buyer's Bird Dog—hard-to-find services and items; 250 words. Interview—Q&A format; 500 words. El Camino Real— potpourri-humor, vignettes, new products and services; 250 words maximum, photo and art. Query or send complete ms. Pays 3¢/word; $15 maximum. Open to suggestions from freelancers for new columns/departments; address to Knute Berger.

How To Break In: "All items must strictly and definitely have a real and believable Peninsula angle. We define the Peninsula as running bayside and coastside from the city/county line of San Francisco to and including San Jose."

PENNSYLVANIA ILLUSTRATED, Box 657, Camp Hill PA 17011. Editor-in-Chief: Albert E. Holliday. Audience is 35-50 years old, some college education, interested in self-improvement, civic and state affairs, history. Bimonthly magazine; 68 pages. Estab: 1976. Circ: 20,000. Pays on publication. Buys first North American serial rights. Submit seasonal/holiday material 6 months in advance. Simultaneous, photocopied and previously published submissions OK. SASE. Reports in 2-3 weeks. Free sample copy and writer's guidelines.

Nonfiction: Expose; how-to (any general interest subject); informational; historical; humor; interview (with prominent Pennsylvanians); nostalgia; profile; travel; new product (made in Pennsylvania); personal experience (unique); and photo feature. Buys 5-7 mss/issue. Query. Length: 500-2,000 words. Pays $50-200.

Photos: Purchased with or without accompanying ms or on assignment. Captions required. Query. Pays $5-10 for 5x7 b&w glossies or semiglossies; $25-50 for 2¼x2¼ color transparencies.

PERIODICAL OF ART IN NEBRASKA, University of Nebraska at Omaha, P-A-N, U.N.O., Annex 21, Box 688, Omaha NE 68101. (402)554-2771. Editor-in-Chief: Pat Gray. Emphasizes "literature and the arts in Nebraska." For students, writers and artists. Quarterly tabloid; 24 pages. Estab: 1974. Circ: 5,000. Payment is at the end of the publishing year. Purchases all rights. Phone queries OK. SASE. Submit seasonal/holiday material 3 months in advance. Reports in 3 months. Free sample copy.

Nonfiction: Interview; nostalgia; personal opinion; and profile on arts in Nebraska only. Buys 8 mss/year. Submit complete ms. Length: 1,000-6,000 words. Pays in surplus divided at end of year.

Fiction: Experimental; humorous; mainstream; western; and serialized novels. Buys 4 mss/year. Submit complete ms. Length: 1,000-6,000 words. Surplus divided at end of year.

Poetry: Avant-garde, free verse, haiku, traditional. Buys 60/year. Limit submissions to 5 at a time. No length requirement.

PHILADELPHIA MAGAZINE, 1500 Walnut St., Philadelphia PA 19102. Editor: Alan Halpern. For sophisticated middle- and upper-income people in the Greater Philadelphia/ South Jersey area. Magazine. Established in 1908. Monthly. Circulation: 115,000. Buys all rights. Buys over 100 mss/year. Pays on publication, or within 2 months. Free writer's guidelines for SASE. Reports in 4 weeks. Queries and mss should be sent to Polly Hurst, Administrative Editor. Enclose S.A.S.E.

Nonfiction and Photos: "Articles should have a Philadelphia focus, but should avoid Philadelphia stereotypes — we've seen them all. Life styles, city survival, profiles of interesting people, business stories, music, the arts, sports, local politics, stressing the topical or unusual. No puff pieces. We're in the 'new journalism' tradition — exposes, fast-moving, first-person accounts — and we're a steady award winner, so quality and professionalism count. We offer lots of latitude for style, but before you make like Norman Mailer, make sure you have something to say." Length: 1,000 to 7,000 words. Pays $75 to $500. Photos occasionally purchased with mss at additional payment of $35 to $150.

PHOENIX MAGAZINE, 4707 N. 12th St., Phoenix AZ 85014. (602)248-8900. Editor: Anita J. Welch. For professional, general audience. Monthly magazine. Estab: 1966. Circ: 60,000. Buys all rights, but will reassign rights to author after publication. Buys about 60 mss a year. Payment on publication. Will send sample copy to writer for $1. February issue: Real Estate; March issue: Arizona Lifestyle; August issue: Annual Phoenix Progress Report; June issue: Salute to Summer. Submit special issue material 3 months in advance. Reports in 1 month. Query first or submit complete ms. Enclose S.A.S.E.

Nonfiction and Photos: Predominantly features on some aspect of Phoenix life; urban affairs, arts, life style, etc. Subject should be locally oriented. Informational, how-to, interview, profile, historical, photo, successful local business operations. Length: 1,000 to 3,000 words. Pays $50 to $100, but payment is negotiable. Photos are purchased with ms with no additional payment, or on assignment.

PITTSBURGH MAGAZINE, Metropolitan Pittsburgh Public Broadcasting Inc., 4802 5th Ave., Pittsburgh PA 15213. (412)622-1300. Editor-in-Chief: Herb Stein. "The magazine is purchased on newsstands and by subscription and is given to those who contribute $17 or more a year to public TV in western Pennsylvania." Monthly magazine; 80 pages. Estab: 1970. Circ: 60,000. Pays on publication. Buys all rights, but may reassign following publication. Phone queries OK. Submit seasonal/holiday material 2 months in advance. SASE. Reports in 6 weeks. Sample copy $1.50; free writer's guidelines.

Nonfiction: Expose, historical, how-to, humor, informational, inspirational, interview, nostalgia, personal experience, personal opinion, profile and travel. Buys 6 mss/issue. Query or send complete ms. Length: 2,500 words. Pays $50-250.

Photos: Purchased with accompanying ms or on assignment. Captions required. Uses b&w and color. Query for photos. Model release required.

Columns/Departments: Travel; Humor; Nostalgia. "All must relate to Pittsburgh or Western Pennsylvania."

For '78: Holiday and seasonal articles and themes are valuable. Each January is an "At Home" issue—decorating, building, furnishing, etc.

ST. LOUISAN, 7110 Oakland Ave., St. Louis MO 63117. (314)781-8787. Editor: Greg Holzhauer. For "those interested in the St. Louis area, recreation issues, etc." Established in 1969. Monthly. Circulation: 20,000. Buys all rights, but will reassign rights to author after publication; buys second serial (reprint) rights. Buys 60 mss a year. Payment on publication. Will not consider photocopied submissions. Submit seasonal material 4 months in advance. Reports on material in 2 months. Query first or submit complete ms. Enclose S.A.S.E.

Nonfiction and Photos: "Articles on the city of St. Louis, metro area, arts, recreation, media, law, education, politics, timely issues, urban problems/solutions, environment, etc., generally related to St. Louis area. Looking for informative writing of high quality, consistent in style and timely in topic." Informational, how-to, personal experience, interview, profile, humor, historical, think pieces, expose, nostalgia, personal opinion, travel. Length: 1,000 to 5,000 words. Pays $100 to $200. 8x10 b&w glossies purchased on assignment. "Shooting fee plus $10 to $20 per print used. All color on individual basis."

SAM HOUSTON'S METROPOLITAN MAGAZINE, 108 Westheimer, Houston TX 77006. (713)523-4473. Editor-in-Chief: Harla D. Kaplan. For Houston and Houstonians; audience is middle and upper income, age 25 and up, with a high school education and higher. Monthly magazine; 68 pages. Estab: 1976. Circ: 30,000. Pays on publication. Buys all rights. Submit seasonal/holiday material 3 months in advance. SASE. Reports in 1-2 months. Sample copy $1.25.
Nonfiction: Expose (any and all aspects of Houston); informational; interview (must be a noteworthy Houstonian); profile and travel (in Texas, U.S. or foreign). Buys 7-8 mss/issue. Submit complete ms. Length: 2,000-3,500 words. Pays $25-150.
Columns/Departments: Destinations (local and foreign travel articles); A La Carte (local restaurants and foods); and Focus (profiles of interesting Houstonians). Buys 3 mss/issue. Send complete ms. Length: 1,500-2,500 words. Pays $25-100.

SAN ANTONIO MAGAZINE, Greater San Antonio Chamber of Commerce, Box 1628, San Antonio TX 78296. (512)227-8181. Editor-in-Chief: Sammye Johnson. Emphasizes quality of life articles about San Antonio. Monthly magazine; 88 pages. Pays on publication. Buys all rights, but may reassign following publication. Phone queries OK. Photocopied submissions OK. SASE. Reports in 2 months. Free sample copy and writer's guidelines.
Nonfiction: "The magazine's purpose is to inform, educate and entertain readers about the quality of life in San Antonio. We're looking for articles that reflect life in San Antonio today." Expose; informational; historical; humor; nostalgia; personal opinion; profile (personality profiles of people who are interesting, colorful and quotable—must be a San Antonian or have ties to the city); travel; personal experience; and photo features. Buys 65 mss/year. Query or send complete ms. Length: 800-3,000 words. Pays $50-300.
Photos: Purchased with mss or on assignment. Captions required. Query. Pays $10-25 for 8x10 b&w glossies. Prefers to pay according to the number of photos used in an article, a bulk rate.
Columns/Departments: Personality profiles of a San Antonian who is involved in the arts, in education, in the medical field, etc., who is interesting, colorful, quotable. Buys 12/year. Query. Length: 1,000-1,800 words. Pays $100.
How To Break In: "The best way is to be a resident of San Antonio and, therefore, able to write on assignment or to query the editor personally. Again, we are looking for material which is related to the city of San Antonio and its people. We consider all possible angles and tie-ins."

SAN FERNANDO VALLEY LIFE MAGAZINE, Marcom/West, Inc., Box 8268, Van Nuys CA 91409. (213)892-4381. Editor-in-Chief: R. Pistol. For the 1.3 million people of the San Fernando Valley, middle and upper income, higher educated; varied interests. Monthly magazine; 80 pages. Estab: 1976. Circ: 30,000. Pays on publication. Buys one-time rights. Submit seasonal/holiday material 3 months in advance. Previously published submissions OK. SASE. Free sample copy and writer's guidelines.
Nonfiction: Historical (on San Fernando Valley and area, or trends, etc); how-to (home and garden material, food, hobbies and crafts, home improvement); informational (any topic of current interest); interview (regional, well-known or unique persons); new product (home, garden or consumer related); nostalgia (topics of current general interest); personal experience (if valley resident, and of very special interest); personal opinion (topics of current general interest); photo feature (valley locations, people editorial or feature); profile; travel (any location in the world); health/nutrition; business; fashion; law; leisure time; senior citizens; and sports. Buys 12 mss/issue. Submit complete ms. Length: 300-4,000 words. Pays $5-$300.
Photos: Purchased with or without accompanying ms, or on assignment. Captions required. Send contact sheet or transparencies. Pays $5-25 for 5x7 or larger b&w prints; $10-75 for any size color transparencies. Model release required.
Columns/Departments: The Arts; Business; Consumer; Dining Out; Enterprises; Entertainment; Fashion; Health & Nutrition; Home & Garden; Law; Leisure/Hobbies; People; Senior Citizens; Sports; Travel; and Calendar of Events. Not all departments run every month. Buys 8 mss/issue. Submit complete ms. Length: 250-1,500 words. Pays $7.50-80. Open to suggestions for new columns/departments.

THE SAN GABRIEL VALLEY MAGAZINE, Miller Books, 409 San Pasqual Dr., Alhambra CA 91801. (213)284-7607. Editor-in-Chief: Joseph Miller. For upper-middle income people who dine out often at better restaurants in Los Angeles County. Bimonthly magazine; 52 pages. Estab: 1976. Circ: 3,400. Pays on publication. Buys simultaneous, second serial (reprint) and one-time rights. Phone queries OK. Submit seasonal/holiday material 1 month in advance. Simultaneous, photocopied and previously published submissions OK. SASE. Reports in 2 weeks. Sample copy $1.
Nonfiction: Expose (political); informational (restaurants in the valley); inspirational (success stories and positive thinking); interview (successful people and how they made it); profile (political leaders in the San Gabriel Valley); and travel (places in the valley). Buys 2 mss/issue. Length: 500-10,000 words. Pays 5¢/word.
Columns/Departments: Restaurants, Education, Valley News and Valley Personality. Buys 2 mss/issue. Send complete ms. Length: 500-1,500 words. Pays 5¢/word.
Fiction: Historical (successful people) and western (articles about Los Angeles County). Buys 2 mss/issue. Send complete ms. Length: 500-10,000 words. Pays 5¢/word.
How To Break In: "Send us a good personal success story about a valley or a California personality."

SANDLAPPER—The Magazine of South Carolina, Greystone Publishers, Inc., Box 1668, Columbia SC 29202. Editor-in-Chief: Bob Rowland. "We reach an affluent, educated audience interested in the state of South Carolina, its past and present." Monthly magazine; 72 pages. Estab: 1968. Circ: 25,000. Pays on publication. Buys all rights, but may reassign following publication. Submit seasonal/holiday material 6-8 months in advance. Photocopied submissions OK. SASE. Reports in 2 weeks. Free sample copy and writer's guidelines.
Nonfiction: Harry Hope, Articles Editor. Historical (sound, articulate insights into South Carolina history); humor (frustrations of daily living); nostalgia; profiles (of living South Carolinians); photo feature; folk heritage; and leisure/recreation. Buys 10 mss/issue. Query. Length 1,500-3,000 words. Pays $50-350.
Photos: Purchased with accompanying ms. Captions required. Send contact sheet. Pays $6-10 for 5x7 or larger glossy finish b&w; $12-35 for 35mm or 2¼x2¼ transparencies. Maximum payment is for cover.
Columns/Departments: Dining Out (notable restaurants around the state); Folkroots (folk heritage material); Styles in Living (notable South Carolina homes); Leisure Living; and Bookshelf (book reviews relating to South Carolina or Southern experience). Buys 6 mss/issue. Query. Length: 300-500 words. Pays $50 maximum.
Fiction: Franklin Ashley, Fiction Editor. "We are interested in Southern regional fiction, with themes, characterization, 'sense of place'—all inherent in the genre. The writer should avoid melodrama, triviality, cliches, schmaltz, and anything that smacks of 'Lil Abner.'" Buys 12 mss/year. Submit complete ms. Length: 1,500-4,000 words. Pays $150-250.
Poetry: Eugene Platt, Poetry Editor. Avant-garde, free verse, traditional. "No patriotic, religious, or inspirational verse." Buys 20/year. Length: 50 lines maximum. Pays $10-15.

SEATTLE BUSINESS MAGAZINE, Seattle Chamber of Commerce, 215 Columbia St., Seattle WA 98104. (206)447-7266. Editor-in-Chief: Ed Sullivan. Emphasizes regional socio-economic affairs. For business and government leaders, civic leaders, regional businessmen, educators, opinion makers, and the general public. Bimonthly magazine; 68 pages. Estab: 1900. Circ: 5,750. Pays on publication. Buys all rights, but may reassign following publication. Submit seasonal/holiday material 2 months in advance. Previously published submissions OK. SASE. Reports in 2 weeks. Free sample copy.
Nonfiction: Informational (socio-economic affairs) and technical. Buys 1-2 mss/issue. Query. Length: 500-2,500 words. Pays $50-300.
Photos: Purchased with accompanying ms or on assignment. Captions required. Pays $50-100 for b&w photos. Total purchase price for ms includes payment for photos. Model release required.
How To Break In: "The freelancer must be able to write—and have a basic awareness of and sympathy for—the interests and problems of the business community as these relate to the community at large."

SOUTH CAROLINA MAGAZINE, Box 89, Columbia SC 29202. (803)796-9200. Monthly. Buys all rights. Pays on publication. Reports in about 1 week. Will send free sample copy on request. Enclose S.A.S.E.
Nonfiction and Photos: Matters of interest to South Carolinians about state history, places, people, education, art, etc. Length: 500 to 1,000 words. Pays 3¢ a word. Photos purchased with mss. Glossy prints, 8x10 or 5x7. Pays $5.

SOUTH CAROLINA WILDLIFE, P. O. Box 167, Columbia SC 29202. (803)758-6291. Editor: John Culler. For South Carolinians interested in hunting, fishing, the outdoors. Magazine; 64 (8½x11) pages. Established in 1953. Every 2 months. Circulation: 85,000. Not copyrighted. Buys 10 mss a year. Pays on acceptance. Will send free sample copy to writer on request. Reports in two weeks. Submit complete ms. Enclose S.A.S.E.

Nonfiction and Photos: Articles on outdoor South Carolina with an emphasis on preserving and protecting our natural resources. Length: 800 to 4,000 words. Pays $100 to $500. Pays $15 for b&w glossies purchased with or without ms, or on assignment. Pays $25 for color used inside; $50 for color on back cover; $100, front cover.

SOUTHERN EXPOSURE, P. O. Box 230, Chapel Hill NC 27514. (919)929-2141. Editor: Bob Hall. For Southerners interested in "left-liberal" political perspective and the South; all ages; well-educated. Magazine; 100 to 230 (8x11) pages. Established in 1973. Quarterly. Circulation: 4,000. Buys all rights. Buys 20 mss/year. Pays on publication. Will consider photocopied and simultaneous submissions. Submit seasonal material 2 to 3 months in advance. Reports in 1 to 2 months. "Query is appreciated, but not required." Enclose S.A.S.E.

Nonfiction and Photos: "Ours is probably the only publication about the South *not* aimed at business or the upper-class people; it appeals to all segments of the population. *And,* it is used as a resource—sold as a magazine and then as a book—so it rarely becomes dated." Needed are investigative articles about the following subjects as related to the South: women, labor, black people, the economy. Informational interview, profile, historical, think articles, expose, personal opinion, and book reviews. Length: 6,000 words maximum. Pays $50 average per article, $100 maximum. "Very rarely purchase photos, as we have a large number of photographers working for us." 8x10 b&w preferred; no color. Payment negotiable.

Fiction and Poetry: "Fiction should concern the South, i.e., black fiction, growing up Southern, etc." Length: 6,000 words maximum. Pays $50-100. All forms of poetry accepted, if they relate to the South, its problems, potential, etc. Length: open. Pays $15-100.

THE STATE, P.O. Box 2169, Raleigh NC 27602. Editor: W.B. Wright. Monthly. Buys first rights. Will send a free sample copy on request. Pays on acceptance. Deadlines 1 month in advance of publication date. Enclose S.A.S.E.

Nonfiction and Photos: "General articles about places, people, events, history, general interest in North Carolina. Also reports on business, new developments within the state. Emphasis on travel in North Carolina; (devote features regularly to resorts, travel goals, dining and stopping places)." Will use humor if related to region. Length: average of 1,000 to 1,200 words. Pays $25 average, $15 minimum. B&w photos purchased with mss. Pays average of $5; minimum of $3.

TEXAS MONTHLY MAGAZINE, Box 1569, Austin TX 78767. Editor: William Broyles. For Texans (in or out of state) with educated interests in politics, culture and lifestyles. Monthly magazine. Estab: 1973. Circ: 200,000. Pays on acceptance. Buys all rights, but may reassign following publication. Submit seasonal/holiday material 4 months in advance. Simultaneous (if so notified) and photocopied submissions OK. SASE. Reports in 2-6 weeks. Free writer's guidelines.

Nonfiction: Subjects must be of interest to an educated Texas readership. Informational; how-to; personal experience; interview; profile; and expose. Length: 1,200-7,500 words. Pays $250-800.

Photos: Purchased with accompanying ms. Pays $30 for b&w photos.

Columns/Departments: Travel; consumer; urban problems; and science. Length: 2,500 words maximum. Pays $150-250.

TEXAS PARADE, P.O. BBx 12037, Austin TX 78711. Editor: Kenneth E. Lively. Monthly. Circulation: 50,000. Buys first North American serial rights. Payment on publicaation. Will send free sample copy to writer on request. Submit seasonal material 6 weeks in advance. Reports in 1 month. Query first or submit complete ms. Enclose S.A.S.E.

Nonfiction and Photos: Articles on people, politics, travel, business, history and sports with a Texas angle. Length: 1,500 to 3,000 words. Pays $175-250. B&w and color photos purchased with mss. Captions required. Also Texas-angled photo stories. Pays $10 minimum.

TOWN & GOWN MAGAZINE, P.O. Box 77, State College PA 16801. (814)238-5051. Editor: Terry Dunkle. For local residents and surrounding townships. Magazine; 70 (6x9) pages. Established in 1966. Monthly. Circulation: 16,000. Rights purchased vary with author and material. Usually buys all rights. Buys about 30 mss a year. Pays on publication. Will send sample copy to writer for 50¢. Will consider photocopied submissions. No simultaneous submissions. Submit seasonal material 3 months in advance. Reports on material accepted for publication in

2 weeks. Returns rejected material in 1 month. Query first, with writing sample and/or clippings. Enclose S.A.S.E.

Nonfiction and Photos: "Local history (Pennsylvania State and State College area) told in an anecdotal, crisp and entertaining way. Profiles of local personages. 'People' is our subject. We do not like pieces that are so laboriously fashioned that all the life in them is extinguished. That is not to say, however, that the writer can skimp on research. Save postage; don't bother sending in articles that have no distinct connection with Centre County, Pennsylvania." Length: 1,000-3,500 words. Pays 1.2¢/word. "Especially interested in short, photojournalistic contributions to Othertainment, a column about unusual ways to entertain oneself in the region." B&w photos purchased with or without mss, or on assignment. Pays $2.50 for inside use; $10 for cover use.

TULSA MAGAZINE, 616 S. Boston, Tulsa OK 74119. (918)585-1201. Editor: Larry Silvey. Audience is primarily medium to upper income level Tulsans. Monthly. Circulation: 6,000. Not copyrighted. Pays on publication. Will send sample copy for 25¢. Deadlines are at least 6 weeks prior to publication date, which is normally on the first Thursday of each month. Reports immediately. Query first. Enclose S.A.S.E.

Nonfiction and Photos: Articles must revolve around people or how subject affects people and must have a Tulsa area slant. Style desired is informal and lively. 1,000 to 4,000 words. Payment is negotiable, $50 to $75, depending on length, research. Photos usually taken by staff or on assignment. May be purchased with mss.

UPCOUNTRY, The Magazine of New England Living, 33 Eagle St., Pittsfield MA 01201. (413)447-7311. Managing Editor: William H. Tague. For people who are interested in the country life of New England. Estab: 1973. Newsprint tabloid published 12 times a year and carried as a monthly supplement by daily newspapers in New England. Circ: 240,000. Buys all rights, but will reassign rights to author after publication. Buys 100 to 150 mss a year. Payment on acceptance. "Prefer written or telephone query in advance of sending material, although we consider everything received." Enclose S.A.S.E.

Nonfiction and Photos: "The magazine deals with life in New England as a whole, and country living, in particular; not as a fantasy, but as a reality. We look for articles on specific topics of current interest to our readership. Questions, specific examples, etc., are all desirable. Above all, articles must deal with New England subjects. New England writers strongly preferred. Articles concerned with moving to and living in the country; coping with country living; rural medicine, taxation, political issues affecting country life; gardening, music, art, theater, birdwatching, outdoor sports, restaurants, country inns, restorations, preservations, etc. Articles on how to come to terms with our environment; profiles of noteworthy people, interesting characters, socio-economic profiles of towns; short (1,200 words maximum) humorous pieces. How-to articles with a New England setting, on subjects relating to country or small town living." Length: 700-3,000 words. Pays $30-150. B&w negatives or 8x10 prints, and color transparencies. Payment varies, but pays a minimum of $10 for b&w negatives and prints; $25 to $75 for color transparencies for covers.

Poetry: Poetry considered, but sparingly used. Traditional forms preferred. Pays $15 minimum.

How To Break In: "We are looking for first-rate writing. This means writing that has clarity, precision, wit, grace, relevance, originality, insight, vividness, logic, freshness and truth."

VANCOUVER MAGAZINE, 1008 Hornby St., Vancouver, B.C., Canada V6Z 1V7. (604)685-5374. Editor: M.F. Parry. For an upper income, urban audience in Vancouver. Monthly magazine; 80-96 pages. Estab: 1967. Circ: 85,100. Rights purchased vary with author and material. Buys first serial rights or second serial (reprint) rights. Buys about 120 mss/year. Pays on acceptance. Free sample copy. Will consider photocopied and simultaneous submissions. Reports in 2 weeks. Query first or submit complete ms. Enclose S.A.E. and International Reply Coupons.

Nonfiction and Photos: City-oriented features, consumer self-help; arts and political columns; sports, life style, entertainment. Some personality profiles on assignment. Also, informational, how-to, personal experience, interview, historical and travel articles, as well as think pieces. Article length: 600 to 4,000 words. Pays 7¢ to 10¢ a word. Column material length: 1,000 words. Pays minimum of $85. B&w glossies (5x7 minimum) and Kodachromes purchased with mss. Pays $25-100.

VERMONT LIFE MAGAZINE, 61 Elm St., Montpelier VT 05602. (802)828-3241. Editor: Brian Vachon. Magazine; 64 pages. Established in 1946. Quarterly. Circulation: 130,000. Buys first rights. Buys about 60 mss a year. "Query is essential." Enclose S.A.S.E.

Nonfiction: Wants articles on Vermont, those which portray a typical and, if possible, unique,

attractive aspect of the state or people. Style should be literate, clear and concise. Subtle humor favored. No nature close-ups and stories, Vermont dialect attempts, or an outsider's view on visiting Vermont. Word length averages 1,500 words. Payment averages 10¢ to 20¢ per word.
Photos: Buys photographs with mss and with captions only. Prefers b&w, 8x10 glossies or matte prints, except on assignment. Color submissions must be 4x5 or 35mm transparencies. Buys one-time rights, but often negotiates for re-use rights also. Rates on acceptance; b&w, $10; color, $75 inside, $200 for cover. Gives assignments but not on first trial with photographers. Query first.

THE WASHINGTONIAN MAGAZINE, 1828 L St., N.W., Washington DC 20036. Editor: John A. Limpert. For active, affluent, well-educated audience. Monthly magazine; 250 pages. Estab: 1965. Circ: 85,000. Buys all rights. Buys 75 mss/year. Pays on publication. Simultaneous and photocopied submissions OK. Reports in 4-6 weeks. Query or submit complete ms. Enclose S.A.S.E.
Nonfiction and Photos: *"The Washingtonian* is written for Washingtonians. The subject matter is anything we feel might interest people interested in the mind and manners of the city. The style, as Wolcott Gibbs said, should be the author's—if he is an author, and if he has a style. The only thing we ask is thoughtfulness and that no subject be treated too reverently. Audience is literate. We assume considerable sophistication about the city, and a sense of humor." Buys how-to's, personal experience, interviews, profiles, humor, coverage of successful business operations, think pieces, and exposes. Length: 1,000 to 7,000 words; average feature, 3,000 words. Pays 10¢ a word. Photos rarely purchased with mss.
Fiction and Poetry: Department Editors: John Limpert (fiction); Ellen Phillips (poetry); Both must be Washington-oriented. No limitations on length. Pays 10¢ a word for fiction. Payment for poetry is negotiable.

WESTCHESTER ILLUSTRATED, 16 School St., Yonkers NY 10401. (914)472-2061 or (212)295-4485. Editor-in-Chief: Peter Porco. Emphasizes life in Westchester County, New York for sophisticated, college-educated, 25-49-year-old suburbanites living within the New York Metropolitan area. "Interests range from participatory sports to the newest county budget, from the safety and convenience of Westchester's highways to the meaning of the latest cinema trends, from where to get the best cheesecake in the county to what their famous and not-so-famous neighbors are up to." Monthly magazine; 80 pages. Estab: 1976. Circ: 28,000. Pays 45 days after publication. Buys all rights, but will reassign following publication. Phone queries OK. Submit seasonal/holiday material 3 months in advance. Simultaneous and photocopied submissions OK. SASE. Reports in 3-5 weeks. Sample copy $1; free writer's guidelines.
Nonfiction: Expose (government: bureaucracies, courts, police, administrations, etc.; commercial: price-fixing, quasi-public companies, etc.; social: education, charities, fads etc.); historical (interesting, offbeat, humorous history, but also little-known history); how-to (start an apartment rental business; how to find a good, trustworthy auto mechanic in Westchester; how to pick out a good local private school; etc.); humor; informational (such as "what the new state environmental law means to local communities," "what happens when you serve jury duty in White Plains, Rye, Pleasantville," etc.); interview (of local politicians, celebrities, everyday people doing unusual things, artists, business people, etc.); new product (but only if the inventor lives in Westchester); personal experience (if the experience centers around an issue and the writer has interviewed many others with similar experiecnes); personal opinion (only in Letters to the Editor); photo feature (not much copy needed; photos must do all the work, while copy explains details not apparent in photo); profile (we prefer lots of personality—people who do offbeat things, don't take themselves too seriously); technical; travel (query first); and sports ("we love features on participatory sports—doing and playing are big with us —and leisure"). Buys 4-5 mss/issue. Query or send complete ms. Length: 500-4,000 words. Pays $20-200.
Photos: Photos purchased with or without accompanying ms or on assignment. Captions required. Pays $5-40 for minimum 5x7 b&w glossy or matte photos; $50-75 for standard size color transparencies (for cover only and usually on assignment). Send query and contact sheet. Model release required.
Columns/Departments: Emporium (a shopper's guide, compilation of special buys and bargains—$5-10 for 100-300 words); Locals (looks at our neighbors—$20-50 for 500-1,300 words); Music (realistic appraisal and shop talk relating do music featured in the local clubs, lounges, discos, etc.—also reviews of new records of any kind of music); Movies (looking for stories about movies made in Westchester, stars who live here, the commercial movie-theater economy, local filmmaking workshops); Books; First Cracks (Charles Stein, Editor—series of short items that take an irreverent look at interesting, offbeat humorous goings-on in West-

chester). Query or submit complete ms. Length: 150-1,500 words, except where specified. Pays $5-50. Open to suggestions for new columns/departments.

How To Break In: "*Westchester Illustrated* hopes to reach a tone that is slick, witty and sophisticated all at once. We like to laugh at Westchester's 'sacred' institutions, be irreverent now and then, and even poke fun at ourselves whenever we can. We're also concerned about the quality of life in Westchester. Freelancers should study the magazine, pick an area they're comfortable with, and write. In style, we like humor, naturalness, an unpretentious manner. In serious articles, emphasize the future of an issue—its trends, implications, etc. In almost all writing, use many quotes, anecdotal, digressionary openings, and finish up with a strong image or statement."

WESTCHESTER MAGAZINE, County Publications, 437 Ward Ave., Mamaruneck NY 10543. (914)698-8203. Editor-in-Chief: Vita Nelson. Emphasizes general interests in Westchester County and the metropolitan area. Monthly magazine; 96 pages. Estab: 1969. Circ: 30,000. Pays on publication. Buys all rights, but may reassign following publication. Submit seasonal/holiday material 3-4 months in advance. Simultaneous, photocopied, and previously published (occasionally) submissions OK. SASE. Reports in 5 weeks. Sample copy $1.25.

Nonfiction: Expose; informational (new phenomena, attitudes, new sports, hobbies, current fads); interview; profile; new product; and personal experience (only to make a point on a broader issue). Buys 5 mss/issue. Query. Length: 2,000 words minimum. Pays $75-100.

THE WESTERN RESERVE MAGAZINE, Box 243, Garrettsville OH 44231. (216)527-2030. Editor-in-Chief: Mary Folger. Managing Editor: Betty Clapp. Emphasizes historical, where-to-go, what-to-do, crafts and collectibles for Northeastern Ohioians with an interest in the region and all it has to offer an upper middle class readership. Published 8 times a year; 64 pages. Estab: 1973. Circ: 10,000. Pays on publication. Buys all rights, but may reassign following publication. Phone queries OK. Submit seasonal/holiday material 3 months in advance. Photocopied submissions OK. SASE. Reports in 1 month. Sample copy $2; free writer's guidelines.

Nonfiction: Historical (Northeastern Ohio); how-to (crafts with history); humor (if Northeastern Ohio historical slant); informational; interview (especially Northeastern Ohio historian, writer, artist, craftsman, etc.); photo feature (Western Reserve slant); profile (of famous or infamous Western Reserve person); and travel.

Photos: Purchased with accompanying ms. Uses b&w; "if sending old photo, we recommend copy—we try not to lose anything, but it can happen." Offers no additional payment for photos accepted with accompanying ms. Total purchase price for ms includes payment for photos. Model release required.

Columns/Departments: "Where to go, what to do" in Ohio and Western Pennsylvania. "New writers can break into *WRM* here and club public relations chairmen are welcome." Buys 6 (full-length "where to go, what to see" columns) per year. Send complete ms. Pays $30 for full-length article. Open to suggestions from freelancers for new columns/departments; address to Mary Folger.

Fiction: Historical (if Northeastern Ohio orientation). Buys 4 mss/year. Send complete ms. Length: 2,000 words maximum. Pays $20-50.

Poetry: "Excellence is only criterion—Betty is particular." Buys 15 poems/year. Limit submissions to batches of 3. Pays $10 minimum.

How To Break In: "Our goal is to help preserve the heritage of the Western Reserve. We need *good* copy and the ability to produce it is all that's needed to break in. "Heritage" is the key here—need both history and contemporary if the contemporary preserves local heritage."

WESTWAYS, P.O. Box 2890, Terminal Annex, Los Angeles CA 90051. (213)746-4410. Managing Editor: N.J. Kockler. Editorial Chief: Frances Ring. For "fairly affluent, college-educated, mobile and active Southern California families. Average age of head of household is 42; median income of family is $15,000. Monthly. Buys first rights. Buys approximately 250 mss a year. Pays on acceptance for mss; on publication for most photos. Submit seasonal material at least 4 to 6 months in advance. Reports in 4 to 6 weeks. Query preferred. Enclose S.A.S.E.

Nonfiction: "Informative articles, well-researched and written in fresh, literate, honest style." This publication "covers all states west of the Rockies, including Alaska and Hawaii, western Canada and Mexico. We're willing to consider anything that interprets and illuminates the American West—past or present—for the Western American family. Employ imagination in treating subject. Avoid PR hand-out type style and format, and please know at least something about the magazine." Subjects include "travel, history, modern civic, cultural, and sociological aspects of the West; camping, fishing, natural science, humor, first-person adventure and experience, nostalgia, profiles, and occasional unusual and offbeat pieces. One article a month on foreign travel." Length: 1,000 to 3,000 words. Pays 10¢ a word and up.

Photos: Buys color and b&w photos with or without mss. Prefers 8x10 b&w glossies. Often publishes photo essays. Pays $25 minimum "for each b&w used as illustration;" $25 to $200 per transparency.
Poetry: Publishes 12 to 15 poems a year. Length: up to 24 lines; "occasionally longer." Pays $25.

WESTWORLD, P.O. Box 6680, Vancouver, B.C., Canada V6B 4L4. (604)732-1371. Editor: Bill Mayrs. Most readers are B.C. residents interested in travel and B.C. Magazine; 72 pages. Established in 1975. Every 2 months. Circulation: 180,000. Buys one-time rights. Buys 30 to 40 mss a year. Pays on publication. Will send sample copy to writer on request. Write for copy of guidelines for writers. Submit seasonal (holiday) material 3 months in advance. Reports in 1 to 2 months. Query first or submit complete ms. Enclose S.A.E. and International Reply Coupons.
Nonfiction and Photos: "Articles of information, travel, historical interest, on B.C. and the 3 prairie provinces. *Westworld* is primarily a regional publication, written for people who want to hear about what they are familiar with, but with some new information or angle, plus a little on exotic faraway places. More on prairies welcome. We do not use stories on the U.S. Auto-touring stories only in our 'Weekend Adventures' format (will supply samples). Also some overseas travel. Perhaps some travel on non-Pacific destinations; something *good* for Christmas; more informative articles that are not entirely historical or travel." Length: 1,500 to 2,500 words for informational and historical articles; 1,000 to 2,500 for those used with photos; 1,000 to 1,500 words for overseas travel articles. No additional payment for 5x7 b&w glossies and color transparencies used with mss.

WICHITA, Wichita Area Chamber of Commerce, 350 W. Douglas, Wichita KS 67202. (318)265-7771. Managing Editor: Gene Dickinson. Coordinating Editor: Marge Setter. Emphasizes business and community assets. Bimonthly magazine; 36 pages. Estab: 1967. Circ: 8,000. Pays 50% on acceptance, balance on publication. Buys all rights, but may reassign following publication. Submit seasonal/holiday material 2 months in advance. Simultaneous, photocopied, and previously published submissions OK. SASE. Reports in 3 weeks. Free sample copy.
Nonfiction: Informational (articles on new management techniques); interviews (with nationally known business leaders); and articles related to Wichita, past and present. Buys 2-3 mss/year. Query. Length: 300-800 words. Pays $50-175.
Photos: Purchased on assignment only. Captions required. Query. No additional payment for 5x7 b&w glossies. Model release required.
How To Break In: "Determine a topic or person that will be of specific interest to Wichita business persons, or send a list of possible topics and/or individuals that the writer has access to for interviews."

WINDOW OF VERMONT, L.L.B. Corp., Warren VT 05674. (802)496-2223. Editor-in-Chief: Mary K. Kerr. For "youngsters to oldsters, those who have that common desire to know and experience as much as possible about our unique state, Vermont." Monthly tabloid; 24 pages. Estab: 1969. Circ: 42,000. Pays on publication. Buys all rights but may reassign following publication. Phone queries OK. Submit seasonal/holiday material 2 months in advance. Simultaneous, photocopied and previously published submissions OK. SASE. Reports in 4 weeks. Free sample copy and writer's guidelines.
Nonfiction: Informational; historical; humor; interview; nostalgia; profile; travel; personal experience; and photo feature. "We will consider nearly any subject and approach, but the article must be definitely 'Vermont oriented'." Buys 6 mss/issue. Submit complete ms. Length: 1,000-2,000 words. Pays $15-25.
Photos: Purchased with or without accompanying ms. Pays $5-10 for 8x11 b&w glossy prints or any size color transparencies. Model release required.
How To Break In: "Imagine what the 'Vermontophile' would like to know—about our past, our present and, in some cases, our future—our people, our towns, our farms, our way of life—and of course, our mountains and valleys, lakes and streams. Once you have this feel for what our readers want, start submitting. Chances are, we'll develop a lasting working relationship."

WINDSOR THIS MONTH, Box 1029, Station A, Windsor, Ont., Canada N9A 6P4. (519)256-7162. Editor: Linda Steel. A city magazine with emphasis on leisure and current trends for the contemporary, active person interested in modern lifestyles and upbeat activities in the Windsor area. Monthly magazine; 32-40 pages. Estab: 1974. Circ: 20,000. Pays on publication. Buys all rights. Submit seasonal/holiday material 3 months in advance. Photocopied submissions OK. SASE. Reports immediately.

Nonfiction: "Articles pertaining to events or personalities of interest to the Windsor and Essex County area. These may be feature articles, humor, nostalgia, business how-to's and interviews with VIP's. Also interested in seeing articles pertaining to changing lifestyles. Emphasis is on local slant with possible exceptions of how-to's. Length: 1,000 words minimum for informational, profiles, humor, nostalgia and articles on successful business operations. 5,000 words minimum for feature articles. 500 words minimum for new product pieces." Pays $25-75 for informational, how-to, interviews, nostalgia and successful business operations. $25-50 for profiles; $20 for humor; $25 for new product pieces.

WISCONSIN TRAILS, Box 5650, Madison WI 53705. (608)288-5564. Editor: Jill Weber Dean. For readers interested in Wisconsin, its natural beauty, history, personalities, recreation, and the arts. Magazine; 44 pages. Established in 1960. Quarterly. Circulation: 28,000. Rights purchased vary with author and material. Buys 30-40 mss/year. Pays on publication. Will send free sample copy to writer on request. Write for copy of guidelines for writers. Will consider photocopied submissions. Submit seasonal material at least 1 year in advance. Reports in 1 month. Query or send outline. SASE.
Nonfiction: "Our articles focus on some aspect of Wisconsin life; an interesting site or event, a person or industry, or history and the arts. We do not use first-person essays (reminiscences are sometimes OK), ecstasies about scenery, or biographies about people who were born in Wisconsin, but made their fortunes elsewhere. No cartoons, crosswords, or fillers. Poetry exclusively on assignment." Length: 1,500 to 3,000 words. Pays $50-250, depending on length and quality.
Photos: Purchased without mss or on assignment. Captions preferred. B&w photos usually illustrate a given article. Color is mostly scenic. Pays $10 each for b&w on publication. Pays $50 for inside color; pays $100 for covers and center spreads. Transparencies; 2¼x2¼ or larger are preferred.
How To Break In: "Be talented; study the magazine to learn what sort of things we want; write a literate query letter; send a few samples of your writing so we'll be confident of your ability to develop the article outlined in your query."

YANKEE, Dublin NH 03444. (603)563-8111. Editor-in-Chief: Judson D. Hale. Managing Editor: John Pierce. Emphasizes the New England region. Monthly magazine; 176 pages. Estab: 1935. Circ: 700,000. Pays on acceptance. Buys all, first North American serial or one-time rights. Submit seasonal/holiday material at least 4 months in advance. Simultaneous and photocopied submissions OK. SASE. Reports in 2 weeks-1 month. Free sample copy and writer's guidelines.
Nonfiction: Historical (New England history, especially with present-day tie-in); how-to (especially for "Forgotten Arts" series of New England arts, crafts, etc.); humor; interview (especially with New Englanders who have not received a great deal of coverage); nostalgia (personal reminiscence of New England life); photo feature (prefer color, captions essential); profile; travel (N.E. only, with specifics on places, prices, etc.); current issues; nature; antiques to look for; food. Buys 50 mss/year. Query. Length: 1,500-3,000 words. Pays $25-500.
Photos: Purchased with accompanying ms or on assignment. (Without accompanying ms for "This New England" feature only; color only). Captions required. Send prints or transparencies. Pays $15 minimum for 8x10 b&w glossies. $100/page for 2¼x2¼ or 35mm transparencies; 4x5 for cover or centerspread. Total purchase price for ms includes payment for photos.
Columns/Departments: New England Trip (with specifics on places, prices, etc.); Antiques to Look For (how to find, prices, other specifics); At Home in New England (recipes, gardening, crafts). Buys 10-12 mss/year. Query. Length: 1,000-2,500 words. Pays $150-350.
Fiction: Deborah Stone, Fiction Editor. Adventure (currently doing some WW II stories about New Englanders); historical; humorous; mystery. Buys 12 mss/year. Send complete ms. Length: 2,000-3,000 words. Pays $400-500.
Poetry: Jean Burden, Poetry Editor. Free verse and modern. Buys 3-4 poems/issue. Send poems. Length: 32 words maximum. Pays $25 for all rights. Annual poetry contest with awards of $150, $100, and $50 for 1st, 2nd and 3rd prizes.

YANKEE MAGAZINE'S GUIDE TO NEW ENGLAND, 143 Newbury St., Boston MA 02116. (617)266-0813. Editor-in-Chief: Georgia Orcutt. Emphasizes travel and leisure for a readership from New England area and from all states in the union. Biannual magazine; 160-176 pages. Estab: 1971. Circ: 110,000. Pays on acceptance. Buys first North American serial rights. Submit seasonal/holiday material 6 months in advance. Simultaneous and photocopied submissions OK. SASE. Reports in 2 weeks. Sample copy $1.50; free writer's guidelines.
Nonfiction: Informational (places to discover on a vacation, tours to take, special restaurants,

related pieces); travel (New England towns/cities, specific things to see, places to stay). Buys 10-15 mss/issue. Query. Length: 500-2,500 words. Pays $50-300.

Photos: Bob Orlando, Art Director. Purchased with or without accompanying ms or on assignment. Send contact sheet or transparencies. Pays $10-75 for b&w 8x10 glossies; $25-150 for 35mm or 2¼x2¼ color transparencies.

How To Break In: "Send us a letter letting us know where you have been in New England and what ideas you think best fit our publication. Please don't send in suggestions if you have not bothered to obtain a copy of the magazine to see what we are all about! Send a query letter for your ideas, and explain why you think you are qualified to write about a given subject. Include samples."

Religious Publications

Educational and inspirational material of interest to a general audience (including students, church members, workers and leaders) within a denomination or religion is the primary interest of publications in this category. Publications intended to assist lay and professional religious workers in teaching and managing church affairs are classified in Church Administration and Ministry in the Trade Journals section. Religious magazines for children and teenagers will be found in the Juvenile, and Teen and Young Adult classifications. Jewish publications whose main concern is with matters of general Jewish interest (rather than religious interest) are listed in the Jewish Publications category.

A.M.E. REVIEW, 468 Lincoln Drive, N.W., Atlanta GA 30318. Editor-Manager: William D. Johnson. For the ministerial majority. Quarterly magazine; 68 to 70 (6x9) pages. Established in 1880. Circulation: 5,000. Not copyrighted. Payment on publication. Will send sample copy to writer for $1. Reports in 10 days. Query first or submit complete ms. Enclose S.A.S.E.

Nonfiction and Photos: Uses material on personal experiences and personal achievements of a religious nature; ministerial profiles, human interest articles, pulpit reviews and book reviews (religious and racial). Length: 2,500 words. Pays 10¢ a word. B&w (3x5) photos are purchased with or without accompanying mss. Pays $2.50.

Fiction: Mainstream, fantasy, humorous, religious. Length: open. Pays 8¢ a word.

Poetry: Free verse and light verse for the Poets' Corner. Length: open. Pays $5.

Fillers: Short humor with a religious slant. Pays $2 per line up to 4 lines.

ABBA, A JOURNAL OF PRAYER, Box 8516, Austin TX 78712. Editor: Eutychus Peterson. For theologians and seminarians. Magazine; 82 pages. Published irregularly. Estab: 1976. Circ: 700. Buys all rights. Buys about 24 mss/year. Pays on acceptance. Will send sample copy to writer for $2.50. Will consider photocopied submissions. No simultaneous submissions. Submit seasonal material 6 months in advance. Reports in 1 week on mss accepted for publication. Submit complete ms. SASE.

Nonfiction: Historical articles (on theology—not churches); how-to (hear God speak); informational (on prayer, meditation and God in us); inspirational (but not didactic); interviews (with theologians and religious writers); profiles (on theologians); and scholarly works on theology. Buys 24 mss/year. Send complete ms. Length: 5,000 words maximum. Pays 1¢/word ($50 maximum).

Photos: Purchased with or without mss. Captions are not used. Pays $3.33-9.99/b&w 5x7 glossy. "Photos must be art; they are used to add beauty to the magazine."

Columns/Departments: Reviews of books and periodicals. Query or submit complete ms. Length: 25-5,000 words. Pays 1¢/word ($50 maximum).

Fiction: Stories on religious subjects. Do not have to be explicitly religious. Experimental; fantasy; humorous; and science fiction. Buys 12/year. Send complete ms. Length: 5,000 words maximum. Pays 1¢/word ($50 maximum).

Poetry: Avant-garde; traditional; free verse; and haiku. Buys 60/year. Submit at least 6 at a time. Length: 75 words maximum. Pays $3.33-9.99.

How To Break In: "Two things are required: A continuing hour-by-hour consciousness of something greater than self in life, and the ability to express it in words which will appeal to highly educated persons interested in theology. All material must wrest me away from the commonplace, toward God."

AMERICA, 106 W. 56th St., New York NY 10019. (212)581-4640. Editor: Joseph A. O'Hare. Published weekly for adult, educated, largely Roman Catholic audience. Usually buys all rights. Pays on acceptance. Reports in two or three weeks. Write for copy of guidelines for writers. Enclose S.A.S.E.
Nonfiction and Poetry: "We publish a wide variety of material on politics, economics, ecology, and so forth. We are not a parochial publication, but almost all of our pieces make some moral or religious point. We are not interested in purely informational pieces or personal narratives which are self-contained and have no larger moral interest." Articles on literature, current political and social events. Length: 1,500 to 2,000 words. Pays $50 to $75. Poetry length: 10 to 30 lines. Address to Poetry Editor.

AMERICAN REVIEW OF EASTERN ORTHODOXY, Box 447, Indian Rocks Beach FL 33535. (813)595-4415. Editor: Robert Burns, Jr. Principally for clergy, students, seminarians, prominent laity of Eastern Orthodox, Roman Catholic, Espiscopal background. Religious news magazine; 32 (6x8) pages. Established in 1954. Published every 2 months. Circulation: 3,000. Not copyrighted. Buys about 6 mss a year. Pays on acceptance. Will send sample copy to writer for $1. Will consider photocopied and simultaneous submissions. Reports immediately. Submit complete ms. Enclose S.A.S.E.
Nonfiction and Photos: News, short items of religious topical interest. Eastern Orthodox items principally. American view, rather than old country view. Photos and terse descriptive matter dealing with the subject are necessary. News exposes. Informational, interview, historical, and photo articles. Length: 500 to 2,500 words. Pays $10 to $25. Photos purchased with ms with no additional payment. Purchased without accompanying ms for $5 minimum. Captions required. Clear b&w glossies.

THE ANNALS OF SAINT ANNE DE BEAUPRE, Basilica of St. Anne, Quebec, Canada G0A 3C0. (418)827-4538. Editor-in-Chief: E. Lefebou. Managing Editor: Jean-Claude Nadeau. Emphasizes the Catholic faith for the general public, of average education; mostly Catholic; part of the audience is made up of people who came to The Shrine of St. Anne de Beaupre. Monthly magazine; 32 pages. Estab: 1976. Circ: 72,000. Pays on acceptance. Buys first North American serial rights. Phone queries OK. Submit seasonal/holiday material 2 months in advance. SASE. Reports in 3-4 weeks. Free sample copy and writer's guidelines.
Nonfiction: Humor (short pieces on education, family, etc.); inspirational; interview; personal experience. Buys 10 mss/issue. Query. Length: 700-1,700 words. Pays $25-35.
Photos: Purchased with or without accompanying ms. Submit prints. Pays $5-15 for b&w glossies; $25-40 for color transparencies. "We buy very few color photos." Total purchase price for ms includes payment for photos.
Columns/Departments: Query. Length: 700-1,700 words. Pays $25-35. Open to suggestions from freelancers for new columns/departments.
Fiction: Religious (Catholic faith). Buys 1 ms/issue. Query. Length: 700-1,700 words. Pays $25-35.
Poetry: Light verse. Buys 12 poems/year. Limit submissions to batches of 6. Pays $5 minimum.
Fillers: Jokes, gags, anecdotes, short humor. "We buy few fillers." Pays $5 minimum.
For '78: Reports on human rights, problems of development vs. church, and Latin America and Africa.

ASPIRE, 1819 E. 14th Ave., Denver CO 80218. Editor: Jeanne Pomranka. For teens and adults: "those who are looking for a way of life that is practical, logical, spiritual, or inspirational." Monthly; 64 pages. Established in 1914. Circulation: 2,900. Buys all rights, but may reassign to author after publication providing credit given *Aspire*. Buys 100 mss a year. Pays on publication, or shortly thereafter. Will send a sample copy to a writer for 13¢. Submit seasonal material 6-7 months in advance. Reports in 2 weeks. Enclose S.A.S.E.
Nonfiction: Uses inspirational articles that help to interpret the spiritual meaning of life. Needs are specialized, since this is the organ of the Divine Science teaching. Personal experience, inspirational, think pieces. Also seeks material for God at Work, a department "written in the form of letters to the editor in which the writer describes how God has worked in his life or around him. Teen Talk includes short articles from teenagers to help other teenagers find meaning in life." Recently published articles include "Sowing and Reaping" and "Peace Beyond Understanding." Length: 100-1,000 words. Pays maximum 1¢/published word.
Fiction: "Anything not opposed to Divine Science teaching." Length: 250 to 1,000 words. Pays maximum 1¢ per published word.
Poetry: Traditional, contemporary, light verse. "We use very little poetry." Length: average 8 to 16 lines. Pays $2 to $4.

BAPTIST HERALD, 1 S. 210 Summit Ave., Oakbrook Terrace, Villa Park IL 60181. (312)495-2000. Dr. Reinhold J. Kerstan. For "any age from 15 and up, any educational background with mainly religious interests." Established in 1923. Monthly. Circulation: 10,000. Buys all rights. Payment on publication. Occasionally overstocked. Will send a free sample copy to a writer on request. Submit seasonal material 3 to 4 months in advance. Enclose S.A.S.E.
Nonfiction and Fiction: "We want articles of general religious interest. Seeking articles that are precise, concise, and honest. We hold a rather conservative religious line." Buys personal experience, interviews, inspirational, and personal opinion articles. Length: 700 to 2,000 words. Payment is $5 to $10. Buys religious and historical fiction. Length: 700 to 2,000 words. Pays $5 to $10.

BAPTIST LEADER, Valley Forge PA 19481. (215)768-2158. Editor: Vincie Alessi. For ministers, teachers, and leaders in church schools. Monthly; 64 pages. Buys first rights, but may reassign rights to author after publication. Pays on acceptance. Will send free sample copy to a writer on request. Read magazine before submitting. Deadlines are 8 months prior to date of issue. Reports immediately. Enclose S.A.S.E.
Nonfiction: Educational topics and social issues. How-to articles for local church school teachers. Length: 1,500 to 2,000 words. Pays $25 to $40.
Photos: Church school settings; church, worship, children's and youth activities and adult activities. Purchased with mss. B&w, 8x10; human interest and seasonal themes. Pays $10-15.

BRIGADE LEADER, Box 150, Wheaton IL 60187. Editor: Don Dixon. Managing Editor: Richard Mould. For men associated with Christian Service Brigade clubs throughout U.S. and Canada. Quarterly magazine; 32 pages, (8½x11). Buys all rights; but will sometimes reassign rights to author after publication; second serial (reprint) rights. Buys 4 mss a year. Payment on acceptance. Submit seasonal material 4 months in advance. Will consider photocopied submissions. Reports in 2 months. Query first. Enclose S.A.S.E.
Nonfiction and Photos: "Articles about men and things related to them. Relationships in home, church, work. Specifically geared to men with an interest in boys. Besides men dealing with boys' physical, mental, emotional needs—also deals with spiritual needs." Informational, personal experience, inspirational. Length: 800 to 1,200 words. Pays 1¢ minimum a word. Photos purchased with or without ms. Pays $7.50 for b&w.

CALVINIST-CONTACT, 90 Niagara St., St. Catherines, Ontario, Canada L2R 4L3. (416)682-5614. Editor: Keith Knight. Christian weekly newspaper. No rights purchased. Enclose S.A.E. and International Reply Coupons.
Nonfiction: "Any material as long as it is suitable for our publication, which has as its aim the practical application of the principles of the Bible as the only true guide in life."

CANADIAN CHURCHMAN, 600 Jarvis St., Toronto, Ont. M4Y 2J6, Canada. Editor: Jerrold F. Hames. For a general audience; Anglican Church of Canada; adult, with religio-socio emphasis. Monthly tabloid newspaper; 28 to 32 pages. Established in 1874. Circulation: 280,000. Not copyrighted. Buys 10 to 12 mss a year. Payment on publication. Will consider photocopied submissions and simultaneous submissions. Query first. Enclose S.A.E. and International Reply Coupons.
Nonfiction: "Religion, news from churches around the world, social issues, theme editions (native rights, abortion, alcoholism, etc.). Newsy approach; bright features of interest to Canadian churchmen. Prefer rough sketch first; freelance usually on assignment only. Our publication is Anglican-slanted, progressive, heavily socially oriented in presenting topical issues." Informational, interview, spot news. Length: 750 to 1,200 words. Pays $35 to $100.

CATHOLIC LIFE, 9800 Oakland Ave., Detroit MI 48211. Editor-in-Chief: Robert C. Bayer. Emphasizes foreign missionary activities of the Catholic Church in Burma, India, Bangladesh, the Philippines, Hong Kong, Africa, etc., for middle-aged and older audience with either middle incomes or pensions. High school educated (on the average), conservative in both religion and politics. Monthly (except July or August) magazine; 32 pages. Estab: 1954. Circ: 18,200. Pays on publication. Buys all rights, but may reassign following publication. Submit seasonal/holiday material 3-4 months in advance. Simultaneous submissions OK. SASE. Reports in 2 weeks. Free sample copy and writer's guidelines.
Nonfiction: Informational; inspirational (foreign missionary activities of the Catholic Church; experiences, personalities, etc.). Buys 30 mss/year. Query or send complete ms. Length: 800-1,400 words. Pays 4¢/word.

How To Break In: "Freelancers should first inquire as to the specific approaches we would require in dealing with the missionary topics...also, whether areas of operation the writer has in mind would be of any appeal to us. Once the writer has written a few articles and submitted the illustrative photos, he would get the feel of the magazine."

CATHOLIC NEAR EAST MAGAZINE, Catholic Near East Welfare Association, 1011 First Ave., New York NY 10022. (212)826-1480. Editor: Virginia Rohan. For a general audience with interest in the Near East, particularly its religious and cultural aspects. Magazine; 24 pages. Established in 1974. Quarterly. Circulation: 180,000. Buys first North American serial rights. Buys about 16 mss a year. Pays on acceptance. Will send sample copy to writer on request. Write for copy of guidelines for writers. Photocopied submissions OK if legible. Submit seasonal material (Christmas and Easter in different Near Eastern lands or rites) 6 months in advance. Reports on material accepted for publication in 3 to 4 weeks. Returns rejected material in 2 weeks. Query first or submit complete ms. Enclose S.A.S.E.
Nonfiction and Photos: "Cultural, territorial, devotional material on the Near East, its peoples and religions, (especially Eastern Rites) including profiles of noted personalities in Asia. Style should be simple, factual, concise. Articles must stem from personal acquaintance with subject matter, or through up-to-date research. No preaching or speculations." Length: 800-1,400 words. Pays 10¢/word. No additional payment for excellent quality b&w glossies used with mss. Captions required. Pays $10 to $15 for color slides or transparencies. All photos must relate to the accompanying ms.

CHICAGO STUDIES, Box 665, Mundelein IL 60060. (312)566-6401, Ext. 61. Editor: George J. Dyer. For Roman Catholic priests and religious educators. Magazine; 112 pages. Established in 1962. Published 3 times/year. Circ: 8,500. Buys all rights. Buys 30 mss a year. Pays on acceptance. Will send sample copy to writer for $1. Will consider photocopied submissions. Submit complete ms. Reports within 6 weeks. Enclose S.A.S.E.
Nonfiction: Nontechnical discussion of theological, biblical, ethical topics. Articles aimed at a nontechnical presentation of the contemporary scholarship in those fields. Length: 3,000 to 5,000 words. Pays $35 to $100.

CHRIST FOR ALL, REACH OUT, Division of Home Missions, Assemblies of God, 1445 Boonville Ave., Springfield MO 65802. Editor: Ruth Lyon. For members and friends of the Assemblies of God who are interested in Home Missions; young adults through senior citizens. Magazine; 8 (8½x11) pages. *Christ for All* established in 1973; *Reach Out* in 1970. Published every 2 months. Circulation: 35,000. Buys all rights. "Our magazines are quite limited in what we could accept from freelance writers. Most of our work is maintained through contributions of interested churches and friends." Pays on publication. Will send free sample copy to writer on request. Write for copy of guidelines for writers. No photocopied or simultaneous submissions. Submit seasonal material 4 to 6 months in advance. "If we can't use material and we think another department can, we usually let them see it before replying. Otherwise, as soon as we reject it, we return it." Query first. Enclose S.A.S.E.
Nonfiction and Photos: "All material must have some religious value. Home Missions subjects related to ethnic groups, Teen Challenge, chaplaincies, New Church Evangelism. Has to be slanted to and acceptable to members of the Assemblies of God, and the material is restricted to Assemblies of God Home Missions. These magazines are promotional and informative in nature, as well as inspirational. They exist for the purpose of informing people about our Home Missions ministries and promoting these ministries. Studying the magazines will give the writer a 'feel' of what we need. We would be interested in a story about the outstanding work of some A/G home missionary as seen through the eyes of the writer." Length: 500-800 words. Pays 2¢/word minimum. B&w and color photos purchased at price set by the contributor. "Must be related to our mission work on Indian reservations, among the deaf or blind; ethnic or minority groups in general. Some pictures can be general, especially scenic or depicting culture or native life.
Fiction: Related to seasonal holidays. Length: 500 to 800 words. Pays minimum of 2¢/word.

THE CHRISTIAN ATHLETE, Fellowship of Christian Athletes, 812 Traders National Bank Bldg., 1125 Grand Avenue, Kansas City MO 64106. (816)842-3908. Editor: Gary Warner. For "general audience of all ages interested in athletics, especially as it involves the perspective of the Christian faith. Large segment includes high school, college and professional athletes and coaches." Established in 1959. Monthly. Circulation: 50,000. Buys first rights only. Buys 15 to 25 mss a year. Payment on publication. Will send free sample copy and editorial guidelines to writer on request. Uses sport in season and profiles of athletes. Submit seasonal material four months in advance. Reports in one to two weeks. Enclose S.A.S.E.

Nonfiction: Personal testimonies and profiles. Articles related to athletics and the Christian faith. Heart of magazine is personal profile of athlete or coach with spiritual perspective the center of article. Wants stories "with masculine approach; strong, fast-paced articles and profiles. Articles related to issues in athletics and society. Message and place of Jesus Christ focal point. We're one of the only magazines we know of dealing in two worlds of athletics and Christianity. Not a straight sport magazine or specifically religious publication but one which bridges both worlds. Avoid the trite 'goody-goody' articles. Want the Christian perspective included with a man's warts showing. Don't want the sickeningly sweet Sunday school pap." Uses informational, how-to (sport), personal experience, interview, profile, inspirational, humor, and think articles. Length: 200 to 2,500 words. Pays $10 minimum per article.

Photos: Photos used with mss and on assignment, captions optional. B&w 5x7 or 8x10. Pays $10 minimum for b&w photos. "We can take an excellent sports photo showing emotion, drama, conflict, agony, defeat, joy, etc., and build free verse, Scripture verse, etc., around it."

Poetry and Fillers: Uses free and light verse. Also uses clippings and short humor. No payment for poetry and fillers.

THE CHRISTIAN CENTURY, 407 S. Dearborn St., Chicago IL 60605. (312)427-5380. Editor: James N. Wall. For college-educated, ecumenically minded, progressive church people, both clergy and lay. Weekly magazine; 24-32 pages. Estab: 1884. Circ: 30,000. Pays on publication. Usually buys all rights. Query appreciated, but not essential. SASE. Reports in 3 weeks. Free sample copy.

Nonfiction: "We use articles dealing with social problems, ethical dilemmas, political issues, international affairs, and the arts, as well as with theological and ecclesiastical matters. We focus on concerns that arise at the juncture between church and society, or church and culture." Length: 2,500 words maximum. Payment varies, but averages $20/page.

CHRISTIAN HERALD, 40 Overlook Dr., Chappaqua NY 10514. (914)769-9000. Editor-in-Chief: Kenneth L. Wilson. Managing Editor: Jane Campbell. Emphasizes religious living in family and church. Monthly magazine; 64 pages. Estab: 1878. Circ: 255,000. Pays on acceptance. Buys all rights, but may reassign following publication. Submit seasonal/holiday material 5-6 months in advance. Photocopied submissions OK. SASE. Sample copy $1; free griter's guidelines.

Nonfiction: Expose; how-to; informational; inspirational; interview; profile; and religious experience. Buys 50-75 mss/year. Query or send complete ms. Length: 1,000-2,500 words. Pays $50 minimum.

Photos: Purchased with or without accompanying ms. Send transparencies. Pays $10 minimum for b&w; $25 minimum for 2¼x2¼ color transparencies.

Columns/Departments: I Protest, a personal opinion column. Buys 5/year. Send complete ms. Length: 1,000-2,000 words. Pays $50 minimum.

Poetry: Light verse, traditional, religious and inspirational. Buys 30 poems/year. Length: 4-20 lines. Pays $10 minimum.

CHRISTIAN HERITAGE, Box 176, Hackensack NY 07602. (201)342-6202. Editor: Rev. Stuart P. Garver. Published monthly except July and August for Protestant evangelicals with an interest in development inside the Roman Catholic Church. Buys first North American serial rights. Reports promptly as a rule; sometimes needs a month in the summer. Enclose S.A.S.E.

Nonfiction: Prefers readable, nonpedantic treatment of Church-State affairs, both historical and current. Interested in fact-filled and interpretive articles on effect of government policies on organized religion. Also in the market for true stories from lives of former clerics who have gone on to successful careers in other fields. Absolutely rejects all anti-Catholic material. Length: 2,200 to 2,500 words. Pay is $15 to $35.

CHRISTIAN LIFE MAGAZINE, Gundersen Dr. and Schmale Rd., Wheaton IL 60187. Editor: Robert Walker. For leadership groups in religious circles. Monthly. Buys all rights. Payment on publication. Reports in 2 weeks to 1 month. Query first for longer articles requiring lengthy research. Enclose S.A.S.E.

Nonfiction and Photos: Devotional and missionary articles, features on Christian organizations, accounts of spiritual aid through Christian witness, church building and remodeling. Sunday school teaching techniques. Christian family life, current events in Christian life, and development of schools and colleges. In all articles, Jesus Christ should be exalted and not individual personalities. It is best to read the magazine first to become familiar with approach (a sample will be sent on request). Major features should be 2,500 to 3,000 words. Shorter articles on how problems were overcome or needs met in areas of Sunday school,

church building and management, and family relationships are usually 1,500 to 2,000 words. Pays up to $175 for article and pix on publication. Clear, action photos with articles and news stories at $3 to $5. For shorter, back-of-book articles, pays $50.
Fiction: Well-plotted stories built upon significant problems faced by Christians in their life and walk with the Lord. Should be solved by overt character action. 2,500 to 2,800 words preferred. Pays $50 for short-shorts.

CHRISTIAN LIVING, Mennonite Publishing House, 616 Walnut Ave., Scottdale PA 15683. (412)887-8500. Editor: J. Lorne Peachey. For Christian families. Monthly. Buys first or second rights. Pays on acceptance. Reports in 2 weeks. Submit complete ms. Enclose S.A.S.E.
Nonfiction and Photos: Articles about Christian family life, parent-child relations, marriage, and family-community relations. Material must address itself to one specific family problem and/or concern and show how that problem/concern may be solved. If about a family activity, it should deal only with one such activity in simple, direct language. All material must relate to the adult members of a family, not the children. Length: 1,000 to 1,500 words. Pays up to $30. Additional payment for b&w photos used with mss.
Fiction and Poetry: Short stories on the same themes as above. Length: 1,000 to 2,000 words. Poems related to theme. Length: 25 lines. Pays up to $30 for fiction; minimum of $5 for poetry.

CHRISTIANITY & CRISIS, 537 W. 121st St., New York NY 10027. (212)662-5907. Editor: Wayne H. Cowan. For professional clergy and laymen; politically liberal; interested in ecology, good government, minorities and the church. Journal of 12 to 16 pages, published every 2 weeks. Established in 1941. Circulation: 10,000. Rights purchased vary with author and material. Usually buys all rights, but may reassign to author after publication. Buys 5 to 10 mss a year. Payment on publication. Will send free sample copy to writer on request. Will consider photocopied and simultaneous submissions. Reports on material in 3 weeks. Enclose S.A.S.E.
Nonfiction: "Our articles are written in-depth, by well-qualified individuals, most of whom are established figures in their respective fields. We offer comment on contemporary, political and social events occurring in the U.S. and abroad. Articles are factual and of high quality. Anything whimsical, superficial, or politically dogmatic would not be considered." Interested in articles on bio-medical ethics, new community projects; informational articles and book reviews. Length: 500 to 5,000 words. Pays $25 to $50.
How To Break In: "It is difficult for a freelancer to break in here but not impossible. Several authors we now go to on a regular basis came to us unsolicited and we always have a need for fresh material. Book reviews are short (800 to 1,500 words) and may be a good place to start, but you should query first. Another possibility is Viewpoints which also runs short pieces. Here we depend on people with a lot of expertise in their fields to write concise comments on current problems. If you have some real area of authority, this would be a good section to try."

CHRISTIANITY TODAY, 465 Gundersen Dr., Carol Stream IL 60187. Editor-in-Chief: Harold Lindsell. Emphasizes religion. Semimonthly magazine; 55 pages. Estab: 1956. Circ: 130,000. Pays on acceptance. Buys all rights, but may reassign following publication. Submit seasonal/holiday material 6-8 months in advance. SASE. Reports in 4 weeks. Free sample copy and writer's guidelines.
Nonfiction: Historical and informational. Buys 4 mss/issue. Query or send complete ms. Length: 1,000-2,000 words. Pays $100 minimum.
Columns/Departments: Ministers' Workship (practical and specific, not elementary ideas; how something *has* worked, not how it *ought* to work). Buys 12 mss/year. Send complete ms. Length: 900-1,100 words. Pays $60 maximum.

THE CHURCH HERALD, 1324 Lake Dr., S.E., Grand Rapids MI 49506. Editor: Dr. John Stapert. For a general audience in the Reformed Church in America. Publication of the Reformed Church in America. Magazine; 32 pages. Estab: 1826. Biweekly. Circ: 74,000. Rights purchased vary with author and material. Buys all rights, first serial rights, or second serial (reprint) rights. Buys about 30 mss a year. Pays on acceptance. Will send free sample copy to writer on request. Write for copy of guidelines for writers. Will consider photocopied and simultaneous submissions. Submit material for major Christian holidays 2 months in advance. Reports in less than 2 weeks. Submit complete ms only. Enclose S.A.S.E.
Nonfiction and Photos: "We expect all of our articles to be helpful and constructive, even when a point of view is vigorously presented. Articles on subjects such as Christianity and culture, government and politics, forms of worship, the media, ethics and business relations, responsible parenthood, marriage and divorce, death and dying, challenges on the campus, drug addiction, alcoholism, Christian education, human interest stories within the church, good news of God's

blessings, praise, etc. Articles by or about a well-known and respected Christian doctor, attorney, businessman, teacher, judge, nurse or labor leader, showing how he faces his responsibilities, deals with his problems, and finds a Christian solution, with quotes and anecdotes to illustrate. We are also looking for material that will help us to build a somewhat younger readership, particularly readers in their teens and twenties." Length: 400 to 1,400 words. Pays 2¢ to 3¢ per word. Photos purchased with or without accompanying ms. Pays 15/8x10 b&w glossy.

Fiction, Poetry, and Fillers: Religious fiction. Length: 400 to 1,400 words. Pays 2¢ to 3¢ per word. Traditional forms of poetry. Length: 30 lines maximum. Pays $5 to $15. Jokes and short humor. Length: about 80 words.

THE CHURCHMAN, 1074 23rd Ave., N., St. Petersburg FL 33704. (813)894-0097. Editor: Edna Ruth Johnson. For people who think; who care about mankind. Magazine, (8x11). Established in 1804. Monthly, October through March; bimonthly, April through September. Circulation: 10,000. Not copyrighted. Uses about 12 mss a year. Pays in contributor's copies. Will send free sample copy to writer on request. Will consider photocopied submissions. No simultaneous submissions. Reports within a month. Submit complete ms. Enclose S.A.S.E.

Nonfiction: Sociological, religious and, sometimes, political material. Although founded by Episcopal leadership, this publication is interdenominational, inter-faith, and relevant to today's troubled world. Inspirational, historical, think pieces, expose. Length: 500 to 1,000 words.

COLUMBIA, P.O. Drawer 1670, New Haven CT 06507. Editor: Elmer Von Feldt. For Catholic families; caters particularly to members of the Knights of Columbus. Monthly magazine. Established in 1920. Circulation: 1,200,000. Buys all rights. Buys 50 mss a year. Payment on acceptance. Will send free sample copy to writer on request. Write for copy of guidelines for writers. Submit seasonal material 6 months in advance. Reports in 4 weeks. Query first or submit complete ms. Enclose S.A.S.E.

Nonfiction and Photos: Fact articles directed to the Catholic layman and his family and dealing with current events, social problems, Catholic apostolic activities, education, ecumenism, rearing a family, literature, science, arts, sports and leisure. Length: 1,000 to 3,000 words. Glossy photos (8x10) b&w are required for illustration. Articles without ample illustrative material are not given consideration. Payment ranges from $200 to $400, including photos. Photo stories are also wanted. Pays $15 per photo used and 10¢ per word.

Fiction and Humor: Written from a thoroughly Christian viewpoint. Length: 3,000 words maximum. Pays $300 maximum. Humor or satire should be directed to current religious, social or cultural conditions. Pays up to $100 for about 1,000 words.

COMMONWEAL, 232 Madison Ave., New York NY 10016. (212)683-2042. Editor: James O'Gara. Edited by Roman Catholic laymen. For college-educated audience. Special book and education issues. Biweekly. Circ: 24,000. Buys 75 mss a year. Pays on acceptance. Will send a sample copy to a writer on request. Submit seasonal material 2 months in advance. Reports in 3 weeks. "A number of our articles come in over-the-transom. I suggest a newcomer either avoid particularly sensitive areas (say, politics) or let us know something about you (your credentials, tearsheets, a paragraph about yourself)." Enclose S.A.S.E.

Nonfiction: "Articles on timely subjects: political, literary, religious." Original, brightly written mss on value-oriented themes. Buys think pieces. Length: 1,000 to 2,500 words. Pays 2¢ a word.

Poetry: Department Editor: John Fanel. Contemporary and avant-garde. Length: maximum 150 lines ("long poems very rarely"). Pays $7.50 to $25.

THE COMPANION OF ST. FRANCIS AND ST. ANTHONY, Conventual Franciscan Friars, 15 Chestnut Park Rd., Toronto, Ontario, Canada M4W 1W5. (416)924-6349. Editor-in-Chief: Rev. Nicholas Weiss. Emphasizes religious and human values for a mostly middle-age and older readership. Monthly magazine; 32 pages. Estab: 1926. Circ: 8,000. Pays on acceptance. Buys all rights, but may reassign following publication. Phone queries OK. Submit seasonal/holiday material 2 months in advance. Simultaneous and photocopied submissions OK. SASE. Reports in 3 weeks. Free sample copy and writer's guidelines.

Nonfiction: Historical; how-to (medical and psychological coping); informational; inspirational; interview; nostalgia; profile; and travel. Buys 6 mss/issue. Send complete ms. Length: 1,000-2,000 words. Pays 2¢/word.

Photos: Photos purchased with or without accompanying ms. Captions required. Pays $5-10 for 5x7 (but all sizes accepted) b&w glossies and color photos. Send prints. Total purchase price for ms includes payment for photos.

Fiction: Adventure; humorous; mainstream and religious. Buys 1 ms/issue. Send complete ms. Length: 1,000-1,500 words. Pays 2¢/word.

How To Break In: "Mss on human interest with photos are given immediate preference."

THE CONGREGATIONALIST, 801 Bushnell, Beloit WI 53511. (608)362-4821. Editor: Dr. Louis B. Gerhardt. "This is the publication of the National Association of Congregational Christian Churches. Readers tend to be members of our churches, or generally spiritually oriented people." Monthly magazine; 24 pages (8½x11). Established in 1840. Circulation: 10,000. Rights purchased vary with author and material. Usually buys all rights. Buys 80 to 160 mss a year. Payment on publication. Will send free sample copy to writer on request. Write for copy of editorial guidelines for writers. Submit Thanksgiving, Christmas, Lent and Easter material at least 3 months in advance. Will consider photocopied and simultaneous submissions. Reports in 3 to 4 weeks. Submit only complete ms. Enclose S.A.S.E.

Nonfiction: Articles and miscellaneous features affirming the goodness of man and his spiritual nature. "We accept a wide range of religious views, and welcome views on controversial subjects not generally covered in religious magazines." Length: 300 to 2,500 words. Pays $15 to $50.

Fiction: Experimental, mainstream, religious, and historical fiction on any theme. Length: 300 to 2,500 words. Pays $15 to $50.

Poetry and Fillers: Traditional forms, blank verse, free verse, avant-garde forms, light verse, and religious poetry. Length: 2 lines minimum; no maximum. Pays $5 minimum. Pays $5 to $15 for religious puzzles.

CONTACT, United Brethren Publishing, 302 Lake St., Box 650, Huntington IN 46750. (219)356-2312. Editor-in-Chief: Stanley Peters. Managing Editor: Dennis Miller. For conservative, evangelical Christians, young and old. Weekly magazine; 8 pages. Circ: 7,000. Pays on acceptance. Buys simultaneous, second serial (reprint) and one-time rights. Submit seasonal/holiday material 6 months in advance. Simultaneous photocopied and previously published submissions OK. SASE. Reports in 4-6 weeks. Free sample copy and writer's guidelines.

Nonfiction: Historical; how-to; humor; informational; inspirational; personal experience and photo feature. Buys 2 mss/issue. Send complete ms. Length: 150-1,200 words. Pays 1¢/word maximum.

Photos: Photos purchased with or without accompanying ms. Pays $6.50 for 5x7 or 8x10 b&w glossies.

Fiction: Adventure, historical; humorous; and religious. Buys 30 mss/year. Send complete ms. Length: 600-1,200 words. Pays 3/4¢/word.

Fillers: Jokes, gags, anecdotes, puzzles and short humor. Buys 2 fillers/issue. Length: 25-250 words. Pays 50¢

THE COVENANT COMPANION, 5105 N. Francisco Ave., Chicago IL 60625. (312)784-3000. Editor-in-Chief: James R. Hawkinson. Emphasizes Christian life and faith. Bimonthly (monthly issues July and August) magazine; 32 pages. Circ: 28,500. Pays on publication. Buys all rights, but may reassign following publication. Submit seasonal/holiday material 3 months in advance. Simultaneous, photocopied and previously published submissions OK. SASE. Reports in 2 months. Sample copy 25¢.

Nonfiction: Humor; informational; inspirational (especially evangelical Christian); interviews (Christian leaders and personalities); and personal experience. Buys 15-20 ms/year. Length: 500-1,100 words. Pays $10-15.

CROSS AND CROWN, Aquinas Institute of Theology, 2570 Asbury, Dubuque IA 52001. (319)556-7593. Editor: Rev. Christopher Kiesling, O.P. For all who are genuinely interested in spiritual advancement. Buys all rights, but right to reuse the material is assigned back without charge if credit line is given to *Cross and Crown.* Payment on publication. Query first or submit complete ms. Enclose S.A.S.E.

Nonfiction: Articles that present a serious examination of important truths pertinent to the spiritual life, but placed in the context of today's world. Scriptural, biographical, doctrinal, liturgical, and ecumenical articles are acceptable. Length: 3,000 to 4,000 words. Pays 1¢ per word.

DAILY MEDITATION, P.O. Box 2710, San Antonio TX 78299. Editor: Ruth S. Paterson. Issued bimonthly. Rights purchased vary with author and material. Very occasionally buys reprint material. Gives permission to writers to resubmit to others after publication. Payment on acceptance. Will send sample copy to writer on request. Reports within 60 days. Submit complete ms. Enclose S.A.S.E.

Nonfiction: Uses metaphysical teachings, inspirational articles (seasonal articles 6 months in advance), nonsectarian religious articles (emphasis on how to apply principles to reader's life). Length: 750, 1,250 and 1,650 words. (Exact word count must be stated on ms.) Pays ½¢ to 1½¢ a word.
Poetry: Along same lines as above. Length: 16 lines maximum. Pays 14¢ per line.

DAILY WORD, Unity Village MO 64065. Editor: M. Smock. Published by the Unity School of Christianity. A monthly manual of daily studies. Copyrighted. Buys a limited number of short articles and poems. Writer must have an understanding of Unity teachings. Reports in 2 to 3 weeks. Enclose S.A.S.E.
Nonfiction and Poetry: To 1,000 words. Pays 3¢ a word and up. Poetry to 16 lines. Pays 25¢ a line and up.

DECISION MAGAZINE, 1300 Harmon Place, Minneapolis MN 55403. (612)332-8081. Editor: Roger C. Palms. Conservative evangelical monthly publication of the Billy Graham Evangelistic Association. Magazine; 16 pages. Estab: 1960. Circ: 4,000,000. Buys all rights unless otherwise arranged. Pays on publication. Reports within 2 months. Enclose S.A.S.E.
Nonfiction: Uses some freelance material; best opportunity is in testimony area (1,600 to 2,000 words). Also uses short narratives, 400 to 750 words. "Our function is to present Christ as Savior and Lord to unbelievers and present articles on deeper Christian life and human interest articles on Christian growth for Christian readers. No tangents. Center on Christ in all material." Pays $40 minimum per article.
Poetry: Uses devotional thoughts and short poetry in Quiet Heart column. Also has feature section which uses verse poems, free verse, brief narrative, illustration. No "preaching" or negativism. Positive, Christ-centered. Pays $5 to $25, depending on length of poem and on what page of magazine it appears.
Fillers: Uses fresh quotations from known or unknown individuals, devotional thoughts. Pays $3 per item.

THE DISCIPLE, Box 179, St. Louis MO 63166. Editor: James L. Merrell. Published by Christian Board of Publication of the Christian Church (Disciples of Christ). For ministers and church members, both young and older adults. Semimonthly. Circ: 85,500. Buys all rights, but may reassign rights to author after publication, upon request. Payment on publication. Payment for photos made at end of month of acceptance. Will send a sample copy to a writer for 25¢. Write for copy of guidelines for writers. Will consider photocopied and simultaneous submissions. Submit seasonal material at least 6 months in advance. Reports in 2 weeks to 3 months. Enclose S.A.S.E.
Nonfiction: Articles and meditations on religious themes; short pieces, some humorous. Length: 500-800 words. Pays $5-15. Also uses devotionals of 200-500 words for "A Faith for Today" page. Pays $10.
Photos: B&w glossies, 8x10. Occasional b&w glossies, any size, used to illustrate articles. Pays $5-10. Pays $15-25 when used for covers. No color.
Poetry: Uses 3 to 5 poems per issue. Traditional forms, blank verse, free verse and light verse. All lengths. Themes may be seasonal, historical, religious, occasionally humorous. Pays $3-5.

EMPHASIS ON FAITH & LIVING, 336 Dumfries Ave., Kitchener, Ontario, Canada N2H 2G1. Editor: Dr. Everek R. Storms. Official organ of The Missionary Church. For Church members. Magazine is published twice a month in U.S.A. but serves the Missionary Church in both the U.S. and Canada. Estab: 1969. Circ: 10,000. Not copyrighted. Buys "only a few" mss a year. Will consider photocopied and simultaneous submissions. Uses a limited amount of seasonal material, submitted 3 months in advance. Reports in 1 month. Submit only complete ms. Enclose S.A.S.E.
Nonfiction: Religious articles, presenting the truths of the Bible to appeal to today's readers. "We take the Bible literally and historically. It has no errors, myths, or contradictions. Articles we publish must have this background. No poetry, please. Especially would like articles covering the workings of the Holy Spirit in today's world." Length: approximately 500 words— "not too long". Pays $5 to $10 per ms.

ENGAGE/SOCIAL ACTION, 100 Maryland Ave., N.E., Washington DC 20002. (202)488-5632. Editor: Allan R. Brockway. For "United Methodist and United Church of Christ clergy and lay people interested in-depth analysis of social issues, particularly the church's role or involvement in these issues." Established in 1973. Monthly. Circulation: 9,000. Rights purchased vary with author and material. May buy all rights and reassign rights to author after publication. Buys about 30 mss a year. Pays on publication. Will send free sample copy to

writer on request. Write for copy of guidelines for writers. Will consider photocopied submissions, but prefers original. Returns rejected material in 2 to 3 weeks. Reports on material accepted for publication in several weeks. Query first or submit complete ms. Enclose S.A.S.E.
Nonfiction and Photos: "This is the social action publication of the United Methodist Church and the United Church of Christ published by the Board of Church and Society of the United Methodist Church. We publish articles relating to current social issues as well as church-related discussions. We do not publish highly technical articles or poetry. Our publication tries to relate social issues to the church—what the church can do, is doing; why the church should be involved. We only accept articles relating to social issues, e.g., war, draft, peace, race relations, welfare, police/community relations, labor, population problems. Reviews of books and music should focus on related subjects." Length: 1,500 words maximum. Pays $35 to $50. 8x10 b&w glossy photos purchased with or without mss. Captions required. Pays $15.

ETCETERA, 6401 The Paseo, Kansas City MO 64131. (816)333-7000, Ext. 277. Editor: J. Paul Turner. Published by the Church of the Nazarene for the 18-23-year-old college/university student. Monthly magazine. Circ: 18,000. Pays on acceptance. Buys first rights or second rights. Submit seasonal material 6 months in advance. SASE. Free sample copy.
Nonfiction: Articles which speak to students' needs in light of their spiritual pilgrimage. How they cope on a secular campus from a Christian life style. First-person articles have high priority since writers tend to communicate best that which they are in the process of learning themselves. Style should be evangelical...material should have "sparkle." Wesleyan in doctrine. Buys interviews, profiles, inspirational and think pieces, humor, photo essays. Length: 1,500 words maximum. Pays 2¢/word.
Photos: B&w glossies. Pays $5 to $15. Interested in photo spreads and photo essays.

THE EVANGELICAL BEACON, 1515 E. 66th St., Minneapolis MN 55423. (612)866-3343. Editor: George Keck. For Evangelical and conservative Protestant audience. Issued biweekly. Rights purchased vary with author and material. Buys first rights, second serial (reprint) rights, or all rights. Pays on publication. Will send free sample copy to a writer on request. Reports on submissions in 4 to 6 weeks. Enclose S.A.S.E.
Nonfiction and Photos: Devotional material, articles on the church, people and their accomplishments. "Crisp, imaginative, original writing desired — not sermons put on paper." Length: 500 to 1,500 words. Pays 2¢ per word. Prefers 8x10 photos. Pays $5 and up.
Fiction and Poetry: "Not much fiction used, but will consider if in keeping with aims and needs of magazine." Length: 100 to 2,000 words. Pays 2¢ a word. "In poetry, content is more important than form." Length: open. Pays $2.50 minimum.

EVANGELICAL FRIEND, Box 232, Newburg OR 97132. (503)538-7345. Editor: Jack Willcuts. Managing Editor: Harlow Ankeny. Readership is evangelical Christian families, mainly of the Quaker church denomination. Monthly magazine; 28 pages. Estab: 1967. Circ: 11,400. Pays on publication. Buys all rights, but may reassign following publication. Phone queries OK. Submit seasonal/holiday material 3-4 months in advance. Simultaneous, photocopied, and previously published submissions OK. SASE. Reports in 4 weeks. Free sample copy and writer's guidelines.
Nonfiction: Historical (church related); how-to (church growth methods, Christian education ideas, etc.); inspirational (Biblically based); interview; personal experience (spiritual); personal opinion (on various controversial subjects that relate to the church, etc.); photo feature (unusual people doing unusual Christian-related services). Buys 2-3 mss/year. Query. Length: 300-1,800 words. Pays $10-25.
Photos: Purchased on assignment. Send contact sheet. Pays $8-20 for b&w glossy or matte finish photos.

EVANGELIZING TODAY'S CHILD, 23033 N. Turkey Creek Rd., Morrison CO 80465. (303)697-8600. Editor: B. Milton Bryan. Bimonthly. Circulation: 33,000. Interdenominational, international, evangelical Christian publication for Sunday school teachers, Christian education directors and other children's workers reaching children with the Gospel. Usually buys all rights, with remuneration to authors upon use by other publications. Pays on publication. Will send editorial guide to writer on request. Query first. Reports in two months. Enclose S.A.S.E.
Nonfiction and Fillers: "Feature articles focus on problems and trends of interest to *evangelical* Christian education personnel, as well as children's workers. Must be Biblically and educationally sound." Length: 1,500 to 3,000 words. The "Resource Center" includes short, practical ideas for Sunday school teachers and children's workers, plus Bible puzzles and drills with meaningful themes. Pays 2-2½¢/word.

FRIAR, Butler NJ 07405. Editor: Father Rudolf Harvey. For Catholic families. Established in 1954. 11 times a year. Not copyrighted. Pays on acceptance. Enclose S.A.S.E.
Nonfiction: Uses articles and features on current problems or events; profiles of notable individuals; trends in sociology and education. Length: 1,800 to 3,000 words. Minimum payment of $15.

FRIDAY FORUM (OF THE JEWISH EXPONENT), 226 S. 16th St., Philadelphia PA 19102. (215)893-3745. Editor: Phyllis Zimbler Miller. For the Jewish community of Greater Philadelphia. Newspaper supplement. Established in 1971. Monthly. Circulation: 70,000. Usually buys all rights, but will reassign rights to author after publication. Buys about 40 mss a year. Pays after publication. Will send free sample copy to writer on request. Will consider photocopied submissions. No simultaneous submissions. Submit special material 6 months in advance. Reports on material accepted for publication in 2 months. Returns rejected material in 1 month. Enclose S.A.S.E.
Nonfiction and Photos: "We are interested only in articles of Jewish themes, whether they be historical, thought pieces, Jewish travel sites, photographic essays, or any other nonfiction piece on a Jewish theme. Topical themes are appreciated." Length: 6 to 12 double-spaced pages. Pays $25 minimum. 8x10 b&w glossies purchased on assignment. Captions required.
Poetry: Traditional forms, blank verse, free verse, avant-garde forms, light verse; must relate to a Jewish theme. Length varies. Pays $10 minimum.

GOOD NEWS, The Forum for Scriptural Christianity, Inc., 308 E. Main St., Wilmore KY 40390. (606)858-4661. Editor-in-Chief: Charles W. Keysor. For United Methodist lay people and pastors, primarily middle age and middle income; conservative and biblical religious beliefs; broad range of political, social and cultural values. Bimonthly magazine; 76 pages. Estab: 1967. Circ: 15,000. Pays on acceptance. Phone queries OK. Submit seasonal/holiday material 6 months in advance. Simultaneous, photocopied and previously published submissions OK. SASE. Reports in 2 months. Sample copy $1. Free writer's guidelines.
Nonfiction: Historical (prominent people or churches from the Methodist/Evangelical United Brethren tradition); how-to (to build faith, work in local church); humor (good taste); inspirational (related to Christian faith); personal experience (case histories of God at work in individual lives) and any contemporary issues as they relate to the Christian faith and the United Methodist Church. Buys 36 mss/year. Query. Pays $10-35.
Photos: Photos purchased with accompanying ms or on assignment. Captions required. Uses fine screen b&w glossy prints. Total purchase price for ms includes payment for photos. Payment negotiable.
Columns/Departments: Good News Book Forum. Query. Open to suggestions for new columns/departments.
Fillers: Clippings, jokes, gags, anecdotes, newsbreaks and short humor. Buys 20 fillers/year. Pays $5-10.

GOOD NEWS BROADCASTER, Box 82808, Lincoln NE 68501. (402)474-4567. Editor: Theodore H. Epp. Interdenominational magazine for adults from 16 years of age. Monthly. Circ: 210,000. Buys first rights. Buys approximately 45 mss/year. Pays on acceptance. Will send a sample copy and an author guide sheet to a writer on request. Send all mss to Thomas S. Piper, Managing Editor. Submit seasonal material at least 6 months in advance. Reports in 1 month. Query preferred, but not required. Enclose S.A.S.E.
Nonfiction and Photos: Articles which will help the reader learn and apply Christian biblical principles to his life. From the writer's or the subject's own experience. "Especially looking for true, personal experience 'salvation', church missions, 'youth' (16 years and over), 'parents', and 'how to live the Christian life' articles." Nothing dogmatic, or preachy, or sugary sweet, or without Biblical basis. Details or statistics should be authentic and verifiable. Style should be conservative but concise. Prefers that Scripture references be from the New American Standard Version or the Authorized Version. Length: maximum 1,500 words. Pays 3¢/word, more in special cases. Photos sometimes purchased with mss. Pays $7-10 for b&w glossies; $25-50 for color transparencies.
How To Break In: "The basic purpose of the magazine is to accomplish one of two things—to present Christ as Saviour to the lost or to promote the spiritual growth of believers by explaining the Bible and how it is relevant to life, so don't ignore our primary purposes when writing for us. Nonfiction should be Biblical and timely; at the least Biblical in principle. Write about ways to enrich family living, give solutions to people's problems, aids to help Christians live their daily experiences while working or relaxing — on the job, at home, in church, at school, in the community, or on the home or foreign mission field. Communicate spiritual truths in a positive way and without preaching at anyone or dogmatically telling the reader

what he has to do. Show a clear progression of thought throughout the article. Use illustrations of your own experiences or of someone else's when God solved a problem similar to the reader's. Be so specific that the meanings and significance will be crystal clear to all readers. We prefer third person articles as a rule."

GOSPEL CARRIER, Messenger Publishing House, Box 850, Joplin MO 64801. (417)624-7050. Editor-in-Chief: Roy M. Chappell, D.D. Managing Editor: Mrs. Marthel Wilson. Denominational Sunday school take home paper for adults, ages 20 through retirement. Quarterly publication in weekly parts; 104 pages. Circ: 3,500. Pays quarterly. Buys simultaneous, second serial and one-time rights. Submit seasonal/holiday material 1 year in advance. Simultaneous, photocopied, and previously published submissions OK. SASE. Reports in 3 months. Sample copy 50¢; free writer's guidelines.
Nonfiction: Historical (related to great events in the history of the church); informational (may explain the meaning of a Bible passage or a Christian concept); inspirational (must make a Christian point); nostalgia (religious significance); and personal experience (Christian concept). Buys 50-80 mss/year. Pays ½¢/word.
Photos: Purchased with accompanying ms. Send prints. Pays $2 for b&w glossies.
Fiction: Adventure, historical; romance; and religious. Must have Christian significance. Buys 13-20 mss/issue. Submit complete ms. Length: 800-2,000 words. Pays ½¢/word.
Fillers: Short inspirational incidents from personal experience or the lives of great Christians. Buys 52-80/year. Length: 200-500 words. Pays ½¢/word.

GOSPEL HERALD, 616 Walnut Ave., Scottdale PA 15683. (412)887-8500. Editor: Daniel Hertzler. Issued weekly (50 issues per year) for adult lembers of the Mennonite Church. Buys first and second rights. Pays on acceptance. Enclose S.A.S.E.
Nonfiction: "Articles discuss theological and practical Christian issues affecting Mennonite readers." Recently published articles include "Depression in the Church" and "Christ and Life's Transitions". Length: 300 to 1,500 words. Pays minimum of 1½¢ per word.

GUIDEPOSTS MAGAZINE, 747 Third Ave., New York NY 10017. Editorial Director: Arthur Gordon. *Guideposts* is an inspirational monthly magazine for all faiths in which men and women from all walks of life tell how they overcame obstacles, rose above failures, met sorrow, learned to master themselves, and became more effective people through the direct application of the religious principles by which they live. Buys all rights, but will reassign rights to author on request, after publication. Enclose S.A.S.E.
Nonfiction and Fillers: Articles and features should be written in simple, anecdotal style with an emphasis on human interest. Short features up to approximately 250 words ($10 to $25) would be considered for such *Guideposts* features as "Fragile Moments," and other short items which appear at the end of major articles. Short mss of approximately 250 to 750 words ($25 to $100) would be considered for such features as "Quiet People" and general one-page stories. Full-length mss, 750 to 1,500 words ($200 to $300). All mss should be typed, double-spaced and accompanied by a stamped, self-addressed envelope. Inspirational newspaper or magazine clippings often form the basis of articles in *Guideposts*, but it is unable to pay for material of this type and will not return clippings unless the sender specifically asks and encloses postage for return. Annually awards scholarships to high school juniors and seniors in writing contest.
How To Break In: "The freelancer would have the best chance of breaking in by aiming for a 1-page or maybe 2-page article. That would be very short, say 2½ pages of typescript, but in a small magazine such things are very welcome. A sensitively written anecdote that could provide us with an additional title is extremely useful. And they are much easier to just sit down and write than to have to go through the process of preparing a query. They should be warm, well-written, intelligent, and upbeat. We like personal narratives that are true and have some universal relevance, but the religious element does not have to be hammered home with a sledge hammer." Address short items to Van Varner.

THE HERALD, SPO 11, Asbury Theological Seminary, Wilmore KY 40390. Editor: Frank Bateman Stanger. For middle-income people who attend evangelical churches. Monthly magazine; 24 pages. Estab: 1888. Circ: 5,000. Not copyrighted. Buys about 15 mss a year. Pays on acceptance. Will send sample copy to writer on request. Will consider photocopied and simultaneous submissions. Submit seasonal (Christmas and Easter) material 4 months in advance. Reports in 1 month. Submit complete ms. Enclose S.A.S.E.
Nonfiction: Articles Editor: G. Wayne Rogers. Bible-based material dealing with the Christian life, the work of the church, etc. Inspirational anecdotes, personal experience, interviews, informational articles. Christmas and Easter material must be written from a religious point of view. Length: open. Pays $15 to $35.

Poetry: Traditional forms of poetry, blank verse, free verse. Must have religious theme. Length: open. Pays $10 minimum.

HIGH ADVENTURE, 1445 Boonville Ave., Springfield MO 65802. (417)862-2781, Ext. 264. Editor: Johnnie Barnes. For boys and men. 16 (8½x11) pages. Established in 1971. Quarterly. Circulation: 35,000. Rights purchased vary with author and material. Buys approximately 10 to 12 mss a year. Pays on publication. Will send free sample copy to writer on request. Write for copy of guidelines for writers. "All articles submitted are held in our files. When the decision is made to use an article in a specific issue, then a check will be sent to the author for the article." Query first or submit complete ms. Enclose S.A.S.E.
Nonfiction, Fiction, Photos, and Fillers: Camping articles, nature stories, fiction adventure stories, and jokes. Nature study and campcraft articles about 500 to 600 words. Buys how-to, personal experience, inspirational, humor, and historical articles. Pays $10 per page. Photos purchased on assignment. Adventure and Western fiction wanted. Length: 1,200 words. Puzzles, jokes and short humor used as fillers.

INSIGHT, The Young Calvinist Federation, Box 7244, Grand Rapids MI 49510. (616)241-5616. Editor-in-Chief: Rev. James C. Lont. Managing Editor: Doris Rikkers. For young people, 15-19, Christian backgrounds and well exposed to the Christian faith. Monthly (except June and August) magazine; 32 pages. Estab: 1921. Circ: 22,000. Pays on publication. Buys simultaneous, second serial (reprint) and first North American serial rights. Phone queries OK. Submit seasonal/holiday material 6 months in advance. Simultaneous, photocopied and previously published submissions OK. SASE. Reports in 4 weeks. Free sample copy and writer's guidelines.
Photos: Photos purchased without accompanying ms or on assignment. Pays $10-25 for 8x10 b&w glossies; $50-100 for 35mm or larger color transparencies. Total purchase price for ms includes payment for photos.
Fiction: Humorous; mainstream and religious. "I'm looking for short stories that are not preachy but that lead our readers to a better understanding of how their Christian beliefs apply to their daily living. They must do more than entertain—they must make the reader think or see something in a new light." Buys 1 ms/issue. Send complete ms. Length: 1,000-3,000 words. Pays $35-100.
Poetry: Free verse; light verse and traditional. Buys 5 poems/year. Length: 4-25 lines. Pays $10-25.
Fillers: Jokes, gags, anecdotes, puzzles and short humor. Buys 4 fillers/year. Length: 50-300 words. Pays $10-35.

INSIGHT, Review and Herald Publishing Association, 6856 Eastern Ave., Washington DC 20012. Editor-in-Chief: Donald John. "Our audience is 16-25 years old, including high school, college, graduate students, and young marrieds. We are directed primarily to Seventh-day Adventist young adults." Weekly magazine; 24 pages. Estab: 1970. Circ: 50,000. Pays on acceptance. Buys first North American serial rights. Submit seasonal/holiday material 3 months in advance. Photocopied and previously published submissions OK. SASE. Reports in 6 weeks. Sample copy and writer's guidelines for postal costs.
Nonfiction: How-to (we like practical Christian help for problems in school, dating, marriage, relating to God and man); historical (use mostly unique features about early Adventist pioneers or events); inspirational (we need factual-based stories); interview (with people who have an influence on the lives of young Christians); personal opinion (need intelligent essays that present God's character in new and enlightening ways, also discussion of problems of living in today's world); personal experience (conversion and witnessing stories handled in a fresh way); and photo feature. Buys 3 mss/issue. Query or submit complete ms. Length: 300-1,800 words. Pays 2-4¢/word.
Photos: Byron Steele, Photo Editor. Purchased without accompanying ms. Pays $50-125 for 8x10 b&w glossies. Query. Model release required.
Columns/Departments: Critique (review of books that have a religious or moral message). Buys 12 mss/year. Query. Length: 300-800 words. Pays 2-4¢/word. Open to suggestions for new columns or departments.
Fiction: Religious (well-written parables and allegories in harmony with our Bible doctrine). Buys 10 mss/year. Query or submit complete ms. Length: 300-1,000 words. Pays 2-4¢/word.
Poetry: Free verse, haiku, light verse, traditional, inspirational. Buys 20/year. Limit submissions to batches of 5. Length: 10-12 lines. Pays $2-10.

INTERACTION, 3558 S. Jefferson, St. Louis MO 63118. Editor: Mervin Marguardt.

Monthly, except July and August. Usually buys all rights. Will accept simultaneous submissions of articles and short stories, if noted. Payment on publication. Usually reports in 6 weeks. SASE.

Nonfiction and Photos: Accepts practical articles that are directed to Sunday school teachers and leaders, as well as articles on various aspects of general education and pieces directed to teachers as persons. Articles should be written in a popular, readable style. Preferred length: 1,000 to 1,500 words. Pays $20 to $50 per article, depending on length and quality. Buys 5x7 or larger b&w photographs with mss for $5 to $10 each.

Fiction: Considered if it makes a point which will aid the church school teacher to gain new perspectives of, or insights for, the teaching of the faith. Preferred length: 1,000 to 1,500 words. Pays $20 to $50 per short story.

Poetry: Accepts very little; published only occasionally. Poetry should be short, of a religious nature. Pays $5 to $15.

INTERLIT, David C. Cook Foundation, Cook Square, Elgin IL 60120. (312)741-2400, ext. 142. Editor-in-Chief: Gladys J. Peterson. Emphasizes Christian communications journalism for missionaries, broadcasters, publishers, etc. Quarterly newsletters; 20 pages. Estab: 1964. Circ: 9,000. Pays on acceptance. Buys all rights, but may reassign following publication. Photocopied submissions OK. SASE. Reports in 2 weeks. Free sample copy.

Nonfiction: Informational; interview and photo feature. Buys 7 mss/issue. Length: 500-3,000 words. Pays 2-4¢/word.

Photos: Purchased with accompanying ms or on assignment. Captions required. Query or send prints. Uses b&w. Offers no additional payment for photos accepted with ms.

LIBERTY, A Magazine of Religious Freedom, 6840 Eastern Ave., N.W., Washington DC 20012. (202)723-0800, ext. 745. Editor: Roland R. Hegstad. For "responsible citizens interested in community affairs and religious freedom." Bimonthly. Circulation: 500,000. Buys first rights. Buys approximately 40 mss a year. Pays on acceptance. Will send a sample copy to a writer on request. Write for copy of guidelines for writers. Will consider photocopied submissions. Submit seasonal material 6 to 8 months in advance. Reports in 1 week. Query not essential, but helpful. Enclose S.A.S.E.

Nonfiction: "Articles of national and international interest in field of religious liberty, church—state relations. Current events affecting above areas (Sunday law problems, parochial aid problems, religious discrimination by state, etc.). Current events are most important; base articles on current events rather than essay form." Buys how-to's, personal experience and think pieces, interviews, profiles. Length: maximum 2,500 words. Pays $75 to $150.

Photos: "To accompany or illustrate articles." Purchased with mss; with captions only. B&w glossies, color transparencies. Pays $15 to $35. Cover photos to $150.

LIGHT AND LIFE, Free Methodist Publishing House, 999 College Ave., Winona Lake IN 46590. Managing Editor: G. Roger Schoenhals. Emphasizes religion for a cross section of adults. Published 20 times yearly. Magazine; 16 pages. Estab: 1867. Circ: 60,000. Pays on publication. Buys all rights, but may reassign following publication. Submit seasonal/holiday material 6 months in advance. Previously published submissions OK. SASE. Reports in 4 weeks. Sample copy and writer's guidelines for SASE.

Nonfiction: Each issue uses a lead article (warm, positive first-person account of God's help in a time of crisis; 1,500 words); a Christian living article (a fresh, lively, upbeat piece about practical Christian living; 750 words); a Christian growth article (an in-depth, lay-level article on a theme relevant to the maturing Christian; 1,500 words); a discipleship article (a practical how-to piece on some facet of Christian discipleship; 750 words); news feature (a person-centered report of a "good news" event showing God at work at the local, conference, or denominational level of the Free Methodist Church; 500 words, 2 photographs); and a back page article (contents must be brief and attractive; poem, parable, or 400-word article, profound and unforgettable). Buys 90 mss/year. Submit complete ms. Pays 2¢/word.

Photos: Purchased without accompanying ms. Send prints. Pays $7.50-20.00 for b&w photos. Offers no additional payment for photos accepted with accompanying ms.

LIGUORIAN, Liguori MO 63057. Editor: Rev. G.F. Gibbons. For families with Catholic religious convictions. Monthly. Circ: 450,000. Not copyrighted. Buys 75 mss a year. Pays on acceptance. Submit seasonal material 4 months in advance. Returns rejected material in 6 to 8 weeks. Enclose S.A.S.E.

Nonfiction and Photos: "Pastoral, practical, and personal approach to the problems and challenges of people today. No travelogue approach or unresearched ventures into controversial areas." Length: 400 to 1,500 words. Pays $35 to $100. Photos purchased with mss; b&w glossies.

THE LITTLE FLOWER MAGAZINE, Marylake, Route 4, Box 1150, Little Rock AR 72206. Editor-in-Chief: Fr. John Michael, O.C.D. Assistant Editor: Br. Adam, O.C.D. For Catholic readership. Bimonthly magazine; 32 pages. Estab: 1921. Circ: 30,000. Pays on publication. Simultaneous, photocopied and previously published submissions OK. SASE. Free sample copy and writer's guidelines.
Nonfiction: Simple, factual discussions of Christian living, prayer, social action, the thinking of important religious writers. "It is important that factual or doctrinal articles be about a very, very specific topic. We cannot use articles about religion in general. For example, we can always use articles on St. Therese of Lisieux; a good article could be written by referring to a good biography such as Ida Goerres' *The Hidden Face,* and concentrating on some specific topic, such as Therese's relations to nineteenth century attitudes toward women; her approach to meditation; her relationship to her superior. Since few of our readers are familiar with current religious literature, it is relatively easy to draw material from good works on specific passages in the Bible, on prayer, on current social questions, on the liturgy, etc." Avoid sentimentality and overly personal presentation. Length: 1,250-1,700 words.

LIVING MESSAGE, P.O. Box 820, Petrolia, Ontario, NON IRO, Canada. Editor: Rita Baker. For "active, concerned Christians, mainly Canadian Anglican." Publication of the Anglican Church of Canada. Established in 1889. Monthly except July and August. Circulation: 15,000. Not copyrighted. Payment on publication. Will send free sample copy to writer on request. Will consider photocopied submissions. Submit seasonal material 5 months in advance. Reports on material in 4 weeks. Submit complete ms. Enclose S.A.E. and International Reply Coupons.
Fiction, Nonfiction and Photos: "Short stories and articles which give readers an insight into other lives, promote understanding and stimulate action in areas such as community life, concerns of elderly, handicapped, youth, work with children, Christian education, poverty, the 'Third World', etc. No sentimentality or moralizing. Readers relate to a warm, personal approach; uncluttered writing. 'Reports' or involved explanatory articles are not wanted. The lead-in must capture the reader's imagination. A feeling of love and optimism is important." Length: up to 2,000 words. Pays $5 to $25. 8x10 b&w prints (with article). Pays $5. Fiction length: 1,000 to 1,500 words. Pays $10 to $20.

LOGOS JOURNAL, Logos International Fellowship, Inc., 201 Church St., Plainfield NJ 07060. (200)754-0745. Senior Editor: Howard Earl. Managing Editor: Carey Moore. For readership interested in charismatic renewal. Bimonthly magazine; 64 pages. Estab: 1971. Circ: 56,000. Pays on publication or acceptance (if assigned). Buys all rights, but may reassign following publication and first North American serial rights. Submit seasonal/holiday material 3 months in advance. Photocopied submissions OK. SASE. Reports in 10 weeks. Sample copy $1. Free writer's guidelines.
Nonfiction: Historical (Church and Holy Spirit); how-to (deal with personal growth from evangelical perspective); humor (please!); informational; inspirational (Jesus centered only); interview (on query only); personal experience; personal opinion (for an Opinion section) and photo feature (query). Buys 40 mss/year. Query. Length: 800-2,000 words. Pays $80-200.
Photos: Photos purchased with accompanying ms. Pays $15-25 for 2¼x2¼ color transparencies or 5x7 b&w glossies.
Columns/Departments: Opinion ("informed person addressing subject significant and thought-provoking to a sizable element of the church today.") Buys 1 ms/issue. Query. Length: 800-1,000 words. Open to suggestions for new columns/departments.
Poetry: Avant-garde; free verse; haiku; light verse and traditional. Limit submissions to batches of 6. Length: 4-50 lines.

THE LOOKOUT, 8121 Hamilton Ave., Cincinnati OH 45231. (513)931-4050. Editor: Mark A. Taylor. For the adult and young adult of the Sunday morning Bible school. Issued weekly. Buys first rights. Pays on acceptance. Sample copy and guidelines for writers 50¢. Reports in 1 month. Study publication before submitting material. Enclose S.A.S.E.
Nonfiction: Chiefly methods or news-type articles on phases of educational work of the local church, or articles dealing with personal or family problems of Christian life or work. Length: 1,000 to 1,500 words. Pays $25 to $35.
Photos: Upright glossies, size 8x10. Human interest or scenic shots of exceptionally good composition for cover use. Sharp b&w contrasts. Pays $7.50 to $15.
Fiction: Short-short stories of 1,000 to 1,200 words. To be acceptable, fiction must be char-

acterized by effective storytelling style, interesting quality—capable of catching and holding the reader's interest. Pays up to $35 for short stories.

THE LUTHERAN, 2900 Queen Lane, Philadelphia PA 19129. (215)848-6800. Editor: A. P. Stauderman. General interest magazine of the Lutheran Church in America. Twice monthly, except single issues in July and August. Buys first rights. Pays on acceptance. Will send a sample copy to a writer on request. Write for copy of guidelines for writers. Enclose S.A.S.E.
Nonfiction: Popularly written material about human concerns with reference to the Christian faith. "We are especially interested in articles in 4 main fields: Christian ideology; personal religious life, social responsibilities; Church at work; human interest stories about people in whom considerable numbers of other people are likely to be interested." Write "primarily to convey information rather than opinions. Every article should be based on a reasonable amount of research or should exploit some source of information not readily available. Most readers are grateful for simplicity of style. Sentences should be straightforward, with a minimum of dependent clauses and prepositional phrases." Length: 500 to 2,000 words. Pays $75 to $200.
Photos: Buys pix submitted with mss. Good 8x10 glossy prints. Pays $10 to $20. Also color for cover use. Pays up to $100.

LUTHERAN FORUM, 155 E. 22nd St., New York NY 10010. (212)254-4640. Editor: Glenn C. Stone. For church leadership, clerical and lay. Magazine; 40 (8½x11¼) pages. Established in 1967. Quarterly. Circulation: 5,500. Rights purchased vary with author and material. Buys all rights, but will sometimes reassign rights to author after publication; first North American serial rights; first serial rights; second serial (reprint) rights; simultaneous rights. Buys 8 to 10 mss a year. Pays on publication. Will send sample copy to writer for 70¢. Will consider photocopied and simultaneous submissions. Returns rejected material at once. Reports on ms accepted for publication in 4 to 6 weeks. Query first or submit complete ms. Enclose S.A.S.E.
Nonfiction: Articles about important issues and developments in the church's institutional life and in its cultural/social setting. Payment varies; $10 minimum. Length: 1,000 to 3,000 words. Informational, how-to, personal experience, interview, profile, think articles, expose, personal opinion. Length: 500 to 3,000 words. Pays $15 to $50.
Photos: Purchased with mss or with captions only. Prefers 8x10 prints. Uses more vertical than horizontal format. Pays $7.50 minimum.
How To Break In: "Send something for our On The Way to the Forum feature. Material for this is usually humorous or offbeat in a gentle way and should have some relation to the life of the Church at some level. Ideal length is 700 to 1,000 words. Payments range from $10 to $20."

THE LUTHERAN JOURNAL, 7317 Cahill Rd., Edina MN 55435. Editor: The Rev. Armin U. Deye. Conservative journal for Lutheran church members, middle age and older. Quarterly magazine; 32 pages, (8½x11). Estab: 1937. Circ: 105,000. Not copyrighted. Buys 12-15 mss a year. Payment on publication. Will send free sample copy to writer on request. Submit Christmas, Easter, other holiday material 4 months in advance. Will consider photocopied and simultaneous submissions. Reports in 8 weeks. Submit complete ms. SASE.
Nonfiction and Photos: Inspirational, religious, human interest, and historical articles. Interesting or unusual church projects. Informational, how-to, personal experience, interview, humor, think articles. Length: 1,500 words maximum; occasionally 2,000 words. Pays 1¢ to 1½¢ a word. B&w and color photos purchased with accompanying ms. Captions required. Payment varies.
Fiction and Poetry: Experimental, mainstream, religious, and historical fiction. Must be suitable for church distribution. Length: 2,000 words maximum. Pays 1¢ to 1½¢ a word. Traditional poetry, blank verse, free verse, related to subject matter of magazine.

THE LUTHERAN STANDARD, 426 S. 5th St., Minneapolis MN 55415. (612)332-4561. Editor: Dr. George H. Muedeking. For families in congregations of the American Lutheran Church. Established in 1842. Semimonthly. Circulation: 520,000. Buys first rights or multiple rights. Buys 30-50 mss/year. Pays on acceptance. Will send free sample copy to a writer on request. Reports on submissions in 3 weeks. Enclose S.A.S.E.
Nonfiction and Photos: Uses human interest, inspirational articles, especially about members of the American Lutheran Church who are practicing their faith in noteworthy ways, or congregations with unusual programs. "Should be written in language clearly understandable to persons with a mid-high school reading ability." Also publishes articles that discuss current social issues and problems (crime, draft evasion, etc.) in terms of Christian involvement and solutions. Length: 650 to 1,250 words, with pictures. Pays 4¢ and up per word. Photos used with mss.

Fiction: "We are particularly interested in getting substantive fiction with a positive Christian theme." Tie-in with season of year, such as Christmas, often preferred. Length: limit 1,200 words. Pays 4¢ per word.

Poetry: Uses very little poetry. The shorter the better; 20 lines. Pays $10 per poem.

LUTHERAN WOMEN, 2900 Queen Lane, Philadelphia PA 19129. Editor: Terry Schutz. 11 times yearly. Circ: 45,000. Official magazine for Lutheran Church Women. Acknowledges receipt of manuscript and decides acceptance within two months. Prefers to see mss 6 months ahead of issue, at beginning of planning stage. Can consider up to 3 months before issue. (December issue is nearly completed by September 1). Buys first rights. Pays on publication. Enclose S.A.S.E.

Nonfiction: Anything of interest to mothers, young or old, professional or other working women, relating to the contemporary expression of Christian faith in daily life, community action, international concerns. Family publication standards. Length: 1,500 to 2,000 words. Some shorter pieces accepted. Pays $30 to $40.

Photos: Purchased with or without mss. Women; family situations; religious art objects; overseas situations related to church. Should be clear, sharp, b&w. No additional payment for those used with mss. Pays $5 for those purchased without mss.

Fiction: Should show deepening of insight; story expressing new understanding in faith; story of human courage, self-giving, building up of community. Not to exceed 2,000 words. Pays $30 to $40.

Poetry: "Biggest taboo for us is sentimentality. We are limited to family magazine type contributions regarding range of vocabulary, but we don't want almanac-type poetry." No limit on number of lines. Pays $10 minimum per poem.

MARIAN HELPERS BULLETIN, Eden Hill, Stockbridge MA 01262. (413)298-3691. Editor: Bro. Robert M. Doyle, M.I.C. For average Catholics of varying ages with moderate religious views and general education. Quarterly. Established in 1947. Circulation: 625,000. Not copyrighted. Buys 18 to 24 mss a year. Payment on acceptance. Will send free sample copy to writer on request. Reports in 4 to 8 weeks. Submit seasonal material 6 months in advance. Enclose S.A.S.E.

Nonfiction and Photos: "Subject matter is of general interest on devotional, spiritual, moral and social topics. Use a positive, practical, and optimistic approach, without being sophisticated. We would like to see articles on the Blessed Virgin Mary." Buys informational, personal experience, inspirational articles. Length: 300 to 900 words. Pays $25-35. Photos are purchased with or without mss; captions optional. Pays $5 to $10 for b&w glossies.

MARRIAGE & FAMILY LIVING, St. Meinrad IN 47577. (812)357-6677. Editor: Ida M. Stabile. Monthly magazine. Circ: 48,000. Pays on acceptance. Buys first North American serial rights. SASE. Reports in 3-4 weeks. Sample copy 25¢.

Nonfiction: Uses 3 different types of articles: 1) Articles aimed at enriching the husband-wife and parent-child relationship by expanding religious and psychological insights or sensitivity. (Note: Ecumenically Judeo-Christian but in conformity with Roman Catholicism.) Length: 1,000-2,000 words. 2) Informative articles aimed at helping the couple cope, in practical ways, with the problems of modern living. Length: 2,000 words maximum. 3) Personal essays relating amusing and/or heartwarming incidents that point up the human side of marriage and family life. Length: 1,500 words maximum. Pays 5¢/word.

Photos: Julie Christie, Department Editor. B&w glossies (8x11) and color transparencies purchased with mss. Pays $125 for 4-color cover photo; $50 for b&w cover photo; $35 for 2-page spread in contents, $30 for 1 page in contents; $10 minimum. Photos of couples especially desirable. Model releases required.

MARYKNOLL MAGAZINE, Maryknoll NY 10545. Editor: Moises Sandoval. Foreign missionary society magazine. Monthly. Pays on acceptance. Will send free sample copy to a writer on request. Query before sending any material. Reports within several weeks. Enclose S.A.S.E.

Nonfiction: Articles and pictures concerning foreign missions. Articles developing themes such as world hunger, environmental needs, economic and political concerns. Length: 800 to 1,500 words. Send an outline before submitting material. Pays $50 to $150.

Photos: "We are a picture/text magazine. All articles must either be accompanied by top quality photos, or be such that we can get the photos." Pays $15 to $25 for b&w; $25 to $50 for color. Payment is dependent on quality and relevance.

THE MENNONITE, 600 Shaftesbury Blvd., Winnipeg, Canada R3P OM4. (204)888-6781. Editor: Bernie Wiebe. For a "general readership—age span—15 to 90 years; education—from grade school to Ph.D's; interests—themes dealing with the Christian response to such issues as the family, ethics, war and peace, life style, renewal, etc." Established in 1881. Weekly except in July and August. Circulation: 16,000. Rights purchased vary with author and material. May buy first and second serial rights. Buys 100 to 125 mss a year. Payment on publication. Will send a free sample copy to writer on request. Submit seasonal material 3 months in advance. Reports in 2 months. Enclose S.A.E. and International Reply Coupons.

Nonfiction, Photos, Fiction, and Poetry: General subject matter is "articles on Bible study, social and political issues faced by Christians, creative responses to the challenges of 20th century life; some poetry on a variety of subjects; a small amount of fiction. *The Mennonite* is a publication of an historic peace church which pays special attention to ways and means of attempting to resolve conflict at various levels of life—family, community, national and international." Buys personal experience, inspirational, think, and personal opinion articles. Length: 500 to 1,500 words. Pays 1½¢ to 2½¢ a word. Purchases photos without mss and captions are optional. Pays $5 to $10 for 5x7 or 8x10 b&w glossies. Buys religious fiction. Length: 800 to 1,500 words. Pays 1½¢ to 2½¢ a word. Buys religious poems in traditional, blank, or free verse. Length: 2 to 40 lines. Pays 35¢ a line.

MENNONITE BRETHREN HERALD, 159 Henderson Hwy., Winnipeg, Manitoba, R2L 1L4, Canada. Editor: Harold Jantz. Family publication. Biweekly. Circu: 9,600. Pays on publication. No copyrighted. Sample copy 40¢. Reports within the month. Enclose SAE and International Reply Coupons.

Nonfiction and Photos: Articles with a Christian family orientation; youth directed, Christian faith and life, current issues. 1,500 words. Pays $10 to $30 for accepted ms. Photos purchased with mss; pays $3.

THE MESSAGE MAGAZINE, Southern Publishing Association of Seventh-Day Adventists, Box 59, Nashville TN 37202. Editor: W. R. Robinson. International religious journal for people of Black origin. Monthly July-October; bimonthly November-June. Pays on acceptance or publication. Buys all rights. SASE. Free sample copy and writer's guidelines.

Nonfiction: Need articles on current events of interest to Blacks; social problems such as divorce, sex, adultery, drugs, diet, family, marriage, abortion, etc. Subjects should be examined in the light of the Holy Scriptures. New approach to doctrinal subjects such as law vs. grace, Godhead, the birth, death, and resurrection of Christ, Second coming, millennium, the Sabbath, immortality, etc. Short, inspirational themes and unusual human interest stories welcome, but must be creative, original, warm—not the usual run-of-the-mill types. When possible, all articles should be geared to Black audience. All references should be fully documented. Length: 500-1500 words. Pays $25 for minor articles; $35 for major.

Poetry: Market is small. Buys about ten poems/year. Short poetry up to 12 lines. Free verse welcome. Not a lot of nature poems needed. Should tell of divine truths of the Christian experience—struggle and victory and praise. Pays $10 maximum.

THE MESSENGER OF THE SACRED HEART, 833 Broadview Ave., Toronto, Ont., Canada M4K 2P9. Editor: Rev. F. J. Power, S.J. For "adult Catholics in Canada and the U.S. who are members of the Apostleship of Prayer." Monthly. Circulation: 21,000. Buys first rights. Buys about 12 mss a year. Pays on acceptance. Will send a sample copy to a writer on request. Submit seasonal material 3 months in advance. Reports in 1 month. Enclose S.A.E. and International Reply Coupons.

Nonfiction: Department Editor: Mary Pujolas. "Articles on the Apostleship of Prayer and on all aspects of Christian living;" current events and social problems that have a bearing on Catholic life, family life, Catholic relations with non-Catholics, personal problems, the liturgy, prayer, devotion to the Sacred Heart. Material should be written in a popular, nonpious style. Length: 1,800 to 2,000 words. Pays 2¢ a word.

Fiction: Department Editor: Mary Pujolas. Wants fiction which reflects the lives, problems, preoccupations of reading audience. "Short stories that make their point through plot and characters." Length: 1,800 to 2,000 words. Pays 2¢ a word.

THE MIRACULOUS MEDAL, 475 E. Chelten Ave., Philadelphia PA 19144. Editorial Director: Rev. Robert P. Crowley, C.M. Quarterly. Buys first North American serial rights. Buys articles only on special assignment. Pays on acceptance. Will send free sample copy on request. Normally reports in 2 days. SASE.

Fiction: Should not be pious or sermon-like. Wants good general fiction—not necessarily religious, but if religion is basic to the story, the writer should be sure of his facts. Only restriction is that subject matter and treatment must not conflict with Catholic teaching and practice.

Can use seasonal material. Christmas stories. Length: 2,000 words maximum. Pays 2¢ and up per word. Occasionally uses short-shorts from 750 to 1,250 words.
Poetry: Maximum of 20 lines, preferably about the Virgin Mary or at least with religious slant. Pays 50¢ a line and up.

MODERN LITURGY, Box 444, Saratoga CA 95070. Editor: William Burns. For artists and musicians, creative individuals who plan group worship services; teachers of religion. Magazine: 32 pages. Established in 1973. Eight times a year. Circ: 10,000. Buys all rights, but may reassign rights to author after publication. Buys about 10 mss a year. Pays on publication. Sample copy $2; free writer's guidelines. No photocopied or simultaneous submissions. Reports in 6 weeks. Query first. Enclose S.A.S.E.
Nonfiction and Fiction: Articles (historical and theological and practical), example services, liturgical art forms (music, poetry, stories, dances, dramatizations, etc.). Practical, creative ideas and art forms for use in worship and/or religious education classrooms. Length: 750 to 2,000 words. Pays $5 to $30.

MOODY MONTHLY, 820 North LaSalle, Chicago IL 60610. Editor: Jerry B. Jenkins. For "Church-oriented Christian families, high school and college graduates, some with Bible school training, special interest in the Bible and in the Protestant evangelical world." Monthly magazine. Circ: 300,000. Buys all rights. Buys 8-12 mss/year. Pays on acceptance. Will send a sample copy to a writer on request. Write for copy of guidelines for writers. Submit seasonal material 4 months in advance. Reports in 1 week. Query. "Cannot read unsolicited mss." Enclose S.A.S.E.
Nonfiction and Fiction: Wants material which is warm, evangelical and clearly relevant to daily life of the individual Christian. Personal experience articles (factual and anecdotal development), solid treatment of contemporary Christian problems, seasonals, and non-promotional features on aspects of Christian work; "news of the Christian world, developments in Christian education, personality sketches, Bible exposition, family-oriented anecdotal material. 'How I Did It' stories of Christians in difficult situations." Family department needs "warm, practical material clearly relevant to parents, either fiction or nonfiction." Length: 1,000 to 2,000 words. Pays $225 maximum.
Photos: B&w glossies; 35mm color. Pays $25-200.
Fillers: Inspirational anecdotes, people-centered stories. Length: 200 to 800 words. Pays 10¢/word.

NATIONAL CATHOLIC REGISTER, 1901 Avenue of the Stars, #1511, Los Angeles CA 90067. (213)533-4911. Editor-in-Chief: Patrick Riley. Emphasizes "covering the Catholic Church." Weekly newspaper; 8 pages. Estab: 1929. Circ: 70,000. Pays on publication. Buys all rights, but may reassign following publication. Phone queries OK. Submit seasonal/holiday material 6 weeks in advance. SASE. Reports in 12 days. Free sample copy and writer's guidelines.
Nonfiction: Informational, interview, and profile. Buys 2 mss/issue. Query. Length: 800-1,000 words. Pays $50-150. "We are primarily looking for stringers all over the U.S. We are interested in news stories on any activity which affects the Catholic community. We are not interested in stories about festivities or fund-raising parties."
Photos: Purchased with accompanying ms or on assignment. Captions required. Pays $10-25 for 8½x10 flat or glossy b&w prints. Query.

NEW CATHOLIC WORLD, Paulist Press, 1865 Broadway, New York, NY 10023. (212)265-8181. Managing Editor: Robert Heyer. Bimonthly magazine; 52 pages. Estab: 1865. Circ: 12,700. Pays on publication. Buys all rights, but may reassign following publication. Submit seasonal/holiday material 6 months in advance. SASE. Reports in 4 weeks. Free sample copy.
Nonfiction: Inspirational and informational; personal experience and personal opinion. Query. Length: 1,000-2,000 words.
Photos: Photos purchased without accompanying ms. Pays $7-15 for b&w photos.
Poetry: All kinds. Buys 30/year. Pays $20.

NEW COVENANT MAGAZINE, Charismatic Renewal Services, Inc., Box 617, Ann Arbor MI 48107. (313)761-8505. Editor-in-Chief: Bert Ghezzi. Managing Editor: Randy Cirner. Emphasizes the charismatic renewal of Christian churches. Ecumenical, with a higher percentage of Roman Catholic readers. Monthly magazine; 36 pages. Estab: 1971. Circ: 67,000. Pays on publication. Buys all rights. Phone queries OK. Submit seasonal/holiday material 8 months in advance. Photocopied and previously published submissions OK. SASE. Reports in 3-4 weeks. Free sample copy.

Nonfiction: Historical; informational (coverage of recent and upcoming events in the charismatic renewal); inspirational; interview and personal experience (life testimonials relating to the charismatic experience). Buys 8 mss/year. Send complete ms. Length: 1,000-3,000 words. Pays 2½-3½¢/word.

Photos: Gerry Rauch, Photo Editor. Photos purchased with or without accompanying ms or on assignment. Pays $10-35 for 8x10 b&w glossies. Send contact sheet and prints. No additional payment for photos accepted with accompanying ms. Model release required.

THE NEW ERA, 50 E. North Temple, Salt Lake City UT 84150. (801)531-2951. Editor: Brian K. Kelly. For young people of The Church of Jesus Christ of Latter-Day Saints (Mormon); their church leaders and teachers. Monthly magazine; 51 pages. Established in 1971. Circulation: 160,000. Buys all rights, but will reassign rights to author after publication. Buys 100 mss a year. Payment on acceptance. Will send sample copy to writer for 35¢. Will consider simultaneous submissions. Submit seasonal material 6 months to a year in advance. Reports in 30 days. Query preferred. Enclose S.A.S.E.

Nonfiction and Photos: "Material that shows how The Church of Jesus Christ of Latter-Day Saints is relevant in the lives of young people today. Must capture the excitement of being a young Latter-Day Saint. Special interest in the experiences of young Latter-Day Saints in other countries. No general library research or formula pieces without the *New Era* slant and feel." Uses informational, how-to, personal experience, interview, profile, inspirational, humor, historical, think pieces, travel, spot news. Length: 150 to 3,000 words. Pays 2¢ to 5¢ a word. Also seeks material for the FYI column (For Your Information) which uses news of young Latter-Day Saints around the world. Uses b&w photos and color transparencies with mss. Payment depends on use in magazine, but begins at $10.

Fiction: Experimental, adventure, science fiction and humorous. Must relate to their young Mormon audience. Pays minimum 3¢ a word.

Poetry: Traditional forms, blank verse, free verse, avant-garde forms, light verse and all other forms. Must relate to their editorial viewpoint. Pays minimum 25¢ a line.

NEW WORLD OUTLOOK, 475 Riverside Dr., Room 1328, New York NY 10027. (212)678-6031. Editor: Arthur J. Moore, Jr. For United Methodist lay people; not clergy generally. Monthly magazine; 50 pages (9x11¼). Established in 1911. Circ: 40,000. Buys all rights, but will reassign to author after publication; buys first North American serial rights. Buys 15 to 20 mss a year. Payment on publication. Will send free sample copy to writer on request. Write for copy of guidelines for writers. Query first or submit complete ms. Enclose S.A.S.E.

Nonfiction: "Articles about the involvement of the Church around the world, including the U.S., in outreach and social concerns and Christian witness, not solely of 1 denomination. Write with good magazine style. Facts, actualities important. Quotes. Relate what Christians are doing to meet problems. Specifics. We have too much on New York and other large urban areas. We need more good journalistic efforts from smaller places in U.S. Articles by freelancers in out-of-the-way places in the U.S. are especially welcome." Length: 1,000 to 2,000 words. Usually pays $50 to $150.

NORTH AMERICAN VOICE OF FATIMA, Fatima Shrine, Youngstown NY 14174. Editor: Steven M. Grancini, C.R.S.P. For Roman Catholic readership. Circulation: 19,000. Not copyrighted. Pays on acceptance. Will send free sample copy to a writer on request. Reports on submissions in 2 weeks. Enclose S.A.S.E.

Nonfiction, Photos, and Fiction: Inspirational, personal experience, historical and think articles. Religious and historical fiction. Length: 700 words. B&w photos purchased with mss. All material must have a religious slant. Pays 1¢ a word.

OBLATE WORLD AND VOICE OF HOPE, P.O. Box 96, San Antonio TX 78291. (512)736-3186. Editor: John A. Hakey, O.M.I. For people interested in the missions and the work of the Oblate Fathers in Texas, Mexico, the Philippines, Latin America, the Orient and the Arctic. Quarterly. Circulation: 50,000. Not copyrighted. Buys very few mss a year. Payment on acceptance. Will send a free sample copy to a writer on request. Will consider photocopied submissions. Submit seasonal material 4 months in advance. Reports in a month. Enclose S.A.S.E.

Nonfiction and Photos: "We accept stories about the Oblates in the above mentioned missions. Once in a while a very short seasonal story (Christmas or Easter) may be accepted. All material should be sent to the editor." Buys informational, interview, and photo articles. Length: 600 to 1,200 words. Pays 2¢ a word. Purchases photos with mss and captions are optional. B&w only.

THE OTHER SIDE, Box 12236, Philadelphia PA 19144. Co-editors: John Alexander, Alfred Krass, Mark Olson. A magazine of Christian discipleship, radical in tone and outlook, with a definite point of view but open to other opinions. Published 9 times/year. Estab: 1965. Circ: 4,700. Pays on publication. Buys first serial, second serial and simultaneous rights. SASE. Reports in 1-2 weeks. Sample copy $1.

Nonfiction: "Articles are not encouraged unless they are highly creative descriptions of personal experiences relative to Christian discipleship amidst current issues of society or interviews or profiles which don't just 'grind an axe' but communicate personality." Length: 250-1,750 words. Pays $10-25.

Photos: "Shots depicting 'the other side' of affluence or the juxtaposition of affluence and poverty are needed." Photo essays on social issues will be considered. Pays $10-25 for b&w photos.

Fiction: "Short pieces of creative writing on hard social issues. A Christian perspective should be clear." Length: 300-1,800 words. Pays $10-20.

OUR FAMILY, Oblate Fathers of St. Mary's Province, Box 249, Battleford, Sasketchewan, Canada S0M 0E0. (306)937-2131. Editor-in-Chief: A.J. Reb Materi, O.M.I. For average family men and women of high school and early college education. Monthly magazine; 32 pages. Estab: 1949. Circ: 10,800. Pays on acceptance. Buys all rights but may reassign following publication, simultaneous, second serial (reprint), first North American serial, and one-time rights. Phone queries OK. Submit seasonal/holiday material 4 months in advance. Simultaneous, photocopied and previously published submissions OK. SASE. Reports in 2-4 weeks. Sample copy 25¢; free writer's guidelines.

Nonfiction: Humor (relating to family life or husband/wife relations); inspirational (anything that depicts people responding to adverse conditions with courage, hope and love); personal experience (with religious dimensions); and photo feature (particularly in search of photo essays on human/religious themes and on persons whose lives are an inspiration to others).

Photos: Photos purchased with or without accompanying ms. Pays $15-25 for 5x7 or larger b&w glossies and color photos (which are converted into b&w). Total purchase price for ms includes payment for photos. Model release required.

Fiction: Humorous and religious. "Anything true to human nature. No moralizing or sentimentality." Buys 1 ms/issue. Send complete ms. Length: 750-3,000 words. Pays 3¢/word minimum.

Poetry: Avant-garde; free verse; haiku; light verse and traditional. Buys 4-10 poems/issue. Length: 3-30 lines. Pays $2-10.

Fillers: Jokes, gags, anecdotes and short humor. Buys 2-10 fillers/issue.

OUR SUNDAY VISITOR, Noll Plaza, Huntington IN 46750. (219)356-8400. Editor: Albert J. Nevins. For general Catholic audience. Weekly. Circ: 400,000. Buys all rights. Buys about 200 mss a year. Pays on acceptance. Will send a sample copy to a writer on request. Submit seasonal material 2 months in advance. Reports in 1 week. Query first. Enclose S.A.S.E.

Nonfiction: Uses articles on Catholic related subjects. Should explain Catholic religious beliefs in articles of human interest; articles applying Catholic principles to current problems, Catholic profiles, etc. Payment varies depending on reputation of author, quality of work and amount of research required. Length: 1,000 to 1,200 words. Minimum payment for major features is $100 and a minimum payment for shorter features is $50 to $75.

Photos: Purchased with mss; with captions only. B&w glossies, color transparencies, 35mm color. Pays $125 for cover photo story, $75 for b&w story; $25 per color photo. $10 per b&w photo.

PENTECOSTAL EVANGEL, The General Council of the Assemblies of God, 1445 Boonville, Springfield, MO 65802. (417)862-2781. Editor-in-Chief: Robert C. Cunningham. Managing Editor: Richard G. Champion. Emphasizes news of the Assemblies of God for members of the Assembly and other Pentecostal and charismatic Christians. Weekly magazine; 32 pages. Estab: 1913. Circ: 260,000. Pays on publication. Buys all rights, but may reassign following publication, simultaneous, second serial (reprint) and one-time rights. Submit seasonal/holiday material 6 months in advance. Simultaneous, photocopied and previously published submissions OK. SASE. Reports in 3 months. Free sample copy and writer's guidelines.

Nonfiction: Informational (articles on home life which convey Christian teachings); inspirational; and personal experience. Buys 8 mss/issue. Send complete ms. Length: 500-2,000 words. Pays up to 2¢/word.

Photos: Photos purchased without accompanying ms. Pays $7.50-15 for 8x10 b&w glossies; $10-35 for 35mm or larger color transparencies. Total purchase price for ms includes payment for photos.

Poetry: Religious and inspirational. Buys 1 poem/issue. Limit submissions to batches of 6. Pays 15¢-30¢/line.

PENTECOSTAL TESTIMONY, 10 Overlea Blvd., Toronto Ont. M4H 1A5 Canada. Editor: Joy E. Hansell. Monthly. For Church members plus general readership. Established in 1920. Circulation: 18,000. Not copyrighted. Payment on publication. Will send free sample copy to writer on request. Write for copy of editorial guidelines for writers. Submit seasonal material at least 3 months in advance. Query first. Enclose S.A.E. and International Reply Coupons.
Nonfiction: Must be written from Canadian viewpoint. Subjects preferred are contemporary public issues, events on the church calendar (Reformation month, Christmas, Pentecost, etc.) written from conservative theological viewpoint. Pays 1¢ per word for originals. Preferred lengths are 800 to 1,200 words.
Photos: Occasionally buys photographs with mss if they are vital to the article. Also buys b&w photos if they are related to some phase of the main topic of the particular issue. Should be 8x10 b&w prints. Payment is $6 to $10 for cover photos.
Fiction: Might use youth-slanted fiction. Same theological slant, same lengths, same payment as nonfiction.
Poetry: Rarely uses. Pays $2.50 for short poems and sonnets.

PRESBYTERIAN RECORD, 50 Wynford Dr., Don Mills, Ontario, Canada M3C 1J7. (416)429-0110. Editor: Rev. Dr. DeCourcy H. Rayner. For a church-oriented, family audience. Monthly magazine. Established in 1876. Circ: 89,500. Buys 10 mss/year. Pays on publication. Will send free sample copy to writer on request. Submit seasonal material 3 months in advance. Reports on manuscripts accepted for publication in 2 weeks. Returns rejected material in 4 weeks. Query first. S.A.E. and Canadian stamps.
Nonfiction and Photos: Material on religious themes. Check a copy of the magazine for style. Also, personal experience, interview, and inspirational material. Length: 800 to 1,600 words. Pays $20 to $50. Pays $5 to $12 for b&w glossy photos. Captions required. Uses positive color transparencies for the cover. Pays $30.

PURPOSE, 616 Walnut Ave., Scottdale PA 15683. Editor: David E. Hostetler. For adults, young and old, general audience with interests as varied as there are persons. "My particular readership is interested in seeing Christianity work in tough situations and come out on top." Monthly magazine. Established in 1968. Circulation: 21,500. Buys first serial rights; second serial (reprint) rights; simultaneous rights. Buys 200 mss a year. Payment on acceptance. Will send free sample copy to writer on request. Write for editorial guidelines for writers. Submit seasonal material 5 months in advance. Will consider photocopied and simultaneous submissions. Reports within 6 weeks. Submit only complete ms. Enclose S.A.S.E.
Nonfiction and Photos: Inspirational articles from a Christian perspective. "I want material that goes to the core of human problems—morality on all levels, or lack of it in business, politics, religion, sex, and any other area—and shows how Christian answers resolve some of these problems. I don't want glib, sweety-sweet, or civil religion pieces. I want critical stuff with an upbeat. *Purpose* is a story paper and as such wants truth to be conveyed either through quality fiction or through articles that use the best fiction techniques to make them come alive. Our magazine has an accent on Christian discipleship. Basically, this means we think our readers take Christianity seriously and we do not accept a compartmentalized expression of faith. Christianity is to be applied to all of life and we expect our material to show this. We're getting too much self-centered material. By that, I mean many writers see religion as a way of getting their needs met with very little concern for how the other fellow may be affected by their selfishness. I would like to see articles on how people are intelligently and effectively working at some of the great human problems such as overpopulation, food shortages, international understanding, etc., motivated by their faith." Length: 200 to 1,200 words. Pays 1¢ to 3¢ per word. Photos purchased with ms. Captions optional. Pays $5 to $35 for b&w, depending on quality. Normal range is $7.50 to $15. Must be sharp enough for reproduction; prefers prints in all cases. Can use color for halftones at the same rate of payment.
Fiction, Poetry, and Fillers: Humorous, religious, and historical fiction relating to the theme of magazine. "Should not be moralistic." Traditional poetry, blank verse, free verse, and light verse. Length: 3 to 12 lines. Pays 25¢ to 50¢ per line. Jokes, short humor, and items up to 400 words. Pays 1¢ minimum per word.
How To Break In: "We are a good market for new writers who combine Christian perceptions with craftsmanship. We are looking for articles which show Christianity slugging it out where people hurt but we want the stories told and presented professionally. Good photographs help place material with us."

QUEEN, (formerly *Queen of All Hearts*), Montfort Missionaries, 40 S. Saxon Ave., Bay Shore NY 11706. (516)665-0726. Editor-in-Chief: James McMillan, S.M.M. Managing Editor: Roger Charest, S.M.M. Emphasizes doctrine and devotion to Mary. Bimonthly magazine; 40 pages.

Estab: 1950. Circ: 10,000. Pays on acceptance. Buys all rights, but may reassign following publication. Phone queries OK. Submit seasonal/holiday material 3 months in advance. Photocopied submissions OK. SASE. Reports in 1 month. Free sample copy.

Nonfiction: Expose (doctrinal); historical; informational; inspirational and interview. Buys 5 mss/issue. Send complete ms. Length: 1,500-2,000 words. Pays $20-40.

Fiction: Religious. Buys 1 ms/issue. Send complete ms. Length: 1,500-2,000 words. Pays $30-40.

Poetry: Free verse and traditional forms. Marian poetry only. Buys 2/issue. Limit submissions to batches of 2. Pays in free subscription for 2 years.

REVIEW FOR RELIGIOUS, 612 Humboldt Building, 539 N. Grand Blvd., St. Louis MO 63103. (314)535-3048. Editor: Daniel F. X. Meenan, S.J. Bimonthly. For Roman Catholic religious men and women. Pays on publication. Reports in about 4 weeks. Enclose S.A.S.E.

Nonfiction: Articles on ascetical, liturgical and canonical matters. Length: 2,000 to 10,000 words. Pays $6 a page.

ST. ANTHONY MESSENGER, 1615 Republic St., Cincinnati OH 45210. Editor-in-Chief: Jeremy Harrington. For a national readership of Catholic families, most of them have children in grade school, high school or college. Monthly magazine; 59 pages. Estab: 1893. Circ: 250,000. Pays on acceptance. Buys first North American serial rights. Submit seasonal/holiday material 4 months in advance. SASE. Free sample copy and writer's guidelines.

Nonfiction: How-to (on psychological and spiritual growth; family problems); humor; informational; inspirational; interview; personal experience (if pertinent to our purpose); personal opinion (limited use; writer must have special qualifications for topic); profile. Buys 20 mss/year. Length: 1,500-3,500 words. Pays 7¢/word.

Fiction: Mainstream and religious. Buys 12 mss/year. Query. Length: 2,000-3,500 words. Pays 7¢/word.

How To Break In: "The freelancer should ask why his/her proposed article would be appropriate for us, rather than for *Redbook* or *Saturday Review*. We treat human problems of all kinds, but from a religious perspective."

ST. JOSEPH'S MESSENGER & ADVOCATE OF THE BLIND, Sisters of St. Joseph of Peace, St. Joseph's Home, Box 288, Jersey City NJ 07303. Editor-in-Chief: Sister Ursula Maphet. For older Catholics interested in the blind and family life. Quarterly magazine; 30 pages. Estab: 1900. Circ: 71,000. Pays on acceptance. Buys all rights, but may reassign following publication. Submit seasonal/holiday material 3 months in advance (no Christmas issue). Simultaneous and previously published submissions OK. Reports in 3 weeks. Free sample copy and writer's guidelines.

Nonfiction: Humor; inspirational; nostalgia; personal opinion; and personal experience. Buys 24 mss/year. Submit complete ms. Length: 300-1,500 words. Pays $3-15.

Fiction: "Fiction is our most needed area." Romance; suspense; mainstream; and religious. Buys 30 mss/year. Submit complete ms. Length: 600-1,600 words. Pays $6-25.

Poetry: Light verse, traditional. Buys 25/year. Limit submissions to batches of 10. Length: 50-300 words. Pays $5-20.

Fillers: Jokes, gags, anecdotes. Buys 30/year. Length: 25-150 words. Pays $5-10.

SAINTS' HERALD, P.O. Box HH, Independence MO 64055. (816)252-5010. Editor: Paul A. Wellington. Issued monthly. This is the family magazine of the Reorganized Church of Jesus Christ of Latter-Day Saints. Reports in 2 weeks. Enclose S.A.S.E.

Nonfiction: Wants articles on current religious topics, church members and historical articles of 1,500 words. No payment.

Photos: Pays up to $10 on acceptance for good 8x10 pictures concerning the church.

Fiction: Relating to current religious problems, challenges, trends. Length: 1,500 words.

SANDAL PRINTS, 1820 Mt. Elliott, Detroit MI 48207. Editor: Rev. Allen Gruenke, OFM Capuchin. For people who are interested in the work of the Capuchins. Estab: 1952. Circ: 8,000. Not copyrighted. Payment on acceptance. Will send free sample copy to writer on request. Reports on material accepted for publication in 1 week. Returns rejected material immediately. Query first. Enclose S.A.S.E.

Nonfiction and Photos: Material on the contemporary apostolates and life style of Capuchins (especially in the Midwest). "We do not use any general religious material; no topical subjects or themes accepted." Length: 2,500 words. Pays $25 to $50. Pays $5 per b&w photo.

How To Break In: "Write about actually living Capuchins and their work. Query before writing the first word."

SCOPE, 426 S. Fifth St., Minneapolis MN 55415. (612)332-4561, Ext. 397. Editor: Dr. Lily M. Gyldenvand. For women of the American Lutheran Church. Monthly. Circulation: 325,000. Buys first rights. Buys 200 to 300 mss a year. Occasionally overstocked. Pays on acceptance. Will send a sample copy to a writer on request. Submit seasonal material 4 to 5 months in advance. Reports in 2 to 3 weeks. Enclose S.A.S.E.

Nonfiction and Photos: "The magazine's primary purpose is to be an educational tool in that it transmits the monthly Bible study material which individual women use in preparation for their group meetings. It contains articles for inspiration and growth, as well as information about the mission and concerns of the church, and material that is geared to seasonal emphasis. We are interested in articles that relate to monthly Bible study subject. We also want articles that tell how faith has affected, or can influence, the lives of women or their families. But we do not want preachy articles. We are interested in any subject that touches the home. The possibilities are limitless for good, sharp, stimulating and creative articles." Length: 700 to 1,000 words. Pays $10 to $50. Buys 3x5 or 8x10 b&w photos with mss or with captions only. Pays $7 to $10.

Poetry and Fillers: "We can use interesting, brief, pithy, significant, or clever filler items, but we use very little poetry and are very selective." Pays $5 to $15.

How To Break In: "Examine a copy of *Scope* and submit a well-written manuscript that fits the obvious slant and audience."

SEEK, Standard Publishing, 8121 Hamilton Ave., Cincinnati OH 45231. (513)931-4050, Ext. 164. Editor: J. David Lang. For young and middle-aged adults who attend church and Bible classes. Sunday School paper; 8 pages. Established in 1970. Quarterly, in weekly issues. Circulation: 60,000. Rights purchased vary with author and material. Prefers first serial rights. Buys 100 to 150 mss a year. Pays on acceptance. Will send free sample copy to writer on request. Write for copy of guidelines for writers. No photocopied submissions. Submit seasonal (Christmas, Easter, New Year's) material 9 to 12 months in advance. Reports in 30 to 60 days. Query first or submit complete ms. Enclose S.A.S.E.

Nonfiction and Photos: "We look for articles that are warm, inspirational, devotional, of personal or human interest; that deal with controversial matters, timely issues of religious, ethical, or moral nature, or first-person testimonies, true-to-life happenings, vignettes, emotional situations or problems; communication problems, and examples of answered prayer. Article must deliver its point in a convincing manner, but not be patronizing or preachy. Must appeal to either men or women. Must be alive, vibrant, sparkling, and have a title that demands the article to be read. We will purchase a few articles that deal with faith or trials of blacks or other racial groups. Always need stories of families, marriages, problems on campus, and life testimonies." Length: 400 to 1,200 words. Pays 1½¢ to 2¢ a word. B&w photos purchased with or without mss. Pays $7.50 minimum for good 8x10 glossies.

Fiction: Religious fiction and religiously slanted historical and humorous fiction. Length: 400 to 1,200 words. Pays 1½¢ to 2¢ a word.

Fillers: Bible crossword puzzles, jumbles and hidden word puzzles are used as fillers. Pays $10 minimum.

THE SIGN, Union City NJ 07087. (201)867-6400. Editor: Rev. Arthur McNally, C.P. Magazine; 56 pages. 10 issues per year. Buys all rights. Will send free sample copy to a writer on request. Reports in 3 weeks. Enclose S.A.S.E.

Nonfiction and Photos: Prime emphasis on religious material: prayer, sacraments, Christian family life, religious education, liturgy, social action — especially "personal testimony" genre. Length: 3500 words maximum. Pays $75 to $300. Uses photos and artwork submitted with articles.

Fiction: Uses, at most, 1 story per month. Length: 3500 words maximum. Pays $200 to $300.

How To Break In: "Written suggestions, outlines, or completed manuscripts welcomed. Telephone inquiries discouraged."

SIGNS OF THE TIMES, 1350 Villa, Mountain View CA 94042. Editor: Lawrence Maxwell. Seventh-Day Adventist. For religiously inclined persons of all ages and denominations. Monthly. Buys first rights only. Reports in 1 week to several months. Enclose S.A.S.E.

Nonfiction: Uses articles of interest to the religiously inclined of all denominations. Most material furnished by regular contributors, but freelance submissions carefully read. Sincerity, originality, brevity necessary. Lengths: 700 to 1,800 words.

SISTERS TODAY, The Liturgical Press, St. John's Abbey, Collegeville MN 56321. Editor-in-Chief: Rev. Daniel Durken, O.S.B. Associate Editor: Sister Mary Anthony Wagner, O.S.B. For religious women of the Roman Catholic Church, primarily. Monthly magazine; 65 pages. Estab: 1929. Circ: 18,000. Pays on publication. Buys all rights, but may reassign following publication. Submit seasonal/holiday material 4 months in advance. SASE. Reports in 1 month. Free sample copy.

Nonfiction: How-to (pray, live in a religious community, exercise faith, hope, charity etc.); informational; inspirational and interview. Also articles concerning religious renewal, community life, worship and the role of Sisters in the world today. Buys 6 mss/issue. Query. Length: 500-3,000 words. Pays $5/printed page.

Poetry: Free verse; haiku; light verse and traditional. Buys 3 poems/issue. Limit submissions to batches of 4. Pays $5.

SOCIAL JUSTICE REVIEW, 3835 Westminister Place, St. Louis MO 63108. (314)371-1653. Editor: Harvey J. Johnson. Issued monthly except for combination of July-August issues. Not copyrighted; "however special articles within the magazine may be copyrighted, or an occasional special issue has been copyrighted due to author's request." Query first. Enclose S.A.S.E.

Nonfiction: Wants scholarly articles on society's economic, religious, social, intellectual and political problems with the aim of bringing Catholic social thinking to bear upon these problems. 2,000 to 3,000 words. Pays about 1¢ a word.

SPIRITUAL LIFE, 2131 Lincoln Rd., N.E., Washington DC 20002. (202)832-6622. Editor: Rev. Christopher Latimer, O.C.D. "Largely Catholic, well-educated, serious readers. High percentage are priests and religious, but also some laymen. A few are non-Catholic or non-Christian." Quarterly. Circulation: 17,000. Buys first rights. Buys about 20 mss a year. Pays on acceptance. Will send a sample copy to a writer on request. Write for copy of guidelines for writers. "Brief autobiographical information (present occupation, past occupations, books and articles published, etc.) should accompany article. Follow *A Manual of Style* (University of Chicago)." Reports in 2 weeks. Enclose S.A.S.E.

Nonfiction: Serious articles of contemporary spirituality. Quality articles about man's encounter with God in the present-day world. Language of articles should be college-level. Technical terminology, if used, should be clearly explained. Material should be presented in a positive manner. Sentimental articles or those dealing with specific devotional practices not accepted. "*Spiritual Life* tries to avoid the 'popular,' sentimental approach to religion and to concentrate on a more intellectual approach. We do not want first-person accounts of spiritual experiences (visions, revelations, etc.) nor sentimental treatments of religious devotions." Buys inspirational and think pieces. No fiction or poetry. Length: 3,000 to 5,000 words. Pays $50 minimum. "Four contributor's copies are sent to author on publication of article." Book reviews should be sent to Brother Edward O'Donnell, O.C.D., Carmelite Monastery, 514 Warren St., Brookline MA 02146.

STANDARD, 6401 The Paseo, Kansas City MO 64131. Adult story paper of the Nazarene Publishing House. Copyrighted. Weekly. Will accept second rights and simultaneous submissions. Pays on acceptance. Write for copy of guidelines for writers. Reports in about 60 days. Enclose S.A.S.E.

Fiction: "Stories should vividly portray definite Christian emphasis or character-building values, without being preachy. Setting, plot, and action should be realistic." Length: 2,000 to 3,000 words. Pays $20 per 1,000 words.

SUNDAY DIGEST, 850 N. Grove Ave., Elgin IL 60120. Editor: Darlene McRoberts. Issued weekly for Christian adults. Buys all rights. Pays on acceptance. Will send free sample copy to a writer on request. Write for editorial requirements pamphlet. Reports on submissions in 4 weeks. Enclose S.A.S.E.

Nonfiction and Photos: Needs articles applying the Christian faith to personal and social problems, articles of family interest and on church subjects, personality profiles, practical self-help articles, personal experience articles and inspirational anecdotes. Length: 500 to 1,800 words. "Study our product and our editorial requirements. Have a clear purpose for every article or story—use anecdotes and dialog—support opinions with research." Pays 3¢ per word minimum. Photos purchased only with mss. Pays about $10 each, depending on quality. Negatives requested (b&w). Return of prints cannot be guaranteed.

Fiction: Occasionally uses fiction that is hard-hitting, fast-moving, with a real woven-in, not "tacked on," Christian message. Length: 1,000 to 1,500 words. Pays 3¢ per word minimum.

Poetry: Occasionally used if appropriate to format. Pays 5¢ per word minimum.

Fillers: Anecdotes of inspirational value, jokes and short humor; must be appropriate to format and in good taste. Length: up to 500 words. Pays 5¢ per word minimum.

How To Break In: "Since we use many first-time writers, there is no real difficulty in 'breaking in'. Our decisions are based more on quality of writing and subject. All mss are considered on an equal basis as far as authors are concerned."

SUNDAY SCHOOL LESSON ILLUSTRATOR, The Sunday School Board, 127 9th Ave., N., Nashville TN 37234. Editor: William H. Stephens. For members of Sunday School classes that use the International Sunday School Lessons and other Bible study lessons, and for adults seeking in-depth Biblical information. Quarterly. Circ: 60,000. Buys all rights. Buys 25 mss/ year. Pays on acceptance. Will not consider photocopied submissions. Submit seasonal material (for Christmas and Easter) 1 year in advance. Reports in 2 weeks. Query first or submit complete ms. Enclose S.A.S.E.
Nonfiction and Photos: Journalistic articles and photo stories researched on Biblical subjects, such as archaeology and sketches of biblical personalities. Material must be written for laymen but research quality must be up-to-date and thorough. Should be written in a contemporary, journalistic style. Pays 2½¢/word. B&w and color photos purchased with ms or on assignment. Captions required. Pays $7.50 to $10.
Fiction and Poetry: Limited amount of religious fiction. Traditional forms of poetry. Pays 2½¢ a word for fiction; $3 to $20 for poetry, depending on length.

THE TEXAS METHODIST/UNITED METHODIST REPORTER, Box 1076, Dallas TX 75221. (214)748-6491. General Manager/Editor: Spurgeon M. Dunnam III. For a national readership of United Methodist pastors and laypersons. Weekly newspaper. Circ: 400,000. Pays on acceptance. Not copyrighted. SASE. Free sample copy and writer's guidelines.
Nonfiction: "We welcome short features, approximately 500 words, focused on United Methodist persons, churches, or church agencies. Write about a distinctly Christian response to human need or how a person's faith relates to a given situation." Pays 3¢/word.
Photos: Purchased with accompanying ms. "We encourage the submission of good action photos (5x7 or 8x10 b&w glossies) of the persons or situations in the article. Pays $10.
Poetry: "Poetry welcome on a religious theme; blank verse or rhyme." Length: 2-12 lines. Pays $2.
Fillers: Cross-word, word-find and other puzzles on religious or biblical themes. Pays $5.

THESE TIMES, Southern Publishing Association, Box 59, Nashville TN 37202. (615)889-8000. Editor: Kenneth J. Holland. For the general public; adult. Magazine; 36 pages. Established in 1891. Monthly. Circulation: 207,000. Rights purchased vary with author and material. May buy first North American serial rights, second serial (reprint) rights or simultaneous rights. Buys about 50 mss a year. Pays on acceptance. Will send free sample copy to writer on request. Write for copy of guidelines for writers. Will consider photocopied and simultaneous submissions. Will accept cassette submissions. Submit seasonal material 6 months in advance. Reports on material accepted for publication in 2 weeks. Returns rejected material in 1 week. Query first. Enclose S.A.S.E.
Nonfiction and Photos: Material on the relevance of Christianity and everyday life. Inspirational articles. How-to; home and family problems; health. Drugs, alcohol, gambling, abortion, Bible doctrine. Marriage; divorce; country living or city living. "We like the narrative style. Find a person who has solved a problem. Then, tell how he did it." Length: 250 to 2,500 words. Pays 6¢ to 10¢ a word. B&w and color photos are purchased with or without ms, or on assignment. Pays $20 to $25 for b&w; $75 to $150 for color.

TODAY'S CHRISTIAN PARENT, (formerly *Today's Christian Mother*), 8121 Hamilton Ave., Cincinnati OH 45231. (513)931-4050. Editor: Mrs. Wilma L. Shaffer. Quarterly. Rights purchased vary with author and material. Buys first North American serial rights and first serial rights. Payment on acceptance. Will send free sample copy to a writer on request. Reports on submissions within 1 month. Enclose S.A.S.E.
Nonfiction: Devotional and inspirational articles for the family. Also articles concerning the problems and pleasures of parents of preschool children, and Christian child training. Length: 600 to 1,200 words. Also can use some handcraft and activity ideas for preschoolers. Study magazine before submitting. Pays minimum of 1½¢ per word.
How To Break In: "Write about familiar family situations in a refreshingly different way, so that help and inspiration shine through the problems and pleasures of parenthood."

"TRUTH ON FIRE!" The Bible Holiness Movement, Box 223 Sta. A, Vancouver, BC V6C 2M3. (604)683-1833. Editor-in-Chief: Wesley H. Wakefield. Emphasizes Evangelism and Bible teachings. Bimonthly magazine; 32 pages. Estab: 1949. Circ: 4,000. Pays on acceptance. Buys all rights, but may reassign following publication. Simultaneous, photocopied and previously published submissions OK. SASE. Reports in 2 weeks. Free sample copy and writer's guidelines.

Nonfiction: "Evangelical articles; articles dealing with social reforms (pacifism, civil rights, religious liberty); expose (present-day slavery, cancer, tobacco, etc.), first person testimonies of Christian experience; doctrinal articles from Wesleyan interpretation. Must observe our evangelical taboos. Nothing favoring use of tobacco, alcohol, attendance at dances or theatres; nothing pro-abortion, pro-divorce-remarriage; no hip or slang. Also, we do not accept Calvinistic religious or right-wing political material. Would like to see material on Christian pacifism, anti-semitism, present-day slavery, marijuana research, religious issues in Ireland, and religious articles." Length: 300-2,500 words. Pays $5-35.

Photos: Photos purchased with or without accompanying ms. Pays $5-15 for 5x7 b&w photos. "Subjects should conform to our mores of dress (no jewelry, no makeup, no long-haired men, no mini-skirts, etc.).

Fillers: Newsbreaks, quotes. Length: 30-100 words. Pays $1-2.50.

TWIN CIRCLE, 1901 Avenue of the Stars, #1511, Los Angeles, CA 90067. (213)553-4911. Editor-in-Chief: Mrs. Geraldine Frawley. Emphasizes the Catholic community. Weekly tabloid; 20 pages. Estab: 1968. Circ: 60,000. Buys all rights, but may reassign following publication. Phone queries OK. Submit seasonal/holiday material 8 weeks in advance. Previously published submissions OK. SASE. Reports in 6 weeks. Free sample copy and writer's guidelines.

Nonfiction: How-to (problem solving, interpersonal relationships), interview, profile. Buys 4 mss/issue. Query. Length: 600-800 words. Pays $25 minimum.

Photos: Purchased with accompanying ms or on assignment. Captions required. Pays $10-25 for 8½x10 flat or glossy b&w prints. Query. Model release required.

THE UNITED CHURCH OBSERVER, 85 St. Clair Ave. E., Toronto 7, Ont., Canada. (416)925-5931. Editor: A.C. Forrest; Associate Editor: Patricia Clarke. For families in the United Church of Canada. Monthly. Not copyrighted. Pays on publication. Will send a sample copy to a writer for 50¢. Reports in 1 month. Query first. Enclose S.A.E. and International Reply Coupons.

Nonfiction: Wants general interest articles on all subjects of interest to church people. No homiletics. Material must have some church connection. Well-researched articles on developments in religion. Also deal in international affairs. Bright, journalistic style is necessary. Preferred lengths are 1,500 to 2,500 words. Thorough knowledge of the subject, authority and topnotch writing are looked for. Pays $50 minimum.

Photos: Buys photographs with mss and occasional picture stories. Use both b&w and color; b&w should be 8x10; color, prefers 4x5 transparencies but can work from 2¼x2¼ or 35mm. Payment varies.

UNITED EVANGELICAL ACTION, Box 28, Wheaton, IL 60187. (312)665-0500. Editor-in-Chief: Billy A. Melvin. For 35-50-year-old pastors and church leaders, including denominational executives. Quarterly magazine; 32 pages. Estab: 1942. Circ: 8,500. Pays on publication. Buys all rights. Phone queries OK. SASE. Reports in 4 weeks. Free sample copy and writer's guidelines.

Nonfiction: Anita Moreland, Nonfiction Editor. Informational (new trends in evangelical denominations or missions or on practical help to local churches and pastors) and interviews. Buys 2 mss/issue. Query. Length: 1,500-2,500 words. Pays 2-5¢/word.

UNITY MAGAZINE, Unity Village MO 64065. Editor: Thomas E. Witherspoon. Publication of Unity School of Christianity. Magazine; 66 (7x10) pages. Established in 1889. Monthly. Circulation: 275,000. Rights purchased vary with author and material. May buy first serial rights or second serial (reprint) rights. Buys 200 mss a year. Pays on acceptance. Will send free sample copy to writer on request. Write for copy of guidelines for writers. No photocopied or simultaneous submissions. Submit seasonal material 6 to 8 months in advance. Reports in 2 weeks. Submit complete ms. Enclose S.A.S.E.

Nonfiction and Photos: "Inspirational articles, metaphysical in nature, about individuals who are using Christian principles in their living." Personal experience and interview. Length: 3,000 words maximum. Pays minimum of 2¢ a word. 4x5 or 8x10 color transparencies purchased without mss. Pays $75-100.

Poetry: Traditional forms, blank verse, free verse. Pays 50¢/line.

VANGUARD: VISION FOR THE SEVENTIES, 229 College St., Toronto, Ontario, Canada M5T 1R4. Estab: 1970. 6 times/year. Circ: 2,500. "Copyright is held jointly by author and

publisher." Reports in 3 weeks. Query first. Enclose S.A.E. and International Reply Coupons.
Nonfiction: "*Vanguard* does not pay its contributors, but we welcome articles on any range of subjects: politics, economics, education, arts, urban affairs, etc., written from a Christian perspective and contributing to the development of a radical Christian consciousness and life style. Contributions are reviewed by our editorial committee."
How To Break In: "This is an idea magazine, reaching a highly educated and culturally aware audience. Freelance writers who are not recognized experts in a field should query the editor for assignments. A summary of writer's educational and journalistic background should accompany all queries."

VERONA FATHERS MISSIONS, 2104 St. Michael St., Cincinnati OH 45204. (513)921-4400. Editor: Fr. Joseph Bragotti, FSCJ. Mainly for Catholic lay and clergy interested in foreign missions efforts of the Verona Fathers. Also grade and high school librarians; churches. Bimonthly magazine; 24 pages. Estab: 1950. Circ: 24,000. Pays on publication. Will send sample copy to writer on request. Reports on material accepted for publication in 30 days. Returns rejected material immediately. Query first. Enclose S.A.S.E.
Nonfiction and Photos: Background information and human interest articles on the developing countries of Africa and Latin America. Should be written in a popular and simple style and reflect a positive outlook on efforts in religious and social fields. Informational, personal experience, interview, inspirational, travel articles. Pays $50. B&w photos purchased on assignment. Payment to be agreed upon with the photographer/writer, but begins at $10.

VISTA, Wesleyan Publishing House, Box 2000, Marion IN 46952. Address submissions to Editor of Sunday School Magazines. Publication of the Wesleyan Church. For adults. Weekly. Circulation: 63,000. Not copyrighted. "Along with mss for first use, we also accept simultaneous submissions, second rights, and reprint rights. It is the writer's obligation to secure clearance from the original publisher for any reprint rights." Pays on acceptance. Will send a sample copy to a writer on request. Editorial deadlines are 9 months in advance of publication. Reports in 6 weeks. Enclose S.A.S.E.
Nonfiction and Poetry: Devotional, biographical, and informational articles with inspirational, religious, moral, or educational values. Favorable toward emphasis on: "New Testament standard of living as applied to our day; soul-winning (evangelism); proper Sunday observance; Christian youth in action; Christian education in the home, the church and the college; good will to others; worldwide missions; clean living, high ideals, and temperance; wholesome social relationships. Disapprove of liquor, tobacco, theaters, dancing. Mss are judged on the basis of human interest, ability to hold reader's attention, vivid characterizations, thoughtful analysis of problems, vital character message, expressive English, correct punctuation, proper diction. Know where you are going and get there." Length: 500 to 1,500 words. Pays 2¢ a word for quality material. Also uses verse. Length: 4 to 16 lines. Pays 25¢ a line.
Photos: Purchased with mss. 5x7 or 8x10 b&w glossies; portraying action, seasonal emphasis or scenic value. Various reader age-groups should be considered. Pays $1 to $2.50 depending upon utility.
Fiction: Stories should have definite Christian emphasis and character-building values, without being preachy. Setting, plot and action should be realistic. Length: 1,500-2,500 words; also short-shorts and vignettes. Pays 2¢ a word for quality material.

THE WAR CRY, The Official Organ of the Salvation Army, 546 Avenue of the Americas, New York NY 10011. (212)691-8780. Editor: Lt. Col. William Burrows. For "persons with evangelical Christian background; members and friends of the Salvation Army; the 'man in the street'." Weekly. Circulation: 290,000. Buys all rights. Buys approximately 200 mss a year. Pays on acceptance. Will send a sample copy to a writer on request. Submit seasonal material for Christmas and Easter issues at any time. "Christmas and Easter issues are 4-color. Rate of payment for material used in these issues is considerably higher than for weekly issue material." Reports in 2 months. SASE.
Nonfiction: Inspirational and informational articles with a strong evangelical Christian slant, but not preachy. Prefers an anecdotal lead. In addition to general articles, needs articles slanted toward most of the holidays, including Mother's Day, Father's Day, Columbus Day, Washington's and Lincoln's birthdays, etc. Length: approximately 1,000 words. Pays $15 to $35.
Photos: Occasionally buys pix submitted with mss, but seldom with captions only. B&w glossies. Pays $5-20.
Fiction: Prefers complete-in-one-issue stories. Stories should run 1,500 to 2,000 words and have a strong Christian slant. May have Salvation Army background, but this is not necessary and may be detrimental if not authentic. Can have modern or Biblical setting, but must not run

contrary to Scriptural account. Principal Bible characters ordinarily should not be protagonists. Pays 2¢/word.

Poetry: Religious or nature poems. Uses very little poetry "except on Christmas and Easter themes." Length: 4 to 24 lines. Pays $2.50 to $15.

Fillers: Inspirational and informative items with a strong Christian slant. 1¢ to 2¢ per word.

WORLD ENCOUNTER, 2900 Queen Lane, Philadelphia PA 19129. (215)848-6800, Ext. 373. Editor: Rev. William A. Dudde. For persons who have more than average interest in, and understanding of, overseas missions and current human social concerns in other parts of the world. Quarterly magazine; 32 pages. Estab: 1963. Circ: 8,000. Buys all rights, but will reassign rights to author after publication. Buys 10 mss a year. Payment on publication. Will send free sample copy to writer on request. Will consider photocopied, cassette and simultaneous submissions, if information is supplied on other markets being approached. Reports in 1 month. Query first or submit complete ms. Enclose S.A.S.E.

Nonfiction and Photos: "This is a religious and educational publication using human interest features and think pieces relating to the Christian world mission and world community. Race relations in southern Africa; human rights struggles with tyrannical regimes; social and political ferment in Latin America; resurgence of Oriental religions. Simple travelogues are not useful to us. Prospective writers should inquire as to the countries and topics of particular interest to our constituents. Material must be written in a popular style but the content must be more than superficial. It must be theologically, sociologically and anthropologically sound. We try to maintain a balance between gospel proclamation and concern for human and social development. We focus on what is happening in Lutheran groups. Our standards of content quality and writing are very high." Length: 500 to 1,800 words. Pays $25 to $150. B&w photos are purchased with or without accompanying mss or on assignment. Pays $10 to $20. Captions required.

How To Break In: "Contact Lutheran missionaries in some overseas country and work out an article treatment with them. Or simply write the editor, outlining your background and areas of international knowledge and interest, asking at what points they converge with our magazine's interests."

WORSHIP, St. John's Abbey, Collegeville MN 56321. (612)363-3765. Editor: Rev. Aelred Tegels, O.S.B. "For readers concerned with the problems of liturgical renewal. The readership is largely Roman Catholic with a growing percentage of readers from the other Christian churches." Bimonthly; 96 pages. Serves as organ of the North American Academy of Liturgy, and, as such, regularly devotes its July issue to the proceedings of the annual meeting of the Academy. Buys all rights. Pays on publication. Reports in 2 to 3 weeks. Enclose S.A.S.E.

Nonfiction: "*Worship* magazine is engaged in an ongoing study of both the theoretic and the pastoral dimensions of liturgy. It examines the historical traditions of worship in their doctrinal context, the experience of worrhip in the various Christian churches, the finding of contemporary theology, psychology, communications, cultural anthropology, and sociology in so far as these have a bearing on public worship. Since the Second Vatican Council, *Worship* magazine has been fully ecumenical in its editorial board and policies as well as in its contributors and contents. Study a recent issue." Length: 3,000 to 5,000 words. Pays 1¢ to 2¢ a word.

Retirement Publications

DYNAMIC MATURITY, 215 Long Beach Blvd., Long Beach CA 90801. Editor: Hubert Pryor. Managing Editor: Carol Powers. "DM is the official publication of AIM—Action for Independent Maturity. AIM members are the 50 to 65 age bracket, pre-retirees." Estab: 1966. Bimonthly. Circ: 190,000. Rights purchased vary with author and material. May buy all rights with the possibility of reassigning rights to author after publication; or first serial rights, or second serial (reprint) rights. Buys 95 mss a year. Payment on acceptance. Will send a free sample copy to a writer on request. Submit seasonal material 4 months in advance. Reports in 1 week. Query first or submit complete ms. "Submit only 1 ms at a time." Enclose S.A.S.E.

Nonfiction and Photos: General subject matter is "health for middle years, pre-retirement planning, second careers, personal adjustment, well-developed hobbies, 'people in action' with useful activities, exciting use of leisure, financial preparation for retirement. We like the 'you' approach, nonpreachy, use of lively examples. We try to slant everything toward our age group, 50 to 65. We do not want pieces about individuals long retired. Prefer not seeing poetry, nostalgia, 'inspirational' preachments." Buys how-to, personal experience, profile, humor, or travel articles. Length: 1,000 to 2,000 words. Pays up to $400 per article. Photos purchased with and without mss for covers. Captions required. Pays $15 to $25 for professional quality b&w photos (5x7, 8x10). Pays $100 maximum for professional quality color photos (35mm or 2¼x2¼ transparencies).

MATURE LIVING, The Sunday School Board of the Southern Baptist Convention, 127 Ninth Ave. N., Nashville, TN 37234. (615)251-2191. Editor-in-Chief: John Warren Steen. A Christian magazine for retired or about-to-be-retired senior adults. Monthly magazine; 52 pages. Estab: 1977. Pays on acceptance. Buys all rights, but may reassign following publication. Phone queries OK. Submit seasonal/holiday material 11 months in advance. Photocopied and previously published submissions OK. SASE. Reports in 2-6 weeks. Free sample copy and writer's guidelines.

Nonfiction: How-to (easy, inexpensive craft articles made from easily obtained materials), informational (safety, consumer fraud, labor-saving and money-saving for senior adults), inspirational (poems and inspirational paragraphs with subject matter appealing to elders), interviews, nostalgia, personal experience, profile and travel. Buys 4-5 mss/issue. Send complete ms. Length: 400-1,400 words. Pays $10-35.

Photos: Photos purchased with accompanying ms. Pays $5-15 for any size b&w glossies. Model release required.

Fiction: Everyday living, humor and religious. Buys 1 ms/issue. Send complete ms. Length: 875-1,400 words. Pays 2½¢/word minimum.

Poetry: Free verse, light verse and traditional. Buys 6-7 poems/issue. Length: 4-24 lines. Pays $5-15.

Fillers: Short humor, religious or grandparent/grandchild episodes. Length: 50-125 words. Pays $5 minimum.

How To Break In: "We want warmth. Presentations don't have to be moralistic or religious, but must reflect Christian standards. Use case histories and examples. Don't write down to target audience. Speak *to* senior adults on issues that interest them. They like inspirational, good-samaritan, and nostalgic articles. We'll buy some light humor and some travel. We'll continually need medium length character studies of unusual people—especially those who have triumphed over adverse circumstances."

MATURE YEARS, 201 Eighth Ave., S., Nashville TN 37202. Editor: Daisy D. Warren. For retired persons and those facing retirement; persons seeking help on how to handle problems and privileges of retirement. Established in 1954. Quarterly. Rights purchased vary with author and material; usually buys all rights. Buys about 50 mss a year. Payment on acceptance. Write for copy of guidelines for writers. Submit seasonal material 1 year in advance. Reports within 6 weeks. Submit complete ms. Enclose S.A.S.E.

Nonfiction, Fiction and Photos: "*Mature Years* is different from the secular press in that we like material with Christian and church orientation. Usually we prefer materials that have a happy, healthy outlook regarding aging, although advocacy (for older adults) articles are at times used. Each issue is developed on a specific theme and the majority of theme-related articles are solicited. However, many freelance materials are used. Articles dealing with all aspects of preretirement and retirement living. Short stories and leisure-time hobbies related to specific seasons. Examples of how older persons, organizations, and institutions are helping others. Writing should be of interest to older adults, with Christian emphasis, though not preachy and moralizing. No poking fun or mushy, sentimental articles. We treat retirement from the religious viewpoint. How-to, humor and travel also considered." Length for nonfiction: 1,200 to 2,000 words. 8x10 b&w glossies purchased with ms or on assignment. "We buy fiction for adults. Humor is preferred. Please, no children's stories and no stories about depressed situations of older adults." Length: 1,000 to 2,000 words. Payment varies.

MODERN MATURITY, American Association of Retired Persons, 215 Long Beach Blvd., Long Beach, CA 90801. Editor-in-Chief: Hubert C. Pryor. Managing Editor: Ian Ledgerwood. For readership over 55 years of age. Bimonthly magazine; 64 pages. Circ: 10 million. Pays on acceptance. Buys all rights. Submit seasonal/holiday material 6 months in advance. Photocopied submissions OK. SASE. Reports in 2 weeks. Free sample copy and writer's guidelines.

Nonfiction: Historical; how-to; humor; informational; inspirational; interview; new product; nostalgia; personal experience; personal opinion; photo feature; profile and travel. Query or send complete ms. Length: 1,000-1,500 words. Pays $100-500.

Photos: Photos purchased with or without accompanying ms. Pays $25 minimum for 8x12 b&w glossies and color slides or prints.

Fiction: Buys some fiction, but must be suitable for older readers. Buys 2-3 mss/year. Send complete ms. Length: 1,000-1,500 words. Pays $50 minimum.
Poetry: All types. Length: 40 lines maximum. Pays $5-50.
Fillers: Clippings, jokes, gags, anecdotes, newsbreaks, puzzles (find the word, not crossword) and short humor. Length: 200-500 words. Pays $5.

NEW ENGLAND SENIOR CITIZEN/SENIOR AMERICAN NEWS, Prime National Publishing Corp., 470 Boston Post Rd., Weston MA 02193. Editor-in-Chief: Ira Alterman. For men and women aged 65 and over who are interested in travel, finances, retirement life styles, special legislation, etc. Monthly newspaper; 24-32 pages. Estab: 1970. Circ: 32,000. Pays 2-4 weeks after publication. Buys all rights. Submit seasonal/holiday material 1 month in advance. Photocopied and previously published material OK. SASE. Reports in 3-4 weeks. Sample copy 50¢.
Nonfiction: How-to (anything dealing with retirement years); informational; historical; humor; inspirational; interview; nostalgia; profile; travel; personal experience; photo features; and articles about medicine relating to gerontology. Buys 2-6 mss/issue. Submit complete ms. Length: 750-1,500 words. Pays 25¢/column inch.
Photos: Purchased with or without ms, or on assignment. Captions required. Submit prints. Pays $5 for 5x7 or 8x10 b&w glossies. Model release required.
Columns/Departments: Humor and Elderly Viewpoints. Buys 2-3/issue. Submit complete ms. Length: 500-1,000 words. Pays 25¢/column inch. Open to suggestions for new columns and departments.
Fiction: Adventure; historical; humorous; mystery; romance; suspense; and religious. Submit complete ms. Length: 750-1,500 words. Pays 25¢/column inch.
Poetry: Traditional forms. Limit submissions to batches of 1-2. Length: 500 words maximum. Pays 25¢/column inch.
Fillers: Jokes, gags, anecdotes; newsbreaks; and short humor. Submit complete ms. Length: 50-100 words. Pays 25¢/column inch.
How To Break In: "Remember that companionship is the theme we seek to pursue. Clean, typed, top-quality copy aimed at satisfying that need would be of great interest."

NRTA JOURNAL, 215 Long Beach Blvd., Long Beach CA 90801. (213)432-5781. Editor: Hubert Pryor. Publication of the National Retired Teachers Association. For retired teachers. Bimonthly. Buys all rights. Pays on acceptance. Will send a sample copy to a writer on request. Reports in 4 weeks. Enclose S.A.S.E.
Nonfiction and Fiction: Service pieces for the retired teacher relating to income, health, hobbies, living; Americana, nostalgia, reminiscence, personality pieces, inspirational articles, current trends. "Also in market for pieces on cultural leaders, cultural subjects and Christmas and other holiday material." Buys fiction occasionally. Length: 1,000 to 1,500 words for nonfiction; 1,500 words maximum for fiction. Pays $100 to $500.
Photos: "Special consideration for picture stories, photographic portfolios, etc." Pays $25 and up each; much more for color and covers.
Fillers: Puzzles, jokes, short humor. Pays $10 and up.

RETIREMENT LIVING, 150 E. 58 St., New York NY 10022. (212)593-2100. Editor-in-Chief: Roy Hemming. Associate Editor: Helen Alpert. "A service-oriented publication (no nostalgia) for pre-retirees (age 55 up) and retirees (age 65 and up). Readers are alert, active, forward-looking, interested in all aspects of meaningful living in the middle and later years." Monthly. Buys all rights. Buys 35 to 100 mss per year. Pays on publication. Will send a sample copy for 75¢ and 18¢ postage. Write for copy of guidelines for writers (enclose S.A.S.E.). Submit seasonal and holiday material 6 months in advance. Reports in 6-8 weeks. Queries preferred, but will look at complete ms. No phone inquiries. "Manuscripts must be accompanied by S.A.S.E.; otherwise not returned."
Nonfiction and Photos: "We like factual articles with a strong service value or how-to with names and rources for reader follow-up. Personal experiences, humor, income ideas, money management, unusual hobbies, self-fulfillment." Unusual travel stories, directly relevant to older people, only. Length: 500 to 1,500 words. Pays $50 to $150 an article; $20 to $25 for spot news. "We reserve all rights to edit and rewrite to our style and space requirements. Photos and color slides must be of professional quality." Pays $15 minimum.
How To Break In: "Profile a dynamic person in your community whose recent retirement activities or retirement plans are unusual and could prove meaningful or instructive to another person."

Science Publications

Publications classified here aim at laymen interested in technical and scientific developments and discoveries, applied science, and technical or scientific hobbies. Journals for professional scientists, engineers, repairmen, etc., will be found in Trade Journals.

ASTRONOMY, AstroMedia Corp., 411 E. Mason St., 6th Floor, Milwaukee WI 53202. (414)276-2689. Editor-in-Chief: Stephen A. Walther. Managing Editor: Penny Oldenberger. Emphasizes the science of astronomy. Monthly magazine; 80 pages. Estab: 1973. Circ: 65,000. Pays on publication. Buys all rights. SASE. Reports in 6-8 weeks. Sample copy $1.50; free writer's guidelines.
Nonfiction: How-to articles (build a telescope; grind a mirror); informational (latest research; what you can observe using a specific type or size of equipment, etc.). "We do not accept articles on UFO's, astrology, or religion." Buys 40-50/year. Submit complete ms. Length: 1,500-3,000 words. Pays 3-7¢/word.
Photos: Purchased with or without mss, or on assignment. B&w and color. Send prints and transparencies. Pays $7.50-10/b&w; $10 minimum for color.
Columns/Departments: Astro News and Astronomy Reviews (books). Buys 50-100/year. Query. Length: 150-500 words. Pays $1.25-1.75/typeset line. Open to suggestions for new columns/departments.

CB YEARBOOK, 229 Park Ave., S., New York NY 10003. (212)673-1300. Editor-in-Chief: Julian S. Martin. For anyone getting started in electronics as a hobby. Magazine; 114 pages. Established in 1968. Annually. Circulation: 315,000. Buys all rights. Pays on acceptance. Reports in 2 to 3 weeks. Query first. Enclose S.A.S.E.
Nonfiction: "We like new and exciting ideas. No padding; straight from the hip writing. Factual, with no puff. There will be a need for good stories on Citizens' Band Radio. Use our current issue as a style manual. Ask the question, is my next writing effort suitable for the issue I hold now?" How-to, personal experience, think pieces and technical articles. Length: open. Pays $100 to $250.

ELECTRONICS HOBBYIST, 229 Park Ave., S., New York NY 10003. (212)673-1300. Editor-in-Chief: Julian S. Martin. For "guys who like to build electronic projects from simple one-transistor jobs to complex digital clocks." Magazine; 104 pages. Established in 1964. Semi-annually. Circulation: 125,000. Buys all rights. Buys about 40 mss a year. Pays on acceptance. Will send sample copy to writer on request. No photocopied or simultaneous submissions. Reports in 2 to 3 weeks. Query first. Enclose S.A.S.E.
Nonfiction: Construction projects only. "Write a letter to us telling details of proposed project." Length: open. Pays $100 to $250.

ELEMENTARY ELECTRONICS, 229 Park Avenue S., New York NY 10003. (212)673-1300. Editor-in-Chief: Julian S. Martin. For electronics hobbyists, amateur radio operators, short-wave listeners, CB radio operators and computer hobbyists. Bimonthly magazine; 96 pages. Estab: 1950. Circulation: 250,000. Buys all rights. Buys 350 mss a year. Payment on acceptance. Will send sample copy to writer on request. Will not consider photocopied or simultaneous submissions. Reports on material accepted for publication in 2 to 4 weeks. Returns rejected material as soon as rejected. Query first. Enclose S.A.S.E.
Nonfiction and Photos: Construction articles are most needed; also, theory and feature articles related to hobby electronics. How-to and technical articles. "The writer should read our book and decide whether he can be of service to us; and then send us a precis of the story he wishes to submit." Length: as required to tell the story. Pays $150 to $250. No additional payment for photos used with mss. "For our column, CB's Buzzin Bee, we will pay up to $25 for short personal accounts of experiences with Citizens' Band radio. Ideally, each item will be 400 to 500 words long and accompanied by a b&w glossy photo."
How To Break In: "I would make three suggestions. First, how-to pieces are always winners. The same goes for construction projects. But they must be to fulfill some need, not just for the sake of selling. Finally, installation stories are very good—something that you buy and where the installation takes some degree of know-how that can be illustrated with step-by-step photos. The author will have to take the photos as he does the job. Theory pieces are tougher — you have to really know us and sense our needs and the sorts of things our readers want to learn about. Feeling and timing are key. We are about 98% freelance and most of our material originates in queries. Please read the magazine first!"

FREY SCIENTIFIC COMPANY CATALOG, 905 Hickory Lane, Mansfield OH 44905. Published annually. Buys all rights. Buys 70-100 rhymes/year. Pays "on acceptance, between October 1 and February 1. Rhymes that arrive after the latter date are held and paid for about November 1, the start of our next publication season." Enclose S.A.S.E.

Poetry: "We use humorous quatrains and limericks in our annual school science materials catalog, which is sent to every high school and college in the U.S. Each rhyme—limerick, quatrain, or couplet—is matched as best as possible to the appropriate section of our catalog. Rhymes pertaining to physics are included in the physics section, biology in the biology section, chemistry in the chemistry section, earth science to earth science, etc." Interested in buying material from writers "who can combine, in a single rhyme, our requirements of proper rhyme construction, distinct scientific reference, and humor. Generally, we will waive any of the three requirements if the rhyme is strong in the other two." Pays $5 per rhyme.

HAM RADIO MAGAZINE, Greenville NH 03048. (603)878-1441. Editor: James R. Fisk. For amateur radio licensees and electronics experimenters. Special May issue: antenna. Established in 1968. Monthly. Circ: 50,000. Buys all rights. Buys 10 mss/month. Pays on acceptance. Will send free sample copy to writer on request. Write for copy of guidelines for writers. Submit special issue material 6 months in advance. Reports in 1 month. Query helpful, but not essential. Enclose S.A.S.E.

Nonfiction and Photos: "Technical and home construction articles pertaining to amateur radio. Stress is placed on new developments. Technical articles of interest to the radio amateur, or home construction articles pertaining to amateur radio equipment. Experience has shown that writers who are not licensed amateur radio operators cannot write successfully for this publication." Length: 500 to 5,000 words. Pays approximately $35 per magazine page. Sharp, clear glossy prints (4x5 to 8x10) purchased with accompanying mss. "Don't wish to see any fiction or operating news."

MECHANIX ILLUSTRATED, 1515 Broadway, New York NY 10036. (212)869-3000. Editor: Robert G. Beason. Recreation Editor: Bill D. Miller. Home and Shop Editor: Burt Murphy. Managing Editor: Paul M. Eckstein. Special issues include boating (spring), new cars (October). Monthly magazine; 106 (8⅛x10⅞) pages. Buys all rights except for picture sets. Pays on acceptance. Write for copy of guidelines for writers. Reports promptly. Query first. Enclose S.A.S.E.

Nonfiction: Feature articles about science, inventions, novel boats, planes, cars, electronics, recreational vehicles, weapons, health, money management, unusual occupations, usually with mechanical or scientific peg, but not too technical. Recently published articles include "A Hang Glider with an Engine", "Good News for the *Next* Heating Season" and "We Trust VW's New Diesel Rabbit." Length: 1,500 words. Pays $400 minimum. Also uses home workshop projects, kinks, etc., for Home and Shop section. Pays $75 to $500, and higher in exceptional circumstances. "We offer a varied market for all types of do-it-yourself material, ranging from simple tips on easier ways to do things to major construction projects. Boatbuilding, furniture construction, painting, photography, electronics, gardening, astronomy, concrete and masonry work or any type of building construction or repair are just a few of the subjects that interest." Pays minimum of $15 for a tip submitted on a postcard without an illustration. Pays $20 to $25 for an illustrated and captioned tip.

Photos: Photos should accompany mss. Pays $400 and up for transparencies of interesting mechanical or scientific subjects accepted for cover; prefers 4x5, but 2¼ square is acceptable. Inside color: $300 for 1 page, $500 for 2, $700 for 3, etc. Pays $30 for single (b&w) feature photos involving new developments, etc., in the field, Home and Shop tips illustrated with 1 photo, $25. Captions are required. B&w picture sets, up to $350. Requires model releases.

Fillers: Pays $75 for half-page fillers.

How To Break In: "If you're planning some kind of home improvement and can write, you might consider doing a piece on it for us. Good how-to articles on home improvement are always difficult to come by. Aside from that, no particular part of the book is easier to break into than another because we simply don't care whether you've been around or been published here before. We don't care who you are or whether you have any credentials — we're in the market for good journalism and if it's convincing, we buy it."

OCEANS, 240 Fort Mason, San Francisco, CA 94123. Editor-in-Chief: Keith K. Howell. For people interested in the sea. Bimonthly magazine; 72 pages. Estab: 1969. Circ: 50,000. Pays on publication. Buys one-time rights. Phone queries OK. Submit seasonal/holiday material 3 months in advance. Simultaneous and photocopied submissions OK. SASE. Reports in 8 weeks. Sample copy 50¢. Free writer's guidelines.

Nonfiction: "Want articles on the worldwide realm of salt water; marine life (biology and ecology), oceanography, maritime history, geography, undersea exploration and rtudy, voyages, ships, coastal areas including environmental problems, seaports and shipping, islands, food-fishing and aquaculture (mariculture), peoples of the sea, including anthropological materials. Writer should be simple, direct, factual, very readable (avoid dullness and pedantry, make it lively and interesting but not cute, flip or tongue-in-cheek; avoid purple prose). Careful research, good structuring, no padding. Factual information in good, narrative style. Our mag is more serious than the common run of diving mags; less technical than *Scientific American.* We do not want articles on scuba; adventuring, travel tend to be overworked. Prefer no sport fishing, boating, surfing, other purely sport-type matter. Diving okay if serious in purpose, unusual in results or story angle. We want articles on rarely visited islands, ports, or shores which have great intrinsic interest, but not treated in purely travelogue style. Can use more on environmental concerns." Length: 1,000-5,000 words. Pays $60/page.

POPULAR ELECTRONICS, 1 Park Ave., New York NY 10016. (212)725-3566. Editor: Arthur P. Salsberg. For electronics experimenters, hi-fi buffs, computer hobbyists, CB'ers, hams. Monthly. Estab: 1954. Circ: 400,000. Buys all rights. Buys about 100 ms/year. Pays on acceptance. Write for copy of guidelines for writers. Will not consider photocopied or simultaneous submissions. Reports in 2 to 4 weeks. Query first. Enclose S.A.S.E.
Nonfiction and Photos: "State-of-the-art reports, tutorial articles, construction projects, etc. The writer must know what he's talking about and not depend on 'hand-out' literature from a few manufacturers or research laboratories. The writer must always bear in mind that the reader has some knowledge of electronics." Informational, how-to, and technical articles. Length: 500 to 3,000 words. Pays $60 to $125 per published page with photo illustration. B&w glossies preferred.
Fillers: Electronics circuits puzzles. Length: 500 to 1,000 words. Pays $25 to $75.

POPULAR MECHANICS, 224 W. 57th St., New York NY 10019. (212)262-4815. Editor: John A. Linkletter. Executive Editor: Sheldon Gallager. Managing Editor: Daniel C. Fales. Home and Shop Editor: Harry Wicks. Magazine; 200 pages. Monthly. Circ: 1,671,216. Buys all rights. Pays promptly. Query first. Enclose S.A.S.E.
Nonfiction: "Our principal subjects are automotive (new cars, car maintenance) and how-to (woodworking, metalworking, home improvement and home maintenance). In addition, we use features on new technology, sports, electronics, photography and hi-fi." Exciting male interest articles with strong science, exploration and adventure emphasis. Looking for reporting on new and unusual developments. The writer should be specific about what makes it new, different, better, cheaper, etc. "We are always looking for fresh ideas in home maintenance, shop technique, and crafts, for project pieces used in the back part of the book. The front of the book uses articles in technology and general science, but writers in that area should have background in science." Lengths: 300 to 2,000 words. Pays $300-$600 and up.
Photos: Dramatic photos are most important, and they should show people and things in action. Occasionally buys picture stories with short text block and picture captions. The photos must tell the story without much explanation. Topnotch photos are a must with Craft Section articles. Can also use remodeling of homes, rooms and outdoor structures. Pays $25 minimum.
Fillers: How-to-do-it articles on craft projects and shop work well-illustrated with photos and drawings. The writer must provide the drawings, diagrams, cutaways, and/or photos that would be appropriate to the piece. Finished drawings suitable for publication are not necessary; rough but accurate pencil drawings are adequate for artist's copy. Pays $15.

POPULAR SCIENCE MONTHLY, 380 Madison Ave., New York NY 10017. Editor: Hubert P. Luckett. For the well-educated adult male, interested in science, technology, new products. Monthly magazine; 175 pages. Established in 1872. Circulation: 1,750,000. Buys all rights. Buys several hundred mss a year. Payment on acceptance. Write for copy of guidelines for writers. Will not consider photocopied or simultaneous submissions. Submit seasonal material 3 to 4 months in advance. Reports in 2 to 3 weeks. Query first. Enclose S.A.S.E.
Nonfiction and Photos: "*Popular Science Monthly* is a man's magazine devoted to exploring (and explaining) to a nontechnical but knowledgeable readership the technical world around us. We are a 'thing'-oriented publication: things that fly or travel down a turnpike, or go on or under the sea, or cut wood, or reproduce music, or build buildings, or make pictures, or mow lawns. We are especially focused on the new, the ingenious, and the useful. We are consumer oriented and are interested in any product that adds to a man's enjoyment of his home, yard, car, boat, workshop, outdoor recreation. Some of our 'articles' are only a picture and caption long. Some are a page long. Some occupy 4 or more pages. Contributors should be as alert to

the possibility of selling us pictures and short features as they are to major articles. Freelancers should study the magazine to see what we want and avoid irrelevant submissions." Length: 2,000 words maximum. Pays a minimum of about $150 a published page. refers 8x10 b&w glossies. Pays $20.

Fillers: Uses shortcuts and tips for homeowners, home craftsmen, car owners, mechanics and machinists.

How To Break In: "Probably the easiest way to break in here is by covering a news story in science and technology that we haven't heard about yet. We need people to be acting as bird-dogs for us out there and we are willing to give the most leeway on these performances. What impresses us the most in a freelance piece—when we're thinking about uncovering a good contributor for the future—is the kind of illustrations the writer supplies. Too many of them kiss off the problem of illustrations. Nothing impresses us more than knowing that the writer can take or acquire good photos to accompany his piece. We probably buy the most freelance material in the do-it-yourself and home improvement areas."

RADIO-ELECTRONICS, 200 Park Ave. S., New York NY 10003. (212)777-6400. Editorial Director: Larry Steckler. Managing Editor: Art Kleiman. For electronics professionals and hobbyists. Monthly. Circ: 173,000. Buys all rights. Pays on acceptance. Send for "Guide to Writing." Reports on submissions in 2 weeks. Enclose S.A.S.E.

Nonfiction: Interesting technical stories on electronics, TV and radio, written from viewpoint of the TV service technician, serious experimenter, or layman with technical interests. Construction (how-to-build-it) articles used heavily. Unique projects bring top dollars. Cost of project limited only by what item will do. Emphasis on "how it works, and why." Much of material illustrated with schematic diagrams and pictures provided by author. Pays about $60 to $100 per magazine page.

Photos: Purchased with mss. Model releases required. Payment included in article price. 8x10 glossy.

How To Break In: "The simplest way to come in would be with a short article on some specific construction project. Queries aren't necessary; just send the article, 5 or 6 typewritten pages."

SCIENCE SIGEST, Hearst Magazines Division, Hearst Corp., 224 W. 57th St., New York NY 10019. (212)262-4161. Editor-in-Chief: Daniel E. Button. Emphasizes sciences and technologies for all ages with a scientific bent. Monthly magazine; 100 pages. Estab: 1937. Circ: 150,000. Pays on acceptance. Buys all rights. Submit seasonal/holiday material 3 months in advance. Simultaneous and previously published submissions OK. Reports in 1 month. Free sample copy and writer's guidelines.

Nonfiction: Informational (authentic, timely information in all areas of science); interview (with outstanding authorities in various fields of science); photo feature (usually single photos with adequate cutlines); profile; and technical (not overly so). Buys 30 mss/year. Query. Length: 750-1,500 words. Pays $50-500.

Photos: Purchased with or without accompanying ms or on assignment. Captions required. Query. Pays $25-100 for 8x10 b&w photos; $50-300 for color. Total purchase price for ms includes payment for photos. Model release required.

Fillers: Anecdotal or nostalgic. Query. Length: 50-250 words. Pays $25-50.

How To Break In: "We have, as of early 1977, changed much of the approach, tone, and content of the magazine. It is imperative that the writer familiarize himself thoroughly with this form. Don't submit or query on the basis of old recollections, assumptions, contacts, or published references. We are specifically open to second rights from other periodicals."

SCIENCE NEWS, Science Service, Inc., 1719 N. St., NW, Washington DC 20036. Editor-in-Chief: Kendrick Frazier. For scientists and science-oriented laymen. Weekly magazine; 16 pages. Estab: 1922. Circ: 155,000. Pays on acceptance. Buys all rights. SASE.

Nonfiction: Profile and technical news. Buys 4 mss/year. Query or send complete ms. Pays $75-200. "We are primarily staff-written for two reasons: (1) Being a weekly newsmagazine, we work very close to deadline. Communications and coordination are crucial. Everyone must note what we've previously reported on the same subject and then add what's new. (2) Quality control. We have really gotten burned in the past by freelance articles that were factually inaccurate. We are occasionally in the market for prepublication excerpts from books, especially those involving a thoughtful, humanistic approach toward science, by noted scientists of established reputation; but again this is seldom."

How To Break In: "Acceptance occurs when the writer is either 1) covering a newsworthy scientific meeting that for some reason we have no reporter at or 2) has a topical news-feature article (1,500-1,800 words) on a specific science topic that we haven't already covered. For this to work for us, the writer must be vary familiar with *Science News* (suitable for scientists and the scientifically interested lay public) and for the subjects we already cover thoroughly. These include, generally, physics, astronomy, the space sciences and medical sciences. Articles must have both news and science value."

SCIENTIFIC AMERICAN, 415 Madison Ave., New York NY 10017. Articles by professional scientists only.

73 MAGAZINE, Peterborough NH 03458. (603)924-3873. Publisher: Wayne Green. For amateur radio operators and experimenters. Monthly. Buys all rights. Pays on acceptance. Reports on submissions within a few weeks. Query first. Enclose S.A.S.E.
Nonfiction and Photos: Articles on anything of interest to radio amateurs, experimenters, and computer hobbyists — construction projects. Pays approximately $20 per page. Photos purchased with ms as illustrations.

Science Fiction, Speculative Fiction and Fantasy Publications

ANALOG SCIENCE FICTION & SCIENCE FACT, 350 Madison Ave., New York NY 10017. Editor: Ben Bova. For general future-minded audience. Monthly. Buys all English serial rights. Pays on acceptance. Reports within 3 to 4 weeks. Query first. Enclose S.A.S.E.
Fiction: Stories of the future told for adults interested in science and technology; central theme usually interaction of strong characters with science or technology-based problems. Length: 3,000 to 60,000 words. Serials only on consultation with Editor. Pays 3¢ to 4 ¢ a word for novelettes and novels, 5¢ a word for shorts under 7,500 words.
Nonfiction and Photos: Needs illustrated technical articles. Length: 5,000 words. Pays 5¢ a word. Buys photos with mss only. Pays $5 each.

FANTASY & TERROR, Atalanta Press, Box 5688, University Station, Seattle WA 98105. (206)324-4003. Editor: Jessica Amanda Salmonson. "Readers are generally of a high intellect to grasp fantasy's complexity." Twice a year. Established in 1973. Buys all rights, but will reassign rights to author after publication. Buys over 50 mss a year. Payment on acceptance. Will send sample copy to writer for $1.50. No carbon copies or photocopies. Reports on material accepted for publication within 30 days. Returns rejected material in 10 days. Submit complete ms. Enclose S.A.S.E.
Fiction: Publishes a wider variety of fantasy-oriented material than any other fantasy publication. Any kind of fantasy will be considered, except science fiction. Epic, heroic and hardcore fantasy especially desired. "Fantasy, and the horror sub-genre in particular, suffers an outlandish number of overworked cliches, all of which should be avoided. Vampires, pacts with devils, magic mirrors, haunted houses, ad infinitum, simply won't sell here." Length: 2,000 to 15,000 words. Pays ½¢ per word and up, maximum $100 per story.

GALAXY, Universal Publishing and Distributing Corp., Box 418 Planetarium Station, New York NY 10024. Editor-in-Chief: James Patrick Baen. Managing Editor: Elaine Ingeborg Will. Emphasizes science fiction for young, science-oriented, high I.Q. types. Monthly magazine; 160 pages. Estab: 1950. Circ: 100,000. Pays on publication. Buys first World serial rights. Phone queries OK. Simultaneous, photocopied and previously published submissions OK. SASE. Reports in 4-8 weeks. Sample copy $1; free writer's guidelines.
Nonfiction: Technical (recent developments and speculations in science and technology with emphasis on areas with dramatic social impact). Buys "very few"/year. Send outline. Length: 3,000-6,000 words. Pays 2½-5¢/word.
Fiction: Science fiction. Buys 70 mss/year. Length: 20,000 words maximum. Pays 2½-5¢/word. "No stories that end with some variation of: 'And it was *earth* — and the alien was God!'"

ISAAC ASIMOV'S SCIENCE FICTION MAGAZINE, Davis Publications, Inc., Box 13116, Philadelphia PA 19101. (215)382-5415. Editor-in-Chief: George H. Scithers. Emphasizes science fiction. Quarterly magazine; 192 pages. Estab: 1976. Circ: 100,000. Pays on acceptance. Buys first North American serial rights and foreign serial rights. Photocopied submissions OK. SASE. Reports in 2-3 weeks. Writer's guidelines for SASE.
Fiction: Science fiction only. "At first, each story must stand on its own; but as the magazine

progresses, we want to see continuing use of memorable characters and backgrounds." Buys 12 mss/issue. Submit complete ms. Length: 100-12,500 words. Pays 3-5¢/word.

STARWIND, The Starwind Press, P.O. Box 3346, Columbus OH 43210. Editor: Elbert Lindsey, Jr. For a college-educated audience (18 to 35) interested in science fiction and fantasy. Magazine; 50 to 60 pages. Established in 1973. Twice a year (fall and spring). Circulation: 2,500. Rights purchased vary with author and material. May buy first North American serial rights or second serial (reprint) rights. Buys about 25 mss a year. Pays on publication. Will send sample copy to writer for $2. Write for copy of guidelines for writers. Will consider photocopied submissions. No simultaneous submissions. Reports on material accepted for publication in 4 to 6 weeks. Returns rejected material in 6 to 8 weeks. Submit complete ms. Enclose S.A.S.E.

Nonfiction: "Interested in analyses of works of well-known science fiction authors and genres in sf and fantasy, or interviews with sf authors or publishers. Reviews of sf books. Also interested in articles dealing with current developments or research in space exploration or colonization, artifical intelligence, genetics, bioengineering, or other subjects. Emphasis should be on extrapolations which are of interest to readers of science fiction." Length: 4,000-20,000 words. Pays ½¢ a word.

Fiction: "Classic hardcore sf, heroic fantasy, supernatural mystery and suspense, occult horror, and some space opera and softcore sf. Particularly interested in stories with non-stereotyped women protagonists. Our prime requisite is good storytelling that is logically constructed. We consider works of unknown writers for all types of material we publish. We prefer not to see extremely short stories with trick endings, rather than well-developed plot." Length: 2,000 to 20,000 words. Pays ½¢ a word.

WEIRDBOOK, Box 35, Amherst Branch, Buffalo NY 14226. Editor-in-Chief: W. Paul Ganley. Emphasizes weird fantasy (swords & sorcery, supernatural horror, pure fantasy) for a readership teen-age and up. Semiannual magazine; 64 pages. Estab: 1968. Circ: 650. Pays on publication. Buys first North American serial rights and right to reprint as part of entire issue. Photocopied submissions OK. SASE. "Best time to submit is in December or May if quick response is desired." Sample copy $2.50; writer's guidelines for SASE.

Fiction: Adventure (with weird elements); experimental (maybe, if in fantasy or horror area). Buys 6 mss/year. Submit complete ms. Length: 20,000 words maximum. Pays ¼¢/word.

WHISPERS, Box 904, Chapel Hill NC 27514. Editor: Dr. Stuart David Schiff. For intelligent adults with an interest in literate horror, terror, fantasy, and heroic fantasy. Many readers collect first edition books and the like in these fields. Magazine; 64 (5x8½) pages. Established in 1973. An approximate quarterly schedule. Circ: 3,000. Buys first North American serial rights only. Buys 15 to 20 mss a year. Pays half of fee on acceptance; balance on publication. Will consider photocopied submissions. No simultaneous submissions. Reports in 3 months. Submit complete ms. SASE.

Fiction: Stories of fantasy, terror, horror, and heroic fantasy. Does not want to see science fiction. No rocket ships, futuristic societies, bug-eyed monsters or the like. Authors whose work is most related to their needs include H. P. Lovecraft, Lord Dunsany, Edgar Allan Poe, Algernon Blackwood, Robert Bloch, Fritz Leiber, Ray Bradbury, and Clark Ashton Smith. Length: 500 to 8,000 words. Pays 1¢ a word.

Social Science Publications

HUMAN BEHAVIOR, Manson Western Corp., 12031 Wilshire Blvd., Los Angeles CA 90025. Editor-in-Chief: Marshall Lumsden. Emphasizes human behavior for college educated audience. Monthly magazine; 80 pages. Estab: 1972. Circ: 100,000. Pays on acceptance. Buys all rights, but may reassign following publication. Photocopied and previously published submissions OK. SASE. Reports in 2 months.

Nonfiction: News, trends, reports on current research and personalities in the behavioral sciences. Buys 5 mss/issue. Query or submit complete ms. Length: 1,800-5,000 words. Pays $150-500.

Photos: Purchased on assignment. Captions required. Query or send contact sheet. Pays $25-50 for b&w photos.

IMPACT OF SCIENCE ON SOCIETY, Unesco, 7 place de Fontenoy, 75700 Paris, France. (1)577-16-10. Editor-in-Chief: J.G. Richardson. Emphasizes science and technology for development and the science-society interrelationship. For an audience concerned with the problems of management of higher education throughout the world. Quarterly magazine; 96 pages. Estab: 1950. Pays on acceptance. Usually buys all rights, but may reassign following publication. Photocopied submissions OK. "Indicate if return of submissions is desired. We pay the postage." Reports in 2 weeks. Free sample copy.

Nonfiction and Science: Publishes articles of 5,000 words; illustrated. Would like to see mss dealing with "science/technology as tools for solving urban problems." Also open to suggestions for new columns or departments. Informational, how-to and profile. Length: 2,000 to 6,500 words. Pays $100 to $325. Interview and humor. Length: 2,500 to 4,500. Pays $125 to $225. "Think" pieces. Length: 2,500 to 6,500. Pays $125 to $325. Photographic presentations. Length: 500 to 1,000 words. Pays $150 to $250. Technical. Length: 2,000 to 6,500 words. Pays $125 to $325. Does not want to see any mystical explanations for scientific phenomena or utopian solutions to problems of world development.

PARAPSYCHOLOGY REVIEW, 29 W. 57th St., New York NY 10019. (212)751-5940. Editor: Betty Shapin. Emphasizes psychical research, parapsychology, research and experiment pertaining to extrasensory perception. For the scientific community, academic community, lay audience with special interest in psychical research and the paranormal. Estab: 1953. Bimonthly. Circ: 2,500. Buys all rights, but will reassign to author following publication. Buys 40-50 mss/year. Pays on acceptance. Will send sample copy to writer for $1. Reports in 1 to 2 weeks. Query first or submit complete ms. Enclose S.A.S.E.

Nonfiction: Articles, news items, book reviews in this general subject area. Must approach psychical research in scientific, experimental fashion. Length: 500-3,000 words. Pays $50 minimum.

PERSONAL GROWTH, P.O. Box 1254, Berkeley CA 94701. (415)548-1004. Editor: James Elliott. For psychologists and well-informed lay persons. Most of them have been to (or led) 1 or more encounter groups. Monthly magazine; 24 pages (7x8½). Established in 1964. Circulation: 5,000. Buys all rights, but will reassign rights to author after publication. Buys 12 mss/year. Pays on acceptance. Sample copy to writer for 2 first class postage stamps; free writer's guidelines. Will consider photocopied, cassette, and simultaneous submissions. Reports in 3-4 weeks. Query. SASE.

Nonfiction: "Anything on personal growth; the human potential movement, psychotherapy, humanistic psychology, etc. Use simple, informal language (not abstract journalese); material should be heavily researched with plenty of examples. We're like *Psychology Today* but with emphasis on personal growth. Taboos are personal accounts of group experiences; articles about the power of positive thinking; articles on 'how religion helped me'; anything featuring the medical model (i.e., 'curing' people). Particularly interested in existensialism, phenomenology and new psychotherapies—also little-known ideas of such famous psychotherapists as Freud, Jung, and Adler—guided imagery and fantasy." Informational, how-to, interview. Length: 200 to 5,000 words. Pays $15 to $200.

PSYCHOLOGY TODAY, 1 Park Ave., New York NY 10016. (714)453-5000. For social scientists and intelligent laymen concerned with society and individual behavior. Monthly. Buys all rights. Each ms will be edited by staff and returned to author prior to publication for comments and approval. Author should retain a copy. Reports within 1 month. Address all queries to Articles Editor. Enclose S.A.S.E.

Nonfiction: Most mss written by scholars in various fields. Primary purpose is to provide the nonspecialist with accurate and readable information about society and behavior. Technical and specialized vocabularies should be avoided except in cases where familiar expressions cannot serve as adequate equivalents. Technical expressions, when necessary, should be defined carefully for the nonexpert. References to technical literature should not be cited within article, but 10 to 12 general readings should be listed at end. Suggested length: 3,000 words. Payment is $500.

THE SINGLE PARENT, Parents Without Partners, Inc., 7910 Woodmont Ave., Washington DC 20014. (310)654-8850. Editor-in-Chief: Barbara C. Chase. Emphasizes marriage, family, divorce, widowhood, and children. Distributed to members of Parents Without Partners, plus libraries, universities, phychologists, psychiatrists, etc. Average age is mid-40's, 60% female. Published 10 times/year. Magazine; 48 pages. Estab: 1965. Circ: 155,000. Pays on publication. Rights purchased vary. Phone queries OK. Submit seasonal/holiday material 3 months in advance. Simultaneous, photocopied and previously published submissions OK. SASE. Reports in 6-8 weeks. Free sample copy and writer's guidelines.

Nonfiction: How-to (home/auto fix-it for single parents); informational (money management, daycare); interviews (with professionals in the field); personal experience (adjustment to widowhood or divorce by adults and children) and travel (for single parents). Buys 4-5 mss/issue. Query. Length: 1,000-6,000 words. Pays $25-50.
Photos: Purchased with accompanying ms. Query. Pays $10-50 for any size b&w glossies. Model release required.
Rejects: "No first-hand accounts of bitter legal battles with former spouses. No poetry or general interest material."

TOGETHER (formerly *Sexology*), 200 Park Ave., S., New York NY 10003. Editor: Jack Nichols. For a lay readership. Monthly magazine; 80 pages. Estab: 1933. Circ: 200,000. Pays on acceptance. Buys all rights, first serial rights or second serial (reprint) rights. SASE. Reports in 4 weeks. Sample copy will be sent to any writer sending a query, if the query is accepted.
Nonfiction: "We are seeking articles to bring to the public authoritative and frank information that will help them integrate their sexual natures with the rest of their lives. We solicit themes reflecting the best of new consciousness/feminist perspectives, indicating infusion of these into practical situations. Such themes must be solidly educational or informative and, at the same time, entertaining and easily read and understood. Our editorial aim is to provide helpful, accurate guidance and advice. We eschew sensationalism, but any solid attempt to bring information to our public is reviewed. We regularly cover 'how to' themes with specific advice on promoting compatability, including sexual acts. We seek anatomic articles (medical) about sexuality, psychological, elderly, singles, new scientific breakthroughs, sociological/philosophical perspectives, other cultures, customs (in sex and relationship) and modern appraisals of the relationship/sex theme." Query first, with outline. Length: 1,800-2,000 words. Pays $175 minimum.

TRANSACTION/SOCIETY, Rutgers University, New Brunswick NJ 08903. (201)932-2280, ext. 83. Editor: Irving Louis Horowitz. For social scientists (policymakers with training in sociology, political issues and economics). Established in 1963. Every 2 months. Circulation: 55,000. Buys all rights, but may reassign rights to author after publication. Pays on publication. Will send sample copy to writer on request. Write for copy of guidelines for writers. Will consider photocopied submissions. No simultaneous submissions. Reports in 4 weeks. Query first. Enclose S.A.S.E.
Nonfiction and Photos: Articles Editor: Eliot Werner. Photo Editor: Jim Colman. "Articles of wide interest in areas of specific interest to the social science community. Must have an awareness of problems and issues in education, population, urbanization that are not widely reported. Articles on overpopulation, terrorism, international organizations." Payment for articles is made only if done on assignment. No payment for unsolicited articles. Pays $200 for photographic essays done on assignment.

VICTIMOLOGY: An International Journal, Box 39045, Washington DC 20016. Editor-in-Chief: Emilio C. Viano. "We are the only magazine specifically focusing on the victim, on the dynamics of victimization; for social scientists, criminal justice professionals and practitioners, social workers and volunteer and professional groups engaged in prevention of victimization and in offering assistance to victims of rape, spouse abuse, child abuse, natural disasters, etc." Quarterly magazine. Estab: 1976. Circ: 2,500. Pays on publication. Buys all rights. SASE. Reports in 6-8 weeks. Sample copy $5; free writer's guidelines.
Nonfiction: Expose; historical; how-to; informational; interview; personal experience; profile; research and technical. Buys 10 mss/issue. Query. Length: 500-5,000 words. Pays $5-50.
Photos: Purchased with accompanying ms. Captions required. Send contact sheet. Pays $15-30 for 5x7 or 8x10 b&w glossies.
Poetry: Avant-garde; free verse; light verse; and traditional. Length: 30 lines maximum. Pays $10-25.
How To Break In: "Focus on what is being researched and discovered on the victim, the victim-offender relationship, treatment of the offender, the bystander-witness, preventive measures, and what is being done in the areas of service to the victims of rape, spouse abuse, neglect and occupational and environmental hazards."

Sport and Outdoor Publications

The publications listed in this category are intended for active sportsmen, sports fans, or both. They buy material on how to practice and enjoy both team and individual sports, material on conservation of streams and forests, and articles reporting on and analyzing professional sports.

Writers will note that several of the editors mention that they do not wish to see "Me 'n Joe" stories. These are detailed accounts of one hunting/fishing trip taken by the author and a buddy—starting with the friends' awakening at dawn and ending with their return home, "tired but happy."

For the convenience of writers who specialize in one or two areas of sport and outdoor writing, the publications are subcategorized by the sport or subject matter they emphasize. Publications in related categories (for example, Hunting and Fishing; Archery and Bowhunting) often buy similar material (in this case articles on bow and arrow hunting). Consequently, writers should read through this entire Sport and Outdoor category to become familiar with the subcategories and note the ones that contain markets for their own type of writing.

Publications concerned with horse breeding, hunting dogs, or the use of other animals in sport are classified in the Animal category. Publications dealing with automobile or motorcycle racing will be found in the Automotive and Motorcycle category. Outdoor publications that exist to further the preservation of nature, placing only secondary emphasis on preserving nature as a setting for sport, are listed in the Nature, Conservation, and Ecology category. Newspapers and Magazine Sections, as well as Regional magazines are frequently interested in conservation or sports material with a local angle. Camping publications are classified in the Travel, Camping, and Trailer category.

Archery and Bowhunting

ARCHERY WORLD, 225 E. Michigan, Milwaukee WI 53202. Editor: Glenn Helgeland. For "archers—average education, hunters and target archers, experts to beginners." Subject matter is the "entire scope of archery—hunting, bowfishing, indoor target, outdoor target, field." Bimonthly. Circ: 89,000. Buys first serial rights. Buys 30 to 35 mss a year. Pays on acceptance "or as near to it as possible." Will send a free sample copy to a writer on request. Tries to report in 2 weeks. Query first. Enclose S.A.S.E.
Nonfiction: "Get a free sample and study it. Try, in ms, to entertain archer and show him how to enjoy his sport more and be better at it." Wants how-to, semitechnical, and hunting where-to and how-to articles. "Looking for more good technical stories and short how-to pieces." Also uses profiles and some humor. Length: 1,000 to 2,200 words. Payment is $50 to $150.
Photos: B&w glossies purchased with mss and with captions. "Like to see proofsheets and negs with submitted stories. We make own cropping and enlargements." Color transparencies purchased for front cover only. Will look at color prints "if that's the only photo available." Pays $5 minimum for b&w; $50 minimum for color.

BOW AND ARROW, P.O. Box HH/37249 Camino Capistrano, Capistrano Beach CA 92624. Editor: Jackie Farmer. For archery competitors and bowhunters. Bimonthly. Buys all rights, "but will relinquish all but first American serial rights on written request of author." Pays on acceptance. Will send free sample copy to a writer on request. Reports on submissions in 6 weeks. Study publication. Author must have some knowledge of archery terms. Query first. Enclose S.A.S.E.
Nonfiction: Articles: bowhunting, major archery tournaments, techniques used by champs, how to make your own tackle, and off-trail hunting tales. Likes a touch of humor in articles. Also uses one technical article per issue. Length: 1,500 to 2,500 words. Pays $75 to $150.
Photos: Purchased as package with mss; 5x7 minimum or submit contacts with negatives (returned to photographer). Pays $75 to $100 for cover chromes, 35mm or larger.

BOWHUNTER MAGAZINE, P.O. Box 5377, Fort Wayne IN 46805. (219)432-5772. Editor: M. R. James. For readers of all ages, background and experience. All share 2 common passions—hunting with the bow and arrow and a love of the great outdoors. Magazine published every 2 months; 64 pages. Established in 1971. Circulation: 85,000. Buys all rights, but may reassign rights to author after publication. Buys 55 mss a year. Payment on acceptance. Will send free sample copy to writer on request. Write for copy of guidelines for writers. No photocopied or simultaneous submissions. "We publish a special deer hunting issue each August. Submit seasonal material 6 to 8 months in advance." Reports within 4 to 6 weeks. Query first or submit complete ms. Enclose S.A.S.E.

Nonfiction, Photos and Fillers: "Our articles are written for, by and about bowhunters and we ask that they inform as well as entertain. Most material deals with big or small game bowhunting (how-to, where to go, etc.), but we do use some technical material and personality pieces. We do not attempt to cover all aspects of archery — only bowhunting. Anyone hoping to sell to us must have a thorough knowledge of bowhunting. Next, they must have either an interesting story to relate or a fresh approach to a common subject. We would like to see more material on what is being done to combat the anti-hunting sentiment in this country." Informational, how-to, personal experience, interview, profile, humor, historical, think articles, expose, nostalgia, personal opinion, spot news, new product, and technical articles. Length: 200 to 5,000 words. Pays $25 to $150. Photos purchased with accompanying ms or without ms. Captions optional. Pays $10 to $25 for 5x7 or 8x10 b&w prints; $50 for 35mm or 2¼x2¼ color. Also purchases newsbreaks of 50 to 500 words for $5 to $25.

How To Break In: "The answer is simple if you know bowhunting and have some interesting, informative experiences or tips to share. Keep the reader in mind. Anticipate questions and answer them in the article. Weave information into the storyline (e.g., costs involved, services of guide or outfitter, hunting season dates, equipment preferred and why, tips on items to bring, etc.) and, if at all possible, study back issues of the magazine. We have no set formula, really, but most articles are first-person narratives and most published material will contain the elements mentioned above."

Basketball

BASKETBALL WEEKLY, 19830 Mack Ave., Grosse Point MI 48236. (313)881-9554. Publisher: Roger Stanton. Editor: Larry Donald. 19 issues during season, September-May. Circ: 40,000. Buys all rights. Pays on publication. For free sample copy, send a large S.A.S.E. Reports in 2 weeks. Also include S.A.S.E. with submissions and queries.

Nonfiction, Photos and Fillers: Current stories on teams and personalities in college and pro basketball. Length: 800 to 1,000 words. Payment is $30 to $50. 8x10 b&w glossy photos purchased with mss. Also uses newsbreaks.

HOOP, Professional Sports Publications, 310 Madison Ave., New York NY 10017. (212)697-1460. Editor: Pamela Blawie. 32-page color insert that is folded into the local magazines of each of the NBA teams. Buys all rights, but will reassign rights to author after publication, if author so requests. "For the most part, assignments are being made to newspapermen and columnists on the pro basketball beat around the country." Will send sample copy to writer for $1. Reports within 1 week. Enclose S.A.S.E.

Nonfiction: Features on NBA players, officials, personalities connected with league. The NBA, founded in 1946-47, is the older of the 2 established professional basketball leagues. Length: 800 to 900 words. Pays $50 per article.

How To Break In: "The best way for a freelancer to break in is to aim something for the local team section. That can be anything from articles about the players or about their wives to unusual off-court activities. The best way to handle this, is to send material directly to the P.R. person for the local team. They have to approve anything that we do on that particular team and if they like it, they forward it to me. They're always looking for new material — otherwise they have to crank it all out themselves."

Bicycling

BICYCLING!, Capital Management Publications, 119 Paul Dr., Box 4450, San Rafael CA 94903. (415)472-4711. Editor-in-Chief: Gail Heilman. Emphasizes bicycles. Monthly magazine; 80 pages. Estab: 1962. Circ: 120,000. Pays on publication. Phone queries OK. Submit seasonal/holiday material 5-6 months in advance. Photocopied submissions OK. SASE. Reports in 5 weeks. Free sample copy; writer's guidelines for SASE.

Nonfiction: How-to (repairing a bike or components, planning a tour, etc.); humor; informational; interview and profile (famous current names in the bicycling world); personal experience and travel. Buys 6 mss/issue. Query. Length: 750-2,000 words. Pays $30 minimum.

Photos: Purchased with or without accompanying ms. Captions required. Query or send contact sheet or transparencies. Pays $10-15 for 8x10 b&w glossies; $20-50 for 35mm color transparencies. No additional payment for photos accepted with accompanying ms.

Columns/Departments: Point of View (any subject on which the writer has a strong, perhaps controversial, position or opinion. Buys 1/issue. Length: 750-1,000 words. Pays $15-45.

Fillers: Clippings. Buys 1/issue. Length: 25-150 words. Pays $1/column inch.

BIKE WORLD, Box 366, Mountain View CA 94040. Editor: Bill Anderson. For bicyclists aged 5-80 interested in training, technical subjects, sophisticated touring stories at the non-beginner level. Monthly magazine; 50 pages. Estab: 1972. Circ: 20,000. Not copyrighted. Buys 100 mss/year. Pays on publication. Free sample copy. Submit seasonal material (winter, summer and spring tours; training in winter; riding the rollers, etc.) 2 months in advance. Reports immediately. Query first or submit complete ms. Enclose S.A.S.E.

Nonfiction and Photos: Technical and touring material; physiology and race topics. "All material must be at a level beyond the beginning 'how-to'." Must be tightly written and avoid the "joys of cycling" approach. Tour stories should make the reader feel he would have a good time. Avoid chronological accounts of events that don't involve the reader. "We are more into athletics than ecology or 'romantic bikeology'." Does not want to see material on "how I bought my first 10-speed, or the Rutabaga Canners annual road race, or a peanut butter and flat tire account of a tour to Michigan's world famous glacial moraines." Would like to see material on tours that turn others on without trying to; technical articles that people can use. How to train and tour, etc. Anything of interest to cyclists who enjoy the sport. Length: open. Pays $15-20/published page; more if quality deserves it. B&w photos are purchased with or without accompanying mss or on assignment. Pays $6 for 5x7 or larger. Must have snappy contrast and be in focus. Captions required. Pays $50 for color slides used for cover. Ektachrome-X or K-II with intensity of action, mood, scenery, etc.

Fillers: News bits, technical tips. Length: 25-300 words. Pays $5 to $10.

Boating

BAY & DELTA YACHTSMAN, Recreation Publications, 2019 Clement Ave., Alameda CA 94501. (415)865-7500. Editor: Michael Dobrin. Emphasizes recreational boating for small boat owners and recreational yachtsmen in the Northern California region. Monthly tabloid newspaper; 56 pages. Estab: 1965. Circ: 17,000. Pays on publication. Buys all rights. Phone queries OK. Submit seasonal/holiday material 2 months in advance. Photocopied submissions OK. SASE. Reports in 1 month. Free writer's guidelines.

Nonfiction: Historical (nautical history of Northern California); how-to (modifications, equipment, supplies, rigging etc., aboard both power and sailboats); humor (no disaster or boating ineptitude pieces); informational (government, legislation as it relates to recreational boating); interview; new product; nostalgia; personal experience ("How I learned about boating from this" type of approach); personal opinion; photo feature (to accompany copy); profile and travel. Buys 10-15 mss/issue. Query. Length: 750-2,000 words. Pays $1/column inch.

Photos: Photos purchased with accompanying ms. Captions required. Pays $5 for 8x10 b&w glossy or matte finish photos. Total purchase price for ms includes payment for photos.

Fiction: Adventure (sea stories, travel—must relate to San Francisco Bay region); fantasy; historical; humorous and mystery. Buys 5 mss/year. Query. Length: 500-1,750 words. Pays $1/columns inch.

How To Break In: "Think of our market area: the waterways of Northern California and how, why, when and where the boatman would use those waters. Think about unusual onboard application of ideas (power and sail), special cruising tips, etc. Write for a knowledgeable boating public."

BOATING, 1 Park Ave., New York NY 10016. (212)725-3972. Editor: Richard L. Rath. For sail and powerboat enthusiasts, informed boatmen, not beginners. Publishes special Boat Show issue in January; Fall show issue in September; New York National Boat Show issue in December; Miami National Boat Show issue in February; annual maintenance issue in April. Monthly. Circulation: 200,000. Buys first periodical rights or all rights. Buys 100 mss/year. Pays on acceptance. Submit seasonal material 6 to 8 months in advance. Reports in 2 months. Query first. Enclose S.A.S.E.

Nonfiction: Uses articles about cruises in powerboats or sailboats with b&w or color photos, that offer more than usual interest; how-to-do-it pieces illustrated with good b&w photos or drawings; piloting articles, seamanship, etc.; new developments in boating; profiles of well-known boating people. The editor advises, "Don't talk down to the reader. Use little fantasy, emphasize the practical aspects of the subject." Length: 300-3,000 words. Payment is $25-$500, and varies according to subject and writer's skill. Regular department "Able Seaman" uses expertise on boat operation and handling; about 1,100 to 1,500 words; pays $150-300/piece.

Photos: Art Director: Shelley Heller. Buys photos submitted with mss and with captions only. 8x10 preferred, b&w. Interested in photos of happenings of interest to a national boating audience. Pays $20 to $25 each. Also buys color transparencies for both cover and interior use, 35mm slides or larger preferred. Pays $100 to $300 for one-time usage, "but not for anything that has previously appeared in a boating publication."

Fillers: Uses short items pertaining to boating that have an unusual quality of historical interest, timeliness, or instruction. Pays $50 to $100.

How To Break In: "From a time-invested standpoint, it would make sense for the beginning writer to try a short filler subject for us, rather than to go for the jackpot. Unless, of course, he has a great story or article that will sell itself. Acceptability of a piece for our magazine hinges at least as much on the quality of the writing as it does on the subject matter. One man will take a trip around the world and produce bilge water for a manuscript; another, like E. B. White, will row across Central Park Lake and make it a great adventure in the human experience. There's no substitute for talent."

BOATING NEWS, Tyrell Publishing, 26 Coal Harbour Wharf, 566 Cardero St., Vancouver, B.C., Canada V6G 2W6. (604)684-1643. Editor-in-Chief: Don Tyrell. Emphasizes leisure boating. Monthly newspaper; 16 pages. Estab: 1970. Circ: 21,000. Pays on acceptance. Buys one-time rights. Phone queries OK. Submit seasonal/holiday material 1 month in advance. Simultaneous ("if not in same area") and photocopied submissions OK. SASE. Reports in 2 weeks. Free sample copy and writer's guidelines.

Nonfiction: Historical; how-to (boat repair, navigation, etc.); humor (about boats); interview (with prominent people); personal experience, photo feature and technical. Buys 20 mss/year. Query. Length: 500-1,000 words. Pays $25 minimum.

Photos: Purchased with or without accompanying ms. Captions required. Query or submit prints. Pays $10-25 for 5x7 b&w glossy photos. Model release required.

Columns/Departments: Cruising, Foreign News, Regional News. Query. Length: 500-1,000 words. Pays $25. Open to suggestions for new columns/departments.

BOATMASTER, B.A.S.S. Publications, Box 3543, Montgomery AL 36117. (205)277-9132. Editor-in-Chief: Dave Ellison. Emphasizes boating, strongly related to fishing. Magazine; every 2 months; 96 pages. Estab: 1976. Circ: 100,000. Pays on acceptance. Buys all rights, but may reassign rights to author following publication. Phone queries OK. Submit seasonal/holiday material 6 months in advance. SASE. Reports in 4 weeks. Free writer's guidelines.

Nonfiction: Expose (which expose improper exploitation of the nation's waterways); how-to and informational (how boaters can keep their rigs running correctly; how to buy a new boat, camper, trailer; how to prevent boat theft; buying insurance for boats; successful fishing methods, both fresh and saltwater; family camping in boats; vacations in boats); interviews (with race drivers; how their methods and techniques can help the 'average' boater; with successful fresh and saltwater anglers); travel (where to go with your boat and what to do when you get there; stress on fishing. No travelog type articles); personal experience (adventure stories usually dealing with a tragedy or near-tragedy); photo features (of unusual boating events); and technical (how to service boat motors, how to get more miles per gallon of gas). Buys about 20 mss/issue. Query. Pays $150-500.

Photos: Purchased with accompanying ms. Captions required. Send prints and transparencies. No additional payment made for 8x10 b&w glossies or 35mm or 2¼x2¼ transparencies.

Fiction: Must deal with boating in some form. Adventure, humorous, mystery, suspense. Buys 3 stories/year. Query. Length: 2,500-3,500 words. Pays $150-350.

Fillers: Clippings, jokes, anecdotes. Must be boating/fishing related. Length: 30-300 words. Pays $5-50.

How To Break In: "With clean copy, double-spaced, an obvious knowledge of subject, excellent pictures (action preferred), superb research, good, hard-hitting leads."

Rejects: "Me and Joe" articles; technical articles written so that an engineering degree is required to understand them; travelogs, rehashes of old articles; fuzzy pix, weak leads, wordy sentences.

CANOE MAGAZINE, The Webb Co., 1999 Shepard Rd., St. Paul MN 55116. (612)647-7450. Editor: Peter A. Sonderegger. For an audience ranging from the weekend recreational canoeist to Olympic caliber flatwater, racing, marathon, poling and sailing canoe and kayak enthusiasts. Bimonthly magazine; 48 pages. Estab: 1973. Circ: 40,000. Buys all rights, but may reassign rights to author after publication. Buys about 30 mss a year. Pays on acceptance. Free sample copy and writer's guidelines. Reports in 30 days. Query or submit complete ms. Enclose S.A.S.E.

Nonfiction and Photos: Articles Editor: P.A. Sonderegger. "We publish a variety of canoeing and kayaking articles, but strive for a balanced mix of stories about trips and competitive events to interest all participants in the sport, whether purely recreational or competitive. Also interested in any articles dealing with conservation issues which may adversely affect the sport. Writing should be readable rather than academic; clever rather than endlessly descriptive. Diary type first-person style not desirable. A good, provocative lead is considered a prime ingredient. For the past year, we have been receiving an excessive number of articles about canoeing experiences in Canadian waters. We want stories about trips in the contiguous 50 states that canoers/kayakers of average ability can identify with. We are consistently interested in use of American waterways and legislation which affect that use. Also interested in articles about safety and training or expansion of the sport to greater number of people." Length: 2,000 words maximum. Pays $25-$150. Will also consider book reviews. Length: 200 to 300 words. Payment is negotiable, but begins at $25. B&w and color purchased with accompanying ms, or on assignment. Pays $15 minimum for b&w; $25 minimum for color. Size: 35mm or larger.

CRUISING WORLD, P.O. Box 452, Newport RI 02840. (401)847-1588. Editor: Murray Davis. For all those who cruise under sail. Monthly magazine; 112 pages. Estab: 1974. Circ: 70,000. Rights purchased vary with author and material. May buy first North American serial rights or first serial rights. Pays on publication. Write for copy of guidelines for writers. Will consider photocopied submissions. No simultaneous submissions. Reports in about 6 weeks. Query first or submit complete ms. Enclose S.A.S.E.

Nonfiction and Photos: Article and Photo Editor: Nim Marsh. "We are interested in seeing informative articles on the technical and enjoyable aspects of cruising under sail. Also subjects of general interest to seafarers." Length: 500 to 3,500 words. Pays $50 minimum. "We also have a short feature section (500 words maximum) and a book review column." Payment for these varies, but begins at $10. B&w prints (5x7) and color transparencies purchased with accompanying ms. Pays $5 minimum for b&w; $15 minimum for color.

Poetry: Traditional forms, blank verse, free verse, light verse. All forms should relate to cruising. Pays $10 minimum.

MOTORBOAT MAGAZINE, 38 Commercial Wharf, Boston MA 02110. (617)723-5800. Editor: Peter L. Smyth. For powerboat owners and devotees. Established in 1973. Monthly. Buys first North American serial rights. Buys 50 mss per year. Payment on acceptance. Will send free sample copy to writer on request. Write for copy of guidelines for writers. Will consider photocopied submissions. Will not consider simultaneous submissions. Reports on material in 4 weeks. "Queries are welcome, but the editor reserves the right to withhold his final decision until the completed article has been reviewed." Enclose S.A.S.E.

Nonfiction and Photos: "We are the only magazine devoted purely to motorboating and use informative, educational articles which instruct the reader without treating him as a novice. Subject matter may cover any aspect of motorboating including profiles, technical stories, maintenance, sportfishing, cruising and seamanship. Houseboat articles with the emphasis on in-land cruising are welcome, as well as big boat cruising stories and articles dealing with mechanical subjects (engines). But, no sailing, please." Length: 2,500 words maximum. Pays $150 to $500. 8x10 b&w glossies purchased with mss. Color (35mm or larger) used on cover. Pays $300 to $400 for color used on cover.

OUTDOORS, Outdoors Bldg., Columbia MO 65201. (314)449-3119. Editor-in-Chief: Lee Cullimore. Emphasizes outdoor boating for families—fishermen, water skiers, men, women, children—boat campers. Monthly magazine; 36 pages. Estab: 1958. Pays on acceptance. Buys one-time rights. Submit seasonal/holiday material 3 months in advance. SASE. Reports in 3 weeks. Free sample copy and writer's guidelines.

Nonfiction: Historical (boating oriented); how-to (fishing, boating); informational (boat camping, hints, tips); profile (of areas, boating oriented); and travel (fishing and boating locations). Buys 8 mss/issue. Query. Length: 1,200 words maximum. Pays $25-150.

Photos: Purchased with or without (occasionally) accompanying ms. Captions required. Send contact sheet or transparencies. Uses 8x10 b&w glossies and 35mm or larger color transparencies. Total purchase for ms includes payment for photos.

POWERBOAT MAGAZINE, 15917 Strathern St., Van Nuys CA 91406. Editor: Bob Brown. For performance-conscious boating enthusiasts. January, Boat show issue; March, Jet drive issue; June, Water ski issue; October, Outboard issue; November, Stern Drive issue. Monthly. Circulation: 50,000. Buys all rights or 1-time North American serial rights. Pays on publication. Will send free sample copy on request. Reports in 2 weeks. Query required. Enclose S.A.S.E.

Nonfiction and Photos: Uses articles about power boats and water skiing that offer special interest to performance-minded boaters, how-to-do-it pieces with good b&w pictures, developments in boating, profiles on well-known boating and skiing individuals, competition coverage of national and major events. Length: 1,500 to 2,000 words. Pays $100 to $150 per article. Photos purchased with mss. Prefers 8x10 b&w. 2¼x2¼ color transparency preferred for cover; top quality vertical 35mm considered. Pays $50 to $100 for 1-time use.

SAIL, 38 Commercial Wharf, Boston MA 02110. (617)227-0888. Editor: Keith Taylor. For audience that is "strictly sailors, average age 35, better than average education." Special issues: "Cruising issues, fitting-out issues, special race issues (e.g., America's Cup), boat show issues." Monthly. Buys first North American serial rights. Buys 100 mss a year. Pays on publication. Will send a free sample copy to a writer on request. Submit seasonal or special material at least 3 months in advance. Returns rejected material in 2 weeks. Acknowledges acceptance of material in 1 month. Enclose S.A.S.E.

Nonfiction: Wants "articles on sailing: technical, techniques, and feature stories." Interested in how-to, personal experience, profiles, historical, new product, and photo articles. "Generally emphasize the excitement of sail and the human, personal aspect." Length: 1,000 to 2,000 words. Payment is $50 to $300.

Photos: B&w glossies purchased with mss. Payment is $10 to $25. Color transparencies purchased. Payment is $35 to $200, $300 for covers.

SAILING MAGAZINE, 125 East Main St., Port Washington WI 53074. (414)284-2626. Editor: William F. Schanen III. For readers mostly between ages of 35 and 44, some professionals. About 75% of them own their own sailboat. Monthly magazine; 64 pages. Estab: 1966. Circ: 25,000. Not copyrighted. Buys 12 mss/year. Pays on publication. Write for copy of guidelines for writers. Will consider photocopied and simultaneous submissions. Reports within 1 month. Query first or submit complete ms. Enclose S.A.S.E.

Nonfiction and Photos: Micca Leffingwell Hutchins, Managing Editor. "Experiences of sailing whether curising, racing or learning. We require no special style. We're devoted exclusively to sailing and sailboat enthusiasts, and particularly interested in articles about the trend toward cruising in the sailing world." Informational, personal experience, profile, historical, travel, and book reviews. Length: open. Payment negotiable. B&w photos purchased with or without accompanying ms. Captions required. Pays $10 for each 8x10 b&w glossy used; also flat fee for series.

SEA, 1499 Monrovia St., Newport Beach CA 92663. (714)646-4451. Editor: Chris Caswell. For pleasure boat owners, power and sail, cruising and racing. Monthly magazine. Circ: 200,000 in 4 regional editions: Western (13 Western states); Eastern (seaboard from North Carolina to Canada); Southern (Florida/Gulf Coast); and Inland (Great Lakes/Midwest). Pays on acceptance. Buys first serial rights. SASE. Reports in 30 days. Free sample copy and writer's guidelines.

Nonfiction: "Two types are needed: Articles of regional interest for each area as well as technical and cruising stories for the national section. Need how-to tips, places to visit by boat, maintenance, personality profiles, fishing, racing, and history articles. Once a writer is established with us, we'll make regular assignments." Length: 500-4,000 words. Pays $50-600.

Photos: B&w glossies and 35mm or larger color transparencies purchased with mss or with captions. Pays $500 maximum. Pays $200 for cover photos.

SPYGLASS, Spyglass Catalog Co., 2415 Mariner Square Dr., Alameda CA 94501. (415)769-8410. Managing Editor: Dick Moore. Emphasizes all aspects of sailing. "For sailors of all ages interested in the perfection of the activity, the betterment of the sailboat, the best available gear and how to apply it." Annual magazine; 400 pages. Estab: 1973. Circ: 20,000. Pays on publication. Buys first North American serial rights. Phone queries OK. Submit material 4 months prior to year's end. Previously published submissions OK. SASE. Reports in 1 month. Sample copy $1.

Nonfiction: Historical (old salts, old boats, old seaports); how-to (any build-it-yourself, repair-it-yourself, remodel-it-yourself, or rig-it-yourself hints on any facet of sailing); informational (on sailing technique, new developments in construction of the sailboat, navigation, racing or cruising); interview (or profile on noted naval architects, boatbuilders, racing or cruising personalities); personal experience (anything that is educational or has some hard lessons to be learned. No travelogues, but better ways to cruise); photo essays (emphasizing innovative apparatus utilizing stock equipment, or custom set-ups), and technical (any aspect of sails, boat construction, electronics and racing tactics). Buys 20 mss/year. Query. Length: 750-3,500 words. Pays 7½¢/word.

Photos: Photos purchased without accompanying ms. Captions required, except for full-page filler photos which should be either action or aesthetic shots. Pays $10-15 for b&w and color photos. Total purchase price for ms includes payment for photos.

How To Break In: "First, include a basic outline with the query. Too often a proposed subject melds into an overworked area of sailing. Because it's an annual, each piece must 'last' all year. We have a keen interest in the practical 'how-to' pieces. Also, we are a West Coast-based publication with a national readership and need more input from the Great Lakes, Gulf Coast and Eastern boating scene."

WOODENBOAT, Box 268, Brooksville ME 04617. Editor-in-Chief: Jonathan Wilson. Managing Editor: Jacqueline Michaud. Readership is composed mainly of owners, builders, and designers of wooden boats. Bimonthly magazine; 100 pages. Estab: 1974. Circ: 20,000. Pays on publication. Buys first North American serial rights. Submit seasonal/holiday material 6 months in advance. Photocopied and previously published submissions OK. SASE. Reports in 2-3 months. Sample copy $1.75; writer's guidelines for SASE.
Nonfiction: Historical (detailed evolution of boat types of famous designers or builders of wooden boats); how-to (repair, restore, build or maintain wooden boats); informational (technical detail on repairs/restoration/construction); new product (documented by facts or statistics on performance of product); personal opinion (backed up by experience and experimentation in boat building, restoring, maintaining, etc.); photo feature (with in-depth captioning and identification of boats); and technical (on adhesives and other boat-building products and materials, or on particular phases of repair or boat construction). Buys 60 mss/year. Submit complete ms. Length: 1,200-3,500 words. Pays 5¢/word.
Photos: Purchased with or without (only occasionally) accompanying ms. Captions required. Send prints, negatives or transparencies. Pays $10 for 8x10 high contrast B&w glossies; $15 minimum for color transparencies.
Columns/Departments: Newsfront (seeking news on developments and contemporary trends of wooden boat construction); and Book Reviews (on wooden boats and related subjects). Buys 1 mss/issue. Length: 300-800 words. Pays 5¢/word. Open to suggestions for new columns/departments.
How To Break In: "Because we are bimonthly, and issues are scheduled well in advance, freelancers should bear in mind that if their material is accepted, it will inevitably be some time before publication can be arranged. We seek innovative and informative ideas in freelancers' manuscripts, and the degree to which research and careful attention has been paid in compiling an article must be apparent. We're not looking for scholarly treatises, rather detailed and thought-out material reflecting imagination and interest in the subject."

YACHTING, Yachting Publishing Corp., 50 West 44th Street, New York NY 10036. (212)391-1000. Editor: William W. Robinson. For yachtsmen interested in powerboats and sailboats. Monthly. Circulation: 128,000. Buys North American serial rights only. Reports on submissions in 3 weeks. Enclose S.A.S.E.
Nonfiction and Photos: Nuts-and-bolts articles on all phases of yachting; good technical pieces on motors, electronics, and sailing gear. "We're overloaded with cruising articles —everyone seems to be going around Cape Horn in a bathtub." Length: 3,000 words maximum. Pays 10¢ per word. Article should be accompanied by 6 to 8 photos. Pays $25 each for b&w photos, "more for color when used." Will accept a story without photos, if story is outstanding.

Bowling and Billiards

BOWLERS JOURNAL, Suite 3734, 875 N. Michigan, Chicago IL 60611. (312)266-7171. Editor: Mort Luby. For "bowling fans of all ages." Magazine; 80 pages. Established in 1913. Monthly. Circulation: 16,200. Rights purchased vary with author and material. Buys 20 to 30 mss a year. Payment on publication. Will send sample copy to a writer for 50¢. Query first. Enclose S.A.S.E.
Nonfiction and Photos: Features about top bowlers and proprietors with unusual operations or who use unique promotions. Seeks "provocative, controversial, lively material and does not want articles on handicapped bowlers or proprietors with children's programs. Buys interviews, profiles, nostalgic and personal experience articles. Length: 1,000 to 2,000 words. Payment: $50 to $100. Buys 8x10 b&w glossies and 35mm or 4x5 color transparencies with mss. Captions required. Pays $5-10 for b&w; $20 to $30 for color.

BOWLING, 5301 S. 76 St., Greendale WI 53129. (414)421-6400. Ext. 230. Editor: Robert R. Reeve. Official publication of the American Bowling Congress. Monthly. Established in 1934. Rights purchased vary with author and material. Usually buys all rights. Pays on publication. Reports within 30 days. Enclose S.A.S.E. for return of submissions.
Nonfiction and Photos: "This is a specialized field and the average writer attempting the subject of bowling should be well-informed. However, anyone is free to submit material for approval." Wants articles about unusual ABC leagues and tournaments, personalities, etc., featuring male bowlers. Length: 500 to 1,200 words. Pays $25 to $100 per article; $10 to $15 per photo.

How To Break In: "Submit feature material on bowlers, generally amateurs competing in local leagues, or special events involving the game of bowling. Should have connection with ABC membership."

THE WOMAN BOWLER, 5301 S. 76th St., Greendale WI 53129. (414)421-9000. Editor: Mrs. Helen Latham. Emphasizes bowling for women bowlers, ages 8-90. Monthly (except for combined May/June, July/August issues) magazine; 48 pages. Estab: 1936. Circ: 135,000. Pays on acceptance. Buys all rights. Phone queries OK. Submit seasonal/holiday material 2 months in advance. Photocopied and previously published submissions OK. SASE. Reports in 1 month. Free sample copy and writer's guidelines.
Nonfiction: Historical (about bowling and of national significance); interview; profile; and spot news. Buys 25 mss/year. Query. Length: 1,000 words maximum (unless by special assignment). Pays $15-50.
Photos: Purchased with accompanying ms. Identification required. Query. Pays $5-10 for b&w glossies. Model release required.

Football

ALL SOUTH CAROLINA FOOTBALL ANNUAL, P.O. Box 3, Columbia SC 29202. (803)796-9200. Editor: Sidney L. Wise. Associate Editor: Doug Murphy. Issued annually, August 1. Buys first rights. Pays on publication. Deadline for material each year is 10 weeks preceding publication date. Query first. Enclose S.A.S.E.
Nonfiction and Photos: Material must be about South Carolina high school and college football teams, players and coaches. Pays 3¢ minimum a word. Buys photos with ms. Captions required. 5x7 or 8x10 b&w glossies; 4x5 or 35mm color transparencies. Uses color on cover only. Pays $5 minimum for b&w; $10 minimum for color.

FOOTBALL NEWS, 19830 Mack Ave., Grosse Pointe MI 48236. (313)881-9555. Editor: Roger Stanton. For avid grid fans. Weekly tabloid published during football season; 24 pages. Estab: 1939. Circ: 100,000. Not copyrighted. Buys 12 to 15 mss a year. Payment on publication. Will send sample copy to writer for 25¢. Reports in 1 month. Query first. Enclose S.A.S.E.
Nonfiction: Articles on players, officials, coaches, past and present, with fresh approach. Highly informative, concise, positive approach. Interested in profiles of former punt, pass and kick players who have made the pros. Interview, profile, historical, think articles, and exposes. Length: 800-1,000 words. Pays $35-75/ms.

Gambling

LAS VEGAS TODAY, Las Vegas Valley Publishing Co., Inc., Box 3936, North Las Vegas NV 89030. (702)642-2567. Editor: Elliot S. Krane. "Our readers are people who visit Las Vegas and people who work in the industry. We buy more material aimed at the latter. They are interested in gambling, and they want hard facts about how the gambling business works." Weekly tabloid; 32 pages. Estab: 1975. Circ: 40,000. Pays on acceptance. "Locally, we buy first-time rights, but will accept simultaneous or reprint rights if the piece hasn't been published in a competing publication." Phone queries OK. Submit seasonal/holiday material 2 months in advance. Photocopied and previously published submissions OK. SASE. Reports in 2 weeks. Free sample copy and writer's guidelines.
Nonfiction: Informational, interview, nostalgia, profile, new product, photo feature. Buys 4 mss/issue. Query. Length: 800-2,500 words. Pays $25.
Photos: Purchased with accompanying ms for no extra payment. Captions required. Submit 5x7 b&w glossy prints.
How To Break In: "We write about the great names of gambling, the great issues of the gambling industry, the giants of the resort hotel industry and the people who work in Las Vegas casinos who have interesting backgrounds or jobs—particularly top amateur athletes or ex-pros in the gambling business. We'll look at stories without pix, but you have a much better chance of success if you have good b&w photos."
Rejects: We absolutely do not use interviews with show business stars, unless those stars are identified closely with Las Vegas. We don't want any 'how to win at craps.'" We would like instead, a profile on the guy who invented your particular system."

WINNING (formerly *Gambling Quarterly*), Box 412, Station F, Toronto, Ontario, Canada. (416)366-9701. Editor: Donald W. Valliere. For gamblers and racing fans of all ages, both sexes, throughout the United States and Canada. Bimonthly magazine, 64-80 pages. Estab: 1974. Circ: 65,000. Buys all rights, but may reassign to author following publication. Buys 18-

24 mss/year. Payment on acceptance. Will send free sample copy to writer on request. Query first or submit complete ms. Reports "as soon as possible." Enclose S.A.E. and International Reply Coupons.

Nonfiction and Photos: "Articles on how to gamble, personalities, travel, humor, latest developments in gambling; all aspects. Interviews and photo stories. Writers must be well acquainted with subject." Buys informational, how-to, interview, profile, historical, think articles, expose, nostalgic articles. Recent articles include "How to Read Between the Lines in a Harness Program", "Lots on Slots" and "Secrets of a Big City Bookie". Length: 1,000-3,000 words. Pays $75-200. Photos purchased with or without ms. Captions optional. Pays $7.50 for b&w; $25 to $35 for color.

General Sports Interest

AAU NEWS, Amateur Athletic Union of the United States, AAU House, 3400 W. 86th St., Indianapolis IN 46268. (317)297-2900. Editor: Martin E. Weiss. Asssociate Editor: Pete Cava. Emphasizes amateur sports. Monthly magazine; 16 pages. Estab: 1925. Circ: 15,000. Pays on publication. Buys one-time rights. Phone queries OK. SASE. Reports in 2 weeks. Free sample copy.

Nonfiction: "General subject matter is profiles of top amateur athletes and athletic volunteers or leaders. Reports on AAU championships, previews of coming seasons, etc. Buys interviews, profiles, photo features, sport book reviews and spot news articles. Length: 1,000 words maximum. Pays $10-50.

Photos: Photos purchased with or without accompanying ms or on assignment. Captions required. Pays $5-25 for 8½x11 b&w glossies; $10-25 for any size color transparencies. No additional payment for photos accepted with accompanying ms. Model release required.

How To Break In: "By staying within the framework of AAU sports: Basketball, baton twirling, bobsledding, boxing, diving, gymnastics, handball, horseshoe pitching, judo, karate, luge, powerlifting, physique, swimming, synchronized swimming, taekwondo, track and field, volleyball, water polo, weightlifting, wrestling and trampoline and tumbling; also AAU Junior Olympics and all matters pertaining to Olympic development in AAU sports."

BUFFALO FAN, P.O. Box 294, Buffalo NY 14240. (716)885-1500. Editor: Richard L. Hirsch. For Buffalo sports fans, men and women, all ages. Magazine; 64 pages. Established in 1974. Buys all rights. Buys about 40 mss/year. Pays on acceptance. Sample copy $1. Will consider photocopied submissions. No simultaneous submissions. Reports on material accepted for publication in 1 week. Returns rejected material as soon as possible. Query first. Enclose S.A.S.E.

Nonfiction and Photos: "Features on subjects of interest to those who follow sports and recreation in Western New York. There must be some Western New York angle to every story." Informational, personal experience, profiles, humor, historical articles, think pieces, nostalgia. Length: 1,000 to 2,000 words. Pays $40 to $75. B&w and color photos purchased with or without accompanying ms, or on assignment. Payment varies, but pays a minimum of $10 for b&w; a minimum of $25 for color.

OUTDOOR CANADA, Suite 201, 181 Eglinton Ave., E., Toronto, Ontario M4P 1J9, Canada. Editor: Sheila Kaighin. For anyone interested in the Canadian outdoors, including armchair sports people and white water canoeists. A family magazine for readers aged 8 to 80. Magazine; 64 to 80 (8¼x11) pages. Estab: 1973. Published 7 times/year. Circ: 41,300. Rights purchased vary with author and material. May buy all rights or first North American serial rights. Buys about 50 mss a year. Pays on publication. Will send sample copy to writer for $1. Will consider photocopied submissions. No simultaneous submissions. reports on material accepted for publication in 2 months. Returns rejected material within 3 weeks. Submit complete ms. Enclose S.A.E. and International Reply Coupons.

Nonfiction and Photos: "Ours is a family magazine, as opposed to a male-oriented magazine. We want a positive approach toward the outdoors. Writers must have a thorough knowledge of the Canadian outdoors, since ours is a totally Canadian publication." Informational, how-to, personal experience, humor, photo articles. Length: 600 to 3,000 words. Pays $50-125. Color transparencies or 8x10 b&w glossies are purchased with or without mss. Pays $25-50. Captions required.

REFEREE, Mano Enterprises, Inc., Box 161, Franksville WI 53126. (414)632-8855. Editor-in-Chief: Barry Mano. For well-educated, mostly 26-50-year-old male sports officials. Bimonthly magazine; 48 pages. Estab: 1976. Circ: 15,000. Pays either on acceptance or publication. Buys all rights. Submit seasonal/holiday material 3 months in advance. Photocopied and previously published submissions OK. SASE. Reports in 4 weeks. Free sample copy.

Nonfiction: How-to; informational; humor; interview; profile; personal experience; photo feature and technical. Buys 54 mss/year. Query. Length: 1,850-3,000 words. Pays $75-150. "No general sports articles."

Photos: Tom Hammill, Photo Editor. Purchased with or without accompanying ms or on assignment. Captions required. Send contact sheet, prints, negatives or transparencies. Pays $10-20 for 8x10 b&w prints; $25-50 for 35mm or 2¼x2¼ color transparencies.

Columns/Departments: The Arena (bios) and Guest Editorial (controversial topics). Buys 24 mss/year. Query. Length: 1,200-1,800 words. Pays $50 minimum.

Fillers: Rudy Mano, Fillers Editor. Jokes, gags, anecdotes, puzzles, sport shorts. Query. Length: 50-200 words. Pays $10-15.

SPORTING NEWS, 1212 N. Lindbergh Blvd., St. Louis MO 63166. "We do not actively solicit freelance material."

SPORTS ILLUSTRATED, Time & Life Bldg., Rockefeller Center, New York NY 10020. Outside Text Editor: Bob Ottum. Primarily staff-written, with small but steady amount of outside material. Weekly. Reports in 2 to 3 weeks. Pays on acceptance. Buys all rights or North American serial rights. Enclose S.A.S.E.

Nonfiction: Material falls into two general categories: regional (text that runs in editorial space accompanying regional advertising pages) and long text. Runs a great deal of regional advertising and, as a result, considerable text in that section of the magazine. Regional text does not have a geographical connotation; it can be any sort of short feature (600 to 2,500 words): historical, humor, reminiscence, personality, opinion, first-person, but it must deal with some aspect of sports, however slight. Long text (2,000 to 5,000 words) also must have sporting connection, however tenuous; should be major personality, personal reminiscence, knowing look into a significant aspect of a sporting subject, but long text should be written for broad appeal, so that readers without special knowledge will appreciate the piece. Wants quality writing. Pays $250 minimum for regional pieces, $750 minimum for long text. Smaller payments are made for material used in special sections or departments.

Photos: "Do not care to see photos until story is purchased."

How To Break In: "One possibility would be an item for the section, As I Saw It. These can be as short as 950 words; can be a personal experience or a happening in sports which occurred prior to the inception of the magazine in 1954."

SPORTSHELF NEWS, P.O. Box 634, New Rochelle NY 10802. Editor: Irma Ganz. For "all ages interested in sports." Established in 1949. Bimonthly. Circulation: 150,000. Pays on acceptance. Query first required. Enclose S.A.S.E.

Nonfiction: Subject matter is exclusively sports. Buys how-to articles. Payment varies, "averages about $50 for 1,000 words."

TEXAS OUTDOOR GUIDE, Alchemy Corp., Box 55573, Houston TX 77055. (713)682-5180. Managing Editor: Stan Slaton. Emphasizes outdoor sports. Bimonthly magazine; 84 pages. Estab: 1968. Circ: 100,000. Pays on publication. Buys all rights but may reassign following publication. Phone queries OK. Submit seasonal/holiday material 3 months in advance. SASE. Reports in 3 months. Free sample copy and writer's guidelines.

Nonfiction: How-to (sporting ideas, hunting and fishing tips, etc.); interview, new product and photo feature. Buys 30 mss/year. Query. Length: 1,000-3,000 words. Pays $50-500.

Photos: Purchased with accompanying ms or on assignment. Captions required. Considers b&w or color. Query. Total purchase price for ms includes payment for photos. Model release required.

WOMENSPORTS MAGAZINE, Charter Publications, 230 Park Ave., New York NY 10017. (212)983-3200. Editor-in-Chief: LeAnne Schreiber. Managing Editor: Claudia Dowling. Emphasizes women and sports for a college-educated readership, middle income, ages 16-35. Monthly magazine; 64 pages. Estab: 1974. Circ: 200,000. Pays on acceptance. Buys all rights. Submit seasonal/holiday material 4 months in advance. Simultaneous and photocopied submissions OK. SASE. Reports in 4 weeks. Sample copy $1; free writer's guidelines.

Nonfiction: Expose (sports organizations and promoters mishandling of their responsibilities to the sport or individual athlete); how-to (participate in given sport or be a savory spectator); informational; historical (Foremother is regular section-bio/personality of famous former athletes); humor (sports humor based on fact and date rather than fantasy); interview; nostalgia; personal opinion (800-1,000 word essay for "Last Word" section); photo feature (esp. historical) and profile. Buys 10 mss/issue. Query. Length: 1,000-3,500 words. Pays generally $100 per 1,000 words with variation for amount of research required.

Photos: Gail Tauber, Photo Editor. Purchased with or without accompanying ms or on assignment. Captions required. Pays $25 minimum for b&w or color prints. Query for photos or send contact sheet. "We will not take the responsibility for originals sent in unsolicited."
Columns/Departments: Aces (athletes at peak, 1,500-2,000 words); Foremothers (former athletes, 1,500-2,000 words); Last Word (opinion/essay, 800-1,000 words); On the Books (book reviews, 1,500-2,000 words). Buys 25 mss/year. Query. Pays $100 minimum.
Fillers: Cutler Durkee, Fillers Editor. Jokes, gags, anecdotes, newsbreaks and puzzles. Buys 20 mss/year.

Golf

CAROLINA GOLFER, P.O. Box 3, Columbia SC 29202. (803)796-9200. Editor: Sydney L. Wise. Associate Editor: Doug Murphy. Bimonthly. Buys first rights. Payment on publication. Will send free sample copy to a writer on request. Reports in 3 to 8 weeks. Enclose S.A.S.E.
Nonfiction and Photos: Articles on golf and golfers, clubs, courses, tournaments, only in the Carolinas. Stories on the various courses should be done "in the manner that would give the reader a basic idea of what each course is like." Length: 1,200 to 1,500 words. Pays according to quality of ms; 3¢ minimum per word. Buys photos with mss. 5x7 or 8x10 b&w glossies. Color should be 4x5 or 35mm transparencies. Pays $5 minimum for b&w; $25 for color transparencies used for cover.

COUNTRY CLUB GOLFER, 2171 Campus Dr., Irvine CA 92715. (714)752-6474. Editor: Edward F. Pazdur. For country club members and club golfers; professional, affluent, college-educated. Magazine; 60 pages. Established in 1972. Monthly. Circulation: 55,000. Buys all rights, but may reassign rights to author after publication. Buys about 6 mss a year. Pays on publication. Will send sample copy to writer for $1. Will consider photocopied and simultaneous submissions. Reports in 10 days. Query first with 1-page outline. Enclose S.A.S.E.
Nonfiction and Photos: Editorial material is confined to country club activities, primarily golf. Anything reflecting country club life styles will be considered; golfing or social activities, etc. No specific style, but prefers informative articles slanted toward the more mature, affluent golfer. Informative features on fashions for country clubs, as well as on how to entertain, give parties, etc. Tips on golfing better. "But, we are not heavily golf instruction oriented since we are the *Esquire* of golf for more mature golfers." Length: open. Pays minimum of $75. No additional payment for b&w glossies or 35mm transparencies purchased with mss. Captions required.
Poetry: Traditional and avant-garde forms of poetry; must be golf-related. Length: 4 to 16 lines. Pays $5 to $10.
How To Break In: "We frequently need to assign writers abroad to write a feature on golfing resorts. For European assignments, writer must also play golf, and be an experienced photographer."

FORE, 3740 Cahuenga Blvd., North Hollywood CA 91604. Editor: Will Hertzberg. Mailed quarterly to the 73,000 members of the Southern California Golf Association. Submit complete ms. Reports in 2 weeks. Enclose S.A.S.E.
Nonfiction and Photos: "Although we do not use a great deal of freelance material, and our rate of payment is low, we are always interested in seeing editorial and photographic material of interest to Southern California golfers. Edited primarily for amateurs, but can always use strong personality profiles and features on professionals as well. Other areas covered include resort/travel with a golf orientation, new equipment, instruction, rules, handicapping, professional and amateur tournament coverage, etc. Rates vary but usually run about $50 per article (1,000 words up), with high-quality b&w photos bringing $15 each. Pay more for color."

GOLF DIGEST, 495 Westport Ave., Norwalk CT 06856. (203)847-5811. Editor: Nick Seitz. Emphasizes golfing. Monthly magazine; 130 pages. Estab: 1950. Circ: 860,000. Pays on publication. Buys all rights. Phone queries OK. Submit seasonal/holiday material 4 months in advance. Photocopied submissions OK. SASE. Reports in 4-6 weeks. Free writer's guidelines.
Nonfiction: Expose; how-to; informational; historical; humor; inspirational; interview; nostalgia; personal opinion; profile; travel; new product; personal experience; photo feature; and technical; "all on playing and otherwise enjoying the game of golf." Buys 6 mss/issue. Query. Length: 1,000-2,500 words. Pays 20¢/edited word minimum.
Photos: Pete Libby, Photo Editor. Purchased without accompanying ms. Pays $10-150 for 5x7 or 8x10 b&w prints; $25-300 for 35mm color transparencies. Model release required.
Columns/Departments: John P. May, Column/Department Editor. Junior & Senior Golf. Buys 2-6 mss/issue. Length: 500-1,000 words. Pays 20¢/edited word. Open to suggestions for new columns/departments.

Poetry: Lois Haines, Poetry Editor. Light verse. Buys 1-2/issue. Length: 4-8 lines. Pays $10-25.
Fillers: Lois Haines, Fillers Editor. Jokes, gags, anecdotes. Buys 1-2/issue. Length: 2-6 lines. Pays $10-25.

GOLF JOURNAL, Chilton Co., Chilton Way, Radnor PA 19089. (215)687-8200. Editor: Mike Bartlett. For golfers of all ages and both sexes. Official publication of the U.S. Golf Association. Magazine: 54 pages. Established in 1948. 10 times/year. Circ: 70,000. Buys all rights. Buys about 30 mss a year. Payment on acceptance. Will send free sample copy to writer on request. Will not consider photocopied or simultaneous submissions. Reports in 2 weeks. Query first. Enclose S.A.S.E.
Nonfiction and Photos: "As the official publication of the United States Golf Association, our magazine is strong on decisions on the rules of golf, USGA championships, history of the game, and on service articles directed to the club golfer. All facets of golf, its history, courses, and clubs. Instructions. Humor." Length: 500 to 2,000 words. Pays maximum of $300. Pays a minimum of $15 for b&w photos. Captions required.

GOLF MAGAZINE, Times Mirror Magazines, Inc., 380 Madison Ave., New York NY 10017. (212)687-3000. Editor-in-Chief: John M. Ross. Emphasizes golf for males, ages 25-65, college educated, professionals. Monthly magazine; 80-100 pages. Circ: 650,000. Pays on acceptance. Buys all rights. Submit seasonal/holiday material 3 months in advance. Photocopied submissions OK. SASE. Reports in 4 weeks. Sample copy $1.25.
Nonfiction: How-to (improve game, instructional tips); informational (news in golf); humor; profile (people in golf); travel (golf courses, resorts); new product (golf equipment, apparel, teaching aids); and photo feature (great moments in golf; must be special. Most photography on assignment only). Buys 4-6 mss/year. Query. Length: 1,200-2,500 words. Pays $350-500.
Photos: Purchased with accompanying ms or on assignment. Captions required. Query. Pays $25-50 for 8½x11 glossy prints (with contact sheet and negatives); $50 minimum for 3x5 color prints. Total purchase price for ms includes payment for photos. Model release required.
Columns/Departments: Golf Reports (interesting golf events, feats, etc.). Buys 4-6 mss/year. Query. Length: 250 words maximum. Pays $35. Open to suggestions for new columns/departments.
Fiction: Humorous, mystery. Must be golf-related. Buys 2-4 mss/year. Query. Length: 1,200-2,000 words. Pays $350-500.
Poetry: Light verse. Buys 4-6/year. Limit submissions to batches of 6. Length: 7-15 lines. Pays $20.
Fillers: Short humor. Length: 20-35 words. Pays $5-10.
How To Break In: "Best chance is to aim for a light piece which is not too long and is focused on a personality or is genuinely funny. Anything very technical that would require a consumate knowledge of golf, we would rather assign ourselves. But if you are successful with something light and not too long, we might use you for something heavier later. Probably the best way to break in would be by our Golf Reports section in which we run short items on interesting golf feats, events and so forth. If you send us something like that, about an important event in your area, it is an easy way for us to get acquainted."

Guns

THE AMERICAN SHOTGUNNER, P.O. Box 3351, Reno NV 89505. Editor: Bob Thruston. Monthly tabloid magazine; 48 pages. Estab: 1973. Circ: 108,000. Buys all rights. Buys 24-50 mss/year. Pays on publication. Will send free sample copy to writer on request. Write for copy of guidelines for writers. Submit special material (hunting) 3 to 4 months in advance. Reports on material accepted for publication in 30 days. Returns rejected material immediately. Submit complete ms. Enclose S.A.S.E.
Nonfiction and Photos: All aspects of shotgunning, trap and skeet shooting and hunting, reloading; shooting clothing, shooting equipment and recreational vehicles. Emphasis is on the how-to and instructional approach. "We give the sportsman actual material that will help him to improve his game, fill his limit, or build that duck blind, etc. Hunting articles are used in all issues, year round." Length: open. Pays $75 to $250. No additional payment for photos used with mss. "We also purchase professional cover material. Send transparencies (originals)."
Fillers: Tips on hunting, shooting and outdoor themes; short humor. Pays minimum of $10.

BLACK POWDER TIMES, P.O. Box 842, Mount Vernon WA 98273. (206)424-3881. Editor: Fred Holder. For people interested in shooting and collecting black powder guns, primarily of the muzzle-loading variety. Tabloid newspaper; 16 pages. Estab: 1974. Monthly. Not copyrighted. Pays on publication. Will send sample copy to writer for 50¢. Will consider photocopied and simultaneous submissions. Reports on material accepted for publication in 2 to 4 weeks. Returns rejected material in 2 weeks. Query first. Enclose S.A.S.E.

Nonfiction: Articles on gunsmiths who make black powder guns, on shoots, on muzzle-loading gun clubs, on guns of the black powder vintage, and anything related to the sport of black powder shooting and hunting. Emphasis is on good writing and reporting. As an example of recently published material, see "Spring Rendezvous at Camus Meadows" and "Bad Luck Flintlock Hunt". Informational, how-to, personal experience, interview, profile, historical articles and book reviews. Length: 500 to 2,000 words. Pays 2¢ a word.

COLT AMERICAN HANDGUNNING ANNUAL, ITHACAGUN HUNTING & SHOOTING ANNUAL, Aqua-Field Publications, Inc., 342 Madison Ave., New York NY 10017. (212)682-0220. Editor and Publisher: Stephen Ferber. For outdoor sportsmen. Magazines; 100 pages. Established in 1974. Annually. Circ: 150,000. Buys all rights, but may reassign rights to author after publication. Buys all of its mss from freelance writers. Pays on acceptance or on publication; varies with contributor. Will send sample copy to writer for 50¢. No photocopied or simultaneous submissions. Submit seasonal (fall) material in the spring. Reports in 2 weeks. Query first or submit complete ms. Enclose S.A.S.E.

Nonfiction and Photos: Original how-to articles on hunting, shooting, and hand-loading. No "me and Joe" stories. "Just good writing with investigative approach to journalism." Emphasis is on interesting and authoritative material with an original approach and good photos. Length: 1,500 to 2,500 words. Pays $150 to $250. Nuts & Bolts column uses how-to material or pieces on new techniques. Length: 1,000 words. Pays $100. No additional payment for b&w glossies (8x10) used with mss. Pays $10 to $15 for b&w's purchased without mss. Pays $50 for color transparencies (35mm or 4x5) purchased with mss.

GUN WEEK, Amos Press, Box 150, 911 Vandemark Rd., Sidney OH 45365. (513)492-4141. Editor-in-Chief: James C. Schneider. News Editor: Marianne R. Sailor. Emphasizes gun hobby; sports, collecting and news. Weekly newspaper; 28 pages. Estab: 1966. Circ: 50,000. Pays on publication. Buys first North American serial rights. Phone queries OK. Submit seasonal/holiday material 6 weeks in advance. Simultaneous and photocopied submissions OK. SASE. Reports in 6 weeks. Free sample copy and writer's guidelines.

Nonfiction: Historical (history of firearms or how they affected an historical event); how-to (dealing with firearms, construction, care, etc.); informational (hunting, firearms, legislative news on the west coast); interview (gun-related persons, heads of college shooting programs, etc.); new product (firearms, ammunition, cleaners, gun-related products, hunting accessories); photo feature (conservation interests); profile (hunters, gun buffs, legislators, conservationists, etc.); technical. Buys 500 mss/year. Query and send complete ms. Length: 125-3,000 words. Pays 50¢/column inch.

Photos: Purchased with or without accompanying ms. Captions required. Send contact sheet, prints and/or slides. Pays $3 minimum for 5x7 or 8x10 b&w glossies; $5 minimum for 35mm color slides. (50¢/column inch with manuscript). Total purchase price for ms includes payment for photos. Model release required.

Columns/Departments: Buys 150-300 mss/year. Query or submit complete ms. Length: 500-1,500 words. Pays $20-35. Open to suggestions from freelancers for new columns/departments; address to James C. Schneider. "Our freelance writers are writing under one designated column, 'Muzzle Loader'—Don Davis, etc. We are looking for possible columnists in firearms collecting, history, hunting and conservation."

Fillers: Clippings, jokes, gags, anecdotes, facts. Send fillers. Length: 25-100 words.

GUN WORLD, Box HH, 34249 Camino Capistrano, Capistrano Beach CA 92624. Editorial Director: Jack Lewis. For ages that "range from mid-twenties to mid-sixties; many professional types who are interested in relaxation of hunting and shooting." Established in 1960. Monthly. Circulation: 129,000. Buys all rights but will reassign them to author after publication. Buys "50 or so" mss a year. Payment on acceptance. Will send a free sample copy to a writer on request. Will not consider photocopied submissions. Submit seasonal material 4 months in advance. Reports in six weeks, perhaps longer. Enclose S.A.S.E.

Nonfiction and Photos: General subject matter consists of "well-rounded articles—not by amateurs—on shooting techniques, along with anecdotes; hunting stories with tips and knowledge integrated. No poems or fiction. We like broad humor in our articles, so long as it does not reflect upon firearms safety. Most arms magazines are pretty deadly and we feel shooting can be fun. Too much material aimed at pro-gun people. Most of this is staff-written and most shooters don't have to be told of their rights under the Constitution. We want articles on new development; off-track inventions, novel military uses of arms; police armament and training techniques; do-it-yourself projects in this field." Buys informational, how-to, personal experience, and nostalgia articles. Pays $250 maximum. Purchases photos with mss and caption required. Wants 5x7 b&w.

GUNS & AMMO MAGAZINE, Petersen Publishing Company, 8490 Sunset Blvd., Los Angeles CA 90069. Editor-in-Chief: Howard E. French. Managing Editor: E.G. Bell. Emphasizes the firearms field. Monthly magazine; 108 pages. Estab: 1958. Circ: 400,000. Pays on publication. Buys all rights. Submit seasonal/holiday material 4 months in advance. SASE. Reports in 1 month. Free writer's guidelines.
Nonfiction: Informational and technical. Buys 7-10 mss/issue. Send complete ms. Length: 1,200-3,000 words. Pays $125-350.
Photos: Purchased with accompanying ms. Captions required. Uses 8x10 b&w glossies. Total purchase price for ms includes payment for photos. Model release required.

GUNS MAGAZINE, 8150 N. Central Park Ave., Skokie IL 60076. Editor: J. Rakusan. Estab: 1955. Monthly for firearms enthusiasts. Circulation: 135,000. Buys all rights. Buys 100 to 150 mss a year. Pays on publication. Will send free sample copy to a writer on request. Reports in 2 to 3 weeks. Enclose S.A.S.E.
Nonfiction and Photos: Test reports on new firearms; how-to on gunsmithing, reloading; round-up articles on firearms types. Historical pieces. Does not want to see anything about "John and I went hunting" or rewrites of a general nature or controversy for the sake of controversy, without new illumination. Length: 1,000 to 2,500 words. Pays $75 to $175. Major emphasis is on good photos. No additional payment for b&w glossies purchased with mss. Pays $50 to $100 for color; 2¼x2¼ minimum.

HANDLOADER MAGAZINE, P.O. Box 3030, Prescott, AZ 86301. (602)445-7814. Editor: Neal Knox. Bimonthly for gun enthusiasts who reload their ammunition. Buys first North American serial rights only. Pays on publication. Reports in two weeks. Query with outline required. Enclose S.A.S.E.
Nonfiction and Photos: Fresh, informative, knowledgeable, technical articles on handloading ammunition. Style: serious and simple. Length: 1,500 to 3,000 words. Pays $75 to $200, including photos (8x10 glossies preferred) and/or illustrations.

THE RIFLE MAGAZINE, P.O. Box 3030, Prescott AZ 86301. (602)445-7814. Editor: Neal Knox. Bimonthly. For advanced rifle enthusiasts. Pays on publication. Buys North American serial rights. Reports in 30 days. "A detailed query will help, and is preferred." Enclose S.A.S.E.
Nonfiction and Photos: Articles must be fresh and of a quality and style to enlighten rather than entertain knowledgeable gun enthusiasts. Subject matter must be technical and supported by appropriate research. "We are interested in seeing new bylines and new ideas, but if a writer doesn't have a solid knowledge of firearms and ballistics, he's wasting his time and ours to submit." Length: 1,500 to 3,000 words. Pays $75 to $200. Photos should accompany ms. Buys ms and photos as a package.

SHOOTING TIMES, News Plaza, Peoria IL 61601. Executive Editor: Alex Bartimo. "The average *Shooting Times* reader is 29 years old. He has an above average education and income. He is probably a semiskilled or skilled or professional worker who has an avid interest in firearms and the shooting sports." Special reloading issue in February; handgun issue in March. Monthly. Circ: 153,000. Buys all rights. Buys 85 to 90 mss/year. Pays on acceptance. Free sample copy and writer's guidelines. Submit seasonal or special material 4 or 5 months in advance. Reports in 4 to 5 weeks. Query first. Enclose S.A.S.E.
Nonfiction and Photos: "Presents a well-balanced content ranging from nontechnical through semitechnical to technical stories covering major shooting sports activities—handguns, rifles, shotguns, cartridge reloading, muzzle loading, gunsmithing, how-to's, and hunting, with a major emphasis on handguns. Hunting stories must be 'gunny' with the firearm(s) and ammunition dominating the story and serving as the means to an end. Articles may run from 1,000 to 2,000 words and must be accompanied by 10 to 12 b&w glossies, 8x10, including 1 or 2 'lead' pictures." Payment is $150 to $300.

Horse Racing

AMERICAN TURF MONTHLY, 505 8th Avenue, New York NY 10018. Editor: Howard Rowe. For "horse racing bettors." Buys 50 to 100 mss a year. Enclose S.A.S.E.
Nonfiction: General subject matter is "articles, systems and material treating horse racing."

Approach should be "how to successfully wager on racing. It is the only publication in the country devoted exclusively to the horse bettor. We have a staff capable of covering every facet aside from system articles." Length: 1,500 to 3,000 words. Pays $40 minimum.

THE BACKSTRETCH, 19363 James Couzens Highway, Detroit MI 48235. (313)342-6144. Editor: Ruth A. LeGrove. For thoroughbred horse trainers, owners, breeders, farm managers, track personnel, jockeys, grooms and racing fans which span the age range from very young to very old. Publication of United Thoroughbred Trainers of America, Inc. Quarterly magazine, approximately 92 pages. Established in 1962. Circulation: 20,000. Rights purchased vary with author and material. Payment on publication. Will send sample copy to writer for 50¢. Will not consider photocopied submissions. Will consider simultaneous submissions. Reporting time varies, but returns rejected material immediately. Submit only complete ms. Enclose S.A.S.E.
Nonfiction: "Mostly general information. No fiction. Articles deal with biographical material on trainers, owners, jockeys, horses and their careers, historical track articles, etc. Unless his material is related to thoroughbreds and thoroughbred racing, he should not submit it. Otherwise, send on speculation. Payment is made after material is used. If not suitable, it is returned immediately. We feel we have more readable material in *The Backstretch*, and we vary our articles sufficiently to give the reader a variety of reading. Articles of a historical nature or those not depending on publication by a certain date are preferable. No special length requirements. Payment depends on material."

TURF & SPORT DIGEST, 511 Oakland Ave., Baltimore MD 21212. Editor-in-Chief: Sean McCormick. For an audience composed of thoroughbred horseracing fans. Monthly magazine; 64 pages. Estab: 1924. Circ: 19,000. Buys all rights, but may reassign following publication. Phone queries OK. Submit seasonal/holiday material 3 months in advance. Photocopied submissions and previously published work OK. SASE. Reports in 3 weeks. Free sample copy.
Nonfiction: Historical, humor, informational and personal experience articles on racing; interviews and profiles (racing personalities). Buys 4 mss/issue. Query. Length: 300-3,000 words. Pays $60-220.
Photos: Purchased with or without mss. Send contact sheet. Pays $15-25/b&w, $100/color.

Hunting and Fishing

ALASKA HUNTING AND FISHING TALES, Box 4-EEE, Anchorage AK 99509. Published irregularly. Buys first North American serial rights. Pays on publication. SASE.
Nonfiction and Photos: True first-person hunting, fishing, or adventure stories from Alaska or adjacent Canada. "Material must have an Alaskan setting, and the general requirements in fact are the same as for *Alaska* magazine." Length: maximum 5,000 words; prefers 2,000 to 3,000 words. "Good photos are a must." Pays $25 to $100.

ALASKA MAGAZINE, Box 4-EEE, Anchorage AK 99509. (907)243-1484. Editor: Robert A. Henning. For wide range of persons interested in fishing, hunting, skiing, camping, gardening, bicycling and photography in Alaska and the North. Wide range of ages. Latest survey shows majority are college-educated and middle income. Monthly magazine; 104 pages, (8½x11). Established in 1935. Circulation: 174,837. Rights purchased vary with author and material. Buys all rights; buys first North American serial rights; buys first serial rights. Payment on publication. Will send sample copy to writer for $1. Submit only complete ms. Enclose S.A.S.E.
Nonfiction and Photos: Marty Loken, Managing Editor. "Articles about the life and events in Alaska, Yukon, northern B.C. Material should be based on writer's actual experience in the North." Buys informational, how-to, personal experience, interview, humor, historical, photo, travel articles. Length: 100 to 3,000 words. Pays $10 to $200. 8x10 b&w photos purchased with ms with no additional payment. Also purchased without ms. 8x10 b&w glossies or Ektachrome and Kodachrome; 35mm color. Pays $10 minimum for b&w; $15 minimum for color. "Photos should accompany all mss."

AMERICAN FIELD, 222 W. Adams St., Chicago IL 60606. Editor: William F. Brown. Issued weekly. Buys first publication rights. Payment made on acceptance. Will send sample copy on request. Reports usually within 10 days. Enclose S.A.S.E.
Nonfiction and Photos: Always interested in factual articles on breeding, rearing, development and training of hunting dogs, how-to-do-it material written to appeal to upland bird hunters, sporting dog owners, field trialers, etc. Also wants stories and articles about hunting trips in quest of upland game birds. Length: 1,000 to 2,500 words. Pays $50 to $200. Uses photos submitted with manuscripts if they are suitable and also photos submitted with captions only. Pays $5 minimum for b&w.
Fillers: Infrequently uses some 100- to 250-word fillers. Pays $5 minimum.

THE AMERICAN HUNTER, 1600 Rhode Island Ave., N.W., Washington DC 20036. Editor: Ken Warner. For sport hunters who are members of the National Rifle Association; all ages, all political persuasions, all economic levels. Established in 1973. Circulation: over 100,000. Buys first North American serial rights "and the right to reprint our presentation." Buys 200 mss a year. Payment on acceptance. Will send free sample copy to writer on request. Write for copy of guidelines for writers. Would prefer not to see photocopied submissions or simultaneous submissions. Reports in 1 to 3 weeks. Query first or submit complete ms. Enclose S.A.S.E.
Nonfiction and Photos: "Factual material on all phases of sport hunting and game animals and their habitats. Good angles and depth writing are essential. You have to *know* to write successfully here." Not interested in material on fishermen, campers or ecology freaks. Length: open. Pays $25 to $900. No additional payment made for photos used with mss. Pays $10 to $25 for b&w photos purchased without accompanying mss. Pays $20 to $100 for color.

THE AMERICAN RIFLEMAN, 1600 Rhode Island Ave., N.W., Washington DC 20036. Editor: Ken Warner. Monthly. Official journal of National Rifle Association of America. Buys first North American serial rights, including publication in this magazine, or any of the official publications of the National Rifle Association. Residuary rights will be returned after publication upon request of the author. Pays on acceptance. Free sample copy and writers' guidelines. Reports in 1-4 weeks. Enclose S.A.S.E.
Nonfiction: Factual articles on hunting, target shooting, shotgunning, conservation, firearms repairs and oddities accepted from qualified freelancers. No semifictional or "me and Joe" type of yarns, but articles should be informative and interesting. Will not consider anything that "winks" at lawbreaking, or delineates practices that are inimical to the best interests of gun ownership, shooting, or good citizenship. Articles should run from one to four magazine pages. Pays about $100-600.
Photos: Full-color transparencies for possible use on cover and inside. Photo articles that run one to two magazine pages. Pays $35 minimum for inside photo; $100 minimum for cover; payment for groups of photos is negotiable.

CAROLINA SPORTSMAN, Box 2581, Charlotte NC 28201. (803)796-9200. Editor: Sidney L. Wise; Associate Editor: Doug Murphy. Bimonthly. Buys all rights. Pays on publication. Will send free sample copy to a writer on request. Reports on submissions in 3 to 8 weeks. Enclose S.A.S.E.
Nonfiction and Photos: Sports stories in quick-moving, vivid, on-the-spot style, dealing with hunting, fishing, camping, backpacking, conservation and other outdoor activities in the Carolinas. Length: 600 to 2,000 words. Pays 3¢ minimum per word, depending on ms. B&w glossy photos and color transparencies are purchased with mss, with additional payment.
Fillers: Sport topics. Length: 25 to 50 words. Pays $5 minimum.

DAIWA FISHING ANNUAL, Aqua-Field Publications, Inc., 342 Madison Ave., New York NY 10017. (212)682-0220. Editor and Publisher: Stephen Ferber. For outdoor sportsmen. Magazine; 100 pages. Established in 1974. Annually. Circ: 150,000. Buys all rights, but may reassign rights to author after publication. Buys all of its mss from freelance writers. Pays on acceptance or on publication; varies with contributor. Will send sample copy to writer for 50¢. No photocopied or simultaneous submissions. Submit seasonal material (spring) during prior winter. Reports in 2 weeks. Query first or submit complete ms. Enclose S.A.S.E.
Nonfiction and Photos: Original how-to articles on fishing. Must be good writing with an investigative approach to journalism. No "me and Joe" stories. All material must be interesting and authoritative, with an original approach and good photos. Length: 1,500 to 2,500 words. Pays $150 to $250. Nuts & Bolts column pieces on new techniques or how-to's. Length: 1,000 words. Pays $100. No additional payment for b&w glossies (8x10) used with mss. Pays $10 to $15 for b&w's purchased without mss. Pays $50 for color transparencies (35mm or 4x5) purchased with mss.

FIELD AND STREAM, 383 Madison Ave., New York NY 10017. Editor: Jack Samson. Monthly. Buys all rights. Reports in 4 weeks. Query. SASE.
Nonfiction and Photos: "This is a broad-based outdoor service magazine. Editorial content ranges from very basic how-to stories that tell either in pictures or words how an outdoor technique is done or device made. Articles of penetrating depth about national conservation, game management, resource management, and recreation development problems. Hunting, fishing, camping, backpacking, nature, outdoor, photography, equipment, wild game and fish recipes, and other activities allied to the outdoors. The 'me and Joe' story is about dead, with minor exceptions. Both where-to and how-to articles should be well-illustrated." Prefers color

to b&w. Submit outline first with photos. Length, 2,500 words. Payment varies depending upon the name of the author, quality of work, importance of the article. Pays 18¢ per word and up. Usually buys photos with mss. When purchased separately, pays $150 and up for color.
Fillers: Buys "how it's done" fillers of 500 to 1,000 words. Must be unusual or helpful subjects. Payment is $250.

FISH AND GAME SPORTSMAN, P.O. Box 737, Regina, Sask., Canada S4P 3A8. (306)523-8384. Editor: J. B. (Red) Wilkinson. For fishermen, hunters, campers and others interested in outdoor recreation. "Please note that our coverage area is Alberta and Saskatchewan." Quarterly magazine; 64-112 pages. Estab: 1968. Circ: 16,000. Rights purchased vary with author and material. May buy first North American serial rights or second serial (reprint) rights. Buys about 50 mss a year. Payment on publication, or within a 3-month maximum period. Will send sample copy to writer for $1. Write for copy of editorial guidelines. "We try to include as much information on all subjects in each edition. Therefore, we usually publish fishing articles in our winter magazine along with a variety of winter stories. If material is dated, we would like to receive articles 4 months in advance of our publication date." Will consider photocopied submissions. Reports in 4 weeks. Submit only complete ms. Enclose S.A.E. and International Reply Coupons.
Nonfiction and Photos: "It is necessary that all articles can identify with our coverage area of Alberta and Saskatchewan. We are interested in mss from writers who have experienced an interesting fishing, hunting, camping or other outdoor experience. We also publish how-to and other informational pieces as long as they can relate to our coverage area. Too many writers submit material to us which quite frankly we don't believe. We call these puff stories and generally after reading the first page or two they are returned to the writers without further reading. Our editors are experienced people who have spent many hours afield fishing, hunting, camping etc., and we simply cannot accept information which borders on the ridiculous. The record fish does not jump two feet out of the water with a brilliant sunset backdrop, two-pound test line, one-hour battle, a hole in the boat, tumbling waterfalls, all in the first paragraph. We are more interested in articles which tell about the average guy living on beans, guiding his own boat, stalking his game and generally doing his own thing in our part of western Canada than a story describing a well-to-do outdoorsman traveling by motorhome, staying at an expensive lodge with guides doing everything for him except landing the fish, or shooting the big game animal. The articles that are submitted to us need to be prepared in a knowledgeable way and include more information than the actual fish catch or animal or bird kill. The story should discuss the terrain, the people involved on the trip, the water or weather conditions, the costs, the planning that went into the trip, the equipment and other data closely associated with the particular event in a factual manner. We like to see exciting writing, but leave out the gloss and nonsense. We are very short of camping articles and how-to pieces on snowmobiling, including mechanical information. We generally have sufficient fishing and hunting data but we're always looking for new writers. I would be very interested in hearing from writers who are experienced campers and snowmobilers." Length: 1,500 to 3,000 words. Pays $40 to $175. Photos purchased with ms with no additional payment. Also purchased without ms. Pays $7 per 5x7 to 8x10 b&w print; pays $75 for 35mm minimum transparencies.

FISHING AND HUNTING NEWS, Outdoor Empire Publishing Company, Inc., 511 Eastlake Ave. E., Box C-19000, Seattle WA 98109. (206)624-3845. Managing Editor: Vence Malernee. Emphasizes fishing and hunting. Weekly tabloid; 16 pages. Estab: 1944. Circ: 112,000. Pays on acceptance. Buys all rights, but may reassign following publication. Submit seasonal/holiday material 3 months in advance. Photocopied submissions OK. Free sample copy and writer's guidelines.
Nonfiction: How-to (fish and hunt successfully, things that make outdoor jaunts more enjoyable/productive); photo feature (successful fishing/hunting in the western U.S.); informational. Buys 70 mss/year. Query. Length: 100-1,000 words. Pays $10 minimum.
Photos: Purchased with or without accompanying ms. Captions required. Submit prints or transparencies. Pays $5 minimum for 8x10 b&w glossies; $10 minimum for 35mm or 2¼ color transparencies. Model release required.

FISHING WORLD, 51 Atlantic Ave., Floral Park NY 11001. Editor: Keith Gardner. Bimonthly. Circ: 250,000. Buys first North American serial rights only. Pays on acceptance. Will send a free sample copy to a writer on request. Will consider photocopied submissions. Reports in 2 weeks. Query first. Enclose S.A.S.E.
Nonfiction and Photos: "Feature articles range from 1,500-2,000 words with the shorter preferred. A good selection of color transparencies should accompany each submission. Subject mat-

ter can range from a hot fishing site to tackle and techniques, from tips on taking individual species to a story on one lake or an entire region, either freshwater or salt. However, how-to is definitely preferred over where-to, and a strong biological/scientific slant is best of all. Where-to articles, especially if they describe foreign fishing, should be accompanied by sidebars covering how to make reservations and arrange transportation, how to get there, where to stay. Angling methods should be developed in clear detail, with accurate and useful information about tackle and boats. Depending on article length, suitability of photographs and other factors, payment is up to $250 for feature articles accompanied by suitable photography. Color transparencies selected for cover use pay an additional $150. Black-and-white or unillustrated featurettes are also considered. These can be on anything remotely connected with fishing. Length to 1,000. Payment $25-$100 depending on length and photos. Detailed queries accompanied by photos are preferred. Cover shots are purchased separately, rather than selected from those accompanying mss. The editor favors drama rather than serenity in selecting cover shots."

FUR-FISH-GAME, 2878 E. Main, Columbus OH 43209. Editor: A. R. Harding. For outdoorsmen of all ages, interested in fishing, hunting, camping, woodcraft, trapping. Magazine; 64 (8½x11) pages. Established 1925. Monthly. Circ: 190,000. Rights purchased vary with author and material. May buy all rights with the possibility of reassigning rights to author after publication; first serial rights or second serial (reprint) rights. Buys 150 mss/year. Pays on acceptance. Sample copy 50¢; free writer's guidelines. Photocopied submissions OK. No simultaneous submissions. Reports in 4 weeks. Submit complete ms. Enclose S.A.S.E.
Nonfiction and Photos: Articles on outdoor-related subjects. Articles on hunting, fishing, trapping, camping, boating, conservation. Must be down-to-earth, informative and instructive. Informational, how-to, personal experience, inspirational, historical, nostalgia, personal opinion, travel, new product, technical. Length: 2,000 to 3,000 words. Pays $50 to $75. Also buys shorter articles for Gun Rack, Fishing, Dog and Trapping departments. Length: 1,000 to 2,000 words. Pays $20 to $35. No additional payment for 8x10 b&w glossies used with ms.

GRAY'S SPORTING JOURNAL, Box 190, Brookline MA 02146. (617)731-8691. Editor: Ed Gray. Managing Editor: Ted Williams. For "the contemplative outdoorsman—the educated hunter and fisherman who gets as much enjoyment from reading high-quality literature about his sport as he does from a day in the field." Magazine; 96 to 112 pages. Estab: 1975. 7 times/year. Buys first North American serial rights. Will send sample copy to writer for $3. Write for copy of guidelines for writers. Will consider photocopied and simultaneous submissions. Submit seasonal material 2 months in advance. Reports in 6 to 8 weeks. SASE.
Nonfiction and Photos: "We want articles on hunting and fishing — experiences and thoughts. We prefer an anecdotal approach and literary merit rather than basic instruction. Questions of style and focus can be settled in response to a query. Our magazine is set up on a seasonal basis. Each issue is directed toward a specific aspect of the hunting and fishing world which, itself, revolves around the seasons." Personal experience articles and think pieces. Length: 2,000 to 4,000 words. Pays $500-1,000. B&w glossies and color transparencies purchased with or without ms, or on assignment. Pays $25 minimum for b&w; $50 minimum for color.
Rejects: How-to, where-to-go, me-and-Joe articles.

ILLINOIS WILDLIFE, P.O. Box 116—13005 S. Western Ave., Blue Island IL 60406. (312)388-3995. Editor: Ace Extrom. For conservationists and sportsmen. "Tabloid newspaper utilizing newspaper format instead of magazine type articles." Monthly. Circulation: 35,000. Buys one-time rights. Pays on acceptance. Will send a sample copy to a writer for 25¢. Reports in 2 weeks. Enclose S.A.S.E.
Nonfiction and Photos: Want "material aimed at conserving and restoring our natural resources." How-to, humor, photo articles. Length: "maximum 2,000 words, prefer 1,000-word articles." Pays 1¢ per word. B&w glossies. Prefers 5x7. Pays $5.

MARYLAND CONSERVATIONIST, Tawes State Office Building C-2, Annapolis MD 21401. Editor: Raymond Krasnick. For "outdoorsmen, between 10 and 100 years of age." Bimonthly. Circulation: 8,000. Not copyrighted. Buys 20 to 30 mss a year. Pays on publication. Will send a free sample copy to a writer on request. Reports within 30 days. Query first. Enclose S.A.S.E.
Nonfiction: "Subjects dealing strictly with the outdoor life in Maryland. Nontechnical in content and in the first or third person in style." How-to, personal experience, humor, photo, travel articles. Overstocked with material on pollution and Maryland ecology. Length: 1,000 to 1,500 words. Payment is 5¢ a word.

Photos: 8x10 b&w glossies purchased with mss. Payment is $15/photo, $35/slide used with article, $10/b&w photo appearing in photo essay. Color transparencies and 35mm color purchased for covers. Payment is $50.

MICHIGAN OUT-OF-DOORS, Box 30235, Lansing MI 48909. (517)371-1041. Editor-in-Chief: Kenneth S. Lowe. Emphasizes outdoor recreation, especially hunting and fishing; conservation; environmental affairs. Monthly magazine; 116 pages. Estab: 1947. Circ: 100,000. Pays on publication. Buys first North American serial rights. Phone queries OK. Submit seasonal/holiday material 6 months in advance. Photocopied and previously published (if so indicated) submissions OK. SASE. Reports in 1 month. Sample copy 50¢; free writer's guidelines.
Nonfiction: Expose, historical, how-to, informational, interview, nostalgia, personal experience, personal opinion, photo feature and profile. "Stories *must* have a Michigan slant unless they treat a subject of universal interest to our readers." Buys 15 mss/issue. Send complete ms. Length: 300-2,100 words. Pays $5-100.
Photos: Purchased with or without accompanying ms. Pays $10 minimum for any size b&w glossies; $50 maximum for color (for cover). Offers no additional payment for photos accepted with accompanying ms.

ONTARIO OUT OF DOORS, 7 Guardsman Rd., Thornhill, Ont., Canada L3T 2A1. Editor-in-Chief: Burton J. Myers. For "the serious Ontario outdoorsman." Monthly magazine; 100 pages. Estab: 1968. Circ: 30,000. Pays on acceptance. Buys first North American serial rights. Submit seasonal/holiday material 3 months in advance. Photocopied submissions OK. Reports in 1 month. Free sample copy and writer's guidelines.
Nonfiction: Expose (wildlife management, conservation), how-to (new techniques for hunting and fishing), informational (related to the out-of-doors), interview (with topical political leaders who affect the outdoors), photo feature (wildlife management), and travel (where to fish and hunt in Ontario). Buys 240 mss/year. Query. Length: 1,000-2,500 words. Pays $25-125.
Photos: Purchased with accompanying ms. Captions required. Send prints or transparencies. Pays $5-25 for 8x10 b&w glossies; $100-125 for transparencies used as cover. Total purchase price for ms includes payment for photos ("except for cover photo when accompanying article.")
Fillers: Mike Bolton, Associate Editor. Newsbreaks. Buys 120 mss/year. Length: 100-500 words. Pays $20.
How To Break In: "The magazine is aimed toward providing information of interest to Ontario's outdoor enthusiasts. Articles should be provincial, not national, in scope."

OUTDOOR LIFE, 380 Madison Ave., New York NY 10017. Editor: Lamar Underwood. For the active sportsman and his family, interested in fishing and hunting and closely related subjects, such as camping, boating and conservation. Buys first North American serial rights. Pays on acceptance. Query first. Enclose S.A.S.E.
Nonfiction and Photos: "What we publish is your best guide to the kinds of material we seek. Whatever the subject, you must present it in a way that is interesting and honest. In addition to regular feature material, we are also interested in combinations of photos and text for self-contained 1-, 2-, or 4-page spreads. Do you have something to offer the reader that will help him or her? Just exactly how do you think it will help? How would you present it? Material should provide nuts and bolts information so that readers can do likewise. We are interested in articles in which the author is actually a reporter interviewing and gathering information from expert sportsmen. Good geographic balance in these articles is essential. We also like spectacular personal adventure and ordeal pieces and we will even assign a staff man to help with the writing if the story really interests us." B&w photos should be professional quality 8x10 glossies. Color photos should be original positive transparencies and 35mm or larger. Comprehensive captions are required. Pays $500-1,000 for 3,000 words, depending on quality, photos and timeliness.
How To Break In: "We are the only magazine of the big three outdoor sports publications with regional sections and that's probably the best in for a writer who is new to us. Check the magazine for one of the six regional editors who would be responsible for material from your area and suggest an item to him. Our regional news pieces cover things from hunting and fishing news to conservation topics to new record fish to the new head of a wildlife agency. You have an advantage if you can provide us with quality photos to accompany the story. These pieces range from 300 to 1,000 words. In addition to the news section of the regionals, the Yellow Pages also include a regional feature each month. Emphasis in the regional features is *not* on species hunted or fished across the country (deer, bass), but rather on regional species (e.g. cutthroat trout in the West; garfish in the Southeast or searun white perch in the North-

east, etc.). The major function of these features is to provide specific information that will be of value to a sportsman who goes in pursuit of the subject species. 'Me and Joe' stories are out. Lively, first-person description of a trip should be considered a 'stepping stone' only for the author to branch out and tell the reader how and where he can also make such a trip in his own area. A regional feature should also give readers information on the natural history of a species: e.g., its habits, its range, its history in the region, and so on. Pay for regional features is $300 minimum for 2,500 to 3,000 words plus photographs (b&w preferred). Another opportunity for writers is the magazine's food page. These articles include a short introduction about the subject species, perhaps an anecdote, and from three to five *tested* recipes. Articles on preparation (smoking, freezing, etc.) of fish and game will also be considered." Pays $50 for 2 to 4 double-spaced manuscript pages and photos.

THE OUTDOOR PRESS, N. 2012 Ruby St., Spokane WA 99207. (509)328-9392. Editor: Fred Peterson. For sportsmen: hunters, fishermen, RV enthusiasts. Weekly tabloid newspaper; 16 pages. Estab: 1966. Circ: 6,000. Rights purchased vary with author and material. Usually buys first North American serial rights. Buys about 63 mss a year. Pays on acceptance. Will send sample copy to writer for 25¢. Will consider photocopied and simultaneous submissions. Submit seasonal material 2 months in advance. Reports on material accepted for publication in 2 weeks. Returns rejected material in 2 weeks. Query first or submit complete ms. Enclose S.A.S.E.
Nonfiction and Photos: How-to-do-it stories; technical in detail. Would like to see material on Indian fishing rights conflicts, crabs, clams, salmon, fly fishing. Does not want anything on ecology. Length: 750 to 4,000 words. Pays $20 to $750. Also looking for material for their columns on guns, dogs, camping, RV's, fishing. Length: 1,000 words. Pays $5 to $200. B&w photos (5x7 or larger) purchased with or without ms, or on assignment. Pays $10 to $200. Captions required.

OUTDOORS TODAY, Outdoors Today, Inc., 569 Melville, St. Louis MO 63130. Editor: Gary Dotson. For outdoorsmen: hunters, fishermen, campers, boaters. Newspaper tabloid; 12-24 pages. Estab: 1970. Weekly. Circulation: 90,000. Buys all rights, but will reassign rights to author after publication. Buys over 200 mss/year. Pays on 10th of month following publication. Will send free sample copy to writer on request. Will consider photocopied and simultaneous submissions. Submit seasonal material 30 days in advance. Reports on material accepted for publication in 60 days. Returns rejected material immediately. Submit complete ms. Enclose S.A.S.E.
Nonfiction and Photos: Outdoor-oriented material dealing with the midwestern United States. Emphasis on area news, i.e., opening of deer season in Missouri; pheasant season roundups by state, etc. Informational, how-to, personal experience, interview, profile, inspirational, humor, historical, think pieces, expose, nostalgia, personal opinion, lake features, photo and travel features. Length: 500 to 750 words. Pays $15 to $100. No additional payment for first photo used with mss. Additional payment for other photos used.
How To Break In: "Deal with news. Be factual and offer readers information they may not already know."

PENNSYLVANIA GAME NEWS, Box 1567, Harrisburg PA 17120. (717)787-3745. Editor-in-Chief: Bob Bell. Emphasizes hunting in Pennsylvania. Monthly magazine; 64 pages. Estab: 1929. Circ: 210,000. Pays on acceptance. Phone queries OK. Submit seasonal/holiday material 6 months in advance. Photocopied submissions OK. SASE. Reports in 1 month. Free sample copy and writer's guidelines.
Nonfiction: Historical, how-to, informational, personal experience, photo feature and technical. "Must be related to outdoors in Pennsylvania." Buys 4-8 mss/issue. Query. Length: 2,500 words maximum. Pays $250 maximum.
Photos: Purchased with accompanying ms. Pays $5-20 for 8x10 b&w glossies. Model release required.

PETERSEN'S HUNTING, Petersen Publishing Co., 8490 Sunset Blvd., Los Angeles, CA 90069, (213)657-5100. Editor-in-Chief: Ken Elliot. Emphasizes sport hunting. Monthly magazine; 84 pages. Estab: 1973. Circ: 135,000. Pays on publication. Buys all rights. Submit seasonal/holiday material 6 months in advance. SASE. Reports in 2 months. Sample copy $1.25. Free writer's guidelines.
Nonfiction: How-to (how to be a better hunter, how to make hunting-related items), personal experience (use a hunting trip as an anecdote to illustrate how-to contents). Buys 3 mss/issue. Query. Length: 1,500-2,500 words. Pays $200-300.

Photos: Photos purchased with or without accompanying ms. Captions required. Pays $15 minimum for 8x10 b&w glossies; $50-150 for 2¼x2¼ or 35mm color transparencies. Total purchase price for ms includes payment for photos. Model release required.

SALMON TROUT STEELHEADER, P.O. Box 02112, Portland OR 97202. Editor: Frank W. Amato. For sport fishermen in Oregon, Washington, and California. Bimonthly. Buys first serial rights. Pays on publication. Will send free sample copy on request. Reports in 2 weeks. Query first. Enclose S.A.S.E.
Nonfiction and Photos: Articles on fishing for trout, salmon, and steelhead. How-to's and where-to's. Length: 1,000 to 2,500 words. B&w photos purchased with mss. Pays $40-150.

SALT WATER SPORTSMAN, 10 High St., Boston MA 02110. (617)426-4074. Editor-in-Chief: Frank Woolner. Managing Editor: Rip Cunningham. Emphasizes saltwater fishing. Monthly magazine; 100 pages. Estab: 1937. Circ: 115,000. Pays on acceptance. Buys first North American serial rights. Phone queries OK. Photocopied submissions OK. SASE. Reports in 4 weeks. Free sample copy and writer's guidelines.
Nonfiction: How-to, personal experience, technical and travel (to fishing areas). Buys 8 mss/issue. Query. Length: 2,500-3,000 words. Pays 5¢/word.
Photos: Purchased with or without accompanying ms. Captions required. Uses 5x7 or 8x10 b&w prints. Pays $200 minimum for 35mm, 2¼x2¼ or 8x10 color transparencies for cover. Offers no additional payment for photos accepted with accompanying ms.

SOUTHERN ANGLER'S GUIDE, SOUTHERN HUNTER'S GUIDE, P.O. Box 2188, Hot Springs AR 71901. Editor: Don J. Fuelsch. Covers the southern scene on hunting and fishing completely. Today, the magazine has become a massive tome of excellent data. Buys all rights. Issued annually. Query first. Enclose S.A.S.E.
Nonfiction: Hunting, fishing, boating, camping articles. Articles that have been thoroughly researched. Condensed in digest style. Complete how-to-do-it rundown on tricks and techniques used in taking various species of fresh and saltwater fish and game found in the southern states. Interested in new and talented writers with thorough knowledge of their subject. Not interested in first person or "me and Joe" pieces. Length is flexible, 750 and 1,800 words preferred, although may run as high as 3,000 words. Pays 5¢ to 30¢ a word.
Photos: Buys photographs with mss or with captions only. Fishing or hunting subjects in southern setting. No Rocky Mountain backgrounds. B&w only—5x7 or 8x10 glossies.

SPORTS AFIELD, With Rod & Gun, 250 West 55 St., New York NY 10019. Editor: David Maxey. For people of all ages whose interests are centered around the out-of-doors (hunting and fishing especially) and related subjects. Monthly magazine; 175 pages. Estab: 1887. Circ: 200,000. Buys first North American serial rights. Buys 90 mss/year. Pays on acceptance. Free writer's guidelines. Photocopied and simultaneous submissions OK. "Our magazine is very seasonal and material submitted should be in accordance. Fishing in spring and summer; hunting in the fall; camping in summer and fall." Submit seasonal material 3 months in advance. Reports within 30 days. Query first or submit complete ms. Enclose S.A.S.E.
Nonfiction and Photo: "Informative how-to articles, and dramatic personal experiences with good photos on hunting, fishing, camping, boating and related subjects such as conservation and travel. Use informative approach. More how-to, more information, less 'true-life' adventure. General hunting/fishing yarns are overworked. Our readers are interested in becoming more proficient at their sport. We want brief, concise, how-to pieces and first-class writing and reporting." Buys how-to, personal experience, interview, nostalgia, and travel. Length: 500 to 2,000 words. Pays $600 or more, depending on length and quality. Photos purchased with or without ms. Pays $25 minimum for 8x10 b&w glossies. Pays $50 minimum for 2¼ or larger transparencies; 35mm acceptable.
Fillers: Mainly how-to-do-it tips on outdoor topics with photos or drawings. Length: self-contained 1 or 2 pages. Payment depends on length. Regular column, Almanac, pays $10 and up depending on length, for newsworthy, unusual or how-to nature items.

THE TEXAS FISHERMAN, Voice of the Lone Star Angler, Cordovan Corporation, 5314 Bingle, Houston TX 77092. Editor: Marvin Spivey. For freshwater and saltwater fishermen in Texas. Monthly tabloid; 40 (10¼x14) pages. Estab: 1973. Circ: 65,000. Rights purchased vary with author and material. Usually buys second serial (reprint) rights. Buys 6 to 8 mss per month. Payment on publication. Will send free sample copy to writer on request. Write for copy of guidelines for writers. Will not consider photocopied submissions. Will consider simultaneous submissions. Reports in 4 weeks. Query first. Enclose S.A.S.E.

Nonfiction and Photos: General how-to, where-to, features on all phases of fishing in Texas. Strong slant on informative pieces. Strong writing. Good saltwater stories (Texas only). Length: 2,000 to 3,000 words, prefers 2,500. Pays $35 to $100 depending on length and quality of writing and photos. Mss must include 8 to 10 good action b&w photos or illustrations. **Fillers:** Short how-to items. Pays $25.

TURKEY CALL, Wild Turkey Bldg., Box 467, Edgefield SC 29824. (803)637-3106. Editor: Gene Smith. An educational publication for the wild turkey enthusiast. Bimonthly magazine; 24-40 pages. Estab: 1973. Circ: 15,000. Buys all rights. Buys 20 mss/year. Pays on publication. Free sample copy when supplies permit. No photocopied or simultaneous submissions. Reports in 3 weeks. Query first or submit complete ms. Enclose S.A.S.E.
Nonfiction and Photos: "Feature articles dealing with the history, management, restoration, harvesting techniques and distribution of the American wild turkey. These stories must consist of accurate information and must appeal to the dyed-in-the-wool turkey hunter, as well as management personnel and the general public. While there are exceptions, we find the management slanted article particularly well suited to us." Length: 1,500-2,500 words. Pays $30 minimum. "How-to and where-to-go articles, along with 'how the wild turkey became re-established' articles of most any length, with specific information and practical hints for success in harvest and management of the wild turkey are what we are seeking. We use color transparencies for the cover; full of action, atmosphere or human interest. We want action photos submitted with feature articles; mainly b&w. For color, we prefer transparencies, but can use 35mm slides. We prefer 8x10 b&w glossies, but will settle for smaller prints, if they are good quality. For contacts, we must have the negatives and contact prints. We want action shots, not the typical 'dead turkey' photos. We are allergic to posed photos. Photos on how-to should make the techniques clear." Pays $10 minimum for b&w.

VIRGINIA WILDLIFE, P.O. Box 11104, Richmond VA 23230. (804)786-4974. Editor: Harry L. Gillam. Monthly. For sportsmen, outdoor enthusiasts. Pays on acceptance. Buys first North American serial rights, second serial rights (reprint) rights. Will send sample copy on request. Query first. Enclose S.A.S.E.
Nonfiction: Uses factual hunting and fishing stories especially those set in Virginia. Boating and gunning with safety slant. Conservation projects. Conservation education. New ways of enjoying the outdoors. Factual articles with photos on conservation issues facing Virginians. Especially needs power boating articles. Slant should be to enjoy the outdoors and do what you can to improve it and keep it enjoyable. Material must be applicable to Virginia, sound from a scientific basis, accurate and easy to read. Length: prefers 800 to 1,500 words. Pays 1½¢ to 3¢ per word.
Photos: Buys photos with mss and photo stories with captions. Should be color transparencies or 8x10 glossies. Pays $5-10/photograph.

WESTERN OUTDOORS, 3939 Birch St., Newport Beach CA 92660. (714)546-4370. Editor-in-Chief: Burt Twilegar. Emphasizes hunting, fishing, camping, boating for 11 Western states only. Monthly magazine; 88 pages. Estab: 1966. Circ: 127,000. Pays on publication. Buys one-time rights. Phone queries OK. Submit seasonal/holiday material 4-6 months in advance. Photocopied submissions OK. SASE. Reports in 4-6 weeks. Sample copy 50¢; free writer's guidelines.
Nonfiction: How-to (catch more fish, bag more game, improve equipment, etc.); informational; photo feature and technical. Buys 130 mss/year. Query or send complete ms. Length: 1,000-1,500 words maximum. Pays $80-150.
Photos: Purchased with accompanying ms. Captions required. Uses 8x10 b&w glossies; prefer Kodachrome II 35mm. Send prints or transparencies. Offers no additional payment for photos accepted with accompanying ms.

WESTERN WASHINGTON FISHING HOLES, Snohomish Publishing Company Inc., 114 Avenue C, Snohomish WA 98290. (206)568-4121. Editors: Milt Keizer, Terry Sheely, John Thomas. For anglers from 8-80, whether beginner or expert, interested in the where-to and how-to of Washington fishing. Magazine published every two months; 52 pages. Estab: 1974. Circ: 3,200. Pays on publication. Buys first North American serial rights. Submit seasonal/holiday material 30-60 days in advance. SASE. Reports in 3 weeks. Free sample copy and writer's guidelines.
Nonfiction: How-to (angling only); informational (how-to). Buys 8-12 mss/year. Query. Length: 800-1,200 words. Pays $25-60.
Photos: Purchased with accompanying ms. Captions required. Send prints. Buys 5x7 b&w

glossies or 35mm color transparencies with article. Offers no additional payment for photos accepted with accompanying ms. Model release required.
Fillers: How-to (only). Buys 4-6 fillers/year. Query. Pays $10 maximum.
For '78: "Would like to see some pieces on striped bass, shad fishing at mouth of Columbia River and Olympic Peninsula steelheading."

Martial Arts

AMERICAN JUDO, United States Judo Association, 6417 Manchester Ave., St. Louis MO 63139. Managing Editor: Jack Murray. Emphasizes Judo for a readership of judo instructors, teen-agers, and young adults. Bimonthly tabloid; 20 pages. Estab: 1960. Circ: 20,000. Pays on publication. Buys all rights, but may reassign following publication. Phone queries OK. Submit seasonal/holiday material 3 months in advance. Photocopied submissions OK. SASE. Reports in 3 weeks. Sample copy 50¢; free griter's guidelines.
Nonfiction: How-to (technical articles on technique or officiating); and photo feature (minimum of 6 photos). Buys 3 mss/year. Query. Length: 750-1,000 words. Pays $15-25.
Photos: Purchased with accompanying ms. Captions required. Uses 5x7 or larger b&w glossies. Total purchase price for ms includes payment for photos.
Columns/Departments: "Champions in Review" (a personality profile of an outstanding competitor). Buys 1/issue. Query. Length: 500-750 words. Pays $10-20. Open to suggestions for new columns/departments.

BLACK BELT, Rainbow Publications, Inc., 1845 W. Empire, Burbank CA 91504. (213)843-4444. Editor-in-Chief: Han Kim. Emphasizes martial arts for both practitioner and layman. Monthly magazine; 72 pages. Estab: 1961. Circ: 75,000. Pays on publication. Buys all rights. Submit seasonal/holiday material 6 months in advance. Simultaneous and photocopied submissions OK. SASE. Reports in 4 weeks. Free sample copy.
Nonfiction: Expose, how-to, informational, interview, new product, personal experience, profile, technical and travel. Buys 6 mss/issue. Query or send complete ms. Length: 100-1,000 words. Pays 4¢-10/word.
Photos: Purchased with or without accompanying ms. Captions required. Send transparencies. Pays $4-7 for 5x7 or 8x10 b&w or color transparencies. Total purchase price for ms includes payment for photos. Model release required.
Fiction: Historical. Buys 1 ms/issue. Query. Pays $35-100.
Fillers: Send fillers. Pays $5 minimum.

KARATE ILLUSTRATED, Rainbow Publications, Inc., 1845 W. Empire Ave., Burbank CA 91504. (213)843-4444. Editor-in-Chief: Han Kim. Emphasizes Karate and Kung Fu. Monthly magazine; 64 pages. Estab: 1969. Circ: 67,000. Pays on publication. Buys all rights. Submit seasonal/holiday material 6 months in advance. Simultaneous and photocopied submissions OK. SASE. Reports in 4-6 weeks. Free sample copy.
Nonfiction: Expose; historical; how-to; informational; interview; new product; personal experience; personal opinion; photo feature; profile; technical and travel. Buys 6 mss/issue. Query or submit complete ms. Pays $35-150.
Photos: Purchased with or without accompanying ms. Submit 5x7 or 8x10 b&w or color photos. Total purchase price for ms includes payment for photos.
Columns/Departments: Reader's Photo Contest and Calendar. Query. Pays $5-25. Open to suggestions for new columns/departments.
Fiction: Historical. Query. Pays $35-150.
Fillers: Newsbreaks. Query. Pays $5.

OFFICIAL KARATE, 351 W. 54th St., New York NY 10019. Editor: Al Weiss. For karatemen or those interested in the martial arts. Established in 1968. Monthly. Circulation: 100,000. Rights purchased vary with author and material; generally, first publication rights. Buys 60 to 70 mss a year. Payment on publication. Will send free sample copy to writer on request. Will consider photocopied submissions. Reports on material accepted for publication in 1 month. Returns rejected material within 2 weeks. Query first or submit complete ms. Enclose S.A.S.E.
Nonfiction and Photos: "Biographical material on leading and upcoming karateka, tournament coverage, controversial subjects on the art ('Does Karate Teach Hate?', 'Should the Government Control Karate?', etc.) We cover the 'little man' in the arts rather than devote all space to established leaders or champions; people and happenings in out-of-the-way areas along with our regular material." Informational, how-to, interview, profile, spot news. Length: 1,000 to 3,000 words. Pays $50 to $150. B&w contacts or prints. Pays $5.

Miscellaneous

BACKPACKER, 65 Adams St., Bedford Hills NY 10507. Editor-in-Chief: Lionel A. Atwill. Managing Editor: Ellen Ramirez. Emphasizes backpacking, cross country skiing, nature photography for backpackers and wilderness enthusiasts. Bimonthly magazine; 100 pages. Estab: 1973. Circ: 120,000. Pays either on acceptance or within 90 days of acceptance. Buys all rights, but may reassign following publication. Submit seasonal/holiday material 1 year in advance. Previously published submissions OK. SASE. Reports in 4 weeks. Sample copy $2.50; writer's guidelines for SASE.

Nonfiction: How-to (repair and make equipment); historical (mountain profiles; conservationists who have made a mark on the world); interview (wildlife photographers, leaders in conservation or land management); new product (prefer short release, not article); nostalgia (backpacking in the past, Indians, early explorers, etc.); personal experience (trips that may illustrate universal points); photo feature; and profile (mountains). Buys 5 mss/issue. Query. Length: 500-3,000 words. Pays $50-500.

Photos: Purchased with or without accompanying ms or on assignment. Captions required. Query. Pays $5-100 for 8x10 b&w photos; $25-200 for 35mm and larger transparencies. Model release usually required.

Columns/Departments: Movable Feasts (recipes for backpackers); Equip & Go (making your own equipment); and Write Time (reader action on conservation issues that may effect backpackers). Buys 2/issue. Submit complete ms. Length: 25-200 words. Pays $5.

How To Break In: "We receive some 3,000 freelance submissions a year. Many of them are rejected because the author is not familiar with *Backpacker* magazine. Generalized articles just don't work here; our readers are terribly sophisticated backpackers and can spot writing by someone who does not intimately know his subject within ten seconds. Articles on trips must have an angle. We don't want to see diaries: where you went, what you took, when you ate, etc."

BACKPACKING JOURNAL, Davis Publications, 229 Park Ave. S., New York NY 10003. (212)673-1300. Editor-in-Chief: Andrew J. Carra. Managing Editor: Lee Schreiber. Emphasizes hiking and backpacking. Quarterly magazine; 96 pages. Estab: 1975. Circ: 45,000. Pays on acceptance. Buys all rights, but may reassign following publication. Submit seasonal/holiday material 4-6 weeks in advance. SASE. Reports in 2 months. Sample copy $1.60.

Nonfiction: Expose (government, parks service, trail organizations); historical (biographies of conservationists, etc.); how-to; humor; informational; interview; new product; personal experience; personal opinion; profile; technical; travel; and equipment. Buys 12-15 mss/issue. Length: 500-3,000 words. Pays $50-250.

Photos: Purchased with or without accompanying ms. Query or send transparencies. Uses 8x10 b&w glossies or 35mm transparencies. Pays $200-250 for cover. Offers no additional payment for photos accepted with accompanying ms.

Columns/Departments: Opinion. Buys 2 mss/issue. Query. Length: 1,000-2,000 words. Pays $150-200.

Fillers: Jokes, gags, anecdotes, newsbreaks, and short humor. Query. Length: 100-500 words. Pays $25-50.

COLEMAN'S CAMPING ANNUAL, Aqua-Field Publications, Inc., 342 Madison Ave., New York NY 10017. (212)682-0220. Editor and Publisher: Stephen Ferber. For outdoor sportsmen. Magazine; 100 pages. Established in 1974. Annually. Circulation: 150,000. Buys all rights, but may reassign rights to author after publication. Buys all of its mss from freelance writers. Pays on acceptance or on publication; varies with contributor. Will send sample copy to writer for 50¢. No photocopied or simultaneous submissions. Submit seasonal material (spring) during prior winter. Reports in 2 weeks. Query first or submit complete ms. Enclose S.A.S.E.

Nonfiction and Photos: Original how-to articles on camping. Must be good writing with an investigative approach to journalism. No "me and Joe" stories. All material must be interesting and authoritative, with an original approach and good photos. Length: 1,500 to 2,500 words. Pays $150 to $250. Nuts & Bolts column pieces on new techniques or how-to's. Length: 1,000 words. Pays $100. No additional payment for b&w glossies (8x10) used with mss. Pays $10 to $15 for b&w's purchased without mss. Pays $50 for color transparencies (35mm or 4x5) purchased with mss.

GAMEKEEPER AND COUNTRYSIDE, Gilbertson & Page Limited, Corry's, Roestock Lane, Colney Heath, St. Albans, Hertfordshire AL4 0QW England. Editor-in-Chief: Edward Askwith. Emphasizes field sports for gamekeepers, members of shooting syndicates, landowners, farmers, fly fishermen, coarse fishermen, naturalists, conservationists, fox hunters, harriers, beaglers. Monthly magazine; 36 pages. Estab: 1896. Circ: 6,478. Buys first British serial rights. Simultaneous and photocopied submissions OK. Previously published work OK. SAE and International Reply Coupons. Reports in 2-3 weeks. Sample copy $1.

Nonfiction: How-to articles (field sports techniques, keepering techniques, shoot management); informational (natural history case histories and experiences); interviews. Buys 180-200 mss/year. Submit nonreturnable photocopy of ms (not the original). Length: 400-1,300 words. Pays $8-50.

Photos: Purchased with or without ms. Pays $5-10 for half-plate or 8x10 b&w glossy. Model release required.

GEORGIA SPORTSMAN MAGAZINE, Box 741, Marietta GA 30061. Editor: John Spears. Emphasizes hunting and fishing and outdoor recreational opportunities in Georgia. Monthly magazine; 64 pages. Estab: 1976. Circ: 30,000. Pays on publication. Phone queries OK. Submit seasonal/holiday material 4 months in advance. Simultaneous, very legible photocopied and previously published submissions OK. Source must be identified for previously published work. SASE. Reports in 4 weeks. Sample copy $1; free writer's guidelines.

Nonfiction: Expose, how-to, informational; historical (acceptable on a very small scale) humor; interviews with fishermen or hunters known statewide; nostalgia (antique weapons such as percussion guns) and articles concerning major legislation and environmental issues affecting Georgia. Length 1,000-2,000 words. Pays 7¢/word minimum.

Photos: B&w and color purchased with or without mss or on assignment. Pays $100 for cover use.

Fillers: Newsbreaks (explanation of source must accompany them) and illustrations. "We are always in the market for illustrations depicting outdoor scenes. Send samples." Newsbreak length: 500 words average. Pays 7½¢/word minimum.

HANDBALL, United States Handball Association, 4101 Dempster St., Skokie IL 60076. (312)673-4000. Editor-in-Chief: Terry Muck. For active handball players from 15 to 70. Bimonthly magazine; 70 pages. Estab: 1951. Circ: 15,000. Pays on publication. Buys all rights, but may reassign following publication. Phone queries OK. Submit seasonal material 2 months in advance. SASE. Reports in 2 months.

Nonfiction: How-to (instructional); historical (I remember so and so); humor (funny experiences with handball); and personal opinion (handball improvement). "Our biggest demand is for instructional articles, with first person types second." Buys 1-3 mss/issue. Send complete ms. Length: 1,000-2,000 words. Pays $100-200.

Photos: Purchased without accompanying ms. Captions required. Send prints. Pays $10-50 for any size b&w glossies. Total purchase price for ms includes payment for photos. No additional payment for photos accepted without accompanying ms.

HOCKEY ILLUSTRATED, 333 Johnson Ave., Brooklyn NY 11206. Editor: Jim McNally. For young men and women interested in hockey. Estab: 1960. Published 6 times a year. Circ: 150,000. Buys all rights, but will reassign rights to author after publication. Buys 65 mss a year. Payment on acceptance. Will not consider photocopied submissions. Submit seasonal material 3 months in advance. Reports immediately on material accepted for publication. Returns rejected material in 1 month. Query first. Enclose S.A.S.E.

Nonfiction and Photos: Controversial hockey pieces, player profiles, in-depth interviews, humor; informational, personal experience, historical, expose, personal opinion. Length: 1,500 to 2,000 words. Pays $100 to $150. Pays $10 for 8x10 glossy b&w purchased with ms, without ms or on assignment. Captions required. Color: pays $150 for cover; $50 to $75 for inside use for 35mm.

Fiction: Fantasy, humorous, historical. Length: 500 to 1,000 words. Pays $50 to $75.

How To Break In: "We have a new department called The Man Behind the Player, which is, of course, the player himself, but viewed from some interesting off-the-ice aspect of his life. The idea is that he's not all ice and skates and sticks and pucks. Recent pieces we've done have been about physical ailments the fans would not know about, religious devotion, a player who preferred to play Lacrosse. These are only 360 words each and I want to run four an issue, so it's an ideal slot for a newcomer. A brief query, just a note really, on the player and what the special angle is, will be enough. We pay approximately $25 for each item. Another opportunity for the new writer is our news item department, Off the Ice. We use lots of little bits and pieces here for which there is no pay. But I'll be grateful and willing to work with a writer who comes in this way."

PADDLE WORLD, 370 Seventh Ave., New York NY 10001. Managing Editor: Marilyn Nason. For amateur paddle tennis players. Magazine; 36 or more pages. Estab: 1975. Published 5 times/year. Circ: 15,000. Buys all rights. Buys 5 mss/year. Pays on publication. Will send sample copy to writer for $1.25. Reports in 8 to 10 weeks. Query first, briefly stating credentials. Enclose S.A.S.E.

Nonfiction: Articles on interesting installations, tournaments, "names" who play platform tennis for fun. Length: open. Pays $2 per printed page minimum.

RACING PIGEON PICTORIAL, Coo Press, Ltd., 19 Doughty St., London, England WCIN 2PT. Editor-in-Chief: Colin Osman. Emphasizes racing pigeons for "all ages and occupations; generally 'working class' backgrounds, both sexes." Monthly magazine; 32 pages. Estab: 1970. Circ: 13,000. Pays on publication. Buys all rights, but may reassign following publication. Submit seasonal/holiday material 3 months in advance. Photocopied and previously published submissions OK. Reports in 5 weeks. Sample copy $2; free writer's guidelines.

Nonfiction: Michael Shepard, Articles Editor. How-to (methods of famous fanciers, treatment of diseases, building lofts, etc.); historical (histories of pigeon breeds); informational (practical information for pigeon fanciers); interview (with winning fanciers); and technical (where applicable to pigeons). Buys 4 mss/issue. Submit complete ms. Length: 6,000 words minimum. Pays £5/page minimum.

Photos: Rick Osman, Photo Editor. Purchased with or without accompanying ms or on assignment. Captions required. Send 8x10 b&w glossy prints or 2¼x2¼ or 35mm color transparencies.

RODEO NEWS, Box 8160, Nashville TN 37207. (615)226-1633. Managing Editor: Marty Martins. Emphasizes the rodeo industry as a sport, business and entertainment. Basically, a young, rural audience actively involved in rodeo as contestants, livestock contractors, producers, managers, sponsors, and rodeo fans. Monthly (except for bimonthly publication in December/January) magazine; 48 pages. Estab: 1961. Circ: 12,500. Pays on publication. Buys all rights, but may reassign following publication. Phone queries OK. Simultaneous and photocopied submissions OK. SASE. Reports in 3 weeks. Free sample copy and editorial guidelines.

Nonfiction: Exposes (on the government and management of rodeo at all levels of competition); how-to (on any contest event or other aspect of rodeo. A recent 4-part series covered athletic taping for the rodeo cowboy); informational (concerning rodeo as a sport, business or entertainment); historical. ("Our 'Rodeoing Back Then' monthly feature covers early day rodeo, circa 1900-1949"); humor (funny incidents happening at or around rodeos); interviews (with current champions or other top contenders or with rodeo businessmen, i.e., stock contractors, sponsors, etc.); photo features (less emphasis on copy length; more on visuals, covering rodeo or related activities). Buys about 25 mss/year. Send complete ms. Length: 400-2,000 words. Pays 3¢/word.

Photos: Purchased with or without mss. Send prints. Pays $3 for 8x10 or 5x7 b&w glossies. Pays $5 for 8x10 color prints.

Fillers: Find the Word rodeo-related puzzles. Buys about 11/year. Length: 40-200 words. Pays 2¢/word or $10 flat fee.

How To Break In: "A freelancer does not have to be a former rodeo contestant to break into this market, but some knowledge of the sport and its jargon (as for any sports coverage) is important. Our April issue is devoted to 'Women in Rodeo' each year, which may provide a slant for some writers."

RODEO SPORTS NEWS, 2929 W. 19th Ave., Denver CO 80204. Dditor: Randy Witte. For avid fans of professional rodeo. Tabloid newspaper; 16 to 32 pages. Established in 1952. Annual. Circulation: 31,000. Buys all rights, but will reassign rights to author after publication. Buys 8 to 10 mss a year. Mostly staff-written. Pays on 15th of month following publication. Will send free sample copy to writer on request. Reports in 2 weeks. Query first or submit complete ms. Enclose S.A.S.E.

Nonfiction and Photos: "We are almost completely staff-written, but we do buy freelance articles on individual members of the Professional Rodeo Cowboys Association, Inc.; biographical sketches on their rodeo careers. Keep in mind that we are highly specialized." Length: 6 to 7 typewritten, double-spaced pages. Pays minimum of $20. Uses 1 color photo per issue. Prefers transparencies. Pays $25. Pays $100 for color in the annual edition. Only 8x10 b&w glossies are considered. Pays $30. Captions required.

RUNNER'S WORLD MAGAZINE, World Publications, Box 366, Mountain View CA 94040. (415)965-8777. Editor-in-Chief: Joe Henderson. Managing Editor: Kevin Shafer. Emphasizes the sport of running, primarily long distance running; for avid runners, coaches, equipment manufacturers and salesmen, race promoters, etc. Monthly magazine; 85 pages. Estab: 1966. Circ: 63,000. Pays on publication. Buys all rights, but may reassign following publication.

Submit seasonal/holiday material 3-4 months in advance. Previously published submissions OK. SASE. Reports in 1 week. Free sample copy and writer's guidelines.

Nonfiction: Expose; historical (where-are-they-now articles, primarily); how-to (improving one's own running and health); humor; informational; inspirational; interview (Q&A format); personal experience; personal opinion (featured in column "Runner's Forum"); technical and profile. Buys 15-20 mss/issue. Query. Length: 1,000 words maximum. Pays $20-50.

Photos: Photos purchased with or without accompanying ms or on assignment. Pays $5-25 for 5x7 or 8x10 b&w glossies; $50-100 for 35mm or 2¼x2¼ color transparencies. Query and send photos. Total purchase price for ms includes payment for photos.

Columns/Departments: Runner's Forum (1,000 words maximum) and Technical Tips (short how-to articles, 1,000 words maximum). Buys 8 mss/issue. Pays $10 flat fee/ms.

SIGNPOST MAGAZINE, 16812 36 Ave., W., Lynnwood WA 98036. Editor-in-Chief: Louise Marshall. About hiking, backpacking, and other muscle-powered travel sports of interest to residents of the Pacific Northwest and Western Canada. Published in half-tab format in newsprint. Established in 1966. Bimonthly. Will consider any rights offered by author. Buys 10 mss a year. Payment on publication. Will send free sample copy to writer on request. Will consider photocopied submissions. Reports in 3 weeks. Query first or submit complete ms. Enclose S.A.S.E.

Nonfiction and Photos: "Most material is donated by subscribers or is staff written. Payment for purchased material is low, usually less than $10. Part of the reward has to be a sense of helping *The Signpost.*"

SKATEBOARD WORLD, Hi-Torque Publications, 16200 Ventura Blvd., Encino CA 91436. (213)981-2317. Editor-in-Chief: Jill Sherman. Primarily for skateboard enthusiasts. Monthly magazine; 160 pages. Estab: 1977. Circ: 250,000. Pays on publication. Buys all rights. Phone queries OK. Submit seasonal/holiday material 3 months in advance. SASE. Reports in 4 weeks.

Nonfiction: How-to (skateboard tricks); informational (skateboarding); interview (skaters out of southern California area); new product; nostalgia (riders from clay-wheel days); photo feature (especially out of California or USA locales); and profile (pro-am riders). Buys 72 mss/year. Submit complete ms. Length: 200 words. Pays $25-100.

Photos: Purchased with or without accompanying ms or on assignment. Captions required. Send contact sheet, prints, or transparencies. Pays $10-40 for any size b&w photo; $15-40 for 35mm Kodacolor transparencies. Model and photographer release required.

Columns/Departments: New Faces (any riders or personalities new to the skateboard world). Buys 36/year. Length: 200-1,000 words. Pays $25-100. Open to suggestions for new columns/departments.

SOUTHERN OUTDOORS MAGAZINE, B.A.S.S. Publications, 1 Bell Rd., Montgomery AL 36117. (205)277-3940. Editor-in-Chief: Bob Cobb. Managing Editor: Tom Gresham. Emphasizes outdoor activities such as hunting and fishing. Published 8 times/year; 80 pages. Estab: 1940. Circ: 175,000. Pays on acceptance. Buys all rights, but may reassign following publication. Phone queries OK. Submit seasonal/holiday material 6 months in advance. SASE. Reports in 4 weeks. Free sample copy and writer's guidelines.

Nonfiction: How-to (on fishing or hunting that will educate the reader without being dry); informational (conservation issues, where-to, equipment); interview ("Question Box" feature in each issue). Buys 70 mss/year. Query. Length: 1,800-2,500 words. Pays $250-400.

Photos: Purchased with or without accompanying ms. Captions required. Pays $10 minimum for 8x10 b&w glossies or 35mm and larger color transparencies. Send contact sheet or transparencies. Offers no additional payment for photos accepted with accompanying ms. Total price for ms includes payment for photos.

Columns/Departments: "Question Box"—interviews with sportsmen on successful fishing, hunting and/or camping techniques. Buys 6 mss/year. Send complete ms. Length: 800-1,500 words. Pays $100-150. Open to suggestions from freelancers for new columns/departments; address to Tom Gresham.

Fillers: Newsbreaks. Send fillers. Length: 100-500 words. Pays $10-50.

How To Break In: Superficial writing won't cut it here. Research the subject well, work the story over several times, shoot good photos and you have a good chance of selling *Southern Outdoors.*

Rejects: Travel articles not pertaining specifically to outdoor activities. "Me and Joe" stories. Inform the reader; don't entertain him. Articles without photos. Good photos are a *must!*

STRENGTH & HEALTH Magazine, S&H Publishing Co., Inc., Box 1707, York PA 17405. (717)848-1541. Editor-in-Chief: Bob Hoffman. Managing Editor: John Grimek. Emphasizes Olympic weightlifting and weight training. Bimonthly magazine; 74 pages. Estab: 1932. Circ: 100,000. Pays on publication. Buys all rights, but may reassign following publication. Submit seasonal/holiday material 4-5 months in advance. SASE. Reports in 2 months. Free sample copy.
Nonfiction: Bob Karpinski, Articles Editor. How-to (physical fitness routines); interview (sports figures); and profile. Buys 15 mss/year. Submit complete ms. Length: 1,500-3,000 words. Pays $50-100.
Photos: Sallie Sload, Photo Editor. Purchased with accompanying ms. Captions required. Query. Pays $5-10 for b&w glossy or matte finish; $50-100 for 2x2 color transparencies (for cover). Model release preferred.
Columns/Departments: Robert Denis, Department Editor. Barbells on Campus (weight training program of college or university; captioned photos required, at least one photo of prominent building or feature of campus; In the Spotlight (profile of a championship caliber weightlifter, training photos as well as "behind the scenes" shots). Buys 1-2/issue. Submit complete ms. Length: 1,500-2,500 words. Pays $50-100.

TRACK & FIELD NEWS, Box 296, Los Altos CA 94022. Managing Editor: Garry Hill. For anyone interested in the sport of track and field. Magazine; 64 (8x10) pages. Established in 1947. Irregular monthly; 9 times first half of year. Circulation: 25,000. Not copyrighted. Buys 10 to 20 mss a year. Pays on publication. Will send free sample copy to writer on request. Will consider photocopied submissions and (if advised) simultaneous submissions. Reports on material accepted for publication in 10 days. Returns rejected material as soon as possible, if requested. Query first. Enclose S.A.S.E.
Nonfiction and Photos: Generally, news-oriented material (current track news), with features angled to those who are making the news and current issues. Knowledge of the sport is almost mandatory. "We are very factually oriented and have an audience that is composed of the cognoscenti. Be realistic. Tell it like it is." Informational, how-to, personal experience, interview, profile, historical, think pieces, personal opinion, technical articles. Length: 500 to 4,000 words. Pays minimum of $10 per published page. B&w (8x10) glossies purchased without ms. Pays $5-15. Captions required.

THE WORLD OF RODEO, Rodeo Construction Agency, Box 660, Billings MT 59103. Editor-in-Chief: Dave Allen. "We reach all of these facets of rodeo: All-girls rodeo, little britches and high school rodeo, Canadian rodeo, oldtimers rodeo. Audience age: 17-60." 18 times/year. Tabloid; 16-20 pages. Estab: 1977. Circ: 15,000. Buys all rights. Phone queries OK. Submit seasonal/holiday material 1 month in advance. Simultaneous and previously published submissions OK. SASE. Reports in 2-3 weeks. Free sample copy and writers' guidelines.
Nonfiction: Expose (personality); historical (oldtimers and famous rodeo animals); humor (pertaining to cowboys); informational (reports on current rodeo events); interview (with controversy or strong message); photo feature (emphasis on quality rodeo action and/or drama); profile (short in-depth sketch of person or persons); Buys 15/issue. Query or submit complete ms. Length: 500-1,000 words. Pays $15-100.
Photos: Purchased with or without mss. Captions required. Send prints. Pays $5/8x10 b&w glossy with good contrast; $35-50/2¼x2¼, 35mm or 8x10 matte or glossy with good color balance.
Poetry: Free verse and light verse. Limit submissions to batches of 3. Length: 15-25 lines. Pays $5-10.

Mountaineering

CLIMBING MAGAZINE, Box E, 310 Main Street, Aspen CO 81611. (303)925-3414. Editor: Michael Kennedy. For "mountaineers of the U.S. and Canada." Published 6 times a year. Established in 1970. Circulation: 3,000. Rights purchased vary with author and material. Buys 48 mss a year. Payment on publication. Will send free sample copy to a writer on request. Will consider photocopied submissions. Reports in 2 weeks. Query first or submit complete ms. Enclose S.A.S.E.
Nonfiction and Photos: General subject matter concerns "technical rockclimbing, mountaineering, and ski touring. Articles can be highly technical—our audience is select. Articles with general appeal also sought with a conservationist slant. We try to be a forum for all mountaineers. We would like to see articles on rock preservation, women in climbing, and attitudes toward mechanization of mountaineering." Buys informational, how-to, personal experience, interviews, profile, inspirational, humor, historical, think, personal opinion, photo, travel,

mountaineering book reviews, spot news, new product and technical articles. "Regular column that seeks freelance material is called 'Routes and Rocks,' which consists of personal accounts of climbs." Length: 500 to 4,000 words. Pays about $4 to $45, according to length. Photos purchased with or without mss, on assignment; and captions are optional. Pays $5 per photo used; $30 for cover. Either b&w or color transparencies (35mm or 2¼x2¼) accepted. Magazine does b&w conversions from transparencies.

Fiction: Buys experimental, mainstream, adventure, humorous, historical, condensed novels, and serialized novels. Length: 1,000 to 3,000 words. Pays $5 minimum.

Poetry: Buys traditional and avant-garde forms, and free, blank, and light verse. Pays $5 minimum.

MOUNTAIN GAZETTE, 2025 York St., Denver CO 80205. (303)388-0974. Editor: Gaylord T. Guenin. A general magazine on mountain subjects from outdoor activities to politics and the environment. Also an emphasis on travel to remote mountain regions of the world. Monthly magazine; 36-42 pages (9x14). Estab: 1966. Circ: 17,500. Buys first North American serial rights. Pays on acceptance. Will send sample copy with guidelines for $1. Reports in 2 weeks to several months. Strongly urges query letter but will look at ms. Enclose S.A.S.E.

Nonfiction: "We're interested in articles on almost any mountain subject, from mountaineering to politics to bluegrass music, but seek the unusual in treatment. Length varies from 1,500 to 6,000 words, but will occasionally consider longer manuscripts." Pays $50 to $300.

Photos: Purchased with or without mss. B&w 8x10 prints only. "Our photography is more often artistic than journalistic." Pays $10-75.

Fiction: Length 500 to 8,000 words. Payment $50 to $300.

Poetry: Traditional forms, free verse, and avant-garde forms. Should relate, however metaphorically, to the mountains. Pays $1 a line.

Skiing and Snow Sports

CHICAGOLAND SNOWMOBILER, Multi-Media Publications, Inc., 222 W. Adams St., Chicago IL 60606. (312)236-5550. Managing Editor: Paul Hertzberg. Emphasizes snowmobiling. Published 6 times yearly (Sept.-Feb.). Tabloid; 32 pages. Estab: 1972. Circ: 19,000. Pays on publication. Buys all rights, but may reassign to author following publication. Phone queries OK. Submit seasonal/holiday material 2 months in advance. Free sample copy.

Nonfiction: How-to (technical features on repairing snowmobiles), humor (winter related), travel (snowmobile travel features in the Midwest). Buys 15 mss/year. Submit complete ms. Length: 1,000-5,000 words. Pays 90¢/column inch.

NORTHWEST SKIER, 903 N.E. 45th St., Seattle WA 98105. (206)634-3620. Publisher: Ian F. Brown. Biweekly. Circ: 15,000. Not copyrighted. Pays on publication. Will send sample copy to writer for 50¢. Reports on submissions immediately. Enclose S.A.S.E. for return of submissions.

Nonfiction: Well-written articles of interest to winter sports participants in the Pacific Northwest and Western Canada, or pieces of a general scope which would interest all of the winter sporting public. Character studies, unusual incidents, slants and perspectives. All aspects of winter sports covered in magazine; not just skiing. Must be authoritative, readable and convincingly thorough. Humor accepted. "Politics are open, along 'speaking out' lines. If you're contemplating a European trip or one to some other unusual recreation area, you might query to see what current needs are. When submitting article, consider pictures to supplement your text." Length: 250 words and up. Pays $10 minimum per article.

Photos: Purchased both with mss and with captions only. Wants strong graphics of winter sports scene. Doesn't want posed shots. 8x10 glossies, both b&w and color. Furnish separations. Pays $2 minimum per photo.

Fiction: Uses very little and use depends on quality and uniqueness. Will use humorous fiction and short-shorts. Length: 250 words and up. Pays 75¢ per column inch.

POWDER MAGAZINE, Surfer Publications, Box 1028, Dana Point CA 92629. (714)496-6424. Editor-in-Chief: Neil Stebbins. Magazine; 5 times/year; 100 pages. Estab: 1972. Circ: 100,000. Pays on publication. Buys first North American serial rights. Phone queries OK. Submit seasonal/holiday material 2-3 months in advance. Simultaneous, photocopied, and previously published submissions OK. SASE. Reports as soon as possible. Free sample copy and writers' guidelines.

Nonfiction: Expose (inside insights into personalities, organizations, their motives and actions); how-to (emphasize advanced skiing techniques); informational (preferably personality oriented or illustrated by adventures); historical (again, only if the work has personality interest to supplement facts and dates); humor (satire, hyperbole, fiction, whatever, but must be in good taste); inspirational (not religious, but philosophic or psychologically stimulating concept articles will be considered); interviews (even with unknown personalities or local characters, as well as ski celebrities); personal opinion (guest editorials are a regular feature); travel (as long as it's not dry, stuffy, bored, or typically informative); new product (short news release items will be considered if products are exceptional); photo features (high quality slides and b&w will be accepted); and technical articles (only if interesting for an expert audience), Buys 5-10/issue. Query or submit complete ms. Length: 300-3,000 words. Pays 6-10¢/word.

Photos: Purchased with or without ms or on assignment. Query or send contact sheets or negatives or transparencies. Pays $200 for b&w and 35mm slides or large format transparencies.

Fiction: "Our fiction requirements correspond to our nonfiction types, with emphasis on originality, style, competence, interest and applicability to our format and involvement with skiing." Buys 2/year. Query or submit complete ms. Length: 250-3,000 words. Pays 6-10¢/word.

Fillers: Clippings, jokes, gags, anecdotes, newsbreaks, short humor. Buys 2/year. Query or send complete ms. Length: 1,000 words maximum. Pays 6-10¢/word.

SKATING, United States Figure Skating Association, Sears Crescent, Suite 500, City Hall Plaza, Boston MA 02108. (617)723-2290. Editor-in-Chief: Gregory R. Smith. Managing Editor: Roy Winder. Monthly magazine; 56 pages. Estab: 1923. Circ: 26,500. Pays on publication. Buys all rights. Phone queries OK. Submit seasonal/holiday material 3 months in advance. Photocopied and previously published submissions OK. SASE. Reports in 1 month. Free sample copy and writer's guidelines.

Nonfiction: Historical; how-to (photograph skaters, train, exercise); humor; informational; interview; new product; personal experience; personal opinion; photo feature; profile (background and interests of national caliber skaters); technical and competition reports. Buys 4 mss/issue. Query or send complete ms. Length: 500-1,000 words. Pays $25.

Photos: Valerie Bessette, Photo Editor. Photos purchased with or without accompanying ms. Pays $5 for 8x10 or 5x7 b&w glossies and color slides. Query.

Columns/Departments: European Letter (skating news from Europe); Ice Abroad (competition results and report from outside of U.S.); Book Reviews; People; Club News (what individual clubs are doing) and Music column (what's new and used for music for skating). Buys 2 mss/issue. Query or send complete ms. Length: 100-500 words. Pays $25. Open to suggestions for new columns/departments.

Fillers: Newsbreaks, puzzles (skating related) and short humor. Buys 1 filler/issue. Query. Length: 50-250 words. Pays $25.

SKI, 380 Madison Ave., New York NY 10017. (212)687-3000. Editor: Richard Needham. 7 times/year, September through spring. Buys first-time rights in most cases. Pays on publication. Reports within 1 month. Enclose S.A.S.E.

Nonfiction: Prefers articles of general interest to skiers, travel, adventure, how-to, budget savers, unusual people, places or events that reader can identify with. Must be authoritative, knowledgeably written, in easy, informative language and have a professional flair. Cater to middle to upper income bracket readers who are college graduates, wide travelers. Length: 1,500 to 2,000 words. Pays $100 to $250.

Fiction: Fiction is seldom used, unless it is very unusual. Pays $100 to $250.

Photos: Buys photos submitted with manuscripts and with captions only. Good action shots in color for covers. Pays minimum $150. B&w photos. Pays $25 each; minimum $150 for photo stories. (Query first on these.) Color shots. Pays $50 each; $100 per page.

How To Break In: "We're putting out a *Guide to Cross Country Skiing* for which we will be needing individual text and photo stories on cross-country ski touring and centers. We're looking for 1,000 to 2,000 words on a particular tour and it's an excellent way for us to get acquainted with new writers. Could lead to assignments for *Ski*. Photos are essential. Another possibility is our monthly column, Ski People, which runs 300- to 400-word items on unusual people who ski and have made some contribution to the sport. Another column, Personal Adventure, was begun recently. For this feature, we welcome 2,000- to 2,500-word 'It Happened to Me' stories of unique (humorous, near disaster, etc.) experiences on skis. Payment is $100."

SKIERS DIRECTORY, Ski Earth Publications, Inc., 38 Commercial Wharf, Boston MA 02110. Editor-in-Chief: Neil R. Goldhirsh. Managing Editor: Carol Silverblatt. Emphasizes skiing for travelers. For male and female traveling skiers age 20-50. Annual magazine; 296 pages. Estab: 1973. Circ: 97,000. Pays on publication. Buys all rights, but may reassign following publication. Photocopied submissions OK. SASE. Reports in 2 weeks. Sample copy $2.50. Free editorial guidelines.

Nonfiction: General interest articles for traveling skiers; special aspect of a resort, etc. How to do anything regarding skiing (how to take a ski vacation; how to repair your skis, etc.) Informational articles on skiing resorts, races. Personality interviews. Personal experience articles dealing with memorable skiing. Travel articles on new places to see and explore. Query or submit complete ms. Length: 1,500 words minimum. Pays $350 maximum.

Photos: No additional payment for b&w and color used with mss. Model release required.

How To Break In: "Since our magazine is published only once a year, every article must be very special. Any story that is very well-written, informative, with a new angle, will receive top consideration."

SKIING MAGAZINE, Ziff-Davis Publishing Co., 1 Park Ave., New York NY 10016. Editor-in-Chief: Alfred H. Greenberg. Managing Editor: Robert Morrow. Published 7 times/year (September-March). Magazine; 175 pages. Estab: 1949. Circ: 450,000. Pays on acceptance. Buys all rights. Submit seasonal/holiday material 3 months in advance. Simultaneous and photocopied submissions OK. SASE. Sample copy $1.

Nonfiction: "This magazine is in the market for any material of interest to skiers. Material must appeal to and please the confirmed skier. Much of the copy is staff prepared, but many freelance features are purchased provided the writing is fast-paced, concise, and knowledgeable." Buys 10 mss/year. Submit complete ms. Length: 1,500-3,000 words. Pays 10¢/word.

Photos: Ed Sobel, Photo editor. Purchased with or without accompanying ms or on assignment. Send contact sheet or transparencies. Pays $100/full page for 8x10 b&w glossy or matte photos; $125/full page for 35mm kodachrome transparencies. Total purchase price for ms includes payment for photos. Model release required.

SNOTRACK, Market Communications, Inc., 225 E. Michigan Ave., Milwaukee WI 53202. (414)276-6600. Editor-in-Chief: Bill Vint. Emphasizes snowmobiling for "almost exclusively northern snowbelt residents; a pickup truck and C.B. radio group." Published 6 times yearly (October-April) magazine; 56 pages. Estab: 1971. Circ: 60,000. Pays on publication. Buys one-time rights. Phone queries OK. Submit seasonal/holiday material 60-90 days in advance. SASE. Reports in 2-3 weeks. Free sample copy and writer's guidelines.

Nonfiction: How-to (make your own accessories, repairs); informational (great places to go snowmobiling); interview (prominent snowmobile personalities and their influence in the sport); photo feature (snowmobile adventures; how-to-make-it; other activities); and technical (how a snowmobile works, how to make it work better). Buys 2-3/issue. Query. Length: 1,500-3,000 words. Pays $50-150.

Photos: Purchased with or withour accompanying, ms or on assignment. Captions required. Send contact sheet and negatives. Pays $15-25 for 8x10 b&w glossies; $50-100 for 35mm or larger color transparencies.

Fillers: Clippings. Buys 10-20/year. Pays $1.

SNOW GOER, 1999 Shepard Rd., St. Paul MN 55116. (612)437-2536. Editor: Don Rankin. For snowmobilers. Published monthly September through January. Magazine, 60 to 104 pages. Established in 1968. Circulation: 500,000. Buys all rights. Pays on acceptance. Free sample copy. Submit special issue material 4 months in advance. Reports within 2 weeks. Query first or submit complete ms. Enclose S.A.S.E.

Nonfiction and Photos: Features on snowmobiling with strong secondary story angle, such as ice fishing, mountain climbing, snow camping, conservation, rescue. Also uses about 25% mechanical how-to stories, plus features relating to man out-of-doors in winter. "'Me and Joe' articles have to be quite unique for this audience." Length: 5,000 words maximum. Pays $100 to $400. Photos purchased with mss and with captions to illustrate feature articles. 5x7 or larger b&w; 35mm color. Payment usually included in package price for feature.

SNOWMOBILE WEST, 521 Park Ave., Box 981, Idaho Falls ID 83401. Editor: Loel H. Schoonover. For owners of snowmobiles; all ages. Magazine; 48 pages. Estab: 1974. Published four times during winter. Circ: 15,000. Buys first North American serial rights. Buys 10 mss/year. Pays on publication. Free sample copy and writer's guidelines. Reports in 2 months. Query first. Enclose S.A.S.E.

Nonfiction and Photos: Articles about trail riding in the Western U.S.A. Informational, how-to, personal experience, interview, profile, travel. Length: 500 to 2,000 words. Pays 3¢ a word. B&w (5x7 or 8x10) glossies and color transparencies (35mm or larger) purchased with mss. Pays $5 for b&w; $10 for color.

Soccer

SOCCER AMERICA, Box 23704, Oakland CA 94623. (415)549-1414. Editor-in-Chief: Lynn Berling. For a wide range of soccer enthusiasts. Weekly magazine; 32 pages. Estab: 1971. Circ: 6,000. Pays on publication. Buys all rights, but may reassign following publication. Phone queries OK. Submit seasonal/holiday material 14 days in advance. Simultaneous, photocopied and previously published submissions OK. SASE. Reports in 1 month. Free sample copy and writer's guidelines.

Nonfiction: Expose (why a pro franchise isn't working right, etc.); historical; how-to; informational (news features); inspirational; interview; photo feature; profile and technical. Buys 1-2 mss/issue. Query. Length: 200-2,000 words. Pays 1¢/word.

Photos: Photos purchased with or without accompanying ms or on assignment. Captions required. Pays $5-15 for 5x7 or larger b&w glossies. Query. Total purchase price for ms includes payment for photos.

Columns/Departments: Book Reviews. Buys 25 mss/year. Send complete ms. Length: 200-1,000 words. Pays 1¢/word. Open to suggestions for new columns/departments.

How To Break In: "A consistent contributor (stringer) via local or regional news from an area gets most favorable attention."

SOCCER WORLD, Box 366, Mountain View CA 94042. (415)965-8777. Editor: Bob Anderson. For U.S. soccer enthusiasts, including players, coaches, and referees. Predominantly high school players and adult coaches. Monthly magazine; 32 pages. Estab: 1974. Circ: 16,000. Buys all rights, but will reassign rights to author after publication. Buys 75 mss a year. Payment on publication. Will send free sample copy to writer on request. Write for copy of guidelines for writers. Will consider photocopied submissions. No simultaneous submissions. Reports on material accepted for publication within 2 months. Returns rejected material as soon as required. Query first. Enclose S.A.S.E.

Nonfiction and Photos: "Articles are primarily of the how-to variety, but we usually include a personality feature with each issue. The foremost consideration is always practical value, i.e., Can a player, coach, or referee improve his performance through the information presented? We are interested in anything on soccer skills and techniques." Length: 1,000 words. Pays $10 to $25 per published page. Pays $2.50 to $15 for 5x7 (or larger) b&w glossies; snappy contrast. Pays $50 for 35mm (or larger) color transparencies for cover use. Must be high impact and vertical format.

Swimming and Diving

SKIN DIVER, 8490 Sunset Blvd., Los Angeles CA 90069. (213)657-5100. Editor/Publisher: Paul J. Tzimoulis. Circ: 166,000. Buys only 1-time rights. Pays on publication. Acknowledges material immediately. All model releases and author's grant must be submitted with mss. Manuscripts reviewed are either returned to the author or tentatively scheduled for future issue. Time for review varies. Mss considered "accepted" when published; all material held on "tentatively scheduled" basis subject to change or rejection up to time of printing. Submit complete ms. Enclose S.A.S.E.

Nonfiction and Photos: Stories and articles directly related to skin diving activities, equipment or personalities. Features and articles equally divided into following categories: adventure, equipment, underwater photography, wrecks, treasure, spearfishing, undersea science, travel, marine life, boating, do-it-yourself, technique and archaeology. Length: 1,000 to 2,000 words, well illustrated by photos; b&w at ratio of 3:1 to color. Pays $35 per printed page. Photos purchased with mss; b&w 8x10 glossies; color: 35mm, 2¼x2¼, or 4x5 transparencies; do not submit color prints or negatives. All photos must be captioned; marked with name and address. Pays $35 per published page for inside photos; $100 for cover photos.

SURFER, P.O. Box 1028, Dana Point CA 92629. (714)496-5922. Editor: Kurt Ledterman. For late teens and young adults. Slant is toward the contemporary, fast-moving and hard core enthusiasts in the sport of surfing. Bimonthly. Rights purchased vary with author and material. Payment on publication. Sample copy $1. Reports on submissions in 2 weeks. Enclose S.A.S.E.

Nonfiction: "We use anything about surfing if interesting and authoritative. Must be written from an expert's viewpoint. We're looking for good comprehensive articles on any surfing spot —especially surfing in faraway foreign lands." Length: open. Pays 5-10¢/word.

Photos: Buys photos with mss or with captions only. Likes 8x10 glossy b&w proofsheets with negatives. Also uses expert color 35mm and 2¼ slides carefully wrapped. Pays $10-40/b&w; $25-125/35mm transparency.

SWIMMING WORLD, 8622 Bellanca Ave., Los Angeles CA 90045. (213)641-2727. Editor: Robert Ingram. For "competitors (10 to 24), plus their coaches, parents, and those who are involved in the enjoyment of the sport." Estab: 1959. Monthly. Circ: 34,000. Buys all rights, but may reassign rights to author after publication. Buys 10 to 12 mss a year. Payment on publication. Will send free sample copy on request. Reports in 1 to 2 months. Query first. Enclose S.A.S.E.

Nonfiction: Articles of interest to competitive swimmers, divers and water poloists, their parents and coaches. Can deal with diet, body conditioning, medicine, as it applies to competitive swimming. Nutrition, stroke and diving techniques, developments in pool purification. Psychology and profiles of athletes. Must be authoritative. Does not want results of competitions. Length: 1,500 words maximum. Pays $50 maximum.

Photos: Photos purchased with mss. Does not pay extra for photos with mss. 8x10 b&w only. Also photos with captions. Pays $2 to $3.

THE WATER SKIER, Box 191, Winter Haven FL 33880. (813)324-4341. Editor: Thomas C. Hardman. Published 7 times/year. Circ: 18,500. Buys North American serial rights only. Buys limited amount of freelance material. Pays on acceptance. Will send free sample copy to a writer on request. Reports on submissions within 10 days. Enclose S.A.S.E.

Nonfiction and Photos: Occasionally buys exceptionally offbeat, unusual text/photo features on the sport of water skiing. Pays $25 and up per article.

Tennis

TENNIS, 495 Westport Ave., Norwalk CT 06856. Publisher: Howard R. Gill, Jr. Editor: Shepherd Campbell. For persons who play tennis and want to play it better. Monthly magazine. Estab: 1965. Circ: 400,000. Buys all rights. Pays on publication. SASE.

Nonfiction and Photos: Emphasis on instructional and reader service articles, but also seeks lively, well-researched features on personalities and other aspects of the game, as well as humor. Query. Length varies. Pays $100 minimum per article, considerably more for major features. $15 to $50 per 8x10 b&w glossy or color transparency.

TENNIS ILLUSTRATED, The Action Group, 4222 Campus Dr., Newport Beach CA 92660. Editor-in-Chief: Lois Wayne. Emphasizes tennis and racquet sports. Monthly magazine; 80 pages. Estab: 1972. Circ: 600,000. Pays 2 weeks after publication. Buys all rights, but may reassign following publication. Submit seasonal/holiday material 3 months in advance. Simultaneous and photocopied submissions OK. SASE. Reports in 2 months. Writer's guidelines $1.

Nonfiction: Exposes (public court construction; money in tennis organizations); historical (development of tennis); how-to (technical advice on phases of tennis); humor; informational (travel); all types of interviews; profiles, photo features and technical articles. Submit complete ms. Length: 300-1,500 words. Pays 10¢/word.

Photos: Purchased without mss. Captions required. Pays $25 maximum for 8x10 b&w glossy prints, or contact sheet and negative; $25-60 for 35mm color slides. Model released required.

Columns/Departments: Material related to the health aspects of the game; travel; the psychology of the game and how it affects a tennis player; coverage of tennis programs. Buys 25/year. Submit complete ms. Pays 10¢/word. Open to suggestions for new columns/departments.

Fiction: Must be pertinent to tennis or athletics and have strong human interest. Buys 2/issue. Submit complete ms. Length: 500-800 words. Pays 10¢/word.

Fillers: Clippings, jokes, gags, anecdotes, newsbreaks, short humor related to tennis. Buys 12/year. Pays 10¢/word.

TENNIS USA, Chilton Co., Chilton Way, Radnor PA 19089. (215)687-8200. Official publication of the United States Tennis Association for members and those with a serious interest in the sport. Editor: Bob Gillen. Monthly magazine. Estab: 1937. Circ: 100,000. Buys all rights. Pays on acceptance. Will send free sample copy to writer on request. Query first. Enclose S.A.S.E.

Nonfiction and Photos: "Writer must have in-depth knowledge of the subject necessary to do an interesting, innovative piece." Features and news stories on tennis events and personalities; instructional articles on how to improve skills; testing and review articles on new equipment, court construction and other technical aspects of the sport; fashion and travel features. Pays $100 to $300.

Teen and Young Adult Publications

The publications in this category are for young people aged 12 to 26. Publications aimed at 2- to 12-year-olds are classified in the Juvenile category.

ALIVE! FOR YOUNG TEENS, P.O. Box 179, St. Louis MO 63166. (314)371-6900. Editor: Darrell Faires. A publication of the Christian Church (Disciples of Christ) for youth in junior high school. Monthly. Circulation: 19,000. Not copyrighted. Payment on publication. Will send sample copy to writer for 25¢. Submit seasonal material 9 months in advance. "Youth are strongly encouraged to be 'co-creators' of the magazine by their contribution of articles, poems, etc." Reports usually within 4 weeks. Enclose S.A.S.E.
Nonfiction: "We seek to affirm and celebrate the aliveness of young teens, and to call them to new 'alive-ability.' We seek to stimulate the thinkings, feelings and doings of youth so that they come alive to the creative possibilities of themselves and their world. Emphasis on first-person articles, articles about outstanding youth, or youth programs, projects and activities (with photos)." Length: 1,500 words maximum. Pays 2¢ a word.
Photos: 8x10 b&w glossies preferred; mostly of youth (preferably junior high age) and youth activities. Pays $5 to $10.
Fiction: Should be related to real life issues of young teens. "We don't like fiction which is too moralistic or preachy; characters who do not come across as real, believable, contemporary persons." Length: 1,500 to 2,000 words. Pays 2¢ per word.
Poetry: Personal insight, affirmation and humorous verse. 16 lines maximum. Pays 25¢ per line.
Fillers: Short humor and puzzles pay 2¢ per word or $3 to $10 per item.

AMERICAN GIRL MAGAZINE, Girl Scouts USA, 830 3rd Ave., New York NY 10022. Editor-in-Chief: Cleo Mitchell Paturis. Monthly magazine; 72 pages. Estab: 1924. Circ: 650,000. Pays on acceptance. Buys all rights for one year. Submit seasonal/holiday material 4 months in advance. SASE. Reports in 2 weeks. Free sample copy and writer's guidelines.
Nonfiction: "We like articles about teens or subjects that teens would be interested in." Query. Length: 500-1,200 words. Pays $75-150.
Fiction: Mainstream; mystery; and adventure. Length: 800-1,200 words. Pays $75-150.
How To Break In: "This is a very tight market now, money is low. Any writer who's trying to make it in this tight economy should think to himself/herself whether the story might be available to me through some other channel. Writers query me all the time about material I can get through the Girl Scout's PR people free. I'm still buying several freelance pieces per issue, but you've got to provide me with something that I wouldn't have any other way of knowing about, and that wouldn't be available to me through some other source."

AMERICAN NEWSPAPER CARRIER, American Newspaper Boy Press, 915 Carolina Ave., N.W., Winston-Salem NC 27101. Editor: Charles F. Moester. Buys all rights. Pays on acceptance. Will send list of requirements on request. Reports in 10 days. Enclose S.A.S.E.
Fiction: Uses a limited amount of short fiction, 1,500 to 2,000 words. It is preferable, but not required, that the stories be written around newspaper carrier characters. Before writing this type of fiction for this market, the author should consult a newspaper circulation manager and learn something of the system under which the independent "little merchant" route carriers operate generally the country over. Stories featuring carrier contests, prize awards, etc., are not acceptable. Humor and mystery are good. Stories are bought with the understanding that *American Newspaper Carrier* has the privilege of reprinting and supplying the material to other newspaper carrier publications in the U.S., and such permission should accompany all mss submitted. Pays $15 and up for stories.

THE BLACK COLLEGIAN, 3217 Melpomene Ave., New Orleans LA 70125. (504)522-2372. Editor: Kalamu Ya Salaam. For black college students and recent graduates with an interest in black cultural awareness, sports, fashion, news, personalities, history, trends, current events, and job opportunities. Published bimonthly during school year; 60-page magazine. Estab: 1970. Circ: 188,000. Rights purchased vary with author and material. Usually buys first North American serial rights. Buys 15 mss a year. Payment on publication. Will send free sample copy to writer on request. Write for copy of guidelines for writers. Will consider photocopied and simultaneous submissions. Submit special material (Career Issue in September; Travel Issue in January; History Issue in November; Jobs Issue in March; Entertainment Issue in May) 2 months in advance. Returns rejected material in 1 month. Query first. Enclose S.A.S.E.
Nonfiction and Photos: Material on careers, sports, fashion, black history, news analysis. Arti-

cles on problems and opportunities confronting black college students and recent graduates. Informational, personal experience, profile, inspirational, humor, think pieces, nostalgia, personal opinion, travel. Length: 1,000 to 3,000 words. Pays $20 to $50. Department and column material includes book and record reviews, how-to, interviews, historical, expose. Length: 2,000 words. Pays $20. B&w photos or color transparencies purchased with or without mss. 5x7 preferred. Pays $5 for b&w; $10 to $50 for color.

BOYS' LIFE, Boy Scouts of America, National Headquarters, North Brunswick NJ 08902. Editor: Robert E. Hood. For boys 8 to 18. Monthly. Circulation: 2,000,000. Publishes 200-240 freelance mss/year, almost all assigned on the basis of a query. Pays on acceptance. Send queries to Articles Editor; fiction mss to Fiction Editor. Enclose S.A.S.E.
Nonfiction and Photos: "Study several issues of the magazine carefully. We assign columns of 350-600 words; major articles of 1,000-1,500 words; photo features with 300 words of text accompanying an adequate selection of b&w prints or color transparencies; short how-to features with photos or drawings. Payment for columns and how-to features is $150 minimum. Major articles payment is $350 minimum. Photo rates are A.S.M.P. and up, depending upon difficulty of assignment. Only the best and most positive material interests us."
Fiction: "Interesting plot, sound characterization, conflict, action, humor, or suspense and clear, literate writing interest us. Most stories deal with boys in their teens, but main characters may be men of any age when the story situation demands. Stories must be factually accurate. Short stories from 2,500 to 3,200 words. Short-shorts of 1,000 words. Payment for fiction is $350 minimum."

BREAD, 6401 The Paseo, Kansas City MO 64131. Editor: Dan Ketchum. Teens' magazine with a point of view that attempts to mold as well as reflect the junior and senior high school Christian teen, sponsored by the youth organization of the Church of the Nazarene. Monthly. Pays on acceptance. Accepts simultaneous submissions. Buys second rights. Will send free sample copy and editorial specifications sheet on request. Reports on submissions in 6 weeks. Enclose S.A.S.E.
Nonfiction: Helpful articles in the area of developing the Christian life; first person, "this is how I did it" stories about Christian witness. Length: up to 1,500 words. Articles must be theologically acceptable and make the reader want to turn over the page to continue reading. Should not be morbid or contain excessive moralizing. Looking for fresh approach to basic themes. The writer should identify himself with the situation but not use the pronoun "I" to do it. Also go easy on "you" (unless the second approach is desired). The moral or application should not be too obvious. Also needs articles dealing with doctrinal subjects, written for the young reader. Pays a minimum of 2¢ per word. Works 6 months ahead of publication.
Photos: 8x10 b&w glossies of teens in action. Payment is $10 and up. Also considers photo spreads and essays. Uses 1 color transparency per month for cover.
Fiction: "Adventure, school, and church-oriented. No sermonizing." Length: 1,500 words maximum. Payment is a minimum of 2¢ a word.

CAMPUS AMBASSADOR MAGAZINE (CAM), 1445 Boonville Ave., Springfield MO 65802. Editor: Dave Gable. For students on secular campuses only. Published by Christ's Ambassadors Department, Assemblies of God. Published 6 times a year (October, November, January through April); magazine, 16 pages, (7x10). Circulation: 12,000. Buys all rights, but will reassign rights to author after publication. Buys 6 mss a year. Payment on acceptance or on publication. "It varies according to type of material." Will send free sample copy to writer on request. Submit Christmas and Easter material 6 months in advance. Will consider photocopied submissions. Reports in several weeks. Enclose S.A.S.E.
Nonfiction: College-age slanted, religious nonfiction on personal evangelism, missions, Bible doctrines, Christianity and the sciences, devotional material. 400 to 1,200 words. Pays 2½-3½¢/word.
Photos: Purchased with mss. Prefers 5x7 b&w glossy. Payment varies according to quality and use.
Poetry: Must have spiritual significance and collegiate relevance. Very little used. Length: 50 lines maximum. Pays 20¢ per line.

CAMPUS NEWS, Box 614, Corte Madera CA 94925. Editor: Wm. Whitney. A biweekly newspaper aimed at the university student. Estab: 1971. Circ: 25,000. Rights purchased vary with author and material. May buy all rights, but may reassign rights to author after publication; first North American serial rights, first serial rights, second serial (reprint) rights or simultaneous rights. Buys 30-40 mss/year. Pays on publication. Sample copy 25¢. Photocopied submissions OK. Submit seasonal material 4 months in advance. Reports in 2-4 weeks. Query first for columns, reviews and fiction. Submit complete ms for nonfiction. SASE.

Nonfiction and Photos: Department Editors: Paul R. Williams (articles); R.W. Whitney (photos). "Reviews of records and films, how-to articles, columns and articles telling of activities or happenings of interest to the college student. Concerts and events such as film festivals, summer activities; travel. Approach should be casual, open, pointed. We do not want to see the radical diatribe type of article. We prefer exposes to be tempered with fact and logic." Length: 200-1,500 words. Pays 25¢-60¢/column inch. 8x10 b&w glossy photos purchased with or without mss. Captions required. Pays $2.

Fiction: Department Editor: R.W. Whitney. Experimental, mainstream. Length: 500-1,500 words. Pays 10¢-60¢/column inch.

Poetry and Fillers: Department Editors: Paul R. Williams (poetry); R.W. Whitney (fillers). Traditional forms, blank verse, light verse, free verse, avant-garde forms. Length: 24 lines maximum. Newsbreaks, puzzles, jokes, short humor. Length: 200 words maximum. Pays 10¢-60¢/column inch.

CHRISTIAN ADVENTURER, Messenger Publishing House, Box 850, Joplin MO 64801. (417)624-7050. Editor-in-Chief: Roy M. Chappell, D.D. Managing Editor: Mrs. Marthel Wilson. A denominational Sunday school take-home paper for teens, 13-19. Quarterly; 104 pages. Circ: 3,500. Pays quarterly. Buys simultaneous, second serial (reprint) and one-time rights. Submit seasonal/holiday material 1 year in advance. Photocopied and previously published submissions OK. SASE. Reports in 4-6 weeks. Sample copy 50¢. Free writer's guidelines.

Nonfiction: Historical (related to great events in the history of the Church); informational (explaining the meaning of a Bible passage or a Christian concept); inspirational; nostalgia; and personal experience. Buys 13-20 mss/issue. Send complete ms. Length: 500-1,000 words. Pays ½¢/word.

Photos: Photos purchased with accompanying ms. Pays $2 for any size b&w glossies.

Fiction: Adventure; historical; religious and romance. Buys 13-20 mss/issue. Length: 800-2,000 words. Pays ½¢/word.

Fillers: Puzzles (must be Bible based and require no art). Buys 13-20 fillers/issue. Length: 200-500 words. Pays ½¢/word.

CHRISTIAN LIVING FOR SENIOR HIGHS, David C. Cook Publishing Co., 850 N. Grove, Elgin IL 60120. (312)741-2400. Editor-in-Chief: Marlene D. LeFever. "Geared toward senior high teens who attend Sunday school." Quarterly magazine; 8 pages. Estab: 1895. Pays on acceptance. Buys all rights. Phone queries OK. Submit seasonal or holiday material 18 months in advance. SASE. Reports in 3-5 weeks. Free sample copy and writer's guidelines.

Nonfiction: How-to (youth projects), historical (with religious base), humor (from Christian perspective), inspirational (non-preachy) interview (some connection to teens and Christianity), personal experience (Christian), and photo feature (Christian subject). Buys 20 mss/issue. Submit complete ms. Length: 1,200-1,800 words. Pays $60-75.

Photos: Kathleen Johns, Photo Editor. Photos purchased with or without accompanying ms or on assignment. Send contact sheet, prints or transparencies. Pays $10-35 for 8½x11 b&w photos; $50 minimum for color transparencies. Model release required.

Fiction: Adventure (with religious theme), historical (with Christian perspective), humorous, mystery, and religious. Buys 5 mss/issue. Submit complete ms. Length: 1,200-1,800 words. Pays $60-75. "No preachy experiences."

CIRCLE K MAGAZINE, 101 E. Erie St., Chicago IL 60611. Executive Editor: Mike Wujcik. "Our readership consists almost entirely of college students interested in the concept of voluntary service. They are politically and socially aware and have a wide range of interests." Published 5 times yearly. Magazine; 16 pages. Estab: 1967. Circ: 11,000. Pays on acceptance. Buys first North American serial rights. Submit seasonal/holiday material 4 months in advance. SASE. Reports in 4 weeks. Free sample copy and writer's guidelines.

Nonfiction: Informational (general interest articles on any area pertinent to concerned college students); interview (notables in the fields of sports, entertainment, politics); and travel (from a student's angle; how to budget, what to take, where to go, etc.). Buys 7-10 mss/year. Query or submit complete ms. Length: 1,500-2,500 words. Pays $50-125.

Photos: Purchased with accompanying ms. Captions required. Query. Total purchase price for ms includes payment for photos.

How To Break In: "This can be a good market for beginning young writers who can really write. We can't compete with the big magazines in payment, but we give the articles good graphic treatment and are willing to form continuing relationships with good, reliable writers."

CO-ED, Scholastic Magazines, Inc., 50 W. 44th St., New York NY 10036. For girls and boys ages 13 to 18. Monthly. Buys all rights. Pays on acceptance. Will send free sample copy on request. Query first. Enclose S.A.S.E.

Fiction: "Stories dealing with problems of contemporary teenagers. (We prefer stories about older teenagers, 16, 17, 18 years old.) Emphasis on personal growth of one or more characters as they confront problems with friendships, dating, family, social prejudice. Suggested themes: finding identity, reconciling reality and fantasy, making appropriate life decisions. Although we do *not* want stories with a preachy, moralistic treatment, we do look for themes that can be a starting point for class discussion, since our magazine is used as a teaching tool in home economics classrooms. Try for well-rounded characters and strong, logical plots. Avoid stereotyped characters and cliched, fluffy romances. If girls with conventional 'feminine' interests are portrayed, they should nonetheless be interesting, active and realistic people. Humor, sports and adventure stories in colorful local or foreign settings." Length: 3,000 words maximum. Pays $300 maximum.

EVANGEL, Free Methodist Publishing House, 999 College Ave., Winona Lake IN 46590. (219)267-7161. Editor-in-Chief: Vera Bethel. Audience is 65% female, 35% male; married, 25-31 years old, mostly city dwellers, high school graduates, mostly non-professional. Weekly magazine; 8 pages. Estab: 1897. Circ: 35,000. Pays on acceptance. Buys simultaneous, second serial or one-time rights. Submit seasonal/holiday material 3 months in advance. Simultaneous and previously published submissions OK. SASE. Reports in 4 weeks. Free sample copy and writer's guidelines.

Nonfiction: Interview (with ordinary person who is doing something extraordinary in his community, in service to others); profile (of missionary or one from similar service profession who is contributing significantly to society); personal experience (finding a solution to a problem common to many; coping with handicapped child, for instance, or with a neighborhood problem. Story of how God-given strength or insight saved a situation). Buys 100 mss/year. Submit complete ms. Length: 300-1,000 words. Pays 2¢/word.

Photos: Purchased with accompanying ms. Captions required. Send prints. Pays $5-10 for 8x10 b&w glossy prints; $2 for snapshots.

Fiction: Religious themes dealing with contemporary issues dealt with from a Christian frame of reference. Story must "go somewhere." Buys 50 mss/year. Submit complete ms. Length: 1,200-1,800 words. Pays 2¢/word.

Poetry: Free verse, haiku, light verse, traditional, religious. Buys 50/year. Limit submissions to batches of 5-6. Length: 4-24 lines. Pays 35¢/line.

How To Break In: "Seasonal material will get a second look (won't be rejected so easily) because we get so little."

EXPLORING, Boy Scouts of America, Route 130, North Brunswick NJ 08902. Editor: Dick Pryce. Executive Editor: Annette Stec. For "ages 14 to 21. High school, some college age. Members of co-ed BSA Exploring program. Interests are education, colleges, careers, music, sports, cars, fashions, food, camping, backpacking." Published every 2 months. Rights purchased vary with author and material. May buy first North American serial rights or first serial rights. Buys about 40 mss a year. Pays on acceptance. Free sample copy and writer's guidelines if large SASE is enclosed. Reports in 2 weeks. Query. SASE.

Nonfiction and Photos: Interested in material slanted toward the interests of their audience, plus profiles on young adults in the news, government and entertainment personalities, consumer information. "We prefer to feature young adults involved in the BSA Exploring program over those involving non-Explorers, but do not eliminate the latter. Write *for* young adults, not at them. Keep articles exciting and informational. Support opinions with quotes from experts. We prefer not to see anything on hang gliding, martial arts, air ballooning or gliding." How-to, personal experience, interviews, profiles, humor, historical and travel. Length: 750-2,000 words. Payment is $150 to $500. B&w and color photos purchased with mss or on assignment.

Fiction: Department Editor: Annette Stec. Mainstream, mystery, suspense, adventure, western, science fiction; humorous and historical fiction. Length: 1,000 to 2,500 words. Pays $150 to $500.

FACE-TO-FACE, 201 Eighth Ave. S., Nashville TN 37202. (615)749-6219. Editor: Sharilyn S. Adair. For United Methodist young people, ages 15 to 18 inclusive. Published by the Curriculum Resources Committee of the General Board of Discipleship of The United Methodist Church. Quarterly magazine; 48 pages. Established in 1968. Circulation: 30,000. Rights purchased vary with author and material. Buys first North American serial rights, or simultaneous rights. Buys about 8 mss a year. Payment on acceptance. Submit Christmas, Easter and summertime material 8 to 9 months in advance. Reports in 1 to 2 months. Query first, if you prefer, by outlining any article or story ideas. Enclose S.A.S.E.

Nonfiction: "Our purpose is to speak to young person's concerns about their faith, their purpose in life, their personal relationships, goals, and feelings. Articles and features (with photos) should be subjects of major interest and concern to high school young people. These include home and family life, school, extracurricular activities, vocation, etc. Satires, lampoons, related to the themes of an issue are also used." Length: 1,800 words maximum. Pays 3¢ a word minimum.

Photos: Uses 8x10 b&w glossies with high impact and good contrast. Pays $15 for one-time use of b&w. "We buy stock photos and those especially taken to illustrate articles."

Fiction: Must deal with major problems and concerns of older teens—such as finding one's own identity, dealing with family and peer-group pressures, and so forth. No straight moral fiction or stories with pat answers or easy solutions are desired. Prefer unresolved endings. Story must fit themes of issue. No serials. Length: 2,500 to 3,000 words. Pays 3 ¢ per word.

Poetry: Related to the theme of an issue. Free verse, blank verse, traditional and avant-garde forms. Length: 10 to 150 lines. Pays 25¢ per line.

FREEWAY, Scripture Press, 1825 College Ave., Wheaton IL 60187. Publication Editor: Anne Harrington. For "Christian high school and college Sunday school class kids." Established in 1943. Weekly. Circulation: 80,000. Buys all rights, "but passes along reprint fees to author, when material is picked up after publication." Buys 100 mss a year. Will send free sample copy to a writer on request. Write for copy of guidelines for writers. Will not consider photocopied submissions. Reports on material accepted for publication in 4 to 6 weeks. Returns rejected material in 2 to 3 weeks. Query first or submit complete ms. Enclose S.A.S.E.

Nonfiction and Photos: "Mostly person-centered nonfiction with photos. Subject must have had specific encounter with Christ. Direct tie-in to faith in Christ. No simply religious or moral stories; subjects must be specifically Christ-centered. Christian message must be woven naturally into a good, true, dramatic, human interest story. Current interest is in the occult, Satanism, witchcraft and battles by Christians against grief, tragedy, danger, etc." Thought articles on Biblical themes. Length: 500 to 1,500 words. Pays $15 to $75. Pays $3-25 for 5x7 and 8x10 b&w photos.

Fiction: Same themes, lengths and rate of payment as nonfiction.

GROUP, Thom Schultz Publications, Box 481, Loveland CO 80537. (303)669-3836. Editor-in-Chief: Thom Schultz. For members and leaders of high-school-age Christian youth groups; average age 16. Tabloid, published 8 times a year; 24 pages. Estab: 1974. Circ: 10,000. Pays on publication. Buys all rights, but may reassign following publication. Phone queries OK. Submit seasonal/holiday material 5 months in advance. Simultaneous, photocopied and previously published submissions OK. SASE. Reports in 3-4 weeks. Free sample copy and writer's guidelines.

Nonfiction: How-to (fund-raising, membership building, worship, games, discussions, activities, crowd breakers, simulation games); informational; (drama, worship, service projects); inspirational (issues facing young people today); interview and photo feature (group activities). Buys 3 mss/issue. Query. Length: 500-3,000 words. Pays 1¢/word and up.

Photos: Photos purchased with or without accompanying ms or on assignment. Captions required. Pays $2.50-25 for 8x10 b&w glossies and 35mm color transparencies.

Columns/Departments: Try This One (short ideas for games; crowd breakers, discussions, worships, fund raisers, service projects, etc.). Buys 6 mss/issue. Send complete ms. Length: 500 words maximum. Pays $5. Open to suggestions for new columns/departments.

Fiction: Religious (believable stories relating to youth groups). Also scripts for skits and miniplays. Buys 2 mss/year. Query or send complete ms. Length: 500-3,000 words. Pays 1¢/word and up.

For '78: Special Easter, Thanksgiving and Christmas issues.

GUIDE, 6856 Eastern Ave., Washington DC 20012. (202)723-3700. Editor: Lowell Litten. A Seventh-Day Adventist journal for junior youth and early teens. Magazine; 32 pages. Established in 1953. Weekly. Circulation: 61,000. Buys first serial rights. Buys about 500 mss/year. Pays on acceptance. Will "occasionally" consider photocopied and simultaneous submissions. Reports in 1 month. Enclose S.A.S.E.

Nonfiction and Poetry: Wants articles and stories of character-building and spiritual value. All stories must be true and include dialogue. Should emphasize the positive aspects of living — faithfulness, obedience to parents, perseverance, kindness, gratitude, courtesy, etc. "We do not use stories of hunting, fishing, trapping or spiritualism." Length: 1,500 to 2,500 words. Pays 2¢

to 3¢. Also buys serialized true stories. Length: 10 chapters. Buys traditional forms of poetry; also some free verse. Length: 4-16 lines. Pays 50¢-$1/line.

HI-CALL, Gospel Publishing House, 1445 Boonville Ave., Springfield MO 65802. (417)862-2791, Ext. 261. Editor-in-Chief: Dr. Charles W. Ford. Managing Editor: Kenneth D. Barney. Sunday school take-home paper for church-oriented teenagers, 12-19. Weekly magazine; 8 pages. Estab: 1954. Circ: 160,000. Pays on acceptance. Buys all rights but may reassign following publication, simultaneous or second serial (reprint) rights. Submit seasonal/holiday material 12 months in advance. SASE. Simultaneous and previously published submissions OK. SASE. Reports in 3 weeks. Free sample copy and writer's guidelines.
Nonfiction: Historical; humor; informational; inspirational and personal experience. "All pieces should stress Christian principles for everyday living." Buys 125 mss/year. Send complete ms. Length: 500-1,000 words. Pays 1-2¢/word.
Photos: Photos purchased with or without accompanying ms or on assignment. Pays $10 for 8x10 b&w glossies; $15-35 for 35mm or 4x5 color transparencies.
Fiction: Adventure (strong Biblical emphasis, but not preachy); humorous; mystery; religious; romance; suspense and western. Buys 130 mss/year. Send complete ms. Length: 1,200-1,800 words. Pays 1-2¢/word.

HIS, 5206 Main St., Downers Grove IL 60515. (312)964-5700. Editor: Linda Doll. Issued monthly from October to June for collegiate students, faculty administrators, and graduate students belonging to the evangelical Christian faith. Buys all rights. Payment on acceptance. Reports within 10 days, or as work permits. Enclose S.A.S.E.
Nonfiction: Articles dealing with practical aspects of Christian living on campus, relating contemporary issues to Biblical principles. Should show relationships between Christianity and various fields of study, Christian doctrine, and missions. Mss up to 1,500 words. Pays 1¢ a word. Reports in 3 months.
Photos and Poetry: Uses b&w singles. Pays $10 per photo. Also uses photo series in which $6 per photo is paid. No color. Rarely accepts illustrated articles. Photos should be original and creative. Poetry occasionally bought. Pays $5 to $10.

IN TOUCH (formerly *Encounter*), Wesleyan Publishing House, Box 2000, Marion IN 46952. For senior teens, ages 15-18. Weekly. Special issues for all religious and national holidays. Not copyrighted. Pays on acceptance. Submit holiday/seasonal material 9 months in advance. SASE. Reports in 6 weeks. Free sample copy.
Nonfiction: Features of youth involvement in religious and social activity; true life incidents and articles on Christian growth. Avoid implied approval of liquor, tobacco, theatres, and dancing. Length: 500-800 words. Pays 2¢/word.
Fiction: Stories with definite Christian emphasis and character-building values, without being preachy. Mystery stories. Setting, plot and action should be realistic. Length: 1,200 words minimum. Pays 2¢/word.
Photos: Purchased with accompanying ms, portraying action or the teenage world, or with seasonal emphasis. Pays $1-10 for 5x7 or 8x11 b&w glossies.
Poetry: Religious and/or seasonal, expressing action and imagery. Length: 4-16 lines. Pays 25¢/line.

JUNIOR BOWLER, 5301 S. 76th St., Greendale WI 53129. (414)421-4700. Official publication of American Junior Bowling Congress. Editor: Marilyn Jeppesen. For boys and girls ages 21 and under. Established in 1946 as *Prep Pin Patter*; in 1964 as *Junior Bowler*. Monthly, November through April. Circulation: 89,000. Buys all rights. Pays on publication. Reports within 10 days. Query first. Enclose S.A.S.E.
Nonfiction and Photos: Subject matter of articles must be based on tenpin bowling and activities connected with American Junior Bowling Congress only. Audience includes youngsters down to 6 years of age, but material should feature the teenage group. Length: 500 to 800 words. Accompanying photos or art preferred. Pays $30 to $100 per article. Photos should be 8x10 b&w glossies related to subject matter. Pays $5 minimum.
How To Break In: "We are primarily looking for feature stories on a specific person or activity. Stories about a specific person generally should center around the outstanding bowling achievements of that person in an AJBC sanctioned league or tournament. Articles on special leagues for high average bowlers, physically or mentally handicapped bowlers, etc. should focus on the unique quality of the league, *Junior Bowler* also carries articles on AJBC sanctioned tournaments, but these should be more than just a list of the winners and their scores. Again, the unique feature of the tournament should be emphasized."

KEYNOTER MAGAZINE, 101 E. Erie St., Chicago IL 60611. (312)943-2300. Ext. 226. Executive Editor: John A. Mars. An organizational publication of Key Club International. For a high school audience, male and female, 15 to 18, members of Key Club, a Kiwanis International sponsored youth organization; service oriented. Published 7 times a year; magazine, 16 pages. Circulation: 90,000. Not copyrighted. Buys about 10 mss a year. Payment on acceptance. Will send free sample copy to writer on request. Prompt reports on material accepted for publication. Returns rejected material in about a month. Query first. Enclose S.A.S.E.

Nonfiction and Photos: "Topical material directed to mature, service-oriented young men and women. We publish articles on current social concerns and entertaining, though not juvenile, articles. Most of our readers are intelligent and leaders in their communities and schools. Articles should be timely and informative, without talking down to the reader. We also use features on concern areas (aging, consumer protection, etc.). All material should be applicable to all geographic areas covered by our magazine. Keep in mind that our audience is Canadian as well as American. We don't take political or religious stands, so nothing in that area, unless it is strictly informational." Length: 1,200 to 2,500 words. Pays $75 minimum. Additional payment is not usually made for b&w photos used with mss. Payment for those purchased on assignment varies with use and quality.

LIVE, 1445 Boonville Ave., Springfield MO 65802. (417)862-2781. Editor: Gary L. Leggett. For young people and adults in Assemblies of God Sunday Schools. Weekly. Special issues during Easter, Thanksgiving, and Christmas use articles of a devotional nature. Circulation: 225,000. Not copyrighted. Buys about 100 mss a year. Payment on acceptance. Will send free sample copy to writer on request. Write for copy of editorial guidelines for writers. Submit seasonal material 12 months in advance. Reports on material within 6 weeks. Enclose S.A.S.E.

Nonfiction and Photos: "Articles with reader appeal, emphasizing some phase of Christian living, presented in a down-to-earth manner. Biography or missionary material using fiction techniques. Historical, scientific or nature material with a spiritual lesson. Be accurate in detail and factual material. Writing for Christian publications is a ministry. The spiritual emphasis must be an integral part of your material." Length: 1,000 words maximum. Pays 1¢ to 2¢ a word, according to the value of the material and the amount of editorial work necessary. Color photos or slides purchased with mss, or on assignment. Pay open.

Fiction: "Present believable characters working out their problems according to Bible principles; in other words, present Christianity in action, without being preachy. We use very few serials, but we will consider 4- to 6-part stories if each part conforms to average word length for short stories. Each part must contain a spiritual emphasis and have enough suspense to carry the reader's interest from one week to the next. Stories should be true to life, but not what we would feel is bad to set before the reader as a pattern for living. Stories should not put parents, teachers, ministers or other Christian workers in a bad light. Setting, plot and action should be realistic, with strong motivation. Characterize so that the people will live in your story. Construct your plot carefully so that each incident moves naturally and sensibly toward crisis and conclusion. An element of conflict is necessary in fiction. Short stories should be written from one viewpoint only." Length: 1,200 to 2,000 words. Pays 1¢ to 2¢ per word.

Poetry: Buys traditional, free, and blank verse. Length: 12 to 20 lines. Pays 20¢ per line.

Fillers: Brief, purposeful, usually containing an anecdote, and always with a strong evangelical emphasis.

LOOKING AHEAD, 850 N. Grove, Elgin IL 60120. (312)741-2400. Editor: Marlene D. LeFever. For junior high school age students who attend Sunday School. Special Christmas, Easter and Thanksgiving issues. Established in 1895. Weekly. Buys all rights, but may reassign rights to author after publication. Buys 50 to 75 mss per year. Pays on acceptance. Will send free sample copy to writer on request. Write for editorial guidelines sheet. Rarely considers photocopied or simultaneous submissions. Submit seasonal material 1 year in advance. Reports on mss accepted for publication in 1½ to 2 months. Returns rejected mss in 3 to 4 weeks. Query first for nonfiction with statement of writer's qualifications. Submit only complete ms for fiction and poetry. Enclose S.A.S.E.

Nonfiction, Fiction and Photos: Photo Editor: William Patton. Wants "very short stories (1,500 to 1,800 words); articles reporting on teen involvement in church/community projects; special how-to mss on earning money, dealing with difficult situations and emotional needs of the age level." All mss should present a Christian approach to life. "Because it is used as part of a dated Sunday school curriculum, articles follow a weekly theme." Pays $60 for nonfiction. Length for fiction: 1,200 to 1,500 words. Pays $60 for fiction. Photos purchased with or without ms or on assignment. Captions optional. Pays $15 for b&w 8x10 glossies. Pays $50 for color transparencies. Color photos rarely used.

THE MODERN WOODMEN, 1701 First Ave., Rock Island IL 61201. (309)786-6481. Editor: Robert E. Frank. For members of Modern Woodmen of America, a fraternal insurance society. Magazine published every 2 months; 24 to 32 pages. Established in 1883. Circulation: 325,000. Not copyrighted. Payment on acceptance. Will send free sample copy to writer on request. Write for copy of editorial guidelines for writers. Will consider photocopied and simultaneous submissions. Reports in 3 to 4 weeks. Submit only complete ms. Enclose S.A.S.E.

Nonfiction, Fiction, Photos, and Poetry: "Nonfiction may be either for children or adults. Fiction should be slanted toward children up to age 16. Our audience is broad and diverse. We want clear, educational, inspirational articles for children and young people. We don't want religious material, teen romances, teen adventure stories." Buys informational, how-to, historical, and technical articles. Length: 1,500 to 2,000 words. Pays $35 per ms. Mainstream, and historical fiction. Length: 1,500 to 2,500 words. Pays $35. B&w photos purchased with ms. Captions optional. Prefers vertical, b&w glossy photos for cover use. Payment varies with quality and need. "Narrative poetry is all we use; we are not in the market for short poems as fillers and we do not have a poet's page. Pay $35 minimum, since we only buy poetry that can be given a full-page treatment."

PROBE, Baptist Brotherhood Commission, 1548 Poplar Ave., Memphis TN 38104. (901)272-2461. Editor-in-Chief: Mike Davis. For "boys age 12-17 who are members of a missions organization in Southern Baptist churches." Monthly magazine; 32 pages. Estab: 1970. Circ: 45,000. Pays on acceptance. Buys one-time rights. Phone queries OK. Submit seasonal/holiday material 6 months in advance. Simultaneous submissions OK. SASE. Reports in 1 month. Free sample copy and writer's guidelines.

Nonfiction: How-to (crafts, hobbies); informational (youth, religious especially); inspirational (personalities); personal experience (any first person by teenagers —especially religious); photo feature (sports, teen subjects). Buys 12 mss/year. Submit complete ms. Length: 500-1,500 words. Pays 2½¢/word.

Photos: Purchased with accompanying ms or on assignment. Captions required. Query. Pays $10 for 8x10 b&w glossy prints. No additional payment for photos accepted with accompanying ms.

PROTEEN, (formerly *Reachout*), Light and Life Press, 999 College Ave., Winona Lake IN 46590. (219)267-7161. Editor-in-Chief: Vera Bethel. Emphasizes Christian living for young teens—ages 12-15. Weekly magazine; 4 pages. Estab: 1950. Circ: 25,000. Pays on acceptance. Buys "any rights the writer offers to sell." Submit seasonal/holiday material 6 months in advance. Simultaneous, photocopied and previously published submissions OK. SASE. Reports in 1 month. Free sample copy and writer's guidelines.

Nonfiction: How-to (hobbies, crafts); informational (nature, animal); historical (short articles on the life of admirable historical characters); inspirational (Christian living, handling personal problems); and personal experience (projects, unusual accomplishments of young people, experiences as a Christian). Buys 1 ms/issue. Submit complete ms. Length: 300-1,000 words. Pays 2¢/word.

Photos: Purchased with or without accompanying ms. Send contact sheet or prints. Pays $10-15 for 8x10 glossy b&w prints.

Fiction: Adventure; historical; mystery; and religious. Buys 1 ms/issue. Submit complete ms. Length: 1,000-1,800 words. Pays 2¢/word.

Fillers: Jokes, gags, anecdotes, word and bible puzzles. Pays 2¢/word.

REFLECTION, Pioneer Girls, Inc., Box 788, Wheaton IL 60187. Editor-in-Chief: Sara Robertson. Managing Editor: Francis Price. Emphasizes Christian education with an emphasis on subjects related to today's girl in today's world. Bimonthly magazine; 32 pages. Estab: 1961. Circ: 12,000. Pays on acceptance. Buys first, second, and simultaneous rights. Submit seasonal/holiday material 6 months in advance. Simultaneous and previously published submissions OK. SASE. Reports in 4 weeks. Sample copy and writer's guidelines $1.

Nonfiction: How-to (crafts geared especially to teenage girls); humor; inspirational; interview; and personal experience. Buys 8 mss/issue. Length: 800-1,500 words. Pays $15-30.

Fiction: Adventure; fantasy; historical; humorous; mystery; religious; romance; and suspense. Buys 12 mss/year. Length: 900-1,500 words. Pays $20-35.

Fillers: Jokes, gags, anecdotes, puzzles, short homor. Buys 12/year. Submit complete ms. Pays $5-15.

SCHOLASTIC SCOPE, Scholastic Magazines, Inc., 50 W. 44th St., New York NY 10036. Editor: Katherine Robinson. Circulation: 1,324,451. Buys all rights. Issued weekly. 4th to 6th grade reading level; 15 to 18 age level. Reports within 4 to 6 weeks. Query first. Enclose S.A.S.E.

Nonfiction and Photos: Articles about teenagers who have accomplished something against great odds, overcome obstacles, performed heroically, or simply done something out of the ordinary. Prefers articles about people outside New York area. Length: 400 to 1,200 words. Payment is $50 per magazine page. Photos purchased with articles. Pays $25 for every photo used.

Fiction and Drama: Problems of contemporary teenagers (drugs, prejudice, runaways, failure in school, family problems, etc.); relationships between people (inter-racial, adult-teenage, employer-employee, etc.) in family, job, and school situations. Strive for directness, realism, and action, perhaps carried through dialogue rather than exposition. Try for depth of characterization in at least one character. Avoid too many coincidences and random happenings. Although action stories are wanted, it's not a market for crime fiction. Looking for material about American Indian, Chicano, Mexican-American, Puerto Rican, and Black experiences among others. Occasionally uses mysteries and science fiction. Length: 400 to 1,200 words. Uses plays up to 3,000 words. Pays $150 minimum, except for short-shorts. Pays $100 for 500 to 600 words.

SEVENTEEN, 850 Third Ave., New York NY 10022. Managing Editor: Ray Robinson. Monthly. Circulation: 1,550,000. Buys all rights for nonfiction and poetry. Buys first rights on fiction. Pays on acceptance. Reports in about 2 weeks. Enclose S.A.S.E.

Nonfiction and Photos: Articles and features of general interest to young women who are concerned with the development of their own lives and the problems of the world around them; strong emphasis on topicality and helpfulness. Send brief outline and query, summing up basic idea of article. Also like to receive articles and features on speculation. Length: 2,000 to 3,000 words. Pays $100 to $500 for articles written by teenagers but more to established adult freelancers. Articles are commissioned after outlines are submitted and approved. Fees for commissioned articles generally range from $500 to $1,350. Photos usually by assignment only. Tamara Schneider, Art Director.

Fiction: Deborah Pines, Fiction Editor. Top-quality stories featuring teenagers—the problems, concerns, and preoccupations of adolescence, which will have recognition and identification value for readers. Does not want "typical teenage" stories, but high literary quality. Avoid oversophisticated material; unhappy endings acceptable if emotional impact is sufficient. Humorous stories that do not condescend to or caricature young people are welcome. Best lengths are 2,500 to 3,000 words. Occasionally accepts 2- or 3-part stories such as mysteries and science fiction with adolescent protagonist and theme. Pays $50 to $300. Conducts an annual short story contest.

Poetry: By teenagers only. Pays $5 to $25. Submissions are non-returnable unless accompanied by S.A.S.E.

How To Break In: "The best way for beginning teenage writers to crack the *Seventeen* lineup is for them to contribute suggestions and short pieces to the Free-For-All column, a literary format which lends itself to just about every kind of writing: profiles, puzzles, essays, exposes, reportage, and book reviews."

THE STUDENT, 127 Ninth Ave. N., Nashville TN 37234. Editor: W. Howard Bramlette. Publication of National Student Ministries of the Southern Baptist Convention. For college students; focusing on freshman and sophomore level. Published 12 times during the school year. Circ: 25,000. Buys all rights. Will buy first rights on request. Payment on acceptance. Will send sample copy to writer on request. Mss should be double spaced on white paper with 70-space line, 25 lines per page. Prefers complete ms rather than query. Reports usually in 6 weeks. Enclose S.A.S.E.

Nonfiction: Contemporary questions, problems, and issues facing college students viewed from a Christian perspective. The need to develop high moral and ethical values. The struggle for integrity in self-concept and the need to cultivate interpersonal relationships directed by Christian love. Length: 1,500 to 1,800 words. Satire and parody on college life, humorous episodes; emphasize clean fun and the ability to grow and be uplifted through humor. Length: 1,500 words maximum. Pays 2½¢ a word after editing with reserved right to edit accepted material.

Poetry: Related to student interests and needs. Length: 30 lines maximum. Pays approximately 35¢ per line.

TEEN MAGAZINE, 8490 Sunset Blvd., Hollywood CA 90069. Editor: Roxanne Camron. For teenage girls. Monthly magazine; 100 pages. Estab: 1957. Circ: 900,000. Buys all rights. Predominantly staff written. Freelance purchases are limited. Reports in 6 to 8 weeks. Enclose S.A.S.E.

Fiction: Department Editor: Kathy McCoy. Stories up to 3,500 words dealing specifically with teenagers and contemporary teen issues. More fiction on emerging alternatives for young women. Experimental, suspense, humorous, and romance. Length: 2,000 to 3,000 words. Pays $100 to $150.

TEENS TODAY, Church of the Nazarene, 6401 The Paseo, Kansas City MO 64131. (816)333-7000. Editor-in-Chief: Dr. Chester Galloway. Managing Editor: Roy F. Lynn. For senior high teens, ages 14-18 attending Church of the Nazarene Sunday school. Weekly magazine; 16 pages. Circ: 67,000. Pays on acceptance. Buys all rights, but may reassign following publication. Submit seasonal/holiday material 10 months in advance. Simultaneous, photocopied and previously published submissions OK. SASE. Reports in 6-8 weeks. Free sample copy and writer's guidelines.
Nonfiction: How-to (mature and be a better person in Christian life); humor (cartoons); personal experience and photo feature. Buys 1 ms/issue. Send complete ms. Length: 500-1,500 words. Pays $10-30.
Photos: Photos purchased with or without accompanying ms or on assignment. Pays $10-25 for 8x10 b&w glossies; $15-50 (sometimes $100) for 8x10 color glossies or any size transparencies. Additional payment for photos accepted with accompanying ms. Model release required.
Columns/Departments: To Be Whole (helping teens be well-rounded persons, build self-worth); Direction (specific instructions gained from a passage of scripture); Last Word (the everyday life of teens—350 words maximum); and Review (review of contemporary youth reading). Buys 2 mss/issue. Send complete ms. Length: 350-1,000 words. Pays 2¢/word. Open to suggestions for new columns/departments.
Fiction: Adventure (if Christian principles are apparent); humorous; religious and romance (keep it clean). Buys 1 ms/issue. Send complete ms. Length: 1,500-2,500 words. Pays 2¢/word.
Poetry: Free verse; haiku; light verse and traditional. Buys 15 poems/year. Pays 20-25¢/line.
Fillers: Puzzles (religious). Buys 15 fillers/year. Pays $5-10.

TIGER BEAT MAGAZINE, 7060 Hollywood Blvd., #800, Hollywood CA 90028. (213)467-3111. Editor: Sharon Lee. For young teenage girls and subteens. Median age: 13. Monthly magazine; 84 (8½x11) pages. Established in 1960. Circulation: 500,000. Buys all rights. Buys 10 mss per year. Payment on acceptance. Will send free sample copy to writer on request. Query first. Enclose S.A.S.E.
Nonfiction and Photos: Stories about young entertainers; their lives, what they do, their interests. Quality writing expected, but must be written with the 12 to 16 age group in mind. Length: depends on feature. Pays $50 to $100. Pays $15 for b&w photos used with mss: captions optional. $50 for color used inside; $75 for cover. 35mm slides preferred.
How To Break In: "We're mostly staff-written; a freelancer's best bet is to come up with something original and exclusive that the staff couldn't do or get."

VENTURE MAGAZINE, Box 150, Wheaton IL 60187. Editor: Paul Heidebrecht. Publication of Christian Service Brigade. For young men 12 to 18 years of age. Most participate in a Christian Service Brigade program. Monthly magazine. Estab: 1959. Circ: 55,000. Rights purchased vary with author and material. Buys all rights, but will sometimes reassign rights to author after publication. Buys 6 mss a year. Payment on publication. Will send sample copy to writer for $1. Submit seasonal material 6 to 7 months in advance. Reports within 6 weeks. Query first. Enclose S.A.S.E.
Nonfiction and Photos: "Family-based articles from boys' perspective; family problems, possible solutions. Assigned articles deal with specific monthly themes decided by the editorial staff. All material has an emphasis on boys in a Christian setting." Length: 400 to 1,200 words. Pays $25 to $75. No additional payment is made for 8x10 b&w photos used with mss. Pays $15 for those purchased on assignment.
Fiction: "Some religious-oriented fiction dealing with religious related experiences or purposes. No far-out plots or trite themes and settings. Length: 800 to 1,200 words. Pays $25-75.

VISIONS, Our Sunday Visitor, Noll Plaza, Huntington IN 46750. (219)356-8400. Editor: Robert P. Lockwood. For Catholic junior high school (age 11 to 14) students of above average intelligence. Magazine; 12 (8½x11) pages. Established in 1974. 27 weeks during the school year. Circ: 42,000. Buys all rights. Will reassign after publication for resale. Buys about 10-20 mss a year. Pays on publication. Will send free sample copy to writer on request. No photocopied or simultaneous submissions. Reports in 3 weeks. Query first or submit complete ms. Enclose S.A.S.E.
Nonfiction: "*Visions* is a Catholic religious educational publication. It is meant to give each

student a knowledge of Catholic beliefs and an understanding of his/her heritage as a Catholic. Though most of our material is catechetically oriented, we do accept profile pieces, articles on liturgy or doctrine applied to the Catholic scene. If you're selling sermons, meditations, or poetry, look elsewhere." Length: 500 to 700 words, "but don't be afraid to go longer if the subject warrants the attention." Pays $30 to $75, depending on length and value.

How To Break In: "Give me a profile piece on a known or unknown Catholic doing some good in this world. Or, give me an article about young Catholics (true to life) and their experiences. Or a good liturgical piece."

WIND, The Wesleyan Church, Box 2000, Marion IN 46952. (317)674-3301, Ext. 146. Executive Editor: David Keith. Managing Editor: Robert E. Black. For teen readers. Monthly newspaper; 8 pages. Circ: 7,000. Buys first rights or second (serial) reprint rights. Buys 15-20 mss/year. Pays on publication. Will send free sample copy to writer on request. Write for copy of guidelines for writers. Will consider photocopied and simultaneous submissions. Submit seasonal material at least 3 months in advance. Reports in 10 days to 2 weeks. Query or submit complete ms. Enclose S.A.S.E.

Nonfiction: "Our publication attempts to promote Bible study, personal piety and aggressive evangelism. We attempt to appeal not only to youth within the church, but also to unchurched youth. We publish short, inspirational articles, full-length articles and features. Themes may include spiritual life, personal problems or areas of concern; personality and character development, relationships with others; moral issues such as drugs, etc.; seasonal, historical and informative articles." Length: 1,000 words maximum. Pays 2¢ a word for first rights; 1¢ a word for second rights.

Fiction: Religious short stories. "We do not use a great amount of fiction, but will occasionally print a piece that fits a theme. Please, no 'easy way out' endings. Be realistic. Even problems that are solved can leave a scar. Sometimes a problem is never solved, but is for the purpose of teaching a lesson. Be honest." Length: 1,000 words maximum. Pays 2¢ a word for first rights; 1¢ a word for second rights.

Poetry: Related to theme. Pays 25¢ a line.

WORKING FOR BOYS, Box A, Danvers MA 01923. Editor: Brother Jerome, C.F.X. For junior high, parents, grandparents (the latter because the magazine goes back to 1884). Quarterly magazine; 28 pages. Estab: 1884. Circulation: 24,258. Not copyrighted. Buys 50 mss a year. Payment on acceptance. Will send free sample copy to writer on request. Submit special material (Christmas, Easter, sports, vacation time) 6 months in advance. Reports in 1 week. Submit only complete ms. Address all mss to the Associate Editor, Brother Alois, CFX, St. John's High School, Main St., Shrewsbury MA 01545. Enclose S.A.S.E.

Nonfiction and Photos: "Conservative, not necessarily religious, articles. Seasonal mostly (Christmas, Easter, etc.). Cheerful, successful outlook suitable for early teenagers. Maybe we are on the 'square' side, favoring the traditional regarding youth manners: generosity to others, respect for older people, patriotism, etc. Animal articles and tales are numerous, but an occasional good dog or horse story is okay. We like to cover seasonal sports." Buys informational, how-to, personal experience, historical and travel. Length: 500 to 1,000 words. Pays 3¢ a word. 6x6 b&w glossies purchased with ms for $10 each.

Fiction: Mainstream, adventure, religious, and historical fiction. Theme: open. Length: 500 to 1,000 words. Pays 3¢ a word.

YOUNG AMBASSADOR, The Good News Broadcasting Association, Inc., Box 82808. Lincoln NE 68501. (402)474-4567. Editor-in-Chief: Melvin A. Jones. Managing Editor: Robert H. Sink. Emphasizes Christian living for church-oriented teens, 12-15. Monthly magazine; 52 pages. Estab: 1946. Circ: 90,000. Buys second serial (reprint) and first North American serial rights. Phone queries OK. Submit seasonal/holiday material 6 months in advance. Previously published submissions OK. SASE. Reports in 3 weeks. Free sample copy and writer's guidelines.

Nonfiction: Historical; how-to (church youth group activities); informational; inspirational; interview; personal experience and photo feature. Buys 2 mss/issue. Query or send complete ms. Length: 500-2,000 words. Pays 3¢/word. "Material that covers social, spiritual and emotional needs of teenagers. Interviews with teens who are demonstrating their Faith in Christ in some unusual way. Biographical articles about teens who have overcome obstacles in their lives."

Photos: Photos purchased with or without accompanying ms. Pays $5-7 for b&w photos; $25-50 for color transparencies. Query. Total purchase price for ms includes payment for photos.

Columns/Departments: Life as a Missionary Kid; Teen Scene (teen activities) and Book Reviews. Buys 2 mss/issue. Query. Length: 300-2,000 words. Pays 3¢/word.

Fiction: Adventure; historical; mystery; religious and suspense. "All submissions must relate to teenagers living the Christian life". Buys 45 mss/year. Query or send complete ms. Length: 500-2,000 words. Pays 3¢/word. "Stories of interest to early teenagers with strong, well-developed plot and a definite spiritual tone. Prefer not to see 'preachy' stories. Seasonal stories needed. Should have a realistic, contemporary setting and offer answers to the problems teens are facing."
Fillers: "Submitted by teens." Jokes and puzzles. Query. Length: 200-750 words. Pays 3¢/word.

YOUNG ATHLETE, Box 513, Edmonds WA 98020. (206)774-3589. Editor-in-Chief: Dan Zadra. Managing Editor: Bob Hinz. Emphasizes youth and amateur sports, recreation and health, ages 10-20. "Also, large peripheral readership of coaches, physical education teachers and athletic directors who work with these athletes." Bimonthly magazine; 76 pages. Estab: 1975. Circ: 175,000. Pays on publication. Buys all rights, but may reassign following publication. Submit seasonal/holiday material 3½ months in advance. Simultaneous, photocopied and previously published submissions OK. SASE. Reports in 5 weeks. Sample copy 50¢. Free writer's guidelines.
Nonfiction: "Interested in any sports-related ms that enlightens, encourages, instructs, challenges or inspires young readers, without preaching or talking down. We cover every sport possible—from marbles to football—from sandlot to the Olympic Games. Want personality features. Length: 250 words for inspirational mss about boys and girls who have achieved in sports at the local level; 800-1,200 words for mss giving insights into the aspirations, philosophies and training techniques of well-known 'Olympic class' amateur athletes; 1,000-1,800 words for mss giving nostalgic glimpses into the early lives, development and eventual rise to fame of today's great professional athletes. Personality features should be liberally spiced with recent quotes from the athlete. How-to mss should be loaded with accurate details. Interested in interpretive articles on new trends in youth or amateur sports; delightful photo stories of little children in various sports; laudatory reports of new and worthwhile sports programs, leagues or organizations for youth." Buys 50 mss/year. Query. Pays $25-200.
Photos: Bob Honey, Photo Editor. Photos purchased with or without accompanying ms. Captions required. Pays $5-15 for b&w photos; $7.50-30 for color photos. Query.
How To Break In: "Writing style should be lively, fast-paced, directly involving and easy to understand. Avoid hero worship, cynicism or 'winning at any cost' philosophy. Our posture: Winning is fine, but participation, personal growth, health, fun and fair play for everyone are what it's all about."

YOUNG MISS, 52 Vanderbilt Ave., New York NY 10017. Editor: Rubie Saunders. Monthly, except June and August, for girls 10 to 14. Buys all rights. Pays on acceptance. Will send editorial requirement sheet to a writer, if S.A.S.E. is enclosed with request. Query on nonfiction. Reports on submissions in 3-4 weeks. All mss must be typed, double-spaced. Enclose S.A.S.E.
Nonfiction: No food, fashion or beauty articles are wanted, but practically everything else goes. Hobbies, unusual projects, self-improvement (getting along with parents, brothers, etc.); how-to articles on all possible subjects. Length: about 1,500 words. Pays $50 minimum. Do not submit illustrations. Rough sketches may accompany a how-to article.
Fiction: "All fiction should be aimed at girls 10 to 14, with the emphasis on the late 12- to 14-year olds. Stories may be set in any locale or time—urban, western, foreign, past, contemporary, or future. Boys may be involved, even in a romantic way, as long as it is tastefully done. Mystery and adventure stories are also welcomed. Stories of today are particularly desirable. Especially interested in fiction with an urban setting dealing with the *real* problems today's young teens face. Overstocked on stories about middle income, small town girls who seem to have no problems greater than getting a date for a school dance or adjusting to a new neighborhood." Length: 2,000 to 2,300 words. Pays $50 minimum.
Fillers: Crossword puzzles and short quizzes on general information and personality subjects. Pays $10 to $25. Occasionally uses how-to fillers; currently overstocked on these.

YOUNG WORLD, The Saturday Evening Post Co., Youth Division, P.O. Box 567B, Indianapolis IN 46206. (317)634-1100. Editor: Julie Plopper. For young people 10 to 14 years old. Monthly, except June/July and August/September. Buys all rights. Pays on publication. Will send sample copy to writer for 50¢. Write for copy of guidelines for writers. Submit seasonal material at least 8 months in advance. Minimum reporting time is 10 to 12 weeks. Mss will not be returned unless accompanied by sufficient postage and S.A.E.
Nonfiction and Photos: Historical, scientific, contemporary articles, and articles dealing with community involvement. "We are particularly interested in articles about young people doing

things: community projects, sports, business enterprises. Also good are informational, how-to, interview, profile, and humorous articles and photo features. We are always interested in contemporary craft projects with clear directions and photos of the finished product. Articles based on interviews with sports or entertainment personalities or teenagers who have accomplished significant things are welcome." Length: 900 words maximum. Pays approximately 3¢ a word. Photos are purchased with accompanying ms. Captions required. Pays $2.50 for each b&w; $5 for color.

Fiction: Adventure, mystery, humor, suspense, westerns, science fiction, romance, and historical fiction. Length: 1,800 words maximum; slightly shorter preferred. Limited number of two-part suspense stories accepted; total word limit 3,500 words. Pays about 3¢ a word.

Poetry: Humorous poetry for young teenagers. Traditional forms, blank and free verse, and light verse. Theme is open. No length limits. No fixed rate of payment.

Puzzles: All types desired; math or word. Should be difficult enough for this age group. No fixed rate of payment.

YOUTH ALIVE!, 1445 Boonville Ave., Springfield MO 65802. Editor: Carol A. Ball. "Official youth organ of the Assemblies of God, slanted to high school teens." Monthly. Circulation: 15,000. Buys some first rights, but "we are interested in multiple submissions, second rights, and other reprints." Pays on acceptance. Will send a free sample copy to a writer on request. Reports in 6 weeks. Enclose S.A.S.E.

Nonfiction, Photos, and Poetry: "Purpose is to provide news of the Pentecostal youth scene, to inspire to Christlike living, and to be used as a witnessing tool. We can use photo features, photos, interviews, biographical features, reports on outstanding Christian youth, how-to-do-it features, some fiction, some poems, humor, news, motivational articles, seasonal material (4 months prior to special day), personal experiences. Avoid cliches, unexplained theological terms, sermonizing, and 'talking down' to youth. Read *Youth Alive!* to get our style, but don't be afraid to submit something different if you think we might like it." Length of articles: 300 to 1,200 words. Payment is 1½¢ a word minimum. Teen-slanted human interest photos purchased with mss. 8x10 b&w glossies or color transparencies. Payment is $10-30. Payment for poetry is 20¢ a line.

YOUTH IN ACTION, Free Methodist Church, 901 College Ave., Winona Lake IN 46590. (219)267-7621. Editor-in-Chief: David Markell. For junior high and high school youth. Monthly magazine; 32 pages. Estab: 1956. Circ: 4,000. Pays on publication. Buys one-time rights. Phone queries OK. Simultaneous, photocopied and previously published submissions OK. SASE. Reports in 4 weeks. Free sample copy and writers' guidelines.

Nonfiction: Alice Wallace, Articles Editor. How-to (subjects dealing with religious themes such as prayer, Bible study, etc.); humor (any subject relevant to teens); inspirational (anything of a religious nature); interviews (with people who are in situations that would relate to our themes); personal experience (which would illustrate a spiritual truth); personal opinion and photo features (on issues and subjects that relate to our theme); profiles; (well-known people, especially teenagers who have become Christians). Buys 10-12/year. Send complete ms. Length: 500-2,000 words. Pays 1½-2¢/word.

Photos: Purchased with or without ms or on assignment. Send 8½x11 prints. Pays $7-15/b&w; $15-25/color.

Fiction: Humorous subjects that relate to teenage interests. Religious themes "along our denominational standards". Buys 5/year. Send complete ms. Length: 500-2,000 words. Pays 1½-2¢/word.

Poetry: Avant-garde and traditional forms; free verse, haiku, light verse. Buys 10/year. Pays $5 minimum.

Theater, Movie, TV, and Entertainment Publications

For those publications whose emphasis is on music and musicians, see the section on Music Publications. Nonpaying markets for similar material are listed in the Literary and "Little" Publications category.

ADAM FILM WORLD, 8060 Melrose Ave., Los Angeles CA 90046. (213)653-8060. Editor: Edward S. Sullivan. For fans of X- and R-rated movies. Magazine; 96 (8x11) pages. Established in 1966. Every 2 months. Circulation: 250,000. Buys first North American serial rights. Buys about 18 mss per year. Pays on publication. Will send sample copy to writer for $1.50. No photocopied or simultaneous submissions. Reports on mss accepted for publication in 1 to 2 months. Returns rejected material in 2 weeks. Query first. Enclose S.A.S.E.

Nonfiction and Photos: "All copy is slanted for fans of X- and R- movies and can be critical of this or that picture, but not critical of the genre itself. Our main emphasis is on pictorial layouts, rather than text; layouts of stills from erotic pictures. Any article must have possibilities for illustration. We go very strong in the erotic direction, but *no* hard-core stills. We see too many fictional interviews with a fictitious porno star, and too many fantasy suggestions for erotic film plots. No think pieces wanted. We would consider articles on the continuing erotization of legitimate films from major studios, and the increasing legitimization of X- and R-films from the minors." Length: 1,000 to 3,000 words. Pays $80 to $210. Most photos are bought on assignment from regular photographers with studio contacts, but a few 8x10 b&w's are purchased from freelancers for use as illustrations. Pays minimum of $10 per photo.

How To Break In: "Send brief, capsule suggestion for unique, authentic, article or layout idea on erotic films, based on factual research, interviews, contacts."

AFTER DARK, 10 Columbus Circle, New York NY 10019. (212)399-2400. Editor: William Como. For an audience "20 to 55 years old." Monthly. Circ: 360,000. Buys first rights. Buys about 30 mss/year. Pays on publication. Sample copy $2. Submit seasonal material 4 months in advance. Reports in 3 to 4 weeks. Query first, including copies of previously published work. Enclose S.A.S.E.

Nonfiction and Photos: Articles on "every area of entertainment—films, TV, theater, nightclubs, books, records." Length: 2,500 to 3,000 words. Pays $75 to $150. Photos with captions only. B&w glossies, color transparencies. Pays $20 to $50.

How To Break In: "The best way to crack *After Dark* is by doing a piece on some new trend in the entertainment world. We have people in most of the important cities, but we rely on freelancers to send us material from out-of-the-way places where new things are developing. Some of our contributing editors started out that way. Query first."

AFTERNOON TV, 2 Park Ave., New York NY 10016. Monthly. For soap opera viewers. Reports at once. Enclose S.A.S.E.

Nonfiction and Photos: Interviews with afternoon TV stars. Pays $100 for eight-page story. Minimum length: 4 typewritten pages. Photos purchased with mss. Pays up to $15 per photo.

How To Break In: "We're a very tough market to break into. Everything we do is interviews with daytime TV performers which makes us a market as specialized as *Popular Mechanics.* If a writer has some credits elsewhere and has done personality pieces before, the best way to break in here would be with a story about a lesser star in one of the New York soaps. We have a West Coast editor and a regular staff of writers out there, and besides, New York has 11 soaps while there are only three in California. The interview doesn't have to be with a performer we've never interviewed before, but it should have some new angle."

AMERICAN FILM, American Film Institute, Kennedy Center, Washington DC 20566. (202)833-9300. Editor: Hollis Alpert. For film professionals, students, teachers, film enthusiasts. Monthly magazine; 80 pages. Established in 1975. Circulation: 25,000. Buys First North American serial rights. Buys 20 to 30 mss a year. Copyrighted. Payment on acceptance. Will send sample copy to a writer for $1. Will consider photocopied submissions, but not simultaneous submissions. Submit seasonal material 3 months in advance. Reports in 1 to 2 weeks. Query first. Enclose S.A.S.E.

Nonfiction: In-depth articles on film and television-related subjects. "Our articles require expertise and first-rate writing ability." Buys informational, profile, historical and "think" pieces. No film reviews. Length: 2,000 to 3,000 words. Pays $250 to $500.

AMERICAN SQUAREDANCE, (formerly *Square Dance*), Burdick Enterprises, Box 788, Sandusky OH 44870. Editors-in-Chief: Stan & Cathie Burdick. Emphasizes squaredancing. Monthly magazine; 100 pages. Estab: 1945. Circ: 11,500. Pays on publication. Buys all rights. Submit seasonal/holiday material 3-4 months in advance. SASE. Reports in 1 week. Free sample copy.

Nonfiction: How-to; informational; historical; humor; inspirational; interview; nostalgia; personal opinion; profile; travel; personal experience; photo feature; and technical. All articles must have dance theme. Buys 18 mss/year. Submit complete ms. Length: 1,000-2,500 words. Pays $10-25.

Photos: Purchased with accompanying ms. Captions required. B&w glossy prints. Pays $2-10.

Fiction: Fantasy; historical; humorous; romance; suspense; science fiction; and western. Must have dance theme. Buys 6 mss/year. Length: 1,500-2,500 words. Pays $10-30.
Poetry: Haiku, light verse, traditional. Must be on a dance theme. Buys 6 poems/year. Limit submissions to 3 at a time. Pays $5-10.
Fillers: Crossword and word puzzles with dance theme. Buys 4/year. Pays $5.

APPLAUSE: San Diego Magazine of the Arts, 2461 5th Ave., San Diego CA 92101. Editor: Lee Massey. Managing Editor: Nancy Sprague. Distributed at performances of the San Diego opera, symphony and other cultural events. Monthly magazine; 52 pages. Circ: 60,000. Pays on publication. Buys all rights, but may reassign following publication. Submit seasonal/holiday material 3 months in advance. SASE. Reports in 2 weeks. Sample copy $1; writer's guidelines for SASE.
Nonfiction: "Primary editorial emphasis is on the San Diego opera, symphony and Old Globe Theatre. We look for articles that will get an 'I-didn't-know-that' reaction from our readers. We also cover other aspects of both performing and visual arts. Our pages are open to your suggestions." Length: 3,000-5,000 words. Pays $1.04/column inch.

BLACK STARS, Johnson Publishing Company, Inc., 820 S. Michigan Ave., Chicago IL 60605. (312)786-7668. Managing Editor: Ariel Perry Strong. Emphasizes entertainment. Monthly magazine; 74 pages. Estab: 1971. Circ: 350,000. Pays on publication. Buys all rights, but may reassign following publication. Seasonal/holiday material should be submitted 3 months in advance. SASE. Reports in 3 weeks. Sample copy $1-2; free writer's guidelines.
Nonfiction: Personal experience and photo feature. "Only articles on black entertainers." Buys 600 mss/year. Query. Length: 4,500 words maximum. Pays $100-200.
Photos: Purchases 8x10 b&w or transparencies. Query, submit prints or transparencies.

CANADIAN THEATRE REVIEW, Room 222, Administrative Studies Bldg., York University, 4700 Keele St., Downsview, Ontario M3J 1P3, Canada. (416)667-3768. Editor: Don Rubin. For critics, actors, educators, audiences. Quarterly magazine; 152 (6x9) pages. Established in 1973. Circ: 3,000. Buys first rights. Payment on publication. Sample copy $3. Reports within 4 weeks. Query, send an outline of article, or submit complete ms. Enclose S.A.E. and International Reply Coupons.
Nonfiction: Essays relating to the theatre. Reviews. Canadian orientation. "We're the only national publication covering Canadian theatre." Also uses historical documentation relating to the Canadian theatre as it existed in the past and regional essays by leading members of the theatrical community. Length: 1,000 to 5,000 words. Pays $35 to $100. Regular features are theme articles, Carte Blanche (free-form essays) and a playscript. Pays $35 for Carte Blanche and $100 for playscript.
Drama: Rates vary for plays by Canadians.

CHANNEL ONE, 1229 N. Highland Ave., Los Angeles CA 90038. Editor: Robert L. Smith. For upper middle-class professional-managerial type of readership; 25-35 years of age. Quarterly magazine. Circ: 100,000. Pays on publication. Buys all rights, but may reassign following publication. SASE. Reports in 15 days.
Nonfiction: Articles with a television, stereo, video tape theme or background. Stories of human interest covering the broad field of electronic communication. Informational, interview, profiles, humor, expose and nostalgia articles. Pieces on program research, TV content, electronic gadgets for the home in the 1980's, future of cable TV, pay TV, etc. Stereo update pieces. "Articles should be helpful, positive, interesting and entertaining on the consumer level." Length: 1,000-1,800 words. Length for reviews: 1,000-1,500 words. Pays $50-100.
Photos: Purchased with or without ms. Captions required. Pays $5 for b&w; $15-35 for color.
Columns/Departments: Showbus uses short items of no more than 1,000 words. Pays $50.
Fiction: Must be related to the electronic media. Length: 1,000-1,800 words. Pays $50-100.
Poetry: Traditional forms and free verse related to magazine's theme. Pays $5-25.

CINEFANTASTIQUE, P.O. Box 270, Oak Park IL 60303. (312)383-5631. Editor: Frederick S. Clarke. For persons interested in horror, fantasy and science fiction films. Magazine; 48 pages. Established in 1970. Quarterly. Circ: 6,000. Rights purchased are all magazine rights in all languages. Pays on publication. Free sample copy, if *Writer's Market* is specified. Photocopied submissions OK. No simultaneous submissions. Reports on material accepted for publication in 4 weeks. Returns rejected material "immediately." Enclose S.A.S.E.
Nonfiction: "We're interested in articles, interviews and reviews which concern horror, fantasy and science fiction films." Potential contributors should request a sample copy to understand requirements. Pays 10¢/column line. Line varies from 30-40 spaces.

DANCE MAGAZINE, 10 Columbus Circle, New York NY 10019. (212)977-9770. Editor: William Como. Monthly. For the dance profession and members of the public interested in the art of dance. Buys all rights. Pays on publication. Sample copy $2. Query suggested. Enclose S.A.S.E.

Nonfiction: Personalities, knowledgeable comment, news. Length: 2,500 to 3,000 words. Pays $25 to $50.

Photos: Purchased with articles or with captions only. Pays $5-15.

How To Break In: "Do a piece about a local company that's not too well known but growing; or a particular school that is doing well which we may not have heard about; or a local dancer who you feel will be gaining national recognition. Query first."

DANCE SCOPE, American Dance Guild, 1619 Broadway, Room 603, New York NY 10019. Editor-in-Chief: Richard Lorber. Emphasizes dance and related performing/visual/musical arts. For performers, university teachers and students, general public audiences, other artists, arts administrators, critics, historians. Semiannual magazine; 80 pages. Estab: 1965. Circ: 5,000. Pays on publication. Buys all rights. Submit seasonal or holiday material 6 months in advance. Photocopied submissions OK. SASE. Reports in 1 month. Sample copy $2.

Nonfiction: Informational (contemporary developments, trends, ideas); historical (synthesis of ideas, not narrowly academic); inspirational (documentation and think pieces); interviews (with commentary, intros, etc.); personal experience (with broad relevance). Buys 12 mss per year. Query. Length: 1,500-3,000 words. Pays $20-50.

Photos: No additional payment for b&w glossies used with mss. Captions required. Query. Model release required.

How To Break In: "With good ideas, good thinking, good writing; original, imaginatively handled material, synthesizing intuition, information and inquiry."

Rejects: "Promo pieces".

DRAMATICS MAGAZINE, International Thespian Society, 3368 Central Pkwy, Cincinnati OH 45225. (513)541-7379. Editor-in-Chief: S. Ezra Goldstein. For theatre arts students, teachers and others interested in theatre arts education. Magazine published bimonthly in September, November, January, March and May. 48 pages. Estab: 1929. Circ: 50,000. Pays on acceptance. Buys first North American serial rights. Phone queries OK. Submit seasonal/holiday material 3 months in advance. Simultaneous, photocopied and previously published submissions OK. SASE. Reports in 3 weeks. Sample copy $1; free writer's guidelines.

Nonfiction: Historical; how-to (technical theatre); informational; interview; photo feature; profile and technical. Buys 30 mss/year. Submit complete ms. Length: 2,500 words minimum. Pays $15-50.

Photos: Purchased with accompanying ms. Uses b&w photos. Query. Total purchase price for ms includes payment for photos.

Columns/Departments: Technicalities (theatre how-to articles); Tag Line (editorials on some phase of the theatre) and Promptbook (entertainment arts news relevant to an educational magazine). Buys 15 mss/year. Send complete ms. Length: 250-1,000 words. Pays $15-40.

Fiction: Drama (one-act plays). Buys 5 mss/year. Send complete ms. Pays $40-50. "We print one short one-act play each issue. Subject matter must be suitable for high school production, run about 30 minutes when produced, and must never have been published before."

DRAMATIKA, 390 Riverside Dr., Suite 10B, New York NY 10025. Editors: John and Andrea Pyros. Magazine; 40 pages. For persons interested in the theater arts. Estab: 1968. Published 2 times/year. Circ: 500-1,000. Buys all rights. Buys 6-12 mss/year. Pays on publication. Will send sample copy to writer for $1. Will consider photocopied submissions. Will also consider simultaneous submissions "if advised." Reports in 1 month. Enclose S.A.S.E.

Drama and Photos: Wants "performable pieces — plays, songs, scripts, etc." Will consider plays on various and open themes. Length: 20 pages maximum. Pays about $25 per piece; $5-10 for smaller pieces. B&w photos purchased with ms with extra payment. Captions required. Pays $5. Size: 8x11.

E W TV GUIDE, Entertainment West, 101 Townsend, San Francisco CA 94107. (415)957-1277. Editor-in-Chief: William Whitney. Emphasizes television programming and stars. Distributed to television audiences through local trade media. Weekly tabloid; 16-24 pages. Estab: 1971. Circ: 50,000. Pays on publication. Buys one-time rights. Submit seasonal or holiday material 3 months in advance. Simultaneous, photocopied, and previously published submissions OK. SASE. Reports in 2-4 weeks. Sample copy 25¢.

Nonfiction: Kerry Pappalardo, Nonfiction Editor. Expose, informational, humor, interview, photo feature, and profile. Buys 5-6 mss/issue. Send complete ms. Length: 500-2,000 words. Pays 2-10¢/word.

Photos: Photos purchased with or without accompanying ms or on assignment. Pays $2-5 for 5x7 b&w glossies. Total purchase price for ms includes payment for photos. Model release required.

Fillers: Clippings, jokes, gags, anecdotes, puzzles. Buys 2-5 fillers/issue. Submit complete ms. Length: 200-500 words. Pays $5-15.

FILM COMMENT, 1865 Broadway, New York NY 10023. Editor: Richard Corliss. For film students, teachers and scholars. Has select group of writers which usually fills its needs. Query before sending mss. Enclose S.A.S.E.

FILM QUARTERLY, University of California Press, Berkeley CA 94720. (415)642-6333. Editor: Ernest Callenbach. Issued quarterly. Buys all rights. Pays on publication. Query first. Enclose S.A.S.E.

Nonfiction: Articles on style and structure in films, articles analyzing the work of important directors, historical articles on development of the film as art, reviews of current films and detailed analyses of classics, book reviews of film books. Length: 6,000 words maximum. Must be familiar with the past and present of the art; must be competently, although not necessarily breezily, written; must deal with important problems of the art. Payment is about 1½¢ per word; higher for material on films not in ordinary theatrical release.

FM GUIDE, 20 Hampton Rd., Box 1592, Southampton NY 11968. (516)283-2360. Editor: Bonnie P. Barton. For the hi-fi and radio enthusiast; especially interested in classical music. Publication of FM Music Program Guide Inc. Magazine; 64 pages. Established in 1965. Monthly. Circulation: 100,000. Buys all rights. Buys about 36 mss per year. Pays on publication. Will send free sample copy to writer on request. No photocopied or simultaneous submissions. Reports on mss accepted for publication in 2 months. Returns rejected material in 6 months. Enclose S.A.S.E.

Nonfiction and Photos: Publishes "radio-oriented nonfiction and hi-fidelity information, equipment stories, general interest in the musical world. Write within a musical interest framework. We cater to radio listeners with guides to programming and composers." Length: informational, 1,200 to 2,500 words; manufacturer profile, 800 to 1,200 words. Pays $25 to $100. Photos purchased with ms with no additional payment. Captions optional.

MODERN MOVIES' HOLLYWOOD EXPOSED, Magazine Management Company, 575 Madison Ave., New York NY 10022. (212)838-7900. Editor-in-Chief: Sherry Romeo. Emphasizes tv and movie stars for a teen to mid-twenties readership who are interested in photos, gossip and stories/interviews with their favorite stars. Published every two months. Magazine; 72 pages. Estab: 1968. Circ: 200,000. Pays on acceptance. Buys all rights. Prefers phone queries. Submit seasonal/holiday material 10-12 weeks in advance. Simultaneous submissions OK. SASE. Reports in 1-3 weeks.

Nonfiction: Expose (scandal, gossip); humor (anecdotes about meeting stars, "round-up articles" on things that happened to stars); interview ("our most-wanted category; most likely to sell us"); nostalgia (very limited use) and photo feature. Buys 100 mss/year. Query or send complete ms. Length: 250-3,000 words. Pays $50-200.

Photos: Purchased with or without accompanying ms or on assignment. Identification required. Query, submit contact sheet, prints or transparencies. Pays $25 minimum for 8x10 b&w glossies; $50-300 for 2¼x2¼ or 35mm transparencies (no color prints bought at this time). Model release required.

Fillers: Jokes, gags, anecdotes, puzzles, star crosswords and diacrostics. Send fillers. Pays $25 minimum.

MODERN SCREEN MAGAZINE, 1 Dag Hammarskjold Plaza, New York NY 10017. Editor: Joan Thursh. Monthly. No fiction or verse. Buys first serial rights. Payment on acceptance. Will consider photocopied submissions. Reports in two weeks. Will send sample copy on request. Query first. Enclose S.A.S.E.

Nonfiction: Uses true articles on movie stars, TV stars, show business personalities and figures who attract world attention. Length: up to 1,000 words. Pays a minimum of $100.

Photos: Buys singles and photo series in b&w and color. Buys pix submitted with mss. Uses contacts up to 8x10. Pays $20 and up.

How To Break In: "We're starting a new section which will contain something along the lines of news briefs —but briefs which are heavily slanted toward a specific personality and which will hold up two-and-a-half to three months after they're published. It would be a good way to break in since we have been tending to stick with the people we know for features. The best way to describe these briefs would be to say they will be like little features, but about people or incidents that can't really be blown up into a full-length story. Interesting information about less important people. But it should be written with a feature story slant. Otherwise if you feel you have a good interview or a good contact, write and tell me what you've got. No need to query for the briefs."

MOVIE LIFE, Ideal Publishing Co., 575 Madison Ave., New York NY 10022. (212)759-9704. Editor: Seli Groves. "Basically, for women, from 9 to 90, interested in peeking at the private lives of entertainment stars." Established in 1938. Monthly. Circulation: 225,000. Buys all rights. Buys about 150 mss a year. Payment on publication. Will not consider photocopied or simultaneous submissions. Reports on material in 3 to 6 weeks. Query first. Enclose S.A.S.E.
Nonfiction and Photos: Feature articles on well-known movie and television personalities. Interviews. Length: 1,500 to 2,000 words. Pays $125 to $200. 8x10 b&w photos purchased with accompanying mss for $25, or without extra payment, depending on the article and photos.
How To Break In: "Let's suppose Elvis comes to town. Check with the local paper to find out who is handling publicity for him. Then see if you can arrange an interview. Also, please get a letter from the press person acknowledging that such an interview actually took place. I'm afraid to say, we sometimes get accounts of meetings which never happened, so we do have to check. You should read our magazine and become familiar with the style. We like first-person accounts and can help out with the style if the facts are good. Our stories tend to be very personal —more visceral then intellectual. Don't be blunted by what you think I might not like. And don't overlook doing some library research for some interesting background on your subjects."

MOVIE MIRROR, TV PICTURE LIFE, PHOTO SCREEN, 355 Lexington Ave., New York NY 10017. Editor of *Movie Mirror:* Joan Goldstein. Editor of *TV Picture Life:* Connie Berman. Editor of *Photo Screen:* Marsha Daly. Monthlies. Buys 10 to 12 mss a month. Pays on acceptance. Submit complete ms. Reports promptly. Enclose S.A.S.E.
Nonfiction: "The most desired sort of story is the fresh and strongly angled, dramatically told article about the private life of a leading motion picture or television star. Categories of stories popular with readers (they've changed little over the years): romantic love, weddings, married life, babies, parent/child relationships, religion, health, extra-marital affairs, divorces, dangerous moments survived, feuds. The major difference in fan mag writing then and now is the increased frankness permissible in today's articles. When many stars talk forthrightly about living together without marriage, bearing children out of wedlock, personal sexual inclinations, etc., fan magazine editors have little choice but to go along with contemporary trends. The object, no matter the category of article, is to tell the reader something she did not already know about a favorite performer, preferably something dramatic, provocative, personal. Our readers are female (over 90% of them), youngish (under 45), and often are wives or daughters of bluecollar workers. It is our purpose to bring a bit of vicarious excitement and glamour to these readers whose own lives may not be abundantly supplied with same. Stars they want to read about now are: (TV) Dean Martin, Mary Tyler Moore, Redd Foxx, Carol Burnett, Peter Falk, William Conrad, and the leads of 'All In The Family,' 'The Waltons,' 'M*A*S*H,' and 'Maude'; (Movies) Elvis Presley, Liz Taylor, Barbara Streisand, Liza Minnelli, Paul Newman, Steve McQueen, John Wayne, Robert Redford. While most of our manuscripts are written by top magazine and newspaper writers in Hollywood and New York, we have an open-door policy. Any writer able to meet our specific editorial needs will get a 'read' here. Until we know your work, however, we would have to see completed manuscripts rather than outlines. Writers outside the two show biz meccas might keep in mind that we are particularly interested in hometown stories on contemporary celebrities. Average length for articles is 2,000 words. Pay starts at $75, going considerably higher for genuine scoops."

MOVIE STARS, Magazine Management Co., 575 Madison Avenue, New York NY 10022. Editor: Ann Hamilton. For anyone from their teens to their sixties who's interested in the lives of top TV and screen personalities. Estab: 1935. Buys all rights. Buys 100 mss/year. Pays on publication. Query. SASE.
Nonfiction and Photos: General subject matter consists of "human interest articles on movies and television personalities." Pays $150 for a 7- to 8-page article. Pays $25 per b&w photo.
How To Break In: "Submit an interview with a secondary character on a popular TV series, or a featured actor in several films, whose face has become known to the public. It is best if you query first, presenting your interview idea and including some personal information about yourself—a resume and some previously published material, for example"

MOVIE WORLD, Magazine Management Co., 575 Madison Ave., New York NY 10022. (212)838-7900. Editor: Jan Musacchio. Fan magazine covering TV and movie fields. Monthly. Buys all rights. Pays on acceptance. Query first on angle and title on unassigned material. Enclose S.A.S.E.
Nonfiction and Photos: "News stories concerning top TV and movie personalities may be submitted in interview or third-person format, although the interview preferred. Articles with melodramatic, emotional impact are acceptable, but writing must be clear, witty, and fresh in its approach. Mss should be gossipy and fact-filled and aimed toward working class adults." Length: 1,500 to 2,500 words. Pays up to $200 for exclusive interviews. Pays up to $35 for b&w and up to $1,000 for color used for cover material.

PERFORMING ARTS IN CANADA, 52 Avenue Rd., Toronto, Ont., Canada. (416)921-2601. Chairman, Editorial Advisory Board: Arnold Edinborough. For "well-educated persons with special interest in theater, music, dance." Quarterly. Circ: 40,000. Buys first rights. Buys 30 to 40 mss a year. Pays 2 weeks following publication. Will send a sample copy to a writer for 50¢. Reports in 3 to 6 weeks. Query first. Enclose S.A.E. and International Reply Coupons.
Nonfiction: "Inspiring and stimulating articles covering Canadian performing arts." Material for department "What's Going On." Length: 200-1,200 words. Pays $25-1,000.

PHOTOPLAY, 205 East 42nd St., New York NY 10017. Editorial Director: David Ragan. For women, ages 18 to 50. Monthly. Buys all rights. Pays on publication. Will send a sample copy to a writer on request. Reports in 2 weeks. Query first. Enclose S.A.S.E.
Nonfiction and Photos: Uses strongly angled stories on "stars"—in all entertainment media, all walks of life—that would appeal to women of all ages. Pays $200 minimum. Buys pix of "stars" with or without ms. Payment varies with pix subject and exclusivity. Pays $25 minimum for b&w; $150 minimum for color.

PHOTO SCREEN, Sterling's Magazines, Inc., 356 Lexington Ave., New York NY 10017. (212)391-1400. Editor: Marsha Daly. Emphasizes TV and movie news of star personalities. Monthly magazine; 75 pages. Estab: 1960. Circ: 300,000. Pays on publication. Buys all rights. SASE. Reports in 6 weeks.
Nonfiction: Exposes (on stars' lives); informational (on Hollywood life); interviews (with stars); photo features (on stars' personal lives). Buys 5-6 mss/month. Query. Pays $75-200.
Photos: Olivia Z. Atherton, Department Editor. Purchased without ms; mostly on speculation. Pays $25-35 for 8x10 b&w (glossy or matte); $50 minimum for color. Chromes only; 35mm or 2¼x2¼.

PLAYBILL MAGAZINE, 151 E. 50th, New York NY 10022. Issued monthly; free to theatergoers. Buys first and second U.S. magazine rights. Enclose S.A.S.E.
Nonfiction: The major emphasis is on current theater and theater people. On occasion, buys humor or travel pieces if offbeat. Wants sophisticated, informative prose that makes judgments and shows style. Uses unusual interviews, although most of these are staff written. Style should be worldly and literate without being pretentious or arch; runs closer to *Harper's* or *New Yorker* than to *Partisan Review*. Wants interesting information, adult analysis, written in a genuine, personal style. Humor is also welcome. Between 1,000 and 2,500 words for articles. Pays $100 to $400 each.
How To Break In: "We're difficult to break into and most of our pieces are assigned. We don't take any theater pieces relating to theater outside New York. We also have short features on boutiquing, fashions, men's wear, women's wear. The best way for a newcomer to break in is with a short humorous or satirical piece or some special piece of reporting on the Broadway theater — no more than 700 to 1,000 words. A number of people have come in that way and some of them have subsequently received assignments from us."

PRE-VUE, P.O. Box 20768, Billings MT 59104. Editor-Publisher: Virginia Hansen. "We are the cable-TV guide for southern Montana; our audience is as diverse as people who subscribe to cable TV." Weekly magazine; 32 to 40 pages. Established in 1969. Circulation: 15,000. Not copyrighted. Payment on publication. Will send free sample copy to writer on request. Will consider photocopied submissions, if they are legible. Will consider simultaneous submissions, but prefers the first look. Submit seasonal material (any holiday, but with a regional tie-in) 2 months in advance. Reports in 8 weeks. Query. Submit complete poetry mss. SASE.
Nonfiction and Photos: "Subject matter is general, but must relate in some way to television or our reading area (southern Montana). We also use articles on history, profiles, etc. Since we are the only cable-TV and entertainment guide in a weekly magazine format in our area, a prospec-

tive contributor might do well to read back issues. We would like articles to have a beginning, middle and end; in other words, popular magazine style, heavy on the hooker lead. We're interested in holidays and special events in our reading area." Informational, how-to, personal experience, interview, profile, inspirational, humor, historical, think pieces, nostalgia, travel, TV or book reviews, spot news, successful business operations, new product. Feature length: 500-800 words. Shorts: 50-200 words. Pays minimum of 2¢/word. 8x10 (sometimes smaller) b&w photos purchased with mss or on assignment. Pays $3 to $6. Captions required. Department Editor: Virginia Hansen.

Poetry: Traditional forms, blank verse, free verse, light verse. Length: 2 to 8 lines. Pays $2.

Fillers: Short humor, local history and oddities. Length: 50-200 words. Pays minimum of 1¢ per word.

PROLOG, 104 N. St. Mary, Dallas TX 75204. (214)827-7734. Editor: Mike Firth. For "playwrights and teachers of playwriting." Quarterly newsletter; 8 pages. Estab: 1973. Circ: 200. Not copyrighted. Buys 4 to 16 mss per year. Pays on acceptance or publication; "may hold pending final approval." Sample copy 50¢. Will consider photocopied and simultaneous submissions. Reports on mss accepted for publication in "over 3 months." Returns rejected material in 1 or 2 months. Enclose S.A.S.E.

Nonfiction: Wants "articles and anecdotes about writing, sales and production of play scripts. Style should be direct to reader (as opposed to third-person observational). "Does not want to see general attacks on theater, personal problems, problems without solutions of general interest. Pays ½¢/word.

SCREEN AND TV ALBUM, Ideal Publishing Corp., 575 Madison Ave., New York NY 10022. Editor: Ann Hamilton. Entertainment news magazine published every 2 months. Audience ranges from sub-teens to mature people in their 60's and "we try to fill the magazine with personalities appealing to these various ages." Buys all rights. Buys 4 to 6 mss a year. Pays on publication. Will send sample copy to writer for 75¢. Query first. Reports within 10 days. Enclose S.A.S.E.

Nonfiction and Photos: Stories concerning popular personalities of film, TV and recording industries must be of human interest, concerned with some personal, not professional, aspect of personality's life. "Give me your ideas on a story, plus your sources for same. Interviews (caution) will be checked through from this end with the personality before any such article is purchased. Check the new TV shows, the new films, and write about them." Interview and photo articles. Length: 1,000 to 3,500 words. "Payments arranged per article prior to transfer of material from writer to editor. I will quote price or discuss asked-for payment." Please query Ms. Sheila Steinach on any photo submission.

How To Break In: "One thing you might try to do is take a look at the second banana on a hit TV show and see what he's doing. We're interested in new personal angles —perhaps he was adopted and is willing to talk about it. We're using longer pieces now and more photos. The main thing a freelancer has to prove to me is that he is dependable, can meet deadlines, can take positive editorial criticism, and is accurate."

SCREEN STORIES, Magazine Management Co., 575 Madison Ave., New York NY 10022. For women, ages 21 to 50. Monthly. Circ: 150,000. Buys approximately 100 mss a year. Pays on publication. Query. SASE.

Nonfiction: Stories about the personal lives of the stars. Buys interviews, personal experience articles. Pays $75 to $300.

THE SOAP BOX, Box 1129, Manassas VA 22110. Publisher: Bruce H. Joffe. Editor: Vickie Pollock Murphy. For daytime drama fans. Monthly tabloid; 32-48 pages. Estab: 1975. Circ: 125,000. Buys all rights. Buys 80 to 120 mss per year. Pays on publication. Will send free sample copy to writer on request. Write for editorial guidelines sheet. Will consider photocopied and simultaneous submissions. Reports in 2 months. Query first. Enclose S.A.S.E.

Nonfiction, Photos and Fillers: "We're looking for creative writers who can deal intelligently with the soap opera as art form, instrument for social reform, and emotional catharsis." Does not want to see stories about stars of the serials — who they date, what they eat, etc. Wants "witty, insightful articles that are not dry or condescending." Pays $1-50 for nonfiction. Length: 250-1,000 words. Also buys material for "Storyline Reports," which reports on each serial and speculates on what is to come in the drama. Length: 250-500 words. Pays $15. Photos purchased with ms with no additional payment, without ms, or on assignment. Captions optional. Pays $5 per b&w glossy; any size. No color. Also buys newsbreaks and short humor. Pays $1 to $5.

SUPER-8 FILMAKER, PMS Publishing Co., 3161 Fillmore St., San Francisco CA 94123. Editor-in-Chief: Bruce Anderson. Emphasizes filmmaking in Super-8, for amateur and professional filmmakers, students and teachers of film. Magazine (8 times a year); 66 pages. Estab: 1973. Circ: 46,000. Pays on publication. Buys all rights. Submit seasonal/holiday material 8 months in advance. SASE. Reports in 1 week. Sample copy $1.25; free writer's guidelines.
Nonfiction: How-to; informational and technical (dealing with filmmaking only); interview (with Hollywood filmmakers). Buys 5 mss/issue. Query. Length: 2,000-3,000 words.
How To Break In: "We are a consumer publication, not a trade publication. Articles written for *Super-8 Filmaker* should contain technical information, but they should not be written in technical terminology. All technical terms and concepts should be defined simply and concisely."

TAKE ONE, Box 1778, Station B., Montreal H3B 3L3. Que., Canada. (514)843-7733. Managing Editor: Phyllis Platt. Editor: Peter Lebensold. For anyone interested in films in modern society. Not a fan magazine. Bimonthly. Circulation: 25,000. Buys about 150 mss a year. Buys North American serial rights. Pays on publication. Will send free sample copy on request. Reports in 3 weeks. Query preferred. Enclose S.A.E. and International Reply Coupons.
Nonfiction and Photos: Interviews, articles, photo stories, reviews. Anything having to do with film. Articles on directors, actors, etc. On new or classic films, on aspects of the industry, current or historical, on aesthetic developments. Anything of interest in this broad area of the communication arts. No taboos at all. Style should be lively, informed and opinionated rather than "newspaperese." Length: 700 to 5,000 words; 1,000 words maximum, reviews. Pays about 2¢ per word. Purchases photos with mss. Events, people in film and/or (occasionally) TV. 8x10 b&w glossy. Pays $5 minimum for photos, but tries to get most photos free from film distributors.
Fiction: Very rarely buys fiction. Query first. Maximum 5,000 words. Rarely uses short-shorts under 2,000 words. Must deal with some aspect of film. No taboos. Pays about 1¢ per word.
Poetry: Rarely published. Must deal with some aspect of film. No taboos. Pays $10 minimum.
How To Break In: "Most writers who have been published in our magazine started out by sending us a review, interview or article on some subject (a film, a filmmaker) about which they cared passionately and (more often than not) had —as a result of that caring —a particular degree of expertise. Often they just happened to be in the right place at the right time (where a film was being made, where a filmmaker was making a public appearance or near where one lived)."

TELEVISIONS MAGAZINE, Washington Community Video-Center, Inc., Box 21068, Washington, D.C. 20009. (202)331-1566. Editor-in-Chief: Nick DeMartino. Managing Editor: Larry Kirkman. Emphasizes communications systems for video producers, TV consumers, persons interested in television, film media and their social impact. Quarterly tabloid; 24 pages. Estab: 1975. Circ: 20,000. Pays on publication. Buys all rights, but may reassign following publication. Submit seasonal/holiday material 4-6 months in advance. Simultaneous and photocopied submissions OK. SASE. Reports in 2 months. Free sample copy.
Nonfiction: Expose (investigations in media area); historical; how-to (utilization of video hardware); humor; informational (what people are doing in the field); interview; new product; personal experience; profile and technical. Buys 16 mss/year. Query or send complete ms. Length: 50-1,200 words. Pays $25-200. "*Televisions* charts the media revolution; where is media going, how is it controlled; consumer video, video discs, how to produce and get programming funded, use of media in social services, museums, schools. Media reform. We review books and video programs, run long features, and a variety of shorts and columns. Our publication is written from the consumer point of view."
Photos: Purchased with accompanying ms; no additional payment.

THEATER ACROSS AMERICA, 104 N. St. Mary, Dallas TX 75214. (214)827-7734. Editor: Mike Firth. For adults interested in theater. Most have experience with theater in school; some with professional experience. Magazine; 12 to 24 pages. Established in 1975. Published 5 times per year. Circulation: 500. Rights purchased vary with author and material. Usually buys first serial rights. Buys 5 to 30 mss per year. Pays on acceptance for publication. "May hold after advising author." Will send sample copy to writer for $1. Will consider photocopied and simultaneous submissions. Submit seasonal material 5 months in advance. Reports on mss accepted for publication in 4 to 6 months. Returns rejected material in 1 month. Enclose S.A.S.E.
Nonfiction, Photos and Fillers: Wants mss containing useful information about theater; experiences which have a general application for others in theater, technical, organizational, financial. Does not want material that is too academic. Would like to see mss on summer the-

ater, Christmas or holiday shows, working with festivals. Buys informational, how-to, personal experience, humor, photo, book reviews, successful business operations, new product, merchandising techniques, technical mss. Length: 50 to 1,250 words. "Word rates will be the same for all items and will depend on number of subscribers. We will start at 1¢ a word and go up with the number of subscribers." Open to suggestions for new columns or departments. Photos purchased with mss with extra payment and purchased without mss "on occasion." Captions required. No color. Pays $5 minimum for b&w. Size: 5x7 glossy or larger. Also buys anecdotes and short humor. Length: 25 to 150 words. Pays "same as for articles."

TV AND MOVIE SCREEN, 355 Lexington Ave., New York NY 10017. (212)391-1400. Editorial Director: Roseann C. Hirsch. Editor: Kathy Loy. Managing Editor: George W. Anderson. For people interested in television and show business personalities. Magazine; 74 pages. Monthly. Circulation: 500,000. Rights purchased vary with author and material. Usually buys all rights. Buys 65 mss a year. Pays on publication. Query first. Reports immediately. Enclose S.A.S.E.
Nonfiction and Photos: Celebrity interviews and angle stories; profile articles. Punchy, enticing and truthful. Length: 1,000 to 1,500 words. Pays $100 to $150. Photos of celebrities purchased without ms or on assignment. Pays $25 each.

TV DAWN TO DUSK, 575 Madison Ave., New York NY 10022. Editor: Jean Thomas. For daytime television viewers. Established in 1970. Monthly. Circ: 200,000. Buys all rights. Pays on publication. Query. SASE.
Nonfiction: Personality pieces with daytime TV stars of serials and quiz shows; main emphasis is on serial stars. Also interested in some women's interest material. Buys interviews, personality pieces, round-up articles, how-to's, profiles, and personal experience articles related to daytime TV only. Length: approximately 1,500 words. Pays $150 minimum.
How To Break In: "The key thing for breaking in here is to have access to one of the daytime TV personalities. Try to choose a character whose story line is evolving into a bigger and more important role. But query first; don't waste your time doing a story on a character who will be going off the show soon. For writers who don't have this kind of access, the best bet is a career retrospective of one of the major characters who has been on for years. You'll need to check a library for clippings."

TV GUIDE, Radnor PA 19088. Executive Editor: Roger Youman. Published weekly. Study publication. Query first (with outline) to Andrew Mills, Assistant Managing Editor. Enclose S.A.S.E.
Nonfiction: Wants offbeat articles about TV people and shows. This magazine is not interested in fan material. Also wants stories on the newest trends of television, but they must be written in layman's language. Length: 200 to 2,000 words.
Photos: Uses professional high-quality photos, normally shot on assignment, by photographers chosen by *TV Guide*. Prefers color. Pays $150 day rate against page rates—$250 for 2 pages or less.

TV MIRROR, 205 East 42nd St., New York NY 10017. Editor: Patricia Canole. For women of all ages. Pays on publication. Reports immediately. Query first. Enclose S.A.S.E.
Nonfiction and Photos: "As the largest 'fan' magazine in the TV field (and radio to a lesser extent), we publish each month 12 or so personal articles about the private lives of television's most popular performers, i.e., stars of such shows as 'M*A*S*H,' 'Rhoda,' 'Maude,' 'All in the Family,' etc., as well as many of the daytime television dramas. Love, marriage, family life, religion, these are the broad human-interest areas which produce the stories preferred by *TVM*. Except for standard staff-written features, all stories are from freelancers, usually based in Hollywood or New York. But we are a wide-open market to any writer who can meet our requirements. It is possible that a writer who lives, for example, in the home town of a major TV star could click at *TV Mirror* by doing an in-depth 'home-town report' on this celebrity, derived from interviews with his former teachers, friends, employers, family members, etc." Length: prefers 2,000 to 3,000 words. Pays 10¢ a word and up. Photos are bought from top-quality freelance photographers.

TV PRE-VUE MAGAZINE, Box 20768, Billings MT 59104. Editor-in-Chief: Valerie Hansen. Managing Editor: Virginia Hansen. Emphasizes television viewing. Weekly magazine; 32 pages. Estab: 1969. Circ: 13,000. Pays on publication. Buys all rights, but may reassign following publication. Submit seasonal/holiday material 2 months in advance. Reports in 3 months. Sample copy 25¢.

Nonfiction: Historical; humor; informational (on TV shows or personalities); interview and profile. Buys 12 mss/year. Query or submit complete ms. Length: 500-800 words. Pays 2-3¢/word.

Photos: Purchased with accompanying ms. Query. Pays $3 for b&w photos. ($12 if used for cover).

Poetry: Haiku, light verse and traditional. Buys 20/year. Limit submissions to batches of 5. Length: 4-8 lines.

Fillers: Anecdotes and profiles. Buys 12/year. Length: 100 words. Pays 2¢/word.

TV RADIO TALK, 575 Madison Ave., New York, NY 10022. Monthly. Buys first rights. 100% freelance. Reports in three weeks. Query first. Enclose S.A.S.E.

Nonfiction and Photos: "Uses interview and third person stories on TV stars, movie stars, record personalities and others who are famous. The stories should be factual. We do not print fiction. We like stories that are fresh and exclusive. There should be conflict in any story suggestion. The slant is usually for the star. The writing should fit the subject; if a love story, tender; if a scoop, exciting." Length: up to 2,000 words. Pays maximum of $200 on publication. Pays $20 up for photos; any size.

TV STAR PARADE, 575 Madison Ave., New York NY 10022. (212)759-9704, Ext. 18. Editor: Diane Simon. For "males and females of all ages interested in private lives of TV and movie stars." Monthly. Circulation: 400,000. Buys all rights. Payment on publication. Submit seasonal material 2 months in advance. Reports in 2 to 3 weeks. Query first required with basic outline of proposed feature. Enclose S.A.S.E.

Nonfiction and Photos: General subject matter consists of interviews, "backstage stories," romance, etc. Approach should be a "chatty style with special attention to dialog, quotes from the stars. We like to use as many real interviews as possible. We never publish made up quotes or interviews. We do not want angles that have been dredged up time and again just to fill space. Interested in timely material." Buys informational, personal experience, interviews, profile, nostalgia, photo articles. "I would appreciate new ideas for columns." Length: "5 to 7 typewritten pages." Pays $150 to $200. Photos are purchased without mss and on assignment. Captions are optional. Wants candid b&w. Pays $25 per photo on publication.

VIDEOGRAPHY, United Business Publications, 750 3rd Ave., New York NY 10017. (212)697-8300. Managing Editor: Peter Caranicas. For "people who use video in education and industry. Operators and producers of cable TV." Monthly magazine; 72 pages. Estab: 1976. Circ: 10,000. Pays on publication. Buys all rights, but may reassign following publication. Phone queries OK. Submit seasonal/holiday material 3 months in advance. SASE. Reports in 3 weeks. Free sample copy and writer's guidelines.

Nonfiction: How-to (using video, producing programs); informational (state-of-the-art articles); interview (video and tv personalities); and profile (equipment and producer). Buys 40 mss/year. Query. Length: 1,500-2,500 words. Pays $50.

Photos: Purchased with accompanying ms. Captions required. Query. Uses any size b&w glossy prints or color transparencies. Offers no additional payment for photos accepted with ms.

WEEKDAY TV, Ideal Publishing Corp., 575 Madison Ave., New York NY 10022. (212)759-9704. Editor: Seli Groves. Bimonthly. Buys all rights. Payment on publication. Query first. Enclose S.A.S.E.

Nonfiction: "Features daytime television stars. Soap opera stars and game show hosts are the subjects of most of the articles. Also use behind the scenes type articles and plot synopses of the soap operas from time to time. All story submissions must be the result of interviews, not articles written from clips and previously published information." Pays $100 to $200, depending on length and quality of article.

How To Break In: "Interview soap stars, then query us with your story ideas. Keeping up with the soap opera plots and cast changes is mandatory. Avid soap watchers are needed to write plot synopses and nostalgia pieces."

Travel, Camping, and Trailer Publications

Publications in this category tell campers and tourists where to go, where to stay, how to get there, how to camp, or how to select a good vehicle for travel or shelter. Publications that buy how-to camping and travel material with a conservation angle are listed in the *Nature, Conservation, and Ecology* classification. *Newspapers and Weekly Magazine Sections*, as well as *Regional Publications*, are frequently interested in travel and camping material with a local angle. *Hunting and fishing and outdoor publications* that buy camping how-to's will be found in the *Sport and Outdoor* category. *Publications dealing with automobiles or other vehicles maintained for sport or as a hobby will be found in the* Automotive and Motorcycle *category. Many publications in the* In-Flight *category are also in the market for travel articles and photos.*

ATLANTIC TRAVELER, 151 First Ave. N.W., or P.O. Box 1677, Largo FL 33540. Editor: Robert E. Lansing. For people who travel, "with emphasis on middle class fairly well-to-do people from 25 on up." Tabloid newspaper; 28 pages. Established in 1975. Monthly. Circulation: 60,000. Rights purchased vary with author and material. Buys 80 to 100 mss per year. Will send sample copy to writer for $1. Write for editorial guidelines sheet. No photocopied submissions. Will consider simultaneous submissions. Submit seasonal material 2 months in advance. Reports on mss accepted for publication in 1 month. Returns rejected material in 2 months. Enclose S.A.S.E.
Nonfiction and Photos: "Need stories about places of tourist interest in the midwest, south, east in the U.S., Canada west to Winnipeg, Mexico, Caribbean, Central America, upper South America. Also anything travel related. Especially want Canadian stories. Part of our effort is devoted to tying together Canadians in the U.S. and Canada." Would like to see mss on the Olympics in Montreal and recreation places in Canada. Buys informational, personal experience, interview, profile, humor, historical, "think" pieces, nostalgia, photo, and travel mss. Length: 500 to 1,000 words. Pays $5 to $500. Open to suggestions for new columns and departments. Photos purchased with accompanying ms with no additional payment, with ms with extra payment or on assignment. Captions required. No color. Any size. Pays $5 minimum.

AWAY, 888 Worcester St., Wellesley MA 02181. (617)237-5200. Editor: Gerard J. Gagnon. For "members of the ALA Auto & Travel Club, interested in their autos and in travel. Ages range from approximately 20 to 65. They live primarily in New England." Slanted to seasons. Quarterly. Circulation: 230,000. Buys first serial rights. Pays on acceptance. Will send a sample copy to a writer on request. Submit seasonal material 6 months in advance. Reports "as soon as possible." Although a query is not mandatory, it may be advisable for many articles. Enclose S.A.S.E. for return of submissions or reply to queries.
Nonfiction and Photos: Articles on "travel, tourist attractions, safety, history, etc., preferably with a New England angle. Also, car care tips and related subjects." Would like a "positive feel to all pieces, but not the Chamber of Commerce approach." Buys both general seasonal travel and specific travel articles, for example, travel-related articles (photo hints, etc.); outdoor activities; for example, gravestone rubbing, snow sculpturing; historical articles linked to places to visit; humor with a point, photo essays. "Would like to see more nonseasonally oriented material. Most material now submitted seems suitable only for our summer issue. Avoid pieces on hunting and about New England's most publicized attractions, such as Old Sturbridge Village and Mystic Seaport." Length: 800 to 1,500 words. "preferably 1,000 to 1,200." Pays approximately 10¢ per word. Photos purchased with mss; with captions only. B&w glossies. Pays $5 to $10 per b&w photo, payment on publication based upon which photos are used.
How To Break In: "New writers stand the same chance as experienced writers in getting published in *Away*. If the need, the quality, the content, the approach, and the timeliness are there, we buy the piece, regardless of whether it's the writer's first sale or the writer's 1000th sale. It should be emphasized that all writers would be wise to learn their market before sending material to *Away* or any other publication."

CAMPING JOURNAL, Davis Publications, 229 Park Ave., S., New York NY 10003. (212)673-1300. Editor-in-Chief: Andrew J. Carra. Managing Editor: Lee Schreiber. Emphasizes family outdoor recreation for active families who enjoy spending approximately 15-20 nights a year camping, particularly on weekends. Magazine, published 8 times a year; 64-80 pages. Estab: 1962. Circ: 281,000. Pays on acceptance. Buys all rights, but may reassign following publication. Submit seasonal/holiday material 4-5 months in advance. SASE. Reports in 6 weeks. Sample copy 75¢. Free writer's guidelines.
Nonfiction: How-to (make equipment yourself, set up campsites, etc.); humor; informational; interview; personal experience; photo feature and travel. "Articles should include campground info, facilities, routes, costs, etc." Buys 80-100 mss/year. Query. Length: 500-3,500 words. Pays $75-300.

Photos: Michele S. Kay, Photo Editor. Photos purchased with or without accompanying ms. Captions required. Uses 5x7 minimum b&w photos and 35mm color transparencies. Total purchase price for ms includes payment for photos.

Fillers: Michele S. Kay, Fillers Editor. Jokes, gags, anecdotes and newsbreaks. Buys 20 fillers/year. Length: 500 maximum. Pays $35-75.

CHEVRON USA, P.O. Box 6227, San Jose CA 95150. (408)296-1060. Editor: Marian May. For members of the Chevron Travel Club. Quarterly. Buys North American serial rights. Pays for articles on acceptance. Pays for photos on publication. Will send a sample copy to a writer on request. Reports in 4 to 6 weeks. Prefers mss on speculation. Enclose S.A.S.E.

Nonfiction: Travel in western, eastern and southern U.S. —close-to-home trips or areas readily accessible by plane, train, bus. Historical emphasis—famous trails, towns, landmarks. Pictorials with nature and environmental themes. Family activities—sports, handcrafts. Each piece should have specific slant—tied to season, unusual aspect. In general, prefers specific subjects well-detailed rather than sketchy. Length: 500 to 1,500 words. Pays 15¢ a word and up.

Photos: Subject matter same as nonfiction. No empty scenics. Majority of photos must have active people in them. Prefers 2¼ square or 4x5, top quality 35mm. Pays $150 full page for color, minimum $75. For b&w, pays $50 full page, $35 minimum.

Fillers: Anecdotal material. Must be about travel, personal experiences. Must be original. Length: about 200 to 250 words. Pays $25 each.

DESERT MAGAZINE, Box 1318, Palm Desert CA 92260. (714)346-8144. Editor: William Knyvett. Emphasizes Southwest travel and history. For recreation-minded families—middle class income, RV owners, bikers and backpackers. Monthly magazine; 48 pages. Estab: 1937. Circ: 40,000. Pays on publication. Buys first North American serial rights. Submit seasonal or holiday material 6 months in advance. SASE. Reports in 4 weeks. Free sample copy and writer's guidelines.

Nonfiction: Historical, informational, personal experience, travel. Buys 8 articles/issue. Query. Length: 500-2,500 words. Pays $20-100.

Photos: Photos purchased with or without accompanying ms. Captions required. Pays $5 for 8x10 b&w glossies; $25 for inside color photos; $35 for 4x5 color cover photos. "2¼x2¼ preferred over 35mm."

DISCOVERY MAGAZINE, Allstate Plaza, Northbrook IL 60062. Editor: Alan Rosenthal. For motor club members; mobile familes with above average income. "All issues pegged to season." Established in 1961. Quarterly. Circ: 940,000. Buys first North American serial rights. Buys 40 mss a year. Payment on acceptance. Will send free sample copy to writer on request. Write for copy of guidelines for writers. Submit seasonal material 8 to 12 months in advance. Reports in 3 weeks. Query first. Enclose S.A.S.E.

Nonfiction and Photos: "Primarily travel subjects. Also automotive and safety. First-person narrative approach for most travel articles. Short pieces on restaurants must include recipes from the establishment." Travel articles and photos often are purchased as a package. Rates depend on how the photos are used. Color transparencies (35mm or larger) are preferred. Photos should show people doing things; captions required. Send transparencies by registered mail, with plenty of cardboard protection. Buys one-time rights for photography. Color photos are returned after use. Length: 1,000 to 2,500 words. "Rates vary, depending on type of article, ranging from $200-400 for full-length features." Photos purchased with accompanying mss; captions required. Photos also purchased on assignment.

Fillers: True, humorous travel anecdotes. Length: 50 to 150 words. Pays $10.

FAMILY MOTOR COACHING, Corporation Famoco, Inc., Box 44144, 8291 Clough Pike, Cincinnati OH 45244. (513)474-3622. Editor: Dan LeHockey. For middle-aged or older readers; well-traveled, well-educated and affluent. Bimonthly magazine; 150 pages. Estab: 1964. Circ: 30,000. Pays on publication. Buys first North American serial rights. Submit seasonal/holiday material 3 months in advance. Simultaneous and photocopied submissions OK. Previously published work acceptable if so advised. SASE. Reports in 2-4 weeks. Free sample copy.

Nonfiction: How-to; informational (must deal with motor homes and camping); and travel (places to see while traveling in motor homes; camping facilities, etc.). Buys 4-5/issue. Query. Length: 1,000-3,000 words. Pays $50-400.

Photos: Purchased with ms. B&w and color. Query. No additional payment.

How To Break In: "We welcome any interesting ideas or suggestions for articles from freelancers. An interested, potential contributor should send a specific and detailed query, giving us his/her qualifications for treating the subject."

HANDBOOK AND DIRECTORY FOR CAMPERS, 1999 Shepard Rd., St. Paul MN 55116. (612)647-7290. Editor: John C. Viehman. For families whose members range in age from infancy to past retirement, and whose leisure interests are aimed primarily at outdoor recreation and travel with recreational vehicles providing the means to enjoyment of this new life style. Established in 1971. Annual. Circulation: 1,650,000. Buys all rights, but will reassign rights to author after publication. Buys 6 to 12 mss a year. Payment on acceptance. Will send free sample copy to writer on request. Write for copy of guidelines for writers. Will consider photocopied submissions. Reports in 30 days. Query first. Enclose S.A.S.E.
Nonfiction: "General articles on outdoor living and travel including how to prepare for trip and ways to gain more enjoyment from the going, staying, and coming home portions of it. In all cases, emphasis should be on the positive, fun aspects of travel and camping, not on the problems sometimes encountered. Writing should be readable rather than academic, clever rather than endlessly descriptive, tight rather than verbose. A good lead is considered essential. First-person articles and stories about personal experiences are not acceptable. We try to emphasize that camping is not only fun in itself, but is the means to all kinds of peripheral activities not normally available to the average family. Editorial slant is consistently on the enjoyment aspects of the experience." Informational, how-to, profile, humor, historical, nostalgia, photo, and travel articles. Length: 700 to 1,500 words. Pays $75 to $275.
Photos: Purchased with accompanying mss or on assignment. Captions optional. Uses color; 35mm and larger. Pays $200 for cover; $50 each for inside use.

LEISUREGUIDE, 1515 N.W. 167th St., Miami FL 33169. Editor-in-Chief: Andrew Delaplaine. An in-room hotel guide book emphasizing information for travelers in Chicago, the Florida Gold Coast (Palm Beach to Miami), and South Carolina's Grand Strand (Myrtle Beach). Annual hard-covered magazine; 140-150 pages. Estab: 1971. Circ: 110,000. Pays on publication. Buys all rights, but may reassign following publication. Submit seasonal/holiday material 3 months in advance. Photocopied submissions and previously published work OK. SASE. Reports in 2 weeks. Sample copy $2.
Nonfiction: Informational (of interest to sophisticated transients in our cities); historical (of interest to our transient reader—usually of light, humorous vein); travel (articles concentrated on the cities in which we publish); photo feature (must be color of very high quality and concentrate on some aspect of interest to the cities served). Buys 50 mss/year. Query. Length: 1,000-3,500 words. Pays $100-500.
Photos: Purchased without mss or on assignment. Query. "A good shot can come from any locale, but be appropriate (because of its general nature) to any of our editions." Pays $10-75 for b&w; $20-125 for color.
Rejects: "We almost never accept the general 'traveler' article to be found in publications such as in-flight magazines. Our articles must relate specifically to the three areas we serve and tell the readers something about these areas."

THE LUFKIN LINE, Lufkin Industries, Inc., P.O. Box 849, Lufkin TX 75901. Editor: Miss Virginia R. Allen. For men in oil and commercial and marine gear industries; readers mostly degreed engineers. Each issue devoted to different areas where division offices located; that is, West Coast, Canada, Mid-Continent, Rocky Mountain, Texas, Gulf Coast, International. Established in 1924. Quarterly. Circulation: 12,000. Not copyrighted. Buys 4 to 8 mss a year. Payment on acceptance. Will send free sample copy to writer on request. Write for copy of guidelines for writers. Will not consider photocopied submissions. Submit seasonal material 3 to 4 months in advance. Reports in 1 month. Query first. Enclose S.A.S.E.
Nonfiction and Photos: "Travel articles. Subjects dealing with U.S. and Canada, and (rarely) foreign travel subjects. Product articles staff written. Length: 1,000 to 1,200 words. Pays $50 per ms with illustrating photos. Color transparencies of seasonal subjects are purchased for inside front cover; pays $30. Illustrations for travel articles may be color prints or transparencies (no smaller than 2¼x2¼). No b&w photos are purchased. Color photos for travel articles may be secured from state tourist or development commissions.

METRO EAST OUTDOOR NEWS, Delaware Valley Outdoor News, Inc., 1150 York Rd., Box 136, Abington, PA 19001. (215)884-6515. Editor-in-Chief: Charles E. Myers. Emphasis on recreation vehicle camping and travel. Monthly (except Dec. and Feb.) tabloid; 32 pages. Estab: 1973. Circ: 40,000. Pays on publication. Buys simultaneous, second serial (reprint) and regional rights. Submit seasonal/holiday material 3-4 months in advance. Simultaneous, photocopied and previously published submissions OK. SASE. Reports in 1 month. Free sample copy and writer's guidelines.
Nonfiction: Historical (when tied in with camping trip to historical attraction or area); how-to

(selection, care, maintenance of RVs, accessories and camping equipment); humor; personal experience and travel (camping destinations within 200 miles of Philadelphia-D.C. metro corridor). Buys 75 mss/year. Query. Length: 1,200-2,000 words. Pays $40-75.

Photos: Photos purchased with accompanying ms. Captions required. Uses 5x7 or 8x10 b&w glossies. Total purchase price for ms includes payment for photos.

Columns/Departments: RV Handyman (RV maintenance, repair and improvement ideas) and Camp Cookery (ideas for cooking in RV galleys and over campfires. Should include recipes). Buys 10 mss/year. Query. Length: 1,000-2,000 words. Pays $40-75.

How To Break In: "Articles should focus on single attraction or activity or on closely clustered attractions within reach on the same weekend camping trip rather than on types of attractions of activities in general. We're looking for little-known or offbeat items. Emphasize positive aspects of camping: fun, economy, etc."

THE MIDWEST MOTORIST, 201 Progress Pkwy., Maryland Heights MO 63043. Editor: Martin Quigley. For "the typical rural type to the best educated in the Midwest." Publication of The Auto Club of Missouri. Bimonthly. Circulation: 280,000. Not copyrighted. Payment on acceptance. Will send free sample copy to writer on request. Reports in 2 to 6 weeks. Query first. Enclose S.A.S.E.

Nonfiction and Photos: "Features of interest to our motoring public. Articles cover important auto-oriented consumer issues as well as travel and auto interest pieces. We seek serious, well-documented consumer and ecology pieces, and are also interested in lighter material, focusing on unusual places to visit." Length: about 1,200 words. Pays $50 to $200. B&w glossy photos purchased with mss. No color.

MINNESOTA AAA MOTORIST, Minnesota State Automobile Association, 7 Travelers Trail, Burnsville MN 55337. (612)890-2500. Editor: Ron D. Johnson. For professional people, educated farmers and businessmen and women interested in travel. Monthly magazine. Established in 1957. Circulation: 260,000. Buys first North American serial rights. Buys 20-30 mss/year. Pays on acceptance. Free sample copy and writer's guidelines. Reports in 3 weeks. Submit complete ms. Enclose S.A.S.E.

Nonfiction and Photos: "Nonfiction articles on domestic and foreign travel, motoring, car care, which are well written and interesting. We have our own auto consultant for articles on automobile safety." Wants "well-written, interesting articles on places throughout the world, where our readers would like to go. Submissions should be readable and entertain and educate our readers. Our emphasis is on the quality, not the quantity, of work." Buys how-to's, personal experience articles, interviews, humor, historical and travel articles, photo essays. Length: 800 to 1,000 words. Pays $150 minimum. Good b&w, 8x10, glossy photos purchased with mss. Pays $15 per photo.

MOBILE LIVING, P.O. Box 1418, Sarasota FL 33578. Editor: Frances Neel. Bimonthly. Buys first rights only. Pays on publication. Will send a free sample copy to a writer on request. Reports on submissions within 1 month. Enclose S.A.S.E.

Nonfiction: Articles on recreational vehicle experiences and travel via recreational vehicles. In travel articles, include names of parks to stay at while seeing the sights, etc. Hobbies involving recreational vehicles and how-to-do-it articles that apply to a general audience also wanted. Length: 1,500 words maximum. Pays 1¢ per word.

Photos: With captions and illustrating articles. B&w glossies only. Returned after use. Pays $3 each.

MOTOR NEWS—MICHIGAN LIVING, Automobile Club of Michigan, Auto Club Dr., Dearborn, MI 48126. (313)336-1504. Editor-in-Chief: Len Barnes. Emphasizes travel and auto use. Monthly magazine; 48 pages. Estab: 1922. Circ: 800,000. Pays on acceptance. Buys first North American serial rights. Phone queries OK. Submit seasonal/holiday material 3 months in advance. SASE. Reports in 4-6 weeks. Free sample copy and writer's guidelines.

Nonfiction: Marcia Danner, Nonfiction Editor. How-to; informational; and travel. Buys 30 mss/year. Send complete ms. Length: 800-2,000 words. Pays $75-200.

Photos: Photos purchased with accompanying ms. Captions required. Pays $25-150 for color transparencies; total purchase price for ms includes payment for b&w photos.

How To Break In: "In addition to descriptions of things to see and do, articles should contain accurate, current information on costs the traveler would encounter on his trip. Items such as lodging, meal and entertainment expenses should be included, not in the form of a balance sheet but as an integral part of the piece."

MOTORHOME LIFE & CAMPER COACHMAN, Trailer Life Publishing Co., Inc., 23945 Craftsman Rd., Calabasas CA 91302. (213)888-6000. Editor: Denis Rouse. For owners and prospective buyers of motorhomes, mini-motorhomes, campers, camping-converted vans. Established in 1962. Published every 2 months. Circulation: 100,000. Buys all rights. Buys about 50 mss a year. Pays on publication. Will send sample copy to writer for $1. Write for copy of guidelines for writers. Submit seasonal material 3 months in advance. Reports in 1 month. Enclose S.A.S.E.

Nonfiction and Photos: "Articles which tell the owner of a self-propelled RV about interesting places to travel, interesting things to do. Do-it-yourself improvements to chassis or coach are heavily emphasized. Human interest and variety articles sought as well. All material must be tailored specifically for our audience. We cover only self-propelled recreational vehicles —no trailers." Informational, personal experience, humor, historical, personal opinion, travel, new product, and technical articles. Length: 2,500 words maximum. Pays $75-200. Photos purchased with accompanying ms with no additional payment.

NATIONAL MOTORIST, National Automobile Club, 1 Market Plaza, #300, San Francisco CA 94105. (415)777-4000. Editor-in-Chief: Jim Donaldson. Emphasizes motor travel in the West. Bimonthly magazine; 32 pages. Estab: 1924. Circ: 318,000. Pays on acceptance for article, layout stage for pix. Buys first publication rights. Submit seasonal/holiday material 3 months in advance. Reports in 1 week. Free sample copy.

Nonfiction: How-to (care for car, travel by car, participate in outdoor sports and hobbies); historical (interesting history and significant historical personalities behind places and areas readers might visit); humor (occasionally buys a story treating something in motoring from a humorous angle); profile (of someone with unusual skills or engaged in some interesting and unusual art, hobby or craft); and travel (interesting places and areas to visit in the 11 western states). Buys 5-8 mss/issue. Query. Length: "around 500 words *or* around 1,100 words." Pays 10¢/word and up.

Photos: Purchased with accompanying ms. Captions optional, "but must have caption info for pix." Send prints or transparencies. Pays $15 and up for 8x10 b&w glossies; $25 and up for 2¼x2¼ or 4x5 color transparencies. Model release required.

NORTHEAST OUTDOORS, 95 North Main St., Waterbury CT 06702. (203)757-8731. Editor: John Florian. Monthly. Circulation: 20,000. Buys all rights. Pays on publication. Will send free sample copy to writer on request. "Queries are not required, but are useful for our planning and to avoid possible duplication of subject matter. If you have any questions, contact the editor." Deadlines are on the 5th of the month preceding publication. Reports in 15 to 30 days. Enclose S.A.S.E.

Nonfiction and Photos: Interested in articles and photos that pertain to outdoor activities in the Northeast. Recreational vehicle tips, maintenance and care are prime topics, along with first-person travel experiences in the Northeast while camping. "While the primary focus is on camping, we carry some related articles on outdoor topics like skiing, nature, hiking, fishing, canoeing, etc. In each issue we publish a 'Favorite Trip' experience, submitted by a reader, relating to a favorite camping experience, usually in the Northeast. Payment for this is $20 and writing quality need not be professional. Another reader feature is 'My Favorite Campground'. Payment is $10. Our pay rate is flexible, but generally runs from $20 for short, simple articles, $30 to $40 for features without photos, and up to $60 for features accompanied by 2 or more photos. Features should be from 300 to 1,000 words. Premium rates are paid on the basis of quality, not length. For photos alone we pay $7.50 for each 8x10 b&w print we use. Photo layouts bring $40."

OHIO MOTORIST, P.O. Box 6150, Cleveland OH 44101. Editor: A. K. Murway, Jr. For AAA members in 5 northeast Ohio counties. Estab: 1909. Monthly. Circ: 221,000. Buys one-time publication rights. Buys 30 mss a year. Payment on acceptance. Will send free sample copy to writer on request. Submit seasonal material 2 months prior to season. Reports in 2 weeks. Submit complete ms. Enclose S.A.S.E.

Nonfiction and Photos: "Travel, including foreign; automotive, highways, etc.; motoring laws and safety. No particular approach beyond brevity and newspaper journalistic treatment. Articles for travel seasons." Needs fuel crisis material. Length: 2,000 words maximum. Pays $50-200/article including b&w photos. 8x10 b&w photos preferred. Purchased with accompanying mss. Captions required. Pays $8 to $20 for singles, although "rarely" purchases singles.

Poetry: Light verse. Length: 4 to 6 lines. Pays $7.50 to $12.

PACIFIC BOATING ALMANAC, Box Q, Ventura CA 93001. (805)644-6043. Publisher/Editor: William Berssen. For "boat owners in the Pacific Southwest." Established in 1965. Published in 3 editions to cover the Pacific Coastal area. Circ: 36,000. Buys all rights. Buys 12 mss/ year. Pays on publication. Sample copy $5.25. Submit seasonal material 3 to 6 months in advance. Reports in 4 weeks. Query first. Enclose S.A.S.E.

Nonfiction and Photos: "This is a cruising guide, published annually in 3 editions, covering all of the navigable waters in the Pacific coast. Though we are almost entirely staff-produced, we would be interested in well-written articles on cruising and trailer-boating along the Pacific coast and in the navigable lakes and rivers of the western states from Baja, California to Alaska inclusive." Pays $50 minimum. Pays $10 for 8x10 b&w glossies.

RV VAN WORLD, 16200 Ventura Blvd., Encino CA 91416. Editor: Chris Hosford. Associate Editor: D. Tiffany Ford. For custom/recreational van owners/campers. Established in 1973. Monthly. Circulation: 80,000. Buys all rights. Payment on publication. Will send free sample copy to writer/photographer on request. Write for copy of editorial and photo requirements. Submit seasonal material at least 4 months in advance. (Winter material needed in mid-summer.) Reports on material in 1 to 2 weeks. Query first. Enclose S.A.S.E.

Nonfiction and Photos: No travel articles of any kind are used. How-to articles related to custom-van enthusiast-type and/or repair or maintenance. Semitechnical, and technical articles related to custom vans and/or van camping. Simple, straightforward style. Any technical material must be accurate. No personal experience used as a rule, although there may be the odd exception if story merits special consideration. Length: about 2,000 words, or more. Pays $40 per printed magazine page (with 50 percent photos). Can use negatives and contact sheets; crisp focus, clean background. Captions must accompany articles. Use separate sheet(s) keyed to numbers of photos. Buys complete editorial package; copy and photos as single unit. No additional payment for photos. Color transparencies; 35mm or larger. No color prints of any type accepted.

SUNBOUND, Webb Company, 1999 Shepard Rd., St. Paul MN 55116. Editor-in-Chief: Don Picard. Managing Editor: Jerry Bassett. Emphasizes family travel involving Florida for summer and winter tourists. Quarterly magazine; 32 pages. Estab: 1973. Circ: 25,000. Pays on acceptance. Buys all rights, but may reassign following publication. Phone queries OK. Submit seasonal/holiday material 6 months in advance. Simultaneous and photocopied submissions OK. SASE. Reports in 3 weeks. Free sample copy and writer's guidelines.

Nonfiction: Historical (travel, places to see orientation); informational (travel, leisure); interview (leisure, travel, strong personality); nostalgia (as relates to travel, leisure); photo feature (travel and leisure) and travel. All topics must relate to Florida. Buys 3-4 mss/issue. Query. Length: 1,500-2,000 words. Pays $100-250.

Photos: Purchased with or without accompanying ms or on assignment. Query. Pays $25 for 8x10 b&w glossies; $75 for 35mm or larger color transparencies. Model release may be required.

TRAVEL, 51 Atlantic Ave., Floral Park NY 11001. (516)352-9700. Editor: Barbara M. Lotz. For middle-aged active travelers. Monthly magazine; 90 pages. Estab: 1901. Circ: 600,000. Buys first North American serial rights. Buys about 100 mss per year. Pays on acceptance. Will send free sample copy to writer on request. Write for editorial guidelines sheet. Will consider photocopied submissions. No simultaneous submissions. Submit seasonal material 6 months in advance. Reports on mss accepted for publication in 2 weeks. Returns rejected material "immediately." Enclose S.A.S.E.

Nonfiction, Fillers and Photos: Wants travel pieces, mostly destination-oriented; some service. Does not want to see mss on overworked destinations. Would like to see more "off-the-beaten-path travel pieces." Length: 1,500 to 2,500 words. Pays $150 for ms with b&w photos. Pays $200 to $300 for ms with color photos. Also buys short travel pieces with 1 or 2 photos, and short humor. Length: 500 to 1,000 words. Pays $25 to $65. Photos purchased with accompanying ms with no additional payment. Captions required. Pays $100 for cover shots. Size: 5x7 minimum for b&w glossy; 35mm or larger color transparency. No dupes. Submit slides in vinyl sheets.

TRAVEL AND LEISURE, 1350 Avenue of the Americas, New York NY 10019. (212)586-5050. Editor-in-Chief: Pamela Fiori. Monthly. Circulation: 800,000. Buys first North American serial rights. Pays on acceptance. Reports in 1 week. Query first. Enclose S.A.S.E.

Nonfiction and Photos: Uses articles on travel and vacation places, food, wine, shopping, sports. Most articles are assigned. Length: 1,000 to 2,500 words. Pays $750 to $1,500.

Photos: Makes assignments to photographers. Pays expenses.

How To Break In: "New writers might try to get something in one of our regional editions

(East, West, South, and Midwest). They don't pay as much as our national articles, but it might be a good way to start. We use a lot of these pieces and they need be no more than 500 to 800 words, 1,000 tops. They cover any number of possibilities from traveling a river in a certain state to unusual new attractions."

TRAVELIN' VANS, 13510 Ventura Blvd., Sherman Oaks CA 91423. (213)990-2510. Editor: Jim Matthews. For van owners and their families. Magazine; 64 pages. Established in 1976. Monthly. Circulation: 80,000. Buys all rights, but may reassign rights to author after publication. Buys 25 to 35 mss per year. Pays on publication. Free sample copy and editorial guidelines. Submit seasonal material 3 months in advance. Reports on mss accepted for publication in 10 days. Returns rejected material in 14 days. Query first. Enclose S.A.S.E.
Nonfiction and Photos: Wants mss about methods of customizing, feature articles on outstanding vans, coverage of "van happenings" rallies, charity activities, special purpose vans and related subjects. Wants how-to and semi-technical mss. "Keep in mind our audience at all times. Generally thought of as a youth group, they are very solid reliable citizens who spend hours and countless dollars making their vans unique and comfortable." No travel articles unless specifically related to van events. "Never, never any emphasis on antisocial behavior." Would like to see mss on van events in many areas of the country far from Southern California. Buys informational, how-to, profile and nostalgia. Length: 1,200 to 1,600 words. Pays $35 per page in finished book. "Approximately 50% photos." Photos purchased with ms with no additional payment. Captions required. B&w primarily; color of outstanding vans.

TRAVELORE REPORT, 225 S. 15th St., Philadelphia PA 19102. Editor: Ted Barkus. For affluent travelers; businessmen, retirees, well educated; interested in specific tips, tours, and value opportunities in travel. Monthly newsletter; 4 pages, (8½x11). Established in 1972. Circulation: 10,000. Buys all rights, but will reassign rights to author after publication. Buys 25 to 50 mss a year. Payment on publication. Will send sample copy to writer for $1. Submit seasonal material 2 months in advance. Enclose S.A.S.E.
Nonfiction and Fillers: "Brief insights (25 to 200 words) with facts, prices, names of hotels and restaurants, etc., on offbeat subjects of interest to people going places. What to do, what not to do. Supply information. We will rewrite if acceptable. We're candid—we tell it like it is with no sugar coating. Avoid telling us about places in United States or abroad without specific recommendations (hotel name, how much, why, how long, etc.)." Pays $5.

WISCONSIN AAA MOTOR NEWS, 433 West Washington Ave., Madison WI 53703. (608)257-0711. Editor: Hugh P. (Mickey) McLinden. Aimed at audience of domestic and foreign motorist-travelers. Monthly. Circ: 225,600. Buys all rights. Pays on publication. Reports immediately. Enclose S.A.S.E. for return of submissions.
Nonfiction and Photos: Domestic and foreign travel; motoring, safety, highways, new motoring products. Length: 500 words maximum. Pays $25 minimum. Photos purchased with mss or with captions only. B&w glossy. Pays $10 minimum.

WOODALL'S TRAILER & RV TRAVEL (formerly *Trailer Travel*), 500 Hyacinth Place, Highland Park IL 60035. (312)433-4550. Editor: Kirk Landers. For recreational vehicle owners and enthusiasts whose interests include travel-camping in North America, and buying, maintaining and customizing their vehicles. Magazine; 125 pages. Established in 1936. Monthly. Circ: 300,000. Rights purchased vary with author and material. Usually buys all rights, but may reassign rights to author after publication. Buys about 75 mss a year. Pays on acceptance. Will send sample copy to writer on request. Write for copy of guidelines for writers. No photocopied or simultaneous submissions. Submit seasonal material 4 to 6 months in advance. Reports in 4 weeks. Query first or submit complete ms. Enclose S.A.S.E.
Nonfiction and Photos: "Travel guides and narratives providing comprehensive views of great camping areas. Also, humor, profiles (especially of those who live and work on the road); recipe and menu ideas; money-saving tips; vehicle maintenance and improvement; insurance, equipment, etc. Our greatest joy is a thoroughly researched article in which facts, figures, quotes and conclusions are presented in clear, concise prose, and in a logical sequence. We avoid material that is slanted exclusively to the raw beginner. Would consider winter camping ideas; pieces on rainy day recreation for families; RV retirement; new, uncrowded, warm weather retreats for winter migrants." Recently published "Big Bend Diary." Length: 1,000 to 3,000 words. Pays $150 to $300; more on assignment. Seasonal photo essays are used when good color is available. B&w and color purchased with or without mss. Pays $25 minimum for b&w; $50 minimum for color. Captions required.
How To Break In: "A background in this special interest field is a must; so is a familiarity with

our editorial style and format. The ripest subject areas are probably well-researched travel material, profiles, and humor. Also, writers with a specific field of expertise — be it bird-watching, interior decorating, engineering or what have you — tend to do well with us by presenting their credentials and a few article ideas in a query. We don't always like their ideas, but if their credentials are right, we often come back to them with our own suggestions."

Union Publications

OCAW UNION NEWS, P.O. Box 2812, Denver CO 80201. (303)893-0811. Editor: Jerry Arch-uleta. Official publication of Oil, Chemical and Atomic Workers International Union. For union members. Monthly tabloid newspaper; 12 pages. Established in 1944. Circulation: 180,000. Not copyrighted. Payment on acceptance. Will send free sample copy to writer on request. Reports in 30 days. Query first. Enclose S.A.S.E.
Nonfiction and Photos: Labor union materials, political subjects and consumer interest articles, slanted toward workers and consumers, with liberal political view. Interview, profile, think pieces and exposes. Most material is done on assignment. Length: 1,500 to 1,800 words. Pays $50 to $75. No additional payment is made for 8x10 b&w glossy photos used with mss. Captions required.

UTU NEWS, United Transportation Union, 14600 Detroit Ave., Cleveland, OH 44107. (216)228-9400. Editor-in-Chief: Jim Turner. For members of the union (250,000) working in the crafts of engineer, conductor, firemen and brakemen on North American railroads. Weekly newspaper; 4 pages. (Also one monthly tabloid; 8 pages). Estab: 1969. Pays on publication. Buys all rights. Phone queries OK. Reports at once.
Photos: Current news shots of railroad or bus accidents, especially when employees are killed or injured. Captions required. Pays $15 minimum for any size 8x10 b&w glossies.

Women's Publications

The publications listed in this category specialize in material of interest to women. Other publications which occasionally use material slanted to women's interests can be found in the following categories: Alternative, Child Care and Parental Guidance; Confession, Education, Farm, Food and Drink; Hobby and Craft; Home and Garden; Religious, and Sport and Outdoor publications.

AAUW JOURNAL, 2401 Virginia Ave. N.W., Washington DC 20037. (202)785-7700. Publication of American Association of University Women. Editor: Jean Fox. For women of all ages who have at least a B.A. degree. Published 5 times annually as a newspaper; twice as a magazine; 12 to 16 pages, newspaper; 48 pages, magazine. Circulation: 190,000. Buys first serial rights. Buys about 10 mss a year, but this varies. Pays on publication. Will send sample copy to writer for $1. Query first; "send sample of work first." Enclose S.A.S.E.
Nonfiction and Photos: "Material used in our journal is usually related to broad themes which AAUW is concerned with. For the next two years, these concerns include the Equal Rights Amendments, laws and public policies affecting women, redefining the goals of education; women as agents of change and the 'politics' of food. No special style or approach necessary. Emphasis on women and their efforts to improve society. B&w photos are purchased on assignment. Captions optional. Pay is minimal since we are a nonprofit organization." Pays $100 maximum.

THE AUSTRALIAN WOMEN'S WEEKLY, Australian Consolidated Press Ltd., 54 Park St., Sydney, NSW, Australia 2000. Editor-in-Chief: Ita Buttrose. For women, mainly ages 14 and older. "25% of our readership is male, they are from all walks of life." Weekly. Estab: 1933. Circ: 830,000. Pays on acceptance or publication. Buys Australian first serial rights. SASE. Sample copy $1.50.
Nonfiction and Fiction: Buys informational; how-to; personal experience; interview; profile; inspirational; humor; historical; "think" pieces; nostalgia; personal opinion; photo; travel; spot news; successful business operations; new product; film, book and theater reviews. Length: 1,000 to 3,000 words. Pays $60 minimum. "We don't have a maximum payment. Depends on article and standard of writing." Publishes all fiction: experimental, mainstream, mystery, suspense, adventure, western, science fiction, fantasy, humorous, romance, historical, condensed novels, serialized novels. Payment: negotiated.

Photos: Purchased with accompanying ms with or without additional payment. Also purchased without accompanying ms. Captions required. Payment: negotiated. Buys 6x8 glossy prints (preferably), and 2¼ or 35mm transparencies.

Fillers: Buys jokes, gags, anecdotes, short humor. Length: open. Payment: negotiated. Also open to suggestions for new columns or departments.

BEAUTY HANDBOOK, 420 Lexington Ave., New York NY 10017. (212)687-2113. Editor-in-Chief: Eileen Dougherty. Emphasizes beauty, grooming and exercise. Quarterly magazine; 84 pages. Estab: 1975. Circ: 1½ million. Pays on publication. Buys all rights. Submit seasonal/ holiday material 4 months in advance. Simultaneous, photocopied, and previously published submissions OK. SASE. Reports in 2 weeks. Free sample copy.

Nonfiction: G. Shakel, Articles Editor. Uses articles on beauty, health, exercise, etc. Buys 40 mss/year. Query. Length: average 300 words. Payment negotiable.

Photos: John McAuliffe, Photo Editor. Purchased with or without accompanying ms or on assignment. Captions required. Query. Submit contact sheet, prints, negatives or transparencies. Offers no additional payment for photos used with ms. Model release required.

BRANCHING OUT, New Woman's Magazine Society, Box 4098, Edmonton, Alberta, Canada T6E 4T1. (403)433-4021. Editor-in-Chief: Sharon Batt. For Canadian women. "The majority are professional, well-educated women with a variety of interests (art, literary, political, feminist); 25-50 years of age. Bimonthly magazine; 48 pages. Estab: 1973. Circ: 4,000. Pays on publication. Buys first North American serial rights. Phone queries OK. Photocopied submissions OK. SAE and International Reply Coupons. Sample copy $1.25; free writer's guidelines.

Nonfiction and Photos: Photo features with 4-5 photographs in a series. Buys 60-70/year. Query. Length: 500-3,500 words. Pays $5-7.50, but first contribution is paid for by a complimentary subscription. B&w photos purchased with or without mss. Query. Pays $5 for first contribution (no smaller than 5x7); $7.50 for subsequent contributions.

Columns/Departments: Material for all columns and features should take a feminist point of view. Book reviews and columns on law and films. Query. Length: 300-1,500 words. Complimentary subscription for first contribution; pays $5-7.50 for later ones.

Fiction: "High quality fiction by Canadian women. Experimental and mainstream. Fiction must be good, not sentimental, tightly constructed, high quality writing." Submit complete ms. Length: 1,000-5,000 words. Same rate of payment as nonfiction.

Poetry: Avant-garde, free verse, haiku. Buys 3-4/issue. Limit submissions to batches of 8. Pays $5 minimum after first contribution.

BRIDE'S MAGAZINE, The Conde Nast Bldg., 350 Madison Ave., New York NY 10017. (212)692-5032. Editor: Barbara D. Tober. For the first or second-time bride in her early twenties, her family and friends, the groom and his family. Magazine published 6 times/year. Estab: 1934. Circ: 300,000. Buys all rights. Buys about 35 mss/year. Pays on acceptance. Free writer's guidelines. Reports in 6-8 weeks. Query or submit complete ms. Enclose S.A.S.E.

Nonfiction: Department Editor: Peyton Bailey. "We want articles on current psychological or sociological topics closely linked to marriage today. Keep in mind contemporary reappraisals of marriage roles but remember that each couple deserves the freedom to choose their life styles. Topics should be well-defined; material well-organized with a bright introduction and optimistic conclusion. Include interviews with authorities and/or young couples. First- or second-person narrative, roundtable, or quiz. Our primary concern is to help the bride with both her wedding and her marriage." Length: 1,500-2,500 words. Pays $300-500.

How To Break In: "Send us a well-written article that is both easy to read and offers real help for the bride as she adjusts to her new role. Nothing on wedding and reception planning, or etiquette, as these are written by staff."

CHATELAINE, 481 University Ave., Toronto M5W 1A7, Canada. (416)595-1811. Editor: Doris McCubbin Anderson. Managing Editor: Mildred Istona. For "Canadian women, from age 20 up, mainly homemakers, with or without outside jobs." Monthly. Buys first world serial rights in English and French (the latter to cover possible use in *Chatelaine's* sister French-language edition, edited in Montreal for French Canada). Pays on acceptance. Reports in 2 to 4 weeks. Query first, with a 1- or 2-page outline. Enclose S.A.E. and International Reply Coupons.

Nonfiction: "Subjects wanted are important national Canadian articles examining all and any facet of Canadian life, especially as they concern or interest Canadian women. Length: 2,000 to 3,600 words. Pays $600 minimum. "We also seek full-length personal experience articles with deep emotional impact. For all serious articles, deep, accurate, thorough research and rich detail are required."

Fiction: Department Editor: Almeda Glassey. Canadian settings, situations and characters much preferred, strong human stories with real character impact; stories reflecting women's new independence. The central character should be a woman. Very little demand for stories where the central character is a child (though children can be important secondary characters), or animal stories. Length: 3,000 to 4,000. No short-shorts. Payment starts at $400.

COSMOPOLITAN, 224 West 57th St., New York NY 10019. Editor: Helen Gurley Brown. Managing Editor: Jim Watters. For career women, ages 18 to 34. Monthly. Circ: 2,465,145. Buys all rights. Pays on acceptance. Not interested in receiving unsolicited manuscripts. Most material is assigned to established, known professional writers who sell regularly to top national markets, or is commissioned through literary agents.

Nonfiction and Photos: Not interested in unsolicited manuscripts; for agents and top professional writers, requirements are as follows: "We want pieces that tell an attractive, 18- to 34-year-old, intelligent, good-citizen girl how to have a more rewarding life—'how-to' pieces, self-improvement pieces as well as articles which deal with more serious matters. We'd be interested in articles on careers, part-time jobs, diets, food, fashion, men, the entertainment world, emotions, money, medicine and psychology, and fabulous characters." Uses some first-person stories. Logical, interesting, authoritative writing is a must, as is a feminist consciousness. Length: 1,200 to 1,500 words; 3,000 to 4,000 words. Pays $200 to $500 for short pieces, $1,000 to $1,750 for longer articles. Photos purchased on assignment only.

Fiction: Department Editor: Harris Dienstfrey. Not interested in unsolicited manuscripts; for agents and top professional writers, requirements are as follows: "Good plotting and excellent writing are important. We want short stories dealing with adult subject matter which would interest a sophisticated audience, primarily female, 18 to 34. We prefer serious quality fiction or light tongue-in-cheek stories on any subject, done in good taste. We love stories dealing with contemporary man-woman relationships. Short-shorts are okay but we prefer them to have snap or 'trick' endings. The formula story, the soap opera, skimpy mood pieces or character sketches are not for us." Length: short-shorts, 1,500 to 3,000 words; short stories, 4,000 to 6,000 words; condensed novels and novel excerpts. "We also use murder or suspense stories of about 25,000 to 30,000 words dealing with the upper class stratum of American living. A foreign background is acceptable, but the chief characters should be American." Has published the work of Agatha Christie, Joyce Carol Oates, Evan Hunter, and other established writers. Pays about $1,000 and up for short stories and novel excerpts, $4,500 and up for condensed novels.

EVE, 210 E. 35 St., New York NY 10016. (212)689-9730. Editor-in-Chief: Diane Masters Watson. For the fashion-minded woman, aged 27-33. Monthly magazine; 100 pages. Estab: 1977. Circ: 250,000. Pays on publication. Buys all rights, but may reassign following publication, or may buy second serial (reprint) rights. Phone queries OK. Submit seasonal/holiday material 3 months in advance. Simultaneous, photocopied, and previously published submissions OK. SASE. Reports in 4 weeks. Sample copy, $1.95 plus postage.

Nonfiction: "I need deeper articles, some sexually oriented, but there's also room for a couple of light pieces to please the readers in Nebraska and Milwaukee." Length: about 3,000 words. Pays $200 minimum.

FAMILY CIRCLE MAGAZINE, 488 Madison Ave., New York NY 10022. (212)593-8000. Editor: Arthur Hettich. For women/homemakers. Monthly. Usually buys all rights. Pays on acceptance. Reports in 6 weeks. Query. "We like to see a strong query on unique or problem-solving aspects of family life, and are especially interested in writers who have a solid background in the areas they suggest." Enclose S.A.S.E.

Nonfiction: Women's interest subjects such as family and social relationships, children, humor, physical and mental health, leisure-time activities, self-improvement, popular culture, travel. Service articles. For travel, interested mainly in local material, no foreign or extensive travel. "We look for human stories, told in terms of people. We like them to be down-to-earth and unacademic." Length: 1,000 to 2,500 words. Pays $250 to $2,500.

Fiction: Occasionally uses fiction relating to women. Buys short stories, short-shorts, vignettes. Length: 2,000 to 2,500 words. Payment negotiable. Minimum payment for full-length story is $500.

Fillers: Short, women's service type or family oriented. Short humor, how-to, or inspirational. 500 words. Pays $100 and up.

FARM WIFE NEWS, 733 N. Van Buren, Milwaukee WI 53202. (414)272-5410. Managing Editor: Judy Borouski. For farm and ranch women of all ages; nationwide. Estab: 1970. Circ:

175,000. Copyrighted. Buys over 400 mss a year. Pays on publication. Sample copy $1; free writer's guidelines. Will consider photocopied submissions. Submit seasonal material 4 to 6 months in advance. Reports in 4 to 6 weeks. Query first or submit complete ms. Enclose S.A.S.E.

Nonfiction and Photos: "We are always looking for good freelance material. Our prime consideration is that it is farm-oriented, focusing on a farm woman or a subject that would appeal especially to her." Uses a wide variety of material: articles on vacations, daily life, sewing, gardening, decorating, outstanding farm women, etc. Topic should always be approached from a rural woman's point of view. Informational, how-to, personal experience, interview, profile, inspirational, humor, think pieces, nostalgia, personal opinion, travel, successful business operations. Length: 1,000 words maximum. Departments and columns which also use material are: A Day in Our Lives, Our Favorite Vacation, Besides Farming, Farm Woman on the Go, Country Crafts, Sewing and Needlecraft, Gardening, Decorating, I Remember When, Farm Nature Stories. Pays $20 to $100. B&w photos are purchased with or without accompanying mss. Color slides and transparencies are also used. They look for scenic color photos which show the good life on the farm. Captions required. Payment depends on use, but begins at $10 for b&w photos; at $25 for color slides or transparencies.

Fiction: Mainstream, humorous. Themes should relate to subject matter. Length: 2,000 words maximum. Pays $40 to $75.

Poetry: Traditional forms and light verse. Length: open. Pays $15 for most poetry; more for long pieces. Must relate to subject matter.

Fillers: Word puzzles and short humor. Pays $15 to $30.

THE FEMINIST ART JOURNAL, 41 Montgomery Place, Brooklyn NY 11215. Editors-in-Chief: Cindy Nemser and Chuck Nemser. Emphasizes women in the arts. Readers are college educated, with a strong interest in the visual and performing arts; many are artists or professionals in the art field; mostly women subscribers. Quarterly magazine; 40-50 pages. Estab: 1972. Circ: 10,000. Pays on publication. Buys all rights, but may reassign following publication. SASE. Reports in 2-3 weeks. Sample copy $2. Free writer's guidelines.

Nonfiction: Expose (of sexism in the art establishment, etc.); historical (solidly researched profiles of women artists, composers, filmmakers etc., of the past); how-to (practical advice for women artists); informational (reports on women artists' caucuses, co-op galleries, etc.); interview and profile. Buys 50 mss/year. Query or send complete ms. Length: 1,200-2,000 words. Pays $25 maximum.

Photos: Photos used with accompanying ms. Captions required. Uses b&w photos. No additional payment for photos accepted with accompanying ms. "Most of our photos are reproductions of art works supplied by galleries or museums to our writers."

Poetry: "Use only poems of exceptional quality that deal with art and/or feminism. Limit submissions to batches of 3. Pays $10-25.

GLAMOUR, 350 Madison Ave., New York NY 10017. (212)692-5500. Editor-in-Chief: Ruth Whitney; Managing Editor: Phyllis Starr Wilson. Monthly. "From a freelance writer we buy first North American serial rights. For our columns we often hold all rights or first North American serial rights." Query first. Enclose S.A.S.E.

Nonfiction: Fashion, beauty, decorating and entertaining, and travel are staff-written, but there is a need for current interest articles; helpful, informative material, humorous or serious, on all aspects of a young woman's life (18 to 35 years old); medicine, mental health, social, economic and emotional problems. Freelancers might study the magazine for style, approach. Length: 2,000 to 3,000 words. Short pieces bring $300 to $500. Pays $750 minimum for regular article.

GOOD HOUSEKEEPING, Hearst Corp., 959 Eighth Ave., New York NY 10019. Editor-in-Chief: John Mack Carter. Managing Editor: Mary Fiore. Mass women's magazine. Monthly; 200 pages. Estab: 1885. Circ: 5,000,000. Pays on acceptance. Rights very with author and material. Phone queries OK. Submit seasonal/holiday material 6-8 months in advance. SASE. Reports as soon as possible.

Nonfiction: Expose; how-to; informational; humor; inspirational; interview; nostalgia; personal experience; photo feature; profile and travel. Buys 8-10 mss/issue. Query. Length: 1,000-5,000 words. Pays $500-5,000.

Photos: Herbert Bleiweiss, Art Director. Photos purchased with or without accompanying ms or on assignment. Captions required, (pic information only). Pays $50-250 for b&w photos; $50-350 for color photos. Query. Model release required.

Columns/Departments: Robert Liles, Features Editor. Light Housekeeping (humorous short-short prose and verse) and The Better Way (ideas and depth research). Query. Pays $25-350. "Only outstanding material has a chance here."

Fiction: Naome Lewis, Fiction Editor. Romance; mainstream; suspense; condensed novels and serialized novels. Buys 3 mss/issue. Send complete ms. Length: 1,000 words (short-shorts)-10,000 words (novels); average: 4,000 words. Pays $1,000.

Poetry: Leonhard Dowty, Poetry Editor. Light verse and traditional. Buys 3 poems/issue. Pays $25 minimum.

Fillers: Robert Liles, Features Editor. Jokes, gags, anecdotes, and short humor, cartoons, and epigrams. Pays $25-100.

HADASSAH MAGAZINE, 50 W. 58th St., New York NY 10022. Editorial Director: Helen G. Lusterman. Executive Editor: Jesse Zel Lurie. For members of Hadassah. Monthly, except combined issues (June-July and August-September). Circ: 345,000. Buys U.S. publication rights. Pays on publication. Reports in 6 weeks. Enclose S.A.S.E.

Nonfiction: Primarily concerned with Israeli, the American Jewish community and American civic affairs. Length: 1,500 to 3,000 words. Pays 10¢ a word.

Photos: "We buy photos only to illustrate articles, with the exception of outstanding color from Israel which we use on our covers. We pay $100 and up for a suitable color photo."

Fiction: Short stories with strong plots and positive Jewish values. Length: 3,000 words maximum. Pays 10¢ a word.

How To Break In: "We read all freelance material that comes in. We do not publish poetry. Best way to break in is to go to your library and study a half dozen back issues."

HARLEQUIN, 240 Duncan Mill Road, Don Mills, Ontario, Canada M3B 1Z4. Editor: Beth McGregor. Emphasizes romance and escape reading; for men and women of all ages, all walks of life. Monthly magazine; 72 pages. Estab: 1973. Circ: 125,000. Pays on acceptance. Buys second serial (reprint) and first North American serial rights. Submit seasonal/holiday material 6 months in advance. Simultaneous, photocopied and previously published submissions OK. SASE and International Reply Coupons. Reports in 3-4 weeks. Free sample copy and writer's guidelines.

Nonfiction: How-to (crafts and home-oriented items); humor (clean, light reading); inspirational; nostalgia; personal experience (triumph over adversity, emotional experiences—prefer photos here); profile (photos required) and travel (armchair traveler material). Buys 3-5 mss/year. Query. Length: 1,000-4,000 words. Pays $50-200.

Photos: Photos purchased with or without accompanying ms. Captions required. Pays $15-25 for b&w photos; $35-75 for 2¼x2¼ and 4x5 color photos. Model release required. "Mostly purchase scenic and travel pics."

Fiction: Humorous (light and clean); romance (upbeat, no promiscuity or premarital sex). Buys 2-5 mss/year. Send complete ms. Length: 1,000-4,500 words. Pays $75-150.

Poetry: Light verse, haiku and traditional. Buys 40 poems/year. Length: 30 lines maximum. Pays $10.

How To Break In: "I can't emphasize enough the clean, wholesome, inoffensive route all our material takes."

HARPER'S BAZAAR, 717 Fifth Ave., New York NY 10022. Editor-in-Chief: Anthony Mazzola. For "women, late 20's and above, middle income and above, sophisticated and aware, with at least 2 years of college. Most combine families, professions, travel, often more than one home. They are active and concerned over what's happening in the arts, their communities, the world." Monthly. Rights purchased vary with author and material. May buy first North American serial rights. No unsolicited mss. Query first. Enclose S.A.S.E.

Nonfiction and Photos: "We publish whatever is important to an intelligent, modern woman. Fashion questions plus beauty and health—how the changing world affects her family and herself; how she can affect it; how others are trying to do so; changing life pattern and so forth. Query us first."

HERS, I.P.E. Magazines Ltd., King's Reach Tower, Stamford St., London SE1 9LS, England. Editor: Jean Anderson. For British readers; young, married women, low income interested in self-identification through first-person real-life stories. Buys 30-40 mss/year from American/Canadian writers. Monthly magazine; 64 pages. Estab: 1965. Circ: 150,000. Pays on acceptance. Buys all rights. Submit seasonal/holiday materal 4 months in advance. SAE and International Reply Coupons. Reports in 6 weeks. Free sample copy and writer's guidelines.

Photos: Bruce Moir, Photo Editor. Uses 35mm or 2¼x2¼ color transparencies. Model release required.

Fiction: Miss Eloise Logan, Fiction Editor. Confessions. Buys 12 mss/issue. Send complete ms. Length: 1,500-5,000 words. Pays £10-15.

IN TOUCH: THE JOURNAL OF PERSONAL POSSIBILITIES, (formerly *The Successful Woman*), P.O. Box 3471, Santa Barbara CA 93105. (805)967-7914. Editor: Barbara Hinrichs. For women from all walks of life who want to reinforce a winning self-image. Newsletter; 12 pages. Established in 1974. Monthly. Circulation: 1,000. Buys all rights, but may reassign rights to author after publication. Buys 50 to 100 mss per year. Pays on publication. Will send sample copy to writer for $1. Will consider photocopied and simultaneous submissions. Reports on mss accepted for publication "immediately." Enclose S.A.S.E.

Nonfiction: "We try to develop each issue around a theme and include book reviews and other resources that tie in with the central theme. Need short articles about women who are living their lives in creative ways. We consider ourselves feminist — with a positive attitude toward solving the problems encountered by women in both their personal and professional lives. Our top concern is always to turn women on to developing their own potential. Our aim is to inspire — no dreary stories about people who are concerned about anything less than excellence. Not interested in hearing about small thinkers." Length: 500 to 750 words. Pays $5. Regular column on women's business enterprises. Length: 500 words. Pays $5. Also uses clippings, but no payment is made.

LADIES' HOME JOURNAL, 641 Lexington Ave., New York NY 10022. Editor: Lenore Hershey. Pays on acceptance. Issued monthly. Query first for nonfiction. SASE.

Nonfiction: "Articles that address themselves to the many issues, emotions, concerns and joys women face today — as wives, mothers, citizens, workers, and as human beings. Factual information, concrete advice, humor, and first-person 'shared experience' approaches are welcomed. Send queries to Kathleen D. Fury, Articles Editor."

Fiction: "We are sorry to announce a new policy under which we will no longer consider short stories sent through the mail. We do not have facilities that permit proper handling. Please do not send in manuscripts as we will be unable to return them."

LADY'S CIRCLE MAGAZINE, Lopez Publications, Inc., 21 West 26th St., New York NY 10010. Editor: Shirley Howard. For homemakers. Monthly. Buys all rights. Pays on publication. Reporting time varies from 1 week to 3 months. Query first, with brief outline. Enclose S.A.S.E.

Nonfiction and Photos: Particularly likes first-person or as-told-to pieces about health and doing good. Also how homemakers and mothers make money at home. Hobbies and crafts. Also articles on baby care, home management, gardening, as well as problems of the homemaker. Also, stories of people who have overcome illnesses or handicaps. Articles must be written on specific subjects and must be thoroughly researched and based on sound authority. Length: 2,500 words. Pays $125. Pays $15 for good b&w photos accompanying articles.

McCALL'S, 230 Park Ave., New York NY 10017. Editor: Robert Stein. "Study recent issues." Monthly. Circulation: 6,500,000. Pays on acceptance. "All mss must be submitted on speculation and *McCall's* accepts no responsibility for unsolicited mss." Reports in 4 to 6 weeks. Query first. Enclose S.A.S.E.

Nonfiction: Department Editor: Helen Markel. No subject of wide public or personal interest is out of bounds for *McCall's* so long as it is appropriately treated. The editors are seeking meaningful stories of personal experience. They are on the lookout for new research that will provide the basis for penetrating articles on the ethical, physical, material and social problems concerning readers. They are most receptive to humor. *McCall's* buys between 200 and 300 articles a year, many in the 1,000- to 1,500-word length. Miss Lisel Eisenheimer is Editor of Nonfiction Books from which *McCall's* frequently publishes excerpts. These are on subjects of interest to women: biography, memoirs, reportage, etc. Address queries for "Right Now" column to Mary McLaughlin. Subjects can be education, medicine, social and community affairs (new ideas and trends), problems being solved in new ways, ecology, women doing interesting things, women's liberation, any timely subject. Short pieces with a news or service angle. Length: 300 to 500 words. Payment is up to $300. The magazine is not in the market for new columns. Almost all features on food, household equipment and management, fashion, beauty, building and decorating are staff-written.

Fiction: Department Editor: Helen DelMonte. "Again the editors would remind writers of the contemporary woman's taste and intelligence. Most of all, fiction can awaken a reader's sense of identity, deepen her understanding of herself and others, refresh her with a laugh at herself, etc. *McCall's* looks for stories which will have meaning for an adult reader of some literary sensitivity. *McCall's* principal interest is in short stories; but fiction of all lengths is considered." Length: about 4,000 words. Length for short-shorts: about 2,000 words. Payment begins at $1,250.

How To Break In: "Your best bet is our monthly newsletter section, Right Now. It's an eight-page section and we buy a lot of freelance material for it, much of that from beginning writers. Some people have gone on from Right Now to do feature material for us. We use 500- to 700-word items in Right Now, many of them how-to's or with a practical intent of some kind. We pay $200 to $250. The stories must have a certain immediacy to suburban housewives in their thirties and forties. New trends, new developments, new ideas. Each idea must have a fresh approach."

MADEMOISELLE, 350 Madison Ave., New York NY 10017. Editor-in-Chief: Edith Raymond Locke. Directed to college-educated women between the ages of 18 to 25. Circulation: 807,352. Reports on submissions in 3 to 4 weeks. Buys first North American serial rights. Pays on acceptance. Prefers written query plus samples of work, published or unpublished. Enclose S.A.S.E.
Nonfiction: Department Editor: Mary Cantwell, Managing Editor. Particular concentration on articles of interest to the intelligent young woman that concern the arts, education, careers, European travel, current sociological and political problems. Articles should be well-researched and of good quality. Prefers not to receive profile articles of individuals or personal reminiscences. Length: "Opinion" essay column, 1,300 words; articles, 1,500 to 6,000 words. Pays $300 for "Opinion" essay column; articles $100 minimum.
Photos: Department Editor: Roger W. Schoening. Commissioned work assigned according to needs. Photos of fashion, beauty, travel; career and college shots of interest to accompany articles. Payment ranges from no-charge to an agreed rate of payment per shot, job series, or page rate. Buys all rights. Pays on publication for photos.
Fiction: Department Editor: Mary Elizabeth McNichols. High-quality fiction by both name writers and unknowns. Length: 1,500-3,000 words. Pays $300 minimum. Uses short-shorts on occasion. "We are particularly interested in encouraging young talent, and with this aim in mind, we conduct a college fiction contest each year, open to men and women undergraduates. A $500 prize is awarded for each of the two winning stories which are published in our August issue. However, our encouragement of unknown talent is not limited to college students or youth. We are not interested in formula stories, and subject matter need not be confined to a specific age or theme." Annually awards 2 prizes for short stories.
Poetry: Department Editor: Mary Elizabeth McNichols. Must be of very high literary quality, under 65 lines. Pays $25 minimum. Annually awards 2 prizes for poetry.

MODERN BRIDE, 1 Park Ave., New York NY 10016. Executive Editor: Cele G. Lalli. Bimonthly. Buys all rights. Pays on acceptance. Reports in 2 weeks. Enclose S.A.S.E.
Nonfiction: Uses articles of interest to brides-to-be. "We prefer articles on etiquette, marriage, planning a home, and travel from honeymoon point of view. *Modern Bride* is divided into three sections: the first deals with wedding dresses; the second with home furnishings; the third with travel. We buy articles for all three; we edit everything, but don't rewrite without permission." Length: about 2,000 words. Payment is about $200 minimum.
Poetry: Occasionally buys poetry pertaining to love and marriage. Pays $15 to $25 for average short poem.

MS. MAGAZINE, 370 Lexington Ave., New York NY 10017. Editor-in-Chief and Publisher: Patricia Carbine. Editor: Gloria Steinem. For "women predominantly; varying ages, backgrounds, but committed to exploring new life styles and changes in their roles and society." Established in 1972. Monthly. Circulation: over 400,000. Rights purchased vary with author and material. Pays on acceptance. Will consider photocopied submissions. Submit seasonal material at least 3 months in advance. Reports in 4-6 weeks. Query first for nonfiction only, "with ideas and outline, and include samples of previous work." Address to Query Editor. Submit complete ms for fiction. Enclose S.A.S.E.
Nonfiction: "Articles, features on the arts, women's minds, women's bodies that relate to exploring new life styles for women and changes in their roles and society. We are a how-to magazine—how a woman may gain control of her life. We are hoping to change the status quo —to treat women as human beings, and not to insult their personhood with down-putting editorializing or insensitive advertising. We encourage women to live their lives as unique people, not role players. We would like more input on what women are doing politically in their communities." Buys informational articles, how-to's, personal experience articles, interviews, profiles, inspirational articles, humor, historical articles, think articles, exposes, personal opinion pieces, photo articles, new product articles, coverage of successful business operations, and art, book, and film reviews. Length varies. Pays $100 to $500. Send to Manuscript Editor.
Photos: Purchased with mss, without mss, or on assignment. Payment "depends on usage." Address to Art Department.

Fiction, Poetry and Fillers: Personal experience, fantasy, humorous, historical; condensed novels, serialized novels. Length: 3,000 words maximum. Pays up to $500. Address to Fiction Editor. Traditional forms, blank verse, free verse, avant-garde forms and light verse, relating to magazine subject matter. Address to Poetry Editor. "We accept nonfiction filler length material only for the Gazette section of the magazine; news from all over." Length: filler length to 3,000 words maximum. Pays up to $500.

How To Break In: "The Gazette section which features short news items is the easiest way to get published here. We use a lot of material from all over the country on politics, the women's movement, human interest material, women profiles. Regional material from outside New York stands the best chance, but nothing is a sure bet. We get a lot of material we can't use from people who don't understand the kind of orientation we seek. It is possible to move from the Gazette to do other work for *Ms*."

NATIONAL BUSINESS WOMAN, 2012 Massachusetts Ave. N.W., Washington DC 20036. (202)293-1100. Editor: Louise G. Wheeler. For "all mature, educated, employed women." Established in 1919. 11 times a year. Buys all rights and second serial rights. Buys 10 or 12 mss a year. Payment on acceptance. Will send a sample copy to a writer for $1. Will consider photocopied submissions. Reports in 6 weeks. Enclose S.A.S.E.

Nonfiction: "Originality preferred. Written specifically for members of the National Federation of Business and Professional Women's Clubs, Inc. No fiction or poems." Buys informational, think, and successful business operations articles. Length: 1,000 to 1,200 words. Pays $10 to $35.

NEWS LADY, *Chicago Daily News*, 401 N. Wabash, Chicago IL 60611. A column for women. Copyrighted. Pays on publication. Reports in 3 weeks, "sometimes longer." Enclose S.A.S.E. and Social Security number.

Nonfiction: Essays on topics of interest. "We prefer essays from people in the *Daily News* trading zone (Illinois, southern Wisconsin, northern Indiana), but we will accept particularly good essays from all over the U.S. We are trying to get essays with a greater degree of sophistication about women's lib, consumerism, and social problems. We're interested in humor, especially family humor. Please, no reporting or didactic essays." Length: 500 to 600 words. Pays $25 savings bond.

PLAYGIRL ADVISOR, 1801 Century Park East #2310, Los Angeles CA 90067. (213)277-6275. Executive Editor: Robert Edward Brown. Emphasizes human sexuality for 18-35-year olds who are interested in exploring "the complexities of human sexuality and the rest of their lives." Monthly magazine; 100 pages. Estab: 1976. Circ: 300,000. Pays on publication. Buys first North American serial rights. Phone queries OK. Submit seasonal/holiday material 6 months in advance. Simultanesou, photocopied and previously published submissions OK. SASE. Free writer's guidelines.

Nonfiction: Humor; informational; interview; personal experience; personal opinion; photo feature. "All material focuses on sexuality." Buys 5 mss/issue. Query. Length: 1,000-4,000 words. Pays $100/thousand words.

Photos: Karen Davidson, Photo Editor. Photos assigned on speculation. Pays $50-250 for b&w photos per assignment. Model release required.

Fiction: Erotica and humor. Must focus on sexuality. Buys 6 mss/year. Send complete ms. Length: 750-4,000 words. Pays $100/thousand words.

How To Break In: "Send query along with a sample of work—either published or unpublished. No articles that do not fit into an educationally erotic format...and no sado-masochism or bondage themes, please."

PLAYGIRL MAGAZINE, 1801 Century Park East, Los Angeles CA 90067. (213)553-8006. Editor-in-Chief: Joyce Dudney Fleming. For an aware, contemporary female audience of all ages, today's multi-faceted women in all occupations, who are interested in a wide range of subjects. Monthly magazine; 136 pages. Established in 1973. Circulation: 1,100,000. Rights purchased vary with author and material. May buy all rights or first North American serial rights. Buys about 100 mss/year. Payment on acceptance. Will send sample copy to writer for $1.75. Will consider photocopied submissions. Will not consider simultaneous submissions. Submit seasonal material for all of the traditional holidays 5 months in advance. Reports in 1 month. Query first for nonfiction. Submit complete ms for fiction. Enclose S.A.S.E.

Nonfiction and Photos: "*Playgirl* does not believe in limiting women's horizons, as most women's magazines do. We use material on any area of concern to women, not just the traditional areas of home and children. Must be totally professional. We are most concerned with literary quality and slant. Articles must be well-researched and tightly written and must demonstrate a respect for the intelligence of our readers." Uses informational, how-to, personal experience, think pieces, nostalgia, and career articles. Length: 1,500-3,000 words. Pays $250/1,000 words. B&w and color photos are purchased on assignment only.

Fiction: "Stories may be sexually oriented, but not salacious. Female characters should be three-dimensional and portrayed realistically." Experimental, mainstream, mystery, suspense, erotica, fantasy, humorous, romance, excerpts from novels. Length: 1,000 to 5,500 words. Rates vary.

REDBOOK MAGAZINE, 230 Park Ave., New York NY 10017. Issued monthly. Rights purchased vary with author and material. Reports in 6-8 weeks. Pays on acceptance. SASE.

Nonfiction: Articles relevant to the magazine's readers, who are young women in the 18- to 34-year-old group. Also interested in submissions for "Young Mother's Story." "We are interested in stories offering practical and useful information you would like to share with others on how you, as a mother and a wife, are dealing with the changing problems of marriage and family life, such as the management of outside employment, housework, time, money, the home and children. Stories also may deal with how you, as a concerned citizen or consumer, handled a problem in your community." Please don't hesitate to send it because you think your spelling or punctuation may be a bit rusty; we don't judge these stories on the basis of technicalities and we do make minor editing changes. For each 1,000 to 2,000 words accepted for publication, we pay $500. Mss accompanied by a large, stamped, self-addressed envelope, must be signed (although name will be withheld on request), and mailed to: Young Mother's Story, c/o *Redbook Magazine.* Stories do not have to be typed, but we appreciate it when they are legibly written." Length: articles, 3,500 to 4,500 words; short articles, 2,000 to 2,500 words.

Fiction: Anne Mollegen Smith, Fiction Editor. Uses a great variety of types of fiction, with contemporary stories appealing especially to women in demand. Short stories of 3,500 to 5,000 words are always needed. Also short-shorts of 1,400 to 1,600 words. Payment for short-shorts begins at $850, and at $1,000 for short stories.

How To Break In: "It is very difficult to break into the nonfiction section, although two columns —Young Mothers and To Be a Woman —which publish short personal experience pieces (1,000 to 1,500 words) do depend on freelancers. Our situation for the fiction department is quite different. We buy a quarter of our short stories cold from writers whose articles come in brown envelopes in the mail. Another 40% are repeats from writers who were originally unsolicited and less than half are from agented writers. We buy about 50 stories a year. This is clearly the best way to break into *Redbook* and we even sometimes ask successful fiction people to do a nonfiction piece, say, essay for our Christmas issue. Most of the stories we're proud of —the fresh material which gives *Redbook* fiction its distinctiveness —are from people we've discovered through the unsolicited mail. So when we open each brown envelope, it is with a great deal of hope. We read everything that comes in and try to give a reading the day it arrives. Still the odds are very difficult, since we do get a great deal of submissions. The short shorts (8½ pages or even shorter) have the very best chance."

SPHERE MAGAZINE, 500 N. Michigan Ave., Chicago IL 60611. Editor: Joan Leonard. Monthly. Study several issues of the publication and query first. Enclose S.A.S.E. Unsolicited mss not accepted.

VIVA, 909 Third Ave., New York NY 10022. For predominantly female audience between 18 and 27. Monthly. Pays within 30 days following publication. Usually reports in 2 to 6 weeks. Submit complete ms. Enclose S.A.S.E.

Fiction: Department Editor: Pat Rotter. Experimental, mainstream, suspense, adventure, erotica, humorous and science fiction. Writers must consider the nature of the magazine before submitting material. Should have strong narrative structure. Avoid mediocrity and the cliche. Length: 1,000 to 4,000 words. Pays about 25¢ per word.

VOGUE, 350 Madison Ave., New York NY 10017. Editor: Grace Mirabella. Issued monthly. For highly intelligent women. Query first. Enclose S.A.S.E.

Nonfiction: Feature Editor: Leo Lerman. Uses articles and ideas for features, 2,000 to 2,500 words. Fashion articles are staff-written. Material must be of high literary quality, contain good information. Pays $300 and up, on acceptance.

W, *Women's Wear Daily,* 7 East 12th St., New York NY 10003. Completely staff-written newspaper.

THE WOMAN, Reese Publishing Co., Inc., 235 Park Ave. S., New York NY 10003. Editor-in-Chief: Diana Lurvey. For women who are now or have been married who may or may not work outside the home but their primary interest is their families; community service minded. Bimonthly magazine; 130 pages. Estab: 1965. Circ: 250,000. Pays on acceptance. Buys all rights, but may reassign following publication. Submit seasonal/holiday material 5 months in advance. SASE. Reports in 2 weeks. Sample copy 75¢.
Nonfiction: Expose; historical; how-to (sewing, money-saving, handling specific child care problems); inspirational; nostalgia; personal experience and personal opinion. Buys 15 mss/issue. Query or send complete ms. Pays $50 minimum.

WOMAN'S DAY, 1515 Broadway, New York NY 10036. Editor: Geraldine Rhoads. 13 issues/year. Circulation: over 8,000,000. Buys first and second North American serial rights. Pays on acceptance. Reports within 2 weeks on queries; longer on mss. Submit detailed queries first to Rebecca Greer, Articles Editor. Enclose S.A.S.E.
Nonfiction: Uses articles on all subjects of interest to women—marriage, family life, child rearing, education, homemaking, money management, travel, family health, and leisure activities. Also interested in fresh, dramatic narratives of women's lives and concerns. Length: 500 to 3,000 words, depending on material. Payment varies depending on length, whether it's for regional or national use, etc.
Fiction: Department Editor: Eileen Herbert Jordan. Uses little fiction; high-quality, genuine human interest romance and humor, in lengths between 1,500 and 3,000 words. Payment varies. "We pay any writer's established rate, however."
Fillers: Brief (500 words maximum), factual articles on contemporary life, community projects, unusual activities are used—condensed, sprightly, and unbylined—in "It's All in a Woman's Day" section. "Neighbors" column also pays $25 for each letter and $5 for each brief practical suggestion on homemaking or child rearing. Address to the editor of the appropriate section.

WOMAN'S WORLD, Greamly Press, 1808 West End Ave., Suite 1500, Nashville TN 37203. Editor-in-Chief: Owen Taylor. For "women, 29-55 years old, entering or re-entering the job market. High school, some college education." Monthly magazine; 88 pages. Estab: 1970. Circ: 300,000. Pays on publication. Buys one-time rights. Submit seasonal/holiday material 4 months in advance. Simultaneous, photocopied, and previously published submissions OK. SASE. Reports in 4 weeks. Free sample copy and writer's guidelines.
Nonfiction: Judith Gregg, Articles Editor. Expose (instances of working women losing ground legally); how-to (on running a household while working, advancing on the job); informational (new career innovations, day care center trends, etc.); humor (geared to working women, no housewife stuff), interview (people involved in the practical side of the woman's movement); profile (needs profiles of women who have made good after 30), travel (practical family ideas); new product (must help working women); personal experience (women who have overcome adversity in returning to work). photo feature. Buys 5-7 mss/issue. Query. Length: 1,500-3,000 words. Pays 8¢/word and up.
Photos: Debra Ferguson, Photo Editor. Purchased with accompanying ms or on assignment. Captions required. Query. Pays $10-50 for 8x10 b&w; $20-80 for 120mm color transparencies. Model release required.
Columns/Departments: Peggy Gregg, Department Editor. "Currently working with regulars." Open to suggestions for new columns or departments.
Poetry: Anna Taylor, Poetry Editor. Free verse, light verse. Buys 2-3 poems/issue. Limit submissions to batches of 5. Length: open. Pays $10-100.
Fillers: Lynn Haber, Fillers Editor. Clippings, short humor. Length: 500-1,000 words. Pays $5-30.
For '78: *"Woman's World* before now has been a monthly cookbook, but the emphasis is changing. We are looking for a core of freelancers out of New York. *WW* already has enough people on standby in the Big Apple."

WOMEN IN BUSINESS, The ABWA Co., Inc., 9100 Ward Parkway, Kansas City MO 64114. Editor: Rita R. Rousseau. For working women in all fields and at all levels; largely middle-aged women in traditional "women's" fields. Magazine; published 9 times a year (combined issues in March/April, July/August and November/December); 24 pages. Estab: 1949. Circ: 95,000. Pays on acceptance. Buys all rights, but may reassign following publication. Submit seasonal/holiday material 3 months in advance. SASE. Reports in 4 weeks. Free sample copy and writer's guidelines.
Nonfiction: How-to (any topic that would help a woman to advance in her career; psychological, self-help, new technological developments, news that affects working women, etc.)

and travel (practical tips on business or personal travel). Buys 1 ms/issue. Query or send complete ms. Length: 600-1,800 words. Pays 5¢/word maximum.

Photos: Photos purchased with accompanying ms. Captions required. Pays $20 maximum ($35 for cover) for 8x10 b&w glossies; $75 maximum (for cover) for color transparencies.

Columns/Departments: Your Personality (pop psychology); The Management Woman (tips for managers); Personal Business (i.e. insurance, taxes); Books Briefly (books of business interest or of special interest to women) and Business Communication (effective speaking, writing, proper forms of letters, etc.). Buys 4 mss/year. Query or send complete ms. Length: 600 words. Pays 5¢/word maximum.

WOMEN STUDIES ABSTRACTS, Rush Publishing Co., Inc., Box 1, Rush NY 14543. Editor-in-Chief: Sara Stauffer Whaley. Educational publication for women (libraries, professors of women's studies, psychologists, college administrators). Quarterly magazine; 100 pages. Estab: 1972. Circ: 1,500. Pays on acceptance. Buys all rights but may reassign following publication. Phone queries OK. Simultaneous, photocopied, and previously published submissions OK. SASE. Reports in 4 weeks. Sample copy $4.50.

Nonfiction: "Bibliographical articles or bibliographies with introduction only. Must be non-sexist, non-racist material written from scholarly knowledge of our field. Must be very accurate in biographical citations." Query. Pays $50-150, "plus percentage of reprints, if made."

WOMEN TODAY, Eve Publishing Corp., 210 E. 35th St., New York NY 10016. Editor-in-Chief: Diana Masters Watson. For an 18-40-year-old female audience. Monthly magazine; 100 pages. Estab: 1977. Circ: 250,000. Pays on publication. Buys all rights, but may reassign following publication, or second serial (reprint) rights. Phone queries OK. Submit seasonal/holiday material 3 months in advance. Simultaneous, photocopied, and previously published submissions OK. SASE. Reports in 4 weeks. Sample copy $1 plus postage.

Nonfiction: "The topics are limitless—travel, exercise, weight control—any topic a woman might be interested in talking about. Can be first person or third person. And this is an excellent market for reprints, and they don't have to come from the big magazines—a hometowm publication is just fine." Payment "depends on the length and quality and the amount of polishing that has to be done. Reprints bring $100-125. Original mss will get more." Length: 2,500-3,000 words.

WOMEN TODAY, Today Publications & News Service, Inc., National Press Building, Washington DC 20045. (202)628-6663. Editor-in-Chief: Myra E. Barrer. Emphasizes equal rights for women. For professional women. Biweekly newsletter; 4-8 pages. Estab: 1971. Pays on publication. Buys all rights. Phone queries OK. Photocopied submissions OK. SASE. Reports in 1 week. Free sample copy.

Nonfiction: How-to (on women's equity, i.e. "how to petition your legislator"); informational (hard news coverage) and technical. Query or send complete ms. Length: 100-300 words. Pays $10.

How To Break In: "By demonstrating authority. We use only current news useful to our readership, which means our writers must be at least a step ahead of most of the country's leaders in this field."

Opportunities and Services

Audiovisual Markets

Because producers of "software"—the trade term for nonprint materials like records, filmstrips, tape cassettes, etc., as opposed to "hardware," which refers to the machines on which they are viewed or played, frequently have highly individualized editorial requirements, freelance writers are encouraged to seek firm assignments from audiovisual producers before writing or submitting finished scripts. A good query letter should outline the writer's credentials (as an educator, specialist in some subject, or professional scriptwriter), include a sample of his writing, and give details of his proposed script or series of scripts.

Many of the companies currently active in the audiovisual field are working with staff writers and do not actively seek freelance contributions. Those who are interested in staff positions will find a more complete list of audiovisual producers in the excellent *Audiovisual Market Place* (published by R.R. Bowker).

Software producers pay on a flat fee or royalty basis, depending on the company and the quality of the writer's material. The sponsored film production company, operating on a contract basis to produce audiovisuals for the government, business or private organizations, offers a flat fee payment, which varies according to the nature of the project and the writer's credentials. If a company produces and markets its own audiovisual products (usually to the elementary and secondary school and college markets), payment is most often according to a royalty contract with the writer, but a flat fee is sometimes paid. The flat fees vary widely, but royalty agreements usually approximate the ones offered for school texts. Based on the net money the publisher receives on sales, this is 3% to 5% for elementary and secondary school materials and 8% to 12% for college textbooks. A few producers offer an even higher percentage, some going as high as 18.75% for college materials.

A/V CONCEPTS CORP., 263 Union Blvd., West Islip NY 11795. Director of R&D: Mrs. D.M. Bogart. Produces material for elementary school up, in developmental and remedial programs. Buys all rights. Free catalog. "Authors must receive a set of our specifications before submitting materials. All material we acquire is to be written with a controlled vocabulary and must meet readability formula requirements. Contributors must be highly creative and highly disciplined." Produces filmstrips with stories printed on them that the students read as they view the filmstrip.
Needs: Education (reading materials). Pays $75 on acceptance.

ABINGDON PRESS (Audio-Graphics Line), 201 8th Ave., S., Nashville TN 37202. For religious professionals, groups and lay persons. Buys all rights. Will send a catalog and editorial guidelines to writer on request. Looking for "people with established reputations whose names help sell the product." Query first. "Study the market. Don't submit vague plans."
Religion: Multimedia kits and prerecorded tapes and cassettes. "Study materials for religious education, educational programs for religious professionals and how-to and self-help programs

for religious groups. Most of these programs produced as sets of 1, 2, or 4 audio-cassettes in a box or album accompanied by a printed guide." Offers 7½ to 10% on retail price.

ACI, MEDIA, INC., 35 W. 45th St., New York, NY 10036. Contact: Production Manager. Curriculum oriented information geared toward K-9 grades. Copyrighted. Will send catalog to writer on request. Audiovisual project assigned to qualified writers and educators outside of permanent editorial staff if they "have a good knowledge of the medium (filmstrips) and have close contact with the educational system." Submission requirements include scripts, resume and completed filmstrip. Average length of a filmstrip is 65 frames, 6 minutes.
Education: Needs silent filmstrips, motion pictures (16mm), multimedia kits and slides. Pays $200 per script.

AERO PRODUCTS RESEARCH, INC., 11201 Hindry Ave., Los Angeles CA 90045. (213)641-7242. Contact: J. Parr. Aviation/aeroscience/aerospace education material for pilot training and schools (private and public schools from K through college). Copyrighted. SASE.
Education: "Developing and editing both technical and nontechnical material. Charts, silent filmstrips, models, multimedia kits, overhead transparencies, phonograph records, prerecorded tapes and cassettes, slides and study prints. Royalty arrangements are handled on an individual project basis. Writers should have flight instructor and ground school instructor experience."

KEN ANDERSON FILMS, Box 618, Winona Lake IN 46590. (219)267-5774. President: Ken Anderson. Produces material for church-related libraries with evangelical bias; films for all ages, with particular interest in children and teenagers. Prefers true stories; rarely purchases fiction, but will consider for the younger ages. No objections to previously published material. Buys motion picture rights. Free catalog. "We cannot guarantee consideration for material unless a brief one-page story synopsis is included. Other than that, writers may send rough material, a collection of anecdotes, published material, a book or whatever form the material may be in as long as it's good film material. We like to maintain a very warm attitude toward writers and will try to give careful consideration either to queries or to full-blown material. We only produce 4-6 films/year, so our quantity needs are limited." Produces sound filmstrips; motion pictures and tapes and cassettes.
Needs: Religious material only. "We are constantly looking for good material which is positively Christian and relates realistically to today's lifestyles." Pays "as low as $100 for basic story idea which the author could then market elsewhere. But general payment runs more between $250-1,000, depending upon story quality and adaptability for audiovisual production."

ANIMATION ARTS ASSOCIATES, INC., 2225 Spring Garden St., Philadelphia PA 19130. (215)563-2520. Contact: Harry E. Ziegler, Jr. Copyrighted. For "government, industry, engineers, doctors, scientists, dentists, general public, military." Send "resume of credits for motion picture and filmstrip productions. The writer should have scriptwriting credits for training, sales promotion, public relations." Enclose S.A.S.E.
Business: Produces 3½-minute, 8mm and 16mm film loops; 16mm and 35mm motion pictures (ranging from 5 to 40 minutes), 2x2 or 4x5 slides and teaching machine programs for training, sales, industrial and public relations. Fee arrangements dependent on client's budget.

HAL MARC ARDEN AND COMPANY, Executive Offices: 240 Central Park South, New York NY 10019. President: Hal Marc Arden. Copyrighted. "Writer must have experience in writing for motion pictures. Scripts are not solicited, but we welcome resumes." Query first. Enclose S.A.S.E. for response to queries.
General: "Specialize in sponsored production only: documentary, educational, public service." Produces silent and sound filmstrips, 16mm motion pictures, multimedia kits, phonograph records, prerecorded tapes and cassettes, and slides. "No royalties. Fee negotiated."

AUGUST FILMS, INC., 321 W. 44th St., New York NY 10036. Produces sound filmstrips; Super 8, 16mm and 35mm motion pictures; prerecorded tapes and cassettes; 35mm slides, and video tapes. Copyrighted. Prospective writer should have had previous experience and expertise in the desired format or style. Enclose S.A.S.E.
General: Producing all kinds of audiovisual materials — from medical, educational, industrial, to feature films. Pays $75 to $100 per minute (up to 10 minutes) for educational and industrial films. Pays flat fee for longer feature films; amount depending on budget.

BACHNER PRODUCTIONS, INC., 501 Madison Ave., New York NY 10022. Produces 16mm film loops; 16mm and 35mm motion pictures, and video tape programs. Not copyrighted. Does not accept unsolicited material. Prospective writer usually must have experience in subject related to proposed film. Also needs knowledge of videotape or film requirements. Sometimes will use good writer without specialized experience and then supply all necessary research. Enclose S.A.S.E.

General: Produces training and sales films and documentaries. Subject matter and style depend upon client requirements. "Sometimes clients supply outlines and research from which our writers work. Usually pay Writer's Guild scale, depending on usage and what is supplied by us. Price varies with assignments."

BARR FILMS, 3490 E. Foothill Blvd., Pasadena CA 91107. "For all age levels; grades K through college level as well as in the public library market to the same age span and adult audience. We also have interest in materials aimed at business and industry training programs." Not copyrighted. Will send a catalog to a writer for $1. Query first. "We will assign projects to qualified writers. We would require previous experience in film writing and would want to see samples of films previously written and completed for sale in the market." Enclose S.A.S.E.

General: "We produce and distribute 16mm films in all curriculum and subject areas. We prefer a semi-dramatic form of script with a moral or informational point. The length of our films is 10 to 20 minutes. We will also consider pure informational subjects with voice over narration. Fees are entirely negotiable, but we normally pay approximately in the area of $500 per script. We will accept film treatments and/or completed visual and dialogue scripts. Please inquire prior to sending your materials to us."

BOARD OF JEWISH EDUCATION OF NEW YORK, 426 W. 58th St., New York NY 10019. (212)245-8200. Contact: Yaakov Reshef. Produces material for Jewish schools, youth groups, temples and synagogues; for audience from kindergarten to old age. Free catalog. "We prefer a treatment before a script is submitted." Produces sound filmstrips; motion pictures (16mm); multimedia kits; tapes and cassettes; "and hope to add video programs in the near future."

Needs: General; education; religion and information. "Generally, length up to 20-25 minutes maximum; most material geared to 10-12 years old and up. Jewish background needed." Pays $300 and up.

ROBERT J. BRADY CO., Routes 197 & 450, Bowie MD 20715. Director, Product Development: C.R. McCarthy. Produces material for professionals and paraprofessionals in medical, allied health, nursing, emergency medicine, fire service, vocational and business fields. Buys all rights. Free catalog. "We are always anxious to develop new writers who can blend both book skills and audiovisual skills. Since most of our writing needs would be commissioned, all submissions should be in the form of resumes, sample materials, and client and title lists." Query. Produces sound filmstrips; motion pictures; overhead transparencies; audio tapes and cassettes; slides (size 35mm); and books and manuals.

Needs: Educational (35mm sound/slide programs, 35mm sound filmstrips—instructional); subject areas: business (training, skills, general); medicine (allied health, nursing, emergency medicine); and fire service training. Pays $400-1,200/script.

THE CHAMBA ORGANIZATION, 230 W. 105 St., New York NY 10025. President: St. Clair Bourne. For "the new hip, activist-oriented audience; the general audience (PG), and in the educational film market, we aim at high school and adult audiences, especially the so-called 'minority' audiences. Assignments are given solely based upon our reaction to submitted material. The material is the credential." Query first. Enclose S.A.S.E.

General: "I concentrate primarily on feature film projects. However, I am always interested in a unique feature-length documentary film project. We prefer submission of film treatments first. Then, if the idea interests us, we then negotiate the writing of the script." Payment is negotiable, according to Writer's Guild standards.

COMPRENETICS, INC., 340 N. Camden Dr., Beverly Hills CA 90210. Contact: Ira Englander. Target audience varies from entry-level hospital and health workers with minimal academic background to continued education programs for physicians and health professionals. Material is copyrighted. Query first. Enclose S.A.S.E.

Education and Medicine: Sound filmstrips, 16mm motion pictures, prerecorded tapes and cassettes. "Films are often programmed with response frames included. Subject areas are primarily in the health and medical field. We currently assign all of our writing responsibilities to outside personnel and intend to continue this arrangement in the future. Our in-house staff normally does subject matter research and content review which is provided for a writer. Writer is then required to provide us with rough outline or film treatment for approval. Due to a somewhat complex review procedure, writers are frequently required to modify through three or four drafts before final approval is granted. Payment is negotiable for each project." $1,000 to $2,500 per script.

CONCORDIA PUBLISHING HOUSE, PRODUCT DEVELOPMENT DIVISION, 3558 S. Jefferson Ave., St. Louis MO 63118. (314)664-7000. For preschool through adult; institutional and home use. Material is copyrighted. Will send a catalog to writer on request. Writer must have demonstrated skills in writing producible material for the audio and visual fields. Competence in the content area is necessary. Initial query is preferred in view of existing production commitments and necessity to maintain a satisfactory product mix. Enclose S.A.S.E.

Education and Religion: Silent and sound filmstrips, 16mm motion pictures, multimedia kits, overhead transparencies, phonograph records, prerecorded tapes and cassettes, 35mm slides and study prints. Content areas relate to the requirements of religious and moral guidance instruction. Emphases may be curricular, quasi-curricular or enriching. Writing fees are negotiated in consideration of such factors as type of production, configuration, complexity of assignment, research required, field tests and production deadlines.

DAVID C. COOK PUBLISHING CO., 850 N. Grove Ave., Elgin IL 60120. Contact: Editor, School Products Division. Produces material for grade school children, K-8. Buys all rights. Free catalog. Produces study prints.

Needs: Education (various topics with pictures and stories for children; manual for teachers). Pays $35-75.

CREATIVE VISUALS, Division of Gamco Industries, Inc., Box 1911, Big Spring TX 79720. (915)267-6327. Director, New Product Development: Judith Rickey. Free catalog and author's guidelines. "We want you, as a potential author, to submit the following information. First, provide a list of your educational degrees and majors. Explain your teaching experience, including subjects taught, grades taught, and the number of years you have taught. Please describe any writing experience, and, if possible, include a sample of your published educational material currently on the market. We ask for this information because we have found that our best authors are usually experienced classroom teachers who are writing in their subject area. Once we have information about your background, we will ask you for the subject and titles of your proposed series." Produces sound filmstrips; overhead transparencies; tapes and cassettes; and study prints.

Needs: Education (grades K-12, all subjects areas). Payment by royalty; usually 7-10% of net sales.

DIVISION OF AUDIOVISUAL ARTS, NATIONAL PARK SERVICE, Harpers Ferry Center, Harpers Ferry WV 25425. (304)535-6371. Asst. Chief: Rick Krepela. Produces material for visitors to National Parks. "Most material becomes public domain after purchase and since the writer does not retain any rights, we purchase all rights." Free catalog of films only. "Potential writers should list their credits and areas of specialization (history, ecology, etc.). We do not buy any 'spec' material. Assignments are given to writers where work or credits are known to us and who have made their availability known." Produces motion pictures (16mm and 35mm); multimedia kits; tapes; videotapes and sound/slide programs.

Needs: "Varies according to park and the particular interpretive program for that park. "Covers history, anthropology, geology, etc." Pays $300 and up for audio messages; $1,200 for sound/slide scripts; and $1,800 and up for motion picture scripts.

MARK DRUCK PRODUCTIONS, 300 E. 40th St., New York NY 10016. Produces audiovisuals for "mostly industry audiences or women's groups." Produces 16mm motion pictures, multimedia kits and video tape industrials. Subjects: retail items, drugs, travel, industrial products, etc. Material is sometimes copyrighted. "The whole production belongs to the client." No unsolicited scripts; only resumes, lists of credits, etc. The freelance writer must have some expertise in the subject, and in writing A/V scripts. Enclose S.A.S.E.

General: Pays minimum of $500 per reel. No maximum. Writer will be expected to produce outline, treatment, and shooting script.

EDUCATIONAL DIMENSIONS GROUP, Box 126, Stamford CT 06904. Managing Editor: Vincent J. Amato. Produces material for K-12 levels. Catalog $1. Query. Produces sound filmstrips; multimedia kits and slides (size 2¼x2¼).

Needs: 40-80 frames geared to proper grade level; all educational disciplines. Pays $100 minimum for consultation. Script writing fees vary.

EDUCATIONAL IMAGES, Box 367, Lyons Falls NY 13368. (315)348-8211. Executive Director: Dr. Charles R. Belinky. Produces material for schools, K-college and graduate school, public libraries, parks, nature centers, etc. Buys all AV rights. Free catalog. "We are looking for complete AV programs. This requires high quality, factual text and pictures." Query. Produces silent and sound filmstrips; multimedia kits; and slides.
Needs: Science and education. Slide sets and filmstrips. Pays $100 minimum plus percentage royalties.

EMC CORPORATION, 180 E. Sixth St., St. Paul MN 55101. Book Editor: Carol Spencer. Editor-in-Chief: Northrop Dawson Jr. Produces material for children, teen-agers—primary grades through high school. Buys world rights. Catalog for SASE. "Writer, via submitted sample, must show capability to write appropriately for the medium." Query. Produces filmstrips (sound); multimedia kits and tapes and cassettes.
Needs: "No standard requirements, due to nature of educational materials publishing—subject area, grade level, instructional objectives, etc." Payment varies.
For '78: "Math materials, consumer education, special education (as related to language, arts and math especially), low vocabularly but high interest fiction and nonfiction for problem readers at secondary grade levels."

FAMILY FILMS/COUNTERPOINT FILMS, 14622 Lanark St., Panorama City CA 91402. Contact: Paul R. Kidd, Director of Product Development. For all age levels from preschool through adult. Copyrighted. Will send a catalog to writer on request. Query first. "Majority projects are assigned and developed to our specifications. Writers may submit their credentials and experience. Some experience in writing film and filmstrip scripts is desired. A teaching credential or teaching experience valuable for our school materials. Active involvement in a mainstream church desirable for our religious projects."
Education and Religion: "Sound filmstrips, 16mm motion pictures and prerecorded tapes and cassettes for schools, universities, public libraries, and for interdenominational religious market. Motion pictures vary from 10 minutes to 30 to 40 minutes. Filmstrips about 50 to 60 frames with running time of 7 to 10 minutes. Emphasis on the human situation and person-to-person relationships. No royalty arrangements. Outright payment depends on project and available budget. As an example, usual filmstrip project requires 4 scripts, for which we pay $150 to $250 each. Motion picture scripts through final draft, $1,200-1,500."

GIRL SCOUTS OF THE U.S.A., 830 Third Ave., New York NY 10022. For girls and adults involved in the Girl Scout movement; the general public. Will send catalog to writer on request. Query first. All projects are generated within the organization, which is not seeking proposals, treatments, or manuscripts. Credentials for writer would depend on project. Enclose S.A.S.E.
General: All audiovisuals deal with some aspect of Girl Scout movement: program, training, administration, public relations, etc. Sound filmstrips, 16mm and 8mm motion pictures, multimedia kits, overhead transparencies, phonograph records, prerecorded tapes and cassettes, 35mm slides, and flip charts. "We work on fee basis only; the amount negotiable in terms of the assignment."

GOLDSHOLL ASSOC., 420 Frontage Rd., Northfield IL 60093. (312)446-8300. President: M. Goldsholl. Buys all rights. Free catalog. Query. Produces sound filmstrips; motion pictures (16/35mm); multimedia kits; tapes and cassettes, and slides (size 35mm).
Needs: PR films for industry. Pays 5-10% of budgets. Also interested in short stories to be made into screenplays, filmscripts (original). "Describe before sending."

HANDEL FILM CORP., 8730 Sunset Blvd., West Hollywood CA 90069. Contact: Production Department. For variety of audiences, depending on film. Material becomes property of Handel Film Corp. if acquired. Submit only upon request. Do not send in unsolicited material. Query first. Enclose S.A.S.E.
Education and Documentary: 16mm motion pictures, approximately half-hour films for science, history and other areas. Payment is negotiable.

HAYES SCHOOL PUBLISHING CO., INC., 321 Pennwood Ave., Wilkinson PA 15221. (412)371-2373. 2nd Vice President: Clair N. Hayes III. Produces material for school teachers, principals, elementary and junior high school students. Buys all rights. Catalog for SASE. Query. Produces charts; workbooks, teachers handbooks, posters, bulletin board material, and liquid duplicating books.
Needs: Education material only ("will consider all types of material suitable for use in elementary schools and Sunday school classes."). Pays $25-2,500.

HESTER & ASSOCIATES, INC., 11422 Hines Blvd., Dallas TX 75229. (214)241-4859. President: Stew Hester. Produces material for school population—kindergarten through post graduate. Buys "exclusive or non-exclusive" rights. Free catalog. "Would prefer an outline of the idea; then we can respond if there is a relevance to our needs." Query. Produces film loops (S8mm); sound filmstrips; multimedia kits; tapes and cassettes; slides (size 35mm); and work books (with and without tapes).
Needs: Education ("Our major efforts at present are sales to school...usually workbooks and activity books in math, art and science.") Pays royalties, 5-15%.

IMPERIAL INTERNATIONAL LEARNING CORP., Box 548, Kankakee IL 60901. Contact: Jim Hargrove, Director of Product Development. Produces material for schools, K-high school. Free catalog. Query. Buys considerable freelance material, but generally on assignment basis only. "Writers seeking assignments should query first. Letter should include a summary of background and professional writing experience, and, if possible, a writing sample suitable for elementary school children, to be held on file." Reports in 6 weeks. Produces sound filmstrips (35mm); tape-centered instructional packages; paperback books; and multimedia kits.
Needs: Education (most interested in seeing materials in the areas of language arts, reading, math, early childhood, special education, and career education); audiovisual software appropriate for elementary school students. "We have seen a strong marketing trend in the last two years toward skill-oriented programs that teach the basics in fresh and imaginative ways. Therefore, most freelance writers we've worked with recently are also educators familiar with elementary school curricula, especially reading and math." Pays flat fee within 90 days after acceptance of ms or reprinted contract.

INSGROUP, INC., 16052 Beach Blvd., Huntington Beach CA 92647. For industrial, military (both enlisted and officer), public school (K through graduate level), police, nursing, and public administrators. Material is copyrighted. Criteria for writers are determined on a project by project basis. Query first, with resumes and be prepared to submit copies of previous efforts. Enclose S.A.S.E.
General: Charts, silent and sound filmstrips, multimedia kits, overhead transparencies, prerecorded tapes and cassettes, 35mm slides, study prints, teaching machine programs, and videotapes. Insgroup develops objective-based validated audiovisual instructional programs both for commercial customers and for publication by Insgroup. These programs cover the entire range of subject areas, styles, formats, etc. Most writing is on a fee basis. Royalties, when given, are 5% to 8%.

INSTRUCTIONAL DYNAMICS INCORPORATED, 450 E. Ohio St., Chicago IL 60611. For early learning through college level. Material is copyrighted. Will send catalog to writer on request. "Writer should have valid background and experience that parallels the specific assignment. Would like to have vita as first contact. We keep on file and activate as needs arise. We use a substantial group of outside talent to supplement our in-house staff." Enclose S.A.S.E.
Education: Silent filmstrips, sound filmstrips, multimedia kits, overhead transparencies, phonograph records, prerecorded tapes and cassettes, 2x2 slides, study prints and hard copy. "Requirements for these vary depending upon assignments from our clients. Payment depends on contractual arrangements with our client and also varies depending on medium or multimedia involved."

INSTRUCTOR CURRICULUM MATERIALS, 7 Bank St., Dansville NY 14437. (716)335-2221. Editorial Director: Margie H. Richmond. "U.S. and Canadian school supervisors, principals, and teachers purchase items in our line for instructional purposes." Buys all rights. Will send a catalog to a writer on request. Writer should have "experience in preparing materials for elementary students, including suitable teaching guides to accompany them, and demonstrate knowledge of the appropriate subject areas, or demonstrable ability for accurate and efficient research and documentation. Please query." Enclose S.A.S.E. for response to queries.
Education: "Elementary curriculum enrichment, all subject areas. Display material, copy, and illustration should match interest and reading skills of children in grades for which material is intended. Production is limited to printed matter: posters, charts, duplicating masters, resource handbooks, teaching guides." Length: 6,000 to 12,000 words. "Standard contract, but fees vary considerably, depending on type of project."

KEN-DEL PRODUCTIONS, INC., 111 Valley Rd., Richardson Park, Wilmington DE 19804. (302)655-7488. Contact: Ed Kennedy. For "elementary junior high, high school, and college level, as well as interested organizations and companies." Will assign projects to qualified writers. Query first. Enclose S.A.S.E. for response to queries.

General: Wants material for "topics of the present (technology, cities, traffic, transit, pollution, ecology, health, water, race, genetics, consumerism, fashions, communications, education, population control, waste, future sources of food, undeveloped sources of living, food, health, etc.); topics of the future; how-to series (everything for the housewife, farmer, banker, mechanic, on music, art, sports, reading, science, love, repair, sleep—on any subject)." Produces sound filmstrips; 8mm, 16mm, and 35mm motion pictures; 16mm film loops; phonograph records; prerecorded tapes and cassettes; slides.

LYCEUM PRODUCTIONS, INC., P.O. Box 1018, Laguna Beach CA 92652. Contact: Patty Lincke. For grade levels from elementary school through college. Copyrighted. Rights purchased are subject to negotiation. Query first. No assignments are made. Enclose S.A.S.E.
Education: Produces sound filmstrips. "Most of our filmstrips provide curriculum support and enrichment in subject areas including natural science, ecology, science, social studies, language arts, art, history and citizenship. Many titles are interdisciplinary. Some titles span wide age groups while others may be more limited in scope. Whatever the concept of the filmstrip, it should stimulate the student to explore dhe subject more fully. Please submit an idea or an outline before sending a manuscript or transparencies. Completed material will only be considered if it has been requested upon the basis of a previous query. Our contracts provide for royalties based on sales with an advance upon acceptance. The possibilities for the unknown freelancer are difficult."

MAGNETIX CORPORATION, 770 W. Bay St., Winter Garden FL 32787. (305)656-4494. President: John Lory. Produces material for the general public. Buys all rights. "Personal contact must be made due to wide variety of very specific scripts we require. Must have ability to dramatize our subjects using sound effects, etc." Produces tapes and cassettes.
Needs: General (20-30 minute audio program with sound effects written to be sold to general public as a souvenir with some educational value.) Pays $300 and up.

ARTHUR MERIWETHER, INC. Box 457, Downers Grove IL 60515. For elementary and high school students. Material is copyrighted. Will send catalog to writer for 75¢. "Prior professional experience is required. Query first. Background as an educator is often helpful." Enclose S.A.S.E.
Education: "We prefer items applying to language arts, English, history, sociology and drama studies to be used as a supplement to regular curriculum materials." Filmstrips (silent and sound), motion pictures, multimedia kits. and prerecorded tapes and cassettes. Games for learning also considered. Pays 5% to 10% royalty.
Religion: "Will consider filmstrip scripts that deal with subjects of contemporary religious importance for elementary and high school religious education groups. Liberal approach preferred. Professional quality only. Scripts purchased outright, or royalty arrangement."
Business: Business-oriented mss or scripts on marketing and staff training.

MRC FILMS, Division of McLaughlin Research Corp., 71 W. 23rd St., New York NY 10010. Executive Producer: Larry Mollot. "Audience varies with subject matter, which is wide and diverse." Writer "should have an ability to visualize concepts and to express ideas clearly in words. Experience in motion picture or filmstrip script writing is desirable. Write us, giving some idea of background. Submit samples of writing. Wait for reply. We will always reply, one way or another. We are looking for new talent. No unsolicited material accepted. Work upon assignment only." Query first. Enclose S.A.S.E. for response to queries.
General: "Industrial, documentary, educational, and television films. Also, public relations, teaching, and motivational filmstrips. Some subjects are highly technical in the fields of aerospace and electronics. Others are on personal relationships, selling techniques, ecology, etc. A writer with an imaginative visual sense is important." Produces silent and sound filmstrips, 16mm motion pictures, prerecorded tapes, cassettes. "Fee depends on nature and length of job. Typical fees: $500 to $1,000 for script for 10-minute film; $1,000 to $1,400 for script for 20-minute film; $1,200 to $2,000 for script for 30-minute film. For narration writing only, the range is $200 to $500 for a 10-minute film; $400 to $800 for a 20-minute film; $500 to $1,000 for a 30-minute film. For script writing services by the day, fee is $60 to $100 per day."

NEBRASKA ETV COUNCIL FOR HIGHER EDUCATION, Box 83111, Lincoln NE 68501. (402)472-3611. Senior Producer—ITV: Darrell Wheaton. Produces material for educational/ instructional television programs for college students for use in college classrooms. Free catalog. "Only persons experienced in preparing material for college level instructional film need inquire. Copies of previous materials must be available for consideration. We need full scripts

in production format including all dialogue and production suggestions, typed in a split column form, preferably." Query. Produces motion pictures (16mm); tapes and cassettes; and video tapes.
Needs: "Requirements are specifically tailored to the particular lesson under development; the organization prepares material in most areas of study." Pays $50-2,000.

NYSTROM, 3333 Elston Ave., Chicago IL 60618. For kindergarten through 12. Material is copyrighted. Will send catalog to writer on request. Required credentials depend on topics and subject matter and approach desired. Query first. Enclose S.A.S.E.
Education: Charts, sound filmstrips, models, multimedia kits, overhead transparencies, and realia. Social studies, earth and life sciences, career education, reading, and language arts. Payment varies with circumstances.

OUR SUNDAY VISITOR, INC., Audiovisual Department, Noll Plaza, Huntington IN 46750. Contact: Margaret Schultz. For students (K to 12), adult religious education groups, and teacher training. Copyrighted. Will send catalog to writer on request. Query first. "We are looking for well-developed total packages only. Programs should display up-to-date audiovisual technique and cohesiveness." Enclose S.A.S.E.
Education and Religion: "Broadly speaking, material should deal with religious education, including liturgy and daily Christian living, as well as structured catechesis. Must not conflict with sound Catholic doctrine. Should reflect modern trends in education. Word lengths may vary." Produces charts, sound filmstrips, overhead transparencies, phonograph records, prerecorded tapes and cassettes and 2x2 slides. Royalties vary from 5% to 10% of price received, depending on the product and its market. Fee arrangements also; for example, so many dollars per each 100, 500, or 1,000 sets or projects produced at time of production.

OUTDOOR PICTURES, Box 277, Anacortes WA 98221. (206)293-3200. Contact: Ernest S. Booth. "We would like to find qualified persons to design filmstrips, take the original photos or prepare the artwork, write the scripts and submit to us the entire package ready to produce. We make the internegative master then return the originals to you. We copyright all such materials, but allow you the right to sell any of the originals to others on a one-time basis."
Needs: "We are interested in all subjects that schools will buy. You should look at audiovisual catalogs and examine existing filmstrips, and work closely with one or more teachers in the grade level where your material would be used. We pay 10% royalty on the retail price of the production. Before you begin, write us for a set of guidelines and a free catalog of our filmstrips."

PACE FILMS, INC., 411 E. 53rd St., New York NY 10022. Contact: Mr. R. Vanderbes. For "TV and theatrical audience in the U.S. and worldwide." Buys all rights. Writing assignments are handled through agencies, but independent queries or submissions are considered. Enclose S.A.S.E. for response.
General: "Documentaries and feature motion pictures for TV and theaters." Pays "Writers Guild of America minimums and up."

PARAMOUNT/OXFORD FILMS, A Subsidiary of Paramount Pictures Corp., 5451 Marathon St., Hollywood CA 90038. For general audiences. Material is copyrighted. Will send catalog to writer on request. Query first. Enclose S.A.S.E.
Education: 16mm motion pictures. "Because we are distributors as well as producers of educational films and filmstrips, much of our activity concerns post production work on films acquired and the marketing of these. For films which we produce, scripts are usually written on assignment by staff or educational script writers known to us; educational films have special requirements to meet school curriculum requirements. Therefore, the opportunity for freelance writers here is limited, except for those living in the area, with the know-how for school scripts. However, if a writer has information on an unusual subject which could be of interest to schools, or a fresh approach to something which could fit into the less structured areas such as language arts or interpersonal relationships, it wouldn't hurt to query us. Also we are beginning to consider the kind of films suitable for business sponsorship, and in some instances we sell to college, adult, church, health and vocational groups. Pay ranges from $500 to $1,000 for 10 to 20 minutes (pages) with rewrite fairly certain to be required."

THE PERFECTION FORM CO., 8350 Hickman Rd., Des Moines IA 50322. Editor-in-Chief: Wayne F. DeMouth. Produces sound filmstrips, cassette programs and learning packages for use in secondary language arts and social studies education. Reports in 30 days. Write for catalog.

Filmstrips: Prefers length of 10-18 minutes, with 100 to 135 frames. Interpretive biographies and studies of historical epochs. Usually pays $500 for script (depending on amount of time needed for editorial revision).

How To Break In: "Writers should study our products carefully before trying to submit their material."

PHOTOCOM PRODUCTIONS, Box 3135, Pismo Beach CA 93449. Contact: B.L. Pattison. Produces material for junior and senior high school students; all subjects taught in public schools are considered for production. Buys all rights. "A list of 6-10 usable topics wins us over every time." Produces sound filmstrips; multimedia kits and slides.

Needs: Educational (high school audience; fast paced; accurate; 50-60 frames, 10-15 minutes long. No racial or sexual bias.). Pays 10% royalties without illustrations; 15% with all pix supplied by author.

PLAYETTE CORPORATION, 301 E. Shore Rd., Great Neck NY 11023. Contact: Sidney A. Evans. For "all school levels, teachers, and libraries." Not copyrighted. Writer must have "a complete and thorough knowledge of the subject with practical applied usage. Material must have been classroom tested before submission." Query first. SASE. No phone calls.

Education and Foreign Languages: Requirements "depend on subject selected." Charts, silent filmstrips, sound filmstrips, multimedia kits, overhead transparencies, phonograph records, prerecorded tapes and cassettes, slides, study prints, and foreign language training aids and games. "Payment for each subject on a separate basis."

PRODUCERS GROUP LTD., One IBM Plaza, Suite 2519, Chicago IL 60611. (312)467-1830. For general audiences. Material is copyrighted. "Make yourself known to us. We do, on some occasions, go outside for help. There is very little point in submitting scripts unless we have a specific project in hand. First, we get the assignment; then we go into creative work. We're probably not the best market for freelance submissions. Unsolicited mss are wasteful, inappropriate. We're too specialized. When and if writer has proven record, we match project to writer's skills, expertise. Originate most of our own creative material here. We prefer any writer to have at least a B.A., or equivalent experience. Must have a record in a-v writing, and hopefully, production. We require clean shooting script, with all visuals completely designated." Query first. Enclose S.A.S.E.

Education: Film loops and sound filmstrips, 8mm and 16mm motion pictures, and multimedia kits. Business-oriented multimedia shows, educational motion pictures, and talk demonstrations. Editorial requirements vary according to assignments. Usually aim toward higher levels of educational background for business communications; aim toward specific age groups for educational films, as required. Usual lengths are 20 minutes. Again, varied according to end use. Standard fee is 10% of gross production budget. No royalty arrangements under this schedule. Straight buyout.

PROFESSIONAL RESEARCH, INC., 660 S. Bonnie Brae St., Los Angeles CA 90057. Vice-President: Richard J. Sternberg, M.D. Produces material for medical/surgical/dental/health care institutional patients, doctors, nurses, allied health professionals. "Looking for writers with experience in development of educational media for health care markets. Only require a few writers each year who must have familiarity with biological and medical/dental sciences, as well as have experience in AV writing." Query. Produces motion pictures (16mm); multimedia kits; and video tapes.

Needs: Medicine (patient education films: live action and animation, lay language, 20 minutes or less; continuing education: content and format adapted to meet subject and audience needs.). Pays $350 minimum (first draft) — $1,000 (completed script maximum).

For 78: Self-paced instructional packages.

PUBLISHERS INVESTORS, INC., 747 Third Ave., New York NY 10017. (212)688-8830. Administrative Assistant: Carol Herrod. Produces material for elementary and secondary students. "Include a list of firms which have used material of the writer. Send samples with all inquiries." Produces silent and sound filmstrips; multimedia kits; phonograph records; and tapes and cassettes.

Needs: Educational (primarily elementary school material). Pays $25 minimum.

Q-ED PRODUCTIONS, INC., P.O. Box 1608, Burbank CA 91507. (213)843-8040. For grade levels kindergarten through 12. Material is copyrighted. Buys all rights. Will send a catalog to writer on request. "We are interested in reviewing completed filmstrip packages (4 to 6 filmstrips in a set) for distribution on royalty basis, or outright buy. Knowledge of the field and experience as a writer of filmstrips and films for education required. Also, demonstrated ability in research required. We look for the new approach. Unique ways of imparting information so that children will want to learn more and on their own. Definitely not interested in didactic, mundane approaches to learning." Query first. Send queries to Henry Spitzer, Vice President/ Production. Enclose S.A.S.E.

Education: Grade levels K-12. Interested in core curriculum materials. Historically strong in values. Materials should be inquiry oriented, open-ended, strong objectives (cognitive, affective, psycho-motor). Royalties open on original materials. Fees range from $450 for a 10-minute film or filmstrip.

REGENTS PUBLISHING COMPANY, INC., Two Park Ave., New York NY 10016. Contact: Julio I. Andujar, President. For foreign language students, in school and at home. Copyrighted. Will send catalog to writer on request. Query with description of material, table of contents and sample portions. Enclose S.A.S.E. for reply. No unsolicited mss. "It would be helpful if writer has done previous audiovisual work, has taught or is currently teaching."

Education: English as a second language. Spanish, French, German. Supplementary materials, cultural aspects of wide appeal in foreign language classes. Vocabulary within the range of foreign language students. Sound filmstrips, multimedia kits, phonograph records, prerecorded tapes and cassettes. Pays 6% of list price.

RHYTHMS PRODUCTIONS, Whitney Bldg., Box 34485, Los Angeles CA 90034. Contact: R.S. White. "Our audience is generally educational, with projects ranging from early childhood through adult markets." Copyrighted. Query first. "We need to know a writer's background and credits and to see samples of his work." Enclose S.A.S.E. for response to queries.

Education: Books, sound filmstrips, 16mm motion pictures, multimedia kits, phonograph records, prerecorded tapes and cassettes, and study prints. "Our firm specializes in creative productions, so though content is basic to the productions, a creative and imaginative approach is necessary." Usually pays $250 for filmstrip scripts.

RIDDLE VIDEO AND FILM PRODUCTIONS, INC., 507 Fifth Ave., New York NY 10017. (212)697-5895. President/Executive Producer: William Riddle. For "general public, young and old alike. Also for theater distribution." Material may be copyrighted or not copyrighted. Write for copy of guidelines for writers. Writer "must be experienced and well-qualified in the subject in order to handle work assignments satisfactorily. We must see a sample of his or her work." Query first. Enclose S.A.S.E. for response to queries.

General: "Story boards and scripts are needed." Produces 8mm, 16mm and 35mm film loops; silent filmstrips; sound filmstrips; kinescopes; models; 8mm, 16mm, and 35mm motion pictures; multimedia kits; prerecorded tapes and cassettes; slides; study prints; videotape productions. Pays "standard going rates, with bonus on super work performed."

HOWARD W. SAMS & CO., INC., Education Division, 4300 W. 62nd St., Indianapolis IN 46268. (317)291-3100. Contact: John Obst, Managing Editor. Query first. Enclose S.A.S.E.

Education: Seeking scripts for "industrial arts, vocational/technical, business education, and career education subjects at the junior and senior high school, technical school and junior college levels." Payment by royalty arrangement.

SAVE THE CHILDREN, 48 Wilton Rd., Westport CT 06880. (203)226-7272. Producer: Andrew Mollo. Generally buys all rights, "but it depends on project. We use work only written for specific assignments." Produces motion pictures (16mm); tapes and cassettes; slides (size 2x2); and posters and displays.

Needs: General (radio and TV); and education (high school, college and adult). Pays $250-500 minimum/assignment.

SEVOTE GROUP, 484 Waterloo Court, Oshawa, Ontario, Canada L1H 3X1. (416)576-0250. General Manager: Bob Stone. Produces material for educational (K-8) and secondary schools. Buys all rights. Catalog for SASE. "We are looking for new projects. Send very brief outline of concept first." Query. Produces silent and sound filmstrips; motion pictures (16mm); multimedia kits; phonograph records; tapes and cassettes; and video tapes.

Needs: Education ("we specialize in the vocal and instrument instruction field.") Pays $500 minimum.

SPENCER PRODUCTIONS, INC., 507 5th Ave., New York NY 10017. (212)697-5895. Contact: Bruce Spencer. For high school students, college students, and adults. Occasionally uses freelance writers with considerable talent. Query first. Enclose S.A.S.E.

Satire: 16mm motion pictures, prerecorded tapes and cassettes. Satirical material only. Pay is negotiable.

BILL STOKES ASSOCIATES, 5642 Dyer St., Dallas TX 75206. Contact: Bill Stokes. Audience varies with projects undertaken; everyone from children to board chairmen. Rights purchased from author as payment for work performed. Writer must have experience in script writing, ability to visualize, good research habits, with recent reel or portfolio. Jobs are let on closed contract basis only. Query first. Enclose S.A.S.E.
General: Super 8mm, 16mm and 35mm film loops, sound filmstrips, 16mm and 35mm motion pictures, multimedia kits, phonograph records, prerecorded tapes and cassettes, and 35mm slides. All materials and requirements contingent upon clients' needs. "We produce sales meetings, industrial films, educational films, animated films, slide shows, filmstrips, multimedia programs, etc., covering a wide range of subjects and applications. Writer must be sufficiently acquainted with av and motion picture production formats to write within specific budget requirements." No royalties are paid. Contract basis only.

SUMMERHILL MEDIA LTD., Box 156, Station Q, Toronto, Ontario, Canada M4T 2M1. Editor-in-Chief: Ian A. Stuart. Will send free catalog to writer on request. Query first, with outline. Reports in 2 weeks. Enclose S.A.S.E.
Education and General: Produces documentary and educational films, for which scripts and ideas in outline form are sought. Also produces supplementary booklets. Would like to receive queries on films about police training; psychology (elementary level); and health in adolescence. Pays $250 fee.

SUMMIT PICTURES INTERNATIONAL LTD., 1040 W. North Las Palmas Ave., Hollywood CA 90038. Contact: Martin Green. For general audience. Material is copyrighted. Occasionally uses freelance writers. Query first. Enclose S.A.S.E.
General: 16mm and 35mm motion pictures. Films, feature length, used for commercials, and industrial documentaries. Also television productions, musicals and variety shows. Payment is flexible, and negotiable.

SWIMMING WORLD, 8622 Bellanca Ave., Los Angeles CA 90045. (213)641-2727. Produces 8mm film loops, 8mm motion pictures, 35mm slides. "Our audience includes swimmers, age 10 through 25, their parents, coaches and administrators involved in the sport; high school through college level." Copyrighted. Will send copy of guidelines for writers. Query first. Enclose S.A.S.E.
Sports: Competitive swimming, diving and water polo. "Must be able to shoot good instructional films and action slides." Pays $150 for 20-minute 8mm color instructional films, plus royalty; but payment depends on project.

TALCO PRODUCTIONS, 279 E. 44 St., New York NY 10017. (212)697-4015. President: Alan Lawrence. Produces material for TV programming; for some schools; and whatever else clients might request. Buys all rights. "We maintain a file of writers and call on those with experience in the general category of the program we are producing. We do not select unsolicited ms. We prefer to receive a writer's resume listing credits. If his experience merits, we will be in touch when a project seems right." Produces sound filmstrips; motion pictures; videotapes; phonograph records; tapes and cassettes; and slides.
Needs: General (client oriented productions to meet specific needs); education (peripheral market); business (public relations, documentaries, industrial); foreign language (we sometimes dub shows completed for clients for a specific market). Payment runs $500 and up; usually Writers Guild minimums apply.

TELSTAR PRODUCTION INC., 366 N. Prior Ave., St. Paul MN 55104. Program Consultant: Dr. Victor Kerns. Produces video material for adult, college level audience, in industry and continuing education. Buys video recording rights. Query. Produces instructional video tapes.
Needs: Education (curricular materials for small group or independent study); business (training and development material); and medicine (para-medical topics). Pays $100 plus royalties.

BOB THOMAS PRODUCTIONS, 23 Broad St., Bloomfield NJ 07003. (201)429-9000. President: Robert G. Thomas. Buys all rights. "Send material with introductory letter explaining ideas. Submit outline or rough draft for motion picture or business matter. If possible, we will contact the writer for further discussion." Enclose S.A.S.E.

Business, Education, and General: "We produce 3 types of material for 3 types of audiences: 8mm film loops in sports and pre-teen areas (educational); 8mm and 16mm motion pictures for business (educational, distributed by agencies); 35mm motion pictures for entertainment for a general audience (theater type). General subject matter may be of any style, any length. For the future, 35mm theatrical shorts for distribution." Payment "depends on agreements between both parties. On 8mm and 16mm matter, one fee arrangement. On 35mm shorts, percentage or fee."

VIDEO FILMS INC., 2211 E. Jefferson Ave., Detroit MI 48207. (313)393-0800. President: Clifford Hanna. For "adult, industrial audience." Query first, with resume of credentials. Enclose S.A.S.E.

Industry: Produces filmstrips, 8mm and 16mm motion pictures, prerecorded tapes and cassettes, and slides. Payment "negotiable."

VISUAL TEACHING, 79 Pine Knob Terrace, Milford CT 06460. Contact: James A. Cunningham. For elementary through college level; most junior high level. Copyrighted. Will send a brochure to writer on request. Query first. "Writers should have a good knowledge and background in biology. We prefer to work with people that have developed a complete story of some aspect in nature accompanied by 2x2 color photos."

Science: "Texts to accompany 2x2 slide sets. 20 slides per set. Approximately 1,000 words. So far, all our topics have been nature and science. We would consider other topics if photographic materials were available or could be obtained. Our usual format is to use 20 2x2 color slides to teach some lesson in nature. The slides must be top quality and it is best that they all be taken by the same photographer. The descriptions are usually written on a general audience level since they are directed mainly toward teachers, not biologists. Writers furnish slides (their own), royalty of 10%."

VOCATIONAL EDUCATION PRODUCTIONS, California Polytechnic State University, San Luis Obispo CA 93407. (805)546-2623. Director: Steven C. LaMarine. Produces material for junior and senior high school students, junior college and some university level classes; all dealing with various aspects of agriculture—crop science, horticulture, mechanics, etc. Buys all rights. Free catalog. "A simple query letter will suffice, but it helps to know prior experience, subject matter of interest; specific topics that we may be interested in developing. We prefer to work with writer-photographers and arrange for a complete package of materials to be developed."

Needs: Produces silent and sound filmstrips; microfilm; multimedia kits; overhead transparencies; tapes and cassettes, and slides (size 35mm). "We usually furnish script development pages for the typing of final drafts, just to make it easier to work with the script. Total length of our filmstrips is about 10 minutes, or 50-70 frames. Avoid talking down to viewer. Technical accuracy is an absolute must." Pays $200/script for a series of 3-6; $400-600 for a single script.

JERRY WARNER & ASSOCIATES, 8455 Fountain Ave., #309, Los Angeles CA 90069. For business, government, schools, and television audiences. Copyright depending on client situation. "We buy full rights to writers' works for sponsored films. Writer must be a professional screenwriter or within the discipline of the special area of subject matter. Do not submit single copy material. Have material registered for datemark, or Writers Guild protection. We accept no responsibility for unsolicited mss." Will answer inquiries within the boundaries of production interest. Enclose S.A.S.E.

Business and General: Sound filmstrips, motion pictures, multimedia kits, and prerecorded tapes and cassettes. Sponsored business and government films; training, public information, public relations, sales promotion, educational, report films. Royalties are paid on proprietary films that writers take equity in rather than full fee, participations. "We read concepts for educational and documentary films and properties for feature films, but do not solicit scripts as a general rule. Fees vary and depend upon individual client or agency. We frequently pay from $50 to $75 per day for research periods and from $500 to $1,500 per reel of script. The wide variance is indicative of how each project has different scope and must be approached on the basis of talent requirement."

Authors' Agents/Literary Services

At any gathering of two or more writers who are establishing themselves in the literary community, the issue of authors' agents invariably pops into the conversation. Frequently overheard are questions like "Do I really *need* an agent? How do I get a good one? What can an agent *do* for me?"

Briefly, an authors' agent is the person responsible for any business concerning the sale of a client's written material. It's an agent's job to stay on top of the field—to know *who* needs *what,* and what is the highest price they're willing to pay for it. In short, an agent is the personal door-to-door salesman of a writer's goods.

It's best that the beginning writer market his own work. This is a good way to become familiar with the field, and there is much to be learned from personal contact between editor and writer. This open-door communication proves invaluable when an editor has an assignment that could be right for a writer with whom he has established a good rapport and working relationship.

Normally a top agent *won't* consider taking on a writer without a proven track record. After all, the agent lives off of a 10-20 percent commission of his clients' sales, and unless a writer is producing quality work prior to signing with the agent, the investment in time and promotion isn't worth the risk. Some agencies charge prospective clients *reading fees* (ranging from around $25 for short stories and articles, to over $100 for novels and stage plays) to insure them some compensation should the material prove unsaleable. In such cases, the listing in *Writer's Market* for the agency states this, and generally gives the amount of the fees.

Once a writer is selling regularly to the major markets, he may want to acquire an agent, thus relieving him of the task of marketing his work, and freeing him to concentrate on other projects, such as books. Agents prefer to represent authors who are primarily doing books as the royalties on book sales are greater than the fees received on magazine sales, and so the agent gets a larger commission.

Be careful in signing any contract with an agent. Be sure you know what rights he's handling for your material, and check to see that there are no charges for services other than those you have contracted for (such as editing or marketing fees or charges for criticism). Some agencies legitimately charge for these services (at about the same prices as are charged for reading fees; sometimes higher for in-depth evaluation), but always take special care to be aware of "hidden" costs or extra charges.

The listings in the following category include information as to what kinds of materials the agency is willing to handle, what percentage the agent receives as his commission, and what fees for reading, evaluating, or critiquing, if any, are charged. Other lists of agents can be obtained from The Society of Authors' Representatives, 101 Park Ave., New York City 10017, and from the Writers Guild of America, West (primarily agents who handle TV and movie material), 8955 Beverly Blvd., Los Angeles 90048.

DOMINICK ABEL LITERARY AGENCY, 498 West End Ave., New York NY 10024. (212)877-0710. Estab: 1975. Obtains new clients through recommendations, solicitation, and blind submissions. Will read unsolicited mss, queries and outlines. SASE. Agent receives 10% commission.
Will Handle: Novels, nonfiction books and syndicated material.

ADAMS, RAY & ROSENBERG, 9200 Sunset Blvd., Los Angeles CA 90069. Estab: 1963. Obtains new clients through recommendation only. Will not read unsolicited mss. Agent receives 10% commission.
Will Handle: Novels (motion picture, publication and TV rights), motion pictures, stage plays (film rights), and TV scripts.

DOROTHY ALBERT, 162 W. 54th St., New York NY 10019. Estab: 1959. Obtains new clients through recommendations of editors, educational establishments, contacts in the film industry, and inquiries. Writers should send letter of introduction, description of material, and list of previous submissions, if any. Will not read unsolicited mss; will read unsolicited queries and outlines. SASE. Agent receives 10% on domestic sales; 20% on foreign.

Will Handle: Novels, nonfiction books, motion pictures (completed, no treatments), stage plays (musicals), TV scripts, juvenile and how-to. No poetry, short stories, textbooks, articles, documentaries, or scripts for established episode shows. "We are interested in novels which are well-plotted suspense; quality drama, adult fiction and human relations. The writer should have some foreknowledge of structure and endurance, whether it be motion pictures, television, or books."

AMERICAN PLAY CO., INC., 52 Vanderbilt Ave., New York NY 10017. (212)686-6333. President: Sheldon Abend. Estab: 1889. Obtains new clients through private referrals and unsolicited submissions. Will read unsolicited mss for a fee of $55-65. "We refund the readers' fee if we license the author's mss." Will read unsolicited outlines and queries. "We waive a reading fee when the writer has been published within the last 7 years." SASE. Agent receives 10% commission on U.S. sales; 20% on foreign.
Will Handle: Novels, nonfiction books, motion pictures, stage plays and TV scripts.
Criticism Services: "We have three readers critiquing the new mss, and take a master composite critique and supply a copy to the writer and the publishing and producing companies."

CUTTY ANDERSON ASSOCIATES, INC., 521 5th Ave., New York NY 10017. Executive Senior Associate: H.M. Rothstein. Estab: 1974. Obtains new clients through personal recommendations and some advertising in professional publications. Will not read unsolicited mss; will read unsolicited queries and outlines. SASE. Made 100 sales in 1976, 150-200 in 1977. Agent receives 10-15% on domestic sales, 20% on foreign and media rights.
Will Handle: Magazine articles and fiction, novels, textbooks, nonfiction books, poetry, motion pictures, stage plays, TV and radio scripts, syndicated material. "We run heavily into journalistic style features and investigative materials."

AUTHOR AID ASSOCIATES, 340 E. 52nd St., New York NY. 10022. (212)758-4213. Editorial Director: Arthur Orrmont. Estab: 1967. Obtains new clients through word-of-mouth, referrals, listings and advertisements. Will read unsolicited mss for fees (available upon request); will read unsolicited queries and outlines. SASE. Agent receives 10% commission on domestic sales; 20% on foreign.
Will Handle: Magazine articles and fiction, novels, nonfiction books, textbooks, poetry (collections only), motion pictures, stage plays, TV scripts and juvenile fiction and nonfiction.
Criticism Services: Will critique all materials. Fees available on request.

AUTHORS' ADVISORY SERVICE, 51 E. 42nd St., New York NY 10017. (212)687-2971. Literary Agent: Marcy Ring. Estab: 1975. Obtains new clients through recommendations, listings in *LMP* and *Writer's Market;* also some direct solicitation. Will read unsolicited mss for $100 (up to 100,000 words). "Reading fee is refundable against commission if work is sold." SASE. Made 100 sales in 1976. Agent receives 10% commission.
Will Handle: Magazine articles and fiction, novels, nonfiction books, poetry, stage plays, and juvenile fiction and nonfiction.
Criticism Services: Will critique material as above. Charges $100 for mss up to 100,000 words, combined rate offered for 2 or more mss (i.e., 2 for $150, 3 for $200). "Rule of thumb: $1/page."

THE BALKIN AGENCY, 403 W. 115th St., New York NY 10025. President: Richard Balkin. Estab: 1973. Obtains new clients through recommendations, over-the-transom inquiries, and solicitation. Will not read unsolicited mss; will read unsolicited queries, or outlines and 2 sample chapters. SASE. Made 18 sales in 1976, 20 in 1977, will make 25 in 1978. Agent receives 10% commission on domestic sales, 20% on foreign.
Will Handle: Magazine articles (only as a service to clients who primarily write books), textbooks (college only), nonfiction books, and professional books (on occasion).
Recent Sales: *Middle Eastern Literature,* by L. Hamalian (New American Library); *Film/Cinema/Movie,* by G. Mast (Harper & Row); and *The Programmable Pocket Calculator,* by H. Mullish (John Wiley & Sons).

THE JOSEPH A. BARANSKI LITERARY AGENCY, 427 Borden, West Seneca NY 14224. Contact: Dennis A. Baranski at the Midwest office, Box 4527, Topeka KS 66604. Estab: 1972. "Most new authors are obtained through recommendations and referrals. We do some advertising in quest of previously unpublished writers with potential." Will read unsolicited mss

subject to a reading fee of $15 for short stories and articles; $35 for full-length works. "This fee will be assessed to writers who have not met a $2000 sales requirement in the last 12 months." Will read unsolicited queries and outlines. SASE. Agent receives 10% commission on domestic sales; 20% on foreign sales.
Will Handle: Fiction and nonfiction books, stage and screen plays, magazine articles, short stories and some poetry. "Concentrate on submitting professionally prepared material. The basics of proper paper, clear type, and standard ms format are very important in this highly competitive field. Study your specific market with regard to the length of your ms. We deal on an international basis representing over 150 clients on three continents. We hope to expand our facilities to handle a maximum of 300 clients by 1979. We will begin an expanded search for new writing talent in the fall of 1978. We are especially interested in works dealing with provocative social and political issues as well as mystery fiction."

LOIS BERMAN, 145 E. 52nd St., New York NY 10022. Estab: 1971. Obtains new clients primarily by referral. Will not read unsolicited mss; will read unsolicited queries. SASE. Agent receives 10% commission.
Will Handle: Stage plays, screenplays and scripts for TV films. "The authors I represent are writers of dramatic material—freelance or on assignment."

BLOOM, BECKETT, LEVY & SHORR, 449 S. Beverly Dr., Beverly Hills CA 90212. (213)553-4850. Estab: 1977; "however, the forerunner of the firm has been in existence for fifteen years." Obtains new clients by recommendations of writers, directors, producers, and studio executives. Also by reading unsolicited motion picture screenplays. Will read unsolicited mss. SASE. Made approximately 200 sales in 1976, 250 in 1977; will do 250 in 1978. Agent receives 10% commission.
Will Handle: "We will read only completed motion picture screenplays. This may include screenplays for feature films as well as television. We will not read outlines, treatments, or scripts for eposodic or situation comedy television."
Recent Sales: *Citizen's Band*, by P. Brickman (Paramount Studios); *The Spell*, by B. Taggert (NBC); and *The Strongest Man in the World*, by D.D. Vowell (CBS).

GEORGES BORCHARDT, INC., 145 E. 52nd St., New York NY 10022. (212)753-5785. Estab: 1967. Obtains new clients "mainly through authors already represented by us who refer others." Potential clients "must be highly recommended by someone we know." Will not read unsolicited mss; will read unsolicited queries from established writers. Made approximately 180 U.S. book sales in 1976, 220 in 1977. Agent receives 10% commission.
Will Handle: Magazine articles and fiction, novels, and nonfiction books.
Recent Sales: *Dickens*, by E. Johnson (Viking); *How to Enjoy Ballet*, by D. McDonagh (Doubleday); and *The Public Burning*, by R. Coover (Viking).

AARON BOWMAN COMPANY (formerly Aaron Bowman Enterprises), 2813 Willow, Granite City IL 62040. (618)451-1620. Chief Agent: Aaron Bowman. Estab: 1972. Obtains new clients through *Writer's Market*. Will read unsolicited mss for a fee of $100. SASE. Made 17 sales in 1976. Agent receives 10% commission. "Reading and analysis fee is returned upon sale of ms."
Will Handle: Novels, textbooks, nonfiction books and poetry books.
Criticism Services: "We critique all material not submitted to publishers, a service included in the $100 reading/analysis fee required with all mss."

BRANDT & BRANDT, 101 Park Ave., New York NY 10017. (212)683-5890. Estab: 1914. Obtains new clients through recommendations of clients and editors. Will not read unsolicited mss; will read unsolicited queries and outlines. Agent receives 10% commission.
Will Handle: Magazine articles and fiction, novels, nonfiction books, motion pictures, and stage plays.

BROOME AGENCY, INC./BROOME LITERARY SERVICE, Box 3649, Sarasota FL 33578. President: Sherwood Broome. Estab: 1957. Obtains new clients "mainly by response to our ads in *Writer's Digest*, plus our listing in *Writer's Market*." Will read unsolicited mss. SASE. Agent receives 10% commission on domestic sales, 15% on Canadian, 20% on foreign.
Will Handle: Magazine articles and fiction, novels, and nonfiction books.
Criticism Services: Will critique short stories, articles, novels, and nonfiction books. Submissions must be in professional format. Charges $25 minimum for short stories and articles (to 5,000 words); $175 minimum for book length mss (to 37,500 words). Rates increase according to length and complexity.

JAMES BROWN ASSOCIATES, INC., 22 E. 60th St., New York NY 10022. (212)355-4182. Estab: 1949. Potential clients "must be professional, not necessarily published." Will read unsolicited queries. SASE. Agent receives 10% commission on domestic sales, 20% on British and translation countries.
Will Handle: "We handle writers concentrating on books." For writers represented will handle all rights, foreign, performance, etc., and magazine articles and fiction.

SHIRLEY BURKE AGENCY, 370 E. 76th St., New York NY 10021. (212)861-2309. Estab: 1948. Obtains new clients through recommendations. Potential clients must have published at least one book. Will not read unsolicited mss; will read unsolicited queries. SASE. Agent receives 10% commission.
Will Handle: Magazine fiction, novels, and nonfiction books.

CHARLES R. BYRNE LITERARY AGENCY, 1133 Avenue of the Americas, 28th Floor, New York NY 10036. (212)221-3145. President: Charles R. Byrne. Estab: 1974. Obtains new clients through recommendations from publishers/editors, other agents, and from present clients. Will read unsolicited mss for a fee "depending on length of mss." Will read unsolicited queries and outlines. SASE. Made 20 sales in 1976, 25-30 in 1977; will do 30 in 1978. Agent receives 10% commission on domestic sales; 20% on foreign.
Will Handle: Novels, textbooks (a limited number), nonfiction books, young adult novels and nonfiction books.
Recent Sale: *The Naming of America,* by A. Wolk (Thomas Nelson, Inc.).

RUTH CANTOR, LITERARY AGENT, 156 5th Ave., New York NY 10010. Estab: 1951. Obtains new clients through recommendations by writers, publishers, editors, and teachers. Potential clients "must be of proven competence as a writer. This means either some publishing record or a recommendation from someone likely to be a competent critic of his work—a teacher of writing, another writer, etc." Will not read unsolicited mss; will read unsolicited queries and outlines. SASE. "Send a letter giving publishing history and writing experience, plus concise outline of proposed project or of ms you want to send. Do not phone." Made 5 sales in 1976. Agent receives 10% commission on domestic sales; 20% on foreign.
Will Handle: Novels, nonfiction books and children's books.
Recent Sales: *Perky,* by G. Bond (Western); *This Savage Land,* by B. Womack (Fawcett); and *Abigail Scott Dunaway,* by D. Morrison (Atheneum).

HY COHEN LITERARY AGENCY, LTD., 111 W. 57th St., New York NY 10019. (212)757-5237. President: Hy Cohen. Estab: 1975. Obtains new clients through recommendations. Will read unsolicited mss, queries and outlines. SASE. Agent receives 10% commission.
Will Handle: Magazine articles and fiction, novels, and nonfiction books.
Recent Sales: *The Franklin Scare,* by J. Charyn (Arbor House); *Blood Money,* by R. Lund (William Morrow); and *The Great Waltz,* by A. Rothberg (Putnam).

COLLIER ASSOCIATES, 280 Madison Ave., New York NY 10016. (212)685-5516. Owner: Lisa Collier. Estab: 1976. Obtains new clients through recommendations of existing clients, editors, friends, and through various listings. Will read unsolicited queries and outlines. SASE. Made 28 sales in 1976, 50 in 1977; will make 75 in 1978. Agent receives 10% commission on domestic sales; 15% on British; and 20% on foreign.
Will Handle: Novels and nonfiction books. "Not interested in travel, astrology, occult or porno."
Recent Sales: *The Secret Life of Henry Ford,* by F.S. Leighton (Bobbs-Merrill); *The Southern Almanac,* by H. Rottenberg (Hammond); and *Unexpected Holiday,* by P. Schwartz (Dell).

BILL COOPER ASSOCIATES, INC., 16 E. 52nd St., New York NY 10022. (212)758-6491. Estab: 1963. Obtains new clients through recommendations and personal pursuit. Will read unsolicited mss. SASE. Marketing fee "subject to submitting source." Made 12 sales in 1976, 15-20 in 1977; will make 20-25 in 1978. Agent receives 10% commission.
Will Handle: Novels, nonfiction books, motion pictures, stage plays, and TV scripts (game shows, situation comedies; only original concepts for series, with fully developed presentation of theme, characters, and a pilot script).
Recent Sales: *Rocky Marciano,* by E. Skehan (Houghton Mifflin); and *Rebellion of the White Rose,* by R. Hanser (G.P. Putnam's Sons).

HAROLD CORNSWEET LITERARY AGENCY, Box 3093, Beverly Hills CA 90212. Estab: 1961. Obtains new clients through *Writer's Market,* writers' referrals and literary department

recommendations of studios. Will read unsolicited mss for a fee of $25-35, depending on length; will read unsolicited queries and outlines. SASE. Made six sales in 1976, 10 in 1977; will make 8-10 in 1978. Agent receives 10% commission.
Will Handle: Novels, nonfiction books, motion pictures, stage plays, and TV and radio scripts. "We specialize in motion picture and TV screenplays."

CREATIVE ENTERPRISES, Box 377, Centreville VA 22020. (703)830-3711. Director: Joyce Wright. Estab: 1975. Obtains new clients through recommendations of other writers, writer's organizations, and *Writer's Market.* Will read unsolicited mss for $100; will read unsolicited queries and outlines. SASE. "Prefer that new authors send a comprehensive chapter outline, background data on himself, and the first four chapters of his ms when querying." Agent receives 10% commission.
Will Handle: Novels and nonfiction books. Will also handle magazine articles and fiction, motion pictures, and TV scripts for established clients. Specializes in how-to, self-help, and career guidance.
Criticism Services: Will critique novels, self-help books, biographies of historical or literary figures, and career guidance books. Mss must be neatly typed, double-spaced, with 1" margins at top, bottom and sides, author's name in left-hand corner, number in right-hand corner. Prefers photocopies for editorial comments. Charges $100 flat fee.
Recent Sales: *A Matter of Revenge,* by C. Demaine (Playboy Press); *The Malthusian Knot,* by R. Bryce (Major Books); and *The Dancing Floor,* by M. McNamara (Crown Publishers).

CREATIVE WRITERS AGENCY, INC., Box 2280, Satellite Beach FL 32937. (305)773-3622. President: John C. Roach, Jr. Estab: 1971. Obtains new clients through *Writer's Market,* authors' recommendations, and advertisements. Will read unsolicited mss. SASE. Charges unpublished authors $300 marketing fee (returnable upon sale of material); no marketing fee for published authors. Made two sales in 1976, three in 1977; will make six or more in 1978. Agent receives 10% commission; 15% for movie rights.
Will Handle: Novels, textbooks, nonfiction books, motion pictures, stage plays and TV scripts. Specializes in material adaptable to motion pictures.
Criticism Services: Novels, textbooks, nonfiction books, motion pictures, stage plays and TV scripts. Charges $25 for mss under 25,000 words; $50 over 25,000 words; $100 over 75,000 words.
Recent Sales: *Starring John Wayne,* by G. Fernett (Neptune Books); *Dos Compadres,* by D. Bostick (Neptune Books); and *Ghost of the Java Cosat,* by W. Winslow (Coral Reef Publishing, Inc.).

RICHARD CURTIS LITERARY AGENCY, 156 E. 52nd St., New York NY 10022. (212)935-1606. Vice President: Martha Millard. Estab: 1969. Obtains new clients through word-of-mouth, referrals by editors, and advertising in *Writer's Digest.* Potential clients "must be selling regularly to major publishers in today's market." Will read unsolicited mss up to 7,500 words for $25; $50 if above 7,500 words. Will read unsolicited queries. SASE. Agent receives 10% commission on domestic sales; 20% on foreign.
Will Handle: Magazine articles and fiction, novels, textbooks, nonfiction books, motion pictures, stage plays, TV scripts and syndicated material.
Criticism Services: Will critique material as above. Charges $25 for mss to 7,500 words; $50 for mss over 7,500 words.
Recent Sales: *The Pack,* by D. Fisher (Warner Bros.); *Help Your Mate Lose Weight,* by Dr. M. Walker (Pyramid Books); and *Zandra,* by W. Rotsler (Doubleday & Co.).

ANITA DIAMANT: THE WRITERS WORKSHOP, INC., 51 E. 42nd St., New York NY 10017. (212)687-1122. President: Anita Diamant. Estab: 1917. Obtains new clients through recommendations by publishers or other clients. Potential clients must have made some professional sales. Will not read unsolicited mss; will read unsolicited queries. SASE. Made 115 sales in 1976. Agent receives 10% commission.
Will Handle: Magazine articles and fiction, novels, nonfiction books, motion pictures, and TV scripts.
Recent Sales: *Male Mid-life Crisis,* by H. Still; *Dr. Solomon's,* by Dr. Neil Solomon (Putnam's); and *Sword of the Golden Stud,* by L. Harner (Fawcett).

PATRICIA FALK FEELEY, INC., AUTHORS' REPRESENTATIVE, 52 Vanderbilt Ave., New York NY 10017. Estab: 1975. Obtains new clients through referrals by clients and editors and by inquiries. Will not read unsolicited mss; will read unsolicited queries and outlines.

SASE. Made approximately 30 sales in 1976. Agent receives 10% commission on domestic sales, 15% on British; 20% on foreign.
Will Handle: Novels and nonfiction books.
Recent Sales: *Marvin & Tige,* by F. Grass (St. Martin's Press); *Case Closed,* by J. Thomson (Doubleday); and *The Junk Food Junkie's Book of Haute Cuisine,* by Sullivan/Gibbs (Popular).

BARTHOLD FLES LITERARY AGENCY, 507 5th Ave., New York NY 10017. Contact: Barthold Fles or Vikki Power. Estab: 1933. Obtains new clients through recommendations of clients and editors, scouting tips, and writers' conferences. Will not read unsolicited mss. Agent receives 10% commission on domestic sales; 15% on British; and 20% on foreign.
Will Handle: Novels and nonfiction books. Specializes in intermediate and teenage juveniles; no picture books.

THE FOLEY AGENCY, 34 E. 38th St., New York NY 10016. (212)686-6930. Estab: 1956. Obtains new clients through recommendations. Will read unsolicited queries. SASE. Made approximately 50 sales in 1976. Agent receives 10% commission.
Will Handle: Novels and nonfiction books.

PEGGY LOIS FRENCH AGENCY, 26051 Birkdale Rd., Sun City CA 92381. (714)679-6325. Estab: 1952. Obtains new clients through word-of-mouth and solicitations. Will read unsolicited mss and queries. SASE. Charges $2.50/1,000 words, lesser fee ($1.95/1,000 words) for mss over 50,000 words. Teleplays and screenplays are priced according to length; plays by the number of acts; novels or short stories by the number of words. "We do not have a reading fee for the established professional who has credits with a major publisher or film producer." Agent receives 10% commission.
Will Handle: Magazine fiction, novels (juvenile and adult), nonfiction books, motion pictures, stage plays and TV scripts.

FULP LITERARY AGENCY, 62 Maple Rd., Amityville NY 11701. (516)842-0972. Agency Representative: M.L. Fulp. Estab: 1976. Obtains new clients through referrals. Will read unsolicited mss, queries or outlines. SASE. Charges $25 marketing fee for all material once client is accepted. Made 2 sales in 1977. Agent receives 10% commission.
Will Handle: Magazine articles and fiction, novels, and nonfiction books. "I like to receive mss from minority writers and females."
Recent Sale: "The Facts," *(Sexology).*

JAY GARON-BROOKE ASSOCIATES, INC., 415 Central Park W., New York NY 10025. President: Jay Garon. Estab: 1951. Obtains new clients through referrals only for new authors; correspondence from published authors. Will not read unsolicited mss; will read unsolicited descriptive letters. Made over $2 million worth of sales in 1976. Agent receives 15% commission.
Will Handle: Novels, nonfiction books, motion pictures, and juvenile material.
Recent Sales: *Gallow's Way,* by D. Winston (Simon & Schuster); *Fire-Dawn,* by V. Coffman (Arbor House); and *Forbidden City,* by A. Esler (William Morrow).

MAX GARTENBERG, LITERARY AGENT, 331 Madison Ave., New York NY 10017. (212)661-5270. Estab: 1954. Obtains new clients through referrals and solicitations. Will not read unsolicited mss; will read unsolicited queries. SASE. Agent receives 10% commission.
Will Handle: Novels and nonfiction books.
Recent Sales: *Miss Margaret Ridpath and the Dismantling of the Universe,* by D. Robertson (G.P. Putnam's Sons); *The War Against the Automobile,* by B. Bruce-Briggs (E.P. Dutton); and *The Complete Book of Home Decorating,* by A.M. Watkins (Charles Scribner's Sons).

LUCIANNE GOLDBERG LITERARY AGENT, 255 W. 84th St., New York NY 10024. Estab: 1974. Obtains new clients through referrals by clients and/or contacts in the publishing media. Will not read unsolicited mss; will read unsolicited queries and outlines. SASE. Charges marketing fee for phone, messenger, photocopies, typing (deducted from first sale). Made six sales in 1976, 15 in 1977; will make 20 in 1978. Agent receives 10% commission.
Will Handle: Novels, nonfiction books, and motion pictures.
Recent Sale: *It Didn't Start with Watergate,* by V. Lasky (Dial).

GRAHAM AGENCY, 317 W. 45th St., New York NY 10036. Owner: Earl Graham. Estab: 1971. Obtains new clients through queries and recommendations. "Will accept any playwright

whose work I feel is saleable, and occasionally will work with a writer whose initial effort may not be saleable, but whom I feel is talented, and whose work I feel merits encouraging." Will read unsolicited queries. Agent receives 10% commission.
Will Handle: Full-length stage plays (including musicals) only.

VANCE HALLOWAY AGENCY, Box 518, Pearblossom CA 93553. (714)249-3818 or 327-9653. Agent: Vance Halloway. Estab: 1954. Free reading of unsolicited mss to 60,000 words; will read unsolicited queries and outlines. SASE. Agent's commission "depends on transaction. All contracts are directed to agency and commissions are deducted from advances and royalty payment." Charges marketing fee "only if I cannot foresee an immediate sale."
Will Handle: Novels, nonfiction books, and stage plays. "Book properties that are geared for possible series like our Death Merchant, Kung Fu, and Murder Master series, contracted to this agency."
Criticism Services: Will criticize commercially slanted material. Submit precis and sample chapters. Fee depends on amount of labor required.
Recent Sales: *Last Stage to Benbow,* by Wagoner (Major Books); *Terror,* by Shiloh (Nu-Triumph) and *Hell in Hindu Land,* by Rosenberger (Pinnacle).

HEINLE AND HEINLE ENTERPRISES, 29 Lexington Rd., Concord MA 01742. (617)369-4858. Senior Member: Charles A.S. Heinle. Estab: 1973. Obtains new clients through word-of-mouth, *Writer's Market,* activities as resident agents at Cape Code Writer's Conference, and recommendations by clients. "We are less concerned that a writer is unpublished, as long as we believe in the writer and the future." Will not read unsolicited mss; will read unsolicited queries and outlines. SASE. Made two sales in 1976, 3-4 in 1977; will make 5-9 in 1978. Agent receives 10% commission.
Will Handle: Magazine fiction, novels, textbooks, and nonfiction books. "We are most interested in materials with a New England theme, past, present, and future, but of course, good writing is the main consideration. We handle some textbooks in the foreign language area, and some reference materials as bibliographies in selected fields."
Recent Sales: *Vida y Voces,* by Smith, et al (Rand McNally); *French Periodical Index,* by Jean-Pierre Ponchie (F.W. Faxon Co.); and *American English by the Audio-Visual Method,* by Girard & Quellet (Didier Canada).

HOME CRAFT UNLIMITED, 4276 Sandburg Way, Irvine CA 92715. Director: Molli Nickell. Estab: 1969. Obtains new clients through referrals from clients and *Writer's Market.* Will read unsolicited mss for approximately $50. "Usually advise authors on how to market their own work." Charges $25/hour for consultation.
Will Handle: Books, articles or syndicated material relating to creative fields: how-to's, interviews with creative people, new media, money makers in crafts, career opportunities in creative fields.
Criticism Services: Will critique material as above. Fee "depends on work—we request writers to query first with SASE—then we advise what to send, plus fee."

L.H. JOSEPH AND ASSOCIATES, 8344 Melrose Ave., Suite 23, Los Angeles CA 90069. (213)651-2322. Estab: 1954. Obtains new clients through inquiries. "We are licensed artist's managers and signatories to the Writer's Guild of America, West." Will read unsolicited mss, queries and outlines. "We prefer letters of inquiry outlining the proposed project, but will consider complete mss." SASE. Agent receives 10% commission.
Will Handle: Novels, textbooks, nonfiction books (in any field), motion pictures, stage plays and TV scripts.
Criticism Services: Will critique submissions only if so requested. Charges $75. Send check with ms.

JSL ASSOCIATES, Box 23040, San Jose CA 95153. (408)225-6902. Contact: Lynn Roberts. Estab: 1975. Obtains new clients through *Writer's Market,* referral by other clients, teachers, writer's groups or Writers Guild of America listings. "We have great success with previously unpublished/unproduced authors. We ask that the work be professional quality, that the desire to work is there, and the willingness to learn." Will read unsolicited mss, queries, or outlines. SASE. Agent receives 10% commission on domestic sales; 15% on foreign.
Will Handle: Magazine articles and fiction, novels, textbooks, nonfiction books, motion pictures, stage plays, TV and radio scripts, syndicated material, juvenile material, and artwork. "We are willing to consider and evaluate any material, except porno."
Criticism Services: "We are going to be working with a former editor/teacher in setting up a small criticism service for those who want it made available. Fees will be made available upon

request. Mss must be typed double-spaced, and must specify that it is being submitted for criticism rather than general reviewing."
Recent Sales: *Killed in the Ratings,* by B. DeAndrea (Harcourt Brace Jovanovich).

VIRGINIA KIDD WITH JAMES ALLEN LITERARY AGENTS, Box 278, Milford PA 18337. (717)296-6205. Estab: 1965. Potential client "must be a published writer; should have earned at least $1,000 (from writing) during the previous year." Will not read unsolicited mss. "I cannot take on *anyone* with no track record. If someone has a special reason for wanting me to handle them, write me a letter explaining why and enclose SASE. I'm not actively looking for new authors—my lists are full." Agent receives 10% commission on domestic sales, 15% on dramatic sales, 20% on overseas sales.
Will Handle: Magazine articles and fiction, novels, textbooks, nonfiction books, motion pictures, TV and radio scripts and science fiction.

DANIEL P. KING, LITERARY AGENT, 5125 N. Cumberland Blvd., Whitefish Bay WI 53217. (414)964-2903. Estab: 1974. Obtains new clients through listings in *Writer's Market,* and referrals from clients. Will not read unsolicited mss; will read unsolicited queries. Made 54 sales in 1976, 50-100 in 1977. Agent receives 10% commission.
Will Handle: Magazine articles and fiction, novels, nonfiction books, and syndicated material. "While I handle general material, I specialize in crime literature (fact or fiction)."

BERTHA KLAUSNER INTERNATIONAL LITERARY AGENCY, INC., 71 Park Ave., New York NY 10016. (212)685-2642. President: Bertha Klausner. Estab: 1938. Obtains new clients through recommendation. Will read unsolicited mss; charges reading fees. Will read unsolicited queries and outlines. SASE. Agent receives 10% commission on domestic sales.
Will Handle: Novels, textbooks, nonfiction books, stage plays, and TV and motion picture scripts. "We represent world rights for all subsidiaries and are represented by our own agents throughout the world."
Criticism Services: Will critique novels and plays. Request rate card.
Recent Sales: *Memoirs of the Nijinsky Family,* by I. Nijinsky (Holt, Rinehart & Winston); and *Shakespeare,* by R. Payne (Harper & Row).

LUCY KROLL AGENCY, 390 West End Ave., New York NY 10024. (212)877-0627. Estab: 1954. Obtains new clients through recommendations. Will not read unsolicited mss; will read unsolicited queries and outlines. SASE. Agent receives 10% commission.
Will Handle: Novels, nonfiction books, motion pictures, and stage plays.

MICHAEL LARSEN/ELIZABETH POMADA LITERARY AGENTS, 1029 Jones St., San Francisco CA 94109. (415)673-0939. Estab: 1972. Obtains new clients through personal recommendations, *Literary Market Place, Writer's Market,* and advertising. Will read unsolicited mss for $25 (refundable immediately upon acceptance); no reading charge for published writers. Will read unsolicited queries and outlines. SASE. Agent receives 10% commission on domestic sales; 20% on foreign.
Will Handle: Novels, nonfiction books, motion pictures, stage plays, and TV scripts. "We request the original copy of the ms, typed double-spaced with pica type on 8½x11 paper; unbound, preferably boxed, with writer's name, address and phone number on the title page."
Recent Sales: *Fairytales,* b C. Freeman (Arbor House and Bantam); *The Voices of Guns,* by P. Avery/V. McLellan (Lorimer Productions); and *The Anti,* by R. McCammon (Avon).

DONALD MacCAMPBELL, INC., 12 E. 41st St., New York NY 10017. (212)683-5580. Estab: 1938. Obtains new clients through letter or phone inquiries or recommendations from clients. Submit descriptive inquiry with SASE. Agent receives 10% commission.
Will Handle: Novels and nonfiction books.

BETTY MARKS, 51 E. 42nd St., New York NY 10017. (212)687-1122. Estab: 1970. Obtains new clients through word-of-mouth recommendations of authors, other agents, editors, and friends. Will read unsolicited mss for $100 up to 100,000 words, if author is previously unpublished. Will read unsolicited queries and outlines. SASE. Made 55 sales in 1976; 75 in 1977. Agent receives 10% commission.
Will Handle: Magazine articles and fiction, novels, nonfiction books, poetry, stage plays, TV scripts, juvenile fiction and nonfiction.
Criticism Services: Will critique material as above. Mss must be typed double-spaced, pages unbound, standard professional format. Charges $100 for mss to 100,000 words; $150 for two mss; $200 for three mss; 50¢/page for shorter material ($25 minimum).

Recent Sales: *Watch It, Dr. Adrian,* by B. Litzinger (Putnam's); *Pending Investigation,* by R. McLaughlin (Berkley); and *A Goldmine of Money Making Ideas,* by M. Brunner (Lorenz Press).

SCOTT MEREDITH LITERARY AGENCY, INC., 845 3rd Ave., New York NY 10022. (212)245-5500. President: Scott Meredith. Estab: 1941. Obtains new clients "through listings such as *Writer's Market;* recommendations by clients; and direct mail advertising. Also, many promising authors are recommended to us by editors, publishers and producers." Will read unsolicited mss, queries, and outlines. "We charge a single fee for all services, including readings, criticism, assistance in revision if required, and marketing. The fee is $50 for fiction or articles to 10,000 words ($1/1,000 words thereafter); $75 for book mss below 10,000 words ($1/thousand words thereafter); $100 for book mss from 10,000-150,000 words; $150 for book mss 150,000-250,000 words; $250 for mss above 250,000 words; $100 for plays or screenplays; $75 for syndicate packages of 3-6 sample columns. SASE. Made 7,200 sales in 1976. Agent receives 10% on domestic sales; 20% on foreign. "If a writer has sold to a major book publisher in the past year or has begun to make major national magazine or television sales with some regularity, we drop fees and proceed on a straight commission basis."
Will Handle: "We handle material in all fields except single poems and single cartoons, though we do handle book-collections of poetry and cartoons."
Recent Sales: *The Saint and the Psychopath,* by Norman Mailer (Little, Brown); *In The Blood,* by Gerald Green (Putnam); *Inventing America,* by Garry Wills (Doubleday); and *The Masters Way to Beauty,* by George Masters and Norma Lee Browning (Dutton).

ROBERT P. MILLS, LTD., 156 E. 52 St., New York NY 10022. President: Robert P. Mills. Estab: 1960. Obtains new clients through recommendations "of someone I know, or if the writer has a respectable publishing history." Will not read unsolicited mss; will read unsolicited queries. SASE. Agent receives 10% commission.
Will Handle: Magazine articles and fiction, novels, nonfiction books, motion pictures, and syndicated material.
Recent Sales: *The Body Language of Sex Power and Aggression,* by J. Fast (M. Evans & Co.); *Twister,* by J. Bickham (Doubleday & Co.); and *Pele's Autobiography,* by Pele, with R.L. Fish (Doubleday & Co.).

HOWARD MOOREPARK, 444 E. 82nd St., New York NY 10028. (212)737-3961. Estab: 1946. Obtains new clients through recommendations. Will read unsolicited mss. SASE. Agent receives 10% commission.
Will Handle: Magazine articles, novels, and nonfiction books.
Recent Sales: *Love's Triumphant Heart,* by V. Ashton (Fawcett); *The Gladiators,* by A. Quiller (Pinnacle) and *Way of the Mystics,* by M. Smith (Oxford UP).

MULTIMEDIA PRODUCT DEVELOPMENT, INC., 170 S. Beverly Dr., Beverly Hills CA 90212. (213)276-6246. President: Jane Jordan Browne. Estab: 1971. Obtains new clients through recommendations and word-of-mouth. "Multimedia handles only works of professional writers who make their living as authors. The rare exceptions are celebrity autobiographies and the 'new idea' nonfiction book." Will read unsolicited mss for $150; will read unsolicited queries and outlines. SASE. Made 77 sales in 1976, 105 in 1977; will make 150 in 1978. Agent receives 10% commission on domestic sales; 20% on foreign.
Will Handle: Novels, textbooks, nonfiction books, motion pictures, and TV scripts.
Criticism Services: "Will critique all material. Submissions for criticism must be submitted with the fee and SASE. All material must be typed double-spaced." Charges $150 for standard-length novels or nonfiction books; $50 for jevenile books of 50 pages or less; $75 for screenplays; and $50 for teleplays of ½-1 hour. "Although Multimedia provides criticism services, the fees are meant to discourage any non-professionals from approaching the agency."
Recent Sales: *Hearts and Minds: the Common Journey of Simone de Beauvoir and Jean-Paul Satre,* by A. Madsen (William Morrow); *Evel on Tour,* by S. Saltman and M. Green (Dell); and *Sawed-off Justice,* by L. Franklin and M. Green (Permut Presentations).

N.C.T., Box 11623, Chicago IL 60611. Contact: Ronald Nielsen. Estab: 1970. Will read unsolicited mss, queries or outlines. "We do not charge a reading fee. For new writers we charge a criticism fee; no fee for established writers. A writer should have been nationally published, and published at the rate of 6 magazine articles per year, or should have published at least one book." SASE. Agent receives 10-30% commission "depending on the item and market, by negotiation."
Will Handle: Magazine articles and fiction, juvenile articles and fiction, novels, nonfiction

books, textbooks, poetry, syndicated material, photo essay material and photo books. "We handle everything if the material is quality. If a writer has not had a book published, but has a good record in the magazine area, we will consider such a writer. Query first on material. Tell use something of your background and interests, as reflected in one or two projects."

CHARLES NEIGHBORS, INC., 240 Waverly Pl., New York NY 10014. (212)924-8296. Estab: 1966. Obtains new clients "mostly through recommendations of existing clients, but also from editors, other agents, and occasionally from *Writer's Market.*" Will not read unsolicited mss; will read unsolicited queries and outlines. SASE. Made 25 sales in 1976, 35 in 1977; will make 50 in 1978. Agent receives 10% commission.
Will Handle: Magazine articles and fiction, novels, nonfiction books, motion pictures, and juvenile material.
Recent Sales: *The Grab,* by M. Katzenbach (William Morrow); *The Girl with the Jade Green Eyes,* by John Boyd (Viking); and *The Commuter Lines,* by S. Fischer (Hawthorn).

B.K. NELSON LITERARY AGENCY, 210 E. 47th St., New York NY 10017. (212)755-9111. Estab: 1969. Obtains new clients "by word of mouth. Often a publisher will call and ask if I have an author for a special project, and I go out and get one. I am also listed in trade books such as *Writer's Market* and get many inquiries as a result." Will read unsolicited mss for $45/60,000 words. Will read unsolicited queries and outlines. Made 25 sales in 1976, 40 in 1977. Agent receives 10% commission on domestic sales; 20% on foreign.
Will Handle: Novels, nonfiction books, motion pictures and biographies.
Criticism Services: Will critique "that which I think has potential (which I can determine from a query and description)." Submissions must be on 8½x11 white paper, double-spaced, about 250 words/page, numbered. Charges $45/60,000 words; $25 if there is a re-read of the re-write.
Recent Sales: *Instant Genius,* by W.W. Lynch (Drake); *Family Guide to Haircutting,* by S. Fodera (Drake); and *Whales,* by B. McNally (Albert Lewis Publisher, Inc.).

NICHOLAS LITERARY AGENCY, 161 Madison Ave., New York NY 10016. Owner: Georgia Nicholas. Estab: 1934. Obtains new clients through The Writers Guild, *LMP,* and recommendations. Will not read unsolicited mss; will read unsolicited queries and outlines and published books for reprint. SASE. Charges a one-time marketing fee of $100. Agent receives 10% commission.
Will Handle: Novels, nonfiction books, motion pictures, stage plays, TV and radio scripts.
Recent Sale: *Winning with Biorhythm,* by C.M. Wolfe (Ace Books).

NORTHEAST LITERARY AGENCY, 69 Broadway, Concord NH 03301. (603)225-9162. Editor: Victor Levine. Estab: 1973. Obtains new clients through listings *(Literary Market Place, Writer's Market);* recommendations from editors, clients; and display advertising. Will read unsolicited mss. SASE. "There is a one-time agency charge of $35, refundable from earned commissions. Depends on writer's credits; if extensive and/or national in scope, there is no agency charge. The charge, payable with first submission, covers our reading of *all* future mss. Time-frame is deliberately open-ended. We're hopeful it will help writers develop into valued clients....good for us as well as them. We promise a sympathetic reading and fast response. In return, we ask that writers don't dump on us soiled and otherwise unmarketworthy mss." Made 45 sales in 1976, 75 in 1977; will make 125 in 1978. Agent receives 10% commission on domestic sales; 20% on foreign.
Will Handle: Magazine articles and fiction, novels, textbooks, nonfiction books, poetry, motion pictures, stage plays, TV and radio scripts, and juvenile fiction/nonfiction (including picture book mss). "Particularly interested in juveniles (all kinds) and all genres in popular fiction (Gothics, romances, science fiction, etc.). Be up-front with us. Tell us where you're at in terms of your writing career: what you've done in the past, what you're presently working on; the direction you wish to go. Please be specific. We prefer to see complete mss, but will read partials by arrangement."
Recent Sales: "Shooting Stars," by J. Waugh (*Cricket* magazine); "Retiring in Mexico," by J. Budd *(Retirement Living);* and *A Spirit of Giving,* by D. Collins (Broadman).

O'NEILL & KRALIK LITERARY CONSULTANTS, Box 461, Birmingham MI 48012. Manager: Michael O'Neill. Obtains new clients through *Writer's Market,* referrals, etc. Will read unsolicited mss for $15; will read unsolicited queries and outlines. SASE. Charges "minimal marketing fee under certain conditions." Agent receives 10% commission.
Will Handle: Magazine articles and fiction, novels, nonfiction books, poetry, and all secondary markets connected with novels. "Our specialty is the young and coming writer. After several years of this, the big houses are beginning to look to us for new writers of significant stature.

We expect this trend to continue and increase. We are most receptive to new writers and suggest that they query us."
Criticism Services: Novels and stories. Charges $150 for novels (to 150,000 words, thereafter $1/1,000 words); $35 for stories. Special arrangements are available.

RAY PEEKNER LITERARY AGENCY, 2625 N. 36th St., Milwaukee WI 53210. Contact: Ray Puechner. Estab: 1973. Obtains new clients through referrals from clients and editors, some from queries. Will not read unsolicited mss; will read unsolicited queries. SASE. Made 40-50 book sales in 1976. Agent receives 10% commission.
Will Handle: Novels, nonfiction books, and young adult material.
Recent Sales: *The American Farm,* by G. Paulsen (Prentice Hall); *Gateway to Limbo,* by C. Lampton (Doubleday); and *The Crescent and the Cross,* by D. Theis (Thomas Nelson).

MARJORIE PETERS & PIERRE LONG LITERARY AGENTS, 5744 S. Harper, Chicago IL 60637. (312)752-8377. Estab: 1955. Obtains new clients through recommendations. Will not read unsolicited mss. SASE. Agent receives 10% commission on domestic sales; 20% on foreign.
Will Handle: Magazine articles and fiction, novels, textbooks, nonfiction books, poetry, and stage plays. "Our agency specializes in fiction and serious poetry. We do not handle serious (non-humorous) sociological/political exposition."
Criticism Services: Will critique novels, short stories, poetry, articles, essays, expository books, stage plays. Submissions must be typed double-spaced, with a 1-inch margin all around. Charges $100 for novels of 200 pages or less, $50 for short stories, articles or essays of 15 pages or less, $5 per page of poetry, and $35 an act for stage plays.
Recent Sales: *Good Girls Don't Get Murdered,* by P. Parker (Scribner's); "Translations of Freud," by F. Brull (*Psychotherapy Journal*); and "La Paloma," by J.W. Dickson (*Silver Foxes*).

THE WALTER PITKIN AGENCY, 11 Oakwood Dr., Weston CT 06883. President: Walter Pitkin. Estab: 1973. Obtains new clients by referral or direct application. Will read unsolicited queries and outlines. "Writers must write an intelligent letter of inquiry and convince us of ability to write marketable material. Inquiry should include some personal background, plus a statement of what it is that the agency would be trying to place. We will solicit the ms if we like the inquiry." SASE. Agent receives 10% commission.
Will Handle: Novels and nonfiction books. Also "almost any other material for clients who write books."

SIDNEY E. PORCELAIN AGENCY, Box J, Rocky Hill NJ 08553. (609)924-4080. Authors' Representative: Sidney Porcelain. Estab: 1951. Obtains new clients through word-of-mouth and referrals. Will read unsolicited mss, queries and outlines. SASE. Made 30 sales in 1976. Agent receives 10% commission.
Will Handle: Magazine articles and fiction, novels, nonfiction books, and TV scripts.
Recent Sales: *Captive Passions,* by F. Michaels (Ballantine); *Walks Far Women,* by C. Stuart (Dial); and *Bride of Belvale,* by H. Rich (Dell).

PORTER, GOULD & DIERKS, 215 W. Ohio St., Chicago IL 60610. (312)644-5457. Estab: 1958. Obtains new clients "usually by internally generated book ideas that we go out and find the authorship to work on them. We also rely on screening publications to watch for promising writing talent. And, we get many referrals from long-term contacts with critics and magazine/ newspaper people who recommend us." Will read unsolicited mss for $50; will read unsolicited queries and outlines. SASE. Agent receives 10% commission.
Will Handle: Magazine articles and fiction, novels, textbooks (selectively), nonfiction books, poetry (highly selective), motion pictures, TV scripts (if the writer has credits), and syndicated material. "We are interested in any marketable writing, but do not encourage cookbooks or travel books unless the writer has a national reputation."
Recent Sales: *Small World, Long Gone,* by Carlson (Chicago Review Press); *Daggers for the Dancing,* by Dierks (Chicago Review Press); and *Professional and the Depression,* by Graubert (Regnery).

QED LITERARY AGENCY, 7032 Willis Ave., Van Nuys CA 91405. President: Vincent J. Ryan. Estab: 1966. Obtains new clients "on the recommendation of established authors, but also through *Writer's Market.*" Will read unsolicited mss for $35; will read unsolicited queries, outlines, and sample chapters free of charge. SASE. Agent receives 15% initial commission, descending with increasing sales volume.

Will Handle: Scholarly nonfiction only. "Mss must be book-length. Subject areas include philosophy, anthropology, theology, sociology, psychology, phenomenology, linguistics, ethnology, archaeology, natural history, ecology, history, and historical fiction. Authors should submit abstract or outline, table of contents, and possibly 1-2 chapters of ms. Do not send complete ms initially. Include information about the number of pages and tables and illustrations. Make submissions on exclusive basis. If in process of writing, may submit ms piecemeal."

RELIGIOUS WRITERS' AGENCY, 908 N. Nottawa St., Sturgis MI 49091. (616)651-6423. Director: Pastor Gregory L. Jackson. Estab: 1976. Obtains new clients through queries. "I deal with religious writing only. Previous publication and formal training in religious studies (divinity degree, etc.) help, but are not absolutely necessary." Will read unsolicited mss, queries and outlines. SASE. Charges $20 marketing fee. "My costs are charged whether the article is accepted or not." Made two sales in 1976, 5-10 in 1977; will make 10 in 1978. Agent receives 10% commission on book sales.
Will Handle: Magazine articles and fiction, textbooks, nonfiction books, and scholarly journal articles.
Criticism Services: Religious articles and books, popular and scholarly. Charge $2/page.
Recent Sales: "Community of Believers," by Dr. T. Hommes (*Emmanuel*); "Refractions," by Dr. T. Hommes (*Emmanuel*); and *"Luther Was a Family Man,"* by Gregory Jackson (*The Lutheran*).

BARBARA RHODES LITERARY AGENCY, 60 Sutton Place S., New York NY 10022. (212)486-0077. Owner: Barbara Rhodes. Estab: 1968. Obtains new clients through recommendation or inquiry letters. Will not read unsolicited mss; will read unsolicited queries. SASE. Made 15 sales in 1976, 20 in 1977. Agent receives 10% commission.
Will Handle: Novels, nonfiction books, and stage plays.
Recent Titles: *A Collapsible Man,* by L.J. Clancy (St. Martin's Press); *TV Test Patterns,* by J. Walders (Doubleday & Co.); and *Nobody Home,* by J.L. Paul (W. Norton).

RHODES LITERARY AGENCY, 436 Pau St., Suite 6, Honolulu HI 96815. (808)946-9891. Director: Fred C. Pugarelli. Estab: 1971. Obtains new clients through advertising in *Writer's Digest,* referrals, and recommendations. Will read unsolicited mss for $10 (300-1,500 words); $25 (over 1,500 words); fee for material over 5,000 words is by arrangement. Will read unsolicited queries and outlines for $5. SASE. Made seven sales in 1976, 10-20 in 1977; will make 20-40 in 1978. Agent receives 10% commission on domestic sales; 15% on Canadian; 20% on foreign.
Will Handle: Magazine articles and fiction, novels, textbooks, nonfiction books, poetry, motion pictures, stage plays, TV and radio scripts, photos, religious, and juvenile material; photos.
Criticism Services: Will critique any material. Charges $10 for up to 1,500 words; $25 for 1,500-5,000 words; $50 over 5,000 words.
Recent Sales: "Corruption in Grandpa's Beer Hall," by Robert Andrea (*Aim* magazine); "The Power of Negative Thinking," by P.W. Lovinger (*Aim* magazine); and "Where to Dine in Hawaii," by M. Lambert *(The Waikiki News).*

JAMES SELIGMANN AGENCY, 280 Madison Ave., New York NY 10016. (212)679-3383. Contact: James F. Seligmann or Nina Seidenfeld. Obtains new clients through recommendation, personal contact, or solicitation. Will not read unsolicited mss; will read unsolicited queries and outlines. SASE. Agent receives 10% commission.
Will Handle: Novels and nonfiction books.
Recent Sales: *Onassis: An Extravagant Life,* by F. Brady (Prentice-Hall); *The Jennifer Project,* by C.W. Burleson (Prentice-Hall); and *The Sexual Abuse of Children,* by F. Rush (Scribner's).

EVELYN SINGER LITERARY AGENCY, Box 163, Briarcliff Manor NY 10510. Agent: Evelyn Singer. Estab: 1951. Obtains new clients through recommendations or if writer has earned $10,000 from freelance writing. Will not read unsolicited mss. SASE. Agent receives 10% commission.
Will Handle: Novels, nonfiction books and children's books (no picture books). "I handle all trade book materal. Please type (double-spaced) neatly—do not send hand-written queries. Give any literary background pertinent to your material."

ELYSE SOMMER INC., Box E, 962 Allen Ln., Woodmere NY 11598. (516)295-0046. President: Elyse Sommer. Estab: 1952. Obtains new clients through recommendations of authors, editors, and through executives and administrators of various organizations. Will read unsolicited queries and outlines. SASE. Agent receives 10% commission.

Will Handle: Nonfiction books. "My specialty at the moment is the nonfiction book, particularly in the hobby area; also health and fitness and general lifestyle improvement. This specialty derives from my own involvement as a writer of how-to books, which has caused me to limit activities to specialty areas."

Recent Sales: *Pillows as Art & Craft*, by R. Adams (Crown); *Miniature Room Book (#2)*, by H. Ruthberg (Chilton Books); and *Running*, by Fanning (Simon and Schuster).

PHILIP G. SPITZER LITERARY AGENCY, 111-25 76th Ave., Forest Hills NY 11375. (212)263-7592. Estab: 1969. Obtains new clients through recommendations of editors and clients. "No previous publication necessary, but potential clients must be working on a book." Will read unsolicited queries and outlines. SASE. Made 30-35 sales in 1976. Agent receives 10% commission on domestic sales; 15% on British; 20% for foreign language sales.

Will Handle: Novels, nonfiction books, motion pictures. For clients also writing books, will handle magazine articles and fiction. Specializes in general nonfiction; particular interest in sports and politics. "Because I am a one-man office I can take on few new clients. I will often decline projects I think might be salable, and this should not be taken as a reflection on the author or his presentation."

Recent Sales: *The Menace of Atomic Energy*, by Ralph Nader and John Abbotts (W.W. Norton); *Superfolks*, by R. Mayer (Dial Press); and *Promises to Keep: Carter's First 100 Days*, by R. Shogan (Crowell).

C.M. STEPHAN, JR., 918 State St., Lancaster PA 17603. Estab: 1971. Obtains new clients through advertising and referral. "Writing must display potential or be competitive. We prefer to work with talented newcomers." Will read unsolicited mss for fee of $10 ($1/1000 words for book length); will read unsolicited queries. SASE. Made two sales in 1976, five in 1977. Agent receives 10% commission.

Will Handle: Magazine articles (personality interviews only), magazine fiction, and novels. "Quality writing, self-discipline and the ability to compromise are desirable assets."

Criticism Services: "Agency charges one fee to read/evaluate; no other charges are involved."

LARRY STERNIG LITERARY AGENCY, 742 Robertson St., Milwaukee WI 53213. (414)771-7677. Estab: 1953. "I am rarely able to take on new clients; too busy with the pros I now represent." Will not read unsolicited mss. Made several hundred sales in 1976. Agent receives 10% commission.

Will Handle: Magazine articles and fiction, novels and nonfiction books.

Recent Sales: *Velvet Shadows*, by A. Norton (Fawcett); *Echoes of Evil*, by I. Comfort (Doubleday); and *The Doll with Opal Eyes*, by J. DeWeese (Doubleday).

ELLEN STEVENSON & ASSOCIATES, Box 96, Port Credit, Mississauga, Ont., Canada L5G 4L5. President: Ellen Kelly. Estab: 1973. Obtains new clients through recommendations, clientele references, and *Writer's Market*. Will not read unsolicited mss; will read unsolicited queries. Charges reading and evaluating fees for beginners. SASE. Made 190 sales in 1976, 25 in 1977; will do 100 in 1978. Agent receives 10% commission.

Will Handle: Novels and nonfiction books. "We specialize in how-to and self-help books, 35,000 words and up."

Criticism Services: Book-length novels, and nonfiction (how-to and self-help). Charges $30 for mss under 25,000 words; $40 for mss of 25,000-60,000 words; $50 for mss of 60,000-75,000 words; and $75 for mss of 75,000 words and up.

Recent Sales: *How to Make Soft Animal Toys*, by C. Dorion (Seagull Books); *The Booze Game*, by Robert Skimin (Seagull Books); and *Murder for Fun*, by E. Kelly (Highway Press).

TWIN PINES LITERARY AGENCY, 123-6 S. HIghland Ave., Apt. 4, Ossining NY 10562. (914)941-1431. Executive Director: Martin Lewis. Estab: 1970. Obtains new clients through word-of-mouth. Will read unsolicited mss for $25. Will read unsolicited queries and outlines. SASE. Charges $100 marketing fee; $75 refundable if ms is not accepted. Agent receives 10% commission.

Will Handle: Magazine articles and fiction, novels, textbooks, nonfiction books, motion pictures, stage plays, and TV scripts. "Interested only in commercially oriented material."

Criticism Services: Will critique any material. Charges $50.

AUSTIN WAHL AGENCY, LTD., 332 S. Michigan Ave., Suite 1440, Chicago IL 60604. (312)922-3329. Contact: Thomas Wahl or George Elias. Estab: 1935. Obtains new clients through recommendation, referrals and solicitation. Will not read unsolicited mss; will read unsolicited queries and outlines. Agent receives 10% on domestic sales; 20% on foreign. "We sometimes make special deals to attract *name* literary figures."

Will Handle: "We do not limit ourselves into categories. We manage the careers of our clients in all areas of their artistry." Magazine articles and fiction, novels (especially those with motion picture potential), textbooks, nonfiction books, technical and reference works, motion pictures ("one of our specialties"), stage plays, TV scripts and syndicated material.

WIESER & WIEJER, INC., 52 Vanderbilt Ave., New York NY 10017. (212)867-5454. Principals: George or Olga Wieser. Estab: 1975. Obtains new clients through referrals from publishers and clients. Writers must be published, and must be working authors. Will read unsolicited mss for a fee of $100; will read unsolicited outlines. SASE. Made $50,000 worth of sales in 1976. $150,000 in 1977. Agent receives 20% commission.

Will Handle: Novels, nonfiction books, motion pictures, and TV scripts.

Criticism Services: General fiction and nonfiction. Mss must be typed double-spaced, and securely bound. "We will evaluate and criticize a complete ms for $100, which will be deducted from our commission if we place the work."

Recent Sales: *The Vintners*, by V. Banis (St. Martins's Press); *Arrest Sitting Bull*, by D.C. Jones (Scribner's); and *The Thrill of Victory*, by B. Sugar (Hawthorn Books).

WRITERS HOUSE, INC., 132 W. 31st St., New York NY 10001. Literary Agents: Judith Ehrlich, Albert Zuckerman and Felicia Eth. Estab: 1973. Obtains new clients through referrals by publishers or other clients. Will not read unsolicited mss; will read unsolicited queries and outlines. SASE. Made 95 sales in 1976, 120 in 1977; will make 140 in 1978. Agent receives 10% commission.

Will Handle: Novels, textbooks, nonfiction books, cartoon and art books, and juvenile fiction and nonfiction.

Recent Sales: *Sky High*, by T. Murphy (Putnam's); *Delta Blood II*, by B. Johnson (Avon); and *The Eye Book*, by Dr. John Eden (Viking).

THE ZALONKA AGENCY, 28 Stanton Rd., Suite 6, Brookline MA 02146. (617)566-6815. Director: J.N. Porter. Estab: 1975. Obtains new clients through word-of-mouth, small ads, and suggestions from authors and editors. Writer must be previously published. Will read unsolicited mss for a fee of $25-200, depending on length. Will read unsolicited queries and outlines. SASE. Made 2-3 sales in 1976; 5-6 in 1977. Agent receives 10% commission on books, 15% on articles, and 20% on foreign sales.

Will Handle: Magazine articles, novels, textbooks, nonfiction books, scholarly works and almanacs. "I especially cater to books dealing with sociology, psychology, and contemporary social problems as well as books dealing with Judaica, Hebraica, and the Middle East. I'm looking for well-written books dealing with contemporary social issues. Never send entire ms. Always send query letter with outline and sample of five pages, along with a short biography and history of ms. I welcome new authors, especially in the nonfiction, contemporary issues genre."

Criticism Services: Nonfiction only, especially social sciences, social problems, Jewish history, the middle East, anything dealing with World War II, religion, politics, and current events. Mss must be typed, double-spaced, one-side only, and numbered. "I will not only criticize the ms, but will also do partial editing, i.e., spelling, grammar, syntext, etc." Charges $2/page.

Recent Sales: *Fourteen Israeli Poets*, (Schocken Books); and *The Nazis Of America (Present Tense* magazine).

Contests and Awards

Unless otherwise noted, the following contests and awards are conducted annually. For information on irregular and "one shot" competitions, see The Markets column in *Writer's Digest* magazine.

Some of the listed contests and awards do not accept entries or nominations direct from writers. They are included because of their national or literary importance. When a competition accepts entries from publishers only, and the writer feels his work meets its requirements, he may wish to remind his publisher to enter his work.

To obtain specific deadline information, required entry blank, or further information, write directly to the address in the individual listing. Enclose SASE.

A.I.P.-U.S. STEEL FOUNDATION SCIENCE WRITING AWARD, Press Relations Division, American Institute of Physics, 335 E. 45 St., New York NY 10017. Awards $1,500, a certificate, and a symbolic device to stimulate and recognize distinguished writing that improves public understanding of physics and astronomy. Journalists must be professional writers whose work is aimed at the general public. Write for details and official entry form.

AAAS-WESTINGHOUSE SCIENCE WRITING AWARDS, Grayce A. Finger, 1515 Massachusetts Ave., N.W., Washington DC 20005. (202)467-4483. Awards three $1,000 prizes to recognize outstanding writing on the natural sciences, and their engineering and technological applications (excluding medicine), in newspapers and general circulation magazines.

AAFP JOURNALISM AWARDS, American Academy of Family Physicians, 1740 W. 92nd St., Kansas City MO 64114. (816)333-9700. Contact: Charlotte Krebs. Annual. Estab: 1969. Purpose: To recognize the most significant and informative reporting and writing on family practice and health care. Only unpublished submissions are eligible. Award: First prize, $1,000 cash and certificate; second, $750 cash and certificate; third, $250 cash and certificate. Deadline: Mid-November. Contest rules and entry form for SASE.

ACTF STUDENT PLAYWRITING AWARDS, American College Theatre Festival, John F. Kennedy Center for the Performing Arts, Washington DC 20566. (202)254-3437. The William Morris Agency awards a cash prize of $2,500 and an agency contract to the author of the best student written play produced as part of the annual American College Theatre Festival.

HERBERT BAXTER ADAMS PRIZE, Committee Chairman, American Historical Association, 400 A St. S.E., Washington DC 20003. Awards $300 annually for an author's first book in the field of European history.

ADIRONDACK-SPA—HARIAN FICTION AWARD, Box 189, Clifton Park NY 12065. Publisher: Harry Barba. Sponsor: Adirondack-Spa Writers & Educators Conference and The Harian Press. Annual. Estab: 1976. Purpose: to encourage the writing and publishing of fiction strong in characterization and plot and written in a functionally suitable style; to encourage writing with a social context (without being "preachy"), quality stories that communicate a moral texture. Writing of resolution is preferred. Unpublished submissions only. Award: first prize, $300; each of two runners-up, $100. "If no manuscript is of sufficient merit, we reserve the right to defer awards. All submitted mss will be considered for publication." Deadline: September 1. Contest rules and entry forms for SASE.

AMATEUR POETRY CONTEST, Poetry Press, Editor, Don Peek, Box 736, Pittsburg TX 75686. Prizes of $50, $25, and $10 will go to top 3 poems. Poems should be between 4 and 16 lines. Enclose S.A.S.E.

AMATEUR RADIO BITING BUG AWARD, Harter Road, Morristown NJ 07960. (201)538-3081. Judge: Ray Collins. Annual. Estab: 1976. Purpose: for best article about amateur radio published in a U.S. non-amateur radio publication.
Categories: National publication; and regional or local publication. Award: $200 and a plaque

(category I); $100 and a plaque (category II). Deadline: January 31, 1979 (for works published from January-December 1978). Contest rules and entry forms for SASE.

AMERICAN ACADEMY AND INSTITUTE OF ARTS AND LETTERS AWARDS, American Academy and Institute of Arts and Letters, 633 W. 155 St., New York NY 10012. Executive Director: Margaret M. Mills. Annual awards include the Richard and Hinda Rosenthal Award ($2,000 for the best novel of the year, which, though not a commercial success, is a literary achievement); the Academy Institute Awards ($3,000 awarded to 10 non-members to further their creative work).

AMERICAN DENTAL ASSOCIATION SCIENCE WRITERS AWARD, Science Writers Award Committee, 211 E. Chicago Ave., Chicago IL 60611. Awards $1,000 for best newspaper article and $1,000 for best magazine article which broadens and deepens public understanding of dental health, dental treatment, or dental research. Write for entry rules.

AMERICAN OSTEOPATHIC ASSOCIATION JOURNALISM AWARDS, 212 E. Ohio St., Chicago IL 60611. (312)944-2713. Association Director, PR; Nancy Bernstein. Annual. Estab: 1956. Purpose: to recognize the growing corps of journalists who report and interpret osteopathic medicine to the scientific community and the general public. Published submissions only. Award: $1,000 for first prize; two additional prizes of $500 each. Deadline: March 1 (for works published from January 1-December 31). Contest rules and entry forms for SASE.

AMERICAN PENAL PRESS CONTEST. Individual awards in writing categories and photography. Sweepstakes awards in 3 categories. "Only prison publications and individual entries published in prison publications are eligible." Sponsored by Southern Illinois University School of Journalism, Carbondale IL 62901. Entries considered between October 1 and September 30. Established in 1964. Write for rules and entry forms.

AMERICAN PSYCHOLOGICAL FOUNDATION NATIONAL MEDIA AWARDS, Mona Marie Olean, Public Information Officer, American Psychological Association, 1200 Seventeenth St., N.W., Washington DC 20036. Special citations in five categories (television/film, radio, magazine writing, newspaper reporting, books/monographs) to recognize and encourage outstanding, accurate reporting which increases the public's knowledge and understanding of psychology. A Grand Prix winner will be selected from the winners of the five categories and receive a $1,000 award.

ANIMAL LAW WRITING AWARD, Prof. Henry Mark Holzer, Chairman, Reviewing Committee, Society for Animal Rights, Inc., 400 East 51 St., New York NY 10022. Awards $300 to the author of an exceptionally meritorious published book or article in the field of animal law.

ASCAP-DEEMS TAYLOR AWARD, Eight prizes of $500 each. Four are awarded for the best nonfiction books, and four for the best nonfiction articles, published in the United States (in English) on music and/or its creators. Sponsored by the American Society of Composers, Authors and Publishers, 1 Lincoln Plaza, New York NY 10023. Entries are considered between January 1 and March 1. Estab: 1967. Rules available from ASCAP.

ATLANTIC FIRSTS, 8 Arlington St., Boston MA 02116. (617)536-9500. Continuously. Purpose: First major publication of fiction in *The Atlantic* by an unestablished author. Submissions must be unpublished. Award: Professional fees are paid for the stories. Prizes of $750 and $250 are awarded for the most distinguished contributions of the preceding period. Rules and entry form available for SASE.

AVIATION/SPACE WRITERS ASSOCIATION WRITING AWARDS, Aviation/Space Writers Association, Cliffwood Rd., Chester NJ 07930. Awards $100 and engraved scroll for writing on aviation and space, in 9 categories: newspapers over 200,000 circulation, newspapers under 200,000 circulation, magazines (special interest); magazines (general interest); television (news documentary); radio (news documentary); books (general nonfiction); books (technical/training); still photography.

BANCROFT PRIZES, Committee, 311 Low, Columbia University, New York NY 10027. Awards 2 prizes of $4,000 for books in American history (including biography) and diplomacy.

GEORGE LOUIS BEER PRIZE, Committee Chairman, American Historical Association, 400 A St., S.E., Washington DC 20003. Awards $300 for the best first book by a young scholar in the field of European international history since 1895.

MIKE BERGER AWARD Committee, Columbia University, Morningside Hts., New York NY 10027. The award, given to writers whose work best reflects the style of the late Meyer Berger, carries a cash prize of $1,500.

CLAUDE BERNARD SCIENCE JOURNALISM AWARDS, 100 Vermont Ave., Suite 1100, Washington DC 20005. (202)347-9565. Director of Public Relations: Bettie W. Payne. Sponsor: National Society for Medical Research. Annual. Estab: 1967. Purpose: to recognize responsible science reporting which has made a significant contribution to public understanding of basic research in the life sciences, including but not limited to experimental medicine.
Categories: Newspapers (daily, weekly and monthly); and magazines of general interest. Published submissions only. Award: $1,000 and certificate for each category. Deadline: February 15 (for works published during the previous calendar year). Contest rules and entry forms on request.

BEST SPORT STORIES AWARDS, 1315 Westport Lane, Sarasota FL 33580. (813)959-6139. Co-Editor: Edward Ehre. Sponsor: E.P. Dutton & Co., Publisher. Annual. Estab: 1944. Purpose: for best magazine sport story, best coverage sport story and best feature sport story. Published submissions only. Award: $250 for each category. Deadline: December 15. Contest rules and entry forms for SASE.

ALBERT J. BEVERIDGE AWARD, Committee Chairman, American Historical Association, 400 A St., S.E., Washington DC 20003. Awards $1,000 for the best book published in English on American history of the U.S., Canada, and Latin America.

BITTERROOT MAGAZINE POETRY CONTEST. Write Menke Katz, Editor-in-Chief, *Bitterroot,* Blythebourne Sta., P.O. Box 51, Brooklyn NY 11219. Awards cash prizes for poems of any genre.

IRMA SIMONTON BLACK AWARD, 610 W. 112th St., New York NY 10025. Contact: Book Award Committee, Publications Division. Sponsor: Bank Street College of Education. Annual. Estab: 1972. Purpose: for excellence of text and graphics in a book for young children published during the preceding calendar year. Published submission only. Award: author and illustrator receive a scroll; winning entry carries an award seal designed by Maurice Sendak. Deadline: end of February (for works published during the preceding year). Contest rules and entry forms for SASE.

HOWARD W. BLAKESLEE AWARDS, Chairman, Managing Committee, American Heart Association, 7320 Greenville Ave., Dallas TX 75231. Awards $500 honorarium and a citation to each winning entry, which may be a single article, broadcast, film, or book; a series; or no more than five unrelated pieces. Entries will be judged on the basis of their accuracy and significance, and on the skill and originality with which knowledge concerning the heart and circulatory system and advances in research or in the treatment, care and prevention of cardiovascular disease are translated for the public. Send for official entry blank and more details.

BOLLINGEN PRIZE IN POETRY, Yale University Library, New Haven CT 06520. (203)436-0236. Biennial award of $5,000 to an American poet whose published book of poetry represents the highest achievement in the field of American poetry.

BOSTON GLOBE-HORN BOOK AWARDS, Sarah Gagne, Children's Book Editor, The Boston Globe, Boston MA 02107. Awards $200 to a book with outstanding text, and $200 to a book with outstanding illustrations. Up to 3 honor books in each category may be designated by the judges. Books may be fiction or nonfiction. No textbooks. Books must be submitted by publisher.

BOWLING WRITING COMPETITION, American Bowling Congress, Public Relations, 5301 S. 76th St., Greendale WI 53129. $1,800 in gift certificate prizes divided equally between 4 divisions — two each in Feature and Editorial. Categories separated by daily newspaper/national publication entrants and bowling publication entrants. Top prize $200 in four divisions for published bowling stories. First through fifth place in each division.

BROOKLYN ART BOOKS FOR CHILDREN CITATIONS. Awards a citation for the recognition and encouragement of the creation of books for children which are both works of art and literature. Sponsored by the Brooklyn Museum, 188 Eastern Pkwy., Brooklyn NY 11238, and the Brooklyn Public Library, Grand Army Plaza, Brooklyn NY 11238. No deadlines. Established in 1972.

EMIL BROWN FUND PREVENTIVE LAW PRIZE AWARDS, Louis M. Brown, Administrator, University of Southern California Law Center, Los Angeles CA 90007. Awards $1,000 for a praiseworthy leading article or book, and $500 for student work in the field of Preventive Law published in a law review, bar journal or other professional publication.

BULTMAN AWARD, Chairman, Department of Drama, Loyola University, New Orleans LA 70118. Awards $100 for original, unpublished and professionally unproduced plays under one hour in length, written by college students and recommended by teacher of drama or creative writing. Mss must be securely bound and accompanied by SASE, or they will not be returned. Deadline: December 1, annually.

THE CANADIAN ILLUSTRATOR'S AWARD, The Amelia Frances Howard-Gibbon Medal is awarded to the illustrator of a children's book of merit written by a Canadian, published in Canada during the previous calendar year. Sponsored by the Canadian Library Association, 151 Sparks St., Ottawa, Ontario, Canada K1P 5E3. Deadline: February 1. Established in 1971.

CAROLINA QUARTERLY FICTION — POETRY CONTEST, P.O. Box 1117, Chapel Hill, NC 27514. Fiction: Awards $150 first prize, $100 second and $50 third for unpublished manuscripts up to 6,000 words. Poetry: $100 for first, $70 second and $30 third; no limit to length. Entrant may not have published a book-length ms in field of entry.

RUSSELL L. CECIL WRITING AWARDS IN ARTHRITIS, The Arthritis Foundation, 3400 Peachtree Rd., N.E., Atlanta GA 30326. Awards $1,000 in each of four categories (newspaper, magazine, radio, and television) to recognize and encourage the writing of news stories, articles and radio and television scripts on the subject of arthritis.

CHILDREN'S BOOK AWARD, Child Study Association of America/Wel-Met, 50 Madison Ave., New York NY 10010. Given to a book for children or young people which deals realistically with problems in their world. The book, published in the past calendar year, must offer an honest and courageous treatment of its theme.

CHILDREN'S SCIENCE BOOK AWARDS, E. 63rd St., New York NY 10021. (212)838-0230. Public Relations Director: Ann E. Collins. Sponsor: The New York Academy of Sciences. Annual. Estab: 1971. Purpose: for the best general or 'trade' books on science for children. **Categories:** Younger Category books for children under 7 years; and Older Category books for children between 7 and 14 years. Published submissions only. Award: $250 for each category. Deadline: November 30 (for works published from December 1-November 30 each year). Contest rules and entry forms for SASE.

CHRISTOPHER AWARDS, William J. Wilson, Associate Director, 12 E. 48th St., New York NY 10017. Awards bronze medallions for motion pictures (producer, director, writer), network television (producer, director, writer), and books (author, editor, illustrator, photographer) to recognize individuals who have used their talents constructively, in the hope that they, and others, will continue to produce high quality works that reflect sound values.

COLLEGIATE POETRY CONTEST, *The Lyric,* 307 Dunton Dr., SW, Blacksburg VA 24060. Editor: Leslie Mellichamp. Annual. Purpose: for the best original and unpublished poem of 32 lines or less, written in the traditional manner, by U.S. or Canadian undergraduates. Award: 1st prize, $100; 2nd prize, $50; and a number of honorable mentions at $25 each. Also $100 to the library of the college in which the winner of the first prize is enrolled, provided that library is on the list of subscribers to *The Lyric.* Deadline: June 1. Contest rules and entry forms for SASE.

COMMUNITY CHILDREN'S THEATRE OF KANSAS CITY MISSOURI PLAYWRITING FOR CHILDREN AWARD, Mrs. John Keller, 5416 101st Terrace, Overland Park KS 66207. Awards $500 for the best drama for children. Write for details. Enclose S.A.S.E.

CONSERVATION NEWS AWARD. Awards a pewter plate mounted on a walnut plaque along with an honorarium (amount varies). Usually about $200. Award is given in recognition of outstanding efforts in communicating the story of natural resource conservation through the written word in newspapers or magazines. Sponsored by the Soil Conservation Society of America, 7515 N.E. Ankeny Rd., Ankeny IA 50021. Entries must be postmarked by no later than Dec. 31. Enclose S.A.S.E. with correspondence.

ALBERT B. COREY PRIZE IN CANADIAN-AMERICAN RELATIONS, Office of the Executive Secretary, American Historical Association, 400 A St., S.E., Washington DC 20003. The Canadian Historical Association and American Historical Association jointly award $1,000 for the best book on the history of Canadian-United States relations, or on the history of both countries.

COUNCIL ON INTERRACIAL BOOKS FOR CHILDREN PRIZES, For more information, write Contest Director, Council on Interracial Books for Children, 1841 Broadway, New York NY 10023. Enclose S.A.S.E. Awards $500 prizes for children's book mss by minority writers. Deadline: December 31.

CPCU-HARRY J. LOMAN FOUNDATION COMMUNICATIONS AWARD, Box 566, Media PA 19063. Awards $1,000 for the best written communication promoting better understanding of the economic and social functions of the property/casualty insurance business. Eligible are editorials, articles or series published in a national business or financial publication directed toward the national business community, not primarily the insurance industry.

DESIGN FOR LIVING CONTEST, 14531 Stephen St., Nokesville VA 22123. (703)791-3672. Charles A. Mills, Awards Chairman. Sponsor: The March Society. Annual. Estab: 1974. Purpose: awarded to the author of a critical essay submitted in response to a social/political question formulated annually by the awards committee. Published or unpublished submissions OK. Award: 1st prize $50; 2nd prize $25. Entries will be considered for publication in the *Journal of the March Society* at the standard rate of payment. Deadline: April 15th. Contest rules and entry forms for SASE.

THE DEVINS AWARD, University of Missouri Press, Columbia MO 65201. For poetry. Write for submission details.

DOG WRITERS' ASSOCIATION OF AMERICA ANNUAL WRITING COMPETITION, Awards given for excellence in writing about dogs in newspapers, magazines, books, club publications. Separate categories for juniors. Open to all. Details from Sara Fath, Secretary, Kinney Hill Rd., Washington Depot CT 06794. (203)868-2863.

JOHN H. DUNNING PRIZE IN AMERICAN HISTORY, Committee Chairman, American Historical Association, 400 A St. S.E., Washington DC 20003. Awards $300 in even-numbered years for an outstanding monograph in manuscript or in print on any subject relating to American history.

DUTTON ANIMAL BOOK AWARD, E. P. Dutton, 201 Park Ave. S., New York NY 10003. Offers a guaranteed minimum $15,000, as an advance against earnings, for an original book-length manuscript concerning a living creature (only Man and Plants are excluded as subjects); fiction or nonfiction. Write for details.

EDUCATION WRITERS AWARD, James G. Trulove, Director of Communications, American Association of University Professors, Suite 500, One Dupont Circle, Washington DC 20036. Awards a citation to recognize outstanding interpretive reporting of issues in higher education, through newspapers, magazines, radio, television and films. Write for entry details. Enclose S.A.S.E.

EDUCATOR'S AWARD, Miss LeOra L. Held, Executive Secretary, Delta Kappa Gamma Society International, P.O. Box 1589, Austin TX 78767. Awards $1,000 to recognize women and their contribution to education which may influence future directions in the profession. Previously published books may be in the fields of research, philosophy, or any other area of learning which is stimulating and creative.

EPILEPSY FOUNDATION OF AMERICA JOURNALISM AWARD, 1828 L St., NW, Suite 406, Washington DC 20036. (202)293-2930. Editor, National Spokesman: Ann Scherer. Annual. Estab: 1972. PUrpose: for articles which generate better understanding of epilepsy and those who suffer from it. Published submissions only. Award: $500 plus plaque. Deadline: 2nd week in December (for works published from December 1, 1977-Novemver 30, 1978). Contest rules and entry forms for SASE.

THE EXPLICATOR LITERARY FOUNDATION, INC., 3241 Archdale Rd., Richmond VA 23235. (804)272-6890. Treasurer: J.E. Whitesell. Annual. Estab: 1956. Purpose: encouragement of *explication de texta* in books. Published submissions only. Award: $200 and bronze plaque. Deadline: April 1. Contest rules and entry forms for SASE.

JOHN K. FAIRBANK PRIZE IN EAST ASIAN HISTORY, Committee Chairman, American Historical Association, 400 A St. S.E., Washington DC 20003. Awards $300 in odd-numbered years for an outstanding book on the history of China proper, Vietnam, Chinese Central Asia, Manchuria, Mongolia, Korea, or Japan, since the year 1800.

FLORIDA THEATRE CONFERENCE ANNUAL PLAYWRITING CONTEST, Craig Hartley, 2232 N.W. 19th Lane, Gainesville Fl 32605. Provides cash award of $250 minimum. Scripts must be submitted by playwrights living in Florida or enrolled in Florida colleges or universities. Musicals, children's plays and collaborations permitted.

THE FORUM AWARD, Atomic Industrial Forum, Inc., 7101 Wisconsin Ave., Washington DC 20014. Mary Ellen Warren, Administrative Assistant. Annually. Estab: 1967. Conducted to encourage factual news coverage of all aspects of peaceful nuclear applications and to honor significant contributions by the print and electronic news media to public understanding of peaceful uses of nuclear energy. Total of $1,000 in prize money is available in each category (print media and electronic media). Nominees must be professional members of the print or electronic media. Entry must have been available to and intended for the general public.

FREEDOMS FOUNDATION AT VALLEY FORGE AWARDS, Awards Administration, Freedoms Foundation at Valley Forge, Valley Forge PA 19481. Awards honor medal and honor certificates for the most outstanding individual contribution supporting human dignity and American freedom principles in fields of journalism, television and radio. Write for further details.

FRIENDS OF AMERICAN WRITERS JUVENILE BOOK AWARDS, Chairman for 1977-79: Mrs. John Biella, 3470 N. Lake Shore Drive, Chicago IL 60657. Awards for a book published during current year, with a Midwestern locale or written by a native or resident author of the Middle West. Up to 2 other awards to runners up and also an award to illustrator. Books submitted by publishers only.

CHRISTIAN GAUSS AWARD, Phi Beta Kappa, 1811 Q St., N.W., Washington DC 20009. Awards $2,500 for a book of literary criticism or scholarship published in the United States. Books submitted by publishers only.

GAVEL AWARDS, 1155 E. 60th St., Chicago IL 60637. (312)947-4164. Staff Director, Special Events: Dean Tyler Jenks. Sponsor: American Bar Association. Annual. Estab: 1958. Purpose: for outstanding public service by newspaper, television, radio, magazines, motion pictures, theatrical producers, book publishers, wire services and news syndicates in increasing public understanding of the American system of law and justice. Published submissions only. Award: silver Gavel and certificate of merit. Deadline: for books, Feb. 1; all others, March 1 (for works published from January 1-December 31, 1978). Contest rules and entry forms for SASE.

GOETHE HOUSE—P.E.N. TRANSLATION PRIZE, P.E.N. American Center, 156 Fifth Ave., New York NY 10010. (212)255-1577. Awards $500 for the best translation from the German language into English, published during the calendar year under review.

GOLDEN RAINTREE AWARD, 205 W. Highland Ave., Milwaukee WI 53203. (414)273-0873. Managing Editor: Jan Celba. Sponsor: Raintree Publishers Limited. Annual. Estab: 1976. Purpose: for mss that reflect outstanding achievement in juvenile literature. Unpublished submissions only. Award: $100 cash and Golden Raintree Seal, in addition to negotiated publication fee for ms. Deadline: December 31.

GUIDEPOSTS MAGAZINE YOUTH WRITING CONTEST, 747 Third Ave., New York NY 10017. For high school juniors or seniors or students in equivalent grades overseas. Awards $3,000 scholarship for the best first-person story telling about a true memorable or moving experience they have had. Second prize of $2,000; third, $1,000; fourth, $800; fifth, $700; and sixth through twentieth, $500. Top winner's story is published in *Guideposts*.

JOHN HANCOCK AWARDS FOR EXCELLENCE IN BUSINESS AND FINANCIAL JOURNALISM, T-54, John Hancock Place, Box 111, Boston MA 02117. (617)421-2770. Co-

ordinator: Jean Canton. Sponsor: John Hancock Mutual Life Insurance Co. Annual. Estab: 1967. Purpose: for excellence in business and financial journalism.
Categories: Syndicated and news service writers; writers for national magazines of general interest; writers for financial-business newspapers and magazines; writers for newspapers with circulation above 300,000; writers for newspapers with circulation 100,000 to 300,000; and writers for newspapers with circulation under 100,000. Published submissions only. Award: $1,000 for each category. Deadline: January 31 (for works published January 1-December 31). Contest rules and entry forms for SASE (after Oct. 31).

CLARENCE H. HARING PRIZE, Committee Chairman, American Historical Association, 400 A St. S.E., Washington DC 20003. Awards $500 every five years to the Latin American who, in the opinion of the committee, has published the most outstanding book on Latin-American history during the preceding 5 years. Next awarded in 1981.

HEADLINERS AWARDS, Elaine Frayne, Exeeutive Secretary, National Headliners Club, Convention Hall, Atlantic City NJ 08401. Presents awards for reporting, writing, photography, TV and radio broadcasting. Annual contest.

HEALTH JOURNALISM AWARDS, 2200 Grand Ave., Des Moines IA 50312. (515)243-1121. Director of Public Affairs: Dr. R.C. Schafer. Sponsor: American Chiropractic Association. Annual. Estab: 1976. Purpose: to recognize journalists whose works suggest solutions to basic health problems.
Categories: Newspapers; consumer magazines; television; radio; trade, professional or special interest publications; and audiovisuals. Published submissions only. Award: $200 and plaque to winner in each category; plaques to runner-up in each category. Deadline: March 1 (for works published previous year, from January 1-December 31). Contest rules and entry forms for SASE.

ERNEST HEMINGWAY FOUNDATION AWARD, P.E.N. American Center, 156 Fifth Ave., New York NY 10010. Awards $6,000 for the best first-published book of fiction, either novel or short story collection, in the English language by an American author.

SIDNEY HILLMAN PRIZE AWARD, Sidney Hillman Foundation, Inc., 15 Union Square, New York NY 10003. Awards $750 annually for outstanding published contributions in nonfiction, fiction, radio and television dealing with themes relating to the ideals which Sidney Hillman held throughout his life. Such themes would include the protection of individual civil liberties, improved race relations, strengthened labor movement, advancement of social welfare, economic security, greater world understanding and related problems. Deadline: January 31.

HOUGHTON MIFFLIN LITERARY FELLOWSHIP, Houghton Mifflin Co., 2 Park St., Boston MA 02107. Awards $2,500 grant and $5,000 as an advance against royalties to help authors complete projects of outstanding literary merit. Candidates should submit at least 50 pages of the actual project (fiction or nonfiction), an informal description of its theme and intention, and a brief biography.

THE HUMANITAS PRIZE, Executive Director, The Human Family Institute, P.O. Box 861, Pacific Palisades CA 90272. (213)454-8769. Awards $10,000 for the thirty-minute teleplay, $15,000 for the sixty-minute teleplay, and $25,000 for the teleplay of ninety minutes or longer previously produced on national network commercial television, aired during prime time hours. To promote a greater appreciation of the dignity of the human person, to deepen the human family's understanding of themselves, of their relationship with the human community, and to their Creator, to aid individuals in their search for meaning, freedom and love; to liberate, enrich and unify the human family. Submission should be made by someone other than the writer of the produced play (for example, the program producer). Write for details and entry form.

INGAA-MISSOURI BUSINESS JOURNALISM AWARDS, William McPhatter, Director, Neff Hall, School of Journalism, Columbia MO 65201. Awards $1,000 in each of four categories to honor excellence in reporting and interpreting business, economic, trade and financial news. To encourage a greater public understanding of the American economic system through coverage of U.S. business in newspapers and magazines. Write for complete details and entry form.

INTERNATIONAL POETS AND PATRONS NARRATIVE CONTEST, 312 Ohio St., Momence IL 60954. (815)472-6305. Contest Chairman: Catherine N. Fieleke. Sponsor: Poets and Patrons of Chicago, Inc. Annual. Estab: 1973. Purpose: for best narrative poem (poem must tell a story—40 lines maximum, any form, any subject). Unpublished submissions only. Award: 1st prize, $25; 2nd prize, $10. Deadline: September 1.

INTERNATIONAL READING ASSOCIATION PRINT MEDIA AWARD. Entries must focus on the field of reading and are judged on the basis of journalistic quality which includes clear and imaginative writing that lifts the material out of the routine category. In-depth studies of reading activities, accounts of outstanding reading practices, relevant reading research reportage, and/or day-to-day coverage of reading programs in the community. Sponsored by the International Reading Association. Entries or requests for additional information should be sent to Charles R. Putney, Public Information Officer, International Reading Association, 800 Barksdale Rd., Newark DE 19711. Deadline: January 2. Established in 1960. Rules and entry forms available at the address above.

IOWA SCHOOL OF LETTERS AWARD FOR SHORT FICTION, English-Philosophy Bldg., University of Iowa, Iowa City IA 52242. Awards $1,000 for a book-length collection of short stories by a writer who has not yet published a volume of fiction.

JOSEPH HENRY JACKSON/JAMES D. PHELAN LITERARY AWARD, 425 California St., Suite 1602, San Francisco CA 94104. (415)982-1210. Assistant Coordinator: Susan Kelly. Sponsor: The San Francisco Foundation. Annual. Estab: 1935 (Phelan contest); 1957 (Jackson contest). "The two competitions were combined in 1957 and are now administered simultaneously. One can compete for one or both depending on eligibility." Purpose: to award the author of an unpublished, partly completed book-length work of fiction, nonfictional prose, short story or poetry (Jackson); to award the author of an unpublished, incomplete work of fiction, non-fictional prose, short story, poetry or drama (Phelan). Award: Both $2,000. Deadline: January 15. Contest rules and entry forms can be obtained by calling the above number.

JACKSONVILLE UNIVERSITY PLAYWRITING CONTEST, Davis Sikes, Director, College of Fine Arts, Jacksonville University, Jacksonville FL 32211. (904)744-3950. Awards prizes up to $1000 and premiere production of previously unpublished plays, plus playwright's expenses in residence, for original 1-act and full-length plays. Deadline: January 1. Write for contest rules. Enclose S.A.S.E.

JEWISH BOOK COUNCIL AWARD FOR A BOOK OF JEWISH THOUGHT, National Jewish Welfare Board, 15 E. 26th St., New York NY 10010. Awards $500 and a citation to the author of a published book dealing with some aspect of Jewish thought, past or present, which combines knowledge, clarity of thought, and literary merit.

JEWISH BOOK COUNCIL AWARD FOR A BOOK ON THE NAZI HOLOCAUST, National Jewish Welfare Board, 15 E. 26 St., New York NY 10010. Awards $500 and a citation to the author of a published nonfiction book dealing with some aspects of the Nazi holocaust period. Books published in English, Yiddish, and Hebrew are acceptable.

JEWISH BOOK COUNCIL AWARD FOR BOOKS OF POETRY, National Jewish Welfare Board, 15 E. 26 St., New York NY 10010. Awards $500 and a citation to the author of a book of poetry of Jewish interest. Books published in English, Yiddish, and Hebrew are acceptable.

JEWISH BOOK COUNCIL JUVENILE AWARD, National Jewish Welfare Board, 15 E. 26 St., New York NY 10010. Awards $500 and a citation to the author of a published Jewish juvenile book.

JEWISH BOOK COUNCIL WILLIAM AND JANICE EPSTEIN FICTION AWARD, National Jewish Welfare Board, 15 E. 26 St., New York NY 10010. Awards $500 and a citation to the author of a published book of fiction of Jewish interest, either a novel or a collection of short stories, which combines high literary merit with an affirmative expression of Jewish values.

ANSON JONES AWARD. $250 cash and engraved plaque in each of eight categories. For excellence in communicating health information to the public through Texas newspapers, magazines, radio and television. Sponsored by the Texas Medical Association, 1801 North Lamar Blvd., Austin TX 78701. (512)477-6704. Entries are considered between December 1 and November 30. Established in 1956. Rules and entry forms available from the Communication Department at TMA (address above).

FRANK KELLEY MEMORIAL AWARD, American Association of Petroleum Landmen, P.O. Box 1984, Fort Worth TX 76101. Awards $250 and a plaque in appreciation for excellence in reporting oil and gas industry information to the general public. Previously published newspaper articles only.

THE ROBERT F. KENNEDY JOURNALISM AWARDS, Committee Chairman, 1035 30th St., N.W., Washington DC 20007. The awards ($1,000 first prize, possible additional grand prize of $2,000, honorable mentions and citations) honor journalists and broadcasters whose work has illuminated the problmes of the disadvantaged in the United States. Write in December for complete details and entry form for next year's competition.

LUCILLE LOY KUCK OHIOANA AWARD. 3 prizes of $250, $150 and $50 for literary excellence. Sponsored by the Martha Kinney Cooper Ohioana Library Association, 1105 Ohio Departments Bldg., Columbus OH 43215. Deadline: February 1. Rules and entry forms may be obtained from the Martha Kinney Cooper Library Association.

HAROLD MORTON LANDON TRANSLATION AWARD, The Academy of American Poets, 1078 Madison Ave., New York NY 10028. Awards $1,000 biennially to American poet for a published translation of poetry from any language into English. Translation may be a book-length poem, collection of poems, or a verse drama translated into verse. Send published books (no manuscripts) to the Academy.

NORMAN LEAR AWARD FOR ACHIEVEMENT IN COMEDY PLAYWRITING, Executive Producer, American College Theatre Festival, John F. Kennedy Center for the Performing Arts, Washington DC 20566. (202)254-3437. Awards $2,500 and a professional assignment to write a complete teleplay for one of the series produced by Norman Lear, a trip to Los Angeles with all expenses paid to participate in story conferences and membership in the Writers Guild of America with the Writers Guild Foundation paying the usual initiation fee of $200, for the best student comedy play produced for the annual American College Theatre Festival.

LEVI'S ANNUAL RODEO PRESS COMPETITION, Levi Strauss & Co., IRWA Rodeo Press Contest, 2 Embarcadero Center, San Francisco CA 94106. Enclose S.A.S.E. Categories: rodeo news stories, rodeo feature stories and rodeo photography.

JERRY LEWIS/MDA WRITING AWARDS, Horst S. Petzall, Director, Department of Public Health Education, Muscular Dystrophy Association, 810 Seventh Ave., New York NY 10019. Awards $1,000, $500, and $250, along with award plaques, to those writers whose work fosters better understanding of muscular dystrophy and related neuro-muscular diseases, and contributes to public support of the effort to conquer these afflictions. Previously published articles, feature stories, editorials or poetry, as well as commentaries, documentaries, dramas, or public-service announcements aired on radio or television, are eligible.

ELIAS LIEBERMAN STUDENT POETRY AWARD. For details, send S.A.S.E. to Elias Lieberman Student Poetry Award, Executive Secretary, Poetry Society of America, 15 Gramercy Park, New York NY 10003. For the "best unpublished poem by a high school or preparatory school student of the USA." Deadline: January 15.

DAVID D. LLOYD PRIZE, Chairman of the Committee, Professor Thomas C. Blaisdell, Jr., Department of Political Science, 210 Barrows Hall, University of California, Berkeley CA 94720. Awards $1,000 biennially for the best published book on the period of the presidency of Harry S. Truman. Books must deal primarily and substantially with some aspect of the political, economic, and social development of the U.S., principally between April 12, 1945 and January 20, 1953, or of the public career of Harry S. Truman. Publication period: January 1-December 31.

THE GERALD LOEB AWARDS, UCLA Graduate School of Management, Los Angeles CA 90024. (213)825-7982. Assistant Dean: Gerald F. Corrigan. Annual. Estab: 1957. Purpose: for distinguished business and financial journalism.
Categories: Single article in a newspaper with daily circulation above 350,000; single article in a newspaper with daily circulation less than 350,000; single article in a national magazine; and

syndicated column or editorial. Published submissions only. Award: $1,000 for each category. Deadline: February 15 (for works published from January 1-December 31). Contest rules and entry forms for SASE.

MAN IN HIS ENVIRONMENT BOOK AWARD, E. P. Dutton, 201 Park Ave. S., New York NY 10003. Offers a guaranteed minimum $10,000 as an advance against earnings for an original single work of adult nonfiction on an ecological theme, dealing with the past, present or future of man in his environment, natural or man-made. Write for details.

HOWARD R. MARRARO PRIZE IN ITALIAN HISTORY, Office of the Executive Secretary, American Historical Association, 400 A St. S.E., Washington DC 20003. Awards $500 for a book or article which treats Italian history in any epoch of Italian cultural history, or of Italian-American relations. Write for submission details.

JOHN MASEFIELD MEMORIAL AWARD, Poetry Society of America, 15 Gramercy Park S., New York NY 10003. Awards $500 for an unpublished narrative poem written in English, not exceeding 200 lines, in memory of the late Poet Laureate of England. Write for submission details enclosing SASE. Deadline: January 15.

EDWARD J. MEEMAN CONSERVATION AWARDS, Scripps-Howard Foundation, 200 Park Ave., New York NY 10017. Awards prizes totaling $10,000 to newspapermen and women on U.S. newspapers in recognition of outstanding work in the cause of conservation, including control of pollution, future technological developments, overpopulation, recycling, conservation of soil, forests, vegetation, wildlife, open space and scenery.

FREDERICK G. MELCHER BOOK AWARD, Doris Pullen, Director, 25 Beacon St., Boston MA 02108. (617)742-2100. Awards $1,000 and bronze medallion for a work published in America judged to be the most significant contribution to religious liberalism. Books submitted by publishers only.

MODERN LANGUAGE ASSOCIATION PRIZES, Committee on Research Activities, 62 Fifth Ave., New York NY 10011. Awards the annual James Russell Lowell Prize, $1,000, for an outstanding literary or linguistic study, a critical edition of an important work, or a critical biography by a member of the Association published in book form. The committee also awards an annual prize for an outstanding article in the *PMLA,* the William Riley Parker Prize.

FRANK LUTHER MOTT-KAPPA TAU ALPHA RESEARCH AWARD IN JOURNALISM, Dr. William H. Taft, Chief, Central Office KTA, School of Journalism, University of Missouri, Columbia MO 65201. Awards $250 and hand-lettered scroll for the best book published during the previous year.

NAEBM DIRECTORS' AWARD. Sponsored by the National Association of Engine and Boat Manufacturers, 666 Third Ave., P.O. Box 5555, Grand Central Station, New York NY 10017. For outstanding contribution by a professional communicator to the sport of boating and allied water sports. Candidates must be nominated by an NAEBM member or director. Submissions must include a statement by the nominator and at least six samples of the individual's work for the 12-month period ending Oct. 1 of each year.

NATIONAL ASSOCIATION OF BANK WOMEN AWARDS FOR DISTINGUISHED JOURNALISM, 111 E. Wacker Dr., Chicago IL 60601. (312)644-6610. Contact: Public Relations Department. Annual. Estab: 1974. Purpose: to recognize and honor journalists whose writings have contributed to a better understanding of the role of executive women in the banking industry now and in the future.
Categories: 1) U.S. newspaper or periodical; and 2) bank-sponsored publication. Published submissions only. Award: $300 cash plus a certificate of recognition for each category. Deadline: June 1, 1978 (for works published during previous year). Contest rules and entry forms for SASE.

NATIONAL BOOK AWARDS, administered by the National Institute of Arts and Letters, 633 W. 155 St., New York NY 10032. Awards $1,000 in each of seven categories for literature written or translated by American citizens and published in the U.S. to honor outstanding creative writing. Categories include biography and autobiography, children's literature, contemporary thought, fiction, history, poetry and (every two years) translation. Deadline: November 15.

THE NATIONAL FOUNDATION FOR HIGHWAY SAFETY AWARDS, Box 3059, Westville Station, New Haven CT 06515. Annual. Estab: 1962. Purpose: to emphasize driving safety. Published submissions only. Award: U.S. Savings Bond and plaques offered to editors, reporters, cartoonists, television and radio directors. Deadline: January 31 (for works published during the year). Contest rules and entry forms for SASE.

NATIONAL HEADLINER AWARDS, Elaine Frayne, Executive Secretary, National Headliners Club, Convention Hall, Atlantic City NJ 08401. Awards the Headliner Medal for outstanding achievement in journalism. Open to all material published or broadcast during the year in newspapers, magazines, syndicates, radio and television, to recognize men and women who exemplify the responsibilities and traditions of the journalistic profession.

NATIONAL HISTORICAL SOCIETY BOOK PRIZE IN AMERICAN HISTORY, Board of Judges, Box 1831, Harrisburg PA 17105. Awards $1,000 for a first book published by an author, to encourage promising historians, young and old, in producing the sound but readable history that is so necessary for portraying our past to the general public.

NATIONAL PRESS CLUB AWARD FOR EXCELLENCE IN CONSUMER REPORTING, Stan Cohen, Chairman, Consumer Awards, National Press Bldg., Washington DC 20045. Provides the Consumer Reporting Award, and Certificates of Recognition in 11 categories. For members of the working press. Deadline for entries: May 15.

NATIONAL SOCIETY OF PROFESSIONAL ENGINEERS JOURNALISM AWARDS, 2029 K St., N.W., Washington DC 20006. (202)331-7020. PR Director: Bill Wanlund. Annual. Estab: 1966. Purpose: for contributing to public knowledge and understanding of the role of engineering and technology in contemporary life. Published submissions only. Award: Three awards of $500, $300 and $200. Deadline: January 15 (for works published during the previous year). Contest rules and entry forms for SASE.

ALLAN NEVINS PRIZE, Professor Kenneth T. Jackson, Secretary-Treasurer, Society of American Historians, 610 Fayerweather Hall, Columbia University, New York NY 10027. Awards $1,000 and publication of winning manuscript for the best written doctoral dissertation in the field of American history, dealing historically with American arts, literature, and science, as well as biographical studies of Americans in any walk of life.

CATHERINE L. O'BRIEN AWARD, c/o Ruder & Finn, Inc., 110 E. 59th St., New York NY 10022. (212)593-6321. Vice President: Jill Totenberg. Sponsor: Stanley Home Products, Inc. Annual. Estab: 1960. Purpose: for achievement in women's interest newspaper reporting. Published submissions only. Award: First prize; $500 and $1,000 journalism scholarship; second prize: $300 and $750 journalism scholarship; third prize: $200 and $500 journalism scholarship. Annual deadline: January 31 (for works published from January-December of calendar year). Contest rules and entry forms available on request.

EARL D. OSBORN AWARD, Robert Francis Kane Associates, Inc., Public Relations, 12 E. 41st St., New York NY 10017. Sponsor: EDO Corporation. Annual. Estab: 1970. Purpose: for best writing in any medium (press, magazine, radio or TV) on general aviation. Published submissions only. Award: $500 and trophy. Deadline: February (for works published during the previous calendar year). Contest rules and entry forms for SASE.

P.E.N. TRANSLATION PRIZE, Chairman, Translation Committee, P.E.N. American Center, 156 Fifth Ave., New York NY 10010. Awards $1,000 for the best translation into English from any language published in the United States. Technical, scientific, or reference works are not eligible. Sponsored by the Book-of-the-Month Club.

FRANCIS PARKMAN PRIZE, Professor Kenneth T. Jackson, Secretary, Society of American Historians, 610 Fayerweather Hall, Columbia University, New York NY 10027. Awards $500 and a bronze medal to recognize the author who best epitomizes the Society's purpose— the writing of history with literary distinction as well as sound scholarship. Books must deal with the colonial or national history of the United States. Books submitted by publishers only.

THE DREW PEARSON PRIZE FOR EXCELLENCE IN INVESTIGATIVE REPORTING, The Drew Pearson Foundation, 1156 15 St. N.W., Washington DC 20005. Awards $5,000 for significant investigative reporting by newspaper reporters, authors of books and magazine articles and journalists involved in radio and television.

PENNEY-MISSOURI MAGAZINE AWARDS, School of Journalism, University of Missouri, Columbia MO 65201. Awards Director: Ruth D'Arcy. Annual. Estab: 1966. Purpose: for excellence in magazine coverage that enhances lifestyle in today's society.
Categories: Contemporary living; consumerism; health; personal lifestyle; expanding opportunities, and excellence in smaller magazines. Published submissions only. Award: $1,000 in each category. Deadline: May 1 (for works published from January 1-December 31). Write for centest rules and entry forms.

PFIZER AWARD, c/o Isis Editorial Office, MHT 5214, Smithsonian Institution, Washington DC 20560. (202)381-5691. Sponsor: History of Science Society, Inc. Annual. Estab: 1958. Purpose: to recognize and reward the best published work related to the history of science in the preceding year, written by an American or Canadian author. Published submissions only. Award: $1,000 and a medal. Deadline: May 1 (for work published during the previous year).

PLAYWRITING FOR CHILDREN'S THEATRE, 5416 W. 101st Terrace, Overland Park KS 66207. Contact: Mrs. John B. Keller. Sponsor: Community Children's Theatre of Kansas City. Annual. Estab: 1951. Purpose: to encourage the writing of outstanding original scripts which are suitable for production by adults for grade school children. Unpublished submissions only. Award: $500. Deadline: First week of January. Contest rules and entry forms for SASE.

EDGAR ALLAN POE AWARDS, Mystery Writers of America, Inc., 105 E. 19 St., New York NY 10003. Awards Edgar Allan Poe statuettes in each of nine categories: best mystery novel published in America, best first mystery novel by an American author, best fact crime book, best juvenile mystery, best paperback mystery, best mystery short story, best mystery motion picture, best television mystery, and best mystery book jacket.

THE POETRY CENTER DISCOVERY-THE NATION CONTEST, The Poetry Center of the 92nd St. YM-YWHA, 1395 Lexington Ave., New York NY 10028. Awards $50 to each of 4 winners, invites each winner to read at The Poetry Center in a special program and publishes one poem by each winner in *The Nation.* Open to poets whose works have not yet been published in book form. Write for details. Enclose S.A.S.E.

POETS CLUB OF CHICAGO NATIONAL SHAKESPEAREAN SONNET CONTEST. 3 prizes of $50, $25 and $10. Sponsored by the Poets Club of Chicago. Mail three copies of only one Shakespearean sonnet, typed on 8½x11 paper, to Anne Nolan, c/o Nolan Boiler Co., 8531 S. Vincennes, Chicago IL 60620. Deadline: September 1. Sonnet must be unpublished and must not have won a cash award in this contest previously. No author identification is to appear on the copies. Enclose a separate envelope with the poet's identification on a card inside it. No poems will be returned. SASE must accompany all inquiries.

PRIZE IN PHOTOGRAPHIC HISTORY, Prize Committee, Photographic Historical Society of New York, Box 1839, Radio City Station, New York NY 10019. Awards $100 to an individual who has written, edited, or produced an original work dealing with the history of photography. Books, magazine articles and monographs are eligible.

PULITZER PRIZES, Secretary, Advisory Board on the Pulitzer Prizes, 702 Journalism, Columbia University, New York NY 10027. Awards $1,000 in categories of journalism, letters, and music for distinguished work by United States newspapers, and for distinguished achievement in literature.

PUTNAM AWARDS, G. P. Putnam's Sons, 200 Madison Ave., New York NY 10016. Awards $7,500 advance against royalties for outstanding fiction and nonfiction book manuscripts. Nominations are made by the editors of G.P. Putnam's Sons from mss already under contract to the house.

ERNIE PYLE MEMORIAL AWARD, Scripps-Howard Foundation, 200 Park Ave., New York NY 10017. Awards $1,000 and a plaque for newspaper writing which exemplifies the style, warmth, and craftsmanship of Ernie Pyle.

REGINA MEDAL, Catholic Library Association, 461 W. Lancaster Ave., Haverford PA 19041. Awards a silver medal for continued distinguished contribution in literature for children.

RELIGIOUS ARTS GUILD ONE-ACT PLAY COMPETITION, 25 Beacon, Boston MA 02108. (617)742-2100. Executive Secretary: Barbara M. Hutchins. Biannual. Estab: 1950. Unpublished submissions only. Award: $200. Deadline: January 15. Contest rules and entry forms for SASE.

RICHMOND CHILDREN'S THEATRE PLAYWRITING AWARD. For details, write Playwriting Contest, 6317 Mallory Dr., Richmond VA 23226. Semi-annually awards $250 first prize for best children's play. Second prize: $125. Third prize: $75.

DOROTHY ROSENBERG ANNUAL POETRY AWARD, 25 Beacon, Boston MA 02108. (617)742-2100. Executive Secretary: Barbara M. Hutchins. Sponsor: Religious Arts Guild. Annual. Estab: 1970. Unpublished submissions only. Award: First prize, $50; second prize, $25. Deadline: March 31. Contest rules and entry forms for SASE.

ST. LAWRENCE AWARD FOR FICTION, *Fiction International*, Department of English, St. Lawrence University, Canton NY 13617. Awards $1,000 to the author of an outstanding first collection of short fiction published by an American publisher during the current year. Editors, writers, agents, readers, and publishers are invited to suggest or submit eligible books.

SATURDAY REVIEW ANNUAL TRAVEL PHOTO CONTEST, 488 Madison Ave., New York NY 10022. Awards travel prizes for b&w or color prints and color transparencies. For amateur photographers only. Entries judged on photographic quality, originality of subject treatment and "sense of place." Write for contest rules.

HENRY SCHUMAN PRIZE, c/o Isis Editorial Office, MHT 5214, Smithsonian Institution, Washington DC 20560. (202)381-5691. Sponsor: History of Science Society, Inc. Annual. Estab: 1955. Purpose: for original prize essay on the history of science and its cultural influences, open to graduate and undergraduate students in any American or Canadian college. Unpublished submissions only. Papers submitted must be 5,000 words in length, exclusive of footnotes, and thoroughly documented. Award: $250. Deadline: July 1.

ROBERT LIVINGSTON SCHUYLER PRIZE, Committee Chairman, American Historical Association, 400 A St. S.E., Washington DC 20003. Awards $500 every five years for recognition of the best work in the field of Modern British, British Imperial, and British Commonwealth history written by an American citizen.

SCIENCE IN SOCIETY JOURNALISM AWARDS, Administrative Secretary, National Association of Science Writers, Box H, Sea Cliff NY 11579. Two awards of $1,000 and engraved medallions to recognize investigative and interpretive reporting about physical sciences and the life sciences and their impact for good and bad. Write for complete details and entry blank.

SCIENCE-WRITING AWARD IN PHYSICS AND ASTRONOMY, Director, Public Relations Division, American Institute of Physics, 335 E. 45 St., New York NY 10017. A single prize of $1,500, a certificate and stainless steel Moebius strip is awarded annually to an author whose work has improved public understanding of physics and astronomy. Entries must be the work of physicists, astronomers or members of AIP member and affiliated societies. Co-sponsored by the United States Steel Foundation.

SERGEL DRAMA PRIZE, The Charles H. Sergel Drama Prize, The University of Chicago Theatre, 5706 S. University Ave., Chicago IL 60637. Awards $1,500 biennially for best original play. Write for details and entry blank. Contest deadline is July 1 of the contest year. Entry blanks are available by February of the contest year.

SIGMA DELTA CHI DISTINGUISHED SERVICE IN JOURNALISM AWARDS, 35 E. Wacker Dr., Suite 3108, Chicago IL 60601. Awards bronze medallions and plaques in 16 categories for outstanding achievements in journalism during the calendar year. Write for details and required entry form.

THE SMOLAR AWARD, Council of Jewish Federations and Welfare Funds, Inc., 575 Lexington Ave., New York NY 10022. Awards a plaque to recognize outstanding journalists in North America whose work appears in English language newspapers substantially involved in the coverage of Jewish communal affairs and issues in the United States and Canada. Write for details and required entry form.

SOCIETY OF COLONIAL WARS AWARD, Awards Committee, 122 E. 58 St., New York NY 10022. Awards bronze medallion and citation to recognize contributions of outstanding excellence in the field of literature, drama, music or art relative to colonial Americana (1607-1775).

SPECIAL OLYMPICS AWARDS. For radio and television broadcasters, newspaper and magazine reporters and feature writers, news photographers, athletes, coaches and sports organizations who during the previous calendar year have made the most distinguished contributions to local, national, or international Special Olympics program. The award is presented at an annual luncheon and consists of a specially designed award. Sponsored by Special Olympics, Inc., and The Joseph P. Kennedy, Jr. Foundation. For information write: Special Olympics Awards, Joseph P. Kennedy, Jr. Foundation, 1701 K St., N.W., Suite 205, Washington DC 20006. Established in 1973.

SPUR AWARDS, Western Writers of America, Inc., Nellie S. Yost, Secretary, 1505 West D St., North Platte NE 69101. Awards the Spur Award Trophy for the best western nonfiction book, western novel, western juvenile nonfiction book, western juvenile fiction book, western television script, motion picture script, and western short material. Write for current details and submission rules.

STANLEY DRAMA AWARD, Wagner College, Staten Island NY 10301. Awards $800 for an original full-length play or musical which has not been professionally produced or received tradebook publication. Must be recommended by a theatre professional (e.g., director, actor, agent, playwright, producer, etc.). Consideration will also be given to a series of two or three thematically connected 1-act plays. Write for applications.

THOMAS L. STOKES AWARD, The Washington Journalism Center, 2401 Virginia Ave. N.W., Washington DC 20037. Awards $1,000 and a citation for the best analysis, reporting or comment appearing in a daily newspaper on the general subject of development, use and conservation of energy and other natural resources in the public interest, and protection of the environment.

THE WALKER STONE AWARDS FOR EDITORIAL WRITING, Scripps-Howard Foundation, 200 Park Ave., New York NY 10017. Awards $1,000 and a certificate for first prize, and $500 honorable mention prize to newspaper men and women in the field of editorial writing, exemplifying general excellence, forcefulness of writing to a purpose, effectiveness as measured by results, and importance of the expression in the public interest.

JESSE STUART CONTEST, *Seven,* 115 South Hudson, Oklahoma City OK 73102. Awards $25, $15, $10, and $5 for the best unpublished poems in the Jesse Stuart tradition; any form or free verse; any length. Write for submission details. Enclose S.A.S.E.

THEATRE ARTS CORPORATION NATIONAL PLAYWRITING CONTEST, Contest Coordinator, Box 2677, Sante Fe NM 87501. (505)982-0252. Awards $500 for original and unproduced plays in each of several categories such as plays in mime and plays for children. The contest is supported by a grant from the National Endowment for the Arts in Washington DC. Write for required rules and entry form. Enclose S.A.S.E.

THE PAUL TOBENKIN MEMORIAL AWARD, Graduate School of Journalism, Columbia University, New York NY 10027. Awards $250 and a certificate for outstanding achievement in the field of newspaper writing in the fight against racial and religious hatred, intolerance, discrimination and every form of bigotry.

TRA ECLIPSE AWARDS. Award consists of an "Eclipse Trophy and $500 'added money.'" Given for an outstanding newspaper story on thoroughbred racing and an outstanding magazine story on thoroughbred racing. Sponsor: Thoroughbred Racing Associations. Contact: TRA Service Bureau, 522 Fifth Ave., New York NY 10036. Deadline for entry: October 31, annually. Starting date for entry: November 1, annually. Established in 1971. No entry blank necessary. Submit copy of published article showing date of publication.

UNICO NATIONAL LITERARY AWARD CONTEST. Sponsored by UNICO National, Italian-American service organization. Write for details to UNICO National, 72 Burroughs Pl., Bloomfield NJ 07003. Awards a total of $3,000 to winners. To be eligible, author must be of Italian lineage and between the ages of 18 to 35.

UNIROYAL HIGHWAY SAFETY JOURNALISM AWARDS, Attn. David E. Kuhnert, PR Manager, Uniroyal, Inc., 1230 Avenue of the Americas, New York NY 10020. Recognizes outstanding journalistic achievements that create a greater public awareness of the need for constant caution on the highways. The five top winners — one each from the categories of newspapers, general magazines, trade publications, radio and television — receive plaques and are provided $1,000 scholarships to give to journalism schools of their choice. Runners-up are awarded certificates of excellence.

UNITED STATES INDUSTRIAL COUNCIL EDUCATIONAL FOUNDATION EDITORIAL AWARDS COMPETITION, P.O. Box 2686, Nashville TN 37219. Awards $100 to $300 for editorials, published in a daily or weekly newspaper, which best interpret the spirit and goals of the free enterprise system in the United States and which describe and analyze the achievements of this system.

VESTA AWARDS CONTEST, American Meat Institute, P.O. Box 3556, Washington DC 20007. Awards an engraved cast bronze statuette of Vesta, mythological goddess of hearth and home, for excellence in the presentation of news about food by daily newspaper food editors and writers. The annual contest is open to any editor or writer regularly employed by a daily newspaper and who is responsible for production of pages or columns dealing with food.

VETERANS' VOICES AWARDS, Hospitalized Veterans' Writing Project, Inc., 5920 Nall, Room 106, Mission KS 66202. The Hospitalized Veterans' Writing Project, which publishes *Veterans' Voices* offers cash prizes for unpublished articles, stories, poems, light verse, and patriotic essays by hospitalized veterans of the U.S. Armed Forces, plus poetry prizes, $5.00; prose, $10.00; special awards are Joseph Posik Award, $50.00 each edition; Gladys Feld Helzberg Poetry Award, $25.00 each edition; two Charlotte Dilling Awards given in June each year for essays on "Why a Two-Party System" or "Why the Veterans Should Vote" — $125.00 first prize — $75.00 second. Also Beginners' Awards, $5.00 extra for regular prose or poetry. Manuscripts received all year long. Sample copy of *Veterans' Voices*, $1.

LUDWIG VON MISES MEMORIAL ESSAY CONTEST, Intercollegiate Studies Institute, Inc. and National Federation of Independent Business, 14 S. Bryn Mawr Ave., Bryn Mawr PA 19010. $1,000 first prize, $500 second prize, $100 each to five runners-up. Open to high school and college students. Annual contest. Write for contest entry form. Deadline: July 1.

WAGNER MEMORIAL POETRY AWARD. For details, send S.A.S.E. to Wagner Memorial Award, c/o Secretary, Poetry Society of America, 15 Gramercy Park, New York NY 10003. Awards $250 for the best poem of any style or length. Deadline: January 15.

EDWARD LEWIS WALLANT BOOK AWARD, Dr. Lothar Kahn, Central Connecticut College, New Britain CT 06150. Awards $125 and citation for a creative work of fiction published during the current year which has significance for the American Jew.

WATUMULL PRIZE IN THE HISTORY OF INDIA, Committee Chairman, American Historical Association, 400 A St. S.E., Washington DC 20003. Awards $1,000 biennially for the best book originally published in the United States on any phase of the history of India.

BERTHA WEISZ MEMORIAL AWARD, 16000 Terrace Rd., #208, Cleveland OH 44112. (216)451-3331. Editor: Julius Weiss. Sponsor: Weiss Philatelic-Numismatic Features. Even numbered years. Estab: 1973. Purpose: for best stamp column and coin column in a newspaper with over 50,000 circulation. Contest judged on originality, research and news of subject. Published submissions only, (and from writers, not from readers). Award: $50 Bond and plaque for both categories. Deadline: December 31 (for works published from January 1-December 1). Contest rules for SASE.

WESTERN WRITERS OF AMERICA GOLDEN SPUR AWARD, Nellie Yost, 1505 West D., North Platte NE 69101. Annual. Estab: 1952.
Categories: Best western novel; best western historical novel; best western nonfiction book; best western juvenile; best western TV show; best western film script; best western short subject

(fiction or nonfiction). Published submissions only. Award: Golden Spur Award given at annual convention banquet. Deadline: December 31 (for works published in that year). Contest rules and entry form for SASE.

THE WALT WHITMAN AWARD, Sponsor, The Academy of American Poets, Inc., 1078 Madison Ave., New York NY 10028. Annual. Estab: 1974. Purpose: for a book-length (50-100 pp.) manuscript of poetry by an American citizen who has not previously published a book of poems. (The winning poet may have published a chapbook or a small edition of a book of poems, and may have published poems in magazines.) Award: $1,000 cash and publication of winning ms by a major publisher. Deadline: manuscripts received between September 15 and November 15. Send SASE in late summer for contest rules and required entry form.

WILMETTE CHILDREN'S THEATRE PLAYWRITING CONTEST, 1200 Wilmette Ave., Wilmette IL 60091. Awards $300 and $200 for the winning original plays, to encourage authors to increase the material available for production with child actors or with both child actions and adults.

THOMAS J. WILSON PRIZE, Harvard University Press, 79 Garden St., Cambridge MA 02138. Awards $500 to the author of a first book by a beginning author accepted by Harvard University Press during the calendar year and judged outstanding in content, style, and mode of presentation.

LAURENCE L. WINSHIP BOOK AWARD, The Boston Globe, Boston MA 02107. (617)929-2644. The $1,000 book award is open to books of fiction or science written by American authors and submitted by U.S. publishing companies. Books must contain a New England angle either in theme, atmosphere or origin of the author.

LeROY WOLFE WRITING AWARDS, Cystic Fibrosis Foundation, 3379 Peachtree Rd. N.E., Atlanta GA 30326. (404)262-1100. Contact: Public Relations Department. Annual. Estab: 1975. Awards $1,000 in each of two categories: magazine and newspaper. To recognize outstanding writing of published news and feature stories on cystic fibrosis and other children's lung-damaging diseases. Write for details and entry blank.

AUDREY WOOD AWARD IN PLAYWRITING, Kenneth Baker, The American University, Washington DC 20016. (202)686-2315. Awards $500 and production of play for the best original (unproduced) script of any length. Annual deadline: March 1.

WORLD OF POETRY CONTEST. Sponsored by *World of Poetry,* a monthly newsletter for poets. Write for details to *World of Poetry,* Box 27507, San Francisco CA 94127. Awards a $1,500 first place prize; $500 second place; plus 49 other cash or merchandise awards. Poems of all styles and any subject matter are eligible.

CAPTAIN DONALD T. WRIGHT AWARD, Southern Illinois University, Edwardsville IL 62025. Contact: Edmund C. Hasse. Sponsor: Southern Illinois University Foundation. Annual. Estab: 1971. Purpose: for distinguished journalism in maritime transportation.
Categories: Newspaper and magazine articles; books; photos and photo essays; tapes; and videotapes and films. Published submissions only. Award: bronze plaque featuring modern and historic forms of river transportation. Deadline: August 1 (for works published within the last two years). Contest rules for SASE.

WRITER'S DIGEST CREATIVE WRITING CONTEST, Write *Writer's Digest,* 9933 Alliance Rd., Cincinnati OH 45242. (513)984-0717. Awards 300 prizes worth over $5,000 (in cash value) for the best article, short story, and poetry entries. Deadline: midnight, May 31. Nonfiction, Fiction, and Poetry: All entries must be original, unpublished, and not previously submitted to a *Writer's Digest* contest. Length: short story, 2,000 words maximum; article, 2,500 words maximum; poetry, 16 lines maximum. Entries must be typewritten, double-spaced, on 8½x11 paper with the author's name and address in the upper left corner. An entry form must accompany each entry. Each contestant is entitled to submit one entry in each category. All entries may be submitted elsewhere after they are sent to *Writer's Digest.* No acknowledgment will be made of receipt of mss. Mss will not be returned and enclosure of S.A.S.E. will disqualify the entry. Announcement of this contest is made yearly in the March through June issues of *Writer's Digest.* Winners announced in October issue.

WRITERS GUILD OF AMERICA WEST AWARDS, Allen Rivkin, Public Relations, Writers Guild of America West, 8955 Beverly Blvd., Los Angeles CA 90048. Awards plaques in screen, television, and radio categories for best written scripts, to members only.

YOUTH MAGAZINE'S CREATIVE ARTS AWARDS, Rm. 1203, 1505 Race St., Philadelphia PA 19102. Awards $25 each to all entries selected for publication in the Creative Arts issue of *Youth*. Categories are creative writing, artwork, photography and sculpture. Entrants must be between ages of 13-19. Deadline: May 1.

Gag and Humor Markets

Markets in this section include information about cartoonists who are looking for gags, as well as other markets for humorous material. Submissions to cartoonists should be made on 3x5 slips of paper. Briefly suggest the scene and add the gagline. For convenience in identifying the gag, include some identifying code number at the upper left-hand side of the gag slip. Your name and address should be typed on the reverse side of the gag slip in the upper left-hand corner.

It should be noted that payment is usually not made for cartoon gags until the cartoonist has sold the cartoon and received his payment. Most of the listings for cartoonists indicate the number of gags they will consider as a single submission. The usual average is 10 to 20. Cartoonists usually return gags in 1 to 3 weeks. Individual listings cite the variations in reporting time, but cartoonists may want to keep ideas they've converted into cartoons for many years. They try to get them circulated everywhere, and in some cases, they may even resubmit them.

Originality is essential, but switching with a fresh idea is allowable. Allowances are made for coincidence since many gag men frequently come up with similar ideas. But submissions of "many that have been done before" will "turn off" the knowledgeable cartoonist and editor.

RAE AVENA, 36 Winslow Rd., Trumbull CT 06611. Cartoonist since 1965. Likes to see all types of gags. Has sold to *National Enquirer, New York Times,* and Pyramid Publications (paperbacks). "Gagwriters should send around 12 gags. Keep descriptions short." Pays 25% commission. Returns rejected material "as soon as possible." Enclose S.A.S.E. for return of submissions.

DOROTHY BOND ENTERPRISES, 2450 N. Washtenaw Ave., Chicago IL 60647. "Been in the cartooning industry since 1944, and have successfully hit all bases. Have sold panels and comic strips to top syndicates and single cartoons to publications in almost every field. When we receive your gag, it is carefully reviewed and, if we think it's salable, it is drawn up at once and sent on its quick way to a wide list of top cartoon buyers. If we reject your gag, it is returned to you within 3 days. Unsold, retained gags are returned to you within 3 months. We are happy to see all gags, with the exception of pornography, cannibal, monkey or elephant gags. Any common topic with a new, funny slant sells quickly. Also, more women should enter the gagwriting field because the many top magazines welcome submissions with a woman's funny viewpoint. And cartoons *should* be funny since they are meant to amuse and entertain. Bitterness and cruelty should be left out. Be professional and type your gags on 3x5 cards with your name and address on the back, and always enclose S.A.S.E. We send you 40% of the sale check the same day we receive it."

BILL BOYNANSKY, Apt. 13/20, Ansonia Hotel, 2109 Broadway, New York NY 10022. (212)787-2520. Estab: 1936. Purchased over 300 gags last year. Submit 15-20 gags at one time. Pays "25% for regular, 35% for captionless; all others—regular payment." Reports in 3 days to 2 months. SASE.
Needs: General, male, female, sexy, girlie, family, children's, adventure, medical. "Prefer to see captionless gag ideas on all subject matter, but no beginners; only those who know their business. I prefer to deal with cartoonists by letter or phone because it saves me time. However, I will respect and consider all mail replies."

JOE BUSCIGLIO, 420 W. North Bay, Tampa FL 33603. Cartoonist since 1941. Query first. State experience and if you are currently selling. General and family gags only. No sex. Pays 25% commission on sale. Currently selling to newspapers, trade journals, and house organs; also "ad" type art and some editorial panels. Will return promptly if material (gags) not adequate. Enclose S.A.S.E. No returns otherwise.

COMEDY UNLIMITED, 2 Edgemar, Daly City CA 94014. Contact: Jim Curtis. "We are always looking for fresh, new premise ideas for unique and creative standup comedy monologues, as well as skits involving two or three people, plus clever and original sight gags, bits, and pieces of business. We also buy original one-liners tailored especially for any of the following: comedians, public speakers, singers, magicians, or jugglers. Since we build everything from night club acts to humorous corporate speeches, it would be advisable not to submit any material until you have sent an S.A.S.E. and request our current projects list to find out exactly what we're most interested in buying during any given quarter. Keep in mind we are exclusively concerned with material intended for oral presentation." If S.A.S.E. is not enclosed with submission, all material will be destroyed after being considered, except items purchased. Pays $1 to $3 per line, on acceptance, and considerably more for zany, new premise ideas and sight gags. Reports in 2 weeks.

A. CRAMER, 1909 Quentin Rd., Brooklyn NY 11229. Cartoonist since 1942. Wants family gags. Gags must have funny situations. Sells to the major markets. Prefers batches of 15 to 20. Pays 25% commission. Enclose S.A.S.E. for return of submissions.

CREATIVE CARTOON SERVICE, 3109 West Schubert Ave., Chicago IL 60647. Contact: Peter Vaszilson. Cartoonist since 1965. "Creative Cartoon Service is an art brokerage service, arranging for sale of artwork between cartoonists, gagwriters and publishers. Please inquire before submitting your work to us." Enclose S.A.S.E. for response to queries.

DON CRESCI, 7 Jeanette St., Mocanaqua PA 18655. Cartoonist since 1965. Interested in general, medical, grocery slant (manager's viewpoint), offbeat, office, sophisticated, girlie slant, fishing, and golf gags, for use in all types of publications. Sold to *Medical Economics, Argosy, Saturday Evening Post, Progressive Grocer* and *Wall Street Journal.* Pays 30% commission. Returns rejected material same day received. Enclose S.A.S.E.

THOMAS W. DAVIE, 1407 S. Tyler, Tacoma WA 98405. Cartoonist since 1960. Interested in general gags, medicals, mild girlies, sports (hunting and fishing), business and travel gags. Gags should be typed on 3x5 slips. Prefers batches of 5 to 25. Sold to *Medical Economics, Sports Afield,* King Features, *Chevron USA, Rotarian, Saturday Evening Post, Ladies' Home Journal, Playgirl* and *Boys' Life.* 25% commission. Returns rejected material within 4 weeks. Enclose S.A.S.E.

LEE DeGROOT, P.O. Box 115, Ambler PA 19002. Began selling cartoons in 1956. Now interested in receiving studio greeting card ideas only. "I draw up each idea in color before submitting to greeting card publishers. Therefore, giving the editors a chance to visualize the idea as it would appear when printed...and thus increasing enormously the chances of selling the idea. Writer's percentage is 25% of selling price."

GEORGE DOLE, Box 3168, Sarasota FL 33578. Estab: 1952. Has sold to *Playboy, Parade, Penthouse.* Submit 12 gags at one time. Pays 25% commission. Reports in 1 week. SASE.
Needs: General, male, female, sexy, girlie, family, children's, sports, medical. Must be sophisticated, funny, etc., and submitted on standard index cards.

JOHN DUNCAN, 4845 Santa Ana, #10, Cudahy CA 90201. Cartoonist since 1975. Interested in general, family, children's, sports, animal gags. No girlie gags and unfunny situations. Has sold to *Alive, On The Line* and other major markets. Wants no more than 20 gags per batch. Pays 25% commission. Held about 100 gags from freelance writers last year. "I didn't buy any." Returns rejected material in 2 days. Doesn't return unsold gags. Enclose S.A.S.E.

JAMES ESTES, 1103 Callahan, Amarillo TX 79106. "Primarily interested in seeing good, funny material of a general nature. Always interested in a good strip idea. Most themes are acceptable, but the usual taboos apply. Submit on 3x5 cards or paper, 10 to 20 gags per submission; clear, concise ideas set down without excessive wordiness. Wholesome, family, general material wanted. I don't do sexy, girlie cartoons at all and it's a waste of gagwriters' postage to send that type gag." Has been selling cartoons for 7 years. Currently selling to *Changing Times, Wall Street Journal, Saturday Review, Physician's Management, Reader's Digest, Medical Economics, Boys' Life, National Enquirer, Saturday Evening Post* and *The Christian Science Monitor,* including several farm magazines, horse and western magazines. Returns rejected material as quickly as possible, usually in 2 to 3 days. Pays 25% of what cartoon sells for. Enclose S.A.S.E. for return of submissions.

MAL GORDON, 7 Elmwood St., Worcester MA 01602. Cartoonist since 1950. Interested in gags for cartoons for major or middle markets. "Gag must be good enough for at least $25 markets before I'll draw it up." 25% commission, when cartoon is sold. Sold to *Golf Digest, Writer's Digest, ADA News, The Rotarian, Golf Journal* and *Tennis U.S.A.* Reports in 10 days. Enclose S.A.S.E.

RANDY HALL, 1121 N. Tulane, Liberal KS 67901. (316)624-2431. Estab: 1974. Purchased 400 gags last year. Has sold to *New Woman, American Legion, VFW Magazine, Medical Times, Modern Medicine, Channels, Wallace's Farmer, Farmer/Stockman, Christian Century, Instructor, Massachusetts Teacher, King Features.* Submit 10-25 gags at one time. Pays 25% commission. Returns rejects the same day received, but "keeps gags going forever if there's a chance of selling them." SASE.
Needs: General, male, female, sexy, girlie, family, industrial, professional, children's, sports, medical, farm, religious, antique, education. "Must be original. I see far too much plagiarism. If it's not original, don't send it. Be consistent and don't send me 25th-round rejects. I like to get first looks occasionally, too."

CHARLES HENDRICK JR., Old Fort Ave., Kennebunkport ME 04046. (207)967-4412. Estab: 1942. Purchased 100 gags last year. Sells to local markets. Submit 10 gags at a time. Pays 50% of commission. Reports in 10-30 days. SASE.
Needs: General family, trade (hotel, motel, general, travel, vacationers). Safe travel ideas—any vehicle. Gags must be clean; no lewd sex.

DAVID R. HOWELL, 338 North E St., Porterville CA 93257. (209)781-4999. Estab: 1974. Purchased 50 gags last year. Has sold to *Writer's Digest, New Woman, Modern Medicine, Easyriders, Road King, Inside Detective, Western Horseman, American Machinist, California Dental Survey, Graphic Arts Monthly.* Submit 6-10 gags at one time. Pays 25-30% commission. Returns rejected gags same day as received. SASE.
Needs: General, female, family, trade (printing), professional, children's, medical, dental, horses. "I need gags that depend on the drawing to show idea; very original—not old, wornout type ideas. No girlies, or suggestive or offensive gags. I do a weekly panel for local paper on the printing and graphic arts trade. Have sold many cartoons to *Graphic Arts Monthly* which very much warrants my need for gags on the printing and graphic arts industry."

HUMOR HOUSE, Box 118, Northville MI 48167. Humor service for specialized publications and advertisers. Wants cartoon gags and inked roughs on banking subjects, family, office, general. Pays $5 for gags, $10 to $20 for inked roughs. Gags should be on 3x5 slips with coded numbers. Buys all rights and pays within 2 weeks after acceptance. Fast return of material. Enclose S.A.S.E. for return of submissions.

LARRY (KAZ) KATZMAN, 101 Central Park, W., Apt. 4B, New York NY 10023. (212)724-7862. Estab: 1949. Purchased over 100 gags last year. Has sold to *Modern Medicine, Medical Economics* and "Nifty Nellie" (syndicated feature). Submit 12-15 gags at one time. Pays 25% commission. Reports in 1 week. SASE.
Needs: "I use only medical (doctor, nurse, hospital) gags; no others." Must be submitted on numbered, separate slips.

JEFF KEATE, 1322 Ensenada Dr., Orlando FL 32807. Cartoonist since 1936. Interested in general situation and timely gags, sports gags (all sports in season) for "Time Out" sports panel. "Be funny. No puns, No oldies. No old hat situations." Has sold all of the major publications over the past 30 years. Currently doing syndicated newspaper cartoon panels for Field Newspaper Syndicate. Pays 25% commission. Bought close to 200 gags from freelancers last year. Holds unsold gags for "approximately 2 years unless gagwriter requests gag back sooner." Returns rejected material immediately. Enclose S.A.S.E. for return of submissions.

STEVE KELL, 733 Waimea Dr., El Cajon CA 92021. (714)440-5749. Estab: 1969. Purchased 25 gags last year. Has sold to *Penthouse, Oui, Playgirl, Saturday Evening Post, New Woman.* Submit 10-15 gags at one time. Pays 25% commission. Returns rejects in 1 week, but holds gags for 2-3 years. SASE.
Needs: General, male, female, sexy, girlie, medical, science fiction, farm. Material should be "fresh, surprising, funny, clean, neat, no misspellings."

REAMER KELLER, Box 3557, Lantana FL 33462. (305)582-2436. Estab: 1935. Purchased 400 gags last year. Has sold to all publications. Pays 25% commission. Reports in 2-12 months. SASE.

Needs: General, sexy, girlie, family, children's, medical. Prefers captionless ideas or very short captions. Does not want to see topical or general gags.

MILO KINN, 1413 S.W. Cambridge St., Seattle WA 98106. Cartoonist since 1942. Interested in medical gags, male slant, girlie, captionless, adventure, and family gags. Wants anything that is funny. Sells trade journals, farm, medical, office, and general cartoons. Sold to *Medical Economics, Modern Medicine, Farm Wife News, Private Practice, Wallace's Farmer,* etc. Pays 25% commission. SASE.

FRANK J. LEWIS, 2867 Gloucester Ct., Woodbridge VA 22191. (703)221-1789. Estab: 1957. Has sold to *Extra, Potomac News, Army Times* and *Navy Times.* Submit no more than 10 gags at one time. Pays 30% commission. Reports in 1 week. SASE.
Needs: "Looking for gags with political accent on anything from the Washington scene to small town politics to include social, environmental or economics. Also willing to work in conjunction with a writer on a strip idea."

LO LINKERT, 1333 Vivian Way, Port Coquitlam, B.C., Canada V3C 2T9. Cartoonist since 1957. Interested in clean, general, male, medical, family, office, outdoors gags; captionless ideas; greeting card ideas. "Make sure your stuff is funny. No spreads." Wants "action gags— not two people saying something funny." Has sold to *National Enquirer, Parade, Maclean's, Playgirl, Field and Stream,* and others. Prefers batches of 10 to 15 gags. Pays 25% commission; $25 for greeting card ideas. Returns rejected material in 1 week. Enclose S.A.E. and International Reply Coupons for return of submissions or 13¢ U.S. postage.

ART McCOURT, 3819 Dismount, Dallas TX 75211. (214)339-6865. Estab: 1952. Purchased all of his gags last year. Has sold to *Arizona Republic, Wallace's Farmer, Independent Banker, Prairie Farmer, American Legion, Mechanix Illustrated* and King Features. Submit 10-15 gags at one time. Pays 25% commission. Reports in 1 week. SASE.
Needs: "Something unique and up-to-date." Does not want to see anything on "crowds, TV, mothers-in-law or desert islands".

MASTERS AGENCY, Box 427, Capitola CA 95010. George Crenshaw, Editorial Director. Actively purchasing gags for "Belvedere", syndicated by Field Enterprises. Also purchasing gags for "Gumdrop", syndicated by United Features. Pays $10 per gag. Will send sample proofs on request. SASE.

RAY MORIN, 140 Hamilton Ave., Meriden CT 06450. (203)237-4500. Estab: 1959. Purchased about 12 gags last year. Has sold to *Boys' Life, Wall Street Journal,* McNaught Syndicate and King Features. Submit 7-10 gags at one time. Pays 25% commission. Holds gags "indefinitely", trying to redraw the cartoon from a different angle. SASE.
Needs: General, family, children's, medical.

IRV PHILLIPS, 2807 East Sylvia St., Phoenix AZ 85032. Interested in general, pantomime, and word gags. Submit on 3x5 cards. Pays 25% commission; $10 minimum on syndication. Also looking for beginning gagwriters to work with beginning cartoonists from his classes at Phoenix College. Enclose S.A.S.E. for return of submissions.

DOM RINALDO, 29 Bay 20 St., Brooklyn NY 11214. Estab: 1960. Purchased 70 gags last year. Has sold to *Penthouse, Oui, Hustler, Beaver, Gallery, Pub, Cheri* and King Features. Submit 10 gags at one time. Pays 25% commission on first 3 sold, 40% thereafter. Reports in 1 day to 1½ years. SASE.
Needs: General, male, female, sexy, girlie, family, professional, children's, adventure, science fiction. "They must be on numbered 3x5 cards for easy filing. The picture should be as funny as the caption. If you see most of my gags in certain magazines, aim your gags for one of them. I have not had much luck with medical gags or sports."

LEE RUBIN, 9 Murray Ave., Port Washington NY 11050. Interested in gags concerning eyesight, eyeglasses and optometrists. Submit maximum of 25 gags at a time. Pays 40% commission. Bought about 33 gags last year. Reports in 1 month. May hold gags for 2 months. Enclose S.A.S.E.

FRANK ("DEAC") SEMATONES, 5226 Mt. Alifan Dr., San Diego CA 92111. (714)279-7178. Estab: 1950. Purchased "hundreds of gags" last year. Has sold to *National Enquirer* and male

and girlie magazines. Pays 25% commission. Reports "immediately, but will keep unsold gags going forever unless return is requested." SASE.
Needs: Male, sexy, girlie. Must be new, fresh and funny. Would like to see ideas for "Eve's Eden," panel-a-day feature. "Adam and Eve gags, but *not* girlie or sexy."

JOSEPH SERRANO, Box 42, Gloucester MA 01930. Cartoonist since 1950. Seasonal and social comment preferred. Has sold to most major and middle markets. Pays 25% commission. Enclose S.A.S.E. for return of submissions.

HARRY SEVERNS, 1623 Boyd, St. Joseph MO 64505. Interested in gags for telephone, medical, farm, sports. No girlie or general gags. Prefers batches of 12 to 15 gags. Pays 30% commission. Has sold to *Modern Medicine, Private Practice, Dakota Farmer* and *Telebriefs.* Enclose S.A.S.E. for return of submissions.

JOHN W. SIDE, 335 Wells St., Darlington WI 53530. Cartoonist since 1940. Interested in "small town, local happening gags with a general slant." Pays 25% commission. Will send a sample cartoon to a gagwriter for $1. Does not return unsold gags. Returns rejected material "immediately." Enclose S.A.S.E. for return of submissions.

JOHN STINGER, Box 202, New Hope PA 18938. Cartoonist since 1967. Interested in general, family, and general business gags. Interested in business-type gags first. Would like to see more captionless sight gags. Currently doing a syndicated panel on business, for which funny ideas are needed. Has sold to *Argosy, True, Industry Week* and other major markets. "Index cards are fine but please keep short." Pays 25% commission; "more to top writers." Bought about 50 gags last year. Can hold unsold gags for as long as a year. SASE.

BOB THAVES, P.O. Box 67, Manhattan Beach CA 90266. Cartoonist for over 20 years. Interested in gags "dealing with anything except raw sex. Also buy gags for syndicated (daily and Sunday) panel, 'Frank & Ernest.' Prefer offbeat gags (no standard, domestic scenes) for that, although almost any general gag will do." Will look at batches containing any number of gags. Pays 25% commission. Returns rejected material in 1 to 2 weeks. May hold unsold gags indefinitely. Enclose S.A.S.E. for return of submissions.

MARVIN TOWNSEND, 631 West 88th St., Kansas City MO 64114. Full-time cartoonist for over 20 years. Interested in gags with a trade journal or business slant. "Religious and children gags also welcome. Captioned or captionless. No general gags wanted. Don't waste postage sending worn-out gags or nonprofessional material." Sells to trade and business publications and church and school magazines. Prefers batches of 12 gags. Pays 25% commission. Enclose S.A.S.E. for return of submissions.

BARDOLF UELAND, Halstad MN 56548. Estab: 1969. Has sold to *Parade, Legion, New Woman,* King Features, McNaught Syndicate. Submit 12-15 gags at one time. Pays 25% commission. Reports in 1-3 days, but holds unsold gags indefinitely unless return is requested. SASE.
Needs: General, family, medical and farm gags. No sex.

ART WINBURG, 21 McKinley Ave., Jamestown NY 14701. Cartoonist since 1936. Will look at all types of gags; general, family, trade and professional journals, adventure, sports, medical, children's magazines. Gagwriter should "use variety, be original, and avoid old cliches." Would prefer not to see gags about "smoke signals, flying carpets, moon men, harems, or cannibals with some person in cooking pot." Has sold to *National Star, VFW Magazine, Physician's Management, American Legion, New Woman, Highlights for Children.* Pays 25% commission. Returns rejected material "usually within a week, sometimes same day as received." Will return unsold gags "on request. Always a possibility of eventually selling a cartoon." Enclose S.A.S.E. for return of submissions.

ANDY WYATT, 9418 N. Miami Ave., Miami Shores FL 33150. (305)756-1439. Cartoonist since 1960. Interested in general, topical, family, business and mild sexy. "I like visual gags, but any good gag is okay. Pays 25% commission. Bought "over 100" gags from gagwriters last year. Will send a sample cartoon to a gagwriter on request, if S.A.S.E. is enclosed with request. Returns rejected material in "1 to 2 weeks if I definitely can't use; sometimes longer if I feel there's a possibility." May hold unsold gags "until I sell, unless a writer specifies he wants gags back at a certain time." Enclose S.A.S.E. for return of submissions.

Government Information Sources

Information and statistics on just about any subject are provided by the administrative, judicial, and legislative offices of the United States government. Often a writer can locate a fact that has eluded his library research by writing a letter to the proper government agency and asking them to supply it or suggest where it might be available. The government offices in the following listings have indicated a willingness to assist writers with research in their areas of expertise. For a more comprehensive directory of government offices, see *A Directory of Information Resources in the United States in the Federal Government* (available from the U.S. Government Printing Office).

Most of the agencies listed here issue booklets about their operations. Copies of these are available (often at no cost) by request, from the individual agencies. The research done by these government offices is usually published in booklet or book form by the U.S. Government Printing Office. Details on getting copies of this material are given in the entry for that office.

ACTION, 806 Connecticut Ave., N.W., Washington DC 20525. Contact: Director of Public Affairs.
Purpose: Federal agency established to administer volunteer programs in the United States and overseas. Programs include Peace Corps, VISTA, Foster Grandparent Program, Retired Senior Volunteer program, and University Year for Action.
Services: Provides writers with photos of *ACTION* program volunteers on their assignments. Writers may also obtain copies of news releases, bibliography of Peace Corps materials, bios and photos of senior personnel, and assistance in obtaining additional information sources within the agency.

ADMINISTRATIVE CONFERENCE OF THE UNITED STATES, 2120 L St. N.W., Suite 500, Washington DC 20037. Contact: Office of Chairman. Purposes are to identify the causes of inefficiency, delay and unfairness in administrative proceedings affecting private rights and to recommend improvements to the President, the agencies, the Congress and Courts. *Volumes I, II and III* of the *Recommendations and Reports of the Administrative Conference of the U.S.,* published in July 1971, June 1973, and June 1975 respectively, contain the official texts of the recommendations adopted by the Assembly, and may be obtained from Superintendent of Documents, U.S. Government Printing Office, Washington DC.

AGRICULTURAL MARKETING SERVICE, U.S. Department of Agriculture, Washington DC 20250. Contact: Director, Information Division. Responsible for market news, standardization and grading, commodity purchases, marketing agreements and orders, egg inspection, and specified regulatory programs. Provides various marketing services for nearly all agricultural commodities. Provides publications, photos, a catalog of available publications, and other assistance to writers.

AGRICULTURE, DEPARTMENT OF, Independence Ave. between 12th and 14th Sts. S.W., Washington DC 20250. (202)447-5247. Contact: Director of Communication. Directed by law to acquire and diffuse useful information on agricultural subjects in the most general and comprehensive sense. Performs functions relating to research, education, conservation, marketing, regulatory work, nutrition, food programs, and rural development.

AIR FORCE, DEPARTMENT OF THE, Established writers seeking information for use in articles concerning any aspect of the U.S. Air Force should contact its Magazine and Book Branch by writing: SAF/OIPM, The Pentagon, Room 4C914, Washington, DC 20330, or calling (202)697-4065/695-7793. This branch also provides a referral service to those authors engaged in historical research on the Air Force. The Air Force also has field offices in New York City, 663 Fifth Ave., (212)753-5609; Chicago, 219 South Dearborn Ave., Room 246-D, (312)353-8300, and Los Angeles, 11000 Wilshire Blvd., Room 10114, (213)824-7517.

AMERICAN BATTLE MONUMENTS COMMISSION, 4C014 Forrestal Bldg., 1000 Independence Ave., S.W., Washington DC 20314. Contact: Col. William E. Ryan, Jr., Director of Operations.
Purpose: "The principal functions are to commemorate the services of the American Forces where they have served since April 6, 1917; to design, construct, operate, and maintain permanent American military burial grounds."
Services: "By writing to the commission, writers may obtain reference information concerning the cemeteries, photographs, individual cemetery booklets, and a general information pamphlet which briefly lists and describes the cemeteries under our care. The commission publishes an information newsletter and periodically updates it as required. A copy of the newsletter may be obtained by writing to the commission."

AMERICAN FOREST INSTITUTE, 1619 Massachusetts Ave., N.W., Washington DC 20036. Contact: Information Services Division. Information and statistics for writers relating to America's forest resources.

ARMY, DEPARTMENT OF THE, The Pentagon, Washington DC 20310. Contact: Office, Chief of Public Affairs.

BUREAU OF MINES, U.S. Department of the Interior, 2401 E St., N.W., Washington DC 20241. Contact: R.O. Swenarton, Chief, Office of Mineral Information.
Purpose: "(1) Research on better ways of recovering, processing, using and recycling minerals, and (2) Gathering and publication of statistical and other data on the mineral industries." Programs include mine productivity research; mine health and safety research; research on mining and the environment; research on metallurgy and nonmetallics, including recycling; mineral industry developments, trends and forecasts.
Services: Provides photos (mostly of the Bureau's own research activities) obtainable from Division of Production and Distribution, Bureau of Mines, 4800 Forbes Ave., Pittsburgh PA 15213. "Minerals and Materials—A Monthly Survey" can be obtained from the Editor, Bureau of Mines, 2401 E St., N.W., Washington, D.C. 20241. "The Bureau of Mines is a good source of information on two main subjects: Its own research programs, and mineral industry developments and trends. Most of the Bureau's publications cover these two areas; we have very few that treat current industry practice on a relatively non-technical level (for example, we do not issue publications on "How Coal is Mined" for a high school audience). The Bureau has a staff of experts on all major mineral commodities, from aluminum to zinc, and these specialists frequently assist authors in research projects."

CENSUS, BUREAU OF THE, U.S. Department of Commerce, Washington DC 20233. Contact: Public Information Officer. Conducts and reports results of censuses and surveys of U.S. population, housing, agriculture, business, manufacturing, mineral industries, construction, foreign trade and governments. Statistical information is available for each state, county, city, metropolitan area, and for portions of cities and metropolitan areas in the U.S. A special reference pamphlet to help librarians and library users quickly familiarize themselves with the many reports available from the Bureau of the Census is being provided by the Bureau. The pamphlet, *A Visual Aid for Quick Reference to Basic Census Bureau Publications,* may be obtained from the Subscriber Services Section (Publications), Washington DC 20233, for 10¢ per copy.

CENTER FOR DISEASE CONTROL, 1600 Clifton Rd., N.E., Atlanta GA 30333. Contact: Donald A. Berreth, Director, Office of Information.
Purpose: "*CDC* is one of six agencies of the U.S. Public Health Service. It is responsible for surveillance and control of communicable and vector-borne diseases, occupational safety and health, family planning, birth defects, lead-based paint poisoning, urban rat control, smoking and health, and health education. Programs include epidemic and/disease outbreaks, foreign travel (health recommendations and requirements), international activities, training of foreign health workers, etc."
Services: "*CDC* provides reference and background materials and photographs on communicable diseases and other subjects. Publishes the *Morbidity and Mortality Weekly Report* and *Surveillance Reports.* Mailing lists are maintained and anyone may request these publications."

CIVIL SERVICE COMMISSION, 1900 E St. N.W., Washington DC 20415. Contact: Office of Public Affairs. Administers the civil service merit system and is responsible for competitive examinations for entry into Federal civil service. Library at central office of Commission in

Washington DC is outstanding location for research in personnel management. Material does not circulate.

COPYRIGHT OFFICE, Library of Congress, Washington DC 20559. Contact: Office of Information and Publications. Registers claims to copyright and provides copyright searches, free circulars on copyright subjects, and other related services.

DEFENSE CIVIL PREPAREDNESS AGENCY, Information Services, Defense Civil Preparedness Agency, The Pentagon, Washington DC 20301. Contact: Vincent A. Otto, Assistant Director, Information Services. Purpose is to prepare the nation to cope with the effects of nuclear attack and to help state and local governments plan and prepare to cope with these effects. An extensive file of disaster photos and movies regarding disasters and emergency preparedness available. Information and newsletters for the general public are available, many from state or local civil preparedness agencies, and also directly from above address.

DEFENSE, DEPARTMENT OF, Room 2E757, The Pentagon, Washington DC 20301. Contact: Magazines and Books, Defense News Branch, Office of the Assistant Secretary of Defense for Public Affairs. Assists magazine and book editors and writers in gathering information about the Department of Defense and its components.

DEFENSE LOGISTICS AGENCY, Cameron Sta.,, Alexandria VA 22314. Contact: Chester C. Spurgeon, Special Assistant for Public Affairs. Responsible for supply support to the Military Services, administration of defense contracts and various other logistics services. Will provide writers with information on Defense Logistics Agency areas of activity. *Introduction to the Defense Logistics Agency* available upon request.

ECONOMIC ANALYSIS, BUREAU OF, U.S. Department of Commerce, Washington DC 20230. Contact: Public Information Officer. Provides basic economic measures of the national economy (such as gross national product), current analysis of economic situation and business outlook, and general economic research on the functioning of the economy.

ENERGY RESEARCH AND DEVELOPMENT ADMINISTRATION, Washington DC 20545. Contact: Office of Public Affairs.

ENVIRONMENTAL PROTECTION AGENCY, Washington DC 20460. Contact: Public Information Center (PM215). Available literature includes popular booklets and leaflets on water and air pollution, solid waste management, radiation and pesticides control, as well as noise abatement and control. 16mm color films on pollution control and photos of pollution problems available by contacting Communications Division of Office of Public Affairs at above address.

FARM CREDIT ADMINISTRATION, 490 L'Enfant Plaza S.W., Washington DC 20578. (202)755-2178. Contact: Information Division. Responsible for the supervision and coordination of activities of the farm credit system, which consists of federal land banks and federal land bank associations, federal intermediate credit banks and production credit associations, and banks for cooperatives. Writers should confine areas of questions to agricultural finance and farm credit.

FEDERAL COMMUNICATIONS COMMISSION, 1919 M St., N.W., Washington DC 20554. Contact: Samuel M. Sharkey Jr., Public Information Officer.
Purpose: Regulation of all forms of telecommunications, broadcasting, cable, common carrier (telephone, telegraph, satellite), CB, safety or special radio.
Services: All material, except for certain special information (trade secrets, etc.) is available for public inspection. Does not do research for writers. Detailed material is available in FCC public reference rooms in Washington D.C.

FEDERAL JUDICIAL CENTER, Dolley Madison House, 1520 H St. N.W., Washington DC 20005. Contact: Mrs. Sue Welsh, Information Service. Purpose is to further the development and adoption of improved judicial administration in the courts of the United States. Information Service collection consists of books, articles, and periodicals in the field. Reference services and a few bibliographies are available. *The Third Branch,* free monthly newsletter of the federal courts, is also available. Information Service open to the public for research purposes and written requests, within the realm of jurisdiction, will be answered, with first priority to federal judicial personnel.

FEDERAL MEDIATION AND CONCILIATION SERVICE, 2100 K St., N.W., Washington DC 20427. Contact: Norman Walker, Director of Information. Purpose is settlement and prevention of labor-management disputes. Collective bargaining is the general subject of programs. Brochures and annual reports are available.

FEDERAL POWER COMMISSION, 825 N. Capitol St. N.E., Washington DC 20426. Contact: William L. Webb, Director of Public Information. Regulation of interstate aspects of natural gas and electric power industries, and licensing of non-Federal hydroelectric power projects. FPC will provide, free of charge, lists of publications and special reports, and general information on regulatory activities. Media representatives may also receive, upon request, a complimentary copy of non-subscription items on the publications list.

FEDERAL TRADE COMMISSION, Sixth St. and Pennsylvania Ave. N.W., Washington DC 20580. (202)523-3830. Contact: Office of Public Information. The Commission is a law enforcement agency whose mission is to protect the public (consumers and businessmen) against abuses caused by unfair competition and unfair and deceptive business practices; to guide and counsel businessmen, consumers, and federal, state, and local officials, promoting understanding among them and encouraging voluntary compliance with trade laws. Will assist a researcher with reprints, copies of speeches, or other documents pertinent to his subject. Most helpful when a writer's questions are specific rather than general. Publications available include *News Summary*, a weekly roundup of news stories emanating from the Commission.

FISH AND WILDLIFE SERVICE, Room 3240, Interior Bldg., Washington DC 20240. Contact: Office of Public Affairs.

FOOD AND DRUG ADMINISTRATION, 5600 Fishers Lane, Rockville MD 20857. Contact: Wayne Pines, Chief, Press Relations.
Purpose: "To protect consumers in the areas of food (except meat and poultry); medicines, cosmetics, medical devices, biologicals, and electronic equipment emitting radiation."
Services: Press releases available; writers can get on mailing list by writing to the above address. Brochures available on many subjects. Publishes *FDA Consumer* magazine, available by subscription through the Government Printing Office.

FOREST SERVICE, U.S. Department of Agriculture, 12th and Independence Ave. S.W., Washington DC 20250. (202)447-4211. Contact: Diane O'Connor, Office of Information, Room 3227, South Agriculture Bldg., Washington DC 20250. Responsible for management of 187 million acres of land in the national forest system; forestry research, and cooperation with state and private foresters. Works on multiple-use management programs, including forest recreation, timber management, range, watershed, wilderness, fire control, etc. Writers preparing material on specific subjects within the above areas may write the press officer. Photographs available.

GENERAL SERVICES ADMINISTRATION, 19th and F Sts. N.W., Washington DC 20405. Contact: Public Information Officer, (202)566-1231. The General Services Administration (GSA) establishes policy and provides for an economical and efficient system for the management of federal property and records, including construction and operation of buildings, procurement and distribution of supplies, utilization and disposal of property, transportation, traffic and communications management, stockpiling of strategic materials and management of government-wide Automated Data Processing resources program. Writers interested in obtaining government contracts should contact any one of GSA's 13 Business Service Centers across the country for information.

INTERIOR, DEPARTMENT OF THE, Interior Bldg., Washington DC 20240. Contact: Director of Public Affairs. The nation's principal conservation agency, with responsibilities for energy, water, fish, wildlife, mineral, land, park, and recreational resources, and Indian and territorial affairs. Requests for information should be directed to the office most concerned with specific subjects of interest. See listings for individual bureaus and agencies to locate the best source for information.

INTERSTATE COMMERCE COMMISSION, 12th and Constitution Ave., Washington DC 20423. (202)275-7301. Contact: Public Information Office. Has regulatory responsibility for interstate surface transportation by railroads, trucks, buses, barges, coastal shipping, oil pipe lines, express companies, freight forwarders, and transportation brokers. Jurisdiction includes rates, mergers, operating rights, and issuance of securities. Free list of publications available.

JUSTICE, DEPARTMENT OF, Constitution Ave. and 10th St. N.W., Washington DC 20530. (202)739-2014. Contact: Public Information Officer.

LABOR, UNITED STATES DEPARTMENT OF, 3rd and Constitution Ave. N.W., Washington DC 20210. Contact: Office of Information, Publications and Reports.

LAND MANAGEMENT, BUREAU OF, U.S. Department of the Interior. Washington DC 20240. Office of Public Affairs provides information and photos on the management of 473 million acres of National Resource Lands (Public Domain) mostly in 10 western states and Alaska; on forest, range, water, wildlife, and recreation resources; on resource uses including camping, hunting, fishing, hiking, rock-hunting, off-road vehicle use; and on primitive, historic, natural and scenic areas.

LIBRARY OF CONGRESS, Washington DC 20540. Serves as a research arm of Congress and as the national library of the U.S. Maintains reading rooms open to scholars for research on the premises. Provides bibliographic and reference information by mail only in cases where individuals have exhausted library resources of their own region. Such reference information should be sought from the General Reference and Bibliography Division. Free list of Library of Congress publications can be obtained from the Central Services Division. Photoduplicates of materials in the collections (not subject to copyrights or other restrictions) are available at set fees from the Photoduplication Service.

MANAGEMENT AND BUDGET, OFFICE OF, Old Executive Office Bldg., Washington DC 20503. Contact: Information Office.

NATIONAL ACADEMY OF SCIENCES, NATIONAL ACADEMY OF ENGINEERING, NATIONAL RESEARCH COUNCIL, INSTITUTE OF MEDICINE, 2101 Constitution Ave. N.W., Washington DC 20418. Contact: Office of Information. A private organization which acts as an official, but independent adviser to the Federal government in matters of science and technology. For writers on assignment, the Academies often can be helpful by identifying authorities in various scientific disciplines and sometimes by providing state-of-the-art reports on broad scientific and environmental subjects prepared by their committees.

NATIONAL AERONAUTICS AND SPACE ADMINISTRATION, Washington DC 20546. Contact: Public Information Office. Principal functions are to conduct research for the solution of problems of flight within and outside the earth's atmosphere and develop, construct, test, and operate aeronautical and space vehicles; conduct activities required for the exploration of space with manned and unmanned vehicles; arrange for most effective utilization of scientific and engineering resources of the United States with other nations engaged in aeronautical and space activities for peaceful purposes; provide for widest practicable and appropriate dissemination of information concerning NASA's activities and their results.

NATIONAL AIR AND SPACE MUSEUM, Smithsonian Institution, Washington DC 20560. Contact: Librarian, NASM. Purpose is to memorialize the national development of aviation and space flight; collect, preserve, and display aeronautical and space flight equipment of historical interest and significance; serve as a repository for scientific equipment and data pertaining to development of aviation and space flight; provide educational material for historical study of aviation and space flight. The Museum's Historical Library has books, drawings, photos, films, scrapbooks, and oral history tape records on all aspects of aviation and astronautics.

NATIONAL ARCHIVES AND RECORDS SERVICE, Pennsylvania Ave. at 8th St. N.W., Washington DC 20408. Contact: Public Information Officer. The National Archives is the repository for permanently valuable, official records of the U.S. Government. All treaties, laws, proclamations, executive orders, and bills are retained. It is also authorized to accept some private papers which deal with goverment transactions. Administering all presidential libraries from Herbert Hoover to Lyndon Johnson and 15 Federal Records centers across the nation, the National Archives was created to serve the government, scholars, writers, and students. Among its holdings are sound recordings, motion pictures, still pictures, and some artifacts.

NATIONAL CREDIT UNION ADMINISTRATION, 2025 M St., N.W., Washington DC 20456. Contact: C. Austin Montgomery, Administrator.
Purpose: "We have the regulatory responsibility to charter, supervise, examine and insure up to

$40,000 per individual shareholders' account in some 13,000 Federal credit unions, and to provide such insurance to qualifying state-chartered credit unions requesting it."
Services: "Reference information is available upon request. Available free are *Credit Union Statistics, Federal Credit Unions, NCUA Recruitment Brochure, Your Insured Funds, Organizing a Federal Credit Union.* Writers interested in the credit union story are offered assistance in developing their articles."

NATIONAL ENDOWMENT FOR THE ARTS, 2401 E St. N.W., Washington DC 20506. Contact: Office of Program Information. An independent agency of the federal government created to aid and encourage cultural resources in the U.S. through matching grants to nonprofit organizations and nonmatching grants to individuals of exceptional talent in the following areas: architecture and environmental arts, dance, education (does not include art history research projects which are handled through the National Endowment for the Humanities), expansion arts (community based, professionally directed arts programs), folk arts, literature, museums, music, public media (film, television, radio), theatre, visual arts, and special projects. Information brochures and latest annual report are available.

NATIONAL FIRE PREVENTION AND CONTROL ADMINISTRATION, U.S. Department of Commerce, Washington DC 20230. Contact: Peg Maloy, Director of Information Services
Purpose: "To reduce human and property losses from fire, in the United States, by half, within a generation. Programs include fire prevention and control through the National Academy for Fire Prevention and Control; The National Fire Safety and research Office; the National Fire Data Center; and the Public Education Office."
Services: Publishes a monthly newsletter, *Fireword,* bulletins, news releases, public education materials, brochures, reports (such as *Arson; America's Malignant Crime*), annual reports, annual conference proceedings, etc.

NATIONAL MARINE FISHERIES SERVICE, National Oceanic and Atmospheric Administration, Department of Commerce, Washington DC 20235. Contact: Public Affairs Office. Biological and technical research, market promotion programs, statistical facts on commercial fisheries, marine game fish, and economic studies are the responsibilities of this Service.

NATIONAL PARK SERVICE, Room 3043, Interior Bldg., Washington DC 20240. (202)343-7394. Contact: Office of Communications. Tom Wilson, Director. Provides information on more than 290 areas of National Park System which the Service administers. Information available includes park acreage and attendance statistics; data on camping, swimming, boating, mountain climbing, hiking, fishing, winter activities, wildlife research and management, history, archaeology, nature walks, and scenic features. Photos of many areas and activities are available. To obtain publications, contact Division of Public Inquiries, Room 1013, Interior Bldg.; to obtain photos, contact Photo Library, Room 8060, Interior Bldg.

NATIONAL TECHNICAL INFORMATION SERVICE, U.S. Department of Commerce, 5285 Port Royal Rd., Springfield VA 22161.
Purpose: "The National Technical Information Service of the U.S. Department of Commerce is the central source for the public sale of government sponsored reports, and of other analyses prepared by Federal agencies, their contractors or grantees, or by Special Technology Groups. *NTIS* sells research, development and engineering reports."
Services: References are available for use at Information Center and Bookstore, 425 13th St., N.W. Washington DC 20004. Photos are generally available on request. All of our periodicals and newsletters are available for sale on subscription basis or may be viewed at *NTIS* Information Center Bookstore."

NATIONAL TRANSPORTATION SAFETY BOARD, 800 Independence Ave., S.W., Washington DC 20591. Responsibility of this agency is the investigation and cause determination of transportation accidents and the initiation of corrective measures. Work is about 80% in the field of aviation; balance is in selected cases involving highways, railroad, pipeline, and marine accidents. Provides writers with accident reports, special studies involving transportation safety. Case history details of all cases available for review are in the Public Inquiry Section of the Safety Board in Washington DC.

NATIONAL WEATHER SERVICE, National Oceanic and Atmospheric Administration, Department of Commerce, 8060 13th St., Silver Spring MD 20910. Contact: Public Affairs Officer. Reports the weather of the U.S. and its possessions, provides weather forecasts to the general public, and issues warnings against tornadoes, hurricanes, floods, and other weather hazards. Develops and furnishes specialized information which supports the needs of agricultural, aeronautical, maritime, space, and military operations. Some 300 Weather Service offices in cities across the land maintain close contact with the general public to ensure prompt and useful dissemination of weather information. Agency publications may be purchased from Superintendent of Documents, U.S. Government Printing Office, Washington DC 20402.

NUCLEAR REGULATORY COMMISSION, Washington DC 20555. Contact: Office of Public Affairs.

OCCUPATIONAL SAFETY AND HEALTH REVIEW COMMISSION, 1825 K St. N.W., Washington DC 20006. (202)634-7943. Contact: Linda Dodd, Director of Information. An independent agency of the executive branch of the government. Functions as a court by adjudicating contested cases under the Occupational Safety and Health Act of 1970. Operates under the mandates of the Freedom of Information Act. Its files are open to anyone who wishes to inspect them. Publishes press releases and *Rules of Procedure.* Information available on written request.

OUTDOOR RECREATION, BUREAU OF, Department of the Interior, Washington DC 20240. Contact: Office of Communications. Serves as Federal coordinator of public and private outdoor recreation programs and activities; as administrator of the Land and Water Conservation Fund; as conveyor of Federal surplus properties to state and local governments for public recreation use. Provides information on national and statewide outdoor recreation planning; assistance available from other government and private sources; the L&WCF's Federal recreation land acquisition and state grant programs; Congressionally authorized resource studies for potential Federal recreation areas including national trails, wild and scenic rivers, lakeshores and seashores, Federal off-road vehicle regulations; Federal recreation area fee system; and sources of technical assistance, literature and research on outdoor recreation.

PATENT AND TRADEMARK OFFICE, U.S. Department of Commerce, Washington DC 20231. Contact: Public Information Officer. Administers the patent and trademark laws, examines applications, and grants patents when applicants are entitled to them under the law. Publishes and disseminates patent information, maintains search files of U.S. and foreign patents and a Patent Search Room for public use, and supplies copies of patents and official records to the public. Performs similar functions relating to trademarks.

RECLAMATION, BUREAU OF, U.S. Department of the Interior, 18th and C Sts., N.W., Washington DC 20240. Contact: Kathy Wood Loveless, Editor.
Purpose: "Operating in the 17 western states, the Bureau of Reclamation is responsible for water resource development. The agency conserves and supplies irrigation water, avails such water for hydroelectric power, recreation, municipal and industrial use, fish and wildlife enhancement, flood control, and other related uses of water."
Services: "Writers may obtain information services by writing the Public Affairs Office, Bureau of Reclamation, or by telephoning (202)343-4662. Requests for photographs should be addressed to Photography Office, Code 911, Bureau of Reclamation. Publishes pamphlets about various projects which might be useful to writers. These may be obtained by writing the above address, Attention Publications, Code 910.

SECRET SERVICE, 1800 G St. N.W., Washington DC 20223. Contact: Office of Public Affairs.

SECURITIES AND EXCHANGE COMMISSION, 500 N. Capitol St., Washington DC 20549. Contact: Office of Public Information.
Purpose: "To administer the securities laws, which have two basic objectives: (1) to provide investors with financial material and other information on securities and (2) to prohibit fraud in the sale of securities."
Services: Bibliographies of Commissioners are available. Write for Publications List.

SENATE, Senate Office Bldg., Washington DC 20510.

SOCIAL SECURITY ADMINISTRATION, 6401 Security Blvd., Baltimore MD 21235. (301)592-1200. Contact: Michael Naver, Press Officer. Administers the Federal retirement, survivors, and disability insurance programs and health insurance for the aged and certain severely disabled people (Medicare) and a program of supplemental security income for aged, blind, and disabled people. Publications on all social security programs are available free of charge from any social security office, or from the Office of Information, above address. Writers may also obtain statistical and historical information, news releases, photos, biographies of top SSA officials, and other information materials. Cannot provide information about any individual social security record or beneficiary. Under the law, all social security records are confidential.

SOIL CONSERVATION SERVICE, U.S. Department of Agriculture, Washington DC 20250. (202)447-4543. Contact: Hubert Kelley, Director, Information Division. Purpose is to help landowners and operators to use their land and water in the best possible manner. Assists local groups with flood, drought, excessive sedimentation, or other water problems. Main concerns are soil, water, plant, and wildlife conservation; flood prevention; better use of water by individuals and communities; improvement of rural communities through better use of natural resources, and preservation of prime farmland. In addition to material of interest to the agricultural and outdoor media, also has work in urban and educational fields that offer article possibilities. "We provide writers with background materials on all phases of our work; arrange interviews; provide b&w and color photographs. For information, write above address. We publish a variety of general and technical publications on practically all aspects of our programs and on soil and water conservation. Single copies are available without charge from Publications Branch, Information Division, Soil Conservation Service, U.S. Department of Agriculture, Washington DC 20250."

SOUTHEASTERN POWER ADMINISTRATION, U.S. Department of the Interior, Samuel Elbert Bldg., Elberton GA 30635. (404)283-3261. Contact: Miss Mary George Bond, Chief, Division of Administrative Management. Responsible for transmission and disposition of electrical energy generated at reservoir projects under the control of the Corps of Engineers in the southeastern U.S., and for water resources development. Will answer inquiries from writers regarding the bureau.

STANDARDS, NATIONAL BUREAU OF, U.S. Department of Commerce, Washington DC 20234. (301)921-3181. Contact: Chief, Office of Information Activities. The nation's central measurement laboratory, charged with maintaining and refining the standards and technology on which our measurement system is based. Covers the entire spectrum of the physical and engineering sciences. Provides the technical base for federal programs in environmental management, consumer protection, health, and other areas. Bureau publications are available through the U.S. Government Printing Office.

SUPREME COURT, No. 1 First St. N.E., Washington DC 20543. (202)393-1640. Contact: Barrett McGurn, Director of Public Information.

TENNESSEE VALLEY AUTHORITY, 400 Commerce Ave., E12A4 C-K, Knoxville TN 37902. Contact: Louis J. Van Mol Jr., Director of Information.
Purpose: "Regional resource development, including economic development, resource conservation and environmental protection, electric power production, waterway development, flood control, agriculture, recreation, fish and wildlife, forestry."
Services: "Reference information, publications, and photos are available on request. Technical libraries are at Knoxville and Chattanooga, Tennessee, and at Muscle Shoals, Alabama. We can arrange interviews and visits to *TVA* projects for interested writers." Publishes the *TVA Press Handbook* for factual reference; and the *Tennessee Valley Perspective*, a quarterly employee magazine; also various information bulletins on specific programs.

TERRITORIAL AFFAIRS, OFFICE OF, C St. between 18th and 19th N.W., Washington DC 20240. Contact: Director of Territorial Affairs.

TRANSPORTATION, U.S. DEPARTMENT OF, 400 7th St. S.W., Washington DC 20590. Contact: Office of Public Affairs, S-80. "We can supply limited photos and reference material, but we can usually put the writer in touch with the right people in the Department."

TREASURY DEPARTMENT, Room 2313, 15th St. and Pennsylvania Ave. N.W., Washington DC 20220. Contact: Public Information Office.

UNITED STATES CIVIL SERVICE COMMISSION, 1900 E St., N.W., Washington DC 20415. Contact: Director, Office of Public Affairs.

Purpose: "To administer a merit system of Federal employment. Programs include recruiting and examining, personnel investigations, equal employment opportunity, employee development and training, incentive awards, personnel management, employee benefits, intergovernmental personnel programs."

Services: Address inquiries to the Director, Office of Public Affairs. *OPA* will either respond directly, or direct inquiry to appropriate bureau or office within the commission. Publishes *The Civil Service Journal,* a quarterly for Federal and other managers; *The First Line,* a bimonthly newsletter for Federal supervisors; *The Federal News Clip Sheet,* a monthly news clip sheet for editors of Federal employees' newsletters, among others. "There are so many possible topics and approaches, it would be best to deal separately with each idea. Write or call the Office of Public Affairs, talk it over informally with an information specialist, get comments, suggestions, sources, etc., applicable to that idea."

U.S. GEOLOGICAL SURVEY (Department of the Interior), National Center, Reston VA 22092. Contact: Frank H. Forrester, Information Officer.
Purpose: "Major Federal earth science research agency. Through field and lab studies and investigations, obtains fundamental data and makes assessments of the nation's mineral, energy, and water resources. Programs include resource estimates, mapping, studies of surface and ground water, supervision of leases on Federal lands, studies of geologic hazards (earthquakes, volcanoes, landslides, floods, glaciers).
Services: "Our Information Office provides news media services: press releases, backgrounders, news photos, arranges interviews, etc." Publishes no periodicals or newsletters; however a variety of nontechnical leaflets are available, and writers may request press release mailings. "We would be pleased to receive inquiries from any writer on general earth science subjects, including natural resources and environmental monitoring."

U.S. GOVERNMENT PRINTING OFFICE, North Capitol and H Sts., N.W., Washington DC 20401. Contact: David H. Brown, Special Assistant to the Public Printer.
Purpose: Printing and binding services for the Congress, Judicial and Executive branches of the Federal Government; distribution of 25,000 titles of Federal documents to the public. Programs include printing production and innovations; mail order sales program.
Services: "Reference materials or information, etc., can be provided on an individual request basis. Writers may obtain Federal reference publications on a broad range of subjects—available through mail order or in 24 bookstores throughout the country."

U.S. SAVINGS BONDS DIVISION, Department of the Treasury, Washington DC 20226. (202)634-5377. Contact: Carolyn Johnston, Director, Public Affairs Office.
Purpose: "To promote the sale and retention of U.S. Savings Bonds, to help the United States government finance its debts in the least inflationary way possible and to encourage savings."
Services: "Services offered to the extent money and time will allow. For specific, local information on the bond program, writers may contact the state savings bonds director." Publishes informational leaflets, quick reference guides. "The Office of Public Affairs, Savings Bonds, will be happy to work with writers who have specific informational requests."

VETERANS ADMINISTRATION, 810 Vermont Ave. N.W., Washington DC 20420. Contact: Information Service 063. Administers laws authorizing benefits principally for former members and certain dependents of former members of the Armed Forces. Major VA programs include medical care, education and training, compensation, pension, loan guaranty, certain death benefits and insurance. Information is available at 58 VA regional offices. Two basic publications for veterans free from VA 27, Washington DC 20420, are 20-67-1 for Vietnam veterans (*Benefits for Veterans and Servicemen with Service Since Jan. 31, 1955, and Their Dependents*) and 20-72-2 for other veterans (*Summary of Benefits for Veterans With Military Service Before Feb. 1, 1955, and Their Dependents*). A third basic Publication (VA 1S-1 Fact Sheet, *Federal Benefits for Veterans and Dependents*) may be purchased from the Superintendent of Documents, U.S. Government Printing Office in Washington DC 20402. The 1978 edition is 85¢. Specialized pamphlets describing individualized VA benefits are available free from VA 27 and a small booklet describing VA itself (VA: What It Is, Was, and Does), is available from VA 063, both 810 Vermont Ave. N.W., Washington DC 20420.

WOMEN'S BUREAU, Employment Standards Administration, U.S. Department of Labor, 200 Constitution Ave., N.W., Washington DC 20210. Contact: Eleanor Coakley, Information Officer.
Purpose: "To formulate standards and policies which shall promote welfare of wage-earning women, improve their working conditions, increase their efficiency, and advance their oppor-

tunities for profitable employment." Programs include sex discrimination in training and employment, nontraditional jobs for women, special needs of low-income women, minorities, youth, women offenders.

Services: "Supplies its own statistical and other studies, bibliographies and a limited number of photos of women in work situations. Single copies of all materials are available upon request."

Greeting Card Publishers

Greeting card companies have specialized editorial needs, just as magazines and publishing houses do, so the successful greeting card writer must learn what kinds of cards each company buys. Many companies produce only a few kinds of cards; even big companies which produce all the standard kinds of cards may have staff writers to prepare some categories, so they may buy only a few kinds and ideas from freelance writers.

To submit conventional greeting card material, type or neatly print your verses on either 4x6 or 3x5 slips of paper or file cards. For humorous or studio card ideas, either use file cards or fold sheets of paper into card dummies about the size and shape of an actual card. Neatly print or type your idea on the dummy as it would appear on the finished card. Put your name and address on the back of each dummy or card, along with a code number of some type, such as 1, 2, 3, etc. The code number makes it easier for the editor to refer to your idea when writing to you, and also helps you in keeping records. Always keep a file card of each idea. On the back of each file card, keep a record of where and when the idea was submitted. Submit from 10 to 15 ideas at a time (this makes up a "batch"); be sure to include a stamped, self-addressed return envelope. Keep the file cards for each batch together until the ideas (those rejected) come back. For ideas you write that use attachments, try to get the actual attachment and put it on your dummy; if you cannot, suggest the attachment. For mechanical card ideas, you must make a workable mechanical dummy. Most companies will pay more for attachment and mechanical card ideas.

The listings below give the publishers' requirements for verse, gags, or other product ideas. Artwork requirements are also given for companies that are interested in buying a complete card from a greeting card specialist who can supply both art and idea.

Brief descriptions for the many types of greeting cards and terms used within the listings are as follows:

Contemporary card: upbeat greeting; studio card belonging to the present time; always rectangular in shape.

Conventional card: general card; formal or sentimental, usually verse or simple one-line prose.

Current needs list: see Market Letter.

Cute card: informal, gentle humor; slightly soft feminine-type card in which the text is closely tied to the illustration.

Everyday card: for occasions occurring every day of the year, such as birthdays and anniversaries.

Humorous card: card in which the sentiment is expressed humorously; text may be either verse or prose, but usually verse; illustrations usually tied closely to the text, and much of the humor is derived from the illustration itself; often illustrated with animals.

Informal card: see Cute card.

Inspirational card: slightly more poetic and religious sounding card within the conventional card line; purpose is to inspire, and is usually poetical and almost Biblical in nature.

Juvenile card: designed to be sent to children up to about age 12; text is usually written to be sent from adults.

Market letter: current needs list; list of categories and themes of ideas and kinds of cards an editor currently needs; some companies publish monthly market letters; others only when the need arises.

Mechanical: card that contains an action of some kind.

Novelty: refers to ideas that fall outside realm of greeting cards, but sent for the same occasion as greeting cards; usually boxed differently and sold at different prices from standard greeting card prices.

Other Product Lines: booklets, books, bumper stickers, buttons, calendars, figurines, games, invitations and announcements, mottoes, note papers, placemats, plaques, postcards, posters, puzzles, slogans, stationery, and wall hangings.

Pop-up: a mechanical action in which a form protrudes from the inside of the card when the card is opened.

Promotions: usually a series or group of cards (although not confined to cards) that have a common feature and are given special sales promotion.

Punch-outs: sections of a card, usually Juvenile, that are perforated so they can be easily removed.

Risque: card that jokes about sex.

Seasonal card: published for the several special days that are observed during the year; Christmas, Easter, Graduation, Halloween, etc.

Sensitivity card: beautiful, sensitive, personal greeting.

Soft line: gentle me-to-you message in greeting form.

Studio: contemporary cards using short, punchy gags in keeping with current humor vogues and trends; always rectangular in shape.

Topical: ideas or cards containing subjects that are currently the topic of discussion.

Visual gags: a gag in which most, if not all, the humor depends upon the drawing or series of drawings used in the card; similar to captionless cartoons.

Study the various types of cards available at your local card shops to see what's currently selling. Another excellent source for learning to write for the greeting card publishers is the complete handbook on writing and selling greeting cards—*The Greeting Card Writer's Handbook,* edited by H. Joseph Chadwick (*Writer's Digest*).

AMBERLEY GREETING CARD CO., P.O. Box 37902, Cincinnati OH 45222. (513)242-6630. Editor: Herb Crown. Buys all rights. Send for list of current needs. Submit ideas on regular 3x5 cards. "We always take a closer look if artwork (a rough sketch on a separate sheet of paper that shows how the card would appear) is submitted with the gag. It gives us a better idea of what the writer has in mind." Do not send conventional cards. Reports in 3 to 4 weeks. May hold ideas for approximately 2 weeks. Enclose S.A.S.E. for return of submissions.

Humorous, Studio and Promotions: Buys all kinds of studio and humorous everyday cards, "including odd captions such as promotion, apology, etc. Birthday studio is still the best selling caption. We never get enough. We look for belly laugh humor, not cute. All types of risque are accepted. No ideas with attachments. We prefer short and snappy ideas. The shorter gags seem to sell best. We are in special need of get well and hospital studio." Would prefer not to see Easter, Mother's Day, and Father's Day ideas. Pays $25. Occasionally buys promotion ideas. Payment negotiable, "depending entirely upon our need, the quantity, and work involved."

Other Product Lines: Promotions, plaques, mottoes, postcards, buttons, and bumper stickers. "Humor is what we look for in other product lines." Pays $25 for mottoes and bumper stickers.

AMERICAN GREETINGS CORPORATION, 10500 American Rd., Cleveland OH 44144. Buys all rights. Pays on acceptance. "A tough, but worthwhile market to crack. Always willing to review new concepts. Newcomers welcomed, but freelancers are competing with a large, professional staff of in-house writers. Always research the card racks before submitting ideas. Like to see total card-line concepts as well as individual card ideas." Reports in 4 weeks. Enclose S.A.S.E.

Conventional: Considers holiday material, but chances are always better with everyday occasions. No limits on the type of material used, as long as it's of professional quality, and salable. Most sales made are by copy which captures some fundamental aspect of people-to-people sentiment. Verse, or prose; any length. Material should be directed to Editor, General Editorial.

Soft Touch: "'Conversational' is the word to describe our style here. We are looking for sincere and simple (but not trite) ways to say 'Happy Birthday', 'Get better soon', 'I love you" and 'I'm glad we're friends'. We look at any idea, any time, and are in the market for the captions mentioned above." Direct material to Soft Touch Editor.

Humorous: "Our humorous line ranges from whimsical compliments to zap-em punch lines. Besides the usual birthday, get well and friendship directions, we're in the market for family captions, especially mother, father, brother, sister, daughter and son. We don't buy *much* here, but we're always interested in new and original approaches." Send ideas to Humor Editor.

Studio: "We're looking for funny and fresh material — try for the unexpected inside line. We look at anything, any time — birthdays, get well, friendship, holiday," These ideas should be addressed to Studio Editor.

Juvenile: "Our juvenile cards range from baby's first birthday to young adult. We don't buy many freelance verses, but we are always interested in concept directions in the things-to-do or novelty areas." Juvenile concepts should be directed to the Juvenile Editor.

Other Product Lines: Calendars, books and promotional concepts.

BARKER GREETING CARD CO., Rust Craft Park, Dedham MA 02026. Humorous Director: Bill Bridgeman. Submissions should be typed or neatly printed on separate 3x5 cards or folded paper. Name, address and a code number should be on back of each idea submitted. SASE must accompany each batch. Artwork on ideas is not necessary. Reports in 1-3 weeks. Buys all rights. Pays on acceptance. Send SASE for Market Letter.

Needs: Studio card ideas for all everyday and seasonal captions; special need for card ideas involving the use of mechanicals and attachments. Some risque (sex and physical humor) ideas are also needed. Specific needs are detailed in their periodic Market Letter. Seasonal needs include Christmas, Hanukkah, Valentine's Day, St. Patrick's Day, Mother's Day, Father's Day, graduation, Halloween and Thanksgiving. Everyday captions are birthday, friendship and get well. "All verse should be as concise as possible." Promotions, mottoes, etc., may be submitted at any time.

Payment: Humorous and studio, $25.

BRILLIANT ENTERPRISES, 117 W. Valerio St., Santa Barbara CA 93101. Editor: Ashleigh Brilliant. Buys all rights. Will send a catalog and sample set for $1. Submit seasonal material any time. "Submit words and art in black on 5½x3½ horizontal, thin white paper. Regular bond okay, but no card or cardboard." Does not want to see "topical references, subjects limited to American culture, or puns." Reports "usually in 10 days." Enclose S.A.S.E.

Other Product Lines: Postcards. "All our cards are everyday cards in the sense that they are not intended only for specific seasons, holidays, or occasions." Messages should be "of a highly original nature, emphasizing subtlety, simplicity, insight, wit, profundity, beauty, and felicity of expression. Accompanying art should be in the nature of oblique commentary or decoration rather than direct illustration. Messages should be of universal appeal, capable of being appreciated by all types of people and of being easily translated into other languages. Since our line of cards is highly unconventional, it is essential that freelancers study it before submitting." Limit of 17 words per card. Pays $25 for "complete ready-to-print word and picture design."

COLORTYPE SERVICES OF LOS ANGELES, INC., 4374 E. La Palma Ave., Anaheim CA 92807. Reports in 4 to 6 weeks. Enclose S.A.S.E.

Sensitivity and Studio: Friendship and nature themes only. No everyday general cards. Body humor and risque. Brevity is important. Contemporary themes only. Payment negotiable, but conforms with established schedules.

CREATIVE PAPERS, INC., Box 448, Jaffrey NH 03452. Director: Lew Fifield. "Send photocopies that we can keep, simply because we do not have the time to write to each individual that submits work. If work is submitted to be returned, include a cover note and SASE." Reports in 4 weeks. Buys all reproduction rights to the concept of existing art, or reproduction rights for a specified product, or the original art and exclusive reproduction rights. Pays on acceptance. Free information sheet and registration form available for postcard request.

Needs: "We are looking for a fresh approach to copy ideas—clever, sophisticated. We are interested in verse and *good* poetry that expresses popular sentiments, and 1- and 2-line copy and card ideas." Especially interested in material for Christmas, Valentine's Day, get well, Easter, birthday, love, sorry, thank you, congratulations, thinking of you, best wishes and invitations. Does not want to see copy for studio cards. Seasonal/holiday material must be submitted a year in advance. "We prefer simple verse rather than long, melodramatic verses— copy that is intelligent and thoughtful." Open for new ideas for posters, puzzles, gift books, greeting books, postcards, games, calendars and buttons.

Payment: Soft line, sensitivity, humorous, conventional, inspirational, informal, juvenile, invitations, announcements, $10.

CUSTOM CARD OF CANADA, LTD., 1239 Adanac St., Vancouver, B.C., Canada V6A 2C8. (604)253-4444. Editor: E. Bluett. Submit ideas on 3x5 cards or small mock-ups. Reports in 3-6 weeks. Buys all rights. Pays on acceptance. Current needs list available for SASE and 10¢.

Needs: All types, both risque and non-risque. "The shorter, the better." Birthday, belated birthday, get well, anniversary, thank you, congratulations, miss you, new job, etc. Seasonal ideas needed for Christmas by March; Valentine's Day (September); graduation (December); Mother's Day and Father's Day (December).

Payment: Studio, etc., $25 minimum.

THE DRAWING BOARD, INC., 256 Regal Row, Dallas TX 75221. Editorial Director: Jimmie Fitzgerald. Type ideas on 3x5 cards with name and address on back of each, along with code number and SASE. Reports in 2 weeks. Buys all rights. Pays on acceptance. Current needs list available for SASE.

Needs: Studio, general, humorous, clever, good prose for everyday and seasonals. Birthday, cheer, friendship, anniversary, baby, congratulations, Christmas, Easter, St. Patrick's, graduation, Mother's Day, Father's Day, Thanksgiving, Halloween, Valentine's Day. Good strong prose for all seasonals and everyday. No sex humor.

Payment: Humorous, studio, conventional, inspirational, informal, juvenile, invitations, announcements, $30-40.

THE EVERGREEN PRESS, P.O. Box 4971, Walnut Creek CA 94596. (415)825-7850. Editor: Malcolm Nielsen. Buys all rights. Pays on publication. Write for specifications sheet. Submit Christmas material any time. "Initial offering may be in the rough. Will not publish risque or 'cute' art." Reports in 2 weeks. Enclose S.A.S.E.

Conventional, Inspirational, and Studio: Interested in submissions from artists. Publishes everyday cards in a "very specialized series using verse from Shakespeare, for example. Our major line is Christmas. We avoid the Christmas cliches and attempt to publish offbeat type of art. For Christmas cards, we do not want Santa Claus, Christmas trees, wreaths, poodle dogs or kittens. We don't want sentimental, coy or cloying types of art. For everyday greeting cards we are interested in series of cards with a common theme. We are not interested in single designs with no relation to each other. We can use either finished art which we will separate or can use the artist's separations. Our studio lines are a complete series with a central theme for the series. We do not try to compete in the broad studio line, but only with specialized series. We do not purchase verse alone, but only complete card ideas, including verse and art." Payment for art on "royalty basis, depending on the form in which it is submitted."

Other Product Lines: Bookplates, note papers, invitations, children's books, stationery. Payment negotiated.

D. FORER AND CO., 511 E. 72 St., New York NY 10021. Editor: Barbara Schaffer. Buys all rights. Pays on acceptance. Sometimes holds material up to 3 weeks. Enclose S.A.S.E.

Informal and Humorous: Anniversary, thank you, new home, birthday, get well, engagement, and general cards. A hint of risque. Cute humor. "We read all occasions all year round; Valentine, Christmas, Father's Day, Mother's Day. We prefer 3-to-4 line verse. Pay $20 for verse, $50 for humorous ideas."

Other Product Lines: Promotions, mottoes, postcards.

FRAN MAR GREETING CARDS, LTD., Box 1057, Mt. Vernon NY 10550. (914)664-5060. Editor: Stan Cohen. Submit ideas in small batches (no more than 15 in a batch) on 3x5 sheets or cards. SASE. Reports in 2 weeks. Buys all rights. Pays on acceptance. Current needs list available for SASE.

Needs: Risque and soft humor, informal, studio and humorous. "Prefer copy with a little punch inside. Long copy is not desirable. No juvenile, sympathy, or religious ideas. Presently not using seasonal material" Seeks material for all everyday categories (birthday, get well, friendship) and special titles (relative birthday, general birthday, thank you, engagement, etc.).

Payment: Soft line, $15-35. Humorous, studio, informal, juvenile, invitations, announcements, $15-25.

Other Product Lines: Promotions, $15-50; mottoes, $15-25; plaques, $15-50. "Ideas for plaques should be short and strictly friendship." Also interested in novelty stationery and novelty items pertinent to stationery area.

GIBSON GREETING CARDS, INC., 2100 Section Rd., Cincinnati OH 45237. Editorial Director: Laurie Kohl. Submit ideas on file cards, 10-15 at one time. SASE. Address materials to editor of appropriate line (Vivian Kuhn, seasonal; Alice Davidson, everyday, studio, humorous; Jean Timberlake, jubenile, cute; and June Daugherty, ancillary products). Reports in 2-3 weeks. Buys all rights. Pays on acceptance. Free information sheet for writers; write to editorial department.

Needs: Humorous, studio, conventional everyday and seasonal, cute and juvenile. "For humorous and studio, we look for short, original, punchy, funny, sendable, contemporary ideas. We can't use attachments or very tricky hand folds, but are always interested in clever use of a simple fold. For the other lines, we look for a different idea and/or an original way of expressing the usual sentiments. Prose, or rhymed verse. We'd like to see more good, fresh, humorous material—short, clever ideas with good illustration possibilities for an unexpected ending inside. Also, good conventional rhymed verse, both everyday and seasonal, a fresh approach, with good rhyme and meter, and contemporary wording with different rhyming words. We do not purchase inspirational material; we use Helen Steiner Rice's material for our inspirational line. However, we do purchase religious verse and prose for the major sending situations and seasons. We can't use poetry, except as it ties in with a direct message and greeting card category. Send ideas for all the usual seasons; Christmas and Valentine's Day are the largest, followed by Mother's and Father's Day, and Easter. Need various family categories and combination relatives for all of these (except, no family categories for studio). We work about 1½ years ahead of season. Need everyday cards for general and family birthdays; illness, cheer are our greatest needs; then, wedding anniversaries (largest categories are general and for various relatives), wedding, sympathy. We'd like to see more combinations of material; rhymed verse plus prose; 2- or 3-part prose; quotes with prose or rhymed verse, etc. Most conventional verse runs 4 to 8 lines, but can run to 16 or even 20, for a special 'page-2'."

Payment: Soft line (only very different sentiments), $10; sensitivity (rarely purchased), $20; humorous (needs good, short humor for relatives), $25-50; studio ("we like fresh, funny material you could send to anyone"), $50; conventional prose, $20; invitations, $20 minimum; announcements, $20 minimum. Also considers material for mottoes ("only new, original material, generous and humorous") pays $20.

VIVIAN GREENE, INC., 15240 N.W. 60th Ave., Miami Lakes FL 33014. President: Vivian Greene. Buys all rights. SASE. Pays on acceptance.
Needs: Only humorous, whimsical comic cards.
Payment: Humorous/studio, $25-150.
Other Product Lines: Gift books, $100-300. Greeting books, $75-300.

HALLMARK CARDS, INC., 25th and McGee, Kansas City MO 64141. Reports in 2 weeks. Tip sheets and needs list mailed on request. SASE.
Needs: Humorous, clever ideas, softer humor and rebus type writing, for contemporary studio cards and humorous, illustrated cards. No artwork.
Payment: $55 for an idea needing minor or no change in editorial content; $40 for an idea needing major or complete change in editorial content.

INTERMART, INC., Box 432, Cambridge MA 02139. (617)963-4400. President: V.G. Badoian. Reports in 2 months. Buys all rights. Pays on acceptance.
Needs: Will consider ideas and material for all types of cards, promotions, mottoes, posters, puzzles, figurines, gift books, greeting books, plaques, postcards, games. Copy limited to 4 lines. Payment by negotiation prior to acceptance begins at $100.

KALAN, INC., 7002 Woodbine Ave., Philadelphia PA 19151. President: Al Kalan. SASE. Reports in 1 week. Copyrighted. Pays on acceptance.
Needs: Ideas for good humor studios and adult (X-rated) studios; primarily birthday. Short verse preferred.
Payment: Humorous, $10-20.
Other Product Lines: Posters, $10-20.

ALFRED MAINZER, INC., 39-33 29th St., Long Island City NY 11101. (212)786-6840. Editor: Arwed Baenisch. Buys all rights. Enclose S.A.S.E.
Conventional, Inspirational, Informal, and Juvenile: All types of cards and ideas. Traditional material. All seasonals and occasionals wanted. Payment for card ideas negotiated on individual basis only.

THE MAKEPEACE COLONY, INC., Box 111, Stevens Point WI 54481. (715)344-2636. President: James L. Murat. "Contact us before submitting material." SASE. Reports in 4-12 weeks. Rights purchased vary. Pays on acceptance or on publication, depending on the product.
Needs: "We occasionally purchase soft humor, friendship and other related greeting card and poster lines, plus occasionally some poetry."

Payment: Soft line, sensitivity, humorous, conventional, inspiration; $10 minimum. Greeting books and plaques, $10 minimum.

MARK I, 1700 W. Irving Park Rd., Chicago IL 60613. Editor: Alex H. Cohen. Buys all rights. Reports within 2 weeks. Enclose S.A.S.E. for return of submissions.
Sensitivity, Humorous, Studio, Invitations, and Announcements: "The verse should fit the cards; humorous for the studio cards; sensitive for the 'tenderness' line. Also interested in Christmas, (both sensitivity and studio) and Valentine's Day (sensitivity only), Mother's Day and Father's Day (studio). Verse should be short and direct, typewritten on one side of 3x5 card." Length: 3 to 4 lines. Pays $25 for studio ideas; $25 for verse; $25 for sensitivity ideas; $25 for humorous ideas, and $125 to $150 for photographs.
Other Product Lines: Wall plaques and poster verse.

MILLER DESIGNS, INC., 9 Ackerman Ave., Emerson NJ 07630. Editor: Whitney McDermot. Buys all rights. Submit seasonal ideas any time. Reports in 3 to 4 weeks. Enclose S.A.S.E.
Soft Line, Humorous, Conventional, Informal and Juvenile: Birthday, anniversary, get well, friendship, bon voyage, birth, as well as ideas for invitations and announcements. Mechanicals if possible, whimsical ideas, clever, witty, and humorous. Also buys Christmas, Easter, Valentine's Day and Mother's Day. Prefers 1 line for front of card and no more than 2 lines for the inside. Pay is open.

NORCROSS, INC., 950 Airport Rd., West Chester PA 19380. (215)436-8000. Art Services Manager: Nancy Lee Fuller. Submit ideas on 3x5 cards with writer's name on each card and SASE. Reports in 3 weeks. Buys all rights. Pays on acceptance. Current needs list available on request.
Needs: Conventional verse and prose in any category (up to 8 lines). All types of humor for all occasions (prose and verse) with or without mechanicals. Risque is OK, short of X-rated type. Especially interested in general, relative and love prose and humorous verse (relative and all-occasion). Ideas for all seasonals also sought. Seasonal schedule available on request. No juvenile or X-rated material.
Payment: Regular verse, $11/line; short prose, $12 minimum; studio/humor, $25/idea minimum.

PATTIES PRINTS, INC., Box 341601, Coral Gables FL 33134. President: Robert Shea. Query first with samples (5x7 minimum). Verses should be submitted on individual index cards, with sender's name and address on the back. Reports in 3-4 weeks. Buys all rights. Pays on publication.
Needs: "Looking for strong new ideas in whimsical areas to promote friendship, birthday and get well wishes. Verses should be short (1-2 lines), sincere, but not sentimental. Open to all areas and ideas, except religious themes." Also seeking material for anniversary, wedding, engagement, thank you, travel, baby, etc. Special interest in the juvenile line for ages 3-8, as well as seasonals for Valentine's Day and Christmas.
Payment: Soft line, conventional, informal, juveniles, invitations, announcements, $15.

QUALITY INDUSTRIES, 550 Devon St., Philadelphia PA 19138. (215)438-5850. Vice President: John D. Harrison Jr. Reports in 2-3 weeks. Buys all rights. Pays "at the end of each year".
Needs: General, poetic, religious, humorous ideas. Nothing risque. No seasonals.
Payment: Soft line, sensitivity, humorous, conventional, inspirational, $25.
Other Product Lines: Ideas and copy for bookmarks and wall hangings. Pays $25.

RUNNING STUDIO, INC., 1020 Park St., Paso Robles CA 93446. (805)238-2232. Editors: John and Dennis Running. Submit ideas on 3x5 cards. SASE. Reports in 2 weeks. Buys all rights. Pays on acceptance.
Needs: Captions and sentiments for two quality card lines: A contemporary, studio line and a more formal, elegant line. "We're looking for humorous, catchy, and ligh-hearted captions for all everyday occasions to go with cute and whimsical art, all in good taste. These should be clever and can be punchy, but not sarcastic or heavy gags. No Christmas. Our second line of pretty and elegant designs need soft, meaningful and more sincere type sentiments. Sensitive, traditional expressions in everyday language for all card sending occasions plus Easter, Valentine, graduation, Mother's Day and Father's Day."
Payment: $20 minimum.

RUST CRAFT GREETING CARDS, INC.,Rust Craft Park, Dedham MA 02026. (617)329-6000. Editorial Director: Karen Middaugh. Submit ideas on individual coded cards (one for each sentiment). Submit around 20 at a time to save postage costs, and enclose SASE. Reports in 2-3 weeks. Buys all rights. Pays on acceptance.

Needs: "New material needed most for masculine relations and double relatives, but will purchase material for any title if it is fresh and original, and usable to our market. We're trying to use more imagery in our line, as well as more additional copy for value at higher prices." Also needs ideas for all major seasons (Christmas, Easter, etc.). Particularly need good material for Father's Day and graduation. "Send ideas all year long. Freelancers should request our market letter to find out upcoming needs for particular seasons, however. We buy ideas for any season at any time, if they are good ones." Does not want to see humorous and studio ideas. Rejects short prose unless it is very distinctive and expresses an idea that is very original. Also rejects highly traditional verse that sounds like copy already on the greeting card racks. Verse length: No longer than 24 lines. Juvenile material: 12 lines.

Payment: Sensitivity, $10-25; conventional and inspirational, $15-40; informal, $15-30; juvenile $15-40 invitations and announcements, $10-25. Usable quotations (must be in public domain), $5-10; short book copy, (16 pages of verse or prose), $50-75; negotiable rates for promotional ideas and copy.

Other Product Lines: Mottoes, $15-30; posters, $15-45; greeting books, $50-75; plaques, $15-30; postcards, $15-25; calendars, $30-50. "Generally shorter material preferred. Need material which is cute and light in tone, but inspirational in message. Copy that suggests a design is also good. Can be verse or prose, and we do use some very long inspirational copy in the general style of *Desiderata*."

SANGAMON COMPANY, Route 48 West, Taylorville IL 62568. Editor: Stella Bright. Buys all rights. Reports in 2 weeks. Enclose S.A.S.E.

Everyday and Humorous: Verse for "everyday" and all seasons; also cute and humorous gags. Payment depends on quality, usually $1.50 a line for verse, and up to $20 for gags. Length: 4 to 8 lines.

STRAND ENTERPRISES, 1809½ N. Orangethorpe Pk., Anaheim CA 90630. (714)871-4744. President: S. S. Waltzman. SASE. Reports in 2 weeks. Buys all rights. Pays on acceptance.

Needs: Notecards that express one's feelings about love and friendship; philosophical and inspirational; faith; on marriage; children, human relationships; nature in short, poetic form (not too deep), prose or statement. Not over 16 lines.

Payment: Soft line, sensitivity, humorous, inspirational, $5-15.

Other Product Lines: Seeking ideas for humorous posters. Pays $15-25.

VAGABOND CREATIONS, 2560 Lance Drive, Dayton OH 45409. Editor: George F. Stanley, Jr. Buys all rights. Submit seasonal material any time; "we try to plan ahead a great deal in advance." Submit on 3x5 cards. "We don't want artwork—only ideas." Reports within same week usually. May hold ideas 3 or 4 days. Enclose S.A.S.E. for return of submissions.

Soft Line and Studio: Publishes contemporary cards. Studio verse only; no slams, puns, or reference to age or aging. Emphasis should be placed on a strong surprise inside punch line instead of one that is predictable. Also prefers good use of double entendre. "Mildly risque." Purchases copy for Christmas, Valentine's and graduation. Wants "one short line on front of card and one short punch line on inside of card." Pays $10 "for beginners; up to $15 for regular contributors."

Other Product Lines: Interested in receiving copy for mottoes and humorous buttons. "On buttons we like double-entendre expressions—preferably short. We don't want the protest button or a specific person named. We pay $10 for each button idea." Mottoes should be written in the "first person" about situations at the job, about the job, confusion, modest bragging, drinking habits, etc. Pays $10 for mottoes.

VISUAL CREATIONS, 25 Hamilton Dr., Novato CA 94947. Editor: David Lieberstein. Buys all rights. Send for current needs list. Sometimes holds material for 3 to 6 weeks. Enclose S.A.S.E.

Informal, Studio, Soft Line and Promotional: Short, simple, original and clever messages for birthday, anniversary, friendship, get well, invitations. "Only ideas pertaining to everyday general occasions. No other seasons. And no photographs." 2 lines only. Buys all year. Seeking original artwork ideas for promotional card line. Pays $25 per verse. Professional only. No strained humor, rhymes, poetry or "love" verse. "For our new studio line, we want original, humorous gags, slightly risque, to go with funny animals or graphic ideas." Pays $25/verse.

Picture Sources

There are many sources of photographs which may have just the illustration you're looking for. Some of these libraries, museums, agencies, and other organizations are included in the list which follows. Many offer free use of photos or charge only a modest fee. In addition, stock photo companies and agencies representing groups of photographers have photographs filed by subject on almost every conceivable topic. Fees for the one-time use of such photographs may vary from $25 for a b&w to several hundred dollars for the one-time reproduction of a color transparency.

Another source for photography (stock or "to order") is the membership of ASMP —The Society of Photographers in Communications. Some members are included below, and a complete list appears in the ASMP Membership Directory, which gives the name, address, and specialties of over 700 professional photographers. It is available from ASMP, 60 East 42nd St., New York NY 10017.

Writers seeking further details from any of the sources below should be sure to enclose an S.A.S.E. with their inquiry.

Several of the photo agencies say they charge "ASMP rates." These are minimum fees set by ASMP as a basis for negotiation, and actual charges may be higher, depending on use. For a practical, complete guide to ASMP rates and policies, *Business Practices and Photography Guide* is available from ASMP for $5.

ASMP also sets minimum fees for photographers working on a day rate. These are outlined in the Membership Directory.

Remember that the following listings are for agencies and institutions whose main concern is the *supplying* of photographs to writers and others. For a major directory of markets for your photography see *Photographer's Market* available from *Writer's Digest Books*.

JOSEPH ABELES STUDIO, 351 W. 54th St., New York NY 10019. (212)247-7860. Manager: Joseph Abeles. Photos of theatrical personalities, stage photographs of plays, musicals, Broadway and Off-Broadway. "Magazine rates and book rates $50 each. All are original photographs. No copies."

ALASKA PICTORIAL SERVICE, Box 6144, Anchorage AK 99502. Contact: Steve McCutcheon. 60,000 b&w, 70,000 color. "All subjects pertaining to Alaska from geomorphology to politics, from scenery to ethnical. We do not ship to individuals: only to recognized business firms, publishing houses, AV productions, governmental bodies, etc." B&w and color. Reproduction rights offered depend upon type of rights the publisher wishes or the advertising agency requires. Fees: minimum $50 b&w; minimum $150 color. "We do not charge a service or search fee unless the project has been cancelled, then only minimum ($15-50) depending upon the time the search required and the cost of transportation. We will accept certain types of assignments."

J. C. ALLEN AND SON, P.O. Box 2061, West Lafayette IN 47906. Contact: J. O. Allen or Chester Allen. 50,000 b&w negatives; 10,000 5x7 transparencies. "Specialize in agricultural illustrations made throughout the Corn Belt States; crops from soil preparation to harvest; livestock of all types. B&w prints are sold for one-time use unless special arrangements are made. Transparencies are usually rented but can be purchased. As long as customer attempts to be reasonable, we accept the rate established by a magazine or book publisher. Advertising use fees vary and are quoted after we know the details."

ALPHA PHOTOS ASSOCIATES, 251 Park Ave. S., New York NY 10010. Manager: Ann Schrieber. One million photos in "almost every conceivable category." Offers "any rights client is willing to purchase. Pictures can even be bought for outright purchase if desired." Fees depend on use.

ALPINE PHOTOGRAPHY, W. Summit Rd., East Route, Monticello UT 34535. (801)587-2553. Contact: Lee Miller. 5,000 photos on file on purchase basis for all rights.

Subjects: Nature, scenics, scientific, snow crystals, winter recreation, farming, ranching, livestock, outdoor life. B&w (8x10) and 35mm color transparencies.
Reproduction fee: $5-500. Prints made to order/$1-35.

ALUMINUM COMPANY OF AMERICA, Alcoa Building, Pittsburgh PA 15219. Contact: A.T. Post, Manager, Financial Communication. Many thousands of photos in "color and b&w on practically everything concerning aluminum —mining, refining, smelting, fabricating, products, uses, etc." Offers worldwide rights. No fees.

THE AMERICAN MUSEUM OF NATURAL HISTORY, Photography Department, Central Park West at 79th St., New York NY 10024. The Photography Department has a library of about 16,000 color transparencies and over 500,000 b&w negatives available for reproduction. Collection includes anthropology, archaeology, primitive art, botany, geology, mineralogy, paleontology, zoology, and some astronomy. Fees and other information will be supplied on request.

AMERICAN PETROLEUM INSTITUTE, 2101 L St., N.W., Washington DC 20037. Contact: Earl A. Ross, Manager, Print Media. Photos pertaining to petroleum. B&w glossies. For non-commercial, non-advertising use only. Credit line required.

AMERICAN STOCK PHOTOS, 6842 Sunset Blvd., Hollywood CA 90028. (213)469-3908. Contact: Al Greene or Yvonne Binder. Nearly 2 million photos. "All subjects: contemporary and historical. Mostly b&w; some color transparencies 4x5 or larger." Offers any rights desired. Only restrictions are limited to previous sales; i.e., 1 year calendar exclusive. Fees: "based on public exposure. $25 minimum."

AMERICAN TRUCKING ASSOCIATIONS, INC., 1616 P St., N.W., Washington DC 20036. (202)797-5236. Contact: News Service Department, Media and Public Relations Division. B&w photographs of different types of trucks (twin trailers, auto carrier, livestock, etc.) and trucks in various situations (traffic, urban, night, etc.). Limited number of color prints available for non-commercial use only. No fees but credit line and return of pictures required. (Pictures not available for advertising purposes.)

ANIMALS ANIMALS, 203 W. 81st St., New York NY 10024. (212)580-9595. Contact: Nancy Henderson. "Hundreds of thousands of pictures of animals from all over the world in their natural habitat in color and in b&w. Mammals, reptiles, amphibians, fish, birds, invertibrates, horses, dogs, cats, etc. One-time use, world rights, foreign language. Service fee of $25 if no sale is made —applicable only on lengthy requests. All uses, if unusual, are negotiable. We follow the ASMP guidelines."

APPEL COLOR PHOTOGRAPHY, Twin Lakes WI 53181. (414)877-2303. Contact: Thomas H. Appel. "Multi-thousands of color photographs" available for purchase. "Will sell any rights." Stocks historicals, points of interest, travel, general scenes, national parks, juveniles, human interest, outdoor sports (specialists in sports spectaculars), spectator sports, wildlife, girls, food, flowers, still lifes, young adult activities, gardens, farms, sunsets, lighthouses, covered bridges, grist mills, bridges, churches, industry, national phenomena, etc; U.S. and some foreign. Return required. Fees vary upon use and nature of publication.

ARIZONA PHOTOGRAPHIC ASSOCIATES' INC., 2350 W. Holly, Phoenix AZ 85009. (602)258-6551. Contact: Dorothy McLaughlin. 250,000 photos available for purchase. Reproduction rights, advertising rights, first rights, second rights, editorial rights and all rights available. A collection from A-Z (animals-zoo) at ASMP code of minimum rates.

ART REFERENCE BUREAU INC., Box 137, Ancram NY 12502. Contact: Donald R. Allen, President, or Janet L. Snow. Have "access to over a million subjects in European locations. Painting, sculpture, graphics, architecture, archaeology, artifacts principally from European locations. B&w glossy photos may be purchased. Color transparencies supplied on 3-month loan only. We clear reproduction rights for any material supplied. Fees vary with the sources who supply material to us."

ARTISTRY INTERNATIONAL, Box 800, San Anselmo CA 94960. (415)457-1482. Contact: Dave Bartruff. 100,000 photos available on sale basis only. Reproduction rights, advertising rights, editorial rights, first rights, all rights. Subjects: World wide subjects for editorial use; color transparencies. Standard ASMP rates.

ASSOCIATED PICTURE SERVICE, Northside Station, Box 52881, Atlanta GA 30355. (404)948-2671. Contact: Buford C. Burch. 25,000 photos on sale basis only. Reproduction rights, advertising rights, second rights, first rights, all rights. Subjects: Nature, historical points, city/suburbs, scenics. Holding fee: $1/day/transparency after 14 days.

ASSOCIATION OF AMERICAN RAILROADS NEWS SERVICE, American Railroads Building, 1920 L St., N.W., Washington DC 20036. Contact: J. Ronald Shumate. B&w glossies on railroad subjects. No fees. Credit line required.

AUSTRIAN INFORMATION SERVICE, 31 E. 69th St., New York NY 10021. Contact: Library Limited. B&w photos of Austria. No fees but credit line and return of pictures required.

AUTHENTICATED NEWS INTERNATIONAL, 170 Fifth Ave., New York NY 10010. (212)243-6995. Managing Editor: Sidney Polinsky. Approximately 1½ million photos, b&w and color. Photo agency for all types of domestic and foreign news photos, stock photos on all subjects, including politics, pollution, geo-thermal and solar energy, etc. 50% commission on all photos sold; b&w and color. Credit line and return of photos required.

AUTOMOBILE PHOTO ARCHIVES, 206 W. 94th St., New York NY 10025. Contact: George A. Moffitt. 2,000 photos on file; loan basis only. Reproduction rights, advertising rights, editorial rights and all rights available. Subjects: Automotive; old, classic, postwar cars shown with personalities (movie stars, etc.). Both standard cars and custom American and European. Fees: $10 service charge. Holding fee of $1/photo after 21 days. B&w additional $35 for editorial; $50 for advertising use.

ROYCE BAIR, PHOTOGRAPHER, 1481 S. Main St., Salt Lake City UT 84115. (801)467-0322 or 561-0054. 5,000 photos available for purchase of reproduction rights only; very little material is sold outright. Subjects: Western states (primarily Utah and Idaho): agriculture, industries, outdoor recreation, scenics. "I follow ASMP guidelines and business practices. I also accept assignment photography." Fees: Prints, $4/print, plus reproduction fee. Holding fee: $1/photo after 14 days.

THE BANCROFT LIBRARY, University of California, Berkeley CA 94720. Contact: Curator of Pictorial Collections. Portraits, photographs, original paintings and drawings, prints and other materials illustrating the history of California, western North America, Mexico. Researchers must consult card indexes and book catalogs to the collection. The Library cannot make selections. Photographic reference copies are available for purchase; negatives and transparencies on a loan basis only. "Commercial users of our pictorial resources are asked to make a donation comparable to the per-unit prices charged by commercial picture agencies for similar materials." Credit line required: "Courtesy, The Bancroft Library." Rights vary with material.

BILLY E. BARNES, 313 Severin St., Chapel Hill NC 27514. (919)942-6350. 65,000 photos (b&w and color) available for one-time use only. Subjects: civil rights activities, poverty problems, education, people shots, rural scenes, industrial, youth in vocational education, scenics. "Shots on file are stock from 20 years of assignments for national magazines, company publications, audiovisual firms, etc." Will send 7-page descriptive index of stock files to prospective buyers; also available for special assignment. Fees: $35/b&w; $75/color transparency. Decreasing rate for multiple frame purchases. Special assignment $150/day in North Carolina; $200 outside of state.

BBM ASSOCIATES, Box 24, Berkeley CA 94710. (415)653-8896. Contact; Clinton Bond. 300,000 "b&w and color pictures ranging over all subject areas; emphasis on the San Francisco Bay area with a bit of everything from the rest of the world. Specialties: ecology, ethnic, children, nature, political, and radical photography." 1-time North American usage. Subsequent fees for additional reproduction. Fees: "Standard ASMP with consideration for certain budget problems."

RICHARD BELLAK — PHOTOGRAPHER, 127 Remsen St., Brooklyn NY 11201. (212)858-2417. About 10,000 photos on a wide variety of people-oriented subjects including migrant workers, Appalachia, children, elderly people, blacks in rural Alabama, youth scenes, third world people. B&w and color. Usually offers one-time, non-exclusive reproduction rights. Minimum fee for b&w is usually $50; $100 minimum for color. Unused photos may not be held longer than 10 days. All photos must be returned undamaged.

THE BETTMAN ARCHIVE, INC., 136 E. 57th St., New York NY 10022. Contact: Research Department. 6,000,000 photos on file (b&w and color). Available on loan only. All rights. All subjects. Holding fee, reproduction fee and service charge vary with material and use.

BIOMEDICAL PHOTO LIBRARY, Camera M.D. Studios, Inc., 122 E. 76th St., New York NY 10021. (212)628-4331. Contact: Library Division. 100,000 biomedical color transparencies and b&w negatives. The biomedical photos illustrate about 30 specialty areas of medicine, such as dermatology, allergy and rheumatology, dentistry, veterinary medicine, botany, entomology and other biological sciences. Also, photos of about 60 sites of normal human anatomy are availabe of adults and children, males and females plus matching skeletal views and, where possible, matching normal x-rays. The 132-page catalog, illustrated in color and b&w, costs $5.75 plus postage.

BLACK STAR, 450 Park Ave. S., New York NY 10016. (212)679-3288. President: Howard Chapnick; Executive Vice-President: Benjamin J. Chapnick. Represents 120 photographers for assignment work. Color and b&w photos of all subjects. Two million photos in collection. One-time use or negotiations for other extended rights. $75 minimum per b&w, $150 minimum per color. Assignment rates quoted on request.

BLACKSTONE-SHELBURNE NEW YORK, INC., 3 W. 30 St., New York NY 10001. (212)736-9100. President: Ira Fontaine. 180,000 sets of negatives. Photos (portraits) of person-alities, businessmen, dignitaries.

DR. BLOCK COLOR PRODUCTIONS, 1309 N. Genesee Ave., Hollywood CA 90046. Con-tact: Mrs. Fred Block. 3,300 color slides, 2x2. "Large collection in the art field. We have sold reproduction rights to publishers for prints in book publications." Credit line requested. Fee: "about $60 for single slide for reproduction." Requests return of originals. Request sheet avail-able of detailed list of photos and prices.

THE BOSTONIAN SOCIETY, The Old State House, 206 Washington St., Boston MA 02109. (617)523-7033. 10,000 photos on file for purchase. Rights for one-time usage. Subjects: People, places and events relative to Boston, mostly of the 19th century, but some 20th century mate-rial. Fees: $25 for reproduction. Prints made to order: $5. Photocopies: 75¢/page.

PHILIP BRODATZ, 100 Edgewater Drive, Coral Gables FL 33133. (305)858-2666. B&w and color pictures of nature, trees, scenics in USA and Caribbean Islands; clouds, water. "Textures" of many kinds. Rights offered for use in books or advertising. Fees depend on use —"whether for book illustration or advertising and one-time use or repeated use. From $25 up."

BROOKLYN PUBLIC LIBRARY, Grand Army Plaza, Brooklyn NY 11238. (212)636-3178. Contact: Elizabeth L. White, Brooklyn Librarian. The History Division's Brooklyn Collection contains about 2,300 b&w photos of Brooklyn buildings and neighborhoods. Also has photo-graph file of the Brooklyn Daily Eagle, covering photographs used from c. 1905 to 1955; it contains thousands of prints of national as well as local news subjects. Some of these are wire service photos and many have been retouched. The photographs cannot be borrowed, but appointments can be made (with a week's notice) for the user to bring his own equipment to photograph prints. Permission to use the wire service photos must be obtained from that ser-vice. There is no other charge or rental fee for use of these photos, but a credit line to the Brooklyn Public Library: Brooklyn Collection is required.

BUFFALO AND ERIE COUNTY HISTORICAL SOCIETY, 25 Nottingham Court, Buffalo NY 14216. (716)873-9644. Contact: Curator of Iconography. "Our emphasis is historical and regional; nineteenth and twentieth century materials of the Niagara Frontier. Reproduction fee depends on project. Publications are generally $15/item/edition." Credit line required.

BUREAU OF TRAVEL DEVELOPMENT, DELAWARE STATE VISITORS SERVICE, State of Delaware, 630 State College Rd., Dover DE 19901. Contact: Donald Mathewson, Tourism Coordinator. Approximately 2,000 photos. "Historic buildings and sites. Indoor-out-door photos of museums. Camping, boating, fishing, and beach scenes. Auto, flat and harness racing. State park nature scenes. Historic churches, monuments, etc." B&w and color. Rights offered unlimited, except credit line required in some cases. No fees charged. "Released on a loan only basis. Must be returned after use."

GUY BURGESS, PHOTOGRAPHER, 202 Old Broadmoor Road, Colorado Springs CO 80906. (303)633-1295. Contact: Guy Burgess. 1,800 5x7 color transparencies of garden scenes, plant portraits. 1-time use. Fees: $100 to $250. Return required.

CALIFORNIA STATE LIBRARY, Library and Courts Bldg., P.O. Box 2037, Sacramento CA 95809. Contact: Kenneth I. Pettitt, California Section Head Librarian. California historical pictures, portraits of Californians (mostly early residents) in b&w only. "Photocopies of specific pictures may be ordered by mail. Selection should be done at the library by the researcher. Names of private researchers, who work on a fee basis, are available. Fees for photocopies vary according to type and size of print. Credit line required."

CAMERA CLIX, INC., 404 Park Ave. S., New York NY 10016. (212)684-3526. Manager: Kent McKeever. Photos of children, florals, animals, historic points, sports, major American cities, scenics, art reproductions, and human interest. "Our emphasis is the calendar and greeting card type of photograph." Large format color transparencies. Rights offered are negotiable. Fees depend on usage and area of distribution. Return of prints, and credit line, are required.

CAMERA HAWAII, INC., 206 Koula Street, Honolulu HI 96813. (808)536-2302. Contact: Photo Librarian. Estimated over 50,000 color and b&w pictures of Hawaii; cross section of all islands, scenics, travel, aerial and general. Also selection of photos from New Zealand, Sydney, Bali, Manila, Taiwan, Hong Kong, Korea, Tokyo and parts of Japan, Guam; minor file of other areas such as Tahiti, West Coast; Washington, New York, Boston area; Quebec, Niagara Falls; spring flowers in Washington, Capitol, New York scenes and others. Usually offers one-time rights, but subject to negotiation according to needs. Fees dependent upon usage and rights required. Minimums generally in line with ASMP standards.

CAMERA M D STUDIOS INC., Library Division, 122 E. 76 St., New York NY 10021. (212)628-4331. Manager: Carroll H. Weiss. Over 100,000 photos of the health and biological sciences. Offers all rights. Credit line, tearsheets and return of prints required. ASMP rates.

CAMERIQUE STOCK PHOTOS, Box 175, Blue Bell PA 19422. (215)272-7649. Contact: Orville Johnson. B&w photos and color transparencies on a variety of subject matter. Selection can be sent on ten-day approval. One-time reproduction fee varies with importance of use, media, circulation, etc. Fee quoted on receipt of this information. Credit line required. Return of pictures required in 10 days, unless extended.

WOODFIN CAMP AND ASSOCIATES, 50 Rockefeller Plaza, New York NY 10020. Contact: Midge Keator or Woodfin Camp. Over 100,000 photos representing general geographic coverage of most countries in the world, with particular emphasis on India, Africa, Russia, Western Europe, South America, Southeast Asia, and the U.S. B&w and color. Fees depend on usage, beginning at $50 per b&w; $150 for color. Usually offers one-time, non-exclusive North American rights. Since most photos were produced from reportage assignments, there are no model releases for the subjects. Requests must be as specific as possible regarding the type of photo needed and its intended use, and rights required.

CANADIAN CONSULATE GENERAL, 1251 Avenue of the Americas, New York NY 10020. (Territory comprises Connecticut, New Jersey, and New York State only.) Contact: Photo Librarian. 8x10 b&w glossies of Canadian scenes and the people of Canada are available, gratis, on a loan basis from the Canadian Consulate General at the above address. Credit line required. Return of pictures requested.

CANADIAN PACIFIC, Windsor Sta., Montreal, P.Q., Canada H3C 3E4. (514)861-6811. Contact: F.E. Stelfox. "We can provide b&w and color photos of all kinds in various sizes from 4x5 to wall murals. Wide selection of historical subjects in b&w of the steam-loco era—ships, rail, logging, oil drilling, hotels, air, containerization. Senic views of Canada, cites, and numerous other subjects." Fees and credit line required.

CANADIAN PRESS, 36 King St. E., Toronto, Ontario, Canada M5C 2L9. (416)364-0321. 600,000 photos of current and historic Canadian personalities and life; mostly b&w. Canadian agents for Wide World Photos, Inc. Offers one-time rights. Charges $20 to $35 for b&w, depending on publication's circulation.

WILLIAM CARTER, PHOTOGRAPHER AND WRITER, 535 Everett Ave., Palo Alto CA 94301. (415)326-1382 or 328-3561. Contact: William Carter. About 30,000 photos on a variety of worldwide subjects, particularly U.S. Middle West, western ghost towns, children, show horses, Middle East, special subjects. Fees negotiable.

WALTER CHANDOHA, RFD, Annandale NJ 08801. (201)782-3666. 100,000 color and b&w pictures of "cats, dogs, horses and other animals. Nature subjects, weather situations, trees and leaves, flowers (wild, domestic, tropical); growing vegetables and fruits; sunsets, clouds, sky and scenics; water, conservation." Offers non-exclusive, limited exclusive, exclusive rights and outright purchase. Fees: Minimum $50 for b&w, minimum $150 for color and up to $3,500, depending on use. "We do not deal with authors direct; we prefer to work with their publishers."

CHICAGO HISTORICAL SOCIETY, Clark St. at North Ave., Chicago IL 60614. (312)642-4600. Contact: John S. Tris. 500,000 photos on file on Chicago history. "Collection is in the public domain. We exercise proprietary rights and sell or rent photographic copies of items in the collection." Print fee: $10 (b&w); $40 (color transparency). Holding fee: $10/week/item. "In certain instances, i.e., advertising, $75." Photocopies: 15¢ plus 50¢ service charge. Copy negative: $15 (30-day rental).

CINCINNATI HISTORICAL SOCIETY, Eden Park, Cincinnati OH 45202. Contact: Edward Malloy, Picture Librarian. Over 750,000 photos and slides of Cincinnati and Cincinnati-related material; general pictures on subjects such as World War I, urban decay, Ohio River transportation. B&w and color slides. One-time use, with fee for commercial use.

JOE CLARK, H.B.S.S. PHOTOGRAPHY, 8775 W. 9 Mile Rd., Oak Park MI 48237. (313)399-4480. 15,000 color and b&w photos on file for sale or loan. Rights vary with material and author. Subjects: city and farm subjects, Michigan, Tennessee, Ohio, Kentucky, Detroit, down South, people, pets, children, landscapes. Fees vary with material and use.

COAST GUARD NEWS & PHOTO CENTER, Third Coast Guard District, New York NY 10004. (212)264-4996. Contact: Photographic Officer. Photos available on loan. Reproduction rights available. Collection is in the public domain. Subjects: U.S. Coast Guard, search and rescue, marine safety, aids to navigation, recreational boating, oil pollution abatement, lighthouses, etc. Generally no charge to qualified sources for publication. Modest charges for personal collections, etc. Credit line required. Fees: Prints made to order, $1.25/b&w; $3-50/color. Photocopies, $3.15/b&w; $6-25/color.

BRUCE COLEMAN INCORPORATED, 15 E. 36 St., New York NY 10016. (212)683-5227. Contact: Norman Owen Tomalin. 300,000 photos available for sale or leasing. Reproduction rights, advertising rights, editorial rights, first rights, all rights. Subjects: Everything but spot news. Fees: $30 minimum service charge. $1/week minimum holding fee. ASMP reproduction fees.

COLLEGE NEWSPHOTO ALLIANCE, 342 Madison Ave., New York NY 10017. (212)697-1136. Manager: Ted Feder. 100,000 b&w photos and color transparencies of college life including political activity, people, current economic and social trends, urban and rural subjects, ecology. Offers one-time to world rights. Fees depend on the reproduction rights and size of reproduction on the page; average $50 for b&w, $125 for color.

COMPSCO PUBLISHING CO., 663 Fifth Ave., New York NY 10022. (201)962-4114 or (212)757-6454. Contact: Ernst A. Jahn. 40,000 photographs on travel, buildings, scenery, people, workmen, railways, roads in Mexico, Central America, South America, USA, Alaska, all Canada with Yukon Territory and British Columbia, Holland, Germany, Easter Islands, Tahiti, South Africa, Tunisia, Jamaica, Finland, Russia, Middle East Arab World, Robinson Crusoe Islands, Galapagos Islands, San Blas Islands, Windward Islands, Grenadine Islands, Greece, and Rhodos Islands. 35mm b&w, color. One-time rights. $10 holding fee after 21 days. One-time reproduction fee: $125 for color; $35 for b&w. Credit line and return of transparencies required.

CONSOLIDATED EDISON COMPANY OF NEW YORK, INC., 4 Irving Place, New York NY 10003. Contact: William O. Farley, Director, Public Information. Single copies of prints available on electric, gas, steam generation and distribution facilities. No fees.

CONTACT PRESS IMAGES, INC., 135 Central Park West, New York NY 10023. Contact: Robert Pledge. (212)799-9570. Photos available on a loan basis for all rights. Subjects: Photojournalistic editorial photography (color and b&w) on major personalities, situations, trends, events, countries of the world; political, economics, sociological and cultural points of view. Service charge: $25. Holding fee: $50. Minimum reproduction fee: $50. Prints made to order: $10.

JERRY COOKE INC., 161 E. 82 St., New York NY 10028. (212)288-2045. Manager: Nancy Henderson. B&w and color photos of children, scenic views, sports, travel, industrial, China, U.S.S.R. and most continents. Rights and fees negotiable.

CULVER PICTURES, INC., 660 First Ave., New York NY 10016. (212)684-5054. Contact: R. B. Jackson. "Widely known in historical field, with over 8 million b&w photos, old prints, engravings, posters, paintings, movie stills covering every imaginable subject. We like to work with writers but cannot send material until acceptance of article or story by magazine or publisher is final. We have found that we cannot tie up pictures on speculative ventures." One-time reproduction fee varies; $25 to $300 (for cover use). Credit line and return of pictures required.

DANDELET INTERLINKS, 126 Redwood Rd., San Anselmo CA 94960. (415)456-1260. Contact: Lucile Dandelet. West Coast stock selection and worldwide assignments. B&w and color. Charges for selection and overlong holding fees. One-time reproduction fee depends on use and rights bought. Assignment rates per ASMP. Credit line and return of pictures required.

ALFRED DE BAT PHOTOGRAPHY, 4629 N. Dover Street, Chicago IL 60640. (312)271-9553. 50,000 pictures of "foreign travel, U.S. travel, Chicago area scenes and activities. Mainly color —some b&w." Offers world, North American, first, one-time, and stock rights. Charges standard ASMP rates.

LEO DE WYS INC., 60 E. 42nd St., New York NY 10017. (212)986-3190. Contact: Diana Ross. "We represent over 400 photographers from around the world, each with their own specialty; freelancers and staffers from companies and magazines." 500,000 (plus) photos included in collection. Scenics, education, science, religion, natural science, agriculture, music, dance, sculpture, celebrities, sports, government, foreign countries, industry, medicine, human interest photos. B&w and color photos available. Charge for making a selection is $25 outside New York state. Holding fee: $1 per photo per day, after 3 weeks. No service charge for 1 to 4 subjects. $25 for 5 or more subjects. Outright purchase price: "high." Reproduction fee: $35 minimum for b&w; $100 minimum for color. Selection on approval or in person. Prints must be returned. Credit line and tearsheets required.

DR. E. R. DEGGINGER, APSA, P.O. Box 186, Convent NJ 07961. Contact: E. R. Degginger. About 80,000 color transparencies on wide range of subject matter including pictorial and nature photography: scenics, travel, industry, science, abstracts, sports, all facets of the natural world. 35mm color. Rights to be negotiated. Charges $125 for one-time usage; covers are higher.

DESIGN PHOTOGRAPHERS INTERNATIONAL, INC., 521 Madison Avenue, New York NY 10022. (212)752-3930. Contact: Alfred W. Forsyth. "Over 1½ million pictures. Comprehensive contemporary collection of worldwide subjects in color and b&w." Offers one-time reproduction rights "unless other specific terms are agreed upon and additional fee is paid for said additional rights." Fees vary "depending on media and specific use."

A. DEVANEY, INC., 40 E. 49th St., New York NY 10017. (212)755-7580. Contact: George Marzocchi. Types of photos available: scenics, seasonal, U.S. and foreign cities, industrials, farming, human interest, religious, etc. B&w and color transparencies; no color prints. Holding fee after 10 days. 1-time reproduction fee depends on use. Credit line required for editorial use only. Return of pictures required except for those used.

DIVISION OF MICHIGAN HISTORY, Department of State, 3423 N. Logan St., Lansing MI 48918. Contact: David J. Olson, State Archivist. Files of original and reproduction prints and negatives accumulated over a period of time and depicting all phases of the Michigan scene. Approximately 100,000 photo items in the collection. The cost of an individual print varies according to the size and finish of the print desired. In those cases where the Division of Michigan History does not have a negative, an additional charge is made for a copy negative, which remains in the collections of the Division of Michigan History. In advance of placing any order, there is a charge of $1 as a service fee, payable to the State of Michigan. Checks and money orders are to be made payable to the State of Michigan. The service fee paid is solely for the cost of handling the order, and does not include the right to further reproduction or publication. If the Commission grants the right to production, the credit line "From the collections of the Michigan History Division" is requested; and, when used in publication, 2 copies of the article, publication or book are requested for inclusion in the Division's research library.

IRVING DOLIN PHOTOGRAPHY, 124 Ludlow St., New York NY 10002. (212)473-4006. Contact: Irving Dolin. Several thousand pictures. "All types of auto racing, in b&w and color. Racing drivers. Files date from 1948. Most are 35mm." Prefers to sell one-time rights; depends upon fee paid. Minimum b&w fee is $35 for one-time editorial use.

DONDERO PHOTOGRAPHY, Box 1006, Reno NV 89504. Contact: Mike Ritter. "Thousands of color and b&w pictures of all western activity in the four seasons; celebrities, mainly entertainment; gambling; legalized prostitution —mood —unidentifiable subjects." Offers one-time rights on stock pictures; exclusive rights when shooting on assignment. Fees: "one-time publication rights for area publications and small newspapers, $10 for b&w, $25 for color; standard space rates for national publications."

DRAKE WELL MUSEUM, R.D. 3, Titusville PA 16354. (814)827-2797. Contact: Jane Elder. 6,000 photographs of the 19th and 20th century petroleum industry. Reproduction rights or advertising rights. Collection is in the public domain. Available for purchase. Charges $10/hour for making selection. Print fee: $2-5. Prints made to order: $5. Photocopies: $5. Copy negative: $5.

EASTFOTO AGENCY, 25 W. 43 St., New York NY 10036. (212)279-8846. Manager: Leah Siegel. 900,000 color and b&w photos on all aspects of life in E. Europe, China, Vietnam, etc. Industrial, political, historical, entertainment, news photos. Offers one-time rights, North American, world in English, world rights in translation. Fees vary according to usage. Minimum of $50 for 1-time use of b&w photos; $125 for color.

EDITORIAL PHOTOCOLOR ARCHIVES, 342 Madison Ave., New York NY 10017. (212)697-1136. B&w photos; color transparencies: 35mm, 2¼x2¼ formats. Subjects include foreign countries and cultures, ecology, children, works of art, family life, human activities, nature. Fees vary depending on use. Generally the b&w fee is $50 and color is $125.

EKM COMMUNICATIONS, 43205 Lenfesty, Mt. Clemens MI 48043. (313)469-1354. Over 100,000 photos available for purchase. Rarely loans photos. Rights vary with material and use. All subject categories: People, animals, medical research, foreign countries, nature, Indians, sports, etc. "We also have photographers around the world who will accept assignments." Reproduction: $50 minimum. Prints made to order: $2/8x10, $3.50/11x14.

ENTHEOS/NORTHWEST, Bainbridge Island WA 98110. (206)842-3641. Contact: Steven C. Wilson. 100,000 photos in collection, "all 35mm color and 16mm color movie footage. Western U.S. and Canada, Alaska, the Arctic; nature, animals, plants, man." Rights to be negotiated with each purchase; varies from exclusive to one-time educational book rights. Fees: $100 minimum per photo for one-time book rights.

EUROPEAN ART COLOR SLIDES, Peter Adelberg, Inc., 120 W. 70th St., New York NY 10023. (212)877-9654. Contact: Peter Adelberg. About 6,000 photos. "Archives of original color transparencies photographed on-the-spot from the original art object in museums, cathedrals, palaces, etc. Prehistoric to contemporary art; all media. Transparencies instantly available from New York office." Charges selection and holding fees. One-time reproduction fee varies from $55 and up for b&w to $75-100 and up for color. Credit line and return of pictures required.

FIELD MUSEUM OF NATURAL HISTORY, Roosevelt Rd. at Lake Shore Dr., Chicago IL 60605. No catalogue of photos available so it is necessary in ordering photos either to inspect the Museum albums or to write, giving precise specifications of what's wanted. Prices and requirements for permission to reproduce available on request. Write to Division of Photography.

FLORIDA CYPRESS GARDENS, INC., Box 1, Cypress Gardens FL 33880. (813)324-2111. Contact: Bert Lacey, Director of Public Relations. Photos of flowers, plants, scenics, boating, water skiing, fishing, camping, pretty girls. One-time reproduction fees; $300 without credit line or no charge with credit line. Return of pictures required. Cypress Gardens also has a staff of photographers that can take pictures in above categories. Prices available on request.

FLORIDA NEWS BUREAU, 410-C Collins Bldg., Tallahassee FL 32304. (904)488-2494. Contact: Tim Olsson. Photographs on all areas and phases of Florida; b&w available to freelancers, b&w and color transparencies to publications. "To receive the greatest value for the tax money that supports our operation, we apply the following guidelines in filling photographic requests: 1) requests direct from publications get first priority; 2) requests from freelancers who have established a record of cooperation with us (tearsheets, credit lines and other acknowledgments) receive second priority; and 3) requests from unknown freelancers are handled on a 'time available' basis. A freelancer who has not worked with us previously should allow plenty of time on photo requests." No fees but credit line and return of transparencies required.

FORD FOUNDATION PHOTO LIBRARY, 320 E. 43 St., New York NY 10017. (212)573-4815. Over 10,000 in contact sheets. Primarily b&w. All related to projects supported by the Foundation: agricultural research, family planning, reproductive biology, public and higher education, community development. Use restricted to bona fide publications; photos must be for use in context of project. No fees; only print costs.

HARRISON FORMAN WORLD PHOTOS, 555 Fifth Ave., New York NY 10017. (212)697-4165. Contact: Harrison Forman. "Over 700,000 Kodachromes on countries throughout the world. Our files are cross-filed by subjects such as: religions of the world, art and architecture, housing, flora, fauna, dances, children, education, agriculture, handicrafts, native rituals, imports and exports, transportation, natural resources, mountains, rivers, jungles, deserts, glaciers, ancient civilization, historical monuments. Special recent coverage on China with over 7,000 Kodachromes. China inventory includes color pix of light and heavy industries, art and architecture, consumer products, education, acupuncture, children, communes, transportation, irrigation products, cities, towns, villages and many more. Thousands of b&w pix of Asia dating from early 1930's. Rates vary, depending on editorial use, publication, reproduction rights offered. Our rates are in conformance with standards of ASMP. Credit line, tearsheets and return of photographs required. We are founder/members of PACA (Picture Agency Council of America)."

FOTOS INTERNATIONAL, 130 West 42nd Street, New York NY 10036. (212)695-0353. Contact: Baer M. Frimer. B&w and color transparencies "covering the entertainment field in all its phases—motion pictures (international); television, radio, stage." 1-time reproduction rights.

FOUR BY FIVE, INC., 342 Madison Ave., New York NY 10017. (212)697-8282. Manager: Joanna Ferrone. Quality stock photos of people, scenics, travel, and concept. Full-color catalogs available on subscription. Free sample. Fees depend on usage and exposure.

FRANKLIN PHOTO AGENCY, 39 Woodcrest Ave., Hudson NH 03051. (603)889-1289. Photographs available of flowers, gardens, trees, plants, wildflowers, etc.; foreign countries; interiors and exteriors of homes, scenics (all seasons), antique cars, insects and small animals, dogs (all breeds), fish pictures, horses (all breeds), fishing and hunting scenes, some sports. Mostly 4x5 color. One-time reproduction and rental fees vary according to use and quantities printed, etc. Not less than $50 minimum. Credit line requested and return of pictures required.

FREE LIBRARY OF PHILADELPHIA, Print and Picture Department, Logan Square, Philadelphia PA 19103. Contact: Robert F. Looney. Photographs available on a wide range of subjects. Original prints: historical and fine arts. Also clippings, plates, news photos. Specialties: portrait collection (300,000 items), Philadelphia history (9,000 items), Napoleonica (3,400 items), fine prints (1,000 items). "Unfortunately we cannot send out samples of literature or groups of pictures from which selections may be made." Photocopies: $3.50 each. Credit line required for original material only.

FREELANCE PHOTOGRAPHERS GUILD, 251 Park Ave. S., New York NY 10010. Contact: Fred Korn. Photos of all countries, U.S.A., and major cities, human interest, subjects from accidents to zoot suits. 5,000,000 b&w, color photos. Reproduction fee depends on usage; $40-1,200 for b&w, $125-2,500 for color.

FREEPORT MINERALS COMPANY, 161 E. 42nd St., New York NY 10017. (212)687-8100. Contact: E.C.K. Read, PR Division. Color and b&w mining and shipping photos of sulphur (including world's only offshore sulphur mine), kaolin, copper, potash, phosphates, Australian nickel-cobalt operations. Usually no restrictions on rights offered. No fees charged.

FREER GALLERY OF ART, Smithsonian Institution, Washington DC 20560. Contact: Mrs. Willa R. Moore. Photographs of Near and Far Eastern paintings, bronzes, porcelains, wood and stone sculptures, jades, and some Whistler paintings. B&w photos and Ektachromes. $1.75 for 8x10 photos, $50 for 8x10 Ektachromes. Request to reproduce must be made in writing to the Director.

LAWRENCE FRIED PHOTOGRAPHY LTD., 330 East 49th St., Studio 1A, New York NY 10017. (212)371-3636. Contact: Lawrence Fried. "500,000 subjects, ranging from travel throughout the world, international and domestic political figures, society, theatre (stage and film), sports, editorial and commercial illustration, military, medical, personalities in b&w and color." Rights offered flexible, "depending on negotiation in each individual case." Fees: minimum b&w, $75; minimum color, $135.

EWING GALLOWAY, 342 Madison Ave., New York NY 10017. Photo agency offering all types, both b&w and color. Prices are based on how and where a photo will be used.

GAMMA-LIAISON PHOTO AGENCY (formerly Liaison Photo Agency), 150 E. 58th St., New York NY 10022. (212)355-7310. Contact: Michael DeWan. One million b&w and color photos available for purchase or loan. Reproduction rights, advertising rights, first rights, second rights, editorial rights, all rights. Subjects: political, social, economic, religious, cultural events, newsmakers, politicians; celebrities of stage, screen and society. Human interest features, children, animals, nature, sports, fashion. Fees: $35 for making selection; $2/photo/day holding fee, after standard holding time. Reproduction fee varies with photo and photographer, but generally $75 minimum/b&w; $125 minimum/color.

GENERAL PRESS FEATURES, 130 W. 57 St., New York NY 10019. (212)265-6842. Manager: Gabriel D. Hackett. Still photo archives, written and illustrated features. Photos of all subjects; lists available. Over 100,000 photos: historic and documentary, social changes (U.S. and Europe), music, fine arts, artists, Americana; pictorials (U.S. and France, Switzerland). Towns, landscapes, politicians, statesmen, celebrities. Both color and b&w. Rights offered open to negotiation. Fees are ASMP minimum code rates. Discount on larger orders.

A. JOHN GERACI, 279 E. Northfield Rd., Livingston NJ 07039. (201)992-0202. 100,000 photos available for reproduction rights, advertising rights, first rights, second rights, or editorial rights. On loan basis only. Subjects: Medical, dermatology, sports, fencing, tennis, travel, people. Fees: $20 for making selections; $20/service charge. $10 print fee. Holding fee: (over 10 days) $10/day. Copy negative, $25.

GERALD PHOTOS, Route 2, Box 103, Molalla OR 97038. (503)829-6982. Contact: Y.D. Gerald. 5,000 photos on file on sale or loan basis for rights which vary with author and material (usually one-time reproduction rights). Subjects: landscapes, flowers, travel/tourist (such as Lake Crescent in Washington National Olympic Park); city scenes, buildings, animals; all in the Northwest area. Credit line and return of original required. Charge for making selection: $5. Reproduction fee: $20/b&w; $40/color. Will take on individual assignments on request.

GLOBE PHOTOS, 404 Park Ave. S., New York NY 10016. (212)689-1340. Contact: Elliot Stern. 10,000,000 photos of all subjects. B&w and color. Offers first rights, all rights, second rights; depends on the price. $35 minimum for b&w, $125 minimum for color. Credit line, tearsheets and return of prints required.

GOVERNMENT OF SASKATCHEWAN, Photographic/Art Division, Room 3, Legislative Building, Regina, Saskatchewan, Canada. Contact: Ray W. Christensen. A large variety of photographs of all aspects of life in Saskatchewan available as prints in black and white and color, available to publishers only; supplies photos directly to publications, but not to freelance writers. Credit line required.

PETER GOWLAND, 609 Hightree Road, Santa Monica CA 90402. (213)454-7867. Contact: Peter Gowland. Over 3,000 photos catalogued and over 100,000 photos in total collection. "Beautiful women —heads, full-lengths, bathing suits, some nudes —in both b&w and color." Non-exclusive rights offered. Fees: b&w, $50/picture for circulation under 100,000, $75/picture for circulation over 100,000; color, $100-500 depending on use.

THE GRANGER COLLECTION, 1841 Broadway, New York NY 10023. (212)586-0971. Contact: William Glover, Director. A general historical picture archives encompassing the people, places, things, and events of the past in b&w prints and color transparencies. Holding fee varies and 1-time reproduction fee depends on use, but minimum fee is $35. Credit line and return of pictures required.

GREATER PROVIDENCE CHAMBER OF COMMERCE, 10 Dorrance St., Providence RI 02903. Contact: Bruce L. Wolff, Vice President, Communications. Photos of Providence in b&w; limited 35mm color slides. Credit line and return of photos required.

HAROLD V. GREEN, 570 St. John's Blvd., Pointe Claire, Quebec, Canada. (514)697-4110. Contact: H. Green. Approximately 20,000 photos. "Wide spectrum of natural history and general biology photos. Also botanical and some zoological photomicrographs. Mainly 35mm color." One-time reproduction rights usually; other rights by agreement. Fees: $50 to $150, color; $25 to $75, b&w.

AL GREENE & ASSOCIATES, 1333 S. Hope St., Los Angeles CA 90015. "100,000 scenics and points of interest around the world. Mostly color on scenics and farming, otherwise b&w." Offers normal one-time reproduction rights, exclusive rights available at additional charge. Fees: $25 minimum.

ARTHUR GRIFFIN, 22 Euclid Ave., Winchester MA 01890. (617)729-2690. Contact: Arthur Griffin. 50,000 color photos of New England and other states; Orient, the Scandinavian countries, Canada and South America; mostly scenics. All islands of the West Indies. Majority are 4x5 transparencies. Offer all rights. ASMP rates.

AL GROTELL, Underwater Photography, 170 Park Row, New York NY 10038. (212)349-3165. 5,000 photos on file including 35mm color transparencies. Available on loan for 60 days. Subjects: Natural history, including underwater scenes, sponges, corals, fish, molluscs, crustaceans, echinoderms, sunken ships, divers, mostly from the Caribbean; marine ecology. Fees vary with material and use.

JUDSON B. HALL, PHOTOGRAPHER, R.F.D. 3, Putney VT 05346. (802)387-6670. "Approximately 10,000 b&w pictures of Marlboro Music Festival—Rudolf Serkin, Alexander Schneider, Pablo Casals and others. Feature material on sugaring, lumbering, education, animals, seasons, Vermontiana, Sweden in 1963, Kiruna, Vasteras, Stockholm; color photos of Europe, Marlboro, Vermont scenes." Rights negotiable according to ASMP. Fees: b&w stock $35 minimum; color editorial, $100 minimum.

HARPER HORTICULTURAL SLIDE LIBRARY, 219 Robanna Shores, Seaford VA 23696. (804)898-6453. Contact: Pamela Harper. 12,000 photos available on loan basis. Can be purchased in some instances. All rights available. Subjects: Garden plants, garden scenes, trees and shrubs, vines, wildflowers, bulbs, perennials, Alpines, etc. Fees: $20 for making selection; minimum of $20 reproduction fee. Duplicates available from $1.50 each.

HAWAII VISITORS BUREAU, 2270 Kalakaua Ave., Honolulu HI 96815. (808)923-1811. Contact: Photo Librarian. Photographs in b&w, 35mm, and 2¼x2¼ color available on evidence of firm assignment. B&w usually no charge, depends on quantity; color on loan. Credit line and return of color required.

HEDRICH-BLESSING, LTD., 11 W. Illinois St., Chicago IL 60610. (312)321-1151. Contact: Gary Knaus. 750,000 photographs in b&w and color of residential interiors and exteriors, commercial and industrial buildings, interiors and exteriors; scenics of mountains, lakes, woods, mostly without people. City views and historic architecture, especially in Chicago. 1-time reproduction fees for editorial use: color, $100 minimum; b&w, $40 minimum. $25/hour research fee required (deductible). Credit line frequently required. Return of pictures required for color.

HEILPERN PHOTOGRAPHERS INC., Box 266, Blue Hills Station, 151 Homestead Ave., Hartford CT 06112. Contact: George R. Garen. Approximately 35,000 aerial photographs, mostly b&w, "of every type of subject, from close-ups of modern buildings and highway intersections to over-all views of cities." One-time reproduction rights. $40 for 7x7 contact print, $9.50 additional for two 8x10 enlargements of entire negative or any portion.

KEN HEYMAN, 64 E. 55th St., New York NY 10022. (212)421-4512. Contact: Natalie Smith or Ken Heyman. "Over 15,000 b&w and color photos of family types—50 countries around the world; general emphasis on people. Also USA in categories: art, America, education, medicine, research, work, industry, American people, cities, poverty—rural and urban; agriculture, youth, military, space, sports; some personalities." Generally offers one-time, non-exclusive North American (or world) rights. Fees: b&w, $50 minimum; color, "proportionately higher." Quantity discounts available.

THE HISTORIC NEW ORLEANS COLLECTION, 333 Royal St., New Orleans LA 70130. (504)523-7146. Contact: Research Department. Over 25,000 pictorial items available on loan basis to sister institutions with necessary insurance and professional staff. Reproduction rights available. Manuscripts Division contains family papers and other original manuscripts and supporting materials (broadsides, sheet music, newspapers); extensive library of rare books, pamphlets, and major Louisiana studies. Pictorial Division consists of engravings, lithographs, photographs, paintings, maps, original framings and artifacts. These materials cover almost every facet of New Orleans history, including architecture, culture, people, and river life, from the 17th to 20th century (largely 19th century). Reproduction fee: $30/item. Prints made to order: $3/8x10 b&w print. Color $7. Slides also available at $3.

HISTORICAL PICTURES SERVICE INC., 17 N. State St., Room 1700, Chicago IL 60602. Contact: Jeane Williams. Approximately 3,500,000 b&w photos, photocopies, and photostats of engravings, drawings, photos, paintings, cartoons, caricatures, and maps, covering all important persons, places, things and events. Pictures sent on 60-day approval. 1-time, North American, world rights, or multiple use. 1-time reproduction fee: $35 average, but varies with use. Credit line and return of pictures required.

ILLINOIS STATE HISTORICAL LIBRARY, Old State Capitol, Springfield IL 62706. (217)782-4836. Contact: Janice Petterchak, Curator of Prints and Photographs. 100,000 photos on file. Rights vary with author and material. Subjects: Illinois history, (people, places and events), Abraham Lincoln, the Civil War. Fees: Prints made to order, $5-7.50/8x10 b&w glossies. Photocopies, 20¢.

THE IMAGE BANK, 88 Vanderbilt Ave., The Penthouse, New York NY 10017. (212)371-3636. Contact: Larry Fried. 500,000 color transparencies available on sale or loan basis. Reproduction rights, advertising rights, second rights, editorial rights. Extremely varied collection. Fees: $35, service charge. $1/day/transparency, holding fee. Reproduction fee varies. "Contact us as early as possible in the creative stages of your project."

IMAGE PHOTOS, Main St., Stockbridge MA 01262. (413)298-5500. Contact: Clemens Kalischer. 500,000 photos available for purchase or loan. Reproduction rights, first rights, second rights and editorial rights offered. Subjects: The arts, architecture, education, farming, human activities, nature, religion, personalities, abstractions, etc. New England, western Europe, India. Fees: $50-250/b&w; $75-1,500/color.

INTERNATIONAL MUSEUM OF PHOTOGRAPHY, George Eastman House, 900 East Ave., Rochester NY 14607. Contact: Martha Jenks, Archives; Roberta DeGolyer, Print Service. Collection spans the history of photography — 1839 to present day. Original prints do not leave the museum, except for approved traveling exhibitions. Reproduction prints must be returned, and a credit line is required. Work is listed by photographer, not subject. "Rates determined by circulation." Fee: $15 to $200, 1-time reproduction.

INTERPRESS OF LONDON AND NEW YORK, 400 Madison Ave., New York NY 10017. (212)832-2839. Manager: Jeffrey Blyth. Photos of personalities; specializing in photojournalism. Topical or unusual picture stories.

LOU JACOBS, JR., 13058 Bloomfield St., Studio City CA 91604. Contact: Lou Jacobs, Jr. About 25,000 b&w negatives and 5,000 color slides. "All manner of subjects from animals to industry, human interest to motion picture personalities, action, children, scenic material from national parks and various states." Offers first rights on previously unpublished material; one-time reproduction rights on the remainder, except for exclusive rights by agreement. Fees: b&w minimum $50 each up to five, and $40 each for five or more; color is $150 each for one to five and $125 each for more than five.

ERNST A. JAHN, 18 Blackrock Terrace, Ringwood NJ 07456. (201)962-4114. 40,000 photos available on purchase or loan basis for reproduction rights, advertising rights, second rights, editorial rights, first rights or all rights. Subjects: International and U.S.A. coverage ranging from general scenery, cities, new buildings, ships, railways, cattle, festivals, general human interest and special studies on the flying squirrel; local and tropical animals. Reproduction fee: $125/color; $25/b&w. Holding fee: $10 after 21 days.

JUDGE STUDIO, 610 Wood St., Pittsburgh PA 15222. "500 to 1,000 old city views of Pittsburgh and air views; industrial, coal towns, bridges; all b&w prints." Offers one-time reproduction rights. $50 fee charged for 1-time.

YORAM KAHANA PHOTOGRAPHY, 1909 N. Curson Place, Hollywood CA 90046. (213)876-8208. Contact: Yoram Kahana or Peggy Halper. 150,000 photos, mostly 35mm transparencies, some b&w. Available on loan basis only. Fees depend on the kind of reproduction rights bought. Subjects: Personalities (screen, TV, rock, jazz, pop; at home sessions, portraits, and in performance); travel (emphasis on people, crafts, folkways, families; strongest in Central America, Kenya, Israel, West Coast). Detailed stock list free to qualified clients. Follows ASMP guidelines for terms of loan, sale and fees.

CURT W. KALDOR, 603 Grandview Dr., South San Francisco CA 94080. (415)583-8704. Several thousand photos of scenic views and city-suburbs; street scenes, aircraft, people, architectural, railroads, shipping and boating, redwoods and timbering, and others. Offers all types of rights up through complete purchase. Charges a flat fee for purchase of reproduction rights. That fee is based on type of usage.

KANSAS STATE HISTORICAL SOCIETY, 10th and Jackson Sts., Topeka KS 66612. (913)296-3165. Contact: Nancy Sherbert. 80,000 photos of Indians, the American West, railroads, military, Kansas and Kansans. Reproduction rights, advertising rights, first rights, second rights. Collection is in the public domain. B&w glossy or matte finish fee: 75¢ (4x5); $1.35 (5x7); $2.75 (8x10); $3 (11x14); $8.50 (16x20). Minimum order $1. "Color transparencies will be made in special cases where such work is feasible for $7." Mounting charge: 75¢/sq. fet. Copy fee of $1.50 if a new negative is required. Credit line required.

KENTUCKY DEPARTMENT OF PUBLIC INFORMATION, Advertising and Travel Promotion, Capitol Annex, Frankfort KY 40601. (502)564-4930. Contact: W. L. Knight, Director. B&w and color photos of scenic, historic; parks, recreation, events. No fees, but credit line and return of pictures required. General information and editorial material available on most areas.

KEYSTONE PRESS AGENCY, INC., 170 Fifth Ave., New York NY 10010. (212)924-4123. Contact: Walter Schrenck-Szill, Managing Editor. Singles and feature sets of news, political, scientific, business, human interest, animals, inventions, education, recreation, underwater, scenics, explorers, personalities, odds, pop and hippies, art, pretty girls, medical, sports, and many more. B&w and color. Pictures must be returned within two weeks; longer period for free holding must be negotiated. One-time reproduction fee for b&w, $50 minimum. Credit line and return of pictures required.

JOAN KRAMER AND ASSOCIATES, 5 N. Clover, Great Neck NY 11021. (212)246-7600 or (212)532-9095. Contact: Joan Kramer. Over 100,000 photos including abstracts, boats, travel shots from U.S.A. and other countries, children, ethnic groups, fisheye shots, nature, people shots, scenics, teenagers, winter scenes and zoos. B&w (8x10) and color (35mm). Rights negotiable. Fees are based on budget available and photo use.

JAMES W. LA TOURRETTE, PHOTOGRAPHER, 170 N. E. 170th St., North Miami Beach FL 33162. Contact: James W. LaTourrette. About 4,000 b&w and color pictures. "2¼ and 35mm underwater color transparencies of the waters in the Florida Keys and Bahama Islands. Some 4x5 color scenics. Motor sports events; boat races, sports car races; scenics, eastern U.S., West Coast, Everglades wildlife and plants." Offers one-time rights. Fees: b&w 8x10 prints, $15 to $25; color transparencies, $25 to $50. "Color to be returned after use."

HAROLD M. LAMBERT STUDIOS, INC., Box 27310, Philadelphia PA 19150. (215)224-1400. Contact: R. W. Lambert. Complete photo service has over 750,000 b&w photos on hand to cover all subjects from babies to skydiving, plus 125,000 color transparencies covering same subjects. Rental fee varies according to use. "Average rates: $15 minimum editorial use with credit line; $35 minimum (b&w); $125 (color); minimum promotional rate."

LAS VEGAS NEWS BUREAU, Convention Center, Las Vegas NV 89109. (702)735-3611. Contact: Don Payne, Manager. B&w, color, both stills and 16mm, available from files or shot on assignment for accredited writers with bona fide assignments. Return of color required.

LATIN AMERICA PHOTOS, 121 Hubinger St., New Haven CT 06511. (203)389-4397. Contact: David Mangurian. More than 45,000 color and b&w 35mm photos on a wide variety of subjects from most Latin American countries including agriculture, archaeology, education, folk arts, food, Indians, industry, mining, scenics, sports, rural and urban life and social conditions. Stock list available upon request. Normally charges standard ASMP rates for nonexclusive, one-time use, but rates may be negotiated depending on publication, use and quantity purchased. Will answer queries about pictures available, but will not loan pictures for articles being submitted on speculation. All requests must be specific to receive attention, including intended use. Credit line and return of all pictures required.

FRED LEWIS, 390 Ocean Pkwy., Brooklyn NY 11218. (212)282-9219. Over 3,000 scenics, animals, night photography, travel, experimental, etc. Color transparencies; 2¼ and 35mm. Offers one-time rights and full rights. Fees range from $100 to $2,000, depending on use.

FREDERIC LEWIS, INC., 35 E. 35th St., New York NY 10016. (212)685-0122. Contact: Irwin Perton. More than 1 million b&w and color photos of "people, places, things, events, current and historical subjects." Offers "whatever rights are required by user." Fees: b&w, $45 minimum; color, $125 minimum.

LICK OBSERVATORY, University of California, Santa Cruz CA 95064. Contact: Administrative Office. Users of astronomical photographs should make their selections from the standard list in the current catalogue of Astronomical Photographs available as slides or prints from negatives obtained at Lick Observatory, since it is not possible to supply views of other objects or special sizes. B&w, 2x2, 8x10, and 14x17. Catalogues are free upon written request. Information concerning color materials is contained in the calalogue. Purchasers are reminded that permission for use of Lick Observatory photographs for reproduction or commercial purposes must be obtained in writing in advance from the Director of the Observatory. Fee: 60¢-$6 for b&w.

LIGHTFOOT COLLECTION, Box 554, Greenport NY 11944. (516)477-2589. Contact: Fred S. Lightfoot. Over 30,000 photos for reproduction rights, advertising rights, editorial rights, first rights. Collection is in the public domain. Subjects: Americana (1854-1920), city, town, village and country scenes. Architecture, transportation, industrial culture, famous people, wars, agriculture, mining, fabrics. Foreign photos on file also. Reproduction fee: $15 minimum. Prints made to order: $5. Photocopies: $5.

LINCOLN FARM, 140 Heatherdell Rd., Ardsley NY 10502. (914)693-4222. Contact: Harold Loren. 5,000 photos of children (7-16) in summer camp activities. Available for purchase or loan at cost of handling and postage. Reproduction rights, editorial rights, all rights.

LINCOLN PICTURE STUDIO, 225 Lookout Dr., Dayton OH 45419. Contact: Lloyd Ostendorf. Photographs in b&w, Civil War era, 1850-1870; photographs of American scenes, people, places; special collection of photographs of Abraham Lincoln, his family, friends and notables of his day. Selecting photographs for an author or publisher is often done with only a small fee for cost of prints and mailing. The reproduction fee ($50 each) is payable when user holds them for reproduction and publication. Credit line and return of photos required.

THE LONG ISLAND HISTORICAL SOCIETY, 128 Pierrepont St., Brooklyn NY 11201. Contact: James Hurley, Executive Director. Photographs in b&w on a wide variety of subjects concerning history of Long Island. All negatives retained by the Society. Credit line required.

LOUISIANA STATE LIBRARY, Box 131, Baton Rouge LA 70821. (504)389-6120. Contact: Mrs. Harriet Callahan. This is a collection pertaining to the state of Louisiana and persons prominent in Louisiana history. Most of the photographs are b&w. It does contain color pictures during the past 5 years. This is a non-circulating, historical collection. Credit line and return of pictures required.

THOMAS LOWES, PHOTOGRAPHER, 491 Delaware Ave., Buffalo NY 14202. (716)883-2650. Contact: Liz Mohring. Over 50,000 photos — yachting and boating, tall ships, Americana (people, landscapes, historic objects and landmarks), hot air ballooning, rodeos, ghost towns, Indian crafts and missions. Farming (people and equipment), Canadian provinces. Color transparencies (35mm). Fees depend on publication.

BURTON McNEELY PHOTOGRAPHY, P.O. Box 338, Land o' Lakes Fl 33539. (813)996-3025. Contact: Burton McNeely. "About 10,000 color only: recreation, travel, romance, girls, underwater, and leisure time activities." Offers any and all rights. "Fees are based on the use of the photos, such as circulation of magazine or type of book. Minimum one-time rate for any published use is $125."

MAGNUM, 15 W. 46th St., New York NY 10036. Joan Liftin, Director of library; Lee Jones, Editor. Over 1,000,000 photos. Photojournalistic reportage, documentary photography, feature and travel coverage; mainly from the thirties. B&w and color. Standard American Society of Magazine Photographers fees.

THE MAYTAG COMPANY, 403 W. Fourth St., N., Newton IA 50208. Contact: Ronald L. Froehlich, Manager, Public Information. Photos of home laundry settings; kitchens; anything in area of laundry appliances, laundering, kitchen appliances, use of dishwashers, disposers; laundering procedures. Also available are industrial shots, in-factory assembly line photos. Both b&w and color (laundry and kitchen settings), transparencies, slides. Credit line and return of color transparencies required.

MEMORY SHOP, 109 E. 12th St., New York NY 10003. Contact: Mark Ricci. "Four million photos. Specializing in movie memorabilia." Offers one-time repro rights. Fees: $5 to $15.

LOUIS MERCIER, 342 Madison Ave., New York NY 10017. Stock photographs; color scenics USA and worldwide; personalities, fashion, food, industry, and the arts. Fees: $35 minimum for b&w; $100 for color depending on use.

MERCURY ARCHIVES, 1574 Crossroads of the World, Hollywood CA 90028. Over a million photos. "Woodcuts and engravings on all subjects; pre-1900. We operate as a stock photo rental service." Full rights offered. Fees: vary per picture on a 1-time and 1-use basis. Research/service fee charged when pictures not used for reproduction.

THE METROPOLITAN MUSEUM OF ART, Fifth Ave., at 82nd St., New York NY 10028. Contact: Photograph and Slide Library. History of art from ancient times to the present. B&w photos: 4x5 and 8x10 for sale; color transparencies: mostly 8x10, rental, for purposes of publication only. New publication: *Color Transparencies for Rental,* $3 plus tax. These cover only paintings and other objects in the Museum's collections. Research must be done by user. Copy photo price schedule available. Fee: $5-10/8x10 photo. Credit line required. Return required on color transparencies only; photographs made to special order are sold outright with one-time reproduction rights included.

MIAMI SEAQUARIUM, 4400 Rickenbacker Causeway, Miami FL 33166. Contact: Zoe Todd. Photos in b&w and color of the Seaquarium and a variety of sea creatures. The Miami Seaquarium makes photographs available to all writers and editors free of charge, providing either the Seaquarium is given a credit line ("Miami Seaquarium Photo"), or the Seaquarium is mentioned in the caption. Tearsheets required. Return required for color only.

MINISTRY OF INDUSTRY AND TOURISM, Hearst Block, Parliament Bldgs., Toronto, Ontario, Canada. Contact: Bruce Reed. "About 40,000 color transparencies and b&w photos of outdoors and travel, fishing, hunting, boating, camping. To be used for travel articles only. Would appreciate a credit line." No fee.

MINNESOTA HISTORICAL SOCIETY, Audio-Visual Library, 690 Cedar, St. Paul MN 55101. (612)296-2489. Contact: Bonnie Wilson. 150,000 photos available for purchase. Reproduction rights offered. Minnesota persons, places and activities. Emphasis on Indians, agriculture, mining, lumbering, recreation, transportation. Reproduction fee: $10-25. Print fee: $2.50. Photocopies: 25¢. Copy negative: $2. Credit line required.

MISSISSIPPI DEPARTMENT OF ARCHIVES & HISTORY, Box 571, (100 S. State St.,) Jackson MS 39205. (601)354-6218. Contact: Jo Ann Bomar. Subjects: Civil War prints from *Harper's Weekly* and Frank Leslie's *Weekly* (some hand-colored); prominent Mississippians, historic spots and other Mississippi scenes, historic buildings and antebellum mansions, the Mississippi River and steamboats. Fees: $3.50 for positive photostat; $3/8x10 glossy. Credit line required.

MISSOURI HISTORICAL SOCIETY, Jefferson Memorial Bldg., Lindell & Debaliviere, St. Louis MO 63112. (314)361-1424. Contact: Ms. Gail R. Guidry. 100,000 photos on Missouri and western life, the World's Fair, early St. Louis, early aviation; the Lindbergh Collection and Steamboat Collection. Reproduction rights available. Reproduction fee $15/photo. Print fee: $7.50/8x10 b&w. "Always write it out of state and request prints. No telephone orders processed. Collection seen upon appointment."

GEORGE A. MOFFITT, COLLECTION, 306 W. 94th St., New York NY 10025. Contact: George A. Moffitt. Photos of pre-war American and Continental standard and custom cars of the movies (with stars that owned them); cars shown with public figures of the past; custom body builders' renderings; antique cars of early American production; racing car scenes, b&w and color; also post-war photos of American and Continental production. 1-time reproduction fee for editorial use: $30, b&w; $100, color.

MONTANA DEPARTMENT OF HIGHWAYS, Montana Travel Promotion Unit, Helena MT 59601. Contact: Josephine Brooker, Director. Scenic, historic, recreational, official (state seal, flag, etc.) photos in 8x10 glossy b&w and 35mm. 2¼ square, 4x5 color transparencies. Writer receives a memo invoice with shipment of photos. If photos are returned within reasonable time, in same condition, invoice is canceled. Credit line required. Return of pictures required for color only. Editorial material also available.

MONTGOMERY PICTURES, Box 722, Las Vegas NM 87701. (505)425-3146. Contact: Mrs. C.M. Montgomery. "6,000 4x5 color transparencies and 10,000 35mm color transparencies of animals, birds, reptiles, flora, scenics, state and national parks, ghost towns, historic, Indian and petroglyphs." 1-time reproduction rights in one country preferred; all other rights by negotiation. Fees: "ASMP rates, where applicable. Otherwise, the publisher's current rates; but not less than $25 per transparency."

THE MUSEUM OF MODERN ART, Film Stills Archive, 11 W. 53rd St., New York NY 10019. (212)956-4209. Contact: Mrs. Mary Corliss. Approximately 3,000,000 b&w stills on foreign and American productions, film personalities, and directors. Duplicates of original stills are sold at a cost of $6/still. Credit line required.

MUSEUM OF NEW MEXICO, P. O. Box 2087, Santa Fe NM 87503. (505)827-2559. Contact: Photo Archives. 80,000 photos available: archaeology, anthropology, railroads, Southwestern Americana, Southwestern Indians. Some 19th-Century foreign holdings including Oceania, Japan, Middle East. Copy prints $2 and up. Reproduction/publication fees and credit lines required. Catalogs and photographer indexes available.

MUSEUM OF SCIENCE, Science Park, Boston MA 02114. Contact: Bradford Washburn. Contact prints of Alaskan and Alpine mountains and glaciers. All b&w. Copy prints, $5 and up. One-time reproduction fees: $25 each for use on ½-page or less; $50 each for use on 1 page; $75 each for use as a double-page spread. Credit line required.

MUSEUM OF THE AMERICAN INDIAN, Broadway at 155th St., New York NY 10032. Contact: Carmelo Guadagno. The Photographic Archives of the Museum include negatives, b&w prints, and color transparencies from Indian cultures throughout the Western hemisphere. The various categories present a selection of everyday customs, ceremonial paraphernalia, costumes and accessories, dwellings and physical types from a majority of areas. B&w photos, 35mm and 4x5 color transparencies. 2,200 Kodachrome slides; list available for $1. Send stamp. 1-time editorial reproduction fee is $20 for b&w and $40 for color. Credit line required. Folder of information available; send stamp.

MUSEUM OF THE CITY OF NEW YORK, Fifth Ave. at 103rd St., New York NY 10029. (212)534-1672. Contact: Esther Brumberg. 22,000 photos on file for sale only. All rights. Subjects: New York City; all aspects of life and history; street scenes, furniture, toys, costumes, theatre, fires, police, social history, etc. Reproduction fee: $10. Print fee: $5. Prints made to order: $5 from existing negatives. Photocopies: 25¢ each.

THE MUSICAL MUSEUM, S. Main St., Deansboro NY 13328. (315)841-8774. Contact: Arthur H. Sanders. Unlimited number of photos on file for all rights on purchase or loan basis. "We now have a staff photographer, who will take photos of items needed from vast collection of musical antiques." Prints or photocopies available.

HANS NAMUTH, LTD., 157 W. 54th St., New York NY 10019. About 5,000 b&w and color photos of people (American artists) available for purchase. Reproduction rights available. Fee: $50-150 service charge.

NATIONAL AIR AND SPACE MUSEUM, Smithsonian Institution, Washington DC 20560. Contact: Catherine D. Scott, Librarian. 900,000 photos. Aviation and space; both b&w and color. Fees: $3.50 per 8x10 b&w glossy or matte. Color, $10. Credit must be given to NASM. Checks are made payable to the Smithsonian Institution.

NATIONAL ARCHIVES AND RECORDS SERVICE, 8th and Pennsylvania Ave., N.W., Washington DC 20408. (202)523-3054. Contact: William H. Leary. Five million photos available for purchase. "Most are in the public domain and may be freely reproduced." Subject: "Pictorial records (primarily b&w) from some 130 Federal agencies illustrating all aspects of American history from the colonial period to the recent past, and many aspects of life in other parts of the world. Included are several large collections such as the Mathew Brady Civil War photographs, the picture file of the Paris branch of the N.Y. Times (1923-1950), and the Heinrich Hoffmann files illustrating activities of the Nazi party in Germany (1923-45)."

NATIONAL CATHOLIC NEWS SERVICE, 1312 Massachusetts Ave., N.W., Washington DC 20005. Contact: Robert A. Strawn. 20,000 photos on purchase basis only. Rights vary with material and usage. Subjects: Catholic-related news and feature and historical material. Fees vary with usage.

NATIONAL COAL ASSOCIATION, 1130 17th St. N.W., Gashington DC 20036. (202)628-4322. Contact: Herbert Foster. 2,000 photos, "mostly b&w shots of bituminous coal production, transportation and use, and reclamation of mined land. Some color transparencies of coal production, many showing land reclamation. Most are modern —no historical pix." Allows free editorial use. No fees. "Credit line to NCA."

NATIONAL FILM BOARD PHOTOTHEQUE, Tunney's Pasture, Ottawa, Ontario K1A 0M9 Canada. (613)593-5826. Contact: G. Lund or C. McDonald, Photo Librarian. About 300,000 b&w photos and color transparencies "illustrating the social, economic and cultural aspects of Canada." Photos purchased for 1-time use only. Pictures can be purchased for editorial and commercial use. Fees vary according to the purpose for which the photos are required.

NATIONAL GALLERY OF ART, Washington DC 20565. (202)734-4215. Contact: Ira Bartfield, Photographic Services. Photographs available of major portion of objects in the Gallery's collections, from medieval to present times, including paintings, drawings, etchings, engravings, sculpture and renderings of American folk-art objects. B&w glossy prints, 8x10. Charge: $2 prepaid. Color transparencies available of many objects; rental fee to cover 3-month loan of transparencies. For details of charges, please write for further information. Permission to reproduce objects will be granted for scholarly publications after receiving written request. Permission is not granted for advertising purposes.

NATIONAL LIBRARY OF MEDICINE, 8600 Rockville Pike, Bethesda MD 20014. Contact: Chief, History of Medicine Division. Photographs available on the history of medicine (portraits, institutions, scenes), not related to current personalities, events, or medical science. B&w and color. Copy prints: 8x10, $3 and up. Credit line required. Prices vary according to service provided, and are subject to change without notice. No pictures sent out on approval.

NATIONAL PHOTOGRAPHY COLLECTION, Public Archives of Canada, 395 Wellington St., Ottawa, Canada K1A ON3. (613)992-3884. Contact: Reference Officers. 4,500,000 photos, "all Canadian subjects: documenting the political, economic, industrial, military, social and cultural life of Canada from 1850 to the present. B&w negatives and prints; color transparencies. On unrestricted or non-copyright material, reproduction rights are normally granted upon request after examination of a statement of purpose, or legitimate use in publication, film or television production, exhibition or research." Fees: b&w 8x10 print, $3.

NEBRASKA STATE HISTORICAL SOCIETY, 1500 R St., Lincoln NE 68508. Contact: Marvin F. Kivett, Director. Photographs available of historical subjects pertaining to Nebraska and trans-Missouri west; agriculture; steamboats; Indians. B&w 8x10 glossy prints $2.50. Credit line required.

NEIKRUG GALLERIES, INC., 224 E. 68th St., New York NY 10021. (212)288-7741. Contact: Mrs. Marjorie Neikrug. Collection of antique photos offered for reproduction. Photographic portfolios viewed; by appointment only.

NEVILLE PUBLIC MUSEUM, 129 S. Jefferson, Green Bay WI 54301. Contact: James L. Quinn, Director. Historical photographs available pertinent to northeastern Wisconsin, especially Green Bay area in b&w and some contemporary color. Photos available at cost only for educational purposes. Museum credit line required.

THE NEW JERSEY HISTORICAL SOCIETY, 230 Broadway, Newark NJ 07104. Contact: Howard W. Wiseman, Curator. Photos available of historical New Jersey houses, buildings, streets, etc., filed by the name of the town (must know the name of town; not filed by subject matter). Charge for making selection: $1.25. 1-time reproduction fee $10 each. Print fee: about $15, depending on job. Copy negative: $5. Credit line required.

THE NEW YORK BOTANICAL GARDEN LIBRARY, Bronx Park, New York NY 10458. Contact: Charles R. Long, Administrative Librarian or Helen Schlanger, Photo Librarian. "Collection being reorganized. Limited access." B&w photos (original and copy), glass negatives, film negatives, clippings, postcards, old prints, original drawings and paintings. Subjects: botany, horticulture; portraits of botanists and horticulturists; pictures from seed catalogues. One-time reproduction fee $35 per print for original b&w photos, $100 for original 35mm color. Credit line required.

NEW YORK CONVENTION AND VISITORS BUREAU, 90 E. 42nd St., New York NY 10017. (212)687-1300. Contact: John P. MacBean. B&w glossies, and color, of New York City's sightseeing attractions and services. No factories, industrial sites, etc. Only city sights; no N.Y. State photos. Please give us specific requests (such as "Statue of Liberty") rather than "a selection of photos." Photos may be used in any legitimate news or feature sense to illustrate copy on the city. No fees, but credit line requested.

THE NEW-YORK HISTORICAL SOCIETY, 170 Central Park W., New York NY 10024. (212)873-3400. Contact: Print Room. About 300,000 photos. Subjects: American history, with emphasis on New York City and New York State; portraits. Seventeenth century to early 20th century. B&w original and copy photos, daguerrotypes, Stereograms, fine-art prints, original cartoons, architectural drawings, business ephemera, glass negatives, posters, postcards, illustrated maps and broadsides. Some material available for editorial reproduction. No loans. Charges print fees and reproduction rights fees.

NEW ZEALAND EMBASSY, 19 Observatory Circle N.W., Washington DC 20008. Contact: Information Officer. A limited number of photos of a general nature about New Zealand. No fees, but credit line and return of pictures requested.

NEWARK MUSEUM, 49 Washington St., Newark NJ 07101. Contact: W.T. Bartle. Photos available on American art (18th, 19th and 20th centuries; painting and sculpture); Oriental art (especially Tibet, Japan, and India); decorative arts (furniture, jewelry, costumes). 8x10 b&w photos. Fee: $2.50 for copy prints; $10, one-time reproduction fee. 4x5 transparencies. $60 sale or $35 for 3-month rental, including reproduction fee. Credit line required.

NEWSWEEK BOOKS, 444 Madison Ave., New York NY 10022. Collection of about 8,000 photos on art of all kinds, architecture, American and world history. B&w and color. Offers reproduction rights for 1-time, non-exclusive use. Charges $35 to $50 for b&w; up to $150 for color.

NICHOLSON PHOTOGRAPHY, 1503 Brooks Ave., Raleigh NC 27607. (919)787-6076. Contact: Nick Nicholson. 20,000 photos available for sale. Reproduction rights, advertising rights, first rights, second rights, editorial rights, all rights. Subjects: scenics, travel, leisure activity, cities, general interest. "All fees negoiated and based on rights requested plus usage. No standard rate. All material in 35mm color transparency form; b&w prints available as conversions from color slides."

NORTH CAROLINA DIVISION OF ARCHIVES AND HISTORY, 109 E. Jones St., Raleigh NC 27611. (919)733-7952. Contact: Archives Branch. 300,000 photos on file. Most are in the public domain. Subjects: "Most of the photographs in our custody pertain to North Carolina history and culture. Holdings include extensive number of pictures depicting buildings and places in North Carolina that have been nominated for or placed on the National Register of Historic Places." None are available for sale or loan, but prints can be made to order, $2-8/b&w; cost, plus 15%/color. "Orders should be placed at least 2 weeks in advance. Detailed research cannot be done by mail or by telephone."

NORTH CAROLINA MUSEUM OF ART, Raleigh NC 27611. (919)733-7568. Contact: Head, Collections Research and Publications Branch. 8x10 b&w glossies; 2x2 color slides; 4x5 color transparencies on permanent collections. Fees: $1.50 for glossies; 75¢ for original slides; 50¢ for duplicate slides; $35 for transparencies. Permission to publish is required.

NOTMAN PHOTOGRAPHIC ARCHIVES, McCord Museum, 690 Sherbrooke St., W., Montreal, Quebec, Canada. (514)392-4781. Contact: Stanley Triggs. 600,000 photos. "Portraits, landscapes, city views, street scenes, lumbering, railroad construction, trains, Indians, fishing, etc." Offers 1-time non-exclusive publication rights. Fees: $25 for most publications. "Photographs on loan only —to be returned after use."

NYT PICTURES, 229 W. 43rd St., New York NY 10036. (212)556-1243. Contact: Raphael Paganelli. This is the photo syndicate of the *New York Times* with almost 3 million photos available. Reproduction rights, advertising rights, editorial rights, all rights. Subjects: Personalities, politics, news and special events. Fee: $12.50/photo print. Reproduction fee: $40 minimum, dependong on use of photos. "Photo research in archives by non-staff members not permitted. Photo research service in archives available at cost of $25/hour or fraction thereof."

OREGON HISTORICAL SOCIETY, 1230 S.W. Park Ave., Portland OR 97205. Contact: Janice Worden, Photographs Librarian. Several hundreds of thousands —300,000 catalogued photos. "All subjects in geographical range: Pacific Northwest (Oregon, Washington, Idaho, British Columbia), Alaska, North Pacific. Most b&w prints and negatives; also color transparencies and negatives, engravings, lantern slides (color and b&w), etc. Virtually all material is available for publication; credit line required." Fees vary according to use.

ORGANIZATION OF AMERICAN STATES, Photographic Records, Graphic Services Unit, 19th St., and Constitution Ave., N.W., Washington DC 20006. (202)381-8700. Contact: C.L. Headen. 35,000 b&w photos available on a loan basis only. Reproduction rights, advertising rights, editorial rights, and all rights offered. Collection is in the public domain. Subjects: Agriculture, antiquities, art, cities and towns, education, historical, industry, minerals, native activities, natural history, political, portraits, public welfare recreation, topography, transportation, Latin America, Barbados, Jamaica, Trinidad, and Tobago. Fee: $2/print. Credit line required. Return of pictures *not* required.

OUTDOOR PIX & COPY, 5639 N. 34th Ave., Phoenix AZ 85017. (602)973-9557. Contact: James Tallon. About 70,000 photos included in this collection. Photos of scenics, education, natural science, agriculture, sports, travel, wildlife, foreign countries (Mexico and Canada), human interest. "Strong on nature, hunting, fishing, camping, recreation. More than 500 selected shots of elk; 2,000 shots of cowboys on cattle drive; thousands of bird shots; lots of plant close-ups including cactus blossoms; national parks and monuments (Western); lots of sealife including fighting elephant seals. "95 percent of the people who write me for pictures find something they are looking for." 35mm color only. Rights vary with material and its use. Selection on approval. Slides must be returned unless all rights are purchased. Credit line and tearsheets appreciated. Outright purchase price: negotiable. Reproduction fee: $50 minimum. "Selections are mailed to prospective buyers within 48 hours, usually the same day requests come in. List of categories available on request."

PACIFIC AERIAL SURVEYS, (formerly Pacific Resources, Inc.), Box 2416, Airport Station, Oakland CA 94614. Contact: Jack E. Logan. 200,000 aerial photographs of western U.S. only. B&w, color. Outright purchase price: b&w 8x10, $50; color transparency, $100. 1-time reproduction fee: b&w, $30; color, $75. Credit line and return of pictures required.

PAN AMERICAN AIRWAYS, Pan Am Bldg., New York NY 10017. Attn: Photo Library. Contact: Ruth Keary, Manager, Film. Photos of Pan Am equipment (airplanes, etc.) and destination photos. B&w and color. Photos supplied for use within travel context. Charges reproduction fee (lab costs) to supply duplicates, whether b&w or color. Fee varies depending upon what is required.

PEABODY MUSEUM OF SALEM, East India Square, Salem MA 01970. (617)745-1876. Contact: Curators of the various departments. 1 million photographs available for sale. Principally maritime history and ethnology of non-European peoples; natural history. B&w and color. Reproduction, advertising and editorial rights. Credit line required. Send for free price list and descriptive brochure. Selection charge depends on research needed; reproduction fee negotiable; print fee $4 and up; photocopies 20¢/page.

PENGUIN PHOTO, 663 Fifth Ave., New York NY 10022. (212)758-7328. Contact: Mrs. Ena Fielden. Over 50,000 photos in b&w and color. Accent is on the field of entertainment: film, stage, music, dance, radio, and TV. "Photos are for strictly editorial use only." Prevalent current fees. "Photos are on loan from collection."

ROBERT PERRON, 104 E. 40th St., New York NY 10016. (212)661-8796. Photos of nature, aerials of coastal scenes, architecture, interiors, energy saving houses. About 10,000 in collection. Offers 1-time rights. Fees: $50 for b&w, $150 for color, editorial.

PHELPS & THOMPSON, INC., STOCK PHOTOGRAPHY (formerly Libra Stock Photographs), 1315 Peachtree St., N.E., Atlanta GA 30309. Contact: Katie Phelps. Sells the use of 50,000 photos including scenics, world travel, education, famous people, faces, sports, human interest, spot news, agriculture, industry, architecture, city skylines, wildlife, miscellaneous people, family scenes, interiors, business situations, seasonal photos, studio, children. Advertising rights, editorial rights, all rights. Service charge: $15-25. Holding fee: $1/photo/day after 14 days. "Rates in accordance with ASMP Guide to Business Practices in Photography. Have 8x10 b&w prints, mostly 35mm color transparencies. Some 2¼x2¼, 4x5, 8x10 color transparencies. No color prints."

PHILADELPHIA MUSEUM OF ART, Rights and Reproduction Department, Box 7646, Philadelphia PA 19101. 250,000 photos and color transparencies. "Paintings, prints, furniture, silver, sculpture, ceramics, arms and armor, coffers, jades, glass, metal objects, ivory objects, textiles, tapestries, costumes, period rooms; photos of works of art in our museum." 8x10 b&w and 5x7 and 4x5 color transparencies. Fees: $5 for 8x10 b&w; $30 rental fee for color transparencies. Reproduction fees are based on usage.

ALLAN A. PHILIBA, 3408 Bertha Dr., Baldwin NY 11510. (212)371-5220 or (516)623-7841. 25,000 photos on file. Travel specialists in color photography. Subjects: the Far East, Europe, South America, U.S.A., North Africa and the Caribbean. Fees vary with use and material.

PHOTO MEDIA, LTD., 105 E. 19th St., New York NY 10003. Contact: David Hayum. Over 50,000 color photos available for leasing. Offers all rights subject to negotiated agreement. Subjects: Human interest, people, children, activities, paperbacks, food, crime, mystery, music, records, couples, animals, etc. Service charge: $25 minimum. Holding fee: $25 minimum. Reproduction fee: $200-2,500.

PHOTO RESEARCHERS, INC., 60 E. 56th St., New York NY 10022. (212)758-3420. Contact: Sam Dasher, Natural History & National Audubon Society Collection or Marcia Mammano, General Library. Includes The National Audubon Society Collection and Rapho Division. More than 1,500,000 award-winning color transparencies and b&w prints. Special editing services. Nature, wildlife, "beautiful people;" all subjects and locations. "Noted photographers available for assignments."

PHOTO TRENDS, 1472 Broadway, New York NY 10036. Contact: R. Eugene Keesee. "About 500,000 b&w and color (mostly 35mm) photos. Subjects: children, education, news photos from England, Sweden, South Africa, Spain and Italy, Hollywood candids from circa 1943 to date, scientific subjects such as photomicrographs, people in places around the world, scenics around the world, wonders and disasters occurring on planet Earth." For editorial, offers "usually North American rights only. World rights available for 95% of the materials." Fees: ASMP rates.

PHOTO WORLD, 251 Park Ave. S., New York NY 10010. (212)777-4210. Manager: Selma Brackman. Photos of personalities, history, World War II, and all other subjects; some specialties. 1,000,000 photos in collection. Rights offered negotiable. Fees depend on reproduction rights.

PHOTOGRAPHY BY HARVEY CAPLIN, Box 10393, Albuquerque NM 87114. (505)898-2020. Contact: Harvey Caplin. 60,000 b&w and color on the following subjects; Cattle, sheep, Indians, scenics, national parks and monuments, industry, history and agriculture. Offers first rights or all rights. Fees: $250 minimum for outright purchase; $60 minimum (color) and $30 minimum (b&w) reproduction fee. Catalog available on request with representative selection of the types of photographs immediately available. Credit line required.

PHOTOGRAPHY COLLECTION, Special Collections Division, University of Washington Libraries, Seattle WA 98195. (206)543-0742. Contact: Curator of Photography. Collection of

200,000 images devoted to history of photography in Pacific Northwest and Alaska from 1860-1920. Most early photographers of the two regions are represented, including Eric A. Hegg (Gold Rush), Wilhelm Hester (Maritime), and George T. Emmons (Anthropology). Special topical assemblies maintained for localities, industries and occupations of Washington Territory and State, for Seattle history, for Indian peoples and totem culture, for ships, whaling and for regional architects and architecture. No printed catalog available; will provide xeroxes of selected views (at 10¢ each) upon receipt of specific statements of needs. Fees by arrangement. Picture credits required for publication and television uses.

PHOTOGRAPHY FOR INDUSTRY (PFI), 850 Seventh Ave., New York NY 10019. (212)757-9255. Contact: Charles E. Rotkin. Over 100,000 photos available on loan basis only. Reproduction rights, advertising rights, first rights, second rights and editorial rights available. Industrial stock color and low level aerial photographs (Europe, U.S.A. and Asia). Fees: ASMP rates or higher.

PHOTOPHILE, 2311 Kettner Blvd., San Diego CA 92101. (714)234-4431. Contact: Linda L. Rill, Graphics Editor. Color only; 80,000 available. B&w conversion service also available. Strong agencies (heaviest in California, the western states and Mexico). Europe "strong" (with new material being added on a constant basis); good files on education; complete San Diego coverage, excellent natural science material; broad range of sports; worldwide architecture. Rights purchased vary with material and its use. Fee: $350 to $1,500 for outright purchase; $15 service charge (if unused); reproduction, $85 to $500 for color. Credit line and tearsheets required. Prints must be returned. "We have a research service available for total projects, regardless of where the photos, prints, etc., come from, including other agencies, museums or governmental sources. An hourly rate of $15, plus expenses, is charged for outside sources work only."

PHOTOVILLAGE, 117 Waverly Place, #5E, New York NY 10011. (212)260-6051 or 541-7720. Contact: Geoffrey R. Gove. Collection of over 50,000 photos, geographic coverage, as well as Americana, ecology, sports, special effects, cover graphics, personalities. B&w and color. Offers non-exclusive reproduction rights. Minimum fee of $50 for b&w; $150 minimum for color. Will shoot to order for $150 minimum purchase.

PICTORIAL PARADE, INC., 130 W. 42 St., New York NY 10036. (212)695-0353. Contact: Baer M. Frimer. Photos of all subjects.

PICTUREMAKERS, INC., 1 Paul Dr., Succasunna NJ 07876. (201)584-3000. President: Bill Stahl. Photos of all subjects.

ENOCH PRATT FREE LIBRARY, 400 Cathedral St., Baltimore MD 21201. Contact: Maryland Department. B&w 8x10 glossies of Maryland and Baltimore: persons, scenes, buildings, monuments. "Copy prints at nominal fees." Credit line required.

PUBLIC ARCHIVES OF CANADA, 395 Wellington St., Ottawa 4, Ont., Canada. Contact: Georges Delisle, Chief, Picture Division. Photos available on Canadiana: historical views, events; portraits. B&w only. Print fee, minimum charge $2.75. Credit line required.

QUEENS BOROUGH PUBLIC LIBRARY, Long Island Division, 89-11 Merrick Blvd., Jamaica NY 11432. (212) 739-1900. Contact: Davis Erhardt. 20,000 b&w original photos, glass negatives, clippings, postcards, old prints. Subjects: Long Island history, all phases. "Many are historical in nature, dating back to the 1890-1920 period." Print and reproduction fees charged. Credit line required.

REFLEX PHOTOS INC., 186 Fifth Ave., New York NY 10010. (212)684-0448. Manager: Lawrence Woods. Over 50,000 b&w photos; 15,000 color transparencies. Life in b&w and color. Offers 1-time rights, first rights, exclusive rights, translation rights, distribution rights and promotion rights. Service charge, holding fee, losses and damage protection negotiable, beginning at $15. Credit line required.

RELIGIOUS NEWS SERVICE, 43 W. 57th St., New York NY 10019. Contact: Jim Hansen, Photo Editor. Over 200,000 items on file. "Religious and secular topics. Largest collection of religious personalities in world. Also fine selection of scenics, human interest, artwork, seasonals, social issues, history, cartoons, etc. RNS can be called on for almost all photo needs, not just religious topics." B&w only. Offers 1-time rights. Fees variable.

REMINGTON ART MUSEUM, 303 Washington St., Ogdensburg NY 13669. (315)393-2425. Contact: Mildred B. Dillenbeck, Curator. Photos of Frederic Remington paintings, watercolors, drawings, and bronzes. B&w prints and color transparencies available. The largest and most complete collection of works by Remington. Charges rental and 1-time reproduction fee. "$6 photographer's fee for b&w; $35 photographer's fee for color." Credit line and return of pictures required.

REPORTS INTERNATIONALE AGENCY, Box 4574, 1350 Santa Fe, Denver CO 80204. Contact: Robert Johnson. 20,000 color photos. "Strong 35mm Kodachrome inventory of the Rocky Mountain states, Canada and the Southwest, Florida, New England, Seattle, Central America, Mexico and France. Scenics, people, flowers, nature, the sciences; mountain sports a specialty." Reproduction rights, advertising rights, editorial rights, first rights and all rights. Reproduction fee: $25 minimum.

RHODE ISLAND DEPARTMENT OF ECONOMIC DEVELOPMENT, Tourist Promotion Division, One Weybosset Hill, Providence RI 02903. Contact: Leonard J. Panaggio, Assistant Director. 2,500 to 5,000 photos. Subjects deal primarily with those used in the promotion of tourism and the state of Rhode Island. Industrial and general picture file includes 8x10 b&w photos, 35mm color transparencies. Color transparencies must be returned. Any pictures or color transparencies can be used for editorial purposes. Any and all of material is available.

RICHARDS COMMERCIAL PHOTO SERVICE, 734 Pacific Ave., Tacoma WA 98402. (206)627-9111. Contact: Ed Richards. "Thousands of b&w and color photos of children, people, animals, farms, forests, all types of industry." Rights offered: "any required." Fees: $25 minimum.

H. ARMSTRONG ROBERTS, 4203 Locust St., Philadelphia PA 19104. (215)386-6300. 420 Lexington Ave., Room 509, New York NY 10017. (212)682-6626. Tina Veiga, Manager. 203 N. Wabash Ave., Room 818, Chicago IL 60601. (312)726-0880. Howard Cox, Manager. Over one-half million stock photographs of all subjects in color and b&w. Also historical file. Catalog and/or 10-day fee approval submissions available. Research and holding fees not generally charged. Reproduction fees vary according to nature and extent of media.

LEONARD LEE RUE, III, R.D. #2, Box 88A, Blairstown NJ 07825. (201)362-6616. Contact: Leonard Lee Rue, III or Barbara Dalton. 500,000 photos on file on sale basis only for reproduction rights or advertising rights. Subjects: Wildlife of the world, nature, outdoor activities, sports, native people; one of the largest files on wildlife in the country. Reproduction fee: $25-35/b&w; $85-125/color. Prices can be negotiated.

S & S PHOTOGRAPHY, Box 8101, Atlanta GA 30306. Manager: Ed Symmes. Photos of all subjects. "Mostly color transparencies of nature, tropical fish, horticulture, bonsai, scenics." About 5,000 photos in collection. Offers "from 1-time only to world rights." Fees depend on usage and rights purchased.

SAN FRANCISCO MARITIME MUSEUM, Foot of Polk St., San Francisco CA 94109. Contact: Isabel Bullen. Photos of West Coast shipping, deep-water sail, steamships, etc. Mostly b&w, some color (contemporary ships). Print fee: $4 (8x10 glossy). Textbooks repro fee is $7.50. Credit line required.

SANFORD PHOTO ASSOCIATES, 219 Turnpike Road, Manchester NH 03104. Contact: Mrs. Gene Tobias Sanford, Stockfile Manager. Over 100,000 photos in collection. "Color (primarily 4x5 transparencies), 35mm, 2¼, some 8x10 transparencies; color negatives — mostly New England scenics and varied all-occasion type photographs. B&w 8x10 scenics and miscellaneous subjects. Our files in both b&w and color cover a wide range of subjects: flowers, children, animals, houses, industry, pollution, soft focus, some other areas in U.S. and many foreign countries. Usually one-time reproduction rights, but more specifically this would depend on whatever the use." Fees: (minimum for 1-time reproduction use) 8x10 b&w, $35; color, $125.

SCALA FINE ARTS PUBLISHERS, INC., 28 W. 44th St., New York NY 10036. Contact: Nancy Palubniak, Assistant Manager. Photos of art objects. "Chronologically, the range is from the caveman to the present; geographically, we cover all Europe, the Near East, and India with a specialty collection from Japan and a small selection of Mayan and Incan objects." Photos available of "paintings, sculpture, architecture, tapestry, pottery, manuscript illumination, and a wide variety of other art styles." Has archive of scientific subjects; "the main topics covered include botany, zoology, geography, geology, biology, medicine, marine life (with special emphasis on underwater), and a wide range of photographs of farming, industry, living conditions, etc., around the world. We represent the famous Alinari collection in the United States. These b&w photographs for rental include objects of art from Greece, Italy, Germany, France, and numerous other countries." B&w photos; color transparencies, 35mm to 8x10. Fee: "varies according to the usage. We will submit photos on approval."

SEKAI BUNKA PHOTO, 501 Fifth Ave., Room 2102, New York NY 10017. (212)490-2180. Manager: Carla Young. Over 100,000 color and b&w photos of Japan and the Far East for usage in New York branch, including modern scenes, historical art treasures, temples/shrines, architecture, costume, manners, etc. Expanding to similar coverage, especially of people and their life styles in the United States and Europe (including calendar pin-ups) for sale in Japan through Tokyo office. B&w are quality 5x7 or larger glossy and color are usually 2¼x3¼, 4x5 or larger. Usually offers 1-time rights, non-exclusive usage, although other rights are negotiable. Discounts from basic prices for quantity use in same work. Basic price minimums (generally $65 for b&w and $125 for color) vary depending upon usage, quantity; other factors depending upon final fee negotiations. Available for special assignments in Japan and Far East.

THE SHAKER MUSEUM, Shaker Museum Rd., Old Chatham NY 12136. Contact: Peter Laskovski, Director. Photographs of Shaker buildings and members; museum galleries; some furniture and other artifacts; B&w only. Charge for making selection $1. Print fees: for first requested copy if not in files, $12, including one 8x10 print; second prints, or if from negative in files, $6. Negative of any requested copy stays in files. Billed by photographer. Credit line required.

ANN ZANE SHANKS, 201 B East 82nd St., New York NY 10028. "About 5,000 items. Stock picture file, color and b&w of people —from the very young to the very old. Celebrities, scenes, hospitals, travel, and interracial activities." Offers first or second rights. Fees: $50 minimum, b&w; $150 minimum, color. Credit line requested.

RAY SHAW, Studio 5B, 255 W. 90th St., New York NY 10024. (212)873-0808. Worldwide editorial photo feature and annual report specialist. Animals, ballet, children, inspirational, American Indians, Mennonites, foreign countries: Algeria, Canada, Denmark, Egypt, England, France, Germany, India, Iran, Israel, Jordan, Lebanon, Luxembourg, Mexico, Morocco, Switzerland, Syria, Tunisia, Yugoslavia, etc.

SHOSTAL ASSOCIATES, INC., 60 E. 42nd St., New York NY 10017. (212)687-0696. Contact: David Forbert. Over 1 million photos available on rental basis. Reproduction rights, advertising rights, first rights, second rights, editorial rights, all rights. All subjects, U.S. and foreign. Fees vary with material and usage.

SICKLES PHOTO-REPORTING SERVICE, Box 98, 410 Ridgewood Rd., Maplewood NJ 07040. (201)763-6355. Contact: Gus Sickles, Jr. "Negatives on file cover a period of about the past 40 years, relating to business, industry, agriculture, etc., but we are basically an assignment service, rather than a supplier of stock photos." Offers all rights. Fee: ASMP rates "or will quote".

SISTO ARCHIVES, 3531 South Elmwood Avenue, Berwyn IL 60402. Contact: John A. Sisto. Over 3 million "historical photos and old prints, over four thousand subject categories." B&w and color available. "The photographs may be reproduced in the manner specified on our invoice. They may not be syndicated, rented, loaned, or re-used in any manner without special permission." Fees: "minimum $25, maximum $500."

SKYVIEWS SURVEY INC., 50 Swalm St., Westbury NY 11590. (516)333-3600. Over 100,000 photos of aerial subjects in northeast region of United States. B&w, color transparencies and slides. Catalogued geographically and by subject. Publication use rights vary with material and its use. Fees range from $37.50 to $200 and over. Credit line and tearsheets required.

DICK SMITH PHOTOGRAPHY, P. O. Box X, North Conway NH 03860. (603)356-2814. "10,000 b&w and 5,000 4x5 color transparencies. Scenics, tourist attractions, geologic and geographic features, farming, animals, lakes, mountains, snow scenes, historic sites, churches, covered bridges, flowers and gardens, aerials, Atlantic coast, skiing, fishing, camping, national parks. These are mostly of New England, but I do have some of the South and West." Offers usually 1-time rights for the specific use. Fees: minimum b&w $35, minimum color $100.

GEMINI SMITH, INC. (formerly Bradley Smith Photography), 5858 Desert View Dr., La Jolla CA 92037. (714)454-6321. Contact: Elisabeth Girard. 5,000 photos on file. Reproduction rights, advertising rights, all rights. B&w and color. Subjects: Paintings and sculptures of the world (all periods, prehistoric to modern); folkways and scenics (Japan, Spain, Mexico, United States, West Indies, India); circus; personalities of the 40's and 50's. Holding fee: $15. Reproduction fee: $75/half-page b&w; $250/full page color.

SOPHIA SMITH COLLECTION, Women's History Archive, Smith College, Northampton MA 01060. Contact: Mary-Elizabeth Murdock, Ph.D., Director. About 5,000 photos emphasizing women's history and general subjects; abolition and slavery, American Indians, outstanding men and women, countries (culture, scenes), U.S. military history, social reform, suffrage, women's rights. Mainly b&w or sepia. Offers U.S. rights, 1-time use only. Print fee based on cost of reproduction of print plus intended use. *Picture Catalog* including fee schedule available for $6 postpaid.

SMITHSONIAN INSTITUTION, National Anthropological Archives, Washington DC 20560. (202)381-5225. There are approximately 50,000 b&w negatives pertaining to North American Indians, including prominent individuals and scenes of life. Most were made between 1860 and 1930. Collections include about 14,000 photographs of anthropological subjects throughout the world. Print fees: 8x10, $3.50 plus mailing charges; advance payment required. Reproduction fee: $10 to $100. Credit line required.

HOWARD SOCHUREK, INC., 680 Fifth Ave., New York NY 10019. (212)582-1860. 250,000 photos on purchase basis only. Reproduction rights, advertising rights, first rights, second rights, editorial rights and all rights available. Subjects: Thermography, ultrasound, science, medical illustration, travel, journalism, U.S.S.R. Fees: Service charge, $50. Reproduction fee: $50/b&w minimum; $150/color minimum.

SOUTH DAKOTA STATE HISTORICAL SOCIETY, Soldiers Memorial, Pierre SD 57501. (605)224-3615. Contact: Mrs. Bonnie Gardner. Photos of Indians, especially Sioux, frontiersmen, life in Dakota Territory, early mines and mining, various other frontier subjects. B&w glossy, matte. Fees: $2 for 5x7; $4 for 8x10. Credit line required.

SOVFOTO/EASTFOTO, 25 W. 43rd St., New York NY 10036. Contact: Leah Siegel. Over 900,000 photos. Photographic coverage from the Soviet Union, China and all East European countries. B&w and color. Fees vary, depending on use. Minimum charge for b&w photos is $50 for 1-time use. Minimum fee for color is $125.

HUGH SPENCER PHOTOS, 3711 El Ricon Way, Sacramento CA 95825. Contact: George H. Spencer. 5,000 b&w, 3,500 35mm color. Plants and animals, biological sciences, birds, mammals, insects, reptiles, amphibians, marine life; ferns, wild flowers, trees, mosses, lichens, fungi, etc. Photomicrographs of plant tissues, sections, algae, protozoa. Offers non-exclusive rights on all subjects. Fees: "$25-37.50 for b&w; $75 to $100 for color, or will negotiate."

BOB AND IRA SPRING, 18819 Olympic View Drive, Edmonds WA 98020. (206)776-4685. "40,000 color transparencies and 40,000 b&w outdoor scenes of the Pacific Northwest, Canada, Alaska, and a comprehensive collection (including industry, homes, schools, scenics) of Japan and Scandanavian countries." Also has a large collection on birds and animals; mostly b&w. Offers 1-time use or outright sale.

TOM STACK & ASSOCIATES, 2508 Timber Lane, Lindenhurst IL 60046. (312)356-2500. 1,000,000 color transparencies and 500,000 b&w photos. Mammals, birds, amphibians, reptiles, insects, marine life including invertrabrates from all around the world, especially endangered species or hard to find and rare species. Flowers and all types of plants, children candids, people from all walks of life and occupations. Boating and marine scenes, farm and country, girls and nudes, romantic couples, foreign geographical locales, all types of sports, old movie stills, etc. Reproduction rights, advertising rights, editorial rights, first rights, all rights. Holding fee: Over 30 days, $1/day. Reproduction fee: ASMP rates.

STATEN ISLAND HISTORICAL SOCIETY, 302 Center Street, Staten Island NY 10306. (212)351-1611. Contact: Raymond Fingado. 10,000 photos, "mostly Staten Island scenes, houses, landscapes. However, we own the famed Alice Austen Collection —excellent shots of New York City street scenes circa 1895 to 1910, waterfront scenes of old sailing ships, Quarantine Station, famous old steamships, immigrants, life of the society set on Staten Island." Primarily b&w. "Usually 1-time publication rights for each picture." Fees are "flexible, but generally average $30 per plate —sometimes, but rarely lower and sometimes higher. Negotiated according to the nature of the project."

STEAMSHIP HISTORICAL SOCIETY OF AMERICA, 414 Pelton Ave., Staten Island NY 10310. Secretary: Alice S. Wilson. Library and photo files now at: Steamship Historical Society Collection, University of Baltimore Library, 1420 Maryland Ave., Baltimore MD 21201. (301)727-6350, ext. 455 or 447. Contact: James Foster. More than 10,000 pictures of ships; ocean, coastal, inland, etc. B&w. Write for current print prices. Inquiries involving lengthy research, $5 per hour. 1-time reproduction fee for commercial use, $5 per picture. Credit line required.

STOCK, BOSTON, INC. 739 Boylston St., Boston MA 02116. Contact: Mike Mazzaschi. Over 100,000 photos on all subjects. Edited stock. Foreign and domestic. B&w and color. All rights available; 1-time use normally. Fees for reproduction vary by use. Credit line and return of photographs required.

SWEDISH INFORMATION SERVICE, 825 Third Ave., New York NY 10022. (212)751-5900. Information Officer: Anne-Marie Sandstedt. Photos of all Swedish subjects except tourism. About 15,000 photos; mostly b&w, some color. Free reproduction. Photos must be returned after use.

SWISS NATIONAL TOURIST OFFICE, 608 Fifth Ave., New York NY 10020. Contact: Walter Bruderer, Public Relations Director. No fees, but credit line and return of pictures required.

SYGMA, 322 W. 72nd St., New York NY 10023. (212)595-0077. Contact: E. Laffont. Sells reproduction and editorial rights to photos on file. Subjects: International news, feature stories, films, politics, social interest. Reproduction fee: $50/b&w minimum; $100/color minimum.

TAURUS PHOTOS, 118 E. 28th St., New York NY 10016. (212)683-4025. Contact: Ben Michalski. 100,000 photos available on loan basis only. Reproduction rights, advertising rights, first rights, second rights, editorial rights, all rights. Subjects: Animals, children, medical, mood, nature, background scenes, sunsets, fishing, marine life, photomicrography, people, scenics. Reproduction rights, advertising rights, first rights, second rights, editorial rights, all rights. Fees: Standard ASMP rates. No research fee.

MAX THARPE PHOTO LIBRARY, 520 N.E. 7th Ave., #3, Ft. Lauderdale FL 33301. (305)763-5449. (Summer address: Box 1508, Statesville NC 28677. (704)872-0471.) 10,000 photos and 20,000 negatives available for sale or rental. Reproduction rights, advertising, rights, second rights and editorial rights offered. Subjects: Human interest, children, teenagers, candid scenes, mountains, sea. B&w and color, aimed mainly for use in Christian publications. Fee varies with material and usage.

THEATRE COLLECTION, New York Public Library, 111 Amsterdam Ave., New York NY 10023. (212)799-2200. Theatre production shots, cinema stills, portraits of theatre personnel; circus, radio, television. This is a research collection and no material is available on loan. Only reproduction through New York Public Library Photographic Service. Print fees on request. Credit line required.

THEPHOTOFILE, Pier 17, San Francisco CA 94111. (415)397-3040. Contact: Gerald L. French. 200,000 photos on file. Price depends on the following usage: reproduction rights, advertising rights, editorial rights, first rights or all rights. Subjects: agriculture, animals, art, disasters, entertainment, flowers, food, industry, people, military, missions (California), recreation, religion, transportation, sports, U.S.A., foreign countries, California, San Francisco. Fees: $35 search/service fee which is waived if purchase is made.

THIGPEN PHOTOGRAPHY, Box 9242, 1442 South Beltline, Mobile AL 36609. (205)666-2851. Contact: Roy M. Thigpen. About 3,000 stock photos; 1½ million job negatives. "Aerial views, architectural, historic, iron-lace, marine and yachting, sports, fishing, hunting; sea-life 'Jubilee' (exclusive coverage of this unusual phenomenon)." Rights offered "negotiable." Fees: "dependent on use."

BILL THOMAS, PHOTOJOURNALIST, R. 4, Box 411B, Nashville TN 47448. (812)988-7865. 60,000 color transparencies available for purchase. Reproduction rights, advertising rights, first rights, second rights, editorial rights. Subjects: travel, outdoor recreation, wildlife, nature, all North America oriented. "We shoot only color transparencies, 35mm or 2¼, mostly latter. Maximum holding time of 3 months unless by arranged agreement." Transparency fee: $50 minimum.

LESTER TINKER PHOTOGRAPHY, 426 County Rd. 223, Durango CO 81301. Contact: Lester Tinker. "B&w and color photos of scenes of the west. Good selection of Rocky Mountain wildflower photos and various historic areas." Fees: $25 minimum for b&w; $100 minimum for color. Credit line requested. Except in cases of outright purchase, all transparencies must be returned.

TRANSWORLD FEATURE SYNDICATE, 141 E. 44 St., New York NY 10017. (212)986-1505. Manager: Mary Taylor Schilling. Photos of children, special events, beauty heads, personalities, photojournalism.

TRANS-WORLD NEWS SERVICE, Box 2801, Washington DC 20013. (202)638-5568. Bureau Chief: G. Richard Ward. Director of Photography: Paul Malec. 18,000 photos of all subjects. B&w and color. Maintains considerable background motion picture footage on the Washington area as well as travel footage on a worldwide basis. 1-time rights only, except on custom photos. Fee varies from $5 to $100 depending on subject and usage.

TREVES WORKSHOP FEATURES, 67-02D 186th Lane, Fresh Meadows NY 11365. (212)969-3170. Contact: Ralph Treves. About 20,000 b&w photos. "Home improvement ideas, use of power tools, all home workshop procedures and materials (electric wiring, cabinetmaking, wall paneling, painting and wallpapering, plumbing, wide range of home repairs)." Offers 1-time use or by negotiation. Fee: $15 to $25 for stock photo, 8x10 print.

UNDERWOOD & UNDERWOOD NEWS PHOTOS INC., 3 W. 46th St., New York NY 10036. (212)586-5910. Manager: Milton Davidson. 5 million photos of all subjects and personalities. B&w and color. Service and holding charge when applicable.

UNION PACIFIC RAILROAD, 1416 Dodge Street, Omaha NE 68179. Contact: Mr. Barry B. Combs, Director of Public Relations. 15,000 color transparencies and many b&w's on national parks and monuments, cities and regions covered by the railroad. Also photos on railroad equipment and operations, and western agriculture and industry. No fees, but credit line required.

UNIPHOTO, 2350 Wisconsin Ave., N.W., Washington DC 20007. (202)333-0500. Contact: William L. Tucker. 100,000 photos available for purchase only. Reproduction rights, advertising rights, first rights, all rights and editorial rights available. A full service photography agency with access to more than 100 photographers across the U.S. Also markets and syndicates feature stories (text and photos) to publications. Query or send samples. Rates vary with material and use. Coordinates photo assignments across the U.S.

UNITED NATIONS, UN Plaza and 42 St., New York NY 10017. Contact: Marvin Weill, Distribution Officer. More than 130,000 selected negatives on the work of the United Nations and its Specialized Agencies throughout the world. In addition to meeting coverage, illustrations primarily represent the work of the United Nations in economic and social development and human rights throughout the world. B&w and color. May not be used for advertising purposes and must be used in a United Nations context. B&w photos, if credited to the United Nations, are currently available for reproduction free of charge, although it is expected one will be instituted in the near future. There is a non-refundable service fee of $5 per color transparency. In addition, there is a fee of $25 for each color photograph published. Unused transparencies must be returned, in usable condition, within 30 days.

UNITED PRESS INTERNATIONAL (Compix Division), 220 E. 42 St., New York NY 10017. Contact: Library Photo Sales Manager. Over 5 million negatives plus b&w print file of 2 million, plus a color transparency file of over 100,000. "Period covered (various collections) from Civil War to present time. Worldwide newsphotos, personalities, human interest and features. Photo Library contains the combined files of Acme Newspictures, International News photos, United Press news photos and the Rau Collection." B&w and color. Rights offered for editorial, advertising, and private use. "Fees range upward from a minimum of $35, depending on usage."

U.S. AIR FORCE CENTRAL STILL PHOTO DEPOSITORY (AAVA) (MAC), 1221 South Fern Street, Arlington VA 22202. Approximately 300,000 exposures with a corresponding visual print file for research use. "The collection consists of b&w and color still photos, negatives and transparencies depicting the history and progress of the U.S. Air Force. This coverage includes equipment, aircraft, personnel, missiles, officer portraits, unit insignia, etc." Fees: 75¢ to $6.50 for b&w; $1 to $17.50 for color.

U.S. COAST GUARD, Public Information Office, Governors Island, New York NY 10004. (212)264-4996. Contact: Public Information Officer. Primarily b&w photos available. Subjects: U.S. Coast Guard, search and rescue, marine safety, aids to navigation, recreational boating, bridge construction work, oil pollution abatement, lighthouses, etc. Generally no charge to qualified sources for publication. Modest charges for personal collections, etc. Credit line required.

U.S. COAST GUARD HEADQUARTERS, 400 7th St., S.W., Room 8315, Washington DC 20590. Contact: Chief, Public Affairs Division. 100,000 photos of "vessels, light stations, other shore stations, rescues, Alaskan Patrols, Arctic, Antarctic, boating safety, and various others illustrating the multi-roles of the Coast Guard. Mostly 8x10 b&w glossies are available; some 35mm color transparency slides. Generally no fee when photos are to be used for publication. There is a fee of $1.25 for each 8x10 b&w glossy for mere personal use. Color is not available for personal use. If for publication, the Coast Guard credit line must be used. The number of photos selected must be kept within reason. Photos not used are requested to be returned."

U.S. DEPARTMENT OF AGRICULTURE, Photography Division, Office of Communication, Washington DC 20250. Contact: Chief, Photography Division. 500,000 or more photos; some very technical, others general. B&w and color (mostly 35mm color) on agricultural subjects. Print fee: $2.70 per 8x10, 30¢ for duplicate 35mm color. Credit line requested. "Slide sets and filmstrips ($13 and up) available on Department programs."

U.S. DEPARTMENT OF THE INTERIOR, Bureau of Reclamation, Room 7444, C St. between 18th and 19th Sts., N.W., Washington DC 20240. Contact: Commissioner, Att'n Code 910. B&w and 35mm color photos available on water-oriented recreation, municipal and industrial water supply, irrigation, agriculture, public works construction, processing of agricultural products, Western cities and scenery, hunting, fishing, camping, boating in the western U.S. "Staff is too limited to permit search for supplying requests for speculative inquiries. However, we are able to respond to requests from publications and from freelancers with assignments for articles." No fees, but credit line requested and return of color pictures required.

UNIVERSITY MUSEUM OF THE UNIVERSITY OF PENNSYLVANIA, 33rd and Spruce Sts., Philadelphia PA 19104. (215)386-7400, Ext. 213. Contact: Ms. Caroline G. Dosker. Over 100,000 photos available for purchase on loan basis. Reproduction rights offered. Subjects: anthropological, archaeological and ethnological. Fees: prints made to order: $15/first print; $7.50/each additional. Credit lines required.

UTAH STATE HISTORICAL SOCIETY, 603 E. South Temple, Salt Lake City UT 84102. (801)533-5755. Contact: Mrs. Margaret D. Lester. B&w historic photos on everything pertaining to Utah and Mormon history; industry, architecture, biography, Indians, drama and theater, athletics, musical bands, orchestras, etc. Photos are made to order; allow 10 days to two weeks for delivery. Photos are not sent on approval; they may not be returned once they are made. Print fees: 5x7 glossy prints, fees subject to change. Credit line required.

VAN CLEVE PHOTOGRAPHY, INC., Box 1366, Evanston IL 60204. (312)764-2440. Contact: Barbara Van Cleve. Approximately 2 million photos of all subjects from around the world in color and b&w. "Our color range from 35mm transparencies up to 8x10 color transparencies, B&w photographs are 8x10. Generally we market 1-time reproduction rights." Fees: minimum $35 for b&w used editorially; minimum $75 for color used editorially.

VISUALWORLD, Box 804, Oak Park IL 60303. (312)524-0405. Contact: D. Peterson. 10,000 photos on file for use on loan basis only. Reproduction rights, advertising rights, editorial rights and first rights available. "Material is leased under agreement, the terms of which are standard (by and large) among stock photograph suppliers." Fees: Reproduction, $35, b&w;

$60-125, color (single editorial use). Print, $4/8x10 b&w. Photocopies, $2.50 (deductible from order).

JOHN WARHAM, Zoology Dept., University of Canterbury, Private Bag, Christchurch, New Zealand. "About 30,000 color (35mm to 5x4) and b&w photos of natural history subjects: birds, mammals, insects from Australia, New Zealand, the Subantarctic and Antarctic and U.K." Normally one-time, non-exclusive rights offered. Fees: $25 b&w, $100 plus for color.

ALEX WASINSKI STUDIOS, 16 W. 22nd St., New York NY 10010. (212)989-0455. Contact: Alex Wasinski. Collection of about 2,500 scenics, cityscapes (day and night), TV and film personalities; fashion, food, moody landscapes, boats, etc. B&w and color. 1-time reproduction rights. Fees for b&w begin at $200; at $250 for color. Maximum is usually $500 for 4x5 color slides.

ROBERT WEINSTEIN HISTORIC PHOTO COLLECTION, 1253 S. Stanley Ave., Los Angeles CA 90019. (213)936-0558. Contact: Robert Weinstein. Photos available on maritime (sailing vessels largely) and western Americana, late 19th century. B&w. Fees subject to mutual agreement; dependent on use.

WEST VIRGINIA DEPARTMENT OF COMMERCE, Advertising Division, State Capitol, Charleston WV 25305. Contact: Judith Vannatter. Photos on West Virginia subjects in 8x10 b&w glossy prints, color in 35mm. Also offers free information on West Virginia attractions and facilities. No fees, but credit line desired and return of color pictures required.

WESTERN HISTORY DEPARTMENT, Denver Public Library, 1357 Broadway, Denver CO 80203. (303)573-5152, Ext. 246. Contact: Mrs. Eleanor M. Gehres. B&w photos on the social, economic, political, and historical developments of the U.S. west of the Mississippi River, especially the Rocky Mountain states. Large holdings of Indians, railroads, towns, outlaws, irrigation, livestock, and forts. "The Department is continually adding to the collection, increasing the holdings by several thousand annually." Prints are not available to lend for consideration purposes. The Department is willing to make selections on the subjects needed. About 280,000 items in the collection. Print fees: $3.50 for 4x5 b&w; $4.50 for 8x10 b&w; $5.25 minimum for 35mm color; $23.50 for 4x5 color. Postage and packaging are extra.

WHALING MUSEUM, 18 Johnny Cake Hill, New Bedford MA 02740. Contact: Richard C. Kugler, Director. This museum adheres to the fee schedules recommended by the Association of Art Museum Directors. Permission to reproduce Whaling Museum material will only be granted publications protected by copyright. Such copyright, where it applies to Museum material, is understood to be waived in favor of the Whaling Museum. Credit line and return of pictures required.

THE WHEELWRIGHT MUSEUM, Box 5153, Santa Fe NM 87502. Contact: Director. Photos available in b&w and color. Copy prints, $1-15. Original work, $5-35. 1-time reproduction fee: $25, b&w; $75, color. Credit line required.

WHITNEY MUSEUM OF AMERICAN ART, 945 Madison Ave., New York NY 10021. Contact: Rights and Permissions. Color transparencies. Rentals: $50 per 3 months; $10 per month thereafter. B&w photographs are also available for reproduction and reference purposes. Credit line and return of ektachromes required.

WIDE WORLD PHOTOS, INC., 50 Rockefeller Plaza, New York NY 10020. Contact: On Approval Section. About 50 million photos. "All subjects in b&w, thousands of them in color. Wide World Photos is a subsidiary of The Associated Press." Offers national, North American, and world rights. Fees start at $35.

MARGARET WILLIAMSON, 175 E. 79th St., New York NY 10021. Collection of about 10,000 photos on European travel, as well as worldwide ice skaters. B&w and color. Charges fee according to use.

THE HENRY FRANCIS DU PONT WINTERTHUR MUSEUM, Wintherthur DE 19735. Contact: Ms. Karol A. Schmiegel, Assistant Registrar. B&w photos and color transparencies of furniture, silver, ceramics, prints, paintings, textiles, and other decorative art objects made or used in America from 1640 to 1840. Selection of photos should be made from Winterthur publications or from photo files in Registrar's Office at the Museum. Fee: $10 for b&w print; charge includes print and 1-time use. Credit line required.

WOLFE WORLDWIDE FILMS, 1657 Sawtelle Blvd., Los Angeles CA 90025. About 11,000 35mm color slides, "basically travel, covering what the tourist sees." Offers non-exclusive worldwide rights. Fees vary, but are dependent upon quantity used, ranging from $50 for one slide down to $15 for a large quantity for reproduction.

GERALD WOLFSOHN PHOTOGRAPHY, 9554 S. W. 82nd St., Miami FL 33173. (305)274-9552. "Slide file of western landscapes, New York scenes, South Florida scenes, Key West, gulls, and other subjects. Specialized forensic photography on request." Fees: $50 for 1-time use. Credit line required.

WOLLIN STUDIOS, 151 E. Gorham St., Madison WI 53703. (608)256-3993. Contact: William Wollin. Thousands of color and b&w photos of Wisconsin buildings, activities, scenes. Rights offered: "Any desired, single to exclusive." Fees: $25 and up for b&w, $50 and up for color.

WYOMING STATE ARCHIVES AND HISTORICAL DEPARTMENT, Barrett Bldg., Cheyenne WY 82002. Contact: Historical Research and Publication Division. Historical information on Wyoming history (fur trade era to present). Sources include catalogued library, manuscript collection, historical collections, maps, microfilmed Wyoming newspapers (1867 to present); biographical files. Fees: 10¢/xeroxed copy page; 15¢/facsimile (from microfilm) copy page. Credit required for publication of material provided.

KATHERINE YOUNG AGENCY, 140 E. 40th St., New York NY 10016. Contact: Katherine Young. Over 50,000 general world coverage photos (strong African coverage) plus European and Japanese news and feature service, historic landmarks, architecture, scenics, people, children and family situations, monuments, animals, flowers, churches and temples. Some historic prints of personalities as well as portraits of famous people. B&w and color. Offers U.S., North American and world rights; 1-time use with further option. Standard American Society of Magazine Photographers fees. Special arrangements negotiable.

Play Producers

Producers of Broadway, Off-Broadway, and Off-Off-Broadway plays are listed below. Entries are also given for resident professional companies, amateur community theaters, and theater workshops in the United States. Non-paying theater workshops are included in this list because the experience and exposure offered by these outlets can introduce talented new playwrights and give them a better chance for commercial production of their plays.

ALLEY THEATRE, 615 Texas Ave., Houston TX 77002. A resident professional theatre; large stage seating 798; arena stage seating 296. Wants good plays, with no length restriction. Not interested in musicals. Royalty arrangements vary. Send complete script. Enclose S.A.S.E. Reports in 6 to 8 weeks. Produces 6 to 8 plays a year.

AMERICAN STAGE FESTIVAL, Box 225, Milford NH 03055. Producing Director: T.C. Lorden. Plays performed at summer festival (professional equity company) for audience of all ages, interests, education and sophistication levels. Produces 6 plays/year. Query with synopsis. 5% standard royalty; "sometimes an additional stipend to playwright if Festival wishes to retain some continuing rights to the script." SASE. Reports in 1 month.
Needs: "The Festival can do comedies, musicals, and dramas. However, the most frequent problems come from plays not fitting into the resident acting company system (all men, all young, all black, for examples) and/or which are bolder in language and action than a general mixed audience will accept. We emphasize plays which move; long and philosophical-discussion oriented plays are generally not done." Length: 2- or 3-acts.

THE BACK ALLEY THEATRE, 617 F St., N.W., Washington DC 20001. Producing Director: Naomi Eftis. Produces quality plays including 6 premieres each year of works by new and established playwrights. Submit complete script. Royalties negotiable. SASE. Reports in 6 months.
Needs: "Any length, any type, serious, comic, experimental. Space is limited and we like to take successful productions into the parks and nearby communities, so small casts and modest set demands are a factor in choosing scripts. We do favor plays that deal with social issues and contemporary problems such as women's rights, minorities, etc. Recently premiered Martin Duberman's *Payments*. "General contract involves percentage for 1-3 years on playwright's future earnings from final date of last performance of our production."

BARTER THEATRE, Main St., Abingdon VA 24210. Producer: Rex Partington. Looks for good plays, particularly comedies. Two or three acts, preferably, but will consider good quality plays of shorter length. Pays 5% royalties. Send complete script only. Enclose S.A.S.E.

THE BOLTON HILL DINNER THEATRE, 1111 Park Ave., Baltimore MD 21201. Manager: A.L. Dersett. Professional dinner theatre. Public audience, middle aged, who prefer comedy. No more than 10 characters in cast. 2-act, 3-act, comedy and revue material. Payment is negotiable. Rarely copyrights plays. Send complete script only, with S.A.S.E. Produces about 10 plays a year.

BROWN UNIVERSITY, Program in Theatre Arts, Box 1897, Providence RI 02912. Plays will be produced for summer theater or during academic year. For students and university-related, sophisticated audience. Uses 1, 2 and 3 act plays. Pays $100. Not copyrighted. Produces 8 to 12 plays a year. Send complete script only. Reports in 2 months. Enclose S.A.S.E.

GERT BUNCHEZ AND ASSOCIATES, INC., 7730 Carondelet, St. Louis MO 63105. Contact: Gert Bunchez, President. "We feel that the time is propitious for the return of stories to radio. It is our feeling that it is not necessary to 'bring back' old programs, and that there certainly should be contemporary talent to write mystery, detective, suspense, soap operas, etc. We syndicate radio properties to clients and stations. Requirements are plays with sustaining lead characters, 5 minutes to 30 minutes in length, suitable for radio reproduction. Disclaimer letter must accompany scripts. Rates from $100 per script if acceptable for radio production and actually produced." Enclose S.A.S.E.

CENTER THEATRE GROUP/MARK TAPER FORUM, 135 N. Grand Ave., Los Angeles CA 90012. (213)972-7353. Literary Manager: David Copelin. Plays to be performed in the Mark Taper Forum, a 750-seat resident theater with a thrust stage; or in the Forum/Laboratory, a 99-seat flexible space. For "an intelligent, sensitive open-minded audience of all ages and classes who are interested in serious classic and contemporary interpretations of the real world." Produces up to 20 plays/year. Submit complete script. Pays 5% of gross receipts less ticket broker commissions for plays performed in the Mark Taper Forum; $100 for plays performed in the Forum/Laboratory. SASE. Reports in 2-3 months.
Needs: "Imaginative contemporary comedies or dramas on any topic, but if the topic has been done to death the writing had better be extraordinary, or the insight and passion unusual. Social issues with a poet's consciousness, and the inner life of man theatricalized." Length: 2- or 3-acts. "Smaller casts are easier but not always necessary. Our stage has minimal wings and flies—so heavy sets/changes are hard. But if the writing is exciting, we'll do what we can. No plays about Gary Gilmore, please, or Richard Nixon. Most naturalist plays are of little interest. The sensitive artist vs. the crass world is a conflict we're heartily bored with. No leftover Bicentennial-contest winners."

THE CHANGING SCENE THEATER, 1527½ Champa St., Denver CO 80202. Year-round productions in theater space. Cast may be made up of both professional and amateur actors. For public audience; age varies, but mostly youthful, and interested in taking a chance on new and/or experimental works. No limit to subject matter or story themes. Emphasis is on the innovative. "Also, we require that the playwright be present for at least one performance of his work, if not for the entire rehearsal period. We have a small stage area, but are able to convert to round, semi-round, or environmental. Prefer to do plays with limited set and props." 1-act, 2-act, and 3-act. Also interested in musicals. "We do not pay royalties, or sign contracts with playwrights. We function on a performance share basis of payment. Our theater seats 78, the first 35 seats go to the theater, the balance is divided among the participants in the production. The performance share process is based on the entire production run, and not determined by individual performances. We do not copyright our plays." Send complete script. Enclose S.A.S.E. Reporting time varies; usually several months. Produces approximately 10 to 15 new plays a year.

CHELSEA THEATER CENTER, 30 Lafayette Ave., Brooklyn NY 11217. Artistic Director: Robert Kalfin. Looking for full-length plays "that stretch the bounds of the theater in form and content. No limitations as to size of cast or physical production." Pays $500 for a 6-month option for an off-Broadway production." Works 10 months in advance. Query first with synopsis. Enclose S.A.S.E. for reply to queries.

ALFRED CHRISTIE, 405 E. 54th St., New York NY 10022. "The theatre is a summer stock theatre and many of the people in the audience are on vacation, most are over age 30." Professional cast. Two-act or three-act plays. "We would like funny situation, contemporary farces or light comedies. Scripts that are sensational in theme, that can compete with today's frank and modern films are also possible. Also, we do children's shows. We like a well-written play with interesting switches or avant-garde scripts that are based on reality and make sense. We would expect the author to copyright the play but if the show moves on to other theatres or Broadway or to a film, etc., we would like a small percentage of the action. We want no family situation shows, no period plays involving many period costumes. We prefer small cast, single-set shows, but if a script is good we would do a larger cast and multiple set production." Produces 6 to 10 full productions and several children's plays yearly. Payment varies. A percentage or a flat fee is possible. "Does the author want to come and work with the people and on the play?" Send synopsis or complete script. "We like scripts by April of each year because we must arrange publicity, hire actors, etc." Enclose S.A.S.E. for return of submissions.

THE CLEVELAND PLAY HOUSE, Box 1989, Cleveland OH 44106. Robert Snook, New Scripts Department. Plays performed in professional LORT theater for the general public. Produces 10 plays/year. Submit complete script. Buys stock rights, and sometimes first class options. Payment varies. SASE. Reports in 6 months.
Needs: "No restrictions. Vulgarity and gratuitous fads are not held in much esteem." Length: 3-acts.

DAVID J. COGAN, 350 Fifth Ave., New York NY 10001. (212)563-9555. Produces 3-act plays. Chiefly interested in contemporary topical material. Looks for special qualities of character development, comedy. Pays royalties on production; percentage of box office. Gives average advance of $2,500. Charges $15 reading fee. Send complete script. Reports in 1 to 2 months. Enclose S.A.S.E.

JEAN DALRYMPLE, 130 W. 56th St., New York NY 10019. Producer: Jean Dalrymple. Plays performed on Broadway, off-Broadway, Show Case or summer theatres for the general public. Produces 1 play/year. Submit through agent only. Royalty as per Dramatists Guild contract. SASE. Reports in 2 weeks-1 month.
Needs: "Comedy or suspenseful drama. 2-3 acts at most; regular play format. No pornography."

THE DURHAM SUMMER THEATER, Paul Creative Arts Center, University of New Hampshire, Durham NH 03824. Contact: John C. Edwards, Managing Director. Plays will be produced by professional company with student apprentices, for summer theater. General public audience. Produces comedies, musicals, children's theater involvements (with or without music), narrative theater adaptations of novels, short stories. "Full company size: 60. Proscenium stage — opening 40'; depth 60'. Studio Theater — flexible for round, thrust, proscenium — 20' x 40'." Length requirements: 2-act and 3-act. Payment negotiated with author. Send synopsis or complete script. Reports in 6 weeks. Produces 5 major, 3 minor plays each year (including children's).

EARPLAY,Vilas Communication Hall, 821 University Ave., Madison WI 53706. Produces radio dramas for National Public Radio Stations in the United States; jointly sponsored by the Corporation for Public Broadcasting, National Endowment for the Arts, University of Wisconsin Extension, and Minnesota Public Broadcasting. Scripts are accepted throughout the year with primary interest in plays demonstrating strong character treatment, imaginative use of sound, and clear and compelling plot lines. All work which makes creative use of the medium will be considered. Because of broadcast schedules, the 1-hour play is best suited for production. Payment: $2,000 for 60 minutes, first rights; $1,000 for 60 minutes, previously performed. Not interested in the following: drama aimed at children, religious drama, educational/instructional material. Send S.A.S.E. for writers' fact sheet to obtain complete submission details. It takes 2 to 3 months for a script to be given thorough consideration. Enclose S.A.S.E. with all submissions and inquiries.

EAST CAROLINA PLAYHOUSE, East Carolina University, Greenville NC 27834. Plays will be performed at the University Theatre, for the general public. All types and lengths of plays considered. Not copyrighted. Send complete script only. Reports usually in 6 weeks to 2 months. Enclose S.A.S.E.

ZELDA FICHANDLER, c/o Arena Stage, 6th and M Sts., S.W., Washington DC 20024. Wants original plays preferably (but not necessarily) submitted through agents. "Plays with relevance to the human situation—which cover a multitude of dramatic approaches—are welcome here." Pays 5 percent of gross. Reports in 6 months. Enclose S.A.S.E.

H.D. FLOWERS, II, Box 2054, South Carolina State College, Orangeburg SC 29117. (803)536-7123. Summer educational theater for college and community audience. Plays with black themes are needed. Style does not matter. Will consider 1-, 2- and 3-act plays. Pays $50 to $75 per performance. Produces 4 to 6 plays a year. Send complete script only. Enclose S.A.S.E.

FOLGER THEATRE GROUP, 201 E. Capitol St., Washington DC 20003. Produced in professional theatre, AEA LORT Contract, for general public. All kinds of plays. "Since we produce 2 Shakespeare productions a season, we would rather not read Shakespearean adaptations or treatments." No limitations in cast, props; stage is small but flexible. Any length play. Payment negotiable. Send complete script or submit through agent. Enclose S.A.S.E. Reports "as soon as possible, usually 8 to 10 weeks." Produces 3 new plays a year, and various Shakespearean productions.

GALWAY PRODUCTIONS, c/o New Jersey Shakespeare Festival, Madison NJ 07940. Director: Paul Barry. Looks for controversial plays on any subject. Pays standard Dramatists Guild royalty percentage. All scripts must be free and clear of subsidiary rights commitments. No musicals or one-acts. Submit synopsis or full-length play. Enclose S.A.S.E.

WILLIAM GARDNER, Academy Festival Theatre, Barat College, Lake Forest IL 60045. Plays will be performed by a professional cast during summer theater. Audience: well-educated, intelligent, 3-act plays considered. Pays 6% for new scripts. Not copyrighted. "We ask certain vested rights." Submit through agent only. Enclose S.A.S.E. Reports in 6 weeks to 6 months. Produces about 4 plays per year.

JAMES GLASS, Box 56, Cecilwood Theatre, Fishkill NY 12524. (914)896-6273. Producer: James Glass. Plays performed in professional equity summer theater. Twenty-ninth year of operation. Produces 6-8 plays/year. Submit complete script. Pays flat fee or percentage. SASE. Reports in 1 month.
Needs: Intelligent comedies. Casts of 2-7; contemporary settings, single set, uncomplicated props. "No plays with filthy language or over-sexed subjects." Length: 2- or 3-acts.

HARWICH JUNIOR THEATRE, Box 168, West Harwich MA 02671. President: Robert Doane. Plays performed in summer theatre with semi-professional and amateur casts for children. Produces 6 plays/year. Query with synopsis. Pays $10-15/performance. SASE. Reports in 1 year.
Needs: "We produce plays for children; adventure stories and fairy tales." Length: 2- or 3-acts; 1½ hours maximum.

CHARLES HOLLERITH, JR., 18 W. 55th St., New York NY 10019. Produces Broadway and off-Broadway plays for the general public. Pays Dramatist Guild rates. Submit through agent only. Reports in 2 weeks. Produces 1 play a year. Length: open. Copyrighted.

HONOLULU THEATRE FOR YOUTH, P.O. Box 3257, Honolulu HI 96801. Artistic Director: Wallace Chappell. Produces plays of "1 hour without intermission. Plays are produced in Honolulu in various theater buildings; also, an annual tour in theater buildings on Neighbor Islands, state of Hawaii. Casts are amateur with professional direction and production; adult actors, with children as needed. Plays are produced for school children, grades 2 through 12, individual plays directed to specific age groups; also public performances." Interested in "historical (especially American) plays, plays about Pacific countries and Pacific legends, and Asian legends and Asian history. Plays must have strong character with whom young people can identify, with stress on action rather than exposition, but not at the expense of reality (i.e., not slapstick). Plays should be reasonably simple technically and use primarily adult characters. Fairy tales (especially mod versions) are at the bottom of the priority list, as are elaborate musicals requiring large orchestras. Casts up to 15, preferably. Technical requirements should be reasonably simple, as sets have to be built at one place and trucked to the theater." Produces 5-6 plays/year. Royalty fee is based on number of performances. Query first with synopsis only. Reports in 1 to 2 months. Enclose S.A.S.E. for reply to queries.

WILLIAM E. HUNT, 801 West End Ave., New York NY 10025. Interested in reading scripts for stock production, off-Broadway and even Broadway production. "Small cast, youth-oriented, meaningful, technically adventuresome; serious, funny, far-out. Must be about people first, ideas second. No political or social tracts." Pays royalties on production. Off-Broadway, 5%; on Broadway, 5%, 7½% and 10%, based on gross. Reports in "a few weeks." Enclose S.A.S.E.

IRON SPRINGS CHATEAU, c/o Mrs. Doug Jensen, 1805 Mesa Rd., Colorado Springs CO 80904. Professional cast will perform plays at a summer theater, for a general audience. Melodrama only. Cast limitation of 8. Drops preferred to sets or flats. Looking for 3-act plays only; 90-minute length. Rate of payment is "$125 to $300 per show." Send complete script only. Enclose S.A.S.E. Reports in 1 week. Produces 4 plays a year.

JON JORY, Producing Director, Actors Theatre of Louisville, 316 W. Main St., Louisville KY 40202. Actors Theatre of Louisville is a resident professional theatre operating under a L.O.R.T. contract for a 35-week season from September to June. Subscription audience of 16,000 from extremely diverse backgrounds. "Plays with a strong story line and a basically positive life view. We are not interested in situation comedies or 'absurdists' work. We are particularly interested in new musicals and small cast straight plays. No one-acts. No more than 12 to 15 actors. There are 2 theatres, one a 640-seat thrust and one seating 200. Multiple set shows are impossible here." Payment is negotiated. Asks for financial participation in the play's future only when a work has been specifically commissioned. SASE. Reports in 2 to 3 months. Produces 2 plays a year.

LORETTO-HILTON REPERTORY THEATRE, 130 Edgar Rd., St. Louis MO 63119. Regional repertory theatre, professional equity company, for general public. Plays varied in themes. Interested in any play suitable for a subscription audience of over 17,000. Royalty payments negotiable; usually between 4% and 5% of gross. Send complete script. Enclose S.A.S.E. Reports within 4 months during the winter season; closed over the summer. Produces 5 plays a year, only one of them an original production.

THE MAGIC THEATRE, INC., 1618 California St., and Building 314, Fort Mason Arts Complex, San Francisco CA 94109. "Oldest experimental theatre in California; established in 1967. General Director: John Lion, Administrative Director: L. Ann Wieseltier. For public audience, generally college educated. General cross section of area with an interest in an alternative theatre. Plays produced in San Francisco, California; produced in the off-Broadway manner. Cast is part equity, part non-equity. The director of the Magic Theatre's concept leans toward the Surrealist movement in the arts. Its main resident playwrights are Michael McClure and Sam Shepard. For the past 5 years has had Rockefeller funding for playwright-in-residence program. The playwright should have an approach to his writing with a specific intellectual concept in mind or a specific theme of social relevance. We don't want to see scripts that would be television or 'B' movie oriented. 1-act or 2-act plays considered. Playwright usually co-pyrights own script. Our productions vary as to degrees of technical complexity. We pay 5% of gross, $100 advance." Produces 10 plays/year. Enclose S.A.S.E.

MANHATTAN THEATRE CLUB, Stephen Pascal, Literary Director, 321 E. 73 St., New York NY 10021. A three theatre, performing arts complex classified as off-off Broadway, using professional actors. "We have a large, diversified audience which includes a large number of season subscribers. We want plays about contemporary problems and people. No special requirements. No verse plays or historical dramas or large musicals. Very heavy set shows or multiple detailed sets are out. We prefer shows with casts not more than 10. No skits, but any other length is fine." Payment is negotiable. Query first with synopsis. Enclose S.A.S.E. Reports in 6 months. Produces 20 plays/year.

CHRISTIAN H. MOE, Theater Department, Southern Illinois University, Carbondale IL 62901. Plays will be performed in a university theater (either a 580-seat theater or an experimental theater which can seat 100 to 150). Cast will be non-equity. Audience is a public one drawn from a university community with disparate interests. Largest percentage is a student and faculty audience. Student age range is roughly from 16 to 25. Also a children's theatre audience ranging from pre-school to 13 years. No restriction on subject matter. "Since we do 3 to 4 children's plays each year, we are interested in children's theatre scripts as well as adult. We prefer full-length plays since we have many student one-acts, the best of which it is our first obligation to produce. Small cast plays are preferred. This applies to children's plays also. A limited budget prohibits lavish set or property demands." 2-act, 3-act, and 50-to-60-minute children's plays. Payment is standard; no set figure. Normally pays $15 per performance for a children's play. Special arrangements made for plays that tour. Query first with synopsis. Enclose S.A.S.E. Usually reports in 3 months. Produces 14 plays a year.

DOUG MOODY MYSTIC SOUND STUDIO'S MYSTIC MUSIC CENTRE, 6277 Selma Ave., Hollywood CA 90028. For home entertainment, all ages. Works produced on phonograph albums and cassette tapes. "We are looking for works capable of being performed within one hour, non-visual. Can be musical. Can rely on sound effects to replace visual effects. Think about the medium!" Payment depending upon royalties to artists and musical copyright royalties. Buys phonograph and audio rights. Query first with synopsis only. Enclose SASE.

OLD LOG THEATER, Box 250, Excelsior MN 55331. Producer: Don Stolz. Produces 2-act and 3-act plays for "a professional cast. Public audiences, usually adult. Interested in contemporary comedies. Small number of sets. Cast not too large." Produces about 14 plays a year. Payment by Dramatists Guild agreement. Send complete script only. Enclose S.A.S.E. for return of submissions.

OMAHA COMMUNITY PLAYHOUSE, 6915 Cass St., Omaha NE 68132. (402)553-4890. Contact: Christopher Rutherford, Artist-in-Residence. Plays performed by an amateur cast in either studio or proscenium theater for an adult, scholastically minded, theatre-oriented audience. Produces 10 plays/year. "Works to be submitted in bound ms form and professional appearance." Does not copyright plays. SASE. Pays $35 for first performance; $25 for each performance thereafter. Some residencies available. Reporting time varies according to need and current demand.
Needs: "Any subject or theme dealt with in a competent manner; hopefully the play will also be of an entertaining nature. Prime consideration given to smaller (2-15) cast shows and prefer-

ence toward simpler demands on our limited budgets for sets, costumes, musicians. Do not send musicals without *complete* score."

OPERA VARIETY THEATER, 3944 Balboa St., San Francisco CA 94121. Director: Violette M. Dale. Plays to be performed by professional and amateur casts for a public audience; all ages, generally families; upper educational level. Submit complete script. "Everyone (cast, author, technical people, publicity, etc.) receives equal percentage." SASE. Reports in 6 months. **Needs:** "Prefer musicals (but must have singable, tuneful material; arranged, ready to cast). Plays or music on most any theme that conservative audiences would enjoy. Must have substantial, believable plot and good characterizations. Must be simple to produce; fairly small cast, easy setting, etc. (small backstage area limits cast, props, staging, etc.). Emphasis is on entertainment rather than social reform." Length: 1- , 2- or 3-acts. "No vulgarity in language or action; no wordy preaching."

OTTERBEIN COLLEGE THEATRE, Westerville OH 43081. Contact: Dr. Charles W. Dodrill. Plays will be performed by the Otterbein College Theatre cast, with a professional guest actor; also summer theatre. For a central-Ohio public. Will not use radical plays. Should be 3-act plays. Not copyrighted. Reports in 6 weeks. Produces 11 plays each year. Send synopsis or complete ms. Enclose S.A.S.E.

JOSEPH PAPP, New York Shakespeare Festival, 425 Lafayette St., New York NY 10003. (212)677-1750. Gail Merrifield, Director of Play Development. Interested in full-length plays and musical works. No restrictions as to style, historical period, traditional or experimental forms, etc. New works produced at the Public Theater (Anspacher, Newman, Other Stage, Little Theater, Martinson and Luesther Halls), Lincoln Center (Beaumont and Newhouse Theaters), Mobile Theater; occasionally at the Delacorte Theater in Central Park. Standard option and production agreements. Reports in 4 to 6 weeks. Enclose S.A.S.E.

THE PLAYWRIGHTS' LAB, 3800 Park, Minneapolis MN 55407. "Plays given readings and semi-professional productions. A staff of 6 playwrights-in-residence reads and critiques plays. Reports in 6 months. 1-act plays have best chance and please send S.A.S.E. A minimum royalty-stipend is available. The lab has operated for more than 5 years and in that time has produced some 60 plays by more than 30 playwrights."

POET'S REPERTORY THEATRE, Box 203, Brookhaven NY 11719. (516)928-7865. Both a tour program and a resident theater program. The tour program plays for any host organization, especially libraries, churches, public schools, colleges, arts conferences, private homes. Resident theater wing plays in four permanent locations twice each year, three performances per production per location. Audiences are both public and private, and are composed of all interests, intelligences, and educational levels. Shorter plays are wanted for tour program, 5 minutes to 55 minutes. Some longer plays for the resident theater program. No restriction on subject or theme. Small casts, preferably no more than 3 for the shorter plays to be toured (although 4 or 5 might get by), and 5 for the longer plays. Avoid extremes of age (no parts for children or the elderly); the play should be able to be cast with persons who are in the age range of 18 to 50. The play should not rely for its impact upon tricky lighting or scenery. No nudity, no on-stage sexual intercourse. 1-act, 2-act, 3-act, or skits considered. "Royalty payments may range between $5 and $20 per performance for shorter plays; about $40 for longer plays. It should be stressed that we are in the context of the experimental and art theater movement and will only use material that is within that context." Send synopsis or complete script. Enclose S.A.S.E. Reports usually in 3 to 5 weeks. Produces about 12 plays a year.

REPERTORY THEATER OF AMERICA/ALPHA-OMEGA PLAYERS, Box 1296, Rockport TX 78382. Booking Manager: John R. Hancock. Plays performed on the college and country club circuit (professional national tour); also local churches and civic groups. For a private audience, college age and over; majority are college graduates; wide range of geographic and religious backgrounds and taste. Produces 4 plays/year. Query with synopsis. Pays $10-20/ performance; averages approximately 100 performances per play per year. SASE. Reports in 3 weeks.
Needs: "Comedies that are fast-paced and adaptable to a dinner theater setting. Adaptations of works by well-known American authors, especially short stories. Historical drama featuring famous religious figures." Length: 2-acts; total running time 1½ hours. No plays with casts larger than 4 (2 men, 2 women, or 3 men and 1 woman); no sound facilities, minimum props. "No guerrilla theater, obscenity, intellectualizing, or bad writing."

ST. CLEMENTS, 423 W. 46 St., New York NY 10036. Plays will be produced at St. Clement's, an off-off Broadway theater; all productions are fully professional for public performances; audiences expect off-off Broadway to be somewhat experimental or innovative. 1-act, 2-act, or 3-act plays. "Our productions are presented under the terms of the Equity Showcase Code. There are no royalties. It is a showcase for the playwrights." Send complete script or submit through agent. Enclose S.A.S.E. Reports in 3 to 6 months. Produces 4 or 5 major plays a year and 10 or 12 readings.

SAN JOSE STATE UNIVERSITY THEATRE, Theatre Arts Department, San Jose State University, 125 S. 7th St., San Jose CA 95192. (408)277-2763. Director of Theatre: Dr. Howard Burman. Plays performed in university theatre by an amateur cast for a public audience, university educated. Produces 1 original play/year. Submit complete script. Pays $500 for Harold C. Crain Award winner. $50 for first performance; $35 for each additional performance of other scripts. SASE.
Needs: "All new scripts of substance and ideas regardless of style, subject or theme. Length: 2-3 acts.

SCORPIO RISING THEATRE FOUNDATION, 426 N. Hoover St., Los Angeles CA 90004. For an audience of selected theatre buffs. "Scorpio Rising Theatre is a repertory theatre dedicated to the works of new playwrights, and winner of Los Angeles drama critics' Circle Award. Looking for all kinds of plays, but prefer contemporary themes. We don't want any situation comedies or Broadway type musicals. Simple cast, props, stage, etc. 1-act, 2-act, 3-act, but open to all." Also interested in developmental work with playwrights-in-residence. Buys amateur performance rights. Payment to be negotiated. Produces 12 plays a year. Send script to Louise Newmark. Send complete script only. Reports in 1 to 2 months. Enclose S.A.S.E. for return of submissions.

SCRANTON THEATRE LIBRE, INC., 512-514 Brooks Bldg., Scranton PA 18503. Executive Director: John J. White. Plays performed by semiprofessional casts for the general public. Produces 6 plays/year. Submit synopsis or complete script. Payment varies. SASE. Reports in 3 months.
Needs: "Only original scripts of any kind; any format."

SEATTLE REPERTORY THEATRE, P.O. Box B, Queen Anne Station, Seattle WA 98109. Plays will be produced on either main stage, or in second theatre, with professional casts in both cases. The second house performs younger, more avant-garde and special interest plays. Audience for main stage is middle class; high percentage of college graduates; ages ranging from teens to advanced middle age. Plays for second house, particularly, will involve novel forms of stage, experiments in style; particular interest in works that explore new ways to use language. In main house, more conventional plays with themes related to present time. Almost any format is acceptable providing the writing is of high quality. No limitations in cast, but prefers 3-act plays. Payment depends on the plays; a guarantee against a percentage of the gross, usually starting at 4%. "When negotiating a new script, we retain a financial interest in subsequent productions of the play for a specified period of time." Send synopsis, with a dozen or so pages of script to give feeling of style, etc. Enclose S.A.S.E. Reports in about 3 months. Produces about 12 plays a year.

LORAINE SLADE, General Manager, Virginia Museum Theatre, Boulevard and Grove Ave., Richmond VA 23221. For public, well-educated, conservative, adventurous audiences. Professional repertory theatre. Looking for biography, experimental styles. Standard format of presentation. Light comedies, musicals. 2-act and 3-act plays considered. Payment is negotiable. For a premiere, theatre requires share in future income. Produces one new script a year. Send complete script only. Reports in 3 to 5 months. Enclose S.A.S.E. for return of submissions.

CHARLES STILWILL, Managing Director, Community Playhouse, Box 433, Waterloo IA 50704. (319)291-4421. Plays performed at Waterloo Community Playhouse with a volunteer cast. "We have 5,260 season tickets holders. Average attendance at main stage shows is 5,663; at studio shows 1,657. We try to fit the play to the theatre. We try to do a wide variety of plays." Looking for good plays with more roles for women than men. "Our public isn't going to accept nudity, too much sex, too much strong language. We don't have enough black actors to do all black shows. We have done plays with as few as 3 characters, and as many as 54. On the main stage we usually pay between $300 and $500. In our studio we usually pay between $50 and $300." Send synopsis or complete script. Enclose S.A.S.E. Reports negatively within 3 months, but acceptance takes longer because they try to fit a wanted script into the balanced season. Produces 6 plays a year: 1 musical, 3 comedies, 2 dramas.

JOE SUTHERIN, c/o St. Bart's Playhouse, 109 E. 50th St., New York NY 10022. Plays will be produced at St. Bart's Playhouse, a 350-seat community theater. "I am also looking for material to produce in other (professional) situations." For public/commercial "sophisticated" audience. Looking for revue, comedy material, or writer who likes to do same. Does not want to see material that relies heavily on sex, four-letter words, etc., to make it viable. Payment varies. Copyright negotiable. Send synopsis or complete script. Enclose S.A.S.E. Reports in "3 months if I'm not snowed under." Produces 2 to 4 plays per year; (also 2 musicals).

TACONIC THEATRE COMPANY, Rhinebeck NY 12572. Director: Michael T. Sheehan. Plays performed at 1) staged readings; 2) summer and winter stock; 3) professional workshop/ studio productions; and 4) possibly full-scale production for a contemporary audience, 20-70 age range; college graduates, middle to upper income; sophisticated. Produces 4-6 plays/year. Submit complete script. No payment for staged readings series; pays $5-25 per use of skits and less than full-length plays; $25-50 for full-length. SASE. Reports in 2-4 weeks.
Needs: Cabaret style (satire, comedy, etc.) themes/subjects about the American experience; small cast and simple technical requirements. "Nothing overtly political, sexual or antagonistic. Try to avoid need for flying scenery, heavy projections, and complicated props and costumes."

THEATER WORLD PUBLISHING CO., 8707 Terrace Dr., El Cerrito CA 94530. (415)525-9341. Editor/Publisher: Frank Anderson. Plays performed in high schools, community colleges, and church groups, in smaller towns and rural areas. Audience is comprised of families with conservative, middle-America values. Publishes 20 plays/year. Submit complete script, or send SASE for free guidelines. 10-50% royalty. Reports in 90 days.
Needs: "Broad comedy; principally, our need is for wholesome treatments of up-to-date themes with emphasis on action and broad humor. Length: mainly 3-acts; some 1-acts. Prefers casts of 14-23, predominantly female. No sex, sexual innuendos or offensive language, smoking or drinking on stage, or controversial subject matter regarding morals, politics, or religion. No adaptations.

THEATRE AMERICANA, P.O. Box 245, Altadena CA 91001. Attn: Playreading Committee. In operation for 43 seasons. For public general audience. Local theatre. Showcase for unknowns in all phases of theater. Awards for best director, set designer, actors, as well as best play. Looking for plays with quality and originality. Any subject matter. Selections not made on the basis of any set structure, but if new forms are used, they must work successfully from an audience viewpoint. 2-act or 3-act plays, 1½ to 2 hours playing time. Not interested in trite material; pornography for shock value unacceptable. Modern verbiage in a valid characterization not censored. Musicals should include piano arrangements. Plays with a Christmas theme or setting are welcomed. No royalties can be paid, but the 4 original plays produced each year are eligible to compete for the $300 C. Brooks Fry Award. Authors copyright own plays. Send complete script only. Reporting time is "very slow. Read year-round. Play finalists retained until May, when 4 are selected for next season's production." Enclose S.A.S.E. for return of submissions.

THE THEATRE IN SEARCH OF PLAYWRIGHTS PROJECT, Theatre Arts-University Theatre, Virginia Polytechnic Institute and State University, Blacksburg VA 24061. "Plays produced as part of Major Production Series-Theatre Arts-University Theatre and as part of studio theatre series. Casts are students, with occasional guest performers drawn from faculty or from visiting performers." Adult audience in university community. Should be full length, previously unproduced scripts of interest to adult audiences. Fresh, attractive, controversial subject matter is desired. Uses 2- and 3-act plays. Offers royalties of $50 for first performance; $25, additional performances; negotiated rates for musical scripts. "We prefer copyrighted material." Send complete script only. Playwright's biography or resume requested. Follow standard play-duplication service procedures. Use tight binders or covers. Reports in 1 month. Produces about 15 plays a year. Enclose S.A.S.E.

THEATRE RAPPORT, 8128 Gould Ave., Hollywood CA 90040. Artistic Director: Crane Jackson. Equity company. Produces plays of 1, 2, and 3 acts. Produces gutsy, relevant plays on highly artistic level and true subjects. No unjustified homosexuality, nudity or profanity; realistic acceptable. For a sophisticated, educated, non-fad, conservative (although venturesome) audience looking for something new and different. Not avant-garde, but a strong point of view is an asset. Approach must be unique. All plays must be West Coast premieres. Pays 20% of gross. Send complete script. Response if interested. All mss read, but none are returned. Produces 6 plays a year.

THEATRE UNDER THE STARS, 1999 W. Gray, Houston TX 77019. Contact: Frank Young. Professional stock theatre in Houston. Possible New York production following Houston run. For the general public. Musical comedies only, including musical dramas and operettas. No grand opera. Product must be commercial. "Any material will be considered if well done." Will consider any length. Payment negotiated. Not all plays are copyrighted. Enclose S.A.S.E. Produces 10 plays each year.

UNIVERSITY AND FESTIVAL THEATRE, John R. Bayless, Business Manager, 137 Arts Bldg., The Pennsylvania State University, University Park PA 16802. (814)863-0381. For general audience 18 to 60 years of age. Produced at either of the Pavilion of Playhouse Theatres located at University Park. University Theatre is an amateur/education program; the Festival Theatre is an equity/student theatre program offered during the summer. Any kind of play is considered. Usually does not copyright plays. For a straight play, pays between $25 and $50 per performance. Produces 12 to 16 plays a year. Send complete script only. Reports in 1 month. Enclose S.A.S.E.

YALE REPERTORY THEATRE, Literary Manager, 222 York St., New Haven CT 06520. Resident professional theatre. For University-oriented audience, but with appeal to a larger community. No limitations of age or special interests, but emphasis on an audience with serious perceptual intelligence, receptive to experiment and innovation. No limitations on subject matter or theme, but not interested in Broadway-type plays, conventional musicals, domestic dramas, etc. "We are generally limited to what the imagination can summon up on a small thrust stage with no flies and little wing space, but we have other stages available for projects with more ambitious physical requirements. Full-evening works preferred." Offers standard L.O.R.T. author contract. Copyright remains with author. "We retain limited residual rights and a small percentage of author's proceeds on subsequent sales of the work." Send complete script. Enclose S.A.S.E. Reports in about 4 months. Produces 7 or 8 full professional productions a year, plus a variety of student full productions, workshops, and cabaret productions.

Play Publishers

Markets for the playwright's work are several: play publishers, whose names and addresses follow; play producers, listed in the Play Producers section; television producers, and motion picture producers. Film producers, like television producers, will not look at scripts submitted directly by the writer. They must be submitted through recognized literary agents. A list of these appears in the Authors' Agents section.

Publications which do not primarily publish plays but occasionally may publish dramatic material in some form are listed in the Juvenile, Literary and "Little", and Theater, Movie, TV, and Entertainment categories in the Consumer Publications section. The playwright should also check the Book Publishers for additional play markets.

BAKER'S PLAY PUBLISHING CO., 100 Chauncy St., Boston MA 02111. Editor: John B. Welch. Plays performed by amateur groups; high school, children's theatre, churches and community theatre groups. Submit complete script. Copyrighted. Pay varies; outright purchase price to split in production fees. $75 for 1-act plays that need work. SASE. Reports in 2-3 months.
Needs: "1-acts (specifically for competition use). Quality children's theater scripts. Chancel drama for easy staging—voice plays ideal. Long plays only if they have a marketable theme. Include as much stage direction in the script as possible." Emphasis on large female cast desired.

CONTEMPORARY DRAMA SERVICE, Box 457, Downers Grove IL 60515. Editor: Arthur Zapel. Plays performed in churches and school classrooms with amateur performers for age level high school to adult; church material for young children, 8-12 years old. Publishes 25-30 plays/year. Submit synopsis or complete script. Usually buys all rights. 10% royalty up to an agreed maximum. Will negotiate for complete rights. SASE. Reports in 1 month.
Needs: "In the church field we are looking for chancel drama for presentation at various holidays: Thanksgiving, Mother's Day, Christmas, Easter, etc. School drama materials can be reader's theatre adaptations, drama rehearsal scripts, simple dialogues and short action plays. We like a free and easy style. Nothing formal. Short sentences and fast pace. Humor also welcomed where possible." Length: 1-act, skits, or short games. Casts not to exceed 9 players.

DODD, MEAD & COMPANY, 79 Madison Ave., New York NY 10016. Executive Editor: Allen T. Klots. Only interested in "playwrights after professional production, who promise to contribute to the literature of the theater." Royalty negotiated. Buys book rights only. Reports in about 4 weeks. Enclose S.A.S.E.

DAVID EASTWOOD, P.O. Box 266, Lake George NY 12845. Plays will be for professional casts in summer theater. Audience: public, tourists. Would like to see "Neil Simon-type comedies." Send synopsis. No drama. Maximum of 8 characters; 2 sets. Will consider 3-act plays; 2½ hours in length. Payment is flexible. Not copyrighted. Query first with synopsis only. Enclose S.A.S.E.

ELDRIDGE PUBLISHING CO., Drawer 209, Franklin OH 45005. (513)746-6531. Editor/General Manager: Kay Myerly. Plays performed in high schools and churches; some professional—but most are amateur productions. Publishes plays for all age groups. Publishes 20-25 plays/year. Send synopsis or complete script. Buys all rights "unless the author wishes to retain some rights." Pays $75-100 for 1-act plays; $350 for 3-acts. SASE. Reports in 60-90 days.
Needs: "We are looking for good straight comedies which will appeal to high and junior-high age groups. We do not publish anything which can be suggestive. Most of our plays are published with a hanging indentation—2 ems. All stage, scenery and costume plots must be included." Length: One-acts from 25-30 minutes; 2-acts of around 2 hours; and skits of 10-15 minutes.

SAMUEL FRENCH, 25 W. 45th St., New York NY 10036. (212)582-2470. Willing at all times to read mss of books concerning the theater, as well as mss of plays. Wants plays that are "original, imaginative. Interested in character. No motion picture scenarios, verse plays, single-shot TV plays, Biblical plays, or children's plays on subjects already published." Accepts 10 to 15 mss a year from freelancers. No reading fee. In addition to publishing plays, also acts as agents in the placement of plays for Broadway production, and of program series for television production. Payment on royalty basis. Send complete script. Reports in 8 to 10 weeks. Enclose S.A.S.E. for return of submissions.

HEUER PUBLISHING CO., 233 Dows Building, P.O. Box 248, Cedar Rapids IA 52406. Amateur productions for schools and church groups. Audience consists of junior and senior high school students and some intermediate groups. Needs 1- and 3-act plays. Prefers comedy, farce, mystery, mystery/comedy. Uses 1-act plays suitable for contest work, (strong drama). "Suggest potential authors write for our brochure on types of plays." Taboos include sex, controversial subjects and family scenes. Prefers 1 simple setting and non-costume plays. Current need is for plays with a large number of characters, (16 to 20 characters). 1-act plays should be 30 to 35 minutes in length; 3-act, 90 to 105 minutes. Most mss purchased outright, with price depending on quality. Minimum of $500 usually. Copyrighted, however, contract stipulates amateur rights only, so author retains professional rights to TV, radio, etc. Query first with synopsis only. Enclose S.A.S.E. Reports in 1 week to 10 days. Publishes 5 to 20 plays a year.

PERFORMANCE PUBLISHING CO., 978 N. McLean Blvd., Elgin IL 60120. Editor: Virginia Butler. 1-, 2-, and 3-act plays for stock, summer, college, high school, grade school, and community theaters. "We publish plays for all segments of the market. For the non-Broadway market, plays for and about high school students are usually the most remunerative. We're looking for comedies, mysteries, dramas, farces, etc., with modern dialogue and theme. Generally, a great deal more experience can be obtained by limiting oneself to 1-acts until one has had at least one work published. We don't want X-rated material. 50% high school, 15% children's theatre, 35% college, community stock and church theater plays desired. We offer royalty contract on industry standard terms. We usually copyright plays in the name of the author and in general acquire all publication and stage rights with exception of first-class professional rights, which remain the author's property, as do radio, film, TV, etc." Publishes approximately 40 plays a year. No insured, certified or registered scripts accepted. Author should retain a copy of any script mailed. Not responsible for manuscripts. Enclose S.A.S.E. Reports in 3 months.

PIONEER DRAMA SERVICE, 2172 S. Colorado Blvd., Box 22555, Denver CO 80222. (303)759-4297. Publisher: Shubert Fendrich. Plays are performed by high school, junior high and adult groups, colleges and recreation programs for audiences of all ages. Publishes 15 plays/year. Submit synopsis or complete script. Buys all rights. Pays "usually 10% royalty on copy sales; 50% of production royalty and 50% of subsidiary rights with some limitations on first-time writers." SASE. Reports in 30-60 days.
Needs: "We are looking for adaptations of great works in the public domain or plays on subjects of current interest. We use the standard 1-act and 3-act format, 2-act musicals, melodrama in all lengths and plays for children's theater (plays to be done by adult actors for children). Length: 1-acts of 15-30 minutes; 2-acts of 90 minutes; 3-acts of 2 hours; and children's theater of 1 hour. "We do not want plays with predominantly male casts, or highly experimental works. Plays should be mature without being obscene or profance."

PLAYS, The Drama Magazine for Young People, 8 Arlington Street, Boston MA 02116. Associate Editor: Sylvia E. Kamerman. Publishes approximately 90 1-act plays each season. Interested in buying good plays to be performed by young people of all age groups—junior and senior high, middle grades, lower grades. In addition to comedies, farces, melodramas, skits, mysteries and dramas, can use plays for holidays and other special occasions, such as Book Week, National Education Week. Adaptations of classic stories and fables, historical plays, plays about other lands, puppet plays, plays for all-girl or all-boy cast, folk tales, fairy tales, creative dramatics, plays dramatizing factual information and on such concepts as good government, importance of voting, involvement and participation as citizens, and plays for conservation, ecology or human rights programs are needed. Prefers one scene; when more than one is necessary, changes should be simple. Mss should follow the general style of *Plays*. Stage directions should not be typed in capital letters or underlined. Every play ms should include: a list of characters, an indication of time, a description of setting; an "At Rise," describing what is taking place on stage as curtain rises; production notes, indicating the number of characters and the playing time, describing the costumes, properties, setting and special lighting effects, if any. Playwrights should not use incorrect grammar or dialect. Characters with physical defects, speech impediments should not be included. Desired lengths for mss are: Junior and Senior high—20 to 25 double-spaced ms pages (25 to 30 minutes playing time). Middle Grades—12 to

15 pages (15 to 20 minutes playing time). Lower Grades—6 to 10 pages (8 to 15 minutes playing time). Pays "good rates on acceptance." Reports in 3 to 4 weeks. Enclose S.A.S.E. for return of submissions.

SUNLIGHT/SHADOW PUBLICATIONS, 10924 Oak St., Kansas City MO 64114. Editor: Dr. Richard S. Dunlop. Plays performed "in discriminating high schools, colleges, and community theaters with non-professional casts whose commitment is to excellence. Submit complete ms, "prefer readable photocopy; author should not send his original copy." Controls all rights; author keeps the copyright. 50% royalty on production. SASE. Reports in 1 month.

Needs: "We seek 1-act and full length plays of outstanding quality, with no restrictions as to subject matter, except that the theme and plot must be significant. We want plays that challenge the player and his audience. At the same time, we assume that theatre does not have to be pointlessly crude, incomprehensibly vague, or generally offensive in order to be challenging. Strong characterizations are very important—the performer must have something competent to work with. Set simplicity is desirable, but the writer needn't limit himself to space and platforms. Length: 1-, 2-, or 3-acts. "We're not interested in children's theatre, routine religious pieties, or empty-headed 'high-school plays.' We prefer complete acting scripts, edited on the basis of performance experience. We will consider plays which have not been produced, but those which have been de-bugged will get preference."

Syndicates

Syndicates sell editorial copy to publishers on a commission basis, with the author receiving 40 to 60 percent of the gross proceeds. Some syndicates, however, pay the writer a salary or a minimum guarantee. Writers of top syndicated columns may earn $50,000 or more per year. The aspiring syndicate writer must first make sure his work won't be competing in an already flooded field. Second, he must select a syndicate which will properly promote his material. The larger syndicates, of course, usually have better promotional facilities. (A list of syndicates which includes all the titles of the columns and features they handle appears in the *Editor and Publisher Syndicate Directory* ($5) published at 850 Third Avenue, New York NY 10022.) It's best to query the syndicate editor first, enclosing a half-dozen sample columns or feature ideas and a self-addressed, stamped envelope. Some writers self-syndicate their own material. The writer here earns 100% of the proceeds but also bears the expense of soliciting the clients, reproducing and mailing the features, billing, etc. See the chapter "How to Syndicate Your Own Column" in the *Writer's Digest* book, *The Creative Writer*.

AMERICAN FEATURES SYNDICATE, 964 Third Ave., New York NY 10022. Editor: Robert Behren. Copyrights material. Will consider photocopied submissions. Reporting time "varies." Enclose S.A.S.E. for return of submissions.
Nonfiction: Travel and true adventure. Buys single features and article series. Does not contract for columns. Length: 1,000 to 5,000 words. Pays $100 to $750. Usual outlets are newspapers and regional magazines, including some trade publications.

AP NEWSFEATURES, 50 Rockefeller Plaza, New York NY 10020. General Executive: Dan Perkes. Enclose S.A.S.E. for return of submissions.
Nonfiction and Photos: Buys article series or column ideas "dealing with areas of science, social issues that can be expanded into book form. Do not usually buy single features." Length: 600 to 1,000 words. Pays minimum $25.

ARKIN MAGAZINE SYNDICATE, 761 N.E. 180th St., North Miami Beach FL 33162. Editor: Joseph Arkin. "We regularly purchase articles from several freelancers, most of whom belong to ABWA, for syndication in trade and professional magazines." Submit complete ms. SASE. Reports in 3 weeks. Buys all North American magazine and newspaper rights.
Needs: Magazine articles (nonfiction; 800-1,800 words, directly relating to business problems common to several (not just one) business firms, in different types of businesses); and photos (purchased with written material). "We are in dire need of the 'how-to' business article." Will consider article series; "will buy after we make placement, all submissions are on speculation." Pays 3-10¢/word; $5-10 for photos; "actually line drawings are preferred instead of photos."
Tips: "The first and foremost requirement is to know what a trade or professional magazine is as compared to consumer or other types of media."

AUTHENTICATED NEWS INTERNATIONAL, ANI, 170 Fifth Avenue, New York NY 10010. (212)243-6995. Editor: Sidney Polinsky. Syndication and Features Editor: Dan Dougherty. Supplies material to national magazines, newspapers, and house organs in the United States and important countries abroad. Buys exclusive and non-exclusive rights. Reports in 3 months. Enclose S.A.S.E.
Nonfiction and Photos: Can use photo material in the following areas: hard news, photo features, ecology and the environment, science, medical, industry, education, human interest, the arts, city planning, and pertinent photo material from abroad. 750 words maximum. Prefers 8x10 b&w glossies, color transparencies (4x5 or 2¼x2¼, 35mm color). Where necessary, model releases required. Pays 50% royalty.

AUTO NEWS SYNDICATE, Box 2085, Daytona Beach FL 32015. Editor: Don O'Reilly. Unsolicited material is acknowledged or returned within a few days, "but we cannot be responsible for loss." Enclose S.A.S.E.

Nonfiction and Photos: Syndicated articles, photos on automotive subjects and motor sports. Newspaper articles ("Dateline: Detroit" and "Inside Auto Racing"). Magazine articles. Radio broadcasts ("Inside Auto Racing"). 50% commission. "Payment is made between acceptance and publication." No flat fees.

BUDDY BASCH FEATURE SYNDICATE, 771 West End Ave., New York NY 10025. Publisher: Buddy Basch. Buys all rights. Will consider photocopied submissions. Query first or submit complete ms. Reports in 1 week to 10 days. Enclose S.A.S.E.
Nonfiction, Humor, Photos, and Fillers: News items, nonfiction, humor, photos, fillers, puzzles, and columns and features on travel and entertainment. "Mostly staff written at present. Query first."

BETTER WORLD EDITORIAL PRODUCTIONS, 809 F St., San Diego CA 92101. Editor: Ross Freiermuth. Buys material for syndication in rural weekly newspapers. Submit complete ms. SASE. Photocopied submissions OK. Reports in 2 weeks. Buys all rights, first rights, and second serial (reprint) rights.
Needs: News items (insights into current events—but not so timely that they become outdated before they are marketed); and photos (purchased with written material). "We're looking for weekly columns on subjects of current interest: social improvement, politics, health, ecology, child development, etc." Pays 50% of the price of finished, camera-ready copy sold. "We sell copy by the column inch. When we set a feature into type, we offer it to about 1,500 weekly publications, at a cost of 12-15¢/column inch." Pays "on purchase of the article from a newspaper. We mail checks monthly."
Tips: "Our market is rural weekly newspapers. Collectively they represent as large a readership as any of the daily newspapers. Writers who are considering this market should put themselves in the shoes of the editor of a small town paper."

CANADIAN SCENE, Suite 305, 2 College St., Toronto, Ont., Canada. M5G 1K3. Editor: Miss Ruth Gordon. Query first. Submit seasonal material 3 months in advance. Reports in 1 week. Pays on acceptance. Enclose S.A.E. and International Reply Coupons for reply to queries.
Nonfiction: "Canadian Scene is a voluntary information service. Its purpose is to provide written material to democratic, foreign language publications in Canada. The material is chosen with a view to directing readers to an understanding of Canadian political affairs, foreign relations, social customs, industrial progress, culture, history, and institutions. In a 700-word article, the writer can submit almost any subject on Canada, providing it leaves the newcomer with a better knowledge of Canada. It should be written in a simple, tightly knit, straightforward style." Length: 500 to 1,000 words. Pays 3¢ a word.

CHICAGO TRIBUNE-NEW YORK NEWS SYNDICATE, INC., 220 East 42nd St., New York NY 10017. Editor: Don Michel. Supplies material to Sunday supplements and newspapers in North America and abroad. Buys worldwide rights, where possible; must have North American rights to be interested. Submit at least 6 samples of any submission for continuing feature. Enclose S.A.S.E. for return of submissions.
Columns, Puzzles: No fiction. Material must be extremely well-written and must not be a copy of something now being marketed to newspapers. Length varies, though columns should generally be 500 words or less. Pay varies, depending on market; usually 50-50 split of net after production on contractual material.

COLLEGE PRESS SERVICE, 1764 Gilpin St., Denver CO 80218. (303)388-1608. Edited by a 5-person collective. Buys 15-20 mss/year for syndication to college and alternative community newspapers. Query with samples and credits. SASE. Photocopied submissions OK. Reports in 4-6 weeks.
Needs: News items (300-500 words with national angle; emphasize college interest); and fillers (100-200 words, no special slant). Pays $15-20.

COLUMBIA FEATURES, INC., 36 West 44 St., New York NY 10036. Editor: William H. Thomas. Buys all rights and world rights, all media. Will consider photocopied submissions. Submit complete ms. Pays on a regular monthly basis for continuing column or contract. Reports in 2 to 4 weeks. Enclose S.A.S.E. for return of submissions.
Humor and Puzzles: Cartoons, comic strips, puzzles, and columns on a continuing basis. Features for special sections: family, home, women's, Sunday supplements. No single features, except series of 6 to 12 parts, about 750 to 1,000 words each article. Lengths vary according to features. Columns: 500 to 750 words. Pays 50% usually.

COMMUNITY AND SUBURBAN PRESS SERVICE, 100 E. Main St., Frankfort KY 40601. Managing Editor: Mike Bennett. Buys second serial (reprint) rights. Pays on acceptance. Enclose S.A.S.E. for return of submissions.

Humor and Photos: Cartoons, gag panels, human interest photos. 8x10 glossy photos purchased without features. Captions required. Pays $15 per cartoon or photo.

CONTEMPORARY FEATURES SYNDICATE, INC., Box 1258, Jackson TN 38301. Editor: Lloyd Russell. Associate Editor: Kathy L. Turner. Currently has 3 columns in syndication; buys several dozen mss/year for syndication to newspapers (columns) and magazines (single features). Submit complete ms and credits. SASE. Photocopied submissions OK "if not submitted elsewhere also." Reports in 6-8 weeks, sometimes longer. Buys all rights.

Needs: News items (not looking for hard news, but rather the story behind the news); fiction (occasional short story, but no longer fiction); fillers (no rehash of the history book; entertain and inform; usually handled on consignment); and photos (purchased with or without written material or on assignment. Captions required). "We believe our product is a line of 'human interest' features and we want to read about people and their relationships." Article series considered if "there is a story too long to be easily and completely told in one article. Have something to say rather than just lots of words." Pays 50% commission on sales; minimum guarantee of $25 for full-length features to magazines; photos bring $5 minimum. Usually pays on acceptance.

Tips: "Be professional. Be patient. And be realistic. Quality material is a must. Selling *any* material takes time to get the top dollar and the best treatment. No one should expect to get rich or famous overnight. It's all summed up in the abused term 'hard work'. That's what it is all about, and that's what it takes."

CRUX NEWS SERVICE, Shickshinny PA 18655. Editor: Thourot Pichel. Does not copyright material. Buys "very few" features a year from freelancers. Will consider photocopied submissions. Enclose S.A.S.E. for return of submissions.

Nonfiction: "History and political only." Buys single features. Does not buy article series or columns. Pays "nominal standard."

CURIOUS FACTS FEATURES, 440 Glenview Dr., Lebanon OH 45036. Editor: Donald Whitacre. Buys all rights. Pays on publication. Reports in 2 weeks. Enclose S.A.S.E.

Nonfiction: Uses "oddities" of all types including strange animals, strange laws, people, firsts, etc. Length: 50 to 100 words. Pays $10 to $15.

DIDATO ASSOCIATES, 280 Madison Ave., New York NY 10016. Rights purchased vary with author and material. Will consider photocopied submissions. Query first or submit complete ms. Pays on acceptance, or on publication. Reports immediately. Enclose S.A.S.E.

Nonfiction: Quizzes which have a behavior science or psychology angle. Must have solid research references by behavior scientists or related professionals. Single feature examples: your clothes tell your personality; study reveals sex attitudes of teenagers; depression linked up with job blahs; terrorists are suicidal personalities, survey shows. Length: 500 to 2,000 words. Pays negotiable rates. Especially needs news-related story ideas and leads in outline form of about 100 words; also with one or more research references. Pays $10 to $50 for leads and psychology quizzes.

DORN-FREDRICKS PUBLISHING CO., 35 East 35 St., Suite 7-H, New York NY 10016. Editor: Dona Davis Grant. Buys all rights, worldwide, foreign rights. Query first. Enclose S.A.S.E.

Nonfiction, Humor, Poetry, and Fillers: Gossip columns of worldwide interest; material for feminine markets; fashion, beauty, etc. Single features include: "Harvest Time of Life" (column), "Mighty Mixture" (column), "Famous Mothers," "Your Key to Courage," "How the West Was Won," "Crafts" and "Homemaker's New Ideas." Interested in humor columns of approximately 800 words. Famous personalities, and beauty. Column length: 800 words. Pays 3¢ a word minimum, depending on name value.

EDITORIAL CONSULTANT SERVICE, P.O. Box 120, Babylon NY 11702. Director: Art Ingoglia. Rights purchased vary with author and material. May buy first rights or second serial (reprint) rights. Pays on publication. Handles copyrighted material "on occasion." Query first. Reports in 2 to 4 weeks. Enclose S.A.S.E.

Nonfiction and Photos: Special feature material pertaining to new and antique automobiles, buses, trucks. "Single features are often purchased dealing with subjects of special interest to the auto owner or to the auto trade. No articles considered without prior query to editor."

Payment on a percentage basis of 25% to 50%. 8x10 b&w photos purchased with features. Captions required. Payment varies.

Tips: "We prefer in-depth queries. Rarely are articles considered that have not been requested (on the basis of a query) by our editors. We are particularly looking for fresh column ideas that *Editorial Consultant Service* can handle on an exclusive basis. The query must be comprehensive and it should outline the major theme of the article or column."

ENTERPRISE SCIENCE NEWS, 230 Park Ave., New York NY 10017. Editor: David Hendin. Buys all rights. Pays on acceptance. Query first. Reports in 2 to 4 weeks. Enclose S.A.S.E. for reply to queries.

Nonfiction: "We only buy from professional science-medical writers." Wants feature-type newspaper stories on scientific subjects of current interest. The science should be interesting and applicable to the reader. Must be clear, concise, accurate and objective. Stories with good art receive preference. Length: 700 to 1,200 words. Pays $30 to $500, "depnding on author, length and type of story, quality of writing, whether commissioned or not, etc."

Photos: Bought with features only.

FACING SOUTH, Box 230, Chapel Hill NC 27514. (919)929-2141. Co-Editors: Jennifer Miller and Kathleen Doble. Buys 52 columns/year for syndication to newspapers. Query or submit complete ms. SASE. Reports in 5 weeks. Buys all rights.

Needs: "650-700-word columns focusing on a southern individual, allowing that person to tell a story. Each week a different writer does a column, although we will use more than one column by the same writer—just spread them over several months." Pays $50. "Writers must send for our guidelines before attempting a column." No payment for photos; "we just need some kind of a snapshot that our artist can use to do an illustration."

FIELD NEWSPAPER SYNDICATE, 401 N. Wabash Ave., Chicago IL 60611. Editor: Richard Sherry. Supplies material to newspapers. Buys all rights. Reports in 4-5 weeks. Enclose S.A.S.E. for return of submissions.

Nonfiction: Article series "only on highly promotable topics by pros with top credentials." No single features. Contracts for columns. Syndicates columns such as Ann Landers, Sylvia Porter, Joseph Kraft, Evans and Novak, and Erma Bombeck. Interested in columns on "service, do-it-yourself, commentary." Length: 750 words maximum. Pay varies according to newspaper sales.

GLOBAL COMMUNICATIONS, 303 Fifth Ave., Suite 1306, New York NY 10016. President: Timothy Green Beckley. "We supply material to publications in the U.S. and overseas." Rights purchased vary with author and material. Usually buys second serial (reprint) rights or simultaneous rights. Buys about 600 features a year. Will consider photocopied submissions. Send complete ms. Reports in 2 weeks. Enclose S.A.S.E.

Nonfiction, Fiction and Fillers: "Our interests are varied and include almost every area. Short fiction doesn't move very well. We go in for straight reporting and investigative pieces." Writing should be colorful, to the point, good news angle. "In addition to original material for U.S. and foreign syndication, we are always looking for previously published pieces which the writer owns foreign rights to. Our material goes to publications in about 13 foreign countries. Our standard commission is 1/3 on all sales. However, sometimes we do purchase outright. Writers should send tearsheets and a letter stating they have rights to sell outside U.S. from original publisher." Currently, best markets include celebrity interviews and profiles, true psychic/UFO pieces (must be well researched), adult fiction and nonfiction, human interest and, in general, "anything that is a bit unusual." Sometimes will purchase material outright for $35 to $500, but 95% of material is handled on a commission basis. Mainly buys adult (sex) fiction; also adventure, Western, erotica, science fiction, religious. Length: 2,000 to 5,000 words. Buys fillers: jokes, gags, anecdotes, short humor. Pays $5 to $25. Buys all rights. No poetry. "We try to give help and advice when possible and are always looking for 'newcomers' to work with. We have about a dozen stringers who send us stories constantly. Always room for more."

Photos: Photos purchased with accompanying ms with no additional payment. Or purchased with or without ms with extra payment. Captions required. Pays $15 minimum for b&w (8x10) and $25 minimum for color slides.

Columns: "Psychic Celebrities" and "Saucers and Celebrities." Materials for these columns are purchased outright. Payment: $50. Buys all rights. No byline.

DAVE GOODWIN & ASSOCIATES, P.O. Drawer 54-6661, Surfside FL 33154. Editor: Dave Goodwin. Rights purchased vary with author and material. May buy first rights or second serial (reprint) rights. Will handle copyrighted material. Buys about 25 features a year from freelancers. Query first or submit complete ms. Reports in 3 weeks. Enclose S.A.S.E.

Nonfiction: "Money-saving information for consumers: how to save on home expenses; auto, medical, drug, insurance, boat, business items, etc." Buys article series on brief, practical, down-to-earth items for consumer use or knowledge. Rarely buys single features. Currently handling "Insurance for Consumers." Length: 300 to 5,000 words. Pays 50% on publication.

HARRIS & ASSOCIATES PUBLISHING DIVISION, 247 South 800 East, Logan UT 84321. (801)753-3587. President: Dick Harris. Rights purchased vary with author and material. May buy all rights or first rights. Does not purchase many mss per year since material must be in their special style. Pays on publication; sometimes earlier. Not necessary to query. Send sample or representative material. Reports in less than 30 days. Enclose S.A.S.E.
Nonfiction, Photos, and Humor: Material on driver safety and accident prevention. Humor for modern women (not women's lib); humor for sports page. "We like to look at anything in our special interest areas. Golf and tennis are our specialties. We'll also look at cartoons in these areas. Will buy or contract for syndication. Everything must be short, terse, with humorous approach." Action, unposed, 8x10 b&w photos are purchased without features or on assignment. Captions are required. Pays 5¢ minimum per word and $15 minimum per photo.

HOLLYWOOD INFORMER SYNDICATE, Box 49957, Los Angeles CA 90049. Editor: John Austin. Purchases mss for syndication to newspapers in San Francisco, Philadelphia, Detroit, Montreal, London, and Sydney. Query or submit complete ms. SASE. Reports in 4-6 weeks. Buys first rights or second serial (reprint) rights.
Needs: News items (column items concerning entertainment (motion picture) personalities and jet setters for syndicated column; 750-800 words). Also considers series of 1,500-word articles; "suggest descriptive query first." Pay negotiable. Pays on acceptance "but this is also negotiable because of delays in world market acceptance."

INTERNATIONAL EDITORIAL SERVICES/NEWSWEEK, INC., 444 Madison Ave., New York NY 10022. Vice President: R.J. Melvin. Offers on speculation to listing of Newsweek worldwide associates first sights on second serial (reprint) rights. Offers 50 to 100 features, over 1,000 photos and graphics a year. Will consider photocopied submissions. Query first. Reports within 3 months. Enclose S.A.S.E.
Nonfiction and Photos: News items, backgrounders, personalities in the news. News-related features suitable for international syndication. Prefers approximately 1,200 words for features. Pays 50% on publication. Photos purchased with features. Pays $25-75 for b&w if purchased separately.

INTERPRESS OF LONDON AND NEW YORK, 400 Madison Ave., New York NY 10017. (212)832-2539. Editor: Jeffrey Blyth. Buys British and European rights mostly, but can handle world rights. Will consider photocopied submissions. Query first or submit complete ms. Pays on publication, or agreement of sale. Reports immediately or as soon as practicable. Enclose S.A.S.E.
Nonfiction and Photos: "Unusual stories and photos for British and European press. Picture stories, for example, on such 'Americana' as a five-year-old evangelist; the 800-pound 'con-man,' the nude-male calendar; tallest girl in the world; interviews with pop celebrities such as Yoko Ono, Bob Dylan, Sen. Kennedy, Valarie Perrine, Priscilla Presley, Bette Midler, Liza Minelli; cult subjects such as voodoo, college fads, anything amusing or offbeat. Extracts from books such as Earl Wilson's *Show Business Laid Bare*, inside-Hollywood type series ('Secrets of the Stuntmen,' 'My Life with Racquel Welch'). Real life adventure dramas ('Three Months in an Open Boat,' 'The Air Crash Cannibals of the Andes'). No length limits—short or long, but not too long. Payment varies; depending on whether material is original, or world rights. Pay top rates, up to several thousand dollars, for exclusive material. Photos purchased with or without features. Captions required. Standard size prints, suitable for radioing if necessary. Pay $50 to $100, but no limit on exclusive material."

KEISTER ADVERTISING SERVICE, Strasburg VA 22657. Editor: G. Walton Lindsay. Buys approximately 25-30 mss/year for syndication to newspapers. Query with samples/credits. SASE. Reports in 1-2 months. Buys all rights.
Needs: "Our copy is limited to about 150 words and deals with human-interest illustrations that lead casually but persuasively into a plea for church membership and attendance. Style should compete with rest of newspaper and not be of a 'preachy' sermonette-like nature." Photos purchased without features; captions required. Pays $15-20/item. Pays on acceptance.

KING FEATURES SYNDICATE, 235 E. 45th St., New York NY 10017. Supplies material to newspapers. Rights purchased vary with author and material. May buy all rights or second serial (reprint) rights. Submit new features and photos to Allan Priavex, Executive Editor. Reports in 2 weeks. Enclose S.A.S.E. for return of submissions.

Nonfiction and Photos: Topical nonfiction, humor, fillers, puzzles, cartoons and comic strips. Buys photo features and article series. Contracts for columns. Length: 500 to 750 words. Pays in commission percentage.

KNOWLEDGE NEWS & FEATURES SYNDICATE, Kenilworth IL 60043. (312)256-0059. Executive Editor: Dr. Whitt N. Schultz. Rights purchased vary with author and material. Usually buys all rights. Will consider photocopied submissions. Query first. Reports in 10 days. Enclose S.A.S.E.

Business Features, Photos and Nonfiction: News items; humor; fillers; business, knowledge and education articles; "success stories." Buys article series. May buy single features. Will contract for columns for syndication. Length: 1,000 minimum for features; 500 minimum for columns. Payment negotiable. Photos purchased with features and also on assignment. Captions required. Buys 8x10 glossy photos. Payment negotiable.

Tips: "Clear, crisp, concise, urgent writing—easy to read—open—spotlight success, inspiration; positive news features."

NATIONAL CATHOLIC NEWS SERVICE, 1312 Massachusetts Ave., N.W., Washington DC 20005. Editor: Richard W. Daw. "Individual judgments are made" as to copyrighting material. "We are served by a number of stringers as well as freelancers. We provide a daily service and have a fairly constant market. Inquiries are welcomed, but they should be both brief and precise. Too many inquiries are coy and/or vague. Will consider photocopied submissions." Pays on publication. Reports in 2 to 3 weeks. Enclose S.A.S.E. for reply to queries.

Nonfiction: Short news and feature items of religious or social interest, particularly items with a Catholic thrust. Buys single features and article series. Feature examples: FCC plagued by letters about non-existent petition from atheist; clown tours America as God's Good Humor Man; bishop lives in house heated 20 degrees cooler than White House. Series examples: Moral implications and religious involvement in capital punishment issue; Catholic schools and integration. Contracts for columns: "This is a highly competitive market and we are extremely selective. Our columns range from labor concerns to the liturgy." Length for single features: no minimum, maximum of 800 words. Article series: maximum of 3 parts, about 700 words each. Columns: open in length; generally, the shorter the better. Generally pays a maximum of 5¢ a word for news and feature copy. Buys book reviews at a rate of 3¢ a word for a maximum of 500 words. Does not buy *unsolicited* reviews, but welcomes queries. "We market primarily to more than 100 Catholic weekly newspapers. We also serve foreign Catholic agencies and U.S. Catholic weekly newspapers."

Photos: Purchased with or without features. Captions required. News and feature photos of interest to Catholic periodicals. "We operate a photo service that mails to clients four times a week." Pays from $5 to $15 for each photo, depending on quality and originality.

NATIONAL FEATURES SYNDICATE, 1066 National Press Bldg., Washington DC 20045. (202)737-7747. West coast office: 948 N. Croft Ave., Hollywood CA 90069. (213)654-8055 or (213)654-1565. Editor: Fred Rosenblatt. Reports in 1 week or less. Pays on acceptance. Enclose S.A.S.E.

Nonfiction: Inside stories of politics and economics of health industry. Buys singles as well as column ideas.

NCT FEATURES, Box 11623, Chicago IL 60611. Contact: Neesa Sweet. *"NCT Features* is a feature service supplying over 120 magazines and newspapers throughout the country with feature material. Our clients include newspaper feature departments, Sunday magazine sections, travel and sports sections, sponsored publications, consumer publications and general interest magazines. SASE. Buys all rights.

Needs: "We deal in a wide variety of topics: travel pieces, adventure, consumer articles, personality profiles, how-to's, sports, column ideas, recreation features, topical stories, comic strips, science, food, history, and anything else that is different and unusual. Articles vary from 500-3,000 words, and price depends on the article and the market. We are particularly on the lookout for story-photo packages—first class words and pictures on unusual exotic and hard hitting topic areas. Photography is handled on a commission basis. Transparencies should be 35mm or larger submitted in plastic viewing files, with the photographer's name and caption information on each slide."

NEW YORK TODAY, INC., NEWS SERVICE, 850 7th Ave., Suite 1200, New York NY 10019. Editor: Ray Wilson. Query first. Enclose S.A.S.E.

Nonfiction: Food, restaurants, entertainment, travel and astrology material for newspapers, radio, television and magazines. Authoritative stories on wine. "We buy something that fits into our scheme of things. Criswell Predicts, Ray Wilson on Broadway, Bob Dana on Wine and Food, and Travel by Hermes, are a few examples of columns we now handle." Length: 750 words. "We have no established rate of payment. We use writers on assignment basis only if our staff cannot cover. Other material is submitted for our approval through query. Then we contact the writer."

NEWS FLASH INTERNATIONAL INC., 508 Atlanta Ave., North Massapequa NY 11758. Editor: Jackson B. Pokress. Supplies material to Observer newspapers and Champion sports publications. "Contact editor prior to submission to allow for space if article is newsworthy." Will consider photocopied submissions. Pays on publication. Enclose S.A.S.E. for reply to queries.
Nonfiction: "We have been supplying a 'ready-for-camera' sports page (tabloid size) complete with column and current sports photos on a weekly basis to many newspapers on Long Island as well as pictures and written material to publications in England and Canada. Payment for assignments is based on the article. It may vary. Payments vary from $20 for a feature of 800 words. Our sports stories feature in-depth reporting as well as book reviews on this subject. We are always in the market for good photos, sharp and clear, action photos of boxing, football and baseball. We cover all major league ball parks during the baseball and football seasons. We are accredited to the Mets, Yanks, Jets and Giants. During the winter we cover basketball and hockey and all sports events at the Nassau Coliseum."
Photos: Purchased on assignment; captions required. Uses "good quality 8x10 b&w glossies; good choice of angles and lenses." Pays $7.50 minimum for b&w photos.

NEWSPAPER ENTERPRISE ASSOCIATION, 230 Park Ave., New York NY 10017. Deputy Editorial Director: David Hendin. Supplies material to "more than 600 daily newspapers." Buys world rights. Will handle copyrighted material. Buys 50 to 75 features a year from freelancers. Query first; send samples. Reports in 2 weeks. Enclose S.A.S.E. for reply to queries.
Nonfiction: "Science-oriented material; investigative reports; good ideas well-executed. We seldom purchase single features. We are interested in well-researched series on topics of particular interest to general audiences. We contract for columns and distribute material on practically all subjects. Do not want to see any Ann Landers type columns or humor columns." Length: 600 to 900 words. Pays $15 to $500.

NORTH AMERICAN NEWSPAPER ALLIANCE, 1200 Park Ave., New York NY 10017. Executive Editor: Sidney Goldberg. Editor: Sheldon Engelmayer. Supplies material to leading U.S. and Canadian newspapers, also to South America, Europe, Asia and Africa. Rights purchased vary with author and material. May buy all rights, or first rights, or second serial (reprint) rights. Pays "on distribution to clients." Query first or submit complete ms. Reports in 2 weeks. Enclose S.A.S.E.
Nonfiction and Photos: In the market for background, interpretive and news features. Life style trends, national issues that affect individuals and neighborhoods. The news element must be strong and purchases are generally made only from experienced, working newspapermen. Wants timely news features of national interest that do not duplicate press association coverage but add to it, interpret it, etc. Wants first-class nonfiction suitable for feature development. The story must be aimed at newspapers, must be self-explanatory, factual and well condensed. It must add measurably to the public's information or understanding of the subject, or be genuinely entertaining. Broad general interest is the key to success here. Length: 300 to 800 words. Rarely buys columns. Looking for good 1-shots and good series of 2 to 7 articles. Where opinions are given, the author should advise, for publication, his qualifications to comment on specialized subjects. The news must be exclusive to be considered at all. Length: 800 words maximum. Rate varies depending on length and news value. Minimum rate $25, but will go considerably higher for promotable copy. Buys 8x10 glossy photos when needed to illustrate story, pays $5 to $10.

NUMISMATIC INFORMATION SERVICE, Rossway Rd., RR 4, Box 232, Pleasant Valley NY 12569. Editor: Barbara White. Purchased 10 features in 1976 for syndication in newspapers. Query or submit complete ms. SASE. Photocopied submissions OK. Reports in 1-2 weeks. Buys all rights.
Needs: News items (columns concerning coins and coin collecting); fiction (maximum 500 words including technical aspects of numismatics, background data); fillers (on individual coins or the entire field of numismatics) and photos (purchased with written material; captions required). Pays $5/500-word article; 50¢/photo.

OCEANIC PRESS SERVICE, 4717 Laurel Canyon Blvd., N. Hollywood CA 91607. Editor: J. Taylor. Buys material from 15-20 writers/year (using their previously published stories and articles) for syndication to newspapers, magazines, and book publishers. Query. SASE. Reports in 2-4 weeks. Buys all rights, second serial (reprint) rights or foreign reprint rights.
Needs: Fiction; fillers; and photos (purchased with or without written material or on assignment. Captions required.) Buys single (one-shot) features or article series if "previously published articles or worldwide interest." Pays 50% commission on sales; minimum guarantee of $25. Photos bring $10-40 for b&w; $20-75 for color. Pays "when money is received from the publisher."

PACIFIC NEWS SERVICE, 604 Mission St., Room 1001, San Francisco CA 94105. (415)986-5690. Editors: Sandy Close, Clark Norton, Jon Stewart and Frank Maurovich. Associate Editor: Rosa Gustaitus. Buys approximately 300 mss/year from between 100-200 writers for syndication to newspapers ranging from major dailies to weeklies and monthlies, including the college and ethnic press and national magazines. Query or submit complete ms. SASE. Photocopied submissions OK. Reports in 1 week. Rights purchased vary with author and material; buys first or second serial (reprint) rights.
Needs: News items (uses news stories, features and analyses of issues and trends that are ignored or poorly covered by major media outlets; stories that look behind the news to help illuminate long-range trends in U.S. foreign policy or domestic politics. Style must be suitable for major newspaper readership: clear, concise and without undocumented opinion and rhetoric. Length about 1,000 words. Welcomes submissions from freelancers and others with specialized knowledge on subjects of importance, foreign and domestic, to U.S. readers); and photos (purchased with written material. Captions required). "We need articles examining the outlook for America's third century; top-notch reporting on the future of cities, the search for social justice." Buys occasional article series, but prefers single features. Pays 50% commission on sales; minimum guarantee $40. Photo brings $5-10. Pays on publication.
Tips: "Write for a broad-ranged audience. *PNS* is subscribed to by 150 newspapers across the country, from *The WAshington Post* to *SF Examiner.* Document every assertion. Look for the national angle in any local story or the U.S. angle in any foreign story."

PUNGENT PRAYER, 709 E. Elm St., West Frankfort IL 62896. Editor: Rev. Phil E. Pierce. Supplies material to newspapers. "Copyright registration optional with author." Buys first or second serial (reprint) rights. Buys up to 40 features a year from freelancers. Will consider photocopied submissions. Reports in 3 weeks. Pays on publication. Enclose S.A.S.E. for return of submissions.
Nonfiction and Poetry: Prayers or prayer stories. Colorful prayers. Prayers concerning holidays — national or religious. Unusual prayers concerning life crisis experiences; humor or pathos. Prayers by or for children. Accounts of answered prayers. Poems that are prayers or prayer stories. "Prayers must appeal to secular readers (non-churchmen); therefore, most ordinary prayers must be rejected, but items with human interest are welcome." General religious items *not* acceptable. Length: 300 words (nonfiction); 38 lines (poetry). Pays $2 to $10.

THE REGISTER AND TRIBUNE SYNDICATE, INC., 715 Locust St., Des Moines IA 50304. President: Dennis R. Allen. Buys material for syndication in newspapers. Submit complete ms. SASE. Photocopied submissions preferred. Reports in 6 weeks. Buys all rights.
Needs: News items (nonfiction); and photos (purchased with written material). Buys article series "from 500-700 words on current topics such as the metric system, motorcycles, self-improvement programs, seasonal series for Christmas and Easter. Pays in royalties. Pays on publication.

RELIGIOUS NEWS SERVICE, 43 W. 57th St., New York NY 10019. Editor-in-Chief: Lillian R. Block. Managing Editor: Gerald Renner. Supplies material to "secular press, religious press of all denominations, radio and TV stations." Enclose S.A.S.E. for return of submissions.
Nonfiction and Photos: "Good news stories on important newsworthy developments. Religious news." Will buy single features "if they have news pegs. Most of our article series are produced by our own staff." Length: 200 to 1,000 words. Pays 2¢ a word. Photos purchased with and without features and on assignment; captions required. Uses b&w glossies, preferably 8x10. Pays $5 minimum.

SAWYER PRESS, P.O. Box 46-578, Los Angeles CA 90046. Editor: E. Matlen. Buys all rights. Buys 50 cartoons a year. Will consider photocopied submissions. Submit complete cartoons only. Reports in 1 week. Enclose S.A.S.E.
Cartoons: Editorial cartoons suitable for college newspapers. Sophisticated social commentary.

Royalty or outright purchase; varies with quality of material. Also looking for Barbarella/John Wiley/Stanton type of illustrating and cartoon strips, b&w and color.

BP SINGER FEATURES, INC., 3164 W. Tyler Ave., Anaheim CA 92686. (714)527-5650. Editor: Jane Sherrod. "We work with 20-30 freelancers/year, using their previously published stories and articles," for syndication to newspapers, magazines and book publishers. Query. SASE. Reports in 3 weeks. Buys all rights, second serial (reprint) rights, and foreign reprint rights. Uses very few originals, many reprints and hundreds of books.
Needs: Fiction, fillers, and photos (purchased with or without written material or on assignment. Captions required). Wants photo interviews with celebrities, previously published books and short stories of good quality. Pays 50% commission on sales; minimum guarantee $25. Photos bring $10-40 for b&w; $20-75 for color. Pays "when money is received from the publisher."

SOCCER ASSOCIATES, P.O. Box 634, New Rochelle NY 10802. Editor: Irma Ganz Miller. Buys all rights. Query first. Reports at once. Enclose S.A.S.E.
Nonfiction and Photos: Buys very little. Currently syndicating "Soccer Shots" and special soccer coverage. Pays $25 to $100.

TEENAGE CORNER, INC., 4800 Ellinda Circle, N.W., Canton OH 44709. Editor: David J. Lavin. Buys no rights. Payment on publication. Reports in 1 month. Enclose S.A.S.E.
Nonfiction: Buys material on teenage problems and situations. Length: 300 to 500 words. Pays $5 to $10.

UNITED FEATURE SYNDICATE, 200 Park Ave., New York NY 10017. Managing Editor: Sidney Goldberg. Supplies material to newspapers throughout the world. Will handle copyrighted material. Buys 25 to 50 series per year, preferably 3 to 7 articles (world rights preferred). Buys first and/or second rights to book serializations. Query first with outline. Reports in 3 months. Enclose S.A.S.E. for reply to queries.
Nonfiction, Comic Strips and Puzzles: News, features, series, columns, comic strips, puzzles. Current columnists include Jack Anderson, Marquis Childs, Henry Taylor, Virginia Payette, Barbara Gibbons. Comic strips include Peanuts, Nancy, Tarzan. Rates negotiable for one-shot purchases. Standard syndication contracts are offered for columns and comic strips.

UNITED PRESS INTERNATIONAL (UPI), 220 E. 42nd St., New York NY 10017. Editor-in-Chief: H.L. Stevenson. "We seldom, if ever, accept material outside our own ranks."

U.S. NEWS SERVICE, Suite 1006, International Bldg., 1800 K St., N.W., Washington DC 20006. Bureau Chief: Walter Fisk. Buys all rights. May handle copyrighted material. May not return rejected material. Enclose S.A.S.E. for return of submissions.
Nonfiction, Humor, Fiction, Photos, Fillers, and Poetry: Buys single features and column ideas. Length varies. Payment varies. 8x10 single weight glossies purchased with features, without features, and on assignment. Captions required.

UNIVERSAL PRESS SYNDICATE, 6700 Squibb Rd., Mission KS 66202. Editor: James F. Andrews. Buys syndication rights. Reports normally in 4 weeks. Enclose S.A.S.E. for return of submissions.
Nonfiction: Looking for features—columns for daily and weekly newspapers. "Any material suitable for syndication in daily newspapers." Currently handling the following: Doonesbury by G.B. Trudeau, Garry Wills column, etc. Payment varies according to contract.

UNIVERSAL TRADE PRESS SYNDICATE, 37-20 Ferry Heights, Fair Lawn NJ 07410. (201)797-5873. Editor: Leon D. Gruberg. Buys first trade paper rights only. Query first. Enclose S.A.S.E. for reply to queries.
Nonfiction: Buys merchandising features in all fields; knitwear merchandising at the retail level; features on knitting mill operations. Length: 1,250 words. Pays 65%.

DOUGLAS WHITING LIMITED, 930 De Courcelle St., Montreal H4C 3C8, Que., Canada. Editor: D.P. Whiting. Supplies material to "all major dailies in Canada and many in the United States." Buys all newspaper rights. No query required. Reports in 4 to 6 weeks. Enclose S.A.E. and International Reply Coupons.
Nonfiction: Science panels, contest promotions, puzzle features and feature columns. "The freelancer should look for ideas and content that are unique. Too much of the sample material received by us is very similar to established syndicated features. Bear in mind, too, that we are a

Canadian syndicate. Most of the material received is too American." Does not buy single features. Length: 150 to 250 words, daily columns; 700 to 1,000 words, weekly columns. "Usually author's share is 40% of net after production costs are deducted. Costs do not include our sales calls and promotion material."

WOMEN'S NEWS SERVICE, 200 Park Ave., New York NY 10017. Editor: Sidney Goldberg. Buys 300 features/year for syndication for newspapers. Query or submit complete ms. SASE. Reports in 3 weeks. Buys all rights, first rights, or second serial (reprint) rights.

Needs: News items (news features, backgrounders, sidebars to events in the news of interest to women's and lifestyles pages; best length is 400-600 words); fiction (outline of plot and description of characters, with one sample chapter); fillers (news-pegged fillers preferred, 100-150 words; of interest to women's and lifestyle pages) and photos (purchased with written material; captions required). Considers "series of 3-6 articles, 700 words or so each. Series should be pegged on news event or a trend, unless service oriented." Pays minimum of $150 for series; $25 minimum for one-shots "higher depending on importance or interest;" $5-15 for fillers. Photos bring $5-15 for b&w glossies.

Tips: "Put your headline material in your lead, keep your stories short; avoid folksy essays, type accurately with plenty of space for editing. If we like your one-shots and use them frequently, we'll be open to a percentage arrangement."

WORLD-WIDE NEWS BUREAU, 309 Varick St., Jersey City NJ 07302. Editor: Arejas Vitkauskas. Enclose S.A.S.E. for return of submissions.

Nonfiction: "Our multiple writeups (separate, and in our weekly columns), start in greater New York publications, then go simultaneously all over the U.S.A. and all over the world where English is printed. News from authors, or literary agents, or publishers on books planned, or ready, or published. Anything from poetry and children's books, to space technology textbooks. We cover over eighty different trade fields."

ZODIAC NEWS SERVICE, 950 Howard St., San Francisco CA 94103. Editor: Jon Newhall. Supplies material to AM and FM stations across the U.S. "We only require exclusive rights for 72 hours." Buys about 1,000 features a year from freelancers. "We purchase 3 each day. Please mail in material (typed) and include phone number for additional information." Will consider photocopied submissions. "If we accept an item for use, it is sent out within 48 hours." Pays on publication. Enclose S.A.S.E.

Nonfiction: "We want exclusive, short news stories suitable for radio reporting. Our audience is young, disenchanted with the establishment. All news stories must be national, not regional or local in interest. Features must be short. We have done radio features (150 to 200 words at most) on ecology problems such as Black Mesa and the Big Sky development, on war protests, on drugs, on rock musicals, on bizarre, offbeat human interest anecdotes and results of psychological studies." Does not buy article series or column features. Length: 200 words "at most, but the shorter, the better." Pays $10 per item, as a rule.

Writers' Clubs

The following clubs are local or regional, nonprofit social or professional groups. They are listed geographically by state, then club name within the state. Writers are requested to enclose a self-addressed stamped envelope when writing any club about membership, meeting times, or further information.

To obtain information on starting a writer's club, consult the booklet *How To Start/Run a Writer's Club* (Writer's Digest).

Alabama

ALABAMA STATE POETRY SOCIETY, Mrs. Virginia Farnell, President, 1427 Westmoreland Ave., Montgomery AL 36106.

CREATIVE WRITERS OF MONTGOMERY, Gary Earl Heath, Secretary, 3816 Governors Dr., #H-233, Montgomery AL 36111.

HUNTSVILLE WRITERS' CLUB, Georgette Perry, 2519 Roland Rd., S.W., Huntsville AL 35805.

Arkansas

ARKANSAS PIONEER BRANCH, NATIONAL LEAGUE OF AMERICAN PEN WOMEN, Ms. Swann Kohler, 819 N. Arthur, Little Rock AR 72205. Estab: 1921. Meets monthly.

AUTHORS, COMPOSERS AND ARTISTS' SOCIETY, Peggy Vining, Counselor, 6817 Gingerbread Lane, Little Rock AR 72204.

OZARK CREATIVE WRITERS, INC., Lida W. Pyles, President, P.O. Box 391 Eureka Springs AR 72632.

POETS' ROUNDTABLE OF ARKANSAS, Roberta E. Allen, 6604 Kenwood Rd., Little Rock AR 72207.

California

CALIFORNIA STATE POETRY SOCIETY, Southern California Chapter, 11143 McGirk Ave., El Monte CA 91731. President: Nelle Fertig. Estab: 1974. Meets monthly.

CALIFORNIA WRITERS' CLUB, 2214 Derby St., Berkeley CA 94705. Secretary: Dorothy V. Benson. Estab: 1905. Meets monthly, except July and August. "Membership is open to prize-winning and published writers."

CONTINENTAL WRITERS WORKSHOP, Lori Colwell, 9859 Continental Dr., Huntington Beach CA 92646.

CUPERTINO WRITERS' WORKSHOP, 10117 N. Portal Ave., Cupertino CA 95014. Den Mother: Phyllis Taylor Pianka. Estab: 1972. Meets senimonthly.

DALY CITY CREATIVE WRITERS' GROUP, Margaret O. Richardson, President, 243 Lakeshire Dr., Daly City CA 94015. Estab: 1965.

FALLBROOK WRITERS' WORKSHOP, 1541 Green Canyon Rd., Fallbrook CA 92028. President: Helen B. Hicks.

FICTIONAIRES, 3315 Romelle, Orange CA 92669. Secretary: Loy LeFevre. Estab: 1963. Meets monthly. Membership limited to 20 members.

FOUNTAIN VALLEY WRITERS WORKSHOP, Clara Schultz, 8815 Hummingbird Ave., Fountain Valley CA 92708.

LONG BEACH WRITERS' CLUB, 1641 Chelsea Rd., Palos Verdes Estates CA 90274. President: Alice Dawson.

LOS ESCRIBIENTES, 107 Rancho Alipaz, 32371 Alipaz St., San Juan Capistrano CA 92675. Contact: Nora Collins. Estab: 1971. Meets semimonthly.

MOUNTAIN-VALLEY WRITERS, 18140 Hawthorne, Bloomington CA 92316. Secretary: Pat Wolfe. Estab: 1969. Meets semimonthly. Membership limited to published writers.

NORTHERN CALIFORNIA CARTOON & HUMOR ASSOCIATION, Walt Miller, Secretary, 609 29th Ave., San Mateo CA 94403.

PROFESSIONAL WRITERS LEAGUE OF LONG BEACH, Box 20880, Long Beach CA 90801. Director: Howard E. Hill. Estab: 1970. Meets monthly.

RIVERSIDE WRITERS' CLUB, 7194 Potomac, Riverside CA 92504. President: Frances Seraly. Estab: 1927. Meets monthly.

SAN DIEGO WRITERS WORKSHOP, Box 19366, San Diego CA 92119. President: Chet Cunningham. Estab: 1962. Meets semimonthly.

SAN FRANCISCO WRITERS WORKSHOP, Dean Lipton, Moderator, Louis Lurie Room, Main Library, McAllister and Larkin Sts., San Francisco CA 94102.

SHOWCASE WRITERS CLUB, Larry Stillman, 7842 Barton Dr., Lemon Grove CA 92045.

SOUTHWEST MANUSCRIPTERS, 560 S. Helberta Ave., Redondo Beach CA 90277. Founding Member: Reb Battles. Estab: 1949. Meets monthly.

SPELLBINDERS LITERARY GUILD, Box 10623, Santa Ana CA 92706. Estab: 1970. Meets monthly. "Prospective members must submit a sample of their work—published or unpublished—to our reading committee. Interested parties may come to one meeting as guests before submitting."

SURFWRITERS, 905 Calle Miramar, Redondo Beach CA 90277. Director: LaVada Weir. Estab: 1958. Meets monthly. Currently there is a waiting list for membership.

TIERA DEL SOL WRITERS' CLUB, 9750 Ramo Ct., Santee CA 92071. Estab: 1970. Meets semimonthly.

WRITER'S CLUB OF PASADENA, 231 S. Hudson, Pasadena CA 91101. Secretary: Willard C. HYatt. Estab: 1922. Meets monthly.

WRITERS' CLUB OF WHITTIER, 14560 Rimgate Dr., Whittier CA 90604. President: Mrs. Betty Lee Campbell. Estab: 1953. Meets weekly.

WRITERS' WORKSHOP WEST, 17909 San Gabriel Ave., Cerritos CA 90701. Estab: 1962. Meets semimonthly.

Colorado

BURNING MOUNTAIN WRITERS CLUB, 80 Wildwood Ln., Glenwood Springs CO 81601. President: June Woods.

ROCKY MOUNTAIN WRITERS GUILD, INC., 2969 Baseline Rd., Boulder CO 80303. President: Dr. James D. Hutchinson. Estab: 1967. Meets monthly. Applicants must be published writers.

WE WRITE OF COLORADO, Elaine C. Zimmerman, Box 942, Arvada CO 80001.

WEST ROCKIES WRITERS CLUB, Box 355, Clifton CO 81520. President: Eva Carter.

Dictrict of Columbia

WASHINGTON AREA WRITERS, 2313 S. Culpeper St., Arlington VA 22206. President: Terrence Miller. Estab: 1973. Meets monthly.

WRITERS LEAGUE OF WASHINGTON, Box 449, Silver Spring MD 20907. Secretary: Ms. L. M. O'Connor. Estab: 1917. Meets monthly.

Florida

WEST FLORIDA WRITERS GUILD, Ferd Chappa, President, Box 4547, Pensacola FL 32507.

Georgia

DIXIE COUNCIL OF AUTHORS AND JOURNALISTS, 4221 N. Shallowford Rd., Apt. 7, Chamblee GA 30341. Director: Harold R. Random. Estab: 1961. Meets 6 times/year.

Illinois

FRIENDS OF AMERICAN WRITERS, Mrs. Stanley E. Gwynn, President, 5901 Sheridan Rd., Chicago IL 60660.

JUVENILE FORUM, 3403 45th St., Moline IL 61265. Host: David R. Collins. Estab: 1975. Meets monthly.

KANKAKEE AREA WRITERS GROUP, 1359 Blatt Blvd., Bradley IL 60915. Secretary: Daisy Cahan. EStab: 1967. Meets semimonthly.

OFF CAMPUS WRITERS WORKSHOP, 373 Ramsay Rd., Deerfield IL 60015. Chairman: Carol Spelius. Estab: 1945. Meets weekly.

QUAD CITY WRITERS CLUB, 2725 30th Ave., Rock Island IL 61201. President: Guy Thomas. Estab: 1953. Meets monthly.

SHAGBARK SCRIBES, Ivan Sparling. Room 314C, Illinois Central College, East Peoria IL 61632.

SKOKIE'S CREATIVE WRITERS ASSN., Leo Friedman, 5256 Foster, Skokie IL 60076.

WRITERS' STUDIO, 125½ 18th St., Rock Island IL 61201. President: Betty Mowery. Estab: 1967. Meets weekly.

Indiana

CENTRAL INDIANA WRITERS' ASSOCIATION, Cheryl B. Denk, Director, R.R. 5, Box 35B, Franklin IN 46131.

FLAME'S WRITERS' CLUB, INC., Box 8264, Merrillville IN 46410. President: O. Kiro.

POETS' STUDY CLUB OF TERRE HAUTE, Esther Alman, President, 826 S. Center St., Terre Haute IN 47807.

SOUTH BEND WRITERS' CLUB, 609 Preston Dr., South Bend IN 46615. President: Jim Sullivan.

Iowa

CHRISTIAN WRITERS OF OMAHA, 2907 Avenue F, Council Bluffs IA 51501. President: Mildred Barger. Estab: 1975. Meets monthly.

JASPER COUNTY WRITERS, INC., 106½ N. Second Ave., E., Newton IA 50208. Contact: Betty Allen.

Kansas

UNIVERSAL WRITERS GUILD, INC., Box 2274, Kansas City KS 66110. Estab: 1971. Meets monthly.

WICHITA LINE WOMEN, Jacquelyn Terral Andrews, 2350 Alameda Pl., Wichita KS 67211.

Kentucky

KENTUCKY STATE POETRY SOCIETY, 1043 Everett Ave., #56, Louisville KY 40204. Membership Chairman: Andrey Wood.

LOUISVILLE WRITERS CLUB, Beverly Giammara, 2205 Weber Ave., Louisville KY 40205. Estab: 1952. Meets semimonthly.

Louisiana

SHREVEPORT WRITERS CLUB, L. Chandler, 630 W. 74th St., Shreveport LA 71106.

Maine

YORK WRITERS, 160 Goodwin Rd., Eliot ME 03903. Secretary: Lillian H. Crowell. Meets monthly.

Maryland

WORDSMITHS: The Creative Writing Group of the Social Security Administration, 6724 Ransome Dr., Baltimore MD 21207. Chairman: Robert Hale. Estab: 1971. Meets biweekly. "Basically for employees of the Social Security Administration, but we do accept anyone."

Massachusetts

MANUSCRIPT CLUB OF BOSTON, 770 Boylston St., Boson MA 02199. Contact: Dr. Ruth E. Setterberg. Estab: 1911. Meets semimonthly.

PIONEER VALLEY SCRIPTORS, Maxine Englehardt, P.O. Box 1745, Springfield MA 01101.

SOCIETY OF CHILDREN'S BOOK WRITERS, New England Region, 31 School, Hatfield MA 01038. Director: Jane Yolen. Estab: 1972. Meets annually.

TWELVE O'CLOCK SCHOLARS, Box 14, West Hyannisport MA 02672. Contact: Mrs. Marion Vuilleumier. Estab: 1952. Meets semimonthly.

Michigan

ANN ARBOR WRITERS WORKSHOP, Mitzi Rachleff Crandall, 19 Heatheridge, Ann Arbor MI 48104.

CHRISTIAN SCRIBES, Box 280, Gobles MI 49055. Director: Elisabeth McFadden. Estab: 1968. Meets 8 times/year.

DETROIT WOMEN WRITERS, 915 E. 5th, Royal Oak MI 48067. Membership chairperson: Vera Henry. Estab: 1900. Meets semimonthly.

POETRY SOCIETY OF MICHIGAN, S. Geneva Page, 256 Burr St., Battle Creek MI 49015.

UPPER PENINSULA OF MICHIGAN WRITERS, Mrs. Donald Thornton, Secretary, 1101 Wells St., Iron Mountain MI 49801.

Minnesota

A.A.U.W. WRITER'S WORKSHOP, Minneapolis Branch, American Association of University Women, 2115 Stevens Ave., Minneapolis MN 55427. President: Jane Thomas. Estab: 1932. Meets semimonthly.

EASTSIDE FREELANCE WRITERS OF MINNESOTA, Marlys B. Oliver, 139 Birchwood Ave., White Bear Lake MN 55110.

MESABI WRITERS CLUB, Archie Hill, Mesabi Community College, Virginia MN 55792.

MINNEAPOLIS WRITER'S WORKSHOP INC., Louise N. Johnson, Executive Board, 545 Northeast Mill St., Minneapolis MN 55421.

MINNESOTA AUTHORS GUILD, Box 2337 Loop Station, Minneapolis MN 55402. President: R. Thomas Holden. Estab: 1920. Meets semimonthly.

MINNESOTA CHRISTIAN WRITER'S GUILD, 4137 11th Ave., S., Minneapolis MN 55407. Secretary: Joyce Ellis. Estab: 1951. Meets monthly.

PEPIN PEN CLUB, Donna Rosen, Secretary, Pepin Apts. A101, Lake City MN 55041.

Missouri

CARTHAGE WRITERS GUILD, Route 2, Carthage MO 64836. President: Mary Brady Bussinger. Estab: 1960. Meets bimonthly.

MISSOURI WRITERS' GUILD, 1840 Cliff Dr., Columbia MO 65201. President: Vivian Hansbrough. Estab: 1915. Meets annually. "Any Missourian who has met at least one of the following requirements shall be eligible for membership: authorship or co-authorship of a published book; sale of three articles, stories or poems; sale of three briefs, stories, articles, or comparable materials to an educational publisher; sale of one serial or novelette to a periodical; sale of one play; or sale of one motion picture screenplay, radio or TV script."

NATIONAL LEAGUE OF AMERICAN PENWOMEN, ST. LOUIS BRANCH, Barbara L. Wolfe, President, 6918 Mackenzie Rd., St. Louis MO 63123. (314)481-6840.

ST. LOUIS WRITERS' GUILD, 2935 Russell Blvd., St. Louis MO 63104. President: Charles Guenther. Estab: 1920. Meets monthly, September-May.

WRITER'S GROUP, Communiversity, c/o University of Missouri, K.C., 5100 Rockhill Rd., Kansas City MO 64110.

Montana

THE STRUGGLERS' CLUB, Jennie Hutton, Ekalaka MT 59324.

Nebraska

NEBRASKA WRITERS GUILD, Box 187, Ogallala NE 69153. Contact: Robert F. Lute III.

NORTHEAST NEBRASKA WRITERS, Box 161, Battle Creek NE 68715. Contact: Kathleen Ageton.

OMAHA WRITERS' CLUB, 517 S. 51st St., Omaha NE 68105. President: Cathy Nelson. Estab: 1945. Meets monthly.

New Jersey

NEW JERSEY POETRY SOCIETY, INC., P.O. Box 217, Warton NJ 07885.

WRITER'S ASSOCIATION OF NEW JERSEY, 9 David Ct., Edison NJ 08817. President: Mary Kuczkir. Estab: 1975. Meets monthly.

WRITERS' WORKSHOP, Mrs. Jack Fleishman, E-12, Rocky Brook Rd., East Windsor NJ 08420.

New Mexico

ROSWELL WRITERS GUILD, 1104 Avenida Del Sumbre, Roswell NM 88201. Publicity Chairman: Lois Reader. Estab: 1972. Meets monthly. "We also have two workshops on the second Tuesday evening and the second Friday afternoon meeting."

New York

BROOKLYN CONTEST AND FILLER WRITING CLUB, Selma Glasser, 241 Dahill Rd., Brooklyn NY 11218.

NEW YORK POETRY FORUM, Dr. Dorothea Neale, Director, 3064 Albany Crescent, Apt. 54, Bronx NY 10463.

THE NIAGARA FALLS ASSOCIATION OF PROFESSIONAL WOMEN WRITERS, 721 2nd St., Youngstown NY 14174. President: Mrs. Victor E. Sandberg. Estab: 1937. Meets monthly. "Full membership is limited to published writers who have been paid for their work. Associate members must be published even though unpaid. Membership is also limited to those in both New York and Canada who are within commuting distance."

WOMEN POETS SHARE, Noreen McDonald, 43 Monell Ave., Islip, Long Island NY 11751.

North Carolina

CHARLOTTE WRITERS CLUB, 3114 Airlie St., Charlotte NC 28205. President: Deane Ritch Lomax. Estab: 1922. Meets monthly.

Ohio

GREATER CANTON WRITERS' GUILD, Malone College, 515 25th St., N.W., Canton OH 44706. President: Sandra Shrigley. Estab: 1966. Meets monthly.

LUNCH-BUNCH, Norma Sundberg, 1740 Mechanicsville Rd., Rock Creek OH 44084.

MANUSCRIPT CLUB OF AKRON, Catherine Montgomery, 1319 Pitkin Ave., Akron OH 44310. Estab: 1929. Meets monthly.

MEDINA COUNTY WRITER'S CLUB, Carol J. Wilcox, 3219 Country Club Dr., Medina OH 44256.

SIGMA TAU DELTA, Beta Beta Chapter, 1167 Addison Rd., Cleveland OH 44103. President: Bernice Krumhansl. Estab: 1926. Meets monthly October-June. Applicants "must have had the equivalent of one year of college English composition, or special writing workshops. This might be waived for a published author."

TRI-STATE WRITERS, (formerly Queen City Writers), Michael A. Banks, Box 112, Milford OH 45150.

VERSE WRITERS' GUILD OF OHIO, Jennifer Groce, President, 2384 Hardesty Drive S., Columbus OH 43204.

WOMAN'S PRESS CLUB, RR 2, Box 353, Walton KY 41094. President: Kathryn Evans McKay. Estab: 1888. Meets monthly, except January, from October-June. "Membership is by invitation and requires evidence of written work already published and paid for."

Oklahoma

SHAWNEE WRITERS ASSOCIATION, 1225 Sherry Lane, Shawnee OK 74801. Director: Ernestine Gravley. Estab: 1968. Meets monthly.

STILLWATER WRITERS, 513 S. Knoblock St., Stillwater OK 74074. Secretary: Florence French. Estab: 1932. Meets monthly. Membership limited to 15-18 members.

WRITERS GROUP OF CUSHING, South Kings Hwy., Cushing OK 74023. President: Mazie Cox Read. Estab: 1968. Meets monthly.

Oregon

WESTERN WORLD HAIKU SOCIETY, 4102 N.E. 130th Place, Portland OR 97230. Founder: Lorraine Ellis Harr. Estab: 1972. Meets semiannually.

WRITER'S WORKSHOP, 114 Espey Rd., Grants Pass OR 97526. Director: Dorothy Francis. Estab: 1970. Meets weekly.

Pennsylvania

HOMEWOOD POETRY FORUM, Mary Savage, Inner City Services, Homewood Branch Carnegie Library, 7101 Hamilton Ave., Pittsburgh PA 15206.

LANCASTER AREA WRITERS' FELLOWSHIP, Route 6, Lancaster PA 17603. Director: John K. Brenneman. Estab: 1960. Meets bimonthly.

LEHIGH VALLEY WRITERS' GUILD, Einar Bredland, Ph.D., President, 2840 College Dr., Allentown PA 18104.

THE PITTSBURGH BRANCH OF BOOKFELLOWS, 3461 Harrisburg St., Pittsburg PA 15204. Contact: Ralph Watson/Carsten Ahrens.

THE SCRIBBLERS, Box 522, Hatboro PA 19040.

WILLIAMSPORT WRITERS FORUM, 2318 Dove St., Williamsport PA 17701. Contact: Cynthia Hoover.

WRITERS WORKSHOP OF DELAWARE COUNTY, Barbara Ormsby, 402 Milmont Ave., Milmont Park PA 19033.

Rhode Island

RHODE ISLAND WRITERS' GUILD, 51 Homer St., Providence RI 02905. Secretary: R.M. Eddy.

South Dakota

SIOUXLAND CREATIVE WRITERS' CLUB, Mrs. Larry Ells, 1905 S. Lake Ave., Sioux Falls SD 57105.

Texas

ABILENE WRITERS GUILD, 502 E.N. 16th, Abilene TX 79601. President: Juanita Zachry. Estab: 1967. Meets monthly.

AMERICAN POETRY LEAGUE, 3915 S.W. Military Dr., San Antonio TX 78211. President: Dr. Stella Woodall. Estab: 1922. Meets monthly.

BEAUMONT CHAPTER OF THE POETRY SOCIETY OF TEXAS, Violette Newton, 3230 Ashwood Lane, Beaumont TX 77703.

CHRISTIAN WRITERS' LEAGUE, 1604 E. Taylor, Harlinger TX 78550. Contact: Jean H. Dudley.

CREATIVE WRITING WORKSHOP, Pauline Neff, 10235 Best Dr., Dallas TX 75224.

NATIONAL LEAGUE OF AMERICAN PEN WOMEN, SAN ANTONIO BRANCH, Dr. Stella Woodall, Organizer and Charter President, 3915 S.W. Military Dr., San Antonio TX 78211.

PANHANDLE PEN WOMEN, Box 616, Pampa TX 79065. Director: Evelyn Pierce Nace. Estab: 1920. Meets bimonthly. "Active members must be published writers; associate members are seriously interested in writing, but have not yet been published. Meetings and opportunities are open to both active and associate members."

SOUTH PLAINS WRITERS ASSOCIATION, Box 10114, Lubbock TX 79408. Director: Arline Harris. Estab: 1955. Meets monthly, September-May.

STELLA WOODALL POETRY SOCIETY, Dr. Stella Woodall, President, 3915 S.W. Military Dr., San Antonio TX 78211.

WRITER'S CLUB OF PASADENA, 2204 Cherry Lane, Pasadena TX 77502. Marketing and Library Chairman: June Caesar. Estab: 1966. Meets monthly.

Utah

SEVIER VALLEY CHAPTER OF THE LEAGUE OF UTAH WRITERS, Marilyn A. Henrie, 68 E. 2nd St., South, Richfield UT 84701.

WASATCH WRITERS, UTAH LEAGUE OF WRITERS, 497 E. 400 North, Bountiful UT 84010. Contact: Steve Stumph.

Vermont

THE "NEW" WRITER'S CLUB, Richard J. Frazier, Fair Haven VT 05743.

Virginia

POETS TAPE EXCHANGE, Frances Brandon Neighbours, Director, 109 Twin Oak Dr., Lynchburg VA 24502.

THE WRITERS ASSOCIATION OF TIDEWATER, 76 Algonquin Rd., Hampton VA 23661. Publicity Chairman: Christine Sparks. Estab: 1976. Meets every three weeks.

Washington

LEAGUE OF WESTERN WRITERS, Philip Lewis Arena, President, 5603 239th Pl. S.W., Mountlake Terrace WA 98043.

POETRY LEAGUE OF AMERICA, Philip Lewis Arena, Poetry Manager, 5603 239th Pl., S.W., Mountlake Terrace WA 98043.

TACOMA WRITERS CLUB, Clydelle Smith, 3806 E. 104th St., Tacoma WA 98406.

WRITERS AND ILLUSTRATORS CO-OP, 2102 Sullivan Dr., N.W., Gig Harbor WA 98335. Secretary: Wayne O. Clark. Estab: 1972. Meets monthly.

West Virginia
MORGANTOWN POETRY SOCIETY, 673 Bellaire Dr., Morgantown WV 26505. Publicity Chairman: Kimberly Dunham.

Wisconsin
GENEVA AREA WRITER'S CLUB, Route 3, Box 193, Delavan WI 53115. President: Clarice L. Moon. Estab: 1971. Meets monthly.

SHEBOYGAN COUNTY WRITERS CLUB, Marion Weber, 1929 N. 13 St., Sheboygan WI 53081.

THE UPLAND WRITERS, Mrs. Harry Johns, 213 W. Chapel, Dodgeville WI 53533.

Wyoming
WYOMING WRITERS ASSOCITION, Carolyn Charkey, President, 1922 Seymour, Cheyenne WY 82001.

Canada
CANADIAN AUTHORS ASSOCIATION, 22 Yorkville Ave., Toronto, Ontario, Canada M3W 1L4.

Canal Zone
CROSSROADS WRITERS, A. Grimm Richardson, Secretary, Box 93, Gatun, Canal Zone.

Writers' Colonies

Alabama

CREEKWOOD COLONY FOR THE ARTS, For application write: Charles Ghigna, Poet-in-Residence, Box 88, Hurtsboro AL 36860. (205)667-7720. Established in 1974. For poets and authors. Cost: $35 weekly. The Colony consists of an 1840 ante-bellum mansion located on 100 acres of woodland in southeast Alabama. Open year-round. The colony accommodates 8 residents. No application deadline. Length of each residency may vary from 1 to 3 weeks or more according to individual needs and availability. Xeroxed copies of published work along with date, volume, number and title of magazine are requested with each application.

Massachusetts

CUMMINGTON COMMUNITY OF THE ARTS, Cummington MA 01026. (403)634-2172. Director: Alan Newman. Founded 1923. Open to 30 adults and 12 children (summer); 15 adults (winter).
Purpose/Programs: "A place and atmosphere in which artists can work. A retreat in nature and community living (we share some maintenance and housekeeping tasks and eat dinner together). Artists come from various disciplines, age groups, and parts of the country. Aside from some group responsibilities, each artist is free to make his own schedule and priorities. Eligibility is based "on excellence of work as judged by admissions committees. Fees: $200/month (September-June); $750 for adults, $375 for children in summer session (July-August).

FINE ARTS WORK CENTER, 24 Pearl St., Provincetown MA 02657. (617)487-9960. Contact: Program Coordinator. Founded 1968. Open to 20 members at one time.
Purpose/Programs: "To give young artists and writers who have finished their formal education time off to work and develop their talents outside an academic situation, but not isolated from their peers as well as older writers and artists. We give grants from $100-200 per month to approximately 20 writers and artists. Visual artists receive studios and some writers are given studio apartments. Lengh of stay is October 1-May 1. Open during winter only. There is a visiting program of readings and lectures by distinguished writers and artists. Write for application." Eligibility is based on samples of work. $10 application fee.

New Hampshire

MILDRED I. REID WRITERS' COLONY. Contact: Mildred I. Reid (at the colony), Contoocook NH 03229. (603)746-3625. Established in 1956. Cost: $75 to $90 weekly includes private room, private conferences, class conferences, food. Fiction, nonfiction, plays, poetry. Length of stay: 1 to 11 weeks, starting June 27 to September 1. No application deadline, but early reservations desirable. Scholarship available for woman acting as hostess half-time or full-time. No more than 12 writers per week accepted.

New Mexico

D.H. LAWRENCE SUMMER FELLOWSHIP. Apply to: Gene Frumkin, D.H. Lawrence Committee, English Dept., Rm. 217, Humanities Bldg., University of New Mexico, Albuquerque NM 87131. (505)277-6347. The fellowship is awarded annually and provides a creative person working in any medium with free housing (capacity 4 persons) at the D.H. Lawrence Ranch, plus a $700 stipend. Applications should include a curriculum vitae, work samples, and two or three letters of recommendation. Length of stay: up to 3 months, summers only. Apply by January 1.

HELENE WURLITZER FOUNDATION OF NEW MEXICO. Contact: Henry A. Sauerwein, Jr., Executive Director, Box 545, Taos NM 87571. (505)758-2413. Established in 1954. For all creative artists in every field. Free housing; residents supply their own food. No financial assistance available. Length of stay: 3 to 12 months. Open year-round. Room for 12 persons. No application deadline.

New York

MacDOWELL COLONY. For admissions, contact: The MacDowell Colony, 145 W. 58th St., #12C, New York NY 10019. Estab: 1907. For writers, sculptors, printmakers, photographers, filmmakers, painters and composers. Cost: $49/week; fellowships available. Length of stay: 1-3 months. Open all year. Accommodates 32 residents (summer); 22 (winter). Application deadlines: 6 months in advance, except June through August, when applications must be in by January 31.

MILLAY COLONY FOR THE ARTS, INC. Apply to Ann-Ellen Lesser, Project Director, Steepletop, Austerlitz NY 12017. (518)392-3103. Established in 1973. For writers, composers and visual artists. Room, board and studio space provided. Length of stay is variable. Open all year. Studio and living facilities for 5 residents. This is the former home of the poet Edna St. Vincent Millay. "Admissions committees of professional artists review applications, looking for talent and seriousness of purpose." Applications may be obtained by writing the Admissions Office at the colony, at above address.

YADDO. Contact: Curtis Harnack, Executive Director, Yaddo, Box 395, Saratoga Springs NY 12866. Began operation in 1926. Room and studio space at no cost, but voluntary contributions expected. Length of stay: 1 to 2 months. Open year-round, but primarily in summer, May through Labor Day. Literary merit, rather than popular appeal is criterion for admission. Applicants must submit work and 2 letters of recommendation. February 15 is annual deadline for applications. Open to persons of any age and nationality who have already published some work. Visual artists and composers also use Yaddo facilities.

Texas

DOBIE-PAISANO FELLOWSHIP. Contact: Audrey Slate, Dobie-Paisano Project, University of Texas at Austin, Main Bldg. 101, Austin TX 78712. (512)471-7213. Established in 1967. For persons born or living in Texas or those whose work is identified with the region. Free housing in the former Dobie ranch, plus a $6,000 stipend for 1 year, or 2-$3,000 awards for 6-months each. Length of stay: 12 months or 6 months. 1979-80 fellowships are for writers; 1978-79 for visual artists. Year begins August 1.

Virginia

VIRGINIA CENTER FOR THE CREATIVE ARTS AT SWEET BRIAR. Contact: William Smart, Director, Box 45, Sweet Briar College, Sweet Briar VA 24595. (804)381-5693. Established in 1971. For writers, painters, sculptors and composers. Cost: $70 per week, with some financial aid available. Two summer sessions. Year-round facilities may be available in 1977.

Writers' Conferences

The following writers' conferences are usually held annually. Contact the conference direct for details about staff, workshops, manuscript criticism opportunities, fees, accommodations, length of conference and dates planned for the current year. Always enclose a self-addressed, stamped envelope when requesting any information.

Alabama

ALABAMA WRITERS' CONCLAVE, Mrs. Carl Morton, 2221 Woodview Dr., Birmingham AL 35216.

Arkansas

ARKANSAS WRITERS' CONFERENCE, 510 East St., Benton AR 72015. Director: Anna Nash Yarbrough. Held each June for published and unpublished writers.

California

CABRILLO MYSTERY WRITERS' CONFERENCE, Community Services, Cabrillo College, 6500 Soquel Dr., Aptos CA 95003. Director: Dr. Timothy Welch. Held each September for published and unpublished writers.

CALIFORNIA WRITERS CONFERENCE, Dorothy Benson, 2214 Derby St., Berkeley CA 94705.

LA JOLLA SUMMER WRITERS' CONFERENCE, University Extension, Q-O14, University of California, La Jolla CA 92093. Director: David Hellyer. Held each August for published and unpublished writers.

LONG BEACH WRITERS CONFERENCE, Howard E. Hill, Director, Box 20880, Long Beach CA 90801.

PASADENA ANNUAL WRITERS' CONFERENCE, 1191 E. Mendicino, Altadena CA 91001. Director: Helen Hinkley Jones. Held each May for published and unpublished writers.

SEMINAR FOR FREELANCE WRITERS, Community Services, Canada College, 4200 Farm Hill Blvd., Redwood City CA 94061. Director: Gladys Cretan. Held each May for published and unpublished writers.

WRITERS' CONFERENCE AT JULIAN, CALIFORNIA, 14560 Ringate Dr., Whittier CA 90604. President: Betty Lee Campbell. Held each April for published and unpublished writers.

WRITERS CONFERENCE IN CHILDREN'S LITERATURE, P.O. Box 296, Los Angeles CA 90066.

WRITERS' FORUM, Pasadena City College, Office of Continuing Education, 1570 E. Colorado Blvd., Pasadena CA 91106.

Colorado

UNIVERSITY OF COLORADO WRITERS CONFERENCE, Bureau of Conferences and Institutes, University of Colorado, 217 Academy, 970 Aurora Ave., Boulder CO 80302. Held each June.

Connecticut

CONNECTICUT WRITERS' LEAGUE CONFERENCE, Box 78, Farmington CT 06032. Chairman: Eugene L. Belisle. Held each May for anyone interested in writing.

WESLEYAN-SUFFIELD WRITER-READER CONFERENCE, Jeanne B. Krochalis, Graduate Summer School, Wesleyan University, Middletown CT 06457.

District of Columbia

GEORGETOWN UNIVERSITY WRITERS CONFERENCE, Georgetown University School for Summer and Continuing Education, Washington DC 20057. Director: Dr. Riley Hughes. Held on campus each July (abroad, each June) for published and unpublished writers.

WRITER'S CONFERENCE, Myra Sklarew, Director, The American University, Department of Literature, Room 215, Gray Hall, Washington DC 20016.

Florida

FLORIDA SUNCOAST WRITERS' CONFERENCE, Dr. Ed Hirshberg, Director, FSWC, Department of English, University of South Florida, Tampa FL 33620.

SOUTHEASTERN WRITERS ASSOCIATION, INC., Mrs. Jos. E. Buffington, Executive Secretary, 393 S. Coconut Palm Blvd., Tavernier FL 33070.

Georgia

DIXIE COUNCIL CREATIVE WRITING WORKSHOP, Harold R. Random, Director, 4221 N. Shallowford Rd., Apt. 7, Chamblee GA 30341.

Illinois

CHRISTIAN WRITERS INSTITUTE CONFERENCE AND WORKSHOP, Gundersen Drive and Schmale Rd., Wheaton IL 60187.

ILLINOIS WESLEYAN UNIVERSITY WRITERS' CONFERENCE, Illinois Wesleyan University, Bloomington IL 61701. Director: Mrs. Bettie W. Story. Held each July for published and unpublished writers.

INTERNATIONAL BLACK WRITERS CONFERENCE, INC., 4019 S. Vincennes Ave., Chicago IL 60053. Director: Alice C. Browning. Held each June for published and unpublished writers.

McKENDREE WRITERS' CONFERENCE, Lynn Grove, President, McKendree Writers' Association, McKendree College, Lebanon IL 62254.

MISSISSIPPI VALLEY WRITERS' CONFERENCE, 3403 45th St., Moline IL 61265. Director: David R. Collins. Held each June for published and unpublished writers.

WRITING '78, 125½ 18th St., Rock Island IL 61201. Secretary: Velvet Fackeldey. Held each March for published and unpublished writers.

Indiana

INDIANA UNIVERSITY WRITERS' CONFERENCE, Ballantine 464, Bloomington IN 47401. Director: Roger Mitchell. Held each June/July for published and unpublished writers.

MIDWEST WRITERS' WORKSHOP, English Department, Ball State University, Muncie IN 47306. Director: Dick Renner. Held each August for published and unpublished writers.

OHIO RIVER WRITERS' WORKSHOP, Evansville Arts & Education Council, 22 Chandler Ave., Evansville IN 47713.

Kentucky

CREATIVE WRITING CONFERENCE, Department of English, Eastern Kentucky University, Richmond KY 40475. Director: William Sutton. Held each June for published and unpublished writers.

WRITING WORKSHOP FOR PEOPLE OVER 57, Council on Aging, University of Kentucky, Lexington KY 40506. Director: C.R. Hager. Held each August for published and unpublished writers over 57 years of age.

Maine

MAINE WRITERS WORKSHOP, G.F. Bush, Director, Box 82, Stonington ME 04681.

SEACOAST WRITERS CONFERENCE, 160 Goodwin Rd., Eliot ME 03903. Registrar: Mrs. Lillian H. Crowell. Held each October for published and unpublished writers.

STATE OF MAINE WRITERS' CONFERENCE, Box 296, Ocean Park ME 04063.

Massachusetts

CAPE COD WRITERS' CONFERENCE, Box 111, West Hyannisport MA 02622. Executive Secretary: Mrs. Pierre Vuilleumier. Held each August for published and unpublished writers.

SCBW NEW ENGLAND CHILDREN'S LITERATURE CONFERENCE, 31 School St., Hatfield MA 01038. Director: Jane Stemple. Held each April for published and unpublished writers.

SCRIPTORS' CONFERENCE, Box 1745, Springfield MA 01101. Secretary: Maxine Englehardt. Held each summer for published and unpublished writers.

Michigan

CHRISTIAN SCRIBES WRITERS' CONFERENCE, Box 280, Cobles MI 49055. President: Elisabeth McFadden. Held each October or November for anyone interested in writing, but "we prefer Christian-oriented writers".

CLARION WRITERS' WORKSHOP IN SCIENCE FICTION & FANTASY, Justin Morrill College, Michigan State University, East Lansing MI 48824. Director: Dr. R. Glenn Wright. Held each summer.

CRAFTSMANSHIP OF CREATIVE WRITING CONFERENCE, Conferences and Institutes, Oakland University, Rochester MI 48063. Assistant Director: Douglas Alden Peters. Held each October for published and unpublished writers.

DETROIT WOMEN WRITERS, Oakland University, Division of Continuing Education, Rochester MI 48063. Contact: Barbara Hoffman.

UNIVERSITY OF MICHIGAN CONFERENCE ON TEACHING TECHNICAL AND PROFESSIONAL WRITING, Humanities Department, College of Engineering, University of Michigan, Ann Arbor MI 48109.

Minnesota

UPPER MIDWEST WRITERS' CONFERENCE, Leslie Russell, Bemidji State University, Bemidji MN 56601.

Missouri

MISSOUR PRESS WOMEN SPRING MEETING, Mildred Planthold Michie, Route 1, Town of Piney Park, St. Clair MO 63077.

Nebraska

CHRISTIAN WRITERS CONFERENCE, 4514 Hascal, Omaha NE 68106. Co-Chairman: Joan Deems. Held each October for published and unpublished writers.

OMAHA WRITERS' CLUB SPRING CONFERENCE, 517 S. 51st Ave., Omaha NE 68105. President: Cathy Nelson. Held each May for published and unpublished writers.

New Hampshire

MILDRED I. REID WRITERS' COLONY, Contoocook NH 03229.

New Jersey

COMEDY AND HUMOR WORKSHOP, 74 Pullman Ave., Elberon NJ 07740. Director: George Q. Lewis. Held each June, July and August for published and unpublished writers.

NEW JERSEY WRITERS' ANNUAL CONFERENCE, 9 David Ct., Edison NJ 08817. President: Mary Kuczkir. Held each October for published and unpublished writers.

WILLIAM PATERSON COLLEGE WRITERS' CONFERENCE, Wayne NJ 07470.

New York

ADIRONDACK-SPA WRITERS & EDUCATORS CONFERENCE, Box 189, Clifton Park NY 12065. Director: Dr. Harry Barba. Held each July for published and unpublished writers.

CHAUTAUQUA WRITERS' WORKSHOP, Summer School Office, Box 28, Chautauqua NY 14722.

CHRISTIAN WRITERS WORKSHOP, Don Booth, 6853 Webster Rd., Orchard Park NY 14127.

CORNELL UNIVERSITY CREATIVE WRITING WORKSHOP, Cornell University Summer Session, 105 Day Hall, Ithaca NY 14853. Dean: Charles W. Jermy, Jr. Held each July-August for published and unpublished writers.

CREATIVE WRITING WORKSHOP, Niagara County Community College, 3111 Saunders Settlement Rd., Sanborn NY 14132.

NATIONAL CRITICS INSTITUTE OF THE EUGENE O'NEILL MEMORIAL THEATER CENTER, Suite 1012, 1860 Broadway, New York NY 10023. Director: Ernest Schier. Held mid-July to mid-August each year for practicing arts writers and critics whose work is published regularly in newspapers or magazines.

NATIONAL PLAYWRIGHTS CONFERENCE OF THE EUGENE O'NEILL MEMORIAL THEATER CENTER, Suite 1012, 1860 Broadway, New York NY 10023. Coordinator: Nancy Quinn. Held mid-July to mid-August each year for published and unpublished writers.

NEW YORK HOLIDAY WORKSHOP, 20 Plaza St., Brooklyn NY 11238. Director: Pauline Bloom. Held each October for published and unpublished writers.

POETRY WORKSHOPS, The Poetry Center, YMHA, 1395 Lexington Ave., New York NY 10028.

ST. LAWRENCE UNIVERSITY FICTION INTERNATIONAL WRITERS' CONFERENCE, Joe David Bellamy, St. Lawrence University, Canton NY 13617.

TECHNICAL WRITERS' INSTITUTE, B.F. Hammet, Director, Rensselaer Polytechnic Institute, Troy NY 12181.

UNIVERSITY OF ROCHESTER WRITERS' WORKSHOP, Dean Robert Koch, Writers' Workshop, Harkness Hall 102, University of Rochester, Rochester NY 14627.

WRITERS' SEMINAR, 6007 Lockport Rd., Niagara Falls NY 14305. Held each May for published and unpublished writers.

North Carolina

MARTHA'S VINEYARD WRITERS WORKSHOP, Thomas Heffernan, Director, Box F9, 1020 Peace St., Raleigh NC 27605.

TAR HEEL WRITERS' ROUNDTABLE, Box 5393, Raleigh NC 27607. Director: Bernadette Hoyle. Held each August for published and unpublished writers.

WESTERN NORTH CAROLINA CHRISTIAN WRITERS' CONFERENCE, Box 188, Black Mountain NC 28711. Director: Yvonne Lehman. Held each August for published and unpublished writers.

Ohio

CUYAHOGA WRITERS' CONFERENCE, Cuyahoga Community College Eastern Campus, 25444 Harvard Rd., Cleveland OH 44122. Director: Mrs. Margaret Taylor. Held each April or May for published and unpublished writers.

MANUSCRIPT CLUB OF AKRON'S ANNUAL WORKSHOP, Catherine Montgomery, 1319 Pitkin Ave., Akron OH 44310.

MIAMI UNIVERSITY CREATIVE WRITING WORKSHOP, Upham Hall, Miami University, Oxford OH 45056. Director: Milton White. Held each May or June for published and unpublished writers.

MIDWEST WRITERS' CONFERENCE, Barbara Akins, Director, Malone College, 515 25th St., N.W., Canton OH 44706.

OHIO POETRY DAY, Ray Buckingham, President, 385 N. Sandusky St., Apt. 15, Delaware OH 43015.

WRITER'S WORKSHOP, Dr. Joseph LaBriola, Director, Sinclair Community College, 444 W. Third St., Dayton OH 45402.

Oklahoma
OKLAHOMA WRITERS FEDERATION ANNUAL CONFERENCE, Ernestine Gravley, 1225 Sherry Lane, Shawnee OK 74801.

UNIVERSITY OF OKLAHOMA ANNUAL SHORT COURSE ON PROFESSIONAL WRITING, Leonard Logan, Oklahoma Center for Continuing Education, University of Oklahoma, 1700 Asp Ave., Norman OK 73037.

Oregon
HAYSTACK WRITERS' WORKSHOP, Dona Beattie, Box 1491, Portland OR 97207.

WILLAMETTE WRITERS CONFERENCE, Ms. Martha Stuckey, 2218 N.E. 8th, Portland OR 97212.

Pennsylvania
PHILADELPHIA WRITERS CONFERENCE, Emma S. Wood, Registrar, Box 834, Philadelphia PA 19105.

ST. DAVIDS CHRISTIAN WRITERS' CONFERENCE, R. #2, Cochranville PA 19330. Registrar: Edna Mast. Held each June for published and unpublished writers.

South Carolina
WINTHROP COLLEGE WRITERS CONFERENCE, Director of Public Service, Joynes Center for Continuing Education, Winthrop College, Rock Hill SC 29733.

Texas
ABILENE WRITERS GUILD WORKSHOP, Pat Carden, 2809 Darrell Dr., Abilene TX 79606.

PANHANDLE PEN WOMEN AND WEST TEXAS STATE UNIVERSITY WRITERS' ROUNDUP, 6209 Adirondack, Amarillo TX 79106. Director: Dolores Spencer. Held each March or April for published and unpublished writers.

PATRIOTIC POETRY SEMINAR, 3915 S.W. Military Dr., San Antonio TX 78211. President-Director: Dr. Stella Woodall. Held each October for published and unpublished writers.

SOUTH TEXAS PRO-AM WRITERS' RALLY, 7010 Mark Dr., San Antonio TX 78218. Director: Peggy Bradbury. Held each October or November for published and unpublished writers.

SOUTHWEST WRITERS' CONFERENCE, Sherman L. Pease, Director, Continuing Education, University of Houston, 4800 Calhoun, Houston TX 77004.

TEXAS WRITERS ROUNDTABLE, Hill Country Arts Foundation, Box 176, Ingram TX 78025. Executive Director: Richard Mace. Held each May for published and unpublished writers.

Utah
LEAGUE OF UTAH WRITERS' ROUNDUP, 448 E. 775 North, Bountiful UT 84010. President: Dora Flack. Held each September for published and unpublished writers.

ROCKY MOUNTAIN WRITERS' CONVENTION, Special Courses and Conferences, 118 HRCB, Brigham Young University, Provo UT 84602. Director: Gary R. Bascom. Held each July for published and unpublished writers.

USU MAGAZINE ARTICLE WRITER'S WORKSHOP, Dick Harris, Director, Utah State University, Logan UT 84321.

WESTERN WRITERS' CONFERENCE, Conference and Institute Division, UMC 01, Utah State University, Logan UT 84322.

Vermont
BREAD LOAF WRITERS' CONFERENCE, Middlebury College, Middlebury VT 05753. Director: Robert Pack. Held each August for published and unpublished writers.

GREEN MOUNTAINS WRITERS WORKSHOP, Johnson State College, Johnson VT 05656. Director: Roger Rath. Held each July for published and unpublished writers.

Virginia
VIRGINIA HIGHLANDS FESTIVAL CREATIVE WRITING DAY, Westwood Estates, Abingdon VA 24210. Chairman: Mrs. William W. Eckridge. Held each August for unpublished writers.

Washington
CENTRUM SUMMER SEASON OF THE ARTS, Fort Worden State Park, Port Townsend WA 98368.

FORT WORDEN POETRY SYMPOSIUM, Jim Heynen, Coordinator, Fort Worden State Park, Port Townsend WA 98368.

PACIFIC NORTHWEST WRITERS CONFERENCE, 51 164th Ave., N.E. Bellevue WA 98008. Contact: Executive Secretary. Held each July for published and unpublished writers.

Wisconsin
MIDWEST WRITERS' CONFERENCE, Dr. Wayne Wolfe, University of Wisconsin-River Falls, River Falls WI 54022.

OUTDOOR WRITERS ASSOCIATION OF AMERICA ANNUAL CONFERENCE, 4141 W. Bradley Rd., Milwaukee WI 53209. Held each June.

Canada
THE BANFF CENTRE, School of Fine Arts, P.O. Box 1020, Banff, Alberta T0L 0C0 Canada.

SUMMER WRITERS' WORKSHOP AT NEW COLLEGE, UNIVERSITY OF TORONTO, Gerald Lampert, Director, Suite 8, 165 Spadina Ave., Toronto, Canada M5T 2C4.

Foreign
EUROPEAN HOLIDAY WRITERS'WORKSHOP, 20 Plaza St., Brooklyn NY 11218. Director: Pauline Bloom. Held each September for published and unpublished writers.

COSTA RICA AND GUATEMALA HOLIDAY WRITERS' WORKSHOP, Pauline Bloom, 20 Plaza St., Brooklyn NY 11238.

SUMMER IN FRANCE, Hazel Kley, Paris American Academy, 9, rue des Ursullnes, 75005 Paris, France.

Writers' Organizations

National organizations for writers listed here usually require that potential members have attained a professional status. Local or regional writers' clubs which are more social in nature are listed in the Writers' Clubs section. SASE must be enclosed with all correspondence with these organizations.

ACADEMY OF AMERICAN POETS, 1078 Madison Ave., New York NY 10028. Established in 1934. President: Mrs. Hugh Bullock. Purpose of the Academy of American Poets is to encourage, stimulate, and foster the production of American poetry. Awards prizes, conducts poetry workshops, readings and other literary events.

AMERICAN ACADEMY AND INSTITUTE OF ARTS AND LETTERS, 633 W. 155 St., New York NY 10022. Executive Director: Margaret M. Mills. An honor society of 250 U.S. artists, writers, and composers from which 50 are elected as members of the Academy. The Institute was founded in 1898 and the Academy in 1904. Both organizations are chartered by Congress. In December 1976, the organizations merged.

AMERICAN AUTO RACING WRITERS AND BROADCASTERS ASSOCIATION, 922 N. Pass Ave., Burbank CA 91505. (213)842-7005. Established in 1955. Executive Director: Mr. Dusty Brandel. An organization of writers, broadcasters and photographers who cover auto racing throughout the U.S. Aims primarily to improve the relationship between the press and the promoters, sanctioning bodies, sponsors, and participants in the sport. Dues: $10 annually, full membership; $25 annually, associate membership.

THE AMERICAN GUILD OF AUTHORS AND COMPOSERS, 40 W. 57th St., New York NY 10019. (212)757-8833. Established in 1931. Executive Director: Lewis M. Bachman. President: Ervin Drake. This organization was formed to provide better royalty contracts from music publishers. AGAC collects royalties and audits for its members and charges 5% commission (but not exceeding $1,400 in 1 year). A regular member is a composer who has had at least 1 song published or recorded by a recognized company. Dues he pays are based on the size and activity of his catalog. Associate members are songwriters who have not yet published. Dues: $25 annually (associate members) $50-300 annually (regular members).

AMERICAN SOCIETY OF COMPOSERS, AUTHORS AND PUBLISHERS (ASCAP), 1 Lincoln Plaza, New York NY 10023. (212)595-3050. Director of Public Relations: Walter Wager. ASCAP licenses the right to perform in public for profit in the U.S. the copyrighted musical works of its 25,000 members and the members of affiliated societies in more than 60 countries. Any composer or lyricist of a copyrighted musical work may join if he or she has had at least 1 musical work regularly published, or recorded or performed in an ASCAP-licensed establishment. Associate membership is open to any writer who has had 1 work copyrighted. Annual dues: $10 for writers; $50 for publishers. No dues for associate members.

AMERICAN SOCIETY OF JOURNALISTS AND AUTHORS, INC., (formerly Society of Magazine Writers, Inc.), 123 W. 43rd St., New York NY 10036. Established in 1948. President: Patrick M. McGrady Jr. Initiation fee: $25. Annual dues for residents of New York and environs: $60. Annual dues for those residing 200 or more miles from New York: $45. For further information, contact Mrs. Dorothea H. Lobsenz, Administrative Secretary.

AMERICAN SOCIETY OF NEWSPAPER EDITORS, Box 551, 1350 Sullivan Trail, Easton PA 18042. Executive Secretary: Mr. Gene Giancarlo. Established in 1922. Serves as a medium for the exchange of ideas. Membership is limited to directing editors (managing editors, executive editors, associate editors, editors of editorial pages, etc.) of daily newspapers in the U.S. Dues: $200 annually.

THE AMERICAN SOCIETY OF WRITERS, 890 National Press Bldg., Washington DC 20045. Contact: Robert D. Shelley. Founded 1973.
Purpose: "To provide an organization with its attendant benefits, privileges and services to

assist writers in all disciplines of the literary arts, to promote and further established writers and to foster and encourage unpublished writers. Awards and prizes are given to recognize achievement among members." Fees: $15/year.

AMERICAN TRANSLATORS ASSOCIATION, P.O. Box 129, Croton-on-Hudson NY 10520. Executive Secretary: Mrs. Rosemary Malia. Established in 1959 as a national professional society to advance the standards of translation and to promote the intellectual and material interest of translators and interpreters in the United States. Welcomes to membership all those who are interested in the field as well as translators and interpreters active in any branch of knowledge.

ASMP-THE SOCIETY OF PHOTOGRAPHERS IN COMMUNICATIONS, 60 E. 42nd St., New York NY 10017. (212)661-6450. Executive Director: Arie Kopelman. Established to promote and further the interests of professional photographers in communications media such as journalism, corporate, advertising, fashion, books, etc. Acts as a clearinghouse for photographic information on markets, rates, and business practices of magazines, advertising agencies, publishers and electronic media; works for copyright law revision; offers legal advice, through counsel, to members concerning questions of rights, ethics and payment. Membership categories include Sustaining, General, Associate, and Student.

ASSOCIATED BUSINESS WRITERS OF AMERICA, P.O. Box 135, Monmouth Junction NJ 08852. Executive Director: William R. Palmer. Members are skilled in one or more facets of business writing (advertising copy, public relations, ghost writing, books, reports, business and technical magazines, etc.). "Members" are full-time writers. "Associates" hold other jobs. Does not place mss for its members. Provides directory profiling members to prospective mss buyers (at $5). Free membership lists mass-mailed to potential buyers. Dues: $40 annually; $10 initiation fee.

AUTHORS GUILD, 234 W. 44th St., New York NY 10036. Established in 1912. Executive Secretary: Peter Heggie. Basic functions and purposes are to act and speak with the collective power and voice of 4,700 writers in matters of joint professional and business concern; to keep informed on market tendencies and practices, and to keep its members informed; to advise members on individual professional and business problems as far as possible. Those eligible for membership include any author who shall have had a book published by a reputable American publisher within 7 years prior to his application; any author who shall have had 3 works (fiction or nonfiction) published by a magazine of general circulation, either national or local, within 18 months prior to application. Annual dues: $35.

AUTHORS LEAGUE OF AMERICA, INC., 234 West 44th St., New York NY 10036. Established in 1912. Administrative Assistant: Kim Tsang Bogart. The Authors League membership is restricted to authors and dramatists who are members of the Authors Guild, Inc., and the Dramatists Guild, Inc. Matters of joint concern to authors and dramatists, such as copyright and freedom of expression, are in the province of the League; other matters, such as contract terms and subsidiary rights, are in the province of the guilds.

AVIATION/SPACE WRITERS ASSOCIATION, Cliffwood Rd., Chester NJ 07930. (201)879-5667. Executive Secretary: William F. Keiser. Established in 1938. Founded to establish and maintain high standards of quality and veracity in gathering, writing, editing, and disseminating aeronautical information. The AWA numbers 1,100 members who work for newspapers, press services, TV, radio, or other media and specialize in writing about aviation or space. Dues: $10, initiation fee; $30, annual dues.

BOXING WRITERS ASSOCIATION, c/o Marvin Kahn, Secretary-Treasurer, N.Y. State AS Athletic Commission, 270 Broadway, New York NY 10007. Established in 1922.

CONSTRUCTION WRITERS ASSOCIATION, 202 Homer Building, Washington DC 20005. Established in 1958. CWA offers its members a forum for the interchange of information, ideas and methods for improving the quality of reporting, editing and public relations in the construction field. It also provides contact between the membership and news-making officials in government, contracting firms, equipment manufacturers and distributors, consulting firms, and other construction trade and professional groups. Any person principally engaged in writing or editing material pertaining to the construction industry for any regularly published periodical of general circulation is eligible for membership. Any public information or public relations specialist who represents an organization or agency the existence of which depends in whole or in part on the construction industry is also eligible. Annual dues: $20.

COUNCIL FOR THE ADVANCEMENT OF SCIENCE WRITING, INC., Northwestern University, Evanston IL 60201. (312)383-0820. Executive Director: W. J. Cromie, 618 N. Elwood, Oak Park IL 60302. Organization purpose is to increase the quality of coverage of science, medicine, technology and related areas in print and broadcast media. Membership is limited to scientists and communicators appointed by CASW board of directors.

DIRECT MARKETING WRITERS GUILD, INC., 15 W. 44th St., New York NY 10038. (212)354-2255. Contact: Michael Fabian. Founded 1964.
Purpose: "To provide a forum for learning the arts of the direct marketing writer's profession; a place where writers meet writers, and privately discuss problems and new achievements in the industry." Eligibility requires that 60% of prospective member's income comes from 1) direct response writing; 2) as a result of supervising writers; 3) as a result of employing direct response writers. Fees: $25/year if within 50 miles of New York City; $15 if more than 50 miles outside of New York.

DOG WRITERS' ASSOCIATION OF AMERICA, INC., 3 Blythewood Rd., Doylestown PA 18901. President: John T. Marvin. Secretary: Sara Futh, Kinney Hill Rd., Washington Depot CT 06794. The association aims to promote and to encourage the exchange of ideas, methods and professional courtesies among its members. Membership is limited to paid dog writers, editors and/or publishers of newspapers, magazines and books dealing with dogs. Annual dues: $12.

THE FOOTBALL WRITERS ASSOCIATION OF AMERICA, Box 1022, Edmond OK 73034. Secretary-Treasurer: Volney Meece. Membership is mainly sports writers on newspapers and magazines who cover college football, plus those in allied fields, chiefly college sports information directors. Dues: $7.50 annually.

GARDEN WRITERS ASSOCIATION OF AMERICA, INC., Gladys Reed Robinson, Membership Chairman, 680 Third Ave., Troy NY 12182. (518)235-3307. Dues: $12.50 annually. Student membership: $5 annually.

INTERNATIONAL ASSOCIATION OF BUSINESS COMMUNICATORS, 870 Market St., Suite 469, San Francisco CA 94102. Executive Director: John N. Bailey. Established in 1970. Dedicated to the advancement of its members and to the advancement of the communication profession. Membership limited to those active in the field of the business of organizational communication.

MARIANIST WRITERS' GUILD, Marianist Community, University of Dayton, 300 College Park Ave., Dayton OH 45469. (513)229-3430. Executive Secretary: Louis J. Faerber, S.M., Ph.D. Established in 1947. Membership is limited to Marianists in America who have had at least 3 works published nationally since 1947.

MOTOR SPORTS PRESS ASSOCIATION (of Northern California), c/o Harriet Gittings, Box 484, Fremont CA 94537. Established in 1963 for the advancement of motor sports and motor sports journalism in Northern California, for the interchange of ideas and information; to provide a body to authenticate legitimate motor sports journalists, photographers, and radio and TV broadcasters, whether fully employed, part-time employed, or freelancing in Northern California. Annual dues: $12.

MUSIC CRITICS ASSOCIATION, INC., c/o Richard D. Freed, Executive Secretary, 6201 Tuckerman Lane, Rockville MD 20852. President: Elliott W. Galkin. The purposes of the Association are to act as an educational medium for the promotion of high standards of music criticism in the press in America, to hold meetings where self-criticism and exchange of ideas will promote educational opportunities, and to increase the general interest in music in the growing culture of the Americas. Membership is open to persons who regularly cover musical events in the U.S. and Canada. Annual dues: $15.

MYSTERY WRITERS OF AMERICA, INC., 105 E. 19th St., New York NY 10003. Established in 1944. Executive Secretary: Gloria Amoury. An organization dedicated to the proposition that the detective story is the noblest sport of man. Membership includes active members who have made at least one sale in mystery, crime, or suspense writing; associate members who are either novices in the mystery writing field or nonwriters allied to the field; editors, publishers, and affiliate members who are interested in mysteries. Annual dues: $35 for U.S. members; $10 for Canadian and overseas members.

THE NATIONAL ACADEMY OF TELEVISION ARTS AND SCIENCES, 291 South La Cienega Blvd., Beverly Hills CA 90211. President: John Cannon. A nonprofit membership organization of professionals working in the television industry. Active members must have worked actively and creatively in television for at least 2 years. Dues: $15 to $30 annually, according to chapter.

NATIONAL ASSOCIATION OF EDUCATIONAL BROADCASTERS, 1346 Connecticut Ave., N.W., Washington DC 20036. Established in 1925. President: James A. Fellows. A professional society of individuals in educational telecommunications; composed of men and women who work in public broadcasting, instructional communications and allied fields. Annual dues: $35.

NATIONAL ASSOCIATION OF GAGWRITERS, 74 Pullman Ave., Elberon NJ 07740. (201)229-9472. Contact: George Quipp Lewis. Estab: 1945.
Purpose: "To discover, develop, encourage, and showcase future funny men and women; to provide guidance; to coordinate careers in comedy; to promote a national sense of humor and happiness; to maintain a high standard of comedic creativity." Fees: $25/year.

NATIONAL ASSOCIATION OF HOME AND WORKSHOP WRITERS, 27861 Natoma Rd., Los Altos Hills CA 94022. President: R.J. DeCristoforo. Prospective members contact: Bob Brightman, 5 Sussex Rd., Great Neck NY 11020. (506)482-2074. Founded 1973.
Purpose: "An informal association of writers and editors in the field of home and workshop writing. We specialize in how-to activities. Members must have had at least 12 pages published in the previous year. Associate members are also welcome (part-time writers, non-voting) as well as folks interested in the how-to field. A bimonthly newsletter goes to all members, and membership list is used by industry to contact suitable writers for instruction booklets, tool use, and for general how-to projects." Fees: $25/year (full membership); $15/year (associate membership).

NATIONAL ASSOCIATION OF SCIENCE WRITERS, INC., Box H, Sea Cliff NY 11579. (516)671-1734. Established in 1934. Administrative Secretary: Rosemary Arctander. This organization was established to "foster the dissemination of accurate information regarding science through all media normally devoted to informing the public. In pursuit of this goal, NASW conducts a varied program to increase the flow of news from scientists, to improve the quality of its presentation, and to communicate its meaning and importance to the reading public. Anyone who is actively engaged in the dissemination of science information, and has two years or more experience in this field, is eligible to apply. There are several classes of membership. Active members must be principally engaged in reporting science through media that reach the public directly: newspapers, mass-circulation magazines, trade books, radio, television and films. Associate members report science through special media: limited-circulation publications and announcements from organizations such as universities, research laboratories, foundations and science-oriented corporations. Lifetime membership is extended to members after they have belonged to NASW for 25 years. Honorary membership is awarded by NASW to outstanding persons who have notably aided the objectives of the association." Annual dues: $25.

NATIONAL LEAGUE OF AMERICAN PEN WOMEN, INC., 1300 17th St., N.W., Washington DC 20036. Established in 1897. "Professionally qualified women engaged in creating and promoting letters, art, and music" are eligible for membership. Women interested in membership must qualify professionally and be presented for membership and endorsed by two active members in good standing in the League. The League holds branch, state, and national meetings. Dues: Initiation fee $5. Annual branch dues plus $15 national dues. For further information, write to national president at address given above.

NATIONAL PRESS CLUB, National Press Bldg., 529 14th St. N.W., Washington DC 20045. Initiation fee: $25-125. Dues: $40 to $244 annually, depending on membership status.

NATIONAL TURF WRITERS ASSOCIATION, Willco Bldg., Suite 317, 6000 Executive Blvd., Rockville MD 20852. Secretary/Treasurer: Tony Chamblin. Membership limited to newspaper or magazine writers who regularly cover thoroughbred racing, sports editors of newspapers which regularly print thoroughbred racing news and results, and sports columnists who write columns on thoroughbred racing. Dues: $10 annually.

NATIONAL WRITERS CLUB, INC., 1365 Logan, Suite 100, Denver CO 80203. (303)861-1234. Established in 1937. Executive Director: Donald E. Bower. "Founded for the purpose of informing, aiding and protecting freelance writers worldwide. Associate membership is available to anyone seriously interested in writing. Qualifications for professional membership are publication of a book by a recognized book publisher; or sales of at least three stories or articles to national or regional magazines; or a television, stage, or motion picture play professionally produced." Annual dues: $17.50, associate membership; $22, professional membership; plus $5 initiation fee.

NEWSPAPER FARM EDITORS OF AMERICA (NFEA), 4200 12th St., Des Moines IA 50313. (515)243-4518. Established in 1953. Executive Secretary: Glenn Cunningham. Writers employed by newspapers, farm editors and farm writers for national wire services are eligible for membership. Dues: $20 annually.

NEWSPAPER FOOD EDITORS AND WRITERS ASSOCIATION, Established in 1973. President: Eleanor Oatman, St. Paul Dispatch & Pioneer Press, St. Paul MN 55101. To encourage communication among journalists devoting a substantial portion of their working time to the furthering of public's knowledge of food; to uphold and foster professional ethical standards for such persons; to increase their knowledge about food and to encourage and promote a greater understanding among fellow journalists and those who manage news dissemination organizations. Dues: $25 annually.

OUTDOOR WRITERS ASSOCIATION OF AMERICA, INC., 4141 W. Bradley Rd., Milwaukee WI 53209. (414)354-9690. Estab: 1927. Executive Director: Edwin W. Hanson. A nonprofit professional and educational organization comprised of newspaper and magazine writers, editors, photographers, broadcasters, artists, cinematographers, and lecturers engaged in the dissemination of information on outdoor sports such as hunting, boating, fishing, camping, etc., and on the conservation of natural resources. Its objectives are "providing a means of cross-communication among specialists in this field, promoting craft improvement, obtaining fair treatment from media, and increasing general public knowledge of the outdoors. Among other subjects, the membership deals extensively in current environmental issues." Requires that each member annually have published a specified quantity of paid material. Sponsorship by an active member of the OWAA is required for membership applicants. Dues: $25, initiation fee; $25, annual fee.

P.E.N., American Center, 156 Fifth Ave., New York NY 10010. (212)255-1977. Estab: 1921. Executive Secretary: Mel Mendelssohn. A world association of poets, playwrights, essayists, editors, and novelists, the purpose of P.E.N. is "to promote and maintain friendship and intellectual cooperation among men and women of letters in all countries, in the interests of literature, the exchange of ideas, freedom of expression, and good will." P.E.N. has 82 centers in Europe, Asia, Africa, Australia, and the Americas. "Membership is open to all qualified writers, translators, and editors who subscribe to the aims of International P.E.N." To qualify for membership, an applicant must have "acknowledged achievement in the literary field, which is generally interpreted as the publication by a recognized publisher of 2 books of literary merit. Membership is by invitation of the Admission Committee after nomination by a P.E.N. member."

PEN AND BRUSH CLUB, 16 E. 10th St., New York NY 10003. Established in 1893. President: Evelyn Chard Kelley. "The Pen and Brush Club is a club of professional women, writers, painters, graphic artists, sculptors, and craftsmen, with a resident membership limited to 350 active members in these fields. Exhibits are held in the galleries of the clubhouse by painters, sculptors, graphic artists, and craftsmen."

POETRY SOCIETY OF AMERICA, 15 Gramercy Park, S., New York NY 10003. (212)254-9628. Executive Secretary: Charles A. Wagner. The oldest and largest group working for an appreciation of poetry and for wider recognition of the work of living American poets, the Society has a membership of traditionalists and experimentalists. Dues: $18 annually.

RELIGION NEWSWRITERS ASSOCIATION, 1100 Broadway, Nashville TN 37202. (615)255-1221. Established in 1949. President: W.A. Reed. First Vice President: Ms. Marjorie

Myer, 1150 15th St. N.W., Washington DC 20071. Officers and members of RNA comprise 125 reporters who cover news of religion for the secular press in the United States and Canada.

ROCKY MOUNTAIN OUTDOOR WRITERS AND PHOTOGRAPHERS, 1111 Morningside Dr., N.E., Albuquerque NM 87110. Contact: D. Harper Simms. Founded 1973.
Purpose: "RMOWP is a select regional organization of professional writers, photographers, artists, and lecturers residing in Arizona, Colorado, Idaho, Montana, New Mexico, Utah, or Wyoming. The organization was founded with the purpose of improving and expanding outdoor writing, photography, and other communication forms." Fees: $10 initiation, $10/year (active; $10 initiation fee; $5/year associate; $25 minimum for supporting members.

SCIENCE FICTION WRITERS OF AMERICA, C. L. Grant, Executive Secretary, 44 Center Grove Rd., Apt. H-21, Dover NJ 07801. (201)361-3089. Membership is limited to established science fiction writers in the country. Purposes are to inform writers of matters of professional benefit, to serve as an intermediary in disputes of a professional nature, and to act as central clearinghouse for information on science fiction and science fiction writers. Dues: $12.50 annually.

SOCIETY FOR TECHNICAL COMMUNICATION, 1010 Vermont Ave. N.W., Suite 421, Washington DC 20005. (202)737-0035. Established in 1953. Executive Director: Curtis T. Youngblood. Dedicated to the advancement of the theory and practice of technical communication in all media, the STC aims primarily for the education, improvement, and advancement of its members. Dues: $20 annually.

SOCIETY OF AMERICAN SOCIAL SCRIBES, c/o The Plain Dealer, 1801 Superior Ave., Cleveland OH 44114. (216)523-4500. Secretary: Mary Strassmeyer. "The Society of American Social Scribes is a nonprofit organization dedicated to serving the interest of the reading public, to promote unbiased, objective reporting of social events and to promote journalistic freedom of movement. It endeavors to upgrade the professional integrity and skill of its members to work to increase the pleasures of the reading public, to support all legitimate efforts toward developing the education of its members, and to help its members offer greater service to their readers. Membership is limited to those regularly engaged as salaried society editors or devoting a substantial or regular part of their time to society coverage and the balance to other strictly editorial work. Society writers on daily newspapers with circulations of 200,000 or more and magazine writers and authors of books on the subject are also eligible for membership." Annual dues: $15.

SOCIETY OF AMERICAN TRAVEL WRITERS, 1120 Connecticut Ave., Suite 940, Washington DC 20036. (202)785-5567. Established in 1956. President: Henry E. Bradshaw. Dedicated to serving the interest of the traveling public, to promote international understanding and good will, and to further promote unbiased, objective reporting of information on travel topics. Active membership is limited "to those regularly engaged as salaried travel editors, writers, broadcasters, or photographers actively assigned to diversified travel coverage by a recognized medium or devoting a substantial or regular part of their time to such travel coverage to satisfy the Board of Directors; or to those who are employed as freelancers in any of the above areas with a sufficient steady volume of published work about travel to satisfy the Board. Associate membership is limited to persons regularly engaged in public relations or publicity within the travel industry to an extent that will satisfy the Board of Directors. All applicants must be sponsored by 2 active members with whom they are personally acquainted." Dues: $50 initiation fee for active members, $100 initiation fee for associate members; $35 annual dues for active members, $75 annual dues for associate members.

SOCIETY OF CHILDREN'S BOOK WRITERS, Box 296, Los Angeles CA 90066. President: Stephen Mooser. Founded 1968.
Purpose: "The Society of Children's Book Writers is the only national organization designed to offer a variety of services to people who write or share a vital interest in children's literature. The SCBW acts as a network for the exchange of knowledge between children's writers, editors, publishers, illustrators and agents." Fees $25/year.

SOCIETY OF PROFESSIONAL JOURNALISTS, SIGMA DELTA CHI, 35 E. Wacker Dr., Chicago IL 60601. Established in 1909. Executive Officer: Russell E. Hurst. Dedicated to the highest ideals in journalism. Membership extends horizontally to include persons engaged in the communication of fact and opinion by all media and vertically to include in its purposes and fellowship all ranks of journalists. Dues: $20 annually.

SOCIETY OF THE SILURIANS, INC., 45 John St., New York NY 10028. (212)233-1897. Secretary: James H. Driscoll. Established in 1924. Primarily a fraternal organization. Membership totals 700. Men and women are eligible for full membership if their history in the New York City media dates back 25 years, for associate membership after 15 years, whether or not they are still so engaged. Dues: $10 annually.

UNITED STATES HARNESS WRITERS' ASSOCIATION, INC., P.O. Box 10, Batavia NY 14020. Established in 1947. Executive Secretary: William F. Brown, Jr. 435 members. Involved in media coverage of harness racing and/or standardbred breeding. Dues: $25 annually.

WASHINGTON INDEPENDENT WRITERS ASSOCIATION, INC., 1057 National Press Building, Washington DC 20045. Executive Director: Patricia Altobello. Established in 1975. Purposes are to further the common goals of reputable writers and to combat unfair practices which hamper work, and to help establish ethical guidelines for the conduct of the profession. Full membership is open to persons who have written and published for compensation 5,000 words or its equivalent during the previous year or who have authored a book commercially published within the preceding 5 years. Associate membership is open to persons with serious interest in the independent writing profession or other independent media professions. Offers workshops and meetings, an annual directory, a monthly newsletter, legal, contract and tax information, an assignment referral service, group hospitalization and a major medical plan. Its committees work on market information, problems of professional relations and development.

WESTERN WRITERS OF AMERICA, INC., 1505 W. "D" St., North Platte NE 69101. Contact: Nellie Yost. Writers eligible for membership in this organization are not restricted in their residence, "so long as their work, whether it be fiction, history, adult, or juvenile, book-length or short material, movie or TV scripts, has the scene laid west of the Missouri River."

WOMEN IN COMMUNICATIONS, INC., National Headquarters, 8305-A Shoal Creek Blvd., Austin TX 78758. (512)452-0119. Estab: 1909 as Theta Sigma Phi. President: Anne Hecker. A professional society for women in journalism and communications. Application fee: $32. Dues: $20 annually.

WRITERS GUILD OF AMERICA, Writers Guild of America, *East*, 22 W. 48th St., New York NY 10036. Writers Guild of America, *West*, 8955 Beverly Blvd., Los Angeles CA 90048. A labor organization representing all screen, television, and radio writers. Initiation fee: $300 (West), $300 (East). Dues: $12.50 per quarter (East), $10 per quarter (West), and 1% of gross earnings as a writer in WGA fields of jurisdiction.

Glossary

All rights. Author gives the publisher complete rights for any use of his material and forfeits any further use of that same material by himself.

Alternative culture. The life styles, politics, literature, etc., of those persons with cultural values different from the current "establishment."

Assignment. Editor asks a writer to do a specific article for which he usually names a price for the completed manuscript.

B&w. Abbreviation for black and white photograph.

Beat. A specific subject area regularly covered by a reporter, such as the police department or education or the environment. It can also mean a scoop on some news item.

Bimonthly. Every two months. See also semimonthly.

Biweekly. Every two weeks.

Blue-pencilling. Editing a manuscript.

Caption. Originally a title or headline over a picture but now a description of the subject matter of a photograph, including names of people where appropriate. Also called cutline.

Chapbook. A small booklet, usually paperback, of poetry, ballads or tales.

Chicago Manual of Style. A format for the typing of manuscripts as established by the University of Chicago Press (Chicago, 60637, revised 12th edition, $12.50).

Clean copy. Free of errors, cross-outs, wrinkles, smudges.

Clippings. Of news items of possible interest to trade magazine editors.

Column inch. All the type contained in one inch of a newspaper column.

Contributors' copies. Copies of the issues of a magazine in which an author's work appears.

Copy. Manuscript material is often called copy by an editor before it is set in type.

Copy editing. Editing the manuscript for grammar, punctuation and printing style as opposed to subject content.

Copyright. A means to protect an author's work. Under the present law, a copyright is valid for the length of the author's life, plus 50 years.

Correspondent. Writer away from the home office of a newspaper or magazine who regularly provides it with copy.

El-hi. Elementary to high school.

Epigram. A short, witty, sometimes paradoxical saying.

Erotica. Usually fiction that is sexually oriented; although it could be art on the same theme.

Fair use. A provision of the Copyright Law that says short passages from copyrighted material may be used without infringing on the owner's rights.

There are no set number of words. A good rule of thumb: "Does my use of this copyrighted material impair the market value of the original?"

Feature. An article giving the reader background information on the news. Also used by magazines to indicate a lead article or distinctive department.

Filler. A short item used by an editor to "fill" out a newspaper column or a page in a magazine. It could be a timeless news item, a joke, an anecdote, some light verse or short humor, a puzzle, etc.

First North American serial rights. The right to first publish an article, story or poem in a copyrighted newspaper or magazine in the U.S. or Canada.

Flesch formula. Developed by Rudolph Flesch, attempts to determine by a mathematical formula the "readability" of writing. Its theory is based on a "write-as-you-talk" idea and the formula measures the number of syllables in a 100-word passage of writing, the number of words per sentence and the percentage of "personal" words, such as personal pronouns, names of people, spoken dialogue, etc. See Rudolf Flesch's *The Art of Readable Writing,* for more details.

Format. The shape, size and general makeup of a publication; that is, for example, 8½x11″ offset printed glossy publication. May sometimes also be used to apply to the general plan of organization of an article as preferred by an editor.

Formula story. Familiar theme treated in a predictable plot structure—such as boy meets girl, boy loses girl, boy gets girl.

Gagline. The caption for a cartoon, or the cover teaser line and the punchline on the inside of a studio greeting card.

Ghostwriter. A writer who puts into literary form, an article, speech, story or book based on another person's ideas or knowledge.

Glossy. A black and white photograph with a shiny surface as opposed to one with a non-shiny matte finish.

Gothic novel. One in which the central character is usually a beautiful young girl, the setting is an old mansion or castle; there is a handsome hero and a real menace, either natural or supernatural.

Honorarium. A token payment. It may be a very small amount of money, or simply a byline and copies of the publication in which your material appears.

Horizontal publication. Usually a trade magazine, published for readers in a specific job function in a variety of industries. For example, *Purchasing Magazine.* (See also vertical publication.)

House organ. A company publication: internal—for employees only; external for customers, stockholders, etc., or a combination publication to serve both purposes.

Illustrations. May be photographs, old engravings, artwork. Usually paid for separately from the manuscript. See also "package sale."

Imagery. Poetry that lends itself to visualization.

International Postal Reply Coupons. Can be purchased at your local post office and enclosed with your letter or manuscript to a foreign publisher to cover his postage cost when replying.

Invasion of privacy. Cause for suits against some writers who have written about persons (even though truthfully) without their consent.

Kill fee. A portion of the agreed-on price for a complete article that was assigned but which was subsequently cancelled.

Libel. A false accusation; or any published statement or presentation that tends to expose another to public contempt, ridicule, etc. Defenses are truth; fair comment on a matter of public interest; and privileged communication—such as a report of legal proceedings or a client's communication to his lawyer.

Little magazines. Publications of limited circulation, usually on literary or political subject matter.

MLA Style Sheet. A format for the typing of manuscripts established by the Modern Language Association (62 Fifth Ave., New York NY 10011). 2nd edition, $2.

Model release. A paper signed by the subject of a photograph (or his guardian, if a juvenile) giving the photographer permission to use the photograph, editorially or for advertising purposes or for some specific purpose as stated.

Ms. Abbreviation for manuscript.

Mss. Abbreviation for more than one manuscript.

Multiple submissions. Some editors of non-overlapping circulation magazines, such as religious publications, are willing to look at manuscripts which have also been submitted to other editors at the same time. See individual listings for which editors these are. No multiple submissions should be made to larger markets paying good prices for original material, unless it is a query on a highly topical article requiring an immediate response and that fact is so stated in your letter.

Newsbreak. A newsworthy event or item. For example, a clipping about the opening of a new shoe store in a town might be a newsbreak of interest to a trade journal in the shoe industry. Some editors also use the word to mean funny typographical errors.

Novelette. A short novel, or a long short story; 7,000 to 15,000 words approximately.

Offprint. Reprints of a published article, story, poem.

Offset. Type of printing in which copy and illustrations are photographed and plates made, from which printing is done; as opposed to letterpress printing directly from type metal and engravings of illustrations.

One-time rights. Is a phrase used by some publications, especially newspapers, to indicate that after they use the story, the writer is free to resell it elsewhere, outside their circulation area, after they've published it. It is not the same as "first rights" since they may be buying one-time rights to a story that has already appeared in some other publication outside their area.

Outline. Of a book is usually a one-page summary of its contents; often in the form of chapter headings with a descriptive sentence or two under each one to show the scope of the book.

Package sale. The editor wants to buy manuscript and photos as a "package" and pay for them in one check.

Page rate. Some magazines pay for material at a fixed rate per published page, rather than so much per word.

Payment on acceptance. The editor sends you a check for your article, story or poem as soon as he reads it and decides to publish it.

Payment on publication. The editor decides to buy your material but doesn't send you a check until he publishes it.

Pen name. The use of a name other than your legal name on articles, stories, or books where you wish to remain anonymous. Simply notify your post office and bank that you are using the name so that you'll properly receive mail and/or checks in that name.

Photo feature. A feature in which the emphasis is on the photographs rather than any accompanying written material.

Photocopied submissions. Are acceptable to some editors instead of the author's sending his original manuscript. See also multiple submissions.

Piracy. Infringement of copyright.

Plagiarism. Passing off as one's own, the expression of ideas, words of another.

Primary sources. Of research are original letters and documents, as opposed to published articles, books, etc.

Pseudonym. See pen name.

Public domain. Material which was either never copyrighted or whose copyright term has run out.

Publication not copyrighted. Publication of an author's work in such a publication places it in the public domain, and it cannot subsequently be copyrighted. Poets especially should watch this point if they hope to republish their work elsewhere.

Query. A letter of inquiry to an editor eliciting his interest in an article you want to write.

Reporting times. The number of days, weeks, etc., it takes an editor to report back to the author on his query or manuscript.

Reprint rights. The right to reprint an article, story, or poem that originally appeared in anothe publication.

Retention rights. You agree to let a magazine hold your article or story or poem for a length of time to see if they can find space to publish it. Since this keeps you from selling it elsewhere (and they might subsequently decide to return it), we don't advocate this practice.

Round-up article. Comments from, or interviews with, a number of celebrities or experts on a single theme.

Royalties, standard hardcover book. 10% of the retail price on the first 5,000 copies sold; 12½% on the next 5,000 and 15% thereafter.

Royalties, standard mass paperback book. 4 to 8% of the retail price on the first 150,000 copies sold.

Runover. The copy in the back of a magazine continued from a story or article featured in the main editorial section.

SAE. Self-addressed envelope.

SASE. Self-addressed, stamped envelope.

Sample copies. Will be sent free to writers by some editors; others require sample copy price and/or postage. See individual listings.

Second serial rights. Publication in a newspaper or magazine after the material has already appeared elsewhere. Usually used to refer to the sale of a part of a book to a newspaper or magazine after the book has been published, whether or not there was any first serial publication.

Semimonthly. Twice a month.

Semiweekly. Twice a week.

Serial. Published periodically, such as a newspaper or magazine.

Shelter books. Magazines that concentrate on home decoration.

Short-short story. Is usually from 500 to 2,000 words.

Short story. Averages 2,000 to 3,500 words.

Simultaneous submissions. Submissions of the same article, story or poem to smaller magazines with non-competing circulations and whose editors have agreed to accept same.

Slant. The approach of a story or article so as to appeal to the readers of a specific magazine. Does, for example, this magazine always like stories with an upbeat ending? Or does that one like articles aimed only at the blue-collar worker?

Slanted. Written in such a way to appeal to a particular group of readers.

Slides. Usually called transparencies by editors looking for color photographs.

Speculation. The editor agrees to look at the author's manuscript but doesn't promise to buy it until he reads it.

Stringer. A writer who submits material to a magazine or newspaper from a specific geographical location.

Style. The way in which something is written—short, punchy sentences or flowing, narrative description or heavy use of quotes or dialogue.

Subsidiary rights. All those rights, other than book publishing rights included in a book contract—such as paperback, book club, movie rights, etc.

Subsidy publisher. A book publisher who charges the author for the cost to typeset and print his book, the jacket, etc., as opposed to a royalty publisher which pays the author.

Syndication rights. A book publisher may sell the rights to a newspaper syndicate to print a book in installments in one or more newspapers.

Tabloids. Newspaper format publication on about half the size of the regular newspaper page. A group of publications in this format on major newsstands, such as *National Enquirer*.

Tagline. An editorial comment on a filler, such as those in *The New Yorker*. In some contexts, it is also used to mean a descriptive phrase associated with a certain person, such as newscaster Walter Cronkite's "That's the way it is . . ."

Tearsheet. Pages from a magazine or newspaper containing your printed story or article or poem.

Think piece. A magazine article that has an intellectual, philosophical, provocative approach to its subject.

Third world. Usually refers to the undeveloped countries of Asia and Africa, but used by some to mean underprivileged or underdeveloped minorities anywhere in the world.

Thirty. Usually shown as -30- means "the end" on newspaper copy. It is a remainder from the days when newspaper telegraphers used it as a symbol for the end of a story transmission.

Transparencies. Positive color slides; not color prints.

Uncopyrighted publication. Such as most newspapers or small poetry and literary magazines. Publication of an author's work in such publications puts it in the public domain.

Unsolicited manuscripts. A story or article or poem or book that an editor did not specifically ask to see, as opposed to one he did write the author and ask for.

Vanguard. In the forefront.

Vanity publisher. Same as subsidy publisher. One who publishes books for an author who pays the production cost himself.

Vertical publication. A publication for all the people in a variety of job functions within the same industry, such as *Aviation Week and Space Technology or Hospitals*.

Vignette. A brief scene offering the reader a flash of illumination about a character as opposed to a more formal story with a beginning, middle and end.

Index

Books of Interest From Writer's Digest

Writing and Selling Science Fiction, edited by C.L. Grant. A comprehensive handbook to an exciting but oft-misunderstood genre. Eleven articles by top-flight sf writers on markets, characters, dialogue, "crazy" ideas, world-building, alien-building, money and more. 191 pp. $7.95.

The Craft of Interviewing, by John Brady. Everything you always wanted to know about asking questions, but were afraid to ask — from an experienced interviewer and editor of *Writer's Digest.* The most comprehensive guide to interviewing on the market. 256 pp. $9.95.

The Mystery Writer's Handbook, edited by Lawrence Treat. A howtheydunit to the whodunit, newly written and revised by members of the Mystery Writers of America. Includes the four elements essential to the classic mystery. A clear and comprehensive handbook that takes the mystery out of mystery writing. 275 pp. $8.95.

A Guide to Writing History, by Doris Ricker Marston. How to track down Big Foot — or your family Civil War letters, or your hometown's last century — for publication and profit. A timely handbook for history buffs and writers. 258 pp. $8.50.

The Confession Writer's Handbook, by Florence K. Palmer. A stylish and informative guide to getting started and getting ahead in the confessions. How to start a confession and carry it through. How to take an insignificant event and make it significant. 171 pp. $6.95.

A Complete Guide to Marketing Magazine Articles, by Duane Newcomb. "Anyone who can write a clear sentence can learn to write and sell articles on a consistent basis," says Newcomb (who has published well over 3,000 articles). Here's how. 248 pp. $6.95.

The Creative Writer, edited by Aron Mathieu. This book opens the door to the real world of publishing. Inspiration, techniques, and ideas, plus inside tips from Maugham, Caldwell, Purdy, others. 416 pp. $6.95.

Handbook of Short Story Writing, edited by Frank A. Dickson and Sandra Smythe. You provide the pencil, paper, and sweat — and this book will provide the expert guidance. Features include James Hilton on creating a lovable character; R.V. Cassill on plotting a short story. 238 pp. $6.95.

A Treasury of Tips for Writers, edited by Marvin Weisbord. Everything from Vance Packard's system of organizing notes to tips on how to get research done free, by 86 magazine writers. 174 pp. $5.95.

One Way to Write Your Novel, by Dick Perry. For Perry, a novel is 200 pages. Or, two pages a day for 100 days. You can start — and finish — your novel, with the help of this step-by-step guide taking you from the blank sheet to the polished page. 138 pp. $6.95.

The Poet and the Poem, by Judson Jerome. A rare journey into the night of the poem — the mechanics, the mystery, the craft and sullen art. Written by the most widely read authority on poetry in America, and a major contemporary poet in his own right. 482 pp. $7.95 ($4.95 paperback).

Writing and Selling Non-Fiction, by Hayes B. Jacobs. Explores with style and know-how the book market, organization and research, finding new markets, interviewing, humor, agents, writer's fatigue and more. 317 pp. $7.95.

The Beginning Writer's Answer Book, edited by Kirk Polking, Jean Chimsky, and Rose Adkins. "What is a query letter?" "If I use a pen name, how can I cash the check?" These are among 500 questions most frequently asked by beginning writers — and expertly answered in this down-to-earth handbook. Cross-indexed. 168 pp. $7.95.

Writing Popular Fiction, by Dean R. Koontz. How to write mysteries, suspense thrillers, science fiction. Gothic romances, adult fantasy, Westerns and erotica. Here's an inside guide to lively fiction, by a lively novelist. 232 pp. $7.95.

Art & Crafts Market, edited by Lynne Lapin and Betsy Wones. Lists 4,498 places where you can show and sell your crafts and artwork. Galleries, competitions and exhibitions, craft dealers, magazines that buy illustrations and cartoons, book publishers and advertising agencies — they're all there, complete with names, addresses, submission requirements, phone numbers and payment rates. 672 pp. $10.95.

Photographer's Market, edited by Melissa Milar and William Brohaugh. Contains what you need to know to be a successful freelance photographer. Names, addresses, photo requirements, and payment rates for 1,616 markets. Plus, information on preparing a portfolio, basic equipment needed, the business side of photography, and packaging and shipping your work. 408 pp. $9.95.

The Cartoonist's and Gag Writer's Handbook, by Jack Markow: Longtime cartoonist with thousands of sales reveals the secrets of successful cartooning — step by step. Richly illustrated. 157 pp. $7.95.

The Greeting Card Writer's Handbook, by H. Joseph Chadwick. A former greeting card editor tells you what editors look for in inspirational verse ... how to write humor ... what to write about for conventional, studio and juvenile cards. Extra: a renewable list of greeting card markets. Will be greeted by any freelancer. 268 pp. $6.95.

Writing For Children and Teen-Agers, by Lee Wyndham. Author of over 50 children's books shares her secrets for selling to his large, lucrative market. Features: the 12-point recipe for plotting, and the ten commandments for writers. 253 pp. $8.95.

Writer's Digest. The world's leading magazine for writers. Monthly issues include timely articles, interviews, columns, tips to keep writers informed on where and how to sell their work. One year subscription, $12.

(Add 50¢ for postage and handling. Prices subject
to change without notice.)
Writer's Digest Books, 9933 Alliance Road, Cincinnati, Ohio 45242.

Notes

Notes

Notes

Notes